02/02

310.⁰⁰

02/02

Cases in Corporate **Acquisitions, Buyouts, Mergers, & Takeovers**

ISSN 1526-5927

Cases in Corporate Acquisitions, Buyouts, Mergers, & Takeovers

Kelly **Hill**, editor

GALE GROUP

Detroit
San Francisco
London
Boston
Woodbridge, CT

CASES IN Corporate Acquisitions, Buyouts, Mergers, and Takeovers

Gale Group Staff

Editorial: Kelly Hill, Editor; Theresa J. MacFarlane, Contributing Editor; Amy Suchowski, Contributing Editor; Keith Jones, Managing Editor

Product Development: Renée D. McKinney, New Product Development

Technical Support: Theresa A. Rocklin, Manager; Magdalena Cureton, Programmer / Analyst

Production: Mary Beth Trimper, Director; Evi Seoud, Assistant Production Manager

Product Design: Cynthia Baldwin, Manager; Pamela A. E. Galbreath, Senior Art Director

Copyright Notice

ISBN 0-7876-3894-3
ISSN 1526-5927
Printed in the United States of America

CONTENTS

H

I

J

K

L

M

N

INTRODUCTION AND USER'S GUIDE

Mergers and acquisitions have become an increasingly important aspect of doing business in the United States and abroad. *Cases in Corporate Acquisitions, Buyouts, Mergers, and Takeovers (CCA)* serves as a one-stop source for valuable and in-depth information on a wide range of M&A activity. It includes approximately 300 entries, each on an important (but not necessarily successful) merger from the past 100 years. Most are high profile mergers, such as America Online's purchase of Netscape, Daimler Benz's acquisition of Chrysler, or MCI's merger with WorldCom.

CCA is written so that it is accessible and relevant to users from a variety of backgrounds. Whether the user is a student fresh out of high school or a veteran business student, *CCA* contains a great deal of valuable information to help guide the researcher's efforts.

Content and Arrangement

Designed for ease of use, *CCA* is organized alphabetically by the names of the companies involved (e.g., America Online & Netscape, DaimlerBenz & Chrysler, and MCI & WorldCom). Each entry may include the following sections:

Companies Affected: includes nationalities of companies and the years these companies were formed.

Contact Information: address, phone and fax numbers, and, if available, web page and e-mail address.

Financials: revenue (sales unless otherwise indicated) and number of employees.

Executive Officers: primary executives of the company.

Major Players: names of major people involved in the action, their corporate affiliations, and brief biographies.

Overview of the Merger/Acquisition: a snapshot of the activity.

History: background information for each company involved.

Market Forces Driving the Merger: comments on the impetus for the activity.

Approach and Engagement: who approached whom and why.

Products and Services: lists the primary products and/or services offered by the company.

Changes to the Industry: discusses the effects of the merger on the industry.

Review of the Outcome: includes such items as corporate growth/dissolution or loss of jobs.

Further Research: suggests articles and books for additional information on the merger/acquisition.

Indexes

General Index: contains alphabetical references to companies, institutions, organizations, people, and relevant legislation. Each index term is followed by page numbers that easily direct the user to both main topics (indicated by bolded page numbers) as well as to all secondary reference terms as mentioned above.

Industry Index: contains references to industries included in the text. Each industry is followed by page numbers that point the user to essays representing those industries.

Acknowledgements

The staff at The Gale Group would like to thank the following individuals for their advice and suggestions for the generation of the Cases in Corporate Acquisitions topic list: Julie Jersyk, Bibliographic Services Librarian at Northeastern University; Judith M. Nixon, Management & Economics Librarian at the Graduate School of Management & Economics, Purdue University; and Rita Ormsby, Reference Librarian and Instructor at The William and Anita Newman Library, Baruch College (The City University of New York).

Comments and Suggestions

Comments and suggestions, including ideas for future essays, are welcome. We invite readers to send us their thoughts at:

Editor
Cases in Corporate Acquisitions, Buyouts,
    Mergers, and Takeovers
27500 Drake Rd.
Farmington Hills, MI 48331-3535
Phone: 800-347-4253
Fax: 800-339-3374

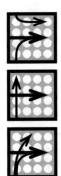

ADOBE SYSTEMS & ALDUS

nationality: USA
date: September 1, 1994
affected: Adobe Systems Inc., USA, founded 1982
affected: Aldus Corp., USA, founded 1984

Adobe Systems Inc.
345 Park Ave.
San Jose, CA 95110-2704
USA

tel: (408) 536-6000
fax: (408) 537-6000
web: http://www.adobe.com

Overview of the Merger

The $450 million merger of Adobe Systems Inc. and Aldus Corp. in September of 1994 secured Adobe's position as the world's fourth largest PC software manufacturer behind Microsoft, Novell, and Lotus. In the retail segment of the PC software market, Adobe secured a five percent share, second only to the 22% claimed by Microsoft. The joining of desktop publishing leader Aldus with the maker of Adobe Acrobat created a market leader in design and illustration software, image editing, and electronic document technology.

The merger was delayed twice by Federal Trade Commission (FTC) investigations, and to meet FTC antitrust guidelines, Adobe was ordered to release all marketing and sales rights to Aldus FreeHand to Altsys by January 15, 1995. After the merger was finalized, Adobe laid off roughly 20% of its workforce due to administrative overlap, particularly overseas.

History of Adobe Systems

In 1982, Charles Geschke and John Warnock left their research scientist positions at Xerox and established Adobe Systems Inc. to market their new PostScript computer language; the language, which communicated to printers how to reproduce digital images on paper, would play a major role in the growth of the desktop publishing industry and the laser printer boom. Although Adobe's founders were initially planning to market PostScript via a high-end electronic document processing system they would develop, their focus changed when they secured a contract from Apple computer to create a controller board and software for Apple's LaserWriter printer. The printer, the first to make use of the PostScript printer language, was shipped in 1985. In 1986, Adobe listed shares publicly for the first time.

In 1987, Adobe established Adobe Systems Europe. The firm also diversified into the PC market by tailoring PostScript for IBM operating systems. Two years later, Adobe expanded into the Pacific Rim by founding a sales unit there. The purchase of OCR Systems and Nonlinear Technologies in 1992 marked the beginning of an expansion period for Adobe. In 1993, the company bought both AH Software

The Business

Financials

Revenue (1998): $894 million

Employees (1998): 2,680

SICs / NAICS

sic 7372 - Prepackaged Software

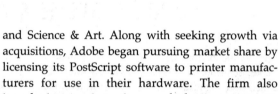

and Science & Art. Along with seeking growth via acquisitions, Adobe began pursuing market share by licensing its PostScript software to printer manufacturers for use in their hardware. The firm also launched its Acrobat software, which allowed users to create and send electronic documents—including graphics, special fonts, and photos—online via portable document format (PDF).

In 1994, Adobe, lacking a desktop publishing application to go with its PostScript printing language, began merger discussions with Aldus Corp. hoping to gain access to PageMaker, the leading desktop publishing application for both Macintosh and Windows platforms. The merger was finalized later that year.

Adobe completed its second major acquisition in 1995 with the $31.5 million purchase of Frame Technology Corp., maker of the Unix-based FrameMaker desktop publishing program. The move into longer text-intensive documents proved disastrous: Adobe didn't understand Frame's enterprise market, and the unit began to lose money. By July of 1996, Adobe's stock prices had plummeted more than 50% to $33 per share, from a high of roughly $74 per share earlier that year.

Hoping its 1995 purchase of Word Wide Web toolmaker Ceneca Communications would prove more lucrative, the company shifted focus in 1996 to Internet publishing and converted its popular PDF into an Internet format. Sales neared the $1 billion mark in 1997, and Windows-based Adobe software generated more revenue than its Mac-based counterparts for the first time. Sluggish sales in 1998 spurred Adobe to lay off roughly 10% of its workforce. Also, competitor Quark Inc. made an unsolicited bid for Adobe, which it later withdrew.

History of Aldus Corp.

In February of 1984, Paul Brainerd founded Aldus Corp., naming his desktop publishing firm after Aldus

Manutius, a pioneering 15th-century Venetian mass book printer. Roughly a year later, Brainerd released PageMaker 1.0 (Macintosh), the first version of the program that would later be credited for revolutionizing the desktop publishing industry.

Aldus became a multi-product company in 1987 with the launch of Aldus FreeHand. During the year, the company also formed Aldus Europe Ltd., released PageMaker 1.0 (Windows) and PageMaker 2.0 (Macintosh), and offered 2.24 million shares of common stock. Aldus FreeHand, Aldus Persuasion, and Aldus PageMaker 3.0 were all launched in 1988. By 1990, Aldus had passed the half-million mark for installed programs. The firm acquired Silicon Beach Software, established Aldus France, and founded the Aldus Developers Association. A year later, Aldus created its Imaging Support Services program and acquired the marketing rights to PhotoStyler and PressWise, as well as the publishing rights to PageAhead.

In 1992, Aldus Japan was founded, and Aldus announced the formation of its consumer division. By 1993, the company employed more than 1,000 workers and boasted annual sales in excess of $200 million. Aldus was acquired by Adobe in a $450 million stock swap in September of 1994. The merger created a $500 million software maker with the ability to create, display, and print documents electronically.

Market Forces Driving the Merger

Adobe's PostScript printer language triggered the rapid growth of laser printers in the early 1990s. Ironically, this success was at the root of Adobe's falling profits in 1992. That year, the intense popularity of laser printers had finally driven prices down, and although the volume of printer sales increased, revenue per printer declined dramatically for Adobe. Sales increased to $266 million from $229 million the year prior, but net income fell to $43 million from $51 million.

As a result, Adobe CEO Warnock launched the "Triple A" plan, which called for accretion, Acrobat, and acquisition. To address the issue of accretion, or expansion, Adobe began manufacturing several new PostScript printer models as a means of gaining access to new markets. Acrobat, the second component of Warnock's plan, was released in June of 1993. The new portable document format (PDF) software allowed users to transmit documents without having to use the ASCII format, which stripped text of most coding. The immediate success of Acrobat boosted 1993 net income to a record high of $57 million, which allowed Adobe to pursue the third goal of the "Triple A" plan: acquisition.

Recognizing that the desktop publishing industry had little competition (mainly Quark and Corel), Warnock knew that an acquisition like Aldus Corp. would secure a large chunk of market share for his firm. The technologies of the two firms were complementary as Adobe did not have a desktop publishing application to go with its PostScript printing language or its electronic document management software. Aldus was also ready for a merger. Profits were down to a paltry $9.5 million, compared to $23.8 million in 1991, and Aldus CEO Paul Brainerd was ready to retire when Warnock approached the firm. Despite the financial struggles of Aldus, Warnock believed that the company's product line and its successful penetration of European markets would serve Adobe well.

Approach and Engagement

It didn't take long for Warnock and Brainerd to hammer out a deal. In March of 1994, Aldus and Adobe announced a $450 million merger agreement in which Adobe would exchange one share of common stock for each of the 13.9 million shares of outstanding Aldus common stock. In response to the announcement, Competitor Altsys Corp. filed an antitrust lawsuit with the Federal Trade Commission (FTC), charging that the merger would undermine the marketing of a version of its FreeHand graphics software, a product Altsys had developed and licensed to Aldus. The FTC's investigation of the charge marked the first case in which the FTC challenged a merger of two software companies.

By July, the FTC had reached a settlement agreement with Adobe and Aldus which required Aldus to release all rights to FreeHand graphics software back to Altsys by July of 1995. The settlement also mandated that the merged company seek FTC approval before acquiring a stake in any firm involved in Macintosh-based professional graphics software or when purchasing software or software licenses worth more than $2 million.

When the merger was finalized, roughly six months after its announcement, Adobe CEO Warnock pointed out that the real work was just beginning for Adobe: "More than any other company in the software business, Adobe is now poised to unleash the power of the computer as a communications tool. It's time to begin integrating our products to form the world's most productive digital tools for the creation, exchange, delivery, and use of information."

Products and Services

According to Aldus CEO Brainerd, the newly merged company had an unmatched depth of desktop

The Officers

Co-Chairman of the Board and Chief Executive Officer:
John E. Warnock

Co-Chairman and President: Charles M. Geschke

Exec. VP, Worldwide Products and Marketing: Bruce R. Chizen

Exec. VP, Worldwide Field Operations: Fred Snow

and electronic publishing software products: "Together, Adobe and Aldus can generate tremendous momentum to meet customer requirements. The new company will have the largest, most respected typeface library, the world's top-selling page layout solution, and best-of-breed illustration, photo-editing, presentation, image retrieval, and video-production applications."

Upon completion of the merger, Adobe reorganized into three units: System Products, Application Products, and Consumer Products. Because product overlap with the merger was minimal, only a few products were discontinued, including Aldus' Photostyler for Windows—an image editor similar to Adobe's Photoshop for Windows—and Hitchcock, a video editor distributed by Aldus.

Adobe's bungled 1995 acquisition of the FrameMaker desktop publishing program from Frame Technology Corp. led it to shift focus in 1996 to Internet publishing software and develop a version of its PDF that was Internet-compatible. Along with leading products Adobe Acrobat, Adobe Illustrator, Adobe PageMaker, Adobe Photoshop, Adobe PostScript, and Adobe Type Library, the company began manufacturing and marketing the following World Wide Web tools: Adobe ImageReady and Adobe ImageStyler, two Web authoring programs; and Adobe PageMill, a Web page creation program. Other products included Adobe After Effects, a 2-D animation program; Adobe Photo Deluxe, photo personalization software; Adobe Premiere, a film and video editor; and Adobe Print Gear, a home and small office printing program.

Changes to the Industry

According to a July 1995 article in *MacWEEK*, larger software companies like Adobe pursued mergers to maintain strength in a market dominated by Microsoft. The larger these companies got, the tougher it was for small start-ups to break into mainstream

The Players

Co-Chairman and CEO of Adobe Systems Inc.: John E. Warnock. While earning a Ph.D. in electrical engineering at the University of Utah, John Warnock began working for various computer technology firms, including IBM. In the early 1980s, he was hired by Xerox as head scientist for their new graphics and imaging lab in Palo Alto, California. It was there that he and his supervisor, Charles Geschke, created the PostScript computer language to tell printers how to reproduce a digitized image on paper. When Xerox declined to market the new product, Warnock and Geschke left Xerox to found Adobe Systems in 1982. While at the helm of Adobe, Warnock collected numerous awards for both his entrepreneurial success and his technical innovation, including "Entrepreneur of the Year" from Ernst & Young, Merrill Lynch, and *Inc. Magazine*, as well as the "Lifetime Achievement Award for Technical Excellence" from *PC Magazine*. In 1998, *Computer Reseller News* named Warnock one of the "Ten Revolutionaries of Computing."

Co-Chairman and President of Adobe Systems Inc.: Charles M. Geschke. In 1980, after working as a principal scientist in Xerox's Computer Science Laboratory, Dr. Charles Geschke established the Imaging Sciences Laboratory for the firm. As director of computer science, graphics, image processing, and optics research, Geschke hired John Warnock to serve as head scientist in his lab. While working together, Geschke and Warnock developed the PostScript computer language, which later became the foundation of Adobe Systems' success.

President and CEO of Aldus Corp.: Paul Brainerd. Paul Brainerd's founding of Aldus Corp. in 1984 heralded the launch of the desktop publishing revolution. In 1985, the University of Minnesota journalism graduate introduced PageMaker to the market; his product brought desktop publishing to the masses. During his ten years as president of Aldus, Brainerd transformed the small start-up into a firm with $250 million in annual revenues and roughly 1,000 employees. Upon completion of the 1994 merger with Adobe Systems, Brainerd accepted a non-operating position as a member of the board of directors.

markets, like desktop publishing. The Adobe-Aldus joining added to a consolidation trend that forced smaller vendors to pursue niche markets. Both Adobe and Aldus started out by tapping into unexplored niche markets; to remain competitive, both had to grow and consolidate. After the merger Adobe gained a top spot in the PC software market—with the likes of Microsoft, Novell, and Lotus—and its size made the road for desktop publishing newcomers an even more difficult one.

The merger changed the focus of the industry itself as well. The acquisition of Aldus' PageMaker program added steam to Adobe's electronic publishing plans. Recognizing that laser printing, the mainstay of the traditional desktop publishing market, would became less lucrative for Adobe as long as electronic publishing continued to grow, the company helped to pioneer the shift towards electronic publishing with its plans to integrate PageMaker and Acrobat.

Review of the Outcome

A 1994 *Computer Weekly* company profile of Adobe offered this analysis of the merger's outcome: "With few competitors on the desktop publishing landscape—bar Quark and Corel—the horizon for Adobe looks pretty rosy. Now CEO of the fourth largest PC software manufacturer in the world, Warnock has achieved a unique feat. Adobe is successfully positioned on the rostrum behind Microsoft, Novell, and Lotus, but without having to compete with any one of them directly."

While the results of the merger were mainly positive for Adobe, the firm did encounter a few bumps along the road to integration. Although 1994 sales jumped by almost 15% to $598 million after the merger, annual net income for Adobe plummeted to $6.3 million, compared to $57 million in 1993. The company also laid off roughly 20% of its workforce, following finalization of the merger, to reduce overlap in administration and operations personnel, which mainly occurred overseas. Within a year of the transaction, however, Adobe had recovered. Stock reached a record high of $70.25 per share, and net income bounced back to roughly $93 million on increased sales of $760 million. The company's future struggles, including its difficult acquisition of Frame Technology Corp. and slower sales in 1998, were mainly the result of increased competition in the industry and, according to some analysts, problems with product strategy.

Research

"Aldus Corp.," in *Notable Corporate Chronologies*, The Gale Group, 1999. Lists major events in the history of Aldus Corp., including the merger.

"Adobe Systems Inc. Briefing Book," in *The Wall Street Journal Online*, available at http://www.wsj.com. This section of *The Wall Street Journal Online* offers a company overview, stock charts, links to archived articles, financials, and press releases.

Adobe Systems Inc. Home Page, available at http://www.adobe.com. Official World Wide Web Home Page for Adobe Systems Inc. Includes news, financial, product, historical, and employment information.

Button, Kate. "On a Roll: Adobe Systems," in *Computer Weekly*, 27 October 1994. Offers a company profile of Adobe which details the reasons for and the outcome of the merger with Aldus.

Casselman , Grace. "Adobe, Aldus Merger Forms Mammoth Publishing Venture," in *Computer Dealer News*, 6 April 1994. Discusses the merger itself and how it might benefit resellers.

"Financial: Adobe Systems Inc. Announces 1994 Earnings; Results Effect of Business Combination with Aldus Corp.," in *EDGE: Work-Group Computing Report*, 9 January 1995. Covers Adobe's financial results following the merger.

"Merger: Adobe & Aldus Complete Merger," in *EDGE: Work-Group Computing Report*, 5 September 1994. Details the financial aspects of the merger, as well as the resulting layoffs.

Parkinson, Kirsten L. "Merger Will Change Layout of DTP; Adobe to Move into Electronic Publishing," in *MacWEEK*, 12 September 1994. Analyzes the effects the merger might have on the desktop publishing industry as a whole.

————. "Mergers Reshape Industry's Future," in *MacWEEK*, 4 April 1994. Discusses the causes and effects of consolidation in the software industry.

Richards, Kathleen. "Adobe/Aldus Merger: Graphical Interface: Combined Company Second in Retail Software Dollars," in *Computer Retail Week*, 3 October 1994. Discusses Adobe's market share in the retail market segment following the merger, Adobe's leading products following the merger, and which products might be dumped as a result of the merger.

Stafford, Jim. "Adobe's Acrobates," in *PC Week*, 29 July 1996. Comments on Adobe's botched acquisition of Frame Technology Corp.

Vizard, Michael. "Adobe to Drop PhotoStyler in Wake of Merger," in *PC Week*, 21 November 1994. Explains Adobe's rationale for discontinuing two Aldus products.

Yoder, Stephen Kreider. "Merger of Adobe, Aldus Nears Approval by FTC; Terms Are Modified Slightly," in *The Wall Street Journal*, 28 July 1994. Covers the antitrust investigation by the FTC, as well as the FTC's ruling on the merger.

ANNAMARIE L. SHELDON

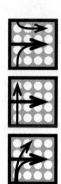

AEROSPATIALE & DASSAULT AVIATION

Aerospatiale SA
37, boulevard de Montmorency, Cedex 16
Paris, F-75781
France

tel: 33-1-42-24-24-24
fax: 33-1-42-24-20-93
web: http://www.aerospatiale.fr

Dassault Aviation SA
9 Rond Point des Champs Elysees
Paris, F-75008
France

tel: 33-1-47-41-7921
fax: 33-1-40-83-9938
web: http://www.dassault-avaition.fr

nationality: France
date: 1999
affected: Aerospatiale SA, France, founded 1936
affected: Dassault Aviation SA, France, founded 1919

Overview of the Merger

As part of France's aerospace industry overhaul, French President Jacques Chirac announced in 1996 plans to privatize Aerospatiale and merge it with Dassault Aviation. Negotiations between the two companies stalled several times in 1996 and 1997. In December of 1998, the French government stepped up its consolidation efforts by transferring its 46% share of Dassault to Aerospatiale; meanwhile, Aerospatiale was hammering out the details of its impending merger with Largardere's defense unit, Matra Hautes Technologies. Upon completion of the merger, Aerospatiale-Matra will become the world's fifth largest aerospace firm. When Aerospatiale-Matra and Dassault combine operations, they will employ a total of 66,000 employees and generate roughly $18 billion in revenues.

History of Aerospatiale SA

In 1936, the French government merged the operations of Farman, Hanriot, Potez, Marcel Bloch, Louis Bleriot, Dyle et Bacalan, Loire Nieuport, Liore Olivie, and Dewoitine into six geographically based aviation companies: Societes Nationales de Constructions Aeronautiques de Committee (SNCAC), du Sud-Ouest (SNCASO), du Sud-Est (SNCASE), du Midi (SNCAM), du Nord (SNCAN), and de L-Ouest (SNCAO). An armistice was signed with the Germans in 1940 which required all French airline companies to begin making products for the German war effort. The resulting Allied bombing of French factories retarded the country's further development of its aviation technology. A year later, the government reduced the number of nationalized companies to two: SNCASO and SNCASE.

Though development and progress were slowed during World War II, new projects such as France's first airplane, Triton, were completed in secret. In 1946, the reestablished French airplane industry first tested Triton. In 1955, in addition to creating the durable and popular Noratlas and Fouga Magister airplanes, French aerospace companies developed the Djinn, a piston-driven helicopter, and the Alouette I and II with turbo engines. A year later, the Durandel supersonic airplane was developed, along with the Griffon II and its combined turbo/ram-jet propulsion system, which eventually led to ballistic propulsion systems technology.

In 1959, the initial six nationalized air interests were reorganized into the Societe pour l'Etude et la Realisation d'Engins Balistiques (SEREB), Sud-Aviation, and Nord-Aviation. Three years later, as a result of SEREB's ballistic missile technology, the French government-sponsored space launch program began. The Strategic Ballistic Sea-to-Surface Missile for National Defense also helped in forming France's nuclear policies.

The 1960s marked a decade of firsts for the French aviation industry. The GIE Airbus Industrie program began in 1963 in conjunction with British, Spanish, and West German airlines and aviation interests. In November of 1965, France became the third nation to launch a satellite independently when Aerospatiale's Diamant blasted off. French aviation companies were also working with German companies to develop the Milan and Hot antitank missiles. The most noteworthy accomplishment of the decade took place when France and Great Britain's Condorde, the first supersonic passenger aircraft, made its first flight in 1969.

In 1970, the French government consolidated its three aerospace companies, Sud-Aviation, Nord-Aviation, and SEREB, into Societe Nationale Industrielle Aerospatiale to avoid unnecessary redundancies in marketing and development. As a result, management for the new aerospace company was reorganized. During the early 1970s, Aerospatiale improved its line of helicopters with Ecureuil, the Super-Puma, and the Dauphin. Plans originally developed at SEREB to design the country's first strategic nuclear missiles were carried out, and 18 of the missiles were installed in land bases. Aerospatiale also did most of the design work for the Ariane space launchers, the result of a combined European space program.

In 1973, heavy losses in the aircraft division prompted talks of lay-offs and cutbacks, but the French government gave Aerospatiale a $100 million advance in capital and guaranteed another $26 million in public bond issues. The company still lost $100 million, partly due to the Concorde; orders were low because its price had risen to $65 million and oil price increases made the supersonic jet even more expensive to operate. The company posted losses again in 1974 due mainly to stagnant sales in the aircraft division. The firm's other divisions—helicopter, missile, and space—fared better.

The French government formed the Societe de Gestion des Participations Aeronautiques (Segopa) from the merger of Avions Marcel Dassault-Breguet Aviation and Aerospatiale, the government's two avi-

The Business

Financials - Aerospatiale SA
Revenue (1998): $9.8 billion

Employees (1998): 36,647

Financials - Dassault Aviation SA
Revenue (1997): $3.5 billion

Employees (1997): 12,000

SICs / NAICS
sic 3721 - Aircraft

sic 3483 - Ammunition Except for Small Arms

sic 3761 - Guided Missiles & Space Vehicles

sic 3663 - Radio & T.V. Communications Equipment

naics 336411 - Aircraft Manufacturing

naics 332993 - Ammunition (except Small Arms)
      Manufacturing

naics 336414 - Guided Missile and Space Vehicle
      Manufacturing

ation interests, in 1979. Two years later, Aerospatiale entered into a joint venture, Eurosam, with French industrial giant Thomson and Italian national airline Alenia. In 1982, Aerospatiale's aircraft division and Alenia formed a 50/50 joint-venture, ATR, to make small aircraft called ATR 42s and ATR 72s.

A joint venture with Thomson called Cosyde began designing defense systems in 1986. In the mid-1980s, Aerospatiale's helicopter division, which exported more helicopters than any other company in the world, held about 33% of the world market, compared to the eight percent held by MBB, the helicopter division of Deutsche Aerospace Airbus (DASA). The space division of Aerospatiale was chosen to implement development and production of Hermes, a spacecraft similar to the U.S. space shuttles. Two of the firm's subsidiaries, Sogerma and Socea, merged to become Sogerma-Socea. In 1989, Sextant Avionique was formed in a complex joint venture between ATEV and a group of companies (Crouzet, EAS, Stena, Siela) working with Thomson-CSF's general aviation division; ATEV, a 50/50 joint venture between Aerospatiale and Thomson, held just over 54% in Sextant. Aerospatiale also formed Unilaser to oversee all of its laser operations. Aircraft orders, on the rise since the early 1980s, continued to grow.

The Officers

Aerospatiale SA

Chairman: Yves Michot

Chief Executive Officer: Philippe Camus

Chief Financial Officer: Francois Auque

Exec. VP, Human Resources: R. Chabod

VP, Communications and External Relations: P. Bayle

Dassault Aviation SA

Chairman and Chief Executive Officer: Serge Dassault

Sr. Exec. VP, International Operations: Pierre Chouzenoux

Exec. VP, Economic and Financial Affairs: Charles
Edelstenne

Exec. VP, Engineering, Research, and Cooperation: Bruno
Revellin-Falcoz

Exec. VP, Industrial and Social Affairs: Michel Herchin

Aerospatiale and Dassault formed Hermespace France in 1990. The unit owned 43.5% of Euro-Hermespace, a joint venture with DASA and Alenia to develop the Hermes spacecraft. That year, Aerospatiale's helicopter operations joined with MBB to make Tigers and NH90s. Space Systems-Loral was formed by Aerospatiale, Alcatel, Alenia, and U.S.-based Loral Corp. to make satellites. French and British aerospace interests began researching the financial and technological aspects of improving upon the Concorde to make the ATSF (Future Supersonic Transport Aircraft), and the AGV, which would carry passengers at speeds up to 15,000 kilometers/hour. Also, Sogerma-Socea took control of Maroc Aviation operations.

Euromissile, 50% owned by Aerospatiale, began manufacturing Thomson-CSF's ground-to-air missiles and moved its operations from the U.S. to Europe in 1991. Another business venture with DASA, Alcatel Espace, and Alenia joined with Airod and Ofema companies to supply work and materials for French helicopters in Malaysia. The ATR joint venture made a bid for Boeing's Canadian subsidiary De Havilland, but the European Commission squashed the acquisition on the grounds that ATR would have a monopoly on 20-70 seat passenger planes. The helicopter divisions of Aerospatiales and DASAs merged to form Eurocopter Holdings.

In 1992, the French government owned over 93% of Aerospatiale's stock. Over 1,000 jobs were eliminated due to a decrease in military orders caused by the end of the Cold War. The S-45 and Hades lines of nuclear missiles were discontinued. Credit Lyonnais SA, a French government-owned bank, boosted Aerospatiale's capital by purchasing 20% of its stock. By the mid-1990s, the firm was considered a world leader in the development and manufacture of aerospace equipment, as well as Europe's most diversified aerospace firm.

However, European governments continued to reduce defense spending causing extensive job cuts at Aerospatiale throughout the decade. As a result, the firm began shifting its attention from aerospace technology to other ventures, such as high speed railroads and air-traffic control networks. In 1995, the missile and satellite operations of Aerospatiale and Daimler-Benz Aerospace AG of Germany were combined in a post Cold War consolidation effort. In 1996, plans for a merger of Aerospatiale and Dassault, including the privatization of Aerospatiale, were announced. Cost cutting efforts paid off for Aerospatiale in the form of a positive debt-to-equity ratio for the first time in several years. In late 1998, the French government transferred its 46% share of Dassault to Aerospatiale and announced its intention to merge Aerospatiale with Lagardere's aerospace operations, Matra Hautes Technologies, by the middle of 1999.

History of Dassault Aviation SA

In 1919, while working in a converted garage, aeronautical engineer Marcel Bloch developed his first product, the Eclair, a variable pitch propellor that allowed for high maneuverability. The Spad VII, XII, and XIII series of fighter planes used an improved Eclair propellor during World War I. Roughly a decade later, Bloch made the MB 60, a plane that served the airmail industry well for long flights. In 1931, Bloch improved on the MB 60 with the MB 120 Colonial, a plane capable of carrying passengers and freight. The MB 80, Bloch's first all metal plane, was designed in 1932 and used as a medical evacuation aircraft.

Throughout the 1930s and 1940s, Bloch constructed several new products, including the MB 200, which was designed with high wings and twin engines. The MB 210, originally designed as a seaplane, sold miserably, but with the addition of fixed or retractable landing gear, about 200 were sold to various European air forces. Bloch also developed, but did not produce, the MB 300 Pacific, designed to satisfy Air France's need for a long distance passenger plane. Instead, he worked to develop the MB 220, which was soon produced in mass quantities. Air France used the 220 almost exclusively for its midrange, European passenger flights.

In 1937, Bloch's aircraft manufacturing operations were nationalized by the newly empowered "Popular Front" party. One of the six state-controlled aviation interests, Societe Nationale de Constructions Aeronautiques de Sud-Ouest (SNCASO), took over Bloch's factories. Later that year, the MB 150 fighter plane flew for the first time. Along with the 151s, 152s, and 155s, the 150s comprised France's air force for several years. The MB 160, an experimental four-engine plane, established new records for freight carried and distance flown. An alternate version, the MB 161 Languedoc, was used by French and Polish airlines and the French Navy.

The first of more than 1,000 aircraft in the MB 174 series were produced in 1938. With oblique wing ribs and other engineering innovations, the 174s had extraordinary altitude and speed capabilities. In 1939, Bloch's MB 140 was developed, but its plans and prototype were destroyed at the advent of World War I to prevent the Germans from gaining access to the technology. Germany offered to make Bloch an "honorary Aryan" if he would build planes for them; after refusing the offer, Bloch went into hiding. The Germans arrested and imprisoned Bloch in 1944 before sending him to the Buchenwald concentration camp where he contracted diphtheria. Fortunately, the Allied forces freed the survivors at Buchenwald the following year. During the war, Bloch's brother, Darius-Paul, had distinguished himself during the French resistance efforts and earned the nickname "tank" or "char d'assault." Respect for his brother's efforts prompted Marcel Bloch to change his last name to Dassault and his company's name to Avions Marcel Dassault.

After recruiting young engineers to help refurbish his war torn company, Dassault was able to work on plans that originated in secret during the German occupation. One of these projects, the MD 315 liaison airplane, required the construction of a new facility in Merignac near Bordeaux. At this time, Dassault began his policy of allowing subcontractors to make some parts, but he reserved the tooling, final assembly, and flight testing for his firm. The first MD 315s were completed in 1949, and Dassault made its first jet fighter plane, the MD 450 Ouragan, or Hurricane. Two years later, Dassault used the Ouragan body as the basis for the Mystere I jet. In 1952, with an American pilot in the cockpit, the Mystere II broke the sound speed barrier in a level flight; it was the first European plane to do so. The first Mirage fighter-interceptor aircraft, the MD 550 Mystere Delta, was produced in 1955. In 1956, the French Air Force gained interceptor, ground attack, reconnaissance, and training aircraft capable of Mach 2 before any other air force in the world when the Mirage III made its first flight.

The Breguet 1001 fighter/bomber was introduced

The Players

Chairman Aerospatiale SA: Yves Michot. Aerospatiale hired Yves Michot in 1984 as vice president of military programs. The following year, he was promoted to corporate vice president of civilian and military programs. Two years later, he accepted the post of corporate executive vice president. Michot added chief operating officer duties to his plate in 1989; in 1995, he took over as president of helicopter operations. The French Council of Ministers appointed Michot chairman of the board in August of 1996, handing him the task of steering the merger of Aerospatiale and Dassault.

Chairman and CEO of Dassault Aviation SA: Serge Dassault. Founder Marcel Dassault decided in the mid-1960s to turn Dassault's electronics operations into a full-fledged company, l'Electronique Marcel Dassault, to make flight electronics. He chose his son, Serge Dassault, to head up the new business. When Marcel Dassault died in 1986, Serge Dassault was appointed chairman of the board by company directors. As leader of the second largest aerospace firm in France, Dassault became a powerful figure in France's aviation industry. His position was weakened in 1996, however, by his implication in Belgium's Augusta affair, which involved allegations of bribery used to secure an electronic defense systems contract with the Belgian air force.

and set a speed record in 1957. Dassault was also given the honor of developing the Etendard IVM, the aircraft destined to be the first plane taking off from France's first aircraft carrier, the Clemenceau. A year later, Dassault was elected to France's Parliament as a representative of the Beauvais region. The firm began manufacturing Etendard IVMs for use on the Clemenceau and the Foch.

The strategic bomber, Mirage IV, made its first flight as Europe's first aircraft capable of sustaining speeds up to Mach 2 by the end of the decade. To manufacture electronic equipment suitable for such a plane, Dassault improved its own department of electronics; the division was soon transformed into a complete electronics company, l'Electronique Marcel Dassault, to make flight electronics and, later, automatic teller machines. France became responsible for its own military development when it backed out of NATO in 1966; this move helped Dassault immeasurably. Pan Am decided to rename the Mystere 20 "Falcon," a name that was eventually used in English speaking countries.

In 1968, Avions Marcel Dassault merged with Breguet Aviation to become Avions Marcel Dassault-Breguet Aviation. The transaction gave Dassault a hand in Breguet's Jaguar tactical support and combat plane sold in France, the United Kingdom, and elsewhere. Dassault-Breguet's 20 factories controlled 35% of France's aerospace industry. The Mercure, built with $280 million in credit to compete with Boeing's 737, flew for the first time in 1971. Two years later, Dassault-Breguet entered a joint venture with Dornier to make Alpha Jet trainers in France and West Germany. In 1976, authorities discovered that Herve de Vathaire, the firms's financial director, had embezzled Ffr8 million. Documents implicating Dassault for tax evasion also surfaced during the investigation.

By the end of the decade, socialist and communist party politicians had gained enough influence in France's Parliament to initiate nationalization plans for the country's aviation interests. The French government paid about $128.5 million for a 21% holding, 33% voting interest, and veto power over Dassault's business decisions. In 1980, Dassault-Breguet bought out Pan Am's share in Falcon Jet Corp. to make it a wholly owned subsidiary. The following year, the French government bought an additional 25% of Dassault-Breguet stock to increase its voting power to 63%.

In 1985, the Committee Nationale d'Etudes Spatiales chose Dassault-Breguet to be a subcontractor to Aerospatiale in the Hermespace program intended to develop a space shuttle. The company's name was officially changed to Dassault Aviation in 1990. As part of a continued defense industry downsizing effort in the mid-1990s, the French government announced plans to merge Dassault with Aerospatiale SA in 1996. After anticipating problems with the wide scope of France's aviation consolidation efforts, however, the government decided in 1997 to postpone the merger until the Airbus restructuring taking place was completed. In December of 1998, the French government transferred its 46% share of Dassault to Aerospatiale, which was in the process of merging with Lagardere's Matra Hautes Technologies.

Market Forces Driving the Merger

Defense industry performance took a worldwide tumble after the end of the Cold War. Sluggish sales and shrinking orders prompted widespread industry consolidation throughout the 1990s. To compete with the emerging U.S. defense giants, such as Boeing Co. and Lockheed Martin Corp., European companies were forced to consider growth via merger as a means of staying competitive. For example, Aerospatiale and Daimler-Benz Aerospace AG of Germany combined their missile and satellite operations in 1995 hoping to streamline operations and reduce costs.

In June of 1996, French President Jacques Chirac met with German chancellor Helmut Kohl to discuss further consolidation of the Franco-German defense industry. A merger between Aerospatiale and Dassualt that included the privatization of Aerospatiale would pave the road for possible future consolidation with other European aerospace firms.

Also, although four times larger than Dassault, Aerospatiale had been losing money throughout the early 1990s. After cropping its workforce by 17% and lightening its debt equity ratio from 16:4 to 3:4, Aerospatiale was better positioned for consolidation than it had been in years.

Looking to further improve Aerospatiale's performance, to shore up France's position in the worldwide defense market, and to contribute to Europe's defense industry cooperation efforts, French President Jacques Chirac decided in 1996 to merge his country's two leading aircraft manufacturers. Although, Dassault executives reacted negatively to Chirac's order, most analysts believed that a merger would benefit Dassualt, whose future had been uncertain after it spent years developing its Rafale combat aircraft, which was still flying only as a prototype at the time of the merger decree. Allowing Dassault to diversify into commercial transport sector would supply the firm's design bureau with needed workload.

Approach and Engagement

When Dassault executives reacted negatively to the merger order, Chirac threatened to nationalize Dassault if the privately held firm resisted consolidation. Aerospatiale CEO Michot and Serge Dassault became locked in a power struggled over who would emerge as leader of the merged group. Also of concern to the Dassault family was the size of their stake in the combined company. French tax law required that individual equity in a company must be greater that 25% to avoid being added to taxable personal net worth.

Further complicating the transaction were complicated plans for combining the two workforces. For example, Dassault's design bureau was to remain separate and its employees would be granted more benefits than their colleagues. Also, Aerospatiale's Toulouse-based Airbus facility would not be made to merge.

In 1997, new Socialist Prime Minister Lionel Jospin temporarily reversed plans to privatize Aerospatiale; by the end of the year, the French government, anticipating problems with the wide scope of France's aviation consolidation efforts, decided to postpone the merger until the Airbus restructuring taking place was completed. Also, problems such as how to integrate Dassault's Rafale combat aircraft and the Aerospatiale's Eurofight had yet to be solved. Most analysts agree that the merger will happen and that its outcome will be positive; speculation now focuses more on its timing than its likelihood.

In July of 1998, Aerospatiale and Largardere's defense unit, Matra Hautes Technologies, agreed to merge into the world's fifth largest aerospace firm. Terms of the agreement stipulated that Aerospatiale would be privatized, and Lagardere would end up holding a 33% stake in the new firm, which would list on the stock exchange upon completion of the transaction, scheduled for mid-1999. In December of 1998, the French government escalated its Aerospatiale/Dassault consolidation efforts by transferring its 46% share of Dassault to Aerospatiale.

Products and Services

Prior to its merger with Matra Hautes Technologies, Aerospatiale was reorganized into two segments: Aircraft, which comprised Airbus, ATR, Socata, Sogerma, and Eurocopter; and Space and Defense, which included Strategic Missiles and Launch Vehicles, Tactile Missiles, and Systems Engineering and Information Technology. Both Strategic Missiles and Launch Vehicles and Tactile Missiles were scheduled to be spun off as wholly owned subsidiaries in early 1999.

The aerospace conglomerate comprised more than 30 companies, including subsidiary Arianespace, which created the Ariane 5 rocket to launch commercial satellites. Exports made up roughly 75% of total revenues. Along with its 40% stake in airline manufacturer Airbus Industrie, Aerospatiale owned 46% of Dassault Aviation. Dassault derived more than 85% of its sales from aircraft exports, including its Falcon business jets and Mirage combat jets. Other sectors included space programs—the firm designed the Ariane 5 rocket's telemetry system and firing equipment—computing, and electronics.

Changes to the Industry and Review of the Outcome

By transferring its 46% stake in Dassault to Aerospatiale, the French government brought the two firms closer to a merger than ever before. The French Ministry of Defense pointed to the consolidation move as an effort to "further the implementation of a concerted strategy for the French aerospace industry in the prospect of alliances with the main European manufacturers which seem necessary in the short term." Eventually joining these two firms will give the French industry added negotiation muscle with other European defense concerns over the long haul as well, according to Defense Deputy Jean-Michel Boucheron.

Reflecting what has become a widely accepted view of the merger, Aerospatiale CEO Michot describes the impending deal as a "technological, commercial, and strategic necessity." Consolidation is key if France wants to compete in the European and/or worldwide defense markets. When the Aerospatiale/Matra Hautes Technologies merger is finalized and Aerospatiale-Matra and Dassault finally combine operations, the aerospace giant will employ a total of 66,000 employees and generate roughly $18 billion in revenues as the fourth largest aerospace firm in the world.

Research

"Aerospatiale," in *Notable Corporate Chronologies*, The Gale Group, 1999. Lists major events in the history of Aerospatiale.

Aerospatiale Home Page, available at http://www.aerospatiale.fr Official World Wide Web Home Page for Aerospatiale. Includes news, financial, product, and historical information.

"Aerospatiale Won't Be Privatized," in *Industry Week*, 8 August 1997. Discusses French Prime Minister Lionel Jospin's decision to not privatize Aerospatiale.

Clarke, Hilary. "An Arms Plot Thriller that Rivals Fiction," in *The European*, 16 May 1996. Details the indictment of Serge Dassault for alleged bribery activities in Belgium's Augusta scandal.

"Dassault Aviation SA," in *Notable Corporate Chronologies*, The Gale Group, 1999. Lists major events in the history of Dassault Aviation SA.

Dassault Aviation SA Home Page, available at http://www.dassault-avaition.fr Official World Wide Web Home Page for Dassault Aviation SA. This site includes news, financial, product, and historical information.

"French Aerospace Industry Accelerates Consolidation, Aviation Week Reports," in *Business Wire*, 15 May 1998. Announces the French government's decision to transfer its 46% stake in Dassault to Aerospatiale.

MacRae, Duncan. "The Not-So-Urgent Merger," in *Interavia Business & Technology*, December 1997. Covers the various reasons for the merger's long delay.

Moxon, Julian. "Dassault/Aerospatiale Marriage Moves Closer," in *Flight International*, 5 June 1996. Outlines the reasons for the merger, including potential alliances with the German aerospace industry.

Sparaco, Pierre. "French Aerospace in Merger Hustle," in *Aviation Week & Space Technology*, 11 November 1998.

Comments on the merger between Aerospatiale and Matra Hautes Technologies.

Tillier, Alan. "The Uneasy Marriage of Dassault," in *The European*, 2 February 1996. Analyzes Dassault's objections to the merger with Aerospatiale.

Verchere, Ian. "French Aerospace Merger Still Waiting for Clearance," in *The European*, 6 March 1997. Discusses major hurdles being faced in the Dassault/Aerospatiale merger negotiations.

"Yves Michot Named Chairman of Aerospatiale," in *Defense Daily*, 8 August 1996. Provides a brief history of Yves Michot's career at Aerospatiale.

ANNAMARIE L. SHELDON

AETNA & U.S. HEALTHCARE

nationality: USA
date: July 1996
affected: Aetna Life and Casualty Co., USA, founded 1853
affected: U.S. Healthcare Inc., USA, founded 1975

Aetna Inc.
151 Farmington Ave.
Hartford, CT 06156

tel: (860)273-0123
fax: (860)275-2677
web: http://www.aetna.com

Overview of the Merger

The joining of health insurer Aetna Life and Casualty Co. with health maintenance organization (HMO) U.S. Healthcare Inc. marked the largest consolidation move in the history of the health management industry. In fact, the $8.9 billion merger was larger than the combined value of all managed care transactions that took place during the three years preceding it. The deal also reflected a new trend in the healthcare industry: bundling managed care capabilities with traditional indemnity products. Completed in July of 1996, the merger created the second largest managed health care provider in the U.S.

History of Aetna Inc.

Lawyer Eliphalet Bulkeley founded Connecticut Mutual Life Insurance in 1846. Agents secured control of the company and usurped Bulkeley the following year. Along with a group of businessman, Bulkeley then established Aetna Life Insurance Co. in 1853; the fledgling firm was a spin off from Aetna Fire Insurance Co. and legally separated from Aetna Insurance Co.

In 1868, Aetna became the first company to offer renewable term life insurance policies. Throughout the late 1800s and early 1900s, the firm diversified into accident, health, workers' compensation, automobile, and property insurance. In 1913, Aetna sold its first group policy to a New York fabric manufacturer. The firm soon began offering ocean and marine insurance; by 1922, it was largest multiple insurance provider in the U.S.

World War I provided the company with opportunities to offer insurance to servicemen and their families. In 1922, Aetna organized a rehabilitation clinic to speed its clients recovery from injuries. The Great Depression took a toll on the firm because insurance companies proved to be a major source of cash to policyholders. Aetna directors, officers, and employees took a 10% pay reduction, but no employees were dismissed. The company recovered during World War II by providing workmen's compensation and liability insurance for the Manhattan Project, which produced the first atomic weapon. At that time, Aetna began insuring the construction of aircraft carriers.

The Business

Financials

Revenue (1998): $20.6 billion

Employees (1997): 40,300

SICs / NAICS

sic 6331 - Fire, Marine & Casualty Insurance

sic 6311 - Life Insurance

sic 6321 - Accident & Health Insurance

sic 6324 - Hospital & Medical Service Plans

naics 524126 - Direct Property and Casualty Insurance Carriers

naics 524113 - Direct Life Insurance Carriers

naics 524114 - Direct Health and Medical Insurance Carriers

In the 1960s, Aetna gained recognition by insuring the lives of the first seven astronauts, paying the first U.S. Medicare claim, and joining with an Italian company, Assicurazioni Generali, to provide insurance to businesses in more than 70 countries. In 1967, Aetna Life and Casualty became the parent company for the corporation; a year later, it was listed on the New York Stock Exchange, and diversification began in earnest.

In 1981, Aetna Life and Casualty reorganized along market lines: Commercial, Employee Benefits, Personal Finance Security, and Diversified Business operations were formed. The following year the company acquired 87% of Federated Investors, the second-largest manager of money markets and mutual funds in the U.S., and oil services operation Geosource. Both acquisitions were later divested when Aetna's leaders realized the company's focus was becoming too scattered.

In 1989, CIGNA sold rights to the "Aetna" name—acquired in an earlier merger involving Aetna Insurance Co.—eliminating the confusion over two "Aetnas." Roughly 8,000 jobs were cut in 1991, and the firm began divesting peripheral operations, such as its auto insurance arm. To capitalize on the burgeoning retirement savings market, Aetna established AE Trust Co. as a means of offering pension trustee services to clients. After deciding to focus more closely on its health insurance operations, Aetna divested its property/casualty operations to Travelers Corp. in 1996. Aetna also purchased U.S. Healthcare Inc. for a record

$8.9 billion and became Aetna Inc., one of the largest health insurance providers in the U.S.

The firm sold its behavioral managed care operations to Magellan Health Services in 1997 and its individual life insurance unit to Lincoln National in 1998. That year, Aetna also negotiated its $1 billion purchase of New York Life Insurance Co.'s health care business, NYLCare, and initiated merger discussions with the healthcare operations of Prudential Insurance. The American Medical Association challenged the deal, citing antitrust concerns. However, the purchase was approved and finalized in early 1999, propelling Aetna into the number one spot among HMO firms in the U.S., with more than 22 million members.

History of U.S. Healthcare Inc.

In 1975, Leonard Abramson borrowed $2.5 million from the federal government to start his own health maintenance organization (HMO). A year later, the Commonwealth of Pennsylvania granted Abramson a license to operate his business, called the Health Maintenance Organization of Pennsylvania, or HMO-PA. The company qualified for federal certification as a non-profit, community-based operation, with less than 20,000 members enrolled.

In 1982, HMO-PA converted to a profit-earning entity and took United States Health Care Systems, Inc. as its official name. With 126,000 members, it was the fastest growing HMO in the country. The following year, the firm made its first public stock offering and used the acquired funds to expand geographically into New Jersey. Following another stock offering in 1984, United States Health Care bought 51% of Chicago Health Care Systems and formed HMO Great Lakes.

Although the firm reduced its prices in an effort to attract members, it still failed to meet its enrollment goals. Profits fell along with stock prices. Fortunately, United States Health Care received permission to provide healthcare programs to senior citizens eligible for Medicare benefits, and in 1985, the firm formed an alliance with the Lincoln National Corp., an Indiana-based insurance holding company. As a result year-end profits reached a record high of $24.5 million. The company changed its name in 1986, simplifying it to U.S. Healthcare, Inc. Lincoln National and U.S. Healthcare launched an HMO called HealthWin; U.S. Healthcare later sold its stake in this venture back to Lincoln. In 1987, a pharmaceutical subsidiary called U.S. Bioscience, Inc. was created to do cancer drug research and development. Dental services were also offered through U.S. Healthcare. Stock prices that year dropped sharply, and the firm posted a significant loss.

Hoping to return to profitability, the firm instituted a physician quality incentive program and created its Corporate Health Administrator subsidiary to serve another segment of the medical services market. In 1989, six former members of the company's Pennsylvania plan filed suit, charging U.S. Healthcare with defrauding its enrollees by failing to inform them that plan doctors were discouraged from referring patients to specialists. The company maintained that its operations complied with all state and federal regulations. Membership reached one million and sales were up to $1 billion.

U.S. Healthcare created U.S. Quality Algorithms Corp. in 1990 to study medical practice patterns and the billing of contracted healthcare providers. Hoping to increase its customer services efficiency, the company banned memos and meetings during the business day and eliminated the use of titles within the organization. Mental health and substance abuse subsidiary U.S. Mental Health Systems was also established that year.

By the mid-1990s, U.S. Healthcare was one of America's largest HMOs, serving 1.3 million members in eight northeastern states. The firm developed its "Primary Care Office Report Card" to assist customers in choosing a primary care physician. U.S. Healthcare also changed its physicians' contracts so that physician-patient communication was encouraged. The revision was made in an effort to quell public concern about the HMO's so-called 'gag rules' prohibiting physicians from discussing treatments not covered by the HMO or from referrals to specialists not in their HMO.

In 1996, the company was ordered to pay a $1.6 million fine to Brokerage Concepts Inc. for violating antitrust laws. The company was found guilty of using its market position to pressure a contracting pharmacy into subscribing to its services. Later that year, U.S. Healthcare merged with Aetna Life and Casualty Co. to become Aetna Inc. The $8.9 billion transaction created a new leader in the managed health care sector.

Market Forces Driving the Merger

The Aetna/U.S. Healthcare merger was announced amidst a flurry of consolidation in both the health insurance and managed care markets. Securities Data Co. estimated the value of healthcare consolidation in 1996 at roughly $77 billion. The reason for the increase in activity was twofold. HMOs found themselves unable to continue raising prices each year. As a result, they began looking for ways to increase unit growth and reduce costs, both potential outcomes of consolidation. At the same time, tradi-

The Officers

Chairman of the Board, President, and Chief Executive Officer: Richard L. Huber

Vice Chairman and Chief Financial Officer: Alan J. Weber

Exec. VP and President, Aetna U.S. Healthcare: Michael J. Cardillo

Exec. VP and President, Aetna International: Frederick C. Copeland Jr.

Exec. VP and President, Aetna Retirement Services: Thomas J. McInerny

tional insurance firms were rapidly losing ground to managed care companies, which had enrolled one fifth of all Americans in their plans by the mid-1990s. Many insurance firms began either exiting the industry—Travelers, Metropolitan and Lincoln all sold their medical operations—or seeking ways to diversify into managed care.

The success of "point of service" managed care was also a factor in the market. This healthcare option offered members out-of-network benefits via a discounted preferred provider organization (PPO), similar to the more traditional indemnity insurance model. Companies began to realize that a certain chunk of their market was willing to pay for the ability to choose doctors and hospitals. The most successful firms, it seemed, would need to offer a wide range of products to clients, particularly large employers who wanted to offer employees several health care options. One of the first mergers to reflect this trend took place in 1995 when HMO United Healthcare bought MetraHealth, formed in 1994 when Travelers Insurance and Metropolitan Life Insurance merged their struggling indemnity healthcare operations, for $2 billion.

Aetna already offered successful indemnity services. To enter managed care, however, the firm needed to purchase a solid HMO company. U.S. Healthcare, a leader in managed care, boasted in excess of two million members, state-of-the-art information systems, and highly regarded cost controlling measures, as evidenced by 1995 earnings of $381 million on only $3.6 billion in revenues, compared to Aetna's $474 million in net income from a whopping $13 billion in sales. A merger with U.S. Healthcare would also allow Aetna to retain its large corporate accounts via a managed care option it previously couldn't offer.

The Players

Chairman and CEO of Aetna Life and Casualty Co.: Ronald E. Compton. At the age of 20, Ronald E. Compton began a career at Aetna that would span four decades. He gradually worked his way up through the firm until he was appointed president in 1988. Three years later, Compton took over as chairman and CEO. While at the helm, he steered Aetna away from property/casualty operations and towards the more lucrative managed health care market by orchestrating two of the firms most noteworthy transactions: the $4 billion divestiture of Aetna's property/casualty line to Traveler's Corp. in late 1995, and the $8.9 billion merger with health maintenance organization U.S. Healthcare in 1996. Compton headed up the newly merged firm, known as Aetna Inc. On March 1, 1998, Compton retired; he was succeeded by current Aetna chairman, president, and CEO Richard L. Huber.

Chairman and CEO of U.S. Healthcare Inc.: Leonard Abramson. In 1975, Leonard Abramson founded his own health maintenance organization (HMO), which later became U.S. Healthcare Inc., one of the first managed care companies in the U.S. The 32-year-old entrepreneur was soon steering one of the country's leading HMOs; his hands-on management style, along with his dedication to capped provider contracting and gatekeeping, earned his company recognition as a model among other HMO companies. While negotiating his firm's merger with Aetna, Abramson agreed to relinquish control of U.S. Healthcare, accepting a $1 billion compensation package—which made him Aetna's largest individual stockholder—a seat on the new company's board, and consulting duties.

U.S. Healthcare recognized that it would also benefit from a consolidation move. The HMO had cut its fees in 1995 to retain market share in the increasingly competitive market, and it was facing rising medical expenses; in fact, medical spending had jumped from 68.2% of total costs in 1994 to 77% when the merger was negotiated. The firm needed to tighten its clinical management of providers, and according to managed care investment bank Sherlock, the merger would allow U.S. Healthcare to ask doctors and hospitals to control medical spending and "blame that on Hartford [Aetna], rather than accepting the blame themselves." U.S. Healthcare also believed it would benefit from Aetna's broad national distribution system, including a wide base of corporate customers, and the firm's marketing and administrative competence.

Approach and Engagement

In the early 1990s, Aetna's property/casualty business held a ninth place spot its market segment, while Aetna's health insurance company ranked second or third in its sector. Concluding that his firm would benefit from a more centralized focus, Aetna CEO Compton began reorganizing Aetna in 1995 by divesting property/casualty operations to Travelers Corp. The $4 billion Aetna secured from the deal allowed the company to begin its diversification into managed care.

Believing that the growing HMO market had only just begun its climb, Compton began hunting for a managed care acquisition, and he and U.S. Healthcare CEO Abramson began negotiations in early 1996. Aetna and U.S. Healthcare officially announced their intent to merge on April 1, 1996, the same day that the Travelers deal secured regulatory approval. According to the terms of the deal, U.S. Healthcare shareholders would receive roughly $57 per share, a 24% premium over the firm's closing price of $45.88 the day prior to the deal's announcement. U.S. Healthcare shareholders would own 22% of the combined company; Aetna shareholders, 78%. Aetna Life and Casualty and U.S. Healthcare would retain their names, operating as units of Aetna Inc. Both boards overwhelmingly approved the deal, which was finalized during July of 1996.

Products and Services

After its merger, Aetna continued to refine its focus on managed care operations. Aetna's subsidiaries, in 1999, included Aetna International, Aetna U.S. Healthcare, Aetna Retirement Systems, and U.S. Quality Algorithms. The company offered group and individual healthcare plans, such as indemnity insurance, PPOs, and HMOs; annuities; individual retirement and asset management services; group pensions and pension plan management services; group life insurance for U.S. customers; and individual life insurance for international clients. Future product plans included continuing to reducing emphasis on life insurance operations and pulling away from the Medicare-based business.

Changes to the Industry

Most analysts believed that the Aetna/U.S. Healthcare deal would spark future consolidation among both traditional insurance companies and

HMOs. According to John Ward of Ward Financial Group, "there are other life insurance companies that are looking to make investments in the managed care business. They may or may not choose to make a big investment to follow suit, but at a minimum it will cause them to revisit their strategy just by the sheer size of the transaction." And industry analyst Ken Laudan of Hambrecht & Quist pointed out that HMOs, "now have kind of an implied mandate that they're going to have to develop this regional strength as well, and the only way to do that is acquisition."

To stay competitive in the late 1990s, indemnity and managed care firms needed to grow via merger as a means of levying concessions from doctors and hospitals, producing the capital to invest in new technologies, and offering large employers inexpensive and comprehensive services. As a result, following the Aetna/U.S. Healthcare merger, several similar billion dollar transactions were finalized in the industry. For example, PacificCare Health Systems Inc. became the fifth largest HMO in the U.S. when it bought FHP Corp. for $2.2 billion in February of 1997. Also, Cigna Corp. paid $1.7 billion for managed care provider Healthsource Inc. in March of 1997. Finally, Foundation Health Corp. took forth place among U.S. HMOs when it purchased Health Systems International for roughly $3 billion in April of 1997.

Future consolidation was certainly in the cards for Aetna. After its 1996 overhaul, the firm sold both its behavioral managed care operations and its individual life insurance unit and purchased New York Life Insurance Co.'s health care business, NYLCare, as well as the healthcare operations of Prudential Insurance. At the beginning of 1999, Aetna was the largest HMO firm in the U.S., with over 22 million members.

Review of the Outcome

Combining Aetna's national reach with the managed care expertise of U.S. Healthcare seemed a synergistic marriage, and by August of 1997, stock prices had climbed from $75 per share when the deal was first announced to $144 per share. Many analysts, though, believed that Aetna and U.S. Healthcare faced a difficult task in blending their two disparate corporate cultures. U.S. Healthcare was known for its aggressive sales tactics and management style, while Aetna was recognized for friendly member service.

Acknowledging that U.S. Healthcare was better at controlling costs, Aetna decided to follow the HMO's management style, hoping to realize an estimated $300 million in savings within 18 months of the merger. Consolidating this quickly, however, caused problems for Aetna with both patients and doctors; the

firm had laid off a number of employees, and a number of claims went unprocessed for quite some time. Earnings tumbled a bit, and stock prices dropped back to roughly $75 by the end of 1997. As a result, the firm decided to integrate its next purchase, NYLCare, more gradually.

Research

"Aetna Inc.," in *Notable Corporate Chronologies,* The Gale Group, 1999. Lists major events in the history of Aetna Inc., including the merger.

Aetna Inc. Home Page, available at http://www.aetna.com. Official World Wide Web Home Page for Aetna Inc. Includes news, financial, product, historical, and employment information.

"Aetna Life & Casualty Co.," in *Best's Review-Life-Health Insurance Edition,* September 1996. Details the terms of the merger after both boards approved the deal.

"Aetna Taps Vice Chairman as New President, CEO," in *Best's Review-Life-Health Insurance Edition,* September 1997. Focuses on the appointment of Aetna's new president and CEO, Richard L. Huber, after Ronald Compton announced his retirement.

Gonzales, Angela. "Aetna Scores, Doctors Sour," in *The Business Journal-Serving Phoenix & the Valley of the Sun,* 9 August 1996. Discusses reactions to U.S. Healthcare founder Leonard Abramson's compensation package for the merger, which was announced at the same time doctors' reimbursements were cut by Aetna.

Greenwald, Judy. "Aetna, U.S. Healthcare Deal to Blend Breadth with Savvy," in *Business Insurance,* 8 April 1996. Explains how both Aetna and U.S. Healthcare will benefit from the merger.

Hayes, Jan. "Health: The Merger Frenzy Continued, and HMOs Got Burned By Some Unexpected Cost Increases," in *Forbes,* 13 January 1997. Offers an overview of consolidation activity in the healthcare industry.

Johnsson, Julie. "Insurer-HMO Mega-Merger," in *American Medical News,* 22 April 1996. Compares the Aetna/U.S. Healthcare deal to similar mergers in the healthcare insurance industry.

Prince, Michael. "Ronald Compton: CEO Bets Future Success on Being a Specialist, Not Generalist," in *Business Insurance,* 3 November 1997. In an interview, Compton explains the reasons for Aetna's shift in focus to managed care.

Schachner, Michael. "The Men Behind Aetna Inc.," in *Business Insurance,* 8 April 1996. Profiles both Ronald E. Compton and Leonard Abramson, leaders of Aetna and U.S. Healthcare, respectively, at the time of the merger.

Smart, Tim. "Aetna's Booster Shot: An $8.9 Billion Merger Makes it No. 1 in Managed Care," in *Business Week,* 15 April 1996. Discusses the anticipated results of the merger.

———. "Moving Mount Aetna: What It Will Take to Make the U.S. Healthcare Merger Pay," in *Business Week,* 10 February 1997. Discusses potential problems with the merger and what both companies need to do to realize the benefits of consolidation.

"U.S. Healthcare, Inc.," in *Notable Corporate Chronologies*, The Gale Group, 1999. Lists major events in the history of U.S. Healthcare Inc., including the merger.

"Yet More the Same Medicine: Aetna and U.S. Healthcare," in *The Economist*, 6 April 1996. This article explains why the Aetna/U.S. Healthcare merger is significant.

JEFF ST. THOMAS

AIRTOUCH & MEDIAONE

nationality: USA
date: 1998
affected: AirTouch Communications Inc., USA, founded 1984
affected: MediaOne Group Inc., USA, founded 1984

AirTouch Communications Inc.
1 California St.
San Francisco, CA 94111
USA

tel: (415)658-2000
fax: (415)658-2034
web: http://www.airtouch.com

Overview of the Merger

AirTouch Communications and U S West Media began jointly operating their domestic cellular businesses in 1994. Plans to officially merge the units fell apart in August of 1997 after the two companies failed to meet the deadline to qualify for the "Morris Trust" tax exemption, which was being dismantled by Congress. U S West Media (by then renamed MediaOne Group) and AirTouch renegotiated a deal in early 1998 which allowed AirTouch to double its cellular coverage via the $5.7 billion purchase of MediaOne's New Vector cellular operations. Upon completion of the transaction, AirTouch's stake in PrimeCo, a personal communications services (PCS) joint venture established in 1994 between Bell Atlantic Corp., NYNEX, AirTouch, and Media One, jumped from 25% to 50%. AirTouch also leapt over SBC Communications Inc. into the number two spot among U.S. cellular service providers, behind AT&T Wireless Services

History of AirTouch

PacTel Corp. was established as a subsidiary of Pacific Telesis Group in 1984. It founded PacTel Cellular to provide telecommunications services to the Los Angeles Olympic Games. Within a year, PacTel Cellular provided cellular telephone service to 15,000 subscribers in southern California. In 1986, Pacific Telesis Group acquired Communications Industries, which was reorganized to form PacTel Paging. The following year, PacTel opened an international subsidiary offering regional paging services in Bangkok, Thailand.

In 1991, PacTel began regional marketing of pagers, reaching nontraditional users of wireless telecommunications by opening retail outlets, and formed a joint venture to provide international long-distance communications service to Japan. That same year, Pacific Telesis Group formed PacTel Teletrac to provide tracking services on stolen vehicles for commercial automobile and truck fleets.

In a move designed to take advantage of changes in telecommunications regulations, PacTel Cellular announced its intention in 1992 to spin off from PacTel Corp. to form an independent company called AirTouch Communications.

The Business

Financials

Revenue (1999): $5.41 billion

Employees (1999): 12,642

SICs / NAICS

sic 4812 - Radiotelephone Communications

naics 513322 - Cellular and Other Wireless
    Telecommunications

naics 513321 - Paging

AirTouch pioneered the use of Code Division Multiple Access (CDMA) digital cellular technology, which increased the company's call-handling capacity by 2,000%. The firm invested $50 million to install CDMA technology in California and Georgia and patented its microcell transceiver which improved cellular service in obstructed areas, including major cities.

AirTouch's initial public offering in 1993 raised $1.38 billion, the third largest IPO in American corporate history. (Pacific Telesis retained an 88% interest in the company.) In 1994, the spin-off of AirTouch from Pacific Telesis was completed. AirTouch formed a joint venture with Belgacom, the Belgian state telecommunications company, to provide mobile communications services, and acquired a nationwide two-way radio frequency paging license at a Federal Communications Commission auction, gaining access to new paging systems and services. That year, the firm introduced AirTouch One Number Service, enabling customers to consolidate multiple numbers, and Display Messaging, equipping cellular phones to accept messages while in use. AirTouch also formed a joint cellular venture with U S West and diversified into personal communications services (PCS) by establishing PrimeCo, a PCS joint venture with Bell Atlantic Corp., NYNEX, and U S West.

In 1995, AirTouch announced its intention to invest $275 million in Globalstar, a satellite-based mobile telephone system scheduled to begin operation in 1998. The company also divested PacTel Teletrac and launched cellular operations in Italy and Spain via its new AirTel subsidiary. By the following year, the company had expanded operations into Brazil, the Czech Republic, Poland, and Taiwan; international sales accounted for 25% of the corporate total. U S West Cellular adopted the AirTouch brand name in anticipation of a planned merger of the two compa-

nies, which was called off in 1997 after Congress voted to eliminate the "Morris Trust" tax exemption on large corporate transactions. In 1996, AirTouch also acquired the outstanding interest in Cellular Communications Inc.; forged informal ties with Vodafone of the United Kingdom to increase penetration of European cellular telecommunications markets; and offered paging services in New York City.

Targets of a 1997 class action price fixing lawsuit in Southern California, both AirTouch and L.A. Cellular agreed to a $165 million settlement. In 1998, AirTouch and MediaOne (formerly U S West Media) rekindled their merger plans. AirTouch paid $5.9 billion for the New Vector cellular operations of MediaOne, including its stake in PrimeCo, to become the second largest wireless service provider in the U.S. Late in the year, Bell Atlantic bid $45 billion for AirTouch; Vodafone topped the offer with a $60 billion bid in early 1999, to which AirTouch tentatively agreed.

History of MediaOne Group

The AT&T monopoly was ordered to disband in 1982 after lengthy antitrust litigation. As a result, AT&T Corp. kept its long distance business, but divested its 23 Bell operating companies, which were organized into seven regional Bell operating companies. One of those seven companies, U S West, was formed in 1984; it consisted of Mountain Bell, Northwestern Bell, and Pacific Northwest Bell, as well as the New Vector cellular phone operation. To better serve its customers, the three Bell companies consolidated operations in 1988. That year, the firm expanded internationally via an investment in a French cable television operator. Further international growth ensued, along with diversification into domestic cable television ventures.

In 1991, U S West and TCI agreed to merge their European cable television and telephone operations. Congress lifted restrictions on information services (put in place during the 1984 Bell restructuring); shortly thereafter, U S West diversified in to directory publishing. Two years later, U S West acquired a 25% stake in Time Warner Entertainment and a 13% stake in Time Warner Japan for $2.5 billion. In 1994, the firm purchased two Atlanta, Georgia-based cable operators for roughly $1.2 billion, as well as United Kingdom-based Thomson Directories. U S West also formed a joint cellular venture with AirTouch Communications and diversified into personal communications services (PCS) by establishing PrimeCo, a PCS joint venture, with Bell Atlantic Corp., NYNEX, and AirTouch.

The firm split its stock in 1995 into two groups: U S West Communications Group, which housed local telephone services, and U S West Media Group, which comprised cellular, cable, and directory operations. Both units continued to operate under the U S West Inc. umbrella. U S West Media paid $11.7 billion for Continental Cablevision, Inc. in 1997 and renamed the company MediaOne, which later combined its cable/Internet operations with those of Time Warner. U S West Cellular adopted the AirTouch brand name in anticipation of a planned merger of the two companies, which was called off in August of 1997 after Congress voted to eliminate the "Morris Trust" tax exemption on large corporate transactions.

After synergies between media and phone operations failed to emerge, U S West decided in 1997 to officially split in two. In early 1998, AirTouch and U S West Media, by then the third largest U.S. cable operator, rekindled their merger plans. The firm divested its New Vector cellular operations, as well as its stake in PrimeCo, to AirTouch for $5.7 billion and announced plans to focus on broadband communications. In June of 1998, U S West Media, which transferred its directory operations to U S West Communications and changed its name to MediaOne Group, and U S West Communications became separate public companies.

Market Forces Driving the Merger

According to technology research firm Yankee Group, the number of worldwide cellular phone users will triple by 2005. While many regional players have secured chunks of market share, most analysts predict that the larger mobile telephony firms will be better poised to capitalize on this explosive growth. The reason for this is fairly straightforward: industry competition heated up significantly in 1997, which forced companies like AirTouch to lower rates. In fact, according a February 1998 *Forbes* article, AirTouch's average monthly bill dropped 38% between 1992 and 1997.

To boost earnings in the face of continually declining rates, companies must secure new customers quickly. Acquiring New Vector cellular operations from MediaOne would allow AirTouch to shore up its position in the U.S. wireless market by nearly doubling its existing base of 3.9 million customers and increasing its reach to 17 states. According to AirTouch CEO Ginn, "With this acquisition, AirTouch casts a strong vote of confidence in our industry's future and reinforces our commitment to wireless. By adding the U.S. wireless interests of U S West Media Group, we'll significantly bolster our operating scale and expand our footprint."

U S West saw the divestiture of its New Vector domestic cellular operations to AirTouch as a neces-

The Officers

Chairman and Chief Executive Officer: Samuel Ginn

President and Chief Operating Officer: Arun Sarin

Exec. VP and Chief Financial Officer: Mohan S. Gyani

Sr. VP, Legal and External Affair, and Secretary: Margaret G. Gill

Sr. VP, Marketing: Brian R. Jones

sary step for its restructuring. Acknowledging that the hoped for synergies between cable and telephone had never really emerged, the firm decided in 1997 to officially split in two: U S West Communications would oversee all telephone operations, and U S West Media (later renamed MediaOne) would take over cable holdings and cellular operations. MediaOne then decided to simplify its structure and refocus on core operations, namely broadband communications technology and international wireless telephony. The capital raised from the New Vector sale would allow MediaOne to pursue its goal of offering high-speed Internet, cable television, and telephone services over a single line via broadband networking.

Approach and Engagement

U S West and AirTouch began joint management of their cellular operations in July of 1994. On April 17, 1997, AirTouch agreed to pay $2.3 billion and assume $2.2 billion in debt for the New Vector cellular operations of U S West Media. The deal seemed likely to prove favorable to both firms: AirTouch stock jumped four percent to 24.50 per share and U S West Media stock climbed 2.4% to 17.625 per share when the transaction was announced. However, Congress had recently repealed the "Morris Trust" tax exemption on large corporate transactions, setting a deadline of April 16th for all firms hoping to take advantage of the tax break. AirTouch and U S West Media appealed unsuccessfully for a one-day deadline extension, and rather than pay taxes on the deal, the two firms decided to fall back on the terms of their 1994 agreement and renegotiate at a later date.

Despite the setback, AirTouch continued to perform well; most industry analysts believed the finalization of the transaction was simply a matter of time. In 1997, AirTouch stock closed at a new high of roughly $42 per share. In early 1998, AirTouch agreed to pay $1.6 billion in preferred stock and $2.7 billion in common stock, as well as to assume $1.4 billion of debt for the domestic cellular operations of U S West Media.

The Players

Chairman and CEO of AirTouch: Sam Ginn. In 1994, Pacific Telesis CEO Sam Ginn became chairman and CEO of AirTouch, which was formed when Pacific Telesis spun off its cellular phone and paging operations, known as PacTel Cellular, into an independent company. Ginn oversaw his firm's acquisition of the New Vector cellular operations of MediaOne (formerly U S West Media) in 1998.

Chairman and CEO of MediaOne Group: Charles M. Lillis. At the age of 31, Charles Lillis earned his Ph.D. at the University of Oregon in 1972. After working as a business professor at Washington State University, a general manager for General Electric, and the dean of the University of Colorado Business School, Lillis joined U S West as a vice president of strategic marketing in 1985. Before being tapped to run U S West Media Group in April of 1995, Lillis served the firm as executive vice president and chief planning officer, as well as president of U S West Diversified Group. Lillis is credited for steering the U S West Media (renamed MediaOne Group) divestment of its New Vector cellular operations to AirTouch and narrowing his firm's focus to broadband communications.

The agreement was not subject to shareholder approval and the transaction closed mid-year.

Products and Services

In 1998, AirTouch offered cellular telephone services, paging, and personal communications services (PCS) in the United States and 12 other countries. AirTouch Cellular included Cellular Communications Inc. and CMT Partners, a 50-50 joint venture with AT&T Wireless. Internationally, AirTouch owned minority stakes in the following cellular operations: Spain's Airtel Movil, Belgacom Mobile, Cellular Communications India Ltd., Central Japan Digital Phone Co., Japan's Digital TU-KA, Sweden's Europolitan, Japan's Kansai Digital Phone Co., Germany's Mannesmann Mobilfunk GmbH, Romania's MobilFon, Omnitel-Pronto Italia, Poland's Polkomtel, India's RPG Cellcom Ltd., South Korea's Shinsegi Telecommunications, Portugal's Telecel, and Tokyo Digital Phone Co.

Upon completion of the merger, AirTouch's stake in PrimeCo Personal Communications, LP jumped from 25% to 50%. AirTouch also owned six percent of the Globalstar satellite-based network service; 10% of International Digital Communications, a long-distance provider; 49% of Northstar Paging Holdings Ltd., based in Canada; 18% of Sistelcom-Telemensaje SA, a paging equipment and services provider based in Spain; and 51% of Telechamada-Servico de Chamada de Pessoas SA, a paging equipment and services provider based in Portugal.

Review of the Outcome

The transition period following the acquisition was an unusually smooth one for both entities, mainly because New Vector had operated under the AirTouch brand name for quite some time. AirTouch secured 2.2 million new cellular customers across 12 states, as well as 62,000 new PrimeCo subscribers, and most New Vector employees retained their positions.

AirTouch usurped SBC Communications Inc. as the number two U.S. cellular service provider with roughly 6.1 million cellular customers, behind AT&T Wireless Services Inc., which boasted 8.19 million subscribers. At the time, analysts predicted that widespread industry consolidation in the late 1990's and early in the next century would leave only a handful of leading wireless players standing. Accordingly, Bell Atlantic bid $45 billion for AirTouch in late 1998; Vodafone topped the offer with a $60 billion bid in early 1999, to which AirTouch tentatively agreed.

Consolidation like this, according to industry consultant Steve Sazegari, will benefit customers, as well as wireless corporations themselves: "Eventually, we'll see two or three national wireless entities providing services. For larger corporations that's a plus. They can go to one vendor and get more coverage at more competitive prices." A February 1998 *Computerworld* article explained that many analysts also believed the AirTouch/New Vector deal will "help clear rate confusion, improve coverage, and perhaps reduce prices." For example, the larger firm will be able to offer national discounts and comprehensive services, rather than the fragmented options currently available to many subscribers. Wireless industry analyst Andrew Seybold believes that expanded coverage will dramatically reduce roaming charges as well.

Research

AirTouch Communications Home Page Available at http://www.airtouch.com. Official World Wide Web Home Page for AirTouch Communications. Includes access to annual reports, news, product, and employment information.

"AirTouch Communications Inc.," in *Notable Corporate Chronologies*, The Gale Group, 1999. Covers major historical milestones in the history of AirTouch Communications.

"AirTouch Takes Over U S West Cellular in $5 Billion Transaction," in *Communications Daily*, 21 April, 1997. Outlines planned acquisition details prior to the "Morris Trust" tax exemption glitch.

"AirTouch to Buy U S West Wireless Properties," in *Communications Daily*, 30 January, 1998. Discusses the second attempt by AirTouch to purchase the cellular operations of U S West.

Bouvet, Stephen. "It's Getting Final: AirTouch to Acquire U S West Wireless Properties," in *Mobile Phone News*, 2 February 1998. Details the terms of the 1998 deal between AirTouch and U S West.

Burrows, Peter. "U S West Scouts a New Frontier," in *Business Week*, 18 May 1998. Describes the split of U S West into two separate companies, as well as each firm's new focus.

Cauley, Leslie. "U S West, AirTouch Fail on Exemption," in *The Wall Street Journal*, 30 July 1997. Explains how U S West and AirTouch failed to meet the deadline for the "Morris Trust" tax exemption, and why the deal fell through.

Gibbons, Kent. "U S West Will Split Cable, Phone," in *Multichannel News*, 3 November 1997. Examines the reasons for the split of U S West into two separate companies and the divestment of the New Vector cellular operations.

Girard, Kim. "AirTouch Deal May Clarify Rates," in *Computerworld*, 2 February 1998. Discusses the likely outcome of AirTouch's acquisition of the cellular operations of U.S. West Media.

LaFranco, Robert. "Mobile Telephony: The Sky's the Limit," in *Forbes*, 23 February 1998. Examines the cellular market and the role large companies, including AirTouch, will play in its growth.

Landler, Mark. "AirTouch to Get Cellular Units from U S West in Stock Deal," in *The New York Times*, 19 April 1997. Details reactions to the planned deal 1997 deal between AirTouch and U S West.

MediaOne Group Home Page Available at http://www.mediaonegroup.com. Official World Wide Web Home Page for MediaOne Group. Includes current and archived press releases, historical information, news, product, and employment information.

SAMIT AYERS

AKZO & NOBEL INDUSTRIES

Akzo Nobel NV
Velperweg 76, Postbus 9300
Arnhem, NL-6800 SB
The Netherlands

tel: 85 664433
fax: 85 663250
web: http://www.akzonobel.com

nationality: The Netherlands
date: February 1994
affected: Akzo NV, The Netherlands, founded 1899
affected: Nobel Industries AB, Sweden, founded 1864

Overview of the Merger

Dutch chemical group Akzo NV paid $2.28 billion for financially floundering Swedish chemicals manufacturer Nobel Industries AB in February of 1994. The merger created Akzo Nobel, the world's leading paint manufacturer and the ninth largest chemical company. The new company, headquartered in Arnhem, the Netherlands, also usurped Imperial Chemical Industries PLC as the largest coatings maker in the world. Combined revenues reached roughly $10 billion, operations spanned 50 countries, employees totaled 70,000 people, and products included basic and specialty chemicals, salt, manmade fibers, coatings, and healthcare products.

History of Nobel Industries

In 1863, Alfred Nobel (of the Nobel prize) invented the blasting cap, which made it possible to control the detonation of nitroglycerin. A year later, with the help of J.W. Smitt, a Stockholm merchant, Nobel established Nitroglycerin Ltd. to manufacture the liquid. Nobel invented dynamite in 1867; nine years later, the company created blasting gelatine. In 1887, smokeless gunpowder was added to the company's product line.

Nobel acquired A.B. Bofors-Gullspang, a Swedish munitions factory, in 1894. A year later, Alfred Nobel died. In the mid 1930s, the company gained international recognition when it produced the 40-mm anti-aircraft gun used by both the U.S. and the U.K. during World War II. Following the war, Bofors continued to manufacture armaments primarily for the Swedish government.

In 1965, Nitroglycerin Ltd. changed its name to Nitro Nobel. Five years later, KemaNord chemical group acquired Nitro Nobel and changed its name to KemaNobel. After purchasing numerous shares in Bofors and KemaNobel during the 1970s and early 1980s, businessman Erik Penser gained control of Bofor. In 1984, Penser took over KemaNobel and merged it with Bofor to form Nobel Industries.

Swedish defense electronics firm Pharos was acquired in 1986. That year, Bofor was accused of allegedly paying $60 million in kickbacks to middlemen in connection with a sale to India, but the charges were later dropped. In 1990, Pharos bought the Spectro-Physics subsidary of Ciba-Geigy and the U.K.'s Continental Microwave; the unit then changed its name to Spectra-Physics. The Gillette Company also agreed to sell its European skin and hair care operations to a unit of Nobel.

A year later, when Penser neared financial collapse, all of his holdings were taken over by government bank Securum. Although he eventually fought to regain control of Nobel, Penser lost; in 1992, the company divested its consumer goods operations to Henkel, the German chemicals group, to offset the estimated $1 billion loss posted the year before. Also, Nobel requested that Gamlestaden, Penser's finance company, repay the $319 million it had lent them last year. In 1993, Nobel's defense electronics unit was sold to Celsius Industrier AB who had purchased the company's interest in Swedish Ordnance the year prior. A year later, Netherlands-based Akzo NV purchased Nobel from Securum and formed Akzo Nobel NV.

History of Akzo NV

Germany's Vereingte Glanzstoff-Fabriken, a coatings and rayon manufacturer, was established in 1899. Twelve years later, Nederlandsche Kunstzijdebariek, a rayon maker known as NK, was founded. The two firms merged into Algemene Kunstzijde-Unie, or AKU, in 1929. In 1967, Koninklijke Zout-Ketjen and Koninklijke Zwanenberg Organon merged to form Koninklijke Zout-Organon (KZO). Two years later, AKU merged with KZO, which owned U.S.-based International Salt, to form Akzo.

After spending nearly two decades growing its chemicals, coatings, and pharmaceuticals operations, Akzo launched a major restructuring to cut costs and streamline operations. The firm divested its paper treatment chemicals business to Nobel Industries in 1993. During that year, Akzo also sold its paper coatings division to Morton; acquired the coil coating units of The Dexter Corp.; and established a joint venture with Harcros, called Ackros, to develop PVC additives and similar chemicals.

In 1994, Akzo and Nobel Industries merged to form Akzo Nobel. The company continued to perform well financially, but the accelerating costs of raw material and a poor exchange rate prompted layoffs, closings, and the sale of both the U.S. salt business and the polyethylene packaging resin operations. Some of the firm's rayon operations were relocated to Poland.

The Business

Financials

Revenue (1998): $14.56 billion

Employees (1998): 68,900

SICs / NAICS

sic 2892 - Explosives

sic 2891 - Adhesives & Sealants

sic 2851 - Paints & Allied Products

sic 2812 - Alkalies & Chlorine

sic 2841 - Soap & Other Detergents

sic 3825 - Instruments to Measure Electricity

sic 3845 - Electromedical Equipment

sic 2833 - Medicinals & Botanicals

sic 2834 - Pharmaceutical Preparations

sic 2844 - Toilet Preparations

sic 2816 - Inorganic Pigments

sic 3843 - Dental Equipment & Supplies

naics 325181 - Alkalies and Chlorine Manufacturing

naics 325611 - Soap and Other Detergent Manufacturing

naics 334514 - Totalizing Fluid Meter and Counting Device Manufacturing

naics 334510 - Electromedical and Electrotherapeutic Apparatus Manufacturing

naics 325411 - Medicinal and Botanical Manufacturing

naics 325412 - Pharmaceutical Preparation Manufacturing

naics 325131 - Inorganic Dye and Pigment Manufacturing

naics 339114 - Dental Equipment and Supplies Manufacturing

In 1996, sales in the pharmaceutical segment dipped due to safety warnings issued by European officials related to the Akzo Nobel's birth control bills. That same year, Akzo Nobel released fertility drug Puregon and anti-depressant Remeron. The firm's least lucrative business, fibers, was consolidated into a joint venture with Sabanci, based in Turkey, in 1997. The following year, Akzo Nobel acquired the decorative coatings operations of BASF, known as BASF deco. The firm also bought specialty chemicals manufacturer Courtaulds, based in the U.K., and changed the unit's name to Akzo Nobel UK. Later that year, Akzo Nobel combined its fiber operations with Akzo

The Officers

Chairman: Cees J. A. van Lede

Deputy Chairman: Herman A. van Karnebeek

Group Director, Fibers, and Chief Financial Officer: Fritz Frohlich

Group Director, Pharmaceuticals: Paul K. Brons

Group Director, Coatings: Ove Matteson

Group Director, Chemicals: Rudy M.J. van der Meer

Nobel UK and announced its intention to spin off the new division, named Acordis, in 1999.

Market Forces Driving the Merger

In the mid-1990s, many major paint and coatings players began narrowing their focus and divesting peripheral operations. At the same time, these firms sought acquisitions in key growth markets to increase sales, to grow product lines as a means of upping market share, and to gain access to new customer bases. For example, Imperial Chemical Industries PLC (ICI) decided to hone its broad coatings focus to architectural and automotive refinish markets. As a result, the firm began pursuing relevant acquisitions and divesting non-core units, such as its powder coatings business and its U.S. industrial coatings business.

Akzo completed a restructuring similar to ICI's before it merged with Nobel. The firm divested its paper treatment chemicals to Nobel (not realizing that it would soon merge with Nobel and gain the leverage to succeed in that field) and a portion of its automotive OEM holdings to PPG; purchased a coil coatings business; and established a PVC additives joint venture. Akzo hadn't made a major purchase in quite a while, and according to chemicals analysts at S.C. Warburg & Co., acquiring Nobel would "strengthen the former Akzo's position in chemicals and coatings, which would jointly account for two-thirds of Akzo Nobel's expected 1994 total turnover, further diluting the former Akzo's exposure to low-growth commodities."

Both firms believed their product lines were complimentary; for example, Nobel's wood coatings would mesh well with Akzo's decorative paints, and Akzo's salt and chloralkalai holdings would eliminate Nobel's need to purchase the materials. The merger would provide opportunities for an increased presence in the plastic coatings and powder coatings markets in Europe and the industrial wood finishes and coil coatings markets in North America. While the companies also saw opportunities to reduce costs via increased productivity, as chemicals analyst Bert Zijlmans of F. van Lanschot Bankiers NV pointed out, "the big advantage to both companies of this merger is not the potential for cutting costs, but the opportunities for expanding markets for products like bleaching and paper chemicals and specialty chemicals, as well as coatings."

Approach and Engagement

Sweden's government was pleased to find a buyer for Nobel; state-owned bank Securum had saved the firm from financial ruin in 1991. Most of Nobel's difficulties were the result of problematic Scandinavian real estate holdings, and the firm needed to reduce its debt. In November of 1993, Akzo agreed to purchase the non-real estate holdings of Nobel from the Swedish government for $2.28 billion, or roughly 40 million new Akzo shares, with the stipulation that the government would retain a 20% stake in the newly merged firm for one year following the transaction.

Several analysts balked at the price, believing it too steep for the troubled firm, but Akzo management, which was hoping to avert any counter bids, maintained that the price was reasonable. The firm pointed out that the chemical and coatings operations of Nobel, when separated from the real estate holdings, had performed better than Akzo in the year prior to the merger. Other elements of the transaction also favored Akzo: Securum would pay Akzo over $500 million in cash; the bank also agreed to retain debt burdens for Nobel's 88% stake in Spectra-Physics AB, its 11% share of Celsius Industries AB, and its biotechnology operations. Shareholders granted approval on January 27, 1998, and the deal was finalized by the end of the following month.

Products and Services

After the merger, chemicals and coating operations made up 67% of total revenues and 64% of operating income; coatings accounted for nearly 33% of sales, mainly due to the success of Akzo Nobel's decorative paint operations in Western Europe. Pharmaceuticals earned 17% of total sales, although the segment accounted for roughly 40% of operating income. Fibers contributed 16% to turnover.

Currently, the chemicals segment of the company oversees operation of energy plants and produces the following products: pulp and paper chemicals, base chemicals, functional chemicals, salt, catalysts, and polymers. The coatings group manufactures paints, inks, and other decorative coatings; automotive finishes; and industrials resins and coatings. Pharmaceutical products include birth control, fertility, and menopause drugs; home pregnancy test kits; veterinary drugs; hospital and laboratory supplies; raw materials for pharmaceuticals; and over-the-counter medicines. The least lucrative segment, fibers, was spun off in 1999; it makes flooring and roofing materials, industrial and textile fibers, industrial non-woven fibers, and porous materials and membranes.

Changes to the Industry

The Akzo/Nobel deal created a new leader in the worldwide paint and coating markets. When the merger was completed, Akzo became the largest supplier of pulp bleaching chemicals and the second largest supplier of paper chemicals in the world; the firm landed ninth among worldwide chemical firms. Akzo Nobel's greater size and scope also afforded the firm enhanced negotiating power with suppliers in the industry.

To remain competitive among the largest multinational players in the paint and coatings industry, like Akzo Nobel, other firms found that additional consolidation was necessary. By 1998, the 10 largest paint and coatings companies in the U.S. held roughly 80% of the total market, while the top European and Asian firms had secured roughly 30% of their markets. While U.S. firms were setting the trend in industry consolidation, their international counterparts were determined to follow in their footsteps believing that larger national and global suppliers were better equipped to serve large multinational clients. For example, ICI acquired the European home improvement operations of Williams Co., based in Britain, and Valspar bought businesses in Australia and Ohio.

Perhaps most indicative of the consolidation trend in the paint and coatings industry was Akzo Nobel's $3.1 billion purchase of specialty chemicals manufacturer Courtaulds, based in the U.K., in 1998. According to Akzo Nobel executive Ove Mattsson, the acquisition was necessary for the firm to retain its competitive edge and eventually meet its goal of securing a 20% market share. "To be a worldwide leader, you need to have almost a 20-25% market share in your niche."

Review of the Outcome

The 1994 merger produced immediate benefits for Akzo Nobel. Sales grew by 26%, from a combined $8.5 billion in 1993 (while the companies were still separate) to a total of $12.8 billion in 1994. Net income also rose from $283 million to $680 million, a 34% jump, during the same time frame. Company executives pointed to product and productivity synergies as the

The Players

Chairman of Akzo Nobel: Cees J.A. van Lede. Law graduate Cees J.A. van Lede worked for Shell during the late 1960s and for McKinsey & Company during the early and mid-1970s. In 1977, he took over as chairman of Koninklijke Nederhorst Bouw BV, a Netherlands-based construction firm. When Hollandse Beton Group acquired Nederhorst in 1982, Van Lede accepted a seat on its board. Between 1984 and 1991, he served as chairman of the Federation of the Netherlands Industry. In 1991, Van Lede was elected to Akzo's Board of Management; he took over as vice chairman in 1993. From 1991 to 1994, Van Lede also worked as vice president of the Union of Industrial and Employers' Confederations of Europe. He succeeded Aarnout Loudon as chairman of Akzo in 1994, assuming responsibility for integrating Nobel and Akzo.

Chairman of Akzo NV: Aarnout Loudon. Former Banker Aarnout Loudon was tapped by Akzo in 1981 to steer the firm. During his 11-year tenure as head of Akzo, Loudon orchestrated three full reorganizations which eventually moved the firm away from commodity fibers and towards specialty chemicals. He announced his retirement in 1994, three months after the Akzo/Nobel merger.

Chairman of Nobel Industries AB: Ove Mattsson. Ove Mattsson was running the struggling Nobel Industrier when the Swedish government decided to sell most of it to Akzo NV. Upon completion of the merger, Mattsson accepted a position with Akzo Nobel as group director of coatings operations, the largest segment of the new company.

reason for at least half of the profit growth. Roughly 3,000 positions were eliminated, but the layoffs didn't exceed what Akzo's pre-merger restructuring plans had projected. Stock price in 1994 also reached a new high of 31.88 per share. Although the company's share prices dipped for a while in 1995, due mainly to poor exchange rates and the rising price of raw materials, Akzo Nobel managed to increase sales to a record $13.3 billion and net income to an unprecedented $817 million that year.

Long-term benefits from the merger were realized as well, at least partly because Akzo management yielded to Nobel expertise where it made sense. For example, Nobel's market share in paper and pulp had exceeded that of Akzo, so Nobel management took over that segment. Nobel was also stronger in decorative coatings, particularly in Northern Europe, so Nobel management retained control of their operations, eventually folding in Akzo's assets and employees. According to S.G. Warburg analysts Michael Stone, "This is a rare example of a deal that made sense at the beginning and makes even more sense as time goes by."

Research

"A Fresh Lick of Paint," in *The Economist*, 13 November 1993. Discusses how and why Azko took over Nobel Industries.

"Akzo Looks Forward to Benefits From Merger," in *ECN-European Chemical News*, 3 January 1994. Explains how Akzo will benefit from its merger with Nobel Industries. Includes projected sales percentages for each segment of the combined company.

"Akzo Nobel," in *Notable Corporate Chronologies*, The Gale Group, 1999. Lists major events in the history of Akzo Nobel, including the merger.

"Akzo Nobel Combination Looks Like a Perfect Fit," in *Chemical Marketing Reporter*, 18 April 1994. Explains reasons for the merger, as well as its potential outcomes.

Akzo Nobel Home Page, available at http://www.akzonobel.com. Official World Wide Web Home Page for Akzo Nobel. Includes news, financial, product, and historical information.

"Akzo/Nobel to Oust ICI From Coatings Throne," in *ECN-European Chemical News*, 15 November 1993. Details Akzo Nobel's new position as the world leader in the coatings industry.

D'Amico, Esther. "If Akzo Buys Courtaulds...," in *Modern Paint and Coatings*, June 1998. Discusses how the potential merger between Akzo Nobel and Courtaulds reflects aggressive industry consolidation.

Einhorn, Stephen. "Strategic Moves Driving Mergers: Long-Term Objectives, Regulatory Pressures Seen as Key Factors," in *American Paint and Coatings Journal*, 9 May 1994. Offers an overview of the consolidation movement in the paint and coatings industry, including details about the Akzo/Nobel joining.

La Monica, Paul R. "Industry Winners in the FW International CEO of the Year Contest," in *Financial World*, 20 July 1993. Profiles winners of the CEO of the year award, including Aarnout Loudon, former CEO of Akzo.

"Merger in a Nobel Cause," in *Investors Chronicle*, 12 November 1993. Describes the terms of the transaction, as well as the benefits to Nobel Industries.

Milmo, Sean. "Akzo Nobel Eyes Market Leader Role," in *Chemical Marketing Reporter*, 10 January 1994. Offers an overview of the merger, including the product synergies of the joined operation.

Picker, Ida. "Akzo Nobel's Syb Bergsma: Profiting Through Synergy," in *The M&A Masters in Institutional Investing*, June 1995. Syb Bergsma, the firm's Executive Vice President of Financial Affairs, offers an in-depth look at the various product and production synergies between Akzo and Nobel.

Reier, Sharon. "Akzo: On Second Thought," in *Financial World*, 7 June 1994. Explains why Akzo was willing to pay what some considered a high price for Nobel Industries.

Reisch, Marc. "Akzo and Nobel to Merge in $1.7 Billion Deal," in *Chemical and Engineering News*, 15 November 1993. Covers the announcement by Akzo and Nobel of their intent to merge.

JEFF ST. THOMAS

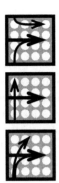

ALLEGHENY LUDLUM & TELEDYNE

nationality: USA
date: August 15, 1996
affected: Allegheny Ludlum Corp., USA, founded 1938
affected: Teledyne, Inc., USA, founded 1960

Allegheny Teledyne Inc.
1000 Six PPG Pl.
Pittsburgh, PA 15222-5479
USA

tel: (412)394-2800
fax: (412)394-3034
web: http://www.alleghenyteledyne.com

Overview of the Merger

In 1996 the specialty metal producer Teledyne Inc. was the target of a hostile takeover attempt by WHX Corp. With its stock prices low and its defenses vulnerable, Teledyne turned to Allegheny Ludlum as a preferred acquirer. Allegheny Ludlum, a leading stainless steel producer, had been interested in certain aspects of Teledyne for many years and took advantage of the timing to merge with the entire company, creating Allegheny Teledyne Inc.

History of Allegheny Ludlum Corp.

Allegheny Ludlum Steel Corp. (ALSC) was formed in 1938 by the merger of two stainless steel makers—Allegheny Steel Co., established in 1898, and Ludlum Steel Co., founded in 1854. The new firm focused on specialty steel. By 1940 its sales reached $37 million, and one decade later they approached $190 million.

ALSC had provided heat-resistant alloys for aircraft engines during World War II. After the war, it turned to production of stainless steel and silicon electrical steel. It developed the industry's first semiautomated system for hot steel. In 1960 Allegheny Ludlum became one of the first U.S. steel companies to engage in overseas steel manufacturing investments with its creation of a Belgian firm.

ALSC acquired True Temper Corp. in 1967, and the following year purchased Jacobsen Manufacturing Co. In 1970 it changed its name to Allegheny Ludlum Industries Inc. The company spun off its steel division in 1976 as a leveraged buyout to existing management. Two years later it bought Wilkinson Match, a producer of consumer products. Allegheny Ludlum decided to divest its specialty metals business, even though those operations generated 70% of company sales.

Richard P. Simmons and Clint Murchison, Jr., organized a management-led leveraged buyout of Allegheny Ludlum for $195 million. Due to stalled last minute negotiations, Murchison backed out and George Tippins took his place in the deal. This leveraged buyout, history's second-largest at that time, was completed on December 26, 1980. Tippins became chairman and Simmons was named president and CEO. In 1981 the company changed its name to Allegheny International, only

The Business

Financials

Revenue (1998): $3.9 billion

Employees (1998): 21,500

SICs / NAICS

sic 3312 - Blast Furnaces & Steel Mills

sic 3316 - Cold-Finishing of Steel Shapes

sic 3322 - Malleable Iron Foundries

sic 3325 - Steel Foundries Nec

sic 3728 - Aircraft Parts & Equipment Nec

sic 3679 - Electronic Components Nec

naics 331221 - Cold-Rolled Steel Shape Manufacturing

naics 331511 - Iron Foundries

naics 331513 - Steel Foundries (except Investment)

naics 336413 - Other Aircraft Part and Auxiliary Equipment Manufacturing

naics 334419 - Other Electronic Component Manufacturing

to change it five years later to Allegheny Ludlum Corp.

The company functioned in stainless and specialty steel. As commodities businesses, they were subject to cyclical fluctuations in the market. The bottom dropped out of the steel market in the early 1980s, and the firm verged on bankruptcy. It recovered in 1984, and began scouting for acquisitions. Through purchases, it gained entry into specialty metals. In 1986 Tippins allowed himself to be bought out by management, relinquishing his 86% share in Allegheny.

Allegheny went public in 1987 to raise capital to pay off debt. That year sales topped the $1 billion mark. Robert Bozzone became president and COO, and Simmons added the post of chairman to his role as CEO. Simmons retired from the latter position in 1990, and was succeeded by Bozzone, followed by Art Aronson in 1994.

In March 1993 it agreed to acquire Athlone Industries Inc. in a stock swap valued at $107 million. This move solidified Allegheny as the largest specialty steel producer, as the deal included Jessop Steel, a leading stainless and tool-steel plate producer.

History of Teledyne, Inc.

In 1960 Henry Singleton, general manager of Litton Industries' electronics equipment division, and his friend George Kozmetsky each invested $225,000 to form Teledyne, Inc., a manufacturer of electric components for aircraft. Singleton became Teledyne's first chairman and president; Kozmetsky was executive vice president. With nearly 450 employees, the company achieved sales of $4 million in its first year. The following year, sales increased to $10 million. Teledyne went public in 1962, using the proceeds to fuel expansion.

After the resignation of Kozmetsky in 1966, the company embarked on an aggressive and diverse acquisition spree, adding more than 100 companies to its holdings. Some were related to the defense business, including engines, aircraft, specialty metals, and computers; the acquisition of Wah Chang Corp., the world's leading producer of hafnium, zirconium, and other exotic metals, fit in this classification. Others were far-flung, including offshore drilling equipment, insurance, and oral hygiene products; an example was its purchase of a 21% stake in United Insurance Co. By 1969, however, Teledyne ceased its aggressive acquisition program to pay off debts.

In 1976, for the sixth time in four years, Teledyne attempted to buy back its stock in order to eliminate the possibility of a takeover attempt. It acquired a 12% stake in Litton Industries, Inc., becoming the largest shareholder of this conglomerate.

By 1981 Teledyne's insurance operations were underperforming, losing $79.2 million before taxes. The following year, Teledyne's stock portfolios dropped $380 million; this unreported loss almost matched the company's earnings of $412 million on sales of $4.3 billion. Part of this problem was its 16% investment in International Harvester, which had lost over $100 million over the past year and a half.

Teledyne spun off the Argonaut Insurance unit as a separate company in 1986. Singleton retired from active management in 1989, and the company became led by William Rutledge as chairman and CEO and by Donald Rice as president. They reorganized the company, centralizing operations and divesting peripheral businesses. Yet the company's stock price remained low.

The company removed itself from the insurance business entirely in 1990 by spinning off Unitrin, the vehicle through which Teledyne held 25% of Litton Industries and 44% of Curtiss-Wright. The following year Teledyne restructured from 130 units to 21 companies, taking a one-time $69 million charge in the process. In August 1994 it sold its electronic systems unit to Litton Industries Inc.

Teledyne's legal troubles began in 1994. In April it paid $112.5 million to settle fraud charges regarding faulty testing of electronic equipment sold to the Pentagon in the 1980s. In July a federal grand jury indicted Teledyne and three international companies for conspiring to export zirconium pellets for use in munitions in the Middle East. In November 1995 Teledyne paid $2 million to settle charges filed by the federal government for inadequately testing electronic equipment installed in military aircraft. On April 19, 1996, just after announcing its proposed merger with Allegheny Ludlum, Teledyne was accused by the U.S. military of concealing shortages, falsifying and destroying documents, and using government parts in commercial airplanes.

Teledyne became the target of a hostile takeover bid by WHX Corp. in late 1994. It rebuffed the bid, but the head of WHX had managed to secure a seat on Teledyne's board. In 1996 WHX again launched a hostile bid, and Teledyne turned to Allegheny Ludlum for assistance.

Market Forces Driving the Merger

Teledyne was vulnerable to a takeover in the mid-1990s. During the previous ten years, declining sales and reduced profits had caused its stock price to drop. A series of costly lawsuits in the early 1990s contributed to the company's problems. Its stock value remained low, despite a strategic reorganization that involved the divestiture of underperforming businesses.

In the right hands, Teledyne had the potential to improve its situation. The Los Angeles-based company was a diverse stainless steel producer with a focus on specialty and high-performance superalloys, tool steels, and titanium alloys. It served the aviation, electronics, industrial, and consumer products industries by manufacturing such products as aerospace castings, construction and mining equipment, and WaterPik oral care devices. Aside from these operations, the company also held a coveted financial asset. Teledyne possessed an $850 million pension-fund surplus, an attractive prize for any company operating an underfunded pension plan.

Meanwhile, Allegheny Ludlum was one of the world's leading producers of stainless flat-rolled steel, including tool steels and high technology alloys. These operations were based in the volatile commodities market. The acquisition strategy of the Pittsburgh-based company had been focused on increasing its core operations in stainless steel. By diversifying into specialty metals, however, Allegheny Ludlum could stabilize its sales and earnings. The specialty market was also more global than the commodities market,

The Officers

Chairman, President, and CEO: Richard P. Simmons

Sr. VP, Human Resources: Judd R. Cool

VP, Investor Relations and Corporate Communications: Richard J. Harshman

Exec. VP, Finance and Administration and Chief Financial Officer: James L. Murdy

and would facilitate the company's goal of international expansion.

Approach and Engagement

Allegheny Ludlum had been interested in certain assets of Teledyne since the 1980s. Two of the desired subsidiaries were Allvac, a titanium and special-alloys producer, and Rodney Metals, a niche producer of ultralight gauge stainless-steel strip. Teledyne rebuffed Allegheny Ludlum's acquisition offers on the grounds that it didn't want to be broken apart.

In 1994 Teledyne became the target of an acquisition offer of another sort. Ron LaBow, chairman of WHX Corp., launched a hostile bid for Teledyne. WHX was the parent company of Wheeling-Pittsburgh Steel Corp., with which Teledyne's specialty metals businesses could mesh. But LaBow was more interested in Teledyne's $850 million pension-fund surplus. Wheeling-Pittsburgh was running a pension-fund shortfall, and would shortly be negotiating its union contracts. Teledyne rejected LaBow's offer and adopted a poison pill defense against future hostile attacks. Through a proxy fight, however, LaBow won a seat on Teledyne's board in 1995.

The bid by WHX spurred Allegheny Ludlum to consider forming a union with Teledyne as a whole, not merely with portions of it. Like WHX, Allegheny Ludlum could use its pension-fund surplus to cover its own $106 million deficit. Of greater appeal, though, were its diverse and global specialty metals businesses, markets into which Allegheny Ludlum had been seeking entry.

In early 1996 LaBow launched a second hostile offer for Teledyne. Before the attack could progress, Allegheny Ludlum appeared on the scene as a white knight. In February Richard Simmons, chairman of Allegheny, suggested a merger, and in March the two companies engaged in formal discussions. Sixteen days later, they had devised a deal, which was announced on April 1, 1996. The news shocked the

The Players

Allegheny Ludlum Chairman: Richard P. Simmons. Richard Simmons earned a bachelor's degree in metallurgy from the Massachusetts Institute of Technology (M.I.T.) in 1953. He took a job as a titanium research metallurgist at Allegheny Ludlum Steel Corp. and became company president in 1972. In 1980 he orchestrated a management-led buyout of Allegheny Ludlum, of which he became chairman and CEO. In 1990 Simmons retired as CEO, maintaining the post of chairman, a role that he held after the company merged with Teledyne in 1996. In 1997 he reacquired the position of CEO upon the retirement of William Rutledge.

Teledyne CEO: William P. Rutledge. William Rutledge began employment at the steelmaking operations of Bethlehem Steel in 1963. He later took a job with Teledyne, where he became president of its metals group. Rutledge was promoted to company president and then chairman and CEO in 1991. He assumed the role of president and CEO upon the formation of Allegheny Teledyne in 1996, and the following year resigned.

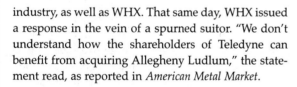

industry, as well as WHX. That same day, WHX issued a response in the vein of a spurned suitor. "We don't understand how the shareholders of Teledyne can benefit from acquiring Allegheny Ludlum," the statement read, as reported in *American Metal Market*.

The $2.25 billion merger would form a new company, Allegheny Teledyne Inc., of which Allegheny Ludlum and Teledyne would be wholly owned subsidiaries. Based in Pittsburgh, the new company would be headed by Richard Simmons as chairman and by William Rutledge as president and CEO.

Under the deal, each share of Allegheny Ludlum would be translated to one share of Allegheny Teledyne, and each share of Teledyne would be converted to 1.925 shares of Allegheny Teledyne. In August shareholders of each company approved the terms, and the merger was completed on August 15, 1996.

Products and Services

The Company operated in four business segments:

Specialty Metals produced metals possessing unique properties, such as corrosion- and heat-resistance, hardness, and malleability. They were used to make products for a broad range of industries including aerospace, oil and gas, automotive, food, chemical processing, transportation, consumer products, power generation, and medical. Companies operating in this segment included Allegheny Ludlum, Allvac, Allvac-SMP Limited, Oremet-Wah Chang, Titanium Industries, and Rome Metals. In 1998 Specialty Metals generated revenues in excess of $2 billion, accounting for 54% of total company revenues.

Aerospace & Electronics businesses served such diverse industries as communications, aerospace, general and commercial aviation, automotive, medical, and industrial manufacturing with a broad spectrum of products and services. These included electronic components and subsystems; sensing, analysis, and instrumentation systems and devices; engineering services; unmanned aerial vehicles and targets; aviation propulsion systems; and high-performance castings. Operating companies were Teledyne Electronic Technologies, Teledyne Brown Engineering, Teledyne Ryan Aeronautical, Teledyne Continental Motors, and Teledyne Cast Parts. Sales in this segment reached just over $1 billion in 1998, accounting for 26% of total company sales.

Industrial businesses made products that were used primarily in basic manufacturing processes in a wide range of industries, including metal, automotive transportation, power generation, construction and building supply, mining, oil and gas, and hydrocarbon/petrochemical processing. Products included cutting tools and tungsten products; nitrogen gas pressure systems; valves, pumps, and boosters; transportable material handlers; mining and construction equipment; and forgings and castings. Companies in this group included Teledyne Metalworking Products, Teledyne Fluid Systems, Teledyne Specialty Equipment, Portland Forge, and Teledyne Cast Parts. In 1998 this segment's revenues reached $515.9 million, or 14% of total company revenues.

Consumer Products made and marketed products primarily designed to promote health and personal comfort and well being. These products included oral health care products, shower heads, residential water filtration devices and systems, and swimming pool equipment. Its operating companies included Teledyne Water Pik and Teledyne Laars. Consumer Products accounted for about six percent, or $247.6 million, of total company sales in 1998.

Changes to the Industry

The merger created a leading manufacturer of specialty metals, complemented by aerospace and electronics, industrial, and consumer products. The businesses of Allegheny Ludlum and Teledyne overlapped in the specialty steel and strip metal segments, strengthening the combined company's operations. The combination extended the company's reach to a broad range of customers, both domestic and international.

In 1997 Allegheny Teledyne announced a divestiture program aimed at eliminating non-core operations while focusing on its specialty chemicals business. That year it shed six businesses that manufactured such products as collapsible packaging tubes, electric heating elements, and plastic compression molds. In 1998 it sold Dynamic Metal Forming and Howell Penncraft. The following year it divested itself of Green River Steel Corp.

At the same time, the company added to its core operations. In 1997 it acquired Oregon Metallurgical Corp., a manufacturer of titanium mill products and castings, as well as a controlling interest in Aerotronics Controls, Inc., a producer of electronic aircraft engine controls. In 1998 it acquired the aerospace division of Sheffield Forgemasters Ltd. That December the firm finally acquired the stainless business of Lukens Inc., for which Allegheny Teledyne had engaged in a yearlong battle with Bethlehem Steel Corp. In the end, Bethlehem successfully acquired Lukens, agreeing to sell its stainless assets to Allegheny Teledyne.

Review of the Outcome

After the merger, the company realized operational synergies. Previously, the subsidiaries of Teledyne operated with a large degree of autonomy, which resulted in a tendency to remain isolated from the other segments, even when the operations were complementary. Under Simmons, these segments engaged in increased exchange with each other and with the subsidiaries of Allegheny Ludlum, resulting in integrated and coordinated production and purchasing. Allegheny Teledyne expected to realize about $108 million in savings from such synergies.

Employment dropped eight percent, from 24,000 in 1996 to 22,000 at year-end 1997. The most significant job-related change, however, occurred at the management level. In February 1997, William Rutledge resigned suddenly. Richard Simmons, who had exited

from day-to-day management of the company, assumed the vacated positions of president and CEO, adding them to his continued in his role as chairman.

In early 1999 Allegheny Teledyne announced a major restructuring that would narrowly define the company's focus on specialized chemicals. The company would accomplish this by spinning off several subsidiaries of its Aerospace & Electronics and Consumer Products divisions. The company's net income in 1998 was $241.2 million on revenues of $3.9 billion.

Research

"Allegheny Teledyne Inc.," in *Notable Corporate Chronologies*, The Gale Group, 1999. Lists major events in the histories of both Allegheny Ludlum and Teledyne, and in the time period since the formation of Allegheny Teledyne.

Allegheny Teledyne Inc. Home Page, available at http://www.alleghenyteledyne.com. Official World Wide Web Page for Allegheny Teledyne. Includes a company history, executive biographies, annual reports, and operational information.

"Allegheny Teledyne Undergoes a Transformation," in *Foundry Management & Technology*, February 1999. Reveals company plans to spin off certain subsidiaries in a reorganization.

"A Merger Creates a Global Specialty-Metals Power," in *New Steel*, August 1997. This informative article details both companies before the merger, the transaction itself, and its internal effects on the newly formed company.

Nolan, Kevin. "Allegheny Teledyne: Merger Abounds with Synergy," in *Metal Center News*, July 1997. Reviews the organizational effects of the merger during the year since its completion.

Robertson, Scott. "A-L, Teledyne Forge $3.2B Merger; Surprise Announcement Greeted with Lots of Conjecture and a Bit of Wonder," in *American Metal Market*, 3 April 1996. Outlines the newly proposed merger, and WHX's reaction to it.

———. "A-L, Teledyne Heading Down Homestretch on Merger," in *American Metal Market*, 19 July 1996. Details the terms of the deal prior to its anticipated closure.

———. "What's Ahead for A-L, Teledyne? Wider Markets, Tighter Focus on High-Value-Added Steels Seen," in *American Metal Market*, 4 April 1996. Describes the gains that Allegheny Ludlum would realize from its union with Teledyne.

"Teledyne Spurns WHX to Merge with Allegheny Ludlum," in *New Steel*, May 1996. Describes the companies' outmaneuvering of WHX in its hostile bid for Teledyne.

DEBORAH J. UNTENER

ALLIED & BENDIX

AlliedSignal Inc.
101 Columbia Rd.
Morristown, NJ 07962
USA

tel: (973)455-2000
fax: (973)455-4807
web: http://www.alliedsignal.com

nationality: USA
date: 1982
affected: Allied Corp., USA, founded 1920
affected: Bendix Corp., USA, founded 1913

Overview of the Merger

When aerospace and automotive company Bendix Corp. launched its $1.5 billion takeover bid for aerospace firm Martin Marietta Corp. in August 1982, the deal already had an unusual twist to it. In the months prior to the offer, Bendix CEO William Agee had gotten divorced and married his secretary, Mary Cunningham. Cunningham's role in major corporate decisions angered Bendix executives, prompting a power struggle. Cunningham's relationship with Agee, as well as her key role in advising Agee during the takeover effort, was later blamed for undermining the firm's negotiations with Martin Marietta.

Using the Pac-Man defense, Martin Marietta counterbid $1.8 billion for Bendix. Because neither firm withdrew its original offer, eventually Bendix and Martin Marietta each acquired controlling stakes in one another. Because Martin Marietta was incorporated in Maryland, where a ten-day waiting period was required prior to a takeover, Bendix, which was incorporated in Delaware and could be taken over immediately, was left vulnerable. To protect itself, Bendix solicited and accepted a $1.9 billion white knight offer from Allied Corp. Bendix and Martin Marietta divested their controlling shares in each other, and Martin Marietta remained independent. The Bendix organization ceased to exist, although Allied retained the Bendix brand name on several products.

History of AlliedSignal Inc.

In 1920, five companies involved in the acid, alkali, coal tar, and nitrogen industries merged to form the Allied Chemical & Dye Corp. Orlando F. Weber was named the company's first president. Eight years later, a synthetic ammonia plant opened near Hopewell, Virginia, and Allied became the leader in ammonia production worldwide.

Regarded as autocratic and extremely secretive, Weber was charged by the Securities and Exchange Commission in 1934 with failing to provide enough information to allow government agencies to access Allied's financial position. A year later, Weber retired and new CEO Fred Emmerich borrowed $200 million to modernize the company's production facilities.

Allied introduced nylon 6 and new refrigerants to the market in 1945. A decade later, the firm began producing heavy denier yarns for use in tire making. Production of yarn for apparel fabrics began in 1956. In 1958, the company's name was changed to Allied Chemical Corp.

Allied acquired Union Texas Natural Gas Corp. in 1962, gaining a reliable raw material source for petrochemical production. Sales reached $1 billion for the first time in 1964. Four years later, new president John T. Conner reorganized Allied, pulling the company out of a number of weak or losing operations. The Union Texas operation was transformed from a raw material source for chemical production into an oil and gas business. Union Texas produced 80% of Allied's net income by the end of the decade.

Allied discontinued its operations in coke, coal, and paving materials in 1980. An electronics company, Eltra Corp., became part of Allied's holdings that year. After being renamed Allied Corp. in 1981, the company acquired Bunker Ramo Corp., an electronics manufacturer, as well as Fisher Scientific Co., a health and scientific products manufacturer. In 1983, Allied bought aerospace and automotive manufacturer Bendix Corp. for $1.9 billion. Two years later, Allied merged with The Signal Companies, Inc., a major producer of oil and gas, to form AlliedSignal Inc. That year, the newly merged firm lost $279 million, the first loss in Allied's history. AlliedSignal then sold 50% of Union Texas.

In 1986, AlliedSignal divested itself of its unprofitable chemical and engineering businesses, known as the Henley Group. A year later, seven additional businesses were sold, allowing AlliedSignal to refocus on three core segments: aerospace, automotive parts, and chemicals. In 1992, AlliedSignal acquired the copperlaminates business of Westinghouse Electric. After purchasing the fluorochemicals business of Netherlands-based Akzo Chemical BV in 1994, AlliedSignal completed the consolidation of its business into four units: Engines, Commercial Avionics Systems, Government Electronic Systems, and Aerospace Equipment Systems.

To respond to a growing heavy-duty truck and diesel equipment market, a new turbocharger plant was constructed in Shanghai, China, in 1995. AlliedSignal divested the majority of its brakes operations in 1996 for $1 billion. The following year, BREED Technologies paid $710 million for AlliedSignal's seatbelt and airbag operations. The firm diversified into

The Business

Financials

Revenue (1998): $15.12 billion

Employees (1998): 70,400

SICs / NAICS

sic 3724 - Aircraft Engines & Engine Parts

sic 5013 - Motor Vehicle Supplies & New Parts

sic 2834 - Pharmaceutical Preparations

sic 3714 - Motor Vehicle Parts & Accessories

sic 2891 - Adhesives & Sealants

sic 2879 - Agricultural Chemicals Nec

naics 336412 - Aircraft Engine and Engine Parts Manufacturing

naics 325412 - Pharmaceutical Preparation Manufacturing

pharmaceuticals with its 1998 purchase of Pharmaceutical Fine Chemicals. In 1999, AlliedSignal secured a $325 million, seven-year contract to run a NASA test site. That year, the firm agreed to merge with Honeywell Inc.

History of Bendix Corp.

In 1913, Vincent Bendix licensed his technique for mass production of triple thread screws, used by the automotive industry in electric starters, to Eclipse Machine Co. A year later, Eclipse began selling integrated starter drives to leading auto makers. A trip to Europe in 1923 proved fruitful to Bendix when he encountered Henri Perrot, an owner of a line of taxicabs, who hired Bendix to develop a more efficient braking system. Later that year, they founded Perot Brake Co. in South Bend, Indiana. In 1924, the new firm changed its name to Bendix Corp. and began listing publicly.

General Motors Corp., the largest customer of Eclipse Machine, helped Bendix finance its purchase of a majority stake in Eclipse in 1928. By that time Bendix had secured 25% of the brake market in the U.S. A move into the aviation industry prompted the firm to change its name to Bendix Aviation Corp. in 1929. Stock prices shot up that year, well over the $26 per share rate of five years earlier.

The Great Depression caused Bendix to halt share dividends in 1932; stock plummeted to less than $5

The Officers

Chairman and CEO: Lawrence A. Bossidy

President and Chief Operating Officer: Frederic M. Poses

Sr. VP and Chief Information Officer: Larry E. Kittelberger

Sr. VP, General Counsel, and Secretary: Peter M. Kreindler

Sr.VP, Human Resources and Communications: Donald J. Kreindler

Sr. VP and Chief Financial Officer: Richard F. Wallman

per share. Development of new automotive systems continued, and the firm was able to begin offering dividends again in 1935. General Motors, which had gained a 25% stake of Bendix by the late 1930s, restructured the firm's subsidiaries into divisions, transforming Bendix from a holding company into an operating company. In 1946, the firm moved its headquarters to Detroit, the heart of the automotive industry.

Because it had become reliant on military production during World War II, Bendix was sent into a tailspin in 1946 after the government canceled $1 billion in contracts. Losses reached $12 million. When the firm began production to support the Korean War effort in 1951, management was careful to treat the work as only temporary. In 1960, the company simplified its name back to Bendix Corp. to better reflect its involvement in several industries.

In the early 1960s, government work accounted for roughly 80% of total revenues at Bendix. To reduce its dependance on automotive and defense work, the firm began diversifying. Headquarters were moved to Southfield, Michigan, in 1971. Two years later, the company paid $27 million for the Autolite spark plug unit of Ford Motor Co., which had been forced to divest its spark plug operations by the Supreme Court. As part of the deal, Ford agreed to purchase the majority of its spark plugs from Bendix for the following ten years.

Bendix bought ASARCO and Bass & Co., two metals processing businesses, in the late 1970s. Early in the next decade, however, the firm began divesting assets, including ASARCO for $336 million and Bass & Co. for $28.8 million. Bendix Forest Products Corp. and United Geophysical Corp. were sold for $425 million and $80 million, respectively. By early 1982, Bendix was sitting on a cash reserve of $500 million. In August, Bendix launched its ill-fated $1.5 billion bid for Martin Marietta Corp., which responded with a bid of its own for Bendix. United Technologies Corp. and Allied Corp. both became involved in the complex

deal. Bendix eventually accepted a $1.9 billion offer from Allied Corp.; the deal was completed in 1983.

Market Forces Driving the Merger

Early in the 1980s, Bendix prepared itself for a major acquisition by selling off peripheral assets and investing the capital into government securities. After building up a cash reserve of $500 million, Bendix spent $100 million for a 7.2% stake in RCA Corp. in March of 1982. Unwilling to allow Bendix—a firm run by a CEO whose romantic relationship with his secretary was at the root of a major managerial power struggle—to gain a larger share, RCA management immediately launched defensive tactics. Bendix then set its sights on Martin Marietta, mainly because sluggish aluminum and cement sales had caused the firm's stock to be undervalued.

Approach and Engagement

On August 25, 1982, Bendix bid $43 per share, or $1.5 billion, for Martin Marietta. Determined to remain independent, Martin Marietta employed the Pac-Man defense by launching a counterbid of $1.7 billion on August 30. According to Bruce Wasserstein, author of *Big Deal: The Battle for Control of America's Leading Corporations*, "if the Pac-Man threat is carried out and the owner doesn't blink, a circular ownership struggle will result. One company might own a majority of the other, and vice versa. The question then arises, who controls whom?" The struggle between Martin Marietta and Bendix turned into a classic example of this defensive stratgy.

Unsure at the time if the Pac-Man defense was sufficient to dissuade Bendix from pursing a takeover, Martin Marietta CEO Thomas Pownall enlisted the help of United Technologies chairman Harry Gray, who agreed on September 7 to enter the bidding for Bendix. Gray and Pownall agreed to split the assets no matter who officially ended up purchasing Bendix.

Negotiations faltered, and on September 20, Bendix announced that it had acquired 70% of Martin Marietta; a few days later, however, Martin Marietta revealed that it was purchasing a controlling 50% of Bendix. Although Bendix had completed its purchase first, it was unable to move quickly to assume control of its board because Martin Marietta was incorporated in Maryland, where a ten-day waiting period was required prior to a takeover. Bendix, on the other hand, was incorporated in Delaware and could be taken over immediately.

Surprised to find itself vulnerable, Bendix bought some time by filing suit in Delaware to prevent Martin Marietta from exercising its voting rights, based on the claim that Martin Marietta had officially become a subsidiary of Bendix. Agee used this breathing room to solicit a white knight offer from Allied Corp., and on September 22, Bendix accepted an $85 per share ($1.9 billion) offer from Allied. However, Martin Marietta went ahead and completed its planned purchase of the Bendix shares, resulting in an ownership structure termed "spaghetti" by Wasserstein. Eventually, Bendix and Martin Marietta divested their controlling shares of each other, although Bendix retained a portion of its Martin Marietta stock. Allied's takeover of Bendix was completed early in 1983.

Products and Services

The 1983 acquisition of Bendix marked Allied's shift towards aerospace operations. The merger with The Signal Companies two years later solidified that focus. Aerospace remained the largest segment of AlliedSignal in 1998, accounting for 32% of total annual revenues. Products included communication and navigation systems; defense electronics; avionics; electric, hydraulic, and pneumatic power systems; engine controls and accessories; flight safety systems; sensors and instrument systems; drilling systems; wheels; and brakes.

Turbine technologies—including aluminum cooling modules, auxiliary power units, ground power units, charged air coolers, engines, and turboshaft engines—brought in 24% of sales in 1998. Transportation products—such as anti-lock brake systems for trucks, Bendix and Jurid friction materials, Prestone antifreeze products, Simoniz wax car care products, and FRAM filters—secured another 16%. Specialty chemicals and electronic solutions garnered 15%, and performance polymers accounted for the remaining 13%. Allied also moved into pharmaceuticals in 1998 via the acquisition of Pharmaceutical Fine Chemicals.

Changes to the Industry

Of the four players caught up in the negotiations, the deal was most lucrative for Allied, which acquired Bendix with minimal effort at a price deemed low by most industry analysts. Although it retained its prized independence, Martin Marietta found itself deep in debt after the dust settled, and United Technologies was forced to look elsewhere for the automotive and industrial assets that it would have secured had it acquired Bendix.

Bendix operated as a subsidiary of Allied until September of 1985, when its operations were absorbed into the divisions of AlliedSignal, which had been formed that year by the merger of Allied and The

The Players

Chairman and CEO of Allied Corp.: Edward L. Hennessy, Jr. Formerly an executive at United Technologies Corp., Edward Hennessy was named CEO of Allied Corp. in 1979. He oversaw the firm's takeover of Bendix Corp. in 1983, as well as its merger with The Signal Companies to form AlliedSignal in 1982. Hennessy was replaced by Lawrence A. Bossidy in 1991.

Chairman and CEO of Bendix Corp.: William A. Agee. William Agee joined Bendix in 1972, after leaving his position at Boise Cascade. In 1976, the 38-year-old Harvard Business School graduate was named chairman of Bendix, succeeding W. Michael Blumenthal, who stepped down to accept the appointment of treasury secretary in the Carter Administration. Agee later foiled Blumenthal's plan to return to Bendix; although his attempt to block Blumenthal's appointment to chairman of Burroughs Corp., by trying to persuade that board to instead allow him to run both firms, was rejected. Agee's later attempts to rid his board of those members closely associated with Burroughs and Blumenthal prompted one board member to resign in protest. Agee became embroiled in a more serious scandal in the early 1980s due to his alleged extramarital affair with his executive assistant Mary Cunningham. Cunningham's involvement in major corporate decisions prompted criticism from several Bendix executives, including executive vice president for strategic planning, Jerome Jacobson. After Jacobson resigned, Agee angered his executive staff by quickly appointing Cunningham as Jacobson's replacement. Mounting pressure eventually forced Cunningham to resign, but prior to her departure, she compiled a list of possible takeover targets for Bendix. When efforts to acquire Martin Marietta Corp. failed, and Bendix was instead acquired by Allied Corp. in 1983, Agee was named president of Allied. He resigned, however, after being passed over for the post of chief operating officer. Morrison Knudsen then hired Agee as CEO and chairman. He was ousted by Morrison Knudsen early in 1995 after his turnaround efforts there faltered.

Signal Companies, Inc. After Signal's aerospace operations were folded into the Bendix unit, aerospace

became the largest segment of AlliedSignal. Many former Bendix assets became part of the AlliedSignal Industrial Group, which was divested the following year. Along with the aerospace assets, AlliedSignal retained the automotive and electronics holdings of Bendix and continued to use the Bendix brand name on various products.

Review of the Outcome

Allied upped its sales from $6 billion to $10 billion with the purchase of Bendix. After the deal was completed, Allied employed 117,000 workers, and Bendix sales accounted for nearly half of annual revenue. According to a September 1983 article in *Aviation Week and Space Technology*, Bendix had "transitioned smoothly into the new parent, Allied Corp. organization, following the tumultuous takeover battle between Bendix and Martin Marietta." In the years to follow, Allied increased its focus on aerospace operations and eventually divested its Union Texas natural gas assets.

Research

AlliedSignal Inc. Home Page, available at http://www.alliedsignal.com. Official World Wide Web Page for AlliedSignal Inc. Includes product and corporate information, news, and annual reports.

"AlliedSignal Inc.," in *Notable Corporate Chronologies*, Gale Research, 1999. Covers major events in the history of AlliedSignal Inc.

"Bendix Corp.," in *International Directory of Company Histories*, vol. I, St. James Press, 1988. Provides a detailed history of Bendix Corp.

Klass, Philip J. "Allied Takes Over Bendix; Martin Stays Independent," in *Aviation Week and Space Technology*, 4 October 1982. Details the terms of the agreement between Allied and Bendix.

———. "Bendix Transitions Smoothly into Allied," in *Aviation Week and Space Technology*, 5 September 1983. Explains how the integration of Bendix into Allied fared.

Wasserstein, Bruce. *Big Deal: The Battle for Control of America's Leading Corporations*, Warner Books, 1998. Offers an overview of the largest mergers in recent American corporate history.

ANNAMARIE L. SHELDON

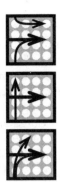

ALLIED WASTE & BROWNING-FERRIS

nationality: USA
date: 1999
affected: Allied Waste Industries, Inc., USA, founded 1987
affected: Browning-Ferris Industries, Inc., USA, founded 1970

Allied Waste Industries
15880 N. Greenway-Hayden Loop, Ste. 100
Scottsdale, AZ 85260
USA

tel: (602)423-2946
fax: (602)423-9242
web: http://www.alliedwaste.com

Overview of the Acquisition

Allied Waste Industries, based in Scottsdale, Arizona, was the third-largest waste services company in North America; Browning-Ferris, headquartered in Houston, Texas, was the second-largest. When Allied Waste acquired Browning-Ferris for $9.1 billion in mid-1999, it tripled in size and moved into the industry's second place spot, behind Waste Management, Inc., with sales of roughly $6.6 billion. Allied Waste Industries CEO Thomas Van Weelden took the helm of the new firm.

History of Allied Waste Industries, Inc.

Allied Waste Industries was established in Houston, Texas, in 1987. Three years later, Allied Waste Industries purchased Sancho. CRX was acquired the following year, and revenues reached $9 million. In 1992, the company bought an Illinois-based waste disposal business. By the early-1990s, the firm had acquired 30 waste hauling firms, and operations spanned sevens states. Due it intense competition from Houston-based waste management leader Browning-Ferris Industries, Allied Waste Industries moved its headquarters to Scottsdale, Arizona in 1993.

The firm expanded via an aggressive non-hazardous waste acquisition program, allowing its units to operate locally. In 1996, Allied Waste Industries scored its biggest purchase to date when it paid $1.6 billion for the non-hazardous solid waste operations of Laidlaw Inc. The Canadian Laidlaw holdings were then divested and the capital used to reduce debt.

Allied Waste Industries moved into the Pacific Northwest in 1998 when it bought Rabanco Cos. The company also paid $1.1 billion for American Disposal Services. In seven years, revenues had grown more than tenfold to $1.7 billion. In 1999, Allied Waste Industries agreed to purchase competitor Browning-Ferris Industries for $9.1 billion.

History of Browning-Ferris Industries, Inc.

In 1966, Tom Fatjo, Jr., bought a garbage truck and entered the waste handling business in Houston, Texas. Increased regulation of the waste handling industry

The Business

Financials

Revenue (1998): $1.57 billion

Employees (1998): 9,500

SICs / NAICS

sic 4953 - Refuse Systems

sic 5093 - Scrap & Waste Materials

naics 562212 - Solid Waste Landfill

naics 562211 - Hazardous Waste Treatment and Disposal

naics 562213 - Solid Waste Combustors and Incinerators

naics 562213 - Solid Waste Combustors and Incinerators

promoted growth of centralized, multi-city waste handlers. Fatjo branched into waste disposal in 1968 and obtained a citywide landfill contract. He also entered into partnership with Louis A. Waters to form Fatjo and Waters.

Fatjo acquired control of Browning-Ferris Machinery Co., a manufacturer of garbage trucks and landfill equipment, in 1969. Between 1967 and 1970, Fatjo and Waters acquired small waste handling firms at an average of one per week. They incorporated as Browning-Ferris Industries, Inc. (BFI) in 1970. The business expanded into paper recycling and established a division to gather suitable paper waste both from its own collection and from outside sources.

BFI signed its first international contract to provide sanitation service in parts of Spain in 1973. By the mid-1970s, BFI operated 157 local waste handling companies. New regulations made opening new landfills prohibitively expensive, while raising operating costs for those already in use. The increased complexity and cost of waste handling discouraged new competitors. BFI divested itself of its paper recycling operations. Price hikes instituted in 1976 boosted earnings by 37%. Full implementation of the 1976 Resource Conservation and Recovery Act tightened control of the disposal of toxic and hazardous substances. BFI won a contract that year to provide waste handling services for the city of Riyadh, Saudi Arabia. After demand for wastepaper waned in the mid-1970s, BFI divested its wastepaper unit, Consolidated Fibers. With revenues in excess of $550 million, BFI by the decade's end was the second-largest waste disposal company in the U.S.

In 1983, disposal of hazardous waste provided

10% of revenues. BFI purchased CECOS International, Inc. and Newco Waste Systems, bringing its total of hazardous waste disposal sites to eight. The following year, the firm came under investigation for monopolistic practices, including price fixing, in seven states. It also formed a joint venture to market trash burning plants. State and federal authorities closed an Ohio-based BFI hazardous waste facility in 1985, and criminal charges were brought against the company for environmental damage in the area. As a result, BFI's hazardous waste division lost money for the first time, but profits for its solid waste and waste-to-energy operations continued to rise.

BFI diversified into the handling of medical waste in 1986 by purchasing two firms operating in that industry. The firm plead guilty to price fixing charges in 1987 and was forced to pay $4.4 million in fines. In 1988, hazardous waste landfills in Louisiana, New York, and Ohio failed to obtain re-certification and were forced to close. Losses in 1990 reached $452 million. Hazardous waste operations were discontinued.

After revitalizing its acquisition program, BFI acquired 110 companies in 1993, more than double that of a year earlier. Along with expansion into western Michigan, the company also moved into San Diego; downtown Chicago; Harrisburg, Pennsylvania; and Augusta, Georgia. BFI also added new contracts in Atlanta, Brighton, New Orleans, New York, Pittsburgh, Ohio, Florida, and Rhode Island. That year, BFI entered the German solid waste market by purchasing a 50% stake in Otto Holding International BV, the third largest solid waste business in Germany. The firm also acquired an Helsinki-based waste company and a number of solid waste operations in Barcelona, Spain.

In 1994, BFI launched a hostile takeover of Attwoods PLC, a British landfill operator with $550 million in annual revenues. Recycling revenues reached $370 million, compared to $9.6 million in 1990. Two years later, the company added ten domestic landfills, expanded landfills in the Netherlands and Italy, and entered the Swiss market. Sluggish revenues in the mid-1990s prompted the firm to divest peripheral operations, such as the tire recycling unit. In 1999, BFI agreed to be acquired by Allied Waste Industries, a smaller competitor.

Market Forces Driving the Acquisition

In the mid-1990s, the Trade Waste Commission broke up an illegal waste hauling and trash cartel in New York City. As a result, the agency denied licenses to more than 50 local garbage hauling operations which were believed to have participated in the illegal activity. This opened up the New York City market, which was considered the largest such market in the U.S. with 200,000 potential customers. In 1998, Browning-Ferris Industries (BFI) was the fourth-largest waste management operator in New York City with 3,000 customers. By purchasing BFI, Allied would gain valuable access to this lucrative market.

Another factor prompting Allied Waste's offer for BFI was the consolidation that had already been occurring in the industry. In 1998, industry leader Waste Management Inc. merged with USA Waste Services Inc., the third largest waste management firm in New York City, and then with Eastern Environmental Services, Inc., the city's second largest garbage hauler after the Waste Management/USA Waste deal was completed. To remain competitive, firms needed to expand geographical reach and gain access to as many markets as possible.

According to a March 1999 *New York Times* article, Allied Waste Industries claimed its move to purchase BFI wasn't part of a consolidation effort, but rather "teaming our management with their assets." BFI had struggled throughout the 1990s mainly due to management missteps such as expanding too rapidly and focusing on recycling, a market that never met growth expectations. In response, the firm slowed its acquisition rate and divested many non-core holdings. With stock hovering around a disappointing $30 per share for several years, many analysts believed BFI was left vulnerable to a buyout.

Approach and Engagement

In July of 1998, Allied Waste Industries approached Browning-Ferris Industries (BFI) about a merger. Hoping to stave off a buyout, BFI management instituted a shareholders' rights program, commonly called a "poison pill," which would make a takeover of the firm difficult without full board approval. After several months of negotiations, the two firms agreed to a friendly buyout.

In February of 1999, Allied Waste Industries announced its $9.1 billion leveraged buyout of BFI. Terms of the agreement stipulated that Allied Waste pay $45 per share in cash and assume roughly $1.8 billion in debt. Allied Waste needed $9.5 billion in senior financing—nearly $7 billion in bank loans and $3 billion in junk bonds—to pay for the purchase and to retain adequate working capital once the deal was finalized.

As one of the largest leverage buyouts in corporate history, the deal attracted several financial institutions, including leveraged lending powerhouse Chase Manhattan and Allied Waste's historical lender, Citigroup. Both firms vied for leading roles in financ-

The Officers

Chairman, President, and CEO: Thomas H. Van Weelden
VP and Chief Operating Officer: Larry D. Henk
VP and Chief Financial Officer: Henry L. Hirvela
VP and Chief Accounting Officer: Peter S. Hathaway
VP, Mergers and Acquisitions: Michael G. Hannon

ing the deal; the negotiations took place in the Manhattan-based law firm of Fried, Frank, Harris, Shriver & Jacobson. After hearing both sales pitches, Allied Waste management appointed Chase administrative agent and named Citibank syndicated agent.

By the end of the March, both firms made filings as stipulated by the Hart-Scott-Rodino Antitrust Improvement Act. In April, as part of a previous agreement between BFI and Allied Waste, BFI sold to Allied Waste its waste services assets in northern New Jersey; Chicago, Illinois; St. Louis, Missouri; and Contra Costa County, California. Allied Waste then sold to BFI waste service assets in Boston, Massachusetts; Atlanta, Georgia; Chicago, Illinois; and the Ohio cities of Dayton, Toledo, Youngstown, Bellefontaine, and Celina.

Products and Services

In 1998, 56% of total revenues at Allied Waste came from collection operations which were organized into 109 collection companies spanning 28 states. The firm's 69 landfill operations brought in 30% of sales; Allied Waste Industries also operated 67 transfer stations and 26 recycling plants. Residential, commercial, and industrial customers totaled 2.2 million.

Browning-Ferris offered collection, recycling, and disposal services to residential, commercial, industrial, and medical waste customers in 1998. Solid waste collection operations accounted for 52% of sales and spanned 46 states, Puerto Rice, and Canada. Landfill sites totaled 90, as did recycling facilities. Browning-Ferris also operated 30 medical waste treatment units.

Review of the Outcome

When Allied Waste completed its $9.1 billion acquisition of Browning-Ferris in mid-1999, it became the second-largest waste management firm in North America, behind Waste Management Inc. While most analysts believe that BFI could benefit from the successful management style of Allied Waste, many are concerned about the size of the transaction. Allied

The Players

Chairman, President, and CEO of Allied Waste Industries, Inc.: Thomas H. Van Weelden. An owner and operator of several solid waste businesses, Thomas Van Weelden was appointed president of Allied Waste Industries in 1992 when the company acquired his Illinois-based waste disposal operation. Five years later, Van Weelden accepted the post of CEO. He succeeded Roger A. Ramsey as chairman on December 31, 1998. When the acquisition of Browning-Ferris was completed in mid-1999, Van Weelden remained at the helm of the combined company.

Chairman of Browning-Ferris Industries, Inc.: William D. Ruckelshaus. In 1988, William Ruckleshaus resigned as head of the Environmental Protection Agency and accepted a position as CEO of Browning-Ferris Industries. He led the struggling firm's restructuring effort in the early 1990s, which involved cutting costs, streamlining operations, exiting the hazardous waste sector, and increasing recycling operations. In 1995, Bruce E. Ranck became CEO, succeeding Ruckelshaus, who remained chairman.

Waste tripled in size when the deal was completed—combined sales totaled nearly $6.6 billion—which may cause the firm various integration problems.

Research

Allied Waste Industries, Inc. Home Page, available at http://www.alliedwaste.com. Official World Wide Web Home Page for Allied Waste Industries, Inc. Includes news, financial, product, employment, historical information.

Barboza, David. "A Trash Hauler is Buying a Much Bigger Rival, a Type of Deal that Makes Wall Street a Bit Nervous," in *The New York Times*, 9 March 1999. Explains why some analysts are leery of the Allied Waste Industries/Browning-Ferris Industries deal.

"Browning-Ferris Industries, Inc." in *Notable Corporate Chronologies*, The Gale Group, 1999. Lists major events in the history of Browning-Ferris Industries, Inc.

Browning-Ferris Industries, Inc. Home Page, available at http://www.bfi.com. Official World Wide Web Home Page for Browning-Ferris Industries, Inc. Includes corporate news, as well as financial, product, and historical information.

Copulsky, Erca. "The Mad, Mad, Mad, Mad War to Finance Allied Waste's LBO," in *Investment Dealers' Digest*, 15 March 1999. Explains why lenders were scrambling to get a piece of the action in financing the LBO by Allied Waste Industries.

Lentz, Philip. "Cartload of Mergers Brings New Firms to Trash Business: No. 1 Hauler Won't Have Monopoly As Out-of-Towners Gain Foothold," in *Crain's New York Business*, 15 March 1999. Details how industry leader Waste Management Inc. has seen increased competition in the lucrative New York City waste management market since the mob-run garbage hauling cartel was broken up. The article also includes a brief explanation regarding how the Allied Waste/Browning-Ferris deal might increase both firms' foothold in the market.

Weidner, David. "Chase to Lead Deal for $9.1B Acquisition," in *American Banker*, 9 March 1999. Offers financial details regarding the leveraged buyout of Browning-Ferris by Allied Waste Industries.

THERA WILLIAMS

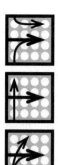

ALLIEDSIGNAL & HONEYWELL

nationality: USA
date: 1999
affected: AlliedSignal Inc., USA, founded 1920
affected: Honeywell Inc., USA, founded 1906

AlliedSignal Inc.
101 Columbia Rd.
Morristown, NJ 07962
USA

tel: (973)455-2000
fax: (973)455-4807
web: http://www.alliedsignal.com

Honeywell Inc.
Honeywell Plaza
Minneapolis, MN 55408
USA

tel: (612)951-1000
fax: (612)951-8537
web: http://www.honeywell.com

Overview of the Merger

Diversified electronics manufacturer AlliedSignal agreed in June of 1999 to merge with Honeywell, an electronic-controls company, to create a firm with a market capitalization of roughly $49 billion and annual sales of $23.5 billion. The new conglomerate, to be called Honeywell, will be one of America's largest; its focus will be aerospace, as well as specialty and electronic chemicals, nylon, and industrial controls. The $14 billion deal, if approved by shareholders and federal regulators, is expected to close by the end of 1999.

History of AlliedSignal Inc.

In 1920, five companies involved in the acid, alkali, coal tar, and nitrogen industries merged to form the Allied Chemical & Dye Corp. Orlando F. Weber was named the company's first president. Eight years later, a synthetic ammonia plant opened near Hopewell, Virginia, and Allied became the leader in ammonia production worldwide.

Regarded as autocratic and extremely secretive, Weber was charged by the Securities and Exchange Commission in 1934 with failing to provide enough information to allow government agencies to access Allied's financial position. A year later, Weber retired and new CEO Fred Emmerich borrowed $200 million to modernize the company's production facilities.

Allied introduced nylon 6 and new refrigerants to the market in 1945. A decade later, the firm began producing heavy denier yarns for use in tire making. Production of yarn for apparel fabrics began in 1956. In 1958, the company's name was changed to Allied Chemical Corp.

Allied acquired Union Texas Natural Gas Corp. in 1962, gaining a reliable raw material source for petrochemical production. Sales reached $1 billion for the first time in 1964. Four years later, new president John T. Conner reorganized Allied, pulling the company out of a number of weak or losing operations. The Union Texas operation was transformed from a raw material source for chemical produc-

The Business

Financials - AlliedSignal Inc.

Revenue (1998): $15.12 billion

Employees (1998): 70,400

Financials - Honeywell Inc.

Revenue (1998): $8.4 billion

Employees (1998): 57,000

SICs / NAICS

sic 3724 - Aircraft Engines & Engine Parts

sic 5013 - Motor Vehicle Supplies & New Parts

sic 2834 - Pharmaceutical Preparations

sic 3714 - Motor Vehicle Parts & Accessories

sic 2891 - Adhesives & Sealants

sic 2879 - Agricultural Chemicals Nec

sic 3823 - Process Control Instruments

sic 3822 - Environmental Controls

naics 334513 - Instruments for Measuring and Displaying Industrial Process Variables

naics 334512 - Automatic Environmental Control Manufacturing

naics 336412 - Aircraft Engine and Engine Parts Manufacturing

naics 325412 - Pharmaceutical Preparation Manufacturing

tion into an oil and gas business. Union Texas produced 80% of Allied's net income by the end of the decade.

Allied discontinued its operations in coke, coal, and paving materials in 1980. An electronics company, Eltra Corp., became part of Allied's holdings that year. After being renamed Allied Corp. in 1981, the company acquired Bunker Ramo Corp., an electronics manufacturer, as well as Fisher Scientific Co., a health and scientific products manufacturer. In 1983, Allied bought aerospace and automotive manufacturer Bendix Corp. for $1.9 billion. Two years later, Allied merged with The Signal Companies, Inc., a major producer of oil and gas, to form AlliedSignal Inc. That year, the newly merged firm lost $279 million, the first loss in Allied's history. AlliedSignal then sold 50% of Union Texas.

In 1986, AlliedSignal divested itself of its unprof-

itable chemical and engineering businesses, known as the Henley Group. A year later, seven additional businesses were sold, allowing AlliedSignal to refocus on three core segments: aerospace, automotive parts, and chemicals. In 1992, AlliedSignal acquired the copperlaminates business of Westinghouse Electric. After purchasing the fluorochemicals business of Netherlands-based Akzo Chemical BV in 1994, AlliedSignal completed the consolidation of its business into four units: Engines, Commercial Avionics Systems, Government Electronic Systems, and Aerospace Equipment Systems.

To respond to a growing heavy-duty truck and diesel equipment market, a new turbocharger plant was constructed in Shanghai, China, in 1995. AlliedSignal divested the majority of its brakes operations in 1996 for $1 billion. The following year, BREED Technologies paid $710 million for AlliedSignal's seatbelt and airbag operations. The firm diversified into pharmaceuticals with its 1998 purchase of Pharmaceutical Fine Chemicals. In 1999, AlliedSignal secured a $325 million, seven-year contract to run a NASA test site. That year, the firm agreed to merge with Honeywell Inc.

History of Honeywell Inc.

In 1906, Mark C. Honeywell founded Honeywell Heating Specialty Co. in Wabash, Indiana. The company, which built water-heating equipment, was one participant in a merger that would later create Honeywell Inc.

A World War I mercury shortage restricted output for Honeywell Heating. In 1914, the firm was renamed Honeywell Heating Specialties and reorganized to include production of automatic temperature controls. Honeywell acquired Jewell Manufacturing's temperature control business in 1922. Five years later the firm merged with Minneapolis Heat Regulator Co. (MHR) to form Minneapolis-Honeywell Regulator Co.; the firm's headquarters were in Minneapolis. MHR's William Sweatt became chairman of the board, and Mark Honeywell was named president. The company incorporated in Delaware and produced 40,000 clocks annually.

Minneapolis-Honeywell established its first foreign subsidiary in Toronto, Canada, in 1930. N.V. Nederlandsche was formed two years later in Amsterdam as the firm's first overseas subsidiary. In 1935, common stock was listed on the New York Stock Exchange. By then, the firm offered both electric and pneumatic temperature control equipment. Honeywell-Brown, Ltd. was created in London.

The firm entered defense production in 1940 as a

manufacturer of precision optical equipment for tank periscopes and artillery sights. Minneapolis-Honeywell's Dutch subsidiary was taken over by the Nazis. In 1941, the firm developed electronic autopilot, the C-1, which became critically important to the war effort. Six years later, a Latin American subsidiary was established in Mexico, along with one in Switzerland. Sales surpassed $100 million in 1950.

In 1955, Datamatic Corp. originated in Newton, Mississippi, as a joint venture between Minneapolis-Honeywell and Raytheon Co. to design, develop, and produce large-scale computer systems. Two years later, the unit installed its first line of mainframe computers, the Datamatic 1000, which sold for $2 million apiece. Raytheon bailed out of the joint project that year, leaving Minneapolis-Honeywell as the sole owner of Datamatic.

In 1964, stockholders approved an official name change to Honeywell Inc. Stock split two-for-one, the fifth split since the company was founded. Honeywell acquired Computer Control Co. in 1966. Sales exceeded $1 billion the following year. In 1969, Honeywell systems contributed to four successful Apollo spaceflights. The firm became the first supplier of digital avionics to commercial airliners with a flight computer for McDonnell Douglas' DC-10.

Honeywell bought General Electric Co.'s computer business in 1970. The result, Honeywell Information Systems Inc., ranked as the second-largest computer company in the world. Sales surpassed $2 billion in 1972, and Honeywell was listed on the London Stock Exchange and the Paris Bourse. Two years later, General Electric's process control operations were acquired. In 1976, Honeywell assumed all marketing support and maintenance responsibility for Xerox computer users worldwide. The firm also won a $16 million contract from Aramco Services for an integrated gas production project in Saudi Arabia. By the end of the decade, Honeywell had introduced fire and smoke detectors to the retail market and had secured a contract from Boeing Co. to develop inertial reference systems for the next generation of 757 and 767 airliners.

The company began a major restructuring in the early 1980s, and a total of 3,500 jobs were eliminated through layoffs, retirement, and transfers. In 1986, Honeywell sold most of its computer division to Group Bull of France and Japan's NEC Corp., creating a three-way joint venture. The firm also bought Sperry Aerospace Group. After experiencing a series of unusual charges related to its defense unit in 1988, Honeywell was forced to absorb serious cost overruns, resulting in a net loss of $435 million. By the decade's end, defense and aerospace contracts

The Officers

AlliedSignal Inc.

Chairman and CEO: Lawrence A. Bossidy

President and Chief Operating Officer: Frederic M. Poses

Sr. VP and Chief Information Officer: Larry E. Kittelberger

Sr. VP, General Counsel, and Secretary: Peter M. Kreindler

Sr. VP, Human Resources and Communications: Donald J. Kreindler

Sr. VP and Chief Financial Officer: Richard F. Wallman

Honeywell Inc.

Chairman and CEO: Michael R. Bonsignore

President and Chief Operating Officer: Giannantonio Ferrari

VP and Chief Financial Officer: Larry W. Stranghoener

VP, Communications: Frances B. Emerson

VP and Secretary: Kathleen M. Gibson

VP and General Counsel: Edward D. Garyson

Vice President and Controller: Philip M. Palazzari

accounted for almost half of Honeywell's sales and contributed significantly to earnings. At the same time, automation systems were getting a boost from the upswing in capital investment.

Company stock split two-for-one in 1990. The Defense and Marine Systems Business, Test Instruments Division, and Signal Analysis Center were spun off into an independent company, Alliant Techsystems Inc. Honeywell entered into an agreement with a West German firm to develop and supply industrial programmable logic controllers for the European industrial market. In 1991, the company launched a $600 million share buyback program. The following year, Minolta Camera Co. agreed to pay Honeywell $96.4 million to settle a suit regarding the use of Honeywell's patented automatic focus technology.

The firm announced plans in 1993 to offer home-control products directly to the homeowner and to market industrial controls in Eastern Europe. In 1994, Honeywell agreed to pay $6.5 million to settle U.S. Labor Department charges that it discriminated against 6,000 female employees between 1972 and 1977. That year the firm was blamed for the crash of USAir Douglas DC-9-31 at Charlotte/Douglas International Airport after the National

The Players

Chairman and CEO of AlliedSignal Inc.: Lawrence A. Bossidy. After graduating from Colgate University with an economics degree, Lawrence Bossidy accepted an entry-level finance management position at General Electric (GE) in 1957. In his 35 years with GE, Bossidy worked as chief operating officer of the credit unit and executive vice president of the services and materials division. He was named vice chairman in 1984 under GE's acclaimed chairman and CEO Jack Welch; he held this post until AlliedSignal tapped him as CEO in July of 1991. Bossidy oversaw AlliedSignal's merger negotiations with Honeywell in 1999, and he plans to serve in the newly merged firm as chairman for one year until his retirement in 2000.

Chairman and CEO of Honeywell Inc.: Michael R. Bonsignore. Electrical engineer Michael Bonsignore began his long career at Honeywell in 1969. After working at the firm's aerospace unit for three years in assorted marketing and business development positions, he was named marketing manager of the marine systems division, eventually taking over as general manager. In 1982, Bonsignore was named president of Honeywell Europe SA, based in Brussels, Belgium. Five years later, he returned to the U.S. to accept the post of executive vice president of international operations, responsible for all non-U.S. activities. After serving as executive vice president and chief operating officer of international operations and home and building control businesses between 1990 and April 1993, Bonsignore was named chairman and CEO. When Honeywell completes its merger with AlliedSignal, Bonsignore will take control of the new firm as CEO.

Transportation Safety Board found that a detection-delay feature in Honeywell's standard wind shear system prevented USAir pilots from making maneuvers necessary to escape the crash. Net income dropped 13%, as the company's sixth restructuring in eight years produced a meager $38 million write-off.

By mid-decade, the firm had divested several of its less profitable units and expanded its building controls division. In 1995, Honeywell agreed to a strategic alliance with China National Petrochemical Corp. (Sinopec) to supply Sinopec with advanced control technology to optimize refining and petrochemical operations at its plants. The following year, Honeywell purchased Duracraft Corp. for $283 million, increasing its presence in the retail market, which accounted for just $80 million of its $6.7 billion in annual sales.

In 1998, after years of litigation, Litton Industries Inc. won a $250 million antitrust suit against Honeywell for monopolizing the commercial airplane guidance and navigation industry; in response, Honeywell filed an appeal. A year later, AlliedSignal and Honeywell agreed to a $14 billion merger.

Market Forces Driving the Merger

As was the case with many major mergers in the 1990s, cost savings was the main impetus for the decision to merge Honeywell and AlliedSignal. "On the cost side, it will follow the brutal 1+1=1 rule, under which the number of staff in any two combining departments is reduced to the size of the larger pre-merger one," wrote *The Economist* about the Honeywell and AlliedSignal deal in June of 1999.

The two firms were also hoping to leverage the strength of Honeywell's cockpit systems and AlliedSignal's leading safety products to increase contracts from aircraft makers who increasingly sought suppliers that were able to provide a broader range of products. According to *Flight International*, the merger agreement also gave "testament to the growing urgency to consolidate the supplier industry following massive mergers among U.S. aerospace and defense price contractors." Previous mergers in those industries included United Technologies Corp.'s $4.3 billion deal with Sundstrand Corp. and the $7 billion purchase of LucasVarity Corp. by TRW Inc.

Both firms also pointed out that the deal would make them less susceptible to the cyclical natures of their industries and generate enough cash flow to fund future acquisitions.

Approach and Engagement

In June of 1999, AlliedSignal and Honeywell announced their merger plans. Shares of each firm jumped 5% on the day that the deal was announced. According to the terms of the tax-free stock swap, Allied will trade 1.875 shares for each Honeywell share. Although AlliedSignal operations will account for roughly 66% of the merged firm's revenues, and headquarters will remain in AlliedSignal's home state of New Jersey, the new company will use the Honeywell name. Honeywell chairman and CEO Michael Bonsignore will take over as CEO. Allied Signal chairman and CEO Lawrence Bossidy will chair the new Honeywell until 2000, when Bonsignore will assume that role as well.

The aviation operations of AlliedSignal will move to Honeywell's operation in Phoenix, Arizona. AlliedSignal Aerospace's leader Robert Johnson will oversee the merged entity's aerospace arm. Giannantonio Ferrari, president and chief operating officer of Honeywell, will oversee all non-aviation activities. Both Johnson and Ferrari will hold the title of chief operating officer. Shareholder approval and regulatory nods are expected by the end of 1999.

Products and Services

Prior to the merger, Aerospace was the largest segment of AlliedSignal, accounting for 32% of total annual revenues. Products included communication and navigation systems; defense electronics; avionics; electric, hydraulic, and pneumatic power systems; engine controls and accessories; flight safety systems; sensors and instrument systems; drilling systems; wheels; and brakes. Turbine technologies—including aluminum cooling modules, auxiliary power units, ground power units, charged air coolers, engines, and turboshaft engines—brought in 24% of sales in 1998. Transportation products—such as anti-lock brake systems for trucks, Bendix and Jurid friction materials, Prestone antifreeze products, Simoniz wax car care products, and FRAM filters—secured another 16%. Specialty chemicals and electronic solutions garnered 15%, and performance polymers accounted for the remaining 13%. Allied also moved into pharmaceuticals in 1998 via the acquisition of Pharmaceutical Fine Chemicals.

Honeywell garnered most of its sales, 41% in 1998, from home and building control operations, including building automation systems, energy management equipment, security control devices, and fire protection gadgets. Industrial products, such as field instrumentation and automation and control products, accounted for 30% of revenues. Space and aviation produced brought in the remaining 29%.

Review of the Outcome

To achieve anticipated cost savings of $500 million, 4,500 positions will be eliminated within 18 months of the merger's completion.

Research

"AlliedSignal Buys Honeywell," in *Chemical Week*, 16 June 1999. Discusses why the two firms decided to merge and what the outcome will likely be.

"AlliedSignal-Honeywell Merger Cuts Jobs," in *United Press International*, 8 June 1999. Predicts the number of layoffs expected as a result of the merger.

AlliedSignal Inc. Home Page, available at http://www.alliedsignal.com. Official World Wide Web Page for AlliedSignal Inc. Includes product and corporate information, news, and annual reports.

"AlliedSignal Inc.," in *Notable Corporate Chronologies*, The Gale Group, 1999. Covers major events in the history of AlliedSignal Inc.

Colvin, Geoffrey. "Honeywell Packs Its Bags," in *Fortune*, 5 July 1999. Explains the terms of the agreement between AlliedSignal and Honeywell.

"Honeywell Inc.," in *Notable Corporate Chronologies*, The Gale Group, 1999. Chronicles major events in the history of Honeywell Inc.

Jasper, Chris. "AlliedSignal-Honeywell Deal Tops Supplier Merger Trend," in *Flight International*, 16 June 1999. Discusses the industry conditions that prompted the deal.

"Old World Charm," in *The Economist*, 12 June 1999. Offers reasons for the merger, as well as possible results.

Palmer, Jay. "Allied Victory; Honeywell's Also a Winner in Deal," in *Barron's*, 14 June 1999. Provides an overview of the terms of the deal, as well as a discussion of how the two firms will likely benefit from it.

ANNAMARIE L. SHELDON

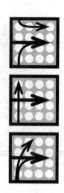

AMERICA ONLINE & NETSCAPE COMMUNICATIONS

American Online Inc.
22000 AOL Way
Dulles, Virginia 20166
USA

tel: 703448-8700
fax: 703918-1400
web: http://www.aol.com

nationality: USA
date: 1999
affected: America Online Inc., USA, founded 1985
affected: Netscape Communications Corp., USA, founded 1994

Overview of the Merger

One of the most noteworthy mergers in the history of the online industry was announced in late 1998 when America Online Inc. (AOL) agreed to pay $4.2 billion in stock for Netscape Communications Corp. As part of the deal, AOL agreed to purchase $500 million worth of hardware from Sun Microsystems, which will be granted rights to sell and develop Netscape's successful server software. Combining AOL's 60% share of the online market with Netscape's 40% share of the browser market will create a firm large and diverse enough to compete with Microsoft Corp. in the growing electronic commerce software market, which is expected to burgeon into a $4 billion industry by 2002.

History of America Online Inc.

In 1985, Quantum Computer Services, Inc., was formed by Stephen M. Case in partnership with Commodore International, Ltd., a manufacturer of personal computers, and Control Video. Established with $2 million in venture capital, Quantum offered an online service, called Q-Link, exclusively for Commodore computer owners. Two years later, Quantum began offering its services to owners of personal computers manufactured by other companies, including the Tandy Corp. The company also achieved profitability for the first time.

Quantum introduced online services for owners of IBM-compatible personal computers in 1988 and for Macintosh users in 1989. The firm also launched America Online (AOL), a nationwide network for personal computer owners. In 1991, Quantum changed its name to America Online, Inc. and reorganized its operations by consolidating services and focusing efforts on the Macintosh and IBM-compatible computer markets, as well as campaigning to increase its number of subscribers. Later that year, the company entered into a joint venture with the Tribune Co., the owner of the *Chicago Tribune*, in an effort to ease its move into the Midwestern market. AOL created a news and information service designed especially for Chicago by making use of items from the local daily paper.

In 1992, AOL listed itself on the NASDAQ system and offered a two-for-one split of its outstanding shares of common stock. The company also developed a licensing and development agreement with Apple Computer, Inc. which allowed AOL to use its technology in Apple's future information services. By then, the number of subscribers was nearly doubling each year.

AOL launched a Windows version of its online service in 1993 and acquired discounts on telephone usage in exchange for providing long-distance telephone provider Sprint Corp. with a sizable package of stock options. The company also signed agreements with media companies including Knight-Ridder, CNN, *Time* magazine, *Omni* magazine, *Wired* magazine, and Disney Adventures. That year, AOL's subscriber base exceeded 500,000 members, and the firm announced its intention to begin offering Internet access.

In 1994, AOL cemented its second agreement with a major television network when it added NBC Online to its offerings. The company also joined Shopper's Express to provide a grocery and pharmacy ordering and home delivery service. Stock split two-for-one and subscribers exceed one million for the first time.

AOL entered into a joint venture in 1995 with Bertelsmann AG, one of the world's largest media companies, to offer online services in Europe. Stock split twice during the year. The firm also launched Global Network Navigator Internet service and introduced services to Germany. That year, eleven class action lawsuits were filed against AOL by its customers for such practices as billing online time by adding 15 seconds to connection time, rounding up the total to the next minute, and billing for supposedly free areas. Subscribers reached three million.

In 1996, AOL launched services in the United Kingdom and France; introduced America Online Canada, featuring local Canadian content and services; and merged with the Johnson-Grace Co., a leading developer of compression technology and multimedia development and delivery tools. Using the Johnson-Grace technology, AOL was able to deliver data-intensive graphics and audio and video capabilities using narrow-band technologies. The firm inked a partnership with Mitsui & Co., one of the world's largest international trading companies, and Nikkei, a media company, to offer interactive consumer services in Japan with a broad range of localized Japanese language content. Revenues reached $1.1 billion that year, and customers agreed to settle the lawsuits related to AOL business practices. AOL also listed on the New York Stock Exchange and launched an unlimited-use pricing program for $19.95 per month.

The following year, AOL struggled to accommodate the deluge of new users who responded to the

The Business

Financials

Revenue (1998): $2.6 billion

Employees (1998): 8,500

SICs / NAICS

sic 7371 - Computer Programming Services

sic 7375 - Information Retrieval Services

sic 7372 - Prepackaged Software

naics 541511 - Custom Computer Programming Services

naics 514191 - On-Line Information Services

new rate. As a result, representatives of 36 state attorney general offices gathered to discuss consumer complaints about the inability to access AOL's services. AOL announced implementation of a $350 million expansion program that included adding system capacity and hiring 600 new customer service representatives; the firm also decided to scale back its promotion campaign and agreed to give refunds to U.S. customers who were frequently unable to log on.

In 1998, AOL acquired CompuServe Inc., intending to keep its service separate from AOL; the purchase upped AOL's market share to 60%. The firm also raised its unlimited usage rates to $21.95 and formed AOL Investments to hold its interests in electronic commerce. Early in the year, it surpassed the one-million-member mark in Europe. A few months later, AOL agreed to pay $4.2 billion for rival Netscape Communications.

History of Netscape Communications Corp.

James H. Clark, a computer industry veteran who founded Silicon Graphics Inc., and Mark Andreessen, a programmer who helped create Mosaic, a graphic interface program for finding Internet sites, co-founded Mosaic Corp. to sell Internet browsing software in 1994. Because Andreessen had been working for the University of Illinois when he and six colleagues created Mosaic, the university objected to the new firm's name. As a result, the company's name was changed to Netscape.

In 1995, Netscape launched its initial public offering (IPO); although the upstart was not yet profitable, its first day capitalization reached a whopping $2.2 billion. Stock selling for $28 per share jumped to $75 per share on the second day of trading. A consortium

The Officers

Chairman and Chief Executive Officer: Stephen M. Case

Vice Chairman: Kenneth J. Novak

President and Chief Operating Officer: Robert W. Pittman

of Adobe Systems Inc., International Data Group, Knight Ridder, and others purchased an 11% stake in Netscape. Stock peaked at $171 per share that year.

At the beginning of 1996, Netscape held roughly 80% of the Internet browser market and was nearing the $500 million mark in annual sales. The firm gave its Navigator software away for free, making its money via the web server fees it charged firms for helping them establish World Wide Web sites. Netscape's success didn't last long, however. The launch of Microsoft's Internet Explorer had an almost immediate negative impact on Netscape's performance. Stock prices plummeted, and market share slipped away. The firm began charging for its Navigator browser, focusing more intently on corporate markets, and purchasing software vendors, including Kiva Software, DigitalStyle, and Portola Communications.

Losses mounted in 1997, and Netscape slashed 12% of its workforce. Five regional Bell Internet companies agreed to use Netscape Navigator as their default browser; America Online, however, chose Microsoft's Internet Explorer. By 1998, market share was down to roughly 40% and shares were trading at a high of only $44 apiece. Keeping the firm afloat was its server business, which offered corporate clients software that drove World Wide Web sites. Late in the year, Netscape agreed to be purchased by American Online for roughly $4.2 billion.

Market Forces Driving the Merger

In the late 1990s, Netscape was floundering in the wake of stiff competition from Microsoft. The competitor had snatched half of Netscape's Internet browser market share in less than three years, mainly by bundling its Internet Explorer software with its Windows 95 platform. Although the Department of Justice eventually ruled that Microsoft must offer a version of its Windows software unbundled from Internet Explorer, the market domination of the Windows platform afforded the behemoth an easy means of dominating the browser market as well. People who bought new computers simply used the browser software already available to them. Far from

its 1995 peak of 80%, Netscape's market share tumbled from 62% to roughly 40% between January and November of 1998.

A merger with America Online (AOL) would not only offer Netscape a chance to secure a large share of the browser market, particularly if AOL switched its default browser from Internet Explorer to Netscape Navigator; it would also create a new company poised to capitalize on the increasingly lucrative electronic commerce market. AOL, mainly a service company, and Netscape, a software vendor, saw synergistic opportunities in together moving forward in electronic commerce, an industry that would be worth an estimated $4 billion by 2202. Netscape's Netcenter was already one of the leading full-service Web sites, offering users a gateway to the Internet, as well as online shopping and entertainment services. And the two firms' Web sites appeared complimentary as well: AOL users tended to log on during the evening and on weekends; Netcenter targeted a more corporate market, and its traffic was heaviest during weekday business hours.

Many analysts believed that AOL wanted to buy Netscape as a means of targeting corporate clients, a task it had struggled with in the mid-1990s. Netscape's Netcenter site, its browser, and its server software which offered electronic commerce applications would grant AOL access to this chunk of the Internet market. AOL also recognized that adding Netscape to its mix would reposition the firm as the market leader in online media and electronic commerce, fields in which AOL had dabbled. Microsoft was expected to compete extensively in these markets, and joining AOL's services with Netscape's software would create a company that could potentially hold its own against the giant.

Approach and Engagement

In November of 1998, America Online (AOL) offered $4.2 billion in stock for Netscape, which it planned to operate as a wholly owned subsidiary. AOL also agreed to license $500 million in Sun Microsystems' hardware; Sun would then gain access to the sale and development rights to Netscape's most lucrative technology, its server software.

In January of 1999, the antitrust division of the Department of Justice requested additional information regarding the merger between the two firms, citing concerns over how the deal might impact the Internet software and services industry. The merger was filed again, and the two firms still awaited a decision in March of 1999.

Products and Services

Online services accounted for 83% of AOL's $2.6 billion sales in 1998. Advertising made up the remaining 17%. Along with chat rooms, email, bulletin boards, and instant messenger services, AOL offered channels such as AOL Today, Entertainment, Kids Only, Games, Health, Travel, WorkPlace, News, and Computing. Online Shopping available via AOL included Amazon.com, FAO Schwartz, Hickory Farms, JC Penny, Land's End, The Sharper Image, and Tower Records.

Netscape earned 58% of its $448 million in sales in 1998 from products, which were divided into three segments. Netscape Client Software included Netscape AOL Instant Messenger, Netscape Collabra, Netscape Composer, Netscape Conference, Netscape Messenger, Netscape Navigator, Netscape Autoadmin, Netscape Calendar, Netscape IBM Host On-Demand, and Netscape Communicator, which came in standard, enhanced, deluxe, Internet access, publishing, and professional editions. Netscape Commercial Applications housed the firm's electronic commerce software, such as Netscape CommerceXpert, Netscape BuyerXpert, Netscape Ecxpert, Netscape Merchant System, Netscape Publishing Xpert, and Netscape Seller Xpert. Netscape Server Software, the most lucrative segment of the company, offered corporate clients software that powered Web sites: Netscape Suitespot integrated scheduling, group collaboration, messaging, Web server, and information management applications; Netscape Suitespot Hosting Edition added Web server, Web filtering, user directory, and email to the package. The Professional Addition offered users security, intranet, and web filtering functions. The remaining 42% of Netscape's revenues came from Netscape Netcenter, the firm's full-service Web site, which offered shopping, discussion groups, business news, a channel finder, a search engine, and software products online.

The Players

Chairman and CEO of America Online: Stephen M. Case. Hawaii native Stephen Case began his career in marketing by developing new types of pizza for Pizza Hut in the early 1980s. In 1983, he joined the marketing department of Control Video, which ran an online service for Atari users. Two years later he co-founded Quantum Computer Services, which launched the Q-Link online service for Commodore computer users. In 1989, envisioning the creation of a mass market for interactive services and content, Case steered his firm's launch of the America Online service for IBM-compatible and Apple computer users. The firm changed its name to America Online (AOL) in 1991; a year later, when the company went public, Case was named chairman and CEO, a position which he retains today.

President and CEO of Netscape: James L. Barksdale. University of Mississippi graduate James Barksdale worked for Federal Express Corp. as chief information officer from 1979 to 1983, when he was appointed vice president and chief operating officer. Under his tutelage, Federal Express became the first service company to earn the Malcolm Baldrige National Quality Award. He then served as president and chief operating officer of McCaw Cellular between 1992 and 1994. When McCaw merged with AT&T Corp., Barksdale assumed the post of CEO of AT&T Wireless Services. Netscape offered him a board seat in October of 1994, and tapped him as president and CEO in January of 1995. His role at America Online after its merger with Netscape remains to be seen.

Changes to the Industry

"The epic confrontation between Netscape and Microsoft is over, but the epic confrontation between Sun and Microsoft proceeds apace, and the epic confrontation between AOL and Microsoft has barely begun," predicted a December 1998 article in *Time* magazine. When the merger between Netscape and AOL is completed, there is no question that the two firms best poised to capitalize on the electronic commerce industry will be Microsoft and AOL. What remains to be seen is how well AOL can make use of its new purchase. It's also likely that the deal will undercut the antitrust investigation currently surrounding Microsoft's rapid domination of the Web

browser market, particularly if AOL switches its default browser from Internet Explorer to Netscape Navigator, which would give Netscape a market share edge over Microsoft.

Review of the Outcome

Some analysts foresee problems for users of Netscape's high-end server products, mainly because the firm's lucrative server software will be marketed and developed by Sun Microsystems once the deal is finalized. Netscape, suspending its rivalry with Microsoft, sold its servers to both Unix vendors and Windows NT vendors. In fact, Windows NT users made up roughly 40% of Netscape's server market. Because the vehemently anti-Microsoft Sun will be selling Netscape's server software along with its own Solaris Unix operating system, sales to Windows NT users might be compromised.

Another area of concern for analysts is the disparate corporate culture each firm possesses. AOL is mainstream and conservative, while Netscape is less conventional. Executives insist that this won't cause major friction because AOL plans to allow Netscape to retain its own identity.

Despite these unfavorable predictions, AOL performed notably well after the announcement of the deal. The firm beat forecasted profits when its sales quadrupled in the quarter following the release of the news. Electronic commerce revenues jumped 22% from the preceding quarter, and the firm announced a two-for-one stock split.

Research

"America Online, Inc.," in *Notable Corporate Chronologies*, The Gale Group, 1999. Lists major events in the history of America Online.

"DOJ Takes Closer Look at AOL-Netscape Merger," in *Computergram International*, 19 January 1999. Explains why the U.S. Department of Justice delayed the AOL/Netscape merger.

Espe, Eric. "Culture Clash: Author Foresees Trouble for AOL-Netscape Merger," in *The Business Journal*, 12 December 1998. Discusses the potential pitfalls of the merger between AOL and Netscape.

Green, Heather. "Not So Odd a Couple After All," in *Business Week*, 21 December 1998. Offers an overview of how the deal between AOL, Netscape, and Sun Microsystems could impact the electronic commerce industry.

Jastrow, Rosa. "Reaction Ranges From Cautious Optimism to Full Support—Netscape VARs Look for Silver Lining," in *Computer Reseller News*, 14 December 1998. Explains the potential positive outcomes of the Netscape/AOL deal.

Krantz, Michael. "AOL, You've Got Netscape," in *Time*, 7 December 1998. Discusses why the two firms decided to merge and how the deal will impact Internet-related industries.

Lohr, Steve. "Conquering the Internet: America Online Sees Netscape Acquisition as a Big Step Towards Its Ambitious Goals," in *The New York Times*, 24 November 1998. Explains why AOL wants to purchase Netscape.

Netscape Communications Corp. Home Page, available at http://www.netscape.com. Official World Wide Web Home Page for Netscape Communications Corp. Includes news, financial, product, and historical information.

"Merger Fallout," in *Computerworld*, 30 November 1998. Predicts the impact of the AOL/Netscape merger on the Microsoft antitrust case, Netscape's success, and Netscape's server clients.

Mossberg, Walter. "If the Techies Hate the AOL-Netscape Deal, It Must Be Good for Us," in *The Wall Street Journal*, 3 December 1998. Comments on potential synergies between Netscape and AOL, as well as how the deal might be good for consumers.

Swisher, Kara. "AOL Beats Profit Forecasts as Net Quadruples," in *The Wall Street Journal*, 28 January 1999. Explains how AOL has fared since the announcement of the merger.

ANNAMARIE L. SHELDON

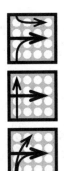

AMERICAN HOME PRODUCTS & AMERICAN CYANAMID

nationality: USA
date: August 1994
affected: American Home Products Corp., USA, founded 1926
affected: American Cyanamid Co., USA, founded 1907

American Home Products Corp.
5 Giralda Farms
Madison, NJ 07940-0874
USA

tel: (973)660-5000
fax: (973)660-7026
web: http://www.ahp.com

Overview of the Merger

The merger of American Cyanamid and American Home Products (AHP) created the fourth largest drug company in the world. What began as a hostile $8.5 billion bid became a friendly takeover when Cyanamid agreed in August of 1994 to become a wholly-owned subsidiary of AHP for $9.7 billion.

History of American Home Products Corp.

A group of executives associated with Sterling Products Inc. and Household Products Inc. consolidated several independent nostrum makers into a holding company, American Home Products (AHP) Corp., in 1926. The new firm sold such medicinal products as Hill's Cascara Quinine, St. Jacob's Oil, Wyeth's Sage and Sulphur, Kolynos dental cream, and Old English No Rubbing Floor Polish.

In 1930, AHP purchased the rights to manufacture a painkiller called Anacin, previously promoted through samples to dentists, which soon became the nation's leading over-the-counter analgesic due to aggressive marketing. Two years later, AHP acquired Wyeth Chemical, a pharmaceutical manufacturer. The firm also purchased sunburn oil that was transformed into Preparation H in 1935. AHP continued to expand via acquisition though the 1940s. By then, AHP had acquired 34 food and drug companies for a total of $25.6 million in cash and stock. In 1946, the firm purchased grocery specialties firm Chef-Boy-Ar-Dee Quality Foods Inc.

By 1971, AHP had spent more money on the promotion of Anacin than any other analgesic manufacturer on a comparable product. A year later, the FTC charged that AHP and two other analgesic makers had promoted their products through unsubstantiated claims; the suit was settled in 1981, and permanent limits were placed on claims deemed misleading.

AHP spent $425 million in 1983 to buy the Sherwood Medical Group, a maker of medical supplies; the purchase placed AHP in a competitive position to capture a large share of the growing medical device market. The firm also introduced

The Business

Financials

Revenue (1998): $13.5 billion

Employees (1998): 52,984

SICs / NAICS

sic 2834 - Pharmaceutical Preparations

sic 2833 - Medicinals & Botanicals

sic 2879 - Agricultural Chemicals Nec

sic 3841 - Surgical & Medical Instruments

sic 2048 - Prepared Feeds Nec

sic 2891 - Adhesives & Sealants

sic 2824 - Organic Fibers-Noncellulosic

naics 325412 - Pharmaceutical Preparation Manufacturing

naics 325411 - Medicinal and Botanical Manufacturing

naics 339112 - Surgical and Medical Instrument Manufacturing

naics 311119 - Other Animal Food Manufacturing

naics 325222 - Noncellulosic Organic Fiber Manufacturing

painkiller Advil that year. In 1985, AHP filed 21 applications with the Food and Drug Administration. Sales exceeded $5 billion for the first time in 1987, and two years later, net income reached $1 billion. AHP's household products unit was divested in 1990.

In 1992, the firm acquired Symbiosis Corp., a leading developer and manufacturer of disposable instruments for laparoscopic and endoscopic surgery, and introduced the Norplant contraceptive system for women. In August of 1994, AHP made a hostile bid for American Cyanamid, seeking to scuttle a multibillion-dollar asset swap discussed by Cyanamid and SmithKline Beecham. When the $9.7 billion merger was completed, AHP became as the third largest worldwide pharmaceutical and health care products manufacturer and the sixth largest agricultural products maker.

To offset debt, AHP divested its Latin American oral-care business to Colgate-Palmolive for $1.04 billion in 1995. Later that year, research and development spending was increased to $1 billion to intensify work on the several drugs. In 1996, AHP introduced Redux, the first weight loss drug to receive FDA approval in roughly 20 years; the firm also refocused on core pharmaceutical operations and divested its food holdings.

Complaints of heart problems linked to taking Redux prompted AHP to recall the drug in 1997; consequently, several lawsuit were filed. AHP also acquired the animal health holdings of Solvay SA that year. In January of 1998, SmithKline Beecham PLC and AHP announced their intention to merge. Less than two weeks later, though, SmithKline Beecham decided Glaxo Wellcome PLC was a more attractive partner and ended its discussions with AHP. Later that year, AHP divested its medical devices holdings and announced plans to merge with Monsanto Co. That merger fell apart in October after executives failed to agree on who would run the new giant.

History of American Cyanamid Co.

Frank Washburn founded American Cyanamid Co. with $5 million in authorized capital in 1907. The company's purpose was to manufacture calcium cyanamide using a process developed in Germany; North American rights were acquired and plant construction began. In 1916, Cyanamid acquired Ammo-Phos Corp., a maker of high grade fertilizer composed of ammonium phosphate and sulfuric acid; Amalgamated Phosphate Company was included in the transaction, marking the beginning of Cyanamid's phosphate mining operations in Brewster, Florida.

During World War I, the cyanide previously supplied by German companies was in great demand. Accordingly, Cyanamid began making cyanide from cyanamide and hydrocyanic acid, which was used in the vulcanization of rubber. The firm diversified into pesticides in 1923 with the purchase of Owl Fumigating Corp., a manufacturer of hydrocyanic acid used to fumigate California citrus trees. In 1929, Cyanamid traded its common stock for holdings in other firms, including heavy chemicals maker Kalbfleish Corp., chemicals manufacturer The Selden Co., dyes and color chemicals maker Calco Chemical Co., and Rezyl Corp., a maker of resins and plasticizers. That year, the firm boasted 30 subsidiaries as one of the most diversified U.S. chemical companies.

With capital raised by the issuing of more than two million shares, Cyanamid launched an acquisition spree that included the purchase of Lederle Laboratories; Davis & Geck, Inc. of Brooklyn, New York; American Powder Co., which complemented the Rezyl lacquer business; Chemical Engineering Corp.; and Chemical Construction Corp. In 1933, General Explosives Corp. and similar operations were bought to augment the explosives production begun by the company during World War I. Cyanamid also contributed to the World War II effort by developing improved sulfa drugs, typhus vaccine, gas gangrene antitoxin, dried blood plasma, and other medicinal products.

Lederle researchers first synthesized vitamin B1 in 1947. A year later, Lederle scientists discovered the broad spectrum antibiotic Aureomycin while conducting experiments on soil samples; the new product was used to combat more diseases than penicillin, and it enabled farmers to produce heavier and healthier livestock. This breakthrough marked the advent of Cyanamid's pharmaceutical and agricultural businesses. In 1952, the firm introduced Malathion, a safe alternative to DDT, which became Cyanamid's leading agricultural product. Tetracycline, a broad spectrum antibiotic, was first produced in 1953; an oral polio vaccine was developed in 1954.

In 1958, the Cyanamid International Division was established to integrate production and marketing efforts outside the U.S. and Canada and to prepare for worldwide expansion. The firm's largest overseas pharmaceuticals facility opened in England that year. Less than two years later, international sales accounted for about 16% of total revenue. The following year, Cyanamid founded its Agricultural Research Center in New Jersey.

Early in the 1960s, Lederle became the first U.S. company licensed to manufacture a live oral polio virus vaccine combining all three Sabin virus strains in a single dosage form; it was marketed under the name Orimune. Cyanamid acquired John H. Breck, Inc., maker of Breck shampoos; Dumas Milner Corp., maker of Pine Sol cleaner; and Formica Corp., a decorative laminates business. The firm was convicted on restraint of trade charges, along with Bristol-Myers Co. and Pfizer Inc., for conspiring to monopolize the marketing and manufacturing of tetracycline. The 81 damage suits filed against Cyanamid were settled for $48.5 million, more than half the firm's net income for 1967. A year later, annual sales reached $1 billion for the first time.

In 1970, Cyanamid entered land development by purchasing The Ervin Co. of North Carolina, Sunstate Builders, Inc. of Florida, and several smaller firms used to form the residential and commercial construction business, Ervin Industries Inc. In its largest consumer products acquisition to date, Cyanamid acquired Sulton, Inc., maker of Old Spice and Pierre Cardin toiletries for men, in 1971.

In 1980, Prowl herbicide was introduced; it soon became the firm's best selling product. Seven years later, Cyanamid diversified into eye care by acquiring Coburn Professional Products. By 1990, all consumer products and operations were divested; the firm refocused on medical, agricultural, fertilizer, and chemical operations. After a prolonged downturn in the U.S. chemicals market, Cyanamid consolidated its chemicals business into a separate division called Cytec Industries in 1991.

The Officers

Chairman, President, and CEO: John R. Stafford
Sr. Exec. VP: Robert G. Blount
Exec. VP: Robert Essner
Sr. VP: David M. Oliveir
Sr. VP: Joseph J. Carr

To help increase its presence in the drug market, the company bought 53% of Immunex Corp., a California-based biotech company, in 1992; Cyanamid combined its anti-cancer operations with those of Immunex. The following year, the firm spun off Cytec to shareholders, completing its transformation from a chemical company to a drug and agricultural products firm. In 1994, American Home Products (AHP) offered a $8.5 billion hostile bid for Cyanamid, seeking to scuttle Cyanamid's negotiations with SmithKline. Cyanamid eventually agreed to become a wholly-owned subsidiary of AHP for $9.7 million.

Market Forces Driving the Merger

A major pharmaceuticals merger trend was launched in 1994 for two major reasons. Firms realized they needed to cut drug development and delivery costs. Intense competition, evidenced by the marginal market shares held by even the largest players in the prescription drug industry, forced firms to funnel huge amounts of cash, up to 30% of total revenues, into sales and marketing efforts. Consolidation allowed these firms to streamline operations and save money. Broader product lines were also seen as necessary for maintaining a competitive edge. Health care providers, particularly managed care companies, had become increasingly concerned with cutting costs and increasing efficiency. Large firms with a broad range of products appealed to these businesses because they could offer volume discounts and one-stop shopping. At the same time, selling larger orders to single customers reduced delivery costs for the drug companies.

Specifically, American Home Products (AHP) wanted Cyanamid's generic drug holdings to bolster its own prescription drug product base, thereby increasing its leverage with managed care operations. Because Cyanamid's consumer brands and over-the-counter products had been marketed on a limited basis, AHP also believed it could improve Cyanamid's sales. Significant cost savings would also be realized if the two firms merged.

The Players

Chairman and CEO of American Home Products Corp.: John R. Stafford. Former Hoffman-LaRoche lawyer John Stafford was appointed chairman and CEO of American Home Products on December 1, 1986. In 1994, he also assumed the role of president. Stafford steered the firm's takeover of American Cyanamid in 1994 and continues to lead AHP today.

CEO of American Cyanamid: Albert J. Costello. Albert Costello began his long career at American Cyanamid as a chemist in the Organic Pigments Department in 1957. In 1991, he assumed the role of president of American Cyanamid. Two years later, he was appointed chairman and CEO. In 1995, not long after American Cyanamid was taken over by American Home Products, W.R. Grace tapped Costello as CEO. He retired from W.R. Grace in late 1998.

According to Wall Street insiders, another factor also prompted AHP to finally make an offer for the firm its had been eyeing for quite some time: Cyanamid and SmithKline Beecham had been discussing an asset swap in which SmithKline Beecham would trade its vaccine and animal health operations for Cyanamid's prescription drug and consumer health businesses. The deal, which AHP was determined to scuttle, would have positioned Cyanamid among world's leading vaccine and animal care firms and broadened SmithKline Beecham's prescription drugs product line.

Approach and Engagement

Although, AHP CEO Stafford and Cyanamid CEO Costello had agreed in 1994 to meet at the end of August to discuss a merger, when news of Cyanamid's talks with SmithKline Beecham reached AHP, the firm decided to make a more assertive move. Hoping to discourage counter offers, AHP launched a hostile bid for Cyanamid early in August of 1994 worth more than 21 times the firm's anticipated annual earnings. The $95 per share cash tender offer, worth an estimated $8.5 billion, valued Cyanamid's stock at 50% more than it was trading for on the New York Stock Exchange then.

AHP then filed suit in a Maine district court to prevent Cyanamid from launching any defensive moves and demanded a copy of its shareholder list, a provision allowed under the laws of Maine, the state where Cyanamid was incorporated. Cyanamid told its shareholders to ignore the offer until its board was able to decide upon a formal response to the offer, a concession allowed by Securities and Exchange Commission regulations. Cyanamid looked to other suitors, including SmithKline Beecham, but AHP's bid was high enough to prevent counter offers. When AHP increased its offer by to $101 per share, Cyanamid agreed to the $9.7 billion deal. To meet FDA antitrust requirements, AHP agreed to divest its diphtheria and tetanus vaccine lines to Chiron Corp.

Products and Services

Pharmaceutical sales accounted for 61% of AHP's $14 billion in sales in 1997. Cyanamid's agricultural products brought in 15%, as did consumer health care products. Medical devices, which were divested in 1998, secured the remaining nine percent.

Pharmaceuticals were divided into eight segments: anti-infective, which consisted of Minocin, Pipracil, Suprax, and pneumonia treatment Zosyn; cardiovascular, which comprised Cordarone, Verelan, and Ziac; mental health, which included Ativan and anti-depressant Effexor; nutritional, which housed Nursoy, Progress, Promil, and S-26/SMA; oncology and hematology, which encompassed BeneFix, Leukine, Neumega, and Novantrone; pain and inflammation, which housed Synvisc; vaccines, which included Acel-Imune, HibTITER, and Orimune; and women's health care products, which consisted of oral contraceptive Alesse, Lo/Orval, estrogen replacement Premarin, and Triphasil. Agricultural products included Acrobat; Counter, an insecticide; Lightning; Odyssey; Pirate; and Prowl and Pursuit, two herbicides. Advil, Centrum, Dimetapp, and Robitussin made up the consumer health care products division.

Changes to the Industry

By 1997, AHP had fully digested Cyanamid and the firm was again on the hunt for new acquisitions. According to Bruce Wasserstein, author of *The Big Deal: The Battle for Control of America's Leading Corporations*, the success of the merger prompted increased industry consolidation. "AHP's sterling performance came despite the fact that the goodwill created by the Cyanamid deal initially reduced AHP's earnings per share. Fundamentally, the market saw the underlying economic sense of the deal, as Jack Stafford had predicted. The dollars-and-cents benefits of consolidation were underscored, only increasing the competition for merger partners." Following AHP's lead, Glaxo Holdings PLC and Wellcome PLC merged in October of 1995; Pharmacia AB and The Upjohn Co. in November of 1995; and Ciba Geigy Ltd. and Sandoz Ltd. into Novartis in 1996. In 1998, major deals between AHP and SmithKline Beecham and AHP and Monsanto failed, but another major consolidation move for AHP seemed imminent.

Review of the Outcome

Analysts initially predicted problems for AHP because its product line was becoming outdated, particularly in the face of stiff competition from newer drugs, and Cyanamid didn't have any new drugs of its own. However, perhaps because AHP divested its Latin American oral-care business for $1.04 billion in 1995 and then increased research and development spending to $1 billion, the merger proved positive. The firm saved an estimated $650 million annually, due, at least in part, to the lay off of 4,300 employees in 1997. And after an initial dip, AHP share prices grew from $28 each before the merger to $75 apiece in 1997.

Research

"American Cyanamid Co.," in *Notable Corporate Chronologies*, The Gale Group, 1999. Lists major events in the history of American Cyanamid Co., including its merger with American Home Products Corp.

"American Home Products Corp.," in *Notable Corporate Chronologies*, Gale Research, 1999. Chronicles major events in the history of American Home Products Corp.

American Home Products Home Page, available at http://www.ahp.com. Official World Wide Web Home Page for American Home Products. Includes news, financial, product, and historical information.

"American Home Products Offers $8.5 Billion for American Cyanamid," in *Chain Drug Review*, 29 August 1994. Discusses the details of the hostile takeover launched by AHP for American Cyanamid.

Harverson, Patrick. "AHP Defends Delicate Chemistry of $9.7bn Acquisition," in *The Financial Times*, 19 August 1994. Details the potential negative impact of the Cyanamid takeover on AHP's bottom line.

Scheid, Jon F. "Cyanamid's Board Endorses AHPC $101 a Share Offer," in *Feedstuffs*, 22 August 1994. Explains the agreement between AHP and American Cyanamid, as well as the potential outcome.

——. "Cyanamid Gets Buyout Bid Amid Swap Rumors," in *Feedstuffs*, 8 August 1994. Discusses the impact of talks between SmithKline Beecham and American Cyanamid on AHP's offer for American Cyanamid.

Wasserstein, Bruce. *Big Deal: The Battle for Control of America's Leading Corporations*, Warner Books, 1998. Offers an overview of the largest mergers in recent American corporate history.

THERA WILLIAMS

AMERICAN HOME PRODUCTS & MONSANTO

American Home Products Corp.
5 Giralda Farms
Madison, NJ 07940-0874
USA

tel: (973)660-5000
fax: (973)660-7026
web: http://www.ahp.com

Monsanto Co.
800 N. Lindbergh Blvd.
St. Louis, MO 63167
USA

tel: (314)694-1000
fax: (314)694-6572
web: http://www.monsanto.com

date: October 1998 (canceled)
affected: American Home Products Corp., USA, founded 1926
affected: Monsanto Co., USA, founded 1901

Overview of the Merger

Monsanto and American Home Products announced in June of 1998 their intent to merge in a stock swap valued at roughly $33 billion. With 75,000 employees and $23 billion in annual revenues, the resulting life science company would have been the world's largest, holding significant chunks of the agricultural chemicals, seed, pharmaceuticals, and nutritional products markets. The firm would have ranked fourth in pharmaceuticals and first in agricultural chemicals and biotechnology. The deal fell apart in October of 1998, however, after executives allegedly clashed over who would end up running the merged company.

History of American Home Products Corp.

A group of executives associated with Sterling Products Inc. and Household Products Inc. consolidated several independent nostrum makers into a holding company, American Home Products (AHP) Corp., in 1926. The new firm sold such medicinal products as Hill's Cascara Quinine, St. Jacob's Oil, Wyeth's Sage and Sulphur, Kolynos dental cream, and Old English No Rubbing Floor Polish.

In 1930, AHP purchased the rights to manufacture a painkiller called Anacin, previously promoted through samples to dentists, which soon became the nation's leading over-the-counter analgesic due to aggressive marketing. Two years later, AHP acquired Wyeth Chemical, a pharmaceutical manufacturer. The firm also purchased sunburn oil that was transformed into Preparation H in 1935. AHP continued to expand via acquisition though the 1940s. By then, AHP had acquired 34 food and drug companies for a total of $25.6 million in cash and stock. In 1946, the firm purchased grocery specialties firm Chef-Boy-Ar-Dee Quality Foods Inc.

By 1971, AHP had spent more money on the promotion of Anacin than any other analgesic manufacturer on a comparable product. A year later, the FTC charged that AHP and two other analgesic makers had promoted their products through unsubstantiated claims; the suit was settled in 1981, and permanent limits were placed on claims deemed misleading.

AHP spent $425 million in 1983 to buy the Sherwood Medical Group, a maker of medical supplies; the purchase placed AHP in a competitive position to capture a large share of the growing medical device market. The firm also introduced painkiller Advil that year. In 1985, AHP filed 21 applications with the Food and Drug Administration. Sales exceeded $5 billion for the first time in 1987, and two years later, net income reached $1 billion. AHP's household products unit was divested in 1990.

In 1992, the firm acquired Symbiosis Corp., a leading developer and manufacturer of disposable instruments for laparoscopic and endoscopic surgery, and introduced the Norplant contraceptive System for women. In August of 1994, AHP made a hostile bid for American Cyanamid Co., seeking to scuttle a multibillion-dollar asset swap discussed by Cyanamid and SmithKline Beecham. When the $9.7 billion merger was completed, AHP became as the third largest worldwide pharmaceutical and health care products manufacturer and the sixth largest agricultural products maker.

To offset debt, AHP divested its Latin American oral-care business to Colgate-Palmolive for $1.04 billion in 1995. Later that year, research and development spending was increased to $1 billion to intensify work on the several drugs. In 1996, AHP introduced Redux, the first weight loss drug to receive FDA approval in roughly 20 years; the firm also refocused on core pharmaceutical operations and divested its food holdings. Complaints of heart problems linked to taking Redux prompted AHP to recall the drug in 1997; consequently, several lawsuit were filed. AHP also acquired the animal health holdings of Solvay SA that year. In January of 1998, SmithKline Beecham PLC and AHP announced their intention to merge. Less than two weeks later, though, SmithKline Beecham decided Glaxo Wellcome PLC was a more attractive partner and ended its discussions with AHP. Later that year, AHP divested its medical devices holdings and announced plans to merge with Monsanto Co. That merger fell apart in October after executives failed to agree on who would run the new giant.

History of Monsanto Co.

John Francisco Queeny's East St. Louis Sulphur Refining Co. burned down the very day it opened in 1899, wiping out his $6,000 life savings. Two years later, Queeny began producing saccharin in a warehouse; the new company was named Monsanto Chemical Works. By 1905, Monsanto was also producing caffeine and vanillin. Sales surpassed $1 million for the first time in 1915.

The Business

Financials - American Home Products Corp.

Revenue (1998): $13.5 billion

Employees (1998): 52,984

Financials - Monsanto Co.

Revenue (1998): $8.64 billion

Employees (1998): 31,800

SICs / NAICS

sic 2834 - Pharmaceutical Preparations

sic 2833 - Medicinals & Botanicals

sic 2879 - Agricultural Chemicals Nec

sic 3841 - Surgical & Medical Instruments

sic 2048 - Prepared Feeds Nec

sic 2891 - Adhesives & Sealants

sic 2824 - Organic Fibers-Noncellulosic

sic 2836 - Biological Products Except Diagnostic

sic 2869 - Industrial Organic Chemicals Nec

naics 325412 - Pharmaceutical Preparation Manufacturing

naics 325411 - Medicinal and Botanical Manufacturing

naics 339112 - Surgical and Medical Instrument Manufacturing

naics 311119 - Other Animal Food Manufacturing

naics 325222 - Noncellulosic Organic Fiber Manufacturing

naics 325414 - Biological Product (except Diagnostic) Manufacturing

naics 325188 - All Other Basic Inorganic Chemical Manufacturing

With the entrance of the U.S. into World War I, Monsanto began to produce strategic products, including phenol, used as an antiseptic, and aspirin. The company's first overseas operations were in a 50% venture with a United Kingdom-based firm that was the world's largest producer of phenol and cresol at the time. In 1927, Monsanto listed publicly on the Chicago Stock Exchange. Two years later, Monsanto had doubled in size and gained entry into key rubber chemical markets by acquiring Rubber Services Laboratories Co. of Akron, Ohio, and Nitro of West Virginia.

Monsanto Chemical Co. incorporated in 1933; by then, the product line had expanded to include the

The Officers

American Home Products Corp.

Chairman, President, and CEO: John R. Stafford

Sr. Exec. VP: Robert G. Blount

Exec. VP: Robert Essner

Sr. VP: David M. Oliveir

Sr. VP: Joseph J. Carr

Monsanto Co.

Chairman and CEO: Robert B. Shapiro

Vice Chairman and Chairman and CEO, G.D. Searle & Co.:
    Richard U. DeSchutter

Vice Chairman: Robert W. Reynolds

President: Hendrick A. Verfaillie

Exec. VP: Pierre Hochuli

manufacture of phosphorus. In April of 1947, the French cargo ship S.S. Grandcamp exploded in a Texas harbor, igniting Monsanto's styrene plant nearby; 512 people, including 145 company employees, were killed and more than 200 were injured.

Monsanto joined with American Viscose in 1949 to form the Chemstranc Corp.; with Monsanto's research in polymers and Viscose's experience in textile marketing, this venture flourished in the new synthetic fiber field. Operations in Spain and Australia also began, as well as synthetic rubber production. The 1955 acquisition of Lion Oil upped Monsanto's assets by more than 50%. A year later, the company laid the foundation of its agricultural group with the commercialization of Randox, an herbicide able to stop weeds before they broke ground.

To reflect the growing diversity of its product line, the company dropped the word "chemical" from its name in 1964. By then, it was involved in nylon and acrylic fiber production, oil and gas exploration, fabricated plastic production, and the manufacture of thousands of specialty and commodity chemicals. That year, in response to increasing environmental concerns, Monsanto introduced biodegradable detergents; in 1976, to decrease pollution of the environment, the firm began phasing out production of polychlorinated biphenyl.

In 1984, Monsanto lost a $10 million antitrust suit to Spray-Rite, a former distributor of Monsanto agricultural herbicides; the U.S. Supreme Court upheld the suit and award, finding that Monsanto acted to fix retail prices with other herbicide makers. Also, Monsanto and seven other manufacturers involved in Agent Orange litigation agreed to a $180 million settlement immediately prior to the beginning of the trial.

The following year, Monsanto divested its petrochemical businesses and purchased G.D. Searle, maker of NutraSweet and the Copper 7 intrauterine device (IUD). Soon after acquiring Searle, disclosures about hundreds of lawsuits over the Copper 7 surfaced. In 1986, sales of IUDs were discontinued in the U.S.

Monsanto introduced Simplesse, an all natural fat substitute, in 1990. Two years later, Maxaquin (lomefloxacin) received approval in the U.S. to be used as the first one-a-day quinolone antibiotic medication. Between 1983 and 1993, Monsanto spent in excess of $300 million to develop bovine somatotropin (EST), a genetically engineered product similar to the hormone produced in cows which controls milk production; the USDA approved the product in 1993 despite objections from dairy farmers and veterinarians.

In 1994, Akzo Nobel NV and Monsanto agreed to merge their rubber and chemical operations into a unit based in Belgium. The companies each owned an equal part of the joint venture. Also, Monsanto purchased Merck & Co.'s specialty chemicals unit, Kelco, for $1.08 billion. A year later, the EPA gave its first ever approval for the growing of plants bioengineered to produce their own pesticide. Monsanto was allowed to plant, but not sell, potatoes, corn and cotton crops that were genetically altered to produce an insecticide. The firm also bought a 49.9% stake in Calgene Inc. for $30 million, as well as certain patent and technology rights.

Dekalb Genetics agreed to jointly research and develop agricultural biotechnology with Monsanto between 1996 and 2006. Both companies obtained licensing revenues for products developed during the cooperative efforts. Monsanto also received a patent for its synthetic genes that allowed plants to create their own insecticides and filed patent infringement suits against rivals Ciba-Geigy AG and Mycogen Corp. for their uses of the gene. That year, the firm also purchased Asgrow Seed, the second largest U.S. soybean-seed marketer, for $240 million; acquired the plant biotechnology assets of W.R. Grace's Agracetus unit; increased its stake in Calgene Inc. to a majority share; and split its stock five-for-one.

In 1997, Monsanto acquired Holden's Foundation Seeds Inc. and its exclusive sales agents, Corn States Hybrid Service Inc. and Corn States International. Monsanto and ArQule Inc. also agreed on a five-year contract to develop new agrochemicals. After its efforts to merge with American Home Products fell through in 1998, the firm launched a multibillion acquisition spree that targeted DeKalb Genetics (the 60% Monsanto did not already own), Delta & Pine Land, Plant Breeding International Cambridge, and Cargill's international seed operations.

Market Forces Driving the Merger

Consolidation activity in the pharmaceuticals market was slow compared to other industries in 1997 and 1998 because most major pharmaceutical companies had the financial resources to develop drugs by themselves. The last merger wave in the industry had taken place in the mid-1990s and resulted in the unions of Glaxo Holdings PLC and Wellcome PLC in October of 1995; Pharmacia AB and The Upjohn Co. in November of 1995; Ciba Geigy Ltd. and Sandoz Ltd. into Novartis in 1996; and American Home Products (AHP) and American Cyanamid Co. in August of 1994.

Industry analysts predicted that as a wave of patent expiry among the largest pharmaceutical players began to break in the late 1990s, many of the firms involved in the merger mania of the mid-1990s, such as AHP, would be seeking new merger and acquisition partners. Consulting firm AT Kearney estimated that between the years 1998 and 2003, expired patents on 42 key drugs would take a $32 billion toll on earnings in the pharmaceutical industry; this was a major cause of the increased merger discussions among pharmaceutical giants during 1998 and 1999.

Several of the industry giants, including AHP, Monsanto, SmithKline Beecham, and Glaxo Welcome were also contemplating mergers as a means of increasing market share, reducing costs, and enhancing research and development budgets. New research dollars would be essential for firms looking to stay competitive in a marketplace where demand, at times, seemed unchecked. In fact, according to Dr. Wang Chong of consulting firm Arthur D. Little, mergers would be necessary for the firms who wanted to remain in the top ten industry tier because to do so would require pharmaceutical companies to introduce at least three new drugs annually. In the late 1990s, only three pharmaceutical businesses were capable of doing this: Johnson & Johnson, Merck & Co., and Pfizer Inc.

AHP and Monsanto believed they could save significantly by consolidating research and development efforts; the dollars saved could also be funneled back into the new company's research and development budget. Most analysts saw the oncology, women's health, cardiovascular, and arthritis pharmaceutical lines of both firms as complementary, and Monsanto

The Players

Chairman and CEO of American Home Products Corp.: John R. Stafford. Former Hoffman-LaRoche lawyer John Stafford was appointed chairman and CEO of American Home Products on December 1, 1986. In 1994, he also assumed the role of president. Stafford steered the firm's takeover of American Cyanamid in 1994 and continues to lead AHP today.

Chairman and CEO of Monsanto Co.: Robert B. Shapiro. Robert Shapiro began working for G.D. Searle & Co. in 1979, where he headed up the firm's NutraSweet operations. In 1985, when Monsanto purchased Searle, Shapiro was retained by his firm's new owner and eventually appointed head of Monsanto's agriculture businesses. In 1994, after serving as president and COO, Shapiro took Monsanto's reigns as chairman and CEO.

would gain access to AHP's strong domestic and international pharmaceutical distribution channels, as well as its deeper marketing and research and development pockets. Merging with Monsanto would also allow AHP to triple its presence in the agricultural chemicals market, surpassing global leader Novartis.

Approach and Engagement

In June of 1998, Monsanto and American Home Products (AHP) agreed to a $33 billion stock swap. Under the terms of the agreement, AHP shareholders would obtain one share in the new firm for each AHP share, and Monsanto shareholders would secure 1.15 shares of the new firm for each Monsanto share. Essentially, AHP would be paying $52.94 per share for Monsanto, a price slightly higher than its market price at the time of the announcement. Executives explained that the lower price reflected that the deal was a merger of equals, not a takeover. In fact, Monsanto CEO Shapiro and AHP CEO Stafford agreed serve as co-CEOs and co-chairs through the integration phase of the merger.

Several analysts saw this agreement as troublesome. According to healthcare analyst Jeffrey J. Kraws, it would be tough for "two CEOs who are used to running companies and who are building very successful franchises—Monsanto in agriculture and American Home more in pharmaceuticals—to all of a sudden relinquish control." Even if the two leaders were each able to give up a bit of power, critics of the deal pointed out that the conservative chief executive of AHP and the more fiscally liberal leader of Monsanto might find it difficult to agree on how to best run the newly merged giant. The deal fell apart in October of 1998, with both firming citing concerns regarding the merger's value for shareholders. However, most analysts believed the true reason was a collision of egos.

Products and Services

Pharmaceutical sales accounted for 61% of AHP's $14 billion in sales in 1997. Agricultural products brought in 15%, as did consumer health care products. Medical devices, which were divested in 1998, secured the remaining nine percent. Pharmaceuticals were divided into eight segments: anti-infective, which consisted of Minocin, Pipracil, Suprax, and pneumonia treatment Zosyn; cardiovascular, which comprised Cordarone, Verelan, and Ziac; mental health which included Ativan and anti-depressant Effexor; nutritional, which housed Nursoy, Progress, Promil, and S-26/SMA; oncology and hematology, which encompassed BeneFix, Leukine, Neumega, and Novantrone; pain and inflammation, which housed Synvisc; vaccines, which included Acel-Imune, HibTITER, and Orimune; and women's health care products, which consisted of oral contraceptive Alesse, Lo/Orval, estrogen replacement Premarin, and Triphasil. Agricultural products included Acrobat; Counter, an insecticide; Lightning; Odyssey; Pirate; and Prowl and Pursuit, two herbicides. Advil, Centrum, Dimetapp, and Robitussin made up the consumer health care products division.

Agricultural products, including herbicides such as Roundup and biotechnology products like NewLeaf, earned Monsanto 42% of its 1997 revenues of $3.12 billion. Pharmaceuticals brought in 32% of the total. This segment was divided into five categories: anti-inflammatory, cardiovascular, central nervous systems, gastrointestinal, and oral contraceptives. Celebra, a promising new arthritis treatment expected to generate significant sales, was scheduled for launch in 1999. Nutrition and Consumer Products, including NutraSweet, Equal, and fat substitute Simplesse, accounted for the remaining sales.

Changes to the Industry and Review of the Outcome

The merger dissolution hit Monsanto harder that it did American Home Products (AHP). The day the deal was called off, AHP stock prices fell from $50 to $45, while Monsanto's tumbled 26.5% from roughly $50 to $37. To recover, Monsanto needed to take more drastic measures than AHP. Accordingly, the firm

secured an additional $2 billion in revolving credit and tripled its SEC shelf registration to $6 billion. Monsanto used the credit line to pursue major seed acquisitions, including DeKalb Genetics ($2.3 billion for the 60% it didn't already own), Delta Pine & Land, Plant Breeding International Cambridge ($525 million), and Cargill's international seed operations ($1.4 billion). Because the transactions raised Monsanto's debt-to-capital ratio to roughly 60%, Standard and Poor's changed Monsanto debt rating from positive to negative.

Some analysts predicted that neither Monsanto nor American Home Products (AHP) would likely pursue a merger in the near future. According to ABN Amro pharmaceutical industry analyst James Keeney, "AHP will likely remain by itself, and the merger sounds a death knell for their involvement in the agricultural chemicals business because they have an untenable position there. I think they'll have to cash out of that business in the next 12 to 24 months." At the same time, however, a 1998 article in *Forbes*, suggested that another deal between AHP and Monsanto, this one a hostile takeover by AHP, could be looming on the horizon.

Research

"American Home Products Corp.," in *Notable Corporate Chronologies*, The Gale Group, 1999. Lists major events in the history of American Home Products Corp.

American Home Products Home Page, available at http://www.ahp.com. Official World Wide Web Home Page for American Home Products. Includes news, financial, product, and historical information.

Blackledge, Cath. "Here Comes Another Drug Pact, Perhaps...," in *The European*, 23 November 1998. Details the major pharmaceutical mergers that were announced and later canceled in 1998.

Chang, Joseph. "AHP and Monsanto Merge to Form Colossal Life Science Firm," in *Chemical Market Reporter*, 8 June 1998. Details the terms of the agreement between AHP and Monsanto and its potential outcome.

———. "AHP, Monsanto Halt Merger Terminating $33 Bn Stock Swap," in *Chemical Market Reporter*, 10 October 1998. Explains why the merger was canceled and predicts what each firm will do in the immediate future.

Fitch, Stephane. "The Next Shoe....," in *Forbes*, 30 November 1998. Predicts that Monsanto might soon be the target of a hostile takeover by AHP.

Fried, Carla. "You'd Think Monsanto Shareholders Would Be Miffed," in *Money*, July 1998. Explains shareholder reaction to the merger price and how the two firms plan to integrate operations.

Gaines, Sallie L. "Deal Off: Monsanto to Follow Own Path," in *Chicago Tribune*, 30 November 1998. Offers an overview of the AHP/Monsanto deal, including why it was called off and what Monsanto will do instead.

Melcher, Richard A. "Monsanto May Be Counting its Chickens," in *Business Week*, 30 November 1998.

Explains how Monsanto CEO Shapiro is steering his firm in the wake of the merger collapse, as well as potential problems he might encounter.

"Monsanto Co.," in *Notable Corporate Chronologies*, The Gale Group, 1999. Lists major events in the history of Monsanto Co.

Monsanto Home Page, available at http://www.monsanto.com. Official World Wide Web Home Page for Monsanto Co. Includes news, financial, product, and historical information.

THERA WILLIAMS

AMERICAN HOME PRODUCTS &
SMITHKLINE BEECHAM

American Home Products Corp.
5 Giralda Farms
Madison, NJ 07940-0874
USA

tel: (973)660-5000
fax: (973)660-7026
web: http://www.ahp.com

SmithKline Beecham PLC
1 New Horizons Ct.
Brentford, Middlesex TW8 9EP
United Kingdom

tel: 44-181-975-2000
fax: 44-181-975-2090
web: http://www.sb.com

date: January 30, 1998 (canceled)
affected: American Home Products Corp., USA, founded 1926
affected: SmithKline Beecham PLC, U.K., founded 1830

Overview of the Merger

The merger of fifth place American Home Products (AHP) and fourth place SmithKline Beecham would have created a new pharmaceutical industry leader—with a six percent share of the worldwide pharmaceuticals market—worth a whopping $125 billion. The new firm's combined over-the-counter sales of $27 billion would have dethroned Bristol-Myers Squibb Co., the current leader in U.S. prescription drugs. However, SmithKline Beecham ended it merger talks with AHP in January of 1998, opting instead to pursue a deal with U.K.-based Glaxo Wellcome PLC; that agreement also fell apart, leaving three of the world's largest pharmaceutical players open for consolidation moves.

History of American Home Products Corp.

A group of executives associated with Sterling Products Inc. and Household Products Inc. consolidated several independent nostrum makers into a holding company, American Home Products (AHP) Corp., in 1926. The new firm sold such medicinal products as Hill's Cascara Quinine, St. Jacob's Oil, Wyeth's Sage and Sulphur, Kolynos dental cream, and Old English No Rubbing Floor Polish.

In 1930, AHP purchased the rights to manufacture a painkiller called Anacin, previously promoted through samples to dentists, which soon became the nation's leading over-the-counter analgesic due to aggressive marketing. Two years later, AHP acquired Wyeth Chemical, a pharmaceutical manufacturer. The firm also purchased sunburn oil that was transformed into Preparation H in 1935. AHP continued to expand via acquisition though the 1940s. By then, AHP had acquired 34 food and drug companies for a total of $25.6 million in cash and stock. In 1946, the firm purchased grocery specialties firm Chef-Boy-Ar-Dee Quality Foods Inc.

By 1971, AHP had spent more money on the promotion of Anacin than any other analgesic manufacturer on a comparable product. A year later, the FTC charged that AHP and two other analgesic makers had promoted their products through unsubstantiated claims; the suit was settled in 1981, and permanent limits were placed on claims deemed misleading.

AHP spent $425 million in 1983 to buy the Sherwood Medical Group, a maker of medical supplies; the purchase placed AHP in a competitive position to capture a large share of the growing medical device market. The firm also introduced painkiller Advil that year. In 1985, AHP filed 21 applications with the Food and Drug Administration. Sales exceeded $5 billion for the first time in 1987, and two years later, net income reached $1 billion. AHP's household products unit was divested in 1990.

In 1992, the firm acquired Symbiosis Corp., a leading developer and manufacturer of disposable instruments for laparoscopic and endoscopic surgery, and introduced the Norplant contraceptive System for women. In August of 1994, AHP made a hostile $8.5 million bid for American Cyanamid Co., seeking to scuttle a multibillion-dollar asset swap discussed by Cyanamid and SmithKline Beecham. To meet FDA antitrust requirements for its proposed buyout of Cyanamid, AHP agreed to divest its diphtheria and tetanus vaccine lines to Chiron Corp. When the takeover was completed, AHP became as the third largest worldwide pharmaceutical and health care products manufacturer and the sixth largest agricultural products maker.

To offset debt, AHP divested its Latin American oral-care business to Colgate-Palmolive for $1.04 billion in 1995. Later that year, research and development spending was increased to $1 billion to intensify work on the several drugs. In 1996, AHP introduced Redux, the first weight loss drug to receive FDA approval in roughly 20 years; the firm also refocused on core pharmaceutical operations and divested its food holdings. Complaints of heart problems linked to taking Redux prompted AHP to recall the drug in 1997; consequently, several lawsuit were filed. AHP also acquired the animal health holdings of Solvay SA that year. In January of 1998, SmithKline Beecham and AHP announced their intention to merge. Less than two weeks later, though, SmithKline Beecham decided Glaxo Wellcome was a more attractive partner and ended its discussions with AHP. Later that year, AHP divested its medical devices holdings and announced plans to merge with Monsanto Co. That merger fell apart in October after executives failed to agree on who would run the new giant.

History of SmithKline Beecham PLC

The SmithKline pharmacy opened in Philadelphia, Pennsylvania, in 1830. In 1846, SmithKline supplied quinine to American soldiers

The Business

Financials - American Home Products Corp.

Revenue (1998): $13.5 billion

Employees (1998): 52,984

Financials - SmithKline Beecham PLC

Revenue (1998): $13.4 billion

Employees (1998): 58,300

SICs / NAICS

sic 2834 - Pharmaceutical Preparations

sic 8071 - Medical Laboratories

sic 2833 - Medicinals & Botanicals

sic 2090 - Miscellaneous Food & Kindred Products

sic 2879 - Agricultural Chemicals Nec

sic 3841 - Surgical & Medical Instruments

sic 2048 - Prepared Feeds Nec

sic 2891 - Adhesives & Sealants

sic 2824 - Organic Fibers-Noncellulosic

naics 325412 - Pharmaceutical Preparation Manufacturing

naics 325411 - Medicinal and Botanical Manufacturing

naics 621512 - Diagnostic Imaging Centers

naics 621511 - Medical Laboratories

naics 339112 - Surgical and Medical Instrument Manufacturing

naics 311119 - Other Animal Food Manufacturing

naics 325222 - Noncellulosic Organic Fiber Manufacturing

during the war with Mexico. The company also supplied spirits of ammonia to U.S. troops in World War I. By the mid-1930s, SmithKline had developed into a major pharmaceuticals firm; it introduced the Benzedrine Inhaler in 1936 and Dexedrine in 1944. In 1976, SmithKline introduced Tagamet, the world's first drug able to heal peptic ulcers; by 1981, it had become the world's number one selling drug.

The following year, SmithKline used its Tagamet revenues to acquire Beckman Instruments, maker of medical supplies such as the pH meter and the spectrophotometer; the firm then changed its name to SmithKline Beckman Corp. In 1987, SmithKline's second leading drug, Dyazide, lost its patent, allowing other companies to make generics. The firm's hypertension drug, Selacryn, was accused of causing liver

The Officers

American Home Products Corp.

Chairman, President, and CEO: John R. Stafford

Sr. Exec. VP: Robert G. Blount

Exec. VP: Robert Essner

Sr. VP: David M. Oliveir

Sr. VP: Joseph J. Carr

SmithKline Beecham PLC

Chairman: Sir Peter Walters, Jr.

Chief Executive Officer: Jan Leschly

Chief Operating Officer and President, Pharmaceuticals
and Consumer Health Care: Jean-Pierre Garnier

Exec. VP and Chief Financial Officer: Andrew Bonfield

damage. SmithKline had to pay $100 million to a child abuse program, and three executives were ordered to do 200 hours of community service as punishment for 36 deaths and 34 counts of failing to immediately inform the FDA of side effects.

In 1847, Thomas Beecham began selling herbal remedies and pills (mostly laxatives) to people in England. A decade later, Beecham was concentrating his efforts on cough tablets and Beecham's Pills, his famous laxatives. He also launched his first advertising campaign, selling his pills through mail order and in the apothecary shop. In 1888, Beecham's pills were distributed in the United States for the first time, and two years later, Beecham established manufacturing operations in New York City.

Financier and land developer Philip Hill acquired the Beecham estate, including the pill business, from the Beecham family in 1924. Four years later, he incorporated the pill operations as Beecham's Pills and acquired new products such as Yeast Vite, Iron Jelloids, Phosferine, and Phylosan; he also acquired new companies such as Prichard and Constance, makers of Amami shampoo, and a toiletries manufacturer.

Beecham continued its expansion efforts throughout the 1930s, buying several companies: toothpaste maker, Macleans Ltd.; County Perfumery, makers of Brylcreem; and an antacid manufacturer, Eno Proprietaries. The company also began making health drinks. Beecham Research Laboratories Ltd. was established to develop new food products and pharmaceuticals in 1944. To reflect its recent product line expansions, Beecham's Pills changed its name to Beecham Group Ltd. the following year. The research

division began focusing exclusively on pharmaceuticals in an effort to propel the company further into the field of medicinal products. By acquiring C.L. Bencard, an allergy vaccine company, Beecham established a strong base for entering the prescription drugs market in 1949.

In 1957, Beecham scientists isolated 6-APA, the penicillin nucleus, a discovery that allowed them to develop all kinds of antibiotics. Two year later, when Beecham's labs produced the world's first partly synthetic penicillins, Broxil (phenethicillin) and Celbenin (methicillin), the problem of bacterial strains immune to widely used vaccines was overcome. The firm acquired Ribena blackcurrant juice, Shloer apple and grape drinks, and PLJ to expand its line of consumer brand health drinks.

Beecham opened a U.S.-based factory designed especially for antibiotics production in 1967. The company bought Horlicks brand milk drinks in 1969 and S.E. Massengill, a U.S.-based feminine hygiene products maker, in 1970. Two years later, the U.K. government forbade the proposed merger of Beecham and the Glaxo Group, its largest competitor, fearing the deal would decrease research efforts in the pharmaceutical industry. By the mid-1970s, the firm was selling its Norval antidepressant and Pollinex allergy vaccine, as well as three new antibiotics: amoxicillin, flucloxacillin, and ticarcillin. In 1977, Beecham paid $76 million for Sucrets brand cough drops and bought Calgon's line of bath products. The company diversified into perfumes in 1979 with the $85 million purchase of U.S.-based Jovan. A year later, Beecham entered the foods market with its purchase of Bovril.

In the early 1980s, Beecham continued its acquisition spree by purchasing J.B. Williams—which gave the firm access to Geritol vitamin supplements, Sominex sleeping pills, and Aqua Velva after shave lotion—for $100 million. Despite sagging ampicillin sales caused by increased competition and government attempts to restrict profits of pharmaceutical companies, Beecham also bought several drug companies in France, West Germany, and Italy. The firm paid $369 million for Norcliff Thayer, makers of Tums and other over-the-counter drugs, and also acquired the cosmetics and fragrance products of BAT in 1985. A year later, the firm began divesting non-core operations.

In July of 1989, Beecham merged with SmithKline Beckman to become SmithKline Beecham PLC, based in London, England. After Merck & Co., the newly merged firm placed number two among world drug companies with $6.9 billion in combined annual sales. In 1990, net income exceeded $1 billion for the first time. A year later, SmithKline Beecham unveiled its first major drug since the merger, Seroxat, an antidepressant.

The company developed several new drugs in the early 1990s, including Relafen, an arthritis drug with $40 million in sales; Paxil, an antidepressant; and Havrix, the world's first hepatitis A vaccine. SmithKline Beecham was number one in acne remedies (Oxy brands), number two in antiulcer drugs, and number three in prescription drugs and toothpaste (Aquafresh). The firm expanded its global distribution network in 1994 when it bought the over-the-counter unit of Sterling Winthrop, and paid $2.3 billion for United HealthCare Corp.'s pharmacy-benefit services unit. SmithKline Beecham then divested its animal health division for $1.5 billion and the U.S. over-the-counter operations of Sterling Winthrop to Bayer AG for $1 billion.

In 1995, over-the-counter sales of Tagamet HB for heartburn and acid indigestion were approved by the FDA. The drug faced direct competition from Johnson & Johnson's Pepcid AC, which was approved for non-prescription use at roughly the same time. SmithKline Beecham and Johnson and Johnson became involved in a $200 advertising war that eventually prompted a New York judge to order both firms to withdraw specific advertisements for their new heartburn drugs, due to their unsubstantiated claims. Later that year, SmithKline Beecham received FDA approval to market its hepatitis A vaccine and to sell a tablet form of Kytril, an anti-nausea drug for cancer patients.

The FDA approved Nicorette gum as an over-the-counter product in early 1996. Also, Hycamtin was approved by the FDA for patients whose ovarian cancer had not responded to other treatments. SmithKline Beecham filed a total of 154 new product approvals in 1996; although new product sales grew by 37%, sales of Tagamet fell 41%. In January of 1997, the firm announced its intention to merge with American Home Products. Less than two weeks later, SmithKline Beecham decided Glaxo Wellcome was a more attractive partner and ended its discussions with American Home Products. SmithKline Beecham and Glaxo Wellcome executives couldn't agree on how to best run the new company, though, and that deal was called off in late February.

Market Forces Driving the Merger

Consolidation activity in the pharmaceuticals market was slow compared to other industries in 1997 and 1998 because most major pharmaceutical companies had the financial resources to develop drugs by themselves. The last merger wave in the industry had taken place in the mid-1990s and resulted in the unions of Glaxo Holdings PLC and Wellcome PLC in October of 1995; Pharmacia AB and The Upjohn Co. in

The Players

Chairman and CEO of American Home Products Corp.: John R. Stafford. Former Hoffman-LaRoche lawyer John Stafford was appointed chairman and CEO of American Home Products on December 1, 1986. In 1994, he also assumed the role of president. Stafford steered the firm's takeover of American Cyanamid in 1994 and continues to lead AHP today.

CEO of SmithKline Beecham PLC: Jan Leschly. Jan Leschly is well known not only in pharmaceutical circles, but also among professional tennis fans. In 1965, Leschly ranked 10th in the world among professional tennis players. Holding degrees in both business and pharmacy, the athlete joined Novo Nordisk A/S, where he worked for seven years, eventually accepting the positions of executive vice president and president of the pharmaceuticals division. Squibb Corp. hired him in 1979 as vice president of commercial development. When Squibb and Bristol-Myers decided to merge in 1988, Leschly was Squibb's president and chief operating officer. Although he was offered a position with the new firm, Leschly resigned. After taking a year off, he emerged to head SmithKline Beecham's pharmaceutical division in June of 1990. Four years later, he assumed the post of CEO, a position he still holds today. In 1994, Leschly also made *Business Week*'s top 25 manager list.

November of 1995; Ciba Geigy Ltd. and Sandoz Ltd. into Novartis in 1996; and American Home Products (AHP) and American Cyanamid Co. in August of 1994.

Industry analysts predicted that as a wave of patent expiry among the largest pharmaceutical players began to break in the late 1990s, many of the firms involved in the merger mania of the mid-1990s, such as AHP, would be seeking new merger and acquisition partners. Consulting firm AT Kearney estimated that between the years 1998 and 2003, expired patents on 42 key drugs would take a $32 billion toll on earnings in the pharmaceutical industry; this was a major cause of the increased merger discussions among pharmaceutical giants during 1998 and 1999.

Consolidation once again appeared imminent as several of the industry giants, including AHP, SmithKline Beecham, and Glaxo Wellcome contemplated mergers as a means of increasing market share, reducing costs, and enhancing research and development budgets. In particular, SmithKline and AHP were hoping to reduce costs by $1-$2 billion and to fund research in new fields, such as genomics. New research dollars would be essential for firms looking to stay competitive in a marketplace where demand, at times, seems unchecked. In fact, according to Dr. Wang Chong of consulting firm Arthur D. Little, mergers would be necessary for the firms who wanted to remain in the top ten industry tier because to do so would require pharmaceutical companies to introduce at least three new drugs annually. In early 1999, only three pharmaceutical businesses were capable of doing this: Johnson & Johnson, Merck & Co., and Pfizer Inc.

Approach and Engagement

American Home Products (AHP) and SmithKline Beecham revealed their potential merger plans on January 20, 1998. This prompted Glaxo Wellcome, which had been eyeing the firm for quite some time, to finally approach SmithKline. By the end of the month, before terms had even been negotiated, SmithKline ended its merger talks with AHP and instead pursued a merger with Glaxo Wellcome; shortly thereafter, this deal also fell apart.

Products and Services

Pharmaceutical sales accounted for 61% of AHP's $14 billion in sales in 1997. Agricultural products brought in 15%, as did consumer health care products. Medical devices, which were divested in 1998, secured the remaining nine percent. Most noteworthy of AHP's pharmaceuticals was Premarin, an estrogen replacement drug, and Leukine, a cancer treatment. Agricultural products included Counter, an insecticide, and Prowl and Pursuit, two herbicides. The consumer health care products segment comprised Advil, Centrum, Dimetapp, and Robitussin.

SmithKline Beecham earned $12.8 billion in revenues in 1997. Pharmaceuticals such as cancer drug Hycamtin and antibiotic Amoxil accounted for 59% of total sales. Consumer healthcare products, including Aquafresh toothpaste, NicoDerm CQ, Nicorette, Philips Milk of Magnesia, Sucrets, Tagamet HB, and Tums, earned 30% of revenue. Finally, clinical laboratories brought in the remaining 11%.

Changes to the Industry

A few months after talks with SmithKline Beecham ended, AHP and Monsanto announced that they were discussing a $34.4 billion merger, which would also create a new drug industry leader, with roughly $23 billion in annual revenues. Critics of the deal pointed out that the conservative chief executive of AHP and the more fiscally liberal leader of Monsanto might find it difficult to agree on how to best run the newly merged giant. Accordingly, the deal fell apart in October of 1998.

Review of the Outcome

Share prices for both AHP and SmithKline Beecham jumped after their merger discussions became public. Although the deal fell through, most analysts believed that because mergers for both firms seemed imminent, their performance wouldn't be adversely affected in the long-term by the terminated negotiations. In fact, some believed that small short-term dips in share price, like the 10% drop AHP experienced after the Monsanto deal was canceled, might prompt the firms to seek consolidation even more aggressively. SmithKline Beecham, however, seemed to pulled its hat out of the ring with the announcement in early 1999 that it would refocus on core operations by divesting its clinical laboratory and diversified pharmaceuticals operations.

Research

"American Home Products Corp.," in *Notable Corporate Chronologies*, The Gale Group, 1999. Lists major events in the history of American Home Products Corp.

American Home Products Home Page, available at http://www.ahp.com. Official World Wide Web Home Page for American Home Products. Includes news, financial, product, and historical information.

"AHP and SB to Merge?," in *Pharmaceutical Business News*, 28 January 1998. Discusses the outcome of the potential merger between AHP and SmithKline Beecham.

Blackledge, Cath. "Here Comes Another Drug Pact, Perhaps...," in *The European*, 23 November 1998. Details the major pharmaceutical mergers that were announced and later canceled in 1998.

"Ecstatic," in *The Economist*, 24 January 1998. Explains how news of the AHP/SmithKline Beecham deal impacted the stock performance of both firms.

Green, Daniel. "A $125bn Urge to Merge," in *The Financial Times*, 24 January 1998. Offers an overview of various reactions to the potential AHP/SmithKline Beecham merger.

———. "Prescription for Future," in *The Financial Times*, 2 February 1998. Explains the planned merger between Glaxo Wellcome and SmithKline Beecham after SmithKline Beecham ended discussions with AHP.

Hensley, Scott. "Drug Giants Talk Marriage: No Provider Perks in American Home-SmithKline Deal," in *Modern Healthcare*, 26 January 1998. Discusses how a merger between AHP and SmithKline Beecham will impact healthcare providers.

"SmithKline Beecham PLC," in *Notable Corporate Chronologies*, The Gale Group, 1999. Lists major events in the history of SmithKline Beecham PLC.

ANNAMARIE L. SHELDON

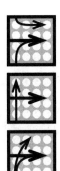

AMOCO & DOME PETROLEUM

nationality: United Kingdom
date: July 14, 1988
affected: Amoco Corp., USA, founded 1889
affected: Dome Petroleum Ltd., Canada, founded 1950

BP Amoco PLC
Brittanic House 1, Finsbury Circus
London, EC2M 7BA
United Kingdom

tel: 44-171-496-4000
fax: 44-171-496-4630
web: http://www.bpamoco.com

Overview of the Merger

When Amoco Corp. purchased Dome Petroleum in 1988 for $4.5 billion, it become the largest natural gas reserves holder in North America. The eighth-largest cross-border deal of the 1980s, Amoco's purchase of Dome marked the firm's first substantial international acquisition and helped decrease its reliance on domestic operations. However, lower-than-expected oil and gas prices plagued Amoco almost immediately after the deal was finalized. By 1993, Amoco Canada Petroleum Co., Ltd.—the unit the Dome holdings were folded into—had lost $1 billion.

History of Amoco Corp.

Standard Oil (Indiana) was established in 1889 as part of John Rockefeller's Standard Oil Trust. Formed outside Whiting, Indiana, the business was located close to the growing midwestern market. The Standard Oil Trust was liquidated by order of the Ohio Supreme Court in 1892; the 20 companies under its jurisdiction reverted to their former status and became subsidiaries of Standard Oil Co. (New Jersey). Roughly 55% of Standard (Indiana) was owned by Standard Oil Co. (New Jersey).

In 1911, after a court battle lasting almost three years, Standard Oil Co. (New Jersey) was ordered to relinquish supervision of its subsidiaries, Standard (Indiana) among them. Once independent, Standard (Indiana) began catering to the burgeoning automobile industry. A year later, the firm opened a service station in Minneapolis. Another service station opened in Chicago in 1913. To get as much gasoline out of each barrel of crude as possible, Standard formulated the cracking process, which doubled yield by separating the oil's molecules. The possibility of cheaper gasoline and a new line of petroleum-based products made the method attractive to other refiners, who then licensed it from Standard (Indiana); this licensing accounted for 34% of Standard (Indiana)'s profits over the next ten years.

By 1918, the firm operated 451 service stations. Along with growing sales of road oil, asphalt, and other supporting products, the automotive industry provid-

The Business

Financials

Revenue (1998): $108 billion

Employees (1998): 96,650

SICs / NAICS

sic 2911 - Petroleum Refining

sic 1311 - Crude Petroleum & Natural Gas

sic 1321 - Natural Gas Liquids

sic 4923 - Gas Transmission & Distribution

sic 1381 - Drilling Oil & Gas Wells

naics 211111 - Crude Petroleum and Natural Gas Extraction

naics 211112 - Natural Gas Liquid Extraction

naics 213111 - Drilling Oil and Gas Wells

ed one-third of all Standard (Indiana) business. During the early 1920s, acquisitions included 33% of Midwest Refining Corp. of Wyoming, 50% of Sinclair Pipe Corp., which improved transportation capacity; and a stake in Pan American Petroleum & Transport Corp. This $37.6 million transaction represented the largest oil consolidation to date in the history of the industry, giving Standard (Indiana) access to one of the world's largest tanker fleets and entry into oil fields in Mexico, Venezuela, and Iraq.

In 1930, the firm consolidated its pipeline systems and crude oil buying assets into the Stanolind Crude Oil Purchasing Corp. The largest oil field in history was discovered in east Texas late in the year. Amoco Chemicals was established in 1945. Three years later, Standard (Indiana) founded a foreign exploration department to head forays into Canada and other countries. By 1952, Standard Oil (Indiana) was considered the nation's largest domestic oil company with 12 refineries in 41 states. International exploration began intensifying during the mid-1950s with the purchase of exploration rights for 13 million acres in Cuba.

In 1957, Standard Oil (Indiana) consolidated nine subsidiaries into four larger companies, including Pan American Petroleum Corp.; Service Pipe Line Corp.; Indiana Oil Purchasing Corp.; and Amoco Chemicals Corp. By 1961, the firm had replaced the brand name of American Oil with Amoco. Foreign exploration by the mid-1960s had expanded to include Mozambique, Indonesia, Venezuela, Argentina, Colombia, and Iran. Standard Oil (Indiana) began production in the Persian Gulf Cyrus field in 1967.

The shah of Iran was overthrown in 1978, and Standard Oil (Indiana) shut down its Iranian facility and evacuated American staff members after all American employees of Amoco Iran Oil Corp. received death threats. After a year of record-breaking production in Iran, the loss resulted in a 35% production decrease in the company's overseas operations. That year, an Amoco tanker, the *Amoco Cadiz*, ran aground off the French coast, leaking 730,000 gallons of oil into the sea. The spill cost $75 million to clean up, and France sued Amoco for $300 million. The suit was settled 12 years later, with a $128 million judgement against the company.

Standard Oil (Indiana) officially changed its name to Amoco Corp. in 1985. The oil price crash in 1986 sliced profits by 63%. Two years later, Amoco purchased Tenneco Oil Company's Rocky Mountain properties for roughly $900 million and Canada's Dome Petroleum for $4.5 billion to become the largest natural gas reserves holder in North America. In 1990, joint ventures in Brazil, Mexico, South Korea, and Taiwan met the growing demand for polyester fibers, helping to generate about 35% of business overseas. The early 1990s marked a period of intense international exploration for Amoco. The firm was the first to venture into mainland China. Despite natural gas discoveries in Trinidad and the Gulf of Mexico, low production in 1995 prompted Amoco to begin divesting peripheral holdings. A restructuring started the previous year called for cutting 3,800 jobs.

In 1997, Amoco, Exxon Corp., Mobil Corp., Royal Dutch/Shell and others merged their oil and natural gas operations in South America with those of Argentina-based Bridas Corp. The venture enabled Amoco to take advantage of the growing energy market in South America and the increased demand for natural gas in Brazil and Chile. In early 1998, Amoco and General Motors Corp. announced a partnership to jointly develop lower emissions gasoline; the agreement was the first of its kind between a petroleum company and an auto maker. Later that year, Amoco and British Petroleum announced their intent to merge; the deal was finalized on December 31, 1998.

History of Dome Petroleum Ltd.

The Canadian petroleum industry took off after Imperial Oil struck oil in Alberta, Canada, in 1947. Jim McCrae, an executive for Dome Mines, decided his firm need to diversify into this fledgling Canadian market. He approached Dome Mines' CEO, Clifford Michel, who was receptive to the idea, and in 1950, Dome Mines hired Jack Gallagher to oversee Dome Mines' petroleum venture in Alberta. To raise capital, Michel approached Loeb, Rhoades, which ended up with a 16% stake in the new unit, eventually called Dome Petroleum. Dome Mines retained a 24% share.

Dome Petroleum listed publicly in 1951 and offered additional shares in 1952, raising a total of $10 million in equity. The firm diversified into natural gas in the early 1950s after finding a gas well in Alberta. In 1957, Dome hired Don Wolcott to exploit that gas field. The following year, he launched construction of a $17 million natural gas liquids recovery plant in Saskatchewan to cull liquid petroleum gases from oil fields in southeastern Saskatchewan. By the end of the decade, Dome had turned down takeover offers from the likes of British Petroleum, Amoco, Shell, and Mobile.

In 1962, Wolcott oversaw construction of Dome's first "straddle plant" near Edmonton. Eight years later, Amoco and Dome jointly built another straddle plant, this one at Cochrane, which gave Dome access to the California market. The company launched its most aggressive natural gas liquids venture in 1972 when it began construction of the Cochin line; at 1,900 miles long, the pipeline was longer than any other used to pump ethylene, propane, butane, and ethane. After wading through six years of engineering and regulatory concerns, the $1.5 billion Cochin line was opened.

In response to the landmark 1968 discovery of oil at Alaska's Prudhoe Bay, Dome decided it needed to venture into the Beaufort Sea. That year, drilling ships built by Dome set sail. A new subsidiary, Canmar, housed Dome's Arctic drilling ventures; by 1978, the unit brought in nearly 10% of annual profits. That year, almost half of the top 50 stocks traded on the Toronto Stock Exchange were related to oil, and Dome was the leader, trading reached $472 million. Shares had reached a record high of $106.75, compared to $60.83 in 1977 and $45 in 1976. In 1979, stock prices jumped another 50% to $223.52. That year, stock split four-for-one.

During the late 1970s, mainly to avoid being taken over as a part of its parent, Dome Mines, Dome Petroleum bought 29.5% of Dome Mines; the firm eventually increased its stake to 38.5%. In 1978, Dome began the acquisition spree that would eventually lead to its downfall. The firm paid $97 million for Canadian Petroleum's stake in TransCanada PipeLines and $360 million for Siebens Oil & Gas. Dome President Bill Richards believed that oil and gas prices would continue to outpace interest rates. Therefore, borrowing money to pay for oil and gas reserves became the strategy driving Dome during the 1980s. The first acquisition of the decade was Dome's $700 million purchase of Kaiser Resources, the oil and gas assets of Kaiser Steel and Aluminum.

The Officers

Co-Chairman: John Brown

Co-Chairman: Larry Fuller

Non-Executive Chairman: Peter Sutherland

Deputy CEO and President, Exploration and Production: Rodney Chase

Deputy CEO and President, Refining and Marketing and Chemicals: Bill Lowrie

Chief Financial Officer: John Buchanan

The Canadian government signed the National Energy Program (NEP) in 1980. The legislation mandated that only Canadian-owned companies would received the largest chunk of federal grants. Because Dome was more than 60% foreign-owned, the firm had to act quickly to avoid being devastated by the NEP. Within a year, Dome had founded Dome Canada and implemented the largest share sale in Canadian corporate history. In May of 1981, Dome bid $65 per share for 20% of Conoco, the ninth largest oil firm in the U.S. Dome sought the shares of Conoco in hopes that it could swap those for Conoco's controlling share of Hudson's Bay Oil & Gas. The $2.6 billion deal, the largest to date in Canadian corporate history, made Dome the largest oil company in Canada. It also boosted Dome's debt from $2.7 billion in 1980 to $5.3 billion in 1981.

In 1982, Citibank loaned Dome $2 billion for its purchase of the remaining shares of Hudson's Bay Oil & Gas. Chairman Jack Gallagher stepped down in 1983, as did president Bill Richards. Dome was saddled with over $7 billion in debt when oil prices took a nosedive in 1986. Management slashed staff and began selling assets, but Dome never recovered. In 1988, Amoco purchase Dome for $4.5 billion in 1988.

Market Forces Driving the Merger

In 1986, crude oil prices fell from $30 per barrel to $10 per barrel in less than six months. Dome Petroleum, already struggling under the weight of a hefty $7 billion in debt, moved precariously close to bankruptcy. For the first time in its history, Dome was vulnerable to a takeover. Losses in 1987 totaled $115 million on sales of $1.7 billion. Amoco was also hurt by the oil crisis—its profits dropped 63% in the wake of the price crash—but the firm was able to recover quickly. By 1987, Amoco's net income was up 82% to $1.4 billion.

The Players

President of Dome Petroleum Ltd.: Bill Richards. Although he had resigned by the time Amoco and Dome had completed their merger, Bill Richards was perhaps the most influential character in Dome's history besides co-founder Jack Gallagher. As a young law school graduate, Richards began working for Dome in the 1950s and became president of the firm in 1974. He steered the majority of Dome's blockbuster acquisitions. Most analysts point to his aggressive acquisition campaign during the 1980s, which saddled Dome with more than $7 billion in debt, as the reason for Dome's ultimate demise and takeover by Amoco.

Chairman and CEO of Amoco Corp.: Richard R. Morrow. Richard Morrow took the helm of Amoco in 1983. He led the firm's first real acquisition spree, beginning with various U.S. assets in the mid-1980s and culminating in its $4.5 billion purchase of Dome Petroleum in 1988. Three years later, he stepped down and was succeeded by Larry Fuller. In 1993, Morrow was elected to serve as temporary chairman of Westinghouse Electric Corp.

By the late 1980s, Amoco was poised for a consolidation move. It had remained on the sidelines during the oil industry's merger frenzy of 1984 which included Mobile's $5.7 billion purchase of Superior Oil; Texaco's $10.8 billion takeover of Getty Oil, which thwarted Pennzoil's earlier $.16 billion offer for 20% of Getty; and Chevron's $13.2 billion takeover of Mesa Petroleum. Richard Morrow, who had taken the helm of Amoco in 1983, was ready to move. After spending $1.5 billion on U.S. acquisitions since his appointment, Morrow was looking towards international expansion. Nearly half of the firm's $3.8 billion exploration budget was earmarked for international ventures in 1988, but Amoco also needed international operations.

Acquiring Dome would give Amoco 212 million barrels of oil reserves, three trillion cubic feet of natural gas, and 11.4 million acres of oil and gas properties at a very attractive price. Amoco would pay a price equal to $5 per barrel, compared to the $11 per barrel it would cost to explore and develop reserves on its own.

Approach and Engagement

Merger negotiations between Amoco and Dome Petroleum began in May of 1997. Almost immediately, TransCanada Pipelines launched a $5.5 billion counter offer, which was turned down by Dome. Amoco upped its original offer of $5.2 billion, mainly in debt assumption, to $5.5 billion in November. Former chairman Jack Gallagher, who owned 2.2% of Dome while terms of the deal were being hammered out, launched a brief, unsuccessful campaign to pressure Amoco to again increase its price.

On July 14, 1988, a Canadian judge ruled that the deal was permissible. Terms of the agreement stipulated that Amoco would pay $555 million in cash, as well as take on roughly $3.5 billion in debt. To appease Canadian concerns about selling out to a U.S. buyer, Amoco agreed to sell 20% of its Dome holdings to Canadian investors within ten years of the deal's completion and to spend a minimum of $2.1 billion in Canadian exploration by 1993.

Products and Services

After the 1998 merger between British Petroleum and Amoco—a decade after the Dome Petroleum takeover—BP Amoco owned in excess of 27,000 service stations throughout the world, including 16,000 U.S. Amoco stations. Oil and gas reserves totaled 14.8 billion barrels. Exploration and production operations spanned 20 countries and included oil and gas exploration, gas processing and marketing, field development, and pipelines and transportation. BP Amoco held a 50% stake in the Trans Alaska Pipeline System. Chemical operations included acetyls and nitriles; derivatives; and polymers and olefins.

The Dome assets had been folded into Amoco Canada Petroleum Co., Ltd. In 1998, the unit produced and marketed natural gas liquids and crude oil in western Canada. Exploration efforts focused on eastern Canada and the Beaufort Sea. The unit also oversaw textile operations in Ontario.

Changes to the Industry and Review of the Outcome

After the deal with Dome Petroleum was completed, Amoco become the largest natural gas reserves holder in North America. However, the deal caused almost immediate problems for Amoco's Canadian unit. By 1993, the subsidiary had lost roughly $500 million. Oil prices, which were expected to reach $31 per barrel by 1992, had only increased to $20 per barrel by 1993. Similarly, the anticipated $3 per thousand cubic feet of natural gas price remained under $2. In response, the firm launched plans to cut properties to 900 by 1996, compared to the 7,200 it operated immediately following its takeover of Dome. Numbering 5,800 after the deal, employees were cut to roughly

2,700 by 1993. According to November 1995 article in, *Oil Daily* Amoco Canada was still being "haunted by the financial ghouls of Dome Petroleum Ltd. as it lost $101 million in the third quarter." Losses since the takeover had mounted to $688 million.

Research

"Amoco Corp.," in *Notable Corporate Chronologies*, The Gale Group, 1999. Lists major events in the history of Amoco Corp.

Boras, Alan. "Amoco Canada Racks Up $101 Million Loss, Blames Troubles on 1988 Acquisition of Dome," in *The Oil Daily*, 2 November 1995. Explains how the Dome acquisition has been a financial drain on Amoco's Canadian unit.

BP Amoco PLC Home Page, available at http://www.bpamoco.com. Official World Wide Web Home Page for BP Amoco. Includes press releases; financial, historical, and product information; and annual reports.

Foster, Peter. *Other People's Money: The Banks, the Government and Dome*, Collins Publishers, 1983. Offers an in-depth look at the rise and fall of Dome Petroleum Ltd.

Jennish, D. "Dome's Light at the End of the Tunnel," in *Maclean's*, 30 November 1987. Explains the terms of the deal between Dome and Amoco.

McKinnon, Ian. "Homecoming in the Oilpatch," in *The Financial Post*, 17 October 1998. Offers a brief history of Dome Petroleum, as well as information on where its top executives are now working.

Therrien, Lois. "Now Amoco Can Really Step on the Gas," in *Business Week*, 1 August 1988. Explains why Amoco is purchasing Dome Petroleum.

ANNAMARIE L. SHELDON

ANHEUSER-BUSCH & CAMPBELL TAGGART

Anheuser-Busch Companies, Inc.
One Busch Place
St. Louis, MO 63118
USA

tel: (314)577-2000
fax: (314)577-2900
web: http://www.anheuser-busch.com

The Earthgrains Co.
8400 Maryland Ave.
St. Louis, MO 63105
USA

tel: (314)259-7000
fax: (314)259-7036
web: http://www.earthgrains.com

nationality: USA
date: November 2, 1982
affected: Anheuser-Busch Companies, Inc., USA, founded 1852
affected: The Earthgrains Co. (formerly Campbell Taggart Inc.), USA, founded 1925

Overview of the Merger

When beer giant Anheuser-Busch paid $560 million for Campbell Taggart, the second-largest baked goods company in the U.S., in November of 1982, it hoped to cash in on anticipated distribution synergies between beer and food products, as well as use its marketing prowess to build a strong brand in what was then a highly fragmented bread market. The beer maker folded Campbell Taggart into its Eagle snack foods unit, which had been established in 1979. The payoff from that unit never materialized, however, and Anheuser-Busch finally put Eagle on the block in 1995. After no suitors came forward, Anheuser-Busch liquidated its Eagle snack food operations and spun off Campbell Taggart as The Earthgrains Co. in 1996.

History of Anheuser-Busch Companies, Inc.

In 1852, George Schneider founded the Bavarian Brewery in St. Louis, Missouri. Eight years later, Eberhard Anheuser, a struggling St. Louis soap manufacturer, bought the Bavarian Brewery. The brewery hadn't turned a profit by 1865, so Anheuser hired his son-in-law, Adolphus Busch, a German immigrant educated in the art of brewing.

Adolphus Busch and restaurateur Carl Conrad created Budweiser, a light beer like those brewed in the Bohemian town of Budweis, in 1878. A year later, the brewery began using the A & Eagle trademark on their beer packaging. In 1896, the premium beer Michelob was introduced. By the turn of the century, Budweiser had become the second American brewer to sell one million barrels annually.

In 1913, the company's name was changed to Anheuser-Busch, Inc. By then operations had been taken over by August Busch, son of Adolphus Busch. When the prohibition period ended in 1933, Busch delivered a case of Budweiser to President Franklin Roosevelt in a carriage drawn by Clydesdale horses, which later become the company's symbol. Beer sales totaled 607,511 barrels that year. By the end of the decade, Anheuser-Busch had become the world's largest brewery.

The company acquired the St. Louis Cardinals baseball team in 1953. Six years later, amusement park Busch Gardens opened in Tampa, Florida. Budweiser Malt Liquor was introduced in 1971, followed by Classic Dark draft beer five years later. The firm introduced two light beers in 1977, and a year later, Anheuser-Busch became the first brewer to sell 40 million barrels in one year.

In 1982, Anheuser-Busch bought baked goods maker Campbell Taggart for roughly $560 million and folded it into its three-year-old Eagle snack foods arm. Bud Light was then introduced to the market, as was O'Doul's non-alcoholic beer. That year, the firm expanded its amusement park holdings with its 1989 purchase of Sea World. Blaming the recession and an increase in the excise tax, the company experienced a 5.2% drop in volume in 1991. Three years later, Bud Light displaced Miller Lite as the second-best-selling beer in the U.S. and also became the best-selling light beer in the country.

Kirin Brewery and Anheuser Busch inked a deal in 1993 to distribute Budweiser in Japan. The firm also acquired an 18% stake in Grupo Modelo, maker of the Corona brand. In 1995, Anheuser Busch won a trademark court case in which it challenged John Labatt Ltd.'s contention that it held the sole right to use the term "ice beer." Labatt had a patented ice-brewing technique and had licensed its technology to other brewers, but the courts ruled that rights to the trademark were separate from the technology patents. That year, Red Hook Ale Brewery, one of the nation's oldest and leading microbrewers, partnered with Anheuser Busch for distribution of its Red Hook's brews. Also that year, the firm sold the struggling St. Louis Cardinals baseball team.

In February of 1996, Anheuser Busch announced that it would close its Eagle Snacks division and take a $206 million after-tax writeoff. As part of its plan to refocus on its core beer business, the firm also sold four of its snack food plants to Frito-Lay, Inc. and spun off its Campbell Taggart baked goods operations as The Earthgrains Co., effectively ending its foray into the food industry. In 1997, the company starting making and selling Kirin beer in the U.S. to bolster its specialty beer segment. The following year, Anheuser Busch upped its stake in Grupo Modelo to roughly 50%. A U.S. Department of Justice investigation of Anheuser Busch's incentive programs for distributors came to an amicable end that year.

History of Campbell Taggart Inc.

Bakers Winfield Campbell and A.L. Taggart founded Campbell Taggart, Inc. in 1925. The firm pursued aggressive growth via acquisition, eventually

The Business

Financials - Anheuser-Busch Companies, Inc.

Revenue (1998): $11.24 billion

Employees (1998): 23,350

Financials - The Earthgrains Co.

Revenue (1998): $1.71 billion

Employees (1998): 18,000

SICs / NAICS

sic 2082 - Malt Beverages

sic 2051 - Bread, Cake & Related Products

sic 2053 - Frozen Bakery Products Except Bread

sic 7996 - Amusement Parks

naics 311213 - Malt Manufacturing

naics 311812 - Commercial Bakeries

naics 311813 - Frozen Cakes, Pies, and Other Pastries Manufacturing

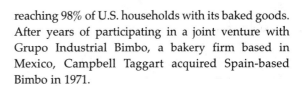

reaching 98% of U.S. households with its baked goods. After years of participating in a joint venture with Grupo Industrial Bimbo, a bakery firm based in Mexico, Campbell Taggart acquired Spain-based Bimbo in 1971.

By the late 1970s, the U.S. Federal Trade Commission had forbidden the company from making any additional U.S. bakery acquisitions. As a result, Campbell Taggart diversified into restaurant operations by purchasing El Chico, a 79-unit struggling Mexican restaurant chain, for roughly $20 million in 1977. The firm was particularly interested in El Chico's frozen and canned Mexican food operations, which accounted for roughly 33% of the chain's total revenues. Within two years of the purchase, 20 new El Chico restaurants were opened. However, Campbell Taggart's lack of experience in the restaurant industry was reflected in the poor performance of the new units. Cost cutting measures hurt sales further, and in November of 1980, the company hired former Steak & Ale executive Richard Rivera to turn El Chico around.

When Anheuser-Busch acquired Campbell Taggart in 1982, it was forced to divest the slowly improving El Chico chain due to laws that prevented the brewer from operating under a retail license. Campbell Taggart, which retained control of El Chico's frozen and canned foods assets, was merged

The Officers

Anheuser-Busch Companies, Inc.

Chairman and President: August A. Busch III

VP and Group Executive: Patrick T. Stokes

Exec. VP and Group Executive: John H. Purnell

VP and Chief Financial Officer: W. Randolph Baker

Group VP and General Counsel: Stephen K. Lambright

The Earthgrains Co.

Chairman and CEO: Barry H. Beracha

CEO, Europate, SA; Exec. Vice President and Managing
    Director, Earthgrains Refrigerated Dough Products:
    Richard W. Witherspoon

President, Worldwide Bakery Products: John W. Iselin Jr.

President and Managing Director, European Bakery
    Products: Xavier Argente

President, U.S. Bakery Products: Barry M. Horner

into the Eagle snack food unit of Anheuser-Busch. Consolidation in the baking industry in the early 1990s heated up, and Campbell Taggart joined the race to acquire regional baking operations. In an effort to streamline operations, Anheuser-Busch began a two-year, $140 million restructuring of the unit in 1993; employees were laid off, peripheral assets were sold, and 13 plants were either sold or closed. In March of 1996, Anheuser-Busch spun off Campbell Taggart as The Earthgrains Co.

The newly independent firm bought Heiner's Bakery Inc. later that year. In 1998, Earthgrains shored up its position in the southeastern U.S. with its $195 million purchase of CooperSmith, a conglomerate of three baking firms, as well as plants in South Carolina and Alabama from Southern Bakeries. Other acquisitions included San Luis Sourdough and a dough maker based in France.

Market Forces Driving the Merger

Brewer Anheuser-Busch began its venture into the food industry in 1979 when it founded its Eagle snack foods unit. "Having prevailed over rival Miller Brewing Co. in the Beer Wars, Anheuser was looking for new areas to spend its gushing cash flow," wrote *Business Week* in a March 1996 article. Although the firm had established a goal of increasing its 32% share in the U.S. beer market to 40% by 1990, management believed that diversification was necessary to prepare

for the eventual saturation of the beer industry. The rationale behind diversification into snack food was simple: synergy. Beer distributors could deliver snack foods to pubs and grocery stores on their normal routes.

Bakery company Campbell Taggart was attractive to Anheuser-Busch for similar reasons. The two firms could share yeast making facilities. Anheuser-Busch had supplied the baking industry with yeast and similar products for several years, so the firm was already familiar with the industry. Also, CEO Busch believed that his firm's marketing might could establish a strong brand in the highly fragmented bread market.

Approach and Engagement

Anheuser-Busch approached Campbell Taggart about a union in July of 1982. In October, shareholders of both firms approved a takeover of Campbell Taggart by Anheuser-Busch in a tax-free stock swap valued at $560 billion.

Roughly half of the 15 million outstanding shares of Campbell Taggart were converted into Anheuser-Busch Series A Convertible Preferred Stock on a one-for-one basis; each Anheuser-Busch preferred share was convertible into .645 a share of Anheuser-Busch common stock. The remaining Campbell Taggart stock was traded for the right to receive $36 per share in cash. Prior to the deal's completion on November 2, 1982, Anheuser-Busch agreed to sell the El Chico restaurant chain of Campbell Taggart to satisfy legal requirements that a brewery not operate under a retail license.

Products and Services

After Anheuser-Busch exited the food industry in 1996, it refocused on two major segments.

Brewed in 11 countries and sold in more than 80 countries, beer accounted for 82% of 1998 sales and included the following brands: American Hop Ale, Azteca, Bud Ice, Bud Light, Budweiser, Busch, Catalina Blonde, Hurricane Ice, Kirin, Michelob, Natural Light, Natural Pilsner, O'Doul's, Red Wolf Lager, Redhook, Rio Cristal, Tequiza, and ZiegenBock Amber.

Busch Entertainment Corp. brought in 7% of annual revenues. Along with theme parks like Adventure Island in Tampa, Florida, and Busch Gardens in Tampa and Virginia, Anheuser-Busch operated the Baseball City Sports Complex in Orlando, Florida; Sea World parks in California, Florida, Ohio, and Texas; Sesame Place, an educational park in Pennsylvania; and Water Country USA in

Virginia. The firm also owned a 20% stake in Spain's Port Aventura.

Other operations included Anheuser-Busch Recycling Corp.; Metal Container Corp.; Anheuser-Busch International, Inc., a foreign licensing unit; Busch Agricultural Resources, Inc. a grain processing operation; Busch Creative Services Corp., a marketing communications business; and Busch Properties, Inc.

Two years after securing its independence, The Earthgrains Co. operated 45 units in the U.S. and 12 in Europe. U.S. bread brands included Bost's, Colonial, Cooper's Mill, Country Recipe, Earth Grains, Grant's Farm, Heiner's IronKids, Kern's, Rainbo, San Luis Sourdough, Signature Line, Smith's, Sun Maid, Sunbeam, and Waldensian. European bread brands included Bimbo, Bimboy, and Siluete. The firm also sold snack cakes and refrigerated dough.

Changes to the Industry

When the deal was completed, Campbell Taggart's operations were folded into Anheuser-Busch's Eagle snack foods unit. The anticipated synergies between food and beer distribution never emerged for Anheuser-Busch, however. According to *Business Week*, "rather than synergy, Anheuser faced a logistical quagmire. A patchwork of Eagle distributors emerged—some also carrying beer, some also carrying Campbell Taggart bread, some independent. And without much product breadth, Anheuser's costs remained high."

In the late 1980s, PepsiCo's Frito Lay business recognized Eagle's weakness and launched a price cutting campaign that put even more pressure on smaller snack foods operations like Eagle. As a result, by the mid-1990s, Frito Lay had upped its market share from 40% to 50%, while Eagle's market share hovered at roughly 5%. In 1995, Eagle posted a $25 million loss on meager sales of $400 million. At the same time, increased competition from Miller Brewing Co. and sluggish beer sales were causing beer profits to languish.

Unwilling to invest further resources it the food industry, Anheuser-Busch decided to refocus on its core beer and amusement park operations and put its Eagle unit on the sales block in October of 1995. However, no serious buyers emerged. In 1996, the beer maker ended up selling four snack food plants to Frito-Lay for $135 million, shutting down Eagle operations (which included a $206 million after-tax write-off), and spinning off the Campbell Taggart baked goods operations as The Earthgrains Co.

The Players

Chairman and CEO of Anheuser-Busch Companies, Inc.: August A. Busch, III. August A. Busch III was elected president of Anheuser-Busch in February of 1974, marking the fourth Busch family generation to run the business. He spearheaded the company's foray into snack foods and baked goods in the late 1970s, including the 1979 establishment of the Eagle snack foods unit and the 1982 acquisition of Campbell Taggart. In 1996, Busch conceded that the move into the foods arena had been a serious misstep, one that cost the company a $206 million charge when it closed its Eagle unit after finding no willing buyers. At roughly the same time, he also oversaw the spin-off of Campbell Taggart operations into The Earthgrains Co., and began refocusing the firm on two core operations: beer and amusement parks.

Chairman of Campbell Taggart Inc.: Bill O. Meade. Bill Meade was chairman of Campbell Taggart in 1982. After his firm was acquired by Anheuser-Busch, he remained at the helm until 1989, when he was succeeded by David S. Leavenworth.

Review of the Outcome

When Anheuser-Busch bought Campbell Taggart in 1982, the bakery was posting annual sales of $1.26 billion. Fourteen years later, immediately prior to its spin-off as The Earthgrains Co., Campbell Taggart's sales had grown to only $1.5 billion, roughly 12% of Anheuser-Busch's sales. Despite efforts to formulate a strong national bread brand, competition from private-label grocery store brands had proven too strong. While the Eagle unit itself failed to earn a profit during its 17-year life span at Anheuser-Busch, Campbell Taggart did reach earnings of roughly $50 million in 1996. In 1998, the firm's first full year of independence, The Earthgrains Co.—the second largest U.S. commercial baker, behind Interstate Bakeries—recorded profits of $36 million on sales of $1.7 billion.

Research

"Anheuser-Busch to Spin off Campbell Taggart Subsidiary," in *Nation's Restaurant News*, 14 August 1995. Details the reasons given by Anheuser-Busch management for spinning off its Campbell Taggart bakery operations.

Anheuser-Busch Companies, Inc. Home Page, available at http://www.anheuser-busch.com. Official World Wide Web Home Page for Anheuser-Busch Companies, Inc. Includes press releases, as well as financial, product, and investor information.

"Anheuser-Busch Companies, Inc.," in *Notable Corporate Chronologies*, Gale Research, 1999. Lists major events in the history of Anheuser-Busch Companies, Inc.

Cole, Robert J. "Busch Holding Talks with Bakery," in *The New York Times*, 4 August 1982. Announces the preliminary merger talks between Anheuser-Busch and Campbell Taggart.

The Earthgrains Co. Home Page, available at http://www.earthgrains.com. Official World Wide Web Home Page for Earthgrains Co. Includes financial, product, historical, and employment information.

Melcher, Richard A. "How Eagle Became Extinct," in *Business Week*, 4 March 1996. Explains why Anheuser-Busch's move into the food industry was unprofitable.

JEFF ST. THOMAS

APPLE COMPUTER & NEXT SOFTWARE

nationality: USA
date: February 4, 1997
affected: Apple Computer Inc., USA, founded 1976
affected: NeXT Software Inc., USA, founded 1985

Apple Computer Inc.
One Infinite Loop
Cupertino, CA 95014
USA

tel: (831)996-1010
fax: (831)996-2113
web: http://www.apple.com

Overview of the Merger

When Apple Computer Inc. took over Steven Job's NeXT Software Inc. for $430 million in February of 1997, the firm hoped to use the NeXTStep operating system to bolster its aging Macintosh software. Securing the consulting services of original co-founder Steven Jobs was an added perk. What the firm didn't anticipate (or maybe it did) was the eventual return of Jobs to the post of Interim CEO. By late 1998, Apple appeared to be recovering from its near death experience, although several hurdles remained. The turnaround wasn't as much the result of Apple's new software as it was the leadership of Jobs.

History of Apple Computer, Inc. and NeXT Software Inc.

In 1976, the Apple Computer Co. was founded by Stephen G. Wozniak and Steven P. Jobs, who placed their home-built computer circuit board, the Apple I, up for sale. The team raised $1,350 towards production costs for the Apple I computers, which were manufactured in Jobs' parents' garage and sold to computer and electronic hobbyists for $666.66. The company also secured its first major agreement with the Byte Shop computer retailer to build 50 units. Apple hired Regis McKenna to develop an advertising strategy. He designed the instantly recognized Apple logo. The "apple" was chosen as an image of health and freshness; a bite was taken out of the apple as a connection to the term "byte." Jobs also consulted with Mike Markkula, a retired electronics engineer who had managed marketing for Intel Corp. and Fairchild Semiconductor Corp. Markkula assisted Jobs in developing a 10-year business plan with a sales goal of $500 million and purchased one-third of the firm for $250,000. By the end of the year, the Apple I was sold through ten U.S. retail stores.

Apple Computer was incorporated in 1977. Business and manufacturing operations were moved to a building in Cupertino, California. The firm introduced the Apple II at the first West Coast Computer Fair; it was the first personal computer to have color graphics capacity, and it came equipped with a keyboard, power supply, and case. When the Apple II was offered for sale to the general public, it came fully assembled with 4K of standard memory and cost $1,298. Annual sales reached

The Business

Financials

Revenue (1998): $5.9 billion

Employees (1999): 8,785

SICs / NAICS

sic 7372 - Prepackaged Software

sic 3571 - Electronic Computers

sic 3572 - Computer Storage Devices

sic 3575 - Computer Terminals

sic 7371 - Computer Programming Services

sic 3577 - Computer Peripheral Equipment Nec

naics 541511 - Custom Computer Programming Services

naics 334111 - Electronic Computer Manufacturing

naics 334112 - Computer Storage Device Manufacturing

naics 334113 - Computer Terminal Manufacturing

naics 334119 - Other Computer Peripheral Equipment
Manufacturing

$1 million that year, and Apple began selling its computers in Europe through independent distributor Eurapple.

In 1978, Apple launched interface cards for connection to printers. Apple's Disk II, the fastest minifloppy disk available, debuted at the Consumer Electronics Show. In only its second year of operation, Apple was recognized as one of the fastest growing firms in America with a tenfold sales increase and a dealer network of roughly 300 distributors. The company decided in 1979 that typewriters could no longer to be used by employees; all text was to be generated by computer. Apple also organized the first Dealer Council, through which Apple could gain dealer input without breaking FTC rules regarding competition; the concept was widely adopted by other personal computer makers. That year, the company also introduced the first Apple printer, the Silentype, and founded the Apple Education Foundation to forward its goal of supplying Apple computer systems to selected schools.

The Apple III was unveiled at the National Computer Conference in 1980. The model, priced at $3,495, was equipped with a new operating system, a built-in disk controller, and four peripheral slots. Apple opened a manufacturing factory in Cork, Ireland, and a European support center in Zeist, the

Netherlands. The Apple II was chosen as the network access machine for EDUNET, an international computer network for higher education and research. Morgan Stanley and Co. and Hambrecht & Quist underwrote an initial public offering of 4.6 million shares of Apple common stock that year at $22 per share. All shares were purchased within minutes of the offering, making it the largest of its kind since Ford Motor Co. went public in 1956.

In 1981, Apple European headquarters began operations in France and England; Jobs became chairman; and the second offering of 2.6 million shares of common stock was completed. The firm also introduced the Apple Language Card, which allowed Apple II users to run programs in Pascal, Fortran, or Pilot; released the IEEE-488 interface card, which enabled Apple II computers to link to over 1,400 scientific and technical instruments; and offered the 5MB Profile hard disk, its first mass storage system. By the following year, over 100 companies were producing personal computers. Apple launched the Apple Dot Matrix printer and became the first personal computer firm to reach $1 billion in annual sales.

After co-founder Wozniak resigned from Apple to launch a new company in the home video industry, Jobs hired John Sculley, former president of Pepsi-Cola Co., as president and CEO in 1983. The firm made the *Fortune* 500 at number 411, and Apple introduced AppleWorks, an integrated package containing word processing, spreadsheet, and database applications all in one, as well as the Apple III Plus computer and the ImageWriter printer. In 1984, the firm aired a landmark commercial, introducing the Macintosh personal computer during the Super Bowl broadcast. The first version of the Macintosh sold for $2,495.

Manufacturing facilities were closed for a week due to excess inventory in 1985, and Sculley announced a major reorganization which reduced the work force by 20% and restructured operations along functional lines. Three of Apple's six manufacturing facilities were closed, and the firm posted its first quarterly loss ever due to the cost associated with the reorganization. The company also denied Microsoft Corp.'s request for Apple to license its products and make the Apple platform an industry standard. After a turbulent power skirmish with Sculley that year, Jobs left Apple to found NeXT Software, Inc., which introduced its NeXTStep operating system three years later.

In 1986, the Macintosh Plus and LaserWriter were unveiled at the AppleWorld Conference in San Francisco. The firm acquired a Cray X-MP/48 supercomputer, valued at about $15.5 million, to simulate future hardware and software architectures and accelerate new product development. Apple also recovered from its financial turbulence to post record profits. A year later, the firm launched a new generation of Macintosh personal computers; announced a two-for-one share split; and created an independent software firm, later known as Claris.

Competition from Microsoft's Windows operating system intensified in the late 1980s, and Apple filed suit in 1988 alleging violation of copyright of its graphical interface; however, Microsoft eventually won the case. Apple reported the first $1 billion quarter in its history that year. Apple and Texas Instruments unveiled the MicroExplorer computer system, an Apple Macintosh II computer equipped with Texas Instruments' Explorer Lisp coprocessor board and advanced software environment; the joint venture was one of Apple's largest value added reseller agreements for the Macintosh family of personal computers. Also, worldwide sales and marketing operations were restructured into three distinct units: Apple USA, Apple Europe, and Apple Pacific.

Sluggish U.S. sales prompted 400 employee layoffs in 1990, as well as price reductions on the Macintosh SE, SE/30, and LaserWriter II printers, and the introduction of a line of low-cost Macintosh personal computers: the Macintosh Classic, the Macintosh LC, and Macintosh IIsi. In 1991, Apple launched low-cost laser printers, including the StyleWriter and Personal LaserWriter LS.; reduced its workforce by roughly 10%; and forged an agreement with IBM Corp. to cooperate on major technology initiatives for the decade as a means of competing with Microsoft. By then, 90% of all computers ran on Microsoft's MS-DOS platform.

After Apple's Newton handheld computer technology, which was to be the basis for new products in the personal digit assistant category, fell drastically short of expectations in 1993, the firm announced additional layoffs. Earnings tumbled a whopping 84%. As a result, the company finally decided to allow the licensing of Macintosh clones in 1994. A year later, the Supreme Court refused to hear Apple's appeal of the 1988 copyright ruling in favor of Microsoft.

Slow sales and expanding surplus inventories in 1995 prompted Apple to lower its prices by up to 25% on six of its models, including its Performa and Power Macintosh computers. Apple lost $1 billion in 1996 as market share continued to dwindle; quality issues forced the firm to recall PowerBook and Performa models. A year later, the firm bought NeXT Software from Steve Jobs, hoping to use the NeXTStep operating system to refurbish its existing Macintosh operating system. Jobs agreed to serve as an advisor to Apple. A cost cutting and restructuring campaign that

The Officers

CEO: Steven P. Jobs

Exec. VP and Chief Financial Officer: Fred D. Anderson

Sr. VP, Worldwide Operations: Timothy Cook

Sr. VP, Worldwide Sales: Mitchell Mandich

Sr. VP, Hardware Engineering: Jonathon Rubinstein

Sr. VP, Service and Support: Sina Tamaddon

year led to more layoffs. When Apple CEO Amelio resigned in mid-1997, Jobs took over as Interim CEO and began working on improving the firm's relationship with Microsoft. Recognizing that licensing agreements were pulling down sales, Jobs revoked most of Apple's major cloning agreements. In 1998, 300 jobs at Claris were eliminated and the unit was renamed FileMaker, Inc. The flawed Newton technology was also abandoned. In August of 1998, Apple released the iMac personal computer; roughly 278,000 units were sold in six weeks. Fourth quarter figures indicated that the company was rebounding.

Market Forces Driving the Merger

Quite simply, Apple's takeover of NeXT Software was born of desperation. Intense competition from Microsoft had drained sales and market share to historical lows, and the Macintosh operating system was aging. The firm had passed up consolidation opportunities with IBM in 1994 and Sun Microsystems in 1996, and several analysts were predicting Apple's extinction. Apple executives seemed unable to control engineers, which bottlenecked new product development; in fact, in 1996, Apple CEO Amelio decided to abandon internal development of a new operating system, instead pinning the firm's future on its merger discussions with Be Inc. and NeXT Software.

NeXT was also struggling; despite increasing software sales which contributed to roughly $50 million in annual revenues, the firm had been posting operating losses since 1993. Although programming professionals regarded the NeXTStep software highly, it had been unable to gain widespread acceptance outside of the corporate market. Agreeing to a merger with Apple would give NeXT access to Apple's end-user markets, including schools and homes.

Approach and Engagement

In 1996, a project manager for NeXT, John Landwehr, heard that Apple was looking for a new

The Players

Chairman and CEO of Apple Computer Inc.: Gilbert Amelio. Gilbert Amelio began earning his reputation as a turnaround specialist in 1971 at Fairchild Semiconductor Corp., where he worked as the manager of the image-capture research department and was charged with the task of improving the division's performance. In 1983, he was appointed president of the Communications System Group of struggling Rockwell International Corp. After three years, Amelio's segment, which had been losing $17 million annually when he took over, earned $12 million in net income. National Semiconductor Corp. tapped Amelio as CEO in 1991, and he led that firm's recovery as well. In January of 1996, Amelio accepted the position of CEO at floundering Apple Computer. Because Apple's market share continued to slide and losses mounted to $1 billion, Amelio resigned his post in July of 1997.

Chairman and CEO of NeXT Software Inc.: Steven P. Jobs. Technology guru Steven Jobs co-founded Apple Computer Inc. in 1976. Credited for co-developing the Apple II computer, spearheading the creation and marketing of the Macintosh computer, and fostering the growth of Apple into a $2 billion firm, Jobs left Apple in 1985 to co-found NeXT Software. President Reagan awarded Jobs the National Medal of Technology that year. A year later, Jobs co-founded computer animation studio Pixar, which produced the award-winning *Toy Story* feature film. *Inc.* magazine named him the Entrepreneur of the Decade in 1989. When Apple acquired NeXT in early 1997, Jobs agreed to act as a consultant for the firm. In July of 1997, however, Apple CEO Gilbert Amelio resigned; Jobs decided to fill in as Interim CEO, and he continues to serves Apple in that capacity today. He also remains chairman and CEO of Pixar.

operating system and pitched the NeXTStep software to Apple's chief technology officer, Ellen Hancock. Although Landwehr approached Apple without the knowledge or approval of NeXT CEO Steve Jobs, executives at both companies found the idea intriguing. Apple was also in negotiations with Be, makers of the Be operating system, at that time. When that deal fell through after the two firms couldn't agree on a price—Be wanted $285 million, while Apple's top offer was

$100 million—the door for NeXT was opened. After several meetings with NeXT, Apple agreed on December 20, 1996 to pay $400 million for the firm. Steven Jobs assented to act as a consultant to Apple. Terms of the deal stipulated that Jobs would receive 1.5 million Apple shares, worth a total of roughly $20 million.

When the transaction took place on February 4, 1997, Apple was forced to create an additional 1.8 million shares, worth roughly $25 million, to offset the lost stock former NeXT employees experienced when the deal was completed. Another $5 million in brokerage fees brought the final purchase price up to $430 million.

Products and Services

Apple's 15 product lines were slashed to four product categories in late 1997. Printers were discontinued, and the Newton technology was abandoned. The company refocused on four product categories: desktop and portable computers for consumers and desktop and portable computers for professionals. These included Macintosh personal computers, including the new iMac; the Macintosh operating system; and Macintosh PowerBook portable computers. The firm also continued to make its personal productivity software, FileMaker Pro.

Changes to the Industry and Review of the Outcome

Apple's losses continued to mount after the merger. In fact, the first quarter following the deal, losses reached $500 million, mainly because of the purchase of NeXT. Analysts predicted dire results for Apple, pointing to the fact that the NeXT software was more geared towards corporate users, not Apple's traditional market. Another concern was the continued inability of Apple executives to control the firm's engineering staff. A February 1997 article in *Fortune* asserted that "anybody who knows Apple Computer knows that the company bought the wrong part of NeXT. NeXT had two parts: the mess of software the company has licensed or developed...and Steve Jobs."

True, Apple didn't buy Jobs, but the firm got him anyway. When Apple CEO Amelio resigned in July of 1997, Jobs stepped in an Interim CEO. Working without pay, Jobs began rebuilding the company he had co-founded and repairing Apple's relationship with Microsoft. Within a month, Apple and Microsoft announced an agreement in which Microsoft would invest $150 million in Apple, as well as release new Macintosh versions of its leading Microsoft Office word processing, spreadsheet, data base and presentation software suite. Apple needed current versions of the popular software to be available for its users.

Jobs then recanted the licenses of several firms who had been creating and marketing Macintosh clones because rather than broadening the Macintosh market, they were simply siphoning sales from Apple. He streamlined the firm's highly unfocused corporate structure and upped the advertising budget to more than $100 million. Jobs hired an inventory specialist who slashed Apple's $400 million inventory to $78 million in less than a year. Distribution was limited to firms who were willing to aggressively market the Macintosh line. Apple also decided to target the consumer market and compete with the likes of Hewlett-Packard Co. and Compaq Computer Corp., rather than directly compete with Microsoft and Intel. Finally, Jobs set to work repairing the company's relationship with major programmers, who had become disenchanted with what they believed was Apple's unreliability.

The restructuring caused some significant problems for Apple, including company rifts due to complaints that the former NeXT employees were favored over the Apple employees and confrontations with former business partner over Apple's retraction of its cloning licenses. However, the overhaul restored Apple to profitability in fiscal 1998. Net income totaled $309 million on sales of $5.9 billion, and the company seemed to be headed in the right direction. According to a November 1998 issue of *Fortune*, Apple's August 1998 release of its iMac was "one of the hottest computer launches ever." The article described the iMac as "the first desktop computer to get the whole industry excited since...well, since the original Macintosh."

Research

"Apple Computer, Inc.," in *Notable Corporate Chronologies*, The Gale Group, 1999. Lists major events in the history of Apple Computer, Inc., including its takeover of NeXT Software Inc.

Apple Computer Home Page, available at http://www.apple.com. Official World Wide Web Home Page for Apple Computer, Inc. Includes news, financial, product, and historical information.

Alsop, Stewart. "Apple's Next Move Misses the Mark," in *Fortune*, 3 February 1997. Explains why the takeover of NeXT Software won't help Apple turn itself around.

Burrows, Peter. "How Apple Took Its NeXT Step," in *Business Week*, 13 January 1997. Details Apple's reasons for pursuing the purchase of NeXT Software.

Burrows, Peter. "Will Apple Slide into High-Tech Irrelevance?, *Business Week*, 17 February 1997. Covers the short-term effects the purchase of NeXT Software had on Apple.

Carlton, Jim. "At Apple, A Fiery Jobs Often Makes Headway and Sometimes a Mess; He Knows How to Market But Clashes with Cloners and Belittles His Foes," in *The Wall Street Journal*, 14 April 1998. Explains the problems that have surfaced since Jobs took over Apple as Interim CEO.

Gomes, Lee. "Next Software, the $400 Million Apple of Apple's Eye, Lacks Operating Profit," in *The Wall Street Journal*, 31 December 1996. Discusses performance of NeXT Software prior to being taken over by Apple.

Gomes, Lee. "Apple Posts $708 Million Loss, Big Revenues Drop," in *The Wall Street Journal*, 17 April 1997. Details the financial performance of Apple following its purchase of NeXT Software.

Kahney, Leander. "NeXT Costs Apple Extra $30M," in *MacWeek*, 17 February 1997. Explains why the final purchase price for NeXT was higher than Apple anticipated.

Kirkpatrick, David. "The Second Coming of Apple," in *Fortune*, 9 November 1998. Offers an overview of the changes Jobs has implemented at Apple since taking over as Interim CEO and the results of those changes.

THERA WILLIAMS

ASEA & BBC BROWN BOVERI

ABB Asea Brown Boveri Ltd.
P.O. Box 8131
Zurich, CH-8050
Switzerland

tel: 41-1-317-7334
fax: 41-1-311-7958
web: http://www.abb.com

nationality: Switzerland
date: January 5, 1988
affected: Asea AB, Sweden, founded 1883
affected: BBC Brown Boveri Ltd., Switzerland, founded 1891

Overview of the Merger

When Swedish electrical group ASEA AB and struggling Swiss competitor BBC Brown Boveri merged in January of 1988, they created a new firm with annual sales of nearly $15 billion. The newly merged ABB Asea Brown Boveri, Ltd., headquartered in Zurich, Switzerland, became one of the largest electrical companies in the world, able to compete with the likes of General Electric Co. and Hitachi. The unconventional merger—in which both firms remained a separate parent, each holding 50% ownership of the ABB—was the largest cross-border deal in Europe during the 1980s.

History of Asea AB

In 1883, Elektriska Aktiebolaget was established in Stockholm, Sweden, by Ludwig Fredholm to manufacture dynamos based on the designs of a young engineer named Jonas Wenstrom, who worked for his brother, Goran Wenstrom. Seven years later, Fredholm arranged to merge Elektriska AB with Goran Wenstrom's company, Wenstroms & Granstroms Elektriska Kraftbolag, creating an electrical equipment manufacturer called Allmanna Svenska Elektriska AB (ASEA).

Ten years later, along with installing electricity at a rolling mill—believed to be the first of its kind in the world—in the Swedish town of Hofors, ASEA build Sweden's first three-phase electrical transmission between the Swedish cities of Hellsjon and Crangesberg. In 1896, one of Sweden's leading inventors and industrialists, Gustaf de Laval acquired a 50% interest in ASEA; he launched a management reorganization that lead the firm into severe financial difficulties; as a result, Enskilda Bank helped ASEA executives oust Laval from control of the company in 1903. The bank also played a major role in ASEA's financial recovery.

Between 1910 and 1914, ASEA established subsidiaries in Great Britain, Spain, Denmark, Finland, and Russia. The firm built the world's largest naturally cooled three-phase transformer in 1932. After several years of negotiations, ASEA and LM Ericsson Telephone Co. signed a pact of non-competition in certain sectors of the electrical market; also, ASEA purchased Elektromekano from Ericsson, gaining full control over a large portion of the electrical equipment market in Sweden.

By 1939, Nazi occupation of Sweden had curtailed ASEA's operations throughout Europe, as well as in Sweden. A trade agreement between the Soviet Union and Sweden was threatened in 1946 by a five-month metal workers strike that prevented ASEA from meeting electrical equipment demand. The following year, ASEA broke into the U.S. market by signing a licensing agreement with Ohio Brass Co. for the local production of surge interrupters. The firm also received sizable orders for the first stage of the massive Aswan Dam project in Egypt.

ASEA reorganized along divisions in the early 1960s, and established an electronics division, which marked the start of ASEA's transition from heavy electrical equipment manufacturer to an electronics company focusing on high technology. In 1968, after receiving an order to build Sweden's first full scale nuclear power station, ASEA merged its nuclear division with state owned Atom-Energi to form ASEA-ATOM.

Percy Barnevik was named ASEA's managing director and CEO in 1980; he immediately launched a reorganization and initiated a major expansion into high technology areas, investing heavily in robotics and other state of the art electronics. Barnevik also turned ASEA's focus to its industrial controls business, with products such as large automation controls. In 1982, ASEA acquired the remaining 50% state interest in ASEA-ATOM.

Scandal rocked the firm in 1985 when a former ASEA vice president was charged by Swedish authorities with tax evasion and violation of foreign exchange regulations in connection with the sale of six sophisticated U.S. computers, with possible military applications, to the Soviet Union; Barnevik insisted that the diversions occurred without management's approval. ASEA completed its merger with BBC Brown Boveri Ltd. in January of 1988 to form ABB Asea Brown Boveri Ltd.

In 1989, ABB formed a joint venture with Westinghouse Electric Corp. ABB initially owned a 45% stake in the new company, but it soon executed its option to buy Westinghouse's share and become the sole owner.

ABB subsidiaries, ABB Mannheim and ABB Combustion Engineering Systems, garnered lucrative contracts in 1992: ABB Mannheim received about $1.25 billion for its participation in the construction of one of the largest hydro electric plants in the world, and ABB Combustion received about $270 million for its participation in a consortium erecting the largest

The Business

Financials

Revenue (1998): $30.87 billion

Employees (1998): 199,232

SICs / NAICS

sic 3621 - Motors & Generators

sic 3625 - Relays & Industrial Controls

sic 3612 - Transformers Except Electronic

sic 3613 - Switchgear & Switchboard Apparatus

sic 3825 - Instruments to Measure Electricity

sic 3822 - Environmental Controls

sic 3823 - Process Control Instruments

sic 3743 - Railroad Equipment

sic 3674 - Semiconductors & Related Devices

sic 3569 - General Industrial Machinery Nec

naics 335312 - Motor and Generator Manufacturing

naics 335314 - Relay and Industrial Control Manufacturing

naics 335311 - Power, Distribution, and Specialty Transformer Manufacturing

naics 335313 - Switchgear and Switchboard Apparatus Manufacturing

naics 334514 - Totalizing Fluid Meter and Counting Device Manufacturing

naics 334512 - Automatic Environmental Control Manufacturing

naics 334513 - Instruments for Measuring and Displaying Industrial Process Variables

naics 333911 - Pump and Pumping Equipment Manufacturing

naics 334413 - Semiconductor and Related Device Manufacturing

naics 333414 - Heating Equipment (except Warm Air Furnaces) Manufacturing

power plant in the People's Republic of China. In 1992, the largest individual contract since ABB's formation was secured from Abu Dhabi for an $800 million combined steam power station and desalination plant. Two years later, the firm entered a joint venture with CTBT, a Vietnamese transformer manufacturer to form ABB Transformers Ltd.

The Officers

Chairman: Percy Barnevik

President and CEO: Goran Lindahl

Exec. VP and Chief Financial Officer: Renato Fassbind

Exec. VP, Oil, Gas, and Petrochemicals: Kjell Almskog

Exec. VP, Automation: Jorgen Centerman

Exec. VP, Products and Contracting: Armin Meyer

In 1995, ABB continued to expand its investments in Eastern Europe and China while closing factories and laying off employees in the U.S. and Western Europe. ABB and DaimlerChrylser merged their transportation operations into a joint venture named Adtranz, which became the world's leading train manufacturer. Contracts secured in the late 1990s included one for eight generators for the Three Gorges hydroelectric power plant in China and another for two power plants in Chile. Earning fell significantly in 1997, prompting CEO Goran Lindahl to move towards a more centralized management structure. In 1999, ABB paid roughly $1.5 billion for Netherlands-based Elsag Bailey Process Automation, an industrial control systems manufacturer.

History of BBC Brown Boveri Ltd.

In 1891, Charles Brown and Walter Boveri founded Brown, Boveri, and Company to manufacture electrical goods in Baden, Switzerland. The firm's name later changed to BBC Brown Boveri Ltd. By 1903, Brown Boveri had established subsidiaries in Germany, France, and Italy; these units developed individually, as if they were domestic companies in the countries in which they operated. Brown Boveri entered into a licensing agreement with the British manufacturing firm Vickers in 1919; Vickers gained the right to manufacture and sell Brown Boveri products throughout the British Empire and in some parts of Europe.

Although successful subsidiaries were also operating in Norway, Australia, and the Balkan peninsula by 1924, Brown Boveri began to suffer from the devaluation of the French franc and the German mark. The firm devalued its capital by 30% to cover the losses. In 1927, Brown Boveri's agreement with Vickers ran out. The advent of the Cold War presented a variety of business opportunities for defense related electrical contractors, but because Brown Boveri's subsidiaries were seen as foreign companies in many of the countries in which they operated, winning contracts involving sensitive technical and other government contracts proved difficult.

In 1970, Brown Boveri began an extensive reorganization: subsidiaries were divided into five groups, and each of these five groups was broken down further into five product divisions, including power generation, electronics, power distribution, traction equipment, and industrial equipment. Four years later, Brown Boveri acquired the British controls and instrument manufacturer George Kent; it was renamed Brown Boveri Kent and incorporated into the parent company's already diverse product line.

Brown Boveri's West German subsidiary in Mannheim, which accounted for nearly 50% of the entire parent company's sales, was one of the first units in the group to rebound from the economic recession of the early 1980s. In 1986, Brown Boveri acquired a significant block of shares in the Mannheim subsidiary, bringing its shareholding to 75%. The following year, the firm introduced Comprex, a supercharging system for diesel engines; it was capable of increasing an engine's horsepower by 35% and delivering up to 50% more torque at lower speeds. Mazda announced its intent to use Comprex in its new diesel passenger model automobiles. Brown Boveri completed its merger with ASEA AB in January of 1988 to form ABB Asea Brown Boveri Ltd.

Market Forces Driving the Merger

In the mid-1980s Brown Boveri's earnings tumbled to 1.5% of total sales, compared to ASEA's 5.5% profit. Most analysts blamed the decline on a general electrical equipment industry downturn. During his tenure at the helm of ASEA between 1980 and 1987, CEO Barnevik had returned the company to profitability, despite the general industry decline. According to an August 1987 article in *Business Week*, he did this mainly by "slashing costs and diversifying into such high-growth businesses such as robotics." A merger with Brown Boveri would offer him a similar challenge.

The deal would also give ASEA the size it needed to compete in the electrical equipment industry. As explained in an August 1987 *Business Week* article, the new company would "have a much broader reach than ASEA alone, which is stronger in Scandinavia. Brown Boveri gives it new muscle in West Germany and Italy. And the merger makes money available for keeping up in key technologies such as superconductors and high-voltage chips."

Approach and Engagement

On August 10, 1987, ASEA AB and BBC Brown Boveri Ltd. announced their intent to merge. Roughly six months later, the deal was finalized. On January 1, 1988, ASEA and BBC Brown Boveri officially merged their two businesses to form ABB Asea Brown Boveri Ltd. Unlike most mergers, the two firms remained separate entities and acted as joint parents of the new firm. ASEA kept its 10% stake in Electrolux Group separate from the deal. Brown Boveri paid ASEA $500 million, which it raised through issuing new shares. ASEA's Curt Nicolin and Brown Boveri's Fritz Leutwiler became joint chairmen of the parent company; Percy Barnevik became the operating company's CEO.

Products and Services

After its 1988 merger, ABB Asea Brown Boveri grew dramatically. By 1999, the energy and engineering parent controlled nearly 1,000 units spanning 140 countries. Operations were divided into eight product/service categories: Power Generation, which included fossil combustion systems and services, district heating, gas turbine power plants, hydro power plants, nuclear power plants and combined-cycle power plants; Power Transmission, which included cables, high-voltage switchgear, power lines, power systems, and power transformers; Power Distribution, which included distribution transformers and medium voltage equipment; Automation, which included instrumentation, drivers, control valves, and motors; Oil, Gas and Petrochemicals; Products and Contracting, such as air handling equipment, low-voltage apparatus, installation material, and service; Financial Services; and ABB Daimler-Benz Transportation, which ABB agreed to sell in 1999.

Changes to the Industry

The merger created a new major player in the electrical equipment industry. ABB Asea Brown Boveri, with combined annual sales of nearly $15 billion, was one of the largest electrical companies in the world, able to compete with the likes of General Electric and Hitachi. By pursuing growth aggressively—the firm acquired more than 100 companies worldwide in the decade following the deal—ABB had positioned itself as a $30 billion world electrical equipment leader by the late 1990s.

Review of the Outcome

Most analysts regarded the unusual deal favorably; immediately following the announcement of the deal, ASEA's stock rose 15.5%, and Brown Boveri's jumped 10%. After the deal was completed, CEO Barnevik moved headquarters to Zurich to ease concerns that the deal was a Swedish takeover. He then began a cost cutting campaign that left corporate staff

The Players

Chairman and CEO of Asea AB: Percy Barnevik. Stanford MBA graduate Percy Barnevik was appointed CEO and managing director of Asea AB at the age of 39 in 1980. He initiated and steered his firm's merger with BBC Brown Boveri in 1987, and then led the new company's growth, mainly via acquisition, into a $30 billion electrical products giant. Barnevik stepped down as CEO in October of 1996, retaining his post as chairman. In April of 1997, Investor, the holding company of Sweden's Wallenburg family, tapped Barnevik as chairman, a position considered one of the most distinguished among Swedish businesses. The following year, *WorldTrade* magazine named Barnevik "Executive of the Decade."

Chairman and CEO of BBC Brown Boveri Ltd.: Fritz Leutwiler. Fritz Leutwiler began a long career in the Swiss banking industry in 1952 when he accepted a position with the Swiss National Bank. Leutwiler took over as chairman of the governors in 1974. By the end of the decade, he was also serving as president of the Bank of International Settlements, a post he resigned from in 1984. Shortly thereafter, Leutwiler decided to exit the state banking sector altogether, and BBC Brown Boveri appointed him chairman in 1985. Not long after BBC Brown Boveri merged with Asea AB in 1988, Leutwiler became joint chairman of the new parent company; four years later, he retired.

numbering only 176 in 1994, compared to 2,000 at the time of the merger. The turn-around specialist also reorganized ABB into 1,300 separate companies. By 1992, sales had reached a record $29.6 billion. The following year, however, sales fell to $28.3 billion due mainly to market downturns in both Japan and Europe.

The pay off for Barnevik's continual focus on growing his firm was significant. "The world's largest electrical engineering group," according to a March 1997 article in *Time* was also "the biggest single investor in Eastern Europe and the former Soviet Union, a Western pioneer in India, and an aggressive player in East Asia and Latin America. For three years running it was voted 'Europe's most respected company' in a poll of executives by the *Financial Times* newspaper."

Research

"ABB ASEA Brown Boveri Ltd.," in *Notable Corporate Chronologies*, The Gale Group, 1999. Lists major events in the history of ABB ASEA Brown Boveri Ltd.

ABB ASEA Brown Boveri Ltd. Home Page, available at http://www.abb.com. Official World Wide Web Home Page for ABB ASEA Brown Boveri Ltd. Includes press releases; financial, historical, and product information; and annual reports.

"The ABB of Management," in *The Economist*, 6 January 1996. Explains the outcome of the merger, as well as Percy Barnevik's role in the success of the company.

Branegan, Jay. "Percy Barnevik," in *Time*, 24 February 1997. Details the career of ABB ASEA Brown Boveri CEO Percy Barnevik, as well as the success of the 1988 merger between ASEA AB and BBC Brown Boveri Ltd.

Childs, B. "Power Surge in Scandinavia," in *Business Week*, 24 August 1987. Covers the reasons for the merger, as well as the details of the agreement.

"Fritz Leutwiler," in *The Economist*, 14 June 1997. An obituary of Fritz Leutwiler, former chairman of BBC Brown Boveri Ltd.

Karlgaard, Rich. "Percy Barnevik," in *Forbes*, 5 December 1994. Details the management style of Percy Barnevik and the effect his leadership has had on ABB ASEA Brown Boveri since the 1988 merger.

ANNAMARIE L. SHELDON

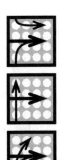

ASHLAND COAL & ARCH MINERAL

nationality: USA
date: July 1, 1997
affected: Ashland Coal, Inc., USA, founded 1975
affected: Arch Mineral Corp., USA, founded 1969

Arch Coal, Inc.
Cityplace One, Ste. 300
St. Louis, MO 63141
USA

tel: (314)994-2700
fax: (314)994-2878
web: http://www.archcoal.com

Overview of the Merger

Ashland, Inc. decided to consolidate its coal businesses in 1997. Publicly traded Ashland Coal and privately held Arch Mineral Corp. joined forces in July of that year to create the largest producer of low-sulfur coal in the eastern U.S., as well as the nation's sixth largest coal company with assets of roughly $1.7 billion and two billion tons in coal reserves. Ashland, Inc. retained a 53% stake in Arch Coal, Inc., the new publicly traded company with annual revenues of nearly $1.3 billion on sales of over 50 million tons of coal. The deal was valued at roughly $341.3 million.

History of Ashland Coal, Inc.

J. Fred Miles founded the Swiss Drilling Co., an Oklahoma Corporation, in 1910. He moved his operation to eastern Kentucky and obtained control of nearly 200,000 acres of oil land in 1916. Two years later, Swiss Oil Co. was incorporated by Miles in Lexington, Kentucky. In 1924, Swiss Oil opened its new Ashland Refining Co. division; two years later, the unit reached $3 million in annual sales. Ashland acquired Tri-State Refining Company in 1930 and Cumberland Pipeline Co., to lessen the firm's dependence on river transport of its crude supplies, in 1931.

In 1936, Swiss Oil and Ashland merged to become Ashland Oil & Refining Co. Ashland merged with Allied Oil Company of Cleveland in 1948. By 1950, the firm was the 19th-largest oil company in the U.S.; Ashland listed on the New York Stock Exchange for the first time that year. In the early 1960s, Ashland increased its petrochemical holdings and acquired a major pipeline system. The company changed its name to Ashland Oil, Inc. in 1970. Also, Ashland Oil Canada, Ltd. was formed. Ashland decided to diversify outside of oil refining by investing in Arch Mineral, a newly formed coal producer, in 1971.

Four years later, the firm established its own coal operation, Ashland Coal, which almost immediately launched an acquisition spree that lasted well into the early 1990s. Most notable among the unit's purchases were Addington Brothers Mining in 1976, Hobert Mining and Construction in 1977, Saarbergwerke in 1981, Coal-Mac in 1989, Mingo Logan in 1990, and Dal-Tex Coal in 1992. Ashland Coal listed publicly for the first time in 1988.

The Business

Financials

Revenue (1998): $1.5 billion

Employees (1999): 4,455

SICs / NAICS

sic 1221 - Bituminous Coal & Lignite-Surface

sic 1222 - Bituminous Coal-Underground

naics 212111 - Bituminous Coal and Lignite Surface Mining

naics 212112 - Bituminous Coal Underground Mining

In 1994, the board of directors decided to change the parent company's name from Ashland Oil to Ashland Inc. to reflect its diversification over the past 13 years into a network of refining, energy, and chemical businesses. Ashland Inc. consolidated its coal holdings—Ashland Coal and Arch Mineral—into Arch Coal, Inc. in 1997. A year later, the new company paid $1.14 billion for the U.S. coal businesses of Atlantic Richfield. Arch Coal was forced to temporarily close its Dal-Tex mine in West Virginia in 1999.

History of Arch Mineral Corp.

Merl Kelce and his brothers merged their family-owned Sinclair Company into the larger Peabody Coal Company in 1955; they succeeded in building the enterprise into a leader in the industry. Ten years later, tired of running a huge organization, the brothers tried to sell the company to Ashland Oil, but they were unsuccessful. In 1968, Kennecott Copper agreed to purchase Peabody Coal for $585 million.

In 1969, still interested in coal, Kelce and longtime associate William "Guy" Heckman formed Sinclair Associates in St. Louis, Missouri, to make selected coal investments. Later in the year, Ashland Oil's CEO requested Kelce's help in evaluating a possible acquisition of Ayshire Collieries. Sinclair Associates also changed its name to Arch Mineral Corp. Kelce acquired a mine in Fabius, Alabama, in 1970, and initiated the purchase of a coal preparation plant, reserves in southern Illinois, and draglines from the Marion Power Shovel Company. With Arch's business firmly underway, tragedy struck that year with the sudden death of Kelce.

Under the leadership of Heckman, the company acquired a Corona, Alabama-based coal reserve; signed a contract to supply George Power; and in exchange for Arch's commitment to supply coal to the government-owned utility, persuaded the Tennessee Valley Authority (TVA) to guarantee the $24.5 million in bonds the company used in the previous year's purchase of the Fabius facility. In 1971, the Hunt brothers, owners of Ashland Inc., acquired a 50% stake in the company. The following year, Arch narrowly won a $58 million bid to purchase the Southwestern Illinois Coal Company. The venture placed the company among the top ten coal producers in the U.S., generating in excess of 12 million tons a year. Also that year, Arch and the Rocky Mountain Energy Company created a joint venture called Medicine Bow Coal Company located 15 miles from Arch's Seminoe I mine in Wyoming.

In 1973, the Fabius mine defaulted on its notes revered to the TVA. In spite of Arch's debt, TVA did not take control of the mines. With the Arab oil boycott causing coal prices to soar in 1974, the company moved firmly in the black with $4.3 million in profits. The Medicine Bow mine opened in 1975, and profits soared to $27 million on sales of $116 million. Many of the firm's original executives resigned amid rumors of disagreements with the new leadership appointed when Heckman became ill in the mid-1970s.

The coal industry was hit in 1977 with a four-month strike; Arch's profits plummeted. In 1979, due to continuing problems with low employee motivation and increased absenteeism, Heckman appointed a new president, R.E. Samples, who began to revitalize morale. In 1984, Arch paid $145 million for troubled U.S. Steel Corp.'s coal business. Operations began winding down at Seminoe I and Medicine Bow in 1985, and the Leahy mine was acquired. The Horse Creek mine opened in 1986, and a year later, after complex negotiations, Arch paid $135 million for Diamond Shamrock Coal.

In the late 1980s, Catenary Coal was created to develop contractor operations on isolated small pockets of Appalachian reserves. Over 23 million tons of coal were produced annually, and the Stansbury mine in Wyoming was added to Arch's operations. In 1991, Arch acquired Blue Diamond Coal. By then, the firm was one of the country's leading and fastest growing coal producers, with mines in Wyoming, Illinois, Alabama, Virginia, West Virginia, and Kentucky. In July of 1997, Arch merged with Ashland Coal to form Arch Coal, headquartered in St. Louis, Missouri.

Market Forces Driving the Merger

Ashland Inc. had wanted to merge its two coal businesses—57%-owned Ashland Coal and 50%-owned Arch Mineral—since the early 1990s. One of the reasons the deal never moved beyond discussions was the questionable performance of certain units of Arch Mineral. For example, the firm's Kentucky division posted a loss in 1991. This prompted the firm to contract an outside productivity consultant for assistance. After closing a plant and implementing other streamlining measures, the Kentucky unit returned to profitability in 1994. The same consultant also helped Arch Mineral save roughly $1 million in its Wyoming division. According to Arch Coal CEO Leer, "the results gained in Kentucky and Wyoming helped Arch Mineral provide a solid foundation and operational base for the merger. Arch Mineral improved its operations, as increased competition in the coal industry fostered an environment favorable toward mergers."

Ashland's falling stock prices in 1996, due at least in part to sluggish performance of the firm's downstream operations, forced Ashland Inc. to take stock of its coal holdings. The firm wanted to take advantage of the economies of scale consolidation would offer. A merger would allow the two companies to reduce costs by eliminating redundancies in operations. And as Ashland Coal CEO claimed, "the two companies fit well together. Arch Mineral has mining properties in southern West Virginia which are located in close proximity to Ashland Coal properties."

Joining the leading producer of low sulfur coal in the eastern U.S. with the second largest producer of coal in the western U.S. would also create the sixth largest U.S. coal company and establish a solid base for growth, which would be necessary to remain competitive in the increasingly cutthroat energy industry. According to an October 1997 article in *Mergers & Acquisitions*, "trends toward greater choices in fuel usage have prompted energy companies of all types to control a diversity of fuel alternatives." Although joining Arch Mineral and Ashland Coal wouldn't immediately result in a much more diverse product line, the larger firm would be better equipped to pursue acquisitions in the late 1990s.

Approach and Engagement

In January of 1997, privately held Arch Mineral and publicly owned Ashland Coal announced their intent to merge. Arch Mineral agreed to change its name to Arch Coal, Inc. Terms of the $341.3 million deal also stipulated that Ashland Coal stockholders would receive one share of Arch Coal common stock for each share of Ashland Coal they held. Holders of Ashland Coal Class B and Class C convertible preferred stock would trade each of those preferred shares in for 20,500 shares of Arch Coal common stock.

Stockholders overwhelmingly approved the deal on June 30, 1997. In fact, of the stockholders who voted, 99% approved the merger. When the transac-

The Officers

Chairman: James R. Boyd

President and Chief Executive Officer: Steven F. Leer

Exec. VP, Mining Operations: Kenneth Woodring

Sr. VP, Chief Financial Officer, and Treasurer: Patrick Kriegshauser

Sr. VP of Law, Human Resources Secretary, and General Counsel: Jeffry Quinn

tion was finalized the next day, Arch had roughly 39.6 million share of common stock outstanding; it also began trading on the New York Stock Exchange. Arch Mineral shareholders owned roughly 52% of Arch Coal; Ashland Coal shareholders owned the remaining 48%. The original parent company of both businesses, Ashland Inc., retained a 53% stake in the new firm.

Products and Services

After the merger was completed, Arch Coal divided its operations into four regions which produced a total of 105.2 million tons of coal in 1997. Central Appalachia produced 41.3 million tons of coal and covered Virginia, West Virginia, and Kentucky. Specific operations included Campbell's Creek, Coal-Mac, Hobet 07, Hobet 21, Lone Mountain, Mingo Logan, Pardee, and Ruffner/Wylo. The Powder River Basin—near Gillette, Wyoming—generated 40.6 million tons of coal and included Black Thunder and Coal Creek. Arch's Western Bituminous Region encompassed Colorado, Utah, and southern Wyoming. Together, Dugout Canyon, Medicine Bow, Seminoe II, Skyline, Sufco, West Elk, and Canyon Fuel Co. (65% owned by Arch), produced 18.4 million tons of coal. Finally, the Conant Mine, which operated in the Illinois Basin, boasted coal production totaling 4.9 million tons.

Review of the Outcome

When the merger was completed, Arch Coal became the largest producer of low-sulfur coal in the eastern U.S.; the firm also boasted significant holdings in Wyoming and Illinois. Arch Coal stock reached a high of 30.50 per share in 1997, compared to a high of 28.38 before the merger, as the firm realized almost immediate earnings and cash flow increases. Arch Coal CEO Leer predicted that "with our merger, the company will be a platform for expansion, through

The Players

Chairman and CEO of Ashland Coal, Inc.: William C. Payne. William Payne was CEO, Chairman, and President of Ashland Coal prior to its merger with Arch Mineral. Upon completion of the transaction in 1997, the 64-year-old coal executive retired.

Chairman and CEO of Arch Mineral Corp.: Steven F. Leer. Before accepting a post at Arch Coal in 1992, Steven Leer served Ashland Coal as senior vice president of marketing and, later, as president. Leer also worked for Valvoline Inc. as senior vice president of operations. As chairman and CEO of Arch Mineral, Leer implemented several productivity enhancements that strengthened the firm's bottom line and prepared it for its 1997 merger with Ashland Coal. When the deal was finalized, Leer took over as Arch Coal's president and CEO.

internal growth and acquisition, and for increasing shareholder value that neither company could achieve individually."

Changes to the Industry

Less than a year after the merger took place, Arch Coal demonstrated that it was indeed a "platform for expansion" with its $1.14 billion purchase of ARCO Coal, the U.S. coal assets of Atlantic Richfield. The deal propelled Arch Coal further up the ladder of coal industry giants, leaving it second only to Peabody Holding Co. Inc. The merger that created Arch Coal resulted in annual coal production of 41.3 million tons and two billion tons of coal reserves. Arch Coal's sub-

sequent purchase of ARCO Coal boosted the firm's annual coal production to 110 million tons; reserves grew to 3.4 billion tons.

Research

"Arch Mineral Corp.," in *Notable Corporate Chronologies*, The Gale Group, 1999. Lists major events in the history of Arch Mineral Corp., including its merger with Ashland Coal, Inc.

Arch Coal Inc. Home Page, available at http://www.arch-coal.com Official World Wide Web Home Page for Arch Coal Inc. Includes news, financial, product, and historical information, as well as annual reports and industry links.

"Ashland, Inc.," in *Notable Corporate Chronologies*, Gale Research, 1999. Lists major events in the history of Ashland Inc., including its investment in Arch Mineral and its creation of Ashland Coal, Inc.

"Ashland Coal, Arch to Merge," in *The Oil Daily*, 1 July 1997. Discusses the merger agreement between Arch Mineral and Ashland Coal, as well as the outcome of the deal.

Blumenfeld, Andrew. "What to Expect from Arch Coal Inc.," in *Coal Age*, May 1997. Offers a brief sketch of causes of the merge and predicts the outcome of the Arch Mineral and Ashland Coal joining.

Collin, Jame. "Ashland Concentrates on Smaller Maneuvers As Analysts Await Big Move on Downstream," in *The Oil Daily*, 8 April 1997. Covers the conditions that prompted the Arch Coal merger, as well as the role of Ashland Inc. in the deal.

"M&A Roundup," in *Mergers & Acquisitions*, September/October 1997. Offers a brief look at several major mergers in 1997, including the Ashland Coal and Arch Mineral deal.

Myers, Todd A. "AAA (Arch-Ashland-ARCO): Arch's Road Map to Success," in *Coal Age*, May 1998. This article offers an overview of Arch Coal's 1998 purchase of ARCO Coal, including how the deal might impact Arch Coal's marketing reach.

"Productivity Gains Assisted Birth of Arch Goal," in *Mining Magazine*, November 1998. Explains how improvements to Arch Minerals's bottom line better positioned it for its merger with Ashland Coal. Includes an interview with Arch Coal CEO Steven Leer.

THERA WILLIAMS

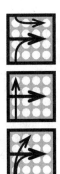

ASTRA & ZENECA

nationality: United Kingdom
date: April 6, 1999
affected: Astra AB, Sweden, founded 1913
affected: Zeneca Group PLC, United Kingdom, founded 1993

AstraZeneca PLC
15 Stanhope Gate
London, W1Y 6LN
United Kingdom

tel: 44 171 304 5000
fax: 44 171 304 5151
web: http://www.astrazeneca.com

Overview of the Merger

The world's third-largest pharmaceutical company was formed in April 1999, when Astra AB joined with Zeneca Group PLC to form AstraZeneca PLC. This Swedish-Anglo company immediately became a major challenger to the industry's heavyweights in several geographic markets, particularly Europe and the U.S. It also assumed leading positions in a number of therapeutic markets, namely anesthesia and gastrointestinal treatments.

History of Astra AB

Astra was formed in 1913 by a group of more than 400 Swedish doctors and apothecaries. The new company released its first products the next year, and the success of the heart medication Digitotal and the nutritional supplement Glokofos enabled it to prosper. A growing product line and a wartime restriction on imports necessitated the addition of new factories to meet demand.

Demand tapered off after World War I, and the Swedish chemical company AB Svensk Fargamnesindistri acquired Astra to boost the drug company's presence. As the price of raw materials continue to lag, however, Astra's expenses were greater than the amount its products could command in the marketplace. Sweden's new socialist decided to nationalize Svensk Fargamnesindistri, but within months the socialist government fell and was succeeded by a government opposed to the nationalization. In 1929 it began seeking a buyer for the company, finally locating a private consortium that purchased the company in 1925.

The new leadership reorganized Astra to suppress its losses, and within a few years it was once again profitable. Newly established research and development facilities produced such important drugs as Hepaforte and Nitropent during the 1930s. Its profitability was once again improved by wartime shortages, and by the end of World War II the company had subsidiaries in the U.S., Argentina, Stockholm, and other European cities.

The blockbuster anesthetic Xylocaine was released in the late 1940s, and remained one of Astra's most successful products for five decades. It stepped up

The Business

Financials

Revenue (1998): $9.1 billion

Employees (1998): 50,000

SICs / NAICS

sic 2834 - Pharmaceutical Preparations

sic 2835 - Diagnostic Substances

naics 325412 - Pharmaceutical Preparation Manufacturing

its research and development activities during in 1950s, releasing a number of successful drugs, including Secergan, Ascoxal, Jectofer, and Citanest. Astra continued to expand in the 1960s, and by 1983 about 80% of its sales originated overseas. Acquisitions and partnerships also diversified Astra into such areas as agriculture, cleaning, and recreational products. By the end of the 1970s, however, it withdrew from those markets to concentrate solely on pharmaceuticals.

With a renewed focus, Astra's pharmaceutical operations continued to develop successful products. By 1984 three products—Xylocaine, Seloken, and Bricanyl—generated over 50% of total revenues. Pretax earnings reached SKr1.5 billion on revenues of SKr6.2 billion in 1988. These results, while bringing attention to Astra by outside investors, failed to impress the Wallenberg family, owner of a 10% stake in Astra. The family began a search for new CEO and president, and in 1988 hired Hakan Mogren.

Mogren began transforming the company into a more aggressive player with greater control over its sales and distribution. By the end of 1997 he had established new subsidiaries and added nearly 1,000 sales representatives. Under Mogren's leadership, Astra also released the ulcer treatment Losec as a direct challenger to Glaxo Pharmaceutical's best-selling Zantac. After only two years at the helm, Mogren boosted sales to SKr9.4 billion.

He continued to strengthen Astra during the 1990s, doubling its sales force to 7,000 and increasing subsidiaries to 40 nations by mid-decade. Losec became the world's best-selling drug in 1996. That year net income reached SKr13 billion on revenues of SKr39 billion.

History of Zeneca Group PLC

Imperial Chemical Industries (ICI) was formed in 1926 through the consolidation of four British chemi-

cal companies to challenge Germany's powerful IG Farben. The end of World War II brought the dissolution of IG Farben, and with it a shift in the balance of power in the industry. ICI emerged as the leader in the U.K., with the DuPont controlling the North and South American markets. These two heavyweights entered into cross-licensing arrangements to operate in the other's territory. The Ryan Anti-Trust Judgment of the 1950s brought an end to that arrangement.

The newly independent company broadened its scope by increasing operations in continental Europe. It also diversified its product offerings, organizing pharmaceuticals as a separate division in the late 1950s, but continued its primary emphasis on heavy chemicals. It achieved growth through numerous acquisitions during the 1970s and 1980s, including that of U.S.-based Beatrice; the top paint manufacturer Glidden, and the agrochemicals producer Stauffer.

By the end of the 1980s, ICI found itself increasingly challenged by the complexities of operating in so many diverse markets. Its lack of a clear focus made it vulnerable to a takeover, a threat that became tangible when Hanson PLC acquired a small stake in ICI. To preempt any such attempt, the company decided to demerge into two units. ICI would continue to operate as a chemical company in traditional markets, while Zeneca would house its pharmaceutical, agrochemical, and specialty products.

Zeneca was established as a subsidiary of ICI on January 1, 1993. That June it was spun off from ICI, and immediately became one of the top 25 U.K. companies in terms of market capitalization, topping even that of its former parent. It was also one of the world's top 20 pharmaceutical companies. Sales for its first year of operation reached GBP4.44 billion, with a profit margin that grew 42% to GBP647 million.

The new company's momentum continued. By 1995 Zeneca was the world's number-two manufacturer of cancer drugs and one of the top six agrochemical firms. Its pharmaceutical unit generated the lion's share of revenues, GBP2 billion of the total GBP4.8 billion, in 1995. It focused on treatments for cancer and disorders of the respiratory, cardiovascular, and central nervous systems. Its best-selling drugs included the cancer treatments Casodex and Arimdex, as well as the asthma drug Accolate. Zeneca also purchased a 50% stake in Salick Health Care, Inc., a U.S.-based provider of cancer treatment.

The company's agrochemicals unit produced such herbicides as Gramoxone, Touchdown, and Surpass. It also worked to develop and produce genetically engineered food and fiber plants. Zeneca's specialties arm manufactured such consumer products as automotive pigments, ink jet dyes, swimming pool fungicides, leather finishes, and water-based resins.

Profits surpassed GBP1 billion for the first time in 1996, when revenues reached GBP5.4 billion. The next year it acquired the remaining 50% of Salick for $234 million. In 1998 Zeneca purchased the U.S.-based fungicides business of Japanese company Ishihara Sangyo Kaisha for GBP303 million.

Market Forces Driving the Merger

The pharmaceutical industry was undergoing a rash of consolidation in the late 1990s, fueled by the patent expiry of blockbuster drugs, the drive to secure an enhanced position in an increasingly global market, and the quest to achieve efficiencies through economies of scale. These pressures impacted European firms in particular. They faced fierce competition from their U.S.-based counterparts, which had richer research and development pipelines as well as a direct presence in the world's largest pharmaceutical market. In 1998, responding to these pressures, two mergers of European pharmaceutical companies were announced. Hoescht AG of Germany agreed to unite its life sciences business with that of Rhone-Poulenc S.A. of France to form Aventis, the world's fourth-largest pharmaceutical firm. A union was also announced between two French companies, Sanofi S.A. and Synthelabo, creating the sixth-largest pharmaceutical firm in Europe. Such consolidations compounded the pressure on the remaining independent pharmaceutical firms, which had little choice but to follow suit.

The pressure of patent expiry loomed large for both Astra and Zeneca. Without patent protection, generic versions could be introduced by competitors, undercutting sales of the original versions. Astra, a Swedish-based pharmaceutical firm, manufactured the world's top-selling drug, the ulcer treatment Prilosec, whose patent was scheduled for expiration in 2001. U.K.-based Zeneca, a leader in cancer medications, also had many imminent patent expirations, including that of its anti-hypertension drug Zestril.

Separately, each company's pipeline held the promise of relatively moderate success, but combined, research and development efforts would provide a greater chance of offsetting the losses due to patent expiration. The companies' product emphases were complementary, as Astra focused on digestive and respiratory ailments while Zeneca was a leader in cancer treatments. A combined company would also propel to the industry's top ranks. It would become Europe's second-largest pharmaceutical company and the world's third-largest, and would hold the top market positions in the gastrointestinal and anesthesia therapeutic areas.

The Officers

Non-Executive Chairman: Percy Barnevik

Executive Deputy Chairman: Sir David Barnes

Executive Deputy Chairman: Hakan Mogren

CEO: Tom McKillop

Executive Director, Chief Financial Officer: Jonathan Symonds

Approach and Engagement

Astra and Zeneca announced their merger agreement on December 9, 1998. The terms of the $35 billion deal called for Astra shareholders to receive 0.5045 shares of the new company, to be named AstraZeneca PLC, in exchange for each Astra share. Zeneca shareholders would own 53.5% of the new company, with Astra shareholders owning the remaining 46.5%.

In anticipation of the merger, Astra had restructured its U.S.-based marketing joint venture with Merck, Astra-Merck Inc. AstraZeneca agreed to buy out Merck for $740 million after the merger, with the option of an additional $950 million at a future date for Merck's remaining interest in existing Astra products.

The European Union granted its conditional approval for the merger in early March 1999. Because of Astra's portfolio of anesthetics, it required Zeneca to return the licensing rights of the local anesthetic Chirocaine to its developing company, Chiroscience. The European Union also insisted that Zeneca locate a third-party distributor for Tenormin in Sweden and Norway, and that Astra divest itself of its European betablocker/diuretic business. The U.S. Federal Trade Commission agreed with those conditions and, having no additional requirements of its own, approved the deal at the end of March.

On April 6, 1999, 96.4% of Astra's shareholders approved the deal, thereby clearing the final hurdle for the merger. AstraZeneca was officially formed on that day.

Products and Services

By late 1999, AstraZeneca developed and manufactured pharmaceuticals for seven primary therapeutic areas.

Cardiovascular treatments included Atacand (candesartan cilexetil), Zestril (lisinopril dihydrate), Ramace (ramipril), Seloken (metoprolol), Tenormin (atenolol), Inderal (propranolol hydrocholoride), Plendil (felodipine), Sular (nisoldipine), Imdur (isosorbide-5-mononitrate), and Canef (fluvastatin).

Central nervous system drugs included Zomig (zolmitriptan), Seroquel (quetiapine), Mysoline (primidone), Vivalan (viloxazine hydrocholoride), and Inderal (propranolol hydrochloride).

Gastrointestinal products included Losec (omeprazole), Entocort (budesonide), and Colazide (balsalazide).

Treatments for Infection included Apatef/Cefotan (cefotetan), Merrem/Meronem (meropenem), and Hibitane (chlorhexidine digluconate).

Oncology medications included Zoladex (goserelin acetate), Nolvadex (tamoxifen citrate), Casodex (bicalutamide), Arimidex (anastrasole), and Tomudex (raltitrexed).

Pain control and Anesthesia products included Diprivan (propofol), Naropin (ropivacaine), Xylocaine (lidocaine), Marcaine/Sensocaine (bupivacaine), EMLA (Eutectic Mixture of Lidocaine and Prilocaine, Carbocaine (mepivacaine), Citanest (prilocaine), and Duranest (etidocaine).

Finally, Respiratory pharmaceuticals included Pulmicort (budesonide), Accolate (zafirlukast), Oxis (formoterol), Bricanyl (terbutaline), and Rhinocort (budesonide).

Changes to the Industry

Completed in less than 90 working days after it was announced, the $35 billion merger formed a leading player in the global pharmaceutical industry. AstraZeneca immediately became the world's third-largest and Europe's second-largest pharmaceutical firm. It also formed the seventh-largest pharmaceutical firm in the lucrative U.S. market, where Astra and Zeneca had previously ranked 13th and 19th, respectively.

AstraZeneca assumed top roles in several therapeutic markets. It ranked number one in both gastrointestinal and anesthesia, number two in oncology, number four in respiratory, and number five in cardiovascular drugs.

The company's combined pipeline positioned it well for future growth. It held 55 new chemical entities in various trial phases. Among the pharmaceuticals in phase III clinical trials were Fasalodex, for advanced breast cancer; Perprazole, a successor to Losec; Budoxis, an asthma medication; and Zendra, for the treatment of stroke.

Review of the Outcome

AstraZeneca's corporate headquarters were located in the U.K., with its research and development operations centered in Sweden. Its non-executive chairman was Percy Barnevik, a large shareholder of the former Astra. Tom McKillop, CEO of Zeneca Pharmaceuticals, took the same role in the new company. Sir David Barnes, Zeneca's CEO, and Hakan Mogren, Astra's president and CEO, became joint deputy chairmen.

The new company expected to realize $1.1 billion in estimated annual savings in three years through efficiencies of operation and economies of scale. Although no major facilities were expected to close, about 6,000 jobs would be lost through redundancies over a three-year period.

On June 30, 1999, AstraZeneca completed the sale of Zeneca's specialty chemicals business for $2.1 billion to a buyout group led by the private equity companies Investcorp and Cinven.

Research

"Astra AB," in *International Directory of Company Histories*, Vol. 20, St. James Press: 1998. Provides a chronology of the company.

"AstraZeneca Merger Completed, Leaps to Third in Pharmaceutical Sales League," in *Marketletter*, 12 April 1999. Announces the completion of the merger.

AstraZeneca PLC Home Page, available at http://www.astrazeneca.com. Official World Wide Web Page for AstraZeneca. Includes product descriptions, financial documents, news releases, executive biographies, and employment opportunities.

Milmo, Sean. "Zeneca and Astra to Merge into a Global Pharma Powerhouse," in *Chemical Market Reporter*, 14 December 1998. Details the merger agreement.

Osborne, Randall. "Astra, Zeneca in $35B Merger Agreement," in *BIOWORLD*, 9 December 1998. Describes the terms of the merger.

"Zeneca Group PLC," in *International Directory of Company Histories*, Vol. 21, St. James Press: 1998. Details the company's history.

LAURA BRYSON

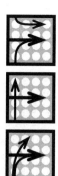

AT&T & MCCAW CELLULAR COMMUNICATIONS

nationality: USA
date: September 20, 1994
affected: AT&T Corp., USA, founded 1877
affected: McCaw Cellular Communications Inc., USA, founded 1937

AT&T Corp.
32 Avenue of the Americas
New York, NY 10013-2412
USA

tel: (212)387-5400
fax: (212)226-4935
web: http://www.att.com

Overview of the Merger

AT&T paid $11.5 billion for McCaw Cellular in September of 1994, gaining much needed access to the burgeoning cellular industry. Deregulation that would give local phone companies permission to compete in long distance markets, while only allowing long distance providers limited access to local markets, loomed large. Recognizing that its competition in the long distance market would likely intensify, AT&T began seeking other avenues of expansion. Purchasing McCaw put AT&T back in direct competition with the Baby Bells for the first time since their spin off from AT&T in 1984.

History of AT&T Corp.

In 1877, a group of three investors, including Alexander Graham Bell, formed the Bell Telephone Company (BTC) to develop the economic potential of the newly invented telephone. A year later, New Haven District Telephone Co. (NHDT), a Bell Telephone Co. licensee, established the world's first telephone exchange and issued the world's first telephone directory. BTC formed the New England Telephone Co. to distribute licensing of company patents.

BTC and NHDT merged to form the National Bell Telephone Company (NBT) in 1879. In 1880, NBT reorganized as the American Bell Telephone Company (ABT), consolidating NBT with the newly-acquired Western Union properties. A year later, ABT acquired Western Electric Manufacturing Co., the main supplier of telegraph equipment for Western Union, to become the exclusive manufacturer of its equipment. ABT created American Telephone and Telegraph Company (AT&T) in 1885 to operate as its long distance subsidiary and to establish a truly national telephone network. Management was eager to have such a subsidiary in service prior to 1893, the expiration date of its original patents.

AT&T provided military phone service in the U.S. during World War I, and set up the American military communication system, comprising radios, telephones, and telegraph lines, in France. In 1921, government regulations were amended to allow for mergers of telephone companies. AT&T began a decade-long period of

The Business

Financials

Revenue (1998): $53.23 billion

Employees (1998): 107,800

SICs / NAICS

sic 4813 - Telephone Communications Except
Radiotelephone

sic 4812 - Radiotelephone Communications

sic 3661 - Telephone & Telegraph Apparatus

naics 513322 - Cellular and Other Wireless
Telecommunications

naics 513321 - Paging

naics 334418 - Printed Circuit Assembly (Electronic
Assembly) Manufacturing

acquisition and expansion. By then, the company was providing service to 64% of all U.S. telephones.

In 1925, AT&T spun off its research and development operations as Bell Telephone Laboratories (BTL), a separate company jointly funded by AT&T and Western Electric. The Federal Communications Commission (FCC) was set up in 1934 to regulate the interstate telephone business, replacing the Interstate Commerce Commission. A year later, the FCC began investigation of AT&T's competitive practices. The firm controlled 83% of U.S. phones and 98% of long distance cables; its Western Electric subsidiary manufactured 90% of the nation's telephone equipment. Assets totaled $5 billion, which made AT&T the largest company in the U.S.

World War II overshadowed the FCC's reports on AT&T's competitive practices. However, the FCC did force AT&T to lower its rates during the war. By the mid 1940s, long distance telephone calls had begun to replace letter writing as the preferred means of communication. In 1949, the prewar FCC report resurfaced, and the U.S. Attorney General sued AT&T for violation of the Sherman Act and asked the firm to separate from Western Electric. Seven years later, the U.S. Attorney General's suit was settled. AT&T and Western Electric were allowed to remain intact, but AT&T had to limit its activities to providing common carrier service, while Western Electric was required to limit itself to supplying equipment to AT&T and fulfilling government contracts.

Both MCI and the U.S. Department of Justice filed an antitrust suit against AT&T in 1974, charging monopoly and conspiracy to monopolize the telecommunications industry. Six years later, a jury found AT&T guilty in the MCI suit and ordered AT&T to pay damages of $1.8 billion. AT&T appealed the decision, and a jury eventually reduced damages to $37.8 million. In 1982, AT&T and the Department of Justice settled their antitrust suit: AT&T agreed to divest itself of its regional operating companies, which would become unregulated, competing businesses.

In 1983, plans for the breakup of AT&T were approved. The company began spinning off BellSouth, Bell Atlantic, NYNEX, American Information Technologies, Southwestern Bell, U S West, and Pacific Telesis to handle regional phone services in the U.S. AT&T retained control of its long distance services, but was no longer protected from competition. Once the split was completed, AT&T reorganized into two divisions: AT&T Communications, which managed the long distance network, and AT&T Technologies, which manufactured and sold telecommunications equipment.

A year after the breakup, the company launched a program of geographic diversification, opening a regional headquarters in Brussels, Belgium, to serve Europe, the Middle East, and Africa, and aggressively seeking joint venture agreements with overseas companies. In 1987, the firm held a 76% share of the U.S. long distance market, down from 91% in 1983. AT&T cut 16,000 employees and assumed a $6.7 billion charge to modernize its network, recording a loss of $1.7 billion in 1988.

Government regulators freed AT&T in 1989 to match the low long distance rates of competitors MCI and Sprint, enabling the company to rebound and show a profit of $2.7 billion, its best figure since the breakup. AT&T paid $7.4 billion to merge with NCR Corp. in 1991. The merger made AT&T the fourth largest computer maker in the U.S. and the seventh largest worldwide; three years later, AT&T changed the NCR unit's name to AT&T Global Information Solutions. In 1993, the firm diversified into cellular telephony with its $12.6 billion purchase of McCaw Cellular.

Congress passed a new telecommunications bill in 1996 that freed AT&T to enter local markets and compete for local telephone service business on a limited basis. In December of that year, AT&T completed its historic split into three separate components: AT&T retained its communications operations; transferred its equipment operations to a new public company, Lucent Technology; and spun off NCR, which had lost $4 billion in the five years it was owned by AT&T. The firm's next major move was also its largest. In early 1999, AT&T paid $59 billion for cable operator TCI Communications, which it renamed AT&T Broadband & Internet Services.

History of McCaw Cellular Communications Inc.

In 1937, John Elroy McCaw opened a radio station in Centralia, Washington, the first ever in the area. Later, intent on building a media empire, he added station KYA in San Francisco and a station in New York City, converting it to an innovative rock and roll format. In 1952, McCaw became one of the first cable television operators. He died suddenly in 1969, and his widow and four sons begin an eight-year process of paying back the money that he borrowed, keeping only one small cable system.

Four years later Craig McCaw took over the business, newly named McCaw Communications Companies Inc., and quickly expanded the company's holdings in the cable television industry from its base as a single system with 4,000 subscribers. The firm entered the radio common carrier field in 1974, by providing paging services to clients. In 1980, McCaw sold a $12 million stake in his company to Affiliated Publications, the parent company of the *Boston Globe*. The firm invested a modest $3.5 million to enter the new cellular telephone industry in 1981 and won all six of its FCC license hearings. As a result, McCaw Cellular Communications, Inc. was incorporated in Washington that year.

Within two years, the volume of requests for cellular licenses had grown so great that the FCC abandoned its system of hearings in favor of a random lottery, introducing an element of chance into the cellular industry. McCaw Cellular purchased mobile phone operator Dominion Cellular late in 1984 and secured licenses to provide cellular phone services in the Colorado cities of Denver and Boulder as well as in Kansas City, Missouri, in 1985. The company also purchased the cellular assets of the Knight-Ridder newspaper chain and paid $120 million for MCI Airsignal, which expanded McCaw Cellular's presence in Denver, Pittsburgh, Sacramento, Fresno, and Salt Lake City.

After acquiring two more cellular firms, Maxcell Telecom Plus and Charisma Communications, McCaw put its cable assets on the block in 1986. Entrepreneur Jack Kent Cooke purchased the cable segment for $755 million the following year. McCaw also acquired Florida Telephone Company and listed publicly in 1987, allowing Affiliated Publications to increase its stake to 45%. By then, the enterprise was the largest U.S. cellular phone operator. In 1988,

The Officers

Chairman and CEO: C. Michael Armstrong

President: John D. Zeglis

Sr. Exec. VP and Chief Financial Officer: Daniel Somers

Exec. VP, Corporate Strategy and Business Development: John Petrillo

Exec. VP, Public Relations: Richard J. Martin

McCaw purchased roughly 10% of Lin Broadcasting. A year later, McCaw offered to buy Lin Broadcasting for $6.5 million. Lin rejected the offer, and after a complicated series of maneuvers, the company succeeded in buying roughly half of Lin's shares.

McCaw sold its cellular telephone properties in the southeastern U.S. to Contel Cellular, Inc. for $1.3 billion in 1990. The firm also forged an agreement in 1991 with PacTel Corp., the third largest cellular operator in the U.S., to join forces in several large urban areas, including San Francisco, Dallas, and Kansas City. That year, McCaw introduced a software program that allowed customers to receive calls outside of their home areas without the use of access codes; the program spawned the North American Cellular Network. The firm also established a joint venture with Southwestern Bell Corp. to establish the trade name Cellular One as a national symbol for independent, or non-wire-line, cellular service. McCaw was acquired by AT&T in 1994 for $11.5 billion; its name was eventually changed to AT&T Wireless Services.

Market Forces Driving the Merger

As part of the 1984 AT&T breakup agreement, AT&T was freed of the 1956 prohibition against entering non-telecommunications ventures; this enabled the firm to move into the computer market. Although the FCC would likely have given AT&T free cellular licenses as part of the 1984 deal, AT&T was more focused on entering the computer industry and capitalizing on what analysts predicted would be a lucrative combination: computers and communication. Viewing the cellular industry's future as low-growth at best, AT&T shelved its cellular operations and began an ill-fated, decade-long foray into computers.

The anticipated computer and communication synergies failed to emerge; in fact, AT&T's gravest misstep, its takeover of NCR Corp. in 1991, cost the company roughly $4 billion in losses. As a result, AT&T began seeking non-computer avenues of expansion. Bundled communication services were being

The Players

Chairman and CEO of AT&T Corp.: Robert Allen. Robert Allen began working for AT&T as a management trainee when he graduated from college in 1957. He climbed his way up the corporate ladder, reaching chairman and CEO status in 1988 after AT&T head James Olson died of cancer. Allan steered AT&T's ill-fated ventures into the computer industry during the late 1980s and early 1990s, including the purchase of NCR, as well as the more lucrative purchase of McCaw Cellular in 1993, and the firm's three-pronged split in 1996. In 1997, Allan agreed to retire early and named John Walter his successor. When AT&T's negotiations with SBC Communications Inc. fell apart in 1997, the board ousted Walter, chose C. Michael Armstrong as its new leader, and forced Allan to resign months earlier than he'd planned.

Chairman and CEO of McCaw Cellular Communications Inc.: Craig O. McCaw. Telecommunications industry trailblazer Craig McCaw took over his family's media company in 1973 and built the firm into the largest cellular operator in the U.S. When AT&T bought McCaw Cellular in 1994, McCaw declined a seat on the board and began pursuing other mobile telephony ventures. The reclusive billionaire rescued personal communications services (PCS) upstart Nextel in 1995 with a $1.1 billion capital infusion. In March of 1998, McCaw accepted the post of CEO at Teledesic LLC, where he was currently serving as chairman.

hailed by analysts as the wave of the future, and AT&T realized it lacked a key component: cellular services. At the same time, deregulation was sweeping the telecommunications industry, and AT&T would soon face increased competition from local telephone companies. According to a December 1994 *Forbes* article, "AT&T considered its options and decided it had only one. The company was too far behind to build businesses from scratch. The Baby Bell were entrenched and controlled 75% of the cellular industry. The customers most likely to be big spenders had already been signed up by established players. So AT&T's best hope was to buy one of them."

Fortunately for Craig McCaw, founder of McCaw Cellular, his firm was one of the only ones AT&T could legally purchase. His flourishing upstart, the largest cellular services provider in the U.S., needed additional resources for its planned nationwide expansion. In 1994, McCaw held 17% of the U.S. cellular market. With roughly 28,000 new customers signing up each day, McCaw believed his firm's potential for growth would be explosive with access to AT&T's deep pockets. McCaw also recognized that linking with AT&T would bolster his efforts to have federal standards passed that would permit all U.S.-based cellular systems to interact.

Approach and Engagement

Craig McCaw first approached AT&T in 1990. The two companies informally negotiated for two years before announcing a joint venture that entailed AT&T purchasing 33% of McCaw for $3.73 billion. The deal would allow AT&T to compete directly with the Baby Bells for the first time since the 1984 breakup; in response, the Bell companies demanded access to long distance markets. Talks faltered several times when AT&T and McCaw disagreed on issues such as how to divide sales from bundled long distance and cellular services, how to determine the extra revenue McCaw would generate from using the AT&T name, and how to choose which technology would be developed collaboratively. Both sides eventually agreed that for the deal to work, AT&T would simply have to take over McCaw.

In August of 1993, AT&T agreed to pay a whopping $12.6 billion in stock for McCaw Cellular. Bell Atlantic, Nynex, and BellSouth Corp. filed an antitrust suit, claiming that the merger of AT&T and McCaw Cellular would give AT&T a monopoly over the cellular equipment market. While a judge eventually found in favor of AT&T, the Department of Justice did impose several restrictions on the deal. In fact, to win Justice Department approval, AT&T and McCaw signed a consent decree that AT&T couldn't market McCaw's cellular services until McCaw had converted at least 60% of its systems to offer equal access to other long distance providers. Prior to the merger, McCaw had used AT&T exclusively. AT&T's share price dipped a bit prior to the acquisition, and when it was completed on September 20, 1994, the final price totaled $11.5 billion.

Products and Services

AT&T's spin-off of NCR in 1996, as well as its separation from Lucent Technologies, left the firm with the following operations: consumer long distance; business long distance; wireless; and local. Of the $53.23 billion AT&T earned in revenues in 1998, $22.94 billion came from consumer long distance sales; $22.63 billion were due to business long distance sales;

$5.4 billion were the result of wireless sales; and $3.54 billion came from other services.

Changes to the Industry

The AT&T/McCaw linkup was finalized just as personal communication services (PCS) technology arrived on the wireless scene. The FTC began planning to auction five new PCS licences per region, which would break up what was essentially a duopoly in the cellular industry. According to Bruce Wasserstein, author of *Big Deal: The Battle for Control of America's Leading Corporations*, these events rocked the cellular industry. "Investors became less sure of the gravity-defying valuations placed on cellular properties. Meanwhile, the cellular companies generally raced to bulk up for the new competitive era."

News of AT&T's planned takeover of McCaw prompted MCI to consider reentering the wireless market. Early in 1994, the firm announced plans to invest over $1 billion in PCS upstart Nextel, but the deal later crumbled. In mid-1994, Bell Atlantic and Nynex announced their intent to join their cellular businesses. AirTouch Communications, Inc. and U S West Inc. also began jointly operating their domestic cellular businesses in mid-1994, a deal that was formally completed in April of 1998.

Review of the Outcome

The acquisition of McCaw Cellular gave AT&T access to the fastest growing market in the telecommunications industry, as well as access to a local market just as deregulation efforts heated up. In December of 1995, to strengthen its wireless holdings, AT&T spent $1.7 billion at a government auction of PCS licenses, gaining access to 80% of the U.S. cellular market. When the Telecommunications Act of 1996 was signed, and long distance and local providers were allowed to compete in one another's markets, AT&T

was better positioned for the new competitive landscape in which bundled services would likely prevail. In 1998, AT&T Wireless remained the largest domestic cellular operation in the U.S.

Research

"Appeals Court Affirms Greene's Decision to Allow Merger Between AT&T/McCaw Via Waiver of MFJ Section I," in *Mobile Phone News*, 27 February 1995. Explains why the merger of AT&T and McCaw Cellular was allowed to proceed despite antitrust concerns.

"AT&T Corp.," in *Notable Corporate Chronologies*, The Gale Group, 1999. Lists major events in the history of AT&T, including its takeover of NCR Corp.

AT&T Home Page, available at http://www.att.com. Official World Wide Web Home Page for AT&T Corp. Includes current and archived news; detailed financial, product, and historical information; and annual reports.

Cauley, Leslie. "The Urge to Merge: The Cellular Industry, Facing Competition From PCS, Is in the Midst of a Major Shake-Up," in *The Wall Street Journal*, 20 March 1995. Offers an overview of the reasons for consolidation in the cellular industry during the mid-1990s.

"Justice Department Drops AT&T-McCaw Complaint," in *Telecommunications Report*, 4 March 1996. Explains how Telecommunications Act of 1996 impacted antitrust concerns about the AT&T and McCaw deal.

Kupfer, Andrew. "AT&T's $12 Billion Cellular Dream," in *Fortune*, 12 December 1994. Offers an in-depth look at the reasons for the merger, as well as at potential outcomes of the deal.

"McCaw Cellular Communications Inc.," in *Notable Corporate Chronologies*, The Gale Group, 1999. Lists major events in the history of McCaw Cellular Communications Inc., including its takeover by AT&T Corp.

Schwartz, Jeffrey. "AT&T Provides Muscle for McCaw," in *Communications Week*, 18 September 1995. In an interview, the president of AT&T's Wireless Services unit details the future of the cellular business.

Wasserstein, Bruce. *Big Deal: The Battle for Control of America's Leading Corporations*, Warner Books, 1998. Offers an overview of the largest mergers in recent American corporate history.

SAMIT AYERS

AT&T & MEDIAONE

AT&T Corp.
32 Avenue of the Americas
New York, NY 10013-2412
USA

tel: (212)387-5400
fax: (212)226-4935
web: http://www.att.com

MediaOne Group
188 Inverness Dr. West
Englewood, CO 80112
USA

tel: (303)858-3000
fax: (303)858-3732
web: http://www.mediaonegroup.com

nationality: USA
date: 2000
affected: AT&T Corp., USA, founded 1877
affected: MediaOne Group, USA, founded 1984

Overview of the Merger

AT&T's staggering $62 billion offer for MediaOne Group has the potential to create the largest cable company in the world. This deal has many facets, including side-deals with Microsoft and Comcast, and has many consumer advocacy groups in an uproar. These groups filed complaints with the FCC and the Department of Justice in May 1999. AT&T's interest in MediaOne further exemplifies the company's growing interest in Internet technology and broadband services, and its expanding goal of becoming the leader in end-to-end communication services. AT&T expects to complete it in the first quarter of 2000.

History of AT&T Corp.

In 1877, a group of three investors, including Alexander Graham Bell, formed the Bell Telephone Company (BTC) to develop the economic potential of the newly-invented telephone. A year later, New Haven District Telephone Co. (NHDT), a Bell Telephone Co. licensee, established the world's first telephone exchange and issued the world's first telephone directory. BTC formed the New England Telephone Co. to distribute licensing of company patents.

BTC and NHDT merged to form the National Bell Telephone Company (NBT) in 1879. In 1880, NBT reorganized as the American Bell Telephone Company (ABT), consolidating NBT with the newly-acquired Western Union properties. A year later, ABT acquired Western Electric Manufacturing Co., the main supplier of telegraph equipment for Western Union, to become the exclusive manufacturer of its equipment. ABT created American Telephone and Telegraph Company (AT&T) in 1885 to operate as its long distance subsidiary and to establish a truly national telephone network. Management was eager to have such a subsidiary in service prior to 1893, the expiration date of its original patents.

AT&T provided military phone service in the U.S. during World War I, and set up the American military communication system, comprising radios, telephones, and telegraph lines, in France. In 1921, government regulations were amended to allow for mergers of telephone companies. AT&T began a decade-long period of acquisition and expansion. By then, the company was providing service to 64% of all U.S. telephones.

In 1925, AT&T spun off its research and development operations as Bell Telephone Laboratories (BTL), a separate company jointly funded by AT&T and Western Electric. The Federal Communications Commission (FCC) was set up in 1934 to regulate the interstate telephone business, replacing the Interstate Commerce Commission. A year later, the FCC began investigation of AT&T's competitive practices. The firm controlled 83% of U.S. phones and 98% of long distance cables; its Western Electric subsidiary manufactured 90% of the nation's telephone equipment. Assets totaled $5 billion, which made AT&T the largest company in the U.S.

World War II overshadowed the FCC's reports on AT&T's competitive practices. However, the FCC did force AT&T to lower its rates during the war. By the mid-1940s, long distance telephone calls had begun to replace letter writing as the preferred means of communication. In 1949, the prewar FCC report resurfaced, and the U.S. Attorney General sued AT&T for violation of the Sherman Act and asked the firm to separate from Western Electric. Seven years later, the U.S. Attorney General's suit was settled. AT&T and Western Electric were allowed to remain intact, but AT&T had to limit its activities to providing common carrier service, while Western Electric was required to limit itself to supplying equipment to AT&T and fulfilling government contracts.

Both MCI and the U.S. Department of Justice filed an antitrust suit against AT&T in 1974, charging monopoly and conspiracy to monopolize the telecommunications industry. Six years later, a jury found AT&T guilty in the MCI suit and ordered AT&T to pay damages of $1.8 billion. AT&T appealed the decision, and a jury eventually reduced damages to $37.8 million. In 1982, AT&T and the Department of Justice settled their antitrust suit: AT&T agreed to divest itself of its regional operating companies, which would become unregulated, competing businesses.

In 1983, plans for the breakup of AT&T were approved. The company began spinning off BellSouth, Bell Atlantic, NYNEX, American Information Technologies, Southwestern Bell, U S West, and Pacific Telesis to handle regional phone services in the U.S. AT&T retained control of its long distance services, but was no longer protected from competition. Once the split was completed, AT&T reorganized into two divisions: AT&T Communications, which managed the long distance network, and AT&T Technologies, which manufactured and sold telecommunications equipment.

The Business

Financials - AT&T Corp.

Revenue (1998): $53.2 billion

Employees (1998): 107,800

Financials - MediaOne Group

Revenue (1998): $2,882 million

SICs / NAICS

sic 4813 - Telephone Communications Except Radiotelephone

sic 4812 - Radiotelephone Communications

sic 3661 - Telephone & Telegraph Apparatus

sic 4841 - Cable & Other Pay Television Services

naics 513322 - Cellular and Other Wireless Telecommunications

naics 513321 - Paging

naics 334418 - Printed Circuit Assembly (Electronic Assembly) Manufacturing

A year after the breakup, the company launched a program of geographic diversification, opening a regional headquarters in Brussels, Belgium, to serve Europe, the Middle East, and Africa, and aggressively seeking joint venture agreements with overseas companies. In 1987, the firm held a 76% share of the U.S. long distance market, down from 91% in 1983. AT&T cut 16,000 employees and assumed a $6.7 billion charge to modernize its network, recording a loss of $1.7 billion in 1988.

Government regulators freed AT&T in 1989 to match the low long distance rates of competitors MCI and Sprint, enabling the company to rebound and show a profit of $2.7 billion, its best figure since the breakup. AT&T paid $7.4 billion to merge with NCR Corp. in 1991. The merger made AT&T the fourth largest computer maker in the U.S. and the seventh largest worldwide; three years later, AT&T changed the NCR unit's name to AT&T Global Information Solutions. In 1993, the firm diversified into cellular telephony with its $12.6 billion purchase of McCaw Cellular.

Congress passed a new telecommunications bill in 1996 that freed AT&T to enter local markets and compete for local telephone service business. In December of that year, AT&T completed its historic

The Officers

AT&T Corp.

Chairman and CEO: C. Michael Armstrong

President: John D. Zeglis

Sr. Exec. VP and Chief Financial Officer: Daniel Somers

Exec. VP, Corporate Strategy and Business Development:
John Petrillo

Exec. VP, Law and Governmental Affairs, and General
Counsel: James Cicconi

MediaOne Group

President, Chairman and CEO: Charles M. Lillis

Exec. VP; President and CEO, MediaOne International: A.
Gary Ames

Exec. VP and Chief Administrative Officer: Roger
Christensen

Exec. VP, General Counsel and Secretary: Frank M. Eichler

Exec. VP, Strategy and Business Development: Douglas D.
Holmes

split into three separate components: AT&T retained its communications operations; transferred its equipment operations to a new public company, Lucent Technology; and spun off NCR, which had lost $4 billion in the five years it was owned by AT&T. AT&T's next three major moves were among the firm's largest. In 1998, AT&T paid cable operators Tele-Communications Inc. (TCI), Cox Enterprises, Inc., and Comcast Corp. $11.3 billion for their joint venture, Teleport Communications Group, a local phone service for businesses. The firm also agreed to join its international assets with those of British Telecommunications PLC to form WorldPartners, in a deal valued at $10 billion. In early 1999, AT&T paid $59 billion for TCI, which it renamed AT&T Broadband & Internet Services. In a bold move, AT&T also announced plans to purchase MediaOne Group for upwards of $60 billion, beating out Comcast's bid. The deal was expected to go through in 2000.

History of MediaOne Group

The AT&T monopoly was ordered to disband in 1982 after lengthy antitrust litigation. As a result, AT&T Corp. kept its long distance business, but divested its 23 Bell operating companies, which were organized into seven regional Bell operating companies. One of those seven companies, U S West, was

formed in 1984; it consisted of Mountain Bell, Northwestern Bell, and Pacific Northwest Bell, as well as the New Vector cellular phone operation. To better serve its customers, the three Bell companies consolidated operations in 1988. That year, the firm expanded internationally via an investment in a French cable television operator. Further international growth ensued, along with diversification into domestic cable television ventures.

In 1991, U S West and TCI agreed to merge their European cable television and telephone operations. Congress lifted restrictions on information services (put in place during the 1984 Bell restructuring); shortly thereafter, U S West diversified in to directory publishing. Two years later, U S West acquired a 25% stake in Time Warner Entertainment and a 13% stake in Time Warner Japan for $2.5 billion. In 1994, the firm purchased two Atlanta, Georgia-based cable operators for roughly $1.2 billion, as well as United Kingdom-based Thomson Directories. U S West also formed a joint cellular venture with AirTouch Communications and diversified into personal communications services (PCS) by establishing PrimeCo, a PCS joint venture, with Bell Atlantic Corp., NYNEX, and AirTouch.

The firm split its stock in 1995 into two groups: U S West Communications Group, which housed local telephone services; and U S West Media Group, which comprised cellular, cable, and directory operations. Both units continued to operate under the U S West Inc. umbrella. U S West Media paid $11.7 billion for Continental Cablevision, Inc. in 1997 and renamed the company MediaOne, which later combined its cable/Internet operations with those of Time Warner. U S West Cellular adopted the AirTouch brand name in anticipation of a planned merger of the two companies, which was called off in August of 1997 after Congress voted to eliminate the "Morris Trust" tax exemption on large corporate transactions.

After synergies between media and phone operations failed to emerge, U S West decided in 1997 to officially split in two. In early 1998, AirTouch and U S West Media, by then the third largest U.S. cable operator, rekindled their merger plans. The firm divested its New Vector cellular operations, as well as its stake in PrimeCo, to AirTouch for $5.7 billion and announced plans to focus on broadband communications. In June of 1998, U S West Media, which transferred its directory operations to U S West Communications and changed its name to MediaOne Group, and U S West Communications became separate public companies.

In the spring of 1999, MediaOne agreed to be bought by AT&T. The proposed deal would give

MediaOne the top position in the cable industry and was expected to be completed in the year 2000.

Market Forces Driving the Merger

The Telecommunications Act of 1996, which allowed local and long distance phone companies, Internet firms, and cable businesses to compete in each other's markets, immediately led way to a hotbed of fierce mergers and acquisitions by the mid- and late-1990s. The first deal to come about after the deregulation was U S West's, $10.8 billion purchase of Continental Cablevision. This was followed by others, including the union of SBC Communications and Pacific Telesis worth $16 billion, and the merger of Bell Atlantic Corp. and Nynex Corp. for $25.6 million. WorldCom Inc. and MCI Communications also forged a $37 billion relationship in 1998.

AT&T completed its purchase of Tele-Communications in March of 1999. The $55 billion deal solidified the company's position among the leaders in Internet services. It also suggested that AT&T would take advantage of recent consolidation in the industry and changing technology. This change in technology was coaxial cable, believed to replace Internet dial-up connections eventually.

According to *PC Week*, "AT&T's cable buying spree was originally intended as an avenue for bypassing the Regional Bell Operating Companies and allowing AT&T to provide local phone services. That strategy, however, has evolved over the past year in an all-out effort by the company to deliver a full menu of phone, Internet, and multimedia entertainment services." Along with this effort came the need to grow in its broadband offerings. However, only 26% of TCI's systems had been upgraded to handle two-way communications, somewhat hindering AT&T's goals.

Approach and Engagement

In April of 1999, AT&T made an unsolicited $62 billion cash and stock offer for MediaOne, one of the largest providers of broadband services in the world, with 72% of its cable systems upgraded to handle two-way communications. The bid towered over Comcast's $60 billion stock swap offer made one month earlier. Comcast bowed out of the bidding in May, only after clinching a side deal with AT&T. The two companies agreed to exchange cable systems and offer competitive local phone service to Comcast customers, potentially increasing its customer base by 2 million and making it the third-largest cable company in the U.S. Comcast would also receive a $1.5 billion termination fee as a result of MediaOne's acceptance

The Players

Chairman and CEO of AT&T Corp.: C. Michael Armstrong. C. Michael Armstrong began working for IBM in 1961. When he was passed over for the CEO slot in 1992, he left IBM and went to work for Hughes Electronics. There, he spearheaded the firm's turnaround via drastic cost cutting, divesting the firm's auto parts and missile operations, and launching the DirecTV satellite service. In 1997, after AT&T's board ousted newly appointed CEO John Walter, Armstrong took over as CEO of AT&T.

Chairman and CEO of MediaOne Group: Charles M. Lillis. Charles Lillis earned his Ph.D. at the University of Oregon in 1972. After working as a business professor at Washington State University, a general manager for General Electric, and dean of the University of Colorado Business School, Lillis joined U S West as a vice president of strategic marketing in 1985. Before being tapped to run U S West Media Group in April of 1995, Lillis served the firm as executive vice president and chief planning officer, as well as president of U S West Diversified Group. Lillis is credited for steering the U S West Media (renamed MediaOne Group) divestment of its New Vector cellular operations to AirTouch and narrowing his firm's focus to broadband communications.

of AT&T's offer. In an *InfoWorld* article, Comcast President Brian Roberts stated, "This is a different outcome than our MediaOne proposal, but it is an elegant win-win result."

AT&T CEO Michael Armstrong also persuaded Bill Gates and Microsoft Corp. to get in on the deal. Not only would this move provide relief to worried investors, as Gate's possessed the uncanny knack of boosting a company's stock, it also had the potential to be lucrative for both parties. Microsoft already owned 11% of Comcast, and agreed to pay $5 billion for 3% of AT&T. In return, Microsoft's Windows CE would become the main operating system for set-top boxes for coaxial cable digital services. Over 7 million (out of 26 million) homes would be using the operating system. Microsoft would also receive MediaOne's 29.9% stake in Telewest, a British cable company. AT&T saw this alliance as a strategic move to further its broadband efforts.

The proposed deal has the potential to create the largest cable company in the U.S., with over 16 million subscribers. Both AT&T and MediaOne plan to complete the deal in the first quarter of 2000, barring any disapproval by the FCC and the Department of Justice.

Products and Services

Prior to the merger, AT&T provided services in over 280 countries across the globe. Its business services accounted for 44% of total sales, consumer services brought in 43%, wireless services claimed 10%, and local services had 3% of total sales. As well as offering local and long distance services, the company also offered an array of diversified services including AT&T Broadband & Internet Services, AT&T Solutions, AT&T Wireless, AT&T Digital PCS, and AT&T Website and WorldNet Services.

MediaOne Group also had operations around the globe. Its U.S. operations accounted for 80% of total sales, its business in the United Kingdom brought in 11%, Central Europe took 7%, and Asia captured the remaining 2% of sales. The company's domestic cable operations were focused in Atlanta, Boston, Chicago, Detroit, Jacksonville, Los Angeles, Miami, and Minneapolis-St. Paul.

Cable and broadband services brought in 86% of sales, while domestic wireless services accounted for 13% of MediaOne's sales. The company also had interests in many cable and wireless operations overseas. Most notable of its operations was its involvement in Road Runner, a venture in high speed data services, and the Time Warner Entertainment Co., focusing on cable programming and broadband communications.

Changes to the Industry

The effects of AT&T's purchase of MediaOne would be far reaching. Not only would AT&T create the largest cable company in the world, Comcast would take third place, and Microsoft would once again have a heads up in Internet service. Advocates of the deal also claimed that the "oligopolisation" of the cable industry would promote competition in two ways: large scale companies could cut prices and costs and Baby Bells would be forced to seek out high speed connectivity on their own. Sandra Kresch, a strategic partner in PricewaterhouseCoopers' entertainment and media interest stated in a *Mediaweek* article that the deal was "essentially the beginning of convergence in being able to marry the telephony and customer-care capability of AT&T with the infrastructure and ability to package video services of the cable industry."

There were many who were concerned, however, that the marriage of AT&T and MediaOne would lessen competition and increase cable and broadband Internet prices. Consumer advocacy groups, such as Consumers Union, Media Access Project, and the Consumer Federation of America, pleaded with the Federal Communications Commission (FCC) and the Justice Department to block the purchase because it does not comply with horizontal ownership rules and violates the Sherman and Clayton antitrust acts. If the deal was allowed to go through, these disenchanted groups believed that consumer interest would be lost, as just 2 or 3 conglomerates would own the entire telephone, cable, and Internet industries.

AT&T insisted that these complaints had no factual basis, and that the merger with MediaOne would not only be beneficial to consumers, it would allow them more choices in Internet and phone services. CEO Armstrong backed up the company's stance in an April 22, 1999, press release, stating "Ever since the Telecommunications Act of 1996 was passed, Americans have been waiting for someone to run another wire to their homes to give them a choice in local phone service and deliver the advanced services they expect in a competitive market. Our earlier acquisition of Tele-Communications, Inc. and now our proposal for MediaOne Group should leave no doubt that we are serious about doing just that."

Review of the Outcome

AT&T's purchase of MediaOne, with an expected completion date of first quarter 2000, will solidify AT&T's leading position in the cable and broadband industry and further the company's goal to be the leading carrier of end-to-end communications for the home and business. MediaOne also stands to gain considerably from the deal, expanding its customer base, as well gaining AT&T's financial stability and access to increased technology in the future. In an April 22nd press release issued by AT&T, Michael Armstrong stated that, "this acquisition is not only an investment in AT&T's future, its also an investment in the future of a competitive communications market in the U.S. Combining AT&T and MediaOne means that far more American consumers will have a choice in local phone service. Together, AT&T and MediaOne will bring broadband video, voice and data services to more communities, more quickly than we could separately or, in MediaOne's case, with any other company."

AT&T expects a gain of up to 12% in revenue growth in its broadband services unit by 2004 as a result of the deal, as well as increases in its wireless, business and data, and video services. These increases represent a shift of focus from business and consumer long distance, to Internet and broadband services. This deal remains under review by the FCC.

Research

"AT&T Cable Deal Under Fire," in *InternetWeek*, 23 August, 1999. Explains consumer advocacy groups disapproval of the proposed purchase of MediaOne.

"AT&T Corp.," in *Notable Corporate Chronologies*, The Gale Group, 1999. Lists major events in the history of AT&T Corp.

AT&T Corp. Home Page, available at http://www.att.com. Official World Wide Web Home Page for AT&T Corp. Includes current and archived news; detailed financial, product, and historical information; and annual reports.

AT&T Press Release, April 22, 1999. Discusses AT&T's bid for MediaOne Group.

"Consumers Oppose AT&T-MediaOne," in *Television Digest*, 23 August 1999. Looks at opposition to the AT&T/MediaOne deal.

Cooper, Jim. "AT&T Trumps Comcast," in *MediaWeek*, 26 April 1999. Discusses AT&T's bid for MediaOne.

Drexler, Michael. "MediaOne Approves AT&T Bid," in *Network World*, 10 May 1999. Explains AT&T's bid and MediaOne's termination notice to Comcast.

Farrell, Mike. "MediaOne Staff Waits on Word," in *Multichannel*, 17 May 1999. Speculates on the outcome of AT&T's proposed deal.

Haney, Clare. "Comcast Ends MediaOne Bid, Agrees to AT&T deal," in *InfoWorld*, 17 May 1999. Discusses AT&T's proposal to purchase MediaOne Group.

MediaOne Group Home Page Available at http://www.mediaonegroup.com. Official World Wide Web Home Page for MediaOne Group. Includes current and archived press releases, historical information, news, product, and employment information.

Rendleman, John. "The Morphing of a New AT&T," in *PC Week*, 10 May 1999. Explains AT&T's deal with Comcast as well as Microsoft in its bid for MediaOne.

CHRISTINA M. STANSELL

AT&T & NCR

AT&T Corp.
32 Avenue of the Americas
New York, NY 10013-2412
USA

tel: (212)387-5400
fax: (212)226-4935
web: http://www.att.com

nationality: USA
date: September 1991
affected: AT&T Corp., USA, founded 1877
affected: NCR Corp., USA, founded 1882

Overview of the Merger

AT&T's $7.5 billion takeover of NCR Corp. in September of 1991 was only one in a string of deals the telecommunications giant had undertaken in an effort to break into the computer market and take advantage of the predicted synergies between the computer and telecommunications industries. The NCR deal, though, proved to be AT&T's most costly error. NCR lost an estimated $4 billion in the five years following its acquisition by AT&T. In December of 1996, AT&T completed its historic split into three separate components: AT&T retained its communications operations; transferred its equipment operations in a new public company, Lucent Technology; and spun off NCR.

History of AT&T Corp.

In 1877, a group of three investors, including Alexander Graham Bell, formed the Bell Telephone Company (BTC) to develop the economic potential of the newly invented telephone. A year later, New Haven District Telephone Co. (NHDT), a Bell Telephone Co. licensee, established the world's first telephone exchange and issued the world's first telephone directory. BTC formed the New England Telephone Co. to distribute licensing of company patents.

BTC and NHDT merged to form the National Bell Telephone Company (NBT) in 1879. In 1880, NBT reorganized as the American Bell Telephone Company (ABT), consolidating NBT with the newly-acquired Western Union properties. A year later, ABT acquired Western Electric Manufacturing Co., the main supplier of telegraph equipment for Western Union, to become the exclusive manufacturer of its equipment. ABT created American Telephone and Telegraph Company (AT&T) in 1885 to operate as its long distance subsidiary and to establish a truly national telephone network. Management was eager to have such a subsidiary in service prior to 1893, the expiration date of its original patents.

AT&T provided military phone service in the U.S. during World War I, and set up the American military communication system, comprising radios, telephones, and telegraph lines, in France. In 1921, government regulations were amended to allow for mergers of telephone companies. AT&T began a decade-long period of acquisition and expansion. By then, the company was providing service to 64% of all U.S. telephones.

In 1925, AT&T spun off its research and development operations as Bell Telephone Laboratories (BTL), a separate company jointly funded by AT&T and Western Electric. The Federal Communications Commission (FCC) was set up in 1934 to regulate the interstate telephone business, replacing the Interstate Commerce Commission. A year later, the FCC began investigation of AT&T's competitive practices. The firm controlled 83% of U.S. phones and 98% of long distance cables; its Western Electric subsidiary manufactured 90% of the nation's telephone equipment. Assets totaled $5 billion, which made AT&T the largest company in the U.S.

World War II overshadowed the FCC's reports on AT&T's competitive practices. However, the FCC did force AT&T to lower its rates during the war. By the mid 1940s, long distance telephone calls had begun to replace letter writing as the preferred means of communication. In 1949, the prewar FCC report resurfaced, and the U.S. Attorney General sued AT&T for violation of the Sherman Act and asked the firm to separate from Western Electric. Seven years later, the U.S. Attorney General's suit was settled. AT&T and Western Electric were allowed to remain intact, but AT&T had to limit its activities to providing common carrier service, while Western Electric was required to limit itself to supplying equipment to AT&T and fulfilling government contracts.

Both MCI and the U.S. Department of Justice filed an antitrust suit against AT&T in 1974, charging monopoly and conspiracy to monopolize the telecommunications industry. Six years later, a jury found AT&T guilty in the MCI suit and ordered AT&T to pay damages of $1.8 billion. AT&T appealed the decision, and a jury eventually reduced damages to $37.8 million. In 1982, AT&T and the Department of Justice settled their antitrust suit: AT&T agreed to divest itself of its regional operating companies, which would become unregulated, competing businesses.

In 1983, plans for the breakup of AT&T were approved. The company began spinning off BellSouth, Bell Atlantic, NYNEX, American Information Technologies, Southwestern Bell, U S West, and Pacific Telesis to handle regional phone services in the U.S. AT&T retained control of its long distance services, but was no longer protected from competition. Once the split was completed, AT&T reorganized into two divisions: AT&T Communications, which managed the long distance network, and AT&T Technologies, which manufactured and sold telecommunications equipment.

The Business

Financials

Revenue (1998): $53.23 billion

Employees (1998): 107,800

SICs / NAICS

sic 4813 - Telephone Communications Except Radiotelephone

sic 3571 - Electronic Computers

sic 4812 - Radiotelephone Communications

sic 7373 - Computer Integrated Systems Design

sic 3578 - Calculating & Accounting Equipment

sic 3575 - Computer Terminals

sic 3571 - Electronic Computers

sic 2759 - Commercial Printing Nec

naics 323119 - Other Commercial Printing

naics 334113 - Computer Terminal Manufacturing

naics 334119 - Other Computer Peripheral Equipment Manufacturing

naics 541512 - Computer Systems Design Services

naics 334111 - Electronic Computer Manufacturing

naics 513322 - Cellular and Other Wireless Telecommunications

naics 513321 - Paging

A year after the breakup, the company launched a program of geographic diversification, opening a regional headquarters in Brussels, Belgium, to serve Europe, the Middle East, and Africa, and aggressively seeking joint venture agreements with overseas companies. In 1987, the firm held a 76% share of the U.S. long distance market, down from 91% in 1983. AT&T cut 16,000 employees and assumed a $6.7 billion charge to modernize its network, recording a loss of $1.7 billion in 1988.

Government regulators freed AT&T in 1989 to match the low long distance rates of competitors MCI and Sprint, enabling the company to rebound and show a profit of $2.7 billion, its best figure since the breakup. AT&T paid $7.4 billion to merge with NCR Corp. in 1991. The merger made AT&T the fourth largest computer maker in the U.S. and the seventh largest worldwide; three years later, AT&T changed the NCR unit's name to AT&T Global Information Solutions. In 1993, the firm diversified into cellular

The Officers

Chairman and CEO: C. Michael Armstrong

President: John D. Zeglis

Sr. Exec. VP and Chief Financial Officer: Daniel Somers

Exec. VP, Corporate Strategy and Business Development: John Petrillo

Exec. VP, Public Relations: Richard J. Martin

telephony with its $12.6 billion purchase of McCaw Cellular.

Congress passed a new telecommunications bill in 1996 that freed AT&T to enter local markets and compete for local telephone service business on a limited basis. In December of that year, AT&T completed its historic split into three separate components: AT&T retained its communications operations; transferred its equipment operations to a new public company, Lucent Technology; and spun off NCR, which had lost $4 billion in the five years it was owned by AT&T. The firm's next major move was also its largest. In early 1999, AT&T paid $59 billion for cable operator TCI Communications, which it renamed AT&T Broadband & Internet Services.

History of NCR Corp.

John Henry Patterson bought a cash register factory in 1882, which he incorporated as National Cash Register (NCR) in 1884. That year, he changed the company's emphasis from manufacturing to sales. In 1906, Charles F. Kettering developed the company's first electric cash register and the Class 100 machine, a low-cost register that remained in production for the next 40 years with only minimal changes. By 1909, NCR controlled 90% of the cash register business in the U.S. Two years later, the American Cash Register Co. filed an antitrust complaint against NCR based on the Sherman Antitrust Act. The company was found guilty of trade restraint and unlawful monopoly in three of the 32 cases; however, a higher court reversed the decision of the antitrust suit.

NCR went public in 1925 and acquired the Ellis Adding-Typewriter in 1929; that year, NCR introduced the Class 3000, the company's first hybrid machine for payroll, billing, and accounting operations. The Great Depression reduced sales and earnings, and the company began the four-year process of reducing its work force by nearly half. By 1931, NCR was nearly bankrupt. The New York bankers who set up the company's stock sale in 1925, Dillon, Read and

Co., began plans to take over NCR. Instead, Edward Deeds, who had sat on the board of 28 companies and helped found the Wright Airplane Co. with Orville Wright, took over and began to turn the company around. A year later, NCR acquired Remington Cash Register. By 1934, the firm was no longer in debt.

When the U.S. War Production Board ordered that the manufacture of all cash registers be stopped in 1942 to conserve metal, NCR continued to rebuild and repair machines. Wartime contracts for fuses and rocket motors covered NCR's overhead, while reconditioning machines provided some profit. NCR also established operations in England, Germany, and Japan in the 1940s.

In 1952, NCR acquired Computer Research Corp., which formed the core of NCR's electronics division. By the end of the decade, the firm had developed its first "small" computer, the 390, which was manufactured by Control Data Corp. In 1968, NCR expanded its base market with the introduction of its third generation of computers, the Century Series, which included a variety of business applications. After sluggish sales prompted a reorganization and sizable layoffs, NCR refocused on computing, particularly retail scanners and ATMs. In 1974, the company officially changed its name from National Cash Register to NCR.

Acquisitions in the late in 1970s and early 1980s included Quanto Corp., a producer of computer output microfilm systems; Comten data communications systems; Gather Group, a supplier of business forms; and Applied Digital Data Systems. The Tower family of computers was introduced in 1983; it became one of the keys to NCR's success in future years. In 1990, NCR developed parallel-processing computer technologies with California-based Teradata. In 1991, AT&T took over NCR; that year, NCR purchased Teradata for $520 million in AT&T stock.

NCR floundered after its takeover by AT&T, eventually racking up nearly $4 billion in losses. In 1996, AT&T spun NCR off to shareholders as an independent, publicly traded company. The firm bought Compris Technologies and Dataworks in 1997. Seeking to strengthen its position in the growing data warehousing market, the firm forged an agreement with Microsoft in 1998 that called for additional integration of NCR's Teradata systems with Microsoft's SQL server technology. Sales that year reached only $6.6 billion, nearly $2 billion less than 1994 revenues.

Market Forces Driving the Merger

As part of the 1984 AT&T breakup agreement, AT&T was freed of the 1956 prohibition against entering non-telecommunications ventures; this enabled the firm to move into the computer market. Hoping to capitalize on what analysts predicted would be a lucrative combination—computers and communication—AT&T paid $254 million for a 25% stake in Olivetti, which agreed to sell AT&T computers in Italy. In 1985, AT&T unveiled its UNIX personal computer, which combined voice and data capabilities. By 1986, due to intense competition from Microsoft's DOS operating system, the UNIX system proved a commercial failure; AT&T's computer operations lost $1.2 billion. Rather than exit the industry altogether, AT&T refocused its computer program on telecommunications-based computers and systems.

In 1987, AT&T joined Sun Microsystems to develop a unified version of the UNIX system and a computer system based on a Sun microprocessor. The investment in computers began to show some return, as the UNIX computer line attracted more customer interest. However, the deal faltered, and AT&T sold its 19.1% stake in Sun later that year. Two years later, AT&T also terminated its agreement with Olivetti. Still determined to find and profit from the anticipated synergies between the computer and communication industries, AT&T began looking to purchase an established computer manufacturer rather than build its own systems. AT&T viewed computers as commodities and believed it could convince its corporate clients to switch computer brands as easily as they did telephone services. The firm also believed its long-term relationships with telecommunications managers would afford a foot in the door with those corporations' systems managers.

Approach and Engagement

AT&T CEO Allen approached NCR CEO Exley in November of 1990. They negotiated for roughly two weeks; when AT&T offered $85 per share for NCR, NCR's board rejected the bid. AT&T countered with a $90 per share hostile takeover bid valued at roughly $6 billion. Angered by the aggressiveness of AT&T, Exley vowed to quit if the takeover was successful. His letter in response to the offer stated, "we simply will not place in jeopardy the important values we are creating at NCR in order to bail out AT&T's failed strategy." To protect against the takeover, the NCR board placed a chunk of shares into an employee retirement trust as a means of blocking AT&T from gaining the 80% vote it needed to dethrone NCR's current board; AT&T sued to have the trust revoked. NCR also lobbied the Federal Communications Commission to investigate AT&T's bid, and attempted to turn public opinion its way by taking out full-page newspaper advertisements.

The Players

Chairman and CEO of AT&T Corp.: Robert Allen. Robert Allen began working for AT&T when he graduated from college in 1957. He climbed his way up the corporate ladder, reaching chairman and CEO status in 1988 after AT&T head James Olson died of cancer. Allan steered AT&T's ill-fated ventures into the computer industry during the late 1980s and early 1990s, including the purchase of NCR, as well as the more lucrative purchase of McCaw Cellular in 1993, and the firm's three-pronged split in 1996. In 1997, Allan agreed to retire early and named John Walter his successor. When AT&T's negotiations with SBC Communications Inc. fell apart in 1997, the board ousted Walter, chose C. Michael Armstrong as its new leader, and forced Allan to resign months earlier than he'd planned.

Chairman and CEO of NCR Corp.: Charles Exley, Jr. NCR tapped former Burroughs executive Charles Exley, Jr. as president in 1976. Three years later, he was appointed CEO of NCR and implemented a reorganization, emphasizing personal computers, fiscal control, and stock repurchasing. When AT&T launched a hostile takeover of NCR in 1990, Exley vowed to quit if the deal was completed. AT&T completed its purchase of NCR in September of 1991, and Exley retired the following year.

In March of 1991, AT&T won its suit to have the employee retirement trust dissolved. Realizing that AT&T would likely gain four seats on the NCR board, Exley once again returned to the negotiating table with Allen. AT&T share prices had increased, which allowed the firm to up its offer to $7.5 billion in stock, a price that valued NCR at more than twice its market capitalization prior to AT&T's initial bid. NCR's board voted to approve the deal, and the transaction was completed in September of 1991.

Products and Services

AT&T's spin-off of NCR in 1996, as well as its separation from Lucent Technologies, left the firm with the following operations: consumer long distance; business long distance; wireless; and local. Of the $53.23 billion AT&T earned in revenues in 1998, $22.94 billion came from consumer long distance sales; $22.63 billion were due to business long distance sales; $5.4

billion were the result of wireless sales; and $3.54 billion came from other services.

Changes to the Industry and Review of the Outcome

The merger caused almost immediate problems for AT&T. NCR's core product, its mainframe computer, was outdated; the corporate cultures of the two firms clashed; and NCR's global operations, mainly in developed countries, were useless to AT&T's telecommunication efforts, which targeted developing countries. While NCR remained profitable in 1992 and 1993, thus boosting AT&T's computer operations out of the red for the first time ever, its shift toward personal computers, necessary to compete with current technology trends, hurt its own lucrative service and consulting operations. Because the newer machines were more dependable, customers sought less support.

When the anticipated synergies from the NCR takeover failed to emerge, AT&T began seeking non-computer avenues of expansion. In 1993, the firm paid $12.6 billion for McCaw Cellular. Five years after the merger, after suffering nearly $4 billion in losses, NCR was cut loose by AT&T in 1996 when management announced a major restructuring that split the company into three parts: AT&T retained its communications operations; equipment businesses were consolidated into a new, publicly traded firm, Lucent Technologies; and computer holdings were spun off as NCR Corp.

Prior to its spin off from AT&T, NCR had begun its move away from personal computers and slashed its workforce by 8,500. Despite these efforts, the firm still had a difficult time once on its own. According to an October 1998 *Forbes* article, "AT&T seized it [NCR] in a hostile takeover in 1991, messed it up, then cast it adrift again. " While some analysts pointed out that NCR was likely headed for rough water in the early 1990s, regardless of its takeover by AT&T, most agreed

that the acquisition made what would have been a difficult time for NCR more like a near death experience.

Research

"AT&T Corp.," in *Notable Corporate Chronologies*, The Gale Group, 1999. Lists major events in the history of AT&T, including its takeover of NCR Corp.

AT&T Home Page, available at http://www.att.com. Official World Wide Web Home Page for AT&T Corp. Includes current and archived news; detailed financial, product, and historical information; and annual reports.

"The End of An Era: NCR Identity Gives Way to AT&T," in *Financial Services Report*, 16 February 1994. Discusses AT&T's decision to change NCR's name to AT&T Global Information Solutions.

"Fatal Attraction," in *The Economist*, 23 March 1996. Details the reasons for AT&T's takeover of NCR, as the well as the negative outcomes of the deal for both companies.

Friedman, Thomas. "Ma Bell M&A Dials a Bad Connection," in *PC Week*, 20 November 1995. Explains how the ill-fated takeover of NCR prompted AT&T's decision to split in three.

Galuszka, Peter. "Still Waiting for the New NCR," in *Business Week*, 15 December 1997. Details the performance of NCR after its spinoff from AT&T.

Keller, John J. "Why AT&T Takeover of NCR Hasn't Been a Real Bell Ringer; Missteps with Balky Unit Result in Growing Losses and Plans for Job Cuts; Will Allen Pull the Plug?," in *The Wall Street Journal*, 19 September 1995. Offers an overview of why AT&T was determined to enter the computer market and how AT&T's takeover of NCR has impacted both firms.

"NCR Corp.," in *Notable Corporate Chronologies*, The Gale Group, 1999. Lists major events in the history of NCR Corp., including its takeover by AT&T Corp.

Upbin, Bruce. "Too Little and Probably Too Late," in *Forbes*, 5 October 1998. Explains what NCR has done to improve its performance since its spinoff from AT&T and offers a prediction for the future of NCR.

Verity, John W. "Is NCR Ready to Ring Up Some Cash?," in *Business Week*, 14 October 1996. Explains why AT&T decided to spin off NCR.

Ziegler, Bart. "NCR Gets Yet Another New Lease on Life," in *The Wall Street Journal*, 30 December 1996. Details NCR's reorganization plans following its departure from AT&T.

SAMIT AYERS

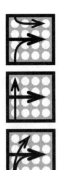

AT&T & TCI

nationality: USA
date: March 9, 1999
affected: AT&T Corp., USA, founded 1877
affected: Tele-Communications Inc., USA, founded 1965

AT&T Corp.
32 Avenue of the Americas
New York, NY 10013-2412
USA

tel: (212)387-5400
fax: (212)226-4935
web: http://www.att.com

Overview of the Merger

AT&T's takeover of Tele-Communications Inc. (TCI), worth a mind boggling $59 billion, joined the leading long distance telephone services provider with the second largest cable operator in the U.S. The deal gave AT&T access to TCI's 11 million customers, a local market the likes of which AT&T hadn't seen since the 1984 Baby Bell spinoffs. Via its new unit, renamed AT&T Broadband and Internet Services unit, AT&T plans to offer integrated telephone, cable television, and Internet services as soon as it completes the costly upgrades of TCI's infrastructure. Whether or not the merger redraws the telecommunications landscape as analysts are predicting remains to be seen, but the deal will likely spark increased consolidation in the industry.

History of AT&T Corp.

In 1877, a group of three investors, including Alexander Graham Bell, formed the Bell Telephone Company (BTC) to develop the economic potential of the newly invented telephone. A year later, New Haven District Telephone Co. (NHDT), a Bell Telephone Co. licensee, established the world's first telephone exchange and issued the world's first telephone directory. BTC formed the New England Telephone Co. to distribute licensing of company patents.

BTC and NHDT merged to form the National Bell Telephone Company (NBT) in 1879. In 1880, NBT reorganized as the American Bell Telephone Company (ABT), consolidating NBT with the newly-acquired Western Union properties. A year later, ABT acquired Western Electric Manufacturing Co., the main supplier of telegraph equipment for Western Union, to become the exclusive manufacturer of its equipment. ABT created American Telephone and Telegraph Company (AT&T) in 1885 to operate as its long distance subsidiary and to establish a truly national telephone network. Management was eager to have such a subsidiary in service prior to 1893, the expiration date of its original patents.

AT&T provided military phone service in the U.S. during World War I, and set up the American military communication system, comprising radios, telephones,

The Business

Financials

Revenue (1998): $53.23 billion

Employees (1998): 107,800

SICs / NAICS

sic 4813 - Telephone Communications Except

    Radiotelephone

sic 4812 - Radiotelephone Communications

sic 3661 - Telephone & Telegraph Apparatus

sic 4841 - Cable & Other Pay Television Services

naics 513322 - Cellular and Other Wireless

    Telecommunications

naics 513321 - Paging

naics 334418 - Printed Circuit Assembly (Electronic

    Assembly) Manufacturing

and telegraph lines, in France. In 1921, government regulations were amended to allow for mergers of telephone companies. AT&T began a decade-long period of acquisition and expansion. By then, the company was providing service to 64% of all U.S. telephones.

In 1925, AT&T spun off its research and development operations as Bell Telephone Laboratories (BTL), a separate company jointly funded by AT&T and Western Electric. The Federal Communications Commission (FCC) was set up in 1934 to regulate the interstate telephone business, replacing the Interstate Commerce Commission. A year later, the FCC began investigation of AT&T's competitive practices. The firm controlled 83% of U.S. phones and 98% of long distance cables; its Western Electric subsidiary manufactured 90% of the nation's telephone equipment. Assets totaled $5 billion, which made AT&T the largest company in the U.S.

World War II overshadowed the FCC's reports on AT&T's competitive practices. However, the FCC did force AT&T to lower its rates during the war. By the mid 1940s, long distance telephone calls had begun to replace letter writing as the preferred means of communication. In 1949, the prewar FCC report resurfaced, and the U.S. Attorney General sued AT&T for violation of the Sherman Act and asked the firm to separate from Western Electric. Seven years later, the U.S. Attorney General's suit was settled. AT&T and Western Electric were allowed to remain intact, but AT&T had to limit its activities to providing common

carrier service, while Western Electric was required to limit itself to supplying equipment to AT&T and fulfilling government contracts.

Both MCI and the U.S. Department of Justice filed an antitrust suit against AT&T in 1974, charging monopoly and conspiracy to monopolize the telecommunications industry. Six years later, a jury found AT&T guilty in the MCI suit and ordered AT&T to pay damages of $1.8 billion. AT&T appealed the decision, and a jury eventually reduced damages to $37.8 million. In 1982, AT&T and the Department of Justice settled their antitrust suit: AT&T agreed to divest itself of its regional operating companies, which would become unregulated, competing businesses.

In 1983, plans for the breakup of AT&T were approved. The company began spinning off BellSouth, Bell Atlantic, NYNEX, American Information Technologies, Southwestern Bell, U S West, and Pacific Telesis to handle regional phone services in the U.S. AT&T retained control of its long distance services, but was no longer protected from competition. Once the split was completed, AT&T reorganized into two divisions: AT&T Communications, which managed the long distance network, and AT&T Technologies, which manufactured and sold telecommunications equipment.

A year after the breakup, the company launched a program of geographic diversification, opening a regional headquarters in Brussels, Belgium, to serve Europe, the Middle East, and Africa, and aggressively seeking joint venture agreements with overseas companies. In 1987, the firm held a 76% share of the U.S. long distance market, down from 91% in 1983. AT&T cut 16,000 employees and assumed a $6.7 billion charge to modernize its network, recording a loss of $1.7 billion in 1988.

Government regulators freed AT&T in 1989 to match the low long distance rates of competitors MCI and Sprint, enabling the company to rebound and show a profit of $2.7 billion, its best figure since the breakup. AT&T paid $7.4 billion to merge with NCR Corp. in 1991. The merger made AT&T the fourth largest computer maker in the U.S. and the seventh largest worldwide; three years later, AT&T changed the NCR unit's name to AT&T Global Information Solutions. In 1993, the firm diversified into cellular telephony with its $12.6 billion purchase of McCaw Cellular.

Congress passed a new telecommunications bill in 1996 that freed AT&T to enter local markets and compete for local telephone service business. In December of that year, AT&T completed its historic split into three separate components: AT&T retained its communications operations; transferred its equipment operations to a new public company, Lucent Technology; and spun off NCR, which had lost $4 billion in the five years it was owned by AT&T. AT&T's next three major moves were among the firm's largest. In 1998, AT&T paid cable operators Tele-Communications Inc. (TCI), Cox Enterprises, Inc., and Comcast Corp. $11.3 billion for their joint venture, Teleport Communications Group, a local phone service for businesses. The firm also agreed to join its international assets with those of British Telecommunications PLC to form WorldPartners, in a deal valued at $10 billion. Finally, in early 1999, AT&T paid $59 billion for TCI, which it renamed AT&T Broadband & Internet Services.

History of Tele-Communications Inc.

Former Texas cattle rancher Bob Magness founded Tele-Communications Inc. (TCI) in 1965 to consolidate his growing interests in cable television companies serving rural areas in Colorado, Montana, Nevada, and Utah. The young company entered a period of major expansion in the late 1960s and early 1970s and incurred additional debt just as interest rates took off. To defray expenses, TCI listed publicly in 1970.

In 1975, the city of Vail, Colorado, sought to secure more cable services from TCI without rate increases, but company president John Malone retaliated by suspending all programming and broadcasting only the names and addresses of city council members until the city relented. After two years of successful legal battles with city cable regulators nationwide, TCI showed a positive cash flow in 1977 and was able to obtain a $77 million loan to refinance corporate debt.

During the late 1970s and early 1980s, TCI declined to enter competition to supply cable television services to urban areas and instead added suburban markets to its traditional base of rural customers. The 1984 Cable Communications Policy Act deregulated cable television, enabling TCI to add Buffalo, Dallas, and Miami to its service area. That year, TCI purchased the ailing Pittsburgh, Pennsylvania-based cable television franchise from Warner-Amex for $93 million and provided the first cable television service to the White House.

In 1985, the company began a program of investment in cable television outlets throughout the United States; the following year, TCI acquired a controlling interest in United Artists Communications and reorganized to decentralize operations. The firm merged with Heritage Communications in 1987, adding 500,000 cable television subscribers to its corporate rolls. Malone moved to reduce the bargaining power

The Officers

Chairman and CEO: C. Michael Armstrong

President: John D. Zeglis

Sr. Exec. VP and Chief Financial Officer: Daniel Somers

Exec. VP, Corporate Strategy and Business Development: John Petrillo

Exec. VP, Public Relations: Richard J. Martin

of producers of cable television programming by providing financial assistance to emerging producers such as Black Entertainment Television and The Discovery Channel. That year, TCI helped underwrite the $1.5 billion purchase of the MGM film library by Ted Turner's SuperStation WTBS.

TCI formed Think Entertainment in 1988 to produce and distribute cable television programming. The company also provided financial assistance to emerging producers including QVC Network and American Movie Classics. The U.S. Department of Commerce threatened antitrust investigations due to increased concentration of ownership within the cable television industry. The 1989 purchase of Storer Communications positioned TCI as the largest supplier of cable television services in the United States. The firm also invested in the Blockbuster Video chain of video rental outlets that year. By the decade's end, TCI owned more than 150 cable companies.

TEMPO Enterprises, a satellite telecommunications services provider, was acquired in 1990. In 1991, TCI launched a public bond issue as part of an effort to restructure corporate debt. Late in the year, the firm purchased the remaining outstanding shares of United Artists Communications, keeping the cable operations and spinning off the theater business. As part of a reorganization, United Artists Communications and Heritage Communications were brought under the operating management of TCI. Interests in networks such as QVC, as well as several cable systems were spun off as Liberty Media. The company also invested in communications infrastructure in Hungary, Ireland, Israel, Malta, New Zealand, Norway, Sweden, and the United Kingdom.

In 1992, TCI acquired Southwest Cablevision. A year later, the firm joined with Comcast in developing Zing, an interactive cable television system. The proposed merger of TCI and Bell Atlantic Corp. came under the scrutiny of the U.S. Senate in 1993. The following year, the Bell Atlantic deal fell through, and TCI purchased its Liberty Media spin-off. Two years

The Players

Chairman and CEO of AT&T Corp.: C. Michael Armstrong. C. Michael Armstrong began working for IBM in 1961. When he was passed over for the CEO slot in 1992, he left IBM and went to work for Hughes Electronics, where he spearheaded the firm's turnaround via drastic cost cutting, divesting the firm's auto parts and missile operations, and launching the DirecTV satellite service. In 1997, after AT&T's board ousted newly appointed CEO John Walter, Armstrong took over as CEO of AT&T.

Chairman and CEO of Tele-Communications Inc.: John Malone. John Malone left AT&T in 1968 to join cable upstart Tele-Communications Inc. (TCI). He served as president of TCI, eventually taking over the reins from founder Bob Magness who died in 1996. When AT&T bought TCI in March of 1999, Malone retained control of Liberty Media, the lucrative cable programming arm of TCI.

later, TCI formed Fox Sports Net, a joint domestic sports programming alliance between Liberty Media and News Corp. Founder Magness died and was succeeded by president John Malone who reorganized the company into four units: domestic cable, programming, new technology, and overseas operations. TCI also acquired Viacom's cable systems. After the Telecommunications Act of 1996 allowed cable, Internet, and telephone firms to compete in one another's markets, TCI and other cable companies launched At Home Corp., a high-speed Internet service provider. In 1998, TCI and AT&T began discussing merger plans; the $59 billion deal was completed in March of 1999.

Market Forces Driving the Merger

The intense pace of merger and acquisition activity in the telecommunications industry during the middle and late 1990s had at its root the passing of the Telecommunications Act of 1996. The bill deregulated the U.S. telecommunications industry, allowing phone companies, both local and long distance, Internet firms, and cable businesses to begin competing in each other's markets. Almost immediately, U.S.-based telecommunications services companies, particularly phone companies and cable operators, began announcing billion dollar mergers, and an industry-wide consolidation trend was launched. While this type of convergence was already taking place on a lim-

ited basis prior to February of 1996, the act opened up unparalleled cross-market penetration opportunities on both a national and an international scale.

The first major deal following the passage of the bill was the $10.8 billion purchase of Continental Cablevision, the third largest cable operator in the United States, by regional telephone operator U.S. West Inc. Roughly a year later, in April of 1997, the second largest phone company in North America was formed when SBC Communications purchased Pacific Telesis for $16 billion. Within months of the transaction, that second place status was usurped by the $25.6 million joining of Bell Atlantic Corp. and Nynex Corp. And just when many analysts thought the merger and acquisition activity in the telecommunications industry had peaked, WorldCom Inc. and MCI Communications Corp. came together in the fall of 1998 for an unprecedented $37 billion.

In an effort to compete with MCI-WorldCom by offering clients increased end-to-end services, including cable television access, AT&T and TCI in 1998 agreed to an historic $48 billion merger. AT&T had been struggling throughout the decade. Faced with falling long distance market share, due to fierce competition, AT&T had to act fast to ensure itself a spot among the industry's leading players; it needed to find new markets. According to Washington-based Legg Mason Precursor Group analyst Scott Cleland, acquiring TCI "was probably the best available move among a host of rotten options." Acquiring TCI would give AT&T the chance to offer video, voice, and data transmissions along the same network. The deal would also give AT&T a much coveted foothold in the $110 billion local market.

At the same time, TCI sorely needed to repair its customer relations, which price increases and shoddy service had badly damaged. The firm was also looking to reduce its $11 billion in network construction debt. A deal with AT&T would offer a much needed infusion of capital, as well as the more popular AT&T brand name.

Approach and Engagement

Almost immediately after taking over as CEO of AT&T in late 1997, Armstrong approached TCI CEO Malone. The two announced a $48 million merger agreement, in June of 1998, which involved the formation of tracking stock to hold AT&T's consumer long distance, cable, and cellular businesses; this would allow investors to purchase shares of AT&T's business segments without requiring AT&T to separate the segments on an operational level. While the tracking stock arrangement was later rejected, the deal moved forward with the Department of Justice's approval in January of 1999, which was conditional on TCI's transfer of its 23.5% stake in Sprint PCS prior to finalization of the merger and divestment of the Sprint PCS shares within five years.

FCC approval followed soon after, minus the unbundling requirements competitors like America Online had hoped for with TCI's broadband Internet access services. Shareholders of both firms overwhelmingly approved the deal in March. TCI shareholders received .7757 of an AT&T common stock share for each share of TCI Group Series A stock and .8533 of an AT&T common stock share for each share of TCI Group Series B stock. Because stock prices for both AT&T and TCI had increased prior to the merger, the deal was valued at $59 billion, which included AT&T's assumption of $11 billion in TCI debt, when it closed on March 9, 1999.

Products and Services

Prior to the merger, AT&T was organized by the following segments: consumer long distance; business long distance; wireless; and local. Of the $53.23 billion AT&T earned in revenues in 1998, $22.94 billion came from consumer long distance sales; $22.63 billion were due to business long distance sales; $5.4 billion were the result of wireless sales; and $3.54 billion came from other services.

The merger with TCI gave AT&T extensive cable holdings, as well as cable programmer Liberty Media Group and a 40% stake in high-speed Internet access provider At Home Corp.

Changes to the Industry

Despite the joining of TCI and AT&T, as well as other cable and telephone firms, the role of cable television technology in the telecommunications industry remains uncertain. While the cable television sector has been the source of intense speculation, the synergies and technologies anticipated by joining cable broadcast companies with other telecommunications operations have yet to come to fruition, mainly because cable networks remain less dependable than telephone lines. According to a July 1998 article in *Multichannel News*, AT&T's plans to use TCI's coaxial cable to gain access to local telephone customers reflects "the same old idea of a single broadband pipe to the home carrying a wide variety of services that has been pursued for decades and continues to be elusive. Over the past few years, a number of Baby Bells and a few media companies have been burned in this pursuit."

AT&T estimates that it will be able to sell local telephony across cable lines in ten markets by the year's end. Critic point out, however, that it will take much longer to complete the upgrading of TCI's out-

moded broadband lines, and cost estimates for the refurbishing range from $9 billion to $20 billion. Although industry analysts disagree over how the deal will bode for AT&T and TCI, as well as for the long-touted convergence in the telecommunications industry, most predict that the merger will likely spark additional consolidation among telephone and cable operators.

Research

"AT&T Corp.," in *Notable Corporate Chronologies*, The Gale Group, 1999. Lists major events in the history of AT&T Corp.

AT&T Corp. Home Page, available at http://www.att.com. Official World Wide Web Home Page for AT&T Corp. Includes current and archived news; detailed financial, product, and historical information; and annual reports.

"AT&T: An Offer You Can't Refuse." in *The Economist*, 6 February 1999. Details the problems AT&T has faced during the decade, as well as the firm's decision to acquire TCI.

Avalos, George. "AT&T Wraps Up Its TCI Merger," in *Knight-Ridder/Tribune Business News*, 10 March 1999. Offers an overview of the AT&T/TCI deal, including its potential results for customers.

Copulsky, Erica. "AT&T/TCI Adapts to Seismic Change Significant for Far More Than Its Size," in *Investment Dealers Digest*, 14 December 1998. Provides an overview of the AT&T/TCI merger, the publication's "merger and acquisition deal of the year."

Elstrom, Peter. "At Last, Telecom Unbound," in *Business Week*, 6 July 1998. Discusses the technological developments the AT&T/TCI deal might spawn.

Fabrikant, Geraldine. "Tracking the Rich Deal of TCI's Chairman is No Easy Job," in *The New York Times*, 27 July 1998. Offers a profile of John Malone, the CEO of TCI, and details his new role at Liberty Media following the merger.

Goldblatt, Henry. "AT&T's Costly Game of Catch-Up," in *Fortune*, 20 July 1998. Details the reasons for AT&T's interest in TCI.

Grover, Ronald. "Every Cable Company is a Cinderella Now," in *Business Week*, 6 July 1998. Discusses the impact the AT&T/TCI merger may have on the telecommunications industry as a whole.

Higgins, John M. "Can AT&T Make TCI Ring a Bell?," in *Broadcasting & Cable*, 30 November 1998. Explains and questions AT&T's narrow focus on the telephone industry, despite its purchase of a cable television giant.

Noll, Michael A. "The AT&T Merger: A $48 Billion Wager," in *Multichannel News*, 27 July 1998. Addresses several potential problems AT&T will face upon completion of its merger with TCI.

"Tele-Communications Inc.," in *Notable Corporate Chronologies*, The Gale Group, 1999. Lists major events in the history of Tele-Communications Inc.

Valovic, Tom. "The AT&T/TCI Deal: A Defining Event in Telecom?," in *Telecommunications*, August 1998. Comments on the impact the AT&T/TCI merger will likely have on the telecommunications industry, including setting the standard for other telephone and cable marriages.

SAMIT AYERS

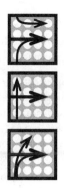

BANC ONE & FIRST CHICAGO NBD

Bank One Corp.
One First National Plaza
Chicago, IL 60670
USA

tel: (312)732-4000
fax: (312)732-3366
web: http://www.bankone.com

nationality: USA
date: October 5, 1998
affected: Banc One Corp., USA, founded 1868
affected: First Chicago NBD Corp., USA, founded 1863

Overview of the Merger

The October 1998 merger of number six Banc One Corp. with number ten First Chicago NBD Corp. created the fifth largest bank holding company in the U.S., as well as the nation's second largest credit issuer, behind Citigroup Inc. The combined company, named Bank One Corp., boasted more than 2,000 nationwide offices and assets in excess of $100 billion. A market capitalization of roughly $72 billion boosted the firm to the number one spot among banks in the midwestern U.S. Although noteworthy, the $21 billion deal was one among several sizable mergers that decade in the commercial banking industry.

History of Banc One Corp.

Sessions and Company was founded in Columbus, Ohio, in 1868. In 1902, businessman A.D. Bartlett founded the People's Banking and Trust Company in Marietta, Ohio. John H. McCoy quit school after the eighth grade to work as a messenger and janitor for the new company. He soon became a friend of Bartlett's and quickly rose through the corporate hierarchy. After Bartlett died in 1922, McCoy took over as bank president.

In 1929, Sessions and Company merged with another small Columbus, Ohio-based bank to form the City National Bank and Trust Company (CNB). The collapse of the New York Stock Exchange signaled the beginning of the Great Depression, and banks began to fail across the United States. McCoy left Peoples Banking and Trust in 1930 to become president of CNB. His first priority was to fully integrate the two banks that formed the company, each of which had continued to operate independently since the merger.

After World War II ended, CNB began to focus on offering consumer banking and financial services to the growing upper and middle classes in the postwar economic boom. When McCoy died in 1958, CNB was the third largest financial institution in Columbus, Ohio. In 1966, CNB became first institution to offer BankAmericard service outside of California, thus pioneering a national credit card program. The following year, the firm formed First Banc as a holding company and embarked on a period of expansion through acquisition.

CNB acquired Farmers Savings and Trust of Mansfield, Ohio, in 1968. The purchase set the standard for future corporate acquisitions, being paid for with a stock swap and leaving existing management in place. Two years later, CNB became the first bank to make available plastic card automated teller machines. CNB bought Citizens Bank and Trust (CBT) of Wadsworth, Ohio, for $2.2 million in 1975. CBT's management proved incompetent and was replaced, but the bank continued to struggle, and CNB was eventually forced to merge CBT into its Bank One subsidiary in Akron, Ohio.

In 1979, First Banc changed its name to Banc One. A year later, Banc One began acquiring larger Ohio-based banks, including the Lake National Bank in Painesville; the Firestone Bank in Akron; and the Winters National Bank in Dayton. By the early 1980s, Banc One employed 7,000 people and boasted $5 billion in assets. Looking to extend corporate holdings outside Ohio, Banc One purchased affiliates in Indiana and Kentucky, including American Fletcher Corporation, which was reorganized to form Banc One Indiana Corp. In 1988, Banc One acquired Marine Corp., a Wisconsin-based bank. The following year, the Federal Deposit Insurance Corporation (FDIC) appointed Banc One to take over operation of the Deposit Insurance Bridge Bank of Dallas, Texas, which was reorganized under Banc One and FDIC auspices to form Bank One Texas NA. Banc One later purchased the FDIC's interest in the joint venture.

Expansion continued into the 1990s with the acquisition of the Bright Banc Savings Association of Dallas, Texas; four Ohio branches of the Pittsburgh, Pennsylvania-based PNC Financial Corp.; Marine Corporation of Springfield, Illinois; Valley National Corp., Arizona's largest bank; Affiliated Bankshares of Colorado; and Team Bancshares of Dallas, Texas. In 1993, Banc One established Banc One Investment Advisors Corp. to standardize and centralize corporate investment services and acquired First Community Bancorp of Illinois, as well as Liberty Mutual Bancorp, Kentucky's third largest bank.

A fall in stock prices, blamed on Banc One's reliance on interest-rate-swap derivatives, forced Banc One to retract its offers for FirsTier Financial Inc. in 1994. That year, the firm made purchases in Wisconsin, Oklahoma, Utah, and Michigan. To gain more control of its scattered holdings, Banc One reversed its long-standing policy of allowing subsidiary banks considerable autonomy of operations and established central control by consolidating all bank holdings under one charter per state. As part of

The Business

Financials

Revenue (1998): $25.59 billion

Employees (1998): 91,310

SICs / NAICS

sic 6712 - Bank Holding Companies

sic 6021 - National Commercial Banks

sic 6022 - State Commercial Banks

sic 6153 - Short-Term Business Credit

naics 551111 - Offices of Bank Holding Companies

the restructuring, Banc One divested its branches in Springfield, Ohio, and its stock transfer unit.

In 1995, Banc One formed a joint venture with Sony Electronics Inc. to create a private-label credit card for use in the purchase of electronic components. Centralization of operations continued. Banc One completed its first multibillion deal by merging with First USA Inc. in 1997 to create the third largest credit card issuing institution in the U.S. That year, the firm sold its corporate automobile club credit card holdings. Banc One and First Chicago NBD merged in October of 1998 to form Bank One, the fifth largest bank in the U.S.

History of First Chicago NBD Corp.

A group of investors led by Edmund Aiken formed the First National Bank of Chicago to take advantage of new regulations contained in the 1863 National Banking Act. In 1882, First National opened the nation's first women's banking department. The bank survived the currency shortage of the late 1880s by importing gold from its corresponding bank in London, England. In 1899, First National established the nation's first pension plan for bank employees.

Expansion began in the early 1900s with the acquisition of Union National Bank and Metropolitan National Bank. First National opened First Trust and Savings Bank as a subsidiary serving noncommercial customers in 1903. Ten years later, the firm became a charter member of the Federal Reserve System, ranking as the third-largest foreign exchange bank in the U.S. First Trust and Savings Bank merged with Union Trust Co. to form the Union Trust and Savings Bank in 1917. The onset of the Great Depression resulted in loss of accounts, but a sound financial base kept the

The Officers

Chairman: Verne G. Istock

Vice Chairman: Richard Lehmann

Vice Chairman: David Vitale

President and CEO: John B. McCoy

Chief Financial Officer: Robert Rosholt

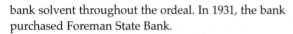

bank solvent throughout the ordeal. In 1931, the bank purchased Foreman State Bank.

The 1950s marked the bank's next major period of sustained growth, as First National focused on innovative business loans. In 1959, the bank opened an office in London to increase international presence and better serve global customers. Continuing its international expansion, First National launched operations in Asia by opening an office in Tokyo, Japan. In 1969, the bank reorganized, changing its name to First Chicago Corp. and making First National Bank of Chicago a principle subsidiary. Although business continued to grow, the percentage of nonperforming loans began to rise, eventually reaching a level twice the national average. Management began tightening its criteria for loan candidates, and by the end of the 1970s, the rate of nonperforming loans dropped. Because it had increased its commitment to fixed-rate loans in 1978, the firm missed out on benefits from the dramatic rise in interest rates in 1979.

In 1983, First Chicago acquired American National Bank and Trust Co., Chicago's fifth-largest bank. Four years later, the firm bought First United Financial Services Inc., a Chicago-based bank holding company, and Beneficial National Bank USA of Wilmington, Delaware, which was renamed FCC National Bank. First National Bank of Chicago became the third-largest issuer of credit cards in the U.S. Many third world countries, including Brazil, suspended foreign loan payments that year, causing First National Bank of Chicago to post losses of $587 million. In 1988, First Chicago increased consumer banking operations with the acquisition of Gary-Coheaton Corp., a bank holding company.

A 1990 Securities Exchange Commission (SEC) investigation of possible illegal trading activities led to the indictments of three First Chicago executives. That year, the firm developed a super-regional banking network centering on Chicago. The Internal Revenue Service demanded $133 million in back payments. Executive bonuses were suspended in 1991, and First Chicago launched a cost-cutting program that includ-

ed widespread staff layoffs. In 1993, the firm divested $1 billion in realty assets; purchased Lake Shore Bancorp Inc. for $304 million; and reorganized its mutual fund portfolio, reducing its range of fund options from 150 to 50.

First Chicago and Detroit-based NBD Bancorp Inc. merged to form First Chicago NBD Corp., the seventh-largest U.S. bank with assets of $120 billion, in 1996. The new firm divested its Ohio operations; formed Pegasus Funds Inc. as a subsidiary mutual fund operation; opened branch offices in Singapore and Beijing; and closed 24 Chicago-area branches and all but nine former NBD branches, laying off more than 1,700 employees. Two years later, First Chicago NBD merged with Banc One Corp., creating the second-largest credit card issuer in the U.S.

Market Forces Driving the Merger

By the 1980s, the bloated commercial banking industry was in need of consolidation. The multitude of banks branches that had been established during growth periods simply lacked customers. Former restrictions on cross-border acquisitions were loosened by several states in the early and mid 1980s, which spawned a consolidation flurry in the 1990s unlike anything the industry had seen before.

Believing that growth was a requirement in the new competitive landscape, many banks pursued a super-regional approach to consolidation in which they acquired competitors in their regions, eliminated redundancies in operations, and closed overlapping branch offices. Along with allowing banks to drastically cut costs, this type of consolidation brought with it the deeper pockets needed to implement technological advances. For example, after the $4.2 billion marriage of NCNB Corp. and C&S/Sovran Corp., which formed NationsBank Corp. in 1992, the new company was able to spend $100 million to automate many banking tasks via a new computer system. The super-regional mergers also helped prepare these banks to compete on a national scale should the federal restrictions on cross-border branching be relaxed. Other super-regional deals during the 1990s included the $4.2 billion merger between BankAmerica Corp. and Security Pacific Corp.; First Union Corp.'s $5.4 billion purchase of First Fidelity in 1995; and First Chicago's acquisition of Detroit-based NBD Bancorp Inc. in 1996 to form First Chicago NBD Corp.

Banc One and First Chicago NBD believed that they could save $930 million annually via their merger, as well as increase sales by $275 million. First Chicago also needed a national partner to grow beyond its regional limitations. NationsBank had expanded into the Midwest in 1996 with its $9.6 billion purchase of Boatmen's Bancshares Inc. and into Florida in 1997 with its $14.8 billion purchase of Barnett Banks, Inc. To compete with this kind of growth, both First Chicago NBD and Banc One needed to expand their reach.

Approach and Engagement

Banc One and First Chicago NBD announced their intent to merge into Bank One Corp. on April 13, 1998. Over the summer, the U.S. Justice Department approved the deal on the condition that both firms divest $1.9 billion of deposits in Indianapolis, Indiana, due to substantial overlap between Banc One and First Chicago NBD in Indiana.

Although share prices for both banks dropped prior to the transaction's closing in September, the "merger of equals" status of the deal protected both firms. Terms of the agreement stipulated that First Chicago NBD shareholders would receive 1.62 shares of Banc One common stock for each share of First Chicago NBD owned. Banc One and First Chicago shareholders overwhelmingly approved the $21 billion deal, which was finalized in October of 1998, leaving Banc One shareholders with roughly 60% of the new company's common stock and First Chicago NBD shareholders with the remaining 40%.

Products and Services

Prior to the merger, Banc One operated more than 1,300 banking units in 12 states and more than 7,750 cash dispensing and ATM machines in 49 states. First Chicago NBD operated more than 1,400 ATM machines, 650 domestic banking offices, and 14 international offices. When the two firms merged into Bank One, products and services were reorganized into four major segments: credit cards; retail and commercial banking; investment management; and consumer finance.

Changes to the Industry

Along with fueling the continued consolidation trend in the commercial banking industry, the Banc One/First Chicago NBD deal will also likely impact the smaller Midwest banks. According to many analysts, when larger mergers take place, smaller banks have an opportunity to target customers by offering more flexible policies than the larger corporations. On the flip side, however, is the larger firm's deeper marketing and technology pockets, which will allow it to cut costs and reach customers in ways simply unavailable to smaller banks.

The Players

Chairman and CEO of Banc One Corp.: John B. McCoy. Banc One Corp. tapped John McCoy as CEO in 1984. He assumed the additional role of chairman in 1987. After the company upped its assets by $15 million in 1992, *American Banker* named McCoy "Banker of the Year." He was considered a leader in the banking industry's consolidation, with roughly 100 acquisitions under his belt by 1993. When Banc One Corp. and First Chicago NBD merged to form Bank One Corp., McCoy accepted the posts of president and CEO of the new firm.

Chairman and CEO of First Chicago NBD Corp.: Verne G. Istock. Verne Istock was hired by NBD Corp. in 1963 as a credit trainee. He was appointed executive vice president in charge of corporate banking in 1982; three years later, he was named a vice chairman. When NBD merged with First Chicago in October 1995, Istock, who was by then chairman of NBD, took the helm as CEO of the new company. Three years later, when First Chicago NBD and Banc One Corp. merged to form Bank One Corp., Istock took over as chairman.

Review of the Outcome

Upon completion of the merger, First Chicago CEO told shareholders, "This merger leverages the many strengths of both companies to create a powerful national banking franchise. With greater economies of scale and skill, we will be an even stronger player in the financial services industry. We will be able to enhance our technological capabilities and will be a major competitive force in credit cards, retail, and business banking across the country."

Quarterly earnings immediately following the merger boded well for the newly joined company. Banc One had improved its bottom line by 39%, while First Chicago NBD had upped its performance by five percent. Management attributed the gains to improved performance by credit card and investment management operations, two of the new firm's core segments.

Research

"Banc One, 1st Chicago NBD Close MegaDeal," in *American Banker*, 5 October 1998. Offers a brief overview of the closing of the transaction between Banc One and First Chicago NBD.

Bank One Corp. Home Page, available at http://www.bankone.com. Official World Wide Web Home Page for Bank One Corp. Includes news, financial, product, and historical information.

"Banc One Corp.," in *Notable Corporate Chronologies*, The Gale Group, 1999. Lists major events in the history of Banc One Corp.

Chase, Brett. "After Merger, NBD Chief's Bonus Doubled While First Chicago Vice Chairman's Fell," in *American Banker*, 3 April 1997. Explains the bonus structure for executives at First Chicago NBD after the 1996 merger.

———. "Banc One Divestiture May Create Potent Rival," in *American Banker*, 4 June 1998. Discusses the forced divestiture of $1.9 billion in Indiana holdings by Banc One and First Chicago NBD.

———. "Resounding Votes of Approval for First Chicago-Banc One," in *American Banker*, 16 September 1998. Offers an overview of management's plans for the newly merged company after the deal received shareholder approval.

———. "Bank One Corp. Units, U.S. Bancorp Report Gains Spurred by Cards, Fees," in *American Banker*, 10 October 1998. This article details the performance of both firms during the first quarter following the merger.

"First Chicago NBD Corp.," in *Notable Corporate Chronologies*, The Gale Group, 1999. Lists major events in the history of First Chicago NBD, including its merger with Banc One Corp.

"Master Builder: A Flair for Marketing Helped Mr. McCoy Expand Banc One in a Highly Competitive Environment," in *American Banker*, 21 January 1998. Details the performance of Banc One CEO and Chairman John B. McCoy during his tenure at the helm of Banc One.

"Mega-Merger Mania Strikes US Banks," in *The Banker*, May 1998. Discusses the significance of the three big 1998 mergers in the banking industry, including the Banc One/First Chicago NBD deal.

Melcher, Richard A. "Is 'Nice, Big, Dull' Good Enough?," in *Business Week*, 12 May 1997. Explains how First Chicago NBD CEO Verne Istock plans to expand in the Midwest as he oversees the integration of First Chicago and NBD.

Vandeveire, Mary. "Small Bankers Cheer Merger Action," in *The Business Journal-Serving Phoenix and the Valley of the Sun*, 17 April 1998. Explains how large mergers in the commercial banking industry, including the Banc One/First Chicago NBD joining, can benefit smaller banks.

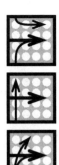

BANCO CENTRAL HISPANOAMERICANO & BANCO SANTANDER

nationality: Spain
date: April 17, 1999
affected: Banco Central Hispanoamericano SA, Spain, founded 1991
affected: Banco Santander SA, Spain, founded 1857

Banco Santander Central Hispano SA
Paseo de la Castellana 24, 7-8 Planta
Madrid, 28046
Spain

tel: 34 91 342 4884
fax: 34 91 342 4880
web: http://www.bsch.es
e-mail: bsch@bsch.es

Overview of the Merger

The adoption of the euro in January 1999 heralded an era of cross-border European banking alliances. The first such union, between Banco Central Hispanoamericano and Banco Santander, formed the largest bank in Spain and the leading foreign financial institution in Latin America, as well as one of the largest financial institutions in Europe as a whole.

History of Banco Central Hispanoamericano SA

Banco Central came into being in Madrid, Spain, on December 6, 1919. It was established by the Marquis of Aldama, the Count of Los Gaitanes, and Juan Nunez Anchustegui to realize the economic growth potential of post-war Spain. It quickly established itself as a major player in emerging industries, particularly coal, iron and steel, shipping, and papermaking. In 1921 Banco Central made its first major acquisition, Banco de Albacete. By the following year, it was operating a national network of 18 branches.

The worldwide and Spanish economic crises of 1929 were evaded by Banco Central due to its investments in heavy industries. This was a two-fold benefit, as its capital resources enabled the firm to purchase its less fortunate competitors. Governmental measures passed in 1931 to alleviate the crisis in Spain's banking industry solidified Banco Central's position. Under the new laws, the Bank of Spain discontinued services to the public, thereby opening a new share of the market to other banks.

By the end of the Spanish Civil War, which placed Francisco Franco in the seat of governmental power, Banco Central was one of the Big Five of the country's banks. In May 1940 the government passed restrictions preventing banks from entering new areas of business, leaving the acquisition of other banks as the only form of growth.

The Business

Financials

Revenue (1999): 236.2 billion euros in assets (est.)

Employees (1999): 106,519 (est.)

SICs / NAICS

sic 6021 - National Commercial Banks

naics 522110 - Commercial Banking

In 1959 the government took further steps to improve Spain's depressed economic condition by joining the International Monetary Fund, the International Bank for Reconstruction and Development, and the Organization for European Economic Cooperation (OEEC). It established a financial stabilization plan that devalued the peseta, restricted government spending, limited government and private credit, improved tax collection, abolished price controls, froze wages, established higher bank rates, and encouraged foreign investment. The International Monetary Fund, the OEEC, the U.S. government, and a group of U.S. banks established a $5.75 million assistance package.

In April and June 1962, laws were passed to reform the Spanish banking industry further. They included the nationalization and reorganization of the Bank of Spain and the reclamation of all currency and credit authority by the government. In effect, the reforms institutionalized the positions of the major Spanish banks, including Banco Central. To comply with these new banking regulations, Banco Central formed Banco de Fomento in 1963 to compete in the newly established industrial bank sector.

During the 1960s the bank continued to invest in developing industries. It created Saltos del Sil, a hydroelectric development in Galicia, Spain; Compania Espanola de Petroleos SA, Spain's first privately owned petroleum company; and Dragados y Construcciones SA, a leader in the construction industry.

By the end of the decade, Spain's fertile economy gave rise to increased banking consumer services, such as credit and checking accounts. By the early 1970s, however, Spanish banks were more conservative than their counterparts throughout Europe. The rise of oil prices and the resulting inflation caused the collapse of many firms and their lending banks. To combat this inflation, the government raised the bank rate, extended business credit, and eliminated restrictions between industrial and commercial banks. Banco Central acquired additional failing financial entities during this period, and by 1975 had doubled the number of its operating offices to more 1,000.

Banco Central continued to expand through acquisitions in the 1980s, purchasing Banco de Granada in 1980, Banco de Credito Inversiones in 1983, and Banco Internacional de Comercio the following year. In 1981 it entered into an alliance with the Luksic Group, thereby becoming the first Spanish bank to establish operations in the Southern Cone of Latin America. By the mid-1980s Banco Central had become the largest bank in Spain, but was considered too inflexible to compete effectively in the liberalized and globalized Spanish economy of the post-Franco era. This posture was partly attributable to the bank's long-time chairman, Alfonso Escamez, who refused to reduce operating costs to improve competitiveness.

In 1988 the cousins Alberto Alcocer and Alberto Cortina joined forces to challenge Escamez for control of Banco Central. By joining with the Kuwait Investment Office, they eventually acquired a 12% stake, earning the group five seats on the 24-member board. After failing to buy them out, Escamez sought to merge the bank with Spain's number-two commercial bank, Banco Espanol de Credito. The new bank would have had consolidated assets in excess of Ptas7 trillion, making it one of the top 25 banks in Europe. The planned merger failed to thwart the cousins, who continued in their pursuit of a voice in the management of the bank by purchasing Banco Espanol's stock. After nine months of battling for Banco Central, the cousins agreed to sell out of Banco Espanol in exchange for the termination of the planned merger. The Kuwait Investment Office then sold its interest, and Escamez remained in control of Banco Central.

Banco Central increased its stake in Sociedad General Azucarera de Espana from 24.8% to about 45% in late 1990. The following June it entered into an agreement to acquire Banco Hispano Americano, and on December 31, 1991, Banco Central Hispanoamericano SA (BCH) was formed. This company immediately became the nation's largest combination banking and industrial group, with a 20% market share.

Before the new company had fully integrated, however, Spain entered into an economic recession. The synergies resulting from combined operations were diluted by an overall drop in profitability. Its industrial holdings, too, heightened the company's vulnerability to economic conditions.

Throughout the ensuing years of wavering profitability, BCH continued its program of acquisition, purchasing majority interests in Cia Inmobiliaria de

Aragon in 1991, Consultoria y Admon de Sistemas Prevision in 1992, Financiera Hispamer SA in 1993, Vitalicio de Pensiones in 1994, Portugal-based Leasefactor SGPS in 1995, and Banco del Sur del Peru in 1996.

Meanwhile, in order to raise capital, BCH divested various properties, including 24.4% of Banco de Valencia in June 1984. That month Angel Corcostegui was brought into the company as CEO. The company embarked on a cost-cutting program, closing branches, reducing its workforce, consolidating administrative offices, and divesting itself of noncore subsidiaries. That July BCH sold 18.7% of Cepsa, Spain's leading private oil company, to Elf Aquitaine, leaving the bank with a 19.5% interest.

In March 1996 BCH sold Banco Central Hispano Puerto Rico to Banco Santander. The firm also entered into an alliance with Cepsa and Endesa, a public utility, to offer telecommunications, oil, gas, and electricity services. Although the accord was terminated in May 1997, the alliance was reborn when BCH increased its interest in Endesa to 3% in early 1998.

Compared to Spain's other leading banks, BCH had fallen behind in Latin American expansion. It began concentrating more resources in that area, agreeing in October 1996 to acquire up to 36% of Columbia-based Grupo Gilinski. Pretax profits increased 141% that year, to Ptas51 billion. BCH operated 2,572 branches and had a workforce of more than 21,600. In November 1997 it linked its computer network with that of Banco Comercial Portugues, forming an international system of collections and payments that granted users of either bank online access to their account information.

History of Banco Santander SA

Banco de Santander SA was founded in 1857 to provide banking services for the Santander region of Spain. The first of the Botin family to chair the bank was Emilio, who took the helm simply because the position fell to him upon regular rotation through the members of the board. Once he took control, however, the succession of the chair ceased to be passed through board members and instead became passed through the Botin family.

Emilio Botin II took control upon his father's death in 1923. The bank was in sore financial straits and was forced to receive a Ptas2 million injection from the Bank of Spain. Emilio II transformed Santander into an aggressive expansionist, extending its reach outside the Santander region for the first time. In 1946 Santander rocked the industry with the acquisition of the far larger Banco Mercantil, Inc., which operated branches in neighboring regions.

The Officers

Co-Chairman: Emilio Botin-Sanz

Co-Chairman: Jose Maria Amusategui

Vice Chairman, Managing Director, and CEO: Angel Corcostegui Guraya

Chief Financial Officer: Jose Luis del Valle

Finding that acquisitions suited its style, the enterprise stepped up the pace of such unions. Between 1948 and 1971, it purchased various banks in Madrid, Catalonia, and Galicia. It also set its sights on international ventures. Banco de Santander focused on Latin America during the 1950s, opening branches in Mexico and Cuba. By the 1970s it had subsidiaries in Argentina, Chile, Costa Rica, the Dominican Republic, Ecuador, Guatemala, Panama, Puerto Rico, and Uruguay. By the 1980s, however, deteriorating economic conditions spurred the firm to exit all Latin American markets except for Chile, Puerto Rico, and Uruguay.

In 1965 Santander formed the industrial bank Banco Intercontinental Espanol through an alliance with Bank of America. Five years later the two banks formed another joint venture, the retail bank Bankinter. This small operation would later serve as a testing ground for the company's innovative products.

Shares of its subsidiary, Banco Comercial Espanol, were offered to shareholders in 1982. Two years later the Spanish Treasury forced the bank to purchase Banco de Murcia and Banco Comercial de Cataluna in an agreement to contribute to the recovery of those banks.

By 1986, having obtained a listing on the London Stock Exchange, Santander had become the sixth-largest bank in Spain. That year 84-year-old Emilio II stepped down as chairman in favor of his son, Emilio III. In 1987 the bank formed an accord with U.S.-based Metropolitan Life Insurance Co. to sell insurance and pension products in Spain. Two years later it acquired a stake in the U.S. insurance firm Kemper Co. to offer investment and management services in the U.S., Europe, and South America. Santander shook up the Spanish banking industry in 1990 by introducing interest-bearing accounts, setting off a period of intense competition for deposits.

Also in 1990 the bank acquired a 10% stake in the Royal Bank of Scotland, an ailing institution that sought a friendly investment to deter takeover

The Players

Banco Santander Chairman: Emilio Botin-Sanz. Emilio Botin III continued family tradition by joining Banco Santander in 1958. According to family legend, he learned about the banking industry by hiding behind curtains while his father discussed business. After graduating from law school, Botin succeeded his father as chairman of Santander in 1986. He led Santander on aggressive expansion in Latin America, earning him the title of *LatinFinance* Man of the Year in 1998. Upon formation of BSCH in 1999, Botin shared the chairmanship with Jose Maria Amusategui until the latter's scheduled retirement in 2002, at which time Botin was slated to continue as sole chairman.

attempts. That year the company also began aggressive expansion in the Americas. In 1991 it paid $28 per share for a 29.99% interest in the U.S.-based First Fidelity Bancorp and set about restructuring that entity. In 1995 its investment was worth $64.29 per share, as First Fidelity merged with First Union Corp. to form the sixth-largest U.S. bank; Santander held 11.4% of the newly formed entity and occupied one seat of its six-member board. In 1997 Santander fully divested its interest in First Union for $2.16 billion—an average return of 43% annually since its original investment.

In 1992 Banco de Santander shortened its name to Banco Santander SA. In April 1994 it acquired 73.45% of Banco Espanol de Credito (Banesto). The program of recovery orchestrated by the Bank of Spain included the installation of new management at Banesto, reduction of bad debts, and divestiture of unprofitable properties. By October of that year, restored investor confidence in Banesto prompted Santander to sell 13% of its stake at a 25% profit.

Santander purchased a 10% stake in Ebro Agricolas, Spain's largest food company, in late 1994. In November it opened a branch in Mexico, becoming the first foreign bank to do so in nearly 70 years. At year's end, Santander had $114 billion in assets and $651 million in net profits. In February 1995 Emilio Botin announced that not only was Santander the nation's largest bank, it had captured nearly a 25% share of Spain's banking market. In March 1995 Santander became the first Spanish bank to receive full authorization from the Federal Reserve Board to conduct investment banking operations in the U.S.

Santander re-entered the Latin American market in the early 1990s, having largely exited that region a decade earlier. The return to the area this time concentrated on investment banking business rather than diversification. In 1995 it acquired interests in Banco Mercantil and Banco Interandino and merged them into Banco Santander Peru the following year. The company also gained a strong foothold in Chile when, in June 1996, it acquired a 51% interest in Banco Osorno y La Union to form Banco Santander Chile, that nation's largest financial institution. In March 1997 Santander acquired a 51% controlling stake in Banco Geral de Comercio, a 77-branch Brazilian bank. In 1998 Geral agreed to acquire 50% of Banco Noroeste to form Brazil's seventh-largest private bank. With this purchase Santander claimed that its Latin American expansion program was complete, save for the occasional small acquisition. By that time Santander was the leading commercial banking enterprise in Latin America.

Market Forces Driving the Merger

On January 1, 1999, much of Western Europe adopted a single currency, the euro. This event opened the door for increased competition from foreign entities. As the Spanish market was smaller than that of such countries as France and Germany, a strong domestic presence didn't necessarily translate into a formidable European presence. Moreover, as competition increased, so did the need for cost-cutting, a benefit that could arise as a result of the union between banks.

The Spanish banking market was overcrowded and increasingly less profitable, as interest rates continued to fall. Spanish banks, ranked by assets, were smaller than other European institutions, yet by market capitalization they were among the continent's largest. However, this strength was vulnerable to falling profits, in which case the banks could become acquisition targets.

Approach and Engagement

On January 15, 1999, after only about a month of negotiation, Banco Santander and Banco Central Hispanoamericano (BCH) announced their merger agreement. Although industry analysts had been expecting European bank consolidation to take place rapidly in the new euro environment, few had not been shocked at this union. Santander, by its own admission, had not been seeking a Spanish partner; in fact, Emilio Botin had dismissed the notion of any further large-scale consolidation in the Spanish banking industry. Banco Central had also been considered to be out of the running for a union, as it had only recently emerged from a difficult merger of its own.

Dubbed a merger of equals, the deal combined Banco Santander, Spain's largest bank, with the third-ranked Banco Central Hispanoamericano. Valued at 10 billion euros, or $11.8 billion, the merger was structured as a stock swap in which five BCH shares were exchanged for three Santander shares. The newly formed company was named Banco Santander Central Hispano SA (BSCH) and emerged as Europe's largest bank based on market capitalization, as well as Latin America's largest foreign financial institution. The new bank was formally created on April 17, 1999, and began trading on the New York Stock Exchange two days later.

Products and Services

Banco Santander Central Hispano began business by operating in six main areas: retail banking in Spain, European banking, Latin American banking, global wholesale banking, asset management and private banking, and industrial portfolios. In Europe its operations included Banco Santander de Negocios, Banco Santander-Portugal, Banesto, Banif, CC-Bank A.G., Hispamer, Open Bank, and Santander Direkt Bank. Its activities in the Americas included Banco de Rio de la Plata, Banco Santa Cruz, Banco Santander Brasil, Banco Santander-Chile, Banco Santander-Colombia, Banco Santander Internacional Miami, Banco Santander Mexicano, Banco Santander Miami, Banco Santander-Peru, Banco Santander-Puerto Rico, Banco Santander-Uruguay, Banco Santander de Venezuela, Banco Santiago, and Grupo Financiero Bital.

Changes to the Industry

Formed in the first bank deal of the new euro era, BSCH threw out the challenge of large-scale consolidation to its rivals. Its assets of 236.2 billion euros dwarfed the next largest Spanish competitor, Banco Bilbao Vizcaya (BBV), with 132.3 billion euros in assets. Industry experts predicted that BBV would quickly respond by entering into a strategic merger deal of its own in order to make a play for the leading market position. Speculation over likely Spanish partnership candidates for BBV included third-placed Argentaria or sixth-placed Banco Popular.

Few analysts predicted that consolidation would be limited to domestic transactions, however. The adoption of the euro opened the door for cross-border deals. The new BSCH, in fact, had not only captured the top domestic position, it had emerged as a leading player in the European market. Its market capitaliza-

tion of just over 31 million euros made it the number-one European bank, although by assets it had just fallen short of breaking into Europe's top ten.

Emerging conditions across Europe set the stage for facilitating such unions. Germany and France, two of Europe's largest banking markets, had only begun the consolidation process, and still had plum opportunities available. The removal of governmental barriers in those countries may have provided the impetus for merger and acquisition activity. France was expected to privatize Credit Lyonnais, which would enable banks to enter into negotiations for stakes in that institution. The European Commission was also expected to rule on the future of the 13 government-controlled Landesbanken, which had enjoyed an unfair advantage in Germany for years.

Review of the Outcome

The newly formed BSCH was headed by co-chairmen Emilio Botin and Jose Maria Amusategui. Amusategui announced his intention of retiring in 2002, at which time Botin would continue as sole chairman. Angel Corcostegui was named vice chairman, managing director, and CEO. The 27-seat board of directors was comprised of 13 members named by Santander, 12 by Banco Central Hispanoamericano, and two independents.

Shortly after the merger was announced, Ana Patricia Botin, daughter of Santander's chairman and considered by many to be Spain's most powerful woman, resigned as director general of Santander. She did so after a Madrid newspaper published a glowing profile of her, touting her as the next in line for the chairmanship. Aware that this article compromised the "merger of equals" spirit, particularly since BCH executives were already sensitive about being overshadowed by Santander, Botin resigned from day-to-day duties, although she retained a seat on the board.

BSCH began operations with a network of 8,681 branches and a workforce of 106,519 employees worldwide. Although overlap made some office closures inevitable, union pressures limited their scope. The new entity planned to maintain the separation of its three main brand names—Banesto, BCH, and Santander—reducing the necessity for closures due to brand overconcentration in a given area. Industry analysts disagreed over the wisdom of maintaining distinctive brands. This strategy would restrict cost savings that could be realized from fully consolidated operations. On the other hand, retention of the brands would make the merger appear virtually seamless to the customers, who would therefore be less likely to change banks at the first sign of service disruption.

Research

"Banco Central," in *International Directory of Company Histories*, Vol. II, St. James Press: 1990. Provides a historical review of the company.

Banco Santander Central Hispano SA Home Page, available at http://www.bsch.es. Official World Wide Web Page for BSCH. This Spanish-language site offers links to related brand Web pages, as well as descriptions of company products, services, and activities.

"BSCH: A Banking Leader for the Europe of the Euro," in *PR Newswire*, 15 January 1999. Describes the terms of the merger deal.

Burns, Richard, and Scott Weeks. "Emilio Botin," in *LatinFinance*, March 1998. Offers a history of Banco Santander.

Shearlock, Peter. "Bank Mergers to Multiply," in *The Banker*, February 1999. Suggests that this merger will trigger a wave of European banking consolidation.

"Spanish Banks: First Mover," in *The Economist*, 23 January 1999. Describes the Spanish banking environment that spurred the deal.

Stewart, Jules. "The Treasurer of Spain," in *EuroBusiness*, May 1995. Profiles Emilio Botin.

Warner, Alison. "Madrid Marches On," in *The Banker*, March 1997. Reports on the expansion of Spanish banks into Latin America.

DEBORAH J. UNTENER

BANK OF MONTREAL & ROYAL BANK OF CANADA

date: December 14, 1998 (canceled)
affected: Bank of Montreal, Canada, founded 1817
affected: Royal Bank of Canada, Canada, founded 1864

Bank of Montreal
119 St. Jacques
Montreal, Quebec H2Y 1L6
Canada

tel: 514877-7373
fax: 514877-7399
web: http://www.bmo.com

Royal Bank of Canada
1 Place Ville Marie
Montreal, Quebec H3B 1Z8
Canada

tel: (514)874-2110
fax: (514)874-6582
web: http://www.royalbank.com

Overview of the Merger

The Bank of Montreal and the Royal Bank of Canada rocked the Canadian banking industry in January of 1998 with news of their $26.6 billion merger plan. The combined bank would have boasted $295 billion in assets and a market valuation of $39 billion, which would have ranked it first in Canada, tenth in North America, and 22nd among the world's largest banks in terms of market capitalization. With 85,000 employees, the new firm would have also become Canada's largest employer. After several months of intense speculation regarding the outcome of the joining of Canada's number three bank with its number one bank, Canadian Finance Minister Paul Martin deemed the merger anticompetitive in December of 1998, rejecting the deal.

History of Bank of Montreal

In 1817, a determined group of nine Canadian merchants accumulated sufficient personal funds to start Montreal Bank. It opened for business without an official charter and relied on American investors for nearly half its initial capital. After proving its worth by helping to fund the building of the Lachine canal, Canada's first canal, the new bank was granted a charter as the Bank of Montreal. Canadians owned all but 15% of the bank's capital.

Bank of Montreal opened its first foreign office, in New York City, in the mid-1800s. In 1864, the bank was appointed to replace Bank of Upper Canada, which continued to verge on bankruptcy, as the Canadian government's official banker. By 1887, Bank of Montreal had branch offices in Winnipeg, Manitoba; Regina, Saskatchewan; Calgary, Alberta; and Vancouver, British Columbia. By the turn of the century, the bank had become the Canadian government's official banker in London, England. After the London securities markets were closed to foreign issues in 1914, the Bank of Montreal and the Canadian government began to float their bond issues on the New York Stock Exchange.

The bank merged with Molson's Bank, a Montreal-based institution with nearly 125 branches, in 1925. Ten years later, the Bank of Canada was created and

The Business

Financials - Bank of Montreal

Revenue (1998): $11.1 billion

Employees (1998): 33,400

Financials - Royal Bank of Canada

Revenue (1998): $12.8 billion

Employees (1998): 60,035

Share (1998): 9% of Canadian mutual fund market

SICs / NAICS

sic 6021 - National Commercial Banks

replaced Bank of Montreal as the government's official banker. In 1972, Bank of Montreal became the last of Canada's five major banks to introduce a credit card program. Hoping to expand internationally, the bank purchased a 25.1% interest in Allgemeine Deutsche Creditanstalt, a medium-sized, West German bank. The latter half of the 1970s marked a period of reconstruction for Bank of Montreal: 50 unprofitable branches were closed, internal pricing policies were revised, and procedures for asset and liability management were modernized. In 1980, the bank installed its first automated teller machine (ATM) in Calgary.

In 1984, the bank finally obtained its entry into the U.S. retail banking market when it acquired Harris Bankcorp, the third-largest bank in Chicago, for $547 million. Bank of Montreal also introduced Gold MasterCard, the first premium credit card in the Canadian market. The following year, the Canadian government deregulated the country's financial system, allowing insurance, banking, and securities brokerage firms to compete in each other's markets. As a result, Bank of Montreal bought Nesbitt Thomson, Inc., the country's fourth-largest brokerage firm.

The bank acquired Burns Fry in 1995, and merged it with its own subsidiary, Nesbitt Thomson, to create Canada's largest investment banking firm, Nesbitt Burns. To better serve its treasury clients, Bank of Montreal and Nesbitt Burns built Canada's largest privately-owned trading floor in Toronto. The bank also opened a branch in Guangzhou, China, to serve small- and medium-sized Canadian and U.S. enterprises looking to finance their trade and investment initiatives in China. The following year, Bank of Montreal launched electronic banking system mbanx; bought a 16% stake in Bancomer, Mexico's second largest bank;

and opened a branch in Beijing. Early in 1998, the bank announced plans for a $26.6 billion merger with Royal Bank of Canada, but the Canadian government nixed the deal late in the year.

History of Royal Bank of Canada

Thomas Kinnear and seven other businessmen in Halifax, Nova Scotia, founded the Merchants Bank in 1864 to support local commerce. Five years later, the bank was incorporated as Merchants Bank of Halifax. To distinguish the bank from two other institutions with similar names, it was renamed the Royal Bank of Canada. By 1910, when the bank acquired the Union Bank of Halifax, over 100 branches were in operation. Two years later, Royal Bank of Canada doubled its assets and its number of operating branches by purchasing Traders Bank of Canada and the Bank of British Honduras.

In 1917, the bank acquired Quebec Bank. After purchasing the Northern Crown Bank and two other banks in British Guiana and Nassau, the Bahamas, in 1918, the Royal Bank of Canada became Canada's second largest bank with 540 branches, as well as a new foreign trade department to handle its growing international presence. Expansion continued into the 1920s with the purchases of Bank of Central and South America and the Union Bank of Canada. During the early 1950s, Royal Bank of Canada fueled Canada's oil and gas exploration efforts by offering banking services in remote locations, such as its oil and gas unit in Calgary, Alberta.

Royal Bank of Canada furthered its international expansion in 1951 by establishing the Royal Bank of Canada Trust Co. in New York. In the early 1960s, the bank diversified into consumer financial services by launching TermPlan, a package of credit and insurance benefits. In 1968, Royal Bank, in partnership with three other banks, introduced Chargex, a credit card that allowed holders to make purchases within a specified credit limit and to obtain cash advances through any of the four participating institutions. In the late 1970s, Royal Bank was reorganized into four groups: two for Canadian retail operations and two for corporate banking and international operations. The bank extended its international network into West Germany, Puerto Rico, and the Bahamas in 1980.

Shortly after the stock market crash in 1987, Royal Bank acquired Dominion Securities, the largest investment house in Canada. Though it was one of the last of Canada's big banks to enter the brokerage market, Royal Bank was able to save a significant amount over pre-cash prices for the new acquisition by waiting. In 1991, Royal Bank acquired McNeil Mantha Inc., an investment banking firm. Four years later, the bank expanded its derivatives operations to a complete, international service with units in New York and Tokyo. The purchase of Westbury Canadian Life Insurance Co. in 1996 marked Royal Bank's largest expansion into the life insurance industry. Early in 1998, Bank of Montreal and Royal Bank agreed to merge; however, due to anticompetitive concerns, the Canadian government rejected the deal in December.

Market Forces Driving the Merger

Executives of both Royal Bank of Canada and Bank of Montreal claimed their merger was necessary if Canadian banks wanted to compete in the global financial marketplace, particularly in the asset management, corporate finance, and mutual fund sectors. Consolidation had swept through the banking industries of most major countries during the nineties, leaving a handful of industry giants poised to dominate the worldwide commercial banking arena. Large foreign banks were also beginning to penetrate Canadian markets. Proponents of the merger pointed to the damage done to the Canadian retail market when foreign retailers, such as U.S.-based Wal-Mart, began competing in Canada; they predicted a similar fate for Canada's banking industry if consolidation wasn't pursued. California-based Wells Fargo had already begun offering small business services to Canadians via a Colorado branch. And Dutch banker ING was targeting Canadian clients by offering higher interest rates on savings accounts than Canadian institutions.

Critics of the merger insisted that foreign competition was no more a threat than it had ever been. According to TD Securities Inc. banking analyst Roy Palmer, "Foreign banks have been able to come here since kingdom come, and none of them have had a particularly good record." The difference in the late 1990s, though, was that American banks, once restricted to local markets, had grown dramatically via consolidation after restrictions were lifted in the 1980s. The smaller American banks had once needed to charge more per services than the large Canadian banks; now that they were operating on a more national scale, they could cut prices to compete with the Canadian banks. Canada's sparse population had also been a deterrent to competitors who believed setting up shop in the nation wouldn't be cost effective. The advent of Internet banking, however, allowed foreign competition access to Canadian customers without the expense of opening a branch there.

The deal would allow Bank of Montreal and Royal Bank of Canada to save roughly $650 million in operating expenses annually. These savings, according to Royal Bank CEO Cleghorn would allow the new company to cut prices. Yet customers feared that the

The Officers

Bank of Montreal

Chairman: Matthew W. Barrett

Vice Chairman, Electronic Financial Services and President, mbanx: Jeffrey S. Chisholm

Vice Chairman, Corporate Services and Organization Development: Gary Dibb

Vice Chairman, Bank of Montreal: Keith O. Dorricott

Vice Chairman and Chairman and CEO, Harris Bankcorp, Inc.: Alan G. McNally

Royal Bank of Canada

Chairman and CEO: John E. Cleghorn

Exec. VP and Chief Financial Officer: Peter Currie

Exec. VP and Chief Information Officer: Martin Lippert

Exex. VP and Chief Risk Officer: Suzanne Labarge

Exec. VP, Human Resources: E. Gay Mitchell

merger would lead to higher prices, fewer choices, and additional industry consolidation. Both banks had already been criticized for high service fees, minimal small business financing opportunities, layoffs, and extravagant salaries for bank executives. Opponents of the deal insisted that the two banks simply wanted to save money, at the expense of employees and customers, as a means of boosting profits.

Approach and Engagement

Royal Bank CEO Cleghorn approached Bank of Montreal CEO Barrett about merging the two banks at a corporate Christmas party on December 19, 1997. They negotiated secretly until January 23, 1998, when they announced the $26.6 billion deal. The terms of the agreement stipulated that Royal Bank shareholders would receive one share of the new stock for each Royal Bank share owned. Bank of Montreal shareholders would get .97 of a share per each Bank of Montreal share they held. Royal Bank shareholders would gain control of 54.9% of the new company, while Bank of Montreal shareholders would own the remaining 45.1%. Cleghorn would take over as CEO, and Barrett would head the executive committee.

Stocks prices for both banks leapt upon the news; Bank of Montreal's share price grew 18% to a record C$67.70; Royal Bank's share price rose to a new high of C$75.75. Intense public debate about the merits and

The Players

Chairman and CEO of Bank of Montreal.: Matthew W. Barrett. At the age of 18, Matthew Barrett left Ireland for London, where he found work as a clerk at the Waterloo branch of the Bank of Montreal. He sailed to Canada in 1967 to accept a position at the firm's headquarters in Montreal. In 1989, Barrett was appointed CEO of the Bank of Montreal. He took over as chairman a year later. When his company's merger with the Royal Bank of Canada was rejected by the Canadian Finance Minister, Barrett remained chairman, but named Anthony Comper CEO.

Chairman and CEO of Royal Bank of Canada: John E. Cleghorn. After working as an accountant and a sugar trader, Canadian John Cleghorn moved into the banking industry in 1966 when he accepted a position at the Canadian unit of New York-based Citicorp. He left Citicorp to join Royal Bank in 1974, where he began climbing the rungs of the corporate ladder. When he was finally given the reins of Royal Bank in 1995, Cleghorn sold the firm's luxury jet, shunned the chairman's private limousine, and got rid of the lavishly adorned private dining rooms atop the bank's headquarters building. Despite his efforts to convince Canadian officials that his firm's merger with Bank of Montreal would be good for Canadian citizens, the deal was rejected late in 1998.

drawbacks of the deal followed. On December 14, 1998, Canadian Finance Minister Paul Martin rejected the merger proposal, along with the Canadian Imperial Bank of Commerce/Toronto Dominion Bank deal. He stated that both deals would "lead to an unacceptable concentration of economic power in the hands of fewer, very large banks."

Products and Services

The Bank of Montreal operated nearly 1,250 branches across Canada in 1998. Via its Nesbitt Burns subsidiary, the bank offered brokerage and trading, investment, and merchant banking services. Its Chicago-based Harris Bank provided retail and investment banking in the U.S. Mortgage banking, document processing, and insurance services were offered through additional subsidiaries.

Through its 1,400-plus domestic units and its 100-plus international offices that spanned 34 countries, Royal Bank of Canada offered individual, corporate, and institutional clients a full range of banking services including: cash management, consumer loans, credit cards, credit lines, debit cards, discount brokerage, equipment financing, foreign exchange, full-service brokerage, global investment management, institutional investment management, insurance, international custody, investment services, and mortgage banking.

Changes to the Industry and Review of the Outcome

After the merger was called off, analysts pointed out that Canadian law prevented either bank from becoming an international acquisition target because shareholders were not allowed to own more than 10% of a bank's stock. Also, Canadian banks were required to be headquartered in the nation itself, and more than half of all directors had to be Canadian citizens. A January 1999 article in *American Banker* stated that, "given the finance minister's ruling, the banks have few alternatives but to expand abroad.

Accordingly, in late 1998, Royal Bank bought First Network Bank of Atlanta, an Internet-based bank, after it was spun off from Security First Technologies. Because it wouldn't have Bank of Montreal's mbanx online banking program, Royal Bank needed an electronic avenue to expansion in the U.S. The bank also purchased New York-based discount broker Bull & Bear Securities, Inc. Most analysts believed Bank of Montreal would also pursue U.S. expansion. According to Eric J. Grubelich, an industry analyst with Keefe, Bruyette & Woods Inc., both firms had "limited growth possibilities in Canada. Logically, the United States makes the most sense for them."

Research

"Bank of Montreal," in *Notable Corporate Chronologies*, The Gale Group, 1999. Lists major events in the history of Bank of Montreal.

Bank of Montreal Home Page, available at http://www.bmo.com. Official World Wide Web Home Page for Bank of Montreal. Includes news, financial, product, and historical information.

Blackwell, Richard. "Royal Bank, B of M Propose $39B Merger," in *The Financial Post*, 24 January 1998. Details the terms of the deal between Royal Bank of Canada and Bank of Montreal.

Elstein, Aaron. "Canada Bars 2 Megadeals, Sees Threat to Competition," in *American Banker*, 15 December 1998. Explains why the Canadian government rejected the Royal Bank/Bank of Montreal and the Canadian Imperial Bank of Commerce/Toronto-Dominion merger proposals.

Kraus, James R. "Canadian Seeks Size to Compete in N. America," in *American Banker*, 22 October 1998. Discusses the impetus behind the deal, as well as why opponents wanted it nixed.

———. "Discouraged at Home, Canada's Big Banks May Be Shopping in U.S. Again," in *American Banker*, 4 January 1999. Predicts what both banks will likely do now that their merger has been rejected.

McQueen, Rod. "Unfinished Business," in *National Post*, 23 January 1999. Details the career of Bank of Montreal CEO Matthew Barrett.

Newman, Peter C. "An Unlikely Partnership: The Bank of Montreal and the Royal Bank Are as Different as Their Chairmen," in *Maclean's*, 2 February 1998. Offers an overview of leadership styles of both CEOs involved in the merger.

Noble, Kimberly. "Big and Bigger: A $39-Billion Deal Challenges Ottawa's Policy on Bank Mergers," in *Maclean's*, 2 February 1998. Provides an in-depth look at the size and scope of the new bank that would result from the merger.

"Royal Bank of Canada," in *Notable Corporate Chronologies*, The Gale Group, 1999. Lists major events in the history of Royal Bank of Canada.

Royal Bank of Canada Home Page, available at http://www.royalbank.com. Official World Wide Web Home Page for Royal Bank of Canada. Includes news, financial, product, and historical information.

ANNAMARIE L. SHELDON

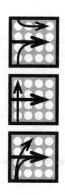

BANQUE NATIONALE DE PARIS & PARIBAS

Banque Nationale de Paris
16 Blvd. des Italiens
Paris, 75009
France

tel: 33 1 40 14 45 46
fax: 33 1 40 14 89 10
web: http://www.bnp.fr

nationality: France
date: August 1999
affected: Banque Nationale de Paris, France, founded 1966
affected: Paribas SA, France, founded 1872

Overview of the Merger

The $17 billion merger of Paribas SA and Societe Generale (SG) would have created SG Paribas, the world's fourth-largest bank in terms of shareholder funds. The deal was scuttled, however, when Banque Nationale de Paris (BNP) bid $37 billion for both Paribas and SG, hoping to form the a new worldwide banking leader with $1.1 trillion in assets. Although BNP successfully secured a controlling stake in Paribas for $13 billion, SG shareholders rejected the bid, leaving both BNP and SG seeking consolidation elsewhere.

History of Banque Nationale de Paris

In 1848, Comptoir d'Escompte was formed in Paris, France, to make credit available to local businesses in the midst of a short-term financial crisis. The firm became a commercial institution after the crisis had passed, greatly expanding its capital and range of activities. Although it did not open domestic branches outside Paris, the bank did establish a presence in London, Brussels, Australia, and French colonies worldwide. In 1880, Comptoir d'Escompte invested heavily in copper and Australian wool and became one of the largest banks in India.

The company had spread itself too thin by 1889, and company president Denfert Rochereau committed suicide. A consortium of French banks stepped in to return the bank to solvency, reorganizing it into a new deposit institution called Comptoir Nationale d'Escompte de Paris (CNEP). CNEP quickly returned to financial health, and although it retained its foreign interests, the bank focused on opening branches in the French provinces. Banque Nationale de Credit (BNC) was founded as a joint venture between Comptoir d'Escompte de Mulhouse (CEM) and Banque Francaise pour le Commerce et l'Industrie (BFCI) in 1913. BNC grew quickly by absorbing several smaller banks and opening many branches in its first year.

When World War I ended, BNC ranked as the fourth-largest bank in France. In 1920, BNC merged with BFCI under the BNC name. CNEP operated 223 branches. The Great Depression crippled BNC, which was heavily involved in long-term loans to industries. Expansion at CNEP slowed. By 1932, BNC's problems had become so acute that the French government and a consortium of banks came forward to assure the bank's solvency. The consortium reorganized BNC as the Banque Nationale pour le Commerce et l'Industrie (BNCI), strictly a deposit bank. Because the Depression had hit small local banks particularly hard, BNCI grew quickly by absorbing troubled institutions of this type.

In 1940, BNCI established an affiliate, the Banque Nationale pour le Commerce et l'Industrie (Afrique). France was conquered by Germany, and French industry was devoted to military production for the German war effort. CNEP and BNCI were nationalized in 1946 as part of the French government's postwar recovery program. This arrangement allowed CNEP to maintain an important role in the French financial system, and the bank was able to grow steadily for the rest of the decade. BNCI also benefitted, developing its overseas network of branches. The following year, BNCI spun off its London office into a subsidiary, the British and French Bank, which established its own international territory and grew rapidly. BNCI grew more rapidly than any other nationalized bank. CNEP expanded at a much slower rate.

In 1965, the French government imposed stringent restrictions on lending in an effort to shrink the national money supply and began discussing a rationalization of the banking system to better concentrate national financial activities. On July 1, 1966, BNCI and CNEP were merged to form the Banque Nationale de Paris (BNP). The merger was mutually beneficial, with CNEP maintaining a strong network of branches in France, and BNCI operating the largest overseas network of any French bank. BNP established the Societe de Garantie des Credits a Court Terme to provide financing to small and medium-sized firms. The newly merged bank also formed, in conjunction with four other European banks, the Societe Financiere Europeene to provide financial and strategic support to international business.

BNP reentered the investment banking business, creating Banexi as its capital unit. The firm also established NATIOVIE as its life insurance subsidiary. In 1972, BNP was one of the first foreign banks allowed to open a branch in Tokyo. The U.S. Federal Reserve Board also allowed the bank to establish the French Bank of California in San Francisco. BNP was the second-largest bank in Europe, controlling $9.2 billion in deposits. Two years later, BNP opened another U.S. affiliate, in Chicago, Illinois. By the end of the decade, branches had been established in Seoul, Korea; Manila, the Philippines; Cairo, Egypt; Los Angeles and Newport Beach, California; Houston, Texas;

The Business

Financials

Revenue (1998): $27 billion

Employees (1998): 56,300

SICs / NAICS

sic 6029 - Commercial Banks Nec

sic 6211 - Security Brokers & Dealers

sic 6021 - National Commercial Banks

sic 6282 - Investment Advice

sic 6082 - Foreign Trade & International Banks

sic 6153 - Short-Term Business Credit

naics 522110 - Commercial Banking

naics 522120 - Savings Institutions

naics 523120 - Securities Brokerage

naics 523930 - Investment Advice

naics 522220 - Sales Financing

naics 522320 - Financial Transactions Processing, Reserve, and Clearing House Activities

naics 522293 - International Trade Financing

Toronto and Vancouver, Canada; Moscow, Russia; and Tehran, Iran.

During the mid-1980s, nationalized deposit banks across Europe begin to enter the investment banking business in an effort to lower their capital-to-loans ratio. BNP was able to prosper in the new environment, having already established a unit called Banexi to conduct investment banking activities. Conservatives took power in France in 1986 and began contemplating privatization of many state-owned companies, including BNP. The following year, BNP acquired a 54% interest in Du Bouzet, a Paris stock brokerage, in anticipation of a new law making it legal for banks to buy into investment firms; organized its own investment subsidiary, the Compagnie d'Investissements de Paris; and purchased Ark Securities Co. of Great Britain, gaining a position in the European equity market.

Socialists come to power in France in 1988, ending the move to privatize industries and halting the law allowing banks to buy investment firms. BNP divested itself of its investment interests and announced plans to issue $400 million in perpetual capital notes and nonvoting certificates of investment

The Officers

Chairman and CEO: Michel Pebereau

President and Chief Operating Officer: Baudouin Prot

Group Exec. VP: Georges Chodron de Courcel

Group Exec. VP: Vivien Levy-Garboua

Exec. VP, Asset & Liability Management: Jean-Francois
    Lepetit

as an alternative means of raising capital. BNP also purchased Chemical Bank Home Loans Ltd., a British mortgage loan provider. In 1989, BNP entered into an alliance with Union des Assurance de Paris, the largest insurer in France, to form one of the nation's most powerful financial groups. The bank also opened an office in Budapest to assist joint ventures involving French and Hungarian companies and moved its capital market operations to London.

After five years of growth, the French banking industry slowed in the early 1990s, and the bank moved to offset the rising cost of funds by widening its margins on medium- and long-term loans. BNP joined with Dresdner Bank to provide financial support to eastern European countries following the fall of Communism in the mid-1990s. In 1996, after Compagnie d'Investissements de Paris (CIP) shareholders demanded that BNP, which owned 84% of the company, take measures to improve CIP share prices, BNP offered to buy out CIP shares at a 30% premium. In 1999, BNP launched a bid for both Paribas SA and Societe Generale. Although Societe Generale rejected the offer, BNP did acquire Paribas.

History of Paribas SA

In 1863, Banque de Credit et de Depot des Pays-Bas (BCDPB) was established in Amsterdam, Netherlands. The following year, BCDPB opened a branch in Paris, France. Banque de Paris (BP) was founded in Paris in 1866. Four years later, BP and BCDPB collaborated to finance bond issues of the Chemins de Fer Meridionaux and the East Tennessee Railroad. BCDPB opened a branch in Geneva, Switzerland, and absorbed the Banque Bischoffsheim-Hirsch of Brussels, Belgium.

On February 11, 1872, BCDPB and BP merged to form the Banque de Paris et de Pays-Bas (BPPB), with headquarters in Paris. The new bank had initial capitalization of Fr62.5 million and issued loans enabling France to liberate territories lost in the Franco-Prussian War. In 1877, Ernest Dutilleul became the

first chairman of BPPB. The bank's primary backers and customers were large French industrial concerns, and BPPB specialized in financing railroad and industrial ventures worldwide. Two years later, the bank participated in the creation of the Banque Hypothecaire de France and the Compagnie Generale du Gaz pour la France et l'Etranger.

Late in the century, BPPB branched into the mining industry, participating in the creation of the Volga and Urals Metallurgical Company in Russia. The bank also founded a venture to study the prospects for railroad construction in China and entered the utility business, financing the establishment of the Societe Franco-Suisse pour l'Industrie Electrique.

BPPB entered into a partnership with Omnium Lyonnaise and Societe Centrale pour l'Industrie Electrique to construct and operate electric-powered public transportation systems in St. Petersburg, Russia, in 1912. With the advent of World War II, the firm began collecting U.S. securities placed in France before the war in order to resell them as a means of improving the bank's balance of payments. BPPB also underwrote loans to the French government to help finance the war effort. When the war ended, BPPB refocused on financing overseas railroad and industrial ventures. In 1920, the bank established Compagnie Standard Franco-Americaine as a joint venture with U.S.-based Standard Oil Co. and formed an investment group to gain control of Steana Romana, operator of the Romanian oil industry.

BPPB became a major competitor among French international banks when it participated in 1924 in the formation of the Compagnie des Francais Petroles. The following year, the bank helped to form syndicates to explore the mineral wealth of Ethiopia, Tunisia, Burma, and Indochina. In 1935, BPPB reorganized the Societe Andre Citroen, in conjunction with Michelin and Lazard, following its liquidation. When World War II began, BPPB was once again forced to curtail its international activities until Allied forces liberated Paris in 1944. When the war officially ended, the bank resumed control of its assets in the U.S.

During the 1950s, anticolonial insurrections in Algeria and Indochina resulted in heavy losses for BPPB during the decade, and the bank began withdrawing from its Asian investments. Share capitalization reached Fr2.2 billion. In 1954, Viet Minh defeated the French, ending French colonial rule in Indochina, which was divided into North and South Vietnam. All BPPB investments in North Vietnam were nationalized. In 1957, BPPB acquired the Banque des Pays de l'Europe Centrale, raising capitalization to Fr6.5 billion. Three years later, the bank created Paribas Corp.

in New York City to conduct investment banking activities in the U.S.

BPPB stock was traded for the first time in 1961 on the exchanges in London, Paris, Frankfurt, Dusseldorf, Brussels, Antwerp, and Geneva. The bank created Banque de Paris et des Pays-Bas Ltd. in London, England, and the Banque de Paris et des Pays-Bas pour le Grand-Duche du Luxembourg in the mid-1960s. By the end of the decade, BPPB had also established an international financial operations division; diversified into issuance of eurobonds; created Sofracorp as a joint venture with the government of the Soviet Union; and reorganized, creating Compagnie Financiere de Parbas (CFPPB) as a holding company with four operating subsidiaries: Banque de Paris et des Pays-Bas; OPFI, to manage the company's industrial and financial holdings; OPB, to manage banking and financial holdings in France; and Paribas International, to operate the company's foreign banking operations.

CFPPB created Banque Ameribas in Luxembourg as a joint venture with the Bank of America in 1971. Paribas Corp. expanded, opening a representative office in Tokyo, Japan, and merging with SG Warburg to form Warburg Paribas SA in 1973. The following year, Warburg Paribas merged with American investment firm A.G. Becker to form the Becker and Warburg Paribas Group (BWPG). CFPPB opened branches in Oman, Bahrain, Japan, Indonesia, and the Philippines in 1975. New ventures were created in Spain, Italy, West Germany, and England in an effort to transfer as many assets as possible outside France following a government announcement favoring nationalization of CFPPB. The bank continued its overseas expansion in 1978, establishing branches in New York City, Grand Cayman Island, Hong Kong, and Bahrain.

Socialists under Francois Mitterand came to power in France in 1981, and CFPPB sold its Swiss and Belgian subsidiaries to prevent them from becoming nationalized. French government filed suit against CFPPB, claiming the bank's sale of subsidiaries prior to nationalization was illegal. When CFPPB's management team resigned in 1982, the French government dropped its suit. CFPPB was then nationalized and reorganized into six departments: Banking, International, Export Finance Delegation, Capital Markets, Industrial Finance, and Administration and Financial Control. In 1984, CFPPB established Paribas Asset Management (PAM) to manage its asset management activities. Three years later, the bank was privatized, with capitalization of Fr2.7 billion.

In 1990, the bank reorganized, replacing its board of directors with a supervisory board and a board of management, and split its banking activities into

The Players

Chairman and CEO of Banque Nationale de Paris: Michel Pebereau. After graduating from France's Ecole National d'Administration, Michel Pebereau worked for the French treasury, as well as for two ministers of finance. In 1981, the Socialist party moved into office, dashing Pebereau's aspirations of securing the Treasury directorship. As a result, he launched a career in the banking industry by joining Credit Commercial de France, where he took the reins in 1988. By the early 1990s, Pebereau had doubled the bank's profits. In 1993, the struggling Banque Nationale de Paris tapped Pebereau as CEO; within five years, Banque Nationale de Paris was the nation's most profitable bank. After unsuccessful attempts to merge with Union des Assurances de Paris, Compaigne de Suez, Credit Industriel & Commercial, and Credit Lyonnais, Pebereau launched his double-barreled bid for Paribas and Societe Generale, hoping to become the leader of the world's largest bank. Instead, Banque Nationale de Paris ended up only with Paribas. Many analysts pointed to the strained relationship between Pebereau and Societe Generale CEO Daniel Bouton as the three-way deal's major stumbling block.

Chairman and President of Paribas SA: Andre Levy-Lang. Ecole Polytechnique graduate Andre Levy-Lang began working for U.S.-based Schlumberger Ltd. in 1962. During his twelve-year tenure at the oil services firm, Levy-Lang worked in both the U.S. and France. He also earned his Ph.D. in business from Stanford University. Because he wanted to raise his children in France, Levy-Lang left Schlumberger in 1974, taking a position with Cie. Bancaire, the retail financial services unit of Paribas. Eight years later, he was named chairman of Cie. Bancaire. Levy-Lang took over Paribas as CEO in 1990. Within eight years, the unprofitable bank boasted an annual net income exceeding $1 billion. He orchestrated his firm's negotiations with Societe Generale in early 1999 and unsuccessfully fought the subsequent bid for both Paribas and Societe Generale by Banque Nationale de Paris. When Banque Nationale de Paris took over Paribas, 61-year-old Levy-Lang retired.

European Banking and International Banking divisions. Two years later, CFPPB reorganized into four departments: Specialized Commercial Banking; Capital Markets; Asset Management; and Advisory Services. This move was intended to expand the range of services offered by the bank. In 1999, CFPPB—by then renamed Paribas SA—agreed to merge with Societe Generale to form the world's fourth-largest bank. That deal was scuttled, however, by Banque Nationale de Paris, which bid for both Paribas and Societe Generale. Eventually, Paribas was acquired by Banque Nationale de Paris.

Market Forces Driving the Merger

On January 1, 1999, the standard European currency, the euro, was launched, eradicating major economic trade barriers between European countries. Consequently, companies began expanding outside of their domestic markets, and competition from international competitors intensified. Recognizing the lack of a major France-based global banking player, as well their vulnerability to foreign takeovers, many of France's leading banks began pursuing mergers as a means of shoring up their position in the new global marketplace. According to a May 1999 article in *Business Week*, French banks were "under pressure to cut costs, boost profits, and bulk up by merging just like their euro zone rivals." Traditionally poorer performers than other European banks, the lower market valuation of French banks made them particularly attractive targets.

Hoping to take advantage of economies of scale, Societe Generale and Paribus announced on February 2 their intent to merge—via a $17.2 billion deal—into the world's fourth-largest bank, with shareholder funds totaling $24 billion. SG Paribas would have usurped Credit Agricole as the largest bank in France and created the first French bank able to compete on global scale with giants such as Deutsche Bank AG and Swiss UBS. Hoping to prevent the deal, Banque Nationale de Paris moved in with an offer of its own for both Paribas and Societe Generale, hoping to become create a global banking behemoth—the world's largest—with assets of $1.1 trillion.

Approach and Engagement

In March, Banque Nationale de Paris (BNP) launched a $37 billion hostile bid for Societe Generale and Paribas. In response, Societe Generale increased its offer for Paribas to $19 billion. BNP also eventually upped its offer by $2 billion. While the three banks wrangled through negotiations, shares at each dropped significantly. On June 21, Societe Generale was blocked by French banking authorities when it

tried to once again up its bid for Paribas. Banque de France Governor Jean-Claude Trichet ordered the three banks to reach some sort of compromise.

In July, Paribas' board of directors turned down the BNP offer, finding it inadequate. However, in August, BNP won the six-month proxy battle for Paribas when it secured 65.2% of the voting shares of Paribas. BNP was also turned down by Societe Generale's board of directors, yet the bank managed to acquire a sizable chunk of Societe Generale's shares. Although BNP was shy of getting the one-third of voting shares it needed to gain control of Societe Generale, management remained undaunted. The 31.8% share it had secured would likely be adequate in the long run. According to an August 1999 article in *American Banker*, "Under French law, an investor with one-third of voting shares can block any major resolution. BNP, they say, can easily reach that threshold by buying SocGen shares in the open market."

A decree by French authorities, however, undermined that plan. Although France's government support the three-way union, Societe Generale CEO Daniel Bouton refused to consider a deal with BNP, pointing to the fact that his shareholders had rejected the offer. After several attempts to convince Societe Generale to take part in the three-way merger, Trichet finally relented. "With the eyes of France's European Union partners on him, Trichet caved in rather than be accused of subverting market forces," wrote *Business Week* in September 1999. On August 28, he ordered BNP to divest its 31.8% stake in Societe Generale.

Products and Services

Banque Nationale de Paris operated roughly 2,000 retail units in France in 1999. Domestic sales accounted for 40% of total revenues. International banking operations, which spanned 76 countries, secured nearly 50% of sales. Besides traditional financial services, the bank offered factoring, equipment leasing, real estate rentals, and insurance services.

Paribas offered international investment banking services to businesses in 60 different countries. The banking holding company also offered real estate, insurance, and consumer and business financing.

Review of the Outcome

Although BNP secured control of Paribas, the assets its had really wanted, those of Societe Generale, remained independent. Most analysts believed that both BNP and Societe Generale would continue to pursue merger deals that would position them as leaders among the world's largest banks.

Research

"Big French Bank Mergers are Delayed," in *United Press International*, 22 June 1999. Explains the negotiations among Societe Generale, Paribas, and Banque Nationale de Paris.

Banque Nationale de Paris Home Page, available at http://www.bnp.fr. Official World Wide Web Page for Banque Nationale de Paris. Available in both French and English, this Web site houses news releases, branch locations, banking services, and financial and investor information.

"Banque Nationale de Paris," in *Notable Corporate Chronologies*, The Gale Group, 1999. Offers a summary of events in the history of Banque Nationale de Paris.

"BNP's Boss: The Man Who May Be King," in *Business Week*, 5 July 1999. Details the career of Michel Pebereau.

"Commentary: A Defeat for BNP, a Victory for Banking Reform," in *Business Week*, 13 September 1999. Explains why French authorities forced BNP to divest its shares of Societe Generale.

"Compagnie Financiere de Paribas," in *Notable Corporate Chronologies*, The Gale Group, 1999. Offers a summary of events in the history of Paribas.

"France's Societe Generale and Paribas to Merge," in *Xinhua News Agency*, 1 February 1999. Describes the merger agreement between Paribas and Societe Generale.

Kamm, Thomas. "Paribas Says No to Offer from BNP," in *The Wall Street Journal Europe*, 12 July 1999. Covers the rejection of BNP's offer by the board of directors of Paribas.

Kraus, James R. "BNP Sweeps Majority of Paribas, Comes Close to Controlling SocGen," in *American Banker*, 17 August 1999. Details the outcome of the proxy battle for control of both Paribas and Societe Generale.

"Paribas CEO Quits in Wake of BNP Hostile Bid's Success," in *American Banker*, 26 August 1999. Covers the career of Paribas CEO Andre Levy-Lang.

"Yes, But Who Won," in *The Economist*, 21 August 1999. Speculates on the outcome of BNP's purchase of Paribas.

ANNAMARIE L. SHELDON

BAT INDUSTRIES & FARMERS GROUP

Zurich Financial Services
Mythenquai 2
Zurich, 8022
Switzerland

tel: 41-1-205-2121
fax: 41-1-205-3618
web: http://www.zurich.com

nationality: Switzerland
date: December 1988
affected: BAT Industries PLC, United Kingdom, founded 1902
affected: Farmers Group, Inc., USA, founded 1928

Overview of the Merger

The $5.2 billion takeover of Farmers Group, the third-largest automobile and home insurer in North America (based on annual sales of $5.4 billion), by Britain's BAT Industries, the largest tobacco multinational operation in the world, marked the sixth-largest cross-border deal of the 1980s. The success of BAT's hostile bid in the highly regulated and conservative U.S. insurance industry came as a shock to many industry analysts who questioned how the British firm would perform in the cutthroat $190 billion U.S. property/casualty insurance market. The deal was the largest takeover to date in the U.S. insurance industry.

In 1998, the firm merged its financial services operations, including the Farmers Insurance unit, with Zurich Insurance Co. to form Zurich Financial Services, the third-largest insurance company in Europe.

History of BAT Industries PLC

In 1901, several small independent British tobacco companies banded together to form the Imperial Tobacco Company Ltd. when James (Duke) Buchanan of the American Tobacco Co. made a bid for the U.K. market. After a prolonged trade war that proved expensive for both Imperial and American Tobacco, a truce was called and the two rival merchants agreed to not conduct business in each other's domestic markets. This deal also initiated the creation of a jointly owned company, British American Tobacco PLC (BAT), to handle the export trade and overseas manufacturing interests of both originating companies.

With Duke as chairman, BAT had its greatest success in China with a massive billboard campaign in 1907, followed two years later by the distribution of millions of free samples. In 1911, the U.S. Supreme Court ruled that American Tobacco was a monopoly and ordered it to disband. As a result, American Tobacco canceled most of its covenants with BAT and Imperial, and sold all of its shares in the company. With most of its interests sold to British investors, BAT then listed on the London Stock Exchange.

During World War I, BAT began distributing cigarettes in increasing numbers to troops abroad, as many had switched to cigarettes from the less convenient pipe. Duke retired in 1923 and was succeeded by Sir Hugo Cunliffe-Owen as chairman. He quickly restructured BAT China Ltd. into independent regional units and lobbied the Chinese government to minimize the taxation of tobacco. By then, BAT's world sales had grown to 50 billion cigarettes per year. The company entered the U.S. market, previously monopolized by American Tobacco, with the 1927 purchase of Brown and Williamson, a small tobacco producer in North Carolina.

Sir Hugo stepped down in 1945 after successfully weathering the storm of communist revolution in China, during which time all of BAT China Ltd.'s assets had been nationalized. In the early 1960s, BAT acquired a minority interest in two companies: Mardon Packaging International, a maker of cigarette packaging, and Wiggins Teape Ltd., a large specialty paper manufacturer. In 1972, the treaty of Rome brought the U.K. into the EEC, and with it, an end to the agreement between BAT and Imperial Tobacco. The companies exchanged brands once again, each retaining full ownership of its original brands in the U.K. and western Europe only.

With the public's growing concern over smoking in the mid-1970s, BAT began acquiring non-tobacco businesses, changed its name to BAT Industries, and became a holding company for several smaller operating companies. Establishing itself as the world leader in the manufacture of carbonless paper, BAT acquired Appleton Papers in 1978. Other purchases included Pegulan, a home-improvement company in West Germany; two fruit juice companies in Brazil; and pulp producers in Portugal and Brazil. By the decades's end, BAT had entered the department store chain industry with the purchases of West Germany's Horten Stores; Kohl's and Department Stores International in the U.K.; the British catalog store Argos; and Gimbels and Saks Fifth Avenue in the U.S.

Imperial sold its remaining BAT shares in 1980. Two years later, BAT made a friendly bid for the Marshall Field department store chain. The firm diversified into insurance with its 1984 purchase of Eagle Star, based in Britain. Meanwhile, it sold British American Cosmetics, International Stores, Kohl's Food Stores, and Mardon Packaging. In 1985, BAT acquired Britain's Hambro Life Assurance, which later became Allied Dunbar. The following year, Gimbels, Kohl's, Batus, and Pegulan were put up for sale. At that time only 50% of pre-tax profit came from tobacco operations. In 1988, BAT won its $5.2 billion bid for Farmers Group, a U.S. insurance firm.

The Business

Financials

Revenue (1998): $39.1 billion

Employees (1998): 68,876

SICs / NAICS

sic 2111 - Cigarettes

sic 2121 - Cigars

sic 6311 - Life Insurance

sic 6351 - Surety Insurance

sic 6331 - Fire, Marine & Casualty Insurance

sic 6733 - Trusts Nec

naics 312221 - Cigarette Manufacturing

naics 312229 - Other Tobacco Product Manufacturing

naics 524113 - Direct Life Insurance Carriers

naics 524126 - Direct Property and Casualty Insurance Carriers

Responding to a hostile takeover bid by Hoylake Investments, BAT restructured in 1989. It spun off its British retailers and sold its paper operations, retaining only tobacco and financial services. In 1991, BAT gained control of Pecs, Hungary's largest cigarette maker, and signed a letter of intent to negotiate a joint venture in the Ukraine. Three years later, BAT agreed to acquire the U.S. tobacco business of American Brands, Inc. for $1 billion.

Mounting anti-tobacco pressure and slow growth in the insurance industry in the late 1990s prompted BAT to restructure. In 1998, the firm refocused on its tobacco operations by merging its financial services operations, including the Farmers Insurance unit, with Zurich Insurance Co. to form Zurich Financial Services, the third-largest insurance company in Europe. Two holding companies were formed to oversee Zurich Financial. Zurich Group shareholders owned 57% of the new firm through Zurich Allied AG; BAT shareholders owned 43% through Allied Zurich PLC.

History of Farmers Group, Inc.

Farmers Group was founded in 1928 as an automobile insurance firm called Farmers Insurance Exchange. As the automobile industry grew, so did demand for additional insurance coverage.

The Officers

Chairman and CEO: Rolf Huppi

Vice Chairman: Earl Cairns

Chief Operating Officer: David Allvey

Chief Financial Officer: Gunther Gose

CEO, Zurich U.S.: Constantine Iordano

Eventually, the Fire Insurance Exchange and Truck Insurance Exchange were founded to service home and commercial insurance needs. In 1988, Farmers was acquired by tobacco giant BAT Industries, which eventually merged its insurance and financial holdings with Zurich Insurance Co. to form Zurich Financial Services. In 1998, Farmers was the third-largest writer of both private passenger automobile and homeowners insurance in the U.S.

Market Forces Driving the Merger

British tobacco giant BAT Industries entered the insurance industry in 1984 when the firm acted as a white knight to save Eagle Star, an insurer based in the United Kingdom, from a hostile takeover effort by the German insurance behemoth Allianz. After hearing that Eagle Star had rejected the first bid of Allianz as too low, BAT chairman Patrick Sheehy made a friendly offer to Eagle Star chairman Sir Denis Mountain. The amount of the offer was nearly identical to that offered by Allianz, but Mountain accepted BAT's bid on the grounds that the two firms were more compatible. Within three years of the acquisition, BAT was realizing substantial benefits from its diversification. Net income for the first half of 1987 grew 26%, and BAT attributed half of this gain to its Eagle Star operations. The firm had also added to its Eagle unit Hambro Life Assurance, based in Britain, in 1985. This purchase increased Eagle's contribution to BAT's total annual profits from 11% in 1985 to 19% in 1986.

BAT wanted to continue to lessen its dependence on tobacco in the late 1980s, and the success of its Eagle financial services and insurance unit compelled the firm to pursue additional insurance acquisitions. Farmers Group, the ninth-largest property/casualty insurer in the U.S., was attractive to BAT because it would offer the firm coveted access to the lucrative U.S. market. According to an August 1988 article in *The Financial Times*, Farmers was also less vulnerable to the cyclical nature of the U.S. market due to its unusual structure. "As the fee-remunerated manager of three mutual insurance exchanges, Farmers itself

carries no underwriting risk, while the low expenses it enjoys by using a direct sales force of 14,000 agents had traditionally made it highly competitive on price. A further indication of the advantages it enjoys is that while conventional US property/casualty insurers are expecting a substantially higher tax bill in 1989 as a result of the U.S. Tax Reform Act, the corporate tax rate of Farmers is actually falling."

Approach and Engagement

During the summer of 1988, BAT launched its hostile takeover bid for Farmers Group. The U.S. insurer sought the help of state legislators in California, including Senator Alan Cranston, in turning away the British suitor. After Farmers turned down a $63 per share bid, BAT upped the offer to $72 per share, or $5.2 billion, and gave Farmers until August 19th to make a decision. Shareholders jumped at the lucrative offer, and BAT and Farmers signed a definitive agreement for their merger in late August. CEO Leo Denlea agreed to remain at the helm of the Farmers, which would be folded into BAT's Eagle Star financial services and insurance unit. After the deal cleared the last of its regulatory hurdles, it was finalized in December of 1988.

Products and Services

By the late 1990s, BAT had merged its insurance and financial services assets with those of Zurich Insurance Co. to form Zurich Financial Services. Premiums accounted for 68% of sales at the new firm; investment income brought in 17%; and management fee income secured 5%.

Along with the Farmers Group property/casualty and life insurance operations, Zurich Financial operated the following U.S. subsidiaries: non-life insurers Colonial American Casualty, Empire Fire and Marine, and Zurich American Group, as well as asset manager Scudder Kemper Investments, Inc. U.K. units included life insurer and asset manager Allied Dunbar, life and non-life insurer Eagle Star, non-life insurer General Surety & Guarantee, and Threadneedle Asset Management. Operations in Italy included non-life insurer Erbasei SpA, life insurer Minerva Vita, reinsurer SIAR, and asset manager Zeta Finanza.

Zurich also operated retail financial service provider Canada Trust; non-life and life insurer Caudal, in Spain; reinsurance holding company Centre Holdings, in Ireland; non-life insurer Metropole, in Portugal; non-life insurer Zurich Biztosito Rt., in Hungary; life and non-life insurer Zurich Handlowy, in Poland; non-life insurer Zurich Insurance Co., in Russia; non-life insurer Zurich

Kosmos, in Austria; non-life insurer Zurich Pojistovna, in the Czech Republic; non-life insurer Zurich Protector Forsikring AS, in Norway; life insurer Zurich Vie, in Belgium; reinsurance holding company Zurich-Agrippina Beteiligungs-AG, in Germany; and non-life insurer Zuritel, in France.

Review of the Outcome

To stave off a $21 billion hostile takeover bid from Hoylake Investments that emerged soon after the purchase of Farmers was complete, BAT announced a major restructuring designed to boost its stock performance. The firm launched plans to divest its retail and paper operations and refocus on tobacco and insurance. In 1990, Marshall Field was sold to Dayton Hudson for $1 billion, and Saks was sold to Investcorp for $1.5 billion.

Analysts pointed out that California regulators had helped BAT scuttle the takeover bid by speaking out against yet another shift in the control of Farmers Group. Surprised by BAT's successful bid for Farmers, many U.S. insurance authorities increased their vigilance of foreign takeovers.

Part of the bid by Hoylake had involved a $4.5 billion offer for Farmers Group by France's AXA-Midi. According to an October 1990 article in *Financial Times*, AXA-Midi was "lucky to escape from what would, after the current slump in market conditions, have proved a costly or even disastrous decision."

The stagnation of the insurance industry, coupled with increasing anti-tobacco sentiment, prompted BAT's decision in 1998 to refocus solely on tobacco operations. As a result, the firm merged its financial services and insurance operations—including the Farmers assets—with Zurich Insurance Co. to form Zurich Financial Services.

Research

"BAT Industries PLC," in *Notable Corporate Chronologies*, The Gale Group, 1999. Offers a history of BAT Industries PLC.

Bunker, Nick. "An Unslaked Thirst for Acquisition," in *Business Week*, 26 August 1988. Explains why BAT Industries pursued the takeover of Farmers Group, a U.S. insurance company.

——. "BAT Clears the Last Fence on Farmers," in *Business Week*, 13 December 1988. Announces the completion of the merger of BAT and Farmers Group.

The Players

Chairman and CEO of BAT Industries PLC: Patrick Sheehy. Long-time BAT Industries employee Patrick Sheehy played an integral role in the firm's diversification into the department store market in the 1970s. In 1982, he was appointed chairman. While at the helm of BAT, Sheehy decided to add a fourth component to his company's tobacco, department store, and paper operations. BAT acted as a white knight in 1984, saving British insurer Eagle Star from a hostile bid by Germany's Allianz AG. Sheehy then orchestrated BAT's takeover of U.S.-based Farmers Group in 1988, one of the largest cross-border deals of the decade.

Chairman and CEO of Farmers Group, Inc.: Leo E. Denlea, Jr. Leo Denlea was head of Farmers Group in 1988 when BAT Industries launched its takeover effort. After the deal was completed, Denlea continued to run Farmers, remaining CEO until March of 1997 and chairman until February 1998. At that point he was succeeded by Martin D. Feinstein.

Farmers Group, Inc. Home Page, available at http://www.farmersinsurance.com. Official World Wide Web Page for Farmers Group, Inc. Includes product, historical, and employment information, as well as annual reports.

Graham, George. "End of the Takeover Trail," in *Financial Times*, 22 October 1990. Discusses the attempt by Hoylake Investments to take over BAT Industries, which included efforts by AXA-Midi to acquire Farmers Group.

Melcher, Richard A. "Take That Jimmy Goldsmith," in *Business Week*, 9 October 1989. Details how BAT was able to stave off the hostile takeover bid of Hoylake Investments, led by Sir James Goldsmith, by refocusing on tobacco and insurance and by divesting paper and retailing operations.

"A Sweeter Offer for Farmers Group," in *Business Week*, 22 August 1988. Outlines the increased offer by BAT for Farmers Group, as well as the regulatory process.

Zurich Financial Services Home Page, available at http://www.zurich.com. Official World Wide Web Page for Zurich Financial Services. Includes product and corporate information, news, and annual reports.

JEFF ST. THOMAS

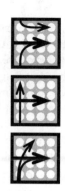

BAXTER TRAVENOL &
AMERICAN HOSPITAL SUPPLY

Baxter Internatonal Inc.
One Baxter Pkwy.
Deerfield, IL 60015
USA

tel: (847)948-2000
fax: (847)948-3948
web: http://www.baxter.com

Allegiance Corp.
1430 Waukegan Rd.
McGaw Park, IL 60085
USA

tel: (847)689-8410
fax: (847)578-4437
web: http://www.allegiance.net

nationality: USA
date: June 1985
affected: Baxter Internatonal Inc., USA, founded 1931
affected: Allegiance Corp., USA, founded 1922

Overview of the Merger

Baxter Travenol's takeover of American Hospital Supply Corp. (AHS) for roughly $5 billion in June of 1985 created the world's largest hospital supply company with more than 120,000 products. Within three years of the merger, Baxter held roughly 25% of the U.S. hospital supply market. Eleven years later, Baxter (by then called Baxter International) spun off most of its AHS holdings as Allegiance Corp.

History of Baxter International Inc.

In 1931, the Don Baxter Intravenous Products Corp. was founded. The company began distributing intravenous solutions commercially to hospitals in the midwestern U.S. A year later, American Hospital Supply became the sole distributer of Baxter's IV solutions. Baxter expanded into Canada by establishing Baxter Laboratories of Canada, Ltd. in 1937. Two years later, Baxter diversified into blood collection with its development of the first sterile, vacuum type blood collection and storage unit, the Transfuso-Vac container, which extended blood storage life from a few hours to 21 days. In 1941, the firm introduced the Plasma-Vac container, the first product to allow for the separation of plasma from whole blood and for plasma storage for later use. By the end of the decade, Baxter had established a pharmaceutical specialities division, Travenol Laboratories, to develop and market chemical compounds and medical equipment.

Hyland Laboratories, the first U.S. company to make human plasma commercially available, was acquired in the early 1950s. Baxter expanded overseas for the first time by founding Baxter Laboratories of Belgium to better serve European customers. In 1956, Baxter launched the first commercially built artificial kidney. Five years later, the firm listed on the New York Stock Exchange for the first time. When American Hospital Supply acquired a competing IV solutions company in 1962, Baxter terminated its 30-year distribution contract with the firm.

In 1970, the U.S. Food and Drug Administration approved the Viaflex plastic container, a product which allowed healthcare professionals to administer Baxter's IV solutions without exposure to outside contaminants. Four years later, Baxter introduced the mini-bag plastic container, which used pre-mixed medicated doses to give pharmacists more control over IV therapy procedures. Baxter changed its name to Baxter Travenol in 1976 to better reflect the scope of its products. In the late 1970s, sales exceeded $1 billion for the first time, and Baxter had achieved a record 24 years of uninterrupted growth in earnings per share.

The company launched its continuous ambulatory peritoneal dialysis machine in 1979. The following year, Baxter introduced the CS-3000 blood separator. Genentech, Inc. and Baxter agreed in 1983 to jointly to develop, manufacture, and market human diagnostics products. In 1985, Baxter acquired American Hospital Supply Corp., creating the largest and most diversified health care products company in the world.

Two years after the American Hospital acquisition, Baxter bought Caremark, Inc., the largest home health care company in the U.S., to gain access to of the fastest growing component of the health care industry. To project a more unified image, Baxter Travenol changed its name to Baxter International Inc in 1988. In 1989, Clintec Nutrition (purchased by Baxter in 1986) was reorganized as a 50/50 joint venture with Nestle S.A. of Switzerland to develop, market, and distribute clinical nutrition products worldwide. The following year, Baxter launched InterLink Access System, the first needle free system for IV therapy procedures. Although annual sales eclipsed $8 billion for the first time, net income plummeted to $40 million, prompting Baxter to launch a major restructuring.

The firm continued to struggle during the early 1990s. Amidst shareholders calling for his ousting, CEO Loucks ordered another restructuring and urged his top managers to buy twice their annual salary worth of stock. Baxter spun off Caremark, retaining the unit's lucrative dialysis machine division, in 1992. The firm then divested its medical diagnostics business in 1994. A U.S. district judge approved a $4.2 billion class action settlement, the largest ever, which concluded the majority of litigation between women and several manufacturers of breast implants, including Baxter. The company also purchased Intramed Laboratories, Inc., an endoscopes maker. Baxter and Rhone-Poulenc Rorer attempted unsuccessfully to negotiate a joint settlement of up to $160 million with hemophiliacs who contracted AIDS from the companies' blood-clotting medications.

The firm's legal battles mounted in 1995 when

The Business

Financials - Baxter Internatonal Inc.

Revenue (1998): $6.59 billion

Employees (1998): 42,000

Financials - Allegiance Corp.

Revenue (1998): $4.57 billion

Employees (1998): 25,000

SICs / NAICS

sic 3841 - Surgical & Medical Instruments

sic 3842 - Surgical Appliances & Supplies

sic 5047 - Medical & Hospital Equipment

naics 339113 - Surgical Appliance and Supplies Manufacturing

naics 339112 - Surgical and Medical Instrument Manufacturing

nearly 50 federal lawsuits and several suits in state courts were filed against Baxter for cases of hepatitis C allegedly contracted through the treatment of immunodeficiency with Gammagard. In an effort to boost its share price, the company launched a two-year $500 million repurchase of its shares. Late in the year, breast implant litigation was reopened because initial claims exceeded the settlement amount by about $3 billion. Baxter, Bristol-Myers Squibb Co., and Minnesota Mining and Manufacturing Co. agreed to offer an increased settlement to better cover the claims. The firm then diversified into cardiovascular perfusion services via its 1995 purchases of PSICOR and SETA.

In 1996, Baxter split itself into two companies: Baxter International Inc. consisted of high growth medical technology and international businesses; and a spin-off healthcare cost management company, named Allegiance, comprised Baxter's cost management and U.S. distribution and surgical products operations. In 1997, the company paid $236 million for Research Medical Inc. to strengthen its position in the open heart surgery devices market and $161 million for Austrian blood plasma maker Immuno International AG to shore up its position in Europe. Baxter acquired the blood therapy unit of Switzerland's Bieffe Medital in 1998, as well as biotechnology company Somatogen and anesthesia drug maker BOC Group PLC.

The Officers

Baxter Internatonal Inc.

Chairman: Vernon R. Loucks, Jr.

President and Chief Executive Officer: Harry M. Janser
Kraemer, Jr.

Sr. VP and Chief Financial Officer: Brian P. Anderson

Sr. VP, Portfolio Strategy: Arthur F. Staubitz

Sr. VP, Human Resources: Michael J. Tucker

Allegiance Corp.

Chairman and Chief Executive Officer: Lester B. Knight

President and Chief Operating Officer: Joseph F. Damico

Sr. VP and Chief Financial Officer: Peter B. McKee

Sr. VP and Chief Information Officer: Kathy Brittain White

Sr. VP, Secretary, and General Counsel: William L. Feather

History of Allegiance Corp.

Foster McGaw, a hospital supply salesman, established American Hospital Supply Corp. (AHS) in Chicago, Illinois, in 1922. Ten years later, the firm secured its first distribution contract with Don Baxter Intravenous Products Corp. AHS achieved profitability for the first time in 1940; the Baxter contract brought in half of total revenues that year. The advent of World War II prompted a surge in the demand for hospital supplies; as a result, AHS opened two regional distribution units in 1944.

AHS established manufacturing operations in the late 1940s. In 1954, the firm purchased V. Mueller, a surgical instrument manufacturer. AHS founded American Dade to manufacture diagnostic tests and laboratory equipment in 1956 and American Convertors to make disposable surgical drapes and gowns in 1961. The following year, AHS and Baxter terminated their 30-year distribution agreement after AHS purchased a competing intravenous solutions operation.

In 1981, AHS purchased disposable oxygenators manufacturer Bentley Laboratories. When Medicare reform prompted caps on hospital procedure and treatment costs, AHS launched a plan to diversify outside of hospital supplies to health care services. When its efforts to merge with Tennessee-based hospital operator Hospital Corporation of America crumbled, AHS agreed to be purchased by Baxter in 1985. Integration of the two firms proved problematic, and Baxter spun its AHS holdings off eleven years later,

minus the lucrative AHS cardiovascular equipment unit, as Allegiance Corp. Allegiance continued to distribute Baxter's intravenous solutions throughout the U.S., while Baxter promoted Allegiance's products abroad.

Toronto-based MDS Inc. and Allegiance merged their Canadian businesses in 1997 to form the largest supplier of health care products in Canada. With only seven percent of sales coming from outside the U.S., Allegiance also launched an international expansion that included purchasing Netherlands-based SOHO Holding B.V., a surgical kit manufacturer, and establishing units in Belgium, Italy, Spain, and Switzerland. A year later, Allegiance bought surgical services consultant Higman Healthcare; inked an agreement to supply the national healthcare network of Kaiser Permanente; and agreed to purchase International Medical Products Group, a surgical supplies manufacturer based in Holland. Cardinal Health bought Allegiance in 1999.

Market Forces Driving the Merger

After Medicare legislation passed in the early 1980s limited hospital treatment costs, American Hospital Supply (AHS) began looking to expand from health care supplies to health care services. As a result, Hospital Corporation of America, a hospital operator based in Tennessee, made a bid for AHS in June of 1985. Although the deal offered little in the way of cost cutting potential, merging the two firms would allow for the vertical integration of customer and supplier, giving AHS access to the heath care services market.

Baxter Travenol was also interested in AHS. Because both Baxter and AHS operated in the hospital supply and medical equipment sectors, a merger would offer cost saving opportunities, as well as a chance to boost market share in an increasingly competitive market. Baxter needed the stronger domestic distribution operations AHS possessed; at the same time, Baxter's international presence would boost the reach of AHS. And the core products of both firms—AHS's medical products and Baxter's blood, renal, and intravenous therapy offerings—were complementary.

Approach and Engagement

To accomplish its goal of merging with AHS, Baxter had to subvert the $3.6 billion merger agreement between AHS and Hospital Corp. Because the deal included defensive tactics, such as reciprocal stock options, a hostile takeover would cost Baxter more than it was willing to spend. Baxter needed to convince shareholders to vote against the Hospital Corp. deal and in favor of a merger with Baxter.

Fortunately for Baxter, the AHS/Hospital Corp. deal did have weaknesses. Several institutional investors of AHS were unhappy with the idea of a takeover by Hospital Corp. because cost savings would be minimal. And many AHS customers who competed directly with Hospital Corp. had threatened to pull their accounts from AHS once the company merged with Hospital Corp. Share prices for both AHS and Hospital Corp. had dropped following the merger's announcement.

Recognizing that AHS investors might be looking for a better option than a takeover by Hospital Corp., Baxter launched a "bear-hug" of AHS, offering $50 per share, substantially more than Hospital Corp.'s original $36.50 per share offer. The cost savings potential of the merger allowed Baxter to outbid Hospital Corp. In a letter, Baxter had explained to AHS shareholders that it was not willing to launch a hostile takeover. Therefore, it needed to bid high enough to thwart a counter offer from Hospital Corp. The tactic worked; Baxter eventually paid $51 per share for AHS, as well as a breakup fee to Hospital Corp.

Products and Services

After the 1996 spin off of its AHS holdings as Allegiance Corp., Baxter reorganized in 1997 into four product groups: IV Systems and Medical Products, which earned 34% of total sales and included infusion pumped, needle-free IV therapy products, IV containers, and surgical glue; Blood Therapies, which brought in 29% of revenues and included automated platelet collection products, manual blood collection systems, a plasma-based immune system booster, and an anti-hemophilic factor; Renal Products, which secured 23% of sales and included a peritonal dialysis solution, an automated dialysis machine, and infusion and drainage systems; and Cardiovascular Products, which accounted for the remaining 14% of revenues and included a heart valve, a vascular surgery catheter, an oxygenator, and a heart pressure catheter. Of Baxter's $6.1 billion in 1997 revenues, roughly 50% were international. In 1998, Baxter halted testing of its highly anticipated blood substitute due to problems with the product. The firm added a heart-assist device to its cardiovascular line that year after the FDA granted approval for its use by patients waiting for a heart transplant.

In 1997, Allegiance was the largest supplier of medical products in the U.S. with more than 300,000 medical, surgical and laboratory product offerings. Respiratory products included oxygen masks, suction catheters, and ventilator circuits. Surgical products ranged from drapes, gloves, and gowns, to sterile surgical procedure kits and stainless steel surgical instru-

The Players

Chairman and CEO of Baxter International Inc.: Vernon R. Loucks, Jr. Marine Corps veteran and Harvard graduate Vernon Loucks worked as a senior management consultant for George Fry and Associates in the early 1960s. In 1966, he was hired by Baxter as an assistant to the president and CEO. After working as a senior manager in both U.S. and international units of the firm, Loucks was elected to Baxter's board of directors in 1975. A year later, he accepted the posts of president and chief operating officer. Loucks took over as CEO in 1980 and chairman in 1987, titles he continues to hold today.

Chairman and CEO of American Hospital Supply Corp.: Karl Bays. When American Hospital Supply (AHS) founder Foster McGaw retired in 1970, salesman Karl Bays took over as CEO. Bays attempted to broaden his firm's scope to include health care services, but when his efforts to merge with Hospital Corp. of America fell through, AHS was acquired by Baxter in 1985; Bays eventually stepped down.

ments. The firm also offered cost management consulting services. Because international sales only accounted for seven percent of total revenue, Allegiance launched an international acquisition spree that year.

Changes to the Industry and Review of the Outcome

Baxter's acquisition of American Hospital Supply (AHS) immediately increased sales by over $3 billion to $5.54 billion. In 1988, Baxter had secured 25% of the U.S. hospital supply market. By 1990, sales surpassed $8 billion for the first time; a year later, net income reached an all-time high of $591 million. Yet assimilation of the two firms proved difficult. According to Bruce Wasserstein, author of *Big Deal: The Battle for Control of America's Leading Corporations*, "Baxter faced a difficult task bringing its two hospital supply divisions together into an efficient whole. Integration problems proved to be a costly distraction."

Ten years after the merger, mainly to raise capital and narrow its focus, Baxter decided to spin off its $4.6 billion AHS hospital supply holdings, minus cardiovascular equipment, as Allegiance Corp. The distribution business had struggled almost continuously while owned by Baxter, and Wall Street analysts had been calling for the split for years. Immediately following the spin-off, Baxter shares tumbled a bit to roughly $45, where they hovered for months. Allegiance stock, on the other hand, jumped 50% to roughly $25 per share during the same time period. According to Allegiance CEO Lester Knight, "Within Baxter, we were constantly competing for resources. Most of the resources went toward the high-tech side, whose returns and rapid growth really pushed our economic decision making." Allegiance's surprising performance was attributed to three major strategies: refocusing on distributing of its own medical products, offering cost management consulting services, and cutting distribution costs by 20%.

Research

Allegiance Corp. Home Page, available at http://www.allegiance.net. Official World Wide Web Home Page for Allegiance Corp. Includes news, financial, product, and historical information.

"Baxter International Inc.," in *Notable Corporate Chronologies*, The Gale Group, 1999. Lists major events in the history of Baxter International, including its takeover of American Hospital Supply and its subsequent spinoff of the AHS operations into Allegiance Corp.

Baxter International Inc. Home Page, available at http://www.baxter.com. Official World Wide Web Home Page for Baxter International Inc. Includes news, financial, product, and historical information.

"Industry Continues to Struggle As Baxter Names Its Distribution Company," in *Health Industry Today*, July 1996. Explains why Baxter decided to undo its 1985 merger with American Hospital Supply.

Lumsdon, Kevin. "Breaking Up Isn't Hard to Do," in *Hospitals & Health Networks*, 5 September 1996. Details Baxter's split into two separate companies: Baxter International and Allegiance Corp.

Oloroso, Arsenio. "About That Spinoff, Vern; Oops: Baxter Stock Lags While Allegiance Flies," in *Crain's Chicago Business*, 20 January 1997. Discusses the performance of both Baxter and Allegiance following the spin off.

Wasserstein, Bruce. *Big Deal: The Battle for Control of America's Leading Corporations*, Warner Books, 1998. Offers an overview of the largest mergers in recent American corporate history.

SAMIT AYERS

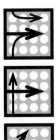

BELL ATLANTIC & GTE

nationality: USA
date: 1999
affected: Bell Atlantic Corp., USA, founded 1984
affected: GTE Corp., USA, founded 1918

Bell Atlantic Corp.
1095 Avenue of the Americas
New York, NY 10036
USA

tel: (212)395-2121
fax: (212)395-1285
web: http://www.bellatlantic.com

GTE Corp.
1255 Corporate Dr.
Irving, TX 75038
USA

tel: (972)507-5000
fax: (972)507-5002
web: http://www.gte.com

Overview of the Merger

The joining of GTE Corp. and Bell Atlantic Corp. will create an industry behemoth with estimated combined annual revenues of $53 billion and a market capitalization of roughly $125 billion. As the second largest phone company in North America—behind AT&T Corp.—the newly merged firm will serve in excess of 60 million access lines and 63 million local phone customers in 38 states. It will also be the largest wireless provider in the U.S., with 10.6 million customers. International reach will grow to 30 countries.

History of Bell Atlantic Corp.

In 1982, the U.S. Department of Justice ended a 13-year antitrust suit against the world's largest corporation, AT&T Corp. Pursuant to a consent decree, AT&T would maintain its manufacturing and research facilities, as well as its long distance operations; however, the firm was required to divest itself of 22 local operating companies, which would be divided among seven regional holding companies. In 1984, Bell Atlantic, one of these companies, opened for business. Bell Atlantic served the northern Atlantic states and owned seven telephone subsidiaries.

Early in its first year of operation as an independent company, Bell Atlantic formed Bell Atlanticom Systems to market traditional cordless and decorator telephones, wiring components, and home security and healthcare systems. The firm also introduced Alex, a cellular telephone service. Later in 1984, Bell Atlantic acquired Texas-based Telecommunications Specialists, Inc. and New Jersey-based Tri-Continental Leasing Corp., a computer and telecommunications equipment provider.

Bell Atlantic continued its rapid expansion with the purchase of MAI's Sorbus Inc., the second-largest U.S. computer service firm, and a related company, MAI Canada Ltd., in 1985. The company also launched the first working system of Integrated Services Digital Network (ISDN) architecture in the nation. Net income reached a record $1 billion that year, and Bell Atlantic decided to target medium-sized customers, offering everything from information services equipment and data processing to computer maintenance.

The Business

Financials - Bell Atlantic Corp.

Revenue (1998): $31.56 billion

Employees (1998): 141,000

Financials - GTE Corp.

Revenue (1998): $25.4 billion

Employees (1998): 120,000

SICs / NAICS

sic 4813 - Telephone Communications Except Radiotelephone

sic 4812 - Radiotelephone Communications

sic 3661 - Telephone & Telegraph Apparatus

sic 2741 - Miscellaneous Publishing

sic 3571 - Electronic Computers

sic 3669 - Communications Equipment Nec

naics 513322 - Cellular and Other Wireless Telecommunications

naics 513321 - Paging

naics 334418 - Printed Circuit Assembly (Electronic Assembly) Manufacturing

naics 334111 - Electronic Computer Manufacturing

In 1986, stock split two-for-one, and Bell Atlantic became the first of the Baby Bells to be listed on Standard & Poor's 100 Stock Index. Acquisitions that year included the real estate assets of Pitcairn Properties, Inc.; Technology Concepts Inc., a firm focused on telecommunications and computer software; and Greyhound Capital Corp., which was later renamed Bell Atlantic Systems Leasing International, Inc. Bell Atlantic and Telefonica de Espana agreed to jointly implement database and software systems for managing telephone facilities in Spain.

Bell Atlantic bought Pacific Computer Corp., Jolynne Service Corp., and National Funding Corp., a medical and commercial leasing firm, in 1987. That year, the firm became the first in the nation to implement Signaling Systems 7 (SS-7), the key to evolving intelligent network technology, with the conversion of two New Jersey Bell central offices. A year later, Bell South and Bell Atlantic were accused of misconduct in bidding attempts to win government contracts. Bell Atlantic also divested MAI Canada Ltd., along with some of the assets of Sorbus, Inc., and purchased the European computer maintenance operations of Bell Canada Enterprises, the assets of CPX Inc., and Dyn Service Network. Bell Atlantic Mobile Systems announced the formation of Bell Atlantic Paging to market pagers and paging service in its region. By the end of the decade, Bell Atlantic had also established a European headquarters in Belgium.

U.S. West and Bell Atlantic agreed in 1990 to help modernize Czechoslovakia's telephone operations. That year, Ameritech and Bell Atlantic acquired Telecom Corp. of New Zealand for $2.5 billion. Bell Atlantic Mobile Systems extended its network in rural-service areas, making Delaware the first state in the nation to offer border-to-border cellular phone service. Bell Atlantic and STET, the Italian phone company, formed a joint venture in Italy in 1991. Bell Atlantic also joined Belle Meade International Telephone, Inc. in a joint venture to set up a communications system in the Soviet Union. The purchase of Metro Mobile gave Bell Atlantic the most extensive cellular phone coverage on the East Coast.

In 1994, Bell Atlantic and three other Baby Bells launched a battle to end the consent decree that prevented them from entering the long-distance markets and manufacturing phones and switches. The following year, a federal judge allowed Bell Atlantic and six other regional Bell companies to offer long-distance services to their cellular customers. The company also founded Bell Atlantic Internet Solutions, a new Virginia-based unit which offered business and residential Internet products and services such as e-mail, Web hosting, and high-speed dedicated access to customers in Washington, Philadelphia, and New Jersey. A $33 billion deal to merge with cable giant Tele-Communications Inc. fell through in 1994 after the FCC lowered cable television subscriber rates.

To strengthen its position in Mexico, Bell Atlantic invested $1 billion in Grupo Iusacell, a Mexican wireless communications company, in 1993; three years later, the company paid $50 million for a controlling stake. Bell Atlantic and NYNEX Corp. established Bell Atlantic NYNEX Mobile, a joint cellular service and paging operation, in 1995. In August of 1997, Bell Atlantic acquired NYNEX in a $25.6 billion deal, one of the largest of the decade. The following year, the company secured conditional approval to offer long distance services in New York and agreed to a $53 billion merger with GTE Corp.

History of GTE Corp.

In 1918, John O'Connell, John A. Pratt, and Sigurd Odegard purchased the Richland Center Telephone Company (RCTC), serving 1,466 rural telephone users in Richland County, Wisconsin, for $33,500. The three men shared the belief that telephone service could be more efficiently provided if local exchanges were managed centrally. Two years later, RCTC was merged into the Commonwealth Telephone Company (CTC), a holding company. CTC immediately purchased three additional local exchanges.

Odegard, in conjunction with two partners, set up Associated Telephone Utilities Company (ATUC) as a holding company. In 1926, ATUC absorbed CTC and launched an aggressive program of expansion in the West by purchasing the Associated Telephone Company of Long Beach, California. By 1929, ATUC managed 340 local exchanges, operating over 500,000 telephones in 25 states. At the time of the stock market crash, the company's revenues had reached nearly $17 million.

In 1930, ATUC established Associated Telephone Investment Company (ATIC) as a wholly owned subsidiary to support the parent company's continued acquisition program. One of the new company's first actions was to purchase large blocks of ATUC stock in an attempt to drive up the value. The campaign failed, and a loan of $1 million was arranged to help defray the company's debt. ATUC also faced financial difficulties, as telephone use fell by 16%, mainly due to the Great Depression. ATUC moved its headquarters from Chicago, Illinois, to New York City. In 1933, ATIC dissolved, and ATUC passed into receivership.

ATUC reorganized as General Telephone Corporation (GTC) in 1935, operating a network created by the consolidation of 12 telephone networks. The following year, GTC formed General Telephone Directory Company (GTDC) to publish directories for the parent company's entire service area. In 1939, GTC began listing on the New York Stock Exchange.

The firm secured huge government contracts during World War II, although the manufacture of telephones for civilian use was banned. War-related research and development projects gave rise to many discoveries with civilian applications, including coaxial cables and transistors. In 1950, GTC expanded into the manufacture of telephone and electrical equipment by purchasing Leich Electric Co. and Leich Sales Corp. By the early 1950s, the firm operated 15 telephone units in 20 states. Acquisitions included San Angelo Telephone Co.; Theodore Gary and Co., the second-largest independent telephone company and maker of telephone equipment in the U.S.; Anglo-Canadian Telephone Company; a majority interest in Compania Dominicana de Telefonos; minority interests in British Columbia Telephone Co. and Philippines Long Distance Telephone Co.; and Peninsular Telephone Company (PTC) of Florida. By

The Officers

Bell Atlantic Corp.

Chairman and CEO: Ivan G. Seidenberg

Co-President and Chief Operating Officer: James G. Cullen

Co-President and Chief Operating Officer: Lawrence T. Babbio, Jr.

Chief Financial Officer and Sr. Exec. VP, Strategy and Business: Frederic V. Salerno

Exec. VP, Strategy and Corporate Development: Alexander Good

GTE Corp.

Chairman and CEO: Charles R. Lee

Vice Chairman: Michael T. Masin

President: Kent B. Foster

Sr. Exec. VP, Market Operations: Thomas W. White

Exec. VP, Finance, and Chief Financial Officer: Daniel P. O'Brien

the end of the decade, GTC operated more than 3.3 million telephones.

In 1959, the firm merged with Sylvania Electric Products to form General Telephone & Electronics Corporation (GT&E), while retaining the Sylvania brand name. The merger added 45 electronics manufacturing plants and annual sales of $333 million to the parent company's telephone service network. A majority interest in Lenkurt Electric Co. was also acquired that year. In 1960, GT&E bought a majority interest in British Columbia Telephone Co. GT&E Laboratories was formed to conduct research and development activities. Company stock split 3-for-1.

Sylvania began full-scale production of color television picture tubes in 1963, and acquired contracts to supply electronic switching equipment to the U.S. Defense Department's global communications system. In 1967, GT&E acquired Hawaiian Telephone Co. (HTC). The firm also founded GT&E Data Services Inc. and divested itself of its interest in the Philippine Long Distance Telephone Co. IT&T filed an antitrust suit against GT&E, challenging the company's acquisition of HTC, and eventually attempting to force GT&E to divest itself of all telephone companies acquired since 1950, as well as the electronics manufacturing operations of Sylvania. In response, GT&E countersued IT&T, claiming that IT&T had violated

The Players

Chairman and CEO of Bell Atlantic Corp.: Ivan Seidenberg. Ivan Seidenberg began his career in the telecommunications industry in the 1960s. Before taking over as chairman and CEO of NYNEX, he served the firm as vice president of government affairs, president of NYNEX Worldwide Information and Cellular Services Group, and vice chairman. When NYNEX merged with Bell Atlantic in 1997, Seidenberg was slated to eventually take the helm at Bell Atlantic. He was named CEO of Bell Atlantic on June 1, 1998 and chairman on December 31, 1998.

Chairman and CEO of GTE Corp.: Charles R. Lee. Charles Lee launched his career at United States Steel Corp. in 1964. After holding several financial and management posts there, he began working for Penn Central Corp. in 1971, where he worked his way up to the position of senior vice president of finance. He accepted a similar appointment at Columbia Pictures Industries Inc. in 1980, and he left that firm in 1983 to join GTE Corp. At GTE, Lee was named president and chief operating officer in December of 1988. Three year later, was appointed CEO and chairman, roles he officially took on in May of 1992.

antitrust laws in its acquisition of telephone and electronics manufacturing concerns. Both suits were later dropped. The firm purchased Northern Ohio Telephone Co. (NOTC) in 1968.

In the early 1970s, GT&E established GTE Satellite Corp.; moved corporate headquarters to Stamford, Connecticut; bought the Philco brand name; established a joint venture with AT&T to create satellites; and acquired television manufacturers in Israel and Canada, as well as a telephone company in West Germany. The firm reorganized in 1976, creating GTE Products Group to manage manufacturing and marketing operations, including all company activities outside the U.S., and GTE Communications Products to manage the operations of Sylvania Electronics, Lenkurt Electric, Automatic Electric, and GTE Information Systems. In 1979, GT&E bought Telenet Communications Corp., a leader in the field of packet switching technology, a precursor of the electronic bulletin board.

GT&E divested its consumer electronics businesses, including Sylvania and Philco, in 1980. Two years later, the firm changed its name to GTE Corp. and formed GTE Mobilnet Inc. to produce and market cellular phones and related equipment. Following the lead of AT&T, GTE broke down its operations along regional lines. In 1983, GTE acquired the long distance unit of Southern Pacific Communications Co. and Southern Pacific Satellite Co., which were renamed GTE Sprint Communications (Sprint) and GTE Spacenet Corporation (GTESC), respectively. The acquisition of Sprint made GTE the third-largest provider of long-distance telephone services in the U.S.

GTE embarked on a new corporate strategy in the mid-1980s, emphasizing the development of core businesses including telecommunications, lighting, and precision materials. GTESC launched its first satellite, and the company offered its first cellular phone service. In 1985, GTE secured a $4.3 billion contract from the U.S. Army to develop a battlefield communications system called Mobile Subscriber Equipment (MSE). The following year, Sprint and GTE Telenet became part of US Sprint, which was equally owned by GTE and United Telecommunications. GTE purchased Airfone Inc., a domestic manufacturer of aircraft telecommunications systems, and Rotaflex PLC, a British manufacturer of lighting equipment. Stock split 3-for-2 in 1987.

The firm developed the first roaming cellular telephone service, which enabled callers to receive calls from outside their cellular service area, in 1988. That year, GTE sold United Telecommunications a controlling interest in US Sprint, retaining 19.9% of stock in the company. The following year, however, GTE sold its remaining interest in US Sprint to United Telecommunications. The firm then reorganized into six operating groups in an effort to streamline operations. In 1989, GTE introduced the first nationwide cellular phone network.

In 1991, GTE and Contel Corp. merged, forming a corporate giant worth $6.6 billion. One year later, GTE sold its worldwide electrical products operations to OSRAM, owned by Siemens, for $1.1 billion. The firm also launched World Class Network (WCN), which offered bundled services for data transmission. Revenues from cellular services grew 41%, as GTE secured 754,000 new cellular customers. GTE and SBC Communications Inc. agreed to market cellular services in each other's territories.

After the Telecommunications Act of 1996 was passed, GTE began offering long-distance services. In 1997, the firm bought Internet service provider BBN for $625 million and agreed to acquire MCI Communications Corp. for $28 billion. WorldCom Inc. outbid GTE, however, with a $37 billion offer for MCI.

In early 1999, Bell Atlantic and GTE agreed to a $53 billion merger of equals. GTE also agree to pay $3.3 billion for roughly 50% of the wireless assets of Ameritech Corp.

Market Forces Driving the Merger

The Telecommunications Act of 1996 spawned an unprecedented consolidation trend in the telecommunications industry. The bill deregulated the market, allowing phone companies, both regional and long distance, cable, and Internet companies to begin competing in each other's markets. The first major deal following the passage of the bill was the $10.8 billion purchase of Continental Cablevision, Inc., the third largest cable operator in the United States, by regional telephone operator U S West Inc. Roughly a year later, in April of 1997, the second largest phone company in North America was formed when SBC Communications bought Pacific Telesis for $16 billion. Within months of the transaction, that second place status was overthrown by the $25.6 million marriage of Bell Atlantic Corp. and NYNEX Corp.

Recognizing that it needed to grow to stay competitive, GTE offered $28 billion in 1997 for MCI Communications. However, in a move that rocked the telecommunications industry, upstart WorldCom outbid GTE with a $37 billion offer for MCI. That deal, perhaps more than any of the others, reflected the quest of telecommunications industry giants to offer a full range of services to clients, including Internet access and related online services. Formed in early 1997 by the purchase of MFS Communications and UUNET Technologies by LDDS WorldCom, WorldCom was the first telecommunications company to offer local, long distance, and international telephone service, Internet access, and data services on a single international fiber network. This grouping of services, known as bundling, was at the core of the industrywide consolidation.

In an effort to compete with MCI-WorldCom by offering clients increased end-to-end services, including cable television access, AT&T Corp. and cable television giant Tele-Communications Inc. in 1998 agreed to an historic $48 billion merger. It was in this climate that Bell Atlantic and GTE decided to come together. With $21 billion in sales and 20 million access lines in 1997, GTE paled in comparison to the new industry giants. After combining assets with Bell Atlantic, those numbers would jump to $53 billion in annual revenues and 61 million telephone lines spanning 40 states. Management of both firms predicted a cost savings of $2 billion within three years of the deal's completion.

Although the increase in size and cost savings were both major factors in the deal, many analysts also looked favorably on the potential product synergies a merger would bring. According to an August 1998 article in *EDGE, on & about AT&T*, the deal would join "Bell Atlantic's sophisticated network serving its dense, data-intensive customer base with GTE's national footprint, advanced data communications capabilities and long distance experience." And because GTE had already moved into the long distance arena—since it had never enjoyed monopoly status, GTE faced fewer FCC restrictions than the Baby Bells—Bell Atlantic would finally gain entrance to the lucrative market the Baby Bells had yet to enter.

Approach and Engagement

In July of 1998, Bell Atlantic and GTE announced their intent to merge. According to the terms of the agreement, Bell Atlantic CEO Seidenberg and GTE CEO Lee will jointly run the company until 2002, when Seidenberg will step down. Management from both sides decided to structure the deal as a merger of equals in the hopes that GTE will be able to retain its long distance operations. If the $53 billion deal passes numerous regulatory hurdles, GTE shareholders will receive 1.22 shares of Bell Atlantic stock for each GTE share owned.

Products and Services

Local phone service brought in 43% of Bell Atlantic's total revenues in 1998. Network integration accounted for 24%. Wireless services, offered in 25 states via Bell Atlantic Mobile, secured 11%. Print and electronic directory publishing (namely, 600 Yellow Pages directories) earned 8%. Other services, including Internet access, long distance, video, and data, brought in the remaining 14%. International operations spanned 21 countries.

GTE served roughly 21 million local phone customers in 28 states in 1998. The firm also offered long distance services to 1.7 million customers nationwide; wireless phone services via its GTE Wireless unit; and air-to-ground services for airline passengers through its GTE Airfone subsidiary. The BBN unit provided Internet access, hosting, and related online services to clients. GTE Government Systems constructed command, control, and intelligence systems for government agencies. Local services accounted for 19% of total sales; network access, 18%; directory publishing, 11%; and external services, such as wireless services, 49%.

Changes to the Industry and Review of the Outcome

While the impact of the merger on the telecommunications industry itself, as well as the effects on each of the firms remains to be seen, most analysts agree that the combined entity will have the resources to challenge the industry's leading players. According to an October 1998 article in *Business Communication Review*, "A united GTE and Bell Atlantic, with its combination of local, long distance, and data services, should be able to compete more effectively against a WorldCom that already has UUNet Technologies, MFS Communications and MCI, not to mention AT&T, Teleport, and TCI, or Sprint, or the massive entity being pieced together by SBC."

Research

"Bell Atlantic and GTE Agree to Merge," in *EDGE, on & about AT&T*, 3 August 1998. Offers an overview of the planned merger between GTE and Bell Atlantic.

"Bell Atlantic and GTE Outline Their Merger of Equals in Mailing to Shareowners," in *PR Newswire*, 14 April 1999.

Covers the details of the terms of the agreement between Bell Atlantic and GTE.

"Bell Atlantic Corp.," in *Notable Corporate Chronologies*, The Gale Group, 1999. Lists major events in the history of Bell Atlantic Corp.

Bell Atlantic Corp. Home Page, available at http://www.bellatlantic.com. Official World Wide Web Home Page for Bell Atlantic Corp. Includes current and archived news; detailed financial, product, and historical information; and annual reports.

"GTE Corp.," in *Notable Corporate Chronologies*, The Gale Group, 1999. Lists major events in the history of GTE Corp.

GTE Corp. Home Page, available at http://www.gte.com. Official World Wide Web Home Page for GTE Corp. Includes news, as well as financial, product, and historical information.

Jackson, Susan. "Take a Number if You Want to Grab GTE," in *Business Week*, 28 July 1997. Explains why GTE makes an attractive merger partner for major telecommunications firms.

Mulqueen, John. "GTE and the New Industry Realities," in *Business Communications Review*, October 1998. Explains the reasons for the merger between GTE and Bell Atlantic.

ANNAMARIE L. SHELDON

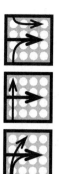

BELL ATLANTIC & NYNEX

nationality: USA
date: August 15, 1997
affected: Bell Atlantic Corp., USA, founded 1984
affected: NYNEX Corp., USA, founded 1984

Bell Atlantic Corp.
1095 Avenue of the Americas
New York, NY 10036
USA

tel: (212)395-2121
fax: (212)395-1285
web: http://www.bellatlantic.com

Overview of the Merger

The $25.6 billion joining of Bell Atlantic and NYNEX in August of 1997 created the largest regional Bell company in the U.S. The second merger of two regional Bell firms following the Telecommunications Act of 1996, the deal created a company that served 39 million phone lines in 13 states and more than four million cellular customers. With $50 billion in assets and $29.2 billion in annual revenues, Bell Atlantic remained second only to AT&T in the North American telephone industry.

History of Bell Atlantic Corp.

In 1982, the U.S. Department of Justice ended a 13-year antitrust suit against the world's largest corporation, AT&T Corp. Pursuant to a consent decree, AT&T would maintain its manufacturing and research facilities, as well as its long distance operations; however, the firm was required to divest itself of 22 local operating companies, which would be divided among seven regional holding companies. In 1984, Bell Atlantic, one of these companies, opened for business. Bell Atlantic served the northern Atlantic states, and owned seven telephone subsidiaries.

Early in its first year of operation as an independent company, Bell Atlantic formed Bell Atlanticom Systems to market traditional cordless and decorator telephones, wiring components, and home-security and healthcare systems. The firm also introduced Alex, a cellular telephone service. Later in 1984, Bell Atlantic acquired Texas-based Telecommunications Specialists, Inc. and New Jersey-based Tri-Continental Leasing Corp., a computer and telecommunications equipment provider.

Bell Atlantic continued its rapid expansion with the purchase of MAI's Sorbus Inc., the second-largest U.S. computer service firm, and a related company, MAI Canada Ltd., in 1985. The company also launched the first working system of Integrated Services Digital Network (ISDN) architecture in the nation. Net income reach a record $1 billion that year, and Bell Atlantic decided to target medium-sized customers, offering everything from information services equipment and data processing to computer maintenance.

The Business

Financials

Revenue (1998): $31.56 billion

Employees (1998): 140,000

SICs / NAICS

sic 4813 - Telephone Communications Except
Radiotelephone

sic 4812 - Radiotelephone Communications

sic 3661 - Telephone & Telegraph Apparatus

naics 513322 - Cellular and Other Wireless
Telecommunications

naics 513321 - Paging

naics 334418 - Printed Circuit Assembly (Electronic
Assembly) Manufacturing

In 1986, stock split two-for-one, and Bell Atlantic became the first of the Baby Bells to be listed on Standard & Poor's 100 Stock Index. Acquisitions that year included the real estate assets of Pitcairn Properties, Inc.; Technology Concepts Inc., a firm focused on telecommunications and computer software; and Greyhound Capital Corp., which was later renamed Bell Atlantic Systems Leasing International, Inc. Bell Atlantic and Telefonica de Espana agreed to jointly implement database and software systems for managing telephone facilities in Spain.

Bell Atlantic bought Pacific Computer Corp., Jolynne Service Corp., and National Funding Corp., a medical and commercial leasing firm, in 1987. The year, the firm became the first in the nation to implement Signaling Systems 7 (SS-7), the key to evolving intelligent network technology, with the conversion of two New Jersey Bell central offices. A year later, Bell South and Bell Atlantic were accused of misconduct in bidding attempts to win government contracts. Bell Atlantic also divested MAI Canada Ltd., along with some of the assets of Sorbus, Inc., and purchased the European computer maintenance operations of Bell Canada Enterprises, the assets of CPX Inc., and Dyn Service Network. Bell Atlantic Mobile Systems announced the formation of Bell Atlantic Paging to market pagers and paging service in its region. By the end of the decade, Bell Atlantic had also established a European headquarters in Belgium.

U.S. West and Bell Atlantic agreed in 1990 to help modernize Czechoslovakia's telephone operations.

That year, Ameritech Corp. and Bell Atlantic acquired Telecom Corp. of New Zealand for $2.5 billion. Bell Atlantic Mobile Systems extended its network in rural-service areas, making Delaware the first state in the nation to offer border-to-border cellular phone service. Bell Atlantic and STET, the Italian phone company, formed a joint venture in Italy in 1991. Bell Atlantic also joined Belle Meade International Telephone, Inc. in a joint venture to set up a communications system in the Soviet Union. The purchase of Metro Mobile gave Bell Atlantic the most extensive cellular phone coverage on the East Coast.

In 1994, Bell Atlantic and three other Baby Bells launched a battle to end the consent decree that prevented them from entering the long-distance markets and manufacturing phones and switches. The following year, a federal judge allowed Bell Atlantic and six other regional Bell companies to offer long-distance services to their cellular customers. The company also founded Bell Atlantic Internet Solutions, a new Virginia-based unit which offered business and residential Internet products and services such as e-mail, Web hosting, and high-speed dedicated access to customers in Washington, Philadelphia, and New Jersey. A $33 billion deal to merge with cable giant Tele-Communications Inc. fell through in 1994.

To strengthen its position in Mexico, Bell Atlantic invested $1 billion in Grupo Iusacell, a Mexican wireless communications company, in 1993; three years later, the company paid $50 million for a controlling stake. Bell Atlantic and NYNEX Corp. established Bell Atlantic NYNEX Mobile, a joint cellular service and paging operation, in 1995. In August of 1997, Bell Atlantic acquired NYNEX in a $25.6 billion deal, one of the largest of the decade. The following year, the company secured conditional approval to offer long distance services in New York and agreed to a $53 billion deal with GTE Corp., which would make Bell Atlantic the largest local phone company in the U.S.

History of NYNEX Corp.

Separation of regional operating companies from AT&T was completed in 1984, and NYNEX Corp. was formed to manage AT&T's former network in New York, Rhode Island, Massachusetts, Vermont, New Hampshire, Maine, and portions of Connecticut. It also shared revenues generated by long-distance calls between northern New Jersey and New York City with Bell Atlantic, another AT&T spin-off. A year later, the firm's subsidiary, NYNEX Business Information Systems, signed a three-year contract to market Wang computers and information processing products in the Northeast, and joined with NEC Corp. to market an information management service.

NYNEX then established the NYNEX Credit Co. to provide financial services to its subsidiary operations. The company also entered into a technology exchange agreement with Nippon Telephone and Telegraph and formed a joint venture with Citicorp and RCA Corp. to create a videotex company. Despite spending $1.9 billion to upgrade its equipment, NYNEX was criticized for modernizing more slowly than the other Baby Bells.

In 1986, the firm began making non-phone acquisitions, including LIN Broadcasting Corp.'s New York City radio paging operations and IBM's chain of 80 computer stores in 33 states; NYNEX Business Centers Co. was established to operate the retail computer outlets. NYNEX entered the international long distance market that year by forming a $400 million joint venture to lay a transatlantic fiber optic cable. The company began selling its white pages phone listings on computer disc in 1987. That year, the firm also purchased business Intelligence Services, Ltd., a London, England-based banking software, consulting, and financial services firm with branches in 13 countries, and secured a three-year, $400 million contract with Northern Telecom to provide equipment to New England and New York Telephone.

NYNEX acquired AGS Computers, Inc. in 1988 to expand its professional services and software production capabilities. The U.S. government launched an investigation of NYNEX's subsidiary, NYNEX Material Enterprises Company, which was eventually required to refund $45 million to customers who were overcharged for telephone equipment. NYNEX Mobile Communications sold its New York radio paging operations in 1989 to focus on developing its cellular phone business. New England entered a period of recession, and NYNEX pushed to gain a foothold in the international long distance business by purchasing a 50% interest in the phone system of Gibraltar and signing international telecommunications consulting contracts with firms in the United Kingdom, France, Taiwan, Australia, South Korea, and Singapore. NYNEX also joined in the creation of a British cable television network.

In 1991, NYNEX introduced online yellow pages covering its service area and became one of four partners hired to assist in the expansion of Indonesia's telephone system. Cost cutting measures included divesting retail computer operations; announcing plans to reduce management personnel by 10% within two years; and cutting non-managerial staff by more than 10% via retirement incentives. Net income plummeted by more than 33% to an all-time low of $601 million, due to costs incurred in modernizing equipment.

The Officers

Chairman and CEO: Ivan G. Seidenberg

Co-President and Chief Operating Officer: James G. Cullen

Co-President and Chief Operating Officer: Lawrence T. Babbio, Jr.

Chief Financial Officer and Sr. Exec. VP, Strategy and Business: Frederic V. Salerno

Exec. VP, Strategy and Corporate Development: Alexander Good

NYNEX, Ameritech Corp., and Pacific Telesis Group each acquired a two percent interest in Qualcomm Corp., a research and development cellular phone technology company, in 1992. The firm also purchased a 10% interest in TelecomAsia and launched plans to lay a fiber optic cable connecting the eastern U.S. with Japan via England and the Middle East. In 1995, Bell Atlantic and NYNEX merged their cellular operations. The following year, the two firms unveiled their plans to merge; the deal was finalized in August of 1998.

Market Forces Driving the Merger

The Federal Communications Commission (FCC) decree forcing cable companies to cut cable subscription rates by 10% in 1993 and by another seven percent in 1994 forced many telephone companies seeking growth via cable acquisitions to regroup. Bell Atlantic and Tele-Communications Inc. (TCI) nixed their merger plans after TCI announced that the new legislation would reduce its cash flow by roughly 10%. Although the anticipation of convergence—voice, video, and data transmissions along a single network—remained high, analysts viewed the outright acquisition of large cable operators a bit more skeptically.

According to Bruce Wasserstein, author of *Big Deal: The Battle for Control of America's Leading Corporations*, "enthusiasm for convergence waned even further in 1995 and 1996, as another major development unfolded in Washington. The Telecommunications Act of 1996...radically redrew the boundaries of the entire telecommunications industry. As a result, phone companies retrenched. Plain old telephone service, long and long-distance, was seen as the best opportunity for future growth." Roughly one year after the passing of the Act, the second largest phone company in North America was formed when SBC Communications Inc. purchased Pacific Telesis

The Players

Chairman and CEO of Bell Atlantic Corp.: Raymond W. Smith. Carnegie Mellon graduate Raymond Smith joined AT&T in 1959 as an engineer. He left his post as finance director of AT&T to join Bell Atlantic during the 1984 Baby Bells spinoffs. After working as president and chief financial officer, Smith was appointed chairman and CEO in 1989. While at the helm of Bell Atlantic, Smith earned several awards, including "CEO of the Year" from CNBC, "Top Manager" from *Business Week*, and "Chief Executive of the Year" from the International Television Association. He is credited for propelling Bell Atlantic to its current position as the largest local telecommunications firm in the U.S. On June 1, 1998, Smith retired from Bell Atlantic and accepted the position of chairman of Rothschild North American Inc.

Chairman and CEO of NYNEX Corp.: Ivan Seidenberg. Ivan Seidenberg began his career in the telecommunications industry in the 1960s. Before taking over as chairman and CEO of Nynex, he served the firm as vice president of government affairs, president of NYNYEX Worldwide Information and Cellular Services Group, and vice chairman. When NYNEX merged with Bell Atlantic in 1997, Seidenberg was slated to eventually take the helm at Bell Atlantic. He was named CEO of Bell Atlantic on June 1, 1998 and chairman on December 31, 1998.

for roughly $16 billion. Months later, Bell Atlantic and NYNEX threatened to usurp that second place status with their landmark $25.6 million deal.

NYNEX recognized that it needed to merge as a means of staying competitive in the less tightly regulated telecommunications industry. Criticized for poor customer service and an aging infrastructure, the regional Bell firm wasn't likely to fare well against competitors who moved into its northeastern U.S. market. A merger between NYNEX and Bell Atlantic would also offer both firms substantial cost savings opportunities. Because the regions the two firms served butted up against each other, eliminating overlaps, merging operations, and expanding and upgrading infrastructure would be less expensive than doing so across a much more disjointed area.

The back-to-back locations would also position the newly merged firm as a viable contender in the long distance market once local firms were allowed to compete with long distance providers. Approximately $20 billion in annual long distance calls began or ended in the two regions; Bell Atlantic wanted to shore up its position as a means of one day competing for this considerable chunk of the long distance market.

Approach and Engagement

Bell Atlantic and NYNEX began discussing merger plans after the passage of the Telecommunications Act of 1996. They originally decided to pursue a merger of equals, in which a new holding company would be founded to dole out new stock in return for the outstanding shares of both firms. Because the ownership of both firms would change, approval would be necessary from each of the thirteen states in the regions of both NYNEX and Bell Atlantic.

Rather than face thirteen separate regulatory hurdles, shareholders of both companies agreed to modify the terms of their merger to change the legal structure to an acquisition of NYNEX in which Bell Atlantic would own more than 50% of the new firm; therefore, regulatory approval would not need to be sought in the seven states in which Bell Atlantic already operated. Early in August of 1997, the FCC approval the $25 billion merger; the transaction was finalized on August 15, 1997.

Products and Services

After the merger, Bell Atlantic served thirteen states: Connecticut, Delaware, Maine, Maryland, Massachusetts, New Jersey, New Hampshire, New York, Pennsylvania, Rhode Island, Vermont, Virginia, and West Virginia. Local phone service in these states brought in 43% of Bell Atlantic's total revenues in 1997. Network integration accounted for 24%. Wireless services, offered in 25 states via Bell Atlantic Mobile, secured 11%. The firm also boasted wireless operations in Mexico, Italy, the Czech and Slovak Republics, Greece, and Indonesia, as well as stakes in wireless businesses in New Zealand, Asia, and the United Kingdom. Print and electronic directory publishing (namely, 600 Yellow Pages directories) earned eight percent. Other services, including Internet access, long distance, video, and data, brought in the remaining 14%. International operations spanned 21 countries.

Changes to the Industry

Bell Atlantic was still pursuing access to the long distance market in 1998. The firm estimated that it would only need to spend roughly $200 million on new equipment to be able to handle the long distance customer base it hoped to secure once the FCC gave its approval. Most of the technology was already in place, and analysts predicted that if the firm was successful enough to snare one quarter of the long distance customers in its regional away from the likes of AT&T and MCI, it would gain $2 billion in additional revenue with minimal cost.

The anticipated deregulation spawned other major deals as well. In 1998, SBC Communications Inc. announced its intent to takeover Ameritech Corp. for $52 billion; the new firm will become the U.S. local telephone industry leader if the deal clears regulatory hurdles. Not to be outdone, Bell Atlantic approached GTE Corp. in July of 1998, inking a $53 billion takeover of the local and long distance provider. If the merger is given the green light, Bell Atlantic will then emerge as the nation's number one local phone company.

Review of the Outcome

When the Bell Atlantic/NYNEX merger was completed, Bell Atlantic became the second largest telecommunications firm in North America—behind AT&T—with annual sales of $30 billion. The firm's reach expanded to 39 million phone lines in 13 states; cellular customers exceeded four million; and assets reached $50 billion. In anticipation of its entrance into the long distance market upon receipt of FCC approval, Bell Atlantic cropped its workforce from 31.5 to 30.6 employees per phone line, and planned additional downsizing efforts. However, a deal NYNEX had forged with the union in 1994 resurfaced: due to a restructuring that was designed to increase productivity, NYNEX had offered roughly 14,000 clerical staff members and line installers (nearly one-third of its workforce) lucrative buyout options. The NYNEX contract expired in August of 1998, leaving Bell Atlantic with a potential labor shortage.

Also, many analysts pointed out that while the deal might have been good for Bell Atlantic's bottom line, it didn't seem to offer customers any benefits. According to a June 1998 survey done by *Network World*, the customers they queried had seen no measurable improvement in customer service or technology and no reduction in prices in the year following the merger.

Research

"Bell Atlantic Corp.," in *Notable Corporate Chronologies*, The Gale Group, 1999. Lists major events in the history of Bell Atlantic Corp.

Bell Atlantic Corp. Home Page, available at http://www.bellatlantic.com. Official World Wide Web Home Page for Bell Atlantic Corp. Includes current and archived news; detailed financial, product, and historical information; and annual reports.

Bernstein, Aaron. "Oops, That's Too Much Downsizing," in *Business Week*, 8 June 1998. Explains how a 1994 NYNEX union contract might lead to labor shortages for Bell Atlantic.

"FCC Gives Green Light to Bell Atlantic-Nynex Merger," in *PC Week*, 18 August 1997. Offers an overview of the Bell Atlantic/NYNEX merger.

Gallant, John. "Has Merger Mania Benefited Telco Customers? Not in Bell Atlantic's Region," in *Network World*, 8 June 1998. Explains the results of a customer satisfaction survey issued one year after the merger.

Golden, Ed. "Long Distance Will Be the Initial Main Focus of the Newly Merged Company," in *InfoWorld*, 25 August 1997. Details Bell Atlantic's plans to break into the long distance market following its merger with NYNEX.

"NYNEX Corp.," in *Notable Corporate Chronologies*, Gale Research, 1999. Lists major events in the history of NYNEX Corp.

Rockwell, Mark. "Combined Bell Atlantic/Nynex Moves Forward," in *InternetWeek*, 1 September 1997. Discusses the immediate outcome of the Bell Atlantic/NYNEX deal for both firms.

Woolley, Scott. "Changing the Smother Culture," in *Forbes*, 4 May 1998. This article explains the desire of the regional Bell firms to enter the long distance market and predicts that Bell Atlantic will be the first firm to do so.

ANNAMARIE L. SHELDON

BELL ATLANTIC & TCI

Bell Atlantic Corp.
1095 Avenue of the Americas
New York, NY 10036
USA

tel: (212)395-2121
fax: (212)395-1285
web: http://www.bellatlantic.com

AT&T Broadband & Internet Services
5619 DTC Pkwy.
Englewood, CO 80111-3000
USA

tel: (303)267-5500
fax: (303)779-1228
web: http://www.tci.com

date: February 1994 (canceled)
affected: Bell Atlantic Corp., USA, founded 1984
affected: AT&T Broadband & Internet Services (formerly Tele-Communications Inc.), USA, founded 1965

Overview of the Merger

One of the largest regional telephone operators in the U.S., Bell Atlantic, and the second largest cable company in the nation, Tele-Communications Inc. (TCI), agreed to a $33 billion merger in October of 1993. The deal would have created the largest communications, information, and entertainment company in the world with more than 22 million customers and a foothold in 59 of the largest 100 U.S. markets. After the Federal Communications Commission ordered cable companies to reduce their rates by seven percent in early 1994, Bell Atlantic demanded a discounted price from TCI to reflect what would likely be a significant dip in cash flow. TCI refused, and the deal crumbled in February of 1994.

History of Bell Atlantic Corp.

In 1982, the U.S. Department of Justice ended a 13-year antitrust suit against the world's largest corporation, AT&T Corp. Pursuant to a consent decree, AT&T would maintain its manufacturing and research facilities, as well as its long distance operations; however, the firm was required to divest itself of 22 local operating companies, which would be divided among seven regional holding companies. In 1984, Bell Atlantic, one of these companies, opened for business. Bell Atlantic served the northern Atlantic states, and owned seven telephone subsidiaries.

Early in its first year of operation as an independent company, Bell Atlantic formed Bell Atlanticom Systems to market traditional cordless and decorator telephones, wiring components, and home-security and healthcare systems. The firm also introduced Alex, a cellular telephone service. Later in 1984, Bell Atlantic acquired Texas-based Telecommunications Specialists, Inc. and New Jersey-based Tri-Continental Leasing Corp., a computer and telecommunications equipment provider.

Bell Atlantic continued its rapid expansion with the purchase of MAI's Sorbus Inc., the second-largest U.S. computer service firm, and a related company, MAI Canada Ltd., in 1985. The company also launched the first working system of

Integrated Services Digital Network (ISDN) architecture in the nation. Net income reach a record $1 billion that year, and Bell Atlantic decided to target medium-sized customers, offering everything from information services equipment and data processing to computer maintenance.

In 1986, stock split two-for-one, and Bell Atlantic became the first of the Baby Bells to be listed on Standard & Poor's 100 Stock Index. Acquisitions that year included the real estate assets of Pitcairn Properties, Inc.; Technology Concepts Inc., a firm focused on telecommunications and computer software; and Greyhound Capital Corp., which was later renamed Bell Atlantic Systems Leasing International, Inc. Bell Atlantic and Telefonica de Espana agreed to jointly implement database and software systems for managing telephone facilities in Spain.

Bell Atlantic bought Pacific Computer Corp., Jolynne Service Corp., and National Funding Corp., a medical and commercial leasing firm, in 1987. The year, the firm became the first in the nation to implement Signaling Systems 7 (SS-7), the key to evolving intelligent network technology, with the conversion of two New Jersey Bell central offices. A year later, Bell South and Bell Atlantic were accused of misconduct in bidding attempts to win government contracts. Bell Atlantic also divested MAI Canada Ltd., along with some of the assets of Sorbus, Inc., and purchased the European computer maintenance operations of Bell Canada Enterprises, the assets of CPX Inc., and Dyn Service Network. Bell Atlantic Mobile Systems announced the formation of Bell Atlantic Paging to market pagers and paging service in its region. By the end of the decade, Bell Atlantic had also established a European headquarters in Belgium.

U.S. West and Bell Atlantic agreed in 1990 to help modernize Czechoslovakia's telephone operations. That year, Ameritech Corp. and Bell Atlantic acquired Telecom Corp. of New Zealand for $2.5 billion. Bell Atlantic Mobile Systems extended its network in rural-service areas, making Delaware the first state in the nation to offer border-to-border cellular phone service. Bell Atlantic and STET, the Italian phone company, formed a joint venture in Italy in 1991. Bell Atlantic also joined Belle Meade International Telephone, Inc. in a joint venture to set up a communications system in the Soviet Union. The purchase of Metro Mobile gave Bell Atlantic the most extensive cellular phone coverage on the East Coast.

In 1994, Bell Atlantic and three other Baby Bells launched a battle to end the consent decree that prevented them from entering the long-distance markets and manufacturing phones and switches. The following year, a federal judge allowed Bell Atlantic and six

The Business

Financials - Bell Atlantic Corp.

Revenue (1998): $31.56 billion

Employees (1998): 140,000

Financials - AT&T Broadband & Internet Services

Revenue (1998): $7.35 billion

Employees (1998): 37,000

SICs / NAICS

sic 4813 - Telephone Communications Except Radiotelephone

sic 4812 - Radiotelephone Communications

sic 3661 - Telephone & Telegraph Apparatus

sic 4841 - Cable & Other Pay Television Services

naics 513322 - Cellular and Other Wireless Telecommunications

naics 513321 - Paging

naics 334418 - Printed Circuit Assembly (Electronic Assembly) Manufacturing

other regional Bell companies to offer long-distance services to their cellular customers. The company also founded Bell Atlantic Internet Solutions, a new Virginia-based unit which offered business and residential Internet products and services such as e-mail, Web hosting, and high-speed dedicated access to customers in Washington, Philadelphia, and New Jersey. A $33 billion deal to merge with cable giant Telecommunications Inc. fell through in 1994.

To strengthen its position in Mexico, Bell Atlantic invested $1 billion in Grupo Iusacell, a Mexican wireless communications company, in 1993; three years later, the company paid $50 million for a controlling stake. Bell Atlantic and NYNEX Corp. established Bell Atlantic NYNEX Mobile, a joint cellular service and paging operation, in 1995. In August of 1997, Bell Atlantic acquired NYNEX in a $25.6 billion deal, one of the largest of the decade. The following year, the company secured conditional approval to offer long distance services in New York and agreed to a $53 billion deal with GTE Corp., which would make Bell Atlantic the largest local phone company in the U.S.

The Officers

Bell Atlantic Corp.

Chairman and CEO: Ivan G. Seidenberg

Co-President and Chief Operating Officer: James G. Cullen

Co-President and Chief Operating Officer: Lawrence T. Babbio, Jr.

Chief Financial Officer and Sr. Exec. VP, Strategy and Business: Frederic V. Salerno

Exec. VP, Strategy and Corporate Development: Alexander Good

AT&T Broadband & Internet Services

Chairman: Leo C. Hindery, Jr.

Vice Chairman: Jerome H. Kern

Sr. VP, Employee Relations: Grace de Latoure

Exec. VP, Secretary, and General Counsel: Stephen M. Brett

History of Tele-Communications Inc.

Former Texas cattle rancher Bob Magness founded Tele-Communications Inc. (TCI) in 1965 to consolidate his growing interests in cable television companies serving rural areas in Colorado, Montana, Nevada, and Utah. The young company entered a period of major expansion in the late 1960s and early 1970s and incurred additional debt just as interest rates took off. To defray expenses, TCI listed publicly in 1970.

In 1975, the city of Vail, Colorado, sought to secure more cable services from TCI without rate increases, but company president John Malone retaliated by suspending all programming and broadcasting only the names and addresses of city council members until the city relented. After two years of successful legal battles with city cable regulators nationwide, TCI showed a positive cash flow in 1977 and was able to obtain a $77 million loan to refinance corporate debt.

During the late 1970s and early 1980s, TCI declined to enter competition to supply cable television services to urban areas and instead added suburban markets to its traditional base of rural customers. The 1984 Cable Communications Policy Act deregulated cable television, enabling TCI to add Buffalo, Dallas, and Miami to its service area. That year TCI purchased the ailing Pittsburgh, Pennsylvania-based cable television franchise from Warner-Amex for $93 million and provided the first cable television service to the White House.

In 1985, the company began a program of investment in cable television outlets throughout the United States; the following year TCI acquired a controlling interest in United Artists Communications and reorganized to decentralize operations. The firm merged with Heritage Communications in 1987, adding 500,000 cable television subscribers to its corporate rolls. Malone moved to reduce the bargaining power of producers of cable television programming by providing financial assistance to emerging producers such as Black Entertainment Television and The Discovery Channel. That year, TCI helped underwrite the $1.5 billion purchase of the MGM film library by Ted Turner's SuperStation WTBS.

TCI formed Think Entertainment in 1988 to produce and distribute cable television programming. The company also provided financial assistance to emerging producers including QVC Network and American Movie Classics. The U.S. Department of Commerce threatened antitrust investigations due to increased concentration of ownership within the cable television industry. The 1989 purchase of Storer Communications positioned TCI as the largest supplier of cable television services in the United States. The firm also invested in the Blockbuster Video chain of video rental outlets that year. By the decade's end, TCI owned more than 150 cable companies.

TEMPO Enterprises, a satellite telecommunications services provider, was acquired in 1990. In 1991, TCI launched a public bond issue as part of an effort to restructure corporate debt. Late in the year, the firm purchased the remaining outstanding shares of United Artists Communications, keeping the cable operations and spinning off the theater business. As part of a reorganization, United Artists Communications and Heritage Communications were brought under the operating management of TCI. Interests in networks such as QVC, as well as several cable systems, were spun off as Liberty Media. The company also invested in communications infrastructure in Hungary, Ireland, Israel, Malta, New Zealand, Norway, Sweden, and the United Kingdom.

In 1992, TCI acquired Southwest Cablevision. A year later, the firm joined with Comcast in developing Zing, an interactive cable television system. The proposed merger of TCI and Bell Atlantic fell through in 1994 after the FCC lowered cable television subscriber rates. That year, TCI purchased its Liberty Media spinoff. Two years later, TCI formed Fox Sports Net, a joint domestic sports programming alliance between Liberty Media and News Corp; reorganized into four units: domestic cable, programming, new technology, and overseas operations; and acquired Viacom's cable systems. After the Telecommunications Act of 1996 allowed cable, Internet, and telephone firms to compete in one another's markets, TCI and other cable companies launched At Home Corp., a high-speed Internet service provider. In 1998, TCI and AT&T began discussing merger plans; the $59 billion deal was completed in March of 1999, and TCI was renamed AT&T Broadband and Internet Services.

Market Forces Driving the Merger

In the early 1990s, the Baby Bells were faced with new competition from "alternate access" companies like MFS Communications, which were building fiberoptic cables that linked corporate clients in major markets directly to long distance networks. This type of infrastructure allowed companies to completely circumvent the regional Bell companies. Long distance provider MCI announced its intention in 1993 to pour $2 billion into such a system, and several cable firms revealed similar plans.

Coupled with this unprecedented competition was the maturity of the local telephone service market. Growth potential for the regional Bell companies was minimal. Consequently, many of the regional Bell companies began looking for avenues of expansion outside their core operations. According to a March 1994 article in *Fortune*, most regional Bell companies were pursuing strategic links with cable television operators as a means of equipping their systems to handle both video and phone transmissions. The firms had "emerged as powerful contenders in the race to network the nation with vast new digital and TV systems."

Southwestern Bell was the first of the Baby Bells to acquire a cable operator with its 1993 purchase of Hauser Communications for $680 million. Later in the year, Southwestern Bell agreed to funnel $1.6 billion in Atlanta-based Cox Cable, and analysts began speculating that the firm was pursuing a deal with Cablevision Systems Corp. Nynex Corp. announced its intent to invest $1.2 billion in Viacom Inc. to help the firm acquire Paramount Communications Inc. At the same time, rumors began circulating about a major link-up between telephone company U S West Inc. and cable operator Time Warner Inc.

Approach and Engagement

Amidst this flurry of activity, Bell Atlantic and TCI began their own merger discussions, which led to an agreement for the most noteworthy transaction of the early 1990s: a $33 billion stock swap between one of the largest regional Bell companies and the second

The Players

Chairman and CEO of Bell Atlantic Corp.: Raymond W. Smith. Carnegie Mellon graduate Raymond Smith joined AT&T in 1959 as an engineer. He left his post as finance director of AT&T to join Bell Atlantic during the 1984 Baby Bells spin offs. After working as president and chief financial officer, Smith was appointed chairman and CEO in 1989. While at the helm of Bell Atlantic, Smith earned several awards, including "CEO of the Year" from CNBC, "Top Manager" from *Business Week*, and "Chief Executive of the Year" from the International Television Association. He is credited for propelling Bell Atlantic to its current position as the largest local telecommunications firm in the U.S. On June 1, 1998, Smith retired from Bell Atlantic and accepted the position of chairman of Rothschild North American Inc.

Chairman and CEO of Tele-Communications Inc.: John Malone. John Malone left AT&T in 1968 to join cable upstart Tele-Communications Inc. (TCI). He served as president of TCI, eventually taking over the reins from founder Bob Magness who died in 1996. When AT&T bought TCI in March of 1999 and renamed it AT&T Broadband and Internet Services, Malone retained control of Liberty Media, the lucrative cable programming arm of TCI.

place U.S. cable operator. It seemed that voice, video, and data services would be brought together on a nationwide scale for the first time, heralding convergence in the telecommunications industry.

Almost as quickly as it flared, the consolidation activity between telephone and cable operators was snuffed in 1994 when the FCC ordered cable companies to reduce their rates by seven percent in addition to the ten percent reduction called for in 1993. Cable stocks tumbled on the news, and TCI announced that the price cut would likely slash its cash flow by $150 million annually. Bell Atlantic CEO Smith demanded that TCI lower the price of their impending merger to reflect TCI's lower valuation, but TCI CEO Malone refused to grant a discount. In February of 1994, the TCI/Bell Atlantic deal was nixed, and the two firms went their separate ways.

Products and Services

Local phone service brought in 43% of Bell Atlantic's total revenues in 1997. Network integration accounted for 24%. Wireless services, offered in 25 states via Bell Atlantic Mobile, secured 11%. Print and electronic directory publishing (namely, 600 Yellow Pages directories) earned eight percent. Other services, including Internet access, long distance, video, and data, brought in the remaining 14%. International operations spanned 21 countries.

Along with its extensive cable holdings, TCI (renamed AT&T Broadband and Internet Services after its 1999 takeover by AT&T) owned cable programmer Liberty Media Group and a 40% stake in high-speed Internet access provider At Home Corp. in 1997.

Changes to the Industry

When the deal between TCI and Bell Atlantic crumbled, most Wall Street analysts predicted that other cable and phone companies would pursue large mergers more cautiously. According to a February 1994 article in *MEDIAWEEK*, "strategic partnerships and minority ownership agreements—as opposed to full-blown mergers—may be the best way to navigate in the future." Analysts pointed to U.S. West's $2.5 billion investment in the cable systems of Time Warner as a deal that might resemble more closely the structure of future transactions. However, the Telecommunications Act of 1996 sparked yet another round of activity between telephone companies and cable operators, two of the most noteworthy being the $10.8 billion purchase of Continental Cablevision, the third largest U.S. cable operator, by U.S. West and the mind blowing $59 billion takeover of TCI by AT&T in early 1999.

Review of the Outcome

Because TCI had continued to struggle with cash flow shortages, as well as increasing competition since the FCC restricted cable rates, most analysts believed Bell Atlantic was better off without the firm. In fact, because it had remained flexible throughout the mid-1990s, Bell Atlantic was better poised to pursue its

$25.6 billion deal with NYNEX in 1997, which doubled its size. When that merger was completed, Bell Atlantic became the second largest telecommunications firm in the U.S.—behind AT&T—with annual sales of $30 billion. The firm's impending $53 billion deal with GTE, slated for mid-1999, will catapult Bell Atlantic to the leading spot among local phone company in the U.S.

Research

"Bell Atlantic Corp.," in *Notable Corporate Chronologies*, The Gale Group, 1999. Lists major events in the history of Bell Atlantic Corp.

Bell Atlantic Corp. Home Page, available at http://www.bellatlantic.com. Official World Wide Web Home Page for Bell Atlantic Corp. Includes current and archived news; detailed financial, product, and historical information; and annual reports.

"Bell Atlantic, TCI and Liberty Media to Merge," in *Video Marketing News*, 18 October 1993. Offers an overview of the planned merger between TCI and Bell Atlantic.

"Bell Atlantic's Seidenberg to Succeed CEO Smith June 1," in *Telecommunications Reports*, 4 May 1998. Explains Bell Atlantic CEO Smith's decision to step down and what the board's expectations are for the new CEO, Ivan Seidenberg.

Burgi, Michael. "FCC Dinged Bell/TCI Merger," in *MEDIAWEEK*, 28 February 1994. Covers the impact of the FCC's seven percent cable subscriber rate reduction in 1994 on the TCI/Bell Atlantic merger.

Jeffrey, Don. "Big Gets Bigger: TCI Links with Bell Atlantic," in *Billboard*, 23 October 1993. Explains why TCI and Bell Atlantic decided to merge.

Kupfer, Andrew. "The Baby Bells Butt Heads," in *Fortune*, 21 March 1994. Offers a detailed account of how the TCI/Bell Atlantic deal went sour and how the nixed deal will impact the telecommunications industry.

"Tele-Communications Inc.," in *Notable Corporate Chronologies*, The Gale Group, 1999. Lists major events in the history of Tele-Communications Inc.

Ziegler, Bart. "What Collapse of TCI Merger Means for Deals," in *The Wall Street Journal*, 25 February 1994. Predicts how the failed TCI/Bell Atlantic merger will impact future deals between cable operators and telephone companies.

ANNAMARIE L. SHELDON

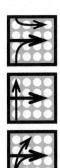

BERGEN BRUNSWIG & IVAX

date: April 1997 (canceled)
affected: Bergen Brunswig Corp., USA, founded 1888
affected: IVAX Corp., USA, founded 1985

Bergen Brunswig Corp.
4000 Metropolitan Dr.
Orange, CA 92868-3598
USA

tel: (714)385-4000
fax: (714)385-1442
web: http://www.bergenbrunswig.com

IVAX Corp.
4400 Biscayne Blvd.
Miami, FL 33137-3227
USA

tel: (305)575-6000
fax: (305)575-6298
web: http://www.ivax.com

Overview of the Merger

The proposed $1.65 billion merger between California-based Bergen Brunswig Corp. (BBC) and Florida-based IVAX Corp., announced in November 1996, marked the first attempted joining of a leading pharmaceutical wholesaler with a generic drug maker. The new firm, named BBI Healthcare, would have boasted a valuation of $3.2 billion and 12,000 employees. After Wall Street criticized the deal, stock for both firms plummeted, and the deal was canceled in April 1997. BBC filed suit against IVAX for alleged breach of contract; IVAX asserted that BBC had canceled the deal for no tangible reason. The suit was dropped in August of 1997 when both firms settled for undisclosed terms.

History of Bergen Brunswig Corp.

In 1888, Lucien Brunswig and F.W. Braun opened F.W. Braun and Company (FWB), a wholesale apothecary, in Los Angeles, California. Two years later, in San Diego, FWB established its first branch office. Brunswig purchased Braun's interest in FWB, becoming sole owner of the company, in 1907. FWB then changed its name to the Brunswig Drug Company (BDC).

The company opened outlets in Arizona and Mexico in the early 1920s and established a new manufacturing facility for laboratory products, packaged drugs, and cosmetics. Sales reached record levels despite a general slump in the U.S. economy.

In the 1940s, demand for pharmaceuticals boomed in light of the discovery of wonder drugs such as sulfa antibiotics and penicillin. BDC stock was publicly traded for the first time in 1949. That year, BDC merged with Coffin-Redington Company, a San Francisco-based manufacturer of pharmaceuticals, beginning a period of rapid expansion for the company. In 1952, BDC acquired Smith-Faus Drug Co. The firm also absorbed the Hazeltine & Perkins Drug Co. and purchased the Western States Wholesale Drug Co. Acquisitions from 1965 to 1968 included E.V. Irving Co.; Flexco Pharmaceuticals; the R.L. Scherer Co.; Rabin-Winters Corp.; Kip, Inc.; Hibbard Medical and Surgical Supply Co.; Kny-Scheerer Corp.; New

The Business

Financials - Bergen Brunswig Corp.

Revenue (1998): $17.12 billion

Employees (1998): 5,400

Financials - IVAX Corp.

Revenue (1998): $637.9 million

Employees (1998): 3,580

SICs / NAICS

sic 5122 - Drugs, Proprietaries & Sundries

sic 2834 - Pharmaceutical Preparations

sic 5047 - Medical & Hospital Equipment

naics 325412 - Pharmaceutical Preparation Manufacturing

Jersey Wholesale Drug Co.; Crown Surgical Manufacturing Corp.; and Rheinhold-Schuman, Inc.

In 1928, Emil P. Martini opened a retail drug store in Hackensack, New Jersey. Roughly twenty years later, Martini consolidated his stores to form the Bergen Drug Company. Bergen began to compete directly with BDC after opening an office and warehouse in Fresno, California, in 1956. The company also purchased Drug Service Inc. of Bridgeport, Connecticut. By 1960, Bergen ranked among the largest wholesalers of pharmaceuticals in the U.S., supplying more than 5,000 pharmacists and hospitals. Acquisitions in 1964 included Garde Drug Co., Wilton Laboratories, and Marett and Co. In 1969, Bergen and BDC merged to form Bergen Brunswig Corp. (BBC). The new company continued the frantic pace of acquisition maintained by its two predecessor companies, purchasing 13 pharmaceutical and medical supply companies during the year.

BBC instituted its Good Neighbor Pharmacy program, designed to make independent pharmacists competitive with retail chain stores and other mass merchandisers, in 1972. Seven years later, the firm became the exclusive distributor of Rexall brand products. In 1980, BBC acquired the drug distribution operations of the Wilsey Bennett Company, gaining a foothold in the Washington, Oregon, and Oklahoma markets. The U.S. pharmaceuticals industry entered a period of rapid growth—BBC experienced dramatic rises in earnings due to the aging of the population and the popularity of two of its products, Zantac, an antiulcer medication, and Epogen, used by kidney

dialysis patients. Stock split five-to-four in 1983. During the mid-1980s, BBC acquired the Stanley Drug Co. of San Antonio, Texas; the Allen Co. of Florida; Synergex Corp. of California; Davis Brothers Drug Co. of Denver, Colorado; Berry Wholesale Drug Co. of Tennessee; the Southwestern Drug Corp. of Texas; and the Los Angeles Drug Co.

In 1988, BBC divested Bergen Brunswig Medical Supply Company for $42.7 million. By 1990, net earnings were 316% higher than three years prior. In 1992, the firm acquired the pharmaceutical distribution operations of the Dr. T.C. Smith Co. of Asheville and Raleigh, North Carolina. That year, BBC also took over Durr-Fillauer Medical Inc., later divesting the Durr-Fillauer Orthopedic unit. The firm purchased Healthcare Distributors of Indiana, Inc. in 1993 and Southeastern Hospital Supply Corp. in 1994. BBC and Apple Computer Inc. jointly launched a new multimedia communication, production information, and electronic ordering system for Bergen Brunswig's pharmacy customers. Also that year, BBC secured a multi-year contract worth $2 billion to be the sole drug distributor for Columbia/HCA Healthcare Corp., the largest hospital-care provider in the country.

In 1995, BBC acquired Biddle & Crowther Co., the leading northwest distributor of medical-surgical supplies, and folded it into the Durr Medical subsidiary. The company formed a new subsidiary, IntePlex Inc., to integrate its product lines and information services for large, managed-care customers. By then, BBC was the sole national pharmaceutical distributor of both drugs and medical-surgical supplies. As part of its plan to more closely integrate the medical-surgical division with the rest of the company, BBC changed the Durr Medical subsidiary's name to Bergen Brunswig Medical Corp. in 1996. Oncology Supply Co. was acquired that year.

The company's $1.6 billion planned merger with IVAX Corp. fell apart in 1997. Another major deal—a $2.6 billion buyout of BBC by Cardinal Health, the second largest wholesale pharmaceutical distributor in the U.S.—was nixed by the FTC in 1998 due to anticompetitive concerns. Acquisition efforts heated up again in the late 1990s, including BBC's purchase of the Stadtlanders Drug Distribution unit of Canada-based Counsel Corp. in 1999.

History of IVAX Corp.

Dermatologist Phillip Frost founded IVAX Corp. in 1985 to serve as a holding company for pharmaceutical and chemical concerns. A year later, IVAX acquired U.S.-based generic drug distributor Goldline Laboratories; the purchase formed the core of what would become the most lucrative segment of the company's operations: generic drugs. In 1988, IVAX listed publicly for the first time. The purchase of U.K.-based Norton Healthcare marked the company's first international foray.

IVAX diversified into veterinary products in 1992. Stock split three-for-two in December of that year. The following year, the company acquired Johnson Products, gaining entrance to the cosmetics market for the first time. IVAX also purchased competitor Zenith Laboratories, the largest U.S. generic drug manufacturer. In 1995, a planned merger between Hafslund Nycomed, a Norwegian drug company, and IVAX crumbled. IVAX's planned merger with Bergen Brunswig also fell apart two years later. The firm's growth rate, an astonishing 40% between 1990 and 1994, began to slow.

After posting losses in both 1996 and 1997, IVAX divested its specialty chemicals and intravenous operations and spun off its veterinary products unit. Carson, Inc. bought Johnson Products from IVAX in 1998. That year, IVAX announced that it would change its name to IVX BioSciences.

Market Forces Driving the Merger

Managed care providers were pressuring pharmaceutical wholesalers in the mid-1990s to cut drug prices. As a result, firms began looking for ways to reduce costs. BBC saw a merger with IVAX as a means of cutting overhead, as well as gaining access to the generic drug market, which was more lucrative than its non-generic counterpart. According to a December article in *Drug Store News*, the merger was "intended to create a company with the clout and efficiencies of a wholesaler and the higher profit levels enjoyed by a generic drug manufacturer. By linking the manufacturing and distribution processes and eliminating duplicative functions, executives at the company [BBC] believe they will be able to push down costs and increase profits." IVAX's European healthcare holdings, particularly Norton Healthcare, would also give BBC access to the international pharmaceutical arena.

IVAX was also ready to make a deal. It's $2.5 billion merger with Hafslund Nycomed, a $1.3 billion Norwegian generic drug manufacturer, fell apart in 1995 after delays in new product launches hurt IVAX's quarterly earnings, causing stock prices to plummet 20% in a single month. The firm remained the leading generic drug maker in the world in 1996 with sales of $1.2 billion. Yet increased competition and falling drug prices were taking a toll on its bottom line. By merging with pharmaceuticals distributor BBC, IVAX would be able to increase efficiency by linking its drug production directly to demand.

The Officers

Bergen Brunswig Corp.

Chairman: Robert E. Martini

President and CEO: Donald R. Roden

Exec. VP, Chief Financial Officer, and President, Bergen Brunswig Specialty: Neil F. Dimick

Exec. VP and Chief Information Officer: Linda Burkett

Exec. VP and Chief Procurement Officer: Charles J. Carpenter

IVAX Corp.

Chairman and CEO: Phillip Frost

Vice Chairman and President: Neil Flanzraich

Vice Chairman, Technical Affairs, and President and CEO, DVM Pharmaceuticals: Jane Hsiao

Deputy CEO and CEO, Norton Healthcare: Issac Kaye

Approach and Engagement

In November of 1996, IVAX and BBC announced their intent to merge into a new company, named BBI Healthcare, which would be based in Miami, Florida. IVAX would close its distribution centers and transfer its drugs to the distribution facilities of BBC. The medical supply units of both companies would be merged.

When news of the deal hit Wall Street, share prices for both companies dropped dramatically. BBC shares tumbled 16% to $27.50, and IVAX shares dove 20% to $12.75. According to HKS & Co. analyst Hemant Shah, how the deal was announced prompted the unfavorable response. "It was one of the most ill-presented mergers I've ever seen. The deal was announced in the morning and the companies never explained to analysts why they were doing it until three hours after the market opened. That was a big mistake. Wall Street had a knee-jerk negative reaction to it."

Besides the initial confusion, what bothered investors most was the price to which IVAX had agreed—$13.76 per share, well below the $15.88 per share the firm had been trading at prior to the deal. The discounted prices raised questions about IVAX's future performance. Industry analysts also questioned the wisdom of a drug distributor purchasing a generic drug maker, something that the pharmaceutical industry hadn't seen before. IVAX would likely lose the segment of its customers who competed directly with BBC once the deal was finalized.

The Players

President and CEO of Bergen Brunswig Corp.: Donald R. Roden. Donald Roden began working for Hoffman La Roche Laboratories in 1969. After holding sales and marketing positions there for three years, he accepted a post as marketing director at a unit of Marion Laboratories. From there Roden went on to serve as vice president of operations at pharmaceutical benefits management pioneer PAID Prescriptions and as group vice president for a unit of Bergen Brunswig. Between 1977 and 1989, he ran his own healthcare management consulting and communications company, Pracon Inc. When Pracon was bought out by Elsevier Ltd., Roden accepted a position with Elsevier, eventually taking over as CEO of Reed Elsevier Medical's North American operations. Bergen Brunswig tapped him as president and chief operating officer in 1995. When negotiations with IVAX began, Roden was elected CEO of Bergen Brunswig, a position he officially took on in 1997.

Chairman and CEO of IVAX Corp.: Phillip Frost. Dermatologist Phillip Frost bought Key Pharmaceuticals in 1972 and began growing the company via acquisition. In 1986, Schering-Plough paid him $800 million for the firm. Intending to make a similar profit with a firm of his own making, Frost founded IVAX Corp. in 1985. He is currently chairman and CEO of IVAX.

In April of 1997, BBC dissolved the deal and filed a lawsuit against IVAX charging breach of contract. IVAX insisted that BBC broke off the deal for no good reason. Four months later, the two firms reached a settlement; terms were undisclosed.

Products and Services

After divesting peripheral operations throughout the late 1990s, IVAX in 1999 focused on three core segments: specialty generic drugs, which accounted for roughly 50% of 1998 revenues; respiratory products, including the Easi-Breathe inhaler; and oncology pharmaceuticals, including cancer treatment Paxene. International operations spanned the Netherlands, Germany, the United Kingdom, Ireland, and China.

In 1999, Bergen Brunswig Corp. (BBC) distributed pharmaceuticals and medical-surgical supplies—including home health care supplies and equipment,

personal health products, oncology products, proprietary medicines, sundries and toiletries, and cosmetics—to chain and independent pharmacies, hospitals, health maintenance organizations, nursing homes, clinics, and physician groups nationwide. The company was organized into four main divisions: Bergen Brunswig Drug Co.; Bergen Brunswig Medical Corp.; IntePlex; and Bergen Brunswig Specialty Co., which included Integrated Commercialization Solutions and Bergen Brunswig Specialty Healthcare Group.

Changes to the Industry and Review of the Outcome

When his firm's merger with BBC fell through, Frost decided IVAX needed to retrench, and he began divesting non-core operations. Analysts believed the future looked bleak for IVAX in the wake of the crumbled BBC deal. Along with two failed mergers in recent years, the company lacked a blockbuster drug to counteract the effects of falling drug prices. Consecutive losses in 1996 and 1997 were the impetus behind the firm's major overhaul: IVAX divested its specialty chemicals and intravenous operations, as well as the Johnson Products unit. Stock prices in 1997 reached an all time low, closing at $6.75, less than half of where they had traded prior to the announcement of the merger with BBC. In 1998, revenues were barely half what they had been in 1996.

As analysts predicted, BBC fared much better than IVAX in the late 1990s. Not only did stock bounced back to expected levels, but the firm also nearly merged with the second largest wholesale pharmaceutical distributor in the U.S., Cardinal Health. After the FTC halted the transaction, BBC launched an acquisition spree that boosted its 1998 revenues significantly.

Research

"Bergen Brunswig Corp.," in *Notable Corporate Chronologies*, The Gale Group, 1999. Lists major events in the history of Bergen Brunswig Corp.

Bergen Brunswig Corp. Home Page, available at http://www.bergenbrunswig.com. Official World Wide Web Home Page for Bergen Brunswig Corp. Includes news, financial, product, and historical information.

"Bergen Brunswig/Ivax to Merge as BBI," in *Pharmaceutical Business News*, 21 November 1996. Explains the reasons for the Bergen Brunswig and IVAX merger.

"Bergen Ends Ivax Deal," in *American Druggist*, April 1997. Offers a brief look at why the agreement between Bergen Brunswig and IVAX fell apart.

"Bitter Ending to a Troubled Deal," in *Mergers & Acquisitions*, May-June 1997. Explains why it's difficult to complete a merger in the healthcare industry and why the merger between IVAX and Bergen Brunswig was canceled.

Fried, Lisa I. "Bergen, IVAX Confront a Changing Market," in *Drug Store News*, 9 December 1996. Covers the industry conditions that prompted IVAX and Bergen Brunswig to consider a merger.

Hensley, Scott. "A Mysterious Breakup: IVAX, Bergen Brunswig Headed to Court After Deal Collapses," in *Modern Healthcare*, 21 April 1997. Discusses the breach of contract lawsuit filed by Bergen Brunswig after the merger with IVAX was halted.

IVAX Corp. Home Page, available at http://www.ivax.com. Official World Wide Web Home Page for IVAX Corp.

Includes news, financial, product, and historical information.

Reingold, Jennifer. "Play It Again, Sam: Ivax Shareholders Have Been Waiting Four Years for Phil Frost to Sell Out," *Financial World*, 11 March 1996. Explains how and why Phillip Frost founded IVAX and why shareholders would like a buyout offer.

Sparks, Debra. "Ivax: The Morning After," in *Financial World*, 16 December 1996. Offers a look at why IVAX and Bergen Brunswig share prices plummeted in the wake of their merger announcement.

THERA WILLIAMS

BERKSHIRE HATHAWAY & GENERAL RE

Berkshire Hathaway Inc.
1440 Kiewit Plaza
Omaha, NE 68131
USA

tel: (402)346-1400
fax: (402)346-3375
web: http://www.berkshirehathaway.com

nationality: USA
date: December 21, 1998
affected: Berkshire Hathaway Inc., USA, founded 1955
affected: General Re Corp., USA, founded 1921

Overview of the Merger

Berkshire Hathaway Inc., the holding company with higher priced stock than any other firm listed on the New York Stock Exchange, paid $22 billion for General Re Corp., the largest reinsurer in the U.S., in December of 1998. Combining the $16.9 billion market capitalization of General Re with Berkshire Hathaway's $98.1 billion resulted in the creation of an insurance behemoth—the world's largest—with a market capitalization near $120 billion. Upon completion of the deal, Berkshire Hathaway also boasted the largest net worth of any company in the U.S. and the second largest in the world, behind Royal Dutch/Shell Group. As a wholly owned subsidiary of Berkshire Hathaway, General Re kept its insurance operations separate from those of its new parent company.

History of Berkshire Hathaway Inc.

Hathaway Manufacturing Co. was incorporated in Massachusetts in 1888. A year later, Berkshire Cotton Manufacturing Co. was also incorporated in Massachusetts. In 1929, after merging with several other New England textile makers, Berkshire Cotton changed its name to Berkshire Fine Spinning Associates, Inc. The new operation accounted for 25% of the fine-cotton-textile production in the U.S. In 1955, Berkshire Fine Spinning merged with Hathaway Manufacturing to form Berkshire Hathaway Inc., a new company with more than 10,000 employees, 14 plants, and nearly six million square feet of plant space.

Within three years of the merger, as a result of the company's poor financial performance, Berkshire Hathaway closed its extensive operations in Adams, Massachusetts, and sold its curtain plant in Warren, Rhode Island, to the Pilgrim Curtain Co. By 1961, the company had shut down seven of its plants and cut its work week to fours days at several locations. Three more plants were closed in Rhode Island in 1962.

In 1965, Buffet Partnership. Ltd., led by investor Warren Buffet, purchased enough stock to control the company. Under new leadership, Berkshire soon diversified into the insurance business with the purchases of National Indemnity

Co. and National Fire & Marine Insurance Co. for a total of $8.5 million. Sun Newspapers, based in Omaha, Nebraska, was also acquired during the late 1960s, as was Illinois National Bank & Trust Co. of Rockford.

Berkshire entered the candy industry for the first time in 1970 when it bought a controlling interest in Blue Chip Stamps, owner of chocolate maker and retailer See's Candies. The firm also acquired Wesco Financial Corp., a savings and loans operator, that year. Insurance operations grew in 1971 with the formation of Cornhusker Casualty Co. and Lakeland Fire and Casualty Co. as part of the National Indemnity Group, as well as the purchase of Home & Automobile Insurance Co. In 1972, the firm formed Texas United Insurance Co., which was later merged into National Indemnity. The National Fire & Marine subsidiary acquired its only wholly owned subsidiary, Redwood Fire & Casualty Insurance Co., in 1976. A year later, Berkshire acquired Cypress Insurance Co. and formed Kansas Fire & Casualty Co. The company made another move into the newspaper business by purchasing, through Blue Chip Stamps, the *Buffalo Evening News*.

In 1978, the firm established another insurance company, Continental Divide Insurance Co., and through a merger with Diversified Retailing Co., acquired Columbia Insurance Co. and Southern Casualty Insurance Co. Because of a requirement of the Bank Holding Company Act of 1969, Berkshire spun off Illinois National Bank & Trust in 1980. Sun Newspapers was also divested. In 1983, the firm acquired the share of Blue Chip Stamps it didn't already own and diversified into furniture with the purchase of a 90% stake in Nebraska Furniture Mart, the largest U.S. home furnishings store. Also, National Indemnity Co. of Florida was formed and added to the National Indemnity group.

When Capital Cities Communications, Inc. bought the American Broadcasting Company in 1985, Berkshire bought 18% of the new company, Capital Cities/ABC Inc., for nearly $516 million. Growth continued in 1986 with the following acquisitions: Scott Fetzer Co., the producer of World Book Encyclopedia; Kirby Homecare; and 84% of Fecheimer Bros. Co., a uniform manufacturer and distributor. Two years later, Berkshire listed on the New York Stock Exchange, becoming the highest-priced stock available.

Stakes in The Gillette Co., USAir Group, Champion International Corp., and jewelry store Borsheim's were added to the mix in 1989. Berkshire's purchase of 6.3% of Coca-Cola Co., made the firm Coke's second-largest shareholder. In 1991, H.H. Brown Shoe Co. was purchased. The firm became the

The Business

Financials

Revenue (1998): $13.83 billion

Employees (1998): 45,000

SICs / NAICS

sic 6351 - Surety Insurance

sic 6719 - Holding Companies Nec

second largest shareholder of General Dynamics Corp. after buying 15% of its outstanding stock in 1992. That year, Berkshire's stock became the first listed security to pass the $10,000-per-share mark in the history of the New York Stock Exchange. Acquisitions included Lowell Shoe Inc. and a majority stake in Central States Indemnity Co. of Omaha.

In 1993, the firm increased its footwear holdings via its acquisition of Dexter Shoe Co. A year later, Berkshire bought 4.96 million shares of McDonald's Corp. Acquisitions in 1995 included Helzberg's Diamond Shops, Inc., and R.C. Willey Home Furnishings. GEICO Corp. became an indirect wholly owned subsidiary of Berkshire in 1996. The company authorized a new, cheaper class of stock known as "Baby Berkshire" to be issued and traded on the New York Stock Exchange at $1,100 a share, compared to its class A stock at $33,800 a share. The firm also nearly doubled its stake in McDonald's and acquired FlightSafety International that year. In December of 1998, Berkshire paid $22 billion in stock for General Re, the largest reinsurance company in the U.S.

History of General Re Corp.

In 1921, General Casualty and Surety Reinsurance Corp. was formed by the merger of Norwegian Globe and Norwegian Assurance, two insurance companies under the direction of Robert Iberstein. The new company began operations in New York with a capital fund of $800,000. In 1923, after Iberstein and his board resigned, James White took over the firm, renaming it General Reinsurance Corp. Soon after the leadership shift, the company began offering what would become its core focus: property and casualty reinsurance.

After a stock swap merger with Mellon Indemnity Corp. in 1945, General Reinsurance held a near monopoly in the fledgling reinsurance—insurance for insurers—market. A year later, the firm began offering management consulting services. For the next

The Officers

Chairman and CEO: Warren E. Buffett

Vice Chairman: Charles T. Munger

VP and Chief Financial Officer: Marc D. Hamburg

VP: Robert H. Bird

VP: Stanford Lipsey

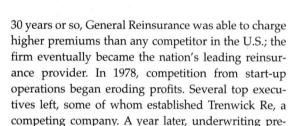

30 years or so, General Reinsurance was able to charge higher premiums than any competitor in the U.S.; the firm eventually became the nation's leading reinsurance provider. In 1978, competition from start-up operations began eroding profits. Several top executives left, some of whom established Trenwick Re, a competing company. A year later, underwriting premiums dropped for the first time in the corporation's history. CEO Harold Hudson, Jr. organized General Re Corp., a holding firm which acquired General Reinsurance and its subsidiaries, in 1980.

Efforts to invest in other insurance companies heated up with the purchase of the United Kingdom's Trident Insurance Group, which was later sold in 1985, and Monarch Insurance Co. of Ohio. By then, General Re was the fourth largest reinsurance company in the world. Overseas expansion began in earnest in 1994 when General Re and Colonia Konzern AG, the world's fifth-largest reinsurer, formed a joint venture. That year, *Institution Investor* named General Re the largest reinsurance firm in the world, based on total assets of $18.5 billion.

In 1995, General Re purchased New England Asset Management. A year later, the firm acquired National Re, based in Connecticut. The joint venture between General Re and Colonia Konzern established operations in China in 1997. In December of 1998, Berkshire Hathaway acquired General Re for $22 billion.

Market Forces Driving the Merger

During the 1990s, airlines crashes, such as the TWA Flight 800 accident, and weather disasters took a toll on reinsurance companies. The industry was also becoming increasingly global, and to compete, firms began consolidating. When General Re and Berkshire Hathaway began discussing their merger, Munich Re had already purchased American Re, and Ace had acquired Tempest Reinsurance.

The bullish market, higher costs, and more financially stable and geographically diverse competition

played a factor in the merger, according to some analysts. Recognizing that the success of the stock market in the late 1990s—a success that many analysts criticized as overvalued—was largely the result of the number of people investing in it, and wanting to dilute his reliance on common stock, Berkshire Hathaway CEO Buffet was looking to do some low-profile stock selling. One way to do this was to purchase a large bond portfolio, like the one General Re possessed. In his firm's 1997 annual report, Buffet explained that Berkshire Hathaway had been changing its "bond/stock ratio moderately in response to the relative values that we saw in each market, a realignment we have continued in 1998." The merger with General Re would allow Berkshire Hathaway to reduce the percentage of stocks as investment assets from 77% to roughly 60% and increase the percentage of bonds as an investment assets from 10% to 30%.

General Re executives pointed to the fact a merger would give the firm access to the deep pockets of Berkshire Hathaway, allowing General Re to write more reinsurance policies. According to a June 1998 article in *The Economist*, however, General Re didn't need more capital. "The acquisition may reveal more about the weakening position of Berkshire Hathaway's existing reinsurance operations." Berkshire Hathaway's National Indemnity subsidiary, which focused mainly on catastrophic business, needed to diversifying into other areas of reinsurance. General Re, which underwrote mostly non-catastrophic reinsurance, would afford Berkshire Hathaway access to new markets.

Approach and Engagement

In June of 1998, Berkshire Hathaway agreed to pay $22 billion in stock for General Re; the price was 29% higher than General Re's current share price of $220.25. According to the terms of the agreement, General Re would continue to operate separately from Berkshire Hathaway's reinsurance operations due to their different target markets.

As the deal approached closing, Berkshire Hathaway stock declined nine percent, due mainly to the fact that General Re shares would no longer trade on the New York Stock Exchange and be removed from the Standard & Poor's 500 index one the deal was finalized; because mutual fund mangers who held only S&P 500 stock would be unable to keep the Berkshire shares received from the stock purchase, those managers were forced to sell their General Re holdings.

Shareholders of both firms approved the merger in September of 1998. In October, the Union Needeltrades, Industrial and Textile Employees

(Unite) surprised the reinsurance industry by filing an antitrust lawsuit to block the merger, but the litigation was later dismissed. The tax-free deal was completed on December 21, 1998. General Re shareholders received either .0035 Class A share or .105 Class B share for each share of General Re common stock owned.

Products and Services

The diverse assets of Berkshire Hathaway in 1998 included property and casualty insurance and reinsurance (which accounted for approximately 65% of total revenues), shoes, aviation training, candy, home cleaning systems, newspapers, and home furnishings. Major equity investments included an eight percent stake in Coca-Cola and a nine percent stake in Gillette. The company also owned the following insurance subsidiaries: GEICO Corp.; 82% of Central States Indemnity Co. of Omaha; 80% of Kansas Banker's Surety Co.; and National Indemnity Co.

Prior to its takeover by Berkshire Hathaway, General Re was organized into four segments: North American property-casualty reinsurance, including General Reinsurance which brought in roughly 50% of total revenues, and National Re; international property-casualty reinsurance, including a 78% stake in Germany's Cologne Re, which was the firm's second largest operating unit; life and health reinsurance; and financial services, including reinsurance brokerage via the Herbert Clough unit, real estate management and derivative products. International sales accounted for roughly 40% of total revenues.

Changes to the Industry

While the effects of a merger this size on the reinsurance industry remain to be seen, Beran, Stearns & Co. analyst Michael Smith asserted, "I think we now have to rethink the issue of consolidation in the industry, because it's quite clear that anybody can be acquired. I think the general view is that companies like General Re would be the ones that would remain independent, and now it looks like almost anyone can be acquired."

Review of the Outcome

Immediately following the merger's completion, Berkshire Hathaway's stock recovered from its premerger decline and climbed 11.75%. The deal created the world's largest insurer with a market capitalization of nearly $120 billion. Berkshire Hathaway was boosted to the number two spot among the world's largest firms in terms of net worth, second only to Royal Dutch/Shell Group.

The Players

Chairman and CEO of Berkshire Hathaway Inc.: Warren E. Buffett. After studying at Columbia Business School during the early 1950s, Warren Buffett began working in 1956 as an independent money manager. He began buying major shares of companies he believed were trading below their value and was soon earning significant returns. In 1969, Buffet became chairman of Berkshire Hathaway. Two years later, he sold off his investment ventures in 1971 for $25 million and a controlling stake in Berkshire Hathaway. It was then that Buffett began running the firm. In his thirty years at the helm of Berkshire Hathaway, the firm's share price has grown a stunning 27% annually.

Chairman and CEO of General Re Corp.: Ronald E. Ferguson. Ronald Ferguson had served as chairman and CEO of General Re for several years at the time of its takeover by Berkshire Hathaway in December of 1998. When the deal was finalized, he remained head of the General Re subsidiary and joined Berkshire Hathaway's board of directors.

Research

Adams, Christopher. "General Re Ensured a Future," in *The Financial Times*, 22 June 1998. Explains the industry conditions that led to the Berkshire Hathaway and General Re merger.

"Berkshire Hathaway Inc.," in *Notable Corporate Chronologies*, The Gale Group, 1999. Lists major events in the history of Berkshire Hathaway Inc.

Berkshire Hathaway Inc. Home Page, available at http://www.berkshirehathaway.com. Official World Wide Web Home Page for Berkshire Hathaway Inc. Includes current and archived press releases; financial and product information; and annual reports.

"Berkshire Merger Threatened By Union Lawsuit," in *Journal of Commerce*, 30 October 1998. Details the surprising antitrust lawsuit filed by the Union Needletrades, Industrial and Textile Employees.

"Buffett's New Policy: Reinsurance," in *The Economist*, 27 June 1998. Explains why Berkshire Hathaway CEO Buffet pursued the deal with General Re.

"General Re Corp.," in *Notable Corporate Chronologies*, The Gale Group, 1999. Lists major events in the history of General Re Corp.

Grant, James. "The Buffett Dilemma: If He Starts to Sell, Who's Going to Buy?," in *Money*, October 1998. Discusses why Buffett wanted to dilute his holding company's reliance on common stock and how that desire led to the merger.

Greenwald, Judy. "Berkshire Hathaway to Acquire General Re," in *Business Insurance*, 22 June 1998. Covers the terms of the agreement between General Re and Berkshire Hathaway.

Silverman, Gary. "Buffett's $22 Billion Hedge: Buying General Re Gives Him Elbow Room if Stocks Fall," in *Business Week*, 6 July 1998. Explains how the deal will reduce Berkshire Hathaway's dependence on common stock assets.

SAMIT AYERS

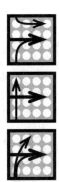

BERTELSMANN & DOUBLEDAY

nationality: Germany
date: 1986
affected: Bertelsmann AG, Germany, founded 1835
affected: Doubleday & Co., USA, founded 1897

Bertelsmann AG
Carl-Bertelsmann-Strasse 270
Gütersloh, D-33311
Germany

tel: 49-52-41-80-0
fax: 49-52-41-751-66
web: http://www.bertelsmann.de

Overview of the Merger

In 1986, German publishing and media giant Bertelsmann AG bought Doubleday & Co., the eighth-largest U.S. publishing company in the U.S., for $475 million. Bertelsmann folded the new purchase into its American publishing arm, which it later renamed Bantam Doubleday Dell Publishing Group Inc. The Doubleday unit struggled in the late in 1980s, posting significant losses in 1988 and 1989. In 1991, however, the firm began a turnaround, due in large part to the success of author John Grisham. A year later, Bantam Doubleday Dell earned profits of roughly $38 million on sales of $640 million. Its success in the U.S. publishing market prompted Bertelsmann to pursue another major acquisition in the late 1990s. The firm paid $1.4 billion for Random House Inc. in July of 1998, thereby becoming the largest commercial book publisher in the world.

History of Bertelsmann AG

After his brother's death in 1819, Carl Bertelsmann set up as a bookbinder in his hometown, Gütersloh, Germany, where he printed and bound hymn books for the churches in the area. In 1835, Bertelsmann incorporated his bookbinding and printing business as C. Bertelsmann Verlag. Upon his death in 1850, Bertelsmann left his wife and son, Heinrich, the bookbinding business and a considerable fortune.

In 1853, the first edition of *Missionsharfe* (Missionary Harp), the firm's first bestseller, was printed; circulation of this hymnal eventually exceeded two million copies. Because the firm ran its own printing press, Bertelsmann was able to expand from a small publisher of denominational literature to a publisher of historical and philological books, as well as novels.

Heinrich Bertelsmann's daughter, Friederike, married Johannes Mohn in 1881. When Bertelsmann, who had no sons, died in 1887, the Mohn family took ownership of the business. Mohn expanded printing operations as a means of increasing book production without incurring outside costs. Disheartened by Germany's defeat in World War I and the ensuing revolution, which brought about the kaiser's

The Business

Financials

Revenue (1998): $16 billion

Employees (1998): 57,807

SICs / NAICS

sic 2731 - Book Publishing

sic 3652 - Prerecorded Records & Tapes

sic 5961 - Catalog & Mail-Order Houses

sic 2732 - Book Printing

sic 2711 - Newspapers

sic 2752 - Commercial Printing-Lithographic

sic 2721 - Periodicals

sic 2789 - Bookbinding & Related Work

sic 2791 - Typesetting

sic 2741 - Miscellaneous Publishing

sic 4833 - Television Broadcasting Stations

sic 4832 - Radio Broadcasting Stations

naics 323117 - Book Printing

naics 334612 - Prerecorded Compact Disc (except Software), Tape, and Record Reproducing

naics 323110 - Commercial Lithographic Printing

naics 323121 - Tradebinding and Related Work

naics 323122 - Prepress Services

naics 513111 - Radio Networks

naics 513112 - Radio Stations

abdication in 1918, Mohn passed on the responsibility for the business to his son, Heinrich. In 1923, despite the family wealth, inflation nearly forced the Bertelsmann printing and publishing house to close. For the first time in the company's history, no new employees were hired, and positions were cut.

In 1939, despite his opposition to Hitler and the National Socialist Party in Germany, Heinrich Mohn successfully traded with the German air force, supplying millions of cheap books and pamphlets. At the start of World War II in Europe, Bertelsmann had roughly 400 printers, typesetters, and publishers in Gutersloh, but the right to print religious texts was revoked. British forces bombed Gutersloh in 1945, destroying most of the company's buildings and equipment with the exception of a few expensive printing machines; despite this, operations continued.

In 1947, Reinhard Mohn returned home to Gutersloh after spending two years in an American prisoners-of-war camp. Though he was the third-oldest brother, he assumed control of the publishing company from his aging father because his oldest brother was killed in the war, and the next oldest brother remained imprisoned in Russia for another two years.

In response to the drastic decline in book consumption among Germans, Reinhard Mohn established Bertelsmann Lesering, a book club that offered discounts and benefits to members, in 1950. Mohn also invited the West German retail booksellers to join the Lesering in return for a certain number of free books every year. Within four years, Bertelsmann Lesering boasted one million members. In 1969, Bertelsmann acquired a minority stake in Gruner+Jahr, a publishing company based in Hamburg; ten years later, Bertelsmann increased its stake to 74.9%. The company also made its first step into the American book publishing industry with the acquisition of a majority stake in Bantam Books, the leading paperback publisher in the U.S., and diversified into recording by purchasing the Arista recording label from Columbia Pictures.

Bertelsmann increased its stake in Bantam to 100% in 1981. RCA and Bertelsmann merged their record labels in 1985 to form RCA/Ariola International. The following year, Bertelsmann offered $333 million to General Electric, which had recently bought out RCA, for RCA's 75% stake in RCA/Ariola International. The purchase made Bertelsmann the third-largest recording company in the world. Bertelsmann then paid $475 million for one of the largest U.S. book publishers, Doubleday, which owned Dell paperbacks, book clubs, and a string of retail book shops. These and other strategic acquisitions throughout the decade positioned Bertelsmann as the global leader among media and communication companies by the late 1980s.

Fortune magazine ranked Bertelsmann as the world's largest publishing company in 1991. Two years later, Bertelsmann agreed to found a joint cable television channel with Tele-Communications Inc. (TCI) for national distribution of music and videos in the U.S. A restructuring that year reshuffled operations into four product segments: books; industry, which included printing, paper, distribution and services; entertainment, and Gruner+Jahr, the magazine and newspaper arm of the company.

Diversifying into Internet services for the first time, Bertelsmann acquired a minority stake in America Online in 1995, and the two companies formed an alliance with Germany's Deutsche Telekom AG. Bertelsmann began secret negotiations to purchase Random House from Advance Publications, Inc. in November of 1997. The record-setting deal was finalized in July of 1998, and Bertelsmann consolidated its North American book operations, including Bantam Doubleday Dell, under the Random House name shortly thereafter.

Market Forces Driving the Merger

In the mid-1980s, according to Bruce Wasserstein, author of *Big Deal: The Battle for Control of America's Leading Corporations,* "a new global thirst for 'software' developed. Movies, compact discs, books, and television shows were sought-after commodities on the global market. As this global pipeline mushroomed, the companies involved began to look across borders for opportunities. For American content companies, the goal was to develop foreign distribution platforms. However, the more dramatic development was a growing international interest in owning American content providers." Bertelsmann was a global leader in the push for a foothold in the U.S. In 1985, the firm announced its intent to spend up to $1 billion to strengthen its foothold in the U.S. media industry.

Bertelsmann's first major move was to buy the remaining 75% stake of the RCA/Ariola record label from General Electric Co. for $333 million. That deal made Bertelsmann the third-largest recording company in the world. Before that purchase was finalized, Bertelsmann also agreed to pay $475 million for troubled Doubleday & Co. After two years of falling profits and dwindling market share, Doubleday management had decided to put the firm on the block. The acquisition of Doubleday would position Bertelsmann as the second-largest book publisher in the U.S.

Approach and Engagement

In 1985, Doubleday earned a paltry $7 million in profits on sales of $472.3 million. Management changes and new editorial procedures had also caused problems for Doubleday. For example, best-selling author Barbara Taylor Bradford left the firm after accepting a contract with competitor Random House. As a result, the Doubleday family, which owned a controlling stake in the firm, decided to sell the company. Doubleday's publishing operations were separated from the company's New York Mets assets, which had earned a more impressive $19.8 million in profits on revenues of $43 million.

According to a December 1986 article in *The Wall Street Journal,* several leading U.S. publishers—including Simon & Schuster Inc. and Random House Inc.—turned down the opportunity to buy Doubleday, believing the price to be too high for the struggling

The Officers

Chairman and CEO: Thomas Middelhoff

Chairman of Supervisory Board: Mark Wossner

Deputy Chairman of Executive Board and Chairman, Gruner+Jahr AG: Gerd Schulte-Hillen

Chief Financial Officer: Siegfried Luther

firm. Confident that access to the U.S. market was worth a high price, Bertelsmann agreed to pay $475 million, plus special payments that would bring the combined purchase price to more than $500 million.

Products and Services

In 1998, Bertelsmann was the world's third-largest media company, behind Time Warner and Walt Disney. All trade book publishing operations previously housed within Bantam Doubleday Dell Publishing Group—including Bantam Books, Dell Publishing, Crown Publishing, Ballantine Publishing, Knopf Publishing, Doubleday, and Broadway Books—were consolidated under the Random House name after Bertelsmann completed the takeover of Random House in 1998. Book publishing accounted for roughly 30% of Bertelsmann's total revenues.

BMG Entertainment, which housed all Bertelsmann music, television, and radio holdings, including the RCA/Ariola record label, was the most lucrative of Bertelsmann's segments, securing 33% of total revenues. Besides RCA/Ariola International, BMG Entertainment included Arista, Austria, BMG Australia, BMG Classics, BMG Japan, BMG Music Canada, BMG Music Publishing, BMG Music Service, BMG Special Products, BMG Studios, Buddha Records, Bugjuice, Deconstruction Records, Peeps, Republic, Victor, Sonopress, TwangThis! and the Windham Hill Group.

Other non-book publishing segments included Bertelsmann Multimedia Group, which spearheaded online book sales plans; Bertelsmann Industrie, the printing arm of the company; Bertelsmann Book, the direct marketing consumer book club business; and Gruner+Jahr, magazine and newspaper publishing operations.

By the late 1990s, Bertelsmann's push into the U.S. had paid off. U.S. sales accounted for nearly 31% of total revenues. Sales in Germany were 31% of the firm's annual total as well.

The Players

Chairman and CEO of Bertelsmann AG: Mark Wossner. Mark Wossner began working in printing and industrial plant industries in the 1960s. He joined Bertelsmann as an assistant to chairman Reinhard Mohn. When Mohn stepped down in 1981 after 30 years at the helm of Bertelsmann, he named Wossner his successor. Wossner was the first non-family member to head up the German publishing and media giant. He guided the firm's push into the U.S. in 1986, when Bertelsmann bought both RCA/Ariola International and Doubleday & Co. In 1997, Wossner announced his retirement, appointing Thomas Middelhoff his replacement.

President and CEO of Doubleday & Co.: James T. McLaughlin. Long-time Doubleday employee James McLaughlin accepted the post of president of Doubleday's troubled Dell unit in 1981. After he marshaled Dell's return to profitability, McLaughlin was appointed an executive vice president of Doubleday. He succeeded Nelson Doubleday, grandson of the founder, as president and CEO in October of 1985. When Bertelsmann bought Doubleday in 1986, McLaughlin ceded control of Doubleday operations to Alberto Vitale.

Changes to the Industry and Review of the Outcome

Upon completion of the acquisition, Bertelsmann folded the Doubleday assets into its American publishing operations, which were renamed Bantam Doubleday Dell Publishing Group Inc. The Doubleday unit struggled in the late in 1980s, posting significant losses in 1988 and 1989 after expansion efforts failed. In 1991, however, the firm began its turnaround with the release John Grisham's best seller, *The Firm*. A year later, Bantam Doubleday Dell earned profits of roughly $38 million on sales of $640 million.

Rather than dousing the market with copies of Grisham's next book, *The Pelican Brief*, Doubleday management shipped only enough copies to keep bookstore shelves stocked. The tactic kept the return rate to a minimal 3%, compared to the standard 30% in returns eaten by most major publishers, helping to boost Doubleday's profits further.

Its success in the U.S. publishing market prompted Bertelsmann to pursue another major acquisition in the late 1990s. In July of 1998—in the largest merger in the publishing industry to date—Bertelsmann paid $1.4 billion for Random House Inc., becoming the largest commercial book publisher in the world.

Research

"Bertelsmann AG," in *Notable Corporate Chronologies*, The Gale Group, 1999. Lists major events in the history of Bertelsmann AG.

Bertelsmann AG Home Page, available at http://www.bertelsmann.de. Official World Wide Web Home Page for Bertelsmann AG. Available in both German and English, this site includes news, financial, product, and historical information.

"Bertelsmann Plans to Raise $600 Million for Purchases," in *The Wall Street Journal*, 6 November 1986. Explains how Bertelsmann will finance its two major U.S. acquisitions—RCA and Doubleday-Dell.

"Coming to America: The Sequel," in *Economist*, 16 November 1991. Offers an in-depth look at Bertelsmann's struggles in the U.S. entertainment market.

Guyon, Janet. "Doubleday & Co. Names McLaughlin President and Chief," in *The Wall Street Journal*, 13 September 1985. Details management changes at Doubleday & Co. prior to its takeover by Bertelsmann.

Landler, Mark. "An Overnight Success—After Six Years," in *Business Week*, 19 April 1993. Discusses how Bertelsmann finally found success in the U.S. book and music markets.

Landro, Laura. "Bertelsmann to Pay About $500 Million for Doubleday but Not Including Mets," in *The Wall Street Journal*, 29 December 1986. Covers reasons for Bertelsmann's purchase of Doubleday & Co., as well as the potential problems Bertelsmann will face as it tries to revive the Doubleday operations.

Wasserstein, Bruce. *Big Deal: The Battle for Control of America's Leading Corporations*, Warner Books, 1998. Offers an overview of the largest mergers in recent American corporate history.

THERA WILLIAMS

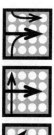

BERTELSMANN & RANDOM HOUSE

nationality: Germany
date: July 1, 1998
affected: Bertelsmann AG, Germany, founded 1835
affected: Random House Inc., USA, founded 1925

Bertelsmann AG
Carl-Bertelsmann-Strasse 270
Gutersloh, D-33311
Germany

tel: 49-52-41-80-0
fax: 49-52-41-751-66
web: http://www.bertelsmann.de

Overview of the Merger

Proclaimed the "shocker of the decade" by *Publisher's Weekly*, the estimated $1.4 billion merger of Bertelsmann AG and Random House Inc. created the largest commercial book publisher in the world. Despite heated protests from the Association of Authors' Representatives and the Authors' Guild that the merger would give Bertelsmann too much control over the $21 billion U.S. book publishing industry, the FTC cleared the largest merger in industry history in May of 1998. Within three months the deal was finalized, and Bertelsmann upped its share of the U.S. book market from roughly six percent to an estimated 11% to 15%.

History of Bertelsmann AG

After his brother's death in 1819, Carl Bertelsmann set up as a bookbinder in his hometown, Gutersloh, Germany, where he printed and bound hymn books for the churches of the area. In 1835, Bertelsmann incorporated his bookbinding and printing business as C. Bertelsmann Verlag. Upon his death in 1850, Bertelsmann left his wife and son, Heinrich, the bookbinding business and a considerable fortune.

In 1853, the fist edition of *Missionsharfe* (Missionary Harp), the firm's first best-seller, was printed; circulation of this hymnal eventually exceeded two million copies. Because the firm ran its own printing press, Heinrich was able to expand beyond being a small publisher of denominational literature to publishing historical and philological books, as well as novels.

Heinrich Bertelsmann's daughter, Friederike, married Johannes Mohn in 1881. When Bertelsmann, who had no sons, died in 1887, the Mohn family took ownership of the business. Mohn expanded printing operations as a means of increasing book production without incurring outside costs. Disheartened by Germany's defeat in World War I and the ensuing revolution which brought about the kaiser's abdication in 1918, Mohn passed on the responsibility for the business to his son, Heinrich. In 1923, despite the family wealth, inflation nearly forced the Bertelsmann printing and publishing house to close. For the first time in the company's history, no new employees were hired, and positions were cut.

The Business

Financials

Revenue (1998): $16 billion

Employees (1998): 57,807

SICs / NAICS

sic 2731 - Book Publishing

sic 3652 - Prerecorded Records & Tapes

sic 5961 - Catalog & Mail-Order Houses

sic 2732 - Book Printing

sic 2711 - Newspapers

sic 2752 - Commercial Printing-Lithographic

sic 2721 - Periodicals

sic 2789 - Bookbinding & Related Work

sic 2791 - Typesetting

sic 2741 - Miscellaneous Publishing

sic 4833 - Television Broadcasting Stations

sic 4832 - Radio Broadcasting Stations

naics 323117 - Book Printing

naics 334612 - Prerecorded Compact Disc (except Software), Tape, and Record Reproducing

naics 323110 - Commercial Lithographic Printing

naics 323121 - Tradebinding and Related Work

naics 323122 - Prepress Services

naics 513111 - Radio Networks

naics 513112 - Radio Stations

In 1939, despite his opposition to Hitler and the National Socialist Party in Germany, Heinrich Mohn successfully traded with the German air force, supplying millions of cheap books and pamphlets. At the start of World War II in Europe, Bertelsmann had roughly 400 printers, typesetters, and publishers in Gutersloh, but the right to print religious texts was revoked. British forces bombed Gutersloh in 1945, destroying most of the company's buildings and equipment with the exception of a few expensive printing machines; despite this, operations continued. In 1947, Reinhard Mohn returned home to Gutersloh after spending two years in an American prisoners of war camp. Though he was the third oldest brother, he assumed control of the publishing company from his aging father because his oldest brother was killed in the war, and his second oldest brother remained imprisoned in Russia for another two years.

In response to the drastic decline in book consumption among Germans, Reinhard Mohn established Bertelsmann Lesering, a book club which offered discounts and benefits to members, in 1950. Mohn also invited the West German retail booksellers to join the Lesering in return for a certain number of free books every year. Within four years, Bertelsmann Lesering boasted one million members. In 1969, Bertelsmann acquired a minority stake in Gruner+Jahr, a publishing company based in Hamburg; ten years later, Bertelsmann increased its stake to 74.9%. The company also made its first foray in American book publishing with the acquisition of a majority stake in Bantam Books, the leading paperback publisher in the U.S., and diversified into recording by purchasing the Arista recording label from Columbia Pictures.

In 1981, Bertelsmann increased its stake in Bantam to 100%, making it a wholly owned subsidiary. Five years later, Bertelsmann paid $475 million for one of the largest U.S. book publishers, Doubleday, which owned Dell paperbacks, book clubs, and a string of retail book shops; the firm also paid $330 million to acquire the remaining 75% of RCA's record division to become the third largest recording company in the world. These and other strategic acquisitions throughout the decade positioned Bertelsmann as the global leader among media and communication companies by the late 1980s.

Fortune magazine ranked Bertelsmann as the world's largest publishing company in 1981. Two years later, Bertelsmann agreed to found a joint cable television channel with Tele-Communications, Inc. (TCI) in the U.S. for national distribution of music and videos. Diversifying into Internet services for the first time, Bertelsmann acquired a minority stake in America Online in 1995, and the two companies formed an alliance with Germany's Deutsche Telekom AG. Bertelsmann began secret negotiations to purchase Random House from Advance Publications, Inc. in November of 1997. The deal was finalized in July of 1998, and Bertelsmann consolidated its North American book operations, including Bantam Doubleday Dell, under the Random House name shortly thereafter.

History of Random House Inc.

Bennett Cerf bought the Modern Library from his boss in 1925. After Cerf and a partner started publishing, at random, luxury editions of the less expensive Modern Library books, they chose the name Random House for their company. Over the next two decades, the company grew via diversified product lines and expanded geographical reach. In the 1930's Random

House entered the children's books arena for the first time; Random House of Canada was established in 1944; and three years later, Random House published its first reference book, *American College Dictionary*.

Random House acquired U.S. publishing house Alfred Knopf Inc. in 1960 and Pantheon Books, a New York-based publisher of works from abroad, in 1961. As it continued to grow, the company strengthened its presence in the reference book market with the release of the first edition of *Random House Dictionary of the English Language* in 1966. To gain access to a broader readership, Random House acquired mass market paperback publisher Ballantine Books in 1973.

In 1965, RCA Corp. had purchased Random House with the goal of integrating electronics and publishing. After struggling to integrate the two companies, RCA sold Random House to privately owned Advance Publications in 1980 for $60 million. Intense growth followed the change in ownership. Random House purchased Fawcett Books in 1982; established Villard Books, a new hardcover imprint, in 1983; bought Times Books from the New York Times Co. in 1984; and acquired Fodor's Travel Guides in 1986. A year later, Random House moved into Europe for the first time with the purchase of Chatto, Virago, Bodley Head & Jonathon Cape, Ltd., a London-based publishing group, to which it added Century Hutchinson Ltd. in 1989 and the trade division of Reed Books in 1997. The London operations were eventually consolidated into a single group named Random House UK.

Growth continued through the late 1980s with the acquisition of Crown Publishing Group in 1988. Random House entered the electronic publishing arena in 1993 by purchasing the electronic publishing division of Bantam Doubleday Dell from German publishing giant Bertelsmann AG. Four years later, Bertelsmann initiated negotiations with Advance Publications to purchase Random House. In July of 1998, the estimated $1.2 billion transaction was finalized.

Market Forces Driving the Merger

Many analysts questioned Bertelsmann's decision to purchase Random House at a time when most large publishers were looking to dump their book publishing operations. In fact, many major players—including News Corp., which owned HarperCollins, and Time Warner, which owned Warner Books and Little, Brown—were seeking either joint ventures or outright sales while Bertelsmann was negotiating its acquisition. The reason for this, according to an April 1998 *Business Week* article, was waning consumer book sales, which fell 3.4% to $5.4 billion in 1997, mainly due to exorbitant best selling author fees and returns on unsold books.

The Officers

Chairman and Chief Executive Officer: Thomas Middelhoff

Chairman of Supervisory Board: Mark Woessner

Deputy Chairman of Executive Board and Chairman,
    Gruner+Jahr AG: Gerd Schulte-Hillen

Chief Financial Officer: Siegfried Luther

According to Bertelsmann CEO Middelhoff, though, the deal with Random House made sense because, unlike Advance Publications, book publishing was Bertelsmann's core focus. With profits high at Bantam Doubleday Dell (particularly when compared to the profits of competing book publishers), total book club membership in Europe and North America exceeding 35 million people, and plans to begin online book sales in the works, Middelhoff believed an acquisition like Random House would help solidify Bertelsmann's position as the world's leading commercial book publisher.

Fortunately, for Bertelsmann, Advance Publications was ready to sell Random House. The book publishing unit's revenues had never measured up to its sister unit's sales. Selling Random House would allow Advance to refocus on its magazine, newspaper, and cable operations. At the same time, Advance's aging CEO, S.I. Newhouse, was getting ready to retire and wanted to shore up his firm's bottom line for his third-generation successors.

Approach and Engagement

Middlehoff approached Newhouse for the first time at his 70th birthday party in November of 1997. Wanting to protect the market value of both companies, especially if negotiations broke down, the two CEOs kept the negotiations secret while they worked out a deal over the next three months. They also wanted to curtail antitrust concerns, as well as negative reactions to the sale of the largest group of English language titles to a German publishing giant, until after terms were finalized.

When the deal was announced in March of 1998 both the Association of Authors' Representatives and the Authors' Guild argued that the merger would give Bertelsmann far too much control over the $21 billion U.S. book publishing industry. By their estimates, Bertelsmann would control in excess of 36% of the U.S. adult trade book market. Their antitrust complaint to the FCC asserted that the 10% market share figure Bertelsmann was using reflected total book

The Players

Chairman and Chief Executive Officer: Thomas Middelhoff. After earning an MBA in Munster, Germany, Thomas Middelhoff began his career by accepting a position as a research assistant at the University of Munster's Institute of Marketing in 1980. In 1986, Middelhoff completed his doctoral dissertation on new media and information technology and was hired by Mohndruck Graphische Betriebe GmbH as a managing assistant. Shortly after securing a position as managing director for Mohndruck in 1989, Middelhoff accepted a position as managing director of Calendar Publishing Co. A year later, he was appointed to Bertelsmann's board of the industry division. In 1994, Middelhoff became a member of Bertelsmann's executive board, as well as head of corporate development and coordinator of the firm's multimedia operations. America Online, Inc. tapped Bertelsmann to serve on their executive board in 1995. A few months after the completion of Bertelsmann's July 1998 merger with Random House Inc., Middelhoff took over as chairman and CEO of Bertelsmann AG, a position the supervisory board had slated him for in July of 1997.

Chairman and CEO, Random House Inc.: Peter Olson. Publishing executive Peter Olson joined Bertelsmann in 1988 as chairman and CEO of the firm's North American Book Group, including Bantam Doubleday Dell Publishing Group and Doubleday Direct, the largest direct marketing consumer book club in the U.S. After Bertelsmann bought Random House in 1998 and regrouped its North American book operations under the Random House name, Olson was appointed chairman and CEO of the new unit; he replaced former Random House CEO Alberto Vitale, who accepted a position as chairman of the supervisory board.

sales, including textbooks and professional books, which targeted completely different markets than trade books.

The FTC delayed the deal twice, but eventually dismissed the antitrust complaints and granted approval for the merger to proceed in May of 1998. By July, the transaction was finalized. Addressing concerns raised by authors and agents that the merger would limit publishing options, new Random House CEO Olson declared in a statement routed to employees upon completion of the merger, "Our new company will draw and build upon the strengths of two great publishing traditions, providing authors, their agents, our booksellers, the international literary and media community, our colleagues, and our readers with an unprecedented diversity of publishing choices and an unstinting commitment to publishing excellence and autonomy."

Products and Services

At the time of the merger, Bertelsmann was the world's third largest media company, behind Time Warner and Walt Disney. The firm's non-book publishing subsidiaries included BMG Entertainment, which housed all Bertelsmann music, television, and radio holdings; Bertelsmann Multimedia Group, which spearheaded online book sales plans; Bertelsmann Industrie, the printing arm of the company; Bertelsmann Book, the direct marketing consumer book club business; and Gruner+Jahr, magazine and newspaper publishing operations.

When the merger was finalized, all trade book publishing operations—including Bantam Books, Dell Publishing, Crown Publishing, Ballantine Publishing, Knopf Publishing, Doubleday, and Broadway Books— were consolidated under the Random House name. Book publishing accounted for roughly 40% of Bertelsmann's total revenues.

Changes to the Industry

The largest merger in the history of the publishing industry gave control of roughly one third of all hardcover bestsellers and half of the leading paperback books in the U.S. to one industry giant. Bertelsmann's share of the total U.S. book market ranged from seven percent to 15%, depending on the source, but the merger boosted its share of the global trade publishing market to a significant 20-23%, according to *Publisher's Weekly*.

A March 1998 *Financial Times* article described Bertelsmann's purchase of Random House as "particularly beneficial to publishers of trade books, bringing the scale both to reduce units costs and to be in more advantageous bargaining positions with retailers and authors' agents." The joining of the German media behemoth with the leading U.S. publishing house also advanced the globalization of the publishing industry to a degree never before seen. And analysts predicted that as Bertelsmann continued its vertical integration efforts via the joining of book club, book publishing, and online book sales operations, barriers between these industry segments would become increasingly blurred.

Review of the Outcome

The $1.4 billion merger boosted sales at Bertelsmann from $12.8 billion in 1997 to roughly $16 billion 1998. The merger's long-term results, however, for both Random House and Bertelsmann are yet to be realized. Most analysts predict a favorable outcome: Bertelsmann gained an impressive catalog of titles which broadened its product base for retail, book club, and online sales; at the same time, Random House attained access to distribution channels that its previous owner, Advance Publications, lacked.

Research

Baker, John F. "Bertelsmann Buy of Random Completed," in *Publishers Weekly*, 6 July 1998. Offers an overview of the merger's progression, as well as information on executive appointments.

"Bertelsmann AG," in *Notable Corporate Chronologies*, The Gale Group, 1999. Lists major events in the history of Bertelsmann Corp.

Bertelsmann AG Home Page, available at http://www.bertelsmann.de. Official World Wide Web Home Page for Bertelsmann AG. Available in both German and English, this site includes news, financial, product, and historical information.

Dugan , I. Jeanne. "Boldly Going Where Others Are Bailing Out: Why Does Betelsmann Think It Can Profit With Random House?" in *Business Week*, 6 April 1998. Discusses the reasons behind the merger and current industry conditions.

Garrity, Brian. "Lazard Banker Pens Publishing Epic," in *Investment Dealer's Digest*, 14 December 1998. Covers the secret negotiations that took place between Bertelsmann and Advance Publications before the merger was announced.

Milliot, Jim. "A Problem With Market Share and Antitrust?" in *Publishers Weekly*, 30 March 1998. Details estimated market share figures for Bertelsmann after the merger.

———. "Authors, Agents Challenge Random/BDD Merger: Complaint to FTC Charges Combination Would Dominate Trade Market, Affect Authorship," in *Publishers Weekly*, 27 April 1998. This article outlines the antitrust and cultural objections raised after the merger was announced.

Random House, Inc. Home Page, available at http://www.randomhouse.com. Official World Wide Web Home Page for Random House, Inc. Includes news, financial, product, historical, and employment information.

Waters, Richard. "Bertelsmann Purchase Set to Open a Whole New Chapter," in *The Financial Times*, 25 March 1998. Analyzes the effects the merger will have on the publishing industry.

ANNAMARIE L. SHELDON

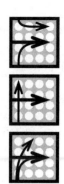

BERTELSMANN & RCA/ARIOLA INTERNATIONAL

Bertelsmann AG
Carl-Bertelsmann-Strasse 270
Gutersloh, D-33311
Germany

tel: 49-52-41-80-0
fax: 49-52-41-751-66
web: http://www.bertelsmann.de

nationality: Germany
date: 1986
affected: Bertelsmann AG, Germany, founded 1835
affected: RCA/Ariola International, USA, founded 1985

Overview of the Merger

In 1986, German publishing and media giant Bertelsmann AG bought the 75% of RCA/Ariola International it didn't already own from General Electric, which had acquired RCA earlier that year. When the $333 million deal was completed, Bertelsmann became the third largest recording company in the world. Bertelsmann then established the Bertelsmann Music Group (BMG) to house all of its radio, television, and music holdings, including the RCA/Ariola record label. The unit struggled, particularly in the U.S., where its market share remained a paltry 10% in 1992. That year, BMG fell from third to fourth place among leading U.S. record companies. By the end of the decade, however, BMG had become Bertelsmann's strongest segment.

History of Bertelsmann AG

After his brother's death in 1819, Carl Bertelsmann set up as a bookbinder in his hometown, Gutersloh, Germany, where he printed and bound hymn books for the churches of the area. In 1835, Bertelsmann incorporated his bookbinding and printing business as C. Bertelsmann Verlag. Upon his death in 1850, Bertelsmann left his wife and son, Heinrich, the bookbinding business and a considerable fortune.

In 1853, the fist edition of *Missionsharfe* (Missionary Harp), the firm's first bestseller, was printed; circulation of this hymnal eventually exceeded two million copies. Because the firm ran its own printing press, Heinrich was able to expand beyond being a small publisher of denominational literature to publishing historical and philological books, as well as novels.

Heinrich Bertelsmann's daughter, Friederike, married Johannes Mohn in 1881. When Bertelsmann, who had no sons, died in 1887, the Mohn family took ownership of the business. Mohn expanded printing operations as a means of increasing book production without incurring outside costs. Disheartened by Germany's defeat in World War I and the ensuing revolution which brought about the kaiser's abdication in 1918, Mohn passed on the responsibility for the business to his son, Heinrich. In 1923, despite the family wealth, inflation nearly forced the Bertelsmann printing and publishing house to close. For the first time in the company's history, no new employees were hired, and positions were cut.

In 1939, despite his opposition to Hitler and the National Socialist Party in Germany, Heinrich Mohn successfully traded with the German air force, supplying millions of cheap books and pamphlets. At the start of World War II in Europe, Bertelsmann had roughly 400 printers, typesetters, and publishers in Gutersloh, but the right to print religious texts was revoked. British forces bombed Gutersloh in 1945, destroying most of the company's buildings and equipment with the exception of a few expensive printing machines; despite this, operations continued. In 1947, Reinhard Mohn returned home to Gutersloh after spending two years in an American prisoners of war camp. Though he was the third oldest brother, he assumed control of the publishing company from his aging father because his oldest brother was killed in the war, and his second oldest brother remained imprisoned in Russia for another two years.

In response to the drastic decline in book consumption among Germans, Reinhard Mohn established Bertelsmann Lesering, a book club which offered discounts and benefits to members, in 1950. Mohn also invited the West German retail booksellers to join the Lesering in return for a certain number of free books every year. Within four years, Bertelsmann Lesering boasted one million members. In 1969, Bertelsmann acquired a minority stake in Gruner+Jahr, a publishing company based in Hamburg; Ten years later, Bertelsmann increased its stake to 74.9%. The company also made its first foray into the American book publishing industry with the acquisition of a majority stake in Bantam Books, the leading paperback publisher in the U.S., and diversified into recording by purchasing the Arista recording label from Columbia Pictures.

Bertelsmann increased its stake in Bantam to 100% in 1981. RCA and Bertelsmann merged their record labels in 1985 to form RCA/Ariola International. The following year, Bertelsmann offered $333 million to General Electric, who had recently bought out RCA, for RCA's 75% stake in RCA/Ariola International. The purchase made Bertelsmann the third largest recording company in the world. Bertelsmann then paid $475 million for one of the largest U.S. book publishers, Doubleday, which owned Dell paperbacks, book clubs, and a string of retail book shops. These and other strategic acquisitions throughout the decade positioned Bertelsmann as the global leader among media and communication companies by the late 1980s.

The Business

Financials

Revenue (1998): $16 billion

Employees (1998): 57,807

SICs / NAICS

sic 2731 - Book Publishing

sic 3652 - Prerecorded Records & Tapes

sic 5961 - Catalog & Mail-Order Houses

sic 2732 - Book Printing

sic 2711 - Newspapers

sic 2752 - Commercial Printing-Lithographic

sic 2721 - Periodicals

sic 2789 - Bookbinding & Related Work

sic 2791 - Typesetting

sic 2741 - Miscellaneous Publishing

sic 4833 - Television Broadcasting Stations

sic 4832 - Radio Broadcasting Stations

naics 323117 - Book Printing

naics 334612 - Prerecorded Compact Disc (except Software), Tape, and Record Reproducing

naics 323110 - Commercial Lithographic Printing

naics 323121 - Tradebinding and Related Work

naics 323122 - Prepress Services

naics 513111 - Radio Networks

naics 513112 - Radio Stations

Fortune magazine ranked Bertelsmann as the world's largest publishing company in 1991. Two years later, Bertelsmann agreed to found a joint cable television channel with Tele-Communications Inc. (TCI) for national distribution of music and videos in the U.S. A restructuring that year reshuffled operations into four product segments: books; industry, which included printing, paper, distribution and services; entertainment, and Gruner+Jahr, the magazine and newspaper arm of the company.

Diversifying into Internet services for the first time, Bertelsmann acquired a minority stake in America Online in 1995, and the two companies formed an alliance with Germany's Deutsche Telekom AG. Bertelsmann began secret negotiations to purchase Random House from Advance Publications, Inc. in November of 1997. The record-setting deal was finalized in July of 1998, and Bertelsmann consolidat-

The Officers

Chairman and CEO: Thomas Middelhoff

Chairman of Supervisory Board: Mark Wossner

Deputy Chairman of Executive Board and Chairman,
     Gruner+Jahr AG: Gerd Schulte-Hillen

Chief Financial Officer: Siegfried Luther

ed its North American book operations, including Bantam Doubleday Dell, under the Random House name shortly thereafter.

Market Forces Driving the Merger

According to Bruce Wasserstein, author of *Big Deal: The Battle for Control of America's Leading Corporations*, U.S. music, book, and media companies were seeking international distribution outlets, while foreign companies sought access to the U.S. market at roughly the same time. "International interest in American music boomed starting in the mid-1980s. With strong distribution networks outside the United States, a number of international media companies saw an opportunity to expand to become global power. A position in the U.S. was the missing critical link. The companies began to shop for U.S. record companies, sparking a consolidation of the record business." Bertelsmann was the first major media company to launch a push into the U.S. record market.

Approach and Engagement

In August of 1985, RCA and Bertelsmann agreed to merge their record labels—RCA Records and Ariola, respectively—to form RCA/Ariola International. The $850 million group, 75% owned by Bertelsmann and 25% owned by RCA, also owned the Arista and Hansa record labels. Neither firm was permitted to divest its stake in the venture without the consent of the other.

When General Electric bought RCA in June of 1986, it agreed to divest the 75% stake in RCA/Ariola to Bertelsmann in September. Bertelsmann agreed to pay a portion of the $333 million price in cash. The remainder was financed through a seven-year bond issue and bank credits. The firm also launched its first stock issue as a means of rasing capital.

Products and Services

In 1998, Bertelsmann was the world's third largest media company, behind Time Warner and Walt Disney. BMG Entertainment, which housed all Bertelsmann music, television, and radio holdings, including the RCA/Ariola record label, was the most lucrative of Bertelsmann's segment, securing 33% of total revenues. Besides RCA/Ariola International, BMG included Arista, BMG Australia, BMG Classics, BMG Japan, BMG Music Canada, BMG Music Publishing, BMG Music Service, BMG Special Products, BMG Studios, Buddha Records, Bugjuice, Deconstruction Records, Peeps, Republic, Victor, Sonopress, TwangThis! and the Windham Hill Group.

Other non-book publishing segments included Bertelsmann Multimedia Group, which spearheaded online book sales plans; Bertelsmann Industrie, the printing arm of the company; Bertelsmann Book, the direct marketing consumer book club business; and Gruner+Jahr, magazine and newspaper publishing operations. All trade book publishing operations—including Bantam Books, Dell Publishing, Crown Publishing, Ballantine Publishing, Knopf Publishing, Doubleday, and Broadway Books—were consolidated under the Random House name after Bertelsmann completed the takeover of Random House in 1998. Book publishing accounted for roughly 30% of Bertelsmann's total revenues.

By the late 1990s, Bertelsmann's push into the U.S. had paid off. U.S. sales accounted for nearly 31% of total revenues. Sales in Germany were 31% of the firm's annual total as well.

Changes to the Industry

The RCA/Artista takeover ignited a wave of consolidation in the worldwide record industry. A year later, Sony acquired CBS Records. PolyGram paid $500 million for A&M Records in 1989. Geffen Records, the last major independent U.S. record firm, was purchased by MCA for $545 million in 1990. After the dust settled, six major global record companies remained standing—Time Warner, MCA, Bertelsmann, Sony, Thorn-EMI, and Philips.

Review of the Outcome

Bertelsmann became the third largest recording company in the world upon its acquisition of the RCA/Ariola record label from General Electric. Within months of the deal, the firm had also acquired Doubleday Dell, a leading U.S. book publisher, for 475 million. However, the U.S. purchases didn't immediately pay off for the firm. By 1992, U.S. sales accounted for 21% of total revenues, but only 10% of net profits.

The Bertelsmann Music Group (BMG), created to house all of the firm's radio, television, and music holdings, including RCA/Ariola International, was barely breaking even and had gone through three presidents in its short six-year history. It hadn't boasted a hit album since *Dirty Dancing* in 1987. The unit struggled, particularly in the U.S., where its market share remained a paltry 10% in 1992. That year, BMG fell from third to forth place among leading U.S. record companies. Although the Arista record label had begun bolstering BMG's performance by 1993— due largely to Whitney Houston's hit soundtrack from *The Bodyguard*, which sold 20 million copies—the RCA label itself continued to undercut the unit's bottom line. By the late 1990s, however, RCA had signed some blockbuster deals itself. BMG became Bertelsmann's most lucrative segment, and analysts finally deemed the RCA/Arista purchase a success.

Research

"Bertelsmann AG," in *Notable Corporate Chronologies*, The Gale Group, 1999. Lists major events in the history of Bertelsmann AG.

Bertelsmann AG Home Page, available at http://www.bertelsmann.de. Official World Wide Web Home Page for Bertelsmann AG. Available in both German and English, this site includes news, financial, product, and historical information.

"Bertelsmann Plans to Raise $600 Million for Purchases," in *The Wall Street Journal*, 6 November 1986. Explains how Bertelsmann will finance its two major U.S. acquisitions—RCA and Doubleday-Dell.

"Coming to America: The Sequel," in *Economist*, 16 November 1991. Offers an in-depth look at Bertelsmann's struggles in the U.S. entertainment market.

The Players

Chairman and CEO of Bertelsmann AG: Mark Wossner. Mark Wossner began working in printing and industrial plant industries in the 1960s. He joined Bertelsmann as an assistant to chairman Reinhard Mohn. When Mohn stepped down in 1981 after thirty years at the helm of Bertelsmann, he named Wossner his successor. Wossner was the first non-family member to head up the German publishing and media giant. He guided the firm's push into the U.S. in 1986, when Bertelsmann bought both RCA/Ariola International and Doubleday-Dell. In 1997, Wossner announced his retirement, appointing Thomas Middelhoff his replacement.

Landler, Mark. "An Overnight Success—After Six Years," in *Business Week*, 19 April 1993. Discusses how Bertelsmann finally found success in the U.S. book and music markets.

Landro, Laura. "GE Will Sell Unit of RCA to Bertelsmann," in *The Wall Street Journal*, 9 September 1986. Covers why General Electric agreed to sell the RCA record unit to Bertelsmann, as well as the terms to which both firms agreed.

Wasserstein, Bruce. *Big Deal: The Battle for Control of America's Leading Corporations*, Warner Books, 1998. Offers an overview of the largest mergers in recent American corporate history.

THERA WILLIAMS

BOEING & MCDONNELL DOUGLAS

Boeing Co.
7755 E. Marginal Way S.
Seattle, WA 98108
USA

tel: (206)655-2121
fax: (206)544-1581
web: http://www.boeing.com

nationality: USA
date: August 1, 1997
affected: Boeing Co., USA, founded 1916
affected: McDonnell Douglas Corp., USA, founded 1920

Overview of the Merger

The 1997 merger of Boeing Co. and McDonnell Douglas Corp. created the largest aerospace firm in the world. Boeing—which had held the title of the world's largest maker of commercial jets since 1958—instantly became the world's largest military aircraft manufacturer. The company laid further claim as NASA's leading contractor, largely due to the merger and its 1996 acquisition of the space and defense units of Rockwell International Corp. Despite doubling its annual revenue to $45.8 billion, versus $22.7 billion in 1996, the company posted a net loss of $178 million in 1997, its first loss in 50 years. Top executives at Boeing blamed production problems for the company's poor performance.

History of Boeing Co.

Bill Boeing, a Seattle lumberman, learned to fly in 1915, under the wing of Glenn Martin, one of the founders of the Lockheed Martin Corp. The next year, Boeing and naval officer Conrad Westervelt founded Pacific Aero Products and built its first plane—the B&W. The company changed its name to Boeing Airplane Company in 1917. Early airborne machines included flying boats, torpedo bombers, and military observers used in World War I. Boeing built more fighter planes than any other maker in the 1920s.

In 1927, federal legislators forced the Post Office to hire private airlines to carry mail cross-country. Not only did Boeing build mail planes; it also won the contract to fly mail between Chicago and San Francisco. Boeing specifically designed the Model 40-powered by Frederick Rentschler's new air-cooled engine-to carry 500 pounds of mail and as many as four paying passengers to make the flights even more profitable. That year Boeing bought Pacific Air Transport.

In 1928, Boeing put all of its manufacturing and transportation operations under the umbrella of Boeing Airplane and Transport Corp. Boeing merged with Rentschler's company the following year to form United Aircraft and Transport. Acquisitions included Sikorsky Aviation and Stout Air Services. By adding other carriers and routes, United became one of the first carriers to offer regularly scheduled coast-to-coast passenger and cargo service. New federal airmail rules in 1934 forced the company to sell its carrier business, now known as United Airlines. The remaining manufacturing concerns became Boeing Airplane.

Boeing began to amass a formidable fleet. Pan Am travelers could cross the ocean in the deluxe Boeing Clipper, a flying boat, or rise above stormy weather in the Boeing Stratoliner, the first passenger plane with a pressurized cabin. The company delivered more than 12,000 B-17 Flying Fortresses to the allied forces during WWII.

Three years after European maker de Havilland introduced the world's first commercial jet in 1949, "Boeing risked the net worth of the company to develop the Dash 80-a prototype of the 707 jetliner," according to corporate lore. The Boeing 727 rolled off the assembly line in 1964 and the 737, the world's best-selling jetliner, in 1967. The 747, the first jumbo jet, finally arrived in 1974, after the company nearly went bankrupt in 1971 owing to a world recession. The world fuel shortage and competition from the newly formed European consortium, Airbus Industrie, prompted Boeing to develop the efficient 757 and 767 in the late 1970s. The 777 wide-body jet touched down in 1995.

In the midst of the full-blown jet age, Boeing helped build the rockets for the Apollo space program. Boeing also built Lunar Orbiters and the Lunar Rover moon buggy in the 1960s. The company changed its name to The Boeing Company in 1961 to reflect its growing diversity. Although commercial aircraft would still bring in the vast majority of the company's revenues, several acquisitions over the next three decades fueled the company's continued thrust into other businesses, including data communications, artificial intelligence, and defense electronics.

Boeing survived a series of ups and downs. In 1995, Singapore Airlines placed a $12.7 billion jetliner order, but a 69-day labor strike cost the company $2 billion in lost revenue. The next year, Boeing won $11 billion in jetliner contracts from three firms: Malaysian Airline, General Electric Co., and United Airlines. In 1996, in a strategic move to stabilize the turbulent jetliner business, Boeing bought the space and defense units of Rockwell International. The next year, Boeing signed a $9 billion deal to create a satellite network for Teledesic Corp., a firm partly owned by Microsoft co-founder Bill Gates. Effective August 1997, Boeing merged with McDonnell Douglas in a $16.3 billion stock swap.

History of McDonnell Douglas

In 1915, Donald Douglas signed on as chief engineer at the Glenn Martin Company, a forerunner to

The Business

Financials

Revenue (1998): $56.15 billion

Employees (1998): 231,000

SICs / NAICS

sic 3728 - Aircraft Parts & Equipment Nec

sic 3721 - Aircraft

sic 3761 - Guided Missiles & Space Vehicles

sic 3812 - Search & Navigation Equipment

naics 336413 - Other Aircraft Part and Auxiliary Equipment Manufacturing

naics 336411 - Aircraft Manufacturing

naics 336414 - Guided Missile and Space Vehicle Manufacturing

naics 334511 - Search, Detection, Navigation, Guidance, Aeronautical, and Systems

Lockheed Martin Corp. Douglas quit five years later to start the Davis-Douglas Company. Working out of the back of a Los Angeles barbershop, the company built its first airplane—the Davis Douglas Cloudster—that David Davis planned to fly in the first nonstop transcontinental flight; after failing, Davis left the firm, which then became the Douglas Co. in 1921.

The company earned a reputation for speedy and reliable flying machines. The U.S. Army bought four Douglas biplanes in 1924 to complete the first round-the-world flight. The company changed its name to Douglas Aircraft in 1928. Douglas turned to the growing commercial market in the 1930s. Rollouts included the DC-1 through the DC-5. The fast and efficient DC-3 handled roughly 90% of worldwide air passenger traffic by 1939.

Douglas planes saw plenty of action during World War II, when aircraft factories switched to military production. Douglas cranked out tons of attack aircraft, including the Dauntless dive bomber, the aerial hero in the Battle of Midway.

Douglas airliners continued to rule the skies until the dawn of the jet age. The company trailed behind de Havilland, which made the first jet in 1949, and Boeing, which hopped on board with the Dash 80 jet

The Officers

Chairman and Chief Executive Officer: Phillip M. Condit

President and Chief Operating Officer: Harry C. Stonecipher

Sr. VP and Chief Financial Officer: Boyd E. Givan

Sr. VP, Secretary, and General Counsel: Theodore J. Collins

in 1952. The first Douglas jetliner—the DC-8—debuted in 1958. Never able to catch up to Boeing jetliners, Douglas openly sought a buyer after a 1966 deficit. The next year, the company accepted a $68.7 million merger bid from St. Louis-based McDonnell Aircraft, a leading carrier-based aircraft maker that started out in 1939 as an airplane parts supplier. Known for Phantom and Banshee fighters, McDonnell also made missiles and spacecraft.

The new McDonnell Douglas Corporation soared. The DC-10 jumbo jet of 1970, along with the Boeing 747, made air travel affordable for the masses. McDonnell Douglas bought Hughes Helicopter in 1984 and thus added the AH-64 Apache attack chopper to its growing fleet. Airliner orders hit record levels for McDonnell Douglas in 1988 and 1989, but defense spending cutbacks after the Cold War hurt the company in the 1990s.

McDonnell Douglas planned to sell 40% of its commercial airliner business to Taiwan Aerospace in 1991, but the deal fell through in 1992. That year, aircraft orders dropped, and the company began layoffs. In 1994, McDonnell Douglas elected its first non-family member, Harry Stonecipher, as President and CEO. The company also won a $400 million contract to launch satellites for Motorola's Iridium project. McDonnell Douglas signed several multibillion-dollar military contracts in 1995, but also took a $1.8 billion charge against the development of the MD-11. In 1996, the U.S. Air Force ordered $14.5 billion worth of C-17 airlifters. That same year, the company lost a $950 million NASA contract to the newly merged Lockheed Martin Corp., then the world's largest aerospace and defense contractor. Late in 1996, Stonecipher began merger talks with Boeing. The $16.3 billion deal was finalized in 1997.

Market Forces Driving the Merger

In 1996, Boeing waged an 18-month overhaul of its entire production system, completely revamping the way it built planes. At the same time, aircraft orders unexpectedly took off from a dead stop. Boeing frantically tried to keep up with the greatest demand for new planes in the history of the jet age while in the midst of the most complex business redesign effort in the world. Further adding to its plight, the company had to cope with a parts shortage caused by its earlier cutbacks that had driven many of its former vendors out of business. The shortage forced Boeing to shut down two production lines, causing a $1.6 billion charge against company earnings. "I've described it as trying to change the tire on my car while going 60 miles an hour," said Boeing CEO Condit in a July 1998 *Time* magazine article titled "Is Boeing Out of Its Spin?"

A merger with McDonnell Douglas would secure for Boeing factory space, trained workers, and increased capacity to handle the load. The strength of McDonnell Douglas' military aircraft business would also counterbalance Boeing's highly cyclical commercial jetliner business, allowing the company to better pull resources to projects as needed.

Approach and Engagement

McDonnell Douglas CEO Stonecipher asked for and received board authorization to negotiate a merger with Boeing Co. in late 1996. Part of the push came when McDonnell Douglas lost a $950 million NASA contract to newly merged Lockheed Martin, then the world's largest aerospace firm. Stonecipher admitted in a June 1997 article in *Interavia Business & Technology*, "Douglas is not dead but dying." Welcoming a chance to further ramp up production and balance its air force, Boeing CEO Condit hashed out a deal with Stonecipher in less than a week in December 1996. When the Boeing-McDonnell Douglas merger went through, Condit remained CEO, and Stonecipher became President and COO of Boeing.

In 1997, the Associated Press reported that FTC commissioners approved the merger after concluding that McDonnell Douglas could no longer compete in the commercial aircraft market on its own. The Pentagon voiced no opposition because the two companies did not directly compete for military contracts.

An *Interavia Business & Technology* article summed up the overseas reaction to the pending merger and the perceived threat to European consortium Airbus: "After a lot of last minute arm-twisting, posturing, brinkmanship, statesmanship and last-minute concessions from both sides, the EU [European Union] finally put its seal of approval on the Boeing/McDonnell Douglas merger." Shareholder approval of the merger followed soon afterwards, and Boeing began operations as a single company on August 4, 1997, with a backlog of over $100 billion. "The Europeans were alarmed about 20-year agreements Boeing had struck with American Airlines, Delta, and Continental to buy only Boeing planes," according to *U.S. News & World Report*. These pacts, the Europeans argued, unfairly shut out Airbus. To avoid antitrust sanctions, Boeing was forced to dismantle the agreements.

Products and Services

The newly formed Boeing Co. divided its business into three units: Boeing Commercial Airplane Group; Information, Space & Defense Systems; and the Shared Services Group.

The Commercial Airplane Group blew past the competition, snaring more than 60% of the world's $65 billion-a-year jetliner market. The main fleet included the 717 (the former MD-95), 737, 747, 757, 767, and 777 jetliners in a variety of passenger and cargo configurations for short or long haul, and low or high capacity. The company also made the MD-80, MD-90, and MD-11 jets.

Boeing derived 40% of its 1997 revenue from Information, Space & Defense Systems. (By comparison, the unit accounted for 29% in 1995.) Products included the F-18 Super Hornet fighter and the C-17 military transport planes. The company also served as the prime contractor on the NASA Space Station and collaborated on a number of programs, such as the F-22 Raptor fighter plane with Lockheed Martin, the V-22 Osprey tilt-rotorcraft with Bell Helicopter Textron, and the RAH-66 Comanche helicopter with Sikorsky. The U.S. government accounted for roughly 70% of the unit's sales. Foreign sales represented 22%; Boeing fighter planes served in the air forces of Australia, Canada, Finland, Israel, Kuwait, Spain, Switzerland, and Saudi Arabia.

The Shared Services Group arranged purchasing and logistical support for Boeing's larger projects and programs and across business unit lines. The group aimed to streamline procedures and gain economies of scale for a wide ranges of services, including travel planning and information management.

Changes to the Industry

The merger of McDonnell Douglas and Boeing took place in an industry spinning from widespread consolidation. The commercial jet market, in particular, essentially became a duopoly. The newly pumped-up Boeing could lay original claims on 77% of all jetliners in service, up from 55% in the pre-merger days. In 1996, Boeing snagged roughly 60% of the $65 billion market, McDonnell Douglas scraped by with about 4%, and the rest went to Airbus Industrie, the

The Players

Chairman and CEO of Boeing: Phillip M. Condit. Phillip Condit earned his pilot's license at the age of 18 and has since proved to be in aviation for the long haul. In 1965— fresh from earning a master's degree in aeronautical engineering from Princeton University and flying high from a newly awarded patent for the design of a flexible aircraft wing—Condit went to work for Boeing on its Supersonic Transport program and eventually logged more than 30 years of service at Boeing in nearly 20 assignments ranging from vice president of sales and marketing to chairman of the board.

President and CEO of McDonnell Douglas Corp.: Harry C. Stonecipher. Harry C. Stonecipher has spent 40 years in the aerospace industry. He held powerful positions at General Electric and Sundstrand before assuming the command of McDonnell Douglas Corp., one of the world's largest defense and space contractors. In 1987, Stonecipher left GE to be an executive vice president at Sundstrand, a worldwide leader in the design and manufacture of technology-based products for aerospace and industrial markets. By 1991, he had collected the titles of CEO, president, and chairman. His noteworthy accomplishments at Sunstrand included marked improvements in quality control, a better relationship with the union workforce, and the repair of the company's badly damaged reputation with the U.S. Department of Defense. In 1994, McDonnell Douglas tapped Stonecipher as President and CEO; he was the first non-family member to run the company in its 75-year history. He became president and COO of Boeing upon the 1997 merger with McDonnell Douglas.

European consortium. During the production crisis that sparked the merger—ironically, these problems were soon compounded by the McDonnell Douglas deal—Airbus had started openly shooting for half the market by hitting on Boeing's former customers. In July 1998, U.S. Airways announced plans to buy 30 more Airbus jets, beefing up a prior order of 400 Airbus jets. The announcement closely followed two record-breakers for the European consortium: Spanish airline, Iberia, ordered 76 jets and three Latin American airlines jointly ordered 179 jets.

Both Boeing and Airbus were hurt in 1997 when Pacific Rim carriers canceled aircraft orders, citing the Asian financial crisis. Air travel in China, however, was growing an average of 20% annually throughout the 1990s. Following its merger with McDonnell Douglas, Boeing continued to bank on a solid future with China, where it had sold $18.5 billion worth of planes over the past 27 years and held 72% of the market. In fact, Boeing had inherited a major McDonnell Douglas contract to provide MD-90 aircraft to Shanghai.

Review of the Outcome

Fortune magazine dubbed the merger "The Sale of the Century." But, given the production problems and delivery delays, Wall Street slashed the value of Boeing shares 26% in the nine months following the merger. In *Business Week*'s Global 1000, which ranks companies worldwide by market value, Boeing took a nose dive, placing "75" in 1998 versus "63" in 1997, a year in which U.S. companies saw their stocks rise 37% overall.

In a May 1998 *Forbes* article, Boeing CEO Condit admitted that his focus on Boeing's recently acquired defense operations—both Rockwell and McDonnell Douglas—had cost the commercial airline operations of Boeing dearly. "Obviously, knowing what I know now, I should have been spending more time watching [the commercial] part of the store."

The outlook brightened in June of 1998. Boeing reported a record 61 deliveries that month and expected to deliver an average of 50 planes a month for the rest of 1998, at a time when established carriers continued to replenish aging fleets with more efficient aircraft, and new carriers were gearing up for more air travelers. According to aerospace analyst Joseph Campbell of Lehman Brothers, "it's good to know Boeing can get the planes out the door, but now it must boost its net profit margins, currently under 3%." Shortly after the news release, Boeing stock rose near-ly $4 a share. The company posted revenues in excess of $56 billion in 1998.

Research

Banks, Howard. "Slow Learner," *Forbes*, 4 May 1998. Details the production errors of Boeing in the months following the Rockwell and McDonnell Douglas acquisitions.

Bernstein, Aaron. "Lost in Space at Boeing," *Business Week*, 27 April 1998. In the wake of the merger, Boeing and McDonnell Douglas executives clash.

Boeing Home Page, available at http://www.boeing.com. Official World Wide Web Home Page for Boeing Co. Includes access to the 1997 Annual Report, news, financial, and employment information. Researchers can also find information and images of past and present Boeing military, commercial, and civilian airplanes.

Condom, Pierre. "The Duopoly," in *Interavia Business & Technology*, September 1997. Examines the effect of the Boeing/McDonnell Douglas merger on Airbus Industrie and explains how the three companies' products and management styles worked with one another within a favorable airplane market.

Cook, William J. "Surfeit in Seattle: As Orders Pour In, Boeing Stumbles," in *U.S. News & World Report*, 17 November 1997. In the wake of its much-celebrated merger, Boeing experiences production problems as orders pour in.

Greenwald, John. "Is Boeing Out of Its Spin?," in *Time*, 13 July 1998. A year after the merger with McDonnell Douglas, this article investigates whether the Boeing Company is finally on track.

Holland, Kelley. "Boeing Production Takes Wing," in *Business Week*, 13 July 1998. Examines the resurgence in production numbers at Boeing. Orders are being filled and customers and management are finally content.

Sutton, Oliver. "Boeing Completes MDC Merger, Unveils New Corporate Structure," in *Interavia Business & Technology*, September 1997. The merger between Boeing and McDonnell Douglas is finally a reality. This article details the new company's corporate structure and examines the role of Philip Condit in the merger.

Wilson, J.R. "Anatomy of a Merger," in *Interavia Business & Technology*, June 1997. Explores the reason behind the merger between Boeing and McDonnell Douglas Corporation: to satisfy Boeing's need for additional facilities, trained workers, and greater capacity to help decrease a massive backlog of orders.

BRIDGESTONE & FIRESTONE

nationality: Japan
date: May 1988
affected: Bridgestone Corp., Japan, founded 1931
affected: Firestone Tire & Rubber Co., USA, founded 1900

Bridgestone Corp.
10-1, Kyobashi 1-chome
Chou-ku, Tokyo 104-8340
Japan

tel: 03-3567-0111
fax: 03-3535-2553
web: http://www.bridgestone.co.jp

Overview of the Merger

Japan's Bridgestone Corp. paid $2.65 billion for Firestone Tire & Rubber Co., the third-largest U.S. tire maker, in May of 1988. The deal marked the largest purchase to date of a U.S. company by the Japanese. Bridgestone's struggles with its Firestone operations after the deal was finalized prompted industry analysts to speculate that Bridgestone had gotten so caught up in winning the heated bidding war with Italy's Pirelli, it forgot to look closely at the condition of Firestone.

History of Bridgestone Corp.

Japanese entrepreneur Shojiri Ishibashi founded Bridgestone Ltd., in Kurume, Japan, in 1931. The firm began producing tires and other items made from rubber. In 1942, the company's name was changed to Nippon Tire Co., Ltd. With the advent of World War II, the firm began supplying military requirements. In 1951, Nippon Tire was renamed Bridgestone Tire Co., Ltd.

In 1963, Bridgestone established in Singapore its first overseas factory. Four years later, another factory was built in Thailand. The firm, as a leading supplier of sporting goods as well as tires, established The Bridgestone Sports Co., Ltd. in 1972. Items produced included golf balls, clubs, and tennis rackets. The following year, an Indonesian factory was opened. In 1976, a sales company was established in Hamburg, Germany, in partnership with Japanese firm Mitsui. The new enterprise, called Bridgestone Reifen GmbH, was intended to increase tire sales in the important West German market.

Bridgestone Singapore ceased operations following the government's lifting of tariff protection for locally made tires in 1980. Four years later, the firm changed its name to Bridgestone Corp. In 1987, Bridgestone approached Goodyear with proposals for a merger of the two tire manufacturers, but negotiations eventually failed. The following year, Bridgestone acquired Firestone for $2.65 billion; the sale brought with it 54,000 employees and two headquarters. Efficiency measures were instituted in 1989, including the streamlining of North American production and marketing through integration of operations at Firestone, which were renamed

The Business

Financials

Revenue (1998): $17.07 billion

Employees (1998): 97,767

SICs / NAICS

sic 3011 - Tires & Inner Tubes

sic 3069 - Fabricated Rubber Products Nec

sic 5013 - Motor Vehicle Supplies & New Parts

sic 5014 - Tires & Tubes

sic 5033 - Roofing, Siding & Insulation

sic 3751 - Motorcycles, Bicycles & Parts

sic 3086 - Plastics Foam Products

sic 3444 - Sheet Metal Work

naics 326211 - Tire Manufacturing (except Retreading)

naics 326299 - All Other Rubber Product Manufacturing

naics 336991 - Motorcycle, Bicycle, and Parts
Manufacturing

naics 332322 - Sheet Metal Work Manufacturing

Bridgestone/Firestone, Inc. and Bridgestone (U.S.A.), Inc.

By 1990, the firm's international sales network included a chain of retail outlets called Cockpit; the stores sold car audio equipment and accessories such as wheels and well tires. Large scale restructuring and investment continued as Bridgestone pursued its ambition to become the world's leading tire manufacturer. The company's 1,550 auto service facilities in North America, formerly called Mastercare, were renamed Tire Zone in 1992. Firestone began selling the competing Michelin brand tire, and the revolutionary "Runflat" tire was introduced.

President Clinton criticized Bridgestone for hiring 2,300 permanent replacements during a strike by the United Rubber Workers (URW). Many of the union workers were not expected to get their jobs back. In August of 1995, the URW ended a 10-month strike at Bridgestone and accepted a contract that included wage reductions of $5.34 per hour and lower health and pension benefits. Also that year, Bridgestone developed a polyurethane material that decreased vibration and noise transfer from the engine of a vehicle to the passenger compartment. The product was lightweight and expanded when heated, enabling it to fill any space and take any shape.

In 1996, hundreds of members of the United Steel Workers of America (USWA) descended on Indianapolis, Indiana, to symbolically drop a black flag on the Bridgestone Corp. at the Indianapolis 500. The union was staging a high-profile campaign, asking consumers to boycott the company's products and services, including tires, sporting goods, and Firestone MasterCare auto centers. In an effort to curtail Japanese imports, Bridgestone constructed a factory in South Carolina in 1997. The following year, the firm unveiled a tire designed to perform best when worn down.

History of Firestone Tire & Rubber Co.

Firestone Tire & Rubber Co. was founded in August of 1900 by 31-year-old inventor and entrepreneur Harvey S. Firestone, who had discovered a new way of making carriage tires. He launched operations with 12 employees in Akron, Ohio. The firm got its first big break when Henry Ford chose Firestone tires for the first mass-produced automobiles in the U.S.

In the firm's first major publicity campaign, Firestone entered and won the first Indy 500 in 1911. Cars driven on Firestone tires eventually won 50 checkered flags. During the 1920s, Firestone leased one million acres in Liberia for rubber plantations and created a chain of automotive supply and service centers. After World War II ended, Firestone diversified into the synthetic rubber and automotive components industries. The firm also began its overseas push. Domestic growth continued with the acquisition of two U.S.-based tire manufacturers: Dayton Tire & Rubber and Seiberling. Although considered a leading tire manufacturer in the U.S., by the 1970s, Firestone was in trouble. A bloated inventory, coupled with a recall in 1978 of Firestone 500 steel-belted radial tires, had taken a toll on the company. Sales totaled $5.3 billion.

John Nevin was hired as president the following year, and he began a major restructuring that included paring down inventory, closing several plants, upgrading the plants that did remain in operation, diversifying into the car rental and automotive services industries, and laying off 8,500 of the firm's 107,000 workers. Headquarters were eventually relocated from Ohio to Chicago, Illinois. By the late 1980s, only five of 17 North American plants continued to operate. Firestone's work force had been whittled to 55,000, roughly half of its size when Nevin took over.

Bridgestone and Italy's Pirelli SpA began a bidding war for Firestone—which held 14% of the U.S. tire market, behind Uniroyal Goodrich Tire Co.'s 17% and Goodyear Tire & Rubber Co.'s 30%—in 1988. Firestone eventually accepted Bridgestone's $2.65 billion offer. In 1989, Bridgestone merged its U.S. operations with Firestone to form Bridgestone/Firestone, Inc.

Market Forces Driving the Merger

In the early 1980s, Japanese tire maker Bridgestone was beginning to recognize that it could no longer rely on Japanese manufacturers to resist importing U.S. and European tires, which were considered higher quality products. Also, Honda Motor Co. Ltd. and Nissan Motor Co. Ltd. began to build plants in the U.S. and Europe; consequently, they sought locally made tires. To secure a portion of this business for itself, Bridgestone needed access to those markets. Rather than spend the time and money building its own factories, the firm decided to buy a foreign tire manufacturer.

Bridgestone began its move into the U.S. market in January of 1983 by buying a Nashville, Tennessee-based plant belonging to Firestone for $52 million. Bridgestone turned the failing plant around, setting the stage for the acquisition of Firestone later in the decade. Firestone CEO Nevin approached Bridgestone about a merger in December of 1984 and again in July of 1986, but he was turned down by the Japanese company both times. When Germany's Continental AG forged a joint venture with two Japanese firms, Toyo Tire and Rubber Co. and Yokohama Rubber Co., Bridgestone decided the time had come to pursue a major international deal.

Prior to approaching Firestone, Bridgestone initiated negotiations with Goodyear, the leading U.S. tire maker, in 1987; however, those talks broke down when Goodyear demanded a price Bridgestone was unwilling to pay. Determined to find a U.S. production base for tire making, particularly heavy-duty radial truck tires, Bridgestone then solicited Firestone. Not only would a merger give Bridgestone access to the lucrative U.S. market; Firestone's operations in Portugal, France, Spain, and Italy offered Bridgestone an opportunity to shore up its European foothold as well.

Firestone was well positioned for a merger, as its performance in the late 1980s was better than it had been in several years due to the streamlining efforts of CEO John Nevin. According to a May 1988 article in *The New York Times*, Nevin believed that the deal would "enhance the value of Firestone stock," as well as job security and both product quality and diversity. However, critics of the deal pointed to the $20 million stock option profit Nevin secured for himself, arguing that the merger negotiations were fueled by corporate greed. Consumer advocate Ralph Nader stated, "Nevin takes this dilapidated Firestone company and closes what he calls inefficient plants. He watches

The Officers

President, Chairman, and CEO: Yoichiro Kaizaki

Exec. VP, Advisor to the President, and Director of Product Planning Division: Tadakazu Harada

Exec. VP, Chairman and CEO of Bridgestone/Firestone, Inc.: Masatoshi Ono

Exec. VP, Advisor to the President: Katsuyoshi Shibata

Exec. VP, Chairman, CEO, and President of Bridgestone/Firestone Europe S.A.: Takeshi Uchiyama

stock go up and its profits resume, and he sells out to the Japanese. That's called undermining the trust of people who took cutbacks to let the company recover."

Approach and Engagement

On February 16, 1988, Bridgestone bid $1.25 billion for 75% of Firestone. When Firestone accepted, Italy's Pirelli, which had conducted informal merger talks with Firestone since 1986, and France's Michelin joined forces to launch a $1.9 billion, or $58 per share, counterbid for full ownership of the U.S. tire maker on March 7. As a result, Firestone stock jumped to $63 per share.

Bridgestone upped its offer to $2.65 billion, or $80 per share, a price which Firestone eventually accepted. Shareholders approved the deal on April 25, and two days later, when the tender offer was completed, Bridgestone owned 96% of Firestone. In early May, Firestone and Bridgestone Acquisition Corp., a Bridgestone subsidiary formed during negotiations, officially merged to finalize the transaction.

Products and Services

In 1998, U.S. sales accounted for 44% of total profits, while Japanese sales secured 39%, and European sales brought in 11%. Bridgestone products were organized into seven segments:

Accounting for 79% of total revenues, **Tires and Tubes** included. tires and tubes for passenger cars, trucks, buses, construction and mining vehicles, commercial vehicles, agricultural machinery, aircraft, motorcycles and scooters, racing cars, utility carts, subways, and monorails.

Automotive Parts included wheels for passenger cars, trucks, buses, and rubber chains.

The Players

Chairman and CEO of Firestone Tire & Rubber Co.: John J. Nevin. John Nevin began his career in the automotive industry at Ford Motor Co. in 1954. He had worked his way up to marketing vice president in 1971 when Zenith Radio Corp. lured him away by offering him the position of president. While at Zenith, Nevin launched an unsuccessful antidumping lawsuit against Japanese television manufacturers, who he claimed were undercutting U.S. manufacturers. Firestone hired him as president in 1979, and the Harvard Business School graduate set to work streamlining the floundering tire maker. Nevin oversaw the firm's merger negotiations with both Bridgestone and Pirelli in 1988. Bridgestone completed its purchase of Firestone in May of that year, and on December 31, Nevin retired. He had secured $20 million in stock option profits for himself during negotiations.

Industrial Rubber Products included steel cord conveyor belts, canvas conveyor belts, belt-related commodities, braided hoses, hydraulic hoses, industrial cord hoses, synthetic hoses, air springs, dampers, noise-insulating systems, water stoppers, waterproof sheets for civil engineering, rubber crawlers, inflatable rubber dams, multi-rubber bearings, marine products, and vibration-isolating rubber for vehicles, railway cars, and industrial machinery.

Chemical Products included building materials such as FRP panel water tanks, unit flooring systems, panel roof tiles, steel fiber for concrete reinforcement, roofing materials, and bathroom fixtures; thermal insulating polyurethane foam products for general building and housing; office equipment components; flexible polyurethane foam products for bedding, furniture, vehicles, and industry; and ceramic foam.

Sporting Goods included golf balls, golf clubs, tennis shoes, tennis rackets, tennis balls, and golf swing diagnostic systems. The two remaining product groups were **Bicycles** and **Other**, which included weighing systems.

The Bridgestone/Firestone U.S. subsidiary operated 36 manufacturing facilities and sold over 50 million tires per year at 1,500 retail outlets across the nation. Employees at the unit totaled 45,000.

Changes to the Industry

Bridgestone's purchase of Firestone marked the first noteworthy international deal between two major tire makers. The deal illuminated the need for the tire industry to keep pace with the globalization of the automotive market. Accordingly, in September of 1989, France's Michelin announced its impending purchase of Uniroyal Goodrich, the second-largest U.S. tire maker.

Review of the Outcome

A few months after the deal was completed, Bridgestone announced its intent to spend $1.5 billion over the next three years refurbishing 28 Firestone plants, as well as the firm's distribution arm. In August of 1989, Bridgestone merged its North American operations with those of Firestone to create Bridgestone/Firestone, Inc. George W. Aucott was named successor to Firestone CEO John J. Nevin, who had announced his retirement when the deal with Bridgestone was completed. However, when Uniroyal and Michelin announced their plans to merge, Bridgestone CEO Akira Yeiri decided the parent company needed to speed the integration of the two firms. As a result, Bridgestone chairman Teiji Eguchi stepped in to head up the North American operations.

Although company officials denied it, industry analysts began speculating that Bridgestone had severely underestimated the work needed to bring Firestone up to snuff. Some approximated that $2.5 billion, in addition to the planned $1.5 billion, would be necessary complete the overhaul of Firestone operations. According to an August 1990 article in *Business Week*, "When Bridgestone officials arrived in Akron, they found a company a far worse condition than they expected. Chairman John J. Nevin...had shuttered tire factories while shifting investment into auto service centers." Along with low productivity at Firestone's tire factories, economic downturns in Europe and Latin America also eroded earnings. Losses totaling $350 million at Firestone caused Bridgestone's profits to tumble 76% to $67 million on revenues of $11.7 billion in 1989. Bonuses for officers were nixed.

In early 1990, Bridgestone announced a hiring freeze; roughly 150 employees accepted early retirement options, and another 250 workers were laid off. Also, the original three-year upgrade plan was stretched to four years. Profits at Bridgestone fell to $33.2 million that year, due mainly to the $400 million in losses posted by Firestone. Although earnings began a slow climb in 1991, culture clashes and labor disputes at Bridgestone/Firestone continued to plague the parent company. In 1997, Bridgestone wrote off the costs related to its purchase of Firestone, causing profits to dive 44% despite record sales.

Research

Bridgestone Corp. Home Page, available at http://www.bridgestone.co.jp.com. Official World Wide Web Page for Bridgestone Corp. Includes product, corporate, and employment information, as well as current news and annual reports.

"Bridgestone Corp.," in *Notable Corporate Chronologies*, The Gale Group, 1999. Covers major events in the history of Bridgestone Corp.

"Bridgestone Corp.," in *International Directory of Company Histories*, St. James Press, Vol. V, 1992. Offers a detailed look at the history of Bridgestone Corp.

Bridgestone/Firestone, Inc. Home Page, available at http://www.firestone.com. Official World Wide Web Page for Bridgestone/Firestone, Inc. Includes product, corporate, historical, and employment information, as well as current news and annual reports.

Hicks, Jonathan P. "Firestone's Chief; John J. Nevin; After the Bridgestone Deal, What's Next?" in *The New York Times*, 1 May 1988. Details the career of John Nevin.

Schiller, Zachary. "Japan Vs. Europe: Firestone May Be Just the Appetizer," in *Business Week*, 21 March 1988. Explains why both Japanese and European tire companies are vying for a foothold in the U.S.

———. "Why Bridgestone's Chairman Is Making Tracks to Akron," in *Business Week*, 20 November 1989. Discusses why Bridgestone decided to speed up integration efforts.

———. "So Far, America Is a Blowout for Bridgestone," in *Business Week*, 6 August 1990. Covers the performance of Firestone since its takeover by Bridgestone.

"When the Bridge Caught Fire," in *The Economist*, 7 September 1991. An in-depth case study of Bridgestone's purchase of Firestone.

ANNAMARIE L. SHELDON

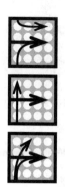

BRISTOL-MYERS & SQUIBB

Bristol-Myers Squibb Co.
245 Park Ave.
New York, NY 10154-0037
USA

tel: (212)546-4000
fax: (212)546-4020
web: http://www.bms.com

nationality: USA
date: October 4, 1989
affected: Bristol-Myers Co. , USA, founded 1858
affected: Squibb Corp., USA, founded 1887

Overview of the Merger

Right on the heels of the $16 billion SmithKline Beckman Corp. and Beecham Group PLC merger, the October 1989 joining of Bristol-Myers Co. and Squibb Corp. created a new industry powerhouse that quickly challenged the second place status of SmithKline Beecham PLC. The $12.7 billion marriage of Bristol-Myers, the 12th largest pharmaceutical firm in the world, and Squibb, the 14th largest, created Bristol-Myers Squibb Co. The new firm boasted combined revenues of $4.5 billion and a $600 million annual research and development budget.

History of Bristol-Myers Co.

In 1887, William Bristol and John Myers each invested $5,000 into the Clinton Pharmaceutical Co., a failing drug manufacturing firm in Clinton, New York, and began selling medical preparations by horse and buggy to local doctors and dentists. Within two years, the workforce had increased from six to nine employees. Because it needed better shipping facilities, the firm moved to Syracuse, New York, a major railroad center. In 1898, the company moved its headquarters to Brooklyn, New York, for better access to customers in Pennsylvania and New England; a year later, the firm incorporated as Bristol-Myers Co.

It wasn't until 1900 that Bristol-Myers reached profitability for the first time. The firm had benefitted from the increasing number of physicians who wrote prescriptions to be filled at a pharmacy, rather than dispensing products themselves. In 1903, Bristol-Myers introduced its new toothpaste, Ipana, which was the firm's first dental product to include a disinfectant that protected against the effects of bleeding gums.

During the early 1920s, the firm shifted focus from its ethical drug business to its specialty products, including Ipana and other toiletries, antiseptics, and cough syrups. In 1924, company shares were first made available for sale; five years later, Bristol-Myers stock was listed on the New York Stock Exchange. The firm became part of Drug, Inc., a recently formed holding company which became the largest manufacturer of proprietary and medicinal products and operated the largest chain of retail stores in the world at the time. Bristol-Myers flourished as part of the conglomerate despite the Depression; however, the other companies in Drug, Inc. did not fare as well, so Drug, Inc. voluntarily split up in 1933.

During World War II, Bristol-Myers reentered the ethical pharmaceuticals industry and acquired Cheplin Laboratories in Syracuse, a small maker of acidophilus milk (milk fermented by bacteria for supposed therapeutic qualities). Because of Cheplin's fermentation expertise and the need for penicillin, Bristol-Myers was brought into the war effort. At war's end the new acquisition was renamed Bristol Laboratories; it focused on penicillin and other antibiotic production.

The late 1950s marked a period of expansion for Bristol-Myers. Acquisitions included Clairol, maker of hair-coloring products; Drackett, a household products manufacturer; and Mead Johnson, a producer of infant formula and children's vitamins. By this time, an over-the-counter (OTC) version of Johnson & Johnson's Tylenol had taken a significant portion of Bristol-Myers's previously strong hold on the analgesics market; a string of new product failures in the mid 1960s drained finances and depressed the company's stock value. In an effort to turn his firm around, CEO Richard Gelb launched a spending program; Zimmer Manufacturing Co., a producer of orthopedic and surgical products, was the first such acquisition.

A 1977 National Cancer Institute report linking an ingredient used in hair colorants, 2-4 DAA, and cancer in laboratory rats prompted Bristol-Myers introduce a new line of hair dyes, as well as reformulate the original line. The following year, the firm acquired Unitek Corp., a dental equipment supplier. Between 1975 and 1980, Bristol-Myers launched 11 new drugs for treatment of cancer and other diseases; though none were breakthrough drugs, they contributed over $200 million in sales. A series of ten-year-old antitrust suits alleging that Bristol-Myers and Beecham Group PLC improperly obtained a patent on the antibiotic ampicillin were finally settled in 1982.

An agreement with John Co. enabled Bristol-Myers to introduce Nuprin, a new nonprescription form of ibuprofen pain reliever, in 1984. That year, the firm entered the market for drugs used to treat anxiety and depression, and built a multi-million dollar research facility in Wallingford, Connecticut. In 1985, Oncogen, a joint venture between Genetic Systems Corp. (GSC) and Syntex Corp. to manufacture products for cancer treatment, invited the firm to join in exchange for a $12 million contribution. After a chief competitor acquired a biotechnology interest, Bristol-Myers negotiated an agreement with GSC manage-

The Business

Financials

Revenue (1998): $18.3 billion

Employees (1998): 54,700

SICs / NAICS

sic 2834 - Pharmaceutical Preparations

sic 2833 - Medicinals & Botanicals

sic 2844 - Toilet Preparations

sic 3842 - Surgical Appliances & Supplies

sic 2842 - Polishes & Sanitation Goods

naics 325412 - Pharmaceutical Preparation Manufacturing

naics 325411 - Medicinal and Botanical Manufacturing

naics 322291 - Sanitary Paper Product Manufacturing

naics 325612 - Polish and Other Sanitation Good
   Manufacturing

ment to buy GSC and Oncogen for $300 million, unaware that GSC already had negotiated a similar deal with Syntex. Syntex threatened to sue but withdrew its offer in exchange for a $15 million compensation package from Bristol-Myers and for marketing rights to selected GSC and Oncogen products.

After a second incident of tampering with capsule type pain relief products caused two deaths in 1986, Bristol Myers recalled Excedrin and all of its nonprescription capsule products, including Comtrex cold relief medication. OTC capsules were phased out completely and replaced by caplets, a specially coated, capsule shaped pill. During the late 1980s, Bristol-Myers continued to grow as a maker of prescription pharmaceuticals and attempted to lessen its dependence on consumer products by focusing on AIDS research. The firm obtained an exclusive license to produce and test two new AIDS drugs, dideoxyadenosine (DDA) and dideoxyionosine (DDI), and received FDA approval to test an experimental AIDS vaccine on humans.

In October of 1989, Bristol-Myers merged with Squibb Corp. to become Bristol-Myers Squibb Co., the second largest pharmaceutical company in the U.S. Two years later, the FDA approved five new drugs, including Pravachal, a cardiovascular drug, and VIDEX, for treating AIDS. Prior to FDA approval, VIDEX was distributed to patients free; following

The Officers

Chairman and CEO: Charles A. Heimbold Jr.

Exec. VP and President, Worldwide Medicines Group:
    Kenneth Weg

Sr. VP; Chief Financial Officer; and Director, Global
    Business Services: Michael F. Mee

Sr. VP, Human Resources: Charles G. Tharp

approval, Bristol-Meyers Squibb continued to supply the drug to those who could not afford it.

In 1994, a U.S. district judge gave final approval to a $4.2 billion class action settlement, the largest ever, which concluded the majority of litigation between women and several manufacturers of breast implants, including Bristol-Myers Squibb. Also that year, the Food and Drug Administration withdrew eight of the company's liquid antibiotics from the market, after foreign objects were found in some of the bottles. Acquisitions included the U.S. marketing rights to Glucophage, a drug used for the treatment of diabetes; UPSA, a French drug company which focused mainly on pain treatment research; and Matrix Essentials, owner of professional hair care and beauty product lines such as Systeme Biolage and Vavoom.

In an effort to strengthen its generic drug market share in Europe, Bristol-Myers Squibb acquired A/S GEA Faraceutisk Fabrik in 1995. Facing the expiration of patents on both Capoten and Taxol that year, the company announced a $500 million expense reduction for 1996 to bolster profits. Also, Calgon Vestal Laboratories, a skin care and infection control products company, was purchased, and Serzone, a new antidepressant drug with minimal side effects, was made easily accessible. In 1996, Bristol-Myers Squibb founded Apothecon Generic Development and Manufacturing Group, a new unit devoted solely to generic pharmaceuticals, as a means of increasing the company's product line and enhancing its domestic and international rank within the growing generic drugs market. Blockbuster drug Pravachol, used to lower cholesterol, was introduced that year. Bristol-Myers Squibb continued researching cancer and AIDS treatments in the late 1990s, including Platinol, a possible treatment for cervical cancer.

History of Squibb Corp.

In 1858, Squibb Corp. was formed by Dr. Edward Squibb in Brooklyn, New York, to developed methods

of manufacturing ether and chloroform. In 1891, he turned the family business over to his sons. Sales by the end of the 1920s had reached nearly $15 million. The firm was called upon during World War II to supply penicillin and morphine.

In 1952, Squibb's business was joined with that of Mathieson Chemical Corp. The following year, the Squibb/Mathieson operations joined with Olin Industries to form Olin Mathieson Chemical Corp. Squibb became an independent company again in 1968, and changed its name to Squibb Corp. Soon afterwards, the firm expanded its product line by acquiring Beech-Nut Corp., makers of baby food and Life Savers candy.

During the later 1970s, Squibb strengthened its position in the cardiovascular drugs segment by launching Capoten and Corgard. In 1982, Denmark-based Novo and Squibb agreed to jointly sell insulin. In October of 1989, Bristol-Myers Co. and Squibb merged, via a $12.7 billion deal, to become Bristol-Myers Squibb Co., the second largest pharmaceutical company in the U.S.

Market Forces Driving the Merger

Throughout the 1980s, pharmaceutical firms were able to stay a step ahead of inflation by upping prescription costs and launching blockbuster new drugs. The industry was among the most profitable in America at that time. By the decade's end, however, many firms faced patent expiry on major drugs. Increased competition was also eroding profits. For example, SmithKline Beckman's best-selling drug, Tagamet, was facing direct competition from Glaxo's anti-ulcer medication Zantac.

To remain competitive, firms needed to develop new drugs, which required deep research and development pockets. According to Bruce Wasserstein, author of *Big Deal: The Battle for Control of America's Leading Corporations*, "Drug companies already spent a much higher percentage of revenues on R&D than other kinds of companies. The expectation was that a major drug company would need to spend more than $500 million a year on research to be successful. Few companies in the industry could afford that level of expenditure on their own." The first major deal indicative of this trend was the SmithKline Beckman and Beecham Group joining, which formed SmithKline Beecham, the world's second largest pharmaceutical firm. The marriage spawned the first major consolidation spree in the pharmaceutical industry.

Realizing they would both need to pursue a large merger to compete in the future, Bristol-Myers and Squibb began eyeing each other shortly after the

SmithKline Beecham deal was announced. Analysts pointed out that while other firms had pursued consolidation to make up for shortcomings or to broaden product offerings, both Bristol-Myers and Squibb were in good shape in the late 1980s. According to an August 1989 *Business Week article*, both firms were "well positioned and fast-growing." And there was relatively little overlap: Squibb was strongest in ethical drug development, while Bristol-Myers had more expertise in the OTC and consumer products markets. Besides anticipated product synergies, the two firms would boast an annual research and development budget of $600 million, second only to Merck & Co.

Approach and Engagement

As early as 1986, Bristol-Myers CEO Richard Gelb had expressed interest in a merger with Squibb, which was run by his old friend Richard Furlaud. It wasn't until mid-1989, though, that Furlaud was also willing to give the idea consideration. Both men had reached their mid-60s, and they decided that if a merger was going to happen, it needed to be sooner than later. On July 27, 1989, Bristol-Myers and Squibb announced their intent to merge. The initial stock swap was worth $11.5 billion. Gelb agreed to takeover the new firm as chairman and CEO; Furlaud accepted a secondary role as president and head of pharmaceutical operations. When the deal was finalized on October 10, 1989, it was worth $12.7 billion. The increase in value was due to higher stock prices, which were mainly the result of positive reaction by analysts to the merger's announcement.

Products and Services

By 1998, pharmaceuticals—including anti-infectives Amikin, Cefzil, Duricef, Fungizone, Maxipime, and Velosef; cardiovascular drugs Avapro, Capoten, Corgard, Monopril, Pravachol, and Sotacor; antibiotic Azactam; cancer treatments Paraplatin, Platinol, Taxol, and VePesid; central nervous system drugs BuSpar and Serzone; and AIDS drugs Videx and Zerit—accounted for roughly 60% of total revenues at Bristol-Myers Squibb.

Medicinal devices, such as orthopedic implants and wound care products, brought in 11% of sales, as did nutritional products. Nutritional products included follow-up infant formulas Alacta, Enfapro, and Next Step; standard infant formulas Enfamil, Lactofree, and Prosobee; nutritional supplements Boost, Choco Milk, Isocal, Nutrament, Sustacal, and Sustagen; and vitamins. Beauty care products, mainly hair care products like shampoo, conditioner and coloring, secured 10%. Consumer medications, including Bufferin, Comtrex, Excedrin, Sea Breeze, and Vagistat-1, made up the remaining eight percent.

The Players

Chairman of Bristol-Myers Co.: Richard L. Gelb. In 1972, Richard Gelb, the eldest son of the founders of Clairol—which had recently been acquired by Bristol-Myers—accepted the position of CEO at Bristol-Myers. Charged with the task of bringing the firm out of its first major slump, Gelb launched a successful spending and advertising program designed to turn Bristol-Myers around. When Bristol-Myers and Squibb merged in 1989, 65-year-old Gelb took over as chairman and CEO. He was succeeded by Charles Heimbold as CEO in 1994 and chairman in 1995.

Chairman of Squibb Corp.: Richard M. Furland. When Bristol-Myers and Squibb began discussing merger plans in 1989, 66-year-old Richard Furland was serving as CEO of Squibb. He agreed to hand the reins over to his old friend Richard Gelb, who was CEO of Bristol-Myers at the time, and take on leadership of the new firm's pharmaceutical business.

Changes to the Industry

Many analysts credited the SmithKline Beecham deal, which created the second largest drug company in the world with combined sales of $6.9 billion, and the Bristol-Myers Squibb union, which created a firm with annual sales of $4.5 billion, for sparking the first wave of pharmaceutical industry consolidation. In 1990, France's Rhone-Poulenc spent $2 billion for U.S.-based Rorer Group Inc. and Dow Chemical Co. began its lengthy takeover of Marion Laboratories. The firms that chose not to merge, such as Merck & Co., pursued strategic joint ventures with other leading players. Despite the flurry of consolidation during the late 1980s and early 1990s, each of the top five companies in the pharmaceuticals industry held less than 5% of worldwide market share, leaving the industry open for future consolidation.

Review of the Outcome

After the deal was completed, pharmaceuticals made up nearly half of the new company's total revenues. The deeper research and development pockets afforded the firm a steady pace of new pharmaceutical products. Within two years, the FDA had approved five new drugs, including Pravachal, a cardiovascular drug, and VIDEX, an AIDS treatment.

Research

Bristol-Myers Squibb Co. Home Page, available at http://www.bms.com. Official World Wide Web Home Page for Bristol-Myers Squibb Co. Includes news, financial, product, and historical information.

"Bristol-Myers Squibb Co.," in *Notable Corporate Chronologies*, The Gale Group, 1999. Lists major events in the history of Bristol-Myers Squibb Co., including the merger between Bristol-Myers and Squibb.

Wasserstein, Bruce. *Big Deal: The Battle for Control of America's Leading Corporations*, Warner Books, 1998. Offers an overview of the largest mergers in recent American corporate history, including the merger of Bristol-Myers and Squibb.

Weber, Joseph. "Filling Bristol-Myers' Prescription," in *Business Week*, 14 August 1989. Offers a detailed account of the reasons for the merger and the terms of the deal.

JEFF ST. THOMAS

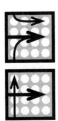

BRITISH AEROSPACE &
MARCONI ELECTRONIC SYSTEMS

nationality: United Kingdom
date: 1999
affected: British Aerospace PLC, United Kingdom, founded 1977
affected: The General Electric Company PLC (parent of Marconi Electronic Systems),
United Kingdom, founded 1886

British Aerospace PLC
Warwick House, PO Box 87, Farnborough
Aerospace Center
Farnborough, Hampshire GU146YU
United Kingdom

tel: 44-125-237-3232
fax: 44-125-238-3000
web: http://www.bae.co.uk

The General Electric Company PLC
One Bruton St.
London, W1X 8AQ
United Kingdom

tel: 44-171-493-8484
fax: 44-171-493-1974
web: http://www.gec.com

Overview of the Merger

The proposed merger between British Aerospace PLC and Marconi Electronic Systems, both British companies, shook up the European defense industry. The $12.3 billion deal, announced in January 1999 and expected to be completed by November, would form the first European defense company large enough to compete with the U.S. giants Lockheed Martin, Boeing, and Northrop Grumman. It would become the world's third-largest defense and aerospace firm and second-largest defense contractor.

Its entry into the industry's top ranks wasn't celebrated by Europe, however—quite the opposite, in fact, as Britain, France, and Germany criticized the move as the death of the formation of European Defence and Aerospace Co. (EDAC). The resulting company, they argued, would be too large to become a partner with any European contenders. More specifically, the merger agreement quashed the proposed mergers of the partners to other European companies. British Aerospace had been close to a union with Germany's DaimlerChrysler Aerospace (DAMA), while Marconi Electronic Systems had been in talks to join with France's Thomson-CSF.

History of British Aerospace PLC

In the post-World War II environment, the number of British aviation companies exceeded the market. To increase their competitiveness, both with each other and with the larger U.S. manufacturers, the British government began consolidating them. In 1960 it merged Vickers-Armstrong, English Electric, and Bristol Aeroplane to form the British Aircraft Corp. (BAC). At the same time, the government formed Hawker-Siddeley Aviation Co. by merging Armstrong Whitworth, A.V. Roe, Folland Aircraft, Gloster Aircraft, and Hawker Aircraft companies.

In 1962 BAC and France's Aerospatiale formed a joint venture to produce the Concorde, a supersonic passenger jet. Three years later, however, with the British aerospace industry still unable to compete effectively, Parliament member Lord Plowden urged the government to merge Rolls-Royce and Bristol-Siddeley to form

The Business

Financials - British Aerospace PLC

Revenue (1998): GBP 28.1 billion

Employees (1998): 47,900

Financials - The General Electric Company PLC

Revenue (1999): GBP 7.6 billion

Employees (1999): 84,000

SICs / NAICS

sic 3721 - Aircraft

sic 3724 - Aircraft Engines & Engine Parts

sic 3761 - Guided Missiles & Space Vehicles

sic 4813 - Telephone Communications Except
Radiotelephone

sic 4812 - Radiotelephone Communications

sic 3812 - Search & Navigation Equipment

naics 336411 - Aircraft Manufacturing

naics 336412 - Aircraft Engine and Engine Parts
Manufacturing

naics 336414 - Guided Missile and Space Vehicle
Manufacturing

naics 513310 - Wired Telecommunications Carriers

naics 513322 - Cellular and Other Wireless
Telecommunications

naics 334511 - Search, Detection, Navigation, Guidance,
Aeronautical, and Systems

a single company for the manufacture of aircraft engines. This proposal for restructuring was carried out in 1966. As part of that merger agreement, Hawker-Siddeley's 50% share in Bristol-Siddeley was sold to Rolls-Royce.

In 1969 England was invited to join Airbus Industrie, a newly established European commercial aircraft consortium, but the financial risk of competing directly against Boeing, McDonnell-Douglas, and Lockheed seemed imprudent to BAC. It decided not to participate, but Hawker-Siddeley became a subcontractor to manufacture wings for Airbus' A-300s.

At about this time, BAC, Messerschmitt-Bolkow-Blohm of Germany, and Aeritalia of Italy formed a partnership called Panavia Aircraft GmbH to make the Tornado combat aircraft. BAC also formed a joint venture, SEPECAT, with Breguet Aviation to manufacture Jaguar jet fighters.

The commercial failure of the Tornado and Jaguar produced another financial drain on BAC, and Lord Plowden's proposal to merge BAC and Hawker-Siddeley was resurrected in 1975. The British government nationalized both BAC and Hawker-Siddeley the following year. In April 1977 Parliament approved the rationalization of Britain's aerospace interests— British Aircraft Corp., Hawker-Siddeley Aviation Company, and Scottish Aviation, Ltd.—into a single state-owned company, British Aerospace (BAe). The new company was divided into an aircraft division and a dynamics division.

British Aerospace incorporated and began trading on the London Stock Exchange in April 1978. The following January BAe agreed to join the Airbus consortium by pledging to invest $500 million over a four-year period in exchange for a 20% share in the development of A-310s.

Privatization of BAe began in December 1979 with its incorporation as a private limited company. BAe was partially privatized in February 1981, when the British government's stake was reduced to 48.4%. Profits that year registered at GBP 71 million despite development costs of GBP 50 million for A-310s and the renamed BAe 146s.

BAe acquired Sperry Gyroscope for GBP 42 million in May 1982. Two years later Thorn-EMI PLC announced its intention to take over BAe, an offer that was rejected by BAe. At the same time the General Electric Company of the U.K. announced that it, too, was interested in acquiring BAe. This proposal was also rejected by BAe on the grounds that its terms were too vague.

The British government offered its 48% stake in BAe for public sale to institutional investors in May 1985. That year BAe underwent reorganization along functional lines, and eight divisions were established to maximize efficiency.

BAe embarked on an aggressive diversification strategy in the late 1980s. In 1987 alone it purchased Royal Ordnance PLC, a maker of guns, ammunition, vehicles, rocket motors, and other defense products, for GBP 190 million; Steinheil Optronik GmbH, manufacturer of optical equipment, for GBP 17 million; Ballast Nedam Groep NV, a civil and marine engineering company based in the Netherlands, for GBP 47 million; a 24% stake in Systems Designers PLC, maker of computer goods, which was later renamed SD-Scicon PLC; and an initial investment in Reflectone Inc., producer of flight simulators and trainers.

In August 1988 BAe paid GBP 140 million for The Rover Group PLC, an automobile, van, 4-wheel drive, and military vehicle manufacturer in the U.K. The next year the company contributed to the establishment of the National Remote Sensing Centre Ltd. with several other communications, aerospace, and Earth observation interests to work with the European Space Agency. BAe also purchased Arlington Securities PLC, a property developer and manager, for GBP 378 million.

BAe founded Microtel Communications Ltd. in April 1990. The following month it obtained a 76% stake in the Liverpool airport and formed British Aerospace (Liverpool Airport) Ltd. to manage and develop it into a major international airport. Other acquisitions included a 49% stake in Kelsey Instruments Ltd. and a 51% share in Satellite Management International Ltd. Annual sales in 1990 exceeded GBP 10 billion for the first time, with net income of GBP 278 million.

Previously a division of British Aerospace Defence Ltd., British Aerospace (Systems and Equipment) Ltd. (BASE), began trading as a separate company on the London Stock Exchange in January 1991. As the primary contractor for Saudi Arabia's Al Yamamah project to develop naval systems and helicopter programs, BASE held the U.K.'s largest export contract.

BAe purchased Heckler & Koch GmbH of Germany, a munitions and general engineering company, in March 1991. That July it traded its Microtel subsidiary for a 30% stake in Hutchinson Telecommunications (UK) Ltd., a mobile telephone maker and servicer.

John Cahill was named company chairman in April 1992. By that time BAe had evolved into an unwieldy conglomerate consisting of seven core activities: defense, Rover, Airbus, commercial property development, corporate aircraft, regional aircraft, and satellite communications. Cahill began a restructuring to concentrate the company's focus on the first four of those seven businesses. In late 1992 BAe took a GBP 1 billion write-off to close a plant for the production of regional aircraft and laid off 3,000 employees. It posted a loss of GBP 970 million for the year.

In June 1993 BAe sold British Aerospace Corporate Jets Inc. and Arkansas Aerospace Inc. to the U.S. based-Raytheon Co. That December it also divested itself of Ballast Nedam. The company sold its 80% interest in the Rover car unit to BMW for $1.2 billion in 1994, the same year that it sold its satellite business to Matra Marconi Space for $87 million.

In 1995 Dassault and BAe entered into plans to

The Officers

British Aerospace PLC

Chairman: Sir Richard Evans

Vice Chairman: Richard Lapthorne

CEO: John Weston

Executive Director: Mike Turner

Financial Director: George Rose

The General Electric Company PLC

Chairman: Sir Roger Hurn

CEO: Lord Simpson

Vice-Chairman: M. Lester

Vice-Chairman: Sir Charles Masefield

Finance Director: J.C. Mayo

establish a joint venture company for the research and development of military aircraft. BAe's pretax profits for the year rose 13% to GBP 234 million. BAe and Hutchinson Whampoa Ltd. formed Orange PLC, a mobile telephone operator, in January 1996. BAe and the Matra unit of France's Lagardere SCA merged their guided missile businesses to form Matra BAe Dynamics, and BAe beat out Lockheed Martin Corp. for a $6.21 billion contract with Britain's Royal air force.

In October 1997 BAe announced that it would purchase from Siemens AG the Siemens Plessey businesses operating in the U.S. and Australia. That December it agreed to participate in a cross-border venture that would create European Defence and Aerospace Co. (EDAC), although no timetable had been set up for its formation.

As part of a plan to establish a foundation for the EDAC, BAe entered into merger discussions with DASA, a unit of DaimlerChrysler. Those plans, however, were scuttled when BAe agreed to merge with another U.K. company, General Electric Company PLC, in January 1999.

History of The General Electric Company PLC

The General Electric Apparatus Company was formed in London, England, by two German immigrants, Hugo Hirst and Gustav Byng, in 1886. The new company produced such devices as telephones, electrically activated bells, ceiling roses, switches, and fittings. In 1889 The General Electric Company Ltd. (GEC) was established as a private company.

The Players

British Aerospace PLC Chairman: Sir Richard Evans. Born in Blackpool in 1942, Richard Evans joined the Ministry of Transport and Civil Aviation at age 18. After moving through several other government posts, he joined the Military Aircraft Division of British Aircraft Corp. in 1969. Evans was appointed to the board of British Aerospace in 1987, and three years later was named its CEO. He was knighted in 1996, and became chairman of BAe in May 1998

General Electric Company PLC Chairman: Sir Roger Hurn. Sir Roger Hurn was appointed to the company's board of directors in December 1998. Prior to that position, he served as chairman of Smiths Industries PLC. Hurn also serves as a non-executive director for Imperial Chemical Industries PLC, as deputy chairman of Glaxo Wellcome PLC, and as chairman of the Court of Governors of the Henly Management College.

Light bulbs were added to its product line in 1893, the same year that the company developed the use of china as an insulating material for switches. In 1896 GEC installed its first commercial alternating current (AC) motor in Liverpool, and three years later won its first contract for a power-generating station.

During the early 1900s intense demand for consumer and commercial electrical equipment enabled GEC to experience rapid growth. It expanded internationally, organizing branches in Europe, Japan, Australia, South Africa, and India. In 1910 the company created a subsidiary operation devoted exclusively to telephone system technology. GEC established the country's first separate industrial research laboratory in 1919.

GEC's most significant contribution to the World War II effort was the production of radar equipment. Throughout the postwar period, GEC becomes involved in the production of nuclear energy, semiconductors, and computers. By 1949, after studying television technology for over a decade, the company had achieved a relay-link of television picture and sound.

The company continued to expand through acquisitions and joint ventures. In 1961 GEC acquired Radio and Allied Industries. Through a hostile bid in 1967, GEC acquired the Associated Electrical Industries, Ltd., which encompassed Metropolitan-

Vickers, BTH, Edison Swan, Siemens Brothers, Hotpoint, and W.T. Henley. The next year GEC merged with English Electric, which was comprised of Elliott Bros., The Marconi Co., Ruston and Hornsby, Stephenson, and Hawthorn & Vulcan Foundry. In 1974 it acquired Yarrow Shipbuilders, followed five years later by Avery.

Sales surpassed GBP 5 billion in 1986, with about 20% coming from the Americas. By that time GEC had become Britain's largest manufacturing company and one of its leading exporters.

GEC launched a takeover attempt of the British aerospace firm Plessey in 1986, but was thwarted. Two years later the company joined forces with West Germany's Siemens to renew its acquisition of Plessey. In 1989 this takeover was approved by the British government, contingent upon GEC's pledge to refrain from sending national security secrets overseas. The acquiring companies agreed, and GEC and Siemens gained control of Plessey later that year.

Also in 1989 GEC joined with France's Compagnie Generale d'Electricite to combine their power-generating equipment into a GBP 4 billion joint venture known as GEC ALSTHOM.

During the early 1990s GEC intensified its move away from domestic electrical products and toward defense electronics. To that end, the firm acquired the defense operations of Ferranti International, a British electronics firm, in 1990. By 1993 GEC employed more than 145,000 workers and recorded sales of GBP 6.45 billion.

In 1995 GEC succeeded in its battle against British Aerospace for control of Vickers Shipbuilding and Engineering Ltd. (VSEL), a submarine maker. Although GEC paid a high price, $1.3 billion, for VSEL, the company believed that the strategic advantages brought by the acquisition would be considerable, since it effectively made GEC the monopolistic supplier of large warships to the British navy.

George Simpson became managing director in 1996 and orchestrated the company's reorganization. As part of this strategy, GEC sold a number of non-core businesses, including Express Lifts, Satchwell Controls, AB Dick, the Wire and Cables Group, Marconi Instruments, and GEC Plessey Semiconductors. In June 1998 it acquired TRACOR, a U.S. defense electronics company, and merged it into Marconi Electronic Systems (MES). GEC also increased its telephone network switching operations by acquiring Siemens' 40% stake in GPT Holdings.

In January 1999 GEC agreed to separate from MES and merge the defense company with British Aerospace, thereby quashing MES's proposed merger with France-based Thomson-CSF. With this proposed exit from the defense industry, GEC quickly positioned itself to become a leader in telecommunications, its new core business. It acquired RELTEC, a U.S. network equipment manufacturer, for $2.1 billion in March 1999. This purchase was followed by its agreement two months later to purchase Fore Systems, Inc., a U.S. maker of Internet switches, for $4.5 billion. Later that year GEC and France's Aerospatiale-Matra agreed to join with DaimlerChrysler Aerospace in establishing Astrium, Europe's largest space company.

Market Forces Driving the Merger

Consolidation in the defense industry was occurring at a rapid rate during the 1990s in response to drastically reduced government defense budgets. Most of this consolidation took place between U.S. firms, creating such giants as Lockheed Martin Corp., Boeing Co., and Northrop Grumman. With each successive merger, the size and scope of the industry's leaders expanded, raising competition and compounding the necessity of unions for the industry's smaller players.

The pressures of this competitive landscape crossed America's borders, impacting the global defense industry. At this time, European countries were embarking on new accords encouraging transborder cooperation, trade, and business ventures. Their defense companies, however, were somewhat slow to embrace this new culture.

In December 1997 the British, French, German, and Italian governments called their respective defense companies to break across national borders by forming a single European concern capable of competing against the U.S. leaders. This giant, dubbed the European Defence and Aerospace Co. (EDAC), would serve as a local supplier on the Continent and as a rival to U.S. companies in other parts of the world.

This governmental appeal was not acted upon immediately, as the French government still held a stake in its defense companies, thereby making them less attractive as partners to other European companies. After France made certain concessions for their privatization, however, the European defense concerns took to the negotiating tables.

British Aerospace (BAe) entered into talks with DaimlerChrysler Aerospace (DAMA) for a $21 billion (GBP 14 billion) merger of equals. Although those talks had stalled over the price of the deal and questions of management, the companies were still in negotiations. Meanwhile, The General Electric Company PLC (GEC) had engaged in discussions to merge its defense unit, Marconi Electronic Systems, with Thomson-CSF, a French firm. When talks between GEC and Thomson-CSF broke down over acceptable structure and control of the resulting company, GEC put Marconi on the auction block.

Sale of this British company on the open market posed a threat to British Aerospace. If it were to be acquired by a foreign company, particularly one of the American giants, British Aerospace would face stiff competition in its local market. "BAe simply couldn't afford the strategic risk of having Lockheed in its backyard dressed up in a Union Jack," commented Chris Avery, a defense analyst at Paribas, in *Time International*.

Aside from merely the defense of its territory, BAe perceived in Marconi operations both similar, such as shipbuilding, and complementary, particularly Marconi's electronics expertise. Moreover, a combined company would be in a position to mingle with such U.S. leaders as Lockheed Martin, Boeing, and Northrop Grumman.

Approach and Engagement

British Aerospace (BAe) and Marconi Electronic Systems shocked the industry, not to mention their respective proposed partners, with their own merger announcement on January 19, 1999. The accord, which the companies formally agreed to on April 27, called for a $12.3 billion (GBP 7.7 billion) merger of equals. Under its terms, The General Electric Company PLC (GEC) shareholders would receive 0.42 shares in BAe for each share of GEC. The resulting company, which would retain the British Aerospace name, would be 63.3% owned by BAe shareholders, with its remaining 36.7% stake in the hands of GEC holders.

The companies predicted that combined operations would result in annual cost savings of GBP 275 million for the first three years. The new company would have a workforce approaching 100,000 employees in the U.K., Australia, France, Germany, Italy, Saudi Arabia, Sweden, and the U.S.

On June 28, 1999, the deal cleared its first regulatory hurdle when it received the approval of the European Commission.

Products and Services

In mid-1999 British Aerospace was made up of five main groups. Commercial Aircraft consisted of British Aerospace Airbus, British Aerospace Aviation Services, British Aerospace Asset Management-Brabazon Ltd., and British Aerospace Regional Aircraft. The Defence Systems Group encompassed Defence Systems, Land & Sea Systems, British

Aerospace Systems & Equipment, British Aerospace Royal Ordnance, and CORDA Ltd. Military Aircraft & Support Systems included British Aerospace Military Aircraft & Aerostructures, British Aerospace Customer Support, British Aerospace Training Services, and British Aerospace Systems & Services. The New Business segment was made up of International Marketing & Sales Organisation, British Aerospace Australia Holdings Ltd., and British Aerospace North America Inc. The final segment, Other Business Units, was comprised of British Aerospace Virtual University, Farnborough Business Aviation Ltd., and BAe Properties Ltd.

Marconi Electronic Systems, which had turnover of GBP 3.5 billion in 1999, operated in avionics and naval systems, as well as under the company names of Alenia Marconi Systems, Matra Marconi Space, and Thomson Marconi Sonar.

In anticipation of the demerger of Marconi Electronic Systems, The General Electric Company, PLC reorganized into three operating divisions. Communications, which became the focus for the new company, operated in the sector of telecommunications and intelligent networking equipment and solutions, including optical networks, access products, support services, secure communications, and fibre optic cables. The Systems segment conducted business as three companies for the collection, management, and communication of digital information: Picker International, which focused on medical systems; Gilbarco, which operated in commerce systems; and Videojet, which conducted business in data systems. The third division, Capital, encompassed GEC's miscellaneous operations, from white goods and weighing technology to software systems and air movement systems; its operating companies included GDA, Avery Berkel, Woods, EEV, EASAMS, Fibreway, and Comstar.

Changes to the Industry

If the proposed merger receives the requisite regulatory approval, it is expected to close by November 1999. At that time, British Aerospace would be propelled to the top ranks of the global defense and aerospace industry. With revenues of nearly $20 billion, it would rank as the third-largest defense and aerospace firm, behind Lockheed Martin and Boeing, and a leading defense contractor, second only to Lockheed.

Their jilted partners were resentful of the deal between BAe and Marconi. DAMA terminated its attempt to merge with BAe, claiming that BAe's increased size would make their union more of a takeover of the German company than a merger of equals. Moreover, the price that BAe was paying for

Marconi would be passed, in part, to DAMA's shareholders.

DaimlerChrysler also viewed the BAe-Marconi deal as the end of the plans for a European Aerospace and Defence Co. (EADC), again pointing to the increased size of BAe. "The dream is over for the EADC," said Juergen Schrempp, DaimlerChrysler's chairman, in an April issue of *Flight International*.

DASA did not remain independent for long, however, On June 11, 1999, it acquired Contrucciones Aeronauticas (CASA), a Spanish state-owned defense company.

Thomson-CSF, too, brushed off the dust of its merger plans and entered into talks with other potential partners. By June 1999 it had begun negotiations with Raytheon, the fourth-largest defense company in the U.S.

With its proposed merger with BAe, GEC was shedding its defense electronics business, leaving analysts wondering about the direction of the remaining company. Within weeks of the merger announcement, GEC provided the answer—it intended to position itself as a leading telecommunications company. In March 1999 it paid $2.1 billion to acquire Reltec, a U.S. network equipment manufacturer. Two months later it agreed to pay $4.5 billion for Fore Systems, Inc., the U.S. maker of a leading switch for Internet traffic.

Research

"All-U.K. Merger Sends European Defence into Disarray," in *Flight International*, 27 January 1999. Describes the proposed deal in terms of its impact on the European industry.

British Aerospace PLC Home Page, available at http://www.bae.co.uk. Official World Wide Web Page for British Aerospace. Includes product and operational information, press releases, a company history, executive biographies, financial news, and press releases.

"British Aerospace PLC," in *International Directory of Company Histories*, Vol. 24, St. James Press, 1999. Profiles of the history of the company.

"Defence Merger Paves Way for Trans-Atlantic Deals," in *South China Morning Post*, 13 June 1999. Details the consolidation moves made by other European defense companies after the announced deal between BAe and Marconi.

Doyle, Andrew. "DASA Sounds Death Knell for Single European Company," in *Flight International*, 7 April 1999. Reports DaimlerChrysler's response to the merger deal.

The General Electric Company PLC Home Page, available at http://www.gec.com. Official World Wide Web Page for The General Electric Company PLC. It includes product and financial information, press releases, and a company history.

Wallace, Charles. "European Shakeout: The Anglo-British Merger of BAe and Marconi Has Called into Question the Development of an Integrated Aerospace and Weapons Industry in Europe," in *Time International*, 1 February 1999. Describes the terms and motivation for the proposed merger, and Europe's reaction to it.

Wilson, Richard. "GEC Sheds Its Historical Baggage as a New Era Starts to Take Shape," in *Electronics Weekly*, 28 April 1999. Discusses the efforts made by GEC to focus on telecommunications.

DEBORAH J. UNTENER

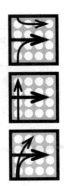

BRITISH AMERICAN TOBACCO &
ROTHMANS INTERNATIONAL

British American Tobacco PLC
Globe House, 4 Temple Pl.
London, WC2R 2PG
United Kingdom

tel: 44 171 845 1000
fax: 44 171 240 0555

nationality: United Kingdom
date: June 7, 1999
affected: British American Tobacco PLC, United Kingdom, founded 1902
affected: Rothmans International PLC, United Kingdom, founded 1890

Overview of the Merger

British American Tobacco and Rothmans International merged in June 1999 to create the world's second-largest tobacco company. Their combined market share put the new company in striking distance of overtaking Philip Morris as the leading international tobacco concern.

History of British American Tobacco PLC

When James Buchanan Duke's American Tobacco Co., which claimed 90% of the U.S. market, made a bid for the U.K. market in 1901, several small independent British tobacco companies banded together to form the Imperial Tobacco Company Ltd. The next year, after a prolonged price war between these two concerns, a truce was called and the two rival merchants agreed to not conduct business in the other's domestic market. This deal also initiated the creation of a jointly owned company, British American Tobacco Co. (BAT) to handle their export trade and overseas manufacturing interests outside of the U.S. and the U.K.

In 1911 the U.S. Supreme Court ruled that American Tobacco was a monopoly and must disband. As a result, American Tobacco canceled most of its covenants with BAT and Imperial, and sold off all of its shares. The collapse of this agreement also opened the U.S. market to BAT, which had gained a listing on the London Stock Exchange.

The company restructured BAT China Ltd. into independent regional units in 1923, and began lobbying the Chinese government to minimize the taxation of tobacco. Two decades later, however, the company lost all of its operations in China, as the Communist Revolution forcibly nationalized all of BAT China Ltd.'s assets.

In 1927 BAT entered the U.S. market with the purchase of Brown & Williamson, a small tobacco producer in North Carolina. In 1962 it acquired a minority interest in two companies: Mardon Packaging International, maker of cigarette packaging, and Wiggins Teape Ltd., a large specialty paper manufacturer.

The treaty of Rome in 1972 brought the U.K. into the European Commission, and with it, an end to the agreement between BAT and Imperial Tobacco. The companies regained full ownership of their original brands in the U.K. and western Europe. During the 1970s, the public's growing concern over smoking prompted BAT to hedge its bets by diversifying outside the tobacco industry. To reduce its image as a tobacco concern, it changed its name to BAT Industries PLC in 1976, becoming a holding company for several smaller operating companies.

Acquisitions in 1978 included Appleton Papers, a manufacturer of carbonless paper; Pegulan, a home-improvement company in West Germany; two fruit juice companies in Brazil; and pulp producers in Portugal and Brazil. The next year it entered the department store chain industry with the purchase of West Germany's Horten Stores, Kohl's and Department Stores International in the U.K., the British catalogue store Argos, and Gimbels and Saks Fifth Avenue in the U.S. BAT bought the Marshall Field department store chain in 1982. It acquired the British firm Hambro Life Assurance in 1985 and the U.S. insurance concern Farmers Group three years later.

As a result of a hostile takeover bid by Sir James Goldsmith's Hoylake Investments in 1989, BAT retreated from its diversification program. It spun off its British retailers and sold its paper operations, leaving the company with only tobacco and financial services. BAT acquired the U.S. tobacco business of American Brands, Inc. for $1 billion in 1994. Two years later it gained access to a 50% Mexican market share by acquiring Cigarrera de Moderna for $1.7 billion.

In December 1997 the European Union announced a ban on all cigarette advertising. Effective in early 1999 in most cases, the EU gave into pressure from the tobacco industry by extending the deadline another nine years for Formula One auto racing sponsorship. This provided BAT with a marketing loophole. It sidestepped the impending ban by purchasing a Formula One team just days before the EU made its official announcement, thereby gaining an effective advertising medium for years to come. "It can call its car the BATmobile if it wants to," wrote *The European*. "Given sufficient incentives, it could probably get its driver to change his name to Lucky Strike."

The U.S. public became increasingly litigious against tobacco companies in the late 1990s. In 1995 Brown & Williamson became the second such company to lose a smoking-related damage suit, and was ordered to pay $750,000 to a Florida plaintiff. In 1998,

The Business

Financials

Revenue (1998): $28.8 billion

Employees (1998): 101,081

SICs / NAICS

sic 2111 - Cigarettes

naics 312221 - Cigarette Manufacturing

the same year that brought the overturning of that verdict, another Florida suit was filed against Brown & Williamson. This time the company became the first tobacco company to be ordered to pay punitive damages to a smoker; this verdict also was overturned in 1999. In 1998 BAT joined with its U.S. competitors to settle for $206 billion all pending lawsuits filed by 46 U.S. states. That year the company also had to contend with litigation arising outside the U.S. borders. In May 1998 Guatemala became the first non-U.S. country to sue American tobacco companies, including BAT, for smoking-related illnesses.

In 1998 BAT separated its financial services arm and merged it with Zurich Insurance to form Allied Zurich. In June 1999 BAT merged with Rothmans International, giving the combined company a 16% global market, just behind Philip Morris Co.'s 17% grip. It also announced that it was engaged in talks to acquire the remaining 58% of Imasco Ltd., owner of Imperial Tobacco Ltd.

History of Rothmans International PLC

Louis Rothman opened a small tobacco kiosk in London, England, in 1890. His hand-rolled cigarettes were popular, and he soon built a reputation as a supplier of tobacco products to wealthy businessmen and aristocrats. Rothman opened a full-fledged store on Pall Mall in London, and introduced the Pall Mall brand of cigarettes. It also operated three kiosks in England and began to expand overseas. By 1902 its products were exported to South Africa, the Netherlands, India, and Australia.

In 1903 Rothman incorporated his company as Rothmans of Pall Mall, and was selected to provide tobacco products to the British royal family. He invented the menthol cigarette in 1906, and developed a better filter that allowed smokers to smoke without getting loose tobacco on their lips.

The Officers

Chairman: Martin F. Broughton

Deputy Chairman: Kenneth H. Clarke

Managing Director: Ulrich G.V. Herter

Finance Director: Keith S. Dunt

Legal Director and General Counsel: Stuart P. Chalfen

Operations Director: John Jewell

During World War I Rothmans lost sales of its specialty blends of Turkish tobacco to cheap, mass-produced cigarettes made from Virginia tobacco. In 1916 the company reorganized and moved to enter the mass market for cigarettes. Five years later it launched Rothmans Diary Service, through which customers received discounts for large orders of cigarettes. In 1926 it created Rothmans (India) Ltd. as a subsidiary.

Despite the onset of the Great Depression in 1929, the company prospered as exports to China and South America increased. That year it reincorporated as Rothmans Limited, a public company. Capital raised from stock sales enabled it to open new stores in Glasgow, Scotland, and in Manchester and Bristol, England.

Rothmans Limited acquired Martins of Picadilly and associated companies in 1937, thereby securing its sources of tobacco leaf throughout World War II. After the war, it sought funding for overseas expansion. In 1951 it entered into a joint venture with Dr. Anton Rupert's Rembrandt Group of South Africa to manufacture Rothmans cigarettes for that country's domestic market. Three years later Rothmans Limited acquired control of Rembrandt Group.

In 1958 Rembrandt Group acquired Carreras and Marcianus Ltd., a leading British manufacturer of tobacco products, and then merged it with Rothmans Limited to form Carreras Rothman Ltd. A period of hostile takeovers in the tobacco industry began in the 1970s. To forestall takeover bids, Carreras Rothman consolidated its global tobacco interests, including Martin Brinkman of West Germany, Tabacofina of Belgium, and Turmac of the Netherlands, to form Rothmans International Ltd. in 1972.

Rothmans International began to diversify, acquiring Rothmans of Pall Mall Canada and its interest in the Carling O'Keefe brewery in 1978. That year it also sold a 25% interest to Philip Morris, the world's second-largest cigarette maker. In 1983 it acquired an interest in Cartier Monde, maker of jewelry, watches,

and other luxury items. Five years later it acquired an additional GBP 18.4 million of stock in Dunhill Ltd., bringing its interest in the company to 55%. Rupert's Rembrandt Group of companies reorganized as the Compagnie Financiere Richemont, which held a 33% interest in Rothmans International.

In 1991 it acquired P.J. Carroll and Company, thereby expanding company operations into the Republic of Ireland. That year it entered into a joint venture with the China Tobacco Corp. to produce Rothmans and Dunhill cigarettes in the People's Republic of China. By 1994 Rothmans was one of the five largest tobacco companies in the world. In 1995 Cie Financiere Richemont AG of South Africa and Rembrandt Group of Switzerland, owner of a 61% interest in Rothmans International, moved to acquire the remaining 39% of the Rothmans International. In 1999 it merged with British American Tobacco.

Market Forces Driving the Merger

By the late 1990s, British American Tobacco (BAT) was confident that tobacco was a high-growth industry, a view contrary to the company's position since the 1970s. Then, it maintained its tobacco operations primarily as a moneymaker for its diverse holdings, as increasingly health conscious and litigious attitudes in the West threatened the future of tobacco companies. In 1998 BAT and its U.S. rivals agreed to make a massive settlement to all 46 U.S. states that still had pending lawsuits against the companies. Believing that it had thereby wiped out its obligations in one fell swoop, BAT sought to get on with business and strengthen its position in emerging markets.

BAT was the second-largest international cigarette company, behind Philip Morris (the two were both dwarfed, however, by the state-owned Chinese National Tobacco Corp., which held an impenetrable hold on China, its only market). With the right purchase, BAT could edge up to Philip Morris and have a better shot at capturing the industry's lead position.

Approach and Engagement

On January 11, 1999, BAT and Rothmans International announced a GBP 5.3 billion ($21 billion) stock swap that would combine the second-largest and fourth-largest international tobacco companies, respectively. The merged firm, which would retain the British American Tobacco name, would produce 950 billion cigarettes per year. This would give it a 16% global market share, behind Philip Morris' 17% hold, which reflected production of one trillion cigarettes annually. (Chinese National Tobacco sold 1.6 trillion cigarettes per year.)

The first, and most substantial, regulatory barrier that the companies encountered was the Australian Competition and Consumer Commission. On March 31, 1999, the ACCC announced its objection to the merger on antitrust grounds, since the new company would have a 62% market share in that country. In June the companies agreed to sell a portfolio of cigarette-related operations in Australia to Imperial Tobacco Group PLC for A$325 million, thereby reducing the combined market share to 44%.

The European Commission granted its approval to the merger in March, and BAT's shareholders did likewise in April. On June 7, 1999—weeks earlier than expected—the union was completed.

Products and Services

The merger brought together the leading cigarette brands of British American Tobacco and Rothmans. International brands included: Benson & Hedges, Dunhill, Capri, GPC, Hollywood, Jan III Sobieski, John Player Gold Leaf, Kent (outside the U.S.), Kool, Lucky Strike, Misty, Pall Mall, Peter Stuyvesant, Rothmans, State Express 555, Viceroy, and Winfield. Local and regional brands consisted of Carlton, du Maurier, GPC, Kool, and Player's in the U.S. and Canada; Barclay, HB, and Prince in the United Kingdom; Belmont, Boots, Derby, Free, and Hollywood in Latin America; and Gold Flake in India.

Changes to the Industry

The newly formed company immediately captured a 16% share of the international market, right behind Philip Morris' 17% grasp. The combined strengths of the merged companies positioned British American Tobacco to make a strike for the industry's top spot. The former BAT had developed a variety of cigarette brands that were marketed to select countries, while Rothmans possessed strong premium brands, including Dunhill, Peter Stuveystant, and Winfield, that had a more dispersed presence in the global market.

As part of that increased global presence, the new company gained Rothmans' leading positions in 22 new companies, including South Africa, Malaysia, and Nigeria. It also reintroduced BAT to China, where it had not had a presence since the Chinese government seized its operations in 1949.

Soon after the announcement of this merger, analysts speculated as to which tobacco companies would be the next to unite. Some suggested that recently privatized companies, such as Spain's Tabacalera or France's SEITA, would aggressively seek partners.

RJR Nabisco, owner of RJ Reynolds, disclosed that it was considering selling its international tobacco operations. Even BAT positioned itself as open to future merger deals, referring in a January issue of *The Economist* to the union with Rothmans as merely "this week's" deal.

In fact, on June 7—the day of the merger's completion—BAT revealed that it was in discussions to acquire the 58% of Imasco Ltd. that it didn't already own. This Canadian-based company owned Imperial Tobacco Ltd., which held a 60% share of Canada's cigarette market. Ironically, it was BAT's merger with Rothmans that opened up the possibility of such a purchase. As part of the terms set by Canadian regulators for approval of BAT's union with Rothmans, the company had agreed to sell its Rothmans Canada business within one year of the merger's completion. Without this divestiture, the Imasco proposal would have been unlikely to receive approval, as it would have raised antitrust flags.

Review of the Outcome

The new company expected to achieve savings of GBP 250 million annually from combined operations in the areas of sales, distribution, manufacturing, and administration. BAT and Rothmans brought 50 and 30 factories to the combined company, respectively, some of which were undoubtedly to be closed, particularly in the countries where they overlapped.

Research

"Australia's Regulator: Imperial Tobacco Lifts Competition," in *The Wall Street Journal*, 2 June 1999. Announces Australia's ultimate approval of the merger.

"BAT Industries PLC," in *Notable Corporate Chronologies*, The Gale Group, 1999. Provides an overview of the company's history.

"BAT and Rothmans to Merge," in *World Tobacco*, January 1999. Details the merger agreement.

"Got a Match?" in *The Economist*, 16 January 1999. Briefly describes the market gains expected to result from the merger.

Hawkins, Paula. "BAT Drives a Hole through New Ban," in *The European*, 11 December 1997. Discusses BAT's purchase of a Formula One racing team to overcome an advertising ban.

"Rothmans International PLC," in *Notable Corporate Chronologies*, The Gale Group, 1999. Profiles the history of the company.

Stecklow, Steve, and Christopher J. Chipello. "BAT is in Talks to Acquire Remaining 58% of Imasco," in *The Wall Street Journal*, 8 June 1999. Reveals BAT's interest in acquiring the ownership of Imperial Tobacco.

RICHARD BARROW

BRITISH PETROLEUM & AMOCO

BP Amoco PLC
Brittanic House 1, Finsbury Circus
London, EC2M 7BA
United Kingdom

tel: 44-171-496-4000
fax: 44-171-496-4630
web: http://www.bpamoco.com

nationality: United Kingdom
date: December 31, 1998
affected: British Petroleum Company PLC, United Kingdom, founded 1909
affected: Amoco Corp., USA, founded 1889

Overview of the Merger

British Petroleum, Britain's largest company, completed the largest ever foreign takeover of a U.S. company on December 31, 1998, with its $53 billion purchase of Amoco Corp., the fifth leading oil firm in the U.S. The new company, BP Amoco PLC, is the third largest oil company in the world—behind Royal Dutch/Shell Group and Exxon Corp.—boasting a market capitalization in excess of $140 billion.

History of British Petroleum Company PLC

Anglo-Persian Oil Co. was formed in 1909, one year after the first oil discovery in the Middle East. Three years later, the new firm signed a ten-year marketing agreement with Royal Dutch/Shell Group. In 1914, Anglo-Persian signed a long-term agreement with the British Admiralty for the supply of fuel oil, which the Royal Navy used as a replacement for coal. The U.K. government invested two million British pounds in the company and received a majority shareholding in return.

The company established a wholly owned oil tanker subsidiary in 1915. Two years later, Anglo-Persian bought British Petroleum Co., the U.K. marketing subsidiary of the European Petroleum Co.; established a refinery in Swansea, Wales, to produce petroleum products for the U.K.; and opened a research laboratory in Sunbury, U.K. By the early 1920s, Anglo-Persian owned more than 30 oil tankers. The firm began forming subsidiaries in many European countries, as well as in Africa and Asia, following the expiration of its agreement with Shell.

During the late 1940s, Anglo-Persian diversified into petrochemicals. In 1954, the company was renamed the British Petroleum Company (BP). That year, BP signed an agreement with the Iranian government, whereby BP held a 40% interest in a newly created consortium of Western oil companies formed to undertake oil exploration, production, and refining in Iran. With the United Kingdom's nationalization depriving the company of two-thirds of its production, BP increased its output in Iraq and Kuwait and built new refineries in Europe, Australia, and Aden.

In 1968, BP acquired the U.S. east coast refining and marketing operations of Atlantic Richfield. After searching for oil in Alaska throughout the decade, BP made a major discovery at Prudhoe Bay on the North Slope in 1969. By then, BP owned over half of the biggest oil fields in the United States. The firm exchanged some of its Alaskan reserves for a 25% stake in Standard Oil of Ohio. The following year, the Forties field, the first major commercial oil find in British waters, was discovered.

BP discovered gas in the British waters of the North Sea in 1969; the firm also diversified into the coal industry in the U.S., Australia, and South Africa. After a seven-year struggle to develop the Prudhoe Bay oil field and construct the 800-mile Trans Alaska Pipeline System, the project was finally completed in 1977. In 1978, BP increased its stake in Standard Oil of Ohio to 55%. Substantial European assets were also acquired from Union Carbide Corp. and Monsanto Co. Following the world recession in the late 1970s, BP was forced to close down or sell off parts of its chemicals businesses beginning in 1980. BP acquired Selection Trust, a U.K.-based mining finance house, in what was considered the largest takeover bid to date on the London stock market.

In 1987, the U.K. government sold its remaining shares in BP as part of the firm's privatization program. BP also acquired the shares of Standard Oil of Ohio it didn't already own, merging the unit with its other U.S. interests to form BP America; the acquisition propelled BP past Mobil to the number three spot among worldwide oil leaders. Other purchases during the latter half of the decade included Purina Mills, manufacturer of domestic livestock feed, and Britoil, one of the largest independent oil exploration and production companies in the U.K.

Having diversified away from its traditional role as an integrated oil company heavily dependent on Middle Eastern oil production, BP began selling its non-core businesses, including its coal interests and mining assets, in 1990. A year later, the firm acquired 93% of Spain's Petromed. BP suffered its first quarterly loss ever in 1992, and company managers ousted CEO Robert Horton. His replacement, John Browne, launched a restructuring which included cutting the workforce by 10% and liquidating assets, including the firm's 57% share of BP Canada and gas stations in California and Florida. By 1995, the firm had refocused on four core operations: oil exploration and production, oil refining and marketing, chemicals, and nutrition.

Atlantic Richfield and BP, co-owners of two major North Slope producers, agreed in 1996 to make more than $2.6 billion in Alaskan investments by the year

The Business

Financials

Revenue (1998): $108 billion

Employees (1998): 96,650

SICs / NAICS

sic 2911 - Petroleum Refining

sic 1311 - Crude Petroleum & Natural Gas

sic 1321 - Natural Gas Liquids

sic 4923 - Gas Transmission & Distribution

sic 1381 - Drilling Oil & Gas Wells

naics 211111 - Crude Petroleum and Natural Gas Extraction

naics 211112 - Natural Gas Liquid Extraction

naics 213111 - Drilling Oil and Gas Wells

2000. In 1998, the Purina Mills unit was divested. BP and Amoco also began merger discussions that year; the deal was completed on December 31, 1998. Months later, BP Amoco and Atlantic Richfield announced their planned $26.8 billion merger.

History of Amoco Corp.

Standard Oil (Indiana) was established in 1889 as part of John Rockefeller's Standard Oil Trust. Formed outside Whiting, Indiana, the business was located close to the growing midwestern market. The Standard Oil Trust was liquidated by order of the Ohio Supreme Court in 1892; the 20 companies under its jurisdiction reverted to their former status and became subsidiaries of Standard Oil Co. (New Jersey). Roughly 55% of Standard (Indiana) was owned by Standard Oil Co. (New Jersey).

In 1911, after a court battle lasting almost three years, Standard Oil Co. (New Jersey) was ordered to relinquish supervision of its subsidiaries, Standard (Indiana) among them. Once independent, Standard (Indiana) began catering to the burgeoning automobile industry. A year later, the firm opened a service station in Minneapolis. Another service station opened in Chicago in 1913. To get as much gasoline out of each barrel of crude as possible, Standard formulated the cracking process, which doubled yield by separating the oil's molecules. The possibility of cheaper gasoline and a new line of petroleum-based products made the method attractive to other refiners, who then licensed it from Standard (Indiana); this licensing accounted for 34% of Standard (Indiana)'s profits over the next ten years.

The Officers

Co-Chairman: John Brown

Co-Chairman: Larry Fuller

Non-Executive Chairman: Peter Sutherland

Deputy CEO and President, Exploration and Production:
Rodney Chase

Deputy CEO and President, Refining and Marketing and
Chemicals: Bill Lowrie

Chief Financial Officer: John Buchanan

By 1918, the firm operated 451 service stations. Along with growing sales of road oil, asphalt, and other supporting products, the automotive industry provided one-third of all Standard (Indiana) business. During the early 1920s, acquisitions included 33% of Midwest Refining Corp. of Wyoming, 50% of Sinclair Pipe Corp., which improved transportation capacity; and a stake in Pan American Petroleum & Transport Corp. This $37.6 million transaction represented the largest oil consolidation to date in the history of the industry, giving Standard (Indiana) access to one of the world's largest tanker fleets and entry into oil fields in Mexico, Venezuela, and Iraq.

In 1930, the firm consolidated its pipeline systems and crude oil buying assets into the Stanolind Crude Oil Purchasing Corp. The largest oil field in history was discovered in east Texas late in the year. Amoco Chemicals was established in 1945. Three years later, Standard (Indiana) founded a foreign exploration department to head forays into Canada and other countries. By 1952, Standard Oil (Indiana) was considered the nation's largest domestic oil company with 12 refineries in 41 states. International exploration began intensifying during the mid-1950s with the purchase of exploration rights for 13 million acres in Cuba.

In 1957, Standard Oil (Indiana) consolidated nine subsidiaries into four larger companies, including Pan American Petroleum Corp.; Service Pipe Line Corp.; Indiana Oil Purchasing Corp.; and Amoco Chemicals Corp. By 1961, the firm had replaced the brand name of American Oil with Amoco. Foreign exploration by the mid-1960s had expanded to include Mozambique, Indonesia, Venezuela, Argentina, Colombia, and Iran. Standard Oil (Indiana) began production in the Persian Gulf Cyrus field in 1967.

The shah of Iran was overthrown in 1978, and Standard Oil (Indiana) shut down its Iranian facility and evacuated American staff members after all American employees of Amoco Iran Oil Corp. received death threats. After a year of record-breaking production in Iran, the loss resulted in a 35% production decrease in the company's overseas operations. That year, an Amoco tanker, the *Amoco Cadiz*, ran aground off the French coast, leaking 730,000 gallons of oil into the sea. The spill cost $75 million to clean up, and France sued Amoco for $300 million. The suit was settled 12 years later, with a $128 million judgement against the company.

Standard Oil (Indiana) officially changed its name to Amoco Corp. in 1985. The oil price crash in 1986 sliced profits by 63%. Two years later, Amoco purchased Tenneco Oil Company's Rocky Mountain properties for roughly $900 million and Canada's Dome Petroleum for $4.5 billion to become the largest natural gas reserves holder in North America. In 1990, joint ventures in Brazil, Mexico, South Korea, and Taiwan met the growing demand for polyester fibers, helping to generate about 35% of business overseas. The early 1990s marked a period of intense international exploration for Amoco. The firm was the first to venture into mainland China. Despite natural gas discoveries in Trinidad and the Gulf of Mexico, low production in 1995 prompted Amoco to begin divesting peripheral holdings. A restructuring started the previous year called for cutting 3,800 jobs.

In 1997, Amoco, Exxon Corp., Mobil Corp., Royal Dutch/Shell and others merged their oil and natural gas operations in South America with those of Argentina-based Bridas Corp. The venture enabled Amoco to take advantage of the growing energy market in South America and the increased demand for natural gas in Brazil and Chile. In early 1998, Amoco and General Motors Corp. announced a partnership to jointly develop lower emissions gasoline; the agreement was the first of its kind between a petroleum company and an auto maker. Later that year, Amoco and British Petroleum announced their intent to merge; the deal was finalized on December 31, 1998.

Market Forces Driving the Merger

In the late 1990s, waning demand for oil, coupled with overproduction, caused oil prices to bottom out. Most of the largest oil firms had already completed restructuring efforts which included slashing workforces and minimizing capital requirements. Needing to cut costs even further, the biggest players in the oil industry began seeking consolidation. British Petroleum (BP) and Amoco were two of the first firms to pursue such a move.

Rock bottom oil prices weren't Amoco's only struggle though. According to a December 1998 article in *Crain's Chicago Business*, "Amoco struggled to maintain its standing among its global competitors while lagging in key benchmarks such as return on capital. Saddled with a dependence on domestic reserves, its attempts to strike big fields overseas were spotty." In 1997, U.S. production accounted for 78% of Amoco's $32 billion in revenues. Without a stronger international presence, Amoco wouldn't be able to compete in the industry's top tier. A merger with BP—a firm that had relied on international production for well over 50% of its 1997 total sales of $72 billion—would give Amoco an unprecedented international presence.

One of Amoco's most appealing assets, according to BP CEO John Browne, was the firm's natural gas operation in Trinidad. Many analysts believed natural gas would play an increasingly key role in the oil industry as its demand continued to outpace demand for oil. Natural gas accounted for only 18% of BP's total production in 1997, compared to 50% of Amoco's production that year. A merger would strengthen BP's position in the natural gas sector.

The two firms believed a merger would also allow them to save $2 billion by the year 2000. These savings would come from product synergies, among other things. For example, Amoco was one of the world leaders in polypropylene production, an area where BP was admittedly weak. Conversely, Amoco lacked in polyethylene production, one of BP's strongest operations. By combining assets, Amoco and BP would reach nearly $13 billion in chemical sales.

Approach and Engagement

Amoco CEO Larry Fuller and BP CEO John Browne began merger negotiations in mid-1998. The two firms announced their $53 billion deal on August 11, 1998. According to the terms of the agreement, the new company, headquartered in London, would be named BP Amoco PLC. Fuller and Browne agreed to jointly run BP Amoco as co-chairmen.

BP shareholders overwhelmingly approved the merger on November 25, 1998; several days later, Amoco shareholders followed suit. The U.S. Federal Trade Commission granted permission for the merger with the stipulation that BP Amoco divest a total of 134 gas stations by June 29, 1999. Due to overlap, BP needed to sell stations in Columbia and Charleston, South Carolina; Charlotte, North Carolina; Jackson and Memphis, Tennessee; and Savannah, Georgia. Amoco had to dispense units in Tallahassee, Florida, and Pittsburgh, Pennsylvania. BP Amoco was also required to divest nine terminals, as well as allow in excess of 1,600 independent gas stations to swap suppliers.

The deal was completed on December 31, 1998,

The Players

Chairman and CEO of British Petroleum Company PLC: John Browne. John Browne's involvement with British Petroleum began the day he was born. The son of a British Petroleum engineer, Browne held several posts at the firm, eventually taking over as chairman in 1996. Credited for tightening the focus of BP and dramatically improving the firm's performance, Browne was knighted by Queen Elizabeth II in 1998. When BP merged with Amoco in 1999, Browne agreed to take on the new role of co-chairman.

Chairman and CEO of Amoco Corp.: Larry Fuller. Cornell University graduate Larry Fuller began working for Amoco in 1961. He held several key management positions within the firm which culminated in his appointment as chairman in 1991. When Amoco and British Petroleum merged in 1999, Fuller became co-chairman of BPAmoco.

and shares were listed on the London Stock Exchange. American Depository Shares were listed on the New York Stock Exchange, and trading began January 4, 1999.

Products and Services

After the merger, BP Amoco owned in excess of 27,000 service stations throughout the world, including 16,000 U.S. Amoco stations. Oil and gas reserves totaled 14.8 billion barrels. Exploration and production operations spanned 20 countries and included oil and gas exploration, gas processing and marketing, field development, and pipelines and transportation. BP Amoco held a 50% stake in the Trans Alaska Pipeline System. Chemical operations included acetyls and nitriles; derivatives; and polymers and olefins.

Changes to the Industry

According to industry analyst Larry Goldstein, the merger between BP and Amoco sparked a consolidation wave that more than likely "forced Exxon into the merger game. They probably would have preferred to stay on the sidelines." In December of 1998, just as the BP/Amoco deal was nearing completion, Exxon and Mobil announced a whopping $77 billion deal. Total and Petrofina also threw their hats into the consolidation ring that month. Not to be outdone, BP Amoco and Atlantic Richfield unveiled their $25 billion merger plan in March of 1999, less than three months after the BP/Amoco deal was completed.

Review of the Outcome

Among oil producers, the newly merged firm was the largest in the U.S. and the world's third largest. BP Amoco was also the leading natural gas producer in North America. Despite the sluggishness of oil stocks in early 1999, on the first day of trading, BP Amoco shares rose 35.5 cents to $15.25 per share. Fuller and Browne immediately began working on eliminating redundancies in an effort to meet their goal of $2 billion in savings by the year 2000. Analysts estimated that roughly 6,000 jobs would be cut, but by March of 1999, according to an article in *Time*, BP Amoco had cut 10,000 jobs.

Research

"Amoco Corp.," in *Notable Corporate Chronologies*, The Gale Group, 1999. Lists major events in the history of Amoco Corp.

"BP-Amoco Finish Merger After FTC Approval," in *The Oil and Gas Journal*, 11 January 1999. Discusses the details of the closing of the merger, as well as the immediate impact on stock prices.

BP Amoco PLC Home Page, available at http://www.bpamoco.com. Official World Wide Web Home Page for BP Amoco. Includes press releases; financial, historical, and product information; and annual reports.

"British Petroleum Company PLC," in *Notable Corporate Chronologies*, The Gale Group, 1999. Profiles major events in the history of British Petroleum Company PLC.

Crown, Judith. "Year's Biggest Stories, 1 of 10: British Oil Giant Guzzles Amoco in $53-Bil Deal," in *Crain's Chicago Business*, 21 December 1998. Explains why the two firms decided to merge.

———. "The Duke of Oil," in *Crain's Chicago Business*, 25 January 1999. Details the career of British Petroleum CEO John Browne.

Knott, David. "Majors' Merger Rash," in *The Oil and Gas Journal*, 7 December 1998. Explains how the BP and Amoco deal sparked an oil industry consolidation trend among the leading players.

Mack, Toni. "Catching up to Exxon," in *Forbes*, 13 March 1995. A snapshot of the career of Larry Fuller at Amoco Corp.

Palmeri, Christopher. "A Good Match in the Oil Patch," in *Forbes*, 21 September 1998. Covers the anticipated synergies between BP and Amoco.

Pellegrini, Frank. "Gas Guzzling Continues with BP-Arco Merger," in *Time*, 29 March 1999. Gives a brief overview of the industry conditions that led to the BP/Amoco merger, as well as its initial outcome.

ANNAMARIE L. SHELDON

BRITISH PETROLEUM & STANDARD OIL OF OHIO

nationality: United Kingdom
date: June 1987
affected: British Petroleum Company PLC, United Kingdom, founded 1909
affected: Standard Oil of Ohio, USA, founded 1911

BP Amoco PLC
Brittanic House 1, Finsbury Circus
London, EC2M 7BA
United Kingdom

tel: 44-171-496-4000
fax: 44-171-496-4630
web: http://www.bpamoco.com

Overview of the Merger

When British Petroleum secured full ownership of Standard Oil of Ohio in 1986, the firm surpassed Mobil Corp. as the third largest oil company in the world—behind Royal Dutch/Shell Group and Exxon Corp.—with combined assets of $48 billion. The $7.7 billion merger was the ninth-largest deal of the 1980s, as well as the second-largest cross-border transaction that decade. At the time, it was also the third-largest acquisition ever completed in both U.S. and British corporate history.

History of British Petroleum Company PLC

Anglo-Persian Oil Co. was formed in 1909, one year after the first oil discovery in the Middle East. Three years later, the new firm signed a ten-year marketing agreement with the Royal Dutch-Shell group. In 1914, Anglo-Persian signed a long-term agreement with the British Admiralty for the supply of fuel oil, which the Royal Navy used as a replacement for coal. The U.K. government invested two million British pounds in the company and received a majority shareholding in return.

The company established a wholly owned oil tanker subsidiary in 1915. Two years later, Anglo-Persian bought British Petroleum Co., the U.K. marketing subsidiary of the European Petroleum Co.; established a refinery in Swansea, Wales, to produce petroleum products for the U.K.; and opened a research laboratory in Sunbury, U.K. By the early 1920s, Anglo-Persian owned more than 30 oil tankers. The firm began forming subsidiaries in many European countries, as well as in Africa and Asia, following the expiration of its agreement with Shell.

During the late 1940s, Anglo-Persian diversified into petrochemicals. In 1954, the company was renamed the British Petroleum Company (BP). That year, BP signed an agreement with the Iranian government, whereby BP held a 40% interest in a newly created consortium of Western oil companies formed to undertake oil exploration, production, and refining in Iran. With the United Kingdom's nationalization depriving the company of two-thirds of its production, BP increased its output in Iraq and Kuwait and built new refineries in Europe, Australia, and Aden.

The Business

Financials

Revenue (1998): $108 billion

Employees (1998): 96,650

SICs / NAICS

sic 2911 - Petroleum Refining

sic 1311 - Crude Petroleum & Natural Gas

sic 1321 - Natural Gas Liquids

sic 4923 - Gas Transmission & Distribution

sic 1381 - Drilling Oil & Gas Wells

naics 211111 - Crude Petroleum and Natural Gas Extraction

naics 211112 - Natural Gas Liquid Extraction

naics 213111 - Drilling Oil and Gas Wells

In 1968, BP acquired the U.S. east coast refining and marketing operations of Atlantic Richfield. After searching for oil in Alaska throughout the decade, BP made a major discovery at Prudhoe Bay on the North Slope in 1969. By then, BP owned over half of the biggest oil field in the United States. The firm exchanged some of its Alaskan reserves for a 25% stake in Standard Oil of Ohio. The following year, the Forties field, the first major commercial oil find in British waters, was discovered.

BP discovered gas in British waters of the North Sea in 1969; the firm also diversified into the coal industry in the U.S., Australia, and South Africa. After a seven-year struggle to develop the Prudhoe Bay oil field and construct the 800-mile Trans Alaska Pipeline System, the project was finally completed in 1977. In 1978, BP increased its stake in Standard Oil of Ohio to 55%. Substantial European assets were also acquired from Union Carbide Corp. and Monsanto Co. Following the world recession in the late 1970s, BP was forced to close down or sell off parts of its chemicals businesses beginning in 1980. BP also acquired Selection Trust, a U.K.-based mining finance house, in what was considered the largest takeover bid to date on the London stock market.

In 1986, the U.K. government sold its remaining shares in BP as part of the firm's privatization program. BP also acquired the shares of Standard Oil of Ohio it didn't already own, merging the unit with its other U.S. interests to form BP America; the acquisition propelled BP past Mobil to the number three spot among worldwide oil leaders. Other purchases during the latter half of the decade included Purina Mills,

manufacturer of domestic livestock feed, and Britoil, one of the largest independent oil exploration and production companies in the U.K.

Having diversified away from its traditional role as an integrated oil company heavily dependent on Middle Eastern oil production, BP began selling its non-core businesses, including its coal interests and mining assets, in 1990. A year later, the firm acquired 93% of Spain's Petromed. BP suffered its first quarterly loss ever in 1992, and company managers ousted CEO Robert Horton. His replacement, John Browne, launched a restructuring which included cutting the workforce by 10% and liquidating assets, including the 57% share of BP Canada and gas stations in California and Florida. By 1995, the firm had refocused on four core operations: oil exploration and production, oil refining and marketing, chemicals, and nutrition.

Atlantic Richfield and BP, co-owners of two major North Slope producers, agreed in 1996 to make more than $2.6 billion in Alaskan investments by the year 2000. In 1998, the Purina Mills unit was divested. BP and Amoco also began merger discussions that year; the deal was completed on December 31, 1998. Months later, BP Amoco and Atlantic Richfield announced their planned $26.8 billion merger.

History of Standard Oil of Ohio

In 1911, after a court battle lasting almost three years, John D. Rockefeller's Standard Oil trust was ordered by the U.S. Supreme Court to disband into 34 independent companies. Standard Oil of Ohio (SOHIO) was among the new companies, as was Standard Oil of New York, which eventually became Exxon Corp.; Standard Oil of California, which evolved into Chevron Corp.; and Standard Oil of Indiana, which grew into Amoco Corp.

Needing more of a foothold in the U.S. oil industry, British Petroleum (BP) exchanged some of its Alaskan reserves for a 25% stake in Standard Oil of Ohio in 1969. Roughly ten years later, BP increased its stake in SOHIO to a controlling 55%. The lucrative Alaskan assets boosted profits dramatically, prompting SOHIO management to seek diversification. The firm's non-oil acquisitions between 1979 and 1981 ranged from animal feed, ceramics, and hybrid corn seed to copper—including Kennecott Copper, which was sold in 1989—and gold. When falling oil and copper prices in the mid-1980s undercut SOHIO's earnings, BP decide to take a more active role in running the firm. In 1985, in an effort to reign in the buying spree and refocus SOHIO on core operations, BP fired SOHIO chairman Alton W. Whitehouse, replacing him with BP executive Robert Horton.

The new chairman launched a restructuring that included posting a $410 million charge on roughly 50% of the unused property owned by SOHIO and laying off 15% of the firm's exploration employees. In April of 1986, BP announced its intent to acquire the shares of SOHIO it didn't already own and merge the unit with its other U.S. interests to form BP America. The $7.7 billion deal was finalized in June of that year.

Market Forces Driving the Merger

British Petroleum (BP) began its takeover of Standard Oil of Ohio (SOHIO) in 1969 by purchasing a minority stake in the firm. According to a 1996 *Crain's Cleveland Business* article, "BP needed a U.S. base from which to expand its American operations, and Standard Oil needed, well, oil, and a chance to bolster its finances and grow."

In 1978, BP upped it ownership to 55%, gaining control of SOHIO. When oil prices jumped in 1987, BP decided it was time to make a move for full ownership. According to BP CEO Walters, as quoted in an April 1987 *Business Week* article, "we have confidence that the oil price has stabilized and that $18 is the right level for stability." Walters also pointed out that the deal would help strengthen BP's North American position.

In addition, acquiring the remaining 45% of SOHIO would boost BP past Mobil Corp. to the third place spot among worldwide oil leaders. BP would gain access to SOHIO's $1.8 billion in cash flow, boosting its own annual capital budget to $3.5 billion.

Approach and Engagement

On April 1, 1986, British Petroleum launched a 20-day tender offer for full control of Standard Oil of Ohio (SOHIO). The $70 per share offer meant BP would have to take on $5 billion in debt to finance what would amount to a $7.4 billion purchase. Several SOHIO shareholders filed suit, claiming that the offer was too low. When BP countered with a $71.50 per share offer, raising the price of the merger to $7.7 billion, the suits were dismissed. In June of 1986, after BP completed its takeover of SOHIO, the firm merged its new wholly owned subsidiary with its BP North America Petroleum operations to form BP America. SOHIO retained its headquarters in Cleveland, Ohio.

Products and Services

Roughly 12 years after BP took over SOHIO, the firm merged with Amoco Corp. to become BP Amoco. Once that deal was completed, BP Amoco owned in excess of 27,000 service stations throughout the world, including 16,000 U.S. Amoco stations. Oil and gas reserves totaled 14.8 billion barrels. Exploration and

The Officers

Co-Chairman: John Brown

Co-Chairman: Larry Fuller

Non-Executive Chairman: Peter Sutherland

Deputy CEO and President, Exploration and Production: Rodney Chase

Deputy CEO and President, Refining and Marketing and Chemicals: Bill Lowrie

Chief Financial Officer: John Buchanan

production operations spanned 20 countries and included oil and gas exploration, gas processing and marketing, field development, and pipelines and transportation. BP Amoco held a 50% stake in the Trans Alaska Pipeline System. Chemical operations included acetyls and nitriles; derivatives; and polymers and olefins.

Review of the Outcome

The integrating of operations proved to be a smooth one, mainly because BP already controlled operations at SOHIO. Although higher stock prices immediately following the deal reflected enthusiasm among industry analysts for the merger, BP's presence in the U.S. never strengthened as much as anticipated. In fact, by 1996, BP America employees totaled only 15,000, compared to 40,000 in 1987, and operations had shrunk considerably. In December of 1998, BP boosted its U.S. foothold via acquisition once again when it bought another of the Standard Oil originals, Amoco Corp., an oil firm that earned nearly 80% of total revenues from U.S. oil production in 1997.

Research

BP Amoco PLC Home Page, available at http://www.bpamoco.com. Official World Wide Web Home Page for BP Amoco. Includes press releases; financial, historical, and product information; and annual reports.

"British Petroleum Company PLC," in *Notable Corporate Chronologies*, The Gale Group, 1999. Lists major events in the history of British Petroleum Company PLC.

Marino, Jim. "BP Takeover Blind-Sided the Venerable Standard Oil," in *Crain's Cleveland Business*, 30 September 1996. Explains why BP wanted full control of SOHIO, as well as how BP's American operations have fared since the takeover.

Miller, Sarah. "Why BP is Going All Out for All of Standard Oil," in *Business Week*, 13 April 1987. Covers why BP decided to pursue full control of SOHIO.

SAMIT AYERS

BRITISH TELECOMMUNICATIONS &
MCI WORLDCOM

British Telecommunications PLC
BT Centre, 81 Newgate St.
London, EC1A 7AJ
United Kingdom

tel: 44-171-356-5000
fax: 44-171-356-5520
web: http://www.bt.com

MCI Communications Corp.
515 E. Amite St.
Jackson, MS 39201-2702
USA

tel: (601)360-8600
fax: (601)974-8350
web: http://www.mciworldcom.com

date: February 1997 (canceled)
affected: British Telecommunications PLC, United Kingdom, founded 1981
affected: MCI Communications Corp., USA, founded 1968

Overview of the Merger

Announced in 1996, the $24.7 billion merger of British Telecommunications PLC (BT) and MCI Communications Corp. would have created Concert PLC. The new firm, headquartered in both London and Washington, D.C., would have seen sales of $42 billion, profits of $4.7 billion, 43 million customers spanning 72 countries, and 183,000 employees. The deal would also have been the largest transatlantic merger in history, creating the world's first global communications company. However, when MCI revealed that losses from failed attempts to penetrate the local phone market in 1997 would be twice as large as estimated, BT shareholders balked and demanded a lower price. This offered other suitors an opportunity to outbid BT, and the MCI/BT deal fell apart after MCI accepted a higher offer from WorldCom Inc.

History of British Telecommunications PLC

The Post Office Act of 1969 changed the status of the United Kingdom Post Office by transforming it into a state public corporation under the Secretary of State for Industry. The telecommunications services remained in the Post Office as a part of the Post Office Telecommunications division. The British Telecommunications Act of 1981 separated telecommunications from the Post Office and set up a new autonomous, yet state-owned, body known as British Telecommunications Corp. (BT).

In 1982, the government announced its intention to privatize BT. The following year, in a duopoly policy, the British government decided not to license any company except BT and Mercury Communications Ltd. to carry telecommunications services over fixed links. Under the 1984 Telecommunications Act, BT became privatized when it was registered in the U.K. as a public limited company. The government retained a 48.6% stake in the new company. BT's main activity was to supply telecommunications services to the 55 million people in the U.K. The firm's performance and development were conditioned by an official regulatory body, the semi-independent Office of Telecommunications (Oftel), which monitored BT's pricing, accounting, investment policies, and quality of services; issued licenses to additional competitors; and facilitated the interconnection of rival services to the BT network.

In 1985, BT launched a pilot integrated services digital network (ISDN) that offered data, voice, text, and image network services at high speed. A year later, the firm purchased Mitel Corp., a Canadian phone equipment manufacturer. Local communications services and national networks divisions were merged to form the BTUK Division in 1988. BT diversified into mobile telephony in 1989 by acquiring a 20% interest in McCaw Cellular Communications Inc., a U.S. mobile cellular telephone operator. Also that year, BT purchased U.S.-based Tymnet, one of the largest value-added network services (VANS) companies in the world, and consolidated some of its own international services under a new company, BT Tymnet Inc.

A restructuring in 1991 replaced the firm's three former operating divisions—BTUK, comprising local communications services and national networks; British Telecom International (BTI); and CSD, Communication Services Division—with two major divisions that dealt directly with customers: Personal Communications and Business Communications. International and U.K. networks were brought together into a new Worldwide Networks Division. Mobile communications and operator services comprised a new Special Business Division. After the British government reviewed its duopoly policy, it recommended that BT and its rival, Mercury Communications, should face greater competition in local, trunk, and international services.

BT set up a subsidiary, Syncordia Corp., in Atlanta, Georgia, to start a global telecommunications network that offered comprehensive services to multinational corporations. In 1992, the firm sold its stake in McCaw Cellular to AT&T Corp. and divested Mitel Corp. BT acquired 20% of MCI Communications Corp. for $4.2 billion in 1993. That year, the British government sold nearly its entire remaining stake in BT for $7.43 billion. In 1994, BT folded Syncordia into the new BT/MCI venture.

By 1995, deregulation had taken its toll on BT's market share; more than 150 firms had started telecommunications operations in the U.K. over the past five years. In 1996, BT and MCI announced their intent to merge into Concert Communications Services; however, before the deal was completed, WorldCom outbid BT for MCI. BT was awarded a $1.5 billion ten-year contract by the U.K. Ministry of

The Business

Financials - British Telecommunications PLC

Revenue (1998): $26.14 billion

Employees (1998): 129,200

Financials - MCI Communications Corp.

Revenue (1998): $17.6 billion

Employees (1998): 77,000

SICs / NAICS

sic 4813 - Telephone Communications Except Radiotelephone

sic 4812 - Radiotelephone Communications

sic 4822 - Telegraph & Other Communications

sic 4899 - Communications Services Nec

naics 513322 - Cellular and Other Wireless Telecommunications

naics 513321 - Paging

Defence in 1997 to provide an advanced national fixed telecommunications network for the U.K. armed forces. The following year, BT and AT&T established a joint venture to offer data, voice, and video services on a global scale.

History of MCI Communications Corp.

John Goeken and William G. McGowan founded Microwave Communications Inc. (MC), a microwave radio system to handle telephone calls between Chicago, Illinois, and St. Louis, Missouri, in 1968. The following year, the FCC granted MC authorization to begin operations, but the company was given no assurance that it could expand its network or connect with existing AT&T lines. AT&T sued MC, blocking the new company from providing service.

MC hired Kenneth Cox in 1971 to spearhead its legal drive to dismantle AT&T's monopoly on telephonic communications. The firm also received final approval to begin providing services along the Chicago-St. Louis route. In 1972, MC issued public stock, raising more than $100 million in capital, and secured an additional $72 million in bank loans to begin construction of its Chicago-St. Louis line of microwave towers. The following year, MC reorganized as MCI Communications Corp. (MCI), and began providing commercial private line service between

The Officers

British Telecommunications PLC

Chairman: Sir Ian Vallance

Deputy Chairman: Sir Colin Marshall

Chief Executive Officer: Sir Peter Bonfield

Chief Financial Officer: Robert P. Brace

President and Chief Executive Officer, BT Worldwide:
   Alfred Mockett

MCI Communications Corp.

Chairman: Bert C. Roberts, Jr.

President and CEO: Bernie J. Ebbers

Vice Chairman and Chairman, UUNet WorldCom: John
   Sidgmore

Chief Financial Officer: Scott Sullivan

VP, Human Resources: Dennis Sickle

Chicago and St. Louis. It faced financial difficulty and was forced to appeal to the FCC to be allowed to route FX calls through AT&T's switched network.

In 1974, MCI filed a civil antitrust suit against AT&T seeking damages. Corporate losses averaged $1 million per month for the next two years. The firm also launched its own long distance service for businesses, Execunet, in direct competition with AT&T. The U.S. Justice Department filed an antitrust suit designed to break up AT&T's system of Bell Telephone companies. In 1976, MCI won the right to use AT&T switching equipment, but AT&T raised its tariffs, ensuring that MCI's service remained more expensive; in response, MCI filed another suit against AT&T, but a judge later found that AT&T's tariff system was fair. After another judge ruled, in 1980, in favor of MCI in its civil antitrust suit against AT&T, MCI entered the personal long distance business, becoming a full-scale competitor with AT&T. Company revenues begin to rise rapidly, nearing $1 billion by 1981.

AT&T finally settled the Justice Department's antitrust suit by agreeing to divest itself of its Bell Telephone subsidiaries in 1984. In the mid-1980s, MCI became the first U.S. company other than AT&T to offer international long distance service. In 1985, IBM agreed to purchase an 18% interest in MCI, which used the capital to expand its national network and launch an aggressive new marketing campaign. That year, AT&T reduced its rates, crippling MCI's earnings and causing the company's stock to plummet 65%.

MCI bought Virginia-based Satellite Business Systems, a long distance and data transmission company, in 1986. Two years later, the firm acquired RCA Global Communications, a company providing worldwide fax, telex, and high-speed data transmission services.

Purchases in the early 1990s included 25% of INFONET Services Corp., a provider of international data services; TelecomUSA, the fourth-largest long distance company in the U.S.; and Overseas Telecommunications Inc., an international leader in digital satellite services. In 1991, MCI introduced its Friends and Family discount long distance service for residential customers; the program was adapted for corporate use the following year. By this time MCI's domestic network had become fully digital. The Federal Aviation Administration awarded MCI a $558 million contract for air traffic control communications systems in 1992. The firm also agreed to provide service to companies including Nissan and Hong Kong Bank.

An FCC audit in 1995 revealed that the Bell spin-off companies had passed $116.5 million in lobbying expenses to MCI, and MCI asked federal regulators to order repayment. In 1996, MCI and British Telecommunications (BT) agreed to form a joint venture called Concert. The deal fell apart, however, when WorldCom outbid BT in 1997. MCI and WorldCom completed their $37 billion deal in the fall of 1998 to form MCI WorldCom, the second largest long distance provider in the U.S.

Market Forces Driving the Merger

By 1995, deregulation in the United Kingdom had taken its toll on British Telecom (BT). Because of the 150 firms that had started telecommunications operations in the U.K. between 1990 and 1995, BT's share of the U.K. residential telephone market had fallen to 93%, down from 99% in 1991; likewise, its business market share had dropped to 83%, down from 94% in 1991. Since 1990, BT had also cut more than 100,000 jobs. After talks with Cable & Wireless, the second largest telecommunications firm in Britain, fell through in 1995, BT decided that its reliance on domestic sales was a weak spot; the firm began seeking international diversification as means of bolstering its performance.

When BT and MCI began merger talks in 1996, domestic sales at BT accounted for 70% of total revenues. BT hadn't pursued a merger with European firms because many national governments were still disinclined to allow foreign firms to compete with their national telecommunications operators. The U.S. market was considered liberal by comparison, and BT wanted to establish a foothold in the lucrative telecommunications industry there.

At the same time, MCI needed the financial muscle of a firm like BT. According to a November 1996 *New York Times* article, BT's financial prowess would "enable the new company to penetrate the local calling market in the U.S.," which at that time was worth $100 billion per year. Since the passing of the Telecommunications Act of 1996—which deregulated the U.S. telecommunications industry, allowing phone companies, both regional and long distance, to begin competing in each other's markets—the race among long distance providers likes MCI and AT&T for local access had intensified. Consolidation was seen by many analysts as a necessary step for firms hoping to land at the top of the global telecommunications heap.

Approach and Engagement

The deal between BT and MCI had at its roots BT's $4.2 billion purchase of a 20% stake of MCI in 1993. On November 3, 1996, the two firms announced their $24.7 billion merger plan and filed an application with the FCC for approval to form Concert Communications Services, which would serve as the parent company of both BT and MCI. Senior executives would be realigned in the following manner: Sir Ian Vallance, current chairman of BT, would become co-chairman of Concert with Bert Roberts, current MCI chairman. Sir Peter Bonfield, CEO of BT, would be Concert's CEO. Gerald Taylor would move from CEO of MCI to president and COO of Concert.

In August of 1997, MCI revealed that losses from failed attempts to penetrate the U.S. local phone market would be twice as large as estimated—nearly $800 million. BT shareholders balked and demanded a lower price. Both sides returned to the negotiations table, and MCI agreed to cut its price by 20% via increased cash payment and decreased share exchange. The newer deal was valued at roughly $18 billion. The lower price offered other suitors an opportunity to outbid BT. On October 1, 1997, WorldCom Inc. launched a successful $37 billion bid for MCI, causing the MCI/BT deal to crumble.

Products and Services

Of British Telecom's $26 billion in 1998 revenues, 31% was secured via domestic telephone calls. Telephone exchange line rentals brought in 19%; international calls accounted for 10%. Both private circuits and mobile communications earned 7% of total sales. Other services included Internet access and directory publishing. International operations included BT France SNC; BT North America Inc.; BT Telecomuni-

The Players

CEO of British Telecommunications PLC: Sir Peter Bonfield. Peter Bonfield spent most of his career in the United States before being appointed CEO of British Telecommunications (BT). In 1995, he spearheaded his firm's efforts to merge with Cable & Wireless PLC, the second largest telecommunications firm in Britain; however, talks came to a halt after the two companies could not agree on a price. When BT and MCI were negotiating their merger, which would have formed Concert PLC, Bonfield was slated to become CEO of the new firm. After merger negotiations fell through in 1997, Bonfield retained his spot as CEO of BT.

Chairman and CEO of MCI Communications Corp.: Bert C. Roberts, Jr. Telecommunications executive Bert Roberts became president and chief operating officer of MCI Communications Corp. in 1985. Seven years later, he took over as chairman and CEO. He is credited for leading MCI's transformation from a small start-up to one of the world's largest long distance providers, with more than $20 billion in annual revenues. When MCI merged with WorldCom in 1998, Roberts was named chairman of the new firm, MCI WorldCom Inc.

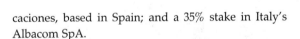

caciones, based in Spain; and a 35% stake in Italy's Albacom SpA.

MCI WorldCom, the product of MCI's 1998 merger with WorldCom Inc., offered the following products in 1999: local, long distance and cellular phone services; paging services; 800 services; calling cards; conference calling; debit cards; Internet access to businesses via the WorldCom fiber optic network; and Internet access to consumers through a venture with the CompuServe unit of America Online.

Review of the Outcome

According to a November 1997 article in *Financial World*, British Telecom (BT) was viewed as a "flabby and directionless competitor afraid—or simply unable—to pull the trigger on a deal that would catapult it into the ranks of the global elite." As the firm's market share continued to decline in the face of intense domestic competition, analysts predicted that a BT linkup with GTE might be in the works.

However, the firm instead decided to purse an alliance with AT&T, whereby the two firms would jointly produce data, voice, and video services on a global scale.

Research

"British Telecommunication PLC," in *Notable Corporate Chronologies*, The Gale Group, 1999. Lists major events in the history of British Telecommunication PLC.

British Telecommunication PLC Home Page, available at http://www.bt.com. Official World Wide Web Home Page for British Telecommunication PLC. Includes current and archived news; financial, product, and historical information; and annual reports.

"MCI and British Telecom Cut Merger Value by 20%, to $18 Billion," in *Communications Daily*, 25 August 1997. Explains how the two firms revised their agreement after MCI posted higher than expected losses.

"MCI Communications Corp.," in *Notable Corporate Chronologies*, The Gale Group, 1999. Lists major events in the history of MCI Communications Corp., including its failed merger with British Telecommunication PLC.

MCI WorldCom, Inc. Home Page, available at http://www.mciworldcom.com. Official World Wide Web Home Page for MCI WorldCom, Inc. Includes current and archived news; financial, product, and historical information; and annual reports.

Moss, Nicholas. "BT Holds the Line on MCI," in *The European*, 21 August 1997. Covers the concerns BT shareholders had regarding the planned takeover of MCI.

Mulligan, Thomas S. "BT to Buy MCI in Biggest Deal of Its Kind," in *Los Angeles Times*, 4 November 1996. Explains why BT and MCI wanted to merge.

"Snatching BT's Bride," in *The Economist*, 4 October 1997. Explores WorldCom's role in the dissolution of the BT/MCI deal.

Winnifrith, Tom. "Life After MCI: What is British Telecom's Next Move?" in *Financial World*, November 1997. Discusses why BT needed to merge with MCI and what the failed deal means for the future of BT.

ANNAMARIE L. SHELDON

BURLINGTON NORTHERN & SANTA FE PACIFIC

nationality: USA
date: September 1995
affected: Burlington Northern Inc., USA, founded 1849
affected: Santa Fe Pacific Corp., USA, founded 1859

Burlington Northern Santa Fe Corp.
2650 Lou Menk Dr.
Fort Worth, TX 76131
USA

tel: (817)333-2000
fax: (817)333-2377
web: http://www.bnsf.com

Overview of the Merger

In June of 1994, Burlington Northern and Santa Fe Pacific announced their intent to merge in a $2.7 billion stock deal. Union Pacific Corp., the largest rail company in the U.S., launched a $3.4 billion counter offer; despite the fact that the bid was higher than Burlington Northern's offer, Santa Fe Pacific quickly rejected the deal, which eventually led to a lawsuit that was later dismissed by a Delaware Chancery Court. The $4 billion merger between Burlington Northern and Santa Fe Pacific in September of 1995 created the largest railroad company in the U.S. with 33,000 miles of track spanning 27 states and two Canadian provinces.

History of Burlington Northern Inc.

In 1849, the Aurora Branch Railroad (ABR) was founded in Aurora, Illinois, by Stephen F. Gale. A year later, ABR became the second railroad to serve Chicago, Illinois. The U.S. Congress ceded 2.5 million acres of land for railroad development in Illinois in 1851. ABR consolidated with the Central Military Tract Railroad and the Peoria and Oquawka Railroad to better position the company in the bidding for the federal land. In 1852, investors led by John Murray Forbes took over operation of ABR, which changed its name to the Chicago and Aurora Railroad Company (CARC). The company then bought the Northern Cross Railroad, thereby adding additional track.

CARC changed its name to the Chicago, Burlington, and Quincy Railroad Company (CB&Q) in 1855. Three years later, poor wheat and corn crops in Illinois reduced CB&Q's freight tonnage carried by 25%, and passengers carried by 20%, resulting in a 40% drop in revenues. Management instituted a cautious reinvestment plan. The Civil War brought rapid growth and development in the railroad industry, and the company recovered. In 1867, CB&Q laid its first steel rails, replacing iron ones. Express mail service operations were launched in 1884. By 1890, the company operated 5,160 miles of track, twice as much as in 1880.

In 1889, Union Pacific and Great Northern Railroads (GNR) sought a merger with CB&Q. Two years later, GNR purchased 61% of CB&Q's stock, and CB&Q became a subsidiary of GNR.

The Business

Financials

Revenue (1998): $8.9 billion

Employees (1998): 42,900

SICs / NAICS

sic 4011 - Railroads-Line-Haul Operating

sic 4111 - Local & Suburban Transit

sic 4013 - Switching & Terminal Services

naics 482111 - Line-Haul Railroads

naics 485112 - Commuter Rail Systems

naics 485111 - Mixed Mode Transit Systems

naics 482112 - Short Line Railroads

The U.S. government nationalized all railroads during World War I, setting rates and traffic flows and guaranteeing revenues equal to the average of the three previous years: $33.3 million. In 1920, government control of CB&Q ended, and the Transportation Act passed, easing restrictions on railroad mergers. The Interstate Commerce Commission (ICC) rejected a proposed restructuring of the relation between the GNR and the CB&Q in 1930. Three years later, the Emergency Transportation Act passed, eliminating duplication of services between competing lines and promoting financial reorganization of railroads.

In 1934, CB&Q began operating the diesel-electric Zephyr locomotive, cutting travel times in half. World War II brought massive increases in rail traffic, enabling CB&Q to continue expansion. In 1960, GNR, CB&Q, and the Northern Pacific railroads contemplated a merger; the ICC approved the deal eight years later. GNR, CB&Q, and Northern Pacific, along with two smaller railroads, merged to form Burlington Northern Inc. (BN) in 1970. BN then diversified into nonrailroad industries, focusing on national resources and airfreight.

BN and Union Pacific sought control of Peninsula Terminal Co. of Portland, Oregon, in 1972, but the U.S. Supreme Court refused to allow the purchase. The following year, BN proposed a merger with the Chicago, Milwaukee, and St. Paul & Pacific Railroad, but the ICC refused to let the deal proceed. Between 1980 and 1985, BN acquired the St. Louis-San Francisco Railway; El Paso Natural Gas Company, a diversified energy concern; and Southland Royal Company, a producer of oil and gas. In 1988, BN reversed its trend toward diversification, spinning off its energy-producing subsidiaries into Burlington Resources Inc., a separate, publicly held corporation; the firm also sold off its trucking subsidiary, Burlington Motor Carriers, Inc.

BN began a reorganization to replace its traditional pyramidal management system with a "matrix" system in 1994. Poor performance led the company to suspend the coastal barge service in Mexico that year. BN agreed in 1995 to acquire Santa Fe Pacific for $4 billion in stock, creating a 33,000-mile railway system. The newly merged company was named Burlington Northern Santa Fe Corp. (BNSF). Also that year, Southern Pacific Rail Corp. and Union Pacific Railroad Co. entered into an agreement with Burlington to ensure long-term rail competition west of the Mississippi River following Burlington's merger with Santa Fe Pacific.

BNSF acquired Washington Central Railroad Co. in 1996. Two years later, the firm divested its stake in petroleum products pipeline outfit Santa Fe Pacific Pipeline Partners. Stock split three-for-one that year.

History of Santa Fe Pacific Corp.

In 1859, Cyrus Kurtz Holliday established Atchison and Topeka Railroad Co. The company was renamed Atchison, Topeka & Santa Fe Railroad Co. (ATS) in 1863 to reflect its growing lines. When the Civil War ended, the firm resumed construction that had ceased due to capital shortages. By 1880, the rail system had reached Albuquerque, New Mexico; seven years later, a line extended to Los Angeles, California.

As the turn of the century neared, the railway system of ATS had grown to nearly 9,000 miles. Headquarters were moved to Chicago in 1904. By 1930, the company owned in excess of 13,000 miles of railway track. In 1968, Santa Fe Industries was established to serve as a holding company for ATS.

During the 1980s, ATS managed to ward off a hostile takeover by corporate raider Michael Dingman. Southern Pacific and Santa Fe began negotiating a merger in 1983. The new company was the second largest railway operator in the U.S., behind Burlington Northern. The Interstate Commerce Commission (ICC) eventually deemed the deal anticompetitive. As a result, ATS divested Southern Pacific in 1989; ATS then changed its name to Sante Fe Pacific.

Burlington Northern agreed in 1995 to acquire Santa Fe Pacific for $4 billion in stock, creating a 33,000-mile railway system. The newly merged company was named Burlington Northern Santa Fe Corp. (BNSF).

Market Forces Driving the Merger

According to a July 1994, *Financial Times* article, one of the fastest growing segments of the railway market during the mid-1990s was intermodal (shipping freight containers and truck trailers using a combination of water, rail, and motor carriers) traffic. To take advantage of this growth, Burlington Northern and Santa Fe Pacific wanted to merge as a means of "boosting the number of long distance destinations" they could offer.

The synergies between Santa Fe's current intermodal business, Burlington Northern's coal hauling operations, and both firm's grain and chemical traffic seemed promising to most analysts as well. And Burlington Northern would gain access to southern California, the southwestern U.S. and Mexico, while Santa Fe Pacific would gain entrance to the northern Midwest and the Pacific Northwest. As explained in a December 1995 article in *Purchasing*, "the merger will provide shippers with single-line service from the Midwest to California and to the Pacific Northwest, across the Southeast and the Pacific Northwest, and between the Gulf of Mexico and Canada." With roughly $7 billion in annual revenue, the new firm would dominate rail cargo in the western U.S.

Approach and Engagement

In June of 1994, Burlington Northern and Santa Fe Pacific announced their intent to merge in a $2.7 billion stock deal. The months following the announcement were anything but smooth. The Coalition of Utah shippers filed statements with the Surface Transportation Board protesting the proposed merger (although shipping associations representing nine other Western states had no objection to the move). Union Pacific Corp., the largest rail company in the U.S., launched a $3.4 billion counter offer in October of 1994; despite the fact that the bid was higher than Burlington Northern's offer, Santa Fe Pacific quickly rejected the deal, claiming that Union Pacific was simply looking to prevent its deal with Burlington Northern. Shareholders were also concerned that a merger with Union Pacific would be rejected by regulators.

Union Pacific then lowered its offer, but guaranteed the deal with a voting trust, which meant that Union Pacific assumed all the risk if the deal fell apart. Union Pacific also filed suit with the Delaware Chancery Court in an effort to force Sante Fe into further negotiations. Union Pacific's final cash bid of $18.50 per share was lower than the $20 per share in cash and stock offered by Burlington Northern, but the voting trust mechanism made the offer more attractive—Union Pacific was willing to pay without

The Officers

Chairman, President and CEO: Robert D. Krebs

Sr. VP and Chief Operating Officer: Matthew K. Rose

Sr. VP and Chief Financial Officer: Denis E. Springer

Sr. VP, Coal and Agricultural Commodities Business:
Gregory T. Swienton

Sr. VP, Intermodal and Automotive Business Group:
Charles L. Schultz

Sr. VP, Law and Chief of Staff: Jeffrey R. Moreland

Sr. VP, Merchandise Business: Douglas J. Babb

waiting for ICC approval of the deal. However, the ICC changed its policy in January of 1995; instead of taking up to 31 months to rule on a merger, the commission decided to shorten this time frame considerably, which lessened the attractiveness of the Union Pacific offer.

On January 30, 1995, the Delaware Chancery Court dismissed Union Pacific's suit, and its effort to block the Burlington Northern takeover of Santa Fe Pacific crumbled. In March, Burlington Northern and Santa Fe shareholders approved the deal. ICC approval followed in July with the stipulation that competitors Union Pacific and Southern Pacific be allowed to use Santa Fe lines for a fee as a means of maintaining competition. In September of 1995, Burlington Northern paid $4 billion in cash and stock for Santa Fe Pacific. The two firms merged to form Burlington Northern Santa Fe Corp. (BNSF).

After the deal was completed, Western Fuels Corp., Western Coal Traffic League, and Southwestern Public Services Corp. filed suit with the U.S. Court of Appeals demanding that the ICC reconsider its permission to allow the merger. The case was later dismissed.

Products and Services

By 1998, intermodal traffic accounted for 28% of the $8.9 billion in sales achieved by Burlington Northern Santa Fe Corp. (BNSF) that year. Coal traffic secured 25%; transport of agricultural commodities, 12%; transport of metals and minerals, 8%; transport of forest products, 7%; transport of consumer goods, 6%; and transport of automotive products, 4%. BNSF owned in excess of 34,000 miles of railway track spanning 28 states in the U.S., as well as in Manitoba and British Columbia, Canada.

The Players

Chairman and CEO of Burlington Northern Inc.: Gerald Grinstein. After spending 15 years as partner in Seattle, Washington-based law firm, which included a stint as chief counsel to the U.S. Senate Commerce Committee, Gerald Grinstein joined Burlington Northern in 1985. He was appointed chairman and CEO in 1990, posts he held until his firm merged with Santa Fe Pacific in 1995. When the merger was completed, Grinstein retired.

Chairman, CEO, and President of Santa Fe Pacific Corp.: Robert D. Krebs. Robert Krebs was instrumental in preparing Santa Fe Pacific for its 1995 merger with Burlington Northern. He is credited for pulling the struggling railroad company out from under $3.5 billion in debt between 1988 and 1990. His drastic overhaul of the firm doubled share prices in 1991. When the merger with Burlington Northern was completed, Krebs took over as chairman, president, and CEO, all positions he retains today.

Changes to the Industry

The merger between Burlington Northern and Santa Fe Pacific created a new leader in the U.S. railway industry. As a result, a flurry of consolidation activity followed the completion of the deal. Most noteworthy was Union Pacific's agreement to purchase Southern Pacific in late 1995. The $5.4 billion deal superceded the BNSF transaction; Union Pacific ended up with more than 34,000 miles of track across 25 states, as well as Canada and Mexico, and reclaimed its spot as the leading U.S. railroad company in 1996.

In October of 1996, Conrail Inc. and CSX Corp. announced the largest consolidation move in the railroad industry to date with their planned $8.4 billion merger. The deal fell through; however, a few years later, Norfolk Southern and CSX jointly acquired Conrail.

Review of the Outcome

Immediately following the deal, BNSF reduced its network by 4,000 miles and cut 1,000 management personnel to reduce operating expenses and increase efficiency. The firm faced delays in integrating as smoothly and as quickly as planned. Part of the problem had to do with the consolidation of dispatching operations, but shortages of motive power and delays in integrating information systems also played a role. Although sales in 1995 jumped to $6.18 billion from nearly $5 billion in 1994, net income plummeted to $92 million from $426 million during the same time period.

In an effort to solve these problems as quickly as possible, the firm earmarked an additional $200 million in capital expenditures, mainly for locomotives. Earnings in 1996 bounced back to $889 million. BNSF also completed the consolidation of its information systems and began using a new inventory, billing, and scheduling systems program on July 4, 1997. Net income in 1998 eclipsed $1 billion for the first time in company history.

Research

"Burlington Northern Santa Fe Corp.," in *Notable Corporate Chronologies*, The Gale Group, 1999. Lists major events in the history of Burlington Northern Santa Fe Corp., including the merger of Burlington Northern and Santa Fe Pacific in 1995.

Burlington Northern Santa Fe Corp., available at http://www.bnsf.com. Official World Wide Web Home Page for Burlington Northern Santa Fe Corp. Includes press releases; financial, historical, and product information; and annual reports.

Kaufman, Lawrence H. "Rail Giants BN, Santa Fe Plan Merger," in *Journal of Commerce and Commercial*, 1 July 1994. Details the initial merger agreement between Santa Fe Pacific and Burlington Northern.

MacDonald, Mitchell E. "UP Offer Complicates BN/Santa Fe Merger Plans," in *Traffic Management*, November 1994. Explains the counter offer by Union Pacific for Santa Fe Pacific, as well as the response of Santa Fe shareholders.

Minahan, Tim. "Merger Mania Drives Rumors of Coast-to-Coast Rail Lines," in *Purchasing*, 14 December 1995. Covers the impact of the BNSF merger on the U.S. railway industry.

Tomkins, Richard. "U.S. Frontiers Blurred After Railway Merger," in *The Financial Times*, 7 July 1994. Offers a brief overview of the reasons Santa Fe Pacific and Burlington Northern wanted to merge.

SAMIT AYERS

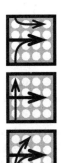

BURROUGHS & SPERRY

nationality: USA
date: 1986
affected: Burroughs Corp., USA, founded 1886
affected: Sperry Corp., USA, founded 1910

Unisys Corp.
Unisys Way
Blue Bell, PA 19424
USA

tel: (215)986-4011
fax: (215)986-2312
web: http://www.unisys.com

Overview of the Merger

The $4.8 billion merger of mainframe specialist Burroughs Corp., manufacturer of the "A" series of computers, with number cruncher Sperry Corp., maker of the 1100 mainframe computer line, created the second-largest computer firm in the nation. The new firm was named Unisys Corp., a synthesis of the words "United Information Systems." The 1986 deal was the culmination of efforts by CEO Michael Blumenthal to compete with industry giant IBM Corp. in the mainframe computer market. After the growing popularity of personal computers in the late 1980s gouged a huge hole in the mainframe computer sector, Unisys posted a $639 million loss in 1989. According to most analysts, the firm's heavy debt load and shaky stock performance in 1997 stemmed from the ill-fated deal.

History of Burroughs Corp.

William Seward Burroughs invented the first recording adding machine, which he called the arithmometer, in 1886. He founded the American Arithmometer Co. that year. In 1892, Burroughs secured a patent for his adding machine, and the following year, he won the Franklin Institute's John Scott Medal for his invention. Five years later, Burroughs died of tuberculosis. His company was incorporated as Burroughs Adding Machine Co. in 1905.

The firm acquired both Universal Adding Machine and Pike Adding Machine in 1908. By 1915, Burroughs offered 90 different types of data-processing machines which, with the help of interchangeable parts, could be modified into 600 different configurations. The Moon-Hopkins Billing Machine was acquired in 1921.

The first major shift in the data processing market was launched with the introduction of the first electronic computer in 1946. By the late 1940s, sales at Burroughs neared the $100 million mark. To better reflect its more diverse product line, the firm renamed itself Burroughs Corp. In 1956, the firm unveiled its first commercial electronic computer and also acquired ElectroData Corp., a leading maker of high-speed computers. Burroughs diversified into automated office machines and introduced the Sensitronic electronic bank bookkeeping machine by the end of the decade.

The Business

Financials

Revenue (1998): $7.2 billion

Employees (1998): 33,200

SICs / NAICS

sic 3571 - Electronic Computers

sic 7371 - Computer Programming Services

sic 7372 - Prepackaged Software

naics 334111 - Electronic Computer Manufacturing

naics 541511 - Custom Computer Programming Services

The company began selling magnetic inks and automatic check sorting equipment in 1960. The following year, Burroughs introduced the B5000 Computer, which was less expensive and easier to use than other mainframes at the time.

The U.S. Dept. of Defense awarded Burroughs a contract to build the Illiac IV supercomputer in the late 1960s. Due to cost-cutting measures instituted mid-decade, the B6500 computer proved unreliable, and plans for the B8500 computer were scrapped when engineers realized they could not produce reliable components cost-effectively. Burroughs diversified into the facsimile market in 1972 when it acquired Graphic Services for $30 million. Three years later, the firm acquired Redactron, maker of automatic typewriters and computer equipment.

In 1981, a lawsuit was filed by 129 customers alleging product unreliability and difficulty getting equipment repaired. Also, Burroughs acquired Memorex and System Development Corp. to better compete with IBM. In 1986, Burroughs merged with Sperry Corp. to form Unisys Corp. The following year, Unisys sold its Memorex division and Sperry's marine division. Also divested were the firm's computer equipment and service holdings, valued at over $8.8 million.

In 1988, Unisys bought Timeplex Inc., a high-tech communications equipment company for $300 million; purchased Convergent Technologies, maker of office workstations, for $351 million; and sold its South African marketing and sales subsidiary to Mercedes Information Technologies for $28 million. Federal prosecutors brought charges of fraud against Unisys executives for bribing Defense Department officials to yield classified procurement documents and for making illegal campaign contributions to members of Congress, activities that allegedly occurred at Sperry before the merger.

Unisys acquired File-Tek, Inc. in 1989, to make use of File-Tek's Unix-based storage systems for the financial industry. After recording a net loss of $639 million, the firm moved into the small- and mid-sized computer market, adopting AT&T's popular Unix operating system as the standard configuration for Unisys machines. Unisys also began manufacturing its own personal computers. By 1990, demand for mainframe computers had fallen drastically, and the company posted a loss of $436 million. Shareholders dividends were suspended that year.

The Timeplex subsidiary was divested in 1991. Ten thousand new layoffs were announced that year, which reduced Unisys to half its size. The firm was also found guilty of using bribery to secure U.S. defense contracts and ordered to pay up to $190 million in damages, penalties, and fines. Sales fell to $8.7 million, resulting in a loss of $1.4 million. Unisys moved further away from mainframe operations that year, choosing to diversify into consulting in hopes of bolstering sales.

In 1994, Unisys was awarded a $127 million three-year contract with the Savings Bank of the Russian Federal, one of the largest banks in the world. The following year, the firm acquired Topsystems International, a European software firm, and incorporated it into Usoft, its new independent software unit; sold its internal CAD organization to Cadence Designs Systems; and divested its aerospace and defense operations to Loral for $862 million.

More layoffs were announced in 1996. The state of Massachusetts sued Unisys for breach of contract, seeking to have the company prohibited from receiving state contracts. Several other states followed suit, alleging shoddy performance by Unisys. The firm joined Bell Communications Research Inc. (Bellcore) to develop a network management system that would allow real-time monitoring of telephone networks. Unisys also introduced ClearPath 61000 services for support of Pentium processors. Unisys and Oracle launched Oracle 7 for the Open Parallel Unisys Service (OPUS). A plan to divide Unisys into three separate companies—computer manufacturing, consulting, and services—was dismissed by shareholders.

In 1997, Lawrence Weinbach was appointed president, CEO, and chairman. He launched a debt reduction plan by using cash to pay off $800 million of the burden. Another plan to split Unisys was rejected. The following year, Unisys agreed to contract Hewlett-Packard Co. for manufacturing and assembling its personal computers and low-end servers.

History of Sperry

Sperry Gyroscope Co. was established in 1910 by Elmer Sperry to manufacture and market navigational equipment. The firm's name was change to Sperry Corp. in 1933 to reflect a broader product line. In 1955, Sperry merged with Remington Rand, maker of ENIAC, "the world's first large-scale, general-purpose computer" and UNIVAC, the "world's first business computer."

In 1960, Sperry launched its 1100 computer series. Five years later, the firm introduced the first multi-processor computer, the 1108. In 1971, Sperry acquired the computer operations of RCA Corp. Sperry unveiled its cache memory disk subsystem in 1976. Ten years later, the 2200 Series—considered the precursor of the ClearPath HMP IX system—was shipped. Also that year, Sperry and Burroughs Corp. merged to form Unisys Corp.

Market Forces Driving the Merger

Efforts to compete with IBM began in 1959 when Burroughs president John Coleman negotiated a partnership agreement between Burroughs and RCA in an effort to pool financial resources to catch up with IBM. Unfortunately, Coleman died before the plan was realized. Burroughs then acquired Memorex for $85.2 million, and System Development Corp. for $9.6 million to better compete with IBM. These acquisitions helped to boost sales by $1 billion.

According to a January 1991 article in *Economist*, Blumenthal's reasons for pursuing the merger with Sperry were straightforward. "Together, the two firms would be able to cut manufacturing, administrative, and service costs. Together they would generate profits large enough to pursue the sort of expensive, innovative research neither could afford on its own. Together, they might even be able to challenge the mighty IBM, whose sales were ten times larger than either company's."

Approach and Engagement

In 1985, Burroughs launched a $4.8 billion takeover bid for Sperry. To finance the deal, Burroughs borrowed $2.5 billion. The following year, Burroughs and Sperry merged to form Unisys Corp. The name was chosen by the employees of both companies to synthesize the words "United Information Systems." Burroughs CEO Michael Blumenthal took the helm of the new firm.

Products and Services

By 1998, Unisys had shifted its focus from mainframe computers and defense electronics to systems integration and support services, which accounted for roughly 66% of total revenues. Services included consulting, distributed computing support, document imaging, outsourcing, remote network management, hardware and software maintenance, Y2K services, and Windows NT support. Hoping to capitalize on the market's shift from mainframe computers to networks, Unisys spent considerable effort in the 1990s developing new products. For example, the firm's ClearPath enterprise servers were designed to incorporate mainframe, Microsoft Windows NT, and UNIX systems within a single platform. Other products included Aquanta servers, notebooks, and personal computers; software; and storage systems.

The Officers

Chairman, President and CEO: Lawrence A. Weinbach

Sr. VP and Chief Financial Officer: Robert H. Brust

Sr. VP, Secretary, and General Counsel: Harold S. Barron

Sr. VP, Major Accounts Sales, and Chief Marketing Officer: Joseph W. McGrath

Exec. VP, Worldwide Human Resources: David O. Aker

Changes to the Industry

The merger created the second-largest computer firm in the nation. Initially, the deal was considered successful, and some analysts predicted that IBM might move towards a takeover of Unisys. However, it soon became apparent that IBM's speed to market and superior marketing tactics were seriously outpacing Unisys' efforts. Ironically, many engineers insisted that Unisys systems were more reliable—it was the slow integration of Burroughs and Sperry lines that caused the firm so many problems. According to the January 1991 issue of *Economist*, "Burroughs and Sperry computers worked to incompatible standards, making it impossible for the merged firm to ever reap the promised economies of scale of cost savings. Since Unisys cannot phase out either of its inherited product lines without abandoning customers, it has had to keep spending precious R&D money on both."

While the firm slowly put together software that made both product lines compatible, share prices fell in 1991 to a mere one-fifth of their price in 1990. In fact, it wasn't until 1994, when CEO James Unruh hired Paul Lutz that the merging of the two mainframe lines—Sperry's 2200 series and Burroughs "A" series—began in earnest. With only one mainframe line to focus on, Unisys would only have to create a

The Players

Chairman and CEO of Burroughs Corp.: W. Michael Blumenthal. W. Michael Blumenthal, former Bendix chairman, joined Burroughs as executive vice president in 1979. He replaced veteran executives, phased out adding machine and calculator product lines, and improved repair services. Sales reached $2.8 billion that year. He soon took over operations of the firm and launched a merger with Sperry Corp. in 1986, which resulted in the formation of Unisys Corp. After demand for mainframe computers declined drastically, and Unisys lost $436 million in 1990, shareholder dividends were suspended, and Blumenthal resigned.

single version of upgrades to keep its products up to date, an advantage IBM had capitalized on for years. The cost savings was estimated at 20% of the firm's total research and development budget.

Review of the Outcome

In the first year following the deal, the newly merged firm closed plants, cut its workforce by 24,000, and lost $43 million. Immediately prior to the deal, Burroughs had employed 67,000 workers and Sperry's staff had numbered 60,500. By 1993, Unisys had slashed its staff to 50,000. The firm had also narrowed its product offerings and closed seven of its 15 plants.

Unisys posted a loss in 1997, due to a $1 billion charge CEO Lawrence Weinbach took mainly to write off the value of the 1986 merger. A February 1997 article in *Fortune* described the ill-fated venture as the conversion of "two condos of weakness into a structure of instability called Unisys."

Research

England, Robert Stowe. "A Bet Against: Whither Mainframes? At Unisys, James Unruh is Betting the Company That Their Future is Bleak," in *Financial World*, 1 August 1995. Explains why Unisys CEO James Unruh decided to shift his firm's focus away from mainframe computers in the mi-1990s.

Laberis, Bill. "James Unruh Face to Face: Unisys' President and CEO Speaks Out About the Merger That Created His Company" in *Compuerworld*, 8 February 1993. Unisys CEO Unruh offers his perspective on the 1986 merger of Burroughs Corp. and Sperry Corp.

"Largest Merger Ever," in *Fortune*, 24 November 1986. Details the immediate outcome of the merger and speculates about a possible takeover attempt of Unisys by IBM.

Loomis, Carol J. "Ten Years After," in *Fortune*, 17 February 1997. Offers an overview of the major deals that took place in 1986, as well as the outcome of each.

"One Merger That Didn't Work," in *Economist*, 19 January 1991. Discusses the performance of Unisys Corp. since the 1986 deal.

"Unisys Appoints Former Executive at Andersen Worldwide as its Chairman," in *The New York Times*, 24 September 1997. Explains how Unisys' new CEO plans to reduce the firm's debt and deal with other problems stemming for the 1986 merger.

Unisys Corp. Home Page, available at http://www.unisys.com. Official World Wide Web Home Page for Unisys Corp. Includes press releases; financial, historical, and product information; and annual reports.

"Unisys Corp.," in *Notable Corporate Chronologies*, The Gale Group, 1999. Lists major events in the history of Unisys Corp., including the merger of Burroughs Corp. and Sperry Corp. in 1986.

ANNAMARIE L. SHELDON

CADBURY SCHWEPPES & A&W BRANDS

nationality: United Kingdom
date: September 9, 1993
affected: Cadbury Schweppes PLC, United Kingdom, founded 1790
affected: A&W Brands, USA, founded 1919

Cadbury Schweppes PLC
25 Berkeley Sq.
London, W1X 6HT
United Kingdom

tel: 44-171-409-1313
fax: 44-171-830-5200
web: http://www.cadburyschweppes.com

Overview of the Acquisition

Cadbury Schweppes acquired A&W Brands in September of 1993 for $334 million. Along with securing the rights to the world's best selling root beer, Cadbury Schweppes gained popular soft drink brands Vernors, Squirt and Country Time, and upped its U.S. soft drinks market share beyond 5% for the first time in the firm's history. The deal prompted a flurry of consolidation activity in the U.S. soft drink industry during the mid-1990s.

History of Cadbury Schweppes PLC

In 1790, German jeweler Jacob Schweppe, along with two partners, founded Schweppe, Paul & Gosse to make artificial mineral water. Two years later, Schweppe went to London, England, to establish the company's English operations. After his partners left the business in 1793, Schweppe renamed his company Schweppes. In 1798, Schweppe coined the term "soda water" when he applied it to one of his aerated water products. His soda water sold better than most other brands because of its high carbonation. Schweppes introduced its first lemonade product in 1834.

By the late 1870s, Schweppes had developed and introduced ginger ale and tonic water. In 1885, Schweppes introduced its first carbonated lemonade drink. The firm listed publicly in 1897. All of Schweppes' overseas business was merged into one British subsidiary in 1923. By the mid-1950s, Schweppes had begun licensing foreign companies to bottle and market its products, and the firm had become the PepsiCo licensee in the U.K. In 1960, Schweppes acquired Hartley's, Moorhouse, and Chivers, three jams and jellies makers.

In 1831, John Cadbury's retail business expanded so much that he moved into a larger building; products included drinking cocoa and chocolate. Cadbury Brothers was formed in 1847 when Benjamin Cadbury joined his brother John as a partner. In 1880, Cadbury Bros. hired European master confectioner, M. Frederic Kinchelman, to demonstrate how to make such things as nougats, pistache, pate d'abricot, and avelines. The following year, Cadbury's Australian subsidiary placed the company's first overseas order. The firm build a new plant in 1905, and

The Business

Financials

Revenue (1998): $6.89 billion

Employees (1998): 38,656

SICs / NAICS

sic 2086 - Bottled & Canned Soft Drinks

sic 2087 - Flavoring Extracts & Syrups Nec

sic 2064 - Candy & Other Confectionery Products

naics 312111 - Soft Drink Manufacturing

George Cadbury, Jr., developed a new chocolate making recipe and technique, which produced a smoother chocolate called Dairy Milk; the product became the most popular molded chocolate in the U.K.

Cadbury bought J.S. Fry & Sons, a major English chocolate company, in 1919. The following year, the firm opened its first factory in Canada. Factories in Australia and New Zealand soon followed. Cadbury Fry, a new subsidiary, began production in Ireland in 1933. Five years later, Cadbury opened a factory in South Africa. The first Cadbury factory in India opened in 1947. By the mid 1950s, Cadbury, Cadbury Fry, and competitor Rowntree made up 51% of the British candy market. Cadbury diversified into sugar-candy with the purchase of confection company Pascall Murray in 1962; to further broaden its product line, the firm bought Typhoo Tea in 1968.

In January of 1969, Schweppes bought out Cadbury's shareholders with $290 million of its stock, and the companies merged into Cadbury Schweppes PLC. Some operations were consolidated, but distribution remained separate due to the control held by bottling franchises. Acquisitions during the early 1970s included Jeyes Ltd., Groovy Beverages, Courtney Wines International, and Pepsi Cola South Africa. After purchasing Connecticut-based candy company Peter Paul for $58 million, Cadbury Schweppes founded Peter Paul Cadbury. U.S. market share was then 10%.

Cadbury Schweppes bought Duffy-Mott Inc., U.S. maker of Mott's applesauce, apple juice, and vegetable drinks, in 1982. Two years later, the company bought Cottees General Foods, expanding its coffee business in Australia with the Maxwell House and Hag brands. Also, 60 million shares of company stock were released in the U.S. that year. Because Coca-Cola's products were dominant in Britain, Cadbury Schweppes sold its PepsiCo franchise in order to get Coke licensing in Britain in 1985. The Jeyes unit was divested and a home soft drink dispenser company, Sodastream Holding Ltd., was purchased.

In 1986, the firm purchased the rights to Canada Dry and Sunkist soft drinks from RJR Nabisco for $230 million to become the world's largest non-cola soft drink company. Coca-Cola paid Cadbury Schweppes $90 million for Canada Dry's Canadian business. Cadbury Schweppes then bought 30% of Dr. Pepper in a deal that included Shearson Lehman Brothers and Texas-based investment company Hicks & Haas. Management decided that Hershey Foods' strong name and distribution network would help sell Cadbury products, so Cadbury's U.S. confectionery business was sold for $300 million as a franchise.

The firm acquired Crush International, including the Orange Crush and Hires brand names, from Proctor & Gamble for $220 million; the 1989 purchase boosted Cadbury Schweppes share of the soft drink market to nearly 5% in the U.S. and over 15% in Canada. Also acquired was TriNaranjus, the number one non-carbonated fruit drink in Spain, and Bassett Foods. Acquisitions in 1990 included Oasis, part of Perrier's soft-drinks business; the French bottling rights for Gini, a Crush International brand name; and the Trebor Group, into which Cadbury Schweppes consolidated its U.K. sugar confectionery businesses. A joint venture called Cadbury Egypt began production of chocolates that year. In 1991, the firm bought Mexico's largest mineral water company, Aguas Minerales. A&W Brands was purchased in 1993.

Cadbury Schweppes spent $1.7 billion to buy Dr. Pepper/Seven Up Co. in 1995. The following year, the firm opened a $30 million chocolate factory near Beijing. To better compete with PepsiCo and Coca-Cola, both of which were aggressively buying root beer brands and other non-cola drinks, the company reorganized its North American beverage unit. In 1996, Cadbury Schweppes made several international candy acquisitions, including Bim Bim, based in Egypt.

Cadbury Schweppes sold its 51% stake of British bottler Coca-Cola & Schweppes Beverages Ltd. (formed in 1987) to Coca-Cola Enterprises for $1 billion in 1997. That year, the company agreed to jointly purchase two independent bottlers with investment firm Carlyle Group to create American Bottling, the second largest bottler of Dr. Pepper and Seven Up products in the U.S. In 1998, Cadbury Schweppes agreed to divest its soft drink and concentrate operations outside the U.S. to Coca-Cola Co. for $1.85 billion. To secure a leading position in Poland's chocolate market, the firm acquired Wedel, the best selling confectionary brand in Poland, in 1999.

History of A&W Brands

In 1919, after purchasing a formula for root beer from a pharmacist in Arizona, entrepreneur Roy Allen sold his first mug of what would soon be known as A&W Root Beer in Lodi, California. The soft drink was a combination of herbs, spices, barks, and berries. Three years later, Frank Wright joined Allen in his venture, and the two partners used the initials of their last names to coin the name "A&W."

Wright left the business in 1924, and Allen launched a franchise system. He also applied for trademarks for the A&W name and logo that year. By 1933, more than 170 franchised units had been opened across the western U.S. When Allen retired in 1950—by this time roughly 450 units were in operation—he sold his business to Gene Hurtz, who renamed it A&W Root Beer Co. Thirteen years later, J. Hungerford Smith Co. bought A&W. In 1966, Boston-based United Fruit Co. purchased J. Hungerford Smith Co., which was then acquired by AMK Corp. in 1970. AMK founded United Brands Co., which included the A&W assets. The following year, AMK established a new subsidiary, A&W Beverages Inc.

The unit launched A&W Sugar-free Root Beer in 1974. The Squirt soft drink brand was acquired in 1986; Vernors, in 1987. In September of 1993, Cadbury Schweppes acquired A&W Brands for $334 million.

Market Forces Driving the Acquisition

To compete with giants Coke and Pepsi in the early 1990s, smaller firms had been consolidating as a means of increasing market share in the non-cola beverage industry segment. Cadbury Schweppes started shoring up its position on August 20, 1993, with its purchase of additional shares of Dr. Pepper/Seven Up Companies, Inc., upping its stake in the firm to 25%. The firm then began eyeing A&W Brands, maker of the world's best selling root beer.

According to an October 1993 article in *Forbes*, A&W held 30% percent of the root beer market. The acquisition would allow Cadbury Schweppes to edge forward in U.S. soft drink market share; it also offered additional advertising resources to A&W, which was facing increased competition by Barq's Inc., who had grown its supermarket root beer sales by 5% since 1991.

Cadbury Schweppes had also been trying to decrease its reliance on chocolate confectionery products due to that market's saturation in the U.K. The more fragmented non-cola soft drink market offered more growth potential for the firm.

The Officers

Chairman: Sir Dominic Cadbury

Deputy Chairman: T.O. Hutchinson

Group Chief Executive: J.M. Sunderland

President and Chief Operating Officer, American Bottling
    Co.: Richard Beardon

President, Dr. Pepper/Seven Up: Todd Stitzer

Group Finance Director: David Kappler

Approach and Engagement

On September 9, 1993, Cadbury Schweppes agreed to pay $334 million for A&W Brands; the $24.50 per share price was worth 21 times the earnings of A&W Brands in 1992. To pay for the acquisition, as well as for its increased stake in Dr. Pepper/Seven Up, Cadbury Schweppes launched a $499 million stock offering of one share per nine current shares. The A&W operations were then folded into the Cadbury Beverages North America unit of Cadbury Schweppes.

Products and Services

In 1997, soft drinks accounted for 47% of sales at Cadbury Schweppes. They included 7UP, A&W, Aguafiel, Canada Dry, Clamato, Cottee's, Dr. Pepper, Mott's, Sunkist, and Squirt. The remaining 53% percent of revenues came from confectionary products, such as Bim Bim, Bouquet d'Or, Cadbury, Chappies, La Pie Qui Chante, Peter Paul, Poulain, Stani, Trebor Allan, Trebor Bassett, and York. U.S. sales secured 35% of the total; United Kingdom sales, 25%; European sales, 19%; and Asian sales, 14%.

Changes to the Industry

Cadbury Schweppes' purchase of A&W Brands was the first in a string of acquisitions in the U.S. soft drink market in the mid-1990s. According to a December 1995 *Beverage World* article, "what started in the summer of '93 when Cadbury decided to love the frosty mug taste of A&W, snowballed in late '94 when Quaker made Snapple its own, and continued while more big names swallowed suitable counterparts." Cadbury Schweppes took part in another large deal in 1995 when it purchased the shares of Dr. Pepper/Seven Up it didn't already own. Tropicana and Dole also announced their hookup.

The A&W deal was also most likely a major factor in Coca Cola's mid-1990s purchase of Barq's Inc., the

The Players

Chairman of Cadbury Schweppes PLC: Sir Dominic Cadbury. Dominic Cadbury began working for Cadbury Schweppes in 1964 and became a board member ten years later. He held many positions before being appointed managing director of the UK Confectionery Division in 1980. Three years later, he accepted the post of group chief executive. Cadbury Schweppes named him chairman in May 1993, and he oversaw the acquisition of A&W Brands a few months later.

Chairman of A&W Brands: Monroe L. Lowenkron. Monroe "Lou" Lowenkron began his career at Pepsi, working for 14 years in the national accounts and syrup sales department; he was eventually appointed national sales manager of syrup sales. In 1968, he moved to Canada Dry as national accounts manager. After eleven years, he secured the post of vice president of sales and marketing. A&W Brands hired Lowenkron as CEO in 1980, a post he retained until the firm was acquired by Cadbury Schweppes in 1993. G. Heileman Brewing tapped Lowenkron as CEO in 1995.

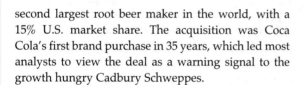

second largest root beer maker in the world, with a 15% U.S. market share. The acquisition was Coca Cola's first brand purchase in 35 years, which led most analysts to view the deal as a warning signal to the growth hungry Cadbury Schweppes.

In 1996, the world's largest bottler, Coca-Cola Enterprises, dropped A&W root beer and Sunkist in favor of competing Coke products such as Barq's root beer and Minute Maid. This prompted the formation of American Bottling, a joint venture between Cadbury Schweppes and investment firm Carlyle Group.

Review of the Outcome

When the acquisition was completed, Cadbury Schweppes became the North American market leader in root beer, creme soda, and ginger ale. In the year following the deal, sales grew 8% and profits jumped 14.9%. Management pointed to the firm's A&W purchase as the reason for the improved U.S. performance.

By 1997, 35% of Cadbury's total earnings and 21% of its sales came from the U.S. beverage market. Because its soft drink market share in Europe remained low, the firm decided in 1998 to divest its European soft drink holdings, minus those in France and South Africa, to Coca Cola for $1.85 billion. The move, when completed, will allow Cadbury Schweppes to refocus on its U.S. soft drink and worldwide confectionary operations.

Research

"A&W History," available at http://www.a-wrootbeer.com/History/history1.htm. Offers a detailed look at the history of A&W Brands, as well as A&W Restaurants.

Benezra, Karen. "Coke Challenges Cadbury with Barq's Buy, But Faces Challenge of Maintaining Bite," in *Brandweek*, 3 April 1995. Explains why Coca-Cola purchased Barq's Inc.

"Cadbury Results Lifted by Overseas Expansion," in *Eurofood*, April 1995. Explains how Cadbury Schweppes fared in the year following its purchase of A&W Brands.

"Cadbury Schweppes PLC," in *Notable Corporate Chronologies*, The Gale Group, 1999. Lists major events in the history of Cadbury Schweppes PLC, including its takeover of A&W Brands.

Cadbury Schweppes PLC Home Page, available at http://www.cadburyschweppes.com. Official World Wide Web Home Page for Cadbury Schweppes PLC. Includes press releases; financial, historical, and product information; and annual reports.

Clash, James M. "A Root Beer Pubic Float?," in *Forbes*, 11 October 1993. Offers a look at how the purchase of A&W Brands by Cadbury Schweppes might affect number two root beer maker Barq's, Inc.

Prince, Gregory. "Come Together," in *Beverage World*, December 1995. Details the consolidation activity in the soft drink industry in 1995.

SAMIT AYERS

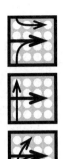

CADBURY SCHWEPPES & DR. PEPPER/SEVEN UP

nationality: United Kingdom
date: 1995
affected: Cadbury Schweppes PLC, United Kingdom, founded 1790
affected: Dr. Pepper/Seven Up Companies, Inc., USA, founded 1885

Cadbury Schweppes PLC
25 Berkeley Sq.
London, W1X 6HT
United Kingdom

tel: 44-171-409-1313
fax: 44-171-830-5200
web: http://www.cadburyschweppes.com

Overview of the Acquisition

When Cadbury Schweppes acquired Dr. Pepper/Seven Up Companies in late 1995 for $1.7 billion, it tripled its stake in the U.S. soft drinks market, jumping into the number three spot behind giants Coke and Pepsi. The 16.1% share of the market held by Cadbury Schweppes upon completion of the deal was the largest third-place position the market had seen in decades. In 1998, after finding itself unable to secure adequate soft drink market share outside the U.S., Cadbury Schweppes agreed to divest its non-U.S. soft drink holdings—excluding France and South Africa operations—to Coca Cola Co. for $1.85 billion.

History of Cadbury Schweppes PLC

In 1790, German jeweler Jacob Schweppe, along with two partners, founded Schweppe, Paul & Gosse to make artificial mineral water. Two years later, Schweppe went to London, England, to establish the company's English operations. After his partners left the business in 1793, Schweppe renamed his company Schweppes. In 1798, Schweppe coined the term "soda water" when he applied it to one of his aerated water products. His soda water sold better than most other brands because of its high carbonation. Schweppes introduced its first lemonade product in 1834.

By the late 1870s, Schweppes had developed and introduced ginger ale and tonic water. In 1885, Schweppes introduced its first carbonated lemonade drink. The firm listed publicly in 1897. All of Schweppes' overseas business was merged into one British subsidiary in 1923. By the mid-1950s, Schweppes had begun licensing foreign companies to bottle and market its products, and the firm had become the PepsiCo licensee in the U.K. In 1960, Schweppes acquired Hartley's, Moorhouse, and Chivers, three jams and jellies makers.

In 1831, John Cadbury's retail business expanded so much that he moved into a larger building; products included drinking cocoa and chocolate. Cadbury Brothers was formed in 1847 when Benjamin Cadbury joined his brother John as a partner. In 1880, Cadbury Bros. hired European master confectioner, M. Frederic

The Business

Financials

Revenue (1998): $6.89 billion

Employees (1998): 38,656

SICs / NAICS

sic 2086 - Bottled & Canned Soft Drinks

sic 2087 - Flavoring Extracts & Syrups Nec

sic 2064 - Candy & Other Confectionery Products

naics 312111 - Soft Drink Manufacturing

Kinchelman, to demonstrate how to make such things as nougats, pistache, pate d'abricot, and avelines. The following year, Cadbury's Australian subsidiary placed the company's first overseas order. The firm build a new plant in 1905, and George Cadbury, Jr. developed a new chocolate making recipe and technique, which produced a smoother chocolate called Dairy Milk; the product became the most popular molded chocolate in the U.K.

Cadbury bought J.S. Fry & Sons, a major English chocolate company, in 1919. The following year, the firm opened its first factory in Canada. Factories in Australia and New Zealand soon followed. Cadbury Fry, a new subsidiary, began production in Ireland in 1933. Five years later, Cadbury opened a factory in South Africa. The first Cadbury factory in India opened in 1947. By the mid 1950s, Cadbury, Cadbury Fry, and competitor Rowntree made up 51% of the British candy market. Cadbury diversified into sugar-candy with the purchase of confection company Pascall Murray in 1962; to further broaden its product line, the firm bought Typhoo Tea in 1968.

In January of 1969, Schweppes bought out Cadbury's shareholders with $290 million of its stock, and the companies merged into Cadbury Schweppes PLC. Some operations were consolidated, but distribution remained separate due to the control held by bottling franchises. Acquisitions during the early 1970s included Jeyes Ltd., Groovy Beverages, Courtney Wines International, and Pepsi Cola South Africa. After purchasing Connecticut-based candy company Peter Paul for $58 million, Cadbury Schweppes founded Peter Paul Cadbury. U.S. market share was then 10%.

Cadbury Schweppes bought Duffy-Mott Inc., U.S. maker of Mott's applesauce, apple juice, and vegetable

drinks, in 1982. Two years later, the company bought Cottees General Foods, expanding its coffee business in Australia with the Maxwell House and Hag brands. Also, 60 million shares of company stock were released in the U.S. that year. Because Coca-Cola's products were dominant in Britain, Cadbury Schweppes sold its PepsiCo franchise in order to get Coke licensing in Britain in 1985. The Jeyes unit was divested and a home soft drink dispenser company, Sodastream Holding Ltd., was purchased.

In 1986, the firm purchased the rights to Canada Dry and Sunkist soft drinks from RJR Nabisco for $230 million to become the world's largest non-cola soft drink company. Coca-Cola paid Cadbury Schweppes $90 million for Canada Dry's Canadian business. Cadbury Schweppes then bought 30% of Dr. Pepper in a deal that included Shearson Lehman Brothers and Texas-based investment company Hicks & Haas. Management decided that Hershey Foods' strong name and distribution network would help sell Cadbury products, so Cadbury's U.S. confectionery business was sold for $300 million as a franchise.

The firm acquired Crush International, including the Orange Crush and Hires brand names, from Proctor & Gamble for $220 million; the 1989 purchase boosted Cadbury Schweppes share of the soft drink market to nearly 5% in the U.S. and over 15% in Canada. Also acquired was TriNaranjus, the number one non-carbonated fruit drink in Spain, and Bassett Foods. Acquisitions in 1990 included Oasis, part of Perrier's soft-drinks business; the French bottling rights for Gini, a Crush International brand name; and the Trebor Group, into which Cadbury Schweppes consolidated its U.K. sugar confectionery businesses. A joint venture called Cadbury Egypt began production of chocolates that year. In 1991, the firm bought Mexico's largest mineral water company, Aguas Minerales. A&W Brands was purchased in 1993.

Cadbury Schweppes spent $1.7 billion to buy Dr. Pepper/Seven Up Co. in 1995. The following year, the firm opened a $30 million chocolate factory near Beijing. To better compete with PepsiCo and Coca-Cola, both of which were aggressively buying root beer brands and other non-cola drinks, the company reorganized its North American beverage unit. In 1996, Cadbury Schweppes made several international candy acquisitions, including Bim Bim, based in Egypt.

Cadbury Schweppes sold its 51% stake of British bottler Coca-Cola & Schweppes Beverages Ltd. (formed in 1987) to Coca-Cola Enterprises for $1 billion in 1997. That year, the company agreed to jointly purchase two independent bottlers with investment firm Carlyle Group to create American Bottling, the second largest bottler of Dr. Pepper and Seven Up products in the U.S. In 1998, Cadbury Schweppes agreed to divest its soft drink and concentrate operations outside the U.S. to Coca-Cola Co. for $1.85 billion. To secure a leading position in Poland's chocolate market, the firm acquired Wedel, the best selling confectionary brand in Poland, in 1999.

History of Dr. Pepper/Seven Up Companies, Inc.

Dr. Pepper brand soft drink was created by pharmacist Charles Alderton at Wade B. Morrison's Old Corner Drug Store in Waco, Texas, in 1885. Within five years, Dr. Pepper was being bottled throughout Texas. The company employed Fargo Express to haul syrup from Waco. In 1923, Morrison and Waco bottler Robert Lazenby formed the Artesian Manufacturing and Bottling Co., which later changed its name to Dr. Pepper Co.

In 1929, C.L. Grigg, owner of the Howdy Co. and maker of Howdy Orange Drink, introduced his new lemon-lime soda, later known as Seven-Up. Seven years later, Grigg changed his company's name to The Seven-Up Co. Seven-Up stock was offered publicly in 1967. In 1978, Philip Morris bought Seven-Up Co., and profits began to drop.

In 1986, Dallas investment firm Hicks and Haas bought Seven-Up Co. for $240 million and Dr. Pepper for $416 million. Two years later, Dr. Pepper Co. and Seven-Up Co. merged to form Dr. Pepper/Seven-Up Companies, Inc., the third largest manufacturer of soft drinks in the U.S., second only to Coca-Cola and Pepsi. The new company's managers consolidated operations at Seven-Up's St. Louis plant by selling property and laying off staff. I.B.C. Root Beer was acquired in 1990.

Dr. Pepper/Seven-Up sued Coca-Cola in 1992 for allegedly disseminating lies among bottlers to prevent them from doing business with Seven-Up. The following year, Cadbury Schweppes increased it small stake in the company to 25%. Despite initial resistance by Dr. Pepper/Seven-Up to a takeover, in late 1995, Cadbury Schweppes acquired Dr. Pepper/Seven-Up for $1.7 billion.

Market Forces Driving the Acquisition

To compete with giants Coke and Pepsi in the mid-1990s, smaller firms had been consolidating as a means of increasing market share in the non-cola beverage industry segment. For example, Quaker bought out Snapple in early 1995 for roughly $1.7 billion. Cadbury Schweppes had been upping its North American soft drinks market share throughout the late

The Officers

Chairman: Sir Dominic Cadbury

Deputy Chairman: T.O. Hutchinson

Group Chief Executive: J.M. Sunderland

President and Chief Operating Officer, American Bottling Co.: Richard Beardon

President, Dr. Pepper/Seven Up: Todd Stitzer

Group Finance Director: David Kappler

1980s early 1990s through acquisitions such as its $334 million purchase of A&W brands in 1993. The firm had also increased its small stake in Dr. Pepper/Seven Up to 25% that year.

Acquiring Dr. Pepper/Seven Up would give the firm increased access to the lucrative U.S. soft drink market, which accounted for 34% of the world market. And the deal would mean roughly 60% of revenues at Cadbury Schweppes would come from soft drink products. According to a January 1995 article in *Mergers & Acquisitions*, Cadbury Schweppes was looking to decrease its reliance on chocolate confectionery products due to that market's saturation. "The chocolate industry is static in mainland Europe, while there is still fragmentation in the market for soft drinks excluding colas."

Despite the lagging performance of the Seven Up brand, most analysts believed Dr. Pepper/Seven Up was in good shape for a takeover. Under the leadership of CEO John Albers, Dr. Pepper had doubled its domestic sales growth between 1990 and 1995 and reduced debt via two leveraged buyouts.

Approach and Engagement

Cadbury Schweppes purchased a small stake in Dr. Pepper (renamed Dr. Pepper/Seven Up after the 1988 merger) in 1986. On August 20, 1993, Cadbury Schweppes increased its holding in Dr. Pepper/Seven Up to 25%. Dr. Pepper/Seven Up instituted a shareholder rights plan in September in an effort to ward off a takeover. The firm also refinanced its debt with a $625 million loan from Bankers Trust Co. In 1994, the two firms began discussing an acquisition by Cadbury Schweppes of the share of Dr. Pepper/Seven Up it didn't already own. They eventually agreed on a $33 per share price, which totaled $1.7 billion. Cadbury Schweppes named its new U.S. soft drinks arm Dr. Pepper/Cadbury North America. Former Dr. Pepper/Seven Up CEO John Albers took over as CEO

The Players

Chairman of Cadbury Schweppes PLC: Sir Dominic Cadbury. Dominic Cadbury began working for Cadbury Schweppes in 1964 and became a board member ten years later. He served the firm in many capacities before being appointed managing director of the UK Confectionery Division in 1980. Three years later, he accepted the post of group chief executive. The firm tapped Cadbury in May of 1993 as chairman, a position he continues to hold today.

Chairman of Dr. Pepper/Seven Up Companies, Inc.: John R. Albers. John Albers joined Dr. Pepper in 1971 as vice president of advertising. After working his way up through the ranks, Albers was elected president and COO in December 1984. The firm appointed him CEO in August 1986. Albers led his firm through its merger with Seven-Up Co. in 1988 and its purchase by Cadbury Schweppes in late 1995. When the deal was completed, he remained CEO of the Dr. Pepper/Seven Up operations.

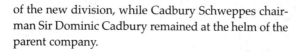

of the new division, while Cadbury Schweppes chairman Sir Dominic Cadbury remained at the helm of the parent company.

Products and Services

In 1997, soft drinks accounted for 47% of sales at Cadbury Schweppes. They included 7UP, A&W, Aguafiel, Canada Dry, Clamato, Cottee's, Dr. Pepper, Mott's, Sunkist, and Squirt. The remaining 53% percent of revenues came from confectionary products, such as Bim Bim, Bouquet d'Or, Cadbury, Chappies, La Pie Qui Chante, Peter Paul, Poulain, Stani, Trebor Allan, Trebor Bassett, and York. U.S. sales secured 35% of the total; United Kingdom sales, 25%; European sales, 19%; and Asian sales, 14%.

Changes to the Industry and Review of the Outcome

Cadbury Schweppes landed in third place in the U.S. soft drink market after the deal was completed. Earnings at Cadbury's North American beverage unit jumped 139% to $379 million on sales of $1.7 billion in the year following the merger. Sales of Dr. Pepper and its diet and caffeine-free versions increased, and the brand accounted for 45% of the company's overall beverage volume in the U.S. In contrast, the struggling

Seven Up brand held only 2.8% of the soft-drink market, versus the 4.9% held by Coca-Cola Co.'s Sprite beverage. This prompted Cadbury Schweppes to change Seven Up's "Uncola" logo in a $25 million campaign by increasing its television air time, creating new packaging for the product, and launching the jingle "It's an up thing."

In 1996, Cadbury Schweppes decided to change the name of Dr. Pepper/Cadbury North America to Dr. Pepper/Seven Up, Inc. to capitalize on name recognition. The unit was then split into two firms, according to CEO Brock, to "keep Dr. Pepper on a roll" and facilitate "an even more bottler-focused organization." Dr. Pepper would oversee all distribution within Coke and Pepsi systems, while Seven Up would handle the non-cola and non-Dr. Pepper distribution.

By 1997, 35% of Cadbury's total earnings and 21% of its sales came from the U.S. beverage market. Because its soft drink market share in Europe remained low, the firm decided to divest its European soft drink holdings, minus those in France and South Africa, to Coca Cola for $1.85 billion. The move, when completed, will allow Cadbury Schweppes to refocus on its U.S. soft drink and worldwide confectionary operations.

Research

Benezra, Karen. "Fizz or Fizzle?," in *Brandweek*, 13 October 1997. Explains how Dr. Pepper and Seven Up managers are planning to increase sales and market share in the late 1990s.

"Cadbury Returns to Base," in *Marketing*, 17 December 1998. Covers why Cadbury Schweppes decided to sell its non-U.S. soft drink operations to Coca Cola Co.

"Cadbury Schweppes PLC," in *Notable Corporate Chronologies*, The Gale Group, 1999. Lists major events in the history of Cadbury Schweppes PLC, including its takeover of Dr. Pepper/Seven Up Companies, Inc.

Cadbury Schweppes PLC Home Page, available at http://www.cadburyschweppes.com. Official World Wide Web Home Page for Cadbury Schweppes PLC. Includes press releases; financial, historical, and product information; and annual reports.

"Dr. Pepper/Seven Up Companies, Inc.," in *Notable Corporate Chronologies*, The Gale Group, 1999. Lists major events in the history of Dr. Pepper/Seven Up Companies, Inc., including its takeover by Cadbury Schweppes PLC.

Jackson, Susan. "Can Cadbury Dodge Big Cola's Bullets?," in *Business Week*, 12 August 1996. Details the obstacles faced by Cadbury Schweppes as the largest competitor of Coca-Cola and PepsiCo.

"New Structure and New Home Built for Dr. Pepper/Seven Up/Cadbury," in *Beverage World*, September 1996. Explains the rationale behind the name change of Cadbury Schweppes U.S. soft drink operations.

Prince, Greg W. "Cadbury Buys Pepper/Seven Up and Everything Changes (Again)," in *Beverage World Periscope Edition*, 28 February 1995. Offers a look at the industry conditions in the U.S. beverages market during the mid-1990s.

West, Louise. "Cadbury Schweppes Gulps Down Dr. Pepper," in *Mergers & Acquisitions International*, 30 January 1995. Explains why Cadbury Schweppes wanted to increase its U.S. soft drink holdings rather than pursue growth in the European confectionary industry.

SAMIT AYERS

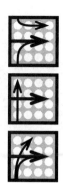

CADENCE DESIGN & VALID LOGIC

Cadence Design Systems, Inc.
2655 Sealy Ave., Bldg. 5
San Jose, CA 95134
USA

tel: (408)943-1234
fax: (408)943-0513
web: http://www.cadence.com

nationality: USA
date: 1991
affected: Cadence Design Systems, Inc., USA, founded 1988
affected: Valid Logic Systems, Inc., USA, founded early 1980s

Overview of the Acquisition

Computer-aided design (CAD) software supplier Cadence Design acquired Valid Logic, a struggling developer and marketer of computer-aided engineering (CAE) software, for $200 million in stock in 1991. The largest deal to date for Cadence, the acquisition pushed the firm ahead of rival Mentor Graphics Corp. to the number one spot among electronic design automation (EDA) firms in the world, with a 24% market share and combined sales of roughly $390 million. Costs associated with the merger were blamed for the $22.4 million loss posted by Cadence Design at the end of 1991.

History of Cadence Design Systems, Inc.

Glen M. Antle founded ECAD Inc. in August of 1982 to develop and market an integrated computer-aided design (CAD) software program, Dracula, which hit the market in April 1983. A year later, ECAD purchased Simon Software, a maker of a unique circuit simulation software program designed specifically for the metal oxide semiconductor chip design process. The Santa Clara, California-based firm diversified into printed circuit board design and layout with its 1987 acquisition of Omnicad Corp. That year, ECAD listed publicly for the first time, selling 1.5 million common shares to raise $11.3 million. By the end of the decade, international marketing efforts had paid off, and the firm operated units in France, West Germany, the United Kingdom, Taiwan, and Hong Kong.

In 1983, SDA Systems Inc. was established in San Jose, California, by James Solomon, a former manager at National Semiconductor Corp. Backed by his former employer and General Electric Co.—each firm put up $1.5 million in start-up financing—Solomon founded SDA to recruit the engineering talent needed to develop design software. Two years later, SDA became the first company to introduce a software product that allowed users to link software from various venders in a common user interface database. Sales in 1987 tripled to $18 million, and the firm earned its first profit. The October 1987 stock market crash thwarted SDA's plans to conduct its initial public offering that year.

In June of 1988, ECAD and SDA merged to form Cadence Design Systems. The $72 million stock swap produced a new firm with $78 million in sales, $15 million in profits and 433 employees. Cadence Design raised $1.6 million via a stock offering. The firm expanded its software products, launching versions for industry giants like Hewlett-Packard Co. and NEC Corp. With a 15.4% market share in 1989, Cadence Design was the world's largest chip design software maker. To strengthen its presence in the lucrative Japanese market, Cadence Design established Cadence Design Systems K.K. in Tokyo. By the end of the year, sales in Japan accounted for 30% of total revenues.

Cadence Design shifted gears in 1989, looking to gain access to the more lucrative systems design software market, which represented the largest component of the electronic design automation (EDA) industry, rather than remaining focused solely chip design. The firm began pursuing systems design acquisitions, including Tangent Systems Corp., Gateway Design Automation Corp., and Automated Systems Inc. By the end of 1990, Cadence Design was the second-largest supplier of EDA Software. Amadeus, a comprehensive systems design software package, was introduced that year. The firm moved into the first place spot in 1991, with a 24% market share, after purchasing Valid Logic Systems Inc. for $200 million in stock.

Cadence Design paid $13 million in stock for Comdisco Systems Inc., a designer of software for digital signal processing and communication applications, in 1993. That year, the firm established a consulting arm, called Spectrum Services, and divested the Automated Systems unit. Substantially lower sales prompted Cadence Design to initiate a restructuring that included hiring new managers and redoubling international sales efforts. In 1994, Cadence Design purchased Redwood Design Automation and merged it with Comdisco to form the Alta Group. Unisys Corp. and Cadence Design forged an agreement in 1995, which stipulated that Cadence would oversee chip design for Unisys.

Cadence Design moved into the system-on-a-chip (SOC) market in 1997 by acquiring High Level Design Systems and Cooper & Chyan Technology, Inc. The following year, the company bought Ambit Design Systems, Inc. and Lucent Technologies' Bell Labs Design Automation Team. Sales reached $1 billion for the first time, setting an EDA industry record.

History of Valid Logic Design Systems, Inc.

Valid Logic Design Systems emerged in the early 1980s as one of the "Little Three." Along with Daisy

The Business

Financials

Revenue (1998): $1.216 billion

Employees (1998): 4,000

SICs / NAICS

sic 7372 - Prepackaged Software

Systems and Mentor Graphics, Valid Logic was considered a forerunner of the computer-aided engineering (CAE) industry. In 1982, Daisy Systems pioneered the first CAE System, which stood apart from computer-aided design (CAD) systems due to its ability to simulate and assess an electronic component's performance prior to its actual production.

The "Little Three" held 83% of the $260 million CAE market in 1984, with sales at Valid Logic reaching $48 million. Analysts predicted that the industry would swell to $2 billion over the next four years, and competition between the three firms intensified. By 1986, Valid Logic found itself struggling to keep pace with Mentor, which had focused on developing software compatible with standard computers rather than building its own hardware. Customers unwilling to wait for Valid Logic to develop such software flocked to Mentor. Although sales grew 9% to $61 million in 1985, the firm lost $7.1 million. In May of 1987, Valid Logic and Telesis Systems Corp. merged. Four years later, Valid Logic was acquired by Cadence Design Systems.

Market Forces Driving the Acquisition

In the late 1980s, Cadence Design had positioned itself as the leading chip CAD provider. However, the $179 million chip design market paled in comparison to the $880 million systems design market, the largest segment of the $1.05 billion EDA market. Because the EDA market was growing at a rate of 25% yearly, Cadence Design CEO Joseph Costello decided to implement a strategy designed to catapult Cadence Design to the top of the EDA heap by 1992. To do that, he figured Cadence Design would need to be a leader in the system design tools sector.

In March of 1989, Cadence Design purchased Santa Clara, California-based Tangent Systems Corp., a supplier of integrated circuit layout design software and gate-array products, from Intergraph Inc. Eight months later, the firm acquired Gateway Design Automation Corp., a Lowell, Massachusetts-based designer of Verilog simulation software. Automated

The Officers

Chairman: Donald L. Lucas

President and CEO: H. Raymond Bingham

Exec. VP, Worldwide Sales and Marketing: John F. Olson

Exec. VP, Engineering: Shane V. Robison

Systems Inc., a printed circuit board design software supplier and fabrication services provider located in Milwaukee, Wisconsin, was added to the mix in April of 1990. Along with growth via acquisitions, Cadence Design funneled large chunks of cash into research and development and established systems design and analog design divisions. With sales of $231.4 million, Cadence Design earned the number two standing among EDA suppliers in 1990.

In 1991, Cadence Design began eyeing Valid Logic, the third-largest EDA supplier. Along with gaining access to Valid Logic's combined system-level design technology and printed circuit board-layout program Allegro, a merger with Valid Logic would allow Cadence Design to move into first place in the EDA industry. The deal would also give much needed marketing resources to Valid Logic, which had been losing ground to competitors since the late 1980s despite the view by many industry experts that the firm had developed superior technology.

Approach and Engagement

Cadence Design and Valid Logic began negotiating a merger agreement in 1991. According to the terms of the pooling of interests agreement, owners of Valid Logic common stock would receive .323 of a share of Cadence Design common stock for each Valid Logic share held, while holders of Valid Logic preferred stock would receive .323 of a share of Cadence Design Series A-1 convertible preferred stock. Shareholders granted approval late in December, and the deal was completed on December 31, 1991.

Cadence Design CEO Costello remained at the helm of the firm. Valid Logic chairman and CEO W. Douglas Hajir was named vice chairman. Valid Logic president and chief operating officer L. George Klaus was appointed executive vice president and chief operating officer.

Products and Services

In the late 1990s, Cadence remained the worldwide leader among EDA software suppliers. Products accounted for 58% of sales and included Valid Logic's Allego, a printed circuit board layout design package; Specctra, another board layout product; Alta, a design test program; Diva and Dracula, two design verification programs; Silicon Ensemble, place and route software; Vampire, deep sub-micron verification software; Verilog, a simulation tool; and Virtuoso, an basic layout and design editing, design compaction, and layout synthesis package. Product maintenance brought in 24% of sales. Services, including component design, engineering, and testing, as well as design process reengineering and developer training, secured the remaining 18%.

Changes to the Industry

When Cadence Design completed its takeover of Valid Logic, it usurped Mentor Graphics as the world's leading EDA supplier. Rather than sparking additional industry consolidation, however, the deal seemed to have the opposite effect. According to *International Directory of Company Histories*, "lower revenues in 1993 were also seen as part of an industry trend confronting both of the larger EDA companies, Cadence and Mentor. In addition to financial losses, both companies also suffered defections of engineers and executives to start-up firms. A perception had emerged that the broad-line suppliers of EDA software were no longer on the cutting edge of technology in the fields of electronics systems design and high-level design automation. Furthermore, the EDA market had matured and was nearing saturation at the higher end." This trend prompted Valid to shore up its support and consulting services, which helped the firm stand out from the multitude of start-up competitors.

Review of the Outcome

Over $50 million in merger-related costs and restructuring expenses caused the firm to post a $22.4 million net loss in 1991, despite increased sales. Cadence Design and Valid Logic spent the next year integrating their product lines. Roughly 10% of the workforce was laid off.

Research

Brandt, Richard. "Mentor Graphics Becomes the 'Big One'," in *Business Week*, 6 July 1987. Describes the competitive industry conditions for Valid Logic in the late 1980s.

Cadence Design Systems, Inc. Home Page, available at http://www.cadence.com. Official World Wide Web Page for Cadence Design Systems, Inc. Includes product, corporate, historical, and employment information, as well as current news and annual reports.

"Cadence Design Systems, Inc.," in *International Directory of Company Histories*, Vol. 11, St. James Press, 1996. Details the history of Cadence Design Systems, Inc.

"Cadence/Valid Merger Approved," in *Business Wire*, 30 December 1991. Describes the terms of the agreement between Cadence Design and Valid Logic.

Levine, Jon B. and Andrea Gabor. "Why the Giants Can't Catch Silicon Valley's 'Little Three'," in *Business Week*, 25 March 1985. Explains how Valid Logic has emerged as one of three start-up companies to pioneer computer-aided engineering technology.

Pollack, Andrew. "A Fun Chief at Cadence Is Serious Merger Man," in *The New York Times*, 4 October 1991. Details the career of Cadence Design CEO Joseph B. Costello.

JEFF ST. THOMAS

CAMPEAU & ALLIED STORES

O&Y Properties Corp.
40 King St. W, No. 2700
Toronto, ON M5H 3Y2
Canada

tel: (416)365-2500
fax: (416)365-2510
sic 5311 - Department Stores

nationality: Canada
date: December 31, 1986
affected: O & Y Properties Corp. (formerly Campeau Corp.), Canada, founded 1968
affected: Allied Stores Corp., USA, founded 1929

Overview of the Merger

The $3.6 billion leveraged buyout of Allied Stores Corp., the sixth-largest department store in the U.S., by Canada's Campeau Corp. in 1986 was the beginning of the end for the Toronto-based real estate operation. Roughly two years after the deal was completed, Campeau paid $6.7 billion for the even larger Federated retail group. Hefty interest payments on an overwhelming $8 billion debt load, coupled with a weak retail market in the late 1980s, forced both Allied and Federated into Chapter 11 bankruptcy. After Campeau posted a loss in 1990 of $1.74 billion, the second-largest annual loss in Canadian corporate history, Robert Campeau was forced to resign from the company he had founded and run for over 20 years. In 1992, Federated and Allied emerged from bankruptcy as Federated Department Stores, Inc. The real estate assets of Campeau began operating that year as Camdev Corp.

History of Campeau Corp.

French Canadian Robert Campeau founded Campeau Corp. in 1968 by combining seven of his real estate operations into one organization. Campeau's efforts to diversify into television via the purchase of Bushnell Communications from Western Broadcasting Co. were thwarted in 1974 when the Canadian Radio-Television Commission blocked the transaction, finding that Campeau was unqualified to operate a television station. Campeau faced rejection again in 1980 when his attempt to acquire Royal Trustco, the leading real estate trust operation in Canada, was blocked when several Canadian corporations purchased the majority of Royal Trustco's stock.

In 1981, Campeau began seeking a major U.S. acquisition. Five years later, he initiated friendly merger discussions with Allied CEO Thomas Macioce, who was only interested in divesting five shopping centers at the time. Determined to land a major deal, Campeau began seeking backing for a hostile takeover, which he completed on December 31, 1986. In March of the following year, Campeau conducted a $1.2 billion junk bond and preferred stock offering as a means of whittling down the hefty debt it had incurred via the $3.6 billion leveraged buyout of

Allied. On April 1, 1988, Federated Department Stores, three times larger than Allied, accepted a $73.50 per share, or $6.6 billion, offer from Campeau.

Within a year of the purchase, it became clear that Campeau had seriously miscalculated the sales his retail operations would garner. Exorbitant interest payments on nearly $8 billion in debt brought Campeau Corp. to its knees. In 1990, the board of Campeau filed for Chapter 11 bankruptcy for both Allied and Federated. Shortly thereafter, the board ousted Campeau himself and began selling assets to pay off debts on which the firm had defaulted. In 1992, what was left of the real estate assets of Campeau began operating as Camdev Corp., which changed its name to O&Y Properties in 1997.

History of Allied Stores Corp.

In 1935, Allied Stores Corp. was created as a successor to Hahn Department Stores, which was organized in 1929 as a holding company to bring the advantages of chain stores to independent, family-owned department stores. Units included Jordan Marsh Co., based in Boston Massachusetts; The Bon Marche, based in Seattle, Washington; Joske Bros. Co., based in San Antonio, Texas; and Maas Bros. Co., based in Tampa, Florida. When the Great Depression took a toll on the retailer, Allied looked to real estate baron B. Earl Puckett to improve performance.

The firm enhanced the quality of its customer relations by offering credit, a "pay when you can" policy, in 1940 and building a reputation for community involvement in times of crisis. Puckett's pursuit of vigorous growth via acquisitions had propelled Allied to the number one spot among department store holding companies by the mid-1940s.

In 1950, Allied opened Northgate in Seattle, the country's first regional shopping center offering one-stop convenience to meet the shopping needs of residents in several communities. The next year, Allied acquired the New Jersey-based Stern Brothers. Because Puckett hadn't given much thought to how his purchases could be best integrated into Allied or to how they would position Allied in the future, the firm found itself struggling amidst a time of prosperity for other retailers. Although strong in Florida, the Pacific Northwest, and Boston, Massachusetts, Allied lacked a foothold in the nation's leading markets, including Chicago, Illinois; Los Angeles and San Francisco, California; and Washington, D.C.

Puckett resigned in 1959; his successor, Theodore Schlesinger, tried to undue some of the damage wrought by the firm's haphazard expansion in the 1940s and 1950s. In 1960, Allied acquired Mabley &

The Players

Founder and CEO of Campeau Corp.: Robert Campeau. Robert Campeau began his real estate career at the age of 25, when he sold a house he had initially been building for his family for a sizable profit. His real estate ventures in Ottawa, Ontario, flourished in the 1950s and 1960s, and homes built by Campeau became known in Canada as high quality residences. After establishing Campeau Corp. in 1968, Campeau began efforts to diversify. Deciding to look for growth in the U.S., Campeau spearheaded efforts in the early 1980s to penetrate the U.S. department stores market. His highly leveraged buyouts of Allied Stores and Federated Department Stores proved disastrous; both firms ended up declaring bankruptcy, and Campeau was dethroned by his board of directors in August 1990.

CEO of Allied Stores Corp.: Thomas Macioce. Thomas Macioce took over as CEO of Allied Stores in 1971. Having just completed his transformation of Allied into an upscale retailer, Macioce resisted the initial efforts of a takeover by Campeau Corp. in 1986. Campeau succeeded, however, and although Macioce was named chairman of Campeau, he resigned in January of 1987.

Carew Co. Two years later, Allied added William H. Block Co., based in Indianapolis, Indiana, to its mix. Schlesinger moved the firm into discounting by launching Almart, a chain of discount stores, in the mid 1960s. Allied reached $1 billion in sales for the first time in 1967.

Thomas Macioce took the reins from Schlesinger in 1971. He began selling off the Almart stores, reducing store size, and placing more of an emphasis on high-margin soft goods like clothing rather than on hard goods, such as furniture and housewares. In 1978, revenues surpassed the $2 billion mark. Wanting to revamp Allied's image as a more upscale retailer, Macioce began acquiring pricey clothing chains, such as Brooks Brothers and Ann Taylor. By the mid-1980s, Macioce had remade Allied into a profitable operator of fashionable department and specialty stores.

Campeau Corp.—which posted sales of $153 million in 1985, compared to $4.1 billion in sales by Allied that year—acquired Allied in 1986 through a leverage buyout. In 1987, Federated Department Stores bought Allied's Block chain from Campeau. The following year, Campeau acquired Federated in another huge leveraged buyout, this one worth $6.6 billion.

Staggering under a takeover-related debt of over $8 billion, Campeau, along with Federated and Allied, filed for reorganization under Chapter 11 of the U.S. Bankruptcy Code in 1991. Divisional consolidations merged Federated and Allied's Florida operations under the Burdines name. Under the watchful eye of Allen Questrom, the new Federated Department Stores, Inc. emerged from Chapter 11 in 1992, operating approximately 220 department stores in 26 states, recording annual sales of more than $7 billion, and employing about 81,000 people. In addition, Federated's stock was listed on the New York Stock Exchange.

Federated and R.H. Macy & Co., Inc. merged in 1994, creating the nation's largest department store chain. The next year, Federated acquired Broadway Stores for about $575 million in stock plus assumed debt. Federated discarded the Bullock's name and converted 21 of its stores into Macy's stores. The company was added to Standard and Poor's 500 stock index.

The latter half of the 1990s were marked by creativity and change. Burdines started Internet sales in 1996. In 1998, Federated had to shell out over $10.6 million to pacify complaints concerning illegal collections of credit card debt. By 1999, the firm had launched the macys.com web site, purchased Fingerhut, an e-commerce and order fulfillment company, and purchased a 20% stake in the Wedding Channel.

Market Forces Driving the Merger

Since the 1970s, Robert Campeau had been seeking ways to bolster his Canada-based real estate operation. After failing at efforts to move into television and to acquire the largest real estate trust business in Canada, Campeau set his sights on the U.S. retailing market. He believed access to American retailing would be the first step to assembling a U.S. commercial real estate empire as stores owned by Campeau would afford ready-made tenants for shopping centers developed by the realtor. According to a February 1987 article in *Business Week*, Campeau planned to "fashion a retail dynamo out of Allied" by decentralizing the retail giant, divesting its 16 more sluggish units, and refocusing on the best performing chains.

Approach and Engagement

Campeau approached Allied in the spring of 1986. When amicable discussions over the next few months didn't produce a merger agreement, Campeau realized he would need to launch a hostile takeover. *International Directory of Company Histories* wrote that, "To the naked eye, the prospect of Campeau buying out Allied seemed like a herring trying to swallow a whale...with Wall Street feverish and wild-eyed over leverage buyouts, however, Campeau assumed that he could borrow as much as he needed to do the job. He was right." The firm secured $3 billion in loans from a group of banks headed by First Boston and Citibank.

Allied rejected Campeau's first offer and sought protection from potential white knight Edward DeBartolo, Sr., a well known shopping center financier. Campeau responded by upping his offer to $66 per share. Unwilling to wait any longer, on October 24, Campeau canceled his offer and bought 53% (25.8 million shares) of Allied for $67 per share, or $1.73 billion, on the open market. Defeated, Allied agreed to a final $69 per share offer, $44 of which would be in cash and $25 of which would be in debt securities. According to the terms of the agreement, the deal needed to be completed by December 31 for both firms to secure certain taxes benefits. Early in December, Campeau agreed to change its offer to $69 per share, all in cash, if the transaction was finalized by the end of the month. Shareholders approved the deal on December 31.

Products and Services

By the late 1990s, Federated Department Stores, which encompassed the assets of both Federated and Allied, had become the nation's largest department store retailer with 355 locations in 35 different states. Macy's, Rich's, Bloomingdale's, Stern's, and Lazarus were all part of the Federated family.

Changes to the Industry and Review of the Outcome

When the deal was completed, Campeau laid off 400 New York-based Allied employees to save an estimated $35 million annually. To pay down debt, the firm divested $2 billion in Allied operations, including Garfinckel, Miller & Rhoads, Miller's, Bonwit Teller, Block's and Plymouth Shops. In the first year following the merger, Campeau reduced the number of Allied stores by more than 50%, paring 684 units to 274. Seventeen of the firm's 21 departments were unloaded, and remaining operations were organized into six autonomous divisions which were charged with the major task of cutting costs. Sales dropped from $4.14 billion to $3.5 billion in 1987, but debt was slashed from $4.3 billion to $2 billion. Campeau had also conducted a $1.2 billion junk bond and preferred stock offering in March as a means of whittling down his firm's hefty debt.

Within two years of the Allied takeover, Campeau began eyeing Federated, a struggling department store giant three times the size of Allied. On January 25, 1988, Campeau launched a $4.2 billion, or $47 per share, bid for Federated. After Federated turned down the offer, Campeau upped the price to $66 per share. In February, R.H. Macy & Co. topped Campeau with a $73.50 per share bid of its own for Federated. The battle ended on April 1; Federated agreed to accept $73.50 per share, or $6.6 billion, from Campeau, which agreed to sell three chains—Bullock's, Bullock's Wilshire, and I. Magnin—to Macy for $1.1 billion.

To finance the huge leveraged buyout, Campeau secured $4 billion in credit from First Boston, Dillon Reed, and Paine Webber, along with a consortium of banks led by Japan's Sumitomo group and Citibank. Edward DeBartolo offered Campeau a $480 million loan in return for a minority stake in Federated; Bank of Montreal and Banque Paribas fronted a high-interest, one-year $500 million loan; the Reichmann brothers, real estate developers in Toronto, bought $260 million in Campeau stock; and Campeau itself was required to produce $1.4 billion in equity, most of which turned out to be disguised debt. To raise the remaining capital, Campeau sold the profitable Brooks Brothers chain to Marks & Spencer PLC for $750 million.

When the deal was completed, additional layoffs dampened employee morale, which had already been badly damaged at Allied in the two years since its takeover. Allied's headquarters were moved to Cincinnati, Ohio, to be consolidated with Federated. Federated and Allied were then reorganized as subsidiaries of Federated Stores, Inc., a new U.S. holding company of Campeau Corp.

A sluggish retail market in the late 1980s, coupled with the costly interest payments Campeau was bound to as a result of its two major leveraged buyouts, debilitated the firm. Campeau's inexperience in the retail sector had led him to miscalculate the sales Allied and Federated would generate. In 1988, Campeau sold off the Gold Circle, Ann Taylor, and MainStreet operations. To make matters worse, a $1.2 billion Federated stock offering in October failed to generate anticipated capital. In the first half of 1989, Allied and Federated posted a combined loss of $306.3 million. The Reichmann brothers offered to loan $250 million to bolster the retail operations, and they con-vinced Campeau to put Bloomingdale's on the block. In January of 1990, after no buyers had come forth for Bloomingdale's, the firm's board of directors seized control of retail operations from Campeau and placed Allied and Federated into Chapter 11 bankruptcy. That year, Campeau posted a loss of $1.74 billion, the second-largest annual loss in Canadian corporate history.

Unfortunately, even the core real estate assets of Campeau were troubled. When the company defaulted on loans to DeBartolo and the Reichmann brothers, the board ousted founder Robert Campeau and stripped his firm of its retail assets. What was left of Campeau Corp.'s operations began operating as Camdev Corp., a real estate firm which later changed its name to O&Y Properties. In 1992, Allied and Federated surfaced from bankruptcy under the name Federated Department Stores, Inc.

Research

"Allied Stores Takeover Cleared," in *The New York Times*, 1 January 1987. Discusses the terms of the agreement.

Barmash, Isadore. "Life with Campeau; Allied's Year of Constant Change," in *The New York Times*, 14 February 1988. Details the changes that took place at Allied during the year following its takeover by Campeau Corp.

Brown, Michael. "Lehman Completes Restructuring for Federated in Just Two Years," in *Investment Dealers Digest*, 21 December 1992. Discusses how Federated and Allied reorganized during their bankruptcy in the early 1990s.

"Campeau Corp.," in *International Directory of Company Histories*, Vol. 11, St. James Press, 1994. Lists major events in the history of Campeau Corp.

Cook, Dan. "Is Campeau In Over His Head at Allied Stores?" in *Business Week*, 9 February 1987. Explains why Campeau pursued a takeover of Allied.

"Federated Department Stores, Inc.," in *Notable Corporate Chronologies*, The Gale Group, 1999. Lists major events in the history of Federated Department Stores, Inc. and Allied Stores, Inc.

Hawkins, Chuck. "Can Campeau's Wizardry Keep the Merry-Go-Round Spinning," in *Business Week*, 22 August 1988. Discusses what Campeau will need to do to make its takeover of Federated a success.

Simon, Bernard. "US Retail Venture Costs Campeau Dollars 1.74Bn," in *Financial Times (London)*, 21 June 1990. Covers the losses experienced by Campeau Corp. since its move into the U.S. retail market.

JEFF ST. THOMAS

CANAL PLUS & NETHOLD

Canal Plus
85/89 quai Andre Citroen, Cedex 15
Paris, 75711
France

tel: 33-1-44-25-10-00
fax: 33-1-44-25-12-34
web: http://www.cplus.fr

nationality: France
date: March 1997
affected: Canal Plus, France, founded 1984
affected: NetHold BV, The Netherlands, founded 1991

Overview of the Merger

When France's pay television channel, Canal Plus, took over the Dutch subscription television service NetHold BV—jointly owned by The Richemont Group and M-Net International Holdings—it became the largest pay television operation in Europe. The $2 billion deal, finalized in March of 1997, created an industry leader with roughly 8.5 million subscribers and a strong foothold in not only France and the Netherlands, but also in Italy, Germany, Spain, Scandinavia, and Benelux.

History of Canal Plus

In 1984, Andre Rousselet, president of France's largest advertising firm, Havas, launched Canal Plus, a subscription television channel offering an alternative to the programming available on France's three government-owned channels. At first, subscriptions were low, and Canal Plus lost Fr330 million during its first full year of operation.

Several politicians asked that the new commercial channel's broadcasting license be canceled, but Rousselet's friendship with President Francois Mitterand prevented that from happening. In fact, Mitterand secured a government concession which briefly granted Canal Plus a monopoly on subscription television. By the end of the year, however, private commercial television stations were allowed by the French government, and Canal Plus began facing competition.

By beefing up its offerings with well known American comedies and French dramas, Canal Plus was able to boost its subscriber base. To avoid paying cable companies to broadcast shows, Canal Plus used an existing broadcast channel, along with decoders. The new station was exempt from government regulations that restricted the number of nights per week that films could be broadcast and required a three-year waiting period between box office release and a film's debut on television.

Within two years of its inception, Canal Plus broke even. The company began to grow at a pace of 25% annually. Subscription renewal rate was nearly 95%, which Canal Plus attributed to its bank account debit system. In 1987, Canal Plus offered its stock publicly for the first time. Stock prices jumped from Fr275 to Fr575 by the end of the year. Profits reached $100 million in 1988, and Canal Plus held a 15% market share in France. The company attempted to form an alliance with Telecine Romandie, but the Swiss government intervened and prohibited the venture.

By the end of the decade, Canal Plus owned 33% of a channel introduced in Belgium; formed an alliance with Prisa, a media company establishing a private commercial television station in Spain; and, in a joint venture with Bertelsmann AG and the Kirch Group, launched Germany's first national pay television channel. Subscribers in France reached three million. In 1990, the firm launched Canal Horizons in Africa. The Canal Plus channel became the most successful subscription channel in Europe and was second only to Home Box Office, Inc. (HBO) worldwide.

In the early 1990s, Canal Plus was paying $100 million annually to purchase rights to American movies. To reduce these costs, the firm diversified into film production by acquiring a 5% share of Carolco Pictures for $30 million and by launching Studio Canal Plus, a Hollywood production company. Canal Plus also agreed to help fund Regency International, the independent production company of Arnon Milchan, producer of *Pretty Woman*. A year later, the company was forced to write off the $30 million it invested in Carolco after the studio declared bankruptcy. Although the charge lowered stock prices, Canal Plus continued to invest in film production and became the largest purchaser in Europe of American movie rights.

As a means of bolstering European film production, roughly 10% of the firm's revenues were invested in French films in 1992. Satellite broadcasting helped Canal Plus reach the locations in France that had no access to the cable network. The four million subscriber mark was surpassed, long considered the point of saturation in the French market. Also that year, BSkyB and Canal Plus agreed to jointly offer digital, multichannel pay television programming to the European market.

Despite growing revenues, profits began to fall in 1994 as competition intensified. In 1995, Canal Plus launched a pay television channel in Poland and continued work on a digital satellite service which would debut in France and then be expanded to serve Germany. After Twentieth Century Fox acquired Carolco, Canal Plus divested its 17% stake in the studio. Despite the start-up costs associated with the launch of Canalsatellite Numerique in 1996, profits continued to rise.

The Business

Financials

Revenue (1998): $2.89 billion

Employees (1998): 3,816

SICs / NAICS

sic 4841 - Cable & Other Pay Television Services

sic 7812 - Motion Picture & Video Production

In 1997, PolyGram sold exclusive rights for its films to Canal Plus for pay television broadcasting. In a $2 billion deal, Canal Plus and Dutch-based NetHold B.V. merged into Europe's largest pay television operator, with 8.5 million subscribers. Norway's Telenor CTV and Canal Plus formed a joint venture to merge two direct-to-home platforms into Canal Digital, a new television platform for Norway. A year later, America Online, Bertelsmann, and Canal Plus agreed to an Internet joint venture.

History of NetHold BV

While running The Richemont Group, the Swiss conglomerate under which his family's tobacco empire operated in South Africa, Anton Rupert developed an interest in the media industry. In 1991, Richemont helped fund South African pay television operator M-Net's purchase of FilmNet, a pay-television group based in Sweden. Richemont also bought a 25% share of Italian pay television operator Telepiu. Richemont's media assets formed the core of what would soon become known as NetHold BV.

In 1995, Richemont and M-Net International Holdings (MIH) decided to merge their pay television operations into NetHold, a global pay television group. Assets included a 20% stake in M-Net; FilmNet and its distributer, MultiChoice; ProNet, a program buyer; Irdeto, a decoding operation; and a minority stake in commercial television network Mediaset.

Within a year, the company had become the third-largest pay television operator in Europe. Subscribers reached 2.7 million and spanned 45 countries in Europe, Africa, and the Middle East. NetHold and Sweden's TV4 inked a joint venture for film production, film purchasing, and digital technology research and development. Also that year, NetHold paid roughly $500 million for 1.1 million digital IRDs. The purchase signaled the firm's shift from analog to digital technology, and in November of 1996, NetHold launched digital television in Sweden, Denmark, Finland, and Norway.

The Officers

Chairman and CEO: Pierre Lescure

Deputy Chairman and Chief Operating Officer: Marc-Andre Feffer

Sr. Exec. VP, Commercial Activities: Bruno Delecour

Sr. Exec. VP, Programming: Alain de Greef

Sr. Exec. VP, Group Subsidiaries: Vincent Grimond

Sr. Exec. VP, Finance: Laurent Perpere

Sr. Exec. VP, International: Michel Thoulouze

Richemont and M-Net International Holdings agreed in 1996 to sell NetHold to Canal Plus. The $2 billion deal, completed in early 1997, created the largest pay television service in Europe.

Market Forces Driving the Merger

In the mid 1990s, the push for digital satellite television services—to replace standard analog technology—across Europe intensified. Because digital start-up costs were high, media companies needed to team up to afford the new technology. Major players like DIRECTV International, France's Canal Plus, England's BSkyB, the Netherland's NetHold, and Germany's Kirch Group began seeking alliances in their quest to dominate Europe's digital satellite television services market. Many analysts predicted a link-up between DIRECTV International and NetHold.

In 1996, NetHold had already lost $140 million due to its recent digital technology spending spree. According to a January 1997 article in *Economist*, increased competition and the risks inherent in the new technology of the pay television industry also prompted NetHold chairman Rupert, who was used to operating in less competitive and more stable markets, to consider a sale. However, it wasn't DIRECTV International who sought the firm's digital technology assets and customer base. Instead, France's Canal Plus emerged as the main contender.

Canal Plus CEO Lescure believed the benefits to his station would be twofold: "the combination of relatively immature pay-TV markets where NetHold is present and the introduction of digital tv offers superb opportunities both to increase our subscriber base, and to distribute our programming software across a wider territory."

Approach and Engagement

On September 6, 1996, Canal Plus and NetHold announced their $2 billion merger. According to the terms of the agreement, Canal Plus would pay $45 million in cash and 6.1 million new Canal Plus shares for nearly all of NetHold's equity. Canal Plus also agreed to assume NetHold's $300 million debt, as well as the $350 million debt of Mediaset, an Italian media company partly owned by NetHold.

In March of 1997, the takeover of NetHold was finalized. Co-owner of NetHold, Richemont Group, gained a 15% stake in Canal Plus. M-Net International Holdings (MIH), owner of the other half of NetHold, ended up with a 5% stake in Canal Plus, as well as NetHold operations in the Middle East, Greece, Cyprus, and Africa, including the MultiChoice television operations in Africa, one of NetHold's most lucrative operations. Richemont and MIH retained three seats on the board of directors of Canal Plus.

Products and Services

Following the merger, Canal Plus boasted 8.5 million subscribers. Of those, 51% were located in France; 21% in Spain; 12% in Italy; 5% in Germany; 4% in Belgium; 3% in both Poland and the Netherlands; and 1% in Africa. Pay television services included Canal J, a children's programming channel; Canal Jimmy; C:Direct, a software download service; Cine Ciefil, a black and white films channel; Cine Cinemas; Comedie!; Demain!, a career channel; Eurosport; Forum Planete and Planete, two documentary channels; MCM, a music channel; Monte Carlo TMC, a general interest channel; Paris Premiere, a fashion and entertainment channel; Seasons, a hunting and fishing channel; and Spectacle, a home shopping channel.

Canal Plus also operated Le Studio Canal, a movie production studio that produced nearly 90% of all French films. It also owned 51% of Antennes Tonna, a cable and satellite equipment manufacturer; 97% of Canal Plus Image, a distributor of television programming; 85% of NC Numericable, a cable television operator; 71% of Ellipse Programme, a television producer; and 70% of Canalsatellite. Pay television assets included Canal Plus Nederland, Sweden's Canal Plus Television and a 90% interest in Italy's TELE Plus.

Changes to the Industry

When the takeover was completed, Canal Plus became the largest pay television operator in Europe. By gaining strong market share throughout Europe, the firm positioned itself for growth in many key territories. For example, Canal Plus gained access to NetHold's alliance with Kirch, which strengthened its position in Germany. Because Canal Plus had already been aligned with Kirch's major competitor, Bertelsmann, the firm was in a unique position to align itself with whichever firm later appeared stronger in Germany's digital television arena. The NetHold takeover also gave Canal Plus a stake in Italy's Telepiu just as digital satellite television was taking off in Italy.

Review of the Outcome

Even prior to the deal's completion, 50 NetHold employees were laid off. NetHold's Multichoice pay service in Poland was canceled in favor of Canal Plus Polska. Scandinavia and Benelux lost NetHold's Super Sports channels.

Analysts acknowledged that Canal Plus had acquired new territories and subscribers via its takeover of NetHold. At the same time, however, they pointed to the unprofitability of most NetHold operations as a reason for concern. According to industry analyst Yves Gauthier, as quoted in a September 1996 article in *Multichannel News*, "Canal Plus bought itself market share throughout Europe. But none of those markets will be profitable for several years." Canal Plus expected NetHold to double its number of subscribers to 3 million by the year 2000, when the unit was expected to finally break even.

Research

Atkinson, Claire "The Race to Conquer Europe," in *Broadcast*, 5 July 1996. Discusses the industry conditions leading up to the takeover of NetHold BV by Canal Plus.

"Canal Plus," in *Notable Corporate Chronologies*, The Gale Group, 1999. Lists major events in the history of Canal Plus.

Canal Plus Home Page, available at http://www.cplus.fr. Official World Wide Web Home Page for Canal Plus. Available in both French and English, this site includes news, financial, product, and historical information.

Dinerman, Ann S. "Recreated NetHold Quickly Gaining Ground," in *Video Age International*, March-April 1996. Offers a company profile of NetHold BV.

"France's Canal+ Does $1.8 Billion Merger Deal with Rival NetHold," in *Broadcasting & Cable*, 16 September 1996. Offers an overview of the terms of the deal between Canal Plus and NetHold.

Mahoney, William. "Canal Plus-NetHold Deal Sends Ripples Around Europe," in *Multichannel News*, 16 September 1996. Explains the impact of the Canal Plus/NetHold deal on the television industry in Europe.

Short, David. "Canal Plus Turns on the Pressure," in *The*

The Players

Chairman and CEO of Canal Plus: Pierre Lescure. Pierre Lescure began his media career in France's radio industry. After working for RTL, Radio Monte Carlo, and Europe 1, Lescure moved into television when he accepted a post with France 2, a public television channel. He moved from there to Canal Plus in 1983. Three years later, Lescure was appointed managing director of Canal Plus. He was eventually named president of the channel, and when its founder, Andre Rousselet, stepped down in February of 1994, Lescure took over as chairman and CEO. He led the firm's takeover over NetHold in 1997 and remains at the helm of Canal Plus today.

Chairman of NetHold BV: Johann Rupert. A member of the second-wealthiest family in South Africa, Anton Rupert took over the family tobacco business—which had been founded by his father in 1955—in the 1980s. An interest in the media industry prompted Rupert to join a group, including South African pay television operator M-Net, in purchasing FilmNet, a pay-television group based in Sweden, in 1991. Three years later, Rupert bought a 25% share of Telepiu, a pay-television operation in Italy. In 1995, Rupert and M-Net International Holdings decided to merge their pay television operations into NetHold, and Rupert took over as chairman of the station. Within a year, the company had become the third-largest pay television operator in Europe. Despite the venture's success, Rupert agreed that year to sell his pay television holdings to Canal Plus. When the deal was completed in early 1997, Rupert exited the media industry and returned to running the family tobacco business. He is currently CEO of Richemont Group, the Swiss conglomerate that holds the Rupert family's tobacco and other assets.

European, 3 April 1997. Details the changes that have taken place at Canal Plus since its takeover of NetHold.

Vermuelen, Amanda. "A NetHold Gem Than Canal Plus Passed Up," in *Multichannel News*, 30 September 1996. Discusses the performance of MultiChoice Africa, a unit of NetHold that Canal Plus did not acquire.

JEFF ST. THOMAS

CHAMPION INTERNATIONAL & ST. REGIS PAPER

Champion International Corp.
One Champion Plaza
Stamford, CT 06921
USA

tel: (203)358-7000
fax: (203)358-6444
web: http://www.championpaper.com

nationality: USA
date: November 1984
affected: Champion International Corp., USA, founded 1893
affected: St. Regis Paper Co., USA, founded 1901

Overview of the Merger

When paper and forest products industry giant Champion International swooped in to save St. Regis Paper—the leading newsprint producer and the sixth-largest paper company in the U.S.—from a hostile takeover by publisher Rupert Murdoch, it became the number one paper company in the U.S. The $1.8 billion merger allowed Champion to focus on pulp and paper production.

History of Champion International Corp.

In 1893, Champion Coated Paper Co. was founded in Hamilton, Ohio, by Peter Thomson. Twelve years later, Reuben Robertson, son-in-law of Thomson, founded Champion Fibre Co. in Canton, North Carolina. The two companies merged to form Champion Paper and Fibre Co. in 1935.

Champion profited when the paper industry shifted into high gear to meet wartime demands. However, by the late 1950s, the firm was struggling. In 1960, Champion's president, Reuben Robertson, Jr., died. His father, Reuben Robertson, Sr., resigned Champion's chairmanship in the wake of his son's death. Karl Bendetsen, the company's first non-family president, took over at a time when the firm was in severe financial trouble. Almost immediately, Bendetsen cut costs, declaring the company "no longer paternalistic in any sense of the word."

By 1967, profits had risen by 41% and *Forbes* declared Champion "one of the best managed companies in the entire paper industry." Champion merged with U.S. Plywood Corp. to form U.S. Plywood-Champion Papers, Inc. Bendetsen was named CEO of the new firm. Acquisitions over the next few years included Drexel Enterprises, a furniture business; Trend Enterprises, a carpet company; and Path Fork Harlan Coal.

In 1972, the company's name was changed to Champion International Corp. When Bendetsen reached mandatory retirement age, Thomas Willers was chosen as his successor. Within two years of his appointment, Willers was forced to resign because the board of directors disliked his plans to take Champion into the chemicals industry. Andrew Sigler was appointed CEO and chairman; he divested sev-

256

eral non-core operations, including carpet and furniture operations.

Champion bought Hoerner Waldorf Corp., the fourth-largest U.S. paperboard and corrugated-box manufacturer, in 1977. In 1984, Champion paid $1.8 billion for St. Regis Corp. When the paper industry slumped in 1989, stock prices begin to fall. By the early 1990s, Champion had divested its office products operations; 57 container, packaging, and paperboard plants; the specialty paper plant in Columbus, Ohio; and timber holdings in several western states, ostensibly to raise needed cash.

Champion agreed to pay $6.5 million in 1993 to settle a claim that a plant in Canton, North Carolina, had pumped toxins into the Pigeon River. Net income jumped in 1995 to $772 million, compared to $63 million last year. Champion bought back two million shares from Loews Corp. for $105 million, began newsprint paper collection operations in Georgia and Tennessee; and licensed its newly developed beach filtrate recycling technology to Wheelabrator Technologies. The following year, the firm announced its intent to divest its newsprint and paper recycling operations. Quebecor's Donohue paid $450 million to Champion for three recycling and two newsprint units in 1998. Also, Conservation Fund, an environmental protection group based in the U.S. agreed to buy 300,000 acres of northeastern U.S. forest from Champion for roughly $75 million.

History of St. Regis Paper Co.

In 1901, St. Regis Paper Co. was founded in upstate New York. Operating as a small newsprint manufacturer, St. Regis tapped the vast supply of spruce Adirondack forests. In 1913, Congress lifted the protective tariff on newsprint, and Canadian businesses began saturating the industry. In response, St. Regis began manufacturing lightweight paper for catalogs, directories, and magazines, as well as other forms of paper. The firm also bought timberlands and built and acquired pulp paper mills.

St. Regis bought a majority stake in Taggert Corp., which it incorporated into its new Kraft and Converting Products Division, in the late 1920s. The firm also diversified into the multiwall bag sector with its acquisition of Bates Valve Bag Co.; to house this unit, St. Regis established the Multiwall Packaging Division.

The boom in the U.S. economy after World War I fueled the company's growth in the white paper market. Making its first foray into the western U.S., St. Regis bought a kraft pulp mill in Tacoma, Washington, in 1930. Over the next ten years, president Roy K.

The Business

Financials

Revenue (1998): $5.65 billion

Employees (1998): 24,000

SICs / NAICS

sic 2621 - Paper Mills

sic 2679 - Converted Paper Products Nec

sic 2656 - Sanitary Food Containers

sic 2676 - Sanitary Paper Products

sic 2411 - Logging

sic 2611 - Pulp Mills

sic 2657 - Folding Paperboard Boxes

sic 2421 - Sawmills & Planing Mills-General

sic 2672 - Coated & Laminated Paper Nec

sic 2671 - Paper Coated & Laminated-Packaging

naics 322121 - Paper (except Newsprint) Mills

naics 322231 - Die-Cut Paper and Paperboard Office Supplies Manufacturing

naics 322215 - Non-Folding Sanitary Food Container Manufacturing

naics 322291 - Sanitary Paper Product Manufacturing

naics 113310 - Logging

naics 322212 - Folding Paperboard Box Manufacturing

naics 321912 - Cut Stock, Resawing Lumber, and Planing

naics 322222 - Coated and Laminated Paper Manufacturing

naics 322221 - Coated and Laminated Packaging Paper and Plastics Film Manufacturing

Ferguson began implementing the following policies: integrating raw material and production facilities, furthering mechanical and engineering research, and focusing on pulp, paper, and allied products. By the early 1940s, St. Regis was the world's leading multiwall bag maker. The firm moved into the southern U.S. when it bought Florida Pulp & Paper Co., based in Pensacola, in 1948. A mill was constructed in Jacksonville in 1953. That year, the firm also diversified into the corrugated container market, initiating a string of acquisitions that eventually included Pollock Paper Co., General Container Corp., Superior Paper Products, Ajax Box Co., Pacific Waxed Paper Co., Growers Container Corp., Gummed Products Co., and Rhinelander Paper Co.

The Officers

Chairman and CEO: Richard E. Olson

Vice Chairman and Executive Officer: Kenwood C. Nichols

Exec. VP: Joseph K. Donald

Exec. VP: L. Scott Barnard

Exec. VP: Burton G. MacArthur, Jr.

In 1957, St. Regis expanded its western holdings by acquiring J. Neils Lumber Co., based in Portland, Oregon, and St. Paul and Tacoma Lumber Co. Merger discussions with RCA Corp. fell apart in 1969. Over the next several years, St. Regis ventured into the insurance and energy industries in an effort to boost profitability. The firm fended off hostile takeover efforts by corporate raiders in early 1984; however, management recognized that the company could no longer remain independent and agreed to a $.8 billion merger with Champion International later that year.

Market Forces Driving the Merger

Profits at seven leading forest products firms tumbled 55% between 1979 and 1983. Falling prices, coupled with rising costs, caused a slowdown in new home construction and paper manufacturing markets, and forest products firms were left vulnerable to hostile takeovers. In the early 1980s, Sir James Goldsmith had made a hefty profit by liquidating Diamond International Corp., wetting the appetites of other corporate raiders. The vulnerability of one major industry player, Crown Zellerbach Corp., served as a prime example of how these firms became targets. Because its major timber assets were significantly undervalued due to the economic downturn, potential buyers were simply unwilling to offer Crown Zellerbach a fair prices for those reserves. St. Regis was in a similar situation in 1984. According to a February 1985 *Business Week* article, the firm's stock was valued at $30 per share, roughly 25% less than its book value, in 1983. "This discrepancy between St. Regis' real value and its stock price gave raiders a rich opportunity. They alone were willing to pay more than the stock price to get at St. Regis' undervalued assets. Their aim: to break up the company and convert the pieces into cash at today's prices."

When St. Regis came under attack from corporate raiders in early 1984, Champion Paper swooped in with a white knight offer for two reasons. Champion CEO Andrew Sigler, an outspoken critic of the type of hostile takeovers popular in the early 1980s, wanted

the operations of St. Regis to continue, rather than see the firm's valuable paper and timber holdings divided and sold to the highest bidder. Also, Champion was looking to increase its U.S. paper operations, and St. Regis boasted a solid footing in the newsprint sector, as well a leading position in publications-grade paper, a market Champion had yet to penetrate. The firm's 500,000 timberland acres in Texas would also complement the 500,000 acres already owned there by Champion.

Approach and Engagement

St. Regis fought off hostile overtures by Sir James Goldsmith, the Bass brothers, Loews Corp., and Laurence A. Tisch. The firm's defensive measures included buying off the raiders, as well as negotiating to sell key assets and threatening buy Colonial Penn Group Inc. to make itself less attractive. It wasn't until publisher Rupert Murdoch made clear his intention to buy the firm for its newsprint operations and sell off the rest that St. Regis took a serious look at the white knight offer made by Champion International back in February of 1984 when St. Regis first came under attack.

In August of 1984, when it looked like Murdoch was close to tendering, St. Regis contacted Champion. The $1.83 billion agreement was negotiated in a single day. Shareholders of both companies approved the deal in November, and it was completed shortly thereafter. Each remaining St. Regis share was converted into 2.85 shares of Champion common stock.

Products and Services

By 1998, pulp and paper products accounted for 83% of sales, while wood products brought in the remaining 17%. Paper and board products included coated and uncoated free sheet paper, coated and uncoated groundwood paper, kraft paper, and unbleached linerboard. Pulp products included bleached softwood kraft pulp, market pulp, and recycled pulp. The firm also sold three wood products: chips, lumber and studs, and plywood. U.S. sales accounted for 85% of total revenues; Canada, 10%; and Brazil, 5%.

Review of the Outcome

When the deal was completed, Champion became the number one forest products company in the U.S. At the end of 1984, despite taking an after-tax $150 million charge related to the merger, Champion posted a $6 million loss for the year. The firm was also saddled with the $1 billion in debt it had assumed to finance the purchase; consequently, all previous expansion plans were put on hold. Frustrated, Champion CEO Sigler implemented a plan to slice debt by $750 million. The non-core assets of St. Regis, including its energy and insurance holdings, were divested. Roughly 2,000 employees lost their jobs when seven wood products plants in the western U.S. were closed. After swallowing the operations of St. Regis, Champion was able to shift its focus from wood products to paper and pulp production, which eventually became the firm's core business.

Research

Champion International Corp. Home Page, available at http://www.championpaper.com. Official World Wide Web Page for Champion International Corp. Includes product and corporate information, and news.

"Champion International Corp.," in *Notable Corporate Chronologies*, The Gale Group, 1999. Offers a history of Champion International Corp.

"Champion Merger," in *The New York Times*, 21 November 1984. Offers a brief overview of the terms of the transaction between Champion International and St. Regis Paper.

Lueck, Thomas. "Building a New Empire Out of Paper," in *The New York Times*, 12 August 1984. Explains why Champion CEO Andrew Sigler offered to acquire St. Regis Paper.

Priest, Alice L. "Champion Struggles to Make the St. Regis Merger Work," in *Business Week*, 25 February 1985. Discusses how Champion had fared since its takeover of St. Regis.

———. "How Time Ran Out at St. Regis," in *Business Week*, 25 February 1985. Explains why St. Regis was vulnerable to corporate raiders.

Sharp, Kathleen. "A Regional Report: The Pacific Northwest; An Exodus From the Timberlands," in *The New York Times*, 16 June 1985. Presents an overview of the state of the forest products industry in the early 1980s.

JEFF ST. THOMAS

The Players

Chairman and CEO of Champion International Corp.: Andrew C. Sigler. A long-time sales and marketing employee of Champion International, Andrew Sigler was appointed CEO and chairman of the firm in 1974 after the board of directors ousted CEO Thomas Willers because they were unhappy with his plans to diversify into chemicals. He immediately launched a divestiture program, selling off several of Champion's non-forest operations. Adamant in his opposition to the highly leveraged buyouts popular in the early 1980s, Sigler led Champion's white knight rescue of St. Regis Paper from corporate raider Rupert Murdoch in 1984. Despite occasional criticism from shareholders for putting his employees needs ahead of profits, Sigler continued to lead Champion until his retirement in 1996.

Chairman and CEO of St. Regis Paper Co.: William R. Haselton. William Haselton began working for St. Regis Paper in 1953 as a chemical engineer. He worked his way up the corporate ladder, eventually landing the appointment of CEO. In 1981, Haselton was elected chairman of the company. He successfully fended off hostile takeover attacks by Sir James Goldsmith and other raiders early in 1984, eventually seeking refuge in a merger with Champion International. Upon completion of the deal, Haselton was appointed vice chairman of Champion.

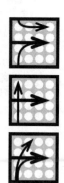

CHASE MANHATTAN & CHEMICAL BANK

The Chase Manhattan Corp.
270 Park Ave.
New York, NY 10017
USA

tel: (212)270-6000
fax: (212)552-5928
web: http://www.chase.com

nationality: USA
date: March 31, 1996
affected: The Chase Manhattan Corp., USA, founded 1799
affected: Chemical Banking Corp., USA, founded 1824

Overview of the Merger

The Chemical Bank/Chase Manhattan merger created an entity with bank offices in 52 countries and over $300 billion in assets. The newly formed company retained the Chase Manhattan moniker to capitalize on its strong foreign market name recognition. Chemical Banking Corp., the surviving entity, took over a majority of management operations, including more than 50% of board positions. The $10 billion stock swap deal allowed Chase to reduce inflated operating expenses. The new Chase expanded banking services, as market trends forced banks to broaden their offerings.

History of The Chase Manhattan Bank Corp.

The Manhattan Corp. was founded in 1799 to challenge the dominance of the Bank of New York and the Bank of the United States. Besides its banking operations, The Manhattan Corp. was chartered to supply water to the city of New York. With a liberal corporate charter, the bank was able to branch into several various projects. It offered financing in the early 1800s for East India trade and in 1859 funded bond payments on the Erie Canal.

In 1877 John Thompson founded Chase National Bank. It was named in honor of Salmon P. Chase, Secretary of the Treasury under President Lincoln. Chase National Bank flourished into one of the largest holders of individual depositor accounts by 1900, signifying its rapid success. Then in 1911, under the new leadership of Albert Henry Wiggin, it began doing business on Wall Street. Wiggin expanded banking services to include trusts, securities, and stock underwriting. By 1917 he made Chase National Bank a major player in the equities markets. He also arranged mergers in which Chase National Bank absorbed seven other banks including the Equitable Trust Corp., making it the largest bank in the world by 1930. Wiggin was forced to resign in 1932. A congressional investigation eventually charged him with selling Chase stock short during the market crash and illegally maneuvering funds to bypass stock transaction laws.

Chase had neglected the domestic consumer branch market in the decade following World War II. It merged with The Manhattan Corporation in 1955 to capitalize on its many branched system throughout New York City. David Rockefeller, who was former vice president of Chase National Bank, was assigned to further develop the newly formed Chase Manhattan Corp. He was eventually named chairman of the board in 1969.

During Rockefeller's tenure Chase Manhattan was involved in several controversial, but financially successful dealings. In 1965, civil rights groups accused Chase of supporting the apartheid regime by purchasing a major share in South Africa's second-largest bank. Activists urged people and businesses to withdraw funds. The following year, Rockefeller decided to open a branch in Saigon, Vietnam. The building was specifically designed to withstand mortar and explosive attacks. By the mid-1970s, Chase's best Middle East customer was the Shah of Iran, with annual deposits reaching $2.5 million. Hostages were taken in 1979 at the U.S. Embassy in Tehran, Iran, when Rockefeller convinced the U.S. government to freeze all U.S. held Iranian assets.

In 1982 the Oklahoma based Penn Square failed, and Chase suffered huge loan losses. This failure haunted Chase until 1993. The company acquired Nederlandse Credietbank N.V. in Amsterdam and Lincoln First Bank in Rochester, New York, in 1984. The following year, Chase purchased six Ohio savings-and-loan institutions and opened its first full-service bank outside New York. In 1986 Chase acquired Continental Bancor and restructured its New York branch system. As a result, 6,000 employees were laid off.

To help combat 1987 losses of $894.5 million, Chase introduced the customer certificate of deposit with interest tied to stock market gains. Also Chase began a series of acquisitions, securing banks in New York, Maryland, Florida, and Arizona.

In 1990 Labrecque was appointed chairman, and realigned Chase's long-term goals to focus on six core businesses: credit cards, mortgage services, regional banking, transaction services, global private banking, and global corporate finance and management. In 1992 Chase sold all 13 of its Ohio banks branches.

Chemical Banking Corp. and The Chase Manhattan Corp. announced in 1995 their merger, which created the nation's largest bank. The merger allowed the two banks to improve their respective service weaknesses and use the combined assets for further growth.

The Business

Financials

Revenue (1998): $32.59 billion

Employees (1998): 69,033

SICs / NAICS

sic 6712 - Bank Holding Companies

sic 6021 - National Commercial Banks

sic 6022 - State Commercial Banks

naics 551111 - Offices of Bank Holding Companies

History of Chemical Banking Corp.

Founded in 1824, the New York Chemical Manufacturing Co. formed a banking division called Chemical Bank. When the New York Chemical charter expired in 1844, it liquidated chemical manufacturing operations and reincorporated as a bank. Chemical Bank was one of the largest and strongest U.S. banks by 1900. By 1907, however, Chemical Bank was losing 100 accounts per year. A resurgence occurred during World War I due to effective management and a marketwide upturn in business. By 1919 the bank's stock increased by nearly $200 per share. The following year Chemical Bank merged with Citizens National Bank, upping its assets to nearly $200 million.

Between 1955 and 1971, Chemical Bank merged with Continental Bank and Trust Co., Corn Exchange Bank, and New York Trust Co. Chemical also formed Chemical New York Corporation in 1968 to expand services into other financial markets.

In 1982 Chemical introduced Pronto, the first electronic home banking system for consumers and small businesses. A joint venture with Chemical, AT&T, and Bank of America in 1985 further developed electronic services. In 1987, while suffering from foreign loan losses, Chemical acquired Horizon Bankcorp and Texas Commerce Bancshares. The Texas Commerce merger was the largest interstate bank merger in U.S. history.

Chemical Banking Corp. and Manufacturer's Hanover merged in 1991, joining the nation's sixth and ninth largest banks respectively. Roughly five years later, Chemical Banking Corp. and The Chase Manhattan Corp. merged to create the nation's largest bank.

The Officers

Chairman and Chief Executive Officer: Walter V. Shipley

President and Chief Operating Officer: Thomas G. Labrecque

Vice Chairman of the Board and Financial Officer: Mark J. Shapiro

Vice Chairman of the Board and Director: William B. Harrison, Jr.

Market Forces Driving the Merger

The 1995 announcement of the Chase/Chemical merger signaled a new era of large mega-mergers which would eventually dominate the industry. Analyst Henry Dickson of Smith Barney stated there were several key forces driving banks to grow larger and larger. First, technological advances allowed companies to handle increased volume. Revenue and financial service diversity was also becoming more important to investors than asset size. Additionally, increased stock prices gave investors more money to work with, which meant more banks became targets for acquisition.

In 1995 Chase Manhattan sought a merger partner after a series of poor earnings. The 1994 economic crash of Mexico negatively affected Chase's capital market income. First quarter trading revenues in 1995 were down to $94 million from $224 million reported for the same time in 1994. Contributing to their 29% first quarter earnings loss, Chase's securities trading and underwriting sales were down by $94 million, while operating expenses increased. Chase needed to cut costs and increase market strength. By merging, Chase hoped to eliminate redundant services, use the increased asset base to gain a market advantage, and enter more market sectors. At the same time, Chemical Bank wanted to use the Chase name for greater involvement in foreign markets.

Approach and Engagement

With Chase suffering losses, it became a prime merger or takeover target. Chase originally discussed a merger with The Bank of America. The latter ceased talks shortly thereafter, stating the deal would be too costly. In August of 1995, Chase Manhattan and Chemical Banking Corp. announced a merger of equals between the two firms, which would create the largest bank in the United States with approximately $300 billion in assets. Walter V. Shipley would take over as the new Chase Manhattan chairman and chief

executive officer, while Thomas Labrecque would become president and chief operating officer.

The new Chase Manhattan Corp. had to grapple with one overriding challenge: size. For the merger to be a success, Chase needed to create a computer system that could accommodate the bank's size, maintain customer service during the transition and afterward, and finally, eliminate smaller branches and redundant services. Initially the size of the merger attracted much press attention, which helped advertise the name.

Conversely, the mega-bank size made consumers leery that customer service quality would suffer. Many consumer groups feared Chase would abandon smaller bank branches in low-income areas. Inner City/Community on the Move filed a lawsuit with the New York Supreme Court after the Federal Reserve Board approved the deal. During the case, the Federal Reserve Board accidentally released a confidential list of 200 proposed branches slated for closure. Inner City's fears seemed justified when many low-income neighborhood branches appeared on the list, but the document did not impact the outcome. State Supreme Court Judge, Beatrice Shainsuit, eventually rejected the community group's argument, and the merger was allowed to continue. The deal was completed on March 31, 1996.

Products and Services

After the merger was completed, Chase increased its international presence, servicing 52 countries. Branches operated in Hong Kong, Panama, and the Caribbean. With its strong foreign presence, Chase became the world's largest U.S. dollar clearing agent. In the late 1990s, Chase remained a minor player in consumer branch banking, focusing instead on electronic commerce.

In New York, Chase led middle-market lending. As the nation's largest auto loan financier, 42% of Chase's 1997 sales came from loans. Credit card services accounted for 4%, while securities interest made up 13% of total revenue.

Changes to the Industry

Chemical Banking Corp. hoped to capitalize on the already well established Chase name in the overseas market, but the firm also launched a $45 million national advertising campaign. To counteract public and industry impressions that such a large bank could only offer impersonal, slow, and unsatisfactory customer service, Chase was pitched as "The Relationship Company." Chase inherited the sports and event marketing opportunities which Chemical had begun, including sponsorship of the U.S. Open tennis tournament.

Successful computer integration, uninterrupted customer services, downsizing, and aggressive marketing campaign proved to competitors that a merger on such a grand scale could be done successfully. The new bank remained the nation's largest until 1998 when Nation'sBank merged with The Bank of America, further highlighting the broad range of financial services banks needed to offer to stay competitive.

Chase became a leader in online commerce with the introduction of its Internet banking services in 1997. An advanced online service launched in March 1999, designed as a nationwide branch for 24 hour personal banking, attracted 400,000 customers. A $2.5 million investment in technological services signified Chase's decision to turn away from traditional branch investments and put itself at odds with competitor trends.

Review of the Outcome

The Chemical/Chase merger created the largest U.S. bank with assets of roughly $300 billion. Chemical Banking's Walter Shipley drew upon his previous merger experience to lead the new bank's formation. The 1991 Chemical/Manufacturer's Hanover merger transition had dragged on for two years. The new Chase completed the transition period within six months, due to strict management timelines and enormous staff support. Instead of merging the two separate computer systems, the new operating systems were based around individual computer suites. Seven days after the merger was signed, the bank's 1,500 traders were already using an integrated system. By mid-July the bank shifted to one payment system and general ledger. By September 1, 1996, every branch, teller and consumer contact point was integrated. Transitional work was done after hours to prevent any disruptions to customer service and branch banking. During the integration process, Chase Manhattan downsized 8,000 employees and closed 400 New York area branches.

Research

"Chase Manhattan," in *Investor's Chronicle*, 27 October 1995. Details Chase's negative earnings and losses prior to announced merger with Chemical.

"Chase Manhattan Corp.," in *Notable Corporate Chronologies*, The Gale Group, 1999. Lists major events in the history of Chase Manhattan Corp.

Chase Manhattan Corp. Home Page, available at http://www.chase.com. Official World Wide Web Home Page for The Chase Manhattan Corp. Includes current and archived news; detailed financial, product, and historical information; and annual reports.

The Players

President and Chief Operating Officer of The Chase Manhattan Corp.: Thomas G. Labrecque. After serving in the Navy, Thomas G. Labrecque joined Chase Manhattan Corp. in 1964. He worked his way up the ranks and became the associate secretary of planning to the executive office by 1970. After being named Chase's Treasury Department executive vice president in 1974, he was the driving force that brought Chase into the retail banking market. Two years later, he was appointed to the management committee. Thomas Labrecque then served as vice chairman and chief operations officer in 1980. From 1981 to 1990, Labrecque served as president, and in 1991 he was named chairman and chief executive officer. After the 1996 Chase and Chemical Banking Corp. merger, he was named president and chief operations officer.

Chairman and Chief Executive Officer of Chemical Banking Corp.: Walter V. Shipley. Walter Shipley began his career with Chemical Banking Corp. in 1956. He became senior vice president in 1979, and was appointed president and a director in 1982. From 1983 until the 1991 Manufacturer's Hanover merger, Shipley served as chairman and CEO. When the merger was completed, he accepted the post of president. Three years later, he was appointed chairman and CEO. When Chemical and Chase Manhattan Corp. merged in 1996, Shipley retained the chairman and CEO positions.

"Chemical Banking Corp.," in *Notable Corporate Chronologies*, The Gale Group, 1999. Lists major events in the history of Chemical Banking Corp.

Davis, Stephen. "Why Tom Labrecque Isn't CEO of Bank of America," in *Institutional Investor*, 11 November 1995. Details reasons why the Chase and Bank of America merger proposal fell through.

Kraus, James. "Chase Profits Off 29%; Surge For Bank of New York," in *American Banker*, 18 April 1995. Reports on Chase's pre-merger 1st quarter earnings.

Lefton, Terry. "Cutting to the Chase," in *Brandweek*, 17 April 1997. Highlights Chase's merger transition period and marketing campaign.

Moyer, Liz. "As Others March to Megadeals, Chase Hears A Different Drummer," in *American Banker*, 19 August 1998. Highlights Chase's decision to focus more on electronic commerce.

Radign, Joseph. "Shake, Rattle and Roll: Bank Mergers Create

Concern," in *U.S. Banker*, September 1995. Discusses market trends impacting 1995 merger activity.

Seiberg, Janet. "New York's Approval of Chase Merger Upheld," in *American Banker*, 22 May 1996. Review of court case that attempted to block Chase/Chemical merger.

———. "Red-faced Fed Trying to Undo Damage After Releasing Chase List of Closings," in *American Banker*, 13 May 1996. Reports on Federal Reserve Board accidental release of confidential merger documents to community activist group trying to block merger.

Talmor, Sharona. "Milestone Managers," in *The Banker*, October 1996. Explains completion of Chase Manhattan and Chemical Banking Corp. merger.

SEAN C. MACKEY

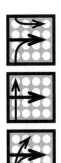

CHEVRON & GULF OIL

nationality: USA
date: March 1985
affected: Chevron Corp., USA, founded 1879
affected: Gulf Oil Corp., USA, founded 1904

Chevron Corp.
575 Market St.
San Francisco, CA 94105
USA

tel: (415)894-7700
fax: (415)894-0583
web: http://www.chevron.com

Overview of the Merger

The largest deal to date in U.S. corporate history, the $13.2 billion takeover of Gulf Oil Corp. by Chevron Corp. in March of 1985 was also one of the messier brawls in the oil industry consolidation war. The battle for Gulf Oil began when Mesa Petroleum began secretly buying shares of the firm in 1983. Increasingly vocal criticism of Gulf Oil management by Mesa CEO T. Boone Pickens added to the pressure on the firm's board. A buyout offer in 1984 from Atlantic Richfield led the board to auction Gulf Oil to the highest of three bidders: Atlantic Richfield, leverage buyout firm Kohlberg Kravis Roberts & Co. (KKR), and Chevron. The victor, Chevron, struggled for several years with the debt it took on to finance the deal.

History of Chevron Corp.

In 1879, California oil prospector Frederick Taylor and a group of investors founded the Pacific Coast Oil Co. after Taylor discovered the state's most productive oil well. Following its incorporation, the firm developed a method for refining the heavy California oil into an acceptable grade of kerosene, the most popular lighting source in use at the time. By the turn of the century, Pacific Coast maintained a team of producing wells in Newhall, California; a refinery at Alameda Point across the San Francisco Bay; railroad tank cars; and an ocean-going tanker, the *George Loomis*. Although John D. Rockefeller's Standard Oil and Pacific Coast were fierce competitors, one of Pacific Coast's best customers was Iowa Standard, which purchased large quantities of kerosene.

Jersey Standard, increasingly attracted to business near the West Coast in order to accommodate crude sales activities for its Asian subsidiaries, purchased Pacific Coast's stock for $761,000, with an arrangement for Pacific Coast to produce, refine, and distribute oil for marketing and sale by Iowa Standard representatives. Iowa Standard's W.H. Tilford and H.M. Tilford assumed leadership of Iowa Standard and Pacific Coast, respectively. At that time, Pacific Coast also began construction of California's largest refinery at Point Richmond on San Francisco Bay, as well as a set of pipelines to bring oil from its San Joaquin Valley wells to the refinery.

The Business

Financials

Revenue (1998): $26.18 billion

Employees (1998): 39,191

SICs / NAICS

sic 1311 - Crude Petroleum & Natural Gas

naics 211111 - Crude Petroleum and Natural Gas Extraction

Pacific Coast saw its crude production rise steeply over the next decade. In 1906, Jersey Standard united its two West Coast subsidiaries into a single entity officially called Standard Oil Co. (California), commonly known as Socal. Recognizing the future importance of the West, Jersey Standard increased the new company's capital from $1 million to $25 million. Socal added a second refinery at El Segundo, California, and pursued the growing markets for kerosene and gasoline in both the western U.S. and Asia.

Socal's refineries used approximately 20% of California's entire crude production, much more than its own wells could supply. To keep its refineries and pipelines full, Socal bought crude from Union Oil, in return handling a portion of the marketing and sale of Union kerosene and naphtha. Socal maintained almost complete control of the market, supplying 95% of the kerosene and 85% of the gasoline and naphtha purchased in California, Alaska, Nevada, Oregon, Washington, Hawaii, and Alaska. When necessary, Socal took advantage of its dominant position, curbing competition by deep price-cutting.

In 1911, Pacific Coast's crude production reached 2.6 million barrels annually. However, the firm was producing a mere 2.3% of California's crude, forcing partner Iowa Standard to buy most of its crude from outside suppliers like Union Oil and Puente Oil. After achieving several breakthroughs in the refining of California's heavy crude into usable kerosene, Socal became the state leader in kerosene production. That year, the Standard Oil Trust was ordered by the U.S. Supreme Court to dissolve, breaking its monopolistic control of the oil industry. Socal emerged as an independent company engaged in the four major segments of the petroleum industry: production, refining, pipelines, and marketing

Over the next several years, Socal completed a series of successful oil strikes, and by 1919, the firm accounted for 26% of nationwide crude production. In 1930, Socal engineers struck oil in Bahrain. Six years later, recognizing the need to access markets larger than its own foreign holdings, Socal sold 50% of drilling rights in Saudi Arabia and Bahrain to the Texas Co., later known as Texaco Inc.. This joint venture produced an entity known as California Texas Oil Co., or Caltex. Eventually, Socal and Texas Co. agreed to jointly market their products under the Caltex brand name, and they soon began pursuing markets in Europe and the Far East, especially Japan.

In 1948, Socal and Texas Co. sold 40% of the Saudi Arabia-based operations of Caltex, which had become known as Arabian American Oil Co., or Aramco, to Socony and Jersey Standard, later known as Mobil Corp. and Exxon Corp., respectively. By the end of the decade, Socal had become one of the few U.S. firms with $1 billion in assets.

Throughout the 1950s, Socal secured one-third of its crude production from Aramco; Saudi Arabia accounted for about two-thirds of the firm's reserve supply. Although other oil fields were discovered in Sumatra and Venezuela, Socal remained dependent on its Aramco concession for crude. By selling its cheap Middle Eastern oil in Europe and Asia, Socal was able to achieve profit increases throughout the 1960s. To market its gasoline in the southeastern U.S., the firm bought Standard Oil Co. of Kentucky.

Responding to the emerging problems in oil politics, Socal merged all of its domestic marketing into a single unit, Chevron USA, in 1981. The firm also began streamlining measures, including the laying off of employees. It also increased its domestic exploration efforts while moving into alternative sources of energy such as shale, coal, and uranium. Socal bid $4 billion for full ownership of AMAX Inc., a leader in coal and metal-mining, but the firm was forced to settle for a 20% stake. In 1984, Socal changed its name to Chevron Corp. That year, Chevron met its short-term oil needs by purchasing the Gulf Corp. for $13.1 billion, the largest purchase to date in the history of U.S. business.

Tenneco Inc. sold its oil and gas properties in the Gulf of Mexico to Chevron for $2.5 billion in 1988; the deal positioned Chevron as a leader in the U.S. natural gas industry. In 1992, Chevron embarked on a $20 billion, 40-year joint venture with the Kazakhstan government to develop large oil reserves in that country at Tengiz and Korolev, which were expected to produce 700,000 barrels per day in 20 years.

The company sold its refinery in Philadelphia, Pennsylvania, to Sun Co. for $170 million in 1994. Production began at new wells in Chevron's Kokongo oil field, located near Cabinda Island off the coast of Angola. To meet new California state environmental standards in 1995, Chevron temporarily halted production at its refinery in Richmond, California, which underwent a $1 billion conversion to production of reformulated gasoline. That year, Chairman Kenneth Derr admitted that Chevron's $700 million investment in the Tengiz oil field had failed to pay off.

NGC Corp. bought the natural gas assets of Chevron for $3 billion in 1996; as a result, Chevron gained a 25% stake of NGC, which later changed its name to Dynegy. Other activities that year included pioneering the use of fiber optic cables to monitor oil field production; discovering reserves of 500 million barrels of oil beneath Chevron land near the Cusiana oil field in Colombia; beginning production at its N'Kossa oil field off the coast of the Congo; and selling its North Sea operations to Oryx for $140 million. The firm also announced plans to abandon its California offshore oil and gas operations within four years due to lack of profitability.

After securing its first onshore oil exploration contract with the People's Republic of China in 1997, Chevron launched construction of a petrochemical plant in Saudi Arabia. Shell Oil bought all of Chevron's United Kingdom-based gas stations that year. In 1998, the U.S. Environmental Agency fined Chevron $540,000 for discharging wastewater into the San Pablo Bay. A planned merger with Texaco dissolved in 1999, and Atlantic Richfield and Chevron inked an agreement to jointly produce oil and gas in the Permian Basin.

History of Gulf Oil Corp.

Backed by Pittsburgh's wealthy Mellon family, J. M. Guffey founded the J. M. Guffey Petroleum Co. in Texas in 1901. William Larimer Mellon ousted Guffey the following year, and five years later, the firm's name was changed to Gulf Oil.

The firm grew via exploration throughout the first half of the century. Major discoveries in both Louisiana and Oklahoma propelled it to a position among the leading U.S. oil players. Gulf ventured into Kuwait after World War II ended. When that country experienced an oil shortage in the 1970s, Gulf Oil's performance dipped. Rumors that Gulf had engaged in domestic and international government payoffs totaling $12 million circulated that decade. The scandal resulted in the resignation of chairman Bob R. Dorsey, as well as other executives.

In the mid-1970s, Gulf Oil decided to branch into other areas to reduce its reliance on oil. However, plans to buy insurer CNA were dropped when understatements of liabilities surfaced, prompting management's decision to hold off on diversification for a while.

The Officers

Chairman and CEO: Kenneth T. Derr

Vice Chairman, Worldwide Refining, Marketing, Chemicals, and Coal Mining: James N. Sullivan

Vice Chairman, Worldwide Oil and Gas Exploration and Production: David J. O'Reilly

In 1977, Gulf Oil paid $455 million for Kewannee Oil Corp. Two years later, the firm acquired Canada's Amalgamated Bonanza Petroleum Ltd. for $120 million. That year, Gulf Oil offered roughly $2 billion for Belridge Oil Co. The firm's bid, however, was topped by a $3.6 billion offer from Shell Oil Co. Efforts to acquire Tenneco were also thwarted by more generous bidders, and Gulf Oil's offer for Marathon Oil Co. was later abandoned.

Gulf Oil offered $5 billion for Cities Service in June of 1982, topping an earlier offer by Mesa Petroleum. Within two months, however, Gulf Oil backed out the deal, which prompted Cities Service to file a breach of contract lawsuit. Three years later, Chevron acquired Gulf Oil for a record $13.3 billion, becoming the third-largest oil firm in the U.S.

Market Forces Driving the Merger

As California crude production began to slow down in the 1960s, Chevron (then known as Socal) grew increasingly dependent on Middle Eastern oil. Although a strike in Louisiana began producing 27.9 million barrels per year, the increase in reserves was only a temporary reprieve. Saudi Arabian oil provided three-quarters of Chevron's proven reserves in the early 1970s. In 1973, OPEC began to seize control of oil in the Middle East, prompting a four-fold increase in base price. Socal could rely on its Saudi partner only for a small price advantage over the general rate, and it was no longer in legal control of sufficient crude to supply its worldwide or domestic demand.

In the late 1970s, U.S. firms began hunting for acquisitions as a means of bolstering falling reserves. Gulf Oil's $2 billion bid for Belridge Oil Co. in the late 1970s was quelled by Shell Oil Co.'s $3.6 billion offer. The next major battle—which involved Conoco Inc., Dome Petroleum Ltd., Cities Service Co., and Seagram Company Ltd.—was eventually settled in September of 1981, when DuPont Co. paid $7.8 billion for Conoco, completing the largest merger in U.S. corporate history.

The Players

Chairman and CEO of Chevron Corp.: George M. Keller. George Keller began working for Chevron (then known as Socal) in 1948. He held several positions at the firm, including a stint as a refinery designer, before securing the top spot in the late 1970s. As chairman, Keller orchestrated the consolidation of all U.S. marketing operations into Chevron USA, as well as his firm's official name change to Chevron. He spearheaded the $13.2 billion acquisition of Gulf Oil in 1985 and oversaw integration of the two firms until his retirement on January 1, 1989. Keller was succeeded by Kenneth T. Derr.

Chairman of Gulf Oil Corp.: James E. Lee. James Lee took was appointed chairman of Gulf Oil in 1981. Along with executive vice president Harold Hammer, Lee directed Gulf Oil's $5 billion bid for Cities Service in June of 1982. After pulling Gulf out of that deal, Lee began steering his firm into exploration in Alaska, the Gulf of Mexico, and offshore California. Those efforts paid off when Gulf Oil was able to fully replace the U.S. reserves it pumped in 1984, nearly twice its reserves replacement when Lee took over. When it appeared that Mesa Petroleum was gearing up to launch a hostile takeover bid for Gulf Oil, Lee began searching for white knight offers. A wild proxy battle ensued, with Chevron emerging as the victor. When Chevron's takeover of Gulf Oil was completed, Lee resigned.

After a decade of sporadic attempts to lessen its dependence on the Middle East, as well as several years of watching rampant consolidation among its chief competitors, Chevron decided to make a move of its own by bidding for Gulf Oil in the same year that Mobile paid $5.7 billion for Superior Oil and Texaco bought Getty Oil for $10.8 billion. Despite a record of shaky management, a substantial base of oil reserves made Gulf Oil appealing to Chevron. Also, according to a January 1985 *Business Week* article, both firms stood to benefit "by pooling geological data and applying Chevron's oil-recovery technology to Gulf's fields."

Approach and Engagement

Gulf Oil chairman James Lee had been searching for a white knight offer since February of 1984. In mid-1983 Mesa Petroleum chairman T. Boone Pickens—who in 1982 had lost the battle for Cities Service to Gulf Oil, which later backed out of its agreement to buy Cities Service—had begun secretly buying Gulf Oil stock. He acquired 4.9% of the firm's stock, staying just below the 5% line to avoid the legal obligation for public filing. Pickens then formed a group of investors, known as Gulf Investors Group, to acquire additional shares of Gulf Oil. When Gulf Investors finally made its mandatory public filing, it owned 9% of Gulf Oil. To defend itself against what seemed like an impending hostile takeover bid from Mesa, Gulf Oil held a special shareholder meeting in December of 1983, at which a decision was reached to switch the firm's state of incorporation from Pennsylvania to Delaware, where state laws would make it more difficult for Mesa to infiltrate Gulf Oil's board.

Increasingly vocal criticism of Gulf Oil's management by Pickens put pressure on the firm's board. Recognizing Gulf Oil's vulnerability, Atlantic Richfield moved in and offered $70 per share for the firm. Defeated, management decided to hold an auction. On March 4, 1984, Atlantic Richfield, leveraged buyout firm Kohlberg Kravis Roberts & Co. (KKR), and Chevron made their bids for Gulf Oil. Chevron's all-cash offer of $80 per share beat out Atlantic Richfield's $72 per share offer, as well as KKR's $87.50 per share cash-and-stock bid.

The U.S. Federal Trade Commission (FTC) gave conditional approval for the deal in April. Six months later, the FTC granted final approval contingent upon the divestiture of several Chevron assets, including 5,600 gas stations across the southeastern U.S., as well as 29 wholesale terminals and a Louisiana-based refinery. Chevron and Gulf Oil were ordered to operate as separate entities until those divestitures were completed. In March of 1985, when all but one of the divestitures were completed, the FTC allowed the transaction to proceed.

Products and Services

Gulf Oil was folded into the Chevron's petroleum operations, which accounted for 90% of total sales in 1998; Chemicals secured the remaining 10%. Operations included Gulf Oil Great Britain; a 50% stake of Caltex, an oil refining and marketing business; a 28% stake in natural gas operation Dynegy; Pittsburgh & Midway Coal Mining Co.; and a 40% stake in Kazakhstan's Tengizchevroil, an oil exploration company.

Changes to the Industry

The takeover of Gulf Oil—which boasted $20 billion in assets, $30 billion in annual sales, and 40,000 employees—nearly doubled Chevron's proven reserves from 1.1 billion bbl. to 1.8 billion bbl. The new third-place giant in the U.S. oil industry, Chevron was also the leading domestic retailer of gasoline and the second-largest oil company in terms of assets. As the largest deal in U.S. corporate history, Chevron's $13.2 billion purchase of Gulf Oil raised the bar for future consolidation.

Review of the Outcome

Although the acquisition of Gulf Oil solved a short-term oil reserves shortage problem for Chevron, many analysts questioned its timing, since oil prices had begun tumbling, making it difficult for Chevron to sell off assets quickly. Consequently, Chevron was unable to pare down its debt, which had swelled to $15.5 billion upon completion of the purchase, as quickly as it wanted. By the onset of the Gulf War, which provided temporary relief from declining oil prices, Chevron was struggling under a debt load of $12 billion. In the early 1990s, Chevron rid itself of Gulf's Canadian operations and all of Gulf's gas stations in the northeast and southeast U.S., laying off 16,000 workers. Two years later, as part of a restructuring program, 4,400 Chevron employees opted for early retirement. The firm also launched plans to streamline operations and lay off about 700 employees at the refinery at Port Arthur, Texas.

Chevron Corp. was fined $700 million in 1996 after a jury decided that Gulf Oil should pay $228.9 million plus interest to Cities Service for nixing its merger plans with the firm in 1982. Despite an appeal in March of 1999, a trial court upheld the verdict.

Research

"Approval on Sale Asked by Chevron," in *The New York Times*, 22 November 1984. Explains the divestitures Chevron is completing to secure final FTC approval for its takover of Gulf Oil.

Chevron Corp. Home Page, available at http://www.chevron.com. Official World Wide Web Home Page for Chevron Corp. Includes press releases, as well as financial, product, and investor information.

"Chevron Corp," in *Notable Corporate Chronologies*, The Gale Group, 1999. Details the history of Chevron Corp.

"Chevron-Gulf," in *The New York Times*, 15 March 1985. Announces final FTC approval for the Chevron/Gulf deal.

"Chevron Files Final Brief in Cities Service Case," in *PR Newswire*, 11 May 1999. Explains the outcome of the lawsuit filed by Cities Service after Gulf Oil backed out of a merger agreement in 1982.

Fisher, Lawrence M. "New Chief at Chevron Sees Greater Expansion," in *The New York Times*, 23 August 1988. Announces the retirement of Chevron chairman George M. Keller and offers a brief look at his career.

Wasserstein, Bruce. *Big Deal: The Battle for Control of America's Leading Corporations*, Warner Books, 1998. Offers an overview of the largest mergers in recent American corporate history.

Wilson, John W. "The Chevron-Gulf Merger: Does It Still Make Sense?," in *Business Week*, 21 January 1985. Questions the reasons behind the deal and discusses problems Chevron might face as a result of taking over Gulf Oil.

ANNAMARIE L. SHELDON

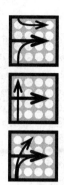

CITICORP & QUOTRON SYSTEMS

Citigroup Inc.
153 E. 53rd St.
New York, NY 10043
USA

tel: (212)559-1000
web: http://www.citi.com

nationality: USA
date: 1986
affected: Citicorp, USA, founded 1812
affected: Quotron Systems Inc., USA, founded 1960

Overview of the Merger

New York-based banking giant Citicorp paid $680 million in 1986 for Quotron Systems, the largest provider of stock market quotes in the U.S., with nearly 100,000 subscribers. Intense competition from Dow Jones & Co., Reuters Holdings PLC, as well as upstarts like Bloomberg Financial Markets, had slashed that customer base to 30,000 by 1994.

In 1991, Citicorp took a $400 million restructuring charge to overhaul Quotron. Two years later, the Quotron unit posted a $35 million loss and Citicorp reported a $179 million charge on its Quotron assets. Determined to unload the failing financial data services unit, Citicorp sold Quotron to Reuters in 1994 for a meager $12.8 million. As part of the deal, Citicorp also agreed to pay Reuters $80 million to cover operating losses for two years. The ill-fated acquisition cost Citicorp more than $1 billion.

History of Citicorp.

In 1791, First Bank of the United States began operation. After the War of 1812, Colonel Samuel Osgood took over the struggling New York branch of First Bank and formed City Bank of New York.

City Bank gained a national charter in 1865 to become the National City Bank of New York (NCB) and adopted the wire abbreviation: Citibank. After attaining the national charter, NCB began distributing national currency and broker government bonds. Citibank gained a reputation of conservative banking practices and was the largest New York City bank, with assets totaling $29.7 million by 1893.

After the Federal Reserve Act of 1913 opened global markets to U.S. banks, Citibank opened a branch in Argentina and purchased Britain's International Banking Corp. Concurrently, national acquisitions of Commercial Exchange Bank, Second National Bank, and the 1926 purchase of People's Trust Company aided in making Citibank the first United States bank to reach $1 billion in assets.

After World War II, Citibank expanded its corporate banking operations and, under the leadership of Walter B. Wriston, took an aggressive approach to commercial lending. Wriston developed and implemented the certificate of deposit in order to increase capital. He additionally acquired First National Bank of New York, and renamed it First National City Bank of New York. In the mid-1970s, Citibank changed its name to Citicorp, and passed its former moniker on to First National City Bank of New York.

Citicorp suffered great losses on bad loans to Third World countries in the late 1970s and early 1980s. Political upheavals in Poland and Iraq caused drastic debt restructuring, while global energy prices raised interest rates too high for low-yield commercial banks to function.

Wriston retired as chairman in 1984 and was succeeded by John S. Reed. Reed oversaw the firm's $680 million purchase of Quotron Systems Inc. in 1986. Loans to Third World countries still plagued Citicorp, and in 1991, company stock fell to a twenty-year low of $8 per share.

The following years bestowed repeated financial blows. Citicorp's automated mortgage system approved too many bad loans, and the Federal Reserve Bank of New York placed service restrictions to ensure Citicorp's longevity. In 1993 Citicorp finally announced a 355% earnings increase in the third quarter, due in part to the introduction of consumer pictures on credit cards for fraud protection and the announcement of a co-branded Visa credit card with Ford Motor Co. A year later, the firm finally divested its floundering Quotron Systems unit to Reuters for $12.8 million, a price roughly fifty times lower than it paid.

Citicorp reorganized upper management ranks in April 1997, placing William I. Campbell over retail businesses while Reed retained leadership of all other operations. One year later, Travelers and Citicorp completed a $70 billion merger deal, forming Citigroup Inc., the world's largest financial services institution. In 1999, Citigroup acquired Mellon Bank's $1.9 billion credit card business to become the largest credit card issuer in the world. Other acquisitions that year included the $558 million loan portfolio and 128 branch offices of Associates First Capital Corp., and Financiero Atlas, a Chilean consumer finance company with $460 million in assets. Citigroup also bought a majority stake in Sears, Roebuck and Co.'s Homelife furniture chain. These purchases reflected Citigroup's quest to become a financial services supermarket.

History of Quotron Systems Inc.

Quotron Systems was launched in 1960 and introduced the U.S. market to the first electronic stock sys-

The Business

Financials

Revenue (1998): $76.4 billion

Employees (1998): 173,700

SICs / NAICS

sic 6020 - Commercial Banks

sic 6311 - Life Insurance

sic 7374 - Data Processing & Preparation

sic 7375 - Information Retrieval Services

naics 514191 - On-Line Information Services

tem. The firm had little competition during its first years of operation and built up a large client base. In 1984, the Quotron 1000, which offered electronic stock quotes as well as calculation functions, was unveiled.

Two years later, Citicorp paid $150 million for Quotron. Shortly thereafter, Shearson Lehman Hutton canceled its five-year, $150 million contract with a joint venture that had previously been formed by AT&T Corp. and Quotron. The lost business was a sign of trouble to come. By the mid-1980s most electronic stock quote operations were using personal computer-based quote terminals. Quotron, however, stuck to its original technology. In the early 1990s, when Quotron finally acknowledged its mistake and forged an agreement with IBM Corp. to implement PC technology, the firm had already lost significant market share and several major clients.

Quotron's F/X trader, the firm's first new product in six years, was launched in 1990, and it secured new customer for the firm. However, intense competition from smaller competitors such as Bloomberg Financial Markets—which had entered the real-time stock, bond, and foreign exchange quote market after technology prices had fallen—had already undercut earnings and market share. Between 1988 and 1991, Quotron slashed in prices by roughly 65%. Citicorp had already spent $1 billion on the unit, but Quotron had yet to earn a profit since its takeover by the New York-based bank. Rumors that Citicorp was seeking suitors for the unit began to circulate, but no offerings for Quotron emerged.

In 1993, Quotron lost $35 million. A year later, Reuters American Holdings Inc., the U.S. unit of Reuters Holdings PLC, paid $12.8 million for the floundering firm.

The Officers

Co-Chairman and Co-CEO: Sanford I. Weill

Co-Chairman and Co-CEO: John S. Reed

Vice Chairman: Deryck C. Maughan

Vice Chairman: Paul J. Collins

Market Forces Driving the Merger

Citicorp pursued its takeover of electronic stock quote provider Quotron Systems in 1986 as part of its plan to become a leading financial information services provider. According to an April 1989 article in *Business Week*, Quotron's customer base of 100,000, the largest in the U.S., was very appealing to Citicorp and "induced Citicorp, in 1986, to pay $680 million for the stock quotation company—an extremely rich $8,500 per Quotron terminal, more than three times the average annual revenues the terminals generate."

Approach and Engagement

Citicorp paid $680 million for Quotron Systems in January of 1986. After spending more than $1 billion to overhaul the financial services unit, Citicorp finally sold Quotron in 1994 for $12.8 million to Reuters American Holdings Inc., the U.S. operation of Reuters Holdings PLC. As part of the deal, Citicorp agreed to pay an additional $80 million to Reuters to cover the anticipated operating losses of Quotron for the next two years.

Products and Services

In 1999, Citigroup and its subsidiaries offered credit, long-term care, and life insurance, in addition to mutual funds, commercial and personal loans, and subprime lending. Despite the diversity of its non-banking services, Citigroup also offered traditional branch banking. Subsidiaries Primerica and Citibank teamed up to sell checking accounts door-to-door.

Because it had acquired Quotron to gain access to its U.S. customer base, rather than its antiquated technology, Reuter's had phased out much of Quotron's technology by the mid-1990s.

Changes to the Industry

As technology prices fell in the late 1980s and early 1990s, smaller competitors began to enter the $4 billion electronic stock, bond, and foreign exchange quote industry, undercutting larger competitors like Quotron and Reuters Holdings, who had once enjoyed near monopoly status. In 1991, Automatic Data Processing boasted 70,000 terminals, compared to Quotron's 60,000, and Bloomberg Financial Markets had snagged 14,000 terminals for itself. Although Reuter's still dominated the worldwide market with 200,000 terminals, the firm's profit growth in 1991 slowed to 6.3%, compared to 31% in 1989 and 13% in 1990.

As explained in a February 1992 *Business Week* article, a few large electronic stock quote players had "called the shots" from the early 1960s, when the industry emerged, to the late 1980s. "Once a brokerage house formed a relationship with a vendor, it wasn't easy to get a divorce." In the early 1990s, however, access to affordable technology had given customers more control.

Review of the Outcome

Citicorp's purchase of Quotron was plagued from day one. Shortly after the deal was finalized, Quotron lost a $150 million, five-year contract from Shearson Lehman Hutton. Because Quotron had yet to shift to personal computer-based quote terminals, it began losing market share and major customers to more technologically savvy competitors. For example, Automated Data Processing lured Merrill Lynch away from Quotron in the late 1980s and eventually usurped Quotron as the largest U.S. electronic stock quote provider. As a result, Citicorp was forced to foot the bill for Quotron's technology upgrade in the early 1990s.

Between 1988 and 1991, Quotron reduced prices by roughly 65%. In 1991, Citicorp posted a $400 million restructuring charge to overhaul Quotron. A year later, despite Citicorp's $1 billion outlay to refurbish the unit, Quotron remained unprofitable. It posted a $35 million loss in 1993, and Citicorp took a $179 million writedown on its Quotron assets. Because Citicorp was also struggling with a bloated bad loan portfolio and a lethargic corporate banking market, many analysts predicted that the sale of Quotron was only a matter of time and was likely to occur as soon as it found a buyer willing to take on the struggling operation.

Reuters emerged as Quotron's only suitor in January of 1994. Although it recognized that most of Quotron's technology was outdated, Reuters viewed the purchase of Quotron as a means of gaining access to a large, albeit dwindling, number of clients in a short amount of time and for a highly reduced price. The deal would also increase its presence in the U.S., a market the firm had found difficult to penetrate.

When Reuters offered to pay $12.8 million for the operation, a price sharply lower than the $680 million Citicorp had paid for Quotron in 1986, Citicorp jumped at the chance to rid itself of the struggling unit. The firm even agreed to compensate Reuters for the operating losses Quotron was likely to realize over the next two years. Because it had long been criticized for not recognizing when to exit a venture and for trying to hang on to all of its assets, the decision to sell Quotron was viewed by most analysts as a welcome shift in management strategy at Citicorp.

Research

"A Blip on the Screen," in *Chief Executive*, April 1994. An interview with Retuers Holdings CEO Peter Job. Includes his views on the pending acquisition of Quotron Systems.

"Citicorp," in *Notable Corporate Chronologies*, The Gale Group, 1999. Lists major events in the history of Citicorp.

Citigroup Home Page, available at http://www.citi.com. Official World Wide Web Home Page for Citigroup. Includes current news, press releases, financial information, and annual reports.

Gullo, Karen. "Citi Will Sell Quotron to Reuters, Cut Costs; Strong Profits Forecast; Stock Rises," in *American Banker*, 14 January 1994. Discusses Citicorp's reasons for selling Quotron.

Meeks, Fleming. "Rich Prospects, Poor Technology," in *Forbes*, 3 April 1989. Details Quotron's loss of market share to Automatic Data Processing in the late 1980s.

Roman, Monica. "Shootout in Tickertown," in *Business Week*, 24 February 1992. Offers a detailed overview of the electronic stock, bond, and foreign exchange market, including the performance of Quotron since its takeover by Citicorp.

The Players

Chairman and CEO of Citicorp: John S. Reed. MIT graduate John Reed worked his way up Citicorp's ranks to become CEO in 1984. In the 1970s, Reed had laid the systems information structure for Citicorp, and he oversaw the group's ill-fated purchase of Quotron Systems in 1986. Reed's most impressive contribution to the company was his risky decision to pursue individual consumer accounts in the late 1980s, while others sought big commercial clients. The risk paid off, and many competitors followed suit. At the same time, he was criticized for making chancy loans to land developers, Third World countries, and heavily indebted companies that allowed non-performing assets to exceed the firm's equity capital in 1990. When Citicorp completed its landmark $70 billion merger with Travelers Group in October of 1998, Reed agreed to share leadership responsibilities with Travelers Group CEO Sanford Weill.

"Quotron Sale Has a Cost for Citicorp; Seller Will Pay to Meet Unit's Losses," in *The New York Times*, 2 April 1994. Details the terms of the agreement between Reuters and Citicorp regarding the sale of Quotron.

JEFF ST. THOMAS

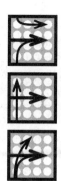

CITICORP & TRAVELERS

Citigroup Inc.
153 E. 53rd St.
New York, NY 10043
USA

tel: (212)559-1000
web: http://www.citi.com

nationality: USA
date: October 8, 1998
affected: Citicorp, USA, founded 1812
affected: Travelers Group, USA, founded 1864

Overview of the Merger

The proposed $70 billion stock swap merger of Travelers Group and Citicorp was finalized on October 8, 1998, at $37.4 billion after both company's stocks plummeted. The merged entity was renamed Citigroup, and became the largest worldwide financial services company with nearly $700 billion in assets.

History of Travelers Group

In 1864 James G. Batterson opened The Travelers Insurance Co. It paid its first death claim on a policy later that same year when a train conductor fell between two rail cars. Travelers created an umbrella of insurance coverage which branched from accident and life into automobile, health, aviation, workers' compensation and group life insurance. By 1870 the red umbrella had already become the company's logo.

In 1915 Louis F. Butler became the third leader of Travelers after the death of Sylvester Dunham. That same year 17 Travelers policyholders were killed when a German submarine sank the Lusitania cruiseliner.

After Butler's death in 1929, Edmund Zacher took control of Travelers and transferred the company's money from equities into U.S. government bonds. Two days later the stock market crashed, but Zacher's choice for a safer investment kept the company afloat.

By 1938 Travelers' combined assets reached $1 billion. In the latter part of the 1950s, Travelers began basing automobile insurance premiums on a driver's safety record instead of vehicle horsepower. In keeping with its name, many famous travelers were covered by the company. Travelers issued the first air travel policy for President Woodrow Wilson, and in the 1960s, issued space travel insurance to *Apollo 11* astronauts for the first moon landing.

Travelers increased its size and scope from 1960 until the Citicorp merger with several acquisitions, beginning with The Phoenix Insurance Co. in 1966. In the 1980s Travelers purchased Keystone Life Insurance Co., and Bankers and Shippers

Insurance Co. The firm's stake in the securities sector grew dramatically with the 1984 purchase of Moseley, Hallgarten, Estabrook and Weeden, and also Dillion, Reed, and Co. two years later.

When real estate soured in the late 1980s, Travelers sold its home mortgage and relocation units, but was financially weak going into 1990. That weakness attracted the attention of Sanford Weill, whose Primerica eventually acquired Travelers. In October of 1998, Travelers and Citicorp completed a $37.4 billion merger.

History of Citicorp.

In 1791 First Bank of the United States began operation. After the War of 1812, Colonel Samuel Osgood took over the struggling New York branch of First Bank and formed City Bank of New York.

City Bank gained a national charter in 1865 to become the National City Bank of New York (NCB) and adopted the wire abbreviation: Citibank. After attaining the national charter, NCB began distributing national currency and broker government bonds. Citibank gained a reputation of conservative banking practices and was the largest New York City bank with assets totaling $29.7 million by 1893.

After the Federal Reserve Act of 1913 opened global markets to U.S. banks, Citibank opened a branch in Argentina, and purchased Britain's International Banking Corp. Concurrently, national acquisitions of Commercial Exchange Bank, Second National Bank and the 1926 purchase of People's Trust Co. aided in Citibank being the first United States bank to reach $1 billion in assets.

After World War II, Citibank expanded its corporate banking operations, and under the leadership of Walter B. Wriston, took an aggressive approach to commercial lending. Wriston developed and implemented the certificate of deposit in order to increase capital. He additionally acquired First National Bank of New York, and renamed it First National City Bank of New York. In the mid-1970s Citibank changed its name to Citicorp, and passed the former moniker on to First National City Bank of New York.

Citicorp suffered great losses on bad loans to Third World countries in the late 1970s and early 1980s. Political upheavals in Poland and Iraq caused drastic debt restructuring, while global energy prices raised interest rates too high for low-yield commercial banks to function.

Wriston retired as chairman in 1984 and was succeeded by John S. Reed. Loans to Third World countries still plagued Citicorp, and in 1991, company-

The Business

Financials

Revenue (1998): $76.4 billion

Employees (1998): 173,700

SICs / NAICS

sic 6020 - Commercial Banks

sic 6311 - Life Insurance

stock fell to a twenty year low of $8 per share. The following years bestowed repeated financial blows. Citicorp's automated mortgage system approved too many bad loans, and the Federal Reserve Bank of New York placed service restrictions to ensure Citicorp's longevity. In 1993 Citicorp finally announced a 355% earnings increase in the third quarter, due in part to the introduction of consumer pictures on credit cards for fraud protection and the announcement of a co-branded Visa credit card with Ford Motor Co.

Citicorp reorganized upper management ranks in April 1997 placing William I. Campbell over retail businesses, while Reed retained leadership of all other operations. One year later, Travelers and Citicorp announced a merger deal creating the largest global financial services institution.

Market Forces Driving the Merger

A press release issued by Citigroup summarized many reasons for the sweep of industry mergers including the Citicorp/Travelers deal. Citigroup stated: "Today major financial companies need not only customer, product and geographic diversity, but also unprecedented capital strength to deal with the economic upheavals that can occur." Rapid deregulation governing financial acquisitions, cross-selling potential, and the breakdown of geographic barriers on global markets also made the risk of becoming too big to manage worth taking for many corporate executives.

Banking mergers had increasingly challenged the relevancy of long-standing anti-trust legislation. Many banks argued that these regulations impeded competition in the exploding global market. In a joint statement, Citigroup's Chairmen Reed and Weill justified their need to merge because, "U.S. financial services companies must be able to offer customers the same array of products and services that their international competitors are now free to provide if we are to maintain our nation's leadership position around the

The Officers

Co-Chairman and Co-CEO: Sanford I. Weill

Co-Chairman and Co-CEO: John S. Reed

Vice Chairman: Deryck C. Maughan

Vice Chairman: Paul J. Collins

world. This is particularly critical given the rapid pace of consolidation by global competitors."

Increased earning potential by cutting operating costs and the ability to exploit cross-selling opportunities with customers made mergers among diversified financial institutions very attractive. The 1997 restructuring of Citicorp's management showed the firm's desire to streamline operations. Additional redundancies and weaknesses were addressed by the consolidation of the firm's international capital markets, corporate finance and multinational finance operations under its Global Banking Unit. Citicorp also sold its fixed-rate loan portfolio to Glendale Federal Bank. The proposed Travelers merger would allow Citicorp the chance to further streamline while concurrently expanding services.

Approach and Engagement

In April 1998 Travelers' Sandy Weill and Citicorp's John Reed announced the stock swap merger. The new company, called Citigroup, retained Travelers' red umbrella as its company logo. Travelers shares were converted equally into Citigroup shares. Citicorp shareholders received two-and-a-half to one share of original stock. Weill and Reed agreed to share leadership of the new firm. The price, originally $70 billion, fell to $37.4 billion after both company's stocks plummeted upon news of the deal.

Citigroup entered the NYSE under Citicorp's former symbol: CCI. Eventually the firm's stock was represented by the symbol C, which was abandoned by Chrysler after it merged with Daimler-Benz.

The Federal Reserve Board approved the merger in October, despite it being technically illegal, stating that Citigroup must, within two years, divest itself of non-banking subsidiaries that provided insurance underwriting, mutual fund distribution, and real estate investment. The deal was finalized on October 8, 1998. Congress was left to decide, after the fact, whether or not to repeal the Glass-Steagall Act of 1933 which outlawed the merger of insurance and security companies with banks.

Products and Services

The new firm's large global presence allowed it to cross-sell services. Citigroup and its subsidiaries were able to provide credit, long-term care, and life insurance, in addition to mutual funds, and commercial and personal loans. The company also entered subprime lending markets. Despite the diversity of its non-banking services, Citigroup also offered traditional branch banking and became the largest global credit card issuer. Subsidiaries Primerica and Citibank teamed up to sell checking accounts door-to-door.

In 1999 Citigroup acquired Mellon Bank's $1.9 billion credit card business. The firm's first quarter 1999 report showed a 75% increase in U.S. credit card earnings. Additional purchases included the $558 million loan portfolio and 128 branch offices from Associates First Capital Corp., and Financiero Atlas, a Chilean consumer finance company with $460 million in assets. Citigroup also bought a majority stake in Sears, Roebuck and Co.'s Homelife furniture chain. These acquisitions reflected Citigroup's desire to become a financial services supermarket.

Citigroup informed Visa in February of 1999 that it was shifting its massive credit card business to MasterCard. The main reason for the switch was due to marketing conflicts and Citigroup's demand for slashed fees. Citigroup paid Visa nearly $75 million in membership dues and fees during 1998.

Changes to the Industry

The largest impact of the Citicorp/Travelers merger is yet to be realized. The direct challenge to Depression era anti-trust regulations has forced Congress to reexamine laws never designed to handle financial services like electronic global commerce. Because European banks are able to integrate financial and securities services, U.S. firms have found it more difficult to increase their presence in the global market. If Congress deregulates banking laws, U.S. competitors will quickly follow Citigroup's lead.

When the deal was completed, Citigroup began aggressively cross-selling to current and potential customers. Financial services firms merged at a breakneck pace during the 1990s creating large—but increasingly fewer—potential merger partners. The ability to expand sales among pre-existing clients may well ensure Citigroup's longevity, especially as merger candidates become more scarce.

Testifying before the House Commerce Subcommittee on Finance, Federal Reserve Board Chairman Allen Greenspan declared his support for the affiliation of financial and insurance services. Greenspan stated that, "the long-term stability of U.S.

financial markets, and the interests of the American taxpayer would be better served by no financial modernization bill rather than one that allows the proposed new activities to be conducted by the bank." Treasury Secretary Robert Rubin, however, strongly disagreed and was supported by President Clinton.

In addition to the growth of their core consumer businesses, including credit cards, Citigroup offered customers complete financial services. With its subsidiary, Commercial Credit, the financial services firm was able to provide loans and home equity products to more than one million national customers. Co-CEO Reed drew upon his technological savvy to lead Citigroup into e-commerce and trade. To compete against discount brokerages on the Internet, Salomon Smith Barney began offering fee-based trading services.

Janet Spencer, a consultant at Delta Consulting Group, stated that Reed and Weill were "setting a new precedent. I think to run an organization, particularly one the size of Citigroup, one person can't do it alone." If Reed and Weill successfully co-manage Citigroup through the long term, they may create a new paradigm for future leaders of merging companies.

Review of the Outcome

The merger of Citicorp and Travelers Group created Citigroup, the world's largest financial services institution, with an asset base of nearly $700 billion, branches in 45 countries, and 100 million customers in 100 countries. Critics of the deal were quick to point out that the two CEOs were known for noticeably dissimilar leadership styles and personalities; however, Weill and Reed quickly proved their compatibility in December 1998, announcing 10,400 job cuts. Next the co-CEOs integrated Travelers' Salomon Smith Barney unit with Citibank's corporate banking services.

Citigroup also began divesting non-banking services to comply with U.S. laws. The elimination of service redundancies, coupled with subsequent mergers to strengthen core businesses, caused revenues to surge in the first quarter of 1999. Stock split three-for-one and gained $1.69, raising the company's quarterly dividend.

Research

"Citicorp," in *Notable Corporate Chronologies*, The Gale Group, 1999. Lists major events in the history of Citicorp.

Citigroup Home Page, available at http://www.citi.com. Official World Wide Web Home Page for Citigroup. Includes current news, press releases, financial information, and annual reports.

The Players

Chairman and CEO of Travelers Group: Sanford I. Weill. In 1960 Sanford "Sandy" Weill started a successful brokerage firm with three friends. During the 1970s Carter, Berlind, Weill and Levitt absorbed several other brokerages including Shearson, Hamill and Lob, Rhoades, Hornblower. Weill sold the brokerage firm to American Express in 1981. He eventually became the number two man at Amex under CEO James Robinson III. Weill and American Express did not meld well together. After an unsuccessful attempt to purchase Amex subsidiary, Fireman's Fund, he left the company in 1985. Thus began the low point of Weill's career, which included the public humiliation surrounding his proposed bid at becoming CEO of BankAmerica. Things turned around for Weill when he bought Control Data spin-off Commercial Credit. Shortly thereafter, Commercial Credit acquired Primerica with its Smith Barney brokerage subsidiary, and Shearson Co. In 1993 he acquired a 27% stake in Travelers Corp., eventually buying the remainder in 1994. Three years later, Weill purchased Salomon Brothers.

Chairman and CEO of Citicorp: John S. Reed. John Reed, an MIT graduate, worked his way up Citicorp's ranks to become CEO in 1984. Reed's most impressive contribution to the company was his risky decision to pursue individual consumer accounts in the late 1980s, while others sought big commercial clients. The risk paid off, and many competitors followed suit. Additionally, in the 1970s, Reed laid the systems information structure for Citicorp.

"Citigroup To Split Stock, Raise Dividend," in *The Washington Post*, 20 April 1999. Announces that Citigroup stock split during the first quarter of 1999.

Cooper, Ron. "Out Takes," in *Investment Dealers' Digest*, 12 October 1998. Discusses the various financial services news including the merger of Travelers and Citicorp.

"Greenspan: Rewrite Banking Bill," in *USA Today*, 28 April 1999. Details House Commerce Subcommittee on Finance discussions regarding revised financial services legislation.

Kaback, Hoffer. "Sandy Weill, Pragmatic Dreamer: Travelers Group CEO Sanford Weill Talks About His Approach To Dealmaking, Governance, and Life In and Out of the Spotlight," in *Directors & Boards*, Spring 1998. Interview with Sandy Weill one week after the merger was announced. Discusses successes of Weill's ability to make deals and management of board of directors.

Keegan, Jeffrey. "New Citigroup Gets OK From Fed, Now It's

Up To Congress," in *Investment Dealers' Digest*, 28 September 1998. Discusses the bill before Congress that would reform financial service laws.

Kulkosky, Edward. "Citi-Travelers Deal Magnifies Risks," in *American Banker*, 8 June 1998. Discusses analysts concerns for the Citicorp and Travelers merger.

Lamiell, Patricia "Citigroup to Slash 10,400," in *The Associated Press*, 12 December 1998. Details Citigroup's job cuts and plans for streamlining operations.

"A Merger Chain Reaction," in *US Banker*, May 1998. Summary of the mega-mergers announced in April 1998, including the Citicorp/Travelers deal.

Moyer, Liz. "Megariddle: Are Two Heads Better Than One?," in *American Banker*, 8 June 1998. Discusses the unique co-chairperson and co-CEO precedent that Reed and Weill set, and highlights benefits and pitfalls of sharing leadership.

Nash, Kim S. "Reed Shifts From Programmer To CEO," in *Computerworld*, 13 April 1998. Details John Reed's career with Citicorp, beginning as a computer programmer and rising to become CEO. Discusses the highlights of his career.

"Travelers Inc.," in *Notable Corporate Chronologies*, The Gale Group, 1999. Lists major events in the history of Travelers Group.

Zuckerman, Sam. "Citigroup's Move From Visa to MasterCard Could Reshape Industry Action Seen As Bid To Shift Power, Bank Identity from Card Associations to Banks," in *San Francisco Chronicle*, 11 February 1999. Highlights Citigroup's reasons for leaving long-time credit card company Visa for smaller competitor MasterCard.

SEAN C. MACKEY

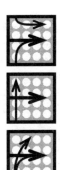

COASTAL & AMERICAN NATURAL RESOURCES

nationality: USA
date: May 15, 1985
affected: Coastal Corp., USA, founded 1955
affected: American Natural Resources Co., USA, founded 1905

Coastal Corp.
Coastal Tower, 9 Greenway Plaza
Houston, TX 77046-0995
USA

tel: (713)877-1400
fax: (713)877-6752
web: http://www.coastalcorp.com

Overview of the Acquisition

Coastal Corp. CEO Oscar Wyatt was thwarted twice in his efforts to score a major natural gas pipeline acquisition in the early 1980s. After taking measures to strengthen his Texas-based diversified energy firm for another takeover battle, Wyatt launched a $2.27 billion hostile bid in 1985 for American Natural Resources (ANR), based in Detroit, Michigan. With net income of $196 million on sales of $3.5 billion in 1984, ANR was one of the largest and most profitable interstate natural gas pipelines businesses in the U.S. When ANR initially balked at the offer, Wyatt upped the bid to $2.5 billion—twice ANR's book value—and ANR accepted. The deal increased Coastal's annual sales to more than $9 billion and its assets to more than $7 billion.

History of Coastal Corp.

In 1955, Oscar Wyatt mortgaged his automobile and used the capital to purchase an equity interest in Wymore Oil Co., which was renamed the Coastal States Oil and Gas Co. (CSOG). The new company boasted 68 miles of pipeline and 78 employees. Wyatt began making a name for himself in the energy market by purchasing gas produced by small drillers, shipping and repacking it, and selling it at an increased price. A controversial aspect of Wyatt's method was his willingness to purchase as much gas as a producer was able to pump, a tactic at odds with the industry norm, which was established to moderate purchases as a means of ensuring that oil fields would last for 20 years.

By 1958, CSOG operated 423 miles of pipeline. That year, the firm created South Texas Natural Gas Gathering Co., a wholly owned subsidiary supplying natural gas to the Transcontinental Gas Pipeline and the Texas Illinois Natural Gas Pipeline. As part of this arrangement, CSOG built a 289-mile long addition to the South Texas pipeline system. The following year, the firm entered into a joint venture to construct a liquid hydrocarbon extraction plant, enabling it to remove and sell usable petrochemicals from natural gas piped through its network.

The Business

Financials

Revenue (1998): $7.36 billion

Employees (1998): 13,200

SICs / NAICS

sic 4612 - Crude Petroleum Pipelines

sic 4613 - Refined Petroleum Pipelines

sic 1311 - Crude Petroleum & Natural Gas

sic 2911 - Petroleum Refining

sic 1231 - Anthracite Mining

sic 1221 - Bituminous Coal & Lignite-Surface

sic 1222 - Bituminous Coal-Underground

naics 211111 - Crude Petroleum and Natural Gas Extraction

naics 212113 - Anthracite Mining

naics 212111 - Bituminous Coal and Lignite Surface Mining

naics 212112 - Bituminous Coal Underground Mining

CSOG began planning construction of the 346-mile long Lo-Vaca Pipeline in Texas in 1960. Two years later, the firm created Lo-Vaca Gathering Co. to administer the newly completed Lo-Vaca Pipeline. It also acquired petroleum shipping, refining, and drilling interests of the Sinclair Oil Co. CSOG listed on the New York Stock Exchange for the first time in 1963. The firm began operating its first wholly owned hydrocarbon extraction facility the following year. By mid-decade, construction began on pipelines for gathering and transporting natural gas products to end-users, and refining accounted for 43% of revenues. The sole provider of natural gas to the Texas cities of Corpus Christi, San Antonio, Austin, Laredo, and Brownsville, CSOG acquired 965 miles of pipeline from United Gas Pipeline Co., and a further 543 miles of pipeline by purchasing the Rio Grande Valley Gas Co. for $26 million in the late 1960s. The refinery at Corpus Christi became the first in the world to make use of isobutane pyrolysis technologies.

In 1970, CSOG entered into a joint venture with Texas Utilities Co., forming North Texas Gas Gathering Systems to connect west Texas gas reserves with Dallas, Texas. The Organization of Petroleum Exporting Countries (OPEC) cut production in 1971, causing prices of petroleum products to increase by 70% in the U.S. In 1973, CSOG acquired the Colorado Interstate Gas Co. (CIGC) for $182 million, which, in

addition to gas drilling, refinery, and pipeline holdings, managed nearly 700 retail outlets. After absorbing CIGC, the firm reorganized as Coastal States Gas Corp. (CSGC), marking a shift in corporate focus away from pipeline operations. Also that year, CSGC acquired the Southern Utah Fuel Co., a coal mining concern, and the Union Petroleum Corp., which was renamed Belcher New England, Inc.

Further moves by OPEC in 1974 caused gas prices to quadruple in the U.S., leaving CSGC in serious trouble given the company's long-term contracts to supply cities with natural gas at fixed prices. Wyatt resorted to drastic measures to recover CSGC's position, at one point cutting off gas supplies to San Antonio and Austin, and seeking regulatory approval to renege on his contracts and raise the price of gas delivered to cities served by the company. In response, customers sued the company, with total damages sought reaching $1.6 billion. CSGC acquired the Belcher Oil Co., one of the largest distributors of fuel oils in the southeastern U.S., in 1977. By the end of the decade, the firm had settled its litigation by spinning off the Lo-Vaca pipeline subsidiary as Valero Energy Corp. and distributing 55% of the new company's stock.

The firm changed its name to The Coastal Corp. in 1980. Revenues topped $5 billion. Three years later, Coastal failed in its efforts to purchase Texas Gas Resources for $550 million when a white knight rescued Texas Gas. Similarly, Coastal's attempt to purchase Houston Natural Gas was thwarted in 1984. In 1985, Coastal completed a hostile takeover of American Natural Resources for $2.4 billion in cash.

The firm negotiated a deal in 1987 to acquire Libyan oil, dodging U.S. trade sanctions against Libya by having the oil sent to its refinery in Hamburg, West Germany. The following year, Coastal concluded an agreement with the China National Chemicals Import and Export Corp. (Sinochem), whereby Sinochem and Coastal shared in the operation of Coastal's Pacific Refining Co. This deal marked the first investment in U.S. energy assets by the People's Republic of China. Coastal's $2.6 billion bid in 1989 to purchase Texas Eastern was topped by an offer from Panhandle Eastern Corp.

General economic downturn adversely affected Coastal's refinery interests, as did the onset of the Persian Gulf War. Sales and profits began to rise in 1992, and construction began on the 155-mile long Empire State Pipeline. Coastal sold its interest in five production oil and gas fields in Tierra del Fuego, Argentina, for $68 million in 1994. Coastal Electric Services Co. was formed as a wholly owned subsidiary providing electrical power marketing services.

The firm also acquired an aromatics plant owned by Kemtec Petrochemical of Quebec to produce paraxylene, a fuel additive.

Due to low profit margins in refining during a period of low fuel prices, Coastal closed its Aruba refinery for maintenance in 1995. That year, the company opened a branch office in Caracas, Venezuela, in an effort to take advantage of investment opportunities in that country. The Aruba subsidiary acquired Esso Petrolera SA, formerly a division of Exxon Corp. Also, Coastal entered into a joint venture with the government of the People's Republic of China to build a power plant in Suzhou.

In 1996, the firm auctioned its coal operations to lessen corporate debt and increase focus on petroleum exploration, production, and pipeline operations. Coastal also cut back on its unbranded fuels operations in the southeastern United States; entered into a joint venture with the government of the Philippines to build a pipeline on Luzon Island; and consolidated several of its operations to create Coastal Field Services Co., a provider of natural gas gathering and processing services. In 1998, Chevron Corp., Mobil Corp., and Coastal joined forces to buy roughly $200 million in crude oil.

Market Forces Driving the Acquisition

In the early 1980s, changes in U.S. federal regulation designed to foster competition in the gas industry radically altered the competitive landscape for natural gas pipeline companies. Gas prices were deregulated, allowing gas producers the freedom to charge whatever they chose. Coastal CEO Oscar Wyatt saw the ensuing upheaval in the industry as an opportunity for quick growth. Wanting his firm to acquire existing pipeline rather than take the time to build its own, Wyatt launched a $550 million hostile bid for Texas Gas Resources in 1983. Although, the deal was foiled by the appearance of CSX Corp. as a white knight, Coastal realized a profit of $26.4 million on the transaction. The following year, Coastal's $1.3 billion bid for Houston Natural Gas Corp. was thwarted when Houston employed the Pac-Man defense and made a bid of its own for Coastal. Coastal earned a profit of $42 million on the venture. (In the competitive atmosphere promoted by deregulation, the mere threat of a takeover by Coastal sent stock prices soaring, allowing Coastal to earn a hefty return on its initial investment in a company, even after a deal went sour.)

Undaunted, Wyatt began seeking a third target. "The two failed attempts had only whetted his appetite," wrote Bruce Wasserstein in *Big Deal: The Battle for Control of America's Leading Corporations*. They had also left Wyatt well positioned for a deal; in each

The Officers

Chairman, President, CEO, and Chief Financial Officer:
    David A. Arledge

Exec. VP, Administration: Coby C. Hesse

Sr. VP and General Counsel: Carl A. Corrallo

Sr. VP, Finance: Donald H. Gullquist

Sr. VP, Marketing: Dan J. Hill

case, substantial profits from the failed deals had lined his pockets. To further increase his chances of success, "Wyatt restructured the charter of Coastal so that it was immune to takeover itself, a "Death Star" not subject to the Pac-Man defense." He also raised $600 million via junk bonds to use for acquisitions. While Coastal was readying itself for another strike, U.S. regulators had decided in 1985 to allow independent companies to sell gas, a practice previously restricted to pipeline companies. Natural gas marketing start-ups began popping up, prompting a wave of industry consolidation.

Early that year, when Coastal began eyeing takeover candidates, American Natural Gas (ANR) appeared an attractive target. With net income of $196 million on sales of $3.5 billion in 1984, ANR was one of the largest and most profitable interstate natural gas pipelines businesses in the U.S. The firm had recently spun off Michigan Natural Gas Co., and the divestiture had left ANR vulnerable to attack. The Detroit pipeline company would bolster Coastal's presence in the Midwest.

Approach and Engagement

Suspicious that Coastal Corp. was eyeing it as a takeover target, American Natural Resources (ANR) bought two million of its own shares in February of 1985 in an effort to bolster its stock prices and ward off a hostile bid. However, Coastal CEO Oscar Wyatt had already acquired a 4.4% stake in ANR when share prices were lower, and investors who were looking to make a profit had accumulated large chunks of ANR cheaply as well.

On March 4, 1985, Coastal bid $60 per share, or $2.27 billion, in cash for ANR. When ANR began soliciting white knight offers, Coastal upped its bid to $65 per share, or $2.5 billion. On March 12, ANR accepted the increased offer, and the next day, both parties met in Detroit to work out the details of the transaction. Wyatt agreed to place four ANR executives on Coastal's board. Most ANR employees were to be retained and the Detroit headquarters would remain

The Players

Chairman and CEO of Coastal Corp.: Oscar S. Wyatt, Jr. During World War II, Oscar Wyatt served the U.S. Air Force as a bomber pilot. After earning a mechanical engineering degree from Texas A&M University, Wyatt mortgaged his automobile and used the capital to purchase an equity interest in a small oil business, which he slowly transformed into a leading diversified energy firm known as The Coastal Corp. Wyatt pled guilty in 1980 to violating federal statutes banning gas price fixing and was fined $40,000. As a result of his misdeeds, Coastal was forced to pay a total of $10 million in penalties, which was partly to blame for a loss the following year of $96.4 million. Wyatt then initiated a restructuring in which corporate debt was reduced by $400 million, and greater efficiencies of production, including retooling of refineries, were realized. The efforts enabled Coastal to return to profitability in 1984. A year later, he orchestrated his firm's $2.5 billion takeover of American Natural Resources, an initially hostile deal that turned amicable. Wyatt lost out to Panhandle Eastern Corp. in a 1989 battle for Texas Eastern Corp. In the early 1990s, Wyatt drew intense public criticism by strenuously opposing U.S. involvement in the Persian Gulf crisis. In 1995, Wyatt stepped down as CEO to make room for successor David A. Arledge. He handed over the chairmanship to Arledge in 1997.

Chairman and CEO of American Natural Resources Co.: William T. McCormick, Jr. Cornell University graduate William McCormick earned a doctorate degree in nuclear engineering from the Massachusetts Institute of Technology. He was hired by American Natural Resources (ANR) in 1978 as vice president of strategic and financial planning. Four years later, he took over as president. McCormick was elected CEO and chairman of ANR in late 1984. He oversaw the firm's negotiations with Coastal Corp. in 1985. Shortly before the takeover of ANR by Coastal was completed, McCormick was tapped by Consumers Power Co. as chairman, CEO, and president.

operational for at least two years. The acquisition was completed on May 15, 1985. Although McCormick was slated to remain chairman of ANR, he resigned later in 1985 to accept a post elsewhere.

Products and Services

ANR remained one of Coastal's largest regulated natural gas systems, along with Colorado Interstate Gas Co., in 1998. Natural gas was the second-largest segment of the firm's operations that year, accounting for 18% of total sales. Activities included domestic gathering, processing, storage, and transportation. The refining, marketing, and chemicals segment of Coastal brought in 71% of sales; exploration and production, 6%; coal, 3%; and power, 2%.

Changes to the Industry

Critics of the acquisition questioned whether Coastal's willingness to take on the debt necessary to finance the purchase of ANR was wise. Coastal's Wyatt insisted his firm could pay down the debt quickly by using the increased cash flow the deal would bring, and investors seemed to agree. According to a May 1985 article in *Business Week*, despite what many analysts considered a high price paid for American Natural Resources (ANR) by Coastal, "ANR's stable cash flow allowed Wyatt to borrow nearly the full purchase prices while boosting Coastal's debt to more than 80% of capital. Despite that load, Coastal's own stock rose. Thus, the ANR deal made every other pipeline more vulnerable by showing how easily a takeover could be financed."

Before the ANR/Coastal was completed, its impact on further industry consolidation was evident. In May of 1985, InterNorth Inc. and Houston Natural Gas Corp. inked a $2.3 billion deal to create a 37,000-mile pipeline system, the longest in the U.S.

Review of the Outcome

Initially, the purchase of ANR increased Coastal's annual sales to more than $9 billion and its assets to more than $7 billion. Within three years of the acquisition, Coastal's cash flow had grown to $575 million, nearly double its total in 1985, enabling the firm to reduced its debt by roughly $1 billion.

Research

"ANR Agrees to New Coastal Bid," in *Financial Times (London)*, 15 March 1985. Announces the terms of the agreement between American Natural Resources and Coastal Corp.

"Coastal Corp.," in *Notable Corporate Chronologies*, The Gale Group, 1999. Covers major events in the history of Coastal Corp.

Coastal Corp. Home Page, available at http://www.coastal-corp.com. Official World Wide Web Page for Coastal Corp. Includes product and corporate information, news, and annual reports.

"Consumers Power Elects," in *The New York Times*, 26 September 1985. Details the career of William T. McCormick.

Ivey, Mark. "The Man Who Strikes Fear in the Heart of the Oil Patch," in *Business Week*, 6 November 1989. Discusses the career of Oscar Wyatt.

———. "The Oil Patch's Slickest Takeover Yet," in *Business Week*, 1 April 1985. Explains why Coastal pursued the purchase of ANR.

Norman, James R. "In Natural Gas, It's Buy or Be Bought," in *Business Week*, 20 May 1985. Offers an overview of the industry conditions that precluded the Coastal/ANR deal.

Wasserstein, Bruce. *Big Deal: The Battle for Control of America's Leading Corporations*, Warner Books, 1998. Offers an overview of the largest mergers in recent American corporate history.

THERA WILLIAMS

COASTAL & TEXAS EASTERN

Coastal Corp.
Coastal Tower, 9 Greenway Plaza
Houston, TX 77046-0995
USA

tel: (713)877-1400
fax: (713)877-6752
web: http://www.coastalcorp.com

date: April 1989 (canceled)
affected: Coastal Corp., USA, founded 1955
affected: Texas Eastern Corp., USA

Overview of the Acquisition

To defend itself against the $42 per share ($2.5 billion) all-cash hostile bid made by Coastal Corp. in January of 1989, Texas Eastern Corp. used a poison pill it had previously adopted to its full advantage. Recognizing that it sooner or later would likely be legally forced to dissolve its pill, Texas Eastern's board agreed to pull the pill in March. The move bought the firm plenty of time to consider other offers, while reducing the likelihood of a lawsuit requiring the pill's redemption. In February, Panhandle Eastern Corp. topped Coastal's offer with a bid of $53 per share ($3.2 billion) in cash and stock, which Texas Eastern eventually accepted.

History of Coastal Corp.

In 1955, Oscar Wyatt mortgaged his automobile and used the capital to purchase an equity interest in Wymore Oil Co., which was renamed the Coastal States Oil and Gas Co. (CSOG). The new company boasted 68 miles of pipeline and 78 employees. Wyatt began making a name for himself in the energy market by purchasing gas produced by small drillers, shipping and repacking it, and selling it at an increased price. A controversial aspect of Wyatt's method was his willingness to purchase as much gas as a producer was able to pump, a tactic at odds with the industry norm, which was established to moderate purchases as a means of ensuring that oil fields would last for 20 years.

By 1958, CSOG operated 423 miles of pipeline. That year, the firm created South Texas Natural Gas Gathering Co., a wholly owned subsidiary supplying natural gas to the Transcontinental Gas Pipeline and the Texas Illinois Natural Gas Pipeline. As part of this arrangement, CSOG built a 289-mile long addition to the South Texas pipeline system. The following year, the firm entered into a joint venture to construct a liquid hydrocarbon extraction plant, enabling it to remove and sell usable petrochemicals from natural gas piped through its network.

CSOG began planning construction of the 346-mile long Lo-Vaca Pipeline in Texas in 1960. Two years later, the firm created Lo-Vaca Gathering Co. to administer the newly completed Lo-Vaca Pipeline. It also acquired petroleum shipping, refining, and drilling interests of the Sinclair Oil Co. CSOG listed on the New York

Stock Exchange for the first time in 1963. The firm began operating its first wholly owned hydrocarbon extraction facility the following year. By mid-decade, construction began on pipelines for gathering and transporting natural gas products to end-users, and refining accounted for 43% of revenues. The sole provider of natural gas to the Texas cities of Corpus Christi, San Antonio, Austin, Laredo, and Brownsville, CSOG acquired 965 miles of pipeline from United Gas Pipeline Co., and a further 543 miles of pipeline by purchasing the Rio Grande Valley Gas Co. for $26 million in the late 1960s. The refinery at Corpus Christi became the first in the world to make use of isobutane pyrolysis technologies.

In 1970, CSOG entered into a joint venture with Texas Utilities Co., forming North Texas Gas Gathering Systems to connect west Texas gas reserves with Dallas, Texas. The Organization of Petroleum Exporting Countries (OPEC) cut production in 1971, causing prices of petroleum products to increase by 70% in the U.S. In 1973, CSOG acquired the Colorado Interstate Gas Co. (CIGC) for $182 million, which, in addition to gas drilling, refinery, and pipeline holdings, managed nearly 700 retail outlets. After absorbing CIGC, the firm reorganized as Coastal States Gas Corp. (CSGC), marking a shift in corporate focus away from pipeline operations. Also that year, CSGC acquired the Southern Utah Fuel Co., a coal mining concern, and the Union Petroleum Corp., which was renamed Belcher New England, Inc.

Further moves by OPEC in 1974 caused gas prices to quadruple in the U.S., leaving CSGC in serious trouble given the company's long-term contracts to supply cities with natural gas at fixed prices. Wyatt resorted to drastic measures to recover CSGC's position, at one point cutting off gas supplies to San Antonio and Austin, and seeking regulatory approval to renege on his contracts and raise the price of gas delivered to cities served by the company. In response, customers sued the company, with total damages sought reaching $1.6 billion. CSGC acquired the Belcher Oil Co., one of the largest distributors of fuel oils in the southeastern U.S., in 1977. By the end of the decade, the firm had settled its litigation by spinning off the Lo-Vaca pipeline subsidiary as Valero Energy Corp. and distributing 55% of the new company's stock.

The firm changed its name to The Coastal Corp. in 1980. Revenues topped $5 billion. Three years later, Coastal failed in its efforts to purchase Texas Gas Resources for $550 million when a white knight rescued Texas Gas. Similarly, Coastal's attempt to purchase Houston Natural Gas Corp. was thwarted in 1984. In 1985, Coastal completed a hostile takeover of American Natural Resources for $2.4 billion in cash.

The Business

Financials

Revenue (1998): $7.36 billion

Employees (1998): 13,200

SICs / NAICS

sic 4612 - Crude Petroleum Pipelines

sic 4613 - Refined Petroleum Pipelines

sic 1311 - Crude Petroleum & Natural Gas

sic 2911 - Petroleum Refining

sic 1231 - Anthracite Mining

sic 1221 - Bituminous Coal & Lignite-Surface

sic 1222 - Bituminous Coal-Underground

naics 211111 - Crude Petroleum and Natural Gas Extraction

naics 212113 - Anthracite Mining

naics 212111 - Bituminous Coal and Lignite Surface Mining

naics 212112 - Bituminous Coal Underground Mining

The firm negotiated a deal in 1987 to acquire Libyan oil, dodging U.S. trade sanctions against Libya by having the oil sent to its refinery in Hamburg, West Germany. The following year, Coastal concluded an agreement with the China National Chemicals Import and Export Corp. (Sinochem), whereby Sinochem and Coastal shared in the operation of Coastal's Pacific Refining Co. This deal marked the first investment in U.S. energy assets by the People's Republic of China. Coastal's $2.6 billion bid in 1989 to purchase Texas Eastern was topped by an offer from Panhandle Eastern Corp.

General economic downturn adversely affected Coastal's refinery interests, as did the onset of the Persian Gulf War. Sales and profits began to rise in 1992, and construction began on the 155-mile long Empire State Pipeline. Coastal sold its interest in five production oil and gas fields in Tierra del Fuego, Argentina, for $68 million in 1994. Coastal Electric Services Co. was formed as a wholly owned subsidiary providing electrical power marketing services. The firm also acquired an aromatics plant owned by Kemtec Petrochemical of Quebec to produce paraxylene, a fuel additive.

Due to low profit margins in refining during a period of low fuel prices, Coastal closed its Aruba refinery for maintenance in 1995. That year, the company opened a branch office in Caracas, Venezuela, in

The Officers

Chairman, President, CEO, and Chief Financial Officer:
   David A. Arledge

Exec. VP, Administration: Coby C. Hesse

Sr. VP and General Counsel: Carl A. Corrallo

Sr. VP, Finance: Donald H. Gullquist

Sr. VP, Marketing: Dan J. Hill

an effort to take advantage of investment opportunities in that country. The Aruba subsidiary acquired Esso Petrolera SA, formerly a division of Exxon Corp. Also, Coastal entered into a joint venture with the government of the People's Republic of China to build a power plant in Suzhou.

In 1996, the firm auctioned its coal operations to lessen corporate debt and increase focus on petroleum exploration, production, and pipeline operations. Coastal also cut back on its unbranded fuels operations in the southeastern United States; entered into a joint venture with the government of the Philippines to build a pipeline on Luzon Island; and consolidated several of its operations to create Coastal Field Services Co., a provider of natural gas gathering and processing services. In 1998, Chevron Corp., Mobil Corp., and Coastal joined forces to buy roughly $200 million in crude oil.

Market Forces Driving the Acquisition

Federal deregulation of natural gas prices in the early 1980s, designed to promote competition in the industry, radically altered the competitive landscape for natural gas pipeline companies. Not only were gas producers granted the freedom to charge whatever they chose, but U.S. regulators also decided in 1985 to allow independent companies to sell gas, a practice previously restricted to pipeline companies. According to Bruce Wasserstein, author of *Big Deal: The Battle for Control of America's Leading Corporations*, "companies had varying success dealing with the new environment. Some floundered around for a few years until they found their stroke. Others took advantage of the uncertainly to build strong competitive positions. A spate of deals resulted, and the industry consolidated."

Texas Eastern found itself among those firms struggling in the wake of the deregulation. Oscar Wyatt, CEO of Coastal Corp., made his first swipe at Texas Eastern in 1984, when he purchased a small stake in the firm. To defend itself against a takeover, Texas Eastern spent $1 billion for oil field and liquid

gas operation Petrolane Inc. that year. Ironically, that acquisition weakened Texas Eastern to the degree that by the mid-1980s, the firm was once again vulnerable to a hostile attack. By 1985, share prices had plummeted to 75 cents, compared to $4.35 in 1981. Although Texas Eastern brought in new management and improved its performance, by the late 1980s it was clear to CEO Dennis Hendrix that the firm would be unable to remain independent much longer.

Coastal set its sights once again on Texas Eastern in 1989. Coastal had spent the last few years integrating American Natural Resources, a natural gas pipeline business it had bought in 1985 for $2.5 billion. That acquisition boosted Coastal's cash flow, allowing the firm to continue seeking growth via acquisition. It was Texas Eastern's operations in the northeastern U.S. that were most attractive to Coastal, which had yet to penetrate that market. The addition of Texas Eastern would also position Coastal as the second-largest natural gas pipeline network in the U.S.

Approach and Engagement

On January 16, Coastal launched a hostile bid for Texas Eastern of $2.6 billion, or $42 per share, a 40% premium over the firm's current trading price of $30.25 per share. Coastal then filed a lawsuit in Houston designed to prevent Coastal from using its poison pill. The pill stipulated that in the event of a hostile offer for more than 30% of the firm's stock, all stockholders except the original bidder were able to buy stock at a considerably discounted price. Recognizing that a judge would likely force the firm to redeem its pill, Texas Eastern decided to preempt the lawsuit by agreeing to pull the pill on March 15. The move bought the firm plenty of time to consider other offers, and the likelihood of a judge forcing an earlier dissolution of the pill was slim.

Within a few weeks, Texas Eastern's shares had jumped to $50 apiece. On February 20, Panhandle Eastern Corp. moved in with a white knight bid of $53 per share, or $3.2 billion in cash and stock. Set to expire on March 20, the offer by Panhandle stipulated that the firm would pay $53 per share in cash for 80%, roughly 48.65 million share, of Texas Eastern's stock, as well as trade between 2.038 and 2.304 shares of its own stock for each remaining share of Texas Eastern. Shareholders voted to accept the new offer, and Coastal eventually removed itself from the running. Later that year, Texas Eastern was acquired by Panhandle Eastern.

Products and Services

In 1998, the refining, marketing, and chemicals segment of Coastal brought in 71% of sales. Natural gas—including domestic gathering, processing, storage, and transportation—was the second-largest segment of the firm's operations that year, accounting for 18% of total sales. Exploration and production brought in 6%; coal, 3%; and power, 2%.

Changes to the Industry and Review of the Outcome

After he the lost the battle for Texas Eastern to Panhandle Eastern, Coastal CEO Wyatt "decided natural gas properties had become overpriced in the market. He turned to investing money in building new pipes and expanding Coastal's network internally," wrote Wasserstein. Coastal's defeat later appeared to many analysts as a boon for the firm, as hazardous land mines discovered on Texas Eastern properties caused Panhandle's stock to tumble 60% in the year following the deal.

In the early 1990s, Panhandle struggled under the debt it had taken on to finance its purchase of Texas Eastern. Panhandle had increased its debt to $5 billion, planning to pay that down by selling off $1.7 billion in Texas Eastern assets. However, increased competition and a natural gas price free-fall eroded profits, preventing the firm from paying off the debt as quickly as it wished.

Research

Andrews, N. "Coastal Bid for Texas Eastern," in *The New York Times*, 17 January 1989. Announces Coastal's hostile bid for Texas Eastern and discusses Wall Street's reaction to the bid.

Coastal Corp. Home Page, available at http://www.coastal-corp.com. Official World Wide Web Page for Coastal Corp. Includes product and corporate information, news, and annual reports.

"Coastal Corp.," in *Notable Corporate Chronologies*, The Gale Group, 1999. Covers major events in the history of Coastal Corp.

Hayes, Thomas C. "Texas Eastern Sets Sale of $1.4 Billion in Assets," in *The New York Times*, 2 March 1989. Details moves by Texas Eastern to smooth its purchase by Panhandle Eastern.

Ivey, Mark. "The Lasso Is Tightening around Texas Eastern," in *Business Week*, 30 January 1989. Explains why Texas Eastern may not be able to remain independent.

The Players

Chairman and CEO of Coastal Corp.: Oscar S. Wyatt, Jr. During World War II, Oscar Wyatt served the U.S. Air Force as a bomber pilot. After earning a mechanical engineering degree from Texas A&M University, Wyatt mortgaged his automobile and used the capital to purchase an equity interest in a small oil business, which he slowly transformed into a leading diversified energy firm known as The Coastal Corp. Wyatt pled guilty in 1980 to violating federal statutes banning gas price fixing and was fined $40,000. As a result of his misdeeds, Coastal was forced to pay a total of $10 million in penalties, which was partly to blame for a loss the following year of $96.4 million. Wyatt then initiated a restructuring in which corporate debt was reduced by $400 million, and greater efficiencies of production, including retooling of refineries, were realized. The efforts enabled Coastal to return to profitability in 1984. A year later, he orchestrated his firm's $2.5 billion takeover of American Natural Resources Co., an initially hostile deal that turned amicable. Wyatt lost out to Panhandle Eastern Corp. in a 1989 battle for Texas Eastern Corp. In the early 1990s, Wyatt drew intense public criticism by strenuously opposing U.S. involvement in the Persian Gulf crisis. In 1995, Wyatt stepped down as CEO to make room for successor David A. Arledge. He handed over the chairmanship to Arledge in 1997.

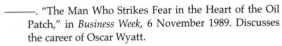

———. "The Man Who Strikes Fear in the Heart of the Oil Patch," in *Business Week*, 6 November 1989. Discusses the career of Oscar Wyatt.

McCormick, Jay. "Panhandle Offers $3.2 Billion for Texas Eastern," in *USA Today*, 21 February 1989. Details the white knight offer made by Panhandle Eastern.

Wasserstein, Bruce. *Big Deal: The Battle for Control of America's Leading Corporations*, Warner Books, 1998. Offers an overview of the largest mergers in recent American corporate history.

THERA WILLIAMS

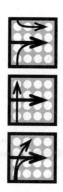

COLUMBIA HEALTHCARE &
HOSPITAL CORP. OF AMERICA

Columbia/HCA Healthcare Corp.
One Park Plaza
PO Box 550
Nashville, Tennessee 37202-0550
USA

tel: (615)327-9551
fax: (615)320-2331
web: http://www.columbia-hca.com

nationality: USA
date: February 1994
affected: Columbia Healthcare Corp., USA, founded 1987
affected: Hospital Corp. of America, USA, founded 1960

Overview of the Merger

The February 1994 joining of Columbia Healthcare Corp. and Hospital Corp. of America created Columbia/HCA Healthcare Corp., the largest hospital chain and healthcare provider in the nation. The $5.7 billion stock swap deal created an industry leader that owned and operated 190 hospitals with over 42,000 beds in 26 states and two foreign countries. According to Columbia leader Richard Scott and Hospital Corp. head Thomas Frist, the deal was in response to anticipated healthcare reform. "The direction of healthcare delivery in the future will focus on quality results and cost efficient operations. We believe this transaction strengthens our efforts towards this goal," the two announced in a statement following the merger. Combined annual revenues were estimated at $10 billion, and the new company was expected to save $130 million in purchasing expenditures within three to five years after the merger.

History of Columbia Corp.

A $250,000 investment made by Richard L. Scott and Richard Rainwater gave birth to the healthcare giant, Columbia Healthcare Corp., in 1987. Scott had been eager to enter the healthcare industry and to create a national healthcare provider network, but had been unsuccessful until he teamed up with Rainwater. With help of Rainwater's investment firm and Citicorp, the pair was able to purchase two El Paso hospitals for $60 million. Both of the hospitals were poorly run and in dire need of reform and repair. Scott and Rainwater started to repair the damage both to the buildings themselves and within the management structure. They earned the goodwill of the hospitals' physicians as well. Accomplishing the restructuring of the two hospitals led to the formation of the El Paso Healthcare System, Ltd. The group of physician investors who participated in the deal eventually gained a 40% share in EPHS. This marked the beginning of the trend in physician shareholding.

Just five months after its formation, Columbia began to consolidate its El Paso operations. EPHS purchased the Landmark Medical Center and the Stanton

Medical Building. The Landmark was operating in the red, which prompted Scott to close it and transfer its patients and equipment to existing hospitals that they owned. The move increased revenue from $3.5 million to $8.9 million in 1988. EPHS went on to open Sun Towers Behavioral Health Center, an 80-bed free-standing psychiatric facility in December of 1988. The behavioral health program from Sun Towers Hospital was transferred to the new facility, expanding the bed count. In the first year of operations, the facility recorded earnings of $2.5 million and increased the average daily census from 11 to 45 patients. This put them even closer to their goal of becoming a full-service operation.

EPHS continued to expand and opened a Lifecare Center, which combined an outpatient wellness center as well as a cardiopulmonary rehabilitation facility. In 1989, the firm started a medical service program called One Source, which it marketed to local employers. The program gave discounts to members at EPHS facilities. In just one year, One Source had over 15,000 members and revenue topping $6.5 million. By the end of the 1980s, EPHS was riding the wave of success as its average daily census increased from 174 to 303 patients, and in two years, revenue skyrocketed from $113 million to $135 million.

Columbia continued to flourish into the 1990s as EPHS acquired two diagnostic imaging centers, began construction on a 296,000-square-foot medical building, and planned for the development of an oncology center. They broke into the Miami market, as well as Corpus Christi, Texas, by purchasing the Victoria hospital and four others. Along Scott's trail of triumph, he gained respect and forged limited partnerships with physician investors. Columbia was later criticized for its strategy of forming relationships with physicians as investors due to concerns that they might have a tendency to over-treat patients in an efforts to increase their profits.

Scott took Columbia public after its acquisition of Smith Laboratories and Sutter Corp. Columbia also entered into a joint venture with Medical Care America of Dallas to build a $50 million hospital in Corpus Christi. Revenues had nearly reached $500 million when Columbia made a $22 million cash purchase of HEI Corp. Columbia then acquired Coral Reef hospital through a limited partnership for $18 million in cash and notes and Southside Community Hospital for $4.5 million. With the $185 million acquisition of Basic American Medical, Columbia now had 24 hospitals, over $1 billion in assets, and revenue of $800 million.

By 1993, Scott was itching to launch Columbia as a national healthcare provider. The announcement of

The Business

Financials

Revenue (1998): $18.68 billion

Employees (1997): 295,000

SICs / NAICS

sic 8062 - General Medical & Surgical Hospitals

sic 8063 - Psychiatric Hospitals

the planned merger with Galen Healthcare would make Columbia the largest non-governmental hospital chain in the United States. The $3.2 billion stock-swap merger raised revenues to over $5 billion, brought the number of hospitals to 94, introduced the firm to 15 new markets, and gave it a presence in 19 states, as well as England and Switzerland. One month later, Scott stunned the industry by announcing his intentions to merge with Hospital Corporation of America. The companies united in February of 1994 in a stock swap worth $5.7 billion and formed Columbia/HCA Healthcare Corp., the largest hospital chain in the United States.

The newly merged firm began to eye the non-profit market. Joint ventures included Cedars Medical Center of Miami and university medical schools and teaching hospitals including the University of Miami, Tulane, Emory, the Medical College of Virginia, and the Medical University of South Carolina. In May of 1994, Columbia/HCA purchased Medical Care America, Inc., the largest provider of outpatient surgery services, for $860 million. In October of that year, Healthtrust was acquired for $5.6 billion. With 311 facilities, Columbia/HCA became the 12th largest employer in the United States, and revenues exceeded $14 billion.

By 1996, the firm had grown to 340 hospitals, 125 outpatient surgery centers, and 182 home health agencies. The firm's aggressive approach to growth started to have a negative impact on its image. The Columbia/HCA empire began to falter as the government launched a federal investigation into the Medicare billing practices of the company. Scott was forced to step down as CEO, and Frist took command in 1997. He immediately announced a new focus on patients, rather than mergers and acquisitions. Frist also ended the practice of selling physicians ownership stakes in Columbia/HCA's hospitals. In an effort to focus on core operations, he began divesting the firm's home care business and almost three dozen of its outpatient surgery centers.

The Officers

Chairman and CEO: Thomas F. Frist, Jr.

President and Chief Operating Officer: Jack Bovender, Jr.

VP, Finance and Treasurer: David G. Anderson

VP, Operations and Finance: Rosalyn S. Elton

Sr. VP, Administration and Human Resources: Neil
Hemphill

History of Hospital Corp. of America

The Hospital Corp. of America got its start in 1960 when Thomas Frist, Sr., along with ten investors, built the Park View Hospital in Nashville, Tennessee. Eight years later, the company was formed to own and manage hospitals with Frist, Sr., as president and Jack C. Massey as chairman. In 1969, the company went public with stock that rose from $18 to $40 per share in the very first day of trading. The next year, John A. Hill became president and Frist, Sr., became vice chairman and chief medical officer. HCA began assembling a board of governors, with prominent physicians from the HCA network of hospitals.

By 1973, the Hospital Corp. of America became the world's largest publicly owned hospital-management company, with 51 hospitals and 7,900 beds. That same year, it entered the international market with the management of the King Faisal Specialist Hospital and Research Centre in Riyadh, Saudi Arabia. The company continued to grow as it expanded into Central America and launched its management contracts division, HCA Management Corp. and Parthenon Insurance Corp. The firm celebrated its 10th anniversary in 1978 with ownership of 100 hospitals and 28,000 employees. Thomas F. Frist, Jr., was named president and CEO of HCA and Donald S. MacNaughton was appointed chairman and CEO.

The early 1980s were marked by growth for HCA. It acquired General Health Services and Hospital Affiliates International, gaining control of about one-fifth of all privately owned U.S. hospitals. Revenues exceeded $4 billion, and the firm also bought Kansas-based Wesley Medical Center. By 1987, reorganization plans were in the works in order to streamline HCA, which was then worth $4.9 billion. The firm sold 104 rural general hospitals to a new employee-owned company called Health-Trust. In March of 1989, Frist, Jr., and other senior managers took the company private via a $4.9 billion leveraged buyout in an effort to restructure without fear of takeover. This reform led to a new and improved HCA that went public in February of 1992.

The following year, HCA was back on track with sales of $4.2 billion and 68,000 employees. In an effort to pare down its debt, the firm began to sell its psychiatric centers—which were a drain on profits and small contributors of revenue—to better focus on its 73 market-leading hospitals. In 1994, HCA announced its plan to merge with Columbia Healthcare Corp. to form a new company, Columbia/HCA, the largest hospital chain in the United States, with $10 billion in annual revenues.

Market Forces Driving the Merger

Healthcare reform was causing a consolidation trend in the hospital industry. The need for quality, cost efficient care forced many companies to form alliances or consolidate to remain competitive. Many merged to create negotiating leverage for managed care contracts. The merger of Columbia Healthcare Corp. and HCA proved to government regulators that the free market could provide healthcare reform faster and more efficiently than the government.

In the early 1990s, hospitals were scurrying to form relationships that would keep them afloat in the ever-changing industry. They knew in order to survive they would have to provide a competitively priced range of services. There was a sink or swim mentality among the smaller hospitals, which would have to forge bonds with other providers in order to supply the range of services needed to remain a player. Outpatient surgery facilities, home health care, and extensive physician affiliations were all needed for a firm to successfully secure contracts from HMOs and insurers. Managed care companies and HMOs were directing patients to select hospitals that could provide the most cost-efficient services. "Health care reform is leading companies to the decision that they have to make acquisitions if they want to increase volume. The only way to combat the profit slippage that will result from lower prices dictated by reform is to go out and acquire. It's a proven, reliable way to increase revenue," said Kurt Kammer, an analyst in Washington, D.C. Although reform was taking place throughout the healthcare industry, hospitals were the hardest hit segment. Fewer medical procedures required overnight stay, which meant hospitals had more beds than they actually needed.

Approach and Engagement

Due the reform shaking up the healthcare industry, HCA leader Frist was looking for a way to remain an industry leader. He sought out Columbia Healthcare Corp. for its strong presence and the leadership style of president, Richard J. Scott. "At this stage in my career, I don't have the energy to take

HCA to the next level", said Frist. He felt that Scott's track record of remarkable success would benefit HCA.

The merger, which took place in February of 1994, created Columbia/HCA Healthcare Corporation, an $11 billion company. The new company owned and operated 197 hospitals in 26 states. The strategy employed by Frist and Scott was to attract more patients in an effort to bring down unit prices and then use those lower prices to attract even more patients. With larger volumes Scott was sure that they would be able to offer lower prices with better quality. The large company would also be able to negotiate discounts with suppliers since they would be purchasing over $2 billion a year in supplies. These discounts were projected to save $80 to $100 million per year. Frist and Scott planned on becoming the largest, most competitive healthcare giant in the industry.

Products and Services

With over 190 hospitals and 42,000 beds in 26 states and two foreign countries, the merger that formed Columbia/HCA created the nation's largest healthcare provider. The newly merged company was able to provide a broad range of services from birthing rooms to outpatient surgery centers to home health care. Columbia/HCA wanted to provide everything a customer would need in one location so that customer would not have to look elsewhere for services. It also increased ventures with teaching hospitals and medical schools in an effort to become a full service provider.

Columbia/HCA also made things easier and more efficient for insurers and HMOs by offering services in many markets where insurers' national clients had operations. They were set on creating local networks city by city so that healthcare buyers would see them as the logical provider; this would be a major trump card when negotiating contracts with them. "Our goal is to create a vehicle in which they (the insurers and HMOs) don't have to talk to as many people," said Scott.

Changes to the Industry

The Clinton health plan that would cut Medicaid and Medicare by almost $3 billion in the next five years took its toll on hospital revenue in the industry. Proposed caps on premium increases were also pressuring hospitals to cut costs or go under. Health care reform was here to stay due to the changing state and federal legislation and the pressure of managed care. Change was a necessity if companies were going to remain a part of the industry, and cutting costs were going to have to be part of any corporate plans.

The Players

Chief Executive Officer of Columbia Healthcare Corp.: Richard Scott. After graduating from the University of Missouri and Southern Methodist Law School, Richard Scott launched his career in his early twenties at the Dallas, Texas-based law firm of Johnson & Gibbs. While working at the firm, Scott realized that healthcare institutions were typically undervalued, a discovery that prompted him to consider a career change. After putting his law career on the back burner, Scott began to negotiate the purchase of Hospital Corporation of America. After the deal fell apart in 1987, he sought out Richard Rainwater to form Columbia Healthcare Corporation that year. Columbia became an aggressive force in the healthcare industry as Scott began to mow down the competition with merger after merger. He saw potential in the changing industry as his company grew from two El Paso hospitals to national healthcare provider status in 1993. That same year, he shocked the industry again by announcing the plans to merge with Hospital Corporation of America. He was named CEO of the new company, Columbia/HCA Healthcare Corporation, the largest hospital chain the U.S. In 1997, Scott was indicted in the investigation of illegal medicare billing practices and was forced to resign.

President and CEO of Hospital Corp. of America: Dr. Thomas F. Frist, Jr. After obtaining his B.A. from Vanderbilt University in Nashville and M.D. degree in 1965 from the Washington University of Medicine in St. Louis, Thomas Frist co-founded the Hospital Corporation of America with his father and Jack C. Massey. The company that had started from just one hospital had grown to see revenues of over $29 million per year and in 1978, Frist was named president and chief operating officer of HCA. The 1990s marked a season of change for Frist and HCA with the merger of Columbia and HCA in February of 1994. Frist served as chairman of the combined company, Columbia/HCA. His position changed to vice chairman after another merger—with HealthTrust, Inc.—took place in 1995. In 1997, Frist took over Columbia/HCA as chairman and CEO when Richard Scott was forced to step down due to a federal investigation into billing practices.

As major changes were happening on a large scale in the industry around them, Columbia/HCA had to contend with major changes of its own. Its peers began to grow cold to Scott's arrogance and business practices. "Some hospitals that are considered inefficient competitors will be acquired simply to eliminate them. We've bought eight hospitals in the last five years solely to shut them down and consolidate them into our operations," Scott said. It was this mentality that began the downfall of the reputation of Columbia/HCA. As quality, cost efficient patient care was becoming a must in the industry, Scott focused on growth and dominance instead of his customers and patients. His reign finally ended in 1997 when he was indicted on fraudulent billing practices by the federal government.

Thomas Frist, Jr., took over and began to reform the company. Instead of focusing on national branding, the company would focus on community patient care. It halted $300 million worth of new hospital building projects. "Patients are the reason we are all here. It is caring for them that unites every one of us," Frist said. "We are no longer in the branding business. We are in the people business. Compassion, kindness, honesty, integrity, fairness, loyalty, respect and dignity are our essential and timeless values." Frist developed a plan to restructure the company with major changes including eliminating annual cash incentive compensation for all employees, selling the company's home care division, and discontinuing ownership sales in hospitals to physicians.

Review of the Outcome

When the $5.7 billion stock-swap merger of Columbia/HCA was completed, the largest hospital chain was formed in the United States. With revenues over $10 billion, an increase in stock value, and an increase in employees from 157,000 in 1994 to 240,000 in 1995, Columbia/HCA was playing the healthcare reform game and winning. Columbia emerged as the dominant partner, grabbing seven of the eleven board seats, with Richard J. Scott at the helm. His aggressive corporate culture dominated the new company in its first several years.

Research

Columbia/HCA Healthcare Corp. Home Page, available at http://www.columbia-hca.com. Official World Wide Web Home Page for Columbia/HCA Healthcare Corp. Includes current and archived news, detailed financial information, and information on its leadership team.

"Columbia/HCA Healthcare Corp.," in *International Directory of Company Histories*, Vol. 15, St. James Press: 1996. Narrates the history of Columbia/HCA.

"Columbia/HCA Healthcare Corp.," in *Notable Corporate Chronologies*, The Gale Group, 1999. Lists major events in the history of Columbia/HCA.

"Columbia, HCA Merge into Largest Hospital Chain," in *American Medical News*, 25 October 1993. Offers an overview of the Columbia/HCA merger and others in the industry.

Gold, Jacqueline S. "Hospital Corp. of America: Deleveraging is Beautiful," in *Financial World*, 28 September 1993. Explains HCA's re-entry into the public market.

Foubister, Vida; Tokarski, Cathy. "Dr. Frist Seeks Doctors' Help in Rebuilding Columbia/HCA," in *American Medical News*, 8 September 1997. Explains Frist's plans for Columbia/HCA after the forced resignation of Scott.

Freany, Margie. "Reform May Force Hospital Mergers," in *Baltimore Business Journal*, 22 October 1993. Explains recent trends in mergers within the hospital industry.

"Frist Launches a New Cultural Direction for Columbia/HCA," in *PR Newswire*, 3 November 1997. Explains Frist's plans for change within Columbia/HCA.

Limbacher, Patricia B. "First 100 Days Busy for Frist; What Comes Next?," in *Modern Healthcare*, 3 November 1997. An overview of Frist's first 100 days in office.

McCue, Michael J. "A Premerger Profile of Columbia and HCA Hospitals," in *Health Care Management Review*, Spring 1996. Discusses the reasons behind the merger of Columbia and HCA.

Tanner, Lisa. "Columbia's Richard Scott Well Positioned For Reform," in *South Florida Business Journal*, 9 July 1993. Details on reform in the industry.

Walsh, Matt. "More Patients, Please," in *Forbes*, 10 October 1994. Comments on Frist's desire to merge with Columbia.

CHRISTINA M. STANSELL

COMPAQ COMPUTER & DIGITAL EQUIPMENT

nationality: USA
date: June 11, 1998
affected: Compaq Computer Corp., USA, founded 1982
affected: Digital Equipment Corp., USA, founded 1957

Compaq Computer Corp.
20555 State Hwy. 249
Houston, TX 77070
USA

tel: (281)370-0670
fax: (281)514-2656
web: http://www.compaq.com

Overview of the Merger

The computer industry saw the largest merger in its corporate history completed in June of 1998 when Compaq Computer paid $8.45 billion in cash and stock for Digital Equipment Corp. Compaq, mainly a manufacturer and marketer of personal computers, became one of IBM's biggest competitors after it swallowed Digital Equipment's more diverse products and services, including its Alpha architecture, Digital Unix operating system, and 22,000 consultants. The merger was almost immediately labeled a success by industry analysts, but problems with the integration of Digital Equipment and Tandem Computers—acquired by Compaq for $4 billion in 1997— eventually led to the ousting of eight-year Compaq chairman and CEO Eckhard Pfeiffer.

History of Compaq Computer Corp.

Compaq Computer was founded in 1982 by Joseph R. Canion, James Harris, and William H. Murto, three senior managers from Texas Instruments, along with Ben Rosen, president of Sevin-Rosen Partners, a high technology venture capital firm in Houston. The following year, the company launched its initial public offering on NASDAQ, raising $67 million. Compaq's revenues reached $111.2 million, a record in U.S. business history for first-year sales.

In 1984, Compaq's personal computers were introduced in Europe. The firm's speed to market of 6 to 9 months, rather than the industry average of 12 to 18 months, enabled it to introduce and ship the Deskpro PC six months after IBM announced the idea for it. Annual sales, a total of $329 million, set another record. Compaq shipped 149,000 PCs worldwide that year and entered the European market with companies in Germany, the United Kingdom, and France.

Intel and Compaq began working together to develop a new microprocessor in 1985. A year later, Compaq joined the Fortune 500; it was the only company to do so in less than four years of operation. In 1987, the first European manufacturing facility opened in Scotland. The collaboration between Intel and Compaq resulted in Compaq's introduction of the Deskpro 386, which performed over three times faster than IBM's fastest PC. The following year, the company introduced its

The Business

Financials

Revenue (1998): $31.16 billion

Employees (1998): 71,000

SICs / NAICS

sic 3571 - Electronic Computers

sic 5734 - Computer & Software Stores

sic 3674 - Semiconductors & Related Devices

sic 7372 - Prepackaged Software

sic 7375 - Information Retrieval Services

naics 334111 - Electronic Computer Manufacturing

naics 334413 - Semiconductor and Related Device Manufacturing

naics 514191 - On-Line Information Services

laptop computer, the SLT/286, which became an immediate success. Compaq was also added to the Standard & Poor's Composite Index of 500 stocks that year.

By the end of the 1980s, Compaq held the number-two position in the European business PC market. In 1989, the firm introduced its first notebook PC, the Compaq LTE; acquired the Wang facility in Stirling, Scotland, for service operations; continued expansion in Latin America and launched the first Compaq server using Extended Industry Standard Architecture (EISA), a hardware design that Compaq developed to increase the speed of PCs and enable them to perform more complex operations.

In 1990, Compaq opened new subsidiaries in Austria, Finland, and Hong Kong, and authorized dealers in Germany, Hungary, the former Yugoslavia, Argentina, Mexico, and Trinidad. International sales accounted for over half of the company's total revenue. Compaq entered the Japanese marketplace in 1991. That year, the firm introduced a new line of computers, the Deskpro/M, and the first worldwide systems Integrator, EDS. A restructuring resulted in a 14% reduction in workforce and the consolidation of operations into two divisions: the Personal Computer Division and the Systems Division.

After losing $70 million, company co-founder and CEO Canion was forced to resign; he was replaced by executive vice president Eckhard Pfeiffer. The last remaining company founder, Harris, also left the company. Eight of the company's 10 most important dealer chains merged into four, prompting Compaq to authorize computer consultants and discount chains to sell its products. In 1992, sixteen new products, including the company's first printer product, were introduced. Layoffs continued and a computer training program was introduced in China. Sales of desktop PCs accounted for almost 90% of Compaq's revenue.

Compaq and PictureTel agreed to collaborate on video conferencing in 1993. The following year, Compaq began placing warning labels on its keyboards in response to growing concerns about repetitive-stress injuries among computer users. The firm also introduced Compaq Contura 400, a mid-range notebook computer. In 1996, Compaq stepped up the use of its human-factors laboratory to refine keyboards and pointing devices and generally make its products easier to use. The firm paid $4 billion for Tandem Computers Inc. in 1997. Less than a year later, merger negotiations began with Digital Equipment Corp. The $8.45 billion deal was completed in June of 1998.

Compaq launched an effort to increase its Internet presence in 1999. The firm announced plans for an initial public offering of Internet search engine unit Alta Vista, previously part of Digital Equipment, and purchased electronic commerce service Shopping.com for $220 million to make Alta Vista more competitive with Yahoo Inc. and Lycos.

History of Digital Equipment Corp.

Computer company Digital Equipment Corp. was founded in 1957 by two MIT engineers, Kenneth Olsen and Harlan Anderson, in Maynard, Massachusetts. The following year, the new company introduced its systems modules. In 1960, Digital Equipment launched the PDP-1, the world's first small, interactive computer. DECUS, the Digital Equipment Computer Users Society, was established in 1961. It became the world's largest computer society dedicated to one manufacturer.

In 1963, the first European sales and service office opened in Munich, Germany. The first Canadian sales office opened in Ottawa, Ontario. Digital Equipment also introduced the world's first minicomputer, the PDP-5, designed by Gordon Bell, and the PDP-1 operating system, the first timesharing system. Subsidiaries in Australia and the United Kingdom were formed in 1964. That year, Digital Equipment unveiled its first 36-bit computer, the PDP-6. The firm launched the PDP-8, the world's first mass-produced minicomputer, in 1965.

Digital Equipment launched its initial public stock offering in 1966. During the late 1960s, manufacturing operations began in San German, Puerto Rico; Japanese headquarters opened in Tokyo; European headquarters opened in Geneva, Switzerland; and stock split three-for-one. Production started at a new plant in Westfield, Massachusetts, for peripheral and metal products in 1970. The firm also began trading on the New York Stock Exchange that year. Products launched during the 1970s included MPS, the firm's first microprocessor; the LSI-11, the firm's first 16-bit microcomputer, the 36-bit DECSYSTEM-20, the lowest-priced general purpose timesharing system on the market; and VAX-11/780, the first member of the VAX computer family. Stock split three-for-one in 1976, and by 1977, sales exceeded $1 billion.

In 1978, Digital Equipment's first retail computer store opened in Manchester, New Hampshire. Two years later, the firm opened a software engineering facility in Nashua, New Hampshire, and introduced VAX-11/750, the second member of the VAX family and the industry's first Large Scale Integration (LSI) 32-bit minicomputer. In 1982, the third member of the 32-bit computer family, the VAX-11/730, was launched, as was a complete range of personal computers.

During the 1980s, Digital Equipment expanded into Brazil via an agreement with Elebra Computadores. The firm also became the first company to register a new semiconductor chip, the MicroVAX II chip, under the Semiconductor Protection Act of 1984. Stock split two-for-one in 1986. That year, Digital Equipment purchased Trilogy Technology Corp. In 1987, Cray Research, Inc., the leading producer of supercomputers, agreed to market and develop products that linked its computer environments with those of Digital Equipment. A similar agreement with Apple Computer, Inc. was inked in 1988.

By the end of the 1980s, international sales accounted for over half of all revenues. In 1990, Digital Equipment established its first direct investment in Eastern Europe, Digital Equipment (Hungary) Ltd., a joint venture company based in Budapest. More than 20 new computers, peripherals, and software products were introduced that year, and the firm acquired the financial services business of Data Logic, Ltd., a leading London-based supplier of UNIX-based software for trading rooms.

Digital Equipment and Asea Brown Boveri Inc. in 1991 formed a new company, EA Information Systems, Inc., based on ABB's Engineering Automation Software Division, a leading supplier of 3-D plant design. Digital and Microsoft announced an

The Officers

Chairman and Acting CEO: Benjamin M. Rosen

Vice Chairman: Frank P. Doyle

Vice Chairman: Robert Ted Enloe III

Sr. VP and Group General Manager, Enterprise Computing: John T. Rose

Sr. VP and Group General Manager, Commercial PC Group: Michael J. Winkler

Sr. VP and Group General Manager, Worldwide Sales & Marketing: Michael D. Heil

alliance allowing Microsoft Windows users to retrieve and exchange data with local area network servers running Digital PATHWORKS software. The firm also acquired the Information Systems Division of Philips Electronics and established Digital Equipment Enterprise to manage the small and medium enterprise market in Europe.

Digital Equipment and Intel Corp. forged a major distribution relationship in 1992. The company acquired BASYS Automation Systems and 800-SOFT-WARE, one of the largest PC software and accessories distribution companies. In 1994, Digital Equipment announced plans to eliminate at least 20,000 jobs over the next two years. In a restructuring aimed at regaining a competitive edge, the firm divested its contract manufacturing unit to SIC Systems Inc. and refocused on core capabilities.

The European Commission investigated Digital Equipment's offices in Britain, Germany, and the Netherlands in 1995 after receiving reports of anti-competitive practices. In 1996, the firm collaborated with MCI and Microsoft Corp. to develop e-mail, group-ware business communications, and other services to manage corporate data networks or Intranets. In the largest acquisition in the computer industry, Digital Equipment was acquired by Compaq Computer Corp. for $8.45 billion in 1998.

Market Forces Driving the Merger

Second to none in news making deals in the computer industry during the late 1990s was Compaq Computer Corp., which completed record setting acquisitions two years in a row. Compaq's $4 billion purchase of Tandem Computers Inc., the largest transaction in the computer hardware industry in 1997, doubled Compaq's sales force and secured Windows NT server technology, which allowed the company to

The Players

Chairman and CEO of Compaq Computer Corp.: Eckhard Pfeiffer. After Compaq Computer lost $70 million in 1991, company co-founder and CEO Joseph R. Canion was forced to resign; this opened the door for executive vice president Eckhard Pfeiffer, who had worked for the firm since 1983. Pfeiffer was lauded for parlaying the $3 billion firm into a $20 billion powerhouse by the late 1990s. He steered the firm's $4 billion purchase of Tandem Computers in 1997 and its $8.45 billion takeover of Digital Equipment Corp. in 1998. When Compaq had difficulty digesting its new holdings, however, the board ousted Pfeiffer in April of 1999.

Chairman and CEO of Digital Equipment Corp.: Robert B. Palmer. Texas Tech University graduate Robert Palmer founded Mostek, a semiconductor operation in the 1970s. His firm was later purchased by United Technologies. Digital Equipment appointed Palmer head of semiconductor operations in 1985. At Digital Equipment, Palmer eventually earned top spots as both president and CEO of Digital. He was appointed chairman of the corporation in 1995.

begin offering clients more fully integrated products. Less than a year later, Compaq and Digital Equipment Corp. announced their $8.45 billion merger, the largest ever in the computer industry. Both deals reflected the growing trends in the marketplace for consolidation and diversification, which were the result of growing demand for fully integrated products and the increasing tendency, particularly on the part of business clients, to seek dealers who could services all of their computing needs.

According to an acquisition investment bank based in New York, worldwide mergers and acquisitions increased in all major computer industry sectors during 1997. During the year, 4,040 transactions, valued at a total of $242.8 billion, were completed, measuring a 25% increase in transactions and a 17% growth in transaction value from 1996. A November 1998 article in *Forbes* states that Digital Equipment, "once number two only to IBM in the computer trade, had been slipping for years." To remain competitive in the rapidly consolidating industry, the company needed to merge. At the same time, Compaq needed to broaden its product offerings to reduce its dependence on personal computer sales. By acquiring Digital Equipment, Compaq would gain access to the firm's $3 billion storage data operations, as well its $6 billion computer services unit.

Approach and Engagement

On January 26, 1998, Compaq launched a $9.6 billion takeover bid for Digital Equipment. Shareholders approved the deal in June, as did the FCC. The transaction was finalized on June 11, 1998, when Compaq issued a $4.5 billion cash payment to Digital Equipment, as well as 141 million Compaq shares. For each Digital Equipment common share, stockholders received $30 in cash and .945 shares of Compaq stock. Digital common stock stopped trading on the New York Stock Exchange that day. To finance the deal, Compaq took a $5.4 billion charge.

Products and Services

In 1997, commercial PCs accounted for 37% of total sales at Compaq; enterprise products brought in another 37%; consumer PCs secured 16%; and services garnered the remaining 13%. Products included desktop PCs, including the Presario, Prosignia, and Deskpro lines; notebook computers, including the Armada, Presario, and Prosignia lines; the Alpha operating system and Alpha chips; the C-Series of handheld computers; monitors; networking and communications equipment; parallel-processing computers; printers; servers and server software; storage products, and workstations. Compaq also offered the following services: consulting; outsourcing; project management; system design; and system integration.

After the merger, Compaq's discontinued Digital's personal computer line. The firm sought to move beyond making and selling personal computers and to offer increased computer services to clients. In 1999, Compaq began shifting its focus to Internet related ventures such as its Alta Vista search engine unit and the recently acquired Shopping.com.

Changes to the Industry

Compaq's purchase of Digital Equipment created a worldwide leader in multi-user storage systems and a new noteworthy competitor of IBM. The firm was the largest personal computer maker in the world and the third largest computer seller. According to an August 1998 article in *Computer Dealer News*, the deal transformed Compaq "overnight into a full-line computer supplier." The piece goes on to explain that "the only other company with an indisputable claim to that distinction is IBM. Hewlett-Packard Co. can make a case for it, but even HP, while its name carries weight in the midrange and PC arenas, is not as strong as Digital (and neither DEC nor HP is as strong as IBM) in the big-iron market, and can't compare to Compaq or IBM in the PC industry."

Review of the Outcome

In November of 1998, a *Forbes* article stated, "In swallowing ailing Digital Equipment Corp., Compaq Computer risked indigestion—or worse. In fact, Digital has been a tasty meal for the acquirer." Compaq cut 5,000 jobs and divested several unprofitable Digital holdings. Overall sales increased to $31 billion, compared to $24.6 billion in 1997. Earnings jumped 14%. Also, revenue from computer services operations grew from $462 million in 1997 to $3.7 billion in 1998, and profit margins for the segment jumped from 23% to 32% during the same time period.

Despite all the good news, however, the fact remained that margins for Compaq's core business—computer products—tumbled 6% to 22% in 1998, mainly due to increased competition and lower prices. When Compaq announced that its first quarter 1999 profits would be 50% lower than anticipated, the firm's stock tumbled 22%. Many analysts began questioning whether Compaq had effectively integrated its Digital Equipment holdings. In April of 1999, Compaq's board overthrew chairman and CEO Eckhard Pfeiffer, replacing him with Benjamin Rosen.

Research

Black, George. "Death for Digital," in *Computer Weekly*, 18 June 1998. Explains how the Compaq/Digital deal will affect both firms, as well as the computer industry.

Buckler, Grant. "Employees Lose Out in Compaq/DEC Deal," in *Computer Dealer News*, 10 August 1998. Details how the merger between Compaq and Digital will affect employees.

"Compaq Computer Corp.," in *Notable Corporate Chronologies*, The Gale Group, 1999. Lists major events in the history of Compaq Computer Corp.

Compaq Computer Corp. Home Page, available at http://www.compaq.com. Official World Wide Web Home Page for Compaq Computer Corp. Includes current and archived news; financial, product, and historical information; and annual reports.

Damore, Kelley. "Eckhard Pfeiffer," in *Computer Reseller News*, 17 November 1998. Covers the career of Eckhard Pfeiffer and the impact the executive has had at Compaq Computer.

"Digital Equipment Corp.," in *Notable Corporate Chronologies*, Gale Research, 1999. Lists major events in the history of Digital Equipment Corp.

Fisher, Daniel. "Bon Appetit!" in *Forbes*, 2 November 1998. Covers the first-year results of the merger for Compaq.

Kerber, Ross. "Critics Say Compaq Computer Hasn't Integrated Disparate Pieces," in *Knight-Ridder/Tribune Business News*, 20 April 1999. Explains why critics are concerned about Compaq's integration of Digital.

ANNAMARIE L. SHELDON

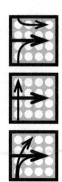

CONAGRA & BEATRICE

ConAgra Inc.
One ConAgra Dr.
Omaha, Nebraska 68102-5001
USA

tel: (402)595-4000
fax: (402)595-4707
web: http://www.conagra.com

nationality: USA
date: August 14, 1990
affected: ConAgra Inc., USA, founded 1919
affected: Beatrice Co., USA, founded 1895

Overview of the Merger

The $1.34 billion transaction that marked the joining of ConAgra Inc. and Beatrice Co. in 1990 brought together such popular brand names as Armour, Morton, Banquet, Hunt's, Wesson, Peter Pan, and Orville Redenbacher. ConAgra was able to move into the dry foods market for the first time, becoming the nation's second largest food company. Sales increased to over $20 billion as a result of the merger.

History of ConAgra Inc.

In 1919, Nebraska Consolidated Mills Corp. was officially formed in Grand Island, Nebraska, when Alva Kinney brought together four grain milling firms to take advantage of increasing grain production in the Midwest. At first, Kinney concentrated on milling the bumper postwar wheat crops at his four locations. He soon added a mill in Omaha, moving his company's headquarters there as well. The new mill doubled Nebraska Consolidated's capacity. In 1926, the Brown Mill in Fremont, Nebraska, was acquired to further bolster capacity. The Omaha mill was destroyed by fire in 1931; a larger version was later rebuilt.

Having run a profitable and relatively quiet company for the past 17 years, Kinney retired as president in 1936. R.S. Dickinson, Kinney's successor, continued the simple but successful policy of milling grain in Nebraska. A new mill was constructed at Grand Island, Nebraska, doubling that location's original capacity. By 1942, Dickinson began using the company's profits to expand. Other thriving milling operations, such as General Mills and Pillsbury, were expanding both the number of plants and the number of products offered, and Nebraska Consolidated followed the same trend. Dickinson opened a flour mill and an animal feed mill in Alabama and promoted research into new types of prepared foods that make use of flour.

The new feed mill allowed Nebraska Consolidated to take advantage of river transportation of Midwestern grain to Southeastern markets. By 1947, the Alabama expansion proved profitable, but the company found it difficult to gain a foothold in the prepared-foods market. Cake mixes, though only a small proportion of the total flour market, accounted for as much as $140 million a year in retail sales. Flour sales and production began to shift away from family flour to bakery flour. To remain competitive, the company made its first major move into the grocery product field with the development of Duncan Hines cake mixes in 1951. Unable to increase its share of the highly-competitive cake mix market, Nebraska Consolidated eventually decided to get out of prepared foods and branch into basic commodities such as grain and feed. To facilitate this, the Duncan Hines brand was sold to Procter & Gamble for almost $1 million.

The new president of Nebraska Consolidated, Allan Mactier, used the proceeds from the sale of Duncan Hines to expand aggressively in 1956. The company built the first major grain processing plant in Puerto Rico through its subsidiary, Caribe Corp. The $3 million plant processed flour, cornmeal, and animal feeds at Catano in San Juan harbor. By 1961, the Puerto Rican milling operation began to turn a profit. The island plant exported 15% of its volume to the Caribbean Islands and Latin America. Funds were budgeted for a desperately needed grain elevator addition, and construction was underway on a poultry pathological laboratory to provide free services to local poultry growers. Only 25% of the poultry consumed in Puerto Rico was raised on the island; Nebraska Consolidated hoped to boost that figure.

The 1960s were marked by expansion, beginning with the purchase of the Georgia-based Dalton Poultry Co. in 1963. Consisting of a feed mill, hatchery, and broiler grow-out operation, along with a processing plant that employed 170 people and produced 6,000 ice-packed broilers an hour, the poultry company allowed Nebraska Consolidated to enter the chicken business. The next year, five feed manufacturing plants in Nebraska and Iowa were acquired with the purchase of Nixon and Co. By 1965, the company began expanding into the European market by forging a partnership with Bioter-Biona S.A., a Spanish producer of animal feed and animal health products.

In 1971, Nebraska Consolidated Mills changed its name to ConAgra, Inc. This new name meant "in partnership with the land" and better reflected the growing firm's sphere of activity. Two years later, ConAgra was listed on the New York Stock Exchange. Purchases for that year included the Kasco dog food plant and the Geisler Pet Products Corp. Heavy losses in commodity speculations in 1975 brought the firm to the brink of bankruptcy. To aid in the financial crisis, ConAgra's first high-profile CEO, former Pillsbury executive Charles Harper, was named president with a mandate to turn the ailing company around. Over

The Business

Financials

Revenue (1998): $23.84 billion

Employees (1998): 82,169

SICs / NAICS

sic 2879 - Agricultural Chemicals Nec

sic 0723 - Crop Preparation Services for Market

sic 2011 - Meat Packing Plants

sic 2013 - Sausages & Other Prepared Meats

sic 2099 - Food Preparations Nec

sic 2092 - Fresh or Frozen Prepared Fish

sic 2048 - Prepared Feeds Nec

sic 2032 - Canned Specialties

sic 2033 - Canned Fruits & Vegetables

sic 2041 - Flour & Other Grain Mill Products

sic 2015 - Poultry Slaughtering & Processing

naics 115114 - Postharvest Crop Activities (except Cotton Ginning)

naics 311119 - Other Animal Food Manufacturing

naics 111998 - All Other Miscellaneous Crop Farming

naics 311911 - Roasted Nuts and Peanut Butter Manufacturing

naics 311423 - Dried and Dehydrated Food Manufacturing

naics 311991 - Perishable Prepared Food Manufacturing

naics 311212 - Rice Milling

naics 311823 - Dry Pasta Manufacturing

naics 311941 - Mayonnaise, Dressing, and Other Prepared Sauce Manufacturing

naics 311942 - Spice and Extract Manufacturing

naics 311999 - All Other Miscellaneous Food Manufacturing

naics 311613 - Rendering and Meat By-product Processing

naics 311612 - Meat Processed from Carcasses

naics 311611 - Animal (except Poultry) Slaughtering

naics 311712 - Fresh and Frozen Seafood Processing

naics 311422 - Specialty Canning

naics 311421 - Fruit and Vegetable Canning

naics 311211 - Flour Milling

naics 311615 - Poultry Processing

the next couple years, Harper sold off non-essential operations to reduce debt. He also began buying agri-

The Officers

Chairman and CEO: Bruce C. Rohde

Exec. VP, Chief Financial Officer, and Corporate Secretary: James P. O'Donnell

Exec. VP and Chief Administrative Officer: Gerald B. Vernon

Sr. VP and Controller: Kenneth W. Difonzo

Sr. VP, Mergers and Acquisitions: Dwight J. Goslee

Sr. VP, Human Resources: Owen C. Johnson

Sr. VP, Trading and Procurement Management: Michael D. Walter

cultural businesses at the low end of their profit cycles in order to turn them around.

With a focus on growth, ConAgra expanded into fertilizers, acquiring United Agri Products, a distributor of herbicides and pesticides, in 1978. Higher grain prices, Harper reasoned, would mean increased demand for such chemicals. In an attempt to counter the cyclical profit pattern of basic agricultural commodities, Harper also entered areas that didn't mesh well with the company's traditional orientation—pet accessories, Mexican restaurants, and fabrics and crafts retailing. By 1980, originally intending to stick with ConAgra's emphasis on basic commodities rather than try to compete with the packaged-food giants, Harper purchased Banquet Foods Corp., claiming that the acquisition was not an entry into prepared foods but a way to increase ConAgra's chicken capacity. The company's chicken production did increase by a third, which brought it from eighth to fifth place among chicken producers.

ConAgra achieved sales of $1 billion for the first time in 1981, and the company went on a buying spree. The firm bought Singleton Seafood, the largest shrimp processor in the country, and Sea-Alaska Products. The next year, ConAgra purchased the Peavey Corporation, a Minneapolis-based flour miller and grain trader, which gave the company 16.3% of the nation's wheat-milling capacity and a system of grain exporting terminals. Political barriers to U.S. grain depressed Peavey's profits, and the acquisition took a few years to prove profitable. In 1982, during a low in the poultry cycle, ConAgra made a move to take first place in the chicken industry by forming Country Poultry, Inc. After a year in business, Country Poultry was delivering more than a billion pounds of brand-name broilers to markets, making it the biggest poultry producer in the country.

ConAgra went on to purchase Armour Food Corp., a processor of red meats such as hot dogs, sausage, bacon, ham, and lunch meats. The acquisition also included Armour's line of frozen gourmet entrees, called Dinner Classics, which complimented Banquet's line of frozen foods. As with many of his other acquisitions, Harper bought Armour in a down cycle for book value ($182 million). By waiting to complete the deal until Armour closed several plants, Harper painlessly eliminated about 40% of Armour's major union members. Armour was then reorganized to emphasize new marketing strategies and refocus product lines.

Harper continued to expand the company, and in 1986, the ConAgra Turkey Corp. was formed. Harper also increased ConAgra's presence in frozen foods by purchasing the Morton, Patio, and Chun King brands. By 1983, Peavey had reaped a $16.4 million profit on sales of $1.2 billion, a promising upward trend. Three years later, ConAgra bought Trident Seafoods and O'Donnell Usen Fisheries, the producer of Taste O'Sea frozen seafood products, thus positioning the company to compete against the leading frozen seafood brands, Mrs. Paul's Kitchens, Gorton's, and Van de Kamp's. That same year, another poultry company, Longmont Foods, was acquired, further strengthening the company's position in the field. The company expanded further into red meats with its purchase of E.A. Miller, Inc., a western producer of beef products, and Montfort of Colorado in 1987. The Montfort deal, for $365 million in stock, made ConAgra the third-largest U.S. beef producer. ConAgra became a leader in meat processing by acquiring 50% of Swift Independent Packing, a processor of beef, pork, and lamb.

By 1988, Armour, as a whole, was still proving unprofitable for ConAgra, but the Dinner Classics line was doing well. Cook Family Foods, Ltd., a producer of branded smoked ham products, merged with ConAgra that same year. In 1989, ConAgra completed the acquisition of Pillsbury's grain merchandising division. ConAgra and W. Jordan Millers Ltd. formed a 50-50 joint venture to process and distribute oat products for human consumption in the United Kingdom and Europe. The joint venture was called Cereal Millers Europe Ltd.

The following year, ConAgra purchased the food giant, Beatrice Co., gaining such brands as Orville Redenbacher (popcorn), and Hunt's (tomato sauces and related products). This huge purchase placed ConAgra in the number two position in the U.S. food industry, behind Philip Morris' Kraft General Foods. The next year, the company acquired Golden Valley Microwave Foods and entered into a joint agreement with an exporter of foods to Eastern Europe called

Chilewich Partners. ConAgra also acquired Arrow Industries that year.

With sales of approximately $9.5 billion, ConAgra employed 43,000 people by 1994. Philip Fletcher, the new CEO of the company, had successfully cut costs and stressed cooperation among the food units. ConAgra's stock rose 13% between January and July. In 1995, ConAgra contracted with Specialty Foods Corp. to produce the Healthy Choice bread brand; at the same time, ConAgra's Golden Valley Microwave Foods Inc. division was producing the Healthy Choice brand of microwave popcorn. Licensing deals were said to be driving the Healthy Choice brand's 31% annual growth rate, and the company began supporting the Healthy Choice brand with $44 million of advertising in 1996.

The latter half of that year was not one of the company's better times. ConAgra, Hormel, and several other companies agreed to settle a fish price-fixing case brought against them by the Federal Trade Commission for a total fine of $21 million. Despite strong earnings growth, ConAgra had to cut 6,500 jobs, close several plants, and take a pre-tax charge of $505 million in its fiscal fourth quarter of 1996 as part of a restructuring program that was being implemented. Nevertheless, by the end of fiscal 1997, the company had experienced an increase of 14% per share and had 83,169 employees in 32 countries.

History of Beatrice Co.

In 1886, George Haskell worked as a bookkeeper for the Fremont Butter and Egg Co. When the company went out of business in 1891, Haskell and business partner Bosworth purchased Fremont's Beatrice Nebraska plant. With $40,000 in capital, the Beatrice Creamery Company was formed in 1895. Three years later, the company's headquarters were moved to Lincoln, Nebraska. The company was incorporated that year with $100,000 in capital.

Beatrice continued its growth spurt despite drought and economic troubles. The company focused on distributing its fresh butter to hotels, restaurants, and grocery stores. Beatrice entered the cold storage industry, a likely fit due to the refrigeration plants needed in the butter making process. At that time, farmers had to go to a skimming station every day to sell their cream, and then go right back to the farm with the skim milk for their livestock feed. Beatrice battled that inefficiency by purchasing cream separators.

In the early 1900s, the company developed its first trademark, Meadow Gold. Considered quite innovative, Beatrice pasteurized churning cream on a large

The Players

Chairman and CEO of ConAgra, Inc.: Charles M. Harper. This University of Chicago graduate began his career at General Motors Corp. in Detroit, Michigan, in 1950. He then went on to join Pillsbury Co. in 1954, where he worked for twenty years as director of industrial engineering, vice president of research and development, and eventually executive vice president and COO. In 1974, he began work with ConAgra, where he soon took over as chairman and CEO, steering the firm's extensive growth throughout the 1980s, as well as its 1990 purchase of Beatrice. Harper went on to become CEO of RJR Nabisco in May 1993. He retired from that company in December 1995.

President and CEO of Beatrice Co.: Frederick B. Rentschler. Rentschler, a Harvard Business School graduate, started work as a salesman for the Armour Dial Company upon graduation. Through hard work and perseverance noted by his peers, he became president of the company within 15 years. Rentschler then took the reins of Hunt-Wesson, owned by Norton Simon, but was forced out in 1984, when Norton Simon was purchased by Esmark, which was then acquired by Beatrice. The next year, however, when Beatrice was bought by Donald P. Kelly with the help of investment firm Kohlberg, Kravis, Roberts & Co., Rentschler's expertise and business savvy was called upon to help run the company. In 1987, he was named CEO. In 1990, he left Beatrice to become CEO of Northwest Airlines.

scale and became the first company to package butter in sealed cartons. In 1907, an ice cream plant was opened in Topeka, Kansas. The ice cream proved to be very popular. In 1912, the company was the first to advertise butter, and then again in 1931, the first to advertise ice cream. The company went on to open a fluid milk plant in Denver, Colorado, and began to distribute milk, buttermilk, and cottage cheese. Beatrice was also the first to use aluminum foil to make bottle caps for milk. It introduced homogenized milk in 1930.

The dairy industry was hit hard during the Depression and then again by World War II. Prices drastically dropped during the Depression, and the government demanded 30% of all butter and rationed the rest. Prices froze, and business was limited, but

Beatrice prevailed. In 1941, the 40th anniversary of the Meadow Gold brand of butter, the company was producing 70 million pounds of butter. The company continued to expand by purchasing La Choy, a producer of oriental foods, in 1943. By 1946, the company had renamed itself the Beatrice Food Co.

Three years later, the company was able to report a gain in net sales for the 10th year in a row and a tripling of total sales. The company had survived the hard times that had put so many businesses to rest. In 1952, Clinton Haskell, president since 1928, died. He had transformed the regional butter maker into a nationally known producer and distributor of well-known brands throughout the U.S. William Karnes took the helm and continued Haskell's quest for growth and diversity. He began to acquire companies and expanded into different markets. From candy and vegetables to furniture, luggage, and chemicals, Beatrice was leaving its mark on several industries and becoming attractive on Wall Street.

By the end of the 1970s, however, the diversity of the product lines Beatrice offered was taking its toll on the company. Karnes retired in 1976, and Wallace Rasmussen took over. The newly named CEO only had three years to run the company before mandatory retirement at 65. Despite concerns that the firm was becoming unmanageable, he continued making acquisitions, including Culligan and Tropicana Products. When James Dutt became CEO in 1980, he began to sell companies in an effort to create a more focused, coherent business. However, he shocked Wall Street in 1981, when he bought Buckingham Corp. and the Coca-Cola bottling Company of Los Angeles. As a result, Beatrice's advertising and marketing budget went from $160 million to $800 million a year. The company name was changed to Beatrice Companies in June of 1984.

Continuing his efforts to become a global marketer, Dutt went on to purchase Esmark, a food and consumer products giant, for $2.7 billion. By 1985, Dutt had severed relations with many of his peers and had increased Beatrice's already large debt load. That year, the board demanded his resignation. William Granger, Jr., replaced Dutt with the intent to reduce debt, but before he could put his plan into action, Donald Kelly, a former chairman of Esmark, took Beatrice private with the help of Kohlberg, Kravis, Roberts & Co., a leveraged buyout firm. The $6.2 billion deal reorganized Beatrice as the wholly owned subsidiary of BCI Holdings Corp.

Selling off assets became Kelly's top priority. He sold Avis, the number two car rental company in the U.S., for $250 million just twelve days after taking over. In 1987, he created E-II Holdings, a spin-off of 15 consumer goods and specialty food companies. Kelly was named CEO of the new company as well as chairman of BCI. Later that year, he changed BCI's name to Beatrice Co. Kelly then sold E-II to American Brands, Inc., a tobacco company, for $800 million, and began to divest other parts of Beatrice. He sold Playtex for $1.25 billion, the Los Angeles Coca-Cola bottler for $1 billion, International Foods for $985 million, and Tropicana for $1.2 billion.

In 1988, Kelly stepped down and appointed Frederick Rentschler, a former Esmark executive, to take over. In 1990, Beatrice Co. was acquired by ConAgra, a food industry giant looking to dive into the packaged and dry goods industry. ConAgra planned to use the company's expertise in that area to expand even further.

Market Forces Driving the Merger

"By operating across the food chain," a favorite saying of Harper, CEO of ConAgra at the time of the merger, the company was able to benefit from various trends in the food industry. Keeping the company diverse was a focus that prompted ConAgra to acquire Beatrice Co. This move would allow them to grow and compete against rivals like Philip Morris, who was also growing through acquisition.

The company was also on the rebound after losing a bid to acquire Holly Farms Corp. Through the acquisition, ConAgra would gain considerable shelf space by entering the dry food market. "We've had an objective for a long time, a number of years, to find a way for a solid entry into the dry part of the grocery store. We've been very weak there," Harper said in an interview with the *Washington Post*.

Approach and Engagement

Kohlberg, Kravis, Roberts & Co. was looking for a buyer for Beatrice Co., a firm that it owned through a leverage buyout. KKR searched for over a year before ConAgra CEO Harper and investment banker Eric Gleacher discussed the potential acquisition in a Colorado chairlift in January of 1990. The talk prompted a meeting between Harper and KKR.

Details of the acquisition were polished when ConAgra visited Beatrice sites to become familiar with the firm's financials. Negotiators were able to come up with a plan that would benefit both KKR and ConAgra: 50% of the price paid by ConAgra would be issued in stock rather than cash. The stock would be tax-free, which was attractive to KKR investors, and it would keep the debt-to-equity ratio low for ConAgra.

After two months of review, the FTC approved

ConAgra's $1.34 billion cash and stock acquisition of Beatrice in August of 1990. The transaction included $626 million in cash, $355 million in ConAgra common stock, and $335 million in convertible preferred stock. KKR retained 15% of ConAgra's stock.

Products and Services

After the merger, ConAgra became the second largest food processor in the nation. Already a leader in the frozen food and processed meat market, the deal brought together brand names such as Armour, Morton, Banquet, Chun King, La Choy, Healthy Choice, Hunt, Wesson, Peter Pan, Swift Premium, Eckrich, Butterball, and Orville Redenbacher. With Beatrice's advertising budget at $70 million, more than five times that of ConAgra, the brands were expected to produce record profits.

In 1998, refrigerated foods accounted for 52% of the firm's $23.8 billion in revenues. Food inputs and ingredients brought in 25%, and groceries and diversified products secured the remaining 23%.

Changes to the Industry

Many outside forces had an affect on all industries in the early 1990s. Faltering economies and the Persian Gulf War were halted mergers and acquisitions throughout the world. Leveraged buyouts were becoming more popular, especially in the supermarket, food, and retail industries. Only strategic buyers were able to continue on paths of growth. ConAgra's acquisition of Beatrice was one of the eleven largest in 1990, proving ConAgra to be a strategically sound organization. When the deal was completed, ConAgra boasted a strong foothold as the number two contender in the food industry and earned a spot among the top twenty industrial corporations in the nation.

Review of the Outcome

Second quarter revenue for ConAgra was up in December of 1990 by 38% to $5.33 billion. Net income also increased to $88.3 million due, in part, to the acquisition. By the fourth quarter of that year, earnings were up to $99.4 million and results were positive in all segments of the company.

With the merger, the company gained control of a large amount of shelf space in grocery stores. Increased interest in low fat food was a trend that would prove to be long lasting and ConAgra planned to build its Healthy Choice line of frozen foods into a major brand.

"ConAgra paid $1.36 billion, but in one swoop added $4.3 billion in sales and leading brand names in the three Beatrice divisions: Hunt-Wesson, Swift-Eckrich and Beatrice Cheese," wrote *Prepared Foods* in September of 1994. "Of equal importance was the strong sales and distribution network Beatrice and Hunt-Wesson had developed. It immediately benefitted existing ConAgra products and became the conduit for bringing the products of future ConAgra acquisitions to regional and national penetration."

Research

Bailey, Jeff. "What Makes ConAgra, Once on the Brink of Ruin, a Wall Street Favorite?," in *Wall Street Journal*, 13 June 1990. Discusses market trends and details of ConAgra's past and future acquisitions.

"Beatrice Company, "in *International Directory of Company Histories*, Vol. II, St. James Press, 1990. Lists major events in the history of Beatrice.

"ConAgra, Inc.," in *Notable Corporate Chronologies*, The Gale Group, 1999. Lists major events in the history of ConAgra.

ConAgra, Inc. Home Page, available at http://www.conagra.com. Official World Wide Web Home Page for Conagra, Inc. Includes product information, as well as historical and financial information.

"ConAgra Concludes Acquisition of Beatrice," in *PR Newswire*, 14 August 1990. Lists details of the acquisition.

"ConAgra Earnings Rose in Fourth Quarter," in *Journal of Commerce*, 12 July 1991. Reports financial information about ConAgra.

"ConAgra Net Surges," in *The New York Times*, 26 December 1990. Lists earning information on ConAgra's second quarter.

Cuff, Daniel. "Beatrice Executive to Refocus on Food," in *The New York Times*, 26 May 1987. Details the career of Frederick Rentschler.

———. "Beatrice Chief Leaving to be Head of NWA," in *the New York Times*, 20 June 1990. Provides information on Frederick Frenschler.

Fusaro, Dave. "Wealthy Choices: ConAgra Blitzes the Competition," in *Prepared Foods*, September 1994. Discusses ConAgra's performance in the mid-1990s.

Gibson, Richard. "ConAgra Agrees to Buy Beatrice For $1.34 Billion,"in *Wall Street Journal*, 8 June 1990. Relates the initial discussions between ConAgra and KKR.

Kleinfield, N.R. "Some Familiar Faces in the Buyout Crowd," in *The New York Times*, 30 October 1988. Comments on the career of Henry Kravis.

Mitchell, Russell. "ConAgra: Out of the Freezer," in *Business Week*, 25 June 1990. Discusses ConAgra's entry into the dry food market.

Potts, Mark. "ConAgra to Acquire Beatrice," in *The Washington Post*, 8 June 1990. Details the events leading up to the merger.

Shapiro, Eben. "ConAgra Who?" in *The New York Times*, 12 June 1990. Describes ConAgra's acquisition history.

"The Spotty Market for M&A," in *Mergers and Acquisitions*, May 1990.

CHRISTINA M. STANSELL

CONSECO & KEMPER

Conseco, Inc.
11825 N. Pennsylvania St.
Carmel, IN 46032
USA

tel: (317)817-6100
fax: (317)817-2847
web: http://www.conseco.com

Kemper Corp.
One Kemper Drive
Long Grove, IL 60049-0001
USA

tel: (847)320-2000
fax: (847)320-2494
web: http://www.kemperinsurance.com

date: November 20, 1994 (canceled)
affected: Conseco, Inc., USA, founded 1983
affected: Kemper Corp., USA, founded 1912

Overview of the Merger

In June of 1994, Conseco made a $3.25 billion bid for Kemper Corp. Outbidding GE's hostile offer of $2.2 billion, Kemper accepted the bid where shareholders were slated to receive $67 per share in cash and Conseco stock. The approved bid would create one of the nation's largest insurance companies with over $85 billion in assets. The offer raised Kemper stock by 6% up to $62.625 per share, and Conseco closed at $51 per share, up $.50.

The golden offer began to tarnish however, when faith in Conseco's ability to finance the deal began to dwindle. The company's effort to reduce debt by unloading its large stakes in three insurance companies failed when insufficient funds were received from the transaction. By October, the acquisition was delayed due to lack of financing. Kemper stock had fallen to $52.625 per share and Conseco's tumbled to $32.25. On November 20th, the deal was abandoned by both parties. Conseco's stock had fallen 27% during the financial fiasco.

History of Conseco, Inc.

Former Aetna employee Stephen C. Hilbert acquired the struggling Executive Income Life Insurance Company for $1.3 million in 1982. He folded the company into his newly established Security National Corp., a company set up to manage the life insurance companies that Hilbert planned to acquire and streamline. He also created Security National of Indiana to develop and market new life insurance services and products. Both companies were headquartered in Carmel, Indiana.

Within one year, the seasoned insurance veteran was able to return Executive Income Life to profitability by tightening operations and cutting excess costs. In 1983, Security National acquired Consolidated National Life Insurance Company. In December of that year, Security National Corp. and Security National of Indiana were merged to form Conseco. There were 25 employees and assets were valued at $3 million.

By 1985, Conseco had assets worth $102 million. The company paid $25 million for Lincoln American Life Insurance Co. and moved the new unit's headquarters from Memphis, Tennessee, to the Carmel headquarters complex. A few months later, Conseco conducted its initial public offering, and, in 1987, bought Western National Life Insurance Co. for $262 million. Assets soared to $3.4 billion, and employees now totaled roughly five hundred.

By moving the bulk of operations to the growing Carmel headquarters, Conseco was able to reduce its workforce by nearly 10 percent in 1988. The company continued to grow and in June 1989, purchased National Fidelity Life Insurance Company, based in Dallas, Texas, for $68 million. Its operations were soon transferred to Carmel. Assets reached $5.2 billion that year.

Conseco rallied in the early 1990s and forged ahead on its growth spurt. To make room for its rapid expansion in Carmel, Conseco constructed a 40,000-square-foot data processing center in 1990. To fund future acquisitions, Hilbert established Conseco Capital Partners (CCP), a limited partnership including many solidly financed firms. CCP bought Great American Reserve Insurance Company for $135 million and Jefferson National Life Group for $171 million. The company continued to seek inefficient, over-staffed companies to purchase. To turn these firms around, Conseco not only cut staff, but also used high-ly efficient information and data processing systems to consolidate marketing, investment, and product development procedures.

In 1991, CCP acquired Beneficial Standard Life for $141 million. Despite recessionary economic conditions, Conseco's assets soared to $11.8 billion and employees number 1,100. The company enlarged its headquarters and opened the Conseco Annuity Center in Dallas, Texas. The next year, the company founded Conseco Capital Management, Inc. (CCM) to offer financial and investment advisory services to insurers. CCP acquired Bankers Life and Casualty Company, a leading individual health insurance policy writer, for $600 million. Net income jumped 46% that year to $170 million.

In 1992, Conseco made one of the first of a few ill-fated investments in non-core ventures when it paid $15 million for a 31% stake of Eagle Credit Corp., a firm which offered financing to Harley-Davidson dealers and their clients. The next year, Conseco secured a controlling share of MDS/Bankmark, an annuity and mutual funds firm. Net income swelled 75% to $297 million, and assets were worth $16.6 billion. The firm also invested $5 million in Rick Galles Racing, an IndyCar racing team. In 1994, Conseco established CCP II to focus on securing acquisitions of companies valued at a minimum of $350 million. The earlier CCP partnership was renamed CCP Insurance,

The Business

Financials - Conseco, Inc.

Revenue (1998): $43,559.9 million

Employees (1998): 14,000

SICs / NAICS

sic 6311 - Life Insurance

sic 6719 - Holding Companies Nec

naics 524113 - Direct Life Insurance Carriers

naics 551112 - Offices of Other Holding Companies

Financials - Kemper Corp.

Revenue (1997): $9.83 billion

Employees (1997): 9,500

SICs / NAICS

sic 6311 - Life Insurance

sic 6321 - Accident & Health Insurance

sic 6331 - Fire, Marine & Casualty Insurance

sic 6282 - Investment Advice

sic 6211 - Security Brokers & Dealers

naics 524113 - Direct Life Insurance Carriers

naics 524114 - Direct Health and Medical Insurance Carriers

naics 524126 - Direct Property and Casualty Insurance Carriers

naics 524128 - Other Direct Insurance Carriers (except Life, Health and Medical)

naics 523999 - Miscellaneous Financial Investment Activities

Inc. and started functioning as a holding company for Conseco, CCP II and CCM. Conseco also spun off Western National Life Insurance.

The company's good fortune began to falter—in 1994, a $3.25 billion merger deal with Kemper Corp. fell apart due to lack of funds necessary to complete the deal. The merger blunder did not stop Hilbert from accomplishing other goals, however. He established Conseco Entertainment to act as a holding company for anticipated investments in the entertainment industry. CCP II went on to acquire Statesman Group,

The Officers

Conseco, Inc.

President and CEO: Stephen C. Hilbert

Exec. VP and Chief Financial Officer : Rollin M. Dick

Exec. VP, Corporate Development, President and CEO,
    Conseco Private Capital Group: Ngaire E. Cuneo

Sr. VP, Chief Accounting Officer and Treasurer: James S.
    Adams

Sr. VP, Investments; President and CEO, Conseco Capital
    Management: Maxwell E. Bublitz

Kemper Corp.

Chairman and CEO: David B. Mathis

President and Chief Operating Officer: William D. Smith

Exec. VP and Chief Financial Officer: Walter L. White

Inc. for $350 million. In 1995, Conseco Global Investments was formed, and Conseco acquired the shares of CCP it did not already own.

In 1996, acquisitions included Wells & Company of Indianapolis, Indiana, Life Partners Group, American Travellers Corp., and TransportHoldings, Inc. CCP II was dissolved as Conseco became able to fund its own acquisitions. Stock split two-for-one, and Conseco was named to the Fortune 500 list and added to the Dow Jones Life Insurance Index. The year 1997 was equally successful as Conseco was added to the Standard & Poor's 500 Index. Growth continued with the purchases of Capitol American Financial Corp., Colonial Penn Life Insurance, Pioneer Financial Services, Inc., and Washington National Corp..

The company continued to do well and in 1998, Conseco and Green Tree Financial Corp., a leading manufactured housing lender, agreed to merge in a $7.6 billion transaction. The deal signaled Conseco's commitment to expand operations outside the insurance arena. The company also became a sponsor of the Indiana Pacers, and the team's new arena was named the Conseco Fieldhouse. In 1999, the company began to focus on lower income clients.

History of Kemper

In November of 1912, insurance salesman James S. Kemper founded the Lumbermen's Mutual Casualty Company (LMC), after he convinced a group of lumber industry leaders in Chicago, Illinois, that recent changes in state law regarding industrial acci-

dents placed them at increased risk of paying compensation to injured workers. The next year, LMC became one of the first companies to issue automobile insurance. The company also formed the National Underwriters (NU) insurance exchange to provide supplementary fire insurance policies to the lumber industry. By 1919, the company expanded opening offices in Philadelphia, Boston, and Syracuse, New York.

LMC and NU established their home offices in Chicago, Illinois, where NU receptionists began to answer incoming calls with "Kemper Insurance." In 1923 the company established two subsidiary operations and began conducting business in Canada. Three years later, Kemper founded the American Motorists Insurance Company (AMICO), which became a part of his insurance operations but had no financial connection with NU or LMC.

Kemper's insurance companies fared well during the Depression, even expanding its product lines by acquiring Glen Cove Mutual Insurance Company (GCMI), a New York-based issuer of boiler and machinery surety bonds and inland marine insurance policies. Kemper reorganized GCMI as American Manufacturers Mutual Insurance Company (AMMIC). In 1936,he established the Traffic Institution at Northwestern University to promote safe driving. By 1948, the Kemper companies had established two more subsidiary operations.

Kemper moved into the life insurance business in 1954, forming The Fidelity Life Asssociation. The company established an automated billing system to cut office expenses throughout the group. In 1957, Kemper began advertising on national television through the sponsorship of sporting events, and offered ocean marine policies for the first time. The company also installed computers to process actuarial data. Kemper began work to establish a non-operating holding company to coordinate activities of the Kemper group of companies in 1959. Two years later, the Federal Kemper Life Insurance Company was formed.

The 1960s were progressive years for the company. In 1962, American Protection Insurance Company joined the Kemper group, and in 1964, the company began offering Highly Protected Risk coverage for commercial properties. Kemperco was incorporated in Delaware to act as a non-operating holding company for the property, casualty, and life insurance operations of Kemper group in 1967. The new company's stock was publicly traded, with LMC retaining a controlling interest. The following year, Kemperco established the National Loss Control Service Corp. (NATLSCO) to offer consulting services in fire protection, safety, industrial hygiene, air pollution, and boiler and mechanical inspection services. The company diversified, acquiring a 40% interest in Extel Corp., a manufacturer of telecommunications devices. In 1969, Kemper entered the reinsurance business, forming the Kemper Reinsurance Company.

In 1970, Kemperco acquired Supervised Investors Services, which was reorganized as Kemper Financial Services, to manage the company's investment portfolio. By the next year, assets managed by Kemperco's financial services operations reached $2 billion, and investment income reached $14 million, a 400% increase over its 1967 level. In 1972, Kemperco reported a 13% volume increase to $329 million, mainly through acquisitions. The next year brought about financial changes when the OPEC oil embargo touched off runaway inflation in the U.S. As a result, Kemperco's net income dropped to $18.9 million for the year. The company began a corporate identity program, establishing one and five-year internal performance objectives. In 1974, Kemperco changed its name to the Kemper Corp. (KC). Despite Kemper's efforts, profits continued to drop by 37%, and net income fell to $12.6 million. Income from insurance premiums accounted for 90% of corporate revenues at the time.

KC instituted a new market-sensitive approach to the insurance industry, and continued to diversify in response to the maturing of its traditional insurance markets. Despite these moves, the company suffered its worst year ever, with net income falling 26% to $9.3 million. By 1977, the company began to rebound, recording profits exceeding $57 million on sales of $808 million. KC's assets topped $1.3 billion. In 1977, James S. Kemper, Jr., resigned as company CEO and was succeeded by Joseph E. Luecke. KC's performance slipped once again, with a record of fifty loss of properties valued at more than $1 million. Total claims filed against the company for the year topped $1 billion.

Kemper embarked on a strategy of diversification into reinsurance and financial services during the 1980s, purchasing Gibraltar Financial (GF) Savings and Loan California. GF recorded huge losses, however, leading to a loss of $10 million for the year by the company as a whole. In 1981, James S. Kemper, Sr., died, and KC announced plans to invest $20 million in expansion of its life insurance operations. GF continued to drag down the performance of KC, which also suffered a decline in revenues obtained from property and casualty premiums due to a rise in U.S. interest rates, and the company posted a loss of $30 million for the year.

The company continued its diversification into the financial services industry by acquiring the Loewi

The Players

Chairman and CEO of Conseco Inc.: Stephen C. Hilbert. After attending Indiana State University, Stephen C. Hilbert began his career in the insurance industry as an agent for Aetna Life Insurance Company in 1967. He left the company in 1970 to work for United Home Life Insurance, but returned to Aetna after five years. He remained an agent until 1979, when he departed from the company to form Conseco. Hilbert saw a need in the industry for a centralized holding company, and he grasped the opportunity to create the firm. He is credited with taking the company from $3 million in assets to one worth over $83 billion, making it one of the nation's largest financial service companies. Hilbert was recognized as one of the top executives in the industry in 1989 by *National Underwriter* magazine and in 1995 was given the award of "Entrepreneur of the Year," in Indiana.

Chairman of Kemper Corp.: David B. Mathis. After graduating from Lake Forest College, David B. Mathis joined forces with Kemper in 1960. He worked his way up the ladder to sales manager and in 1970, went to work in Europe for the company. In 1978, he was named president of Kemper International Insurance Company. One year later he took on the role of general manager of Kemper National's national/international department. In 1982, he became president and CEO of Kemper Reinsurance. He continued up that ladder and, in 1992, he was elected chairman and CEO of Kemper Corp. Mathis was credited with being a leader in the industry and seeing his company through reorganizations and growth.

Financial Companies of Milwaukee, Bateman Eichler Hill Richards of Los Angeles, and Prescott, Ball & Turben (PBT) of Cleveland, Ohio. KC's operating earnings from property and casualty operations fell by 51%, but the performance of the company's life insurance, reinsurance, and investment services operations improved by 38%. In 1984, KC expanded into the investment services business, acquiring Burton J. Vincent, Chelsey & Company, a Chicago-based dealer in regional securities. The next year, operating earnings in the company's property and casualty operations improved significantly, and KC acquired an 80% interest in Boettcher & Company, a Denver, Colorado-based regional brokerage firm. KC also began to divest itself of its holdings in GF.

In 1986, KC created Kemper Financial Companies as a holding company for its financial services operations and sold a 12% interest in the new company to its employees for $88 million. The next year, the stock market crash caused problems in the financial services industry in general, but KC's operations posted earnings 25% above the previous year's level. Reorganization of KC continued with the sale of most of the company's accident and health insurance operations. Its property and casualty business continued to improve.

By 1988, the diversification process was complete, and the company posted record net income of $220 million on revenues of $2.4 billion on the strength of its success in financial and investment services, life insurance, and reinsurance. Property and casualty business declined once again, and KC withdrew from offering automobile insurance in the state of Massachusetts. It created Kemper Clearing Corp. to clear securities trades for all of KC's brokerage businesses.

In 1989, LMC purchased AMICO from KC and reduced its ownership of KC from 48% to 38%. Banco Santander, Spain's fourth-largest bank, purchased a 3% interest in KC, and the two companies formed a joint venture to provide investment and management services in the U.S., Europe, and South America. The following year, the Kemper companies reorganized. All companies not affiliated with KC formed Kemper National Insurance Companies (KNI), with David B. Mathis succeeding Luecke as president and CEO of KC, and Gerald L. Maatman becoming president and CEO of KNI. In 1991, KC consolidated its financial and investment services in the Chicago area to concentrate its attention on retail brokerage services. It formed Kemper Risk Management (KRM) as a joint venture with LMC. KC's mortgage and real estate portfolios began to attract the attention of regulatory bodies.

KC reported a net income loss of $8 million in 1992 due primarily to $61 million in losses attributed to the company's securities brokerage and reinsurance operations. KC subsidiary PBT was assessed $137 million in damages connected with a fraud and racketeering suit brought against the company by Continental Grain. Judgement in the case, however, was stayed pending appeal of the case. With rumors circulating of a Kemper buyout in 1995, three executives resigned, including chairman and chief executive, Charles Kierscht. Stephen Timbers was selected to replace him.

Kemper agreed to an acquisition by Zurich Insurance Co., a Swiss outfit, for $2 billion. GE's financial unit attempted a hostile takeover, but finally dropped its bid, as did Conseco Inc., who had outbid

GE, allowing Zurich to negotiate an amicable acquisition. In 1995, KC Divested itself of its unit Kemper Securities Inc. through an employee stock ownership program, and the new company took the name Everen Capital Corp. The transaction was a condition for KC's takeover by Zurich Insurance Company. In January of 1996, Zurich Insurance completed its acquisition of Kemper Corp., which took on the name of Kemper Financial Services Inc.

Market Forces Driving the Merger

The interest in Kemper reflected the increase of consolidation in the insurance industry as well as the surge of demand for financial services. Kemper's large portfolio of mutual funds, its two life insurance subsidiaries, and its security brokerage, were widely appealing to companies looking to expand. Kemper was seen to be able to enhance a company's position in a fee based market.

Conseco's profits were faltering and its stock had lost one third of its value. The company was losing out to competitors, investors were not seeing returns, and Hilbert, the company's founder, was pressured to make positive changes. Rising interest rates were taking a bite out of profit and Conseco set its eyes on Kemper. Management felt that the joining of the two companies would be a sound business move by expanding product lines in insurance and money management. According to an article in *The Washington Post*, "Kemper could enhance Conseco's position in the fee-based businesses, such as mutual funds and securities brokerage." Conseco felt pressure to bid on the company, especially when GE Capital threw its hat in the ring when it offered $60 per share for Kemper.

Approach and Engagement

On March 14, 1994, GE Capital announced a $2.2 billion, $55 a share bid for Kemper. The offer was rejected three days later even though Kemper was experiencing increased pressure from shareholders to sell itself. GE raised its bid in May to $60 a share, and Conseco decided to get into the game and put its own bid of $65 a share on the table. GE dropped its bid upon the emergence of Conseco's offer, and Kemper accepted on June 27th. Kemper left the bidding open until July 6th, with Conseco set to receive $25 million if the company accepted another offer.

The deal called for shareholders to receive $56 in cash and $11 worth of Conseco stock per each share. Conseco planned to keep the Kemper name, but sell its two life insurance companies, along with its real estate holding for $1.35 billion to Conseco Capital Partners. The financing included $750 in junk bonds, a confidence letter from Morgan Stanley & Company, stating that the bonds were sellable, a $1.22 billion loan from Citicorp, an investment of $550 million by Conseco Capital Partners, and the issuance of nine million shares of common stock. Conseco planned on selling one or more of its own life insurance holdings in order to decrease debt generated from the offer. Relations between Stephen Hilbert, chairman of Conseco, and David Mathis, CEO of Kemper, were good as both felt the acquisition would benefit the two companies.

On October 26, Conseco revealed that the offer had to be delayed due to financing problems. The sale of Bankers Life Holding Corp., CCP Insurance Inc., and Western National Corp., which would have helped finance the bid, did not attract buyers. One week later, the company lowered its bid to $60 a share. Less than one month later, the deal was called off due to the lack of financing and the decrease in Conseco share value.

Products and Services

In 1998, Conseco's insurance and fees were 82% of total sales, almost $6,400 million. Its financial segment accounted for $1,390 million in sales. The company had over 26 different operations such as American Life and Casualty, Bankers National Life, Colonial Penn Life, Green Tree Financial, and Washington National. Assets totaled $43,600 million, with operations in Carmel, Indiana; Chicago, and Philadelphia, including 185 sales offices in the U.S.

Kemper posted $9,834 million in assets in 1997. Worker's compensation was 52% of total sales at $1,173 million. General Liability accounted for 16% with $351 million in sales. Other services included property insurance, commercial auto, marine, and bond and burglary. The company dealt with risk management, excess casualty coverage, ISO 9000 registration services, commercial and environmental services, and global coverage within its subsidiaries.

Changes to the Industry

With interest rates on the rise, the financial service industry was not faring well. Stock prices were declining and it was an unstable time to try to sell. The bid by Conseco in June of $67 could in no way be negotiated for just six months later. Analysts predicted that if Kemper wanted to sell, the most it would see would be $50 a share.

Conseco was reeling from its attempted takeover of Kemper as well. With the company stock declining by 41% six months after the offer, American General Corp. purchased Conseco's 40% ownership of Western National Corp. for $274 million. The cash from the sale would give the company much needed funds to repurchase some of its stock.

Review of the Outcome

Conseco lost over $23.3 million in the bid for Kemper and saw its stock plummit to $32.50 per share. In an effort to increase earnings, the company paid $460 million for 40% of Bankers Life Holding Corp., and $268 million for 51% of CCP Insurance Inc., to acquire 100% interest in the two companies. Assets in 1995 were up to $17,297.5 million from $10,811.9 in 1994. Assets continued to grow and were at $43,599 million in 1998. At the company's annual meeting in May of 1999, Hilbert went over the company's goals for the upcoming year. The company wanted to see growth in insurance and accumulation collections by 8%, additional growth in managed financed receivables by 25%, and to reach $100 billion in managed financial assets.

Kemper's shareholders were upset at the failed bids by GE and Conseco, and were pressuring Mathis to take action. A group led by Zurich Insurance offered the company $47.50 a share in cash and $2 per share in preferred stock in April of 1995. The deal was approved by shareholders in November of 1995. Net income increased that year to $169 million from $25 million in 1994. By 1997, assets for the company were at $9,833 million and net income was $222.1 million.

Research

"American General in Deal to Buy Conseco Unit," in *The New York Times*, 3 December 1994. Provides information on American General's purchase of Conseco's 40% interest in Western National Corp..

"Conseco, Inc.," in *Notable Corporate Chronologies*, The Gale Group, 1999. Lists major events in the history of Conseco Inc.

Conseco Inc. Home Page, available at http://www.conseco.com. Official World Wide Web Home Page for Conseco Inc. Includes current news, executive information, and financial information.

Cook, Bob. "Conseco Pays $728 Million for First Post-Kemper Acquistions," in *Investment Dealers Digest*, 6 March 1995. Explains two acquisitions of two life insurance companies followed failed bid to takeover Kemper.

"Kemper Corp.," in *Notable Corporate Chronologies*, The Gale Group, 1999. Lists major events in the history of Kemper Corp.

Lipin, Steven. "Kemper Agrees to be Acquired by Group Headed by Zurich Insurance," in *Wall Street Journal*, 11 April 1995. Discusses the buyout bid made by Zurich.

Norris, Floyd. "Takeover of Kemper is Dropped," in *The New York Times*, 21 November 1994. Details the failed bid and Kemper's reaction.

Quint, Michael. "Conseco Bid for Kemper is Accepted," in *The NewYork Times*, 28 June 1994. Comments on the bid made by Conseco for Kemper.

Steinmetz, Greg. "Conseco Makes $2.68 Billion Bid to Buy Kemper," in*Wall Street Journal*, 24 June 1994. Explains GE's withdrawal of offer and Conseco's bid.

CHRISTINA M. STANSELL

CONSOLIDATED FOODS & GENTRY

Sara Lee Corp.
3 First National Plz.
Chicago, IL 60602-4260
USA

tel: (312)726-2600
fax: (312)726-3712
web: http://www.saralee.com

date: 1965 (canceled)
affected: Consolidated Foods Corp., USA, founded 1939
affected: Gentry, Inc., USA

Overview of the Acquisition

Consolidated Foods acquired Gentry Inc., a Los Angeles, California-based maker of dehydrated onion and garlic products, in 1951. The minor deal received little press until 1965 when the U.S. Supreme Court found that the purchase violated section seven of the Clayton Antitrust Act. Because Consolidated Foods bought large quantities of products from food processors, who used garlic and dehydrated onions when preparing and packaging their products, Consolidated Foods had the power to influence food processors to buy Gentry products, thus limiting competition. As a result of the verdict, Consolidated Foods sold Gentry to Basic Food Materials in 1967. *Federal Trade Commission v. Consolidated Foods Corporation* remains the dominant reciprocity case.

History of Sara Lee Corp.

Nathan Cummings borrowed $5.2 million to buy C.D. Kenny Co., a small wholesaler of coffee, tea, and sugar, in 1939. Two years later, C.D Kenny Co. was incorporated. In 1942, after completing the purchase of Sprague, Warner & Co., a distributor of canned and packaged food, the company changed its name to Sprague Warner-Kenny Corp. The firm then launched an aggressive acquisition campaign that would become the hallmark of its expansion strategy over the next several decades.

After acquiring several grocery chains in 1945, Sprague Warner-Kenny changed its name to Consolidated Grocers Corp. Consolidated went public in 1946, and sales that year increased $123 million over the previous year. In 1951, the firm bought Gentry, Inc., a maker of dehydrated onion and garlic spices. In 1954, stockholders voted to change the company's name to Consolidated Foods Corp. to reflect its diverse presence in food processing, packaging, and distribution. In 1956, the firm acquired the Kitchens of Sara Lee, a five-year-old maker of frozen baked goods that was founded by Charles Lubin and named after his daughter. That year, Consolidated also entered the retail food business by acquiring 34 Piggly Wiggly supermarkets.

International expansion began in 1960 with Consolidated's purchase of a controlling interest in a Venezuelan vinegar company. The firm increased its global expansion two years later, acquiring the Dutch canner Jonker Fris. In 1961, the company bought the Eagle supermarket chains. In compliance with an order by the Federal Trade Commission, Consolidated divested its Eagle and Piggly Wiggly supermarkets in 1966 and its Gentry unit in 1967. The company expanded outside the food industry by acquiring Oxford Chemical Corp.; it also purchased E. Kahn's Sons Co., its first meat company. Sales topped $1 billion for the first time in 1967.

Acquisitions in 1968 bought Consolidated entry into several new industries including apparel. The firm also acquired Bryan Foods, Inc., in 1968 and Aris Gloves, later renamed Aris Isotoner, the following year. Hillshire Farm and Rudy's Farm were acquired in 1971. Consolidated entered the personal care business the next year by purchasing Erdal, a Dutch company later renamed Intradal.

Durable goods accounted for nearly two-thirds of corporate profits in 1975. For this reason the company began focusing on non-food merchandise, believing that federal restraints on the food industry would continue to impede growth in that area. That year, John H. Bryan became CEO, and initiated the divestiture of more than 50 small companies purchased in the 1960s. Sales for 1975 reached $2.4 billion.

In 1978, Consolidated acquired Chef Pierre, a frozen desserts manufacturer, and invested in Douwe Egberts, a coffee, tea, and tobacco company based in Holland. The next year, the firm completed the hostile takeover of Hanes Corp., a family-owned undergarment manufacturer whose brands included L'eggs, Bali, and Hanes. Consolidated also acquired Superior Tea and Coffee Co., a distributor of coffee and tea for the foodservice industry, as well as Gallo Salame, Inc., a manufacturer of Italian sausage products.

The Spanish household products company Productos Cruz Verde was purchased in 1980 and contributed to the company's record sales of $5 billion that year. Two years later, Consolidated acquired meat processor Standard Meat Co. and added to its meat holdings with the 1984 purchase of Jimmy Dean Meat Co. For $330 million, the firm acquired the foreign subsidiaries of Nicholas Kiwi Limited, an Australian maker of various shoe care products, medicines, cleaners, and cosmetics.

Consolidated changed its name to Sara Lee Corp. in 1985, using one of its most prominent brand names to enhance public awareness of the company. That year, the company purchased Coach Leatherware Co., a manufacturer of high-quality leather handbags and

The Business

Financials

Revenue (1999): $20 billion

Employees (1998): 139,000

SICs / NAICS

sic 2095 - Roasted Coffee

sic 2053 - Frozen Bakery Products Except Bread

sic 2013 - Sausages & Other Prepared Meats

sic 2251 - Women's Hosiery Except Socks

sic 2252 - Hosiery Nec

sic 2254 - Knit Underwear Mills

sic 2322 - Men's/Boys' Underwear & Nightwear

sic 2342 - Bras, Girdles & Allied Garments

sic 2341 - Women's/Children's Underwear

sic 2842 - Polishes & Sanitation Goods

sic 5963 - Direct Selling Establishments

sic 5046 - Commercial Equipment Nec

naics 311920 - Coffee and Tea Manufacturing

naics 311813 - Frozen Cakes, Pies, and Other Pastries Manufacturing

naics 311613 - Rendering and Meat By-product Processing

naics 315111 - Sheer Hosiery Mills

naics 315119 - Other Hosiery and Sock Mills

naics 315192 - Underwear and Nightwear Knitting Mills

naics 315221 - Men's and Boys' Cut and Sew Underwear and Nightwear Manufacturing

naics 315231 - Women's and Girls' Cut and Sew Lingerie, Loungewear and Nightwear Manufacturing

naics 325612 - Polish and Other Sanitation Good Manufacturing

naics 311612 - Meat Processed from Carcasses

naics 454390 - Other Direct Selling Establishments

naics 421440 - Other Commercial Equipment Wholesalers

other accessories. In 1987, Sara Lee acquired Akzo Consumenten Produkten, a maker of food, household, and personal care products in Holland. Sara Lee was one of the largest U.S. multinationals, with foreign revenues reaching nearly $2 billion that year.

The company continued to increase its global presence by purchasing a 25.1% interest in Delta-Galil,

The Officers

Chairman and CEO: John H. Bryan

President and Chief Operating Officer: C. Steven McMillan

Exec. VP: Frank L. Meysman

Sr. VP and Chief Financial Officer: Judith A. Sprieser

Sr. VP: James R. Carlson

a leading Israeli textile company, in 1988; it also gained entry into the men's sock market by purchasing Adams-Millis Corp. In 1989, Sara Lee acquired Dim, S.A., the leading producer of hosiery and underwear in France and of Champion athletic knitwear in the U.S. Also that year, Sara Lee acquired Hygrade Products, maker of Ball Park hot dogs, and completed the divestiture of its food service operations.

In 1991, the company sold its European over-the-counter drug business to Roche Holding AG. That year Sara Lee purchased Playtex Apparel, Inc., a manufacturer of intimate apparel, and Rinbros, a Mexican-based maker of men's and boys' underwear. Acquisitions in 1992 included BP Nutrition's Consumer Foods Group, Giltex Hosiery, Bessin Corp., the furniture care operations of SC Johnson Wax, and certain properties of Mark Cross, Inc. The European bath and body care business of SmithKline Beecham PLC was purchased in 1993.

A restructuring in 1994 called for the closure of several factories and the loss of 8,500 jobs. That year Imperial Meats was acquired, and Sara Lee's sales exceeded $15 billion. In 1997, the company initiated its "de-verticalization" plan, a restructuring that included the divestiture of non-core businesses and the elimination of 90 manufacturing and distribution facilities.

In July 1998, Sara Lee divested its international tobacco operations by selling Amphora, Drum, and Van Nelle to Imperial Tobacco for $1.1 billion. Later that year, the company acquired the Continental Coffee Products Co. from Quaker Oats Co. Sara Lee recalled certain hot dogs and packaged meats that were linked to 24 deaths due to food poisoning. In June 1999, the company announced its planned merger with Chock Full o' Nuts Corp.

Approach and Engagement

Prior to its purchase by Consolidated Foods Corp., Gentry Inc. held roughly 32% of the U.S. market for dehydrated onion and garlic. Seven years after the acquisition, in 1958, the firm had increased that

market share to 35%. After an initial antitrust investigation, the Federal Trade Commission (FCC) ruled in 1962 that the acquisition violated antitrust regulations. According to Irwin M. Stelzer in *Selected Antitrust Cases*, the FTC found the deal problematic because "merely as a result of its connection with Consolidated, and without any action on the latter's part, Gentry would have an unfair advantage over competitors enabling it to make sales that otherwise might not have been made." Officials were concerned that because Consolidated Foods was a major customer of food products processors, those food processors who used garlic and dehydrated onions when preparing and packaging their products might be influenced to buy those products from Gentry as a means of securing a mutually beneficial, or reciprocal, arrangement.

In 1964, that decision was reversed by the U.S. Circuit Court of Appeals, which pointed to the fact that although Gentry's had upped its share of the dehydrated onion market by roughly 7%, its share of the dehydrated garlic market had fallen 12%. The Court of Appeals believed that even if the two firms had blatantly attempted to forge reciprocal purchasing agreements, the decline in dehydrated garlic market share indicated that those efforts had failed; therefore, competition hadn't been diminished.

Finally, in 1965, the U.S. Supreme Court reversed the judgement of the court of Appeals and handed down its decision that the transaction had indeed violated section seven of the Clayton Antitrust Act. The Court explained that "post-acquisition evidence here tends to confirm, rather than cast doubt upon, the probable anticompetitive effect which the Commission found the merger would have...Gentry, in a rapidly consolidating market, was able to increase its share of onion sales by 7% and hold its losses in garlic to a 12% decrease," wrote Stelzer. Thus, Consolidated Foods was ordered to divest Gentry.

Products and Services

In the mid-1960s, food processing accounted for 41% of sales and 46% of profits at Consolidated Foods. The firm's supermarket unit brought in 20% of sales and 10% of profits, as did wholesaling efforts. Food service operations secured 10% of sales and 13% of profits. Finally, non-food operations garnered 9% of sales and 21% of profits.

By the late 1990s, the firm—by then renamed Sara Lee Corp.—had evolved into a global consumer packaged goods company operating in more than 40 countries. It was divided into five business segments.

Sara Lee Foods was the world's leading packaged

meats company, offering such brands such as Ball Park, Bryan, Hillshire Farm, Jimmy Dean, and Justin Bridou. In 1999, this unit had sales of $5.2 billion.

The **Coffee and Tea** segment, which contributed $2.6 billion in sales in 1999, included such brands as Douwe Egberts, Maison du Cafe, Marcilla, and Merrild.

Household and Body Care, accounting for $2 billion in sales, included branded household and body care products branded as Sanex, Duschdas, Badedas, Radox, Delial, and others. This segment also housed Sara Lee's Direct Selling division, which distributed cosmetics, fragrances, jewelry, toiletries, and apparel products directly to consumers' doors.

The **PYA/Monarch Foodservice Division**, with 1999 sales of $2.7 billion, was the fourth-largest full-line foodservice company in the U.S. It distributed paper supplies, foodservice equipment, and dry, refrigerated, and frozen foods to institutional customers and restaurants.

Branded Apparel, with sales of $7.4 billion in 1999, was comprised of three subsegments. Intimate Apparel and Accessories offered such brands as Bali, Dim, Hanes Her Way, Just My Size, Playtex, and Wonderbra, as well as the newly licensed Ralph Lauren Intimates collection. Knit Products offered the Hanes, Hanes Her Way, Champion, Dim, Just My Size, Rinbros, Abanderado, and Princesa brands. Legwear, the U.S. leader in sheer hosiery, offered Hanes, L'eggs, Donna Karan, and DKNY brands.

Changes to the Industry and Review of the Outcome

In 1967, Consolidated Foods sold Gentry, Inc. to Basic Food Materials. Although another Federal Trade Commission ruling had forced the divestiture of 109 Eagle and Piggly-Wiggly supermarkets and 30 Mays drug stores in 1966, Consolidated Foods continued on its path of growth via acquisition.

The *Federal Trade Commission v. Consolidated Foods Corporation* has served as a key case in antitrust litigation since 1965, and it remains the most important reciprocity case today.

The Players

Founder and Chairman of Consolidated Foods Corp: Nathan Cummings. Canadian-born Nathan Cummings began working in his father's shoe store early in the 1900s. He borrowed $5.2 million in 1939 to buy C.D. Kenny Co., a wholesaler of sugar, coffee, and tea that would evolve into Consolidated Foods. After spending nearly 30 years growing his firm into a leader the U.S. food industry and overseeing numerous acquisitions, including the 1951 purchase of Gentry, Inc., Cummings retired in 1968. He remained the firm's largest shareholder until he died, at the age of 88, in 1985.

Research

Briet, William and Kenneth G. Elzinga. *The Antitrust Casebook*, Dryden Press, 1982. Covers key antitrust cases, including *Federal Trade Commission v. Consolidated Foods Corporation*.

"Consolidated-Foods; OBIT/Nathan Cummings, Founder of Consolidated Foods," in *Business Wire*, 20 February 1985. Details the career of Nathan Cummings.

"Consolidated Foods Told to Divest Itself of Gentry," in *The New York Times*, 1 December 1962. Briefly describes the initial ruling by the Federal Trade Commission.

"Court Reverses F.T.C. on Food Merger Rule," in *The New York Times*, 26 March 1964. Details the ruling by the Court of Appeals that reversed the Federal Trade Commission's finding.

"Food Corporation Is Still Growing," in *The New York Times*, 8 October 1967. Covers the dealings of Consolidated Foods over the past several years.

Sara Lee Corp. Home Page, available at http://www.saralee.com. Official World Wide Web Home Page for Sara Lee Corp. Includes news releases, financial data, product information, and an historical review of the company.

"Sara Lee Corp.," in *Notable Corporate Chronologies*, The Gale Group, 1999. Offers a chronology of Sara Lee's history.

Stelzer, Irwin M. *Selected Antitrust Cases*, Richard D. Irwin, Inc., 1966. Covers key antitrust cases, including *Federal Trade Commission v. Consolidated Foods Corporation*.

JEFF ST. THOMAS

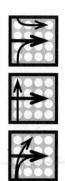

COOPER INDUSTRIES & MCGRAW-EDISON

Cooper Industries, Inc.
600 Travis, Ste. 5800
Houston, TX 77002-1001
USA

tel: (713)209-8400
fax: (713)209-8995
web: http://www.cooperindustries.com
e-mail: info@cooperindustries.com

nationality: USA
date: May 31, 1985
affected: Cooper Industries, Inc., USA, founded 1833
affected: McGraw-Edison Co., USA

Overview of the Acquisition

McGraw-Edison, a manufacturer of electrical and industrial products, became a wholly owned subsidiary of Cooper Industries, a maker of tools, hardware, compression and drilling equipment, and other electrical and electronic products, on May 31, 1985. The $1.4 billion acquisition was the largest in Cooper's history, nearly doubling its size and positioning it among the world's largest lighting manufacturers.

History of Cooper Industries, Inc.

In 1833, Brothers Charles and Elias Cooper build a foundry in Mount Vernon, Ohio, called C. & G. Cooper Co., to manufacture plows, maple syrup kettles, hog troughs, sorghum grinders, and wagon boxes. In 1852, Cooper shipped its first steam-powered compressors for blast furnaces when the railroad linked Mount Vernon to the rest of the nation. Its products included wood-burning steam locomotives and steam-powered blowing machines for charcoal blast furnaces. Cooper became the first company in the West to produce the new, highly efficient Corliss engine in 1869.

With the discovery of gas at the turn of the century, along with the development of the oil industry, Cooper began to make a gradual change to natural-gas internal-combustion engines. During World War I, the firm began building high-speed steam-hydraulic forging presses for government arsenals, munitions plants and shipyards, as well as giant gas engines and compressors and triple-expansion marine engines. Needing additional production facilities to meet the mounting orders for large natural-gas engine compressor units, Cooper merged with Bessemer Gas Engine Co., based in Pennsylvania, in 1929.

Recognized as the largest builder of gas engines and compressors in the U.S., Cooper-Bessemer Corp. opened a sales office in New York at the beginning of the Great Depression. Sales dropped more than 90% in 1931, reflecting the near halt of construction on long-distance pipelines and in American shipyards. By the end of the decade, the firm had slowly revived by continuing to improve products and by entering new markets, including developing a diesel to replace steam-powered railroad engines.

During World War II, Cooper-Bessemer became a major producer of diesel engines for military vessels of all kinds; the firm also increased production of locomotive engines. With net sales at an all time high in 1944, Cooper-Bessemer listed publicly on the New York Stock Exchange for the first time. Looking to sell its products worldwide, Cooper-Bessemer opened its first sales-service branch outside of the U.S., in Caracas, Venezuela. The company also developed the "turbo flow" high-compression gas-diesel engine. In 1947, Cooper-Bessemer introduced the GMW engine, which delivered 2,500 horsepower and could be shipped in one assembled unit.

By the early 1950s, sales had exceeded $50 million, surpassing the company's wartime high. At that time, Cooper-Bessemer's shipments were almost solely to markets supported by the Korean War effort. In 1954, a seven-week strike, a nationwide recession, and the Supreme Court's ruling that producers selling gas to interstate pipelines must submit to the Federal Power Commission's jurisdiction, all contributed to a 38% decrease in net sales. Revenues bounced back to a record high of $61.2 million in 1956, due to revitalized demand. Cooper-Bessemer began seeking avenues of diversification to decrease its vulnerability to the cyclical energy market.

In 1960, the firm unveiled the world's first industrial jet-powered gas turbine. Four years later, Cooper-Bessemer formed a wholly-owned British subsidiary, Cooper-Bessemer (U.K.), Ltd. and opened an office in Beirut. Acquisitions such as Kline Manufacturing, Ajax Iron Works, and the Pennsylvania Pump and Compressor Co., helped boost sales from $68 million to $117 million during the first half of the 1960s. To reflect its diversity, the company changed its name to Cooper Industries in 1965. Two years later, Lufkin Rule Co. joined Cooper's holdings. The firm bought Crescent Niagara Corp. in 1968.

Cooper branched into aircraft services with the purchase of Dallas Automotive, Southwest Airmotive Corp., and Standard Aircraft Equipment in 1970. White Motor Co. was acquired in 1976. Three years later, the company purchased Dallas-based Gardner-Denver Co.; the deal was one of the ten largest in U.S. business history at the time. Sales exceeded $1 billion.

Diversifiying into electrical components for the first time, Cooper acquired Crouse-Hinds Co. of Syracuse and Belden Corp. in 1981. Four years later, the firm merged with McGraw-Edison Co., a maker of electrical energy-related products. Sales for the year surpassed $3 billion. In 1989, Cooper purchased Champion Spark Plug Co., the world's largest maker

The Business

Financials

Revenue (1998): $3.6 billion

Employees (1998): 28,100

SICs / NAICS

sic 3563 - Air & Gas Compressors

sic 3531 - Construction Machinery

sic 3541 - Machine Tools-Metal Cutting Types

sic 3542 - Machine Tools-Metal Forming Types

sic 3545 - Machine Tool Accessories

sic 3546 - Power-Driven Handtools

sic 3645 - Residential Lighting Fixtures

sic 3646 - Commercial Lighting Fixtures

naics 333912 - Air and Gas Compressor Manufacturing

naics 333512 - Machine Tool (Metal Cutting Types) Manufacturing

naics 333513 - Machine Tool (Metal Forming Types) Manufacturing

naics 333515 - Cutting Tool and Machine Tool Accessory Manufacturing

naics 333991 - Power-Driven Hand Tool Manufacturing

naics 335121 - Residential Electric Lighting Fixture Manufacturing

naics 335122 - Commercial, Industrial and Institutional Electric Lighting Fixture Manufacturing

of spark plugs for combustion engines, and Cameron Iron Works.

Three Canadian operations were purchased in 1991. The following year, Brazilian hand tool maker Ferramentas Belzer do Brasil joined Cooper's holdings. Cooper added Abex Friction Products to its mix in 1994. In July of 1995, the firm divested its ailing petroleum and industrial equipment business by spinning it off to its shareholders and exchanging 85.5% of its stock in the unit, called Cooper Cameron, with shareholders in return for 9.5 million of its own shares. The 1996 acquisitions of two electrical products manufacturers, CEAG of Germany and Cutler-Hammer of Brazil, in addition to an automotive parts producer, Trichamp of South Africa, expanded international operations. Growth in the electrical sector continued in 1997 via eight acquisitions, including Menvier-

The Officers

Chairman, President, and CEO: H. John Riley, Jr.

Exec. VP, Operations: Ralph E. Jackson, Jr.

Sr. VP and Chief Financial Officer: D. Bradley McWilliams

Sr. VP, General Counsel, and Secretary: Diane K. Schumacher

Sr. VP, Human Resources: David R. Sheil, Jr.

Swain Group, an emergency lights and alarm manufacturer. Cooper also sold its automotive operations to Federal-Mogul. Efforts to purchase United Kingdom-based lighting products manufacturer TLG fell through in 1998. That year, Cooper bought Apparatebau and Hundsbach, two German electrical products firms. A restructuring eliminated 1,000 jobs and 12 plants.

Market Forces Driving the Acquisition

Cooper began its foray into the electrical products industry in 1981 when it acted as a white knight, rescuing Crouse-Hinds Co., based in Syracuse, New York, from InterNorth Inc. with a $700 million stock bid. Along with Crouse-Hinds came Belden Corp., a wire and cable manufacturer Crouse-Hinds had been in the process of purchasing. The impetus behind the acquisition was Cooper's desire to reduce its reliance on the cyclical gas and oil industry. The firm had been pursuing diversification away from energy-related businesses since the late 1950s. The Crouse-Hinds assets not only doubled Cooper's size, they also acted as a major buffer when gas and oil demand dipped in the early 1980s. Although energy-related sales slid 60% at Cooper, strong electrical components sales helped minimize the damage.

In the mid-1980s, Cooper began eyeing McGraw-Edison, a maker of lighting fixtures, fuses, and power distribution equipment. Such an acquisition would allow Cooper to increase its electrical products operations and target the primary power supply industry. According to Robert B. Dyer, a vice president of Cooper, purchasing McGraw-Edison would afford both firms "an outstanding opportunity to combine a very well-regarded set of product lines. We have a number of common lines of distribution that go well together to the marketplace."

Approach and Engagement

In March of 1985, when Cooper Industries CEO Robert Cizik approached McGraw Edison about a possible deal, McGraw Edison CEO Edward Williams told Cizik his firm was not for sale. However, later that month, McGraw Edison and Forstmann Little & Co. announced a merger plan. Cooper Industries blocked what would have been the largest leveraged buyout in U.S. corporate history when it countered Forstmann Little's $1.3 billion bid for McGraw-Edison with a $65 per share, or $1.1 billion, offer of its own. Cooper also agreed to assume roughly $300 million in McGraw-Edison debt, bringing the total purchase price to $1.4 billion.

Forstmann Little dropped its bid, rather than up its offer, and Cooper's tender offer for the 16.9 million outstanding shares of McGraw-Edison began on March 27. The deal was completed on May 31, 1985, when McGraw-Edison became a wholly owned subsidiary of Cooper. Cizik remained at the helm of Cooper, and Williams accepted the vice chairmanship.

Products and Services

By the late 1990s, electrical products had become the focus of the company. Cooper was organized into two divisions. The electrical products group accounted for roughly 75% of sales and included Arrow Hart wiring devices, Buss fuses, Crouse-Hinds electrical fixtures, and Halo lighting systems. The tools and hardware group included Apex sockets, Crescent wrenches, Plumb hammers, and Weller soldering equipment.

Review of the Outcome

McGraw-Edison, with annual sales of $1.7 billion in 1984, nearly doubled the size of Cooper Industries, whose own sales had reached $2 billion prior to the deal. The transaction also pushed Cooper into the ranks of the world's largest lighting manufacturers and raised Cooper's debt-to-capital ratio from 50% to 54%. By the end of 1985, through the divestiture of non-core assets, as well as layoffs, Cooper had reduced that ratio to 49%.

Cooper added to its electrical products holdings in 1988 with the purchase of RTE Corp., a maker of electrical distribution equipment. By the end of the decade, Cooper manufactured more than one million products in 145 plants.

Research

Cooper Industries, Inc. 1985 Annual Report. Describes the state of Cooper Industries in the year of its acquisition of McGraw Edison.

Cooper Industries, Inc. Home Page, available at

http://www.cooperindustries.com. Official World Wide Web Page for Cooper Industries, Inc. Offers news releases, financial and product information, and employment information.

"Cooper Industries, Inc.," in *Notable Corporate Chronologies*, The Gale Group, 1999. Provides an overview of the history of the company.

Cuff, Daniel F. "Cooper Tops Bid to McGraw," in *The New York Times*, 26 March 1985. Details Cooper Industries counter offer for McGraw-Edison.

———. "Forstmann Drops Its Bid for McGraw," in *The New York Times*, 28 March 1985. Explains why Forstmann backed out of the running for McGraw-Edison.

"Edward J. Williams to Retire as Vice Chairman of Cooper Industries," *Southwest Newswire*, 17 December 1985. Covers the career of Edward J. Williams.

"John Riley Elected President and CEO of Cooper; Chairman Robert Cizik to Retire in April 1996," in *PR Newswire*, 1 August 1995. Covers the career of Robert Cizik.

JEFF ST. THOMAS

COSTCO & PRICE

Costco Companies, Inc.
999 Lake Dr.
Issaquah, WA 98027
USA

tel: (425)313-8100
fax: (425)313-8103
web: http://www.costco.com

nationality: USA
date: October 1993
affected: Price Co., USA, founded 1976
affected: Costco Wholesale Corp., USA, founded 1983

Overview of the Merger

The merger of San Diego, California-based Price Co. and Kirkland, Washington-based Costco Wholesale Corp. in October 1993 created the second-largest warehouse chain in the U.S., behind the Sam's Club chain of Wal-Mart, Inc. The newly formed Price/Costco, Inc. (later renamed Costco Companies, Inc.) boasted annual sales of $16 billion and operated 195 stores in the U.S., compared to the 282 stores operated by Sam' Club.

History of Costco Wholesale Corp.

In September of 1983, The Cost Club opened its first wholesale warehouse, in Seattle, Washington. Cofounder Jeffrey H. Brotman acted as chairman, while his partner, James D. Sinegal, oversaw operations as president. Although sales reached $102 million in 1984, the firm lost $3.3 million. After changing its name to Costco Wholesale Corp., the firm conducted its initial public offering. Costco also opened its first two Canadian locations, one in Edmonton, Alberta, and one in Vancouver, British Columbia.

The firm added fresh foods to its product line in 1986. Stores were opened in Minnesota and Wisconsin. The following year, sales exceeded $1 billion for the first time; net income totaled $5.1 million. Costco opened a store in Honolulu, Hawaii, in 1988.

The firm moved into the northeastern U.S. by opening two stores in Massachusetts in 1990. That year, Costco added home improvement and green nursery products to selected warehouses. Stock split two-for-one in 1991, and Costco completed a public offering of 3.45 million shares of common stock. Proceeds of approximately $200 million were used to fund expansion and to reduce debt. The company also opened eleven Sandwich/Pizza Shops, 19 One-Hour Photo Labs, and four Print Shops and was restructured into two divisions: West Coast and East Coast operations.

In 1992, Costco sold $300 million 5.75% convertible subordinated debentures, netting proceeds of $297 million. Sales of $6.5 billion were 25% higher than the previous year's; net income had jumped 34% to $113.3 million. Within a decade of its founding, Costco had become one of the top four operators of wholesale retail outlets in the U.S. with approximately four million members at its 100 stores in 15 U.S. states and Canada. In October of 1993, Costco merged with rival Price Club, becoming Price/Costco Inc. The following year, Price/Costco spun off its commercial real estate operations as Price Enterprises.

Price/Costco sent coupon books to two million non-members in order to compete with other discount chains in 1995. As a means of keeping costs under control, the firm engaged in no other advertising efforts. That year, Price/Costco opened 19 new stores. In 1996, Price/Costco and Price Enterprises resolved a two-year-old lawsuit stemming from the merger that created Price/Costco and the spin-off of Price Enterprises Inc. Price Enterprises agreed to eliminate some non-compete restrictions and transfer certain intangible assets as a result of the agreement. Also that year, Price/Costco launched a service that allowed customers to shop for a new car online. In 1997, the firm changed its name to Costco Companies, Inc., and stock prices jumped roughly 69% to $41.

History of Price Co.

In 1976, Sol Price, Rick Libenson, and Giles Bateman founded the Price Co. (PC) to operate a membership-only, cash-and-carry merchandising warehouse store in San Diego, California. Members paid a flat fee of $25 to shop in the store, which featured items priced at 10% above cost. The new firm lost $16 million during its first year of operation. Two years later, PC opened a second Price Club store, this one in Phoenix, Arizona. Four more stores had been opened in California and Arizona by the end of the decade.

PC became a public company in 1980 and continued to show improved performance as rising inflation drove customers to seek lower-cost retail outlets for a number of goods. Net income doubled in fiscal 1983 to $15 million, on sales of $641 million. That year, two new competitors entered the discount warehouse retailing arena: Costco, based in Seattle, Washington; and Arkansas-based Wal-Mart, Inc. PC responded by accelerating its pace of expansion. Net income nearly doubled again in 1984, reaching $29 million on sales of $1.15 billion. PC opened five new stores in California, one in New Mexico, and two in Virginia; created a subsidiary, Price Club East, Inc., to manage its expansion in the eastern U.S.; and sold $74 million in debentures to raise capital for continued expansion.

By the mid-1980s, PC was the largest discount retail warehouse store operator in the U.S., although

The Business

Financials

Revenue (1998): $24.3 billion

Employees (1998): 63,000

SICs / NAICS

sic 5141 - Groceries-General Line

sic 5182 - Wines & Distilled Beverages

sic 5122 - Drugs, Proprietaries & Sundries

that standing was soon overtaken by Wal-Mart's Sam's Club chain. In 1985, the firm opened a store in Glen Burnie, Maryland, and established a subsidiary to develop or lease excess land purchased for building Price Club outlets. PC's policy was to buy inexpensive land in less desirable locations outside major cities. Although PC failed in an attempt to acquire 12 TSS-Seedman stores in New York in 1986, the company continued to expand by opening its first store outside the U.S. in Canada. The collapse of the New York Stock Exchange in October 1987 caused PC's stock value to fall by more than 60%, to $23.50 per share. The company issued a $200 million debenture offering to offset its loss of capital.

In 1988, PC restructured to incorporate its expanded activities and acquired A.M. Lewis, Inc., a wholesale grocery chain operating in California and Arizona. PC shifted the focus of its expansion to Quebec, Canada, and the eastern U.S. Growth continued in 1989, enabling the company to issue its first dividend to stockholders. Also that year, PC opened eight new stores in California, Arizona, New York, and Quebec and piloted two home and office furniture retail outlets in southern California. Sluggish sales soon forced the firm to close the two new home and office furniture outlets.

PC diversified into the lodging and leisure industry in 1990 by entering into a joint venture with Atlas Hotels, Inc., through which PC could design and market travel packages to Price Club customers, and AHI was entitled to draw credit from PC. The company also opened stores in Colorado, and British Columbia, Canada, that year. In 1991, PC entered into a joint venture with retailer Controladora Comercial Mexico to operate Price Club stores in Mexico. The company also issued $250 million in debentures to finance the purchase of land for potential new store locations and to thwart any possible takeover attempts.

The Officers

Chairman: Jeffrey H. Brotman

President and CEO: James D. Sinegal

Exec. VP and Chief Financial Officer: Richard A. Galanti

Exec. VP, International Operations: Franz E. Lazarus

Sr. Exec. VP and Chief Operating Officer: Richard D. DiCherchio

In 1992, when second quarter profits declined 26% from their levels the previous year, stockholders threatened legal action, alleging that PC's management painted an unrealistic picture of corporate prospects at the last annual meeting. A few months later, PC completed its first store closing when it shut down a unit in Richmond, Virginia. Also that year, in an effort to keep up with competitors, Price Clubs stores added bakeries; fresh meat, poultry, and fish; full-service hearing aid departments; and landscaping centers. In October of 1993, PC merged with rival Costco Wholesale to form Price/Costco Inc.

Market Forces Driving the Merger

Between the late 1970s and early 1990s, warehouse club retailing had grown into a $33 billion industry. This growth slowed dramatically in the early 1990s as the market reached saturation. New single market competitors, including PetSmart and Office Depot, were also stealing business from the multiproduct warehouses.

Price Co. (PC) was one of the warehousers most crippled by the squeeze. The firm's efforts to diversify into home and office furniture had fizzled. Also hurting the chain was the minimal expansion it had engaged in during the 1980s, when rivals were gobbling up market share. According to a July 1993 article in *Business Week*, "Throughout the '80s, the Prices refused to expand much beyond their California base. When they finally began to add stores aggressively in 1991, they ran headlong into such rivals as Costco and Wal-Mart's Sam's Clubs." Eleven of the new Price Club stores opened in 1991 were in California, where 29 Price Club stores were already in operation. As a result, the firm found itself cannibalizing its own stores; earnings in 1992 fell roughly 4%, the first decline in over a decade. Stock fell from a 1991 high of $65 per share to $30 per share.

Similar to the major players in many industries nearing saturation, leading warehouse retail chains began pursuing consolidation in the early 1990s. For example, in May of 1993, warehousing giant Wal-Mart, Inc. announced its plans to buy 14 Pace Membership Warehouse units from Kmart Corp. Concern over a merger between Costco and Wal-Mart, which controlled more than half the market, prompted PC to begin negotiations with Costco, which was hoping to avoid a takeover by Wal-Mart. At the same time, Costco did not want to see any alliances forming between Wal-Mart and PC.

Approach and Engagement

Price Co. (PC) head Robert Price and Costco leader James Sinegal had first held merger discussions in 1992, but negotiations ended with bickering over who would run the merged firm. When earnings during the first three quarters of 1993 plummeted 18% and shareholders neared revolt, PC founder Sol Price arranged for a meeting at his home in La Jolla, California, with his son, Robert, and Sinegal.

On June 16, 1993, the two parties agreed to a partial merger, whereby both firms would operate with separate headquarters. As CEO, Sinegal would oversee domestic operations, while Price, as chairman, would head up international operations. Costco shareholders would own 52% of the merged firm, to be named Price/Costco, while PC shareholders would control the remaining 48%. Purchasing and shipping operations would be consolidated and technologies shared.

The all-stock multibillion dollar deal was completed in October of 1993. Costco shareholders received one share in the new company for each Costco share held, while PC shares were worth 2.13 new shares.

Products and Services

By the late 1990s, Costco had surpassed Wal-Mart's Sam's Club as the leading wholesale club operator, with roughly 300 membership warehouses in the U.S., Canada, Mexico, South Korea, Taiwan, and the United Kingdom. U.S. operations accounted for 81% of sales. Products included fresh and dry food, snacks, beverages, health and beauty products, appliances, electronics, jewelry, apparel, cameras, books, furniture, office supplies, pet food, sporting goods, tobacco, toys, and tools.

Review of the Outcome

The merger between Price Co. and Costco Wholesale created Price/Costco, a new industry giant, second only to Sam's Club, owned by Wal-Mart, in terms of stores operated. However, management disputes plagued the firm after the merger was completed. Although the international expansion begun by Price Co. prior to the deal had continued, revenues and profits kept falling. Disputes arose over which direction Price/Costco should take. Robert Price sought to continue his company's real estate interests, whereas Sinegal pushed for further expansion of the warehouse chain. Many analysts believed it was Price's focus on real estate—one reason the firm may not have expanded as quickly as its competitors—that had gotten the warehouse retailer into trouble in the first place.

Price and Sinegal decided upon a partial split in 1994. The commercial real estate assets of Price/Costco, along with four warehouse units and holdings in several international ventures, were spun off as Price Enterprises Inc. Robert Price resigned as chairman to head up the new firm; he was replaced by co-founder Jeffrey Brotman.

After the split, Price/Costco refocused on its warehouse operations, and by the end of 1996, revenues had reached $18 billion. Warehouses in operation totaled 266; they spanned 21 states, Mexico, Canada, the United Kingdom and Korea. The firm adopted the Costco Companies moniker in 1997. By then, it had surpassed Sam's Club as the world's leading warehouse chain.

Research

Barrett, Amy. "A Retailing Pacesetter Pulls Up Lame," in *Business Week*, 12 July 1993. Describes the struggles of Price Co. in the years preceding the merger with Costco.

Costco Companies, Inc. Home Page, available at http://www.costco.com. Official World Wide Web Page for Costco Companies, Inc. Offers news releases, financial and product information, and employment information.

"Costco Wholesale," in *Notable Corporate Chronologies*, The Gale Group, 1999. Provides an overview of the history of the company.

"Driving Costco," in *Business Week*, 12 January 1998. Describes the performance of Costco in the late 1990s.

"Price Club, Costco Merging Discount Stores From Huge Alliance," in *The San Francisco Chronicle*, 17 June 1993. Offers an overview of the general details of the merger.

The Players

President and CEO of Costco Wholesale Corp.: James D. Sinegal. Former Peace Corp. volunteer James Sinegal began his career in membership warehouse retailing at Fedmart, a chain founded by Sol Price in 1954. Sinegal and Price encountered each again when Sinegal began working for Price Co. in the 1970s. After climbing his way up to the post of executive vice president, Sinegal left to co-found competitor Costco Wholesale with Jeffrey H. Brotman in 1983. Ten years later, Sinegal found himself negotiating a merger with Sol Price's son, Robert Price. When Costco Wholesale and Price Co. merged to form Price/Costco, Sinegal took the reins as CEO and president, posts he continues to hold today.

Chairman of Price Co.: Robert Price. Robert Price began working for the Price Co. when his father, Sol Price, founded the first warehouse store in 1976. Twelve years later, Robert took over as chairman when his father resigned. Criticized for expansion efforts deemed "too little, too late" by many industry experts, Price eventually agreed to merge his family business with Costco Wholesale in 1993, taking the back seat to Costco chief executive James D. Sinegal. Management scuffles led to the spin off in 1994 of Price/Costco's commercial real estate assets as Price Enterprises, Inc. Price then resigned as chairman of Price/Costco, choosing instead to head up Price Enterprises.

"The Price Co.," in *Notable Corporate Chronologies*, The Gale Group, 1999. Provides an overview of the history of the company.

Tait, Nikki. "U.S. 'Warehouse Clubs' in Deal to Merge Operations," in *Financial Times*, 17 June 1993. Covers the terms of the transaction.

JEFF ST. THOMAS

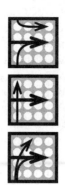

CREDIT SUISSE & FIRST BOSTON

Credit Suisse First Boston
11 Madison Ave.
New York, NY 10010-3629
USA

tel: (212)325-2000
fax: (212)325-8249
web: http://www.csfb.com

nationality: USA
date: December 1988
affected: Credit Suisse Group, Switzerland, founded 1856
affected: First Boston Corp., USA, founded 1933
affected: Credit Suisse First Boston, United Kingdom, founded 1978

Overview of the Merger

Credit Suisse, the third-largest commercial bank in Switzerland, and First Boston Corp.,the oldest investment bank on Wall Street, began their rocky relationship in 1978 when they formed Credit Suisse First Boston (CSFB), a London-based international securities business. The increasing globalization of the financial industry fostered territorial controversy between First Boston and CSFB, which prompted the two firms, along with Credit Suisse, to reformulate their original agreement.

In 1988, Credit Suisse took First Boston private and merged it with Credit Suisse First Boston under the holding company CS First Boston, Inc. The $1.1 billion merger left Credit Suisse with a 44.5% stake in CS First Boston, the maximum allowed by the U.S. Glass-Steagall Act, which prohibited a bank from owning more than 45% of U.S. securities house. Deregulation in the U.S. banking industry allowed Credit Suisse gain to control of CS First Boston (later called Credit Suisse First Boston) in 1990, after the Swiss banking giant pumped $300 million into the firm and took on $470 million in nonperforming loans. As a result, Credit Suisse became the first international owner of a leading U.S. investment bank.

History of Credit Suisse Group

In 1856, Alfred Escher, a young Zurich politician, decided to set up an independent bank called Credit Suisse. He put up Sfr3 million worth of shares on public offer and received Sfr218 million in subscriptions within three days. In 1867, Credit Suisse posted its first and only loss, which was due to a downturn in Switzerland's growing textile industry caused by collapsing cotton prices. By 1871, Credit Suisse, a benefactor of railroad expansion, was the largest bank in Switzerland.

At the beginning of World War I, Credit Suisse operated 13 domestic branch offices. Foreign investment in Switzerland stopped completely; as investors in hostile countries returned Swiss securities, the bank played a crucial role in placing them on the Swiss market. When World War I ended, the bank focused on financing the electrical utilities of the country. In 1924, Credit Suisse helped finance the national railroad's conversion to electricity. By the end of the 1930s, mounting tensions in Europe had prompted Credit Suisse to focus on penetrating English speaking countries; the bank formed the Swiss-American Corp. to focus on U.S. securities. In 1940, Credit Suisse's first foreign branch was opened, in New York City.

At the end of World War II, Credit Suisse remained financially sound despite losing almost half of its employees to war related service. Large amounts of credit remained extended to Swiss authorities who were owed more than Sfr1.7 billion by Germany. Normal banking operations resumed, including issuing paper for foreign debtors. The bank began offering new types of savings accounts and consumer credit cards.

The emergence of a free gold market in the late 1960s enabled Credit Suisse to become a major gold trading house; the acquisition of Valcambi SA, a precious metals refinery, added the manufacturing of ingots and coins to Credit Suisse's activities. By 1970, Credit Suisse operated offices on every continent except Antarctica. In 1977, authorities begin investigating a fraudulent banking and foreign exchange trading scheme at the bank's Chiasso branch which involved more than $1.2 billion. Several top executives resigned. The following year, Credit Suisse First Boston (CSFB), a joint venture with the New York investment bank First Boston, was formed. Michael von Clemm was named chairman and CEO of CSFB; in 1980, he oversaw one of the biggest financial disasters in CSFB's history: the purchase a $150 million issue that eventually cost the bank between $20 million and $40 million in losses.

During the early 1980s, Credit Suisse began shifting its focus from traditional Swiss banking practices to world investment banking and money management. In 1985, Credit Suisse became one of the first major Swiss banks to begin operations in the West German market. A $4 billion bond was floated by General Motors Acceptance Corp. in a joint venture involving CSFB, Credit Suisse, and First Boston. First Boston acted as lead manager, Credit Suisse provided a letter of credit to back the notes, and CSFB placed $400 million of the bonds in Europe.

CSFB and First Boston merged into a new holding company, CS First Boston, in 1988. Credit Suisse owned a 44.5% stake of CS First Boston. The following year, Credit Suisse formed CS Holding as a new parent company to oversee all the group's activities, including CSFB, CS Life (a life insurance carrier), Fides Holding (money management services), Leu Holding, and Electrowatt (electricity, manufacturing, and engineering services). Credit Suisse gained control of CS First Boston in 1990.

The Business

Financials

Revenue (1998): $6.71 billion

Employees (1998): 14,126

SICs / NAICS

sic 6712 - Bank Holding Companies

sic 6029 - Commercial Banks Nec

sic 6311 - Life Insurance

sic 6211 - Security Brokers & Dealers

naics 551111 - Offices of Bank Holding Companies

naics 524113 - Direct Life Insurance Carriers

Union Bank of Switzerland rejected a $47 billion merger proposal by CS Holding in 1996. That year, the firm announced a major restructuring that included consolidating power in Zurich and cutting its workforce by 15% or 5,000 employees. The company planned to condense all subsidiaries into four specialized business units: Swiss domestic banking, worldwide private banking, institutional asset management, and corporate investment banking. In 1997, CS Holding changed its name to Credit Suisse Group. The firm also paid roughly $10 billion for Winterthur Insurance Co.. The deal boosted Credit Suisse's assets to $466 billion, making it nearly as large as Deutsche Bank AG, Europe's biggest bank.

History of First Boston Corp.

The Safety Fund Bank was founded in 1859. Five years later, after entering the national bank system of the U.S., Safety Fund changed its name to First National Bank of Boston. Shortly thereafter, First National took over the Massachusetts National Bank of Boston. The Glass-Steagall Act was passed in 1933, preventing banks from operating in both commercial and investment ventures. Consequently, First National and Chase National Bank merged their securities assets into a new firm called First Boston Corp.

First Boston struggled during the years of the Great Depression. The advent of World War II proved to be a boon for the firm due to the nation's growing need for capital. First Boston became the target of an antitrust investigation in the 1940s. During that decade, the company's agreement to provide the financial backing for an oil refinery in Puerto Rico fell apart. It wasn't until the early 1970s that First Boston

The Officers

Chairman, Credit Suisse First Boston, Credit Suisse, and
  Credit Suisse Group: Rainer E. Gut
Vice Chairman, Credit Suisse First Boston, Credit Suisse,
  and Credit Suisse Group: Robert L. Genillard
CEO: Allen D. Wheat
Chief Financial Officer: Stephen A.M. Hester
Vice Chairman: Didier Pineau-Valencienne

began to experience consistent success, due in large part to the improved treasury bond market. International expansion began in earnest at that time.

In 1978, Credit Suisse and First Boston founded Credit Suisse First Boston (CSFB), a securities house based in London. The structure of the agreement was rather complex; in essence, CSFB and First Boston owned 40% of each other, while Credit Suisse owned roughly 60% of CSFB.

First Boston posted a $100 million loss in 1986 when it miscalculated the success of the bond market. When the stock market crashed in 1987, First Boston lost $60 million on takeover stocks. The firm lost another $50 million in the mortgage sector in 1988. That year, First Boston and CSFB were merged under a new holding company, CS First Boston, Inc., based in New York. Credit Suisse initially owned a 44.5% stake in the new firm.

CS First Boston began investing in Russia in the early 1990s, eventually establishing an office in Moscow. In 1997, Credit Suisse First Boston (India) Securities was founded and an office in South Korea was opened. Barclays PLC agreed to sell a large chunk of its Asian investment banking assets to CS First Boston—which by then was referred to as Credit Suisse First Boston—for $170 million in 1998.

Market Forces Driving the Merger

Despite its almost immediate success in the Eurobond market, Credit Suisse First Boston (CSFB) was plagued with internal problems from its inception in 1978 as a joint venture between Credit Suisse and First Boston. For example, six executives, including three executive directors, left CSFB when Jack Hennessy, formerly of First Boston, was appointed CEO in 1982. Problems at CSFB continued in 1984 when three more executives defected to Merrill Lynch, taking seven employees with them.

In the mid-1980s, CSFB was forced to diversify into mergers and acquisitions, equity sales, and other specialties when its share of the Eurobond market dropped from more than 16% to just over 11%. The firm began 1987 with an estimated $15 million loss on a debt swap with Italy. Also, as the financial industry become increasingly global, executives at First Boston and CSFB began bickering over how to divide both territory and profits. According to an April 1998 article in *The Economist*, "First Bostonians have accused their London offspring of pursuing only deals on which all the profit will accrue to CSFB. CSFB executives, for their part, have snootily considered First Boston to be a spendthrift monster, lacking intellect and knowledge of international markets. Arguments and even refusals to pay up have led to complaints that more time is spent on transatlantic wrangles than on fighting the real opposition."

Boundaries that were once clear—CSFB targeted Europe, while First Boston operated in the rest of the world—had been muddied when "the once-distinct U.S., European, and Japanese capital markets started fusing together," wrote *Business Week* in February of 1987. Although CSFB had been able to stay ahead of its competitors in the European securities market, the firm's top managers recognized that they needed to not only continue the push diversify into other markets, but also to resolve the growing friction between CSFB and First Boston.

Approach and Engagement

In April of 1988, the heads of Credit Suisse, First Boston, and CSFB—Rainer Gut, Peter Buchanan, and Jack Hennessy, respectively—met to discuss their options. The anticipated loosening of the Glass-Steagall Act, which prevented a bank from operating in both commercial and investment markets, would likely allow Credit Suisse to gain control of First Boston if it chose to pursue such a deal. However, management believed that banking on deregulation was risky. Instead, they chose to pursue a more complex transaction in which Credit Suisse would take First Boston private and consolidate it with CSFB under the umbrella of CS First Boston, Inc., a new holding company in which Credit Suisse would hold a 44.5% stake, the maximum allowed at the time. To boost morale, employees would be allowed to own 25% of CS First Boston. To achieve status as a global investment bank, management would also seek a Japanese partner to complement its U.S. and European assets. The $1.1 billion deal was approved by First Boston's board of directors in October and completed in December.

Products and Services

Credit Suisse First Boston operated 60 offices in more than 30 countries in 1998. European sales accounted for 47% of total revenues; U.S. sales brought in 44%; and Asian sales secured the remaining 9%. Products and services were organized into four segments: investment banking, which accounted for 27% of sales; fixed income and derivative products, which garnered 26%; equity, which brought in 21%; and Credit Suisse financial products, which secured 16%.

Changes to the Industry and Review of the Outcome

When the junk bond market collapsed in 1989, CS First Boston found itself holding over $1 billion in nonperforming bridge loans First Boston had made to fund corporate takeovers. As a result, Credit Suisse took over $470 million of the bad loans and infused CS First Boston with $300 million in equity in 1990, gaining control of CS First Boston and becoming the first international owner of a leading U.S. investment bank. CS First Boston CEO Jack Hennessy fired First Boston head William Mayer, replacing him with Archie Cox. Layoffs that year totaled roughly 400, nearly 10% of First Boston's staff.

By 1992, First Boston had not only repaid Credit Suisse for its bailout in 1989, but had also turned itself around due to strong sales in the fixed-income debt sector. Employees were expecting sizable bonuses. However, CSFB's poor performance undercut the overall bonus structure when management decided to divide the pot evenly. Consequently, several angry First Boston employees quit, highlighting the fact that, five years after the merger, the two firms still viewed each other as separate entities.

Integration problems weren't the only issues facing CS First Boston. To achieve its goal of becoming a global investment powerhouse, CS First Boston had searched for a Japanese partner for ten years. Finally, in 1998, Barclays PLC agreed to sell a large chunk of its Asian investment banking assets—including operations in China, Hong Kong, Indonesia, India, Malaysia, Singapore, and Taiwan—as well as its European investment banking operations, to the firm for $170 million.

Research

Bartlett, Sarah and Richard Melcher. "Credit Suisse First Boston: The Honeymoon Is Over," in *Business Week*, April 25, 1988. Explains the outcome of the original joint venture between First Boston and Credit Suisse.

Credit Suisse First Boston Home Page, available at http://www.csfb.com. Official World Wide Web home page of Credit Suisse First Boston. Includes company news, product descriptions, and historical information.

"Credit Suisse Group," in *Notable Corporate Chronologies*, The Gale Group, 1999. Lists major events in the history of Credit Suisse Group.

"CS First Boston; All Together Now?" in *The Economist*, 10

The Players

Chairman and CEO of Credit Suisse Group: Rainer E. Gut. Swiss-born Rainer Gut was named a general partner of New York-based Lazard Freres & Co. in 1968. Three years later, he accepted the posts of chairman and CEO of Swiss American Corp., Credit Suisse's U.S. investment banking affiliate. He became a deputy member of the executive board of Credit Suisse in 1973, achieving full membership status two years later. After stints as both speaker of the board and president of the board, Rainer took over as chairman in 1983. Between 1988 and 1997, he also served as chairman of CS First Boston Inc., which later became commonly known as Credit Suisse First Boston.

Chairman and CEO of First Boston Corp.: Peter T. Buchanan. Peter Buchanan spent more than three decades at First Boston, beginning his career there in the mid-1950s. He took over the struggling firm in the late 1970s and helped reshape it into a leading investment banking player. When Credit Suisse First Boston and First Boston Corp. merged in 1988 to form CS First Boston Inc., later known as Credit Suisse First Boston, Buchanan retired.

CEO of Credit Suisse First Boston: John M. Hennessy. John Hennessy began working for First Boston in 1974. He spent two years as assistant treasury secretary for international affairs. In 1982, he joined the ranks of Credit Suisse First Boston—a securities joint venture forged between Credit Suisse and First Boston in 1978. Soon after Credit Suisse First Boston and First Boston Corp. were merged in 1988 to form CS First Boston Inc., Hennessy took over the new holding company as CEO.

April 1993. Explains the outcome of the First Boston/CSFB merger.

"CS First Boston; As Many Names As a Russian Novel," in *The Economist*, 3 November 1990. Details the performance of First Boston in the 1980s.

Farrell, Christopher. "The Merger That Will Make First Boston a Trinity," in *Business Week*, 24 October 1988. Discusses the complex deal between Credit Suisse, First Boston, and CSFB.

Fidler, Stephen. "Swallowed By Its Offspring," in *Financial Times (London)*, 11 October 1988. Reports the internal problems experienced at CSFB since its founding in 1978.

Melcher, Richard A. "Trying to Patch Up a Family Quarrel in Banking," in *Business Week*, 2 February 1987. Explains why First Boston and CSFB decided to merge.

"A Treaty in Store for CSFB," in *The Economist*, 16 April 1988. Covers the performance of CSFB from its inception in 1978 to its merger with its co-parent, First Boston, in 1988.

ANNAMARIE L. SHELDON

CREDIT SUISSE & WINTERTHUR

Credit Suisse Group
Paradeplatz 8, PO Box 1
Zurich, 8070
Switzerland

tel: 41-1-212-1616
fax: 41-1-333-2587
web: http://www.creditsuisse.com

nationality: Switzerland
date: December 15, 1997
affected: Credit Suisse Group, Switzerland, founded 1856
affected: Winterthur Swiss Insurance Co., Switzerland, founded 1875

Overview of the Merger

When Credit Suisse, the third-largest commercial banking firm in Switzerland, took over Winterthur, a leading Swiss insurer, for $9.5 billion in December of 1997, it became Switzerland's largest financial services business, ahead of rivals Union Bank of Switzerland and Swiss Bank Corp. Combined assets totaled $464 billion. The deal reflected a trend among the largest players in the financial and insurance sectors to combine operations as a way of providing more comprehensive services to large global corporations.

History of Credit Suisse Group

In 1856, Alfred Escher, a young Zurich politician, decided to set up an independent bank called Credit Suisse. He put up Sfr3 million worth of shares on public offer and received Sfr218 million in subscriptions within three days. In 1867, Credit Suisse posted its first and only loss, which was due to a downturn in Switzerland's growing textile industry caused by collapsing cotton prices. By 1871, Credit Suisse, a benefactor of railroad expansion, was the largest bank in Switzerland.

At the beginning of World War I, Credit Suisse operated 13 domestic branch offices. Foreign investment in Switzerland stopped completely; as investors in hostile countries returned Swiss securities, the bank played a crucial role in placing them on the Swiss market. When World War I ended, the bank focused on financing the electrical utilities of the country. In 1924, Credit Suisse helped finance the national railroad's conversion to electricity. By the end of the 1930s, mounting tensions in Europe had prompted Credit Suisse to focus on penetrating English speaking countries; the bank formed the Swiss-American Corp. to focus on U.S. securities. In 1940, Credit Suisse's first foreign branch was opened, in New York City.

At the end of World War II, Credit Suisse remained financially sound despite losing almost half of its employees to war related service. Large amounts of credit remained extended to Swiss authorities who were owed more than Sfr1.7 billion by Germany. Normal banking operations resumed, including issuing paper for foreign debtors. The bank began offering new types of savings accounts and consumer credit cards.

The emergence of a free gold market in the late 1960s enabled Credit Suisse to become a major gold trading house; the acquisition of Valcambi SA, a precious metals refinery, added the manufacturing of ingots and coins to Credit Suisse's activities. By 1970, Credit Suisse operated offices on every continent except Antarctica. In 1977, authorities begin investigating a fraudulent banking and foreign exchange trading scheme at the bank's Chiasso branch which involved more than $1.2 billion. Several top executives resigned. The following year, Credit Suisse First Boston (CSFB), a joint venture with the New York investment bank First Boston, was formed. Michael von Clemm was named chairman and CEO of CSFB; in 1980, he oversaw one of the biggest financial disasters in CSFB's history: the purchase a $150 million issue that eventually cost the bank between $20 million and $40 million in losses.

During the early 1980s, Credit Suisse began shifting its focus from traditional Swiss banking practices to world investment banking and money management. In 1985, Credit Suisse became one of the first major Swiss banks to begin operations in the West German market. A $4 billion bond was floated by General Motors Acceptance Corp. in a joint venture involving CSFB, Credit Suisse, and First Boston. First Boston acted as lead manager, Credit Suisse provided a letter of credit to back the notes, and CSFB placed $400 million of the bonds in Europe.

CSFB and First Boston merged into a new holding company, CS First Boston, in 1988. Credit Suisse owned a 44.5% stake of CS First Boston. The following year, Credit Suisse formed CS Holding as a new parent company to oversee all the group's activities, including CSFB, CS Life (a life insurance carrier), Fides Holding (money management services), Leu Holding, and Electrowatt (electricity, manufacturing, and engineering services). Credit Suisse gained control of CS First Boston in 1990.

Union Bank of Switzerland rejected a $47 billion merger proposal by CS Holding in 1996. That year, the firm announced a major restructuring that included consolidating power in Zurich and cutting its workforce by 15% or 5,000 employees. The company planned to condense all subsidiaries into four specialized business units: Swiss domestic banking, worldwide private banking, institutional asset management, and corporate investment banking.

In 1997, CS Holding changed its name to Credit

The Business

Financials

Revenue (1997): $48.34 billion

Employees (1998): 62,300

SICs / NAICS

sic 6712 - Bank Holding Companies

sic 6029 - Commercial Banks Nec

sic 6311 - Life Insurance

sic 6211 - Security Brokers & Dealers

sic 6321 - Accident & Health Insurance

sic 6331 - Fire, Marine & Casualty Insurance

naics 551111 - Offices of Bank Holding Companies

naics 524113 - Direct Life Insurance Carriers

naics 524114 - Direct Health and Medical Insurance Carriers

naics 524126 - Direct Property and Casualty Insurance Carriers

Suisse Group. The firm also paid roughly $10 billion for Winterthur Swiss Insurance Co.

History of Winterthur Swiss Insurance Co.

In 1875, Colonel Heinrich Rieter and a group of factory owners established Swiss Accident Insurance Co. (SAIC) to insure themselves against workmen's compensations claims by their employees. The following year, SAIC operated branches in Germany, Austria-Hungary, Belgium, Holland, Luxembourg, Denmark, and Norway. The Swiss Factory Act came into effect in 1878, and SAIC began offering liability insurance.

In 1881, company reports noted a disturbing disparity between premium income and the amount paid to settle claims. Two years later, chairman Widmer-Kappeler fled abroad after the company's rapid expansion, coupled with several years of high claims, caused SAIC to record huge losses. Liquidation of the company was discussed by the board of directors, but later rejected. Heinrich Sulzer-Steiner was named head of the company's supervisory board in 1884, and SAIC began a gradual recovery.

By the turn of the century, SAIC offered accident, liability, burglary and guarantee, and property insurance. The company also offered insurance against

The Officers

Chairman: Rainer E. Gut

Vice Chairman and Chief Risk Officer: Hans-Ulrich Doerig

CEO: Lukas Muhlemann

Chief Financial Officer: Richard Thornburgh

CEO, Credit Suisse Asset Management: Phillip M. Colebatch

death from acute infectious illness. In 1910, SAIC opened a branch office in Spain. The Swiss government nationalized the workmen's accident insurance industry in 1918, causing significant losses for SAIC and forcing the company to shift its focus to the writing of individual accident and liability policies in Switzerland. That year, SAIC diversified into automobile insurance, acquiring Agrippina, a German insurance firm that pioneered the writing of automotive policies in 1901.

Hyperinflation in Germany forced German firms to abandon their activities in Switzerland in 1923, enabling SAIC to create Winterthur Life Assurance Co. (WLA) and diversify into life insurance. In 1931, the company moved into a new headquarters complex in Winterthur. Five years later, a branch office in New York City was opened.

SAIC purchased the American Casualty Company (ACC) in 1950 and consolidated its existing North American clients into ACC. ACC was later sold to Continental National American, and SAIC retained only its reinsurance operations in North America. In 1958, SAIC acquired Europeai, a Portuguese company specializing in life and property insurance. Growth continued in 1962 when the firm took over competitor Federal Insurance Co., based in Zurich, Switzerland. Acquisitions over the next several years included Union et Prevoyance (UP) of Belgium and Heimat, an Austrian insurance company.

In 1975, SAIC changed its name to Winterthur Swiss Insurance Co. and began to concentrate on diversifying within the insurance business, particularly into engineering insurance. A year later, the firm forged a joint venture with Norwich Union of the United Kingdom and Chiyoda Fire and Marine of Japan, forming Norwich Winterthur Group and Norwich Winterthur Reinsurance Corp. Ltd. to provide marine insurance and reinsurance. Winterthur established the Winterthur Legal Insurance Co. in 1978 and Itau Winterthur Insurance Company Ltd., to manage Winterthur's South American operations, in 1979.

Winterthur reentered the North American insurance market in 1982 by acquiring the Republic Insurance Group of Dallas, Texas. Five years later, Winterthur purchased a controlling interest in the Neuchatel Insurance Group and a minority holding in the Nordstern insurance group, increasing its presence in the German medical insurance market. In a move that tripled its share of the Italian insurance market, Winterthur purchased the Intercontinentale insurance group of Italy in 1988. The Southern Guaranty Companies of Montgomery, Alabama, were also acquired. By the end of the decade, UP had changed its name to Winterthur-Europe Assurance (WEA) and Winterthur had acquired Transatlantische Gruppe and established the Churchill Insurance Company Ltd., specializing in telephone sales of automobile insurance in the United Kingdom.

Activities in 1990 included purchasing Wisconsin-based General Casualty Group; forging a joint life and health insurance venture with Massachusetts Mutual Life Insurance Co.; turning branches in four European companies over to WEA; and establishing Winterthur-Europe Life Assurance to provide life insurance coverage throughout Europe. Winterthur joined with the American International Group Inc. in 1991 to market employee benefit plans to multinational companies. Four years later, the firm purchased the Italian and Spanish units of Swiss Reinsurance Co. Credit Suisse Group bought Winterthur for $9.7 billion in 1997.

Market Forces Driving the Merger

Credit Suisse had operated in the life insurance market for quite some time before negotiating a merger with Winterthur, but its life insurance unit had performed poorly throughout the 1990s. Rather than viewing this a reason to exit the industry, however, Credit Suisse believed that it needed to find a means of strengthening its insurance operations. According to an August 1997 article in *The European*, Winterthur would "get Credit Suisse out of its flat life insurance business" by allowing the firm to "build on Winterthur's strengths, such as southern Europe."

Unlike traditional mergers, the goal of the deal wasn't cost savings exacted from streamlining operations and laying off employees. Rather, Credit Suisse and Winterthur managers were hoping to position the merged firm as a frontrunner in the emerging "bancassurance" market, in which insurance was sold through bank branches. Winterthur's assets would allow Credit Suisse to meet the insurance and financial needs of "multinational corporations seeking one-stop shopping," wrote *Business Insurance* in August of 1997. For example, Credit Suisse could use its asset management experience to improve the employee benefits packages offered by Winterthur.

On a small scale, Credit Suisse and Winterthur, as well as Swiss Reinsurance Co., had been marketing combined insurance and banking products to business customers since 1995. In fact, Swiss Reinsurance held a 5% stake in Winterthur in 1997, and Credit Suisse owned a 10% chunk of Swiss Reinsurance.

Approach and Engagement

In the five years prior to the merger, Swiss financier Martin Ebner, Winterthur's largest shareholder, had been battling for control of the firm. In August of 1997, his investment firm, BZ Group, owned 30% of Winterthur. Ebner sent a letter to shareholders offering three merger choices: BZ Group, Credit Suisse, or a foreign firm. Credit Suisse and Winterthur announced their agreement to join forces on August 11. Four days later, Credit Suisse shares dropped 10% to $122.8 each; analysts blamed the drop on concerns among European investors that benefits resulting from mergers in the financial industry took years to emerge.

On September 5, shareholders of both firms approved the deal, and shortly thereafter, the European Commission and Swiss Competition Commission gave their nods. By October 16, 9.43 million shares (97.4%) of Winterthur's shares had been tendered to Credit Suisse. Because U.S. and UK approval was still pending, the deadline was extended to November 14. By then 99.2% of the shares had been tendered, exceeding the 98% required to proceed with the agreed upon share exchange, worth roughly $9.5 billion, which was completed on Dec 15. The exchange ratio was one Credit Suisse share for every 7.3 Winterthur shares held. Ebner became the second-largest shareholder of Credit Suisse, with an estimated 6% stake.

Products and Services

Premiums accounted for 36% of sales at Credit Suisse in 1997. Interest brought in 35%. Investment income secured 10%, as did commissions. Trading activities garnered the remaining 9%. Operations in Switzerland, other European countries, and the U.S. each produced roughly one-fourth of annual revenues, while activities in Japan delivered slightly less than one-tenth of the total.

Changes to the Industry

The deal boosted Credit Suisse's assets to $464 billion, making it nearly as large as Deutsche Bank AG, Europe's biggest bank. The firm also became the world's third largest asset manager, behind FMR Corp. and AXA-UAP, as well as Switzerland's largest financial institution, ahead of Union Bank of Switzerland and Swiss Bank Corp. However, that

The Players

Chairman and CEO of Credit Suisse Group: Rainer E. Gut. Swiss-born Rainer Gut was named a general partner of New York-based Lazard Freres & Co. in 1968. Three years later, he accepted the posts of chairman and CEO of Swiss American Corp., Credit Suisse's U.S. investment banking affiliate. He became a deputy member of the executive board of Credit Suisse in 1973, achieving full membership status two years later. After stints as both speaker of the board and president of the board, Rainer took over as chairman in 1983. Between 1988 and 1997, he also served as chairman of CS First Boston Inc. In 1997, Gut oversaw his firm's takeover of Winterthur Insurance Co.

Chairman and CEO of Winterthur Swiss Insurance Co.: Peter Spalti. Peter Spalti assumed control of Winterthur in the early 1980s. In 1989, he was appointed chairman of the board. After negotiating a takeover agreement with Credit Suisse in 1997, Spalti announced his retirement as CEO, effective December 31, 1997. Thomas Wellaur succeeded Spalti, who retained his spot as chairman.

first-place standing was short-lived. Less than a year after the Credit Suisse/Winterthur union, Union Bank of Switzerland and Swiss Bank completed their own megadeal, worth $29 billion, and dethroned Credit Suisse.

Most analysts believed the deal was likely to spark further consolidation as the lines between banking and insurance blurred. Accordingly, rumors of a linkup between Deutsche Bank and Assurances Generales de France began circulating, and although both firms denied any merger plans, Deutsche Bank management did concede that the bank was seeking an insurance acquisition. Also, in October of 1998, U.S.-based insurance giant Travelers Group completed a $37.4 billion stock swap merger with U.S.-based bank holding company Citicorp, creating the largest worldwide financial services institution.

Review of the Outcome

When the deal was completed, Credit Suisse merged its life insurance operations into Winterthur, which became an independent operating company under the umbrella of Credit Suisse Group. Combined customers totaled 15 million. Management expected its employee base of 60,000 to shrink by roughly 500 employees between 1998 and 2000, due mainly to attrition. In 1998, Winterthur divested its reinsurance operations to Partner Reinsurance for $750 million and began tightening its focus to direct insurance operations. By the end of the year, Travelers Property Casualty Corp., the U.S.-based insurance arm of Citigroup, and Winterthur International had forged a joint venture to market combined insurance and financial products to multinational clients.

Research

"Credit Suisse Group," in *Notable Corporate Chronologies*, The Gale Group, 1999. Lists major events in the history of Credit Suisse Group.

Kielmas, Maria. "Swiss Giants Plan to Merge," in *Business Insurance*, 18 August 1997. Offers a detailed look at the reasons underlying the merger, as well as an overview of combined financials.

Parry, John. "Credit Suisse Insures Itself with Winterthur," in *The European*, 14 August 1997. Discusses the performance of Credit Suisse prior to the merger, as well as the firm's reasons for wanting to move into insurance.

"PartnerRe Set to Acquire Winterthur Re This Year," in *Best's Review*, 1 October 1998. Covers Winterthur's plans to exit the reinsurance industry.

Prince, Michael. "Travelers, Winterthur Form a Global Alliance," in *Business Insurance*, 21 December 1998. Describes the joint venture created by Winterthur and Travelers to sell financial and insurance products on an international scale.

Winterthur Swiss Insurance Co. Home Page, available at http://www.winterthur.com. Official World Wide Web home page of Winterthur Swiss Insurance Co. Includes company news, product descriptions, and historical information, including archived press releases.

"Winterthur Swiss Insurance Co.," in *Notable Corporate Chronologies*, Gale Research, 1999. Covers major events in the history of Winterthur Swiss Insurance Co.

ANNAMARIE L. SHELDON

CROWN CORK AND SEAL & CARNAUD METALBOX

nationality: USA
date: February 1996
affected: Crown Cork and Seal Co., USA, founded 1927
affected: Carnaud Metalbox SA, France, founded 1987

Crown Cork and Seal Co.
One Crown Way
Philadelphia, PA 19154-4599
USA

tel: (215)698-5100
fax: (215)676-7245
web: http://www.crowncork.com

Overview of the Merger

In May of 1995, Crown Cork and Seal and France's Carnaud Metalbox announced a cash and stock swap deal of $5.2 billion including $1.2 billion in assumed debt. The European Commission investigated anti-trust issues and required the two companies to divest five tin plate aerosol plants located throughout Europe, reducing their combined 65% market share by 25%.

Prior to the merger, both companies received 80% of their revenues from the country in which they were based. The new Crown Cork and Seal became the world's largest packaging company with revenues exceeding $11 billion. The companies joined together their vast aluminum production operations and expanded their PET and plastic markets with CMB's presence in health and beauty packaging.

History of Crown Cork and Seal Co.

In 1927 Crown Cork and Seal was incorporated in New York City when two packaging companies consolidated services. With the acquisition of Acme Can Co. in 1936 Crown entered the canmaking business. Ten years later it was a pioneer of the aerosol can.

Between 1955 and 1960, CC&S steered global packaging marketing development, with the purchase of "pioneer rights" in many growing industrial countries. These rights allowed CC&S the first chance to develop can and packaging operations in several countries. Since there was little competition, Crown was able to shift outdated equipment overseas and keep overhead costs down.

The appointment of John F. Connelly as CC&S's president in 1957 began a period of fiscal growth and laid the foundation for future expansion. Under his leadership, Crown Cork rebounded from near bankruptcy by stopping production and selling stockpiled discontinued products to consumers. He also eliminated poorly performing products, like aluminum ice cube trays, and terminated nearly 25% of CC&S's employees. Throughout his term, Connelly avoided diversification of products, but expanded current services into more markets. Connelly began

The Business

Financials

Revenue (1998): $8.3 billion

Employees (1998): 38,459

SICs / NAICS

sic 3411 - Metal Cans

sic 3089 - Plastics Products Nec

sic 3466 - Crowns & Closures

sic 3569 - General Industrial Machinery Nec

naics 332431 - Metal Can Manufacturing

naics 332115 - Crown and Closure Manufacturing

naics 333414 - Heating Equipment (except Warm Air Furnaces) Manufacturing

using aerosol cans for a range of services including insecticides, household products and health and beauty aids. By the late 1980s, Connelly managed to keep CC&S nearly debt free, while many competitors were scrambling to sell assets in hopes of cleaning up their balance sheet. Long after competitors had pioneered new markets and developed material sources and technology, CC&S acquired established production equipment at a fraction of the original cost.

In 1981, William Avery was appointed president of CC&S. He became Connelly's protege, upholding the company's fiscal and operational conservatism. Connelly stepped down in 1989 and Avery took the helm. He began a rapid series of acquisitions in the 1990s. One of his first purchases, Constar, launched CC&S to the head of the nation's PET market. Additionally, by 1993, CC&S grew to the nation's fourth largest canmaker with the purchase of aluminum canmaker, Van Dorn, and one year later acquired the can unit of Tri Valley Growers. In Europe, CC&S acquired PET manufacturer Wellstar.

With the announcement of a merger between France's Carnaud Metalbox and CC&S, Avery turned his company into the world's largest packaging manufacturer. Revenues reached over $10 billion, and the company expanded its European, Asian, and Latin American presence.

History of Carnaud Metalbox

In 1897 the Barringer family began producing their own metal boxes for their mustard. Eventually,

the Barringers entered the metal toy industry, which expanded their success. In 1939 the Barringer operations joined with the Metal Box Group of Companies, which soon became known as Sutton Metal Box.

After World War II ended, Sutton expanded toy production and entered the aerosol can market. The company continued to expand its presence in can manufacturing, until its 1989 merger with Carnaud, a French packaging company with plastic and metal operations worldwide. After that deal was completed, the company changed its name to Carnaud Metalbox and focused more intently on growing its new health and beauty packaging operations. By 1995, when Carnaud Metalbox and Crown Cork and Seal announced their merger, Carnaud Metalbox had became Europe's largest packaging manufacturer.

Market Forces Driving the Merger

Crown Cork & Seal and Carnaud Metalbox needed to expand their international business. Prior to the merger CC&S made gains in Latin America and China with expansion of its Buenos Aires aluminum manufacturing plant and a joint venture China. Carnaud held a 3% share of the global health and beauty sector, which CC&S coveted. Both companies were established in different, but complimentary markets. The merger would allow Carnaud to sell production equipment in the U.S. and gain a share in the PET packaging market. CC&S wanted to increase its foreign revenues, especially in health and beauty packaging. Additionally, economies of scale and management efficiencies would reduce overall costs, while CC&S could aggressively focus on research and development to establish long-term growth.

Despite healthy growth in the early 1990s CMB revenues fell in 1993, forcing the company's CEO, Jurgen Hintz, to seek out ways to increase sales. The 1994 proposed merger with Wheaton would have established CMB in the forefront of the United States health and beauty packaging market; however, the deal fell through when Wheaton shareholders became uncomfortable with their weakened control over the combined company.

Approach and Engagement

While Carnaud Metalbox CEO Hintz was busy working out a merger deal with Pechiney, CC&S CEO Avery and major shareholder Seilliere were holding secret negotiations. On May 24, 1995, the companies announced their planned merger, which would create the world's largest packaging company. Avery offered CMB shareholders the option to sell their stock for $46 per share or convert it into CC&S shares. This price was nearly 20% over CMB's current market value.

The European Commission held up the merger for several months as it examined anti-trust concerns. To receive approval the two companies agreed to sell throughout Europe five combined plants which manufactured tin plate cans used for aerosol containers. The divestiture was required to reduce what would have been a daunting 65% share of the aerosol can market to 40%.

When the European Commission approved the deal, 46.7% of CMB shareholders sold their stock for cash, while 53.5% was converted into Crown Cork stock, including the 30% share owned by Seillere's CGIP. In addition to the stock swap, CC&S assumed $1.2 billion in debt. In February of 1996, the two companies were officially joined under the name Crown Cork and Seal Co., with headquarters stationed in a $31 million Philadelphia complex built after the merger to accommodate the company's growth. While Avery remained the chairman and CEO of the company, the office of president was divided into four geographic regions, with a different president responsible for each one. CMB's Tommy Karlsson became the European division president, and Jurgen Hintz eventually left CMB.

Products and Services

The new Crown Cork and Seal was able to expand current operations, grab a larger share of geographic markets, and reduce overhead costs along the way. Since both companies were established in different regions, operation redundancies were at a minimum. Conversely, the merger expanded exponentially the scope of Crown's reach, especially in the PET container industry, which accounted for 20% of the firm's revenues by 1998. Both companies led their home nation's in the plastic container field, and the merger allowed both to increase sales and reduce raw materials cost.

The new Crown Cork and Seal offered extensive plastic and PET products in bottle, jar and preform designs. CC&S offered bottles for food, health, and industrial packaging. In pharmaceuticals, CC&S offered protective sealing, eye-droppers, nasal sprays, inhalers, syringes, and much more. In addition to plastics, the company offered a full range of steel and aluminum cans for food, beverages, aerosol, and a variety of industrial uses.

CMB laid the successful groundwork for CC&S to play a vital role in the fast turnaround world of the health and cosmetics industry. Since most container designs were constantly being changed to increase appeal, CMB had moved older operations and designs to developing markets, allowing the firm to run a product longer and therefore decrease operating costs

The Officers

Chairman and CEO: William J. Avery

Vice Chairman: Michael J. McKenna

President and Chief Operations Officer, American
    Division: John W. Conway

Exec. VP, European Division: Tommy H. Karlsson

per design. The Research and Development branch of the company had sought out new technology and design to meet the demand of established markets. After the merger, CC&S offered unique packaging designs, like the low-profile perfume pump, the Zelvalve dispenser, and a variety of lipstick, mascara, and compact cases.

Changes to the Industry

After the deal was completed, Crown Cork and Seal entered France's bourse stock market. While the new company had assumed sizable short- and long-term debt, CC&S operations in 49 countries with 247 plants worldwide gave it a strong global presence, and the industry was forced to contend with a new worldwide packaging leader.

Review of the Outcome

The 1996 merger strengthened Crown Cork and Seal's global dominance in aluminum can manufacturing. Crown Cork expanded its assets in Europe, and gained the 3% worldwide share of the lucrative health and cosmetic market that CMB had previously secured. CMB's U.S. plant in Virginia began selling a full line of canning and packaging equipment for the manufacturing market. The newly combined company divested itself of 25% of the European tin plate-lined can market, but even after the sale of five plants to U.S. Can for $58 million cash and assumed debt, CC&S retained a 40% worldwide market share.

Increased imports of filled products reduced the demand for cans made by CMB in 1997 and 1998. As a result, Crown Cork and Seal announced plans to layoff 2,700 employees, nearly 7% of its total workforce. The $127 million charge the firm posted as a result of its downsizing effort was a major factor in the $21.9 million loss reported for the three months ended September 30, 1998.

The Players

Chairman and CEO of Crown Cork and Seal Co.: William J. Avery. William Avery joined Crown Cork and Seal (CC&S) in 1959 as a management trainee. CEO Connelly became his mentor, instilling Avery with his fiscal conservatism and tightfisted leadership style. In 1981 Avery was named president. When he took the helm as CEO in 1989, he used the company's savings to launch a buying spree. In ten years he increased revenues and assets with 19 acquisitions, including Constar, the nation's largest polyethylene terephthalate (PET) plastic producer. Thanks to Avery's purchases and expansion, CC&S more than doubled revenues by 1994, with $4.5 billion in sales. In 1995 he arranged the merger with France's Carnaud Metalbox, making CC&S the world's largest packaging manufacturer. Avery retained the chairman and CEO positions after the deal was completed.

President of Compagnie General d'Industrie et de Participation (CGIP): Baron Ernest-Antoine Seilliere. In 1995 Ernest-Atoine Seilliere ran his family businesses under CGIP, a holding company with ventures in auto parts, information technology; it was formerly the majority stockholder of Carnaud Metalbox. Seilliere, a descendant of the French aristocratic Wendel family who once supplied Louis XIV with cannonballs, created the CGIP when he took the helm of his family's dynasty in 1978. When William Avery set his eye on Carnaud Metalbox (CMB), and concurrently, dominance of the European market, he didn't bother to tell CMB's CEO, but instead went to Seilliere. As the president of CMB's majority shareholder, CGIP, Seilliere held all the cards to make a merger possible. The two leaders conducted their negotiations in secret, and announced the proposed merger in May 1995. Seilliere was able to convince shareholders to trade, sell or invest CMB stock into Crown Cork and Seal and was named a director of the new company when the takeover was completed.

Research

"Crown Cork and Seal Company, Inc." in *Notable Corporate Chronologies*, The Gale Group, 1999. Details major events in the company's history.

Crown Cork and Seal Co. Home Page, available at http://www.crowncork.com. World Wide Web Home Page for Crown Cork and Seal Company, Inc. Includes information regarding products and services and offers an archived press release database.

"Crown Cork Seeks Global Gains," in *Sun (Baltimore)*, 12 June 1996. Discusses the bottling equipment sales that the Virginia-based Carnaud Metalbox operation planned to launch after the Crown Cork and CMB merger.

"From Mustard to Metal Box," in *European Cosmetic Markets*, 1 August 1997. Provides an historical overview of Carnaud Metalbox predecessor, Metal Box.

"International Expansion: Crown + CMB = Global Leadership," in *European Cosmetic Markets*, 1 May 1996. Highlights aspects of the Crown/CMB merger including stock swap and purchase options.

"L'avenir C'est Moi," in *The Economist*, 11 January 1997. Discusses Baron Seilliere's business history and position at CGIP.

Lewis, James and Peter Cripps. "How Crown Put Its Seal on a Complex Deal," in *Acquisitions Monthly*, May 1996. Summarizes key points of the Crown Cork/Carnaud Metalbox merger.

Morais, Richard C. "One World," in *Forbes*, 4 December 1995. This article sheds light on the personality and business savvy of Baron Ernest-Antoine Seilliere.

Pidgeon, Ron. "All Systems Go for Crown Cork and Seal," in *Packaging Week*, 22 February 1996. Discusses the outcome of the stock swap and purchase deal after the CMB shareholder meeting where the merger received its final approval.

Regan, Bob. "Crown Cork Bids $5.2 billion for French Aluminum Can Firm," in *American Metal Market*, 24 May 1995. Summarizes aspects of proposed merger of Crown Cork and Seal and CMB.

SEAN C. MACKEY

CUC INTERNATIONAL & HFS

nationality: USA
date: December 1997
affected: CUC International Inc., USA, founded 1973
affected: HFS Inc., USA, founded 1992

Cendant Corp.
9 W. 57th St.
New York, NY 10019
USA

tel: (212)431-1800
web: http://www.cendant.com

Overview of the Merger

On May 27, 1997, CUC International and HFS announced a $14.1 billion stock swap merger of equals that would allow the companies to "bundle" unrelated services marketed to their respective customers. Combined assets and sales would create a company earning nearly $22 billion annually. HFS brought a huge consumer database of 100 million customers, which CUC wanted to use to expand its telephone shopping system and direct marketing programs. Hotel franchising giant HFS would also be able to cross-market its diverse businesses in a variety of new locations and sell directly to CUC members.

CUC International issued nearly 434 million new shares to accommodate the stock swap, with 2.4 shares of its stock being traded for each HFS share. Company shareholders on both sides reacted negatively to the announcement, sending stocks plummeting. Following the news, HFS dropped $3.37 and CUC International lost $1.37. Eventually stockholders relaxed, and in December of 1997, the merger was completed.

History of HFS Inc.

In 1990 Henry Silverman led the Blackstone Group in the purchase of the Howard Johnson and Ramada hotel chains. In the 1980s Silverman had turned Days Inn, once a tiny hotel chain, into the world's third largest franchise. In 1992 he was reacquainted with Days Inn as Blackstone Group purchased the hotel company. Silverman then created a holding company, Hospitality Franchise Systems (HFS), to oversee the three combined hotel operations. When he took HFS public that year, stock began selling for $4 per share; by 1997, stock had increased nearly 2000%, giving investors one of the highest returns in the nation.

Silverman expanded the firm with aggressive acquisitions of many hotel franchises including Travelodge, Super 8, Village Lodge, and Knights Inn. In 1995, after a failed casino deal, the company officially changed its name to HFS. It then diversified into the real estate market with the purchase of four major brokerages: Century 21, Coldwell Banker, ERA, and the vacation time-share mogul, RCI. Within five years, HFS became the world's largest hotel franchiser.

The Business

Financials

Revenue (1998): $5.28 billion

Employees (1998): 35,000

SICs / NAICS

sic 6794 - Patent Owners & Lessors

sic 7514 - Passenger Car Rental

sic 8741 - Management Services

naics 532111 - Passenger Car Rental

HFS further diversified its holdings with the purchase of Avis and PHH, a corporate relocation firm. HFS did not deal in physical assets, but instead sold franchises, with brand name and reservation capabilities, providing an extensive cross-marketing infrastructure between the various operations. HFS sold 75% of its Avis operations to the public during merger negotiations with CUC International.

In May 1996, CEO Henry Silverman announced a planned merger of equals via a $14 billion stock swap with CUC International. The merger was completed in December 1997, with both companies running separate operations under the name Cendant. Less than a year later, authorities discovered that CUC International had falsified accounting records, adding $500 million in revenues and increasing pretax profit margins to look more attractive to investors. CUC International CEO Walter Forbes was forced to resign along with almost all former CUC management personnel. Silverman took over Forbes' chairman position, but lost nearly $1 billion in bonuses, compensation and stock options as the firm suffered tremendous losses due to shareholder upset.

In 1998 Cendant continued HFS's acquisition spree with the purchase of the nation's second-largest tax preparation firm, Jackson Hewitt. Silverman sold former CUC holdings including Hebdo Mag and Match.com. The company suffered a $220 million settlement in a class action lawsuit spawned by the CUC accounting fraud. Conversely, Cendant sued the accounting firm Ernst & Young, the auditor of CUC finances, for gross negligence.

History of CUC International, Inc.

Walter Forbes, along with a group of friends, formed Comp-U-Card in 1973, hoping to create a computer accessed home shopping network.

Unfortunately, not many people owned personal computers at the time, yet Forbes poured a great deal of money into this failing venture, convinced electronic commerce could attract consumers by offering goods at highly discounted rates.

A 1979 attempt at computer accessed shopping proved a failure. Additionally, a television shopping network and electronic kiosks at retail stores, providing pictures and descriptions of products for credit card purchase, were unsuccessful. Since Forbes then had to wait nearly 15 years before his computer commerce dream would become a reality, he needed to find a marketing niche that would turn his hundreds of thousands of dollars into a worthwhile investment. He focused on telephone sales, where consumers could order catalog products by phone using a credit card. The products were offered at remarkably discounted rates, usually only 6-10% over wholesale prices. Comp-U-Card received the customer order, immediately processed the sale, and shipped products from the manufacturer. Since the company had no inventory, retail space, and broker fees, it didn't incur many overhead costs.

Forbes changed the company name to Comp-U-Card (CUC) International in 1982 and took it public one year later. Success came when CUC International entered into "affinity programs," incentives credit card companies offered to customers to increase membership and card usage. Credit card companies began offering CUC International shopping club memberships and service discounts. The first shopping service was called "Shoppers Advantage," which by 1990, cost about $40 annually. Credit card companies received a percentage of the membership fees in return for their mailing lists. From 1983 to 1985, the company increased revenue by nearly $45 million.

In 1986 the company diversified services with the acquisition of Benefit Consultants, which allowed the company to market accidental death insurance through banks and credit unions. By 1987 sales reached $142 million, helped in part by the additional acquisition of Madison Financial Corp., which offered affinity programs to financial institutions. That same year Forbes officially changed the company name to CUC International, Inc.

The success of CUC International was largely due to its ability to retain members—renewal rates reached an impressive 70%—and its strong presence in shopping clubs and newer discount travel, auto, and discount dining memberships. In the first half of the 1990s, CUC acquired many marketing firms including coupon book giant, Entertainment Publications. By 1995 the company had nearly 40 million members and began promoting its services on the

Internet, fulfilling Forbes' lifelong dream of conducting commerce via computer.

In December of 1997, CUC completed its merger with hotel franchiser HFS. The stock swap, valued at $14 billion, created Cendant. Both companies shared customer databases to reach consumers through direct mail and cross marketing programs. Forbes was forced to resign less than one year after the merger when evidence of CUC International's accounting fraud surfaced.

Market Forces Driving the Merger

Increased marketing ability was the driving force behind the HFS and CUC International merger. HFS Hospitality Division CEO John Russell summed up the reason for the merger in a June 1997 interview for *Travel Agent* magazine, "We have to deliver heads in beds to our hotels, and we need to use all avenues to do that." HFS sought a major opportunity to cross market its hotel services to rental car and real estate consumers, and CUC International provided market exposure through its Travel Advantage discount travel club and its strength at direct mail advertising.

HFS's 100 million customer database attracted the attention of direct mail giant CUC International. CUC International hoped to recruit new members via direct mail and by marketing its discount shopping, travel, and dining memberships in the hotel, real estate, and auto rental sectors. Prior to the merger, the two companies had inked a deal where customers calling HFS for a hotel reservation were asked if they were interested in travel discounts. If a customer answered yes, he or she was forwarded to a CUC International salesperson. In the first year of the new program, one million people said yes and joined CUC International membership.

Approach and Engagement

The May 1996 announcement of the merger between CUC International and HFS was not well received by investors. The main goal of the merger was the ability to cross-market products and services, a practice which had not found great success in the past. The deal was set up as a stock swap merger of equals, with each HFS share being exchanged for 2.4 CUC International shares. The new company was named Cendant Corp. Both companies kept their respective headquarters, and ran their operations separately.

Leadership was divided into approximately three year terms. HFS leader Henry Silverman was named president and CEO, and CUC's Walter Forbes became chairman. According to the terms of the deal, on January 1, 2000, the two leaders would switch posi

The Officers

Chairman, President, and CEO: Henry R. Silverman

Vice-Chairman and General Counsel : James E. Buckman

Vice-Chairman; Chairman and CEO, Travel Division: Stephen P. Holmes

Vice-Chairman; Chairman and CEO, Alliance Marketing Division: Michael P. Monaco

tions. After serving terms in each position, both leaders planned to step down to allow for new management. Forbes stepped down prematurely in 1998, however, only a few months after the merger was completed, due to evidence of nearly $500 million in pretax revenue falsely reported on CUC's annual report.

Products and Services

Prior to the merger between HFS and CUC International, the two companies began a joint venture called "Transfer Plus." This testing of cross marketing possibilities proved successful, with HFS customers being transferred to CUC sales reps if they were interested in travel discounts when placing a reservation at the company's hotel franchises. They continued this program after the merger and added many more cross marketing programs.

After the deal was completed, the new firm, named Cendant Corp., became the world's largest hotel franchiser—with chains such as Days Inn, Ramada, Wingate Inn, and Howard Johnson—with a total of 6,000 hotels and over 500,000 rooms. Cendant also boasted an extensive real estate empire, with ownership of Century 21, Coldwell Banker, and ERA. Vacation timeshares were offered through the firm's RCI subsidiary. Cendant was the world's largest relocation service for corporations, federal agencies, and military personnel. Each year the company transferred over 100,000 people.

Through its subsidiary Cendant Mortgage, Cendant became the nation's 6th largest mortgage provider. Via its Welcome Wagon franchise, Cendant offered discounts and databases of local products and services to new home owners using Cendant's relocation services.

In the UK, Cendant owned the largest private car park operation, National Car Park, and automobile assistance company, Green Flag.

The firm's membership clubs included Travel Advantage; Autovantage; Netmarket, an online discount shopping service; Shoppers Advantage; and credit card protection services.

The Players

Chairman and CEO of HFS Inc.: Henry R. Silverman. Henry Silverman began his career after graduating from the University of Pennsylvania law school in 1964. He served as the assistant to Steve Ross, the builder of the Time Warner empire. Silverman eventually worked as the head of the leveraged buyout fund for Reliance Group Holdings and the Blackstone Group. While at Blackstone, he spent $170 million to purchase Ramada and Howard Johnson franchise rights in 1990, creating Hospitality Franchise Systems (HFS) two years later. He quickly expanded his hotel presence with the acquisition of Days Inn, Travelodge, Super 8, Village Lodge, and Knights Inn. By the mid-1990s, Silverman had created the world's largest hotel franchiser. He then expanded into real estate franchises with the purchase of Century 21, ERA, and Coldwell Banker. HFS also purchased Avis, further increasing the products offered to its hotel guests in cross-marketing campaigns. Silverman turned the cross-marketing business strategy into a multi-million dollar empire. Synergy had been disputed as an impossible business tactic after many failed attempts, including the Avis/Sheraton combination. Silverman felt his company could pull it off successfully because HFS owned franchise rights and not material assets. After he proved to franchisers that cross-marketing was successful between the hotel, rental car, and real estate industries, Silverman continued to expand his business with acquisitions. The deal with HFS and CUC International, announced in May of 1996, was the next plausible step. Silverman became the president and CEO, while CUC's Walter Forbes was named chairman. They agreed to switch jobs on January 1, 2000, and retire after five years to allow new management to further develop their legacy. Forbes, however, stepped down in 1998, and Silverman added the title of chairman to his job description.

Changes to the Industry and Review of the Outcome

The $14 billion stock swap merger added a massive cross-marketing wing to the world's largest hotel franchiser, HFS. The merger allowed CUC to expand its discount membership club with access to HFS's 100 million customers with promotions and affinity programs. Using the direct mail and cross marketing

aspects of the merged companies, with over 168 million customers, Cendant—a large holding company with ownership of many franchise rights and discount club memberships—created a successful business based on company synergies, despite investor skepticism.

When accounting fraud evidence surfaced against CUC International, many analysts pointed out that in an era of mergers with larger and larger corporations, due diligence practices were being overlooked in order to achieve financial gains. Cendant stock suffered greatly and fell from a high of $41.35 to $7.50 per share. A class action lawsuit, filed by shareholders, was settled out of court for nearly $220 million. Cendant then sold 20 businesses and slimmed operating costs. Company revenues nearly doubled after the merger, and despite the CUC accounting fiasco, Cendant reported 1998 net income of $540 million.

Research

"All in the Same Bunch," in *The Economist*, 31 May 1997. Discusses the cross-marketing potential of the merger between HFS and CUC International.

Bigness, Jon and Jared Sanberg. "CUC, HFS Agree on $10.9 Billion Merger," in *The Wall Street Journal*, 28 May 1997. Summarizes aspects of the announced merger between the two companies.

Cendant Corp. Home Page, available at http://www.cendant.com. Official World Wide Web Site for Cendant Corp. Includes a descriptions of company services and franchises, press releases, and annual reports.

DeMarrais, Kevin G. "Parsippany, NJ-Based Franchiser Forecasts Significant Growth in 2000," in *Knight Ridder/Tribune Business News*, 27 May 1999. Discusses comments made by chairman, president and CEO, Henry Silverman at a meeting in East Hanover regarding how Cendant plans to move away from the scar left by accounting fraud of predecessor CUC International.

Diamond, Kerry. "HFS: Merger With Direct Marketing Giant Won't Bypass Retailers," in *Travel Agent*, 2 June 1997. Explains how the cross marketing and sales potential of the merger will not eliminate the involvement of travel agents in the hotel reservation industry.

Fink, Ronald. "Hear No Fraud See No Fraud Speak No Fraud," in *CFO, The Magazine for Senior Financial Executives*, October 1998. Discusses lack of due diligence in the merger of HFS and CUC International.

Fox, Justin. "Who the Hell is Henry Silverman?" in *Fortune*, 27 October 1997. Highlights key aspects of Henry Silverman's career.

Mannino, Barbara. "Building and Empire," in *Best's Review, Property-Casualty Insurance Edition.*, April 1998. Summarizes the biography of Henry Silverman and the mergers he directed to parlay HFS into the world's largest hotel franchiser.

Timmons, Heather. "HFS Plan to Merge With Direct Marketer Gets Cool Reception," in *American Banker*, 29 May 1997. Details how investor skepticism with the merger between CUC International and HFS caused a drastic slump in their stocks.

SEAN C. MACKEY

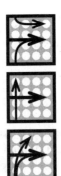

CVS & ARBOR DRUGS

nationality: USA
date: April 1998
affected: CVS Corp., USA, founded 1892
affected: Arbor Drugs, Inc., USA, founded 1963

CVS Corp.
One CVS Dr.
Woonsocket, RI 02895
USA

tel: (401)765-1500
fax: (401)766-2917
web: http://www.cvs.com

Overview of the Merger

In April of 1998, CVS Corp. teamed up with Arbor Drugs Inc. in a $1.48 billion all-stock deal. Arbor, with 207 stores, pushed CVS past competitor Walgreen Co. as the number one prescription drugstore chain in the U.S. Upon completion of the deal, CVS was responsible for dispensing 12% of all retail prescriptions in the nation via its 4,100 stores in 24 states. Combined annual revenues reached $15 billion.

History of CVS Corp.

In 1892, Frank Melville acquired three shoe stores with the plan of developing them into a network of stores. In the early 1900s, Frank and his son John Ward Melville joined with J. Franklin McElwain and established a chain of shoe stores called Thom McAn Shoe Corp., named after Scottish golfer Thomas McCann. By 1931, the company operated 476 shoe stores under the names John Ward, Thom McAn, Rival, and Courdaye; net income reached $1.2 million on sales of $26 million.

The company went public on the New York Stock Exchange in 1936. During the 1950s Thom McAn grew with the acquisition of the Miles Shoes chain. Under the leadership of Francis C. Rooney, the company also expanded into the apparel industry by opening Chess King and by acquiring Foxwood, which was renamed Foxmoor.

The company continued to diversify and in 1969 acquired the Consumer Value Store (CVS) pharmacy chain. Other purchases followed, including Clinton Merchandising Inc., Metro Pants Corporation, and Spotwood Apparel, Inc. In 1975, Marshall's Inc. was also acquired. Through its growth and diversification, the company ranked as the 32nd-largest retailing company in the U.S. with sales surpassing $1.2 billion.

Kenneth Berland became president in 1980 and continued to focus on the company's growth potential. In 1981, the firm purchased Kay-Bee Toys and Hobby Shops, Inc. One year later it acquired Wilson's House of Leather. In 1985, the company partnered with Linens 'n Things, Inc., and also sold the Foxmoor chain.

The Business

Financials

Revenue (1998): $15.27 billion

Employees (1998): 97,000

SICs / NAICS

sic 5912 - Drug Stores & Proprietary Stores

Stanley Goldstein succeeded Berland as president that year and was named chairman and CEO in 1986.

Goldstein spent the first part of the 1990s gobbling up other companies. He targeted Berman's Specialty Stores and Finish Line, People's Drug Stores, the five-store apparel chain of Bob's Stores, and Circus World Toy Stores Inc. With sales of more than $8.7 billion early in the decade, the company also purchased the 29-store chain of Massachusetts-based Thayer Pharmacies, the 128-unit Foot Action chain, and the 136-store K & K toy store chain. In 1993, the company agreed to acquire the 60-unit chain Standard Drug Stores and the Austin Drug chain, which operated nine stores in Long Island, New York.

In 1994 Harvey Rosenthal, president and CEO of CVS, became president and chief operating officer of the parent firm. He began a restructuring plan to focus only on pharmacy operations. In keeping with that plan, he sold Marshall's to The TJX Companies, Inc. for $600 million in 1995. The next year the company changed its name to CVS Corp. and acquired 85% of the Southern drugstore chain, Big B. Inc., for $423.2 million. CVS also planned to close its Thom McAn shoe stores; spun off its footwear businesses as a separate company, Footstar, Inc., to its shareholders; and sold Kay-Bee Toys to Consolidated Stores Corp. for $287.5 million. Wilson's completed a management buyback for $69.7 million that year as well.

CVS became the largest drug store chain in the U.S. by acquiring Revco D.S., Inc. for $2.8 billion in 1997. The company operated 3,888 stores in 24 states and the District of Columbia. Later that year CVS divested itself of the last of its non-drug businesses and sold Bob's Stores to an investor group for $92 million, and divested its remaining 32.5% interest in Linens 'n Things for $147 million. In 1998 CVS acquired Arbor Drugs, Inc., the eighth-largest drug store chain in the U.S., in a $1.48 billion stock swap deal, bringing store count to 4,100 and adding the state of Michigan to its service area.

Along with Elensys Care Services and Glaxo Wellcome, CVS was named in a class action lawsuit

alleging violation of patient confidentiality through the companies' direct-mail drug-marketing campaign. In 1999 CVS purchased Soma.com, an online pharmacy site.

History of Arbor Drugs Inc.

In 1963 Eugene Applebaum opened a drugstore, Civic Drugs, in Dearborn, Michigan. With a goal of becoming a leading chain in Michigan, Applebaum purchased five more stores in the Detroit area throughout the 1970s. In 1974 he incorporated under the name of Arbor Drugs.

Headquartered in Troy, Michigan, Arbor continued to purchase small companies in the 1980s. In 1981 the company purchased Cunningham and five years later acquired the Sentry chain. Arbor went public in 1986 with hopes of increasing revenue in an effort to expand and build more stores in the Michigan area. The company also pioneered 24-hour photo development and was known for its computerized pharmacy network that kept information on customer records and warned of possible dangerous drug interactions or allergic reactions.

Arbor became the target of a Blue Cross Blue Shield of Michigan suit in 1993. The insurance company claimed that Arbor had been overcharging them since 1988. At the same time, investor interest was waning in the company as a result of changes in the federal healthcare system and the general consensus that prescription drug profits would falter. Arbor settled the complaint with Blue Cross out of court, doling out $15 million to the insurance company and $7 million to the government.

Arbor continued to expand despite those problems. In 1994 the company purchased the M&R chain, and by 1996 its distribution center had doubled in size. Between 1996 and 1997 Arbor had opened 30 new stores. With 45% of the market in Detroit and over 200 stores in Michigan, Applebaum sold his chain to CVS Corp. in 1998.

Market Forces Driving the Merger

In keeping with its plan to focus on its drugstore operations, CVS purchased Revco D.S. Inc. in 1997. The move was deemed logical as the recent trend in the industry was to cut costs and gain market share through mergers and acquisitions. Consolidation was sweeping through the drug store industry in the late 1990s, including CVS's purchase of Revco, Rite-Aid Corp.'s acquisition of Perry Drugs and Thrifty Payless, and Eckerd Corp.'s deal with Kerr Drug. Smaller, regional chains were migrating toward larger companies as a means of survival in the rapidly shrinking industry; these stores found it difficult to compete with larger national chains that had the financial means to expand and increase technology. Between 1996 and 1998, drug store giants like CVS, Rite Aid, and Eckerd snatched up 10,000 stores, paved the way for future industry consolidation.

Another motive behind the expansion was the increasing popularity of HMO's. *The Boston Globe* reported, "As health maintenance organizations look to cut costs, many have struck agreements with large drugstore chains to provide prescription drugs at discounted prices to their members. But only the biggest chains have the clout to make such HMO alliances profitable." As a result, regional chains were looking to pair up with larger companies as a means of surviving the cost cutting that forced profits to tumble on prescription medicine.

Arbor Drugs, the nation's eighth largest chain, was a powerful force in the metropolitan Detroit area. With its strong reputation for solid financial performance, Arbor was considered an industry leader by drug store analysts. CVS did not have a presence in that area and wanted to continue to grow after its Revco purchase. By teaming up with Arbor, CVS would also be able to upstage competitor Walgreen's entrance in the Detroit market. By penetrating the Detroit region, the nation's fourth-largest drugstore market, CVS would also be able to bid for prominent auto maker's prescription contracts.

Approach and Engagement

CVS and Arbor Drugs began discussing merger plans in early 1998. According to an article in *The Detroit News*, Eugene Applebaum said the joining of the two companies was "a case of waiting for the right partner," and CVS met all of his "criteria." He also said the deal would benefit stockholders, employees, and customers. In February 1998, CVS announced its intent to join forces with the regional firm in a $1.48 billion stock swap. Two months later, the acquisition was finalized.

Products and Services

After the merger, CVS served 24 states and the District of Columbia. The company had 414 stores in Ohio, 363 in New York, 321 in Massachusetts, 319 in Pennsylvania, 304 in Georgia, 296 in North Carolina, 291 in Indiana, 253 in Virginia, and 225 in Michigan. Along with operations in other states, CVS owned 4,122 stores in the eastern United States.

In 1998, CVS's pharmacy operations accounted for 58% of total sales. Contributing to the other 42% were its front store operations in over-the-counter drugs, greeting cards, beauty items, foods, seasonal merchandise, and photo finishing and film services.

The Officers

Chairman and CEO; President and CEO, CVS Pharmacy: Thomas M. Ryan

President and Chief Operating Officer: Charles C. Conway

Exec. VP, Corporate Development: Lawrence Zigerelli

Exec. VP, Marketing of CVS Pharmacy: Daniel Nelson

Exec. VP, CVS Pharmacy Stores: Larry J. Merlo

Changes to the Industry and Review of the Outcome

CVS's acquisition of Arbor Drugs made it the leading retailer of prescription drugs in the U.S. drug store market. The $1.48 billion stock swap furthered CVS's plans to focus on pharmacy operations and, along with the 1997 purchase of Revco, led to the purchase of Soma.com in June of 1999. Focused on being a leader in the industry, CVS continued to operate in either the first or second market share position in over 80% of it markets in 1999.

CVS opened 382 stores in 1998 and expected to open 440 in 1999. Net sales in the first quarter of 1999 increased by 17.7% to $4.24 billion. In the beginning of 1999, Arbor stores saw little change in keeping with CVS's plans make few changes to the well-managed company.

Research

"CVS Corp.," in *Notable Corporate Chronologies*, The Gale Group, 1999. Lists major events in the history of CVS Corp.

CVS Corp. Home Page, available at http://www.cvs.com. Official World Wide Web Home Page for CVS Corp. Includes historical, financial, and product information, as well as recent news articles.

"DrugStore Merger to Create Giant," in *The Times-Picayune*, 10 February 1998. Discusses benefits to CVS by acquiring Arbor Drugs.

Preddy, Melissa. "CVS Store Chain Buys Troy-based Arbor Drugs," in *The Detroit News*, 10 February 1998. Discusses recent changes in drug store chains and Arbor's deal with CVS.

Reidy, Chris. "CVS to Buy Detroit's Drugstores for $1.48 B," in *The Boston Globe*, 10 February 1998. Explains recent industry trend in purchasing small companies and the benefits of becoming partners with HMO's.

Steinhauer, Jennifer. "CVS to Acquire Arbor Drugs for $1.48 Billion in Stock," in *The New York Times*, 10 February 1998. Lists benefits to Arbor and CVS on proposed deal, as well as recent industry acquisitions.

CHRISTINA M. STANSELL

CYPRUS MINERALS & AMAX

Cyprus Amax Minerals Co.
9100 E. Mineral Circle
Englewood, CO 80112
USA

tel: (303)643-5000
web: http://www.cyprusamax.com

nationality: USA
date: November 1993
affected: Cyprus Minerals Co., USA, founded 1979
affected: AMAX, Inc., USA, founded 1887

Overview of the Merger

To strengthen its coal, copper, and molybdenum operations, while reducing its long-term debt, Amax announced a $1.2 billion stock swap merger agreement with Cyprus Minerals, a leading copper producer and the world's largest lithium supplier, in May of 1993. The new company was named Cyprus Amax Minerals Co., the nation's largest molybdenum operation and second largest copper and coal producer.

Both companies reported losses prior to the merger, but the new company, officially formed in November of 1993, earned nearly $5 billion in assets and $2.7 billion in revenue. Subsidiaries Alumax and Amax Gold were spun off prior to the merger. Additionally, both companies reduced their molybdenum operations to comply with Department of Justice stipulations.

History of Cyprus Minerals Co.

Cyprus Minerals grew out of the 1979 acquisition of Cyprus Mines Corp. by Amoco Minerals. The acquisition gave the company, led by Kenneth J. Barr, the ability to mine copper, talc, calcium carbonate, kaolin, and it opened exploration of molybdenum and gold. The main commodities of Cyprus were coal, copper, and industrial minerals.

In 1980, the Cyprus Coal subsidiary was created to handle mines in Colorado, Pennsylvania, and Kentucky. By 1985, coal accounted for 56% of the company's $706 million in revenues. The company was shortly thereafter spun off with little debt and began purchasing more mines in Colorado, Utah, and Virginia. This increased the company's capacity to more than $18 million tons, and Cyprus reached $32 million in revenues within six months of becoming independent.

In 1986, Cyprus became the third largest worldwide molybdenum producer with the acquisition of the Serrita copper and molybdenum mine. The purchase also expanded the company's copper interests, and Cyprus became the nation's third largest copper producer.

Cyprus Gold explored national and Australian gold prospects in 1986. The findings were positive, and the following year, a $25 million advance was given to the subsidiary to pursue the commodity potential through joint ventures.

In 1988, Cyprus became the largest U.S. producer of molybdenum and expanded copper interests through a series of acquisitions. The following year, copper accounted for 90% for the company's $250.1 million in profits. Additionally in 1989, Cyprus acquired an 82% interest in Foote Mineral Corp., the world's largest lithium producer.

Cyprus increased operating efficiencies with cost-cutting and the expansion and modernization of facilities. The company began a $100 million expansion and upgrade of the Miami site's smelter service in order to make Cyprus self-sufficient in processing and thus reduce production costs.

Kenneth Barr retired in 1991. Board member Calvin A. Campbell, Jr., replaced him as chairman and a year later was also appointed president. A worldwide economic decline negatively affected three of Cyprus' main commodities: copper, coal and molybdenum.

In 1992, Milton Ward was named as Cyprus chairman and CEO and charged with the task of streamlining the company and bringing it out of its financial slump. Known as a vigorous, non-sleeping manager, Ward immediately cut the company's assets and began updating equipment. He slimmed Cyprus' commodities, divesting smaller mining and mineral interests.

Less than one year after taking the helm at Cyprus, Ward announced the planned merger with mining giant Amax to form Cyprus Amax Minerals Co. During the merger preparations, Cyprus, in a joint venture with LAC Minerals Ltd., began developing a mine at the El Abra copper deposit with the Chilean government's mining company, Codelco. The El Abra site provided Cyprus one of the world's largest and lowest-cost copper production developments. With over 880 million tons of high grade ore, easy accessibility, and a major underlying copper sulfide deposit, El Abra became one of Cyprus' greatest investments.

To intensify Cyprus Amax's copper and molybdenum production, and reduce losses due to global price reductions in other commodities, the company sold many operations including subsidiary Amax Gold to Kinross Gold in May of 1998. Additionally, Cyprus Amax sold its lithium carbonate interest to Germany-based Metallgesellschaft AG for $305 million and its coal mining operations to RAG International Mining for $1.1 billion.

The Business

Financials

Revenue (1998): $2.56 billion

Employees (1998): 7,200

SICs / NAICS

sic 1021 - Copper Ores

sic 1221 - Bituminous Coal & Lignite-Surface

naics 212234 - Copper Ore and Nickel Ore Mining

naics 212111 - Bituminous Coal and Lignite Surface Mining

History of Amax, Inc.

American Metal Climax, Inc. was established in 1957 after the merger of American Metal Company Ltd. and Climax Molybdenum Co. The company was nicknamed Amax, and in 1957, that became the official moniker. Company predecessor American Metal Company (Amco), was founded by Berthold Hochschild to trade metals with Germany. World War I forced Amco to focus on American sales, and the company began drawing on molybdenum deposits in Colorado. Molybdenum was found to be an effective hardener for steel, benefitting military production. Amax became one of the largest molybdenum producers after the 1957 merger.

Amax expanded its interests through acquisitions in the early 1960s. The company entered the tungsten market, formed Amax Petroleum, and began aluminum production with the purchase of Kaweenr Co. and Chicago's Apex Smelting Company. In 1963, Amax added aluminum sheet production to its services by joining Hunter Engineering Co. Amax established a new subsidiary, the Amax Aluminum Group, in 1965, and acquired aluminum manufacturer Johnson Foil Company the following year.

In 1969, Amax entered the coal market with the purchase of Ayshihre Collieries of Indiana which later became the subsidiary, Amax Coal Co. A series of acquisitions and joint ventures in the first half of the 1970s forced Amax to sell 50% of its aluminum subsidiary to Japan's Mitsui & Co. Amax CEO Pierre Gousseland turned down repeated attempts by Standard Oil to obtain the remaining 80%. By 1982, during the middle of a metal industry recession, Amax's debt was reported at an astounding $390 million.

The Officers

Co-Chairman, CEO, and President: Milton H. Ward

Co-Chairman, Cyprus Amax Minerals Co.; CEO, Alumax Inc.: C. Allen Born

Sr. VP and Chief Financial Officer: Gerald J. Malys

Sr. VP, Secretary and General Counsel: David C. Wolf

Amax's board of directors asked CEO Gousseland to resign in 1985 due to mismanagement and allegations of unethical behavior. Allen Born took over the CEO position in 1986 and immediately began redefining Amax's mining interests and business operations. He liberally divested smaller mineral concerns, focusing only on efficient money-making ventures. He dumped weak performers, including phosphate, lead and copper and iron.

Born guided Amax back into the aluminum market and persuaded the board to borrow almost $435 million to buy their Japanese partner's share of Alumax. He developed the Amax's Sleeper gold mine in Nevada. In the first part of the 1990s, despite a price slump in aluminum, Born gambled that, in the long term, it would become a highly profitable market. He increased the company's debt in order to upgrade aluminum processing operations, which paid off a few years later.

The increased modernization debt, a drastic fall in copper prices, a steady devaluation in coal, and the high developmental costs of acquired Alaska gold property Fort Knox nearly crippled Amax. To reduce debt and re-establish Amax as a leader in the mining industry, Born agreed to a merger with Cyprus Minerals Co. in 1993. The new firm was named Cyprus Amax Minerals Co.

Market Forces Driving the Merger

The reasons that Milton Ward and Allen Born were placed at the helm of their respective companies also motivated the merger between Cyprus and Amax. Amax needed to reduce its debt and sell its smaller, economically draining interests. Ward was trying to increase Cyprus' share in the copper, gold, and coal markets, while decreasing debt and operating inefficiencies.

Amax CEO Born told his board of directors the merger would allow him to focus on problems impacting the company's aluminum subsidiary, Alumax Inc., especially its $800 million debt. To do this, Born planned to expand Alumax's worldwide products, sell

company assets, and explore new aluminum sources in order to compete with lower cost Russian exports. Additionally, Amax needed help as it posted a $284 million loss in 1992.

Bill Siedenberg, an analyst with Smith Barney Harris Upham & Co., stated that strong placement in the coal market was the main reason for the merger. Estimates for the new Cyprus Amax Minerals suggested the company would be able to produce more than 70 million tons of coal a year. The two firms would also gain an increased presence in the global market, mainly by joining their large gold operations.

Approach and Engagement

In May of 1993, Cyprus Minerals Co. and Amax Inc. announced a merger of equals. Cyprus Minerals was the surviving entity in the $1.2 billion stock swap merger. Both parties were able to walk away from the deal prior to signing the agreement if Cyprus stock fell below $20 per share. The new company was to be named Cyprus Amax Minerals Company, with corporate headquarters in Englewood, Colorado.

The U.S. Department of Justice required the nation's two largest mining companies to divest some of their molybdenum operations prior to the merger. Cyprus sold its idle Thompson Creek mine in Idaho, while Amax dumped its Langeloth, Pennsylvania, roasting plant. Both sites had been idle for several years and were sold to Tonopah Mineral Resources, LLC.

Milton Ward, Cyprus' chairman, CEO, and president, retained the same positions in the new company. Amax CEO Allen Born became co-chairman of Cyprus Amax and CEO of the spun off company, Alumax Inc. Amax contributed five directors to the company's board, while Cyprus provided ten.

Prior to the merger, Amax spun off Alumax Inc. and Amax Gold into publicly traded companies. Amax shareholders received shares in both subsidiaries. Cyprus Amax Minerals gained a 42% stake in Amax Gold, while Amax shareholders received 28%. Amax shares were converted on a two to one basis for Cyprus Amax stock.

Products and Services

After the deal was completed, Cyprus Amax Minerals Co. operated interests in copper, molybdenum, coal, gold, and lithium. After nearly $200 million in renovations and constructions, Cyprus created its own smelting plant and a technologically advanced refinery to help reduce production costs. Copper was used primarily in building wire, plumbing and heating products, and a variety of electrical applications. The El Abra mine, a joint venture with LAC Minerals Inc. and Chile's government-operated Codelco, provided a massive ten-year reserve of nearly 880 million tons.

The merger allowed Cyprus to expand direct and subsidiary molybdenum operations. Additionally, Cyprus Amax became the world's largest producer of lithium carbonate. As the nation's second largest coal producer, Cyprus Amax offered over 80 million tons in 1998. Also, through its subsidiary, Amax Gold Inc., Cyprus increased annual production to approximately 700 ounces by 1998. Operations were located Alaska, Russia, and a large surface gold mine in Chile.

Changes to the Industry

The merger of Cyprus Minerals and Amax created the nation's largest mining firm. Focusing on a core group of minerals, the new Cyprus Amax Minerals became the world's largest producer of lithium, the second largest national coal producer, and the largest shareholder of Amax Gold, Inc. In the cyclical molybdenum industry, the creation of Cyprus Amax, a "molybdenum juggernaut," added a new element of stability to the market according to a July 1995 article in *American Metal Market*. The 1995 molybdenum price tumble to $5-$7 per pound was expected to be checked by "Cyprus' ability to control production and manage inventory," an outcome of the firm's larger size and richer resources.

In order to concentrate on select mining operations, both companies divested various interests after the merger's announcement, allowing for smaller companies to increase their holdings. Amax spun off two subsidiaries prior to the merger's completion, creating Alumax Inc. and Amax Gold. Cyprus Amax Minerals retained a majority share of Amax Gold, which was sold in 1998 to other shareholder, Kinross Gold, after a continued slump in gold prices. Also, aluminum giant Alcoa announced its intent to merge with Alumax that year.

Review of the Outcome

After the merger was completed, Cyprus Amax Minerals minimized debt through service consolidation, job cuts, and combined efforts in four major markets: copper, gold, lithium and molybdenum. In an effort to save $120 million annually, the firm closed its molybdenum sales and marketing offices in Norwalk, Connecticut; shut down operations at its Metec molybdenum processing plant in New Jersey; and laid off 110 employees at its Colorado-based Henderson mines.

The Players

Chairman, CEO, and President of Cyprus Minerals Co.: Milton H. Ward. After obtaining his bachelor's and master's degrees in mining engineering from the University of Alabama, Milton Ward began working as a shaft miner at the San Manuel Copper Company in 1955. After six years and many positions, Ward joined Kerr-McGee in Grants, New Mexico. In charge of the company's five uranium mines, he increased daily production and cut unit costs by 50%. In 1970, Ward moved to Albuquerque and Ranchers Exploration and Development Corp. where he witnessed the largest non-nuclear blast, which formed the Big Mike Mine. Four years later, he joined Freeport Minerals Co. as corporate vice president, which later joined with McMoRan. Together the new corporation was the first to take a subsidiary in the gold market successfully. Ward left an 18 year career at Freeport to try his hand as chairman, CEO, and president of Cyprus Minerals Company in 1992. Ward immediately cut production costs, updated equipment, and narrowed the company's focus to a few main commodities including, coal, copper, molybdenum and lithium. Less than a year after taking over at Cyprus, Ward announced the merger with Amax Inc. When the deal was completed, Ward retained his positions as CEO and president, and shared the role of chairman with Amax's Allen Born. Ward's success in the mining industry and his ability to parlay Cyprus into a strong company led to his being named the Copper Club's 1995 Man of the Year.

Research

Caney, Derek J. "Cyprus and Amax Merger Near Altar; Clears Justice Antitrust Concerns," in *American Metal Market*, 10 November 1993. Discusses how Cyprus and Amax plan to sell molybdenum interests.

————. "Prices, Merger Hit Cyprus Amax Results," in *American Metal Market*, 28 January 1994. Reports on copper and molybdenum sales affecting Cyprus Amax's post-merger revenue.

"Cyprus Amax Minerals Co.," in *Notable Corporate Chronologies*, The Gale Group 1999. Lists major events in the history of Cyprus Minerals Co. and Amax Inc.

Cyprus Amax Minerals Company, *Cyprus Amax Minerals Company Annual Report*, 1998. Annual financial and productivity report.

Cyprus Amax Minerals Company, *Elements of Growth*, 1999. Company overview of services, interests, and operations.

The Players

Chairman and CEO of Amax, Inc.: C. Allen Born. A third generation miner from Durango, Colorado, Allen Born made an impact in the mining industry with his no-nonsense, hands-on approach to management. After college and brief stints at different companies, Born became a metallurgist at the Colorado-based molybdenum mine of Amax. He was eventually transferred to Vancouver to head Amax's Canadian interests, which included tungsten. In 1981, after 14 years with Amax, Born accepted the CEO position of Canadian-based Placer Development Ltd. During his four years there, Born successfully experimented with cost cutting and expanded the company's gold assets. In 1985, Amax CEO Pierre Gousseland asked Born if he would return to his former company and attempt to save it. Born returned to Amax and immediately began selling off the company's poorly performing mineral operations, including phosphate, lead and copper. Born gambled Amax's future by heavily investing in aluminum at a time when the market was slumping. He increased the company's debt with the 50% stock purchase of Alumax and the opening of a new smelting plant in Canada. His hunch paid off, and aluminum eventually gained a healthy position on the commodities market. In 1992, Amax merged with Cyprus Minerals. Born became co-chairman of the new Cyprus Amax Minerals Co. and president and CEO of the company's subsidiary aluminum operation, Alumax. In 1998, Alumax was purchased by Alcoa. The following year, Born announced his retirement from Amax and stepped down as co-chairman.

"Cyprus, Amax Spawn Mega Mining Company," in *Northern Miner*, 31 May 1993. Reports the proposed terms of the merger between Cyprus and Amax.

Fraser, Bruce W. "Allen Born, Amax," in *Financial World* 21 April 1987. Discusses Amax CEO Allen Born's work to turn the struggling company around and highlights points in his career.

Leinster, Colin. "Al Born Digs Amax Out of a Hole; To Save the Giant Mining Company From Bankruptcy, the Durango Kid Shot the Money Losers and Nursed the Winners," in *Fortune*, 27 April 1987. Details Allen Born's impact at Amax and discusses highlights in his career.

"Merger Will Create A Mining Giant," in *The New York Times*, 26 May 1993. Summary of merger deal between Amax Inc. and Cyprus Minerals.

Morris, Kathleen. "H-e-r-e's Milton," in *Financial World*, 30 March 1993. Highlights Milton Ward's career at Cyprus.

Saltzman, Joyce A. "Alcoa Completes Merger with Alumax," in *Business Wire*, 31 July 1998. Summarizes announced merger with Alcoa and Alumax Inc.

Ward, Milton H. "Inside View of Cyprus Amax Merger," in *American Metal Market*, 30 March 1994. Transcript of speech given by Milton Ward discussing the post-merger operations at Cyprus Amax Minerals.

Wells, Garrison. "Mining Merger a One-of-a-kind Deal," in *Denver Business Journal*, 28 May 1993. Discusses the terms of the proposed merger between Amax and Cyprus.

Yafie, Roberta C. "Milton H. Ward, Master Builder," in *American Metal Market*, 16 February 1995. Chronicles the career of Milton Ward, his impact at Cyprus, and the terms of the Cyprus Amax merger.

———. "As Cyprus Swings So Swings the Marketplace," in *American Metal Market*, 20 July 1995. Explains the impact the merger has had on the molybdenum industry.

SEAN C. MACKEY

DAIMLER-BENZ & CHRYSLER

nationality: Germany
date: November 17, 1998
affected: Daimler-Benz AG, Germany, founded 1882
affected: Chrysler Corp., USA, founded 1924

DaimlerChrysler AG
Epplestrasse 225
Stuttgart, D-70546
Germany

tel: 49-711-17-1
fax: 49-711-17-94022
web: http://www.daimlerchrysler.com

Overview of the Merger

The $37 billion merger of Chrysler Corp., the third-largest car maker in the U.S., and Germany's Daimler-Benz AG in November of 1998 rocked the global automotive industry. In one fell swoop, Daimler-Benz doubled its size to become the fifth-largest automaker in the world based on unit sales and the third-largest based on annual revenue. Employees totaled 434,000. Anticipating $1.4 billion in cost savings in 1999, as well as profits of $7.06 billion on sales of $155.3 billion, the new DaimlerChrysler manufactured its cars in 34 countries and sold them in more than 200 countries.

History of Daimler-Benz AG

In 1882, Gottlieb Daimler, a gunsmith who studied engineering in several European countries, joined with researcher Wilhelm Maybach to set up an experimental workshop. They tested their first engines on a wooden bicycle, a four-wheeled vehicle, and a boat. The French rights to Daimler's engines were sold to Panhard-Levassor.

Three years later, Carl Benz circled a track next to his small factory in a three-wheeled automobile run by a gasoline powered, internal combustion engine he had designed. By 1888, Benz had 50 workmen building his three-wheeled car. He began manufacturing a four-wheeled car run by a gasoline powered, internal combustion engine in 1890.

At the turn of the century, Austro-Hungarian Consul-General and businessman Emil Jellinek offered to underwrite Daimler's production of a new high performance car; in return he asked that the vehicle be named after his daughter, Mercedes. In 1906, Ferdinand Porsche replaced Daimler's oldest son, Paul Daimler, as chief engineer at the company's Austrian factory after Paul returned to the main plant in Stuttgart, Germany. Porsche proved to be one of the most influential and prolific automotive designers ever, as he produced 65 designs during his years with Daimler.

The Daimler and Benz companies began coordinating designs and production

The Business

Financials

Revenue (1998): $154.61 billion

Employees (1998): 441,500

SICs / NAICS

sic 6159 - Miscellaneous Business Credit Institutions

sic 7514 - Passenger Car Rental

sic 3711 - Motor Vehicles & Car Bodies

sic 3713 - Truck & Bus Bodies

sic 3519 - Internal Combustion Engines Nec

sic 3721 - Aircraft

naics 336111 - Automobile Manufacturing

naics 336112 - Light Truck and Utility Vehicle
Manufacturing

naics 336399 - All Other Motor Vehicle Parts Manufacturing

naics 336992 - Military Armored Vehicle, Tank and Tank
Component Manufacturing

naics 336211 - Motor Vehicle Body Manufacturing

naics 532111 - Passenger Car Rental

naics 522292 - Real Estate Credit

naics 522293 - International Trade Financing

naics 522294 - Secondary Market Financing

naics 522298 - All Other Non-Depository Credit
Intermediation

in 1924, but they maintained their own brand names. Two years later, Daimler and Benz merged to become Daimler-Benz AG, which began producing cars under the name Mercedes-Benz. The merger allowed the two firms to avoid bankruptcy in the midst of poverty and inflation in Germany after World War I. In 1939, the German government took over that nation's auto industry, appropriating its factories to manufacture trucks, tanks, and aircraft engines for the Luftwaffe during World War II. Daimler-Benz's importance to the German war effort made the company a primary target of air strikes, which destroyed 70% its plants.

At war's end, workers resumed their previous jobs. The sorely damaged factories recovered, and the company again became one of the most successful auto makers in the world. In 1957, convicted war criminal Friedrich Flick raised his personal stake in Daimler-Benz to over 37%, gaining controlling interest as an individual stockholder. Within two years, Flick's

$20 million investment had grown in worth to $200 million, making him Germany's second ranking industrialist. His holdings allowed him to push the firm to buy 80% of its competitor, Auto Union, in order to gain a smaller car for the product line; the acquisition made Daimler-Benz the fifth-largest automobile manufacturer in the world and the largest outside the U.S.

Chairman Joachim Zahn, a lawyer, set aside about $250 million as preparation for the difficult phase Daimler-Benz foresaw in the auto industry in the 1970s. The company also invested in engines powered by inexpensive diesel fuel, a product line that comprised 45% of its output. High labor costs and the increasing value of the deutsche mark (DM) caused the price of Mercedes-Benz cars to rise, and the company began marketing them as "investments."

Daimler-Benz purchased Freightliner, a manufacturer of heavy trucks, just as sales dropped with the onset of the U.S. recession in the early 1980s. The 190 model, a smaller version of the firm's saloon car, was unveiled in 1983. It not only attracted new customers; the updated image of the new model lowered the average age of a Mercedes owner from 45 to 40. In 1985, Daimler-Benz bought 65.6% of Dornier, a privately held manufacturer of spacecraft systems, commuter planes, and medical equipment, for $130 million. A few years later, the firm paid $820 million for 56% of AEG, a high technology maker of electronic equipment such as turbines, robotics, and data processing equipment, as well as household appliances.

Growth via acquisition continued in 1989 with the purchase of a majority stake in Messerschmitt-Bolkow-Blohm, a West German aerospace and defense company that was Germany's member of the G.I.E. Airbus consortium. Messerschmitt was later merged with the operations of Dornier, Motoren-und-Turbinen-Union, and the aerospace aspects of AEG to form Daimler-Benz's Deutsche Aerospace (DASA) division. The following year, DASA formed a joint venture with the Pratt & Whitney division of United Technologies Corp.

Daimler-Benz acquired a stake in Metallgesellschaft AG, the Frankfurt-based international supplier of raw materials and technological services, in 1991. A 34% stake in France's Cap Gemini Sogeti, the world's leading computer services company, was acquired by the newly formed Daimler-Benz Interservices division. Several major stock acquisitions and working agreements with international corporations—such as Fokker of the Netherlands, Germany's Siemens AG, and Sweden's Electrolux—were completed in 1992. That year, Daimler-Benz announced 7,500 layoffs in addition to 20,000 previous job losses. By 1995, 70,000 jobs had been eliminated.

With competitor BMW closing in on the leadership of German luxury car sales, Daimler-Benz relied heavily on a revision of its popular Mercedes 190 compact in 1993. Instead, a $1.05 billion loss was reported, one of the company's worst ever. In 1994, the largest rights issue in German history was completed as Daimler-Benz's one-for-ten offer left U.S. shareholders with over an 8% stake in the company. The entire transaction totaled $1.9 billion.

Daimler-Benz and ABB Asea Brown Boveri Ltd. announced plans to merge their railroad operations into the world's largest supplier of trains and other rail equipment in 1995. Due to German currency's increasing gains against the dollar, as well as restructuring costs, the company announced a startling $1.06 billion loss for the first half of the year and a record $3.84 billion record loss for the full year. Daimler-Benz, for the first time since 1950, withheld a divident from its shareholders in 1996. Extensive layoffs and divestitures, including the sale of the Dornier Leftfahrt GmbH aircraft unit to Fairchild Aircraft Inc., helped return the firm to profitability. In 1998, Daimler-Benz and Chrysler merged to form DaimlerChrysler.

History of Chrysler Corp.

In 1924, the Maxwell Motor Corp., headed up by Walter Chrysler, produced the first Chrysler automobile. Over 32,000 models were sold for a profit in excess of $4 million. The same year, Maxwell-Chrysler of Canada opened in Windsor, Ontario. On June 6, 1925, Chrysler was incorporated when Walter Chrysler took over Maxwell Motor Car. Other accomplishments included the introduction of the Chrysler Four Series 58 with a top speed of 58 mph and the incorporation of Chrysler Corp. of Canada, Ltd. By that time, more than 3,800 dealers were selling Chrysler cars. Ford Motor Co. closed its doors that year to redesign its Model T, previously the fastest automobile at 35 mph.

By 1927, Chrysler had sold 192,000 cars to become fifth in the industry. The company acquired Dodge Brothers, Inc., quintupling its size. Chrysler also began production of the De Soto and the first Plymouth, priced from $675 to $725 in order to appeal to consumers with average incomes. In just two years, Chrysler had grown to become one of the Big Three leading automotive manufacturers. In 1933, Chrysler surpassed Ford, its major competitor, in annual sales for the first time.

The company continued to thrive, and in 1934, Chrysler developed its first automatic overdrive transmission, as well as the industry's first one-piece, curved glass windshield. In 1938, Chrysler established and became minority owner in Chrysler de Mexico.

The Officers

Co-Chairman and co-CEO: Robert J. Eaton

Co-Chairman and co-CEO: Juergen E. Schrempp

Chief Financial Officer, Corporate Finance and
    Controlling: Manfred Gentz

Sr. VP, Engineering and Technology: Bernard I. Robertson

Exec. VP, Product Development and Design: Thomas C.
    Gale

With the onset of the war in 1941, Chrysler converted to war production and began making B-29 bomber engines and anti-aircraft tanks and guns. By 1945, Chrysler had supplied more than $3.4 billion in military equipment to the Allied forces. After the war, the company focused on product development and growth. In 1946, Chrysler began production of the first hardtop convertible. Four years later, the company expanded outside North America by purchasing a majority of Chrysler Australia, Ltd. Electric powered windows were developed as well.

The Hemi, a hemispheric combustion chamber V-8 engine, and Oriflow shock absorbers were designed in 1951. The next year, Lynn A. Townsend became president and brought in an IBM computer system that replaced 700 members of the clerical staff. As primary contractor of the Saturn booster rockets, Chrysler's space division contributed to one of America's first successful space flights. By 1955, drivers of Chrysler products were the first to enjoy all-transistor car radios and the convenience of power steering. The company ended the decade by developing electronic fuel injection as an alternative to carburetors.

In 1960, production of the De Soto ceased. Chrysler introduced its first 5/50 warranty—five years or 50,000 miles on drive train components—in 1963. Safety innovations such as a front seat shoulder harness and a self-contained rear heater/defroster system were developed in 1966, as well as the Air Package, a system for controlling exhaust emissions.

Continual management changes were blamed for a $4 million loss in 1969; the firm was operating at only 68% of its capacity. Chrysler fared no better during the 1970s. After losing $52 million in 1974 and $250 million in 1975, the board tapped former Ford president Lee Iacocca to take over as president and CEO.

In January of 1980, President Jimmy Carter signed the Chrysler Corp. Loan Guarantee Act, which pro-

The Players

Chairman of Daimler-Benz AG: Jurgen Schrempp. High school dropout Jurgen Schrempp began working at Daimler-Benz at the age of 15 as an apprentice mechanic. He left the firm briefly to pursue an engineering degree, which he earned in 1967. After serving as head of customer service in South Africa between 1974 and 1982, Schrempp moved to Ohio, where he held a managerial position for two years. He then returned to South Africa as vice president. In 1985, he was named CEO of Daimler-Benz South Africa. Four years later, he was given the task establishing a new aerospace unit at Daimler-Benz, which he did by folding together the firm's four aerospace assets into a single holding company named DASA. Schrempp succeeded Edzard Reuter as CEO and chairman in 1995. After slashing the firm's workforce by 63,000 employees and paring its 35 units to 23, he began preparing the firm for a major merger. Upon completion of the blockbuster deal with Chrysler in 1998, Schrempp took over as co-chairman and co-CEO of DaimlerChrysler.

Chairman of Chrysler Corp.: Robert Eaton. Robert Eaton began his career in the automotive industry in the 1970s. A graduate of the University of Kansas, he started with General Motors as an engineer. He worked his way up through the company working at various levels of engineering management in several different divisions. In 1986, he was named president of GM Europe, Zurich, and Switzerland. Eaton joined Chrysler in 1992 as vice chairman and chief financial officer. That same year, he took over as CEO when Iacocca resigned. He is credited with reviving the company and leading the way to the highest profits Chrysler had seen. In 1995, he successfully fended off a takeover attempt by Kirk Kerkorian and was named "Industry Leader of the Year" and "Most Valuable Player" by *Automotive News* magazine. Eaton went on to lead the company through its merger with Daimler-Benz in 1998 and was named co-chairman and co-CEO of DaimlerChrysler.

vided the company with $1.5 billion in federal loan guarantees and stipulated that Chrysler sell its corporate jets. In July of that year, Iacocca began appearing in Chrysler's television advertisements in an effort to boost sales. The next year, however, Chrysler reported

a record loss of $1.7 billion, cut inventories by $1 billion, and reduced the white-collar staff by 50%.

Iacocca began pushing for new product development. Production began on K-cars, the Dodge Aries, and the Plymouth Reliant. To cut costs, the cars were all built on the same "platform" that became the basic engine, suspension, and underbody design for all Chrysler's vehicles. In 1982, Iacocca released his autobiography, which became the best selling non-fiction hardcover book in the U.S. Hoping that interest in the company would increase as well, Chrysler paid off its government loan seven years early. In 1983, production of minivans, the Dodge Caravan and Plymouth Voyager, began. Chrysler also reintroduced the convertible.

Turnaround efforts paid off with a record 1984 net profit of $2.4 billion. That year, Chrysler acquired 15.6% in Officine Alfieri Maserati SpA. In 1985, it bought Gulfstream Aerospace for $637 million and began a joint venture, Diamond Star Motors, with Mitsubishi Motors Corp. to build small cars in the U.S. The company also launched a reorganization in 1987 that temporarily laid-off workers in two plants so that inventory could be reduced. Later that year, Chrysler was divided up as a holding company with four divisions: Chrysler Motors, Chrysler Financial, Chrysler Technologies, and Gulfstream Aerospace. The holding company's headquarters moved from Highland Park, Michigan, to Manhattan, New York.

Shareholders approved the acquisition of Renault's 46% stake in American Motors Corp., maker of Jeep and Eagle vehicles, for $800 million. The company also bought Electrospace Systems for $367 million and Nuova Automobil F. Lamborghini SpA. Wanting to be the leader in quality assurance, Chrysler introduced an unprecedented 7-year/70,000-mile power train warranty and a 7-year/100,000 mile outer body rust protection warranty in 1987. All Chrysler vehicles were manufactured with air bag restraint systems, including the Chrysler New Yorker and the Dodge Dynasty, by the end of that year.

In 1988, Chrysler began a joint venture with Fiat SpA to distribute Alfa Romeo cars in North America. The following year, Pentastar Transportation Group, Inc., a rental car subsidiary, was formed when Chrysler purchased Thrifty Rental Car System, Inc., Snappy Car Rental, Inc., Dollar Rent A Car Systems, Inc., and General Rent-A-Car, Inc. to prevent other car companies from owning them. The plan backfired, however, when all four of the rental agencies lost money.

Iacocca started 1989 by implementing a $1 billion cost-cutting program. Chrysler also began a joint venture with Steyr-Daimler-Puch of Austria to produce minivans for Europe. In 1990, Chrysler re-purchased

7.7 million shares of its own stock and Kirk Kerkorian acquired 9.8% to become the company's largest single shareholder.

Chrysler sold Gulfstream for $825 million in 1990. The next year, 35 million new shares were issued at $10. Chrysler also sold 50% of Diamond Star Motors and withdrew from its joint venture with Fiat.

The Jefferson North Assembly Plant, a $1.6 billion investment in Detroit, began production of Jeep Grand Cherokees in the early 1990s. By 1994, plans were underway to more than double Chrysler's export of Jeep Cherokees to Japan. Profits reached a record $3.71 billion. That year, the company announced the recall of 1,600 1994 four-wheel-drive Dodge Dakota trucks to repair a defect that could cause a bolt in the upper suspension to break.

In April of 1995, Kirk Kerkorian bid $55 a share, nearly $20 billion, for the 90% of Chrysler shares he didn't yet own. However, he could not raise the financial backing he needed and his bid failed. As the company's focus turned to safety, it announced that it would replace rear door latches on all of its 1995 minivans and 4.5 million of its 1984-1994 minivans. This prompted criticism from the NHTSA, which accused Chrysler of misleading customers about the safety of its minivans and alleged that the company was attempting to limit its efforts to replace rear door latches on minivans. While asserting that the vehicles were indeed safe, Chrysler agreed to replace all latches at no charge.

In 1995, Chrysler spent $2.1 billion in one-time expenses to retool two key factories for minivan construction and remodel a third factory for the assembly of pickup trucks. The economic turbulence in Mexico that followed the devaluation of the peso cost the company approximately $300 million. The following year, Chrysler and Kerkorian reached a five-year truce: Kerkorian agreed not to initiate a takeover attempt or attempt to increase his shareholdings, and Chrysler appointed a Kerkorian supporter to the board.

Chrysler spun off its Dollar Thrifty Automotive unit at $2.50 per share. Despite record sales in November and December of 1997, overall annual sales declined. In an effort to gain market share overseas and remain competitive in the U.S., the company merged with Daimler-Benz in late 1998 to form DaimlerChrysler.

Market Forces Driving the Merger

The deal between Chrysler and Daimler-Benz was put into motion in the early 1990s, when executives at Daimler-Benz realized that the luxury car market they targeted with the Mercedes line was approaching saturation. Because traditional markets had matured and consumers in emerging markets were typically unable to afford higher-priced autos, "Mercedes began to look for a partner that would both broaden its appeal and give it the scale it needed to survive industry consolidation," wrote *Fortune* in January 1999. Eventually, Daimler-Benz settled on Chrysler because of its broad range of less costly vehicles and its third-place status in the U.S.

The trend of globalization had forced Chrysler to take a look at foreign markets in the mid-1990s. With the majority of sales coming from North America, the company was looking for a way to break into overseas markets. After plans in 1995 to jointly make and market automobiles in Asia and South America with Daimler-Benz fell apart, Chrysler devised Lone Star, a growth plan that called for exporting cars built in North America instead of spending money on building plants overseas. The plan faltered because the firm didn't have enough managers placed in international locations to boost sales as quickly as Chrysler wanted.

Daimler-Benz also pursued growth of its own after the attempts at an alliance with Chrysler crumbled in 1995. The German automaker built a plant in Alabama to manufacture its M-class sport utility vehicle and a small A-class model. Quality control problems with both autos plagued the factory in 1996 and 1997. To make his firm more attractive to suitors, Daimler-Benz CEO Jurgen Schrempp it on the New York Stock Exchange, began using U.S. GAAP accounting guidelines, and reduced the independence of the Mercedes unit by removing its separate board of directors. A merger seemed the company's only option. According to *Fortune*, "overcapacity in the industry kept worsening, making consolidation inevitable, and manufacturers like Toyota and Volkswagen, both of which dwarfed Daimler, were building premium auto brands such as Lexus and Audi that would hold a considerable cost advantage."

Approach and Engagement

Daimler-Benz CEO Schrempp called Chrysler CEO Eaton in January of 1998. They met briefly at Chrysler's headquarters during the North American International Auto Show in Detroit. A deal between Daimler-Benz and Chrysler seemed inevitable until Ford's Alex Trotman contacted Schrempp about a possible alliance. Trotman and Schrempp met in London in March to discuss terms. Prior to a second meeting, however, the deal fizzled after Trotman admitted to Schrempp that the Ford family was unwilling to consider a deal that would reduce its 40% stake of Ford's voting stock.

Schrempp and Eaton rekindled their merger negotiations and the $37 billion deal was officially announced on May 7 in London. According to the terms of the agreement, the new firm—named DaimlerChrysler—would be incorporated in Germany, 58% owned by former Daimler-Benz shareholders, and managed mainly by former Daimler-Benz executives. Schrempp and Eaton agreed to jointly run the company until 2001, when Eaton would retire and Schrempp would gain full control. After more than 98% of Daimler-Benz shares were converted into DaimlerChrysler shares, the new firm was officially listed on worldwide stock exchanges on November 17, 1998.

Products and Services

After the merger, DaimlerChrysler manufactured the following makes of automobiles: Chrysler, Dodge, Eagle, Jeep, Mercedes-Benz, Plymouth, and Smart, a compact car. Chrysler passenger cars made up 41% of total sales; Daimler passenger cars accounted for 24%. Other automotive operations, which secured 17% of sales, included four-wheel drive vehicles, commercial vehicles, trucks, and busses. Services accounted for 9% of sales and encompassed financial, insurance brokerage, information technology, telecommunications, and real estate management. Aerospace operations made up another 6% of total revenues.

Changes to the Industry

The new DaimlerChrysler moved into the fifth place spot among global automakers based on the four million vehicles it was estimated to produce in 1999. Anticipated sales of $155.3 billion positioned the firm as third in the world in terms of revenue. Analysts heralded the deal as the first in a new wave of intense global consolidation among the industry's leading players. Accordingly, DaimlerChrysler stock continued to outperform Ford Motor Co., General Motors Corp., and the Dow Jones Industrial Average in May of 1999, one year after the deal's formal announcement.

Review of Outcome

The new firm faced its first hurdle almost immediately. Standard & Poor's chose not to list DaimlerChrysler in the Standard & Poor's 500 stock index because the firm had become a German entity. Standard & Poor's fund managers were forced to sell their Chrysler shares, and because they were unable to exchange them for DaimlerChrysler shares, the new firm lost a wide shareholder base. On a more positive note, DaimlerChrysler didn't face the expense of spending five to ten years integrating its computer-aided design systems or its financial applications because the two firms already used the same systems.

The success of the merger depends upon how well the two disparate teams mesh. As pointed out by a November 1998 article in *Business Week*, "Where one company is clearly more advanced, decisions are easy: For instance, Daimler will handle fuel-cell and diesel technology, and Chrysler will keep its electric-vehicle project. Other decisions are tougher. Chrysler invented the minivan, but Daimler was far along in developing its own. So the two are hotly debating whether to ditch Daimler's version or offer a separate luxury model."

To achieve the promised $1.4 billion in savings—the anticipated outcome of complementary geographic reach and product lines, but not of the layoffs that typify mergers of this scope—integration efforts began immediately with the financing departments of both firms first on the list. Most analysts consider purchasing likely be the second candidate for cost cutting efforts as DaimlerChrysler works to leverage its size to garner discounts for such commodities as steel and services like transportation. The firm will also be able to manufacture some of the same components for both Chrysler and Mercedes vehicles, although management is careful to point out the importance of maintaining distinct brand identities to avoid undermining the luxury reputation of Mercedes vehicles. In both Europe and North America, Chrysler and Mercedes showrooms will remain separate, although warehousing, logistics, service, and technical training will be combined. Complete integration of purchasing operations is scheduled to take three to five years; merging manufacturing functions will take even longer, as might ironing out anticipated cultural clashes between the Germans and the Americans.

Research

Child, Charles. "DaimlerChrysler: One Year Later, the Winner Is...," in *Automotive News*, 3 May 1999. Compares the performance of DaimlerChrysler stock to other leading industry players.

"Chrysler Corp.," in *Notable Corporate Chronologies*, The Gale Group, 1999. Profiles major events in the history of Chrysler Corp.

"Daimler-Benz AG," in *Notable Corporate Chronologies*, The Gale Group, 1999. Lists major events in the history of Daimler-Benz AG.

DaimlerChrysler AG Home Page, available at http://www.daimlerchrysler.com. Official World Wide Web Home Page for DaimlerChrysler AG. Includes current and archived news, detailed financial information, and historical information.

Flint, Jerry. "A Letter to Jurgen Schrempp," in *Forbes*, 31 May 1998. Predicts integration problems the two firms will likely encounter after the merger is completed.

Jackson, Kelly. "Eaton: The All Stars' All Star," in *Automotive News*, 10 July 1995. Details the career of Robert Eaton.

McGinn, Daniel. "Hands on the Wheel," in *Newsweek*, 12 April 1999. Discusses the reasons for the merger between Daimler-Benz and Chrysler, as well as the challenges the newly merged firm faces.

Miller, Karen. "The Auto Baron," in *Business Week*, 16 November 1998. Details the career of Jurgen Schrempp and how he forged a deal with Chrysler.

Taylor, Alex. "The Germans Take Charge," in *Fortune*, 11 January 1999. Explains how the deal came about and what management will have to do for the new firm to be successful.

ANNAMARIE L. SHELDON

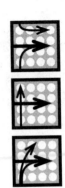

DELOITTE HASKINS & SELLS & TOUCHE ROSS

Deloitte Touche Tohmatsu
International
1633 Broadway
New York, NY 10019-6754
USA

tel: (212)492-2000
fax: (212)492-4154
web: http://www.deloitte.com

nationality: USA
date: October 1989
affected: Deloitte Haskins & Sells, USA, founded 1845
affected: Touche Ross, USA, founded 1899

Overview of the Merger

On the heels of the July 1989 merger of Ernst & Whinney and Arthur Young—the second-and sixth-largest public accounting firms in the world, respectively—into Ernst & Young came the announcement of the deal between Deloitte Haskins & Sells and Touche Ross. In less than a year, the Big Eight of the accounting industry were consolidated into the Big Six. The merger of the group's two smallest firms created Deloitte & Touche, an accounting goliath with nearly $4 billion in annual revenues, only $300 million less than Ernst & Young. In an unusual twist, the United Kingdom arm of Deloitte Haskins & Sells shunned the merger, opting instead to join forces with Coopers & Lybrand, L.L.P., to form the largest accounting consultancy in the U.K.

History of Deloitte Haskins & Sells

In 1845, 25-year-old William Welch Deloitte opened an accounting firm in London, across the street from the bankruptcy court. Deloitte prospered as the advent of joint stock companies gave rise to a need for standardized financial record keeping and financial divulging. In 1849, the Great Western Railway hired Deloitte as an independent auditor. As the first such auditor in accounting history, Deloitte unearthed fraudulent behavior by executives of the Great North Railway and created an investment protection system.

Deloitte was named the first president of the Institute of Chartered Accountants in 1888. His firm expanded into the U.S. for the first time in 1893, acting an auditor for a fledgling soap and candle company that would later become known as Procter & Gamble. The U.S. unit merged with Haskins & Sells, an accountancy firm with 34 offices in operation, in 1924.

The firm changed its name to Deloitte Haskins & Sells in 1978. Five years later, a merger with Price Waterhouse fell through. In 1989, Deloitte Haskins & Sells merged with Touche Ross to form Deloitte & Touche, whittling the Big Seven accounting firms down to the Big Six. The company later called itself Deloitte Touch Tohmatsu to incorporate the name of its Japanese arm, Ross Tohmatsu, founded in 1968. Before the merger was completed, the United Kingdom unit of Deloitte Haskins & Sells opted out of the deal with Touche Ross, instead joining forces with the U.K. operations of Coopers & Lybrand to form Coppers & Lybrand Deloitte, Britain's largest accounting and management consulting firm.

In the early 1990s, Deloitte weathered litigation regarding its activity in the savings and loan scandal, as well as lawsuits filed by insolvent clients. To centralize its consulting activities in the U.S. and the United Kingdom, the firm established Deloitte & Touche Consulting in 1995. The following year, Deloitte diversified into the corporate fraud investigation market. Roughly 1,000 consultants resigned in 1999, forming their own consulting business.

History of Touche Ross

In 1899, George A. Touch (later changed to Touche) formed an accounting firm. The following year, he joined forced with another accountant, John Niven, to found Touch, Niven & Co. in New York. In its early years of operation, the firm landed clients such as R.H. Macy and General Electric Co.

George Touche was knighted in 1917, and he died in 1935. His firm went on to merge with another U.S. accountancy in 1947, forming Touche Ross, which became known as the most unconventional of the Big Eight accounting firms. An alliance with Japan's Tohmatsu, founded in 1968 by Admiral Nobuzo Tohmatsu and Iwao Tomita, resulted in the formation of Ross Tohmatsu. In 1989, Touche Ross merged with the more conservative Deloitte Haskins & Sells to form Deloitte & Touche.

Market Forces Driving the Merger

The merger frenzy in the late 1980s among large accounting houses, including Ernst & Whinney and Arthur Young, as well as Deloitte Haskins & Sells and Touche Ross, according to *Business Week*, exhibited "the accountants' response to the wave of restructuring that their clients have undergone. Clients are disappearing—every time one company takes over another, one accounting firm is out—and those clients that remain demand lower prices on bread-and-butter services such as audits."

As prices on traditional accounting services fell and undermined earnings, firms were diversifying into more lucrative services, such as computer consulting. However, the technology and training required to offer these services was rather expensive. The economies of scale and increased revenue base afforded by consolidation deepened the pockets of accounting firms.

The Business

Financials

Revenue (1998): $9 billion

Employees (1998): 82,000

SICs / NAICS

sic 8721 - Accounting, Auditing & Bookkeeping

sic 8742 - Management Consulting Services

sic 6282 - Investment Advice

naics 541211 - Offices of Certified Public Accountants

naics 541214 - Payroll Services

naics 541219 - Other Accounting Services

naics 541611 - Administrative Management and General Management Consulting Services

naics 541612 - Human Resources and Executive Search Consulting Services

Approach and Engagement

On July 6, 1989, Deloitte Haskins & Sells and Touche Ross announced their intent to merge into Deloitte & Touche. Touche Ross CEO Edward Kangas agreed to head up the firm's international operations, while the chairman of Deloitte Haskins & Sells, J. Michael Cook, agreed to oversee U.S. operations. The deal was completed later in the year.

On October 5, the United Kingdom unit of Deloitte Haskins & Sells surprised most analysts when it distanced itself from the Deloitte & Touche deal by agreeing to merge with the U.K. operations of Coopers & Lybrand. According to the *Financial Times (London)*, Coopers CEO Brandon Gough pursued the deal to save face in the rapidly consolidating industry. "Given the firm's known penchant for being number one, it was clear that many partners were none too pleased at Cooper's sudden relegation to the bottom of the Big Eight pile. By linking up with Deloitte in this way, Mr. Gough preserves his reputation for being tough and unpredictable and redeems himself in the eyes of his merger-hungry partners."

Products and Services

By the late 1990s, Deloitte Touche Tohmatsu International operated roughly 700 offices spanning in excess of 130 countries. Along with accounting and auditing, the firm offered information technology con-

The Officers

Chairman: Edward A. Kangas

CEO: James E. Copeland, Jr.

Chief Operating Officer: J. Thomas Presby

Director, Finance: Gerald W. Richards

Director, Communications: David Read

sulting, management consulting, mergers and acquisitions consulting, tax advice, and financial planning. North American activities accounted for 55% of total revenues. Europe brought in 29%; Asia, 10%; Latin America, 3%; Africa, 2%; and the Middle East, 1%.

Changes to the Industry

The deal condensed the Big Seven into the Big Six, and many analysts predicted increased industry consolidation would follow. Although rumors of various hookups swept through Wall Street during the early 1990s, the next major move didn't take place until 1997, when Price Waterhouse and Coopers & Lybrand announced their intent to merge into a $12 billion accounting behemoth, the largest of the Big Five accounting firms. In response, Ernst & Young and KPMG Peat Marwick agreed to join forces to create an even larger player. A few months later, though, that deal was canceled, with both firms pointing to expensive and time consuming regulatory hurdles as the culprits.

Review of the Outcome

Despite the differing management styles of the flamboyant Touche Ross and the staid Deloitte Haskins & Sells, integration of the two firms was surprisingly smooth. According to a September 1994 article in *Financial World*, Deloitte & Touche performed fairly well in the years following the merger. "While it hasn't been the most successful firm, it has been a sold

middle-of-the-pack performer. Its management consulting practice has been growing at 12% to 15% a year. It has a reasonably strong international presence, particularly in Asia, South America, and Canada." Many analysts contributed the continued success of the firm to the management of Michael Cook, who implemented a program which focused the firm's attention on its top 300 clients.

Research

Cowan, Allison Leigh. "U.S. Accounting Firms Merge in Hope of Overseas Growth," in *The New York Times*, 7 July 1989. Explains the impetus for consolidation among the accounting industry's largest firms.

———. "Vote Supports Merger of Touche and Deloitte," in *The New York Times*, 14 August 1989. Describes the terms of the agreement to merge between Deloitte Haskins & Sells and Touche Ross.

"Deloitte & Touche," in *International Directory of Company Histories*, Vol. 9, St. James Press, 1992. Covers the history of Deloitte & Touche.

Deloitte Touche Tohmastu International Home Page, available at http://www.deloitte.com. Official World Wide Web Home Page for Deloitte Touche Tohmastu International. Includes current and archived news, as well as employment, product, historical, and investor information.

Laderman, Jeffrey M. "When One Plus One Equals No. 1," in *Business Week*, 5 June 1989. Discusses why major accounting firms are planning to merge.

MacDonald, Elizabeth. "Deloitte & Touche's Cook is Retiring," in *The Wall Street Journal*, 3 February 1999. Details the career of J. Michael Cook.

Waller, David. "Coopers and Deloitte Expected to Merge in UK," in *Financial Times (London)*, 4 October 1989. Covers the decision of Coopers & Lybrand to merge its U.K. operations with Deloitte's U.K. arm.

———. "Coopers and Lybrand Will Join Forces with Deloitte," in *Financial Times (London)*, 5 October 1989. Confirms the decision of Coopers & Lybrand to merge its U.K. operations with Deloitte's U.K. arm.

———. "Deloitte Deal Pushes Coopers into Top Slot," in *Financial Times (London)*, 5 October 1989. Details the outcome of the joining of the U.K. operations of both Coopers & Lybrand and Deloitte Haskins & Sells.

JEFF ST. THOMAS

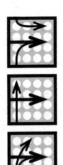

DOMINION RESOURCES & EAST MIDLANDS ELECTRICITY

nationality: USA
date: March 1997
affected: Dominion Resources, Inc., USA, founded 1909
affected: East Midlands Electricity, UK

Dominion Resources, Inc.
120 Tredegar St.
Richmond, VA 23219
USA

tel: (804)819-2000
fax: (804)819-2233
web: http://www.domres.com

Overview of the Merger

In March 1996, Dominion Resources announced plans to purchase East Midlands Electricity for $2.2 billion. The $11 per share offer for the British firm gave Dominion a foothold in the British market, which was subject to several other U.S. takeovers. The deal marked the fourth recent U.S. entry into the British power field and was completed in March 1997. However, Dominion struggled with its British unit, and within a year and a half of the merger, sold it to PowerGen PLC.

History of Dominion Resources, Inc.

Although Dominion Resource's largest subsidiary, Virginia Electric and Power Co. (Vepco) was founded in 1909, the company can trace its roots back to the Appomattox Trustees, established in 1781. The organization, whose members included George Washington and James Madison, was established to oversee navigation on the Appomattox River for rum and tobacco hauling. (Nearly two hundred years later, in 1975, the trustees formed the Upper Appomattox Co.) Ownership changed hands to the Virginia Passenger and Power Co. in 1901. Virginia Railway and Power Co. (VR&P), under the leadership of Frank and Jay Gould, purchased the firm in 1909.

By 1912, VR&P was growing rapidly. The company's president, Thomas S. Wheelwright, oversaw the acquisitions of Richmond Passenger & Power, Richmond Traction Co., and Richmond & Petersburg Electric Railway Co. At the time, transit was the company's main source of revenue at $1.4 million compared to $614,000 for business and home electricity. VR&P continued to purchase other companies such as Norfolk & Portsmouth Traction Co., Richmond Railway and Viaduct Co., and Norfolk & Ocean View Railway Co. The company also bought gas properties in Norfolk, entering the natural gas distribution business. This proved to be a lucrative move during World War I for the company.

VR&P was purchased in 1925 by Stone & Webster, Inc. The holding company of Engineers Public Service was formed to manage the newly acquired company,

The Business

Financials

Revenue (1998): $6.08 billion

Employees (1998): 11,033

SICs / NAICS

sic 4911 - Electric Services

naics 221111 - Hydroelectric Power Generation

naics 221112 - Fossil Fuel Electric Power Generation

naics 221121 - Electric Bulk Power Transmission and Control

naics 221122 - Electric Power Distribution

naics 221113 - Nuclear Electric Power Generation

naics 221119 - Other Electric Power Generation

and its name was changed to Virginia Electric and Power Co. Wheelwright was replaced by Luke C. Bradley after the deal. Vepco grew throughout the latter half of the 1920s and the 1930s through acquisitions. The company's trolley and transit business, however, faltered after the advent of the automobile. Revenues dropped significantly from $290,000 in 1923 to $85,000 in 1931, and electric streetcars were being phased out by motor buses. In 1949, Vepco ran its last streetcar.

Vepco's owner, Engineers Public Service, had to divest itself of all operations, excluding Vepco, in 1940. The Securities and Exchange Commission had sued the company during a period of dissolution in the utilities industry, and as a result, Vepco became independent in 1947. The company merged with Virginia Public Service Co., doubling its service area and becoming one of the largest electric utility companies in the U.S.

Vepco continued on its quest for growth throughout the 1950s. The company snatched up East Coast Electric Co., Hydro-Electric Corp. of Virginia, and Roanoke Utilities Co. In 1955, after a long battle with the U.S. Department of the Interior, Vepco completed the Roanake Rapids dam in North Carolina. With Jack Holtzclaw at the helm, the local power company had grown into an entity that controlled most of the electric utilities of Virginia and parts of North Carolina and West Virginia.

Vepco entered the nuclear energy industry in the 1960s. The company became a member of the non-

profit organization, Carolinas-Virginia Nuclear Power Association, an organization developed to create a prototype for an experimental nuclear reactor. As well as becoming a frontrunner in that industry, Vepco also created one of the first underground residential distribution systems, using lightweight, buried cables. The company's innovative process soon became standard in all residential areas.

The company continued to lead the industry with its creative innovations. Vepco pioneered the worlds first extra-high voltage system, constructed the first 500,000 volt transmission system, and opened one of the largest hydroelectric plants in the world. The company also saw revenues of $215 million in 1965—its property and facilities had doubled in just 10 years. Times changed, however, in the 1970s on account of rising fuel bills, higher interest rates, and inflation. The oil embargo also caused increased costs and greater shortages. In response, Vepco converted its oil stations to coal-fired stations. By 1980, the company was near bankruptcy.

William W. Berry led the company through the 1980s. He pared back nuclear interests, changed management, and implemented a recovery plan. In 1983, he created Dominion Resources to act as a holding company. Dominion's objective was to use Vepco's expertise in unregulated areas. In 1985, Dominion Capital, an investment subsidiary, was formed. Two years later, Dominion created Dominion Lands, a real estate subsidiary. Berry eliminated all plant construction and focused on energy management and coal versus oil.

In 1986, Dominion acquired Potomac Electric Power Co. One year later, a third subsidiary was formed, Dominion Energy. Berry continued to focus on expanding its unregulated business, an effort which earned a 25% return on equity with the formation of out of state plants. Generation sources became privatized, and Dominion was able to bid on sources in West Virginia, California, and South America. In 1988, the company purchased half of Enron Cogeneration. Dominion Energy began seeking joint ventures in order to develop natural gas reserves.

Thomas Capps became CEO of Dominion in 1990. He continued a plan of expansion, and, in 1995, he orchestrated the purchase of three natural gas companies. The next year, the company formed a partnership with Chesapeake Paper Products with a goal of building a $42 million cogeneration plant. In 1997, Dominion entered the British market with the purchase of East Midlands Electricity. Dominion's opportunities in the market did not prove to be viable and in 1998, the company sold its British unit to PowerGen. In 1999, Dominion struck a deal with Consolidated

Natural Gas which would position it as the number one natural gas and electric company in the U.S.

Market Forces Driving the Merger

According to Bruce Wasserstein, author of *Big Deal: The Battle for Control of America's Leading Corporations*, Great Britain represents "a particularly attractive market for U.S. companies because deregulation has proceeded more quickly there. The U.K. companies have already begun offering telecommunications and other services, and are a laboratory for what will happen in the U.S. market. Moreover, U.K. companies have outpaced their U.S. counterparts in terms of growth." Analysts also pointed out that, because of growing competition spawned by looser monopoly protection in the U.S., companies were turning to high-growth markets abroad.

American companies anticipated eventual deregulation in the electric utility industry as well. Forced to position themselves competitively, many turned to the U.K. to do just that. Entergy Corp. bid $2.1 billion for London Electricity , and CalEnergy paid $1.3 billion for Northern Electric. Other British regional deals included Southern Co.'s purchase of South Western Electricity PLC and Central and Southwest Corp.'s $2.5 billion deal with Seeboard PLC. Dominion Resource's competitors were branching out into global relationships, and the company responded by putting its own bid on the table for East Midlands Electricity.

Dominion Resources looked at the deal as a way to complement its U.S. business. By pairing up with East Midlands, the company could be a viable contender in the global market by increasing its worldwide utility markets and by adding 2.3 million people to its customer base. These customers could also become a target for Dominion's other products and services.

Approach and Engagement

Thomas Capp ventured to the U.K. early in November of 1996 to discuss merger plans with East Midlands Electricity. Representatives from the two companies met and in just two hours had sketched out a plan to join forces. East Midlands Electricity was pleased with the offer from the company because it viewed Dominion as a well run and reputable operation and thought the deal represented a fair value to shareholders.

Dominion's newly formed subsidiary, DR Investments, offered $2.2 billion, $11.06 per share, for the British utilities firm. According to a press release issued by Dominion, the company was "delighted that

The Officers

Chairman, President, and CEO: Thomas E. Capps

Exec. VP and Chief Financial Officer: Edgar M. Roach, Jr.

Exec. VP; President and CEO, Virginia Electric and Power: Norman B. Askew

Exec. VP; President, Dominion Capital: David L. Heavenridge

Exec. VP; President, Dominion Energy: Thomas N. Chewning

East Midlands recognizes the benefits to both its shareholders and customers that will arise from the proposed acquisition." The company also looked forward to entering the U.K. market.

Due to the size of the offer, the deal was subject to review under the U.K.'s Fair Trading Act of 1973. The Secretary of State for Trade and Industry, Ian Lang, had to clear the offer to avoid referral to the Monopolies and Mergers Commission. In December, he did just that as Dominion gained just over 50% of East Midland's shares. Dominion completed its purchase in March of 1997.

Products and Services

In 1998, Virginia Power accounted for 70% of total sales with $4.2 billion in sales. Dominion U.K., which ran East Midlands, accounted for 16% of total sales. Dominion Capital and Dominion Energy accounted for the remaining 13% with $409 million and $383 million in sales respectively.

When Dominion sold East Midlands eighteen months after the deal was struck, the company focused on operations in its three subsidiaries. Virginia Power operated two nuclear power plants, four hydroelectric plants, eight fossil fuel plants, and one pumped storage plant in Virginia, West Virginia, and North Carolina. Dominion Energy owned facilities in Illinois and interests in power plants in West Virginia, New York, New Jersey, and California, as well as international operations in Argentina, Belize, and Bolivia. Dominion Capital, its third subsidiary, dealt with financial services and investments.

Changes to the Industry

By June of 1998, seven of the eight regional electricity companies that Americans had purchased recently were for sale. U.S. shareholders were dis-

The Players

Chairman, President and CEO of Dominion Resources, Inc.: Thomas E. Capps. A law graduate from the University of North Carolina at Chapel Hill, Thomas E. Capps began his career with a law firm in North Carolina. He joined Carolina Power and Light Co. in 1970 as the company's senior counsel. In 1974, he teamed up with Boston Edison Co. as vice president and general counsel. After a short stint with the Boston firm, he went to Miami to work for the law firm of Steel Hector and Davis as a senior partner. Capps served as chairman of the executive committee until 1984, when he joined Virginia Power and quickly became executive vice president. In 1986, he was elected president of Dominion Resources, the owner of Virginia Power, and eventually became chairman and CEO as well. Capps, known by his peers as a strong and controversial leader, lead the company through many major acquisitions including East Midlands in 1997 and Consolidated Natural Gas Co. in 1999.

CEO of East Midlands Electricity: Norman Askew. Durham University, Aston, and London Business School graduate Norman Askew worked in the U.S. for TI Aerospace and Titeflex International as managing director and president. He was responsible for aerospace and automotive operations in the U.S., Canada, France, and the United Kingdom. Askew joined East Midlands in 1994 and, as president, oversaw the company's pairing with U.S.-based, Dominion Resources in 1997. In May of that year, he was named president and CEO of Virginia Power, the principal subsidiary of Dominion Resources.

pleased with financial returns and Prime Minister Tony Blair and his Labor government were imposing a windfall-profits tax on the companies that were sold. Dominion paid $156.6 million for the tax imposed on East Midlands. According to industry analysts, most companies were discouraged with their British investments and were looking to other parts of the world for higher returns.

Among the U.S. companies unloading its British concerns was Entergy. In August of 1998, the company was looking for a buyer for London Electric. By this time, analysts were speculating that other U.S. companies would also put their once hot prospects up for sale.

Review of the Outcome

Although net income grew by 34.2% from 1997 to 1998, and stock closed higher than it had ever been at $46.75 in 1998, Dominion Resources was also looking for a buyer for East Midlands. Since its purchase, Dominion had been seeking potential partners and mergers in Great Britain to further its customer reach there, which at the time of the deal was 2.3 million homes and businesses. In a 1998 press release, Thomas Capps commented, "We've been frustrated in our ability to grow our assets in the U.K. When you can't grow, you're better off taking out the capital and redeploying it into assets that you can grow." PowerGen PLC offered $3.2 billion to Dominion for East Midlands to gain 100% control of DR Investments, which was created to purchase East Midlands in 1996. Although Dominion viewed the partnership with the company as a positive learning experience, it accepted the offer and planned to use the profits from the sale to boost operations in eastern United States and in Latin America, as well as to increase gas reserves.

Research

Barrie, Chris. "The Americans Take Power," in *The Guardian London*, 19 December 1996. Discusses the U.S. penetration of the British electricity industry.

Cowe, Roger. "London Electricity for Sale," in *The Guardian London*, 4 August 1998. Explains recent trends in utility industry and U.S. shareholders' discontent with British concerns.

Dominion Resources, Inc. Home Page, available at http://www.domres.com. Official World Wide Home Page for Dominion Resources, Inc. Includes historical, financial, and product information, as well as recent news articles and archived press releases.

"Dominion Resources, Inc," in *International Directory of Corporate Histories*, Vol. V, St. James Press, 1992. Lists major events in the history of Dominion Resources, Inc.

"Dominion to Buy Britain's East Midlands," in *Los Angeles Times*, 14 November 1996. Relates the terms of the deal between Dominion and East Midlands.

Hamilton, Martha. "Dominion to Purchase British Utility," in *The Washington Post*, 14 November 1996. Discusses Dominion's bid and other U.S. bids for British companies.

Hamilton, Martha. "Dominion May Sell British Firm," in *The Washington Post*, 24 June 1998. Reports reasons for Dominion's sale of East Midlands.

Wasserstein, Bruce. *Big Deal: The Battle for Control of America's Leading Corporations*, Warner Books, 1998. Offers an overview of the largest mergers in recent American corporate history.

CHRISTINA M. STANSELL

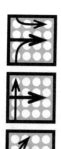

DOW CHEMICAL & UNION CARBIDE

nationality: USA
date: 2000
affected: Dow Chemical Co., USA, founded 1897
affected: Union Carbide Corp., USA, founded 1917

Dow Chemical Co.
2030 Willard H. Dow Ctr.
Midland, MI 48674
USA

tel: (517)636-1000
fax: (517)636-0922
web: http://www.dow.com

Union Carbide Corp.
39 Old Ridgebury Rd.
Danbury, CT 06817-0001
USA

tel: (203)794-5300
fax: (203)794-4336
web: http://www.unioncarbide.com

Overview of the Acquisition

The union of Dow Chemical and Union Carbide, expected to be completed in early 2000, would form the world's second-largest chemical concern, after DuPont. The deal was the product of a consolidation wave in the chemical industry, fueled by a downturn in the commodities market. By acquiring Union Carbide, Dow would strengthen its position in several businesses, particularly polyethylene, while saving an estimated $500 million in annual expenses.

History of The Dow Chemical Co.

In 1889, Herbert Henry Dow persuaded three businessmen to invest in his method for the extraction of bromides and chlorides from brine deposits in Michigan. The next year the Midland Chemical Co. was formed by Dow and J.H. Osborn to manufacture ferric bromide from brine through Dow's process. The company first became profitable in 1894.

The Dow Process Co. was formed in 1895 as a partnership to manufacture bleach. In May 1897, The Dow Chemical Co. was incorporated, taking over the assets of The Dow Process Co. The next year Dow Chemical sold its first product, chlorine bleach. Its sales for its first full year in operation were $15,000, and, in 1899, the company showed a profit for the first time.

In 1900, Dow Chemical absorbed Midland Chemical, which continued to manufacture bromine. Two years later a second Midland Chemical Co. was set up to manufacture chloroform from carbon tetrachloride using A.W. Smith's process. Also in 1902 Dow introduced its bleach internationally. Five years later, Dow, Libbey, and Fostoria formed a new company, Midland Manufacturing, to develop electrolytic potash cell. Dow entered the field of agricultural chemicals in 1910, and three years later it discontinued its manufacture of bleach. In 1914, Midland Chemical formally merged with Dow.

During World War I, Dow diversified into the production of chemicals previously supplied by German companies. The end of the war, however, led to decreased demand, and Dow cut its payroll to 400 employees. Still, in 1920, the

361

The Business

Financials - Dow Chemical Co.

Revenue (1998): $18.4 billion

Employees (1998): 39,000

Financials - Union Carbide Corp.

Revenue (1998): $5.6 billion

Employees (1998): 11,627

SICs / NAICS

sic 2812 - Alkalies & Chlorine

sic 2821 - Plastics Materials & Resins

sic 2822 - Synthetic Rubber

sic 2823 - Cellulosic Manmade Fibers

sic 2843 - Surface Active Agents

naics 325181 - Alkalies and Chlorine Manufacturing

naics 325211 - Plastics Material and Resin Manufacturing

naics 325212 - Synthetic Rubber Manufacturing

naics 325221 - Cellulosic Manmade Fiber Manufacturing

naics 325613 - Surface Active Agent Manufacturing

company was selling $4 million worth of such bulk chemicals as chlorine, calcium chloride, salt, and aspirin.

Dow expanded into new areas during the 1920s. It developed the first commercial synthesis of phenol from chlorobenzel, thereby gaining a significant lead in the U.S. phenol industry. In addition, the advent of the automobile age increased demand for ethylene dibromide due to its anticlogging effect in leaded gasoline. Dow's growth attracted the attention of competitors, and DuPont made an unsuccessful offer to purchase the company.

Dow established its first subsidiary, Jones Chemical Co., in 1928 to extract iodine from brine through Dow's patented process. That year, ethylene was developed by cracking petroleum, and soon opened the way for the development of such products such as styrene and saran. In 1930, with the continuing demand for ethyl dibromide, Dow negotiated for the establishment of Ethyl Dow Corporation. Three years later it formed a joint venture with Ethyl Gas Co. to extract bromine from seawater for ethylene dibromide production.

Dow produced the first styrene in the U.S. at its Midland factories in 1937, introducing the STYRON polystyrene. Two years later it gained its first large manufacturing location outside of Midland, Michigan, by acquiring the Great Western Chemical Co. of Pittsburg, California.

In 1943, Dow joined with Corning Glass Works to form Dow Corning Corp. for the production of organosilicon compounds and materials. Also that year Dow's first agricultural product, 2-4-D herbicide, was added to its product line. Styrofoam brand plastic foam was introduced in 1944. Four years later the company released styrene and butadiene, two vital ingredients in artificial rubber.

In 1952, Dow built a plant in Japan, its first outside of North America. The next year Saran Wrap brand plastic film, made from Dow's saran resin, was introduced as the company's first consumer product. It followed up the success of that product by introducing Handi-Wrap brand plastic film in 1960. Also that year it acquired Pitman-Moore of Indianapolis, Indiana. Dow's sales exceeded $1 billion for the first time in 1964.

Dow diversified into pharmaceuticals in 1960 by acquiring Allied Labs in 1960. Five years later it introduced the Liurgen one-shot measles vaccine. In 1969, the Cordis Dow Corp. was formed to manufacture and market the Dow artificial kidney.

Ziploc storage bags were introduced in 1972. In 1979, with sales of $9.2 billion, Dow was the world's seventh-largest chemical company and the second-largest in the U.S. Sales exceeded $10 billion for the first time in 1980.

In March 1981, Dow acquired Merrell, an ethical pharmaceutical firm, and became the 15th-largest concern in the nation's human health industry. Four years later it acquired the Texize Division of the Morton Thiokol Inc. and the worldwide polymer chemical business of the Upjohn Co.

Dow and Sumitomo Chemical Co., Ltd., announced an agreement in 1988 to form a joint venture in Japan to market and manufacture polycarbonate resins. That year DowBrands, formerly Dow Consumer Products Inc., announced the introduction of two new product lines: Simoniz professional floor care products and Dow bathroom cleaning products. It entered into an agreement with Exxon Chemical Co. to form Dexco Polymers, a 50/50 joint venture for the supply and marketing of styrenic block polymers.

In 1989, it joined with Eli Lilly & Co. to create one of the largest research based agricultural companies in the world, DowElanco, which held both parent companies' plant science businesses, as well as Dow's industrial pest control business. Dow further expanded its human health business by combining with Marion Laboratories, Inc., to form Marion Merrell Dow Inc..

Dow Corning became the center of a controversy over faulty silicone breast implants, and discontinued their production in 1992. Although the company was cleared of charges that the implants were put on the market without proper testing, the Food & Drug Administration banned the implants because Dow Corning and other manufacturers failed to prove that the products were safe. In 1994, Dow agreed to a $4.2 billion settlement to put to rest much of the litigation.

A ruling that exempted Dow Chemical from breast implant litigation, based on the company's claims that it had not participated in Dow Corning's making of implants, was overturned in 1995. Dow Corning filed for Chapter 11 bankruptcy protection, yet a judge ruled that the lawsuits against Dow Corning and Dow Chemical could proceed despite the bankruptcy filing. As a result, for the first time, Dow Chemical was found solely liable in a breast implant case, and was ordered to pay $4.1 million in compensatory damages and $10 million in punitive damages to the plaintiff. In another class action suit, the jury determined that Dow Chemical concealed the health risks of silicone used in the implants, and in 1998 Dow agreed to settle those claims for $3.2 billion.

In 1995, Dow sold its 71% stake in Marion Merrell Dow to Hoechst for $7.1 billion. The next year it purchased INCA International, as well as a stake in Mycogen Corp., a seed developer. Two years later it sold its 80% stake in Destec Energy. It also purchased Eli Lilly's 40% interest in DowElanco, later renamed Dow AgroSciences. In 1998, it purchased the remaining interest in Mycogen, folding it into Dow AgroSciences. That year it also sold it DowBrands consumer products business to S. C. Johnson & Son. Net income that year reached $1.3 billion on revenues of $18.4 billion. In 1999, Dow agreed to purchase both ANGUS Chemical Co. and Union Carbide Corp.

History of Union Carbide Corp.

The first carbon arc streetlight was implemented in 1876 in Cleveland, Ohio. Ten years later the National Carbon Co. was formed to manufacture street light carbons and, later, carbon electrodes for electric furnaces. In 1890, the company produced the first dry cell battery, and in 1894 built one of the nation's first industrial research laboratories.

The Union Carbide Co. was formed in 1898 to manufacture calcium carbide. At that time, electric lighting had become fairly practical, eliminating any expansion hopes for Union Carbide's acetylene light-

The Officers

Dow Chemical Co.

Chairman: Frank P. Popoff

President and CEO: William S. Stavropoulos

Exec. VP and Chief Financial Officer: J. Pedro Reinhard

Exec. VP: Anthony J. Carbone

Exec. VP: Michael D. Parker

Union Carbide Corp.

Chairman, President and CEO: William H. Joyce

VP, Strategic Planning, Investor Relations and Public Affairs: Joseph S. Byck

VP, General Counsel, and Secretary: Bruce D. Fitzgerald

VP, Human Resources: Malcolm A. Kessinger

VP, Chief Financial Officer, and Controller: John K. Wulff

ing business, but its calcium carbide plants were productive. In 1906, it purchased an alloys business and a metals research laboratory, and established a separate division to produce alloys for steelmaking. Under the direction of chief metallurgist Dr. Fredrick M. Becket, the company introduced a line of alloying metals, such as low-carbon ferrochrome, that resulted in the development of modern stainless steels. The discovery in France of a hot metal-cutting flame created a demand for such resources.

In 1911, Union Carbide purchased an interest in Linde Co., an oxygen-producing company. Union Carbide's major competitor during this period was the Prest-O-Lite Co., the largest single purchaser of calcium carbide for automobile acetylene lamps. In 1914, seeking an alternative form of acetylene, Prest-O-Lite consulted scientists from the Linde Air Products Co. and Union Carbide to conduct research on the gas. These cooperative efforts led to the 1917 formation of the Union Carbide & Carbon Corp., which acquired the stock of Linde Air Products, National Carbon, Prest-O-Lite, and Union Carbide Co.

Both the petrochemical industry and Union Carbide's chemical business were established in 1920, when the company completed construction of its first commercial ethylene plant. The combined research efforts of its united companies enabled Union Carbide to develop rapidly. Its new products included ethylene glycol (later marketed as Prestone anti-freeze and coolant); batteries for portable radios; quiet flickerless carbons used for the first sound movies; and ferroal-

The Players

Dow Chemical President and CEO: William S. Stavropoulos. William Stavropoulos, who earned degrees in pharmaceutical chemistry and medicinal chemistry, began working at Dow in 1967 as a research chemist. He was soon named research manager, touching off a period of rapid ascension in company leadership. He became director of marketing for the Dow U.S.A. Plastics Department in 1979, and VP of Dow U.S.A. Plastics and Hydrocarbons eight years later. In 1990, he was named VP of The Dow Chemical Co. He became president and chief operating officer in April 1993, and CEO in November 1995. After guiding Dow through its pending absorption of Union Carbide, Stavropoulos was expected to retire in 2000, having reached the company's traditional retirement age of 60.

Union Carbide Chairman, President, and CEO: William H. Joyce. William Joyce joined Union Carbide as an engineer in 1957. A quarter of a century later he became president of the silicones and urethane intermediates division. In 1985 he was named president of the polyolefins unit. He continued to move up the company ranks, becoming executive VP of operations in 1992, and president and chief operating officer of Union Carbide the next year. After the firm's pending acquisition by Dow is completed, Joyce will serve as vice chairman of the new Dow Chemical.

loys to improve the steels used to build skyscrapers, bridges, and cars. It entered into the graphite business by acquiring the Acheson Graphite Corp. in 1928, and later absorbed Bakelite Corp., a plastics concern, in 1939.

In 1926, the company acquired vanadium interests on the Colorado Plateau, which eventually supplied the uranium for atomic energy. Having demonstrated that gaseous diffusion could be used to separate quantities of uranium-235, Union Carbide and the Manhattan Engineer District entered into a contract in 1943 to operate the Oak Ridge Gaseous Diffusion Plant. That year Linde perfected a refining process for treating uranium concentrates. Union Carbide and Carbon Research Laboratories soon contributed to the development of the atomic weapon itself.

The company expanded following World War II. Polyethylene, a plastic used in squeeze bottles, films,

and sheeting, became its biggest seller. It began venturing into new fields of technology. In the mid-1950s it formed a Metals Division to handle worldwide ore procurement, and Visking Co., a food casings business. With its diverse interests, the company dropped "carbon" from its moniker and took the name Union Carbide Corp. in 1958. As such consumer products as Eveready batteries and Prestone anti-freeze continued to grow, the company established a consumer products division. Early in the 1960s, the Glad line of plastic wraps, bags, and straws was introduced.

Beginning in the late 1960s, Union Carbide decided to sell and dissolve some of its properties in order to concentrate on core industries. Among the businesses sold were Neisler Laboratories, the Stellite, or Materials Systems Division, Ocean Systems, Inc., and The Englander Co. The firm also divested itself of most of its oil and gas interests, a pollution-monitoring devices business, a plastic container line, a fibers business, a jewelry line, and an insect repellant business. With the advent of new strategies came new materials and processes, including molecular sieve adsorbents and catalysts, specialized electronic materials, foamed plastics, biomedical systems, pollution abatement systems, energy conversion, miniature batteries, chemicals to increase food yields, and Thornel carbon-graphite fibers.

Union Carbide approached authorities in India in 1975 with an offer to build a pesticides plant in the city of Bhopal. The plant was built later that year, with Union Carbide holding a 51% interest and private Indian companies owning the remaining 49%. Although the plant was built on the outskirts of the city, an area that was not densely populated, the plant's construction increased the area's population to more than 900,000. In December 1984, a massive disaster at the Bhopal plant led to the death of more than 2,500 people and the injury of thousands more. Called "the worst industrial accident in history" by *Newsweek*, the incident was caused by a deadly leak of methyl isocyanate gas (MIC) into the air.

Following the accident, Bhopal police arrested five senior Indian executives of Union Carbide. Numerous class action suits were filed against the company. Business shut down at the Indian facility, and Union Carbide ceased production and distribution of methyl isocyanate at its plant in Institute, West Virginia. Its stock price plunged 12 points, and its reputation was greatly tarnished. Later, in 1989, it was ordered to pay a $470 million settlement by India's Supreme Court.

In this vulnerable state, it was the target of a 1985 takeover attempt by GAF, a chemicals and roofing materials firm. Union Carbide thwarted this attempt by buying back 55% of its stock, assuming $3 billion in debt in the process. To pare down this load, it began selling various assets. Its battery division, including the Eveready brand, was sold to Ralston Purina Co.; its agricultural products operation was sold to Rhone-Poulenc; its home and auto products business, including the Glad brand, was sold to First Brands. In July 1989, Union Carbide Corp. was transformed into a holding company for Union Carbide Chemicals and Plastics Co., Union Carbide Industrial Gases Inc., and UCAR Carbon Co.

In 1990, Union Carbide sold its urethane polyols and propylene glycols businesses to Arco Chemical, and sold 50% of UCAR Carbon to Mitsubishi. Two years later it spun off Union Carbide Industrial Gases as Praxair, Inc. Also in 1992 it developed UCON Refrigeration Lubricant 488, a lubricant that represented a step forward in the quest to phase out ozone-destroying chlorofluorocarbons.

It sold its 50.9% stake in Union Carbide India Ltd., the nation's largest maker of dry cell batteries, to McLeod Russel in 1994. Investing aggressively in its core businesses, the company began emerging as a leading producer of polyethylene and ethyl glycol. In late 1995, after a drastic, long-term restructuring following the Bhopal tragedy, Union Carbide consolidated its assets in North America and reduced employment from 100,000 in the early 1980s to 12,000.

In January 1996, Union Carbide purchased Shell Oil Co.'s polypropylene plastic assets, which Shell was forced to sell by the U.S. Federal Trade Commission to encourage competition in the polypropylene market. The acquisition gave Union Carbide the remaining 50% of a joint polypropylene business that it ran with Shell.

It entered into a joint venture with Exxon Chemical Co. in 1997 to form Univation Technologies. Company earnings in 1998 were $403 million on revenues of $5.7 billion. In August 1999 Union Carbide entered into an agreement to be purchased by The Dow Chemical Co.

Market Forces Driving the Acquisition

The chemical industry plunged into a sharp downturn in the late 1990s because of a collapse in commodity prices. Companies quickly set about cutting expenses by trimming costs and selling underperforming businesses. When no further gains could be wrung through such efforts, chemical companies began looking toward consolidation as a means of achieving synergies while increasing operations. By mid-1999 three such unions had been announced: Crompton & Knowles agreed to join with Witco;

Rohm and Haas with Morton International; and Eastman Chemical with Lawter International.

Union Carbide had been hit particularly hard by the down cycle, as it had focused on commodity products rather than leveraging itself in the less volatile specialty chemicals industry. In the second quarter of 1999, its earnings plummeted 53%. Yet Union Carbide was still a valuable chemical company, ranking seventh in the U.S. and 21st worldwide.

Dow Chemical, on the other hand, had nearly completed a restructuring that left it more focused on the less cyclical specialty areas. It had divested itself of about $10 billion in underperforming businesses while strengthening its core operations through $5 billion in acquisitions. As a result, Dow was one of the few chemical companies to meet or exceed its earnings expectations. William Stavropoulos, president and CEO, stated that the company's restructuring had been the first step in becoming a world leader. The second phase was to achieve growth through strategic acquisitions in an effort to become a greater challenge to the industry's leader, DuPont.

The operations of Dow Chemical and Union Carbide were complementary, yet not overly redundant. Both were leaders in polyethylene and other polyolefins. A combined company would become the world's largest producer of polyethylene, holding a 20% share of the global market and a 40% share of the U.S. market. More significantly, a combined Dow and Union Carbide would form the world's second-largest chemical company. It would also save an estimated $500 million annually, in part through the anticipated reduction of 2,000 jobs.

Approach and Engagement

William Stavropoulos and William Joyce, friends for 20 years, entered into talks in May 1999, and began negotiating in earnest in late July. On August 3, they announced that they had reached a deal.

Union Carbide would be acquired by Dow Chemical for $9.3 billion in stock and the assumption of $2.2 billion in debt. Each Union Carbide share would be exchanged for 0.537 Dow shares, valued at $66.96 each, a premium of 37% over Union Carbide's trading price. The resulting company would retain the Dow Chemical name. Joyce would become its vice chairman, and Stavropoulos was expected to retire after a brief integration period.

The companies acknowledged that they might be compelled by federal regulators to shed some assets, but did not anticipate any conditions that could not easily be overcome. Barring any regulatory or other barriers, they expected to complete the deal in the first quarter of 2000.

Products and Services

By the turn of the century, The Dow Chemical Company was a developer and manufacturer of chemical, plastic, and agricultural products and services in 168 countries around the world. Its Performance Plastics business offered high-performance polymers and products, including adhesives, sealants and coatings; engineering plastics; epoxy products and intermediates; fabricated products; insite technology licensing; and polyurethanes. Its Performance Chemicals businesses provided specialized products used by customers in a variety of industries, including automotive, consumer products, food processing, pulp and paper, and crop protection. Dow's Plastics division produced polyethylene, polyethylene, terephthalate (PET), polystyrene, and polypropylene for such industries as electronics, durable goods, food service, health care, packaging, and recreation. Its Chemicals and Metals products were used either as processing aids or raw materials for a wide variety of industries, from food processing to automotive. In the Hydrocarbons and Energy business, Dow was the world leader in the production of olefins, ethylene, and styrene.

Union Carbide operated in two business segments. Specialties & Intermediates produced a broad range of products, including specialty polyolefins used in wire and cable insulation; surfactants for industrial cleaners; catalysts for the manufacture of polymers; acrolein and derivatives; water-soluble polymers; cellulose-, glucose- and lanolin-based materials for personal care products; specialty coatings; acrylic and vinyl acrylic latex used in paints and adhesives; solvents; vinyl acetate monomer, and ethylene oxide derivatives. Its Basic Chemicals & Polymers segment converted various hydrocarbon feedstocks, principally liquefied petroleum gases and naphtha, into the basic building-block chemicals ethylene and propylene (also known as olefins), which were in turn converted to polyethylene, polypropylene, and ethylene oxide and ethylene glycol.

Research

"Dow Chemical Co.," in *Notable Corporate Chronologies*, The Gale Group, 1999. Profiles the history of the company.

The Dow Chemical Co. Home Page, available at http://www.dow.com. Official World Wide Web Page for Dow Chemical. Provides financial information, product descriptions, executive biographies, and press releases.

Hamilton, Martha M. "Dow Chemical Acquires Union Carbide," in *The Washington Post*, 4 August 1999. Reveals the terms of the newly announced deal.

Marks, Brenda. "Dow Chemical-Union Carbide Merger to Cut 2,000 Jobs," from *Knight-Ridder/Tribune Business News*, 4 August 1999. Discloses the companies' plans to reduce the workforce to realize savings after the merger.

Tullo, Alex. "Dow-Carbide Merger Boost Polymers," in *Chemical Market Reporter*, 16 August 1999. Details the companies' strengths in certain technologies.

"Union Carbide Corp.," in *Notable Corporate Chronologies*, The Gale Group, 1999. Offers a chronology of the company's history.

Union Carbide Corp. Home Page, available at http://www.unioncarbide.com. Official World Wide Web Page for Union Carbide. Includes product and financial information, news releases, and a company history.

DEBORAH J. UNTENER

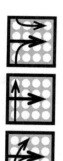

DU PONT & CONOCO

date: September 30, 1981
affected: E.I. du Pont de Nemours & Co., USA, founded 1802
affected: Conoco Inc., USA, founded 1875

E.I. du Pont de Nemours & Co.
1007 Market St.
Wilmington, DE 19898
USA

tel: (302)774-1000
fax: (302)774-7321
web: http://www.dupont.com

Conoco Inc.
600 N. Dairy Ashford
Houston, TX 77079
USA

tel: (281)293-1000
fax: (281)293-1440
web: http://www.conoco.com

Overview of the Merger

In September of 1981, when Du Pont paid $7.8 billion for Conoco, the ninth-largest oil company in the U.S., it completed the largest deal in U.S. corporate history to date and nearly doubled its assets and revenues, as well as its earnings. Acting as a white knight, Du Pont beat out an offer from Mobil Corp. and rescued Conoco—which had been in merger negotiations with Dome Petroleum Ltd., Cities Service Co., and Seagram Company Ltd.—from a hostile takeover bid by Seagram. Although Conoco performed well as a unit of Du Pont, most analysts believed that the firm would be worth much more on its own. Nearly 17 years after moving into the oil industry, Du Pont launched an initial public offering of 30% of Conoco, by then the nation's sixth-largest oil concern, and announced its intent to spin off the remainder of the firm by the end of 1999.

History of E.I. du Pont de Nemours and Co.

In 1802, E.I. du Pont de Nemours and Co. was founded by Eleuthere Irenee du Pont near Wilmington, Delaware. Capitalized at $36,000 with 18 shares of $2,000 each, the company began construction of its first plant for the manufacture of gun powder, commonly known as "black powder." Two years later, the company shipped its first powder.

After 30 years of manufacturing nothing but black powder, De Pont expanded its product line to include refined saltpeter, pyroligneous acid, and creosote. In 1859, the company's first manufacturing venture outside the Wilmington area came with the purchase of the Wapwallopen powder mills in the coal mining region near Wilkes-Barre, Pennsylvania. A new product, gun cotton, was produced for the U.S. Navy in 1982, and two years later, smokeless powder was developed at the request of the U.S. government. In 1899, the company underwent a change from family partnership to incorporation.

In 1902, Du Pont management launched a diversification program, expanding the business through acquisition and research. Eastern Laboratory, one of the first industrial research laboratories in the U.S., was established in Gibbstown, New Jersey. Du Pont branched into new fields such as nitrocellulose solutions and lac-

The Business

Financials - E.I. du Pont de Nemours & Co.

Revenue (1998): $24.76 billion

Employees (1998): 101,000

Financials - Conoco Inc.

Revenue (1998): $22.8 billion

Employees (1998): 16,650

SICs / NAICS

sic 2819 - Industrial Inorganic Chemicals Nec

sic 1311 - Crude Petroleum & Natural Gas

sic 2899 - Chemical Preparations Nec

sic 2833 - Medicinals & Botanicals

sic 2834 - Pharmaceutical Preparations

sic 2892 - Explosives

sic 2879 - Agricultural Chemicals Nec

sic 2298 - Cordage & Twine

sic 2824 - Organic Fibers-Noncellulosic

sic 2821 - Plastics Materials & Resins

naics 325998 - All Other Miscellaneous Chemical Product and Preparation Manufacturing

naics 211111 - Crude Petroleum and Natural Gas Extraction

naics 325199 - All Other Basic Organic Chemical Manufacturing

naics 325411 - Medicinal and Botanical Manufacturing

naics 325412 - Pharmaceutical Preparation Manufacturing

naics 314991 - Rope, Cordage and Twine Mills

naics 325222 - Noncellulosic Organic Fiber Manufacturing

naics 325211 - Plastics Material and Resin Manufacturing

---

quers through the acquisition of International Smokeless Powder Co. By 1906, Du Pont held a 75% share of the U.S. powder market. The company supplied 56% of the national production of explosives, with $60 million in estimated assets, and was one of the nation's largest corporations. As a result, the U.S. government initiated antitrust proceedings against the company.

By 1910, the firm had moved into England, Brazil, and Canada. A 1912 ruling following the U.S. government suit charging violation of the Sherman Anti-

Trust Act led to the division of Du Pont's explosives business into three parts: one for Du Pont, and one each for two new independent corporations, Hercules Powder Co. and Atlas Powder Co.

The outbreak of World War I provided Du Pont a tremendous earning opportunity; by the conflict's end, the company realized profits of $89 million. Through the 1915 purchase of Arlington Co., Du Pont ventured into the field of pyroxylin plastics of nitrocellulose. The firm also entered the rubber coated fabrics field with its purchase of Fairfield Rubber Co. in 1916. Acquisitions by the end of the decade included Harrison Bros. & Co., a producer of acids, heavy chemicals, pigments, dry colors, and paints; a stake in General Motors Corp.; Flint Varnish & Color Works; and the New England Oil, Paint, and Varnish Co.

In 1923, Du Pont acquired the rights to cellophane from French interests. The company made the product moistureproof, thus transforming it from a decorative wrap to a packaging material for food and other products. The company also introduced "Duco" pyroxylin automobile lacquers, tetraethyl lead, and industrial alcohol. Hercules and Du Pont formed a joint venture in 1925 to purchase an explosives facility in Mexico. The firm also developed an ammonia using high-pressure synthesis technology purchased from French and Italian interests; licensed European and Japanese firms to produce and market Duco lacquers; and established Du Pont Rayon de Mexico.

Du Pont developed the first synthetic fiber-forming polymer, the forerunner of nylon, in 1930. The following year, in a joint venture with General Motors, Du Pont developed Freon, a fluorocarbon refrigerant, and neoprene, the first successful general-purpose synthetic rubber. In 1943, Du Pont entered the x-ray and fluoroscopic screen fields through the purchase of the Patterson Screen Co. Two years later, the firm diversified into photographic printing papers via its purchase of Defender Photo Supply Co.

In 1949, Du Pont found itself again being scrutinized by the U.S. Department of Justice, which criticized the firm's stake in General Motors and charged conspiracy, monopoly, and restraint of trade. A subsidiary, Du Pont Far East, was established that year to set up sales offices in the Asia-Pacific region. Dacron polyester fiber was unveiled in 1950. In 1961, the Supreme Court ruled that Du Pont must dispose of its 63 million shares of General Motors stock. The General Motors divestiture began the following year and was completed in January of 1965. By the end of the decade, more than 20 additional international subsidiaries and joint ventures were formed in Europe, Latin America, and the Pacific Rim, including four joint ventures in Japan.

Entering the pharmaceutical market for the first time, Du Pont introduced the antiviral agent Symmetrel in 1966. Three years later, the firm acquired Endo Laboratories, a pharmaceutical manufacturer. In 1970, the analytical instruments division of Bell & Howell was purchased, and two years later, Du Pont began producing low-dose mammography X-ray products. To strengthen its position in the electronic connector and biomedical instrument fields, the company purchased Berg Electronics.

The fibers industry began stagnating from overcapacity in the late 1970s, and Du Pont realized that it had been depending too heavily on those products. However, climbing raw materials costs and declining demand continued to depress the market, prompting Du Pont to concentrate exclusively on repairing its old business rather than creating a new base. This hindered research and development, and plans to phase out dye making were launched. Du Pont was one of the worst hit chemical companies in the economic recession of 1980, but the firm did develop Kevlar, a revolutionary heat and puncture resistant material used for fire resistant clothing, bullet proof vests, cables, and reinforcement belting in tires.

In 1981, Du Pont purchased Conoco, Inc. for $7.8 billion in the largest merger ever in U.S. business history. Other acquisitions during the first half of the decade included New England Nuclear Corp., a producer of radioisotope chemicals and radiopharmaceuticals; the crop protection chemical operations of SEPPIC in France; Solid State Dielectrics, a supplier of dielectric materials used in the manufacture of multilayer capacitors; an interest in Biotech Research Laboratories; a substantial minority position in Haemonetics, the world's leading supplier of automatic blood processing machines; and the carbon fiber technology and composites business of Exxon Corp. Total research and development expenditures exceeded $1 billion.

As part of its program to align the company's industrial departments more closely with major end markets in 1986, Du Pont formed four new departments: Automotive Products, Electronic Products, Imaging Systems, and Medical Products. Du Pont and N.V. Philips of the Netherlands formed a joint venture, Philips Du Pont Optical, to market optical discs in a variety of formats. By 1987, Du Pont was bloated with the many businesses it had acquired over the years. Management returned to its policy of focusing on areas of maximum profit by moving away from commodity production and concentrating instead on oil, health care, electronics, and specialty chemicals.

Problems with quality control, particularly paint flaking on plastic products, cost Du Pont its mirror

The Officers

E.I. du Pont de Nemours & Co.

Chairman and CEO: Charles O. Holliday, Jr.

Exec. VP; Chief Operating Officer, Specialty Fibers, Performance Coatings, and Ploymers: Richard R. Goodmanson

Exec. VP; Chief Operating Officer, Pharmaceuticals, Agriculture, and Nutrition: Kurt M. Landgraf

Exec. VP; Chief Operating Officer, Pigments and Chemicals, Specialty Polymers, Nylon, and Polyester: Dennis H. Reilley

Conoco Inc.

Chairman: Edgar S. Woolard, Jr.

President and CEO: Archie W. Dunham

Exec. VP, Exploration Production: Robert E. McKee III

Exec. VP, Refining, Marketing, Supply, and Transportation: Gary W. Edwards

Sr. VP, Legal; General Counsel: Rick A. Harrington

Sr. VP, Finance; Chief Financial Officer: Robert W. Goldman

housings contract with Ford Motor Co. in 1988. To prevent a takeover, the firm bought back about 8% of its outstanding stock in 1989. The following year, Du Pont began phasing out its Orlon acrylic fiber business; sold its virology blood screening business to Ortho Diagnostics Systems, Inc.; divested two instrument businesses to Ametek, Inc.; dissolved the Philips Du Pont Optical joint venture; and announced plans to spend $500 million over three years to expand production of Lucre, commonly known as spandex.

In the early 1990s, Du Pont sold its electronic connectors business and retreated from pharmaceuticals by putting that division into a joint venture with Merck & Co. The firm also sold half of Consolidation Coal Co. for over $1 billion to Germany's Rehinbraun A.G.

In 1994, Du Pont agreed to settle 220 lawsuits filed by growers alleging crop damage from the company's Benlate fungicide by paying $214 million. The following year, Du Pont paid $8.8 billion to buy back Seagram's 24% stake in Du Pont. That year, a U.S. district judge levied a $115 million fine against Du Pont, finding that the company "cheated" plaintiffs in the first federal court trial regarding Du Pont's Benlate

The Players

CEO of E.I. du Pont de Nemours and Co.: Edward Jefferson. Edward Jefferson was one of the first non-family members to lead Du Pont. A chemist by training, he directed the company into the biosciences and other specialty lines and oversaw the firm's blockbuster purchase of Conoco in 1981.

Chairman of Conoco Inc.: Ralph Bailey. Ralph Bailey was chairman of Conoco during the intense bidding war for the firm in 1980 and 1981. He fended off an offer from Dome Petroleum, negotiated with Seagram and Cities Service, and after Seagram launched a hostile takeover bid, Bailey sought Du Pont as a white knight. When the landmark deal with Du Pont was completed, Bailey stepped down and eventually accepted the chairmanship at United Meridian Corp., a post he held until his retirement in 1995.

fungicide. A Miami jury awarded $4 million in 1996 to six-year-old John Castillo and his parents in their lawsuit against Du Pont and Pine Island Farms Inc. The jury ruled that the boy was born without eyes because his mother was exposed to the Du Pont fungicide Benlate during her frequent walks near the Pine Island Farm in Miami while pregnant. Benlate was suspected in 40 other similar cases throughout the world.

In 1997, DuPont paid $1.7 billion for a 20% stake in Pioneer Hi-Bred International Inc. As part of its shift away from oil and towards biotechnology, the firm launched an initial public offering of 30% of Conoco in 1998, raising $4.4 billion. That year, Du Pont also bought out Merck's 50% stake in joint venture Du Pont Merck Pharmaceutical. The firm's 81 units were consolidated into three segments: foundation, differentiated, and life sciences. A few months later, in early 1999, the three segments were reshuffled into eight business units. Du Pont also bought Germany-based Herberts GmbH, the paint and coatings arms of Hoechst AG, and agreed to pay $7.7 billion for the remaining 80% of Pioneer Hi-Bred International.

History of Conoco Inc.

Continental Oil & Transportation was founded by Isaac Elder Blake in 1875. Ten years later, the firm merged with the Colorado operations of Standard Oil Co. By the early 1900s, Continental had secured nearly 98% of the oil market in the western U.S. In 1911, the Supreme Court forced the Standard Oil monopoly to disband. Two years later, Continental was one of 34 independent oil companies formed as a result of the ruling.

The firm built its first gas station in 1914, diversified into oil production with its 1916 purchase of United Oil, and merged with Mutual Oil in 1924, gaining access to production, refining, and distribution operations. Marland Oil and Continental merged in 1929.

When World War II ended, Continental began constructing an offshore oil exploration barge, the first of its kind in the industry. Along with several other major oil players, Continental completed the world's first drill ship in 1956. By the 1960s, the firm had moved into Africa, South America, and the Middle East by purchasing oil fields. Gas stations in Europe were also acquired.

In 1963, Continental diversified into agricultural products when it bought American Agricultural Chemicals. Moving into the coal industry for the first time, the firm purchased Consolidation Coal three years later. A reorganization in the early 1970s divided operations into two segments: Conoco Chemical and Consol, and Continental changed its name to Conoco in 1980.

Canada's Dome Petroleum offered to buy a 20% stake in Conoco in 1981. In response, Conoco began discussing partnerships with Seagram and Cities Service. When Seagram launched a hostile bid for Conoco, the firm sought white knight suitors, and both Du Pont and Mobil emerged. Concerned that a merger with Mobil might be blocked by the U.S. government on antitrust grounds, Conoco accepted a lower bid from Du Pont. When the $7.8 billion deal was completed, Conoco became a wholly owned subsidiary of Du Pont, but kept its separate headquarters in Texas.

Under Du Pont's umbrella, Conoco made several noteworthy discoveries during the 1980s, including fields in the North Sea and the Gulf of Mexico, and operations grew to span 30 countries. The firm restructured in the early 1990s and decided to focus on 16 key countries. A plan to invest $1 billion in Iranian oil production was curbed by the U.S. government in 1995. Du Pont spun off Conoco as an independent company in 1998, a year of tumbling oil prices. The company launched a streamlining plan that included pruning 6% of its workforce.

Market Forces Driving the Merger

Most analysts point to the 1979 Belridge Oil Co. and Shell Oil Co. merger as the deal that sparked the intense wave of oil industry consolidation in the 1980s. California-based Belridge, partly owned by both Mobil and Texaco, put itself up for sale in the late 1970s after Mobil and Texaco had applied increasing pressure to buy the small firm outright; the firm's founders, who owned 55% of Belridge, rejected the advances of both firms in hopes of a higher offer. When Shell Oil bid $3.6 billion, roughly $500 million more that any other suitor, Belridge accepted, and the largest merger in U.S. corporate history was completed.

Belridge "set off a bruising competitive atmosphere," wrote Bruce Wasserstein in *Big Deal: The Battle for Control of America's Leading Corporations*. "When in May 1981, Conoco—the nation's ninth-largest oil company—became a target, the deal capture public imagination." Dome Petroleum ignited the race for Conoco by offering to purchase a 20% stake in the firm for $65 per share. Dome wasn't looking to own Conoco; rather, it sought the shares of Conoco in hopes that it could swap those for Conoco's controlling interest in Hudson's Bay Oil & Gas. Conoco management paid the offer scant attention, believing it too low. When shareholders approved the $2.6 billion deal, Conoco management was caught by surprise, and Conoco was made more vulnerable to a takeover.

Seagram and Cities Service began merger negotiations with Conoco at roughly the same time. When Conoco sought a white knight to counter a hostile bid from Seagram, Du Pont began eyeing the oil firm. The worldwide oil crisis in the mid-1970s was at the root of Du Pont's decision to move into the oil industry and secure for itself a stable source of crude oil for its petrochemical production. According to a November 1998 article in *Newsweek*, "In 1981 people feared that oil prices were going to the moon, that chemical companies like Du Pont that relied heavily on petroleum feedstocks would lose control of their destinies and that oil exporting companies would rule the earth." Acquiring Conoco would lessen Du Pont's vulnerability to oil price and availability fluctuations.

Approach and Engagement

In response to Seagram's $73 per share offer for 41% of Conoco's stock, Du Pont offered $87.50 per share in cash for 40% of Conoco's stock and 1.6 Du Pont shares for each remaining Conoco share. The counter offer, made in July of 1981, was quickly topped by an offer from Mobil, which eventually offered $120 per share, compared to Du Pont's final bid of $98 per share.

Despite the fact that Mobil's offer was nearly 20% higher than Du Pont's, Conoco shareholders accepted Du Pont's bid, mainly due to the potential antitrust

issues that might have arisen had it agreed to merge with Mobil, the second-largest oil company in the U.S. On August 5, 1981, Du Pont began tendering shares for Conoco's stock, a process that was completed on September 30, 1981.

Products and Services

After Du Pont spun off its Conoco holdings in 1998, it refocused on eight product segments. Performance Coatings and Polymers, which accounted for 17% of sales, included automotive equipment coatings, elastomers, engineering resins, industrial high-performance coatings, and original equipment coatings. Nylon Enterprise, which consisted of nylon fibers, nylon intermediates, and polymers, brought in 16% of sales. Specialty Polymers, such as color proofing systems, flexible laminates, flexographic printing plates, photoresists, and thick films, secured 15% of sales. Pigments and Chemicals, including ammonia, catalysts, cyanides, glycolic acid, industrial diamonds, performance lubricants, and titanium oxide, were responsible for 13% of sales. Specialty Fibers, such as lycra, garnered 12% of sales. Agriculture and Nutrition, including seeds, insect control chemicals, fungicides, herbicides, and biotechnology products, made up 11% of sales. Polyester Enterprise and Pharmaceuticals, the two remaining segments, accounted for 11% and 10% of sales, respectively.

Conoco operated in 40 countries in 1998. Petroleum exploration spanned 15 countries, and the firm sold gas at nearly 8,000 units in Europe, Asia, and the U.S. Other U.S. operations included four refineries and roughly 6,500 miles of pipeline.

Changes to the Industry

According to Bruce Wasserstein, "With Conoco, the Oil Wars exploded, and the 1980s merger boom began." A few months after it lost out to Du Pont, Mobil began pursuing a deal with Marathon Oil Co., the sixteenth-largest oil firm in the U.S. Mobil's $85 per share cash offer for 66% of Marathon's outstanding shares was higher than other bidders, but the firm was once again thwarted by antitrust concerns, when Marathon shareholders accepted a lower offer from U.S. Steel Corp. In 1984, Mobil finally found a merger partner; the firm paid $5.7 billion for Superior Oil Co., the largest independent U.S. oil firm. Also that year, Texaco bought Getty Oil Co. for $10.8 billion, and Chevron Corp. paid $13.2 billion for Gulf Oil Corp.

Review of the Outcome

While Conoco performed well as a wholly owned subsidiary of Du Pont, the fears that had prompted Du

Pont to move into the oil industry never materialized. Most analysts believed Conoco would be better off on its own, and by the mid-1990s, Du Pont had set its sights on the emerging biotechnology industry. As a result, Du Pont launched in 1998 an initial public offering of 30% of Conoco, raising a record $4.4 billion. The firm announced its intent to spin off the remainder of the firm by the end of 1999.

Although Wall Street praised Du Pont for the unusual tax-free "split-off" status of the divestiture, other analysts viewed the deal more skeptically. *Newsweek* criticized Du Pont for buying Conoco when the market favored sellers and divesting the oil firm in a buyers' market, pointing out that an investment in a Standard & Poor's index fund would have provided a much better return on investment.

Research

E.I. du Pont de Nemours and Co. Home Page, available at http://www.dupont.com. Official World Wide Web Home Page for E.I. du Pont de Nemours and Co. Includes news, as well as financial, product, and historical information.

"E.I. du Pont de Nemours and Co.," in *Notable Corporate Chronologies*, The Gale Group, 1999. Lists major events in the history of E.I. du Pont de Nemours and Co.

Plishner, Emily. "The Dilemma," in *FW*, 5 December 1995. Explains why Du Pont is considering spinning off its Conoco unit.

Sloan, Allen. "Buying High, Selling Low?" in *Newsweek*, 9 November 1998. Reports Du Pont's decision to spin off its oil operations as an independent company.

Taylor, Alex. "Why Du Pont Is Trading Oil for Corn," in *Fortune*, 7 June 1999. Covers Du Pont's shift in focus from oil to biotechnology in 1999.

Westervelt, Robert. "DuPont Outlines Terms of Conoco Split," in *Chemical Week*, 31 March 1999. Describes the terms of Du Pont's "split off" of Conoco.

Wasserstein, Bruce. *Big Deal: The Battle for Control of America's Leading Corporations*, Warner Books, 1998. Offers an overview of the largest mergers in recent American corporate history.

THERA WILLIAMS

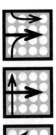

DU PONT & HERBERTS

date: March 1, 1999
affected: E.I. du Pont de Nemours & Co., USA, founded 1802
affected: Herberts GmbH, Germany, founded 1866

E.I. du Pont de Nemours & Co.
1007 Market St.
Wilmington, DE 19898
USA

tel: (302)774-1000
fax: (302)774-7321
web: http://www.dupont.com

Overview of the Acquisition

In March of 1999, when Du Pont paid $1.89 billion in cash for Herberts GmbH, the German-based paint and coatings unit of Hoechst AG, it became the world's leading maker of automotive paints and coatings, with estimated combined sales of $3.7 billion, 14,000 employees, and a 30% market share. Du Pont merged its automotive coatings unit, the leader in North American and South American markets, with Herberts, the largest European supplier of automotive coatings, to form a new unit, Du Pont Performance Coatings.

History of E.I. du Pont de Nemours and Co.

In 1802, E.I. du Pont de Nemours and Co. was founded by Eleuthere Irenee du Pont near Wilmington, Delaware. Capitalized at $36,000 with 18 shares of $2,000 each, the company began construction of its first plant for the manufacture of gun powder, commonly known as "black powder." Two years later, the company shipped its first powder.

After 30 years of manufacturing nothing but black powder, De Pont expanded its product line to include refined saltpeter, pyroligneous acid, and creosote. In 1859, the company's first manufacturing venture outside the Wilmington area came with the purchase of the Wapwallopen powder mills in the coal mining region near Wilkes-Barre, Pennsylvania. A new product, gun cotton, was produced for the U.S. Navy in 1982, and two years later, smokeless powder was developed at the request of the U.S. government. In 1899, the company underwent a change from family partnership to incorporation.

In 1902, Du Pont management launched a diversification program, expanding the business through acquisition and research. Eastern Laboratory, one of the first industrial research laboratories in the U.S., was established in Gibbstown, New Jersey. Du Pont branched into new fields such as nitrocellulose solutions and lacquers through the acquisition of International Smokeless Powder Co. By 1906, Du Pont held a 75% share of the U.S. powder market. The company supplied 56% of the national production of explosives, with $60 million in estimated assets, and was

The Business

Financials

Revenue (1998): $24.76 billion

Employees (1998): 101,000

SICs / NAICS

sic 2819 - Industrial Inorganic Chemicals Nec

sic 1311 - Crude Petroleum & Natural Gas

sic 2899 - Chemical Preparations Nec

sic 2833 - Medicinals & Botanicals

sic 2834 - Pharmaceutical Preparations

sic 2892 - Explosives

sic 2879 - Agricultural Chemicals Nec

sic 2298 - Cordage & Twine

sic 2824 - Organic Fibers-Noncellulosic

sic 2821 - Plastics Materials & Resins

naics 325998 - All Other Miscellaneous Chemical Product
      and Preparation Manufacturing

naics 211111 - Crude Petroleum and Natural Gas Extraction

naics 325199 - All Other Basic Organic Chemical
      Manufacturing

naics 325411 - Medicinal and Botanical Manufacturing

naics 325412 - Pharmaceutical Preparation Manufacturing

naics 314991 - Rope, Cordage and Twine Mills

naics 325222 - Noncellulosic Organic Fiber Manufacturing

naics 325211 - Plastics Material and Resin Manufacturing

one of the nation's largest corporations. As a result, the U.S. government initiated antitrust proceedings against the company.

By 1910, the firm had moved into England, Brazil, and Canada. A 1912 ruling following the U.S. government suit charging violation of the Sherman Anti-Trust Act led to the division of Du Pont's explosives business into three parts: one for Du Pont, and one each for two new independent corporations, Hercules Powder Co. and Atlas Powder Co.

The outbreak of World War I provided Du Pont a tremendous earning opportunity; by the conflict's end, the company realized profits of $89 million. Through the 1915 purchase of Arlington Co., Du Pont ventured into the field of pyroxylin plastics of nitrocellulose. The firm also entered the rubber coated fab-

rics field with its purchase of Fairfield Rubber Co. in 1916. Acquisitions by the end of the decade included Harrison Bros. & Co., a producer of acids, heavy chemicals, pigments, dry colors, and paints; a stake in General Motors Corp.; Flint Varnish & Color Works; and the New England Oil, Paint, and Varnish Co.

In 1923, Du Pont acquired the rights to cellophane from French interests. The company made the product moistureproof, thus transforming it from a decorative wrap to a packaging material for food and other products. The company also introduced "Duco" pyroxylin automobile lacquers, tetraethyl lead, and industrial alcohol. Hercules and Du Pont formed a joint venture in 1925 to purchase an explosives facility in Mexico. The firm also developed an ammonia using high-pressure synthesis technology purchased from French and Italian interests; licensed European and Japanese firms to produce and market Duco lacquers; and established Du Pont Rayon de Mexico.

Du Pont developed the first synthetic fiber-forming polymer, the forerunner of nylon, in 1930. The following year, in a joint venture with General Motors, Du Pont developed Freon, a fluorocarbon refrigerant, and neoprene, the first successful general-purpose synthetic rubber. In 1943, Du Pont entered the x-ray and fluoroscopic screen fields through the purchase of the Patterson Screen Co. Two years later, the firm diversified into photographic printing papers via its purchase of Defender Photo Supply Co.

In 1949, Du Pont found itself again being scrutinized by the U.S. Department of Justice, which criticized the firm's stake in General Motors and charged conspiracy, monopoly, and restraint of trade. A subsidiary, Du Pont Far East, was established that year to set up sales offices in the Asia-Pacific region. Dacron polyester fiber was unveiled in 1950. In 1961, the Supreme Court ruled that Du Pont must dispose of its 63 million shares of General Motors stock. The General Motors divestiture began the following year and was completed in January of 1965. By the end of the decade, more than 20 additional international subsidiaries and joint ventures were formed in Europe, Latin America, and the Pacific Rim, including four joint ventures in Japan.

Entering the pharmaceutical market for the first time, Du Pont introduced the antiviral agent Symmetrel in 1966. Three years later, the firm acquired Endo Laboratories, a pharmaceutical manufacturer. In 1970, the analytical instruments division of Bell & Howell was purchased, and two years later, Du Pont began producing low-dose mammography X-ray products. To strengthen its position in the electronic connector and biomedical instrument fields, the company purchased Berg Electronics.

The fibers industry began stagnating from over-capacity in the late 1970s, and Du Pont realized that it had been depending too heavily on those products. However, climbing raw materials costs and declining demand continued to depress the market, prompting Du Pont to concentrate exclusively on repairing its old business rather than creating a new base. This hindered research and development, and plans to phase out dye making were launched. Du Pont was one of the worst hit chemical companies in the economic recession of 1980, but the firm did develop Kevlar, a revolutionary heat and puncture resistant material used for fire resistant clothing, bullet proof vests, cables, and reinforcement belting in tires.

In 1981, Du Pont purchased Conoco, Inc. for $7.8 billion in the largest merger ever in U.S. business history. Other acquisitions during the first half of the decade included New England Nuclear Corp., a producer of radioisotope chemicals and radiopharmaceuticals; the crop protection chemical operations of SEPPIC in France; Solid State Dielectrics, a supplier of dielectric materials used in the manufacture of multilayer capacitors; an interest in Biotech Research Laboratories; a substantial minority position in Haemonetics, the world's leading supplier of automatic blood processing machines; and the carbon fiber technology and composites business of Exxon Corp. Total research and development expenditures exceeded $1 billion.

As part of its program to align the company's industrial departments more closely with major end markets in 1986, Du Pont formed four new departments: Automotive Products, Electronic Products, Imaging Systems, and Medical Products. Du Pont and N.V. Philips of the Netherlands formed a joint venture, Philips Du Pont Optical, to market optical discs in a variety of formats. By 1987, Du Pont was bloated with the many businesses it had acquired over the years. Management returned to its policy of focusing on areas of maximum profit by moving away from commodity production and concentrating instead on oil, health care, electronics, and specialty chemicals.

Problems with quality control, particularly paint flaking on plastic products, cost Du Pont its mirror housings contract with Ford Motor Co. in 1988. To prevent a takeover, the firm bought back about 8% of its outstanding stock in 1989. The following year, Du Pont began phasing out its Orlon acrylic fiber business; sold its virology blood screening business to Ortho Diagnostics Systems, Inc.; divested two instrument businesses to Ametek, Inc.; dissolved the Philips Du Pont Optical joint venture; and announced plans to spend $500 million over three years to expand production of Lucre, commonly known as spandex.

The Officers

Chairman and CEO: Charles O. Holliday, Jr.

Exec. VP; Chief Operating Officer, Specialty Fibers, Performance Coatings, and Polymers: Richard R. Goodmanson

Exec. VP; Chief Operating Officer, Pharmaceuticals, Agriculture, and Nutrition : Kurt M. Landgraf

Exec. VP; Chief Operating Officer, Pigments and Chemicals, Specialty Polymers, Nylon, and Polyester: Dennis H. Reilley

In the early 1990s, Du Pont sold its electronic connectors business and retreated from pharmaceuticals by putting that division into a joint venture with Merck & Co. The firm also sold half of Consolidation Coal Co. for over $1 billion to Germany's Rehinbraun A.G.

In 1994, Du Pont agreed to settle 220 lawsuits filed by growers alleging crop damage from the company's Benlate fungicide by paying $214 million. The following year, Du Pont paid $8.8 billion to buy back Seagram's 24% stake in Du Pont. That year, a U.S. district judge levied a $115 million fine against Du Pont, finding that the company "cheated" plaintiffs in the first federal court trial regarding Du Pont's Benlate fungicide. A Miami jury awarded $4 million in 1996 to six-year-old John Castillo and his parents in their lawsuit against Du Pont and Pine Island Farms Inc. The jury ruled that the boy was born without eyes because his mother was exposed to the Du Pont fungicide Benlate during her frequent walks near the Pine Island Farm in Miami while pregnant. Benlate was suspected in 40 other similar cases throughout the world.

In 1997, DuPont paid $1.7 billion for a 20% stake in Pioneer Hi-Bred International Inc. As part of its shift away from oil and towards biotechnology, the firm launched an initial public offering of 30% of Conoco Inc. in 1998, raising $4.4 billion. That year, Du Pont also bought out Merck's 50% stake in joint venture Du Pont Merck Pharmaceutical. The firm's 81 units were consolidated into three segments: foundation, differentiated, and life sciences. A few months later, in early 1999, the three segments were reshuffled into eight business units. Du Pont also bought Germany-based Herberts, the paint and coatings arms of Hoechst AG, and agreed to pay $7.7 billion for the remaining 80% of Pioneer Hi-Bred International.

The Players

Chairman and CEO of E.I. du Pont de Nemours and Co.: Charles O. Holliday. University of Tennessee engineering graduate Charles Holliday began working for Du Pont in 1970. He served as engineer, business analyst, and product planner during his first decade at the firm. In 1984, Holliday was named a manager of corporate planning. In the late 1980s, he also worked as the global business director of two key brands, Nomex and Kevlar, before accepting the position of director of marketing of the chemicals and pigments division in 1988. Two years later, Holliday secured the vice presidency of Du Pont's Asia Pacific operations. His position there culminated in the chairmanship in 1995. That year, Holliday became an executive vice president of Du Pont. Two years after being named one of "Tomorrow's CEOs" by *Fortune* in 1996, Holliday was tapped by Du Pont as CEO. On January 1, 1999, he added the role of chairman to his resume.

Chairman of Herberts GmbH: Dr. Jurgen Ritz. In 1969, Jurgen Ritz earned a doctorate degree in chemistry at the Johann Gutenburg University in Mainz. He launched his career by accepting a position as research chemist at Hoechst AG. After holding several management positions in the firm's synthetic resins research unit, Ritz was appointed head of research and development at Herberts GmbH, the paint and coatings subsidiary of Hoechst, in 1981. Seven years later, he returned to Hoechst as the head of regional coordination for North American operations. In 1988, Ritz was named head of the coatings and synthetic resins division, under which Herberts operated. Ritz served as member of the board of directors of Hoechst from 1990 to 1994. On January 1, 1995, he joined the management board of Herberts and assumed the chairmanship three months later. When Du Pont acquired Herberts in 1999, Ritz relinquished his position to Du Pont management.

History of Herberts GmbH

In 1866, Otto Louis Herberts founded a paint and boiling business in Barmen, Germany. Within ten years, Herberts was selling carriage, floor, and decorative paints. The company moved outside of Germany for the first time in 1893, when it opened a unit in Newark, New Jersey.

Between 1896 and 1900, Herberts developed locomotive and wagon paints. A line of paints that dried more quickly was launched in 1909. By 1930, Herberts had expanded its product offerings to include electrical insulation varnishes, furniture paints, and coach refinishing coatings. Nitropon, a vehicle coating process that used nitrocellulose, was also introduced.

A synthetic resins and plasticizers plant was completed in 1940. Nine years later, Herberts launched Plastodur, a paint for plastic walls. In 1956, a distribution operation was set up in Italy, and a marketing and sales office was opened in Scandinavia in 1961. By then, Herberts was making and selling laminate adhesives, laminated panels, non-drip paint, and plastic foil. In 1966, Herberts converted from a sole proprietorship into a limited commercial partnership. International expansion continued, and by the end of the decade, the firms operated subsidiaries in the Netherlands, Belgium, Austria, and Spain.

In 1970, Herberts acquired France's Hadfiels S.A. The following year, the firm purchased Hanbeck N.V., based in Rotterdam, the Netherlands. In 1972, Hoechst AG purchased 51% of Herberts, which by then employed 3,408 workers, and Herberts was soon converted to a private limited company. Four years later, Hoechst secured the remaining 49% of Herberts, which became a wholly owned subsidiary of parent company. Hoechst folded five units—Spies Hecker, Permatex, Hellac, Flamuco, and Flamingo—into the Herberts Group.

Herberts divested its general wood varnish operations in 1982. A year later, building paints operations were spun off as Herberts Baufarben GmbH, an independent unit. The firm exited the plastic surfaces for furniture industry in 1985. Two years later, Herberts bought a stake in HPG Industrial Coatings and took over Hoechst's 25% stake in Central Paints Industrial Inc., based in Taiwan.

In 1990, Herberts unveiled its full line of automotive refinishing products in the U.S. That year, operations in Southeast Asia were launched. Its acquisitions included Portuguese paint and varnish business Valentine S.A. and Italian powder coatings maker Deniel. The firm bought several Becker powder coatings operations across Europe and the U.S. in 1992. Three years later, Herberts completed a new waterbased paints factory. U.S.-based O'Brien Powder Coatings Co. was purchased in 1996. Du Pont agreed to acquire Herberts from Hoechst in 1998 for $1.89 billion; the deal was completed in March of 1999, and Herberts was merged into Du Pont Performance Coatings.

Market Forces Driving the Acquisition

According to Du Pont CEO and chairman, the acquisition of Herberts reflected "Du Pont's intent to establish global leadership positions in our core businesses through selective investments that capitalize on attractive cost positions and technology synergies. This action is similar to those we have taken recently to build stronger global positions for our Lycra elastine and titanium dioxide business. The Herberts acquisition will enable our automotive coatings business to increase its contribution to shareholder value." The merger would join the leading automotive coatings supplier in North and South America with its European counterpart to create the largest automotive coatings business in the world.

However, many analysts asserted that increased market share and an unmatched global presence were not the only reasons fueling this deal. According to a December 1998 article in *Ward's Auto World*, "this deal was perhaps the first sign of strategic positioning by suppliers who are eager to do business with the new DaimlerChrysler AG, now the fifth-largest automaker in the world, as well as to strengthen ties in general with European automakers." Du Pont, who had only a minimal share of Chrysler's coatings work in North America, would gain access to Herbert's extensive contracts with Mercedes-Benz. Du Pont would likely be able to leverage those contracts for increased North American business.

Approach and Engagement

In October of 1998, Du Pont agreed to pay $1.89 million in cash to Hoechst for Herberts GmbH. The U.S. Federal Trade Commission granted its approval in December of that year. In February of 1999, the European Commission also gave the deal its blessing. The transaction was finalized on March 1, 1999. Louis F. Savelli was named president of the new unit, Du Pont Performance Coatings.

Products and Services

In 1998, DuPont reorganized on eight product segments. Performance Coatings and Polymers, which accounted for 17% of sales, included automotive equipment coatings, elastomers, engineering resins, industrial high-performance coatings, and original equipment coatings. The Herberts paint and coatings assets were folded into this segment in 1999.

Nylon Enterprise, which consisted of nylon fibers, nylon intermediates, and polymers, brought in 16% of 1998 sales. Specialty Polymers, such as color

proofing systems, flexible laminates, flexographic printing plates, photoresists, and thick films, secured 15% of sales. Pigments and Chemicals, including ammonia, catalysts, cyanides, glycolic acid, industrial diamonds, performance lubricants, and titanium oxide, were responsible for 13% of sales. Specialty Fibers, such as lycra, garnered 12% of sales. Agriculture and Nutrition, including seeds, insect control chemicals, fungicides, herbicides, and biotechnology products, made up 11% of sales. Polyester Enterprise and Pharmaceuticals, the two remaining segments, accounted for 11% and 10% of sales, respectively.

Changes to the Industry and Review of the Outcome

While the outcome of the deal and its impact on the automotive coatings industry remains to be seen, the new president of Du Pont Performance Coatings, Louis Savelli, predicted, "by combining the complimentary assets, technology, and regional market strengths of Du Pont and Herberts, we will create a much stronger business that can grow profitably and better serve customer needs on a global basis."

Research

"Du Pont Receives EC Approval for Herberts Acquisition," in *PR Newswire*, 8 February 1999. Offers an overview of the approval process for Du Pont's takeover of Herberts.

E.I. du Pont de Nemours and Co. Home Page, available at http://www.dupont.com. Official World Wide Web Home Page for E.I. du Pont de Nemours and Co. Includes news, as well as financial, product, and historical information.

"E.I. du Pont de Nemours and Co.," in *Notable Corporate Chronologies*, The Gale Group, 1999. Lists major events in the history of E.I. du Pont de Nemours and Co.

Herberts GmbH Home Page, available at http://www.agenturcafe.de/herberts. Official World Wide Web Home Page for Herberts GmbH prior to its takeover by Du Pont. Includes news, as well as financial, product, employment, and historical information.

McCracken, Jeffrey. "Du Pont Buy Could Paint Troy as Number 1," in *Crain's Detroit Business*, 2 November 1998. Explains the terms of the deal.

Murphy, Tom. "Du Pont Pushes for Europe: Herberts Deal Could Be a Sign of Things to Come," in *Ward's Auto World*, December 1998. Discusses Du Pont's reasons for acquiring Herberts.

Westervelt, Robert. "DuPont Seals Herberts Deal," in *Chemical Week*, 10 March 1999. Offers a brief look at the finalization of the acquisition.

THERA WILLIAMS

DUKE POWER & PANENERGY

Duke Energy Corp.
422 S. Church St.
Charlotte, NC 28242
USA

tel: (704)594-6200
fax: (704)382-3814
web: http://www.duke-energy.com

nationality: USA
date: June 1997
affected: Duke Power Corp., USA, founded 1899
affected: PanEnergy Corp., USA, founded 1929

Overview of the Merger

Bill Grigg and George Mazanec, PanEnergy's vice chairman at the time, initiated a dialogue in November of 1996 about the future of the energy industry and how their companies could work together. After several months of negotiations, both firm agreed to the following final terms: PanEnergy's stockholders would receive 1.0444 shares of Duke shares per PanEnergy share, in the stock swap valued at $7.7 billion.

This merger, completed in June of 1997, created an integrated energy company with total market capitalization of $23 billion ($17 billion in equity and $6 billion in debt and preferred stock). PanEnergy became a wholly owned subsidiary of Duke Power and the resulting company was named Duke Energy Corp. PanEnergy acquired technology and power producing resources and a broader based market, while Duke Power acquired PanEnergy's marketing expertise in a deregulating industry. The two companies together began providing one-stop shopping for power needs.

History of Duke Power Corp.

Duke Power Corp. was founded in 1899 by Surgeon W. Gill Wylie as the Catawba Power Co. The first hydroelectric plant near Fort Mill, South Carolina, was operational by 1904. Catawba was renamed the Southern Power Co. the following year when it was bought by the American Development Co. Wylie became president.

In 1910 James "Buck" Duke (founder of the American Tobacco Co. and namesake of Duke University) became president of Southern Power. Duke was instrumental in forming several power companies and reorganized Mill-Power to sell heavy electric equipment to the region's textile mills. Three years later, he formed the Southern Public Utility Co. in order to acquire Piedmont-Region Utilities.

Duke established Wateree Electric in 1917, which became Duke Power in 1924. By 1925 the Duke family held about 85% of Duke Power's stock, and by 1935 Duke Power owned all Southern Power's former properties. When the company went public in 1950, Duke interests still owned 67% of Duke Power; they were diluted to 15% when the company began listing on the New York Stock Exchange in 1961.

Duke Power protected itself from the 1970s energy crisis by investing in coal mining and nuclear energy (the first of its three nuclear plants was completed in 1974). Duke Energy Corp. was organized in 1988 to develop projects outside its home region, buying Nantahala Power and Light. Mill-Power was sold in 1990.

The 1990s brought new overseas markets such as an Argentine power station in 1992 and diverse non-energy ventures such as communications and real estate. As the industry moved toward deregulation, Duke Power was looking for a means to stay on top of the market. In June of 1997, the firm paid $7.7 billion for PanEnergy Corp. and changed its name to Duke Energy Corp.

History of PanEnergy Corp.

PanEnergy Corporation started in 1929 as Interstate Pipeline Co. The following year it became Panhandle Eastern Pipeline Co. (PEPL). The firm completed its first pipeline in 1939 from the Texas panhandle to eastern Illinois. In 1951 PEPL began its second line, Trunkline Gas Co., to link with the Gulf Coast, soon extending its system northeast from Illinois to the Indiana-Michigan border.

The energy crunch of the 1970s raised demand for natural gas because the heating oil was more expensive and occasionally short in supply. PEPL forged a 20-year contract for liquified natural gas with Sonatrach, an Algerian supplier, in 1975.

PEPL became the Panhandle Eastern Corp. in 1981. It bought Texas Eastern Corp. in 1989. Two years later it again increased its operations by extending pipelines to the East Coast. Other mergers and alliances helped PanEnergy secure its leading market position in natural gas. This position was reinforced with a merger with Duke Power in 1997.

Market Forces Driving the Merger

Deregulation was the driving force behind the 1997 merger between PanEnergy Corp. and Duke Power Corp. Competition was prompting power companies to pare down costs and find new ways to market power to customers. Power was no longer provided by a local monopoly in a prescribed district or area. Because of this increased competition, new markets had opened.

In 1992 Congress decided to allow anyone who bought power wholesale to buy it from any source,

The Business

Financials

Revenue (1998): $17.61 billion

Employees (1998): 22,000

SICs / NAICS

sic 4911 - Electric Services

sic 4923 - Gas Transmission & Distribution

naics 221111 - Hydroelectric Power Generation

naics 221112 - Fossil Fuel Electric Power Generation

naics 221113 - Nuclear Electric Power Generation

naics 221119 - Other Electric Power Generation

naics 221121 - Electric Bulk Power Transmission and Control

naics 221122 - Electric Power Distribution

and suppliers such as Duke Power were ordered to open their transmission lines to competitors. The retail market—individual businesses and homes—also saw deregulation in the mid-1990s, beginning in California, New England and some Mid-Atlantic states. Eventually, nearly all retail customers would be able to choose their source of power. The global marketplace was also expected to encounter relaxed regulation. Prior to the deal between Duke Power and PanEnergy, a combination of privatization and deregulation had made it possible for the U.S. and other utilities to invest and operate from Finland to Argentina.

William Grigg, CEO of Duke Power, explained that the future of the business lay in five different areas. The first business, power generation, was something Duke Power had already done well, and the cost of production was likely to keep that segment competitive. The second business, bulk transmission, was expected to remain regulated. Local business, however, would probably become a free-for-all as anyone could target any market. The business of energy services would compete on price, reliability, and value added services, and energy services companies might even try to build brand recognition. The final business, brokers and futures traders, would trade electricity futures; many analysts believed this market could become the world's largest commodities market.

The Officers

Chairman and CEO: Richard B. Priory

Exec. VP and Chief Financial Officer: Richard J. Osborne

Exec. VP and Chief Administrative Officer: Ruth G. Shaw

Exec. VP and General Counsel: Richard W. Blackburn

To best capitalize on emerging trends, Grigg first wanted to secure the base of its business with the most cost-effective, customer-focused utility in the Piedmont area. To this end, Duke Power had trimmed its workforce, increased it productivity, and reduced inventories 6% annually in the eight years prior to the merger. Its residential rates were 20% lower in the 1990s than they were in the previous decade. Customer service had also become important in the retail market. A 24-hour, 365-day service had become the industry standard, and Grigg warned, "Once the competition knocks on our customers' doors, it's too late to get competitive."

Duke Power also needed to expand its energy services to encompass efficiency consulting, power plant management, and home security. The merger with PanEnergy would allow the firm to offer "one-stop shopping" for all of the energy of its customers, regardless of fuel. A further area of development essential to Duke Energy's growth was marketing, one of PanEnergy's strengths. PanEnergy also operated in the western U.S., where deregulation in the gas industry has been going on for some tim; the firm's expertise would be valuable to Duke Power when it encountered deregulation on the East Coast.

Approach and Engagement

William Grigg, Duke's chairman and CEO, and George Mazanec, PanEnergy's vice chairman, were attended a board meeting of Associated Electric and Gas Insurance Ltd. where they discussed the changes going on in the industry and how they both might benefit from them. After a period of four months of secret negotiations, a deal was finally agreed upon and announced on November 25, 1996.

Another seven months passed before they secured the necessary approvals. Paul Anderson, chairman and CEO of PanEnergy said "It happened about six months faster than we thought it would." Because the companies had no mutual areas of business, there was little concern over "market power." The deal also wasn't about savings, so customers and shareholders didn't have to worry about extensive layoffs or streamlining of operations. The only concession was to South Carolina PSC, which extracted a promise of no rate increases until the year 2000.

William Grigg announced his retirement at the time of the merger, believing that a new company in a new century needed new leadership. Richard B. Priory became chairman and CEO of the newly formed Duke Energy Corp., and Paul Anderson became president and COO. The company also formed a new board with eleven members from Duke Power and seven from PanEnergy. PanEnergy continued to operated from its base in Houston, Texas.

Products and Services

Duke Power entered the merger as one of the largest investor-owned utilities with a base of 1.8 million customers in North and South Carolina. Duke was also second in sales of unregulated wholesale power with volumes of 14.5 million mw/hr as reported to the Federal Energy Regulatory Commission.

PanEnergy operated 37,000 miles of pipeline serving the Midwest, Mid-Atlantic and NewEngland regions, which accounted for almost 12% of the nation's gas consumption. In addition, a unit of PanEnergy and a unit of Mobil Oil Co. merged, creating one of the largest gas marketers in the country as reported by *Oil and Gas Journal*.

The merger between Duke Power and PanEnergy gave PanEnergy a partner in the electric sector with financial strengths, engineering expertise, and global power asset management skills. When the deal was completed, Duke Energy was able to offer delivery and management of both gas and electricity in multiple regions of the country. According to Grigg, "both Duke Power and PanEnergy realize that the convergence of the gas and electric industries means that a combined company would achieve distinct advantages not available to either on a stand alone basis."

Changes to the Industry

Analysts believed this merger was different from other recent gas and power combinations because of the size of the two firms and because of the standard this merger set for the rest of the industry. The first merger between two companies who lacked distribution companies for their partners, the deal was also a strong move towards a national market share in both the gas and power markets.

Another differentiating factor was the diversity of each company's interests. PanEnergy's interest in Sable Island gas put gas in New England, which suffered from a lack of gas. With a broader base of operations and an expanded range of products and services, the combined company was expected to be better able to negotiate deals for its customers.

Review of the Outcome

Because there was such minimal product, service, and geographic overlap between the two firms, the merger resulted in only 350 layoffs. After the deal was finalized, revenues for Duke Energy rose from $4.7 billion to $17.6 billion. Stock, which at the end of 1996 was at $46.25 per share, rose in 1998 to $64.06 per share.

Business remained as competitive as ever with deregulation, and Duke Energy took some steps to grow both domestically and internationally. In partnership with TEPPCO, Duke Energy inked a deal to expand its distribution business overseas. The company also diversified beyond energy to wireless communications and residential and commercial real estate.

The purchase of three power generating plants in California for $501 million boosted Duke Energy's position in the California market. Acquisitions continued into 1999 when Duke joined Virginia Power and French nuclear fuel manufacturer COGEMA to form a consortium to convert weapons-grade plutonium into usable fuel in civilian nuclear reactors.

Research

Burka, Paul. "Power Surge," in *Texas Monthly*, September 1997. Reports the merging of Texas electric and natural gas utilities in anticipation of deregulation of electricity.

Deogun, Nikhil. "Duke Power's Grigg Has Made His mark by Taking Risks," in *The Wall Street Journal*, 26 November 1996. Profiles William H. Grigg and his achievements at Duke Power company, particularly the acquisition of PanEnergy Corp. Include comments from Robert Bradshaw, a lawyer and friend of Grigg.

Duke Energy Corp. Home Page, available at http://www.duke-energy.com. Official World Wide Web Home page for Duke Energy Corp. Includes news, as well as financial, product, historical, and employment information.

Katz, Marvin. "And They Lived Happily Ever After," in *American Gas*, July 1998. This interview with Paul Anderson outlines the Duke Power/PanEnergy merger and how this was affecting the industry. Compares Duke merger with other deals in the industry.

Lorenzetti, Maureen. "Duke-PanEnergy Is Biggest Deal So Far," in *Platt' Oilgram News*, 26 November 1996. Reports on the acquisition by Duke Power of PanEnergy Corp; includes implications of the merger on the energy services industry.

"PanEnergy Sold in $7.7 Billion Deal," in *Pipeline & Gas Journal*, January 1997. Announces the merger between PanEnergy and Duke Power with reflections from William H. Grigg, Chairman and CEO of Duke Power, and Paul M. Anderson, President and CEO of PanEnergy Corp.

Salpukas, Agis. "A $7.7 Billion Union of Gas, Electricity," in *The New York Times*, 26 November 1996. Covers the details of agreement to merge.

Saunders, Barbara. "Duke/PanEnergy Deal a M&A Strategy Shift," in *Oil & Gas Journal*, 2 December 1996. Analyzes the merger between Duke Power and PanEnergy and its effects on the power industry.

Schobelock, Robin. "Duke Power, PanEnergy in Mega Merger," in *Oil & Gas Investor*, February 1997. Quotes Paul M. Anderson, PanEnergy president and CEO, as to potential of merger for both companies; also outlines financial details of merger.

Stewart, Thomas A. "When Change Is Total, Exciting—and Scary," in *Fortune*, 3 March 1997. Duke Power CEO William Grigg discusses the changes happening in the industry resulting from deregulation and the changes at Duke Power and its way of doing business.

MARTHA KRUPA

EASTMAN KODAK & STERLING DRUG

Eastman Kodak Co.
343 State St.
Rochester, NY 14650
USA

tel: (716)724-4000
fax: (716)724-1089
web: http://www.kodak.com

nationality: USA
date: March 1988
affected: Eastman Kodak Co., USA, founded 1878
affected: Sterling Drug Inc., USA, founded 1901

Overview of the Merger

Acting as a white knight, Eastman Kodak snatched up Sterling Drug in a $5.1 billion deal in March 1988. The joining of the two companies furthered Eastman Kodak's efforts to enter into the pharmaceutical industry and also thwarted Hoffman-La Roche and Co.'s attempts to takeover the drug company. The merger came under tough scrutiny from Wall Street analysts who claimed Kodak overpaid for Sterling, taking on considerable debt as a result. Six years later, the firm decided to refocus on core operations and sold off its pharmaceutical holdings.

History of Eastman Kodak Co.

In 1878, George Eastman invented gelatin dry plates, which could be exposed and developed at the photographer's convenience, unlike cumbersome wet-plate photography. He also invented an emulsion-coating machine for mass-production of dry plates, which he began producing commercially in a rented loft in Rochester, New York, in 1880. One year later, Eastman and Henry A. Strong, a local buggy-whip manufacturer, formed a partnership called Eastman Dry Plate Corp.

In 1883, Eastman developed a new film system that was compatible with almost every plate camera available. The following year, the company's name was changed to Eastman Dry Plate and Film Corp. New products included Eastman Negative Paper; a roll holder for negative paper; and Eastman American Film, the first transparent negative. To take advantage of the growing European photography market, the company opened a wholesale office in London, England, in 1886. Two years later, the name "Kodak," was invented by Eastman and trademarked. Eastman also introduced the first portable camera.

Under the new name of Eastman Corp., the firm incorporated as Eastman Photographic Materials in the United Kingdom to distribute Kodak products from the London headquarters. Eastman and his research assistant, William H. Walker, introduced commercial transparent roll film used in motion picture cameras as well.

In 1891, the company built a manufacturing plant in Harrow, England, and marketed its first daylight-loading camera. The next year, the company was renamed Eastman Kodak Corp. of New York. Eastman also introduced the Pocket Kodak Camera that used roll film and had a small window through which consumers were able to read the number of exposures used. The company also began to supply plates and paper for the newly-discovered X-ray process, as well as marketing the first film especially coated for motion picture use. In addition, Kodak established a wholly-owned subsidiary in France.

At the turn of the century, Eastman Kodak introduced its Brownie Camera, which sold for $1 and used film that cost 15 cents per roll, making the hobby of photography financially accessible to more people. Kodak also created a new developing machine that allowed film processing without a darkroom in 1902. The next year, Kodak Non-Curling film was introduced and remained the standard film for amateur photographers for nearly 30 years. In 1908, the first commercially practical safety film, using cellulose acetate as a base instead of the highly flammable cellulose nitrate, was brought to the market as well.

In 1920, Tennessee Eastman Co. was organized to manufacture wood alcohol, vital to film making. A 1921 court ruling forced Kodak to divest six of the companies it had acquired and to end the practice of requiring Kodak dealers to exclusively sell Kodak products at fixed prices. Two years later, Kodak made amateur motion pictures practical with the introduction of 16 mm reversal film, the 16 mm Cine-Kodak Motion Picture Camera, and the Kodascope projector. The popularity of 16 mm resulted in an international network of Kodak processing laboratories. In 1928, Kodacolor Film was introduced, making color motion pictures a reality for amateur cinematographers as well.

During the 1930s, Kodak introduced its first motion picture film designed especially for sound motion pictures; purchased the Nagel Camera Corp. in Stuttgart, Germany; and diversified into the textile industry by marketing cellulose acetate yarn. In 1932, founder George Eastman committed suicide at the age of 77, bequeathing his entire estate to the University of Rochester.

New product introductions in the 1950s included the low-priced Brownie 8-mm movie camera and the Bantam Microfilmer. Subsidiary Texas Eastman began manufacturing alcohol and aldehydes for the chemical trade. Eastman Chemical Products, Inc. was formed to market products made by Tennessee Eastman and Texas Eastman. Also, the company faced antitrust problems because of its practice of including the cost of processing in the price of film, which was said to

The Business

Financials

Revenue (1998): $13.46 billion

Employees (1998): 86,200

SICs / NAICS

sic 3861 - Photographic Equipment & Supplies

sic 3691 - Storage Batteries

sic 2824 - Organic Fibers-Noncellulosic

sic 3089 - Plastics Products Nec

naics 333315 - Photographic and Photocopying Equipment Manufacturing

naics 325992 - Photographic Film, Paper, Plate and Chemical Manufacturing

naics 335911 - Storage Battery Manufacturing

naics 325222 - Noncellulosic Organic Fiber Manufacturing

naics 326122 - Plastics Pipe and Pipe Fitting Manufacturing

naics 326121 - Unsupported Plastics Profile Shape Manufacturing

naics 337215 - Showcase, Partition, Shelving, and Locker Manufacturing

naics 326199 - All Other Plastics Product Manufacturing

inhibit trade in the photo-finishing industry. A consent decree forced Eastman Kodak to end this practice in 1955.

Kodak High Speed Ektachrome film became the fastest high-speed film on the market in the early 1960s. Sales exceeded $1 billion for the first time in 1962. The company's most successful camera, the Instamatic, was introduced in 1963. The cartridge-loading film brought amateur photography to new heights of popularity.

During the early 1970s, Kodak established Carolina Eastman Corp. to manufacture polyester fibers and yarn; received an Emmy Award for its development of fast color processing for television use; formed Eastman Technology to develop products in areas unrelated to its traditional businesses; acquired Spin Physics, a California-based producer of magnetic heads used in recording equipment; and introduced two Super 8 sound movie cameras. By 1975, sales had surpassed $4 billion. Kodak introduced the Ektaprint Copier-Duplicator, competing directly with Xerox Corp. and IBM Corp. The compa-

The Officers

Chairman and CEO: George M.C. Fisher

President and Chief Operating Officer: Daniel A. Carp

Exec. VP and Assistant Chief Operating Officer: Carl F. Kohrt

Exec. VP and Assistant Chief Operating Officer: Eric L. Steenburgh

Sr.VP, President, Entertainment Imaging: Joerg D. Agin

ny competed with Polaroid Corp. by introducing instant cameras, and while it was able to capture approximately 25% of the U.S. instant camera market, reports of quality flaws stifled sales. The Eastman Chemicals Division introduced Kodapak Polyester Plastic for use in manufacturing beverage bottles in 1978. Company operations were reorganized to consolidate the U.S., Canadian, and international photographic areas into one division.

Kodak entered the clinical chemistry market with the Kodak Ektachem 400 blood analyzer in 1980; however, it was unable to match the reliability of competing products. The company also acquired Atex, Inc., a manufacturer of computer-based publishing systems. In 1981, Kodak was forced to pay $6.8 million in damages to Berkley Photo, which charged the company with illegally monopolizing the photographic market. In 1982, the Kodak disc camera was developed. Tennessee Eastman began operations of the only commercial plant in the U.S. which made industrial chemicals from coal. In 1984, Kodak introduced complete lines of videotape cassettes for all video formats and floppy disks for use in personal computers. The company collaborated with Matsushita Electric Industrial Co. of Japan to create its first electronic product, a camcorder combining an 8 mm video camera and recorder. The firm also reorganized into 17 business units and created a new Life Sciences Group.

In 1985, Kodak purchased Verbatim Corp., a floppy disk manufacturer. The company re-entered the 35 mm camera market that year with a product made by Chinon Industries in Japan. However, a federal appeals court ordered Kodak to abandon the instant camera business in 1986. As a result, the company reduced its work force by 10%. Two years later, the firm acquired Sterling Drug for $5.1 billion. By the end of the decade, Kodak had diversified into the general consumer battery market, with a line of Kodak Supralife alkaline batteries; the health care industry, with the establishment of Eastman Pharmaceuticals

Division; and the electronic still-video market with seven products for recording, storing, manipulating, transmitting, and printing electronic still video images.

Authorities discovered that toxic chemicals from the company's Rochester plant had leaked into the area's groundwater, and in 1990, Kodak admitted that it had violated New York's environmental law. The company was fined $2 million, and it agreed to clean up the site of the Kodak Park manufacturing facility and to reduce the plant's chemical emissions. Polaroid also commenced court action against Kodak for copyright infringement relating to the production of instant cameras. The court eventually awarded Polaroid $873.2 million in damages.

In 1992, Kodak entered a joint R&D project with Canon, Fuji Photo, Minolta, and Nikon, to examine advanced silver-halide photographic systems. One year later, the company released a portable photo CD player. After Kodak decided to refocus on its core businesses, Sanofi purchased the prescription drug operations of the Sterling pharmaceutical unit for $1.68 billion. SmithKline-Beecham PLC purchased the over-the-counter operations of Sterling for $2.93 billion, and the company sold its clinical diagnostics unit to Johnson & Johnson for $1.01 billion. In 1994, the firm was fined another $5 million and forced to allot $60 million to clean up the environmental problems it created in New York four years ago.

Kodak sold its L&F Products unit to Reckitt & Colman PLC for $1.55 billion in 1995. Kodak was forced to pay $23.8 million in damages to eleven service organizations after a federal court ruled that it engaged in monopolistic practices that year. The company also began selling private-label film on the Japanese market. Soon afterwards, Kodak filed a petition alleging that the government of Japan had created tariff and market conditions unfairly benefitting Fuji Photo Film Inc. The Japanese patent office invalidated the magnetic-label patent held by Eastman Kodak, denying the company royalty payments from the use of this technology, and the World Trade Organization did not back Kodak's claims.

In 1996, Kodak assumed control of Eckerd Corp.'s seven regional photo finishing laboratories. The company also sold off its copier sales and service business. With earnings were on the decline, plans to eliminate 20,000 jobs by the year 2000 were announced. Wanting to remain competitive, Kodak looked to partner with Internet companies and in 1998, formed relationships with America Online, Intel Corp., and Adobe Systems Inc. Kodak also teamed up with Ebay.com, an online auction house, to allow Ebay customers to display photos of their merchandise online.

History of Sterling Drug, Inc.

In 1901, William Erhard Weiss and Albert H. Diebold established the Neuralgyline Company in West Virginia. The pair developed an aggressive marketing plan for their pain relieving product, Neuralgine, and the company used money earned from sales to advertise further. By 1907, the firm had enough in profits to purchase the Sterling Remedy Co.

Weiss and Diebold changed the name of the newly acquired company to Sterling Drug. With a product line of Neuralgyline, Danderine, Casaets, and California Syrup of Figs, Sterling jumped at the chance to acquire the American Bayer Co., a German owned company that became available after being seized during World War I. The company assumed a major portion of the world's aspirin market while the American Bayer Co.'s counterpart in Germany, I.G. Farben, was trying to tap into the Latin American market. In 1923, Sterling gave Bayer 50% of its stock in Winthrop Laboratories and a Sterling subsidiary, in trade for Bayer manufacturing information, as well as patent and technical data.

The relationship of Sterling and Farben soon became a target of scrutiny by the U.S. government. With the onset of World War II, the government used Sterling's position to start an economic trade war against Germany in Latin America. Weiss and Diebold, the company's founders, were forced to resign as they were seen as trying to help a German-owned company during the war effort. Under new leadership, Sterling soon became key in the offensive attack against Farben and its efforts in Latin America.

Through extensive advertising and marketing measures, Sterling claimed victory in the trade-war battle with Germany. Sydney Ross, a Sterling subsidiary, sold more aspirin in one year than Farben did, and Latin Americans had been exposed to over five million advertisements. Even after the war, Sterling continued to battle with the German company and its American subsidiaries. By 1970, Sterling had retained rights to the Bayer trademark for aspirin in the United States. The German company owned the rights outside of the U.S.

By this time, Sterling also owned the pain relievers Cope, Vanquish, Measurin, and Midol. The company had also entered into the consumer market with products such as cosmetics, Beacon Wax, fragrances, and d-con insecticides. In the early 1970s, Sterling began to manufacture its own products. The company developed Talwin, an analgesic, and also marketed Neo-Synephrine, a nasal decongestant; Negram, used to treat urinary tract infections; Sulfamylon, a cream for burns; and pHisoHex, a skin cleanser.

The Players

President of Eastman Kodak Co.: Kay P. Whitmore. MIT graduate Kay Whitmore joined the Eastman Kodak Co. in 1957, as a film engineer. He held various positions in manufacturing and management for the company. Whitmore worked his way up through the ranks and was eventually named president in 1983 and CEO in 1989. He also served as chairman for Eastman Kodak. He is credited for seeing the company through difficult financial times of the 1980s and 1990s, as well as spearheading its foray into the pharmaceuticals industry. In August of 1993, after 37 years of service, Whitmore was forced to resign due to management restructuring. In 1998, he was appointed to the board of directors for TenFold Corp., a software and services company.

Chairman and CEO of Sterling Drug, Inc.: John M. Peitruski. John Peitruski was named president of Sterling Drug in the early 1980s. He led a company wide streamlining and cost cutting effort during his tenure and orchestrated the deal with Eastman Kodak in 1988 as chairman and CEO. After the merger of the two companies, he served as chairman of Eastman Kodak's Sterling unit and as executive vice president of Kodak for a short while. In August of 1988, he resigned from the company.

Although the company was prospering, it saw its share of bad times. The FTC was on its back for a merger with Lehn & Fink, and the FDA ruled that hexachlorophene, which was in pHisoHex, could only be sold through prescription. At the same time, increasing competition in the aspirin market caused Sterling problems. Johnson & Johnson released Tylenol, a non-aspirin product, whose makers claimed it was safer and worked faster than Bayer. Sterling's large market share with Bayer soon dropped with the onset of additional brands such as Bufferin and Excedrin.

In response to the heated competition, Sterling spent over $153 million in advertising in 1973. Clark Wescoe, the new CEO, began to restructure the company. He rearranged Sterling into three divisions: pharmaceuticals, over-the counter-drugs, and consumer goods. The restructuring proved to be profitable and by 1974, sales were $950 million.

In the latter half of the 1970s, the company once again did battle with the FDA when the agency accused Sterling of misrepresenting its pain relieving products in its advertising. In 1982, the company missed a chance to gain market share when Tylenol was removed from store shelves after seven incidences of cyanide poisoning. The company also faced competition from American Home Products and Upjohn when the two gained FDA approval for an over-the-counter version of ibuprofen.

In an effort to increase sales, John M. Pietruski, president of Sterling, began to oversee an increase in product development. The company also began to focus on strengthening and broadening its existing product lines. His efforts did not go unnoticed and soon the company became a takeover target with the onset of consolidation in the pharmaceutical industry in the 1980s. Threatened by a hostile takeover by Hoffman-La Roche & Co. in 1988, Sterling accepted Eastman Kodak's friendly bid for the company. Eastman Kodak completed the deal in 1988 and Sterling Drug was folded into Kodak's operations.

Market Forces Driving the Merger

In 1988, Eastman Kodak was focused on pursuing interests in the pharmaceutical field. The company viewed biotechnology as the wave of the future and wanted to take advantage of its potential to change medicine and agriculture. Kodak already had interests in biotech with over $250 million spent in backing research for small companies. With the Sterling purchase, Kodak would gain the company's sales network, as well as its experience in pushing drugs through the U.S. Food and Drug Administration (FDA).

Kodak had been pursuing diversification for some time. The company had interests in chemicals, copiers, X-rays, and blood analyzers. Kodak felt the threat of film market penetration from electronic and video photography in the future and wanted to broaden its business. In an article in the *Los Angeles Times*, Kodak CEO Kay Whitmore stated that Kodak "wanted another business opportunity. When technological change challenges your basic business, you protect that area and look for new things." Rather than entering the video industry—where penetration was difficult with Sony, Matsushita, and Toshiba already firmly entrenched—Kodak decided to pursue the newer biotechnology industry. In the same article Whitmore went to say, "we felt we had an opportunity with our research and chemical manufacturing base to enter this new technology on even terms with the major pharmaceutical companies. We are in the process of creating a research capability in biotechnol-

ogy and in traditional pharmaceutical research as well."

Approach and Engagement

In following with Kodak's strategy to establish itself in the drug industry, the company was looking for an acquisition to finish its three-part plan which already included the establishment of a pharmaceutical research and development group and joint ventures with small research companies focused on biotech development such as Panlabs, Inc and Enzon, Inc. An opportunity arose for Kodak when Sterling Drug found itself the target of a hostile takeover.

In January of 1988, Hoffman-La Roche, a Swiss drug company, made a play for Sterling with a $4.65 billion bid. Sterling management saw the price as inadequate and was not attracted to the foreign offer. Eastman Kodak stepped in and, acting as a white knight, offered $5.1 billion for the company, promising to keep it intact. Hoffman-La Roche could not top the offer and backed away from Sterling. The friendly $89.50 per share offer was just what Kodak needed to accelerate its entry into the pharmaceutical industry. Leaders from both Kodak and Sterling viewed the deal as being beneficial to both companies as well as Sterling's shareholders. In March of 1988, the transaction was finalized.

Products and Services

Eastman Kodak spent most of the 1990s selling off its non-core businesses and focusing once again on its photography and imaging operations. In 1998, the company had operations in the U.S. as well as the UK, Russia, Mexico, Japan, Indonesia, India, Germany, France, China, Canada, Brazil, and Australia. With sales of $7.164 billion, Kodak's Consumer Imaging division—including products such as cameras, digital media, film, kiosks and scanning systems, photo chemicals and paper, photo processing, projectors, and photo-enhancing software—accounted for 53% of total revenues for the company. Other divisions included Kodak Professional, which was responsible for 14% of total sales, and Health Imaging, which secured 11%. Other imaging services—including applications software, audiovisual equipment, digital cameras, and microfilm products—brought in the remaining 22% of total sales.

Changes to the Industry

Eastman Kodak's purchase of Sterling Drug took place amidst a frenzy of consolidation in the drug industry. Drug companies had several different motives for merging, including using economies to scale to combat the increasing cost of introducing new drugs and strengthening global presence. These companies were also looking to mergers as a way of diversifying existing products lines and gaining marketing skill and expertise in biotech research.

Several other mergers followed the Kodak/Sterling deal. In 1989, Dow Chemical Co. teamed up with Marion Laboratories for $5.5 billion, SmithKline Beckman joined with Beecham Group PLC for $7.7 billion, and Bristol-Myers Co. combined with Squibb Corp. for $12 billion. Small biotech companies were looking for partners as well; they needed to team up with larger pharmaceutical companies in order to finance expensive research. These larger companies were more than happy to scoop up the research firms as the biotech industry was poised to introduce the next wave of important new drugs. Deals included Amgen Inc. and Hoffman-La Roche; Immunex Corp. and Eastman Kodak's Sterling Drug unit; Nova Pharmaceutical and SmithKline Beckman; and California Biotechnology, Inc. and Pfizer Inc.

Review of the Outcome

The deal between Eastman Kodak and Sterling Drug was viewed by many analysts in a negative fashion. Many felt that Kodak overpaid for the drug company, pointing to the firm's hefty debt load of 55% of total capitalization. Stock closed at $45.13 per share in 1988, down from $49 per share in 1987. During the same time period, net income plunged from $1.39 billion in 1988 to $529 million. Strong gains were not seen until Eastman Kodak announced it was restructuring the company and focusing on its core film and imaging businesses in 1994.

According to Bruce Wasserstein, author of *Big Deal: The Battle for Control of America's Leading Corporations*, "Eastman Kodak's struggle with Sterling demonstrated the importance of having a global presence. The company lacked the global drug distribution network to boost international sales." As a result, Kodak struck up a deal with France's Sanofi in 1991, hoping to gain a stronger international foothold. Kodak's pharmaceutical interests continued to struggle, however, and in 1994, Kodak left the drug indus-

try. The company sold its prescription pharmaceutical interests to Snaofi for $1.7 billion, its over-the-counter drugs to SmithKline Beecham for $2.9 billion, and its diagnostic operations to Johnson & Johnson for $1 billion.

Kodak used the earnings from the sales to pay off debt caused by the Sterling deal. After cutting thousands of jobs, restructuring management, and refocusing company's operations, Kodak's net profit margin increased to 8.4% in 1995 from 4.1% in 1994. In 1998, Kodak's stock closed at $72 per share, the second highest price ever, and its 10.4% net profit margin was higher than it had been in over twenty years.

Research

Eastman Kodak Co. Home Page, available at http://www.kodak.com. Official World Wide Web Home Page for Eastman Kodak Co. Includes current and archived news, and detailed financial and product information.

"Eastman Kodak Co.," in *Notable Corporate Chronologies*, The Gale Group, 1999. List major events in the history of Eastman Kodak Co.

Flanigan, James. "Kodak Makes its Move Into Biotechnology with Sterling," in *Los Angeles Times*, 23 January 1988. Lists details of Eastman Kodak's purchase of Sterling Drug.

Freudenheim, Milt. "Drug Makers Try Biotech Partners," in *The New York Times*, 30 September, 1988. Discusses trends in the drug industry and recent mergers.

"Kodak to Acquire Sterling Drug," in *The Toronto Star*, 23 January 1988. Lists details of Hoffman-La Roche's attempt to takeover Sterling.

"Sterling Drug, Inc.," in *International Directory of Company Histories*, Vol. 1, St. James Press, 1988. Relates major events in the history of Sterling Drug, Inc.

Wasserstein, Bruce. *Big Deal: The Battle for Control of America's Leading Corporations*, Warner Books, 1998. Offers an overview of the largest mergers in recent American corporate history.

Wayne, Leslie. "Kodak Agrees to Buy Sterling for $5.1 Billion," in *The New York Times*, 23 January 1988. Explains Kodak's approach to purchasing Sterling.

Williams, Linda. "Perspective on the Drug Firm Merger," in *Los Angeles Times*, 29 July 1989. This article explains the motives behind recent drug mergers.

CHRISTINA M. STANSELL

ELI LILLY & PCS HEALTH SYSTEMS

Eli Lilly & Co.
Lilly Corporate Ctr.
Indianapolis, IN 46285
USA

tel: (317)276-2000
fax: (317)277-6579
web: http://www.lilly.com

nationality: USA
date: November 1994
affected: Eli Lilly & Co., USA, founded 1876
affected: PCS Health Systems, Inc., USA

Overview of the Acquisition

Eli Lilly's $4.1 billion purchase of PCS Health Systems, the largest manager of drug benefit programs in the U.S., from McKesson Corp. in November of 1994 was in response to a growing consolidation trend among large drug makes and pharmacy benefit managers. However, restrictions placed on the deal by the U.S. Federal Trade Commission undermined Eli Lilly's efforts to use PCS to widen its distribution network. As a result, Eli Lilly wrote off $2.4 billion related to the purchase in 1997 and sold PCS to Rite Aid Corp. for $1.5 billion two years later.

History of Eli Lilly & Co.

In 1876, Colonel Eli Lilly, a 38-year-old chemist and Civil War veteran, frustrated by the poor quality medicines available, established a laboratory in Indianapolis and founded his company as a sole proprietorship. That year, the new business established itself with the innovation of gelatin-coated capsules. Eli Lilly began exporting empty gelatin capsules to Japan in the early 1990s.

In 1923, the company introduced insulin for the treatment of diabetes. The drug was derived from the pancreas glands of animals; 6,000 cattle or 24,000 hogs were required for the production of one ounce. Eli Lilly also established a foreign sales division. Three years later, the Eli Lilly Laboratory for Clinical Research was formed. In 1928, liver extract for the treatment of pernicious anemia was developed in association with Drs. Minot and Murphy of Harvard University. Sales in the early 1930s reached $13 million.

Eli Lilly's first international affiliate opened, in the United Kingdom, in 1934. Nine years later, full-scale production of penicillin began. The Eli Lilly International Corp. was formed as a subsidiary of the parent firm to coordinate the expansion of the company's business throughout the world. Sales exceeded $100 million in 1947. In the early 1950s, Eli Lilly researchers isolated the antibiotic erythromycin from a species of mold found in the Philippines. By the decade's end, Eli Lilly had manufactured 60% of the Salk poliomyelitis vaccine; marketed V-Cillin, a penicillin, and Vancocin HC1, an antibiotic; and introduced Darvon, a painkiller.

Elanco Products Co. was formed in 1960 for the production of veterinary pharmaceuticals. Four years later, Eli Lilly introduced Keflin, its first cephalosporin antibiotic. In 1968, Eli Lilly Research Centre Ltd., near London, England, was dedicated. Eli Lilly stock was listed on the New York Stock Exchange for the first time in 1970. Keflex, an oral cephalosporin antibiotic, was introduced in 1971. Eli Lilly paid $38 million for Elizabeth Arden Sales Corp., a New York-based cosmetics firm. In 1972, Dista Products Co. was formed. A year later, Eli Lilly stock was listed on the Zurich, Basel, and Geneva exchanges, and the firm established a Pharmaceutical Division. Sales topped $1 billion in 1974.

Eli Lilly acquired IVAC Corp., maker of vital signs measuring equipment, in 1976. Dobutrex, a heart drug primarily for use in hospitals, was launched in France. By 1980, the firm had acquired Cardiac Pacemakers, Inc.; launched Ceclor, which eventually became the world's top-selling oral antibiotic; and acquired Physio-Control Corp. Sales exceeded $2 billion. In 1982, Oraflex, the American version of Benoxaprofen, was withdrawn from the market due to FDA charges that Eli Lilly suppressed controversial research findings related to the drug. Also that year, the patent on Keflin expired, and Eli Lilly introduced Humulin, a human insulin, which was the first pharmaceutical product produced through recombinant DNA technology.

In 1984, Eli Lilly purchased Advanced Cardiovascular Systems, Inc. The Oraflex controversy continued as the U.S. Justice Department filed criminal charges against Eli Lilly and Dr. William Ian H. Shedden, the former vice-president and chief medical officer of Eli Lilly Research Laboratories. The Justice Department accused the defendants of failing to inform the government of four deaths and six illnesses related to Oraflex. Eli Lilly pled guilty to 25 counts and was fined $25,000; Shedden was fined $15,000. The firms legal troubles mounted in 1985 when Eli Lilly was involved in litigation regarding DES, a drug prescribed to women in the 1940s and 1950s for the prevention of miscarriages. DES was blamed for causing cancer and reproductive problems for the children of women who took it during their pregnancies. As the first and largest manufacturer of diesthylstilbestrol, Eli Lilly was ordered to pay $400,000 to the first male seeking damages in a DES-related case.

Hybritech Inc., a biotechnology company, was acquired for $300 million in 1986. That same year, Eli Lilly stock was listed on the Tokyo stock exchange and Prozac was first marketed in Belgium; the blockbuster antidepressant was introduced to the U.S. market in 1988. By 1990, Eli Lilly had begun marketing Humatrope, a human growth hormone of recombi-

The Business

Financials

Revenue (1998): $9.2 billion

Employees (1998): 29,800

SICs / NAICS

sic 3845 - Electromedical Equipment

sic 3841 - Surgical & Medical Instruments

sic 5122 - Drugs, Proprietaries & Sundries

sic 5961 - Catalog & Mail-Order Houses

sic 2834 - Pharmaceutical Preparations

sic 2833 - Medicinals & Botanicals

sic 2879 - Agricultural Chemicals Nec

naics 422210 - Drugs and Druggists' Sundries Wholesalers

naics 454110 - Electronic Shopping and Mail-Order Houses

naics 325412 - Pharmaceutical Preparation Manufacturing

naics 325411 - Medicinal and Botanical Manufacturing

naics 325320 - Pesticide and Other Agricultural Chemical Manufacturing

naics 334510 - Electromedical and Electrotherapeutic Apparatus Manufacturing

naics 339112 - Surgical and Medical Instrument Manufacturing

nant DNA origin, in the Netherlands; introduced Axid, an antiulcer compound, in the United Kingdom; divested Elizabeth Arden to Faberge; acquired Devices for Vascular Intervention, Inc. and Pacific Biotech, Inc.; listed its stock on the London stock exchange; and established an agri-chemicals joint venture with Dow Chemical Co., called DowElanco. Sales topped $5 billion, and net income reached $1 billion.

In 1992, Eli Lilly and Shionogi & Co., Ltd., of Osaka, Japan, entered into an agreement in principle under which Eli Lilly's gelatin capsule business would be transferred to Shionogi. In exchange, Eli Lilly received cash and the rights to market its human insulin product, Humulin, in Japan. That year, Eli Lilly acquired Origin Medsystems, Inc. In 1994, Eli Lilly acquired pharmacy benefit management company PCS Health Systems from McKesson Corp. for $4.1 billion and sold IVAC Corp. to River Acquisition Corp.

Sales of Prozac had exceeded $2 billion by 1995. In 1996, Eli Lilly placed 52nd in *Business Week*'s Global

The Officers

Chairman: Randall L. Tobias

CEO: Sidney Taurel

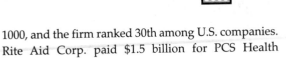

1000, and the firm ranked 30th among U.S. companies. Rite Aid Corp. paid $1.5 billion for PCS Health Systems early in 1999.

Market Forces Driving the Acquisition

Conventional health insurance plans offered by employers made employees responsible for their health care expenses up to a specified deductible. Upon reaching that deductible, the employer, or the insurance company used by the employer, was responsible for treatment costs. This system afforded both doctors and patients the freedom to choose courses of treatment without being concerned about cost.

Rising healthcare costs in the early 1980s prompted employers to seek cheaper alternatives. Health maintenance organizations (HMOs) became popular in the mid-1980s as they offered cheaper coverage by restricting treatment options. These HMO firms organized a network of doctors and hospitals that agreed to follow HMO guidelines when considering treatment options. Because healthcare providers were partially responsible for the costs of procedures and products not included in the HMO parameters, doctors and hospitals could save money by prescribing treatments more selectively.

It was in this cost conscious environment that pharmacy benefits management companies emerged. These companies worked with managed care organizations to suppress the rising costs of pharmaceuticals by purchasing drugs in bulk from manufacturers and encouraging doctors to prescribe the least expensive drug in a given class. By the mid-1990s, U.S. pharmaceutical companies were being pressured on two fronts to reduce prices. Because managed care companies had access to huge numbers of customers, they were in a position to dictate prices to manufacturers. Also, the Clinton Administration posed a threat to the industry's unchecked pricing structure, a freedom pharmaceutical manufacturers in many other countries lacked.

In 1993, to steel itself against what seemed to be inevitable pricing restrictions, Merck & Co., the world's largest drug maker, sought to acquire a pharmacy benefits manager, believing the distribution channel would garner enough new sales to counter-balance the effects of price reductions. Merck's $6.6 billion acquisition of Medco Containment, the nation's leading mail-order pharmacy company, marked the industry's first linkup between a drug manufacturer and distributor. Competing pharmaceutical giants began seeking similar deals. For example, SmithKline Beecham acquired Diversified Pharmaceutical Services, Inc. for $2.3 billion early in 1994. Unwilling to be left behind, Eli Lilly began seeking a pharmacy benefit management company of its own.

Many analysts viewed McKesson Corp.'s PCS Health Systems division as the next likely target. As a result of this speculation, from the time of Medco's July 1993 announcement of its plans to buy Merck to February of 1994, McKesson's stock jumped more than 40%. Although PCS had caused problems in the late 1980s for McKesson—when the firm tried to satisfy the demands of insurance companies to cut costs, it had alienated major clients by reducing reimbursements to drug stores and pharmacies—the prescription benefit manager had dramatically improved its performance by the early 1990s. Sales and earnings were increasing by as much as 50% annually, and the purchase of Integrated Medical Systems Inc. in early 1994 had transformed PCS into a "full-fledged medical-services-management company" wrote *Business Week*.

Approach and Engagement

On July 11, 1994, Eli Lilly announced its intent to pay $4.1 billion to McKesson Corp. for PCS Health Systems Inc. The $76 per share cash and stock offer was set to expire on September 9. However, a request for more information made by the Federal Trade Commission on July 27 prompted Eli Lilly to extend the deadline to September 26. By early September, roughly 36% of McKesson's 41.5 million shares had been tendered.

Although it had approved two similar deals (Merck/Medco and SmithKline Beecham/Diversified Pharmaceutical Services) without restriction, the Federal Trade Commission (FTC) agreed only to approve the deal conditionally, stipulating that Eli Lilly must not prevent PCS from selling any drug approved by an independent committee and that Eli Lilly and PCS must not share information that would give Eli Lilly an advantage over competitors. In November, the tender offer was formally completed, although the FTC didn't grant its final approval of the deal until July 31, 1995.

Products and Services

Sales of antidepressant Prozac accounted for 30% of revenues at Eli Lilly in 1998. Zyprexa, a psychosis treatment, garnered another 16%. Anti-infective drugs—such as antibiotics Ceclor, Dynebac, Keflex, Keftab, Kefurox, Kefzol, Nebcin, Tazidime, and Vancocin—accounted for 13% of sales, as did insulin drugs. Animal health products, including antibiotics and feed additives, brought in 7%. Ulcer treatment Axid and blood clot inhibitor ReoPro both secured an additional 4%; pancreatic cancer treatment Gemzar, 3%; human growth hormone Humatrope, 3%; and osteoporosis drug Evista, 1%.

Changes to the Industry

According to Bruce Wasserstein in *Big Deal: The Battle for Control of America's Leading Corporations*, the FTC scrutiny faced by Eli Lilly and PCS had negative effects on other deals between drug makers and pharmacy benefit managers, even those completed prior to the Eli Lilly/PCS transaction. "The Lilly restriction eventually whipsawed Merck and SmithKline. Government antitrust officials reviewed their deals a second time, after the fact, as is permissible under antitrust regulations. Merck and SmithKline ended up accepting the same restrictions as Lilly. Partly because of these limitations the PBM deals have turned in mixed results."

Review of the Outcome

Of the drug makers that moved into the pharmacy benefit management industry hoping to increase distribution channels, Eli Lilly struggled the most. Integration proved difficult. Unable to use PCS as a means of increasing sales of its own drugs, Eli Lilly finally admitted it had paid too much for the pharmacy benefit manager and posted a $2.4 billion write off on the acquisition in 1997. Two years later, Eli Lilly sold PCS to Rite Aid Corp. for $1.5 billion, nearly $2.5 billion less than it had spent on the firm five years prior. Eli Lilly then announced its intent to refocus on its core business of manufacturing pharmaceuticals.

Research

Dugan, Ianthe Jeanne and Robert O'Harrow, Jr. "Rite Aid Plans to Buy Big Benefits Manager," in *The Washington Post*, 17 November 1998. Explains why Eli Lilly decided to sell its pharmacy benefits management unit and refocus on manufacturing drugs.

Eli Lilly & Co. Home Page, available at http://www.lilly.com. Official World Wide Web Page for Eli Lilly & Co. Offers news releases, financial and product information, and employment information.

"Eli Lilly & Co.," in *Notable Corporate Chronologies*, The Gale Group, 1999. Provides an overview of the history of the company.

"Eli Lilly Extends Its Offer to Buy McKesson," in *The New*

The Players

Chairman and CEO of Eli Lilly & Co.: Randall L. Tobias.
After graduating from Indiana University, Randy Tobias launched his career in telecommunications by accepting an entry-level position at Indiana Bell. He worked his way up through the ranks of the phone company, and when the Bell monopoly was forced to disband in 1984, Tobias headed up AT&T Corp.'s new long distance efforts. Tobias also became known for success in entering international markets. In 1986, Tobias was named vice chairman of AT&T, a post he held until being tapped in June of 1993 by Eli Lilly. His first major move at the helm of Eli Lilly came a year later when Tobias announced the planned acquisition of PCS Health Systems in 1994. After that deal failed to produce the anticipated profits and the firm was forced to take a sizable write-off on the value of PCS, Tobias stepped down as CEO, remaining chairman.

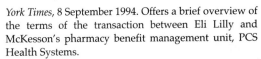

York Times, 8 September 1994. Offers a brief overview of the terms of the transaction between Eli Lilly and McKesson's pharmacy benefit management unit, PCS Health Systems.

Freudenheim, Milt. "Eli Lilly Chief's High-Stakes Gamble," in *The New York Times*, 13 July 1994. Discusses why Eli Lilly wants to purchase PCS Health Systems from McKesson.

"Lilly Bows to the FTC," in *Business Week*, 7 November 1994. Briefly describes the restrictions posed by the Federal Trade Commission on Eli Lilly's purchase of PCS Health Systems.

Mitchell, Russell and Joseph Weber. "And the Next Juicy Plum May Be McKesson?" in *Business Week*, 28 February 1994. Comments on the likelihood of a takeover of McKesson's PCS Health Systems.

Scott, Lisa. "FTC Approves Lilly's PCS Purchase," in *Modern Healthcare*, 7 August 1995. Announces the FTC's final approval of the deal.

Wasserstein, Bruce. *Big Deal: The Battle for Control of America's Leading Corporations*, Warner Books, 1998. Offers an overview of the largest mergers in recent American corporate history.

Waters, Richard. "Eli Lilly Charge to Reflect Lower Value of PCS," in *The Financial Times (London)*, 24 June 1997. Examines the outcome of Eli Lilly's purchase of PCS Health Systems, including its $2.4 billion charge in 1997.

THERA WILLIAMS

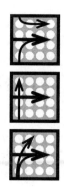

ENSCO INTERNATIONAL & DUAL DRILLING

Ensco International Inc.
2700 Fountain Pl., 1445 Ross Ave.
Dallas, TX 75202-2792
USA

tel: (214)922-1500
fax: (214)855-0080
web: http://www.enscous.com

nationality: USA
date: June 1996
affected: Ensco International Inc., USA, founded 1986
affected: Dual Drilling Co., USA, founded 1950

Overview of the Merger

In January 1996, Ensco International Inc. announced a planned stock swap acquisition of Dual Drilling Co. Both companies signed a letter of intent proposing all Dual common stockholders receive .625 Ensco shares for each Dual Drilling share. The transaction was completed in October of that year, with Ensco's Carl Thorne taking the helm of the larger company. The combined companies created one of the world's largest jackup rigs operations, with an extensive support fleet of supply and hauling vessels.

History of Ensco International Inc.

Ensco International Inc. became the world's leading contract rig operator only after surviving a close call with bankruptcy. The product of many acquisitions, Ensco is the result of Richard Rainwater's first investment in Blocker Energy after he left Bass Brothers Enterprises in 1986.

Blocker Energy Inc. was a contract drilling operation with land and rig services based in Texas. The company incurred increasing debt during the oil slump of the 1980s, as it had taken out loans totaling more than $100,000 in million, which became increasingly difficult to repay. Blocker reported a net revenue loss of $2.87 million in 1985 and a first quarter 1996 loss of $242,000.

Richard Rainwater and his company, BEC Ventures, entered negotiations with Blocker and its creditors in an attempt to acquire the drilling firm. A deal was reached in December 1986, which gave Rainwater 65% of Blocker's outstanding common stock and 400,000 shares of non-cumulative convertible preferred stock. Additionally, Rainwater assumed $12 million of the remaining debt. Blocker's creditors received cash and newly issued stock worth 10% of the $82.4 million outstanding debt.

John Blocker, the company's founder and CEO, retained his position immediately after the acquisition, but was replaced by Carl Thorne in 1987. The company was then renamed Energy Services Co. It became known by its abbreviation ENSCO, and in 1996 the name was again changed to Ensco International, Inc.

History of Dual Drilling Co.

In 1950, Robert Priddy founded Dual Drilling Co. in Wichita Falls. The company was acquired in 1980 by Bechtel Enterprises. Dual's operations were moved in 1983 to Dallas, Texas, where it focused on land and offshore drilling rigs.

The oil bust in the mid-1980s ruined many drilling firms, but Dual survived by doing business with large companies, with a focus on offshore operations. Dual was also one of the few operators to offer twin drilling rigs, which attracted large companies like Exxon Corp.

In June 1990, Dual Drilling announced that its parent company, Bechtel Enterprises, had agreed to sell the drilling group to Mosvold Shipping A.S. of Norway. The deal was approved by U.S. regulators, which added Dual's 17 rigs to Mosvold's three for $170 million. Transocean Drilling A/S announced its desire to acquire Dual from its Norwegian parent company in 1994. Dual formed an oversight committee during the negotiations, which eventually were terminated.

In 1996 Ensco International Inc. acquired Dual Drilling with the approval of Mosvold, creating one of the world's largest jackup rig fleets.

Market Forces Driving the Merger

Ensco International Inc. had been growing successfully since 1987, but so did the worldwide demand for jackup rigs. In order to meet the market needs, provide state of the art equipment, and increase its global exposure, Ensco sought a strategic acquisition target. Since Ensco had been created from the remnants of Blocker Energy in 1987, it had acquired only a few new rigs. Ensco hoped an acquisition would increase fleet size significantly, and Dual's 20 offshore rigs made it the best candidate. Additionally, both companies had rather lopsided fleets that would complement one another. Ensco had 37 support vessels to service only a few rigs, while Dual had a combined total of 34 rigs, including jack up, barge and independent leg operations, with few hauling and supply ships.

L.H. Dick Robertson, CEO of Dual Drilling, stated that the combination would, "create a great opportunity for Dual's stockholders," based upon their equally good reputations for products and services. Both companies could also provide improved services to attract new and larger clients, while also being able to meet any future industry booms.

Approach and Engagement

The public was not made aware of acquisition discussions between Ensco International and Dual

The Business

Financials

Revenue (1998): $813.2 million

Employees (1998): 3,100

SICs / NAICS

sic 1311 - Crude Petroleum & Natural Gas

sic 1381 - Drilling Oil & Gas Wells

naics 213111 - Drilling Oil and Gas Wells

naics 211111 - Crude Petroleum and Natural Gas Extraction

Drilling, until a joint announcement was made in January 1996. Both companies signed a letter of intent to execute a stock swap merger converting each common Dual stock into .625 common shares of Ensco.

At a Dual Drilling stockholder meeting in June 1996, DUAL Invest AS (formerly Mosvold) announced it had entered into an adjoining agreement with Ensco for its 59.6% outstanding shares and voted in favor of the merger. Stockholders approved the deal, and after regulatory approval, operations were combined under the name Ensco International, Inc. with management of the fleet being split between the company's subsidiaries throughout the world.

Products and Services

In the late 1990s, Ensco owned 52 rigs varying from dual drilling, work over barges, API type self-contained platform rigs, and a Gorilla class harsh environment jackup. Ensco's drilling units were split among four geographic subsidiaries located in the United States, the United Kingdom, the Caribbean and Asia. Ensco spent $500 million in rig upgrades since the mid-1990s. Two new offshore rigs were in the process of being built in 1999: a Keppel Fels harsh environment jackup, and a semi-submersible unit for drilling in water over 7,500 feet.

Ensco supported its jackup rigs with an extensive marine transportation fleet including tug, supply and anchor hauling ships. The Ensco Marine Co., a subsidiary of Ensco International, Inc., operated the 37 marine transportation ships. The Six Anchor-Hauling/Tug vessels moved rigs, while 23 large and eight miniature supply ships were based out of Broussard, Louisiana, and provided support to operations in the Gulf of Mexico.

The Players

Chairman, President and CEO of Ensco International Inc.: Carl F. Thorne. Carl Thorne made a career by being at the top of the sometimes rocky oil industry. At Sedco, he worked his way up the ranks to become president of the company's drilling operations. When Blocker Energy was purchased in 1986 by Richard Rainwater's BEC Ventures, Thorne was offered a board position under CEO John Blocker. Rainwater quickly replaced Blocker with Thorne, who took over as chairman and CEO of the renamed Energy Services Co. (later changed to Ensco International Inc.). Thorne's leadership and Rainwater's investment strategies created a successful contract rig operation worth $256 million in annual revenues. When Ensco acquired Dual Drilling Co. in 1996, Thorne was additionally named president.

Venture Capitalist: Richard Rainwater. Richard Rainwater grew up in a middle-class Fort Worth family, where his family ran a wholesale business. He studied mathematics and physics at the University of Texas, and in 1966 he went to Stanford Business School. There he met Sid Bass, heir to Bass Enterprises, but the two didn't become close friends until later. After graduating, Rainwater took an institutional salesman position at Goldman Sachs.

In 1970, Richard Rainwater joined Bass Brothers Enterprises, Inc. as an investment coordinator. His knack for finding successful financial ventures made the Bass family business a $4 billion enterprise, and Rainwater became a multimillionaire. In 1986 Rainwater left the Bass Brothers to form BEC Ventures, which immediately acquired controlling interest of Blocker Energy. Eventually, he reduced his hold on Blocker (now Ensco International) to only 5%. Rainwater was instrumental in Ensco's purchase of Dual Drilling Co. in 1996. He eventually founded Rainwater, Inc. to continue his legacy of venture capitalism.

Changes to the Industry

Ensco International, Inc., became one of the world's largest offshore rig operators via its merger with Dual Drilling. With 34 rigs and 37 marine support vessels, the new fleet was able to meet ever increasing market demands, especially the interests of leading national and worldwide customers. Ensco also gained well needed exposure in the premium jackup market.

Review of the Outcome

After the merger of Dual Drilling and Ensco in 1996, the new Ensco reported record earnings in the first quarter of 1997. Day rates for its rigs jumped to $41,000, compared to $28,000 during the same time period in 1996. The increase was sparked by increased demand for offshore drilling and Ensco's ability to serve a larger share of the market with the its larger fleet. Additionally, Ensco continued its upgrade of all equipment in order to meet the needs of premium customers. With the exception of six units being updated, almost the entire fleet was being utilized within the first six months after the merger.

Ensco's marine support fleet also increased its per day rate from $4,100 in the first quarter of 1996 to $6,800 during the same time period of 1997. The fleet remained busy during the normal seasonal slowdown, which increased ship utilization to 92%, up from 84% in 1996.

Research

Bianco, Anthony and Todd Mason. "The Man Behind A $5 Billion Dynasty," in *Business Week*, 20 October 1986. In-depth article looks at Richard Rainwater's results while at Bass Brothers. Report also gives biographical information on the deal maker and discusses his decision to leave Bass in order to start his own venture capital and investment firm.

Bleakley, Fred R. "The Boom In Restructuring," in *The New York Times*, 9 May 1985. Examines the debt reduction tactics used by Blocker Energy in order to ride out the slump in oil business.

"Block Energy Corp. Completes Restructuring of Debt and Sale of Controlling Interest To New Investor," in *Southwest Newswire*, 12 December 1986. Summarizes the acquisition of Blocker Energy by Richard Rainwater and the stock and debt transactions involved in the deal.

"Dual Drilling to Hold Special Stockholders' Meeting On June 12, 1996," in *Southwest Newswire*, 14 May 1996. Itemizes topics to be voted on by Dual Drilling stockholders, including the proposed merger offer by Ensco International.

Ensco International, Inc. Home Page, available at http://www.enscous.com Official World Wide Web Home Page for Ensco International, Inc. Includes current and archived press releases, as well as detailed financial and product information.

"Ensco International, Inc. to Acquire Dual Drilling Company," in *PR Newswire*, 25 January, 1996. Reports on the joint announcement that the two companies will merge in a stock swap deal, with Ensco as the surviving entity.

"Norwegian Firm to Acquire Dual for $170 Million," in *Dallas Business Journal*, 25 June, 1990. Reviews terms of planned acquisition of Dual Drilling by Mosvold Shipping AS.

SEAN C. MACKEY

ERNST & WHINNEY & ARTHUR YOUNG

nationality: USA
date: July 1989
affected: Ernst & Whinney, USA, founded 1896
affected: Arthur Young, USA, founded 1895

Ernst & Young International
787 Seventh Ave.
New York, NY 10019
USA

tel: (212)773-3000
fax: (212)773-6350
web: http://www.eyi.com

Overview of the Merger

The July 1989 merger of Ernst & Whinney and Arthur Young—the second- and sixth-largest public accounting firms in the world, respectively—created a new global accounting leader and reduced the industry's Big Eight to the Big Seven. The newly merged firm, named Ernst & Young, boasted $4.3 million in combined annual sales, nearly $300 million more than the second place KPMG Peat Marwick. Employees totaled 70,000, and operations spanned 100 countries. That same year, the Big Seven were condensed into the Big Six with the merger of Deloitte Haskins & Sells and Touche Ross into Deloitte & Touche.

History of Ernst & Whinney

In 1986, the firm of Ernst & Ernst was founded by a partnership between Alwin C. Ernst and his older brother, Theodore C. Ernst; it was based in Cleveland, Ohio. Ernst & Ernst took on its first additional partners in 1910. Three years later, income taxes began to be levied in the U.S., and the need for accountants began to swell dramatically. In 1924, Coca-Cola Co. became a client of Ernst & Ernst. British accounting firm Whinney, Smith & Whinney and Ernst & Ernst agreed in 1945 to operate on the other's behalf in their respective markets.

Ernst & Ernst moved into the lucrative New York market via its 1978 merger with S.D. Leidesdorf. In 1979, Whinney Murray & Co. (previously Whinney, Smith, & Whinney) and Turquands Barton Mayhew merged with Ernst & Ernst to become Ernst & Whinney, with operations in the U.S. and Europe. The new firm's audit of Chrysler Corp. paved the way for the bailout offer the auto maker received from the U.S. government.

In 1984, Ernst & Whinney achieved $1 billion in sales. Four years later, the firm eclipsed the $2 billion in revenues mark. In 1989, Ernst & Whinney, by then the second-largest public accounting firms in the world, merged with Arthur Young, the sixth-largest player in the global industry. Although the deal was billed as a merger of equals, most Wall Street analysts viewed it as a bail out of the struggling Arthur Young business by Ernst & Whinney. The new firm initially had 6,100 partners and two CEOs, Ray Groves from Ernst & Whinney and William Gladstone

The Business

Financials

Revenue (1998): $10.9 billion

Employees (1998): 85,000

SICs / NAICS

sic 8721 - Accounting, Auditing & Bookkeeping

sic 8742 - Management Consulting Services

sic 6282 - Investment Advice

naics 541211 - Offices of Certified Public Accountants

naics 541214 - Payroll Services

naics 541219 - Other Accounting Services

naics 541611 - Administrative Management and General Management Consulting Services

naics 541612 - Human Resources and Executive Search Consulting Services

from Arthur Young. Ernst & Young's client list included American Express, Mobil Corp., BankAmerica Corp., Time Inc., Eli Lilley & Co., and Coca-Cola.

In 1992, Ernst & Young received notice that its audits of 23 failed savings and loans accounts—which experienced total losses of over $5.5 billion—were to be investigated by the Office of Thrift Supervision, a government body formed to recover losses from accounting firms that should have discovered improprieties during savings and loan audits. Among the institutions audited was Charles Keating's Lincoln Savings & Loan in Irvine, California; Ernst & Young ended up paying a fine of $400 million to settle accusations that it helped Keating deceive the federal government about the health of Lincoln Savings & Loan.

The firm had moved into consulting by the mid-1990s. In 1996, Ernst & Young acquired Wright Killen & Co., a petrochemicals consulting operation based in Texas. The following year, Ernst & Young faced a whopping $4 billion lawsuit with regards to its ill-fated 1993 reorganization of Merry-Go-Round Enterprises, which failed to prevent the retail chain's insolvency. To settle the case, Ernst & Young agreed to pay $185 million. In October of 1997, KPMG Peat Marwick and Ernst & Young agreed to merge into the largest accounting firm in the world; however, in February of 1998, the deal collapsed. Lawsuits continued to plague Ernst & Young in 1999.

History of Arthur Young

In 1895, Arthur Young founded and headed the Arthur Young accounting firm based in Kansas City, Kansas, after breaking from an earlier union of the firm of Stuart and Young. A year later, Young formed Arthur Young and Co. with his brother Stanley Young. In 1906, Young terminated what had become an unsatisfactory partnership with his sibling.

In 1913, the need for accountants began to swell as income taxes began to be levied in the U.S. By 1983, Young had reached total revenues in excess of $1 billion for the first time.

The Bank of England sued Young in 1985 and collected $44 million after a firm-audited bank collapsed. Although revenues eclipsed $2 billion by 1988, the firm continued to struggle as it faced expensive litigation regarding its audits of failed savings and loan institutions.

In 1989, Young merged with Ernst & Whinney, the world's second-largest accountancy, to form Ernst & Young. Although both sides called the transaction a merger of equals, many observers believed Ernst & Whinney had rescued the floundering Young from near insolvency.

Market Forces Driving the Merger

According to a 1989 *Business Week* article, the merger of Ernst & Whinney and Arthur Young reflected "the accountants' response to the wave of restructuring that their clients have undergone. Clients are disappearing—every time one company takes over another, one accounting firm is out—and those clients that remain demand lower prices on bread-and-butter services such as audits." Because prices on traditional accounting services were falling, and cutting into profits, firms were branching out into more lucrative services, such as computer consulting. However the technology and training necessary to offer such services was quite costly. The economies of scale and increased revenue base realized by a merger would allow the firms to spend more than they would have been able to as independent businesses.

The similar corporate cultures, complementary products lines, and diverse geographic operations of both firms were also cited as reasons for the deal. Difficulties integrating disparate corporate environments were a major cause for concern in many of the largest mergers in the late 1980s; however, that hurdle was simply not an issue for Ernst & Whinney and Arthur Young as both firms were already used to a conservative management style. Product overlap was also not as problematic an issue as might be expected in a merger of two industry leaders, mainly because the two firms targeted different industries; Ernst &

Whinney served manufacturing companies and commercial banks, while Arthur Young's clients tended to be investment banks and technology-based firms. Moreover, the strong presence of Arthur Young on both the East Coast and West Coast of the U.S. would give Midwest powerhouse Ernst & Whinney access to different markets. Internationally, the combined firm would be number one in Japan and a leading force in nearly every European country.

Approach and Engagement

Ernest & Whinney and Arthur Young announced their intent to merge in May of 1989. Partners of both firms approved the deal in July, and it was finalized shortly thereafter. The chairmen and CEOs of both firms—Ray Groves at Ernst and William Gladstone at Arthur Young—agreed to co-chair the new firm, which was named Ernst & Young.

Products and Services

Ernst & Young offered three main types of services: Consulting, Corporate Finance, and Tax Services. The firm was the fourth-largest management consulting practice, with more than 15,500 consultants worldwide. Specific consulting services included business transformation, supply chain management, information technology operations, financial and human resource administration, and business modeling. The Corporate Finance segment offered financial analysis, financing assistance, acquisition candidate evaluation, merger integration, and business valuation. The Tax Services division marketed its services for intercompany transactions, merger and acquisitions, international financing, and reorganizations.

Changes to the Industry

On the heels of the Ernst & Young deal was the merger of Deloitte Haskins & Sells and Touche Ross into Deloitte & Touche. That deal condensed the Big Seven into the Big Six. Wall Street analysts debated about the likelihood of other major mergers in the accounting industry, but the next blockbuster deal didn't come until 1997, when Price Waterhouse and Coopers & Lybrand announced their intent to merge into a $12 billion accounting powerhouse, which became the largest of the Big Five accounting firms. In response, Ernst & Young and KPMG Peat Marwick agreed to join forces to create an even larger player, but they canceled their merger plans a few months later, blaming costly regulatory hurdles.

Review of the Outcome

After the merger was completed, Coca-Cola demanded Ernst & Young drop its PepsiCo account

The Players

Chairman and CEO of Ernst & Whinney: Raymond J. Groves. At 42 years of age, Ray Groves took the reins of Ernst & Whinney as CEO in 1977. He transformed the Midwest-based accounting firm into an international powerhouse based in New York, mainly through growth via mergers and acquisitions. When Ernst & Whinney merged with Arthur Young in 1989, Groves agreed to co-chair the new firm, Ernst & Young, with Arthur Young's leader, William Gladstone. When Gladstone stepped down in 1991, Groves took over as sole chairman and steered the company through the saving and loan litigation that nearly destroyed it. Credited for setting an industry standard with his 1993 settlement agreement with governmental agencies, which helped put the saving and loan scandal to rest, Groves retired in October of 1994, handing leadership of Ernst & Young to Philip Laskawy.

Chairman and CEO of Arthur Young: William L. Gladstone. William Gladstone was head of Arthur Young when merger negotiations with Ernst & Whinney began in 1989. Upon completion of the deal, he took over as co-chairman, along with former Ernst & Whinney chairman and CEO, Ray Groves. Gladstone retired in 1991.

due to conflict of interest concerns regarding the same firm servicing the two competitors. Ernst & Young also closed 76 of its 200 offices. Revenues exceeded $5 billion in the year following the merger, but rumors circulated that the company was near collapse due to savings and loan litigation costs. Cost cutting measures, including more layoffs, were implemented.

Five years after the deal's completion, Ernst & Young remained the undisputed market share leader in the U.S. According to figures listed in a September 1994 *Financial World* article, the firm audited 116 of the nation's 500 largest industrial firms, 61 of the 200 leading electronics businesses, 107 of the 400 biggest insurance agencies, and 22 of the 100 top construction companies. However, sales in 1993 were the second lowest of the Big Six players. Management blamed the flat performance on continued costs of integrating the two firms, as well as on the firm's $400 million savings and loan settlement.

Research

Craig Jr., James L. "Ray Groves: A Leader with a Point of View," in *CPA Journal*, March 1995. Offers an overview of the career of Ernst & Whinney leader Ray Groves.

Ernst & Young International Home Page, available at http://www.eyi.com. Official World Wide Web Home Page for Ernst & Young International. Includes current and archived news, as well as employment, product, and investor information.

"Ernst & Young International," in *Notable Corporate Chronologies*, The Gale Group, 1999. Lists major events in the history of Ernst & Young International.

"Ernst & Young: A Sleeping Giant," in *Financial World*, 27 September 1994. Details the reasons for the lackluster performance of Ernst & Young since its 1989 merger.

Laderman, Jeffrey M. "When One Plus One Equals No. 1," in *Business Week*, 5 June 1989. Discusses why Ernst & Whinney and Arthur Young are planning to merge.

Miller, Tracey L. "Megamerger Deals Throw Profession in Play: For Ernst/KPMG: Business as Usual, But on a Global Scale," in *Accounting Today*, 10 November 1997. Explains why the accounting industry is starting to see megamergers among its largest players, as well as the reasons for mergers among accounting firms in the late 1980s.

ANNAMARIE L. SHELDON

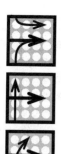

ERNST & YOUNG & KPMG PEAT MARWICK

date: February 1998 (canceled)
affected: Ernst & Young International, USA, founded 1895
affected: KPMG Peat Marwick LLP, USA, founded 1897

Ernst & Young International
787 Seventh Ave.
New York, NY 10019
USA

tel: (212)773-3000
fax: (212)773-6350
web: http://www.eyi.com

KPMG Peat Marwick
345 Park Ave.
New York, NY 10154
USA

tel: (212)909-5000
fax: (212)909-5299
web: http://www.us.kpmg.com

Overview of the Merger

Less than a month after Price Waterhouse and Coopers & Lybrand, L.L.P., announced their intent to merge into a $12 billion accounting powerhouse, Ernst & Young and KPMG Peat Marwick agreed to join forces to create a $16 billion behemoth. The deal, made public in October of 1997, would have resulted in the creation of the world's largest accounting group, with 12,800 partners, 150,200 employees, and operations spanning 151 countries. However, the union was canceled in early 1998, a week after the European Union intensified its investigation of the proposed merger. Management pointed to a lengthy regulatory process, which had the potential to become quite costly, as the reason for the deal's demise, but several industry analysts also blamed unresolved differences in management style and customer opposition to the merger.

History of Ernst & Young

In 1895, Arthur Young founded and headed the Arthur Young accounting firm based in Kansas City, Kansas, after breaking from an earlier union of the firm of Stuart and Young. A year later, Young formed Arthur Young and Co. with his brother Stanley Young. In 1906, Young terminated his unsatisfactory partnership with his sibling. That year, the firm of Ernst & Ernst was founded by a partnership between Alwin C. Ernst and his older brother, Theodore C. Ernst; it was based in Cleveland, Ohio.

Ernst & Ernst took on its first additional partners in 1910. Three years later, income taxes began to be levied in the U.S., and the need for accountants began to swell dramatically. In 1924, Coca-Cola Co. became a client of Ernst & Ernst. British accounting firm Whinney, Smith & Whinney and Ernst & Ernst agreed in 1945 to operate on the other's behalf in their respective markets.

PepsiCo became a client of Young in 1965. In 1979, Whinney Murray (previously Whinney, Smith, & Whinney) and Turquands Barton Mayhew merged with Ernst & Ernst to become Ernst & Whinney, with operations in the U.S. and Europe. The new firm's audit of Chrysler Corp. paved the way for the bailout offer the auto maker received from the U.S. government.

The Business

Financials - Ernst & Young International

Revenue (1998): $10.9 billion

Employees (1998): 85,000

Financials - KPMG Peat Marwick

Revenue (1998): $3.8 billion

Employees (1998): 21,553

SICs / NAICS

sic 8721 - Accounting, Auditing & Bookkeeping

sic 8742 - Management Consulting Services

sic 6282 - Investment Advice

naics 541211 - Offices of Certified Public Accountants

naics 541214 - Payroll Services

naics 541219 - Other Accounting Services

naics 541611 - Administrative Management and General Management Consulting Services

naics 541612 - Human Resources and Executive Search Consulting Services

In 1983, Young reached total revenues in excess of $1 billion for the first time. The following year, Ernst & Whinney also achieved $1 billion in sales. The Bank of England sued Young in 1985 and collected $44 million after a firm-audited bank collapsed. In 1988, both Ernst & Whinney and Young eclipsed the $2 billion in revenues mark. Young continued to face expensive litigation regarding its audits of failed savings and loan institutions.

A year later, the second-largest and the sixth-largest public accounting firms in the world, Ernst & Whinney and Arthur Young, merged to form the world's largest accounting firm, Ernst & Young. Although the deal was billed as a merger of equals, most Wall Street analysts viewed it as a bail out of the struggling Arthur Young business by Ernst & Whinney. The new firm initially had 6,100 partners and two CEOs, Ray Groves from Ernst & Whinney and William Gladstone from Arthur Young. Ernst & Young's client list included American Express, Mobil Corp., BankAmerica Corp., Time Inc., Eli Lilley & Co., and Coca-Cola, who demanded the firm drop its PepsiCo account due to conflict of interest concerns regarding the same firm servicing the two competitors. Consolidation efforts prompted Ernst & Young to close 76 of its 200 offices.

Revenues exceeded $5 billion in the year following the merger, but rumors circulated that the company was near collapse. Cost cutting measures, including layoffs, were implemented. In 1992, Ernst & Young received notice that its audits of 23 failed savings and loans accounts—which experienced total losses of over $5.5 billion—were to be investigated by the Office of Thrift Supervision, a government body formed to recover losses from accounting firms that should have discovered improprieties during S&L audits. Among the institutions audited was Charles Keating's Lincoln Savings & Loan in Irvine, California; Ernst & Young ended up paying a fine of $400 million to settle accusations that it helped Keating deceive the federal government about the health of Lincoln Savings & Loan.

The firm had moved into consulting by the mid-1990s. In 1996, Ernst & Young acquired Wright Killen & Co., a petrochemicals consulting operation based in Texas. The following year, Ernst & Young faced a whopping $4 billion lawsuit with regards to its ill-fated 1993 reorganization of Merry-Go-Round Enterprises, which failed to prevent the retail chain's insolvency. To settle the case, Ernst & Young agreed to pay $185 million. In October of 1997, KPMG Peat Marwick and Ernst & Young agreed to merge into the largest accounting firm in the world; however, in February of 1998, the deal collapsed. Lawsuits continued to plague Ernst & Young in 1999.

History of KPMG Peat Marwick LLP

James Marwick and Roger Mitchell founded Marwick, Mitchell & Co. (MMC) in 1897 to provide accounting services in New York City. By 1905, MMC had diversified into financial services and created a subsidiary banking practice. Marwick met William Peat, owner of a prestigious London, England-based accounting firm, in 1911. The two agreed to merge their companies, forming Peat, Marwick, Mitchell & Co.

In 1925, the merger agreement forming Peat, Marwick, Mitchell & Co. was made permanent, and the company changed its name to Peat, Marwick, Mitchell, & Copartners (PMMC). Twenty-five years later, PMMC absorbed Barrow, Wade, Guthrie & Co., the oldest accounting firm in the U.S. The new company began to focus on development of management consultancy operations.

PMMC reorganized its international operations as PMM & Co. International in the late 1960s. In 1975, several clients brought lawsuits against PMMC, claiming improper practices. The company was forced to submit its books for review by competitor Arthur Young. No improprieties were discovered. PMMC restructured in 1978 to form Peat Marwick International (PMI), which acted as an umbrella company for national member firms.

In 1979, U.S. accounting firms Main Lafrenz and Hurdman Cranstoun merged to form Main Hurdman & Cranstoun (MHC). The new company then merged with a consortium of European accounting firms led by Klynveld Kraayenhoff of the Netherlands and Deutsche Treuhand of West Germany, to form Klynveld Main Goerdeler (KMG), one of the world's largest accounting firms. In 1987, KMG and PMMC merged to form Klynveld Peat Marwick Goerdeler. Although conflicting accounts between the two companies caused KMG's business to fall by 10%, the new company, named KPMG Peat Marwick, immediately ranked as the world's largest accounting firm.

By the end of the decade, KPMG had become the first accounting firm to institute a formal program to evaluate the quality of its services through client surveys. The firm was supplanted as the largest in the U.S. by Ernst & Young. Jon Madonna became president of KPMG in 1990 and immediately reorganized the company's ranks, cutting the management team by 14% while raising salaries. KPMG's administrative structure was also adjusted along interdisciplinary lines, replacing the old tax, audit, and consulting divisions. Revenues increased by only 3% that year.

In 1994, KPMG settled claims brought against it for accounting work performed for savings and loan institutions that later failed by agreeing to pay $128 million to the Resolution Trust Corp. and $58.5 million to the Federal Deposit Insurance Corp. By then, the firm had fallen to fourth place among U.S. accounting firms. Mirroring the trend among the nation's largest accounting firms in 1995, KPMG shifted corporate focus from accounting to management consulting services. The firm formed KPMG Baymark Capital, an investment banking subsidiary able to offer clients services the parent firm was unable to supply due to CPA independence requirements.

To handle peripheral accounting for clients in the southwestern U.S., KPMG opened a new unit in Dallas, Texas, in 1996. The company also acquired the accounting firm of Barefoot, Marrinan and Associates, Inc. In October of the following year, KPMG and Ernst & Young agreed to merge into the largest accounting firm in the world. A few months later, however, the deal crumbled. In 1999, KPMG was implicated in a Medicare/Medicaid fraud scandal with Columbia/HCA Healthcare Corp.

Market Forces Driving the Merger

According to a November 1997 article in *Accounting Today*, mergers among the accounting

The Officers

Ernst & Young International

Chairman: Philip A. Laskawy

CEO: William L. Kimsey

KPMG Peat Marwick

Chairman and CEO: Stephen G. Butler

Deputy Chairman: Robert W. Alspaugh

Chief Marketing Officer: Timothy R. Pearson

Chief Administrative Officer: Michael J. Reagan

industry's "Big Six" players were unavoidable because global firms increasingly sought accountants who were willing to "develop their reach and expertise to keep their business humming in the global marketplace." Ernst & Young and KPMG cited this as the main reason behind their decision to merge into the world's largest accounting firm, pointing out that their multinational clients wanted accountants, auditors, and consultants with as broad a geographic reach as their own. KPMG, which was strongest in Europe, and Ernst & Young, a leader in Japan and the Middle East, would gain access to one another's markets.

Both firms were also looking to increase size as a means of funding the technology necessary to remain competitive in the bourgeoning consulting industry, upon which most major accounting firms were becoming reliant as traditional accounting markets reached saturation. The deeper pockets that would come with consolidation would also lessen each firm's vulnerability to costly litigation. Opportunities for product synergy were a factor in the deal as well. Ernst and Young, a leader in energy and real estate markets, would benefit from KPMG's foothold in governmental and academic industries.

Critics of the merger insisted it was a knee-jerk reaction—based on either fear or ego—to the Price Waterhouse and Coopers & Lybrand deal, announced weeks earlier, which would create the largest accounting firm in the world, with combined sales of $12 billion. Once merged, KPMG and Ernst & Young would usurp Price and Coopers as the global industry leader.

Approach and Engagement

In September of 1997, Ernst & Young approached KPMG Peat Marwick about a possible merger. If a deal with KPMG didn't pan out, Ernst & Young made clear its intention to pursue negotiations with Deloitte

The Players

Chairman of Ernst & Young International: Philip A. Laskawy. Philip Laskawy succeeded Ray Groves as chairman of Ernst & Young in 1994. He steered the firm's ill-fated merger attempt with KPMG Peat Marwick in 1997. Laskawy plans to retire in the year 2000.

Chairman and CEO of KPMG Peat Marwick LLP: Stephen G. Butler. University of Missouri graduate Stephen Butler launched his career with an entry-level position at KPMG Peat Marwick. After being named a partner in 1979, Butler held management positions in both Tennessee and Florida, as well as in Amsterdam, the Netherlands. When he was tapped as chairman and CEO in 1996, Butler was serving as leader of the firm's largest unit, its New York office. He oversaw KPMG's attempted merger with Ernst & Young in 1997 and remains at the helm of KPMG today.

Touche Tohmatsu International. Although Ernst & Young was considered a much stronger global presence than KPMG, the firm found itself granting concession after concession to satisfy KPMG's European parent, including agreeing to locate the new firm's headquarters in Amsterdam.

On October 20, 1997, Ernst & Young and KPMG Peat Marwick announced their intent to merge into a global accounting powerhouse with $16 billion in combined sales. Ernst & Young leader Philip Laskawy agreed to continue as chairman of the newly combined firm until his retirement in 2000. KPMG head Stephen Butler agreed to take over immediately as CEO. Upon Laskawy's retirement, Butler would also take on the role of chairman until his retirement in 2002.

In February of 1998, the European Union revealed its intention to increase antitrust scrutiny of the planned union. A week later, at Ernst & Young's urging, the two firms abandoned their merger plans because, as explained in a joint statement, "the regulatory process, with investigations in the U.S., Europe, Australia, Switzerland, Canada, and Japan, would have taken many months, incurring considerable costs and potentially considerable disruption to client service." Industry analysts greeted the explanation skeptically, pointing to clashes in corporate culture and client dissatisfaction with the deal as the real culprits.

Products and Services

Ernst & Young offered three main types of services: Consulting, Corporate Finance, and Tax Services. The firm was the fourth-largest management consulting practice, with more than 15,500 consultants worldwide. Specific consulting services included business transformation, supply chain management, information technology operations, financial and human resource administration, and business modeling. The Corporate Finance segment offered financial analysis, financing assistance, acquisition candidate evaluation, merger integration, and business valuation. The Tax Services division marketed its services for intercompany transactions, merger and acquisitions, international financing, and reorganizations.

Services offered by KPMG were also organized into three segments. Consulting Services, which grew by nearly 50% and accounted for 40% of total revenues in 1998, included customer management, supply chain management, human resources, and finance. Assurance Services, which brought in 36% of sales, included BMP audit, assurance-based advisory services, information risk management, internal audit services, forensic and litigation services, mergers and acquisitions, corporate finance, appraisal and valuation, corporate recovery, actuarial services, and channel management. Tax Practices, which secured the remaining 24% of sales, included total tax minimization, federal tax, state and local tax, international services, international executive services, personal financial planning, economic consulting services, tax management solutions, and financial capital strategies.

Changes to the Industry

Ironically, the decision by Ernst & Young and KPMG to cancel their merger may well have smoothed the regulatory road for Price Waterhouse and Coopers & Lybrand. Rather than having to consider two major mergers that would have condensed six world accounting leaders into four, antitrust investigators were instead faced with a single deal. After completing the lengthy approval process, the two firms joined forces on July 1, 1998, to form PricewaterhouseCoopers, the world's leading accountancy firm.

Review of the Outcome

The main issue faced by both firms after their merger crumbled was one of credibility. "There was no logic for the deal except that their two biggest rivals were joining forces," wrote *European* in February of 1998. "What is worrying for the two firms' clients—to whom they dispense advice and high fees—is that if these beancounters can't even make a decent decisions on a business they know, what is the point of asking their advice on anything else?"

Research

"Bean-Counters Unite: The Merger of Ernst & Young and KPMG to Create the World's Largest Accountancy Firm Affects Businesses Everywhere, and Not Necessarily for the Better," in *Economist*, 25 October 1997. Discusses why the two firms agreed to merge and what the outcome will likely be.

Ernst & Young International Home Page, available at http://www.eyi.com. Official World Wide Web Home Page for Ernst & Young International. Includes current and archived news, as well as employment, product, and investor information.

"Ernst & Young International," in *Notable Corporate Chronologies*, Gale Research, 1999. Lists major events in the history of Ernst & Young International.

Fox, Harriot Lane. "When a Merger Doesn't Add Up," in *The European*, 23 February 1998. Explains why the merger was doomed from the start.

Kelly, Jim. "Rise and Decline of a Merger," in *The Financial Times*, 19 February 1998. Chronicles the agreement to merge by Ernst & Young and KPMG and their subsequent decision to nix the deal.

"KPMG Merger Called Off," in *Accounting Today*, 23 February 1998. Discusses why the two firms decided to cancel their merger.

KPMG Peat Marwick LLC Home Page, available at http://www.us.kpmg.com. Official World Wide Web Home Page for KPMG Peat Marwick LLC. Includes annual reports, press releases, and investor information.

"KPMG Peat Marwick LLC," in *Notable Corporate Chronologies*, Gale Research, 1999. Lists major events in the history of KPMG Peat Marwick LLC.

Miller, Tracey L. "Megamerger Deals Throw Profession in Play: For Ernst/KPMG: Business as Usual, But on a Global Scale," in *Accounting Today*, 10 November 1997. Explains why the accounting industry is starting to see megamergers among its largest players.

Telberg, Rick. "Butler Named New Peat CEO," in *Accounting Today*, 21 October 1996. Offers a brief overview of the career of Stephen Butler.

ANNAMARIE L. SHELDON

EXXON & ANGLO-AMERICAN OIL

Exxon Corp.
5959 Las Colinas Blvd.
Irving, TX 75039-2298
USA

tel: (972)444-1000
fax: (972)444-1882
web: http://www.exxon.com

nationality: USA
date: January 1930
affected: Exxon Corp. (formerly Standard Oil Company of New Jersey), USA, founded 1882
affected: Anglo-American Oil Company, Ltd., USA, founded 1888

Overview of the Acquisition

The 1911 dissolution of the Standard Oil trust resulted in the loss of the Anglo-American Oil Company, a valuable marketing arm in the U.K., by Standard Oil Company (New Jersey). Jersey continued to supply Anglo-American until 1928, when the last of their contracts expired. Rather than forge another long-term contract, Jersey decided that it would be more economically and strategically beneficial to regain direct control of the British company. After lengthy negotiations, Jersey completed the acquisition in January 1930.

History of Standard Oil Company (New Jersey)

In 1859, John D. Rockefeller formed a business partnership with Maurice B. Clark called Clark & Rockefeller. The merchants dealt in the purchase and resale of grain, meat, farm implements, salt, and other basic commodities. The firm's two partners, having put away a substantial amount of capital, began looking for new ventures in 1863. As a result, they invested in a small oil refinery in Cleveland, Ohio, an area considered the center of refining and shipping for the developing Oil Region. That year, avoiding risky drilling in favor of refining, Clark and Rockefeller joined with oil specialist Samuel Andrews to form Clark & Co.

With excellent railroad connections, as well as the Great Lakes, to draw upon for transportation, the new firm flourished. The discovery of oil brought with it a revolution in methods of illumination, and kerosene soon replaced animal fat as the primary source of light across the country. In 1865, Rockefeller, dissatisfied with his partnership, bought Clark out for $72,000 and created a new company, Rockefeller & Andrews, one of Cleveland's largest refiners. The demand for oil continued to explode in the late 1860s, with Cleveland handling the lion's share of Pennsylvania crude, and Rockefeller & Andrews dominating the Cleveland scene. In 1867, Henry Flagler became a partner in the firm, at that time the world's leading oil refinery.

The size of Rockefeller, Andrews, & Flagler gave it significant leverage in railroad negotiations. Most of the oil refined by the company made its way to New York and the eastern seaboard; 60 carloads per day were generated, allowing the partners to negotiate lucrative rebates from the war-ring railroads.

On January 10, 1870, Rockefeller and his partners incorporated their firm, The Standard Oil Co., as a means of raising the capital needed to enlarge it further. In 1871, facing problems of excess capacity and dropping prices in the oil industry, Rockefeller and Flagler came up with an unprecedented plan for the eventual unification of all U.S. oil refiners into a single company. Rockefeller approached the Cleveland refiners, as well as a number of important firms in New York and elsewhere, with an offer of Standard Oil stock or cash in exchange for their often-ailing plants. By the end of 1872, all 34 Cleveland area refiners had agreed to sell, some freely and for profit, and others under alleged coercion. Due to Standard's great size and the industry's overbuilt capacity, the company was in a position to make offers that competitors could hardly refuse; top dollar was paid for viable companies.

By 1875, Rockefeller had succeeded in absorbing the three next-largest refiners in the nation, located in New York, Philadelphia, and Pittsburgh, and had begun moving into the field of distribution with the purchase of several new pipelines being laid across the country; the threat of monopoly grew with each additional acquisition. Six years after beginning its annexation campaign, Standard Oil controlled $33 million of the country's $35 million annual refining capacity, as well as a significant proportion of the nation's pipelines and oil tankers. At the age of 39, John D. Rockefeller was one of the five wealthiest men in the U.S.

Nine Standard Oil officials were indicted by a Pennsylvania grand jury in 1879 for violating state antimonopoly laws. Though the case was not pursued, it indicated growing resentment toward the massive company and was only the first among many legal battles waged to curb its power.

In 1882, Rockefeller and his eight associates created the Standard Oil Trust, the first such business trust in U.S. history. This move allowed the company to overcome state laws restricting the activity of a corporation to its home state. The trustees were thus virtually unfettered to purchase, establish, dissolve, merge, or divide their companies without government interference. Moreover, the trust's legal structure was a labyrinth that defied comprehension by any outsider who might question it.

Domiciled in New York City, the Standard Oil Trust held all assets of the various Standard Oil companies. Of the nine trustees, Rockefeller held the largest number of shares. Together, the trust's 30 companies controlled 80% of refineries and 90% of oil

The Business

Financials

Revenue (1998): $115.3 billion

Employees (1998): 79,000

SICs / NAICS

sic 2911 - Petroleum Refining

sic 2992 - Lubricating Oils & Greases

sic 1311 - Crude Petroleum & Natural Gas

sic 1321 - Natural Gas Liquids

sic 5541 - Gasoline Service Stations

sic 2865 - Cyclic Crudes & Intermediates

sic 4925 - Gas Production & Distribution Nec

sic 5169 - Chemicals & Allied Products Nec

sic 2869 - Industrial Organic Chemicals Nec

naics 324110 - Petroleum Refineries

naics 324191 - Petroleum Lubricating Oil and Grease Manufacturing

naics 211111 - Crude Petroleum and Natural Gas Extraction

naics 211112 - Natural Gas Liquid Extraction

naics 447110 - Gasoline Stations with Convenience Stores

naics 325110 - Petrochemical Manufacturing

naics 221210 - Natural Gas Distribution

naics 422690 - Other Chemical and Allied Products Wholesalers

pipelines in the U.S. and constituted the leading industrial organization in the world. Its first year's combined net earnings were $11.2 million, of which some $7 million was reinvested toward expansion. Also that year Standard Oil Co. of New Jersey (Jersey), a refining and marketing organization, was incorporated; this firm formed the core of what would eventually become Exxon Corp.

The Sherman Antitrust Act was passed in 1890, largely as a result of Standard's oil monopoly. Its enactment laid the groundwork for the second major legal assault waged against the mammoth firm. Two years later, the Ohio Supreme Court forbade the trust to continue operating Standard of Ohio, and ordered its dissolution. Rockefeller sidestepped the order by transferring the trust's business to other states; the trust was thereby technically dissolved, but still operated as an enterprise headquartered in New York. In

The Officers

Chairman and CEO: Lee R. Raymond

Sr. VP: Rene Dahan

Sr. VP: Harry J. Longwell

Sr. VP: Robert E. Wilhelm

1899, taking advantage of newly liberalized state law in New Jersey, the Standard directors made Standard Oil Co. of New Jersey the main vessel of their holdings, changing its name to Standard Oil Co. (New Jersey).

In 1905, a U.S. congressman from Kansas launched an investigation of Standard Oil's role in the falling price of crude in his state. The commissioner of the Bureau of Corporations, James R. Garfield, decided to investigate the entire national oil industry—which was, in effect, Standard Oil. Garfield's critical report prompted a barrage of state lawsuits against Jersey and, in late 1906, a federal suit was filed charging the company, John D. Rockefeller, and others with running a monopoly.

In 1911, the U.S. Supreme Court upheld a lower court's conviction of the company for monopoly and restraint of trade. The Court ordered Jersey to divest itself of its 33 major Standard Oil subsidiaries, including those eight that subsequently retained the Standard name. Jersey retained an equal number of smaller companies spread around the U.S. and overseas that represented $285 million of the former company's $600 million net value. Notable among the remaining holdings were refineries, producing companies, and foreign marketing affiliates. Absent were the pipelines needed to move oil from well to refinery, much of the former tanker fleet, and access to a number of important foreign markets, including Great Britain and the Far East. Rockefeller stepped down from his position as president, and John D. Archbold took over. His first challenge was to secure sufficient supplies of crude oil for the firm's extensive refining and marketing capacity. Jersey's former subsidiaries continued selling crude to Jersey and, in reality, the dissolution decree had little immediate effect on the coordinated workings of the former Standard Oil group, but the firm set about to find its own sources of crude.

The company spent $17 million in 1919 to buy a 50% stake in Houston-based Humble Oil & Refining Co., a rapidly growing network of Texas producers, that immediately assumed first place among Jersey's

domestic suppliers. The firm listed its stock on the New York Stock exchange for the first time in 1920. Jersey established the Standard Oil Co. of Venezuela the following year. In 1924, the company joined forces with General Motors Corp. to form Ethyl Gasoline Corp. Two years later, Esso, a premium motor fuel, was introduced.

Jersey bought the Venezuelan holdings of Creole Petroleum in 1928. That year Jersey and Socony-Vacuum, prodded by chronic shortages of crude, joined three European companies in forming Iraq Petroleum Co. Also, Jersey, Shell, and Anglo-Persian secretly agreed to limit each firm's share of world production, attempting to limit competition and keep prices at high levels. As with Rockefeller's similar tactics 50 years earlier, it was not clear if the agreement was illegal because its participants were located in a number of different countries, each with its own set of trade laws.

Jersey and Socony-Vacuum merged their Far Eastern affiliates to form Standard-Vacuum Oil Co. in 1933. Uniflo motor oil went on sale the following year. Ten-year-old patent agreements made with Germany's chemical group I.G. Farben expired in 1939. Three years later the U.S. Justice Department brought suit against Jersey, claiming that the patent agreements with I.G. Farben violated antitrust laws and slowed down the development of synthetic rubber. Although it denied any wrongdoing, Jersey signed a consent decree that not only ended the remaining Farben contracts but provided for royalty-free licensing of the patents they covered.

In 1946, Jersey consolidated its Venezuelan properties and operations under Creole Petroleum, the largest crude producer in the Jersey group, as well as most the profitable Jersey company. Two years later, the firm acquired a 30% interest in the Arabian American Oil Co. for $74 million.

During the 1950s, Jersey negotiated a contract with seven other companies to operate the Iranian oil industry. It also established the Esso Education Foundation and made its first major oil discovery in Libya. CEO Eugene Holman initiated the consolidation of Jersey's principal domestic affiliates into a wholly-owned Humble Oil & Refining Co. Greatly increased efficiency resulted, as Humble became the nation's largest producer of crude oil, natural gas, and natural gas liquids, and ranked first in the movement of crude oil and oil products by pipeline, barge and tankers, and in value of oil refined and products sold.

Huge natural gas reserves were discovered in the Groningen province of the Netherlands in 1960. Growing nationalism and an increased awareness of the extraordinary power of the large oil companies led to the formation of the Organization of Petroleum Exporting Countries (OPEC) and to a series of increasingly bitter confrontations between countries and companies over control of the oil. In 1962, Jersey entered the fertilizer manufacturing business in Colombia. The following year production began in the 12% Jersey-owned Murban field in the Sheikdom of Abu Dhabi.

Decentralization of foreign operations began in the mid-1960s at Jersey. Four regional organizations were expanded to coordinate the work of individual affiliates in Europe and Africa, Latin America, the Middle East, and the Pacific and Far East. The larger affiliates—Humble in the U.S., Creole in Venezuela, and Imperial in Canada—continued as regions unto themselves.

Standard Oil Co. (New Jersey) was officially renamed the Exxon Corp. in 1973. Humble and most of the other domestic affiliates were merged into Exxon under new names, all of which included the word Exxon. That year Middle East oil-producing nations imposed an oil embargo on the U.S. in response to American sponsorship of Israel during the Arab-Israeli war. The resulting 400% price increase spawned a prolonged recession. In response, oil firms began exploration into new sources of energy and sought opportunities in other fields. For Exxon, the embargo caused increased corporate sales of the expensive oil, allowing it to double, within two years, its 1972 revenues of $20 billion. By 1980, that figure had soared to $100 billion.

The price of oil peaked in 1981 and began to fall for the remainder of the decade. Exxon's sales dropped sharply, but OPEC's hold on the industry lessened. Having abandoned its forays into other areas, the company refocused on the oil and gas business, cutting its assets and workforce substantially to accommodate the drop in revenue without losing profitability. A joint venture polyethylene plant in Saudi Arabia began operations in 1984. Two years later Exxon entered into a production contract with Hunt Oil Co. in the Yemen Arab Republic.

On March 24, 1989, the oil tanker *Exxon Valdez* crashed in Prince William Sound off the port of Valdez, Alaska, spilling 260,000 barrels of crude oil. The environmental disaster cost Exxon $1.7 billion in 1989, as the company and its subsidiaries were faced with more than 170 civil and criminal lawsuits brought by state and federal governments and individuals. The resulting public relations damage threatened the company's future ability to gain drilling rights in other coastal areas of the U.S. Also that year the firm acquired Texas Canada Inc. for $4.1 billion in the ninth-largest cross-border deal of the 1980s.

A deal between Exxon and the state-owned Indonesian oil company Pertamina to drill the Natuna natural gas field in the South China Sea crumbled in 1993. Exxon reportedly wanted the Indonesian government, independent of Pertamina, to be jointly responsible with Exxon for any environmental damage. The following year an Alaska jury found that Exxon's "recklessness" had caused the 1989 *Exxon Valdez* spill. Although plaintiffs sought damages totaling $16.5 billion, the company was ordered to pay commercial fishermen only $286.8 million.

A meeting between U.S. Vice President Al Gore and Russian Prime Minister Viktor Chernomyrdin coincided with the June 30, 1995, signing of an agreement between Exxon and other oil and gas producers to develop Russian oil fields. Exxon secured an exclusive deal worth $15 billion for drilling off of Sakhalin Island. The company was also part of an oil company consortium that would drill Russia's Arctic Pechora Basin. In 1996, net profits hit a record $6.5 billion. Royal Dutch/Shell and Exxon merged their oil and fuel additives operations. Also that year secret agreements between Exxon and plaintiffs in lawsuits resulting from the *Exxon Valdez* oil spill were made public. The agreements would have reduced Exxon's punitive damages by requiring plaintiffs to return a large portion of the payout to Exxon, but a judge voided the agreements. In late 1998 Exxon and Mobil agreed to merge in an $80 billion deal, one of the largest to date in U.S. corporate history.

History of Anglo-American Oil Company, Ltd.

By the early 1880s, the products of the Standard Oil Company of New Jersey (Jersey) were sold internationally through a network of independent local merchants in foreign companies. Facing increasing competition in such overseas markets as Britain and Russia, Jersey decided to establish its own foreign marketing affiliates, which would be financed more heavily and would therefore be better equipped to compete aggressively. In April 1888, Jersey established the first of its many foreign affiliates, Anglo-American Oil Company, Ltd. Set up in London to increase Jersey's kerosene sales in the U.K., Anglo-American employed both American and British officers.

In 1911, the Standard Oil Trust was dissolved, and with it Jersey's ownership of Anglo-American. Jersey continued to supply its former affiliate through long-term contracts, however.

After World War I, Anglo-American expanded its presence in the U.K. by acquiring other companies and by forming new enterprises. In 1922, it established the Irish American Oil Co. to serve the new Irish Free State. Three years later it acquired the British-Mexican

Petroleum Co., Ltd. In 1927, Anglo-American purchased Glico Petroleum Co., merging it with a subsidiary of British-Mexican to form Redline-Glico Ltd.

When the last of its contracts with Anglo-American expired in 1928, Jersey began negotiating the acquisition of the London firm. Inability to come to terms with Anglo-American's officers and shareholders stalled the talks. Finally, in January 1930 Jersey completed the acquisition of Anglo-American through the Standard Oil Export Corp.

Back in the Standard fold, Anglo-American continued its expansion program. In 1932, it acquired Cleveland Petroleum Products Co., and the next year obtained a stake in Sealand Petroleum Co. A change in U.S. tax law prompted Jersey to acquire direct control of Anglo-American in 1936, and Standard Oil Export Corp. was liquidated. The Anglo-American moniker disappeared when the company was renamed Esso Petroleum Co., Ltd. in the 1950s.

Market Forces Driving the Acquisition

After the dissolution of Standard Oil, Anglo-American Oil Co., the U.K.-based marketing subsidiary of Standard Oil Company of New Jersey, cut its ties with its parent. Until 1928, however, Jersey maintained a link with its former affiliate through long-term supply contracts. When the last contract expired in 1928, Jersey endeavored to reacquire Anglo-American, in large part because the British gasoline market was even larger than that of Germany and France combined. Moreover, direct ownership would better position the company to withstand formidable competition of Russian oil. "Indeed," wrote the authors of New Horizons, "the alternative to the purchase of this former associate was the possible loss of one of Jersey's largest outlets abroad."

Approach and Engagement

After consulting with U.S. and U.K. legal experts, Jersey entered into negotiations to acquire Anglo-American in 1929. It planned to make the purchase through the Standard Oil Export Corp., an association of domestic affiliates that supplied Anglo-American with oil. That corporation was held by Jersey, Humble Oil & Refining Co., Standard Oil of Louisiana, and The Carter Oil Co.

Initially, Anglo-American's officers and shareholders opposed the deal, but after the stock market crashed later that year, the officers recommended the offer. Under its terms, one share of Standard Oil Export would be exchanged for every 5 5/9 shares of Anglo-American.

By January 1930, the majority of Anglo-American's shares had been tendered, and the deal was completed.

Products and Services

Petroleum and natural gas operations accounted for 90% of total revenues at Exxon in 1998. Downstream products and operations included lubricants, refining, and service stations, while upstream operations included oil and gas exploration and production, which spanned more than 30 countries. Chemicals—such as aromatics, fuel and lubricant additives, performance chemicals for oil field operations, plasticizers, polyethylene and polypropylene plastics, solvents, and specialty resins and rubbers—accounted for 9% of sales. The firm also engaged in coal and mineral mining, as well as power generation.

Review of the Outcome

"Anglo-American was the most important of Jersey's European marketing affiliates after 1930," wrote the authors of New Horizons. That company continued the aggressive expansion strategy that it had launched after World War I. It acquired Cleveland Petroleum Products Co., which had four marketing affiliates in the U.K. It also purchased an interest in Sealand Petroleum Co., a subsidiary of Continental Oil Co. By 1938 Anglo-American was selling more than 22 million barrels of oil in the U.K., capturing 27% of that market.

Research

Abels, Jules. The Rockefeller Billions, The Macmillan Co., 1965.

"Exxon Corp.," in Notable Corporate Chronologies, The Gale Group, 1999. Provides a historical review of the company.

Exxon Corp. Home Page, available at http://www.exxon.com. Official World Wide Web Page for Exxon. Includes information on products, services, and finances, as well as news releases and a brief company history.

Larson, Henrietta M., Evelyn H. Knowlton, and Charles S. Popple. New Horizons: History of Standard Oil Company (New Jersey) 1927-1950, Harper & Row, 1971.

Nevins, Allan. Study in Power: John D. Rockefeller, Industrialist and Philanthropist, 2 volumes, Charles Scribner's Sons, 1953.

Tarbell, Ida. History of the Standard Oil Company, Peter Smith, 1904.

Yergin, Daniel. The Prize: The Epic Quest for Oil, Money, and Power, Simon & Schuster, 1991.

CAROLINE C. HOBART

EXXON & MOBIL

nationality: USA
date: 1999
affected: Exxon Corp., USA, founded 1882

Exxon Corp.
5959 Las Colinas Blvd.
Irving, TX 75039-2298
USA

tel: (972)444-1000
fax: (972)444-1882
web: http://www.exxon.com

Mobil Corp.
3225 Gallows Rd.
Fairfax, VA 22037-0001
USA

tel: (703)846-3000
fax: (703)846-4666
web: http://www.mobil.com

Overview of the Merger

The $88 billion merger of Fairfax, Virginia-based Mobil Corp., the world's fourth largest oil company, with the Irving, Texas-based oil industry leader, Exxon Corp., is scheduled for completion in late 1999. Along with its status as the world's largest oil firm, with estimated sales in excess of $200 billion per year, Exxon Mobil will also find itself among the world's largest chemical concerns. To save an estimated $3 billion, Exxon Mobil plans to lay off roughly 9,000 of its 123,000 employees. The deal is the largest to date in U.S. corporate history.

History of Exxon Corp.

In 1859, John D. Rockefeller formed a business partnership with Maurice Clark called Clark & Rockefeller. The merchants dealt in the purchase and resale of grain, meat, farm implements, salt, and other basic commodities. The firm's two partners, having put away a substantial amount of capital, began looking for new ventures in 1863; as a result, they invested in a small oil refinery in Cleveland, Ohio, an area considered the center of refining and shipping for the developing Oil Region. That year, avoiding risky drilling in favor of refining, Clark and Rockefeller joined with oil specialist Samuel Andrews to form Clark & Co.

With excellent railroad connections as well as the Great Lakes to draw upon for transportation, the new firm flourished. The discovery of oil brought with it a revolution in U.S. methods of illumination, and kerosene soon replaced animal fat as the primary source of light across the country. In 1865, Rockefeller, unhappy with his Clark-family partners, bought them out for $72,000 and created a new company, Rockefeller & Andrews, one of Cleveland's largest refiners. The demand for oil continued to explode in the late 1860s, with Cleveland handling the lion's share of Pennsylvania crude, and Rockefeller & Andrews dominating the Cleveland scene. Henry Flagler joined the firm, at that time the world's leading oil refinery, as a partner.

The firm's size gave it significant leverage in railroad negotiations. Most of the oil refined by the company made its way to New York and the eastern seaboard; 60

The Business

Financials - Exxon Corp.

Revenue (1998): $115.3 billion

Employees (1998): 79,000

Financials - Mobil Corp.

Revenue (1998): $53.5 billion

Employees (1998): 41,500

SICs / NAICS

sic 2911 - Petroleum Refining

sic 2992 - Lubricating Oils & Greases

sic 1311 - Crude Petroleum & Natural Gas

sic 1321 - Natural Gas Liquids

sic 5541 - Gasoline Service Stations

sic 2865 - Cyclic Crudes & Intermediates

sic 4925 - Gas Production & Distribution Nec

sic 5169 - Chemicals & Allied Products Nec

sic 2869 - Industrial Organic Chemicals Nec

naics 324110 - Petroleum Refineries

naics 324191 - Petroleum Lubricating Oil and Grease
    Manufacturing

naics 211111 - Crude Petroleum and Natural Gas Extraction

naics 211112 - Natural Gas Liquid Extraction

naics 447110 - Gasoline Stations with Convenience Stores

naics 325110 - Petrochemical Manufacturing

naics 221210 - Natural Gas Distribution

naics 422690 - Other Chemical and Allied Products
    Wholesalers

carloads per day were generated, allowing the partners to negotiate lucrative rebates from the warring railroads.

On January 10, 1870, Rockefeller and his partners incorporated their firm, The Standard Oil Co., to raise the capital needed to enlarge it further. Facing problems of excess capacity and dropping prices in the oil industry in 1871, Rockefeller and Flagler came up with an unprecedented plan for the eventual unification of all U.S. oil refiners into a single company. Rockefeller approached the Cleveland refiners, as well as a number of important firms in New York and elsewhere, with an offer of Standard Oil stock or cash in exchange for their often-ailing plants. By the end of 1872, all 34 Cleveland area refiners had agreed to sell, some freely and for profit, and others under alleged coercion. Due to Standard's great size and the industry's overbuilt capacity, the company was in a position to make offers that competitors could hardly refuse; top dollar was paid for viable companies.

By 1875, Rockefeller had succeeded in absorbing the next three largest refiners in the nation, located in New York, Philadelphia, and Pittsburgh, and had begun moving into the field of distribution with the purchase of several new pipelines being laid across the country; the threat of monopoly grew with each additional acquisition. Six years after beginning its annexation campaign, Standard Oil controlled $33 million of the country's $35 million annual refining capacity, as well as a significant proportion of the nation's pipelines and oil tankers. At the age of 39, John D. Rockefeller was one of the five wealthiest men in the U.S.

Nine Standard Oil officials were indicted by a Pennsylvania grand jury in 1879 for violating state antimonopoly laws. Though the case was not pursued, it indicated growing negative feelings toward the massive company and was only the first among many legal battles waged to curb its power. In 1882, Rockefeller and his associates created the Standard Oil Trust, the first such business trust in U.S. history. This move allowed the company to overcome state laws restricting the activity of a corporation to its home state. Henceforth, the Standard Oil Trust, domiciled in New York City, held all assets of the various Standard Oil companies. Of the nine trustees, Rockefeller held the largest number of shares. Together, the trust's 30 companies controlled 80% of refineries and 90% of oil pipelines in the U.S. and constituted the leading industrial organization in the world. The trust's first year's combined net earnings were $11.2 million, of which some $7 million was reinvested toward expansion. Also that year, Standard Oil Co. of New Jersey (Jersey), a refining and marketing organization, was incorporated; the firm formed the core of what would eventually become Exxon Corp.

The Sherman Antitrust Act was passed in 1890, largely as a result of Standard's oil monopoly. Its enactment laid the groundwork for the second major legal assault waged against the mammoth firm. Two years later, an Ohio Supreme Court order forbid the trust to continue operating Standard of Ohio. As a result, the trust was dissolved. Taking advantage of newly liberalized state law in New Jersey, the Standard directors made Standard Oil Co. of New Jersey the main vessel of their holdings, changing its name to Standard Oil Co. (New Jersey).

In 1905, a U.S. congressman from Kansas launched an investigation of Standard Oil's role in the falling price of crude in his state. The commissioner of the Bureau of Corporations, James R. Garfield, decided to investigate the entire national oil industry—which was, in effect, Standard Oil. Garfield's critical report prompted a barrage of state lawsuits against Jersey and, late in the year, a federal suit was filed charging the company, John D. Rockefeller, and others with running a monopoly.

In 1911, the U.S. Supreme Court upheld a lower court's conviction of the company for monopoly and restraint of trade. The Court ordered the separation from Jersey of 33 of the major Standard Oil subsidiaries, including those which subsequently kept the Standard name. Jersey retained an equal number of smaller companies spread around the U.S. and overseas which represented $285 million of the former company's $600 million net value. Notable among the remaining holdings were refineries, producing companies, and foreign marketing affiliates. Absent were the pipelines needed to move oil from well to refinery, much of the former tanker fleet, and access to a number of important foreign markets, including Great Britain and the Far East. Rockefeller stepped down from his position as president, and John D. Archbold took over. His first challenge was to secure sufficient supplies of crude oil for the firm's extensive refining and marketing capacity. Jersey's former subsidiaries continued selling crude to Jersey and, in reality, the dissolution decree had little immediate effect on the coordinated workings of the former Standard Oil group, but the firm set about to find its own sources of crude.

The company spent $17 million in 1919 to buy a 50% stake in Houston, Texas-based Humble Oil & Refining Co., a rapidly growing network of Texas producers which immediately assumed first place among Jersey's domestic suppliers. The firm listed its stock on the New York Stock exchange for the first time in 1920. The following year, Jersey established the Standard Oil Co. of Venezuela. In 1924, the company joined forces with General Motors Corp. to form Ethyl Gasoline Corp. Two years later, Esso, a premium motor fuel, was introduced.

Jersey bought the Venezuelan holdings of Creole Petroleum in 1928. That year, Jersey and Socony-Vacuum, prodded by chronic shortages of crude, joined three European companies in forming Iraq Petroleum Co. Also, Jersey, Shell, and Anglo-Persian secretly agreed to limit each firm's share of world production to its present relative amount, attempting to limit competition and keep prices at high levels. As with Rockefeller's similar tactics 50 years earlier, it was not clear if the agreement was illegal, because its participants were located in a number of different countries, each with its own set of trade laws.

The Officers

Exxon Corp.

Chairman and CEO: Lee R. Raymond

Sr. VP: Rene Dahan

Sr. VP: Harry J. Longwell

Sr. VP: Robert E. Wilhelm
affected: Mobil Corp., USA, founded 1866

Mobil Corp.

Chairman and CEO: Lucio A. Noto

President and Chief Operating Officer: Eugene A. Renna

Exec. VP and Chief Financial Officer: Harold R. Cramer

Sr. VP and General Counsel: Samuel H. Gillespie III

Jersey and Socony-Vacuum merged their Far Eastern affiliates to form Standard-Vacuum Oil Co. in 1933. Uniflo motor oil went on sale the following year. Ten-year-old patent agreements made with Germany's chemical group, I.G. Farben, expired in 1939. Three years later, the U.S. Justice Department brought suit against Jersey, claiming that the patent agreements with I.G. Farben violated antitrust laws and slowed down the development of synthetic rubber. Although it denied any wrongdoing, Jersey signed a consent decree that not only ended the remaining Farben contracts but provided for royalty-free licensing of the patents they covered.

In 1946, Jersey consolidated its Venezuelan properties and operations under Creole Petroleum, the largest crude producer in the Jersey group, as well as most profitable Jersey company. Two years later, the firm acquired a 30% interest in the Arabian American Oil Co. for $74 million.

During the 1950s, Jersey negotiated a contract with seven other companies to operate the Iranian oil industry; established the Esso Education Foundation; and made its first major oil discovery in Libya. CEO Eugene Holman initiated the consolidation of Jersey's principal domestic affiliates into the wholly owned Humble Oil & Refining Co. Greatly increased efficiency resulted as Humble became the nation's largest producer of crude oil, natural gas, and natural gas liquids and came to rank first in the movement of crude oil and oil products by pipeline, barge and tankers, and in value of oil refined and products sold.

Huge natural gas reserves were discovered in the Groningen province of the Netherlands in 1960

The Players

Chairman and CEO of Exxon Corp.: Lee R. Raymond. Exxon President Lee Raymond replaced Lawrence Rawl as chairman and CEO in 1993. In a public relations blunder in 1998, Raymond criticized the global warming theory, further alienating environmental groups already upset with Exxon over the 1989 *Valdez* oil spill in Alaska. When Exxon and Mobil complete their merger in late 1999, Raymond will take over as chairman and CEO of Exxon Mobil.

Chairman and CEO of Mobil Corp.: Lucio A. Noto. Lucio Noto joined Mobil in 1962 as a regional planner. He worked his way up the ranks of the oil firm, eventually landing the posts of chief operating officer and president. Noto took over as chairman and CEO of Mobil on March 1, 1994, succeeding Allen E. Murray. When Exxon and Mobil complete their merger in late 1999, Noto will take over as vice chairman of the new firm.

. Growing nationalism and an increased awareness of the extraordinary power of the large oil companies led to the formation of the Organization of Petroleum Exporting Countries (OPEC) and to a series of increasingly bitter confrontations between countries and companies over who should control the oil. In 1962, Jersey entered the fertilizer manufacturing business in Colombia. The following year, production began in the 12% Jersey-owned Murban field in the Sheikdom of Abu Dhabi. Decentralization of foreign operations began in the mid-1960s at Jersey. Four regional organizations were expanded to coordinate the work of individual affiliates in Europe and Africa, Latin America, the Middle East, and the Pacific and Far East. The larger affiliates—Humble in the U.S., Creole in Venezuela, and Imperial in Canada—continued as regions unto themselves.

Standard Oil Co. (New Jersey) was officially renamed the Exxon Corp. in 1973. Humble and most of the other domestic affiliates were merged into Exxon via new names, all of which included the word Exxon. That year, Middle East oil-producing nations imposed an oil embargo on the U.S. in response to U.S. sponsorship of Israel during the Arab-Israeli war. The resulting 400% price increase spawned a prolonged recession. In response, oil firms began exploration into new sources of energy and sought opportunities in other fields. For Exxon, the embargo caused increased corporate sales of the expensive oil, allowing it to dou-

ble, within two years, its 1972 revenues of $20 billion. By 1980, that figure had soared to $100 billion.

The price of oil peaked in 1981 and began to fall for the remainder of the decade. Exxon's sales dropped sharply, but OPEC's hold on the industry lessened. Having abandoned its forays into other areas, the company refocused on the oil and gas business, cutting its assets and work force substantially to accommodate the drop in revenue without losing profitability. A joint venture polyethylene plant in Saudi Arabia began operations in 1984. Two years later, Exxon entered into a production contract with Hunt Oil Co. in the Yemen Arab Republic.

On March 24, 1989, the oil tanker, *Exxon Valdez*, crashed in Prince William Sound off the port of Valdez, Alaska, spilling 260,000 barrels of crude oil. The environmental disaster cost Exxon $1.7 billion in 1989 as the company and its subsidiaries were faced with more than 170 civil and criminal lawsuits brought by state and federal governments and individuals. The resulting public relations damage threatened the company's future ability to gain drilling rights in other coastal areas of the U.S. Also that year, the firm acquired Texas Canada Inc. for $4.1 billion in the ninth-largest cross border deal of the 1980s.

A deal between Exxon and state-owned Indonesian oil company Pertamina to drill the Natuna natural gas field in the South China Sea crumbled in 1993. Exxon reportedly wanted the Indonesian government, independent of Pertamina, to be jointly responsible with Exxon for any environmental damage. The following year, an Alaska jury found that Exxon's "recklessness" caused the 1989 *Valdez* spill. Although plaintiffs sought damages totaling $16.5 billion, the company was ordered to pay commercial fishermen only $286.8 million.

A meeting between U.S. Vice President Al Gore and Russian Prime Minister Viktor Chernomyrdin coincided with the June 30, 1995, signing of an agreement between Exxon and other oil and gas producers to develop Russian oil fields. Exxon secured an exclusive deal worth $15 billion for drilling off of Sakhalin Island, and the company was also part of a oil company consortium that would drill Russia's Arctic Pechora Basin. In 1996, net profits hit a record $6.5 billion. Royal Dutch/Shell and Exxon merged their oil and fuel additives operations. Also that year, secret agreements between Exxon and plaintiffs in lawsuits resulting from the Exxon Valdez oil spill in Alaska were made public. A judge voided the illicit contracts, which would have reduced Exxon's punitive damages by requiring plaintiffs to return a large portion of the payout to Exxon. In late 1998, Exxon and Mobil agreed to merge in an $80 billion deal, one of the largest to date in U.S. corporate history.

History of Mobil Corp.

In 1866, carpenter and part-time inventor Matthew Ewing devised an innovative method of distilling kerosene from oil by using a vacuum. Although this production method was less successful than he had hoped, his partner, Hiram Bond Everest, noticed that the gummy residue from this process was suitable as a lubricator. Ewing and Everest took out a patent on behalf of Vacuum Oil Co., which was incorporated on October 4, 1866. Ewing later sold his interest in the company in order to focus on experiments in kerosene. The new company soon enjoyed great success due to the demand for heavy vacuum oil, particularly the Gargoyle 600-W Steam Cylinder Oil, by manufacturers of steam engines and the new internal-combustion engines.

John D. Rockefeller's Standard Oil Co., nicknamed Socony, acquired Vacuum Oil in 1879, paying $200,000 for 75% of its stock. Despite its small size, Vacuum was extended a great degree of latitude by Standard's management. In 1886, Everest led Vacuum on an independent course in foreign sales, opening affiliates in Montreal, Canada, and Liverpool, England. By the turn of the century, Vacuum also had operations in France, Germany, Italy, Hungary, India, Singapore, Japan, Australia, New Zealand, and Cuba.

In 1910, Vacuum's holding company, Standard Oil Co. of New Jersey, invested $500,000 to retool its Bayonne, New Jersey, refinery to include the manufacture of Vacuum's lubricants for export. By that time Standard's subsidiaries controlled nearly all of the foreign market, with Socony's affiliates handling about 30% and Vacuum Oil contributing six percent of the total. Socony's domestic operations included five refineries that produced kerosene, gasoline, and naptha for sale in New York and New England through jobbers and a growing number of new roadside stores known as "gas stations."

In 1911, the U.S. Supreme Court ordered the dissolution of Standard of New Jersey, charging violation of the Sherman Antitrust Act. Among the 33 new companies created as a result were Vacuum and Socony. These newly independent companies were cut off from their former sister companies and spent the next two decades expanding operations to become more self-reliant. Vacuum, which focused on the refinery business, completed construction of a new refinery for export products in 1917. Socony increased its production operations by acquiring 45% of Magnolia Petroleum Co., which owned wells, pipelines, and a Texas refinery, and marketed chiefly in Texas and the Southwest.

Socony purchased the remainder of Magnolia in 1925 and the next year acquired General Petroleum Corp. of California to help supply its large Far East markets. In 1929, Vacuum acquired Lubrite Refining Co. and in 1930, purchased both Wadhams Oil Corp. and White Star Refining Co. Entering the Midwest for the first time in 1930, Socony purchased White Eagle Oil Refining Co., operator of gas stations in 11 states.

Vacuum Oil and Socony merged when Socony purchased the assets of Vacuum in 1931, forming Socony-Vacuum Corp. To supply its Far East markets more efficiently, the firm joined with Standard of New Jersey to form the Standard-Vacuum Oil Co. (Stanvac) in 1933. The next year, Socony-Vacuum Corp. changed its name to Socony-Vacuum Oil Co., Inc. By that time it had become the nation's second-largest oil concern, with nearly $500 million in sales. It also sold a full line of petroleum products in warehouses and gas stations in 43 states, many sporting the Mobil brand name or its winged, red horse logo.

By World War II, Stanvac contributed 35% of Socony-Vacuum's corporate earnings. With 14 refineries and a fleet of 54 ocean-going tankers, Socony-Vacuum's European holdings were vulnerable to intensifying warfare. In 1941, its large refinery in Gravenchon, France, was destroyed. Likewise, a $30 million refinery in Palembang, Indonesia, was burned to prevent Japanese control. German submarines destroyed 32 company ships, killing 432 crew members. Capital losses and declining civilian revenue, however, were replaced by increases in military sales.

Capitalizing on the worldwide recognition of the Mobil gasoline brand, the company changed its name to Socony Mobil Oil Co., Inc. in 1955. Egypt's nationalization of the Suez Canal the following year provided one of the many indications that the company's Middle Eastern dependence would prove to be a liability. The canal was reopened in 1957, creating a surplus of oil and a corresponding drop in prices that forced the company to reorganize. As part of that reorganization, Magnolia Petroleum and General Petroleum merged. Also in 1959, the company formed two chief operating divisions: Mobil Oil Co. for North American operations and Mobil International Co. to serve all other parts of the world.

Mobil Chemical Co. was formed as a subsidiary in 1960 to take advantage of the many discoveries in petrochemicals. Six years later, Socony Mobil Oil Co. was renamed Mobil Oil Corp., and its red horse logo was retired in favor of a bright red "o" within the Mobil moniker.

By 1966, the Middle East supplied 43% of Mobil's crude production. Massive world consumption of oil surpassed production, shifting the market in favor of the Organization of Petroleum Exporting Countries

(OPEC). In 1973, OPEC imposed an embargo on oil shipments to the U.S. for six months and commenced a gradual annexation of U.S.-owned oil properties. The price of oil quadrupled overnight, marking a new era of energy awareness. Sales and profits for all of the major oil companies dramatically increased as an immediate result; Mobil's sales nearly tripled within four years to $32 billion. As its profits reached record heights, Mobil responded to congressional and media criticism by defending the rights of members of the oil industry to conduct business as they deemed appropriate.

However, to protect itself from any anti-oil company backlash, Mobil embarked on a diversification campaign. In 1974, it acquired Marcor, owner of the Montgomery Ward retailer, followed by Container Corp. of America, a paperboard manufacturer. Mobil's hold on these and other extraneous assets was only temporary, and by 1993, the firm had divested numerous underperforming operations.

Mobil Corp. was formed as a holding company for Mobil Oil Corp. and Mobil Chemical in 1976. An unsuccessful attempt to acquire Conoco Inc. in 1981 was followed the next year when a bid for Marathon Oil Co. fell through. In 1984, Mobil purchased Superior Oil Co. for $5.7 billion, gaining extensive reserves of natural gas and oil in Canada and the U.S. Four years later, Mobil discontinued retail gasoline businesses in 20 states, deriving 88% of its retail revenue from the remaining 14 states, and cut its oil-related employment by 20%.

The company made determined efforts to increase exploration activities. By 1991, new discoveries enabled Mobil to increase its oil and natural gas production by 5%, to 1.6 million barrels per day. Later that year, the firm acquired Exxon's Australian facilities and divested its Wyoming coal mine and hundreds of Texas oil wells for a total of $570 million. In 1994, the company signed a production-sharing agreement with Vietnam's state oil company to develop the offshore Blue Dragon field. In October of the following year, Mobil sold its plastics unit, Packaging Corp., maker of Hefty and Baggies products, to Tenneco Inc. for $1.27 billion in order to renew its focus on the core areas of oil, gas, and petrochemicals.

In 1996, Mobil and British Petroleum PLC consolidated their European refining, fuel, and gas station operations in a $5 billion agreement. According to the pact's division of labor, British Petroleum was responsible for the refining, marketing, and distribution, while Mobil handled the lubricant portion of the business. Two years later, Mobil agreed to be acquired by Exxon to form Exxon Mobil, the world's largest petroleum company.

Market Forces Driving the Merger

Decreased demand for oil, along with overproduction, caused oil prices to plummet in the late 1990s. After hitting a high of $35 per barrel in the early 1990s, crude oil prices dropped to $10 per barrel, compared to an average price of $15-$20 per barrel between 1986 and 1998. Most of the oil industry's leading players had already completed restructuring efforts which included slashing workforces and minimizing capital requirements. For example, Mobil had sought joint ventures, including merging its California exploration and production operations with those of CalResources, a unit of Royal Dutch/Shell, as a means of cutting costs. Needing to reduce expenditures even further, the biggest firms in the oil industry began seeking large scale consolidation.

British Petroleum, Britain's largest company, and Amoco Corp., the fifth-largest oil firm in the U.S., were two of the first firms to pursue such a move. In the largest ever foreign takeover of a U.S. company, on December 31, 1998, British Petroleum spent $53 billion to acquire Amoco Corp. The new company, BP Amoco PLC, became the third largest oil company in the world—behind Royal Dutch/Shell Group and Exxon—boasting a market capitalization in excess of $140 billion.

It was only a few months after British Petroleum and Amoco announced their deal in August of 1998 that Mobil and Exxon began eyeing each other. Along with an estimated cost savings of $3 billion annually and a 13% share of the U.S. gasoline market, a merger between the two firms would fill at least one major gap at Exxon. According to industry analyst Rob Harvan, as quoted in *Chemical Market Reporter* in December of 1998, "Exxon was lagging behind in developing new crude reserves, while Mobil has been a very strong player in developing new reserves. With this deal, Exxon finds its need for reserves ameliorated, and the rest of it is pure synergy."

Approach and Engagement

Exxon and Mobil announced their $77 billion merger agreement on December 1, 1998. By May of 1999, the all-stock deal was worth roughly $88 billion, including assumed debt, thanks to a surge in Exxon's share price. Shareholders of both firms approved the deal on May 27, 1999. According to the terms of the transaction, Mobil shareholders will receive $108.17 worth of Exxon stock for each Mobil share held.

Exxon head Lee Raymond will take over as chairman and CEO of Exxon Mobil, while Mobil leader Lucio Noto will serve as vice chairman. Exxon shareholders will own roughly 70% of the new firm; Mobil shareholders will control the remaining 30%.

The European Commission began a hearing on the proposed merger in August. The deadline for a verdict is October 12.

Products and Services

Petroleum and natural gas operations accounted for 90% of total revenues in 1998 at Exxon. Downstream products and operations included lubricants, refining, and service stations, while upstream operations included oil and gas exploration and production, which spanned more than 30 countries. Chemicals—such as aromatics, fuel and lubricant additives, performance chemicals for oil field operations, plasticizers, polyethylene and polypropylene plastics, solvents, and specialty resins and rubbers—accounts for 9% of sales. The firm also engaged in coal and mineral mining, as well as power generation.

A major producer, refiner, and marketer of petroleum, Mobil's exploration and production activities focused on locating, developing, and producing hydrocarbon resources worldwide. In 1998, the company produced the equivalent of 1.7 million barrels of oil per day and had reserves of 7.6 billion barrels of oil equivalent, a 12-year supply.

Mobil's marketing and refining facilities, with refining capacity of 2.2 million barrels of oil per day, operated at a 94% utilization rate in 1998. The firm sold 144 million gallons of refined products daily in more than 15,000 service stations in 50 countries. Additionally, Mobil lubricants were marketed in more than 100 countries.

Mobil Chemical operated 28 chemical facilities located in 10 countries. Its principal products included basic petrochemicals (ethylene, propylene, benzene, and paraxylene), intermediates (ethylene glycol), and a key derivative (polyethylene).

Changes to the Industry

When the merger was announced, many analysts predicted that the transaction would help fan the oil industry's already intense consolidation flames. Accordingly, just a few weeks the merger's announcement, France's Total SA and Belgium's Petrofina SA threw their joined the consolidation frenzy. Also, in March of 1999, BP Amoco and Atlantic Richfield unveiled their $25 billion merger plans.

Review of the Outcome

Along with cementing Exxon's status as the world's largest oil company, the record setting deal, if approved, will also create a chemicals powerhouse and the world's largest privately owned natural gas company. Exxon Mobil plans to save $3 billion annually by laying off close to 9,000 of its 123,000 employees.

Research

"EU Sets Merger Hearings," in *The Oil Daily*, 27 July 1999. Announces the hearing date for the European Commission and the verdict deadline.

"Exxon Corp.," in *Notable Corporate Chronologies*, The Gale Group, 1999. Covers major events in the history of the company.

"Exxon-Mobil Merger Delayed," in *The Oil Daily*, 7 May 1999. Details the increase in the merger's value since its announcement and announces the deal's new projected date of completion.

Link, Janet. "Exxon and Mobil in Largest Merger Ever," in *Chemical Market Reporter*, 7 December 1998. Explains why the two firms decided to merge.

"Lucio A. Noto," in *The Oil and Gas Journal*, 21 February 1994. Profiles the career of Lucio A. Noto.

Mobil Corp. Home Page, available at http://www.mobil.com. Official World Wide Web Page for Mobil. Includes information on products and services, finances, and employment, as well as news releases, biographies, and a company history.

"Mobil Corp.," in *Notable Corporate Chronologies*, The Gale Group, 1999. Covers major events in the history of the company.

Shook, Barbara. "Merged Exxon, Mobil Will Be Powerhouse in Natural Gas Industry," in *The Oil Daily*, 11 December 1998. Details the assets of the merger firm.

Troester, David. "Falling Petroleum Prices Drive Exxon, Mobil Merger," in *Business First of Buffalo*, 14 December 1998. Describes the industry conditions leading up to the merger.

ANNAMARIE L. SHELDON

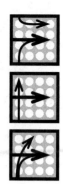

FEDERAL EXPRESS & TIGER INTERNATIONAL

FDX Corp.
6075 Poplar Ave.
Memphis, TN 38119
USA

tel: (901)369-3600
fax: (901)395-2000
web: http://www.fedex.com

nationality: USA
date: December 1988
affected: Federal Express Corp., USA, founded 1971
affected: Tiger International, Inc., USA, founded 1945

Overview of the Merger

The $880 million union of Tiger International, the world's leader in all cargo air carriers, and Federal Express, an overnight express company, created an industry giant with over $4 billion in revenue and expanded services matched only by UPS, United Parcel Service. Federal Express gained the Flying Tiger's routes in the Pacific Rim and Europe, along with the company's sales and network area in that region, making it a leader in the international air cargo industry.

History of Federal Express Corp.

In 1971, recognizing that air passenger traffic was growing so rapidly that parcel service was becoming less important, Frederick W. Smith used a $4 million inheritance and nearly $91 million in capital to buy a used aircraft business in Little Rock, Arkansas. Smith's plan was to provide an overnight delivery service, which he named Federal Express. By April of 1973, Federal Express began operations at Memphis International Airport. The company employed 389 people and used 14 Dassault Falcon airplanes.

The firm began to provide overnight and second-day package delivery services as well as Courier Pak, envelopes for document delivery. The company touted itself as "a freight service company with 550-mile-per-hour delivery trucks." Late in 1973, Fred Smith, the company's founder, president, and CEO, experienced trouble meeting payroll. After General Dynamics rejected his loan request, he flew to Las Vegas and won $27,000 by playing black jack. Payroll demands were met that year, and by 1975, despite suffering a $11.5 million loss during the company's fiscal year, Federal Express began making a profit.

The company started advertising and direct-mail promotion of its services, and by 1976, Federal Express delivered over 9,000 packages on an average night. The business grossed $3.6 million for the year but still owed roughly $49 million to creditors. One year later, along with the UPS strike and competitor REA Express's bankruptcy, the federal deregulation of airlines allowed Federal Express to utilize more flexible flight schedules and larger airplanes, such as Boeing 727s. As a result, the company reported sales of $110 million and profits of $8 million.

In April of 1978, Federal Express became a public company. That December, the company was listed on the New York Stock Exchange. It continued in its new-found wealth, with over 35,000 shipments handled per day and roughly 10,000 employees. One year later, profits increased to $21.4 million. In 1980, the company called itself a "500-mile-an-hour warehouse," with approximately 65,000 packages delivered per night and with destinations in 89 cities. In 1981, the Ally & Gargano agency created the "Federal Express: When it absolutely positively has to be there overnight" television advertisements. The company also announced a new service, overnight delivery of document-size envelopes up to 2 ounces for $9.50. By the end of 1982, Federal Express ranked as the number-one provider of air freight services.

Federal Express achieved $1 billion in revenues in 1983, becoming the first company to reach that goal in fewer than ten years without mergers or acquisitions. The next year, Smith implemented a new facsimile delivery service, ZapMail, promising delivery of documents within two hours at a cost of $35 per document for five pages or less. The company began to make acquisitions, starting with Gelco Express, a package courier based in Minneapolis, Minnesota. Other companies were acquired in the United Kingdom, the Netherlands, and the United Arab Emirates, enhancing Gelco's 84 country span. By 1985, Federal Express opened a European operations center in Brussels, Belgium. Corporate sales reached $2 billion for that year.

In order to put an end to unnecessary travel time and expenses, Federal Express opened regional sorting centers in Oakland, California, and Newark, New Jersey, to control nearby deliveries. The company also began retaining the products of such clients as IBM until asked to ship them. ZapMail services lost about $350 million dollars in 1986, and were subsequently discontinued. The company still netted a profit for the year, however. In 1987, Federal Express acquired Island Courier Company and Cansica Corporation. Smith began to implement a method of gauging efficiency. Service Quality Indicators, by which each region was assessed points for late deliveries, deliveries to incorrect destinations, and lost packages, proved to be quite helpful.

Federal Express was riding the wave of success in the latter half of the 1980s. By 1988, revenues reached $3.9 billion and profits were approximately $188 million. SAMIMA, an Italian company, and three Japanese freight carriers, were purchased. Federal Express also began operations of Business Logistics Services, which provided management of transportation and business operations for other businesses. In 1989, Federal Express bought Tiger International, Inc.,

The Business

Financials

Revenue (1998): $15.87 billion

Employees (1998): 138,000

SICs / NAICS

sic 4513 - Air Courier Services

sic 4215 - Courier Services Except by Air

sic 4522 - Air Transportation-Nonscheduled

naics 481212 - Nonscheduled Chartered Freight Air Transportation

naics 481211 - Nonscheduled Chartered Passenger Air Transportation

owner of the Flying Tigers air cargo delivery service, for $883 million. Problems with government safety requirements and pre-existing debt accompanied the new acquisition, and corporate debt was estimated to be $2.1 billion. By August of 1989, the integration of Flying Tigers and the existing Federal Express fleet was completed, expanding its runway rights into Paris, Frankfurt, Japan, and cities in Asia and South America. International revenues nearly doubled, making it the world's largest full-service, all-cargo airline.

In 1990, Federal Express ended an existing price war by raising its domestic rates for the first time since 1983. It introduced EXPRESS freighter, an international cargo service, and began operation of a new division, Federal Express Aeronautics Corporation, in 1991. The firm decided to sell roughly half of its U.K. operations to Littlewoods, its original owner. One year later, Federal Express ceased all intra-European express services and closed its domestic business in Italy, Germany, France, and the U.K. in order to concentrate on shipping freight to and from Europe.

In fiscal year 1992, Federal Express's sales reached $7.6 billion annually. It had a 45.2% market share of shipments and retained a 33% market share of revenue, compared to 24.8% and 21% for its closest competitors, respectively. Business Logistics opened a headquarters in Singapore. It also signed contracts with Laura Ashley to manage global inventory and transportation management, and with IBM to provide early morning delivery of parts. In 1993, the company planned to spend $35 million for construction of a maintenance facility in Memphis and to add two hangars, an airfield ramp, and taxiing areas. Ranked

The Officers

Chairman, President and CEO: Frederick W. Smith

Exec. VP and Chief Financial Officer: Alan B. Graf, Jr.

Exec. VP, Market Development and Corporate
Communications: T. Michael Glen

Exec. VP and Chief Information Officer: Dennis H. Jones

Sr. VP and Chief Personnel Officer: James A. Perkins

as the world's largest overnight delivery service, Federal Express handled an average of 1.4 million express packages daily.

Contract negotiations with the Air Line Pilots Association began in 1994, as the union asked for significant pay increases, improved benefits, and job security. Federal Express continued introducing new products, and in 1995, the company began to offer same-day delivery service for letters and packages to compete with a similar program initiated by the United Parcel Service. Federal Express also launched service to nine new countries, eight of which were in the former USSR. In August of that year, the company announced a new service that promised delivery by 8 a.m. in most U.S. markets in order to compete with the United Parcel Service's similar early delivery program.

The beginning of 1996 was turbulent, with contract negotiations still going on, and a blizzard that cost the company $20 million. Federal Express kept focused on growth, however, and in February, in an attempt to reach the burgeoning small business and home office market, Federal Express established a co-marketing agreement with OfficeMax that allowed it to put self-service drop boxes at the nationwide retailer's stores. Also, the initial version of InterNetShip, the industry's first Internet shipping service for online customers, was released. By March, Federal Express and the Air Line Pilots Association reached a tentative agreement. The company ended that year by opening an all-cargo route to China becoming the first U.S. cargo carrier allowed to fly in China.

The company merged with Caliber System, a trucking company in 1997. FDX was created as a holding company for Caliber's subsidiary, RPS, which was United Parcel Service's largest ground shipment competitor. By December of 1997, Federal Express reached an agreement with its union pilots that, upon approval by the Federal Express Pilots Association, the agreement would become the only union contract held by any Federal Express employees. The company decid-

ed to outsource large portions of its flight operations to reduce threats of pilot strikes in 1998.

History of Tiger International Inc.

The Flying Tigers group was formed in 1941 during World War II. Volunteers from the U.S. military service joined the group, which was created to protect the Burma Road, the route that brought supplies to the Chinese. The group of men worked from December 18, 1941, to July 4, 1942, defending the road successfully in their P-40 planes painted with sharks' teeth and flying tigers.

A group of men from that organization, including Robert Prescott, formed an airfreight company in June of 1945. Military veterans were able to get government surplus aircraft at special discounts, and the newly formed company adopted the name of the Flying Tiger Line. CEO Prescott led the company through its rocky financial start with the motivation "We're unique, so let's not imitate. Imitation lets you catch up to the guy ahead, but never lets you pass."

The first plane used by the company was a Budd Conestoga with a capacity of more than 7,000 pounds. In 1949 the force was joined by the Curtiss C-46 "Commando," which could carry over 13,000 pounds of cargo. The C-54 was used in the largest and longest airlift ever by a private contractor, to supply the American Occupation Forces in Japan. From 1957 to 1967, the company used the Q507/Constellation, which could carry 43,000 pounds of freight. With the help of this plane, Tiger was able to change the marketing map of the U.S. with the introduction of the first nonstop, transcontinental airfreight schedule. In 1961, the company purchased the first turbine powered Canadair CL-44s. The $55 million addition to its fleet could handle over 65,000 pounds of freight. By 1969, the company upgraded its fleet to jet freighters to allow for a more extensive geographic reach and cargo capacity. The company began to grow at an amazing rate and eventually was known as the industry leader in all cargo shipments.

Tiger International played a key role in both the Korean and Vietnam wars. In the Korean conflict, the company provided air transportation for military personnel and cargo from the U.S. to military bases in the Pacific region. During the Vietnam war, the company was responsible for air transportation and was credited with aiding political refugees just hours before the Communist takeover in South Vietnam. The company also joined forces with the U.S. Postal Service during this time to insure timely delivery of mail.

After the war in Vietnam, the company began to focus on non-government related contracts by starting to push its commercial services. With shipping consisting mostly of Asian imports, Tiger began to receive most of its income from its commercial ventures. The company made this new transition smoothly and a popular industry slogan became "If Tigers can't move it, nobody can." By 1979, the company had pushed Pan Am aside by becoming the globe's largest air cargo carrier. Tiger was also the first company to successfully use the Boeing 747 strictly for air freight. That plane was able to carry over 200,000 pounds of cargo.

In the early 1980s, Tiger added the B747-200F series to its fleet. The company was able to carry large, oddly shaped shipments because of the nose loading capabilities of the plane. Tiger now serviced all continents except Africa. With only 6,000 employees and a closely knit staff, the company had developed a positive can-do attitude that became attractive to companies looking to expand their business. In 1988, Tiger was taken over by Federal Express, signaling the end of an important era in the aviation industry. The Tiger name still held strong for the group of men that first started the organization, and in 1989, Congress commended the group of aviators for 50 years of valued service to the United States.

Market Forces Driving the Merger

With the air freight industry becoming more competitive, Federal Express was searching for ways to remain a leader. Its delivery in Japan was becoming an increasing problem, there was a rising concern over how facsimile machines would affect business, and the company was looking to diversify. By entering the larger cargo market, Federal Express would be able to alleviate some of those concerns.

Tiger International served 21 countries and specialized in heavy cargo, making it an attractive target for takeover by Federal Express. Recent years saw an increase in competition by UPS as well as falling prices in the market. Coupled with the increase use and growing popularity of fax machines, Federal Express saw the need to diversify in order to stay afloat. With the international market expected to grow by 13% in 1989, and domestic delivery only by 8%, the company wanted to push for a larger reach globally. Trying to expand in Japan and the Pacific Rim had been costly and slow, but through Tiger, the company could earn valuable landing rights in those nations much more effectively.

Approach and Engagement

Federal Express and Tiger International began discussing a possible takeover in March of 1988. By December of that year, Federal Express announced its plan to purchase the company for $880 million, and

The Players

Chairman of Federal Express Corp.: Frederick Smith. After serving in Vietnam, Frederick Smith founded Federal Express in 1971 with the money from an inheritance. He saw a need for an overnight service company, and since then has led Federal Express to become one of largest in the industry. Smith was inducted into the International Air Cargo Association's Hall of Fame in 1988. His leadership in the company has remained strong through the 1990s and is credited for the company's success worldwide.

President of Tiger International Inc.: James A. Cronin. University of California at Berkley graduate James Cronin joined Tiger International in 1980. He took on several management roles in the marketing and operations area. In 1987, Cronin was named president and Chief Operating Officer of Flying Tigers, Tiger International's principal subsidiary. Later that year, he was elected president of Tiger International. Cronin is credited with restoring the company to profitability. After Tiger was taken over in 1989 by Federal Express, Cronin worked as a partner for Alfred Checchi Associates, and as a private investigator and consultant for Landair Services Inc. In 1996, he was named Chief Operating Officer and Executive Vice President of Finance of Ascent Entertainment Group.

began offering a tender of $20.875 per share. Tiger's largest shareholder, Saul P. Steinberg's Reliance Group Holdings, agreed to sell its 16.5% stake in the company. *The Los Angeles Times* reported chairman Frederick Smith as stating "The combination of Tiger's international route authorities, highly efficient cargo fleet and strategically located airport facilities will enable Federal Express to accelerate the development of its global distribution network."

Already dominating the $6 billion industry with over 50% of the market share, Federal Express wanted to move aggressively into the foreign arena. Federal Express would have to give up rights to carry small packages from the U.S. to Japan, but planned to take advantage of Tiger's less restrictive cargo rights to the country. Management on both sides felt the merger would result in dramatic operating efficiencies and benefit customers worldwide.

Products and Services

Since Tiger served more than 30,000 cities in 21 countries, Federal Express's customer reach increased significantly after the merger. In March of 1989, the company introduced a low-price next-afternoon service. It was intended for documents and packages up to five pounds and to fill in Federal Express's gap of time between morning and afternoon courier pickups. The new offer would also take advantage of available space on the newly acquired Tiger planes.

In 1999, Federal Express boasted numerous domestic and international services with a presence in the U.S. and more than 200 countries. Federal Express 2Day, 2Day Freight, Express Saver Freight, First Overnight, Overnight Freight, Priority Overnight, SameDay, and Standard Overnight were offered domestically, with U.S. domestic express accounting for 70% of total sales in 1997. International services included Federal Express International Airport-to-Airport, Economy, Express Freight, First SM, MailService, Priority Direct Distribution, Priority Freight, and Priority Plus. International delivery claimed 25% of total sales in 1997.

Changes to the Industry

By the late 1980s, the air cargo industry began to see an increase in traffic and the amount of freight moved. The amount of total freight, mail, and express increased in 1988 by 13.9%. Analysts credited the increase to the cheap U.S. dollar, making U.S. goods attractive and accessible to foreigners. Interest in the Singapore market increased as well, with Federal Express's rival, UPS, planning to use advanced computer operations to reduce the amount of paperwork needed and increase speed of operations. With the acquisition of Tiger's fleet, Federal Express had a strong presence overseas, spurring other companies to advance there as well.

With the anticipated lifting of the European Commission's trade barriers in 1992 and increased trade with the Pacific Rim countries, the aircargo industry was a hotbed of competition. Smaller companies like Pronto Worldwide Couriers Pte. Ltd. were entering the global arena by expanding operations in the U.S. and Europe. Large companies continued to gain strong footholds in the market. Analysts predicted that in less than 5 years, the industry would begin to consolidate, with the smaller companies being gobbled up by larger ones.

Review of the Outcome

After its takeover of Tiger International, Federal Express gained increased access to Heathrow Airport in London, Narita Airport near Tokyo, and South America. It also took over Tiger's 39 planes and 6,500 employees, making it a giant in the air cargo industry. Jeffrey R. Rodek, Federal Express's Vice President in charge of financial planning and control, was named the new president of Tiger International in June of 1989.

Federal Express's net income dropped in fiscal 1989's first quarter to $30.4 million from $66.3 million in the previous year. Revenue increased by 53%, however, to $1.6 billion. The second quarter saw a 29% decline in net profits as well, with revenue increasing from $1.14 billion to $1.72 billion. Net income continued to slide for the company until it made a turnaround in 1993. In 1998 the company boasted $503.1 million in net income.

Research

Adelson, Andrea. "Federal Express to Buy Flying Tiger," in *The New York Times*, 17 December 1988. Details the bid by Federal Express to buy Tiger International.

Bangsberg, P.T. "Air Couriers Battle to Increase Market Shares in Pacific Basin," in *Journal of Commerce*, 29 August 1989. Provides insight on the changing industry and increased interest in Singapore.

———. "Courier Wars Intensify in Singapore," in *Journal of Commerce*, 30 October 1989. Comments the continuing interest the air cargo industry has in that area of the globe.

Breskin, Ira. "Air Cargo Merger Would Create Giant," in *Journal of Commerce*, 19 December 1988. Lists details of merger between Federal Express and Tiger International.

FDX Corp. Home Page, available at http://www.fedex.com. Official World Wide Web Home Page for FDX Corp. Includes product information, financial data, and archived news articles.

"Federal Express Corp.," in *Notable Corporate Chronologies*, The Gale Group, 1999. Lists major events in the history of Federal Express Corp.

"Federal Express to Offer New Service," in *Journal of Commerce*, 8 March 1989. Discusses the emergence of Federal Express's new next afternoon service.

Flying Tiger Line Home Page, available at http://www.flyingtigerline.org. Official World Wide Web Home Page for the Flying Tigers. Includes historical information on Tiger International, including the organization's involvement in World War II.

Gellene, Enise. "A Tiger's Flag Flies for the Last Time," in *Los Angeles Times*, 5 August 1989. Relates Tiger's last day of business in Los Angeles.

"International Air Cargo Association's Hall of Fame," in *Aviation Week and Space Technology*, 9 March 1998. Discusses Fred Smith's induction to the Hall of Fame.

"Tiger International Will Be Purchased by Federal Express," in *Los Angeles Times*, 16 December 1988. Describes details of the merger.

CHRISTINA M. STANSELL

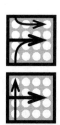

FEDERATED DEPARTMENT STORES & R.H. MACY

nationality: USA
date: December 19, 1994
affected: Federated Department Stores, Inc., USA, founded 1929
affected: R.H. Macy & Co., Inc., USA, founded 1858

Federated Department Stores, Inc.
7 W. Seventh St.
Cincinnati, OH 45202
USA

tel: (513)579-7000
fax: (513)579-7555
web: http://www.federated-fds.com

Overview of the Merger

The $4.1 billion acquisition of R.H. Macy & Co. by Federated Department Stores created the largest department store chain in the U.S., with more than 335 stores and annual sales of $13 billion. Federated saved Macy's from bankruptcy by purchasing its $449.3 million bankruptcy claim in early 1994. The move gave Federated the leverage it needed to complete the deal in December of that year.

History of Federated Department Stores, Inc.

Federated Department Stores was created in 1929 as a holding company for three family-owned departments stores including Abraham & Straus, in Brooklyn; F&R Lazarus & Co., in Columbus; and its subsidiary, Shillito's, in Cincinnati. In the next year, Bloomingdale's joined Federated, and first-year annual sales were over $112 million.

In 1934, chairman Fred Lazarus implemented a new merchandising technique that he had observed in Paris. Garments were arranged by size, then by style, color, and price. One year later, Allied Stores Corp. was founded as a successor to Hahn Department Stores, which was organized in 1928 as a holding company to bring the advantages of chain stores to independent, family-owned department stores. Department store shopping was becoming popular, and by the end of the 1930s, Federated's chairman had convinced President Roosevelt to change the Thanksgiving holiday from the last Thursday to the fourth Thursday in November, extending the Christmas shopping season.

Both Federated and Allied enhanced the quality of their customer relations by offering credit, a "pay when you can" policy, in 1940 and building a reputation for community involvement in times of crisis. Two years later, the plan seemed to pay off when sales volume reached $170.8 million, the highest in retailer history. Allied also acquired The Bon Marche ACU, Inc. that year.

Federated's subsidiary, Shillito's, was the first store to extend credit to black customers in 1946, and the first to employ black salespeople and executives. In 1950, Allied opened Northgate in Seattle, the country's first regional shopping cen-

The Business

Financials

Revenue (1998): $15.66 billion

Employees (1998): 114,700

SICs / NAICS

sic 5311 - Department Stores

ter offering one-stop convenience to meet the shopping needs of residents in several communities. The next year Allied acquired the New Jersey-based Stern Brothers. Burdines of Miami became a division of Federated through an exchange of common stock in 1956, and three years later, Federated acquired Rike's and Goldsmith's, the largest department stores in Dayton and Memphis. By the end of the 1950s, sales were nearly $760 million, a 112% increase over the past ten years.

The years to follow were prosperous. In 1962, William H. Block Co., based in Indianapolis, Indiana, was acquired by Allied. By 1964, Federated's annual net sales had surpassed the $1 billion mark for the first time, and in 1967, Allied also reached $1 billion in sales. Continuing to break down social barriers, Federated's subsidiary, Abraham & Straus (A&S), established BRAG (Black Retail Action Group) to provide technical assistance to minority-owned businesses and scholarships to students in retailing in 1968.

The 1970s were similar to years past, and by 1974 over 240 Federated stores were in operation. Suburban sales were robust, while downtown locations were generating only about 30% of sales. Federated acquired Rich's, Atlanta's leading department store, through an exchange of common stock. In 1978, sales for Allied exceeded $2 billion for the first time.

With the retail industry booming, Federated invested $15 million of its earnings to establish a charitable foundation in 1980. Rikes of Dayton was merged with Shillito's to form Shillito Rikes in 1984, and two years later, Federated's Shillito Rikes and Lazarus divisions merged into a single, billion-dollar corporation operating under the Lazarus name. That same year, Campeau Corp. acquired Allied Stores. In 1987, Federated bought Allied's Block division, incorporating it into Lazarus.

In 1988, Campeau Corp. acquired Federated, moving Allied's headquarters to Cincinnati to be consolidated with Federated. Goldsmith's merged with Rich's, retaining the Goldsmith's name. Federated and Allied were then reorganized as subsidiaries of Federated Stores, Inc., a new U.S. holding company of Campeau Corp. Later, staggering under a takeover-related debt exceeding $8 billion, Federated and Allied filed for reorganization under Chapter 11 of the U.S. Bankruptcy Code. In 1991, divisional consolidations merged Federated and Allied's Florida operations under the Burdines name. Under the watchful eye of Allen Questrom, the new Federated Department Stores, Inc. emerged from Chapter 11 in 1992, operating approximately 220 department stores in 26 states, recording annual sales of more than $7 billion, and employing about 81,000 people. In addition, Federated's stock was listed on the New York Stock Exchange.

Federated and R.H. Macy & Co. merged in 1994, creating the nation's largest department store chain. The next year, Federated acquired Broadway Stores for about $575 million in stock plus assumed debt. Federated discarded the Bullock's name and converted 21 of its stores into Macy's stores. The company was added to Standard and Poor's 500 stock index.

The latter half of the 1990s were marked by creativity and change. Burdines started Internet sales in 1996, and Questrom retired and was replaced by James Zimmerman, who became CEO. In 1998, the company sold Aeropostale and the Charter Clubs stores. That year, Federated also had to shell out over $10.6 million to pacify complaints concerning illegal collections of credit card debt. By 1999, the firm had launched the macys.com web site, purchased Fingerhut, an e-commerce and order fulfillment company, and acquired a 20% stake in the Wedding Channel.

History of R.H. Macy & Co. Inc.

Rowland H. Macy opened a retail store in Manhattan in 1858. Within one year, the store sold $85,000 worth of goods on its cash-only policy. By 1870, sales topped $1 million with items such as dry goods, men's accessories, linens, costume jewelry, silver, and clocks. In 1877, Macy died and left control of the store to his chosen heirs, Robert Valentine and Abiel Laforge.

By the end of the 1880s, ownership had passed to Charles Webster, who partnered with the Straus family, owners of a chinaware business that sold its products through Macy's. Webster went on to sell his half interest to the Straus family, ending the Macy family's line of ownership in 1896. Six years later, the store relocated to 34th Street and Broadway, at Herald Square. The new store cost $4.5 million, and within one year sales approached $11 million.

Nathan Straus became the sole owner of Macy's after buying out his brothers in 1912. The company's success continued, and by 1918, sales reached $36 million. Macy's went on to sponsor New York's Thanksgiving Day Parade in 1924, starting a long-lasting tradition. Under the leadership of Edward Finkelstein, Macy's was considered "the world's largest store" in the 1940's.

The first half of the 1950s brought unwelcome change. In 1951, common stock fell to $2.51 per common share from $3.35 one year earlier. The next year, Macy's posted the first annual loss in its history. Unaccustomed to negative performance, the company finally instituted charge accounts and catered to its suppliers to a greater extent than ever before. By 1955, Bamberger's, a division of Macy's, began a prosperous renaissance under David Yunich. The chain multiplied in suburban New York over the next eight years.

Finkelstein began to implement a strategy that would bring success back into the picture for Macy's. In 1969, Macy's California was bailed out of tough times by Finkelstein, who restored profitability. In 1974, Finkelstein revamped the Herald Square store. Two years later, Macy's experienced its biggest Christmas season ever, with greatly increased annual earnings. Finkelstein became CEO of the New York division in 1978.

Macy's continued to thrive in the 1980s. Bamberger's sales in 1981 reached $799 million. The next year, corporate sales gains of 20.1% topped the industry. In 1984, the company's best year to date, sales rose to $4.07 billion, and net income reached $221.8 million. Macy's common stock was soaring. In 1985, sales were up to $4.37 billion, but net income dropped to $189.3 million. Sales costs rose as a result of advertising expenses and new training programs. Nevertheless, Macy's experienced its second-best year in history.

Finkelstein led the top 350 Macy executives in a leveraged buyout at $70 per share in 1986. Two years later, Macy's added to its debt by purchasing Bullock's, Bullock's-Wilshire, and the I. Magnin chain for $1 billion. With sales faltering in 1989, the company experienced a mediocre Christmas season. By 1990, rumors of bankruptcy began to circulate on account of the firm's $4 billion long-term debt. Late in the year, Macy's took out a full-page ad in *Women's Wear Daily* refuting the rumors. Sales dropped the next year, and Macy's sustained further losses. To cut its deficit, the company bought back $300 million of its bonds for less than 50% of their face value. In January of 1992, Macy's announced an indefinite delay in payments to suppliers. At the month's end, the company had no choice but to declare bankruptcy. In April of that year, Finkelstein was replaced by Myron Ullman III and

The Officers

Chairman and CEO: James M. Zimmerman

Vice Chairman, Finance and Real Estate: Ronald W. Tysoe

President and Chief Merchandising Officer: Terry J. Lundgren

Exec. VP, Law and Human Resources: Thomas G. Cody

Exec. VP, Federated Marketing Services: Joseph Feczo

Mark Handler. Under new management, holiday sales reached $1.2 billion in 1992, and revenue was 3.8% higher than in 1991. By 1993, Macy's was showing its first profit, $147.7 million, since filing for bankruptcy. The company announced it would close eleven stores with low growth potential and that it planned to start a 24-hour television home shopping channel.

Federated Department Stores made a bid for Macy's in 1994, raising anti-trust inquiries from both federal and New York state officials. The Federal Trade Commission approved the merger, and the largest department store chain in the U.S. was created. In 1995, all 21 stores of the Bullock's chain in Southern California, which had retained their name following acquisition by Macy's, took on the Macy's name; the change reflected the effort by Federated to consolidate its merchandising operations under one umbrella. Nine A&S department stores in New York state had their facades remodeled and their names changed to Macy's. In 1996, the Jordan Marsh name was changed to Macy's at 19 New England stores. That same year 40 Broadway stores in Southern California adopted the Macy's name as well.

Market Forces Driving the Merger

Between 1971 and 1991, sales at traditional department stores fell 14%. During the same time period, discount department store chains enjoyed a 10% upswing in business. With industry analysts predicting that this department store shopping downturn would continue in the face of increased competition from discounters, companies like Federated were forced to finance building and development on their own.

Investors were leery of doling out money for traditional department store and shopping center development; therefore, retail companies were forced to consider consolidation. Strategic planning to acquire companies that had existing stores became increasingly commonplace. Federated, which emerged from bankruptcy in 1992, saw an opportunity to acquire

The Players

Chief Financial Officer of Federated Department Stores, Inc.: Ronald W. Tysoe. Ron Tysoe, a graduate of the University of British Columbia, began his career as an assistant to the vice president of Campeau Corp.'s shopping division. He moved upward through the company, and in 1986, was a key advisor in the $3.5 billion acquisition of Allied Stores, Inc. In 1988, Tysoe was again key in the $6.6 billion takeover of Federated Department Stores. By 1990, however, the takeover was in a shambles, with Federated becoming the largest bankruptcy case in history. Federated management sought Tysoe's help in restructuring the company. He joined Federated as chief financial officer and was responsible for the company's emergence from bankruptcy. His skills were called upon to recreate the retail giant, and in 1994, he led Federated's $4.1 billion acquisition of R.H. Macy & Co.

Chairman and CEO of Federated Department Stores, Inc.: Allen Questrom. In 1980, Allen Questrom became the youngest executive to lead Federated's Atlanta-based Rich's division. From 1988 to 1990, he directed Neiman Marcus as president and CEO. In 1990, Questrom went back to Federated as CEO and orchestrated major events that kept the company afloat: the company's rise from Chapter 11, the takeover of R.H. Macy & Co., the acquisition of The Broadway, and the restoration of Federated's competitive edge against such rivals as May Department Stores and J.C. Penney Co. Questrom retired from Federated in 1997, and in May of 1999 he was named chairman and CEO of Barney's New York.

competitor Macy's when the struggling chain sought bankruptcy protection of its own that year. A merger with Macy's would allow Federated to increase its operations to 335 stores.

Approach and Engagement

Federated CEO Allen Questrom and President James Zimmerman turned to Ron Tysoe after their repeated bids for Macy's had been rejected. Tysoe, a bankruptcy wizard, was appointed chief financial officer of the company and given free reign to make the deal. In 1994, he approached Prudential, Macy's

largest secured creditor, with an outstanding loan of $832.5 million and offered his plan for repayment of the loan. Federated agreed to purchase half of the claim against Macy for $110 million in cash and issued a promissory note for $340 million, making the company Macy's largest creditor. Federated, who wanted equity in Macy's in return for the claim, also began negotiations with other creditors. Finally, in December of 1994, the merger was completed when Federated issued 55.6 million shares of common stock and 18 million warrants to Macy's creditors. "We spent many long and difficult months getting to this point. First, in hammering out a merger plan with Macy's and its creditor groups, and most recently in developing an elaborate transition plan," commented James Zimmerman, Federated's president and chief operating officer in a December 1994 article in *Daily News Record*.

Products and Services

When the deal was completed, Federated Department Stores became the nations largest department store retailer with 355 locations in 35 different states. Macy's, Rich's, Bloomingdale's, Stern's, and Lazarus all became part of the Federated family. Questrom focused on private-label merchandising, an area in which Macy's excelled; the unit accounted for 15% of sales, compared to 5% of sales at Federated.

Changes to the Industry

Consolidation was the name of the game in the retail industry in the mid-1990s. Fewer malls were being built, and retailers had to find a way to lower costs and improve margins. Increasing the number of outlets so that purchasing and expenses were spread out was the most popular way of accomplishing those goals. "We believe it is inevitable that eventually only a handful of department store companies will remain as viable competitors in the retail market place. This reality requires that retailers leverage their expenses and do a better job of creating economies so customers can benefit through lower prices for our high-quality goods," Questrom said at a Federated shareholders meeting.

Review of the Outcome

Macy's emerged from bankruptcy when Federated Department Stores merged with the company in December of 1994. The company reported a $57 million loss in the first quarter of 1995 due to a $51 million after tax provision from the consolidation of R.H. Macy & Co. Combined earnings rose 87% and expenses fell from 37.7% of sales to 35.8% of sales. Federated was finally able to reach its target earnings of 11.8%, a goal its had pursued for quite some time. It was the belief of Federated senior management that the merger would also create a more efficient retail operation.

Federated shut down Macy's Close-Out Stores by the end of 1995. Despite the hefty charge against earnings, reported between $15 and $25 million, the company wanted to get rid of the stores since it was policy to clear merchandise in a department store format. Macy's private label was introduced to Burdines, Rich's, Lazarus, and The Bon Marche in 1995.

Research

"Federated Department Stores, Inc.," in *Notable Corporate Chronologies*, The Gale Group, 1999. Lists major events in the history of Federated Department Stores, Inc.

"Federated Department Stores Inc.,"in *Cincinnati Business Courier*, 8 May 1995. Explains the outcome of merger.

"Federated, Macy's Merger to Be Official on Monday," in *Daily News Record*, 14 December 1994. Lists details of merger of Federated and Macy's.

"Federated Plans to Divide Private Label Overseas Sourcing," in *Daily News Record*, 8 December 1994. Discusses plans for overseas product sourcing to be handled by Macy's product development.

Green, Howard. "New Consumer Realities for Retailers," in *Marketing News*, 25 April 1994. Describes recent trends in the retail industry.

Palmieri, Jean. "Federated Closing Close-Out Stores by End of Year," in *Daily News Record*, 5 May 1995. Explains plans for the closing of several Macy stores.

Ryan, Thomas. "Federated Loses $57M in Quarter; Macy Costs Blamed for Most of It," in *WWD*, 11 May 1995. List results for the first quarter earnings of 1995.

Siklos, Richard. "Macy's Holiday Revival," in *The Financial Post*, 24 December 1994. Reports information on Ron Tysoe and events leading up to the merger.

CHRISTINA STANSELL

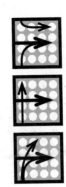

FILIPACCHI MEDIAS &
HACHETTE FILIPACCHI PRESS

Hachette Filipacchi Medias S.A.
149-151 rue Anatole France
Levallois-Perret, 92300
France

tel: 33-1-41-34-60-00
fax: 33-1-41-34-77-77
web: http://www.lagardere.fr/us/

nationality: France
date: June 1997
affected: Filipacchi Medias S.A., France, founded 1957
affected: Hachette Filipacchi Press, France, founded 1826

Overview of the Merger

Hachette Filipacchi Medias was created in 1997 by joining the operations of Hachette and Filipacchi Medias. With majority ownership in Lagardere's hands, the new entity stood as the world's leading magazine and publishing group with combined revenues of over Ffr11 billion.

History of Filipacchi Medias S.A.

In 1957, Daniel Filipacchi combined his interest in jazz and publishing to found Publications Filipacchi. His first acquisition was *Jazz Magazine*. In 1962, Filipacchi along with partner Frank Tenot, launched the monthly *Salut LesCopains*. The company's name was changed to Filipacchi Medias, and the partners created a holding company, Nouvelle Editions Musicales Modernes (NEMM), which was 60% owned by Filipacchi and 40% by Tenot.

Throughout the 1960s, the company continued to grow. It launched *Lui*, modeled after *Playboy*, the men's magazine. Filipacchi's most important move came in 1976, when it acquired *Paris-Match*,which had a circulation of one million copies per week, from the Prouvost publishing group. This purchase catapulted the company into one of the leading positions among French magazine publishers.

In 1980, Filipacchi joined Jean-Luc Lagardere to acquire Hachette, which was currently under the control of holding company Marlis. Filipacchi acquired a 20% stake in Marlis and created a subsidiary, France Editions Publications (FEP), which absorbed Hachette's business. The venture was managed by Filipacchi and Tenot.

Filipacchi remained focused on growth and diversification. In 1984, the company acquired *L'Echo des Savanes* and went public on the Paris secondary market. In a diversification move, it also bought Skyrock, France's third-largest FM radio station. In 1987, Filipacchi Medias launched *Jeune & Jolie* and formed Hachette Filipacchi Regies to handle advertising for both Filipacchi Medias and FEP. The company also made a second public offering and increased its interest in Marlis to 35%. In 1988, Filipacchi added Groupe Interdeco Regie to its advertising business and one year later, formed Hachette Filipacchi Global Advertising and Hachette Interdeco (Espagne).

In 1992, Matra-Hachette restructured, dissolving Marlis and regrouping Matra and Hachette under Groupe Lagardere SCA. FEP changed its name to Hachette Filipacchi Press (HFP). Filipacchi Medias transferred its 35% ownership of Marlis to 34% ownership of HFP. Lagardere retained 100% control of Hachette SA and 66% of HFP. In 1993, Filipacchi was listed on the primary Paris stock exchange. HFP also acquired control of the digital transmissions of cable-based radio station Multiradio. Filipacchi Medias' revenues remained flat in the mid-1990s, despite its purchases.

In 1997, Filipacchi Medias and HFP merged their magazine and newspaper operations to form Hachette Filipacchi Medias (HFM). The deal involved three steps: Hachette SA acquired 39% of NEMM; Hachette SA ceded its 66% control of HFP to Filipacchi Medias; and NEMM merged into Filipacchi Medias, which then assumed the new name. Lagardere held a 67.4% interest, Daniel Filipacchi and Tenot retained 13.1%, and the remaining 19.4% of shares were publicly owned. Gerald de Roquemaurel was named president and director of the new company, which stood as the world's leading magazine publisher, with 160 French and international titles, including *Paris-Match*, *Elle*, *Woman's Day*, *Mirabella*, *Car and Driver*, *Premiere*, *Travel Holiday*, *Eating Well*, and *George*.

Later that same year, the company made plans to expand its film, television and distribution company, possibly into projects based on its magazines. Michael J. Berman, president of Hachette Filipacchi Productions, the company's television and movie arm, sold his half interest in *George*, a political magazine, to Hachette. In 1988, in a venture with Avon Products, Inc., the company launched the bimonthly *Athena: Common Sense, Uncommon Style*, which was to be distributed via newsstands and U.S. Avon sales representatives. In 1999, Hachette Filipacchi Medias published about 200 titles in more than 32 countries across the globe.

History of Hachette Filipacchi Press

In 1826, Louis Hachette acquired the Bretif bookstore, which he renamed the Librarie Louis Hachette. He was successful from the start and, by 1852, expanded to become the first to set up newsstands in French train stations. Throughout the remainder of the decade, the company began book publishing and

The Business

Financials

Revenue (1998): $2.4 billion

Employees (1998): 8,768

SICs / NAICS

sic 2711 - Newspapers

sic 2721 - Periodicals

sic 4832 - Radio Broadcasting Stations

naics 513111 - Radio Networks

naics 513112 - Radio Stations

worked with many well-known popular authors of the time.

During World War I, the company lost many employees to the war effort. It continued to do well, however, and purchased Pierre Lafitte in 1916. After the war, the firm underwent a restructuring and listed publicly for the first time in 1919. Up until World War II, the Librarie Hachette grew internationally, as well as in France. It purchased firms throughout South America and Europe, and its business had tripled since its inception.

German forces tried unsuccessfully to take over the company during World War II. In 1944, Hachette created the Nouvelles Messageries de la Presse Parisienne (N.M.P.P.), a distribution and transport system. The company's book operations also expanded after the war, and along with this, came the creation of the Livre de Poche, which Hachette added to its publishing divisions.

By 1963, the company had become a complex entity, owning many different operations. Its Livre de Poche business became quite popular, offering classics in paperback. In 1970, the company lost rights to distribute Gallimard's books. This had a negative effect on business, but did not stop the firm from introducing the Encyclopedie Generale d' Hachette in 1975. Librarie Hachette's entrance into the dictionary industry was a success and one year later, the company acquired Jean Prouvost, owner of *Tle 7 Jours* and *Paris Match*. In 1977, the company simplified its name to Hachette.

Hachette was facing increased competition in the industry. Despite its recent introduction of a massive distribution center, the company's share price had fallen into takeover range. In 1980, Jean Luc Lagardere-

The Officers

Chairman and CEO: Gerald de Roquemaurel

Chairman, Hachette Filipacchi Magazines: Daniel
    Filipacchi

President: Roger Therond

Exec. VP, Finance: Pascal Bellanger

Exec. VP, Legal: Bernard Mainfroy

gained control of the company along with Filipacchi Medias.

Market Forces Driving the Merger

By 1994, Group Lagardere was comprised of high-tech operations, automobile interests, and Hachette Filipacchi Presse, which comprised the publishing aspects of Jean Luc Lagardere's empire. Within that publishing arm stood many different subsidiaries and units including Filipacchi Medias, Hachette, HFP, and Groupe Lagardere. By combining all units into one entity, Lagardere would be able cut costs, as well as unify the media interests into the world's largest magazine and newspaper publishing group.

Approach and Engagement

According to an April 1997 article in *Mediaweek*, "shares of the French company Filipacchi fell nearly 15% last Thursday after Lagardere low-balled an offer to buy controlling interest in the company." Nevertheless, the deal went through in June 1997. Terms called for a three step process in which Hachette S.A. would acquire 39% of NEMM; Hachette S.A. would turn over its 66% control of HFP to Filipacchi Medias; and NEMM operations would meld into Filipacchi Medias, which would assume the new name of Hachette Filipacchi Medias. Lagardere remained in control of 67.4% of the new company, and Daniel Filipacchi and Frank Tenot kept a 13.1% stake. The remaining 19.4% of shares were sold to the public.

Products and Services

In 1999, Hachette Filipacchi Medias was one of the world's largest magazine and newspaper publishers. Within France, Hachette Filipacchi Medias published 48 different titles and internationally published 155 magazine titles in more than 32 different countries. In the U.S., HFM was the largest foreign magazine publisher offering 27 titles in 17 different markets, with more than 47 million readers. Titles included *Woman's Day*, *Car and Driver*, *Elle*, *George*, *Premiere*, and *Mirabella*. The company also had operations in editorial and printing logistics, advertising, electronic publishing, and film and video.

Review of the Outcome and Changes to the Industry

By unifying all publishing operations into one entity, Lagardere created the world's largest magazine and newspaper publishing company. According to *Mediaweek*, "U.S. magazine-industry watchers downplayed the significance of the merger as an internal debt restructuring."

In 1998, net income for the company was $97.2 million, an increase of 27.4%. Sales also grew 16.9%. HFM acquired Japanese publishing house Fujingaho and Italy's Rusconi in 1999, and projected sales to be FFr15 billion that year.

Research

"Hachette," in *International Directory of Company Histories*, Vol. IV, St. James Press, 1991. Covers the history of Hachette.

"Hachette Filipacchi Medias," in *Notable Corporate Chronologies*, The Gale Group, 1999. Lists major events in the history of Hachette Filipacchi Medias.

"Hachette Filipacchi Medias S.A.," in *International Directory of Company Histories*, Vol. 21, St. James Press, 1998. Covers the history of Hachette Filipacchi Medias S.A.

"Hachette Filipacchi Medias FY Sales," in *AFX News*, 11 February 1999. Lists financial results for HFM in 1998.

"Lagardere Aims to Control Hachette," in *Mediaweek*, 7 April 1997. Briefly describes Lagardere's interest in Hachette.

Lagardere Group Home Page, available at http://www.lagardere.fr/us/. Official World Wide Web Home Page for Lagardere Group. Includes historical, financial, and product information, as well as recent news articles about Lagardere and HFM.

CHRISTINA M. STANSELL

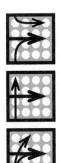

FIRST CHICAGO & NBD BANCORP

nationality: USA
date: January 1996
affected: First Chicago Corp., USA, founded 1863
affected: NBD Bancorp Inc., USA, founded 1933

Bank One Corp.
One First National Plaza
Chicago, IL 60670
USA

tel: (312)732-4000
fax: (312)732-3366
web: http://www.bankone.com

Overview of the Merger

The January 1996 merger of First Chicago Corp. and Detroit-based NBD Bancorp Inc. resulted in a new entity, First Chicago NBD Corp., the seventh-largest U.S. bank with assets of $120 billion. The $5.3 billion merger of equals was one of many significant consolidation moves in the banking industry during 1996.

History of First Chicago Corp.

A group of investors led by Edmund Aiken formed the First National Bank of Chicago to take advantage of new regulations contained in the 1863 National Banking Act. In 1882, First National opened the nation's first women's banking department. The bank survived the currency shortage of the late 1880s by importing gold from its corresponding bank in London, England. In 1899, First National established the nation's first pension plan for bank employees.

Expansion began in the early 1900s with the acquisition of Union National Bank and Metropolitan National Bank. First National opened First Trust and Savings Bank as a subsidiary serving noncommercial customers in 1903. Ten years later, the firm became a charter member of the Federal Reserve System, ranking as the third-largest foreign exchange bank in the U.S. First Trust and Savings Bank merged with Union Trust Co. to form the Union Trust and Savings Bank in 1917. The onset of the Great Depression resulted in loss of accounts, but a sound financial base kept the bank solvent throughout the ordeal. In 1931, the bank purchased Foreman State Bank.

The 1950s marked the bank's next major period of sustained growth, as First National focused on innovative business loans. In 1959, the bank opened an office in London to increase international presence and better serve global customers. Continuing its international expansion, First National launched operations in Asia by opening an office in Tokyo, Japan. In 1969, the bank reorganized, changing its name to First Chicago Corp. and making First National Bank of Chicago a principle subsidiary. Although business continued to grow, the percentage of nonperforming loans began to rise, eventually reaching a level twice the national average. Management began tightening its criteria for loan candidates, and by the end of the

The Business

Financials

Revenue (1998): $25.59 billion

Employees (1998): 91,310

SICs / NAICS

sic 6712 - Bank Holding Companies

sic 6021 - National Commercial Banks

sic 6022 - State Commercial Banks

sic 6153 - Short-Term Business Credit

naics 551111 - Offices of Bank Holding Companies

1970s, the rate of nonperforming loans dropped. Because it had increased its commitment to fixed-rate loans in 1978, the firm missed out on benefits from the dramatic rise in interest rates in 1979.

In 1983, First Chicago acquired American National Bank and Trust Co., Chicago's fifth-largest bank. Four years later, the firm bought First United Financial Services Inc., a Chicago-based bank holding company, and Beneficial National Bank USA of Wilmington, Delaware, which was renamed FCC National Bank. First National Bank of Chicago became the third-largest issuer of credit cards in the U.S. Many third world countries, including Brazil, suspended foreign loan payments that year, causing First Chicago to post losses of $587 million. In 1988, the bank increased consumer banking operations with the acquisition of Gary-Coheaton Corp., a bank holding company.

A 1990 Securities Exchange Commission (SEC) investigation of possible illegal trading activities led to the indictments of three First Chicago executives. That year, the firm developed a super-regional banking network centering on Chicago. The Internal Revenue Service demanded $133 million in back payments. Executive bonuses were suspended in 1991, and First Chicago launched a cost-cutting program that included widespread staff layoffs. CEO Barry Sullivan abruptly resigned, and Richard Thomas was named his successor.

Thomas implemented a reorganization designed to reduce the bank's percentage of non-performing loans. In 1993, the firm divested $1 billion in realty assets; purchased Lake Shore Bancorp Inc. for $304 million; and reorganized its mutual fund portfolio, reducing its range of fund options from 150 to 50.

First Chicago and Detroit-based NBD Bancorp merged to form First Chicago NBD Corp., the seventh-largest U.S. bank with assets of $120 billion, in 1996. The new firm divested its Ohio operations; formed Pegasus Funds Inc. as a subsidiary mutual fund operation; opened branch offices in Singapore and Beijing; and closed 24 Chicago-area branches and all but nine former NBD branches, laying off more than 1,700 employees. Two years later, First Chicago NBD merged with Banc One Corp., creating the second-largest credit card issuer in the U.S.

History of NBD Bancorp Inc.

The National Bank of Detroit (NBD) was founded in Detroit, Michigan, in the midst of the Great Depression, to provide banking services for those who had pulled their money from failing banks. It was capitalized equally by General Motors Corporation and the Reconstruction Finance Corp. (RFC) in 1993. Both General Motors and the RFC sold their stakes in NBD the following decade. After World War II ended, the booming automotive market allowed NBD to expand to suburban areas outside of Detroit.

In 1972, the National Detroit Corp. holding company was established. Two years later, NBD founded NBD Mortgage Co. The firm began purchasing banks in Indiana and Illinois in the 1980s. In 1981, National Detroit Corp. was renamed NBD Bancorp Inc. Via its aggressive acquisition campaign, NBD eventually became the largest banking company in Indiana and Michigan and established a strong foothold in Florida's trust market.

Both First Chicago and NBD acquired several banks during 1990-1995. The two banks merged in 1996, forming First Chicago NBD Corp., the seventh-largest U.S. bank with assets of $120 billion.

Market Forces Driving the Merger

By the 1980s, the swollen commercial banking industry was ready for consolidation. The glut of bank branches established in the U.S. during growth periods simply lacked customers. Former restrictions on cross-border acquisitions were loosened by several states in the early and mid 1980s, which spawned a consolidation flurry in the 1990s unlike anything the industry had ever experienced.

Believing that growth was a requirement in the new competitive landscape, many banks pursued a super-regional approach to consolidation in which they acquired competitors in their regions, eliminated redundancies in operations, and closed overlapping branch offices. Along with allowing banks to drastically cut costs, this type of consolidation brought with it the deeper pockets needed to implement technological advances. For example, after the $4.2 billion marriage of NCNB Corp. and C&S/Sovran Corp., which formed NationsBank Corp. in 1992, the new company was able to spend $100 million to automate many banking tasks via a new computer system. The super-regional mergers also helped prepare these banks to compete on a national scale should the federal restrictions on cross-border branching be relaxed. Other super-regional deals during the 1990s included the $4.2 billion merger between BankAmerica Corp. and Security Pacific Corp. and First Union Corp.'s $5.4 billion purchase of First Fidelity in 1995.

In 1995, the number of mergers and acquisitions in the banking industry decreased to 420, compared to 564 in 1994 and 477 in 1993. However, the collective value of the deals shot up to $73.1 billion, compared to $22.4 billion in 1994. According to a January 1996 article in *American Banker*, "with banking revenues shrinking, technology costs expanding, industry over-capacity, good asset quality and, last but hardly least, a soaring stock market, the perfect conditions were in place in 1995 for a tidal wave of consolidation." First Chicago and NBD Bancorp predicted an annual cost savings of $200 million after the elimination of redundant technologies and jobs. While NBD was looking to expand beyond its upper Midwest region, First of Chicago sought to avoid a takeover.

Approach and Engagement

In August of 1995, First Chicago and NBD Bancorp announced their $5.3 billion intent to merge. According to the terms of the agreement, stockholders of First Chicago would receive 1.81 shares of common stock of First Chicago NBD Corp. in exchange for each share of First Chicago common stock owned. After the merger of equals was finalized, First Chicago stockholders would own 50.1% of the common stock. In addition, the firms conducted a $300 million common stock buyback prior to the merger's completion.

First Chicago CEO Richard Thomas agreed to step down as CEO upon completion of the deal in exchange for keeping the bank's headquarters in Chicago. The newly merged firm was named First Chicago NBD Corp. and began operations in January of 1996.

Products and Services

In 1997, First Chicago NBD operated more than 1,400 ATM machines, 650 domestic banking offices, and 14 international offices. The firm's credit card operations were the fifth-largest in the world. When the firm merged with Bank One in 1998, products and services were reorganized into four major segments:

The Officers

Chairman: Verne G. Istock

Vice Chairman: Richard Lehmann

Vice Chairman: David Vitale

President and CEO: John B. McCoy

Chief Financial Officer: Robert Rosholt

credit cards; retail and commercial banking; investment management; and consumer finance.

Changes to the Industry

Along with fueling the continued consolidation trend in the commercial banking industry, the First Chicago/NBD deal set the stage for the $21 billion First Chicago NBD/Bank One deal in 1998. As cited in the July 1995 issue of *American Banker* by New York-based Gerard Klauer Mattison analyst George Salem, "the First Chicago deal poured gasoline on a fire that was already burning." Two months after First Chicago and NBD completed their deal, Chemical Bank and Chase Manhattan merged into an the largest bank in the U.S. with offices in 52 countries and over $300 billion in assets.

Review of the Outcome

Immediately following the merger, First Chicago NBD cut 2,000 jobs in an effort to achieve predicted annual cost savings of $200 million. The firm's performance in the year following the deal was solid: In 1996, profits jumped 25% to $1.4 billion and return on equity grew to 17%, compared to 14.5% the year prior. Analysts pointed out, however, that stock buybacks were a likely cause of the improvement. Also, credit card margins declined that year in the face of increasing competition.

By 1998, the firm had fallen to the number ten spot among U.S. banks. Needing to shore up its position once again, First Chicago NBD agreed to merge with number six Banc One Corp. to create the fifth largest bank holding company in the U.S., as well as the nation's second largest credit issuer, behind Citigroup Inc.

Research

Bank One Corp. Home Page, available at http://www.bankone.com. Official World Wide Web Home Page for Bank One Corp. Includes news, financial, product, and historical information.

"First Chicago NBD Corp.," in *Notable Corporate Chronologies*, The Gale Group, 1999. Lists major events in the history of First Chicago NBD, including its merger with Banc One Corp.

Kleege, Stephen. "Merger Frenzy Just Beginning: Chase-Chemical Deal Rumored," in *American Banker*, 14 July 1995. Discusses the impact the First Chicago NBD deal will likely have on the U.S. banking industry.

Melcher, Richard A. "Is 'Nice, Big, Dull' Good Enough?," in *Business Week*, 12 May 1997. Explains how First Chicago NBD has performed since its merger in 1996.

"U.S. Banks Get Married for Money," in *The Banker*, August 1995. Details the reasons for the consolidation flurry in 1995 in the U.S. banking industry.

JEFF ST. THOMAS

FIRST UNION & CORESTATES FINANCIAL

nationality: USA
date: April 1998
affected: First Union Corp., USA, founded 1908
affected: CoreStates Financial Corp., USA, founded 1803

First Union Corp.
One First Union Ctr.
Charlotte, NC 28288-0570
USA

tel: (704)374-6565
fax: (704)374-3425
web: http://www.firstunion.com

Overview of the Acquisition

The $16.6 billion purchase of CoreStates Financial by First Union Corp. in April of 1998 was the largest U.S. commercial banking deal to date in the industry's history. It was also considered one of the ten largest U.S. deals of the 1990s, although the slew of multibillion-dollar U.S. corporate mergers in late 1998 and 1999 may well knock it off that list. After the takeover was completed, First Union became the leading banking network on the East Coast, with roughly 2,400 units— 500 of which had belonged to CoreStates Financial—spanning 13 states.

History of First Union Corp.

In 1908, Union National Bank (UNB) was founded in Charlotte, North Carolina, by H. M. Victor. The bank's first headquarters were located in a hotel room, and initial capitalization was provided by the sale of 1,000 shares of stock at $10 per share. Business grew steadily over the next twenty years under Victor's ultraconservative direction.

UNB survived the Depression, and even benefitted from it, as many competing banks become insolvent during the decade. Business boomed during World War II due to increased wartime demand for a wide range of banking products and services. The U.S. economy continued its rapid expansion in the late 1940s. In 1947, UNB became the first Charlotte bank to open a branch office. By the end of the decade, UNB had established a reputation for innovation in provision of customer services, offering flat-fee checking accounts and charge cards.

In 1958, UNB President Carl McCraw Sr. hired C. C. Hope to manage the bank's development of branching networks through merger and acquisition. Later that year, UNB merged with First National Bank and Trust Co. of Asheville, North Carolina, to create the First Union National Bank of North Carolina (FUNBNC). In the mid-1960s, the bank diversified via its acquisition of Cameron-Brown Co., a leading mortgage banking and insurance concern in the southeastern United States. FUNBNC became one of the few U.S. banks able to offer full insurance and mortgage services to customers in all 50 states. The bank continued its aggressive

The Business

Financials

Revenue (1998): $21.54 billion

Employees (1998): 71,486

SICs / NAICS

sic 6712 - Bank Holding Companies

sic 6021 - National Commercial Banks

sic 6022 - State Commercial Banks

sic 6153 - Short-Term Business Credit

naics 551111 - Offices of Bank Holding Companies

merger and acquisition strategy, adding more than 60 local North Carolina banks to its network during the next twenty years.

In December of 1968, FUNBNC underwent a reorganization and formed First Union Corp. as its holding company. The new company was put under the chairmanship of C. C. Cameron, founder of Cameron-Brown. Assets totaled $1 billion. Five years later, Edward E. Crutchfield became president of First Union.

By 1985, assets had reached $8.2 billion. The U.S. Supreme Court approved regional interstate banking that year, and First Union began expanding its operations outside North Carolina. Crutchfield succeeded Cameron as CEO. After merging with Northwestern Financial Corp., First Union became North Carolina's second-largest bank. Over the next nine years, First Union completed 40 mergers and acquisitions of banks in North Carolina, South Carolina, Florida, Georgia, and Tennessee.

The bank issued its own proprietary mutual funds in 1986. The following year, it established a capital partners group to provide merchant banking services in the southeastern United States. First Union listed on the New York Stock Exchange in 1988. Assets exceeded $40 billion in 1990.

Rapid economic growth in the southeastern United States fueled continued growth and expansion by First Union in the early 1990s. Acquisitions in 1992 included Georgia Federal Bank, South Carolina Federal Corp., and Sailors and Merchants Bank and Trust. In 1993, First Union acquired Dominion Bankshares Corp. The bank developed a licensed sales staff to market mutual funds and established a derivatives products division to assist corporate customers

wishing to minimize the impact of interest rate fluctuations on their businesses.

In 1995, First Union acquired Coral Gables Fedcorp for $531 million; Palm Beach Investment Management Corp.; and Columbia First Bank FSB for $222 million. First Union's $5.89 billion purchase of First Fidelity Bancorp. in 1996 was one of the most expensive deals in U.S. banking history. The bank's Corporate Capital Markets Group began offering investment services that year. First Union also received federal approval to offer debt securities services. Credit card processing operations were divested.

To expand its rail car leasing operations, First Union acquired Northbrook Rail Corp. of Illinois in 1996. The bank continued its aggressive acquisition campaign with the purchases of Home Financial Corp. of Hollywood, Florida; Taylor and Clark Insurance Services Inc., a specialist in provision of business insurance policies; Keystone Investments; and Center Financial Corp. of Waterbury, Connecticut. Corporate assets reached $134 billion that year.

In 1997, First Union sold three branches and associated deposits to Consolidated Bank and Trust Company and announced plans to establish self-service banking branches. Rising delinquency rates among credit card users forced First Union to add receivables to the trust backing corporate credit card securities, leaving the company with $100 million in receivables to hold $97 million in securities. First Union became the largest bank in Virginia after it acquired Signet Banking Corp. After receiving Federal Reserve Board approval to underwrite equity deals and preferred stock, First Union diversified into securities.

Deregulation in the investment banking industry continued. In 1998, First Union strengthened its presence in the consumer finance market via its $16.6 billion purchase of CoreStates Financial Corp. The bank also diversified into home equity lending when it acquired the Money Store.

History of CoreStates Financial Corp.

In 1803, George Clymer established the Philadelphia Bank. The state-chartered bank was renamed Philadelphia National Bank (PNB) after it secured a national charter in 1864. A series of mergers in the mid-1920s left PNB securely atop its perch as the leading bank in Philadelphia. In 1926, the number three and number four banks in the city merged to form Franklin-Fourth Street National Bank, which pushed Girard National Bank out of the number two bank spot. That year, number one PBN and number three Girard National Bank also merged. In 1928, PNB took over Franklin-Fourth Street National Bank.

The bank diversified into the retail banking and trust sectors in 1951 when it purchased Ninth Bank and Trust Co. Two years later, PNB extended its reach outside county lines for the first time. Aggressive growth via acquisition continued, including the 1995 merger with First Philadelphia Banking and Trust. That year, PNB became the first bank in Philadelphia to exceed $1 billion in assets. The Bank Holding Act of 1956 granted bank holding companies permission to own more than one bank and to diversify into non-banking industries. The Act prompted PNB to move into commercial finance, international investing, and eventually credit card services.

ATM services were first offered to customers in the early 1970s via PNB's Money Access Services unit. Despite the firm's rapid growth and diverse holdings, earnings in the late 1970s faltered. This poor performance led to a restructuring in 1981, and PNB conducted several other reorganizations throughout the decade. In 1986, the bank made its first out-of-state foray when it moved into the New Jersey market.

Terrence Larson took over as chairman in 1988. He led PNB's 1990 purchase of First Pennsylvania Corp. To better reflects its diverse holdings, PNB changed its name to CoreStates Financial Corp. that year. After a few acquisitions proved difficult to integrate, CoreStates initiated a restructuring in 1994. Bank of Boston and CoreStates agreed to join forces in 1995, but the merger later crumbled. The following year, CoreStates upped its assets by a whopping 50% when it acquired Meridian Bancorp. In 1997, authorities discovered that a unit of Meridian had been embroiled in a "yield burning" tax evasion scandal; although no fines were levied while the IRS examined its rules regarding yield burning, CoreStates began preparations for possible back tax payments.

The bank opened a branch in Seoul that year and refused a takeover bid from Mellon Bank for $18 billion. The following year, however, CoreStates accepted First Union's $16.6 billion bid. The deal was completed in April.

Market Forces Driving the Acquisition

By the 1980s, the distended U.S. commercial banking industry was poised for consolidation. The excess of bank branches established in the U.S. during growth periods simply lacked customers. Former restrictions on cross-border acquisitions were loosened by several states in the early and mid 1980s, which spawned a consolidation flurry in the 1990s unlike anything the industry had ever experienced.

Believing that growth was a requirement in the new competitive landscape, many banks pursued a super-regional approach to consolidation in which

The Officers

Chairman and CEO: Edward E. Crutchfield

Vice Chairman: B.J. Walker

Vice Chairman: Charles L. Coltman

Vice Chairman: G. Kennedy Thompson

President and Chief Operating Officer: John R. Georgius

they acquired competitors in their regions, eliminated redundancies in operations, and closed overlapping branch offices. Along with allowing banks to drastically cut costs, this type of consolidation brought with it the deeper pockets needed to implement technological advances. For example, after the $4.2 billion marriage of NCNB Corp. and C&S/Sovran Corp., which formed NationsBank Corp. in 1992, the new company was able to spend $100 million to automate many banking tasks via a new computer system. Similar deals during the mid-1990s included the $10 billion merger of Chemical Banking Corp. and The Chase Manhattan Corp. in 1996; First Union's $5.4 billion purchase of First Fidelity in 1996, which gave First Union a solid footing in the Northeastern U.S.; and the $14.8 billion deal between NationsBank and Barnett Banks in 1997.

According to Bruce Wasserstein, author of *Big Deal, the Battle for Control of America's Leading Corporations*, "by developing wide branch networks, these super-regionals hoped to position themselves to become national banks. They essentially were gambling that federal bank regulations would be revised to allow cross-border branching. In that event, the super-regionals would be able to leverage their existing retail and wholesale operations across a far larger group of potential customers."

In particular, First Union wanted access to Core States strong presence along the East Coast, as well as its international network. The deal would bolster First Union's already strong regional presence by giving the firm an "unbroken crescent of territory from Connecticut to Florida," according to a December 1997 *Business Week* article, as well as offering the bank its first noteworthy international inroad.

Approach and Engagement

First Union and CoreStates Financial announced their $16.6 billion deal in November of 1997. The price offered by First Union was 5.3 times higher than the book value of CoreStates. Community activists protested the merger on the grounds that it would be

The Players

Chairman and CEO of First Union Corp.: Edward E. Crutchfield. In 1983, Edward Crutchfield became president of First Union. At 32 years of age, he was the youngest president of a major U.S. banking company. Two years later Crutchfield succeeded Cameron as CEO. He steered the acquisition of more than 70 banks over the next 13 years, overseeing his largest deal to date when First Union took over CoreStates Financial Corp. in 1998. Crutchfield retained his top spot after the purchase was completed.

Chairman of CoreStates Financial Corp.: Terrence A. Larson. Long-time CoreStates executive Terrence Larson was appointed chairman of the firm in 1988. Ten years later, when First Union took over CoreStates Financial in April of 1998, Larson took on the roles of vice chairman and head of the First Union's global banking operations. A month later, however, he announced his resignation, effective July 1, 1998. Larson was succeeded by Charles L. Coltman.

unfriendly to lower-income residents in Philadelphia. In response, First Union promised to increase small business and low- and middle-income consumer lending in Philadelphia to the tune of $13 billion. The bank also agreed to create a $1 million charitable foundation and to set aside $40 million for job training and $209 million for severance packages for laid-off employees. Shareholders of both banks approved the takeover in March of 1998.

Pennsylvania Senator Arlen Specter also criticized the deal and began routing legislation designed to curtail banking megamergers and limit post-merger layoffs and branch closings. He dropped his bill on April 13, 1998, after it garnered little support. The First Union/CoreStates Financial transaction was finalized later that month. First Union CEO Crutchfield continued to head up the bank; CoreStates Financial CEO Larson took over global banking operations and began serving as vice chairman. International expansion responsibilities were given to veteran CoreStates Financial executive Michael P. Heavener.

Products and Services

After its purchase of CoreStates Financial was completed, First Union became the leading banking network on the East Coast, with roughly 2,400 units,

500 of which had belonged to CoreStates Financial. Operations spanned 13 states, customers numbered 16 million, and ATMs totaled 3,400.

Traditional banking services included savings and checking accounts, mortgages, consumer loans, and commercial banking services for small- and medium-sized companies. Investment banking services, including mutual funds and investment advice, were offered through the Wheat First Securities unit. Brokerage services were housed in First Union Brokerage Services Inc. First Union also provided corporate financing, such as debt underwriting and asset financing, to clients.

Changes to the Industry

First Union became the sixth largest bank in the U.S. with $237 billion in assets when its purchase of CoreStates Financial was completed. Its deal was overshadowed by the largest merger in U.S. banking history—the $41.5 billion marriage of NationsBank and California-based Bank-America in late 1998. In early 1999, First Union CEO Crutchfield expressed his intent to follow suit and pursue westward expansion.

Review of the Outcome

Once the purchase was completed, First Union laid off 7,300 employees and closed 150 branch offices. Many customers complained about longer lines and increased banking fees. In November of 1998, First Union completed its conversion of the 400-plus CoreState Financial systems without any major glitches. The bank announced its intent to cut its work force by another 7% in 1999; in the first quarter of that year, another 5,850 jobs were eliminated.

Research

"Anti-Megadeal Bill Elicited Big Ho-Hum, Sponsor Says," in *American Banker*, 20 April 1998. Discusses the anti-merger legislation forwarded by Pennsylvania Senator Arlen Specter, including his decision to drop the bill.

Chase, Brett. "First Union Promotes Exec to Fill Void Left By Larsen," in *American Banker*, 12 May 1998. Explains why former CoreStates Financial chairman Terrence Larsen decided to leave First Union.

First Union Corp. Home Page, available at http://www.firstunion.com. Official World Wide Web Home Page for First Union Home Page Corp. Includes news, financial, product, and historical information.

"First Union Corp.," in *Notable Corporate Chronologies*, The Gale Group, 1999. Lists major events in the history of First Union Corp.

Greising, David. "You Paid How Much For That Bank?" in *Business Week*, 1 December 1997. Explains why First Union was willing to pay a high price for CoreStates Financial.

Kraus, James. "1st Union Ready to Flex CoreStates' Global Muscle," in *American Banker*, 12 May 1998. Details how First Union is planning to capitalize on CoreStates's international presence.

Wasserstein, Bruce. *Big Deal: The Battle for Control of America's Leading Corporations*, Warner Books, 1998. Offers an overview of the largest mergers in recent American corporate history.

JEFF ST. THOMAS

FIRST UNION & FIRST FIDELITY

First Union Corp.
One First Union Ctr.
Charlotte, NC 28288-0570
USA

tel: (704)374-6565
fax: (704)374-3425
web: http://www.firstunion.com

nationality: USA
date: January 1996
affected: First Union Corp., USA, founded 1908
affected: First Fidelity Bancorp., USA, founded 1812

Overview of the Acquisition

In January of 1996, North Carolina-based First Union bought New Jersey-based First Fidelity, one of the largest U.S. East Coast banks, with $38 million in assets. The $5.6 billion price was the largest in the banking industry to date. The deal transformed First Union—the ninth largest bank holding company in the U.S., with assets of $87 billion—into a $125 billion bank, the sixth-largest in the U.S. and the leading East Coast financial institution. Many analysts saw this acquisition as a precursor to the deluge of multibillion deals that took place in the U.S. banking industry during the late 1990s.

History of First Union Corp.

In 1908, Union National Bank (UNB) was founded in Charlotte, North Carolina, by H. M. Victor. The bank's first headquarters were located in a hotel room, and initial capitalization was provided by the sale of 1,000 shares of stock at $10 per share. Business grew steadily over the next twenty years under Victor's ultraconservative direction.

UNB survived the Depression, and even benefitted from it, as many competing banks become insolvent during the decade. Business boomed during World War II due to increased wartime demand for a wide range of banking products and services. The U.S. economy continued its rapid expansion in the late 1940s. In 1947, UNB became the first Charlotte bank to open a branch office. By the end of the decade, UNB had established a reputation for innovation in provision of customer services, offering flat-fee checking accounts and charge cards.

In 1958, UNB President Carl McCraw Sr. hired C. C. Hope to manage the bank's development of branching networks through merger and acquisition. Later that year, UNB merged with First National Bank and Trust Co. of Asheville, North Carolina, to create the First Union National Bank of North Carolina (FUNBNC). In the mid-1960s, the bank diversified via its acquisition of Cameron-Brown Co., a leading mortgage banking and insurance concern in the southeastern United States. FUNBNC became one of the few U.S. banks able to offer full insurance and mortgage services to customers in all 50 states. The bank continued its aggressive merger and acquisition strategy, adding more than 60 local North Carolina banks to its network during the next twenty years.

In December of 1968, FUNBNC underwent a reorganization and formed First Union Corp. as its holding company. The new company was put under the chairmanship of C. C. Cameron, founder of Cameron-Brown. Assets totaled $1 billion. Five years later, Edward E. Crutchfield became president of First Union.

By 1985, assets had reached $8.2 billion. The U.S. Supreme Court approved regional interstate banking that year, and First Union began expanding its operations outside North Carolina. Crutchfield succeeded Cameron as CEO. After merging with Northwestern Financial Corp., First Union became North Carolina's second-largest bank. Over the next nine years, First Union completed 40 mergers and acquisitions of banks in North Carolina, South Carolina, Florida, Georgia, and Tennessee.

The bank issued its own proprietary mutual funds in 1986. The following year, it established a capital partners group to provide merchant banking services in the southeastern United States. First Union listed on the New York Stock Exchange in 1988. Assets exceeded $40 billion in 1990.

Rapid economic growth in the southeastern United States fueled continued growth and expansion by First Union in the early 1990s. Acquisitions in 1992 included Georgia Federal Bank, South Carolina Federal Corp., and Sailors and Merchants Bank and Trust. In 1993, First Union acquired Dominion Bankshares Corp. The bank developed a licensed sales staff to market mutual funds and established a derivatives products division to assist corporate customers wishing to minimize the impact of interest rate fluctuations on their businesses.

In 1995, First Union acquired Coral Gables Fedcorp for $531 million; Palm Beach Investment Management Corp.; and Columbia First Bank FSB for $222 million. First Union's $5.6 billion purchase of First Fidelity Bancorp. was one of the most expensive in U.S. banking history. The bank's Corporate Capital Markets Group began offering investment services that year. First Union also received federal approval to offer debt securities services. Credit card processing operations were divested.

To expand its rail car leasing operations, First Union acquired Northbrook Rail Corp. of Illinois in 1996. The bank continued its aggressive acquisition campaign with the purchases of Home Financial Corp. of Hollywood, Florida; Taylor and Clark Insurance Services Inc., a specialist in provision of business

The Business

Financials

Revenue (1998): $21.54 billion

Employees (1998): 71,486

SICs / NAICS

sic 6712 - Bank Holding Companies

sic 6021 - National Commercial Banks

sic 6022 - State Commercial Banks

sic 6153 - Short-Term Business Credit

naics 551111 - Offices of Bank Holding Companies

insurance policies; Keystone Investments; and Center Financial Corp. of Waterbury, Connecticut. Corporate assets reached $134 billion that year.

In 1997, First Union sold three branches and associated deposits to Consolidated Bank and Trust Company and announced plans to establish self-service banking branches. Rising delinquency rates among credit card users forced First Union to add receivables to the trust backing corporate credit card securities, leaving the company with $100 million in receivables to hold $97 million in securities. First Union became the largest bank in Virginia after it acquired Signet Banking Corp. After receiving Federal Reserve Board approval to underwrite equity deals and preferred stock, First Union diversified into securities.

Deregulation in the investment banking industry continued. In 1998, First Union strengthened its presence in the consumer finance market via its $16.6 billion purchase of CoreStates Financial Corp. The bank also diversified into home equity lending when it acquired the Money Store.

History of First Fidelity Bancorp.

In 1812, the State Bank of Newark opened for business, with William Pennington as its first president. The bank prospered during the Civil War, and in 1865, it was granted a national charter and renamed The National State Bank of Newark. By the early 1900s, assets had reached $3.9 million. The bank remained virtually unaffected by the stock market crash; by 1948, assets had grown to over $80 million.

In 1950, National State merged with Orange First National and U.S. Trust Co., becoming one of the largest banks in the state, with assets of over $168 mil-

The Officers

Chairman and CEO: Edward E. Crutchfield

Vice Chairman: B.J. Walker

Vice Chairman: Charles L. Coltman

Vice Chairman: G. Kennedy Thompson

President and Chief Operating Officer: John R. Georgius

lion. Five years later, Lincoln National Bank consolidated with National State. In 1958, the bank purchased Federal Trust Co. By the decade's end, combined assets exceeded $418 million and National State was New Jersey's second largest bank.

The bank formed a parent company, First National State Bancorp., in 1969. In 1984, the largest merger in the banking industry to date brought together Fidelity Union Bancorp. with First National to create First National State Bancorp. with assets of $10 billion. The following year, the newly merged company was renamed First Fidelity Bancorp.

Growth continued with the purchase of Morris County Savings Bank in 1987. Due to major acquisitions—including the purchase of Fidelcor, Inc. in 1988—and a corporate reorganization, First Fidelity had become one of the 25 largest banking companies in the U.S. by 1989. However, the bank hadn't fully integrated its operations, which prompted a government investigation of First Fidelity's asset quality and Wall Street speculation about a potential buyout. In 1990, Anthony Terracciano was named president, CEO, and chairman. In an effort to improve performance, he reduced the workforce by 20%, eliminating 6,000 jobs, and outsourced the bank's data and system functions.

In 1991, Banco de Santander, based in Spain, bought 14% of First Fidelity. The added capital staved off hostile takeover bids for a few years, but First Fidelity recognized its vulnerability and agreed to merge with First Union in 1995. The $5.6 billion takeover was completed in January of 1996.

Market Forces Driving the Acquisition

According to Bruce Wasserstein, author of *Big Deal, the Battle for Control of America's Leading Corporations*, the banking industry's consolidation in the mid-1990s readied banks for possible future deregulation. "By developing wide branch networks, these super-regionals hoped to position themselves to become national banks. They essentially were gam-

bling that federal bank regulations would be revised to allow cross-border branching. In that event, the super-regionals would be able to leverage their existing retail and wholesale operations across a far larger group of potential customers." For example, BankAmerica had ventured east for the first time in 1994 when it spent $1.9 billion to acquire Continental Bank of Illinois. Similarly, acquiring First Fidelity would give First Union access to the lucrative East Coast market.

Many banks also pursued a super-regional approach to consolidation in which they acquired competitors in their regions, eliminated redundancies in operations, and closed overlapping branch offices. These mergers quite often allowed banks to slash expenses. In contrast, however, First Union wasn't looking to cut costs by purchasing First Fidelity. The takeover was more likely to result in increased revenues for First Union, which operated mainly in the southeastern U.S., because it would gain a solid footing a new market. Since overlap in the operations of First Union and First Fidelity was nearly nonexistent, the branch closings and layoffs typical of banking mergers in the 1990s would not occur as a result of the deal.

Approach and Engagement

On June 18, 1995, First Union and First Fidelity announced their intent to join forces. First Union intended to take an earnings charge of $140 million, roughly 50 cents per share, to offset integration costs related to the acquisition. That amount was later upped to $270 million, or 97 cents a share.

The Neighborhood Assistance Corporation of America challenged the deal, claiming First Union had violated the Community Reinvestment Act by keeping activists from taking part in the shareholders' meeting on October 3rd, when the deal was approved. Later in the month, the Federal Reserve board rejected the suit and gave First Union and First Fidelity the nod. The $5.6 billion deal was finalized on January 1, 1998. First Union CEO Crutchfield held his top spot, while First Fidelity CEO Terracciano became president.

Products and Services

After its 1996 purchase of First Fidelity was completed, First Union became the leading banking network on the East Coast with 10 million customers in 13 states. Two years later, after the bank had purchased CoreStates Financial, operations grew to roughly 2,400 units spanning 13 states; customers numbered 16 million and ATMs totaled 3,400.

Traditional banking services included savings and checking accounts, mortgages, consumer loans, and commercial banking services for small- and medium-sized companies. Investment banking services, including mutual funds and investment advice, were offered through the Wheat First Securities unit. Brokerage services were housed in First Union Brokerage Services Inc. First Union also provided corporate financing, such as debt underwriting and asset financing, to clients.

Changes to the Industry

When the deal was completed, First Union, with assets of $125 billion, became the sixth-largest bank in the U.S. and the leading East Coast financial institution. Many analysts saw the acquisition as a precursor to several major deals within First Union's regional. Analysts attributed the merger of UJB Financial Corp. and Summit Bancorp, which created the largest bank in New Jersey, to the First Fidelity takeover. The First Union/First Fidelity deal was also at least partly responsible for the CoreStates Financial/Meridian Bancorp hookup and Fleet Financial Group's acquisition of Natwest Bank N.A. In addition, the banking climate, particularly in New Jersey, became more competitive. According to a January 1997 article in *American Banker*, First Union moved into the state with its marketing guns drawn, and competitors were forced to intensify their own marketing efforts to retain customers.

The merger was also a factor in the deluge of multibillion banking deals that took place across the U.S. during the late 1990s. For example, the $10 billion merger of Chemical Banking Corp. and industry leader Chase Manhattan Corp. was completed two months after First Union's takeover of First Fidelity. In 1997, NationsBank Corp. and Barnett Banks, Inc. completed their landmark $14.8 billion deal to become the third-largest U.S. bank. Not to be outdone, First Union was back on the acquisition trail in 1998. It completed a $16.6 billion purchase of CoreStates Financial in April 1998 to shore up its position on the Eastern Seaboard, strengthen its sixth-place status, and gain access to CoreStates international assets.

Review of the Outcome

The purchase gave First Union a leading position in the East Coast, a market it had yet to tap. The layoffs and branch closings typical of banking mergers didn't happen because the two firms had virtually no geographic overlap prior to the merger. Upon completion of the deal, Standard & Poor's raised First Union's long-term senior debt rating from A2 to A1 and its long-term subordinated debt rating from A3 to

The Players

Chairman and CEO of First Union Corp.: Edward E. Crutchfield. In 1983, Edward Crutchfield became president of First Union. At 32 years of age, he was the youngest president of a major U.S. banking company. Two years later Crutchfield succeeded Cameron as corporate CEO. He steered the acquisition of more than 70 banks over the next 13 years, overseeing his largest deal to date when First Union took over CoreStates Financial Corp. in 1998. Crutchfield retained his top spot after the purchase was completed.

Chairman of First Fidelity Bancorp.: Anthony P. Terracciano. Anthony Terracciano launched his career in banking when he accepted a position at Chase Manhattan Bank in 1964. Terracciano's 23-year tenure at Chase Manhattan culminated in the vice chairmanship. He joined Mellon Bank in 1987 as president and chief operating officer. Three years later, Terracciano left Mellon to accept the top spot at First Fidelity, where he was named president, CEO, and chairman of the struggling firm. He is credited for transforming the $700 million bank into a $5.4 billion powerhouse via an aggressive acquisition campaign during the early 1990s. When First Union bought out First Fidelity in 1996, Terracciano accepted the post of president at First Union. In December of 1997, he retired.

A2. In October of 1996, the bank announced plans to spend $24 million over the next year to refurbish or replace the outdated infrastructure of First Fidelity.

Research

Blanden, Michael. "A State of Merger Mania," in *The Banker*, October 1997. Offers an in-depth look at the consolidation activity in the U.S. banking industry during the mid-1990s.

Cline, Kenneth. "Merging the 'Firsts': Deal Depends on Revenue Growth," in *American Banker*, 28 March 1996. Explains how the First Union/First Fidelity deal differs from most other mergers in the banking industry during the mid-1990s.

First Union Corp. Home Page, available at http://www.firstunion.com. Official World Wide Web Home Page for First Union Home Page Corp. Includes news, financial, product, and historical information.

"First Union Corp.," in *Notable Corporate Chronologies*, The Gale Group, 1999. Lists major events in the history of First Union Corp.

Mastrull, Diane. "How Long Will Terracciano Stay at First Union?" in *Philadelphia Business Journal*, 23 June 1995. Explains the roles of the top executives at First Union following its takeover of First Fidelity, including former First Fidelity CEO Anthony Terracciano.

Matthews, Gordon. "First Union Doubles Charge It Will Take For First Fidelity Acquisition," in *American Banker*, 31 August 1995. Discusses the increased charge First Union took against earnings for its purchase of First Fidelity.

Seiberg, Jaret. "Activists Sue to Block First Union Acquisition of First Fidelity," in *American Banker*, 26 October 1995.

Details the lawsuit filed by Neighborhood Assistance Corporation of America to block the takeover.

———. "Fed Approves 1st Union's Acquisition of 1st Fidelity," in *American Banker*, 27 October 1995. Announces the Federal Reserve Board's approval for First Union's takeover of First Fidelity.

Stoneman, Bill. "Aggressive 1st Union Setting the Tone in New Jersey," in *American Banker*, 30 October 1997. Explains the impact the merger between First Union and First Fidelity had on the banking industry in New Jersey.

ANNAMARIE L. SHELDON

FLEET FINANCIAL GROUP & NATIONAL WESTMINSTER BANCORP

nationality: USA
date: May 1, 1996
affected: Fleet Financial Group, Inc., USA, founded 1791
affected: National Westminster Bancorp (U.S. subsidiary of National Westminster Bank PLC, United Kingdom, founded 1829)

National Westminster Bancorp
One Federal St.
Boston, MA 02110-2010
USA

tel: (617)346-4000
fax: (617)346-0464
web: http://www.fleet.com

Overview of the Acquisition

In May of 1996, Fleet Financial Group, the eleventh-largest bank holding company in the U.S., acquired New Jersey-based National Westminster Bancorp from National Westminster Bank PLC of London, England, for $3.26 billion to become the eighth-largest bank in the U.S. The deal left Fleet with assets of $88 billion and 1,200 branches serving roughly four million households across seven states, from New Jersey to Maine.

History of Fleet Financial Group, Inc.

In 1791, Providence Bank was established in Rhode Island by shipping merchant and former Congressional representative John Brown. Twelve years later, Elkanah Watson, previously an apprentice in the shipping business under John Brown, received a charter for his own financial institution, the State Bank of Albany. In 1886, Samuel Pomeroy Colt, son of the inventor of the Colt revolver, received a charter for the Industrial Trust Co., another predecessor of Fleet Financial. In an acquisition spree that lasted over 20 years, Industrial Trust purchased 29 smaller banks throughout Providence, Rhode Island.

Providence National and Merchants National Bank, the largest bank in Rhode Island, merged in 1926. Roughly 25 years later, Providence National and Union Trust Co., another major Providence-based bank, merged to form Providence Union National Bank and Trust Co. In 1954, Providence Union National and Industrial Trust consolidated operations as Industrial National Bank, still under the original Providence Bank's charter.

On September 18, 1968, Industrial National formed its own holding company, Industrial Bancorp. In this way, Industrial National was able to skirt the regulatory restrictions of the Bank Holding Company Act that would have prevented Industrial National from conducting a range of nonbank financial services. That year, Industrial Bancorp gained a listing on the New York Stock Exchange. Industrial Bancorp changed its name to the Industrial National Corp. in 1970.

The Business

Financials

Revenue (1998): $10 billion

Employees (1998): 36,000

SICs / NAICS

sic 6712 - Bank Holding Companies

sic 6021 - National Commercial Banks

naics 551111 - Offices of Bank Holding Companies

The State Bank of Albany merged with the Liberty National Bank of Buffalo to form the United Bank Corporation of New York (UBNY), a holding company, in 1972. UBNY changed its name to Norstar Bancorp in the early 1980s, around roughly the same time it acquired Northeast Bankshare Association of Maine in the first instance of an interstate bank merger in the U.S. Industrial National changed its name to Fleet Financial Group, and, in 1986, Fleet and Norstar began merger negotiations. On January 1, 1988, the two firms merged, in a $1.3 billion deal, to form Fleet/Norstar Financial Group, Inc. The new company operated nearly 1,000 offices in 40 states.

In 1990, the Federal Deposit Insurance Corp. (FDIC) was eager to dump the Bank of New England (BNE) and its billions of dollars in bad debt. Kohlberg Kravis Roberts (KKR) and Fleet/Norstar joined forces to make an offer, but they battled over the terms of their $625 million bid for BNE until five minutes before the FDIC's deadline. Their bid was accepted, to the amazement of most financial experts, and KKR gained a 15.7% share of Fleet/Norstar's non-voting stock. By acquiring BNE's $15 billion in assets and extensive retail branch network, Fleet/Norstar surpassed Bank of Boston as New England's largest bank. Consolidation resulted in the firing of nearly half of BNE's 11,000 employees. In 1991, Fleet/Norstar formed RECOLL Management Corp. as a wholly owned subsidiary to manage, collect, and liquidate part of the pool of assets acquired by the FDIC from failed banks.

Fleet/Norstar reverted to its old name, Fleet Financial Group, in 1992. Two years later, the firm agreed to a $5.95 million settlement of a class-action lawsuit alleging that the bank used unfair lending practices. Fleet acquired New Bedford Institution for Savings (NBIS) in November of 1995. The company also merged with Shawmut National Corp. in a $3.7

billion deal that boosted its assets to $81 billion, making Fleet the 10th-largest bank in the U.S.

The U.S. Labor Department filed an administrative complaint against Fleet in 1996, accusing the company of firing manager David Conners, who cooperated with the Labor Department in its investigation of Fleet's hiring and promotion practices and lending policies to minorities. Later confronted by allegations of charging black and Hispanic customers exorbitant fees, Fleet agreed to pay $4 million in a settlement with the Justice Department. Although Fleet denied that any discrimination took place, the firm also proposed the development of a diversity program. In May of that year, Fleet acquired U.S.-based National Westminster Bancorp for $3.26 billion to become the eighth largest bank in the U.S.

Acquisitions in the late 1990s included mutual fund manager Columbia Management, discounter brokerage Quick & Reilly, Merrill Lynch Specialists, the U.S. business credit operations of Sanwa Bank, and the credit card operations of Household International, Crestar Financial, and Advanta. In 1999, Fleet announced its intent to merge with BankBoston.

History of National Westminster Bancorp

The earliest predecessor to National Westminster Bank PLC, the parent company of National Westminter Bancorp, was Manchester and Liverpool District Banking Co. (which later became District Bank), first established in 1829. Four years later, National Provincial Bank was organized as a joint-stock company. At that time, the Bank of England was the exclusive bank note issuer for the London area. Although National Provincial's administrative offices were in London, management decided to open its branches outside the 65-mile radius, so the bank could issue its own notes. It wasn't until 1866 that National Provincial finally opened a London banking office, recognizing that a presence in the world's financial capital was worth sacrificing its note-issuing privilege.

By 1835, National Provincial had opened its first branch, in Gloucester, and District Bank had established 17 new branches. That year, London and Westminster Bank was formed as the first joint stock bank in London and the first bank established under the Bank Charter Act of 1833. In 1847, London and Westminster made its first acquisition when it bought Young & Son; the firm later merged with both Commercial Bank of London and Middlesex Bank and bought Unity Joint-Stock Bank.

In 1885, District Bank opened an office in London. By the turn of the century, National Provincial operated roughly 250 offices in England. To compete with regional banks like Lloyds and Midland, London and Westminster merged with London and County Bank, to form London County and Westminster Bank. In 1913, London County and Westminster acquired the Ulster Bank, which had 170 branches throughout Ireland. Five years later, London County and Westminster became London, County, Westminster & Parrs, the fifth largest bank in England, after acquiring Parr's Bank and its 320 offices throughout England. London, County, Westminster & Parrs changed its name to Westminster Bank Ltd. in 1923. During the early 1920s, District Bank opened 130 new branches, and National Provincial acquired several banks: Sheffield Banking Co., Northamptonshire Union Bank, Guernsey Banking Co., Coutts & Co., and Bradford District Bank.

District Bank merged with the County Bank, a Manchester-based firm in 1935, initiating its nationwide expansion. In 1958, National Provincial acquired North Central Finance. A decade later, District Bank, National Provincial Bank, and Westminster Bank merged to form National Westminster Bank Ltd. (NatWest). The new company moved into the U.S. for the first time in 1977 with its purchase of National Bank of North America in New York. In 1982, NatWest became a public limited company (PLC). Five years later, NatWest expanded its American subsidiary, NatWest USA, with the acquisition of First Jersey National Bank.

County NatWest, the bank's investment banking subsidiary, underwrote a stock offering for Blue Arrow PLC, an employment agency. When the stock offering faltered and County NatWest was left with 13.5% of Blue Arrow, the bank concealed its stake by dividing it among itself, its own marketing arm (County NatWest Securities), and Union Bank of Switzerland. An investigation by the Department of Trade and Insurance (DTI) of the role played by County NatWest in the Blue Arrow acquisition found that County NatWest had violated a law requiring a timely report of holdings greater than 5% and that the company's secrecy had deceived both regulators and financial markets about Blue Arrow's true stock value. Several senior executives resigned.

In 1989, NatWest USA acquired another New Jersey-based bank, Ultra Bancorp, gaining 285 branches in the northeastern U.S. and $20 million in assets. U.S. holdings continued to grow with the $500 million purchase of Citizens First Bancorp., a 50-branch New Jersey bank, in 1994. Two years later, Fleet Financial Group acquired NatWest's U.S. assets—by then named National Westminster Bancorp—for $3.26 billion.

The Officers

Chairman and CEO: Terrence Murray

President and Chief Operating Officer: Robert Higgins

Vice Chairman and Chief Financial Officer: Eugene M. McQuade

Vice Chairman and Chief Technical Officer: Michael R. Zucchini

Vice Chairman and Chief Administrative Officer: H. Jay Sarles

Market Forces Driving the Acquisition

Widespread consolidation in the U.S. banking industry during the mid-1990s had at its core the belief that industry deregulation was imminent. Bruce Wasserstein, author of *Big Deal: The Battle for Control of America's Leading Corporations* wrote, "By developing wide branch networks, these super-regionals hoped to position themselves to become national banks. They essentially were gambling that federal bank regulations would be revised to allow cross-border branching. In that event, the super-regionals would be able to leverage their existing retail and wholesale operations across a far larger group of potential customers." For example, BankAmerica moved east of the Mississippi for the first time in 1994 when it spent $1.9 billion to acquire Continental Bank of Illinois. Similarly, First Union bought First Fidelity for $5.6 billion in early 1996 to gain access to the lucrative East Coast market and became the sixth-largest bank in the U.S. and the leading East Coast financial institution.

Many analysts saw the First Union/First Fidelity marriage as the forerunner to several major deals, including the UJB Financial Corp. and Summit Bancorp merger, which created the largest bank in New Jersey; the CoreStates Financial Corp. and Meridian Bancorp hookup; and Fleet Financial Group's acquisition of National Westminster Bancorp. Fleet, which had been pursuing acquisitions aggressively and had just paid $3.4 billion for Shawmut National Bank, found National Westminster's position in the lucrative New York and New Jersey markets appealing. The recent penetration of the New England states by the industry's leading players had put pressure on New England-based banks like Fleet to continue growing or run the risk of being swallowed. Because parent company NatWest was eager to unload its U.S. operations, the price was right for Fleet also. NatWest had realized that remaining a force in the North American market would require hefty investments; as a result, in September of 1995,

The Players

Chairman and CEO of Fleet Financial Group, Inc.: Terrence Murray. Terrence Murray became CEO of Fleet in 1982. He spearheaded the bank's aggressive expansion program over the next several years, including the 1983 purchase of Credico and the 1996 acquisition of National Westminster Bancorp.

NatWest put its U.S. operations on the block. When Fleet offered $3.26 billion, slightly more than book value (compared to the two times book value prices of most other major deals), NatWest accepted.

Approach and Engagement

In December of 1995, Fleet Financial announced its intent to pay $3.26 billion in cash and securities for National Westminster Bancorp, the U.S. unit of National Westminster Bank PLC. The Federal Reserve Board and Office of the Comptroller of the Currency both granted their approval of the deal on April 15, 1996. The transaction was completed on May 1, 1996, when Fleet made a $2.7 billion cash payment to National Westminster. According to the terms of the agreement, additional annual payments—up to $560 million over eight years—would be based upon the earnings of National Westminster Bancorp.

Products and Services

When the deal was completed, Fleet Financial served nearly 6.2 million households through its 1,200 branches and 2,000 ATM machines in Connecticut, Maine, Massachusetts, New Hampshire, New Jersey, New York, and Rhode Island. Commercial customers totaled 40,000. Along with commercial and consumer banking services, Fleet offered mortgage banking, government banking, asset-based lending, equipment leasing, investment management services, and student loan processing.

In 1998, loan interest and fees accounted for 59% of total sales. Non-loan interest secured 9%; investment services, 8%; commissions, 7%; processing, 5%; capital markets, 5%; and credit cards, 4%. Total assets exceeded $20 billion.

Changes to the Industry

The merger helped fuel continued consolidation in the banking industry across the U.S. during the late 1990s. For example, in 1997, NationsBank Corp. and Barnett Banks, Inc. completed a $14.8 billion merger, becoming the third-largest bank in the U.S. The following year, First Union completed a $16.6 billion purchase of CoreStates Financial to shore up its position on the Eastern Seaboard, strengthen its sixth-place status, and gain access to CoreStates international assets. Not to be outdone, Fleet announced its intent to merge with BankBoston Corp. in 1999 as a means of regaining its spot as the eighth-largest U.S. bank.

Review of the Outcome

In the first year following the merger, Fleet was criticized for not generating profits quickly enough from its merger with National Westminster Bancorp, as well as it previous merger with Shawmut National Corp. However, the firm's performance had improved by 1997. Citing cost cuts as a major factor—which produced a savings of $700 million, $100 million more than first estimated—Fleet posted a net income of $328 million in the second quarter of 1997, a 17% increase from the past year.

Research

Dugas, Christine. "Fleet Deposits NatWest into Fold," in USA Today, 20 December 1995. Explains why Fleet wants to buy the U.S. NatWest operations.

"Fleet and National Westminster Receive All Regulatory Approvals on Merger," in PR Newswire, 15 April 1996. Describes the terms of the agreement between Fleet and NatWest.

"Fleet Financial Group Completes Purchase of Natwest Bank N.A.," in PR Newswire, 1 May 1996. Covers the completion of the deal between Fleet and NatWest.

Fleet Financial Group, Inc. Home Page, available at http://www.fleet.com. Official World Wide Web Home Page for Fleet Financial Group, Inc. Includes news, financial, product, and historical information.

"Fleet Financial Group, Inc.," in Notable Corporate Chronologies, The Gale Group, 1999. Lists major events in the history of Fleet Financial Group, Inc.

"Fleet Profits Balloon 17% After Mergers; B of A Up 11%," in American Banker, 17 July 1997. Details Fleet's performance since the merger.

"National Westminster Bank PLC," in Notable Corporate Chronologies, The Gale Group, 1999. Lists major events in the history of National Westminster PLC.

Wasserstein, Bruce. Big Deal: The Battle for Control of America's Leading Corporations, Warner Books, 1998. Offers an overview of the largest mergers in recent American corporate history.

THERA WILLIAMS

FLETCHER CHALLENGE &
RURAL BANKING AND FINANCE

nationality: New Zealand
date: October 1989
affected: Fletcher Challenge Ltd., New Zealand, founded 1861
affected: Rural Banking and Finance Corp., New Zealand, founded 1974

Fletcher Challenge Ltd.
810 Great South Rd.
Penrose, Auckland
New Zealand

tel: 64 9 525 9000
fax: 64 9 525 0559
web: http://www.fcl.co.nz

Overview of the Merger

Fletcher Challenge Ltd., New Zealand's largest private sector company, achieved great success in the early 1980s, based largely on the operational compatibility of its many diverse subsidiaries. Its services in forestry, pulp manufacturing, and construction industries made Fletcher nearly impenetrable to small economic disturbances. Fortunately, this diversity also helped the company weather the turmoil of the 1987 stock market crash that ruined many companies and created huge losses for investors.

The New Zealand government, with joint or full ownership of many commercial enterprises, took the brunt of the country's stock market collapse. In order to offset the losses and debts repayable to businesses, the government was forced to sell some of its operations. Fletcher Challenge's strong financial foundation allowed it to acquire the Petroleum Corp. of New Zealand (Petrocorp) in 1988. A year later, the company acquired 100% of the Rural Banking and Finance Corp., despite opposition from two political groups tied to farming interests. Fletcher Challenge agreed to pay NZ$550 million (US$321.7 million) for the firm, as well as NZ$75 million toward loan loss recoveries as the bank was obligated to repay the government NZ$450 million in debt. In return, the government agreed to guarantee Fletcher Challenge's Eurocommercial paper, valued at US$200 million.

In the second half of 1990, Rural Bank saw earnings slump by 25% to NZ$40.2 million due to lower prices and activity in the agriculture industries. As a result, earnings at Fletcher Challenge dropped by 17.7%. Within two years, Fletcher Challenge had extracted more than NZ$350 million in dividends from Rural Bank, but that was not enough to help the company, as it fought increasing losses. To minimize debt, Fletcher sold Rural Bank to National Bank of New Zealand (NBNZ) for NZ$450 million in 1992. Ownership of Rural was transferred to Britain's Lloyd's Bank, which owned NBNZ.

History of Fletcher Challenge Ltd.

Fletcher Challenge Ltd. was created by the merging of three paper and forestry giants in 1981, but the foundation of New Zealand's largest privately-

The Business

Financials

Revenue (1998): $3.76 billion

Employees (1998): 20,000

SICs / NAICS

sic 1542 - Nonresidential Construction Nec

sic 1521 - Single-Family Housing Construction

sic 1522 - Residential Construction Nec

sic 3241 - Cement-Hydraulic

sic 3310 - Blast Furnace & Basic Steel Products

sic 3275 - Gypsum Products

sic 0800 - Forestry

sic 2499 - Wood Products Nec

sic 2611 - Pulp Mills

sic 2621 - Paper Mills

sic 1311 - Crude Petroleum & Natural Gas

sic 1321 - Natural Gas Liquids

sic 1382 - Oil & Gas Exploration Services

sic 2861 - Gum & Wood Chemicals

sic 2911 - Petroleum Refining

sic 4924 - Natural Gas Distribution

naics 322121 - Paper (except Newsprint) Mills

naics 211111 - Crude Petroleum and Natural Gas Extraction

naics 211112 - Natural Gas Liquid Extraction

naics 325191 - Gum and Wood Chemical Manufacturing

owned company began 120 years earlier. In 1861, John T. Wright and Robert Robertson formed a livestock partnership in Dunedin, New Zealand called Wright Stephenson & Co. By 1906 the firm had opened its first overseas office in London, England, and began publicly trading its stock there and in New Zealand. In the 1920s, the company diversified its operations into fertilizers, breeding stock, land development, department store management, and automobile trading.

In 1908, James Fletcher emigrated to New Zealand from Scotland. The following year, Fletcher and partner Bert Morris formed a building company. Morris stayed with the company until 1912, when he sold his shares to his partner. That same year the company changed its name to Fletcher Brothers, Ltd.,

reflecting the addition of James' brothers, William and Andrew, to the firm. In 1919, the name was again changed to Fletcher Construction Co.

Despite a worldwide depression, Fletcher Construction achieved success in New Zealand by winning bids to build the Post Office of Dunedin, the National Art Gallery, the Wellington railway station, and public housing developments. In 1939, Fletcher opened its own lumber operations to provide building materials, which were scarce due to the start of World War II. The following year, Fletcher's son and namesake, James Fletcher, took the company's stock public under the new name Fletcher Holdings, Ltd. By the age of 28, the young Fletcher was appointed managing director.

Fletcher struck a deal with the New Zealand government to create the Tasman Pulp and Paper Corp. in 1952. Tasman focused primarily on export business and in 1975 began operating two transport ships for exporting commerce to New Zealand's South Island and Australia.

In 1970, Ronald Trotter became chairman of Wright, Stephenson & Co. He led the firm into a merger with National Mortgage Agency of New Zealand Ltd. forming Challenge Corporation, Ltd. The new company expanded into fish and meat exportation. By the end of the decade, Challenge Corp. had assets totaling NZ$7.6 million. In 1979, the government sold its stock in Tasman, leaving Fletcher and Challenge with 56.46% and 28.23%, respectively. The three companies were then merged to Fletcher Challenge Ltd., with Hugh Fletcher appointed as chief operating officer, while Challenge's Ronald Trotter became chairman.

Fletcher Challenge expanded in 1983 by acquiring 96% of British Colombia-based Crown Forest Industry, Ltd. for NZ$421 million. The 1988 merger of Crown Forest and British Columbia Forest Products Ltd. formed Fletcher Challenge Canada, Ltd. In 1992, Fletcher divested nearly $1 billion in these companies as part of debt restructuring. Five years later, the company sold its last stake in solid wood product manufacturing to TAL Acquisition Ltd. for $348 million.

In 1988, Fletcher Challenge paid the government NZ$1.14 billion for ownership of the Petroleum Corp. of New Zealand, the country's largest oil and gas company. Fletcher also obtained an interest in British Petroleum's Maui Field. North American operations grew in 1989, when Fletcher acquired Dinwiddie Construction Co. and an 80% share of A-M Homes, both based in California. The same year, the company purchased the remaining 34% of Wright Schuchart of Seattle, in which it had secured an initial stake in 1987.

As part of governmental debt reduction, New Zealand sold 100% of Rural Banking and Finance to Fletcher in 1989. For three years, the company earned large dividends, but in 1992 it decided to sell the finance firm as part of its own restructuring plan.

History of the Rural Banking and Finance Corp.

In 1974, while serving as the current governmental majority, New Zealand's Labour Party created the Rural Banking and Finance Corp. The state-owned and operated system was designed to offer mortgage and financing to the agricultural center. By the last half of the 1980s, Rural Bank was the largest lender of medium and long-term financing to farming interests. It held 73% of all first farm mortgages and maintained 40,000 clients. In March 1989 it recorded NZ$2.6 billion in loans.

Considered the liberal counterpart of New Zealand's political movements, The Labour Party also helped create the nation's welfare system, and voted to withdraw their country from all alliances with nuclear powers. Ironically, in the 1980s the party began to cut subsidies, and to deregulate commercial activities in order to promote privatization. The 1987 market crash forced the government to sell many of its interests quickly. Fletcher Challenge purchased Petrocorp in 1988 and Rural Bank in 1989, helping ease the nation's loan losses by more than NZ$1 billion.

In 1992, Fletcher Challenge sold Rural Bank to the National Bank of New Zealand, owned by Lloyd's Bank in London, England, for NZ$450 million. Fletcher received NZ$350 million from the new owner and NZ$100 million in dividends from the bank. The deal sparked concern as it was the second sale of a New Zealand bank to an overseas interest within a four week span. Despite selling Rural Bank for less than its purchase price, Fletcher earned NZ$350 million in dividends during its short tenure as owner.

Market Forces Driving the Merger

The stock market crash in October 1987 saw shares plummet 49% below the year-to-date high. New Zealand's interest rates jumped, while the dollar remained strong. The government, in an effort to repay losses and turn the economy around, needed to divest itself of many interests, including Rural Bank. Additionally, the Labour Party in 1984 opened business restrictions in order increase growth in exporting commodities that could be sold more competitively worldwide.

Unencumbered by anti-trust regulations found in the United States, Fletcher Challenge was an empire created by a diverse group of businesses, each with a

The Officers

Chairman: William Wilson

CEO, Fletcher Challenge Ltd. and Fletcher Challenge Paper: Michael Andrews

CEO, Fletcher Challenge Forests: Paul L. Fowler

CEO, Fletcher Challenge Energy: Greig Gailey

CEO, Fletcher Challenge Building: Terry N. McFadgen

product or service that could benefit the others. Fletcher's construction subsidiaries could get better prices on wood from the firm's forestry businesses, while pulp manufacturing helped paper producers. Also, the company's trucks and equipment could run on gas from its petrochemical subsidiary.

New Zealand's export economy was based almost entirely on farming, of which Fletcher Challenge was no exception, with more than 60% of revenues coming from overseas sales. Rural Bank was the largest financier of agricultural business loans and mortgages. Having financial services in this area of the economy could provide high dividends, strong growth, and minimum risk on losses. Fletcher Challenge hoped to make money off of annual dividends, while also exploiting possible benefits for its own export subsidiaries.

Approach and Engagement

The New Zealand government quietly worked on an acquisition deal with Fletcher Challenge Ltd. for Rural Banking and Finance Corp. as part of its intentions to repay loan losses in the wake of the 1987 stock market crash. During this time, many businesses found themselves in serious financial trouble, especially farmers. The latter group accounted for a large majority of Rural Bank's loan and mortgage business. Fletcher Challenge agreed to pay NZ$550 million for the bank and took on the responsibility repaying nearly NZ$450 million in debt the bank owed to the government. In return, Fletcher gained 100% control of Rural Bank.

The Federated Farmers national political lobby group objected to the sale due to the monopolistic power Fletcher would have. The biggest concern was the amount of power the privately owned company wielded upon the national economy as the largest stock and station agent. Fletcher would own the bank to which farmers paid on loans, as well as serve the farmers as a business. Many analysts believed this dual role of Fletcher would leave farmers at a disad-

The Players

CEO of Fletcher Challenge Ltd.: Hugh Fletcher. Hugh Fletcher lived a modest life, especially for the heir and CEO of New Zealand's largest privately-owned company. With an MBA from Stanford, Fletcher joined the ranks of his family's company at the age of twenty-eight. In 1980 he filled the position of CEO, following in his father's and grandfather's footsteps. During his first year at the helm, Fletcher merged the Fletcher Holdings construction business with Tasman Pulp & Paper and Challenge Corp. Fletcher became the chief operating officer of the newly formed Fletcher Challenge Ltd., while Ronald Trotter of Challenge Corp. assumed the CEO duties. After Trotter retired in 1990, Fletcher took the helm and led the company through a massive debt reduction program in early 1990s. In 1992, as part of the restructuring, Fletcher sold Rural Bank to the National Bank of New Zealand, only four years after initially acquiring the agricultural loan and finance firm. He was succeeded in 1997 by William Wilson.

vantage, especially during their economic rebuilding. Federated Farmers tried to block the deal by placing an equivalent NZ$550 million bid for the bank, but did not pledge loan loss repayments as Fletcher did. Fletcher won the bid and in October 1989 took over the bank with loans worth NZ$2.6 billion.

Products and Services

Fletcher Challenge Ltd., based out of New Zealand, acted as the holding company for the Fletcher Challenge Group, with worldwide operations in the forestry, building, energy and paper industries in the late 1990s. The four main subsidiary groups of the firm were traded independently on the New Zealand, Australian, and New York Stock Exchanges.

Fletcher Challenge Forest provided plantation forestry products to New Zealand, Australia, Japan, and the U.S. It managed forests in New Zealand and Argentina, where it sourced out environmentally managed solid wood products.

Fletcher Challenge Building provided plastering materials and plasterboard, wood paneling and doors, aluminum refinement, concrete and steel. Its products served more than two-thirds of the national construction industry. Construction and housing operations

served 43% of the Asian/Pacific markets and 41% of New Zealand.

The **Fletcher Challenge Energy** subsidiary operated oil and gas mining operations in New Zealand, Canada, and Brunei, with assets totaling NZ$1.8 billion. Fletcher's acquisition of Petrocorp in 1988 made the company the leading petrochemical producer in New Zealand, with 68.5% control of the nation's largest extraction area, the Maui Field. The company also operated 40 automobile gas service stations called *Challenge!* in New Zealand.

Fletcher Challenge Paper and Fletcher Challenge Canada Ltd. had international pulp and newsprint operations. On July 13, 1999, Fletcher announced plans to merge Paper with its 58%-owned Challenge Canada Ltd. The new company will become the largest Pacific Rim paper company. Services will be reduced to newsprint and groundwood papers, with some specialty pulp operations. If approved by regulators and shareholders, the new company will produce 2.4 million tons of newsprint annually and 1.1 million tons of pulp products.

Changes to the Industry

Fletcher Challenge's 1989 acquisition of Rural Banking and Finance exemplified the move to privatize New Zealand's industry, which was spawned by the Labour Party's 1984 decision to remove many regulatory restrictions for businesses. The $550 million deal, plus loan loss repayments, helped ease the nation's debt after the 1987 market crash. Rural Bank's operations were virtually unchanged during this time.

Review of the Outcome

For three years, Fletcher Challenge ran Rural Banking and Finance as a subsidiary, earning $350 million in dividends. The bank was not as profitable as Fletcher Challenge had hoped, and in 1992 Fletcher sold it as part of a major debt restructuring. The National Bank of New Zealand purchased Rural Bank, shifting ownership not only to the private sector, but to an overseas company, Lloyd's Bank of England.

Research

"Capital: Market Monitor," in *The American Banker*, 9 August, 1990. Discusses governmental guarantee of Fletcher Challenge's Eurocommercial paper.

"Fletcher Challenge: Eager To Push Its Business Beyond New Zealand," in *Business Week*, 12, October 1981. Comments on the actions and goals of Fletcher Challenge shortly after it was created by the merger of Fletcher Holdings and Challenge. Report also gives some biographical and historical information on key executives and the companies involved.

Fletcher Challenge Ltd. Home Page, available at http://www.fcl.co. Official World Wide Web Home Page for Fletcher Challenge Ltd. Includes current and archived news, and detailed financial, product, and historical information.

"Fletcher Challenge Ltd.," in *Notable Corporate Chronologies*, The Gale Group, 1999. Lists major events in the history of Fletcher Challenge Ltd.

Hall, Terry. "Fletcher Challenge Buys New Zealand Farm Lender," in *Financial Times*, 19 August 1989. Summarizes the deal between Fletcher Challenge and the New Zealand government.

"New Zealand Sells Another Bank to Overseas Owner," from *Xinhua General Overseas News Service*, 30 November 1992. Discusses the sale of Rural Bank to The National Bank of New Zealand, which is owned by Lloyd's Bank of England.

"New Zealand's Rural Bank Sold To Private Ownership," from *Xinhua General Overseas News Service*, 18 August 1989. Details the terms of Fletcher Challenge's purchase of Rural Bank.

—SEAN C. MACKEY

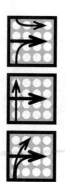

FORD & VOLVO

Ford Motor Co.
The American Rd.
Dearborn, MI 48121
USA

tel: (313)322-3000
fax: (313)322-7896
web: http://www.ford.com

AB Volvo
Goteborg, S-405 08
Sweden

tel: 46-31-59-00-00
fax: 46-31-54-57-72
web: http://www.volvo.com

nationality: USA
date: March 31, 1999
affected: Ford Motor Co., USA, founded 1903
affected: AB Volvo, Sweden, founded 1915

Overview of the Acquisition

Ford Motor Co. secured its rank as the world's number-two automaker with its 1999 purchase of Volvo Car Corp., the automotive business of AB Volvo. This $6.45 billion deal followed the previous year's DaimlerChrysler formation and perpetuated the trend of megamergers within the global auto industry. It also brought the industry one step closer to the consolidation of players into the last remaining Global Six.

History of Ford Motor Co.

Henry Ford built his first steam engine in 1878 and five years later completed his first gasoline-fed, one-cylinder, internal combustion engine. In 1896 he built his first car, called a *Quadricycle*, which he sold to finance the construction of a lighter weight racecar. In 1899 he resigned from Edison Illuminating Co. to form the Detroit Automobile Co. Two years later, however, the company faced bankruptcy due a production rate that was lower than anticipated.

Meanwhile, Ford built two four-cylinder, 80-horsepower racecars in his shed, the *999* and the *Arrow*. When one of Ford's racecars prevailed against Alexander Winton's world champion car, *The Bullet*, his investors agreed to establish a car production company for him to run. Ford's tenure there was short-lived, however, as he spent more time in the development of racecars than in the type of car that the investors planned to produce and sell. He was soon requested to resign.

In 1902 Ford formed a partnership with Alex Malcolmson to design and build a prototype for a new car. Twelve investors raised a sum of $28,000 to finance the company, which was capitalized at $150,000. The next year, the Ford Motor Co. was founded and began production of the Model A. By the end of its first year, the company sold more than 17,000 cars. It soon introduced three new models: the Model B, the Model C, and the Model F, ranging in price from $800 to $2,000.

The Model K, a luxury, six-cylinder car selling for $2,500, was unveiled in 1906 at the insistence of Malcolmson , who urged the company to produce high-priced cars for the elite, believing this market to be more profitable. The car sold poorly, which caused strained relations between Malcolmson and Ford, who believed that inexpensive, practical automobiles for the middle-class was a more profitable market in the long run. Malcolmson resigned later that year.

The Model T was the product of Ford's assembly-line concept that revolutionized manufacturing of all types, including carmaking. Unveiled in 1908, the Model T sold more than 10,000 units in its first year. Its success was attributed to its its reliability and low price, $825. For the first time, automobile ownership was no longer a luxury of the urban rich.

In 1914 Ford became a significant force behind the social revolution among industrial workers when he implemented a minimum wage of $5 for an 8-hour day, twice the current rate. By that time the company employed one-sixth of the nation's labor force and manufactured one-half of the nation's cars.

Ford ventured into truck and tractor manufacturing during World War I. In 1919 trouble with stockholders over the building of a plant prompted Henry and Edsel Ford to purchase all outstanding company stock for $106 million. The company purchased the Lincoln Motor Co. in 1922. After acquiring the Stout Metal Airplane Co., Ford built Tri-Motor airplanes for the nation's first commercial airlines.

After the 15-millionth Model T came off the assembly line in 1927, Henry Ford consented to end its production at the urging of Edsel, who maintained that the car was outdated in comparison to the Chevrolet that General Motors was producing. In 1932 Edsel Ford was appointed president when his father's failing health caused him to step back from day-to-day duties. That year Ford became the first car company to introduce a model with a one-piece block V-8 engine.

In 1938, just as it introduced the Mercury model, Ford's market share fell behind that of GM and Chrysler. Edsel Ford died of cancer in 1943, and Henry resumed the presidency when no clear successor emerged from within the company's managerial ranks. Two years later his grandson, Henry Ford II, became president.

In 1950 Ford usurped Chrysler as the second-largest automobile manufacturer, behind GM. Ford would continue to hold this position through the rest of the century. Shares of Ford stock were offered for public sale for the first time in 1956, the same year that it created an aerospace division. Two years later it introduced the infamous Edsel model. As consumers passed up the Edsel for less expensive cars like the Ford Fairlane, Ford reported a loss of $250 million.

Ford purchased Philco Corp. in 1961 and established a tractor factory the following year. The Ford

The Business

Financials - Ford Motor Co.

Revenue (1998): $144.4 billion

Employees (1998): 345,175

Financials - AB Volvo

Revenue (1998): SEK 212.9 billion

Employees (1998): 79,820

SICs / NAICS

sic 3711 - Motor Vehicles & Car Bodies

sic 3713 - Truck & Bus Bodies

sic 6141 - Personal Credit Institutions

sic 3531 - Construction Machinery

sic 3728 - Aircraft Parts & Equipment Nec

sic 3519 - Internal Combustion Engines Nec

naics 336111 - Automobile Manufacturing

naics 336112 - Light Truck and Utility Vehicle Manufacturing

naics 336120 - Heavy Duty Truck Manufacturing

naics 336211 - Motor Vehicle Body Manufacturing

naics 522291 - Consumer Lending

naics 333120 - Construction Machinery Manufacturing

naics 336413 - Other Aircraft Part and Auxiliary Equipment Manufacturing

naics 333618 - Other Engine Equipment Manufacturing

Mustang was introduced in 1964, and sold more than 100,000 units within the first 100 days of its availability. Targeted to American youth, the car's concept was credited to the general manager of the Ford Division, Lee Iacocca. In 1977 Henry II demoted Iacocca and gave his job to William Clay Ford. As Henry II faced accusations by stockholders of financial mismanagement and bribery, he fired Iacocca, increasing stockholder dissatisfaction with his style of leadership and management. Two years later Henry II stepped down, turning his position as CEO over to Philip Caldwell.

In 1980 Ford experienced a loss of $1.54 billion, the first of a string of losses during the decade. Attributed to the oil crisis of the 1970s, these results called for the closure of 15 plants and the reduction of 33% of the workforce in 1983. The company emerged from the crisis by 1984, when its sales and profits reached record levels.

The Officers

Ford Motor Co.

Chairman: William C. Ford, Jr.

President and CEO: Jacques A. Nasser

Vice Chairman: W. Wayne Booker

Vice Chairman and Chief of Staff: Peter J. Pestillo

Exec. VP and Chief Financial Officer: John M. Devine

AB Volvo

Chairman: Hakan Frisinger

President and CEO: Leif Johansson

Deputy CEO and Exec. VP: Lennart Jeansson

Executive VP: Arne Wittlov

Ford purchased the Versatile agricultural equipment manufacturer in 1987. That year it also bought 74% of the luxury sports car maker Aston Martin; it acquired the remaining 25% in 1994. In 1989 it purchased Jaguar for $2.5 billion, as well as the Associates financial services company.

The company expanded into the car rental business by purchasing Hertz Corp. in 1994 and Budget Rent-A-Car two years later; it sold the latter in 1997. Ford increased its interest in Mazda Motor Corp. to a controlling stake in 1996. This $481 million investment raised Ford's ownership of Mazda to just over one-third, and allowed it to name Henry D.G. Wallace as the first foreign president of a major Japanese corporation.

Ford instituted the largest U.S. auto safety recall in 1996, when it had to repair 8.7 million cars and trucks in order to fix an ignition switch problem that reportedly caused a short-circuit and ignited fires. The recall involved 10 car models built between 1988 and 1993, and costed Ford $50 per vehicle.

It exited from the heavy-duty truck business by selling those operations in 1997 to Freightliner, a unit of Daimler-Benz. The next year it spun off Associates First Capital and sold its interest in Kia Motors. Ford purchased the automaking business of Volvo for $6.45 billion in 1999.

History of AB Volvo

AB Volvo was formed in 1915 as a subsidiary of AB Svenska Kullagerfabriken, a Swedish ball bearing manufacturer. It began the assembly of cars in 1927 and of trucks in 1928. Two years later it acquired the means to safeguard the delivery of engines by purchasing a majority interest in AB Pentaverken. In 1934 Volvo began the production of bus chassis and marine engines. The following year the company gained a listing on the Stockholm Stock Exchange.

Volvo acquired a majority interest in the Swedish precision engineering company Svenska Flygmotor AB, later known as Volvo Aero. In 1942 it purchased Kopings Mekaniska Verkstad AB, Sweden's leading gearbox manufacturer. That year the company produced its first bogie axle, thus increasing the load capacity of its trucks. Its first tractor was unveiled in 1943, and by 1947 Volvo was recognized as one of the largest companies in Sweden.

Volvo entered the 1950s by acquiring AB Bolinder-Munktell, a Swedish manufacturer of farm machinery with its own line of diesel engines. This unit eventually became part of the VME Group, later renamed Volvo Construction Equipment. By 1951 the company concentrated on tractor production, and soon accounted for one out of every five tractors sold in Sweden. Passenger car volume also surpassed that of trucks and buses, partly due to the heavy demand for the Volvo PV 444 model, which had been introduced in 1944.

Volvo became the first manufacturer to introduce turbo-charged diesel engines in trucks and buses. In 1955 the company made its first export to the U.S., and established a North American import company the following year. In 1958 the 100,000th Volvo automobile was exported, and the first Volvo truck was sold in the U.S.

The Volvo Penta Aquamatic inboard boat engine earned accolades in 1959 as the world's first commercially successful solution to the difficulties arising from an inboard engine with an outboard drive. The next year the company formed an insurance company, Forsakrings AB Volvia. In 1966 it unveiled its 140 model, which was named the "Car of the Year."

Pehr Gyllenhammar was named CEO in 1971, and proceeded to lead the company on a campaign to diversify outside of automobiles, where it had slim chance of ever becoming a true leader. Volvo also began adding to its heavy truck holdings.

The VESC, or Volvo Experimental Safety Car, was unveiled in 1972. With low profits and an inability to finance a comprehensive product modernization program, Volvo explored a possible merger in 1977 with Saab-Scania, Sweden's other car manufacturer. Three months following the announcement, however, plans were abandoned due to heavy opposition.

In 1981 Volvo diversified into the oil industry with the acquisition of Beijerinvest Group, a Swedish company with interests in oil, food, finance, and trading. It also bought the truck operations of U.S.-based White Motors, later providing the basis for Volvo GM Heavy Truck Corp. In 1982 it introduced Duoprop, an airplane part featuring two counter-rotating propellers to provide 30% faster acceleration and 10% better fuel efficiency. Two years later Volvo entered into a joint venture with U.S.-based Clark Equipment Co., thereby creating the world's third-largest construction equipment company.

U.K.-based Leyland Bus Group Ltd. was acquired in 1988. Two years later Volvo sold its food and pharmaceutical interests for a share of the government-controlled holding company, Procordia. Also, Volvo initiated a stock swap with Renault SA and began the production of cars in the Netherlands in a joint venture with Mitsubishi Motors and the Dutch government. In the largest industrial overhaul in Swedish history, Volvo spent $2 billion in 1991 to update its plants and develop the 800 series of performance-oriented family sedans.

A failed merger with Renault prompted the resignation of Gyllenhammar. Soren Gyll, his successor, began selling off the company's non-core businesses. In 1995 Volvo acquired the remaining 50% of Volvo Construction Equipment, as well as a 51% stake in Prevost Car Inc., a Canadian bus manufacturer.

The company introduced the Volvo B7R bus chassis and the Volvo 770 truck to the North American market in 1997. Gyll resigned suddenly and was replaced by Leif Johansson. The next year Volvo paid $570 million to acquire the construction equipment business of Samsung Heavy Industries, and also purchased Mexicana de Autobuses, a Mexico-based bus manufacturer.

Volvo sold its automobile operations to Ford Motor in 1999, leaving the company with operations in only heavy-duty vehicles, including heavy trucks, buses, construction equipment, marine and industrial engines, and aerospace vehicles. Flush with capital from the sale to Ford, Volvo bought an unfriendly 20% stake in Scania AB, a Swedish heavy-truck rival.

Market Forces Driving the Acquisition

The global automobile industry in the late 1990s was showing signs of a consolidation trend. Manufacturers throughout the world were feeling the pinch of flat sales, pricing competition, and international overcapacity. In 1998 DaimlerChrysler was formed by the merger of two automotive giants, and erased all doubt that small independent companies would survive on their own for much longer.

The Players

Ford Motor President and CEO: Jacques A. Nasser. Jacques Nasser joined Ford Motor in 1968 and worked his way through the company ranks, eventually becoming president and CEO of the company on January 1, 1999. His love of hard work evoked wariness in Volvo's employees over the possible change in the work environment of that newly acquired Swedish company.

Volvo President and CEO: Leif Johansson. Leif Johansson, CEO of AB Electrolux, one of Europe's leading appliance makers, became president and CEO of Volvo in April 1997. He continued the strategy of the former CEO, Soren Gyll, to divest peripheral businesses in order to focus on vehicle manufacturing.

Analysts and industry players were predicting a shakeout of the industry into the Global Six—General Motors, Ford, DaimlerChrysler, Toyota, Honda, and Volkswagen. These supergiants were expected to achieve their entry in this elite group by securing the acquisitions of their smaller brethren.

As one of those relatively diminutive companies, AB Volvo was actively seeking a partner even though it was far from hurting. It had built a valuable reputation as one of the safest brands available, and had a socially and environmentally responsible corporate image. Yet in the automotive sector, this Swedish concern was slow to institute innovations, and lacked the financial resources to enable it to pick up the pace. Part of its reticence to invest heavily in its auto operations, known as Volvo Car Corp., was that the company's commercial vehicle business accounted for a greater share, 60%, of overall revenues. By divesting its auto business, which would never survive independently anyway, Volvo could focus on increasing its commercial business.

The addition of the Volvo brand to Ford Motor's lineup would increase its luxury car offerings, which at that time consisted of Jaguar, Lincoln, and Aston Martin. It would also attract new classes of luxury car customers—females and consumers under the age of 55. Volvo would also provide Ford with European manufacturing plants, as well as the potential for the exchange of vehicle platforms, or chassis, between the combined company's models.

Approach and Engagement

In the months prior the announcement of a definite deal, rumors were flying about potential partners for Volvo. Ford and Volkswagen had been named as possible suitors, but it was the Italian automaker Fiat SpA that particularly wanted to acquire Volvo. According to reports, Fiat had offered $7 billion for the entire concern, including the commercial vehicles business. Volvo rejected that offer, since it wanted to maintain and develop those operations itself.

Instead, Volvo formed a pact with Ford. Announced on January 28, 1999, the deal called for the purchase of Volvo Car Corp. by Ford for $6.45 billion in cash. According to the terms, Ford would gain the right to use the Volvo brand name on passenger vehicles, including cars, minivans, sports-utility vehicles, and light trucks, while Volvo retained the right to use the Volvo name on all commercial vehicles and non-auto products.

Volvo's shareholders approved the deal on March 8, and regulatory bodies did likewise on March 29. On March 31, 1999, Volvo Car Corp. was transferred to Ford Motor, which paid the Swedish corporation $700 million and SEK 10.2 billion on that day. The remaining balance of $1.6 billion was scheduled to be paid within two years.

Products and Services

Ford Motor created the Premier Automotive Group to hold its luxury brands: Volvo, Aston Martin, Lincoln, and Jaguar. Before the addition of Volvo, Ford's luxury operations sold 250,000 vehicles by mid-1999. With the newly acquired brand, the company expected its global luxury sales to reach 750,000 in the year 2000. Ford's other automotive brands were Ford and Mercury, as well as a 33% interest in Mazda. Additionally, the company operated a Financial Services Sector, consisting of Ford Credit, Hertz, and USL Capital.

After divesting itself of its automotive business, AB Volvo operated in five segments: Volvo Buses, Volvo Trucks, Volvo Construction Equipment Group, Volvo Penta Corp. (marine and industrial engines), and Volvo Aero.

Changes to the Industry

Ford secured its second-place position, behind General Motors, among the world's automotive companies, acquiring a 16% global market share. Its 11.7% share of the European market just edged out GM's 11.5% share, although they both trailed far behind the 18.4% share held by the leader of that market, Volkswagen AG.

A June 1999 issue of the *Detroit Free Press* reported results of a study predicting that Ford would soon overtake GM as the world's leader in terms of both revenue and production. According to Autofacts Group, a unit of PricewaterhouseCoopers, Ford's global production was expected to reach 9.15 million cars and light trucks by 2005, while GM would trail slightly behind with 9.1 million.

Review of the Outcome

Ford vowed to have minimal impact on the operations and culture of Volvo Cars Corp. Still, employees of the newly acquired company were somewhat anxious about being the subordinates of an aggressive American boss, particularly Jacques Nasser, who worked so hard that he shunned vacations. Swedish companies were traditionally run by compromise rather than direct order, and their bosses encouraged a healthy balance of work and play.

No layoffs or closures were announced immediately after the deal, but they were expected to be forthcoming. Additionally, Swedish suppliers admitted that they didn't have the large-scale capabilities to service Ford, and neither could they ever hope to compete against Ford's established suppliers.

Research

"AB Volvo," in *Notable Corporate Chronologies*, The Gale Group, 1999. Profiles the history of the company.

AB Volvo Home Page, available at http://www.volvo.com. Official World Wide Web Page for Volvo. Offers product and financial information, a company history, and press releases.

Carter, Matthew. "Volvo Trembling on Brink of Matrimony," in *The European*, 14 December 1998. Predicts an impending merger for Volvo.

Craig, Charlotte W. "2005 Could Be Ford's Year," in *Detroit Free Press*, 8 June 1999. Reports results of the study predicting that Ford would overtake GM as the industry leader by 2005.

"Ford Motor Co.," in *Notable Corporate Chronologies*, The Gale Group, 1999. Reports significant events in the history of Ford.

Ford Motor Co. Home Page, available at http://www.ford.com. Official World Wide Web Page for Ford. Features product information, annual reports and other financial data, and press releases.

Konrad, Rachel. "Volvo Workers Leery of Ford's Hard-Charging, American Ways," in *Knight-Ridder/Tribunes Business News*, 5 March 1999. Describes Volvo's workplace environment in contrast to that of most large American companies.

"Sale of Volvo Cars Concluded," in *M2 Presswire*, 31 March 1999. Briefly reports the completion of the purchase.

"Swede Success—Ford Uses Ready Cash to Buy up Volvo Cars," in *Ward's Auto World*, February 1999. Details the acquisition agreement.

DAVIS MCMILLAN

FORSTMANN LITTLE & GENERAL INSTRUMENT

nationality: USA
date: August 22, 1990
affected: Forstmann Little & Co., USA, founded 1978
affected: General Instrument Corp., USA, founded 1923

Forstmann Little & Co.
767 Fifth St.
New York, NY 10153
USA

tel: (212)355-5656
fax: (212)759-9059

General Instrument Corp.
101 Tournament Dr.
Horsham, PA 19044
USA

tel: (215)323-1000
fax: (215)443-9454
web: http://www.gi.com

Overview of the Acquisition

On August 22, 1990, Forstmann Little & Co. completed the acquisition of General Instrument for $1.55 billion; the deal was the biggest leveraged buyout of 1990. Under the ownership of Forstmann Little, General Instrument underwent a major restructuring as it split into the three separate companies of CommScope, General Semiconductor, and NextLevel Systems. Less than two years after the purchase was completed, the leveraged buyout company began divesting its share of General Instrument by commencing a series of stock sales. In 1999, Forstmann Little made its final sale of General Instrument stock to Liberty Media Corp., reducing its holding of General Instrument to 1%.

History of Forstmann Little & Co.

Forstmann Little & Co., a leveraged-buyout (LBO) company, was founded in 1978 by Theodore Forstmann and W. Brian Little. Between 1978 and 1995, common stock investors in Forstmann Little controlled companies earned an average net profit of 36%, and bond investors between 1982 and 1995 netted an 18.5% profit. A successful strategy employed by Forstmann Little was to purchase companies at a low interest rate. This allowed the companies more time to develop and pay back debts. Another characteristic that set Forstmann Little apart from other LBO firms was its resistance to the use of junk bonds. So strong was this resistance that from 1988 to the purchase of Gulfstream Aerospace Corp. from Chrysler in 1990, the firm did not acquire a single company.

In 1990, Forstmann Little also spent $1.6 billion to purchase General Instrument Corp., a supplier to the cable television industry. In December of 1994, Forstmann Little purchased Ziff-Davis Publishing Co. for $1.4 billion in cash, and just a year later sold it to Softbank Corp. for $2.1 billion. Even with its share of bankruptcies, Forstmann Little & Co. remained the best performing of all the LBO companies in the late 1990s.

In April of 1998, Forstmann Little announced plans to sell nearly one-half of its holdings in Gulfstream Aerospace to raise $675 million. In May of the following

The Business

Financials

Revenue (1998): $1.98 billion

Employees (1998): 7,350

SICs / NAICS

sic 4813 - Telephone Communications Except
     Radiotelephone

sic 4841 - Cable & Other Pay Television Services

sic 6211 - Security Brokers & Dealers

year, Forstmann Little agreed to divest its remaining 23% stake in Gulfstream to General Dynamics Corp. The firm also divested its remaining 15% stake in General Instrument to Liberty Media Corp. for $650 million in 1999.

History of General Instrument Corp.

In 1923, General Instrument Corp. was founded in New York City by Abraham Blumenkrantz. The corporation had its beginnings in a simple machine shop where variable condensers and other radio components were manufactured. The business expanded over the next 16 years, and went public in 1939.

During the 1940s General Instrument diversified and manufactured components for phonographs, television, and even bombs to support the war effort. In the early 1950s, General Instrument designed and manufactured converter boxes for UHF television broadcasts, which had recently become very popular.

Through the 1950s and early 1960s, the primary interest of General Instrument was supplying materials to support television broadcast bands. This changed in 1967 when General Instrument purchased Jerrold Communications Corp., a supplier of equipment to the cable television industry, and American Totalisator, a major manufacturer of parimutuel gaming equipment; these purchases enabled the company to enter two new and diverse markets. In an attempt to strengthen its gaming and cable television interests in the 1970s, General Instrument sold off unrelated assets and purchased a number of supporting electronics firms.

To further strengthen its position in the cable television market, General Instrument purchased Tocom, a cable television converter manufacturer in 1983. It then purchased the Videocipher encryption system

and all of the cable television equipment operations from M/A COM in 1986. The late 1980s were a time when the scrambling of television broadcasts began for home satellite dishes, and de-scramblers became a necessary piece of equipment. General Instruments had attained a near monopoly of the market with its VideoCipher purchase, and posted $1.3 billion in sales for 1989.

On August 22, 1990, Forstmann Little & Co. purchased General Instrument in a leveraged buyout for $1.6 billion, and Theodore J. Forstmann was named to the General Instrument Board of Directors. In 1991 General Instrument formed the General Instruments Communications division when it merged its VideoCipher and Jerrold Communications holdings. In June of 1992, less than two years after the purchase of General Instrument, Forstmann Little sold off 22 million shares of stock with a reverse leveraged buyout.

General Instrument entered the telecommunications field when it purchased NextLevel, a fiber-optic equipment manufacturer in 1995. That same year, Forstmann Little reduced its interest in General Instrument even further when it sold off 50% of its remaining stock holdings.

General Instrument split into three independent companies in 1997. CommScope, which specialized in cable television services; NextLevel Systems, which specialized in system networks, and General Semiconductor, all of which became separately traded commodities. That same year, NextLevel purchased Telenetworks; the company changed its name back to General Instrument the following year.

As General Instrument diversified into the telecommunications field, revenues increased to a record $1.988 billion in 1998. In April of 1999, General Instrument repurchased 5.3 million shares of its stock, and Liberty Media purchased 10 million shares, both from Forstmann Little. These transactions ended Forstmann Little's nine-year relationship with General Instrument.

Market Forces Driving the Acquisition

Despite sales of $1.3 billion in 1989, profits at General Instrument did not meet expectations due to a recession that was affecting the cable television industry at the time. Corporate growth was dependent on costly research and development, so General Instrument sought available capital, finding it in Forstmann Little.

Forstmann Little's attraction to General Instrument may have been self-serving, according to several industry analysts who pointed out that

Forstmann Little's two-year lapse in acquiring companies may have made the leveraged buyout firm more anxious than usual to complete a purchase. As for why General Instrument was a choice, Theodore Forstmann asserted that he was impressed with General Instrument's domination of the cable television industry. He also believed that General Instrument was in a strong position to profit from any possible equipment upgrades resulting from anticipated governmental regulations of the cable industry.

Approach and Engagement

On July 2, 1990, General Instrument announced its agreement to be taken over by Forstmann Little General Instrument Acquisitions Corp. (FLGIAC), which had been formed for the sole purpose of the merger. General Instrument's stock price rose to $45.12 the day the merger was announced.

Forstmann Little paid $44.50 cash per share in a tender agreement that ran until August 13, 1990. Along with the stock sale, Forstmann Little assumed all of General Instrument's existing debt. This brought the total cost of the merger to $1.6 billion, half of which came from Forstmann Little's buyout fund. The remaining $800 million was lent by a consortium of banks headed up by Continental Bank and Manufacturers Hanover Trust Co.

General Instrument was advised in the merger by Merrill Lynch Capital Markets, while Lazard Freres & Co. and Goldman, Sachs & Co. advised Forstmann Little. Lazard Freres and Goldman, Sachs also acted as dealer managers. On August 22, 1990, Forstmann Little announced that it had completed the acquisition of General Instrument.

Products and Services

In 1999, Forstmann Little's holdings included Department 56, Lear Siegler, Pullman, and Thompson Minwax. The firm continued to operate as one of the most successful leveraged buyout companies in the U.S.

General Instruments was organized into five operating segments. Advanced Network Systems manufactured terminals for two-way communications, as well as analog set-top terminals and other analog cable products. Digital Network Systems manufactured digital set-top terminals and other digital cable products. Transmission Network Systems produced systems for audio, video, and data transfer via cable, while Satellite Data Network Systems designed satellite systems for use by educational institutions and businesses. Finally, NextLevel Communications produced fiber-optic and coaxial products used to integrate telephony into cable networks.

The Officers

Forstmann Little & Co.

CEO and Chief Financial Officer: Theodore J. Forstmann

General Partner: Erskine Bowles

General Partner: Thomas Lister

General Instrument Corp.

Chairman and CEO: Edward D. Breen

Chief Financial Officer and Sr. VP, Finance: Eric M. Pillmore

Sr. VP, Manufacturing and Procurement: Robert D. Cromack

Sr. VP and General Manager, Advanced Network Systems: Daniel M. Maloney

Sr. VP, Secretary, and General Counsel: Robert A. Scott

Review of the Outcome

On October 6, 1990, Frank Hickey was replaced by Donald Rumsfeld as CEO of General Instrument. Over the next two years, General Instrument streamlined by selling off its military applications, transportation electronics applications, video store units, and real estate holdings. With this reduction completed, General Instrument focused only on supplying materials and technology to the cable and satellite television industries.

In April 1992, Forstmann Little reduced its stake in General Instrument when it instituted a reverse leveraged buyout of 22 million shares of General Instrument stock at a cost of $354 million. Forstmann Little retained 63% of the total available stock—the 29 million shares were worth $650 million. That same year, General Instrument's sales rose 15.7% to reach $1 billion.

Two divisions of General Instrument, Jerrold Communications and VideoCipher, combined in 1993 to create General Instrument's communication division. In a surprise move, General Instrument restructured its debt in July of 1993. It prepaid the final $100 million of the subordinated debt issued by Forstmann Little in 1990 eight years early. Debt owed to Continental Bank and Manufacturers Hanover Trust Co. was also refinanced, allowing General Instrument to reduce its interest payments by $25 million per year and funnel that money into research and development. As General Instrument strengthened, Forstmann Little continued to reduce its stock hold-

The Players

CEO of Forstmann Little & Co.: Theodore J. Forstmann. After graduating from Yale, Theodore Forstmann began his financial career by becoming a founding partner of Forstmann Little & Co. in 1978. After acquiring General Instrument in 1990, Forstmann became a member of the General Instrument board. He led his firm's purchase of Gulfstream Aerospace in 1990, and named himself chairman of Gulfstream in 1993. By 1995, Forstmann's net worth was estimated to be $400 million. He retained the positions at Gulfstream and General Instrument until both were divested in 1999.

Chairman and CEO of General Instrument Corp.: Frank G. Hickey. Frank Hickey began his sixteen-year reign as CEO of General Instrument in November of 1974. He ran the company through very prosperous times, including a 266% increase in earnings in 1988, as well as times that were financially troubling. For instance, between 1983 and 1986, stock prices fell from 66.875 to 12.75. Because General Instrument clearly produced a quality product, some analysts speculated that General Instrument's poor record was due to continuing managerial problems. Hickey remained CEO until 1990, when General Instrument was purchased by Forstmann Little & Co.

ings. Roughly 10 million shares were sold for $30.50 in March, and after a sale of stock for $51 in September, Forstmann Little held only 30% of the firm's available stock.

International sales boomed in 1995 as General Instrument targeted overseas markets, but earnings dropped when General Instrument acquired NextLevel, a company that manufactured fiber-optic equipment for $85 million. Soon after the purchase, a Texas jury found NextLevel's founders guilty of illegal use of trade secrets from a previous employer. The damages were assessed at $369 million, and General Instrument's entry into the communications market was delayed. Forstmann Little sold 50% of its stock holdings for $40 a share in April of that same year, reducing its holdings to 15% of the available stock.

General Instruments split into three independent companies in 1997: NextLevel Systems, CommScope, and General Semiconductor. NextLevel Systems grew

when it purchased Telenetworks and accepted an offer worth $4.5 billion to produce 15 million digital set-top cable boxes for a dozen companies. The following year, NextLevel Systems changed its name back to General Instrument and entered into a $180 million contract with Primestar to produce cable decoders. Revenues jumped 12.7%.

On April 5, 1999 Forstmann Little effectively ended its relationship with General Instrument when it sold off all but 1% of its stock holdings. General Instrument purchased 5.3 million of the shares for $148 million and Liberty Media Corp. purchased 10 million shares for $280 million. Commenting on the sale, CEO Edward D. Breen described the association between General Instrument and Forstmann Little as "tremendously successful." He went on to say that "this relationship has brought us through many changes in our industry and in our company, and we thank Forstmann Little for the contributions its partners have made to our success. In particular, we thank Ted Forstmann for being a driving force in making General Instrument the world leader that it is today."

Research

Antilla, Susan. "$1.2B Wins General Instrument," in *USA Today*, 3 July 1990. Details finances surrounding the merger between Forstmann Little and General Instrument.

Cuff, Daniel F. "Business People; Rumsfeld Becomes Chief at General Instrument," in *The New York Times*, 5 October 1990. Offers a look at the history of Donald Rumsfeld.

"Forstmann Little to Acquire General Instrument for $44.50 per Share," in *PR Newswire*, 2 July 1990. Discusses the financial details of Forstmann Little's acquisition of General Instrument.

"Forstmann Little Completes Acquisition of General Instrument; General Instrument Bonds Redeemed," in *PR Newswire*, 22 August 1990. Details the bond redemption involved in the purchase of General Instrument by Forstmann Little.

General Instrument Corp. Home Page, available at http://www.gi.com. Official World Wide Web Home Page for General Instrument Corp. Includes press releases, as well as financial, product, and investor information.

"General Instrument to Repurchase 5.3 Million Shares as Forstmann Little Concludes its Eight Year Investment; Liberty Media Corporation to Purchase 10 Million GI Shares From Forstmann Little," in *PR Newswire*, 5 April 1999. Explores the distribution of available stock as Forstmann Little divests General Instrument.

Goggin, Keith. "Leaner GI to Emerge After Forstmann Little's Reverse LBO," in *Mergers and Acquisitions Report*, 20 April 1992. Provides a financial history of events that led up to Forstmann Little's reverse leveraged buyout of General Instrument.

Kosman, Josh. "Forstmann Little Exits General Instrument," in *BuyOuts*, 17 May 1999. Comments on the finances surrounding the reverse leveraged buyout of General

Instrument, as well as a brief financial history of the partnership.

Parker, Marcia. "General Instrument," in *Pensions and Investments*, 7 January 1991. Presents the financial details and reasons for the purchase of General Instrument by Forstmann Little.

Ringer, Richard. "Company News; General Instrument to Pay Off its Debt Early," in *PR Newswire*, 1 July 1993.

Explores the reasons for the 1993 debt restructuring of General Instrument.

Wayne, Leslie. "$1.6 Billion Buyout by Forstmann," in *New York Times*, 3 July 1990. Discusses the finances surrounding the purchase of General Instrument by Forstmann Little.

DAVE W. SHELDON

FORSTMANN LITTLE & GULFSTREAM AEROSPACE

Forstmann Little & Co.
767 Fifth St.
New York, NY 10153
USA

tel: (212)355-5656
fax: (212)759-9059

Gulfstream Aerospace Corp.
500 Gulfstream Rd.
Savannah, GA 31408
USA

tel: (912)965-3000
fax: (912)965-3011
web: http://www.gulfstreamaircraft.com

nationality: USA
date: February 13, 1990
affected: Forstmann Little & Co., USA, founded 1978
affected: Gulfstream Aerospace Corp., USA, founded 1959

Overview of the Acquisition

In February of 1990, Forstmann Little & Co. agreed to purchase Gulfstream Aerospace from Chrysler Corp. for $825 million. Eight years later, after greatly expanding the scope of Gulfstream's operations, the leveraged buyout company began divesting its share of Gulfstream, ultimately selling it to General Dynamics Corp. for $5.3 billion in 1999.

History of Forstmann Little & Co.

Forstmann Little & Co., a leveraged-buyout (LBO) company, was founded in 1978 by Theodore Forstmann and W. Brian Little. Between 1978 and 1995, common stock investors in Forstmann Little controlled companies earned an average net profit of 36%, and bond investors between 1982 and 1995 netted an 18.5% net profit. A successful strategy employed by Forstmann Little was to purchase companies at a low interest rate. This allowed the companies more time to develop and pay back debts. Another characteristic that set Forstmann Little apart from other LBO firms was its resistance to the use of junk bonds. So strong was this resistance that from 1988 to the Gulfstream purchase from Chrysler in 1990, the firm did not acquire a single company.

In 1990, Forstmann Little also spent $1.6 billion to purchase General Instrument Corp., a supplier to the cable television industry. In December of 1994, Forstmann Little purchased Ziff-Davis Publishing Co. for $1.4 billion in cash, and just a year later sold it to Softbank Corp. for $2.1 billion. Even with its share of bankruptcies, Forstmann Little & Co. remained the best performing of all the LBO companies in the late 1990s.

In April of 1998, Forstmann Little announced plans to sell nearly one-half of its holdings in Gulfstream Aerospace to raise $675 million. In May of the following year, Forstmann Little agreed to divest its remaining 23% stake in Gulfstream to General Dynamics Corp. Also in 1999, the firm divested its remaining 15% stake in General Instrument to Liberty Media Corp. for $650 million.

History of Gulfstream Aerospace Corp.

In 1959, Grumman Corp. developed the world's first business plane, the Gulfstream I. Two hundred of them quickly sold, and a new market for aerospace technology was opened. In 1966, Grumman introduced the Gulfstream II. This business jet could fly faster than commercial jets and could carry sixteen passengers and a full crew. It was such a popular plane that Grumman built an assembly plant in Savannah, Georgia, solely for the manufacture of the GS II.

As the recession of the late 1970s hit, Grumman began redirecting its focus to military aircraft as sales of corporate jets dropped. In 1978, Allen E. Paulson, owner of American Jet Industries, purchased the Gulfstream operations for $52 million and established the Gulfstream Aerospace Corp. He immediately set out to develop and market an even more sophisticated business jet, the GS III. Along with setting his sights on building a better version of the Gulfstream jet, he began manufacturing the parts needed for the jets on site. This eliminated the need for vendors, and helped to greatly increase revenues. From 1980 to 1982, revenues skyrocketed from $187 million to $582 million. It was also during this time that Gulfstream expanded out of Savannah. In 1981, Gulfstream established Gulfstream Aerospace Technologies, a 400,000-square-foot plant in Oklahoma City.

Despite the impressive revenue numbers posted in 1982, profits had dwindled. Research and development costs for developing a new jet had risen ninefold over the previous ten years, and government subsidized competition from other countries drove profits down. Paulson was forced to sell eight million shares of common stock to raise $152 million.

Chrysler Corp. purchased Gulfstream in 1985 and retained Paulson as chair of the new subsidiary. With the infusion of funds from Chrysler Corp., Gulfstream was able to post profits again; in fact, it had its most profitable years under the ownership of Chrysler. Two years after the purchase, production of the GS III ended, and the GS IV was introduced. The GS IV was a faster, almost silent version of the GS III. It was so popular that even with a price of $15.8 million, Gulfstream experienced its largest backlog of orders ever. The company grew again in 1986, as it expanded to Long Beach, California.

A recession hit the American automotive industry in 1990. In a move to streamline its operations, Chrysler sold Gulfstream. With the help of Forstmann Little & Co., Paulson purchased 25 million shares of common stock from Chrysler for $825 million. William C. Lowe was named CEO and president of Gulfstream, and Paulson continued on as chairman.

The Business

Financials

Revenue (1998): $2.42 billion

Employees (1998): 7,740

SICs / NAICS

sic 3721 - Aircraft

sic 3724 - Aircraft Engines & Engine Parts

sic 6211 - Security Brokers & Dealers

naics 336411 - Aircraft Manufacturing

naics 336412 - Aircraft Engine and Engine Parts
  Manufacturing

Along with developing better and faster corporate jets, Lowe concentrated on serving more cost-conscious customers by upgrading the existing GS IIs and IIIs to extend their life spans and to meet FAA noise regulations. He also entered the international military market by producing Special Requirements Aircraft.

The evolution of the Gulfstream line of jets continued. In 1992, the GS V, as well as the GS IV-SP (special performance), were introduced. Both incorporated advanced collision avoidance features, and sales were brisk. By 1995, Gulfstream claimed to have $2 billion dollars in "firm" orders for the GS V alone. More expansion occurred in 1998, as Gulfstream purchased Kimberly-Clark Corp.'s aircraft completion unit for $250 million.

In April of 1998, Forstmann Little announced plans to sell nearly one-half of its holdings in Gulfstream Aerospace to raise $675 million. In May of the following year, Forstmann Little agreed to divest its remaining 23% stake in Gulfstream to General Dynamics Corp.

Market Forces Driving the Acquisition

Chrysler Corp., under the control of Lee Iaccoca, purchased Gulfstream Aerospace in 1985 in an attempt to diversify. With the infusion of funds from Chrysler, GuLfstream was able to expanded its operations to the West Coast by acquiring a plant in Long Beach, California. It also began production of the GS IV, the world's premier business jet, which sold for $15.8 million apiece and set a speed record as it flew around the world. As a result, Gulfstream soon experienced the largest backlog of orders in company his-

The Officers

Forstmann Little & Co.

CEO and Chief Financial Officer: Theodore J. Forstmann

General Partner: Erskine Bowles

General Partner: Thomas Lister

Gulfstream Aerospace Corp.

Chairman and CEO: Theodore J. Forstmann

Vice Chairman: Bryan T. Moss

President and Chief Operating Officer: Bill Boisture

Exec. VP, Chief Financial Officer, and Chief Administrative
      Officer: Chris A. Davis

tory. Under the control of Chrysler, Gulfstream was able to post record profits each year.

With the onset of a recession and increased Japanese automotive competition in 1990, Chrysler posted a $664 million loss in revenues. As a result, the firm streamlined its operations by divesting non-automotive subsidiaries, including Gulfstream Aerospace.

Since he had sold Gulfstream to Chrysler in 1985, Allen Paulson, the aerospace company's CEO and founder, had been eager to purchase his company back. When it was offered up for sale in 1990, he jumped at the chance. Paulson believed that Gulfstream would see improved performance as an independent firm because the freedom would foster the same entrepreneurial atmosphere that had fueled his firm's initial success.

Forstmann Little's attraction to Gulfstream was more self-serving, according to several industry analysts, who pointed out that Forstmann Little's two-year lapse in acquiring companies may have made the leveraged buyout firm unusually eager to complete a purchase. Late in 1989 and early in 1990, Forstmann Little had also been considering the purchase of Learjet Corp.

Approach and Engagement

After pursuing Allen Paulson for some time, Theodore Forstmann finally met with him in January of 1990 to discuss the purchase of Gulfstream Aerospace from Chrysler Corp. Along with the purchase of Gulfstream, the two were interested in the purchase of Learjet Corp. On February 13, 1990, they announced the purchase of all 25 million shares of Gulfstream common stock for the price of $825 million

in cash. According to Chrysler chairman Lee Iaccoca, Chrysler was "happy with the price." The owners of Learjet Corp., Integrated Resources Inc., filed for Chapter 11 bankruptcy protection on the same day the Gulfstream deal was being closed.

Paulson, along with Forstmann Little, provided all of the equity, while Forstmann Little provided all of the subordinated debt. Cash for half of the purchase price was made available by Forstmann Little, while the remainder came in the form of a letter of commitment from Manufacturers Hanover Trust Co.

Products and Services

In 1999, Forstmann Little's holdings include Department 56, Lear Siegler, Pullman, and Thompson Minwax. The firm continued to operate as one of the most successful leveraged buyout companies in the U.S.

In its final year of Forstmann Little ownership, 78% of Gulfstream's $2.43 billion in sales was generated by new aircraft sales. Roughly 12% of total sales came from aircraft services, and the remaining 10% were attributed to pre-owned aircraft sales and services. Along with the production and sale of their trademark Gulfstream IV-SP and V business jets, Gulfstream also produced the C-20H and C-37A for the U.S. Air Force, the C-20G for the U.S. Navy, and the U-4 for the Japanese Air Force. The firm's manufacturing capabilities allowed it to also post substantial sales in the industry segments of spare parts, repairs, engine overhauls, and custom interior modifications.

Review of the Outcome

In 1990, Forstmann Little committed $100 million in equity to the $850 million purchase of Gulfstream Aerospace from Chrysler Corp. Less than one year later, Forstmann Little was forced to direct another $100 million into Gulfstream to keep the aerospace firm out of bankruptcy. In August of 1992, after a failed attempt to execute an initial public offering of Gulfstream, Forstmann Little infused $250 million more into Gulfstream Aerospace. This unexpected investment gave Gulfstream an implied value of $1.3 billion.

GS-V was introduced at the 1992 National Business Aircraft Association Conference and performed well even in the midst of a recession that hit the private jet market rather hard. Due to high development costs of the GS-V, poor management, and stiff competition, Gulfstream posted a $275 million loss in 1993 and came within weeks of defaulting on its loans.

As a result of Gulfstream's loss of market share

and money to competition, Forstmann Little changed the company's management in 1993. William C. Lowe was removed from the chief executive position and Theodore Forstmann was named chairman. The new management team eliminated $40 million in annual operating costs and overhauled Gulfstream's marketing and sales strategies. Once operating costs had been cut and competitive marketing had been put in place to compete with Bombardier Inc. and Dassault Aviation SA of France, Gulfstream addressed its underestimation of GS-V development costs. Forstmann Little converted $450 million of Gulfstream bonds into shares of common stock and reduced the interest costs by $40 million. Not including GS-V research and development, Gulfstream earned $60 million before taxes, and posted record plane sales in 1994.

In 1996, four years after the first attempt to bring about an initial public offering, Forstmann Little successfully conducted an initial public offering of Gulfstream at $24 per share, and raised $888 million before expenses. Forstmann Little's equity in the company was thereby reduced from 100% to 48%. Gulfstream's stock rose 53% over the first four months of 1998. In May of 1998, a second public offering at $43 per share raised nearly $675 million and reduced Forstmann Little's equity in the company to 23%. As news of the sale reached the market, Gulfstream stock dropped $1.9375 to close at $44.875.

In May of 1999, Forstmann Little announced that it would sell its remaining 23% stake in Gulfstream to General Dynamics Corp. At the time, Gulfstream's stock was valued at $4.8 billion. Forstmann Little retained the rights to sell its 8% stake in the company, worth roughly $1.1 billion, after the merger was finalized.

The Players

CEO of Forstmann Little & Co.: Theodore J. Forstmann. After graduating from Yale, Theodore Forstmann began his financial career by becoming a founding partner of Forstmann Little & Co. in 1978. After acquiring Gulfstream Aerospace in 1990, Forstmann named himself chairman in 1993. By 1995, Forstmann's net worth was estimated to be $400 million. He retained the position of chairman of Gulfstream until it was sold to General Dynamics Corp. in 1999.

Chairman and CEO of Gulfstream Aerospace Corp.: Allen E. Paulson. Allen Paulson began his aviation career with Trans World Airlines, where he worked as a mechanic for thirty cents an hour. Paulson left TWA and became head of American Jet Industries, a California based holding company that specialized in converting planes into propjets. In 1978, he paid $52 million to Grumman for the Gulfstream plants and offices. With this purchase he formed and became chairman and CEO of Gulfstream Aerospace Corp. In 1985, Chrysler purchased Gulfstream for $637 million, and five years later, Paulson, along with Forstmann Little & Co., purchased Gulfstream back. Through all of these changes, Paulson remained CEO until 1993, when Theodore J. Forstmann took over as chairman of the firm.

Research

"Forstmann Little & Allen Paulson to Acquire Gulfstream for $825 Million," in *PR Newswire*, 13 February 1990. Discusses financial details surrounding the purchase of Gulfstream Aerospace.

"Forstmann Little to Cut Its Gulfstream Stake in Half," in *The New York Times*, 22 April 1998. Details the financial aspects of Forstmann Little's second sale of Gulfstream Aerospace stock.

Fromson, Brett. "Dealmaker of the Decade; Ted Forstmann Got No Respect in the 80s. Now He's Flying High," in *The Washington Post*, 4 June 1995. Offers a chronological history of Forstmann's relationship with Gulfstream Aerospace.

"Gulfstream Aerospace Corp.," in *International Directory of Company Histories*, Vol. 13, St. James Press, 1995.
Provides a detailed history of Gulfstream Aerospace Corp.

Gulfstream Aerospace Corp. Home Page, available at http://www.gulfstreamaircraft.com. Official World Wide Web Home Page for Gulfstream Aerospace Corp. Includes press releases, as well as financial, product, and investor information.

Huemer, Jason. "Forstmann Little to Refuel Gulfstream Deal with $250 Mil," in *Mergers and Acquisitions Report*, 31 August 1992. Offers an overview of Forstmann Little's attempt to pull Gulfstream out of financial trouble.

Kosman, Josh "Forstmann Little Plans to Land Gulfstream," in *BuyOuts*, 31 May 1999. Discusses the finances surrounding the sale of Gulfstream Aerospace by Forstmann Little, as well as the financial history of the partnership.

DAVE W. SHELDON

FORSTMANN LITTLE & ZIFF-DAVIS

Fosrtmann Little & Co.
767 Fifth St.
New York, NY 10153
USA

tel: (212)355-5656
fax: (212)759-9059

Ziff-Davis Inc.
One Park Ave.
New York, NY 10016
USA

tel: (212)503-3500
fax: (212)503-4599
web: http://www.ziffdavis.com

nationality: USA
date: December 22, 1994
affected: Forstmann Little & Co., USA, founded 1978
affected: Ziff-Davis Inc., USA, founded 1927

Overview of the Acquisition

Leveraged buyout (LBO) firm Forstmann Little & Co. moved into publishing for the first time in 1994 with its $1.4 billion purchase of Ziff-Davis Inc. At that time, this company was the world's largest publisher of computer magazines and a leading provider of computer product information. When Softbank Corp., Japan's largest distributor of computer software and peripherals, offered Forstmann Little $2.1 billion for Ziff-Davis in February of 1996, the LBO abandoned its plans to take the publisher public in three to five years and instead sold it to Softbank.

History of Forstmann Little & Co.

Forstmann Little & Co., a leveraged buyout (LBO) company, was founded in 1978 by Theodore Forstmann and W. Brian Little. Between 1978 and 1995, common stock investors in Forstmann Little controlled companies earned an average net profit of 36%, and bond investors between 1982 and 1995 netted an 18.5% net profit. A successful strategy employed by Forstmann Little was to purchase companies at a low interest rate, thereby allowing the companies more time to develop and pay back debts. Another characteristic that set Forstmann Little apart from other LBO firms was its resistance to the use of junk bonds. So strong was this resistance that from 1988 to the purchase of Gulfstream Aerospace Corp. from Chrysler in 1990, the firm did not acquire a single company.

In 1990, Forstmann Little also spent $1.6 billion to purchase General Instrument Corp., a supplier to the cable television industry. In December of 1994, Forstmann Little purchased Ziff-Davis Inc. for $1.4 billion in cash, and just a year later sold it to Softbank Corp. for $2.1 billion. Even with its share of bankruptcies, Forstmann Little & Co. remained the best performing of all the LBO companies in the late 1990s.

In April of 1998, Forstmann Little announced plans to sell nearly one-half of its holdings in Gulfstream Aerospace to raise $675 million. In May of the following year, Forstmann Little agreed to divest its remaining 23% stake in Gulfstream to General Dynamics Corp. Also in 1999, the firm divested its remaining 15% stake in General Instrument to Liberty Media Corp. for $650 million.

History of Ziff-Davis Inc.

In 1927, William Ziff and Bernard Davis founded Ziff-Davis as a publisher of magazines. Believing that aviation was an important component of America's future as a world leader, Ziff viewed aviation as the next major advance in the transportation industry. This prompted his launch of the company's first special interest magazine, *Popular Aviation*. That magazine's success prompted the firm to offer other publications that appealed to special interests, such as *Popular Photography* in 1937, *Radio News* in 1938, *G.I. Joe* in 1940, *Plastics* in 1948, *Radio and Appliances* in 1948, and *Modern Bride* in 1949.

William Ziff died in 1953. Three years later, his son, Bill Ziff, Jr., purchased the portion of the company owned by Davis. The new owner took over as the post-war U.S. economy was beginning its boom. Ziff believed that as consumer wealth increased, and people began spending more time and money on leisure activities, the special interest and leisure market would flourish. As a result, he increased his company's focus on special interest publishing. Each new magazine was geared toward an up and coming niche market. The company also launched several annual handbooks and buying guides as companion publications. *Sports Car Illustrated* debuted in 1955; it later became known as *Car and Driver*. The following year, *Popular Boating* was released; it was later called *Boating*. In 1958, *HiFi & Music Review* was first published; its name was changed to *HiFi Review* and, later, *Stereo Review*.

As the air transportation industry began burgeoning, Ziff-Davis diversified into travel and tourism publishing by launching various trade publications aimed at travel agents, hotels, and airlines, including *Official Hotel & Resort Guide* in 1962, *Skiing* in 1964, *Business & Commercial Aviation* in 1965, *Cycle* in 1966, *Travel Weekly* in 1967, *Hotel & Travel Index* in 1968, and *Aviation Daily* in 1969. The firm also published a variety of annual buying guides and handbooks as adjuncts to popular titles.

In 1973, Ziff-Davis launched the following publications: *Photomethods*, *Intellectual Digest*, *Meetings & Conventions*, and *Psychology Today*. *Official Meetings Facilities Guide* was first published in 1974. In 1975, a cover story in an issue of *Popular Electronics* featured the first personal computer, the Altair; the article was the first to cover microcomputing for the average consumer.

The Business

Financials

Revenue (1998): $955 million

Employees (1998): 2,889

SICs / NAICS

sic 2721 - Periodicals

sic 2732 - Book Printing

sic 6211 - Security Brokers & Dealers

sic 4841 - Cable & Other Pay Television Services

sic 7389 - Business Services Nec

naics 323117 - Book Printing

In 1985, 12 trade publications were divested to Rupert Murdoch, and 12 consumer magazines were sold to CBS. After being diagnosed with prostate cancer, Ziff transferred control of the family business to his three sons. Ziff-Davis then refocused on the microprocessor, believing that it held the future of business computing. The firm began forging information partnerships and concentrating efforts on publications that served the computer industry. As it had with electronics products, the firm conducted laboratory tests of the products about which it wrote. During this time period, Ziff-Davis began publishing *Creative Computing*, *Color Computer*, *Microsystems*, *Sync*, *Small Business Computing*, *PC Jr*, *PC Magazine*, *PC Week*, *PC Tech Journal*, *MacWeek*, and others.

In 1988, Ziff returned to his post as chairman of the company. The firm began diversifying into electronic services, as well as newsletters and trade show management. In 1993, Ziff retired; he was succeeded by Eric Hippeau, who led efforts to put the firm on the block. A year later, Forstmann Little paid $1.4 billion for Ziff-Davis, which then sold the firm to Softbank Corp. for $2.1 billion in February 1996.

Yahoo! and Ziff-Davis formed a joint venture in 1996, in which the *ZD Internet Life* magazine was renamed *Yahoo! Internet Life*. The following year, Ziff-Davis assumed control of the trade show operations of Softbank. Launched in the mid-1990s, ZDNet.com quickly became a leading computing content Internet site. ZDTV, a 24-hour cable station covering technology, computers, and Internet news, made its debut in 1998.

In April of that year, Ziff-Davis conducted its ini-

The Officers

Forstmann Little & Co.

CEO and Chief Financial Officer: Theodore J. Forstmann

General Partner: Erskine Bowles

General Partner: Thomas Lister

Ziff-Davis Inc.

Chairman and CEO: Eric Hippeau

Chief Financial Officer: Timothy C. O'Brien

Sr. VP, Human Resources: Rayna A. Brown

Sr. VP and General Counsel: J. Malcolm Morris

Sr. VP, Development and Planning: Daryl R. Otte

Sr. VP, Communications: Charlotte Rush

tial public offering and began trading on the New York Stock Exchange. A year later, ZDNet was spun off as in independent company. Ziff-Davis retained an 85% interest in ZDNet.

Market Forces Driving the Acquisition

After Bill Ziff, Jr. retired as chairman of Ziff-Davis in 1993, his successors decided the firm had gone as far as it could on its own in the computer magazine market, and the publishing company was put up for sale. Ziff-Davis needed the deeper pockets of a larger firm to propel future growth and to solidify its position as a leading player in the computer publications arena, both in the U.S. and abroad.

Leveraged buyout (LBO) firm Forstmann Little was able to offer low interest and principal payments. Additionally, according to a company spokesperson, it was able to focus on increasing the actual value of the company, not merely upping its annual returns. According to Eric Hippeau, CEO of Ziff-Davis, "Forstmann Little is the ideal partner to help us take Ziff-Davis to the next level as we build on our leading domestic and international position in computer publishing. Their unique capital structure and focus on growth will be instrumental in helping Ziff-Davis reach its full potential."

At the same time, Ziff-Davis possessed a number of qualities that the LBO looked for in buyout candidates. Ziff-Davis was the most successful computer publishing company and had a profit margin well above that of other computer publishers in the country. Not only was the industry was rather immune to recessions, the company also had a high potential for growth and a strong management team. According to Theodore Forstmann of Forstmann Little, "Ziff-Davis

is an outstanding company, with dominant market share, a highly capable management team and significant growth potential."

Approach and Engagement

Several bidders emerged for Ziff-Davis, including industry giants Reed Elsevier PLC, Hachette Filipacchi Magazines, and K-III Communications Corp.; however, none were willing to bid higher than $1 billion for the computer publisher. On October 27, 1994, Forstmann Little stepped forward with a $1.4 billion cash offer, which Ziff-Davis immediately accepted. Not included in the sale were trade show unit Ziff-Davis Exposition and Conference Co.; Information Access Co., a database collection including roughly 4,000 consumer magazines and trade periodicals; and Interchange Online Network, an electronic publishing system.

According to the terms of the transaction, Ziff-Davis would stay in New York, and CEO Eric Hippeau would remain at the helm of the publisher. The workforce (which totaled 3,300 employees), editorial direction, and organizational structure of Ziff-Davis would be unchanged as a result of the deal.

The acquisition was officially completed on December 22, 1994. Forstmann Little financed roughly $950 million of the purchase price with its own equity and subordinated debt funds, more than the firm had ever spent of its own capital. Bank loans covered the remainder of the cost.

Products and Services

In 1999, Forstmann Little's holdings included Department 56, Lear Siegler, Pullman, and Thompson Minwax. The firm continued to operate as one of the most successful leveraged buyout companies in the U.S.

Publishing accounted for 70% of total sales at Ziff-Davis in 1998. Publications included *Biz/Excite*, *Computer Gaming World*, *Computer Shopper*, *Electronic Gaming Monthly*, *Expert Gamer*, *Family PC*, *Inside Technology Training*, *Inter@ctive Week*, *MacWeek*, *MacWorld*, *Official U.S. PlayStation Magazine*, *PC Computer*, *PC Magazine*, *PC Week*, *Product Reviews*, *Product Testing*, *Sm@rt Reseller*, and *Yahoo! Internet Life*. Trade show operations brought another 28%, and Internet products secured the final 2%.

Changes to the Industry and Review of the Outcome

In January of 1995, Ziff-Davis restructured operations, eliminating 12 out of 18 jobs in creative services, five out of 52 jobs in human resources, six out of 90 jobs in facilities, two out of 46 jobs in ZD Labs, and three executive spots.

When Forstmann Little bought Ziff-Davis, most analysts expected the LBO to take the publishing company public in three to five years. However, Mayayoshi Son, head of Japan's Softbank Corp., had other plans for the computer publisher. Son's quest to push his firm into the number-one spot among worldwide computer magazines led him to approach Theodore Forstmann about purchasing Ziff-Davis. After Forstmann told Son that he wanted at least $2 billion for Ziff-Davis, Son made a $2.1 billion offer, which Forstmann Little accepted in November of 1995. In February of 1996, Forstmann Little sold Ziff-Davis for nearly three-quarters of a billion dollars more than it paid for it, making a 50% return on its investment of little more than one year.

Research

Carmody, Deirdre. "Forstmann to Acquire Ziff-Davis," in *The New York Times*, 28 October 1994. Explains why Forstmann Little made an offer for Ziff-Davis.

"Forstmann Little Completes Acquisition of Ziff-Davis," in *PR Newswire*, 22 December 1994. Discusses financial details regarding the purchase of Ziff-Davis by Forstmann Little.

Huhn, Mary. "Ziff Sold for $1.4 Billion," in *MEDIAWEEK*, 31 October 1994. Reports the terms of the agreement between Ziff-Davis and Forstmann Little.

Manly, Lorne. "Ziff Re-Boots: Ziff-Davis Built Its Empire on Business Computer Titles. But New Owner Forstmann Little Wants to Expand While Paring Down a $500 Million Bank Debt," in *Folio: The Magazine for Magazine Management*, 15 April 1995. Details management's plans to growing Ziff-Davis.

"Softbank Agrees to Buy Ziff-Davis PC Magazine Group," in *The New York Times*, 10 November 1995. Discusses the reasons why Softbank Corp. wanted to buy Ziff-Davis from Forstmann Little.

The Players

CEO of Forstmann Little & Co.: Theodore J. Forstmann. After graduating from Yale, Theodore Forstmann began his financial career by becoming a founding partner of Forstmann Little & Co. in 1978. After acquiring Gulfstream Aerospace in 1990, Forstmann named himself chairman in 1993. By 1995, Forstmann's net worth was estimated to be $400 million. He retained the position of chairman of Gulfstream until it was sold to General Dynamics Corp. in 1999.

Chairman and CEO of Ziff-Davis Inc.: Eric Hippeau. Eric Hippeau worked for International Data Group (IDG) as vice president of computer publications in Latin American between 1975 and 1986. He then took over as publisher of the firm's *InfoWorld* magazine until 1989, when Ziff-Davis hired him to publish *PC Magazine*. The following year, Hippeau was named executive vice president of Ziff-Davis. After a short stint as president and chief operating officer, he took over as chairman and CEO in 1993. Hippeau remained at the helm of Ziff-Davis after its 1994 takeover by Forstmann Little and subsequent sale to Softbank Corp.

Weinberg, Neil. "Bubble, Bubble…," in *Forbes*, 11 March 1996. Offers an overview of the growth of Japan's Softbank Corp. under Masayoshi Son.

Ziff-Davis Inc. Home Page, available at http://www.ziff-davis.com. Official World Wide Web Home Page for Ziff-Davis Inc. Includes press releases, as well as historical, financial, product, and investor information.

DAVE W. SHELDON

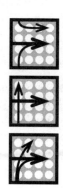

FUJITSU & FAIRCHILD
SEMICONDUCTOR INTERNATIONAL

Fujitsu Ltd.
6-1, Marunouchi 1-chrome
Chiyoda, Tokyo 100-8211
Japan

tel: 81-3-3213-4160
fax: 81-3-3216-9365
web: http://www.fujitsu.co.jp

Fairchild Semiconductor Corp.
333 Western Ave., Mail Stop 01-00
South Portland, ME 04106
USA

tel: (207)775-8100
fax: (207)761-6020
web: http://www.fairchildsemi.com

date: canceled in March 1987
affected: Fujitsu Ltd., Japan, founded 1935
affected: Fairchild Semiconductor Corp., USA, founded 1957

Overview of the Merger

The planned merger between Fujitsu Ltd. and Fairchild Semiconductor would have created one of the first globally powerful semiconductor companies in history. The deal, which would have constituted one of the largest transfers of American technology and research to Japan, was squelched by Fairchild in March of 1987, after heated debate in Washington threatened to prolong, if not cancel, the sale. Many officials felt the deal would have been a breach of national security due to Fairchild's operations with the Pentagon and defense computer systems. Advocates of the deal claimed that those who opposed it did so for political reasons only.

History of Fujitsu Ltd.

In 1935, Fujitsu Ltd. was created as the manufacturing arm of Fuji Electric, a joint venture formed in 1923 by Siemens and Furukawa Electric to modernize Japan's communications network. Fujitsu's initial contracts were for the manufacture of telephone equipment. Two years later, Fujitsu expanded its activities to include production of carrier transmission equipment. World War II placed increasing demands on Japanese industry, however, and Fujitsu shifted exclusively to the production of anti-aircraft weapons by the end of the war.

In 1945, wartime bombing eliminated nearly 50% of Japan's telephone network. The U.S.-led government of occupied Japan forced Fujitsu to reorganize as a publicly held company. By 1952, a coalition led by Eisaku Sato convinced the government of occupied Japan to set up a new public utility, Nippon Telephone and Telegraph (NTT), to complete reconstruction and maintain operation of Japanese telephone services. NTT quickly became a leading consumer of electronic products, and Fujitsu was able to establish a relation as one of the four official suppliers to the new utility.

Fujitsu continued to grow, and in 1954, developed the first Japanese commercial computer. Five years later, the Japanese government erected trade barriers to protect domestic computer manufacturers from competition with transistorized computers introduced by IBM. With government encouragement, Fujitsu embarked on development of a central processing unit and ventured into related areas such as semiconductor production and factory robotics. In 1961, the Japanese government concluded an agreement whereby IBM traded patents to domestic manufacturers in exchange for access to Japanese markets. Alone among Japanese computer manufacturers, Fujitsu did not form any joint agreements with U.S. companies in the aftermath of this agreement.

Throughout the 1960s, Fujitsu continued on its path in computers. In 1962, the company worked to develop a product to compete with the IBM 1401 as part of FONTAC, a government-sponsored program also involving Hitachi and NEC. Although FONTAC failed, it paved the way for more sophisticated attempts at a coordinated national computer industry, such as the Japanese Electronic Computer Company (JECC), a joint venture of 7 Japanese firms. Benefitting from government contracts and loans, JECC increased domestic computer sales by 203%.

By further developing technology created during the FONTAC project, Fujitsu was able to produce the most advanced Japanese computer to date and quickly became JECC's leading supplier in 1965. By 1970, the company's fortunes suffered in the face of the introduction of the IBM 370 computer line. The Japanese government announced a liberalized import policy to take effect in 1975, giving Fujitsu five years to become truly competitive in an international market. To offset this situation, the Japanese Ministry of International Trade and Development instituted an accelerated program of government subsidies for computer research and development.

In 1972, Fujitsu began to produce IBM-plug-compatible computers. Italso purchased a 30% interest in Amdahl Corp., an American computer manufacturer headed by Gene Amdahl, a former IBM engineer who developed his corporation for the purpose of producing a cheaper version of the IBM 370. Fujitsu spun off its factory robotics interests as Fujitsu Fanuc as well. With guaranteed buyers in NTT and JECC, the company was free to follow aggressive strategies for growth. In 1974, the company developed the first plug-compatible computer. Four years later, it entered into a joint venture with Siemens and surpassed IBM Japan as the leading Japanese producer of computers.

In the early 1980s, Fujitsu entered into a partnership with TRW to sell point-of-sale systems, embarked on a joint computer marketing venture with ICL, and released its first supercomputer. In 1985, IBM accused Fujitsu of stealing proprietary operating systems soft-

The Business

Financials - Fujitsu Ltd.

Revenue (1999): $43.9 billion

Employees (1999): 188,000

Financials - Fairchild Semiconductor Corp.

Revenue (1999): $735.1 million

Employees (1998): 6,927

SICs / NAICS

sic 3575 - Computer Terminals

sic 3661 - Telephone & Telegraph Apparatus

sic 3695 - Magnetic & Optical Recording Media

sic 7372 - Prepackaged Software

sic 7371 - Computer Programming Services

naics 334113 - Computer Terminal Manufacturing

naics 334418 - Printed Circuit Assembly (Electronic Assembly) Manufacturing

naics 334613 - Magnetic and Optical Recording Media Manufacturing

naics 541511 - Custom Computer Programming Services

ware. Fujitsu claimed it was entitled to the information under a secret agreement signed in 1983. An arbitrator eventually awarded IBM damages of $237 million from the 1985 suit, but also allowed Fujitsu to inspect IBM-developed software packages for 10 years for a nominal fee.

In 1986, Fujitsu attempted to purchase Fairchild Semiconductor, but its plans were thwarted when the U.S. government blocked the sale to avoid foreign ownership of a defense computer component manufacturer. That action did not stop the firm from purchasing interest in other companies. In 1990, it bought 80% of ICL, a British manufacturer of computer mainframes. ICL then purchased 50% of the European maintenance operations of Bell Atlantic Co. and 100% of Nokia Data Holding, the largest Scandinavian computer manufacturer. In 1995, the company received an order for a supercomputer from Western Geophysical Co., a Texas oil-exploration company, its first from the U.S. It also developed Perclean, a powerful alternative cleaning solvent, enabling the company to completely stop using trichloroethane, which is destructive to the ozone layer.

The Officers

Fujitsu Ltd.

Chairman Emeritus: Takuma Yamamoto

Chairman: Tadashi Sekizawa

Vice Chairman: Michio Naruto

President: Naoyuki Akikusa

Fairchild Semiconductor Corp.

Chairman, President and CEO: Kirk P. Pond

Exec. VP and Chief Financial Officer: Joseph R. Martin

Exec. VP, Chief Administrative Officer, Secretary and
General Counsel: Daniel E. Boxer

Exec. VP: Jerry M. Baker

Exec. VP: W. Wayne Carlson

Fujitsu continued to be Japan's largest computer manufacturer, with a 25% market share, and ranked second in the world behind IBM, in 1996. Fujitsu PC Corp. was launched in the U.S. in an effort to expand its PC business. By 1998, the company was focused on increasing profits. It took many subsidiaries public, in an effort to battle falling demand in the semiconductor market and Asia's weakening economy. The company began a joint venture with Toshiba Corp. and also focused efforts on Internet business with its 1999 purchase of Nifty Serve, a Japanese online provider.

History of Fairchild Semiconductor Corp.

Fairchild Semiconductor Corp. was founded in 1957. Sherman Mills Fairchild gave funds to a group of California scientists, including Robert Noyce and Gordon Moore—founders of Intel Corp.—to develop a new process in transistor manufacturing. The group set out to develop and produce superior semiconductor components.

In 1959, the Planar process was introduced by the group. This development proved to be an historical achievement in semiconductor technology and is used today in the production of transistors and integrated circuits.

In the 1970s, leading engineers had left the company as it was being poorly run and management was faltering. The company was near financial ruin when it was bought by Schlumberger, a French conglomerate, in 1979. The deal proved to be a failure and the French company began to look for a buyer in the mid 1980s.

In 1986, Japanese company Fujitsu made a bid for Fairchild. The deal never went through, however, as it failed to gain approval by the U.S. government. One year later, Schlumberger sold the company to National Semiconductor. Fairchild's new focus was on supercomputer and mainframe computer logic chips.

Fairchild grew through acquisitions in the 1990s. Major purchases included a semiconductor unit of Raytheon Co. for $117 million and a division of Samsung Electronics Co., Ltd. for $450 million. The company was divested in 1997, upon a reorganization effort by National Semiconductor. Sterling Holding Co. bought a 53% stake in the company for $550 million, while National kept a 12% interest. In 1999, Fairchild Semiconductor went public. The company continued to grow and develop logic chips, discrete power and signal components, and analog, mixed signal, and non-volatile memory chips.

Market Forces Driving the Merger

In 1986, the semiconductor industry was facing an uncertain future due to a financially crippling recession. Industry-wide losses totaled over $1 billion, and over 60,000 of the industry's 230,000 jobs had been cut. Worldwide demand had also decreased from an average of 18% per year to just under 13% per year. At the same time, the industry was dealing with a surplus, and the U.S. faced increased international competition, especially from Japan.

New technological trends were also marking change in the industry. New denser, more complex chips were the wave of the future. As a result, companies that had a handle on both semiconductor and electronic systems were projected to have an edge. This need for vertical integration sparked a wave of consolidation throughout the industry. Companies like Motorola Inc. and Toshiba were forming joint ventures for the exchange of technology. However, large companies which had diversified into semiconductors operations, were opting to exit the industry. United Technologies Corp. sold its Mostek unit and Honeywell Inc. also sold its semiconductor unit, Synertek.

The U.S. had also recently signed a semiconductor trade agreement with Japan. This agreement set minimum U.S. prices for Japanese-made chips. The agreement did not cover chips manufactured on American soil, a motivating factor in the recent Japanese interest in U.S. semiconductor operations. Many analysts also felt that Fujitsu looked to Fairchild as a way around the agreement.

Another factor motivating Fujitsu's interest in Fairchild was the increasing purchase power of the yen, as well as declining export profit margins. Buying was a more lucrative option than building in foreign territory. Fairchild had been financially faltering, and its owner, Schlumberger, could not afford to maintain the company's operations. Fujitsu had also been losing money in its semiconductor business, although it remained Japan's largest computer manufacturer. The two companies felt that Fairchild's high speed logic chips and Fujitsu's memory chips would complement each other.

Approach and Engagement

On October 23, 1986, Fujitsu announced that it planned to purchase an 80% interest in Fairchild Semiconductor for $200 million from Schlumberger Ltd., an oilfield services company. Schlumberger would retain a 20% stake in Fairchild, while Fujitsu would meld its operations into Fujitsu Microelectronics.

Upon announcement of the deal, the Reagan administration jumped into action. Even though Fairchild was owned by a foreign interest already, France was not a threat in the technological industry as Japan was. Fairchild, along with its semiconductor operations, dealt with emitter-coupled logic (ECL). The ECL chips played an important role in supercomputers and high-tech Pentagon weapons. A debate broke out by November on whether or not the deal would breach national security. Officials in government defense and state departments were torn on the issue. Some felt that the deal would tighten relations with a defense ally and deter the collapse of Fairchild. According to *The Washington Post*, other defense officials were concerned that, "the deal would leave Japan in control of one of the Pentagon's major suppliers of computer chips and provide that country with a major advantage over American manufacturers in the global competition for the sale and development of high-technology products."

The Committee on Foreign Investment in the United States (CFIUS) did not have the power itself to block the sale. However, U.S. laws that protected U.S. technology were in place. In 1983, the CFIUS caused Japanese concerns to pull away from two deals by raising security concerns; both Nippon Steel Corp. and Kyocera Corp. had backed away from potential U.S. purchases.

In March 1987, Commerce Secretary Malcolm Balridge announced that the Cabinet would be taking over the decision on whether or not to allow the deal to go through. He made his opinion clear on the matter, stating that the deal should be blocked "in retaliation for Japan's refusal to buy American supercomputers for its public agencies and universities," as

The Players

U.S. Secretary of Commerce:Malcolm Baldridge. Former CEO of a brass manufacturing company, Malcolm Baldridge became Secretary of Commerce in 1981 during the Reagan administration. His main focus became U.S. business, as he pushed for deregulation and reform of export controls on trade with Communist countries. He spearheaded several global trade reform efforts as well. Baldridge played an instrumental role in squelching the 1987 planned merger of Fairchild Semiconductor and Fujitsu Ltd. He died later that year, while practicing for a rodeo event.

President and CEO of Fairchild Semiconductor Corp.:Donald W. Brooks. Southern Methodist University graduate Donald Brooks joined Texas Instruments Inc. and worked there as a troubleshooter and senior vice president. After 25 years of service with the company, he was recruited by Fairchild in 1983. He became head of North American operations and was soon elected CEO in 1985. During his tenure, he restored the company to profitability and oversaw negotiations in the failed merger with Fujitsu Ltd. In 1995, Brooks was named president of Taiwan Semiconductor Manufacturing.

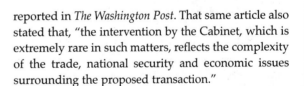

reported in *The Washington Post*. That same article also stated that, "the intervention by the Cabinet, which is extremely rare in such matters, reflects the complexity of the trade, national security and economic issues surrounding the proposed transaction."

In mid-March, Schlumberger announced that it had nixed plans to sell Fairchild to Fujitsu. One reason given by the company reported in *The New York Times* was that, "the rising political controversy in the United States concerning the venture made it unlikely that the sale of Fairchild could be completed within a reasonable time." Analysts also looked to increasing trade friction with Japan, an underlying distrust of Japan, and a fear that the Japanese would take over the chip industry, as causes for the called-off transaction.

Products and Services

In 1998, Fujitsu Ltd. operated in Belgium, China, Columbia, Germany, India, Indonesia, Iran, Jordan, Malaysia, Russia, Thailand, the U.S., Vietnam and

Zimbabwe. Operations in Japan made up 60% of sales in 1999. Information processing brought in 36% of sales, as did services and software; telecommunications secured 12%; and electronic devices accounted for 10%. Computer products included networking equipment, printers and scanners, personal computers, servers, and software. Fujitsu's communications systems included digital microwave products, submarine cable systems, and teleconferencing equipment. The company also produced electronic components, LCD's, semiconductors, air conditioners, and navigation systems.

Fairchild Semiconductor had locations around the globe in 1998, including Maine, California, Utah, South Korea, Malaysia, Hong Kong, and Japan. Asian sales accounted for 33% of total revenues. Fairchild produced logic, discrete, analog, and mixed signal and non-volatile memory chips, as well as providing contract manufacturing. Logic production, the most lucrative of its operations, brought in 38% of total sales.

Review of the Outcome and Changes to the Industry

When the Fujitsu deal fell through, many in the U.S. semiconductor industry breathed a sigh of relief. The transaction's failure eased concerns that if the Japanese company went ahead with the purchase, other Japanese firms would follow, saturating the semiconductor market and taking over American technology.

The battle that ensued in Washington before and after the deal died was harsh. Those who went along with the deal claimed that those who opposed it, did so simply because of unfolding political issues with Japan. Cries of potential national security breeches, they claimed, were only a red herring. After all, Fairchild went under French management when Schlumberger purchased it in 1979, and no one raised an eyebrow.

Late in 1987, Fairchild was eventually sold to National Semiconductor. National paid only half of what Fujitsu had offered for the company.

Research

Auerbach, Stuart. "Cabinet to Weigh Sale of Chip Firm," in *The Washington Post*, 12 March 1987. Explains Cabinet involvement in decision of Fujitsu purchase.

———. "Fujitsu Drops Takeover Bid for California Chip Maker," in *The Washington Post*, 17 March 1987. Reports the dropped bid for Fairchild.

"Fairchild Chip Officer Defends Fujitsu Deal," in *The New York Times*, 27 October 1986. Discusses the career of Donald Brooks and his deal with Fujitsu.

Fairchild Semiconductor International Home Page, available at http://www.fairchildsemi.com. Official World Wide Web Page for Fairchild Semiconductor. Offers news releases, historical information, and financial information.

Fujitsu Ltd. Home Page, available at http://www.fujitsu.co.jp. Official World Wide Web Page for Fujitsu Ltd. Houses news releases, company information, and financial and product information.

"Fujitsu Ltd.," in *Notable Corporate Chronologies*, The Gale Group, 1999. Offers a summary of events in the history of Fujitsu Ltd.

Kehoe, Louise. "Long Shadows in Silicon Valley," in *Financial Times (London)*, 29 October 1986. Discusses recent events in the chip industry.

Pollack, Andrew. "Fujitsu in Deal on Chip Maker," in *The New York Times*, 24 October 1986. Describes Fujitsu's bid for Fairchild.

Rapoport, Carla. "The Pressures That Led to a Switch in Semiconductor Strategy," in *Financial Times (London)*, 29 October 1986. Covers forces driving Fujitsu's bid for Fairchild.

Rempel, William. "The Fairchild Deal," in *Los Angeles Times*, 30 November 1987. Discusses political involvement in the Fujitsu bid for Fairchild.

Schrage, Michael. "Fujitsu Buying Stake in Fairchild," in *The Washington Post*, 25 October 1986. Examines Fujitsu's bid, as well as recent trends in the chip industry.

CHRISTINA M. STANSELL

GENERAL CINEMA & HARCOURT BRACE JOVANOVICH

nationality: USA
date: November 1991
affected: General Cinema Corp., USA, founded 1922
affected: Harcourt Brace Jovanovich Inc., USA, founded 1919

Harcourt General Inc.
27 Boylston St.
Chestnut Hill, MA 02467
USA

tel: (617)232-8200
fax: (617)739-1395
web: http://www.harcourt-general.com

Overview of the Merger

General Cinema's $1.5 billion purchase of Harcourt Brace Jovanovich saved the publishing concern from financial demise in 1991. The deal was drawn out over the course of one year, as a group of Harcourt bondholders rejected several bids by General Cinema. The bargaining paid off, however, and in November of 1991, the acquisition was approved. General Cinema had interests in movie theaters, specialty retailing, and publishing as a result of the deal.

History of General Cinema Corp.

In 1922, Philip Smith Theatrical Enterprises was created by Philip Smith, a young film salesman. The company incorporated in 1939, as movie theaters were growing in popularity across the U.S. Smith continued to look for ways to increase profits, and in 1951, he opened the first mall movie theater at Shopper's World in Framingham, Massachusetts.

By 1960, General Drive-In, formed by Smith Management Co. and Midwest Drive-In, was listed on the New York Stock Exchange and operated over 20 drive-in theaters and 19 indoor theaters. When Philip Smith died one year later, his son, Richard A. Smith, took over the company acting as president and CEO.

Under his leadership, the company began to develop a multi-screen theater. In 1963, General Drive-In introduced the first such theaters in Houston, Texas, and Peabody, Massachusetts. One year later, the company's named was changed to General Cinema Corp. as its focus was shifting away from outdoor theaters.

Smith began to diversify the company, and in 1968, he purchased a 90% interest in the American Beverage Corp. for $18.1 million. Other acquisitions followed, including the Robert H. Snyder Corp. for $5 million. In 1970, the 15 Mann theaters in Minneapolis, Minnesota were bought to increase General Cinema's area theaters to 21. However, the Justice Department ruled that the company had eliminated competition in that area and forced it to sell nine of the newly acquired theaters.

The Business

Financials

Revenue (1998): $4.2 billion

Employees (1998): 12,000

SICs / NAICS

sic 5311 - Department Stores

sic 2731 - Book Publishing

With 412 indoor theater screens and 46 drive-ins, General Cinema was the largest theater operator in the U.S. in 1973. The company was also focused on its bottling operations, and by 1975, it was the largest independent bottler of Pepsi-Cola and Dr. Pepper in the U.S. The firm ended the decade by closing many of its drive-in theaters as popularity diminished. It also introduced Sunkist Orange Soda and bought two radio stations in Boston.

Smith diversified the company even further in the 1980s. His plan continued with the $300 million purchase of $1 million shares of preferred stock in Carter Hawley Hale (CHH) which operated several retail stores including, Broadway, Emporium, Bergdorf Goodman, and Neiman Marcus. The agreement allowed General Cinema representation on CHH's board and provided the firm with an option to buy CHH subsidiary Walden Book Corp. Inc., which it declined.

In 1985, the fiscal year ended with record profits and sales for the twelfth consecutive year and for the twenty-fourth time in the last 25 years. One year later, General Cinema announced that the U.S. government was investigating its beverage business for potential antitrust infractions and its movie theaters for ticket price-fixing. The company also bought $135 million in Cadbury Schweppes PLC stock without informing the Securities and Exchange Commission (SEC). (Normally, companies were to report acquisitions over $15 million so the SEC could investigate for antitrust violations.)

CHH created a chain of specialty retail stores called the Neiman Marcus Group in 1987. General Cinema exchanged its 49% of CHH stock for 60% in the new stores. General Cinema also announced it had purchased 8.7% of Cadbury Schweppes, and group annual sales exceeded $1 billion for the first time. In 1988, the firm invested another $234 million in Cadbury Schweppes and revealed that it might attempt a full acquisition. One year later, all of its bot-

tling businesses were sold to PepsiCo, for about $1.88 billion in cash.

The next decade proved to be one of change for the company. It sold its interest in Cadbury Schweppes for roughly $500 million. With the excess cash flow from the sale of its bottling units, General Cinema announced plans to merge with Harcourt Brace Jovanovich (HBJ). The deal went through in November of 1991; as a result of the merger with the textbook publisher, the company reported an annual loss of $306 million. The firm also had to contend with its lack of communication with the SEC in earlier years. In 1992, the SEC fined General Cinema $950,000 for its Cadbury Schweppes investments, effectively negating its profit from the sale of the stock.

To more accurately reflect its current focus on publishing, General Cinema changed its name to Harcourt General Inc. in 1993. Later that year, the company spun off its movie theater operations to shareholders. Harcourt General also sold its insurance businesses to General Electric for $400 million in 1994. The divestment was initiated to allow the company to continue its efforts to focus on publishing. The company purchased additional stock in Neiman Marcus Group as well, which raised its stake to 58.6%.

In 1997, Harcourt General acquired Churchill Livingstone, the largest health science publisher in Europe, from Peason PLC for roughly $92.5 million. It also merged with National Education Corp., which allowed the company to become a leader in the education industry. One year later, Mosby Inc. was acquired, and Harcourt Health Sciences was formed. The new entity was the world's leading medical publisher.

History of Harcourt Brace Jovanovich Inc.

In 1919, Alfred Harcourt and Donald C. Brace began a publishing firm by the name of Harcourt, Brace & Howe. Will D. Howe, an editor and author, left the company one year later, and the name was changed to Harcourt, Brace & Co. Just three months after incorporation, the company had its first hit publication, *Organizing For Work* by H.L. Gant.

Throughout the 1920s, the company continued to have success in publishing, including *The Economic Consequences of Peace* by John Maynard Keynes. Harcourt also diversified into religious publications as well as college and school textbooks. The company's first employee, Ellen Knowles Eayres, led the firm to implement an equal employment opportunities program for women. She eventually married Alfred Harcourt. Margaret McElderry also worked for the company from 1946 to 1972, in the first children's book department. She is credited for the discovery of many notable authors, including Joan Walsh Anglund and Eleanor Estes.

In 1942, Alfred Harcourt left the company and relinquished control to Donald Brace. During the war, the company published *Men Must Act*, which was offered free in an ad in *The New York Times* to the first 500 respondents. William Jovanovich joined the company in 1947 as a salesman. In 1955, after the deaths of Harcourt and Brace, Jovanovich was named president.

The new leader set forth an aggressive path for the company to follow. By 1960, the company had gone public and merged with World Book Co. to form Harcourt, Brace & World Inc., a leading publisher in elementary, secondary, and college material. Throughout the remainder of the decade, Harcourt continued to grow by acquisition. Deals included several educational filmstrip production companies, farm and trade publications, and Academic Press.

In 1970, Jovanovich was named chairman, and the company changed its name to Harcourt Brace Jovanovich. The company made acquisitions in every year of this decade, with the exception of 1975. Major purchases included The Psychological Corp., the Beckley-Cardy Co., Bay Area Review Course, Bar Review Institute, and Pyramid Communications. In 1976, Harcourt also bought Sea World theme parks. By 1978, the company was publishing more than 2,300 titles and 75 magazines.

At the same time that Jovanovich was making these bold purchases, the company was seeing losses in certain operations. As a result, he reduced the company budget, fired top executives, and reorganized the company. The firm was reorganized into five groups: university and scholarly publishing, school materials and assessment, periodicals and insurance, business publications and broadcasting, and popular enterprises.

In 1980, HBJ bought an insurance broker. During the next two years, the firm also moved eleven new periodical markets. Headquarters moved to Orlando, Florida, in 1982 at a cost estimated near $35 million. The firm continued on its buying spree with the acquisition of several more insurance operations and—once the move to Florida was complete—additional theme parks in the Orlando area, as well as California.

The largest purchase in the HBJ's history came in 1986, when it paid $500 million for the educational and publishing division of CBS Inc.. One year later, the firm had to fend off a takeover attempt from British Printing and Communications Corp. (BPCC). The fight was successful, but costly, as HBJ took on over $2.9 billion in debt to make itself unattractive to

The Officers

Chairman and CEO: Richard A. Smith

President and Co-Chief Operating Officer: Brian J. Knez

President and Co-Chief Operating Officer: Robert Smith

Sr. VP and Chief Financial Officer: John Cook

Sr. VP, General Counsel, and Secretary: Eric P. Geller

BPCC. To whittle down its mounting deficit, the company began selling assets, including two VHF television stations, book clubs, and the corporate jets. The firm also cut theme park jobs. By the end of 1987, the company had sold over $370 million in assets.

In 1989, the company divested all of its theme park operations. HBJ went through another reorganization and Peter Jovanovich, son of William, took over the company. The company was faltering under its debt load and had a 1993 obligation to pay dividends and interest to its bondholders. Left with few options, the company agreed in November of 1991 to be taken over by General Cinema for $1.5 billion.

Market Forces Driving the Merger

General Cinema had a long history of buying assets at low prices and then selling them for huge profits at a later date. When the firm sold its soft drink bottling company to Pepsi-Co in 1989 for $1.88 billion, it was left with cash to spend at a time when most major companies were faltering. Since the sale, Richard Smith had been looking for a third business to add to his movie theater and specialty retail operations. In an article in *The New York Times* Smith commented that HBJ, "filled his demand for a consumer business with sales, marketing and distribution." He went on to say that, "we wanted a protected position. We wanted a brand equity that could be promoted, but where there were reasonably high barriers of entry."

For Harcourt Brace Jovanovich, being bought by a large, financially stable company was an answer to its prayers. The company was swimming in $1.9 billion in debt after its takeover battle with Robert Maxwell and BPCC. A merger with General Cinema would relieve the financial burden, as well as keep the company intact as General Cinema had deep enough pockets to revive HBJ's publishing efforts and save the company from bankruptcy.

Approach and Engagement

General Cinema and HBJ began merger talks in late 1990. In January of 1991, General Cinema

The Players

Chairman and CEO of General Cinema Corp.: Richard A. Smith. Richard A. Smith was elected president and CEO of General Drive-In, later named General Cinema Corp., in 1961. He led the company through several successful ventures including its foray into soft drink bottling. Under Smith's leadership, General Cinema became the largest independent bottler of Pepsi-Cola and Dr. Pepper in the U.S., as well as the largest theater operator in 1973. The company also began operations in specialty retailing under his command. In 1991, he led the purchase of Harcourt Brace Jovanovich and became CEO and chairman of the new company, Harcourt General. In November of 1999, he relinquished his CEO title, but remained chairman.

President and CEO of Harcourt Brace Jovanovich Inc.: Peter Jovanovich. Peter Jovanovich began his career in publishing in 1972, when he joined Macmillan. Following in his father's footsteps, he began to work for Harcourt Brace in 1980 and was appointed president and CEO in January of 1990. After the merger with General Cinema, he resigned his post and took the top position at Macmillan/McGraw-Hill. Five years later, he left the company and joined Addison Wesley Longman as chairman and CEO in 1997.

announced that it had agreed to purchase HBJ for $1.4 billion. The terms included $1.30 per share for Harcourt shareholders and tender offers to the company's debt holders. Peter Jovanovich stated in a *Los Angeles Times* article that, "this merger will help us preserve the company and make it grow." With interest payments due on debt planned to significantly rise by 1992, HBJ saw the deal as its best financial option.

Despite an overwhelming sense of relief that the firm had avoided insolvency, HBJ bondholders were upset over the terms of the deal. General Cinema offered $1.1 billion for five issues of senior and subordinated classes of bonds with a face value of $1.9 billion. While shareholders would profit on the deal, bondholders would have to take a discount. By April, General Cinema had failed to reach an agreement with bondholders and had extended its bid twice. Talks broke off after the second extension passed, but resumed again in August. General Cinema raised its bid to $1.5 billion, giving more to bondholders for their investments, while giving less to shareholders.

The new terms included 75 cents worth of General Cinema stock for every Harcourt share owned, and bondholders received 47 cents to $1 for every $1 dollar in face value for their bonds. (The old offer would have paid out 32 cents to 93 cents per $1 face value.)

In October, bondholders approved the deal. On November 25, 1991, the deal was completed with all regulatory approvals met. Richard Smith stated in *The New York Times*, "we look forward to bringing HBJ into the General Cinema group of companies and providing it with the financial resources to further strengthen it operating businesses."

Products and Services

The new company, Harcourt General, focused on its specialty retailing and publishing interests in 1998. Specialty retailing accounted for 56% of total sales, where publishing efforts brought in the remaining 44%.

Retail operations included Bergdorf Goodman, Neiman Marcus, direct-mail catalog sales, Chef's catalog, and the Neiman Marcus Christmas Book. Publishing concerns were divided into five groups: Harcourt, Inc., Harcourt Health Sciences, Harcourt Higher Learning, Harcourt Professional & Corporate Development, and Harcourt Science & Technology. Harcourt Inc. was responsible for classroom education including assessment products and textbooks. Harcourt Health Sciences dealt with medical publications and nursing and healthcare books. Harcourt Higher Learning included interests in Archipelago; multi-media course materials in chemistry, economics, and physics; distance learning materials for health sciences; business and financial education publishing; behavioral science textbooks; and various other scholastic publications. Harcourt Professional & Corporate Development included assessment and testing materials for professionals such as BAR/BRI Bar Review and CPA review programs. Harcourt Sciences & Technology was comprised of Academic Press, which had operations in life, physical, and social sciences publishing.

Changes to the Industry

The General Cinema/Harcourt deal came after the great merger boom of the 1980s. Richard Smith, therefore, was able to buy the company for a relatively low price, compared to what it would have cost in earlier years. Financially secure, General Cinema was able to rebuild Harcourt into a publishing giant. Under its new name, Harcourt General, the publishing entity was reintroduced to the industry. It soon became one of the world's largest publishing concerns.

The company also spun off its theater interest to focus on publishing and its specialty retailing operations. This move left both industries with viable, financially stable competitors.

Review of the Outcome

In the fourth quarter of 1991, General Cinema reported a loss of $285.9 million as a result of its purchase of HBJ. The loss was expected and did not deter the company from pursuing its aggressive plans in the publishing industry. General Cinema's purchase of HBJ changed both companies operations significantly. The company's name was changed to Harcourt General Inc. in 1993, to reflect its new-found interest in publishing. Theater interests were spun off and insurance assets were sold in an effort to focus on publishing and specialty retailing. Revenue for 1992 reached $3.71 billion, up from $3.58 billion in 1991. Stock price closed at $29.50 in 1992, while it had closed at $20.25 in 1991.

HBJ was saved from certain financial ruin as a result of the deal. Not only did General Cinema's purchase take care of HBJ's financial burden, it allowed the firm to grow and prosper once again. The company now stands as a world leader in publishing.

Research

"$1.4 Million Takeover of Harcourt Set," in *Los Angeles Times*, 24 January 1991. Explains Harcourt's financial situation and benefits of merging with General Cinema.

Brooks, Nancy Rivera. "Harcourt Brace Jovanovich Accepts General Cinema Bid," in *The Washington Post*, 23 August 1991. Comments on General Cinema's increased bid for HBJ.

Cieply, Michael. "General Cinema to Buy HBJ," in *Los Angeles Times*, 25 January 1991. Discusses General Cinema's first bid for HBJ.

Fabrikant, Geraldine. "General Cinema's Big Bet of Harcourt Brace's Revival," in *The New York Times*, 6 January 1992. Reports Richard Smith's acquisition strategy and plans for HBJ.

Fabrikant, Geraldine. "Harcourt Deal Raises Questions," in *The New York Times*, 31 January 1991. Explains General Cinema's bid and financial terms of the deal.

———. "Talks are Suspended on Buyout of Harcourt," in *The New York Times*, 18 April 1991. Describes General Cinema's approach to bondholder dissent of its offer to purchase HBJ.

"Harcourt Brace Jovanovich Inc.," in *International Directory of Company Histories*, Vol. IV, St. James Press, 1991. Covers the history of HBJ.

Harcourt General Inc. Home Page, available at http://www.harcourt-general.com. Official World Wide Web Home Page for Harcourt General Inc. Includes historical, financial, and product information, as well as recent news articles.

"Harcourt General Inc.," in *Notable Corporate Chronologies*, The Gale Group, 1999. Lists major events in the history of Harcourt General Inc.

Kindleberger, Richard. "Buyout Leaves General Cinema with $286m Loss," in *The Boston Globe*, 21 December 1991. Reports fourth quarter results for General Cinema.

McDowell, Edwin. "Harcourt Accepts Bid From General Cinema," in *The New York Times*, 25 January 1991. Discusses HBJ's initial agreement with General Cinema.

CHRISTINA M. STANSELL

GENERAL DYNAMICS &
NEWPORT NEWS SHIPBUILDING

General Dynamics Corp.
3190 Fairview Park Dr.
Falls Church, VA 22042
USA

tel: (703)876-3000
fax: (703)876-3125
web: http://www.generaldynamics.com

Newport News Shipbuilding Inc.
4101 Washington Ave.
Newport News, VA 23607-2770
USA

tel: (757)380-2000
fax: (757)753-8790
web: http://www.nns.com

date: February 1999 (canceled)
affected: General Dynamics Corp., USA, founded 1899
affected: Newport News Shipbuilding Inc., USA, founded 1886

Overview of the Acquisition

On February 18, 1999, General Dynamics Corp. made a $1.4 billion hostile takeover bid to purchase Newport News Shipbuilding Inc. The acquisition would have merged the two largest producers of U.S. warships and submarines. On April 1999, after nearly two months of heated debate in the Senate Armed Services Committee over antitrust issues, the acquisition was blocked.

History of General Dynamics Corp.

In 1899, John Holland gained financial backing from the U.S. government to found the Electric Boat Co., a maker of submarines. Isaac Leopold Rice, a lawyer-financier and battery and electronics magnate, offered to develop the company financially in return for an interest in Electric Boat. Holland soon lost control of the company to Rice, who secured contracts with the U.S. Navy and other foreign naval services.

By 1905, Electric Boat was selling submarines to both Japan and Russia while the two nations were at war with each other. Isaac Rice died in 1915 and was replaced by associate Henry Carse. Under Carse, Electric Boat purchased Electro Dynamics (ship propulsion), Elco Motor Yacht, and New London Ship & Engine (diesel engine and civilian ship manufacturer).

When the U.S. entered World War I, Carse devoted the company's resources to the construction of disposable cargo vessels rather than submarines. After recognizing the greater demand for submarines, he retooled to recommence submarine production; however, by the time production was fully in progress, the war had ended. In 1918, Carse was faced with bankruptcy when the Navy purchased primarily surface ships. As a result, Electric Boat refocused on surface ships.

The U.S. government investigated Electric Boat's business practices in 1941, accusing the firm of profiting from foreign wars. Carse defended the company's actions by responding that Electric Boat was forced to secure agreements with foreign governments since the U.S. Navy had suspended all major contracts for ten years. That same year, the Roosevelt administration reassessed its position on military preparedness when it observed German re-militarization and hostile Japanese activities. The government ordered submarines and PT (patrol/torpedo) boats from Electric Boat, which led to the revival of the company. A serious labor shortage necessitated the hiring of women as welders and riveters.

With the end of the war in 1945, government orders for new vessels were dramatically reduced, and employee count fell from 13,000 to 400. Electric Boat began a reorganization, as well as a plan of diversification into related commercial and defense industries, when it acquired Canadair from the Canadian government for $22 million.

Canadair proved to be of vital importance to the company as demand for aircraft increased throughout the 1940s. Electric Boat continued its diversification in the 1950s when it purchased Convair from Atlas Corp., a manufacturer of civilian and military aircraft. On February 21, 1952, General Dynamics was formed as the parent company to manage the operations of Electric Boat, Canadair, and Convair.

Electric Boat launched the first nuclear submarine, the Nautilus, in 1954. Because of contractual obligations with TWA and Howard Hughes, Convair was unable to introduce its new jetliner and took a $425 million loss on the entire passenger liner program. Financially weakened, General Dynamics agreed in 1959 to merge with Material Services Corp. That year, General Dynamics partnered with Grumman Corp. to bid against the Boeing Co. for production of the F-111 fighter-bombers, with which the U.S. Defense Department planned to replace its fleet of B-52 bombers. The General Dynamics/Grumman model was selected in 1960, and General Dynamics' Fort Worth division was established to build F-111 the following year.

To strengthen its position in the shipbuilding industry, General Dynamics acquired the Quincy Shipbuilding Works from Bethlehem Steel for $5 million in 1963. The Electric Boat division and its chief competitor, Newport News Shipbuilding, were awarded contracts to manufacture Los Angeles class submarines in 1971. Takis Veliotis was hired to manage the Quincy yard and, in 1973, he agreed to build liquefied natural gas tankers in conjunction with Frigitemp, a cold storage engineering firm.

To compete for a $200 million Department of Defense jet fighter contract, General Dynamics developed the prototype for its F-16 in 1973. The F-16 was chosen over Northrop's F-17 Cobra, and it became one of General Dynamics' major product lines. In 1976,

The Business

Financials - General Dynamics Corp.

Revenue (1999): $10 billion

Employees (1999): 44,000

Financials - Newport News Shipbuilding Inc.

Revenue (1998): $1.86 billion

Employees (1998): 18,200

SICs / NAICS

sic 3721 - Aircraft

sic 3731 - Ship Building & Repairing

sic 3795 - Tanks & Tank Components

sic 3519 - Internal Combustion Engines Nec

naics 336611 - Ship Building and Repairing

naics 336992 - Military Armored Vehicle, Tank and Tank Component Manufacturing

naics 333618 - Other Engine Equipment Manufacturing

Canadair was sold back to the Canadian government for $38 million.

Cost overruns (as much as $89 million per vessel) on 18 Los Angeles class submarines prompted a dispute ensued between the Defense Department and Electric Boat in 1977. That year, General Dynamics sought protection under Public Law 85-804, which was originally intended to protect "strategic assets" from bankruptcy due to cost overruns. Veliotis transferred from Quincy to the Groton shipyard, where productivity had deteriorated due to absenteeism and an employee turnover rate of 35%. Management had lost control of inventory, and reconstruction was necessary because of poor workmanship. By the year's end, Veliotis had restored order to the Electric Boat operation.

Veliotis moved from Electric Boat to a seat on the General Dynamics board of directors in 1981 and served as an international salesman. He soon resigned over a dispute in which he claimed he had been promised the position of CEO. Later, Veliotis fled to Greece after an indictment by government prosecutors of illegal business practices.

General Dynamics acquired the tank division of Chrysler Corp. for $336 million in 1982. The unit became a division of General Dynamics called Land Systems. That year, General Dynamics was contracted

The Officers

General Dynamics Corp.

Chairman and CEO: Nicholas D. Chabraja

President and Chief Operating Officer: James E. Turner

Exec. VP: Gordon R. England

Sr. VP and Chief Financial Officer: Michael J. Mancuso

Sr. VP, Law: David A. Savner

Newport News Shipbuilding Inc.

Chairman and CEO: William P. Fricks

Exec. VP, Operations: Thomas C. Schievelbein

Sr. VP and Chief Financial Officer: David J. Anderson

VP and General Counsel: Stephen B. Clarkson

VP and General Manager, Submarines: William G.
    Cridlin, Jr.

by the government to service and maintain TAKX supply ships for the Army's Rapid Deployment Force. Several executives were called to testify before a congressional subcommittee regarding overcharges, which resulted in investigations by the Justice Department and the Internal Revenue Service. After the involuntary resignation of Admiral Rickover, General Dynamics secured a government contract to manufacture several models of boats, including the $500 million Ohio class Trident submarine.

In 1986, General Dynamics acquired Cessna Aircraft Corp. and merged it with one of its subsidiaries. In 1987, Convair became the Space Systems division which manufactured Atlas launch vehicles for military and commercial customers. The firm also sold the Quincy shipyard for $49.5 million and founded a new division called Valley Systems, to gain contracts for the Reagan Administration's Strategic Defense Initiative.

A large reorganization took place in 1992 with a series of sales. Cessna Aircraft was sold to Textron Inc. for $600 million, and the General Dynamics missiles operations, as well as portions of Convair, were sold to Hughes Aircraft Co. Also, Lockheed Corp. acquired the Tactical Military Aircraft operations of General Dynamics for $1.5 billion in cash.

In order to compete in new high technology fields, General Dynamics maintained a strong 12,500-member research and development team. In 1992, its Fort Worth division worked in conjunction with other manufacturers on the Air Force's Advanced Tactical

Fighter and on the preliminary design of the National Aero-Space Plane. The Space Systems division was contracted for the production of superconducting magnets for the Superconducting Super Collider, and Electric Boat manufactured the first nuclear-powered attack and ballistic missile-firing submarines.

General Dynamics eliminated approximately 3,200 positions in its Electric Boat operations in Croton, Connecticut, in 1996. This was due to the large decline in U.S. defense spending. That same year, a U.S. Court of Claims awarded General Dynamics and McDonnell Douglas Corp. $1.74 billion in a suit the two firms had filed against the Department of Defense for termination of its contract to build the Navy A-12 attack jet.

On February 18, 1999, General Dynamics Corp. launched a $1.4 billion hostile bid for Newport News Shipbuilding Inc. A few months later, the Senate Armed Services Committee prohibited the deal, citing antitrust concerns. However, General Dynamics quickly recovered from the setback, and purchased Gulfstream Aeropsace Corp. for $4.8 billion in stock in May 1999.

History of Newport News Shipbuilding Inc.

Railroad magnate Collis P. Huntington founded Chesapeake Dry Dock and Construction Co. in 1886. The company flooded its first dry dock, which was based in Newport News, Virginia, three years later and changed its name to Newport News Shipbuilding and Drydock Co. in 1890.

A long relationship with the Navy began in 1893 when Newport News Shipbuilding was contracted to build three gunboats. Over the next six years, the shipyard won numerous contracts for the production of battleships, as well as commercial vessels such as tugs and passenger steamers. By 1899, the company had a workforce of 4,500, and new vessel contracts exceeded $10.5 million.

Newport News Shipbuilding began submarine production in 1905, but battleship production continued to be its primary focus. During the years of WWI, Newport News built 25 destroyers and continued the production of battleships. The firm also became active in refitting commercial vessels for wartime use.

In response to the shipbuilding lull that occurred at the end of the war, the company diversified its operations to include luxury yachts, railroad freight cars, transmission towers, aqueducts, hydraulic turbines and even traffic lights. The staff was cut to 2,000 by 1922.

In 1933, Newport News launched the first ship

ever built as an aircraft carrier, the USS Ranger. By 1940, seven more carriers were on order, as well as four more cruisers. A group of 17 investment firms bought Newport News for $18 million, and they took the company public.

The company's focus shifted to nuclear power in 1951, and two new subsidiaries were created as a result. The Eastern Idaho Construction Co. was formed to run a reactor test station in preparation for atomic supercarriers, and Newport News Industrial Corp. specialized in land based reactors. The first nuclear powered submarine, the shark, was launched in 1959, and the first nuclear powered aircraft carrier, the Enterprise, was launched the following year.

Aerospace corporations such as General Dynamics moved into the shipbuilding industry in the mid-1960s and presented intense competition for Newport News. By 1968, the competition had taken its toll. Newport News reported a $3.5 million loss in the first half of the year and began to pursue merger opportunities. On September 4, 1968, Tenneco Inc., a conglomerate from Houston, Texas, purchased the company for approximately $123 million.

During the restructuring by Tenneco, the employees unionized under the United Steelworkers Union. OSHA fined Tenneco $766,190, the largest OSHA fine ever, for over 600 cases ranging from excessive noise to unsafe working conditions at Newport News.

Overhauls and repairs became the main revenue sources for Newport News in the early 1970s. By mid-decade, naval contracts accounted for more than 90% of operating revenues. New naval contracts pushed profits to $82 million with revenues of over $1 billion in 1981. Newport News secured a $3.1 billion contract for the construction of two more nuclear powered carriers in 1982, which guaranteed steady work for at least ten more years.

Newport News reduced its reliance on naval contracts when it diversified into cargo ship production and extended its shipbuilding operations to the Middle East. In 1994, the company contracted with Eletson Corp. to build tankers and with the United Arab Emirates to invest in and manage the Abu Dhabi Ship Building Co.

The company committed nearly $100 million to facility expansions in 1994 to accommodate increased contracts, which included a $3 billion agreement for another nuclear powered carrier. Two years later, on December 11, 1996, Tenneco spun off Newport News Shipbuilding. After 28 years, it once again operated as an independent, publicly traded company. In 1999, the Senate Armed Services Committee prevented General Dynamics from taking over the firm.

The Players

Chairman and CEO of General Dynamics Corp.: Nicholas D. Chabraja. Nicholas Chabraja was named chairman and CEO of General Dynamics in 1997. After efforts to take over Newport News Shipbuilding fell through, he oversaw the firm's acquisition of Gulfstream Aerospace Corp. in May 1999.

Chairman and CEO of Newport News Shipbuilding Inc.: William P. Fricks. After graduating from Auburn University in 1966, William Fricks began working in the industrial engineering department of Newport News Shipbuilding. He moved up through senior management quickly and was named president and CEO in 1995. Fricks helped create a backlog of orders in excess of $3 billion and initiated innovative processing strategies that cut ship design and production time in half. On January 16, 1997, Fricks was elected chairman.

Market Forces Driving the Acquisition

General Dynamics initiated a series of layoffs as a result of the reduced military spending in the mid-1990s and shifted its focus to developing new land- and air-based military defense systems. These changes left General Dynamics unable to adequately compete with other major defense contractors such as Raytheon, Lockheed Martin, and Boeing.

In 1997, General Dynamics attempted to strengthen its position as a naval shipbuilder by purchasing NASSCO, the only private builder of naval ships on the west coast. Two years later, General Dynamics viewed a merger with Newport News, the only other nuclear shipyard and submarine manufacturer, as one that would bolster the company in times of shrinking naval contracts and allow for a higher quality product at a lower price. This was also the view of the command deputy of the Navy's Supervisor of Shipbuilding in San Diego, Glenn Cox. According to Cox, "Five to ten years ago you would have had all the shipyards playing cutthroat with each other to gather all the work they could. In today's environment everybody—the Navy, the public shipyards, the private shipyards—is teaming together to deliver a quality product." In fact, Newport News had already entered into a $740 million deal to merge with Avondale when General Dynamics made its move.

Approach and Engagement

Newport News Shipbuilding announced on February 18, 1999, that General Dynamics had made a $1.4 billion bid to acquire all of its outstanding common stock. The offer placed the stock purchase price at $38.50 per share and was contingent upon a series of conditions, which stipulated the necessity of "due diligence and antitrust clearance for the appropriate regulatory authorities in the Department of Justice and Defense."

Resistance to the move came from individuals who were concerned with reduced competition among shipyards and a monopoly in the nuclear submarine field. U.S. Representative Duncan Hunter noted that if the deal went through, competition for nuclear ship work would be wiped out since General Dynamics and Newport News were the only U.S. producers of nuclear submarines. Defense Secretary William Cohen and Senate Armed Services Committee chairman John Warner also opposed the deal on the same grounds. Analysis by the Department of Defense determined that if the sale went through, General Dynamics would possess 95% of the research and development funds from the Navy, as well as 75% of the shipyard engineers.

Cynthia Brown, president of the American Shipbuilding Association in Washington, D.C., supported the purchase on the grounds that with shrinking military expenditures, a large number of shipyards could be maintained. From 1981 to 1999, the number of private shipbuilders shrank from 22 to eight, and the six largest reduced staff from 82,000 to 55,000 from 1991 to 1997. "As long as the rate of shipbuilding is so low, it is going to be very difficult to maintain six major shipbuilders."

The debate continued until April 14, 1999, when the Pentagon blocked the merger. The Pentagon felt that the loss of competition in the nuclear submarine field outweighed the savings that the merger claimed possible. The Pentagon was concerned about competition in the rest of the shipbuilding industry, as well.

Products and Services

In 1999, General Dynamics consisted of four primary divisions: Marine, which produces nuclear submarines and surface ships; Combat Systems, which supplies armored vehicles and ordinance; Aerospace, which designs, develops, manufactures, and markets intercontinental business jets; and Information Systems and Technology, which focuses on communication systems, as well as avionic, maritime, and commercial uses of technology.

Major products include the Seawolf-class nuclear-powered attack submarine, Arleigh Burke-class Aegis destroyer, Abrams M1A2 digitized main battle tank, munitions and gun systems, advanced fiber-optics products, high-speed data processors for satellites, and the Gulfstream IV-SP and Gulfstream V ultra-long range, large cabin business jets. Future projects include the 21st century platforms like the Virginia-class new attack submarine, San Antonio-class amphibious assault ship, DD 21 land attack destroyer, and the Marine Corps Advanced Amphibious Assault Vehicle (AAAV).

Newport News Shipbuilding posted sales of $1.862 billion in 1998. The construction of new vessels accounted for 45% of total annual revenues. The maintenance of vessels already in the fleet secured 39%, and engineering brought in the remaining 16%.

Changes to the Industry

After the Pentagon blocked the deal with Newport News, General Dynamics continued its attempts to strengthen its position as a major player in the military defense industry by purchasing companies in fields other than shipbuilding. In May of 1999, General Dynamics agreed to purchase Gulfstream Aerospace Corp. for $5.3 billion in stock, and on June 23 of 1999, they purchased three defense related businesses from GTE Corp. for $1.05 billion in cash. These two additions were projected to bring in nearly $4 billion in annual revenues and increase annual sales to roughly $9.5 billion.

As predicted by industry analysts, consolidation in the shipbuilding industry continued. Defense contractor Litton Industries Inc. bid to purchase Newport News, as well as Avondale Industries Inc., a New Orleans, Louisiana-based builder of both military and commercial ships. The total offered price for the two was $2.43 billion. When those deals are completed, and the two shipbuilders are merged together, not only will there be one less shipbuilding company, but there will also be one more company with the funds and resources to compete directly with General Dynamics in the marine defense industry.

Review of the Outcome

In addition to blocking the sale, the Pentagon added insult to injury by demanding higher efficiency and savings from Newport News. William Cohen stated, "We decided that the considerable potential savings made possible by the proposed merger were offset by efficiency opportunities at Newport News." As a result, the Pentagon demanded an additional cost savings of $350 million over the next three years from Newport News.

Research

"Defense, Electronics Giant Litton Offers to Buy Shipyards," in *Knight Ridder/Tribune Business News*, 6 May 1999. Examines the details surrounding the offer of Litton to purchase Newport News, as well as Avondale.

General Dynamics Corp. Home Page, available at http://www.generaldynamics.com. Official World Wide Web Home Page for General Dynamics. Includes press releases, as well as financial, product, and investor information.

Muradian, Vago. "General Dynamics Makes "Unsolicited Bid" To Acquire Newport News," in *Defense Daily*, 19 February 1999. Announces the preliminary purchase offer between General Dynamics and Newport News.

"Newport News Shipbuilding and Dry Dock Co.," in *International Directory of Company Histories*, Vol. 13, St. James Press, 1996. Chronicles the history of Newport News Shipbuilding.

Newport News Shipbuilding Home Page, available at http://www.nns.com. Official World Wide Web Home Page for Newport News Shipbuilding. Includes press releases, as well as financial, product, historical and investor information.

Palmer, Jay "Scuttled Deal; Pentagon Nixed Bid For Newport News," in *Barron's*, 19 April 1999. Announces the pentagon's rejection of the General Dynamics bid to purchase Newport News.

"Pentagon Opposes General Dynamics Deal," in *United Press International*, 16 April 1999. Reports the pentagon's rejection of the General Dynamics bid to purchase Newport News.

Seidsma, Andrea "Shipyard Debate is Growing," in *San Diego Business Journal*, 15 March 1999. Explores the positive and negative aspects of shipyard consolidation in the US.

Smart, Tim "General Dynamics To Buy GTE Units; $1 Billion Deal Continues Buying Spree," in *The Washington Post*, 23 June 1999. Explains the details surrounding the purchase of three GTE divisions by General Dynamics.

DAVE W. SHELDON

GENERAL ELECTRIC & RCA

General Electric Co.
3135 Easton Tpke.
Fairfield, CT 06431-0001
USA

tel: (203)373-2211
fax: (203)373-3131
web: http://www.ge.com

nationality: USA
date: June 1986
affected: General Electric Co., USA, founded 1878
affected: RCA Corp., USA, founded 1919

Overview of the Merger

The $6.4 billion cash takeover of RCA Corp. by General Electric Co. in June of 1986 was the largest non-oil merger to date in U.S. corporate history. The combination of General Electric, with sales of $27.95 billion, and RCA, with sales of $10.11 billion, produced a $40 billion powerhouse well positioned in consumer and commercial electronics, defense, broadcasting, and satellite communications.

Reversing its decision in 1930 to force the firms apart, the U.S. Justice Department approved the deal on the condition that RCA's vidicon tube operations, as well as five radio stations, be divested. By the end of the year, GE sold RCA's record assets to Bertelsmann AG, as well as the firm's carpet and insurance businesses, for a total of roughly $1.3 billion. Although the purchase was a major factor in GE's significant growth during the late 1980s and early 1990s, difficulties integrating NBC plagued GE for several years.

History of General Electric Co.

In 1878, the Edison Electric Light Co. was founded to support Thomas Edison's incandescent lamp research. A year later, Edison invented the first practical incandescent lamp. He also constructed his first dynamo, or direct-current generator. Edison secured an incandescent lamp patent in 1880. Trial runs of Edison's first electric railway were made at Menlo Park that year.

Edison Machine Works was established in New York City in 1881. The first full-scale public application of the Edison lighting system occurred in London, England, at the Holborn Viaduct. The first system in the U.S. was at Pearl Street Station, the nation's first central station, which began operation in New York City in 1882. The following year, Thomson-Houston Co. was formed from the American Electric Company, which was founded by Elihu Thomson and Edwin Houston, patent holders of arc lighting.

Edison Electric purchased the Sprague Electric Railway and Motor Co., which built the nation's first large-scale electric streetcar system, in 1889. The company also formed the Edison General Electric Co., the major domestic supplier of electrified railway systems. Thomson-Houston purchased Brush Electric Co. and later merged with Bentley-Knight Electric Railway Co. In 1892, General Electric Co. (GE) was formed through the merger of Edison General Electric Co. and Thomson-Houston Co. A year later GE began its first venture into the field of power transmission with the opening of the Redlands-Mill Creek power line in California.

By the end of the decade, GE had constructed a massive power-transmission line at Niagara Falls; begun electrification of existing rail lines, and built the world's largest electric locomotives (90 tons) and transformers (800 KW). It formed the General Electric Research Laboratory, the nation's first industrial laboratory. Acquisitions in the early 1900s included Sprague Electric Co. and Stanley Electric Manufacturing Co., a maker of transformers.

In 1911, the commercial electric refrigerator was developed. Two years later, GE developed a high-vacuum, hot-cathode X-ray tube, which laid the foundation for medical technology operations at GE. The U.S. Navy commissioned GE to build the first ship powered by turbine motors rather than steam, and the firm introduced a turbine-propelled battleship in 1915. An experimental household refrigerator was developed in 1917. The following year, the Edison Electric Appliance Co. was formed from the merger of GE's heating-device section, Hughes Electric Heating Co., and Pacific Electric Heating Co.

GE established a research staff in 1919 to investigate plastics, which eventually led to the firm's diversification outside electricity. Initial research was devoted to coatings, varnishes, insulation, and other electrical wiring products. That year, GE formed the Radio Corporation of America (RCA) to develop radio technology at the request of the government. Within five years, GE operated two radio stations: WGY, in Schenectady, New York, and KGO in Oakland, California. The "Radiola Superheterodyne" was introduced that year, and GE divested itself of its utilities operations in the wake of federal antitrust action.

In 1927, GE station WGY broadcasted its first television drama. A 1930 antitrust suit launched by the U.S. Justice Department forced GE to divest its stake in RCA. GE introduced its first electric dishwasher and began offering consumer financing of personal appliances in 1932. Six years later, GE developed the fluorescent lamp and a mode of radio transmission known as frequency modulation (FM) as an alternative to the prevailing amplitude modulation (AM). In 1940, GE began broadcasting on FM.

During World War II, GE produced more than 50 different types of radar for the armed forces and over 1,500 marine power plants for the Navy and Merchant

The Business

Financials

Revenue (1998): $99.8 billion

Employees (1998): 293,000

SICs / NAICS

sic 3724 - Aircraft Engines & Engine Parts

sic 3631 - Household Cooking Equipment

sic 3632 - Household Refrigerators & Freezers

sic 3633 - Household Laundry Equipment

sic 3629 - Electrical Industrial Apparatus Nec

sic 3646 - Commercial Lighting Fixtures

sic 3351 - Copper Rolling & Drawing

sic 3645 - Residential Lighting Fixtures

sic 2821 - Plastics Materials & Resins

sic 3511 - Turbines & Turbine Generator Sets

sic 4911 - Electric Services

sic 4833 - Television Broadcasting Stations

sic 6141 - Personal Credit Institutions

sic 6153 - Short-Term Business Credit

naics 336412 - Aircraft Engine and Engine Parts
      Manufacturing

naics 335221 - Household Cooking Appliance
      Manufacturing

naics 335222 - Household Refrigerator and Home and Farm
      Freezer Manufacturing

naics 335224 - Household Laundry Equipment
      Manufacturing

naics 335999 - All Other Miscellaneous Electrical Equipment
      and Component Manufacturing

naics 335121 - Residential Electric Lighting Fixture
      Manufacturing

naics 325211 - Plastics Material and Resin Manufacturing

naics 333611 - Turbine and Turbine Generator Set Unit
      Manufacturing

naics 221113 - Nuclear Electric Power Generation

Marines. After the government discovered that GE controlled 85% of the light bulb industry, a court forced the firm to release its patents to other companies in 1949.

The Officers

Chairman and CEO: John F. Welch, Jr.

Vice Chairman; Chairman and CEO, GE Capital Services:
  Dennis D. Dammerman

Vice Chairman: Eugene F. Murphy

Vice Chairman: John D. Opie

Chief Financial Officer and Sr. VP, Finance: Keith S. Sherin

In 1954, GE designed the J-79, the world's first jet engine to power aircraft at twice the speed of sound. In 1955, the navy launched the submarine *Seawolf*, the world's first nuclear-powered vessel, with a reactor developed by GE. Two years later, GE secured a license from the Atomic Energy Commission to operate a nuclear-power reactor; it was the first licensing of its kind in the U.S. for a privately owned generating station. Consumer appliance operations were boosted after the completion of a new manufacturing site, Appliance Park, which made GE home products, including hair dryers, skillets, electric ovens, self-cleaning ovens, and electronic knives.

GE faced another antitrust suit in 1961 when the Justice Department indicted GE and 28 other companies for price fixing on electrical equipment. GE was fined almost $500,000 and forced to pay damages to utilities that purchased price-fixed equipment; three GE managers received jail sentences and several others were forced to resign. By the end of the decade, the firm had undergone a massive organizational restructuring in an attempt to accommodate its size; the number of distinct operating units within the company was cut from more than 200 to 42, with each new section operating in a particular market.

The 1973 oil embargo led to a world energy crisis; as a result, new opportunities opened for GE as consumers sought electricity as a solution to the energy burden. GE's worldwide diversification enabled it to withstand the worst economic recession since the Great Depression, with earnings dropping only 4%. As plant construction costs skyrocketed and environmental concerns grew, the firm's nuclear power division began to lose money. The divestiture of its computer business left GE with no capacity for manufacturing integrated circuits and the high technology products in which they were used. To counter the perception that it had fallen behind in electronics technology, GE spent $385 million to acquire firms in the field, including Intersil, a semiconductor manufacturer; Calma, a computer-graphics equipment producer; and four software producers.

GE paid $2.2 billion for Utah International, a major coal, copper, uranium, and iron minor and producer of natural gas and oil, in 1976. The new unit, which conducted 80% of its business in foreign countries, contributed 18% to GE's total earnings. A reorganization the next year broke operations into six sectors. Having received no new orders for plants in five years, GE pulled out of the nuclear power business in 1970 except for its provision of services and fuel to existing plants and its continued research on nuclear energy.

A management shakeup in 1981 positioned Jack Welch as president of GE. In 1983, a new GE dishwasher plant was opened in Louisville, Kentucky, as the first phase of a $1 billion investment in major appliances. Common stock split two-for-one that year, and net earnings reached $2 billion for the first time. In 1986, GE acquired RCA for $6.4 billion and RCA's National Broadcasting Co. (NBC), the leading U.S. television network. In a move to prepare for Europe's unified market, GE bought 50% of the European appliance business of Britain's General Electric Company (GEC) in 1989.

A jury awarded Fonar Corp. $100 million in a mid-1990 suit against GE for patent infringement of its diagnostics MRI technology. In 1995, GE Capital expanded its insurance business with the acquisition of Aon Corp., a life insurance firm, for $960 million, bolstering GE Capital to a spot among the nation's largest financial institutions. A year later, GE expanded its international operations by inking a $1 billion agreement to establish power plants in China, Hungary, and Pakistan. Rapid growth continued as GE completed 108 acquisitions for roughly $20 billion in 1998. GE stock grew by 27%, its annual growth rate for the past twenty years, in 1999. Chairman Jack Welch announced his resignation that year.

History of RCA Corp.

Because Marconi Wireless Telegraph Company of America—the only company in the U.S. able to operate transatlantic radio and telegraph communications—was British owned, the U.S. government asked General Electric to establish a company to acquire Marconi in 1919. In October of that year, GE established Radio Corporation of America (RCA), which purchased Marconi. The two companies began cross licensing patents on long distance transmission equipment.

AT&T Corp. bought a share of RCA in 1920 as a means of cross licensing patents with the firm, and a year later, Westinghouse did the same. RCA gained access to Westinghouse's patents in exchange for peddling Westinghouse's wares to the public. That year, RCA began radio broadcasting operations.

In 1926, RCA created National Broadcasting Co. (NBC) to oversee radio operations. The following year, RCA unveiled the first Radiotron tube, which eliminated the need for batteries. RCA acquired the Victor Talking Machine Co. in 1928. At the turn of the decade, the U.S. Justice Department launched an antitrust investigation of RCA, seeking to nullify the firm's many patents. To satisfy antitrust concerns, General Electric, AT&T, and Westinghouse eventually sold their stakes in RCA, which was able to retain its patents.

The firm spent the next forty years growing and diversifying via acquisition. By the 1970s, RCA owned frozen foods vendor Banquet and rental car giant Hertz Corp. In 1965, RCA had purchased Random House Inc. with the goal of integrating electronics and publishing. After struggling to integrate the two companies, RCA sold Random House to privately owned Advance Publications in 1980 for $60 million. The firm's 1981 acquisition of CIT Financial was blamed for RCA downgraded credit in the early 1980s. Edgar H. Griffiths, who had been appointed CEO in 1976, was dethroned by RCA's board of directors in 1981 and succeeded by Thornton Bradshaw.

Between 1976 and 1985, RCA sold off roughly one unit each year, including the 1985 sale of Hertz for $587.5 million, until all diversified subsidiaries were divested, except carpet maker Coronet Industries. General Electric (GE) paid $6.4 billion for RCA in June of 1986 and immediately sold the firm's carpet, record, and insurance assets. The RCA brand name was retained and NBC became a separate division of GE.

Market Forces Driving the Merger

When Jack Welch took the helm of GE in 1981, he immediately began a restructuring that would prepare the firm for its 1986 takeover of GE. His plan called for improving GE's bottom line by slashing costs and selling all businesses except those that were current or potential market leaders. Between 1981 and 1985, divestitures totaled in excess of $5.6 billion and the firm's employee base was lightened considerably—nearly 130,000 workers had been eliminated, some via layoffs and others by the sale of GE units.

Once GE's performance had improved significantly—GE had reported cash reserves of $3 billion, as well as $1 billion in credit—Welch began looking for ways, including the pursuit of strategic acquisitions, to increase revenues. Merger discussions in 1985 with CBS fizzled, and GE's alleged bid for Hughes Aircraft Co. was topped by General Motors Corp.

The Players

Chairman and CEO of General Electric Co.: John F. Welch, Jr. "Jack" Welch became president of GE in 1981; at 49 years of age, Welch was the youngest GE president ever. During his first year at the helm, he led the firm's acquisition of 338 businesses and product lines for $11 billion and the divestiture of 232 units for $5.9 billion. Welch decentralized the company but retained existing systems of classifying divisions by performance. He also oversaw GE's takeover of RCA in 1986. By the time that he announced his resignation in 1999, Welch had increased the market value of GE to $280 billion from $12 billion in 1981.

Chairman and CEO of RCA Corp.: Thornton F. Bradshaw. Former president of Atlantic Richfield Co., Thornton Bradshaw was appointed CEO of RCA in 1981 amidst a managerial scuffle. He continued a divestment campaign started by his predecessor, Edgar Griffiths, and was praised for improving RCA's earnings to the tune of $341 million in 1984, nearly eight times what they had been three years prior. Bradshaw steered the firm's takeover by GE in 1986, and when the transaction was completed, Bradshaw handed over the reins of RCA to GE CEO Jack Welch and retired.

Undaunted, Welch set his sights on RCA, a firm which had recently completed a significant revamping of its own and was also pursuing a major deal. According to Bruce Wasserstein, author of *Big Deal: The Battle for Control of America's Leading Corporations*, "For RCA, the friendly deal with GE represented the culmination of its own restructuring effort. Thornton Bradshaw, a former oil executive, had taken over as chairman of RCA in the same year Welch became chairman of GE. Bradshaw's mission was to stabilize the faltering company. He promptly divested businesses. Hertz, CIT, Gibson Greetings, Banquet Foods, Random House—all were sold to outsiders who did much better with them than RCA. Welch bought the remaining company, including the jewel of its defense business, at a bargain price."

Approach and Engagement

Rumors in early 1985 about a possible takeover of RCA by the likes of Ford Motor Co. and United Technologies Corp. had prompted the firm to implement a poison pill defense tactic as a means of preventing a hostile takeover. Amicable negotiations with GE, however, rendered the pill useless.

On December 12, 1985, GE and RCA officially announced their intent to merge. Shareholders of both firms approved the purchase price of $66.50 per share (twice the book value of RCA), or $6.28 billion in cash. Later, many RCA shareholders voiced their concern over what they believed was too low a price for RCA. They also criticized the cash payment status of the agreement, pointing out that a stock swap would have allowed the deal to proceed free of taxes.

The U.S. Justice Department approved the deal in June of 1986 on the condition that RCA's vidicon tube operations, as well as five radio stations, be divested. Although RCA Corp. was defunct once the deal was finalized, GE retained the RCA brand name. GE CEO Jack Welch remained at the helm of GE, while RCA CEO Thornton Bradshaw retired.

Products and Services

In 1999, GE was segmented into eight groups: GE Capital Services, which offered consumer and business financing and accounted for 50% of the firm's total revenues; industrial products and systems, which brought in 11% of sales; aircraft engines, 10%; power systems, 8%; plastics, 6%; appliances, 5%; technical products and services, 5%; and broadcastings, including NBC, which secured another 5%.

Review of the Outcome

By the end of the 1986, GE had sold RCA's record assets to Bertelsmann AG, as well as the firm's carpet and insurance businesses, for a total of roughly $1.3 billion. After absorbing RCA, almost 80% of GE's earnings came from services and high technology, compared to 50% six years earlier. GE also divested RCA's David Sarnoff Research Center and RCA's television manufacturing business. The firm posted a 21% operating loss in 1989, but sales and earnings in the years following the deal skyrocketed. In 1995, revenues reached $70 billion, compared to $28.3 billion in 1985.

Although the RCA deal was a major factor in GE's significant growth during the late 1980s and early 1990s, difficulties integrating the NBC television network plagued GE for several years. NBC CEO Grant Tinker—credited for parlaying the network into the top spot and mending the management turnover problem at NBC—retired after the deal with GE was completed. His successor, GE's Robert Wright, began his tenure with a cost cutting campaign. The traditional corporate culture of GE clashed with the more inventive atmosphere that characterized NBC and GE's streamlining efforts were publicly lambasted by NBC employees, including late-night talk show host David Letterman.

Research

Abrams, Bill. "General Electric to Acquire RCA for $6.28 Billion; Combined Firm's Revenues Would Top $40 Billion," in *The Wall Street Journal*, 12 December 1985. Explains the reasons for the deal between RCA and GE.

Barnes, Peter W. "NBC Chief Seen Leaving after GE Link," in *The Wall Street Journal*, 21 April 1986. Discusses the decision by Grant A. Tinker to retire from NBC after GE's takeover of RCA is completed.

"General Electric Co.," in *Notable Corporate Chronologies*, The Gale Group, 1999. Lists major events in the history of General Electric Co.

General Electric Co. Home Page, available at http://www.ge.com. Official World Wide Web Home Page for General Electric Co. Includes news, as well as financial, product, and historical information.

"RCA Corp.," in *International Directory of Company Histories*, Vol. II, St. James Press, 1990. Offers a detailed history of RCA Corp., including the firm's takeover by GE.

Roberts, Johnnie L. "RCA Holders Clear $6.28 Billion Sale to GE; NBC Radio Unit May Be Sold," in *The Wall Street Journal*, 2 May 1986. Details shareholders concerns regarding the price GE is paying for RCA, as well as the type of deal being pursued.

Wasserstein, Bruce. *Big Deal: The Battle for Control of America's Leading Corporations*, Warner Books, 1998. Provides an overview of the largest mergers in recent American corporate history.

JEFF ST. THOMAS

GENERAL MILLS & GORTON'S

nationality: USA
date: August 16, 1968
affected: General Mills Inc., USA, founded 1866
affected: Gorton's Corp., USA, founded 1868

General Mills Inc.
One General Mills Blvd.
Minneapolis, MN 55426
USA

tel: (612)540-2311
fax: (612)540-4925
web: http://www.generalmills.com

Overview of the Merger

General Mills' $30 million acquisition of Gorton's came at a time when the company was on an aggressive buying spree and looking for entrance into the prepared frozen foods industry. The deal brought about an investigation by the Federal Trade Commission (FTC), which was concerned that the merger might lessen competition in the frozen seafood industry. General Mills was allowed to go ahead with deal, and on November 2, 1973, the FTC dismissed the complaint for the final time.

History of General Mills Inc.

In 1866, Cadwallader Washburn opened a flour mill in Minneapolis, Minnesota. His business, which soon became the Washburn Crosby Corp., competed with local miller C.A. Pillsbury. In 1869, the two millers joined forces to form the Minneapolis Millers Association. Pillsbury and Washburn both wanted to find a way to make midwestern winter wheat into a higher grade of flour. Eventually, with the help of a French engineer, Washburn not only improved the method but made his product the best flour available in America. When Pillsbury adopted the same technique, Minneapolis became the country's flour-milling center.

In the next 10 years, Washburn made several key introductions, including the Middling's Purifier, an invention which made possible the production of a superior flour made from spring wheat, and implemented the world's first roller mill, which enabled the company to produce flour at faster rates and in greater quantities, thereby increasing the its competitive edge. By 1880, the company was becoming increasingly well known and Washburn's Superlative brand of flour won the gold medal at the Miller's International Exhibition in Cincinnati.

In 1889, Washburn Crosby incorporated. James S. Bell was named president at a time when the available supply of flour was greater than the demand. Bell's merchandising expertise was of extreme importance to the company's advancement and success. In 1893, the company invested in Royal Milling of Great Falls. Washburn Crosby's expansion policy helped the organization stay ahead of its competition, and by the end of the decade, the company had established its first small research laboratory.

The Business

Financials

Revenue (1998): $6.03 billion

Employees (1998): 10,200

SICs / NAICS

sic 5812 - Eating Places

sic 2043 - Cereal Breakfast Foods

sic 2041 - Flour & Other Grain Mill Products

sic 2092 - Fresh or Frozen Prepared Fish

sic 2026 - Fluid Milk

sic 2099 - Food Preparations Nec

sic 2034 - Dehydrated Fruits, Vegetables & Soups

naics 311514 - Dry, Condensed, and Evaporated Dairy
    Product Manufacturing

naics 311511 - Fluid Milk Manufacturing

naics 311423 - Dried and Dehydrated Food Manufacturing

naics 311999 - All Other Miscellaneous Food Manufacturing

naics 311211 - Flour Milling

naics 311712 - Fresh and Frozen Seafood Processing

naics 111998 - All Other Miscellaneous Crop Farming

naics 311911 - Roasted Nuts and Peanut Butter
    Manufacturing

naics 311991 - Perishable Prepared Food Manufacturing

naics 311212 - Rice Milling

naics 311823 - Dry Pasta Manufacturing

naics 311941 - Mayonnaise, Dressing, and Other Prepared
    Sauce Manufacturing

naics 722211 - Limited-Service Restaurants

naics 722212 - Cafeterias

naics 722213 - Snack and Nonalcoholic Beverage Bars

The company began the 20th century with an aggressive growth plan. In 1903, a flour mill was purchased in Louisville, Kentucky, and one was constructed in Buffalo, New York. The company also leased a flour mill in St. Louis, Missouri. By 1906, an unusually large advertising budget of $200,000 was approved, thus elevating Washburn Crosby to one of the nation's leading advertisers.

In 1921, the famous Betty Crocker personality was created by advertising manager Sam Gale, as a fictional spokeswoman. Company correspondence to housewives was sent out with Betty's "signature." In 1923, the company introduced its first Gold Medal Products, including pancake, whole wheat, buckwheat, and cake flours, as well as a wheat flake breakfast food which was eventually marketed as Wheaties. Most of these items failed to gain consumer recognition but contributed to paving the way for future introductions of packaged foods. That same year, $2 million worth of Washburn Crosby preferred stock was offered for public sale.

General Mills was created through the consolidation of the Washburn mill with several other major flour-milling companies around the country, including the Red Star Milling Corp., the Sperry Milling Corp., and the Larrowe Milling Corp., in 1928. Within five months of the consolidation, the new entity was comprised of 27 companies, making General Mills the largest flour milling company in the world. The move was well-timed, giving the company strength to survive and remain prosperous throughout the coming Depression.

Throughout the 1930s and 1940s, General Mills continued to thrive. Bisquick was introduced and soon became one of the company's most popular products, as did Cheerios. In 1937, all subsidiary companies were dissolved, and General Mills operated with five geographic sales divisions, along with Larrowe (producer of feed products), Farm Service (feeds), Star Grain, and American Research Products (vitamins). The company also formed mechanical and chemical development divisions, which helped with the war effort in the early 1940s.

In 1946, General Mills entered the home appliance business. Also introduced over the next year or so were dessert mixes Apple Pyequick. This signaled the start of a product line that was destined to expand significantly over the next two decades. The company turned to decentralization in 1951, reorganizing into five operating divisions including Food, Chemical, Mechanical, Special Commodities, and Farm Service. Two years later, further decentralization occurred with the division of the food segment into Grocery Products, Flour, and Feed.

General Mills began to branch out internationally, with its entrance into the Canadian market with cereals and baking mixes and the Venezuelan, Guatemalan, and Mexican markets with flour products. Although the company's food products were doing well, its ventures into electronics and appliances were failing.

In 1961, General Edwin was appointed president. He reevaluated company output and shook up management positions. With the flour market declining at the rate of 3% per year, Rawlings recognized a shift in consumer preference and responded by planning to close half the flour mills, encouraging commitment to packaged foods, and eventually divesting the electronics, appliances, and formula feeds operations. A short-term, five-year sales decline resulted. In 1964, the soybean division was dissolved, and the electronics division was sold. Rawlings also led the company through a series of acquisitions beginning with the purchase of Morton Foods, Inc. The deal signaled General Mills' entry into the snack food market.

Seven flour mills were sold in 1965, and the firm began a rapid acquisition spree. The Tom Huston Peanut Corp. was acquired, European markets were expanded with the purchase of Tragasol and Smiths, and in 1968, General Mills entered the frozen seafood market with its acquisition of Gorton's, which the Federal Trade Commission (FTC) unsuccessfully attempted to block. The French company, Biscuiterie Nantaise, was purchased as well. The company also entered the fashion business when it bought Monocraft (Monet). General Mills moved aggressively into the toy and game market with the purchase of Rainbow Crafts (makers of Play-Doh), Kenner, and Parker Brothers. In 1969, the FTC issued a consent order blocking General Mills from further acquisitions within the snack-food industry. At the time of purchase, both Morton and Tom Huston were among the top-ten producers of potato and corn chips. The company decentralized its food operations into five divisions: Golden Valley; Betty Crocker; Sperry; Big "G"; and Food Service.

The company continued to enter into new markets with the purchases of Red Lobster, Eddie Bauer, and Travel World. By 1975, however, 73% of acquisitions made within the last 25 years had been divested within a five-year period. The company's profitable core business in consumer foods helped to ease the burden of these failed efforts. In 1977, the chemical division was divested, removing General Mills from the high technology products business. The company also entered the refrigerated yogurt market with the purchase of Michigan Cottage Cheese, and the formation of Yoplait U.S.A., a consumer food group subsidiary. By the end of the decade, General Mills divided its businesses once again into food processing, restaurants, games and toys, fashion, and specialty retailing.

In 1980, General Mills faced another battle with the FTC, which filed an antitrust complaint against several cereal companies following a ten-year investigation. It charged that between 1958 and 1972, cereal manufacturers realized an average after-tax profit of 19.8%, compared to a general manufacturing average of 8.9%. The FTC suggested that Kellogg, General Mills, and General Foods shared a monopoly over the cereal industry. Those charges were dismissed the following year, after the companies involved lobbied

The Officers

Chairman and CEO: Stephen W. Sanger

Vice Chairman: Raymond G. Viault

Exec. VP; CEO, Cereal Partners Worldwide: Stephen R. Demeritt

Sr. VP, Operations: Randy G. Darcy

Sr. VP and General Counsel: Siri S. Marshall

for—and won—congressional favor. Meanwhile, General Mills' restaurant division opened the Olive Garden chain in 1983. By 1985, General Mills had also become the world's largest toy maker.

The company made a bold move in the mid-1980s, divesting items representing over 25% of sales, including toys, fashion, and non-apparel retailing. Although General Mills reported a loss of $72 million due to the divestitures, long-term profits were realized in 1987, when earnings reached $222 million. Core businesses at this point included Big G cereals, Red Lobster restaurants, consumer foods, and specialty-retailing.

By 1990, the company had successfully fended off a takeover attempt, and its specialty retailing businesses were sold. General Mills then refocused on two areas: consumer foods and restaurants. The company began to show a return for its restructuring efforts as stock rose 20%. General Mills also engaged in a price war with other cereal companies. In 1995, Gorton's was sold to Unilever and restaurant interests were spun off. Two years later, the company made its largest purchase ever, when it bought Ralcorp Holdings Inc.'s Chex snack and cereal assets for $570 million. In 1999, the company remained focused on its cereal and other food products, as well as increasing foreign market share.

History of Gorton's Corp.

John Pew & Co., established in 1849, and Slade Gorton & Co., founded in 1868, were leaders in fish industry in Gloucester, New England. Both covered the Atlantic territory and packaged and cured fish. In 1875, the Gorton name became a registered trademark. By 1889, due to the its success, Slade Gorton had over 40 employees and two facilities.

Gorton's cod was the first nationally advertised fish in the U.S., and, by 1901, it sold for nine cents a pound and came wrapped and salted. Slade Gorton and John Pew then merged their companies with Reed & Gamage and David B. Smith & Co. The deal brought together the top fishing businesses in the area with the

The Players

Chairman and CEO of General Mills Inc.: Edwin W. Rawlings. A Harvard Business school graduate, Edwin W. Rawlings finished his 30-year career in the Air Force in 1959, after rising to full general and commander of the Air Materiel Command. Rawlings joined General Mills that year. He quickly rose to top rank as president in 1961 and chairman and CEO in 1967. His move to close nine flour mills in 1965 was a noteworthy event in U.S. flour milling history. Rawlings retired in 1969, one year after the Gorton's deal, and remained a board member until 1976. He died on December 8, 1997.

President of Gorton's Corp.: E. Robert Kinney. Robert Kinney became a director of Gorton's in 1953, when his company, North Atlantic Packaging, teamed up with the frozen seafood company. In 1958, he was named president of Gorton's and embarked on a mission of growth and acquisition. He successfully led the company through its merger with General Mills and became vice president of the company upon the deal's completion. By 1977, Kinney had been elected CEO and chairman of General Mills. He also served on the board of Nashua Corp., a computer products firm. Kinney retired in 1989.

largest fleet of ships on the Atlantic. The new company, Gorton-Pew Fisheries Co. was breaking ground in packaged fish, which soon became a popular item.

The company struggled after World War I, when a shipment of fish sent to Italy was confiscated and never paid for by that government. Other managerial problems prompted Gorton-Pew to declare bankruptcy, and in 1923, the firm was reorganized by William Putnam. Acting as president, he led the company into refrigeration. In 1929, Gorton's purchased the Gloucester Cold Storage and Warehouse Co. and began its foray into the fish freezing industry.

World War II brought about an increased demand for fish due to the meat shortage. In 1944, the company introduced its first fish steak, soon to be a company staple. Five years later, Gorton's made the first refrigerator trailer truck shipment of frozen fish from its home in Gloucester to California.

When Gorton's introduced its fried and frozen codfish in 1952, frozen seafood was finally becoming popular across the United States. The health benefits of fish had not yet been recognized, and despite a significant cost advantage, fish had not been that popular inland. Convenience food saw a huge rise in popularity in the 1950s, and Gorton's fish was among the products that housewives wanted in their freezers.

Robert E. Kinney, the leader of North Atlantic Packing who was now in a joint venture with Gorton's, became a director in the company after the deal and became president in 1958. The company was successful, with sales in the millions and a product line that included main courses, fried and frozen specialties, canned fish, and pickled fish. The company changed its name to Gorton's of Gloucester and began using foreign sources when its demand exceeded what American fisherman could supply.

Throughout the 1960s, Gorton's grew rapidly by acquisition. Purchases included Florida Frozen Foods, Blue Water Seafoods of Cleveland, Riggin & Robbins, and Red L Foods. In 1962, the firm began supplying McDonald's with fish for its filet of fish sandwiches. Gorton's also acquired Blue Water Seafoods of Montreal, Canada; Fulham Brothers; and Connecticut Freeborn Farms, which dealt in frozen hors d'oeuvres.

In 1968, Gorton's became a wholly owned subsidiary of General Mills. With the new financial backing, Gorton's was able to delve into research and development of fish products, as well as introduce new products such as shrimp and chips, ocean snacks, and heat-and-serve entrees. The company was also able to expand and had operations in sixteen different plants across the U.S. by the 1970s.

Under new management, Gorton's stopped its aggressive acquisition strategy. In 1990, the company was the leader in the frozen seafood industry with its creative product line including marinated breaded shrimp, lemon pepper and southern fried fish fillets, and pre-grilled fish. In May 1995, General Mills sold Gorton's to Unilever. The deal gave Unilever entrance to the U.S. frozen food market.

Market Forces Driving the Merger

Under the leadership of General Edwin Rawlings, General Mills was focused on strengthening its position in the foods industry throughout the 1960s. The company had been entering new markets such as snack foods and had acquired companies such as Morton Foods in 1964 and the Tom Huston Peanut Co. in 1966.

By aligning itself with Gorton's, General Mills could enter the frozen fish market, as well as utilize the company's highly successful distribution system to promote new frozen items General Mills was developing. The firm was determined to grow in size by entering many different industries. A deal with Gorton's would accomplish part of that goal.

Approach and Engagement

On March 25, 1968, General Mills announced plans to purchase Gorton's. The deal called for the exchange of one share of General Mill's common stock for 1.4 shares of Gorton's stock. Valued at $28 million, the merger called for approval of Gorton's shareholders after both company's directors agreed on the terms in March.

The two companies completed the deal on August 16, 1968. By that time, the terms had changed to value the transaction at $30 million and included the exchange of 544,711 shares of General Mill's stock for 762,596 of Gorton's common shares. The remaining 365,099 shares of Gorton's were purchased for $9.49 million. General Mills planned to operate Gorton's as a subsidiary with no change to current operations or management.

Products and Services

General Mills sold Gorton's in 1995 to concentrate on its cereal and foods products. With facilities in the U.S. as well as Canada, its products were represented in over 100 different markets. In 1998, the company's cereal brands brought in 35% of total sales. Its Betty Crocker line accounted for 25% of sales; U.S. Convenience Foods took 18%; international operations accounted for 16%; and food service brought in 6% of total sales.

General Mills was also involved in foreign joint ventures with Nestle, PepsiCo, and Bestfoods. Popular cereal brand names included Cheerios, Kix, Wheaties, and Lucky Charms. The company produced dessert and baking mixes as well, such as Bisquick, Gold Medal, and Betty Crocker cakes and frostings. Dinner products included Hamburger Helper and Suddenly Salad, and Lloyd's refrigerated food items. The General Mills snack line boasted brand names such as Pop Secret, Fruit Roll-Ups, Bugles, and Chex snack mix, and General Mills also owned Colombo and Yoplait yogurt.

Changes to the Industry

The same year that General Mills entered the frozen food industry, it made a bold move into the toy industry as well. With its purchase of Rainbow Crafts, Kenner, and Parker Brothers, the food concern shifted from being the largest flour miller in the world to the largest manufacturer of toys across the globe. By the late 1970s, one-third of the company's sales were from its toy operations.

This foray into new markets was popular among food concerns in the 1960s and 1970s. Nestle S. A. ventured into pharmaceuticals and cosmetics, with its purchase of L'Oreal and Alcon Laboratories.

Carnation was diving into many different food products as was Kraft General Foods. The general belief among these companies was that the acquisitions would pay off and increase sagging profits.

Review of the Outcome

The deal with Gorton's brought about an investigation by the Federal Trade Commission (FTC) on July 19, 1970. A complaint was filed stating that the merging of General Mills and Gorton's had the potential to lessen competition in the industry and that General Mills had violated section 7 of the Clayton Act. In November of 1973, the complaint was dismissed upon FTC findings that General Mills had not broken any laws in its transaction with Gorton's.

In 1969, General Mills was ranked number two in ready-to-eat cereals and number one in cake and cookie mixes, as well as frosting and flour. By 1971, sales had risen to $1.1 billion and operating profits topped out at $44 million. General Mills continued to grow, and, between the years of 1950 and 1986, the firm bought 86 companies in several different industries. Seventy-three percent of the purchases made before 1975 were divested in just five years.

Gorton's proved to be a successful venture during the 1970s and 1980s. General Mills began a corporate restructuring in the early 1990s with a focus on its consumer foods. As a result, Gorton's was sold to Unilever in 1995.

Research

"General Mills Inc.," in *Notable Corporate Chronologies*, The Gale Group, 1999. Lists major events in the history of General Mills Inc.

General Mills Inc. Home Page, available at http://www.generalmills.com. Official World Wide Web Home Page for General Mills Inc. Includes historical, financial, and product information, as well as recent news articles.

"General Mills Inc.," in *International Directory of Company Histories*, Vol. 10, St. James Press, 1995. Covers the history of General Mills Inc.

General Mills Inc. Press Release, 16 August 1968. Lists the terms of the purchase of Gorton's.

General Mills Inc. Press Release, 18 May 1995. Details Unilever's purchase of Gorton's.

"General Mills Acquires Gorton's, Awaits FTC Challenge of Merger," in *The Wall Street Journal*, 19 August 1968. Discusses FTC involvement in the Gorton's deal.

"General Mills, Gorton's Agree on Merger Plan," in *The Wall Street Journal*, 26 March 1968. Discusses tentative plans for General Mills to purchase Gorton's.

"Gorton's," in *International Directory of Company Histories*, Vol. 13, St. James Press, 1996. List major events in the history of Gorton's.

CHRISTINA M. STANSELL

GENERAL MOTORS & ELECTRONIC DATA SYSTEMS

General Motors Corp.
100 Renaissance Ctr.
Detroit, MI 48243
USA

tel: (313)556-5000
fax: (313)556-5108
web: http://www.gm.com

Electronic Data Systems Corp.
5400 Legacy Dr.
Plano, TX 75024-3199
USA

tel: (972)604-6000
fax: (972)605-2643
web: http://www.eds.com

nationality: USA
date: June 27, 1984
affected: General Motors Corp., USA, founded 1897
affected: Electronic Data Systems Corp., USA, founded 1962

Overview of the Merger

General Motors acquired Editorial Data Systems (EDS) for $2.5 billion, highest amount ever paid for a computer services firm, in 1986. While EDS was able to streamline several of GM's bloated systems, the anticipated technological synergies between the two firms never emerged. As a result, GM decided to spin off its EDS unit in 1995. Once independent, EDS became the world's largest independent computer-services company, with $25 billion in market value, nearly ten times what GM originally paid for it in 1984.

History of General Motors Corp.

In 1897, Olds Motor Vehicle Co. was founded by Ransom E. Olds when he introduced the first Oldsmobile model, a $1,200, four-seater, luxury vehicle. The Olds operation was the first American factory in Detroit, Michigan, devoted exclusively to the production of automobiles.

Three years later, David Buick built a factory in Detroit under his own name. Max Grabowsky established the Grabowsky Motor Vehicle Co., which later evolved into a large part of the GM Truck and Bus division. In 1902, Cadillac Automobile Co. was formed in Detroit by Henry Leland, a former Oldsmobile employee. The company was named after the French explorer who founded Detroit in 1701. That year, the Buick Motor Car Co. was founded in Detroit and purchased by William Durant. The Oakland Motor Car Co., which later became GM's Pontiac Motor division, was formed in 1907.

In 1908, William Durant launched a plan to consolidate the leading automakers as General Motors Co. Buick, America's leading automobile manufacturer, and Oldsmobile joined GM. A year later, Cadillac and Pontiac were purchased by the young GM Co. By 1910, the Buick/Oldsmobile merger had proved successful, but Durant's buying spree required additional financing. After a number of rejections from financial lenders, Durant finally secured loans worth $15 million under strict conditions. The banks forced Durant to step down, and they took control, setting up their own management team.

In 1911, Chevrolet Motor Co. was established in Detroit by racecar driver Louis Chevrolet and Durant. That year, GM was the first automobile manufacturer to be listed on the New York Stock Exchange; GM Export Co. was formed; and GM combined its previously acquired Rapid Motor and Reliance Motor operations under Pontiac to create GMC, a truck production arm of GM. In 1915, Chevrolet acquired 54.5% of GM, and Durant regained control as president.

GM was incorporated under Delaware state law in 1916. Durant organized United Motors Co., a consolidation of companies that provided parts and services to the automobile industry. GM also expanded into other industries such as refrigerator manufacturing and financing. The following year, GM converted its automobile factories to military materials production sites for the war effort. In 1919, it acquired the assets of Chevrolet, as well as Hyatt Bearings, New Departure, a 60% interest in Fisher Body, and Frigidaire Co., which was divested years later. General Motors of Canada, Ltd. was also established that year.

By 1920, more than 30 companies had been purchased by GM for stock, which fell to $14 a share that year. Banks rescued the corporation by again ousting Durant, and the DuPont family and J.P. Morgan & Co. took control of GM. In 1923, Alfred P. Sloan was named president. He immediately began decentralizing GM management, a move that was later praised by Wall Street analysts for rescuing GM economically after the onset of the Depression. Sloan's tactics were later used as a model for management by many other large businesses.

The first GM vehicle to be produced outside the U.S. was assembled in Denmark in 1924. A year later, Chevrolet surpassed Ford's Model T in popularity, and GM purchased Vauxhall Motors Ltd. of London, England, which was later merged with Germany's Adam Opel. Pontiac became an official division of GM in the early 1930s, as did Packard Electronic Co. when it was acquired by GM.

After the collapse of 450 Michigan banks due to the Depression, GM created the National Bank of Detroit. A 44-day sit-down strike in 1937 at the Fisher Body plant in Flint ended with a victory for the United Auto Workers (UAW) over the right to organize GM workers. The Detroit Diesel Engine division was also established that year.

In 1940, GM produced its 25 millionth car and held 44% of the U.S. automobiles market. The firm began retooling factories for defense weaponry and machinery production for the World War II effort; GM built $12.3 billion worth of military equipment, including ball bearings, tanks, naval ships, fighting

The Business

Financials - General Motors Corp.

Revenue (1998): $161 billion

Employees (1998): 594,000

Financials - Electronic Data Systems Corp.

Revenue (1998): $16.8 billion

Employees (1998): 120,000

SICs / NAICS

sic 3711 - Motor Vehicles & Car Bodies

sic 3663 - Radio & T.V. Communications Equipment

sic 5013 - Motor Vehicle Supplies & New Parts

sic 3724 - Aircraft Engines & Engine Parts

sic 3714 - Motor Vehicle Parts & Accessories

sic 5084 - Industrial Machinery & Equipment

sic 3519 - Internal Combustion Engines Nec

sic 6159 - Miscellaneous Business Credit Institutions

sic 6141 - Personal Credit Institutions

sic 7373 - Computer Integrated Systems Design

sic 7371 - Computer Programming Services

sic 7379 - Computer Related Services Nec

sic 7374 - Data Processing & Preparation

sic 7375 - Information Retrieval Services

naics 541511 - Custom Computer Programming Services

naics 514191 - On-Line Information Services

naics 541512 - Computer Systems Design Services

naics 336111 - Automobile Manufacturing

naics 336112 - Light Truck and Utility Vehicle Manufacturing

naics 336412 - Aircraft Engine and Engine Parts Manufacturing

naics 336399 - All Other Motor Vehicle Parts Manufacturing

planes, bombers, guns, cannons, and projectiles, within five years.

In 1945, a 113-day UAW strike ended only after government intervention. A year later, manufacturing returned to civilian automobile production. Cadillac and Oldsmobile unveiled high compression V8 engines in 1948. Five years later, the Chevrolet Corvette was introduced as the first mass-produced

The Officers

General Motors Corp.

Chairman and CEO: John F. Smith, Jr.

Vice Chairman: Harry J. Pearce

President and Chief Operating Officer: G. Richard
Wagoner, Jr.

Exec. VP and Chief Financial Officer: J. Michael Losh

Sr. VP and General Counsel: Thomas A. Gottschalk

Electronic Data Systems Corp.

Chairman and CEO: Richard H. Brown

President and Chief Operating Officer: Jeffrey M. Heller

Exec. VP and Chief Financial Officer: James E. Daley

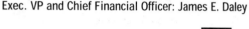

car with a plastic body. GM became the first company in the world to reach an annual profit of $1 billion in 1955. GM and other auto makers experienced a decrease in sales in 1956, coupled with significantly increased import market penetration. The nation's imports had surpassed its exports, and imports accounted for 8% of U.S. car sales.

A recession in the late 1950s prompted a demand for smaller, more fuel-efficient cars. In response, GM unveiled the Buick Special, the Oldsmobile F-85, and the Pontiac Tempest in 1960. A year later, Chevrolet introduced the Chevy II, a new small-sized car. Chevrolet introduced the Camaro, the division's sixth line of cars, in 1966, at roughly that same time that Pontiac launched the Firebird. GM began diversifying its interests in home appliances, insurance, locomotives, electronics, ball bearings, banking, and financing. A two-month UAW strike in 1970 ended with the implementation of retirement benefits for employees with 30 years of service at GM.

In response to tighter federal pollution control guidelines in the early 1970s, GM created the Environmental Activities Staff to monitor the performance of GM products in the environment. GM was adversely affected by the oil embargo, as well as by air pollution control regulations. Its luxury car sales dropped by 35%, as sales of compacts and subcompacts increased; by the mid-1970s, smaller cars accounted for 40% of all car sales in the U.S. Cadillac introduced the Seville and Chevrolet unveiled the Chevette in 1976. GM's U.S. cars were equipped with the catalytic converter that year, and the company launched its redesigned luxury cars, which were about a foot shorter and 100 pounds lighter than older models. GM introduced mid-sized cars from

Chevrolet, Pontiac, Oldsmobile, and Buick in 1977. By the end of the decade, the firm had spent $4.5 billion to meet regulations on pollution control, and market share had reached nearly 50%.

In the early 1980s, GM embarked upon its largest overseas expansion project, opening a plant in Zaragoza, Spain, to manufacture the Opel Corsa, GM's smallest car ever produced. A joint venture between GM and Fanuc Ltd. of Japan resulted in the creation of GMFanuc Robotics Corp. to develop and sell robotic systems. A joint venture with Isuzu Motors Ltd. of Japan was formed to produce a subcompact car to be manufactured in Japan and sold worldwide.

In 1983, GM launched its Saturn project, a development program involving the building of a new family of sub-compact cars in the U.S. from design to assembly. A year later, GM and Toyota Motor Corp., the world's two largest auto makers, formed New United Motor Manufacturing Inc. (NUMMI), a joint venture established to produce a small-sized Chevrolet car at Toyota's California plant. That year, GM acquired Electronic Data Systems (EDS), one of the largest data processing and telecommunications businesses in the world.

GM acquired Hughes Aircraft Co., one of the leading defense electronics companies worldwide, from Howard Hughes Medical Institute in 1985. Managed under the name GM Hughes Electronics (GMHE), the unit was merged with GM's Delco Electronics assets. After tension mounted between GM chairman Roger Smith and EDS founder H. Ross Perot, GM paid Perot $700 million for his EDS stock and seat on the board of directors. In 1986, the firm coordinated its growing European operations into GM Europe, based in Zurich.

GM paid $600 million for half of Swedish car manufacturer Saab in 1989. The following year, GM built the first Saturn car at the assembly plant in Spring Hill, Tennessee. To avoid a strike in 1990, new CEO Robert Stempel signed a three-year labor contract with the UAW calling for greater job and income security. A year later, GM's North American operations lost $7 billion in the firm's worst performance since 1982. Stempel launched the closing of over 20 plants during the next several years, which eliminated over 70,000 jobs.

GM's stock offering in 1992, which raised over $2 billion, was the largest in U.S. history. In 1994, GM recalled nearly five million gas powered pickup trucks because of potentially defective "sidesaddle" fuel tanks. A group of investors paid $1.25 billion for GM's National Car Rental unit in 1995, allowing GM to sharpen its focus on its core auto-making business. Also that year, China's leading car maker, Shanghai

Automotive, picked GM as its partner in a $1 billion deal to build sedans targeted for Chinese company fleets. Fiscal year profits reached $6.9 billion on sales of $168.8 billion, the best performance ever by an American corporation.

A 1996 walkout at GM's brake-parts supplier in Dayton, Ohio, snowballed into the largest shutdown of GM operations since 1970. After 17 days, a settlement was reached, allowing GM to outsource its supplier contracts in the future, even if GM's own unionized plants were bidding for the work. General Motors and Investor AB announced plans to pump $524 million into struggling automaker Saab, in a plan that could give GM a controlling interest in Saab by the year 2000. GM also completed the spinoff of EDS, creating the nation's largest independent computer services company.

As part of its plan to focus even more closely on auto making, GM also divested the defense electronics operations of its Hughes Electronics subsidiary to Raytheon Co. in 1997 and merged the electronic automotive parts operations of Hughes with Delphi Automotive, the leading auto parts maker in the world. A year later, Amoco Corp. and GM announced a partnership to jointly develop lower emissions gasoline; the agreement was the first of its kind between a petroleum company and an auto maker.

North American operations came to a standstill in 1998 in the wake of two UAW walkouts at two Michigan-based GM plants. After losing roughly $2.8 billion as a result of the seven-week strike, GM hired a new labor relations head. In 1999, GM raised $1.6 billion when it spun off 18% of Delphi Automotive in an initial public offering.

The Players

Chairman and CEO of General Motors Corp.: Roger B. Smith. Roger Smith began working for General Motors in the mid-1950s. After serving as a director for 19 years, Smith took over as CEO and chairman of the company in 1981. During Smith's nine-year tenure as CEO, General Motor's U.S. market share tumbled as he led the firm through a mammoth restructuring that included extensive layoffs. Smith also steered the firm's two major acquisitions in the 1980s: the $2.5 billion takeover of Electronic Data Systems in 1984, and the $5.2 billion purchase of Hughes Aircraft in 1985. In 1990, Smith was succeeded by Robert Stempel as CEO. Three years later, he retired as chairman.

Chairman of Electronic Data Systems Corp.: H. Ross Perot. Future presidential candidate H. Ross Perot worked as a salesman for IBM Corp. between 1952 and 1962. When management rejected his proposal to offer electronic data processing management services to customers, Perot resigned to found Electronic Data Systems. He parlayed his upstart into a billion dollar operation and sold it to General Motors in 1984. GM bought Perot's remaining EDS shares in 1986 for $700 million, partly to end conflict between Perot and GM CEO Smith over how best to manage EDS. Two years later, Perot established Perot Systems, a competitor to EDS.

History of Electronic Data Systems Corp.

Electronic Data Systems Corp. (EDS) was incorporated in 1962. Its founder, H. Ross Perot, an IBM salesman, had presented to IBM his idea of providing electronic data processing management services, instead of merely selling computer equipment, in order to service the many companies that were having difficulty finding employees with adequate computer skills to operate new equipment. IBM rejected his proposal, and Ross left IBM to start EDS.

Ross purchased wholesale computer time on an IBM 7070 computer at Southwestern Life Insurance in Dallas, Texas, and secured his first profit by selling the time at retail cost to Collins Radio, his first customer. In 1963, EDS signed its first data processing contract with Mercantile Security Life and its first commercial facilities management contract with Frito Lay. Unlike other service companies offering short-term contracts

of two or three months, EDS agreed to five-year fixed-price contracts. The firm made a profit by setting up a system, providing the staff to operate it, and then gradually removing EDS staff after the client's employees were brought up to speed.

With the passage of Medicare legislation in 1965, EDS entered a new market by organizing Medicare and Medicaid claims processing systems. Within three years, Medicare and Medicaid accounts made up 25% of the firm's total revenues. Dallas Bank was the first financial institution account for EDS, which later became the world's leading provider of data processing services to banks and savings and loans. In 1968, EDS offered stock for public sale, signed its first one-month $1 million contract, and initiated steps towards regional data centers.

In the early 1970s EDS acquired Wall Street Leasing, gaining eight credit unions as customers as a result. (By 1990, credit union accounts totaled 3,000.) Revenues reached $100 million; EDSNET, the EDS communications network, was launched; and EDS established a major health insurance system and pioneered a systems engineering development program. In 1976, F&M Schaefer Corp. filed a lawsuit against EDS claiming that EDS's data processing system was inaccurate and deficient. EDS contended that Schaefer merely wished to avoid paying the $1.2 million that he owed to the company. That year, EDS entered the international market when it secured an account in Saudi Arabia and signed a three-year $41 million contract with the Iranian government to provide computer services and training. EDS also introduced major software applications products worth over $3.5 billion.

The company withdrew operations from Iran in 1971 due to its six-month lag in payments. Perot ordered EDS employees back to the U.S. after several Iranian officials working with EDS were jailed. However, two EDS employees were arrested. Perot then designed a plan that provided his employees safe passage home.

In 1978, EDS paid F&M Schaefer $200,000 in an out-of-court settlement. Morton Meyerson was appointed as president in 1979; Perot stayed on as chairman. EDS expanded business interests, acquiring accounts with hospitals, small banks, and small businesses. EDS bought Potomac Leasing, thereby securing federal government contract work.

Meyerson, appointed CEO in the early 1980s, was recognized by the *Wall Street Transcript* as "The Best CEO in the Computer Services Industry" for three consecutive years. EDS secured an information contract from the federal government, the largest such contract ever awarded, and a ten-year $656 million contract for Project Viable to develop the U.S. Army's computerized administrative system into what is now known as Army Standard Information Management Systems (ASIMS).

In June of 1984, General Motors purchased EDS for $2.8 billion. That year, EDS set up business in the United Kingdom; it subsequently established subsidiaries in Canada, Mexico, Brazil, Venezuela, Australia, New Zealand, France, and Germany. Morton Meyerson resigned in 1985 and Lester M. Alberthal became president and CEO. During the late 1980s, EDS founded a subsidiary in Japan and opened the Paris Information Processing Center. It also forged two significant joint ventures, the first with the Commission for Science and Technology of the Beijing Municipal Government to develop the Beijing International Information Processing Co., and the second with Nippon Information Industry Corp. of Japan

to establish Nippon EDS, which provided computer services and maintained telecommunications operations.

Fortune named EDS the leading company in diversified service in 1988. EDS broadened its international presence to 27 countries and acquired General Data Systems, Ltd. and VideoStar Connection, Inc. In 1990, the company secured a $712 million contract with the Army, Navy, and Defense Logistics Agency. The firm also acquired a 30% stake in Infocel. By 1992, the GM account contributed only 41% of EDS's $8.5 billion in revenues. EDS France and GFI Informatique merged, forming a business that ranked in the top five of France's leading information technology service providers.

Unable to reach an agreement on financial terms, EDS and Sprint called off merger talks in 1994. Pursuing its goal to offer full-service business consulting, EDS acquired *A.T. Kearney* in 1995 for $628 million in cash and stock incentives. The deal merged 1,600 consultants from EDS with Kearney's 1,900, forming one of the world's largest consulting firms. In 1996, GM completed the spin-off of EDS. In return for its independence, EDS paid GM $500 million and agreed to provide GM with discounted computer services for ten years.

A few months after the spin-off, EDS posted a second quarter loss of $850 million, reflecting the costs of job elimination, early-retirement plans, and the write-down of assets. In 1997, the firm won a multiyear $4 billion contract to run the computer systems of BellSouth Telecommunications, ending a 19-month dry spell in which EDS had not been able to secure any contracts worth more than $1 billion. Aberthal was replaced by Richard Brown in 1999. MCI WorldCom and EDS forged a $17 billion agreement that year to use each other's technologies.

Market Forces Driving the Merger

GM spent most of the 1970s developing smaller versions of its luxury, gas guzzling autos. The firm responded successfully to customer demands for more fuel efficient modes of transportation, and its new line of vehicles prospered, boosting sales and earnings for the firm. To further its success, the company embarked on a $40 billion, seven-year plan to produce even more small, fuel efficient cars. According to Bruce Wasserstein, author of *Big Deal: The Battle for Control of America's Leading Corporations*, GM's plan faltered mainly because "oil prices crashed. As a result, customer interest in larger cars was renewed. GM, with its focus on new, fuel efficient models, was hamstrung by dated models. Foreign competition, especially from Japanese manufacturers, grew intense. The benefits of the capital spending program proved more elusive than hoped for."

With market share down to 41%—compared to 50% in the late 1970s—and profits dwindling, GM decided pursue acquisitions for two reasons: to quickly gain access to new technology and to gain a foothold in newer, less cyclical markets. EDS was attractive to GM because it would be able to streamline the firm's bulky data processing and communications systems. The automaker could use EDS as springboard for its diversification into the booming information technology market. EDS would also be able to automate GM's factories.

EDS sought the deal with GM, which was then the largest corporate user of computers, to guarantee access to GM's information technology contracts, worth an estimated $3 billion. Also, to grow, EDS believed that it needed the resources of a larger firm like GM. The increase in sales that would likely result from a marriage with GM, along with access to GM's deeper research and development and marketing pockets, would allow the firm to garner new contracts. EDS would also benefit from GM's international network.

Approach and Engagement

In early 1984, GM and EDS began negotiating GM's takeover of EDS. According to the terms of the agreement, EDS would maintain its own key personnel and management. To pay for part of the $2.5 billion purchase, GM issued EDS $500 million worth (13.6 million shares) of a new GM stock called Class E; its value was linked to EDS's performance, and GM agreed to pay dividends worth 25% of the unit's operating profits each year. GM paid EDS the remaining $2 billion in cash on June 27, 1984, and the deal was completed. EDS CEO Perot was appointed a seat on GM's board of directors.

Products and Services

By 1998, GM had divested EDS, as well the Hughes Aircraft assets it acquired in 1985. As a result, automotive products accounted for 89% of GM's total revenues, while financial services secured the remaining 11%. U.S. operations brought in 69% of total sales; Canada and Mexico, 7%; Europe, 18%; and Latin America, 6%.

GM's car making operations included Buick, Cadillac, Chevrolet, GMC, Holden, Oldsmobile, Europe's Opel/Vauhall, Pontiac, and Saturn. The company also owned 50% of Saab via a joint venture with Investor AB, and 49% of Japanese car maker Isuzu. Car making operations were organized under

two umbrellas: International Operations and North American Operations.

Other GM units included Allison Transmission, Delphi Automotive Systems (which GM began spinning off in 1999), finance and insurance service provider General Motors Acceptance Corp., GM Locomotive Group, and communications equipment provider Hughes Electronics Corp.

Changes to the Industry

Although it gained access to the lucrative GM contracts, EDS found that after its union with GM, many potential customers, who directly competed with GM, were loath to give work to EDS. An August 1995 article in *Economist* explained, "EDS...discovered that most of its sales momentum was coming from other customers, and that any chance of teaming up with new partners was scuppered once they found out that GM shared EDS's bed."

Integration problems and management disputes also plagued the firm. In 1986, GM purchased Perot's remaining shares in stock for over $700 million, removing Perot from his seat on the board of directors and from leadership of EDS.

Despite a run-up in GM's Class E stock and rapid growth by EDS, many analysts criticized the merger, insisting that both firms would be better off on their own. After deciding to refocus on its core automotive operations, General Motors announced plans in 1995 to spin off its EDS unit, positioning EDS as the world's largest independent computer-services company with $25 billion in market value, ten times what GM originally paid for it in 1984. The tax-free plan proposed by the companies would give EDS the independence to pursue strategic alliances and expand into new markets. On June 10, 1996, GM completed the spin-off of Electronic Data Systems, and EDS stock began trading on the New York Stock Exchange. In return for its independence, EDS paid GM $500 million and provide GM with discounted computer services for ten years.

Review of the Outcome

In the 18 months following the deal, as EDS worked towards cutting GM's $6 billion annual data-processing costs by managing the corporation's mammoth data-processing system, GM's class E stock jumped 150%. Revenues at EDS tripled to $3.4 billion within the first full year of the GM acquisition. Profits, however, dropped by 5.5%.

In 1986, EDS personnel increased to 40,000, almost triple the amount in 1984. The firm used its increased capital to expand into telecommunications and factory automation. By 1989, GM's communications network and EDS' EDSNET were consolidated, forming the largest digital private telecommunications network; the task required three years, a staff of 2,000, and over $1 billion.

According to a 1991 article in *Economist*, "the savings EDS wrung out of GM's telecoms network and out of administering the medical scheme for GM's past and present employees" already equaled the price GM had paid for EDS. By 1995, sales at EDS had reached $12 billion. When GE spun off EDS as an independent company, it was worth 10 times its 1984 value.

Research

"Electronic Data Systems Corp.," in *Notable Corporate Chronologies*, The Gale Group, 1999. Lists major events in the history of Electronic Data Systems Corp.

"General Motors Corp.," in *Notable Corporate Chronologies*, The Gale Group, 1999. Profiles major events in the history of General Motors Corp.

General Motors Corp. Home Page, available at http://www.gm .com. Official World Wide Web Home Page for General Motors Corp. Includes news, as well as financial, product, and historical information.

"GM Wheels of Fortune," in *Newsweek*, 17 June 1985. Explains the reasons behind GM's purchase of EDS.

Sloan, Allan. "Roger Smith's Revenge," in *Newsweek*, 28 August 1995. Reports how the Class E stock of EDS has soared since the firm's takeover by GM.

"The $22-Billion Disconnect: Electronic Data Systems," in *The Economist*, 12 August 1995. Discusses GM's reasons for spinning off EDS.

Zellner, Wendy. "No Separation Anxiety at EDS: Free of GM, It Will Have a Chance to Soar Higher," in *Business Week*, 21 August 1995. Predicts what EDS will do once free of GM.

———. "Why EDS Won't Be Sorry to Be Single Again," in *Business Week*, 15 April 1996. Discusses the term of the EDS spinoff by GM.

Wasserstein, Bruce. *Big Deal: The Battle for Control of America's Leading Corporations*, Warner Books, 1998. Offers an overview of the largest mergers in recent American corporate history.

THERA WILLIAMS

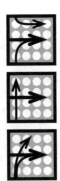

GENERAL MOTORS & HUGHES AIRCRAFT

nationality: USA
date: December 31, 1985
affected: General Motors Corp., USA, founded 1897
affected: Hughes Aircraft Co., USA, founded 1932

General Motors Corp.
100 Renaissance Ctr.
Detroit, MI 48243
USA

tel: (313)556-5000
fax: (313)556-5108
web: http://www.gm.com

Overview of the Merger

On December 31, 1985, General Motors purchased Hughes Aircraft Co., the seventh-largest defense contractor in the U.S., for $5.2 billion in cash and stock. Despite the success of Hughes Aircraft while a unit of GM, many analysts blamed the purchase—along with GM's earlier $2.5 billion acquisition of Electronic Data Services—for preventing GM from focusing on its core automotive operations. In 1997, the firm divested the defense electronics unit to Raytheon Co. for $9.8 billion.

History of General Motors Corp.

In 1897, Olds Motor Vehicle Co. was founded by Ransom E. Olds when he introduced the first Oldsmobile model, a $1,200, four-seater, luxury vehicle. The Olds operation was the first American factory in Detroit, Michigan, devoted exclusively to the production of automobiles.

Three years later, David Buick built a factory in Detroit under his own name. Max Grabowsky established the Grabowsky Motor Vehicle Co., which later evolved into a large part of the GM Truck and Bus division. In 1902, Cadillac Automobile Co. was formed in Detroit by Henry Leland, a former Oldsmobile employee. The company was named after the French explorer who founded Detroit in 1701. That year, the Buick Motor Car Co. was founded in Detroit and purchased by William Durant. The Oakland Motor Car Co., which later became GM's Pontiac Motor division, was formed in 1907.

In 1908, William Durant launched a plan to consolidate leading automakers as General Motors Co. Buick, America's leading automobile manufacturer, and Oldsmobile joined GM. A year later, Cadillac and Pontiac were purchased by the young GM Co. By 1910, the Buick/Oldsmobile merger had proved successful, but Durant's buying spree required additional financing. After a number of rejections from financial lenders, Durant finally secured loans worth $15 million under strict conditions. The banks forced Durant to step down, and they took control, setting up their own management team.

The Business

Financials

Revenue (1998): $161 billion

Employees (1998): 594,000

SICs / NAICS

sic 3711 - Motor Vehicles & Car Bodies

sic 3663 - Radio & T.V. Communications Equipment

sic 5013 - Motor Vehicle Supplies & New Parts

sic 3724 - Aircraft Engines & Engine Parts

sic 3714 - Motor Vehicle Parts & Accessories

sic 5084 - Industrial Machinery & Equipment

sic 3519 - Internal Combustion Engines Nec

sic 6159 - Miscellaneous Business Credit Institutions

sic 6141 - Personal Credit Institutions

sic 7373 - Computer Integrated Systems Design

naics 336111 - Automobile Manufacturing

naics 336112 - Light Truck and Utility Vehicle Manufacturing

naics 336412 - Aircraft Engine and Engine Parts Manufacturing

naics 336399 - All Other Motor Vehicle Parts Manufacturing

naics 541512 - Computer Systems Design Services

In 1911, Chevrolet Motor Co. was established in Detroit by racecar driver Louis Chevrolet and Durant. That year, GM was the first automobile manufacturer to be listed on the New York Stock Exchange; GM Export Co. was formed; and GM combined its previously acquired Rapid Motor and Reliance Motor operations under Pontiac to create GMC, a truck production arm of GM. In 1915, Chevrolet acquired 54.5% of GM, and Durant regained control as president.

GM was incorporated under Delaware state law in 1916. Durant organized United Motors Co., a consolidation of companies that provided parts and services to the automobile industry. GM also expanded into other industries such as refrigerator manufacturing and financing. The following year, GM converted its automobile factories to military materials production sites for the war effort. In 1919, it acquired the assets of Chevrolet, as well as Hyatt Bearings, New Departure, a 60% interest in Fisher Body, and Frigidaire Co., which was divested years later. General Motors of Canada, Ltd. was also established that year.

By 1920, more than 30 companies had been purchased by GM for stock, which fell to $14 a share that year. Banks rescued the corporation by again ousting Durant, and the DuPont family and J.P. Morgan & Co. took control of GM. In 1923, Alfred P. Sloan was named president. He immediately began decentralizing GM management, a move that was later praised by Wall Street analysts for rescuing GM economically after the onset of the Depression. Sloan's tactics were later used as a model for management by many other large businesses.

The first GM vehicle to be produced outside the U.S. was assembled in Denmark in 1924. A year later, Chevrolet surpassed Ford's Model T in popularity, and GM purchased Vauxhall Motors Ltd. of London, England, which was later merged with Germany's Adam Opel. Pontiac became an official division of GM in the early 1930s, as did Packard Electronic Co. when it was acquired by GM.

After the collapse of 450 Michigan banks due to the Depression, GM created the National Bank of Detroit. A 44-day sit-down strike in 1937 at the Fisher Body plant in Flint ended with a victory for the United Auto Workers (UAW) over the right to organize GM workers. The Detroit Diesel Engine division was established that year. In 1940, GM produced its 25 millionth car and held 44% of the U.S. automobiles market. The firm began retooling factories for defense weaponry and machinery production for the World War II effort; GM built $12.3 billion worth of military equipment, including ball bearings, tanks, naval ships, fighting planes, bombers, guns, cannons, and projectiles, within five years.

In 1945, a 113-day UAW strike ended only after government intervention. A year later, manufacturing returned to civilian automobile production. Cadillac and Oldsmobile unveiled high compression V8 engines in 1948. Five years later, the Chevrolet Corvette was introduced as the first mass-produced car with a plastic body. GM became the first company in the world to reach an annual profit of $1 billion in 1955. GM and other auto makers experienced a decrease in sales in 1956, coupled with significantly increased import market penetration. The nation's imports had surpassed its exports, and imports accounted for 8% of U.S. car sales.

A recession in the late 1950s prompted a demand for smaller, more fuel-efficient cars. In response, GM unveiled the Buick Special, the Oldsmobile F-85, and the Pontiac Tempest in 1960. A year later, Chevrolet introduced the Chevy II, a new small-sized car. Chevrolet introduced the Camaro, the division's sixth line of cars, in 1966, at roughly that same time that Pontiac launched the Firebird. GM began diversifying its interests in home appliances, insurance, locomotives, electronics, ball bearings, banking, and financing. A two-month UAW strike in 1970 ended with the implementation of retirement benefits for employees with 30 years of service at GM.

In response to tighter federal pollution control guidelines in the early 1970s, GM created the Environmental Activities Staff to monitor the performance of GM products in the environment. GM was adversely affected by the oil embargo, as well as by air pollution control regulations. Its luxury car sales dropped by 35%, as sales of compacts and subcompacts increased; by the mid-1970s, smaller cars accounted for 40% of all car sales in the U.S. Cadillac introduced the Seville and Chevrolet unveiled the Chevette in 1976. GM's U.S. cars were equipped with the catalytic converter that year, and the company launched its redesigned luxury cars, which were about a foot shorter and 100 pounds lighter than older models. GM introduced mid-sized cars from Chevrolet, Pontiac, Oldsmobile, and Buick in 1977. By the end of the decade, the firm had spent $4.5 billion to meet regulations on pollution control, and market share had reached nearly 50%.

In the early 1980s, GM embarked upon its largest overseas expansion project, opening a plant in Zaragoza, Spain, to manufacture the Opel Corsa, GM's smallest car ever produced. A joint venture between GM and Fanuc Ltd. of Japan resulted in the creation of GMFanuc Robotics Corp. to develop and sell robotic systems. A joint venture with Isuzu Motors Ltd. of Japan was formed to produce a subcompact car to be manufactured in Japan and sold worldwide.

In 1983, GM launched its Saturn project, a development program involving the building of a new family of sub-compact cars in the U.S. from design to assembly. A year later, GM and Toyota Motor Corp., the world's two largest auto makers, formed New United Motor Manufacturing Inc. (NUMMI), a joint venture established to produce a small-sized Chevrolet car at Toyota's California plant. That year, GM acquired Electronic Data Systems Corp. (EDS), one of the largest data processing and telecommunications businesses in the world.

GM acquired Hughes Aircraft Co., one of the leading defense electronics companies worldwide, from Howard Hughes Medical Institute in 1985. Managed under the name GM Hughes Electronics (GMHE), the unit was merged with GM's Delco Electronics assets. After tension mounted between GM chairman Roger Smith and EDS founder H. Ross Perot, GM paid Perot $700 million for his EDS stock and seat on the board of directors. In 1986, the firm coordinated its growing European operations into GM Europe, based in Zurich.

The Officers

Chairman and CEO: John F. Smith, Jr.

Vice Chairman: Harry J. Pearce

President and Chief Operating Officer: G. Richard Wagoner, Jr.

Exec. VP and Chief Financial Officer: J. Michael Losh

Sr. VP and General Counsel: Thomas A. Gottschalk

GM paid $600 million for half of Swedish car manufacturer Saab in 1989. The following year, GM built the first Saturn car at the assembly plant in Spring Hill, Tennessee. To avoid a strike in 1990, new CEO Robert Stempel signed a three-year labor contract with the UAW calling for greater job and income security. A year later, GM's North American operations lost $7 billion in the firm's worst performance since 1982. Stempel launched the closing of over 20 plants during the next several years, which eliminated over 70,000 jobs.

GM's stock offering in 1992, which raised over $2 billion, was the largest in U.S. history. In 1994, GM recalled nearly five million gas powered pickup trucks because of potentially defective "sidesaddle" fuel tanks. A group of investors paid $1.25 billion for GM's National Car Rental unit in 1995, allowing GM to sharpen its focus on its core auto-making business. Also that year, China's leading car maker, Shanghai Automotive, picked GM as its partner in a $1 billion deal to build sedans targeted for Chinese company fleets. Fiscal year profits reached $6.9 billion on sales of $168.8 billion, the best performance ever by an American corporation.

A 1996 walkout at GM's brake-parts supplier in Dayton, Ohio, snowballed into the largest shutdown of GM operations since 1970. After 17 days, a settlement was reached, allowing GM to outsource its supplier contracts in the future, even if GM's own unionized plants were bidding for the work. General Motors and Investor AB announced plans to pump $524 million into struggling automaker Saab, in a plan that could give GM a controlling interest in Saab by the year 2000. GM also completed the spinoff of EDS, creating the nation's largest independent computer services company.

As part of its plan to focus even more closely on auto making, GM divested the defense electronics operations of its Hughes Electronics subsidiary to Raytheon Co. in 1997 and merged the electronic automotive parts operations of Hughes with Delphi

The Players

Chairman and CEO of General Motors Corp.: Roger B. Smith. Roger Smith began working for General Motors in the mid-1950s. After serving as a director for 19 years, Smith took over as CEO and chairman of the company in 1981. During Smith's nine-year tenure as CEO, General Motor's U.S. market share tumbled as he led the firm through a mammoth restructuring that included extensive layoffs. Smith also steered the firm's two major acquisitions in the 1980s: the $2.5 billion takeover of Electronic Data Systems in 1984, and the $5.2 billion purchase of Hughes Aircraft in 1985. In 1990, Smith was succeeded by Robert Stempel as CEO. Three years later, he retired as chairman.

Automotive, the leading auto parts maker in the world. A year later, Amoco Corp. and GM announced a partnership to jointly develop lower emissions gasoline; the agreement was the first of its kind between a petroleum company and an auto maker.

North American operations came to a standstill in 1998 in the wake of two UAW walkouts at two Michigan-based GM plants. After losing roughly $2.8 billion as a result of the seven-week strike, GM hired a new labor relations head. In 1999, GM raised $1.6 billion when it spun off 18% of Delphi Automotive in an initial public offering.

History of Hughes Aircraft Co.

Howard Hughes founded Hughes Aircraft in 1932 to construct new types of airplanes. As part of the World War II effort, the firm began constructing a boat that could also fly and carry troops to various locations. However, the machine wasn't completed until after the war had ended. In the late 1940s, Hughes began remodeling DC-3 planes for business use and diversified into defense electronics.

Frustrated with what they perceived as Howard Hughes' increasingly eccentric behavior, 75 engineers resigned in 1953 and the U.S. Air Force began terminating its contracts with the firm. As a result, Hughes founded the Howard Hughes Medical Institute, into which he shifted the assets of Hughes Aircraft, and hired aviation executive Lawrence Hyland as president. Under a new group of engineers, the firm developed the first laser beam light in 1960, launched the first communications satellite in 1963, and constructed

the Surveyor, which landed on the moon in 1966. Hughes died in 1976, and board of trustees took over the medical institute.

In 1985, General Motors acquired Hughes Aircraft from the Howard Hughes Medical Institute for $2.7 billion. The new unit, operating as a wholly owned subsidiary of GM, designed, manufactured, and marketed electronic systems. The following year, Hughes completed an air traffic control system for South Korea. In 1989, the firm secured a $325 million contract to develop a new air traffic control system for Canada. Hughes purchased Avicom International, an aircraft passenger entertainment, services, and communications provider, in 1990.

Due to declining defense budgets the early 1990s, Hughes announced plans to reorganize its defense electronics operations via downsizing and divesting non-core operations. Hughes acquired the missile operations of General Dynamics Corp. for $62.8 million and 21.51 million shares of stock. The firm also merged with Delco Electronics to form GM Hughes Electronics (GMHE). The company focused on four main segments: automotive electronics, which accounted for 32% of revenues; telecommunications and space, which made up 18%; defense electronics, which brought in 44%; and commercial technologies, which secured the remaining 6%.

To strengthen its international presence, GMHE established Hughes Europe, Hughes Asia/Pacific, and Hughes Middle East in 1992. International sales accounted for 18% of total revenues. Growth in automotive electronics and telecommunications and space operations resulted in an increase in annual revenues to $13.5 billion. In 1993, The DBS-1, GMHE's 100th commercial communications satellite, was launched to broadcast DIRECTV programming, which began in 1994 after the launch of DBS-2. A broadcast center for DIRECTV was completed in Castle Rock, Colorado. GMHE also secured an infrastructure equipment contract from BellSouth Cellular, as well as a $766 million contract from NASA for its Earth Observation System/Data Information System. It divested its commercial airline simulator operations and several electronics components holdings. Delco Electronics Asia/Pacific was founded in Singapore.

A restructuring launched in 1994 reduced corporate staff by one-half and consolidated four aerospace and defense units into one operation. GMHE and Olivetti agreed to jointly expand digital satellite communications in Europe. In 1995, GMHE acquires CAE-Link Corp., a simulation, training, and technical services supplier to the U.S. military and NASA, for $155 million. DIRECTV subscribers totaled 1.2 million, and the service was offered internationally via Galaxy

Latin America and DIRECTV Japan. GMHE changed its name to Hughes Electronics. In December, Hughes Electronics purchased Magnavox Electronic Systems Co. for $382.4 million.

In 1996 Hughes and PanAmSat agreed to merge satellite services operations into PanAmSat Corp., a publicly held company, of which Hughes owned 71.5%. The following year, Hughes acquired the Marine Systems Division of Alliant Techsystems, Inc. for $141 million. GM sold the Hughes Aircraft assets of Hughes Electronics to Raytheon and shifted the auto parts assets of Delco Electronics to Delphi Automotive Systems. Hughes then refocused on telecommunications and space, its fastest growing segment.

Market Forces Driving the Merger

GM spent most of the 1970s developing smaller versions of its luxury, gas guzzling autos. The firm responded successfully to customer demands for more fuel efficient modes of transportation, and its new line of vehicles prospered, boosting sales and earnings for the firm. To further its success, the company embarked on a $40 billion, seven-year plan to produce even more small, fuel efficient cars. However, Bruce Wasserstein, author of *Big Deal: The Battle for Control of America's Leading Corporations*, reported that GM's plan faltered mainly because "oil prices crashed. As a result, customer interest in larger cars was renewed. GM, with its focus on new, fuel efficient models, was hamstrung by dated models. Foreign competition, especially from Japanese manufacturers, grew intense. The benefits of the capital spending program proved more elusive than hoped for."

With market share down to 41%—compared to 50% in the late 1970s—and profits dwindling, GM decided to pursue acquisitions for two reasons: to quickly gain access to new technology and to gain a foothold in newer, less cyclical markets. Hughes Aircraft was attractive to GM because its electronics technology would likely be applicable to auto manufacturing. GM was also interested in diversifying into the high growth space and satellite technologies of Hughes.

At the same time, Hughes was looking for research and development dollars after facing several canceled Department of Defense contracts in 1984. Because it was owned by the Howard Hughes Medical Institute, Hughes Aircraft was required by the IRS to make contributions to the organization. The terminated contracts made it difficult for the firm to meet those obligations as well as pursue its own research and development efforts.

Approach and Engagement

In 1985, GM agreed to pay $5.2 billion to Howard Hughes Medical Institute for Hughes Aircraft Co. To pay for half of its purchase, GM issued a new class of stock, Class H shares, which were separate from traditional GM stock. GM agreed to pay dividends on the Class H stock based on Hughes' earnings, and to offer the stock to the public within three years. The takeover was completed on December 31, 1985, and Hughes Aircraft began operating as a wholly owned subsidiary of GM.

Products and Services

After the Hughes Aircraft assets were divested, automotive products accounted for 89% of GM's total revenues, while financial services secured the remaining 11%. U.S. operations brought in 69% of total sales; Canada and Mexico, 7%; Europe, 18%; and Latin America, 6%.

GM's car making operations included Buick, Cadillac, Chevrolet, GMC, Holden, Oldsmobile, Europe's Opel/Vauhall, Pontiac, and Saturn. The company also owned 50% of Saab via a joint venture with Investor AB, and 49% of Japanese car maker Isuzu. Car making operations were organized under two umbrellas: International Operations and North American Operations.

Other GM units included Allison Transmission, Delphi Automotive Systems (which GM began spinning off in 1999), finance and insurance service provider General Motors Acceptance Corp., GM Locomotive Group, and communications equipment provider Hughes Electronics Corp.

Changes to the Industry

After Hughes (later renamed GM Hughes Electronics after GM merged the unit with its Delco Electronics assets) became a part of GM, it found that many of its customers, direct competitors of GM, were reluctant to do business any longer. The firm's expensive technology was also blamed for a decrease in sales. In June of 1988, Hughes lost two lucrative contracts—a communications satellite project and an air traffic control system upgrade—to a competitor. According to a 1990 article in *Business Week*, after its takeover by GM the firm was "plagued by production problems, high costs, slowing Pentagon spending, and a tangle of federal investigations."

These problems, along with GM's decision to refocus on its core automobile and other commercial operations, prompted GM to sell the original Hughes Aircraft defense electronics assets to Raytheon Co. for $9.8 billion in 1997. Prior to the sale, Hughes was separated from GM's Delco Electronics, and GM also retained the space and telecommunications operations of Hughes.

Review of the Outcome

GM's decision to divest Hughes Aircraft after owning the operation for twelve years belied the fact that Hughes had done quite well under GM after the first few bumpy years. By 1994, Hughes had slashed its workforce of 80,000 to 50,000, and sales and profits had doubled to roughly $14 billion and $1 billion, respectively. The firm dealt with defense spending cuts by strengthening its position in commercial satellite technology. According to an August 1994 article in *Forbes*, GM helped Hughes reduce its dependence on military contracts to 48%, compared to 70% in the late 1980s, by supplying cash and credit, "enabling Hughes to invest over $2 billion in telecommunications and space since 1987." By the mid-1990s, Hughes owned and operated 13 satellites, more than any other competitor in the world.

Research

Banks, Howard. "GM's Hidden Treasure," in *Forbes*, 1 August 1994. Discusses the success of Hughes Aircraft as a unit of GM.

"Can GM Manage It All?" in *Fortune*, 8 July 1985. Explains why GM decided to purchase Hughes Aircraft.

"General Motors Corp.," in *Notable Corporate Chronologies*, The Gale Group, 1999. Lists major events in the history of General Motors Corp.

General Motors Corp. Home Page, available at http://www.gm.com. Official World Wide Web Home Page for General Motors Corp. Includes news, as well as financial, product, and historical information.

"GM and Hughes Aircraft," in *Business Week*, 17 June 1985. Explains GM's reasons for purchasing Hughes Aircraft and details how GM plans to use the new unit.

Grover, R. "The Head Winds Holding Back Hughes Aircraft," in *Business Week*, 12 September 1988. Describes the problems Hughes Aircraft faced after its takeover by GM.

"Hughes Electronics Corp.," in *Notable Corporate Chronologies*, The Gale Group, 1999. Lists major events in the history of Hughes Electronics Corp.

Muradine, Vago. "GM Expected to Announce Sale of Hughes to Raytheon Today," in *Defense Daily*, 16 January 1997. Comments on GM's decision to sell Hughes Aircraft to Raytheon.

Schine, E. "GM and Hughes: Is This Marriage Fizzling?," in *Business Week*, 12 February 1990. Offers an overview of the problems Hughes Aircraft continued to face in the early 1990s.

Wasserstein, Bruce. *Big Deal: The Battle for Control of America's Leading Corporations*, Warner Books, 1998. Provides an overview of the largest mergers in recent American corporate history.

THERA WILLIAMS

GEORGIA-PACIFIC & GREAT NORTHERN NEKOOSA

nationality: USA
date: June 26, 1990
affected: Georgia-Pacific Corp., USA, founded 1927
affected: Great Northern Nekoosa Corp., USA, founded 1898

Georgia-Pacific Corp.
Georgia-Pacific Center, 133 Peachtree St. NE
Atlanta, GA 30303
USA

tel: (404)652-4000
fax: (404)584-1470
web: http://www.gp.com

Overview of the Acquisition

After a hostile battle that later turned friendly, Georgia-Pacific paid $3.74 billion for Connecticut-based Great Northern Nekoosa Corp., a competing producer of pulp, paper, containerboard, lumber, and plywood, as well as the seventh-largest paper products producer in the U.S., in June of 1990. Although the deal propelled Georgia-Pacific to the number one spot among U.S. forest product firms, it also saddled the company with $1.3 billion in debt. Losses in early 1991 prompted Georgia-Pacific to divest several assets, including 80% of Great Northern Paper Inc. to Bowater (which eventually bought the remaining 20%), as means of generating capital to pay down debt. The deal marked the first hostile takeover effort in the paper industry.

History of Georgia-Pacific Corp.

In 1927, Georgia Hardwood Lumber Co. began operating in Augusta, Georgia, as a hardwood lumber wholesaler with $12,000 in start-up funds provided by its founder, Owen Cheatham. Over the next decade, the company began manufacturing lumber and worked to increase its milling capabilities in the southern U.S. By 1938, the company operated five southern sawmills.

Georgia Hardwood became the largest supplier of lumber to the U.S. Army during World War II. After the war ended, the firm purchased a plywood mill in Bellingham, Washington. The mill allowed Georgia Hardwood to take advantage of plywood's growing popularity in the construction industry and gave the company a strong competitive advantage. Additional plywood mills in Washington and Oregon were purchased in 1948. The company changed its name to Georgia-Pacific Plywood & Lumber Co. to reflect more accurately its geographic and operational expansion. Another plywood plant was opened in 1949.

In 1951, the company changed its name to Georgia-Pacific Plywood Co. Two years later, it moved its headquarters from Georgia to Olympia, Washington, as a means of increasing proximity to Owen Cheatham's newly purchased timberland acquisitions in the western and southern states. Company headquarters moved again, in 1954, to Portland, Oregon. Cheatham continued to acquire additional for-

The Business

Financials

Revenue (1998): $13.33 billion

Employees (1998): 45,000

SICs / NAICS

sic 2611 - Pulp Mills

sic 2421 - Sawmills & Planing Mills-General

sic 2411 - Logging

sic 2621 - Paper Mills

sic 2821 - Plastics Materials & Resins

sic 2493 - Reconstituted Wood Products

naics 322121 - Paper (except Newsprint) Mills

naics 322122 - Newsprint Mills

naics 321113 - Sawmills

naics 325211 - Plastics Material and Resin Manufacturing

naics 321219 - Reconstituted Wood Product Manufacturing

est acreage and manufacturing facilities, including Coos Bay Lumber Co. and Hammond Lumber Co. The company's name was changed to Georgia-Pacific Corp. in 1957. The following year, a kraft pulp and linerboard mill opened in Toledo, Oregon, marking Georgia-Pacific's entrance into the paper business. The operation used wood waste from sawmills and plywood plants, an approach that became a worldwide standard.

Georgia-Pacific's first resin adhesive plant opened at Coos Bay, Oregon, in 1959. The operation was intended to supply the resin required for the company's plywood-production business, but it gradually grew large enough to supply resin to other plywood manufacturers as well. The acquisition of W.M. Ritter Lumber Co. in 1961 propelled Georgia-Pacific to the third place spot among U.S. lumber companies. That year, the firm built its first corrugated-container plant in Olympia, Washington. Acquisitions throughout the remainder of the decade included Crossett Lumber Co., Puget Sound Pulp and Timber Co., Vanity Fair Paper Mills, St. Croix Paper Co., Fordyce Lumber Co., Bestwall Gypsum Co., and Kalamazoo Paper Co.

Company founder Owen Cheatham died in 1970. Robert B. Pamplin, who had worked with Cheatham since the company's inception, was named chairman and CEO. Two years later, Georgia-Pacific was required by the Federal Trade Commission to defend its acquisition of 16 small firms in the South that supplied the company with 673,000 acres of the southern pine used to make plywood. Charging that the acquisitions created a monopoly, the FTC issued a consent order forcing Georgia-Pacific to divest 20% of its assets. As a result, the firm spun off Louisiana-Pacific Corp.

Georgia-Pacific purchased the wood-products operations of Boise Cascade at Fort Bragg, California, in 1973. A slump in the housing industry depressed the company's lumber and plywood business, but growth in chemical, pulp, and paper operations resulted in record profits. Exchange Oil & Gas Corp. was acquired in 1975, enabling the company to become more self-sufficient by developing its own reserves of important raw materials required for the operation of its chemical plants. In 1976, Robert Flowerree succeeded Robert Pamplin as chairman and CEO. A 25-year Georgia-Pacific veteran, Flowerree proved instrumental in the firm's diversification into chemicals. Under his leadership, the firm expanded its building products to include roofing materials, which it began to produce in a converted paper mill.

By the late 1970s, Georgia-Pacific drew three-quarters of its sales from the southern and eastern U.S. As a result, the firm moved its headquarters back to Georgia. The relocation caused many employees to leave the company and several senior executives to retire, leaving Georgia-Pacific vulnerable at a critical time, particularly in the growing chemical arena. As a result, Georgia-Pacific divested a large portion of its chemical operations to Georgia Gulf Corp. in 1984. A linerboard mill was acquired, along with several corrugated container plants, and over 300,000 acres of forest from St. Regis Corp. Two paper plants were converted to the production of high-margin products, such as bleached board and copier papers. The firm successfully expanded a wood-products mill in South Carolina and a plant in Florida to produce lattice and fencing materials that were in high demand.

Georgia-Pacific sold Exchange Oil & Gas in 1985, but the company retained its specialty chemicals business, which continued to deliver good returns. The following year, Georgia-Pacific entered another area of the paper market through the introduction of Angel Soft bathroom tissue. Acquisitions in the late 1980s included U.S. Plywood Corp., selected assets of the Erving Distributor Products Co., Brunswick Pulp & Paper Co., and American Forest Products Co.

In June of 1990, Georgia-Pacific paid $3.74 billion for Great Northern Nekoosa Corp., becoming the largest forest products concern in the U.S. The following year, after pleading guilty to tax evasion, Georgia-Pacific paid $5 million in fines. The company also sold

80% of Great Northern Paper Inc. to Bowater for $300 million. Exports to Mexico rose by about 40%, or $40 million, in 1994. That year, Georgia-Pacific sold its roofing manufacturing operations, as well as its envelope making unit.

In 1996, Georgia-Pacific acquired the gypsum wallboard business of Domtar, Inc., of Montreal, Canada. The $350 million deal included nine U.S. manufacturing sites and four Canadian sites, which would enable the company to compete more effectively in North America. To satisfy U.S. Justice Dept. antitrust concerns about the acquisition, Georgia-Pacific sold facilities in Buchanan, New York, and Wilmington, Delaware.

The continued sluggishness of the worldwide paper market in the late 1990s prompted Georgia Pacific to split operations into two separate trading stocks: Georgia-Pacific Group and The Timber Co. The move was designed to protect the timber assets from the cyclical nature of the paper industry. Georgia Pacific Corp. remained in place as a holding company for the two units.

History of Great Northern Nekoosa Corp.

The Northern Development Co. was incorporated in 1898. Renamed Great Northern Paper Co., the firm began producing newsprint in 1900. By the early 1920s, Great Northern Paper was also making corrugated paper. The 1930s marked a progression from the manufacture of wrapping paper to the manufacture of business paper. Over the next thirty years, the firm focused on growing its pulp and paper operations.

Great Northern Paper and Edwards Paper Co. merged in 1970 to form Great Northern Nekoosa Corp. The company began seeking acquisitions as a means of augmenting its manufacturing and distributing capacity. In 1973, Great Northern bought Heco Envelope Co. Two years later, the firm purchased Pak-Well.

Acquisitions during the 1980s included Leaf River Forest Products, in 1981; Barton, Duer & Koch, as well as Consolidated Marketing , Inc., in 1982; Triquet Paper Co., in 1983; Chatfield Paper Co., in 1984; J&J Corrugated Box Corp. and Iowa-based Carpenter Paper Co., in 1986; the forest product operations of Owens-Illinois, in 1987; and Owens-Papers in 1988. Great Northern became an acquisition target itself in 1989 when Georgia-Pacific offered $3.6 billion to buyout the firm. Great Northern resisted the initial overtures by Georgia-Pacific, but eventually agreed to be acquired by the paper and forest products giant in 1990 for $3.74 billion.

The Officers

Chairman, President, and CEO: Alston D. Correll

Chief Financial Officer and Exec. VP, Finance: John F. McGovern

Exec. VP, Timber; President and CEO, Timber Co.: Donald L. Glass

Exec. VP, Pulp and Paperboard: Clint M. Kennedy

Exec. VP, Wood Products and Distribution: Ronald L. Paul

Market Forces Driving the Acquisition

Despite intense competition in the paper industry in the late 1980s, paper products accounted for a larger chunk of profits than wood products for the first time in Georgia-Pacific's history, due to the firm's successful tissue and towel operation, combined with the production of linerboard, kraft, and fine papers. Hoping to further reduce its reliance on the cyclical building products market, Georgia-Pacific began eyeing Great Northern Nekoosa, a competing paper company.

According to *International Directory of Company Histories*, "Great Northern Nekoosa was a particularly attractive candidate for acquisition, owing to its depressed stock price. Georgia-Pacific saw the combination of the two companies as an opportunity to achieve economies of scale and other cost savings." Purchasing Great Northern would also allow Georgia-Pacific to augment its manufacturing capacity at a much lower cost than building its own plants.

Approach and Engagement

Georgia-Pacific launched a hostile $63 per share ($3.6 billion) offer for Great Northern Nekoosa in late 1989. Great Northern rejected the offer and began implementing defensive measures, including distributing roughly $80 million in surplus pension plan assets to employees. After launching and losing several lawsuits designed to block the deal, Great Northern hired Goldman Sachs in February of 1990 to solicit white knight offers. The firm also delayed a planned shareholders meeting from March 2 to March 20. No white knight bidders emerged, however, and Great Northern agreed to a slightly increased $3.74 billion offer from Georgia-Pacific, which didn't include the $1.3 billion in Great Northern debt Georgia Pacific would assume.

Shareholders approved the deal on June 22, 1990, and four days later, the transaction was completed

The Players

Chairman and CEO of Georgia-Pacific Corp.: T. Marshall Hahn, Jr. Marshall Hahn succeeded Robert Flowerree as president of Georgia-Pacific in 1976. Six years later, he was named chief operating officer. In 1983, Hahn replaced Flowerree, who retired earlier than expected, as CEO and chairman of the firm. He orchestrated Georgia-Pacific's controversial takeover of Great Northern Nekoosa Corp. in 1990. After announcing his retirement in 1993, Hahn handed over the reins to A.D. Correll and was named honorary chairman.

when Great Northern Nekoosa became a wholly owned subsidiary of Georgia-Pacific. Georgia-Pacific financed the purchase price via a $2.4 billion unsecured, seven-year term loan and a $1.4 billion unsecured, five-year, revolving credit line.

Products and Services

In the late 1990s, pulp and paper accounted for 43% of Georgia-Pacific's total sales. Pulp and paper products and services were organized into four main segments: Communications Papers, which included business forms, checks, envelopes, office papers, and stationery; Containerboard and Packaging Materials, which included bleach board, corrugated packaging, kraft paper, and linerboard; Market Pulp; and Tissue Papers, such as bathroom tissues, napkins, and paper towels. Tissue brands included Angel Soft, Coronet, Delta, MD, and Sparkle.

Building products and services, which brought in 57% of sales, were organized into five units: Chemicals, which included adhesives, specialty chemicals, and wood resins; Gypsum Products, such as industrial plaster, joint compound, specialty panels, and wallboard; Wood Panels, including hardboard, medium-density fiberboard, oriented strand board, panelboard, particleboard, plywood, and softboard; Lumber; and Distribution.

Changes to the Industry

When the deal was completed, Georgia Pacific became the leading forest products concern in the U.S., worth an estimated $14.1 billion. Because the deal was the first hostile takeover effort in the forest products industry, other leading players, including Champion International Corp. and International

Paper Co., began reviewing their own vulnerability to such an attack.

Review of the Outcome

Georgia-Pacific's debt swelled from $3.8 billion to $6 billion after the takeover of Great Northern Nekoosa was completed, and its debt ratio climbed from 47% to roughly 70%. Part of that deficit was eliminated through the sale of two linerboard mills, at least 30 box plants, and some timberland in the Pacific Northwest, which raised a total of nearly $1 billion. The firm also put its roofing materials business up for sale as a means of generating additional capital to reduce its heavy debt load. Bowater bought 80% of Great Northern Paper Inc. in 1991 and later purchased the remaining 20%.

Critics of the deal argued that the purchase wasn't worth the debt load under which Georgia-Pacific would operate, and the firm's performance in the years following the acquisition validated those concerns. Due to both costly interest payments and falling paper prices, Georgia-Pacific posted a first quarter loss in 1991 of $7 million, its first quarterly loss in nearly a decade. In 1992, the firm lost a whopping $124 million. Operating profits from paper totaled $84 million, compared to $979 million in 1990. Losses were whittled to $34 million in 1993, but it wasn't until 1994 that the firm returned to profitability and began, as stated in a March 1994 article in *Pulp & Paper*, "emerging from the GNN takeover as one of the major world players in both building products and pulp and paper sectors."

Research

Collingwood, Harris. "Great Northern May Have Nowhere to Run," in *Business Week*, 26 February 1990. Details why Great Northern Nekoosa may be forced to accept the takeover bid from Georgia-Pacific.

Ferguson, Kelly. "Georgia-Pacific: Deals, Debt, and Redirection," in *Pulp & Paper*, March 1994. Offers an overview of Georgia-Pacific's performance in the four years after the acquisition.

"Georgia-Pacific Completes Great Northern Nekoosa Merger and $4 Billion Bank Financing," in *PR Newswire*, 26 June 1990. Describes the terms of the transaction.

Georgia-Pacific Corp. Home Page, available at http://www.gp.com. Official World Wide Web Page for Georgia-Pacific Corp. Includes product, corporate, and employment information, as well as current news and annual reports.

"Georgia-Pacific Corp.," in *International Directory of Company Histories*, Vol. 9, St. James Press, 1996. Details the history of Georgia-Pacific Corp. and offers a brief sketch of Great Northern Nekoosa Corp.

"Georgia-Pacific Corp.," in *Notable Corporate Chronologies*, The Gale Group, 1999. Covers major events in the history of Georgia-Pacific Corp.

Hayes, John R. "New Man on the Spot," in *Forbes*, 1 March 1993. Discusses the roles of T. Marshall Hahn and his successor, A.D. Correll, in the acquisition of Great Northern Nekoosa by Georgia-Pacific.

Hicks, Jonathon P. "Georgia Pacific May Laugh Last," in *The New York Times*, 23 May 1991. Describes the performance of Georgia Pacific in the months following the acquisition of Great Northern Neekosa and predicts that the firm will eventually be better off because of the purchase.

THERA WILLIAMS

GILLETTE & BRAUN

The Gillette Co.
Prudential Tower Bldg.
Boston, MA 02199
USA

tel: (617)421-7000
fax: (617)421-7123
web: http://www.gillette.com

nationality: USA
date: December 19, 1967
affected: The Gillette Co., USA, founded 1901
affected: Braun AG, German, founded 1921

Overview of the Merger

Shaving industry giant The Gillette Co. paid $50 million for Germany's Braun AG, a manufacturer of radios, toasters, electric shavers, and other consumer products, in December of 1967. Unhappy with Gillette's growing share of the U.S. shaving market, the U.S. Justice Department filed an antitrust suit, blocking Gillette from integrating the shaving product operations of Braun. A consent decree settled the litigation in 1975; Gillette agreed to spin off Braun's U.S. shaving assets as a separate company, Cambridge Shaver Imports Inc.

History of Gillette Co.

Irritated by dull razor blades, King Camp Gillette originated the disposable razor idea in 1895. Six years later, machinist William Nickerson joined with Gillette to develop the safety razor. The two formed the American Safety Razor Co. to raise the estimated $5,000 needed to begin manufacturing the razor. The firm's name was later changed to Gillette Safety Razor Co.

In 1903, Nickerson constructed a blade sharpening machine, and Gillette began production of the first disposable razor. A year later, Gillette secured a patent for his safety razor. Gillette established its first overseas operations in 1905. By the end of the decade, the firm had adopted a new Gillette diamond trademark and opened a manufacturing plant in Paris, with offices located in Germany, Austria, Scandinavia, and Russia. Gillette sold the majority of his interest in the company in 1910, but he remained president.

In 1914, Nickerson invented a fully automatic sharpening device that replaced the machine Gillette had been using since its founding. To supply the Armed Forces during World War I, the U.S. government ordered 3.5 million razors and 36 million blades in 1917. Branch offices were established in Milan, Brussels, Copenhagen, Geneva, Madrid, and Constantinople by 1920. In November of the following year, the company's patent expired on its safety razor, and the New Improved Gillette razor and Silver Brownie razors were introduced.

In the early 1920s, the company introduced a gold-plated razor, available for

$1, and a woman's version known as the Debutante, for 79 cents. Foreign business accounted for nearly 30% of Gillette's total sales. Marketing efforts heated up in 1926: Gillette signed a contract with the Wm. Wrigley Jr. Co., which granted a complimentary set of razors to each dealer who purchased a box of Wrigley's gum; banks promoted "Shave and Save" by offering a Gillette razor to any new depositor; and businesses begin giving razors away to customers at opening day functions.

In 1928, the owner of a single edge blade firm named the AutoStrop Safety Razor Co. tried to sell Gillette his patented idea for a new method of producing double edge blades. Gillette refused and began producing a new double edge blade of its own. In response, AutoStrop filed a patent infringement suit. Two years later, Gillette and AutoStrop merged.

Falling stock prices prompted the firm to reorganize in the early 1930s. Manufacturing in Brazil began, Gillette resigned the presidency due to failing health, and Gillette's Blue Blade was introduced to the public. In 1933, the company cut prices on some of its products in hopes of raising profits. A year later, the first one-piece razor was launched. International operations accounted for half of earnings.

Brushless shave cream, Gillette's first non-razor or blade-oriented product, was introduced in 1936. Two years later, the Gillette Thin Blade and a $20 electric shaver were offered for the first time. In the early 1940s, the company contributed its time and energy to the war through the manufacture of fuel control units for government planes. The shortage of time being devoted to its civilian consumers caused Gillette to create a new advertisement showing how to preserve razor blades.

During the 1950s, Gillette diversified and took over the Toni Co., a manufacturer of home permanents. In 1955, Gillette changed its name to The Gillette Co. The company bought Paper Mate and began producing office supplies. In 1964, Gillette reorganized into two groups: Gillette Products, which included shaving and men's products, and Diversified Products, which handled all other products. Three years later, the firm bought Braun AG, a manufacturer of electric shavers and appliances. An antitrust suit filed by the U.S. government regarding Gillette's purchase of Braun was resolved in 1975.

Gillette opened a new Paper Mate plant in Santa Monica, California, in 1968. Activities during the 1970s included launching the Trac II twin-blade shaving system and the disposable Cricket lighter; acquiring Buxton, Inc., a producer of quality leather goods; purchasing such brands as Right Guard, Soft & Dri, Adorn, White Rain, and Dry Idea; and introducing the Eraser Mate pen.

The Business

Financials

Revenue (1998): $10 billion

Employees (1998): 43,100

SICs / NAICS

sic 3691 - Storage Batteries

sic 3421 - Cutlery

sic 2844 - Toilet Preparations

naics 335911 - Storage Battery Manufacturing

naics 332211 - Cutlery and Flatware (except Precious) Manufacturing

Oral-B, a maker of dental products, agreed to be purchased by Gillette in 1984. That year, the firm launched its Braun shaver in the U.S. Revlon, Inc. offered to buy Gillette three times in 1987, but the firm turned down each bid. After spending nearly $200 million on its development, Gillette unveiled the Sensor shaving system. In 1990, the U.S. Justice Department blocked Gillette's effort to buy Wilkinson Sword, a smaller competitor. To complete the deal, Gillette agree to purchase only select non-U.S. assets of the firm.

In the early 1990s, Gillette began construction on a factory in Russia. The firm also unveiled the Gillette Series, a line of high-performance male grooming products including shaving preparations, deodorants, and after-shave skin conditioners. In 1994, Gillette reorganized facilities globally and reshuffled 2,000 jobs. About 60 facilities around the world were shut down and multiple-product manufacturing sites were converted to single-product facilities. The firm commanded 40% of the global market for shaving products.

Consumer preference for fresher, lighter scents was the basis for the new range of men's toiletries, called Pacific Light, shipped in 1995. This line also introduced the company's first alcohol-free aftershave and soap-free shower gel. In 1996, Gillette acquired Duracell International Inc. for $7.1 billion in stock. Two years later, Duracell introduced its Duracell Ultra line, and Gillette unveiled its new three-blade razor, a product it spent more than five years developing.

Sales fell as international market economies slumped in 1998; this prompted Gillette to launch a

The Officers

Chairman and CEO: Michael C. Hawley

Chief Financial Officer and Sr. VP, Finance: Charles W. Cramb

Exec. VP, Global Business Management, Gillette Grooming Products, and Duracell: Edward F. DeGraan

Exec. VP, Commercial Operations, Western Hemisphere: Robert G. King

Exec. VP, Commercial Operations, Eastern Hemisphere: Jorgen Wedel

cost cutting plan that included laying off 11% of its employee base, closing 14 plants, shutting down 12 warehouses, and eliminating 30 offices. By 1999, Gillette's new razor was the best selling razor in the U.S.

History of Braun AG

In 1921, Max Braun established an appliances factory in Frankfurt, Germany. Two years later, the operation began making radio parts for the growing radio industry. By the end of the decade, Braun was manufacturing complete radios, and the firm had become one of Germany's leading radio manufacturers.

Braun started making combined radio and phonograph sets in 1932. Four years later, the company unveiled its first battery-operated portable radio. Employees exceeded 1,000 in 1938. During World War II, Braun manufactured radio equipment and other military hardware for the Nazi war effort. After returning to the manufacture of radios for the consumer market in the late 1940s, Max Braun began tinkering with an electric shaver. He had tried some of the earliest models and believed he could improve upon them; as a result, Braun's S50 electric foil shaver was patented in 1949 and mass produced for the first time in 1950.

Max Braun died in 1951, and his two sons assumed control of the company. Within a year, they had expanded the family operation to include electronic photography equipment by developing an electronic flash called Hobby. In a landmark consumer goods deal, Braun agreed in 1954 to license rights to sell its electric shavers in the Western Hemisphere, United Kingdom, and the British Commonwealth countries to Ronson Corp., based in Woodbridge, New Jersey, until 1976. In return, Ronson agreed to leave all other European markets alone. Braun personnel were

granted the equivalent of health care benefits in the mid-1950s. At roughly the same time, the Braun Design, a new line of radio products, was unveiled.

A department devoted solely to product design was established in 1956. That year, the firm launched the first mass-produced automatic 35 millimeter slide projector. In 1959, Braun introduced H1, a compact space heater with an adjoining fan; TP1, a radio combined with a turntable that positioned the needle underneath the records; and Studio 2, a component-based hi-fi set. The "sixtant" electric shaver was created in 1962, and Braun listed publicly for the first time that year. Braun demonstrated T1000, its shortwave receiver, at the Berlin Radio Fair Exhibition in 1963.

In 1966, the firm introduced Permanent, its first lighter. Annual sales had reached roughly $70 million. The following year, concerned that Ronson was making scant effort to market its electric shaver, Braun attempted unsuccessfully to terminate the 1954 licensing agreement with the firm. In December, The Gillette Co. acquired an 85% equity interest in Braun for $50 million and assumed control of the firm.

Market Forces Driving the Merger

In 1957, Gillette held a 40% share of the European shaving market. Wet shaving products accounted for roughly three-fourths of industry sales; dry shaving products made up the remainder. During the early and mid-1960s, electric shavers gained ground on wet shaving merchandise, particulary in Europe and Asia. By 1967, dry shaving goods had close to half of the European shaving market; because Gillette didn't offer an electric razor, its market share there fell from 40% to 30%. To respond to this trend, CEO Vincent Ziegler believed Gillette had two choices if the firm was to remain a leader in the international shaving industry: develop an electric shaver of its own or buy a firm that was already firmly entrenched in the market niche.

The expense of developing a major new product in-house was daunting to Gillette. Although it would have to bid generously to beat out suitors interested in Germany's Braun AG—the third largest European manufacturer of electric razors, with sales in 1966 of $62 million and profits of $2 million—that option would likely be the more cost effective choice. At the time, Braun was soliciting offers from potential partners as a means of securing the capital it needed for continued growth.

Approach and Engagement

Braun was considering offers from the likes of General Electric Co., Philips Electronics NV, and

Siemens AG, when Gillette launched its startling $50 million cash and stock outright purchase offer on October 17, 1967. Roughly 90% of Braun's voting stock was held by brothers Artur and Erwin Braun, while a Swiss investment group controlled the remaining 10%. Believing that Gillette would afford the German firm a fair amount of autonomy, Braun accepted Gillette's offer in December. Combined with nonvoting shares previously acquired, Gillette owned an 85% equity interest in Braun when the purchase of 100% of Braun's common stock and 38% of its preferred stock was completed on December 19. Gillette financed a portion of the deal with $12.5 million in common stock and a cash payment of $27.5 million, which it raised via Gillette International Capital Corp.'s sale of $50 million 15-year, 4.75% debentures. Gillette International also agreed to pay another $10 million in cash.

The deal was subject to regulatory approval, and in February of 1968, the U.S. Department of Justice (DOJ) found that the merger limited potential competition, violating the Clayton Antitrust Act. The DOJ ordered Gillette to halt any further integration of the two firms and sought a court order that would force Gillette to reverse the transaction. Pointing to Gillette's dominant 54% share of the U.S. shaving industry—the second place company, Eversharp Inc. held a much smaller 25% of the market—the DOJ argued that the acquisition of Braun, the third-largest European manufacturer of electric razors, was anticompetitive. To defend itself, Gillette pointed out that Braun's prior agreement with Ronson Corp. prevented it from selling Braun razors in the Western Hemisphere, including the U.S., until 1976.

A consent decree finally brought an end to the suit in 1975. Gillette offered to divest Braun's U.S. shaving operations as a separate company, called Cambridge Shaver Imports Inc., to Becker & Becker Inc. Gillette also agreed to pump a total of $2.5 million into the new firm over the next three years.

Products and Services

In 1998, Gillette blades and razors, including Atra, Custom Plus, Good News, Mach 3, SensorExcel, and Trac II, brought in 30% of sales. Duracell battery sales accounted for nearly 26% of Gillette's total revenues. The unit sold five brands: Duracell, Duracell Ultra, Geep, Mallory, and Rocket. Types of batteries included alkaline, lithium ion rechargeable batteries, nickel metal hydride rechargeable batteries, primary lithium, and zinc air. Duracell operated manufacturing units in the U.S., China, Belgium, and India. Braun appliances, thermometers, and blood pressure monitors secured 17% of sales; toiletries, such as antiperspirants Dry Idea, Right Guard, and Soft & Dri, White

The Players

Chairman and CEO of The Gillette Co.: Vincent C. Ziegler, Jr. While at the head of Gillette Products Group in the early 1960s, Vincent Ziegler spearheaded what would prove to be a highly lucrative effort to market Right Guard spray deodorant products to women as well as men. After writing an unsolicited letter—regarding what he saw as Gillette's need to diversify as a means of maintaining growth—to CEO Carl Gilbert, Ziegler was appointed president in 1965. Within a year, Ziegler had taken over as CEO and chairman. His first major move involved restructuring Gillette along product lines rather than geography. During his nine years at the helm of Gillette, Ziegler's most noteworthy accomplishment was guiding the firm's 1967 takeover of Germany's Braun AG, thus strengthening Gillette's foothold in the growing dry shaving market and positioning the company for global growth. Colman Mockler succeeded Ziegler in 1976.

Chairman of Braun AG: Erwin Braun. In 1951, Erwin Braun and his brother, Artur Braun, took control of the firm their father founded thirty years ago. Eleven years later, they took the company public as a means of generating capital for growth. Erwin Braun acted as the chief negotiator with Gillette in 1967. That year, he also established the International Braun awards for design in engineering. For his "contributions to industrial design," Braun was named an honorary chairman of the Association of German Industry Designers in 1969.

Rain hair care products, Satin Care shaving gel for women, and Gillette Series toiletries for men, 12%; Paper Mate, Parker, Waterman, and Liquid Paper stationery products, 9%; and Oral-B dental hygiene products, 6%.

Gillette operated international manufacturing operations in Belgium, Spain, Germany, the United Kingdom, Brazil, Mexico, South Africa, and France. International sales accounted for 62% of total revenues.

Changes to the Industry and Review of the Outcome

By the mid-1970s, sales from Braun accounted for 20% of total revenues at Gillette. However, the antitrust suit prevented Gillette from integrating Braun's operations into its own, "resulting in costly duplication of some of its manufacturing, marketing, and distribution efforts overseas," according to *The Wall Street Journal* in a June 1975 article.

Gillette executives succeeded in getting Braun's license agreement with Ronson terminated in 1974, two years earlier than the original agreement stipulated. The firm was then able to sell Braun electric shavers in the United Kingdom, the former British Commonwealth countries, and in the Western Hemisphere, excluding the U.S., which was still off limits due to antitrust censures.

Integration efforts began in earnest in the 1980s when Gillette began selling off Braun's peripheral units, including the photography and hi-fi businesses. Focused on electric shavers and small appliances, Braun "emerged as a steady and sometimes spectacular profit maker," wrote Gordon McKibben in *Cutting Edge, Gillette's Journey to Global Leadership.* "By 1996, Braun was a $1.7 billion business, second only to blades and razors as a sales and profit contributor to Gillette as a whole, excluding Duracell. Sales outside Germany accounted for 82 percent of total volume. Prodded by its parent, Braun had moved from parochialism to globalism in a thirty-year stop and start process that accelerated in the mid-1980s. It became Gillette's most conspicuous example of advancing global leadership through acquisition of another company."

Research

"Gillette Buys Control of Braun; Clearance By U.S. Still Pending," in *The Wall Street Journal*, 20 December 1967. Offers an overview of the terms of the transaction between Gillette and Braun.

"Gillette Co. Agrees to Run Braun A.G. Unit As Separate Operation," in *The Wall Street Journal*, 19 February 1968. Discusses the antitrust suit levied by the U.S. Department of Justice regarding Gillette's purchase of Braun.

The Gillette Co. Home Page, available at http://www.gillette.com. Official World Wide Web Page for The Gillette Co. Includes product and corporate information, news, annual reports, and links to home pages of subsidiaries, including Braun.

"The Gillette Co.," in *Notable Corporate Chronologies*, Gale Research, 1999. Offers a history of The Gillette Co.

"Gillette Plan to Create Competitor is Cleared, Settling Antitrust Case," in *The Wall Street Journal*, 31 December 1975. Describes what Gillette agreed to do to settle the eight-year antitrust case.

"Gillette Says U.S. Agrees to Settle Braun Antitrust Suit," in *The Wall Street Journal*, 18 June 1975. Explains how Gillette's inability to integrate Braun has affected the firm's performance.

McKibben, Gordon. *Cutting Edge: Gillette's Journey to Global Leadership*, Harvard Business School Press, 1998. Details the history and growth of Gillette.

ANNAMARIE L. SHELDON

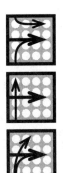

GILLETTE & DURACELL

nationality: USA
date: December 31, 1996
affected: The Gillette Co., USA, founded 1901
affected: Duracell International Inc., USA, founded 1935

The Gillette Co.
Prudential Tower Bldg.
Boston, MA 02199
USA

tel: (617)421-7000
fax: (617)421-7123
web: http://www.gillette.com

Overview of the Merger

When consumer products manufacturer Gillette Co. announced in September of 1996 its intent to purchase battery maker Duracell International Inc. for $7.1 billion in stock, share prices of both firms soared. Within two days of the announcement, Gillette stock prices climbed 8% and Duracell shares jumped a whopping 27%. Wall Street looked favorably upon the deal, which would link Duracell, maker of the world's best selling batteries, with Gillette's major global distribution and marketing networks. By the time the takeover was finalized on December 31, 1996, Gillette shares had grown from $65.13 apiece to $77.75 each, which made the deal even more lucrative for Duracell shareholders.

History of Gillette Co.

Irritated by dull razor blades, King Camp Gillette originated the disposable razor idea in 1895. Six years later, machinist William Nickerson joined with Gillette to develop the safety razor. The two formed the American Safety Razor Co. to raise the estimated $5,000 needed to begin manufacturing the razor. The firm's name was later changed to Gillette Safety Razor Co.

In 1903, Nickerson constructed a blade sharpening machine, and Gillette began production of the first disposable razor. A year later, Gillette secured a patent for his safety razor. Gillette established its first overseas operations in 1905. By the end of the decade, Gillette had adopted a new Gillette diamond trademark and opened a manufacturing plant in Paris with offices located in Germany, Austria, Scandinavia, and Russia. Gillette sold the majority of his interest in the company in 1910, but he remained president.

In 1914, Nickerson invented a fully automatic sharpening machine that replaced the machine Gillette had been using since its founding. To supply the Armed Forces during World War I, the U.S. government ordered 3.5 million razors and 36 million blades in 1917. Branch offices were established in Milan, Brussels, Copenhagen, Geneva, Madrid, and Constantinople by 1920. In November of the following year, the company's patent expired on its safety razor, and the New Improved Gillette razor and Silver Brownie razors were introduced.

The Business

Financials

Revenue (1998): $10 billion

Employees (1998): 43,100

SICs / NAICS

sic 3691 - Storage Batteries

sic 3421 - Cutlery

sic 2844 - Toilet Preparations

naics 335911 - Storage Battery Manufacturing

naics 332211 - Cutlery and Flatware (except Precious)
  Manufacturing

In the early 1920s, the company introduced a gold-plated razor, available for $1, and a woman's version known as the Debutante, for 79 cents. Foreign business accounted for nearly 30% of Gillette's total sales. Marketing efforts heated up in 1926: Gillette signed a contract with the Wm. Wrigley Jr. Co. that granted a complimentary set of razors to each dealer who purchased a box of Wrigley's gums; banks promoted "Shave and Save" by offering a Gillette razor to any new depositor; and businesses begin giving razors away to customers at opening day functions.

In 1928, the owner of a single edge blade firm named the AutoStrop Safety Razor Co. tried to sell Gillette his patented idea for a new method of producing double edge blades. Gillette refused and began producing a new double edge blade of its own. In response, AutoStrop filed a patent infringement suit. Two years later, Gillette and AutoStrop merged.

Falling stock prices prompted the firm to reorganize in the early 1930s. Manufacturing in Brazil began, Gillette resigned the presidency due to failing health, and Gillette's Blue Blade was introduced to the public. In 1933, the company cut prices on some of its products in hopes of raising profits. A year later, the first one-piece razor was launched. International operations accounted for half of earnings.

Brushless shave cream, Gillette's first non-razor or blade-oriented product, was introduced in 1936. Two years later, the Gillette Thin Blade and a $20 electric shaver were offered for the first time. In the early 1940s, the company contributed its time and energy to the war through the manufacture of fuel control units for government planes. The shortage of time being devoted to its civilian consumers prompted Gillette to create new advertisement showing how to preserve razor blades.

During the 1950s, Gillette diversified and took over the Toni Co., a manufacturer of home permanents. In 1955, Gillette changed its name to The Gillette Co. The company bought Paper Mate and began producing office supplies. In 1964, Gillette reorganized into two groups: Gillette Products, which included shaving and men's products, and Diversified Products, which handled all other products. Three years later, the firm bought Braun AG, a manufacturer of electric shavers and appliances. An antitrust suit filed by the U.S. government regarding Gillette's purchase of Braun was resolved in 1975.

Gillette opened a new Paper Mate plant in Santa Monica, California, in 1968. Activities during the 1970s included launching the Trac II twin-blade shaving system and the disposable Cricket lighter; acquiring Buxton, Inc., a producer of quality leather goods; purchasing such brands as Right Guard, Soft & Dri, Adorn, White Rain, and Dry Idea; and introducing the Eraser Mate pen.

Oral-B, a maker of dental products, agreed to be purchased by Gillette in 1984. That year, the firm launched its Braun shaver in the U.S. Revlon, Inc. offered to buy Gillette three times in 1987, but the firm turned down each bid. After spending nearly $200 million on its development, Gillette unveiled the Sensor shaving system. In 1990, the U.S. Justice Department blocked Gillette's effort to buy the United Kingdom's Wilkinson Sword, a smaller competitor.

In the early 1990s, Gillette began construction on a factory in Russia. The firm also unveiled the Gillette Series, a line of high-performance male grooming products including shaving preparations, deodorants, and after-shave skin conditioners. In 1994, Gillette reorganized facilities globally and reshuffled 2,000 jobs. About 60 facilities around the world were shut down and multiple-product manufacturing sites were converted to single-product facilities. The firm commanded 40% of the global market for shaving products.

Consumer preference for fresher, lighter scents was the basis for the new range of men's toiletries, called Pacific Light, shipped in 1995. This line also introduced the company's first alcohol-free aftershave and soap-free shower gel. In 1996, Gillette acquired Duracell International Inc. for $7.1 billion in stock. Two years later, Duracell introduced its Duracell Ultra line, and Gillette unveiled its new three-blade razor, a product it had spent more than five years developing.

Sales fell as international market economies slumped in 1998; this prompted Gillette to launch a cost cutting plan that included laying off 11% of its employee base, closing 14 plants, shutting down 12 warehouses, and eliminating 30 offices. By 1999, Gillette's new razor was the best selling razor in the U.S.

History of Duracell International Inc.

The P.R. Mallory Co. was founded in 1935; the firm coined the Duracell brand name for its batteries. Mallory's business grew steadily for the next several years. In 1966, earnings per share hit a peak of $2.34 before falling sharply with the economic recession. Six years later, sales of electrical and electronic items to businesses provided a boost to the company, complementing consumer sales.

As the recession worsened in the early 1970s, company earnings began to fall sharply. Fortunately, Mallory's debt load was small and, although most of its market was domestic, it was well positioned to take on foreign firms that had lower production costs. *Fortune* magazine ranked Mallory as the 507th-largest company, with $323 million in sales and profits of $10 million, in 1977. Most sales were to individual consumers and to makers of consumer durables, with industry and the military accounting for the rest. The company's ad campaign focused on the use of batteries in toys, and the "copper-top" image it created proved successful in promoting the long life of Duracells.

Competition from Energizer and Panasonic took a toll on Mallory's earnings in the late 1970s. In 1978, Dart Industries bought Mallory for $46 per share, or $215 million, and renamed it Duracell Inc. After gaining control, Dart divested several of Mallory's subsidiaries, but the new owner kept and promoted the Duracell brand.

In 1980, Kraft Inc. and Dart merged. When they split six years later, Kraft kept Duracell. In 1988, Duracell was taken over by Kohlberg Kravis Roberts (KKR), an investment banking firm, for $1.9 billion. The buyout was viewed favorably because no assets were sold and no large layoffs occurred. Alkaline batteries accounted for 80% of Duracell's revenues in 1989. New products included lithium manganese dioxide batteries and the Copper Top Tester, a package that allowed consumers to test the power of batteries. A fierce mass marketing campaign that was part of the buyout agreement paid off. KKR took Duracell public in the spring of that year, and share values rose from $15 to $20 in the first hour of trading.

Duracell held 43% of the U.S. alkaline battery market in the early 1990s. The growth of the cellular telecommunications industry prompted significant

The Officers

Chairman and CEO: Michael C. Hawley

Chief Financial Officer and Sr. VP, Finance: Charles W. Cramb

Exec. VP, Global Business Management, Gillette Grooming Products, and Duracell: Edward F. DeGraan

Exec. VP, Commercial Operations, Western Hemisphere: Robert G. King

Exec. VP, Commercial Operations, Eastern Hemisphere: Jorgen Wedel

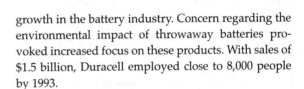

growth in the battery industry. Concern regarding the environmental impact of throwaway batteries provoked increased focus on these products. With sales of $1.5 billion, Duracell employed close to 8,000 people by 1993.

In 1994, India's Poddar Group and Duracell formed a joint venture, called Duracell India Private Ltd., to make and market Duracell's alkaline batteries in India. Duracell also spent $70 million in China to build a factory to manufacture alkaline batteries. International expansion efforts continued throughout the year, and Duracell teamed up with Toshiba Battery Co. of Japan and Varta Batterie AG of Germany to manufacture rechargeable batteries in the United States; this partnership was named 3C Alliance LLP.

Duracell's global growth fueled a run-up in 1995 stock prices. Shares reached a high of $49.37. In 1996, the firm set up distribution networks in Russia in hopes of capitalizing on mushrooming electronics sales there. TDK Corp. signed a deal with Duracell to jointly develop and manufacture ion electrode sets for use in Duracell lithium-ion rechargeable batteries. Duracell also agreed to acquire Sunpower, a South Korean battery brand, and its related sales and distribution operations from STC Corp. for $115 million. That year, the Gillette Co. acquired Duracell for $7.1 billion in stock.

Market Forces Driving the Merger

Between 1990 and 1996, more than 40% of Gillette's sales had come from new products, earnings had increased nearly 17% annually, and return on equity had been approximately 33%. Gillette ranked second in return on sales among U.S. consumer products companies. To continue growing, the firm needed to find a means of expansion that would be likely to produce similar results.

The Players

Chairman and CEO of The Gillette Co: Alfred Zeien. Alfred Zeien was hired by Gillette in 1968. He worked his way up through the ranks, and when CEO Colman Mockler suffered a fatal heart attack in 1991, Zeien stepped in as his replacement. He challenged each unit of the firm to either secure or maintain the leading position in its market. Zeien also led Gillette's diversification into batteries, via its take over of Duracell in 1997. Two years later, Zeien stepped down, making room for his successor, Michael Hawley.

Chairman and CEO of Duracell International Inc.: Charles Perrin. After working for Chesebrough-Ponds for 12 years, including a stint as president of the packaged goods unit, Charles Perrin joined the ranks of Duracell, where he eventually took over as CEO and chairman and led the firm's transformation from a multinational operation to a true global player. When Duracell was taken over by Gillette in 1996, Perrin stepped down. He joined the board of directors of Avon that year and was appointed vice chairman and chief operating officer of Avon in 1997.

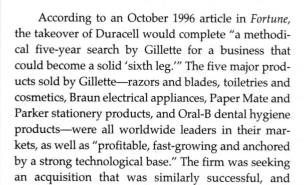

According to an October 1996 article in *Fortune,* the takeover of Duracell would complete "a methodical five-year search by Gillette for a business that could become a solid 'sixth leg.'" The five major products sold by Gillette—razors and blades, toiletries and cosmetics, Braun electrical appliances, Paper Mate and Parker stationery products, and Oral-B dental hygiene products—were all worldwide leaders in their markets, as well as "profitable, fast-growing and anchored by a strong technological base." The firm was seeking an acquisition that was similarly successful, and Duracell fit the bill.

In 1996, Duracell was the largest alkaline battery maker in the world, with nearly 50% of the U.S. market and annual revenues of $2.3 billion. The battery manufacturer, intrigued by Gillette's international prowess, was also interested in a merger. Duracell's international efforts had just begun to reach many major markets outside of the U.S. and Europe, and Gillette's international marketing and distribution resources would give Duracell global reach.

Approach and Engagement

In September of 1996, Gillette agreed to acquire Duracell in a stock-for-stock deal valued at roughly $7.1 billion. Both firms approved a fixed exchange ratio of .904 of a Gillette share for each Duracell share. Within two days of the announcement, Gillette stock prices climbed 8% and Duracell shares jumped a whopping 27%.

Kohlberg, Kravis, Roberts and Company L.P. (KKR), which owned Duracell, and Gillette shareholder Warren E. Buffett butted heads briefly during negotiations. According to a December 1996 article in *Newsweek,* Henry R. Kravis, the head of KKR, demanded a $20 million fee for its negotiation of the deal. Buffett insisted that an $8 million payment was sufficient. After Kravis threatened to back out of the agreement, Buffett relented and agreed to pay KKR the $20 million fee.

Shareholders approved the deal on December 30, 1996, and the transaction was completed on the following day. By then, Gillette shares had grown from $65.13 apiece to $77.75 each, which made the deal even more lucrative for Duracell shareholders. (Because the exchange ratio was fixed, Duracell shareholders received more than the original agreement stipulated.)

Products and Services

In 1998, Duracell battery sales accounted for nearly 26% of Gillette's total revenues. The unit sold five brands: Duracell, Duracell Ultra, Geep, Mallory, and Rocket. Types of batteries included alkaline, lithium ion rechargeable batteries, nickel metal hydride rechargeable batteries, primary lithium, and zinc air. Duracell operated manufacturing units in the U.S., China, Belgium, and India.

Gillette blades and razors, including Atra, Custom Plus, Good News, Mach 3, SensorExcel, and Trac II, brought in 30% of sales; Braun appliances, thermometers, and blood pressure monitors, 17%; toiletries, such as antiperspirants Dry Idea, Right Guard, and Soft & Dri, White Rain hair care products, Satin Care shaving gel for women, and Gillette Series toiletries for men, 12%; Paper Mate, Parker, Waterman, and Liquid Paper stationery products, 9%; and Oral-B dental hygiene products, 6%.

Gillette operated international manufacturing operations in Belgium, Spain, Germany, the United Kingdom, Brazil, Mexico, South Africa, and France. International sales accounted for 62% of total revenues.

Review of the Outcome

By the time the takeover was finalized on December 31, 1996, Gillette shares had grown more than 8% to $77.75 each, which made the stock deal even more rewarding for Duracell shareholders. Gillette renamed its new unit Duracell Global Business Management Group.

Duracell flourished with access to Gillette's deeper international marketing and research and development pockets. Sales in 1997 grew to $2.4 billion and in 1998 to $2.5 billion. In 1998, the firm introduced the Duracell Ultra, a new line of alkaline AA and AAA batteries designed to last up to 50% longer in digital cameras, cell phones, and remote-control devices. Duracell also bought India's Geep, as well as Rocket, the leading battery maker in South Korea.

Research

Duracell Home Page, available at http://www.duracell.com. Official World Wide Web Page for the Duracell unit of Gillette. Includes product information, news, and corporate information.

"Duracell International Inc.," in *Notable Corporate Chronologies*, The Gale Group, 1999. Offers a history of Duracell International Inc.

"The Gillette Co.," in *Notable Corporate Chronologies*, The Gale Group, 1999. Provides a history of The Gillette Co.

The Gillette Co. Home Page, available at http://www.gillette.com. Official World Wide Web Page for The Gillette Co. Includes product and corporate information, news, annual reports, and links to home pages of subsidiaries.

"Gillette-Duracell Merger Approved," in *Business Wire*, 30 December 1996. Discusses the shareholder votes for the merger.

Grant, Linda. "Gillette Knows Shaving—And How to Turn Out Hot New Products," in *Fortune*, 14 October 1996. Explains why Gillette was seeking a major acquisition.

Kerber, Ross. "Buyout Firm Offers Up $1.52 Billion Stake in Gillette," in *Knight-Ridder/Tribune Business News*, 2 April 1999. Describes Kohlberg, Kravis, Roberts and Company's plan to sell over $1 billion worth of Gillette stock.

Maremont, Mark. "How Gillette Wowed Wall Street," in *Business Week*, 30 September 1996. Explains why stock prices surged for both Gillette and Duracell upon news of their plan to merge.

Sloan, Allan. "Battle of the Titans," in *Newsweek*, 9 December 1996. Explains the role of high profile investors Warren Buffet and Henry Kravis in Gillette's takeover of Duracell.

ANNAMARIE L. SHELDON

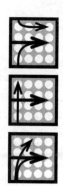

GILLETTE & WILKINSON SWORD

The Gillette Co.
Prudential Tower Bldg.
Boston, MA 02199
USA

tel: (617)421-7000
fax: (617)421-7123
web: http://www.gillette.com

nationality: USA
date: March 1990
affected: The Gillette Co., USA, founded 1901
affected: Wilkinson Sword Company, Ltd., USA, founded 1772

Overview of the Merger

U.S. razor blade industry leader Gillette, which held roughly 50% of the $700 million U.S. market, offered $72 million to Swedish Match AB in December of 1989 for Wilkinson Sword's blade and razor operations. Anticipating antitrust concerns by the European Commission, Gillette excluded all Wilkinson operations in European Community countries from its offer. However, the U.S. Justice Department launched an investigation of the deal, concerned with the fact that Wilkinson, despite holding a mere 3% of the U.S. market, was one of only four suppliers of blades in the U.S. Rather than face expensive and time-consuming litigation, Gillette agreed to axe the U.S. assets of Wilkinson as well and bought the firm's remaining operations in March of 1990 for $65 million. Gillette faced further scrutiny two years later when the European Commission ordered the firm to divest all Wilkinson Sword assets in Western Europe, Eastern Europe, and Turkey. In 1993, Gillette sold those operations to Warner-Lambert for $142 million.

History of Gillette Co.

Irritated by dull razor blades, King Camp Gillette originated the disposable razor idea in 1895. Six years later, machinist William Nickerson joined with Gillette to develop the safety razor. The two formed the American Safety Razor Co. to raise the estimated $5,000 needed to begin manufacturing the razor. The firm's name was later changed to Gillette Safety Razor Co.

In 1903, Nickerson constructed a blade sharpening machine, and Gillette began production of the first disposable razor. A year later, Gillette secured a patent for his safety razor. Gillette established its first overseas operations in 1905. By the end of the decade, Gillette had adopted a new Gillette diamond trademark and had opened a manufacturing plant in Paris, with offices located in Germany, Austria, Scandinavia, and Russia. Gillette sold the majority of his interest in the company in 1910, but he remained president.

In 1914, Nickerson invented a fully automatic sharpening machine that replaced the machine Gillette had been using since its founding. To supply the

Armed Forces during World War I, the U.S. government ordered 3.5 million razors and 36 million blades in 1917. Branch offices were established in Milan, Brussels, Copenhagen, Geneva, Madrid, and Constantinople by 1920. In November of the following year, the company's patent expired on its safety razor, and the New Improved Gillette razor and Silver Brownie razors were introduced.

In the early 1920s, the company introduced a gold-plated razor, available for $1, and a woman's version known as the Debutante, for 79 cents. Foreign business accounted for nearly 30% of Gillette's total sales. Marketing efforts heated up in 1926: Gillette signed a contract with the Wm. Wrigley Jr. Co. which granted a complimentary set of razors to each dealer who purchased a box of Wrigley gum; banks promoted "Shave and Save" by offering a Gillette razor to any new depositor; and businesses begin giving razors away to customers at opening day functions.

In 1928, the owner of a single edge blade firm named the AutoStrop Safety Razor Co. tried to sell Gillette his patented idea for a new method of producing double edge blades. Gillette refused and began producing a new double edge blade of its own. In response, AutoStrop filed a patent infringement suit. Two years later, Gillette and AutoStrop merged.

Falling stock prices prompted the firm to reorganize in the early 1930s. Manufacturing in Brazil began, Gillette resigned the presidency due to failing health, and Gillette's Blue Blade was introduced to the public. In 1933, the company cut prices on some of its products in hopes of raising profits. A year later, the first one-piece razor was launched. International operations accounted for half of earnings.

Brushless shave cream, Gillette's first non-razor or blade-oriented product, was introduced in 1936. Two years later, the Gillette Thin Blade and a $20 electric shaver were offered for the first time. In the early 1940s, the company contributed its time and energy to the war through the manufacture of fuel control units for government planes. The shortage of time being devoted to its civilian consumers spurred Gillette to create new advertisements instructing how to preserve razor blades.

During the 1950s, Gillette diversified and took over the Toni Co., a manufacturer of home permanents. In 1955, Gillette changed its name to The Gillette Co. The company bought Paper Mate and began producing office supplies. In 1964, Gillette reorganized into two groups: Gillette Products, which included shaving and men's products, and Diversified Products, which handled all other products. Three years later, the firm bought Braun AG, a manufacturer of electric shavers and appliances. An antitrust suit

The Business

Financials

Revenue (1998): $10 billion

Employees (1998): 43,100

SICs / NAICS

sic 3691 - Storage Batteries

sic 3421 - Cutlery

sic 2844 - Toilet Preparations

naics 335911 - Storage Battery Manufacturing

naics 332211 - Cutlery and Flatware (except Precious) Manufacturing

filed by the U.S. government regarding Gillette's purchase of Braun was resolved in 1975.

Gillette opened a new Paper Mate plant in Santa Monica, California, in 1968. Activities during the 1970s included the launch of the Trac II twin-blade shaving system and the disposable Cricket lighter; the acquisition of Buxton, Inc., a producer of quality leather goods; the purchase of such brands as Right Guard, Soft & Dri, Adorn, White Rain, and Dry Idea; and the introduction of the Eraser Mate pen.

Oral-B, a maker of dental products, agreed to be purchased by Gillette in 1984. That year, the firm launched its Braun shaver in the U.S. Revlon, Inc. offered to buy Gillette three times in 1987, but the firm turned down each bid. After spending nearly $200 million on its development, the Sensor shaving system was introduced. In 1990, the U.S. Justice Department blocked Gillette's effort to buy Wilkinson Sword, a smaller competitor. To complete the deal, Gillette agree to purchase only select non-U.S. assets of the firm.

In the early 1990s, Gillette began construction on a factory in Russia. The firm also unveiled the Gillette Series, a line of high-performance male grooming products including shaving preparations, deodorants, and after-shave skin conditioners. In 1994, Gillette reorganized facilities globally and reshuffled 2,000 jobs. About 60 facilities around the world were shut down and multiple-product manufacturing sites were converted to single-product facilities. The firm commanded 40% of the global market for shaving products.

The Officers

Chairman and CEO: Michael C. Hawley

Chief Financial Officer and Sr. VP, Finance: Charles W. Cramb

Exec. VP, Global Business Management, Gillette Grooming Products, and Duracell: Edward F. DeGraan

Exec. VP, Commercial Operations, Western Hemisphere: Robert G. King

Exec. VP, Commercial Operations, Eastern Hemisphere: Jorgen Wedel

Consumer preference for fresher, lighter scents was the basis for the new range of men's toiletries, called Pacific Light, shipped in 1995. This line also introduced the company's first alcohol-free aftershave and soap-free shower gel. In 1996, Gillette acquired Duracell International Inc. for $7.1 billion in stock. Two years later, Duracell introduced its Duracell Ultra line, and Gillette unveiled its new three-blade razor, a product it had spent more than five years developing.

Sales fell as international market economies slumped in 1998; this prompted Gillette to launch a cost-cutting plan that included laying off 11% of its employee base, closing 14 plants, shutting down 12 warehouses, and eliminating 30 offices. By 1999, Gillette's new razor was the best selling razor in the U.S.

History of Wilkinson Sword Company, Ltd.

Wilkinson Sword was founded in 1772 by Henry Nock, a well known gun maker who lived in London, England. Five years later, the firm began making bayonets. In 1802, Nock was named master of the Worshipful Company of Gunmakers. Two years later, he was granted the Royal Appointment to King George III. Since then, Wilkinson Sword has held the Royal Warrants as gun or sword maker for the British Sovereign.

Henry Nock died in 1804, and his son-in-law, James Wilkinson, assumed leadership of the business. Noteworthy customers during the 19th century included Queen Victoria, the Prince of Wales, the King of Siam, the King of Naples, the King of Prussia, and Prince N.L. Bonaparte. After Wilkinson retired in 1825, his son, Henry, moved Wilkinson's offices and showroom from London to Pall Mall and diversified operations to include sword making. In 1843, Henry Wilkinson invented a sword blade testing machine

able to test a sword's ability to bend and bear shock loads. Because of its implementation of quality control measures, Wilkinson swords became known worldwide for their strength, balance, and reliability.

By the late 1880s, sword making had become a main focus of operations for the firm. In 1889, the firm became a private limited company and took the name of Wilkinson Sword Company Ltd. Ten years later, Wilkinson diversified into the shaving products market by introducing its first safety razor. By then, the company had also moved into bicycles and typewriters, ventures that took a back seat to shaving products after the turn of the century.

In 1962, Wilkinson launched stainless steel blades, which were an immediate success in the U.S., prompting other shaving industry leaders like Gillette and Schick to launch their own stainless steel line. In 1989, Gillette offered to buy the non-European Community assets of Wilkinson Sword, but the U.S. Justice Department blocked the deal, citing antitrust concerns. Gillette then acquired the non-European Community and non-U.S. operations of the firm for $65 million. In March of 1993, in response to a European Commission ruling, Gillette divested its Wilkinson operations in North America, Turkey, Eastern Europe, and Western Europe to Warner-Lambert Co. for $142 million.

Market Forces Driving the Merger

After staving off three hostile takeover attempts in the 1980s, Gillette was ready to grow by the turn of the decade. Chairman and CEO Mockler had died suddenly, and his successor, Alfred Zeien fashioned a new mission statement: "Our mission is to achieve or enhance clear leadership, worldwide, in the existing or new core consumer product categories in which we choose to compete." As explained by Zeien in *Cutting Edge: Gillette's Journey to Global Leadership*, the firm "would not become involved in any way whatsoever in a core business in which we are neither a worldwide leader or have a plan in place to become a worldwide leader."

Although Zeien didn't take over until after the Wilkinson deal was completed, he had already become a powerful force in the company. His management vision—though not formally adopted until 1991—impacted the firm in the late 1980s, when the deal with Wilkinson was conceived. Gillette was looking for ways to grow its core business: razor blades. The market was considered saturated, and acquisitions were one way to increase mass. Wilkinson, which held 3% of the U.S. market, would give Gillette another brand to market and boost its customer base, as well as increase the firm's presence in several international markets. At the same time, access to Gillette's deeper pockets would allow Wilkinson more marketing leverage in the U.S.

Approach and Engagement

Gillette approached Wilkinson Sword's parent, Swedish Match AB, in December of 1989, offering $72 million for full control of Wilkinson's razor blade business except its operations in European Community (EC) countries. The firm was hoping to secure Wilkinson operations in the U.S., Brazil, New Zealand, Australia, and Austria, as well as in those European countries that weren't members of the EC.

On January 9, 1990, the U.S. Justice Department filed an antitrust suit to block the deal, finding that, as two of only four U.S. blade suppliers, a union between Gillette and Wilkinson Sword would break U.S. monopoly laws. Two months later, Gillette agreed to pay $65 million for the non-U.S. and non-EC assets of Wilkinson. The deal was structured in such a way that Gillette secured a 22.9% stake in Swedish Match (later renamed Eemland).

Products and Services

In 1998, Gillette blades and razors, including Atra, Custom Plus, Good News, Mach 3, SensorExcel, and Trac II, brought in 30% of sales. Duracell battery sales accounted for nearly 26% of Gillette's total revenues. The unit sold five brands: Duracell, Duracell Ultra, Geep, Mallory, and Rocket. Types of batteries included alkaline, lithium ion rechargeable batteries, nickel metal hydride rechargeable batteries, primary lithium, and zinc air. Duracell operated manufacturing units in the U.S., China, Belgium, and India. Braun appliances, thermometers, and blood pressure monitors secured 17% of sales; toiletries, such as antiperspirants Dry Idea, Right Guard, and Soft & Dri, White Rain hair care products, Satin Care shaving gel for women, and Gillette Series toiletries for men, 12%; Paper Mate, Parker, Waterman, and Liquid Paper stationery products, 9%; and Oral-B dental hygiene products, 6%.

Gillette operated international manufacturing operations in Belgium, Spain, Germany, the United Kingdom, Brazil, Mexico, South Africa, and France. International sales accounted for 62% of total revenues.

Changes to the Industry and Review of the Outcome

Less than a year after the purchase of Wilkinson was completed, the European Commission found that the deal violated free competition rules. British regu-

The Players

Chairman and CEO of The Gillette Co: Colman Mockler, Jr. A graduate of the Harvard Business School, Colman Mockler began his corporate career with a brief stint at General Electric. He left that position to accept a post at Harvard as a business researcher. In 1957, Mockler went to work for Gillette as an assistant to the controller. For the next 17 years, he served in various financial administration capacities and was credited with successfully overhauling the firm's international accounting system. Mockler was named president and chief operating officer in 1974 at the age of 44; two years later, he took the helm of Gillette as chairman and CEO. Mockler propelled the firm's sales past $2 billion for the first time in 1980, but stiff competition from other blade makers, as well as economic downturns in many international markets, caused the firm to falter. In response, Mockler began divesting poorly performing and slow growth units; by the end of 1981, more than 12 businesses or product lines—accounting for 7% of total annual revenues—had been sold. He was credited for keeping three hostile takeover bidders at bay during the 1980s and for overseeing the 1990 launch of the Sensor razor, which boosted U.S. razor and blade sales by 54% and worldwide sales by a whopping 71% within three years. Gillette's ill-fated purchase of Wilkinson Sword operations in early 1990 was viewed by many Wall Street analysts as one of Mockler's few missteps. Only two months after announcing his planned retirement, Mockler died of a heart attack on January 25, 1991.

lators asked Gillette to sell its 22.9% stake in Swedish Match in March of 1991. When Gillette failed to respond to the request, the European Commission ordered the firm to sell its share of the firm. The ruling also forced Gillette to divest its Wilkinson Sword assets in Eastern Europe, Western Europe (even those not part of the European Community), and Turkey. As a result, Warner-Lambert bought the Wilkinson operations from Gillette for $142 million in 1993. Gillette retained control of Wilkinson operations in Latin America, Asia, and Australia.

Research

Collingwood, H. "A Nick in Gillette's Buyout Plans," in *Business Week*, 22 January 1990. Explains the suit filed by the U.S. Justice Department to block the acquisition of Wilkinson Sword by Gillette.

———. "Justice Blunts a Gillette Deal," in *Business Week*, 2 April 1990. Discusses Gillette's decision to drop its bid for the U.S. operations of Wilkinson Sword.

"The Gillette Co.," in *Notable Corporate Chronologies*, The Gale Group, 1999. Offers a history of The Gillette Co.

The Gillette Co. Home Page, available at http://www.gillette.com. Official World Wide Web Page for The Gillette Co. Includes product and corporate information, news, annual reports, and links to home pages of subsidiaries.

McKibben, Gordon. *Cutting Edge: Gillette's Journey to Global Leadership*, Harvard Business School Press: 1998. Details the history and growth of Gillette.

"Wilkinson Sword: A New Lease on Life?" in *European Cosmetics Market*, May 1993. Discusses the purchase of Wilkinson Sword by Warner-Lambert Co.

JEFF ST. THOMAS

GLAXO HOLDINGS & WELLCOME

nationality: United Kingdom
date: October 1995
affected: Glaxo Holdings PLC, U.K., founded 1873
affected: Wellcome PLC, U.K., founded 1880

Glaxo Wellcome PLC
Berkeley Ave.
Greenford,, Middlesex UB6 ONN
United Kingdom

tel: 44-171-493-4060
fax: 44-171-408-0228
web: http://www.glaxowellcome.co.uk

Overview of the Merger

When Glaxo Holdings, the second largest drug maker in the world and Wellcome PLC, a leader in antiviral research, joined forces in October of 1995, they completed the biggest corporate takeover in British history, valued at $15 billion, as well as the largest merger in the pharmaceuticals industry to date. The newly formed Glaxo Wellcome PLC usurped Merck & Co. as the world's largest prescription drug company, with a 5.3% share of the global pharmaceuticals market and $12.2 billion in annual worldwide sales. Because both Glaxo and Wellcome faced patent expiry on their blockbuster drugs—Zantac and Zovirax—pushing new drugs through the pipeline became Glaxo Wellcome's major focus.

History of Glaxo Holdings PLC

In 1873, Joseph Nathan formed Joseph Nathan & Co., an importer and exporter of products that included patent medicines. Roughly 35 years later, Nathan & Co. acquired the rights to an American milk drying process. Because the best application of the dry milk was as a baby food ingredient, the company established the Glaxo Baby Food unit. Alec Nathan, the youngest son, moved to London, where he oversaw baby food operations.

The advent of World War I, along with increasing demand for its products, prompted Glaxo to begin construction of Glaxo House, a new headquarters, and to refurbish its manufacturing facilities. In 1923, Glaxo began distribution operations in India and South America. A few years later, the firm purchased the rights to the vitamin D extraction process and began selling vitamin D enriched products that sold with great success. This led to the introduction of the firm's first pharmaceutical product, Ostelin Liquid, which was also the U.K.'s first commercial vitamin concentrate.

In 1935, Glaxo Baby Foods established Glaxo Laboratories Ltd. as its pharmaceutical subsidiary. The firm introduced Adexolin, a vitamin A and D product, and Ostermilk, a vitamin fortified milk drink. After World War II began, Glaxo focused production on penicillin, anesthetics, and vitamin supplements. At roughly the

The Business

Financials

Revenue (1998): $13.24 billion

Employees (1998): 53,068

SICs / NAICS

sic 2834 - Pharmaceutical Preparations

sic 2833 - Medicinals & Botanicals

sic 2836 - Biological Products Except Diagnostic

sic 2879 - Agricultural Chemicals Nec

sic 3841 - Surgical & Medical Instruments

sic 2048 - Prepared Feeds Nec

sic 2891 - Adhesives & Sealants

sic 2824 - Organic Fibers-Noncellulosic

naics 325412 - Pharmaceutical Preparation Manufacturing

naics 325411 - Medicinal and Botanical Manufacturing

naics 325414 - Biological Product (except Diagnostic) Manufacturing

naics 339112 - Surgical and Medical Instrument Manufacturing

naics 311119 - Other Animal Food Manufacturing

naics 325222 - Noncellulosic Organic Fiber Manufacturing

same time, the company adopted the American deep fermentation process of mass-producing penicillin. Glaxo Baby Foods absorbed its parent, John Nathan & Co., to become an independent public company in 1948. Non-core businesses, such as butter importing and fencing exporting, were sold.

Murphy Chemical and Allen and Hanbury's, two veterinary products makers, were acquired in the late 1950s. Among Glaxo's postwar accomplishments were the isolation of vitamin B12, useful in the treatment of pernicious anemia; synthesis of the hormone needed to treat hypothyroidism; development of the U.K.'s first commercial cortisone product; and the discovery of sisal, the source of a steroid used to commercially synthesize a series of corticosteroids. In 1961, Glaxo acquired Edinburgh Pharmaceuticals Industries.

In conjunction with Schering USA, another pharmaceutical research company, Glaxo developed a vital production process that led to the introduction of a new corticosteroid, Betnovate, in 1963. Five years later, Glaxo acquired Europe's biggest drug wholesaler, Vestric, and Farley's Infant Foods. Ventolin,

which soon became the world's leading asthma drug, was introduced in 1969.

In 1972, Glaxo arranged a merger with its competitor, Boots of the U.K., to stave off the takeover attempts of Beecham. Neither the merger nor the takeover could be finalized, however, because the Monopolies Commissioners decided they would impede research and development through lack of competition. That year, Glaxo renamed itself Glaxo Holdings PLC. By the end of the decade, Glaxo had purchased U.S.-based Meyer Laboratories, sold Murphy Chemical, founded a U.S. subsidiary, and introduced Zinacef, an antibiotic produced from imperfect fungi.

In 1980, arguably the most pivotal year in Glaxo's history, the firm introduced Zantac in several European markets to compete with SmithKline's Tagamet, the world's best selling drug at the time. Roche and Glaxo established a joint venture in 1983, in which Roche's underutilized marketing force helped introduce Zantac in the U.S. Glaxo also launched Ceftazidime, an injectable antibiotic. By mid-decade, Zantac held 25% of the prescription market. Based on the drug's success, Glaxo began constructing a $40 million factory in North Carolina. Stock split two-for-one.

Glaxo acquired the research operations of Biogen in 1987. The following year, Glaxo built new plants in the U.K., Italy, and Japan, as well as spending $350 million for a research and development facility in the U.S. Non-core businesses, such as food and animal health lines, were divested. By 1988, Zantac had secured 53% of the antacid market, compared to Tagamet's 29%. The success of the drug propelled Glaxo to the number-two spot among worldwide pharmaceutical companies. Glaxo introduced Zofran, a drug designed to help suppress nausea normally induced by chemotherapy, in 1990. Within a year, Zofran accounted for $484 million of the company's $5.5 billion in annual sales.

Under pressure for charging high prices in the early 1990s, Glaxo cut prices by 15% for U.S. government-funded clinics. In 1995, Zantac received over-the-counter sales approval in the U.K. The company offered a surprise purchase bid to Wellcome PLC for $14.15 billion in cash and securities. Wellcome shareholders reluctantly accepted Glaxo's hostile takeover bid and Glaxo Wellcome PLC, the world's largest prescription drug company, was created.

Following the merger, the FDA approved the marketing of Epivir, Glaxo Wellcome's experimental AIDS drug that increased the effectiveness of AZT. After a dispute with Clinton officials over the legitimacy of an extended patent on Zantac, Glaxo

Wellcome won Senate approval to keep its exclusive rights to market the peptic ulcer treatment in the U.S. Glaxo also agreed to sell its stakes in specific joint ventures to Warner-Lambert for $1.5 billion. The sale of its consumer joint venture—which included non-prescription drugs Sudafed, and Actifed, as well as Neosporin—allowed the company to refocus on its prescription medication operations.

In 1997, Glaxo Wellcome divested its Scotland-based pharmaceuticals manufacturing facility to ChiRex for $66 million. The firm also purchased Spectra Biomedical and formed a genetics unit to house its new operation. Glaxo Wellcome's antidepressant Zyban secured FDA approval as an anti-smoking treatment. SmithKline Beecham ended merger talks with American Home Products Corp. in January of 1998, opting instead to pursue a deal with Glaxo Wellcome; that agreement fell apart after the firms couldn't agree on who would run the new industry giant.

History of Wellcome PLC

Silas Burroughs and Henry Wellcome, two American pharmacists, founded London-based Burroughs Wellcome Co. in 1880. By 1882, the firm had started making its own pharmaceutical products. Henry Wellcome died in 1936. He left his shares in the firm to a charitable trust for medical research, and as a result, the Wellcome Trust, which later became the largest charity in Britain and the world's leading private medical research fund, was set up as a sort of parent company to Wellcome. Wellcome's death sent the firm into a tailspin that lasted over a decade. It wasn't until research and development funding was significantly increased during the 1950s, that Burroughs Wellcome (by then named Wellcome PLC) experienced its first truly successful decade.

In 1981, Wellcome introduced Zovirax, an antiviral medicine used to treat herpes, chicken pox, and cold sores; it soon became the firm's best selling drug. Six years later Retrovir, an antiviral product used mainly to treated HIV, received FDA approval. By the end of the decade Wellcome was the world's leading maker and seller of antiviral drugs, which accounted for nearly half of the firm's total revenues. Another antiviral, Wellferon, was soon developed as a treatment for chronic hepatitis B infections. By 1993, Wellcome's Zorivax was the forth best selling drug in the world.

The Wellcome Trust had divested 21% of its stake in Wellcome PLC in 1986 in an effort to diversify its holdings. In 1992, the Trust sold another 40.5% of the pharmaceutical manufacturer it owned for over two billion pounds. Three years later, Wellcome Trust sold

The Officers

Chairman and CEO: Sir Richard Sykes

Deputy Chairman: Roger Hurn

Exec. Director, Research and Development: James E. Niedel

Exec. Director, Finance and Investor Relations: John D. Coombe

Exec. Director, Legal and Corporate Affairs: Jeremy Strachan

Exec. Director, Europe, Africa, and Middle East: James M.T. Cochrane

off the final 39.5% of Wellcome PLC to Glaxo Holdings PLC.

Market Forces Driving the Merger

Pharmaceutical firms launched a consolidation flurry in 1994 for two main reasons. First, firms needed to reduce drug development and delivery expenses. Fierce competition, evidenced by the marginal market shares held by even the largest players in the prescription drug industry, forced firms to channel massive amounts of cash—up to 30% of total revenues—into sales and marketing efforts. Consolidation allowed these firms to streamline operations and save money.

More diverse product lines had also become crucial for firms looking to maintain or gain a competitive edge. Health care providers, particularly managed care companies, had become increasingly concerned with cutting costs and increasing efficiency. Large firms with a broad range of products appealed to these businesses because they could offer volume discounts and one-stop shopping. At the same time, selling larger orders to single customers reduced delivery costs for the drug companies.

By merging with Wellcome, Glaxo, who relied heavily on its gastrointestinal and respiratory drugs, would increase its product line to include Wellcome's virology and genetics products. According to Robert Ingram, CEO and president of Glaxo Inc., the U.S. arm of Glaxo Holdings, the merged company would be able to offer customers "a product line covering a broad range of therapeutic categories and meet the new trends in customer needs better. It will also benefit from a portfolio that includes product lines in four therapeutic areas that each have annual sales exceed-

The Players

Chairman and CEO of Glaxo Holdings PLC: Sir Richard Sykes. At the age of 17, Richard Sykes began his career in microbiology by accepting a position with a pathology laboratory. He eventually earned a Ph.D. in microbiology from Bristol University. In 1972, Sykes left academia and joined the corporate world when he was hired by Glaxo to head up the firm's antibiotic research unit. Five years later, he went to work for U.S.-based competitor Squibb as assistant director of the company's microbiology research department. In 1979, Squibb appointed Sykes directory of microbiology and associate director of its Institute for Medical Research. By the time Sykes left Squibb, he had earned himself a top spot as vice president of infectious and metabolic diseases.

After his nine-year stint in the U.S., Sykes returned home as deputy head of Glaxo Group Research. He was appointed chairman and CEO of the unit in 1987. After Glaxo's board asked for the resignation of chairman and CEO Paul Girolami, who was deemed too conservative, Sykes was given the top spot at Glaxo in 1993. He was charged with the task of growing the firm via acquisition. After less than a year and a half at the helm of Glaxo, Sykes, who had been knighted in 1994 for his contributions to the British pharmaceutical industry, launched a takeover of Wellcome PLC. When the two firms completed their deal, Sykes became deputy chairman and CEO of Glaxo Wellcome PLC.

ing $1 billion: gastrointestinal, respiratory, antiviral, and antibiotic."

A broader product line would also lessen Glaxo's dependence on Zantac, which accounted for nearly 40% of total revenues and was set to lose its patent protection in mid-1997. During the second half of 1994, Zantac sales had dipped for the first time since the advent of the drug, mainly due to competition from SmithKline Beecham's Tagamet.

Approach and Engagement

On January 23, 1995, Glaxo PLC launched a $15 billion hostile bid for Wellcome PLC. The price was almost double the market price of Wellcome shares. Three days later, Wellcome rejected the offer as too low. However, Sykes secretly negotiated with Wellcome Trust, which owned roughly 40% of Wellcome PLC. He secured the backing of the firm's largest shareholder, and the deal was finalized in October of 1995. Sykes took the helm of the newly merged firm; with a year, all but one of Wellcome's directors had resigned, many of whom felt betrayed by the board of Wellcome Trust.

Products and Services

The merger broadened Glaxo Wellcome's product line, reducing its dependence on a single drug or type of drugs. In 1997, respiratory products accounted for 23% of total revenues; antiviral drugs, 18%; gastrointestinal medicines, 17%; central nervous system treatments, 12%; bacterial infection products, 11%; oncology drugs, 6%; dermatology products, 3%; cardiovascular medicines, 3% and anesthetics, 1%. North American sales brought in 45% of total revenues.

Changes to the Industry

The merger dethroned Merck & Co. from its spot as the world's largest prescription drug company, but Glaxo Wellcome's status as the number one pharmaceuticals firm in the world was short-lived. Other mergers soon followed: Pharmacia AB and The Upjohn Co. merged in November of 1995; and Ciba Geigy Ltd. and Sandoz Ltd. completed a $36 billion deal to form Novartis in 1996. In fact, Glaxo Wellcome and SmithKline Beecham came close to a marriage in 1998, but negotiations crumbled after the two firms disagreed about who would head up the new industry leader.

Consolidation again appeared imminent in the late 1990s as several of the industry giants, including Glaxo Wellcome, American Home Products, and SmithKline Beecham contemplated mergers as a means of increasing market share, reducing costs, and enhancing research and development budgets. New research dollars were becoming essential for firms looking to stay competitive in a marketplace where demand, at times, seemed unchecked. In fact, according to Dr. Wang Chong of consulting firm Arthur D. Little, mergers would be necessary for the firms who wanted to remain in the top ten industry tier because to do so would require pharmaceutical companies to introduce at least three new drugs annually. In early 1999, only three pharmaceutical businesses were capable of doing this: Johnson & Johnson, Merck & Co., and Pfizer Inc.

Review of the Outcome

Glaxo's bid took not only Wellcome by surprise—most industry analysts were shocked as well. Glaxo's shares fell 7% upon the merger's announcement, and critics pointed out that the deal didn't seem to make sense because Wellcome's blockbuster drug, Zovirak, was facing patent expiry in mid-1997, roughly the same time that Glaxo's Zantac would lose patent protection.

Glaxo Wellcome CEO Sykes argued that the new firm would be able to cut costs by up to $1 billion per year and push more new drugs through the pipeline quickly as a means of bracing itself for competition to Zantac and Zovirak. Once the deal was completed, cost cutting began. All Glaxo and Wellcome scientists were forced to reapply for their jobs. Within three years, Wellcome's operations in Greenville, North Carolina, were closed, as was its research and development center in Beckenham, England, and its headquarters in London. A total of 7,500 employees were laid off. Also, Wellcome's 311C90 migraine drug was divested to Zeneca Group PLC, and Glaxo Wellcome sold the U.S. rights to its antihistamine, Semprex-D, to Medeva PLC for $16.5 million. By 1999, the firm had broadened its focus from Zantac and Zovirak to include asthma drugs Ventolin and Serevent, as well as Hepatitis B treatment Zeffix and HIV and AIDS treatments Epivir and Combivir.

Research

Borzo, Greg. "Glaxo Bids $15 Billion to Buy Wellcome, maker of AZT," in *American Medical News*, 13 February 1995. Discusses the reasons for the hostile takeover launched by Glaxo Holdings PLC for Wellcome PLC.

Evans, Richard. "A Giant Battles Its Drug Dependency," in *Fortune*, 5 August 1996. Explains the immediate outcome of the merger between Glaxo Holdings and Wellcome, as well as the obstacles yet to be faced by the new firm.

"Glaxo Completes Wellcome Acquisition," in *Chain Drug Review*, 10 April 1995. Offers an overview of the merger between Glaxo Holdings and Wellcome.

Glaxo Wellcome PLC Home Page, available at http://www.glaxwellcome.co.uk. Official World Wide Web Home Page for Glaxo Wellcome PLC. Includes news, financial, product, and historical information.

"Glaxo Wellcome PLC," in *Notable Corporate Chronologies*, The Gale Group, 1999. Lists major events in the history of Glaxo Wellcome PLC, including its 1995 merger.

Green, Daniel. "The Painful Path From Hostility to Synergy," in *The Financial Times*, 9 April 1996. Discusses the outcome of the merger, including divestitures, layoffs, and closings.

"Sir Richard Sykes," in *Management Today*, December 1995. Offers a detailed sketch of the career of Sir Richard Sykes.

THERA WILLIAMS

SIR JAMES GOLDSMITH & CROWN ZELLERBACH

Fort James Corp.
1650 Lake Cook Rd., PO Box 89
Deerfield, IL 60015-0089
USA

tel: (847)317-5000
fax: (847)236-3755
web: http://www.fortjames.com

nationality: USA
date: July 22, 1985
affected: Crown Zellerbach Corp., USA, founded 1871

Overview of the Acquisition

When Sir James Goldsmith gained control of Crown Zellerbach in July of 1985, despite the firm's use of the "second generation" poison pill, a third generation poison pill emerged to tighten the loophole through which Goldsmith had slipped to gain control of Crown Zellerbach. Within a year of the hostile takeover, Crown Zellerbach was purchased by James River Corp., which eventually merged with Fort Howard Corp. to form Fort James Corp.

History of Crown Zellerbach Corp.

Founded in 1871, Crown Zellerbach had grown into one of the leading forest products companies in the U.S. by the mid-1980s. The concern, based in San Francisco, owned 3.4 million acres of timberland stretching from Los Angeles to the Pacific Northwest. Beneath 640,000 acres of its forestland, it held oil and gas rights. Additionally, the firm operated in the businesses of pulp and paper, plywood, and packaging.

In 1970 C. Raymond Dahl was appointed chairman and CEO. Under his reign, Crown Zellerbach's earnings and morale slumped. Although the company's sales of $790 million ranked Crown Zellerbach the nation's fifth-largest forest products company, its earnings didn't correspond. For the quarter ending September 30, 1981, pretax income registered only $2.2 million, a result that placed the company at the bottom of the industry in terms of performance.

As a result of this poor performance, as well as the resignation of executive vice president Charles LaFollette, the board of directors ousted Dahl. William Creson, president since 1977, was named his successor on October 8, 1981. He immediately announced plans to streamline senior management, consolidate operations, and divest certain assets. The pressure to restore the company to profitability wasn't simply internal, however. Its low stock price made Crown Zellerbach vulnerable to a takeover. In 1986 James River paid $1.6 billion for a majority stake in Crown Zellerbach to become the second-largest U.S. tissue maker.

Market Forces Driving the Acquisition

In the late 1970s, a sluggish U.S. forest products industry caused a slowdown in both new home construction and paper manufacturing. Interest rates began to climb, and firms in need of capital found themselves ensnared in a cycle of growing debt as they paid the increased interest rates.

Crown Zellerbach was hit exceptionally hard in the early 1980s. Because its major timber assets were significantly undervalued due to the economic downturn, potential buyers were simply unwilling to offer the firm a fair prices for those reserves. At the same time, the highly diverse operations of Crown Zellerbach had not been fully integrated. Consequently, CEO William Creson had begun to sell off the company's plywood operations while growing core pulp and paper operations, a process that added to his firm's debt. Although sales in 1983 reached $2.7 billion, profits totaled a mere $87.8 million, and the company's stock price held steady at about $39, compared to a high of $62.75 in 1980.

Approach and Engagement

Aware of its vulnerability to a takeover, Crown Zellerbach's board of directors approved the adoption of the "poison pill" defense on July 18, 1984. This anti-takeover defense had been invented two years earlier, and Crown Zellerbach became the first company to make use of it. The pill's purpose was to activate a stock repurchase in the event of a hostile takeover attempt by allowing shareholders to buy company stock at a discounted price, thereby diluting the investment of the unfriendly suitor. Under the terms of Crown Zellerbach's pill, once an investor acquired 20% or announced its intention to buy 30% of the company's stock, its shareholders would be allowed to purchase $200 worth of stock at the half-off price of $100. These rights would become exercisable once the company was 100% acquired or merged.

Undaunted, Sir James Goldsmith announced on December 12, 1984, that he intended to acquire 25% of Crown Zellerbach's outstanding shares. This financier had recently made offers for other major companies, including Continental Group and St. Regis Paper Company. In 1982 he gained control of Diamond International Corp., another forest products company with large timberland reserves. Reportedly, he was interested in the same assets of Crown Zellerbach and, as he did with Diamond, would break up and sell its non-timberland operations.

By March 12, 1985, Sir James had acquired an 8.6% interest in Crown Zellerbach. On April 1 he issued a "bear hug," a proposal to purchase addition-

The Business

Financials

Revenue (1998): $7.3 billion

Employees (1998): 30,000

SICs / NAICS

sic 2297 - Nonwoven Fabrics

sic 2621 - Paper Mills

sic 2679 - Converted Paper Products Nec

sic 2656 - Sanitary Food Containers

sic 2676 - Sanitary Paper Products

sic 2411 - Logging

sic 2611 - Pulp Mills

sic 2657 - Folding Paperboard Boxes

naics 313230 - Nonwoven Fabric Mills

naics 322121 - Paper (except Newsprint) Mills

naics 322231 - Die-Cut Paper and Paperboard Office Supplies Manufacturing

naics 322215 - Non-Folding Sanitary Food Container Manufacturing

naics 322291 - Sanitary Paper Product Manufacturing

naics 113310 - Logging

naics 322212 - Folding Paperboard Box Manufacturing

al stock at a premium price, thereby putting pressure on the target company's board to accept it out of concern for the best interest of the shareholders. This $1.14 billion offer, at $41.62 per share, was contingent on Crown Zellerbach's withdrawal of its poison pill. Sir James warned that if the company refused to retract the defense he would launch a proxy battle for several seats on its board in order to gain control of the company from within. Chairman William Creson responded that the board "will not be hurried, bullied or intimidated by Sir James Goldsmith," according to *The New York Times*.

On April 10 Sir James extended his formal offer for 70% of the company at a price of $42.50 per share, or $807 million, again hinged upon removal of the pill. This initiated a flurry of lawsuits. On April 15 Crown Zellerbach filed for an injunction against him, while Sir James sued for the company's refusal to give him the list of its shareholders in order to prevent him from waging a proxy battle.

The Officers

Crown Zellerbach Corp.

Chairman and CEO: Miles L. Marsh

Exec. VP and Chief Financial Officer: Ernst A. Haberli

Exec. VP, Operations and Logistics: John F. Rowley

Mead Corp. rode onto the scene as a white knight, or a preferred acquirer, on April 24. This publishing and forest products company offered $50 per share, or $1.36 billion. Crown Zellerbach's rescue was short-lived, however, as the companies discontinued their merger talks the following day, presumably due to Mead's reluctance to increase its already considerable debt load. In light of this collapse, Crown Zellerbach announced on April 25 a major restructuring in which it would break apart into three companies by liquidating its timber assets and spinning off its specialty packaging business. This strategy effectively deterred Sir James, but only temporarily. On April 26 Crown Zellerbach Acquisition Corp., the company Sir James had formed for the purpose of acquiring Crown Zellerbach, withdrew its offer.

Sir James reinitiated his takeover on May 8, when he increased his stake to 19.6% by purchasing a block of shares held by an investor. The next day he gained one seat on the company's board through a shareholder vote at Crown Zellerbach's annual meeting. Two-thirds of the shareholders also approved the company's reorganization plans.

Sir James gave the company until May 13 to revoke its poison pill. On that day he nudged his interest to 19.9%, just shy of the 20% of threshold. He warned Crown Zellerbach that if he triggered the pill the company's hope of enlisting a white knight would be virtually nil, as the costs of merging with Crown Zellerbach would be prohibitive.

On May 14 Sir James became the first hostile bidder to swallow a poison pill, as he increased his stake to over 20%. As it turned out, though, this defensive measure worked for, not against, him in two ways. First, as he had warned, it insulated his interests from acquisition by another company, since Crown Zellerbach was now virtually unmarketable. Second, the pill had no effect on the value of his stake because he intended only to gain control of the company, not to affect a merger. According to the terms of the pill, only when Crown Zellerbach was completely acquired by an outsider could its shareholders purchase stock at a discount.

Crown Zellerbach and Sir James called a truce on May 26, agreeing to cooperate on the company's restructuring plan and to suspend all pending litigation against each other. This truce lasted only six weeks, however, as the two sides failed to reach agreement on the restructuring. By July 10 Sir James held a 26% stake, which he boosted to over 50% by July 22, thereby gaining control of Crown Zellerbach. Three days later he became the company's chairman, while William Creson retained the positions of president and CEO.

Products and Services

Crown Zellerbach was acquired by James River Corp. in 1995. Three years later, James River and Fort Howard Corp. merged to form Fort James Corp., which in 1998 was organized into five operating segments:

Tissue—North American contained such brands as Brawny, So-Dri, and Mardi Gras paper towels; Quilted Northern and Soft 'n Gentle bathroom tissue; and Vanity Fair and Mardi Gras napkins. Its commercial product segment offered the lodging, restaurant, school, hospital, and institutional industries such brands as the Envision line of 100% recycled paper products, and Preference and Acclaim towel and tissue products. This segment reported 1998 income from operations as $864.8 million on sales of $3.4 billion.

The newly-formed **Dixie Division** consisted of the Dixie disposable cup, plate, and cutlery products. This business reported income from operations in 1998 to be $89.1 million on sales of $775.5 million.

Tissue—European contained an assortment of leading brands for a number of countries. In France, it offered Lotus and Moltonel bathroom tissue, and Okay kitchen towels. The Lotus brand made another appearance in the Netherlands. In Spain, its strongest brand was Colhogar bathroom tissue and kitchen towels. Ireland was home of the KittenSoft brand of bathroom tissue and kitchen towels, while Turkey stocked Selpak bathroom tissue and kitchen towels. Finland and Italy were markets for the Embo and Tenderly bathroom tissue brands, respectively. In Greece, it offered the Delica brand of bathroom tissue and kitchen towels. This business segment also produced feminine hygiene products and pharmacy supplies. It also the served the away-from-home market with bathroom and facial tissues, paper towels, and tabletop products for hotels, restaurants, office buildings, and the food service industry. Income from European operations was $236.2 million on sales of $1.87 billion in 1998.

Packaging Operations provided the food industry with folding cartons, paperboard, and extrusion coated products. The company's Qwik Wave product line served the microwave foods market. The packaging segment also met the specialized packaging needs of leading pharmaceutical companies. Income from operations in 1998 was $56.6 million on sales of $717.7 million.

Communications Papers & Fiber included the Eureka! and Eclipse brands of office printing and copying paper, as well as paper for commercial printing and publishing, forms bond, and envelope papers. The Columbia brand was a line of uncoated groundwood printing papers. This segment's income from operations dipped to $2.4 million on 1998 sales of $796.6 million.

Changes to the Industry

According to Bruce Wasserstein, author of *Big Deal: The Battle for Control of America's Leading Corporations*, "A major weakness of the flip-over pill was demonstrated by Sir James Goldsmith's 1985 takeover of Crown Zellerbach...a third-generation pill—the "flip-in, flip-over"—was developed in reaction to Goldsmith's victory." The new pill was different from the one employed by Crown Zellerbach in two ways: it became active if a hostile bidder acquired more than a prescribed amount of stock; and the hostile bidder was barred from purchasing cheaper stock once a pill was activated.

Review of the Outcome

Almost immediately after taking control of Crown Zellerbach, Sir James Goldsmith announced the impending sale of certain assets to James River Corp. On December 16, 1985, James River agreed to pay $766 million for the acquisition. The deal was finalized in May of 1986 after James River exchanged 22.6 million shares for 17.6 million Crown Zellerbach shares not already owned by Sir James.

Research

Chase, Marilyn. "Crown Zellerbach to Shed Timber Assets, Spin off Unit in Bid to Fight Goldsmith," in *The Wall Street Journal*, 26 April 1985. Describes the company's proposed restructuring plan.

Cole, Robert J. "Goldsmith Bids for Zellerbach," in *The New York Times*, 2 April 1985. Relates Sir James' initial offer for Crown Zellerbach.

Diamond, Stuart. "Big Stake in Crown Is Sought," in *The New York Times*, 13 December 1984. Discusses Sir James' intention to acquire up to 25% of Crown Zellerbach.

The Players

Investor: Sir James Goldsmith. Sir James Goldsmith was born in 1933 to a British hotelier and a French mother. He attended Eton College until dropping out of school at age sixteen. In just four years he amassed a fortune by acquiring the French distribution rights to a British rheumatism remedy. From that point, the Anglo-French financier made successive investments and acquisitions, adding to his coffers. After a three-month battle for Crown Zellerbach, Sir James gained control of the company as chairman in July 1985.

Crown Zellerbach Chairman, President, and CEO: William T. Creson. William Creson joined Crown Zellerbach as an executive vice president in 1976, having spent 22 years in the pulp and paper business. After moving through successive positions, he was named company president in 1977. On October 8, 1981, he succeeded C. Raymond Dahl as chairman and CEO, retaining the post of president. After Sir James Goldsmith's acquisition of Crown Zellerbach, Creson turned over the post of chairman to Goldsmith. In August 1998 Creson passed away in his home in Napa, California.

Dobrzynski, Judith H. and Jonathan B. Levine. "One Way or Another, Crown is Going to Topple," in *Business Week*, 29 April 1985. Suggests that Crown Zellerbach's days of independence are numbered.

Fort James Corporation Home Page, available at http://www.fortjames.com. Official World Wide Web Page for Fort James. Includes access to product information, press releases, and investor information.

"James River Corporation of Virginia," in *Notable Corporate Chronologies*, The Gale Group, 1999. Provides an overview of the company until the formation of Fort James.

Tharp, Mike. "Goldsmith Wins Fight for Crown Zellerbach Corp.," in *The Wall Street Journal*, 26 July 1985. Details Sir James' acquisition of control of Crown Zellerbach.

Wiegner, Kathleen K. "Crown of Thorns," in *Forbes*, 9 November 1981. Describes the difficulties faced by Creson as he was appointed to chairman of Crown Zellerbach.

Wasserstein, Bruce. *Big Deal: The Battle for Control of America's Leading Corporations*, Warner Books, 1998. Offers an overview of the largest mergers in recent American corporate history.

PATRICIA ARCHILLA

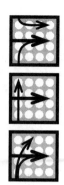

GRAND METROPOLITAN & GUINNESS

Diageo PLC
8 Henrietta Pl.
London, W1M 9AG
United Kingdom

tel: 44-171-927-5200
fax: 44-171-927-4600
web: http://www.diageo.com

nationality: United Kingdom
date: December 17, 1997
affected: Grand Metropolitan PLC, United Kingdom, founded 1931
affected: Guinness PLC, United Kingdom, founded 1759

Overview of the Merger

The 23.8 billion pounds sterling merger of Grand Metropolitan PLC and Guinness PLC—two of the largest distillers in the world—in December of 1997 created the largest wine and spirits company in the world, although its share of the global spirits market was only 5% and of the worldwide wine market only 1%. The new firm, named Diageo PLC, held 18 of the top 100 wine and spirits brands in the world, including Johnnie Walker, the world's best selling whisky; Gordon's gin; Smirnoff vodka; and Baileys liqueur. Non-alcohol assets included Burger King, Haagen-Dazs, Green Giant, and Pillsbury. With a market capitalization of roughly 20.6 billion pounds sterling, Diageo was the eighth-largest company in the United Kingdom and the seventh-largest food and drink supplier in the world.

History of Grand Metropolitan PLC

In 1926, at age 16, Maxwell Joseph quit school and established a property firm, Grand Metropolitan. Joseph struggled during the early years of his business because the English economy was in the midst of a depression. Joseph's business finally got off the ground in the mid-1940s with the purchase of the blitz-damaged Mandeville Hotel in the Marylebone district of London.

Grand Metropolitan began expansion in 1950 through the low-cost purchase and development of new hotels. As the firm's base of operations widened, Joseph acquired more profitable and prestigious hotels; the first was London's Mount Royal Hotel for $2.8 million. In Paris, Joseph purchased the Lotti Hotel; in Cannes, the Carlton Hotel; and in Copenhagen, the Hotel d'Angleterre. Grand Metropolitan went public in 1961, just prior to its purchase of Grand Hotels (Mayfair) Ltd.

Initiating a strategy of diversification, Joseph purchased Express Dairies in 1969. Because the Express Dairies purchase received such strong support from shareholders, within a year Joseph had also acquired Berni Inns, Ron Nagle, and Truman Hanburg; the latter was Grand Metropolitan's first brewery acquisition and also the largest takeover deal in Britain at that time, costing 400 million pounds.

In the early 1970s, Grand Metropolitan purchased the Watney-Mann brewery and the 51% that it didn't already own of Carlsberg, a Danish brewery. After debt peaked at 528 million pounds in 1976, the firm was forced to sell some of its smaller businesses and shares in Carlsberg beer for 5.39 million pounds. The following year, Grand Metropolitan bought a 20% share in Pleasurama, a casino operator, increasing shareholder equity above the level of debt. A series of leveraged buyouts in 1979 included the Savoy Hotel Group, which was sold shortly thereafter because of low returns.

Grand Metropolitan offered $415 million in 1980 for Liggett Group Inc., an American tobacco and liquor company that distributed Grand Metropolitan's J&B Scotch whiskey in the U.S. Liggett mounted a legal battle to thwart Grand Metropolitan. At the same time, Standard Brands entered a competing bid of $513 million. Grand Metropolitan countered with $590 million, a price Standard Brands could not top, and Liggett shareholders accepted the offer. The company's overexposure in the British economy became problematic that year as England entered a period of recession, and the English Monopolies Commission brought charges against Grand Metropolitan for its control over certain markets. In response, Grand Metropolitan made plans to diversify geographically.

In 1981, Grand Metropolitan achieved greater financial stability largely due to Liggett's success selling Bailey's Original Irish Cream and J&B Scotch in the U.S. To generate greater profits from liquor sales in Britain, the firm attempted to enter the retail liquor market. However, because the British government did not permit producers and distributors of liquor to own retail outlets, the company was forced to adopt a different strategy. To circumvent restrictions while drawing a portion of the profits earned from retail liquor and food sales, Grand Metropolitan subleased its bars and restaurants to outside management.

The following year, Grand Metropolitan purchased the Intercontinental Hotel chain, which included 110 hotels, from Pan American World Airways in exchange for $500 million, Grand Metropolitan's Forum Hotel chain, and several other smaller hotel properties. To ease monopoly concerns, Grand Metropolitan pursued the largely unrestricted markets of the U.S. It established a U.S. subsidiary called GrandMet USA Inc. to operate Liggett and three new units: Western Dairy Products, in California; Express Foods Inc., in Vermont; and Dry Milks Inc., in Kentucky. In Britain, Grand Metropolitan divested itself of marginally performing subsidiaries and peripheral companies.

Divestitures during the mid-1980s included CC

The Business

Financials

Revenue (1998): $29 billion

Employees (1998): 77,000

SICs / NAICS

sic 2082 - Malt Beverages

sic 2085 - Distilled & Blended Liquors

sic 2022 - Cheese-Natural & Processed

sic 2024 - Ice Cream & Frozen Desserts

sic 2026 - Fluid Milk

sic 2032 - Canned Specialties

sic 2084 - Wines, Brandy & Brandy Spirits

sic 5812 - Eating Places

naics 311942 - Spice and Extract Manufacturing

naics 311513 - Cheese Manufacturing

naics 311514 - Dry, Condensed, and Evaporated Dairy Product Manufacturing

naics 311422 - Specialty Canning

naics 311999 - All Other Miscellaneous Food Manufacturing

naics 722211 - Limited-Service Restaurants

Soft Drinks Ltd., a bottler and distributer of Coca-Cola in southern England, and Express Dairy. Proceeds from the sales were used to strengthen Grand Metropolitan's hotel and entertainment division, which purchased the profitable Mecca Leisure group. Entering the health care services industry for the first time, Grand Metropolitan acquired Quality Care Inc., a large home health care and medical equipment company, and purchased an interest in Pearl Health Services. Also, the Liggett unit was divested.

In 1987, RJR Nabisco sold Heublein Inc., including Smirnoff vodka, Arrow liqueurs, Harvey's Bristol Cream sherry, and Guinness Stout beer, to Grand Metropolitan for $1.3 billion. Allen Sheppard was appointed CEO. Believing that new opportunities in the health care services industry were minimal, Sheppard advocated the sale of Quality Care. The following year, the Intercontinental chain was sold.

After acquiring Pillsbury Co., which owned Burger King, Green Giant, and Haagen-Dazs, in a hostile takeover in 1989, Sheppard implemented plans to focus on brand name products. Two years later, Grand Metropolitan sold its brewing operations to Foster's

The Officers

Chairman: Tony Greener

Group CEO: John McGrath

Group Director, Strategy: Jim Glover

Group Director, Corporate Affairs: Peter Lipscomb

Group Director, Finance: Philip Yea

Brewing, forming a joint venture with Foster's to manage its 330 pubs under Foster's Courage subsidiary. In 1992, the firm's food sector sold two dairy businesses and bought a frozen food company. The beverages division bought the Greek distillery Kaloyannis Brothers and sold its 20% stake in E. Remy Martin and Cointreau.

Grand Metropolitan paid $2.6 billion for Pet Inc. in 1995 and began integrating Pet's products—including Old El Paso, Progresso, and Van de Kamp's—into a new line of Pillsbury Specialty Brands. That year, Pillsbury recalled all of its Green Giant frozen spinach products after packages were found to contain mice particles and fly larvae.

In 1996, the firm established a joint venture to convert 40 of Japan Tobacco's restaurants into Burger Kings and agreed to a venture with Chinese state-owned Qufu Distillery to form a joint distillery where Grand Metropolitan produced Smirnoff vodka and Gilbey's gin. Due to low profits, Grand Metropolitan began closing down its Burger King restaurants in France in 1997. The firm then announced plans to merge with Guinness PLC to form Diageo, the largest wine and spirits company in the world. The deal was completed in December of 1997.

History of Guinness PLC

In 1759, Arthur Guinness, an experienced brewer, leased an old brewery at James Gate in Dublin, Ireland. Guinness made ales and porters that were sold only in Dublin. The company secured an active trade with local pubs and soon became one of the largest employers in the city. In 1775, the business nearly came to an abrupt end because of a dispute over water rights, as the city decided to eliminate the channel that provided the brewery with water. The dispute was settled by means of a tenant agreement.

In 1798, Guinness began exporting from Dublin, and 15 years later, production output increased by 50%. Extra Superior Porter, later named stout, represented only 4% of Guinness's sales in the 1820s; by

1980, the beer accounted for 82% of sales. In 1886, Guinness became a public company under the name Guinness (Arthur) Son and Co. Ltd. Shares were traded on the London Exchange, and the company raised 6 million pounds.

By the 1920s, Guinness had reached the shores of the Caribbean and of East and West Africa. The new Park Royal facility in England became operational in 1936. Guinness Extra and Draught Guinness were the first products brewed for the British market at this facility. After World War II, the company was divided into Guinness Ireland and Guinness U.K. In 1950, Guinness became the first local firm to market its own lager by introducing Harp lager, which became the most successful product in the growing British lager market.

The firm diversified into healthcare by establishing a pharmaceutical operation, Twyford Laboratories, in 1959. During the 1960s, the company continued to expand into countries with warm climates, and it constructed new breweries in Nigeria, Malaysia, Cameroon, Ghana, and Jamaica. It introduced a new product, Irish Ale, which was exported to France and Britain, and purchased Crooke Laboratories.

In 1970, Guinness went on a purchasing spree, acquiring 270 companies that produced a wide variety of products, from baby bibs to car polish. The firm changed its name to Guinness (Arthur) & Sons PLC in 1980. A year later, Guinness executives appointed the first non-family professional manager, Ernest Saunders, as CEO. He disposed of 160 companies, slashed overhead, and spent heavily to advertise Guinness Stout. In 1984, Sanders decided to reduce brewing to only 50% of Guinness's total volume. He launched a buying spree by acquiring publisher Martin the Newsagent PLC and health spa Champneys.

In 1985, Guinness acquired scotch maker Arthur Bell & Sons PLC and Neighborhood Stores PLC. That year, company profits tripled and share price quadrupled. A year later, Guinness beat out Argyll with a successful 2.5 billion pound hostile takeover bid for Distillers Co., the maker of Johnnie Walker, Gordon's, Tangueray, and other liquors. The company then changed its name to Guinness PLC. A few months later, Saunders and two of his directors were accused of orchestrating an international scheme to artificially raise the value of Guinness shares in order to make the Distillers acquisition possible. He was also charged with manipulating investors to purchase huge amounts of Guinness shares with the understanding that the company would eventually buy them back. Company auditors discovered some $38 million worth of invoices for "services" rendered by various international investors during the Distillers takeover.

The Guinness board asked for Saunders' resignation in 1987, and then brought legal action against him and one of his fellow directors, John Ward. The British government charged Saunders with fraud, claiming that he knowingly destroyed evidence during the Trade and Industry Department investigation. Sir Anthony Tennant became Guinness' new CEO. He refocused the company on brewing and distilling by selling peripheral businesses and purchasing businesses that had the same focus as Guinness.

Acquisitions during the late 1980s included Shenley Co., Buckley's Brewery PLC, Wax SpA in Italy, and Siegenthaler in Switzerland. The firm formed 11 new companies and two new ventures in the Pacific Rim as well as eight joint ventures in Europe. In 1989, Guinness bought 24.1% of French cognac, champagne, perfume, and leather goods maker LMVH Moet Hennessy Louis Vuitton. A year later, LVMH doubled its 12% stake in Guinness to 24%. Guinness acquired All Brand Importers; Schenley Canada; Guinness's Canadian beer distributor, Rymax Corp.; J. Cawsey in Australia; the spirits company of Elders; and the outstanding 25% of Harp Lager from Greene King. That year, Saunders was convicted on criminal charges and sentenced to jail.

In 1991, Guinness purchased 99.3% of La Cruz del Campo SA in Spain for 482 million pounds; the deal marked the largest foreign investment in Spain's history. The firm also acquired 67.5% of Asbach, the German brandy manufacturer, along with its Austrian subsidiary; Inter-American Holdings, a distributor in Mexico; Prestige Beverage, a distiller in Venezuela; U.S.-based Glenmore Distilleries; Californian scotch maker Scoresby; and Pampero Especial. The scandal of 1986 finally ended when the company agreed to pay compensation totaling 92 million pounds to Argyll.

Guinness and LVMH reorganized their cross-shareholdings in 1994, disengaging Guinness from LVMH's perfume and luggage lines while linking it more strongly with the its champagne and cognac business. LVMH reduced its stake in Guinness from 24 to 20% by selling 72 million shares on the open market. The European Commission of Human Rights decided that the United Kingdom government deprived Ernest Saunders of a fair hearing in 1990 when it compelled him to testify against himself. British legal authorities appealed the conviction of Saunders and three other defendants, but it was upheld.

As part of its plan to focus on its premium brands, including Gordon's gin and vodka and Scoresby scotch whisky, Guinness sold North American assets to Canandaigua Wine Co. for $171 million in 1995. A

The Players

Group CEO of Grand Metropolitan PLC: John McGrath. John McGrath began working for Watney Mann & Truman Brewers in 1985. A year later, he was appointed managing director of the Grand Metropolitan unit. McGrath became a member of Grand Metropolitan's board in 1992 and accepted the posts of chairman and CEO of the United Distillers & Vintners subsidiary in 1993. Three years later, he was named group CEO of Grand Metropolitan, a position he retained until the firm merged with Guinness to form Diageo PLC. When the deal was completed in December of 1997, McGrath accepted the position of group CEO of the newly merged firm.

Chairman and CEO of Guinness PLC: Tony Greener. After working for Thames Board Mills, Tony Greener was hired as a retail controller at Dunhill, a small family-owned cigarette, lighter, and pipe business. Within three years, he was appointed managing director. During his ten years at the helm of Dunhill, Greener transformed the firm into a multinational luxury goods conglomerate reliant on smoking-related items for only 10% of total revenues. In 1986, Greener was named non-executive director of the board of directors of Guinness just as the scandal that sent Guinness CEO Ernest Saunders to jail came to light. Between 1987 and 1992, he served as managing director of Guinness subsidiary United Distillers. Greener succeeded Sir Anthony Tennant as CEO of Guinness in 1992 and as chairman a year later. When Grand Metropolitan and Guinness merged to form Diageo PLC in 1997, Greener took the reins as chairman of the new food and drink industry giant.

year later, Guinness announced a 39 million pound charge against 1995 earnings and weak liquor sales in the United States, Europe, and Japan. Seeking to improve its stock price, Guinness repurchased 100 million of its own shares. The firm announced plans to merge with Grand Metropolitan PLC to form Diageo, the largest wine and spirits company in the world, in 1997. The deal was completed by the year's end.

Market Forces Driving the Merger

In the mid-1990s, most industry analysts viewed the global wine and liquor market as highly fragmented. Although the Guinness/Grand Metropolitan merger announcement was met with heated opposition and antitrust concerns, the new firm would only hold 5% of the worldwide liquor market and 1% of the global wine market, despite its status as the leading wine and spirits maker in the world.

Because liquor consumption was declining—in the U.S. it had fallen 40% since 1980—alcoholic beverage companies were forced to consolidate as a means of cutting costs. According to a May 1997 article in *Time* magazine, this explained why "Britain's Guinness and Grand Metropolitan fell into each other's arms like veteran barflies." Because there was little product overlap between the two firms, management predicted a cost savings of 75 million pounds sterling by the year 2001. Geographic overlap was minimal as well: Grand Metropolitan was stronger in North America, while Guinness relied more heavily on Europe and other markets.

Besides cost cutting benefits, both firms viewed their marriage as a means of ensuring long-term growth. By joining their market leading brands, such as Guinness' Bell's and Johnnie Walker scotch and Gordon's gin with Grand Metropolitan's Smirnoff Vodka and Baileys Irish Creme, the firms would be able to plug any holes in their product offerings, as well as capitalize on the number-one status that 18 of their brands would boast.

Approach and Engagement

The 23.8 billion pounds sterling ($53.8 billion) deal between Grand Metropolitan and Guinness was announced in May of 1997. SBC Warburg handled negotiations for Grand Metropolitan, while Lazard Brothers took on that role for Guinness. The two firms agreed to a merger of equals that would create a new company, to be named GMG Brands.

Shortly after the deal was announced, competitor LVMH Moet Hennessy Louis Vuitton offered to merge with Guinness and Grand Metropolitan and outlined a plan to spin off food and brewing operations. Guinness and Grand Metropolitan rejected the deal in July. In June, the European Commission (EC) had expressed antitrust concerns and launched a review of the merger. The EC sent both firms a "statement of objections" in August, and scheduled a hearing for the following month. EC approval was granted in October with several stipulations, including the divestiture of Dewar's Scotch and Ainslie's operations in Europe and the sale of Gilbey's operations in Belgium to an independent distributor.

Shareholders overwhelmingly approved the merger in early December. Although many rejected

the Diageo name, which was developed as a replacement for the GMG Brands name agreed upon earlier, a 97% proxy vote decided in favor of it. On December 15, the U.S. Federal Trade Commission cleared the merger only after Guinness and Grand Metropolitan agreed to divest their worldwide Dewar's Scotch whiskey and Bombay gin operations. The deal was completed on December 17, 1997.

Products and Services

After the merger, Diageo operated in more than 50 countries in North America, Europe, and the Pacific Rim, as well as in other regions. The firm was organized into four main segments: spirits and wine, packaged food, beer, and fast food.

Spirits and wine accounted for 43% of total sales in 1998. Diageo's liquor brands included Baileys, Bell's, Gilbey's, Gordon's, J&B, Johnnie Walker, Pampero, Popov, Rebel Yell, Smirnoff, Tangueray, and White Horse. The firm also distributed Jack Daniels, Jose Cuervo, and Wild Turkey and sold three main wine brands: Blossom Hill, Cinzano, and Glen Ellen.

Packaged food, including Green Giant, Haagen-Dazs, Old El Paso, Pillsbury, Progresso, and Totino's, brought in 31% of sales. Beer brands, which secured 18%, included Alcazar, Draught Guinness, Enigma, Guinness Stout, Harp, Hoffmans, Hudson Blue, Keler, and Kilkenny. The fast food Burger King operations captured the remaining 7%.

Changes to the Industry

As required by the EU and the FCC, Diageo sold its and Dewar's Scotch whiskey and Bombay gin brands to Bacardi for $1.9 billion in 1998. The mature alcohol markets in Europe and the U.S. remained flat, and the Asian economic crisis curtailed what had looked like promising emerging wine and spirits markets elsewhere. Competitor LMVH Moet Hennessy Louis Vuitton reduced what had been an 11% stake in Diageo to 7%.

Review of the Outcome

Shares of both firms rose upon news of the deal in May of 1997. Most analysts believed the combination of best-selling brands boded well for the new industry leader. Initially, the outcome for the new firm seemed promising, particularly as Diageo was able to double its initial cost savings estimate to 150 million pounds, and integration efforts proceeded without a hitch or lost market share. Layoffs totaled roughly 2,000, or 10% of Diageo's total beer, wine, and liquor workforce.

However, a year after the deal was completed, sales had fallen by 7% and profits dropped 4%. The market was flat, and many analysts believed that it would remain so. Compounding the problem, according to a December 1998 article in *Economist*, was the fact that Diageo relied too heavily on secondary brands and lacked a single strong spirits brand that could drive global growth. "Diageo has not been nearly radical enough in directing resources to the brands that make money, and 'fixing or flogging' those that are less profitable." In 1999, perhaps in response to this criticism, Diageo launched a divestiture campaign that included the sale of several whiskey, bourbon, and cordial brands, as well as Spanish brewing operations.

Research

Diageo PLC Home Page, available at http://www.diageo.com. Official World Wide Web Page for Diageo PLC. Includes product information, news, and corporate information.

"Diageo: The Morning After," in *Economist*, 12 December 1998. Offers an in-depth look at the performance of Diageo since the Guinness/Grand Metropolitan merger.

Gilbert, Mervyn. "Rivals Take Aim as Drinks Giant Takes Shape," in *Grocer*, 17 May 1997. Discusses the antitrust concerns raised by rivals of Guinness and Grand Metropolitan after the announcement of their merger.

Greenwald, John. "A Pint of Guinness with That Whopper?" in *Time*, 26 May 1997. Explains why both firms were seeking a merger.

"Guinness and Grand Met in Mega-Deal League," in *Acquisitions Monthly*, June 1997. Discusses the details of the transaction.

"Guinness PLC," in *Notable Corporate Chronologies*, The Gale Group, 1999. Offers a history of Guinness PLC.

"Guinness-Grand Met Merger Wins Approval," in *Nation's Restaurant News*, 8 December 1997. Reviews the shareholder and proxy votes for the merger itself, as well as for the new name of the firm.

"Grand Met, Guinness Reject LVMH Proposal for Merger," in *WWD*, 28 July 1997. Details the offer made to Guinness and Grand Metropolitan by LVMH Moet Hennessy Louis Vuitton for a three-way merger.

"Grand Metropolitan PLC," in *Notable Corporate Chronologies*, The Gale Group, 1999. Offers a history of Grand Metropolitan PLC.

"Spotlight on Grand Met, Guinness Deal," in *The Financial Post*, 30 August 1997. Explains the concerns raised by the European Commission regarding the Guinness/Grand Metropolitan merger.

ANNAMARIE L. SHELDON

GRAND METROPOLITAN & LIGGETT

Diageo PLC
8 Henrietta Pl.
London, W1M 9AG
United Kingdom

tel: 44-171-927-5200
fax: 44-171-927-4600
web: http://www.diageo.com

nationality: United Kingdom
date: August 7, 1980
affected: Grand Metropolitan PLC, United Kingdom, founded 1926
affected: Liggett Group Inc., USA, founded 1822

Overview of the Merger

United Kingdom-based drinks, consumer products, and hotels group Grand Metropolitan paid $590 million for the tobacco, distilling, and pet food group Liggett in 1980 to gain access to the U.S. consumer products market. The deal, which marked the first U.S. acquisition for Grand Metropolitan, as well as its first foray into the cigarette market, did provide Grand Met a base from which to grow its U.S. operations. However, the firm's stint in the tobacco industry itself was rather short-lived. In 1986, Brook Group Ltd. paid $137 million for the tobacco operations of Liggett. Grand Metropolitan retained the Liggett's wine and spirits distribution assets and pet food operations.

History of Grand Metropolitan PLC

In 1926, at age 16, Maxwell Joseph quit school and established a property firm, Grand Metropolitan. Joseph struggled during the early years of his business because the English economy was in the midst of a depression. Joseph's business finally got off the ground in the mid-1940s with the purchase of the blitz-damaged Mandeville Hotel in the Marylebone district of London.

Grand Metropolitan began expansion in 1950 through the low-cost purchase and development of new hotels. As the firm's base of operations widened, Joseph acquired more profitable and prestigious hotels; the first was London's Mount Royal Hotel for $2.8 million; in Paris, Joseph purchased the Lotti Hotel; in Cannes, the Carlton Hotel; and in Copenhagen, the Hotel d'Angleterre. Grand Metropolitan went public in 1961, just prior to its purchase of Grand Hotels (Mayfair) Ltd.

Initiating a strategy of diversification, Joseph acquired Express Dairies in 1969. Because the Express Dairies purchase received such strong support from shareholders, within a year Joseph had also acquired Berni Inns, Ron Nagle, and Truman Hanburg; the latter was Grand Metropolitan's first brewery acquisition and also the largest takeover deal in Britain at that time, costing 400 million pounds.

In the early 1970s, Grand Metropolitan purchased the Watney-Mann brewery and the 51% that it didn't already own of Carlsberg, a Danish brewery. After debt peaked at 528 million pounds in 1976, the firm was forced to sell some of its smaller businesses and shares in Carlsberg beer for 5.39 million pounds. The following year, Grand Metropolitan bought a 20% share in Pleasurama, a casino operator, increasing shareholder equity above the level of debt. A series of leveraged buyouts in 1979 included the Savoy Hotel Group, which was sold shortly thereafter because of low returns.

Grand Metropolitan paid $590 million in 1980 for Liggett Group, an American tobacco and liquor company that distributed Grand Metropolitan's J&B Scotch whiskey in the U.S. To generate greater profits from liquor sales in Britain, the firm attempted to enter the retail liquor market. However, because the British government did not permit producers and distributors of liquor to own retail outlets, the company was forced to adopt a different strategy. To circumvent restrictions while drawing a portion of the profits earned from retail liquor and food sales, Grand Metropolitan subleased its bars and restaurants to outside management.

The following year, Grand Metropolitan purchased the Intercontinental Hotel chain, which included 110 hotels, from Pan American World Airways in exchange for $500 million, Grand Metropolitan's Forum Hotel chain, and several other smaller hotel properties. The firm also began building its U.S. operations and selling poorly performing subsidiaries in Britain.

Divestitures during the mid-1980s included CC Soft Drinks Ltd., a bottler and distributor of Coca-Cola in southern England, and Express Dairy. Proceeds from the sales were used to strengthen Grand Metropolitan's hotel and entertainment division, which purchased the profitable Mecca Leisure group. Entering the health care services industry for the first time, Grand Metropolitan acquired Quality Care Inc., a large home health care and medical equipment company, and as well as an interest in Pearl Health Services. Also, the Liggett tobacco unit was divested in 1986.

In 1987, RJR Nabisco sold Heublein Inc., including Smirnoff vodka, Arrow liqueurs, Harvey's Bristol Cream sherry, and Guinness Stout beer, to Grand Metropolitan for $1.3 billion. Allen Sheppard was appointed CEO. Believing that new opportunities in the health care services industry were minimal, Sheppard advocated the sale of Quality Care. The following year, the Intercontinental hotel chain was sold.

After acquiring Pillsbury Co., which owned

The Business

Financials

Revenue (1998): $29 billion

Employees (1998): 77,000

SICs / NAICS

sic 2082 - Malt Beverages

sic 2085 - Distilled & Blended Liquors

sic 2022 - Cheese-Natural & Processed

sic 2024 - Ice Cream & Frozen Desserts

sic 2026 - Fluid Milk

sic 2032 - Canned Specialties

sic 2084 - Wines, Brandy & Brandy Spirits

sic 5812 - Eating Places

naics 311942 - Spice and Extract Manufacturing

naics 311513 - Cheese Manufacturing

naics 311514 - Dry, Condensed, and Evaporated Dairy Product Manufacturing

naics 311422 - Specialty Canning

naics 311999 - All Other Miscellaneous Food Manufacturing

naics 722211 - Limited-Service Restaurants

Burger King, Green Giant, and Haagen-Dazs, in a hostile takeover in 1989, Sheppard implemented plans to focus on brand name products. Two years later, Grand Metropolitan sold its brewing operations to Foster's Brewing, forming a joint venture with Foster's to manage its 330 pubs under Foster's Courage subsidiary. In 1992, the firm's food sector sold two dairy businesses and bought a frozen food company. The beverages division bought the Greek distillery Kaloyannis Brothers and sold its 20% stake in E. Remy Martin and Cointreau.

Grand Metropolitan paid $2.6 billion for Pet Inc. in 1995 and began integrating Pet's products—including Old El Paso, Progresso, and Van de Kamp's—into a new line of Pillsbury Specialty Brands. That year, Pillsbury recalled all of its Green Giant frozen spinach products after packages were found to contain mice particles and fly larvae.

In 1996, the firm established a joint venture to convert 40 of Japan Tobacco's restaurants into Burger Kings, and agreed to a venture with Chinese state-owned Qufu Distillery to form a joint distillery where Grand Metropolitan would produce Smirnoff vodka

The Officers

Chairman: Tony Greener

Group CEO: John McGrath

Group Director, Strategy: Jim Glover

Group Director, Corporate Affairs: Peter Lipscomb

Group Director, Finance: Philip Yea

and Gilbey's gin. Due to low profits, Grand Metropolitan began closing down its Burger King restaurants in France in 1997. The firm then announced plans to merge with Guinness PLC to form Diageo, the largest wine and spirits company in the world. The deal was completed in December of 1997.

Diageo sold its Dewar's Scotch whiskey and Bombay gin brands to Bacardi for $1.9 billion in 1998. The mature alcohol markets in Europe and the U.S. continued to produce flat sales, and the Asian economic crisis curtailed what had looked like promising emerging wine and spirits markets elsewhere. Competitor LMVH Moet Hennessy Louis Vuitton reduced its 11% stake in Diageo to 7%.

History of Liggett Group Inc.

The Liggett Group was founded when the Liggett family started up a snuff making business in 1822. After George Myers joined the business in 1873 as a partner, the company's name was changed to Liggett & Myers. Cigarette brands such as L&M and Chesterfield earned the firm a top spot among tobacco firms worldwide.

Liggett's decision to avoid the filtered and low-tar cigarette market niches began taking a toll on the firm in the 1950s. The firm held roughly 20% of the U.S. cigarette market in the early 1960s. Operations had diversified from tobacco-based products—which were housed in the Liggett & Myers Tobacco Co. unit—to include liquor distilling and distribution, soft drink bottling, sporting goods, and Alpo pet food. After a deal to divest its faltering cigarette operations in 1978 crumbled, Liggett slashed marketing expenses in both its pet food and tobacco segments as a means of bolstering profits. The firm also introduced a generic cigarette brand. In 1979, Liggett sold its distilling operations for $97.5 million in cash. Sales reached $1 billion.

Grand Metropolitan bought Liggett in 1980 for $590 million. When the low-priced generic cigarette market took off, Liggett was poised as the leader in that category. That success was soon challenged, how-

ever, as industry giants like Philip Morris quickly moved into the burgeoning market. As a result of the increased competition, operating profits for Liggett dropped a whopping 90% to $6.4 million in 1985, compared to $66.7 million a year earlier. The weakened performance undermined Grand Metropolitan's plans to sell Liggett for $325 million to a group of investors that included Liggett management.

In 1986, Grand Metropolitan sold Liggett to Brook Group Ltd. for $137 million, retaining Liggett's pet food operations, which it later sold, and its wine and spirits distribution assets. Liggett's U.S. market share had slipped to 3.9% of the $34 billion U.S. cigarette industry. In 1997, Liggett became the first major tobacco firm to admit publicly to the addictive properties of cigarettes. As the fifth-largest U.S. tobacco firm, Liggett was part of a $205 billion settlement negotiated in 1998 by the industry's leading players and 46 states. By then, Philip Morris had paid Liggett $300 million for its L&M, Chesterfield, and Lark cigarette brands.

Market Forces Driving the Merger

Grand Metropolitan's overexposure in the British economy became problematic in 1980 as England entered a period of recession, and the English Monopolies Commission (EMC) brought charges against Grand Metropolitan for its control over certain markets. Roughly 88% of the firm's $455 million in net income was earned in Britain, prompting the EMC to forbid the firm from making any further significant acquisitions there. In response, Grand Metropolitan made plans to diversify geographically. "With Grand Met straining at the seams of its local market," CEO Maxwell Joseph wanted his firm prepared to "thrust into the largest consumer market in the world: the U.S.," wrote *Business Week* in August of 1981.

Liggett Group could provide Grand Metropolitan access to the U.S. consumer goods market with its footholds in the tobacco, pet food, wine and spirits, sporting goods, and soft drink bottling industries there. To move into the U.S. market, Grand Metropolitan wanted to use Liggett to increase its U.S. sales of spirits and to serve as a foundation for the U.S. food ingredients companies the firm planned to acquire.

Approach and Engagement

Owner of 9.5% of Liggett Group, Grand Metropolitan offered $50 per share, or $415 million, in cash on April 4, 1980, for the remainder of the firm. In response, Liggett mounted a legal battle, initiated on May 1, to thwart Grand Metropolitan. Five days later,

Standard Brands Inc. entered a competing bid of $570 million. Grand Metropolitan countered with $590 million, a price that Standard Brands could not top. The tender offer expired in June, when Grand Metropolitan gained control of 83.2% of Liggett's voting shares. Shareholders gave final approval for the deal on August 7.

Holders of Liggett capital stock were offered $69 per common share of stock, $158.62 per share of convertible preferred stock, and $70 per share of 7% preferred stock. Liggett was removed from the New York Stock Exchange and began operating as a subsidiary of Grand Metropolitan.

Products and Services

In 1998, Diageo (formed in 1997 by the merger of Grand Metropolitan and Guinness) operated in more than 50 countries in North America, Europe, and the Pacific Rim, as well as in other regions. Grand Metropolitan's push into the U.S., launched by its 1980 acquisition of Liggett, had paid off—North American operations accounted for nearly half of total revenues, while European operations brought in 34% of sales. The firm was organized into four main segments: spirits and wine, packaged food, beer, and fast food.

Spirits and wine accounted for 43% of total sales in 1998. Diageo's liquor brands included Baileys, Bell's, Gilbey's, Gordon's, J&B, Johnnie Walker, Pampero, Popov, Rebel Yell, Smirnoff, Tangueray, and White Horse. The firm also distributed Jack Daniels, Jose Cuervo, and Wild Turkey, and sold three main wine brands: Blossom Hill, Cinzano, and Glen Ellen.

The Pillsbury unit accounted for 31% of sales and oversaw the packaged food operations of Diageo. Pillsbury's refrigerated dough products were the best selling in the U.S. and its baking mixes were second only to General Mills. Other brands included Green Giant canned and frozen vegetables, Haagen-Dazs ice cream products, Hungry Jack frozen foods, Jeno's frozen pizza, Matha White baking mixes Old El Paso Mexican food products, Pappalo's frozen pizza, Pillsbury Toaster Strudels, Progresso Italian food products, and Totino's frozen pizza and snack items.

Beer brands, which secured 18% of sales, included Alcazar, Draught Guinness, Enigma, Guinness Stout, Harp, Hoffmans, Hudson Blue, Keler, and Kilkenny. The fast food Burger King operations captured the remaining 7%.

Changes to the Industry

According to an October 1986 article in *Financial Times (London)*, Grand Metropolitan began efforts to "get out the cigarette business almost as soon as it got

The Players

CEO and chairman of Grand Metropolitan PLC: Sir Maxwell Joseph. Maxwell Joseph quit school at the age of 16 to found Grand Metropolitan in 1926. After struggling for several years, Joseph finally got his company up and running in the mid-1940s with the purchase of a war-torn hotel in London. He acquired several more hotels and took his firm public in 1961. Grand Metropolitan's purchase of brewery Truman Hanburg in 1970, which marked the largest takeover deal in Britain at that time, was orchestrated by Joseph. He also led his firm's diversification into tobacco in 1980 by winning a hostile takeover battle for Liggett. Joseph was knighted in 1981, and he died shortly thereafter.

CEO of Liggett Group Inc.: Raymond J. Mulligan. After working for both the Minute Maid Corp. and the Berry Biscuit Co., Raymond Mulligan was hired in 1961 by Allen Products Co. Eight years later, he was named president of the firm, which had been purchased by Liggett in 1964. Mulligan worked his way up the ladder at Liggett and eventually secured the top spot there. When Grand Metropolitan took over Liggett in 1980, Mulligan agreed to retire in two years at the age of 60. Accordingly, Jonathan W. Olds took the reins from him on February 1, 1982.

into it through its acquisition of Liggett's tobacco, liquor, and consumer products businesses in 1980." The firm wanted to exit the industry for two main reasons: first, increased health awareness was making tobacco companies increasingly vulnerable not only to declining cigarette sales, but also to potentially costly litigation; at the same time, Liggett leadership in the low-cost generic brand cigarette market was slipping as larger tobacco players moved into that growing segment and competed with Liggett by slashing prices.

In fact, Liggett's poor performance in 1985 undermined Grand Metropolitan's plan to sell the firm to a management consortium for $325 million. That year, Grand Metropolitan divested its Pinkerton chewing tobacco unit for $138 million and a tobacco operation in Brazil for $28 million. Two years later, Brook Group Ltd. bought the tobacco operations of Liggett for $137 million, completing Grand Metropolitan's exit from the tobacco industry.

Review of the Outcome

To ease monopoly concerns raised by European authorities, Grand Metropolitan pursued the largely unrestricted markets of the U.S. after it purchased Liggett. The firm became more financially stable due to Liggett's success at selling Bailey's Original Irish Cream and J&B Scotch in the U.S. In 1981, the firm established a U.S. subsidiary called GrandMet USA Inc. to operate Liggett and three new units: Western Dairy Products, in California; Express Foods Inc., in Vermont; and Dry Milks Inc., in Kentucky. The increased revenues from its new U.S. base allowed Grand Metropolitan to divest itself of marginally performing subsidiaries and peripheral companies in Britain.

Research

Diageo PLC Home Page, available at http://www.diageo.com. Official World Wide Web Page for Diageo PLC. Includes product information, news, and corporate information.

"Grand Metropolitan: A British Giant Expands into U.S. Consumer Market," in *Business Week*, 24 August 1981. Explains why Grand Metropolitan was looking to move into the U.S. consumer good market.

"Grand Metropolitan PLC," in *Notable Corporate Chronologies*, The Gale Group, 1999. Offers a history of Grand Metropolitan PLC.

Harris, Clay. "GrandMet Sells Liggett Group for 97 M Pounds (Pds) Cash," in *Financial Times (London)*, 29 October 1986. Discusses Grand Metropolitan's decision to divest the Liggett tobacco operations.

Sloane, Leonard. "Liggett Chief Elected," in *The New York Times*, 1 December 1981. Details the career of Raymond Mulligan.

Stevenson, Richard W. "Grand Met in Talks to Sell Liggett," in *The New York Times*, 25 September 1986. Offers an overview of Liggett's performance since its takeover by Grand Met.

"Why a White Knight Likes Liggett," in *Business Week*, 19 May 1980. Details the counter offer launched by Standard Brands for Liggett.

JEFF ST. THOMAS

GRAND METROPOLITAN & PILLSBURY

nationality: United Kingdom
date: January 1989
affected: Grand Metropolitan PLC, United Kingdom, founded 1931
affected: Pillsbury Co., U.S., founded 1869

Diageo PLC
8 Henrietta Pl.
London, W1M 9AG
United Kingdom

tel: 44-171-927-5200
fax: 44-171-927-4600
web: http://www.diageo.com

Overview of the Merger

When Grand Metropolitan PLC, a United Kingdom distilling giant, launched its $60 per share hostile takeover bid for Minnesota-based food company Pillsbury in October of 1988, Pillsbury quickly realized it would be difficult to remain independent. The firm's expansion during the mid-1980s had resulted in growing losses, which left it vulnerable. Although Pillsbury had adopted a poison pill—the issue of a new class of securities to make a takeover prohibitively expensive—to defend against such an attack, Grand Metropolitan's all-cash offer was 50% higher than the current trading value of Pillsbury's stock. Refusing such an offer would likely be considered detrimental to its shareholders.

Pillsbury management instead decided to resist the bid as a means of garnering the highest offer possible. First, the firm rejected the bid as too low. When white knights never materialized, mainly because Grand Metropolitan's offer was so high, Pillsbury then announced its intent to spin off its Burger King holdings, as well as several other non-core holdings, and use the proceeds to distribute a one-time dividend to shareholders. In response, Grand Metropolitan upped its offer to $63 per share. In December of 1988, a Delaware court forced Pillsbury to redeem its poison pill. The final purchase price for Pillsbury was $66 per share, or $5.75 billion—10% higher than the original offer. The deal, completed in January of 1989, was the fourth-largest cross-border deal of the 1980s. It helped shape merger and acquisition law by establishing that a high enough all-cash offer could often force a company to redeem a poison pill.

History of Grand Metropolitan PLC

In 1926, at age 16, Maxwell Joseph quit school and established a property firm, Grand Metropolitan. Joseph struggled during the early years of his business because the English economy was in the midst of a depression. Joseph's business finally got off the ground in the mid-1940s with the purchase of the blitz-damaged Mandeville Hotel in the Marylebone district of London.

Grand Metropolitan began expansion in 1950 through the low-cost purchase

The Business

Financials

Revenue (1998): $29 billion

Employees (1998): 77,000

SICs / NAICS

sic 2082 - Malt Beverages

sic 2085 - Distilled & Blended Liquors

sic 2022 - Cheese-Natural & Processed

sic 2024 - Ice Cream & Frozen Desserts

sic 2026 - Fluid Milk

sic 2032 - Canned Specialties

sic 2084 - Wines, Brandy & Brandy Spirits

sic 5812 - Eating Places

naics 311942 - Spice and Extract Manufacturing

naics 311513 - Cheese Manufacturing

naics 311514 - Dry, Condensed, and Evaporated Dairy
Product Manufacturing

naics 311422 - Specialty Canning

naics 311999 - All Other Miscellaneous Food Manufacturing

naics 722211 - Limited-Service Restaurants

and development of new hotels. As the firm's base of operations widened, Joseph acquired more profitable and prestigious hotels; the first was London's Mount Royal Hotel for $2.8 million. In Paris, Joseph purchased the Lotti Hotel; in Cannes, the Carlton Hotel; and in Copenhagen, the Hotel d'Angleterre. Grand Metropolitan went public in 1961, just prior to its purchase of Grand Hotels (Mayfair) Ltd.

Initiating a strategy of diversification, Joseph purchased Express Dairies in 1969. Because the Express Dairies purchase received such strong support from shareholders, within a year Joseph had also acquired Berni Inns, Ron Nagle, and Truman Hanburg; the latter was Grand Metropolitan's first brewery acquisition and also the largest takeover deal in Britain at that time, costing 400 million pounds.

In the early 1970s, Grand Metropolitan purchased the Watney-Mann brewery and the 51% that it didn't already own of Carlsberg, a Danish brewery. After debt peaked at 528 million pounds in 1976, the firm was forced to sell some of its smaller businesses and shares in Carlsberg beer for 5.39 million pounds. The following year, Grand Metropolitan bought a 20%

share in Pleasurama, a casino operator, increasing shareholder equity above the level of debt. A series of leveraged buyouts in 1979 included the Savoy Hotel Group, which was sold shortly thereafter because of low returns.

Grand Metropolitan offered $415 million in 1980 for Liggett Group Inc., an American tobacco and liquor company that distributed Grand Metropolitan's J&B Scotch whiskey in the U.S. Liggett mounted a legal battle to thwart Grand Metropolitan. At the same time, Standard Brands entered a competing bid of $513 million. Grand Metropolitan countered with $590 million, a price Standard Brands could not top, and Liggett shareholders accepted the offer. The company's overexposure in the British economy became problematic that year as England entered a period of recession, and the English Monopolies Commission brought charges against Grand Metropolitan for its control over certain markets. In response, Grand Metropolitan made plans to diversify geographically.

In 1981, Grand Metropolitan achieved greater financial stability largely due to Liggett's success selling Bailey's Original Irish Cream and J&B Scotch in the U.S. To generate greater profits from liquor sales in Britain, the firm attempted to enter the retail liquor market. However, because the British government did not permit producers and distributors of liquor to own retail outlets, the company was forced to adopt a different strategy. To circumvent restrictions while drawing a portion of the profits earned from retail liquor and food sales, Grand Metropolitan subleased its bars and restaurants to outside management.

The following year, Grand Metropolitan purchased the Intercontinental Hotel chain, which included 110 hotels, from Pan American World Airways in exchange for $500 million, Grand Metropolitan's Forum Hotel chain, and several other smaller hotel properties. To ease monopoly concerns, Grand Metropolitan pursued the largely unrestricted markets of the U.S. It established a U.S. subsidiary called GrandMet USA Inc. to operate Liggett and three new units: Western Dairy Products, in California; Express Foods Inc., in Vermont; and Dry Milks Inc., in Kentucky. In Britain, Grand Metropolitan divested itself of marginally performing subsidiaries and peripheral companies.

Divestitures during the mid-1980s included CC Soft Drinks Ltd., a bottler and distributer of Coca-Cola in southern England, and Express Dairy. Proceeds from the sales were used to strengthen Grand Metropolitan's hotel and entertainment division, which purchased the profitable Mecca Leisure group. Entering the health care services industry for the first time, Grand Metropolitan acquired Quality Care Inc., a large home health care and medical equipment company, and purchased an interest in Pearl Health Services. Also, the Liggett unit was divested.

In 1987, RJR Nabisco sold Heublein Inc., including Smirnoff vodka, Arrow liqueurs, Harvey's Bristol Cream sherry, and Guinness Stout beer, to Grand Metropolitan for $1.3 billion. Allen Sheppard was appointed CEO. Believing that new opportunities in the health care services industry were minimal, Sheppard advocated the sale of Quality Care. The following year, the Intercontinental hotel chain was sold.

After acquiring Pillsbury, which owned Burger King, Green Giant, and Haagen-Dazs, in a hostile takeover in 1989, Sheppard implemented plans to focus on brand name products. Two years later, Grand Metropolitan sold its brewing operations to Foster's Brewing, forming a joint venture with Foster's to manage its 330 pubs under Foster's Courage subsidiary. In 1992, the firm's food sector sold two dairy businesses and bought a frozen food company. The beverages division bought the Greek distillery Kaloyannis Brothers and sold its 20% stake in E. Remy Martin and Cointreau.

Grand Metropolitan paid $2.6 billion for Pet Inc. in 1995 and began integrating Pet's products—including Old El Paso, Progresso, and Van de Kamp's—into a new line of Pillsbury Specialty Brands. That year, Pillsbury recalled all of its Green Giant frozen spinach products after packages were found to contain mice particles and fly larvae.

In 1996, the firm established a joint venture to convert 40 of Japan Tobacco's restaurants into Burger Kings and agreed to a venture with Chinese state-owned Qufu Distillery to form a joint distillery where Grand Metropolitan produced Smirnoff vodka and Gilbey's gin. Due to low profits, Grand Metropolitan began closing down its Burger King restaurants in France in 1997. The firm then announced plans to merge with Guinness PLC to form Diageo, the largest wine and spirits company in the world. The deal was completed in December of 1997.

History of Pillsbury Co.

In 1869, George Pillsbury and his son, Charles, purchased a struggling flour mill in Minneapolis, Minnesota. Twelve years later, they constructed a flour mill on the Mississippi river and named their flour product Pillsbury's BEST. The firm went public in 1927 as Pillsbury Co., and began trading on the New York Stock Exchange.

The firm held the first "Pillsbury Bake-Off" in 1949. By that time, its product line had expanded to include baking mixes, cake mixes, and frosting mixes.

The Officers

Chairman: Tony Greener

Group CEO: John McGrath

Group Director, Strategy: Jim Glover

Group Director, Corporate Affairs: Peter Lipscomb

Group Director, Finance: Philip Yea

Ballard Flour Co. was acquired in 1952, and the legendary "Pillsbury Dough Boy" ad campaign was launched in 1965. Non-food acquisitions in the 1960s included publishing and insurance operations. The firm also moved outside the U.S. for the first time. In 1967, Pillsbury diversified into fast food via its acquisition of Burger King.

Food assets were expanded during the 1970s as the firm refocused on food and divested peripheral holdings. Acquisitions included Totino's, a frozen pizza maker, in 1975; Steak and Ale restaurants in 1976; and canned and frozen vegetable maker Green Giant in 1979. Growth continued in the early 1980s with the introduction of Bennigan's restaurants and the purchase of ice cream maker Haagen-Dazs. In 1988, Grand Metropolitan PLC launched a hostile takeover bid for Pillsbury. Although the firm initially resisted, in December of that year, Pillsbury accepted a $5.75 billion offer. The deal was completed in January of 1989.

Market Forces Driving the Merger

In the late 1980s, Pillsbury was vulnerable to a takeover as a result of its costly expansion efforts during the early 1980s and several abrupt management changes in the mid-1980s. The firm's restaurant operations were floundering. Poor customer service, coupled with the stellar performance of competitor McDonald's, had plagued Burger King for years; an increasingly health conscious society was visiting Steak & Ale less often; and Bennigan's hadn't completed its transformation from a singles' scene to a family eatery.

Even Pillsbury's more lucrative operations weren't free of problems. The high-cost baking mixes division hadn't launched a blockbuster product in years; increased competition in the frozen fish market had undercut sales; and sharp price increases of Totino's frozen pizza had severely hurt the brand's sales. In 1988, Pillsbury earned a meager $69.7 million on sales of $6.1 billion. Share prices hovered at a paltry $35, and many analysts criticized the firm for "resting on its laurels."

The Players

CEO of Grand Metropolitan PLC: Allen Sheppard. A graduate of the London School of Economics, Allen Sheppard worked for two years as a college instructor. In 1958, he took a job at Ford Motor Co. as a financial analyst. Sheppard spent several years in the automotive industry, culminating in his appointment as marketing director at British Leyland in 1971. Four years later, Grand Metropolitan hired Sheppard to run its struggling brewery and pub operation, Watney's. He worked his way up to group managing director of Grand Metropolitan in 1982 and took over as CEO of the group in 1986 and as chairman in 1987. His major accomplishments at the helm of Grand Metropolitan included the takeover of Pillsbury in 1989. After being dubbed "the toughest boss" by London's *Sunday Times* and named a lord in 1994, Sheppard ended his 21-year career at Grand Metropolitan when he retired in 1996.

CEO of Pillsbury Co.: Philip L. Smith. University of Michigan graduate Philip Smith began his career at an advertising firm. In 1966, he was hired by General Foods, where he worked for nearly 20 years. After serving as president of the Maxwell House coffee unit, Smith worked his way up to the post of chief financial officer and, soon afterwards, president. In the early 1980s, he was slated to become CEO of the firm; however, in November of 1985, Philip Morris Companies acquired General Foods. Although Smith did become CEO of General Foods, he worked under Philip Morris chairman Hamish Maxwell. Wanting to head an independent company, Smith accepted the top spot at troubled Pillsbury Co. in October of 1988. His stint there was remarkably short-lived. Almost immediately, Pillsbury was faced with a hostile bid by Grand Metropolitan. Before stepping down, Smith was able to stave off the takeover for several months, which resulted in a purchase price 10% higher than the original offer.

According to an October 1988 article in *Business Week*, Grand Metropolitan CEO Allen Sheppard began eyeing Pillsbury after launching his plan to "shed the company's hotel roots and other sidelines and build a global liquor, food, and retailing titan." The firm had recently divested its Inter-Continental Hotels Corp.

for $2.3 billion and purchased Smirnoff vodka maker Huelein Inc. for $1.2 billion. If it could turn Pillsbury around, Grand Metropolitan would gain coveted access to the U.S. food and retail market.

Approach and Engagement

On October 4, 1989, Grand Metropolitan launched a $5.23 billion ($60 per share) cash offer for Minnesota-based Pillsbury. To reassure the Minneapolis community that it was committed to local development, Grand Metropolitan cast its bid from Minneapolis, rather than from its New York or London offices, and met in person with local officials and the press. Hoping to solicit white knight offers, Pillsbury rejected the bid as being too low, despite the fact that it was double the value of the firm's current trading price. Pillsbury also filed lawsuits, insisting that state laws banned a liquor maker like Grand Metropolitan from retailing food products.

Also in Pillsbury's favor was the fact that it had recently adopted a poison pill by issuing a new class of securities designed to make a takeover too expensive for most potential purchasers. Hoping to circumvent this problem, Grand Metropolitan filed a lawsuit to force Pillsbury to terminate its poison pill, pointing out that its premium, all-cash offer represented no threat to Pillsbury shareholders. An initial Delaware court trial ended on November 7 in Pillsbury's favor, with the judge finding that the firm need not redeem its poison pill while it considered which options would be best for shareholders.

The size of Grand Metropolitan's offer discouraged competitors from counter bidding, prompting Pillsbury to try another defensive tactic: promising to distribute a special dividend to shareholders after spinning off Burger King and other non-core holdings. Pillsbury stockholders shunned the idea and began tendering shares to Grand Metropolitan. The poison pill was still in place, however, so Grand Metropolitan declined the shares. Instead, it increased its offer to $63 per share and extended the deadline. In December of 1988, a second Delaware court verdict, this one in favor of Grand Metropolitan, forced Pillsbury to redeem its poison pill, and negotiations between the two firms were quickly finalized.

In the end, Grand Metropolitan agreed to pay $66 a share, or $5.75 billion, for Pillsbury, a price 10% higher than the original offer. The takeover was completed in January of 1989.

Products and Services

In 1998, Diageo (formed in 1997 by the merger of Grand Metropolitan and Guinness) operated in more than 50 countries in North America, Europe, and the

Pacific Rim, as well as in other regions. The firm was organized into four main segments: spirits and wine, packaged food, beer, and fast food.

Spirits and wine accounted for 43% of total sales in 1998. Diageo's liquor brands included Baileys, Bell's, Gilbey's, Gordon's, J&B, Johnnie Walker, Pampero, Popov, Rebel Yell, Smirnoff, Tangueray, and White Horse. The firm also distributed Jack Daniels, Jose Cuervo, and Wild Turkey and sold three main wine brands: Blossom Hill, Cinzano, and Glen Ellen.

The Pillsbury unit accounted for 31% of sales and oversaw the packaged food operations of Diageo. Pillsbury's refrigerated dough products were the best selling in the U.S. and its baking mixes were second only to General Mills. Other brands included Green Giant canned and frozen vegetables, Haagen-Dazs ice cream products, Hungry Jack frozen foods, Jeno's frozen pizza, Matha White baking mixes Old El Paso Mexican food products, Pappalo's frozen pizza, Pillsbury Toaster Strudels, Progresso Italian food products, and Totino's frozen pizza and snack items.

Beer brands, which secured 18%, included Alcazar, Draught Guinness, Enigma, Guinness Stout, Harp, Hoffmans, Hudson Blue, Keler, and Kilkenny. The fast food Burger King operations captured the remaining 7%.

Changes to the Industry

The takeover helped shape business law by establishing that a high enough all-cash offer could often force a company to redeem a poison pill. Although future legislation has increased the complexity of the poison pill issue with regards to an all cash premium offer, the Pillsbury acquisition remains a key case in merger and acquisition litigation.

Review of the Outcome

Under Grand Metropolitan's tutelage, Pillsbury began dumping non-core holdings and refocusing on food brands. Nearly 550 jobs were cut within six months of the deal's completion. Within a year and a half, Pillsbury's staff had been slashed by 23% and the following assets divested: Steak & Ale restaurants; grain merchandising holdings, including Azteca Corn Products; Bennigan's restaurants; Quik Wok restaurants; and Van de Kamp's and Bumble Bee seafood brands. In 1992, Archer Daniels Midland Co. and Pillsbury established a joint flour milling venture. Archer Daniels eventually took over flour milling operations, while Pillsbury continued to market the products.

By 1993, Pillsbury accounted for nearly 33% of total revenues at Grand Metropolitan. And within five years of the takeover, Pillsbury was only half its 1988 size, yet its $250 million in profits were more than threefold the $69 million earned in 1988. Foodservice operations, which had been transformed into a separate division after the 1989 takeover, had grown to $500 million in sales by 1994, compared to $100 million in 1989.

Besides shifting from commodity products to food products, the firm also moved "beyond its U.S. base into world markets" according to an April 1994 article in *Prepared Foods*. In 1992, Nippon Suisan Kaisha Ltd. and Pillsbury established Green Giant Frozen Foods K.K. in Japan. The firm also expanded into South Africa and Mexico during the mid-1990s. In 1998, Pillsbury bought Puerto Rico's Productos Kikuet, a refrigerated dough firm, and began moving into India in 1999 via a packaged flour operation.

Research

Collingwood, H. "Grand Met Shakes Up Pillsbury," in *Business Week*, 20 March 1989. Discusses Grand Metropolitan's integration efforts immediately following the takeover of Pillsbury.

Diageo PLC Home Page, available at http://www.diageo.com. Official World Wide Web Page for Diageo PLC. Includes product information, news, and corporate information.

Fusaro, Dave. "The Doughboy is Smiling Again," in *Prepared Foods*, April 1994. Offers an overview of the improved performance of Pillsbury five years after its takeover by Grand Metropolitan.

"Grand Metropolitan PLC," in *Notable Corporate Chronologies*, The Gale Group, 1999. Offers a history of Grand Metropolitan PLC.

Howard, Theresa. "Lord Allen Sheppard: Chairman, Grand Metropolitan PLC, London," in *Nation's Restaurant News*, January 1995. Details the career of Allan Sheppard.

Kirkland, R.I. "Grand Met's Recipe for Pillsbury," in *Fortune*, 13 March 1989. Explains Grand Metropolitan's plans to improve Pillsbury's performance.

Maremont, Mark. "Pillsbury Could Be a Grand Coup for Grand Met," in *Business Week*, 17 October 1988. Details why Grand Met is pursuing a takeover of Pillsbury.

Mitchell, R. "A Diet Doctor for the Doughboy," in *Business Week*, 8 August 1988. Offers a look at the vulnerability of Pillsbury to a takeover in the late 1980s.

———. "Pillsbury's 'Trust Me' Defense is Already ...," in *Business Week*, 21 November 1988. Details the defensive tactics employed by Pillsbury in response to Grand Metropolitan's hostile takeover bid.

"Pillsbury Co.," in *International Directory of Company Histories*, Vol. 13, St. James Press, 1996. Offers a history of Pillsbury Co.

Wasserstein, Bruce. *Big Deal: The Battle for Control of America's Leading Corporations*, Warner Books, 1998. Offers an overview of the largest mergers in recent American corporate history.

ANNAMARIE L. SHELDON

GTE & CONTEL

GTE Corp.
1255 Corporate Dr.
Irving, TX 75038
USA

tel: (972)507-5000
fax: (972)507-5002
web: http://www.gte.com

nationality: USA
date: May 1991
affected: GTE Corp., USA, founded 1918
affected: Contel Corp., USA, founded 1961

Overview of the Merger

After James Johnson took over GTE in 1988, he began refocusing the firm on local phone operations. GTE's $6.6 billion takeover of Contel Corp. in 1991 moved the company into the number one spot among U.S. local phone operators, and positioned it as the nation's second-largest cellular phone service provider, behind McCaw Cellular Communications Inc. Despite a purchase price that many Wall Street analysts found a bargain, the deal was viewed skeptically because it pushed GTE further into the cellular phone market, an industry that was considered risky, at a time when GTE hadn't yet completed its reorganization. The acquisition was the largest to date in the U.S. telecommunications market.

History of GTE Corp.

In 1918, John O'Connell, John A. Pratt, and Sigurd Odegard purchased the Richland Center Telephone Company (RCTC), serving 1,466 rural telephone users in Richland County, Wisconsin, for $33,500. The three men shared the belief that telephone service could be more efficiently provided if local exchanges were managed centrally. Two years later, RCTC was merged into the Commonwealth Telephone Company (CTC), a holding company. CTC immediately purchased three additional local exchanges.

Odegard, in conjunction with his two partners, set up Associated Telephone Utilities Company (ATUC) as a holding company. In 1926, ATUC absorbed CTC and launched an aggressive program of expansion in the West by purchasing the Associated Telephone Company of Long Beach, California. By 1929, ATUC managed 340 local exchanges, operating over 500,000 telephones in 25 states. At the time of the stock market crash, the company's revenues had reached nearly $17 million.

In 1930, ATUC established Associated Telephone Investment Company (ATIC) as a wholly owned subsidiary to support the parent company's continued acquisition program. One of the new company's first actions was to purchase large blocks of ATUC stock in an attempt to drive up the value. The campaign failed, and a loan of $1 million was arranged to help defray the company's debt. ATUC also faced financial difficulties, as telephone use fell by 16%, mainly due to the Great Depression. ATUC moved its headquarters from Chicago to New York City. In 1933, ATIC dissolved, and ATUC passed into receivership.

ATUC reorganized as General Telephone Corporation (GTC) in 1935, operating a network created by the consolidation of 12 telephone networks. The following year, GTC formed General Telephone Directory Company (GTDC) to publish directories for the parent company's entire service area. In 1939, GTC began listing on the New York Stock Exchange.

The firm secured huge government contracts during World War II, although the manufacture of telephones for civilian use was banned. War-related research and development projects gave rise to many discoveries with civilian applications, including coaxial cables and transistors. In 1950, GTC expanded into the manufacture of telephone and electrical equipment by purchasing Leich Electric Co. and Leich Sales Corp. By the early 1950s, the firm operated 15 telephone units in 20 states. Acquisitions included San Angelo Telephone Co.; Theodore Gary and Co., the second-largest independent telephone company and maker of telephone equipment in the U.S.; Anglo-Canadian Telephone Company; a majority interest in Compania Dominicana de Telefonos; minority interests in British Columbia Telephone Co. and Philippines Long Distance Telephone Co.; and Peninsular Telephone Company (PTC) of Florida. By the end of the decade, GTC operated more than 3.3 million telephones.

In 1959, the firm merged with Sylvania Electric Products to form General Telephone & Electronics Corporation (GT&E), while retaining the Sylvania brand name. The merger added 45 electronics manufacturing plants and annual sales of $333 million to the parent company's telephone service network. A majority interest in Lenkurt Electric Co. was also acquired that year. In 1960, GT&E bought a majority interest in British Columbia Telephone Co. GT&E Laboratories was formed to conduct research and development activities. Company stock split 3-for-1 that year.

Sylvania began full-scale production of color television picture tubes in 1963, and acquired contracts to supply electronic switching equipment to the U.S. Defense Department's global communications system. In 1967, GT&E acquired Hawaiian Telephone Co. (HTC). The firm also founded GT&E Data Services Inc. and divested itself of its interest in the Philippine Long Distance Telephone Co. IT&T filed an antitrust suit against GT&E, challenging the company's acqui-

The Business

Financials

Revenue (1998): $25.4 billion

Employees (1998): 120,000

SICs / NAICS

sic 4813 - Telephone Communications Except Radiotelephone

sic 4812 - Radiotelephone Communications

sic 3661 - Telephone & Telegraph Apparatus

sic 2741 - Miscellaneous Publishing

sic 3571 - Electronic Computers

sic 3669 - Communications Equipment Nec

naics 513322 - Cellular and Other Wireless Telecommunications

naics 513321 - Paging

naics 334418 - Printed Circuit Assembly (Electronic Assembly) Manufacturing

naics 334111 - Electronic Computer Manufacturing

sition of HTC, and eventually attempting to force GT&E to divest itself of all telephone companies acquired since 1950, as well as the electronics manufacturing operations of Sylvania. In response, GT&E countersued IT&T, claiming that IT&T had violated antitrust laws in its acquisition of telephone and electronics manufacturing concerns. Both suits were later dropped. The firm purchased Northern Ohio Telephone Co. (NOTC) in 1968.

In the early 1970s, GTE established GTE Satellite Corp.; moved corporate headquarters to Stamford, Connecticut; bought the Philco brand name; established a joint venture with AT&T to create satellites; and acquired television manufacturers in Israel and Canada, as well as a telephone company in West Germany. The firm reorganized in 1976, creating GTE Products Group to manage manufacturing and marketing operations, including all company activities outside the U.S., and GTE Communications Products to manage the operations of Sylvania Electronics, Lenkurt Electric, Automatic Electric, and GTE Information Systems. In 1979, GT&E bought Telenet Communications Corp., a leader in the field of packet switching technology, a precursor of the electronic bulletin board.

The Officers

Chairman and CEO: Charles R. Lee

Vice Chairman: Michael T. Masin

President: Kent B. Foster

Sr. Exec. VP, Market Operations: Thomas W. White

Exec. VP, Finance, and Chief Financial Officer: Daniel P.
    O'Brien

GT&E divested its consumer electronics businesses, including Sylvania and Philco, in 1980. Two years later, the firm changed its name to GTE Corp. and formed GTE Mobilnet Inc. to produce and market cellular phones and related equipment. Following the lead of AT&T, GTE broke down its operations along regional lines. In 1983, GTE acquired the long distance unit of Southern Pacific Communications Co. and Southern Pacific Satellite Co., which were renamed GTE Sprint Communications (Sprint) and GTE Spacenet Corporation (GTESC), respectively. The acquisition of Sprint made GTE the third-largest provider of long-distance telephone services in the U.S.

GTE embarked on a new corporate strategy in the mid-1980s, emphasizing the development of core businesses, including telecommunications, lighting, and precision materials. GTESC launched its first satellite, and the company offered its first cellular phone service. In 1985, GTE secured a $4.3 billion contract from the U.S. Army to develop a battlefield communications system called Mobile Subscriber Equipment (MSE). The following year, Sprint and GTE Telenet became part of US Sprint, which was equally owned by GTE and United Telecommunications. GTE purchased Airfone Inc., a domestic manufacturer of aircraft telecommunications systems, and Rotaflex PLC, a British manufacturer of lighting equipment. Stock split 3-for-2 in 1987.

The firm developed the first roaming cellular telephone service, which enabled users to receive calls from outside their cellular service area, in 1988. That year, GTE sold to United Telecommunications a controlling interest in US Sprint, retaining 19.9% of stock in the company. The following year, however, GTE sold its remaining interest in US Sprint to United Telecommunications, completing its exit of the long distance market. The firm then refocused on core local phone service and reorganized into six operating groups in an effort to streamline operations. In 1990, GTE introduced the first nationwide cellular phone network.

In 1991, GTE and Contel Corp. merged, forming a corporate giant worth $6.6 billion. One year later, GTE sold its worldwide electrical products operations to OSRAM, owned by Siemens, for $1.1 billion. The firm also launched World Class Network (WCN), which offered bundled services for data transmission. Revenues from cellular services grew 41%, as GTE secured 754,000 new cellular customers. GTE and SBC Communications Inc. agreed to market cellular services in each other's territories.

After the Telecommunications Act of 1996 was passed, GTE began again offering long-distance services. In 1997, the firm bought the Internet service provider BBN for $625 million and agreed to acquire MCI Communications Corp. for $28 billion. WorldCom Inc. outbid GTE, however, with a $37 billion offer for MCI. In early 1999, Bell Atlantic and GTE agreed to a $53 billion merger of equals. GTE also agreed to pay $3.3 billion for roughly 50% of the wireless assets of Ameritech Corp.

History of Contel Corp.

In 1960, Charles Wohlstetter bought TransAlaska Telephone Co. and incorporated the firm as Telephone Communications Corp. Within a few months, he changed his company's name to Continental Telephone Corp. A year later, Continental bought Illinois-based Millstadt Telephone Co. The young firm went public in 1962, and within a year, net income eclipsed $1 million. When Continental merged with Independent Telephone Corp. in 1964, it doubled in size and became the fourth-largest independent telephone company in the U.S.

Continental acquired Fort Kent Telephone Co. in 1965 and upped its operations to more than 550,000 phones. The following year, the firm became one of the youngest in history to be listed on the New York Stock Exchange. In 1967, Continental pioneered customer dialed person-to-person and collect calls. By the end of the decade, assets exceeded $1 billion.

In 1976, the company launched digital toll services in California; it was the first independent phone operator to offer such services in the U.S. Continental's first fiber optic cable was completed in Virginia in 1980. By then, the firm operated two million phone lines. Two years later, Continental Telephone changed its name to Continental Telecom and began using the Contel logo, which became the firm's official moniker in 1986.

A reorganization in 1985 resulted in the creation of four segments: Telephone Operations, Business Systems, Federal Systems, and Information Systems. Contel also activated its first communications satellite that year. In 1990, the firm bought cellular operations from McCaw Cellular and announced plans to merge with GTE. The blockbuster $6.6 billion deal was finalized the following year.

Market Forces Driving the Merger

GTE's purchase of Contel may never have happened if the firm hadn't been burned by its foray into the long distance market in the early 1980s. Its 1983 purchase of the long distance operations of Southern Pacific Communications Co. for $750 million in cash seemed a smart move at the time. GTE had pursued the Southern Pacific unit in the wake of deregulation efforts in the early 1980s, which led to the break up of the local AT&T monopoly. New rate structures had been put into place for all long distance companies, and MCI, Sprint, and other AT&T competitors would no longer receive discounts for access to AT&T lines. As a result, only the largest companies were likely to survive. This prompted a wave of consolidation in the telecommunications industry and precipitated GTE's move into long distance.

The purchase of Southern Pacific's long distance assets, which were renamed GTE Sprint Communications, made GTE the third-largest provider of long distance telephone services in the U.S.; however, they caused problems for GTE almost immediately. Consecutive billion-dollar cash injections in the unit in 1984 and 1985 failed to increase Sprint's long distance market share from a meager 4%. After posting a $1.3 billion charge in 1986 against its GTE Sprint assets, GTE agreed to merge GTE Sprint with U.S. Telecom, the long distance business of United Telecommunications, to form US Sprint, an equally owned joint venture. James Johnson took the helm of GTE in 1988 and launched a restructuring designed to refocus the firm on core local telephone operations.

After selling its remaining long distance holdings in 1989, Johnson began seeking a means of growing GTE's local phone operations, as well as its cellular holdings. Along with upping GTE's cellular operations by 28%, acquiring Contel would give GTE access to Contel's customer lines which were "tied into sophisticated digital switches." Rather than paying an estimated $500,000 per switch to upgrade its existing network, GTE would be able to "scrap plans for new switches in territories adjoining Contel properties," wrote *Business Week* in September of 1990. Additional savings could be achieved by consolidating overlapping customer service hubs and repair truck operations.

Approach and Engagement

GTE CEO Johnson approached Contel CEO Wohlstetter in May of 1990 about a possible merger of

The Players

Chairman and CEO of GTE Corp.: James L. Johnson. James Johnson, known as "Rocky" to his staff, became president and chief operating officer of GTE in 1986. Two years later, Johnson took over as chairman and CEO, a position he retained until 1992, when he stepped down and accepted the position of chairman emeritus. While holding the reins at GTE, Johnson began a restructuring program that included layoffs and refocusing on core local phone operations. He also led GTE's divestment of its long distance Sprint holdings—a move that proved ill-advised—and also steered the firm's $6.2 billion takeover of Contel Corp. in early 1991, a deal that many analysts dubbed a steal for GTE.

Chairman and CEO of Contel Corp.: Charles Wohlstetter. Charles Wohlstetter began working in New York's financial market as a runner for Wall Street in 1929. After the stock market crash, he moved into brokering. Wohlstetter pursued a screen writing career in Hollywood in the late 1930s, but soon gave that up to resume his financial dealings. In 1962, Wohlstetter founded Continental Telephone, which eventually became known as Contel Corp. and evolved into a group of 30 phone companies serving 30 states and the Caribbean. When GTE acquired Contel in 1991, Wohlstetter became vice chairman, a post he retained until his death on May 24, 1995.

the two firms. Wohlstetter's initial response was cool. In late May, just as his firm's stock reached a 52-week low, Wohlstetter revealed his intent to issue 14.5 million new common shares and use the capital raised to lower Contel's $3.5 billion in debt. Realizing that GTE would need to pay more for Contel if the new shares were issued, Johnson scheduled another meeting with Wholstetter on July 5, at which time GTE agreed to issue 1.27 shares of GTE stock, worth roughly $32.50, for each share of Contel stock owned. Wohlstetter canceled his planned share offering, and the deal with GTE was made public on July 12.

The $6.6 billion price, which included assumption of the $3.5 billion in Contel debt and valued Contel at roughly five times its cash flow, was substantially lower than the typical eight to nine times cash flow prices other telecommunications firms had been drawing. Shareholders criticized Wohlstetter for agreeing to such a low price, pointing out that Contel was significantly more profitable than GTE. Despite these complaints, however, the deal was completed in May of 1991. As part of the agreement, 10% of Contel's stock continued to trade publicly.

Products and Services

After divesting several Contel holdings during the 1990s, GTE served roughly 21 million local phone customers in 28 states in 1998. The firm also offered long distance services to 1.7 million customers nationwide; wireless phone services via its GTE Wireless unit; and air-to-ground services for airline passengers through its GTE Airfone subsidiary. The BBN unit provided Internet access, hosting, and related online services to clients. GTE Government Systems constructed command, control, and intelligence systems for government agencies. Local services accounted for 19% of total sales; network access, 18%; directory publishing, 11%; and external services, such as wireless services, 49%.

Changes to the Industry

By acquiring Contel, GTE gained 155,000 cellular phone customers and became the second-largest cellular provider in the U.S., behind McCaw Cellular Communications Inc. GTE also added Contel's 2.6 million local phone lines to its 18 million lines spanning 40 states and jumped into first place among U.S. local exchange carriers. As the largest merger in U.S. telecommunications history at the time, the deal heightened the pace of future consolidation.

Review of the Outcome

Investor concerns over Contel's debt, as well as GTE's major move into the seemingly unstable cellular phone arena, caused a 20% decline in GTE's stock in the two months following the merger's announcement. The trepidation that had surrounded the deal seemed valid, as two years later GTE was still struggling to service all of its new customers. State authorities in Virginia even launched an investigation of GTE local phone service in response to complaints. The firm's credit ratings were downgraded due to the assumption of Contel's sizable debt. In an effort to counter the ill effects of the deal, GTE sold Contel operations in nine states to Citizens Utilities Co. for $1.1 billion in 1993.

Because 10% of Contel still traded publicly, GTE was compelled by regulators to separate its GTE Mobilenet cellular operations from it Contel cellular operations. Wanting to combine its cellular operations as a means of cutting costs, GTE paid $250 million for the 10% stake in 1995.

Despite its struggles in the years following its purchase of Contel, by the late 1990s, most analysts viewed the deal as a positive one because it strengthened GTE local operations. An October 1998 article in *Business Communications Review* explained, "It may not have been clear back then just how crucial it would be for a carrier to hold an incumbent position in the local loop, but nowadays it's an article of faith: Since the passage of the Telecommunications Act of 1996, the real struggle is over control of the 'last mile.' Not only does GTE have this control, it has proved as adept as any RBOC in fighting to keep newcomers out of its markets."

Research

Gold, Jacqueline S. "GTE: Poor Connection," in *FW*, 26 October 1993. Discusses GTE's struggles since its 1991 takeover of Contel Corp.

"GTE Corp.," in *Notable Corporate Chronologies*, The Gale Group, 1999. Lists major events in the history of GTE Corp.

GTE Corp. Home Page, available at http://www.gte.com. Official World Wide Web Home Page for GTE Corp. Includes news, as well as financial, product, and historical information.

"GTE Raises Offer for Contel Cellular By 13% to $250 Million," in *The Wall Street Journal*, 28 December 1994. Explains why GTE decided to purchase the remaining 10% of Contel's shares.

Keller, John J. "GTE Will Sell Some Systems for $1.1 Billion," in *The Wall Street Journal*, 20 May 1993. Details why GTE is divesting some of its Contel assets.

Mulqueen, John. "GTE and the New Industry Realities," in *Business Communications Review*, October 1998. Explains the reasons for the merger between GTE and Bell Atlantic, and discusses GTE's sale of Sprint .

Vogel, Todd. "GTE: Right Moves, Wrong Results," in *Business Week*, 24 September 1990. Offers an overview of Wall Street's reaction to news of the merger.

———. "Maybe Contel Should Have Phoned Its Bankers," in *Business Week*, 30 July 1990. Discusses the price Contel accepted in comparison to the price typically paid for a U.S. telecommunications firm.

ANNAMARIE L. SHELDON

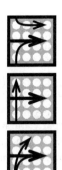

GTE & SPRINT

nationality: USA
date: 1983
affected: GTE Corp., USA, founded 1918
affected: Sprint Corp., USA, founded 1970

GTE Corp.
1255 Corporate Dr.
Irving, TX 75038
USA

tel: (972)507-5000
fax: (972)507-5002
web: http://www.gte.com

Sprint Corp.
2330 Shawnee Mission Pkwy.
Westwood, KS 66205
USA

tel: (913)624-3000
fax: (913)624-3088
web: http://www.sprint.com

Overview of the Merger

In 1983, GTE Corp. paid $750 million in cash for the long distance operations of Southern Pacific Communications Co., which it renamed GTE Sprint Communications. The acquisition made GTE the third-largest provider of long distance telephone services in the U.S., yet it caused problems for GTE almost immediately. Back-to-back billion-dollar capital infusions in the unit in 1984 and 1985 failed to up Sprint's long distance market share from a meager 4%. Consequently, GTE took a $1.3 billion write-off on its purchase of Sprint in 1986 and agreed to merge it with U.S. Telecom, the long distance business of United Telecommunications. Performance problems continued, and in 1989, GTE divested another 30% of Sprint to United Telecommunications, which purchased the final 19.9% of Sprint from GTE in 1992 for $500 million.

History of GTE Corp.

In 1918, John O'Connell, John A. Pratt, and Sigurd Odegard purchased the Richland Center Telephone Company (RCTC), serving 1466 rural telephone users in Richland County, Wisconsin, for $33,500. The three men shared the belief that telephone service could be more efficiently provided if local exchanges were managed centrally. Two years later, RCTC was merged into the Commonwealth Telephone Co. (CTC), a holding company. CTC immediately purchased three additional local exchanges.

Odegard, in conjunction with two partners, set up Associated Telephone Utilities Co. (ATUC) as a holding company. In 1926, ATUC absorbed CTC and launched an aggressive program of expansion in the West by purchasing the Associated Telephone Co. of Long Beach, California. By 1929, ATUC managed 340 local exchanges, operating over 500,000 telephones in 25 states. At the time of the stock market crash, the company's revenues had reached nearly $17 million.

In 1930, ATUC established Associated Telephone Investment Company (ATIC) as a wholly owned subsidiary to support the parent company's continued acquisition program. One of the new company's first actions was to purchase large blocks

The Business

Financials - GTE Corp.

Revenue (1998): $25.4 billion

Employees (1998): 120,000

Financials - Sprint Corp.

Revenue (1997): $14.87 billion

Employees (1998): 64,900

Share (1998): 10% of U.S. long distance market

SICs / NAICS

sic 4813 - Telephone Communications Except Radiotelephone

sic 4812 - Radiotelephone Communications

sic 3661 - Telephone & Telegraph Apparatus

sic 2741 - Miscellaneous Publishing

sic 3571 - Electronic Computers

sic 3669 - Communications Equipment Nec

naics 513322 - Cellular and Other Wireless Telecommunications

naics 513321 - Paging

naics 334418 - Printed Circuit Assembly (Electronic Assembly) Manufacturing

naics 334111 - Electronic Computer Manufacturing

of ATUC stock in an attempt to drive up the stock's value. The campaign failed, and a loan of $1 million was arranged to help defray the company's debt. ATUC also faced financial difficulties, as telephone use fell by 16% as a result of the Great Depression. ATUC moved its headquarters from Chicago, Illinois, to New York City. In 1933, ATIC dissolved, and ATUC passed into receivership.

ATUC reorganized as General Telephone Corporation (GTC) in 1935, operating a network created by the consolidation of 12 telephone networks. The following year, GTC formed General Telephone Directory Co. (GTDC) to publish directories for the parent company's entire service area. In 1939 GTC began listing on the New York Stock Exchange.

The firm secured huge government contracts during World War II, although manufacture of telephones for civilian use was banned. War-related research and development projects gave rise to many discoveries with civilian applications, including coaxial cables

and transistors. In 1950, GTC expanded into the manufacture of telephone and electrical equipment by purchasing Leich Electric Co. and Leich Sales Corp. By the early 1950s, the firm operated 15 telephone units in 20 states. Acquisitions included San Angelo Telephone Co.; Theodore Gary and Co., the second-largest independent telephone company and maker of telephone equipment in the U.S.; Anglo-Canadian Telephone Co.; a majority interest in Compania Dominicana de Telefonos; minority interests in British Columbia Telephone Co. and Philippines Long Distance Telephone Co.; and Peninsular Telephone Co. (PTC) of Florida. By the end of the decade, GTC operated more than 3.3 million telephones.

In 1959, the firm merged with Sylvania Electric Products to form General Telephone & Electronics Corporation (GT&E), while retaining the Sylvania brand name. The merger added 45 electronics manufacturing plants and annual sales of $333 million to the parent company's telephone service network. A majority interest in Lenkurt Electric Co. was also acquired that year. In 1960, GT&E bought a majority interest in British Columbia Telephone Co. GT&E Laboratories was formed to conduct research and development activities. Company stock split 3-for-1.

Sylvania began full-scale production of color television picture tubes in 1963, and acquired contracts to supply electronic switching equipment to the U.S. Defense Department's global communications system. In 1967, GT&E acquired Hawaiian Telephone Co. (HTC). The firm also founded GT&E Data Services Inc. and divested itself of its interest in the Philippine Long Distance Telephone Co. IT&T filed an antitrust suit against GT&E, challenging the company's acquisition of HTC, and eventually attempting to force GT&E to divest itself of all telephone companies acquired since 1950, as well as the electronics manufacturing operations of Sylvania. In response, GT&E countersued IT&T, claiming that IT&T had violated antitrust laws in its acquisition of telephone and electronics manufacturing concerns. Both suits were later dropped. The firm purchased Northern Ohio Telephone Co. (NOTC) in 1968.

In the early 1970s, GTE established GTE Satellite Corp.; moved corporate headquarters to Stamford, Connecticut; bought the Philco brand name; established a joint venture with AT&T Corp. to create satellites; and acquired television manufacturers in Israel and Canada, as well as a telephone company in West Germany. The firm reorganized in 1976, creating GTE Products Group to manage manufacturing and marketing operations, including all company activities outside the U.S., and GTE Communications Products to manage the operations of Sylvania Electronics, Lenkurt Electric, Automatic Electric, and GTE

Information Systems. In 1979, GT&E bought Telenet Communications Corp., a leader in the field of packet switching technology, a precursor of the electronic bulletin board.

GT&E divested its consumer electronics businesses, including Sylvania and Philco, in 1980. Two years later, the firm changed its name to GTE Corp. and formed GTE Mobilnet Inc. to produce and market cellular phones and related equipment. Following the lead of AT&T, GTE broke down its operations along regional lines. In 1983, GTE acquired the long distance unit of Southern Pacific Communications Co. and Southern Pacific Satellite Co., which were renamed GTE Sprint Communications and GTE Spacenet Corporation (GTESC), respectively.

GTE embarked on a new corporate strategy in the mid-1980s, emphasizing the development of core businesses including telecommunications, lighting, and precision materials. GTESC launched its first satellite, and the company offered its first cellular phone service. In 1985, GTE secured a $4.3 billion contract from the U.S. Army to develop a battlefield communications system called Mobile Subscriber Equipment (MSE). The following year, GTE Sprint Communications and U.S. Telecommunications, the long distance unit of United Telecommunications, merged to form U.S. Sprint, which was equally owned by each parent company. GTE purchased Airfone Inc., a domestic manufacturer of aircraft telecommunications systems, and Rotaflex PLC, a British manufacturer of lighting equipment. Stock split 3-for-2 in 1987.

The firm developed the first roaming cellular telephone service, which enabled callers to receive calls from outside their cellular service area, in 1988. The following year, GTE sold United Telecommunications a controlling interest in U.S. Sprint, retaining 19.9% of the company. The firm then reorganized into six operating groups in a effort to streamline operations. In 1989, GTE introduced the first nationwide cellular phone network.

In 1991, GTE and Contel Corp. merged, forming a corporate giant worth $6.6 billion. One year later, GTE sold its worldwide electrical products operations to OSRAM, owned by Siemens, for $1.1 billion. The firm also sold its remaining interest in U.S. Sprint to United Telecommunications and launched World Class Network (WCN), which offered bundled services for data transmission. Revenues from cellular service grew 41%, as GTE secured 754,000 new cellular customers. GTE and SBC Communications Inc. agreed to market cellular services in each other's territories.

After the Telecommunications Act of 1996 was passed, GTE began again offering long distance services (a market it had exited in 1992 with its divestment

The Officers

GTE Corp.

Chairman and CEO: Charles R. Lee

Vice Chairman: Michael T. Masin

President: Kent B. Foster

Sr. Exec. VP, Market Operations: Thomas W. White

Exec. VP, Finance, and Chief Financial Officer: Daniel P. O'Brien

Sprint Corp.

Chairman and CEO: William T. Esrey

President and Chief Operating Officer: Ronald T. LeMay

Exec. VP and Chief Financial Officer: Arthur B. Krause

Exec. VP, External Affairs, and General Counsel: J. Richard Devlin

Sr. VP and Treasurer: Gene M. Betts

of the Sprint holdings). In 1997, the firm bought Internet service provider BBN for $625 million and agreed to acquire MCI Communications Corp. for $28 billion. WorldCom Inc. outbid GTE, however, with a $37 billion offer for MCI. In early 1999, Bell Atlantic and GTE agreed to a $53 billion merger of equals. GTE also agreed to pay $3.3 billion for 50% of the wireless assets of Ameritech Corp.

History of Sprint Corp.

In 1970, Southern Pacific Communications Corp. founded a network to handle the communications of the Southern Pacific Railroad. Twelve years later, United Telecommunications (UT) established a subsidiary operation, U.S. Telecommunications (UST), to provide satellite-based long distance telephone service to businesses. In 1983, GTE Corp. purchased the communications network from Southern Pacific for $750 million in cash and renamed it GTE Sprint Communications (GTESC).

A federal antitrust suit forced AT&T to divest itself of its 22 local Bell Telephone companies in 1984, opening the telephone industry to competition. Many new telephone carriers emerged, hoping to take over a small portion of AT&T's former business by using the AT&T network. That year, GTESC began to lay fiber optic cables. UST president and CEO Bill Esrey announced that his company would establish its own fiber optic cable network in the U.S. and also pursue a merger with GTESC. Two years later, GTESC and UST

The Players

Chairman and CEO of GTE Corp.: Charles R. Lee. Charles Lee launched his career at United States Steel Corp. in 1964. After holding several financial and management posts there, he began working for Penn Central Corp. in 1971, where he worked his way up to the position of senior vice president of finance. He accepted a similar appointment at Columbia Pictures Industries Inc. in 1980, and he left that firm in 1983 to join GTE Corp. At GTE, Lee was named president and chief operating officer in December of 1988. Three year later, was appointed CEO and chairman, roles he officially took on in May of 1992.

Chairman and CEO of Sprint Corp.: William T. Esrey. Bill Esrey was named president and CEO of U.S. Telecommunications, the long distance unit of United Telecommunications, in the early 1980s. He steered the merger of GTE Sprint Communications with U.S. Telecommunications into U.S. Sprint in 1986, and he took the helm of the newly merged firm when the deal was completed. Esrey is credited for propelling Sprint's growth, helping it to maintain its third place spot among long distance telephone service providers in the U.S.

merged to form U.S. Sprint. GTE and UT each retained an equal interest in the new company and invested $2 billion into its development over the next two years. Soon after the deal was completed, Sprint introduced its "pin drop" advertising campaign and placed the first coast-to-coast call across the U.S. using its fiber optic network.

GTE began to withdraw its support from Sprint in the late 1980s. Although Sprint had doubled its customer base since its creation, it was beset with billing difficulties and other customer service problems. As a result, the firm established a 24-hour operator assistance service. Sprint also began offering toll-free calling to its customers. After completing construction of its fiber optic network, Sprint transferred the last of its services from the old lines maintained by GTE and UT.

In 1989, UT purchased 30.1% of Sprint from GTE as part of a campaign to devote more resources to Sprint's development. That year, Sprint won a contract to handle 40% of the federal government's long-dis-

tance business. The firm also acquired a 50% interest in Private Transatlantic Telecommunications Systems, Inc; formed a global marketing alliance with Cable & Wireless PLC of the United Kingdom; and won an ongoing court battle with AT&T, thereby gaining access to millions of customers whose long distance service could previously be provided only by AT&T; the ruling also enabled Sprint to maintain pay phones for the first time. Sprint secured a 50% share of the Hawaiian long distance market when it bought Long Distance/USA, a Hawaii-based firm with bilingual operators for handling calls between the U.S. and Japan.

The following year, Sprint acquired GTE's Telenet unit, which had been equally owned by GTE and UT. The firm also launched a new advertising campaign, featuring actress Candice Bergen. In 1991, Sprint entered into a three-year, $100 million agreement with the Securities Industry Assn. to provide voice and data communications services to its member brokerage and investment firms nationwide. British Waterways and Sprint forged a joint venture to establish a fiber optic network in the U.K. by using rights of way along the British inland canal network. By the early 1990s, Sprint had captured 9% of the $70 billion U.S. long distance telephone business, and accounted for nearly half of UT's annual revenue.

In 1992, UT purchased the remaining 19% of Sprint from GTE, adopting the unit's name for its entire operations. Sprint also established the first Telemail brand electronic messaging system in the People's Republic of China. The following year, the firm completed its TAT-11 fiber optic cable linking the U.S., Great Britain, and France. Its fiber optic network extended throughout Europe and the former Soviet Union, the Middle East, Japan, Hong Kong, and the Philippines.

After France and Germany relaxed international telecommunications regulations, Sprint forged a $4.1 billion pact in 1995 with Deutsche Telecom AG and France Telecom to form a global network offering service to customers outside their home regions. A year later, Deutsche Telecom and France Telecom purchased a 20% stake in Sprint for $3.6 billion. Sprint used the capital to fuel its nationwide personal communications (PCS) network effort. The firm also divested its cellular holdings and its Chicago-based local telephone operations.

In 1997, Sprint diversified into computer network services with its purchase of Paranet. Sprint invested $220 million in EarthLink Network for a $28 stake in the company in 1998. That year, Sprint merged its PCS assets into PCS Group, which it then listed publicly. Sprint's PCS operations extended to Hawaii in 1999 when the firm bought the Hawaiian operations of PrimeCo.

Market Forces Driving the Merger

When MCI gained FCC approval in 1969 to build a new phone line between Chicago and St. Louis, the AT&T long distance monopoly was dealt a blow. The door for long distance competition had finally been wedged open, and soon other competitors were entering the market. For example, Southern Pacific Communications Co. founded the long distance unit that would eventually become known as Sprint.

Deregulation efforts in the early 1980s, led to not only the break up of the local AT&T monopoly, but also to new rate structures for all long distance companies. MCI, Sprint, and other competitors would no longer receive discounts for access to AT&T lines. According to Bruce Wasserstein, author of *Big Deal: The Battle for Control of America's Leading Corporations*, "with new higher access charges, only those with a large enough customer base to sustain continued investment and guarantee sufficient return on investment had the strength to survive. Shaky operators began to look around for partners and a consolidation occurred." This environment prompted GTE to consider purchasing the long distance communications network from Southern Pacific Communications. Although the network was obsolete, its purchase would give GTE easements for laying new cable between major cities in the U.S.

Approach and Engagement

In 1983, GTE acquired the long distance operations of Southern Pacific Communications Co. for $750 million in cash. The operation was renamed GTE Sprint Communications. In 1986, GTE Sprint Communications and U.S. Telecommunications, the long distance unit of United Telecommunications, merged to form U.S. Sprint. GTE and United Telecommunications each retained an equal interest in the new company. Three years later, GTE sold 30.1% of its stake in the unit to United Telecommunications, who bought the remaining 19% in 1992.

Products and Services

GTE served roughly 21 million local phone customers in 28 states in 1998. The firm also offered long distance services to 1.7 million customers nationwide; wireless phone services via its GTE Wireless unit; and air-to-ground services for airline passengers through its GTE Airfone subsidiary. The BBN unit provided Internet access, hosting, and related online services to clients. GTE Government Systems constructed command, control, and intelligence systems for government agencies. Local services accounted for 19% of total sales; network access, 18%; directory publishing, 11%; and external services, such as wireless services, 49%.

Sprint relied on its nationwide long distance services for 57% of its revenue in 1997. Local services, offered to 7.5 million customers in 19 states, brought in 34% of the total. Directory publishing secured the remaining 9%. In 1998, subsidiary PCS Group offered personal communications services to customers. Global One provided wireless services to travelers and international corporations. Via its EarthLink holding, Sprint also offered Internet access to roughly 600,000 U.S. clients.

Changes to the Industry

The acquisition made GTE the third-largest provider of long distance telephone services in the U.S., yet it caused problems for GTE almost immediately. Back-to-back billion-dollar capital infusions in the unit in 1984 and 1985 failed to boost Sprint's long distance market share from a meager 4%. AT&T was simply still too strong a competitor, boasting an 80% market share. Consequently, GTE took a $1.3 billion write-off on its purchase of Sprint in 1986 and agreed to merge it with U.S. Telecom, the long distance business of United Telecommunications.

Despite the firm's speedy expansion from 2.7 million customers to six million during the next two years, performance problems, including customer service glitches, continued. In 1989, GTE decided it could no longer afford the capital expenditures Sprint required, and the firm divested another 30% of its remaining shares in Sprint to United Telecommunications. When Sprint's performance strengthened in the early 1990s, United Telecommunications exercised its option to purchase the final 19.9% of Sprint for $500 million in 1992.

Review of the Outcome

In hindsight, GTE's decision to sell Sprint was a poor one. By the mid-1990s, Sprint was firmly entrenched as the third-largest long distance telephone service provider in the U.S. with a noteworthy 10% market share. An October 1998 article in *Business Communications Review* called the sale of Sprint one of GTE's "most ill-advised moves" and pointed out that the firm had attempted to reverse its error in judgement by entering the long distance market once again in 1996. "The ink was barely dry on the Telecom Act when GTE became a reseller of WorldCom's long distance service."

Research

Goldblatt, Henry. "Why Sprint's on the Block," in *Fortune*, 2 February 1998. Discusses why Sprint is a likely merger candidate for the late 1990s.

"GTE Merges Sprint with US Telecom," in *Time*, 27 January 1986. Explains GTE's decision to sell Sprint to US Telecom.

"GTE Corp.," in *Notable Corporate Chronologies*, The Gale Group, 1999. Lists major events in the history of GTE Corp.

GTE Corp. Home Page, available at http://www.gte.com. Official World Wide Web Home Page for GTE Corp. Includes news, as well as financial, product, and historical information.

Mulqueen, John. "GTE and the New Industry Realities," in *Business Communications Review*, October 1998. Explains the reasons for the merger between GTE and Bell Atlantic and discusses GTE's sale of Sprint .

"Sprint Corp.," in *Notable Corporate Chronologies*, The Gale Group, 1999. Lists major events in the history of Sprint Corp., including its sale to GTE and subsequent divestment.

Sprint Corp. Home Page, available at http://www.sprint.com. Official World Wide Web Home Page for Sprint Corp. Includes corporate news; financial, product, and historical information; and annual reports.

Wasserstein, Bruce. *Big Deal: The Battle for Control of America's Leading Corporations*, Warner Books, 1998. Offers an overview of the largest mergers in recent American corporate history.

JEFF ST. THOMAS

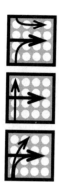

GTE SPRINT COMMUNICATIONS & UNITED TELECOMMUNICATIONS

nationality: USA
date: 1986
affected: GTE Sprint Communications, USA, founded 1983
affected: United Telecommunications, USA, founded 1899

Sprint Corp.
2330 Shawnee Mission Pkwy.
Westwood, KS 66205
USA

tel: (913)624-3000
fax: (913)624-3088
web: http://www.sprint.com

Overview of the Merger

Three years after it paid $750 million in cash for the long distance operation of Southern Pacific Communications Co.—which was renamed GTE Sprint Communications—GTE agreed to merge the unit with U.S. Telecom, the long distance business of United Telecommunications. The 1986 merger resulted in the creation of U.S. Sprint, which was jointly owned by GTE and United Telecommunications. Three years later, United Telecommunications purchased another 30% of GTE's Sprint holdings. In 1992, United Telecommunications took full ownership of U.S. Sprint when it purchased the final 19.9% of the unit for $500 million; the firm then renamed itself Sprint Corp.

History of United Telecommunications Corp.

In 1899, Jacob Brown founded, in Abilene, Kansas, one of the first independent (non-Bell) telephone companies. Six years later, Brown's son, Cleyson, founded Union Electric to sell telephone equipment. Long distance provider Home Telephone and Telegraph was established in 1910. The following year, Cleyson merged his firm with other phone interests and renamed his holdings United Telephone. Missouri and Kansas Telephone purchased a 60% stake in United Telephone.

The Union Electric unit was sold in 1925 to generate capital for telephone operations. That year, the firm incorporated as United Telephone and Electric. The firm continued growth via acquisition through even the Great Depression, but during World War II expansion ground to a halt. It wasn't until 1952 that United Telephone and Electric was able to make another purchase; the firm bought Investors Telephone that year. Cable television, satellite communications, and nuclear power became the company's focus during the next decade. Acquisitions included telephone equipment manufacturer North Electric and Automated Data Services.

In 1971, the company changed its name to United Telecommunications. Florida Telephone was added to the mix three years later. In 1982, United

The Business

Financials

Revenue (1998): $16.02 billion

Employees (1998): 64,900

SICs / NAICS

sic 4813 - Telephone Communications Except Radiotelephone

sic 4812 - Radiotelephone Communications

sic 3661 - Telephone & Telegraph Apparatus

sic 2741 - Miscellaneous Publishing

sic 3571 - Electronic Computers

sic 3669 - Communications Equipment Nec

naics 513322 - Cellular and Other Wireless Telecommunications

naics 513321 - Paging

naics 334418 - Printed Circuit Assembly (Electronic Assembly) Manufacturing

naics 334111 - Electronic Computer Manufacturing

Telecommunications established a subsidiary operation, U.S. Telecommunications , to provide satellite-based long-distance telephone service to businesses. Four years later, GTE Corp. agreed to merge its GTE Sprint Communications long distance unit with U.S. Telecommunications to form U.S. Sprint, jointly owned by GTE and United Telecommunications. GTE sold United Telecommunications a controlling interest of U.S. Sprint in 1989, retaining 19.9% of stock in the company. In 1992, however, GTE sold its remaining interest in U.S. Sprint for $500 million to United Telecommunications, which adopted the Sprint name for its entire operations.

History of Sprint Corp.

In 1970, Southern Pacific Communications Corp. founded a network to handle the communications of the Southern Pacific Railroad. In 1983, GTE Corp. purchased the communications network from Southern Pacific for $750 million in cash and renamed it GTE Sprint Communications. Although the network was obsolete, its purchase gave GTE easements for laying new cable between major cities in the U.S.

A federal antitrust suit forced AT&T to divest itself of its 22 local Bell Telephone companies in 1984, opening the telephone industry to competition. Many new telephone carriers emerged, hoping to take over a small portion of AT&T's former business by using the AT&T network. That year, GTE Sprint Communications began to lay fiber optic cables. U.S. Telecommunications, the long distance unit of United Telecommunications, announced plans to establish its own fiber optic cable network in the U.S. and also to pursue a merger with GTE Sprint Communications.

Two years later, GTE Sprint Communications and U.S. Telecommunications merged to form U.S. Sprint. GTE and United Telecommunications each retained an equal interest in the new company and invested $2 billion into its development over the next two years. Soon after the deal was completed, Sprint introduced its "pin drop" advertising campaign and placed the first coast-to-coast call across the U.S. using its fiber optic network.

GTE began to withdraw its support from Sprint in the late 1980s. Although Sprint had doubled its number of customers since its creation, it was beset with billing difficulties and other customer service problems. As a result, the firm established a 24-hour operator assistance service. Sprint also began offering toll-free calling to its customers. After completing construction of its fiber optic network, Sprint transferred the last of its services from the old lines maintained by GTE and UT. In 1989, UT purchased 30.1% of Sprint from GTE as part of a campaign to devote more resources to Sprint's development. That year, Sprint won a contract to handle 40% of the federal government's long-distance business.

In 1989, the firm acquired a 50% interest in Private Transatlantic Telecommunications Systems, Inc; formed a global marketing alliance with Cable & Wireless of the United Kingdom; and won an ongoing court battle with AT&T, thereby gaining access to millions of customers whose long distance service could previously be provided only by AT&T; the ruling also enabled Sprint to maintain pay phones for the first time. Sprint secured a 50% share of the Hawaiian long distance market when it bought Long Distance/USA, a Hawaii-based firm with bilingual operators for handling calls between the U.S. and Japan.

The following year, Sprint acquired GTE's Telenet unit, which had been equally owned by GTE and United Telecommunications. The firm also launched a new advertising campaign, featuring actress Candice Bergen. In 1991, Sprint entered into a three-year, $100 million agreement with the Securities Industry Assn. to provide voice and data communications services to its member brokerage and investment firms nationwide. British Waterways and Sprint forged a joint venture to establish a fiber optic network in the U.K. by using rights of way along the British inland canal network. By the early 1990s, Sprint had captured 9% of the $70 billion U.S. long distance telephone business and accounted for nearly half of UT's annual revenue.

In 1992, United Telecommunications purchased the remaining 19% of Sprint from GTE, adopting the unit's name for its entire operations. That year, Sprint established the first Telemail brand electronic messaging system in the People's Republic of China. The following year, the firm completed its TAT-11 fiber optic cable linking the U.S., Great Britain, and France. Its fiber optic network extended throughout Europe and the former Soviet Union, the Middle East, Japan, Hong Kong, and the Philippines.

After France and Germany relaxed international telecommunications regulations, Sprint forged a $4.1 billion pact in 1995 with Deutsche Telecom AG and France Telecom, forming a global network to offer service to customers outside their home regions. A year later, Deutsche Telecom and France Telecom purchased a 20% stake in Sprint for $3.6 billion. Sprint used the capital to fuel its nationwide personal communications (PCS) network effort. The firm also divested its cellular holdings and its Chicago-based local telephone operations.

In 1997, Sprint diversified into computer network services with its purchase of Paranet. Sprint invested $220 million in EarthLink Network for a $28 stake in the company in 1998. That year, Sprint merged its PCS assets into PCS Group, which it listed then publicly. Sprint's PCS operations extended to Hawaii in 1999 when the firm bought the Hawaiian operations of PrimeCo.

Market Forces Driving the Merger

When MCI gained FCC approval in 1969 to build a new phone line between Chicago and St. Louis, the AT&T long distance monopoly was dealt a blow. The door for long distance competition had finally been wedged open, and soon other competitors were entering the market. For example, Southern Pacific Co. founded the long distance unit that would eventually become known as Sprint. Deregulation efforts in the early 1980s, led to not only the break up of the local AT&T monopoly, but also to new rate structures for all long distance companies. MCI, Sprint, and other competitors would not receive discounts for access to AT&T lines.

According to Bruce Wasserstein, author of *Big Deal, the Battle for Control of America's Leading Corporations*, "with new higher access charges, only those with a large enough customer base to sustain continued investment and guarantee sufficient return

The Officers

Chairman and CEO: William T. Esrey

President and Chief Operating Officer: Ronald T. LeMay

Exec. VP and Chief Financial Officer: Arthur B. Krause

Exec. VP, External Affairs, and General Counsel: J. Richard Devlin

Sr. VP and Treasurer: Gene M. Betts

on investment had the strength to survive. Shaky operators began to look around for partners and a consolidation occurred." This environment prompted GTE to seek out long distance provider Sprint. What GTE perhaps didn't account for was the strength of industry behemoth AT&T, which held an 80% share of the U.S. long distance market throughout the 1980s.

The acquisition of Sprint made GTE the third-largest provider of long distance telephone services in the U.S., yet it caused problems for the firm almost immediately. Back-to-back billion-dollar capital infusions in the unit in 1984 and 1985 failed to boost GTE Sprint Communication's long distance market share from a meager 4%. Consequently, GTE took a $1.3 billion write-off on its purchase of the Sprint unit in 1986 and agreed to merge it with U.S. Telecom, the long distance business of United Telecommunications and the fourth-largest long distance telephone service provider in the U.S. The result, U.S. Sprint, would be better equipped to compete with AT&T.

Approach and Engagement

In 1986, GTE agreed to merge GTE Sprint Communications with U.S. Telecommunications, the long distance arm of United Telecommunications. The new firm, U.S. Sprint, would be jointly owned by both parent companies. Terms of the deal stipulated that United Telecommunications would pay GTE $230 million. United Telecommunication CEO Esrey was named president and CEO of the new operation.

When GTE decided to put its share of U.S. Sprint up for sale in 1988, United Telecommunication took advantage of its right of first refusal. The firm sold its cellular operations to Centel Corp. for $775 million to raise the capital it would need for the deal. In 1989, United Telecommunications bought 30.1% of U.S. Sprint; the deal included an option to purchase the remaining shares. After Sprint's cash flow and earning improved in the early 1990s, United Telecommunications paid another $500 million for the

The Players

Chairman and CEO of Sprint Corp.: William T. Esrey. Bill Esrey was named president and CEO of U.S. Telecommunications, the long distance unit of United Telecommunications, in the early 1980s. He steered the merger of GTE Sprint Communications with U.S. Telecommunications into U.S. Sprint in 1986 and he took the helm of the newly merged firm when the deal was completed. Esrey is credited for propelling Sprint's growth, helping it to maintain its third place spot among long distance telephone service providers in the U.S.

remaining 19.9% of Sprint. When the deal was finalized, United Telecommunications renamed itself Sprint Corp.

Products and Services

Sprint relied on its nationwide long distance services for 57% of its revenue in 1997. Local services, offered to 7.5 million customers in 19 states, brought in 34% of the total. Directory publishing secured the remaining 9%. In 1998, subsidiary PCS Group offered personal communications services to customers. Global One provided wireless services to travelers and international corporations. Via its EarthLink holding, Sprint also offered Internet access to roughly 600,000 U.S. clients .

Changes to the Industry

Despite U.S. Sprint's speedy expansion from 2.7 million customers to six million during its first two years of operation, performance problems, including customer service glitches, continued. In 1989, GTE decided it could no longer afford the capital expenditures Sprint required, and the firm divested another 30.1% of its remaining shares in Sprint to United Telecommunications. When Sprint's performance strengthened in the early 1990s, United Telecommunications purchased the final 19.9% of Sprint for $500 million in 1992. Recognizing that it had made a error in judgement, GTE attempted to reenter the long distance market in 1996 via a deal with WorldCom.

Review of the Outcome

What was considered one of GTE's biggest blunders was a boon for United Telecommunications. By the mid-1990s, Sprint was firmly entrenched as the third-largest long distance telephone service provider in the U.S. with a noteworthy 10% market share.

Research

Goldblatt, Henry. "Why Sprint's on the Block," in *Fortune*, 2 February 1998. Explains why Sprint is a likely merger candidate for the late 1990s.

"GTE Is Trying to Solve 2 Problems," in *Business Week*, 27 January 1986. Describes GTE's struggles with its Sprint unit, as well as the firm's problems with its communications equipment business.

"GTE Merges Sprint with US Telecom," in *Time*, 27 January 1986. Details why GTE decided to sell Sprint to US Telecom.

"Sprint Corp.," in *Notable Corporate Chronologies*, The Gale Group, 1999. Lists major events in the history of Sprint Corp., including its sale to GTE and subsequent divestment.

Sprint Corp. Home Page, available at http://www.sprint.com. Official World Wide Web Home Page for Sprint Corp. Includes corporate news; financial, product, and historical information; and annual reports.

Wasserstein, Bruce. *Big Deal: The Battle for Control of America's Leading Corporations*, Warner Books, 1998. Offers an overview of the largest mergers in recent American corporate history.

JEFF ST. THOMAS

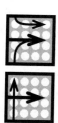

GULF OIL & CITIES SERVICE

date: August 6, 1982 (canceled)
affected: Gulf Oil Corp. (bought out by Chevron Corp. in 1985), USA, founded 1901
affected: Citgo Petroleum Corp. (formerly Cities Service Co.), USA, founded 1910

Gulf Oil Corp.
575 Market St.
San Francisco, CA 94105
USA

tel: (415)894-7700
fax: (415)894-0583
web: http://www.chevron.com

Citgo Petroleum Corp.
One Warren Place
6100 S. Yale Ave.
Tulsa, OK 74136
USA

tel: (918)495-4000
fax: (918)495-4511
web: http://www.citgo.com

Overview of the Merger

When Gulf Oil, the sixth-largest oil firm in the U.S., outbid Mesa Petroleum Co. with a friendly $63 per share offer for Cities Service, the 19th-largest U.S. oil company, it set in motion what would have been one of the largest deals in U.S. corporate history. The $5 billion agreement, inked in June of 1982, was exceeded in value only by the $7.2 billion DuPont/Conoco merger and the $6 billion purchase of Marathon Oil by U.S. Steel.

In August, however, Gulf pulled out of the deal, citing stringent restrictions by the U.S. Federal Trade Commission as the reason. Cities Service, which had paid Mesa Petroleum $225.5 million to repurchase its own shares, filed a breach of contract lawsuit that wasn't resolved until the late 1990s.

History of Gulf Oil Corp.

Backed by Pittsburgh's wealthy Mellon family, J. M. Guffey founded the J. M. Guffey Petroleum Co. in Texas in 1901. William Larimer Mellon ousted Guffey the following year, and five years later, the firm's name was changed to Gulf Oil.

The firm grew via exploration throughout the first half of the century. Major discoveries in both Louisiana and Oklahoma propelled it to a position among the leading U.S. oil players. Gulf ventured into Kuwait after World War II ended. When that country experienced an oil shortage in the 1970s, Gulf Oil's performance dipped. Rumors that Gulf had engaged in domestic and international government payoffs totaling $12 million circulated that decade. The scandal resulted in the resignation of chairman Bob R. Dorsey, as well as other executives.

In the mid-1970s, Gulf Oil decided to branch into other areas to reduce its reliance on oil. However, plans to buy insurer CNA were dropped when understatements of liabilities surfaced, prompting management's decision to hold off on diversification for a while.

In 1977, Gulf Oil paid $455 million for Kewannee Oil Corp. Two years later, the firm acquired Canada's Amalgamated Bonanza Petroleum Ltd. for $120 million.

The Business

Financials - Gulf Oil Corp.

Revenue (1998): $26.18 billion

Employees (1998): 39,191

Financials - Citgo Petroleum Corp.

Revenue (1998): $10.9 billion

Employees (1998): 4,500

SICs / NAICS

sic 1311 - Crude Petroleum & Natural Gas

naics 211111 - Crude Petroleum and Natural Gas Extraction

That year, Gulf Oil offered roughly $2 billion for Belridge Oil Co. The firm's bid, however, was topped by a $3.6 billion offer from Shell Oil Co. Efforts to acquire Tenneco were also thwarted by more generous bidders, and Gulf Oil's offer for Marathon Oil Co. was later abandoned.

Gulf Oil offered $5 billion for Cities Service in June of 1982, topping an earlier offer by Mesa Petroleum. Within two months, however, Gulf Oil backed out the deal, which prompted Cities Service to file a breach of contract lawsuit. Three years later, Chevron acquired Gulf Oil for a record $13.3 billion, becoming the third-largest oil firm in the U.S.

History of Cities Service Co.

Henry L. Doherty founded Cities Service Co. in 1910 as a holding company comprised of three large firms: Denver Gas and Electric, Spokane Gas and Fuel, and Empire District Electric. The new firm grew by purchasing smaller gas utility operations across the U.S., and in 1913, the firm acquired 53 utilities firms. A gas shortage prompted Cities Service to move into exploration in 1915.

After a unit of Cities Service discovered oil in El Dorado, Kansas, the firm established Empire Gas and Fuel to oversee oil production. Within two years, 1,000 wells were in operation. Cities Service served the military effort in World War I by upping its oil production for the tanks and aircraft that ran on the fuel. By the war's end, the company operated seven refineries, and oil refining and production had become one of its a major activities. Gas utilities spanned 20 states, and electric utilities customers numbered 144,000.

As the automotive industry took off in the 1920s, so did demand for petroleum. Although the Great Depression took a toll on the firm, utilities operations kept it afloat during the 1930s. The Public Utilities Act of 1935 ordered all utility holding companies to divest all but one public utility, and Cities Service began selling off its utility subsidiaries. During World War II, Cities Services operated its own tanker fleet, including 13 of its own ships and 18 government-owned oil tankers. The company also began production on what eventually became one of the world's largest oil refineries, in Louisiana.

By the end of the 1950s, Cities Service had completely exited the utilities sector and refocused on oil and gas. The firm adopted the Citgo brand name in 1960s and launched Citgo Premium gasoline. The chaotic 1970s, due to conflict in the Middle East, and a worldwide recession in the early 1980s left Cities Service vulnerable to a takeover. A hostile bid by Mesa Petroleum in 1982 was thwarted when Cities Service agreed to a higher offer from Gulf Oil Corp. When Gulf Oil pulled out of the deal, citing prohibitive Federal Trade Commission hurdles, Cities Service filed suit for damages and eventually won the case several years later. In December of 1982, Occidental Petroleum Corp. paid $4.3 billion for Cities Service to become the 12th-largest oil concern in the U.S. Cities Service began operating as a wholly owned subsidiary of Occidental.

In 1983, Occidental combined the oil refining and marketing units of Cities Service into Citgo Petroleum Corp., which was sold to Southland Corp. Three years later, Southland sold 50% of Citgo to Petroleos de Venezuela, S.A., the Venezuelan state-owned oil company, for $300 million. When Citgo paid $661 million for the remaining 50% of its own stock in January 1990, Petroleos de Venezuela gained full control of the firm. The following year, Petroleos de Venezuela folded its other U.S. unit, Champlin Refining and Chemicals, Inc., into Citgo; the subsidiary was eventually named PDV American, of which Citgo remained operating company.

Market Forces Driving the Merger

Gulf Oil's $2 billion bid for Belridge Oil Co. in the late 1970s was quelled by Shell Oil Co.'s $3.6 billion offer. Industry analysts pointed to the 1979 union of Shell and Belridge as the match that lit the intense consolidation fuse in the oil industry in the 1980s. The next major battle—which involved Conoco Inc., Dome Petroleum Ltd., Cities Service Co., and Seagram Company Ltd.—was eventually settled in September of 1981, when DuPont Co. paid $7.8 billion for Conoco, completing the largest merger in U.S. corporate history. These deals were fueled by a worldwide reduction in reliance on U.S.-based oil during the 1970s, which led to extraordinary increases in oil prices. The boost in prices upped cash flow for most major oil companies. The extra cash, coupled with the likelihood of future oil shortages, led to an ardent clambering for new oil reserves.

Cities Service was considered an attractive target because of its 10.6 million unexplored acres, 300 million bbl. in oil reserves, and three trillion cubic ft. in gas reserves. Like most other oil firms in the early 1980s, Cities Service had seen its North American oil and gas reserves decrease in the previous five years. In fact, they had plunged by roughly 29% despite increased funding of exploration. As a result, the firm's stock had dwindled to roughly $35 per share, leaving the board of directors, as well as shareholders, discontented. In 1981, Cities Service lost $49 million, despite raising its oil prices in the U.S. by 50%.

Although the firm felt confident that it had effectively defended itself against a $45 per share hostile bid by Mesa Petroleum in June of 1982 and wasn't actively seeking a white knight, the board let Gulf Oil know that it would consider a friendly offer. Gulf Oil had also seen its oil and gas reserves fall in the late 1970s and early 1980s. The acquisition of Cities Service would help to bolster reserves, at least on a short-term basis.

Approach and Engagement

When Gulf Oil offered $63 per share, or $5 billion, for Cities Service on June 17, 1982, Mesa Petroleum and Cities Service had been locked in a takeover battle for three weeks. Realizing that the Gulf Oil's bid was simply too high for him to top, Mesa Petroleum CEO Pickens relented. Later that month, he sold his 5% stake in Cities back to the firm for $55 per share. On June 22, Gulf Oil mailed its agreement to Cities Service shareholders, stating that it would pay $63 in cash for 51% of Cities Service stock and that the additional outstanding shares would each be redeemable for a fixed-income security.

In August, Gulf Oil terminated its offer for Cities Service, claiming that it was unable to meet the formidable restrictions posed by the U.S. Federal Trade Commission (FTC). "The FTC's settlement demand would involve very substantial costs to Gulf by reason of the divestitures and associated expenses which make the acquisition unacceptable from a financial standpoint," explained Gulf Oil in a prepared statement.

Within weeks of the deal's announcement, the FTC had secured a temporary restraining order to

The Officers

Gulf Oil Corp.
Chairman and CEO: Kenneth T. Derr

Vice Chairman, Worldwide Refining, Marketing, Chemicals, and Coal Mining: James N. Sullivan

Vice Chairman, Worldwide Oil and Gas Exploration and Production: David J. O'Reilly

Citgo Petroleum Corp.
Chairman: Luis Urdaneta

President and CEO: David J. Tippeconnic

Exec. VP: Roberto V. Mandini

Sr. VP and Chief Financial Officer: Ezra Hunt

Sr. VP, Supply and Marketing: W.A. Devore

block the deal due to its concern that the merger would limit gasoline marketing and jet fuel production and distribution competition in the Southeast and on the East Coast. However, most industry analysts believed that the FTC's requirements were reasonable and that the true cause of the transaction's dissolution was nervousness on the part of Gulf Oil over the price it had agreed to pay.

Products and Services

Three years after it reneged on its deal with Cities Service, Gulf Oil was acquired by Chevron Corp. and folded into the firm's petroleum operations, which accounted for 90% of total sales in 1998. Chemicals secured the remaining 10%. Operations included Gulf Oil Great Britain; a 50% stake of Caltex, an oil refining and marketing business; a 28% stake in natural gas operation Dynegy; Pittsburgh & Midway Coal Mining Co.; and a 40% stake in Kazakhstan's Tengizchevroil, an oil exploration company.

Cities Service, later known as Citgo Petroleum, operated 14,000 independent retail gasoline stations in the U.S. Along with gasoline, the firm refined and marketed jet fuel, diesel fuel, lubricants, heating oils, and waxes. Citgo also operated asphalt refineries in New Jersey and Georgia and crude oil refineries in Louisiana and Texas.

Changes to the Industry and Review of the Outcome

In August of 1982, after Gulf Oil rescinded its $63 per share offer for the firm, Cities Service found itself

The Players

Exec. Vice President of Gulf Oil Corp.: Harold H. Hammer. After working for a few years as a trainee for U.S. Steel, Harold Hammer established H. H. Hammer Inc., a management consulting operation, in the 1950s. While running his new firm, Hammer attended night school, eventually earning both an MBA and a law degree. In the 1960s, he worked as vice president of Control Data Corp., ultimately steering the company's purchase of Commercial Credit Corp. in 1968. Hammer left Control Data to become chief financial officer of Gulf Oil, and in the early 1970s, he was ostracized by upper management when company auditors revealed that the firm had taken part in domestic and international political payoffs. Hammer eventually secured the third-place spot of executive vice president at Gulf Oil and led the firm through a series of acquisitions in the late 1970s. He orchestrated the $5 billion offer for Cities Service, one of the largest deals in U.S. corporate history, in June of 1982. Gulf Oil suddenly backed out of the deal a few weeks later, and when Gulf Oil was acquired in 1985 by Chevron Corp., Hammer retired.

Chairman of Gulf Oil Corp.: James E. Lee. James Lee was appointed chairman of Gulf Oil in 1981. Along with executive vice president Harold Hammer, Lee directed Gulf Oil's $5 billion bid for Cities Service in June of 1982. After pulling Gulf out of that deal, Lee began steering his firm into exploration in Alaska, the Gulf of Mexico, and offshore California. Those efforts paid off when Gulf Oil was able to fully replace the U.S. reserves it pumped in 1984, nearly twice its reserves replacement when Lee took over. When it appeared that Mesa Petroleum was gearing up to launch a hostile takeover bid for Gulf Oil, Lee began searching for white knight offers. A wild proxy battle ensued, with Chevron emerging as the victor. When Chevron's takeover of Gulf Oil was completed, Lee resigned.

Chairman and CEO of Cities Service Co.: Charles J. Waidelich. Oil executive Charles Waidelich was named president of Cities Service in 1971. By the time the firm was locked in a battle for control with Mesa Petroleum in the early 1980s, he had succeeded Robert V. Seller as chairman and CEO. Waidelich successfully defended his firm against Mesa Petroleum by inking an agreement to be acquired by Gulf Oil in August of 1982. After that deal dissolved, Waidelich began searching for a new buyer. When Occidental Petroleum acquired Cities Service in December of 1982, Waidelich resigned.

reeling. Mesa Petroleum's earlier assault had spotlighted Cities Service's weaknesses, and the firm's options were scant. According to an August 1982 article in *The Washington Post*, the company had little choice but to "sell out to another firm—at fire-sale prices—or to sell its assets piecemeal and go out of business." Cities Service filed suit against Gulf Oil for damages related to the $225.5 million it paid to Mesa to repurchase its own shares after the deal with Gulf was announced. Also, many Wall Street brokerage firms suffered sizable losses on the stock they had purchase in anticipation of the deal.

In December of 1982, Occidental Petroleum paid $53 per share for Cities Service, which began operating under the Citgo name as a wholly owned subsidiary of Occidental. Cities Service's base of 22,500 employees was eventually slashed to a scant 4,000.

Chevron Corp., which acquired Gulf Oil in 1985 to become the third-largest oil company in the U.S., was fined $700 million in 1996 after a jury decided that Gulf Oil should pay $228.9 million plus interest to Cities Service for nixing its merger plans with the firm. Chevron appealed the verdict, but in March of 1999, a trial judge approved the judgment.

Research

"Chevron Files Final Brief in Cities Service Case," in *PR Newswire*, 11 May 1999. Explains the outcome of the lawsuit filed by Cities Service after Gulf Oil backed out of a merger agreement in 1982.

"Citgo Petroleum Co.," in *International Directory of Company Histories*, Vol. 4, St. James Press, 1991. Details the history of Citgo Petroleum Co.

Citgo Petroleum Co. Home Page, available at http://www.citgo.com. Official World Wide Web Home Page for Citgo Petroleum Co. Includes press releases, as well as financial, product, and investor information.

"Cities May Give Gulf Problems, Not Solutions," in *Business Week*, 5 July 1982. Predicts the outcome of the merger of Gulf Oil and Cities Service.

Cole, Robert J. "Gulf's Resident Merger Master," in *The New York Times*, 27 June 1982. Details the career of Gulf Oil's Harold H. Hammer.

Potts, Mark. "Gulf Oil Corp. Drops Bid for Cities Service," in *The Washington Post*, 7 August 1982. Announces Gulf Oil's termination of plans to take over Cities Service.

———. "Occidental May Make New Cities Service Bid," in *The Washington Post*, 18 August 1982. Discusses the struggles of Cities Service after Gulf Oil ended plans to take over the firm.

ANNAMARIE L. SHELDON

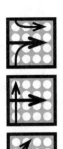

GULF + WESTERN & PARAMOUNT PICTURES

nationality: USA
date: October 19, 1966
affected: Gulf + Western Corp., USA, founded 1956
affected: Paramount Pictures Corp., USA, founded 1912

Viacom International Inc.
1515 Broadway, 51st Fl.
New York, NY 10036
USA

tel: (212)258-6000
web: http://www.viacom.com
e-mail: info@viacom.com

Overview of the Merger

Houston, Texas-based conglomerate Gulf + Western paid roughly $125 million for struggling film producer Paramount Pictures in October of 1966. Paramount formed the core of Gulf + Western's increasingly important entertainment assets. Twenty-three years later, after the firm had refocused on two core businesses—entertainment and communications—Gulf + Western adopted the Paramount name. Viacom acquired Paramount in 1994, and the firm began concentrating on a single industry: entertainment.

History of Gulf + Western Corp.

After experimenting in the import-export business, Austrian-born Charles George Bluhdorn began searching for a publicly traded company whose stock he could use to buy other companies. In 1956, he secured a controlling interest in Michigan Plating & Stamping and joined its board of directors. The next year, Bluhdorn merged Michigan Plating with Beard & Stone Electric Co., a Houston-based auto parts distributor.

In 1958, in deference to the company's location on the Gulf of Mexico and to Bluhdorn's belief that most of its growth would originate in the West, where automobile sales were rapidly increasing, the firm changed its name to Gulf + Western Corp.

Having acquired a number of private auto parts distributors and warehouses, Gulf + Western's annual sales approached $200 million in the mid-1960s. Bluhdorn embarked on a diversification campaign, and in just a matter of days, the company purchased a large amount of stock in New Jersey Zinc, a large mining and chemical company.

The struggling Paramount Pictures Corp. became Bluhdorn's next target in 1966. Gulf + Western acquired 23 companies in 1968, including Consolidated Cigar, E.W. Bliss, Universal American, Brown Co., and Associates Investment Co. Sales surpassed the $1 billion mark for the first time, reaching $1.3 billion and producing net income of $69.8 million. Five years later, Gulf + Western acquired Madison Square Garden.

The Business

Financials

Revenue (1998): $12.1 billion

Employees (1998): 111,700

SICs / NAICS

sic 4841 - Cable & Other Pay Television Services

sic 4833 - Television Broadcasting Stations

sic 7822 - Motion Picture & Tape Distribution

sic 7812 - Motion Picture & Video Production

sic 2731 - Book Publishing

sic 7996 - Amusement Parks

naics 513210 - Cable Networks

naics 513120 - Television Broadcasting

naics 512120 - Motion Picture and Video Distribution

naics 512110 - Motion Picture and Video Production

naics 511130 - Book Publishers

naics 713110 - Amusement and Theme Parks

In 1969, the company's fast-paced acquisition program ended when Wall Street analysts, congressmen, and the media charged Gulf + Western with manipulating accounting procedures to inflate its earnings. As a result, the company's stock dropped 30 points, costing shareholders $500 million and further reducing its dismal price earnings.

In 1975, Gulf + Western acquired Simon & Schuster Inc. The company's regulatory problems continued that year when the U.S. Securities and Exchange Commission (SEC) charged that the company's operations in the Dominican Republic illegally withheld over $38 million in profits owed to the Dominican Republic government. In 1980, the company reached a settlement with the SEC over this matter, whereby Gulf + Western agreed to pay $39 million over seven years to fund a social and economic development program in the Dominican Republic.

In 1978, as the company's poor public image continued, Gulf + Western spent $3.3 million to print its annual report in *Time* magazine, hoping to raise its price earnings ratio. The next year, the SEC initiated a second investigation, accusing Bluhdorn and executive vice president Don. F. Gatson of misconduct. Among its charges were allegations that the two executives allowed the company's pension fund to make "inappropriate" investments in companies where they

had personal investments. This investigation was settled in 1981, with no restitution called for under the terms of the agreement.

Bluhdorn died of a heart attack in 1983 and was succeeded as CEO by Martin S. Davis. Davis quickly streamlined the company's operations, focusing on the areas of entertainment and communications. Within months, Consolidated Cigar was sold, as were 50 other units, including operations in chemicals, concrete equipment, and mechanical presses.

Gulf + Western acquired the remaining 73% of Esquire, Inc., as well as the publishers Prentice-Hall and Ginn & Co., in 1984. Divestitures continued, and the company sold its consumer and industrial products to Wickes Co. for $1 billion in cash in 1985. Four years later, Gulf + Western changed its name to Paramount Communications Inc.. Also that year, the company made an unsuccessful bid for Time Inc.

In 1991, Paramount purchased the television station operator TVX, renaming it Paramount Stations Group, and started a pay-per-view programming and distribution venture with Capital Cities / ABC. It also purchased the Macmillan Computer Publishing division in late 1991 for $157.5 million. The company's revenues increased to $4.3 billion in 1992, due in large part to the success of such movies as *The Addams Family*, *Star Trek VI*, and *Wayne's World*.

Paramount began bypassing television networks in 1993 by taking its TV series, *The Untouchables* and *Deep Space Nine*, directly into the first-run syndication market. The following year, Paramount was the prize in a heated takeover battle between Viacom Inc. and QVC, and in July of 1994, Paramount was acquired by Viacom. Before the battle was over, Paramount acquired Macmillan Inc., thereby becoming the nation's second-largest book publisher. Viacom sold the reference and educational publishing operations of Simon & Schuster to Pearson PLC for $4.6 billion in 1998. The firm retained its profitable consumer publications businesses.

History of Paramount Pictures Corp.

In 1912, Adolph Zukor acquired the U.S. rights to *Queen Elizabeth*, a French Sarah Bernhardt film. After the movie debuted successfully at New York's Lyceum Theatre, Zukor established Famous Players in Famous Plays as a movie production business. Within a year, Famous Players was producing 30 films annually. Zukor and Jesse Lasky, owner of Jessie L. Lasky Feature Play Co., joined forces to create Famous Players-Lasky, an equally owned partnership, in 1916. That year, Zukor purchased a controlling stake in Paramount Co., the film distribution business that had been serving both Famous Players and Lasky since 1914.

During the next five years, the firm produced nearly two pictures a week. Famous Players-Lasky adopted the simpler Paramount name during that time and began making purchases in an effort to create a large chain of theaters. Zukor traveled to France and England in 1924, where he established the Paris Paramount and the London Plaza theaters. Also, Paramount's distribution unit began international expansion, opening studios in London, Berlin, and Bombay.

The number of theaters in operation reached 2,000 by the 1930s, and Paramount established the Publix Theaters division to house them. The firm also changed its name to Paramount-Publix. Paramount had funded its rapid growth by paying theater owners with Paramount stock, which could be cashed in on specific dates for a predetermined price. During the Great Depression, however, the firm was unable to pay what it owned on the stock. After extensive layoffs and salary cuts, Paramount-Publix declared bankruptcy in 1933.

Two years later, the firm emerged as Paramount Pictures, Inc. The success of Mae West comedies and Bing Crosby musicals boosted profits to $3 million in 1936. During the late 1940s, the U.S. government ordered Paramount to sell off its domestic theater assets. As a result, profits plummeted to $6 million in 1950, compared to $20 million in 1949.

In the early 1960s, a downturn in the feature film production industry took a toll on Paramount. After a brief stint producing television programs, the firm had exited that market. Efforts to lease old movies were garnering poor profits. As a result, dissident shareholders threatened a proxy fight in 1965. A year later, Gulf + Western paid $125 million for Paramount.

Market Forces Driving the Merger

Gulf + Western founder and CEO Charles Bluhdorn began seeking diversification for his automotive parts firm in 1965. After searching for a business with a sizable cash reservoir—necessary for future acquisitions—Bluhdorn settled on New Jersey Zinc, a mining and chemical firm whose managers and controlling owners were disputing how to best spend a large cash accumulation. Via an $84 million loan from Chase Manhattan Bank, Bluhdorn purchased a controlling stake in the firm. He decided the surplus cash would be best spent purchasing, on the cheap, companies with assets that were likely undervalued. Gulf + Western could then borrow heavily against those assets and use the funding for future acquisitions.

The Officers

Chairman and CEO: Sumner M. Redstone

Deputy Chairman and Exec. VP: Philippe P. Dauman

Deputy Chairman and Exec. VP: Thomas E. Dooley

Chairman and CEO of the Blockbuster Entertainment Group: John F. Antioco

Chairman and CEO of Simon & Schuster: Jonathan Newcomb

In 1966, Paramount Pictures emerged as an attractive target. Although the firm had been struggling with its feature film production operations—like most large movie businesses in the mid-1960s—Paramount's considerable real estate holdings and downtown movie theaters in Canada were quite valuable. Also, Paramount was receptive to being acquired by a larger firm because such a deal would likely "eliminate the possible threats of any more proxy fights. Paramount could concentrate on its job of making movies under the protective umbrella of highly successful Gulf & Western," wrote *The Wall Street Journal* on July 5, 1966, calling the merger a "major effort to revitalize Paramount."

Approach and Engagement

Although Gulf + Western CEO Charles Bluhdorn joined the board of Paramount Pictures on March 24, 1966, his firm didn't being began its actual dealings with Paramount until the following month when it purchased 143,000 shares, or a 9% stake, in the movie company from two dissident directors, Herbert J. Siegel and Ernest H. Martin, who then resigned. Gulf + Western paid $83 per share, $9.50 higher than Paramount's closing price of $73.50 a few days earlier, to become the largest shareholder of Paramount. Gulf + Western president John H. Duncan and executive vice president David N. Judelson replaced Siegel and Martin.

In June, Gulf + Western acquired another 50,000 Paramount shares, upping its stake in the firm to 12%. Three months later, a group of Chicago investors sold 108,427 shares of Paramount stock to Gulf + Western for $80 apiece. The transaction left Gulf + Western with an 18.5% stake in Paramount (301,427 shares). It was then that the two firm announced their intended stock swap, in which each Paramount share would be exchanged for 1.458 Gulf + Western shares, .389 of a Gulf + Western Series B cumulative convertible preferred share, and .21 of a new Gulf + Western sinking fund cumulative preferred share.

The Players

Founder and CEO of Gulf + Western Corp.: Charles George Bluhdorn. Austrian immigrant Charles Bluhdorn began his U.S. career by importing coffee from Brazil and Africa. After his business, Fortune Coffee Co., suffered from the instability in the coffee industry, Bluhdorn began seeking a business operating in a less cyclical market. Intrigued by the burgeoning automotive parts industry, Bluhdorn bought a controlling stake in Michigan Plating & Stamping Co. in 1956, securing for himself a spot on the firm's board of directors. Bluhdorn spent the next several years overseeing his businesses (renamed Gulf + Western in 1958). When Gulf + Western took over Paramount Pictures in 1966, Bluhdorn named himself chairman of that firm. In the 1970s, a U.S. Securities and Exchange Commission charged Bluhdorn and executive vice president Don. F. Gatson with misconduct, alleging that they had allowed the company's pension fund to make "inappropriate" investments in companies in which the two executives had made personal investments. The case was later dropped. While flying home from a business trip in 1983, the 56-year-old Bluhdorn died of a heart attack.

Exec. Vice President of Paramount Pictures Corp.: George Weltner. In 1965, Paramount's executive vice president, George Weltner, spearheaded a proxy battle to overthrow current management, including chairman Barney Balaban, who had led the company for 30 years. The move was successful in that it prompted Gulf + Western to launch a takeover bid for Paramount.

Paramount shareholder Pauline Low publicly opposed the merger, filing a lawsuit which alleged the deal was "unfair" to stockholders. Within a few days, the case had been dismissed by a New York state judge. Shareholders of both firms approved the deal on October 19, and Paramount began operating as a subsidiary of Gulf + Western.

Products and Services

In 1998, Paramount's parent, Viacom, operated in six business segments:

Entertainment housed the company's operations in the production and distribution of motion pictures and television programming, as well as its television stations, international channels, movie theater operations, and music publishing. This segment was comprised of Paramount Pictures, Paramount Television, Spelling Entertainment Group Inc., and the Paramount Stations Group. It generated revenues of $4.8 billion.

Networks encompassed basic cable and premium subscription television program services. Channels included MTV, MTV2, Nickelodeon, Nick at Nite, Nick at Nite's TV Land, VH1, Showtime, The Movie Channel, and Flix. This segment also held the company's interests in Comedy Central, Sundance Channel, and UPN (United Paramount Network). Total revenues for the segment reached $2.6 billion in 1998.

The **Video** segment consisted of Blockbuster Video, a retailer in home videos and games; it produced $3.9 billion in 1998 revenues. The **Parks** segment, comprised of the five regional Paramount Parks, achieved $421 million in revenues. **Publishing** encompassed such consumer publishing imprints as Simon & Schuster, Pocket Books, Scribner, and The Free Press; this unit generated sales of $564 million. Finally, **Viacom Online Services**, the company's interactive businesses, produced revenues of $13.7 million.

Changes to the Industry

Paramount formed the core of Gulf + Western's entertainment assets, which eventually became the conglomerate's most important operations. In 1989, twenty-three years after the merger with Paramount, Gulf + Western changed its name to Paramount Communications Inc. Under the auspices of Martin Davis, the firm had refocused on two core businesses: entertainment and communications. In 1994, entertainment giant Viacom acquired Paramount, tightening focus further to core entertainment assets.

Review of the Outcome

The $125 million purchase of Paramount boosted Gulf + Western into the ranks of the nation's top manufacturing companies. Sales that year increased from $180 million to nearly $450 million, and earnings nearly tripled. Near bankruptcy at the time of the merger, Paramount benefitted from the deal as well; the movie company posted record high box office revenues in 1972.

Research

"Gulf & Western Gains 2 More Seats on Board of Paramount Picture," in *The Wall Street Journal*, 19 April 1966. Explains why two Gulf + Western executives replaced two Paramount board members.

"Gulf + Western, Inc.," in *International Directory of Company Histories*, Vol. I, St. James Press, 1988. Offers a detailed history of Gulf + Western, Inc.

"Gulf & Western Purchases 108,427 Paramount Shares," in *The Wall Street Journal*, 14 September 1966. Details Gulf + Western's increasing control of Paramount.

"Gulf & Western Says It Has Raised Holding in Paramount to 12%," in *The Wall Street Journal*, 30 June 1966. Details Gulf + Western's increasing control of Paramount.

"Holders Vote Merger of Paramount Pictures into Gulf + Western," in *The Wall Street Journal*, 20 October 1966. Announces shareholder approval for the deal; details terms of the transaction.

"Paramount Holder Loses Court Bid to Bar Merger," in *The Wall Street Journal*, 18 October 1966. Explains the lawsuit filed by an angry shareholder hoping to block the merger, as well a judge's dismissal of the case.

"Paramount Pictures Corp.," in *International Directory of Company Histories*, Vol. II, St. James Press, 1989. Offers a detailed history of Paramount Pictures Corp.

"Paramount Says Merger Formula Allows Highest Payment to Shareholder," in *The Wall Street Journal*, 4 October 1966. Details the financial terms of the stock swap agreement.

Penn, Stanley. "Revitalizing Paramount Pictures Is Main Gulf & Western Aim After Merger in Fall," in *The Wall Street Journal*, 5 July 1966. Describes the reasons for the merger between Gulf + Western and Paramount.

"Two Dissidents at Paramount Sell Stock, Quit Board," in *The Wall Street Journal*, 18 April 1966. Covers Gulf + Western's first purchase of Paramount stock.

Viacom International Inc. Home Page, available at http://www.viacom.com. Official World Wide Web Page for Viacom. Includes a description of operations, news releases, executive biographies, annual reports, investor information, and links to company home pages.

—ANNAMARIE L. SHELDON

GULF + WESTERN & PRENTICE-HALL

Viacom International Inc.
1515 Broadway, 51st Fl.
New York, NY 10036
USA

tel: (212)258-6000
web: http://www.viacom.com
e-mail: info@viacom.com

nationality: USA
date: December 21, 1984
affected: Gulf + Western Corp., USA, founded 1956
affected: Prentice-Hall, Inc., USA, founded 1913

Overview of the Acquisition

In December of 1984, Gulf + Western paid $710 million for Prentice-Hall, the largest college textbook publisher in the U.S., climbing over the back of McGraw-Hill, Inc. to become the nation's leading publisher. Already a sizable contender in the publishing industry, thanks to its purchase of Simon & Schuster in 1975, Gulf + Western posted roughly $4 billion in annual sales prior to the deal. Adding the $500 million in yearly revenues of Prentice-Hall nearly doubled the publishing operations of Gulf + Western, a conglomerate in the midst of refocusing operations on two core businesses: communications and entertainment.

History of Gulf + Western Corp.

After experimenting in the import-export business, Austrian-born Charles George Bluhdorn began searching for a publicly traded company whose stock he could use to buy other companies. In 1956, he secured a controlling interest in Michigan Plating & Stamping and joined its board of directors. The next year, Bluhdorn merged Michigan Plating with Beard & Stone Electric Co., a Houston-based auto parts distributor.

In 1958, in deference to the company's location on the Gulf of Mexico and to Bluhdorn's belief that most of its growth would originate in the West, where automobile sales were rapidly increasing, the firm changed its name to Gulf + Western Corp.

Having acquired a number of private auto parts distributors and warehouses, Gulf + Western's annual sales approached $200 million in the mid-1960s. Bluhdorn embarked on a diversification campaign, and in just a matter of days, the company purchased a large amount of stock in New Jersey Zinc, a large mining and chemical company.

The struggling Paramount Pictures Corp. became Bluhdorn's next target. Paying $125 million for the movie company in 1966, Gulf + Western immediately became one of the nation's top manufacturing companies. Sales that year increased from $180 million to nearly $300 million—almost tripling earnings to $17 million.

Gulf + Western acquired 23 companies in 1968, including Consolidated Cigar, E.W. Bliss, Universal American, Brown Co., and Associates Investment Co. Sales surpassed the $1 billion mark for the first time, reaching $1.3 billion and producing a net income of $69.8 million. Paramount became a success story. Nearly bankrupt when purchased, it recorded its highest box-office revenues in history during 1972. Five years later, Gulf + Western acquired Madison Square Garden.

In 1969, the company's fast-paced acquisition program ended when Wall Street analysts, congressmen, and the media charged Gulf + Western with manipulating accounting procedures to inflate its earnings. As a result, the company's stock dropped 30 points, costing shareholders $500 million and further reducing its dismal price earnings.

In 1975, Gulf + Western acquired Simon & Schuster Inc. The company's regulatory problems continued that year when the U.S. Securities and Exchange Commission (SEC) charged that the company's operations in the Dominican Republic illegally withheld over $38 million in profits owed to the Dominican Republic government. In 1980, the company reached a settlement with the SEC over this matter, whereby Gulf + Western agreed to pay $39 million over seven years in order to fund a social and economic development program in the Dominican Republic.

In 1978, as the company's poor public image continued, Gulf + Western spent $3.3 million to print its annual report in *Time* magazine, hoping to raise its price earnings ratio. The next year, the SEC initiated a second investigation, accusing Bluhdorn and executive vice president Don. F. Gatson of misconduct. Among its charges were allegations that the two executives allowed the company's pension fund to make "inappropriate" investments in companies where they had personal investments. This investigation was settled in 1981, with no restitution called for under the terms of the agreement.

Bluhdorn died of a heart attack in 1983, and was succeeded as CEO by Martin S. Davis. Davis quickly streamlined the company's operations and focused on the areas of entertainment and communications. Within months, Consolidated Cigar was sold, as were 50 other units, including operations in chemicals, concrete equipment, and mechanical presses.

Gulf + Western acquired the remaining 73% of Esquire, Inc., as well as the publishers Prentice-Hall and Ginn & Co., in 1984. Divestitures continued, and the company sold its consumer and industrial products to Wickes Co. for $1 billion in cash in 1985. Four

The Business

Financials

Revenue (1998): $12.1 billion

Employees (1998): 111,700

SICs / NAICS

sic 4841 - Cable & Other Pay Television Services

sic 4833 - Television Broadcasting Stations

sic 7822 - Motion Picture & Tape Distribution

sic 7812 - Motion Picture & Video Production

sic 2731 - Book Publishing

sic 7996 - Amusement Parks

naics 513210 - Cable Networks

naics 513120 - Television Broadcasting

naics 512120 - Motion Picture and Video Distribution

naics 512110 - Motion Picture and Video Production

naics 511130 - Book Publishers

naics 713110 - Amusement and Theme Parks

years later, Gulf + Western changed its name toParamount Communications Inc. Also that year, the company made an unsuccessful bid for Time Inc.

In 1991, Paramount purchased the television station operator TVX, renaming it Paramount Stations Group, and started a pay-per-view programming and distribution venture with Capital Cities/ABC. It also purchased the Macmillan Computer Publishing division in late 1991 for $157.5 million. The company's revenues increased to $4.3 billion in 1992, due in large part to the success of such movies as *The Addams Family*, *Star Trek VI*, and *Wayne's World*.

Paramount began bypassing television networks in 1993 by taking its TV series, *The Untouchables* and *Deep Space Nine*, directly into the first-run syndication market. The following year, Paramount was the prize in a heated takeover battle between Viacom Inc. and QVC, and in July of 1994, Paramount was acquired by Viacom. Before the battle was over, Paramount acquired Macmillan Inc., thereby becoming the nation's second-largest book publisher. Viacom sold the reference and educational publishing operations of Simon & Schuster to Pearson PLC for $4.6 billion in 1998. The firm retained its profitable consumer publications businesses.

The Officers

Chairman and CEO: Sumner M. Redstone

Deputy Chairman and Exec. VP: Philippe P. Dauman

Deputy Chairman and Exec. VP: Thomas E. Dooley

Chairman and CEO of the Blockbuster Entertainment
    Group: John F. Antioco

Chairman and CEO of Simon & Schuster: Jonathan
    Newcomb

History of Prentice-Hall, Inc.

New York University professor Charles Gerstenberg and his student, Richard Ettinger, founded Prentice-Hall in 1913. The firm eventually grew into the leading publisher of college textbooks in the U.S. Sales had neared the $500 million mark by the mid-1980s, when Prentice-Hall moved into personal computer software and personal computer book publishing. In December of 1984, Gulf + Western purchased the firm for $710 million, merging it into its Simon & Schuster publishing unit. Pearson bought Simon & Schuster's educational and reference publishing assets, including Prentice-Hall, in 1998.

Market Forces Driving the Acquisition

In the decade prior to Gulf + Western's bid for Prentice-Hall, a wave of consolidation had swept through the publishing and entertainment industries. Gulf + Western made its first major move into publishing when it took over Simon & Schuster in 1975. MCA, Inc. bought Putnam; Hearst Corp. acquired William Morrow; and Harper & Row purchased J.B. Lippincott. In early 1984, Macmillan, Inc. snagged Scriber Book Cos. and Random House Inc. added to its mix the book publishing operations of New York Times Co.. Early that year, Gulf + Western paid $180 million for the 73% of textbook publisher Esquire Inc. it didn't already own and $100 million for Ginn & Co.

It was in this consolidation happy environment that Gulf + Western first approached Prentice-Hall. According to a November 1984 article in *Newsweek*, acquiring the college textbook publisher was "part of Martin Davis's grand plan to reshape Gulf + Western. While Charlie Bluhdorn snatched up firms manufacturing everything from auto parts to mattresses and built a large stock portfolio, Davis wants to concentrate on the firm's entertainment and communications group, using Paramount Picture and Simon and Schuster as a base."

Acquiring the nation's largest textbook publisher would give Gulf + Western the leading position in the industry's most profitable segment. The firm would also gain entrance to promising new niche markets, such as education and business software publishing and information publishing for data banks. According to Martin Davis in a letter sent to Prentice-Hall, the deal would allow his firm to become "a major force in virtually every important segment of the book publishing business."

Approach and Engagement

Gulf + Western made its first swipe at Prentice-Hall in September of 1993 when CEO Martin Davis offered $60 per share for the 12.5% stake owned by majority shareholder Richard P. Ettinger, Jr. When Ettinger, son of Prentice-Hall's cofounder, refused to sell, Davis attempted to purchase the company outright via a $63.78 per share offer made by a third party.

On November 5, 1984, Davis and Prentice-Hall president Donald Schaefer met for the first time to discuss a merger deal. Despite Schaefer's reluctance to consider a takeover, which Davis initially pitched at $68 per share, later that day Gulf + Western launched a $70 per share, or $695.3 million, cash tender offer for the 10 million outstanding shares of Prentice-Hall. The bid reflected a significant premium over Prentice-Hall's current share price of $45; however, the firm's stock jumped to $70 upon the deal's announcement. Gulf + Western agreed to allow Prentice-Hall management to remain in place, operating the publisher as a separate entity.

Prentice-Hall's board of directors rejected the offer on November 8, finding it too low. The firm also took defensive measures, such as upping dividends and instituting "golden parachute" contracts—sizable payments which would be activated by a change in managerial control—for its highest executives.

On November 26, Prentice-Hall agreed to Gulf + Western's increased bid of $71 per share, or $710 million. By December 10, the expiration date of the tender offer, shareholders had tendered 95% of their common shares to Gulf + Western. The transaction was completed on December 21.

Products and Services

In 1998, Viacom, parent of Paramount (formerly Gulf + Western), operated in six business segments:

Publishing encompassed such consumer publishing imprints as Simon & Schuster, Pocket Books, Scribner, and The Free Press. Prentice-Hall had recently been divested when the firm sold off its reference and educational publishing operations. This unit generated sales of $564 million in 1998.

Entertainment housed the company's operations in the production and distribution of motion pictures and television programming, as well as its television stations, international channels, movie theater operations, and music publishing. This segment was comprised of Paramount Pictures, Paramount Television, Spelling Entertainment Group Inc., and the Paramount Stations Group, and generated revenues of $4.8 billion in 1998.

Networks encompassed its basic cable and premium subscription television program services. These networks included MTV, MTV2, Nickelodeon, Nick at Nite, Nick at Nite's TV Land, VH1, Showtime, The Movie Channel, and Flix. This segment also held the company's interests in Comedy Central, Sundance Channel, and UPN (United Paramount Network). Total revenues in 1998 for the Network segment reached $2.6 billion.

The Video segment consisted of Blockbuster Video, a retailer in home videos and games; it produced $3.9 billion in revenues in 1998. The Parks segment, comprised of the five regional Paramount Parks, achieved $421 million in 1998 revenues. Finally, Viacom Online Services, the company's interactive businesses, produced 1998 revenues of $13.7 million.

Changes to the Industry

When the deal was completed, Gulf + Western usurped McGraw-Hill as the largest publisher in the U.S. Although it eventually lost its first-place standing, Gulf + Western continued increasing its publishing holdings as part of its effort to focus on two core businesses: entertainment and communications. The firm's efforts to acquire Time Inc. fell through in 1989. Two years later, Gulf + Western—by then renamed Paramount—paid $157.5 million for Macmillan's computer publishing unit. In 1994, Paramount acquired Macmillan Inc., moving up to second-place among the nation's book publishers. That year, entertainment giant Viacom acquired Paramount. A shift in focus to core entertainment assets prompted Viacom to divest the reference and educational publishing operations of Simon & Schuster, including Prentice-Hall, Allyn & Bacon, and Globe Fearon, to Pearson PLC for $4.6 billion in 1998.

Review of the Outcome

Second-quarter interest payments at Gulf + Western jumped to $31.3 million in 1985, compared to $17.5 million in the same period a year earlier, a direct effect of the purchase of Prentice-Hall. As a result, Gulf + Western's net earnings that quarter tumbled 33% to $46 million, compared to $68.4 million in 1984.

The Players

Chairman of Gulf + Western Corp.: Martin S. Davis. Martin Davis, a former publicist, took the helm of the bloated Gulf + Western in 1983. His efforts to refocus the company on communications and entertainment, included the 1985 purchase of publisher Prentice Hall. By 1987, Davis had sold off nearly $2.6 billion in assets and stocks. Two years later, Gulf + Western changed its name to Paramount Communications and made an unsuccessful attempt to take over Time Inc. Four years later, Davis found himself on the receiving end of such an attempt when QVC launched an unfriendly bid to wrest Paramount from its merger agreement with Viacom. Adding insult to injury was the fact that such a deal would place Paramount in the hands of Barry Diller, whose clashes with Davis had spurred Diller to resign from Paramount in 1983. Ultimately, Viacom succeeded in its bid for Paramount, at which point Davis resigned, although he gained a seat on the board of Viacom's parent, National Amusements, Inc. In 1994, Davis established Wellspring Associates, L.L.C., a buyout group specializing in investing in undervalued companies in need of dramatic restructuring. By early 1998, Wellspring had made investments in the bankrupt Discovery Zone, the hockey equipment manufacturer SLM International, and Lionel Trains, a toy company acquired in 1995.

Offsetting that downturn, however, was the increase in operating income realized by the publishing arm of Gulf + Western due to the addition of Prentice-Hall's operations, which were eventually merged into Gulf + Western's Simon & Schuster unit.

Research

Broder, John. "Earnings: Gulf & Western Net Drops 33% In 2nd Quarter," in *Los Angeles Times*, 7 March 1985. Discusses the immediate impact of the deal on Gulf + Western's performance.

"G&W Completes Prentice Hall Merger," in *The Washington Post*, 22 December 1984. Announces the completion of the Gulf + Western/Prentice-Hall deal.

"Gulf + Western, Inc.," in *International Directory of Company Histories*, Vol. I, St. James Press, 1988. Offers a detailed history of Gulf + Western, Inc.

Lieberman, D. and R. Grover. "Gulf & Western," in *Business Week*, 14 September 1987. Details the career of Martin S. Davis.

Nicholson, Tom. "A Bidding War for the Books," in *Newsweek*, 19 November 1984. Offers a detailed look at the efforts of Gulf + Western to acquire Prentice-Hall.

Potts, Mark. "Prentice-Hall Rejects Bid from G&W," in *The Washington Post*, 9 November 1984. Describes the negotiations between Gulf + Western and Prentice-Hall.

————. "Prentice-Hall Accepts New G&W Bid," in *The Washington Post*, 27 November 1984. Describes the negotiations between Gulf + Western and Prentice-Hall.

Prentice-Hall, Inc. Home Page, available at http://www.prenticehall.com. Official World Wide Web Page for Prentice-Hall, Inc. Includes product, corporate, historical, and employment information.

Sanoff, Alvin P. "Behind Merger Mania in Book Publishing," in *U.S. News & World Report*, 10 December 1984. Discusses the industry conditions prior to the acquisition.

Viacom International Inc. Home Page, available at http://www.viacom.com. Official World Wide Web Page for Viacom. Includes a description of operations, news releases, executive biographies, annual reports, investor information, and links to company home pages.

ANNAMARIE L. SHELDON

GULF + WESTERN & SIMON & SCHUSTER

nationality: USA
date: June 1975
affected: Gulf + Western Corp., USA, founded 1956
affected: Simon & Schuster Inc., USA, founded 1924

Viacom International Inc.
1515 Broadway, 51st Fl.
New York, NY 10036
USA

tel: (212)258-6000
web: http://www.viacom.com
e-mail: info@viacom.com

Overview of the Acquisition

Gulf + Western's $10.5 million purchase of trade book publisher Simon & Schuster in June of 1975 marked the conglomerate's first major foray into publishing. With access to the deeper pockets of Gulf + Western, later renamed Paramount Communications Inc., Simon & Schuster was able to diversify into the publishing industry's textbook and information services segments. In 1998, the firm was divided in two by Viacom International, which had purchased Paramount Communications four years earlier; the parent company retained Simon & Schuster's consumer publishing businesses and sold the reference and educational publishing operations of Simon & Schuster to Pearson PLC for $4.6 billion.

History of Gulf + Western Corp.

After experimenting in the import-export business, Austrian-born Charles George Bluhdorn began searching for a publicly traded company whose stock he could use to buy other companies. In 1956, he secured a controlling interest in Michigan Plating & Stamping and joined its board of directors. The next year, Bluhdorn merged Michigan Plating with Beard & Stone Electric Co., a Houston-based auto parts distributor.

In 1958, in deference to the company's location on the Gulf of Mexico and to Bluhdorn's belief that most of its growth would originate in the West, where automobile sales were rapidly increasing, the firm changed its name to Gulf + Western Corp.

Having acquired a number of private auto parts distributors and warehouses, Gulf + Western's annual sales approached $200 million in the mid-1960s. Bluhdorn embarked on a diversification campaign, and in just a matter of days, the company purchased a large amount of stock in New Jersey Zinc, a large mining and chemical company.

The struggling Paramount Pictures Corp. became Bluhdorn's next target. Paying $125 million for the movie company in 1966, Gulf + Western immediately became one of the nation's top manufacturing companies. Sales that year increased

The Business

Financials

Revenue (1998): $12.1 billion

Employees (1998): 111,700

SICs / NAICS

sic 4841 - Cable & Other Pay Television Services

sic 4833 - Television Broadcasting Stations

sic 7822 - Motion Picture & Tape Distribution

sic 7812 - Motion Picture & Video Production

sic 2731 - Book Publishing

sic 7996 - Amusement Parks

naics 513210 - Cable Networks

naics 513120 - Television Broadcasting

naics 512120 - Motion Picture and Video Distribution

naics 512110 - Motion Picture and Video Production

naics 511130 - Book Publishers

naics 713110 - Amusement and Theme Parks

from $180 million to nearly $300 million—almost tripling earnings to $17 million.

Gulf + Western acquired 23 companies in 1968, including Consolidated Cigar, E.W. Bliss, Universal American, Brown Co., and Associates Investment Co. Sales surpassed the $1 billion mark for the first time, reaching $1.3 billion and producing a net income of $69.8 million. Paramount became a success story. Nearly bankrupt when purchased, it recorded its highest box office revenues in history during 1972. Five years later, Gulf + Western acquired Madison Square Garden.

In 1969, the company's fast-paced acquisition program ended when Wall Street analysts, congressmen, and the media charged Gulf + Western with manipulating accounting procedures to inflate its earnings. As a result, the company's stock dropped 30 points, costing shareholders $500 million and further reducing its dismal price earnings.

In 1975, Gulf + Western acquired Simon & Schuster Inc. The company's regulatory problems continued that year when the U.S. Securities and Exchange Commission (SEC) charged that the company's operations in the Dominican Republic illegally withheld over $38 million in profits owed to the Dominican Republic government. In 1980, the compa-

ny reached a settlement with the SEC over this matter, whereby Gulf + Western agreed to pay $39 million over seven years in order to fund a social and economic development program in the Dominican Republic.

In 1978, as the company's poor public image continued, Gulf + Western spent $3.3 million to print its annual report in *Time* magazine, hoping to raise its price earning ratio. The next year, the SEC initiated a second investigation, accusing Bluhdorn and executive vice president Don. F. Gatson of misconduct. Among its charges were allegations that the two executives allowed the company's pension fund to make "inappropriate" investments in companies where they had personal investments. This investigation was settled in 1981, with no restitution called for under the terms of the agreement.

Bluhdorn died of a heart attack in 1983, and was succeeded as CEO by Martin S. Davis. Davis quickly streamlined the company's operations by focusing on the areas of entertainment and communications. Within months, Consolidated Cigar was sold, as were 50 other units, including operations in chemicals, concrete equipment, and mechanical presses.

Gulf + Western acquired the remaining 73% of Esquire, Inc., as well as the publishers Prentice-Hall, Inc. and Ginn & Co., in 1984. Divestitures continued, and the company sold its consumer and industrial products to Wickes Co. for $1 billion in cash in 1985. Four years later, Gulf + Western changed its name to Paramount Communications Inc. Also that year, the company made an unsuccessful bid for Time Inc.

In 1991, Paramount purchased the television station operator TVX, renaming it Paramount Stations Group, and started a pay-per-view programming and distribution venture with Capital Cities/ABC. It also purchased the Macmillan Computer Publishing division in late 1991 for $157.5 million. The company's revenues increased to $4.3 billion in 1992, due in large part to the success of such movies as *The Addams Family*, *Star Trek VI*, and *Wayne's World*.

Paramount began bypassing television networks in 1993 by taking its TV series, *The Untouchables* and *Deep Space Nine*, directly into the first-run syndication market. The following year, Paramount was the prize in a heated takeover battle between Viacom Inc. and QVC, and in July of 1994, Paramount was acquired by Viacom. Before the battle was over, Paramount acquired Macmillan Inc., thereby becoming the nation's second-largest book publisher. Viacom sold the reference and educational publishing operations of Simon & Schuster to Pearson PLC in 1998. The firm retained its profitable consumer publications businesses.

History of Simon & Schuster Inc.

Richard L. Simon and M. Lincoln Schuster established Simon & Schuster in January of 1924. The firm's first publication, *The Crossword Puzzle Book* sold more than 100,000 copies in its first year of print. Simon & Schuster's next big hit came two years later when it published *The Story of a Philosophy*, by Will Durant, a best seller in both 1926 and 1927. In 1935, Josephine Johnson's *Now in November*, a Simon & Schuster publication, won the Pulitzer Prize.

Simon & Schuster agreed to fund 49% of Robert F. de Graff's launch of Pocket Books, a line of cheap paperback reprints. During World War II, roughly 25,000 Pocket Books, priced at 25 cents each, were shipped overseas. To meet demand while paper was rationed, Simon & Schuster paid other less successful publishing houses for any paper supplies that went unused. In 1942, Simon & Schuster launched the Little Golden Books line of hardcover children's books, a joint venture with Western Printing and Lithographing Co.

In 1944, Field Enterprises paid $3 million for Simon & Schuster, which remained fairly autonomous. Pocket Books began publishing original and hard cover books, the most famous of which was *Baby and Child Care* by Dr. Benjamin Spock, printed for the first time in 1946. When Marshall Field, head of Field Enterprises died in 1957, the original owners of Simon & Schuster—who had stayed with the firm as managers—were able to buy the firm back for $1 million, only one-third of what they had sold it for over a decade ago. The firm sold its stake in Little Golden Books to Western Printing in 1958.

The firm conducted its initial public offering in 1966 and was eventually listed on the New York Stock Exchange. That year, Simon & Schuster gained full control of Pocket Books. After negotiations with several potential merger partners fell through, Simon & Schuster agreed to a $10.5 million takeover offer made by conglomerate Gulf + Western in 1975.

Market Forces Driving the Acquisition

Simon & Schuster began seeking a partner as a means of expansion in 1970. In May of that year, the firm negotiated a deal with Norton Simon Inc., a conglomerate that had ventured into magazine publishing. After those talks ceased, Simon & Schuster and Kinney National Service Inc. began discussing a merger. Simon & Schuster eventually backed away from those negotiations, hoping to find a more attractive price. Textbook publisher Harcourt Brace Jovanovich and Simon & Schuster agreed to merge in 1974, but the deal was nixed the following year after issues arose over who would run the company. Simon

The Officers

& Schuster was looking for a buyer, but the firm wasn't willing to relinquish total control to an outsider.

At roughly the same time, Gulf + Western was shopping for new markets to penetrate. According to a February 1975 *Business Week* article, the firm's goal of "getting into publishing" was a fairly common trend among large conglomerates, including International Telephone and Telegraph Corp. and RCA Corp.

Approach and Engagement

Gulf + Western launched a one-to-eight stock swap bid for the 3.5 million outstanding shares of Simon & Schuster in February of 1975. The 430,000 shares offered by Gulf + Western were worth roughly $11 million. On April 3, the firm adjusted its offer to one Gulf + Western share for every ten Simon & Schuster shares. The 350,000 Gulf + Western shares were valued at a total of $10.5 million, based on the stock's closing price of roughly $30 per share that day. In June, shareholders approved the deal, which included stipulations that executive vice president Richard E. Snyder be named president of Simon & Schuster and that Leon Shimkin remain chairman.

Products and Services

In 1998, Viacom, parent of Paramount (formerly Gulf + Western) and Simon & Schuster, operated in six business segments:

Entertainment housed the company's operations in the production and distribution of motion pictures and television programming, as well as its television stations, international channels, movie theater operations, and music publishing. This segment was comprised of Paramount Pictures, Paramount Television, Spelling Entertainment Group Inc., and the Paramount Stations Group, and generated revenues of $4.8 billion in 1998.

The Players

Founder and CEO of Gulf + Western Corp.: Charles George Bluhdorn. Austrian immigrant Charles Bluhdorn began his U.S. career by importing coffee from Brazil and Africa. After his business, Fortune Coffee Co., suffered from the instability in the coffee industry, Bluhdorn began seeking a business operating in a less cyclical market. Intrigued by the burgeoning automotive parts industry, Bluhdorn bought a controlling stake in Michigan Plating & Stamping Co. in 1956, securing for himself a spot on the firm's board of directors. Bluhdorn spent the next several years overseeing his businesses, which was renamed Gulf + Western in 1958. When Gulf + Western took over Paramount Pictures in 1966, Bluhdorn named himself president of that firm. He oversaw his firm's first major foray into publishing in 1975 when he orchestrated the purchase of Simon & Schuster. Later in the decade, a U.S. Securities and Exchange Commission charged Bluhdorn and executive vice president Don. F. Gatson with misconduct, alleging that they had allowed the company's pension fund to make "inappropriate" investments in companies in which the two executives had made personal investments. The case was later dropped. In 1983, while flying home from a business trip, the 56-year-old Bluhdorn died of a heart attack.

Chairman of Simon & Schuster Inc.: Leon Shimkin. Leon Shimkin served as the business manager of Simon & Schuster during the company's formative years. He became an equal partner with founders Richard L. Simon and M. Lincoln Schuster in the mid-1930s. In 1939, the three men contributed equally to finance 49% of the startup costs of Pocket Books, a series of low cost paperback reprints which quickly became the first mass marketed paperback line in the world. When Simon died in 1960, Schuster and Shimkin divided his stock equally, becoming co-owners of the publishing house. Six years later, Schuster retired and sold his shares to Shimkin. As sole owner, Shimkin's first move was to take the company public. In 1973, he appointed Seymour Turk president, retaining for himself the role of chairman. Between 1970 and 1974, Shimkin negotiated the sale of Simon & Schuster. After nixing plans with several firms, including Harcourt Brace Jovanovich Inc., Shimkin finally agreed to an offer by Gulf + Western in 1975. He remained chairman of Simon & Schuster for several years.

Publishing encompassed such consumer publishing imprints as Simon & Schuster, Pocket Books, Scribner, and The Free Press; this unit generated sales of $564 million in 1998.

Networks encompassed its basic cable and premium subscription television program services. These networks included MTV, MTV2, Nickelodeon, Nick at Nite, Nick at Nite's TV Land, VH1, Showtime, The Movie Channel, and Flix. This segment also held the company's interests in Comedy Central, Sundance Channel, and UPN (United Paramount Network). Total revenues in 1998 for the Network segment reached $2.6 billion.

The **Video** segment consisted of Blockbuster Video, a retailer in home videos and games; it produced $3.9 billion in revenues in 1998. The **Parks** segment, comprised of the five regional Paramount Parks, achieved $421 million in 1998 revenues. Finally, **Viacom Online Services**, the company's interactive businesses, produced 1998 revenues of $13.7 million.

Changes to the Industry

The deal sparked increased industry consolidation as many of the industry's leading players began to see that size seemed synonymous with success. Not only did consolidation bring with it economies of scale, but larger firms could also afford new technology, marketing campaigns, etc. During the late 1970s and early 1980s, MCA, Inc. bought Putnam; Hearst Corp. acquired William Morrow; and Harper & Row purchased J.B. Lippincott. In early 1984, Macmillan Inc. snagged Scriber Book Cos. and Random House Inc. added to its mix the book publishing operations of New York Times Co.

Review of the Outcome

By the early 1980s, Simon & Schuster had seen its sales grow to $210 million, compared to $44 million in 1975. This performance helped propel sales at Gulf + Western to roughly $4 billion in 1983. As a result, Gulf + Western continued to increase its publishing assets. Early in 1984, Gulf + Western paid $180 million for the 73% of textbook publisher Esquire Inc. it didn't already own, doubling Simon & Schuster's employee count and catapulting firm into the sixth place spot among U.S. book publishers. The conglomerate also paid $100 million for educational publisher Ginn & Co.. In December of that year, Gulf + Western paid $710 million for Prentice-Hall, the largest college textbook publisher in the U.S. When the operations of Prentice-Hall, which secured nearly $500 million in yearly revenues, were merged into Simon & Schuster, the firm overthrew McGraw-Hill, Inc. as the nation's leading publisher.

Although Simon & Schuster eventually lost its first-place standing, the firm continued pursuing publishing acquisitions as part of Gulf + Western's effort to focus on two core businesses: entertainment and communications. In 1986, elementary textbook publisher Silver Burdett Co. was purchased for $125 million. Negotiations for the purchase of Time Inc. fell apart in 1989. Two years later, Gulf + Western—by then renamed Paramount—paid $157.5 million for Macmillan's computer publishing unit. In 1994, Paramount acquired Macmillan Inc., moving up to second-place among the nation's book publishers. That year, entertainment giant Viacom acquired Paramount. A shift in focus to core entertainment assets prompted Viacom to divest the reference and educational publishing operations of Simon & Schuster, including Prentice-Hall, Allyn & Bacon, and Globe Fearon, to Pearson PLC for $4.6 billion in 1998.

Research

"G&W's Publishing Deal," in *Business Week*, 10 February 1975. Offers a brief look at Gulf + Western's initial offer for Simon & Schuster.

"Gulf + Western, Inc.," in *International Directory of Company Histories*, Vol. I, St. James Press, 1988. Provides a detailed history of Gulf + Western, Inc.

"Simon & Schuster Inc.," in *International Directory of Company Histories*, Vol. II St. James Press, 1989. Offers a detailed history of Simon & Schuster Inc., including details regarding its takeover by Gulf + Western.

"Simon & Schuster Picks Snyder as President," in *The Wall Street Journal*, 24 June 1975. Covers changes in management at Simon & Schuster after the deal was completed.

Sanoff, Alvin P. "Behind Merger Mania in Book Publishing," in *U.S. News & World Report*, 10 December 1984. Discusses the industry conditions in the decade following Gulf + Western's purchase of Simon & Schuster.

Viacom International Inc. Home Page, available at http://www.viacom.com. Official World Wide Web Page for Viacom. Includes a description of operations, news releases, executive biographies, annual reports, investor information, and links to company home pages.

ANNAMARIE L. SHELDON

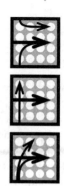

HALLIBURTON & DRESSER INDUSTRIES

Halliburton Co.
3600 Lincoln Plaza
500 N. Akard St.
Dallas, TX 75201-3391
USA

tel: (214)978-2600
fax: (214)978-2611
web: http://www.halliburton.com

nationality: USA
date: September 30, 1998
affected: Halliburton Co., USA, founded 1919
affected: Dresser Industries Inc., USA, founded 1880

Overview of the Acquisition

When energy services titan Halliburton Co. paid $7.7 billion to acquire oil field equipment manufacturer Dresser Industries in September of 1998, it surpassed Schlumberger Ltd. as the world's largest oil field services company. The joining of the two Dallas, Texas-based firms resulted in a behemoth with annual revenues exceeding $17 billion.

History of Halliburton Co.

In 1919, Erle Halliburton established the Better Method Oil Well Cementing Co. and moved his family to Burkburnett, Texas, to introduce his services to the oil industry. After Texas showed little interest in his methods, Halliburton transferred his operations to Oklahoma and organized the Halliburton Oil Well Cementing Co. By 1921, 17 trucks carried Halliburton's crews and equipment to drilling sites in Louisiana, Arkansas, and other oil-rich areas.

The firm incorporated in 1924. By then, Halliburton had successfully patented all of its new processes and devices, leaving the oil industry unable to function without its services. Halliburton and his wife held 52% of company stock, and the Magnolia, Texas, Gulf, Humble, Sun, Pure, and Atlantic oil companies jointly owned the remaining 48%. In 1929, the company moved into Canada and launched a new product line of oil well apparatus. Four new branches opened in 1932, enabling Halliburton to send 75 cementing and well-testing crews to sites in seven states. The company also began to mount equipment on ships and barges. By the end of the decade, Halliburton had acquired Perkins Cementing Co., extending operations to the West Coast and the Rocky Mountain region, and established a South American subsidiary in Venezuela.

The firm served the World War II effort by making gun-mount bearings for the U.S. Navy, as well as parts for the B-29 bomber and jigs, fixtures, and dies for the Boeing airplane. In 1948, Halliburton shares were offered on the New York Stock Exchange for the first time. The following year, Halliburton licensed a new process called Hydrafrac, designed to increase well productivity. By the mid-1950s, drilling activity had increased dramatically, and Halliburton operated nearly 200 centers in the U.S., as well as 32 service locations in Canada, subsidiaries in Venezuela and Peru, and operations in Mexico, Saudi Arabia, Sumatra, Italy, Germany, Australia, and Cuba.

In 1957, Welex Jet Services was acquired, along with Jet Research Center and Freightmaster, a maker of rail car couplings. To offset a slump in the oil industry, Halliburton continued its acquisition program, buying Otil Engineering Corp. in 1959. Brown & Root, internationally known for the construction of military bases, petrochemical plants, and offshore platforms, became a subsidiary of Halliburton in 1962. By 1965, Halliburton was comprised of 16 units which were organized into three main segments: oil-field services and sales; engineering and international construction; and specialty sales and service.

The company's marine capabilities expanded in 1968 with the acquisition of Texas-based Jackson Marine Corp. and the purchase of an 80% interest in the Taylor Diving and Salvage Co. in New Orleans. Along with offshore exploration, Halliburton also found success with hydraulic cushioning for railroad cars, electronics and explosives for the defense and aerospace industries, and pollution control products. In 1976, to offset the slowdown of offshore exploration in the North Sea, Brown & Root and competitor Raymond International teamed up in a $22 million bridge construction project in Louisiana.

The economic recession of the early 1980s, coupled with drastically lower oil prices, prompted net income to tumble. A 1985 lawsuit alleging that Brown & Root had mismanaged a south Texas nuclear power plant construction project cost the company $750 million in settlement fees. The following year, Halliburton downsized, slashing employees from 115,000 to 65,000. Acquisitions late in the decade included Texas Instrument Inc.'s Geophysical Services (GSI); Geosource, another geophysical service company; and Gearhart Industries, which was merged with Welex to form Halliburton Logging Services.

In 1991, the firm opened an office in Moscow. Brown & Root was chosen as the prime contractor for an $8 billion luxury resort near Nagoya, Japan. An additional 800 jobs were slashed in 1992. Stock split two for one in 1996. That year, Halliburton paid $557 million for Landmark Graphics Corp. In 1997, Amoco Corp. filed suit against Landmark Graphics for patent infringement. In October of 1998, Halliburton acquired Dresser Industries Inc., an oil field equipment maker, in a $7.7 billion deal.

History of Dresser Industries Inc.

In 1880, Solomon Dresser opened a small business in Bradford, Pennsylvania, called S.R. Dresser Co., to

The Business

Financials

Revenue (1998): $17.35 billion

Employees (1998): 107,800

SICs / NAICS

sic 1629 - Heavy Construction Nec

sic 1389 - Oil & Gas Field Services Nec

sic 3533 - Oil & Gas Field Machinery

naics 213112 - Support Activities for Oil and Gas Field Operations

naics 333132 - Oil and Gas Field Machinery and Equipment Manufacturing

provide supplies to the oil industry. He soon was awarded a patent for his cap packer, a device that prevented crude oil from mixing with other fluids in a well. In 1884, offices opened in Allentown and Clarendon, Pennsylvania, as well as in Bolivar, New York. The following year, Dresser introduced a leak proof pipe coupling. In 1884, Standard Oil Co. ordered nine of the company's sleeves, or elongated couplings, on a trial basis. Before long, orders were pouring in from Ohio and Pennsylvania.

The firm incorporated in 1905 as the S.R. Dresser Manufacturing Co. Two years later, a new Bradford plant began producing stain-resistant steel couplings to replace inferior iron ones. Solomon died in 1911, leaving his son-in-law, Fred Miller, in charge. In 1928, with no one to succeed the aging Miller, the family sold the company to W.A. Harriman & Co., an investment-banking firm that took Dresser public.

A subsidiary opened in Toronto in 1931. Two years later, Dresser bought Bryant Heater Co. In 1937, the firm acquired New York-based Clark Brothers Co., an engineering firm that manufactured gas engines, compressors, and pumping equipment for the oil and gas industries. Dresser then merged its operations with Clark to become Dresser Manufacturing Co. By the end of the decade, Dresser's product line had grown to nearly 130 items, assets exceeded $2 million, sales reached nearly $6 million, and employees totaled 700.

During the early 1940's Dresser purchased a 50% stake in the Van der Horst Corporation of America; became involved with the secret Manhattan Project, which was engaged in research to develop the atomic

The Officers

Chairman: William E. Bradford

Vice Chairman: Donald C. Vaughn

CEO: Richard B. Cheney

President and Chief Operating Officer: David J. Lesar

Exec. VP and Chief Financial Officer: Gary V. Morris

bomb; and changed its name to Dresser Industries. In an effort to shift its product line emphasis from capital goods to expendable ones needing frequent replacement, Dresser acquired Security Engineering, a maker of drilling bits, in 1945. Four years later, Magnet Cove Barium Corp. of Houston, Texas, joined the company as a subsidiary.

In 1950, Dresser formed Dresser Vaduz, a subsidiary based in Liechtenstein, to execute and monitor all foreign license agreements, and to funnel profits between the different companies, keeping Dresser's profits overseas where they couldn't be taxed by the U.S. government. By the end of the decade, subsidiaries were operating in Canada, Britain, Mexico, Peru, Brazil, and Venezuela.

Dresser acquired Harbison-Walter, a maker of heat-resistant bricks, and Symington-Wayne, a maker of gas station and railroad equipment, in 1969. Following an oil spill in 1970 that affected 200 miles of ocean, Dresser quickly ordered pollution-control plans to be submitted by each Dresser division. The firm bought Lodge-Cottrell, a British maker of electrostatic precipitators for pollution removal from the stack of coal-fired electric utility plants, in 1972. Sales eclipsed $1 billion for the first time in 1973. The following year, Dresser acquired Jeffrey Galion, a manufacturer of mining and construction equipment.

New chairman John J. Murphy began divesting unprofitable companies and diversifying into new areas, including life insurance, finance, and car leasing, in the early 1980s. He also closed five of the company's 18 fire-brick plants. In 1986, a joint agreement was forged with Halliburton Co., a market leader in the drilling fluids field, to form the M-I Drilling Fluids Co. A year later, a 50-50 partnership was established with Ingersoll-Rand, a supplier of compressors, turbines, and electric machinery. Dresser entered into a joint venture with Komatsu of Japan in 1988 to form Komatsu Dresser Co., a heavy equipment manufacturer. The firm also acquired M.W. Kellogg Co., which formed the core of the firm's engineering and construction division.

In the early 1990s, Dresser acquired Mono Group, a maker of pumps; Peabody, a manufacturer of blowers and combustion equipment; and the diamond drill-bit product line of rival Baker Hughes. Dresser and Shaw Industries, Ltd. formed a global pipe coating joint venture in 1996, with Dresser holding a 50.1% share. M.W. Kellogg Co. landed a multi-million dollar ethylene expansion contract from Nova Chemicals (Canada), Ltd. In October of 1998, Halliburton acquired Dresser for $7.7 billion.

Market Forces Driving the Acquisition

In the late 1990s, the petroleum industry struggled in the wake of declining oil and gas prices. While the smaller and mid-sized companies were being squeezed by dwindling sales, the larger firms had the resources to not only weather the downturn, but also to pursue mergers as a means of increasing geographic scope and strengthening international operations.

The bigger companies also sought consolidation as a means of countering the effects of the depressed market and shoring up their position to best take advantage of the opportunities that would likely materialize while the industry recuperated. According to *Offshore* in April 1998, Halliburton viewed the purchase of Dresser Industries as a means of creating an "oilfield services and engineering and construction company with the broadest range of services to the petroleum industry worldwide." By joining its energy services operations with Dresser's oil field equipment manufacturing operations, Halliburton would be able to offer more products and services to its clients. The firm also claimed that the money saved by eliminating overlap and integrating operations would be passed along to clients via lower prices.

Approach and Engagement

Halliburton announced its $7.7 billion offer for Dresser Industries on February 26, 1998. Shareholders of both firms approved the takeover in June. The deal was cleared in both Europe and Canada the following month. In September, the U.S. Justice Department granted approval on the condition that Halliburton divest its PathFinder logging-while-drilling (LWD) and measurement-while-drilling (MWD) operations. The firm had also recently sold its 36% stake in MI Drilling, a drilling fluids company, for $265 million to Smith International Inc. The requirement was issued to ease antitrust concerns that the merger would limit competition in the multibillion U.S. drilling fluid industry, in which Dresser's Sperry-Sun Drilling Services Inc. was a world leader, by securing a 70% market share for Halliburton.

Dresser shareholders received one share of Halliburton common stock for each share of Dresser common stock. To pay for the purchase, Halliburton issued 176 million new shares of its common stock, increasing the number of outstanding shares 439 million. William Bradford, former chairman and CEO of Dresser Industries, was appointed chairman of Halliburton. Halliburton CEO Richard Cheney retained his post.

Products and Services

When the deal was completed, Dresser's engineering and petroleum operations were absorbed into Halliburton, while Dresser's energy equipment operations became a separate Halliburton unit, known as Dresser Equipment Group, which accounted for 16% of sales in 1998. The group included compressors, control products, electric motors, gas and diesel engines, gas and steam turbines, gasoline and diesel dispensing systems, generators, meters, and pumps.

Halliburton's Engineering and Construction Group brought in 32% of sales. It included contract maintenance operations and services, economic and technical feasibility studies, environmental consulting and waste management, remedial engineering and construction for hazardous waste sites, and site evaluations. The largest division, the Energy Services Group, secured 52% of total sales. It housed the Brown & Root Energy Services unit, which engaged in oil and gas, offshore, and sub-sea construction and engineering; the Halliburton Energy Services unit; and Landmark Graphics Corp.

Changes to the Industry

When Halliburton completed its takeover of Dresser Industries, it surpassed Schlumberger Ltd. as the leader in the oil field services industry. Other major players were in the midst of their own consolidation efforts in 1998: Baker Hughes Inc. and Western Atlas Inc. merged that year, as did Schlumberger and Camco Inc. According to a December 1998 article in *World Oil*, "These mergers and acquisitions are perceived to have strengthened the petroleum sector and improved its overall capacity to furnish clients with integrated services, project management expertise, and discrete products/services for offshore and onshore needs." To meet antitrust regulations, Halliburton sold its Pathfinder LWD and MWD unit to Energy Services Inc. in early 1999.

Review of the Outcome

The acquisition nearly doubled Halliburton's size. Integration of the two firms, coupled with a continued decline in the price of oil, prompted

The Players

Chairman and CEO of Halliburton Co.: Richard B. Cheney. After graduating from the University of Wyoming, Richard Cheney launched his political career when he secured a post as a White House aide in 1969. In 1975, he was named Chief of Staff to President Gerald Ford. Between 1978 and 1989, Cheney served as a U.S. Representative from Wyoming. After his four-year stint, from 1989 to 1992, as the U.S. Defense Secretary ended, Richard Cheney left the political arena in 1995 to accept the top spot at Halliburton. He steered the firm's acquisition of Dresser Industries in 1998, retaining his position as CEO.

Chairman and CEO of Dresser Industries Inc.: William E. Bradford. William Bradford earned a geology degree at Centenary College in 1958. In 1963, he became executive vice president of Analytical Logging Corp., which was later acquired by Dresser Industries. During the 1970s, he served in several managerial positions at Dresser units, including product manager of D.A.T.A. Systems and area manager of Mid-Continent. Bradford was appointed senior vice president of Dresser Industries in 1985. Three years later, he took over as president and CEO of Dresser-Rand Co. The board of Dresser Industries elected Bradford president and chief operating officer in 1992, posts he held until December of 1996, when he took the helm as chairman and CEO. When Dresser was acquired by Halliburton in 1998, Bradford was named chairman of Halliburton.

Halliburton to cut more than 9,000 jobs. The firm posted a $14.7 million loss on sales of $17.4 billion in 1998, due mainly to special charges related to the acquisition.

Research

Bellfore, Leslie. "Halliburton and Dresser Industries," in *Offshore*, November 1998. Announces the approval of the deal by the U.S. Department of Justice.

Cawley, Rusty. "Halliburton, Dresser Deal Tops List of Mergers," in *Dallas Business Journal*, 20 March 1998. Offers an overview of the merger agreement.

DeLuca, Marshall. "Halliburton," in *Offshore*, April 1998. Briefly explains why Halliburton and Dresser decided to merge.

"Dresser Industries Inc.," in *Notable Corporate Chronologies*, The Gale Group, 1999. Covers major events in the history of Dresser Industries Inc.

Fletcher, Sam. "Halliburton Reports Loss Due to Special Charges," in *The Oil Daily*, 27 January 1999. Discusses the immediate outcome of the deal.

"Halliburton and Dresser Complete Merger," in *PR Newswire*, 30 September 1998. Offers a detailed look at the terms of the final agreement.

Halliburton Co. Home Page, available at http://www.halliburton.com. Official World Wide Web Page for Halliburton Co. Includes product and corporate information, news, and annual reports.

"Halliburton Co.," in *Notable Corporate Chronologies*, The Gale Group, 1999. Covers major events in the history of Halliburton Co.

McWilliams, Gary. "Dick Cheney Ain't Studyin' War No More," in *Business Week*, 2 March 1998. Details the career of Dick Cheney.

ANNAMARIE L. SHELDON

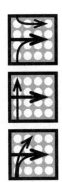

HASBRO INDUSTRIES & MILTON BRADLEY

nationality: USA
date: 1985
affected: Hasbro Industries, Inc., USA, founded 1923
affected: Milton Bradley Co., USA, founded 1860

Hasbro Inc.
1027 Newport Ave.
Pawtucket, RI 02861
USA

tel: (401)431-8697
fax: (401)431-8535
web: http://www.hasbro.com

Overview of the Acquisition

Hasbro acquired Milton Bradley in a two-step transaction valued at $360 million. First, Hasbro offered $50 for each of 3.02 million Milton Bradley shares, about 43% of shares outstanding. It also announced that it would buy 8% of Milton Bradley common stock for $50 per share from the heirs of the late James J. Shea, the previous chairman of Milton Bradley Co. The remaining 49% would be paid for in Hasbro common stock and a new convertible preferred stock at a value of about $50 a share. Milton Bradley Co. became a wholly owned subsidiary of Hasbro Bradley, Inc. The integrated entity had both American and international marketing and manufacturing capabilities.

History of Hasbro, Inc.

Hasbro, Inc. started as a family owned company in Providence, Rhode Island, in 1923. It began with eight family members headed by Henry and Helal Hassenfeld, immigrants from Poland. Known as Hassenfeld Brothers, the company started by selling textile remnants and later manufactured pencil boxes and school supplies.

It wasn't until 1943 that the company expanded to include toys such as paint sets, wax crayons, and doctor and nurse kits. During the '40s and '50s, the company introduced such new toys as Mr. Potato Head, the first toy advertised on television, and acquired the rights to license Walt Disney characters. The introduction of G. I. Joe, in 1964, resulted in tremendous growth. Stephen Hassenfeld also joined the company that year.

On October 10, 1968, Hasbro went public and changed its name to Hasbro Industries, Inc. It continued to diversify by acquiring Romper Room, Inc., now known as Claster Television, Inc., in 1969.

Alan Hassenfeld joined the company in 1970 as Assistant to the President, and later helped to develop international markets as assistant to the President of International Affairs. In 1974, Stephen Hassenfeld became President of Hasbro Industries, Inc. and his father, Merrill, served as CEO until his death in 1979.

The Business

Financials

Revenue (1998): $3.3 billion

Employees (1998): 10,000

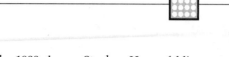

The 1980s began Stephen Hassenfeld's career as Chairman and CEO of Hasbro. His dream was to grow the company through a series of acquisitions including Glenco Infant Items, Inc. and Knickerbocker Toy Co., which held the trademark Raggedy Ann and Andy plush toys. Its greatest acquisition at this time was of the Milton Bradley Co. in 1984. This pushed Hasbro Industries into the Fortune 500 category and into contention with Mattel for first place among toy companies. By 1985, Hasbro had acquired a sales volume of $1.2 billion and had gained access to the game segment of that industry, as well as the European markets that had been developed by Milton Bradley.

In September 1984, Alan Hassenfeld became president of Hasbro Industries. That year also marked the start of the Hasbro Children's Foundation, established to help needy children throughout the world. By this time, Hasbro had united its four subsidiaries—Hasbro Toys, Milton Bradley, Playskool and Playskool Baby—under a parent corporation called Hasbro, Inc.

Alan Hassenfeld was named Chairman and CEO on July 6, 1989, upon the death of his brother Stephen. Under Alan's leadership, Hasbro, Inc. expanded and strengthened in presence in such foreign markets as Spain, Germany, and the Benelux countries.

The 1990s brought the acquisition of Tonka Corp., which included Kenner products and Parker Brothers divisions. This added to Hasbro's product line-up such classic brands as Monopoly, Tonka Trucks, Nerf, Easy-Bake Oven, Clue, and Play-Doh. Hasbro entered the Asian market by purchasing the Nomura Toy Co. Ltd. of Japan and the controlling interest in Palmyra, a leading toy distributor of Southeast Asia.

Hasbro's leadership in the games division improved with the 1994 purchase from Waddingtons of such games as Pictionary and Clue. Hasbro also entered the CD-ROM game market by creating a new division, Hasbro Interactive. Monopoly CD-ROM, an instant success, was followed by CD-ROM versions of the world's most popular board games, including Trivial Pursuit, Scrabble, Yahtzee, Battleship, Risk, and Clue. Hasbro Interactive continued to grow in 1998 with the acquisition of a large portion of Atari's portfolio of the 1980s popular video games.

Hasbro diversified into the candy business through Cap Toys and Oddzon Products Inc. It also renewed and expanded its leasing agreement with Lucas Film for the three "prequels" of the *Star Wars* movie series, the first of which was released in May 1999. Hasbro acquired the rights to action figures, board and video games, as well as the manufacture of handheld electronic games, creative play, and die cast vehicle categories.

History of Milton Bradley Co.

In 1860 Milton Bradley formed a company to produce lithographs for local businesses. Bradley's first big product, however, was The Checkered Game of Life, which he developed while visiting a friend. After selling his entire stock (several hundred copies) of the game to distributors in New York City, orders poured in nationwide. Over the course of the first winter of 1860, he sold 40,000 copies.

Bradley, whose game business was interrupted by the Civil War, began drafting weaponry. He also produced travel versions of such games as Chess, Checkers, Backgammon, Dominoes, and The Checkered Game of Life for soldiers to play during their long hours of inaction. These "Games for Soldiers" kits sold for $1 apiece.

In late 1869, Bradley became involved in the kindergarten movement. He developed exact shades of color for colored paper and paints; these colors—red, orange, yellow, green, blue, and violet—have remained the standard for children's art supplies for decades. Bradley supplied the materials free of charge to the kindergartens in his hometown. Meanwhile, he continued to produce games and puzzles. He became the first American manufacturer of croquet sets. His croquet rules, culled from various oral traditions, became the standard for American play.

In the late 1870s, Bradley's partners insisted that he discontinue the kindergarten work because of the economic depression. Bradley then became director of the company and sold his share in the company to George Tapley, who became president. Milton Bradley died in 1911 and Ralph Ellis succeeded him as director. By 1920, net earnings were $350,000 on $3.5 million in sales. During the '20s and '30s, sales fell, ideas for new games came less frequently, and aging facilities proved unable to keep up with the variety of products being produced. The educational department became the chief source of income, with crayons accounting for one-third of profits.

At the beginning of World War II, sales fell to $2 million and loans totaled $900,000. Under the new management of James J. Shea as President, the company turned to three new products for revitalization:

gunstocks, universal landing gear for fighter planes, and The Game Kit for Soldiers. These products brought in contracts of almost $600,000, and the Game Kits brought in almost $2 million during the war.

In the post-war era, Milton Bradley Co. introduced such new games as Candy Land, Rack-O, and Chutes and Ladders. It profited from new TV programming with companion games like Concentration. It also reintroduced a modern version of The Checkered Game of Life as The Game of Life. At this time educational materials were only 7% of total sales.

In 1968, James Shea, Jr., succeeded his father as President, and earnings rose to $4 million on sales of $69 million. Milton Bradley Co. opened manufacturing facilities in Holland, England, France, and Germany, and the introduction of Battleship and Twister garnered sales of three million copies.

Milton Bradley began acquiring assets and companies in the 1970s beginning with Playskool Mfg. Co., the second-largest manufacturer of preschool toys, and E. S. Lowe Co., maker of Yahtzee. The company introduced Simon, an electronic game, in 1977.

Milton Bradley initially avoided the video game market, thinking that it was an overpriced fad. A later attempt, in 1983, resulted in a $30 million loss. This left shareholders ready for an offer from Hasbro in 1984. Upon completion of that union, Milton Bradley became a subsidiary of Hasbro Industries, and by 1988 accounted for 20% of Hasbro's sales.

Market Forces Driving the Acquisition

Stephen Hassenfeld, chairman and CEO of Hasbro Industries, was looking for a vehicle to move his company to the top of the toy industry. He had been watching Milton Bradley for some time. Milton Bradley, coming off a poor showing in the video game arena, was amenable to an offer. Hasbro's purchase of Bradley would strengthen Hasbro's market on low-tech games and acquire strong foreign markets and manufacturing facilities. Harry Oreinstein, a toy industry expert, said "Very rarely do you find two companies that fit so well with virtually no overlap." Where Milton Bradley was strong overseas, Hasbro had little. Where Milton Bradley was number-one in games, Hasbro was a non-player. By adding Milton , Bradley's Playskool products to Hasbro's lines Hasbro would become second in the market in preschool toys, behind Fisher Price of Quaker Oats Co.

Approach and Engagement

It was a friendly deal, according to Stephen Hassenfeld. "We are paying a full price, not a premi-

The Officers

Chairman and CEO: Alan G. Hassenfeld

Vice Chairman: Harold P. Gordon

President and Chief Operating Officer: Herbert M. Baum

Exec. VP and Chief Financial Officer: John T. O'Neill

Exec. VP Global Operations and Development: Alfred J. Verrecchia

um," he said. "The transaction took place very quickly once it was felt Milton Bradley was going to do a transaction with somebody," Verrecchia of Hasbro reported. It was important not to have confidence on the part of the shareholders and to avoid a bidding war with other companies.

An agreement was produced in only 10 days of negotiations. It was then put before Milton Bradley shareholders for approval. Hassenfeld personally explained the merger to virtually all key managers at Milton Bradley to ease the transition. The result was a new company called Hasbro Bradley, Inc. The name was changed the following year to Hasbro, Inc. when a holding company was formed to incorporate all subsidiaries.

Products and Services

The merger produced a larger product line, reducing the company's dependence on only one or two popular products. A larger base of popular products would protect the company against major losses due to a failed product. Hasbro's G. I. Joe had made Hassenfeld "nervous" because it captured a lion's share of $125 million in sales, but after the merger it accounted for only 17% of total sales.

Hassenfeld decided on more pre-market testing and parent/child input in the company's product line earlier in development. He wanted to improve the quality of its offerings by merging the best of both companies and cutting out the low producers. Milton Bradley would be able to use some of Hasbro's basic popular toys to spin off new games.

Changes to the Industry

The merger between Hasbro Industries, Inc. and Milton Bradley Co. benefited both companies. Each had something to offer the resulting holding company, Hasbro, Inc. Milton Bradley produced low-tech games and toys, basics to the industry, and manufactured and marketed them worldwide. Bradley had branches

The Players

Chairman and CEO of Hasbro Industries, Inc.: Stephen Hassenfeld. A grandson of one of the founding brothers of Hasbro Industries, Stephen Hassenfeld explored diplomacy as a career while in college. After graduating from Johns Hopkins in 1962 with a degree in political science, he decided to join the family business. Named chairman and CEO after working in many positions in the company, he retained those roles after Hasbro bought out Milton Bradley in 1985.

Chairman and President of Milton Bradley Co.: James J. Shea, Jr. James Shea was the second-generation president of Milton Bradley Co. When the firm was acquired by Hasbro in 1985, Shea was appointed chairman of Milton Bradley, which began operating as a wholly owned subsidiary of Hasbro. Roughly three weeks after the deal was completed, Shea resigned.

and subsidiaries in Canada, nine European countries, and Brazil. Licensing agreements also allowed Milton Bradley to manufacture in Australia, Japan, New Zealand, Venezuela, Mexico, and Sweden.

Milton Bradley provided global resources for Hasbro, thereby enabling the company to market versions of Hasbro toys and products to broader markets. This combination of resources put Hasbro, Inc. into the Fortune 500 group with sales in 1984 for the two companies projected at $700 million, possibly surpassing Mattel in California, its closest competitor. Milton Bradley's Playskool subsidiary combined with the best of Hasbro's preschool line to establish Hasbro's greater presence in the preschool toys market.

G. Wayne Miller's *Toy Wars: The Epic Struggle Between G. I. Joe, Barbie and the Companies that Make Them*, chronicles the cutthroat rivalry between the two companies. Miller said that after they acquired all sizeable competitors, Hasbro and Mattel became the only major players in the industry and "a small number of executives determined how the children of the world would play."

Although the Milton Bradley acquisition boosted Hasbro's presence in the toy industry, it could not afford to remain complacent. Alan Hassenfeld was left, at the time of his brother's death, to develop a product to compete with Barbie, enter the video game market, and revitalize G. I. Joe, all while trying to

downsize at the same time. Meanwhile, the toy industry was undergoing strong public scrutiny over the dilemma of how violent toys and television affected children.

Review of the Outcome

The immediate impact of the merger was a rise in stock prices. Milton Bradley stock jumped $2.625 a share at the announcement of the merger, while Hasbro stock gained $1.125. The newly formed Hasbro, Inc. expanded its product line, strengthened its total sales to over $700 million, and acquired new markets for its combined product line.

The only fallout of the merger was James J. Shea, Jr., chairman of the Milton Bradley subsidiary. He resigned less than three weeks after the merger was completed. He was no longer the leader of his own company, and his style of management was dissimilar to that of Hassenfeld, since Stephen Hassenfeld called his management style more "participatory." There was also some dispute over the closing of the Playskool plant in Chicago, which seemed to have contributed to his resignation. While Hassenfeld wanted to keep it open until after the merger, Shea felt that it should close. Ultimately, Hassenfeld agreed and closed the plant, but not until after Shea resigned.

Milton Bradley Co. moved its headquarters to Pawtucket, Rhode Island, into a facility that had been formerly used for distribution. In spite of the shifting of people and resources, the merger went very smoothly.

Research

Allen, Hamilton. "Hasbro to Buy Milton Bradley," in *Providence (RI) Journal*, 5 May 1984. Announces the acquisition of Milton Bradley by Hasbro and the effects on organization, resources, and personnel.

————. "Milton Bradley Purchase, Hot Toys Put Pawtucket Firm Near Industry's Top," *Providence (RI) Journal*, 23 December 1984. Reviews Hasbro/Bradley merger and its effects on Hasbro, Inc.

Fierman, Jaclyn. "Deals in Toyland," in *Fortune*, 11 June 1984. Announces the merger deal between Hasbro and Milton Bradley.

Gilpin, Kenneth N. "A Bit of Diplomacy in the Hasbro Deal," in *The New York Times*, 5 May 1984. Profiles Stephen Hassenfeld, Chairman of Hasbro, Inc.

Hasbro, Inc. Home Page, available at http://www.hasbro.com./history.htm Official World Wide Web Home Page for Hasbro, Inc. Includes product, historical, consumer, and employment information.

"Hasbro, Inc.," in *Notable Corporate Chronologies*, The Gale Group, 1999. Chronicles major events in the history of Hasbro, Inc.

"Hasbro: Merging with Milton Bradley to Get Nearer the No. 1." in *Business Week*, 21 May 1984. Profiles companies and players in merger and analyzes benefits and projects results.

"Hasbro's Urge to Merge, Quality First," in *Chain Store Age, General Merchandize Trends*, March 1985. Evaluates the results of Hasbro-Bradley merger and how it affects products and new releases.

Hays, John R. "Rip van Hasbro," in *Forbes*, 9 September 1996. Reviews the attempted to takeover of Hasbro by Mattel, including interview with Alan Hassenfeld regarding his strategies and a profile of the companies.

Jones, Alex S. "Rival Gets Milton Bradley," in *The New York Times*, 5 May 1984. Details the financial aspects and players of the merger.

Marchetti, Michele. "Battles with Barbie," in *Sales and Marketing Management*, February 1998. Analyzes marketing inside Hasbro, reviews G. Wayne Miller's *Toy Wars* book, and describes the role Alan Hassenfeld plays in the toy market.

"Milton Bradley Co.," in *Notable Corporate Chronologies*, The Gale Group, 1999. Chronicles major events in the history of Milton Bradley.

MARTHA KRUPA

HILTON HOTELS & BALLY ENTERTAINMENT

Hilton Hotels Corp.
9336 Civic Center Dr.
Beverly Hills, CA 90210
USA

tel: (310)278-4321
fax: (310)205-7678
web: http://www.hilton.com

nationality: USA
date: July 1996
affected: Hilton Hotels Corp., USA, founded 1919
affected: Bally Entertainment Corp., USA, founded 1931

Overview of the Merger

In June of 1996, Hilton Hotels Corp. became the largest casino company in the world when it acquired Bally Entertainment Corp. in a $2 billion stock transaction. With ownership of over 15 casinos, Hilton's revenue skyrocketed, net income increased from $82 million in 1996 to $250 million in 1997, and net profit margin jumped from 2.1% in 1996 to 4.7% in 1997. With hotels throughout the U.S. and abroad, Hilton Hotels remained third in the lodging industry, behind only Starwood and Marriott.

History of Hilton Hotels Corp.

In 1919, Conrad Hilton purchased his first hotel, The Mobley, in Cisco, Texas, while traveling to make his fortune in banking. By 1925, the first hotel to carry the Hilton name opened in Dallas. Soon after, Hilton was operating his first property outside of Texas after purchasing the lease of The Sir Francis Drake hotel in San Francisco. The 1942 purchase of two hotels in New York City—The Roosevelt and The Plaza—marked Hilton's move out east. In the mid-1940s, Hilton purchased The Palmer House and The Stevens (now known as the Chicago Hilton & Towers), the latter being the largest hotel in the world at the time. This led to the creation of Hilton Hotels Corp. in 1946 and marked its listing on the New York Stock Exchange.

The 1950s saw Hilton as a front runner in the hospitality industry. The company was able to lease The Waldorf-Astoria in New York, which Conrad Hilton referred to as "the greatest of them all." Hilton also opened its first hotel abroad, the Castellana Hilton in Madrid, marking the beginning of Hilton International Co., a wholly-owned subsidiary. The firm completed the largest real estate transaction in the history of the hotel industry when it purchased The Statler Hotel Co. for $111 million in 1954.

The 1960s and 1970s proved to be years of change for the corporation. Hilton International spun off as a separate corporation with Conrad as president; the corporation's franchising subsidiary, Statler Hilton Inns, was established; and in 1967 Hilton International was acquired by TWA. Hilton also jumped into the gaming market by purchasing the Flamingo and the Las Vegas Hilton. In 1973, Hilton became a leader in computerized referral and reservation systems in the industry by introducing Hiltron and HNSIS. In 1975, Prudential bought a 50% interest in six Hilton hotels for $83.3 million. By the latter part of 1977, Hilton had gained total ownership of the building and land of the illustrious Waldorf-Astoria for $35 million.

Hilton continued on its growth spurt, and in 1982 The Las Vegas Hilton (purchased in 1971) added 391 rooms, becoming the largest hotel in the world with 3,174 guest rooms. Conrad International Hotels was created as the company's new international operating subsidiary. By 1988, Hilton had made its first mark overseas by opening the first Conrad International hotel in the Western Hemisphere; also, La Belle Creole opened on the island of St. Martin in the French West Indies. By 1990, more than 270 hotels and inns in the U.S. were operating under the Hilton name. The very next year, the Hilton Grand Vacations Company, a nationwide system of vacation ownership resorts, was established. The 614-room Conrad Istanbul opened, overlooking the Sea of Maramara, and Conrad Hotels was awarded an exclusive contract to develop a $75 million resort and casino in Punta del Este, Uruguay. As Hilton strived to be the biggest and best, it joined forces with competitors Circus Circus and Caesars World to propose a $2 billion Las Vegas-style gambling facility in Chicago; at the same time, plans were underway to develop the first Vacation Ownership Resorts.

The 1990s began with Hilton as one of America's largest hotel operations with more than 240 properties and over 95,000 rooms nationwide. Just as the corporation seemed unstoppable, a federal jury ordered The Las Vegas Hilton and Hilton Hotels Corp. to pay $6.7 million in punitive and compensatory damages to former Navy lieutenant Paula Coughlin in a case stemming from the Tailhook sexual-harassment scandal in November of 1994. One year later, President and COO Raymond "Skip" Avansino resigned unexpectedly. The move prompted a decision by Hilton's board to cancel a previously announced spinoff of the company's gaming operations in 1996.

Veteran hotelman Stephen Bollenbach left Disney in 1996 to become Hilton's President and CEO. That year, Hilton announced the $2 billion purchase of Bally Entertainment Corp. Despite Bollenbach's reputation as a master dealmaker, continuing efforts to expand floundered and Hilton's plan to take over ITT Corp. failed. In 1998 Hilton and Circus Circus began unsuccessful merger discussions. By the end of 1998, Hilton spun off its gaming operations as Park Place Entertainment Corp., a publicly held company. This new gaming venture won the battle against Mirage

The Business

Financials

Revenue (1998): $1.76 billion

Employees (1998): 38,000

SICs / NAICS

sic 7011 - Hotels & Motels

sic 7999 - Amusement & Recreation Nec

sic 5812 - Eating Places

sic 6794 - Patent Owners & Lessors

naics 721191 - Bed and Breakfast Inns

naics 721199 - All Other Traveler Accommodation

naics 561599 - All Other Travel Arrangement and Reservation Services

naics 711219 - Other Spectator Sports

naics 532292 - Recreational Goods Rental

naics 722211 - Limited-Service Restaurants

naics 722212 - Cafeterias

naics 722213 - Snack and Nonalcoholic Beverage Bars

Resorts in acquiring Starwood's Ceasars casino operations in April of 1999. This acquisition made Park Place the world's largest gaming company.

History of Bally Entertainment Corp.

Lion Manufacturing, later known as Bally Manufacturing Corp., the leading manufacturer of coin-operated amusement equipment, was founded in Chicago by partners Roy Moloney, Joel Linehan, and Charles Wendt in 1931. One year later, Lion introduced the first pinball machine, which offered seven plays for a penny. They company sold more than 50,000 machines in seven months. In 1938, Lion's first slot machine hit the market, and the company began producing shavers, ballpoint pens, sewing machines, the first humidifiers, and cola dispensing machines.

In 1942, Bally switched production during World War II to detonator fuses and gun-sights for bombers. During peak war production, Lion manufactured 6,000 fuses a day, seven days a week. Bally received the Army-Navy Award for its efforts. After the war in 1955, Lion began producing soft drink and coffee dispensers and was going strong until the death of co-founder Roy Molony in 1957, which spawned a period of instability.

The Officers

Chairman: Barron Hilton

President and CEO: Stephen F. Bollenbach

Exec. VP and President of Hotel Operations: Dieter H. Huckestein

Exec. VP, Chief Financial Officer, and Treasurer: Matthew J. Hart

Exec. VP, General Counsel, and Secretary: Thomas E. Gallagher

---

In 1960, Lion sold its coffee machine business to Seeburg, America's largest jukebox manufacturer, and focused on developing its existing line of gaming machines. Lion sales manager William O'Donnell and his investment partners purchased the company in 1963. Lion developed a new slot machine called Money Honey, which combined mechanical play with electric pay-out techniques. This became the template for electronic video games that emerged several years later. On March 18, 1968, Lion Manufacturing was renamed Bally Manufacturing Corp., in honor of its first pinball game. Bally continued to maintain its primary manufacturing facilities in Chicago and in Dublin, Ireland. Bally's stock went public on March 4, 1969; the company acquired Midway Manufacturing, a producer of arcade games, that year.

In 1970, Bally added three new foreign distributing companies in Finland, Norway, and Austria, and formed Bally France S.A. The company began expanding its interest in Europe and moved into Australia and the Far East. In 1972 it purchased almost all of the assets and business of Gunter Wulff Apparatebau, a German company that produced gaming machines, and Empire Distributing, a Chicago company, and its affiliates. The company established arcades in 300 stores and opened game rooms in several shopping malls and existing arcades. Product distribution spread throughout Scandinavia, Eastern and Western Europe, Australia, Africa, and South America. Bally formed a new subsidiary, Original Equipment Motors Inc., to produce motors for Bally and Midway machines. In 1973, Bally purchased Advance Automatic Sales Co., Diemasters, Great Lakes Acceptance, and Paliner, an electronics equipment manufacturer. The firm acquired American Amusements Inc., a chain of shopping-mall game arcades, and renamed it Aladdin's Castle in April of 1974.

By 1975, Bally common stock began trading on the New York Stock Exchange. Bally Distributing was acquired for $9.5 million in cash and stock. The Aladdin's Castle subsidiary expanded by purchasing LeMans Speedway family amusement centers in 1976. In 1977, Bally purchased a casino hotel and introduced a programmable home video game, while disposing of subsidiaries in Finland, Sweden, and Guam. Manufacturing facilities in Belgium were closed that year. The company also acquired electronics firm Dave Nutting Associates Inc. In 1978, the state of New Jersey began requiring licensing of casino operators just as Bally began construction on a large hotel and casino complex in Atlantic City that was to be called Bally's Park Place. Williams Electronics, a competing producer of slot machines, filed suit against Bally claiming that the company had a monopoly on slot machine sales. The New Jersey Gaming Commission required William O'Donnell to resign and put his stock into a blind trust due to speculation that he had past business dealings with figures involved in organized crime. O'Donnell denied the allegations; nevertheless, Robert Mullane replaced him as chairman.

By 1980, the New Jersey State Casino Control Commission granted Bally a license to sell slot machines in New Jersey and Bally's Park Place received a plenary license. Bally opened a major manufacturing and office complex in Illinois, and acquired the Land of Oz Inc., an amusement arcade operating company. This was also the year that Bally introduced Space Invaders, a popular video game destined to generate considerable revenue. Bally had 221 arcade centers open around the country; the firm's booming video arcade business became its largest single market for the year. In 1981, Bally introduced Pac-Man, assembled and distributed under license from Japan's Namco. Pac-Man and Ms. Pac-Man became the most popular such games in history. Bally also opened its first European arcade and introduced a microprocessor-based series of slot machines.

With an eye toward diversification, Bally acquired Six Flags Corp., an operator of theme parks. This move was prompted by an expected slowdown in the video game market, as well as increased Japanese competition. Bally also bought Scientific Games Development, a designer and supplier of computerized lottery games. In 1982, Bally introduced Baby Pac-Man, a game combining both video and pinball playing fields.

Bally purchased Health and Tennis Corp. of America and Lancer Yacht Corp. in 1983. Revenue generated by amusement games dropped by 60%, but Bally held steady, having successfully anticipated this change. Bally began focusing on the fitness industry, and in 1984, Bally purchased Lifecycle Inc., a manufacturer of exercise bikes, renaming it Bally Fitness Products. The Six Flags subsidiary acquired another theme park, while Scientific Games emerged as Bally's fastest growing division. Through Scientific Games, Bally won the California State Lottery contract, worth roughly $40 million. Bally also won contracts to supply lottery ticket machines in Oregon, Missouri, and West Virginia, and purchased MGM Grand Hotels.

In 1987, real estate mogul Donald Trump, holding almost 10% of Bally stock, threatened a takeover. Bally bought Trump out and increased its holdings through acquisition of the Golden Nugget casino in Atlantic City, renaming it Bally's Grand. Bally's Marketing Corp. was created to market the casino properties. Bally became the world's largest owner and operator of fitness centers. To increase focus on this segment, the firm sold amusement game manufacturing businesses in 1988. Ownership in U.S. Health, was increased to over 70%.

Bogged down by high yield debt, Bally decided to restructure organizationally and financially after missing an $18.4 million interest payment on its Nevada casinos. The company backed out of a deal to buy the London Clermont Club. Operations began at Bally's relocated slot machine manufacturing facility in Las Vegas. In 1991, Bally's Grand subsidiary bondholders filed a bankruptcy petition. Domestic and foreign gaming machine operations were consolidated into Bally Gaming, a holding company, and 30% of its stock became public. In 1992, Bally's Grand filed for reorganization for its Nevada casinos. That year, financier Robert Brennan became Bally's majority shareholder, but he later sold his shares. Hilton Hotels bought Bally Reno for $83 million.

In 1994, Bally Manufacturing Corp., the leading operator of casino hotels and the largest operator of fitness centers in the U.S., changed its name to Bally Entertainment Corp. The next year, Bally spun off Bally's Health & Tennis Corp. In 1996, Bally agreed to be acquired by Hilton Hotels Corp. for $2 billion in stock.

Market Forces Driving the Merger

The mid-1990s marked a consolidation period in the gaming industry. Five years before, many states had legalized gaming, which prompted the upstart of many gaming operations. Since then, however, the number of cities rejecting casinos grew. Larger companies were looking to penetrate existing markets. The major players—Hilton, Mirage Resorts Inc., Circus Circus, MGM Grand Inc, and ITT Corporation—were expected to survive by forming partnerships and buying out smaller companies. According to Hilton CEO Bollenbach, "there will be further consolidation in the

The Players

President and CEO of Hilton Hotels Corp: Stephen F. Bollenbach. Stephen Bollenbach, a graduate of California State University, Northridge, began his career with Ludwig Group as a financial manager. Between 1968 and 1980, he worked his way up through the company, until he landed the position of vice president of finance and assistant to the chief operating officer. After leaving the Ludwig Group, Bollenbach began an illustrious career as the chairman and CEO of Southwest Savings and Loan, where he played a key role in the acquisition of five savings and loan associations. He then moved on to the Holiday Corp. and took on the role of chief financial officer. His efforts resulted in a 250% increase in company stock value in just two years. From 1990 to 1992, Bollenbach worked as CEO of the Trump Organization where he worked closely with Donald Trump to restructure and refinance the assets and companies owned by Trump. It seemed all of Bollenbach's ventures turned to gold, and this "King Midas" of the financial world had just begun to scratch the surface. In 1993 he became President and CEO of Host Marriott Corp. His creative efforts lead to the restructuring of Marriott Corp. and the creation of Host Marriott and Marriott International. As senior vice president and chief financial officer of The Walt Disney Co., Bollenbach led the firm's acquisition of ABC/Capital Cities, the second largest acquisition in U.S. history. In 1996, Bollenbach became president and CEO of Hilton Hotels; he was the first non-family member to head up the firm. Once again his deal making skills proved noteworthy as the acquisition of Bally Entertainment Corp. in June made Hilton Hotels the world's largest gaming company. Bollenbach also sits on the board of America West Corp. and K-Mart Corp.

Chairman and CEO of Bally Entertainment Corp.: Arthur M. Goldberg. Known as the "dealmeister of the 1980s," this Rutgers graduate began his career by taking over his family's trucking business, Transco Group. From there he went on to Triangle Industries and International Controls. In 1989, he left his vice chairman position of the New Jersey Sports Authority when he saw an opportunity with Bally Manufacturing. New to the gaming industry, he was made CEO of the company when he proposed a turnaround plan that was credited with saving the company from bankruptcy, raising its share price by 118.3% in 1995, and bolstering its revenue and income. In 1996, when Hilton Hotels Corp. acquired Bally Entertainment Corp., Goldberg remained a key player in industry with a seat on the board of the combined company.

gaming industry, the opportunities for growth in the new jurisdictions are not going to be there."

In the beginning of the 1990s, smaller companies in the gaming industries were able to thrive in smaller towns like St. Louis and in river boats along the Mississippi. Once larger, more experienced companies from Las Vegas and Atlantic City arrived in these towns, smaller companies could not compete. It became strategically sound to buy out competition in these smaller gaming areas. Ceasars World, Casino Magic, Casino America, Players International, and Grand Casino all became targets of larger companies. Being able to promote a company name in smaller cities and in more than one area became attractive to the high rollers in Las Vegas and Atlantic City.

Wanting to remain a powerful force in the gaming and hotel industry, Hilton Hotels was a frontrunner of the industry's consolidation. Hotel owners were intrigued by the benefits of owning casino properties. By mixing casino and convention business, companies could expect to see profit rise. Hilton was also attracted to Bally's assets and growth opportunities, not to mention its foothold in Atlantic City via Bally's Park Place and Bally's Grand. The purchase would make Hilton the largest casino company in the world.

Approach and Engagement

In early 1996, ITT Sheraton and Hilton Hotels began merger discussions with Bally Entertainment. Hilton won the bid, and in July, they completed the stock for stock deal announced in late June. Hilton completed a four-for-one stock split before the acquisition, with Bally shareholders receiving one share of Hilton stock for every share of Bally's stock owned. Hilton also assumed Bally's $1 billion net debt. When shareholders finally approved the $3 billion acquisition in September of 1996, Hilton owned 15 casinos with 18,000 hotel rooms: more than 100,000 rooms in total.

Products and Services

After the merger, Hilton owned 15 casinos in Las Vegas, Reno, New Orleans, Turkey, Ontario, and Australia. Plans to build casinos in Kansas City, and Punta Del Este, Uruguay, were also in the works. The Las Vegas Hilton, which opened in 1997, included a 22,000-square-foot casino. Hilton also gained access to Atlantic City via Bally's Park Place. Other assets included The Grand, Robinsonville, Mississippi, with a dockside casino/hotel, and a New Orleans river boat casino. The "Paris Las Vegas" casino resort was slated to open in 1999.

Changes to the Industry

The acquisition of Bally Entertainment by Hilton Hotels paved the way for the consolidation of the gaming industry. Due to slowdowns in areas of new development, many small casino companies were forced out of the industry as highrollers took over. Larger companies began to invest time and money in the larger gaming areas, Las Vegas and Atlantic City. The big got bigger with deals like ITT Sheraton's and Ceasars World's joint venture with Planet Hollywood International. Circus Circus penned a deal with Four Seasons Regent Hotels and Resorts. Also, hoteliers began to cash in as conventions became a large part of the gaming industry. Hotels could provide quality convention service at professional and upscale standards.

Review of the Outcome

After his firm's acquisition of Bally Entertainment was completed, Hilton Hotels CEO Bollenbach predicted, "this will create the most powerful force in gaming and also create good value for shareholders." He added, "we want to be the largest in the gaming industry. We want to be the winner in the consolidation of the gaming industry." Initial results boded well for the merged firm. Net income for Hilton Hotels leapt from $82 million in 1996 to $250 million in 1997. Stock prices also rose, as did revenue.

Hilton continued to expand, announcing a $4 billion agreement to merge with Promus Hotel Corp., the owners and operators of such hotels as The Doubletree Inn, Hampton Inn, and Embassy Suites, in 1999. Upon completion of that venture, the company will have nearly 1,700 hotels, approximately 290,000 rooms, and 85,000 employees. Hilton estimates that the merger will also result in synergies worth about $55 million.

Research

"Bally Entertainment Corp.," in *Notable Corporate Chronologies*, Gale Research, 1999. Lists major events in the history of Bally Entertainment Corp.

Boisclair, Marc. "After Hilton Bets $2 Billion, Other Casino Owners Wonder: Hold 'em or Fold 'em?" in *Meetings & Conventions*, August 1996. Explains how the gaming industry may be headed for consolidation.

Hilton Hotels Corp. Home Page, available at http://www.hilton.com. Official World Wide Web Home Page for Hilton Hotels Corp. This site includes detailed product, financial, and historical information.

"Hilton Hotels Corp.," in *Notable Corporate Chronologies*, Gale Research, 1999. List major events in the history of Hilton Hotels Corp.

Koss-Feder, Laura. "Hilton Betting on Bally Corp. Deal," in *Hotel and Motel Management*, 3 July 1996. Explains the benefits of the acquisition to Hilton.

McCarthy, Joseph L. "The Player," in *Chief Executive (U.S.),* April 1996. Offers information on Bally Entertainment CEO Arthur Goldberg.

Rundle, Rhonda. "Park Place Entertainment to Purchase Starwood's Ceasars Casino Operations," in *The Wall Street Journal,* 28 April 1999. Offers information on the purchase of Ceasar's casino operation by Park Place Entertainment.

Taub, Stephen. "High Rollers Seek Gaming Companies," in *Financial World,* 13 September 1994. Offers insight on the industry leading up to the merger.

CHRISTINA M. STANSELL

HOECHST & CELANESE

Hoechst AG
Brueningstrasse 50
Frankfurt, D-65926
Germany

tel: 49-69-3050
fax: 49-69-303-665
web: http://www.hoechst.com

nationality: Germany
date: March 2, 1987
affected: Hoechst AG, Germany, founded 1863
affected: Celanese Corp., USA, founded 1904

Overview of the Merger

West German pharmaceutical and chemical giant Hoechst AG bought New Jersey-based Celanese, the eighth-largest U.S. chemical company, for $2.8 billion in March of 1987. The deal was the largest takeover to date of a U.S. company by a West German firm. Hoechst then merged its American Hoechst unit with Celanese to form Hoechst Celanese Corp., the fifth-largest chemicals company in North America, with 24,000 employees. The new firm also earned a spot among the Fortune 100. When Hoechst agreed more than a decade later to merge with Rhone-Poulenc SA to form Aventis, the largest life sciences firm in the world, it began making plans to spin off its chemicals arm as Celanese AG.

History of Hoechst AG

In 1863, Chemist Eugene Lucius founded Lucius & Co. in the town of Hoechst near Frankfurt, Germany. He began with only five employees and equipment consisting of only a three horsepower steam engine and a small boiler. Anilin oil and arsenic acid were combined in the boiler to produce a synthetic fuschia dye. After researcher Adolf Bruening contributed unprecedented research in iodine, adding to Lucius & Co.'s success in the dye and chemical industries, the company changed its name to Lucius & Bruening.

The firm opened a new chemical plant in 1874, and by the early 1880s, the workforce had reached 1,900 employees. In 1883, a company chemist working with quinine discovered Antipyrin, one of the first analgesics. In cooperation with leading researchers Kock and Erlich, Lucius & Bruening produced Novocaine. By the turn of the century the company had introduced Salvarsan, a syphilis cure and the first disease-specific medicine ever manufactured.

In 1906, Lucius & Bruening announced its successful synthesis of adrenaline. Along with other German chemical companies, including Bayer AG and BASF AG, Lucius waged an intense price war against its U.S. rivals in the dye industry in 1914. While domestic business increased during World War I, Lucius lost its share of the American market and all of its U.S. assets. England, France, and the

U.S. dismantled elaborate organizations developed during the war to coordinate chemical production; Germany's, however, remained intact.

Lucius & Bruening successfully isolated insulin in 1923. Two years later, the firm merged with Bayer, BASF, and other German chemical companies to form I.G. Farbenindustrie AG, which became the leading chemical supplier to the Nazi regime. From its onset, IG Farben was active in politics, especially in urging Germany to re-arm itself. In 1933, IG Farben developed its own spy network and placed its directors in the German senate. The company, representing Germany's most important industry, was very influential in the elections supporting Adolf Hitler, whose plans for world domination were compatible with IG Farben's plans to monopolize the international chemical industry.

After the fall of France in 1940, the Nazi regime appointed IG Farben to manage the chemical industries in conquered nations. Five years later, directors of IG Farben were charged with war crimes. Despite the gravity of the accusations and the large amount of evidence extracted from IG Farben's records, no director received longer than a four-year prison sentence. The IG Farben conglomerate was dismantled, and the three main companies were given back their previous holdings. In 1952, Lucius & Bruening reemerged as Hoechst, an independent chemical company in possession of most of its previous facilities, which survived Allied bombing attempts during WW II.

The following year, Hoechst obtained rights, exclusive of the U.S., to manufacture polyester. In 1954, the firm entered into the research and manufacture of polyethylene and polyolefins; two years later, it began manufacturing petrochemicals. Several foreign subsidiaries were established to accommodate overseas production. By the end of the 1960s, Hoechst had acquired a Dutch maker of plastic moldings; established a Trevira polyester plant in Austria, as well as a joint venture in oxo-alcohols in France; and commenced polyestrene production in Spain.

In 1970, Hoechst secured almost the entire diuretic market and became the leader in oral medication for diabetics. The firm also acquired Berger, Jensen & Nicholson (Britain's largest paint producer), Hystron Fibers, and a majority stake in Roussel Uclaf. Successful pharmaceutical products helped to offset losses in the fibers market late in the decade.

In 1980, Hoechst made the largest single investment in its history with the establishment a $100 million plant in Freeport, Texas. The firm actively pursued gaining a larger share in the U.S. drug market by doubling its U.S. sales force and targeting hospitals, the major customers for ethical drugs. During the

The Business

Financials

Revenue (1998): $26.2 billion

Employees (1998): 97,000

SICs / NAICS

sic 2812 - Alkalies & Chlorine

sic 2816 - Inorganic Pigments

sic 2822 - Synthetic Rubber

sic 2821 - Plastics Materials & Resins

sic 2824 - Organic Fibers-Noncellulosic

sic 2833 - Medicinals & Botanicals

sic 2834 - Pharmaceutical Preparations

sic 2835 - Diagnostic Substances

sic 2836 - Biological Products Except Diagnostic

naics 325181 - Alkalies and Chlorine Manufacturing

naics 325131 - Inorganic Dye and Pigment Manufacturing

naics 325182 - Carbon Black Manufacturing

naics 325211 - Plastics Material and Resin Manufacturing

naics 325212 - Synthetic Rubber Manufacturing

naics 325222 - Noncellulosic Organic Fiber Manufacturing

naics 325411 - Medicinal and Botanical Manufacturing

naics 325412 - Pharmaceutical Preparation Manufacturing

naics 325413 - In-Vitro Diagnostic Substance Manufacturing

naics 325414 - Biological Product (except Diagnostic) Manufacturing

decade, Hoechst began investing in genetic engineering through a joint venture with Massachusetts General Hospital. It also purchased the industrial ceramics division of Germany's largest fine china maker, Rosenthal, endeavoring to gain some of Japan's 90% market share in semi-conductor ceramics. Additionally, it acquired New Jersey-based Celanese Corp. for $2.8 billion.

To gain a wider presence in the North American market, Hoechst secured a controlling stake in Celanese Mexicana, the leading private chemical company in Mexico, in 1990. The firm also finalized negotiations with Teijin in Japan for its production and marketing of flame retardant fiber in the Far East. The following year, Hoechst introduced Altace, a hypertension drug, through a co-marketing agreement with The Upjohn Co.

The Officers

Chairman and CEO: Jurgen Dormann

Chief Financial Officer: Klaus-Jurgen Schmieder

President and CEO, Celanese: Knut Zeptner

Member Management Board and Director Personnel:
Ernst Schadow

Member Management Board: Claudio Sonder

Member Management Board: Horst Waesche

Strengthening its position in the European coatings market, Hoechst acquired in 1991 the powder coating business of Beckers in Sweden, the fiber business of Chemiefaser Guben in eastern Germany, and two industrial coating plants from Lacufa. A fall in profits in 1992 prompted streamlining measures, including the closing of several dye and fine chemical plants. Losses in 1993 were at the root of a cost reduction program, which included incentives for early retirement.

In 1995, Hoechst acquired U.S. pharmaceutical company Marion Merrell Dow Inc. for $7.1 billion. The purchase upped the company's U.S. market share from 1% to 4%, making Hoechst the third-largest drug company in the world, with $11 million in annual sales. Also that year, in what was believed to be the largest environmental liability case ever in Germany, Hoechst's insurers paid $21 million to 7,000 people whose cars and houses were damaged by a little-publicized leak from a plant near Cologne. The following year, in the wake of three industrial accidents in four days at its Hoechst and Griesheim (Frankfurt) sites, Hoechst immediately appointed emergency managers at each German site and announced plans to invest $100 million to modernize the measurement and control technology at those two sites.

Multikarsa, based in Indonesia, bought the European operations of Trevira from Hoechst in 1998. The following year, Hoechst sold its paints and coatings unit and announced its intent to spin off industrial chemicals operations as Celanese AG. These divestitures were in preparation for Hoechst's plans to merge with Rhone-Poulenc SA into Aventis SA, the largest life sciences group in the world, by the end of 1999.

History of Celanese Corp.

In 1904, brothers Dr. Camille E. Dreyfus and Dr. Henri Dreyfus began researching cellulose acetate in a small shed in their father's backyard in Basel, Switzerland. Six years later, they opened a factory for the production of cellulose acetate to be used as a non-flammable motion picture film base. In 1917, the U.S. government hired the two brothers to supply acetate lacquer coating to the U.S. military, work that began the following year after a factory was built for that purpose in Cumberland, Maryland.

When World War I ended, the Dreyfus brothers continued their work with cellulose acetate. In 1921, at a factory in England, they produced the first commercial cellulose acetate yarn, or "artificial silk," on the market. Three years later, the plant in Maryland began producing the yarn as well.

By the end of the 1930s, the brothers' business, by then known as Celanese Corp., had diversified into plastics and industrial chemicals. The introduction in the 1950s of synthetic fibers—such as polyester, nylon, and acrylic—reduced the market for cellulose fiber and forced Celanese to begin venturing into new markets such as polyester and nylon, as well as chemicals, plastics, paints, and petroleum. In 1962, Celanese formed a European joint venture with German chemical and pharmaceutical giant Hoechst AG. Twenty-five years later, Hoechst acquired Celanese for $2.8 billion and merged its U.S. operations with Hoechst to form Hoechst Celanese Corp.

Market Forces Driving the Merger

After years of disappointing results due mainly to poor performance in the fibers market, Hoechst's U.S. unit, American Hoechst Corp. reorganized in 1982 into four segments: fibers and film, petrochemicals and plastics, specialty products, and health care and agricultural chemicals. Sales grew from $1.51 billion in 1982 to $1.76 billion in 1984. More importantly, earnings jumped from a paltry $3 million to $53.2 million during the same time period, allowing the firm to pursue a major acquisition. The firm surprised Wall Street in 1986 with its bid for Celanese, a polyester fibers and commodity-based chemicals group with annual sales of $2.5 billion. Analysts questioned why American Hoechst was interested in increasing its reliance on commodity fibers, a market that it had been pulling away from during the past decade.

American Hoechst countered that the acquisition would bring many benefits. First and foremost, the deal would position the unit's German parent company, Hoechst AG, as one of the world's largest chemical producers, with $17.5 billion in annual revenues. The addition of Celanese would also improve Hoechst AG's position in the lucrative U.S. market—a long-time goal of the German firm—and give American Hoechst access to the marketing expertise and well developed sales network of Celanese.

According to a 1989 article in *Financial Times (London)*, "American Hoechst was also too small to develop the managerial and technological resources required to compete in U.S. chemicals. It needed more critical mass to justify the investment and research development necessary to build its business." Moreover, "Celanese was also burdened by problems of size. It was eager to broaden its base of its $3 billion business beyond fibers and commodity chemicals, but its limited resources meant its expansion was restricted to joint venture and equity stakes in other companies where it could not exercise managerial control." Having boosted its profitability after a recent restructuring and stock buyback, Celanese was also apprehensive that it might soon become the target of a hostile bid.

Approach and Engagement

On November 3, 1986, Celanese Corp. announced its agreement to be acquired by Hoechst AG for $2.85 billion. Celanese stock bounded $24 per share to $242.50 upon news of the deal. According to the terms of the agreement, the American Hoechst unit of Hoechst AG would issue a tender offer of $245 for each of the 11.63 million outstanding shares of Celanese. To gain the approval of the U.S. Federal Trade Commission, Celanese agreed to divest its two largest fiber factories within 12 months of the deal's completion. The acquisition was completed on March 2, 1987, when Celanese and American Hoechst merged operations to form Hoechst Celanese Corp. By the end of the year, Ernest H. Drew had taken over as CEO and Dieter zur Loye had been appointed chairman of the new firm.

Products and Services

Two years after the merger was completed, Hoechst Celanese reorganized into five segments: Advanced Materials, which included engineering plastics; Advanced Technology, which involved the research and development specialty products, as well as new business development activities; Chemicals, which comprised specialty and commodity chemicals, Fibers and Film; and Life Sciences, which focuses on pharmaceuticals, animal health, and agricultural crop protection products.

By the late 1990s, the Celanese unit accounted for 15% of total revenues at Hoechst AG. The firm's pharmaceutical arm, Hoechst Marion Roussel, brought in the largest chunk at 25%, due mainly to products like hypertension drug Cadizem and allergy treatment Allegra. Trevira, the technical polymers unit, secured 12%. AgroEvo crop protection products and specialty chemicals both garnered 8%, while Messer and

The Players

Chairman and CEO of American Hoechst Corp.: Jurgen Dormann. Jurgen Dormann began his career at Hoechst AG as a management trainee in 1963. Within a decade, he had worked his way up to head of the corporate staff department. In 1984, he was named a deputy member of the board of management. Dormann was chairman and CEO of American Hoechst prior to its merger with Celanese Corp. in March of 1987. He remained at the helm of the newly merged firm, Hoechst Celanese Corp., until December of that year, when he was named chairman of Hoechst Corp., the holding company of Hoechst AG's U.S. operations, as well as chief financial officer of the parent company. In 1994, Dormann took over as chairman of Hoechst AG.

Chairman and CEO of Celanese Corp: John D. Macomber. After working as a senior partner at McKinsey & Co. for roughly 20 years, John Macomber accepted a post with Celanese Corp. in the mid-1970s. He was eventually appointed chairman and CEO of the firm, and stock prices grew from $24.50 per share to $245 per share during his reign. When Hoechst AG acquired the firm in March of 1987, the 59-year-old executive secured a $2 million "golden parachute" severance package and stepped down to make room for new management.

Herberts each grabbed 5%. Plastics snagged 4%; Ticona, 3%; Hoechst Roussel Vet, an animal heath operation, 2%; and Behring Diagnostics, 1%.

Changes to the Industry and Review of the Outcome

"Given that textile fibers was the only area of activity where the two companies overlapped, the merger was relatively free from the cuts and closures that mar the aftermath of so many acquisitions," wrote *Financial Times (London)*. The 150 layoffs that did occur were due to redundancies in corporate operations, such as finance and human resources.

The immediate success of Hoechst Celanese—the fifth-largest chemicals company in North America and the newest Fortune 100 member—surprised many industry analysts. During its first full year of operation, net income reached $250 million on sales of $5.7 billion, one of the strongest performances realized by any Hoechst group unit that year. Despite increased competition in 1989, sales grew to exceed $6 billion. Hoechst Celanese spent a whopping $546 million in November of 1993 for a 53% stake in Copley Pharmaceuticals Inc., an over-the-counter and generic drugs manufacturer that had realized a sales increase of 80% in 1992 and had 23 new products in the approval pipeline.

The acquisition was intended to parlay Hoechst Celanese into a leader in the burgeoning generic and over-the-counter drug market, yet it seemed a poor decision in hindsight, as lawsuits emerged alleging that tainted batches of Copley's Albuterol asthma drug led to deaths. To bolster its U.S. pharmaceuticals presence, Hoechst AG paid $7.1 billion for Marion Merrell Dow and formed the pharmaceutical arm Hoechst Marion Roussel, which soon accounted for 25% of total revenues. Hoechst Celanese refocused on chemicals, which accounted for 15% of sales in 1997.

In May of 1999, Hoechst announced its intent to purchase the 44% of Celanese Canada that it didn't already own for $306 million. Once the acquisition is completed, Hoechst will spin off its chemical operations as Celanese AG to prepare for its planned merger with Rhone-Poulenc to form Aventis SA, the world's largest life sciences group.

Research

"Celanese Chief Leaving as Hoechst Takes Over," in *The New York Times*, 5 March 1987. Details the career of Celanese CEO John D. Macomber.

Hoechst AG Home Page, available at http://www.hoechst.com. Official World Wide Web Home Page for Hoechst AG. Available in both German and English, this site includes current and archived news, as well as employment, product, and investor information.

"Hoechst AG," in *Notable Corporate Chronologies*, The Gale Group, 1999. Lists major events in the history of Hoechst AG, including its takeover of Celanese Corp.

"Hoechst Celanese Corp.," in *International Directory of Company Histories*, Vol. 13, St. James Press, 1995. Describes the history of Hoechst Celanese Corp., including the merger that formed the company.

"Hoechst to Purchase Rest of Celanese Canada," in *The New York Times*, 20 May 1999. Explains how Hoechst AG is preparing for its merger with Rhone-Poulenc by buying the remainder of Celanese Canada prior to spinning off Celanese to shareholders.

Rawsthorn, Alice. "Laying Down the Ground Rules for a Marriage of Two Cultures: World Chemicals," in *Financial Times (London)*, 1 September 1989. Explains why Hoechst bought Celanese and how the resulting unit, Hoechst Celanese, has fared in the two years since the deal was completed.

Ross, Philip E. "Hoechst Celanese Fills Chief Executive Post," in *The New York Times*, 29 December 1987. Details the management changes at Hoechst Celanese months after its formation.

THERA WILLIAMS

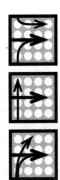

HOECHST & MARION MERRELL DOW

nationality: Germany
date: July 1995
affected: Hoechst AG, Germany, founded 1863
affected: Marion Merrell Dow Inc., USA, founded 1828

Hoechst AG
Brueningstrasse 50
Frankfurt, D-65926
Germany

tel: 49-69-3050
fax: 49-69-303-665
web: http://www.hoechst.com

Overview of the Merger

When German chemical and pharmaceutical giant Hoechst paid $7.2 billion to Dow Chemical Co. for Marion Merrell Dow Inc., the firm increased its share of the U.S. pharmaceutical market from 6% to 24% and doubled its overall drug sales. The deal also propelled Hoechst from the number seven spot among worldwide pharmaceutical firms to third place. Hoechst founded a new unit, Hoechst Marion Roussel (HMR), to house its new purchase, and during its first year of operation, HMR introduced the blockbuster allergy drug Allegra.

History of Hoechst AG

In 1863, Chemist Eugene Lucius founded Lucius & Co. in the town of Hoechst near Frankfurt, Germany. He began with only five employees and equipment consisting of only a three horsepower steam engine and a small boiler. Anilin oil and arsenic acid were combined in the boiler to produce a synthetic fuschia dye. After researcher Adolf Bruening contributed unprecedented research in iodine, adding to Lucius & Co.'s success in the dye and chemical industries, the company changed its name to Lucius & Bruening.

The firm opened a new chemical plant in 1874, and by the early 1880s, the workforce had reached 1,900 employees. In 1883, a company chemist working with quinine discovered Antipyrin, one of the first analgesics. In cooperation with leading researchers Kock and Erlich, Lucius & Bruening produced Novocaine. By the turn of the century the company had introduced Salvarsan, a syphilis cure and the first disease-specific medicine ever manufactured.

In 1906, Lucius & Bruening announced its successful synthesis of adrenaline. Along with other German chemical companies, including Bayer AG and BASF AG, Lucius waged an intense price war against its U.S. rivals in the dye industry in 1914. While domestic business increased during World War I, Lucius lost its share of the American market and all of its U.S. assets. England, France, and the U.S. dismantled elaborate organizations developed during the war to coordinate chemical production; Germany's, however, remained intact.

The Business

Financials

Revenue (1998): $26.2 billion

Employees (1998): 97,000

SICs / NAICS

sic 2812 - Alkalies & Chlorine

sic 2816 - Inorganic Pigments

sic 2822 - Synthetic Rubber

sic 2821 - Plastics Materials & Resins

sic 2824 - Organic Fibers-Noncellulosic

sic 2833 - Medicinals & Botanicals

sic 2834 - Pharmaceutical Preparations

sic 2835 - Diagnostic Substances

sic 2836 - Biological Products Except Diagnostic

naics 325181 - Alkalies and Chlorine Manufacturing

naics 325131 - Inorganic Dye and Pigment Manufacturing

naics 325182 - Carbon Black Manufacturing

naics 325211 - Plastics Material and Resin Manufacturing

naics 325212 - Synthetic Rubber Manufacturing

naics 325222 - Noncellulosic Organic Fiber Manufacturing

naics 325411 - Medicinal and Botanical Manufacturing

naics 325412 - Pharmaceutical Preparation Manufacturing

naics 325413 - In-Vitro Diagnostic Substance
Manufacturing

naics 325414 - Biological Product (except Diagnostic)
Manufacturing

Lucius & Bruening successfully isolated insulin in 1923. Two years later, the firm merged with Bayer, BASF, and other German chemical companies to form I.G. Farbenindustrie AG, which became the leading chemical supplier to the Nazi regime. From its onset, IG Farben was active in politics, especially in urging Germany to re-arm itself. In 1933, IG Farben developed its own spy network and placed its directors in the German senate. The company, representing Germany's most important industry, was very influential in the elections supporting Adolf Hitler, whose plans for world domination were compatible with IG Farben's plans to monopolize the international chemical industry.

After the fall of France in 1940, the Nazi regime appointed IG Farben to manage the chemical indus-tries in conquered nations. Five years later, directors of IG Farben were charged with war crimes. Despite the gravity of the accusations and the large amount of evidence extracted from IG Farben's records, no director received longer than a four-year prison sentence. The IG Farben conglomerate was dismantled, and the three main companies were given back their previous holdings. In 1952, Lucius & Bruening reemerged as Hoechst, an independent chemical company in possession of most of its previous facilities, which survived Allied bombing attempts during WW II.

The following year, Hoechst obtained rights, exclusive of the U.S., to manufacture polyester. In 1954, the firm entered into the research and manufacture of polyethylene and polyolefins; two years later, it began manufacturing petrochemicals. Several foreign subsidiaries were established to accommodate overseas production. By the end of the 1960s, Hoechst had acquired a Dutch maker of plastic moldings; established a Trevira polyester plant in Austria, as well as a joint venture in oxo-alcohols in France; and commenced polyestrene production in Spain.

In 1970, Hoechst secured almost the entire diuretic market and became the leader in oral medication for diabetics. The firm also acquired Berger, Jensen & Nicholson (Britain's largest paint producer), Hystron Fibers, and a majority stake in Roussel Uclaf. Successful pharmaceutical products helped to offset losses in the fibers market late in the decade.

In 1980, Hoechst made the largest single investment in its history with the establishment a $100 million plant in Freeport, Texas. The firm actively pursued gaining a larger share in the U.S. drug market by doubling its U.S. sales force and targeting hospitals, the major customers for ethical drugs. During the decade, Hoechst began investing in genetic engineering through a joint venture with Massachusetts General Hospital. It also purchased the industrial ceramics division of Germany's largest fine china maker, Rosenthal, endeavoring to gain some of Japan's 90% market share in semi-conductor ceramics. Additionally, it acquired New Jersey-based Celanese Corp. for $2.8 billion.

To gain a wider presence in the North American market, Hoechst secured a controlling stake in Celanese Mexicana, the leading private chemical company in Mexico, in 1990. The firm also finalized negotiations with Teijin in Japan for its production and marketing of flame retardant fiber in the Far East. The following year, Hoechst introduced Altace, a hypertension drug, through a co-marketing agreement with The Upjohn Co.

Strengthening its position in the European coatings market, Hoechst acquired in 1991 the powder coating business of Beckers in Sweden, the fiber business of Chemiefaser Guben in eastern Germany, and two industrial coating plants from Lacufa. A fall in profits in 1992 prompted streamlining measures, including the closing of several dye and fine chemical plants. Losses in 1993 were at the root of a cost reduction program, which included incentives for early retirement.

In 1995, Hoechst acquired U.S. pharmaceutical company Marion Merrell Dow Inc. for $7.1 billion. The purchase upped the company's U.S. market share from 1% to 4%, making Hoechst the third-largest drug company in the world, with $11 million in annual sales. Also that year, in what was believed to be the largest environmental liability case ever in Germany, Hoechst's insurers paid $21 million to 7,000 people whose cars and houses were damaged by a little-publicized leak from a plant near Cologne. The following year, in the wake of three industrial accidents in four days at its Hoechst and Griesheim (Frankfurt) sites, Hoechst immediately appointed emergency managers at each German site and announced plans to invest $100 million to modernize the measurement and control technology at those two sites.

Multikarsa, based in Indonesia, bought the European operations of Trevira from Hoechst in 1998. The following year, Hoechst sold its paints and coatings unit and announced its intent to spin off industrial chemicals operations as Celanese AG. These divestitures were in preparation for Hoechst's plans to merge with Rhone-Poulenc SA into Aventis SA, the largest life sciences group in the world, by the end of 1999.

History of Marion Merrell Dow Inc.

In 1828, William S. Merrell, a chemist, opened a small retail drugstore, Western Market Drug Store, in Cincinnati, Ohio. Along with his brother, Ashbel Merrell, William Merrell moved to larger facilities and changed the name of the business to Wm. S. Merrell & Co. Operations in the 1850s included manufacturing as well as wholesale and retail sales. By the end of the decade, Merrell was manufacturing over 1,000 products, including the most indigenous or botanic medicines of any company in the U.S.

In 1876, Merrell became the first company to manufacture salicylic acid, the forerunner of acetylsalicylic acid (aspirin), for the U.S. medical profession. The firm began to diversify in the early 1900s, making fluid extracts, tinctures, tablets, pills, ointments, capsules, elixirs, vitamin pills, and toothpaste. In 1938, Vick Chemical Co. purchased Merrell, which continued operations as a wholly owned subsidiary. Two years later, Cepacol brand mouthwash was introduced and marketed nationally by Merrell.

The Officers

Chairman and CEO: Jurgen Dormann

Chief Financial Officer: Klaus-Jurgen Schmieder

President and CEO, Celanese: Knut Zeptner

Member Management Board and Director Personnel:
    Ernst Schadow

Member Management Board: Claudio Sonder

Member Management Board: Horst Waesche

In 1956, Merrell established an international division to expand its operations and markets outside the U.S. Four years later, Vick Chemical Co. changed its name to Richardson-Merrell Inc. to honor both William Merrell and Vick's founder, Lunsford Richardson. Merrell introduced papaverine hydrochloride, a cerebral vasodilator sold under the brand name Pavabid, in the early 1960s. The drug soon became the firm's best selling product. Merrell was merged in 1971 with the National Drug Co., also owned by Richardson-Merrell, to form the Merrell-National Laboratories Division, which began research to find new compounds for the treatment of cardiovascular disease, central nervous system disorders, and abnormal cell growth.

Dow Chemical Co., based in Midland, Michigan, acquired the domestic and international operations of Merrell-National Laboratories in 1981 to form Merrell Dow Pharmaceuticals Inc. Merrell Dow operated as a division of Dow Chemical and was headquartered in Cincinnati, Ohio. The following year, the blockbuster hypertension drug Cardizem received U.S. Food and Drug Administration (FDA) marketing approval as a calcium slow channel blocker indicated for the treatment of angina. In 1985, the FDA approved Merrell Dow's Seldane brand allergy treatment for marketing in the U.S.; it became the world's top selling nonsedating antihistamine, but the drug was later pulled from shelves when possibly life-threatening side effects were discovered.

Ewing Marion Kauffman founded Marion Laboratories in 1950 as a one-man company operating out of his home in Kansas City, Missouri. Initially, he sold injectable products manufactured by Taylor Pharmacal Co. To raise operating capital, Kauffman persuaded each of seven men to invest $1,000 and purchase a $1,000 bond. In 1952, Marion Laboratories was incorporated. The firm recorded its first profitable year in 1954, and sales exceeded $1 million for the first time in 1959. On August 19, 1965, Marion's stock was

The Players

Chairman and CEO of American Hoechst Corp.: Jurgen Dormann. Jurgen Dormann began his career at Hoechst AG as a management trainee in 1963. Within a decade, he had worked his way up to head of the corporate staff department. In 1984, he was named a deputy member of the board of management. Dormann was chairman and CEO of American Hoechst prior to its merger with Celanese Corp. in March of 1987. He remained at the helm of the newly merged firm, Hoechst Celanese Corp., until December of that year, when he was named chairman of Hoechst Corp., the holding company of Hoechst AG's U.S. operations, as well as chief financial officer of the parent company. In 1994, Dormann took over as chairman of Hoechst AG. He steered his firm's acquisition of Marion Merrell Dow in 1995 and remains at the helm of Hoechst today.

Chairman and CEO of Marion Merrell Dow Inc.: Fred W. Lyons, Jr. After serving as an executive vice president of Marion Laboratories, Fred Lyons was named president and chief operating officer of the firm in 1977. In 1984, he took over as CEO. When Marion merged with Merrell Dow to form Marion Merrell Dow, Lyons accepted the post of president of the newly merged firm, and in 1992, he was named CEO. The 58-year-old Lyons retired when Hoechst took over Marion Merrell Dow in 1995 to form Hoechst Marion Roussel Inc.

made available for public sale with an initial offering of 187,740 shares at $21 apiece. Four years later, the firm began trading on the New York Stock Exchange.

Marion introduced Gaviscon brand antacid tablets, intended for relief of heartburn associated with reflux esophagitis, in 1970. Seven years later, sales exceeded $100 million for the first time. In 1981, Marion divested four subsidiaries whose manufacturing operations ranged from home stairway elevators to vision correction products. Tanabe Seiyaku and Marion announced an agreement in 1984 to jointly develop, license, and market certain Tanabe compounds in the U.S. and Canada. Between 1983 and 1987, stock split four times. In 1988, Marion and Schering-Plough Corp. announced an agreement to jointly develop over-the-counter formulations of Marion's prescription product Carafate. That year, the

firm divested its analytical systems operations and acquired American Biomaterials Corp.

After deciding to refocus on its core pharmaceutical operations in 1989, Marion sold off its scientific products arm and bought a minority equity interest in U.S. Bioscience, a development stage pharmaceutical company focused on cancer treatments. Later that year, Marion and Dow Chemical signed an agreement to merge Marion with Merrell Dow to form Marion Merrell Dow Inc. Joseph G. Temple, Jr. was elected chairman and CEO of the new firm.

Nordic Laboratories Inc. became wholly owned after Marion Merrell Dow acquired the remaining 14.6% of its stock in 1991; it was placed under the management of Marion Merrell Dow (Canada) Inc. That year, the FDA approved the Nicoderm brand nicotine transdermal system for marketing in the U.S. SmithKline Beecham PLC and Marion Merrell Dow jointly created SmithKline Beecham Consumer Brands in 1992 to develop and market over-the-counter drugs in the U.S. Combined sales of all Cardizem brand products surpassed $1 billion. In 1994 the company settled Federal Trade Commission charges that its acquisition of a generic-drug maker last year wrongfully created a monopoly in the U.S. gastrointestinal drug market.

German pharmaceutical company Hoechst AG paid $7.2 billion to acquire Marion Merrell Dow Inc. in 1995. After the deal was completed, Hoechst established a new division, Hoechst Marion Roussel. During its first full year of operation, Hoechst Marion Roussel received FDA approval to market a prescription antihistamine called Allegra. This allergy drug quickly become one of the firm's best seller, replacing Seldane.

Market Forces Driving the Merger

Hoping to parlay itself into a leader in the burgeoning generic and over-the-counter drug market, Hoechst spent a startling $546 million in November of 1993 for a 53% stake in Copley Pharmaceuticals Inc., a U.S.-based over-the-counter and generic drugs manufacturer that had realized a sales increase of 80% in 1992 and had 23 new products in the approval pipeline. The purchase price was 20 times the annual sales of Copley (compared to an industry standard of three or four times sales), but Hoechst justified its offer by pointing to the necessity of securing a strong foothold in the generics market. The recessionary conditions in Germany in 1992 and 1993, coupled with a downturn in the commodity chemicals industry, prompted Germany's largest chemical companies to seek growth in the less cyclical pharmaceutical industry. Because pressure to reduce costs in the pharmaceutical industry was growing, the low cost margin generic drug segment was most attractive to companies like Hoechst. However, the acquisition of Copley caused problems for Hoechst after lawsuits emerged alleging that tainted batches of Copley's Albuterol asthma drug led to deaths. As a result, in the mid-1990s, Hoechst was still looking for its big break into the U.S. pharmaceutical market, particularly the generic drug segment.

According to a March 1995 article in *Business Week*, Hoechst CEO Dormann was also "scrambling to position Hoechst as one of a handful of high-volume drugmakers powerful enough to deal directly with health-maintenance organizations (HMOs) and hospitals in the managed-care era." Although Marion Merrell Dow had few promising products in the pipeline, its sales force was regarded as an industry leader, largely due to the inroads it had made with large HMOs. Hoechst hoped to use Marion Merrell Dow to sell its drugs in the lucrative U.S. market, where even its leading products had languished in the face of aggressive sales and marketing tactics by U.S. pharmaceutical industry leaders.

Approach and Engagement

Hoechst spent the latter half of 1994 informally negotiating its purchase of Marion Merrell Dow with Dow Chemical. On February 28, 1995, Hoechst bid $7.2 billion in cash, or $25.75 per share, for the 71% of Marion Merrell Dow owned by Dow Chemical, as well as the 29% owned by shareholders on the New York Stock Exchange. The price was $500 million less than Dow had paid for the firm in 1989, but Hoechst CEO Dormann believed Dow Chemical's desire to sell Marion Merrell Dow—prompted by an 11% drop in net income in 1994 and dwindling market share, which were both mainly the result of patent expiry on leading drugs—would outweigh its desire to make a profit on the deal. Hoechst also offered $200 million to Dow Chemical for its Latin American operations.

In July of 1995, the U.S. Federal Trade Commission, The European Commission, and Canadian cartel authorities approved the deal. Later that month, the transaction was finalized, and Hoechst established a new pharmaceutical arm, named Hoechst Marion Roussel, to house its new purchase.

Products and Services

By the late 1990s, Hoechst Marion Roussel had become the largest segment of Hoechst AG, accounting for 25% of annual sales, due mainly to products like hypertension drug Cadizem and allergy treatment Allegra. The Celanese chemicals unit accounted for 15% of total revenues. Trevira, the technical polymers unit, secured 12%. AgroEvo crop protection products and specialty chemicals both garnered 8%, while Messer and Herberts each grabbed 5%. Plastics snagged 4%; Ticona, 3%; Hoechst Roussel Vet, an animal heath operation, 2%; and Behring Diagnostics, 1%.

Changes to the Industry and Review of the Outcome

The purchase of Marion Merrell Dow allowed Hoechst AG to up its U.S. pharmaceutical market share from 6% to 24%, double its overall drug sales, and move into the third-place spot among worldwide pharmaceutical groups. Within a year of the deal's completion, Hoechst Marion Roussel had introduced Allegra, which soon became one of the world's leading allergy drugs. By 1997, U.S. operations accounted for 22% of the parent firm's total revenues. Between 1995 and 1998, Hoechst laid off 8,000 employees, nearly 20% of its workforce, due to redundancies related to the acquisition.

Research

"Hoechst's Acquisition Plans for MMD, Syva, Approved," in *Pharmaceutical Business News*, 11 July 1995. Announces that Hoechst had received regulatory approval for its acquisition of Marion Merrell Dow.

Hoechst AG Home Page, available at http://www.hoechst.com. Official World Wide Web Home Page for Hoechst AG. Available in both German and English, this site includes current and archived news, as well as employment, product, and investor information.

"Hoechst AG," in *Notable Corporate Chronologies*, The Gale Group, 1999. Lists major events in the history of Hoechst AG, including its takeover of Celanese Corp.

"Marion Merrell Dow Inc.," in *Notable Corporate Chronologies*, The Gale Group, 1999. Profiles major events in the history of Marion Merrell Dow Inc.

Miller, Karen. "A $7 Billion Passport? Why Hoechst Needs Marion Merrell Dow," in *Business Week*, 20 March 1995. Explains why Hoechst AG wants to purchase the struggling Marion Merrell Dow.

Peaff, George. "Hoechst Bids $7 Billion for Dow Drug Unit," in *Chemical & Engineering News*, 6 March 1995. Discusses the details of the offer made by Hoechst for Marion Merrell Dow.

———. "Hoechst to Cut 8,000 Pharmaceutical Jobs," in *Chemical & Engineering News*, 10 July 1995. Reports on the layoffs that resulted from Hoechst's purchase of Marion Merrell Dow.

Young, Ian. "Big Three Head Down the Generics Road; Seeking Growth in Off-Patent Drugs," in *Chemical Week*, 24 May 1995. Explains the industry and economic conditions that prompted interest by Germany's leading chemical and drug firms in the generic drug market.

THERA WILLIAMS

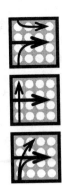

HOLLINGER & SUN-TIMES

Hollinger International Inc.
10 Toronto St.
Toronto, ON M5C 2B7
Canada

tel: (416)363-8721
fax: (416)364-0832
web: http://www.hollinger.com

nationality: Canada
date: March 1994
affected: Hollinger International Inc., Canada, founded 1985
affected: Sun-Times Inc., USA

Overview of the Acquisition

Discussions of an acquisition of Sun-Times Inc. began in 1992 between David Radler and investment banking mogul Leonard Shaykin. Shaykin's banking firm had purchased the *Chicago Sun-Times* in 1986 for $145 million, but the paper was suffering as a result of a national recession and loss of sales to emerging news media. The deal for Sun-Times Inc. also included ownership of suburban Chicago's *Pioneer Press* and *Star* newspapers. Radler and Shaykin reached a deal without negotiations between corporate lawyers, and with little fanfare. Radler stated at a press conference that the deal took so long because both men were simply too busy to finalize it.

Adler & Shaykin agreed to sell the newspaper, along with two smaller Chicago publishing operations, in a $180 million cash deal with American Publishing. Sun-Times Inc. President and CEO Sam McKeel resigned shortly after the acquisition, and Radler filled the top three positions.

History of Adler & Shaykin

The Investment Banking firm Adler & Shaykin was founded in February 1983, with a focus on handling leveraged buyouts (LBOs). The company was formed by the partnership of venture capitalist Fredrick Adler and pioneer LBO financier Leonard Shaykin. Besides his position at Adler & Shaykin, Fredrick Adler was also a senior partner at the New York law firm Reavis & McGrath.

Shaykin joined Citicorp in 1979 and led the bank's Venture Capital Ltd., where he perfected the art of the LBO. The LBO technique is based upon the use of a company's assets for collateral to gain investor financing. During his time there he was credited with creating such companies as Data General, Sci-Tex, and Lexidata.

The banking firm acquired several suffering businesses, including Peterson Outdoor Advertising, Addiction Recovery Corp., and the *Chicago Sun-Times*, in 1986. In 1992, Shaykin and American Publishing president David Radler began friendly discussions regarding a sale of the *Chicago Sun-Times*, which Shaykin purchased for $145 million in addition to a $100 million deal for surrounding smaller newspapers and a direct mail company. The cash deal was finalized in March of 1994.

History of Hollinger Inc.

Conrad Black began his corporate career when he started taking control of the Argus Corp. in 1978. Black founded Hollinger Inc. in 1985 to handle his growing subsidiaries. (Its name came from a mining operation asset of Argus Corp.) In 1985 Black paid $43 million for a 50.1% interest in England's *Daily Telegraph*, which became a wholly owned subsidiary in 1995.

Hollinger Inc. immediately began acquiring small newspapers throughout Canada, England, and the United States. As Hollinger's interests in the U.S. grew, Black formed Chicago-based American Publishing Co. While the company continued to acquire newspapers throughout the United States, Hollinger also purchased Jerusalem Post Publications, the only English-language daily in Israel. When Hollinger Inc. became mired in debt during the last half of the 1980s, Black transferred a large portion of the company's newspaper operations to its Chicago-based subsidiary, capitalizing on the higher values available in the U.S. market. In 1995 Black formed Hollinger International as an umbrella company for American Publishing, based in Chicago.

American Publishing President David Radler negotiated a purchase of the *Chicago Sun-Times* in 1994. The deal, valued at $180 million, put Hollinger near the top of major newspaper publishers. Shortly after the acquisition was completed, American Publishing offered stock in an initial public offering, earning $88 million.

In 1995 Hollinger purchased two daily and 12 non-daily newspapers from Canadian-based Armdale, and 19 paid-circulation papers from Thomson Corp. As news media expanded into cable and computer sectors, Hollinger formed Hollinger Digital in 1997 to handle new investments in the emerging markets. The same year, Hollinger sold its interest in the Australian John Fairfax to a New Zealand company. While Hollinger held a strong interest in Southam, it wasn't until 1999 that the company finally acquired the entire publisher in order to create a nationwide Canadian newspaper to compete against the *Globe and Mail*. The Southam acquisition gave Hollinger control of Montreal's *The Gazette* and the *Ottawa Citizen*.

Market Forces Driving the Merger

Hollinger Inc. found much success with small newspapers, but had never taken charge of a large

The Business

Financials

Revenue (1998): $2.2 billion

Employees (1998): 16,500

SICs / NAICS

sic 2711 - Newspapers

sic 6719 - Holding Companies Nec

naics 551112 - Offices of Other Holding Companies

U.S. operation. After an attempt to purchase the *New York Daily News* fell through, Leonard Shaykin commented to David Radler that Adler & Shaykin "had a much better paper in Chicago if [Hollinger] wanted a major paper in the United States." American Publishing had reported net losses in 1993, and looked to raise assets and sales through acquisition and growth.

What most affected the *Chicago Sun-Times*—and the entire newspaper market—was a national recession and the growth of cable and online media markets. Additionally, the *Chicago Sun-Times* could not accept much color print work, therefore giving the *Tribune* an advantage for investors and advertisers. Despite a daily circulation of 500,000, the *Chicago Sun-Times* saw a 5.5% decline overall from March 1993 to March 1994, and was still running second behind the *Chicago Tribune*. Adler & Shaykin stated that they were earning a "modest" return on their investment, while having recouped most of the purchase costs with the sale of the direct-mail company.

Approach and Engagement

At a press conference in February 1994, the public was made aware of a two-year conversation among friends that led to the $180 million sale of the *Chicago Sun-Times* to American Publishing Company, a Hollinger, Inc. subsidiary. Leonard Shaykin, partner of the investment firm Adler & Shaykin, had conducted weekly calls with David Radler where the discussions mostly focused on sports and a possible acquisition. According to Radler, the proposal "never really varied," it was merely a matter of both parties being too busy to close the deal. The exclusion of corporate lawyers and accountants further made the $180 million offer easy to approve and execute. The Sun-Times Inc. deal, completed in the end of March 1997, also included ownership of Pioneer Press and Star Publications.

The Officers

Chairman and CEO of Hollinger Inc., Hollinger
International, and Hollinger Canadian Publishing
Holdings: Conrad M. Black

President and COO of Hollinger Inc., Chairman and CEO of
American Publishing, The Sun Times and Sterling
Newspapers: F. David Radler

Deputy Chairman: Dixon S. Chant

President of American Publishing Company: Jerry J.
Strader

When David Radler became chairman of the
newspaper he began a series of cost-cutting measures
but did not overturn corporate management. On June
30, 1994, however, president and CEO Sam McKeel
resigned, along with CFO and Treasurer Joseph
Gaynor III, General Manager and EVP Michael Veitch,
and Vice-President and Controller Bernadette Soens.
Job cuts at lower levels followed shortly thereafter,
with an initial 200 jobs phased out as part of an overall cost savings program to help finance the construction of a new plant.

Products and Services

In 1998 Hollinger Inc. was one of the leading
worldwide English-language newspaper publishers.
Since its 1985 purchase of England's *Daily Telegraph*,
Hollinger had grown as holding company of several
subsidiaries, including Hollinger International, Inc.
and American Publishing Co. Hollinger owned, or
had interest in, 114 daily and 330 non-daily newspapers worldwide with a combined daily circulation of
4.3 million.

Through American Publishing, Hollinger
expanded its presence in the U.S. newspaper industry
to include 275 small newspapers and more than 75
weekly and biweekly papers. The 1994 acquisition of
the *Chicago Sun-Times*, the first large American publication with a circulation of 500,000, instantly doubled
Hollinger's total daily volume. The *Chicago Sun-Times*
was the eighth-largest U.S. daily metropolitan publication, and had narrowed the circulation gap between
itself and its largest competitor, *The Chicago Tribune*.

The Toronto-based company currently owned 61
of the 105 daily Canadian papers, plus 30 weekly publications. UniMedia, Sterling, and Southam publishing
companies operated under Hollinger's Canadian
Newspaper Group. Southam published *The Gazette*

and *The Ottawa Citizen*. The 1998 combination of
Southam with the *Financial Post* spawned Hollinger's
first national daily, the *National Post*.

Hollinger's operations abroad included
England's staunchly conservative *Daily Telegraph* with
a 1.1 million daily circulation, making it the largest
broadsheet worldwide. Hollinger also published *The
Jerusalem Post*, Israel's only English-language newspaper.

With the 1997 creation of Hollinger Digital, the
newspaper giant entered the online publishing market
with such news Web sites as the *Electronic Telegraph*
and *The Spectator* magazine.

Changes to the Industry

After Hollinger acquired the *Chicago Sun-Times*,
Conrad Black's newspaper conglomerate nearly doubled its daily circulation overnight. The *Chicago Sun-
Times* was the first large U.S. metropolitan newspaper
that Hollinger owned, having made its previous success by purchasing smaller operations serving small
towns or covering local issues. To handle the company's new stake in the U.S., Hollinger, Inc. formed
Hollinger International, Inc. as an umbrella for its
American Publishing Company subsidiary. To pay
back a $50 million loan to Hollinger for the acquisition
and to help pay off an additional $51 million in relat-
ed expenses, American Publishing offered 33% of its
stock in an initial public offering, netting $88 million.

American Publishing CEO David Radler initially
took over the *Chicago Sun-Times* as chairman.
President and CEO Sam McKeel and a handful of
other top executives left the paper months after the
deal was completed. Radler took over McKeel's positions and set about reducing operating expenses
through job cuts and the tightening of operating
budgets. Despite his history for repairing a company,
then moving on to do the same at the next Hollinger
operation, David Radler has remained in the leadership of the newspaper.

The *Chicago Sun-Times* saw its second-quarter
1994 advertising revenues increase by 14%.
Additionally, a 10-cent increase for rival *Chicago
Tribune* increased the market share of *Chicago Sun-
Times*. Once operating costs were stabilized the company built a new production plant with sorely needed
equipment upgrades.

Review of the Outcome

With the purchase of smaller Chicago-area publications in the *Chicago Sun-Times* deal, American
Publishing's influence increased coverage of local
issues. Despite being owned by the staunch conserva-

tive Conrad Black, the *Chicago Sun-Times* kept its independent and liberal angle. The news medial mogul recognized early in his career that newspapers needed an angle and individual character to be successful, and that what might require changing was operating procedures, not style. The paper increased its circulation to become the eighth-largest U.S. metropolitan daily newspaper.

Research

"American Publishing Plans Initial Public Offering," in *Chicago Sun-Times*, 26 April 1994. Discusses the reasons why the new owner of the *Chicago Sun-Times* offered 33% of its shares in an initial public offering.

Borden, Jeff. "Sun-Times Boss Is a Citizen Pain: Radler Credo: More Cuts Mean More Profits," in *Crain's Chicago Business*, 25 July 1994. Looks at executive resignations at the *Chicago Sun-Times* after its acquisition by American Publishing, and the planned restructuring by David Radler.

———. "Sun-Times Paper Cuts Prick Fears," in *Crain's Chicago Business*, 11 July 1994. Details the resignation of the newspaper's CEO and other executives only months after it was acquired by the American Publishing Co.

Elstrom, Peter J.W. "How Deal Was Done, How Backers Fared," in *Crain's Chicago Business*, 7 March 1994. Examines the terms and negotiations of the American Publishing Company purchase of the *Chicago Sun-Times* in a $180 million dollar deal with Adler & Shaykin.

Fitzgerald, Mark. "Hollinger Buys Chicago Sun-Times," in *Editor & Publisher*, 5 March 1994. Outlines the $180 million acquisition of the newspaper, and Hollinger's commitment to not influence the paper's editorial slant.

Hollinger Inc. Home Page, available at http://www.hollinger.com. Official World Wide Web Home Page for Hollinger Inc. and its subsidiaries. Includes press releases, annual reports, and detailed financial, product, and investor information.

"Hollinger Unit Raises $88 Million in Public Offering," in *Editor & Publisher*, 4 June 1994. Discusses the result of the initial public offering of 33% of American Publishing Company stock.

Newman, Peter C. "A New Image For Conrad's Number 2," in *Maclean's*, 29 September 1997. Article looks at the career of David Radler before and after he took the helm at the *Chicago Sun-Times*.

Waters, Craig. "The Buyout Beat Goes On," in *Inc.*, August 1983. Focuses on Leonard Shaykin and the leveraged buyout methods he used to create his new partnership with Fredrick Adler.

SEAN C. MACKEY

The Players

Chairman and CEO of Hollinger Inc., Hollinger International, and Hollinger Canadian Publishing Holdings: Conrad M. Black. Conrad Black was born in Montreal, Quebec, in 1944. His father, a successful businessman, managed the Argus Corporation from the 1950s until his death in 1976. Black acquired Argus shares and a comfortable inheritance from his father. After combining their stock interests, Black and his brother were able to gain controlling interest of Argus by 1978. By selling off various holdings throughout the first half of 1985, and acquiring the remaining interest held by other shareholders, Black used his growing wealth to obtain a 50.1% interest in England's *Daily Telegraph* for $43 million. The conservative broadsheet became the first of many operations that would build Black's newspaper empire. Black formed Hollinger Inc. as a holding company in 1985 to manage his growing assortment of businesses. Hollinger then began acquiring small-market, local newspapers throughout the U.S. Hollinger formed American Publishing Co. to manage its U.S. operations, which by 1995 had become the nation's second-largest newspaper publisher, due in part to the 1994 acquisition of the *Chicago Sun-Times*. After Hollinger shifted its newspaper businesses under its American Publishing subsidiary, Hollinger International, Inc. was created as a U.S. umbrella company based out of Chicago. Black was named International's chairman and CEO, while American Publishing Co.'s president, David Radler assumed the president and COO positions.

President and COO of Hollinger Inc., Chairman and CEO of American Publishing, The *Chicago Sun-Times* and Sterling Newspapers: F. David Radler. Franklin David Radler began his newspaper career with Conrad Black when they bought the struggling *Sherbrooke Record* in 1969. While Black managed Hollinger's overall assets and investment strategies, Radler became the on-site hatchet man and operating manager for all of the company's acquisitions. Although he had helped turn around several newspapers by cutting jobs and operating costs, Radler never ran the companies as a publisher in the traditional sense until he took over the *Chicago Sun-Times*. After doing his usual cost-cutting tactics, including cutting jobs, Radler began running the newspaper's daily operations. The Montreal-born Radler commuted from Chicago to Vancouver where he worked on other Hollinger matters including the company's first Canadian national newspaper, designed to compete against *The Globe and Mail*.

IBM & LOTUS

International Business Machines
Corp.
New Orchard Rd.
Armonk, NY 10504
USA

tel: (914)499-1900
fax: (914)765-7382
web: http://www.ibm.com

nationality: USA
date: June 1995
affected: International Business Machines Corp., USA, founded 1911
affected: Lotus Development Corp., USA, founded 1982

Overview of the Acquisition

After two attempts to negotiate a merger, IBM CEO Louis Gerstner called Lotus head Jim Manzi to let him know that he was tired of waiting. On June 5, 1995, IBM made a hostile takeover bid for a cash purchase of the Cambridge, Massachusetts, software developer. IBM eventually paid $64 per share in a deal that, valued at $3.5 billion, was the most expensive in the computer industry. It also marked the first hostile takeover bid in IBM's history, highlighting its desire to own Lotus.

History of International Business Machines Corporation

In 1911, The Computer Tabulating Recording Co. (CTR) was formed from the merger of Tabulating Machine Co., International Time Recording Co., and the Computing Scale Company. Then, in 1914, Thomas Watson, Sr. became general manager of CTR after leaving National Cash Register. By the time CTR changed its named to International Business Machines (IBM Corp.) in 1924, the company had expanded into Europe, Canada, and Brazil, and had nearly tripled its sales with the introduction of the printing tabulator.

In 1925, Watson was named CEO and COO. The same year, IBM paid its first stock dividend, at 20%. IBM continued to expand globally with an office in the Philippines and the introduction of products in Japan. By 1928 the company had reached $5.3 million in profits, and a year later, despite the stock market crash, IBM issued a five-percent stock dividend, added employees, and increased engineering development.

In the first part of the 1930s, IBM acquired Electromatic Typewriters, Inc., and in 1935, introduced the first successful electronic typewriter. Ironically, in the midst of anti-competitive investigations led by the Justice Department, the U.S. government simultaneously became one of IBM's largest customers. Eventually, though, the Supreme Court ordered IBM to release card-related restrictions. By 1939, the company had become the country's largest office machine manufacturer, with nearly $50 million in sales.

IBM continued to expanded its governmental support as the war effort demanded increased production. The company created targeting instruments, automatic rifles, and mobile accounting units for U.S. troops. IBM plants earned Army-Navy "E" awards in 1942. By 1944 the company reached nearly $140 million in sales and helped build the Mark I, the first computer.

Throughout the 1940s and 1950s, IBM introduced and modified several products including the Automatic Sequence Controlled Calculator; the first small electronic calculator, called the IBM 603 multiplier; pocket-sized Braille writing devices; the 604 Calculating Punch; the Selective Sequence Electronic Calculator; the IBM Model A and Model A "Executive" typewriters; the 407 Accounting Machine; and, in 1952, its first scientific calculating computer. Even though its top competitor, Rand, was the first to introduce the production computer, IBM's 85% share in the business market allowed it to upgrade its existing customer base, effectively becoming the largest computer manufacturer.

Thomas Watson, Jr., followed his father's footsteps and worked his way up the management ranks, becoming chairman in 1961. Continuing and expanding IBM's commitment to human rights, dedication to the advancements in the government's military and space technology, and employment equality, Watson was awarded the Medal of Freedom, the U.S. government's highest civilian honor. IBM expanded its governmental projects with Russian/English translating services on the Mark I computer, guidance computers for the Gemini space program, tracking systems for NASA's Mercury flights, and assistance on the Apollo space missions.

During the company's rapid growth in computer technology and applications, it was subject to many anti-trust allegations and lawsuits. Three notable suits brought by Control Data Corp., Data Research Corp., and VIP Systems Corp. were all settled out-of-court. In 1982, the Justice Department finally dropped its 13-year antitrust suit after it could not successfully prove any wrong doing.

IBM introduced the personal computer in 1982, becoming the market leader, with $6.6 billion of profit, in 1984. The next year, however, revenues slowed as competitors developed and sold cheaper models based on IBM's design. In 1987, IBM failed in an attempt to market a personal computer with Microsoft's OS/2 operating system. This computer was designed with an interface similar to Apple computers, but was never widely received. As the market shifted from IBM's mainframe technology to personal computers, the company found itself faced with major

The Business

Financials

Revenue (1998): $81.6 billion

Employees (1998): 291,067

SICs / NAICS

sic 3695 - Magnetic & Optical Recording Media

sic 3823 - Process Control Instruments

sic 3674 - Semiconductors & Related Devices

sic 3577 - Computer Peripheral Equipment Nec

sic 7372 - Prepackaged Software

sic 7371 - Computer Programming Services

sic 3571 - Electronic Computers

sic 3575 - Computer Terminals

naics 334413 - Semiconductor and Related Device Manufacturing

naics 334613 - Magnetic and Optical Recording Media Manufacturing

naics 334513 - Instruments for Measuring and Displaying Industrial Process Variables

naics 334111 - Electronic Computer Manufacturing

naics 334113 - Computer Terminal Manufacturing

naics 334418 - Printed Circuit Assembly (Electronic Assembly) Manufacturing

naics 541511 - Custom Computer Programming Services

challenges. Thousands of jobs were eliminated, and company stock fell sharply. In 1991 IBM reported a net loss of $2.8 billion. Under the leadership of CEO John Akers, IBM was restructured into several small businesses, with the main leadership acting as a holding company.

IBM began its turnaround with the release of the laptop computer in 1992 and hired Louis V. Gerstner, Jr., as CEO in 1993. He was an outsider to the company and a novice to the computer industry, but had a proven record of leadership. He immediately instituted drastic changes to speed up IBM's strength, including the removal of several long time top-ranking executives. Gerstner broadened IBM's product scope by developing operating software and focusing on personal computers. In 1995, Gerstner led the hostile takeover of software icon Lotus Development Corp. to expand services into Internet and work-group business applications. IBM also upgraded its line of main-

The Officers

Chairman and CEO: Louis V. Gerstner, Jr.

Sr. VP and Chief Financial Officer: Douglas L. Maine

Sr. VP and General Counsel: Lawrence R. Ricciardi

frames into smaller, faster, and cheaper machines, which attracted record sales. By 1997, IBM's revenue reached $78.5 billion and continued to grow through acquisition of complimentary product and service companies.

History of Lotus Development Corporation

Mitchell D. Kapor founded Lotus in 1982 to develop applications for the emerging personal computer market. Named after the Hindu symbol of enlightenment, Lotus started with eight employees. Kapor partnered with Jonathan Sachs to create the spreadsheet program Lotus 1-2-3, which was a huge success. The company's stock went public in 1983, and sold over two million shares, making nearly $41 million. By the end of the year, Lotus was the second-leading software company, with sales totaling $53 million.

Although Kapor had created a successful product, he was uncomfortable with operational responsibilities. He saw in management consultant Jim Manzi the right person for the job. Manzi was appointed president while Kapor retained the chairman position. In 1986 Kapor left Lotus altogether to pursue other ventures.

When Manzi joined Lotus in 1984, he set out to develop new products besides 1-2-3. Lotus introduced an integrated software package called Symphony in 1985, but the word processing, database, and network-oriented program received poor reviews. That same year Lotus struggled to release Jazz, an Apple compatible spreadsheet program, which ultimately failed as well. By the end of 1985, the company was still soaring on the success of 1-2-3, so Manzi worked to improve it. In 1986 Lotus agreed to create a 1-2-3 program for IBM's mainframe computers and introduced the spreadsheet software to Japan.

By 1988 Lotus commanded 70% of the spreadsheet market, and by 1989 income rose to $68 million. Lotus missed a great opportunity when it decided not to develop programs for rival Microsoft's Windows package. Instead, Lotus developed its own operating system called OS/2, which failed to win customers. Lotus acquired Samna Corp. for $65 million in 1990 for

its Ami Pro word processing program. Even with these acquisitions, the company remained third, behind Microsoft and WordPerfect, in the word processing market.

In 1990 Lotus negotiated a merger with Novell, Inc., the nation's largest computer networking firm, but the deal fell through. That same year, Lotus filed and won a copyright infringement suit against Borland International Inc. for its Quattro Pro spreadsheet program.

In an attempt to combat poor sales in 1991, Lotus was forced to lay off 400 employees. Under pressure to introduce another product to boost sales, Lotus unveiled three products in 1991: a mail package called Open Messaging Interface, Lotus Notes, and another mail program called cc:Mail. The Notes and cc:Mail programs became favorites of IBM and General Motors, and by 1992, revenue had reached $900 million, with 1.5 million copies of cc:Mail sold that year. In 1984, Lotus paid $84 million in common stock for software designer—and Notes creator—Iris Associates.

IBM, in order to expand into greater software markets, purchased Lotus in 1995 in a friendly takeover worth $3.5 billion. Manzi lasted only three months as a subordinate to IBM chief Louis Gerstner before stepping down. Lotus, with 60% of 1998 sales coming from Lotus Notes, continued to expand its work group software development with the purchase of DataBeam and Ubique Ltd., which specialized in collaborative applications.

Market Forces Driving the Acquisition

IBM had been refocusing its sales strategy as competition in the PC markets increased and Microsoft continued to cement its software dominance. Although the company was making large gains in the personal computing field, heavier competition forced IBM to seek growth in other ventures, of which software and Internet-oriented services were the most viable. Lotus' Notes program was proving to be a great product—its sales were climbing and it was a software package that could compete well in a Microsoft dominated market. Notes allowed customers to work in groups simultaneously on projects, something that other products could not do. IBM hoped that this program, when packaged with its own products, would attract increased sales.

"The advantage to IBM? Only Notes..." stated analyst Paul Johnson while discussing reasons for the company's takeover Lotus in *Computer Reseller News*. In a letter to Lotus announcing the takeover bid, IBM CEO Louis Gerstner discussed both companies' mutual interest in a future built on a "collaborative computing environment where people can work and communicate across enterprises..."

Lotus CEO Jim Manzi had turned down several merger offers by IBM because he believed that grouping Notes with one computer manufacturer might eliminate potential sales to other competitors. Still, Lotus would gain IBM's massive financial backing for development and worldwide marketing, in addition to the computer manufacturer's customer base.

Approach and Engagement

Lotus CEO Jim Manzi was not interested in merging with IBM, despite several discussions with the computer giant's Senior Vice President, John Thompson. Shortly after talks failed, Manzi received a phone call on June 5, 1995, which he thought was a prank. It wasn't. It was Louis Gerstner, CEO of IBM, informing Manzi that IBM had just placed a takeover bid worth nearly four times Lotus' current stock rate.

Gerstner had little trouble persuading Lotus' board to accept the healthy cash buyout and to remove its "poison pill" provisions. Originally, IBM offered Lotus $60 per share, but when the deal was finalized a month later, shares went for $64 each, raising the total bill to $3.5 billion. IBM took a one-time, non-cash charge against its earnings in the quarter in which the deal was completed.

The acquisition was finalized at $64 per share, totaling $3.5 billion, and became the largest computer buyout in history. The deal was completed within one month of the public announcement.

Products and Services

Lotus didn't introduce any new products immediately after the buyout. Instead, it used IBM's generous $1.5 million marketing budget to sell Notes, bundling the program with IBM products. Another $1.5 million for research and development eventually led to improved Notes and SmartSuite releases. Former Lotus CEO Jim Manzi had refused to listen to his development team's insistence to embrace the Internet with Notes. After the buyout, however, that became a priority, eventually leading to an IT management software called Domino. Domino was later combined with Notes, allowing further collaborative, assembly-line, and expanded information distribution for users.

Changes to the Industry

IBM's buyout of Lotus in June 1995 expanded the computer manufacturer's share of the software mar-

The Players

Chairman and CEO of International Business Machines Corp.: Louis V. Gerstner, Jr. Louis Gerstner began his career at the consulting firm of McKinsey & Co., Inc. in 1965, after receiving his MBA from Harvard Business School. At 28, he became one of the company's youngest partners. He left to join American Express in 1978, after consulting for the company for many years. Gerstner later became president of American Express, and chairman and CEO of Travel Related Service Company, its largest subsidiary.

In 1989 Gerstner left American Express to take the helm at food and tobacco giant RJR Nabisco. He left the company after only four years, in the midst of his restructuring program, when IBM offered him their Chairman and CEO position. Immediately upon taking the helm, Gerstner replaced three longtime executives, cut jobs, and restructured smaller operations. In 1995 he announced a takeover of Lotus Inc. Under his leadership, IBM turned around from a financial downslide by moving toward personal computers, Internet development, and smaller mainframe designs.

CEO of Lotus Development Corp.: Jim P. Manzi. Jim Manzi took the helm at Lotus in 1984, replacing founder Mitch Kapor. Kapor chose Manzi for his management consultant experience and to help Lotus market its spreadsheet software, moving the company into a new direction. Prior to his appointment as CEO, Manzi worked with Lotus as a management consultant at McKinsey & Co. His education began at Colgate, and included a master's degree in economics at Tufts. Lotus stayed afloat under his leadership, despite crippling competitive losses due to competition from Microsoft. Manzi pushed Lotus into work group programs, which caught the attention of IBM. The merger placed Lotus and Manzi under the leadership of IBM's CEO, Gerstner. Manzi, who was known for his abrasive and demanding personality, lasted only 99 days as Senior Vice President, citing strategy conflicts with IBM as the reason for his departure. He left the company with an estimated $78 million stock profit. After leaving IBM, Manzi started an Internet discount shopping site called Nets.Inc., which offered a variety of consumer goods. The company however, declared bankruptcy in 1997, after it was unable to raise the necessary funds.

ket. During the first year, sales of the Lotus Notes program tripled with the help of IBM's extensive marketing budget and product packaging. As a result of its affiliation with IBM, Lotus lost a major client, Electronic Data Systems Corp. (EDS). Since EDS was a direct competitor with an IBM subsidiary, the Dallas-based integrator switched to Microsoft's Exchange Server.

The merger created the opportunity for Notes to branch into the ever-growing Internet market. IBM's Internet development team, led by Irving Wladawsky-Berger, focused on partnering IBM and Lotus products together for a better advantage in the market, while also eliminating any product redundancies. Additionally, the Internet division established programming that could make current IBM mainframes Internet accessible. Further highlighting IBM's interest in the Internet, the company acquired network management specialist Tivoli Systems in 1996.

Review of the Outcome

Although Lotus remained a separately managed company under IBM, major changes took place in Lotus' upper management ranks after the merger, beginning with the departure of former Lotus CEO Jim Manzi after only three months. Lotus' senior vice president of desktop operations and chief technology officer both resigned as well. Worldwide Services Unit VP June Rokoff stepped down after the merger, but remained an IBM consultant for one year. IBM appointed Michael Zisman as Lotus' chief executive officer, while Jeffery Papows was named chief operating officer.

Despite taking a large one-time charge against revenues for the purchase, IBM still posted a profit increase of more than five percent in 1995. A year after the Lotus buyout, IBM's stock had risen 42%, and by 1998 profits had increased each succeeding year by more than seven percent. At that time IBM was the second-largest software developer, behind Microsoft, with 35% of its annual earnings coming from the services arm.

In the spring of 1999 the Securities and Exchange Commission (SEC) charged a former Lotus secretary, her husband, and several others with insider trading. Regulators had noticed a 90% options increase and wild stock trading prior to the IBM buyout announcement. The SEC hopes to recoup the estimated $1.3 million the illegal trading earned.

Research

"Acquisition: IBM Announces Offer to Acquire Lotus Development Corporation for $60 Per Lotus Share in Cash," in *EDGE: Work-Group Computing Report*, 12 June 1995. Discusses IBM's bid to takeover Lotus shortly after the announcement was made. Highlights terms set forth by IBM and possible ramifications to the industry.

Demarzo, Robert C. "Just Why Is Gerstner Hostile?" in *Computer Reseller News*, 12 June 1995. Examines IBM CEO Louis Gerstner's role in the hostile bid for Lotus.

Gage, Deborah. "Manzi's Independent Nature Made IBM Career a Long Shot," in *Computer Reseller News*, 16 October 1995. Details Manzi's relationship with IBM before and after the takeover of Lotus.

Goldblatt, Henry. "Another Net Loser," in *Fortune*, 9 June 1997. Discusses the bankruptcy of Jim Manzi's Internet shopping mall, his first endeavor after leaving IBM.

Hays, Laurie. "Manzi Quits at IBM and His Many Critics Are Not At All Surprised; Lotus Chief, Tempestuous and Quick to Fire Aides, Leaves Fast—And Rich; Life with 'Louie' Gerstner," in *The Wall Street Journal*, 12 October 1995. Focuses on Jim Manzi's personal attitude and points to reasons why his stay at IBM was doomed from the beginning.

IBM Home Page, available at http://www.ibm.com. Official World Wide Web Home Page for IBM. Includes current news; links to subsidiary companies; detailed financial, product, and historical information; and annual reports.

"IBM," in *Notable Corporate Chronologies*, The Gale Group, 1999. Lists major events in the history of IBM.

"It's Hot! It's Sexy! It's...Big Blue?" in *Business Week*, 4 March 1996. Highlights IBM's performance after the Lotus buyout and discusses the computer giant's market focus on Internet and personal computing business.

"Lotus Development Corporation" in *Notable Corporate Chronologies*, The Gale Group, 1999. Profiles major events in the history of Lotus Development Corp.

McTague, Jim. "It Was Crowded Inside; How A Secretary's Tip Led to an Unusually Deep SEC Probe," in *Barron's*, 7 June 1999. Discusses charges filed against a former Lotus secretary and 24 other people after an extensive four-year investigation by the SEC.

Moltzen, Edward, F. and Barbara Darrow. "What a Difference a Year Makes," in *Computer Reseller News*, 3 June 1996. Comments on IBM's growth and increased sales of Notes software after it purchased Lotus in 1995.

Nulty, Peter and Karen Nickel. "America's Toughest Bosses," in *Fortune*, 27 February 1989. Highlights aspects of select corporate leaders, including Jim Manzi.

Sellers, Patricia and David Kirkpatrick. "Can This Man Save IBM?" in *Fortune*, 19 April 1993. Provides an overview of the life and career of Louis Gerstner.

SEAN C. MACKEY

CARL ICAHN & TRANS WORLD AIRLINES

nationality: USA
date: September 1985
affected: Trans World Airlines, Inc., USA, founded 1925

Trans World Airlines, Inc.
One City Center, 515 N. 6th St.
St. Louis, MO 63101
USA

tel: (314)589-3000
fax: (314)589-3129
web: http://www.twa.com

Overview of the Takeover

In the spring of 1985, Carl Icahn acquired 20% of TWA stock and continued to accumulate shares in order to gain control of the company. That May, Icahn offered a takeover bid valued at $19 in cash and $4 of preferred stock for each share of common stock. The proposal was withdrawn shortly thereafter, and a new bid was eventually made. Icahn was named the company's CEO in September 1985, and led TWA for eight years before selling out of it and stepping down.

History of Trans World Airlines, Inc.

Western Air Express, the predecessor of TWA, was established on July 13, 1925, by Harry Chandler and James Talbot. The airline primarily served as a mail carrier, with flights between Los Angeles and Salt Lake City. The name was changed to Transcontinental and Western Air (TWA) in 1930 after Western merged with Transcontinental Air Transport. TWA was the first to offer coast-to-coast air service.

After Howard Hughes bought the airline in 1939, TWA began offering transatlantic flights between New York and Paris. To highlight its expanded service, the company changed its name to Trans World Airlines and moved its headquarters to New York in 1950. During the first part of the 1960s, Hughes had his stock placed in a voting trust after he failed to meet the terms of a loan for the purchase of 63 jets. TWA subsequently sued Hughes for $115 million for anti-monopoly violations. In 1965 he sold his 6,584,937 shares for $546.5 million.

As the first all-jet airline, TWA began offering worldwide service in 1967. Jet service was expanded two years later when TWA offered the first 747 (1969) and 767 service (1982) to the United States.

In 1983 Trans World Corporation spun off TWA as a publicly traded company. Two years later corporate raider Carl Icahn successfully completed a hostile takeover bid of TWA, gaining operating control. In 1986 Icahn led TWA's acquisition of St. Louis competitor Ozark Airlines. During his first year at the helm, Icahn cut nearly $400 million in operating costs and helped TWA record its first fourth-

The Business

SICs / NAICS

sic 4512 - Air Transportation-Scheduled

naics 481111 - Scheduled Passenger Air Transportation

quarter profit gain since 1968. TWA's stock went private in 1988, with employees owning 10% and CEO Icahn holding the remaining shares, worth $400 million.

Icahn sold TWA's routes from major hubs on the East Coast to American Airlines for $445 million. Despite several attempts to avoid bankruptcy, TWA filed for Chapter 11 reorganization in 1992. Icahn then sold London routes from Baltimore and Philadelphia for $50 million. As Icahn's investment continued its downward spiral, he resigned as chairman and sold his interest in TWA in 1993. As part of the company's reorganization, its main corporate offices were moved from its costly New York site to St. Louis.

TWA filed another bankruptcy reorganization in 1995, after which the airline declared its first operating profit since 1989. Its financial success did not last long, however, as TWA flight 800 crashed into the ocean off Long Island in 1996, killing all 230 passengers. After the tragedy, Gerald Gitner was named TWA's fourth CEO in three years. In 1999 Gitner was elected chairman and was succeeded as CEO by then-president William Compton.

Market Forces Driving the Takeover

By the mid-1980s, TWA had failed to turn a profit in several years. Increasing operational costs and a market slowdown—driven by consumer fears of terrorism—contributed to the company's depressed stock price. Icahn saw such conditions as perfect opportunities to make a great deal of money. He also firmly believed that corporate takeovers helped the economy by removing upper management whose actions had, in his mind, stifled the success of some of the nation's largest corporations.

Approach and Engagement

TWA's undervalued stock prices attracted the attention of Carl Icahn, who began purchasing the company's stock in the first quarter of 1985. By early spring Icahn had acquired nearly 20% the company's stock and continued to buy more.

This method of engagement is typical among corporate raider strategies, through which Icahn had become a multi-billionaire. After gaining control of a large portion of stock, Icahn would launch a hostile proxy fight and force a takeover. Once in command, he would reform management, streamline operations, and sell company assets in order to recoup his investment and make a large profit. The more undervalued the company's stock, the greater the potential for profit.

Throughout his takeover attempt, Icahn suffered several hurdles. First, TWA's board appealed to the U.S. Department of Transportation to block his acquisition of any additional shares on the grounds that TWA would not be a safe airline if it were led by someone without aviation experience. This only temporarily stalled Icahn's first buyout offer of $19 in cash for $4 in preferred stock.

Icahn then lost his financial backing. By the time this matter was straightened out, he had managed to obtain nearly 50% of the company's stock and had successfully worked out a labor agreement with the airline's workers.

Texas Air emerged as a rival bidder for TWA, offering $23 per share at a time when TWA's stock was trading at only $17 per share. TWA's board initially approved the Texas Air's offer, but eventually went with Icahn's sweetened offer of $24 in preferred stock for up to 12 million of the 24 million remaining shares of common stock.

Products and Services

Serving 89 cities throughout the United States, Canada, Europe, Central America, the Middle East, and the Caribbean, Trans World Airlines, Inc. was one of the nation's 10 largest air carriers in 1998. From its main hub in St. Louis, the airline recorded more than 350 departures a day, plus 40 from New York's JFK, and served a total of 24 million passengers.

In 1997 the U.S. Department of Transportation ranked TWA second for domestic on-time arrivals. The following year the last of the company's intercontinental Boeing 747s were replaced by the more efficient 767. That same year the company ordered 24 MD-83 twinjets, and 125 other jets to update its fleet.

TWA was one of the first to offer business-class seating for passengers. These seats have more room and amenities than economy-class, but without the excessive cost and perks of first-class. This new seating helped TWA to record a profit during the first years under the leadership of Carl Icahn.

TWA also offered Getaway programs, which packaged hotel, entertainment, and airfare for week long vacations. The airline permitted customers to make reservations directly via the Internet. Its customers could also earn frequent flyer miles by using the TWA Visa or MasterCard.

Changes to the Industry and Review of the Outcome

Carl Icahn became the CEO of TWA in September of 1985. During his first two years he cut costs, moved TWA's headquarters to smaller, less-expensive sites, and sold several of its routes to competitors, including its prized New York-to-London line. These moves enabled the company to record its first profit in years. He also orchestrated the acquisition of Ozark Airlines in 1986 to increase TWA's St. Louis services. In 1988 TWA went private, and Icahn obtained 90% of the company's stock. By that time, the company was mired in an ever-increasing debt load due to Icahn's investments. It filed the first of its two bankruptcy reorganizations in 1992; the second was filed three years later. Upon his departure in 1993, Icahn loaned the company $190 million to help it stay afloat. In return he was given the right to sell airline tickets, a deal valued at $610 million. Through his travel agency, he sold the tickets at significant discounts, underselling even TWA. In 1995 the airline filed a lawsuit against Icahn for his actions, but lost when the judge declared that Icahn was not in violation of the ticket-selling agreement.

By 1998 it had been a full decade since TWA had turned a profit. Despite fleet upgrades and workforce reductions, the airline reported a $79.1 million loss in the fourth quarter 1998. In 1999 the company planned an additional 1,000 job cuts, mostly through attrition. In an attempt to increase revenues, TWA set about regaining its JFK-to-Heathrow route. The company's CEO, Gerald Gitner, even appealed to President Clinton in February of 1999, stating his concern regarding the anti-trust position afforded to other airlines.

Research

"An End to Flying Fanny Fatigue," in *Time*, 13 May 1985. Highlights the introduction of business-class seating, with more room than economy- but less than first-class.

Flint, Perry. "The Oldest Start-Up," in *Air Transport World*, March 1996. A review of TWA's ability to stay afloat despite filing bankruptcy twice in five years.

"Ichan Sued by TWA," in *Crain's New York Business*. A brief article announcing TWA's lawsuit against former CEO Carl Icahn for selling tickets in violation of their agreement.

Kuitenbrouwer, Peter. "Stone Cold Corporate Raider," in *National Post*, 30 January 1999. Addresses current and previous corporate ventures of Carl Icahn, and reflects on his time at TWA.

The Players

Independent Financier: Carl Icahn Carl Celian Icahn was born to a working class family in 1936 in the Bayswater section of Queens. After attending Princeton University, he began his financial career as a stockbroker trainee. Icahn served as the investor for his uncle and earned his relative a great deal of money. This uncle loaned the young Icahn $400,000 to start his own trading firm, Icahn & Co.

Icahn's early success was attributed to his knack in arbitrage dealings. Later, during the 1980s, he became one of the most well known corporate raiders, and a master at "greenmail." This method of engagement is typical among corporate raider strategies, through which Icahn has become a multi-billionaire. After gaining control of a large portion of stock, Icahn launched a hostile proxy fight and forced a takeover. Once in command, he reformed management, streamlined operations, and sold company assets in order to recoup his investment and make a large profit. The more undervalued the company's stock, the greater the potential for profit.

When Icahn left TWA in 1993, he loaned the ailing company $190 million to keep it afloat during bankruptcy reorganization. In return, he was given the right to sell airline tickets, which held a retail value of $610 million, over the Internet and through his travel agency. Since he needed to recoup only a small portion to make a profit, he undersold the tickets to customers. Even TWA could not compete against the discounted prices, so the airline filed a $100 million lawsuit charging that Icahn violated their agreement. St. Louis County Circuit Judge Kenneth Romines eventually ruled in favor of Icahn, clearing him of any wrongdoing.

In April 1999, Icahn ended his fourth unsuccessful attempt to gain control of RJR Nabisco, the holding company that owns the Nabisco snack food giant, and R.J. Reynolds, the cigarette manufacturer. He tried several times to take over RJR Nabisco in order to split the company into separate food and cigarette operations, but was unsuccessful.

Carl Icahn currently holds interests in several companies, and serves as the chairman and CEO of American Real Estate Partners, L.P., and as chairman for Stratosphere Corporation, a languishing Las Vegas hotel and casino operator. Throughout 1998 and 1999 Icahn took a majority stockholder position of Canadian-based Phillips Petroleum, which fought his involvement and became immersed in a bankruptcy reorganization. Although he failed to gain control of Pan Am airlines, Marvel Entertainment Group (Marvel Comics), and RJR Nabisco, to name a few, he efforts have proved lucrative.

Leinster, Colin. "Carl Icahn's Calculated Bets," in *Fortune*, 18 March 1985. A brief biography of Carl Icahn, highlighting some major deals in his career, his approach to business, and current projects.

Simon, Ellen, "Icahn Exits Proxy Fight with RJR Nabisco, Acknowledges Defeat," from *Knight-Ridder/Tribune Business News*, 29 April 1999. Discusses Icahn's fourth unsuccessful attempt to take over and split the operations of RJR Nabisco.

———. "Investor Gives up Takeover Bid, Sells Nabisco Stake," from *Knight-Ridder/Tribune Business News*, 15 June 1999. Describes the actions of RJR Nabisco after Icahn divested his stock in the company.

"TWA Finalizes Bargain to Become a Private Carrier: Icahn Gains 90% Control Despite Union Opposition," in *Travel Weekly*, 3 November 1988. Discusses TWA's privatization that gave Icahn 90% control of the company.

TWA Home Page, available at http://www.twa.com. Official World Wide Web Home Page for TWA. Includes current news, travel services and reservations, historical information, and press releases.

"TWA Looks to Win Back 'Rightful' Heathrow Slots," in *Travel Trade Gazette UK & Ireland*, 17 February 1999. A brief report on the news that TWA seeks to regain its routes to London's Heathrow airport.

"Trans World Still Making a Loss after a Decade," in *Flight International*, 24 February 1999. Provides a detailed review of TWA's 1998 financial performance.

SEAN C. MACKEY

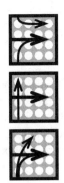

ICN PHARMACEUTICALS & ROCHE HOLDING

date: November 1988 (canceled)
affected: ICN Pharmaceuticals, Inc., USA, founded 1960
affected: Roche Holding AG, Switzerland, founded 1894

ICN Pharmaceuticals, Inc.
3300 Hyland Ave.
Costa Mesa, CA 92626
USA

tel: (714)545-0100
fax: (714)556-0131
web: www.icnpharm.com

Roche Holding AG
Grenzacherstrasse 124
Basel, 4002
Switzerland

tel: 41-61-688-1111
fax: 41-61-691-9391
web: www.roche.com

Overview of the Takeover

In September 1987, executives at Roche Holding were informed that a small California-based drug manufacturing company, ICN Pharmaceuticals, was attempting a hostile takeover by acquiring the voting shares of the company. ICN initially acquired 6.3%, which eventually grew to 8.6%, but its attempt was seen by many as ridiculous. Roche's 16,000 voting shares were valued nearly $2 billion, and ICN had control of about 1,000 shares. Most of the remaining shares were owned by members of the Hoffmann-La Roche family, the founders of Roche, who were unlikely to ever part with their stock.

In November of 1988, ICN sold its 8.6% stake to an unidentified buyer for $209 million, a higher rate than when originally purchased. Jack Scholl, an ICN spokesman, explained that the sale of the stock allowed the company to reverse $15.6 million in unrealized trading losses. Additionally, ICN hoped to use the profits to facilitate a future acquisition.

History of ICN Pharmaceuticals, Inc.

In 1960, Yugoslavian immigrant Milan Panic started International Chemical and Nuclear Corp., which specialized in nucleic acid research. In 1973 the firm's name was changed to ICN Pharmaceuticals.

During the 1980s ICN created a drug called Ribavirin as a treatment for the virus that causes HIV. The Food and Drug Administration (FDA) didn't approve the drug, causing ICN to suffer economic losses in the United States. The drug was made available in Mexico, however, and many AIDS patients traveled there to acquire the drug legally. Eventually the drug received FDA approval as a treatment for a rare infant respiratory illness called RSV.

ICN then tried to gain approval for use of Ribavirin as a stand-alone treatment for Hepatitis C, but it was rejected. Because Panic sold the stock before the announcement was made, he became embroiled in an insider trading scandal that was eventually settled. In 1995 Schering-Plough Corp. licensed Ribavirin from ICN for use as a combined use treatment for Hepatitis C, for which it received FDA approval.

The Business

Financials - ICN Pharmaceuticals, Inc.

Revenue (1998): $838 million

Employees (1998): 13,250

Financials - Roche Holding AG

Revenue (1998): $17.93 billion

Employees (1998): 66,707

SICs / NAICS

sic 2819 - Industrial Inorganic Chemicals Nec

sic 2869 - Industrial Organic Chemicals Nec

sic 3679 - Electronic Components Nec

sic 5122 - Drugs, Proprietaries & Sundries

sic 8731 - Commercial Physical Research

naics 211112 - Natural Gas Liquid Extraction

In 1987 ICN made a futile attempt to take over Roche Holdings by acquiring shares of the firm's voting stock. One year later ICN sold the stock and made a healthy profit. The attempt opened doors in Europe where ICN CEO Panic raised $500 million in capital to continue pushing Ribavirin. In 1997, Roche sold worldwide rights to almost a dozen of its products and a plant in Puerto Rico to ICN.

With his connection to Eastern Europe, Panic was quick to enter the emerging pharmaceutical market as Europe underwent massive changes in the 1980s and 1990s. ICN became the largest drug manufacturer in Russia, with other operations in Poland and Yugoslavia. ICN also became the first company to open a retail pharmacy in Russia. In 1999, however, the Yugoslav and Serbian governments seized ICN's Yugoslavian drug plant and detained several managers, alleging that the company hadn't paid for its share in its subsidiary, ICN Galeinka. After a futile legal attempt to reopen its operations failed, ICN pulled out of Yugoslavia, a market which accounted for 30% of the company's revenues.

History of Roche Holding AG

On October 1, 1896, Fritz Hoffmann-La Roche joined with his ex-business partner Max Carl Traub to form F. Hoffmann-La Roche &amp Co. Ltd. Based in Basel, Switzerland, this chemicals and pharmaceuticals manufacturing company hired Dr. Emil Christoph

Barell as a chemist, whose work would gain Roche its first patent.

Slow business made a financial restructuring a painful necessity, and the young company took on various investors in 1987. This influx of capital enabled Roche to establish subsidiaries in Milan and Grenzach. The following year the company developed its first successful product, the non-prescription cough syrup Sirolin.

In 1904 Roche introduced Digalen, the first consistently safe dosage of digitalis for the treatment of heart diseases. A subsidiary in New York was established the following year to serve as the basis for the company's extensive American marketing and production operations. In 1909 the firm introduced Pantopon, a remedy for a variety of mild conditions. This product would prove to be the company's longest selling product, as it was still marketed in the late-1990s.

By 1911 Roche had expanded worldwide with subsidiaries in Paris, Vienna, London, St. Petersburg, and Yokohama, Japan. During World War I, trade with the neighboring countries Germany and France was closed off, demonstrating the need for Roche to establish its own production facilities. By 1919 the company's financial state was dire, so Fritz Hoffmann-La Roche provided 75% of the SFr4 million needed to restructure Roche as a limited company; Dr. Barell, two associates, and Fritz's brother-in-law provided the remaining 25%. This brother-in-law, Rudolf Adolf Koechler-Hoffmann, became chairman of F. Hoffmann-La Roche Ltd. Co.

Dr. Barell became the company president upon the death of Fritz Hoffmann-La Roche in 1920. That year the introduction of its first hypnotics, such as Somnifen, marked the company's shift from drug extraction to the synthesis of chemical therapeutics.

Due to the financial difficulties incurred as a result of World War I and the threat of another war in Europe, Roche established Sapac Corporation Ltd. in 1927 as a separate company comprised of several of the group's operating units. That year it obtained the commercial right to produce thyroxine, a thyroid hormone. In 1929 Roche transferred its New York operations to Nutley, New Jersey; this became Roche's American headquarters. Sales that year reached SFr50.4 million, up from SFr18.2 million in 1921.

Roche first synthesized ascorbic acid, a source of vitamin C, in 1933, leading to the introduction of the company's first vitamin specialty product, Redoxin. This discovery was followed two years later with the development of synthesized vitamin B1. At the outbreak of World War II, Roche moved its headquarters to Lausanne, Switzerland. The company also consolidated all associated companies outside continental Europe into Sapac.

Roche introduced its first cosmetic, Panteen hair tonic, in 1944. Its success led to the formation of Panteen AG by the end of that same year. In 1949 Roche entered the antimicrobial market with the launch of Gantrisin, a treatment for urinary tract infections. Three years later, to great fanfare, it released Rimifon as a treatment for tuberculosis. This product also led to the development of antidepressants, as mood elation was a side effect of the drug.

In 1953 synthetic vitamin K was launched as Konakion. Two years later Roche established a department of experimental medicine, consisting of its work on pharmacology and chemotherapy. In 1956 it synthesized the cancer drug 5-fluorouracil, which served as the basis for the development of future cancer drugs. Two years later Roche expanded its non-prescription operations by acquiring Laboratoires Sauter SA, whose product line included anti-inflammatories, digestives, adhesive bandages, and suppositories.

In 1960 Roche introduced Librium, a benzodiazepine tranquilizer, that later became America's best-selling prescription drug. The next year the company forayed into tropical disease treatment with the release of Astiban, for the treatment of the parasitic disease schistosomiasis.

Roche had a successful year in 1963. It introduced the hugely successful benzodiazepine tranquilizer Valium. Also that year Roche acquired Givaudan SA, a perfume and flavoring manufacturer that comprised the core of Roche's Fragrances and Flavors division.

In 1965 Dr. Walter Adolf Jann became chairman and CEO, and led the company on a diversification campaign that took it into such new fields as bioelectronics, publishing, agrochemicals, and liquid crystal displays (used in consumer products like clocks and calculators).

The company expanded into diagnostics in 1969 with the formation of a division to develop, produce, and sell equipment and materials that contribute to diagnosis of disease. That year sales of Valium exceeded those of Librium for the first time. That same year, Roche acquired a stake in the agrochemicals firm Dr. R. Maag AG; this company was absorbed into Roche eight years later. By 1971 Roche's vitamins accounted for more than 50% of worldwide production.

In 1973 British authorities insisted upon pricing controls, to which Roche finally relented in 1975. In addition to the negative reaction from this well-publicized battle, Roche suffered several other public relations blows. In 1975 a former Roche employee, Stanley

The Officers

ICN Pharmaceuticals, Inc.

Chairman and CEO: Milan Panic

President and Chief Operating Officer: Adam Jerney

Exec. VP, CFO, and Controller: John E. Giordani

Exec. VP, Secretary, and General Counsel: David C. Watt

Exec. Vice President, Strategic Planning: Bill A. MacDonald

Roche Holding AG

Chairman: Fritz Gerber

Vice Chairman: Rolf Hanggi

Vice Chairman: Andres F. Leuenberger

President and CEO, Hoffmann-La Roche: Patrick J. Zenner

Adams, waged a media war against the company for offering illegal discounts to customers. The following year, a chemical cloud released by its Italian fragrance subsidiary Icmesa caused skin damage to residents of neighboring communities and necessitated the destruction of produce, farm animals, and contaminated buildings. Roche paid over SFr300 million in compensation.

Fritz Gerber was named chairman and CEO in 1978 to improve the company's business and reputation. He set about reversing the diversification efforts of the past in order to focus on core strengths. In 1982 the company formed Roche Biomedical Laboratories by acquiring Biomedical Reference Laboratories, Inc. and Consolidated Biomedical Laboratories, Inc. That year it sold the Panteen cosmetics company to Richardson-Vicks Inc.

In 1981 Roche released Imadyl, its first drug in the rheumatology segment. That year SmithKline's Tagamet drug overtook Valium as the world's best-selling prescription pharmaceutical. In 1982, with few products in the R&D pipeline, and no expected blockbusters, Gerber formed an agreement to market Glaxo Holdings' Zantac product. Rocephin, Roche's first injectable cephalosporin antibiotic, was also introduced. Sales that year were $7.1 billion with net income of $281 million.

Roche Research Foundation was formed in 1983 by merging Roche Study Foundation, Emil Barell Foundation, Fritz Hoffmann-La Roche Foundation, and Roche Foundation for Scientific Exchange and Biomedical Collaboration with Switzerland. The com-

The Players

Chairman, President and CEO of ICN Pharmaceuticals, Inc.: Milan Panic. In the 1950s former bicycling champion Milan Panic left Yugoslavia for the United States where he founded International Chemical and Nuclear Corp. (later named ICN Pharmaceuticals) in 1960. Panic turned ICN into a forerunner in nucleic acid research. As Eastern Europe markets began to emerge in the early 1990s, Panic opened operations in Russia and his former homeland. He then took a nine-month sabbatical from ICN in 1992 to serve as prime minister in Yugoslavia. In 1999 the Serbian Government took control of ICN's Yugoslav drug plant, declaring that ICN never paid for its majority stake in the subsidiary, ICN Galenika.

Chairman of Roche Holding AG: Fritz Gerber. The Italian-born Gerber began his career at Zurich Insurance in 1959 and was appointed chairman in 1977. One year later he accepted the chairman and chief executive positions at Roche. He continued to serve both companies until 1995, when he retired from Zurich. During his tenure at Roche, Gerber reduced costs, refocused research goals, and eliminated diversification programs, leading to a decade of growth at 25% compounded annually. In March 1999, Gerber announced his plan to retire in 2001.

pany acquired American Diagnostics, Inc. in 1984 and Productor Kaspe SA the following year. The U.S. patent for Valium expired in 1985, and as a result the company's pharmaceutical sales were cut in half by competition from cheaper generic imitations.

In June 1986 Roche acquired the licensing rights to market Genentech's treatment for hairy cell leukemia. This product, sold under the name Roferon-A, marked Roche's foray into genetically engineered pharmaceuticals. In 1987, the same year that it thwarted ICN Pharmaceuticals attempted takeover, Roche embarked on a hostile takeover attempt of its own, bidding $4.2 billion for Sterling Drug Inc. It's offer was topped by Eastman Kodak.

Roche Holding Ltd. emerged from a 1989 company restructuring as the holding company for F. Hoffmann-La Roche Ltd., its main operations arm. Acquisitions that year included Eupharma GmbH; Priorin AG; Institut Virion AG and its marketing com-

pany Dinalar AG; Roche Lipid Technologies Ltd.; Givaudan Aromen GmbH; and 60% of Laboratoires ACS.

Roche's Plant Protection Division was divested with the sales of La Quinoleine et ses Derives and Dr. R. Maag to Ciba-Geigy Ltd. in 1990. That September the firm strengthened its presence in biotechnology by acquiring 60% of Genentech, Inc., a U.S.-based research and manufacturing company, for $2.1 billion. That same year, Roche acquired Fritzsche, Dodge & Olcott Inc., a New York-based flavorings and fragrances company.

In 1991 the company paid $821 million for Nicholas, the European over-the-counter drug business of Sara Lee. It also acquired the marketing rights to polymerase chain reaction (PCR) technology from Chiron Corp. Neupogen, a product for treating cancer patients, was introduced that year.

The U.S. Food and Drug Administration (FDA) approved Roche's AIDS treatment dideoxycytidine in 1992. That year Roche ranked first in world vitamin sales and second in fragrances. Roche purchased the struggling drug maker Syntex Corp. for $5.3 billion. It later sold Syntex's women's healthcare product lines and its animal health business.

Roche Biomedical Laboratories merged with National Health Laboratories Holdings in 1995 to form Laboratory Corporation of America, the nation's largest operator of medical lab tests. That year the FDA approved the sale of Roche's AIDS drug, Invirase. Its introduction of CellCept, an agent for the prevention of transplant rejections, marked Roche's entry into the field of transplant medicine.

In 1996 the company bought out Procter & Gamble's interest in their joint venture, thereby gaining control of such products as Aleve and Femstat. That year Roche sold its namatic liquid crystal chemical business to Merck & Co., although it continued to conduct research in that field. Roche strengthened its German over-the-counter position by acquiring Rhone-Poulenc Rorer's vitamin and tonic brands in Europe.

In 1997 Roche acquired Corange Ltd., parent company of Boehringer Mannhelm GmbH, the world's second-largest diagnostics company, for $11 billion. That year it also paid $1 billion to purchase Tastemaker, a flavors company. In 1998 it sold its 84% stake in DePuy Group, a manufacturer of orthopedic products, to Johnson & Johnson for $1.4 billion. In May 1999 the company agreed to pay a fine of $500 million to settle a U.S. Department of Justice claim of vitamin price-fixing. This settlement led to the release of several executives involved in Roche's vitamin operations.

Market Forces Driving Takeover

ICN Pharmaceuticals struggled for years to find a market for its alleged HIV treatment, Ribavirin. The FDA refused its approval as a treatment for viral complication caused by HIV, or as a standalone treatment for Hepatitis C. To find a successful market, ICN CEO Milan Panic went to Europe to raise $500 million in capital funds to promote the drug.

In the hopes of obtaining a new market and an established sales force, ICN became interested in purchasing a foreign pharmaceutical company. ICN settled on Roche, citing the company's marketing strength as the main reason. Because of the minuscule chance that a takeover of Roche was actually possible, market analysts wondered if the real motivation was stock speculation.

Approach and Engagement

ICN Pharmaceuticals began purchasing Roche voting stock in 1987 in hopes of facilitating a hostile takeover. ICN initially acquired 6.3% percent of the stock, apparently unaware of—or unconcerned by—the fact that most of the 16,000 bearer shares were owned by Hoffman-La Roche family members who weren't expect to sell them.

Roche learned of the takeover attempt after ICN disclosed its plan to the Federal Trade Commission. There was little concern regarding ICN's intentions, even when ICN made a second purchase to earn 7.3%. By the middle of 1988, ICN had amassed 8.6% of the stock

Roche's shares jumped dramatically from the time ICN began acquiring the bearer stock. In order to capitalize on the market, ICN sold its shares to an unidentified party for $209 million in November 1988.

Products and Services

In the late 1990s, ICN was the largest pharmaceutical provider in Russia. The firm sold research chemicals, diagnostic products, and drugs, including roughly 70 antibacterial treatments. ICN's blockbuster antiviral drug, ribavirin, was sold in Europe, Canada, and the U.S. In 1999, its plant in Yugoslavia was taken under Yugoslav-Serbian control, which forced the company to abandon operations which made up 30% of its revenue.

In 1998, Roche Holding operated in four main business units:

Roche Pharmaceuticals was divided into two segments. The Prescription sector developed and marketed drugs in the areas of the central nervous system, infectious diseases, oncology, virology, cardiovascular diseases, inflammatory and autoimmune diseases, dermatology, metabolic disorders, and respiratory diseases. Its Nonprescription segment produced such brands as Aleve, Aspro 500, Bepanthen, Bepanthen Plus, Bepanthen Lotion, Berocca Calcium and Magnesium, Elevit Pronatal, Ephynal, Pretuval, Pretuval C, Supradyn, Redoxon, Rennie, and Saridon.

Roche Vitamins and Fine Chemicals produced and sold ingredients that impacted nutrition, health maintenance, and disease prevention in humans and animals. The product range consisted of vitamins, carotenoids, medicinal feed additives, amino acids, feed enzymes, citric acid, polyunsaturated fatty acids, UV filters, emulsifiers, and antitussives.

Roche Diagnostics focused on diagnostic systems for the in-vitro diagnostic market, for the patient self-monitoring sector, and for the research community. It operated four business units: Roche Molecular Biochemicals, Roche Molecular Systems, Roche Laboratory Systems, and Roche Patient Care.

The **Fragrances and Flavors Division** served luxury perfume makers, the cosmetics industry, consumer goods manufacturers, the food and beverages industries, and the pharmaceuticals industry. The Fragrances operation produced ingredients for luxury perfumes, toilet waters, cosmetics, soaps, and other household products. The **Flavors** unit focused on natural and synthetic flavor additives for beverages, foods, pharmaceuticals, oral hygiene products, and animal feeds.

Changes to the Industry

Had ICN been able to acquire Roche, it would have become one of the world's largest pharmaceutical companies. Instead, ten years after the takeover attempt, Roche sold worldwide rights to nearly a dozen products to ICN. In return, ICN agreed to give Roche a 10% equity stake and $15 million in cash and assumed debt. ICN also purchased a Roche manufacturing plant in Puerto Rico as part of the deal.

Review of the Outcome

The acquisition of Roche bearer shares by ICN was unable to force a hostile takeover. ICN was able to amass 8.6% of the stock before selling the shares for $209 million. The sale of the stock helped ICN reverse $15.6 million in unrealized losses in the company's stock portfolio and also provided funds to facilitate another acquisition at a later date.

Research

Buchan, James and John Wicks. "James Buchan and John Wicks On Ambitions of California's ICN," in *Financial Times*, 29 September 1987. Discusses ICN's acquisition of Roche voting shares and projections for expected outcomes. Also gives insight into ICN CEO Milan Panic.

"Company News; Stake in Hoffmann To Be Sold by ICN," in *The New York Times*, 25 March 1988. Describes ICN's sale of its Roche stock in a $209 million deal.

Hall, William. "Gerber To Retire As Roche Chief," in *Financial Times*, 10 March 1999. Announces Fritz Gerber's plan to retire from Roche in 2001 and provides highlights of his career.

Hall, William. "Zurich's Hanggi Goes To Roche," in *Financial Times*, 22 October 1996. Comments on the connection between Zurich and Roche and the appointment of Hanggi as Roche's vice chairman.

Kravetz, Stacy. "ICN To Acquire Roche Holding Product Rights," in *The New York Times*, 24 June 1997. Reports on the deal between Roche and ICN for worldwide rights to Roche products and a manufacturing plant.

"Roche Holding AG," in *Notable Corporate Chronologies*, The Gale Group, 1999. Lists major events in the history of Roche Holding AG and its subsidiaries.

Wicks, John. "US Drugs Group Takes Roche Stake," in *Financial Times*, 23 September 1987. Examines the recent announcement of ICN's plan to force a hostile takeover of Roche.

SEAN C. MACKEY

ING & BARINGS

nationality: Netherlands
date: March 6, 1995
affected: Internationale Nederlanden Groep N.V., Netherlands, founded 1845
affected: Barings PLC, United Kingdom, founded 1792

Internationale Nederlanden Groep N.V.
Strawinskylaan 2631, P.O. Box 810, 1000 AV Amsterdam,
The Netherlands

tel: 31-20-541-54-11
fax: 31-20-541-54-44
web: http://www.inggroup.com

Overview of the Acquisition

Barings bank was acquired in 1995 by Netherlands-based ING Groep NV when disaster struck Barings at its Singapore office. The illegal and covert actions of Nick Leeson, a young derivatives trader, had quickly added up to over $1 billion in losses, instantly bankrupting one of England's oldest merchant banking institutions.

The financial investment group Ernst & Young was placed in charge of Barings' assets, handling all aspects of the company's sale and potential debt reconciliation. The Bank of England first looked into bailing the company out of its trouble, but quickly decided that the losses were too great. Many other financial institutions made offers to purchase parts of Barings services, but only ING Groep offered to assume control of the entire firm, excluding the holding company. Barings was quickly up and running again under ING, which assumed debt in excess of $1 billion.

History of International Nederlanden Groep N.V.

Internationale Nederlanden Groep N.V. (ING)'s earliest predecessor began operations in 1845. The Netherlands Insurance Co. offered services throughout the Netherlands, including Amsterdam. By 1900, Netherlands Insurance Co. had 139 worldwide agencies; it began offering life insurance in 1918. Another parent organization, the Nationale Life Insurance Bank, was established in 1863 and was one of country's only life insurance companies at the time.

A century later, in 1963, The Netherlands Insurance Co. and National Life Insurance Bank merged to form Nationale-Nederlanden (NN). NN had a strong international presence which was further increased by the 1979 acquisition of U.S.-based Life Insurance Company of Georgia and the 1984 purchase of AMFAS Group. By the end of the 1980s, NN was the largest life insurer in The Netherlands.

In 1881, the Dutch government founded the Rijkspostspaarbank, a bank allowing people to create savings accounts in bank operations run out of the nation's post offices. In 1918, another government program, the Postcheque-en Girondienst

The Business

Financials

Revenue (1998): $44.67 billion

Employees (1998): 82,750

SICs / NAICS

sic 6311 - Life Insurance

sic 6399 - Insurance Carriers Nec

sic 6081 - Foreign Banks-Branches & Agencies

sic 6082 - Foreign Trade & International Banks

naics 524113 - Direct Life Insurance Carriers

naics 524128 - Other Direct Insurance Carriers (except Life, Health and Medical)

naics 522293 - International Trade Financing

(giro), was installed. The giro allowed people to use vouchers drawn on their savings accounts in the Rijkspostspaarbank to pay bills and became the standard method of settling accounts. In 1986, the two services were combined to form Postbank. The government was the sole shareholder.

In 1927, Nederlandsche Middenstandsbank (NMB) was formed with the backing of the Dutch government to guarantee its accounts. The financial investment was eventually converted into shares, giving the government an 86% interest. The bank became one of the leading financial institutions in The Netherlands. In 1989, Postbank and NMB merged to form NMB Postbank Group, with the government owning 49% of the company's stock. A year later, the government divested more than half of its shares, as the nation embraced more privatization.

In 1991, insurance giant National-Nederlanden merged with Postbank to form International Nederlander Groep N.V. (ING). The government further divested its shares, only owning 8% after the merger. ING's income grew to over $2 billion in 1993 and 1994, and it made a failed attempt at acquiring Barings Bank. When Barings went bankrupt a year later, however, ING was able to acquire the banking firm for $1 billion, including the assumption of debt.

After acquiring Barings, ING purchased several other companies including Poland's Bank Slaski (1996); investment bank Furman Selz (1997); Equitable of Iowa (1997); Belgium's Banque Bruxelles Lambert (1998); and Guardian Insurance Co. of Canada (1998).

History of Barings PLC

In 1792, Barings Bank opened in London, England, and operated for over two hundred years as a merchant bank. Barings loaned the money to Thomas Jefferson for the Louisiana Purchase and was proud to list the Queen of England as a long time patron. Barings also financed Napoleon during his rise and fall.

In 1890, Barings suffered its first heavy loss when investments in Argentina soured. London, a major financial center at the time, feared the losses would affect the city and other banks. The Bank of England stepped in and set up a guarantee fund to protect Barings and other institutions. The Rothschilds family provided additional backing.

Barings' success for more than two centuries was based on being a relatively small operations dealing with large assets, operating as a staunchly conservative financial institution, and its expertise in researching emerging markets.

In February 1995, Barings collapsed when it discovered that Nick Leeson, a derivatives trader in Singapore, had been concealing a series of financial losses that had accumulated to over $1 billion. The bankrupt bank began seeking buyers, and ING Groep was one of many interested suitors; it eventually acquired Barings operations for $1.59 (1 pound) and the assumption of its hefty debt. ING formed a new unit, ING Barings, which resumed trading on March 9, 1995.

The holding company, Barings PLC, was not acquired, and it was responsible for repaying its investors. In 1997, Barings PLC reached an agreement to settle outstanding claims with Ernst & Young, the executor of the banks assets.

Market Forces Driving the Acquisition

Barings Bank had caught the attention of ING long before its bankruptcy opened the door for an acquisition in 1995. ING had proposed a merger in 1994, which Barings rejected. When Nick Leeson tapped $1.4 billion of Barings' assets in a series of bad derivative trades, he instantly crushed one of England's oldest merchant banks. As a result, Barings needed to be sold off as a means of paying down debt.

ING wanted control of Barings in order to exploit the merchant bank's emerging market investments. Because Barings had established services in Asian and Latin American markets, ING could instantly increase its global presence, which already included Europe and the United States.

Approach and Engagement

When Barings Bank went bankrupt in February of 1995, investment firm Ernst & Young was made the executor of the banks assets and given the responsibility of liquidating assets to pay off debts, assess the total damage caused by Barings trader Nick Leeson, and work with investors to recoup their losses.

Initially, The Bank of England analyzed Barings' situation to see if a bailout was at all possible. It was not long before the Bank of England declared that the losses were too great to support Barings. Consequently, Ernst & Young set out to sell Barings' assets in hopes of recouping investors' money. Barings was up for sale, in whole or part, and many firms were eager to acquire portions of the 200-year-old institution. ABN Amro, Smith Barney, Goldman Sachs and many others offered to purchase parts of Barings. Few companies, however, were interested in acquiring the entire operation.

Within two weeks of Barings' collapse, ING made an offer of $1.59 (1 pound) for ownership of all of the banks operations, including the assumption of nearly $1 billion in debt. The holding company, Baring PLC, which controlled Barings Bank, was not included in the purchase, however, as it was responsible for any legal claims against Barings.

The deal was accepted by Ernst & Young on March 6, 1995. ING immediately took control of the company and renamed it ING Barings. Hessel Lindenberg, an ING executive was sent to London with a team of investigators to oversee the bank's existing operations. The management was left intact until Lindenberg could report on any operational redundancies and expose any possible connections to the Singapore disaster. In order to keep Barings' top management in place, ING agreed to pay nearly $1 million in bonuses.

Products and Services

After the deal, holding company ING Groep added ING Barings to the group of autonomous businesses under its umbrella, including Postbank, Nationale-Nederlanden, ING Bank, and ING Barings. The acquisition of Barings also created many smaller companies including Barings Asset Management, a global emerging market investment firm, and Barings Private Equity Partners, which specialized in venture capital investments.

ING offered banking and investment services to private, commercial, and institutional clients worldwide. Postbank, based in The Netherlands, was one of ING's largest personal banking services. The 1998 acquisition of Banque Bruxelles Lambert opened up

The Players

Derivatives Trader of Barings PLC Singapore Office: Nicholas W. Leeson. Nick Leeson had only a high school education when he took a clerical position for Barings Bank in 1989. He grew up in Watford, a suburb of London, England, and came from a middle class blue-collar family. At Barings, Leeson quickly moved up the ladder and became a derivatives trader and manager at the bank's Singapore office. By 1994, his small Singapore office was the bank's biggest profit center.

Leeson's ego soon got the best of him. Since losing is part of the game, but not something a trader necessarily wants to be known for, Leeson created a false computer record called "Account 88888" in which he dumped losses to hide them. As manager of derivatives trading, he was in a position to oversee the trades and record their performance afterward. Typically, financial institutions assign one person to each task, in order to prevent possible swindling, but Barings failed to do so in this case. By the start of 1995, the account was up to $80 million.

Hoping to recoup his losses, Lesson bet large sums on Nikkei futures called "straddles." When the Kobe earthquake sent Tokyo stocks off kilter, straddling contracts lost huge. Rather than face the consequences, Leeson fled the country through Southeast Asia with his wife. By the time the London office got wind of the disaster, Leeson was nowhere to be found and Account 88888 had reached $1 billion.

Eventually Leeson found himself in a Frankfurt jail, while Singapore and England fought over where to try him. He eventually was convicted and spent four and a half years in a Singapore prison. His actions left Barings bankrupt, and many companies looked into parceling off the bank's services. Eventually Netherlands-based ING purchased the entire firm with the exception of the holding company.

After his release in July 1999, Leeson returned to London with an orange bag carrying all his remaining possessions. He was greeted by a throng of reporters and an injunction freezing all potential assets he might receive from his memoir *Rogue Trader* and a movie based upon his life.

The Players

Chairman and CEO of International Nederlanden Groep N.V.: Aad Jacobs Aad Jacobs was born and raised in Rotterdam, and brought a sense of individual modesty and an emphasis on teamwork to his career. His work ethic earned him the position of chief investment officer of Nationale Nederlander, one of the companies that joined to form Internationale Nederlanden Groep N.V. (ING) in 1991.

A year later, Jacobs, was appointed CEO of ING, after the firm's first CEO failed to get the company heading in the right direction. Jacobs took over while the company was in the midst of an insider trading scandal, and he invited anyone guilty of any wrong doing to confess to all improprieties to him within two weeks. Those who did come forward would keep their job, while those who remained silent would be fired.

Jacobs' modesty could be seen in the investment and growth strategy of ING during his tenure. The company was involved in many different ventures, but invested conservatively, earning the nickname "Mr. 5%" based on its usual investment involvement. One exception, however, was the purchase of bankrupt Barings Bank in 1995. Instead of acquiring a portion of the company, Jacobs bought all of Baring's services and took on more than $1 billion in debt.

In 1998, ING Groep and ING Barings shuffled many top executive positions. ING Baring's vice president, Godfreid van der Lugt, took over as chairman of the subsidiary and eventually of the parent company when Aad Jacobs retired.

the company's presence in Europe's middle-market commercial banking, adding to the services ING offered after the Barings acquisition. ING Barings' biggest asset was its investment banking operations in emerging markets.

ING was also the world's second largest life and health insurer, serving five continents. Other types of coverage include health, disability, auto, home, property/casualty, and reinsurance.

Changes to the Industry

ING's 1995 acquisition of Barings Bank helped create a large worldwide banking, investment, and insurance firm. By assuming Baring's $1 billion dollars of debt, ING increased its asset base from $40 billion to $180 billion overnight.

ING prided itself on running low-profile, nearly autonomous companies, but it gained greater name recognition with the Barings acquisition. Barings itself was left intact after running under the control of ING, but after an investigating of the London office, 21 staff members were fired for allegedly ignoring several warning signs indicating Leeson's disastrous dealings in Singapore. ING and Barings personal banking firms, although similar in operation, were not integrated despite obvious operational redundancies and potential benefits based on economies of scale, further highlighting ING's commitment to let its companies run themselves.

In January 1996, managers of Baring Capital Investors (BCI) acquired their group from ING for an undisclosed amount. BCI became an independent buyout house and changed its name to BC Partners. It started operations with 15 investors advising $940 million in funds.

Review of the Outcome

The structure of Barings remained almost entirely intact after the deal was completed. The newly renamed ING Barings continued operations in all of Barings offices with its focus still on emerging market investments. However, employee departures from the firm after the 1995 collapse weakened Barings dominance in this field.

Longtime ING executive Hessel Lindberg became chairman of ING Barings during its first year. To increase its global investment services, ING acquired the small U.S. firm Furman Selz in 1997. Duetsche Bank, however, raided ING Barings Latin America research department, taking a large chunk of staff and initiating a downturn in ING's overall global investment standings. ING also announced plans to eliminate 1,200 jobs at ING Barings as part of an investment restructuring, after its 1998 earnings were down $170 million, due in large part to a global economic decline.

Nick Leeson spent four and a half years in prison before being released. Peter Barings and many other top officials at Barings were never indicted for any wrongdoing. Ronald Baker, head of Barings derivatives in 1995, was charged with misconduct by the Securities and Futures Authority, but successfully appealed his case, rebutting six charges against him.

Research

"Baring Capital Buys Out ING," in *Venture Capital Journal*, 1 January 1996. Discusses the buyout of Baring Capital

Investors by its former managers, creating an independent investment firm after ING acquired the operations in 1995.

Bray, Nicholas. "Baker, A Former Barings Official, Is Cleared of Misconduct Charge," in *Wall Street Journal*, 12 June 1997. Highlights the legal battles of Ronald Baker after the 1995 collapse of Barings.

Bright, Julia. "Bring ING Barings Back Again; 'It's Been An Extraordinary Year,' Say Hessel Lindenberg, Reflecting on His First 12 Months As Chairman of ING Barings Bank," in *The Director*, April 1996. Discussion with Hessel Lindenberg about the Barings' success following the bankruptcy in 1995.

Copulsky, Erica. "Former Furman Selz Bankers Simmer Over Bonuses, Disorder at ING Barings: People Who Weren't Guaranteed Weren't Paid," in *Investment Dealers' Digest*, 29 March 1999. Article examines ING's troubles with its investment branches, particularly Furman Selz.

"ING Group N.V.," in *Notable Corporate Chronologies*, The Gale Group, 1999. Lists major events in the history of ING Group N.V..

"ING Offers To Pay Nominal Price For Barings In Exchange For Assuming All Liabilities," in *Wall Street Journal*, 3 March 1995. Highlights terms of acquisition offer made by ING for Barings Bank.

Kynaston, David. "1890: A peculiarly British Crisis," in *The Financial Times*, 27 February 1995. Brief overview of a previous time in Barings history where it needed help to bail itself out of a financial loss.

Morais, Richard. "Everyone Was Afraid," in *Forbes*, 9 September 1996. Company profile of ING and its emerging markets investments.

Reid, T.R. "Leeson: Back From the Futures; Broker Who Broke Barings Returns To English Creditors," in *The Washington Post*, 8 July 1999. Discusses the life of Nick Leeson after he single-handedly ruined one of England's oldest banks and spent over four years in a Singapore jail.

Reier, Sharon. "Flying Dutchman: Why Aad Jacobs Decided Holland's ING Would Buy Barings," in *Financial World*, 20 June 1995. Interview and profile of Aad Jacobs.

Smit, Barbara and Tony Patey. "ING Reassures Investors Over Rushed Barings Buy," in *The European*, 10 March 1995. Discusses ING's acquisition of Barings.

SEAN C. MACKEY

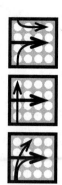

INGERSOLL-RAND & CLARK EQUIPMENT

Ingersoll-Rand Co.
200 Chestnut Ridge Rd.
Woodcliff Lake, New Jersey 07675
USA

tel: (201)573-0123
fax: (201)573-3172
web: http://www.ingersoll-rand.com

nationality: USA
date: April 9, 1995
affected: Ingersoll-Rand Co., USA, founded 1874
affected: Clark Equipment Co., USA, founded 1903

Overview of the Merger

In March 1995, Ingersoll-Rand Co. made an unsolicited takeover bid for Clark Equipment Co. Clark rejected the $78 per share offer, so Ingersoll-Rand starting buying Clark shares at $77 apiece, seeking to gain enough shareholder interest to win a proxy fight. To defend itself, Clark filed a lawsuit, alleging that joining the asphalt paving operations of both firms would violate antitrust laws. A month after the original bid, Clark's stocks grew sharply, devaluing Ingersoll-Rand's original offer. On April 9, 1995, Clark approved an increased offer of $86 per share, becoming a wholly-owned subsidiary of Ingersoll-Rand in a $1.5 billion deal.

History of Ingersoll-Rand Co.

In 1871, Simon Ingersoll patented his invention of the rock drill. He sold the patent to Jose Francisco de Navarro in 1874, who began financing the organization of the Ingersoll Rock Drill Co. A few years later, Ingersoll merged with Sergeant Drill, a company started by one of Navarro's former employees, Henry Clark Sergeant. In 1905, Ingersoll-Sergeant Rock Drill merged with Rand Drill, creating Ingersoll-Rand.

From 1905 to 1915, Ingersoll-Rand added to its core air compressor and rock drill business by manufacturing new products like pneumatic tools, industrial pumps, and jackhammers. In 1925, Ingersoll-Rand assisted in the creation of the first successful diesel locomotive, known as the Central Railroad of New Jersey's No. 1000. The expansion continued after World War II with the acquisition of Aldrich Pump, Torringion, DAMCO, and Schlage Lock.

Ingersoll-Rand became the largest bearing manufacturer in the U.S. with its 1986 purchase of Fafnir Bearings. In 1992, Ingersoll-Rand entered into a partnership with Dresser Industries Inc., creating Ingersoll-Dresser Pump. Ingersoll-Rand acquired Clark Equipment Co., and its many subsidiaries, for $1.5 billion in 1995.

After the merger with Clark, Ingersoll-Rand continued to diversify its services through acquisitions of Master Lock interest, Thermo King, and Harrow industries. For the 1998 Winter Olympic Games in Nagano, Japan, Ingersoll-Rand supplied compressors and other equipment.

History of Clark Equipment Co.

The George R. Rich Manufacturing Co. was formed in 1903, in Chicago, Illinois. The company made only one item, a drill. Two years later, the firm moved its operations to Buchanan, Michigan, and Eugene Clark joined the company. Under Clark, the manufacturer started to flourish and changed its name to Celfor Tool Co., to better reflect its product.

Celfor began to diversify with the 1916 acquisition of Buchanan Electric Steel Co., and its name was again changed to Clark Equipment Co. Sales reached $12 million before the company took its stock public in 1928, earning $3.5 million. After the 1929 market crash, Clark suffered several years of reduced sales. The company blossomed during World War II, with sales reaching $77 million in 1943, due in part to military usage of its heavy duty lift trucks. Between the mid-1950s and the mid-1980s, Clark pursued growth and diversification through acquisitions, including Ross Carrier Co., Hurth Axle SpA, Melroe, Club Car, and Blaw-Knox Construction Equipment.

In 1985, while in the midst of an economic downturn that began after a 1979 sales peak, Clark entered into a 50-50 joint venture with AB Volvo, called VME. By 1994, VME was the fourth largest worldwide construction equipment manufacturer. In 1995, Clark decided to offer its 50% interest in a public stock offering and use the money from the sale to buy back three million of its 17.4 million outstanding Clark Equipment Co. shares. Before the initial public offering could take place, however, Volvo purchased Clark's shares for $573 million. It was the biggest acquisition in Volvo's history, and it received criticism from market analysts who felt VME would function well as a public stock.

Since 1979, Clark had suffered continuous economic losses, due in part to the leadership of former CEO James Rinehart, who stepped down in 1983. After Leo McKernan took control that year, he began reducing operations, cutting jobs, and closing plants. Clark was also forced to sell some of its stock to generate revenue. The mid-1990s marked the end of Clark's slump. Its stock was listed as a star performer on the NYSE, rising 169% between 1993 and 1994.

In the spring of 1994, Clark acquired Blaw-Knox Construction from White Industries, the U.S. subsidiary of Electrolux AB. The $114 million deal gave Clark a strong share of the asphalt paving market. In January 1995, Clark bought Club Car for $237 million,

The Business

Financials

Revenue (1998): $8.29 billion

Employees (1998): 46,600

SICs / NAICS

sic 3533 - Oil & Gas Field Machinery

sic 3531 - Construction Machinery

sic 3537 - Industrial Trucks & Tractors

sic 3714 - Motor Vehicle Parts & Accessories

naics 333132 - Oil and Gas Field Machinery and Equipment Manufacturing

naics 333924 - Industrial Truck, Tractor, Trailer, and Stacker Machinery Manufacturing

naics 336211 - Motor Vehicle Body Manufacturing

gaining control of the nation's largest golf cart manufacturer, with a 35% market share. Clark added a light utility vehicle division to the company upon taking ownership. Clark's success attracted the attention of Ingersoll-Rand which paid $1.5 billion to acquire Clark and its several subsidiaries in 1995. Despite attempts to prevent the takeover, Clark eventually conceded to a deal after Ingersoll-Rand sold off its asphalt paving operations to meet antitrust stipulations.

Market Forces Driving the Merger

A hostile takeover would have appealed to Clark Equipment Co. during the mid-1980s, but the Ingersoll-Rand's offer came about nine years too late. After suffering continued losses from 1979 to 1986, Clark began a slow turnaround through acquisition and restructuring. By 1994, Clark had emerged as a financially sound heavy-equipment manufacturer with products as diverse as golf carts and asphalt pavers. Clark's 1994 revenue was $974 million, with profits reported at $161.9 million. Clark did not need, nor want, to be taken over, but Ingersoll-Rand saw an opportunity and grabbed it.

"[Clark] meets all of the financial and operations criteria we have sought in an acquisition candidate," said Ingersoll-Rand's CEO James Perrella. In addition to its financial strength, Clark's interests were diversified into construction machines, asphalt pavers, skid steer loaders, forklifts, and truck transmissions.

The Officers

Chairman, President, and CEO: James E. Perrella

Exec. VP: Brian D. Jellison

Exec. VP: Steven T. Martin

Clark's Club Car subsidiary was the second largest golf cart manufacturer in the United States. A merger with Clark, would boost Ingersoll-Rand's 1995 sales to nearly $6 billion, from $4.51 in 1994.

Approach and Engagement

In February 1995, Clark Equipment CEO Leo McKernan received a letter from Ingersoll-Rand proposing a tender purchase of $1.34 billion, or $78 per share. After the two companies spent a month trying to negotiate a fair deal, Clark finally rejected Ingersoll-Rand's offer.

Ingersoll-Rand then began more hostile maneuvers, rapidly buying Clark stock at $77 per share. Ingersoll-Rand hoped to gain enough interest in the company to force a proxy fight and vote out Clark's current board. In response to Ingersoll's bid, Clark filed a civil lawsuit, declaring that the companies combined share in the asphalt paver market would violate antitrust regulations. Because only five asphalt paver manufacturers operated in the U.S., joining two would give unfair market share to Ingersoll-Rand. Insisting that the charges were merely a diversionary stall tactic, Ingersoll-Rand pointed out that its asphalt paver products represented less than $10 million of the company's $4.5 billion revenue.

During the takeover negotiations, Clark Equipment's stock grew nearly 50%, which undervalued the original offer. Ingersoll-Rand then increased its offer to $86 per share, or $1.5 billion. Clark accepted the second offer to prevent the possible loss of its board in a proxy fight. Eventually, a court ruled that Ingersoll needed to sell its asphalt paver business in order to fall within antitrust regulations. The paver operations were sold to Champion Road Machinery Ltd., thus clearing the last hurdle for Ingersoll to complete its takeover in April 1995. Clark became a wholly-owned subsidiary, with Clark's cash position of over $430 million used to pay for 33% of the purchase.

Products and Services

In the late-1990s, Ingersoll's subsidiaries were organized into four categories: air/temperature controls, construction equipment, engineered products,

and hardware including locks. Ingersoll earned 40% of its revenue in foreign markets.

Air and temperature control products accounted for 27% of the firm's total sales. Part of the air/temperature controls sector, the Air Compressor Group included Thermo King, a refrigerated transport manufacturer. The company owned a 51% interest in Ingersoll-Dresser Pumps and 49% of Dresser-Rand in joint ventures with Dresser Industries.

The Specialty Vehicles division, part of the construction equipment segment, was most affected by the acquisition of Clark Equipment. Ingersoll-Rand manufactured skid steer loaders via its Melroe subsidiary. Known as Bobcats, these loaders played a major role in the small- and medium-sized construction markets. The Club Car operation, formerly a Clark subsidiary, was the nation's second largest golf cart producer. Clark also added forklift and hydraulic excavators and increased asphalt paving operations.

Water-jet cutting systems, automotive components, ball and roller bearings, centrifugal and reciprocating pumps, door closing devices, locks, and steel doors were all a part of Ingersoll-Rand's engineered products group. These products, in conjunction with the hardware and tools division, made up 47% of company sales. Ingersoll-Rand continued to sell many of the same tools that established the company before 1900, including rock drills and bits, jackhammers, and rotary drills.

Changes to the Industry and Review of the Outcome

Since Clark was already a successfully functioning company, Ingersoll-Rand left the company's structure alone. Clark's corporate headquarters were moved, however, from South Bend, Indiana, to Ingersoll's offices in New Jersey. Clark Equipment was taken off the stock market and became wholly-owned by Ingersoll-Rand. Additional acquisitions after 1995 added to operations and increased sales.

By acquiring Clark, Ingersoll gained control of Blaw Knox Construction Equipment, which held a 50% share of the asphalt paving market and secured sales of $1 million in 1994. After the purchase, Ingersoll-Rand had manufacturing operations on every continent except Antarctica, with 120 facilities worldwide. Ingersoll's 1995 sales increased 27% totaling $5.7 billion.

At the end of 1996, Ingersoll-Rand sold the Clark-Hurth Components division to Toledo, Ohio-based Dana Corp. It was the only operation acquired in the purchase of Clark Equipment that was divested. Ingersoll-Rand's CEO James Perrella stated that

Clark-Hurth did not figure well into the company's long term goals. The amount of the deal was not disclosed.

Ingersoll-Rand's stock price doubled from its 1995 close of $23.43 per share to $47.25 per share in 1998. Profits grew annually by more than 5%, and the firm added 5,000 employees to its roster during that time period.

By 1998, international markets accounted for 40% of company sales. The acquisition of Clark Equipment brought Ingersoll-Rand closer to its goal of achieving 50% of sales internationally by the year 2000.

Research

"$1.3 Billion Bid for Clark Equipment," in *New York Times*, 29 March 1995. Discusses Ingersoll-Rand's first attempt to acquire Clark Equipment. Also looks at per share cost of the deal and Clark's decision to fight the takeover bid.

"After the Takeover," in *Star-Ledger*, 28 April 1995. Looks at Ingersoll's motivation to acquire Clark equipment.

"Asphalt Merger a Go," in *FTC Watch*, 12 June 1995. Discusses the sale of Ingersoll-Rand's asphalt paving operations to a Canadian-based company, clearing any anti-trust concerns preventing the acquisition of Clark Equipment.

"Clark Accepts Ingersoll Bid of $1.5 For Takeover," in *The Wall Street Journal*, 10 April 1995. Discusses Ingersoll's second takeover bid, which Clark accepted to avoid a proxy fight.

"Clark Equipment Co.," in *Notable Corporate Chronologies*, The Gale Group, 1999. Lists major events in the history of Clark Equipment Co.

"Clark Equipment Fights Ingersoll's Bid By Filing Civil Suit On Anti-trust Ground," in *The Wall Street Journal*, 31 March 1995. Discusses the grounds of antitrust concerns Clark Equipment used a basis for its motion to block the takeover bid by Ingersoll-Rand.

"Indiana's Highest-Paid CEOs," in *Indiana Business Magazine*, July 1994. A brief summary of the top chief executive officers of Indiana, including Clark Equipment's Leo McKernan.

Ingersoll-Rand Co. Home Page, available at http://www.ingersoll-rand.com. Official World Wide Web Home Page for Ingersoll-Rand Co. Includes press releases, annual reports, and detailed financial, product, and historical information.

"Ingersoll-Rand Co.," in *Notable Corporate Chronologies*, The Gale Group, 1999. Lists major events in the history of Ingersoll-Rand Co.

Jaffe, Thomas. "Punt," in *Forbes*, 30 June 1986. Discussion of Clark's continued slump in sales.

Ventuono, William C. "The Triumph of the 'Tin Horse'," in *Railway Age*, January 1995. Covers the history of the first successful diesel locomotive in 1925, made jointly by several companies including Ingersoll-Rand.

SEAN C. MACKEY

The Players

Chairman, President and CEO of Ingersoll-Rand Co.: James E. Perrella James Perrella joined Ingersoll-Rand in 1982. As an executive vice president, Perrella ran some of the company's large subsidiary operations including the Torrington Air Compressor division. In 1992, he was named president. Perrella was also appointed chairman and CEO in 1993 when Theodore Black retired. After realizing that many U.S. companies lacked footholds in the global marketplace, including Ingersoll-Rand, he led the company through a major restructuring, turning attention to worldwide consumers. By 1999, the company earned 40% of its revenues from outside the United States. That year, Perrella announced his resignation as CEO, scheduled to take place in October. His planned successor is president and chief operating officer Herbert L. Henkel. Perrella will remain chairman of Ingersoll-Rand, as well as chairman of the National Foreign Trade Council, where he works to increase America's worldwide presence.

CEO of Clark Equipment Co.: Leo J. McKernan Leo McKernan joined Clark Equipment in 1964. He attended several colleges including New York University and the University of Bridgeport while he worked his way up the ranks of the firm. In February 1986, McKernan was named president and chief operating officer, replacing James Rinehart. In May of the same year, McKernan was additionally appointed CEO. He later became chairman. McKernan was given the task of pulling Clark Equipment out of its downward spiral after sales peaked at $1.73 billion in 1979. Under Rinehart's tutelage, the firm had fallen behind competitors in new product development and marketing, as well as foreign production. To strengthen Clark's performance, McKernan began by selling off its accounting division and moving its forklift production offshore, which allowed Clark to close plants in Michigan and Kentucky. By the 1990s, Clark was back on its feet again, considered one of the strongest businesses in South Bend, Indiana. Its financial and market strength attracted the attention of Ingersoll-Rand Co., which made a successful hostile takeover bid in 1995.

INSURANCE COMPANY OF NORTH AMERICA & CONNECTICUT GENERAL

CIGNA Corp.
One Liberty Pl.
Philadelphia, PA 19192-1550
USA

tel: (215)761-1000
fax: (215)761-5515
web: http://www.cigna.com

nationality: USA
date: March 31, 1982
affected: Insurance Company of North America, USA, founded 1792
affected: Connecticut General Corp., USA, founded 1865

Overview of the Merger

In November 1981 Insurance Company of North America (INA) and Connecticut General Corp. announced their plan for a merger of equals, creating CIGNA Corp., the second-largest insurance company in the United States. The $4 billion stock swap deal was directed by investment firm Goldman Sachs and was finalized in March 1982.

Both companies had become successful in different, but complimentary, insurance markets and hoped to capitalize on cross-marketing possibilities. The different management and operational styles were also combined with Connecticut General's Robert Kilpatrick and INA's Ralph Saul sharing the CEO position. Integration proved troublesome, however, and spun CIGNA into a financial downturn, especially in the property/casualty division. Saul eventually stepped down as CEO, and John Cox, a former INA vice president who headed CIGNA'a property/casualty division, resigned shortly thereafter due to frustrations with the new operations.

In 1988 each of CIGNA's 13 divisions began individual restructuring. One by one operations were streamlined and redundancies were eliminated as the firm committed itself to improving customer relations, which had suffered during the first years of the merger.

History of Insurance Company of North America

In Philadelphia's Independence Hall, a group of businessmen met in 1792 to form the Insurance Company of North America (INA). INA began insuring marine cargo and in 1794 issued its first life policy to a sea captain. That same year the company was incorporated and became the first U.S. insurance company to issue coverage of contents destroyed in building fires.

During the first half of the 19th century, INA expanded its insurance agencies throughout the United States. In 1849 an office in California was established, and its premiums were paid in gold dust. Several years later a Pacific Coast Department was created in San Francisco.

INA began offering services worldwide when it set up agencies in Europe and South America in 1887. In the following decade INA became the first U.S. company to write insurance in China, when the Yangtsze Insurance Association, Ltd. became an agent.

INA's marine branch played an important role in the company's success. In 1898, based on statistical research developed by Benjamin Rush, INA began "scientific underwriting" and profits soared as claims declined. In 1920 INA began offering comprehensive transportation policies for ships, railroads, and trucks.

INA continued its foreign ventures in the 1920s by its affiliation with the American Foreign Insurance Association (AFIA), setting up agencies in Asia, South America, India and Europe. In the U.S. INA kept creating new subsidiaries to expand into more insurance branches. INA also created the Securities Company of North America as a holding company for its stock in various subsidiaries.

In 1942 an INA subsidiary wrote accident and health insurance policies for men working on the Manhattan Project, without knowing what the work entailed. Fifteen years later INA was the lead underwriter for the first nuclear power plant in Pennsylvania.

From the 1960s until the beginning of the 1980s INA began slowly combining services and subsidiaries. INA acquired Pacific Employers Group in 1965. A new subsidiary was created in 1977 to handle property/casualty, insurance and reinsurance programs in Canada.

In 1982 INA merged with Connecticut General Corp. to form CIGNA Corp. headquartered in Philadelphia, Pennsylvania. The firm began focusing on group health policies in the mid-1980s due to a 25% jump in those policies in 1984. In 1994 CIGNA's individual insurance earnings exceeded $100 million for the first time. Three years later, the firm bought Healthsource, a managed care firm, for $1.5 billion. CIGNA exited the property/casualty industry in 1999.

History of the Connecticut General Corp.

Connecticut General Life Insurance Co. (CG) was founded in 1865 when the Governor of Connecticut signed a special act incorporating the insurance firm. In 1912 CG began offering individual accident insurance. One year later the company wrote its first group life insurance plan for employees of *The Hartford Courant* newspaper. Its group insurance plans took off,

The Business

Financials

Revenue (1998): $21.4 billion

Employees (1998): 47,700

SICs / NAICS

sic 6300 - Insurance Carriers

sic 6331 - Fire, Marine & Casualty Insurance

sic 6311 - Life Insurance

sic 6321 - Accident & Health Insurance

sic 6320 - Medical Service & Health Insurance

sic 6719 - Holding Companies Nec

sic 6351 - Surety Insurance

naics 524126 - Direct Property and Casualty Insurance Carriers

naics 524113 - Direct Life Insurance Carriers

naics 523999 - Miscellaneous Financial Investment Activities

naics 524126 - Direct Property and Casualty Insurance Carriers

naics 551112 - Offices of Other Holding Companies

and in 1918 CG wrote a plan covering 5,400 employees at Gulf Oil.

As CG expanded its insurance scope, it set up new departments to handle the business. The Accident Department, which was originally designed to provide individual accident coverage, began offering health insurance as well. In 1919 a special reinsurance bureau was set up to handle the influx of business. CG also began offering group accident and sickness coverage that year, further expanding its services.

With the dawn of commercial air travel, CG began offering passengers insurance for flights and also wrote group contracts for airline employees. After World War II began, CG was able to gain a strong advantage in the life insurance market by offering estate planning as a way to market its coverage.

In 1962 CG acquired Aetna Insurance Co., which became CG's property/casualty subsidiary. Due to its increasingly diverse services, CG was forced to create Connecticut General Insurance Corp. in 1967 to oversee operations. After forming the holding company, CG began offering mutual funds, which agents eventually marketed to clients. In 1981 the holding compa-

The Officers

Chairman and CEO: Wilson H. Taylor

President and Chief Operating Officer: H. Edward Hanway

Exec. VP, Human Resources and Services: Donald M. Levinson

Exec. VP and Chief Financial Officer: James G. Stewart

ny became a general business corporation called Connecticut General Corp.

One of CG's investments was an 80% share in the development of a planned community in Columbia, Maryland, in 1963. In 1969 CG established an HMO to serve the Columbia area.

Connecticut General merged with Insurance Company of North America in 1982 forming CIGNA Corp. In 1984, the new firm paid $215 million for AFIA, which provided underwriting to property/casualty insurance in 23 countries. CIGNA further expanded its services with the acquisition of EQUICOR, a leading employee benefits provider, and MCC Companies, a managed mental health care unit, in 1990.

Market Forces Driving the Merger

The merger of Insurance Company of North America (INA) and Connecticut General (CG) to form CIGNA was designed to diversify market sectors, exploit possible cross-marketing sales, increase assets to get an edge on competitors, and most importantly for INA, bail out its struggling property/casualty division, which had suffered major losses in 1981 as the entire market took a downturn under low premium rates. Specifically, INA hoped to boost its sales by cross-marketing property/casualty insurance in conjunction with CG's group employee benefit packages. Called "true group" packages, CIGNA hoped to gain a strong position in this emerging market, despite skepticism of its marketability.

By joining forces, INA and CG would create an asset base of $30 billion. Additionally, the new company's investment portfolio would be worth more than $22 billion, allowing for healthy resources to design, implement, and create new programs to accommodate the increased size of the company, as well as to improve services.

Approach and Engagement

Directors of INA and CG announced their approval of a merger between the firms in November 1981. The new company's name was originally to be North American General Corp., but this was eventually changed to CIGNA, a conglomeration of the abbreviations both of the firm's used. Company shareholders and government regulators approved the deal, which was finalized in March of 1982.

As part of its "merger of equals" approach, INA CEO Ralph Saul and CG CEO Robert Kilpatrick were named co-CEO's of CIGNA. Kilpatrick also became the company's president, responsible for the operations of the many insurance divisions. Saul was appointed chairman, accountable for investments, marketing, and broader company issues.

The deal was hammered out by a third party. Although the companies had been interested in the merger for quite some time, both preferred to leave negotiations to investment firm Goldman Sachs, which received $5 million for its services.

Products and Services

The merger of INA and CG created a huge insurance and investment firm with offices in 70 countries and 14 million clients in the United States alone. The combination of the companies' services helped create a diversified insurance firm with ample cross-marketing potential.

INA's property and casualty division made up nearly 60% of the merged company's annual revenue, while CG's group insurance operations became a major division for CIGNA. Group benefits include benefit packages for employers including medical and dental plans, in conjunction with managed care services.

CIGNA also offered life, accident, and disability insurance to both national and international markets. Its reinsurance division worked to continue those types of coverage, and included high risk insurance underwriting. The financial arm of CIGNA included personal investing planning, corporate investments, discount brokering and retirement plans.

Changes to the Industry

By the end of the 1970s, non-life insurance had taken a drastic downturn, causing INA to show losses of $170 million in its property and casualty markets. This trend continued, and CIGNA averaged a 30% loss in the first and second quarters immediately following the completion of the merger in 1982. CIGNA wanted to use its cross-marketing potential to try to bail out its property and casualty division. At the time of the merger, a new market called "true group" programs, which offered individual home, life, and auto insurance to employees in conjunction with group benefit plans, was taking shape. However, operations didn't move quickly to begin such program, and management grew increasingly frustrated.

In 1983, CIGNA lost another $805 million. That year, vice president John Cox, who headed up property casualty/operations, resigned amidst a management scuffle. His departure was one of several executive resignations. By 1984 the property/casualty branch was underwriting $100 million of monthly losses. Also, despite shifting money from its profitable benefit and investment services divisions to the non-life insurance sector, CIGNA lost most of its special tax benefit.

Angry investors began selling stock, which plummeted from $55 per share to $31 per share. After several attempts to bolster its property/casualty division, including making other property/casualty acquisitions, CIGNA sold off its property/casualty assets to Ace Limited in 1999.

Review of the Outcome

Initially, operations of both firms remained in separate locations. As the merger began to take shape, however, modest job cuts ensued, including 500 layoffs due to INA's headquarters being moved.

The analytical management style of CG didn't work well with INA's shoot from the hip approach. This frustrated top executives of both companies, and their attempts to manage on an equal status proved almost impossible. CIGNA agents also found the joint leadership hard to handle. Used to CG's strong bond with its agents, INA's lack of such a tie caused many CG agents to leave or guide clients to other insurers.

Despite long-term trouble in the property and casualty sector, CIGNA did find success in its employee benefits, financial services, and group health benefits units. A 25% increase of group health policies in 1984 made those operations CIGNA's primary sector. However, the firm continued to struggle in the years following the merger, as many operations were run separately. It wasn't until W.H. Taylor took the helm in 1988 and began leading a series of division-by-division restructuring efforts that the firm began to turn around. By 1995 CIGNA's common stock price had finally exceeded $100 per share, compared to its $55 per share price when the merger took place.

Research

CIGNA Corp. Home Page, available at http://www.cigna.com. World Wide Web home page for CIGNA Corp. Includes press releases, current news, financial information, and annual reports.

"Could CIGNA Be a Merger Casualty?" in *Financial World*, 19

The Players

Chairman and CEO of Insurance Company of North America: Ralph S. Saul. A native of Brooklyn, New York, Ralph Saul earned a B.A. in economics from the University of Chicago and a law degree from Yale. He served in the Navy during World War II and held a variety of positions during his career, including director of the Securities and Exchange Commission, chairman of First Boston Corp. and president of the American Stock Exchange. In 1974 Saul was appointed vice chairman of Insurance Company of North America (INA). Under his leadership INA sold off several assets, including Hospital Affiliates International, Inc. for $615 million. In 1982 he was named co-CEO and chairman of CIGNA, which was created by the merger of INA and Connecticut General. He stepped down from the shared CEO position shortly after the merger, remaining chairman until 1984 when he retired.

CEO of Connecticut General Corp.: Robert D. Kilpatrick. Robert Kilpatrick began his career with Connecticut General in 1954. After working his way up the ranks, he was named senior vice president of the company's group insurance operations. In 1976, Henry Roberts retired as CEO of Connecticut General, and Kilpatrick was named his successor. When INA and Connecticut General merged to form CIGNA in 1982, Kilpatrick became the company's president and co-CEO, with Ralph Saul. After only a few months sharing the lead post, Saul announced he would step down and let Kilpatrick run the newly merged firm by himself. When Saul retired as chairman in 1984, Kilpatrick also took on that role.

September 1984. Discusses the problems faced by CIGNA after the merger, including employee resignations and huge losses in its property/casualty division.

Diamond, David. "One More Grant In Financial Services," in *The New York Times*, 15 November 1981. Profiles the career of Ralph Saul.

Faris William A. and Claire R. Liedell. "Re-engineering With A Small r: The CIGNA Experience," in *Human Resource Planning*, February 1994. Discusses the restructuring program set in place by W.H. Taylor in 1988.

"How INA Will Fit With Connecticut General," in *Business Week*, 19 April 1982. Examines the potential outcome of a new company being formed by the merger of INA and Connecticut General.

"INA/Connecticut General; Self-assured," in *The Economist*, 14 November 1981. Discusses the proposed merger of INA and CG, including reasons for the deal, and offers projections for the performance of the new company.

"Insurance Endorsement," in *Business Week*, 12 April 1976. Briefly announces the appointment of Robert Kilpatrick as president and director of Connecticut General and his eventually placement as CEO on July 1, 1976.

"Only One Boss For CIGNA," in *Business Week*, 31 January 1983. Announcement of Ralph Saul's planned resignation as co-CEO in order to give CIGNA a clearly defined leadership hierarchy to alleviate operational confusion created after the merger.

SEAN C. MACKEY

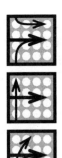

INTERBREW & LABATT BREWING

nationality: Belgium
date: July 27, 1995
affected: Interbrew SA, Belgium, founded 1366
affected: Labatt Brewing Co., Ltd., Canada, founded 1847

Interbrew SA
Vaartstraat 94
Leuven, B-3000
Belgium

tel: 32 16 247111
fax: 32 16 247407
web: http://www.interbrew.com

Overview of the Acquisition

Belgium-based Interbrew SA, one of the world's oldest beer brewers, bought Labatt Brewing Co., the second-largest Canadian beer company, for $2.95 billion in July of 1995. Labatt agreed to the $28.50 per share takeover bid to avoid the hostile overtures of Canada's largest buyout firm, Onex Corp. The deal allowed Interbrew, which became the world's third-largest beer company, to penetrate the North American brewery market for the first time.

History of Interbrew SA

Interbrew SA began as an amalgamation of several breweries, including the Den Horen brewery, which dated back to 1366 and was later named Artois, and the Piedbouef brewery in Liege, Belgium, founded in 1853. The Piedbouef family took over the Brasserie Nord-Europe in Armentieres, France, in 1967. A year later, the Artois and Piedbouef breweries first began their dealings when they founded the Brassico Co. to jointly purchase the Ghlin brewery in Belgium.

In 1977, the Artois brewery agreed to jointly produce and distribute Stella Artois brand beer in the United Kingdom with the Whitbread brewery. Between 1981 and 1986, Artois and Piedbouef jointly purchased holdings in several breweries in Belgium, as well as Italy's Won Wunster. The two companies merged in 1987, creating what was soon known as Interbrew SA, based in Leuven, Belgium.

Interbrew continued its acquisition campaign throughout the remainder of the decade. In 1990, it purchased a minority stake in the Belle-Vue brewery; within a year, Interbrew had acquired full ownership. In 1994, Interbrew established a $23.7 million joint venture with Zhu Jiang, China's third-largest brewery, for the distribution of the Stella Artois brand in Canton, China. By 1995, the firm had expanded its operations to Romania and Bulgaria. As part of its strategy to evolve into a leading international brewer, Interbrew purchased Canada's Labatt Brewing Co. for $2.95 billion that year. Other international purchases continued into the late 1990s.

The Business

Financials

Revenue (1998): $4.2 billion

Employees (1998): 16,700

SICs / NAICS

sic 2082 - Malt Beverages

sic 2084 - Wines, Brandy & Brandy Spirits

sic 5181 - Beer & Ale

sic 7941 - Sports Clubs, Managers & Promoters

naics 711211 - Sports Teams and Clubs

naics 311213 - Malt Manufacturing

History of Labatt Brewing Co.

In 1847, John Kinder Labatt purchased Simcoe Street Brewery, located in Ontario, Canada, in partnership with Samuel Eccles, an experienced brewer. Six years later, Labatt became sole owner and renamed the company John Labatt's Brewery. The founder died in 1866, at age 63, and left the brewery to his wife and son, who renamed the business Labatt & Co. In 1878, Labatt's India Pale Ale won a gold medal at the International Exposition in Paris, France.

Prohibition began in Canada in 1915. Unlike the U.S., where Prohibition was a federal matter, each province worked out its own variation of the general rule and permitted alcoholic beverages to be manufactured locally for export. In 1920, Labatt became one of the first Canadian companies to provide its employees annual vacations with pay. When Prohibition ended in 1926, Labatt was the only brewery of the 15 survivors with its management intact. In 1932, Labatt became one of the first Canadian companies to provide its employees with a group insurance plan.

Despite the promotion of such benefits, in the first kidnap assault in Canadian history, John Labatt III was captured by gangsters in 1934 and held hostage for a week. Although he was released unharmed in Toronto, Labatt retired from public life for the remaining years of his presidency.

The firm launched its initial public offering in 1945 to raise capital for expansion. The following year, Labatt acquired Copland Brewing Co., located in Toronto. After the brewery was renovated, it nearly doubled Labatt's capacity. In 1950, Lucky Lager Ale won the Star of Excellence from the International Food

Institute, Brussels. A year later, Labatt introduced a new light tasting lager called Pilsener Lager Beer. Nicknamed "Blue," the beer eventually evolved into the popular Labatt's Blue brand.

Labatt bought Shea Winnipeg Brewery Ltd., which included Community Hotels and a controlling interest in Kiewel's and Pelisser's, in the early 1950s. The Great West Railway brought the first train into London, Ontario, permitting Labatt to ship beer to Hamilton, Toronto, and Montreal. In 1956, W.H.R. Jarvis became the first non-family president of Labatt, which began expanding into other provinces with the construction of a brewery in Villa La Salle, Quebec. By the end of the decade, Labatt had also formed a Feed Products Department, later known as Miracle Feed, to manufacture animal feed additives using brewing byproducts; introduced Velvet Cream Stout to the Ontario market; and acquired Lucky Lager Breweries Ltd., based in British Columbia.

Acquisitions during the early 1960s included Saskatoon Brewing Co. and Delmar Chemicals Ltd. of Lachine, Quebec. In 1964, Milwaukee-based Schlitz Brewing Co. purchased 39% of Labatt. In response, U.S. Attorney General Robert F. Kennedy filed a civil anti-trust suit preventing Schlitz from exercising voting rights of its Labatt stock. Public reaction to the deal caused sales of Labatt's beer to suffer. The firmed then created John Labatt Ltd. as a holding company, while brewing operations were handled by Labatt Brewing Co., which later changed its name to Labatt Brewing Co. Ltd. Also that year, SKOL International Ltd. was formed by Labatt, Allied Breweries of Great Britain, Pripp Breweries of Sweden, and Unibra of Belgium, to brew and market SKOL beer throughout the world.

John Labatt Ltd. acquired control of Parkdale Wines Ltd. in 1965. Labatt and Guinness Overseas Ltd. jointly formed Guinness Canada Ltd. that year. As a result of the deal, Guinness Stout became the first beer to be brewed under license in Canada. Two years later, Canada's first draft beer in a bottle, Labatt Draft, was produced at the Montreal brewery and distributed throughout Quebec. Full ownership of John Labatt Ltd. was returned to Canada when Schlitz Brewing sold its Labatt shares to three Canadian investment organizations. The firm diversified into dairy and processed foods by purchasing shares in the Ogilvie Flour Mills Co. Labatt also acquired Manning's Inc., a U.S. food service business, as well as a 64% stake in Laura Secord Candy Shops Ltd. from Fanny Farmer Candy Shops Inc.

During the 1970s, Labatt bought over 96% of Columbia Brewing Co. Ltd.; another 32% of the Laura Secord Candy Shops; and a 45% interest in an

American League baseball expansion franchise for Toronto, the Toronto Blue Jays. Labatt's Special Lite, later known as Labatt's Lite, was introduced as Canada's first low-calorie light beer in 1978.

Via an agreement with Anheuser-Busch Inc. of St. Louis, Missouri, Labatt introduced Budweiser and Michelob beer to Alberta, Canada, in 1980. The agreement permitted Labatt to brew Budweiser, the best-selling beer in the world, in Canada, and to market U.S.-produced Michelob there. With sales of $1.5 billion in 1981, Labatt secured the first place spot among Canadian beer brewing companies. Two years later, the firm launched Labatt's Blue Light and John Labatt Classic, Canada's first premium beer. Dairy operations were increased when Labatt acquired Johanna Dairies, the largest table milk processor in the northeastern U.S. Over the next eight years, the firm also bought The Sports Network (TSN) and the promotional rights of the Montreal Expos Baseball Club; introduced John Labatt Classic Light; sold its Canadian wine operations; merged its importing operations with Latrobe Brewing Co., brewer of Rolling Rock beer, to form Labatt Brewing Co. U.S.A.; joined forced with Birra Moretti and Prinz Brau brewing companies to form the largest brewing company in Italy; founded a new broadcast unit, Dome Productions; and secured 50% of New York-based International Talent Group.

In 1991, Labatt bought Maple Leaf Foods Inc.'s Black Diamond cheese business and its dairy division, as well as the Neilson Dairy ice cream business, including Haagen Dazs. A year later, the firm sold its food division, known as JL Foods, to H.J. Heinz. The Miracle Feeds and Ogilvie Mills units were also divested, and Labatt upped its stake in the Toronto Blue Jays by 45%. In 1994, in a move to enter the fast-growing Mexican beer market, Labatt paid $510 million to acquire a 22% interest in the brewing division of Fomento Economico Mexicano SA (Femsa). The following year, to avoid a hostile takeover threat by Onex Corp., Labatt agreed to be acquired by Belgian beer maker Interbrew SA for $2 billion.

Market Forces Driving the Acquisition

In the mid-1990s, shareholders rejected a Labatt management plan, reflecting discontent among institutional investors with the company's recent quest for sports, entertainment, and international beer brewing acquisitions. Stockholders were most upset over Labatt's $510 million purchase of a 22% stake in Femsa Cerveza, one of Mexico's leading beer brewers, in July of 1994. Although the deal seemed promising at the time, as Mexico was considered one of the most attractive beer markets in the world, the crash of the peso roughly a year later forced Labatt to take a $219 mil-

The Officers

Chairman: Paul De Keersmaeker

CEO, Europe, Asia/Pacific, and Africa: Johnny Thijs

CEO, Interbrew Americas: Hugo Powell

Exec. VP and Chief Financial Officer: Jo Van Biesbroeck

Exec. VP, Corporate Affairs: Axel Cogels

lion charge in fiscal 1995. Consequently, the firm's debt-to-equity ratio jumped from 44% to 58%, prompting the Canadian Bond Rating Service to downgrade Labatt's debt outlook to "negative."

According to a May 1995 issue of Business Week, the "financial fallout" wasn't short-term. Labatt CEO Taylor admitted the Mexican acquisition was "likely to hurt Labatt's earnings for the next two years." With shareholders disgruntled, long-term debt at a high of $643 million, and stock at a low of $16 per share, compared to a high of $22 per share in 1992, Taylor announced a plan to divest a portion of the Toronto Blue Jays baseball team holdings, as well as other sports and entertainment assets. He also attempted to adopt a shareholder rights plan, which would allow shareholders to acquire new stock at a 50% discount in the event of a hostile takeover bid. However, shareholders nixed the plan, leaving the firm vulnerable.

Approach and Engagement

Canada's Onex Corp., known as a takeover specialist, launched a $24 per share, or $1.7 billion, hostile takeover bid for Labatt on May 18, 1995. Labatt immediately rejected the all-cash offer, began talking with other potential friendly suitors, and asked shareholders to not tender shares to Onex. Labatt stock fell further due to concerns that the takeover would result in a large tax liability.

After buying time in court, Labatt agreed, on June 6, to be acquired for C$4 billion (US$2.95 billion) by private brewer Interbrew SA, which was looking to extend its geographical reach to the lucrative North American beer market. The C$28.50 per share agreement—$26.25 in cash and $2.25 in interest-bearing notes—included the assumption of $950 million in debt and the stipulation that if Labatt nixed the deal in favor of another suitor, Interbrew would be compensated with $68 million in cash and the right to purchase Labatt's Italian operations for roughly $120 million.

Because Canadian law required that domestic broadcasters be at least 80% Canadian-owned,

The Players

CEO of Interbrew SA.: Hans Meerloo. Hans Meerloo was CEO of Interbrew in 1995, when the firm purchased Labatt Brewing for $2.95 billion as a means of gaining access to the lucrative North American beer market. When the deal was completed, Meerloo was named vice chairman of Interbrew, along with Labatt CEO George Taylor. However, disagreements with shareholders prompted him to resign a few months later.

Chairman and CEO of Labatt Brewing Co: George S. Taylor. George Taylor began his career with Labatt in 1960 at the age of 19. He served the firm in various positions, landing the top spot in 1992. After divesting the Labatt's food and dairy businesses, Taylor pursued growth in three major industries: international beer making, entertainment, and sports. He also launched a marketing blitz that boosted Labatt's Canadian market share four percentage points to 45% and operating profits to $192 million by 1995.

Taylor orchestrated the firm's ill-fated acquisition of the Femsa Cerveza brewery in 1994. Although the purchase gave Labatt entrance to the lucrative Mexican beer market, the ensuing collapse of the peso forced the firm to post a $219 million charge in 1995. Unwilling to wait for the Mexican economy turn around, angry shareholders began criticizing Taylor's judgement. Recognizing Labatt's vulnerability to a hostile takeover, Taylor attempted to put in place a poison pill, but shareholders nixed the plan, sending a public message about their willingness to consider buyout offers. A few months later, Labatt agreed to be taken over by Interbrew. When the acquisition was concluded, Taylor was named vice chairman of Interbrew, and he continued to oversee the operations of Labatt.

Interbrew began seeking suitors for Labatt's broadcasting operations in June. A month later, the Belgian brewer agreed to sell the assets in question to a consortium of Labatt executives and other investors if 67% of Labatt's shares were tendered by the scheduled deadline of July 27.

The deal cleared its regulatory hurdles on July 24, when Interbrew received clearance under the Investment Canada Act for its unit, 3250216 Canada Inc., to acquire all the common shares of Labatt. Antitrust authorities in Canada, the U.S., Belgium, Italy, and the United Kingdom also approved the deal, which was completed by the deadline. When the sale of Labatt's broadcasting operations was complete, Interbrew redeemed for cash the interest-bearing notes it had issued as part of its payment for Labatt.

Products and Services

In the late 1990s, Interbrew sold roughly 120 types of beer, including lagers and premium and specialty beers, in over 80 countries. Operations spanned Belgium, Canada, and South Korea—the firm's three leading markets—as well as Bulgaria, China, Croatia, France, Hungary, the Netherlands, Romania, Russia, Ukraine, the U.S., and Yugoslavia.

Canadian brands included Alexander Keith's, Bud Light, Budweiser, John Labatt Classic, John Labatt Classic Wheat, Kokanee, Labatt .5, Labatt 50, Labatt Blue, Labatt Blue Light, Labatt Canadian Ale, Labatt Crystal, Labatt Extra Dry, Labatt Genuine Draft, and Labatt Ice. Belgian brands included Das and Juliper. The firm sold Rolling Rock in the U.S. through its Latrobe Brewing subsidiary and Dos Equis in Mexico through its FEMSA Cerveza unit.

Changes to the Industry

The acquisition created the world's third-largest beer company. Like many other worldwide beer brewing leaders, Interbrew continued to pursue international expansion. In 1998, the firm bought 50% of South Korea's Oriental Brewery, owned by Doosan Group, for $250 million. Sun Brewing, the largest beer brewer in Russia, and Interbrew agreed to form Russia-based Sun Interbrew in 1999. That year, Interbrew also beat out Adolph Coors Co. with its $378 million bid for Jinro-Coors Brewery, based in Korea.

Review of the Outcome

Interbrew's plans to strip Labatt down to its core brewing operations began during the negotiation process. Shortly after the deal was completed, Interbrew sold off Labatt's broadcast operations, Labatt Communications Inc. (LCI), to an LCI management-led consortium for $605 million. LCI became a new independent company with assets that included Dome Productions, the sports channel TSN, an 80% interest in the Discovery Channel, and a 25% interest in the Viewer's Choice channel.

Divestitures of peripheral assets continued, including the sale of U.K.-based John Labatt Retail in 1996. After trying to sell the Toronto Blue Jays franchise for two years, Interbrew decided in late 1997 to revitalize the struggling team. A year later, however, the team was back on the block, along with Labatt's 48% stake in the SkyDome, which succumbed to a $38 million debt load and declared bankruptcy in 1999.

Research

"Belgian Brewer Presses Case to Buy Labatt," in *The New York Times*, 18 July 1995. Details the terms of the transaction, including Interbrew's planned sale of Labatt's communications assets.

Farnsworth, Clyde H. "Labatt Accepts $2.9 Billion Bid From Large Brewer in Belgium," in *The New York Times*, 7 July 1995. Covers the negotiations from the time of the initial hostile bid by Onex Corp. to Labatt's acceptance of a counter offer by Interbrew.

Interbrew SA Home Page, available at http://www.interbrew.com. Official World Wide Web Page for Interbrew SA. Includes product, corporate, historical, and employment information, as well as current news.

"Interbrew SA," in *Notable Corporate Chronologies*, The Gale Group, 1999. Details the history of Interbrew SA, including its takeover of Labatt.

"Interbrew Receives Court Approval for Labatt Acquisition," in *Canada News Wire*, 24 July 1995. Announces the approval of the deal by several regulatory bodies.

"Labatt Brewing Co.," in *Notable Corporate Chronologies*, The Gale Group, 1999. Details the history of Labatt Brewing Co., including its takeover by Interbrew.

Symonds, William C. "Did Labatt Guzzle Too Much Too Fast?," in *Business Week*, 29 May 1995. Describes the events that caused Labatt's vulnerability.

JEFF ST.THOMAS

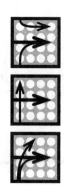

INTERNATIONAL NICKEL & ESB

Inco Ltd.
145 King St. W., Ste. 1500
Toronto, Ontario M5H 4B7
Canada

tel: (416)361-7511
fax: (416)361-7781
web: http://www.incoltd.com

nationality: Canada
date: August 1974
affected: International Nickel Co., Canada, founded 1902
affected: ESB Inc., USA

Overview of the Acquisition

Canada's International Nickel Co., the world's largest producer of nickel, paid $226 million for Philadelphia-based ESB Inc., the world's leading battery maker, in July of 1974. Morgan Stanley & Co. acted on behalf of International Nickel, representing the aggressor in a hostile takeover for the first time ever. Because most established investment banking firms had eschewed hostile takeovers as "dirty business" up until that time, the involvement of Morgan Stanley in the deal attracted a great deal of attention and helped elevate hostile bids to fair game status for other investment banking companies.

History of International Nickel Co.

In 1902, Charles Schwab of U.S. Steel Corp. and others in the industry created International Nickel (Inco), a holding company, by merging the interests of Canadian Copper Co., Orford Copper Co., Anglo-American Iron Co., American Nickel Works, Nickel Corporation Ltd., Vermillion Mining Co. of Ontario, and Societe Miniere Caledonienne. By 1913, Inco had increased its share of the U.S. nickel market to 70%. Three years later, the company formed a Canadian subsidiary, International Nickel Company of Canada, to establish a refinery at Port Colborne and to consolidate the mining interests in Canada.

World disarmament agreements in the early 1920s killed the munitions market, leaving Inco with a huge backlog of nickel. Profits dropped to $1.2 million over the next year. President Robert Crooks Stanley launched a vigorous research and development department to find new uses for nickel during peacetime. Inco effectively blocked the growth of such competitors as British America Nickel, which made a serious bid for the U.S. market in 1923, by lowering its price from 34 cents to 25 cents, a move which drove British America to bankruptcy a year later. In 1928, the company restructured, and the Canadian subsidiary became the parent company. Inco acquired Mond Nickel, a British refiner of nickel and copper ores, in 1929.

With World War II approaching, Inco became the supplier of nickel to both sides, signing a long-term contract with Germany's I.G. Farbenindustrie AG. In a 1945 antitrust suit, the U.S. Department of Justice charged that Inco's agreement with Farben was part of an effort to form a worldwide nickel cartel that, in the process, had supplied Germany with a stockpile of nickel critical to the war. By war's end, Inco's assets were valued at about $135 million, with sales of $148 million. The antitrust action was settled in 1948, when Inco signed a consent decree agreeing to only sell nickel in the U.S. at fair prices.

The nickel shortage became severe in 1950 when the Korean War added a backlog of orders for armor plate, and the U.S. government added nickel to its list of stockpiled metals critical to national defense. The inevitable result was an increase in price and a host of new competitors entering the market. In 1956, after several years of exploration, Inco made a major find in northern Manitoba, a field christened "Thompson" after company chairman John F. Thompson. The site accounted for 30% of sales that year. Although sales fell in 1958, a strike by the Mill, Mine and Smelter Workers Union kept inventories down, preventing a loss for the year.

In 1965, under the leadership of new chairman Harry S. Wingate, Inco's sales hit a record $572 million; net income reached $136 million. A strike by 17,000 workers at Sudbury in 1971, followed by a sharp recession, resulted in nickel sales dropping by 25%. By mid-decade, Inco's share of the free world's nickel sales had slipped below 50%. Hoping to become less reliant on nickel, Inco paid $224 million for ESB Inc., a leading manufacturer of large storage batteries, including the Ray-O-Vac brand, in 1974. Two years later, the company officially changed its name to Inco Ltd. The company's U.K. subsidiary became Inco Europe Ltd., and International Nickel Inc. became Inco United States, Inc.

Sales slipped drastically in 1981, and the company reported a year-end loss of $470 million, its first loss in 50 years. Two years later, Inco sold off its battery operations. Sales in 1984 fell another $500 million as the recession and corporate debt proved a fatal combination. The nickel market finally rebounded in the late 1980s, and Inco earned a profit of $125 million in 1987. Two years later, profits had soared to $753 million, and Inco merged its gold interests with Consolidated TVX Mining.

In the mid-1990s, Inco announced plans to build a $600-700 million smelter plant on a former U.S. naval base in Newfoundland. In April of 1996, Vancouver-based Diamond Fields Resources Inc. accepted a takeover bid from Inco. Exadiam Corp. filed a lawsuit to stop the sale, claiming that it already owned Diamond's assets. A few months later, Inco reached a $34 million settlement with Exadiam, which allowed it to continue its takeover. On August 31, 1996, Inco paid $4.3 billion for Diamond Field, gaining control of nick

The Business

Financials

Revenue (1998): $1.76 billion

Employees (1998): 11,000

SICs / NAICS

sic 2819 - Industrial Inorganic Chemicals Nec

naics 325998 - All Other Miscellaneous Chemical Product and Preparation Manufacturing

el, copper, and cobalt deposits in Newfoundland's Voisey's Bay. The deal was one of the biggest in Canadian mining history.

Market Forces Driving the Acquisition

Fueled by weapon production for the Vietnam War, demand for nickel soared in the late 1960s. As a result, International Nickel (Inco) borrowed money to launch a large-scale expansion. Despite the popularity of less expensive nickel oxides and ferro-nickels being used by competitors, Inco continued to focus on mining the more costly high-grade nickel. When the recession hit in the early 1970s, and nickel sales fell by 25%, Inco's stock plummeted by 50% in just a few months. Staggering under its escalating debt load, Inco realized that it could no longer rely solely on the cyclical nickel industry.

According to Bruce Wasserstein in *Big Deal: The Battle for Control of America's Leading Corporations,* "After the Oil Shock of 1973, Inco management settled on energy as an attractive sector. Eventually, a management committee selected the subcategory of 'packaged energy' as strategically attractive. A failed attempt was made to acquire a British car battery maker. ESB, formerly the Electric Storage Battery Company, the world's largest battery maker and Philadelphia's eleventh largest company, seemed a good second choice." ESB management believed that demand for batteries would grow as worldwide oil supplies dwindled.

Approach and Engagement

Inco first approached ESB on July 18, 1974. Although ESB expressed resistance to the idea of a takeover, Inco took the advice of its investment advisor, Morgan Stanley & Co., and moved forward with a cash bid of $157 million, or $28 per share, compared to ESB's share price of $19.50. Realizing that it would be

The Officers

Chairman and CEO: Michael D. Sopko

President: Scott M. Hand

Exec. VP, General Counsel, and Secretary: Stuart F. Feiner

Exec. VP, Marketing: Peter J. Goudie

Exec. VP, Operations: Peter C. Jones

difficult to justify turning down a bid of that size, ESB enlisted the help of Goldman, Sachs & Co., which advised the firm to begin soliciting other offers from more friendly suitors. On July 22, United Aircraft and Transportation Co. (later known as United Technologies Corp.) counterbid $34 per share for the battery maker. Thinking it had defeated Inco, ESB accepted.

Undaunted, Inco responded by increasing its per share offer to $36, and a bidding war ensued, which Inco eventually won at $41 per share, a price of approximately $227 million. By mid-August, 95% of ESB's shares had been tendered to Inco. The transaction was finalized shortly thereafter.

Products and Services

Inco divested its battery making operations in the early 1980s. By the end of the following decade, the firm was mining nickel, which accounted for roughly three-fourths of sales; copper, which brought in more than one-tenth of sales; cobalt; and precious metals, including gold, silver, and platinum. Inco also produced sulfuric acid and liquid sulfur dioxide. Major operations were located in Canada, Indonesia, Japan, and the United Kingdom, although the firm also operated on a smaller scale in Barbados, China, France, Germany, Guatemala, Hong Kong, India, New Caledonia, Taiwan, Thailand, and the U.S.

Changes to the Industry

According to John Brooks in *The Takeover Game*, "In the world of investment banking, Morgan Stanley was, and for years had been, the glass of fashion and the mold of form." Like most of its competitors, the firm had avoided acting as the aggressor in hostile takeovers. The reason for this, wrote Brooks, was that "until 1974 hostile takeovers had been widely regarded in Wall Street as dirty business, beneath the dignity of the likes of Morgan Stanley." As the most influential investment firm on Wall Street, the firm's decision to represent International Nickel in its quest for ESB set the stage for the future involvement of large investment bankers in less-than-friendly merger and acquisition activity.

Review of the Outcome

The diversification into batteries proved an expensive mistake for Inco. The price the firm had paid for ESB raised the eyebrows of many analysts, who were already concerned about Inco's hefty debt load. Nickel sales remained sluggish, and Inco spend three years engaged in antitrust litigation defending its purchase to authorities concerned about Inco's dominance in the nickel industry. At the time, nickel was a raw material used by battery makers, and antitrust investigators suspected the deal might limit competition.

"More fundamentally, Inco simply seemed ill-matched to manage a consumer goods business," wrote Wasserstein. "The miniaturization revolution that would bring portable calculators and Sony Walkman to America swelled battery usage. However, Inco was conditioned to thinking in terms of selling raw materials in a commodity market. Duracell and others thrashed ESB's Ray-O-Vac line at the checkout counter."

In the early 1980s, Inco acknowledged its mistake, sold its battery operations, and wrote off the deal on which it lost roughly $200 million. The firm also cut its workforce in half and decided to refocus on its core nickel operations, even if it meant hunkering down for several years and waiting for the market to recover. Inco's patience paid off in the late 1980s when demand for nickel saw an upswing. By 1990, net income had neared $800 million.

Research

Brooks, John. *The Takeover Game*, Truman Talley Books/E.P. Dutton, 1987. Traces the history of hostile takeovers in U.S. corporate history, including International Nickel's hostile takeover of ESB in 1977.

Inco, Ltd. Home Page, available at http://www.incoltd.com. Official World Wide Web Home Page for Inco, Ltd. Includes news, financial, product, and historical information.

"Inco, Ltd.," in *Notable Corporate Chronologies*, The Gale Group, 1999. Provides an overview of the history of the company.

"Expert Strategists in the Acquisition Game," in *Business Week*, 14 November 1977. Details the role of Morgan & Stanley and Goldman, Sachs & Co. in the International Nickel and ESB deal.

Madrick, Jeff. *How We Got From the First Hostile Takeover to Megamergers, Corporate Raiding, and Scandal*, Bantam Books, 1987. Covers the history of current merger and acquisition activity, including the ESB/International Nickel deal.

Wasserstein, Bruce. *Big Deal: The Battle for Control of America's Leading Corporations*, Warner Books, 1998. Offers an overview of the largest mergers in recent American corporate history.

JEFF ST. THOMAS

INTERNORTH & HOUSTON NATURAL GAS

nationality: USA
date: July 1985
affected: InterNorth Inc., USA, founded 1930
affected: Houston Natural Gas Corp., USA, founded 1925

Enron Corp.
1400 Smith St.
Houston, TX 77002-7369
USA

tel: (713)853-6161
fax: (713)853-3129
web: http://www.enron.com

Overview of the Merger

In July of 1985, energy transmission and production company InterNorth and Houston Natural Gas Corp., operator of the world's sole transcontinental gas pipeline, merged to form Enron, operator of the largest natural gas pipeline network in the U.S. Despite initial problems with power struggles among management, falling natural gas prices, and a hefty debt load, the highly successful $2.4 billion deal eventually served as a model for future consolidation in the natural gas industry.

History of InterNorth Inc.

In 1930, Northern Natural Gas Co. was organized in Omaha, Nebraska, by three companies: North American Light & Power Co., United Light & Railways Co., and Lone Star Corp. In 1941, United Light & Railways sold its share of Northern to the public. The following year, Lone Star distributed its holdings to its stock holders.

Northern Natural acquired the gas-gathering and transmission lines of Argus Natural Gas Co. in 1944 and soon consolidated the Argus properties into a subsidiary called Peoples Natural Gas Co. In 1947, North American Light & Power sold its shares to underwriters, who in turn offered the stock to the public. Peoples was dissolved as a subsidiary in 1952 and its operations became a division of the parent company. In the mid-1950s, Northern Natural established two subsidiaries: Northern Natural Gas Producing Co., to operate its gas leases and wells, and Northern Plains Natural Gas Co., to bring Canadian gas reserves to the continental U.S. The People's division purchased a natural gas system in Dubuque, Iowa, in 1957.

The firm created two additional subsidiaries in 1960: Northern Gas Products Co., to build and operate a natural gas extraction plant in Bushton, Kansas, and Northern Propane Gas Co., for retail sales of propane. Four years later, Council Bluffs Gas Company of Iowa was acquired and merged into the Peoples division. Northern Natural Gas was sold to Mobil Corp. In 1966, Hydrocarbon

The Business

Financials

Revenue (1998): $31.2 billion

Employees (1998): 17,800

SICs / NAICS

sic 1311 - Crude Petroleum & Natural Gas

sic 2911 - Petroleum Refining

sic 4925 - Gas Production & Distribution Nec

naics 211111 - Crude Petroleum and Natural Gas Extraction

Transportation was formed to own and operate a pipeline system carrying liquid fuel. Acquisitions in 1967 included Propane Corp., a distributor of propane gas in the eastern U.S. and the Caribbean; Mineral Industries Inc., a marketer of automobile antifreeze; National Poly Products; and Viking Plastics of Minnesota. Northern Natural also created Northern Petrochemical Co. to manufacture and market industrial and consumer chemical products.

Plateau Natural Gas Co. became part of the Peoples' division in 1970. The following year, the firm acquired Olin Corp.'s antifreeze production and marketing business. Northern Natural formed UPG Inc. in 1973 to transport and market the fuels produced by Northern Gas Products. Three years later, Northern Arctic Gas Co. was created as a partner in the proposed Alaskan arctic pipeline. Also, Northern Liquid Fuels International Ltd. was formed as a supply and marketing company.

Northern Natural changed its name to InterNorth Inc. in 1980. An attempted hostile takeover of Crouse-Hinds Co., an electrical products manufacturer, was thwarted by Cooper Industries, Inc. Also that year, InterNorth established Northern Overthrust Pipeline Co. and Northern Trailblazer Pipeline Co. to participate in the Trailblazer pipeline and created two exploration and production companies: Nortex Gas & Oil and Consolidex Gas and Oil Ltd. In 1981, the firm established Northern Engineering International Co. to offer professional engineering services. The following year, InterNorth formed Northern Intrastate Pipeline Co. and Northern Coal Pipeline Co., as well as InterNorth International, Inc. to oversee non-U.S. operations. The 1983 purchase of Belco Petroleum Corp. for $770 million expanded oil and gas exploration and production efforts. Chemplex Co., a poly-

ethylene and adhesive manufacturer, was acquired in 1984.

Houston Natural Gas Corp. and InterNorth merged in 1985 to form HNG/InterNorth. The new enterprise began to divest businesses that did not fit in with its long-term goals, including the Peoples division, which was sold for $250 million. In 1986, the firm adopted the name Enron Corp. and sold its chemical subsidiary and its 50% stake in Citrus Corp. The following year, Enron centralized its gas pipeline operations under Enron Gas Pipeline Operating Co. and formed Enron Oil & Gas Co. for exploration and production. By the end of the decade, Enron had also added cogeneration plants to produce electricity and thermal energy from one source in both New Jersey and Texas; signed a 15-year contract to supply natural gas to a cogeneration plant on Long Island; and inked an agreement with Coastal Corp. that allowed the firm to increase the natural production from its Big Piney Field in Wyoming.

In 1990, Enron acquired CSX Energy's Louisiana production facilities. Tenneco Inc. divested its natural gas liquids/petrochemical operations to Enron in 1991. The firm secured a 20-year, $4 billion contract to supply natural gas to a planned upstate New York cogeneration plant in 1992. Three years later, the government of Trinidad and Tobago awarded an offshore oil exploration contract to Enron. Rather than compete against electricity utilities, Enron decided in 1997 to enter the industry with the acquisition of Portland General Electric. The following year, the firm moved into the international water industry when it purchased Wessex Water and folded its operations into Azurix, a newly formed water division. Enron and SK Group agreed in 1999 to jointly distribute natural gas in South Korea. That year, Enron listed Azurix as a public company.

History of Houston Natural Gas Corp.

In 1925, Houston Natural Gas Corp. was founded as a distributor of natural gas in southern Texas. In the mid-1950s, the firm diversified into the developing of oil and natural gas sites, and it acquired Houston Pipe Line Co. in 1956.

Valley Gas Production was added to the mix in 1963. Houston Natural Gas exited the distribution industry in 1976 when it sold its distribution operations to Entex. Acquisitions in 1984 included Transwestern Pipeline, based in California, and Florida Gas Transmission. After skirting a hostile takeover effort by Coastal Corp., Houston Natural Gas agreed in 1985 to merge with InterNorth to form what became known as Enron.

Market Forces Driving the Merger

The deregulation of natural gas prices in the early 1980s by the U.S. government drastically increased competition for natural gas pipeline companies because, for the first time, gas producers were able to charge whatever prices they chose. In 1985, federal regulators also decided that independent companies could sell gas, a practice previously restricted to pipeline companies.

One natural gas firm, Texas Eastern, found itself struggling in the wake of the deregulation. Oscar Wyatt, CEO of Coastal Corp., made his first overtures toward Texas Eastern in 1984, when he purchased a small stake in the firm. In a defensive move, Texas Eastern paid $1 billion for oil field and liquid gas operation Petrolane Inc. that year. According to Bruce Wasserstein, author of *Big Deal: The Battle for Control of America's Leading Corporations,* the famed "Oscar Wyatt was not the only player going after natural gas companies in the mid-1980s. Other strategic purchasers, as well as financial buyers, saw the consolidation potential in the industry." One such buyer, investor Irwin Jacobs, began acquiring shares in InterNorth. This action prompted chairman Sam Segnar to look for a friendly deal. Joining forces with Houston Natural Gas would give the firm a 37,000-mile nationwide natural gas pipeline, the largest in U.S., and thus access to nearly all major U.S. markets.

Approach and Engagement

Segnar approached Houston Natural Gas in May of 1985. After roughly two weeks of negotiations, InterNorth and Houston Natural Gas publicly announced their $2.4 billion merger. Although the two firms initially planned to retain separate headquarters, InterNorth eventually agreed to move from Omaha, Nebraska, to Houston, Texas. Houston Natural Gas CEO Kenneth Lay would serve as president and take over as CEO and chairman of the newly merged firm—to be named HNG/InterNorth until a new named was decided upon—on January 1, 1987, when InterNorth CEO Sam Segnar would retire. The merger was finalized in July of 1985.

Products and Services

By the late 1990s, Enron had become the largest buyer and seller of natural gas in the U.S. The firm marketed electricity through its Portland General Electric subsidiary; other commodities included coal and water. Wholesale energy sales accounted for 87% of total revenues. Non-energy services included risk management services, energy project financing, engineering and construction for energy infrastructure, and consulting. U.S. operations accounted for 81% of sales.

The Officers

Chairman and CEO: Kenneth L. Lay

Vice Chairman: Joseph W. Sutton

President and Chief Operating Officer: Jeffrey K. Skilling

Sr. VP and Chief Financial Officer: Andrew S. Fastow

Sr. VP and Chief Accounting, Information, and Administrative Officer: Richard A. Causey

Changes to the Industry

Despite its status as operator of the largest natural gas pipeline in the U.S., Enron wasn't focused only on the transportation of natural gas. Recognizing the importance of marketing in the deregulating natural gas industry, the firm also moved into trading natural gas when it formed Enron Capital in 1992. "Very quickly, Enron's trading operation became a de facto market maker for natural gas contracts and developed into the nation's leading wholesaler of natural gas," wrote Wasserstein.

Review of the Outcome

In the first year following the merger, the net income of HNG/InterNorth plummeted to $166 million, a drop of 42%, on sales of roughly $10 billion. Management scuffles became apparent even to clients, and Houston Lighting & Power Co., the firm's largest customer, canceled a long-term contract. Hoping to reinvent itself with a new corporate identity, HNG/InterNorth, with the help of consultant Lippincott & Marguiles Inc., settled on a new name for the firm: Enteron. After discovering that the word meant digestive tract, the firm changed the name to Enron, which was approved by a board meeting vote on April 10, 1986.

To help pay down its hefty $4.3 billion in debt—largely the result of the merger—Enron divested 50% of Citrus Corp., 50% of its electricity and steam power operations, and 16% of its exploration and production operations. The newly merged firm also laid off roughly 1,500 employees, or 10% of the workforce, and restructured operations. When Lay took over as CEO in 1987 he "set out to make Enron the leading integrated pipeline company in North America, shedding layers of bureaucracy and expanding the company's pipeline network," stated *Fortune* in August 1996. These efforts paid off handsomely. Between 1988 and 1993, Enron's stock price jumped 217%, compared to an industry average of 44%. Between 1989 and 1992, net income grew roughly 50% to $330 million.

Research

Davis, Jo Ellen. "A Mega-Pipeline with a Massive Identity Crisis," in *Business Week*, 14 April 1986. Describes the problems Houston Natural Gas and InterNorth experienced in the first year after the merger.

"CEO Portrait," in *Philadelphia Business Journal*, 10 July 1998. Details the career of Kenneth Lay.

Enron Corp. Home Page, available at http://www.enron.com. Official World Wide Web Page for Enron Corp. Offers news releases, financial and product information, and employment information.

"Enron Corp.," in *Notable Corporate Chronologies*, The Gale Group, 1999. Provides an overview of the history of the company.

"Enter Enron," in *Economist*, 12 February 1994. Describes the performance of Enron in the nine years since the merger.

Hurt, Harry. "Power Players," in *Fortune*, 5 August 1996. Discusses the management of Enron by Kenneth Lay.

Wasserstein, Bruce. *Big Deal: The Battle for Control of America's Leading Corporations*, Warner Books, 1998. Offers an overview of the largest mergers in recent American corporate history.

THERA WILLIAMS

INTERSTATE BAKERIES & CONTINENTAL BAKING

nationality: USA
date: July 1995
affected: Interstate Bakeries Corp., USA, founded 1930
affected: Continental Baking Co., USA, founded 1849

Interstate Bakeries Corp.
12 E. Armour Blvd.
Kansas City, MO 64111
USA

tel: (816)502-4000
fax: (816)502-4155

Overview of the Acquisition

Interstate Bakeries, the third-largest wholesale bakery in the U.S., acquired Continental Baking Co., the nation's leading wholesale bakery, for $220 million in cash and 16.9 million shares of stock in July of 1995. Continental Baking's parent, Ralston Purina Co., had created a separate, "targeted" stock—a structure devised by Lehman Brothers in 1991—for Continental Baking in 1993. The Interstate/Continental deal marked the first time a company with targeted stock was sold.

History of Interstate Bakeries Corp.

In 1930, baker Ralph Leroy Nafziger founded Interstate Bakeries in Kansas City, Missouri, as a bread wholesaler. Seven years later, Interstate acquired Schulze Baking Co. By 1950, the firm had also purchased Supreme Baking Co., based in Los Angeles, California, and Buffalo, New York-based O'Rourke Baking Co.

Growth via acquisition continued in 1951 when Interstate bought Mrs. Karl's Bakeries, located in Milwaukee, Wisconsin. Diversifying into cake baking, the firm acquired Ambrosia Cake Co., Remar Baking Co., and Butter Cream Baking Co. in 1954. In 1957, Denver, Colorado-based Campbell-Sell Baking Co. was added to the mix. Cake operations were bolstered in 1959 by the purchase of Kingston Cake Bakery of Pennsylvania.

During the first half of the 1960s, purchases included Cobb's Sunlit Bakery, based in Green Bay, Wisconsin; Schall Tasty Baking Co., based in Traverse City, Michigan; Sweetheart Bread Co.; and Hart's Bakeries, Inc. Interstate then underwent a period of consolidation and shut down a few factories, including the Schall Tasty and Butter Cream Baking units. The firm also sold its bakery in Buffalo, New York. In March of 1968, Interstate acquired the Millbrook bread operations of National Biscuit Co., including its fleet of roughly 700 delivery trucks. Expansion into non-baking operations occurred a few months later when Interstate acquired Baker Canning Co., a food processor based in Wisconsin. To reflect its diversified scope, the firm changed its name to Interstate Brands Corp. on July 25, 1969. It had

The Business

Financials

Revenue (1999): $3.45 billion

Employees (1999): 34,000

SICs / NAICS

sic 2051 - Bread, Cake & Related Products

naics 311812 - Commercial Bakeries

grown into the third-largest wholesale baking company in the U.S.

The canning unit was sold in 1974, and Interstate refocused on core baking operations. That year, the firm paid $500,000 for Nolde Brothers Inc. Looking to diversify outside the data processing industry, DPF Inc. offered to buy 43% of Interstate. Although Interstate filed a lawsuit in an effort to block the deal and made plans to purchase diary products processor Farmbest Foods, which would have diluted the stock that could be controlled by DPF to 37%, DPF was ultimately successful. On February 27, 1979, DPF paid $37 million for control of Interstate and moved the firm's headquarters to Hartsdale, New York. Within two years, DPF had exited the data processing industry completely and tightened it focus to baked goods. DPF also adopted the Interstate Bakeries moniker. Despite securing a $50 million tax break, due to the liquidation of the data processing assets, Interstate struggled to get back on solid financial ground.

In 1982, the firm moved its headquarters back to Kansas City. Declining white bread sales, along with increased competition in the baking industry, fueled the firm's downward spiral. Plans to merge with American Bakeries Co. dissolved, and in 1983, Interstate posted its first loss. The following year, losses mounted to $4.2 million. After taking a $21 million write-down and leveraging its pension fund to pay down debt, Interstate began working on bolstering sagging sales. The company stepped up its advertising efforts, particularly of its non-white bread products; introduced several new products; closed five plants; and launched a $110 million campaign to refurbish existing operations. Acquisitions during this time included Purity Baking Co., maker of Sunbeam bread, and Stewart Sandwiches. By the late 1980s, the company was again operating in the black with 1987 earnings of $13.5 million. That year, the newly formed IBC Holding Corp. bought the outstanding shares of Interstate and took the bakery firm private.

IBC's first move was the $132 million acquisition of the Merita/Cotton's Bakeries unit of American Bakeries Co. Bolstered by its new operations, IBC's sales exceeded $1 billion for the first time in 1989. Two years later, IBC Holding changed its name back to Interstate Bakeries and listed publicly, raising $250 million. The firm used the capital to whittle down debt which had ballooned after the Merita purchase.

Operations were decentralized in the early 1990s under the leadership of former Merita president Charles A. Sullivan. In 1995, Interstate paid $220 million in cash, as well as 16.9 million shares of stock, to Ralston Purina Co. for its Continental Baking Co. subsidiary. When the deal was completed, Interstate became the largest bakery wholesale operation in the U.S.

In 1997, Interstate acquired San Francisco French Bread from Specialty Foods and Marie Callender's crouton brand from International Commissary. The following year, the firm bought John J. Nissen Baking and Drake's, a maker of snack cakes owned by Canada's Culinar Inc. Interstate's effort to acquire the reminder of Culinar in 1999 were thwarted by Saputo Group.

History of Continental Baking Co.

In 1849, Ward Baking Co. was established by the Ward family in New York. Two generations later, in 1921, William Ward founded United Bakeries to oversee the Ward family business. United adopted the Continental Baking Co. name in 1924. The following year, Continental acquired Taggart Baking, including the Wonder bread brand, and became the largest baked goods wholesaler in the U.S.

Hotelier ITT Corp. acquired Continental in 1968. Americans became more health conscious in the 1970s, and sales at Continental, particulary of Hostess snack cakes, dwindled. Ralson Purina bought Continental from ITT in 1984. Nine years later, the parent company established a separate class of stock for Continental Bakery. Also that year, Continental and Interstate Bakeries forged their first alliance by exchanging production plants. Interstate bought a Continental bread plant in Tampa, Florida, while Continental bought an Interstate cake production plant in Los Angeles, California. In 1995, Interstate paid roughly $460 million in cash and stock for Continental.

Market Forces Driving the Acquisition

In the early 1990s, when the U.S. federal government issued new dietary guidelines stressing the importance of bread and grains, Interstate saw the popularity of its major product—bread—rise. To capitalize on this increased demand, Interstate began a process of decentralizing operations. Local units were granted more autonomy in an effort increase their efficiency. By mid-decade, the reorganization had paid off, and Interstate was able to pursue an acquisition of considerable size. Continental, the wholesale baked goods industry leader in the U.S., emerged as an attractive target. Its brands included Wonder bread and Hostess snack cakes, and many of its factories were situated in markets Interstate had yet to penetrate. The deal would catapult Interstate to the number one spot among wholesale bakeries.

At the same time, Ralston Purina was ready to sell Continental. According to *Investment Dealers' Digest,* "Continental stock briefly traded as high as 12 in late 1993, but battered by an intensely competitive industry climate and a high cost structure, they were changing hands just above 4 shortly before the divestiture."

Despite increased consolidation in the bread industry, the market was still considered highly fragmented in the mid-1990s, and acquisitions were viewed by many as the only reasonable means of growth. Prior to the announcement of the Interstate/Continental deal came the agreement by CPC International to buy the Entenmann's, Freihofer's, Oroweat, and Boboli operations of the Kraft Foods division of Philip Morris Companies, Inc.

Approach and Engagement

On January 6, 1995, Interstate Bakeries announced its intention to buy Continental Baking for $330 million in cash and 16.9 million shares of common stock. Because Continental's parent, Ralston Purina, had issued a targeted stock for Continental in 1993—spinning off 55% of the unit to its shareholders, yet retaining full ownership—the divestiture was complex. CS First Boston acted as Ralston Purina's advisor. The rules of targeted stocks stipulate that if 80% or more of a targeted subsidiary is sold, the net proceeds, minus taxes and expenses, must be distributed to shareholders. After determining the net proceeds from the sale of its bakery unit, Ralston Purina had three choices: redeem all the targeted stock for the amount of the proceeds, payout the amount of the proceeds in a lump-sum dividend, or issue shares of Ralston Purina stock worth 110% of the total proceeds.

On April 13, 1995, after Continental announced weaker operating results, Interstate reduced its offer for Continental by $110 million to $220 in cash and 16.9 million common shares, a bid worth $461 million. According to the terms of the agreement, Ralston Purina would reduce its 45% stake in Interstate to 15% or less by 1999.

The Officers

Chairman and CEO: Charles A. Sullivan

President and Chief Operating Officer: Michael D. Kafoure

Sr. VP and Chief Financial Officer: Frank W. Coffey

VP, Secretary, and General Counsel: Ray S. Sutton

Sr. VP, Corporate Marketing: Mark D. Dirkes

The U.S. Department of Justice granted conditional approval for the deal on July 20. Concerned that the union might result in higher white bread prices in five major markets—Los Angeles and San Diego, California; Chicago and central Illinois; and Milwaukee, Wisconsin—the approval was contingent upon Interstate's divestiture of either its own brands or the Wonder bread brand in those areas.

Products and Services

In the late 1990s, Interstate Bakeries operated roughly 70 bakeries, spanning 29 states. Products were sold in both grocery stores and convenience stores. The firm also operated 1,500 thrift bakeries, which sold items nearing their date of expiration. Bread brands included Wonder, the best selling bread in the U.S., Home Pride, Holsum, Butternut, Sunbeam, and Merita. Snack cake brands included Dolly Madison, Hostess, and Drake's. Interstate also made croutons, bagels, breakfast pastries, rolls, English muffins, and stuffing.

Changes to the Industry

The purchase of Continental Baking made Interstate Bakeries the leading baked goods wholesaler in the U.S. The firm continued its plan of growth via acquisition with the purchases of San Francisco French Bread and the crouton operations of Marie Callender in 1997 and John J. Nissen Baking and snack cake maker Drake's, a unit of Canada's Culinar, Inc., in 1998. Competitor The Earthgrains Co., spun off from Anheuser-Busch in March of 1996, also pursued growth aggressively, buying Heiner's Bakery Inc. in the same year it achieved independence. In 1998, Earthgrains shored up its position in the southeastern U.S. with its $195 million purchase of CooperSmith, a conglomerate of three baking firms, as well as plants in South Carolina and Alabama from Southern Bakeries. Other acquisitions included San Luis Sourdough and a dough maker based in France.

Interstate began planning another major purchase in 1999, agreeing to acquire the reminder of Culinar,

The Players

Chairman and CEO of Interstate Bakeries Corp.: Charles A. Sullivan. At the age of 60, University of Toledo graduate Charles Sullivan left his post at Seven-Up Indiana, a company he was credited for turning around, to accept a senior vice presidency at American Bakeries Co. In 1982, Sullivan was also named president of American Bakeries Merita bread unit. Four years later, he was appointed executive vice president. When Interstate Bakeries acquired Merita in 1987, Sullivan stayed on to oversee the Merita operations. A little more than a year later, he took over as president and CEO of Interstate Bakeries. Sullivan orchestrated the firm's acquisition of Continental Baking Co. in 1995, its largest deal to date, and remains chairman and CEO of Interstate Bakeries today.

which owned the Hostess trademark in Canada. However, another Canadian firm, Saputo Group, outbid Interstate.

Review of the Outcome

Interstate gained access to blockbuster brands like Wonder and Hostess with the purchase of Continental Bakery, yet "the acquisition also saddled Interstate with Continental's high cost structure," wrote *Financial World* in November of 1995. As a result, earnings dipped 3% in the first quarter of 1996, despite a 72% jump in sales to $471.5 million. Management pointed to the 79% increase in overhead expenses as the culprit. Rising wheat prices also undercut profits.

Interstate CEO Sullivan reacted by reorganizing the firm into three geographic segments—eastern, central, and western—each headed by an executive vice president accountable for Interstate and Continental brands, as well as factories located in the area. Sullivan also began a three-year $100 million cost cutting plan which included streamlining manufacturing and delivery efforts. For example, Hostess cake production was moved to Dolly Madison plants in Georgia, Kansas, and Indiana.

By the first quarter of fiscal 1997, earnings had more than doubled from the previous year and stock reached a 52-week high of $37.35. Debt had also been whittled by $150 million, reducing the firm's debt-to-equity ratio from 51.7% to 37.3%. Improvements continued, and stock split two-for-one on September 23, 1997, after closing at a high of $67.69 the day prior. As part of its antitrust agreement with the U.S. Justice Department, Interstate divested rights to the Weber's white bread brand in California and its Chicago Butternut bakery in 1997.

In July of the same year, Ralson Purina initiated its mandatory reduction of its 45% stake in Interstate Bakeries by issuing $420 million in stock appreciation income linked securities (SAILS), which would convert to Interstate shares in the year 2000.

Research

Davidson, Gordon. "'Lean and Mean' Suits Sullivan," in *Milling and Baking News*, 7 November 1995. Covers the career of Charles A. Sullivan, head of Interstate Bakeries.

"IBC a 'Branded Food Company,' Sullivan Tells Shareholders," in *Milling and Baking News*, 1 October 1996. Describes the performance of Interstate Bakeries in the first year after the merger.

"Interstate Bakeries Corp.," in *International Directory of Company Histories*, Vol. 12, St. James Press, 1996. Details the history of the company.

"Interstate Bakeries to Buy Ralston Purina Unit," in *The New York Times*, 13 April 1995. Announces the initial offer made by Interstate Bakeries for Continental Baking.

"Interstate Board Votes Stock Split, Hikes Dividend," in *Milling and Baking News*, 30 September 1997. Describes the performance of Interstate Bakeries in the second year after the merger.

Pratt, Tom. "First 'Targeted Stock' Issue to Unwind in Continental Sale; Ralston Purina Can Settle Up in Three Ways," in *Investment Dealers' Digest*, 16 January 1995. Discusses the logistics of the first-ever sale of a targeted stock company.

"Shareholders Delight in Sell-Off," in *Mergers & Acquisitions*, March/April 1995. Explains how Continental Bakery shareholders will benefit when Ralston Purina sells the company to Interstate Bakeries.

Stuntz, Michael and Jonathan D. Glater. "Competition and the Profit Margarine," in *The Washington Post*, 24 July 1995. Covers the antitrust stipulations attached to the U.S. Justice Department approval of the deal.

Turcsik, Richard. "Mergers Seen Heating Baked Goods," in *Supermarket News*, 4 September 1995. Describes the industry conditions immediately preceding the deal.

Ward, Judy. "Interstate Bakeries: Not Half-Baked," in *Financial World*, 21 November 1995. Describes the problems faced by Interstate Bakeries immediately following its purchase of Continental Bakeries.

ANNAMARIE L. SHELDON

C. ITOH & ATAKA

nationality: Japan
date: October 1, 1977
affected: C. Itoh & Co., Ltd., Japan, founded 1858
affected: Ataka & Co., Ltd., Japan, founded 1904

Itochu Corp.
5-1 Kita-Aoyama 2-chome, Minato-ku
Tokyo, 107-8077
Japan

tel: 81 3 3497 7295
fax: 81 3 3497 7296
web: http://www.itochu.co.jp

Overview of the Merger

The merger of C. Itoh & Co., Ltd. and Ataka & Co., Ltd.—Japan's fourth and tenth largest *sogo shosha* (trading companies), respectively—was arranged by the Japanese government on October 1, 1977. As a result, C. Itoh & Co. bumped Marubeni Corp. out of the third place spot among Japan's leading trading companies, behind Mitsubishi Corp. and Mitsui & Co.

History of C. Itoh & Co., Ltd.

In 1858, 18-year-old Chubei Itoh organized a wholesale linen business. In 1872, selling cloth to merchants in Okayama and Hiroshima, Itoh opened a larger shop in Osaka. By 1883, the firm was recognized as one of the largest textile wholesale retailers in the area, and a branch opened in Kyota. Two years later, Itoh and his nephew, Tetsujiro Sotoumi, opened a third shop in Kobe and renamed their enterprise The Itoh-Sotoumi Co.

Itoh died in 1903 and left the family business to his son, Chubei Itoh II. In an attempt to bypass the *shokan* (foreign trading agents) called Chosenya that were established in 1898 to handle trade between Japan and the Korean peninsula, Itoh put two company representatives in Korea in 1905 and later opened a branch office in Seoul. By 1919, the company's trading division had grown to twice the size of its parent company. Foreign offices were established in New York, Calcutta, Manila, and four cities in China.

Deep in debt due to the recession, C. Itoh was forced to restructure in 1921. Hundreds of employees were laid off, and the Calcutta branch was closed. Daido Trading was created from a division of C. Itoh Trading. Business improved when an earthquake in 1923 shut down the operations of the company's Tokyo-based competitors. In 1931, the Calcutta branch reopened. By the end of the decade, new offices had been opened in Australia, Thailand, and Indonesia, and the one-man-rule of Chubei Itoh II was replaced by a more consensus-oriented form of management.

The Business

Financials

Revenue (1998): $116 billion

Employees (1998): 8,400

SICs / NAICS

sic 5084 - Industrial Machinery & Equipment

sic 5065 - Electronic Parts & Equipment Nec

sic 5131 - Piece Goods & Notions

In 1941, C. Itoh merged with two trading companies—Marubeni & Co. and Kishimoto & Co.—to form Sanko Kabushiki Kaisha. Three years later, in an effort to rationalize Japanese industry, the government ordered the merger of Sanko, Daido, and a subsidiary of C. Itoh called Kureha Textiles. The new company, called Daiken Manufacturing, existed for a short time before Japan surrendered to Allied forces.

When World War II ended, the military occupation authority SCAP (Supreme Commander of Allied Powers) ordered the dissolution of Japan's *zaibatsu*, or "money cliques." *Zaibatsu* companies included giants such as Mitsui & Co., Mitsubishi Corp., and Sumitomo Corp. Although Daiken (formerly C. Itoh) was too small to be considered a *zaibatsu* company, it was also ordered to disband. In 1949, Kureha, C. Itoh, and Marubeni Corp. became independent companies with separate management groups. Both C. Itoh and Marubeni were granted the authority to operate on both a domestic and an international level.

C. Itoh began exporting Japanese textile products on a barter basis in return for foreign grain in 1950. Trade representatives were dispatched to India, Pakistan, and the U.S. With the United Nations war effort in Korea early in the decade, Japanese companies, including C. Itoh, were contracted to supply food, clothing, and other provisions to U.N. forces in Korea. The company also diversified into petroleum, machinery, aircraft, and automobiles. Many of C. Itoh's military contracts were canceled following the end of the Korean War, and the firm took over the business of smaller companies that were forced into bankruptcy following the recession caused by the demobilization in Korea.

During the 1960s, C. Itoh and other leaders such as Mitsui Bussan, Mitsubishi, and Sumitomo become known as *sogo shosha*, or general trading companies. An international network was created to make the companies more responsive to worldwide business opportunities.

In partnership with Mitsubishi and Nissho Iwai, the company identified an opportunity to develop a nickel and cobalt mine at Greenvale in northeastern Australia in 1971. Two years later, when OPEC countries forced a substantial increase in the price of oil, the C. Itoh Fuel Co. began investing heavily in the development of new technologies for petroleum production. In participation with the government, C. Itoh absorbed a major portion of Ataka, a major trading company facing bankruptcy, in 1977. As a result of the deal, C. Itoh became the third largest Japanese trading firm.

In 1985, C. Itoh established Japan Communications Satellite Company, Inc. (JCSAT) with Mitsui and Hughes Communications to launch and operate communication satellites. The Japan Satellite Communications Network was formed a year later. In 1987, C. Itoh pulled out of the Greenvale Mine project when the demand for non-ferrous metals failed to recover. With NTT, Century Leasing Systems, and Hukuhodo, C. Itoh established Japan Satellite Video in 1988. The following year, JCSAT launched the first of two satellites.

C. Itoh and Toshiba Corp. joined with Time Warner Inc. in 1991 to form Time Warner Entertainment Co. to produce and distribute motion pictures and television programs and to supply and operate cable systems in the U.S. In 1992, the company changed its name to Itochu, to reflect the transliteration of its Japanese name. Itochu also diversified into leasing air conditioners and TVs to hotels, as well as manufacturing and marketing garden fences. Recognized as one of the world's largest companies by the mid-1990s, Itochu was organized into four operating groups: textiles; machinery, aerospace and electronics; basic industries; and consumer industries and real estate.

The firm agreed in 1996 to form a joint insurance policy sales venture with Global Insurance Co.; created a marketing unit in Australia to help domestic companies promote products to the Japanese market via the Internet; and signed a contract, worth 43 billion yen, with Nissho Iwai Co. and Ever Gain Corp. to construct a storage facility on Hong Kong's Kowloon peninsula. Strong importing and exporting operations helped to fuel a 12% sales jump in fiscal 1997.

History of Ataka & Co., Ltd.

Ataka & Co., Ltd. was established in 1904 to import pulp, lumber and sugar. In 1927, the firm changed it focus to steel trading. During the 1960s, leading Japanese companies, including Mitsubishi and Sumitomo, become known as *sogo shosha*, or general trading companies. Ataka was the smallest of the *sogo shosha*. An international network was created among the firms to increase their responsiveness to worldwide business opportunities.

Revenues reached $6.8 billion in fiscal 1975. The following year, however, sales plummeted a whopping $1.7 billion after Canada's Newfoundland Refining Co. defaulted on a huge loan made by a few years earlier by Ataka American Inc. The Japanese government stepped in and arranged a takeover by C. Itoh & Co., the fourth largest member of the *sogo shosha*. The deal was completed in October of 1977.

Market Forces Driving the Merger

In the mid-1970s, Ataka America Inc. made a $90 million loan to John M. Shaheen, who planned to use the credit for upgrades to his oil refinery at Come by Chance, Newfoundland. When Shaheen's Newfoundland Refining Co. declared bankruptcy in 1975 and defaulted on the loan, Ataka was in serious trouble. According to Alexander Young in *The Sogo Shosha: Japan's Multinational Trading Companies*, the firm had been repeatedly warned by Japanese banks and the government to exercise more caution when lending, yet its decision to act as a lender to Shaheen was reflective of a cultural lending style the firm had practiced for years. "Previously, the extension of loans to and investments in group firms, group joint ventures and affiliates, and customers was often made on the basis of promoting friendly and closer business relations than on strict criteria of sound growth, diversification, and earnings. This may have worked in Japan during two decades of rapid economic growth when the *sogo shosha* had nearly unlimited sources of borrowing and good cash flow and when they were backed up by their main banks."

Ataka & Co., however, had learned the hard way that this lending methodology wouldn't work in other parts of the world. The firm neared bankruptcy in 1976, and the Japanese government, unwilling to allow the country's tenth largest trading company to fail, began seeking a merger partner.

Approach and Engagement

The Japanese government began the process of merging Ataka & Co. into C. Itoh & Co. in January of 1976. The transaction was finalized on October 1, 1977, when Ataka's steel and chemical operations were absorbed by C. Itoh & Co.

Products and Services

In the late 1990s, Itochu Corp. was organized into eight operating groups: energy and chemicals, which

The Officers

Chairman: Minoru Murofushi

President and CEO: Uichiro Niwa

Exec. VP; Chairman and CEO, Itochu International; Chairman, Itochu Europe: Jay W. Chai

Exec. VP; President, Textile: Hiroshi Sumie

Exec. VP; President, Energy and Chemical: Masahiso Naitoh

accounted for 26% of sales; food, forest products, and general merchandise, which secured 23%; plant, automobile, and industrial machinery, which brought in 17%; textiles, which garnered 11%; metals and ores, which accounted for 19%; aerospace, electronics, and multimedia, which secured 7%; construction and realty, which brought in 5%; and finance, insurance, and logistics, which garnered the remaining 1%.

The firm operated more than 1,000 subsidiaries and affiliated companies across the globe, although Asian sales accounted for 93% of revenues, with sales in Japan bringing in 80% of that total.

Changes to the Industry

C. Itoh & Co. replaced Marubeni & Co. as Japan's third largest trading company. After witnessing the dissolution of Ataka, & Co., Japanese officials began questioning the highly leveraged capital structure of other *sogo shosha* companies. As a result, the firms became more selective lenders and worked to reduce their debt-to-equity ratios.

Review of the Outcome

The chemical and steel operations of Ataka greatly reduced C. Itoh's reliance on textiles. By the end of the 1970s, textiles generated roughly 20% of total sales. Other acquisitions reduced that number to 11% by the late 1990s.

Research

"Big Japanese Merger," in *Business Week*, 26 January 1976. Briefly describes the plans of the Japanese government to merge the troubled Ataka & Co. into C. Itoh & Co.

"C. Itoh & Co., Ltd.," in *International Directory of Companies Histories*, Vol. 1, St. James Press, 1988. Provides an overview of the history of the company, before it changed its name to Itochu Corp.

Itochu Corp. Home Page, available at http://www.itochu.co.jp. Official World Wide Web

Page for Itochu Corp. Available in English, Japanese, and Chinese, this site offers news releases, financial and product information, and employment information.

"Itochu Corp.," in *Notable Corporate Chronologies*, The Gale Group, 1999. Provides an overview of the history of the company.

Young, Alexander K. *The Sogo Shosha: Japan's Multinational Trading Companies*, Westview Press, 1979. Describes the roots and development of Japan's *Sogo Shosha*, including Ataka & Co. and C. Itoh & Co.

JEFF ST. THOMAS

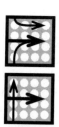

ITT & HARTFORD FIRE INSURANCE

nationality: USA
date: May 1970
affected: International Telephone and Telegraph Corp., USA, founded 1920
affected: Hartford Fire Insurance Co., USA, founded 1810

Hartford Life, Inc.
200 Hopmeadow St.
Simsbury, CT 06089
USA

tel: (860)525-8555
fax: (860)843-3528
web: http://www.thehartford.com

Overview of the Acquisition

In 1970, the merger of International Telephone and Telegraph Corp. and Hartford Fire Insurance Co. was the largest business combination in U.S. history at that time. Hartford was the sixth-largest property and casualty insurance company and had a surplus fund exceeding $400 million. More than anything else, Hartford's large pool of capital funds attracted the attention of ITT's investment bankers. By 1969, ITT had become relatively debt-heavy through acquisitions. At the same time, corporate growth had inflated ITT stocks, allowing ITT to cheaply acquire Hartford by exchanging its inflated stocks for less valuable Hartford stocks. Ultimately, Hartford Fire Insurance Co. was the most profitable and valuable of ITT's acquisitions, providing the necessary funds for continued corporate growth.

The ITT/Hartford merger is historically significant, not only as an instance of early conglomerate development in the U.S., but in a related sense, as the catalyst of debate over the interpretation of antitrust law. Richard McLaren, the head of the antitrust division at the Department of Justice, opposed conglomeration. According to McLaren, large concentrations of corporate assets afforded big businesses undue influences over government policy and unfair advantages in product markets. Competition between companies engaged in the production of unrelated goods and services did not serve as grounds for legal action, however. Therefore, in filing an antitrust suit to block ITT's acquisition of Hartford, McLaren argued that ITT would use its accumulated financial and political power over its subsidiaries to command the purchase of its goods and to stifle competition. Ultimately, in order to retain Hartford, ITT pledged itself to divesting corporations equal in value to its prize insurance company.

History of International Telephone and Telegraph Corp.

Colonel Sosthenes Behn founded International Telephone and Telegraph Corp. in 1920. Throughout its history, the fortunes of ITT were intimately linked to U.S. and global politics. During the 1920s, Behn began acquiring foreign telephone and telegraph companies, first in the Caribbean and Latin America, and then in

The Business

Financials

Revenue (1998): $386 million

Employees (1998): 4,500

SICs / NAICS

sic 6411 - Insurance Agents, Brokers & Service

naics 524291 - Claims Adjusting

naics 524292 - Third Party Administration of Insurance and Pension Funds

naics 524298 - All Other Insurance Related Activities

Europe. Behn also established overseas factories to produce telephonic and telegraphic gear for his foreign acquisitions. The integrated production of goods and provision of services underpinned what Behn conceived of as "The International System." Given that most foreign telephone companies were state-owned and operated, ITT's early growth was accomplished through cooperation with foreign governments and not through independent start-up in the private sector. This necessarily limited the power of ITT over its foreign subsidiaries operating within the jurisdiction of non-U.S. states.

The limited nature of ITT's control over its foreign subsidiaries was revealed in the years preceding World War II. Led by General Franco, for example, the Spanish government froze the assets of the National Telephone Company of Spain (CTNE), an ITT subsidiary, and replaced ITT managers with Franco supporters. In this case, only the intervention of the U.S. State Department and a series of difficult negotiations produced a settlement by which Behn repatriated CTNE profits in the form of dividends. After 1945, Behn initiated a new phase of ITT development by committing ITT to capital repatriation and to the production of high-tech electronic products for the U.S. military. However, ITT's military contracts produced limited returns, and by the mid-1950s, ITT was again relying on its European operations for the bulk of its profit.

Behn died in 1956. Three years later, Harold Geneen took over as CEO. This and the Cuban Revolution marked the beginning of a new phase in ITT history. In 1959, Castro seized control of Cuba Telephone Co., one of Behn's original foreign acquisitions. To Geneen, the loss of Cuba Telephone demonstrated the importance of reducing ITT's dependence on overseas business and the support of foreign governments. Successful corporate risk management, in Geneen's view, required increasing ITT's annual earnings from U.S. operations from the 1959 level of 20% to 50% by 1965. Risk management during the next ten years consisted of repatriating ITT's capital assets to the U.S. and of diversifying ITT's product line to ensure profits during cyclical downturns or slumps in the consumer demand for certain products.

Geneen's diversification plan involved conglomeration through the exchange of relatively valuable ITT stocks for the less valued stocks of stable or declining U.S. companies. Through such exchange, those holding the stock of acquired companies would become ITT stockholders or creditors. Between 1961 and 1968, through hundreds of tender offers and stock exchanges, ITT acquired 50 U.S. corporations with a relatively small capital outlay, given the assets of the acquired companies. These companies included Continental Baking Co., the nation's largest bread and cake baking company; Thorp Finance Corp. and Aetna Finance Co., consumer finance companies; Avis Corp., the second-largest car rental system; Airport Parking Company of America; and Levitt & Sons, the largest U.S. developer of planned residential communities. ITT's largest acquisition was Rayonier, a producer of wood pulp products used in synthetics, with assets of $292 million. Between 1961 and 1968, ITT quadrupled its assets to become the 15th-largest industrial corporation in the United States.

While some analysts argued that Geneen was sacrificing research and development for rapid growth, others pointed out that he was creating a solid nexus of corporations engaged in complementary lines of production. These latter analysts suggested that Geneen, for example, had linked the fortune of Grinnell, a producer of fire prevention equipment, to that of Hartford Fire Insurance Co., which would direct its clients to purchase Grinnell products. In 1969, the complementary relationship between ITT's subsidiaries prompted Richard McLaren, the U.S. Assistant Attorney General, to file an antitrust suit against ITT. In filing suit against ITT for its acquisition of Canteen Corp., Grinnell Corp., and Hartford Fire Insurance Co., McLaren attempted to reinterpret antitrust law, specifically the 1914 Clayton Act, which prohibited certain forms of mergers involving corporations with overlapping product lines. In filing suit against ITT, McLaren cited reciprocity theory, arguing that ITT could use its accumulated financial and political power over its subsidiaries to command the purchase of its goods and to stifle competition.

Geneen sought backing for his corporate policies from powerful allies in Washington, including John

Erlichmann, Nixon's chief domestic advisor, and Secretary of Commerce, Maurice Stans. In August of 1970, Geneen paid regular visits to members of the White House staff for the express purpose of presenting his case. In late December of 1970, a federal judge handling McLaren's suit ruled against the Justice Department, arguing that aggregate concentration fell outside the scope of antitrust law. With McLaren filing for appeal, and with a suit against the Hartford merger still pending, Geneen renewed his efforts with the administration. On April 21, 1971, Nixon ordered McLaren to withdraw his appeal and settle with ITT.

In 1972, Geneen's relations with White House staff members became a matter of public interest when Jack Anderson, a Washington columnist, revealed memoranda produced by ITT executives that suggested that ITT Sheraton had contributed to Richard Nixon's 1972 presidential campaign for the express purpose of influencing judicial proceedings related to McLaren's suit against ITT. By this point, Geneen had already been associated with corruption of political processes. In 1970, he had became the object of public attention when the media exposed his substantial financial contributions towards CIA campaigns against Chile's Marxist president, Salvador Allende, who had pledged to nationalize certain companies, including ITT's foreign subsidiary, Chiltelco.

In the mid-1970s, Geneen experienced not only legal and public relations problems, but also difficulties in managing what had become an unwieldy conglomerate. Geneen's continued commitment to conglomeration raised questions about his ability to change with new circumstances, particularly following sharp increases in interest rates and the onset of inflation, which precluded easy recourse to the sale of ITT stocks, which had declined in value. Instead of adopting a more conservative approach to corporate management, Geneen drew upon the surplus funds of his less debt-heavy companies to pursue continued growth. Geneen did, however, begin targeting growth companies in the energy industry, namely Carbon Industries, Eason Oil, and North Electric.

By the time Geneen stepped down as CEO in 1977, ITT was greatly in need of rationalization. Geneen's successor, Lyman Hamilton, believed that ITT had been overextended, and by 1979, he had shut down or sold off over 30 companies and divisional operations. Profits, however, remained sluggish, and Hamilton was forced to resign as CEO after 19 months. Rand Araskog, Hamilton's successor, was also committed to balancing ITT's budget and developing a core of growth industries around electronics, particularly telecommunications. Arguably, however, decades of corporate expansion and conglomeration had been achieved at the expense of research and

The Officers

Chairman: Ramani Ayer

President and CEO: Lowndes A. Smith

Exec. VP of Investment Products Division and Individual Life Division: Thomas M. Marra

Sr. VP and Chief Actuary: Craig R. Raymond

Sr. VP and General Counsel: Lynda Godkin

development of core industries, and in the early 1980s, ITT had fallen behind in the digital switch technology needed to compete in the telecommunications industry.

In the mid-1980s, acquisitions were largely confined to electronic mail, fiber optics, and telecommunications software. By 1987, ITT was trimming down even in telecommunications, spinning off telephone switching gear and telecommunications operations as joint ventures. By this point, half of ITT's $17.4 billion in annual sales was coming from insurance and financial services.

In June of 1995, ITT announced its plan to divide its holdings into three companies that would be spun off to public stockholders. The division of ITT's $25 billion holdings, finalized in December of 1995, produced ITT Corp., which encompassed Sheraton Hotels, information services, and casinos; ITT Hartford, an insurance company; and ITT Industries, a producer of electronics, and automotive and defense equipment. The history of ITT since 1995 is one of reversing decades of conglomeration. In 1995, ITT Hartford severed its ties with ITT to become Hartford Life, Inc. In 1997, Starwood Hotels & Resorts, a real estate investment group, bought out ITT Corp. ITT Industries, with its numerous subsidiaries, continued to produce defense, aerospace, electronic, and automotive products.

History of Hartford Fire Insurance Co.

In 1810, a group of Connecticut businessmen founded the Hartford Fire Insurance Co. At the time, in the absence of water propulsion systems, fire represented the largest threat to property owners. Twenty-five years later, Hartford's reputation was boosted when Hartford's president, Eliphalet Terry, backed Hartford policies with his personal fortune after a fire had destroyed much of Manhattan. Hartford's sound record in the area of claims payments remained strong throughout numerous such disasters, including the 1906 San Francisco Earthquake. In 1913, the advent of

The Players

Hartford Fire Insurance Co. Chairman: Harry V. Williams. Born in Philadelphia in 1907, Harry Williams studied at the University of Pennsylvania before beginning an executive career at Hartford Fire Insurance Co. Throughout a business career spanning three decades, Williams served as chairman at Hartford Insurance Group, Hartford Fire Insurance Co., Twin City Fire Insurance, Co., and the New York Underwriters Insurance Co. In 1968, under Williams' chairmanship, Hartford Fire Insurance Co. was the fifth biggest property and liability insurance company in the United States. As chairman, Williams was cautious and conservative, converting profits into surplus funds. This strategy made Hartford attractive as an acquisition to ITT, to Williams' dismay. He strongly opposed ITT's attempts to acquire Hartford, but eventually conceded to pressure from the company's directors and stockholders to merge. Despite his opposition to the merger, Williams continued working on the executive board of Hartford after the acquisition in 1970.

ITT President: Harold Geneen. Harold Geneen was born in Bournemouth, England, in 1910; soon afterwards, he and his parents settled in the United States. He took a job as a page at the New York Stock Exchange, where he established a number of important business contacts. In 1934, Geneen accepted a position at Lybrand, Ross Brothers, & Montgomery Co., one of the best-known accounting firms in the country. Between 1934 and 1956, he held positions at various U.S. companies. In the mid-1950s, he accepted a position at Raytheon, an electronics corporation. As vice president, Geneen ceaselessly promoted the unorthodox corporate strategy of product diversification. In 1959, thwarted in his attempts to diversify Raytheon's product line, Geneen accepted the presidency of International Telephone and Telegraph Corp. By then, he was firmly committed to corporate growth through conglomeration, even at the expense of corporate stability. In 1959, after Fidel Castro expropriated Cuban Telephone Co., a subsidiary of ITT, Geneen announced a long-term diversification and capital repatriation plan designed to lessen ITT's dependence on overseas profits. During the next 17 years, Geneen pursued corporate expansion through aggressive conglomeration; at one point in the early 1970s, ITT was acquiring one company per week. After surviving a scandal over his questionable relationships with federal officials that facilitated his company's growth, Geneen began to experience difficulty in managing his unwieldy conglomerate. Geneen stepped down as CEO in 1977 and died 20 years later.

Workmen's Composition and the popularity of the auto led Hartford to establish a new division dedicated solely to casualty insurance. In 1959, Hartford purchased Columbian National Life to round out its portfolio to include, not only fire, property, and casualty, but also life insurance.

By 1968, Hartford had become the fifth-largest property and liability insurance company in the United States. It premiums stood at $969 million, and it possessed $1.9 billion worth of assets. Hartford also had a capital surplus of $400 million, due to the cautious corporate management of Chairman Harry Williams and the Board of Directors. Hartford's surplus capital made the insurance company particularly appealing to International Telephone and Telegraph Corporation, which had become capital-deficient through its aggressive pursuit of conglomeration.

Hartford became particularly vulnerable to a takeover bid in the Spring of 1968, when the casualty insurance business began to falter and the price of Hartford stock declined dramatically. By November, ITT had taken an option on $1.2 million, or six percent, of Hartford's total shares. In December, ITT made a tender offer to purchase the entire company, specifically an offer to exchange inflated ITT stock for Hartford stock of half its value. In May of 1970, although Chairman Harry Williams opposed the merger of ITT and Hartford, the Board of Directors conceded to pressure from stockholders hoping to profit through an exchange of ITT/Hartford stock. ITT's purchase of Hartford for $1.4 billion consummated what was then the largest takeover in U.S. history.

In the years following the merger, ITT Hartford provided capital to fund ITT growth, simultaneously extending its life insurance operations to become one of the industry's fastest-growing firms. In 1995, as a subsidiary of ITT Corp., ITT Hartford began marketing annuities to 34 million AARP members, demonstrating its ability to seek out new markets and sources of profit. At this time, ITT Hartford also began to anticipate federal reforms of the insurance industry designed to cap premiums. Specifically, Hartford executives began to divest parts of its health insurance division in order to free capital for investment in a growing annuity business.

In 1995, ITT furthered its voluntary dismemberment by spinning off Hartford to public stockholders. In 1996, ITT Hartford was renamed the Hartford Financial Service Groups, and severed its connection to ITT. The Hartford Insurance Group began trading its shares on the New York Stock Exchange and expanding its overseas operations, mainly those in South America. Hartford Life, Inc. is currently an independent company, traded on the New York Stock Exchange.

Market Forces Driving the Merger

The ITT/Hartford merger contributed to a trend towards conglomeration in the 1960s. Conglomeration, or the consolidation of companies with diverse lines of production within a single, over-arching corporation was, in the 1960s, an accepted form of corporate risk management. In 1962, *The New York Times* reported that at least 80 U.S. *Fortune* 500 companies were controlled by other corporations, while 1968 alone witnessed 551 conglomerate mergers. Although conglomeration allowed many corporations to both diversify and expand without facing antitrust suits, continued corporate expansion often depleted conglomerates' capital funds and produced debt-heavy balance sheets. For this reason, ITT sought to diversify its holdings and build up its capital reserves by taking over conservatively managed firms that had channeled profits into capital surplus funds rather than corporate expansion. In 1969, Hartford possessed assets worth $1.9 billion, or half of those held by ITT, and excess capital of $400 million. To ITT, whose debt had tripled from $310 million to $932 million between 1964 and 1968, a merger with Hartford, the nation's sixth-largest property, casualty, and fire insurance company, promised numerous benefits.

In return for Hartford's capital reserves, ITT, a large consumer of individual and corporate insurance, offered Hartford a chance to expand its client base through association with a lager affiliate. Moreover, the merger would allow Hartford stockholders to exchange their shares for ITT common stock, which was fetching 30 times more than actual earnings in 1968, at a time when Hartford stock prices were plummeting. As a result, by exchange of inflated ITT stock for Hartford stock, ITT, a company deficient in capital assets, was able to engulf Hartford without much capital outlay.

Approach and Engagement

In the fall of 1968, a sharp decline in the price of its stock made Hartford particularly vulnerable to a corporate takeover. In late 1968, ITT's president, Harold Geneen, accumulated two million shares, or 8%, of Hartford's total outstanding shares to begin a sustained takeover effort. That takeover was formally launched on November 1, 1969, when ITT representatives notified Hartford of ITT's interest in a merger. On November 2, at a meeting with Hartford directors, Geneen expressed a commitment to invigorate Hartford. When Hartford president Harry Williams failed to discuss the terms of a merger, Geneen made a direct takeover bid. On December 23, he offered $750 million in ITT stock—roughly $70 per share for stock that had, weeks before, been worth only half that amount.

In the months preceding Geneen's preliminary takeover bid, Williams had already begun exploring antitrust suit options, and in doing so, found an ally in Richard McLaren, head of the antitrust division of the U.S. Department of Justice. On August 1, 1969, McLaren filed a suit against ITT to prevent its takeover bid. On Oct 1, however, a federal district court denied McLaren's motion for a preliminary injunction to block the takeover, and on November 10, a majority of Hartford stockholders approved the ITT/Hartford merger. In early March of 1970, the combined pressures from ITT and its stockholders proved too much for Hartford's board to bear, and general agreement to merger terms was announced. On May 24, 1970, the Connecticut Insurance Commission approved the merger, and several days later, Hartford accepted ITT's final tender offer.

According to the terms of the merger, ITT issued 21.7 million shares of a new $2.25 cumulative convertible preferred stock for Hartford common stock. ITT would also pay a premium of $28 per Hartford share, or a total of $600 million. The exchange of ITT for Hartford shares began on June 16, 1970 and lasted through December of that year. Ultimately, the ITT/Hartford became the most expensive acquisition by an American corporation to date. Through the merger, ITT gained assets worth $1.9 billion, or almost half of its own assets, and a surplus capital fund of $400 million.

Products and Services

In the late 1990s, Hartford Life was a major provider of employee benefits, group insurance, short- and long-term disability insurance, accidental death and dismemberment coverage, and life and health reinsurance. The company also dealt in individual annuities, including mutual funds; group annuities, like deferred compensation and retirement plan services; and structured settlement contracts. In the 1980s, after losing profits due to slowing sales of death benefit life insurance, Hartford began specializing in variable-rate annuities.

In 1998, premiums on employee benefits accounted for $1.8 billion, or 31% of its sales, the same amount generated by investment products. Corporate-owned life insurance accounted for $1.6 billion, or 27% of its sales. Individual life insurance accounted for $567 million, or 10% of sales.

Changes to the Industry

The ITT/Hartford Fire Insurance Co. merger occurred during a period of intensive conglomeration that left many expanding corporations such as ITT burdened with heavy long-term debt. ITT clearly gained from its acquisition of Hartford Fire Insurance Co., drawing upon Hartford assets of $1.9 billion and surplus capital fund of $400 million to further its own diversification schemes. The benefits of the merger for Hartford were less clear, although not negligible. As late as the 1990s, Wall Street analysts argued that ITT Hartford's stock value had been elevated and maintained through its association with a larger diversified partner. They argued, moreover, that the merger had created a perception that Hartford was expanding its channels of product distribution.

In 1979, ten years after the merger, the Hartford Insurance Group was still a major source of profit despite the fact that, under ITT ownership, it had fallen to seventh position among the largest property-casualty insurers in the US. Investment income at Hartford and ITT's finance companies offset losses in underwriting and yielded operating income of $404 million. In the 1980s, Hartford's management restructured the company to deal less in personal insurance and more in annuities sales. As a result of its corporate restructuring, Hartford Life was well positioned to survive ITT's divestitures and corporate spin-offs in 1995.

Review of the Outcome

ITT's run on Hartford shares drove the value of Hartford stocks up by 50 points in 1969. In the wake of the merger, with its new connections to ITT employees and subsidiaries, Hartford gained new channels of distribution for its individual and corporate policies.

ITT, for its part, clearly benefitted from its access to Hartford's large pool of surplus capital.

The acquisition, however, was costly from both a legal and a financial standpoint. To retain Hartford, its prize acquisition, against antitrust suits filed by the Department of Justice, ITT agreed to divest itself of Canteen Corp. and Avis Corp.. In addition, ITT agreed not to acquire any domestic corporation with assets of $100 million or more without special approval from the Department of Justice. With the announcement of the ITT/Hartford settlement, ITT stock prices declined sharply. However, Hartford's profits more than compensated for divestitures forced by the antitrust suits. Throughout the 1970s and early 1980s, Hartford earnings accounted for no less than 20% of ITT's net earning. These earnings did not offset the long-term consequences of financial overextension at ITT, and in 1995, amidst both analysts' and insiders' suggestions that ITT had spread itself too thinly in pursuing highly diverse lines of production, ITT spun off its Hartford subsidiaries.

Research

Araskog, Rand. *The ITT Wars*, Henry Holt and Company, 1989. Lengthy biographical sketch of the CEO who led ITT's most intensive divestiture efforts.

Goolrick, Robert. *Public Policy Toward Corporate Growth: The ITT Merger Cases*, National University Publications, 1978. A study that outlines the market forces driving conglomeration in the late 1960s and 1970s.

Sampson, Anthony. *The Sovereign State of ITT*, Stein and Day, 1973. A highly critical work that explores ITT's involvement in U.S. foreign policy.

Sobel, Robert. *ITT: The Management of Opportunity*, Times Books, 1982. Provides extensive details related to Harold Geneen's connections to White House staff members during the Nixon years.

ALICE M. RITSCHERLE

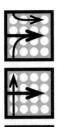

ITT & STARWOOD

nationality: USA
date: February 23, 1998
affected: ITT Corp., USA, founded 1920
affected: Starwood Hotels & Resorts Worldwide, Inc., USA, founded 1991

Starwood Hotels & Resorts
Worldwide, Inc.
777 Westchester Ave.
White Plains, NY 10604
USA

tel: (914)640-8100
fax: (914)640-8310
web: http://www.starwood.com

Overview of the Merger

The 1997 battle for ITT Corp. was one of the nastiest takeovers of the decade. Hilton Hotels Corp. and ITT locked horns for nearly a year in a struggle that was as much a personal contest of wills between their respective chairmen as it was a business deal.

Hilton's President and CEO, Stephen F. Bollenbach, sensed vulnerability in ITT, a diverse hotel and casino company that seemed to be straying from its strength in those areas into risky diversions. Hilton, a hospitality and gaming company in its own right, would benefit from ITT's Sheraton brand name appeal. The combination of the two companies would operate 655 hotels and more than 30 casinos.

To ITT, though, acquisition by Hilton was not desired in the least. Chairman Rand Araskog resisted Hilton's advances, which had begun as informal offers, then as formal tender offers, and finally as an embittered takeover battle that would land ITT in court for its defensive tactics.

As the war was entering its eleventh month, Starwood Lodging rode up as a white knight, a friendly acquirer favored by Araskog. Starwood, which had recently agreed to acquire Westin Hotels, would become the world's largest hotel company, with 650 hotels in 70 countries, and revenues of $10 billion.

History of Starwood Hotels & Resorts Worldwide, Inc.

With backing from the wealthy Burden and Ziff families, Barry Sternlicht founded Starwood Capital Group in 1991. This real estate investment company started out by purchasing troubled apartment complexes and then reselling them for profit. Sternlicht sought to enter the urban hotel industry, and did so by acquiring existing operations rather than undertaking the costly construction of new facilities. After obtaining private funding for the purchase of a 15-unit chain, he strategized to attract investors for the funding of further acquisition.

The Business

Financials

Revenue (1998): $4.9 billion

Employees (1998): 130,000

SICs / NAICS

sic 7011 - Hotels & Motels

naics 721110 - Hotels (except Casino Hotels) and Motels

naics 721120 - Casino Hotels

In 1995 he found the way. The Hotel Investors Trust had a rare and attractive structure known as a paired-share real estate investment trust, which enabled it to record income tax as personal rather than corporate. He purchased the company in 1995, and the next year renamed it as Starwood Lodging Trust while renaming Starwood Capital as Starwood Lodging Corp. The company closed the year with interests in 76 hotels.

Starwood expanded internationally in August 1997 by acquiring several Westin Regina facilities in Mexico. On September 8th it announced an agreement to acquire Westin Hotels & Resorts for $1.8 billion. Upon completion of the acquisition on January 2, 1998, Starwood's two sister companies were renamed. Starwood Lodging Trust became Starwood Hotels & Resorts Trust, and Starwood Lodging Corp. became Starwood Hotels & Resorts Worldwide, Inc.

The company followed up the Westin acquisition with the $14.6 billion purchase of ITT Corp. Completed on February 23, 1998, the merger absorbed ITT's four hotel brands—Sheraton, Caesars, Four Points, and Ciga Hotels. Starwood introduced a new business hotel brand, W Hotels, that fall. It launched its second riverboat casino, *The Glory of Rome*, in November. By end of that year, Starwood operated 690 hotels and casinos in 71 countries, and reported increased revenues of $4.9 billion over the previous year's total of $926 million.

Starwood relinquished its paired-share status in January 1999, reorganizing as a C-Corporation with the trust as a subsidiary. The next month, it announced that it was looking to sell Caesars; Park Place Entertainment Corp. was reportedly showing interest in purchasing the chain.

History of ITT Corp.

The International Telephone and Telegraph Corp. was founded in 1920 by the brothers Louis and Hernand Behn as a holding company for their telephone enterprises, among them the Cuban Telephone Company and the South Puerto Rico Telephone Corp. In 1925 it purchased AT&T's telephone equipment manufacturing company, International Western Electric Corp. During the 1940s it began to focus on such equipment manufacturing operations and international telephone operations, abandoning the U.S. telephone business.

Harold Geneen became chairman in 1959, and in 1963 launched an aggressive acquisition spree that averaged one purchase per month. In 1968 it bought Sheraton Hotels and Continental Baking Corp., producer of such brands as Wonder Bread and Hostess snack cakes. It also made a bid for the ABC television network, but was challenged by the U.S. Department of Justice on antitrust grounds. In 1969 it purchased Hartford Insurance, but the following year it agreed to the government's request to divest its Hartford-sized assets and restrain from purchasing any further U.S. companies with assets greater than $100 million.

Rank Araskog became chairmen in 1979, and proceeded to divest 250 of ITT's overly diverse operations, including most of its telecommunication businesses. In 1992 its assets of $53.9 billion earned it *Fortune* magazine's rank of 18th-largest diversified financial company in the world.

ITT entered the gaming industry with its 1993 purchase of the Desert Inn in Las Vegas. It purchased the European luxury hotel chain Ciga S.p.A. the following year. In 1995 it acquired the Caesars hotel casino brand, as well as a 50% stake in Madison Square Garden. That June the company reorganized as three separate companies: ITT Corp., for hotels, casinos, and information services; ITT Hartford, for insurance; and ITT Industries, for electronics, automotive, and defense operations.

For most of 1997, ITT Corp. was occupied in evading the hostile takeover campaign of Hilton Hotels Corp. With its defenses eroding away and acquisition looking inevitable, ITT turned to Starwood Lodging as a preferred acquirer—its white knight. On February 23, 1998, Starwood completed its $14.6 billion purchase of ITT.

Approach and Engagement

Stephen F. Bollenbach, Hilton's CEO, approached Rand Araskog with informal acquisition offers beginning in October 1996. Throughout the rest of that year, Araskog expressed no interest in negotiating a deal, rejecting each of Hilton's offers. Seeing that informality was getting him nowhere, Bollenbach formally put forward a $55 per share tender offer in January 1997. This offer, which included the assumption of $4 billion in debt, amounted to $10.5 billion. Even though its current share price was only $42, ITT rejected the offer as too low and mobilized defenses. It already had in place a poison pill, a mechanism that triggers devaluation in an investor's stake if he acquires a specified percentage of the company's voting stock. Yet ITT deemed this single defense inadequate.

In order to raise funds to enable it to better resist the takeover, ITT sold extensive assets, upgraded Caesars Palace, and rescheduled the annual shareholder meeting from May to November. In July it announced that it would split into three separate companies that September: ITT Destinations, for hotel and gaming operations; ITT Corp., for telephone directory publishing; and ITT Educational Services, its technical schools divisions. By spinning off hotel and gaming—the operations that Hilton sought—the company would be able to reorganize its structure to make it even more resistant to takeover. Unlike that of the original company, its board of directors would be staggered, that is, elections of directors would come up during different years, making it much more difficult for Hilton to introduce its own slate of directors as an option for ITT shareholders to vote in as a replacement.

Originally calling this split-up a "smoke-and-mirrors scheme," Bollenbach finally gave in and raised its offer in August to $70 per share. Araskog's rejection of this offer prompted Bollenbach to file suit against ITT, alleging two illegal defensive tactics—rejecting the offer and breaking up the company, both without allowing shareholders to vote. On September 29th, a Nevada federal court sided with Hilton and forced ITT to put the split-up to shareholder vote. With its ace now trumped, ITT set November 12th as the date of the annual shareholder meeting, which would determine the company's future with Hilton.

Now that ITT's staggered board maneuver had been foiled, it was possible that shareholders would elect Hilton's slate, a move just a step away from acquisition. With both companies now vying for shareholder support, each turned to the press for a little name-calling and mudslinging. The attacks grew personal. As reported in *Newsweek*, Bollenbach called Araskog a "superweenie," while Araskog spat that, "it'll be a cold day in hell" before he would negotiate with Bollenbach.

On October 20th, just three weeks before the shareholder meeting, Starwood Lodging appeared on the scene. This white knight offered a friendly bid of

The Officers

Chairman and CEO, Starwood Hotels & Resorts: Barry S. Sternlicht

President and CEO, Starwood Hotels & Resorts Worldwide: Richard D. Nanula

Exec. VP, Human Resources: Susan Bolger

Exec. VP, Chief Financial Officer: Ron Brown

Exec. VP, General Counsel: Tom Janson

$82 per share, a package worth $9.8 billion. The $82 share price would be paid as $15 in cash and $67 in stock. ITT believed that if it must be acquired, Starwood was an attractive suitor. That company had two very appealing characteristics (aside from the fact that it wasn't associated with Bollenbach). First, although it was seven times smaller than ITT, its stock price was higher. And second, ITT was one of only five paired-share REITs (real estate investment trusts), structures that allowed the company both to own and manage property.

Bollenbach conceded defeat. Then, on November 4th, he upped Hilton's offer to $80 per share, or $9.3 billion. Although that was $2 less per share than Starwood's bid, it offered more cash—up to $44 per share. ITT's board finally announced that the company was up for sale to the highest bidder. Taking a cue on the matter of cash tender, Starwood raised its bid to $85 per share, $25.50 of which would be in cash. Hilton refused to increase its bid, maintaining that it still offered the better deal, even though Bollenbach had doubts as to whether ITT's shareholders would concur.

His concerns proved well-founded, as a nearly three-quarters majority of shareholders voted on November 12th to re-elect ITT's incumbent directors, effectively dismissing Hilton's bid. Two days later, the board accepted Starwood's $10.2 billion offer.

By February 20, 1998, Starwood and ITT had received the necessary regulatory approval from the Federal Trade Commission, Department of Justice, and the state gaming commissions of Mississippi, New Jersey, and Nevada. The reworked final deal, worth $14.6 billion, was completed three days later.

Products and Services

Starwood offered six hotel brand names, most of which had been acquired through the acquisitions of ITT and Westin.

The Players

ITT Chairman: Rand Araskog. Rand Araskog, a West Point graduate, joined ITT Corp. in the 1960s as a marketer of satellites and defense equipment. Meanwhile, the company's chairman, Harold Geneen, was embarking on an aggressive diversification scheme for the telephone company, taking it in such wild new directions as rental cars, hotels, and snack cakes. Geneen stepped down in 1978, and Araskog, who had by then achieved the rank of president and CEO, succeeded him as chairman. He proceeded to reduce company debt incurred from Geneen's shopping spree by selling off many of those extraneous enterprises. Yet he, too, was not immune to making unusual purchases. In 1994 he apparently got sports fever, joining with Cablevision Systems to purchase Madison Square Garden, the MSG Network, the New York Rangers, and the New York Knicks. Araskog would later be forced to shed those purchases in defense against a takeover by Hilton. When the dust settled almost a year later, Araskog found himself out of a job.

Starwood Chairman and CEO: Barry Stuart Sternlicht. Born in New York City, Barry Sternlicht graduated from Brown University and then earned an MBA from the Harvard Business School in 1986. That year he joined Chicago-based JMB Realty, where he demonstrated his deal-making prowess. He orchestrated the acquisition of Randsworth Trust PLC in 1989, only to watch this portfolio bottom-out with the 1991 collapse of London's real estate market. Sternlicht quit his job in the spring, and that autumn founded Starwood Capital Group. Four years later he purchased Hotel Investors Trust, a real estate investment trust possessing a valuable grandfathered tax status that gave it tremendous advantage in making acquisitions, including the purchase of ITT. Upon completion of that merger, this 37-year-old continued to hold the top seat of Starwood, the largest hotel company in the world.

Sheraton Hotels & Resorts was a brand name established in 1937. Acquired as part of ITT, Sheraton targeted the business traveler. By the beginning of 1998, 314 Sheratons existed in 59 countries.

Westin Hotels and Resorts operated as 113 locations in 23 countries. Starwood had established plans to expand this chain, and by the end of 1997 had begun development of 26 new facilities.

The Luxury Collection consisted of 53 properties in 20 countries. Facilities included in this collection operated under various brands, including St. Regis and the European luxury brand Ciga, but more often they were named distinctly. Examples of such luxury hotels were Prince de Galles, in Paris; Hotel Danieli, in Venice; and The Royal Hawaiian, in Honolulu.

Caesars was one of the world's pre-eminent gaming brands, acquired as part of the ITT package. Among its hotel casino facilities were the well-known Caesars Palace in Las Vegas and Caesars Atlantic City. It also operated casinos in Ontario, Australia, Peru, Egypt, and the Philippines. In addition, Caesars ran two riverboat casinos in the U.S. Its dockside casino in Tunica, Mississippi, was visited by more than one million customers annually. On November 20, 1998, Caesars launched its second riverboat, *The Glory of Rome*. This floating casino was the world's largest, possessing 90,000 square feet of gaming space, and operated just off Harrison County, Indiana. In February 1999, Starwood announced that it is putting Caesars World Inc. up for sale.

Four Points Hotels was the nation's fastest growing mid-sized hotel brand. Geared toward business travelers, these hotels existed in 77 locations in five countries at the end of 1997. By 2000 Starwood expected to have expanded this collection to 500 facilities.

In the autumn of 1998, Starwood debuted a new brand, **W Hotels**. These hotels were designed to offer the business traveler comfortable yet sophisticated accommodations. Trademarks included such perks as an oversized mahogany desk and a chaise lounge.

Changes to the Industry

Now a combination of three successful hotel companies, Starwood integrated the best practices of each. It combined its six hotel brands under Sheraton's Res4 reservation system. From Westin, it drew its exemplary training program. The companies' sales and call centers were combined, as were their distribution, program, and technology systems.

The future of the paired-share real estate investment trust (REIT) became questionable as a result of the Starwood/ITT merger. Bollenbach lobbied the U.S. Congress to examine the fairness of the structure, which he contended gave ITT an unfair advantage in Starwood's acquisitions.

The REIT, created by Congress in 1960, could own property and avoid paying corporate income taxes as long as it paid out 95% of its taxable income as dividends, which are subject only to personal income taxes. These REITs were permitted only to own property, not manage it. The paired-share REIT, of which Starwood was one of only five remaining, utilized a loophole that enabled it both to own and manage properties while still avoiding corporate taxes. These types of REITs were outlawed, yet grandfathered, by Congress in 1984.

In January 1998, the Clinton Administration asked Congress to scrutinize the paired-share structure and consider imposing restrictions on it. Starwood reacted by hiring Bob Dole to lead a public policy advisory committee and by giving George Mitchell, former Senate majority leader, a seat on its board of trustees.

Congress passed legislation closing up this loophole, and on January 6, 1999, shareholders approved the restructuring of Starwood. The company relinquished its paired-share status and reorganized as a C-Corporation, with the trust as a subsidiary.

Review of the Outcome

Starwood barely had a chance to catch its breath after January's completion of the Westin acquisition. Until the ITT acquisition, that $1.6 billion transaction was Starwood's largest purchase to date. The combined portfolio of 220 hotels in 23 countries made Starwood the world's largest hotel company, behind Holiday Inn and Marriott International Inc.

Starwood's rank catapulted to the number one spot with the ITT acquisition. It nearly tripled its holdings, and as of 1998 year-end, Starwood's portfolio consisted of 690 hotels and casinos, with 223,000 rooms in 71 countries. It was the world's largest hotel and gaming company, generating revenues of $4.9 billion. The acquisitions of ITT and Westin were responsible for the bulk of that figure, as Starwood's 1997 revenues were only $933.6 million.

Research

"Do Not Pass Go: The Bid for ITT," in *The Economist*, 8 November 1997. The status of the takeover battle just before the shareholder vote.

Gilpin, Kenneth N. "Shareholders of ITT Reject Hostile Takeover by Hilton," in *The New York Times*, 13 November 1997. ITT's shareholders vote against the Hilton bid, and the board approves the Starwood offer.

Hurt, Harry, III. "Just Like Playing Monopoly," in *U.S. News & World Report*, 17 November 1997. Profiles Barry Sternlicht and the history of Starwood.

"ITT Corp." in *Notable Corporate Chronologies*, The Gale Group, 1999. Profiles the history of the company.

Lowry, Tom. "Hilton Stands Firm on ITT Bid," in *USA Today*, 11 November 1997. The bidding is over, and ITT's fate now rests in its shareholders.

Nigro, Dana. "Hilton Loses to Starwood in Battle for ITT," in *Meetings & Conventions*, December 1997. Short overview of the bidding war for ITT.

Sloan, Allan. "They Deserve Each Other: But There's a Logic to the Ugly ITT-Hilton Fight," in *Newsweek*, 17 November 1997. Hilton's repeated attempts at the hostile takeover of ITT, including the exchange of insults between Bollenbach and Araskog.

Starwood Hotels & Resorts 1997 Annual Report. Lists in-depth financial news and announcements.

Starwood Hotels & Resorts Home Page, available at http://www.starwood.com. Official World Wide Web Page for Starwood Hotels & Resorts. It includes access to a facility directory, summary financial information, and recent news.

Tomkins, Richard. "Court Ruling Clears Way for Hilton," in *The Financial Times*, 1 October 1997. Nevada court knocks down ITT's planned break-up to deter Hilton's takeover.

Vallejo, Maria P. "Starwood Starts Reign," in *Business Travel News*, 23 February 1998. Starwood absorbs the ITT and Westin chains while its paired-share status hangs in the balance.

Warner, Melanie. "How Barry Sternlicht Became the King of Hotels," in *Fortune*, 8 December 1997. The paired-share advantage in Starwood's acquisition of ITT.

DEBORAH J. UNTENER

JAMES RIVER & CROWN ZELLERBACH

Fort James Corp.
1650 Lake Cook Rd.
PO Box 89
Deerfield, IL 60015-0089
USA

tel: (847)317-5000
fax: (847)236-3755
web: http://www.fortjames.com

nationality: USA
date: May 1986
affected: James River Corp. of Virginia, USA, founded 1969
affected: Crown Zellerbach Corp., USA, founded 1871

Overview of the Acquisition

The 1986 acquisition by James River of certain assets of Crown Zellerbach was the outcome of an animated hostile takeover of the Crown by Sir James Goldsmith. This battle was replete with such colorful takeover terms as "bear hug" and "white knight." Most significant was its pioneering of the "poison pill" defensive measure. When Sir James outmaneuvered that defense, the business community hatched the next generation poison pill, closing up the loophole through which he gained control of Crown Zellerbach.

History of James River Corp. of Virginia

In 1969 Ethyl Corp. decided to shed its papermaking business in favor of chemical operations and sold its unprofitable Abermarle mill to two Ethyl engineers for $1.5 million. Brenton S. Halsey and Robert C. Williams named their company James River Paper. The mill's outdated mechanics were ill-suited to modern requirements for commodity grade papermaking, and rather than undergo costly upgrades, the partners decided instead to focus on specialty paper production. They launched into production of the automotive air- and oil-filter paper and managed to squeak out a profit of $166,000 in their company's first year of operation.

James River embarked on an acquisition spree in the early 1970s. Its first purchase was in 1971 of a specialty mill belonging to St. Regis Paper Co. Two years later the firm changed its name to James River Corp. of Virginia upon its initial public offering. It made several more acquisitions in the years that followed. Of special note were its 1978 purchase of Scott Graphics from Scott Paper Co., its foray into industrial film products, and its 1980 purchase of Gulf & Western's 80% interest in Brown Paper, providing James River its first in-house source of wood pulp as well as expansion into the consumer paper market.

Its communications and packaging operations proved to become more profitable than its core industrial product line, which was more subject to market volatility. Consumer product offerings were strengthened in 1982 when James

River bought the Dixie/Northern division of American Can Co. This acquisition brought the strong consumer brands of Dixie cups, Northern toilet paper, and Bolt, Brawny, and Gala paper towels. By the end of that year, net income was $55 million on sales of $1.6 billion.

Expansion through acquisition continued, and in 1984 James River ventured internationally by purchasing GB Papers of Scotland. In 1986 it doubled its size by paying $1.6 billion for a majority stake in Crown Zellerbach Corp., thereby becoming the second-largest U.S. tissue maker.

James River continued its frantic pace of acquisitions and as a result found itself unable to meet its wood pulp needs in 1989. It first purchased pulp from other suppliers and then began examining the feasibility of using recycled fibers to meet its printing and writing paper production needs. By this time, however, the firm had already over extended itself, and posted a 13% decrease in 1990 income. It began divesting itself of less profitable businesses, including specialty papers and non-wovens, and reorganized around consumer products, communications paper, and packaging.

The company slowly experienced recovery. In 1995 its spun off to shareholders Crown Vantage Inc., which held much of its communications paper operations, as well as the specialty paper-based sector of its packaging unit. Miles Marsh was brought into the company as CEO that October, and assumed the additional role of chairman the following January.

In 1996 James River continued to divest noncore businesses, including its flexible packaging operations, the inks division of its packaging unit, foam cup business, and the specialty operations of its North American Consumer Products division. These divestitures enabled the firm to reduce a substantial portion of its long-term debt and to record net income of $157.3 million on 1996 sales of $5.7 billion. By the end of that year, it operated 60 manufacturing facilities across the U.S., Canada, and Europe.

In August 1997 James River merged with Fort Howard Corp. to form the leading tissue manufacturer in North America. Net income in 1998 rose to $550.4 million on sales of $7.3 billion. In April 1999, to strengthen its commitment to focus on its core consumer products businesses, Fort James announced the sale of its packaging business to ACX Technologies, Inc. for $830 million in cash.

History of Crown Zellerbach Corp.

Founded in 1871 Crown Zellerbach (CZ) had grown into one of the leading forest products compa-

The Business

Financials
Revenue (1998): $7.3 billion

Employees (1998): 30,000

SICs / NAICS
sic 2297 - Nonwoven Fabrics

sic 2621 - Paper Mills

sic 2679 - Converted Paper Products Nec

sic 2656 - Sanitary Food Containers

sic 2676 - Sanitary Paper Products

sic 2411 - Logging

sic 2611 - Pulp Mills

sic 2657 - Folding Paperboard Boxes

naics 313230 - Nonwoven Fabric Mills

naics 322121 - Paper (except Newsprint) Mills

naics 322231 - Die-Cut Paper and Paperboard Office Supplies Manufacturing

naics 322215 - Non-Folding Sanitary Food Container Manufacturing

naics 322291 - Sanitary Paper Product Manufacturing

naics 113310 - Logging

naics 322212 - Folding Paperboard Box Manufacturing

nies in the U.S. by the mid-1980s. The concern, based in San Francisco, owned 3.4 million acres of timberland stretching from Los Angeles to the Pacific Northwest. Beneath 640,000 acres of its forestland, it held oil and gas rights. Additionally, the firm operated in the businesses of pulp and paper, plywood, and packaging.

In 1970 C. Raymond Dahl was appointed chairman and CEO. Under his reign, CZ's earnings and morale slumped. Although the company's sales of $790 million ranked CZ the nation's fifth-largest forest products company, its earnings didn't correspond. For the quarter ending September 30, 1981, pretax income registered only $2.2 million, a result that placed the company at the bottom of the industry in terms of performance.

As a result of this poor performance, as well as the resignation of executive vice president Charles LaFollette, the board of directors ousted Dahl. William Creson, president since 1977, was named his successor

The Officers

Chairman and CEO: Miles L. Marsh

Exec. VP and Chief Financial Officer: Ernst A. Haberli

Exec. VP, Operations and Logistics: John F. Rowley

on October 8, 1981. He immediately announced plans to streamline senior management, consolidate operations, and divest certain assets. The pressure to restore the company to profitability wasn't simply internal, however. Its low stock price made CZ vulnerable to a takeover. In 1986 James River paid $1.6 billion for a majority stake in CZ to become the second-largest U.S. tissue maker.

Market Forces Driving the Acquisition

The U.S. forest products industry was in the midst of a recession during the early 1980s. The slump, which began around 1979, drove down new home construction and paper manufacturing. At the same time, it caused interest rates to rise. Companies lacking large cash reserves were forced to borrow at higher interest rates, sinking them deeper into a cycle of debt.

Crown Zellerbach suffered particularly hard during this time. Its major timber reserves were significantly undervalued due to the recession, and the company was able to locate no buyers willing to offer what it believed those assets were worth. Moreover, CZ held a rather diverse array of non-integrated operations. William Creson had begun to pare down the company's plywood operations while boosting its pulp and paper business, taking on more debt in the process. In 1983 CZ earned $87.8 million on sales of $2.7 billion, and its stock price hovered at about 39, down from 62.75 in late 1980.

Approach and Engagement

Aware of its vulnerability to a takeover, Crown Zellerbach's board of directors approved the adoption of the "poison pill" defense on July 18, 1984. This anti-takeover defense had been invented two years earlier, and CZ became the first company to make use of it. The pill's purpose was to activate a stock repurchase in the event of a hostile takeover attempt by allowing the shareholders to buy company stock at a discounted price, thereby diluting the investment of the unfriendly suitor. Under the terms of CZ's pill, once an investor acquired 20% or announced its intention to buy 30% of the company's stock, its shareholders

would be allowed to purchase $200 worth of stock at the half-off price of $100. These rights would become exercisable once the company was 100% acquired or merged.

Undaunted, Sir James Goldsmith announced on December 12, 1984, that he intended to acquire 25% of CZ's outstanding shares. This financier had recently made offers for other major companies, including Continental Group and St. Regis Paper Company. In 1982 he gained control of Diamond International Corp., another forest products company with large timberland reserves. Reportedly, he was interested in the same assets of CZ and, as he did with Diamond, would break up and sell its non-timberland operations.

By March 12, 1985, Sir James had acquired an 8.6% interest in CZ. On April 1 he issued a "bear hug," a proposal to purchase additional stock at a premium price, thereby putting pressure on the target company's board to accept out of concern for the best interest of the shareholders. This $1.14 billion offer, at $41.62 per share, was contingent on CZ's withdrawal of its poison pill. Sir James warned that if the company refused to retract the defense he would launch a proxy battle for several seats on its board in order to gain control of the company from within. Chairman William Creson responded that the board "will not be hurried, bullied or intimidated by Sir James Goldsmith," according to *The New York Times*.

On April 10 Sir James extended his formal offer for 70% of the company at a price of $42.50 per share, or $807 million, again hinged upon removal of the pill. This initiated a flurry of lawsuits. On April 15 CZ filed for an injunction against him, while Sir James sued for the company's refusal to give him the list of its shareholders in order to prevent him from waging a proxy battle.

Mead Corp. rode onto the scene as a white knight, or a preferred acquirer, on April 24. This publishing and forest products company offered $50 per share, or $1.36 billion. CZ's rescue was short-lived, however, as the companies discontinued their merger talks the following day, presumably due to Mead's reluctance to increase its already considerable debt load. In light of this collapse, CZ announced on April 25 a major restructuring in which it would break apart into three companies by liquidating its timber assets and spinning off its specialty packaging business. This strategy effectively deterred Sir James, but only temporarily. On April 26 CZC Acquisition Corp., the company that he had formed for the purpose of acquiring CZ, withdrew its offer.

Sir James reinitiated his takeover on May 8, when he increased his stake to 19.6% by purchasing a block of shares held by an investor. The next day he gained one seat on the company's board through a shareholder vote at CZ's annual meeting. Two-thirds of the shareholders also approved the company's reorganization plans.

Sir James gave the company until May 13 to revoke its poison pill. On that day he nudged his interest to 19.9%, just shy of the 20% of threshold. He warned CZ that if he triggered the pill the company's hope of enlisting a white knight would be virtually nil, as the costs of merging with CZ would be prohibitive.

On May 14 Sir James became the first hostile bidder to swallow a poison pill, as he increased his stake to over 20%. As it turned out, though, this defense measure worked for, not against, him in two ways. First, as he had warned, it insulated his interests from acquisition by another company, since CZ was now virtually unmarketable. Second, the pill had no effect on the value of his stake because he intended only to gain control of the company, not to affect a merger. According to the terms of the pill, only when CZ was completely acquired by an outsider could its shareholders purchase stock at a discount.

CZ and Sir James called a truce on May 26, agreeing to cooperate on the company's restructuring plan and to suspend all pending litigation against each other. This truce lasted only six weeks, however, as the two sides failed to reach agreement on the restructuring. By July 10 Sir James held a 26% stake, which he boosted to over 50% by July 22, thereby gaining control of CZ. Three days later he became the company's chairman, while William Creson retained the positions of president and CEO.

In mid-October 1985 CZ announced discussions over the possible sale of certain assets to James River Corp. These two companies agreed on December 16 to the $766 million acquisition. Under the stock swap, James River would exchange up to 22.6 million shares for about 17.6 million CZ shares not already owned by Sir James. In late April 1986 CZ's shareholders approved the deal, which was completed the following month.

Products and Services

Fort James had five operating segments:

Tissue—North American contained such brands as Brawny, So-Dri, and Mardi Gras paper towels; Quilted Northern and Soft 'n Gentle bathroom tissue; and Vanity Fair and Mardi Gras napkins. Its commercial product segment offered the lodging, restaurant, school, hospital, and institutional industries such brands as the Envision line of 100% recycled paper products, and Preference and Acclaim towel and tis-

The Players

Investor: Sir James Goldsmith. Sir James Goldsmith was born in 1933 to a British hotelier and a French mother. He attended Eton College until dropping out of school at age sixteen. In just four years he amassed a fortune by acquiring the French distribution rights to a British rheumatism remedy. From that point, the Anglo-French financier made successive investments and acquisitions, adding to his coffers. After a three-month battle for Crown Zellerbach, Sir James gained control of the company as chairman in July 1985.

Crown Zellerbach Chairman, President, and CEO: William T. Creson. William Creson joined Crown Zellerbach as an executive vice president in 1976, having spent 22 years in the pulp and paper business. After moving through successive positions, he was named company president in 1977. On October 8, 1981, he succeeded C. Raymond Dahl as chairman and CEO, retaining the post of president. After Sir James Goldsmith's acquisition of Crown Zellerbach, Creson turned over the post of chairman to Goldsmith. In August 1998 Creson passed away in his home in Napa, California.

sue products. This segment reported 1998 income from operations as $864.8 million on sales of $3.4 billion.

The newly-formed **Dixie Division** was comprised of the Dixie disposable cup, plate, and cutlery products. This business reported income from operations in 1998 to be $89.1 million on sales of $775.5 million.

Tissue—European contained an assortment of leading brands for a number of countries. In France, it offered Lotus and Moltonel bathroom tissue, and Okay kitchen towels. The Lotus brand made another appearance in the Netherlands. In Spain, its strongest brand was Colhogar bathroom tissue and kitchen towels. Ireland was home of the KittenSoft brand of bathroom tissue and kitchen towels, while Turkey stocked Selpak bathroom tissue and kitchen towels. Finland and Italy were markets for the Embo and Tenderly bathroom tissue brands, respectively. In Greece, it offered the Delica brand of bathroom tissue and kitchen towels. This business segment also produced feminine hygiene products and pharmacy supplies. It also the served the away-from-home market with bathroom and facial tissues, paper towels, and table-top products for hotels, restaurants, office buildings, and the food service industry. Income from European operations was $236.2 million on sales of $1.87 billion in 1998.

Packaging Operations provided the food industry with folding cartons, paperboard, and extrusion coated products. The company's Qwik Wave product line served the microwave foods market. The packaging segment also met the specialized packaging needs of leading pharmaceutical companies. Income from operations in 1998 was $56.6 million on sales of $717.7 million.

Communications Papers & Fiber included the Eureka! and Eclipse brands of office printing and copying paper, as well as paper for commercial printing and publishing, forms bond, and envelope papers. The Columbia brand was a line of uncoated groundwood printing papers. This segment's income from operations dipped to $2.4 million on 1998 sales of $796.6 million.

Changes to the Industry

Before the acquisition, Crown Zellerbach ranked seventh among the nation's tissue producers, just ahead of James River. Its plants in the Pacific Northwest had annual capacity of 210,000 tons in tissue in business papers, which complemented the similar operations of James River. The added assets nearly doubled the size of James River, raising its sales from $2.5 billion to $4.5 billion. It also enabled James River to jump into the position of the nation's second-largest tissue company, after Scott Paper.

The implications of the acquisition of CZ extended farther into the business community than merely its union with James River. The effectiveness of the poison pill in fending off unfriendly bidders was brought into question. This led to the development of the "flip-in" poison pill, which closed up the loophole that Sir James had not only penetrated but had turned

to his advantage. Like the pill implemented by CZ, once an investor acquired a certain percentage of shares, the pill was triggered. But the difference in this new generation of pill was that the shareholders, except for the triggering investor, could immediately purchase discounted stock—its implementation was not contingent upon 100% acquisition.

Research

Chase, Marilyn. "Crown Zellerbach to Shed Timber Assets, Spin Off Unit in Bid to Fight Goldsmith," in *The Wall Street Journal*, 26 April 1985. Describes the company's proposed restructuring plan.

Cole, Robert J. "Goldsmith Bids for Zellerbach," in *The New York Times*, 2 April 1985. Relates Sir James' initial offer for CZ.

Diamond, Stuart. "Big Stake in Crown Is Sought," in *The New York Times*, 13 December 1984. Describes Sir James' intention to acquire up to 25% of CZ.

Dobrzynski, Judith H. and Jonathan B. Levine. "One Way or Another, Crown is Going to Topple," in *Business Week*, 29 April 1985. Suggests that Crown Zellerbach's days of independence are numbered.

Fort James Corporation 1997 Annual Report, Fort James Corporation, 1998. Provides in-depth financial news and annual overview.

Fort James Corporation Home Page, available at http://www.fortjames.com. Official World Wide Web Page for Fort James. Includes access to product information, press releases, and investor information.

"James River Corporation of Virginia," in *Notable Corporate Chronologies*, The Gale Group, 1999. Provides an overview of the company until the formation of Fort James.

Smith, Timothy K. and Mike Tharp. "James River Set to Buy Crown Zellerbach Lines," in *The Wall Street Journal*, 17 December 1985. Describes the acquisition agreement between James River and Crown Zellerbach.

Tharp, Mike. "Goldsmith Wins Fight for Crown Zellerbach Corp.," in *The Wall Street Journal*, 26 July 1985. Details Sir James' acquisition of control of CZ.

Wiegner, Kathleen K. "Crown of Thorns," in *Forbes*, 9 November 1981. Describes the difficulties faced by Creson as he was appointed to chairman of Crown Zellerbach.

PATRICIA ARCHILLA

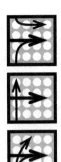

JAMES RIVER & FORT HOWARD

nationality: USA
date: August 13, 1997
affected: James River Corp. of Virginia, USA, founded 1969
affected: Fort Howard Corp., USA, founded 1919

Fort James Corp.
1650 Lake Cook Rd., PO Box 89
Deerfield, IL 60015-0089
USA

tel: (847)317-5000
fax: (847)236-3755
web: http://www.fortjames.com

Overview of the Merger

The 1997 merger of James River Corporation of Virginia and Fort Howard Corp. created a company that became the leading tissue manufacturer in North America. It also usurped Proctor & Gamble Company as the world's second-largest tissue manufacturer. The newly formed company, Fort James Corp., was fast on the heels of the industry's leading company, Kimberly-Clark Corp.

James River's strength was in the consumer paper market—with such brands as Dixie, Northern, and Brawny. These operations were perfectly complemented by Fort Howard's leading position in the commercial and industrial market, as well as its strong presence in tissue manufacturing with such brands as Mardi Gras, Soft'n Gentle, and Green Forest. That company's efficient manufacturing processes, which heavily utilized recycled paper, was an asset and would be beneficial in applications throughout the new company.

History of James River Corporation of Virginia

In 1969 Ethyl Corp. decided to shed its papermaking business in favor of chemical operations, and sold its unprofitable Abermarle mill to two Ethyl engineers for $1.5 million. Brenton S. Halsey and Robert C. Williams named their company James River Paper. The mill's outdated mechanics were ill-suited to modern requirements for commodity grade papermaking, and rather than undergo costly upgrades, the partners decided instead to focus on specialty paper production. They launched into production of the automotive air- and oil-filter paper, and managed to squeak out a profit of $166,000 in their company's first year of operation.

James River embarked on an acquisition spree in the early 1970s. Its first purchase was in 1971 of a specialty mill belonging to St. Regis Paper Company. Two years later the firm changed its name to James River Corporation of Virginia upon its initial public offering. It made several more acquisitions in the years that followed. Of special note were its 1978 purchase of Scott Graphics from the Scott Paper Company, its foray into industrial film products, and its 1980 purchase of

The Business

Financials

Revenue (1998): $7.3 billion

Employees (1998): 30,000

SICs / NAICS

sic 2297 - Nonwoven Fabrics

sic 2621 - Paper Mills

sic 2679 - Converted Paper Products Nec

sic 2656 - Sanitary Food Containers

sic 2676 - Sanitary Paper Products

sic 2411 - Logging

sic 2611 - Pulp Mills

sic 2657 - Folding Paperboard Boxes

naics 313230 - Nonwoven Fabric Mills

naics 322121 - Paper (except Newsprint) Mills

naics 322231 - Die-Cut Paper and Paperboard Office Supplies Manufacturing

naics 322215 - Non-Folding Sanitary Food Container Manufacturing

naics 322291 - Sanitary Paper Product Manufacturing

naics 113310 - Logging

naics 322212 - Folding Paperboard Box Manufacturing

Gulf + Western's 80% interest in Brown Paper, providing James River its first in-house source of wood pulp as well as expansion into the consumer paper market.

Its communications and packaging operations proved to become more profitable than its core industrial product line, which was more subject to market volatility. Consumer product offerings were strengthened in 1982 when James River bought the Dixie/Northern division of American Can Company. This acquisition brought the strong consumer brands of Dixie cups, Northern toilet paper, and Bolt, Brawny, and Gala paper towels. By the end of that year, net income was $55 million on sales of $1.6 billion.

Expansion through acquisition continued, and in 1984 James River ventured internationally by purchasing GB Papers of Scotland. In 1986 it doubled its size by paying $1.6 billion for a majority stake in Crown Zellerbach Corp., thereby becoming this second-largest U.S. tissue maker.

James River continued its frantic pace of acquisitions, and as a result found itself unable to meet its wood pulp needs in 1989. It first purchased pulp from other suppliers, and then began examining the feasibility of using recycled fibers to meet its printing and writing paper production needs. By this time, however, the firm had already over extended itself, and posted a 13% decrease in 1990 income. It began divesting itself of less profitable businesses, including specialty papers and non-wovens, and reorganized around consumer products, communications paper, and packaging.

The company slowly experienced recovery. In 1995 its spun off to shareholders Crown Vantage Inc., which held the much of its communications paper operations, as well as the specialty paper-based sector of its packaging unit. Miles Marsh was brought into the company as CEO that October, and assumed the additional role of chairman the following January.

In 1996 James River continued to divest noncore businesses, including its flexible packaging operations, the inks division of its packaging unit, foam cup business, and the specialty operations of its North American Consumer Products division. These divestitures enabled it to reduce a substantial portion of its long-term debt and to record net income of $157.3 million on 1996 sales of $5.7 billion. By the end of that year, it operated 60 manufacturing facilities across the U.S., Canada, and Europe.

History of Fort Howard Corp.

Austin Edward Cofrin, a former employee of the Northern Paper Company, established the Fort Howard paper mill in 1919. The mill was a moderately-sized business, employing 43 workers in 1920. The cost of a mill to convert timber to pulp was too high, however, so Cofrin began to produce pulp from rags and other recycled items. The company soon earned the nickname "The Fort" due to its policy of closely guarding its production techniques and balance sheets.

By 1946 the company was self-sufficient, generating its own power, operating its own truck fleet, and producing many of its own chemicals. Fort Howard's proprietary de-inking technology enabled the efficient conversion of waste paper into raw materials for papermaking.

The company was forced out of secrecy in the 1960s by securities regulations that called for the company to unseal its records. In 1971 it went public, and sales of the following year topped $100 million. That figure reached $537 million in 1982, as the company's product line included tissue, toilet paper, paper towels, and napkins for the institutional market. Recycled paper accounted for 90% of its pulp requirements.

Fort Howard purchased Maryland Cup Company, maker of disposable tableware, plates, and cups, in 1983, and Lily-Tulip Inc. in 1985. By 1987 the difficulty in assimilating these acquisitions combined with that year's stock market crash caused Fort Howard to struggle to right itself. The company became private again in 1988 through a leveraged buyout, led by the Morgan Stanley Group, that left it struggled with $3.7 million in debt. Despite subsequent divestitures, including its cup unit and its European disposable foodservice operations, the company continued to post net losses due to its debt burden. In 1995 it shed its troublesome private status and made another initial public offering. Sales for the following year totaled $1.6 billion. The company operated three manufacturing plants in the US, one in the U.K., and a joint venture in China.

Market Forces Driving the Merger/Acquisition

For years, James River had been trailing behind Kimberly-Clark and Proctor & Gamble in the worldwide tissue industry. The commodity nature of the pulp and paper industry didn't help matters, and the company was at the mercy of global economies.

The situation was similar for the smaller Fort Howard company, although this firm was somewhat shielded from pulp price fluctuations due to its reliance on recycled raw materials. This company was still struggling under its debt load, and would benefit from a partnership to help lift it.

A marriage between the two companies would create a force that would not only be likely to withstand industry-imposed pressures, but would constitute a formidable competitor to the industry's leaders. The fit would work out nicely. The firms had just enough overlap to combine technologies, which would reduce expenses and increase efficiency. They also brought to the table strengths in different, yet complementary, areas.

James River had such leading consumer brandnames as Dixie cups, Northern tissue, and Brawny paper towels, and the marketing skills to go along with them. It also enjoyed a deeper penetration in international markets, with manufacturing facilities in 10 European countries.

Fort Howard's consumer brands enjoyed a presence of their own, but more important to a merger was the company's low-cost manufacturing base and strength in commercial products.

Approach and Engagement

On May 5, 1997, James River and Fort Howard signed their merger agreement. Under its terms, Fort

The Officers

Chairman and CEO: Miles L. Marsh

Exec. VP and Chief Financial Officer: Ernst A. Haberli

Exec. VP, Operations and Logistics: John F. Rowley

Howard shareholders would receive 1.375 shares of the new company, to be called Fort James Corp., for each share of Fort Howard. James River stack would simply convert to Fort James stock on an equal basis.

The transaction would total $5.8 billion, comprised of a $3.4 billion stock swap and the assumption of $2.4 billion in Fort Howard debt. Miles Marsh, James River's chairman and CEO, would retain those positions at the new company, and Michael Riordan, Fort Howard's chairman and CEO, would become its president and chief operating officer. The 15-seat board of directors would take 11 members from James River and four from Fort Howard.

The two companies estimated that their merger would result in savings approximating $150 million in 1998. They would realize these savings by combining technologies and logistics, increasing purchasing efficiencies, eliminating duplicate workforces and overhead costs, and increasing product quality and productivity. As reported in *Business Wire*, Marsh commented, "From the beginning, we have looked at this as a merger of equals, with both companies contributing important product strengths, strategic assets, and management talent."

On June 6, 1997, that U.S. Department of Justice requested additional information from the companies to facilitate its review of the proposed merger. In early August the agency completed its probe and raised no objections to the merger, just days after the U.K. Office of Fair Trading completed its own investigation.

Separate shareholder meetings were held on August 12, and stockholders of each company endorsed the merger. The $5.8 billion transaction was completed the following day.

Products and Services

Fort James had five operating segments:

Tissue—North American contained such brands as Brawny, So-Dri, and Mardi Gras paper towels; Quilted Northern and Soft'n Gentle bathroom tissue; and Vanity Fair and Mardi Gras napkins. Its commercial product segment offered the lodging, restaurant, school, hospital, and institutional industries such

The Players

Chairman and CEO: Miles L. Marsh. Miles Marsh had served in a variety of executive positions at leading companies before joining James River. Throughout most of the 1980s he held executive posts at the Dart & Kraft Inc., Kraft Inc., and General Foods USA businesses of Philip Morris Companies, Inc. He engineered the turnaround of Pet Inc. during his tenure there as chairman and CEO beginning in 1991. In October 1995, James River benefited from Marsh's experience in consumer products when he joined the company as CEO. He added the post of chairman to his responsibilities in January 1996. Upon the company's merger with Fort Howard, Marsh maintained those roles for the newly formed Fort James Corp.

President and Chief Operating Officer: Michael T. Riordan. Michael Riordan had held a long tenure at Fort Howard. Before joining that company as vice president in 1983, he held management positions at International Mineral & Chemical Corp., Rockwell International, and Rexnord Inc. Riordan was promoted to president and chief operating officer of Fort Howard in 1992. He continued to advance up the corporate ladder, acquiring the rank of CEO in September 1996, as well as chairman in February 1997. He filled the positions of president and chief operating officer of Fort James Corp. upon its creation from James River and Fort Howard in August 1997. Riordan didn't stick with the new company for long, though. In April 1998 he announced his resignation in order to pursue CEO opportunities elsewhere.

brands as the Envision line of 100% recycled paper products, and Preference and Acclaim towel and tissue products. This segment reported 1998 income from operations as $864.8 million on sales of $3.4 billion.

The newly-formed **Dixie Division** was comprised of the Dixie disposable cup, plate, and cutlery products. This business reported income from operations in 1998 to be $89.1 million on sales of $775.5 million.

Tissue—European contained an assortment of leading brands for a number of countries. In France, it offered Lotus and Moltonel bathroom tissue, and Okay kitchen towels. The Lotus brand made another appearance in the Netherlands. In Spain, its strongest brand was Colhogar bathroom tissue and kitchen towels. Ireland was home of the KittenSoft brand of bathroom tissue and kitchen towels, while Turkey stocked Selpak bathroom tissue and kitchen towels. Finland and Italy were markets for the Embo and Tenderly bathroom tissue brands, respectively. In Greece, it offered the Delica brand of bathroom tissue and kitchen towels. This business segment also produced feminine hygiene products and pharmacy supplies. It also served the away-from-home market with bathroom and facial tissues, paper towels, and tabletop products for hotels, restaurants, office buildings, and the food service industry. Income from European operations was $236.2 million on sales of $1.87 billion in 1998.

Packaging Operations provided the food industry with folding cartons, paperboard, and extrusion coated products. The company's Qwik Wave product line served the microwavable foods market. The packaging segment also met the specialized packaging needs of leading pharmaceutical companies. Income from operations in 1998 was $56.6 million on sales of $717.7 million.

Communications Papers & Fiber included the Eureka! and Eclipse brands of office printing and copying paper, as well as paper for commercial printing and publishing, forms bond, and envelope papers. The Columbia brand was a line of uncoated groundwood printing papers. This segment's income from operations dipped to $2.4 million on 1998 sales of $796.6 million.

Changes to the Industry/Review of the Outcome

Wall Street, anticipating a problematic post-merger situation similar to the one created as a result of the 1995 merger between Kimberly-Clark and Scott Paper, felt slightly jumpy about the prospects for Fort James. Yet its fears were unfounded, as the newly formed company experienced little difficulty in transition. Fort James was not only able to live up to its promise of $150 million in savings, it managed to reduce its debt by $50 million on top of that.

During 1990, as the company integrated its operations, it began to review its position in the industry. It was already North America's leading tissue manufacturer, and the world's second-largest tissue maker. Its consumer products operations are not its sole business, however, since it was still involved in the paper making industry as well. The already volatile papermaking business, which made up 15% of its total sales, was prey to a two-pronged industry slump in 1998.

Aggressive Asian pulp and paper suppliers flooded the U.S. market with their products, creating a glut that forced prices down. During the first half of 1998, according to the American Forest and Paper Products Association, such imports from the Far East rose 234% over the same period in 1997.

The second attack on the industry was a weakened demand for U.S. products. Exports were down, in the overall market for white office copying paper—the primary product of Fort James' communications paper line—softened, as large paper customers began increasingly posting documents on the Internet rather than producing hardcopies.

In response, by late 1998, Fort James began considering divesting itself of its communications paper division. Shedding this business wouldn't be a simple undertaking, however, as the mills that produce this paper are the same mills used to produce the company's tissue products. A sale would have to include a partnership or contract to continue its supply of tissue products.

At the same time, the company made steps to strengthen its tissue and packaging operations. It began looking into overseas acquisitions, since the tissue market there is less mature than in the U.S. In May it split its North American Business into Dixie and North American Towel & Tissue, providing each segment with a greater focus. In June the company purchased Canada-based Beckett Technologies, a microwave packaging products manufacturer.

Sales at year-and 1998 remained steady, coming in at $7.3 billion. Net income, however, increased 25 per to $550.4 million. Perhaps this figure provided evidence enough to convince industry watchers that Fort James had successfully made it over the hump of its post-merger assimilation.

Research

"Fort Howard Corporation," in *Notable Corporate Chronologies,* The Gale Group, 1999. Lists major events in the company's history up to its merger with James River.

"Fort Howard, James River to Merge," in *Nonwovens Industry,* June 1997. The merger announcement and a brief summary of the contributing companies' strengths.

"Fort James Corporation," in *International Directory of Company Histories,* Vol. 22. St. James Press, 1998. Profile of the new company, with an emphasis on the history of James River.

Fort James Corporation 1997 Annual Report, Fort James Corporation, 1998. Provides in-depth financial news and annual overview.

"Fort James Corporation Completes Merger," in *PR Newswire,* 13 August 1997. Brief discussion of the new company, including its new logo and leading executives.

Fort James Corporation Home Page Available at http://www.fortjames.com. Official World Wide Web Page for Fort James. Includes access to product information, press releases, and investor information.

"James River Corporation of Virginia," in *Notable Corporate Chronologies,* The Gale Group, 1999. Provides an overview of the company until the date of the merger.

"James River, Fort Howard Agree to Merge; Creating a Preeminent Consumer Products Company," in *Business Wire,* 5 May 1997. Describes the merger agreement, lists the strengths of each of the original companies, and relays comments from the companies' chairman on the proposed deal.

Mullins, Robert. "Fort Pain," in *The Business Journal-Milwaukee,* 23 October 1998. Compares this merger compared to the Kimberly-Clark/Scott Paper merger.

Rewick, C.J. "Tissue-Maker's Tale, a Real Tear Jerker," in *Crain's Chicago Business,* 14 September 1998. Critique of the company's first year in operation.

PATRICIA ARCHILLA

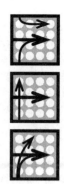

JEFFERSON-PILOT & CHUBB LIFE INSURANCE

Jefferson-Pilot Corp.
100 N. Greene St.
Greensboro, NC 27401
USA

tel: (336)691-3000
fax: (336)691-3938
web: http://www.jpfinancial.com

nationality: USA
date: May 13, 1997
affected: Jefferson-Pilot Corp., USA, founded in 1907
affected: Chubb Life Insurance Company of America, USA, founded in 1991

Overview of the Merger

The timing was right for Jefferson-Pilot's 1997 acquisition of Chubb Life Insurance Company of America (CLICA). For Jefferson-Pilot (J-P), a diverse insurance provider, this subsidiary expanded its life insurance business from a largely regional operation to that of a contender in the national market. CLICA, renamed Jefferson Pilot Financial Insurance Company in 1998, combined with J-P's other life insurance holdings to boost J-P to the rank of the nation's third-largest writer of universal life insurance.

As for The Chubb Corp., the former parent of CLICA, the life insurance market was slipping out of its grasp. This company, also diverse in the insurance industry, found itself increasingly unable to compete against the life insurance giants. After considering possible investment of additional capital into this segment, Chubb instead opted to sell. By exiting that business, Chubb became better able to focus on its core competency—property/casualty insurance.

History of Jefferson-Pilot Corp.

Jefferson Standard Life Insurance set up shop on August 7, 1907, in Raleigh, North Carolina. Named after Thomas Jefferson, the company was founded by brothers P.D. and Charles W. Gold, along with a team of 22 financial backers, for the purpose of strengthening the growth of the South in the post-Reconstruction era by providing an alternative to the large Northern financial institutions. Beginning as a regional door-to-door retailer, the company had over $1 million of insurance in force after its first five months of operation.

The company soon began making acquisitions, starting with Security Life and Annuity Company and the Greensboro Life Insurance Company in 1912. Six years later it had expanded operations into 14 Southern states, and by the following year had $37 million of insurance in force. Jefferson Standard continued to grow, even venturing during the 1920s into newspaper publishing, the first of its media interests; over the years it would also eventually acquire interests in radio and television broadcasting. Conservative leadership enabled the company to withstand the Great Depression and World War II.

In 1945 Jefferson Standard purchased controlling interest in Pilot Life Insurance Company, and the two companies were united in 1968 under the newly-formed holding company Jefferson-Pilot Corporation. By this time, operations in 32 states, the District of Columbia, and Puerto Rico generated $3 billion of insurance in force. Jefferson-Pilot had no intention of slowing down, and in the following decade it diversified into pension and retirement products, tax-sheltered annuities, and financial planning. Fortunately, the company's cautiousness enabled it to avoid what would ultimately prove to be unwise investments in junk bonds and real estate during the 1980s.

Not everyone involved in the company was exuberant about its fortunate position, however. In 1991 two major shareholders, Louise and Donald Parsons, attempted to oust company president W. Roger Soles, citing slow profit growth. They were unsuccessful, but two years later Soles retired and was succeeded by David A. Stonecipher. He immediately set about revitalizing the company, remaking management, trimming off excess fat, and looking for acquisition opportunities. In 1995 Jefferson-Pilot obtained a stronghold in the Midwest and West with its $575 million purchase of Michigan-based Alexander Hamilton Life and its $100 million acquisition of Kentucky Central Life.

History of The Chubb Corp.

Thomas Chubb and his son Percy formed the New York Marine Underwriters syndicate in 1881 through the investment of $1,000 from each of 100 merchants. The following year the partners formed Chubb & Son as an underwriter of ship and cargo insurance. It soon became the agent of London-based Marine Insurance Co. Ltd. and of Sea Insurance Company of England. In 1901 New York Marine Underwriters, Chubb & Son's principal property/casualty affiliate, reorganized as the Federal Insurance Company.

The company diversified in 1921 into underwriting fidelity, surety, and casualty insurance by obtaining majority control of U.S. Guarantee Company. During the rest of that decade it expanded geographically, opening branches in Chicago and Montreal. In 1929 it joined with the Marine Office of America to establish Associated Aviation Underwriters, the nation's largest aviation underwriting concern. It continued diversification via the acquisition of Colonial Life Insurance Company in 1957 and of Pacific Indemnity in 1967. During the latter year, it established The Chubb Corporation as a holding company for its growing portfolio of businesses.

Plans to merge with First National Corp. (now

The Business

Financials

Revenue (1998): $2.6 billion

Employees (1998): 2,200

SICs / NAICS

sic 6311 - Life Insurance

sic 6321 - Accident & Health Insurance

sic 6331 - Fire, Marine & Casualty Insurance

naics 524113 - Direct Life Insurance Carriers

naics 524114 - Direct Health and Medical Insurance Carriers

naics 524126 - Direct Property and Casualty Insurance Carriers

Citigroup) were nixed in 1969 by the U.S. Department of Justice on antitrust grounds. The following year, Chubb ventured into real estate with the acquisition of Bellemead Development Corp. In 1972 it founded Chubb Custom Market as a specialty insurance provider offering coverage for the film, television, and theatrical industries.

Chubb Life Insurance Company of America was formed in 1991 as an intermediate holding company for Chubb Corp's life insurance subsidiaries. In 1997, realizing that its life insurance business could no longer effectively compete with the giants that had arisen during the recent industry consolidation, Chubb decided to exit from that segment of the insurance business.

Market Forces Driving the Merger/Acquisition

Consolidation in the life insurance industry had created large, deep-pocketed giants that dominated the market. For Chubb Corp., a mid-sized company, effective competition would require a large capital infusion into its life insurance business. Such an investment would be difficult to secure and may have threatened the company's, and shareholders', financial security. As Chairman and CEO Dean O'Hare reported in the company's 1996 annual report, "As already-large insurers acquire rival companies of all sizes, they are simultaneously slashing their costs and boosting their sales forces, thus creating a powerful one-two competitive punch against mid-sized players such as Chubb Life."

The Officers

Chairman and CEO: David A. Stonecipher

President, Financial Operations: Dennis R. Glass

Exec. VP, Life Operations: Leslie L. Durland

Exec. VP and General Counsel, Life Operations: John D. Hopkins

Exec. VP, Investments: E. Jay Yelton

Before settling on the decision to sell, Chubb weighed other options for the life insurance unit, such as spinning it off to shareholders or investing additional resources in it. These alternatives were dismissed for three reasons: there was no guarantee that Chubb Life Insurance Company of America (CLICA) would begin to show adequate return on equity; Chubb's shareholders would be responsible for footing the bill of any capital infusion; and suitors had already begun making attractive acquisition overtures for CLICA.

One such suitor was Jefferson-Pilot, which was seeking a point of entry into the northeastern U.S. The company has its roots in the South, where it still maintained a strong following. Acquiring Alexander Hamilton had extended its reach into the Midwest, just as the Chubb subsidiary would do in the Northeast.

Jefferson-Pilot would also gain new products through CLICA. While supplementing its own individual life insurance line, J-P would also acquire variable insurance products. These products are popular with banks, a market that J-P had recently entered by offering its insurance products to customers of Charter One Bank.

Approach and Engagement

In October 1996, The Chubb Corp. retained Goldman, Sachs & Co. to locate a buyer for its life insurance business. It didn't take long to find one, and on February 24, 1997, Chubb entered into a definitive agreement to sell Chubb Life Insurance Company of America (CLICA) to Jefferson-Pilot for $875 million in cash.

Regulatory approval was received rather quickly, and on May 13, 1997, the two companies closed the deal. The Chubb Corp. was paid with $775 million in cash from Jefferson-Pilot as well as $100 million in dividends from CLICA.

Products and Services

Jefferson-Pilot Corp. closed 1998 with an array of individual and group life and health insurance, as well as annuity and investment products. Its Jefferson-Pilot Communications Company subsidiary owned and operated three network-affiliated television stations and 17 radio stations, and produced and syndicated sports programming.

In 1998, the company's Life Insurance business registered a 27% increase in earnings, to $245.2 million. Its Annuity and Investment Product earnings advanced 12 % to $71.1 million. Jefferson-Pilot Communications Company's earnings of $27.5 million were an increase of 17% over the previous year.

Changes to the Industry

In the life insurance market, the major players kept getting bigger and bigger. Consolidation had driven out small- to mid-sized ventures, and Chubb Corp. was no exception. Having the foresight to exit that business before it drained company resources from other lines of business proved to its advantage. By shedding its less profitable businesses—life insurance and real estate operations—Chubb became singularly focused on its greatest strength, that of property and casualty insurance. The company intended to commit to those operations by using the proceeds of the CLICA sale to repurchase about 10% of the company's outstanding stock.

As one of those industry giants in question, Jefferson-Pilot improved its position with the acquisition. After the sale, it became one of the nation's top 15 life insurance companies based on total life premium, one of the top 10 based on life sales, and the third-largest writer of universal life insurance in the U.S.

Review of the Outcome

The newly-formed Jefferson-Pilot Corporation had more than 25,000 sales representatives, nearly two million customers, and over $160 billion of life insurance in force. The Chubb Life companies contributed to that mix an independent sales network of 9,000 agents and 1,300 general agents. Its Chubb Securities subsidiary, which was also acquired during the transaction, brought 1,200 registered broker representatives who also served as life insurance agents.

The new combination proved immediately profitable. Jefferson-Pilot's life insurance arm increased earnings 27% in 1998, from $194 million to $245 million in a single year. Chubb Life Insurance Company of America, now renamed Jefferson Pilot Financial Insurance Company, had been fully integrated in 1998, and earnings for the following year are expected to show even greater growth, as the costs associated with integration would have been completely assumed.

Chairman, CEO, and President David Stonecipher summed up the company's positive outlook in a 1999 press release: "We believe that Jefferson-Pilot has a focused and balanced portfolio of businesses and products, on both the insurance and communications sides of the company, that provide a sound platform for continued solid internal growth."

Research

"After Takeover of Chubb, Jefferson-Pilot May Explore Eastern U.S. Bank Programs," in *Bank Investment Product News*, 3 March 1997. Short article on Jefferson-Pilot's likely expansion of its bank insurance operations.

"Chubb to Sell Life Insurance Subsidiary," in *Business Insurance*, 3 March 1997. Overview of Chubb Corp.'s rationale for executing the sale and the subsequent stock repurchase.

"The Chubb Corporation," in *Notable Corporate Chronologies*, The Gale Group, 1999. Lists major events in the company's history.

The Chubb Corporation Home Page, available at http://www.chubb.com. Official World Wide Web Home Page for The Chubb Corporation. Includes access to the 1997 Annual Report, news, and company history.

Cone, Edward. "Man in a Hurry," in *Business North Carolina*, August 1994. Profile of Jefferson-Pilot's David Stonecipher and his accomplishments since joining the firm.

"Jefferson-Pilot to Acquire Life Insurance Operations of The Chubb Corporation," in *PR Newswire*, 24 February 1997. Press release from the announcement of the acquisition deal.

"Jefferson-Pilot Completes Purchase of Chubb Life," in *PR Newswire*, 13 May 1997. Short summary of the acquisition terms and details.

"Jefferson-Pilot Corporation," in *International Directory of Company Histories*, Vol. 11. Detroit: St. James Press, 1995. Profile of various companies, their history and current operations.

Jefferson-Pilot Home Page, available at http://www.jpfinancial.com. Official World Wide Web Home Page for the Jefferson-Pilot Corporation. Includes access to the 1997 Annual Report, news, and a brief company history.

WILLIAM P. FREEMAN

The Players

Jefferson-Pilot President and CEO: David A. Stonecipher. David Stonecipher's rapid rise to success at Jefferson-Pilot is typical of his life. Born in Tennessee, he attended McCallie prep school before attending Vanderbilt University, from where he graduated in three years. Drawn to both mathematics and business, he found an interesting blend of the two in the field of actuaries. He joined the Life Insurance Company of Georgia in 1962 as an actuarial trainee. There he remained for 30 years, progressively succeeding through the ranks of vice president, senior VP, executive VP, president and chief operating officer, and was finally named CEO in 1991. During his short tenure as president, he increased assets from $1.6 billion to $2.2 billion. In 1993 he was lured by Jefferson-Pilot to replace W. Roger Soles as President and CEO—to the delight of employees and shareholders alike. In characteristic fashion, Stonecipher efficiently put Jefferson-Pilot back on track by introducing new blood into the executive management team, hiring 4,000 additional sales agents, closing nearly half of its field offices, and seeking expansion through acquisitions. Net income in 1993, the year that he came on board, was $219 million; in 1996 this figure had grown to $290.5 million. In 1998 he was elected chairman of the board, while continuing his reign as president and CEO.

The Chubb Corp. Chairman and CEO: Dean R. O'Hare. Dean O'Hare, a New Jersey native, earned a Bachelor's degree in financial management from New York University in 1963. He joined the Chubb Corporation that year as a surety underwriting trainee. Continuing his education, he received an MBA from Pace University in 1969. He was promoted to an officer three years later. In 1981 O'Hare was named chief financial officer—a position that he held until 1994. In the meantime, he had become the company president in 1986, and chairman and CEO two years later.

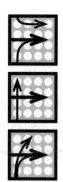

JOHNSON & JOHNSON & CORDIS CORP.

Johnson & Johnson
One Johnson & Johnson Plaza
New Brunswick, NJ 08933
USA

tel: (732)524-0400
fax: (732)524-3300
web: http://www.jnj.com

nationality: USA
date: February 1996
affected: Johnson & Johnson, USA, founded 1886
affected: Cordis Corp., USA, founded 1959

Overview of the Merger

Johnson & Johnson's acquisition of Cordis Corp. had been difficult, but not because of regulatory interference of stockholder objections. Rather, Cordis simply didn't want to be purchased, and had installed a "dead-hand" poison pill defense to prevent its takeover. This defense was soon outmaneuvered, however, and Cordis became a subsidiary of Johnson & Johnson (J&J) in February 1996.

The companies were a natural fit. Cordis had a strong name and a share of the angioplasty medical products market, a market into which Johnson & Johnson wanted to extend its reach. For its part, J&J offered the small company the financial resources to help ensure its continued success and to allow it to venture into new directions.

History of Johnson & Johnson

Johnson & Johnson was founded at a time when the medical and surgical concepts of antiseptics were in their infancy. Doctors regularly operated ungloved and wounds were wrapped in unclean scraps from textile mills. As a result, a great number of patients died from post-surgical infection. When Joseph Lister put forth his theory of germs as the source of infection, much of the scientific and medical community was doubtful. Moreover, Lister's recommended method for sterilization was to spray the operating room with carbolic acid, an impractical and cumbersome procedure for even the largest of hospitals.

Lister's theory convinced Robert Wood Johnson, however. This druggist had attended a lecture by Lister in 1876, and believed that a huge market for practical antiseptic procedures existed. His brothers, James Wood Johnson and Edward Mead Johnson, had established a partnership in 1885, and Robert Wood joined it in 1886. The company followed up its first product, a medicinal plaster, with a soft, absorbent cotton-and-gauze surgical dressing. This mass-produced product was soon shipped throughout the U.S.

Johnson & Johnson (J&J) established a bacteriological laboratory in 1891, and soon developed a method of guaranteeing the sterility of its bandages. It introduced a zinc oxide-based plaster that was stronger and less irritating to the skin than other adhesive bandages.

To secure a source for its increasing need for textile materials, J&J purchased Chicopee Manufacturing Corporation in 1916. Three years later the company expanded internationally by establishing an affiliate in Canada. It ventured overseas in 1924 by forming a Great Britain unit. Two of J&J's best-known brands—Band-Aid and Johnson's Baby Cream—were introduced in the early 1920s.

Robert Wood Johnson's son, also named Robert, was elected company president in 1932. He instituted a decentralized organizational structure in which divisions and affiliates were given autonomy to direct their own operations. He also took J&J into new directions, diversifying into pharmaceuticals, hygiene products, and textiles. The company strengthened its pharmaceutical holdings with its 1959 acquisitions of McNeil Pharmaceutical Company and Cilag-Chemie, as well as its 1961 purchase of Janssen Pharmaceutica.

Beginning in the 1960s, J&J launched aggressive consumer advertising. By 1978 it had captured half of the feminine hygiene products market by taking its advertisements out of women's magazines and putting them on television.

McNeil Pharmaceutical introduced the non-aspirin Tylenol pain reliever in 1960. Originally marketed as a high-priced product, Tylenol entered the mass market upon the introduction of lower-priced competition, Datril, in the mid-1970s. There it not only beat the non-aspirin competition, but also snatched the top position away from Anacin. Tylenol became J&J's best-selling product.

J&J added to its professional healthcare operations over the following years. It acquired Extracorporeal Medical Specialties, a manufacturer of kidney dialysis and intravenous treatment products, in 1977. The firm created Critikon, Inc. in 1979 for critical-care products. It entered the field of eye care and ophthalmic pharmaceuticals with its 1981 acquisition of Iolab Corp., maker of ocular lenses for cataract surgery. In 1983 it formed Johnson & Johnson Hospital Services to develop and implement corporate marketing programs.

In September 1982 tragedy struck when seven people died from ingesting Tylenol capsules that had been laced with cyanide. J&J immediately canceled advertisements and pulled all Tylenol products from store shelves. Company stock dropped 18%, and Datril and Anacin products were in such demand that supplies were back-ordered.

The Business

Financials

Revenue (1998): $23.7 billion

Employees (1998): 93,100

SICs / NAICS

sic 2844 - Toilet Preparations

sic 3842 - Surgical Appliances & Supplies

sic 2834 - Pharmaceutical Preparations

naics 325412 - Pharmaceutical Preparation Manufacturing

naics 339113 - Surgical Appliance and Supplies Manufacturing

naics 322291 - Sanitary Paper Product Manufacturing

naics 325620 - Toilet Preparation Manufacturing

naics 325611 - Soap and Other Detergent Manufacturing

After the Food and Drug Administration (FDA) discovered that the tampering have been done at the retail level rather than during manufacturing, J&J was faced with the challenge of rebuilding its leading product and reputation. It offered exchange and refund programs, as well as high-valued coupons for future purchases. It also redesigned its packaging to include three levels of tamper resistance, two more levels than the FDA had issued in its tamper-resistant packaging guidelines for the entire food and drug industry. Within months, sales approached their former levels; by 1989 Tylenol was generating $500 million in sales.

James Burkes, J&J's chairman and CEO since 1976, earned a spot in the National Business Hall of Fame in 1990 for his savvy, yet honest, handling of this crisis. In 1989 three men filled the company's top posts upon the retirement of Burke and president David R. Clare—Ralph S. Larsen was named chairman and CEO, Robert Campbell became vice chairman, and Robert Wilson was appointed president.

The company continued on the path of expansion throughout the 1980s. It acquired Frontier Contact Lens, later renamed Vistakon, in 1981, and purchased Lifescan, Inc., manufacturer of home blood glucose, in 1986. Three years later it entered into a joint venture with Merck Consumer Pharmaceuticals Company to develop and market over-the-counter (OTC) products.

The next decade began with J&J's expansion into Eastern Europe through the opening of operations in

The Officers

Chairman and CEO: Ralph S. Larsen

Vice Chairman of the Board: Robert N. Wilson

VP, Finance: Robert J. Darretta

VP, Administration: Russell C. Deyo

VP, General Counsel: Roger S. Fine

Moscow, Hungary, Poland, and the former Yugoslavia. The company acquired RoC, S.A. in 1993 and Neutrogena Corp. in 1994; both manufacturers of skin and hair care products. J&J also strengthened its diagnostics business in 1994 by acquiring Clinical Diagnostics from Kodak. Revenues at the end of that year totaled $15.7 billion.

History of Cordis Corp.

William Murphy, an engineer and medical doctor, established Medical Development Corporation in 1957. This medical device company introduced the lumbar puncture tray, a disposable set of needles and tools for spinal taps. Murphy then licensed the concept to Mead John & Company for $300,000, sinking the proceeds into research and development. It was in those operations that Murphy excelled, so he hired John Sterner to manage the company as president in 1959.

By 1960 Murphy had changed his company's name to Cordis ("of the heart") to reflect its primary focus. Cordis became involved in the new field of cardiac pacemakers, devices that stimulate the heart with electrical charges. By the early 1970s Cordis was the nation's second-largest pacemaker manufacturer.

Despite its success, Cordis was still generating a negative net operating cash flow. Research and development remained the company's focus and, consequently, its largest expense. Murphy and Sterner were forced to sell most of their stock just to keep the firm in business.

To make matters worse, flawed circuits from its supplier CTS Corporation, coupled with a 30% internal rejection rate, caused the Food and Drug Administration (FDA) to issue a product advisory against Cordis in 1974. Sales and earnings dropped, and employee salaries were cut by 20%. CTS agreed to invest $5 million into Cordis in exchange for 25% of its stock; Cordis bought back that interest in 1977.

Cordis received another injection from CTS, this time in the form of a company leader. Norman Weldon had served as president of CTS, and assumed that role at Cordis in 1979. He implemented a restructuring of

the company's manufacturing and marketing operations. The reorganization was costly, however, and in 1981 Cordis lost $8.3 million and had $89 million in debt.

Two events in the early 1980s contributed to the company's rebound. In 1982 Cordis won FDA approval for an innovative synchronous pacemaker, which regulates two chambers of the heart instead of just one. At the same time, several competitors became immersed in a kickback scandal. Cordis' sales skyrocketed to $207 million in 1984, and the company became profitable again. It also regained its second-place rank, from which it had been supplanted in 1979.

Cordis then faced another quality control crisis. Company engineers discovered that its lithium-powered pacemaker had a high potential for corrosion and, possibly, leakage. Cordis warned doctors and the FDA of the possibility for corrosion. The close monitoring of the 8,500 patients who had already received the device revealed an even more serious problem—an unforeseen chemical reaction was sapping the power of the batteries. The FDA ordered recalls of Cordis' pacemakers in 1983 and 1985, and barred the firm from testing or selling new products for 18 months.

Sales sank to $80 million in 1986. The pacemaker business had proved troublesome, to say the least, so Cordis sold this division in 1987. That year Weldon resigned and was succeeded by Robert Strauss as president and CEO.

Cordis intensified operations in the catheter business. Its diagnostic cardiac catheters, fine-gauge tubes used in angiography, enabled Cordis to capture 40% of the global angiography market by 1990. Sales this year were $202.6 million, but debt was $31.6 million.

Strauss sought to diversify Cordis into other catheter markets. The therapeutic heart catheter was used in angioplasty, and its market was large and profitable. The company reorganized into product-oriented teams in order to develop a comprehensive line of angioplastic devices. By 1994 Cordis had captured 10% of the nation's angioplasty sales and a third-place 17% of the global market. At the same time, the company had dramatically improved its financial condition. Company debt was reduced to a mere $1.1 million and sales had multiplied to $443 million.

Market Forces Driving the Acquisition

Johnson & Johnson manufactured coronary stents, devices that surgeons use to hold the artery open after angioplasty. By late 1995, it was the only company with FDA clearance to market the stents. J&J became increasingly eager to cement its position in the cardiac medical products market.

In Cordis J&J found an appealing and complementary array of medical products used in angioplasty. Such products, including the balloons that are used in conjunction with J&J's stents, would allow the company to offer a package of coronary devices to customers, becoming a one-stop shop.

For Cordis, a merger with an industry giant such as J&J would secure its continued success. Cordis, for all its achievements, was still a small fish in a big pond. Already established leaders were extending their reach, as the pharmaceutical and health care industries were undergoing intense consolidation. A marriage with J&J made sense. There was just one problem—Cordis wanted to remain independent.

Approach and Engagement

Johnson & Johnson approached Cordis management in September 1995, but was sternly rebuffed. J&J, which had always preserved a friendly approach in its acquisition efforts, went out of character and became aggressive. On October 19, 1995, it launched a hostile bid for Cordis. The transaction would take one of two forms, according to Cordis' preference. A cash transaction would be priced at $100 per share, amounting to $1.6 billion, or a stock-for-stock deal at $105 per share. The latter share price was a 16% premium to Cordis' closing stock price on October 18th. J&J also claimed that it was a 70% premium to Cordis' stock price before rumors of an acquisition bumped it up beginning the previous July.

According to *Genesis Report/Dx*, J&J chairman Ralph Larsen wrote to Cordis' leader Robert Strauss that a merger "will give the combined company a greater breadth of technologically superior products including balloon/stent systems and provide a stronger competitive position in the marketplace."

On October 20th, the day after launching its bid, J&J filed with the Security Exchange Commission (SEC) for permission to begin a proxy fight for Cordis' nine-member board. Under Florida law, if it gained the support of 50.1% of Cordis' shareholders, it could replace that company's board.

As it turns out, Cordis had been prepared for such a maneuver, even before J&J officially made a move. Only a few days prior to the hostile bid, Cordis' board had installed a "dead-hand" poison pill defense. A typical poison pill is an anti-takeover defense that triggers an automatic devaluation of stock in the event that a shareholder acquires a particular percentage of shares. It does not, however, preclude a hostile bidder from replacing the target company's board with members of its own. Such newly installed members could then vote in favor of redeeming or modifying the pill.

The relatively rare dead-hand pill closes off this vulnerability by allowing a vote on redemption only to those members who had been on the board prior to the takeover bid. J&J would thereby be stymied even if it did manage to replace Cordis' board.

J&J responded by filing in court to overturn the poison pill plan. Cordis shareholders also filed lawsuits against Cordis, claiming that by not considering J&J's offer, the directors were preserving their own interests, not those of the shareholders.

Meanwhile, Cordis began searching in earnest for a white knight, a preferred acquirer. Although other companies were certainly interesting Cordis, none stepped up as a third-party bidder. Industry experts surmised that this reluctance stemmed not from intimidation of the size of the bid, but of the size of J&J. No one was willing to enter into a price war with the giant.

Cordis realized that it was fighting a losing battle. With no white knight in sight, it succumbed to pressure and capitulated in early November 1995. It had managed to increase J&J's bid to $109 per share, or $1.8 billion, in stock.

The Federal Trade Commission approved of the deal on the condition that J&J would sell off a piece of Cordis upon the merger. In order to keep its share of the market for cranial shunts, manufactured by both companies, below 85%, Cordis' neurological unit must be divested.

After passing J&J's due diligence review and subsequent vote by Cordis shareholders, the merger was completed in February 1996.

Products and Services

Johnson & Johnson has three main business areas: Consumer, Professional, and Pharmaceutical/Diagnostics.

Consumer operations consisted of skin and hair care, sanitary protection, wound care, oral care, and over-the-counter pharmaceuticals. Brand names included Johnson's Baby Powder, Shampoo, Lotion and Oil; Neutrogena shampoos, soap, and lotions; Tylenol and Motrin; o.b. Tampons; Stayfree sanitary protection products; Reach toothbrushes; Band-Aid Brand Adhesive Bandages; Imodium A-D antidiarrheal; Mylanta antacid products; Monistat 7 for vaginal yeast infections; and Pepcid AC Acid Controller.

Professional products were commonly found in hospitals, clinics, and physicians' offices, and were used by medical professionals for surgery, patient care, wound closure, diagnosis, blood testing, and related medical purposes. Product lines included surgical implants, instruments, needles and sutures; blood glucose monitoring systems; wound closure devices; endoscopic instruments; specialty dressings; orthopedic products for fracture immobilization and joint repair and replacement; contact lenses; and infection control products.

Pharmaceutical/diagnostics products included many leading prescription products, such as Risperdal (risperidone) for schizophrenia, Propulsid (cisapride) for gastrointestinal disorders, Nizoral (ketoconazole) for fungal infections, and Ultram (tramadol HCl) for pain.

Changes to the Industry

The acquisition of the Cordis line of products propelled J&J to the forefront of the interventional cardiology market. Its sales in that market were approximately $1 billion, twice that of its nearest competitors, Boston Scientific Corporation and Guidant Corporation.

The combined company's hold on the stent market proved to be temporary, however. By November 1998 Cordis' share of the market was only 10%, down from 80% in 1997. The company was confident that its new generation of products, likely to receive FDA approval in 1999, would enable it to regain its once-dominant position.

Review of the Outcome

Cordis Corporation became a wholly-owned subsidiary of Johnson & Johnson. Cordis continued to improve its market position, and in 1997 made two acquisitions. In April it gained a line of nitinol-based products by acquiring Nitinol Development Corporation, and in October it merged with Biosense, Inc., a medical sensor technology company based in Israel and headquartered in New York.

Johnson & Johnson continued to involve itself in acquisitions as well. In 1997 it acquired the over-the-counter rights to Motrin from Pharmacia & Upjohn in exchange for Pediacare and several other products. In November 1998 it purchased DuPuy, Inc., a manufacturer of orthopedic products. The following February it completed its acquisition of the dermatology skin care business of S.C. Johnson & Son, Inc.

J&J's sales in 1998 increased 4.7% to $23.7 billion. The company's three operating segments also reported growth. J&J's Consumer segment increased 0.4% to $6.5 billion. The Pharmaceutical and Professional segments each generated revenues of $8.6 billion, an increase of 11.3% and 1.6%, respectively. Cordis Corporation is included in the Professional business,

and its decline in stent sales were offset by strong showings from the segment's other products, such as suture anchors, laparoscopy mechanical closure devices, and the recently acquired DePuy line of orthopedic products.

Johnson & Johnson claimed to be the world's largest and most comprehensive manufacturer of healthcare products serving the consumer, pharmaceutical, diagnostics, and professional markets.

Research

"Acquisitions: Johnson & Johnson Cordis Corp.," in *In Vivo*, 1 November 1995. J&J's offer is a premium to Cordis' stock price.

Chandler, Michele. "Cordis Seeks to Recapture Major Share of the Market it Made," in *Miami Herald*, 2 November 1998. How Cordis plans to recapture its hold on the stent market.

"Cordis Corp.," in *International Directory of Company Histories*, Vol. 19, St. James Press, 1998. Profile of the company through its acquisition by J&J.

"J&J Builds Stent Empire with Cordis Buy," in *Health Industry Today*, 1 December 1995. Brief look at the cardiology product line of a combined company.

"J&J Files Bid to Oust Board of Cordis Corp.," in *The Wall Street Journal*, 23 October 1995. J&J Moves to Replace Cordis' Board of Directors.

"J&J Gets Cordis, Finally," in *In Vivo*, 1 November 1995. Report of Cordis' acceptance of the acquisition offer, and how each company will benefit from a merger.

"J&J Means Business: Puts the Moves of Cordis," in *Genesis Report/Dx*, 1 September 1995. The hostile bid is first offered, and passages of Larsen's letter to Strauss is included.

"Johnson & Johnson," in *International Directory of Company Histories*, Vol. 8, St. James Press, 1994. Profile of the company until its acquisition of Cordis.

Johnson & Johnson Home Page, available at http://www.jnj.com. Official World Wide Web Page for Johnson & Johnson. Includes career and investment information, company news and background, product information, and related company Websites.

"Johnson & Johnson's Hostile Bid for Cordis," in *The New York Times*, 20 October 1995. J&J launches its hostile bid for Cordis.

Nesse, Leslie Kraft. "Change in Cordis' Structure Leads to Increased Sales, Profits," in *South Florida Business Journal*, 10 June 1994. Describes the successful reorganization of Cordis before it was approached by J&J.

"Rift Healed, Cordis Says Yes to J&J," in *Daily Business Review*, 7 November 1995. Cordis submits to the $109 per share merger offer.

"Shareholders Sue Cordis; 'Poison Pill' Plan Rapped," in *Miami Herald*, 25 October 1995. J&J and Cordis' own shareholders file suits against the company.

"Third Parties Drag Their Feet on Cordis," in *Mergers & Acquisitions Report*, 30 October 1995. Suggests possible reasons why Cordis was unable to find a white knight.

DEBORAH J. UNTENER

JOHNSON CONTROLS & HOOVER UNIVERSAL

nationality: USA
date: May 1985
affected: Johnson Controls Inc., USA, founded 1885
affected: Hoover Universal Inc., USA, founded 1913

Johnson Controls Inc.
5757 N. Green Bay Ave.
Milwaukee, WI 53201
USA

tel: (414)228-1200
fax: (414)228-2302
web: http://www.johnsoncontrols.com

Overview of the Merger

Celebrating its 100th year of business, Johnson Controls nearly doubled its revenue with the $490 million purchase of Hoover Universal in 1985. Both major suppliers to the automotive industry, Johnson Controls and Hoover Universal began negotiating their deal after corporate raider Victor Posner, who owned a 20% stake in Johnson Controls, allegedly began threatening a takeover. Upon completion of the deal, however, Posner sold his shares.

History of Johnson Controls, Inc.

Warren Seymour Johnson, a professor at the State Normal School in Whitewater, Wisconsin, produced the first Johnson System of Temperature Regulation, an electric thermostat system which he installed at the school in 1883. Upon receiving a patent for the device, he persuaded William Plankinton to become his financial backer. Their partnership, the Milwaukee Electric Manufacturing Co., allowed Johnson to devote all his time to inventing. In 1885, the company reorganized into Johnson Electric Service Co. and incorporated in Wisconsin.

Johnson continued to invent control devices, as well as designing products such as chandeliers, springless door locks, puncture-proof tires, thermometers, and a hose coupling for providing steam heat to passenger railcars. The creations for which the company received the greatest recognition however, were tower clocks. Johnson had developed a system powered by air pressure that increased the reliability of such clocks.

Johnson's wireless communication exhibit took second place at Paris World's Fair, and as a result, Johnson, his sons, and inventor Charles Fortier began to test a variety of alloys in wireless sets. The men built a 115-foot tower several miles south of Milwaukee, but many attempts to transmit messages to the company's downtown factory were unsuccessful. With Johnson now president of the newly named Johnson Service Co., he sought ways to enter the automotive industry. In 1907, the company was interested in establishing an automobile company, but unable to secure backing. At the same time, Johnson introduced a gasoline-powered engine.

The Business

Financials

Revenue (1998): $12,587 million

Employees (1998): 89,000

SICs / NAICS

sic 3692 - Primary Batteries-Dry & Wet

sic 1796 - Installing Building Equipment Nec

sic 7382 - Security Systems Services

naics 335912 - Primary Battery Manufacturing

naics 561621 - Security Systems Services (except
     Locksmiths)

He became the first person to receive a U.S. contract to deliver mail with a horseless carriage. Ultimately, the company's failure to expand upon its automobile interests was a source of frustration to Johnson until his death in 1911.

Harry W. Ellis was elected president after Johnson's death and decided to concentrate on opportunities for growth in the controls field. He sold all of the company's other businesses, improved the efficiency of factory operations in Milwaukee, and introduced a modern accounting system. In 1912, the company regained rights to sell, install, and service its temperature control and regulation systems throughout the country and established 18 U.S. branch offices, six Canadian offices, and direct agencies in Copenhagen, Berlin, St. Petersburg, Manchester, and Warsaw. During World War I, the company's temperature control business was classified by the War Industry Board as nonessential to the war effort, since it was seen as a means of providing comfort. Johnson contracts dropped off as civilian construction was sharply reduced. The firm looked to the government buildings for business and began seeking contracts to retrofit old buildings with new temperature control systems.

The Great Depression dealt a serious blow to the construction industry, and most new building-control installations in the 1930s aimed for economy. Projects in schools and government buildings were concerned with saving fuel as well. Johnson's new Dual Thermostat, which allowed a building to save fuel by automatically lowering temperatures at times when a building was unoccupied, was in demand. Upon the country's entrance into World War II, Johnson was

classified as part of an essential industry, evidence of the change in the way the public perceived building controls. Johnson's contributions to the war effort included installing temperature and humidity control systems in defense facilities and the engineering of special military products. Under the leadership of company president Joseph A. Cutler, Johnson also made leak detectors that were used to test barrage balloons and manufactured echo boxes, devices that tested radar sets.

After World War II ended, civilian construction boomed and with it, the company's new contracts. Interest in air-conditioning also increased. In 1956, Johnson began to build and install pneumatic control centers that allowed a single building engineer to monitor panels displaying room temperatures, ventilating conditions, water temperatures, and the outdoor temperature. In 1960, the firm purchased a panel-fabrication firm in Oklahoma. Operations at company headquarters in Milwaukee were also expanding, leading to the purchase of an additional building for the brass foundry, metal fabrications, assembly operations, and machining work.

In 1961, the Systems Engineering & Construction Division was established. It provided equipment for all 57 air force Titan II launch complexes and most other major missile programs. The National Aeronautics and Space Administration (NASA) contracted with Johnson throughout the decade for mission-control instrumentation for the Apollo-Saturn program. Despite its good fortune, Johnson, along with competitors Honeywell and Powers Regulator, was charged in a federal antitrust suit with price-fixing of pneumatic temperature control systems. The ensuing consent decree, coupled with new competitors in the controls market, meant increasingly competitive bidding. Also, Johnson occasionally won contracts on which it ended up making little or no profit.

The company was looking to diversify as a means of staying competitive. After realizing that electronics technology could be used to control all aspects of building maintenance, Johnson bought the electronics division of Fischbach & Moore in 1963 to bolster its in-house electronics capability. The next year construction of the company's first foreign manufacturing plant began in Italy. An international division, with subsidiaries in England, France, Australia, Belgium, Italy, and Switzerland, was established.

Because of its increasing involvement in projects requiring exacting quality standards and high-quality components, Johnson acquired Associated Piping & Engineering Co. and Western Piping and Engineering Co. The companies fabricated expansion joints and piping for nuclear and fossil fuel generating plants and many other industrial applications. In 1967, Johnson introduced the T-6000, a solid-state digital data logger that used "management by exception," a system that announced when its variables were outside specified limits so an engineer's attention was only called for when needed. The T-6000 not only performed heating, ventilating, and air-conditioning functions, but also monitored fire/smoke detection, security, and emergency lighting systems.

By the end of the decade, Johnson acquired Penn Controls, a maker of controls for original-equipment manufacturers, distributors, and wholesalers, to gain its own supply of electrical products for installation projects. Penn also had manufacturing plants and subsidiaries abroad, which helped Johnson to expand its international markets.

In 1972, Johnson introduced the JC/80, the industry's first mini-computer system that managed building controls. One of the JC/80s advantages was that operators of the system needed only minimal training. Cutting fuel requirements by as much as 30%, the JC/80 was introduced at the ideal time, just a year before international embargoes on oil would change the way people viewed energy consumption. Two years later, the company changed its name to Johnson Controls. By 1977, Johnson Controls held approximately 35% of the estimated $600 million market for commercial-building control systems. It had 114 branch offices in the U.S. and Canada, and over 300 service centers staffed by 10,000 engineers, architects, designers, and service technicians.

Although Johnson fared well in the boom market for energy-conservation products, new companies were beginning to crowd the building controls field in the latter half of the 1970s. To diversify, the company merged with Globe-Union, the country's largest manufacturer of automotive batteries. The merger doubled Johnson's sales, broadened its financial base, and gave it leadership in a new field. By 1981, sales had surpassed the $1 billion mark. Johnson began taking the lead in the development of controls for "intelligent buildings," which featured state-of-the-art technology to manage energy, comfort, and protection needs.

In 1985, Johnson greatly expanded its automotive business with the acquisition of Hoover Universal, a major supplier of seating and plastic parts for automobiles and a new entrant in the plastic-container industry. Johnson expanded its plastics business by acquiring Apple Container Corp. in 1988, and the soft drink bottle operations of American National Can Co. One year later the company announced a joint venture with Yokogawa Electric Corp. to manufacture control instrumentation and to service industrial automation systems for the North American market. Pan Am

The Officers

Chairman and CEO: James H. Keyes

President and Chief Operating Officer: John M. Barth

Sr. VP and Chief Financial Officer: Stephen A. Roell

VP, Corporate Technology: Steven J. Bomba

VP, Human Resources: Susan F. Davis

World Services, a leading provider of high-tech and other facility-management services for military bases, airports, and space centers was also purchased.

Johnson's battery group acquired Varta, the largest automotive-battery maker in Canada in 1989. The battery division unveiled the EverStart, a new automotive battery that carried its own emergency backup power system. It was hailed as the first real breakthrough in battery technology in decades. By 1990, Johnson claimed leadership market positions in both Europe and the Far East. By mid-year, the company decided to sell off Varta and its car door components business while acquiring several European car seat component manufacturers. Weak domestic auto sales reduced demand for the firm's automotive products, and the three major auto makers accounted for more than 15% of Johnson' sales.

In 1994, Johnson Controls announced tentative plans to close its automotive battery plants in Dallas, Texas, and Owosso, Michigan, as a result of losing its contract to supply Die Hard batteries to Sears, Roebuck & Co. Despite this problem, stock was at an all-time high in 1995, and the company raised its dividend for the 21st year in a row. That year the company paid $585 million for two car seat manufacturers and a supplier of plastic bottles to the soft drink industry. Johnson also opened a $5 million research center for recycling and manufacturing innovations in Manchester, Michigan.

In 1996, Johnson Controls was a finalist for the 1996 PACE awards in the category of "companies with worldwide sales in excess of $500 million." The PACE awards were given out every year by Automotive Magazine and Ernst & Young LLP to automotive suppliers that came up with the best innovations in the industry. One year later the company was able to forge another contract with Sears to make Die-Hard batteries. In 1998, Johnson made three purchases including the Becker Group, Creative Control Designs, and Commerfin SpA. The company planned to sell its plastics machinery division, as well as its industrial battery operations.

The Players

President and CEO of Johnson Controls Inc.: Fred L. Brengel. After graduating from the Stevens Institute of Technology, Fred Brengel went to work for Johnson Controls in 1948 as a sales engineer. He took on such management roles as executive vice president and vice president of sales before being elected president and CEO in 1967. Brengel took on the role of chairman as well, after the merger of Johnson and Hoover Universal. Upon his retirement in 1988, Brengel had successfully seen the company rise from $120 in sales to $2.6 billion. He is credited for overseeing Johnson Controls' growth into one of the largest U.S. manufacturers of automotive seating, batteries, and plastics.

Chairman, President, and CEO of Hoover Universal Inc.: John F. Daly. John Daly began his career in the engineering industry in 1946 working as an executive vice president for Hardie Manufacturing in Michigan. He worked for several other companies, including Internat Steel and Universal Wire Spring, before joining Hoover Ball and Bearing in 1960, where he moved from vice president to president and chief operating officer in 1967. Three years later Daly was elected chairman, president, and CEO of the newly named company, Hoover Universal. In 1986, after Johnson Controls and Hoover Universal merged, Daly became vice chairman of Johnson Controls, a position he held until 1987.

Chairman of Sharon Steel: Victor Posner. Victor Posner, known as a corporate raider in the 1970s and 1980s, had interests in over 40 companies at the peak of his career. The Miami investor's habits included purchasing large stakes in struggling companies, and according to an article in *Forbes*, he "put himself on the payroll as chief executive and chairman and ended up with paychecks that, taken together, made him one of the highest paid executives in America, surpassing even the bosses of Exxon and Ford." Posner's threats to takeover Johnson Controls in 1985 prompted the firm to merge with Hoover Universal. Two years later he was cited for tax evasion. In 1993, Posner and his son were barred by the SEC from heading a publicly owned company.

History of Hoover Universal Inc.

Hoover Universal was founded in 1913 as the Chelsea Steel Ball Co. At the time, the majority of steel balls in the U.S. were imported from Europe. With the onset of World War I, however, imports declined dramatically in the U.S., and Chelsea found itself in an advantageous position. By 1917, the company was paying $2 per month per share in cash dividends, and just three years later sales were over $3 million.

In 1924, the company diversified into the production of ball bearings. Hoover eventually added brass, bronze, and monel to its steel ball line. Along with this diversification came high costs for supplies and labor. Because Hoover had been putting a high percentage of net earnings in cash dividends, earnings were not being reinvested into the company. This allocation of funds was undermining Hoover's ability to compete, grow, and update plants and equipment.

By 1932, sales were at a low of $391,000. Hoover management implemented a plan in hopes of seeing profits rise once again. The company borrowed money, began plant modernization, and increased production to meet demand. By 1955, sales increased 30% although few new customers were added to the company's portfolio. This forced management to reconsider its sales and marketing approach. That same year, Hoover merged with Universal DieCasting and Manufacturing Corp. The move increased Hoover's product line, as well as its number of manufacturing plants. By 1957, the company saw the highest sales and earnings in its 44-year history with net income of over $1.6 million.

The early 1960s were marked by growth and diversification. Hoover acquired Cuyahoga Steel and Wire Co. and Universal Inc., which led to the addition of six new operating divisions and subsidiaries. The company also increased plant capacity to keep up with growing customer demand. Hoover entered the container industry, as well with the introduction of its bleach containers. It formed a new subsidiary, Plas-Tainer, to oversee the development of this new product.

Later in the decade, Hoover acquired Aluminum Extrusions Inc. and Tillsonburg Machine Ltd. Automotive negotiations with General Motors had halted work at the company's Stubnitz Spring Division, which manufactured seat and back springs for cars and trucks. The strike lasted 13,000 work days and involved nearly 400 workers. Sales and earnings suffered, prompting Hoover to make a public offering in March of 1971 to raise capital to pay off debt. During the next five years, Hoover paid $4 million for two acquisitions: Rogate Industries and Mansfield Plastic Products.

The firm joined forces with PepsiCo in 1976 to manufacture plastic bottles for its carbonated drinks. Volkswagen also chose the supplier to make front seat frames for its famous "rabbit" car. By the end of the 1970s, Hoover was the leading producer of automotive seating; the company also supplied structural foam products like sun visors, console covers, and crash pads; die castings such as grills, headlight bezels, door handles, and knobs; injection molded plastic parts including power steering fluid reservoirs, window wiper gears, glove compartments, and gear shift indicators; sealants, coatings, and adhesives used for oil and air filter gaskets; draw-tite hitches, and aluminum products. The company also opened up 11 new plants across the U.S.

Hoover began the 1980s with lagging sales caused by a downturn in the automotive industry, as well as other markets the company served. As a result, Hoover was forced to shut several plants in Michigan and Ohio, two areas severely hurt by the recession. However, the company's precision metal ball business was doing well. Increase in demand for chrome balls used in spindle bearings in automobiles lead to a new plant opening in Georgia and a doubling in size of the company's North Charleston plant.

In 1982, the company purchased American Welding & Manufacturing Co., gaining access to the aerospace industry. In 1983 and 1984, the company saw record growth. The national economy was strengthening, auto sales were on the rise, and the demand for plastic containers led to sales of $845.5 million and a rise in net earning of 13% in 1984. The company acquired Superior Ball, TriCoast Container Corp., and Costruzioni Meccaniche S.P.A. of Italy. In 1985, Hoover Universal teamed up with Johnson Controls in an effort to remain the number one supplier of auto seating in the U.S. industry.

Market Forces Driving the Merger

In 1982, Hoover was lacking a management succession plan with its chairman position wide open. The company recognized the growth potential in the automotive seating industry and wanted to increase its foothold in that market. However, existing management questioned whether the firm was financially and managerially ready for a large acquisition that year. Hoover's higher-ups decided that pursuit of such an acquisition was not in the best interest of the company and looked instead to be taken over by a financially sound automotive seating company. The firm also hoped to find a partner that would help solve its management problems.

Johnson Controls saw Hoover Universal as a means to grow. Its seating and plastics operations had the potential to drive up sales and revenues. Hoover's seating business alone was generating $270 million annually. Johnson was also attracted to Hoover's unique ability to provide completely assembled seating and its "just in time" delivery system, which was attractive to auto makers. In a press release issued by Johnson Controls in March of 1985, the company stated, "as a result of the merger, the combined corporation will become the largest independent manufacturer of seating for cars and light trucks, supplying all U.S. operations of major domestic and foreign auto companies. It will also become the leading supplier to the market for plastic bottles and containers. Hoover Universal will strengthen Johnson Controls' position as a major supplier to the automotive industry and enhance its Battery and Controls Divisions' technical and manufacturing plastics capabilities."

At the same time, analysts speculated that Johnson was worried about impending advances from corporate raider Victor Posner. The investment tycoon owned over 20% of Johnson's shares, and his reputation for taking over companies and depleting cash reserves was well known.

Approach and Engagement

Early in 1984, Hoover Universal approached Johnson Controls CEO Fred Brengel. The two companies sketched out a deal and according to *The New York Times*, "the pact called for Johnson to create a subsidiary to buy 45 percent of Hoover's 13.4 million outstanding shares at $36.50 each, or about $219 million in cash." In May of 1985, the deal was finalized, and Victor Posner sold his interest in Johnson.

Products and Services

After the merger with Hoover in May 1985, Johnson Controls had four core businesses: controls, batteries, automotive, and plastics. These businesses were responsible for manufacturing seats, interiors, and batteries for cars, as well as environmental controls and security systems for buildings, and for providing integrated facility management for businesses. In 1998, 98% of sales came from the automotive components division. Roughly 40% of that came from the big three automakers: Ford, GM, and DaimlerChyrlser.

Johnson Controls had over 250 subsidiaries and operations in the U.S. and 34 other countries. In 1998, U.S. operations accounted for 63% of total sales. Europe accounted for 28% of sales.

Review of the Outcome

After acquiring Hoover, Johnson auctioned off 40% of its assets in an effort to focus on its automotive seating and plastics divisions. Citicorp Venture won the bid for the units, and with the proceeds, Johnson was able to reduce the acquisition debt incurred by the Hoover deal by over $2 million. Johnson also purchased Ferro Manufacturing in July of 1986 and with the two deals, nearly doubled its revenues. In 1986, Johnson reported increased sales—$2.6 billion, up from $2.3 billion in 1985—for the 40th consecutive year. Net income also rose to $95.9 million, compared to $89.7 million in 1985.

Johnson stood as the leading producer of automotive seating in the U.S. after the deal, as well as a strong force the batteries, controls, and plastics sectors. The company continued to grow throughout the remainder of the 1980s and into the 1990s. Net income steadily increased with the exception of 1990 and 1993, rising to $338 million in 1998. Stock prices increased as well, reaching $46.50 in 1998, compared to $17.38 in 1989.

Research

Berman, Phyllis. "A Once-Fearsome Raider," in *Forbes*, 18 May 1998. Covers the career of Victor Posner.

Daniels, Lee. "Johnson Buying Hoover Universal," in *The New York Times*, 5 March 1985. Discusses the merger agreement between Hoover and Johnson Controls.

"Fred Brengel Retires as Officer of Johnson Controls," in *PR Newswire*, 29 September 1988. Covers the career of Fred Brengel.

Hoover Ball and Bearing Annual Report, 1955. Details the major events in the history of Hoover.

Johnson Controls Inc. Home Page, available at http://www.johnsoncontrols.com. Official World Wide Web Home Page for Johnson Controls Inc. Includes historical, financial, and product information, as well as recent news articles.

"Johnson Controls Inc.," in *Notable Corporate Chronologies*, The Gale Group, 1999. Lists major events in the history of Johnson Controls Inc.

"Johnson Controls, Inc. to Acquire Hoover Universal, Inc.," in *PR Newswire*, 4 March 1985. Discusses details of merger with Hoover and benefits to Johnson Controls.

CHRISTINA M. STANSELL

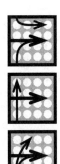

KIRK KERKORIAN, LEE IACOCCA & CHYRSLER

nationality: Germany
date: April 1995
affected: Chrysler Corp., USA, founded 1924

DaimlerChrysler AG
Epplestrasse 225
Stuttgart, D-70546
Germany

tel: (49)711-17-1
fax: (49)711-17-94022
web: http://www.daimlerchrysler.com

Overview of the Merger

Kirk Kerkorian and Lee Iacocca launched a hostile $32 billion takeover bid for Chrysler in April of 1994. Kerkorian, the largest shareholder of Chrysler, with a $2.8 billion stake in the automotive giant, and Iacocca, the former chairman of the company, wanted to take Chrysler private. Kerkorian had been in battle with the company's management for several months, complaining about dividends and claiming that shareholders were not receiving monies owed to them. He accused the company of undervaluing its stock. Instead of selling his stake in the company, he sought out Iacocca mainly for his strong influence, and sold him on his plan to take over the company. Industry experts claimed that the bid was just a ploy to increase the stock price and that the two had no real interest in running the company.

When Kerkorian's first bid with Iacocca failed, he joined forces with Jerome York, former financial executive for Chrysler. The two continued throughout the rest of 1995 with takeover attempts, criticizing the management style of Eaton.

History of Chrysler Corp.

In 1924, the Maxwell Motor Corp., headed up by Walter Chrysler, produced the first Chrysler automobile. Over 32,000 models were sold for a profit in excess of $4 million. The same year, Maxwell-Chrysler of Canada opened in Windsor, Ontario. On June 6, 1925, Chrysler was incorporated when Walter Chrysler took over Maxwell Motor Car. Other accomplishments included the introduction of the Chrysler Four Series 58 with a top speed of 58 mph and the incorporation of Chrysler Corp. of Canada, Ltd. By that time, more than 3,800 dealers were selling Chrysler cars. Ford Motor Co. closed its doors that year to redesign its Model T, previously the fastest automobile at 35 mph.

By 1927, Chrysler had sold 192,000 cars to become fifth in the industry. The company acquired Dodge Brothers, Inc., quintupling its size. Chrysler also began production of the De Soto and the first Plymouth, priced from $675 to $725 in order to appeal to consumers with average incomes. In just two years, Chrysler had grown to become one of the Big Three leading automotive manufacturers. In 1933,

The Business

Financials - Chrysler Corp.

Revenue (1998): $154.6 billion

Employees (1998): 441,500

SICs / NAICS

sic 6159 - Miscellaneous Business Credit Institutions

sic 7514 - Passenger Car Rental

sic 3711 - Motor Vehicles & Car Bodies

sic 3713 - Truck & Bus Bodies

naics 336111 - Automobile Manufacturing

naics 336112 - Light Truck and Utility Vehicle Manufacturing

naics 336992 - Military Armored Vehicle, Tank and Tank Component Manufacturing

naics 336211 - Motor Vehicle Body Manufacturing

naics 532111 - Passenger Car Rental

naics 522292 - Real Estate Credit

naics 522293 - International Trade Financing

naics 522294 - Secondary Market Financing

naics 522298 - All Other Non-Depository Credit Intermediation

Chrysler surpassed Ford, its major competitor, in annual sales for the first time.

The company continued to thrive, and in 1934, Chrysler developed its first automatic overdrive transmission, as well as the industry's first one-piece, curved glass windshield. In 1938, Chrysler established and became minority owner in Chrysler de Mexico.

With the onset of the war in 1941, Chrysler converted to war production and began making B-29 bomber engines and anti-aircraft tanks and guns. By 1945, Chrysler had supplied more than $3.4 billion in military equipment to the Allied forces. After the war, the company focused on product development and growth. In 1946, Chrysler began production of the first hardtop convertible. Four years later, the company expanded outside North America by purchasing a majority of Chrysler Australia, Ltd. Electric powered windows were developed as well.

The Hemi, a hemispheric combustion chamber V-8 engine, and Oriflow shock absorbers were designed in 1951. The next year, Lynn A. Townsend became president and brought in an IBM computer system

that replaced 700 members of the clerical staff. As primary contractor of the Saturn booster rockets, Chrysler's space division contributed to one of America's first successful space flights. By 1955, drivers of Chrysler products were the first to enjoy all-transistor car radios and the convenience of power steering. The company ended the decade by developing electronic fuel injection as an alternative to carburetors.

In 1960, production of the De Soto ceased. Chrysler introduced its first 5/50 warranty—five years or 50,000 miles on drive train components—in 1963. Safety innovations such as a front seat shoulder harness and a self-contained rear heater/defroster system were developed in 1966, as well as the Air Package, a system for controlling exhaust emissions.

Continual management changes were blamed for a $4 million loss in 1969; the firm was operating at only 68% of its capacity. Chrysler fared no better during the 1970s. After losing $52 million in 1974 and $250 million in 1975, the board tapped former Ford president Lee Iacocca to take over as president and CEO.

In January of 1980, President Jimmy Carter signed the Chrysler Corp. Loan Guarantee Act, which provided the company with $1.5 billion in federal loan guarantees and stipulated that Chrysler sell its corporate jets. In July of that year, Iacocca began appearing in Chrysler's television advertisements in an effort to boost sales. The next year, however, Chrysler reported a record loss of $1.7 billion, cut inventories by $1 billion, and reduced the white-collar staff by 50%.

Iacocca began pushing for new product development. Production began on K-cars, the Dodge Aries, and the Plymouth Reliant. To cut costs, the cars were all built on the same "platform" that became the basic engine, suspension, and underbody design for all Chrysler's vehicles. In 1982, Iacocca released his autobiography, which became the best selling non-fiction hardcover book in the U.S. Hoping that interest in the company would increase as well, Chrysler paid off its government loan seven years early. In 1983, production of minivans, the Dodge Caravan and Plymouth Voyager, began. Chrysler also reintroduced the convertible.

Turnaround efforts paid off with a record 1984 net profit of $2.4 billion. That year, Chrysler acquired 15.6% in Officine Alfieri Maserati SpA. In 1985, it bought Gulfstream Aerospace for $637 million and began a joint venture, Diamond Star Motors, with Mitsubishi Motors Corp. to build small cars in the U.S. The company also launched a reorganization in 1987 that temporarily laid-off workers in two plants so that inventory could be reduced. Later that year, Chrysler was divided up as a holding company with four divisions: Chrysler Motors, Chrysler Financial, Chrysler Technologies, and Gulfstream Aerospace. The holding company's headquarters moved from Highland Park, Michigan, to Manhattan, New York.

Shareholders approved the acquisition of Renault's 46% stake in American Motors Corp., maker of Jeep and Eagle vehicles, for $800 million. The company also bought Electrospace Systems for $367 million and Nuova Automobil F. Lamborghini SpA. Wanting to be the leader in quality assurance, Chrysler introduced an unprecedented 7-year/70,000-mile power train warranty and a 7-year/100,000 mile outer body rust protection warranty in 1987. All Chrysler vehicles were manufactured with air bag restraint systems, including the Chrysler New Yorker and the Dodge Dynasty, by the end of that year.

In 1988, Chrysler began a joint venture with Fiat SpA to distribute Alfa Romeo cars in North America. The following year, Pentastar Transportation Group, Inc., a rental car subsidiary, was formed when Chrysler purchased Thrifty Rental Car System, Inc., Snappy Car Rental, Inc., Dollar Rent A Car Systems, Inc., and General Rent-A-Car, Inc. to prevent other car companies from owning them. The plan backfired, however, when all four of the rental agencies lost money.

Iacocca started 1989 by implementing a $1 billion cost-cutting program. Chrysler also began a joint venture with Steyr-Daimler-Puch of Austria to produce minivans for Europe. In 1990, Chrysler re-purchased 7.7 million shares of its own stock and Kirk Kerkorian acquired 9.8% to become the company's largest single shareholder.

Chrysler sold Gulfstream for $825 million in 1990. The next year, 35 million new shares were issued at $10. Chrysler also sold 50% of Diamond Star Motors and withdrew from its joint venture with Fiat.

The Jefferson North Assembly Plant, a $1.6 billion investment in Detroit, began production of Jeep Grand Cherokees in the early 1990s. By 1994, plans were underway to more than double Chrysler's export of Jeep Cherokees to Japan. Profits reached a record $3.71 billion. That year, the company announced the recall of 1,600 1994 four-wheel-drive Dodge Dakota trucks to repair a defect that could cause a bolt in the upper suspension to break.

In April of 1995, Kirk Kerkorian bid $55 a share, nearly $20 billion, for the 90% of Chrysler shares he didn't yet own. However, he could not raise the financial backing he needed and his bid failed. As the company's focus turned to safety, it announced that it would replace rear door latches on all of its 1995 minivans and 4.5 million of its 1984-1994 minivans. This prompted criticism from the NHTSA, which accused

The Officers

Chrysler Corp.

Co-Chairman: Robert J. Eaton

Co-Chairman and Co-CEO: Juergen E. Schrempp

Chief Financial Officer, Corporate Finance and Controlling: Manfred Gentz

Sr. VP, Engineering and Technology: Bernard I. Robertson

Exec. VP, Product Development and Design: Thomas C. Gale

Chrysler of misleading customers about the safety of its minivans and alleged that the company was attempting to limit its efforts to replace rear door latches on minivans. While asserting that the vehicles were indeed safe, Chrysler agreed to replace all latches at no charge.

In 1995, Chrysler spent $2.1 billion in one-time expenses to retool two key factories for minivan construction and remodel a third factory for the assembly of pickup trucks. The economic turbulence in Mexico that followed the devaluation of the peso cost the company approximately $300 million. The following year, Chrysler and Kerkorian reached a five-year truce: Kerkorian agreed not to initiate a takeover attempt or attempt to increase his shareholdings, and Chrysler appointed a Kerkorian supporter to the board.

Chrysler spun off its Dollar Thrifty Automotive unit at $2.50 per share. Despite record sales in November and December of 1997, overall annual sales declined. In an effort to gain market share overseas and remain competitive in the U.S., the company merged with Daimler-Benz in late 1998 to form DaimlerChrysler.

Market Forces Driving the Merger

Starting in 1992 with a profit of over $700 million, Chrysler saw substantial increases over the next two years. In 1993, profit was $3.4 billion and in 1994 it was up to $5.2 billion. The company began to stockpile its cash for a five-year, $23 billion product program and for the event of a possible business downturn. This strategy made the company vulnerable for a takeover, but Eaton, Chrysler's chairman, wanted to hold on to that money.

In 1994 the company's stock peaked at $80 a share due to the success of minivans and new vehicles. The stock remained undervalued, however, due to nega-

The Players

President of Tracinda Corp.: Kirk Kerkorian. Kirk Kerkorian was a prominent figure in the business world. Never having finished high school, Kerkorian began his career in the 1940s as a commercial pilot. He soon founded the Los Angeles Air Service, later known as Trans International Airlines Corporation. In 1969 he purchased controlling interest in MGM, his first takeover, worth $82 million, and became its CEO in 1974. He was responsible for the merger with United Artists that formed MGM/UA in 1981. In keeping with his desire to control his business ventures, he became the leading shareholder of the company. In 1986 he sold MGM/UA to Turner Broadcasting for $1.5 billion. The company was eventually sold back to Kerkorian, and he went on to sell it to Pathe Communications for $1.3 billion. In 1990 Kerkorian set his eyes on Chrysler. With over 10% of the company's stock in his hands, he began to plot with its former CEO, Lee Iacocca, to take over the company. His efforts failed, but the investment mogul walked away with a fortune, roughly 14% of shares worth $3 billion. Kerkorian regained control of MGM in 1996 when he bought it for $1.3 billion.

Chairman of Chrysler Corp.: Robert Eaton. Robert Eaton began his career in the automotive industry in the 1970s. A graduate of the University of Kansas, he started with General Motors as an engineer. He worked his way up through the company, working at various levels of engineering management in several different divisions. In 1986 he was named president of GM Europe, Zurich, and Switzerland. Eaton joined Chrysler in 1992 as vice chairman and Chief Financial Officer. That same year, he took over as CEO when Iacocca resigned. He is credited with reviving the company and leading the way to the highest profits Chrysler had ever seen. In 1995 he successfully fended off a takeover attempt by Kirk Kerkorian and was named "Industry Leader of the Year" and "Most Valuable Player" by *Automotive News* magazine. Eaton went on to lead the company through the merger with Daimler-Benz in 1998 and was named co-chairman of the new company, DaimlerChrysler.

tive publicity concerning safety and quality issues, as well as a lack of foreign interests. The next year, investors pushed down the stock price of all three of the U.S. automakers in anticipation of falling profits due to higher interest rates. Kirk Kerkorian, Chrysler's largest shareholder, was not happy with current stock prices. In November of 1994 he sent a letter to the board asking that certain steps be taken to increase stock price. As a result, Chrysler raised the dividend, announced a $1 billion stock buyback, and allowed Kerkorian to increase his stake in the company to 15%.

Chrysler now had a stockpile of cash worth $7.5 billion, which Kerkorian thought was far too much. Driven by greed, he sought the help of Lee Iacocca, the former chairman of Chrysler, to launch a takeover bid. Iacocca was willing to help since he believed that the company needed to think bigger, market more aggressively, and increase quality. He agreed that Chrysler had too much cash and that investors should be seeing some of that money. Many analysts felt that Iacocca was involved in the deal for revenge on the company that forced him to retire, claiming that he was trying to regain control of the industry. Iacocca denied such claims, stating that he was involved in the transaction as an advisor and was excited at the opportunity to continue his investment with Chrysler as a show of support for the company.

Approach and Engagement

Northwest Airline's co-chairman, Gary Wilson, approached Kirk Kerkorian with an idea of bidding on the Chrysler Corporation. The airline backed out of the deal, but the spark had been lit in the leveraged-buyout mind of Kerkorian. He had been in battle with the company over its undervalued stock for months and considered a takeover as the perfect vehicle to drive up prices.

Just as Robert Eaton, chairman of Chrysler, was about to present a speech at the New York auto show, his advisors briefed him on Kerkorian's plans. Eaton was shocked when he heard that the investment giant had enlisted the help of none other than Lee Iacocca, former chairman of Chrysler. He raced back to Michigan to discuss the offer with his board.

Kerkorian's deal called for him to put up his 36 million shares of Chrysler valued at $55 per share, a total of roughly $2 billion. Iacocca would put in 910,000 shares valued at $50 million. (Share price at the time of the deal was at $39 down from $55 per share.) The two would lobby for bank support of $12 billion, which they planned to add to Chrysler's debt, and look to outside investors for $3 billion. The kicker in the deal was that the duo planned to use $5.5 billion of the company's own cash reserves to finance the takeover.

Eaton took the April 12 bid to his board, which formally rejected it on April 24, 1995. The company said it was not for sale and that such a bid would cripple the company with debt and cause it major harm. Chrysler would be overrun with debt, product development would be hindered, it would be at a disadvantage come the next downturn, and, due to Iacocca's past relationship in foreign markets, future overseas deals could be non-existent.

Kerkorian did not give up that easily. In October of 1995, after his failed attempt with Iacocca, he sought out Jerome B. York, former Chief Financial Officer of Chrysler, to help him. York became vice chairman at Kerkorian's Tracinda Corporation. The two had similar opinions concerning Chrysler's management team, and they began to discredit Eaton. The next couple of months were not pleasant for Eaton, and he was noted with stating that Kerkorian was a disruptive force, one that the company hoped would go away

In 1996 Kerkorian's demands included three seats on the board and a return of the $6.9 billion cash reserve to its shareholders. He had upped his stake to 13.9% from 10%. Amid the attacks by Kerkorian, Chrysler doubled its dividend to $2 per share and initiated a $2 billion buyback program. In January of that year, the company extended its contract with Robert A. Lutz, CEO, until February of 1999 to fend off further advancement made by the raider. Kerkorian finally halted his hostile attacks, and in February of 1996, the automotive giant and investment mogul agreed to a five-year truce.

Products and Services

After months of battling Kerkorian, Chrysler could finally start focusing on pressing company issues. Small world car development and increasing market share in the United States were among its priorities. Chrysler continued to make plans with other automakers, hoping to forge a joint venture in which an all-new small car would be produced for developing countries. The company also focused on making Plymouth its entry-level nameplate. As part of the deal with Kerkorian, Chrysler was solidifying plans to sell its non-automotive operations, Chrysler Technologies Corporation, an aerospace and electronics unit, and its Rental Car Operations.

By 1998 the company manufactured such makes as Chrysler, Dodge, Eagle, Jeep, and Plymouth. These passenger cars made up 41% of total sales that year. Other automotive operations included four-wheel drive vehicles, commercial vehicles, trucks, and

The Players

Former CEO of Chrysler Corp.: Lee Iacocca. After graduating from Princeton, Lido Anthony Iacocca began his career with Ford Motor Company in 1946. His career with the automobile maker was successful as well as controversial, due to strained relations with Henry Ford II. In 1956, Iacocca masterminded the 56/56 deal, whereby a consumer could purchase a 1956 Ford for 20% down and only $56 a month. In 1964 he led the way in the development of the Mustang. Iacocca was named president of the company in 1970. The years to follow were marred by conflicts with Ford II, and in 1978, Iacocca was fired. In November of that year, he teamed up with Chrysler and became CEO of the company. Iacocca was faced with the challenge of restoring the company to profitability. In 1983, he pledged for a government loan guarantee, and with the help of layoffs, cutbacks, and personal advertising, the company got back on its feet. He released his autobiography in 1984, which became a national best seller. In 1992 he retired, naming Robert Eaton to take his place. After leaving Chrysler, he opened the Iacocca Capital Partners bank, participated in joint ventures with Native American investors concerning casinos on tribal lands, and joined the board of Kirk Kerkorian's MGM Grand. In 1995, he teamed up with Kerkorian in an effort to take over Chrysler. The buyout duo was rebuffed, however.

busses. Services, which made up 7% of total sales in 1998, included financial, insurance brokerage, information technology, telecommunications, and real estate management.

Changes to the Industry

The trend of globalization forced Chrysler to take a look at foreign markets in the late 1990s. With most of its sales coming from North America, the company was looking for a way to break into overseas markets. At the same time, Daimler-Benz, based in Germany, was looking for a way to diversify its product line. The two companies merged in 1998, gaining Chrysler a larger European market and exposing Daimler to Chrysler's expertise in product diversification.

Chrysler's export business was increasing as well. International shipments shot up 29% from 161,000 vehicles in 1994, to 208,000 in 1995. A little over half of those were made in the U.S. and Canada. The need for small, inexpensive vehicles in underdeveloped countries became a prominent concern as well. In India, for example, it was more economical for a U.S. company to produce and sell there by forging a relationship with a company that already had operations in that country.

Review of Outcome

Threats of takeover by Kirk Kerkorian were halted when in February of 1996 the battling investment guru and Chrysler came to a five-year truce. After two attempts, one with Iacocca and the other with the help of Jerome York, the heated negotiations stopped. Kerkorian could not find the financial backing he needed for the first attempt, and Chrysler made itself clear that it was not for sale.

In the terms of the truce, Kerkorian gained a board seat for James D. Aljian, a trusted Tracinda executive, and a stock repurchase plan in which Chrysler will spend $2 billion. It also called for certain changes in corporate policies that allowed an investor with cash or fully funded buyout offer to purchase more than 15% of company stock. Iacocca received a total of $53 million and all lawsuits for insider trading, which Chrysler had filed against Iacocca and Kerkorian, were dropped. As part of the deal Kerkorian was forced to reduce his stake in Chrylser to 13.6% or less. He was also promised that management needs would not overpower shareholder interests in the future.

Chrysler's stock closed at 50.88 in 1995 and 68.50 in 1996. The highs were 51.75 and 68.75, respectively, and net income was at $1.6 billion by the end of 1996.

Research

"Chrysler Corp.," in *Notable Corporate Chronologies*, The Gale Group, 1999. Lists major events in the history of Chrysler Corp.

"Chrysler Wants Kerkorian to Hit the Road," in *Ward's Auto World*, June 1995. Provides insight into Eaton's distaste for the takeover bid.

Cook, William. "Driving Defensively," in *U.S. News & World Report*, 23 October 1995. Discusses the emergence of Kerkorian's first takeover bid.

Gardner, Greg. "So Long Kirk, Hello Steve," in *Ward's Auto World*, April 1996. Describes the company's plan after the Kerkorian backed off from takeover attempts.

Jackson, Kelly. "Eaton: The All Stars' All Star," in *Automotive News*, 10 July 1995. Discusses the career of Robert Eaton.

———. "Kerkorian Truce Lets Chrysler Move On," in *Automotive News*, 12 February 1996. Explains the details of the truce between Kerkorian and Chrysler.

Meyer, Michael. "Is This Lee Iacocca's Bid for Revenge?," in *Newsweek*, 24 April 1995. Discusses possible reasons for Iacocca's involvement in the takeover bid.

"Peace Breaks Out between Chrysler, Kerkorian," in *Ward's Auto World*, March 1996. Explains details of the truce.

Sloan, Allan. "Rich and Much Richer," in *Newsweek*, 24 April 1995. Lists reasons for Kerkorian's bid on Chrysler.

Willis, Andrew. "Battle for Chrysler," in *Maclean's*, 24 April 1995. Explains the relationship between Kerkorian and Iacocca.

CHRISTINA M. STANSELL

KIMBERLY-CLARK & SCOTT PAPER

nationality: USA
date: December 13, 1995
affected: Kimberly-Clark Corp., USA, founded 1872
affected: Scott Paper Co., USA, founded 1879

Kimberly-Clark Corp.
351 Phelps Dr.
Irving, TX 75038
USA

tel: (972)281-1200
fax: (972)281-1435
web: http://www.kimberly-clark.com

Overview of the Merger

The 1995 merger between Kimberly-Clark and Scott Paper created the world's leading tissue producer and the second-largest provider of household and personal care products. It also was a competitive coup against Proctor & Gamble (P&G), with which Kimberly-Clark (K-C) had been engaged for years in a battle, often litigious, for market share.

Although K-C and Scott Paper operated in largely the same industry, each contributed strengths where the other was weak. K-C had prowess in facial tissue and personal care products. It was best known for such consumer brands as Kleenex tissue, Kotex feminine napkins, Huggies diapers, and Depend incontinence products. Its Kleenex brand held the leading 47.4% share of the U.S. market for facial tissue. The company had established a strong presence in the U.S. and Latin America, but had been unable to penetrate P&G's grip on the European market.

Scott Paper was a leader in consumer bathroom tissue and household towels. It possessed such well-known consumer brands as Scott tissue, Cottonelle bathroom tissue, and Viva paper towels. These products were in the lower-end price range, a perfect fit with K-C's higher end brands, as many retailers tended to stock products from these two segments, squeezing out the mid-range brands. In addition, Scott had a 20% share of the global commercial "away-from-home" market, an area where K-C was poorly represented. Scott derived about one-third of its revenue from Europe, where it was the leading tissue producer, and would provide K-C with the distribution network to break into that market.

History of Kimberly-Clark Corp.

In 1872 John A. Kimberly, Charles B. Clark, Frank C. Shattuck, and Havilah Babcock entered into a partnership to form Kimberly, Clark and Co. for the production of newsprint from linen and cotton rags. Operations expanded six years later when the partners assumed partial ownership and complete management of the Atlas paper mill in nearby Appleton, Wisconsin. In 1880 the company incorporated as Kimberly & Clark Co.

The Business

Financials

Revenue (1998): $12.3 billion

Employees (1998): 54,700

SICs / NAICS

sic 2676 - Sanitary Paper Products

sic 2621 - Paper Mills

sic 3842 - Surgical Appliances & Supplies

sic 5111 - Printing & Writing Paper

sic 5113 - Industrial & Personal Service Paper

naics 322291 - Sanitary Paper Product Manufacturing

naics 322121 - Paper (except Newsprint) Mills

In 1889 the firm constructed a large complex for the production of pulp and paper on the Fox River. In honor of John Kimberly the town that emerged around this operation was aptly named Kimberly. The company reorganized and incorporated as Kimberly-Clark Co. in 1906.

In 1914 company researchers hit on a product that proved invaluable to its future. In working with a pulp by-product of processed sugar cane, they produced crepe cellulose wadding (tissue). During World War I, this product, called cellucotton, was used to treat and dress wounds as a substitute for scarce surgical cottons. Army nurses discovered a second use for the material, as disposable padding for feminine hygiene needs. The company realized the commercial potential of cellucotton as a product for women, but was reluctant to market it under the Kimberly-Clark name. So, to shield itself from possible negative public relations, it formed the Cellucotton Products Co. to produce and sell the newly introduced Kotex feminine napkin, the first such item of its kind. Although many stores refused to stock or display the item, and magazines refused to advertise it, women drove the sales, demonstrating the huge market for the product.

In 1924 the company introduced Kleenex, a disposable tissue intended for the removal of cold cream. The company expanded internationally the following year by establishing Canadian Cellucotton Products Ltd. In a joint partnership with the New York Times Co., Kimberly & Clark built a newsprint mill in Ontario in 1926; this mill would later become known as Spruce Falls Power and Paper.

The company changed its name and went public in 1928 as the Kimberly-Clark Corp. Two years later, a survey revealed that consumers chose to use Kleenex tissues primarily as disposable handkerchiefs, and the company redirected its marketing strategy to that end. For the first time, the product was promoted for its current use, and within one year Kleenex sales doubled.

After World War II, the company expanded its facilities to meet revived consumer demands. Output was stepped up at existing plants, while new operations were built or acquired. In 1948 Kimberly-Clark began its foray into aviation with the purchase of a six-seat plane to be used as an executive shuttle.

During the 1950s the company established plants in Germany, Mexico, and the U.K. It also made a number of acquisitions, including Munising Paper Co., a manufacturer of saturated base papers; Neenah Paper Co., producer of cotton content correspondence papers; American Envelope Co.; and Peter J. Schweitzer, Inc., making Kimberly-Clark a world supplier of thin papers. In 1955 the company absorbed the Cellucotton Products Co.

In 1968 Kimberly-Clark debuted Kimbies, the first disposable diaper. The product, made of fluff pulp for greater absorbency, was initially considered successful. But eventually its sales declined due to leakage, and the product was withdrawn from the market. In 1969 the company's in-house air travel operation was converted into a profitable venture by offering corporate aircraft maintenance services; this new subsidiary was named K-C Aviation Inc.

Darwin E. Smith became president in 1971. He initiated major changes, including the sale or closure of six paper mills and the sale of over 300,000 acres of land in California. The acquired capital was used to increase the advertising budget and construct additional production facilities.

In 1975 Kimberly-Clark introduced feminine protection panty liners, the first product of its kind, under the trademark name Lightdays. The following year the company withdrew from the coated paper business in the U.S. and disposed of its Kimberly, Wisconsin, paper mill.

The company reentered the diapers market with its 1978 introduction of Huggies. This product was highly absorbent and had a superior fit due to elasticized legs. Huggies would eventually become the company's best-selling consumer product. It unveiled Depends, an incontinence product, in 1980. Nine years later it introduced Huggies Pull-Ups, disposable training pants for toddlers.

In 1984 the company formed Midwest Express Airlines, Inc. as a wholly-owned subsidiary of K-C Aviation, and began commercial flight service between Boston, Dallas, and Appleton and Milwaukee, Wisconsin. The following year, the corporate headquarters was relocated from Neenah to the Dallas area.

Procter and Gamble, producer of Pampers disposable diapers, filed suit against Kimberly-Clark in 1985, claiming patent infringement on its waistband material. A federal grand jury later ruled in favor of Kimberly-Clark, and the two companies began their adversarial relationship.

In 1990 the Spruce Falls Power and Paper Co. was divested in accordance with Kimberly-Clark's decision to exit from fiber-based, commodity class products. Two years later Darwin Smith retired and was succeeded as chairman by Wayne Sanders. That year the company joined with VP-Schickedanz of Germany to form an alliance for the production of consumer paper products. In 1994 its Kimberly-Clark Argentina SA subsidiary combined operations with Descartables Argentinos SA to manufacture personal-care products.

In December 1995 Kimberly-Clark acquired competitor Scott Paper Co. in a $9.2 billion merger, becoming a $12 billion global consumer products company. The following year it spun off Midwest Express Airlines through an initial public offering. In 1996 the company captured a 49% U.S. market share for facial tissue, 29% for bathroom tissue, 17% for household towels; 33% for disposable diapers, 28% for baby wipes, 74% for training pants, 27% for feminine care, and 53% for incontinence care.

In June 1997, the company sold its majority stake in Scott Paper Ltd., its Canadian tissue subsidiary. The following year it agreed to acquire Ballard Medical Products in order to expand its reach in the disposable medical supplies business.

History of Scott Paper Co.

In 1879 the Scott Paper Co. was founded by brothers E. Irvin Scott and Clarence R. Scott in Philadelphia to produce such coarse paper goods as bags and wrapping paper. It soon expanded operations, and by 1890 Scott Paper was the nation's leading producer of bathroom tissue. At the urging of Arthur Hoyt Scott, Irving's son, the company began to marketing toilet tissue under its own label. The company made its first acquisition in 1902, purchasing the Waldorf private label from one of its customers for name-brand toilet tissue.

In 1907 Scott introduced Sani-Towels, the nation's first paper towel. Tradition held that this invention

The Officers

Chairman and CEO: Wayne R. Sanders

Group President: Robert E. Abernathy

Group President, Personal Care Products: Kathi P. Seifert

Group President, Tissue, Pulp and Paper: Thomas J. Falk

Sr. VP and Chief Financial Officer: John W. Donehower

had been inspired by a Philadelphia schoolteacher who found it unsanitary for pupils to share the same cloth towel. Scott Paper went public in 1915. The following year Scott leapt ahead of its competition by selling its bathroom tissue by the sheet.

Thomas McCabe became president in 1927, and began Scott's long-term acquisition of mills, machines, and timberland with the purchase of a Nova Scotia, Canada, pulp mill and its attendant timber holdings. Scott was virtually unaffected during the Great Depression, in large part because the economic climate scarcely affects consumption of the products that Scott produced.

In 1936 it joined with The Mead Corp. to form Brunswick Pulp and Paper Co., which built and operated a pulp mill in Georgia to supply both Mead and Scott. During World War II, Scott continued to prosper despite paper shortages. Its sales in 1948 approached $75 million.

Scott aired the first television commercial for bathroom tissue in 1955. That year the company held a 38% share of the sanitary-paper business, with its closest competitor taking only 11%. Throughout the decade, its Scottie tissues and Scotkins napkins dominated the home paper products market with little competition. But its virtual monopoly of its market began to erode in 1957 with Procter & Gamble's entry into the home paper products market. That company acquired Charmin Paper Mills, a regional producer of facial and toilet tissues, paper towels, and napkins. Scott reacted by lowering its prices.

In 1965 it made its first non-paper acquisition with the purchase of Plastic Coating Corp. and its subsidiary, Tecnifax Corp. Two years later it purchased S.D. Warren, a maker of fine book papers. Within a few years, Warren's profits were eaten up by the general advertising recession and by the cuts in educational funding, which reduced the textbook market. In 1968 it purchased Brown Jordan, a maker of casual furniture, as well as two manufacturers of audio-visual aids.

The Players

Chairman and CEO of Kimberly-Clark Corp.: Wayne R. Sanders. After receiving a degree in civil engineering from the Illinois Institute of Technology, Wayne Sanders acquired an MBA from Marquette University in 1972. Three years later he joined Kimberly-Clark as a financial analyst. From there he worked his way up through various executive positions, becoming a vice president in 1981. Throughout the late 1980s, Sanders received a promotion on virtually an annual basis. In 1990 he became company president and chief operating officer, exchanging the COO position for the CEO role the following year. In 1992 Sanders was elected chairman, retaining his CEO responsibilities.

Chairman and CEO of Scott Paper: Albert J. Dunlap. Albert Dunlap earned a reputation as a turnaround specialist. During the 1980s he revived both Crown Zellerbach and Diamond International. When, after years of struggling, Scott Paper couldn't get in the black, Dunlap was brought in to work his magic. He was hired as CEO on April 19, 1994, and by the end of that month had replaced nine of the 11 members of the executive committee. He embarked on a program of intense cuts, including eliminating one-third of the company's workforce. As part of his reorganization program, Dunlap encouraged Scott's merger with Kimberly-Clark. Upon completion, he resigned and turned the company's management over to its new parent.

With 1969 sales at a record high, but with return on equity standing at only 12%, the company decentralized its management, thereby clearing the decision-making bottleneck that had plagued Scott. The company continued to slip, however, and its market share decreased to 33% from its 1960 hold of 45%. The number of Scott's competitors in the toilet tissue market had increased to 11, and in facial tissue to seven. Both markets were fully mature, growing at only about two percent annually. Between 1972 and 1977 Scott spent more than $600 million on new plants and equipment.

The company turned around with the 1976 launch of Cottonelle, Scott's answer to Charmin. Scott's aging facilities kept production costs high, however, and another capital-spending program was required to upgrade plants and expand capacity. By 1984 the market had settled a little. While Scott's Cottonelle toilet tissue and Viva paper towels still competed with Procter & Gamble's top-quality brands, ScotTissue and ScotTowels captured the midrange market, leaving the higher and lower ends of the market to Procter & Gamble, store brands, and cheaper labels. Profits that year rose 51% to $187 million on sales that increased five percent to $2.8 billion. Scott promptly bought back the 20.5% interest in Scott held by Brascan, Ltd., taking on a $300 million debt in the process, but eliminating any threat of takeover.

In 1989 Scott acquired the White Swan Tissue Division, a maker of sanitary products, from E.B. Eddy Forest Products of Canada. The following year it purchased a 51% stake in the sanitary tissue businesses of Feldmuhle in Germany and the Netherlands. Sales reached a record high for the eighth consecutive year, but earnings dropped 61%. In 1991 it sold its interest in Sanyo Scott, its Japanese joint venture. As part of ongoing cost-cutting efforts, 2,000 workers were laid off, with plans to lay off an additional 3,800 in 1992.

Al Dunlap became chairman and CEO in 1994. He immediately began making dramatic moves, including personally buying $4 million in Scott stock, selling assets, dramatically cutting staff, and closed the company's Philadelphia headquarters. It announced the closure of its tissue manufacturing operations in Fort Edward, New York, and the downsizing of its paper mill in Oconto Falls, Wisconsin. The resulting layoffs were part of the company's plan to reduce its global employment by 25%. In 1994 it announced that 10,500 jobs would be eliminated by the end of the year. After selling off S.D. Warren for $1.6 billion, Scott's 1994 revenues totaled $3.6 billion.

Market Forces Driving the Merger

The tissue paper products industry was breaking out of a depression in which it had been mired for several years. This $8 billion industry was largely dependent on the pulp and paper industry, which was subject to the ups and downs of the commodity market. Prices had been down, which affected the tissue industry in the same way. Competitive pricing had also worked to keep profitability down for tissue products.

Beginning in late 1994, however, fiber costs experienced a sharp rise. As a result, tissue producers began to raise their prices, a sign of a healthy market. With the horizon looking bright for continued paper cost increases, industry players became growingly confident about extending their reach. Often, the most efficient way to do this was to partner with an existing company in the target market.

K-C had acquired its fair share of battle scars against P&G in the ongoing quest for dominance in the diaper market. On several occasions, their disputes landed them in the courtroom. P&G had filed four major patent violation suits against K-C since the mid-1980s. Although the judicial outcome was not always in P&G's favor, the suits did accomplish slight victories outside the courtroom. K-C's market share for diapers dropped from 32% in 1985 to 29% in 1992.

Kimberly-Clark launched an offensive against P&G in 1990. Its Mexican subsidiary, K-C de Mexico, filed a patent infringement suit against P&G de Mexico. This was hardball. Since patent infringement was a criminal offense in Mexico, a prison term was a real possibility for the top executive at the P&G subsidiary. This matter, along with all pending legal disputes between the companies, was settled in April 1992. At the same time, K-C and P&G agreed to settle future disputes through arbitration.

K-C embarked upon a serious effort to penetrate the European diaper market in 1994. A price war between K-C and P&G ensued, with each company accusing the other of initiating it. Regardless of the instigator, however, P&G inadvertently allowed K-C to snag a 30% share of the French market. P&G's tough pricing endangered the future of Peaudouce, the leading French competitor, and it was subsequently acquired by K-C. Likewise, P&G's push in the Argentinean market enabled K-C to acquire a one-third interest in the domestic manufacturer, thereby increasing its market share to 41%.

Despite these segmented victories, K-C was still unable to increase its presence in Europe across the board. A merger with Scott Paper would enable it to benefit from that company's well-established distribution network in that market.

From Scott Paper's point of view, the driving force behind the desire to merge had less external drama than K-C's situation, but was far more important to the company internally. Albert Dunlap had been hired in April 1994 as the company's CEO, and immediately took bold steps to revive the unprofitable company. He instituted a major restructuring, divesting non-core businesses and eliminating about 11,000 of the company's positions, about one-third of its workforce. A merger with a complementary company was part of Dunlap's plan to strengthen its core operations.

Approach and Engagement

On July 17, 1995, Kimberly-Clark and Scott Paper announced their $9.4 billion merger agreement. The resulting company, which would retain the K-C name,

would become the world's leading tissue producer and the second-largest producer of household and personal care products. Wayne Sanders, chairman and CEO of K-C, would retain those positions at the new firm, and Albert Dunlap, chairman and CEO of Scott, would resign. The transaction would take place as a stock swap, in which Scott stockholders received .765 shares of K-C stock for each share of Scott.

On December 12, 1995, stockholders of each company approved the merger. That same day, both the U.S. Department of Justice and the European Commission (EC) granted their conditional approval. The Department of Justice required that K-C close several mills and divest itself of the Scotties facial tissue business and the baby wipes business, including the Baby Fresh, Wash-a-Bye Baby, and Kid Fresh brands. The EC needed additional time to evaluate the European aspect of the merger, but granted its approval for the non-European aspects. On December 13, Kimberly-Clark and Scott Paper were officially united.

On January 16, 1996, the EC granted its final approval, with several conditions. Since the deal would form the largest tissue producer in Europe, with more than twice the market share of its closest rival, it must make some changes in the facial and bathroom tissue market. Among other stipulations, the company must not combine the Kleenex bathroom tissue brand with Scott's Andrex brand in the U.K. and Ireland.

The new company was also bound by Canada's Competition Bureau to divest itself of its 50.1% controlling interest in Toronto-based Scott Paper Ltd., since the combined company would have a 45% control of the domestic tissue market. Likewise, the merger received approval from Mexico's Federal Competition Commission only after it agreed to sell off 67,000 tons per year of capacity, among other similar requirements.

Products and Services

Kimberly-Clark operated in eight consumer business segment. Tissue-Based Products included facial and bathroom tissue, paper towels, and wipers for household and away-from-home use. Personal Care Products included disposable diapers, training and youth pants, feminine and adult incontinence care products, wet wipes, and health care products. Its Family Care brands included Kleenex facial tissue, bathroom tissue, napkins, and paper towels; Cottonelle bathroom tissue and moist wipes; Viva paper towels; Scott bathroom tissue, napkins, and paper towels; and Hi-Dri paper towels. Infant Care consisted of Huggies diapers and baby wipes. Child

Care brands included Huggies Pull-Ups disposable training pants, GoodNites disposable underpants, and Huggies Little Swimmers disposable swimpants. Feminine Care products included Kotex pads, New Freedom Lightdays pantiliners, and Security tampons. Adult Care brands included Depend and Poise products for incontinence.

The Professional Health Care segment served the medical community with non-wovens products designed to resist penetration of blood and liquid-borne and airborne pathogens. Its lines included surgical products, sterilization products, infection control products, patient care products, orthopedic products, and wound care products.

The Away From Home segment served the industrial, hotel, and institutional markets with such washroom and workplace brands as Kleenex, Scott, Surpass, WypAll, and Kimwipes.

The company also operated a variety of additional businesses. Neenah Paper produced premium writing, text, and cover papers. Technical Paper included tape base paper, abrasive base paper, furniture component papers, label base papers, book cover and publishing papers, imaging papers, medical packaging papers, and colored kraft papers; it offered such brands as Munising LP cleanroom paper, Texoprint durable printing paper, Buckskin durable cover stock, Prevail fiber reinforced paper, Kimdura synthetic paper, Duraform latex saturated label, Kimlon compressible press packing, and Kimpreg latex saturated and coated paper. Nonwovens provided products for industrial filtration, as well as materials for making car and boat covers, industrial spill cleaning fabrics, furniture and bedding backing, protective apparel for health care workers, pre-moistened wipes for hand cleaning and disinfecting, and animal care products such as leg wraps.

Changes to the Industry

With the acquisition of Scott Paper, Kimberly-Clark saw its share of the bathroom tissue market jump from five percent to 31%. It more than tripled its share of the paper towel market, grabbing an 18% share. Its 70% dominant position in the Mexican market was a near monopoly. Similarly, it acquired a 56% share of the South Korean market and a 36% share in the Australian market.

The company had plenty of room to grow, however. The global disposable diaper market had barely been tapped, as only 10% of diaper use was of the disposable variety. In Mexico, for example, disposable diaper use was only 30% of total diapers; in Brazil it was only 20%, and in China it was practically nil.

Review of the Outcome

The workforce was significantly reduced as a result of the merger. The combined company eliminated about 6,000 positions, representing 10% of its global workforce. Rather than cutting those positions in waves, Kimberly-Clark decided to make the cuts in a single announcement because "we don't want axes hanging over people's heads," explained Wayne Sanders in *The Wall Street Journal*. About 2,700 of the eliminated positions arose from job redundancy, particularly in such administrative areas as sales and accounting. The remaining 3,300 came from the divestiture of up to 12 manufacturing facilities.

K-C took a $1.4 billion charge related to the merger. About $390 million was employee-related, including severance and relocation expenses. Disposal of facilities required about $285 million, miscellaneous acquisition expenses amounted to $250 million, and write-offs and write-downs cost $475 million.

Research

Glowacki, Jeremy J. "Kimberly-Clark Corp.: Accelerates Global Expansion with Scott Merger," in *Pulp & Paper*, December 1995. Describes the gains in international expansion that K-C will receive by merging with Scott Paper.

"K-C to Acquire Scott Paper, Create Tissue Giant," in *Pulp & Paper*, September 1995. Reports the merger announcement, as well as the strengths that each company would contribute to the union.

"Kimberly-Clark Corp.," in *Notable Corporate Chronologies*, The Gale Group, 1999. Lists major events in the history of the company.

Kimberly-Clark Corp. Home Page, available at http://www.kimberly-clark.com. Official World Wide Web Page for Kimberly-Clark. Includes access to product information, press releases, a company history, executive biographies, and investor information.

Lenzner, Robert, and Carrie Shook. "The Battle of the Bottoms," in *Forbes*, 24 March 1997. Describes the battle for market dominance between Kimberly-Clark and Proctor & Gamble.

Linden, Dana Wechsler. "'You Want Somebody to Like You, Get a Dog,'" in *Forbes*, 28 August 1995. An interview with Scott Paper's turnaround CEO, Albert Dunlap.

Lipin, Steven, and Paulette Thomas. "Kimberly-Clark to Acquire Scott Paper in Stock Deal Valued at About $6.8 Billion," in *The Wall Street Journal*, 17 July 1995. Details the strengths of each of the uniting companies, and the shape of the resulting operation.

"Merger Control: Kimberly/Scott Get All Clear to Create Paper Giant," in *Multinational Service*, 13 February 1996. The European Commission grants its approval of all aspects of the merger.

Murray, Matt. "Kimberly-Clark to Take Charge of $1.4 Billion," in *The Wall Street Journal*, 14 December 1995. Reports the expenses and job eliminations resulting from the recently completed merger.

"Scott Buyout to Mean Loss of 6,000 Jobs, Sale of 12 Plants," in *Pulp & Paper*, February 1996. Briefly discusses the impending plant sales and elimination of company positions.

"Scott Paper Co." in *Notable Corporate Chronologies*, The Gale Group, 1999. Profiles the company from its foundation through its acquisition by Kimberly-Clark.

DEBORAH J. UNTENER

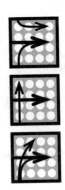

KLYNVELD MAIN GOERDELER &
PEAT, MARWICK, MITCHELL

KPMG International
345 Park Ave.
New York, NY 10154
USA

tel: (212)909-5000
fax: (212)909-5299
web: http://www.kpmg.com

nationality: USA
date: April 1, 1987
affected: Peat, Marwick, Mitchell & Co., USA, founded 1925
affected: Klynveld Main Goerdeler, The Netherlands, founded 1979

Overview of the Merger

The 1987 union of Klynveld Main Goerdeler and Peat, Marwick, Mitchell & Co. was the biggest merger in accounting history at that time. It immediately propelled the resulting company, Klynveld Peat Marwick Goerdeler, to the industry's top spot, as its revenues of $2.7 billion were nearly twice those of the next largest firm, Arthur Andersen & Co. By taking such a swift lead, KPMG touched off a wave of consolidation among the world's largest accounting firms.

History of Klynveld Main Goerdeler

The U.S. accounting firms Main Lafrentz and Hurdman Cranstoun merged to form Main Hurdman & Cranstoun in 1979. The new company then merged with a consortium of European accounting firms led by Klynveld Kraayenhoff of the Netherlands and Deutsche Treuhand of West Germany to form Klynveld Main Goerdeler, which immediately became the world's largest accounting firm. This federation also included Denmark's C. Jespersen, Canada's Thorne Riddel, the United Kingdom's Thomson McLintok, and Switzerland's Fides Revision. By 1985, however, KMG had slipped to the industry's sixth position.

Klynveld Main Goerdeler merged with Peat, Marwick, Mitchell & Co. in 1987 to form Klynveld Peat Marwick Goerdeler (KPMG), which immediately ranked as the largest accounting firm in both the U.S. and the world.

In 1989, Ernst & Young usurped KPMG as the largest accounting firm in the U.S. The next year Jon Madonna became president and immediately reorganized KPMG's management ranks, cutting the management team by 14% while raising the salaries of partners. Its administrative structure was also adjusted along interdisciplinary lines, replacing the previous tax, audit, and consulting divisions. Revenues increased by only 3% that year, however.

KPMG had fallen to fourth place among U.S. accounting firms by 1994. That year it settled the claims brought against it for accounting work performed for savings and loan institutions that later failed. As a result it agreed to pay $128 million to the Resolution Trust Corp. and $58.5 million to the Federal Deposit Insurance Corp.

KPMG mirrored the trend occurring among the nation's largest accounting firms by shifting its corporate focus from accounting to the provision of management consulting services in 1995. It formed KPMG Baymark Capital, an investment banking subsidiary able to offer clients services that the parent firm was unable to provide due to CPA independence requirements.

The firm acquired the bank consultancy firm Barefoot, Marrinan & Associates, Inc. in 1996. In October 1997, KPMG and Ernst & Young agreed to merge, forming the largest of the remaining Big Four, with $18 billion in revenues. However, increased governmental scrutiny over the shrinking pool of the industry's leading players was perceived to be too much of a challenge for the partners, so they terminated their agreement the next year.

In 1998, KPMG paid $75 million to settle claims brought against it over its audit of Orange County, California, which had declared bankruptcy several years earlier. Cisco Systems Inc. announced plans in August 1999 to invest more than $1 billion in KPMG's Internet services business. Stephen G. Butler, CEO since 1996, was named the successor of chairman Colin M. Sharman in September 1999.

History of Peat, Marwick, Mitchell & Co.

In 1897, James Marwick and Roger Mitchell founded Marwick, Mitchell & Co. to provide accounting services in New York City. The firm diversified into financial services in 1905, creating a subsidiary banking practice. Six years later, Marwick and William Peat, owner of a prestigious London accounting firm, agreed to a temporary merger of their companies, forming Peat, Marwick, Mitchell & Co. This alliance was made permanent in 1925, and the company changed its name to Peat, Marwick, Mitchell, & Copartners.

In 1950, Peat Marwick absorbed Barrow, Wade, Guthrie & Co., the oldest accounting firm in the U.S. The new company began to focus on the development of management consultancy operations. In 1972, it reorganized its international operations as PMM & Co. (International). Renamed six years later as Peat Marwick International, this unit acted as an umbrella company for national member firms outside of the U.S.

By 1986, Peat Marwick was one of the world's top accounting firms, second only to Arthur Anderson & Co. The next year it merged with Klynveld Main Goerdeler to form Klynveld Peat Marwick Goerdeler.

Market Forces Driving the Merger

The accounting industry in the early 1980s was ruled by a band of nine firms: Arthur Andersen & Co.;

The Business

Financials

Revenue (1998): $10.4 billion

Employees (1998): 92,000

SICs / NAICS

sic 8721 - Accounting, Auditing & Bookkeeping

sic 7291 - Tax Return Preparation Services

naics 541211 - Offices of Certified Public Accountants

naics 541213 - Tax Preparation Services

Arthur Young & Co.; Coopers & Lybrand; Deloitte Haskens & Sells; Klynveld Main Goerdeler; Peat, Marwick, Mitchell & Co.; Price Waterhouse; Touche Ross; and Ernst & Whinney.

In the late 1970s, accounting firms had set aside their distaste for advertising and stepped into the unfamiliar territory of marketing their services. This heightened competition in the industry, with the firms jockeying ever intently for increased market share and revenues. Globalization, both within the accounting industry and throughout the business world in general, put additional pressure on accounting firms to meet the increasingly demanding needs of clients who expected their accounting firms to be well-versed in international practices and issues. The drive to expand into new directions, to cover a greater geographic area, and to achieve economies of operation also spurred the members of the Big Eight to begin scouting within their ranks for merger partners.

In December 1984, Price Waterhouse and Deloitte Haskins & Sells announced a merger pact. Although this agreement was later terminated, it created intense pressure for the other companies for form similar unions.

Peat, Marwick, Mitchell & Co. had strong U.S. operations but a relatively weak international presence. This deficiency was particularly notable in Europe, where the firm had only 34 offices. Klynveld Main Goerdeler had the opposite difficulty. Its greatest strength was its operations in Europe, where it had 196 offices. In the U.S., however, the company was plagued by relative anonymity. It had been in search of a partner to increase its presence in the U.S., which was one of the leading markets for accounting and financial services. Without that presence "it would have been difficult for us to become No. 1, 2, or even

The Officers

Chairman: Stephen G. Butler

CEO: Paul C. Reilly

Regional Exec. Partner, Europe, Middle East Africa: Colin Holland

Regional Exec. Partner, Americas: Lou Miramontes

Regional Exec. Partner, Asia-Pacific: John Sim

No. 8," admitted Paul H. Boschma, KMG's international chairman, in *Business Week*. "So we decided a megamerger would be the best alternative."

Approach and Engagement

On September 3, 1986, Peat, Marwick, Mitchell & Co. and Klynveld Main Goerdeler announced their agreement to merge, thereby creating the world's largest accounting firm. Since the companies were organized as partnerships rather than publicly traded companies, they required the approval of member firms, not shareholders. On October 9 the companies' American partners, Peat, Marwick, Mitchell & Co. and KMG Main Hurdman, agreed to join, forming Peat Marwick Main & Co. The merger agreement continued to receive partnership approval throughout 1986 and into early 1987. On April 1, 1987, Klynveld Peat Marwick Goerdeler (KPMG) was formed.

Products and Services

KPMG operated from 825 locations in 157 countries, and its worldwide personnel count reached 92,000 in 1998. The firm's core services included audit and accounting, tax, management consulting, corporate finance, and corporate recovery. It served the following industries: banking and finance, building and construction, energy and natural resources, government, health care and life sciences, industrial products, information, communications and entertainment, insurance, retail and consumer products, and transportation. Management consulting was the greatest growth segment in 1998, with its revenues increasing over 30% to $3 billion.

Changes to the Industry and Review of the Outcome

Klynveld Peat Marwick Goerdeler had been born as the leading accounting firm in the world. With rev-

enues of $2.7 billion, it had a comfortable lead over the next largest company, Arthur Andersen, which had revenues of $1.6 billion. The other accounting firms of the Big Seven soon entered into alliances to form a company large enough to challenge or, ideally, supplant KPMG as the market leader.

These other companies were encouraged by KPMG's financial results as well. In the two years since its formation, KPMG had increased its revenues by 44%, to $3.9 billion. At the same time, it had reduced its overhead by trimming partners by 510, employees by 560, and offices by 127.

On July 7, 1989, two large deals were announced. Deloitte Haskins & Sells agreed to merge with Touche Ross & Co. to form Deloitte & Touche, and Ernst & Whinney agreed to combine with Arthur Young & Co. to form Ernst & Young. KPMG had been in existence for only a decade before it, too, began shopping around for another merger partner. In October 1997, it agreed to merge with Ernst & Young, but called off the pact in light of the anticipated difficulty in receiving regulatory approval to proceed. The leapfrogging continued, and on July 1, 1998, PricewaterhouseCoopers took the lead when it was formed through the merger of Price Waterhouse and Coopers & Lybrand.

Research

Greising, David with Leah J. Nathans and Laura Jereski. "The New Numbers Game in Accounting," in *Business Week*, 24 July 1989. Describes the consolidation in the accounting industry in the immediate years after the formation of KPMG.

KPMG International, available at http://www.kpmg.com. Official World Wide Web Page for KPMG International. Includes descriptions of products and services, topical accounting issues, and worldwide office locations.

"KPMG Peat Marwick L.L.P.," in *Notable Corporate Chronologies*, The Gale Group, 1999. Profiles the history of the company.

"KPMG Worldwide," in *International Directory of Company Histories*, Vol. 10, St. James Press, 1995. Provides a historical review of the company.

"Merger Numbers Add Up for Peat Marwick," in *The San Diego Union-Tribune*, 4 September 1986. Details the strengths and weaknesses of the merger partners.

Riley, Barry. "Accountancy: Globalisation Strains Structure," in *Financial Times (London)*, 15 December 1986. Profiles the challenges posed by globalization on accounting houses, with an emphasis on British firms.

Weiss, Stuart and Mark Maremont. "Peat Marwick Merges Its Way to the Top," in *Business Week*, 15 September 1986. Describes the newly announced merger deal.

DAVIS MCMILLAN

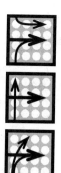

KOHLBERG KRAVIS ROBERTS & BEATRICE

nationality: USA
date: April 1986
affected: Kohlberg Kravis Roberts & Co., USA, founded 1976
affected: Beatrice Companies, USA, founded 1895

ConAgra, Inc.
One ConAgra Dr.
Omaha, NE 68102-5001
USA

tel: (402)595-4000
fax: (402)595-4707
web: http://www.conagra.com

Overview of the Acquisition

The 1986 buyout of Beatrice Companies by Kohlberg Kravis Roberts & Co. marked a turning point for the investment firm. The $6.2 billion leveraged buyout (LBO) was KKR's largest LBO yet, and turned the image of the investment firm from friendly acquirer to hostile raider. Even though the deal wasn't technically hostile, it was close enough to spur Jerome Kohlberg, a founding partner, to resign.

History of Kohlberg Kravis Roberts & Co.

Jerome Kohlberg, Jr., left Bear, Stearns & Co. in 1976 to establish his own investment firm. He brought in cousins Henry Kravis and George Roberts, also Bear Stearns employees, and the three partners formed Kohlberg Kravis Roberts.

They had amassed experience at Bear Stearns in the methods of acquiring companies, and decided to build their company around the leverage buyout (LBO). The LBO consisted of the use of an acquisition target's credit to secure the financing needed to purchase it. The company's assets are then sold off to repay that debt. Finally the company itself is sold, ideally at a large profit on the investment.

KKR developed a profile of the perfect LBO target. It should be undervalued and have a group of managers and/or shareholders that wanted to take the company private. And if it were in a state of leadership transition, all the better.

Despite its lofty goal of taking control of billion-dollar companies, KKR had modest beginnings. Its start-up capital was $120,000, and its office was a dingy, leased suite furnished with leftover desks and cabinets.

The partners immediately took its first steps toward success. One of its first deals was the $23 million buyout of A.J. Industries, a manufacturer of brake drums. After closing several other deals over its first two years, KKR went after its first Fortune 500 company, Houdaille Industries. This machine maker was acquired by KKR for $350 million in April 1979.

The Business

Financials

Revenue (1999): $24.6 billion

Employees (1998): 82,169

SICs / NAICS

sic 2068 - Salted & Roasted Nuts & Seeds

sic 2051 - Bread, Cake & Related Products

sic 2035 - Pickles, Sauces & Salad Dressings

sic 2015 - Poultry Slaughtering & Processing

naics 311911 - Roasted Nuts and Peanut Butter
Manufacturing

naics 311941 - Mayonnaise, Dressing, and Other Prepared
Sauce Manufacturing

naics 311615 - Poultry Processing

After this deal, the LBO gained wide recognition as an effective, and profitable, means of acquiring companies. Competitors to KKR quickly arose, but by this time KKR had established a reputation as an experienced LBO dealmaker, and investors began flocking to KKR's door.

Not all of the company's investments were successful, however. Its 1991 buyout of American Forest Products actually lost money, and its 1987 purchase of Walter Industries resulted in that company's bankruptcy. But these losses were shadowed by the firm's stellar deals. Between 1983 and 1984 KKR spent a total of $28 billion on seven companies, including its first $1 billion deal, for Wometco Enterprises.

The 1986 Beatrice Companies deal changed the image of the company, and with it the image of the LBO itself. By issuing the takeover deal as a virtual "bear hug," the company's board was left with little choice than to capitulate, selling the firm for $6.2 billion. Unhappy with an end to company's nice-guy image, Kohlberg resigned at the conclusion of the transaction.

In 1987, after resigning, Kohlberg sued his ex-partners for reducing his stake in KKR on deals that had been conducted while he was at the company; the suit was later settled quietly. This situation arose from Kohlberg's 1984 leave of absence for brain tumor surgery. Upon his return months later, Kravis and Roberts were unwilling to relinquish the control in the company that they had gained in his absence. They demand-

ed a larger share of profits to go along with their greater roles in KKR, thereby cutting Kohlberg's stake.

KKR bought out Safeway Stores for $4.4 billion in 1986, followed by Owens-Illinois the following year, and Stop & Shop in 1988. The monumental buyout of RJR Nabisco for $31 billion in 1988 garnered huge media attention and set the record as the largest LBO in corporate history.

The nation slid into a recession in 1989, bringing an end to the frenzy of mammoth LBOs. KKR began making more investments than full-scale takeovers. That year it established K-III Communications Corp. to manage its broadcasting and media interests. In September 1992 it invested $300 million in American Re Corp., the third-largest reinsurance company in the U.S.

By mid-1994 KKR had spent $70 billion on over 40 companies. That year it swapped its investment in RJR Nabisco for the acquisition of Borden, Inc. Two years later KKR ventured into Europe, acquiring Reed Regional Newspapers for $324 million. In April 1999 KKR entered into the bidding for the 900-unit chain of Hoyts Cinemas, with the plan to consolidate the U.S. movie theaters into its Regal Cinema chain.

History of Beatrice Company

George Haskell, a former bookkeeper for the Fremont Butter and Egg Company, purchased that defunct company in 1891. Four years later he founded the Beatrice Creamery Company with $40,000 in start-up capital, and the company began producing butter. In 1898 the firm was incorporated as the Beatrice Creamery Company of Nebraska and produced 940,000 pounds of butter.

Early growth was hampered by economic hardship, scarce financing, low prices, and drought. The company survived, however, by distributing fresh butter directly to grocery stores, restaurants, and hotels. It soon ventured into the cold storage business, a peripheral business due to the refrigeration plants required to manufacture butter.

In 1901 the company registered the trademark Meadow Gold for its butter, which it marketed on a national scale in 1912. Beatrice grew steadily through the 1940s. It expanded into other dairy products, and pioneered many innovations in the industry. It was the first to sell packaged butter in sealed cartons, and was one of the first companies to pasteurize churning butter on a large scale.

Beatrice opened an ice cream plant in 1907, and became the first company to advertise ice cream on a national level. It ventured into the distribution of milk, cottage cheese, and buttermilk with the 1923 purchase of a fluid milk plant in Denver. The company also introduced homogenized milk in 1930.

The U.S. government demanded a 30% share of all butter during World War II, and rationed the rest. It also froze milk prices and limited the use of milk fats and solids in ice cream. In 1941 Beatrice produced 70 million pounds of butter.

As part of a program to diversify out of dairy products, it purchased La Choy, a maker of oriental food products, in 1943. Three years later, reflecting its wider focus, the company changed its name to Beatrice Foods Company. The firm's diversification program was further promoted by William Karnes, who became president in 1952. He led the company into expansion and growth not only in the foods industry, but also into such areas as luggage, furniture, and chemicals.

The company's steady growth, however, increasingly fell short of Wall Street expectations. While Beatrice itself was less interested in profitability than growth, its shareholders were not. To appease them Karnes named Wallace Rasmussen as president upon Karnes' retirement in 1976. Rasmussen ignored the wishes of Wall Street, and continued to make acquisitions. Among them were the Culligan water-softening company and the Tropicana Products orange juice producer.

When James Dutt became CEO upon Rasmussen's retirement in 1980, he faced the daunting challenge of streamlining the company to improve profitability. He divested those companies returning under 20%, including Airstream, the trailer producer; Morgan Yacht Corp.; Dannon Company; and the Royal Crown Cola and Seven-Up domestic soft drink franchises.

In 1981, however, he reversed his popular divestiture program by acquiring the Coca-Cola Bottling Company of Los Angeles and Buckingham Corp., the importer of Cutty Sark and other liquors. He defended these purchases by claiming that they fit in with his plan to transform Beatrice into a marketing giant. He quintupled the company's advertising and marketing budget to $800 million. The company also changed its name again, to Beatrice Companies, in 1984.

Dutt then purchased Esmark, a food and consumer products company, in 1984 for $2.7 billion—23 times its earnings. He had acquired a reputation as an autocrat; by mid-1985, 37 of the company's top officers had resigned since Dutt had taken control.

Disappointed in Dutt's leadership methods and unsuccessful marketing expansion, Beatrice's board asked for his resignation in August 1985. William

The Officers

Chairman, President and CEO: Bruce C. Rohde

Exec. VP, CFO, and Corporate Secretary: James P. O'Donnell

Exec. VP and Chief Administrative Officer: Gerald B. Vernon

Chairman, ConAgra Agri-Products: Floyd McKinnerney

Chairman, Lamb-Weston and President, ConAgra Foodservice Sales: Richard A. Porter

Granger, Jr., emerged as an interim CEO, but was soon displaced by Donald Kelly, who joined with Kohlberg Kravis Roberts & Co. to orchestrate the $6.2 billion leverage buyout of the company. Beatrice was reorganized as the wholly owned subsidiary of BCI Holdings Corp.

Kelly lost no time streamlining the company. Only 12 days after taking the helm, he sold Avis for $250 million. He continued to dismantle the firm, selling off E-II, a collection of 15 consumer goods and specialty food companies; Playtex; the Los Angeles Coca-Cola Bottler; International Foods; and Tropicana. In 1987 he changed BCI's name to Beatrice Company to reflect its return to the food industry.

Kelly resigned as CEO in mid-1987 and as chairman in October 1988; Frederick Remtschler was named his successor in both positions. In 1991 Beatrice was purchased by ConAgra, Inc.

Market Forces Driving the Acquisition

During the 1980s the leverage buyout (LBO) was a powerful means of gaining control of a company, and Kohlberg Kravis Roberts & Co. was a master at it. This investment firm sought to increase its wealth by acquiring control of an undervalued, sell off parts of it to repay the debt it had accrued in purchasing it, and then selling the remainder of the newly-private company at a profit.

Beatrice Companies was a prime target for such a buyout. It was flailing about under the mismanagement of CEO James Dutt. His recklessness led the company's board to request his resignation. An interim CEO emerged, but the company's leadership was still shaky.

At this time Donald P. Kelly, leader of Beatrice's recently acquired Esmark subsidiary, approached KKR. He assured the buyout shop that if it could gain

The Players

Kohlberg Kravis Roberts & Co. Founder: Jerome Kohlberg. Jerome Kohlberg put the leveraged buyout (LBO) on the map. He had been skilled in its application as early as the 1960s, as a partner of Bear, Stearns & Co. After success in several LBOs, he recruited Henry Kravis and George Roberts to help him put more deals together. In 1976 the three men left Bear Stearns to form their own LBO specialist, Kohlberg Kravis Roberts. One decade later, however, Kohlberg resigned out of protest to the firm's new-hostile approach to the takeover of Beatrice.

Esmark President: Donald P. Kelly. Donald Kelly, head of the Esmark subsidiary of Beatrice, was the "inside man" behind the leveraged buyout of Beatrice. He assured Kohlberg Kravis Roberts that if that firm were to acquire control of Beatrice, Kelly would be able to improve its condition as its leader. Upon conclusion of the transaction, he held true to his word. As CEO of Beatrice he sold off several non-core pieces and cut frivolous expenses, garnering a handsome profit for KKR. All this he accomplished in remarkably short time. Kelly stepped down as CEO in mid-1987, and resigned as chairman the following year.

control, he would serve as an enthusiastic and effective leader of Beatrice.

Approach and Engagement

On October 16, 1985, KKR offered Beatrice's board $5.6 billion for the company. The board rejected the bid as inadequate, and tried to mobilize a buyout team of its own to deter KKR. The company's managers were unable to secure the necessary backing, however.

KKR's offer, while technically not hostile, was a "bear hug"—a bid so lucrative that it put pressure on the target company's board to accept it in the best interest of its shareholders. Those shareholders put pressure on Beatrice's board as well, given the company's current condition.

Beatrice's board finally accepted KKR's sweetened deal. The $6.2 billion bid consisted of a capital structure made up of bank loans, junk bonds, and equity. In April 1986 the transaction was completed, and Beatrice became part of KKR's BCI Holdings Corp.

Products and Services

In 1998, after ConAgra purchased Beatrice, the company's consumer brands consisted of: La Choy, Wesson, Swiss Miss, Hebrew National, Country Pride, Orville Redenbacher, County Line, Healthy Choice, Hunt's, Eckrich, Butterball, ACT II, Banquet, Amour, Decker, Peter Pan, Swift Premium, Cook's, Van Camp's, and Marie Callender's.

Review of the Outcome

As part of their pact, KKR installed Donald Kelly to the position of CEO. He immediately began cutting expenses by slashing marketing efforts and killing promotional campaigns, including those revolving around auto racing, of which Beatrice's former CEO Dutt had been an enthusiast.

More importantly, however, Kelly restored the company's focus and divested non-core businesses. He sold Avis for $275 million, the Los Angeles Coca-Cola bottling companies for $1 billion, Playtex for $1.25 billion, Tropicana for $1.2 billion, and International Foods for $985 million. He consolidated Beatrice's non-food businesses as E-II Holdings, which was spun off to shareholders; it was later purchased for $800 million by American Brands, which E-II had been pursuing as an acquisition target.

By autumn 1998 Kelly's steady dismantling of Beatrice had earned more than $7.3 billion, already surpassing KKR's purchase price. Upon the sale of Beatrice to ConAgra in 1991, KKR's investment had recouped net proceeds of $2.2 billion.

Research

"Beatrice Company.," in *International Directory of Company Histories*, Vol. II, St. James Press: 1990. Discusses the company's history, through its takeover by KKR.

Burrough, Bryan, and John Helyar. *Barbarians at the Gate: The Fall of RJR Nabisco*, Harper & Row, 1990. Offers a detailed examination of KKR's takeover of RJR Nabisco, and sheds insight into the firm and its major players.

ConAgra, Inc. Home Page, available at http://www.conagra.com. Official World Wide Web Page for ConAgra. Includes product and financial information, a company history, and officer biographies.

"ConAgra Reports Fiscal 1999 Results," from *PR Newswire*, 1 July 1999. Discloses the company's financial results.

Loomis, Carol J. "Has the Beatrice LBO Gone Pffft?" in *Fortune*, 31 July 1989. Speculates that the buyout of Beatrice fell below expectations.

Wasserstein, Bruce. *Big Deal: The Battle for Control of America's Leading Corporations*, Warner Books, 1998. Offers an overview of the largest mergers in recent American corporate history.

SAMANTHA MORRISON

KOHLBERG KRAVIS ROBERTS & BORDEN

nationality: USA
date: December 21, 1994
affected: Kohlberg Kravis Roberts & Co., USA, founded 1976
affected: Borden, Inc., USA, founded 1857

Kohlberg Kravis Roberts & Co.
9 W. 57th St., Ste. 4200
New York, NY 10019
USA

tel: (212)750-8300
fax: (212)750-0003

Overview of the Acquisition

In acquiring Borden Inc. in 1994, Kohlberg Kravis Roberts & Co. killed two birds with one stone: it took a stake in a company that it believed would provide a return on its investment, and it provided a vehicle through which to unload its stake in the languishing RJR Nabisco.

History of Kohlberg Kravis Roberts & Co.

Jerome Kohlberg, Jr., left Bear, Stearns & Co. in 1976 to establish his own investment firm. He brought in cousins Henry Kravis and George Roberts, also Bear Stearns employees, and the three partners formed Kohlberg Kravis Roberts.

They had amassed experience at Bear Stearns in the methods of acquiring companies, and decided to build their company around the leveraged buyout (LBO). The LBO consisted of the use of an acquisition target's credit to secure the financing needed to purchase it. The company's assets are then sold off to repay that debt. Finally the company itself is sold, ideally at a large profit on the investment.

KKR developed a profile of the perfect LBO target. It should be undervalued and have a group of managers and/or shareholders that wanted to take the company private. And if it were in a state of leadership transition, all the better.

Despite its lofty goal of taking control of billion-dollar companies, KKR had modest beginnings. Its start-up capital was $120,000, and its office was a dingy, leased suite furnished with leftover desks and cabinets.

The partners immediately took its first steps toward success. One of its first deals was the $23 million buyout of A.J. Industries, a manufacturer of brake drums. After closing several other deals over its first two years, KKR went after its first Fortune 500 company, Houdaille Industries. This machine maker was acquired by KKR for $350 million in April 1979.

After this deal, the LBO gained wide recognition as an effective, and profitable, means of acquiring companies. Competitors to KKR quickly arose, but by

The Business

SICs / NAICS

sic 6799 - Investors Nec

naics 523910 - Miscellaneous Intermediation

this time KKR had established a reputation as an experienced LBO dealmaker, and investors began flocking to KKR's door.

Not all of the company's investments were successful, however. Its 1991 buyout of American Forest Products actually lost money, and its 1987 purchase of Walter Industries resulted in that company's bankruptcy. But these losses were shadowed by the firm's stellar deals. Between 1983 and 1984 KKR spent a total of $28 billion on seven companies, including its first $1 billion deal, for Wometco Enterprises.

The 1986 Beatrice Companies deal changed the image of the company, and with it the image of the LBO itself. By issuing the takeover deal as a virtual "bear hug," the company's board was left with little choice than to capitulate, selling the firm for $6.2 billion. Unhappy with an end to company's nice-guy image, Kohlberg resigned at the conclusion of the transaction.

In 1987, after resigning, Kohlberg sued his ex-partners for reducing his stake in KKR on deals that had been conducted while he was at the company; the suit was later settled quietly. This situation arose from Kohlberg's 1984 leave of absence for brain tumor surgery. Upon his return months later, Kravis and Roberts were unwilling to relinquish the control in the company that they had gained in his absence. They demanded a larger share of profits to go along with their greater roles in KKR, thereby cutting Kohlberg's stake.

KKR bought out Safeway Stores for $4.4 billion in 1986, followed by Owens-Illinois the following year, and Stop & Shop in 1988. The monumental buyout of RJR Nabisco for $31 billion in 1988 garnered huge media attention and set the record as the largest LBO in corporate history.

The nation slid into a recession in 1989, bringing an end to the frenzy of mammoth LBOs. KKR began making more investments than full-scale takeovers. That year it established K-III Communications Corp. to manage its broadcasting and media interests. In September 1992 it invested $300 million in American Re Corp., the third-largest reinsurance company in the U.S.

By mid-1994 KKR had spent $70 billion on over 40 companies. That year it swapped its investment in RJR Nabisco for the acquisition of Borden. Two years later KKR ventured into Europe, acquiring Reed Regional Newspapers for $324 million. In April 1999 KKR entered into the bidding for the 900-unit chain of Hoyts Cinemas, with the plan to consolidate the U.S. movie theaters into its Regal Cinema chain.

History of Borden, Inc.

In 1851 Gail Borden, Jr., founded the *Telegraph and Texas Register*, which became famous for its "Remember the Alamo" headline. The following year Borden invented a portable bathhouse, a wind-powered wagon (the prairie schooner), an oar-driven steamboat, the lazy Susan, and a nonperishable meat biscuit that pointed the way for other important discoveries such as how to make nonperishable milk. His work on preventing contamination and spoilage of milk paid off in 1856 when his process of heating and condensing milk in a vacuum received a patent as a result of strong recommendations from Texas senator Samuel Houston; Robert McFarlane, editor of *Scientific American*; and John H. Currie, the head of a research facility.

In 1857 Borden established Gail Borden Jr. and Co. to manufacture and distribute condensed milk. It changed its name to New York Condensed Milk Co. the following year upon receipt of a capital infusion from Jeremiah Millbank. The company grew during the U.S. Civil War, as the demand for canned milk increased. Borden's company licenses other companies to manufacture their milk to maintain sufficient production. By 1874 it was the largest producer of condensed milk in the U.S.

The company added fresh, fluid milk, evaporated milk, and caramels throughout the century, and acquired Elgin Condensed Milk Co. in 1894. Five years later the company expanded internationally by purchasing an evaporated milk plant in Ingersoll, Ontario.

The company changed its name to Borden Co. in 1919. By 1928, it had embarked on a program of expansion and diversification. It purchased the Merrell-Soule Co., thereby acquiring the patents for drying milk, and the rights to manufacture KLIM whole milk powder and None Such mincemeat, the company's first non-dairy product. The company also acquired J.M. Horton Ice Cream Co. and the Reid Ice Cream Corp.

In 1929 Borden became the holding company for four operating companies: Borden's Food Products, Borden's Dairy Products, Borden's Ice Cream and

Milk, and Borden's Cheese and Produce. That year it also acquired the Casein Co. of America, the leading maker of glues in the U.S.

Elsie the Cow was introduced as a cartoon character in 1936 to symbolize purity and wholesomeness and to establish nationwide awareness of the company and its products. Because of increased prices for fluid milk and federal regulations restricting Borden from passing the increase on to customers, Borden's profits sank during the Depression. During World War II, however, orders for exportation of condensed and evaporated milk and milk powder increased. The U.S. military also purchased large quantities of synthetic adhesives from Borden for the construction of PT boats.

In 1947 Borden introduced Elmer's Glue-All, the first household adhesive, and Lady Borden ice cream, the first nationally distributed premium ice cream in the U.S. A chemical manufacturing subsidiary in Argentina was formed and Durite Plastics, Inc. was acquired. The company also entered the market of molding compounds made from synthetic thermosetting resins. Three years later it introduced E-Z Cheez mix for cheesecake, initiating operations for supplying flavorings and coatings to other food manufacturers.

Chemical operations increased during the 1950s. In 1953 Borden gained full ownership of its United Kingdom chemical subsidiary and acquired American Polymer Corp., a manufacturer of vinyl, acrylic, and methacrylic products. Chemical operations in Mexico also began that year. In 1955 it acquired several makers of paint, paper, and textile coatings and binders: American Monomer Corp., Monomer-Polymer, Inc., American Resinous Chemicals Corp., and Reslac Chemicals, Inc. Its first polyvinyl alcohol was produced in 1959, marking the near total integration of its chemical business.

In 1961 Borden purchased Wyler & Co., a leading maker of powdered drink mixes and dehydrated soups; Greenwood Foods, Inc., the largest U.S. packager of red cabbage and pickled beets; its second ink company, Hawley-Monk Co.; and Columbus Coated Fabrics Corp., a coated wallcoverings manufacturer. Annual sales eclipsed $1 billion for the first time. Two years later it introduced Cremora non-dairy creamer. That year Borden also acquired Aunt Jane's Foods, Inc., a major packager of pickles; Old London Foods, Inc., the leading maker of melba toast; and Mystick Adhesives Products, Inc., number two in production of pressure-sensitive tapes.

Borden continued its acquisition spree, adding a number of new companies in 1964: Wise Foods, Inc., maker of salty snacks and the leading potato chip maker in the eastern U.S.; the Cracker Jack Co., maker

The Officers

Co-Founder: Henry R. Kravis

Co-Founder: George Roberts

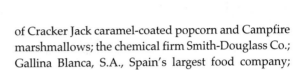

of Cracker Jack caramel-coated popcorn and Campfire marshmallows; the chemical firm Smith-Douglass Co.; Gallina Blanca, S.A., Spain's largest food company; and Wilhelm-Wever GmbH, Germany's largest commercial and retail baker.

Borden entered the hair spray and fragrance markets through the acquisitions of Ozon Products, Inc. and Jean Patou in 1966. It also purchased Krylon, Inc., a leading maker of household spray paints. In 1969 it added the 51-unit BBF, Inc. restaurant chain and Crystal Springs Water Co. The next year it purchased Deran Confectionery and Chicago Almond Products Co., thereby entering the candy and the processed nut businesses, respectively.

The company purchased the Pepsi-Cola Bottling Co. of Indianapolis in 1971, followed by several other Pepsi bottling franchises later in the decade. In 1977, in response to the worldwide energy crisis, Borden founded an Energy Resources Department and began actively exploring for new natural gas sources. Two years later it acquired Creamette Co., Buckeye Potato Chip Co., and Guy's Foods, Inc.

During the 1980s Borden initiated a $1.5 billion development program consisting of selling noncore assets and reinvesting the revenue in growth areas: packaged consumer products and specialty chemicals. It spent $1.9 billion on the acquisition of more than 90 companies. In 1986 Borden began to focus on pasta, snacks, niche grocery, dairy, non-consumer, and film/adhesive products as facilities consolidated and realigned. Annual sales that year exceeded $5 billion. The purchase of the Prince Company in 1987 made Borden the nation's leading pasta maker, with a 33% share of the market.

In 1989 Borden embarked on an effort to establish efficient, low-cost production and aggressive marketing. It set aside a sum of $404 million to brace it against the cost of implementing this plan, which included the closure of 45 older and smaller plants as production and distribution were to be consolidated in the most modern and efficient facilities. Three years later the company announced plans to cut 1,300 jobs, most of them in dairy or Far Eastern operations. By that time Borden was the largest maker of ice cream in the world; it was also the largest maker of synthetic

The Players

Kohlberg Kravis Roberts & Co. Co-Founder: Henry R. Kravis. Henry Kravis, a native of Tulsa, Oklahoma, earned a degree in economics before receiving an MBA from Columbia University. In 1969 he joined the ranks of Bear, Stearns & Co., where he worked with his cousin George Roberts and his mentor Jerome Kohlberg, Jr. In 1976 the three men left Bear Stearns to found Kohlberg Kravis Roberts & Co. Since that time Kravis has orchestrated some of the largest leveraged buyouts (LBOs) in corporate history.

adhesives in the U.S., and Elmer's Glue-All was the world's most popular household glue.

In 1994 Borden sold the bulk of its food service to Heinz for $130 million. After watching Borden's market value decline rapidly in the space of only a couple of years, Kohlberg Kravis Roberts & Co. took over Borden in December 1994 with a plan to revamp the troubled company. At that time Borden reported a $484 million fourth-quarter loss.

Veteran consultant and turnaround leader C. Robert Kidder was named CEO of the company in January 1995. In a continued effort to turn itself around, Borden announced plans to sell part of its dairy business later that year. Divestitures continued, as Borden Foods refocused on the core operations of "grain-based meal solutions." Among such divestitures were its Borden/Meadowgold Dairies business, its Cracker Jack business, its cheese division, and its decorative products business.

Market Forces Driving the Acquisition

Borden Inc., the foods and chemicals conglomerate, experienced poor financial performance for several years. It had attempted a recovery by divesting unprofitable assets, undergoing numerous restructurings, and cutting its workforce. None of the efforts had a lasting impact, however. In 1994 Borden's management instructed the company's brokers to locate a potential buyer for the troubled company.

Meanwhile, Kohlberg Kravis Roberts & Co. was always in the market to make money. This investment firm had acquired fame—and wealth—through such well-publicized leveraged buyouts (LBOs) as that of RJR Nabisco. That controversial acquisition had turned sour in the hands of KKR, reporting six years of dismal returns. Private label competition and anti-

tobacco sentiments had hurt the company. In 1991 KKR had spun off a 60% stake in RJR through an initial public offering.

Ideally, KKR was looking to participate in a transaction that would be both a sound investment and a means of divesting itself of its remaining stake in RJR. In 1994 Borden fit the bill.

Approach and Engagement

On September 1994 Kohlberg Kravis Roberts and Borden entered into an agreement in principle. The deal called for KKR to acquire all of Borden in exchange for $2 billion of KKR's stake in RJR Nabisco, thereby reducing KKR's stake to about 17.5%. In addition RJR would purchase a 20% stake in Borden. On September 23 the companies signed a definitive agreement.

Despite this agreement, Paul Kazarian tried to enter into the bidding. He proposed a vague $2.4 billion deal, to be offered through his company, Japonica Partners L.P. Borden's management never took this offer very seriously, however, since Kazarian had refused to comply with its repeated requests for the specifics of his proposal.

Throughout the proceeding Borden continued to shed assets. It agreed to sell Wise Foods, Campfire Marshmallows, and Coco Lopez, as well as its entire dairy division.

On December 21, 1994, KKR acquired control of Borden. On that day 63.5% of Borden's shares had been tendered, significantly more than the 40% needed to close the deal.

Products and Services

In 1998 Borden operated in three main product segments. Its Borden Foods division encompassed the pasta brands Creamette and Prince, the Classico pasta sauce, and Wyler's brand bouillon and dry soup mixes. Its Chemicals unit contained operations in adhesives, coatings, melamine crystal, resins, and specialty inks. Finally, consumer adhesives were part of the Elmer's Products division.

Review of the Outcome

KKR officially took the reins at Borden on March 15, 1995. At that time two board members tendered their resignations, reportedly due to the changing nature of the company. KKR also officially cut ties with RJR Nabisco, having transferred its remaining stake in that company to Borden.

After KKR's assumption of control, Borden underwent yet another reorganization. That May nine independent business units were established. The planned sale of its Wise snack business was cancelled, and the company decided to retain its dairy operations west of the Mississippi.

Research

"Borden Inc.," in *Notable Corporate Chronologies*, The Gale Group, 1999. Offers a history of the company.

"Borden Rejects Rival Bid from Japonica," in *Milling & Baking News*, 13 December 1994. Reports Borden's rejection of Kazarian's rival acquisition offer.

"Borden Signs Definitive Merger Plan with KKR," in *Milling & Baking News*, 4 October 1994. Describes the merger agreement.

Burrough, Bryan, and John Helyar. *Barbarians at the Gate: The Fall of RJR Nabisco*, Harper & Row, 1990. Offers a detailed examination of KKR's takeover of RJR Nabisco, and sheds insight into the firm and its major players.

"A Kinder, Gentler Barbarian," in *The Economist*, 17 September 1994. Describes KKR's more friendly approach to acquiring Borden than it had used in gaining control of RJR Nabisco.

"A New Life for Borden," in *Prepared Foods*, July 1995. Explains the restructuring at Borden Inc. after the acquisition.

Schiffrin, Matthew. "Milk for Cigarettes?" in *Forbes*, 10 October 1994. Briefly reports the preliminary acquisition agreement.

Wasserstein, Bruce. *Big Deal: The Battle for Control of America's Leading Corporations*, Warner Books, 1998. Offers an overview of the largest mergers in recent American corporate history.

SAMANTHA MORRISON

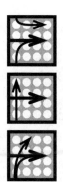

KOHLBERG KRAVIS ROBERTS & RJR NABISCO

Nabisco Group Holdings Corp.
1301 Avenue of the Americas
New York, NY 10019
USA

tel: (212)258-5600
fax: (212)969-9173
web: http://www.rjrnabisco.com

nationality: USA
date: November 30, 1988
affected: Kohlberg Kravis Roberts & Co., USA, founded 1976
affected: Nabisco Group Holdings Corp. (formerly RJR Nabisco Holdings Corp.), USA, founded 1874

Overview of the Acquisition

The $25 billion takeover of RJR Nabisco by Kohlberg Kravis Roberts & Co. was the largest leveraged buyout (LBO) in corporate history, far surpassing Chevron's $13.3 billion takeover of Gulf Oil in 1984. The LBO developed into a bidding war involving several rivals, but the chief contenders were KKR and a management team led by F. Ross Johnson, RJR's president.

History of Kohlberg Kravis Roberts & Co.

Jerome Kohlberg, Jr., left Bear, Stearns & Co. in 1976 to establish his own investment firm. He brought in cousins Henry Kravis and George Roberts, also Bear Stearns employees, and the three partners formed Kohlberg Kravis Roberts.

They had amassed experience at Bear Stearns in the methods of acquiring companies, and decided to build their company around the leveraged buyout (LBO). The LBO consisted of the use of an acquisition target's credit to secure the financing needed to purchase it. The company's assets are then sold off to repay that debt. Finally the company itself is sold, ideally at a large profit on the investment.

KKR developed a profile of the perfect LBO target. It should be undervalued and have a group of managers and/or shareholders that wanted to take the company private. And if it were in a state of leadership transition, all the better.

Despite its lofty goal of taking control of billion-dollar companies, KKR had modest beginnings. Its start-up capital was $120,000, and its office was a dingy, leased suite furnished with leftover desks and cabinets.

The partners immediately took its first steps toward success. One of its first deals was the $23 million buyout of A.J. Industries, a manufacturer of brake drums. After closing several other deals over its first two years, KKR went after its first Fortune 500 company, Houdaille Industries. This machine maker was acquired by KKR for $350 million in April 1979.

After this deal, the LBO gained wide recognition as an effective, and profitable, means of acquiring companies. Competitors to KKR quickly arose, but by this time KKR had established a reputation as an experienced LBO dealmaker, and investors began flocking to KKR's door.

Not all of the company's investments were successful, however. Its 1991 buyout of American Forest Products actually lost money, and its 1987 purchase of Walter Industries resulted in that company's bankruptcy. But these losses were shadowed by the firm's stellar deals. Between 1983 and 1984 KKR spent a total of $28 billion on seven companies, including its first $1 billion deal, for Wometco Enterprises.

The 1986 Beatrice Companies deal changed the image of the company, and with it the image of the LBO itself. By issuing the takeover deal as a virtual "bear hug," the company's board was left with little choice than to capitulate, selling the firm for $6.2 billion. Unhappy with an end to company's nice-guy image, Kohlberg resigned at the conclusion of the transaction.

In 1987, after resigning, Kohlberg sued his ex-partners for reducing his stake in KKR on deals that had been conducted while he was at the company; the suit was later settled quietly. This situation arose from Kohlberg's 1984 leave of absence for brain tumor surgery. Upon his return months later, Kravis and Roberts were unwilling to relinquish the control in the company that they had gained in his absence. They demanded a larger share of profits to go along with their greater roles in KKR, thereby cutting Kohlberg's stake.

KKR bought out Safeway Stores for $4.4 billion in 1986, followed by Owens-Illinois the following year, and Stop & Shop in 1988. The monumental buyout of RJR Nabisco for $31 billion in 1988 garnered huge media attention and set the record as the largest LBO in corporate history.

The nation slid into a recession in 1989, bringing an end to the frenzy of mammoth LBOs. KKR began making more investments than full-scale takeovers. That year it established K-III Communications Corp. to manage its broadcasting and media interests. In September 1992 it invested $300 million in American Re Corp., the third-largest reinsurance company in the U.S.

By mid-1994 KKR had spent $70 billion on over 40 companies. That year it swapped its investment in RJR Nabisco for the acquisition of Borden, Inc. Two years later KKR ventured into Europe, acquiring Reed Regional Newspapers for $324 million. In April 1999 KKR entered into the bidding for the 900-unit chain of Hoyts Cinemas, with the plan to consolidate the U.S. movie theaters into its Regal Cinema chain.

The Business

Financials

Revenue (1998): $17 billion

Employees (1998): 80,400

SICs / NAICS

sic 2064 - Candy & Other Confectionery Products

sic 2052 - Cookies & Crackers

sic 2067 - Chewing Gum

sic 2068 - Salted & Roasted Nuts & Seeds

sic 2035 - Pickles, Sauces & Salad Dressings

naics 311330 - Confectionery Manufacturing from Purchased Chocolate

naics 311340 - Non-Chocolate Confectionery Manufacturing

naics 311821 - Cookie and Cracker Manufacturing

naics 311919 - Other Snack Food Manufacturing

naics 311911 - Roasted Nuts and Peanut Butter Manufacturing

naics 311941 - Mayonnaise, Dressing, and Other Prepared Sauce Manufacturing

History of RJR Nabisco Holdings Corp.

In 1874 Richard Joshua Reynolds, after selling his interest in his father's tobacco business, moved to Winston, North Carolina, the heart of the bright leaf tobacco area. He invested $7,500 in land, and built a small factory to manufacture flat plug chewing tobacco. In the first year of operation, the establishment produced 150,000 pounds of tobacco.

The R.J. Reynolds Tobacco Co. was incorporated in North Carolina in 1879. It faced stiff competition from manufacturers in Winston and its neighboring city of Salem. In 1884 R.J.'s brother, William Neal Reynolds, joined the firm. Initially, Reynolds' products were sold to jobbers who distributed chewing tobacco under their own brand names.

In 1885 R.J. Reynolds introduced Schnapps, his own brand of chewing tobacco, which soon gained popularity. The next year he registered "R.J.R." as his trademark and had an elaborate RJR design affixed to his carriage. These ornate initials became the company's symbol and remained as such until 1961, when they were redesigned.

The company issued its first stock in 1890, with the firm's founder owning nearly 90%. R.J. Reynolds

The Officers

Chairman, President, and CEO: Steven F. Goldstone

Sr. VP, Human Resources and Administration: Gerald I. Angowitz

Sr. VP and General Auditor: A. : Jeffrey A. Kuchar

Sr. VP, Associate General Counsel, and Secretary: : H. Colin McBride

Sr. VP, Strategy and Business Development: Lionel L. Nowell III

was elected president, with his brother serving as vice president. A sales department was created, as was a systematic national advertising program. Reynolds was one of the first companies to introduce saccharin as a sweetening agent in chewing tobacco. The company also adopted many labor-saving devices and experienced a 400% production increase over the next six years.

Reynolds began experimenting with smoking tobacco in 1894 to compete with James Buchanan Duke's profitable brands, and also out of his desire to turn scrap tobacco into a paying product. The next year the company introduced its first smoking tobacco brand, Naturally Sweet Cut Plug.

Although company assets were valued at over $1 million, its considerable expansion late in the decade brought about a need for large amounts of capital. Reluctantly, Reynolds sought help from rival James Duke. Duke's American Tobacco Co. had established a subsidiary, Continental Tobacco Co., in an effort to monopolize the nation's chewing tobacco business. Reynolds sold two-thirds of his stock to Continental, but retained his position as president of the R.J. Reynolds Tobacco Co. Reynolds tried to maintain his independence in Duke's tobacco trust and was determined not to be swallowed up by his rival. Duke extended Reynolds his independence as long as he acquired chewing tobacco companies in the Virginia and Carolina areas for the trust. Reynolds proceeded to buy ten such companies.

R.J. Reynolds demonstrated his independence from the trust in 1905 by producing five brands of smoking tobacco. Two years later Prince Albert smoking tobacco, a unique mixture of burley and flue-cured tobacco, was introduced by Reynolds. The product achieved instant success with the slogan "It can't bite your tongue."

The tobacco trust, like most trusts during this period, proved unpopular. In 1911 a U.S. Circuit Court ordered the dissolution of the American Tobacco Co. Since American was forced to divest itself of all Reynolds stock, R.J. Reynolds and members of his family reacquired some of the firm's stock. During the trust's years, Reynolds had expanded facilities, hired aggressive management, and increased production and sales almost five-fold.

In 1912 R.J. regained control of the company, at a time when Reynolds Tobacco was the smallest of the big four tobacco manufacturers. The company again considered the production of cigarettes because of the great success experienced by its Prince Albert brand. Profits that year reached $2.75 million.

After manufacturing the company's first cigarette, Reynolds decided to produce three different cigarette brands simultaneously to see which one had the greatest public appeal. R.J. personally selected the blend of Turkish, burley, and flue-cured tobaccos, along with the new name of the brand that would prove most popular, Camel. The item became instantly successful due to its blend, low price, and advertising. In 1915, in fact, Reynolds spent more than $2 million in an aggressive national advertising campaign.

William Neal Reynolds assumed the presidency after the death of R.J. Reynolds in 1918. At that time the company employed 10,000 people in 121 buildings in the Winston-Salem area. Four years later its preferred stock was listed on the New York Stock Exchange.

Sales rose to nearly $24 million in 1924, largely because of the phenomenal sale of Camels. The firm's net profits surpassed those of the nation's largest manufacturer, the American Tobacco Co. At that time the majority of the company's voting stock was in the hands of employees. For the past several years, employees had been encouraged, via a company bylaw, to purchase voting stock, and had even been allowed to borrow from surplus funds and profits to do so. In 1927 the company's common stock was listed for the first time.

Bowman Gray, Sr., became chairman in 1931. Under his direction, the firm introduced moisture-proof cellophane as a wrapper to preserve freshness in cigarettes, an innovation other companies soon adopted. The company also began manufacturing its own tinfoil and paper from factories in North Carolina to reduce dependence on foreign supplies, and it developed a new sales policy stressing mass sales based on brand name loyalty and recognition.

In 1948, in a major antitrust suit against the tobacco industry, several Reynolds officers were convicted and fined on charges of monopolistic practices; the company itself was also found guilty. The next year Reynolds introduced a major new cigarette brand,

Cavalier. The product never won a wide acceptance, however, and lost a total of $30 million over five years.

An article entitled "Cancer by the Carton" appeared in *Reader's Digest* in 1952, and the tobacco industry began to experience, for the first time, critical attacks centering on the issue of smoking and health. The next year the Sloan-Kettering Cancer Institute announced that its research showed a relationship between cancer and tobacco. The development of filter-tipped cigarettes was, in part, a response to such health concerns.

Winston, the company's first filter-tipped cigarette, was introduced in March 1954 to compete directly with Brown & Williamson's Viceroy brand. With such catchy slogans as "Winston tastes good like a cigarette should" and "It's what's up front that counts," the cigarette was quickly accepted, selling 40 billion in its first year alone.

Two years later Reynolds began marketing Salem, the industry's first king-size filter-tipped menthol cigarette. The new brand went on to reap tremendous profits, but Camel remained the industry leader for the rest of the 1950s and into the beginning of the next decade.

In 1957 the board of directors responded to increasing health concerns by appointing a diversification committee to study possible investment in non-tobacco areas and to consider expansion of tobacco operations overseas. Alexander H. Galloway became president in 1960 and, along with Chairman Bowman Gray, Jr., led the company into a period of unparalleled growth and diversification. This diversification strategy initially focused on acquisitions in food-related industries. Reynolds bought a controlling interest in Haus Neuerburg, one of West Germany's leading cigarette manufacturers; this purchase also marked the beginning of international tobacco operations for Reynolds.

All cigarette manufacturing became centralized in 1961 with the opening of a massive, modern factory in Winston-Salem, North Carolina. Two years later Reynolds bought Pacific Hawaiian Products.

The U.S. surgeon general issued a report linking smoking with lung cancer and heart disease in 1964. The next year U.S. Congress passed the Cigarette Advertising and Labeling Act, requiring tobacco companies to place health warnings on cigarette packs.

Reynolds acquired Chun King for $63 million in 1966. R.J. Reynolds Foods, a subsidiary, was created to encompass all of the organization's non-tobacco companies. Two years later R.J. Reynolds International was established to develop foreign tobacco markets.

The Players

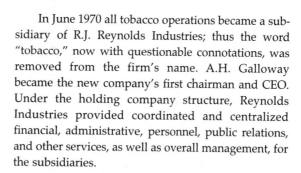

In June 1970 all tobacco operations became a subsidiary of R.J. Reynolds Industries; thus the word "tobacco," now with questionable connotations, was removed from the firm's name. A.H. Galloway became the new company's first chairman and CEO. Under the holding company structure, Reynolds Industries provided coordinated and centralized financial, administrative, personnel, public relations, and other services, as well as overall management, for the subsidiaries.

Later that year Reynolds Industries acquired American Independent Oil Co. (Aminoil), an independent producer and refiner whose principal sales were to other oil companies. Also, Vantage brand cigarettes were first marketed.

In 1971 cigarette advertising was banned from radio and television. Three years later Winston Lights, a low "tar" and nicotine version of the original Winston cigarette, went on sale. The company acquired one of Canada's largest tobacco manufacturers, Macdonald Tobacco Inc., which had been the sole Canadian distributor of RJR cigarette brands.

In addition to governmental pressure, Reynolds faced intense competition, primarily from Philip Morris, and marketing strategies focused on luring customers away from competitors instead of attracting new smokers. Philip Morris' Marlboro brand surpassed Winston in domestic sales in 1976. The next year Reynolds introduced its Real brand cigarette to appeal to the back-to-nature movement, but sales proved disastrous; within three years the product was discontinued.

R.J. Reynolds acquired produce giant Del Monte Corp. in 1979. The next year Reynolds was the first U.S. company to reach an agreement with the People's Republic of China to manufacture and sell cigarettes there. Late in 1980 the firm announced an ambitious $2 billion, ten-year construction and plant modernization plan.

The federal cigarette tax doubled in 1983. Reynolds acquired Heublein Inc., a well-known manufacturer of wines and spirits. It also began manufacturing the novel 25-cigarette-per-pack Century brand. Most consumers, however, preferred the traditional 20-cigarette pack. That year competitor Philip Morris usurped Reynolds as the leader in domestic sales.

In 1984, with the sale of Aminoil to Phillips Petroleum for $1.7 billion, Reynolds completed the divestiture of all transportation and energy operations. Reynols followed that up with one of the largest acquisitions in corporate history, the purchase Nabisco Brands, Inc. for $4.9 billion in 1985. This acquisition raised the corporation's non-tobacco earnings to 40% of its total. F. Ross Johnson, a Nabisco veteran, was appointed president and COO of the new firm, RJR Nabisco.

In 1986 Johnson forced out Wilson and assumed the position of CEO. He continued the policy of returning the company to its core business by selling off more than half the corporation's subsidiaries. Headquarters were moved from Winston-Salem to Atlanta, Georgia. The next year Reynolds began test-marketing a smokeless cigarette, Premier, in response to mounting pressure to make smoking more acceptable; the item was a colossal failure, however. That same year Heublein was sold to Grand Metropolitan.

At a meeting of the board of directors in 1988, Johnson proposed a leveraged buyout to take the company private. The directors, alienated by Johnson's proposal, opened the door to other bidders, and ultimately accepted the $25 billion offer by Kohlberg Kravis Roberts & Co.; this was the largest leveraged buyout in U.S. history.

RJR Nabisco Holdings Corp. was established as the parent company of RJR Nabisco, Inc. After F. Ross Johnson resigned, KKR selected Louis Gerstner, Jr. to take over as CEO. He immediately instituted cost cutting measures, including an 11.5% personnel cutback in tobacco operations. Corporate headquarters relocated to New York and Nabisco's European food business was divested.

In 1990 Del Monte's processed foods operation was sold, along with selected facets of Nabisco. RJR's attempts to target specific consumer groups with new cigarette brands failed. The company did, however, succeed in penetrating the Soviet market.

Sales of the company's three most popular brands, Camel, Winston, and Salem, accounted for 28% of 1991 revenues. By that time debt had been reduced to about $17 billion from $25 billion at the time of the buyout. The company, once again, went public with a new issue of stock; the action put approximately 25% of the firm back in public hands with KKR retaining roughly 65%.

By May 1993 RJR Nabisco was facing cash-flow problems as a result of price competition in the cigarette industry and a proposed increase in the cigarette tax. The firm also lost CEO Louis V. Gerstner, Jr., who resigned to take the top job at IBM. Mike Harper, noted for developing ConAgra into a strong company, took the helm as CEO of RJR Nabisco.

In November 1995 investors Bennett S. LeBow and Carl Icahn purchased 4.8% of RJR Nabisco in a bid to force the company to split its food and tobacco businesses through a proxy battle. The following April, having defeated LeBow and Icahn, RJR Nabisco re-elected its board of directors and rejected a spin-off of its food operations. The company eliminated 6,000 jobs and took a charge of $428 million in 1996. This action was repeated in 1998 due to soft sales, resulting in another 6,500 job cuts and a charge of $530 million.

In May 1999 RJR Nabisco completed the sale of its international tobacco business to Japan Tobacco, Inc. for $8 billion. The following month the company's tobacco and food businesses were split, and RJR Nabisco was renamed Nabisco Group Holdings Corp.

Market Forces Driving the Acquisition

F. Ross Johnson, RJR Nabisco's leader, had been trying to boost the company's depressed stock price for several years. Yet even the dividend hikes and stock buybacks failed to have a lasting impact. In his mind, the only remaining option for turning the company around was to take the company private through a leveraged buyout (LBO). Johnson didn't present his idea to the board, however. Instead he gathered together a team of managers to join him in his scheme.

Approach and Engagement

On October 19, 1988, Ross Johnson announced to RJR Nabisco's board that he and a group of managers intended to take the company private through a leveraged buyout. Their offer was $75 per share, nearly a 30% premium over RJR's current stock price, for a total of $17 billion.

The board was shocked, and then angered at Johnson's gall. Considering him to be nothing more than a raider, the members declined to enter into exclusive negotiations with him. Instead, they publicized the offer, thereby effectively putting RJR on the sales block.

The first rival suitor to emerge was Kohlberg Kravis Roberts. Within a few days it offered $90 per share, or $20.3 billion. Other suitors showed up as well. Forstmann Little briefly entered the fray, but soon dropped out. The First Boston investment firm pulled together a bid of $26.8 billion, but it was dismissed by RJR's board as a frivolous offer.

On November 7 the board announced that all bids were to be submitted by November 18. Both Johnson and KKR jockeyed for position as the higher bidder, alternatively upping their offers to best the other's. After a deadline extension until November 29, the final bids were in the hands of the board. On the following day, KKR was proclaimed the winner, with a bid of $25 billion.

Products and Services

Nabisco's products include the following brand names: SnackWell, Oreo, Teddy Grahams, A1, Triscuit, Breath Savers, CareFree, Now 'N Later, Life Savers, Planters, Chips Ahoy!, Barnum's Animals, and Knox.

Changes to the Industry

As the largest leveraged buyout (LBO) in history, the takeover of RJR Nabisco raised the bar for future buyouts. Yet the enormous price of this deal and the egos of its participants drew criticism and scorn for takeovers and, by extension, the runaway circus of corporate America in general. This battle was the subject of *Barbarians at the Gate: The Fall of RJR Nabisco*, which was later dramatized as a Showtime movie.

Review of the Outcome

After the acquisition, RJR Nabisco Holdings Corp. was established as the parent company of RJR Nabisco, Inc. Over the course of the 14 months after the takeover, most of the company's top managers, including F. Ross Johnson, resigned. Louis V. Gerstner, Jr., president of American Express, was recruited as RJR's new CEO. He immediately began cutting costs in order to reduce the massive buyout debt. Such measures include an 11.5% personnel cutback in tobacco operations, and the elimination of the practice of overstocking retailers with cigarettes. After a year or so, though, the period of transition appeared to be ending, and the company returned to an even keel.

Unfortunately, strong pricing competition from Philip Morris and the increasing liability of tobacco companies kept RJR from experiencing the level of growth that it had anticipated. In October 1994 KKR reduced its ownership of RJR by using part of its stake in the company to purchase Borden Inc. In March 1995 KKR ended its relationship with RJR altogether by divesting the last of its holding in the company.

Research

Burrough, Bryan, and John Helyar. *Barbarians at the Gate: The Fall of RJR Nabisco*, Harper & Row, 1990. Offers a detailed examination of KKR's takeover of RJR Nabisco, and sheds insight into the firms and their major players.

Castro, Janice. "Duel of the Takeover Titans," in *Time*, 7 November 1988. Presents an account of the takeover.

"Corporate America Snuggles up to the Buy-Out Wolves," in *The Economist*, 29 October 1988. Mentions the RJR buy-out in terms of an analysis of the LBO in general.

Greenwald, John. "Where's the Limit? The Biggest Takeover Battle in History Raises Questions about Greed, Debt and the Well-Being of American Industry," 5 December 1988. Presents an analysis of the role of the LBO in corporate America.

"KKR Shed Last of Its Stake in RJR Nabisco," in *The Wall Street Journal*, 23 March 1995. Relates KKR's divestiture of its remaining stake in RJR.

Leinster, Colin. "Greed Really Turns Me Off," in *Fortune*, 2 January 1989. Presents an interview with Henry Kravis about the RJR buyout.

Nabisco Group Holdings Corp.: http://www.rjrnabisco.com. Includes new releases and investor information.

"RJR Nabisco Holdings Corp.," in *Notable Corporate Chronologies*, The Gale Group, 1999. Offers a history of the company.

Saporito, Bill. "How Ross Johnson Blew the Buyout," in *Fortune*, 24 April 1989. Provides a blow-by-blow account of the takeover.

———. "They Cleaned Our Clock," in *Fortune*, 2 January 1989. Presents an interview with Ross Johnson about the RJR buyout.

Wasserstein, Bruce. *Big Deal: The Battle for Control of America's Leading Corporations*, Warner Books, 1998. Offers an overview of the largest mergers in recent American corporate history.

SAMANTHA MORRISON

KOHLBERG KRAVIS ROBERTS & SAFEWAY STORES

Kohlberg Kravis Roberts & Co.
9 W. 57th St., Ste. 4200
New York, NY 10019
USA

tel: (212)750-8300
fax: (212)750-0003

nationality: USA
date: September 6, 1986
affected: Kohlberg Kravis Roberts & Co., USA, founded 1976
affected: Safeway Stores Inc., USA, founded 1926

Overview of the Acquisition

When Safeway Stores Inc., the world's largest grocery store chain, became the target of a hostile takeover by Dart Group Corp. in 1986, it turned to Kohlberg Kravis Roberts & Co. as a preferred acquirer. This investment group, specializing in leveraged buyouts (LBOs), took Safeway private in a $4.25 billion deal. After the transaction, in an effort to reduce the massive debt load incurred from the LBO, Safeway embarked on an aggressive streamlining strategy, laying off 63,000 workers in the process.

History of Kohlberg Kravis Roberts & Co.

Jerome Kohlberg, Jr., left Bear, Stearns & Co. in 1976 to establish his own investment firm. He brought in cousins Henry Kravis and George Roberts, also Bear Stearns employees, and the three partners formed Kohlberg Kravis Roberts (KKR). They had amassed experience at Bear Stearns in the methods of acquiring companies and decided to build their company around the leverage buyout (LBO), which consists of the use of an acquisition target's credit to secure the financing needed to purchase it. The company's assets are then sold off to repay that debt. Finally the company itself is sold, ideally at a large profit on the investment.

KKR developed a profile of the perfect LBO target. It should be undervalued and have a group of managers and/or shareholders that want to take the company private. And if it were in a state of leadership transition, all the better.

Despite its lofty goal of taking control of billion-dollar companies, KKR had modest beginnings. Its start-up capital was $120,000, and its office was a dingy, leased suite furnished with leftover desks and cabinets.

One of its firm's first deals was the $23 million buyout of A.J. Industries, a manufacturer of brake drums. After closing several other deals over its first two years, KKR went after its first Fortune 500 company, Houdaille Industries. This machine maker was acquired by KKR for $350 million in April 1979.

After this deal, the LBO gained wide recognition as an effective, and profitable, means of acquiring companies. Competitors to KKR quickly arose, but by this time KKR had established a reputation as an experienced LBO deal maker, and investors began flocking to KKR's door.

Not all of the company's investments were successful, however. Its 1991 buyout of American Forest Products actually lost money, and its 1987 purchase of Walter Industries resulted in that company's bankruptcy. But these losses were shadowed by the firm's stellar deals. Between 1983 and 1984, KKR spent a total of $28 billion on seven companies, including its first $1 billion deal, for Wometco Enterprises.

The 1986 Beatrice Companies deal changed the image of the company, and with it the image of the LBO itself. By issuing the takeover deal as a virtual "bear hug," the company's board was left with little choice but to capitulate, selling the firm for $6.2 billion. Unhappy with the end of the company's nice-guy image, Kohlberg resigned at the conclusion of the transaction.

In 1987, after resigning, Kohlberg sued his ex-partners for reducing his stake in KKR on deals that had been conducted while he was at the company; the suit was later settled quietly. This situation arose from Kohlberg's 1984 leave of absence for brain tumor surgery. Upon his return months later, Kravis and Roberts were unwilling to relinquish the control in the company that they had gained in his absence. They demanded a larger share of profits to go along with their greater roles in KKR, thereby cutting Kohlberg's stake.

KKR bought out Safeway Stores for $4.25 billion in 1986, followed by Owens-Illinois the following year, and Stop & Shop in 1988. The monumental buyout of RJR Nabisco for $31 billion in 1988 garnered huge media attention and set the record as the largest LBO in corporate history.

The nation slid into a recession in 1989, bringing an end to the frenzy of mammoth LBOs. KKR began making more investments than full-scale takeovers. That year it established K-III Communications Corp. to manage its broadcasting and media interests. In September 1992, it invested $300 million in American Re Corp., the third-largest reinsurance company in the U.S.

By mid-1994, KKR had spent $70 billion on over 40 companies. That year it swapped its investment in RJR Nabisco for the acquisition of Borden, Inc. Two years later, KKR ventured into Europe, acquiring Reed Regional Newspapers for $324 million. In April 1999, KKR entered into the bidding for the 900-unit chain of Hoyts Cinemas, with a plan to consolidate the U.S. movie theaters into its Regal Cinema chain.

The Business

SICs / NAICS

sic 6799 - Investors Nec

naics 523910 - Miscellaneous Intermediation

History of Safeway Stores Inc.

In 1915, M.B. Skaggs purchased his father's 18 x 32 ft. store in American Falls, Idaho, and established Skaggs United Stores. Unlike other stores, which displayed merchandise in barrels or stacked on tables, Skaggs installed easy-to-reach shelves. By 1926, Skaggs operated a chain of 428 grocery stores throughout California and the Pacific Northwest.

Safeway Stores was formed in 1926 through the merger of Skaggs and Safeway, a 338-unit grocery chain in California and Hawaii owned by Merrill Lynch. By year-end, the enterprise was operating 766 stores and was one of the first companies to offer cash-and-carry service. Two years later, the company gained a listing on the New York Stock Exchange. Safeway made acquisitions in Washington DC, Virginia, Maryland, Arkansas, Iowa, Kansas, Missouri, and Texas, increasing the number of stores in operation by the end of 1928 to 2,000—800 of which contained meat markets.

Canada Safeway Ltd. was established in Winnipeg in 1929. Two years later the company merged with the 1,400-store MacMarr chain in the Pacific Northwest. In 1947, sales reached $1 billion for the first time.

Safeway launched a massive building campaign in 1949 to replace more than 1,000 old stores with new, larger models that included such conveniences as dairy sections, self-help meat stands, and frozen food cases. Five years later the firm began offering its employees major medical coverage, a step that helped to cement good labor relations. Charles Merrill's son-in-law, Robert Magowan, was named president of the firm in 1957, just as sales reached $2 billion.

Safeway embarked on an aggressive expansion program. On the domestic front, it expanded into Alaska and Iowa in 1959. International expansion soon followed, as the company entered the United Kingdom by initiating operation of 11 John Gardner Ltd. stores in 1962. The following year, Safeway expanded into the Australian market by acquiring three Pratt Supermarkets in the Melbourne area.

The Officers

Co-Founder: Henry R. Kravis

Co-Founder: George Roberts

General Partner: Edward Gilhuly

General Partner: Perry Golkin

General Partner: James H. Greene, Jr.

Operations in West Germany were established with the 1964 purchase of several Big Bar Basar stores. That year Safeway also opened the first "international" supermarket in Washington DC, stocking food products from all of the world's major cuisines. Sales reached $3 billion in 1966, the same year that Quenten Reynolds succeeded Magowan as president.

The company divested itself of Super S drug stores in 1971 after several unprofitable years. That year it surpassed A&P to become the world's largest food retailer. In 1973, the United Farm Workers (UFW) filed suit against Safeway, demanding that the company pressure lettuce and grape growers to accept the union as the employees' collective bargaining agent. Safeway refused and countersued the union for $150 million, claiming that the UFW had undertaken a campaign of harassment and sabotage.

Legal entanglements continued the following year, as Safeway was named, along with most of its competitors, in a $1.5 billion suit filed by a group of cattlemen for allegedly fixing prices of dressed beef. Safeway agreed to pay the cattlemen $150,000.

Earnings in 1976 and 1977 were depressed, reflecting a management problem that was compounded by the impending retirement of chairman and CEO William Mitchell in 1980. In 1979, after a two-year financial recovery, earnings again declined. Peter Magowan, son of former chairman Robert, was named Mitchell's successor. Once at the helm, Magowan streamlined the company, slashing corporate management by 15%, closing less profitable stores, and consolidating divisions. The firm sold its 130-store Australian operation to Woolworth's Ltd. in 1985. These efforts resulted in a 25% increase in net income, to $231 million, on sales of $19.7 billion in 1985.

The company began offering health-oriented products in 1982, thereby solidifying its concept of one-step shopping. That year it formed a joint venture with the Knapp Communications Corp. to create a string of gourmet food stores called Bon Appetit. In 1983, Safeway installed salad bars in its stores, began offering bulk food items, and launched SNAP (Safeway's Nutrition Awareness Program). By the end of that year it operated 1,953 U.S. stores, 303 of which contained in-store pharmacies.

In 1986, Safeway was taken private via a leveraged buyout by Kohlberg Kravis Roberts & Co., averting a hostile takeover attempt by the Dart Group Corp. Saddled with enormous debt following the buyout, Safeway streamlined its operations, selling a large number of its stores, including its Liquor Barn retail outlets, 59 grocery stores in Texas and New Mexico, and its entire Oklahoma division. It also sold its British operations to the Argyll Group PLC. In 1988, Safeway continued its divestiture program, selling its 99 Houston-area stores to an investment group led by local Safeway management.

The privatization was short-lived, as Safeway returned to a public status in 1990 by offering 11.5 million shares as the newly renamed Safeway Inc. The next year Safeway offered an additional 70 million shares of common stock. Also in 1991, the company retired $565 million in debt and recorded sales of over $15 billion. The Safeway SELECT line of private-label products premiered in 1993. That year Steve Burd, company president since 1992, was named CEO.

New packaging equipment enabled Safeway to increase its output of dairy products by 60% in 1994. That year the company closed six manufacturing plants. By the end of 1995, after converting its private-label products to the Safeway brand, the company had consolidated the number of its private labels from 100 to 12.

Safeway went on an acquisition spree in the mid-1990s. In April 1997, it completed its acquisition of The Vons Companies Inc., a large supermarket operation in southern California, in which Safeway had held a 34.5% stake. Safeway acquired Dominick's Supermarkets, Inc. in October 1998.

Magowan retired as chairman in favor of Steven Burd, president and CEO, in May 1998. That year net income rose to $806.7 million from $621.5 million in 1997, while sales reached $24.5 billion, compared to $22.5 billion the previous year.

In July 1999, the firm commenced a tender offer for Carr-Gottstein Foods Co. and entered into an agreement to acquire Randall's Food Markets, Inc. for $1.8 billion.

Market Forces Driving the Acquisition

In mid-1986, Wall Street was abuzz with rumors that Safeway Stores, the world's largest supermarket chain, would be the target of a takeover bid. The company had been streamlined under the leadership of chairman and CEO Peter Magowan and was attractive to suitors. In May 1986, Dart Group Corp., a takeover instrument for corporate raiders Herbert H. Haft and his son Robert, began purchasing Safeway stock. By July, Dart had acquired 3.6 million shares, or 5.9%, in the grocery store chain.

When Dart's investment was disclosed, Safeway's stock price climbed from its $41 per share price. This prompted the Harts to lay their cards on the table, offering a $58 per share, or $3.6 billion, hostile bid for Safeway. When Safeway declined to enter into negotiations, Dart sweetened its bid to $64 per share, or $3.9 billion, provided that Safeway submit to a friendly acquisition.

Safeway continued to remain silent on the offer, causing analysts, and the Harts, to suspect that it had entered into talks with a white knight suitor. Among the firms named as possible acquirers was Kohlberg Kravis Roberts & Co. This investment firm had a track record of rescuing targets of hostile takeovers by taking them private through leveraged buyouts.

Approach and Engagement

The rumor mill ground to a halt on July 27, 1986, when Safeway and Kohlberg Kravis Roberts (KKR) announced their deal. The two-part leveraged buyout was valued at a total of $4.25 billion. In the first phase of the transaction, the investment group led by KKR and certain Safeway executives, would offer $69 per share in cash for 73% of Safeway's outstanding stock. The remaining interest would later be purchased at $61.60 in bonds plus $7.40 in warrants entitling the holder to purchase shares in the company that would become Safeway's new owner.

Dart Group withdrew its offer on July 31. KKR, through the SSI Holdings company that had been established for the purpose of the buyout, completed the acquisition of 73% of Safeway's stock on September 6, 1986.

Products and Services

Safeway Inc. was one of the largest food and drug retailers in North America based on sales. As of January 2, 1999, it operated 1,497 stores, including 324 Vons stores and 114 Dominick's stores, in the western, southwestern, Rocky Mountain, midwestern, and mid-Atlantic regions of the United States. Its Canadian operations were primarily located in western Canada, in the provinces of British Columbia, Alberta, and Manitoba/Saskatchewan. It also held a 49% interest in Casa Ley, S.A. de C.V. Safeway's retail grocery business accounted for 98% of total company sales.

The Players

Kohlberg Kravis Roberts & Co. Co-Founder: Henry R. Kravis. Henry Kravis, a native of Tulsa, Oklahoma, earned a degree in economics before receiving an MBA from Columbia University. In 1969, he joined the ranks of Bear, Stearns & Co., where he worked with his cousin George Roberts and his mentor Jerome Kohlberg, Jr. In 1976, the three men left Bear Stearns to found Kohlberg Kravis Roberts & Co. Since that time, Kravis orchestrated some of the largest LBOs in corporate history.

Safeway Stores Inc. Chairman and CEO: Peter A. Magowan. Peter Magowan graduated from Stanford University and earned a master's degree from Oxford University. He is the son of Robert Magowan, who served as chairman of Safeway from 1955 to 1971. Peter joined the company in 1968 as a real estate negotiator. He was placed in charge of Safeway's Western division in 1978 and became chairman and CEO of the company in January 1980. Magowan's efforts to streamline operations after taking the helm produced the desired financial results, but the ensuing resignation of several top executives was attributed to his autocratic management style.

Magowan oversaw and participated in the company's leveraged buyout under Kohlberg Kravis Roberts in 1986. He resigned from day-to-day leadership of Safeway in 1993 to become president and partner of the San Francisco Giants baseball club. In May 1998, Magowan retired as chairman of Safeway in favor of Steven Burd, its president and CEO.

Additionally, Safeway held operations in manufacturing, food processing, and distribution. Since its introduction in 1993, its Safeway SELECT brand name encompassed about 900 products. The firm also offered 2,500 products marketed under the Safeway, Lucerne, and Mrs. Wright's banners.

Review of the Outcome

Adding fuel to the fire of discontent over the general concept of the leveraged buyout, the effects of the privatization of Safeway brought little joy to anyone—aside from the investors—involved in the deal. The company sold about 1,000 stores, 45 plants, and entire divisions in several states.

In the aftermath, 63,000 Safeway employees lost their jobs. Although the majority found employment at the stores that had been sold to other grocery chains, full-time employment eluded thousands of others. A handful of laid-off workers made suicide attempts, one of which was successful. In addition, several fatal heart attack-related deaths were attributed to the stress of workers' newfound unemployment, although this correlation was adamantly refuted by Safeway management.

Many of the workers who remained with the company found that the workplace subjected them to increased pressure. Skilled employees were replaced by less experienced, and therefore cheaper, part-time workers. A new system implemented at stores penalized managers if they failed to meet weekly quotas. And Safeway's focus on retiring the debt incurred through the leveraged buyout had come at the expense of investments in store improvements.

These cost-cutting measures did benefit the company's financial and market position, however. By shedding less profitable operations, Safeway recorded greater earnings from remaining divisions. It also occupied a more powerful market position, ranking first or second in the markets where it operated.

Research

"About 73% of Safeway's Stock Was Tendered," in *Los Angeles Times*, 11 September 1986. Briefly announces the completion of the LBO.

Burrough, Bryan and John Helyar. *Barbarians at the Gate: The Fall of RJR Nabisco*, Harper & Row, 1990. Offers a detailed examination of KKR's takeover of RJR Nabisco, and sheds insight into the firm and its major players.

Cole, Robert J. "Safeway Agrees to Buyout Bid," in *The New York Times*, 28 July 1986. Reveals the terms of the newly announced buyout agreement between Safeway and KKR.

Faludi, Susan C. "A Buyout's Bitter Fallout," in *St. Petersburg Times*, 27 May 1990. (Reprinted from *The Wall Street Journal*). Provides an in-depth account of the results of the LBO, with a strong emphasis on the impact on Safeway employees.

Henderson, Nell. "Dart Drops Safeway Takeover Bid," in *The Washington Post*, 1 August 1986. Describes the withdrawal of Dart for Safeway in light of the competing bid by KKR.

Safeway Home Page, available at http://www.safeway.com. Official World Wide Web Home Page for Safeway. Offers news releases, financial information, a store directory, and shopping features such as recipes and advertised sales.

"Safeway Inc.," in *Notable Corporate Chronologies*, The Gale Group, 1999. Offers a history of the company.

SAMANTHA MORRISON

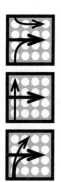

KYOEI STEEL & FLORIDA STEEL

nationality: USA
date: December 21, 1992
affected: Kyoei Steel Ltd., Japan, founded 1947
affected: Florida Steel Corp., USA, founded 1956

AmeriSteel Corp.
5100 W. Lemon St., Ste. 312
PO Box 31328
Tampa, FL 33631-3328
USA

tel: (813)286-8383
fax: (813)207-2251
web: http://www.ameristeel.com

Overview of the Acquisition

Florida Steel, the nation's largest manufacturer of concrete-reinforcing steel bars, was verging on bankruptcy by the early 1990s. In technical default on millions of dollars of debt, which was incurred through its leveraged buyout several years earlier, Florida Steel put itself up for sale in 1992. Kyoei Steel, one of Japan's leading steel bar manufacturers, was seeking to increase its presence in the U.S. market. In a $315.6 million deal, Kyoei Steel acquired Florida Steel in December 1992, making the U.S. company a subsidiary of the Japanese firm.

History of Florida Steel Corp.

Samual L. Flom and Donald F. Taylor founded Florida Steel Products in 1937. For nearly two decades the company flourished by supplying reinforced steel fabricated products to the construction industry. In 1956, however, intense competition from northern steel manufacturers spurred Florida companies to consolidate. That year Florida Steel Corp. was formed through the merger of six of the state's steel companies, including Florida Steel Products.

Later in 1956 the new company initiated construction on the first electric steel mill in Florida. Four years later Florida Steel acquired Easterby & Murnaw, a North Carolina reinforcing steel fabricating firm. This deal also called for the construction of a steel minimill in North Carolina, and groundbreaking took place in 1962. Florida Steel went public on the New York Stock Exchange in 1966.

During the 1970s, the company built its third and fourth electric steel minimills in Indiantown and Baldwin, Florida, respectively. In 1981, it expanded its geographic reach by constructing an electric steel minimill in Jackson, Tennessee.

In 1984, Florida Steel diversified into the epoxy-coated fabricated reinforcing steel business by purchasing one such facility in Tampa, Florida. This marked the beginning of a short-lived acquisition spree for the company. In 1986, it purchased both Stafford Rail Products, based in South Carolina, and Atlas Steel & Wire Co., based in New Orleans. The next year the firm acquired Knoxville Iron and Steel Service Companies, thereby gaining an electric steel minimill and five reinforcing steel fabricating plants.

The Business

Financials

Revenue (1999): $671.5 million

Employees (1999): 1,900

SICs / NAICS

sic 3312 - Blast Furnaces & Steel Mills

naics 331111 - Iron and Steel Mills

naics 331221 - Cold-Rolled Steel Shape Manufacturing

These acquisitions left Florida Steel vulnerable to a takeover. To thwart any such attempt, it went private in August 1988 through a $300 million management-led leveraged buyout. This action established FLS Holdings, Inc. as the company's new parent.

The leveraged buyout was responsible for the near-collapse of Florida Steel. High interest rates caused the company to struggle with the heavy debt load incurred through the buyout, just as the construction industry entered a recession. In January 1992 company executives put Florida Steel up for sale, and Kyoei Steel Ltd. agreed to pay $350 million for it. When the deal closed that December, FLS Holdings and Florida Steel became subsidiaries of the Japanese steelmaker.

Its new owner began implementing resuscitation measures for Florida Steel. In June 1994, it closed the company's melt shop in Tampa, and in September 1995 it closed that city's 12-inch rolling mill. Kyoei also initiated a search for new management, and in June 1994 recruited Phillip Casey as CEO for Florida Steel.

On April 1, 1996, Florida Steel Corp. changed its name to AmeriSteel Corp. to reflect its national focus. The next year the company filed for an initial public offering, but later cancelled those plans. In February 1999, it entered into an agreement to purchase Brocker Rebar Co., Inc., a Pennsylvania-based company. For fiscal 1999, which ended that March, AmeriSteel recorded net income of $25 million on revenues of $671.5 million. The company posted its most profitable quarter in its history on June 30, 1999, when it earned net income of $10.4 million, up from $6.6 million over the same period in the previous year.

On August 4, 1999, Gerdau S.A., Brazil's leading long products steelmaker, agreed to acquire a 75% majority interest in AmeriSteel. Kyoei Steel, which would retain a 15% stake, wanted to sell its controlling interest in order to focus on its operations in Asia.

Market Forces Driving the Acquisition

By early 1992, it had become evident that the leveraged buyout of Florida Steel Corp. in 1988 had been disastrous. A recession in the construction industry had reduced sales for its products. At the same time, the company had assumed a large amount of debt through the buyout. The weight of this burden, heavy enough under normal circumstances, was also compounded by heightened interest rates throughout the banking community. In January 1992, Florida Steel disclosed that it was in technical default on its loans. At that time it began shopping around for a buyer.

Kyoei Steel Ltd. was one of Japan's leading manufacturers of steel bars. This Osaka-based firm had been founded by, and was currently owned by, the Takashima family. In 1973, Kyoei had made its foray into the U.S. by constructing a rolling mill in New York, the first Japanese steel mill built in the country. The company was continually looking to boost its American presence, and it later acquired a mill in Arkansas. When Florida Steel, the nation's leading maker of concrete-reinforcing steel bars, began entertaining sales offers, Kyoei eagerly extended a bid.

Approach and Engagement

On June 29, 1992, Kyoei Steel Ltd. announced its agreement to purchase Florida Steel Corp. The $335 million deal had two components. Kyoei would pay $30 per share, or $15 million, for Florida Steel's common stock, and would pay $24 per share, or $38 million, for its preferred stock. In addition, it would assume the company's debt, which consisted of $146 million in bank loans, $125 million in bonds, and $11 million in industrial revenue bonds. The offer was contingent upon the tender of 90% of Florida Steel's bonds.

The deal was immediately challenged by a shareholder of Florida Steel. On June 30, a lawsuit was filed alleging that its terms favored the holders of common stock, which was primarily held by Florida Steel's officers, directors, and investment bankers, over the holders of its preferred stock.

This lawsuit, as well as a pending investigation into Florida Steel's sale of substandard steel, led Kyoei to reduce the value of the offer. Preferred stock would be purchased for $18 per share, or $29 million, and common stock would be purchased for $19 per share, or $9.4 million. These modifications reduced the total value of the deal by $14.6 million.

On November 22, Kyoei suspended its acquisition of Florida Steel after only 54% of shareholders had tendered their bonds. In response, Florida Steel extended the deadline of the tender offer, and on

November 27 Kyoei announced that nearly 90% of the outstanding bonds had been tendered. On December 21, 1992, the acquisition was completed, at which point Florida Steel became a subsidiary of Kyoei Steel.

Products and Services

In the late 1990s, AmeriSteel utilized raw steel scrap to manufacture a variety of products. Its Steel Mill Group, which operated four steel mills (two in Tennessee, one in North Carolina, and one in Florida), offered angle, channel, flat, rebar and coil, round and wire rod, and square steel. The company's Fabricated Reinforcing Steel Group supplied fabricated concrete reinforcing steel. AmeriSteel's Rail Products Division was the largest producer of railroad spikes in North America, and had plants in Lancaster, South Carolina, and Paragould, Arkansas.

Review of the Outcome

Kyoei Steel initially stated that it had no plans to alter Florida Steel's name, workforce, or management. Yet the debt-ridden U.S. company obviously needed changes to improve operations.

In order to transform Florida Steel into a "world-class steel operation," Kyoei Steel embarked on an executive search in May 1994 to locate and recruit a new chief for Florida Steel. In early June, Phillip E. Casey resigned as vice chairman and chief financial officer of Birmingham Steel Corp. to become CEO of Florida Steel. Later that month the company shut down its Tampa melt shop, which had been struggling since its opening three years earlier.

The reorganization continued in 1995. In February, Florida Steel closed its minimill steel fabricating plants in Woodbridge, Virginia, and Ft. Myers, Florida. That September it shut down its 12-inch rolling mill in Tampa. Among other changes implemented by its new parent, Florida Steel expanded its product offering from an emphasis on reinforcing steel to a near-equal mix with merchant bar and wire rod. It also adopted a new sales and marketing strategy to

The Officers

Chairman and CEO: Phillip E. Casey

VP, Chief Financial Officer, and Secretary: Thomas J. Landa

Group VP, Fabricated Reinforcing Steel: J. Donald Haney

VP, Steel Mill Operations: Dennis Andrew

VP, Human Resources: James S. Rogers

improve its national and international presence. In April 1996, Florida Steel Corp. changed its name to AmeriSteel Corp. as a reflection of this expanded focus.

In August 1999, Kyoei Steel entered into an agreement that would terminate its control of AmeriSteel. It agreed to sell its majority stake in the U.S. company to Gerdau S.A., a Brazilian steelmaker.

Research

AmeriSteel Corp. Home Page, available at http://www.ameristeel.com. Official World Wide Web Home Page for AmeriSteel. Includes news releases, financial data, product information, employment opportunities, and a historical review of the company.

Stengle, Bernice. "Florida Steel Agrees to Cut Its Selling Price," in *St. Petersburg Times*, 25 August 1992. Details the reduction of the price for Florida Steel.

———. "Florida Steel Deal Completed for $350 Million," in *St. Petersburg Times*, 22 December 1992. Announces the completion of the acquisition.

———. "Japanese Firm to Buy Florida Steel," in *St. Petersburg Times*, 30 June 1992. Describes the newly announced deal.

Trigaux, Robert. "Purchase of Florida Steel Hits Obstacle," in *St. Petersburg Times*, 24 November 1992. Details Kyoei's suspension of the acquisition due to a shortage in the number of bonds tendered.

—J.M. WEBER

THE LIMITED & CARTER HAWLEY HALE

The Limited Inc.
3 Limited Pkwy.
Columbus, OH 43230
USA

tel: (614)415-7000
web: http://www.limited.com

date: May 21, 1984 (canceled)
affected: The Limited Inc., USA, founded 1963
affected: Carter Hawley Hale Stores, Inc., USA, founded 1896

Overview of the Acquisition

The Limited made two successive takeover attempts for Carter Hawley Hale Stores during the mid-1980s. Carter Hawley thwarted each attempt by selling its shares to General Cinema, but the debt that the retailer accrued in the process came close to breaking the company. Carter Hawley gained bankruptcy protection in 1991, emerging from under it a year later with the assistance of the Zell/Chilmark investment fund. Within four years, however, the Carter Hawley name ceased to exist, as its specialty stores became the property of General Cinema and its department stores were acquired and renamed by Federated Department Stores.

History of The Limited Inc.

Leslie Wexner dropped out of law school in 1961 in order to work at his parents' women's clothing store in Columbus, Ohio. He and his father held opposing opinions on the operation of the store, and Leslie ventured out on his own two years later. With a $5,000 loan from his aunt, the Kingsdale shopping center of Columbus became the birthplace of Leslie Wexner's first women's clothing store. He named his company The Limited because of the limited amount of merchandise that it made available to customers. Sales that first year hit $160,000.

Due to the success of Wexner's company, his parents closed down their own store and began working for their son in 1965. By the next year, employees numbered 100. In 1968 company sales surpassed the $1 million mark. The following year, with a total of five stores in operation, The Limited went public.

As the shopping mall concept rapidly developed, The Limited chain grew to 100 units by 1976. Two years later, the company purchased Mast Industries, which became The Limited's merchandise procurement arm. In 1980 the chain expanded to open its first Limited Express store, a brand that placed more emphasis on the younger population with trendier designs. Two years later The Limited acquired Lane Bryant, offering larger sized fashions; Victoria's Secret, a lingerie retailer; and Roaman's, a catalog merchandiser.

The Forenza clothing line was created for The Limited in 1984. That year, as its sales exceeded the $1 billion mark, the company gained a listing on the London Stock Exchange. It made an unfriendly bid for Carter Hawley Hale in 1984 and again in 1986, but was thwarted both times by the emergence of General Cinema as a white knight.

In 1985 The Limited obtained Lerner Stores and Henri Bendel. The following year it opened its first Lerner Woman store, which was then merged with Sizes Unlimited, and also formed Limited Credit Services. Net sales rose past $3 billion. In 1987 the firm opened two Limited International Fashion stores and debuted its first Limited Too, a children's clothing store. The company acquired Abercrombie & Fitch in 1988, the same year that it introduced Lingerie Cacique.

The firm sold Lerner Woman to United Retail Group, Inc. in 1989. That year it obtained a charter for Limited Credit Services to become the World Financial Network National Bank and became the first U.S. retailer to transform its credit division in that manner. Victoria's Secret Bath Shops were also launched in 1989, the same year that its Express men's clothing operations were renamed Structure. *Forbes* ranked The Limited first in growth and profitability among specialty apparel companies.

Although the company began the '90s with by unveiling Bath & Body Works, a 1993 slump in the retail industry spurred The Limited to scale back operations and to divest itself of its Brylane catalog business. The following year the company expanded internationally by joining with Next PLC to open four Bath & Body Works stores in the U.K. Sales and profits that year dropped. In response, the company announced plans to renew the organizational structure and management ranks, as well as to consolidate operations as a group of brands rather than a collection of stores.

The Limited expanded into outdoor sporting equipment in 1995 by acquiring Galyan's Trading Co. for $32 million. That year its Intimate Brands unit, which encompassed Victoria's Secret, Bath & Body Works, and Cacique, went public, reducing The Limited's ownership to 83%. The following year the company took Abercrombie & Fitch public, and in 1998 it sold its remaining 84% interest in that firm.

In January 1998 The Limited revealed that it would close its 118-unit Cacique chain. The next month it announced the closure of about 200 underperforming Limited, Lerner, Lane Bryant, and Express stores, as well as the closure of all but one of the six Henri Bendel stores. The company also sold its remaining interest in Brylane.

The Business

Financials

Revenue (1998): $9.3 billion

Employees (1998): 126,800

SICs / NAICS

sic 5611 - Men's & Boys' Clothing Stores

sic 5621 - Women's Clothing Stores

sic 5632 - Women's Accessory & Specialty Stores

sic 5641 - Children's & Infants' Wear Stores

sic 5941 - Sporting Goods & Bicycle Shops

sic 5999 - Miscellaneous Retail Stores Nec

naics 446120 - Cosmetics, Beauty Supplies, and Perfume Stores

naics 448110 - Men's Clothing Stores

naics 448120 - Women's Clothing Stores

naics 448130 - Children's and Infants' Clothing Stores

naics 448190 - Other Clothing Stores

naics 451110 - Sporting Goods Stores

History of Carter Hawley Hales Stores, Inc.

Arthur Letts opened The Broadway store in 1896 in Los Angeles. One of the state's first department stores, this outlet offered a variety of wares in its 600,000 square feet of retail space. In 1919 The Broadway Department Store incorporated in California and then in Delaware seven years later. The company first expanded in March 1931 by acquiring the Hollywood store of B.H. Dyas Corp. This outlet was redesigned and renamed Broadway-Hollywood later that year. In November 1940 the company built the three-story Broadway-Pasadena store. Net income that year reached $231,000 on sales of $15.9 million. In 1945 the post-War economy drove Broadway's net income beyond $1 million on revenues of $31.7 million.

Edward W. Carter became president in 1946. Within months he pioneered the suburban shopping center concept, building The Crenshaw Center outside of Los Angeles. He then sought investors to finance his ambitious expansion plans. In 1949 he sold 195,000 shares to Hale Brothers Stores, Inc., operator of 12 specialty and department stores. Two years later the two corporations merged to form Broadway Hale Stores, Inc.

The Officers

Chairman and CEO: Leslie H. Wexner

Vice Chairman and Chief Administrative Officer: Kenneth B. Gilman

Exec. VP and Chief Financial Officer: V. Ann Hailey

Exec. VP and Chief Human Resources Officer: Arnold F. Kanarick

In 1956 the company paid $10 million to acquire 99.2% of Dohrmann Commercial Co., a diverse provider of retail products and services. Among its home furnishings, appliance, and hotel supply operations, Dohrmann also possessed 16% of the Emporium Capwell Co., owner of the largest department stores in San Francisco and Oakland.

In the early 1960s Broadway-Hale acquired Coulter's, Marston Co., and Korrick's Inc. In order to focus on retailing, it sold Dohrmann Commercial Co. and Dohrmann Hotel Supply, while retaining ownership of the stake in Emporium Capwell. By 1968 Broadway had increased its stake in that profitable company to 50.3% and fully absorbed it two years later.

Broadway expanded aggressively in 1969. That year it acquired Sunset House, a leading mail-order chain; Neiman-Marcus Co., a high-end chain of specialty stores; and Walden Book Co., the nation's largest book retailer. By the end of that year Broadway-Hale was the 13th-largest department store chain in the U.S. and the leading retailer in the West.

In 1971 the company acquired Bergdorf Goodman Co., which operated a single, yet highly respected, store in New York. The following year Carter became CEO and appointed Philip Hawley as president; Prentis Hale remained chairman. Later that year Broadway acquired Holt Renfrew & Co., a 19-store upscale specialty group based in Montreal. In 1974 it purchased a 20% stake in House of Fraser, the owner of Harrod's of London, 135 other British retail stores, and Illium's of Copenhagen. The next year Broadway changed its name to Carter Hawley Hales Stores, Inc. (CHH)

Hawley became CEO in 1977, embarking on a plan to integrate the company's diverse businesses into a single, well-run company. He sold its stake in House of Fraser and then made an unsuccessful bid for Marshall Field & Co. Earnings that year were $42 million on sales of $1.4 billion.

CHH continued its purchasing spree in 1978, when it acquired the 15-unit John Wanamaker chain and the 26-outlet Thalhimer Brothers. Despite the company's massive growth, however, its profit margin that year was only 3.3%. To improve profits, Hawley centralized and standardized store administration and operations, yet earnings still resisted recovery, dropping 17% in 1981, decreasing again in 1982, and stagnating in 1983.

These low earnings made CHH vulnerable to a takeover. In 1984 The Limited, Inc. made an unfriendly bid, which CHH thwarted by selling a large company stake to General Cinema Corp. and by repurchasing a significant chunk of its own stock. The fight was successful, but costly. Two years later The Limited joined with Edward J. DeBartolo Corp. to make another attempt for CHH. Again the company turned to General Cinema to purchase its stock and thwarted the takeover attempt.

Because its debt had grown to devastating levels, CHH divested some assets. It followed up its 1985 sale of Walden Book by selling John Wanamaker in 1987. That year the company split itself into two entities. Department stores, which retained the Carter Hawley Hale Stores corporate name, encompassed The Broadway, Broadway-Southwest, Emporium Capwell, Thalhimer, and Weinstocks stores. Specialty stores, of which General Cinema gained controlling interest by exchanging its stake in CHH, included Neiman-Marcus, Contempo Casuals, and Bergdorf Goodman.

CHH lacked the resources to undertake the remodeling required for its stores. This problem was compounded when a 1989 earthquake damaged 12 Emporium outlets. In October 1990 the company agreed to sell Thalhimer to May Department Stores for $325 million. Much of this capital was used to pare down debt while the rest was earmarked for remodeling.

Circumstances continued to deteriorate, however. The firm's workforce was reduced by 1,000 and its $100 million bank credit line collapsed. In February 1991 CHH sought Chapter 11 bankruptcy protection. The Zell/Chilmark investment fund acquired 70% of the company's stock later that year, and in October 1992 CHH emerged from bankruptcy protection.

David Dworkin succeeded Hawley as CEO in March 1993, and the company changed its name to Broadway Stores, Inc. In 1995 it was purchased by Federated Department Stores, Inc., making Federated the nation's largest department store retailer.

Market Forces Driving the Acquisition

Carter Hawley Hale had adopted a strategy of expansion through acquisition in the 1970s, picking up a number of department and specialty store chains. The diverse operations were run separately, with little attempt to integrate operations and practices. When Philip Hawley became CEO in 1977, he orchestrated a long-term and costly reorganization. Among his centralization efforts was the construction of a $75 million computer center. Despite such moves, CHH's profitability remained depressed. While sales and operations continued to grow, profits declined in 1981 and 1982 and were stagnant in 1983. This financial state of affairs made the firm vulnerable to a takeover attempt.

Meanwhile, The Limited was eager to break into high-fashion retailing. Among the company's operations were its women's clothing stores operating under the names The Limited, Lane Bryant, and Victoria's Secret. The latter two had been acquired in 1982, and the company was still hot on the acquisition trail in 1984.

Approach and Engagement

On April 2, 1984, The Limited announced its $1.1 billion bid for CHH. The two-step deal was contingent upon receipt of 53.6% of the company in a tender offer at $30 per share, followed by a stock swap for the remaining shares. A week later CHH was still silent about the bid, but had filed a civil suit against The Limited, alleging antitrust violations.

Concerned that CHH would divest some of its more profitable assets or seek safety in the arms of a white knight, The Limited sought to persuade shareholders to oust the company's board. Before it could accomplish this feat, however, CHH did precisely what The Limited had feared. On April 17 it sold 23% of its voting shares to General Cinema Corp., the movie theater operator and Pepsi Cola bottler. As part of the pact, General Cinema agreed to vote its shares according to CHH's wishes. This stake, purchased for $300 million, also included the option of purchasing Walden Book Co. at a later date. Many observers believed that in offering up one of its most valuable properties, CHH was adopting a "scorched earth" policy, meaning it would severely damage itself in order to remain independent.

At the same time, CHH bought 18% of its outstanding stock on the open market and announced its intention to purchase additional shares in order to make The Limited's takeover more difficult. The Limited recognized this strategy for what it was and filed suit seeking an injunction against any such future purchases as well as the reversal of the previous acquisition of shares.

The sale of the stake to General Cinema drew the scrutiny of the New York Stock Exchange, whose rules stipulated that the sale of more than 18% of a compa-

The Players

The Limited Chairman and CEO: Leslie H. Wexner. Born on Sept. 8, 1937, Leslie Wexner became an entrepreneur due to disagreements with his father over the operation of the family's clothing store. His father maintained that the highest profits arose from the sale of expensive articles, while Leslie insisted that greater earnings could be realized by selling larger quantities of more reasonably priced sportswear. In 1963 he put his theory to the test, opening the first Limited store. He took his successful retailing concept to the shopping malls, where the company expanded its holdings into a variety of operations.

Carter Hawley Hale Chairman and CEO: Philip M. Hawley. Philip Hawley graduated from the University of California at Berkeley with a degree in economics. After a stint at Merrill Lynch, Hawley started a chain of ice cream parlors. In 1958 he joined Broadway-Hale as a buyer, and in ten years he was named president. His name was added to the company moniker in 1974. Hawley became CEO in 1977 and chairman in 1983. He retired from Carter Hawley Hale in March 1993, at which time he became a private consultant.

ny's interest required shareholder approval, which CHH had not solicited. This scrutiny didn't stop CHH, however, and it increased its stock buyback to 37% by April 24. This move decreased the number of shares outstanding, thereby increasing General Cinema's interest to 33%. It also resulted in the added scrutiny of the Security Exchange Commission, which launched an investigation as to whether or not the repurchase constituted an illegal tender offer.

On April 27 The Limited sweetened its bid to $35 per share and lowered its requirement of a minimum receipt of tendered shares from 20.3 to 15.5 million. CHH again rejected the offer as "inadequate." In early May the company received encouragement in its defensive tactics when a federal judge rejected the SEC's claim regarding the company's stock repurchases. On May 21 The Limited realized that it was fighting a losing battle and withdrew its tender offer. It wasn't giving up the hope of eventually gain control of CHH, however. "I'm a patient man," said chairman Leslie Wexner in *The Wall Street Journal*. "What you've got now is a siege, as opposed to an active battle."

The fight had been costly for CHH, as its stock buyback required the assumption of even more debt. To reduce this load, it sold Walden Book to KMart Corp. for $295 million after General Cinema passed on its option to purchase the chain. In 1985 CHH also sold its Holt Renfrew division.

As warned by Wexner, The Limited's withdrawal had not been a truce, only a temporary lull in the battle. On November 25, 1986, The Limited joined with the Edward J. DeBartolo Corp., the leading developer of shopping centers in the U.S., to make a renewed bid. Their joint company for this purpose, Retail Partner, offered $1.8 billion in cash, or $55 per share, for two-thirds of all voting shares. CHH smugly boasted in a released statement, "This offer certainly proves that we were right before in rejecting the 1984 offer," as reported in *The New York Times*.

When General Cinema signaled that it would not vote against CHH to accept to this offer, Retail Partners modified the terms of the offer to require the receipt of a simple majority stake, thereby reducing General Cinema's clout in the matter. This company responded by raising its stake in CHH, and by December 9 had acquired a 49.1% interest. Retail Partners consequently withdrew its offer, which had been sweetened to $60 per share.

Products and Services

The Limited Inc. operated a number of retail stores: Limited Stores, offering women's sportswear, had sales of $757 million from 551 stores in 1998; Express, geared toward young, stylish women, drew sales of $1.4 billion from its 702 stores; Lerner New York, featuring women's sportswear, generated sales of $940 million from 643 stores; Lane Bryant, offering fashions for full-figured women, accounted for $933 million in sales from its 730 stores; Henri Bendel, which targeted higher-income women, had sales of $40 million from its single Manhattan location; Structure, offering men's sportswear, generated $610 million in sales from its 532 stores; Limited Too, which targeted fashion-conscious girls, had sales of $377 million from its 319 stores; and Galyan's Trading Company, the sporting goods retailer, drew $220 million in sales from its 14 stores.

The Limited also owned 83% of the shares of Intimate Brands, Inc., which consisted of: Bath & Body Works, a personal care products retailer, which had sales of $1.3 billion in 1998; and Victoria's Secret Stores and Victoria's Secret Catalogue, offering intimate apparel, foundations, and related products for women, had sales of $1.8 billion and $759 million, respectively.

Changes to the Industry and Review of the Outcome

Although Carter Hawley Hale had successfully resisted the takeovers, few industry analysts considered the company victorious. Debt levels were higher than ever, leaving CHH with little cash or credit for renovation, which was desperately needed to raise earnings.

In January 1987 CHH sold its John Wanamaker division to Woodward & Lothrop Inc. That August the firm split into two separate companies in order to refine its retail focus. The department store holdings, which retained the Carter Hawley Hale corporate name, consisted of a total of 114 stores under the Broadway, Emporium Capwell, Thalhimers, and Weinstocks names. Its 190 specialty stores, including Neiman-Marcus, Bergdorf Goodman, and Contempo Casuals, were spun off to shareholders. The transaction called for the exchange of one CHH share for $17 in cash, one share of the specialty store business, and one share of the new CHH. General Cinema received a 52% ownership of the specialty store group of in exchange for most of its stake in CHH.

The department stores were aging and sorely in need of renovation. Nature, too, seemed to conspire against CHH, as the San Francisco earthquake of 1989 damaged 12 Emporium stores, forcing their temporary closure. The company recorded a net loss of $26 million that year. In October 1990 it sold Thalhimer to May Department Stores for $325 million, using the proceeds to retire some of its debt and to renovate some of its California outlets.

Continuing its efforts to improve its situation, CHH reduced its workforce by 1,000. As its $100 million credit line from the Bank of America collapsed, the company watched its stock price plunge to $14. On February 11, 1991, CHH was forced to file for bankruptcy protection against its creditors. Later that year the investment fund Zell/Chilmark, a partnership between Samuel Zell and David Schulte, purchased a 75% stake in CHH. On October 8, 1992, CHH emerged from bankruptcy. By early November 1992 its shares were trading for $6.5—a far cry from even the stingiest of The Limited's offers.

In March 1993 David Dworkin succeeded the retiring Philip Hawley as CEO. Dworkin, who was known as the force responsible for the turnaround of the London retailer Storehouse, redefined company goals and replaced 60% of its senior management. CHH changed its name to Broadway Stores, Inc. The company never reacquired its preeminence, however, and in 1995 was purchased by Federated Department Stores. This company, which became the nation's largest department store retailer, converted 56 of

Broadway's stores to the Macy's name and five to Bloomingdale's, while closing or selling Broadway's remaining 21 stores.

Research

Barmash, Isadore. "Carter Hawley Bid by Limited," in *The New York Times*, 3 April 1984. Relates The Limited's initial bid for CHH.

———. "The Limited Gains Ally for Carter Bid," in *The New York Times*, 26 November 1986. Describes The Limited's partnership with DeBartolo in its second bid for CHH.

"Carter Hawley Hales Stores, Inc.," in *International Directory of Company Histories*, Vol. V, St. James Press: 1992. Narrative account of the company's history, through its emergence from bankruptcy in 1992.

Ingrassia, Lawrence, and Roy J. Harris Jr. "General Cinema to Expand into Retailing through Stake in Carter Hawley Spinoff," in *The Wall Street Journal*, 10 December 1986. Describes the termination of The Limited's second bid and CHH's division into two entities.

The Limited, Inc. Home Page, available at http://www.limited.com. Official World Wide Web Page for The Limited. Includes a store locator, annual reports and other financial information, employment opportunities, and hyperlinks to its stores' Web pages.

"The Limited, Inc.," in *International Directory of Company Histories*, Vol. 20, St. James Press: 1998. Profiles the history of The Limited.

Paltrow, Scot J. and William M. Bulkeley. "General Cinema Buys 23% Stake in Carter Hawley," in *The Wall Street Journal*, 17 April 1984. Details General Cinema's initial purchase of CHH stock.

Saporito, Bill. "Makeover for a Plain-Jane Retailer," in *Fortune*, 11 April 1988. Describes CHH's efforts to become a department store retailer after the spinoff of its specialty store operations.

Solomon, Jolie B. "Limited Ends Its Offer for Carter Hawley But Says Control of Retailer Is Still a Goal," in *The Wall Street Journal*, 22 May 1984. Reports The Limited's termination of its tender offer.

DEBORAH J. UNTENER

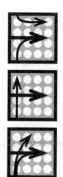

LOCKHEED & MARTIN MARIETTA

Lockheed Martin Corp.
6801 Rockledge Dr.
Bethesda, MD 20817
USA

tel: (301)897-6000
fax: (301)897-6704
web: http://www.lmco.com

nationality: USA
date: March 15, 1995
affected: Lockheed Corp., USA, founded 1916
affected: Martin Marietta Corp., USA, founded 1917

Overview of the Merger

The $10 billion merger of Lockheed Corp. and Martin Marietta Corp. combined the second- and third-largest U.S. defense contractors to form the world's largest weapons maker. On one hand, the 1995 merger stunned the industry. It was the largest defense-related deal since the end of the Cold War, and came quickly on the heels of Martin Marietta's attempted acquisition of Grumman Corp. On the other hand, however, the defense industry had been experiencing a wave of consolidation, and a deal of this magnitude was generally considered to be inevitable.

History of Lockheed Corp.

Allan and Malcolm Loughead engineered and constructed a small ultralight seaplane called the Model G, one of the first "tractor" designs with a forward-mounted engine enclosed in the fuselage. In 1912 the Loughead brothers established the Alco Hydro-Aeroplane Co. with financial backing from Max Mamlock's Alco Cab Co. By the following year, however, the company was forced to dissolve because it was unable to sell any of its planes.

In 1916 the brothers tried again by establishing the Loughead Aircraft Manufacturing Co. in Santa Barbara, California. Tired of having their name mispronounced, they changed the company name to "Lockheed." In 1919, the same year that Malcolm resigned, company engineer Jack Northrop helped the company develop its twin-engine F-1 flying boat. Northrop went on to develop the Vega in 1927. This plane, which became widely known as an explorer's plane, was used by Amelia Earhart to cross the Atlantic. In 1928 Northrop resigned from Lockheed.

The Detroit Aircraft Corp. acquired Lockheed in 1929. Infuriated by the takeover, Allan Loughead resigned and sold his holdings in the company. Under the new management, Lockheed's engineers produced a number of new airplanes, most notably the passenger transport, Orion. In 1932 Detroit Aircraft, in poor financial condition due to the Depression, sold Lockheed to a group of investors for $40,000. Airmail legislation and other congressional acts in 1934 forced the breakup of a number of powerful aviation combines. Lockheed, however, was small enough to escape the notice of regulators.

In 1938, after the German annexation of Austria, British delegates toured the U.S. in search of airplanes to purchase for the Royal Air Force. Lockheed engineers quickly designed a reconnaissance bomber, the Hudson, with powerful engines, a bomb bay, and guns. In the largest military contract awarded before the war, Britain purchased 200 Hudsons for $25 million, marking a turning point in Lockheed's business.

By the end of World War II, Lockheed had produced 19,297 aircraft for the military, nine percent of the nation's total production. It resumed its civilian Constellation project, introduced several versions of the triple-rudder airplane, and maintained numerous military contracts.

In 1953 Lockheed tested a vertical take-off and landing plane, equipped with what was widely recognized as the propulsion mechanism of the next century. Lockheed also undertook plans for a nuclear-powered aircraft, and established its missiles and space division to produce satellites and submarine-launched missiles. In 1960 it introduced the U-2 and the SR-71 spy planes. The latter, nicknamed the Blackbird, was regarded as nearly perfect by most engineers, with a cruising speed of over 2,100 mph at an altitude of over 85,000 ft.

When Boeing announced the development of its 747, and Douglas its DC-10, Lockheed responded with the risky construction project of a commercial wide body jetliner of its own, the 1011 TriStar. In 1970 the TriStar was first flown, but the program was set back due to major problems. Rolls-Royce, the manufacturer of the 1011's engines, went into receivership. Sales of the jetliner quickly dropped, and the company faced a liquidity crisis. In 1971 Lockheed took out a guaranteed government loan to avoid bankruptcy. The Securities and Exchange Commission withheld any action against Lockheed because its guaranteed loan gave the government an active interest in the company's quick financial recovery.

In 1976 an international scandal added to the financial troubles experienced by Lockheed, when it was accused of bribing officials in Iran, Indonesia, Italy, the Netherlands, and Japan. The U.S. government subsequently implemented more stringent anti-bribery laws. Lockheed's management was replaced and the company was restructured under the guidance of Robert Haack, former president of the New York Stock Exchange.

The company acquired Sanders Associates, an electronics maker, in 1986. It later sold its Dialog computer information network, as well as its CADAM and Lockheed DataPlan computer service interests. The poor performance of its Hubble Space Telescope contributed to the company's woes in 1990. That year

The Business

Financials

Revenue (1998): $26.3 billion

Employees (1998): 165,000

SICs / NAICS

sic 3721 - Aircraft

sic 3761 - Guided Missiles & Space Vehicles

sic 3663 - Radio & T.V. Communications Equipment

naics 336411 - Aircraft Manufacturing

naics 336414 - Guided Missile and Space Vehicle Manufacturing

naics 334220 - Broadcasting and Wireless Communications Equipment Manufacturing

Harold Simmons, a Texas billionaire, gathered investors who wanted Lockheed to cease expansion into non-defense projects, spearheading proxy fights. The company survived this attack from Simmons, however, and he consequently sold most of his 19.8% interest in the company at a loss of $42 million.

In 1992 it formed a joint venture with Martin Marietta to acquire LTV Corp.'s missile and aircraft divisions. It also entered into a joint venture with AT&T and Malev Hungarian Airlines to implement non-defense projects. Lockheed, McDermott, and Olin announced the creation of the International Disarmament Corp. In March 1993 it acquired the tactical aircraft business of General Dynamics in exchange for a block of Lockheed's stock. Company sales that year were $13.2 billion.

History of Martin Marietta Corp.

Glenn L. Martin moved in 1905 to Santa Ana, California, where he built and flew his first experimental gliders. In 1917 he established the Glenn L. Martin Co. in Cleveland, Ohio, hiring Donald Douglas as chief designer. After incorporating in Maryland, the company moved to Baltimore in 1929.

In the 1930s the company made significant strides into the airplane industry. It introduced the first U.S.-built bombers and was awarded the Collier Trophy for the B-10 bomber. With backing from Pan Am Airlines, it delivered the first passenger airplane, the Clipper, capable of traveling long distances over water. The M-130 Clipper held 32 passengers and traveled up to 2,500 miles.

The Officers

Chairman and CEO: Vance Coffman

President and Chief Operating Officer: Peter B. Teets

During World War II, Martin supplied thousands of airplanes for the war effort, including the A-30 Baltimore, the B-26 and B-29 bombers, the PBM Mariner flying boat, and the amphibious Mars air freighter. In 1947 the company entered the highly competitive commercial airline market with the M-202. Development of later aircraft, the M-303 and M-404, proved to be a severe drain on company finances.

Chester C. Pearson was hired as president and general manager, with Glenn Martin as chairman, in 1949. The company's orders increased due to demand arising from the Korean War, but the firm continued to lose money. The termination of production of the M-404 airplane and the hiring of hundreds of new and unskilled workers resulted in reduced productivity and income. Two years later, after a loss of $22 million, George M. Bunker and J. Bradford Wharton, Jr. were recruited to take the company's helm. Under their leadership, the company diversified into missiles, electronics, and nuclear systems. In 1953 Martin began designing the Titan, an Intercontinental Ballistic Missile, which evolved into a versatile space launch vehicle. By the following year, the company had eliminated its debt.

In 1960 Martin produced its last airplane, a Navy P5M-2 antisubmarine patrol plane. To diversify its product line, the company merged in 1961 with American Marietta Corp., a supplier of construction materials, to form Martin Marietta Corp. In 1968 it acquired 41% of Harvey Aluminum, later called Marietta Aluminum.

The company's diverse operations in aerospace, chemicals, electronics, aluminum, and construction products enabled it to experience growth during the 1970s. Much of that growth was generated through government contracts. Martin Marietta's aerospace unit received government contracts in 1969 for two *Viking* capsules that would later land on Mars. Four years later, the company was awarded the contract to build the external fuel tank for NASA's space shuttles. In 1979 it won the contract for the MX missile.

In 1982 Bendix Corp. made a hostile takeover bid for Martin Marietta, but the company countered by attempting to take over Bendix, accruing $1.34 billion in debt in the process. To reduce that debt load, Martin Marietta divested itself of its cement, aluminum, and specialty chemicals operations. By 1986 the company had reduced its debt to $220 million.

Martin Marietta's sales in 1989 reached $5.8 billion as a result of increased defense electronics business and orders for Titan launchers. Its *Magellan* spacecraft was launched to map the surface of Venus. In 1992 the company entered into a joint venture with Lockheed to acquire LTV Corp.'s missile and aircraft divisions. The following year it paid $3 billion to acquire General Electric's aerospace business, a producer of radars. Sales in 1993 reached $9.4 billion.

In 1994 it acquired the space systems division of General Dynamics. It also spun off its materials unit as Martin Marietta Materials, Inc. Later that year it agreed to merge with Grumman Corp., but backed down when Northrop Corp. stepped in with its own bid for that company.

Market Forces Driving the Merger

The conclusion of the Cold War had a devastating effect on the U.S. defense industry. The government no longer had reason to stockpile weapons and related equipment, so defense budgets were slashed. As a result, the nation's defense contractors were in fierce competition for the few remaining contracts still offered by the government. Since many of these companies relied on the government as their largest customer, they scrambled to find ways to fill the void from reduced sales in that sector. Most had three choices: exit the business entirely, increase sales in the commercial sector, or join forces with a peer to grab a larger piece of the pie. For many firms, the third option was the most tasteful and viable.

The federal government, too, recognized this to be the most favorable option, and encouraged merger activity in the industry. In 1994 the Clinton Administration orchestrated an agreement between the Pentagon and the Federal Trade Commission to extend more relaxed consideration to such proposed deals. This accord wasn't struck merely to preserve the financial well being of the contractors, however. The government believed that, as the industry's largest customer, it would benefit from consolidation by being the recipient of reduced prices.

It was this combination of a shrinking market and governmental encouragement that spurred the merger of Northrop Corp. and Grumman Corp. in April 1994. Martin Marietta was well familiar with that transaction, as it had engaged in a battle with Northrop for the acquisition of Grumman. Northrop was the eventual winner, as Martin Marietta declined to participate in a bidding war. Still, Martin Marietta knew that sooner or later it would join in the consolidation movement.

Likewise, Lockheed Corp. experienced the urge to merge. For nearly a year, it had sought an acquisition candidate, but found that the most desirable companies were too large to be acquired. Then it hit on the formula of a merger of equals. With the termination of Martin Marietta's acquisition of Grumman, Lockheed viewed that company as a potential partner. The union of the two companies would combine strengths in complementary operations with little overlap. Lockheed was an aerospace leader, particularly in the manufacture of airframes, and produced two well-known fighters, the F-16 and the F-22 stealth. Martin Marietta had a background in aeronautics, and had recently forayed into defense electronics, including avionics, sensors, and subsystems.

Approach and Engagement

In March 1994, just days after Martin Marietta's withdrawal from the battle for Grumman, chairman Norman Augustine received a phone call from his friend, Daniel Tellep, chairman of Lockheed. Tellep suggested a merger of their two companies, and the pair entered into quiet negotiations. In less than six months they had struck a deal. On August 30, 1994, they announced that their respective boards had approved a merger.

The companies cited expansion into civilian markets as a prime reason for the union. Combined, the two firms derived only about 40% of their total business from the non-defense sector. Their synergies in this area, particularly in electronics, would enable them to consolidate research, administration, and computer systems. They estimated that consolidation would save them about $5 billion, which would be invested in R&D and acquisitions. As reported in *Defense Daily*, Augustine stated, "Our long-term plan is to maintain growth in our core defense, civil government and commercial business. We also will marshal our considerable technological and management resources to produce solutions for aerospace, environment, urban, energy and information technology challenges in both the private and public sectors, in the U.S. and abroad."

On January 12, 1995, the Federal Trade Commission (FTC) granted its non-binding consent order to the merger, reserving its final decision until March. As part of its initial consent, the FTC required the companies to agree to several provisions that addressed the Commission's antitrust concerns in the areas of space-based early-warning systems, expendable launch vehicles, and combat aircraft. The combined company would be required to eliminate its exclusivity agreements with suppliers on early-warning systems. Its launch vehicle units would be barred

The Players

Lockheed Chairman and CEO: Daniel M. Tellep. Daniel Tellep earned a B.S. and an M.S. from the University of California at Berkeley. In 1955 he took a job as a principal scientist at Lockheed Missiles & Space Company. After managing programs in thermodynamics, missile reentry systems, and engineering development, he became an executive VP. In 1984 Tellep was appointed president of Lockheed Missiles & Space. In 1987 he became president of Lockheed Corp., and moved up to chairman and CEO in 1989. In 1993 Tellep was selected by the National Management Association as Executive of the Year. In December 1995 he retired as CEO, and was succeeded by Norman Augustine. The following year Tellep reached the mandatory retirement age of 65, and stepped down as chairman in favor of Augustine that December.

Martin Marietta Chairman and CEO: Norman R. Augustine. Norman Augustine earned both a B.S. and an M.S. in aeronautical engineering at Princeton University. He then worked at the Department of Defense, serving as undersecretary of the Army from 1975 to 1977. At Martin Marietta, he orchestrated the celebrated merger with Lockheed Corp. after failing in an attempt to acquire Grumman Corp. Upon formation of Lockheed Martin, Augustine assumed the post of president with the understanding that he would succeed Daniel Tellep as chairman and CEO. In December 1995 he succeeded to CEO, and one year later added the post of chairman to his duties. That year he was named one of *Business Week*'s top 25 managers. Augustine retired as CEO in August 1997 to become an engineering professor at his alma mater. He was succeeded by Vance Coffman, who also succeeded him as chairman in April 1998. Augustine is the author of two books: 1983's *Augustine's Laws*, an analysis of the U.S. aerospace industry, and 1998's *Augustine's Travels*, a commentary on the role of the U.S. executive.

from receiving non-public information garnered through its satellite division. Likewise, its military aircraft operations would not be allowed to access the proprietary information received by its electronics division.

As part of this consent order, former Martin Marietta executives would receive a total of $82.4 million in bonuses. Of that amount, about $31 million would be contributed by the federal government as part of its performance incentive plan with that company. According to *Defense Daily*, a Department of Defense statement reported that, "Mergers often trigger payments to company officials under their employment contracts. As a result of the merger, certain officials are entitled to accelerated payment of deferred compensation and incentive payments." For the most part, taxpayers were oblivious to this payment, but Lockheed shareholders were well aware of it. Some were angered, threatening to vote against the merger. Yet on March 15, 1995, some 90% approved the deal, and the companies were officially united.

In the $10 billion stock swap, Lockheed shareholders received 1.63 shares of the newly formed Lockheed Martin Corp., while Martin Marietta shares were converted on a one-to-one basis. The new company was headquartered at Martin Marietta's base in Bethesda, Maryland. Daniel Tellep, chairman and CEO of Lockheed, assumed the same positions at Lockheed Martin, while Norman Augustine, chairman and CEO of Martin Marietta, became president, scheduled to succeed Tellep upon his retirement in three years.

Products and Services

Lockheed Martin was organized into six major business sectors:

Aeronautics encompassed six lines of business: tactical aircraft; air mobility; modification, maintenance, and logistics; reconnaissance; surveillance and command; and advanced development. Its product offerings included the C130J Hercules, the C5 Galaxy, the F16 Fighting Falcon, the F22 Raptor, the F117 Nighthawk, the JASSM (Joint Air to Surface Stand-off Missile), and the X-33 VentureStar. In 1998 the Aeronautics sector had sales that dropped one percent to $5.99 billion.

Electronics involved the design, development, and manufacture of electronic systems for global defense, civil, and commercial markets. Its core businesses included naval systems, missiles and air defense, aerospace electronics, platform integration, and postal systems. Its product line was diverse, and included electronic defense and sonar systems, advanced combat systems, submarine command and control systems, and missile, rocket, and space systems. This sector was the strongest performer in 1998, as its sales rose four percent to $7.34 billion.

Information & Services provided government and commercial customers with a range of information technology solutions, from complex systems integration projects for the federal government to the operation of electronic toll collection systems on the nation's highways. Sales in this sector in 1998 fell 19% to $5.21 billion.

Space & Strategic Missiles was involved in the design, development, test, and manufacture of a variety of advanced technology systems for space and defense. Chief products included planetary spacecraft and other space systems, space launch systems, and ground systems. In 1998 this sector's sales dropped from $8.3 billion to $7.46 billion.

Global Telecommunications focused on four areas: Global Network Solutions, a provider and operator of wireline, fiber, and wireless telecommunications networks; Global Transport Services and Operations, a provider of global transmission services, wholesale capacity, and end-to-end transport and applications solutions; Network Systems Development, which leveraged network engineering and systems integration expertise, enterprise systems, and communications systems; and Personal Communications Systems, a provider of personal communications solutions to individual businesses and government organizations.

The **Energy & Environment** unit conducted basic and applied research and development to: strengthen the nation's leadership in key areas of science; increase the availability of clean, abundant energy; restore and protect the environment; and contribute to national security.

The Global Telecommunications and Energy & Environment units are consolidated as the company's Energy & Other operations, which achieved 1998 revenues of $255 million.

Changes to the Industry

Lockheed Martin immediately became the world's largest defense contractor, with $22.4 billion in annual sales and $865 million in earnings. It also moved into a position to challenge Boeing as the world's largest aerospace company, as its 1993 sales in that sector totaled $21.8 billion, just behind Boeing's $25 million.

The merger raised the stakes in the defense industry. Lockheed Martin dwarfed even the world's largest defense contractors. First-tier U.S. contractors faced increased pressure to consolidate, thereby perpetuating the industry's shrinking playing field. In fact, Lockheed Martin soon got bumped down to the industry's second-place position. The August 1997 union of Boeing and McDonnell Douglas had captured the top spot.

Review of the Outcome

At the completion of the merger, Lockheed Martin estimated that it would be forced to reduce its workforce by about 30,000 positions. It withheld official determination, however, until it completed a reorganization and integration of the companies' operations. In June 1995 the firm announced that the number of lay-offs would be fewer than originally anticipated, and it would eliminate 15,000 jobs, or 12% of its workforce, over the following two years.

The company continued to participate in the dizzying industry-wide consolidation. In April 1996 it purchased Loral Corp., which was renamed as the Lockheed Martin Tactical Systems, Inc. subsidiary. In July 1997 Lockheed Martin and Northrop Grumman entered into a merger agreement, but Lockheed Martin withdrew its offer the following year after the U.S. Department of Justice announced its intention of blocking the merger in court. In February 1999 Lockheed Martin offered to purchase 49% of COMSAT, a communications satellite company; COMSAT's shareholders were scheduled to vote on the deal in June 1999.

Meanwhile, the company divested itself of several operations. In 1996 it distributed its 81% stake in Martin Marietta Materials, Inc. In January 1997 it received $450 million from the sale of two business units, Armament Systems and Defense Systems, to General Dynamics. That April Lockheed Martin spun off 10 noncore units as L-3 Communications Corp., of which it retained a 34.9% interest. In November 1997 it exchanged its stock in the newly formed subsidiary, LMT Sub, for the stake in Lockheed Martin that had been held by General Electric since 1993. In August 1998 it announced the formation of Lockheed Martin Global Telecommunications, Inc., a wholly owned subsidiary.

The company's financial results for 1998 were the worst since its formation three years earlier. Net earnings dropped 8.5% to $1.18 billion on revenues that fell 6.4% to $26.3 billion. Lockheed Martin attributed the decline to weak sales in space-related and commercial information sectors, as well as to the delay in the signing of a $5 billion military aircraft order with the United Arab Emirates. The U.S. Government remained its largest customer, accounting for about 70% of it 1998 net sales.

Research

Bielski, Tanya. "Stockholders Approve Lockheed, Martin Marietta Merger," in *Defense Daily*, 16 March 1995. Describes the clearing of the final hurdle toward merger, as well as the new company's outlook for the future.

Bollinger, Martin J. "What Lockheed Martin Means to Europe," in *Interavia Business & Technology*, October 1994. Projects the impact that the merger will have on the global defense industry.

"DOD Foots Bill for Some Martin Marietta Bonuses," in *Defense Daily*, 20 March 1995. Reports the $31 million that the U.S. government paid to company executives as part of the merger agreement.

Harrison, Joan. "A Giant Merger of Two Survivors," in *Mergers & Acquisitions*, January-February 1995. Profiles the merging companies.

"Joining Forces: Merger of Lockheed and Martin Marietta Pushes Industry Trend," in *The Wall Street Journal*, 30 August 1994. Anticipates the merger announcement.

"Lockheed Martin is Born," in *Electronic News (1991)*, 20 March 1995. Reports the approval of shareholders for the deal.

"Lockheed Martin Corp.," in *Notable Corporate Chronologies*, The Gale Group, 1999. Profiles the history of both Lockheed and Martin Marietta, and describes major events since the consolidated company's formation.

Lockheed Martin Corp. Home Page, available at http://www.lmco.com. Official World Wide Web Page for Lockheed Martin. Includes product description, officer biographies, annual reports and other financial information, and news releases.

"Lockheed/Martin Marietta Overcome Anti-trust Snag," in *Flight International*, 18 January 1995. Describes the terms of the FTC's initial consent decree.

Muradian, Vago. "Lockheed Martin Posts Sales, Net Earnings Drop in 1998," in *Defense Daily*, 29 January 1999. Provides an in-depth account of the company's annual and quarterly financial results.

O'Toole, Kevin. "A Question of Scale: Will Big Also Be Beautiful, as Consolidation Creates American Aerospace Giants?" in *Flight International*, 4 January 1995. Provides a lengthy analysis of the U.S. and global defense industries in light of the proposed merger.

DEBORAH J. UNTENER

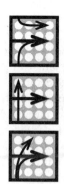

LOCKHEED MARTIN & LORAL

Lockheed Martin Corp.
6801 Rockledge Dr.
Bethesda, MD 20817
USA

tel: (301)897-6000
fax: (301)897-6704
web: http://www.lmco.com

nationality: USA
date: April 23, 1996
affected: Lockheed Martin Corp., USA, founded 1916
affected: Loral Corp., USA, founded 1948

Overview of the Merger

Lockheed Martin Corp.'s 1996 merger with Loral Corp. strengthened the company's position as the world's largest defense contractor. The global defense industry was experiencing a shift in focus from a physical hunk of metal to an electronic blip on a screen. Loral's strong operations in defense electronics and systems integration melded with Lockheed's operations in those areas, while Loral's satellite business, not included as part of the merger, was spun off as Loral Space & Communications Corp.

History of Lockheed Martin Corp.

In 1916 Allan and Malcolm Loughead established the Loughead Aircraft Manufacturing Co. After changing the company name to "Lockheed," the company developed its twin-engine F-1 flying boat with the assistance of company engineer Jack Northrop, who developed the Vega in 1927. The Detroit Aircraft Corp. acquired Lockheed in 1929, and then sold Lockheed to a group of investors in 1932.

Meanwhile, Glenn L. Martin established the Glenn L. Martin Co. in 1917. During the 1930s the company made significant strides into the airplane industry. It introduced the first U.S.-built bombers and delivered the Clipper, the first passenger airplane capable of traveling long distances over water.

In 1938, after the German annexation of Austria, Britain purchased 200 Hudsons for $25 million in the largest military contract awarded before the war, marking a turning point in Lockheed's business. By the end of World War II, Lockheed had produced 19,297 aircraft for the military, nine percent of the nation's total production.

During World War II, Martin supplied such airplanes for the war effort as the A-30 Baltimore and the B-26 and B-29 bombers. In 1947 the company entered the highly competitive commercial airline market with the M-202. Development of later aircraft, the M-303 and M-404, proved to be a severe drain on company finances. The Korean War increased Martin's sales, but it continued to lose money. It recovered in the 1950s by diversifying into missiles, electronics, and nuclear systems.

During that decade Lockheed established a missiles and space division to produce satellites and submarine-launched missiles. In 1960 it introduced the U-2 and the SR-71 spy planes; the latter was nicknamed the Blackbird. That year Martin produced its last airplane, a Navy P5M-2 antisubmarine patrol plane. To diversify its product line, Martin merged in 1961 with American Marietta Corp., a supplier of construction materials, to form Martin Marietta Corp. In 1968 Martin Marietta acquired 41% of Harvey Aluminum, later called Marietta Aluminum.

In 1971, after introducing a problem-riddled TriStar commercial jetliner, Lockheed took out a guaranteed government loan to avoid bankruptcy. In 1976 an international scandal added to the financial troubles experienced by Lockheed, as it was accused of bribing officials in Iran, Indonesia, Italy, the Netherlands, and Japan.

Martin Marietta's diverse operations in aerospace, chemicals, electronics, aluminum, and construction products enabled it to experience growth during the 1970s. In 1982 Bendix Corp. made a hostile takeover bid for Martin Marietta, but the company responded by attempting to take over Bendix, accruing $1.34 billion in debt in the process. To reduce that debt load, Martin Marietta divested itself of its cement, aluminum, and specialty chemicals operations. Martin Marietta's sales in 1989 reached $5.8 billion as a result of increased defense electronics business and orders for Titan launchers.

The poor performance of its Hubble Space Telescope contributed to Lockheed's woes in 1990. It avoided a takeover attempt orchestrated by Texas billionaire Harold Simmons. In March 1993 Lockheed acquired the tactical aircraft business of General Dynamics in exchange for a block of Lockheed stock. That year Martin Marietta acquired General Electric's aerospace business, a producer of radars, and the following year acquired the space systems division of General Dynamics. Later that year it agreed to merge with Grumman Corp. but backed down when Northrop Corp. stepped in with its own bid for that company.

In March 1995 Lockheed and Martin Marietta merged to form Lockheed Martin, the world's largest weapons maker. It continued to be active in mergers and acquisitions. In April 1996 it purchased Loral Corp., which was renamed Lockheed Martin Tactical Systems, Inc.

The Business

Financials

Revenue (1998): $26.3 billion

Employees (1998): 165,000

SICs / NAICS

sic 3721 - Aircraft

sic 3761 - Guided Missiles & Space Vehicles

sic 3663 - Radio & T.V. Communications Equipment

naics 336411 - Aircraft Manufacturing

naics 336414 - Guided Missile and Space Vehicle Manufacturing

naics 334220 - Broadcasting and Wireless Communications Equipment Manufacturing

History of Loral Corp.

Loral Electronics Corp. was founded in 1948 by William Lorenz and Leon Alpert. Focused on producing radar and sonar detection systems, the company aimed to win contracts for advanced airborne radar systems and for U.S. Navy navigation computing. In 1959, the same year that it went public, Loral acquired Willor Manufacturing Corp. and Allor Leasing Corp.

In 1961 Loral formed a division for the development of communications, telemetry, and space navigation systems for satellites. Taking a $15 million loan to finance expansion, Loral specialized in radar receivers by the end of the decade. Despite having won a number of contracts in recent years, including a $3.9 million Navy contract for Doppler navigation radar and a $14 million contract from General Dynamics, the company reported a loss of $3 million in 1971. Unable to make its loan payments, it brought in Bernard Schwartz as president and CEO. He immediately initiated the divestiture of companies not aligned with its core defense electronics businesses.

The defense electronic industry experienced a boom beginning in the Yom Kippur War in 1973, when Egypt used radar-guided weapons to shoot down about 100 Israeli planes. Soon afterward, Loral developed a software-based programmable radar-warning receiver for the F-16 fighter, thereby shaving system reprogramming time from three weeks to only 20 minutes. It also expanded internationally by developing a radar warning and jamming system for Belgium. By 1979 Loral was the nation's largest electronic warfare company.

The Officers

Chairman and CEO: Vance Coffman

President and Chief Operating Officer: Peter B. Teets

In 1980 its position slipped to second place when competitor E-Systems surpassed Loral's $197 million in electronic warfare sales. That year marked the beginning of an acquisition spree by Loral that lasted until 1992, during which time it acquired 13 companies. In 1983 it purchased the electro-optical defense and aerospace operations of Xerox, and two years later acquired the military computer unit of Rolm. In 1986 the company sold its packaging division to Bernard Schwartz.

Loral purchased Goodyear Aerospace Corp. in 1987 for $588 million. In 1989 it sold that unit's aircraft braking and engineered-fabrics divisions for $455 million. That year Loral won a Special Operations Force training and rehearsal contract worth up to $2 billion over the next 15 years. Profits reached $87.6 million on sales of $1.18 billion.

Loral purchased 51.5% of Ford Aerospace in July 1990 for $715 million, thereby doubling its size. The following year it sold 49% of Space Systems-Loral to three European aeronautics firms. In 1992 it purchased the missile operations of LTV. In 1993 it entered into an agreement to develop and manufacture broadcast satellites for Tele-Communications Inc. in order to compete in the direct broadcast satellite television market. In December of that year Loral diversified into systems integration by purchasing most of IBM's Federal Systems Company for $1.5 billion. By the end of 1993 Loral had $2.9 billion in sales, 30 operating divisions, and 28,000 employees.

In April 1994 Loral announced that its Globalstar system, a low-earth orbit satellite telecommunications system , was scheduled to begin operations in 1998. In 1995 the company purchased the aerospace and defense operations of Unisys for $862 million. Later that year, it teamed up with Motorola, TRW, and three other firms to offer international cellular telephone service.

Market Forces Driving the Merger

The defense industry's merger wave was in full force when Lockheed Martin and Loral decided to pair up. A shrinking U.S. defense budget spurred contractors to come together in order to compete effectively for the ever-scarcer government contracts. This merger and acquisition activity was encouraged by the Pentagon, which aimed to keep down the costs that it, as the industry's largest customer, paid for defense products and services. Increasingly, the government's remaining contracts focused on defense electronics, including smart weapons, electronic jammers, and self-protection systems for aircraft.

In 1994 Northrop Corp. acquired Grumman Corp. to form Northrop Grumman Corp. The following year, Lockheed Martin Corp. was formed through the combination of Lockheed Corp. and Martin Marietta Corp. Lockheed Martin immediately became the world's largest defense contractor, yet could not afford to become complacent. At any time, it might have been knocked out of the industry's top spot by a behemoth forged by a combination of its remaining competitors, which were consolidating at a rapid rate.

Defense electronics was the ripest segment of the industry. Consolidation there, too, was occurring rapidly. Hughes Electronics Corp. bought the electronics defense unit of Magnavox in 1995. The following January, Northrop Grumman announced its $3 billion acquisition of the electronics and defense business of Westinghouse.

In order to grow, Lockheed Martin looked to Loral. That company's defense electronics operations would cement Lockheed's hold in that market, particularly in information and business electronics, command and control, and electronic warfare. In addition, Lockheed would strengthen its competitiveness in systems integration, tactical missiles, combat systems, and simulation and training.

Loral, also, would benefit from a merger. By contributing its defense and systems integration businesses to Lockheed, it could turn its attention to the satellite communications business, particularly its Globalstar project. In this segment, it foresaw the greatest potential for growth.

Approach and Engagement

In January 1996, after four months of negotiations, Lockheed Martin and Loral announced their merger agreement. The deal encompassed three main elements. Loral's defense electronics and systems integration businesses would be acquired by Lockheed to form Lockheed Martin Tactical Systems, Inc., a wholly-owned subsidiary of Lockheed. Secondly, Loral's remaining businesses, its satellite communications operations, would form a new company, Loral Space & Communications Corp. This company would hold a 51% interest in Space Systems/Loral, a commercial satellite manufacturer, and a 34% stake in the Globalstar satellite communications project. Finally, Lockheed would acquire a 20% stake in Loral Space for an investment of $344 million.

The $9.1 billion cash transaction would call for $7 billion for the purchase of Loral's shares at $38 each, plus the assumption of $2.1 billion in debt. Additionally, each Loral share would be converted to a single share of Loral Space.

Bernard Schwartz, chairman and CEO of Loral Corp., would retain those positions at the newly formed Loral Space in addition to serving as vice chairman and board member of Lockheed. Loral's president and CEO, Frank Lanza, would become an executive VP and chief operating officer at Lockheed. Daniel Tellep, Lockheed's chairman, and Norman Augustine, its CEO, would retain their positions after the merger.

In April 1996 the European Commission and the U.S. Department of Defense approved the deal. On the 18th of that month, the U.S. Federal Trade Commission granted its consent to the merger, but with several provisions. Lockheed Martin would be barred from increasing its interest in Loral Space. It would also be prevented from providing information to Space Systems/Loral under their technology services agreement. Additionally, Bernard Schwartz, or any other person serving on the boards of both Lockheed and Loral Space, would be banned from obtaining non-public information on Lockheed's competing satellite projects. On April 23, 1996, Lockheed completed the acquisition of Loral's shares.

Products and Services

Lockheed Martin was organized into six major business sectors:

Aeronautics encompassed six lines of business: tactical aircraft; air mobility; modification, maintenance, and logistics; reconnaissance; surveillance and command; and advanced development. Its product offerings included the C130J Hercules, the C5 Galaxy, the F16 Fighting Falcon, the F22 Raptor, the F117 Nighthawk, the JASSM (Joint Air to Surface Stand-off Missile), and the X-33 VentureStar. In 1998, the Aeronautics sector had sales that dropped one percent to $5.99 billion.

Electronics involved the design, development, and manufacture of electronic systems for global defense, civil, and commercial markets. Its core businesses included naval systems, missiles and air defense, aerospace electronics, platform integration, and postal systems. Its product line was diverse, and included electronic defense and sonar systems, advanced combat systems, submarine command and control systems, and missile, rocket, and space systems. This sector was the strongest performer in 1998, as its sales rose four percent to $7.34 billion.

The Players

Lockheed Martin Chairman: Daniel M. Tellep. Daniel Tellep earned a B.S. and an M.S. from the University of California at Berkeley. In 1955 he took a job as a principal scientist at Lockheed Missiles & Space Company. After managing programs in thermodynamics, missile reentry systems, and engineering development, he became an executive VP. In 1984 Tellep was appointed president of Lockheed Missiles & Space. In 1987 he became president of Lockheed Corp., and moved up to chairman and CEO in 1989. In 1993 Tellep was selected by the National Management Association as Executive of the Year. In December 1995 he retired as CEO, and was succeeded by Norman Augustine. The following year Tellep reached the mandatory retirement age of 65, and stepped down as chairman in favor of Augustine that December.

Loral Chairman and CEO: Bernard L. Schwartz. Bernard Schwartz earned a B.S. in finance from City College of New York, from which he later received an honorary Doctorate of Science. In 1972, after serving as president of Leasco, a computer leasing concern, Schwartz was recruited to turn around Loral's financial dire straits. Under his leadership, that company emerged as a leader in defense electronics and satellite communications technology. Before that company's merger with Lockheed Martin, Loral had just experienced its 96th consecutive quarterly earnings increase. Upon the April 1996 merger, Schwartz was made chairman and CEO of the newly formed Loral Space & Communications Corp., as well as vice chairman and board member of Lockheed Martin.

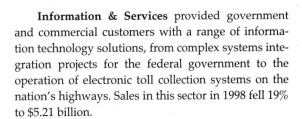

Information & Services provided government and commercial customers with a range of information technology solutions, from complex systems integration projects for the federal government to the operation of electronic toll collection systems on the nation's highways. Sales in this sector in 1998 fell 19% to $5.21 billion.

Space & Strategic Missiles was involved in the design, development, test, and manufacture of a variety of advanced technology systems for space and defense. Chief products included planetary spacecraft and other space systems, space launch systems, and ground systems. In 1998 this sector's sales dropped from $8.3 billion to $7.46 billion.

Global Telecommunications focused on four areas: Global Network Solutions, a provider and operator of wireline, fiber, and wireless telecommunications networks; Global Transport Services and Operations, a provider of global transmission services, wholesale capacity, and end-to-end transport and applications solutions; Network Systems Development, which leveraged network engineering and systems integration expertise, enterprise systems, and communications systems; and Personal Communications Systems, a provider of personal communications solutions to individual businesses and government organizations.

The **Energy & Environment** unit conducted basic and applied research and development to: strengthen the nation's leadership in key areas of science; increase the availability of clean, abundant energy; restore and protect the environment; and contribute to national security.

The Global Telecommunications and Energy & Environment units were consolidated as the company's Energy & Other operations, which achieved 1998 revenues of $255 million.

Changes to the Industry

Lockheed Martin remained the world's largest aerospace and defense company. Its sales in 1996 rose 18%, from $22.9 billion to $26.9 billion, attributable in large part to its merger with Loral. Boeing was a close second, however, with sales of $22.7 billion that year. That company proved to be formidable competition, and in August 1997 united with McDonnell Douglas to regain the industry's top spot.

The merger with Loral brought Lockheed a second type of threat, one that was new to the industry. Just prior to Lockheed's completion of its tender offer for Loral, McDonnell Douglas announced that it would blacklist Lockheed as a supplier. That company's president and CEO, Harry Stonecipher, had doubts as to whether a subsidiary, such as Loral Space, would be capable of working loyally with a competitor of its parent. Industry analysts were mildly surprised at the bluntness of the statement, but were not unduly shocked at the sentiment behind it. Some commented that this perception of a possible conflict of interest was inevitable in the rapidly consolidating defense industry.

Review of the Outcome

Although the merger did call for some job reduction, it didn't create the need for Lockheed to undergo major restructuring, which could have created heavy job loss. On September 1, 1996, the company reorganized into six business sectors. Later that year it unveiled the final phase of the integration of Loral by announcing the closure of eight plants, resulting in the loss of 1,600 jobs.

On June 30, 1997, Lockheed Martin Tactical Systems, the subsidiary that housed the assets gained from Loral, was merged into Lockheed. That July Lockheed entered into a merger agreement with Northrop Grumman, but Lockheed Martin withdrew its offer the following year after the U.S. Department of Justice announced its intention of blocking the merger in court. In February 1999 Lockheed Martin offered to purchase 49% of COMSAT, a communications satellite company; COMSAT's shareholders were scheduled to vote on the deal in June 1999.

Meanwhile, the company divested itself of several operations. In 1996 it distributed its 81% stake in Martin Marietta Materials, Inc. In January 1997 it received $450 million from the sale of two business units, Armament Systems and Defense Systems, to General Dynamics. That April Lockheed Martin spun off 10 noncore units as L-3 Communications Corp., of which it retained a 34.9% interest. In November 1997 it exchanged its stock in the newly formed subsidiary, LMT Sub, for the stake in Lockheed Martin held by General Electric since 1993. In August 1998 it announced the formation of Lockheed Martin Global Telecommunications, Inc. as a wholly owned subsidiary.

The company's financial results for 1998 were the worst since its formation three years earlier. Net earnings dropped 8.5% to $1.18 billion on revenues that fell 6.4% to $26.3 billion. Lockheed Martin attributed the decline to weak sales in space-related and commercial information sectors, as well as the delay in the signing of a $5 billion military aircraft order with the United Arab Emirates. The U.S. Government remained its largest customer, accounting for about 70% of it 1998 net sales.

Research

"FTC Okays Lockheed/Loral Deal, But Restricts Schwartz's Role," in *Satellite News*, 22 April 1996. Details the terms of the FTC's consent.

Leopold, George, Loring Wirbel, and Margaret Ryan. "Loral Sells Defense Arm," in *Electronic Engineering Times*, 15 January 1996. Describes the format of the merger, as well as the formation of Loral Space.

"Lockheed Buys Most of Loral in the Industry's Latest Deal," in *Satellite News*, 15 January 1996. Reveals the details of the proposed merger.

"Lockheed Martin Corp.," in *Notable Corporate Chronologies*, The Gale Group, 1999. Profiles the history of the company.

Lockheed Martin Corp. Home Page, available at http://www.lmco.com. Official World Wide Web Page for Lockheed Martin. Includes product description, officer biographies, annual reports and other financial information, and news releases.

Muradian, Vago. "Lockheed Martin Posts Sales, Net Earnings Drop in 1998," in *Defense Daily*, 29 January 1999. Provides an in-depth account of the company's annual and quarterly financial results.

————. "MDC Stance on Lockheed Martin-Loral Signals Omen for Industry," in *Defense Daily*, 24 April 1996. Describes McDonnell Douglas' announcement to blacklist Lockheed.

O'Toole, Kevin. "Mergers Mould Shape of US Industry," in *Flight International*, 26 February 1997. Provides the financial results of the leading aerospace companies for 1996.

—DEBORAH J. UNTENER

LOCKHEED MARTIN & NORTHROP GRUMMAN

Lockheed Martin Corp.
6801 Rockledge Dr.
Bethesda, MD 20817
USA

tel: (301)897-6000
fax: (301)897-6704
web: http://www.lmco.com

Northrop Grumman Corp.
1840 Century Park E.
Los Angeles, CA 90067
USA

tel: (310)553-6262
fax: (310)201-3023
web: http://www.northgrum.com

date: July 16, 1998 (canceled)
affected: Lockheed Martin Corp., USA, founded 1996
affected: Northrop Grumman Corp., USA, founded 1994

Overview of the Merger

The frenetic pace of consolidation in the U.S. defense industry came to a screeching halt in 1998. The U.S. government, which had been approving—and even encouraging—merger activity in the industry, abruptly modified its stance. After eight months of review and, according to Lockheed Martin and Northrop Grumman, with no advance warning, the Department of Justice filed suit to block the $11.4 merger of these two firms. This decision shocked the companies, the industry, and Wall Street, particularly in light of the government's recent approval of the larger Boeing/McDonnell Douglas merger and its pending review of the Raytheon/Hughes deal. The government, however, maintained that the Lockheed/Northrop proposal introduced the issue of vertical integration, which had not been a factor in the other deals.

History of Lockheed Martin Corp.

In 1916 Allan and Malcolm Loughead established the Loughead Aircraft Manufacturing Co. After changing the company name to "Lockheed," the company developed its twin-engine F-1 flying boat with the assistance of company engineer Jack Northrop, who developed the Vega in 1927. The Detroit Aircraft Corp. acquired Lockheed in 1929, and then sold Lockheed to a group of investors in 1932.

Meanwhile, Glenn L. Martin established the Glenn L. Martin Co. in 1917. During the 1930s the company made significant strides into the airplane industry. It introduced the first U.S.-built bombers and delivered the Clipper, the first passenger airplane capable of traveling long distances over water.

In 1938, after the German annexation of Austria, Britain purchased 200 Hudsons for $25 million in the largest military contract awarded before the war, marking a turning point in Lockheed's business. By the end of World War II, Lockheed had produced 19,297 aircraft for the military, nine percent of the nation's total production.

During World War II, Martin supplied such airplanes for the war effort as the A-30 Baltimore and the B-26 and B-29 bombers. In 1947 the company entered the highly competitive commercial airline market with the M-202. Development of later aircraft, the M-303 and M-404, proved to be a severe drain on company finances. The Korean War increased Martin's sales, but it continued to lose money. It recovered in the 1950s by diversifying into missiles, electronics, and nuclear systems.

During that decade Lockheed established a missiles and space division to produce satellites and submarine-launched missiles. In 1960 it introduced the U-2 and the SR-71 spy planes; the latter was nicknamed the Blackbird. That year Martin produced its last airplane, a Navy P5M-2 antisubmarine patrol plane. To diversify its product line, Martin merged in 1961 with American Marietta Corp., a supplier of construction materials, to form Martin Marietta Corp. In 1968 Martin Marietta acquired 41% of Harvey Aluminum, later called Marietta Aluminum.

In 1971, after introducing a problem-riddled TriStar commercial jetliner, Lockheed took out a guaranteed government loan to avoid bankruptcy. In 1976 an international scandal added to the financial troubles experienced by Lockheed, as it was accused of bribing officials in Iran, Indonesia, Italy, the Netherlands, and Japan.

Martin Marietta's diverse operations in aerospace, chemicals, electronics, aluminum, and construction products enabled it to experience growth during the 1970s. In 1982 Bendix Corp. made a hostile takeover bid for Martin Marietta, but the company responded by attempting to take over Bendix, accruing $1.34 billion in debt in the process. To reduce that debt load, Martin Marietta divested itself of its cement, aluminum, and specialty chemicals operations. Martin Marietta's sales in 1989 reached $5.8 billion as a result of increased defense electronics business and orders for Titan launchers.

The poor performance of its Hubble Space Telescope contributed to Lockheed's woes in 1990. It avoided a takeover attempt orchestrated by Texas billionaire Harold Simmons. In March 1993 Lockheed acquired the tactical aircraft business of General Dynamics in exchange for a block of Lockheed stock. That year Martin Marietta acquired General Electric's aerospace business, a producer of radars, and the following year acquired the space systems division of General Dynamics. Later that year it agreed to merge with Grumman Corp. but backed down when Northrop Corp. stepped in with its own bid for that company.

The Business

Financials - Lockheed Martin Corp.

Revenue (1998): $26.3 billion

Employees (1998): 165,000

Financials - Northrop Grumman Corp.

Revenue (1998): $8.9 billion

Employees (1998): 49,600

SICs / NAICS

sic 3694 - Engine Electrical Equipment

sic 3721 - Aircraft

sic 3728 - Aircraft Parts & Equipment Nec

sic 3761 - Guided Missiles & Space Vehicles

sic 3663 - Radio & T.V. Communications Equipment

sic 3812 - Search & Navigation Equipment

sic 7373 - Computer Integrated Systems Design

sic 7374 - Data Processing & Preparation

naics 334511 - Search, Detection, Navigation, Guidance, Aeronautical, and Systems

naics 336322 - Other Motor Vehicle Electrical and Electronic Equipment Manufacturing

naics 336411 - Aircraft Manufacturing

naics 336413 - Other Aircraft Part and Auxiliary Equipment Manufacturing

naics 336414 - Guided Missile and Space Vehicle Manufacturing

naics 514210 - Data Processing Services

naics 541512 - Computer Systems Design Services

naics 334220 - Broadcasting and Wireless Communications Equipment Manufacturing

In March 1995 Lockheed and Martin Marietta merged to form Lockheed Martin, the world's largest weapons maker. It continued to be active in mergers and acquisitions. In April 1996 it purchased Loral Corp., which was renamed Lockheed Martin Tactical Systems, Inc. In July 1997 Lockheed Martin and Northrop Grumman entered into a merger agreement, but Lockheed Martin withdrew its offer the following year after the U.S. Department of Justice announced its intention of blocking the merger in court.

The Officers

Lockheed Martin Corp.

Chairman and CEO: Vance Coffman

President and Chief Operating Officer: Peter B. Teets

Northrop Grumman Corp.

Chairman, President, and CEO: Kent Kresa

President and CEO, Logicon Inc.: Herbert W. Anderson

President, Integrated Systems and Aerostructures Sector:
  Ralph D. Crosby, Jr.

Chief Human Resources and Administrative Officer:
  Marvin Elkin

VP and Controller: Nelson F. Gibbs

Meanwhile, the company divested itself of several operations. In 1996 it distributed its 81% stake in Martin Marietta Materials, Inc. In January 1997 it received $450 million from the sale of two business units, Armament Systems and Defense Systems, to General Dynamics. That April Lockheed Martin spun off 10 noncore units as L-3 Communications Corp., of which it retained a 34.9% interest.

History of Northrop Grumman Corp.

On December 6, 1929, three former employees of the Loening Aircraft Engineering Co.—Roy Grumman, Jake Swirbul, and Bill Schwendler—established the Grumman Aircraft Engineering Corp. Within three months, the company had a contract to design a U.S. Navy fighter. In 1931 the company unveiled introduced the FF-1, a plane so durable that it earned Grumman the nickname "The Iron Works." The Grumman Goose, the company's first commercial aircraft, was released in 1937.

In 1939 aerospace engineer and innovator Jack Northrop founded Northrop Aircraft, and began working on a "Flying Wing" bomber, which he anticipated would be in demand during World War II. He followed up his early releases with other Flying Wings, the B-35 and the B-49.

In 1945, although Grumman had produced over 17,000 aircraft, the sudden termination of government contracts at the end of World War II resulted in a 27% drop in gross sales. In 1946 they plummeted to almost one-tenth of what they had been two years earlier. By 1947, however, net income and profit margins rose substantially.

During the 1950s Northrop continued its focus on government defense contracts, relying heavily on its F-89 fighter plane and Snark missile system. Grumman accelerated the production of military aircraft following the onset of the Korean War, resulting in a 70% increase in gross sales. In 1954 the F9F-9, the prototype of the first Grumman aircraft to reach supersonic speeds in level flight, made its first flight. In 1958 Grumman released its first corporate jet, the Gulfstream.

Despite repeated efforts to diversify, Northrop Corp. continued to rely on defense contracts during the 1960s. During that decade Grumman Corp. began work on the lunar module for the Apollo space mission and won a contract to build 134 F-14 Tomcats. The costs involved in producing these planes were higher than anticipated, and by 1972 the company was nearly bankrupt. A $75 million loan from the Shah of Iran helped the company to improve its financial position.

During the 1970s Northrop acquired a number of companies. In 1971 alone, it acquired Olson Laboratories, Wilcox Electric, Inc., and World Wide Wilcox, Inc. The following year it acquired Berkeley Scientific Laboratories (later known as Northrop Data Systems, Inc.), a 23% interest in General Energy Resources, Inc., and Page Aircraft Maintenance, Inc., which then changed its name to Northrop Worldwide Aircraft Services, Inc. In 1974 George A. Fuller Co. merged into Northrop. During the 1980s it sold off several of these holdings in an effort to streamline operations.

In 1981 Grumman faced a hostile takeover attempt by LTV Corp., a steel, electronics, and aircraft conglomerate based in Texas. On the grounds that the takeover would reduce competition in the aerospace and defense industries, a U.S. Court of Appeals rejected LTV's bid. By 1991 Grumman's business with the U.S. government accounted for 89% of its sales. Northrop, too, was adversely affected by declining government orders, and was forced to cut 3,000 jobs.

In April 1994 Northrop and Grumman merged to form Northrop Grumman Corp. After completion of this union, the company continued to strengthen the electronics operations that had been held by Grumman prior to the merger. Late in 1994 it bought the remaining shares of Vought Aircraft Co. for $130 million. In 1996 it spent $2.9 billion to purchase the defense and electronics systems business of Westinghouse Electric Corp. In August 1997 it acquired Logicon Inc., a provider of computer systems for scientific and management information. In September 1998 this subsidiary acquired International Research Inc. for $55 million.

In July 1997 it entered into a merger agreement with Lockheed Martin Corp., but this agreement was scrapped a year later, when the U.S. government filed suit to block the deal. As a result of the $186 million in the terminated merger-related charges, Northrop Grumman's 1998 net income was $214 million, down from $407 million in 1997. Sales also dipped, from $9.2 billion to $8.9 billion in the same time frame.

Market Forces Driving the Merger

By 1997 the consolidation wave that engulfed the U.S. defense industry had reduced the number of Tier I prime contractors to three—Boeing, Lockheed Martin, and Raytheon. Although there still remained a number of Tier III companies, those with defense sales below $4 billion annually, Northrop Grumman was the last surviving Tier II player. With annual revenues of about $9 billion, it was finding itself increasingly unable to compete with the leaders, and was eager to join with another company that would enable it to do so.

Lockheed Martin had participated in rapid merger and acquisition activity in recent years, enabling it to lay claim to the industry's top spot. That position was constantly challenged, however, by rivals of increasing size and breadth. In July 1997 Boeing gained governmental approval to merge with McDonnell Douglas, thereby strengthening its position as the world's largest aerospace concern as well as the nation's second-largest defense contractor. Raytheon, the industry's third major player, had recently emerged as the leader in the defense electronics sector, having acquired the defense electronics units of Texas Instruments and agreeing to acquire the defense operations of Hughes Aircraft.

To stave off competitive threats from these two corporations in particular, Lockheed moved to unite with another company. A union with Northrop Grumman appeared in good form. Northrop would provide Lockheed with the capability to build radars in support of the air traffic management market. Through Northrop, Lockheed could expand its space and missiles businesses with the addition of sensor and smart-weapon technology. A merger would provide Lockheed entry into air transport, as Northrop was a leading supplier of commercial airstructures. Moreover, a combined company would realize about $1 billion in savings in the areas of operations, procurement, and research and development.

Approach and Engagement

During the first week of July 1997, the Federal Trade Commission (FTC) approved Boeing's merger with McDonnell Douglas, and the Department of

The Players

Lockheed Martin Chairman: Norman R. Augustine. Norman Augustine earned both a B.S. and an M.S. in aeronautical engineering at Princeton University. He then worked at the Department of Defense, serving as undersecretary of the Army from 1975 to 1977. At Martin Marietta, he orchestrated the celebrated merger with Lockheed Corp. after failing in an attempt to acquire Grumman Corp. Upon formation of Lockheed Martin, Augustine assumed the post of president with the understanding that he would succeed Daniel Tellep as chairman and CEO. In December 1995 he succeeded to CEO, and one year later added the post of chairman to his duties. That year he was named one of *Business Week*'s top 25 managers. Augustine retired as CEO in August 1997 to become an engineering professor at his alma mater. He was succeeded by Vance Coffman, who also succeeded him as chairman in April 1998. Augustine is the author of two books: 1983's *Augustine's Laws*, an analysis of the U.S. aerospace industry, and 1998's *Augustine's Travels*, a commentary on the role of the U.S. executive.

Northrop Grumman Chairman, President, and CEO: Kent Kresa. Kent Kresa, a New York City native, earned several degrees in aeronautics and astronautics: a B.S. in 1959, an M.S. in 1961, and an E.A.A. in 1966. He was involved in ballistic missile defense research and reentry technology at Massachusetts Institute of Technology (M.I.T.) from 1961 to 1968. After working with the Defense Advanced Research Projects Agency, Kresa joined Northrop Corp. in 1975 as a vice president of research and technology. From there he advanced through other executive positions, attaining the roles of company president in 1987, CEO in January 1990, and Chairman in September of that year.

Justice cleared Raytheon's acquisition of Texas Instrument's defense and electronics unit. On July 3 Lockheed Martin and Northrop Grumman announced their merger agreement. Coming on the heels of these other two approved deals, the companies' executives, industry watchers, and investment analysts predicted that the merger would have little difficulty in gaining regulatory approval. Peter Aseritis, a director at CS First Boston/Credit Suisse, told *Defense Daily*, "If the government approved the approximately $48 billion Boeing-McDonnell Douglas merger, it might be hard to deny the far smaller $37 billion Lockheed Martin-Northrop Grumman deal."

The $11.4 billion deal would involve the $8.3 billion purchase of Northrop by Lockheed, plus the assumption of $3.1 billion in debt. Norman Augustine and Vance Coffman, Lockheed's respective chairman and CEO, would retain those positions at the merged company, while Northrop's chairman, CEO, and president, Kent Kresa, would become vice chairman of Lockheed Martin. The union would make the company the $37 billion defense leader and the second-largest aerospace company, behind the $48 billion Boeing.

On August 28, the companies submitted the paperwork that formally requested government approval. One month later, the Department of Justice (DoJ) requested further information, a practice not unusual, especially given the size of the deal under consideration. On February 13, 1996, the companies submitted a document known as a White Paper, which is a response to lingering governmental concerns that were not alleviated by the second informational request. At that point, the government later claimed, the companies should have realized that the merger was facing difficulty in clearing regulatory hurdles. It claimed that the questions outlined in its request for the White Paper brought up the issue of vertical integration, a topic that hadn't been raised earlier. The companies disputed this claim.

The companies and the government also retrospectively disagreed on the circumstances surrounding the shareholder votes, held on February 26, which overwhelmingly supported the merger. Lockheed and Northrop claimed that they had contacted the government prior to that date, asking whether there was any reason to reschedule the votes, but that the government hadn't responded. The government countered that it had clearly indicated that the companies would face objection to the deal unless they crafted a plan to better address its concerns.

On March 6 the government met with the companies to officially disclose its opposition to the merger. The companies were utterly shocked at what they claimed was the first hint of any such opposition. They had assumed that the meeting would be a forum for negotiating final details, such as the divestiture of about $300 million in electronic warfare operations. The government, however, revealed its strenuous concerns regarding vertical integration and aircraft antitrust issues. It wanted the merged company to divest all of Northrop's electronics operations, worth $4 billion, or about half of that company's assets. This amount was the largest divestment ever asked of merging companies.

Specifically, the government raised four primary objections. Vertical integration, or a company's capability to produce the components necessary for the manufacture of the final product, was of key concern. Defense Secretary William Cohen, as reported in *Defense Daily*, stated that the proposed merger "creates unprecedented problems of vertical integration, in our judgment, combining Lockheed Martin's strength in platforms and systems, with Northrop Grumman's considerable electronics and platform capabilities." The government's other objections included antitrust concerns in defense electronics and the aircraft market, and a conflict of interest in systems engineering and technical assistance.

In the weeks following, Lockheed and Northrop filed counter arguments, asserting that the government was operating under a flawed assessment of the competitiveness of the merged company. They pointed out the strong competition in the aircraft and electronics segments that it faced from Boeing and Raytheon, particularly if the latter's acquisition of Hughes' businesses was approved. They also reiterated their commitment to continue purchasing components from subcontractors. Moreover, they calculated that the Pentagon would realize annual savings of at least $700 million from the merged company. Additionally, they offered to divest $1 billion in operations.

The DoJ rejected the companies' arguments and counter offers, and, on behalf of the Department of Defense (DoD), on March 23 filed suit to block the merger. The trial was scheduled to begin on September 8, 1996. The companies announced their intention of fighting the government in court, and issued a joint response with the U.S. District Court. As reported in *Defense Daily*, that statement asserted that "Lockheed Martin and Northrop Grumman take issue with each of the plaintiff's claims as inconsistent with the law, the facts, and the DoD's previously consistent policy favoring consolidation."

However, Lockheed soon decided that the costs of a protracted legal battle were too great, and on July 16, 1998, terminated the merger. Not only would the legal fees become high, expected to reach $15 million per quarter, but the companies had already incurred losses since the beginning of the saga a year earlier. Executives were taken away from their everyday responsibilities to deal with merger-related issues, and other employees found it difficult to focus on the work at hand while contemplating their company's future. Moreover, the companies' stock prices had plummeted since early March, before the government revealed its opposition to the merger. During that time, Northrop's stock price fell from about $137.25 to $97.38, while Lockheed's dropped from $117 to $104. Vance Coffman, Lockheed Martin's chairman and CEO, stated in *Defense Daily* that "we looked at probably a dozen different options in terms of ways to satisfy the government's intent and we could not find a way."

Products and Services

Lockheed Martin was organized into six major business sectors: Aeronautics, which encompassed tactical aircraft; air mobility; modification, maintenance, and logistics; reconnaissance; surveillance and command; and advanced development; Electronics, which involved the design, development, and manufacture of electronic systems for global defense, civil, and commercial markets; Information & Services, which provided government and commercial customers with a range of information technology solutions, from complex systems integration projects for the federal government to the operation of electronic toll collection systems on the nation's highways; Space & Strategic Missiles, which was involved in the design, development, test, and manufacture of a variety of advanced technology systems for space and defense; Global Telecommunications, which focused on the areas of Global Network Solutions, Global Transport Services and Operations, Network Systems Development, and Personal Communications Systems; and Energy & Environment, which conducted basic and applied research and development to strengthen the nation's leadership in key areas of science; increase the availability of clean, abundant energy; restore and protect the environment; and contribute to national security.

Northrop Grumman was organized into three operational segments: Integrated Systems and Aerostructures, which was a systems integration enterprise with capabilities to design, develop, produce, and support fully missionized airborne systems and subsystems; Electronic Sensors and Systems, which designed, developed, produced, and supported advanced electronics products for government, industry, commercial, and personal use; and Information Technology, comprised of Logicon Inc., which provided advanced information technology systems and services to support national security, civil, and industrial needs.

Changes to the Industry

Chins dropped at the news of the government's vow to block the merger in court. Up until the Lockheed Martin/Northrop Grumman deal, the government had shown little resistance to the defense-related mergers that were rapidly shrinking the industry. In fact, the Pentagon had encouraged the DoJ and the FTC to exhibit a more relaxed posture in considering such deals. It had raised little objection to the megamerger of Boeing and McDonnell Douglas, as well as to Raytheon's separate acquisitions of the defense businesses of Texas Instruments and Hughes Aircraft. Suddenly, it seemed, the government had decided that enough was enough.

William Cohen, the U.S. Defense Secretary, contested that interpretation of the government's attitude toward defense-related mergers. "Our policies have not changed as some have alleged," he said in *Defense Daily*. "But the market is now more concentrated than it was four years ago and mergers therefore require us to exercise greater scrutiny. That said, we intend to continue to review mergers on a case-by-case basis. We will continue to support mergers that increase efficiencies and do not raise anti-competitive concerns."

Review of the Outcome

Both Lockheed Martin and Northrop Grumman asserted that they would be able to prosper despite their failed merger. Lockheed revealed that it was considering a stock repurchase to boost its trading value. There was a consensus among industry watchers, however, that Northrop would find it more difficult to go it alone. That company would likely be forced to merge with or be acquired by another firm if it expected to survive against the industry giants. In fact, as the deal with Lockheed collapsed, several U.S. companies expressed interest in pursuing Northrop. Two European companies, GEC-Marconi, of Britain, and Daimler-Benz Aerospace, of Germany, also appeared interested in aspects of Northrop.

Research

"DoJ Says it Gave Companies Ample Warning of Merger Stance," in *Defense Daily*, 15 April 1998. Presents the contradictory claims of the companies and the government regarding the regulatory opposition to the merger.

"Justice, Lockheed Go to Court over Lockheed-Northrop Deal," in *Defense Daily*, 24 March 1998. Details the government's lawsuit to block the merger.

Leon, Jean-Claude. "Then There Were Three," in *Interavia Business & Technology*, July 1997. Suggests that although the Lockheed/Northrop deal may have been the last of the industry's major mergers, the market could still support unions of smaller companies.

"Lockheed Martin Corp.," in *Notable Corporate Chronologies*, The Gale Group, 1999. Profiles the history of both Lockheed and Martin Marietta, and describes major events since the consolidated company's formation.

Lockheed Martin Corp. Home Page, available at http://www.lmco.com. Official World Wide Web Page for Lockheed Martin. Includes product description, officer biographies, annual reports and other financial information, and news releases.

"Lockheed Martin's Board Votes to End Northrop Merger Bid," in *Defense Daily*, 17 July 1998. Details Lockheed's termination of the merger agreement.

Muradian, Vago. "Lockheed, Northrop File Response to Justice's Suit," in *Defense Daily*, 13 April 1998. Reports the companies' statement to the U.S. District Court in response to the government's suit.

"Northrop Grumman Corp.," in *Notable Corporate Chronologies*, The Gale Group, 1999. Profiles the history of both Northrop and Grumman, and describes major events since the consolidated company's formation.

Northrop Grumman Corp. Home Page, available at http://www.northgrum.com. Official World Wide Web Page for Northrop Grumman. Includes product description, annual reports and other financial information, and news releases.

Warwick, Graham. "Augustine's Vision," in *Flight International*, 16 July 1997. Details the benefits that a merged company would realize in its various market segments.

———. "A Merger Too Far?" in *Flight International*, 18 March 1998. Questions the government's attitude toward future defense-related mergers in light of its opposition to the Lockheed/Northrop deal.

DEBORAH J. UNTENER

LTV & JONES & LAUGHLIN

nationality: USA
date: June 25, 1968
affected: Ling-Temco-Vought Corp. (LTV), USA, founded 1946
affected: Jones & Laughlin Steel Co., USA, founded 1902

The LTV Corp.
200 Public Sq.
Cleveland, OH 44114-2308
USA

tel: (216)622-5000
fax: (216)622-1931
web: http://www.ltvsteel.com

Overview of the Acquisition

By 1968, the American steel industry was beset by problems due, in part, to a long-standing neglect of market research and product development. While its Japanese and European competitors staked out powerful positions in the global market and modernized production in the 1950s and 1960s, the American steel industry's profits rested largely on wage controls and the high-volume output of outmoded equipment. By the late 1960s, the entrance of foreign steel onto the American market, followed by the decline and takeover of specific American steel corporations, had catalyzed debates about the immediate efficacy of economic protectionism and, more generally, about the future of American industry.

LTV's acquisition of Jones & Laughlin Steel Corp. was significant, not only as a catalyst of debate over America's relative industrial power, but also as an instance of early conglomerate development in the U.S. Moreover, it served as the basis for a historic legal battle over the interpretation of U.S. antitrust law. Prior to 1968, officials at the Department of Justice had invoked the 1914 Clayton Antitrust Act, the legislation most applicable to the regulation of mergers, only to prosecute those corporations attempting to monopolize single product lines or markets. Given previous interpretations of the Clayton Act, as well as the Nixon administration's overall support of big business, LTV's acquisition of Jones & Laughlin might not have resulted in an antitrust suit had it not been for efforts of Richard McLaren, the head of the antitrust division at the Department of Justice.

McLaren argued that conglomerate development needed to be curbed on the grounds that large concentrations of corporate assets afforded big businesses undue influences over government policy and unfair advantages in developing new product lines. However, he lacked legal precedent for filing a suit to prevent the merger of companies with unrelated product lines. Therefore, he argued against the merger on the grounds of reciprocity. Specifically, he argued that LTV would use its accumulated financial and political power to pressure subsidiaries into purchasing LTV products. This, McLaren argued, would limit LTV's competitors' ability to access certain markets. According to a 1970 settlement outlined by the Justice Department, LTV had to divest itself of a majority share in Braniff Airways and National Car Rentals in order to retain its Jones & Laughlin subsidiary.

The Business

Financials - Jones & Laughlin Steel Co.

Revenue (1998 Net Income): $27 million

Employees (1998): 14,800

SICs / NAICS

sic 3316 - Cold-Finishing of Steel Shapes

sic 3317 - Steel Pipe & Tubes

sic 3411 - Metal Cans

sic 3444 - Sheet Metal Work

naics 332322 - Sheet Metal Work Manufacturing

naics 332431 - Metal Can Manufacturing

naics 332439 - Other Metal Container Manufacturing

History of LTV

In the late 1960s, LTV was one of the largest conglomerates in the United States, having grown steadily throughout its history due to a series of mergers and acquisitions orchestrated by James Ling. Ling, a Dallas-based industrialist, laid the foundations for LTV in 1946 when he established the Ling Electric Co. with $2,000. Initially, the Ling Electric Co. worked with individual clients, repairing faulty doorbells and wall plugs, and wiring new houses. By the early 1950s, however, Ling had greatly expanded his company's client base by bidding on large industrial contracts and selling cable and other electronic hardware. By 1955, Ling Electric Co. was worth $1.5 million.

At that point, Ling incorporated his business. Finding little support among financiers, he obtained authorization to issue 800,000 shares at $2.25 each. Retaining personal ownership of half of these shares, he sold the remaining $205,000 in shares in a somewhat unorthodox fashion, soliciting friends and setting up booths to promote his company at state fairs. Within 90 days, Ling had sold 400,000 shares for a total of $738,000. The price of these shares remained relatively unstable for the next three years, fluctuating rapidly due to his early attempts to expand his company through acquisitions.

Ling's first significant acquisition involved a struggling California company that produced vibration detector equipment for the military. This acquisition marked the entrance of Ling Electronics, as Ling's company became known, into the aerospace industry. It also produced a series of lucrative defense contracts with the U.S. military. In defense-related and aero-

space industries, Ling Electronics faced limited competition, yet James Ling, committed to product diversification as the safest form of corporate risk management, continued to expand Ling Electronics. Some of his most notable acquisitions included the 1956 purchase of L.M. Electronics. In 1960, Ling purchased Altec-Lansing, manufacturers of high-fidelity sound equipment, thereby gaining control of the company's numerous subsidiaries. That year, he also merged his company, renamed Ling-Altec Electronics, with Temco Electronics and Missiles Co., a company specializing in defense contracts with the government. He named the resulting corporation Ling-Temco Corp. In 1961, Ling purchased Chance-Vought, Inc., a manufacturer of planes for the U.S. Navy, to create Ling-Temco-Vought (LTV).

Between 1961 and 1963, Chance-Vought and other LTV subsidiaries maintained slim profit margins, prompting Ling to downsize by reducing LTV's managerial corps from 700 to 166, and by divesting LTV of several unprofitable operations. In 1963, despite the bitterness and anxiety created by his downsizing, Ling became chairman and CEO of LTV. As CEO, Ling decided to decentralize and diversify what had become, by the mid-1960s, a stagnating and overextended corporation. In 1964, he initiated a series of decentralizing moves known collectively as Project Redeployment. Specifically, he disaggregated LTV into three separate divisions, each directed by semiautonomous managers. By increasing the independence of his corporate divisions and subsidiaries, Ling increased both incentives and responsibilities for profit among his managers.

In 1966, despite Ling's downsizing at the managerial level, *Fortune* magazine named LTV the fastest growing company in the U.S. Throughout the late 1950s and the 1960s, Ling established a stake in a wide range of markets and extended LTV's subsidiary holdings to reduce LTV's vulnerability to fluctuations and downturns in the demand for any single product or service. Ling purchased Greatamerica Corp., for example, to gain a bank, an insurance-holding concern, the National Car Rental System, and an 81% interest in Braniff Airways.

Ling aggressively diversified LTV, not only to safeguard its profits against seasonal or cyclical downturns in trading and sales, but also to profit from the inflation of LTV stock and the resale of corporate subsidiaries. LTV typically acquired expensive corporations by exchanging its convertible preferred stock for the common stock of companies targeted for acquisition, or by offering above-market prices for the outstanding stock of targeted corporations. After acquiring Okonite Co., a copper wire and cable manufacturer in 1965; Wilson & Co., a meatpacking interest and a producer of pharmaceuticals and sporting goods in 1967; Greatamerica, the parent of Braniff Airlines and National Car Rental, in 1968; and finally, Jones & Laughlin Steel in 1968, LTV held the 14th spot among *Fortune* magazine's Top 500 corporations in the United States. Between 1965 and 1968, sales rose from $336 million to $2.8 billion.

Although profitable in the short-term, rapid and phenomenal growth precipitated numerous legal and financial problems for the company by the end of the 1960s. In the spring of 1969, Richard McLaren, the head of the antitrust division at the Department of Justice, filed suit against LTV for its acquisition of Jones & Laughlin, making LTV the first major target in a campaign against conglomerates. While the antitrust case was pending, Ling was barred from managing Jones & Laughlin's assets. Early in 1970, the Justice Department initiated a legal settlement by offering LTV the option to retain Jones & Laughlin on the condition that it relinquish its controlling interest in the Okonite Co. and Braniff Airways. By then, Ling had already decided to liquidate the less remunerative holdings of his overextended conglomerate, and in 1971, he divested LTV of Braniff Airways and Okonite Co.

The divestiture of Braniff and Okonite failed to halt the drastic plunge of LTV's profits and stock prices, however. In order to defray LTV's debts, Ling continued to sell off subsidiary holdings in excess of those named in the antitrust settlement. In May of 1970, restive over LTV's legal problems and what seemed to be the disintegration of the company, LTV's creditors and executives forced Ling to step down as board chairman and assume the position of president. Only two months later, after being demoted to vice-chairman of the board, Ling resigned from LTV altogether.

After Ling's resignation, LTV continued to expand, albeit primarily through the acquisition of metal and aerospace companies. In 1977, LTV bought Lykes Corp., a manufacturer of petroleum equipment, and Youngstown Sheet & Tub, a steel producer. After selling Wilson & Co. in 1981, LTV's major subsidiaries included LTV Steel, LTV Aerospace & Defense, and LTV Energy Products. In 1984, LTV augmented its position in the steel market by purchasing Republic Steel Corp. for $770 million. This decision was somewhat ill-timed. By 1986, cheap imported steel was flooding the U.S. market. With water freight shipping becoming cheaper and more efficient, it was often less expensive to import Japanese and European steel to the West Coast than from the Midwest and East Coast, the base of U.S. steel production. To pare costs and bolster its finances, LTV sold Gulf States Steel, most of its nonsteel assets, and its specialty products division

The Officers

Jones & Laughlin Steel Co.

Chairman, President, and CEO, LTV; President LTV Steel:
J. Peter Kelly

Exec. VP: James F. Haeck

Exec. VP: Richard J. Hipple

Exec. VP and Chief Financial Officer: Arthur W. Huge

Exec. VP: Jeffery A. Saxon

in the late 1980s. In 1992, low oil prices led LTV to file for bankruptcy protection. That same year, the company closed several plants and laid off more than 30,000 employees; it also sold its aircraft business to a consortium of U.S.-based companies, namely Loral and Northrop/Carlyle.

In 1993, LTV emerged from bankruptcy with a new stock offering and a relocation of corporate headquarters from Dallas to Cleveland. After 1993, LTV's risk management strategies frequently involved joint ventures, most notably a 1994 venture with Japan's Sumitomo Metal Industries, which had invested $200 million in LTV, and British Steel, to form Trico Steel. LTV expansion after 1993 also assumed a more international aspect, as when LTV joined with Cleveland-Cliffs to produce iron briquettes for steel making in Trinidad and Tobago. In the late 1990s, LTV's domestic sales were sluggish at best, and in 1998, LTV closed its 40-year-old Pittsburgh coke-producing facility and a Cleveland steel finishing operation. LTV simultaneously reduced its steel output, and together with other American steel producers, began filing trade complaints against Russian, Japanese, and South American competitors for dumping steel on the U.S. market. In 1999, LTV ranked as the third largest steel producer in the U.S., behind USX-US Steel and Bethlehem Steel.

History of Jones & Laughlin

Given its evolution from a small family-owned business into the subsidiary of a vast conglomerate, the history of Jones & Laughlin has mirrored that of the U.S. steel industry, and more generally, of American heavy industry as a whole. While operative before the Civil War, Jones & Laughlin Steel Co. incorporated only in 1902. At this point, the company's steel production was based largely in Pittsburgh, the location of Jones & Laughlin's Bessemer converters and basic open-hearth furnaces. In 1909, the company established its famous Aliquippa Works in Woodlawn,

The Players

Jones & Laughlin Chairman and CEO: Charles Milton Beeghly. Having earned a B.A. from Ohio Wesleyan University, Charles Beeghly took a job with Cold Metal Products Co., a business founded by his father in 1926. In 1946, he assumed the vice presidency of Cold Metal Products Co. In 1957, Jones & Laughlin acquired the Cold Metal Products Co., and Beeghly became president of the strip-steel division. One year later, he became the executive vice-president of Jones & Laughlin, and in 1963, he was appointed chairman of the board and CEO.

Although Jones & Laughlin's market share had increased from 4.9 to 5.8 percent between 1957 and 1963, Beeghly feared the effects of rising labor costs and foreign competition and, as CEO, he upheld corporate profits through wage controls and cost-cutting in the areas of research and development. Ultimately, global market conditions and Beeghly's neglect of market research and product development eroded the basis of Jones & Laughlin's financial growth. Shortly before his retirement in 1968, Beeghly presided over the sale of Jones & Laughlin's majority stake to Ling-Temco-Vought Inc. After retiring from Jones & Laughlin, he served as a director of the Dollar Savings and Trust Co. and the Mellon National Bank and Trust Co. Beeghly died on February 18, 1999.

Pennsylvania, a riverside town 26 miles outside of Pittsburgh. The move to Woodlawn had been prompted by, among other things, punitive court fines imposed for damage to neighborhoods near plants on the Monongahela River. The site of integrated facilities for steel production, the plant, located on 475 acres, served as the center of a company town.

By 1914, Jones & Laughlin was poised to assume a dominant position in the steel industry, having captured a large market for finished and unfinished steel products. Military armament during World War I boosted a demand for steel, and by 1920, the company had the capacity to produce over 6 million tons of pig iron, ingots, and finished hot rolled steel products per year. It also had the income to finance the integration of its operations by purchasing the Vesta and Shannopian coal lands, various limestone quarries in West Virginia, and iron ore deposits in Minnesota and in Michigan. In certain respects, Jones & Laughlin was

an unusual steel producer, expanding internally rather than through mergers. In this sense, the company was run in a fairly conservative fashion by the Jones and Laughlin families, which owned the majority of the company's stock and dictated corporate strategy, even after 1923, when Jones & Laughlin was transferred to public ownership.

During the 1930s, Jones & Laughlin began to experience financial difficulties and conflicts with organized labor. Despite the expansion of production capacity and the innovations in chemical processing of the 1920s and 1930s, the onset of the Great Depression marked reductions in workers' hours and cutbacks in research and development. The Great Depression also witnessed workers' successful challenge to Jones & Laughlin's management, which had taken a particularly uncompromising and repressive position in relation to organized labor during and after World War I. In conjunction with prosecuting union leaders at the Aliquippa plant, Jones & Laughlin's managers had routinely leveled charges of communism against workers and labor organizers not affiliated with the company-sponsored union. In 1937, however, the Supreme Court found Jones & Laughlin in violation of the National Labor Relations Act of 1935 for discriminating against members of the Amalgamated Association of Iron, Steel and Tin Workers of America. Later that year, millworkers at Jones & Laughlin voted overwhelmingly to name the Steel Workers Organizing Committee (SWOC) to represent their interests, and relations between labor and management assumed a hostile tone.

In 1936, despite declining revenues, Jones & Laughlin gambled on research and development, opening the Hazelwood Metallurgical Research Laboratory. By 1941, Jones & Laughlin researchers had developed a Bessemer flame-control process that produced more uniform and higher-quality steel. Over the next decade, Jones & Laughlin increased its revenues by licensing new production methods and by contracting to the U.S. military following the onset of World War II. In 1942, lucrative defense contracts allowed Jones & Laughlin, led by Horace Edgar Lewis, to acquire plants in the Midwest and gain access to Great Lakes shipping routes. After World War II, under the leadership of Admiral Ben Moreell and C.L. Austin, Jones & Laughlin entered into new areas of production related to semifinished, hot-rolled and cold-finished steel, and steel wire. In the 1950s, Jones & Laughlin began replacing outdated ovens and mills, and began to replace obsolete Bessemer furnaces with Linz-Donawitz converters, more commonly known as basic oxygen furnaces. Between 1957 and 1963, Jones & Laughlin's market share increased from 4.9 to 5.8 percent.

Modernization steps taken during the 1950s laid the foundation for both increased production and long-term competitiveness. After 1963, however, the conservative management strategies of CEO Charles Milton Beeghly eroded the basis of Jones & Laughlin's long-term profits. Until his retirement in 1968, Beeghly pursued vigorous cost-cutting strategies, reducing workers' wages and cutting back expenditures on product research and development in order to increase Jones & Laughlin's immediate profits and stock prices. This, compounded by oligarchic practices that included price fixing among eight large American carbon and sheet steel firms, worsened the competitiveness of the American steel industry in general and Jones & Laughlin in particular. Retrenchment in research and development, price fixing, and finally a decision in 1965 to erect a $600 million steel mill in Illinois, precisely when Japanese and European steel interests were poised to establish a West Coast market, virtually destroyed Jones & Laughlin's dominance in the steel market. By the late 1960s, the mill in Hennepin Illinois was a huge drain on Jones & Laughlin's finances, given the fact that European and Japanese steel producers could ship steel to California and Alaska more cheaply than Jones & Laughlin. Jones & Laughlin, moreover, had made itself vulnerable to takeover attempts.

In 1968, Ling-Temco-Vought made Jones & Laughlin a subsidiary by purchasing 80% of its stock. With its profits plummeting, Jones & Laughlin discontinued costly modernization programs that might have provided the company with access to the international market and the basis for long-term growth. Extremely pressured by LTV executives to uphold corporate profits, Avery Adams, chairman, president, and CEO of Jones & Laughlin, promoted both increased output and cutbacks in research at a time when the company needed to regain its competitiveness in face of a burgeoning influx of foreign steel. In the 1970s, Jones & Laughlin closed many of its plants and allowed others to remain idle or operate at minimum capacity. By the mid-1980s, it had entered a period of seemingly inevitable demise. In 1984, LTV acquired Republic Steel and shifted the base of its steel production from Pittsburgh to Cleveland while keeping Jones & Laughlin as a division of the LTV Steel Corp.

Market Forces Driving the Merger

LTV's acquisition of Jones & Laughlin reflected a trend toward conglomeratization among U.S. corporations. Undertaken as a corporate risk management strategy, conglomerate development typically involved both decentralization of management and diversification of product lines within a single, over-

The Players

Ling-Temco-Vought Chairman and CEO: James J. Ling. James Ling was born in Hugo, Oklahoma, on December 31, 1922. At age fourteen, Ling dropped out of high school, and after four years of working odd jobs, he settled in Dallas. There he assisted electrical contractors and completed correspondence courses until he qualified as a journeyman electrician. In 1946, he sold his house for capital to establish Ling Electric Co., a small contracting firm that installed and repaired wiring in homes. By the late 1960s the company had grown through acquisitions to become one of the largest conglomerates in the nation.

As chairman and CEO of what became known, in 1961, as Ling-Temco-Vought (LTV), Ling established a niche in the electronic hardware, aerospace, pharmaceutical, communications, and meat and food processing industries; he also made successful bids on large military defense contracts with the government. By 1968, after acquiring such companies as Jones & Laughlin, Ling had boosted LTV to the 14th position among the Top 500 corporations in the U.S. However, his diversification strategies were costly from both a financial and a legal standpoint. In 1969, the Department of Justice filed suit against LTV for its acquisition of Jones & Laughlin. The antitrust suit, as well as the enormous corporate debt created by Ling's expensive acquisitions, generated discontent among LTV's creditors and stockholders, and in May of 1970, Ling was forced to step down as the board chairman and CEO. Two months later, Ling was demoted to the position of vice-chairman of the board, and immediately after, he resigned from LTV.

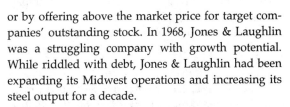

or by offering above the market price for target companies' outstanding stock. In 1968, Jones & Laughlin was a struggling company with growth potential. While riddled with debt, Jones & Laughlin had been expanding its Midwest operations and increasing its steel output for a decade.

For its part, Jones & Laughlin executives had, by the mid-1960s, made their corporation vulnerable to takeover by neglecting to develop new technologies to meet the demands of a rapidly changing global steel market. Up until the mid-1950s, a small number of large American industries produced a majority of the arching corporation. As CEO of LTV, James Ling expanded and diversified his company, typically by exchanging LTV convertible preferred stock for the common stock of companies targeted for acquisition world's steel, and in the absence of powerful foreign competition, minimized investments in technology at the expense of future prosperity. The complacence of U.S. steel concerns was further compounded by price-fixing practices among oligarchic steel magnates, who discouraged smaller firms from interloping through joint agreements to undersell competition.

In the early 1960s, as Japanese and European economies began to recover from the effects of World War II, American steel producers slowly began to support technological development, replacing outdated Bessemer converters with more efficient Linz-Donawitz converters. Innovation, however, had arrived too late. Once foreign steel entered the market, Jones & Laughlin was forced into debt simply to match Japanese and European performance, and high capital outlays were coincidental with the underutilization of overextended facilities. By 1959, the United States was a net importer of steel, not least because it was often more expensive to transport steel to Hawaii, Alaska, and California from the Jones & Laughlin's Midwestern mills than it was from Japan or even Europe. By 1968, Jones & Laughlin had become vulnerable to takeover, and LTV, failing to anticipate an influx of foreign steel, began bidding on the company.

Approach and Engagement

In mid-1968, when Ling-Temco-Vought made its first unofficial bid to buy Jones & Laughlin, rumors of a takeover grossly inflated Jones & Laughlin stock prices. On May 1, 1968, Jones & Laughlin common stock closed at 49 1/8. By May 9 it had reached 62 and by May 10, it had reached 77. The New York Stock Exchange suspended trading of Jones & Laughlin common and preferred stock on May 10. The next day, LTV offered $85 in cash per share for a 63% interest in Jones & Laughlin. By June 25, LTV had acquired 5,001,548 shares for slightly over $425 million. To pay for the 63% interest, LTV drew $200 million from its own funds, $100 million from various Canadian and European sources, and the remaining sum from American banks.

Prior to 1968, conglomerates had escaped prosecution by the antitrust division of the Justice Department. The 1914 Clayton Act, which pertained to monopolies, addressed only acquisitions and mergers involving companies with identical or closely related product lines. On March 24, 1969, however, Richard McLaren, the head of the antitrust division, filed suit against LTV, arguing that, by creating large concentra-

tions of capital assets, conglomerates were gaining unfair advantages in startup industries and exerting unhealthy influences over foreign policy. In filing suit, McLaren aimed to strip LTV of its controlling interest in Jones & Laughlin. On March 27, LTV and the Justice Department announced a temporary agreement by which LTV could purchase up to 81% of Jones & Laughlin stock provided that the latter company remained independent, and that it would sell off its Jones & Laughlin shares if it lost its case. Early in 1970, the Justice Department outlined a permanent settlement that allowed LTV to retain Jones & Laughlin as a subsidiary if it divested itself of controlling interests in the Okonite Co. and Braniff Airways.

Products and Services

In 1968, Ling-Temco-Vought, Inc., was one of the nation's most diversified corporations, a vast conglomerate engaged in steel making, meat and food processing, production and marketing in electronics, communications, aerospace, and pharmaceutical and industrial chemical enterprises. The antitrust suit filed by the Justice Department in early 1970, however, initiated a series of divestments that radically altered LTV's product lines and corporate development. During the 1970s, LTV acquired new subsidiaries, but generally within the steel and aerospace industries. In 1977, LTV bought Lykes Corp., a manufacturer of petroleum equipment, and Youngstown Sheet & Tub, a steel producer. After 1981, LTV's main subsidiaries consisted of LTV Steel, LTV Aerospace & Defense, and LTV Energy Products. In 1984, LTV added to its steel producing holdings by purchasing Republic Steel for $770 million, and in 1993, it entered into a joint venture with Japan's Sumitomo Metal Industries and British Steel to form Trico Steel.

By the late 1990s, LTV was the third-largest steel producer in the United States, ranking behind only USX-US Steel and Bethlehem Steel. Its products included coated sheet steel, cold-and-hot-rolled sheet steel, strip steel, tubular products, and tin products. LTV's tin mills produced primarily tin cans and closures. The company possessed a stake in several joint ventures, including a 50% stake in Trico Steel. In 1998, hot and cold flat-rolled steel accounted for $1.8 billion, or roughly 44%, of LTV's sales. Galvanized products accounted for $1.2 billion, or 28%, of total sales while tin mill products accounted for $395 million, or 9%, of sales.

Changes to the Industry

LTV's acquisition of Jones & Laughlin produced enormous debt for LTV and plummeting profits for both companies. Jones & Laughlin executives and managers, pressured by LTV to maintain profitability, initiated a series of cutbacks that precluded the modernization of plant equipment necessary for survival in a globalizing market. The neglect of market research and product development, combined with an emphasis on increased steel output, further eroded Jones & Laughlin's efficiency and profitability.

Jones & Laughlin's virtual demise by the mid-1980s was caused by a number of interrelated factors, not least of which was its inability to adapt to technological change in the postwar market. This, in addition to conservative managerial decisions fostered by LTV's relationship to its subsidiaries, contributed to Jones & Laughlin's steady decline after the mid-1960s. Finally, the increasing popularity and use of lightweight plastics in the construction of consumer durables greatly diminished the global demand for steel by the 1990s. In that it increased the LTV's debt and discouraged investment in research and development by LTV's subsidiaries, the acquisition contributed to the partial dissolution of LTV, one of America's largest conglomerates, and the near demise of Jones & Laughlin. Whatever the cause of its difficulties, by the 1970s, Jones & Laughlin was shutting down plants one by one, leaving others idle, and demolishing many others.

Review of the Outcome

Jones & Laughlin was one of four major acquisitions made by LTV between 1965 and 1968. The four acquisitions, which included the Okonite Co., Wilson & Co., Greatamerica, and Jones & Laughlin, pushed LTV from the 204th to the 14th place among the top 500 U.S. industrial corporations by 1968. James Ling had initially pursued acquisitions and mergers as a means of inflating LTV stock and decreasing LTV's debts through the public resale of subsidiaries, and in an immediate sense, his strategy paid off. Between 1965 and 1968, LTV's sales rose from $336 million to $2.8 billion.

In a less immediate sense, LTV's acquisition of Jones & Laughlin was costly from both a legal standpoint, and in the long-term, from a financial standpoint as well. To buy Jones & Laughlin, LTV borrowed enormous sums from foreign and domestic banks, increasing its debt to a total of $865 million. By August 1969, LTV was required to pay 9 1/2% in interest on $110 million in loans from 25 major banks. Moreover, the acquisition occurred as the steel industry was entering a period of precipitous decline. Between 1967 and 1969, LTV's earnings plummeted from $33.9 mil-

lion to $27.7 million, while its stocks dropped from 169 1/2 in August of 1967 to 33 1/8 at the end of 1968. LTV lost $65 million in the first quarter of 1969 and $3.3 million in the second quarter. At the end of 1969, LTV reported a net loss of $38.1 million and announced plans for large-scale divestment. Such plans were enforced by the antitrust suit filed by the Department of Justice. By the terms of the suit's 1970 settlement, LTV relinquished its controlling interest in Braniff Airways and Okonite Co. The apparent dissolution of LTV caused great unrest among stockholders, and in May of 1970, James Ling was forced to step down as board chairman.

Some, if not all, of LTV's financial problems of the late 1969 and the early 1970s could be attributed to its acquisition of Jones & Laughlin. During the last quarter of 1968, Jones & Laughlin lost $185,000. In 1969, Jones & Laughlin earned $22.1 million increased its debt by paying $22.3 million in dividends. Jones & Laughlin continued its decline in 1970, losing $1.2 million in the first quarter of the year and passing on the payment of dividends in the second quarter. The steadily declining performance of Jones & Laughlin meant, among other things, dispelled any illusions that LTV would be able to reduce its own debts by drawing on the profits of its steel-producing subsidiary. Although, in 1969, Jones & Laughlin might have possessed great profit potential, it was in need of expensive equipment upgrades, and by assuming the responsibility for inflexible interest payments as the American steel industry was entering a period of steady decline, LTV laid the foundations for long-term debt. In 1976, LTV had a debt of $1.2 billion, much of it acquired through its $426 million cash purchase of Jones & Laughlin stock in 1968.

Research

Hall, Christopher. *Steel Phoenix: The Fall and Rise of the U.S. Steel Industry*, St. Martin's, 1997.

Hogan, William T. *An Economic History of the Iron and Steel Industry in the United States, Volume 5*, Lexington Books, 1971.

Kiers, Luc. *The American Steel Industry: Problems, Challenges, Perspectives*, Westview Press, 1980.

Scheuerman, William. *The Steel Crisis: The Economics and Politics of a Declining Industry*, Praeger, 1986.

Seely, Bruce, ed., *The Encyclopedia of American Business History and Biography: The Iron and Steel Industry in the Twentieth Century*, Facts on File Publications, 1994.

ALICE M. RITSCHERLE

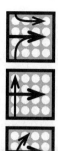

LUCAS INDUSTRIES & VARITY

LucasVarity PLC
46 Park St.
London, W1Y 4DJ
United Kingdom

tel: 44 171 647 0610
fax: 44 171 647 0624
web: http://www.lucasvarity.com

nationality: United Kingdom
date: September 6, 1996
affected: Lucas Industries PLC, England, founded 1875
affected: Varity Corp., USA, founded 1847

Overview of the Merger

LucasVarity, one of the world's largest automotive supplies manufacturers, was formed by the 1996 merger between Lucas Industries PLC and Varity Corp. These two companies came together in order to join forces in the auto industry by becoming a complete systems provider rather than just a parts manufacturer.

Lucas Industries, based in Solihull, England, was a leader in disc brakes and diesel fuel injection systems. Its other automotive operations were the electrical, electronic, and aftermarket segments. Outside the automotive industry, Lucas operated an aerospace division, which had been suffering due to the cyclilcity of the aerospace industry. One of Lucas' main weaknesses was in penetrating the anti-lock braking system (ABS) market, as the company was unable to lower it prices enough to compete with its rivals. It also generated most of its sales in the European market, but had only about 16% of sales coming from North America.

Varity Corporation had a strong hold on the North American market. Based in Buffalo, New York, this company had captured a 25% share of the U.S. ABS market. Yet it was still smaller than such rivals as ITT Automotive and Robert Bosch GmbH. In addition to brakes, Varity also manufactured diesel engines. Its VarityPerkins diesel engines division was the company's only global business.

History of Lucas Industries PLC

Industrialist Joseph Lucas founded the Tom Bowling Lamp Works in 1875. The company was named after the ship's lamp, which was its main product. Five years later, Lucas received a patent for The King of the Road bicycle lamp, a product that would eventually lead to the company's fortune. In 1882 Joseph formed a partnership with his son Harry. Joseph Lucas & Son expanded the range of goods offered in its catalogs, supplying cycle repairers and manufacturers with nearly every product that they might need.

The company incorporated in 1897 as a public company. By now it had become a leader in the industry and had expanded into the automotive parts and accessories market. In 1903 sales and profits began to rise as a result of the Parliamentary Act, which raised the speed limit above walking pace, thereby making the use of cars more attractive. Lucas expanded into ignition equipment with the 1914 acquisition of Thomson-Bennett, a firm specializing in Magnetos; Thomson-Bennett was later renamed the Lucas Electrical Company. The 1916 introduction of British Summer Time (daylight savings) led to a permanent drop in the sale of cycle lamps. At the time that Harry Lucas retired in 1923, the company employed 3,000 workers and recorded a profit of GBP 58,000.

In 1925 Lucas acquired two rivals in the motor accessories business: Rotax and CAV. Five years later it purchased the lighting, starting, and ignition operations of S. Smith & Son. For three years in the early 1930s, Lucas paid Auto-Lite, a U.S. tire manufacturer, $50,000 per year to avoid the British market, promising in return to stay out of the U.S. market. These two companies also agreed to exchange technical information and licenses.

The Bendix Corp. sold two-thirds of its British brake manufacturing subsidiary to Lucas in 1932, along with the licenses allowing Rotax to make such aviation equipment as the inertia starter. Five years later, Lucas acquired the remaining interests of CAV-Bosch, a joint venture it had formed in 1931 for the development of diesel engines. By the end of the 1930s, Lucas had become a leader in ignition equipment, diesel engines, and brakes.

In 1948 the company began work on the RAF's "V Bombers," beginning with the Vickers "Valiant." Three years later it reorganized into divisions, with personnel and finance falling under a renamed holding company, Joseph Lucas (Industries) Ltd.

The Cycle Accessories Division was eliminated in 1962. Six years later, CAV, now the world leader in the manufacture of fuel injection equipment, gained control of rival Simm, giving it 90% of the British fuel pump industry. By the end of the decade Lucas was faced with stiff competition, as the strike that had hit the U.K. components industry had encouraged motor manufacturers to switch to multiple sourcing for their needs.

Lucas' aerospace division began expansion in the late 1960s; by 1970 it had spent over GBP 20 million on acquisitions. In 1971 Rotax, renamed Lucas Aerospace, was forced to lay off 16% of its workforce following the financial collapse of the Rolls-Royce, for which Rotax supplied the engines. Two years later the non-aerospace elements of the former Rotax subsidiary were spun-off as a new company, Lucas Defense Systems.

The Business

Financials
Revenue (1998): $6.6 billion (GBP 4.3 billion)

Employees (1998): 55,946

SICs / NAICS
sic 3714 - Motor Vehicle Parts & Accessories

sic 3720 - Aircraft & Parts

naics 336312 - Gasoline Engine and Engine Parts Manufacturing

naics 336322 - Other Motor Vehicle Electrical and Electronic Equipment Manufacturing

naics 336340 - Motor Vehicle Brake System Manufacturing

naics 336412 - Aircraft Engine and Engine Parts Manufacturing

The company was renamed Lucas Industries in 1974, the same year that it acquired Rotodiesel, a leader firm in the French diesel market. By 1975 one-third of all new cars had brakes manufactured by the Lucas Girling subsidiary. A strike by Lucas toolmakers shut down the entire U.K. car industry in 1977, and in 1981 Lucas recorded its first loss in the company's history. Two years later, however, it again began to show a profit, due in large part to its non-automotive operations.

Lucas Automotive was formed in 1988 to hold all of the company's automotive subsidiaries. During the 1980s, a shrinking British automobile industry forced Lucas to dispose of 14 units, close 25 production sites, and cut its workforce by 35,000. In 1990 Lucas Aerospace acquired a division of Tracor Aviation Inc., renaming it Lucas Aviation Inc. In May 1995 Lucas announced the sale of its troubled U.S. Geared Systems Division.

In 1994 the U.S. Pentagon barred Lucas Industries from future contracts, citing investigators' claims that the company's substandard aircraft parts posed serious safety hazards. Also, the company came under criminal investigation for falsifying the inspection of parts used on many Boeing commercial jets. The following year, the Lucas Western Inc. subsidiary pled guilty to felony charges and was fined $88 million. In 1995 Lucas Industries earned net income of $48.7 million on revenues of $4.7 billion. It had a workforce of 33,361 that year.

The Officers

Chairman: Edmund A. Wallis

CEO: Victor A. Rice

Chief Operating Officer: J. Anthony Gilroy

Group Finance Director: Neil D. Arnold

Sr. VP, Human Relations: J. Howard Chandler

Sr. VP, Corporate Development: Iain D. Duffin

History of Varity Corporation

Daniel Massey, a successful farmer, began the manufacture and repair of simple farm implements in Newcastle, Ontario, Canada, in 1847. Massey's son, Hart, acquired a number of patents in 1851, including one for a lawn mower. The company's growth, particularly in exports, increased dramatically after its exhibition of machines at the 1867 Paris International Exposition.

The company, now known as Massey Manufacturing, acquired the Toronto Reaper and Mower Company in 1881. Ten years later it merged with Harris Company to form Massey-Harris Limited. In 1892 it invested in Verity Plow Co.; in 1914 it acquired the remaining interest in that company. The company expanded its manufacturing operation into the U.S. with the acquisition of New York-based Johnston Harvester Co. in 1910.

The firm expanded into the manufacture of tractors when the use of steam gave way to gasoline and kerosene engines in the 1920s. In 1922 it debuted its first successful combine. Massey-Harris purchased the J.I. Case Plow Works Company of Racine, Wisconsin, in 1928. Ten years later it introduced the self-propelled combine, an invention that revolutionized harvesting methods throughout the world. During World War II, Massey-Harris was contracted to produce hundreds of wings for the wooden Mosquito bomber, tanks, naval gun mounts, and other war material.

In 1953 the Harry Ferguson Company, a tractor manufacturer, merged with Massey-Harris. The newly renamed Massey-Harris-Ferguson Company Ltd. immediately became the second-largest farm machinery manufacturer in the world. In 1957 the company entered the industrial and construction machinery market. Two years later, the company shortened its name to Massey-Ferguson and acquired the diesel engine manufacturer Perkins Engines of England. In 1966 it acquired a 36% interest in Motor Iberica, a major Spanish producer of tractors and trucks. That year it also expanded into the production of construction machines.

When the agricultural machinery market collapsed in 1979, Massey-Ferguson was caught off guard and was nearly destroyed by rising interest rates on an accumulated debt of $1.6 billion. It recorded a loss of $262 million that year. The following year Victor Rice was named CEO, and the company closed a British construction machinery plant and a Scottish combine plant. It returned to profitability in 1984, and purchased Rolls-Royce Diesels International from Vickers PLC. Two years later it purchased Dayton Walther Corp., an Ohio-based motor vehicle components manufacturer.

In 1986 the company adopted Varity Corporation as its new name, a homage to the British inventor William Varity, whose plow company was bought by Massey-Harris in 1892. Varity acquired Kelsey-Hayes Corp., a world leader in antilock braking systems and aluminum wheels, in 1989. Two years later, shareholders approved the reincorporation of Varity as a U.S. business on the grounds that over 75% of shareholders were U.S. residents, and U.S. sales represented the company's largest market. As a result, Varity became a holding company for all of the firm's interests. In 1994 the company abandoned the farm machinery business. Sales for fiscal 1996 totaled $2.4 billion, with net income of $125 million; employees numbered 9,755.

Market Forces Driving the Merger

Lucas Industries and Varity Corp. felt the pinch of industry consolidation in early 1996, when AlliedSignal announced the sale of its hydraulic braking and anti-lock braking system (ABS) businesses to Robert Bosch GmbH. Bosch had already been the leader in that technology, and the positions of Lucas and Varity slipped even farther away from that company. The ABS market was an area in which both companies had been attempting to expand. Varity already held a strong share of the U.S. market, thanks to its ability to offer inexpensive systems. Its Kelsey-Hayes division was the North American leader in rear-wheel light truck ABS, and had captured a healthy share of the North American 4-wheel ABS market. Yet Varity's attempts to expand globally, particularly into Europe and Asia, had not been successful. Lucas, too, had been outmaneuvered in the ABS market, since it had not been able to match the falling prices of its rivals. Moreover, original equipment manufacturers (OEMs) were increasingly expecting parts manufacturers to provide complete systems rather than merely components.

The product lines of Varity and Lucas had little overlap, yet were complementary, especially in the area of fuel injection systems. VarityPerkins had entered into several alliances to attempt to develop such systems. By joining with Lucas it would gain the latest technology, as well as research and development direction, in this market.

Lucas' aerospace business had been in a slump due to decreased demand. The company had come to rely on its automotive operations to generate more of the total revenue, and needed to invest further in those operations to compete against large rivals. Becoming a major player, however, would be difficult if it relied on internal growth alone. A merger or acquisition would be the more effective method of achieving that goal.

Approach and Engagement

On May 31, 1996, Lucas Industries PLC and Varity Corporation announced their $4.9 billion merger agreement. The resulting company, LucasVarity PLC, would be formed via a stock swap. Lucas shareholders would receive about 62% of the company's common stock. The transfer of Varity stock would be a bit more complex. Each Varity share would be converted to 1.38 American Depository Receipts, each of which represented 10 ordinary LucasVarity shares.

LucasVarity would be based in London, England. Sir Brian Pearse, chairman of Lucas Industries, would assume that role at the new company. Victor Rice, chairman and CEO of Varity, would become CEO of LucasVarity.

The new company would be the world's second-largest OEM supplier of braking systems for light vehicles, as well as the second-largest manufacturer of diesel fuel injection systems. It would also become the eighth-largest automotive supplier in the world, outranking TRW Inc. and Dana Corp. Total sales would be $6.7 billion, based on the combined 1995 revenues of Lucas and Varity. It would also realize savings of $100 million per year from efficiencies of scale, as well as another $100 per year in taxes.

On June 7, 1996, England-based BBA, an industrial supplier of brake components, announced that it was abandoning its planned hostile takeover bid for Lucas Industries. BBA believed that its own product line fit better with Lucas than Varity's did, but it didn't want to pursue an acquisition without the support of Lucas' board of directors.

Shareholders of each company overwhelmingly approved the merger in August. On September 6, 1996, the High Court of Justice of England and Wales also approved the deal, and LucasVarity was officially formed.

"They've just created one of the world's largest automotive suppliers, a powerful player," said James

The Players

Honorary Chairman: Sir Brian Pearse. Before joining Lucas Industries, Sir Brian Pearse had been the Finance Director of Barclays Bank PLC. He served in that position from 1987 until 1991, when he was appointed Chief Executive of Midland Bank PLC. In May 1994 he joined the board of Lucas Industries as Deputy Chairman, and was appointed Chairman that November. Sir Brian was acquired a seat on the board of LucasVarity PLC in May 1996, and became chairman of that newly formed company. He held that position until May 1998, when he announced his retirement and his succession by Ed Wallis.

CEO: Victor A Rice. Victor Rice worked at Perkins Group for an entire decade beginning in 1970. He became a Director of Varity Corporation in 1978. Two years later he began his tenure as Chairman and Chief Executive Officer. He held these positions until Varity's merger with Lucas in 1996. Rice became CEO of LucasVarity PLC upon its formation in 1996. He was also named Vice Chairman of TRW Inc. upon that company's acquisition of LucasVarity in 1999.

Carter, a partner in Ernst & Young, as reported in Automotive News. "The new company will be larger than Lear Corp., and that's significant."

Products and Services

LucasVarity Automotive incorporated four main divisions. Light Vehicle Braking Systems supplied braking systems and components, with particular strengths in foundation brakes, actuation, anti-lock braking systems (ABS), and next generation systems such as traction control and vehicle stability control. Diesel Systems served the car, van, truck, bus, agricultural, industrial, and marine sectors with products ranging from mechanical rotary fuel pumps, fuel injectors, and filters, to fully-integrated electronically controlled systems. Electrical and Electronic Systems was a major supplier of advanced electronic controls, wiring, and body electrical systems, focusing on three strategic sectors: interface systems, distribution systems, and control systems. Its fourth main division was Aftermarket Operations, a provider of comprehensive parts, service, technical, and diagnostic support to both vehicle manufacturers and the global independent automotive aftermarket.

Lucas Aerospace provided products and services supporting every major civil and military aerospace program in the Western world, from helicopters to the latest generation of commercial and military jets. Its principal areas of activity were: Engine Controls, fuel systems and other engine management systems for civil and military engines; Power Generation, the integration of electrical power generation, management, and control systems; Flight Controls, which provided primary and secondary flight controls, thrust reversers, and actuation systems on more than 75% of all wide and narrow body jet airliners in production; Cargo Systems, lower deck and main deck systems; Hoists and Winches, airborne hoists and winches for military, civil, and commercial applications; and Missile Actuation, which was a leading supplier of missile actuation systems, with complete in-house capabilities for fin, wing, and thrust vectoring control systems on all missile types.

Changes to the Industry

The 1996 merger did not bring an end to the merger activity involving the companies formerly known as Lucas Industries and Varity. Aside from the various small acquisitions that it engaged in during the years after its formation, LucasVarity would also be a participant in the largest acquisition in the automotive parts industry. In January 1999, Ohio-based TRW Inc. announced its $7 billion cash purchase of LucasVarity; the deal was expected to close during the second quarter of that year. The new company, with $19 billion in sales, would become North America's largest independent auto parts supplier, as well as the fourth-largest of all suppliers.

Review of the Outcome

In December 1996, LucasVarity announced that it would sell 13 non-core businesses and eliminate 8,000 jobs over the course of two years. The sale of these operations accounted for about 5,000 of those positions, with the additional 3,000 eliminated in large part through attrition and voluntary redundancy. In addition, LucasVarity eliminated 50 of its top 150 management positions.

Among the most notable of its divestitures were the sales of VarityPerkins to Caterpillar Inc. in 1998, followed by its Heavy Vehicle Braking division to Meritor Automotive, Inc., in 1999.

In September 1998 the board of directors proposed to move the company from London to Buffalo, New York. There, the board reasoned, LucasVarity would be closer to its peers in the U.S. automotive industry, and would therefore be more competitive in securing investment and acquisition opportunities. Shareholders voted in November on the measure, and it failed by only one percentage point.

In August 1998, LucasVarity reorganized into two units: automotive and aerospace. For the fiscal year ending January 31, 1999, total company sales were GBP 4.3 billion. Automotive operations contributed GBP 3.5 billion, of which braking systems accounted for GBP 1.8 billion. LucasVarity's aerospace division generated GBP 716 million.

Research

Adams, David. "With LucasVarity Merger, TRW Would Be Top Independent Auto Parts Supplier," in *Knight-Ridder/Tribune Business News*, 30 January 1999. Details the newly announced merger of LucasVarity with TRW Inc.

Brooke, Lindsey. "Lucas, Varity to Merge; Form $6.7-Billion Supply Giant," in *Automotive Industries*, June 1996. Describes the union's role as the second-largest supplier of light vehicle brakes.

Ferris, Deebe. "Where LucasVarity is Heading," in *Ward's Auto World*, November 1996. Briefly discusses the newly formed company, and describes the various systems that LucasVarity demonstrated at a recent motor show.

Kisiel, Ralph. "Lucas, Varity Agree to Merge," in *Automotive News*, 3 June 1996. Relates the merger announcement and briefly discusses the strengths and weaknesses of the uniting companies.

"Lucas and Varity Merge, Forming $6.7 Billion Company," in *Defense Daily*, 4 June 1996. Details the stock swap arrangement of the newly announced merger.

"LucasVarity PLC," in *Notable Corporate Chronologies*, The Gale Group, 1999. Provides major events since the company's formation, and profiles Lucas Industries PLC prior to 1996.

LucasVarity PLC Home Page, available at http://www.lucasvarity.com. Official World Wide Web Page for LucasVarity. Includes an financial and investor information, product descriptions, and news releases.

Mortimer, John. "Lucas Looks for Way out," in *The Engineer*, 16 May 1996. Discusses how Bosch's acquisition of AlliedSignal's braking businesses contributed to the Lucas/Varity merger.

Sedgwick, David. "LucasVarity Cuts 50 of Top 150 Managers," in *Automotive News*, 25 November 1996. Reports Rice's trimming of management positions.

———. "LucasVarity to Sell Units, Cut 8,000 Jobs," in *Automotive News*, 9 December 1996. Describes the upcoming business and job eliminations.

———. "Varity and Lucas Seem a Good Fit," in *Automotive News*, 13 May 1996. Discusses the strengths and weaknesses Lucas and Varity, and provides the latest financial data for the two companies.

"Varity Corp.," in *Notable Corporate Chronologies*, The Gale Group, 1999. Profiles the history of Varity until its merger with Lucas.

PATRICIA ARCHILLA

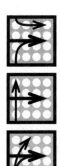

LVMH MOET HENNESSY LOUIS VUITTON & GUCCI

date: August 1999 (canceled)
affected: LVMH Moet Hennessy Louis Vuitton SA, France, founded 1743
affected: Gucci Group N.V., The Netherlands, founded 1923

LVMH Moet Hennessy Louis Vuitton
30, avenue Hoche
Paris, 75008
France

tel: 33 1 44 13 2222
fax: 33 1 44 13 2119
web: http://www.lvmh.com

Gucci Group N.V.
Rembrandt Tower, Amstelplein 1
Amsterdam, 1096 HA
The Netherlands

tel: 31 20 4621700
fax: 31 20 4653569

Overview of the Merger

In early 1999, LVMH Moet Hennessy Louis Vuitton SA, the world's largest luxury goods group, spent $1.4 billion to acquire a 34.4% stake in fashion house Gucci Group N.V. and launched one of the decade's most bitter takeover battles in Europe. Fearing that the luxury goods giant was preparing to slowly take over, Gucci insisted that the firm either make a full offer or agree to legally limit its power. When LVMH declined to do either, Gucci agreed to sell 43% of itself to Pinault-Printemps-Redoute SA by issuing $3 billion in new Gucci shares for $75 each, which would dilute LVMH's stake in Gucci to approximately 22%. In response, LVMH offered $8.7 billion for full control of Gucci. After rejecting LVMH's bid, Gucci completed its deal with Pinault, which planned to merge its recently purchased Yves Saint Laurent assets with Gucci to create a new luxury goods powerhouse. LVMH filed suit against Gucci, hoping to reverse the defensive measures, but a judge later dismissed the case.

History of LVMH Moet Hennessy Louis Vuitton SA

In 1743, Claude Moet established a winery, Moet et Cie, near Epernay. Seven years later, Moet began selling champagne in Germany, Spain, Eastern Europe, and America. Claude died in 1792, leaving the company to his grandson, Jean-Remy Moet, whose friendship with Napoleon and his wine drinking entourage, placed Moet et Cie in the limelight as the most famous wine-maker in the world.

The company was renamed Moet et Chandon in 1832. By the turn of the century, Moet was selling roughly two million bottles per year. Moet introduced the Dom Perignon brand of vintage champagne in the 1930s. Ruinart Pere et Fils, France's oldest champagne house, was acquired in 1962. Nine years later, Moet, by then France's number one champagne producer, and the Hennessy Cognac Co. merged to form Moet Hennessy. The new company's first acquisition was perfume maker Christian Dior.

Moet Hennessy opened the Domaine Chandon winery in Napa Valley, California, in 1973. Five years later, Moet bought Roc, a French cosmetics firm specializing in hypoallergenic make-up. A French rose company, Delbard, also joined

The Business

Financials - LVMH Moet Hennessy Louis Vuitton SA

Revenue (1998): $8.1 billion

Employees (1998): 33,000

Financials - Gucci Group N.V.

Revenue (1998): $1.04 billion

Employees (1998): 1,950

SICs / NAICS

sic 2084 - Wines, Brandy & Brandy Spirits

sic 2085 - Distilled & Blended Liquors

sic 5122 - Drugs, Proprietaries & Sundries

sic 2844 - Toilet Preparations

sic 5099 - Durable Goods Nec

sic 2386 - Leather & Sheep-Lined Clothing

sic 2389 - Apparel & Accessories Nec

sic 2341 - Women's/Children's Underwear

sic 2342 - Bras, Girdles & Allied Garments

naics 315292 - Fur and Leather Apparel Manufacturing

naics 315999 - Other Apparel Accessories and Other Apparel Manufacturing

naics 315212 - Women's, Girls', and Infants' Cut and Sew Apparel Contractors

naics 315211 - Men's and Boys' Cut and Sew Apparel Contractors

the company's holdings. In March of 1987, Louis Vuitton—established in 1854 as a luggage and trunks shop in Paris—acquired champagne maker Veuve Clicquot. Several months later, Louis Vuitton merged with Moet Hennessy in an effort to avoid potential hostile takeover attempts. The combined enterprise was known as LVMH Moet Hennessy Louis Vuitton. By the year's end, LVMH acquired the cognac house of Hine and signed a series of international agreements with the Guinness group to establish a joint distribution network in the U.S., the Far East, and Europe. The Givenchy Couture group was acquired in 1988. Management clashes between Moet Hennessy head Henry Racamier and Louis Vuitton chairman Alain Chevalier led Racamier to solicit the support of investor Bernard Arnault, a move that ultimately proved ill-advised. By the end of the decade, Arnault

had secured a 43% share of LVMH, and he took over as chairman. Both Chevalier and Racamier eventually resigned.

By 1990, LVMH owned a 24% stake in Guinness. The firm also purchased an 11% interest in Spain's Loewe SA, whose leather and fabric fashion goods and accessories were marketed by LVMH. Veuve Clicquot diversified overseas, acquiring a majority interest in Cape Mentelle of Australia and its New Zealand subsidiary, Cloudy Bay. LVMH acquired almost all of the shares in Lanson and Pommery Champagne in 1991; Lanson was sold immediately as it directly competed with other LVMH brands. The following year, the firm launched Dune and Amarige perfumes; acquired a majority interest in the J.G. Monnet cognac house; and purchased an additional stake in Guinness, as well as a 7% interest in Marnier-Lapostolle, maker of Grand Marnier.

Bon Marche sold its Christian Lacroix and Kenzo fashion lines to LVMH in 1993. The firm acquired a controlling interest in Fred, one of top ten jewelers in the world, in 1995. That year, Hubert de Givenchy presented his last collection as designer of the brand bearing his name. In 1996, LVMH acquired the shares of Loewe SA it didn't already own. Also, Louis Vuitton celebrated the centennial of the monogram fabric bearing the distinctive LV initials. DFS Group, the world's largest luxury goods distributor, agreed to a $2.47 billion takeover offer from LVMH in 1997. DFS management remained intact, and the company was managed independently of LVMH.

After buying Sephora and Marie-Jeanne Godard, the two leading perfume retailers in France in the late 1990s, LVMH held a 20% share of France's perfume market. Efforts to gain control of Gucci Group in 1999 were thwarted by defensive measure taken by Gucci management.

History of Gucci Group N.V.

In 1923, Guccio Gucci opened a leather goods store in Florence, Italy. Mussolini's attack on Ethiopia prompted the League of Nations to punish Italy in 1935, and Gucci's leather supply was cut off. As a result, the firm diversified into canvas products, including purses and sacks.

Gucci moved into the U.S. in 1953 by opening a store in New York. Although Gucci lured famous clientele, including Queen Elizabeth and Grace Kelly, to his stores, marketing efforts were rather limited. It was the founder's son, Aldo Gucci, who parlayed Gucci into a worldwide brand name through licensing efforts in the late 1950s and 1960s. Ready-to-wear clothing lines for both men and women were introduced in the mid-1970s.

Bickering among family members, which eventually led to a few minor jail sentences, took a toll on the firm in the 1980s. Investcorp bought 50% of Gucci in 1987 from Paolo Gucci, son of Aldo. The remaining half of the firm was owned by Maurizio Gucci, Paolo's nephew; he took over in 1989. Hoping to make the Gucci name more exclusive, he reduced licensing efforts and limited the number of stores selling Gucci brand products. Sales tumbled. In 1993, Maurizio sold his half of Gucci to Investcorp. New management helped return the firm to profitability, and in 1995, Gucci conducted its initial public offering. A takeover effort by LVMH Moet Hennessy Louis Vuitton in 1999 was thwarted when Gucci sold 42% of itself to Pinault-Printemps-Redoute for $2.9 billion.

Market Forces Driving the Merger

Sluggish cognac sales undercut profits at LVMH in the late 1990s. Net income in 1998 fell 29%, due mainly to poor sales Asia, and the firm announced its intent to reduce cognac operations in favor of the more lucrative luxury goods operations. Gucci Group, which had neared collapse in the mid-1990s, had turned itself around, and its strong leather goods, watches, and fashion product lines were attractive to LVMH.

Approach and Engagement

LVMH began acquiring shares of Gucci in January of 1999. Italian fashion house Prada sold its 9.5% stake in Gucci—acquired in 1998—to LVMH early that year. By March, LVMH had spent $1.4 billion for a 34.4% stake in the fashion house. Suspicious that the luxury goods giant was preparing to slowly take over, without paying shareholders a fair premium, Gucci insisted that the firm either make a full offer or agree to legally limit its power. When LVMH declined to do either, Gucci implemented an employee stock ownership plan; by issuing millions of new shares, Gucci was able to weaken LVMH's influence enough to allow Gucci CEO Domenico De Sole to decline LVMH's request for a seat of Gucci's supervisory board.

On March 19, Gucci shocked the fashion industry when it agreed to sell 43% of itself to Pinault-Printemps-Redoute by issuing $3 billion in new Gucci shares for $75 each, a move which would dilute LVMH's stake in Gucci to approximately 22%. Pinault had recently acquired Yves Saint Laurent and a few beauty product lines from French pharmaceutical giant Sanofi and was hoping to merge them into Gucci to create a new luxury goods player.

The Officers

LVMH Moet Hennessy Louis Vuitton SA

Chairman and CEO: Bernard Arnault

Vice Chairman: Antoine Bernheim

Exec. Committee, Administration: Pierre Gode

Exec. Committee, Finance: Patrick Houel

Exec. Committee, Human Resources: Concetta Lanciaux

Gucci Group N.V.

Chairman, President, and CEO: Domencio De Sole

Creative Director: Tom Ford

Exec. VP and Chief Financial Officer: Robert Singer

President, Gucci America: Patricia Malone

Exec. VP, Sales and Merchandising: Brian Blake

In response, LVMH filed suit in an effort to block the deal and then offered $8.7 billion for full control of Gucci. News of the offer by LVMH caused share prices of all three companies to hit record highs: Gucci gained 6.8%; LVMH, 4.2%; and Pinault, 6.5%. In the *Daily News Record*, a spokesperson for Gucci declared the offer a win for the company because LVMH was "offering the price that Gucci had been asking since LVMH began buying Gucci shares on the stock market earlier this year." The bid was 23 times earnings.

Despite the higher offer, Gucci turned LVMH down in April, citing as cause for concern a condition that if independent shareholders accepted the offer, Gucci would be required to issue enough new shares to give LVMH control of the company. LVMH responded by sending a letter directly to Gucci shareholders explaining the reasons for the condition. In an April 22 hearing in Amsterdam, after examining the defensive tactics used by Gucci, a judge ruled in favor of Gucci, and the deal with Pinault was allowed to stand. In May, LVMH began preparing an appeal. Some analysts predicted that the case could make it to the Dutch Supreme Court.

Products and Services

Cognac and other liquor products, including the Hennessy, Pellisson, and Thomas Hine brand names, accounted for 10% of total sales at LVMH in the late 1990s. Champagne and wines secured 18%; fragrances and cosmetics, 20%; fashion and leather goods, 26%; and retailing, 26%.

Major operations included high fashion career clothing designer Christian Dior; French leather goods

The Players

Chairman and CEO of LVMH Moet Hennessy Louis Vuitton SA: Bernard Arnault. Bernard Arnault paid $15 million for fashion house Christian Dior in 1984. After turning that firm around, he spent the next fifteen years building a fashion, liquor, cosmetics, and retailing giant with sales in excess of $8.5 billion. As a shareholder, Arnault gained control of LVMH in 1989 after securing a 43% stake in the firm. He became chairman and CEO when Henry Racamier stepped down following a legal battle for control of the firm. Arnault's efforts to take over Gucci in 1999 were thwarted when Gucci sold 42% of itself to Pinault-Printemps-Redoute.

Chairman, President, and CEO of Gucci Group N.V.: Domenico De Sole. Harvard graduate Domenico De Sole took over as president of Gucci in 1994 after a highly publicized and dramatic family battle for control of the firm led the Gucci family to sell out to Investcorp. He had worked as president of Gucci America since 1984 and prior to that, served as a partner for Patton, Boggs & Blow, a law firm based in Washington. In De Sole's first four years at the helm of Gucci, sales grew more than fourfold to exceed $1 billion. When LVMH Moet Hennessy Louis Vuitton moved to take over the company in 1999, De Sole masterminded several successful defensive measures, keeping LVMH at bay.

---

maker Louis Vuitton; French couture house Givenchy; French apparel and accessories maker Celine; fashion house Christian Lacroix; leather goods maker Loewe; Italian shoemaker Berluti; perfume retailer Guerlain; Moet Hennessy, the world's largest cognac maker, as well as the maker of Dom Perignon; Duty Free Shoppers; and Sephora, a luxury goods chain.

Gucci sold such products as leather bags and purses, perfume, clothing, scarves, shoes, ties, watches, jewelry, and eyewear.

Changes to the Industry

Gucci's decision to join forces with Pinault as a means of avoiding a takeover by LVMH set the stage for the creation of a new luxury goods industry leader, behind only LVMH and Vendome. Pinault planned to merge its Saint Laurent fashion and fragrances lines, °as well as its Oscar de la Renta, Van Cleef & Arpels, Roer & Gallet, and Fendi brands, into Gucci.

Research

Conti, Samantha. "De Sole: A Formidable Foe," in *Women's Wear Daily*, 22 March 1999. Details the career of Domenico De Sole.

"Gucci Gets the Upper Hand over LVMH," in *Cosmetics International*, 25 June 1999. Explains how Gucci and Pinault plan to create a new luxury goods powerhouse.

"Gucci's the Victor in Takeover War; LVMH May Appeal," in *Women's Wear Daily*, 28 May 1999. Explains the outcome of the suit LVMH filed against Gucci.

"LVMH Fires New Weapon: Letter to Gucci Shareholders," in *Women's Wear Daily*, 16 April 1999. Describes Gucci's reasons for rejecting the bid and LVMH's responses to those concerns.

LVMH Moet Hennessy Louis Vuitton SA Home Page, available at http://www.lvmh.com. Official World Wide Web Page for LVMH Moet Hennessy Louis Vuitton SA. Available in both French and English, this Web site houses news releases, financial information, product information, and more.

"LVMH Moet Hennessy Louis Vuitton SA," in *Notable Corporate Chronologies*, The Gale Group, 1999. Offers a summary of events in the history of LVMH Moet Hennessy Louis Vuitton SA.

"LVMH Offers to Buy All of Gucci," in *Daily News Record*, 22 March 1999. Describes the terms of the offer LVMH made for all of Gucci.

Norton, Leslie P. "In Showdown Over Gucci, LVMH Raises the Stakes," in *Barron's*, 12 April 1999. Offers an overview of the takeover battle for Gucci.

Olive, David. "A Wolf in Cashmere Clothing," in *National Post*, 27 February 1999. Covers the career of Bernard Arnault.

THERA WILLIAMS

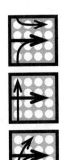

MACANDREWS & FORBES & MARVEL ENTERTAINMENT

nationality: USA
date: 1988
affected: MacAndrews & Forbes Holdings Inc., USA, founded 1984
affected: Marvel Entertainment Group Inc., USA, founded 1939

MacAndrews & Forbes Holdings
35 East 62nd St.
New York, NY 10021
USA

tel: (212)688-9000
fax: (212)572-8400

Marvel Entertainment Group Inc.
387 Park Ave. S.
New York, NY 10016
USA

tel: (212)696-0808
fax: (212)576-8598
web: http://www.marvel.com

Overview of the Merger

Comic book sales were plump in the early 1980s, consuming income from stores that had opened to meet increasing interest in comic book collecting. These stores, generally in malls, were exclusively devoted to comic book sales. Marvel dedicated several special issues to this direct sales market; between 1981 and 1982, such sales accounted for half of the company's income. Marvel made its comic book sales even fatter in 1985 with the introduction of *Star Comics* designed for young children, and by the end of that year, its revenues reached $100 million.

Attracted by Marvel's success, New World Pictures bought Marvel in 1986 for $46 million to capitalize on its comic characters and to gain ownership of its animation studio. Two years later it sold the company, following a series of losses, to the Andrews Group, Inc., a subsidiary of MacAndrews & Forbes Group, for $82.5 million.

History of MacAndrews & Forbes

One of America's top private enterprises, MacAndrews & Forbes has had a successful history in buying struggling companies, revamping them, and then selling them at a higher price.

In 1978 Perelman bought 40% of Cohen-Hatfield Industries, a jewelry store operator that bought a minority stake in the licorice-flavoring producer MacAndrews & Forbes the next year. Two years later Cohen-Hatfield acquired the rest of MacAndrews & Forbes.

This was about the time that Perelman was going through what would later be referred to as a "passing fancy" as a media mogul. Accordingly, MacAndrews & Forbes bought 82% of Technicolor, a motion picture processor that was sold in 1988. Also during the mid-1980s, Perelman renamed his company to reflect its function: MacAndrews & Forbes Holdings.

The Business

Financials - MacAndrews & Forbes Holdings

Revenue (1998):$6 billion

Employees (1998): 29,854

Financials - Marvel Entertainment Group Inc.

Revenue (1998): $335 million

Employees (1998): 1,100

SICs / NAICS

sic 2721 - Periodicals

naics 511120 - Periodical Publishers

In a move that typified holding companies in the mid-1980s—that of buying unrelated organizations—MacAndrews & Forbes acquired control of a Florida-based supermarket chain, Pantry Pride, in 1985. The supermarket company then bought cosmetic giant Revlon for $1.8 million. MacAndrews & Forbes, perhaps to show that it couldn't safely be said to "typify" anything, subsequently acquired two other cosmetics vendors: Max Factor and the fragrance and cosmetic lines of Yves St. Laurent. Revlon's Max Factor unit was sold in 1991 to Procter & Gamble for over $1 billion.

MacAndrews & Forbes acquired 37.5% of TV infomercial producer Guthy-Renker, merged it with seven stations belonging to SCI Television, and created New World Television. This company combined with Genesis Entertainment, a TV syndicator, and New World Entertainment, which had owned Marvel Entertainment Group, to form New World Communications Group, which Perelman took public in 1994.

That was a big year for MacAndrews & Forbes Holdings. Perelman joined with Gerald J. Ford to purchase the nation's fifth-largest savings and loan, Ford Motor Company's First Nationwide. First Nationwide would, in the late 1990s, acquire for $1.2 billion a 31% stake in the nation's number two thrift, California's Golden State Bancorp.

History of Marvel Entertainment Group, Inc.

Now the largest American publisher of comic books, Marvel Entertainment started during the Depression when, by providing action-packed thrillers for ten cents an issue, its comic books were an instant success.

That success, however, roller-coastered. Along with that of other comic book publishers, Marvel's sales slowed in the Fifties following strong sales in the Thirties and Forties, but rebounded in the Sixties when its popular characters were appealing to baby boomers' children. It again sagged in the Seventies, only to bounce back strongly the next decade. The children of the boomers' children were intrigued, as their parents had been, with Marvel comic characters, and the company prospered. Diversifying with licensing agreements and video arrangements that featured its well-known characters proved valuable in the Nineties and added to the company's financial strength.

Martin Goodman, a publisher of pulp magazines in New York, founded Marvel after being convinced by a salesman from Funnies, Inc. to invest in comic books. Funnies, Inc. was a group of writers and artists that produced comic books but didn't publish them.

Both of Marvel's original super-heroes, the Human Torch and the part-man/part-fish Sub-Mariner, were rebels. Angry, snide, and creating havoc everywhere they went, these fantasy creations were immensely appealing to young people. The first issues were successful enough that Goodman was able to form a new company, Timely Productions, to publish *Daring Mystery Comics* and *Mystic Comics*, each of which had its own new string of superheroes.

Expanding on these successes, Timely went on to publish humorous comic books: *Comedy Comics*, *Joker Comics*, and *Krazy Comics*, as well as funny animals that would appeal to a younger audience. Soon it added beauty tips to its Miss America series on dating and dances, and had another popular seller.

The Atlas News Company was created early in the 1950s to capitalize on the comics' popularity. Goodman, through Atlas, was able not only to create comic books, but also to distribute them. But, in the mid-1950s, these comic superhero, war, horror, and teenage figures were blamed for causing violence in society. Comic book sales decreased, and distribution activities became a drain on income.

Then, just as in the comics, a superhero came to the rescue. Actually it was a superhero group, *The Fantastic Four*, that restored Marvel to financial well-being. The Four (the original Human Torch along with Mr. Fantastic, The Thing, and Invisible Girl) and newly created superhero companions *The Avengers* and the *X-Men* were instant successes. Merchandising, television syndication and Saturday morning cartoons followed, providing saturation coverage of the characters' exploits. By 1968 Marvel was selling 50 million comic books a year. Goodman sold Marvel to Perfect Film and Chemical Corporation that year; Perfect Film soon became Cadence Industries Corporation. Within Cadence, Goodman's properties were known as Magazine Management.

In a slump similar to that of the Fifties, Marvel lost ground in the Seventies. To revitalize itself, and without the Comics Code board seal of approval (a censorship board, the Comics Code Authority, had been set up in 1955 to assure that no one would be offended by reading the comics), Marvel published comics featuring vampires and werewolves. It created, for audiences older than its color books appealed to, black-and-white comics, and in 1975 introduced Giant Size X-Men, its most popular franchise ever.

Sales were strong, but profits were not. Rising paper profits and decreasing numbers of retail outlets, hurt revenue. Looking to television and to direct mail to take advantage of The Incredible Hulk and its other popular characters, the company found a waiting market. When it added graphic novels, it once again saw its profit margin grow. By the end of 1985, its revenues had reached $100 million, and the financial market took notice.

Approach and Engagement

The acquisition of Marvel Entertainment Group from New World Entertainment was completed in 1988. New World Pictures, which subsequently underwent a series of corporate transformations, had purchased Marvel in 1986, hoping to capitalize on the publisher's comic characters and its animation studio. New World sold Marvel to the Andrews Group, Inc. (a subsidiary of MacAndrews & Forbes Holdings, which had been formed in 1984) in 1988 for $82.5 million. MacAndrews & Forbes partially controlled New World at the time; it gained control of the rest in 1989. In 1991, Perelman took Marvel public.

Products and Services

MacAndrews & Forbes is a multi-billion dollar holding company; a few well-known names of its many companies include Revlon (cosmetics and personal care products), the Coleman Company (outdoor recreation equipment), New World Communications Group (TV broadcasting, production and distribution) and Consolidated Cigar. Until recently, it also held Sunbeam (small appliances).

Marvel bought Fleer Corporation, which makes trading cards, for $265 million in 1992. It also owns 46% of Toy Biz, Inc., maker of toys, some based on Marvel's comic book characters. It is one of the world's top comic book producers as well as being a leading marketer of its popular characters, and is a leading youth entertainment company. Some of its

The Officers

MacAndrews & Forbes Holdings

Chairman and CEO: Ronald O. Perelman

Vice Chairman: Donald G. Drapkin

Vice Chairman: Howard Gittis

President: Bruce Slovin

Exec. VP: Meyer Laskin

Marvel Entertainment Group Inc.

President and COO: Joseph Calamari

Exec. VP and General Counsel: Pamela Bradford

Exec. VP, Advertising Sales and Promotions: Steve Bobouski

VP, Licensing and Consumer Products: Kenneth Abrams

VP, Administration and Human Resources: Ann Yarmark

operations include publishing of comic books, trading cards, activity stickers and licensing of its characters for consumer products, media and advertising promotions.

Its *Spider-Man* and *X-Men* shows are highly rated weekly animated TV series, and Marvel is one of the largest licensors of characters to software developers. It has a stable of more than 1,500 superheroes and other characters. Toy Biz's Marvel action figures top the charts.

Changes to the Industry

Marvel Enterprises, Inc. was formed on October 1, 1998 upon Marvel Entertainment Group, Inc.'s emergence from bankruptcy and merger with Toy Biz. Toy Biz and Marvel traded business monikers, and Marvel Enterprises has resumed its role as a leading character-based entertainment company. It appointed Winston Fowlkes in February 1999, as publisher of its comics. Mr. Fowlkes was co-founder of comics publisher Voyager Communications, and it was believed that he would help to leverage the popularity of Marvel's characters across film, television, and the Internet.

Review of the Outcome

The New York Times in March 1993 reported that, as part of the deal, MacAndrews & Forbes Holdings could increase its 60% stake of Marvel to 80%. It offered $25 per share, or about $275 million, for the

The Players

MacAndrews & Forbes Holdings Chairman and CEO: Ronald O. Perelman. Ronald Perelman is noted for his ability to turn companies around. At the age of 35, he left Philadelphia and his father's conglomerate, Belmont Industries, to go to New York. He has been shuffling assets astutely ever since. He turned his original investment into an investment empire with sales of roughly $2 billion from such companies as Revlon, National Health Laboratories, and Marvel Entertainment's comics. Mr. Perelman sits on so many big-name boards that sales of many companies can almost be said to be internal shuffling.

additional 20% stake. After the offer was announced, the stock closed at $23.75 per share, an increase of $4.25. The reason for the offer, analysts said, was to help MacAndrews offset some of its losses from savings and loan First Gibraltar.

Following diminishing comic sales, Perelman placed Marvel in bankruptcy in 1996. He lost control of the company in 1997 when a federal judge ruled that Marvel bondholders could foreclose on the 80% of company stock that backed their bonds. The foreclosure allowed the bondholders to oust the Board of Directors, installing a board led by Carl Icahn.

In 1998 the battle for control of Marvel ended when it was acquired by Toy Biz, Inc. In taking control, Toy Biz changed its name to Marvel Enterprises. Earlier, in October 1997, Marvel had sued its banks, Perelman, and the major shareholders of Toy Biz, claiming that those parties were responsible for its financial collapse. The suit asked for $710 million in

collateral from the banks and for them to subordinate their claims. It wanted to get rid of its board, and assessed unspecified financial damages against Perelman and others. It also requested that a bankruptcy reorganization case be moved to the U.S. District Court in Delaware.

Meanwhile, Perelman's New World Communications Group, which sold Marvel to MacAndrews & Forbes Holdings, partnered with Rupert Murdoch's Fox TV in 1994. Murdoch, a naturalized citizen who may be one of the few Americans richer than Perelman, joined his Fox network with New World's seven stations for $500 million and a 20% ownership stake in New World. Fox-owned stations in 1994 reached 25% of the nation's TV households, and New World's were expected to supply another 15%.

Perelman bought his New World shares at $8.47 in March 1994 during New World's rights offerings. Murdoch paid $12.92 for most shares, $15 for others, and a whopping $50 for still others. Does anybody know if King Midas smoked a cigar? If so, perhaps he's been reincarnated as Ron Perelman.

Research

Anderson, Richard W., "BIFF! POW! Comic Books Make a Comeback," *Business Week*, 2 September 1985.

Daniels, Les. *Marvel: Five Fabulous Decades of the World's Greatest Comics*, New York: Harry N. Abrams, 1991.

Henry, Gordon M., "Bang! Pow! Zap! Heroes are Back," in *Time*, 6 October 1986.

"A Marriage of Corporate Celebrities," in *Mergers & Acquisitions*, September 1992.

"Marvel Entertainment Group, Inc.," in *International Directory of Company Histories*, Vol. 10, St. James Press: 1995.

Sloan, Allan, "How You Can Invest With Revlon's Ronald Perelman," in *Money*, July 1994.

BARBARA J. KELLY

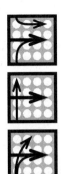

MANPOWER & BLUE ARROW

nationality: USA
date: September 1987
affected: Manpower Inc., USA, founded 1948
affected: Blue Arrow PLC, United Kingdom, founded mid-1900s

Manpower Inc.
5301 N. Ironwood Rd.
Milwaukee, WI 53217
USA

tel: (414)961-1000
fax: (414)961-7081

Overview of the Merger

Manpower Inc. became the target of a hostile takeover attack in August of 1987 when Blue Arrow PLC, a large temporary employment group based in the United Kingdom, bid $1.21 billion, or $75 per share, for the world's leading employment agency. Manpower rejected the offer as too low, prompting Blue Arrow to up its bid to $1.3 billion, or $82.50 per share, an offer Manpower accepted. Six times smaller than Manpower, Blue Arrow tripled its size when the purchase was completed in September. Management shakeups—including a power struggle that resulted in the firing of Manpower head Mitchell Fromstein and a criminal investigation that led to the ousting of Blue Arrow leader Antony Berry—rocked the company over the next two years. When the dust settled, Fromstein emerged as the victor. After he regained control of the firm, he essentially reversed the takeover by selling off Blue Arrow operations.

History of Manpower Inc.

In 1948, law partners Elmer L. Winter and Aaron Scheinfeld founded Manpower, Inc. in Milwaukee, Wisconsin, to meet the need for temporary industrial laborers amid the post-World War II labor shortage. By 1956, Manpower was well established in Wisconsin and began to franchise the company name. After four years of successful franchising efforts in the U.S., Manpower established branches in Europe, South America, Africa, and Asia.

The firm launched its quarterly Employment Outlook Survey, which measured the hiring intentions of employers, in 1962. During the 1970s, Manpower continued to expand and began to diversify throughout the decade, acquiring Nationwide Tax Service of Detroit, Michigan; Gilbert Lane Personnel, Inc. of Hartford, Connecticut; and Manpower Southampton Ltd. of Southampton, England. In 1976, Parker Pen Co. acquired Manpower for $27.2 million. When PPC's sales faltered later in the decade, board member Mitchell Fromstein repurchased a 20% interest in Manpower and became the firm's president and CEO. Sales totaled $300 million.

The Business

Financials

Revenue (1998): $8.81 billion

Employees (1998): 2,015,000

SICs / NAICS

sic 7363 - Help Supply Services

Manpower invested $15 million in Skillware, a computer training program, in 1978. Two years later, Fromstein began changing the focus of the company from providing temporary industrial labor to temporary office help. Market for temporary labor increased dramatically during the decade, as companies sought to avoid the increasing cost of employee benefits. In 1986, Parker Pen divested itself of its writing instruments operations, and the holding company adopted the Manpower name. The following year, Manpower entered into an agreement with IBM, through which Manpower provided on-site training and support services to buyers of IBM systems. Also, Blue Arrow PLC of the United Kingdom purchased Manpower for $82.50 per share. Fromstein was permitted to stay on as president and CEO, although he was soon fired as a result of a personality conflict with Blue Arrow's president, Antony Berry.

Because Berry was heavily invested in U.S. securities, the collapse of the New York Stock Exchange crippled Blue Arrow's finances. Berry and several Blue Arrow directors were investigated for financial impropriety. The investigation discredited Berry, allowing Fromstein to regain control of Blue Arrow in 1989. Less than two years later, Fromstein had adopted the Manpower name for Blue Arrow, moved headquarters back to Wisconsin, and sold Blue Arrow Personnel Services Ltd. for $48.7 million. Manpower then began divesting itself from non-employment Blue Arrow holdings.

In the mid-1990s, Manpower forged a Michigan-based joint venture with Franklin Bank and opened hundreds of new domestic and international branches. The firm remained the world's largest supplier of temporary services, with more than 1,850 offices in 34 countries. Annual sales of $6.88 billion in 1995 reflected an average growth rate of 30% during the last decade. In 1996, the firm increased its European business as many employers turned to temporary help to bypass their country's stringent labor laws. Manpower also secured 200,000 new customers via an alliance with Drake Beam Morin. Inc., the world's largest out-placement service. Overseas expansion continued with the 1998 purchase of Australia-based Kirby Contract Labour.

Market Forces Driving the Merger

Blue Arrow's bid for the much larger Manpower was the "culmination of three years of swift growth since it joined London's Unlisted Securities Market in 1984," stated *Financial Times (London)* in August of 1987. Blue Arrow CEO Antony Berry had propelled the firm's rapid growth since 1984 with an intense acquisition campaign. Adding U.S.-based Manpower to its mix would be a major coup for the United Kingdom-based temporary employment firm, not only because of Manpower's status as the world's largest temporary employment group, but also because of its strength in the rapidly growing U.S. market.

Approach and Engagement

In August 1987, Blue Arrow bid to buy out Manpower at $75 per share. Manpower rejected the offer, and the price of company stock rose from $62.37 to $78 per share. Manpower CEO Fromstein considered making a counter offer for Blue Arrow. At the same time, Adia S.A., an employment company based in Switzerland, threw its hat into the ring by announcing its interest in Manpower. Fromstein also threatened to reject any bid by Blue Arrow lower than $90 per share. However, because of the jump in the firm's stock price, Manpower shareholders favored the takeover and brought suit against Fromstein for making a decision they believed was financially irresponsible.

Recognizing that he couldn't preserve Manpower's independence without risking a drop in stock prices, Fromstein conceded defeat. The three-week battle came to an end when Manpower agreed, on August 21, to Blue Arrow's offer of $82.50 per outstanding share of common stock, a 10% increase over the original offer. The price was roughly 10 times Manpower's book value and 43 times reported earnings. Fromstein was permitted to stay on as president and CEO, and the firm's U.S. operations retained the Manpower name.

Blue Arrow financed the deal via a $1.56 billion rights issue, the largest such offering by a United Kingdom company to date. For every two shares of Blue Arrow stock held, existing shareholders received five new shares of the merged company. New shares were offered for $2.68 each, and the issue tripled Blue Arrow's capitalization.

Products and Services

After selling Blue Arrow Personnel Services Ltd. and most of the remaining Blue Arrow holdings in the early 1990s, Manpower continued to offer temporary employment services on a worldwide scale. In 1999, the firm operated 2,700 offices across 48 countries. Temporary employees—serving clerical, industrial, and technical needs—exceeded two million. Manpower also offered long-term employment services, such as employee screening and training.

Changes to the Industry

The botched deal seemed to leave other temporary employment agencies a bit leery of attempting to merge on such a grand scale. The next large international merger didn't take place until 1996 when France-based Ecco and Switzerland-based Adia merged to form Adecco, which usurped Manpower in the late 1990s as the leading temporary employment group in the world.

Review of the Outcome

On December 6, 1988, the Blue Arrow board fired Fromstein, asserting that he was resisting efforts to integrate the two firms. Insiders pointed to power struggles between Fromstein and Berry as the real reason for Fromstein's ousting.

As the sole leader of Blue Arrow and the recently acquired Manpower operations, Berry floundered. A sports fan, Berry orchestrated Blue Arrow's costly, unauthorized investment in a yacht competing in the America's Cup race. The stock market crash of October 1987 revealed Berry's most serious indiscretion. To generate the capital needed to purchase Manpower, Berry had secured a $1.3 billion loan from England's National Westminster Bank (NatWest), which was to be paid off via the cash raised from stock issue. Blue Arrow shareholders bought 38% of the shares; as underwriter, the bank was responsible for selling the remainder of the shares. According to an April 1991 article in *Financial World*, the bank feared that this situation might concern investors, so it purchased 12% of the shares as a means of upping the amount of shares sold to a more respectable 50%. The transaction itself was legal, but the secrecy surrounding the purchase was viewed by investigators as a calculated effort to deceive potential buyers. A criminal investigation prompted several bank executives to resign; although they were found guilty of misleading the market in a February 1992 ruling, an appeal later cleared their names.

On January 13, 1989, the Blue Arrow board replaced Berry with Fromstein, who had organized the support of Manpower's U.S. franchises. By then,

The Officers

Chairman, President, and CEO: Mitchell S. Fromstein

VP, Chief Financial Officer, Chief Accounting Officer, and Treasurer: Michael J. Van Handel

Exec. VP, the Americas and the Pacific Rim: Terry A. Hueneke

Sr. VP, International Corporate Affairs: Joel W. Biller

Sr. VP, International Marketing: James A. Fromstein

Blue Arrow shares had plunged 46% to $1.54 apiece. Fromstein changed the parent company's name back to Manpower, and he oversaw the sale of Blue Arrow Personnel Services Ltd. for roughly $50 million. By 1991, U.S. ownership of the company had grown from 10% to 60%, and Fromstein was able to return Manpower headquarters to Milwaukee, Wisconsin. The remaining Blue Arrow assets were sold off by mid-decade.

Research

Buchan, James and Phillip Coggan. "Manpower Recommends Raised Dollars 1.3 Bn Bid from Blue Arrow," in *Financial Times (London)*, August 22, 1987. Discusses why Blue Arrow bid for Manpower and what prompted Manpower to accept the offer.

Collingwood, H. "Manpower Gets a Divorce," in *Business Week*, 17 June 1991. Details Manpower's sale of Blue Arrow Personnel Services just four years after Blue Arrow took over Manpower.

"The End of Blue Arrow," in *The Economist*, 16 January 1993. Explains the outcome of the litigation surrounding the failure of Blue Arrow's 1987 rights issue, which was implemented to fund the purchase of Manpower.

Gilbert, Nick. "Manpower Comes Home," in *Financial World*, 30 April 1991. Speculates on why the failure of the Blue Arrow rights issue wasn't revealed to the public.

Hall, William. "Adecco Hopes to Lay the Ghost of Blue Arrow Disaster" in *The Financial Times*, 29 August 1996. Discusses the first major international merger in the temporary services industry since the Blue Arrow takeover of Manpower.

Harris, Clay. "Manpower Chief's Resignation Deal A Blow to Blue Arrow," in *Financial Times (London)*, 7 December 1988. Discusses the departure of Mitchell Fromstein from Blue Arrow.

"Manpower, Inc.," in *Notable Corporate Chronologies*, The Gale Group, 1999. Covers major events in the history of Manpower, Inc.

"Manpower, Inc.," in *International Directory of Company Histories*, St. James Press, Vol. 9, 1994. Offers a detailed look at the history of Manpower, Inc.

Melcher, Richard A. "For Mitchell Fromstein, How Sweet It Is," in *Business Week*, 30 January 1989. Covers the return of Mitchell Fromstein to Blue Arrow and the ousting of Antony Berry.

Phillips, Stephen. "Blue Arrow to Acquire Manpower," in *The New York Times*, 22 August 1987. Announces Manpower's acceptance of Blue Arrow's increased $1.3 billion takeover bid.

THERA WILLIAMS

MARION LABORATORIES &
MERRELL DOW PHARMACEUTICALS

nationality: Germany
date: December 2, 1989
affected: Merrell Dow Pharmaceuticals Inc., USA, founded 1828
affected: Marion Laboratories Inc., USA, founded 1950

Hoechst AG
Brueningstrasse 50
Frankfurt, D-65926
Germany

tel: 49 69 3050
fax: 49 69 303 665
web: http://www.hoechst.com

Overview of the Acquisition

The pressure to consolidate in the pharmaceutical industry was felt by both Marion Laboratories and Merrell Dow Pharmaceuticals in 1989. These two companies were unable to stand independent in a field that was forming, with each successive merger, increasingly powerful rivals. Marion and Merrell Dow each provided the other with valuable strengths. Merrell Dow had strong research and development prospects and an international presence, while Marion had one of the industry's most highly regarded marketing and sales force. In December 1989, the companies were officially united as Marion Merrell Dow Inc.

History of Merrell Dow Pharmaceuticals Inc.

William S. Merrell, a chemist, entered the pharmaceuticals industry in 1828 by opening a small retail drugstore, Western Market Drug Store, in Cincinnati, Ohio. The young company grew steadily, and in 1852 moved into a larger facility. That year Merrell's brother Ashbel joined the business, which took the name Wm. S. Merrell & Co. Its operations had expanded to include manufacturing, as well as wholesale and retail sales. By 1858, it manufactured more than 1,000 products, including the largest number of indigenous and botanic medicines of any company in the U.S.

In 1876, Merrell became the first U.S. manufacturer of salicylic acid, the forerunner of acetylsalicylic acid (aspirin), for the medical profession. The company continued to expand its product line, and in 1914 initiated the manufacture of fluid extracts, tinctures, tablets, pills, ointments, capsules, elixirs, vitamin pills, and toothpaste. Five years later, the firm eliminated the ampersand from its moniker and became known as The Wm. S. Merrell Co.

The Vick Chemical Co. purchased the company in 1938, making Merrell a wholly owned subsidiary. Two years later, Merrell introduced and marketed nationally the Cepacol brand mouthwash.

The Business

Financials

Revenue (1998): $26.2 billion

Employees (1998): 97,000

SICs / NAICS

sic 2812 - Alkalies & Chlorine

sic 2816 - Inorganic Pigments

sic 2822 - Synthetic Rubber

sic 2821 - Plastics Materials & Resins

sic 2824 - Organic Fibers-Noncellulosic

sic 2833 - Medicinals & Botanicals

sic 2834 - Pharmaceutical Preparations

sic 2835 - Diagnostic Substances

sic 2836 - Biological Products Except Diagnostic

naics 325181 - Alkalies and Chlorine Manufacturing

naics 325131 - Inorganic Dye and Pigment Manufacturing

naics 325182 - Carbon Black Manufacturing

naics 325211 - Plastics Material and Resin Manufacturing

naics 325212 - Synthetic Rubber Manufacturing

naics 325222 - Noncellulosic Organic Fiber Manufacturing

naics 325411 - Medicinal and Botanical Manufacturing

naics 325412 - Pharmaceutical Preparation Manufacturing

naics 325413 - In-Vitro Diagnostic Substance
   Manufacturing

naics 325414 - Biological Product (except Diagnostic)
   Manufacturing

Merrell sought to increase its global presence by establishing the Merrell International Division in 1956. Four years later its parent, Vick Chemical Co., changed its name to Richardson-Merrell Inc. to honor William Merrell and Lunsford Richardson, the founder of Vick.

In 1971, Merrell merged with the National Drug Co., also owned by Richardson-Merrell, to form the Merrell-National Laboratories Division. The company initiated research efforts to discover new compounds for the treatment of cardiovascular disease, central nervous system disorders, and abnormal cell growth.

Merrell entered into a licensing agreement in 1976 with Tanabe Seiyaku Co., a Japanese company, to develop and market diltiazem, a family of cardiovascular drugs sold under the brand name Cardizem.

In March 1981, Dow Chemical Co. of Midland, Michigan, acquired the domestic and international operation of Merrell-National Laboratories, Inc. to form Merrell Dow Pharmaceuticals Inc. as a division of Dow Chemical.

The U.S. Food and Drug Administration (FDA) approved Merrell Dow's Seldane brand drug in 1985 for marketing in the U.S. This product would soon become the world's top selling nonsedating antihistamine and the company's leading product. In 1987, Merrell Dow Pharmaceuticals reached $1 billion in sales for the first time and the following year registered revenues of $1.3 billion.

Merrell Dow Pharmaceuticals entered into an agreement to acquire Marion Laboratories in July 1989. That December the deal was concluded, with the formation of Marion Merrell Dow Inc.

The newly formed company announced the discovery of Ornidyl, the first new drug in 40 years for the treatment of African Sleeping Sickness, in 1990. This product was manufactured by Marion Merrell Dow and distributed by the World Health Organization. Sales for its first full year as a new company approached $2.5 billion.

Marion Merrell Dow announced an agreement with F. Hoffmann-La Roche Ltd., based in Basel, Switzerland, in 1991. In the accord, the two would cooperate in the development and marketing of RO 40-5967, a new cardiovascular drug. Later that year, Nordic Laboratories Inc. became a wholly owned subsidiary when Marion Merrell Dow acquired the remaining 14.6% of its stock. Also in 1991, the FDA granted approval for Nicoderm, the first nicotine transdermal patch for smoking cessation.

In 1992, the company announced a partnership with U.K-based SmithKline Beecham Plc calling for the creation of SmithKline Beecham Consumer Brands to develop and market over-the-counter pharmaceutical products in the U.S. That year Marion Merrell Dow also entered into an agreement with Oncogene Science Inc. to develop gene-based cardiovascular drugs. At the end of 1992, company sales exceeded $3.3 billion.

Marion Merrell Dow introduced a three-way therapy for tuberculosis in 1994. The drug, called Rifater, contained a combination of three pharmaceuticals—isoniazid, rifampin, and pyrazinamide—to assist in combating the spread of drug-resistant strains of tuberculosis.

In January 1995, a U.S. Federal Appellate Court dismissed a case against Marion Merrell Dow regarding the drug Bendectin. The court ruled that there was no valid scientific evidence to prove that the anti-nausea medicine many women took during pregnancy caused birth defects.

The German pharmaceutical company Hoechst AG paid $7.2 billion to acquire Marion Merrell Dow Inc. in July 1995, thereby breaking into the U.S. drug market. A new division of Hoechst resulted from the purchase, Hoechst Marion Roussel Inc. The following year, Hoechst Marion Roussel received FDA approval to market the prescription antihistamine Allegra, which would later replace Seldane as the company's best-seller.

History of Marion Laboratories Inc.

Ewing Marion Kauffman, a former salesman for an Illinois pharmaceutical company, established his own business in 1950. Funded with $4,000 in capital, the one-man company was operated out of his basement in Kansas City, Missouri. Initially he sold injectable products manufactured by Taylor Pharmacal Co.

In 1952, Kauffman persuaded seven men to invest $1,000 each and to purchase an additional $1,000 bond, on which no interest was to be paid in order to raise operating capital. That year Marion Laboratories was incorporated. The firm recorded sales of $176,000 and its first profit, of $6,000, in 1954. Five years later, the company achieved annual sales in excess of $1 million for the first time.

Marion introduced papaverine hydrochloride, a cerebral vasodilator sold under the brand name Pavabid, in 1962, and would later prove to be one of the company's best-selling products. The firm went public in 1965, offering 187,740 shares at $21 apiece. Its stock was introduced on the New York Stock Exchange five years later.

During the 1970s, prohibitive costs for research and development spurred Marion to adopt the unique strategy of reformulating and developing drugs that had been rejected by other pharmaceutical companies. The program proved successful, as its earnings were $12 million in 1974, up from $130,000 in 1964.

In 1977, Marion's net sales surpassed $100 million for the first time. That year Fred W. Lyons, Jr., an executive vice president with Marion, was named president and chief operating officer. The company established a consumer products division in 1978, and introduced the Gaviscon brand antacid tablets, intended for relief of heartburn associated with reflux esophagitis.

Over the years, Marion Laboratories had entered into diverse businesses outside of pharmaceuticals. In

The Officers

Chairman and CEO: Jurgen Dormann

Chief Financial Officer: Klaus-Jurgen Schmieder

President and CEO, Celanese: Knut Zeptner

Member Management Board and Director of Personnel: Ernst Schadow

Member Management Board: Claudio Sonder

1981, it divested four such subsidiaries whose manfacturing operations ranged from home stairway elevators to vision correction products: American Stair-Glide Corp., Kalo Laboratories Inc., Marion Health & Safety Inc., and Optico Industries Inc.

In 1982, Marion received federal approval to market two breakthrough drugs: Cardizem, a calcium slow channel blocker intended for the treatment of angina, and Carafate, an ulcer treatment. Both drugs were the product of research originated by Japan-based Tanabe Seiyaku Co. and obtained by Marion through a licensing agreement. In 1984, these two companies entered into a joint venture to develop, license, and market certain Tanabe products in the U.S. and Canada.

Marion Laboratories and Schering-Plough Corp. announced an agreement in 1988 whereby the companies would jointly develop over-the-counter formulations of Carafate. Later that year Marion sold its Analytical Systems division and purchased American Biomaterials Corp.

The heart medication Cardizem accounted for $441 million, the lion's share, of company revenues in 1988. These sales, combined with those from the ulcer medication Carafate, accounted for 90% of Marion's total sales that year. The company's recent regulatory approval for a new version of Cardizen for use by patients with high blood pressure was predicted to increase that product's sales to an estimated $600 million in 1989.

The final year of the decade was marked by aggressive strides by Marion to increase its pharmaceuticals business. In April, it sold its Scientific Products division. Two months later it paid $15 million to acquire a 20% interest in American Bioscience, a development stage pharmaceutical company with research focus on innovative drugs and therapies for the treatment of cancer. Most notable, however, was its agreement in July to be acquired by Merrell Dow Pharmaceuticals Inc. The deal, concluded in December, established Marion Merrell Dow Inc.

The Players

Marion Laboratories Inc. CEO: Fred W. Lyons, Jr. Fred Lyons began his quarter-century career with Marion Laboratories in 1970 by joining the company as vice president and general manager of its pharmaceutical division. Seven years later he succeeded to the presidency of the firm and led it on a prosperous path. Having become CEO in 1984, he orchestrated its acquisition by Merrell Dow in 1989, at which point he became president of the newly formed Marion Merrell Dow. Lyons was named CEO in 1992 and chairman the following year. He again directed his company's acquisition, this time by Hoechst AG in 1995. Lyons retired from the newly formed Hoechst Marion Roussel on April 1, 1996.

Merrell Dow Pharmaceuticals Inc. CEO: Joseph G. Temple, Jr. A Chicago native, Joseph Temple earned a chemical engineering degree from Purdue University. In 1951, he began working in research, sales, and management at Dow Chemical. When the company acquired the pharmaceutical business of Merrell-National Laboratories in 1981, Temple was named president and CEO of the newly formed Merrell Dow Pharmaceuticals. He oversaw his company's acquisition of Marion Laboratories in 1989, becoming chairman and CEO of Marion Merrell Dow. In 1993, Temple resigned, turning the chairmanship over to Fred Lyons.

Market Forces Driving the Acquisition

The pharmaceuticals business was highly lucrative during the late 1980s. Companies were reaping the rewards of their investments in research and development, and the number of break-through drugs boomed. Prices for such products outpaced the rate of inflation, as firms increased their profitability by pushing up prices. In fact, in the U.S., pharmaceuticals was the most profitable industrial sector. With such an appealing environment, newcomers flocked to the industry.

This increase in competition spelled trouble for industry players at the approach of the 1990s. Patent expiry on blockbuster drugs loomed, which meant that rivals would soon become able to introduce generic versions at lower prices. This threat of declining sales and profits heightened the necessity for new

product development, but most companies' research and development pipelines lacked adequate prospects for new best sellers. Even for those that did, the testing and approval process typically took five to 10 years, far longer than would be of immediate benefit to that company's balance sheet in a highly competitive industry.

Consolidation offered a solution, and large pharmaceutical companies scrambled to unite. The merger wave was initiated by Roche Holding Ltd. through its hostile takeover attempt for Sterling Drug Inc. in 1988. Ultimately, that target company was acquired by a white knight, Eastman Kodak. A similar outcome occurred later that year, when A.H. Robbins Co. fell into the arms of American Home Products Corp. to thwart a takeover bid by Sanofi . This consolidation wave continued into 1989, with the merger of SmithKline Beckman and Beecham Group PLC.

As even the largest pharmaceutical companies were joining forces, smaller players had little choice but to follow suit. Marion Laboratories and Merrell Dow Pharmaceuticals were two such firms that fell under such pressure. Marion's top-selling product, the hypertension drug Cardizem, was facing patent expiry in 1992. The company's patent on its second best seller, the ulcer treatment Carafate, had expired in 1986, and although no generic competition had yet arisen, it might emerge at any time. Moreover, since Marion's strategy had been to invest in the development of new products than in their research, the firm was dependent on licensing agreements for new product introduction. As a result, its research and development pipeline was dry. It needed a partner with strengths in that area.

Although the threat was not as immediate as Marion's situation, Merrell Dow was also facing the expiration on the patent of its leading product. Seldane, an allergy medication, was scheduled to become available in generic versions starting in 1994. Unlike Marion Laboratories, however, Merrell Dow had a rich pipeline. Still, Marion would provide Merrell with one of the strongest pharmaceutical marketing forces in the U.S. Marion's strength was in securing licensing agreements, particularly with foreign firms, and developing and marketing the pharmaceuticals in the industry's largest market, the U.S. This potential for increased domestic business would complement Merrell Dow's presence in international markets, where it derived about 85% of its total sales.

Approach and Engagement

Marion Laboratories approached Merrell Dow Pharmaceuticals in early May 1989 to discuss a possible union. Two months later the companies had come to terms, and on July 17 announced an agreement. The two-part deal involved a cash tender of $38 per share, or $2.2 billion, for 39% of Marion's stock. Then, Merrell Dow would increase that stake to 67% by issuing shares of the newly formed company, Marion Merrell Dow Inc., to Marion shareholders, thereby bringing the deal's total value to about $5.5 billion.

Ewing Kauffman, Marion's founder and chairman, would become the new company's chairman emeritus. Joseph Temple, Merrell Dow's CEO, would serve as chairman and CEO, while Fred Lyons, his counterpart at Marion, would become president of the resulting company.

Kauffman pledged the 23% stake held by his family in support of the deal. Marion's other shareholders approved the acquisition on December 1, 1989, and the deal was completed the following day.

Products and Services

Hoechst AG operated in four segments in 1998. The largest, Pharmaceuticals, consisted of Hoechst Marion Roussel. This company accounted for DM13.7 billion, or about 25% of total company revenues, based largely on such successful products as the hypertension drug Cadizem and the allergy treatment Allegra. Hoechst's Agriculture segment consisted of Hoechst Schering AgrEvo, a joint venture of Hoechst and Schering, and was involved in crop protection, crop production, seeds, and environmental health. The third segment, Animal Health, was represented by Hoechst Roussel Vet, which produced antiparasitics, vaccines, antiinfectives, and feed additives. The Industry segment was comprised of the Celanese chemical unit, the Trevira technical polymers unit, and the industry gas producer Messer.

Changes to the Industry

The union of Merrell Dow and Marion Laboratories was a link in the chain of industry consolidation in the late 1980s. It was soon followed by the $12 billion merger of Bristol-Myers Co. and Squibb Corp., paving the way for a number of other mega-deals in the 1990s. Roche acquired Genentech, Inc. in 1990 and Syntex Corp. in 1994, the same year that American Home Products purchased American Cyanamid Co.

Among these deals was the acquisition of Marion Merrell Dow by Germany-based Hoechst AG. This chemical and pharmaceutical giant paid $7.2 billion to relieve Dow Chemical of its struggling pharmaceutical company in July 1995. Despite healthy prospects, Marion Merrell Dow had not been able to perform as expected, a difficulty primarily attributable to patent expiry. With declining market share and an 11% dip in its 1994 net income, Dow Chemical divested itself of this pharmaceutical arm, allowing for the formation of Hoechst Marion Roussel.

Research

Brockinton, Langdon. "It's a Wedding Day for Dow and Marion," in *Chemical Week*, 26 July 1989. Details the terms of the acquisition, as well as the respective strengths of each company.

"Dow Chemical Buys Marion Stock," in *St. Louis Post-Dispatch*, 5 December 1989. Briefly reports the completion of the deal.

Freudenheim, Milt. "Dow Taking Big Stake in Marion," in *The New York Times*, 18 July 1989. Relates the newly announced acquisition offer.

Hoechst AG Home Page, available at http://www.hoechst.com. Official World Wide Web Home Page for Hoechst AG. This German- and English-language site offers news releases, product and financial information, and employment data.

"Marion Laboratories. Inc.," in *International Directory of Company Histories*, Vol. I, St. James Press, 1988. Profiles of the history of the company through the mid-1980s.

"Marion Merrell Dow Inc.," in *Notable Corporate Chronologies*, The Gale Group, 1999. Provides a chronology of the history of the company, including both Marion Laboratories and Merrell Dow.

DEBORAH J. UNTENER

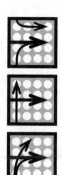

MARKS & SPENCER & BROOKS BROTHERS

Marks & Spencer PLC
Michael House, 37-67 Baker St.
London, W1A 1DN
United Kingdom

tel: 44 171 935 4422
fax: 44 171 487 2679
web: http://www.marks-and-spencer.com

nationality: United Kingdom
date: May 2, 1988
affected: Marks & Spencer PLC, England, founded 1894
affected: Brooks Brothers Inc., USA, founded 1818

Overview of the Acquisition

Marks & Spencer intended to use its 1988 purchase of Brooks Brothers as a springboard into the U.S. retail market. The largest retailer in its British homeland, Marks & Spencer was increasingly becoming squeezed by limited growth opportunities and competitive pressures from expanding foreign chains. In its enthusiasm to acquire the well-respected chain, it paid a hefty price—a price that it would come to regret by the end of the century, when it considered putting Brooks Brothers on the sales block.

History of Marks & Spencer PLC

In 1882 23-year-old Michael Marks fled Poland and arrived in England. He began selling haberdashery, displaying his buttons, thread, and similar wares on a tray tied around his neck. Two years later he borrowed GBP 5 to buy stock from wholesaler Isaac Dewhirst, and by the end of the year Marks had made enough money to take a stall in Leeds Market. Mark's limited English-language skills prompted him to hang a sign reading, "Don't ask the price; it's a penny"; this would become his slogan for years.

Having established a chain of eight penny stalls by 1894, Marks needed a partner for expansion. Tom Spencer, an employee of Dewhirst, joined him to create Marks & Spencer. The partnership became a limited company in 1901, as its stalls numbered 24 and its shops 12. In 1916 Mark's son Simon took the company's helm.

It adopted the policy of buying directly from manufacturers in 1924, putting it in a position to monitor the quality of goods and cut out the expense of going through wholesalers. Two years later, Marks & Spencer became a public company with 125 stores. It introduced the St. Michel brand in 1928 to signify goods produced by the company's specifications. In 1931 it added food products to its offerings, starting with produce and canned goods.

In 1957 the company launched Operation Simplification, which reduced the amount of bureaucratic paperwork and eliminated employee time clocks. This successful program earned it attention at the governmental level, and in 1970 a company representative was recruited by the British government to make its defense procurement operations more efficient. This service was repeated in 1979.

Israel Sieff, Simon Marks' brother-in-law, became chairman in 1964. Oversaturation in the domestic market spurred Marks & Spencer to expand into North America. It entered Canada in 1973 by purchasing three chains—Peoples, D'Allaird's, and Walker's. These outlets were renamed Marks & Spencer Canada, and were stocked with the same British products that were sold in England. This program failed miserably, and eventually Marks & Spencer offered Canadian wares and updated the appearance of the dreary units.

The company expanded into Continental Europe in 1975 with the opening of stores in Paris and Brussels. In 1985 Marks & Spencer introduced its charge card, thereby entering the financial services business. Three years later it entered the U.S. retailing market with the acquisition of the 16-unit Kings Super Markets in New Jersey and upscale clothier Brooks Brothers.

During the 1990s it continued international expansion, opening stores in Hong Kong, Hungary, Spain, and Turkey. It also scaled back its Canadian operations, selling the Peoples chain in 1992 and the D'Allaird's chain in 1996. The next year it acquired the 19-unit U.K.-based Littlewoods chain for $323 million.

In January 1999 the company revealed that its pretax profit for 1999 would be GBP 625 million, 40% lower than the previous year's earnings of GBP 1.75 billion. As a result, Peter Salsbury was appointed CEO in February. Only six weeks into his term, he eliminated 31 executive positions, including three directors. The reorganization also called for the termination of additional staff, as well as a hold on future international expansion.

History of Brooks Brothers Inc.

Henry Sands Brooks established a clothing store in 1818 in New York City. This shop, one of the nation's first to offer ready-made clothing, passed to his sons upon his death in 1833. Henry and Daniel H. Brooks renamed the store H. and D.H. Brooks & Co., and in 1850 again renamed it, to Brooks Brothers.

By 1857, when it opened a second store in New York, Brooks Brothers offered custom and ready-made clothing as well as a variety of piece goods, including cashmeres, velvet, silk, and satin. It had quickly earned a reputation as an upscale outfitter, and counted such Union generals as Grant and Sherman among

The Business

Financials

Revenue (1998): GBP 8.2 billion ($13.9 billion)

Employees (1998): 71,000

SICs / NAICS

sic 5311 - Department Stores

sic 5611 - Men's & Boys' Clothing Stores

sic 5621 - Women's Clothing Stores

sic 6141 - Personal Credit Institutions

sic 6311 - Life Insurance

naics 452110 - Department Stores

naics 448110 - Men's Clothing Stores

naics 448120 - Women's Clothing Stores

naics 522210 - Credit Card Issuing

naics 524113 - Direct Life Insurance Carriers

its customers. President Abraham Lincoln was a regular patron, and wore a Brooks Brothers coat to his second inaugural; he is rumored to have been wearing this coat on the night of his assassination. Throughout the years, Brooks Brothers would prove to be a clothier for numerous U.S. presidents, from Grant to Clinton.

Brooks Brothers manufactured most of its clothing, which was based on British styles. About 1900 it introduced its famous "Sack Suit," a loosely constructed suit with straight-legged trousers and a three-button jacket lacking shoulder pads and tapering at the waist. In 1900 it introduced another Brooks Brothers staple, the pink shirt, as well as its button-down collared shirts. Other English imports were polo coats and shirts, the Shetland sweater, and foulard ties. These fashions were enormously popular with Hollywood celebrities and the Eastern upper crust. The company unveiled its first offering for women—a version of the pink shirt—in 1912, and by the late 1940s the store had established a small women's department.

The company expanded outside New York by opening a Boston store in 1912. Three years later its flagship New York shop completed a series of relocations by settling in at the corner of Madison Avenue and 44th Street. As a privately held company, Brooks Brothers didn't disclose financial figures, but its 1923 pretax earnings were estimated to be in excess of $1

The Officers

Chairman: Sir Richard Greenbury

CEO: Peter Salsbury

Managing Director, U.K Retail: Andres Stone

Managing Director, Overseas Retail: Guy McCracken

million. At some point during the following decade, however, the company lost money; reports varied, but one estimate indicated an operating deficit of $1 million that would require the business to take in $3.6 million annually just to break even.

Julius Garfinckel & Co., Inc., a Washington DC department store operator, purchased 62% of Brooks Brothers in 1946 for $3 million; the remaining 38% continued to be held by the department store John Wanamaker, which had purchased that stake years earlier. Under Garfinckel's management, Brooks Brothers trimmed operating expenses and adopted more aggressive merchandising to boost sales. The company's earnings rose steadily, reaching nearly $798,000 in 1955.

The chain flourished in the 1950s as the "Ivy League" look became vogue. The following decade, however, was a rough storm for the company to weather. Long hair and European fashions became the clothing of choice, even among those men who followed conventional career paths. Brooks Brothers, which had always been extremely reluctant to modify any of its fashions, grudgingly gave a little ground, gradually widening its coat lapels from three inches to 3 7/8 inches.

The chain consisted of 10 stores in 1970. More than 30% of its suits were manufactured at its Long Island plant, with the remainder produced by other manufacturers according to specifications. In 1979 Brooks Brothers expanded internationally, opening a store in Tokyo. By the next year the company operated a 24-unit chain.

The 1980s marked a period of ownership shuffles for Brooks Brothers. In 1980 it was sold to Allied Stores Corp. for $228 million. Six years later Allied sold it and several other properties to Campeau Corp., a Canadian-based retailer and real estate company. In 1988 it passed to Britain's largest retailer, Marks & Spencer, for a remarkable $750 million.

Its new owner introduced computerized systems and mass-merchandising techniques that had been successful in building Marks & Spencer into a model retailer over its existence. In order to attract the younger generation, which considered the traditional Brooks Brothers look too conservative and uptight, the company introduced sportswear and less expensive clothing, and increased its women's department. It made other "revolutionary" changes as well, including the installation of escalators, display of shirts and sweaters on tabletops, and an increased use of color. Through it all, Brooks Brothers was walking a very narrow line between appealing to new customers and retaining long-standing patrons resentful of change.

The chain increased its stores from 83 in 1994 to nearly 100 by 1996. Sales also increased, from GBP 286 million in 1996 to GBP 304 million the following year.

Market Forces Driving the Acquisition

By the late 1980s, Marks & Spencer had about saturated its domestic market. Expansion was a necessity in the retail industry and Britain's largest retailer was not spared. The problems associated with the limitations of its domestic growth were further exacerbated by the infiltration of such foreign competitors as The Gap that threatened to grab a share of Marks & Spencer's core customer base. Reluctantly, it was forced to admit that the U.S. offered fertile ground for the well-oiled retail machine. Still Marks & Spencer was a bit gun-shy about expanding across the Atlantic. Its entry into Canada in 1973 had proved a disaster, and those operations had only begun to show a profit more than a decade later.

Determined to learn from its past mistakes, the retailer sought to purchase and maintain an existing U.S. chain rather than try to apply its British formula to newly established operations. That way, it could institute select streamlining practices yet avoid tinkering with any operations that had already proved successful. In 1987 Marks & Spencer began scouting for attractive U.S. properties.

Approach and Engagement

On February 25, 1988, Campeau Corp. announced its agreement to sell Brooks Brothers to Marks & Spencer for $770 million in order to finance its acquisition of Federated Department Stores. As part of the deal, Marks & Spencer acquired the rights to sell St. Michel branded food at Campeau's 258 department stores.

Industry analysts were shocked at the purchase price, which was more than twice Brooks Brothers' sales of $290 million and 17 times its pretax earnings in 1988. Executives at the British retailer justified the high price based on the Brooks Brothers name and reputation in the men's clothing market. Many analysts remained unconvinced, however. "Brooks Brothers is in a class by itself, but the offer is astronomical," said Howard Davidowitz, New York retailing consultant, in *Business Week*. "For this to work, they'll have to expand Brooks tremendously in sales and in profits."

In April Marks & Spencer announced that it was shaving $20 million off of the price tag, citing financing costs that were higher than anticipated. On May 2, 1988, the transaction was completed for $750 million.

Products and Services

Marks & Spencer was organized into three business units in 1999. U.K. Retail and Overseas Retail both housed the company's retail operations, including the Brooks Brothers, King Super Markets, and Marks & Spencer operations. Its Financial Services arm included the Marks & Spencer Account Card, its Life Assurance & Pensions holdings, its Savings & Investments offerings, its Personal Loans services, and its Personal Reserve service.

Changes to the Industry

Marks & Spencer held high hopes for its new U.S. property. It expanded the 47-unit Brooks Brothers chain outside of its concentration in the Northeast and Midwest, opening seven stores throughout the country, including several in Florida. By 1994 it had also forayed into new retail markets, opening 26 stores in outlet shopping centers. Despite, or due to, these expansion efforts, the company's bottom line didn't respond.

As it completed the acquisition in 1988, Marks & Spencer set the goal of achieving profits of $75 million within five years. By 1990 experts doubted whether Brooks Brothers would achieve that lofty earnings goal. For that year, although sales increased to $322 million, earnings dropped 41%, to $23 million. Profits rebounded in 1992, and in 1993 the chain posted a 16% rise in earnings, to $21.1 million, on sales of $338 million. That encouraging upturn shifted for the worse in 1995, however, when Brooks Brothers' profits plummeted 60% to $92 million. *The Wall Street Journal* wrote that as a result, Marks & Spencer "frostily concedes that the company paid too much when it purchased Brooks Brothers."

Aside from a couple of positive earnings hiccups, the downward spiral continued throughout most of the decade. In May 1999 Marks & Spencer reported its worst results in years: a 41% drop in the company's overall profits, to GBP 655.7 ($1.06 billion) from GBP 1.11 the previous year. Brooks Brothers' profits dropped as well, down 22% to GBP 12.4 million, yet its Japanese branches contributed most of that downfall; U.S. results remained flat compared to the previous year.

The Players

Marks & Spencer Chairman and CEO: Sir Richard Greenbury. Richard Greenbury had worked for Marks & Spencer his entire life. In 1952 he quit school at age 16 in order to support his mother, who had become ill. He began working as a junior management trainee at a Marks & Spencer outlet, earning GBP 4 per week. His hard work caught the attention of the company's leader, Simon Marks. Greenbury became the company's youngest director when he joined the board at age 33. In 1988 he became the firm's first CEO from outside its founding families. He ascended to the chairmanship in 1991, and was knighted the following year. In February 1999, as Marks & Spencer was hip-deep in financial problems, Greenbury passed the reins of CEO to Peter Salsbury. He also announced his retirement as chairman, scheduled for 2000.

In response, Marks & Spencer implemented a restructuring that cut 31 executives and 200 other administrators. In the second phase of workforce reduction, it planned to lay off 15%, or 290, of its store managers. Marks & Spencer also revealed that it was considering the divestiture of both Brooks Brothers and King Super Markets to focus on its domestic and European operations.

Review of the Outcome

The Brooks Brothers purchase provided Marks & Spencer with entry into the U.S., but several snags arose from this American invasion. Brooks Brothers was caught in an ever-gaping time warp that affected even its core clientele, Wall Street executives. The U.S. trend toward workplace casual days, wholly unforeseen by the British retailer, prompted Marks & Spencer to revise its original plan not to tamper with Brooks Brothers' traditional merchandise. It added sportswear to its product offerings, threw splashes of color into its lines, expanded the women's department to encompass an entire floor, and introduced a variety of suit styles in a range of prices. It even began adding pleats to its trousers again, a feature that had been discontinued in the 1960s.

All of these radical changes aimed not only to supply casual day clothing for the executive, but also to attract members of the younger generation who had been turned off by the retailer's stodgy image and merchandise. But Marks & Spencer knew that Brooks

Brothers was no ordinary retailer with an ordinary clientele. It had to tread lightly, lest it disturb or annoy its long-standing—and change-resistant—patron base. The news-breaking installation of an escalator at its flagship store, for example, resulted in a flurry of letters of complaint from customers who wanted the elevator to remain the status quo. Others were quite shaken at Brooks Brothers' new advertising campaign, which incorporated full-page color magazine ads. This, too, brought a mass of angry letters to the company president, as the company had always restricted its marketing to a small sketch run in the same place of *The New York Times* each day.

The response to these seemingly insignificant changes was overshadowed by the effect of more substantive changes. Marks & Spencer closed several plants in favor of outsourcing the manufacturing of clothing, and long-standing customers claimed to notice a difference in the quality. Marks & Spencer also cut the sales staff, reducing the number of personnel available to offer customers personal attention.

Research

Beck, Ernest. "Marks & Spencer's Sees Earnings Fall, Unveils Plans for Broad Restructuring," in *The Wall Street Journal*, 19 May 1999. Reveals the company's plans to cut expenses through a reorganization.

Bhargava, Sunita Wadekar. "What's Next, Grunge Bathrobes?" in *Business Week*, 21 June 1993. Brooks Brothers reverses its downward profits cycle by updating its image.

"Brooks Brothers Inc.," in *International Directory of Company Histories*, Vol. 22, St. James Press: 1998. Provides a historical review of the company, before and after it was acquired by Marks & Spencer.

Brooks Brothers Inc. Home Page, available at http://www.brooksbrothers.com. Official World Wide Web Page for Brooks Brothers. Includes an online store, a brief company history, and a store directory.

Levine, Joshua. "An Escalator? In Brooks Brothers?" in *Forbes*, 9 July 1990. Describes some of the innovations deemed upsetting to Brooks Brothers' veteran customers.

Maremont, Mark. "Marks & Spencer Pays a Premium for Pinstripes," in *Business Week*, 18 April 1988. Offers analysts' reactions to the acquisition deal.

"Marks & Spencer PLC," in *Notable Corporate Chronologies*, The Gale Group, 1999. Profiles the history of the company.

Marks & Spencer PLC Home Page, available at http://www.marks-and-spencer.com. Official World Wide Web Page for Marks & Spencer. It includes news releases, descriptions of products and services, and a store directory.

Parker-Pope, Tara. "Marks & Spencer Takes Its Lumps Abroad," in *The Wall Street Journal*, 24 May 1995. Discloses the company's drop in profits from operations outside of the U.K.

Shenker, Israel. "Marks & Spencer, the 'Uniquely-British Aunty,'" in *Smithsonian*, November 1987. Presents the colorful history of Marks & Spencer.

DEBORAH J. UNTENER

MATSUSHITA ELECTRIC INDUSTRIAL & MCA

nationality: Japan
date: December 1990
affected: Matsushita Electric Industrial Co. Ltd., Japan, founded 1918
affected: MCA, Inc., USA, founded 1924

Matsushita Electric Industrial Co. Ltd.
1006 Oaza Kadoma
Kadoma City, Osaka
Japan

tel: 81-6-6908-1121
fax: 401-6-6908-2351
web: http://www.mei.co.jp.com

Overview of the Merger

The $6.59 billion joining of MCA Inc. and Matsushita Electric Industrial Co. Ltd. was the largest purchase of a U.S. company ever made by a Japanese firm. The deal linked together an American entertainment giant, which produced music, movies, and TV shows, and a Japanese consumer electronics leader. The acquisition came one year after Sony Corp.'s controversial purchase of Columbia Pictures and sparked yet another wave of heated debate concerning Japanese takeovers of American companies.

History of Matsushita Electric Industrial Co. Ltd.

In 1918, Konosuke Matsushita and his brother-in-law, Toshio Iue, founded a company that manufactured electric plugs in Osaka, Japan. Matsushita was able to build up a loyal customer base by incorporating new technologies into his products while keeping prices low. Throughout the 1930s, he also diversified into the production of bicycle lamps, electric heaters, radio sets, electric motors, and dry batteries. In 1935, he incorporated as Matsushita Denki Sangyo (Matsushita Electric Industrial Co., Ltd.) (MEI).

MEI grew powerful during World War II and built up important overseas markets in Taiwan, Korea, and Manchuria. However, at the end of the war, MEI was devastated, having lost its overseas markets and suffered great infrastructural damage from Allied action. In 1946, the government of Japan set price controls and demanded that Matsushita resign due to his wholehearted support of the Japanese war effort. When MEI workers threatened to strike, the government allowed Matsushita to remain in his post.

In 1951, Matsushita went to America for the first time. He set his sights on obtaining a share of the U.S. market. Japanese antimonopoly laws were relaxed after the Korean War, and MEI began a period of acquisition. Included in his deals were a joint venture with Philips, giving the company access to the latest electronics technologies. The company also added new products to its line such as washing machines, televisions, refrigerators, and vacuum cleaners. In 1957, MEI introduced a high quality line of FM radio receivers, tape recorders, and stereo sound

The Business

Financials

Revenue (1998): $59.2 billion

Employees (1998): 275,962

SICs / NAICS

sic 3531 - Construction Machinery

sic 3571 - Electronic Computers

sic 3631 - Household Cooking Equipment

sic 3632 - Household Refrigerators & Freezers

sic 3633 - Household Laundry Equipment

sic 3579 - Office Machines Nec

sic 3651 - Household Audio & Video Equipment

naics 333923 - Overhead Traveling Crane, Hoist, and Monorail System Manufacturing

naics 339942 - Lead Pencil and Art Good Manufacturing

naics 334518 - Watch, Clock, and Part Manufacturing

naics 333313 - Office Machinery Manufacturing

naics 334111 - Electronic Computer Manufacturing

naics 335221 - Household Cooking Appliance Manufacturing

naics 335222 - Household Refrigerator and Home and Farm Freezer Manufacturing

naics 335224 - Household Laundry Equipment Manufacturing

systems developed by JVC, in which they had acquired a 50% interest. The company also entered the television market by the end of the decade.

Throughout the 1960s, MEI concentrated on the domestic market, and soon became Japan's largest producer of home appliances. When labor costs in Japan rose, the company opened its first overseas manufacturing plants in Taiwan and Singapore. By 1965, the company's Panasonic and Technics brands had become well known in North America. The company also extended its product lines to include air conditioners, microwave ovens, and stereo systems.

MEI began to invest heavily in research to develop a video recording system (VCR) in 1970. JVC began to develop a workable video home system (VHS), and the company began obtaining licensing agreements with RCA Corp., General Electric Co., Philips Electronics NV, NEC Corp., Toshiba Corp., and Sanyo

Electric Co. in the early years of the decade in anticipation of the market release of the VHS system. In 1975, Sony, which had refused to share its Betamax technology earlier in the decade, was forced to ask for a compromise in developing VHS, as its Betamax system had lost its market completely. Matsushita refused to cooperate, and Sony was forced to develop its own VHS system.

Matsushita stepped down in 1986 and was replaced by Akio Tanii. He began to reorganize company management, making older engineers into salespeople and turning research and development over to younger minds. He also moved company focus away from consumer electronics to high technologies, including semiconductors and factory automation, business machines, and audiovisual devices. In 1987, MEI entered into a joint venture with Ford Motor Co. and Mazda Motor Corp. to produce heating and cooling units for Mazda cars. The company ended the decade by consolidating its European operations under a central administrative unit located in the United Kingdom and creating a third central administrative unit in Singapore to coordinate overseas company activities in Asia. Continuing its consolidation of overseas affiliates, MEI also formed a central administrative unit in North America in 1989.

In 1990, MEI acquired MCA Inc., a U.S. manufacturer of consumer electronics and owner of Decca Records and Universal Pictures, for $6.1 billion. The company also agreed to manufacture and market IBM computers that year, hoping to improve upon IBM Corp.'s traditional weakness in consumer markets. By 1991, net income had dropped significantly due to declining sales. In 1992, MEI became the first industrial concern to float a global bond issue, seeking $1 billion to reduce corporate debt. In 1996, the company was forced to sell 80% of MCA to Seagram, as a result of cultural incompatibility and further losses in net income. One year later, the company reorganized into five divisions including digital TV systems, optical discs, communications, monitor and display devices, and semiconductors. Net income continued to drop in 1998 as the company halted operations in the North American semiconductor market.

History of MCA Inc.

Jules Stein formed the Music Corporation of America in 1924. He had started booking bands in college and found that it could be quite lucrative. In its first year, MCA grossed over $30,000, and by 1927, the company represented over 40 bands. It was slowly growing into the largest band agency in the U.S., and Stein expanded into booking singers, dancers, and comedians.

In 1936, Stein hired Les Wasserman, who quickly became a strong force in the company. When MCA moved to California in 1937, he became the first agent to negotiate actor contracts in terms of movie earnings, rather than a straight salary. This boosted the company's reputation as its actors were becoming millionaires. By the end of the 1930s, MCA dealt with 60% of Hollywood talent including Ronald Reagan, Jimmy Stewart, and Betty Grable.

In 1945, MCA acquired the Hayward-Deverich Agency, the most illustrious firm in the business. One year later, Wasserman was named president and CEO. He led the company into producing its first television show, *Stars Over Hollywood* in 1949.

MCA began focusing on selling shows to major networks and reruns to local stations throughout the U.S. The company produced its first syndicated show, *Chevron Theatre*, and some key acquisitions. MCA purchased TV rights to Paramount's collection of over 750 films, and in 1959, bought Universal Studios' back lot for over $11 million. The entertainment company also made its first public offering that year and reorganized the company as MCA, Inc. The new company had 20 subsidiaries including Revue Productions, which handled the production of television film series, and MCA Artists, its talent division.

In 1962, MCA bought Decca Records, which owned Universal Pictures. The deal brought about the Justice Department's ruling that the company would have to act as either a talent agency or a film production business. MCA decided to focus on film and divested itself of its talent concerns. It branched out into other operations as well, to make up for lost revenue. The company purchased Spencer Gifts, a retail outlet, and Columbia Savings & Loan.

Throughout the 1970s, MCA released a series of successful films including *Jaws*, *Airport*, *The Sting*, and *The Deer Hunter*. It also produced famous television shows such as *Kojak*, *Quincy*, *The Six Million Dollar Man*, and *The Incredible Hulk*. MCA purchased Yosemite Park & Curry Co., but its plans to build hotels and restaurants on the land prompted the Department of Interior to ban development in national parks. The company also created one of America's largest tourist attractions on the back lot of Universal Studios.

By 1980, MCA had over 20 films, 90 record albums, and over 700 books scheduled to be published. The firm also controlled over 11 hours of television programming a week. Operating income dropped severely in 1981, however, due to several flops such as *Flash Gordon* and *The Great Muppet Caper*, and overbudgeting on *The Blues Brothers*. As a result,

The Officers

Chairman: Masaharu Matsushita

President: Yoichi Morishita

Exec. VP: Kazuhiko Sugiyama

Exec. VP: Masayuki Matsushita

Chairman and CEO, Matsushita Electric Corp. of America: Yoshinori Kobe

management reduced the film budget and implemented tighter controls. That same year, MCA bought 423 acres in Orlando, Florida, where it erected another Universal Studios theme park.

The company seemed to emerge from its financial problems for a few years with hit movies like *E.T.* and *Back to the Future*. The success did not last long, though, and MCA was once again forced to cut costs, employees, and departments. In 1990, Wasserman was looking for a partner and found one in Japan's Matsushita Electric Industrial Co. The Japanese interest purchased MCA for over $6 billion in 1990. The deal only lasted five years, and MCA was sold to Seagram Company Ltd. in 1995 for $5.7 billion. One year later, MCA changed its name to Universal Studios.

Universal Studios sold its publishing interests after teaming up with Seagram. The company also focused on restructuring after purchasing PolyGram, a giant in the music industry in the late 1990s. Universal Music began a venture with BMG called getmusic.com. The Internet deal promoted the company's music and products through its website.

Market Forces Driving the Merger

In the mid-1990s, companies who had control of new technologies such as satellite, cable, videocassettes, were looking to team up with counterparts who could provide the content for these outlets. According to Bruce Wasserstein, author of *Big Deal: The Battle for Control of America's Leading Corporations*, "movies, compact discs, books and television shows were sought-after commodities on the global market. As this global pipeline mushroomed, the companies involved began to look across borders for opportunities. For American content companies, the goal was to develop foreign distribution platforms. However, the more dramatic development was a growing international interest in owning American content providers."

The Players

CEO of Masushita Electric Industrial Co. Ltd.: Akio Tanii. Akio Tanii joined Masushita in 1986. Under his leadership the company expanded its product line to include auto electronics, audiovisuals, housing and air-conditioning products, and factory automation. In 1990, he orchestrated the deal with MCA, and in 1992, began a reorganization process of the company. Tanii stepped down from his post in 1993, after a scandal involving the sale of defective refrigerators that cost the company $416 million. His resignation also came at a time when the company was seeing the worst profits in its history.

CEO of MCA Inc.: Les Wasserman. Les Wasserman joined the entertainment industry in 1936, when he was hired by Jules Stein, MCA's founder. He worked side by side with Stein and was named president in 1946 and eventually chairman and CEO in 1973. Throughout his high profile career, Wasserman masterminded several deals including the purchase of Universal's studio operations, Universal Pictures, and the merger with Matsushita in 1990. He received many career awards including the "Jean Hersholt Humanitarian Award," a star on the Hollywood Hall of Fame, and the "Presidential Medal of Freedom." His career with MCA ended when Matsushita sold the company in 1995.

Chairman of Creative Artists Agency: Michael Ovitz. UCLA graduate Michael Ovitz began his career in entertainment by working at Universal Studios while in college. After working his way through the industry, he went on to become chairman of the Creative Artists Agency, where he brokered both the Columbia/Sony deal and the Matsushita/MCA merger. He joined Disney in 1995 as president, but left in December of 1996, after a fallout with company chairman, Michael Eisner. In 1999, Ovitz created the Artists Management Group and signed big names such as directors Martin Scorsese and Sidney Pollack, as well as actors Claire Danes and Samuel L. Jackson.

For Matsushita, owning an American entertainment company had endless possibilities for profit. Similar to the impetus for Sony's purchase of Columbia, the Japanese company looked to capitalize on the growing interest in American entertainment overseas, as well as match MCA's software to its hardware. Another strong motivation to merge with an entertainment company was that Matsushita's customers would be watching company-owned material on company-manufactured products.

MCA had been looking for a deal for quite some time. Other American entertainment companies had linked up with Japanese counterparts including CBS Records with Sony; The Walt Disney Co. with Touchwood Pacific; Interscope with Nomura Babcock; and Largo Entertainment with Pioneer. The faltering health of CEO Lew Wasserman and a need for cash also fueled the search. The chairman was looking to keep the company strong should he become unable to function at his post in the future, and the deal with Matsushita suited his needs. Cash would be injected into his company and management would stay in place for five years as the Japanese interest did not want to change MCA's core operations.

Approach and Engagement

The bargaining process between Matsushita and MCA was filled with the dramatics typical of a Hollywood-produced movie. On Labor Day weekend in 1990, Michael Ovitz phoned Lew Wasserman with news that he had found a potential buyer for MCA. In the months to follow, private meetings took place in Los Angeles, Honolulu, and Osaka, Japan. Matsushita threatened to rescind its offer when on September 25, 1990, news of the deal was leaked to the press. MCA's stock quickly skyrocketed by $19.50 a share to $54. Matsushita, a typical Japanese company, did not do business publicly and was offended by the leak.

The fact that news of the deal got out before MCA could publicly announce it hurt that firm as well. A Japanese takeover of yet another American entertainment company did not sit well with those who felt Matsushita would begin to censor certain aspects of American film. During October of 1990, both Matsushita and MCA were criticized by employees and analysts. Media involvement in the negotiations became so overwhelming that meetings became completely private with only top management involved.

After months of exhaustive bargaining, MCA finally agreed to Matsushita's $72 per share, $6.59 billion, offer. Under the terms of the deal, MCA management would stay in place for five years, and creative control would remain with MCA. In December 1990, the U.S. courts cleared the way for the largest Japanese purchase of a U.S. interest.

Products and Services

Due to lagging sales and friction between Japanese and American management, Matsushita left the Hollywood entertainment industry in 1995, when it sold an 80% interest of MCA to Seagram. The company was left to focus on its core operations and in 1998 operated over 203 companies in 45 different countries.

In 1998, Matsushita developed products such as air-conditioners, audio appliances, camcorders, CD and CD-ROM players and drives, DVD players, pagers, radios, telephones, TVs, and VCRs. Information and communication equipment accounted for 29% of sales. Video and audio equipment made up 24%, components brought in 20%, home and household equipment and appliances secured 18%, and industrial equipment garnered 9% of total sales.

Changes to the Industry

After the Matsushita/MCA deal, Toshiba formed a joint venture with Time Warner. A recession slowed down the merger deals, however, in the early 1990s, but they sparked up again in 1993. Developments in technology and changes in industry regulations created a wave of change in the media market including Warner and Paramount's creation of their own networks and ABC's merger with Disney. The deals however, were different than those of the 1980s and early 1990s. Japanese interest in American media had slowed dramatically, and large U.S. based companies were teaming up with other American-owned companies.

Review of the Outcome

After the merger, Matsushita kept a low profile in MCA dealings. With its owner in Osaka, Japan, MCA had only one Matsushita representative in its U.S. office. The deal, done in part by MCA's Wasserman in an attempt to create cash flow for MCA, had not yet provided that, and in fact, MCA was floundering due to high operational costs and movies that had flopped at the box office. In 1991, MCA experienced a 10% drop in profits as its owner dealt with a 39% drop.

In Wasserstein's book, he mentioned that, "shortly after the MCA deal, Matsushita and Sony were rocked by a stock market crash that wiped out more than $2.6 trillion in value on the Tokyo Stock Exchange, along with a major recession and real estate crash." From 1991 to 1992, Matsushita's net income dropped to $1.9 billion from $1.8 billion. The Japanese interest was not producing the much needed cash infusion that MCA had hoped for and tensions between the two management teams became strained. Matsushita ignored Wasserman's desire to acquire a record company or television network to boost revenue, and a public battle broke out in 1994.

In 1996, Matsushita broke free of the Hollywood entertainment industry. Eyeing problems that Sony was having with Columbia at the time, it decided to sell its American company. In 1995, Matsushita sold MCA to Seagram for $5.7 billion.

Research

Cieply, Micheal. "The Poker Game to Win MCA," in *Los Angeles Times*, 30 November 1990. Discusses the lengthy negotiations between Matsushita and MCA.

Citron, Alan. "Japan's Thirst for Hollywood is Unquenched," in *Los Angeles Times*, 10 December 1990. Lists Japanese purchases of U.S.-owned companies in the early 1990s.

———. "Judge Clears Way for Matsushita to Purchase MCA," in *Los Angeles Times*, 29 December 1990. Explains the clearing of the Matsushita/MCA deal.

Fabrikant, Geraldine. "Who Gets What From MCA Deal," in *The New York Times*, 1 December 1990. Discuss terms of the merger between MCA and Matsushita.

"Matsushita Electric Industrial Co. Ltd.," in *Notable Corporate Chronologies*, The Gale Group, 1999. Lists major events in the history of Matsushita Electric Industrial Co. Ltd.

Matsushita Electric Industrial Co. Ltd. Home Page, available at http://www.mei.co.jp. Official World Wide Web Home Page for Matsushita Electric Industrial Co. Ltd. This site includes historical, financial, and product information, as well as recent news articles.

"MCA Inc.," in *International Directory of Company Histories*, Vol. II, St. James Press, 1990. Summarizes the history of MCA Inc.

Sanger, David. "The Deal for MCA," in *The New York Times*, 2 December 1990. Explains U.S. reluctance toward another deal with a Japanese company.

Wasserstein, Bruce. *Big Deal: The Battle for Control of America's Leading Corporations*, Warner Books, 1998. Offers an overview of the largest mergers in recent American corporate history.

CHRISTINA M. STANSELL

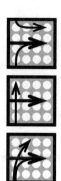

MATTEL & TYCO TOYS

Mattel Inc.
333 Continental Blvd.
El Segundo, CA 90245-5012
USA

tel: (310)252-2000
fax: (310)252-2179
web: http://www.mattel.com

nationality: USA
date: March 27, 1997
affected: Mattel Inc., USA, founded 1944
affected: Tyco Toys, Inc., USA, founded 1926

Overview of the Merger

In 1997 Mattel, already the world's largest toy company, solidified its position by acquiring Tyco Toys, the number three player in the industry. The deal had been hatched by Mattel to widen the gap between it and the second-placed Hasbro, for which Mattel had previously launched a takeover bid. Tyco had built itself into a toy conglomerate, yet was experiencing financial problems in the mid-1990s, and was attracted to Mattel's stability and its leading market position.

History of Mattel Inc.

Mattel Creations was founded in 1944 by Elliott and Ruth Handler as a picture frame manufacturer. Using the wood scraps from those products, the Handlers began designing dollhouse furniture. In the virtually toyless marketplace immediately after World War II, the company drew $100,000 in sales during its first year. Mattel expanded its product line during the rest of the decade, introducing toy banks, play makeup sets, plastic musical instruments, and music boxes. By 1955 sales reached $5 million.

The company broke new ground by advertising on television year-round instead of just during the December holiday season. Its success in later years was fanned by exploiting television Westerns with the production of toy guns. In 1959, however, Mattel took a sharp turn from such rough-and-tumble toys. That year it introduced the Barbie Doll, which would later prove to be the best-selling doll of all time. Ruth Handler conceived the idea while watching her daughter, Barbie, opt to play with adult-looking, rather than baby-looking, paper dolls. The Barbie line soon grew to include a wide array of clothing and accessories, as well as such doll companions as Ken (also named after a child of the Handlers), Midge, Skipper, and Christie.

In 1960 the company unveiled Chatty Cathy, the first talking doll. It introduced Hot Wheels miniature model cars in 1968. The success of its products, as well as a number of acquisitions, propelled Mattel to the world's leading position in the toy industry by the end of the decade.

Several setbacks in the early 1970s tempted the company's chief financial officer to record orders in the sales column, even those orders that were later canceled. When this practice was came to light in 1973, company stock plummeted and the Securities Exchange Commission launched an investigation. Mattel was ordered to restructure, and Ruth Handler and the CFO were sentenced to 41 years in jail, a sentence that was later reduced to 2,500 hours of community service. In the 1980s the Handlers dissolved their ties with the company by cashing in their stock holdings.

By 1980 Mattel owned Ringling Bros., Barnum & Bailey Circus; Shipsted & Johnson's Ice Follies; Western Publishing, the largest publisher of children's books; and the Intellivision video game company. A slump in the latter business caused the company to approach bankruptcy, only to be rescued by a $231 million venture capital investment in 1984. By then, however, it had lost the industry's top spot to Hasbro.

Poor performance of key products caused the company to slip again, until John Amerman became chairman in 1980. He immediately improved Mattel's bottom line by closing plants, reducing the workforce, curbing advertising, and selling off all non-toy businesses. The company also began refocusing on such hot-sellers as Barbie and Hot Wheels. By 1991 the company estimated that 95% of all U.S. girls aged 3-11 owned at least one Barbie. That product line contributed about half of Mattel's $1.85 billion in sales in 1992.

Mattel expanded into other segments of the toy industry such as plush toys, games, boys' action figures, and activity toys, thereby increasing its presence in the industry from 34% to 80%. It forged licensing agreements with the Walt Disney Co. for the rights to its movie characters, with Hanna-Barbera for such characters as Yogi Bear and the Flintstones, with Turner Broadcasting for its Tom and Jerry characters, and with Nickelodeon for the characters appearing on that cable network.

The company also diversified into games with its 1992 acquisition of International Games, Inc., maker of such games as UNO. The following year it cemented its leading position by purchasing Fisher-Price in a stock swap valued at $1.19 billion. In 1994 it acquired J.W. Spear, producer of the Scrabble board game, and Kranso, whose brands included Power Wheels and Wham-O frisbees and hula-hoops. In 1996 it launched an unsuccessful $5.2 billion hostile bid for Hasbro, but

The Business

Financials

Revenue (1998): $4.78 billion

Employees (1998): 29,000

SICs / NAICS

sic 3942 - Dolls & Stuffed Toys

sic 3944 - Games, Toys & Children's Vehicles

naics 339931 - Doll and Stuffed Toy Manufacturing

naics 339932 - Game, Toy, and Children's Vehicle
  Manufacturing

later withdrew. Mattel's net income that year was $372 million on sales of $4.5 billion, of which its Barbie line contributed $1.7 billion.

History of Tyco Toys, Inc.

John N. Tyler founded Mantua Metal Products in 1926, named after his hometown in New Jersey. This home-based business initially produced model trains and accessories that were compatible with existing train sets. During the 1930s Tyler introduced his own brand of toy train kits.

Model trains appealed to both children and adults who fancied the detail work involved in piecing together the kits, but they were not true toys. In the 1940s, however, Mantua expanded into ready-to-run train sets. Produced on a scale smaller than that of sets manufactured by industry leaders Lionel and Marx, the kits were an immediate success. Other model manufacturers followed Mantua's lead, resulting in a price war through which the company prospered.

During the 1960s Tyco, as the company was then known, diversified into electric racecar sets, a logical extension of its train sets. In 1970 the Tyler family sold the company to Consolidated Foods, a subsidiary of Sara Lee Corp. Under the leadership of the food company, Tyco's earnings dropped alarmingly, as the toy business proved to its new owner to be nothing like the food industry. Richard Grey and Harry Pierce, both of whom understood the toy business, were recruited in 1975 to run Tyco, and its financial condition steadily improved.

Tyco was sold in 1981 in a streamlining effort by Sara Lee. The new owner, Savoy Industries, was an

The Officers

Chairman and CEO: Jill E. Barad

Vice Chairman, Mattel and President, Pleasant Co.:
Pleasant T. Rowland

President, Worldwide Manufacturing Operations: Joseph
C. Gandolfo

President, Corporate Operations and General Counsel:
Ned Mansour

Exec. VP, Worldwide Business Planning and Resources:
Francesca Luzuriaga

investment group led by Benson Selzer. His goal was to use Tyco's assets to build a diversified conglomerate, while Grey believed that Tyco's future was firmly rooted in the toy industry. The matter came to a head after Selzer took Tyco public in 1986. Tyco, under Selzer's chairmanship, began to lend money to and make acquisitions from other Selzer companies, some of which were unrelated to the toy business. When Selzer used Tyco's money in 1988 to purchase a Puerto Rican underwear manufacturer in which the Selzer family had an interest, Tyco's shareholder filed suit. The Selzer family sold its nine-percent interest in Tyco in 1991. As quoted in a 1992 *Business Week* article, Grey recalled of the Selzers, "Not everything they did was terrible, but a couple of things were absolutely self-serving."

Tyco began acquiring licenses to popular characters from other companies to capture part of their proven appeal. It made deals with The Children's Television Workshop for the rights to Sesame Street characters and with the Walt Disney Company for those to The Little Mermaid character. In 1993 it became the first to acquire a license from Warner Bros. to produce toys based on such Looney Toons characters as Bugs Bunny and Daffy Duck.

The toy industry at that time was in the midst of a massive consolidation that concentrated a large percentage of the toy market into the hands of the leaders, Hasbro and Mattel. Tyco, too, grew and diversified through acquisitions, and in 1992 it was the third-largest toy manufacturer, up from 22nd in 1986. Of its notable acquisitions were the View-Master/Ideal Group, with its flagship View Master 3D viewer; Illco Toy Co., producer of preschool toys; and Universal Matchbox Group Ltd., maker of die-cast toy cars.

In 1993 it appeared that Tyco had bitten off more than it could chew, however. The acquisition spree, a disappointing performance of a number of key products, and the poor timing of entry into Europe contributed to an operating loss of $57 million, down from a profit of $44 million in 1992. Sales dropped slightly as well, down five percent to $730 million over the same period.

The company reacted by consolidating operations, reducing the workforce by five percent, and shutting down its Italian subsidiary. Despite these efforts, the company posted a loss of $35 million in 1994. Rumors of a takeover abounded. The troubled company appeared to be a ripe acquisition candidate, especially in an industry consolidating at a rapid rate.

Market Forces Driving the Merger

The U.S. toy industry was dominated by two companies that had been engaged in a perpetual dance for leading market share. In 1995 Mattel held the number one position with a 15.6% share, edging out Hasbro's 11.8% share. These two manufacturers left the others far behind. Tyco's 3.2% share earned it the third-place position, followed by Little Tikes' 2.8% and Hallmark's 2.1% share.

With such a considerable lead over the rest of the pack, Mattel and Hasbro were fairly insulated from all competitors except each other. They had built their respective empires in large part through acquisitions, and Hasbro was conceivably only one or two purchases away from usurping Mattel as the industry's leader. Mattel had, in fact, tried to eliminate that threat by launching a takeover for Hasbro in 1996. That bid was terminated by Mattel due to expected opposition by the Federal Trade Commission (FTC).

While the U.S. government quite reasonably challenged that merger attempt, which would have created a behemoth with a 27.4% market share, the acquisition of a smaller company might gain approval. So it looked at the next largest competitor, Tyco Toys. Mattel would benefit from Tyco's product line, particularly the boys' toys segment, an area where Mattel was weak.

Tyco had been in shaky financial straits for several years, and would benefit from Mattel's stability. It would also be in a position to benefit from Mattel's extensive overseas distribution system, as international sales accounted for only about 25% of Tyco's total revenues. Since the U.S. accounted for only about four percent of the world's children, according to Mattel, the global growth potential was significant.

Approach and Engagement

On November 18, 1996, Mattel and Tyco Toys announced their merger agreement. The $755 million deal would take place as a stock swap in which Tyco shareholders would receive approximately 0.49 shares of Mattel stock. That stock, valued at $12.50, represented a 78% premium for Tyco shareholders. Several days later, however, Tyco's preferred shareholders objected to those terms. On November 25, Mattel revised the agreement so that common shares would be converted as planned, but preferred shares would be exchanged on a share-for-share basis.

Just before the end of the year, the FTC made a second request for information from the companies. This sort of request was not uncommon, but did indicate that the agency was considering the deal seriously. Industry watchers suggested that its concerns might have focused on miniature toy vehicles, as Mattel produced Hot Wheels and Tyco made Matchbox cars. Yet those concerns were dismissed, and on March 20, 1997, the FTC cleared the merger, which had been approved by Tyco shareholders two days earlier. On March 27 the transaction was completed.

Products and Services

Mattel designed, manufactured, and marketed a broad variety of children's products on a worldwide basis. In 1999 the company reorganized into five operating segments: Mattel International, Boys/Entertainment, Girls/Barbie, Fisher-Price Brands, and Mattel Media. In 1998, however, Mattel's product lines were grouped into four major categories: Girls, which included Barbie dolls and accessories, collector dolls, software, and the Fashion Magic, American Girl, Cabbage Patch Kids, and Polly Pocket trademarks; Infant and Preschool, which was comprised of Fisher-Price, Disney preschool and plush toys, Power Wheels, Sesame Street, See 'N Say, Magna Doodle, and View-Master; Entertainment, which included Disney, Nickelodeon, games, and puzzles; and Wheels, which was made up of Hot Wheels, Matchbox, Tyco Electric Racing, and Tyco Radio Control products.

Review of the Outcome

As a result of the merger, the companies expected to realize about $700 million in savings. By eliminating duplicate administrative offices and consolidating manufacturing and distribution operations. Mattel cut about 2,700 positions, or 10% of its workforce.

Jill E. Barad succeeded John Amerman as chairman and CEO on January 1, 1997. She proceeded to lead the company on a continuation of its strategy of expansion through acquisition. In June 1998 Mattel purchased Bluebird Toys, from which Mattel had been licensing the Polly Pocket trademarks. The following

The Players

Mattel Chairman and CEO: Jill E. Barad. Jill Barad is one of only two women at the helm of a *Fortune* 500 company. She graduated from New York's Queens College in 1973 with degrees in English and psychology. While attending school, she became a beauty consultant for a cosmetics company. Using her experience in that industry, Barad took a job as an account executive for the Max Factor account at Wells, Rich, Greene/West advertising agency, and was also a brand manager for Coty Cosmetics. She joined Mattel in 1981 as a product manager. Succeeding through executive positions, she became CEO on January 1, 1997, and added the role of chairman of the board on October 8, 1997.

Tyco Toys Chairman and CEO: Richard E. Grey. After graduating from the University of California at Los Angeles, Richard Grey became a manufacturer's representative for Tyco, gaining a thorough knowledge of the business. Named president in 1973, he and his management partner, Harry Pearce, turned the company into the nation's third-largest toy conglomerate. Ironically, Grey's father had encouraged John Tyler, the founder of Tyco, to take a chance on ready-to-run train sets.

---

month it paid $715 million to purchase Pleasant Co., a direct marketer of American Girl brand products; that company's founder and president, Pleasant Rowland, became Mattel's vice chairman.

In December 1998 the company entered into a merger agreement with The Learning Co., which would make Mattel the world's second-largest consumer software company. Mattel's net income in 1998 rose to $332 million on sales that dropped slightly to $4.78 billion.

Acquisitions continued in 1999. In March it agreed to acquire Purple Moon, producer of computer software targeted to girls. This company's products would be incorporated into Mattel Media, a unit established in 1996 to house the company's software operations, and which generated sales of $100 million in 1998. Later in March Mattel entered into a licensing agreement with EMAP Petersen, Inc. to manufacture products based on that company's magazine titles, including *Hot Rod*, *Motor Trend*, and *Teen Magazine*.

In April 1999 Mattel reported a loss, attributed to a decline in the sales of Sesame Street and Mattel

Media products. It announced a restructuring that called for the elimination of about 3,000 jobs, or 10% of its workforce. Meanwhile, it announced the October launch of its Mattel.com Web site, a subsidiary through which it would sell directly to consumers.

Research

Bannon, Lisa. "Mattel Announces Layoffs of 3,000 Ahead of Learning Co. Acquisition," in *The Wall Street Journal*, 16 April 1999. Details Mattel's recent financial problems, culminating in additional job elimination.

Collins, Glenn. "A Surprise in Toyland: Mattel to Buy Tyco," in *The New York Times*, 19 November 1996. Describes the recently announced merger deal, with particular attention to market share of the industry's leaders.

"Mattel, Inc.," in *International Directory of Company Histories*, Vol. 25, St. James Press: 1999. Provides a historical review of the company, including its merger with Tyco.

Mattel Inc. Home Page, available at http://www.mattel.com. Official World Wide Web Page for Mattel. Includes a company history, executive biographies, annual reports, press releases, and product information.

"Mattel's Offer for Tyco Toys Hits a Snag," in *The Wall Street Journal*, 21 November 1996. Describes the objections that Tyco's preferred shareholder had to Mattel's original offer.

"Mattel/Tyco Merger to be Completed by March 31; Integration/Restructuring to Result in $700 Million in Savings over 5 Years, " in *PR Newswire*, 20 March 1997. Announces the FTC's approval of the merger.

"Suddenly, Tyco is Playing with the Big Kids," in *Business Week*, 15 June 1992. Traces Tyco's rise to the rank of third-largest toy company.

"Tyco Toys, Inc.," in *International Directory of Company Histories*, Vol. 12, St. James Press: 1996. Offers a narrative account of the company's history through 1994.

DEBORAH J. UNTENER

MCCAW CELLULAR COMMUNICATIONS & LIN BROADCASTING

nationality: USA
date: March 5, 1990
affected: McCaw Cellular Communications Inc., USA, founded 1937
affected: LIN Broadcasting Corp., USA, founded 1961

AT&T Corp.
32 Avenue of the Americas
New York, NY 10013-2412
USA

tel: (212)387-5400
fax: (212)226-4935
web: http://www.att.com

Overview of the Merger

In one fell swoop, McCaw Cellular cemented its position in 1990 as the nation's leading cellular services provider and raised the bar for future deals in the industry. After numerous attempts to outmaneuver each other, McCaw eventually prevailed over BellSouth in the quest for the acquisition of LIN Broadcasting. The final purchase price of $3.38 billion was the largest ever made in the cellular market to date. It also valued LIN's holdings at $350 per potential customer—twice as high as any cellular purchase before that time.

History of McCaw Cellular Communications Inc.

In 1937 John Elroy McCaw established the area's first radio station, in Centralia, Washington. In the years that followed, he pursued his mission to build a media empire, taking that first step by acquiring station KYA in San Francisco. He then added station WINS in New York City, and converted it into the nation's first rock-and-roll station. Over the course of the next two decades, McCaw held interests in many radio and television stations, and became one of the first cable television operators.

John McCaw died suddenly in 1969, and his widow and four sons began an eight-year process of paying back his loans by selling the company's properties, leaving them with only a 7,000-subscriber cable system. Four years later Craig McCaw assumed control of the business, and soon proved to have inherited his father's initiative and desire to create a national enterprise. By 1980 the firm, now known as McCaw Communications Companies, had 30,000 cable television subscribers in Washington and Alaska.

McCaw entered the radio common carrier field in 1974 by providing paging services to subscribers. After reading AT&T projections for the future of the cellular telephone industry, which was similar to the paging services industry, McCaw decided to take a chance on the new business. Having sold a $12 million stake in the company to Affiliated Publications, the parent company of the *Boston Globe*, McCaw invested a modest $3.5 million in the venture. In 1981 it acquired licenses

The Business

Financials

Revenue (1998): $53.23 billion

Employees (1997): 128,000

SICs / NAICS

sic 4813 - Telephone Communications Except Radiotelephone

sic 4812 - Radiotelephone Communications

sic 3661 - Telephone & Telegraph Apparatus

naics 513322 - Cellular and Other Wireless Telecommunications

naics 513321 - Paging

naics 334418 - Printed Circuit Assembly (Electronic Assembly) Manufacturing

from the Federal Communications Commission for six of the nation's top 30 markets.

In 1984 it initiated an aggressive program for the acquisition of small cellular companies throughout the country. In doing so, McCaw took on huge amounts of debt, certain that the payoff in cellular would be forthcoming. In 1985 it acquired licenses to provide cellular telephone services in the Colorado cities of Denver and Boulder, as well as in Kansas City, Missouri. It also made a major addition to its cellular holdings by purchasing the entire cellular business of MCI, MCI Airsignal, for $120 million. This provided McCaw with a presence in Pittsburgh, Sacramento, Fresno, and Salt Lake City, as well as partial ownership of cellular companies in five other cities. It added two more cellular firms to its interests, Maxcell Telecom Plus and Charisma Communications, in 1986.

McCaw gained additional capital to continue its acquisition campaign by going public and by selling its cable operations to entrepreneur Jack Kent Cooke for $755 million in 1987. That year it acquired the Florida Telephone Co., and Affiliated Publications increased its stake in the company to 45%. By that time McCaw had spent over $1 billion to further its cellular interests. It had acquired licenses for 94 markets with a combined total of 37 million potential customers, making the enterprise the largest U.S. cellular telephone operator.

In February 1988 McCaw made a bid for Mobile Communications Corp., owner of half of the cellular franchises in Houston and Los Angeles, but lost out to BellSouth Corp. That year it purchased a 9.8% stake in LIN Broadcasting. McCaw's revenues reached $311 million, but the company continued to be unprofitable, recording a loss of $297 million. Despite this, most investors recognized the company's intrinsic worth, and McCaw's stock price valued the firm at about $3.5 billion. Affiliated Publications, however, grew tired of waiting for its investment to pay off, and relinquished its holdings in McCaw.

McCaw launched a $6.5 billion unfriendly offer for the remainder of LIN in 1989. To finance this bid, the firm agreed to sell a 22% stake in McCaw to British Telecommunications PLC for about $1.37 billion. After a complicated series of maneuvers with rival bidder BellSouth Corp., McCaw successfully acquired a controlling interest in LIN in March 1990. That year it sold its cellular telephone properties in the southeastern U.S. to Contel Corp. for $1.3 billion.

In 1991 McCaw entered into an agreement with PacTel Corp., the nation's third-largest cellular operator, to join forces in such large urban areas as San Francisco, Dallas, and Kansas City. That year the firm also introduced a software program that allowed subscribers to receive calls outside of their home territory without the customary use of a series of access codes, thereby creating the foundation for the North American Cellular Network. Later in 1991 it announced a joint venture with the Southwestern Bell Corp. to establish the name Cellular One as the national brand for its cellular service.

McCaw entered the field of electronic data transmission in 1992 by forming a partnership with IBM and eight other cellular operators to establish such services over a cellular telephone network. It also announced a strategic alliance with AT&T whereby McCaw would receive $2 billion, use of the AT&T brand name and other marketing considerations, and access to Bell Labs, in exchange for a 33% equity interest.

In 1993, with 2.2 million of the nation's 10 million subscribers, McCaw was the leading provider of wireless communications services in the U.S. By the following year it was growing at a rapid pace, adding approximately 28,000 new subscribers daily. Also in 1994 McCaw was purchased by AT&T for $11.5 billion, resulting in a new company called AT&T Wireless Services. The next year it introduced a new cellular digital packet data service, Air Business.

History of LIN Broadcasting Corp.

LIN Broadcasting Corp. was founded in 1961 as a radio broadcaster in Nashville, Tennessee. Four years later it paid $2 million to acquire WTVP-TV of Decatur, Illinois. The company went public in 1966, the same year that it exchanged $3 million in stock for a controlling interest in Medallion Pictures Corp.'s 375 feature films and cartoons. LIN purchased stations in Texas and Virginia in 1967, and the following year it acquired Adonis Radio Corp., an advertising media buyer. This shopping spree proved costly, as its combined losses for the previous two years amounted to $1 million.

The company went through a succession of leaders in 1969. The Saturday Evening Post Co. purchased the four-percent stake held by LIN's chief, Frederick Gregg, Jr., and installed Martin Ackerman at the helm. Ackerman was ousted by the board of directors within five weeks, however, and Joel Thorpe assumed control. Finally, Donald Pels became the company's leader, just as LIN's losses for the year amounted to $6.5 million.

Pels set about refocusing the company on its broadcasting roots. He began divesting pieces of its diverse collection of holdings, including record and film companies, a talent agency, and art galleries. When he was finished, LIN's remaining assets consisted of radio and television stations. Soon thereafter, Pels became interested in the paging business, which had operating margins of 40%. By the late 1970s LIN had acquired paging businesses in New York and Houston, two of the nation's leading markets. By 1984 it had added three others—Los Angeles, Philadelphia, and Dallas.

McCaw Cellular Communications launched an unfriendly bid for LIN in 1989, and LIN turned to BellSouth Corp. as a white knight. After a lengthy battle, McCaw acquired control of LIN in March 1990.

Market Forces Driving the Merger

By 1989, after only five years in the business, McCaw Cellular had built the largest cellular telephone company in the U.S. by accumulating small operations across the country. McCaw had 50 million POPs, industry lingo for "potential customers," in its territory, more than twice as many as that of its closest rival, Pacific Telesis Group. Yet most of those properties were located in small cities rather than large urban centers. While this geographic dispersion provided a structural foundation for the nationwide system that McCaw strove to build, it lacked the commanding presence in major markets that was vital for a true national system.

LIN Broadcasting, on the other hand, had operations in New York, Los Angeles, Houston, Dallas, and Philadelphia. With 18 million POPs, it was one of the

The Officers

Chairman and CEO: C. Michael Armstrong

President: John D. Zeglis

Sr. Exec. VP and Chief Financial Officer: Daniel Somers

Exec. VP, Corporate Strategy and Business Development: John Petrillo

Exec. VP, Law and Governmental Affairs, and General Counsel: James Cicconi

last remaining independent cellular companies with a significant presence in five of the nation's top 10 cellular markets. "LIN is [McCaw's] only chance to become a national company," said Dennis Leibowitz, of Donaldson, Lufkin & Jenrette Securities Corp., in *Business Week*.

Approach and Engagement

McCaw Cellular acquired a 5.4% stake in LIN Broadcasting in April 1988. At that time, it claimed that the purchase should be considered "purely as an investment in a well-run company, without any unfriendly intent," according to *The Wall Street Journal*. McCaw soon altered this stance, however, as eight months later it announced its intention of seeking regulatory approval to increase its interest in LIN.

On June 6, 1989, having increased its stake in LIN to 9.8%, McCaw launched an unsolicited bid for the balance of LIN's shares. The $120-per-share offer, valued at $5.85 billion, was a 16% premium over LIN's over-the-counter value. It also assigned the extraordinary value of $275-300 per POP—more than twice the going rate for cellular companies. Analysts suspected that McCaw went so high for two reasons: to make the bid irresistible to LIN's shareholders and to enact a preemptive strike against any other potential suitors. On June 20 LIN rejected the offer as "inadequate."

On July 10 McCaw reduced its bid to $110 per share in response to the negative outcome of a lawsuit involving LIN. For three years, that company had tried to force its partner, Metromedia Inc., to sell to LIN its portion of their joint cellular interests in New York and Philadelphia. A New York Court of Appeals rejected LIN's claim, thereby devaluing the company's worth.

McCaw and LIN entered into talks for a sweetened offer, but McCaw broke off negotiations on July 21. Days later, LIN's chairman, Donald Pels, tried to settle the matter once and for all. In a letter to chair-

The Players

McCaw Cellular Communications Chairman and CEO: Craig O. McCaw. Craig McCaw has been hailed as the late-20th century's answer to Theodore Vail, the chairman who built AT&T into a nationwide telephone network by consolidating hundreds of small companies. After earning a degree in history from Stanford University in 1973, McCaw took control of his family's ailing cable television company. This visionary recognized the future of the infant cellular telephone industry and strove to establish a national network. To accomplish this, he set about acquiring cellular companies throughout the U.S., culminating with his purchase of LIN Broadcasting in 1990. AT&T purchased McCaw Cellular in 1994, at which point Craig McCaw took his leave from the company. In March 1998 McCaw added the position of CEO to his responsibilities as chairman of Teledesic LLC.

LIN Broadcasting Chairman and CEO: Donald A. Pels. Donald Pels left his position as executive vice president at Capital Cities Inc. to join LIN Broadcasting in 1969. He trimmed down the overly diversified company and led it first into the paging industry and then into cellular telephony. In 1989 LIN's collection of cellular licenses in large urban centers drew the interest of McCaw Cellular and BellSouth, which both sought to acquire control of the firm. Upon McCaw's eventual victory, Pels stood to gain over $200 million from the sale of his stake in LIN.

man Craig McCaw, Pels wrote that $127.50 per share would be deemed a fair price, and gave McCaw until July 31 to respond. McCaw stood firm, and in early August reiterated its $110 per share offer.

BellSouth Corp. entered the scene on September 10, when LIN announced that it would merge its cellular properties with those of BellSouth. The complex deal called for LIN to spin off its television operations, pay shareholders a $20 dividend, and provide them with a 50% interest in the company made up of their combined cellular operations.

In a ploy reminiscent of a chess maneuver, McCaw moved to increase LIN's vulnerability by forcing it to protect a piece of its property. On October 3 it agreed to purchase Metromedia's New York cellular interests for $1.9 billion, or $275 per POP. For LIN to hang onto those valuable assets, its merger partner,

BellSouth, would have to top that offer. McCaw knew that BellSouth was a conservative company, and would probably be unwilling to dilute its earnings by paying that much for a stake in the relatively risky cellular industry. This put McCaw in a win-win situation, the company believed. Either BellSouth would terminate its merger pact with LIN, thereby clearing the field for McCaw, or the companies would allow McCaw to purchase the New York interests without a fight, in which case it would gain entry into a leading market and, ironically, become a partner of LIN.

McCaw pressed its advantage on October 10. It raised its bid for LIN to $125 per share, but only for the 22 million shares that would give it a 50.3% controlling interest. In addition, it included a "back end" provision, whereby it would be obligated to purchase LIN's remaining shares in July 1994 at a price roughly equivalent to what a third party would have to pay at that time. If it declined to do so, the shares would be placed on the auction block.

Backed into a corner, BellSouth and LIN revised their merger accord on October 27. Most of the original terms remained intact, but the $20 per share dividend was raised to $42 per share. Additionally, LIN would exercise its right as Metromedia's partner to purchase that company's portion of their New York cellular franchise for $1.9 billion, swiping them from McCaw's grasp. Moreover, BellSouth added a back end provision similar to McCaw's, except that it would not be obligated to purchase the outstanding shares. "BellSouth can just sit there and leave public holders hanging on for the next 20 years...but McCaw guarantees an auction price for those assets," said Frederick Moran, president of Moran Asset Management, a large LIN stockholder, in *The Wall Street Journal*.

On November 20 McCaw turned up the heat. It sweetened its bid to $150 per share and threatened to oust LIN's board through a proxy fight at LIN's shareholder meeting in January. In early December LIN sought to bring a close to the merger drama by requesting both McCaw and BellSouth to submit their final offer. BellSouth failed to respond, but McCaw increased its bid to $154.11 per share. On December 4 Pels recommended that LIN's shareholders accept that offer, and on December 11 the two companies reached a definitive agreement. On March 5, 1990, McCaw completed its acquisition of 51.9% of LIN for $3.38 billion.

Products and Services

After spinning off NCR and separating from Lucent Technologies, AT&T operated four business segments: Consumer Long Distance accounted for

$22.94 billion in revenues in 1998; Business Long Distance contributed $22.63 billion in revenues; Wireless brought in $5.4 billion; and $3.54 billion originated from other services.

Changes to the Industry

The acquisition of LIN Broadcasting made McCaw Cellular the undisputed leader of the U.S. cellular telephone industry. With 68 million POPs, many in the nation's leading markets, McCaw was well on track to establishing a nationwide network. Its plan was to integrate independent cellular licensees into its Cellular One network through a franchise arrangement. LIN's all-important licenses in such major cities as New York and Los Angeles provided McCaw with the clout to persuade these smaller companies to join Cellular One.

However, by gaining that leverage through the purchase of LIN, McCaw also increased its debt load to $3.8 billion. According to a December 1989 issue of *Forbes*, "in order to create a national cellular telephone company able to compete with the [national wireline network of the] Bell companies, McCaw had no choice but to strain his company to the bursting point to control LIN." Just prior to the closure of the deal, McCaw had managed to shave $1.3 billion from that burden by selling to Contel Corp. its less desirable interests in Alabama, Kentucky, and Tennessee. The firm had little fear of the remaining balance. McCaw had been willing to carry a continuous large debt load ever since it ventured into the cellular market, confident that those investments would pay off in the future.

The explosive growth in wireless telecommunications foreseen by McCaw occurred shortly after its acquisition of LIN. The field expanded to encompass not only cellular telephones, but also two-way pagers, hand-held computers, and mobile fax machines. The number of U.S. subscribers grew from 3.5 million in 1989 to 10 million in 1994. That year, as McCaw was adding new subscribers at a rate of 28,000 per day, the firm was acquired by AT&T for $11.5 billion.

Review of the Outcome

Aside from the increased debt load carried by McCaw Cellular, the acquisition brought the companies a couple of financial burdens. LIN Broadcasting paid BellSouth a $66.5 million break-up fee as a consequence of their terminated merger accord. Then, in March 1992, the companies agreed to pay $8.5 million to settle shareholder suits alleging unfair stock options that had been extended to LIN's officers and directors as part of the McCaw transaction.

In January 1990, just prior to the closing of the acquisition, details surfaced about the advantageous stock arrangement that LIN's executives had received. Since McCaw purchased only about half of LIN, shareholders could tender an equivalent proportion of their stock. Officers and directors, however, arranged to sell all of their stock, receiving an immediate and lucrative payout. The 1.3 million shares held by Donald Pels, LIN's chairman, were worth over $200 million, "one of the largest sums ever made by an individual as a publicly held media company changed hands," reported *The New York Times*.

Research

"AT&T Corp.," in *Notable Corporate Chronologies*, The Gale Group, 1999. Lists major events in the history of AT&T.

AT&T Corp. Home Page, available at http://www.att.com. Official World Wide Web Home Page for AT&T. Includes news releases, financial data, product information, and a historical review of the company.

Dolan, Carrie, G. Pascal Zachary, and Janet Guyon. "McCaw Offers to Buy LIN for Price of $5.85 Billion," in *The Wall Street Journal*, 7 June 1989. Details McCaw's initial hostile bid for LIN.

Dolan, Carrie, and Julie Amparano Lopez. "McCaw to Buy into Franchise in New York," in *The Wall Street Journal*, 4 October 1989. Relates McCaw's strategic move to force a play by LIN and BellSouth by moving in on LIN's holdings in New York.

Fabrikant, Geraldine. "Lin and BellSouth to Merge Units," in *The New York Times*, 12 September 1989. Details the terms of LIN's merger pact with BellSouth.

———. "Lin Merger's Windfall: A Question of Fairness," in *The New York Times*, 5 January 1990. Details the discrepancies between McCaw's payout to LIN's executives and shareholders.

Hof, Robert D. "The Cellular Bidding War Will Get Even Hotter," in *Business Week*, 19 June 1989. Relates McCaw's hostile bid for LIN and offers the predictions by analysts that other companies will enter into the bidding.

"McCaw Cellular Communications Inc.," in *Notable Corporate Chronologies*, The Gale Group, 1999. Profiles the history of McCaw Cellular.

"McCaw Cellular Purchases a 5.4% Stake in Company," in *The Wall Street Journal*, 14 April 1988. Briefly announces McCaw's initial purchase of an interest in LIN.

McCoy, Charles, Julie Amparano Lopez, and John J. Keller. "McCaw Boosts Offer for LIN to $150 a Share," in *The Wall Street Journal*, 21 November 1989. Describes McCaw's sweetened offer for LIN.

Meeks, Fleming. "Winning is Only the First Step," in *Forbes*, 25 December 1989. Profiles Craig McCaw and describes his vision for the company.

DEBORAH J. UNTENER

MCKESSON & GENERAL MEDICAL

McKesson HBOC, Inc.
McKesson Plz., One Post St.
San Francisco, CA 94104-5296
USA

tel: (415)983-8300
fax: (415)983-7160
web: http://www.mckhboc.com

nationality: USA
date: February 21, 1997
affected: McKesson HBOC, Inc. (formerly McKesson Corp.), USA, founded 1833
affected: General Medical Corp., USA, founded 1950

Overview of the Acquisition

The acquisition of General Medical in 1997 made McKesson the largest health care supply management company in North America. With $13.7 billion in revenues, McKesson was the nation's largest drug wholesaler, and General Medical was the third-largest distributor of medical supplies in the U.S. The deal also marked a return to the industry's drive for consolidation of pharmaceutical wholesalers and medical suppliers, a formula that had proven unsuccessful in the past.

History of McKesson Corp.

John McKesson and Charles Olcott opened a small import and wholesaling shop in New York City's financial district in 1833. Finding success in supplying therapeutic drugs and chemicals to the clipper ships that shuttled goods to and from the New World, the two made their assistant, Daniel Robbins, a partner. After Olcott's death in 1853, the firm was renamed McKesson & Robbins.

In 1926 McKesson & Robbins was sold to Frank D. Coster, who had changed his name from Philip Musica when his family was arrested for bribery connected with their food import business some years earlier. Three years later McKesson & Robbins persuaded many of the nation's largest wholesale drug distributors to become their subsidiaries, resulting in a nationwide network that rivaled the huge drug chains. Profits in 1929 reached $4.1 million on unprecedented sales of $140 million. By 1930 the company had wholesale drug operations in 33 states, serving over 15,000 retail druggists and employing over 6,000 people.

The company established liquor departments through its wholesale subsidiaries with the repeal of Prohibition in 1933. Later, McKesson established its Spirits Import Company.

Coster's secret identity was revealed in 1938 when a company treasurer's concern over the handling of profits led to an investigation of McKesson & Robbins. The next year he committed suicide when the investigation revealed that he had stolen $3 million from McKesson and was paying blackmail fees to a former partner who had discovered his identity. As a result, McKesson & Robbins was forced into bankruptcy, from which it finally emerged in 1941.

By 1955, having formed a chemical department more than 50 years ago, McKesson was distributing more than 1,000 heavy and fine chemicals manufactured by over 100 companies. In 1967 Foremost Dairy of California initiated a hostile takeover of the company. The resulting enterprise was renamed Foremost-McKesson. A computerized order-entry system, called Economost, which revolutionized the drug distribution industry was introduced in 1969. Seven years later Rudolph Drews (who had been fired from Foremost-McKesson two years earlier) failed in a takeover bid of Foremost-McKesson.

That same year the company acquired C.F. Mueller Co., the country's largest pasta maker, and Gentry International, an onion and garlic processor. Foremost-McKesson reorganized into four major operating groups in 1978: drugs and health care, wine and spirits, foods, and chemicals, as well as a small homebuilding division.

In 1981 the company acquired its first chemical recycling plant and initiated plans to build six additional plants across the country. Two years later the dairy, food processing, and homebuilding portions of its business were divested and the company adopted the name McKesson Corp. In addition, it spent $90 million on acquisitions of distributor and distributor-related industries.

By 1985 McKesson was recognized as the country's largest distributor of drug and medical equipment, wine and liquor, bottled water, and car waxes and polishers. An anti-trust suit blocks McKesson's acquisition of Alco Health Services in 1988.

The company won a contract to distribute drugs to nearly 1,000 Wal-Mart Stores in 1989. Two years later Medis, a leading Canadian distributor, was acquired.

In 1995 the company formed a new unit, McKesson Health Systems, to serve the pharmaceutical needs of hospitals and long-term care providers. The new unit specialized in assisting in clinical trials of biotechnology products, and was renamed McKesson BioServices.

Also that year McKesson completed the sale of its PCS Health Systems unit to Eli Lilly & Company for approximately $4 billion. Additionally, it sold its El Salvador subsidiary, Corporacion Bonima S.A., to Bayer A.G. of Germany for $40 million. Meanwhile, the firm acquired Ogden BioServices Corporation to broaden its role in the emerging biotechnology industry.

In 1996 Mark A. Pulido was selected to succeed David E. McDowell as president, chief operating officer, and director. That year the company acquired

The Business

Financials

Revenue (1998): $20.8 billion

Employees (1998): 25,000

SICs / NAICS

sic 5122 - Drugs, Proprietaries & Sundries

sic 5047 - Medical & Hospital Equipment

naics 422210 - Drugs and Druggists' Sundries Wholesalers

naics 421450 - Medical, Dental and Hospital Equipment and Supplies Wholesalers

Automated Healthcare, Inc., of Pittsburgh, for $61 million. McKesson also acquired the pharmaceutical distribution business of FoxMeyer Corporation. In December 1996 it sold its 55% interest in Armor All Products Corp. to The Clorox Co. for $222 million.

The following year McKesson purchased General Medical, the largest U.S. distributor of medical surgical supplies, for about $775 million. It also sold Millbrook Distribution Services, Inc. and Aqua-Vend in order to focus more on health care services.

It entered into an agreement to merge with AmeriSource Health Corp. in 1997, but the Federal Trade Commission blocked the deal in 1998 on antitrust grounds. In early 1999, however, McKesson acquired HBO & Co., a leading health care information provider, for $14 billion. The newly merged entity took the name McKesson HBOC, Inc.

In the wake of the merger, the revelation of accounting inconsistencies at HBO & Company forced McKesson to restate fiscal 1999 results twice. As a result of this and the ensuing shareholder lawsuits, McKesson shuffled top management. Among those to leave were Mark A. Pulido, McKesson's former president and CEO, and Richard H. Hawkins, former executive vice president and chief financial officer, both of whom resigned in June 1999.

In February 1999 the company acquired Kelly/Waldron & Co. and Kelly Waldron/Technologies Solutions, both operating in information services for the pharmaceuticals industry.

History of General Medical Corp.

Richmond Surgical Supply was founded in 1950 as a supplier of medical products to the Richmond,

The Officers

Chairman: Alan Seelenfreund

Co-CEO: John H. Hammergren

Co-CEO: David L. Mahoney

Acting Chief Financial Officer: Heidi Yodowitz

Corporate Sr. VP, Human Resources and Administration: E. Christine Rumsey

Virginia, area. The private company grew gradually, and incorporated in 1965. Throughout its history, it passed into the possession of various owners. In 1993 a group of the firm's management completed a leveraged buyout.

Following that buyout, the company, which had taken the name General Medical Corp., embarked on an aggressive acquisition spree. In 1994 it purchased numerous distribution facilities to serve regional areas. Its acquisition of a Denver facility in March 1994 marked the company's 45 distribution centers. By that measure General Medical ranked as the nation's third-largest distributor of medical supplies, behind Owens & Minor, Inc. and Baxter Hospital Supply.

In addition to distribution facilities, General Medical also scooped up alternate care distributors. In 1994 it purchased F.D. Titus & Sons, Foster Medical Supply, and Randolph Medical, followed the next year by Denver Surgical Supply and Goetze-Niemer. In September 1996 the firm entered into a $100 million agreement to distribute the products of its rival Allegiance Healthcare Corp. to hospital and nonhospital customers.

In 1997, for the first time, General Medical's financial condition was disclosed. As part of its intention to make its initial public offering, the firm was required to issue public filings with the Securities and Exchange Commission. Those statements revealed that General Medical's revenues in 1995 reached approximately $1.5 billion. Its revenues for the first nine months of 1996 were 15.6% higher than those over the same period of time in 1995. The proportion of those sales was 58% from the acute care market, 31% from the physical care market, and 11% from the extended care market. The filings also revealed that General Medical was deep in debt.

Its public offering never took place, however. On the eve of its filing, it entered into an agreement to be purchased by McKesson Inc., a deal that was completed in February 1997.

Market Forces Driving the Acquisition

The consolidation wave that was taking over the pharmaceutical manufacturing industry trickled down into the pharmaceutical and medical supply distribution industries. These wholesalers, serving hospital, clinics, and private practices, had the same dream as players in many other industries—to become a one-stop shop for customers.

This was not a novel idea in the industry. In fact, it had been tried before and had met with failure. The problem for pharmaceuticals and medical suppliers was that large customers and small clients required different vastly different distribution models. While a large client like a hospital might order crates of thermometers, for example, a private practice physician might require only a handful, forcing the distributor to sell only a partial case. But by the mid-1990s the merger fever had hit again, and companies believed that they could overcome the difficulties of distribution with specialized information systems, equipment, and labor skills.

McKesson, a large drug wholesaler, was interested in General Medical to gain access to the nonhospital market, where McKesson was relatively weak. McKesson learned through General Medical's public filing that it was burdened with a heavy debt load, and might therefore appreciate the financial security that McKesson had to offer.

Approach and Engagement

McKesson began making acquisition overtures to General Medical in the winter of 1996. Since General Medical was preparing for its initial public offering, however, it didn't bother entering into negotiations. The company's financial advisors recommended that General Medical continue to plan its IPO as a back-up only if McKesson's offer was unacceptable.

The transaction was negotiated and completed in record time. On January 28, 1997, McKesson and General Medical announced their acquisition agreement. The cash-and-stock offer, worth $347 million plus the assumption of $428 million of General Medical's debt, was completed on February 21, the day before General Medical's planned stock offering.

Products and Services

In 1998 McKesson HBOC, Inc. was the world's largest pharmaceutical supply management and healthcare information technology company. It provided pharmaceutical supply management and information technologies across the entire continuum of healthcare, including market-leading businesses in pharmaceutical and medical-surgical distribution, information technology for healthcare providers, and outsourcing.

McKesson HBOC operated three principal business units:

Pharmaceutical Services included four primary segments. BioServices covered biological material handling, regulatory support/adverse event reporting, kit and label production, validation, kaye portable validator system, customer support and training, pharmaceutical repository, packaging and labeling, patient-specific drug delivery, and adverse event reporting. Healthcare Delivery Systems encompassed HDS, DTC Solutions, distribution services, cost recovery and patient transition programs, patient resource center, treatment ind program management, reimbursement support services, patient assistance programs, trial script pharmacy-based starter supply programs, marketing support programs, and database management and fulfillment services. J Knipper offered flat and fulfillment mail, product recall services, data processing, personalization, lists, and postal/shipping services. Finally, Technology Solutions was comprised of Dynastrat.

Information Technologies offered such systems as Pathways 2000, Clinical Information Systems, HIS Solutions, Physician Solutions, Resource Management, Access Management, Decision Support, Homecare, Managed Care, Clinical Auditing and Compliance, Community Health Management, and Infrastructure.

Supply Management featured four main offers: Automated Healthcare included Packaging Program, Connect-Rx, AcuScan-Rx, AcuDose-Rx Cabinet, ROBOT-Rx, ROBOT-Rx Cartless System, and AcuDose-Rx. BakerAPS, covered Baker Cells, Pharmacy 2000, Autoscript III, Baker Cassettes, and Baker Universal. Health Systems offered UBC Optimization Program, Telestock, Acumax Plus, CoSource Pharmacy Program, EconoLink 5.0 System, EconoLink, EconoLink Data Translator, Electronic Data Interchange (EDI), and SupplyNET. Red Line Extended Care featured FROG, COMETS, ORBITS+, Home Care Products, and Red.e.Net.

Changes to the Industry

After the acquisition of General Medical, McKesson became the leading health care supply management company. Its potential to offer integrated services to both the hospital and nonhospital markets was viewed as industry analysts as a potential trigger for future deals. "Within the next five years, there could be just three to five medical device manufacturers and about that many distributors," suggested Kenneth Abramowitz, a senior health care analyst for Sanford Bernstein & Co., in a 1997 issue of *Health Industry Today.*

Review of the Outcome

Upon its absorption into McKesson, General Medical took the name McKesson General Medical (MGM). It immediately took steps to retool its distribution capacities. It replaced small, outdated warehouses with larger, automated facilities, thereby enabling it to consolidate its warehouses from about 60 to only 46.

Research

Cassak, David. "Do Drugs and Hospital Supplies Mix? in *In Vivo*, June 1997. Describes the changing industry, with a focus on the combination of McKesson and General Medical.

Clark, Don. "McKesson Plans to Buy General Medical for about $347 Million in Cash, Stock," in *The Wall Street Journal,* 29 January 1997.

"McKesson Corp.," in *Notable Corporate Chronologies,* The Gale Group, 1999. Provides an overview of the company.

McKesson HBOC, Inc. Home Page, available at http://www.mckhboc.com. Official World Wide Web Page for McKesson HBOC. Offers new releases, financial and product information, and executive biographies.

"Shroud of Financial Secrecy Lifts: General Medical Goes Public," in *Health Industry Today,* February 1997. Reveals the finances of General Medical in preparation for its IPO.

Speer, Tibbett L. "From Docks to Docs," in *Hospitals & Health Networks,* 5 August 1997. Reviews the difficulties inherent in offering a one-stop shop for drug and medical supplies.

Werner, Curt. "General Medical-McKesson Deal Meets General Approval, Acceptance," in *Health Industry,* 1 March 1997. Describes the completion of the deal, and what each company had to gain from the other.

———. "Mega-Mergers Test Arguments for and against Consolidation," in *Health Industry,* 1 November 1997. Offers opinions on the combination of the drug wholesale and medical supply industries.

PATRICIA ARCHILLA

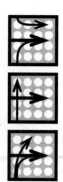

MERCK & MEDCO CONTAINMENT SERVICES

Merck-Medco Managed Care, LLC
100 Summit Ave.
Montvale, NJ 07645
USA

tel: (201)358-5400
web: http://www.merck-medco.com

nationality: USA
date: November 1993
affected: Merck & Co., Inc., USA, founded 1891
affected: Medco Containment Services Inc., USA, founded 1983

Overview of the Merger

The 1993 acquisition of Medco Containment by Merck & Co. united the world's largest pharmaceutical maker with the nation's leading mail-order pharmacy company. The result, Merck-Medco Managed Care, became a vital link in Merck's vertical integration by providing the pharmaceutical giant with the means of distribution.

This was the industry's first such merger between a drug manufacturer and distributor, and it triggered a snowball effect. Other pharmaceutical companies, already under pressure to reduce prices, couldn't afford to allow Merck to increase its lead over them, so they scrambled to enter into similar deals of their own.

Medco Containment was a pharmacy benefits management company (PBM). These companies acted as the link between drug companies and cost-conscious managed care companies. They strove to contain the expense of drugs, and did so in two ways. They purchased drugs in bulk quantities, usually securing discounted prices. They also maintained lists of the various drugs available in a certain class, from which the doctors in the managed care plan were encouraged to make their prescription selections. If a doctor prescribed an expensive drug, the PBM phoned him to encourage the switch to a lower-priced, but equally effective, product. Merck, as well as the other pharmaceutical companies that followed its lead, acquired Medco with the intention of getting more of its products on those preferred drug lists.

In addition, Merck had its eye on Medco's mail-order business and retail pharmacy connections. Its computer database was of particular interest, though. This network, which tracked the sales of drugs and doctors' prescription patterns, recorded about 74 million pharmaceutical transactions each year. It would be a valuable tool for Merck in evaluating the marketplace.

History of Merck & Company Inc.

Merck had its roots in the mid-17th century. In 1668 Friedrich Jacob Merck purchased an apothecary in the German town of Darmstadt. The company, which came to be known as E. Merck AG, was passed down through the family's generations for a century and a half before winding up in the hands of Heinrich Emmanuel Merck in 1827. Having studied with the prominent organic chemist Justus von Liebig, Merck applied Liebig's theories for the firm's production of morphine. Its product line expanded, and by 1855 Merck pharmaceutical products were used throughout the world.

In 1887 the chemist Theodore Weicker traveled to the U.S. from Germany to establish an American branch of E. Merck AG. In 1891 the company that would become known as Merck & Company was formed when George Merck, grandson of Heinrich, entered into a partnership with Weicker. George began supplying chemicals and drugs imported from Germany to New York apothecaries. Its product line included chloral hydrate, iodides, and alkaloids. Sales reached $1 million in 1897.

In 1903 the company ventured into chemical and drug production at its plants in New Jersey and St. Louis. The following year, Weicker sold his interest in the company to George Merck, thereby dissolving their partnership. Weicker used his proceeds to purchase a controlling interest in the competing drug company E.R. Squibb. George's business, now known as Merck & Co., expanded its American product line to include morphine, cocaine, bismuths, and iodides. Sales exceeded $2 million in 1905.

With the U.S. entrance into World War I, George Merck was forced in 1917 to break formal ties with his family and with the company E. Merck AG in Germany. The U.S. government seized E. Merck AG's 80% interest in Merck & Co., allowing George to retain his shares. At war's end, the U.S. sold its seized shares to the public.

In 1927 the company merged with Powers-Weightmann-Rosengarten, a Philadelphia-based producer and distributor of pharmaceutical chemicals known for producing the anti-malarial drug quinine. Two years later, sales surpassed $13 million, enabling the company to invest heavily in research and development.

The two Merck firms, in America and in Germany, entered into an agreement in 1932 providing for the exchange of technical information and the division of world sales territories in order to avoid competing with each other. The following year, George Merck established the Merck Institute for Therapeutic Research, and recruited prominent chemists and biologists to work on the production of new pharmaceuticals. The results paid off in 1934, when Merck perfected the synthesis of the newly isolated vitamin B1, gaining the license to produce and sell it.

The Business

Financials

Revenue (1998): $14.3 billion

Employees (1998): 11,000

SICs / NAICS

sic 5122 - Drugs, Proprietaries & Sundries

sic 5961 - Catalog & Mail-Order Houses

sic 2834 - Pharmaceutical Preparations

sic 2833 - Medicinals & Botanicals

sic 2879 - Agricultural Chemicals Nec

naics 422210 - Drugs and Druggists' Sundries Wholesalers

naics 454110 - Electronic Shopping and Mail-Order Houses

naics 325412 - Pharmaceutical Preparation Manufacturing

naics 325411 - Medicinal and Botanical Manufacturing

naics 325320 - Pesticide and Other Agricultural Chemical Manufacturing

In 1943 a Merck-funded scientist working at Rutgers University discovered streptomycin, a revolutionary antibiotic used for the treatment of tuberculosis and other infections. Because of the drug's potential importance, Merck chose not to claim exclusive patent rights, although it did become its leading producer. The following year, Merck played a role in the development of cortisone, the first steroid. Originally intended to treat arthritis, the drug ultimately was used to treat such diseases as bronchial asthma and rheumatic fever.

As part of the consent decree of an anti-trust suit, Merck's non-compete agreement with its German counterpart was dissolved in 1945. Soon after, domestic and foreign competition intensified as new products flooded the market. Merck found itself ill prepared to engage in direct selling to individual doctors and dentists.

In 1948 Merck announced its discovery of B12, a new vitamin considered highly effective in the battle against serious anemia. By 1953 exports accounted for about 20% of company sales. That year Merck merged with the pharmaceutical firm and longtime customer Sharp & Dohme. This Philadelphia-based company brought with it a well-established overseas distribution network, which became the basis of the new entity, Merck Sharp & Dohme International.

The Officers

Merck Chairman, President, and CEO: Raymond V.
    Gilmartin

Sr. VP and Chief Financial Officer: Judy C. Lewent

Sr. VP and General Counsel: Mary M. McDonald

Merck entered into a joint venture agreement with the Japanese pharmaceutical firm Banyu, forming Nippon Merck-Banyu. In 1958 Merck began the sale of Diuril, an antihypertensive drug that was the first major product in the company's new line of cardiovascular drugs.

The company embarked on a program of diversification in the mid-1960s. Throughout the next several years, the company acquired Calgon Corp., a nationwide provider of water treatment chemicals and services; Baltimore Aircoil, a manufacturer of refrigeration and industrial cooling equipment; and Kelco, a processor of kelp for the production of alginates and specialty chemicals.

Legal troubles began for Merck in the mid-1970s. In 1974 a $35 million lawsuit was filed against Merck and 28 other drug manufacturers and distributors of DES. This drug, a miscarriage preventative prescribed over a twenty-year period, contained a known carcinogen; the defendants were ordered to notify potential victims, provide detection and treatment, and pay billions of dollars in damages. In 1975 the U.S. Securities and Exchange Commission revealed that Merck, along with other U.S. companies, made illegal payments totaling $3.6 million in order to obtain foreign business in 39 African and Middle Eastern countries.

In 1979 the company's Kelco subsidiary acquired Alginate Industries Ltd. of London. Four years later Merck acquired the Spanish pharmaceutical firm Abello SA. That year it also spent $315 million to acquire a majority share in Nippon Merck-Banyu; this was the first such purchase by any U.S. firm operating in Japan.

Merck divested itself of Baltimore Aircoil in 1985, at the same time acquiring the Italian firm Neopharmed. That year biochemist and head of research, Roy Vagelos, was named CEO. In 1986 the company acquired Vestal Laboratories Inc., a manufacturer of skin care products, disinfectants, and germicides. Merck annual revenues totaled $3.5 billion for the year, ranking it second in sales in the U.S. pharmaceutical industry.

In 1990 the firm bought the nonprescription business of ICI America, maker of Mylanta, whose drugs are marketed through Johnson & Johnson. In 1991 Merck entered into a number of joint ventures. Its agreement with Astra AB of Sweden allowed Merck to distribute most of Astra's products. It created DuPont Merck Pharmaceutical Co. in partnership with E.I. du Pont de Nemours & Co.; it would sell its 50% stake in this venture in 1998 for $2.6 billion.

In 1992 Merck employed 38,000 people, maintained 16 research centers, and operated 47 manufacturing facilities in 18 countries. The following year it acquired Medco Containment Service Inc., the nation's largest pharmacy-benefit services company, for $6 billion. Merck's revenues that year exceeded $10 billion for the first time. It created its first joint venture in China in 1994 by teaming up with Hangzhou East China Pharmaceutical. In 1996 it bought Systemed, a mail-order drug and pharmaceutical benefits management company catering to mid-sized customers, those organizations with fewer than 10,000 members.

In 1997 Merck and Rhone-Poulenc merged their animal health businesses to form Merial Ltd., the largest such operation in the world. That year Merck also sold its insecticide and fungicide businesses to Novartis AG. Company revenues in 1998 totaled $26.9 billion, with net income reaching $5.2 billion.

History of Medco Containment Services, Inc.

In the early 1980s, Martin Wygod predicted that the pharmaceuticals industry would begin to experience tremendous growth. An aging population combined with the trend toward shorter hospital stays would increase the demand for drugs. With a small fortune accumulated from a history of buying and selling companies for profit, Wygod acquired National Pharmacies in 1983. This mail order pharmaceutical and vitamin business was purchased from corporate raider Victor Posner for $30 million. That year he formed Porex Technologies, a plastic medical device manufacturer, as a holding company for National Pharmacies.

In 1984 the company, now renamed Medco Containment Services, sold off 20% in a public offering. It began aggressively enrolling such new clients for its mail order company as General Motors, Alcoa, and Georgia-Pacific. The following year it acquired Paid Prescriptions, a retail drug store claim processor for $29 million. This company offered its participants a choice of filling prescriptions at a discount through its network of 40,000 participating drugstores.

Medco generated about 90% of Porex's sales in 1987, and that year it acquired this parent company.

Two years later it acquired Synetic Inc., establishing it as a subsidiary to serve as a holding company for many of Medco's operations, including Porex. In 1990 Medco introduced a controversial program called Prescriber's Choice, wherein Medco would promote a company's drug as the top choice in its category in exchange for deep discounts.

In 1991 the company formed the Medical Marketing Group, Inc. subsidiary, which utilized Medco's computer database to sell to drug companies the data that it had compiled on doctors' prescription patterns. That year Medco acquired American Biodyne, a managed mental health services provider, and bought a 23% share in Comnet Corp. Synetic captured a greater share of the institutional market by purchasing part of Rix Dunnington and Dunnington Super Drug, which provided pharmaceutical services to institutions in the northeastern U.S. Revenues reached $1.8 billion that year.

With Medco offering medications for prices 25% less than retail pharmacies, Wygod described his company as "the Wal-Mart of pills" in the *Wall Street Journal*. By 1993 all but a handful of the major U.S. pharmaceutical firms had signed on with Medco. Later that year, Merck & Company paid $6 billion to acquire Medco, transforming it into a subsidiary, Merck-Medco Managed Care, LLC.

Market Forces Driving the Merger

Managed care had changed the landscape of the pharmaceutical industry. Prior to the 1980s, the extend of healthcare treatment was largely determined by the doctor and patient. Under the traditional health insurance program offered by employers, an employee was responsible for his health care expenses up to a specified deductible. After that threshold was crossed, the employer, or more typically an insurance company, was responsible for the cost of treatment. This allowed doctors and patients to pursue courses of treatment unchecked, as they were typically unconcerned with costs.

With costs of healthcare spinning out of control, employers sought cheaper alternatives. The health maintenance organization (HMO) became popular in the mid-1980s. These organizations offered cheaper coverage by placing checks and balances on the system. They organized a network of doctors and hospitals that had agreed to follow the HMOs' recommendations when providing treatment. Services above and beyond these guidelines were partially paid for by the healthcare provider, thus instilling incentive to prescribe treatments more selectively.

The Players

Former Chairman and CEO of Merck & Co.: Dr. P. Roy Vagelos. Roy Vagelos grew up in close company with Merck researchers. He worked after school at a coffeehouse near the company's laboratory, and later studied chemistry at the University of Pennsylvania. He enrolled in Columbia University's College of Physicians and Surgeons, and in 1965 became chairman of the biochemistry department of the Washington University School of Medicine in St. Louis. Merck recruited him in 1975 to revive its research and development operations. Vagelos did just that, and in the mid-1980s, while its nearest competitor released only five $100 million products, Merck released thirteen. He became chief executive in 1985 and chairman the following year. After retiring from Merck in 1994, he joined Regeneron Pharmaceuticals, Inc. as chairman of the board.

Former Chairman of Merck-Medco Managed Care: Martin J. Wygod. Martin Wygod became a millionaire before his 30th birthday. Starting out as an analyst on Wall Street, he quit his job to establish his own brokerage with $20,000 from his mother. With the $10 million that he garnered by selling his company at age 29, he began acquiring several small firms in the healthcare field. He sold his collection of companies for $180 million and purchased the mail-order pharmaceutical distributor National Pharmacies in 1983. From there his Medco Containment company became the nation's leading mail-order drug company. Wygod was known for his outspokenness on cost reduction, a quality that rubbed Merck & Co., Medco's new parent, the wrong way. He resigned from the company in 1994, and bought Synetic Inc. later that year. This prompted Merck & Co. to file suit against Wygod in March 1999, charging violation of a non-compete agreement.

Pharmacy benefits management companies (PBMs) evolved in this environment. These companies worked with managed care organizations to suppress the rising costs of pharmaceuticals. They purchased drugs in bulk from the manufacturers, and encouraged doctors to prescribe the least expensive drug in a given class. As managed care systems proliferated, so did PBMs.

By the mid-1990s, pharmaceutical companies were under a two-pronged attack to reduce prices. First, managed care companies wielded more clout than ever before, and were in a position to dictate prices to manufacturers. Second, political pressure from the Clinton Administration posed a threat to their unregulated pricing abilities, a liberty that was not enjoyed by pharmaceutical manufacturers in many other countries.

To protect itself against the pricing limitations it saw as imminent, Merck sought to acquire a PBM, hoping that the benefits it would acquire from a distribution channel would offset any potential losses resulting from price reductions.

Approach and Engagement

On July 28, 1993, Merck and Medco Containment announced their merger agreement. Merck-Medco Managed Care would be the first vertically integrated drug company in the U.S. The $6.6 billion deal would be a stock swap, in which Medco stockholders would receive either $39 or 1.2 Merck shares for each Medco share. Medco's chairman, Martin Wygod, would head the new company, which would become a subsidiary of Merck & Co.

On November 5th, the U.S. Federal Trade Commission approved the deal after investigating it for potential antitrust violations. Shareholders subsequently voted for the merger, and the acquisition was completed later that month. "This allows Merck to manage the entire process, from discovery of the drug right down to delivery to the patients' mouths," commented Richard Vietor, drug industry analyst for Merrill Lynch & Co., in *Chain Drug Review*.

Products and Services

PAID Prescriptions, L.L.C. was Merck-Medco's retail pharmacy program. Operating through the Coordinated Care Network of 55,000 participating retail pharmacies, this operation managed 269 million prescriptions in 1998.

Merck-Medco Rx Services was a mail-order pharmacy service located in nine states: Florida, Massachusetts, Nevada, New Jersey, New York, Ohio, Pennsylvania, Texas, and Washington. In 1998 the number of mail service prescriptions reached 53 million, more than doubling the amount in 1991.

Changes to the Industry

"It's a watershed event for the drug industry," remarked medical industry consultant John Wilkerson in *Forbes*, commenting on the formation of Merck-Medco. His prediction proved correct, as a string of similar transactions soon followed.

In 1994 SmithKline Beecham acquired Diversified Pharmaceutical Services for $2.3 billion, followed by Eli Lilly's purchase of PCS Health Systems for $4.1 billion. Bristol-Myers Squibb entered into a joint venture with the distributor Axion Pharmaceuticals Inc. Pfizer entered into two separate alliances with PBMs, Caremark International Inc. and Value Health Inc., the former of which was also joined by Rhone-Poulenc Rorer.

The SmithKline/Diversified deal cleared Federal Trade Commission (FTC) approval as easily as Merck-Medco had, but as more of the deals came down the pike, the government began subjecting them to closer scrutiny. The third proposed drug maker/PBM merger, Lilly/PCS, was required to consent to several conditions before gaining approval from the FTC. PCS's list of favored drugs must include those offered by Lilly's competitors. The companies must also establish a "fire wall" between them so that the parent company would not have access to the prices of competitors' products.

The FTC exercised its option of enforcing the same conditions on the Merck-Medco and SmithKline Beecham/Diversified deals, retroactively. The General Accounting Office, an investigative unit of Congress, revealed that Merck-Medco had eliminated some competing products from its preferred drug list. A company spokesperson confirmed that Merck products were given preferential treatment in some cases, according to a December 1995 issue of *Chain Drug Review*. The FTC officially required Merck in September 1998 to adopt its guidelines. Merck agreed to the terms, claiming that the agreement was merely a formality since the company had been voluntarily following similar policies for three years.

Review of the Outcome

The clash of cultures between the two merging companies resulted in the resignation of Medco's founder, Martin Wygod. Merck was a traditional, conservative company, and Wygod had instilled in his company a spirit of entrepreneurship and cost-consciousness. When Merck's president and COO resigned in 1993, followed by the retirement of its chairman and CEO, P. Roy Vagelos, Wygod appeared to be next in line for succession to Merck's top positions. Yet in mid-1994 Raymond Gilmartin was selected as Merck's new CEO, and Wygod resigned in frustration.

This would not be the last of the company's involvement with Wygod, however. In March 1999 Merck & Co. filed suit against Wygod and three former Medco executives for violating a non-compete agreement by operating Synetic Inc., a distributor of data between doctors and managed care companies.

Merck exited the mental healthcare business in July 1995 by selling Medco Behavioral Care Corp., the nation's second-largest manager of mental healthcare, to Kohlberg Kravis Roberts & Co. for $340 million. In 1996 Merck-Medco purchased Systemed Pharmacy, a Los Angeles-based PBM. By 1998 Merck-Medco had 51 million members through 1,100 plan sponsor clients. The company managed 322 million prescriptions, an 11% increase over the previous year.

Research

Boroughs, Don L. "Merck's Medicine Man," in *U.S. News & World Report*, 21 February 1994. Profiles Martin Wygod and the challenges that he will face in joining the conservative Merck.

"Investigators Question Merck-Medco Practices," in *Chain Drug Review*, 18 December 1995. Reports the investigation by Congress into Merck-Medco's competitive improprieties.

Laskoski, Gregg. "Let's Make a Deal," in *American Druggist*, June 1994. Discusses the industry trend, initiated by Merck/Medco, of drug companies forming alliances with PBMs.

"Medco Containment Services Inc.," in *Notable Corporate Chronologies*, The Gale Group, 1999. Lists major events in the company's history, through its acquisition by Merck.

"Merck Agrees to Bar Medco from Certain Practices" in *Drug Topics*, 7 September 1998. Provides a brief report on the agreement stuck by Merck and the FTC to separate some aspects of their respective businesses.

"Merck & Co., Inc." in *Notable Corporate Chronologies*, The Gale Group, 1999. Profiles Merck, including its acquisition of Medco.

Merck & Co., Inc., 1998 Annual Report. Covers financial highlights and describes company operating segments.

Merck & Co., Inc. Home Page Available at http://www.merck.com. Official World Wide Web Page for Merck. Includes access to product information, press releases, and investor information.

"Merck-Medco Deal Raises Questions," in *Chain Drug Review*, 3 July 1995. Presents opinions from proponents and detractors of the deal.

Nulty, Peter. "1995 National Business Hall of Fame," in *Fortune*, 3 April 1995. Profiles new inductees to the magazine's Hall of Fame, including P. Roy Vagelos.

Rudnitsky, Howard. "Anticipating Hillary," in *Forbes*, 30 August 1993. Offers an analysis of the upcoming merger and of the industry pressures that inspired it.

Silverman, Edward R. "Merck & Co. Sues Founder of Pharmacy-Benefits Manager Medco," in *Knight-Ridder Tribune Business News*, 25 March 1999. Reports on the suit filed by Merck against Wygod and his new company, Synetic.

KIMBERLY N. STEVENS

MERCK & RHONE-POULENC

Merial Ltd.
27 Knightsbridge
London , SW1
United Kingdom

web: http://www.merial.com

nationality: United Kingdom
date: July 31, 1997
affected: Merck & Co., Inc., USA, founded 1891
affected: Rhone-Poulenc SA, France, founded 1928

Overview of the Merger

In July 1997, Merck & Co. and Rhone-Poulenc combined their animal health and poultry genetics businesses to form Merial Ltd. This company, a joint venture equally owned by the two pharmaceutical companies, immediately became the world's leading business dedicated to the development, manufacture, and marketing of veterinary pharmaceuticals and vaccines.

The joining operations were complementary, yet with little overlap. Rhone-Poulenc's contribution, its Rhone-Merieux subsidiary, was the world's sixth-largest animal health company. It was a global leader in vaccines, and focused primarily on products for the pets sector. Rhone-Merieux enjoyed a strong presence in Europe and the Far East.

Merck & Co. contributed its Merck AgVet subsidiary, which ranked as the world's fourth-largest animal health business. Its strengths were in parasiticides, particularly for the farm animal sector. Geographically, Merck AgVet's presence was limited to the U.S.

History of Merck & Company Inc.

Merck had its roots in the mid-17th century. In 1668 Friedrich Jacob Merck purchased an apothecary in the German town of Darmstadt. The company, which came to be known as E. Merck AG, was passed down through the family's generations for a century and a half before winding up in the hands of Heinrich Emmanuel Merck in 1827. Having studied with the prominent organic chemist Justus von Liebig, Merck applied Liebig's theories for the firm's production of morphine. Its product line expanded, and by 1855 Merck pharmaceutical products were used throughout the world.

In 1887 the chemist Theodore Weicker traveled to the U.S. from Germany to establish an American branch of E. Merck AG. In 1891 the company that would become known as Merck & Company was formed when George Merck, grandson of Heinrich, entered into a partnership with Weicker. George began supplying chemicals and drugs imported from Germany to New York apothecaries. Its product line included chloral hydrate, iodides, and alkaloids. Sales reached $1 million in 1897.

In 1903 the company ventured into chemical and drug production at its plants in New Jersey and St. Louis. The following year, Weicker sold his interest in the company to George Merck, thereby dissolving their partnership. Weicker used his proceeds to purchase a controlling interest in the competing drug company E.R. Squibb. George's business, now known as Merck & Co., expanded its American product line to include morphine, cocaine, bismuths, and iodides. Sales exceeded $2 million in 1905.

With the U.S. entrance into World War I, George Merck was forced in 1917 to break formal ties with his family and with the company E. Merck AG in Germany. The U.S. government seized E. Merck AG's 80% interest in Merck & Co., allowing George to retain his shares. At war's end, the U.S. sold its seized shares to the public.

In 1927 the company merged with Powers-Weightmann-Rosengarten, a Philadelphia-based producer and distributor of pharmaceutical chemicals known for producing the anti-malarial drug quinine. Two years later, sales surpassed $13 million, enabling the company to invest heavily in research and development.

The two Merck firms, in America and in Germany, entered into an agreement in 1932 providing for the exchange of technical information and the division of world sales territories in order to avoid competing with each other. The following year, George Merck established the Merck Institute for Therapeutic Research, and recruited prominent chemists and biologists to work on the production of new pharmaceuticals. The results paid off in 1934, when Merck perfected the synthesis of the newly isolated vitamin B1, gaining the license to produce and sell it.

In 1943 a Merck-funded scientist working at Rutgers University discovered streptomycin, a revolutionary antibiotic used for the treatment of tuberculosis and other infections. Because of the drug's potential importance, Merck chose not to claim exclusive patent rights, although it did become its leading producer. The following year, Merck played a role in the development of cortisone, the first steroid. Originally intended to treat arthritis, the drug ultimately was used to treat such diseases as bronchial asthma and rheumatic fever.

As part of the consent decree of an anti-trust suit, Merck's non-compete agreement with its German counterpart was dissolved in 1945. Soon after, domestic and foreign competition intensified as new prod

The Business

Financials

Revenue (1998): $1.8 billion

Employees (1998): 6,500

SICs / NAICS

sic 2834 - Pharmaceutical Preparations

naics 325412 - Pharmaceutical Preparation Manufacturing

ucts flooded the market. Merck found itself ill prepared to engage in direct selling to individual doctors and dentists.

In 1948 Merck announced its discovery of B12, a new vitamin considered highly effective in the battle against serious anemia. By 1953 exports accounted for about 20% of company sales. That year Merck merged with the pharmaceutical firm and longtime customer Sharp & Dohme. This Philadelphia-based company brought with it a well-established overseas distribution network, which became the basis of the new entity, Merck Sharp & Dohme International.

Merck entered into a joint venture agreement with the Japanese pharmaceutical firm Banyu, forming Nippon Merck-Banyu. In 1958 Merck began the sale of Diuril, an antihypertensive drug that was the first major product in the company's new line of cardiovascular drugs.

The company embarked on a program of diversification in the mid-1960s. Throughout the next several years, the company acquired Calgon Corp., a nationwide provider of water treatment chemicals and services; Baltimore Aircoil, a manufacturer of refrigeration and industrial cooling equipment; and Kelco, a processor of kelp for the production of alginates and specialty chemicals.

Legal troubles began for Merck in the mid-1970s. In 1974 a $35 million lawsuit was filed against Merck and 28 other drug manufacturers and distributors of DES. This drug, a miscarriage preventative prescribed over a twenty-year period, contained a known carcinogen; the defendants were ordered to notify potential victims, provide detection and treatment, and pay billions of dollars in damages. In 1975 the U.S. Securities and Exchange Commission revealed that Merck, along with other U.S. companies, made illegal payments totaling $3.6 million in order to obtain foreign business in 39 African and Middle Eastern countries.

The Officers

President-Directeur General: John Preston

Directeur General: Louis Champel

Directeur General Adjoint: Yves Moreau

Secretaire General: Thierry Descollonges

Finances et Administration: Dominique Takizawa

Commercial International: Max Gauphichon

In 1979 the company's Kelco subsidiary acquired Alginate Industries Ltd. of London. Four years later Merck acquired the Spanish pharmaceutical firm Abello SA. That year it also spent $315 million to acquire a majority share in Nippon Merck-Banyu; this was the first such purchase by any U.S. firm operating in Japan.

Merck divested itself of Baltimore Aircoil in 1985, at the same time acquiring the Italian firm Neopharmed. That year Roy Vagelos, biochemist and head of research, was named CEO. In 1986 the company acquired Vestal Laboratories Inc., a manufacturer of skin care products, disinfectants, and germicides. Merck annual revenues totaled $3.5 billion for the year, ranking it second in sales in the U.S. pharmaceutical industry.

In 1990 the firm bought the nonprescription business of ICI America, maker of Mylanta, whose drugs are marketed through Johnson & Johnson. In 1991 Merck entered into a number of joint ventures. Its agreement with Astra AB of Sweden allowed Merck to distribute most of Astra's products. It created DuPont Merck Pharmaceutical Co. in partnership with E.I. du Pont de Nemours & Co.; it would sell its 50% stake in this venture in 1998 for $2.6 billion.

In 1992 Merck employed 38,000 people, maintained 16 research centers, and operated 47 manufacturing facilities in 18 countries. The following year it acquired Medco Containment Service Inc., the nation's largest pharmacy-benefit services company, for $6 billion. Merck's revenues that year exceeded $10 billion for the first time. It created its first joint venture in China in 1994 by teaming up with Hangzhou East China Pharmaceutical. In 1996 it bought Systemed, a mail-order drug and pharmaceutical benefits management company catering to mid-sized customers, those organizations with fewer than 10,000 members.

In 1997 Merck and Rhone-Poulenc merged their animal health businesses to form Merial Ltd., the largest such operation in the world. That year Merck

also sold its insecticide and fungicide businesses to Novartis AG. Company revenues in 1998 totaled $26.9 billion, with net income reaching $5.2 billion.

History of Rhone-Poulenc SA

In 1858 Etienne Poulenc, a French pharmacist, opened an apothecary in Paris and began to manufacture drugs. At the turn of the century, Poulenc's brothers joined his pharmaceutical business to form Etablissement Poulenc-Freres. This new company soon began working with Comptoir des Textiles Artificielles (CTA). In 1922 the firm acquired May and Baker, a pharmaceutical company based in the U.K.

Meanwhile, in 1895, the Societe Chimiques des Usines du Rhone was formed in Lyon, France, for the manufacture of dyestuffs and perfumes. By the end of the century, German companies dominated the European production of chemicals, particularly dyestuffs, so completely that French companies could not profit. As a result, the Usines du Rhone discontinued its dyestuffs operations and was taken over by French banks. In 1919 Usines du Rhone formed a perfume company in Brazil, Rhodia SA; its Rodo perfume garnered almost 75% of the company's profits. In 1922 CTA and Usines du Rhone merged certain operations to form Rhodiaceta. Through the interactions of both Usines du Rhone and Poulenc-Freres with CTA, the two companies developed close ties.

In 1928 they decided to make it official. Societe des Usine Chimiques Rhone-Poulenc was formed that year through the merger of Societe Chimiques des Usines du Rhone and Etablissement Poulenc-Freres. At the same time, it established two subsidiaries: Prolabo, to develop new ways to make artificial textiles, and Specia, to develop specialty pharmaceuticals. The following year, however, worldwide economic difficulties forced Rhone-Poulenc to reduce its number of labs to two and its factories to three.

By the end of World War II, Rhone-Poulenc had suffered from the German occupation and the ensuing supply limitations. Despite the diminished research and development of the previous years, it produced nylon and became the first French company to produce penicillin. In 1953 it began the manufacture of its products in the U.S. Three years later it acquired a health products company, Theraplix.

In 1961 the company established a holding company, Rhone-Poulenc SA, to oversee the operations of its various subsidiaries. In the late 1960s it made several acquisitions: Pechiney-Saint-Gobain, maker of agricultural and basic chemicals; Progil, a chemical company; a 50% interest in Institut Merieux; and a majority stake in the research facility Laboratoire

Roger Bellon. By 1969 Rhone-Poulenc was the largest company in France, and the following year it became the third-largest chemical company in Europe.

In the early 1970s, France's high tariffs limited foreign expansion. Though the company tried to expand globally, its efforts proved ill timed, as little market share was left for which to compete. To add to Rhone-Poulenc's financial woes, the French government's attempts to decrease inflation were detrimental to business, and forced the company to lay off 20,000 employees.

By the latter part of the decade, the company had recovered. In 1979 its U.S. subsidiary, Rhone-Poulenc Inc., acquired 58% of Anken Industries. Two years later, Rhone-Poulenc purchased P.B.U.S.A. Co. and the agricultural chemicals business of Mobil Chemical Corp. In October of that year, the Socialist Mitterand party gained control of the French government and began to nationalize most of the country's companies. When Rhone-Poulenc was nationalized in 1982, the new French government installed Loik Le Floch-Prigent as its chairman. This year the company increased its revenues by making a number of acquisitions. But due to continued unprofitability, it lost its status as the country's largest chemical company. It later discontinued the production of fertilizers and petrochemicals.

In 1983 Floch-Prigent returned profitability to the company for the first time in four years by reducing the workforce and eliminating ailing operations. Two years later Siltec Corp., in which Rhone-Poulenc owned stock, agreed to make silicon wafers with Rhone-Poulenc. It also entered into a joint venture with Mitsui Petrochemical for the manufacture of computer boards.

Jean-Rene Fourtou replaced Floch-Prigent as chairman in 1986. The company's farm chemicals business improved through the acquisition of the agri-chemicals business of Union Carbide Corp. The following year, the company acquired the industrial chemicals business of Stauffer, and Fourtou began advocating privatization. In 1989 net income exceeded FrF 3 billion on sales greater than FrF 73 billion.

In 1990 the company purchased 66% of Rhone-Poulenc Rorer Inc., a merger of R-P's human pharmaceuticals business with U.S.-based pharmaceuticals company, the Rorer Group Inc. This acquisition increased Rhone-Poulenc's North American sales with such products as Maalox, the world's best selling antacid. The following year it formed Pateur Merieux Serums et Vaccins, a joint venture with Merck & Co. for the manufacture of children's multi-vaccines. The company continued a divestiture program of non-core businesses. In 1991 alone its divestitures brought in

more than $700 million. By 1992 Rhone-Poulenc was the world's eighth-largest chemical company, as well as France's largest chemical and veterinary pharmaceutical company.

In December 1993 Rhone-Poulenc became privatized when the French government sold its majority interest. Earlier that year the company had expanded into biotechnology by purchasing 37% of Applied Immune Science in a joint research venture in cell and gene therapy. In 1994 the company acquired Cooperation Pharmaceutique Francaise, the nation's second-largest over-the-counter drug distributor. In 1995 its Rhone-Merieux subsidiary acquired Sanofi's animal health activities in North American, South America, and Asia.

On July 31, 1997, Rhone-Poulenc merged Rhone-Merieux with Merck & Co.'s animal health business to form the world's leader in animal health and poultry genetics. Later that year it acquired full ownership of Rhone-Poulenc Rorer for FrF 27 billion. By the end of 1997, Rhone-Poulenc generated net sales of FrF 90 billion and had a workforce of 68,377.

In January 1998, the company formed Rhodia, one of the world's leaders in specialty chemicals, by combining its chemical operations with its fibers and polymers businesses. It operated in two main businesses: Life Sciences, comprised of pharmaceuticals and animal health units, and Specialty Chemicals, operating as Rhodia. In December of that year, it announced a proposed merger with Hoescht AG to form Aventis SA, expected to be the world's largest life sciences company. In December 1998, the two companies evaluated the feasibility of speeding up the proposed merger to consummate it sometime in 1999, rather than the planned completion target date of 2001.

Market Forces Driving the Merger

The pharmaceutical industry during the mid-1990s was marked by rapid consolidation. Pressures of patent expiry and rising research and development (R&D) costs encouraged companies to engage in mergers, acquisitions, and joint ventures. An alliance would provide ther resources to increase R&D and marketing efforts, while reducing administrative and distribution expenses. By entering into such a deal, a company could propel itself up the ranks of the industy leaders much more quickly than it could by investing resources to expand its current operations.

Both Merck and Rhone-Poulenc were facing impending patent expiry. One such patent, for Merck's Ivermectin animal health drug, was scheduled to expire in 1997. Upon expiration of a patent, competitors became permitted to introduce their own version of the product, thereby reducing the sales for the original patent holder. Lost revenue must be offset by some other source, and a pooling of interests with an ally often provided an attractive avenue.

Approach and Engagement

On December 19, 1996, Merck & Co. and Rhone-Poulenc signed a letter of intent to merge their animal health and poultry genetics businesses by establishing Merial Ltd. The new company would be a 50-50 joint venture based in England. With revenues of about $1.7 billion, it would be the world's leader in animal health. Dr. John Preston, president of Merck AgVet, would become chairman, while Louis Champel, president of Rhone-Merieux, would assume the role of CEO. Merial would be vertically integrated, and responsible for the discovery, manufacture, and marketing of drugs and vaccines for animals.

Merck & Co. would contribute Merck AgVet, including its research, sales, and marketing activities. Rhone-Poulenc's subsidiary, Rhone-Merieux, would bring its R&D, manufacturing, and sales and marketing operations.

Both parent companies would also contribute their poultry genetics businesses. Rhone-Merieux's ISA-Babcock subsidiary would combine with Merck's Hubbard Broiler and British United Turkeys. The resulting operation, Hubbard-ISA, would have revenues of $330 million, making it the global leader in that sector.

In return, Merial would provide its parents companies with production and research developments, including any innovative compounds or technologies.

On July 3, 1997, the European Commission approved the alliance. On July 31, the joint venture was created, and on August 1, 1997, it began operations as Merial Ltd.

Products and Services

Merial's product line included the following brands: Aftobov, a vaccine against foot-and-mouth disease in cattle; Cryomarex, a vaccine against Marek's disease in chickens; Eurican, a combined vaccine associating valences against diseases in young dogs; Eurifel, a combined vaccine associating the chlamydia valence for cats; Eqvalan, an internal antiparasitic for horses; Frontline, an external antiparasitic for cats and dogs; Geskypur, a vaccine against Aujeszky's disease in pigs; Heartgard, and antiparasitic against dirofilariosis in cats and dogs; Ivomec, an internal and external antiparasitic for production animals; Ivomec Eprinex, an internal and external

antiparasitic for cattle; Ketofen Cattle, and anti-inflammatory for cattle; Mucobovin, a vaccine against mucous membrane disease in cattle; Nemovac, a vaccine against infestious head-swelling syndrome in poultry; Rabisin, a vaccine against rabies; and Raboral, a recombinant caccine against rabies in wild animals. Additionally, Merial also produced a Lyme disease vaccine.

Review of the Outcome

Merial immediately captured a 13% share of the $10.7 billion global animal health market. At the end of 1997, its revenues totaled FrF 10.1 billion ($1.7 billion). The company's 6,500 employees worked in 150 different countries, and Merial operated 17 research facilities around the globe. It was the world's leader in veterinary biology, offering a comprehensive line of pharmaceuticals and vaccines to treat and prevent diseases afflicting a number of animal species, including cattle, chickens, pigs, horses, dogs, and cats, as well as wild animals. Merial was also the global leader in poultry genetics, covering meat-producing chickens, laying hens, and turkeys.

In April 1998, Merial announced the sale of its Canadian producer of animal antibacterials and feed-stuffs, J. Webster Laboratories, in order to focus on its pharmaceutical and vaccine businesses. That year, its first full year of operation, Merial generated revenues of $1.8 billion. This increase over the previous year was largely attributable to its Frontline flea and tick combatant, which experienced a 70% jump in sales to capture a 27% share of the U.S. market.

Research

"Commission Green Light for Merial Joint Venture," in *European Report*, 5 July 1997. The proposed joint venture receives approval from the European Commission.

Kamm, Thomas, and Robert Langreth. "Merck, Rhone-Poulenc Agree to Combine Animal-Health Lines, Taking Top Spot," in *The Wall Street Journal*, 20 December 1996. Provides details on the newly-announced merger.

"Merck & Co. Inc.," in *In Vivo*, January 1997. Briefly discusses the companies' contributions to their upcoming joint venture.

"Merck & Co. Inc." in *Notable Corporate Chronologies*, The Gale Group, 1999. Profiles Merck beyond the formation of Merial.

"Rhone-Poulenc and Merck Merge Units," in *Chemical Week*, 19 January 1997. Describes Merial in terms of the strengths of its contributing businesses.

"Rhone-Poulenc SA," in *Notable Corporate Chronologies*, The Gale Group, 1999. Lists major events in the company's history, through its establishment of Merial.

Rhone-Poulenc SA, 1997 Annual Report. Details the company's finances and operating segments.

"R-P, Merck Join Animal Health Units," in *Chemical Market Reporter*, 23 December 1996. Discusses the strengths that Merial will acquire from Rhone-Merieux and Merck AgVet.

Smith, Rod. "Merck, Rhone-Poulenc Set to Complete Animal Health Merger," in *Feedstuffs*, 21 July 1997. Describes the finalized merger deal, including a brief discussion on the combined poultry genetics operations.

"U.S.: Merial's 1998 Turnover," in *Les Echos*, 1 March 1999. Provides year-end financial results for Merial.

—KIMBERLY N. STEVENS

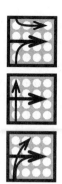

MESA PETROLEUM & CITIES SERVICE

Pioneer Natural Resources Co.
1400 Williams Sq. W.
5205 N. O'Connor Blvd.
Irving, TX 75039-3746
USA

tel: (972)444-9001
fax: (972)969-3559
web: http://www.pioneernrc.com

Citgo Petroleum Corp.
One Warren Place
6100 S. Yale Ave.
Tulsa, OK 74136
USA

tel: (918)495-4000
fax: (918)495-4511
web: http://www.citgo.com

nationality: USA
date: June 1982 (canceled)
affected: Pioneer Natural Resources Co. (formerly Mesa Petroleum Co.), USA, founded 1956
affected: Citgo Petroleum Corp. (formerly Cities Service Co.), USA, founded 1910

Overview of the Merger

In the late 1970s, Mesa Petroleum Co. began eyeing Cities Service Co., the 19th-largest oil firm—20 times the size of Mesa—and the 38th-largest industrial business in the U.S., as a potential acquisition target. Management at Cities Service got wind of the deal, and the larger firm launched a $17 per share bid in May of 1982 for Mesa before the smaller company had a chance to make its planned hostile offer. The preemptive move marked the first use of what came to be known as the "Pac-Man" defense, in which a firm faced with a hostile bidder defended itself by attempting to purchase that suitor.

Although Mesa did make a $45 per share bid for 15% of Cities Service, which would have upped its stake in the firm to 20%, Gulf Oil outbid Mesa with a friendly $63 per share offer for Cities Service in June. Shortly thereafter Gulf pulled out of the deal, prompting Cities Service to file a lawsuit that wasn't resolved until the late 1990s. By the end of the year, Occidental Petroleum had purchased Cities Service for $4.3 billion, becoming the 12th-largest oil company in the U.S.

History of Mesa Petroleum Co.

After resigning from Phillips Petroleum Co. in 1956, geologist T. Boone Pickens founded Petroleum Exploration in 1956. Eight years later, Pickens merged his new firm with the Canadian firm Altair Oil and Gas to form Mesa Petroleum Co. That year, Mesa conducted its initial public offering. The company spent the next decade and a half growing via both exploration and acquisition. In 1979, Mesa created a royalty trust and spun it off to shareholders; as a result, the firm's oil and gas profits were dispersed to shareholders free of corporate profit tax.

In the early 1980s, sales reached $400 million, and Mesa prepared to launch a hostile bid for the much larger Cities Service Co. That deal was thwarted when Cities Service countered with a bid of its own for Mesa, and then accepted a higher offer from Gulf Oil Corp. in a deal that later crumbled. Although Mesa walked away from the Cities Service defeat with a $30 million profit, it soon found itself struggling due to costs related to its intense level of exploration in the Gulf of Mexico. A battle in 1983 for Gulf Oil ended in favor of Chevron Corp., but Mesa earned a $300 million profit on the deal. In late 1984, Mesa began purchasing stock in Phillips Petroleum. Although efforts to take over that firm failed also, Pickens was able to sell his stock back to the firm for another hefty profit.

Mesa's performance began slipping in the late 1980s as natural gas prices tumbled, and the firm began divesting assets. A public offering in 1994 raised $93 million in capital, but growing shareholder dissent led the firm's board of directors to propose the creation of a panel of outside directors. Recognizing Mesa's vulnerability to a hostile takeover, the board adopted a poison pill, which would become active in the event that an investor or group of investors gained more than 10% of the firm's stock. The pill would allow shareholders—aside from the aggressor(s)—to buy common shares at a 50% discount.

By 1996, debt had swelled to $1.2 billion and stock prices were hovering at roughly $2.50 per share, compared to an earlier high of $68.75 per share. Investor Richard Rainwater bought $133 million in stock of the nearly bankrupt Mesa and offered to double that amount in return for four board seats. Pickens reluctantly stepped down, turning his firm over to a new management team. Jon Brumley took over as chairman and CEO.

Brumley launched plans for a $150 million equity offering in 1997. Early that year, Mesa bought Greenhill Petroleum Corp. for $270 million, as well as natural gas assets from MAPCO Inc. In April, Parker and Parsley Development Co. and Mesa completed a $1.9 billion merger to form Pioneer Natural Resources Corp. After oil and gas prices bottomed out, the new firm took an $863 million write down, resulting in a loss of nearly $900 million for the fourth quarter of 1997. A deal in 1998 to sell 425 of its 450 U.S. oil and gas reserves to Costilla Energy fell through, but Prize Energy emerged as a buyer in 1999, agreeing to pay $245 million for 400 U.S. fields.

History of Cities Service Co.

Henry L. Doherty founded Cities Service Co. in 1910 as a holding company comprised of three large firms: Denver Gas and Electric, Spokane Gas and Fuel, and Empire District Electric. The new firm grew by purchasing smaller gas utility operations across the U.S., and in 1913, the firm acquired 53 utilities firms. A gas shortage prompted Cities Service to move into exploration in 1915.

After a unit of Cities Service discovered oil in El Dorado, Kansas, the firm established Empire Gas and Fuel to oversee oil production. Within two years, 1,000 wells were in operation. Cities Service served the military effort in World War I by upping its oil production

The Business

Financials - Pioneer Natural Resources Co.

Revenue (1998): $711.5 million

Employees (1998): 1,016

Financials - Citgo Petroleum Corp.

Revenue (1998): $10.9 billion

Employees (1998): 4,500

SICs / NAICS

sic 1311 - Crude Petroleum & Natural Gas

naics 211111 - Crude Petroleum and Natural Gas Extraction

for the tanks and aircraft that ran on the fuel. By the war's end, the company operated seven refineries, and oil refining and production had become one of its major activities. Gas utilities spanned 20 states, and electric utilities customers numbered 144,000.

As the automotive industry took off in the 1920s, so did demand for petroleum. Although the Great Depression took a toll on the firm, utilities operations kept it afloat during the 1930s. The Public Utilities Act of 1935 ordered all utility holding companies to divest all but one public utility, and Cities Service began selling off its utility subsidiaries. During World War II, Cities Services operated its own tanker fleet, including 13 of its own ships and 18 government-owned oil tankers. The company also began production on what eventually became one of the world's largest oil refineries, in Louisiana.

By the end of the 1950s, Cities Service had completely exited the utilities sector and refocused on oil and gas. The firm adopted the Citgo brand name in 1960s and launched Citgo Premium gasoline. The chaotic 1970s, due to conflict in the Middle East, and a worldwide recession in the early 1980s left Cities Service vulnerable to a takeover. A hostile bid by Mesa Petroleum in 1982 was thwarted when Cities Service agreed to a higher offer from Gulf Oil Corp. When Gulf Oil pulled out of the deal, citing prohibitive Federal Trade Commission hurdles, Cities Service filed suit for damages and eventually won the case several years later. In December of 1982, Occidental Petroleum Corp. paid $4.3 billion for Cities Service to become the 12th-largest oil concern in the U.S. Cities Service began operating as a wholly owned subsidiary of Occidental.

The Officers

Pioneer Natural Resources Co.

Chairman: Jon Brumley

President and CEO: Scott D. Sheffield

Chief Financial Officer and Exec. VP, Finance: M. Garrett Smith

Exec. VP, Worldwide Exploration: Mel Fischer

Exec. VP: Dennis E. Fagerstone

Citgo Petroleum Corp.

Chairman: Luis Urdaneta

President and CEO: David J. Tippeconnic

Exec. VP: Roberto V. Mandini

Sr. VP and Chief Financial Officer: Ezra Hunt

Sr. VP, Supply and Marketing: W.A. Devore

In 1983, Occidental combined the oil refining and marketing units of Cities Service into Citgo Petroleum Corp., which was sold to Southland Corp. Three years later, Southland sold 50% of Citgo to Petroleos de Venezuela, S.A., the Venezuelan state-owned oil company, for $300 million. When Citgo paid $661 million for the remaining 50% of its own stock in January 1990, Petroleos de Venezuela gained full control of the firm. The following year, Petroleos de Venezuela folded its other U.S. unit, Champlin Refining and Chemicals, Inc., into Citgo; the subsidiary was eventually named PDV American, of which Citgo remained operating company.

Market Forces Driving the Merger

The $3.6 billion deal between Belridge Oil Co. and Shell Oil Co. in 1979 ignited the fervent wave of consolidation seen by the oil industry in the 1980s. That deal was soon followed by the battle for Conoco Inc., which was eventually settled in September of 1981, when DuPont Co. paid $7.8 billion for Conoco, completing the largest deal in U.S. corporate history. The motivation for these deals stemmed from a reduced reliance on U.S.-based oil during the 1970s that led to unprecedented price hikes in oil. The increased cash flow that major companies realized during the early 1970s—the result of the increased prices—along with forecasts of future oil shortages, led to an intense scrambling for new oil reserves.

Mesa Petroleum CEO Pickens believed it was cheaper to buy new reserves by acquiring large companies than to explore for new oil. Cities Service had appeared an attractive target to Pickens since the late 1970s, mainly because of its 10.6 million unexplored acres, 300 million bbl. in oil reserves, and three trillion cubic ft. in gas reserves. The firm had also become increasingly vulnerable. During the latter half of the decade, Cities Service had seen its reserves decrease by roughly 20% despite increased funding of exploration. As a result, its stock had languished in the mid-30 range, leaving the board of directors, as well as shareholders, dissatisfied. In 1981, Cities Services lost $49 million, despite a 50% increase in its oil prices in the U.S. By contrast, Mesa Petroleum had earned $106 million on sales of $407 million. While Pickens didn't claim he could prevent the dwindling of reserves, he asserted that the firm could be better managed as a means of increasing shareholder value.

Approach and Engagement

Mesa began acquiring shares of Cities Service in the late 1970s. By May of 1982, the smaller firm owned a 5% stake in its target, and CEO Pickens had lined up four partners who were willing to invest a total of up to $1 billion in a takeover of Cities Service. However, before Mesa could proceed with its hostile offer, planned for June 4, Cities Service launched a surprise $17 per share bid for Mesa on May 28. Two days later, Mesa counterbid $50 per share for Cities Service by making an offer subject to the approval of Cities Service's board of directors. Concerned that the massive debt that Mesa needed to assume to pull off a deal of this scope would lead Pickens to sell off assets after gaining control, the board rejected his offer.

By making its offer first, Cities Service had positioned itself at an advantage; at the time, federal law required a 20-day waiting period for all tender offers, meaning that Cities Service could purchase Mesa two days before Mesa could purchase Cities Service. The bid by the targeted firm for its attacker, later coined the "Pac-Man" defense, became a standard defensive tactic employed by firms engaged in hostile takeover battles.

After Cities Service launched its bid, Mesa's largest investor pulled out of the deal, leaving Pickens grappling to find enough cash for a tender offer. Instead of tendering for all of Cities Service's outstanding stock, Mesa announced a $45 per share bid for 15% of Cities Service. "Given the steep premium over the market price for Cities stock, more than 15 percent of the shareholders might very well tender their shares to Mesa. If that happened, Pickens would have a powerful lever to raise additional cash. Moreover, Mesa would argue that the tender offer was a referendum on incumbent management's performance," explained Bruce Wasserstein in *Big Deal: The Battle for Control of America's Leading Corporations.*

On June 17, Gulf Oil stepped in and offered $63 per share for Cities Service. Realizing that the price was simply too high for him to top, Pickens relented. Later that month, he sold his shares in Cities back to the firm for $55 each, realizing a profit of $30 million.

Products and Services

By the late 1990s, Mesa had merged with Parker and Parsley Development Co. to form Pioneer Natural Resources Corp., an oil and gas exploration firm with 762 million barrels of oil reserves. Pioneer operated mainly in the Gulf Coast, the Permian Basin, and the Midcontinent. Exploration and production also took place in Argentina, Canada, Gabon, and South Africa.

Cities Service, later known as Citgo Petroleum, operated 14,000 independent retail gasoline stations in the U.S. Along with gasoline, the firm refined and marketed jet fuel, diesel fuel, lubricants, heating oils, and waxes. Citgo also operated asphalt refineries in New Jersey and Georgia and crude oil refineries in Louisiana and Texas.

Changes to the Industry

Although Mesa's first run at a major acquisition had ended in failure, the firm secured a $30 million profit for itself when it sold its shares in Cities Service back to the firm. More importantly, CEO Pickens had learned a great deal about maneuvering through a hostile takeover battle. While he never won a major deal, he was able to bring several large firms, including Gulf Oil and Phillips Petroleum, to their knees and fund Mesa's growth with the profits he earned in the wake of his negotiations.

Review of the Outcome

Cities Service faltered in August of 1982 after Gulf Oil rescinded its $63 per share offer for the firm. Mesa Petroleum's attack had exposed Cities Service's shortcomings, and the firm's options were scant. According to an August 1982 article in *The Washington Post*, the company had little choice but to "sell out to another firm—at fire-sale prices—or to sell its assets piecemeal and go out of business." Cities Service filed suit against Gulf Oil for damages related to the $225.5 million it paid to Mesa to repurchase its own shares after the deal with Gulf was announced.

In December of 1982, Occidental Petroleum paid $53 per share for Cities Service, which began operating under the Citgo name as a wholly owned subsidiary of Occidental. What was once a base of 22,500 employees at Cities Service was slashed to a mere 4,000.

The Players

Chairman and CEO of Mesa Petroleum Co.: T. Boone Pickens. Legendary corporate raider T. Boone Pickens graduated from college with a geology degree in the early 1950s. After spending four years at Phillips Petroleum, he left to start his own firm, parlaying his initial $2,500 investment into a firm pulling in annual revenues of $400 million by the early 1980s. Pickens earned his fame by speaking out against oil executives, who he felt were more concerned with perks than producing value for shareholders, and by launching takeover attacks on firms he criticized for being poorly managed. While his bids for companies like Cities Service, Gulf Oil, and Phillips Petroleum in the 1980s never came to fruition, Pickens quite often found his pockets lined with significant profits when white knight suitors came calling and he sold his stock back the firms for cash. Dissident shareholders eventually forced Pickens out of his own firm, which had neared bankruptcy in the mid-1990s.

Chairman and CEO of Cities Service Co.: Charles J. Waidelich. Oil executive Charles Waidelich was named president of Cities Service in 1971. By the time the firm was locked in a battle for control with Mesa Petroleum in the early 1980s, he had succeeded Robert V. Seller as chairman and CEO. Waidelich successfully defended his firm against Mesa Petroleum by inking an agreement to be acquired by Gulf Oil in August of 1982. After that deal dissolved, Waidelich began searching for a new buyer. When Occidental Petroleum acquired Cities Service in December of 1982, Waidelich resigned.

Chevron Corp., which acquired Gulf Oil in 1985, was fined $700 million in 1996 after a jury decided that Gulf Oil should pay $228.9 million plus interest to Cities Service for nixing its merger plans with the firm. Although Chevron appealed the verdict, a trial court upheld the damages award in March of 1999.

Research

"Chevron Files Final Brief in Cities Service Case," in *PR Newswire*, 11 May 1999. Explains the outcome of the lawsuit filed by Cities Service after Gulf Oil backed out of a merger agreement in 1982.

Citgo Petroleum Co. Home Page, available at http://www.citgo.com. Official World Wide Web Home

Page for Citgo Petroleum Co. Includes press releases, as well as financial, product, and investor information.

"Citgo Petroleum Co.," in *International Directory of Company Histories*, Vol. 4, St. James Press, 1991. Details the history of Citgo Petroleum Co.

Cole, Robert J. "Mesa Wins in Court and Bid for Cities Service Advances," in *The New York Times*, 17 June 1982. Describes Mesa's bid for Cities Service.

"Mesa Locks Horns with Cities Service," in *Business Week*, 14 June 1982. Offers an in-depth look at the battle for control between Mesa Petroleum and Cities Service.

"Mesa Petroleum: Despite Defeat, It Still Hankers to Take Over an Oil Giant," in *Business Week*, 25 October 1982. Discusses Mesa Petroleum's plans after its bid for Cities Service was thwarted by Gulf Oil.

Pioneer Natural Resources Co. Home Page, available at http://www.pioneernrc.com. Official World Wide Web Home Page for Pioneer Natural Resources Co. Includes financial, product, historical, and employment information, as well as annual reports.

Potts, Mark. "Occidental May Make New Cities Service Bid," in *The Washington Post*, 18 August 1982. Discusses the struggles of Cities Service after Gulf Oil ended plans to take over the firm.

Wasserstein, Bruce. *Big Deal: The Battle for Control of America's Leading Corporations*, Warner Books, 1998. Offers an overview of the largest mergers in recent American corporate history.

Zellner, Wendy. "T. Boone Pickens is Down, But He Swears He Isn't Out," in *Business Week*, 18 February 1991. Discusses the struggles of Mesa Petroleum in the early-1990s.

Zipf, Peter. "Mesa Triumphant in New Pioneer Firm: Merger With Parker & Parsley Completes Turnaround," in *Platt's Oilgram News*, 8 April 1997. Discusses the activities of Mesa Petroleum in the mid-1990s.

ANNAMARIE L. SHELDON

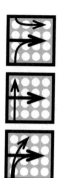

MESA PETROLEUM & PHILLIPS PETROLEUM

date: December 23, 1984 (canceled)

affected: Pioneer Natural Resources Co. (formerly Mesa Petroleum Co.), USA, founded 1956

affected: Phillips Petroleum Co., USA, founded 1903

Pioneer Natural Resources Co.
1400 Williams Sq. W.
5205 N. O'Connor Blvd.
Irving, TX 75039-3746
USA

tel: (972)444-9001
fax: (972)969-3559
web: http://www.pioneernrc.com

Phillips Petroleum Co.
4th and Keeler Streets
Bartlesville, OK 74004
USA

tel: (918)661-6600
fax: (918)661-6279
web: http://www.phillips66.com

Overview of the Acquisition

The takeover attempt for Phillips Petroleum was one of a string of hostile bids launched by T. Boone Pickens and his Mesa Petroleum Co. during the 1980s. The battle was brief, being both initiated and concluded in December 1984. Phillips averted the takeover by paying Mesa to drop its attempt, but its respite was short-lived. Unhappy with the deal that Phillips had cut with Mesa, Carl Icahn, a large shareholder of Phillips, launched his own takeover of Phillips in early 1985. He, too, terminated his attack upon payment by Phillips. These two deals left Phillips loaded with debt, which required several years of streamlining to reduce.

History of Mesa Petroleum Co.

T. Boone Pickens resigned from Phillips Petroleum in 1956 to establish his own oil firm, Petroleum Exploration, with $2,500 in capitalization. The Texas-based company remained independent until 1964, when it merged with Altair Oil and Gas, a Canadian company, to form Mesa Petroleum Co. The new concern went public that same year, gaining access to the capital needed to embark on exploration and acquisition ventures.

The 1980s brought Mesa fame and fortune. In May 1982, having accumulated a 5% stake in Cities Service Co., Mesa launched a hostile takeover of the much larger oil company. Before its offense was fully mobilized, however, Cities caught wind of the proposed bid and turned the tables on Mesa. By using the Pac-Man defense, Cities launched a takeover attempt for its suitor. Cities dropped this counterattack in June, when it agreed to be acquired by Gulf Oil Corp. This deal garnered Mesa a $30 million profit from the sale of its stake in Cities.

Mesa provoked a similar battle later that year by launching a bid for General American Oil Co. (GAO). Phillips Petroleum ultimately gained control of GAO, and Mesa walked away with a $45 million profit from its GAO stock. Mesa again repeated this performance in 1983 by bidding for Gulf Oil. When Chevron Corp. played the role of white knight, Mesa earned $500 million by selling its accumulated stake in Gulf. In another attempt to take over a large oil company, Mesa

The Business

Financials - Pioneer Natural Resources Co.

Revenue (1998): $711.5 million

Employees (1998): 1,016

Financials - Phillips Petroleum Co.

Revenue (1998): $11.8 billion

Employees (1998): 17,300

SICs / NAICS

sic 1311 - Crude Petroleum & Natural Gas

sic 1321 - Natural Gas Liquids

sic 1381 - Drilling Oil & Gas Wells

sic 5541 - Gasoline Service Stations

naics 211111 - Crude Petroleum and Natural Gas Extraction

naics 211112 - Natural Gas Liquid Extraction

naics 213111 - Drilling Oil and Gas Wells

naics 447110 - Gasoline Stations with Convenience Stores

launched a bid for Pickens' previous employer and bidding rival, Phillips Petroleum. That attempt also failed, but Mesa made a handsome profit.

In 1985, Pickens launched an attempt for Unocal Corp., and for the first time was thwarted without gaining a substantial profit. The steps taken by Unocal and its chairman, Fred Hartley, in fending off Pickens resulted in the Unocal Standard, a ruling that redefined the scope of defensive measures permissible against a hostile attack.

The close of the 1980s brought an end to Mesa's takeover bent. Natural gas prices were declining, forcing the company to divest various assets in order to remain solvent. A stock offering that brought in $93 million in 1994 did little to quell shareholder dissatisfaction. By then the company that had made headlines for launching hostile takeover attempts found itself vulnerable to being on the receiving end of such an attack.

In 1996, Mesa's debt load was $1.2 billion and its stock price languished at $2.50, a fraction of its previous high of $68.75. Richard Rainwater invested $133 million in Mesa that year, pledging to double that amount in exchange for four seats on the company's board. Dissident shareholders welcomed this deal, forcing Pickens out of the company in favor of a new management team.

John Brumley, Mesa's new chairman and CEO, planned a $150 million equity offering in 1997. The company returned to an acquisition strategy, but focused on smaller, less hostile deals. It paid $270 million for Greenhill Petroleum Corp. and then purchased the natural gas operations of MAPCO Inc. Pioneer Natural Resources Corp. was formed by the April 1997 merger of Mesa with Parker and Parsley Development Co.

History of Phillips Petroleum Company

Banker brothers Frank Phillips and L.E. Phillips established the Anchor Oil and Gas Company (AOGC) in 1903 in Bartlesville, Oklahoma. The new company's first two wells came up dry, but the third one produced, beginning a long string of successful drilling. Two years later, as it began showing a profit, AOGC sought to make commercial use of natural gas, a by-product of oil drilling that most drillers considered useless and simply burned at the well.

The Phillips brothers decided to leave the oil business in 1917, but the entry of the U.S. into World War I caused the price of crude oil to rise by 250%, so they reincorporated AOGC as the Phillips Petroleum Co. The company started out with 27 employees and assets worth $3 million. Phillips won a patent infringement suit against Union Carbide in 1926, gaining full rights to its process for separating hydrocarbon compounds and further stimulating its research into the commercial possibilities of natural gas. By the following year, Phillips operated more than 2,000 wells in Texas and Oklahoma, producing 55,000 barrels of oil per day, and controlled assets valued at $266 million.

In 1927, the company opened its first refinery in Borger, Texas, and its first gas station in Wichita, Kansas. It used the brand name Phillips 66 for its gas stations as a tribute to Highway 66, as well as claims of the speed that cars could attain by using this product.

In 1930, it acquired the Independent Oil & Gas Co., owned by Wade Phillips, the third Phillips brother. The acquisition greatly expanded the company's refinery and retailing capacities. Phillips also pioneered the commercial use of liquified petroleum gas and began work to prove that different petroleum products could be sent over the same pipeline. Two years later it developed new processes for manufacturing carbon black and butadiene, two ingredients of synthetic rubber. Demand for synthetic rubber products increased when Japan cut off U.S. supply of natural rubber during World War II.

Phillips diversified into foreign oil exploration after the war, purchasing land and mineral rights in

Venezuela, Canada, and Colombia. It established the Phillips Chemical Co. in 1948, and three years later Phillips' chemists discovered Marlex, a chemical compound that serves as a building block for many modern plastics. The first commercial use of the new product was in the manufacture of hula hoops.

The company expanded its network of gas stations beyond the Midwest, opening outlets in Texas and Louisiana in 1952. That year it became the first company to acquire approval to drill for oil in Alaska, and in 1962, in conjunction with three other petroleum companies, Phillips drilled the first offshore oil wells in Alaska. By 1955, its assets were valued at $931 million, with natural gas reserves of 13.3 trillion cubic feet.

By 1967, Phillips operated gas stations in all 50 states. That year William Keeler, a Chief of the Cherokee Nation, became president. He strove to reduce Phillips' dependence on outside sources of oil, stressing acquisition of crude oil producers and increased exploration efforts. Earnings reached a peak of $164 million, but began a steady decline in the coming years.

The company made an unsuccessful attempt to purchase the American Petroleum Corp., a major producer of crude oil, in 1969. The next year it joined other U.S. petroleum producing companies in forming Alyeska Pipeline Service Co. to build the Trans-Alaska pipeline linking the oil fields at Prudhoe Bay with the port of Valdez.

An energy crisis in 1973 touched off a worldwide rise in petroleum prices, causing greatly increased production costs in chemical industries. Phillips divested itself of its service stations in the Northeast and instituted strict controls on corporate planning to improve performance of its chemical subsidiaries. Also that year the company was fined $30,000 for making illegal campaign contributions to Richard Nixon.

In 1975, it sold its remaining West Coast holdings to the Oil Shale Corp., and created Phillips Coal Co. Three years later it sold its interest in Pacific Petroleums Ltd., a holding company for its Canadian oil equity interests. By the end of the decade, its strategy of seeking new reserves outside the U.S. backfired, as the Iranian revolution cut off the company's holdings in that country in 1979.

William Douce became president in 1980. Two years later Phillips acquired substantial new reserves, uncovering an oil field off the California coast in conjunction with Chevron. The next year it purchased General American Oil Co. for $1.1 billion.

The Officers

Pioneer Natural Resources Co.

Chairman: Jon Brumley

President and CEO: Scott D. Sheffield

Chief Financial Officer and Exec. VP, Finance: M. Garrett Smith

Exec. VP, Worldwide Exploration: Mel Fischer

Exec. VP: Dennis E. Fagerstone

Phillips Petroleum Co.

Chairman and CEO: Wayne W. Allen

President and COO: James J. Mulva

Exec. VP, Human Resources, Capital Budgeting and Services: C.L. Bowerman

Exec. VP: K.L. Hedrick

Exec. VP: B.Z. Parker

Corporate raider T. Boone Pickens launched a hostile takeover of Phillips in 1984, withdrawing only when the company bought out his interest. The following year Carl Icahn attempted a hostile takeover of his own, again bowing out only at great expense to Phillips. In 1985, with an enormous debt load as a result of these two battles, Phillips focused on aggressive debt reduction. The company divested itself of Aminoil and Geyser Geothermal in 1986.

These efforts enabled Phillips to record earnings of $650 million in 1988. Its recovery stalled the following year, however, when its plastics plant in Pasadena, Texas, exploded, killing 23, causing $500 million in damage, and halting the company's production of polyethylene. Net profits fell to $219 million. In response, it reduced its workforce by 9,000 and refocused on its core oil and gas businesses. Strong performance by its petrochemical operations offset low oil prices and led a corporate comeback.

In 1991, the company's exploration and production group averaged 215,000 barrels of oil, 160,000 barrels of liquid natural gas, and 1.3 billion cubic feet of natural gas per day. Phillips' net profits were $258 million, but it still carried $3.9 billion in debt from its battles with corporate raiders. The following year the company planned to offer 51% of its gas production and processing assets for sale to the public, but it delayed the offering in hopes of an improved market price.

The Players

Mesa Petroleum Chairman and CEO: T. Boone Pickens. A geology student and native of Oklahoma oil territory, T. Boone Pickens took a job in 1951 with Phillips Petroleum, against which he would later engage in battle. He stayed at the company until 1956, when he resigned to found Petroleum Exploration Co. This firm merged with Altair Oil and Gas to form Mesa Petroleum in 1964. A spree of attempted takeovers during the 1980s earned Pickens a fortune, as well as a dubious reputation as corporate raider. In the latter part of the decade, however, Mesa grew introspective, focusing on its own problems instead of on the perceived mismanagement of its target companies. Disenchanted shareholders ousted Pickens from his own firm in 1996, when Mesa was on the verge of bankruptcy.

Phillips Petroleum Chairman and CEO: William C. Douce. William Douce became president of Phillips Petroleum in 1980. By 1982, when C.J. Silas succeeded him as president, 62-year-old Douce had been promoted to chairman and CEO. He fended off the successive hostile attacks of Pickens and Icahn in the mid-1980s, but secured Phillips' independence only at a great financial strain to the company. In April 1985, Douce retired from Phillips and was replaced by Silas.

Net operating income increased by 43% to $580 million in 1995, the highest level since 1990. The next year the company announced a plan to expand its chain of Phillips 66 service stations and convenience stores, increasing the number of retail units from 300 to 500 over the next three to five years. Also in 1996, Phillips became the first petroleum firm to form a partnership with a South African company when it signed a contract with South Africa National Oil Co. to explore oil and gas reserves in the Indian Ocean off the coast of South Africa.

The company entered the dicyclopentadiene (DCPD) market in 1996, and announced plans to produce 40 million pounds of polyester-grade DCPD per year. Later that year it purchased a subsidiary of Parker and Parsley Petroleum Co. for $78 million. Conoco Inc., the energy subsidiary of DuPont, and Phillips discussed the possibility of combining their U.S. refining, marketing, supply, and transportation operations, but negotiations stalled.

In 1997, the company entered into joint ventures with Qatar General Petroleum and with Petroleos de Venezuele. Two years later, Phillips and Ultramar Diamond Shamrock Corp. terminated discussion of merging their North American oil refining and marketing businesses.

Market Forces Driving the Acquisition

The oil crisis of the 1970s lay at the root of the major consolidation in the oil industry during the 1980s. A demand that outweighed supply put into play two disparate efforts to lessen the impact of the oil shortage: increased exploration and reduced dependence on oil.

Conservation efforts to reduce reliance on oil lowered demand, with the U.S. becoming 32% more oil-efficient by 1985. These efforts were strengthened with the public's realization of the Earth's finite supply of natural resources. Oil demand was reduced even further during the economic recession of the early 1980s.

These forces had a devastating impact on the oil industry. Initially, the companies had enjoyed great success, as their redoubled exploration efforts produced increased profits with every barrel. The industry experienced a boom as prices skyrocketed. The bottom fell out, however, at the hands of conservation and efficiency in the early 1980s. Oil companies had extended their exploration activities beyond demand, and costs associated with exploration exceeded the market value of the oil. As a result, the stock prices of most U.S. oil companies fell far below the intrinsic value of their reserves.

Undervalued stock provided the motivation for consolidation. Sparked by the battle for Conoco Inc. in 1981, the Oil Wars consumed the industry. Mesa Petroleum was one of the most tenacious suitors of its rivals, yet it failed to close any of its hostile deals. It had lost out on both Cities Service and General American Oil in 1982 and was foiled in its pursuit of Gulf Oil the following year. Undeterred and, in fact, richer than ever from such unsuccessful bids, Mesa turned its attention to Phillips Petroleum as its next target.

Approach and Engagement

On December 4, 1984, Mesa Petroleum launched a $9.3 billion takeover bid for Phillips Petroleum. In partnership with Wagner & Brown Co., Mesa already owned 5.7% of Phillips. The partners offered $60 per share for an additional 9.7% stake, and disclosed that they would pursue financing to increase that interest to nearly 21%.

Mesa's threat was very real to William Douce, Phillips chairman, since its offer was 30% higher than Phillips' trading price of $40 per share. Phillips acted immediately to block the bid, persuading an Oklahoma court that Mesa was legally bound to refrain from bidding for Petroleum. In a 1983 standstill accord between Mesa and General American Oil (GAO), Mesa had agreed not to acquire any further interest in GAO. The court agreed with Phillips' contention that this pact extended to include Phillips, which had since acquired GAO.

Although it had won that round, and had also filed to block the deal in two other courts, Phillips knew that a protracted entanglement with Mesa could ultimately result in the loss of its independence. Mesa's track record suggested that even if it failed in its acquisition attempt, a more powerful suitor might finish what Mesa had started. Phillips decided to bring an end to the fight on December 23, 1994, when it reached an agreement with Mesa. Under its terms, Mesa would receive a guaranteed $53 for each of its Phillips shares, giving it a profit of $81 million—a hefty return from a battle that lasted only three weeks.

Products and Services

Pioneer Natural Resources Corp., formed by the merger of Mesa with Parker and Parsley Development Co., had 762 million barrels in oil reserves in the late 1990s. Its activities were concentrated in the Gulf Coast, the Permian Basin, and the Midcontinent, although it also operated in Argentina, Canada, Gabon, and South Africa.

In 1999, Phillips Petroleum operated in four primary business segments. Exploration & Production, its largest operation, was involved in locating and developing oil, natural gas, and natural gas liquids. Gas Gathering Processing & Marketing encompassed the resale of natural gas and natural gas liquids. Refining, Marketing & Transportation acquired and processed crude oil, sold gasoline and other petroleum products, and transported Phillips products through 5,200 miles of pipeline. Finally, Chemicals & Plastics encompassed its global operations in chemicals and plastics.

Changes to the Industry

Although it had eliminated Pickens and Mesa Petroleum as a threat, Phillips' troubles were only beginning. As part of the agreement that gave Mesa $53 per share, Phillips planned to recapitalize the company to reduce the number of outstanding shares, thereby creating more value per share for its stockholders. Management estimated the resulting value of its stock at $53 per share.

Shareholders, however, were not pleased with the deal, claiming that $53 was an overstated value. One such shareholder, Carl Icahn, who held a 4.85% stake, offered $60 per share as part of a leveraged buyout of Phillips. As with Pickens, the company paid him off to drop his takeover, offering a package of securities valued at $53-$57 per share. At this price, Icahn's stock holdings earned him a profit of $52.5 million, to which Phillips added $25 million to cover his takeover-related expenses.

These back-to-back defenses left Phillips saddled with $8 billion in debt. It entered into a period of aggressive debt reduction, as it was paying more in interest on its debt than on oil exploration. By 1988, however, Phillips' profitability had been restored, and it posted earnings of $650 million.

Research

Berg, Eric N. "Pact Ends Mesa's Bid for Phillips," in *The New York Times*, 24 December 1984. Describes the agreement that terminated Mesa's takeover attempt.

Cole, Robert J. "Shares of Phillips Surge," in *The New York Times*, 6 December 1984. Details the newly announced bid by Mesa for Phillips.

Norman, James R. "The Day After at Phillips: Everybody Won, Everybody Lost," in *Business Week*, 18 March 1985. Offers commentary on the outcome of the struggle for Phillips to Pickens, Icahn, and Phillips.

Phillips Petroleum Co. Home Page, available at http://www.phillips66.com. Official World Wide Web Home Page for Phillips Petroleum. Features product and services information, a company history, financial and investor data, and news releases.

"Phillips Petroleum Co.," in *Notable Corporate Chronologies*, The Gale Group, 1999. Profiles the history of the company.

Pioneer Natural Resources Co. Home Page, available at http://www.pioneernrc.com. Official World Wide Web Home Page for Pioneer Natural Resources. Offers information on finances and products, as well as a company history.

Potts, Mark. "Okla. Court Bars Mesa Takeover of Phillips," in *The Washington Post*, 7 December 1984. Relates the court's decision to extend Mesa's standstill agreement with GAO to Phillips.

PATRICIA ARCHILLA

MESA PETROLEUM & UNOCAL

Pioneer Natural Resources Co.
1400 Williams Sq. W.
5205 N. O'Connor Blvd.
Irving, TX 75039-3746
USA

tel: (972)444-9001
fax: (972)969-3559
web: http://www.pioneernrc.com

Unocal Corp.
2141 Rosecrans Ave., Ste. 4000
El Segundo, CA 90245
USA

tel: (310)726-7600
fax: (310)726-7817
web: http://www.unocal.com

date: May 20, 1985 (canceled)
affected: Pioneer Natural Resources Co. (formerly Mesa Petroleum Co.), USA, founded 1956
affected: Unocal Corp., USA, founded 1890

Overview of the Acquisition

The 1985 battle between Mesa Petroleum and Unocal was not only replete with drama, it also produced two notable results. For the first time, Mesa Petroleum and its chairman, corporate raider T. Boone Pickens, walked away from a hostile takeover attempt with no immediate profit. More importantly, however, the battle resulted in the Unocal Standard, a measure of the extent of defensive maneuvers legally permissible for warding off hostile suitors in takeover attempts in the U.S.

History of Mesa Petroleum Co.

T. Boone Pickens resigned from Phillips Petroleum in 1956 to establish his own oil firm, Petroleum Exploration, with $2,500 in capitalization. The Texas-based company remained independent until 1964, when it merged with Altair Oil and Gas, a Canadian company, to form Mesa Petroleum Co. The new concern went public that same year, gaining access to the capital needed to embark on exploration and acquisition ventures.

The 1980s brought Mesa fame and fortune. In May 1982, having accumulated a 5% stake in Cities Service Co., Mesa launched a hostile takeover of the much larger oil company. Before its offense was fully mobilized, however, Cities caught wind of the proposed bid and turned the tables on Mesa. By using the Pac-Man defense, Cities launched a takeover attempt for its suitor. Cities dropped this counterattack in June, when it agreed to be acquired by Gulf Oil Corp. This deal garnered Mesa a $30 million profit from the sale of its stake in Cities.

Mesa provoked a similar battle later that year by launching a bid for General American Oil Co. (GAO). Phillips Petroleum ultimately gained control of GAO, and Mesa walked away with a $45 million profit from its GAO stock. Mesa again repeated this performance in 1983 by bidding for Gulf Oil. When Chevron Corp. played the role of white knight, Mesa earned $500 million by selling its accumulated stake in Gulf. In another attempt to take over a large oil company, Mesa launched a bid for Pickens' previous employer and bidding rival, Phillips Petroleum Co. That attempt also failed, but Mesa made a handsome profit.

In 1985 Pickens launched an attempt for Unocal Corp., and for the first time was thwarted without gaining a substantial profit. The steps taken by Unocal and its chairman, Fred Hartley, in fending off Pickens resulted in the Unocal Standard, a ruling that redefined the scope of defensive measures permissible against a hostile attack.

The close of the 1980s brought an end to Mesa's takeover bent. Natural gas prices were declining, forcing the company to divest various assets in order to remain solvent. A stock offering that brought in $93 million in 1994 did little to quell shareholder dissatisfaction. By then the company that had made headlines for launching hostile takeover attempts found itself vulnerable to being on the receiving end of such an attack.

In 1996 Mesa's debt load was $1.2 billion and its stock price languished at $2.50, a fraction of its previous high of $68.75. Richard Rainwater invested $133 million in Mesa that year, pledging to double that amount in exchange for four seats on the company's board. Dissident shareholders welcomed this deal, forcing Pickens out of the company in favor of a new management team.

John Brumley, Mesa's new chairman and CEO, planned a $150 million equity offering in 1997. The company returned to an acquisition strategy, but focused on smaller, less hostile deals. It paid $270 million for Greenhill Petroleum Corp. and then purchased the natural gas operations of MAPCO Inc. Pioneer Natural Resources Corp. was formed by the April 1997 merger of Mesa with Parker and Parsley Development Co.

History of Unocal Corp.

Lyman Stewart, a 19-year-old Presbyterian evangelist, invested $124 for a one-eighth interest in a Pennsylvania oil lease. Two decades later he abandoned his religious calling for the oil industry. Stewart and partner Wallace Hardison moved to California and formed the Union Oil Co. of California in 1890 through the merger of three oil firms.

In the ensuing decades, Union Oil grew through expansion and innovation. Its Santa Paula refinery contained the first petroleum laboratory in the western region of the U.S. Union Oil constructed the first oil tanker. Its chain of service stations, which marketed the 76 gasoline brand, grew steadily during the 1930s.

Fred Hartley, who had joined the company in 1939, became its president and CEO in 1964. The next year he orchestrated the largest acquisition at that time, paying $900,000 for Pure Oil Co. This acquisition

The Business

Financials - Pioneer Natural Resources Co.

Revenue (1998): $711.5 million

Employees (1998): 1,016

Financials - Unocal Corp.

Revenue (1998): $5.5 billion

Employees (1998): 7,880

SICs / NAICS

sic 1311 - Crude Petroleum & Natural Gas

sic 1321 - Natural Gas Liquids

sic 1381 - Drilling Oil & Gas Wells

sic 5541 - Gasoline Service Stations

naics 211111 - Crude Petroleum and Natural Gas Extraction

naics 211112 - Natural Gas Liquid Extraction

naics 213111 - Drilling Oil and Gas Wells

naics 447110 - Gasoline Stations with Convenience Stores

doubled the size of Union and transformed it from a regional company into a national player.

In the years following World War II, while other companies were conducting exploration in international regions, Union Oil remained committed to domestic ventures. By the end of the 1950s California still provided nearly two-thirds of the company's total production.

Union Oil first discovered natural gas in Alaska in 1959 and acquired drilling rights in the Cook Inlet three years later. The company continued to expand its Alaskan activities, installing the world's first single-legged platform in the Trading Bay Field and constructing the first ice island in the Beauford Sea.

The POCO graphite division had been established by Pure Oil when that company obtained the rights to a specialty material developed for space exploration. POCO's products were first put to practical use in 1977 as part of the radioisotope thermoelectric generators of *Voyager I* and *Voyager II*.

Union Oil adopted its nickname, Unocal, as its corporate moniker in 1983. T. Boone Pickens attempted a hostile takeover of the company two years later. He was thwarted when Unocal repurchased one-third of its stock, thereby running the company's debt load to $5.9 billion. To reduce that burden, Unocal began

The Officers

Pioneer Natural Resources Co.

Chairman: Jon Brumley

President and CEO: Scott D. Sheffield

Chief Financial Officer and Exec. VP, Finance: M. Garrett
Smith

Exec. VP, Worldwide Exploration: Mel Fischer

Exec. VP: Dennis E. Fagerstone

Unocal Corp.

Chairman and CEO: Roger C. Beach

Vice Chairman: John F. Imle, Jr.

Exec. VP, North America Energy Operations, and Chief
Financial Officer: Timothy H. Ling

Exec. VP, International Energy Operations: Charles R.
Williamson

VP, Chief Legal Officer, and General Counsel: Dennis P.R.
Codon

selling off assets, including its landmark headquarters building in Los Angeles and 140 truck stops. It cut capital expenditures, trimmed its workforce by 5%, and reduced its quarterly dividend. Unocal also pulled out of Norway, divested itself of its coal and uranium mines, and exited the retail gasoline business in the Southeast. In addition, it spun off its Midwestern gas stations to UNO-VEN, a joint venture with Petroleos de Venezuela.

Unocal also began to shift its production focus from the U.S. to Asia. In 1996 it completely gave up production in California by selling its oil and gas fields there to Nuevo Energy for $516 million. The next year it sold three refineries, 1,300 service stations, and the rights to the 76 brand to Tosco for $2 billion. Unocal acquired a 29% interest in Tarragon Oil & Gas in 1998.

Market Forces Driving the Acquisition

T. Boone Pickens repeatedly insisted that he wanted to control a large oil company. This, he said, was the motivation behind his string of hostile attacks for companies far larger than his Mesa Petroleum Co. He attributed the fact that he was unsuccessful in each of those attempts to either misfortune or bad timing.

Analysts and oil executives suspected otherwise, however. Although Pickens failed to gain control of

his targets, he always managed to walk away from the battlefield millions of dollars wealthier. Critics claimed that his takeover attempts were bluffs used to force a company to invoke a greenmail defensive tactic.

Greenmail, as defined by Bruce Wasserstein in *Big Deal: The Battle for Control of America's Leading Corporations*, is "a payment to repurchase shares at a premium price in exchange for the acquirer's agreement to forgo a hostile offer." In each of his attacks, from Cities Service to Phillips Petroleum, Pickens had made a hefty profit when his stake was bought out by the target company itself or by its white knight acquirer.

Despite such accusations, Pickens was determined to continue his pursuit of oil companies. Having failed to win Phillips Petroleum in 1984, he turned to Unocal Corp. as his next challenge.

Approach and Engagement

In February 1985, less than two months after abandoning its bid for Phillips Petroleum, Mesa Petroleum acquired a 7.9% stake in Unocal Corp. Aware of what such a stake meant in the hands of T. Boone Pickens, Fred Hartley, Unocal's chairman, launched a preemptive defense against a potential hostile attack. On March 12 Unocal sued its bank, Security Pacific National Bank, for violating its obligations to Unocal by extending credit to Pickens for investment in Unocal. Hartley sent a copy of the lawsuit, along with a letter lambasting corporate raiders and the banks that facilitate them, to the Federal Reserve, various bank directors, and every member of Congress. Under pressure, Security Pacific and two others withdrew from their dealings with Pickens, but were soon replaced by other banks offering credit to Mesa.

Still claiming that it was interested in Unocal stock for investment purposes only, Mesa increased its stake to 13.5% on March 27. But on April 9 Mesa formally launched a $3.4 billion hostile bid for 51% of Unocal at $54 per share in cash. The remaining 49% stake would be purchased through junk bonds valued at $54 per share.

Unocal's board rejected the offer as inadequate and on April 16 unveiled its "Boone bomb." This defense consisted of a self-tender for 49% of its stock at $72 in debt securities. The proposal was unique in that it would become active only if Pickens acquired the 51% stake that he claimed to seek, and then it would exclude Pickens' stake from the repurchase.

Pickens argued that the offer acted against the interest of Unocal's shareholders, since they would gain nothing if Mesa simply terminated its takeover attempt. In response, Unocal refashioned its offer to include the unconditional obligation to repurchase 29% of its shares, still excluding those held by Pickens.

On April 29 a Delaware court agreed with Pickens that a company's shareholders must be treated equally. On appeal, however, the Delaware Supreme Court reversed that decision, ruling that the Unocal offer was "reasonable in relation to the threat that the board rationally and reasonably believed was posed by Mesa's inadequate and coercive two-tier tender offer."

In the face of this defeat, Pickens dropped his bid. On May 20 Mesa and Unocal announced an agreement whereby Pickens would be included in Unocal's self-tender, but only for one-third of his shares. Additionally, Mesa agreed not to buy any more Unocal shares for 25 years.

Products and Services

Pioneer Natural Resources Corp., formed by the merger of Mesa with Parker and Parsley Development Co., had 762 million barrels in oil reserves in the late 1990s. Its activities were concentrated in the Gulf Coast, the Permian Basin, and the Midcontinent, although it also operated in Argentina, Canada, Gabon, and South Africa.

Unocal operated in four business segments during the late 1990s. The North America Energy Operations and International Energy Operations groups were engaged in the exploration and production of crude oil and natural gas and project development in 17 countries around the world; in 1998 Unocal produced 184,000 barrels of petroleum liquids and 1,826 million cubic feet of gas per day, principally from the U.S. Gulf of Mexico region, Thailand, and Indonesia. The Geothermal Operations group was the world's largest producer of geothermal energy, supplying steam for the generation of electricity to power plants with a combined installed capacity of nearly 1,100 megawatts. Unocal Global Trade was an asset-based organization for oil and natural gas commodity trading. Finally, the Diversified Business Group included Unocal Agriproducts (agricultural fertilizers and chemicals), Alaska oil and gas operations, PocoGraphite (specialty graphites), Molycorp (lanthanides and molybdenum), and real estate sales and development.

Changes to the Industry

Since the takeover was unsuccessful, the Mesa/Unocal battle had no impact on the oil industry. It did, however, have repercussions for future takeovers in corporate America. The Unocal Standard became a measure against which exclusionary self-

The Players

Mesa Petroleum Chairman and CEO: T. Boone Pickens. A geology student and native of Oklahoma oil territory, T. Boone Pickens took a job in 1951 with Phillips Petroleum, against which he would later engage in battle. He stayed at the company until 1956, when he resigned to found Petroleum Exploration Co. This firm merged with Altair Oil and Gas to form Mesa Petroleum in 1964. A spree of attempted takeovers during the 1980s earned Pickens a fortune, as well as a dubious reputation as corporate raider. In the latter part of the decade, however, Mesa grew introspective, focusing on its own problems instead of on the perceived mismanagement of its target companies. Disenchanted shareholders ousted Pickens from his own firm in 1996, when Mesa was on the verge of bankruptcy.

Unocal Chairman, CEO, and President: Fred L. Hartley. Fred Hartley was born in Vancouver, Canada, in January 1917. In 1939, after earning a degree in chemical engineering from the University of British Columbia, he became an engineer trainee at Union Oil Co. of California, predecessor of Unocal. Hartley was promoted to vice president of research in 1956 and made a senior vice president four years later.

In 1964 Hartley was named President and CEO, and chairman in 1974. Under his direction, the company was transformed from a local operator into the 12th-largest oil company in the U.S. He is credited with fending off the takeover attempt by Mesa Petroleum in 1985. Three years later Hartley handed the positions of president and CEO to Richard Stegemeier. In 1989 he also stepped down as chairman in favor of Stegemeier, remaining a director and chairman emeritus of Unocal. Hartley died on October 19, 1990, at age 73.

tender offers could be used as a defense against a corporate raider.

Under this standard, a discriminatory defense must pass a two-prong test. First, a company's board must demonstrate that the offer is inadequate and detrimental to established corporate strategy. Second, it must show that its response is in proportion to the threat.

Review of the Outcome

At the time of the cancellation of its takeover bid, Mesa Petroleum's shares in Unocal were estimated to be valued in the mid-30s, far below the $45 average price that the firm had paid. This represented a $100 million loss for Pickens, but only if he sold the shares immediately. Instead, he waited until May 1986 to liquidate his remaining 10% interest, earning a profit of $50 million on his investment.

Unocal, on the other hand, took on an additional $4.4 billion in debt through its defense against Mesa. With the company's debt load hovering at $5.9 billion, it implemented cost-cutting measures that included the divestiture of assets, cutting of capital expenditures, and reduction of its workforce.

Research

Norman, James R. "At Unocal, A Victory 'Without the Champagne'," in *Business Week*, 3 June 1985. Details the expense incurred by Unocal in defeating Mesa.

———. "Is Unocal's 'Boone Bomb' More Than a Bluff?" in *Business Week*, 29 April 1985. Describes Unocal's initial self-tender offer.

Pioneer Natural Resources Co. Home Page, available at http://www.pioneernrc.com. Official World Wide Web Home Page for Pioneer Natural Resources. Offers information on finances and products, as well as a company history.

Potts, Mark. "Pickens Launches $3.4 Billion Bid for Control of Unocal; Hartley Expected to Resist Takeover," in *The Washington Post*, 9 April 1985. Describes the terms of the hostile offer.

Rivera, Nancy, and Debra Whitefield. "Unocal Sues Its Bank over Loans to Pickens; Seeks Help from Fed," in *Los Angeles Times*, 13 March 1985. Details Unocal's attempt to thwart Mesa's potential bid.

Stevenson, Richard W. "Unocal's Costly Independence," in *The New York Times*, 23 December 1986. Describes the efforts taken at Unocal to reduce its debt over the year since the battle was concluded.

"Unocal Corp.," in *International Directory of Company Histories*, Vol. IV, St. James Press: 1991. Provides an historical review of the company.

Unocal Corp. Home Page, available at http://www.unocal.com. Official World Wide Web Home Page for Unocal Corp. Features news releases, employment opportunities, information on products and services, and financial and investor data.

Wasserstein, Bruce. *Big Deal: The Battle for Control of America's Leading Corporations*, Warner Books, 1998. Offers an overview of the largest mergers in American corporate history.

PATRICIA ARCHILLA

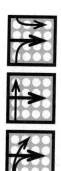

MICHELIN & UNIROYAL GOODRICH

nationality: France
date: May 1990
affected: Michelin Group, France, founded 1889
affected: Uniroyal Goodrich Tire Co., USA, founded 1892

Compagnie Generale des
Etablissements Michelin
12 cours Sablon
Clermont-Ferrand, 63000
France

tel: (33)4-73-98-59-00
fax: (33)4-73-98-59-04
web: http://www.michelin.fr

Overview of the Merger

Michelin's $1.5 billion purchase of Uniroyal Goodrich created the largest tire company in the world. The deal also placed Michelin second in the U.S. market for passenger tires, just behind Goodyear Tire & Rubber Company, with 22% of the market share. Although Michelin's executives enthusiastically supported the transaction for its potential to launch the company into the U.S. market, Michelin floundered in the next year as a result of the increased debt from the deal, plummeting share prices, and elimination of almost 3,000 jobs in France.

History of Michelin Group

In the early 1830s Edouard Daubree and Aristide Barbier formed the Barbier, Daubree farming company in Clermont-Ferrand, France. The new company manufactured sugar, but was pushed into rubber manufacturing by Daubree's wife. By the latter half of the decade, the firm was making rubber balls, hoses, and drive belts.

After the deaths of the original founders in 1886, Edouard and Andre Michelin took over Barbier, Daubree Compagnie. Three years later the two renamed the company Michelin et Compagnie and began innovations in the bike tire industry. In 1891 Edouard developed a detachable tire that could be repaired in just 15 minutes rather than hours. Michelin made history when a bike using their tires won a race, beating the closet opponent by over eight hours. The next year, further innovations enabled the tire to be changed in under two minutes. By 1893 over 10,000 cyclists used Michelin's tires.

Continuing with the development process, Michelin introduced the first pneumatic tire for use by horse-drawn carriages. Soon, over 600 Paris cabs were using the tires, and in 1895 the company developed the tire for cars. The two brothers tested the tires in a 745-mile race from Paris to Bordeaux and back again. The pair placed ninth with their new tires.

In the early 1900s, Michelin needed to distinguish itself from competitors. The brothers introduced the Michelin Man (nicknamed Monsieur Bibendum), a mar-

The Business

Financials

Revenue (1998): $15.3 billion

Employees (1998): 127,241

SICs / NAICS

sic 3011 - Tires & Inner Tubes

sic 5014 - Tires & Tubes

sic 3714 - Motor Vehicle Parts & Accessories

naics 326211 - Tire Manufacturing (except Retreading)

keting character created from a stack of tires. The Michelin Red Guide, a free publication covering travel and tire care, was also introduced. By 1909 the company was publishing an English-language guide to France. Michelin was also diving into foreign operations in the United Kingdom and Italy, and it acquired a rubber plantation in Indo-China in 1905. That same year, the Semelle, a tire with leather treads and steels rivets, was introduced.

Continuing efforts led to the development of the detachable wheel rim, allowing motorists to carry spare Michelin tires, just as the winner of the first Grand Prix did. The company was also developing tires that could be used for trucks. In an attempt to increase its popularity, Michelin offered FrF 100,000 to the first air pilot who could complete a difficult course and land on the peak of Puy de Dome mountain. Michelin introduced itself in the aeronautics industry when the feat was accomplished in 1911.

With the onset of Word War I, Michelin dedicated itself to the war effort. It supplied 100 free bombers, as well as 1,800 at cost, to the French government. In 1917, the company introduced an all-purpose tire named the Roulement Universel. Two years later, all tires began to be treaded with parallel cord plies. Advances in low-pressure tires increased tire life expectancy, and improvements continued in durability and road handling.

Michelin had become the 17th-largest tire vendor in the world by 1930. With ventures in Germany, Belgium, Spain, Italy, and Holland, the company was focusing on the manufacturing process of its tires. The use of vehicles was becoming so popular that Michelin increased the number of countries its road guides covered. It introduced the Pilote, a tire with unparalleled road handling due to its ratio of width to depth, and in 1937 unveiled the Metallic, a tire designed for truck loads.

Michelin took over Citroen, an automobile manufacturer, in 1935. The new company was the largest industrial group in France until 1974, when Peugeot took over Citroen. The Michelin family remained in control of the company during the developing and innovative years.

Andre died in 1931 and Edouard in 1940. Robert Puiseux, Edouard's son-in-law, took the helm in 1940 and led the company through World War II. The period was rough for the family, as members were imprisoned in camps and killed in war efforts. When the Nazis seized many of Michelin's plants, the company sabotaged the tires so that they wouldn't fare well in cold temperatures. Michelin was also key in providing maps to the French government and the U.S. war department.

After the war, the company recovered lost plants, modernized its existing facilities, built new factories, and manufactured wire, wheels, and tooling, along with its tires. In 1946 Michelin created the radial tire, one of its greatest accomplishments. Developed in secret during the war, the company went public with the new tire in 1949, introducing it as the X-tire. Public demand surged and, by 1969, Michelin produced more than 30 million tires per year. The company stayed ahead of its competition by broadening the use of these tires by making them compatible for trucks and agricultural vehicles. The company also introduced tubeless tires.

Focusing on research and development, Michelin opened a testing center in Ladoux, not far from the company's headquarters. Factories were opened in Nigeria, Algeria, and Vietnam. In 1965, the company pushed its way into the U.S. market by joining up with Sears, Roebuck to provide replacement tires for cars. By 1970, under the leadership of Francois Michelin, the company was selling more than 2.5 million tires per year in the U.S. Still concentrating on new product development, it furthered its development of the radial tire. In 1979 its tires were on the Ferrari that won the Formula 1 World Championship.

Radial tires became available for aircraft in 1981 and for motorcycles in 1987. Michelin continued to be a front runner in the industry with its constant technological developments. The M series, introduced in 1985, offered state-of-the-art advances in radial tires. The MXL, part of this line, became the best selling tire in Europe. With the acquisition of Uniroyal Goodrich in 1990, Michelin cemented its place as the number-one leader in the tire industry.

The auto and tire market faced a recession in 1991. Michelin experienced a FrF 5.27 billion loss in 1991 and was forced to cut nearly 15% of its workforce. The company re-grouped, consolidated facilities, and focused on tire production, suspension, and product manufacturing. Throughout the hardships, it followed its passion for research and development, introducing new high-performance tires and a fuel-efficient tire.

The company also focused on new acquisitions. In 1996, it purchased a 90% interest in the rubber manufacturer Taurus, joined forces with Continental, and introduced the first zero-pressure tire, which could run flat for over 50 miles. By 1998, Michelin maintained operations in 170 countries and employed more than 120,000 workers. Global sales reached $15.3 billion, and the famous Michelin man celebrated its 100th anniversary.

History of Uniroyal Goodrich Tire Co.

The U.S. Rubber Company was formed from nine rubber manufacturing firms in 1982. In just three years the company introduced the first pneumatic tire in the U.S. In 1907, U.S. Rubber bought the Canadian Consolidated Rubber Company. It developed the first pneumatic airplane tire and truck tire in 1911. Meanwhile, B.F. Goodrich, the first established rubber company in America, was making a name across the U.S. from its durable tires.

By 1920 the U.S. Rubber Company was selling tires to General Motors. The company was granted the first patents for synthetic rubber research, making it possible for further developments in the use of synthetic rubber for tires. Nevertheless, B.F. Goodrich was the first to introduce a tire made from synthetic rubber. U.S. Rubber fought back, and in 1941 the company developed the all-synthetic rubber tire for automobiles.

Both the company and the industry fared well in the decades after World War II. In 1966 U.S. Rubber Company changed its name to Uniroyal, Inc. Four years later the newly named company opened the first steel-belted radial plant in response to overwhelming demand for radial tires. In 1977 Uniroyal marketed the first hideaway spare tire, and two years later was the first to successfully introduce a puncture-sealant tire named the Royal Seal.

By the 1980s Uniroyal was an attractive company. It had received technological patents for the first non-pneumatic spare tire, and sales were positive. In 1985, B.F. Goodrich and Uniroyal joined forces to meld their auto and truck tire business together. The result was The Uniroyal Goodrich Tire Company. In 1988, Clayton & Dubilier bought Goodrich's 50% interest in the venture in order to financially restructure the company. Although the company struggled after the joint venture with B.F. Goodrich, Clayton & Dubilier was able to reorganize it and to increase profits.

The Officers

Managing Partner and General Partner: Edouard Michelin

Managing Partner and General Partner: Francois Michelin

Managing Partner and General Partner: Rene Zingraff

Director of Finance: Eric Bourdais de Charbonniere

Director of Personnel: Thierry Coudurier

Chairman and President, Michelin North America: Jim Micali

The financially sound company, became attractive to Michelin in 1989. One year later, Uniroyal Goodrich was acquired by the French tire maker. Uniroyal provided Michelin with a large portion of the U.S. tire market, making it the leader in the industry.

Market Forces Driving the Merger

In the past, Michelin had little interest in making private label tires in the U.S., as the company prided itself on producing its premium, upscale tires. Yet with replacement tire sales as the most profitable in the U.S. market, with 50% of those sales coming from various lower-end brands, Michelin needed a method of penetrating that market to remain competitive.

In an article in the *European Rubber Journal*, a Michelin representative stated that the acquisition would allow it to "spread its research and development costs over more units, offer its American and Canadian dealers more tire lines to complement its front-line Michelin products, benefit from the private-brand market, which accounts for more than half the U.S. after-market and about one-third of Uniroyal Goodrich's tire sales, and strengthen its position as an original equipment supplier to U.S. auto makers."

Meanwhile, Uniroyal Goodrich was faltering on account of a flat market, conflicts with General Motors (one of its largest customers), a heavy debt load, and large pension obligations. Analysts felt that without partnering up with a stronger company, Uniroyal would fail in the global market. The company would not be able to afford the capital expenditures needed to remodel plants or to keep up with innovative designs. With such competitors as Bridgestone investing $1.5 billion to upgrade its Firestone plants and Goodyear having over $500 million in its capital budget per year, Uniroyal was not positioned well with its plan to spend $500 million over the next five years. According to an article in *The New York Times*, a

The Players

Managing and General Partner of Michelin Group.: Francois Michelin. In 1989 Michelin joined the company that his ancestors had founded. Although he started as the head of production at a factory in Puy-en-Velay, Michelin was named a managing partner two years later.

Managing and General Partner of Michelin Group: Edouard Michelin. After graduating from Ecole Centrale in Paris, Edouard Michelin joined the company in France in 1989 and received the title of managing partner in 1991. He focused his efforts on U.S. operations.

President and Chief Operating Officer of Uniroyal Goodrich Tire Co.: Sheldon R. Salzman. Salzman joined the United States Rubber Company in 1955. He became a leader in the chemical division, but was asked to run the tire operations in 1979. He is credited with increasing income to $85.3 million in that department. Salzman rejoined the chemical operations briefly, but returned to work in the tire division after Clayton & Dubilier took the company private in 1985. He was named president and Chief Operating Officer of Uniroyal in 1988.

Chairman of Uniroyal Goodrich Tire Co.: B. Charles Ames. As a partner of Clayton & Dubilier, Ames took over as chairman and CEO of Uniroyal Goodrich when B.F. Goodrich sold its 50% stake in the company to the investment firm. He is credited with improving productivity, strengthening management, and increasing marketing efforts. Ames previously worked as chairman and CEO for Acme-Cleveland Corporation.

Uniroyal union official in Wisconsin stated "It would be better for everyone if the company were acquired by some bigger company."

Approach and Engagement

In the latter half of 1988, Michelin executives approached Uniroyal Goodrich and merger talks began. The following year, the pair announced their plan for Michelin to purchase Uniroyal Goodrich for $1.5 billion. The French tire maker would assume $810 million in debt and pay $690 million for the company. The merger was completed in May 1990.

Products and Services

After the merger, Uniroyal Goodrich continued to manufacture and distribute its Uniroyal, B.F. Goodrich, and private label brands. The company operated research and development plants in Troy, Michigan, and Akron, Ohio, and had nine factories: five in the U.S., two in Ontario, and two in Mexico. Michelin operated six plants in the U.S. and three in Canada. After the union of the two companies, Michelin became the largest tire maker in the world, with 24% of the North American market under its control.

In 1997 the Compagnie Generale des Etablissements Michelin maintained offices in over 170 countries, operated six rubber plants in Nigeria and Brazil, and owned 79 manufacturing operations in 18 countries. With tires and wheels accounting for 99% of total sales in 1997, the company focused on such brand names as Michelin, Uniroyal, B.F. Goodrich, Taurus, Riken, Tyremaster, and Pneu Laurent. Among Michelin's products were passenger and truck tires, aircraft tires, two-wheel tires, earthmover tires, agricultural tires, suspension systems, and tourism services.

Changes to the Industry

The tire industry faced heated competition and global consolidation. Michelin's purchase of Uniroyal came on the heels of several other major mergers. Bridgestone Corporation of Japan bought out Firestone Tire & Rubber Company, Continental merged with General Tire & Rubber Company, Pirelli SpA of Italy joined forces with Armstrong Rubber Company, and Sumitomo Rubber Industries Ltd. of Japan purchased Dunlop tires. Goodyear Tire & Rubber Company was the last remaining U.S.-owned tire company after the Michelin deal. Analysts attribute the shift toward foreign ownership of the industry to failing U.S. efforts to effectively modernize facilities, the slow development of radial tires, and inefficient cost structures. The U.S.-based companies were quick to look at buyouts and acquisitions as a means of staying afloat in the market.

Review of the Outcome

The $1.5 billion purchase of Uniroyal Goodrich seemed golden to Michelin at first glance. The French tire maker became the globe's largest producer of tires, increasing its market share to 22%. In the aftermath of deal, however, Michelin's outlook on the future tarnished. By October of 1990, stock had plummeted by 62% after the announcement that the company expected large losses that year. Michelin was forced to cut over 2,260 jobs across France.

Contributing factors included the $800 million debt from the Uniroyal deal, fluctuating prices due to overcapacity, and declining car sales in Europe. First-half results for 1990 were bleak, with $76.8 million in losses.

Analysts criticized the Uniroyal purchase, claiming that it hurt shareholder interest and was financially unsound. Francois Michelin backed the company's deal, stating that it was necessary for gaining increased market share, a feat that would have been much more costly than an acquisition. In 1990 the company posted a staggering $943 million loss. The next year showed improvement, as the company saw a loss of $135 million in net income. By 1992 Michelin had $14 million in net income, but it fell again in 1993 with a $620 million loss. In 1998 the company had 127,241 employees and net income of $670 million.

Research

Browning, E.S. "Michelin, Squeezed by Acquisition of Uniroyal, See Losses, Job Cuts," in *Wall Street Journal*, 26 June 1990. Explains first half results for Michelin in 1990.

Compagnie Generale des Etablissements Michelin Home Page, available at http://www.michelin.fr. Official World Wide Web Home Page for Michelin. Includes current and archived news, detailed financial, product, and historical information, as well as annual reports.

Davis, Bruce. "Michelin Buys Uniroyal Goodrich," in *European Rubber Journal*, November 1989. Offers insight on the purchase of Uniroyal by Michelin.

Greenhouse, Steven. "Michelin Facing Problems as No. 1," in *The New York Times*, 19 October 1990. Explains Michelin's downfall after the deal with Uniroyal.

Hicks, Jonathan. "Tire Company's Uphill Struggle," in *The New York Times*, 13 June 1989. Discusses Uniroyal's battle for financial stability during the latter half of the 1980s.

"Michelin" in *International Directory of Company Histories*, Vol. V, Gale Research 1994. Lists major events in the history of Michelin.

Rivera Brooks, Nancy. "Michelin Group to Buy Uniroyal Goodrich in a Deal Worth $1.5 Billion," in *Los Angeles Times*, 23 September 1989. Discusses the terms of the acquisition.

CHRISTINA M. STANSELL

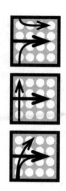

MICROSOFT & INTUIT

One Microsoft Way
Redmond, WA 98052-6399
USA

tel: (425)882-8080
fax: (425)936-7329
web: http://www.microsoft.com

Intuit Inc.

2535 Garcia Ave.
Mountain View, CA 94043
USA

tel: (650)944-6000
fax: (650)944-3699
web: http://www.intuit.com

date: May 20, 1995 (canceled)
affected: Microsoft Corp., USA, founded 1975
affected: Intuit Inc., USA, founded 1983

Overview of the Merger

Microsoft Corp. and Intuit Inc. agreed to merge in October 1994. Microsoft, the world's largest manufacturer of computer software, wanted to improve its position in the personal finance software market. This niche was dominated by a small company known as Intuit, producer of the highly successful Quicken application. For Intuit, ownership by Microsoft would lend it security and the marketing resources to cement its hold on the market. The U.S. Department of Justice (DoJ), however, wouldn't allow it. Microsoft's other antitrust entanglements drew a critical eye to this merger deal, and the two companies' internal correspondence didn't help matters. In April 1995, the DoJ filed suit to block the deal, and Microsoft withdrew its acquisition offer the following month.

History of Microsoft Corp.

The introduction of the Altair 8800, the first commercial microcomputer, in January 1975 reunited two old friends, William Gates and Paul Allen, who approached Altair's manufacturer, Micro Instrumentation and Telemetry Systems, with the proposal of creating a BASIC interpreter for the system. The offer was met with enthusiasm, and six weeks later the newly formed Microsoft firm delivered. Having had the foresight to retain the rights to their program, they soon began customizing it for other computers, such as those produced by Apple Computer and Commodore. Gates designed the operating system—MS-DOS (short for Microsoft Disk Operating System)—for the 1981 breakthrough, the IBM PC.

In 1982 Microsoft broke into the foreign market by opening Microsoft Ltd. in England. It introduced the Microsoft Mouse, a hand-held pointing device used to move the cursor on the computer screen, as well as the word processing program Microsoft Word.

Microsoft's Windows operating system, introduced in 1985, revolutionized computers by making them more user-friendly by way of a graphical user interface, just as the Macintosh had done for Apple's customers the prior year. The company closed the year with sales of $590 million and a workforce of 2,800. In 1986 Microsoft went public, raising $61 million. It released Excel for Windows, a spreadsheet to compete against Lotus 1-2-3, in 1987; by the end of that year it was the largest PC software company in the U.S.

Microsoft improved upon itself with the 1990 launch of Windows 3.0. That year, a price war broke out between IBM and Microsoft over their competing operating systems, Microsoft's DOS 5.0 and IBM's OS/2. In 1991 IBM and Apple announced an alliance to create a new operating system that would allow information to be swapped between the two systems. The move was seen as a way to outflank Microsoft, which was beginning to control the software and operating systems market.

Microsoft's legal troubles began in 1988, when Apple filed suit against the company for stealing the "look and feel" of the Macintosh in its Windows program. In April 1992, the court ruled that the visuals used in Windows 2.03 and Windows 3.0 were not protected under Apple's copyrights. In December of that year, however, the company came under investigation by the Federal Trade Commission (FTC) for allegations of unfair and monopolistic trade practices.

Microsoft and the U.S. Department of Justice reached an agreement in July 1994, when the firm agreed to alter its marketing practices. Critics of this settlement claimed that it failed to curtail the company's alleged anticompetitive practices, and in February 1995 the U.S. District Court rejected the settlement as too lenient. Microsoft and the Department of Justice filed appeals.

History of Intuit Inc.

Necessity, it is said, is the mother of invention. The driving force behind the invention of Quicken was Scott Cook's desire for a computer program to automate the aggravating task of paying bills and managing household finances. Confident that he could apply his background in marketing and technology, this 23-year-old graduate of Harvard business school was determined to launch a software company to do just that.

Cook visited the campus of Stanford University to post an advertisement for a computer programmer. He asked a passing student, Tom Proulx, for directions to a bulletin board. Proulx, it turned out, had done some programming and agreed to write a simple check-balancing program for Cook. In his dorm room, he created the first Quicken program, and the pair founded Intuit around it in 1983.

Intuit was headquartered in Proulx's basement with a staff of seven employees. The upstart company met two hurdles blocking its entry into the market. Its initial strategy was to sell the software to customers

The Business

Financials - Microsoft Corp.

Revenue (1998): $14.48 billion

Employees (1998): 27,055

Financials - Intuit Inc.

Revenue (1998): $592.7 million

Employees (1998): 2,860

Share (1998): 80%

SICs / NAICS

sic 7372 - Prepackaged Software

sic 7375 - Information Retrieval Services

naics 511210 - Software Publishers

naics 514191 - On-Line Information Services

through banks, but Cook dropped this plan when he realized that banks were poorly equipped to sell prepackaged software. The second obstacle was the company's inability to secure a retail distributor due to its anonymity. By 1985 the company was struggling to stay afloat, and the partners watched three of their employees leave when Intuit became unable to pay them. The remaining four still believed in the product, and worked for free for six months.

In 1986 the company risked it all. Intuit was $300,000 in debt and had only $95,000 left in the bank, yet it launched a $125,000 advertising campaign. Cook and Proulx firmly believed that word of mouth would propagate sales, but they needed to get the product into the hands of initial buyers.

The success of the ad campaign caused company sales to explode. By the late 1980s, Quicken became one of the best-selling personal finance applications. Intuit was suddenly able to secure financing from venture capital companies that had rejected it just a couple of years earlier. This infusion of capital enabled Quicken to enter the global marketplace. By 1991, with sales of $55 million, Quicken ranked along with WordPerfect and Lotus 1-2-3 as a top-selling software application.

Intuit used Quicken as a springboard for other product introductions. In 1991 it launched QuickPay, a software program designed to work with Quicken to help small businesses process their payroll. The following year marked the debut of QuickBooks, a small-

The Officers

Microsoft Corp.

Chairman and CEO: William H. Gates III

President: Steve Ballmer

Exec. VP, Chief Operating Officer: Bob Herbold

Chief Technology Officer: Nathan Myhrvold

Intuit Inc.

Chairman of the Executive Committee: Scott D. Cook

Chairman of the Board: Bill V. Campbell

President and Chief Executive Officer: Bill H. Harris

Chief Technology Officer and Senior VP: Eric Dunn

Chief Financial Officer and VP: Greg J. Santora

business bookkeeping program designed to work in conjunction with both Quicken and QuickPay. By 1992 Quicken had captured a 70% share of the personal financial software market.

In 1993 Intuit began to expand out of the stand-alone computer market into electronic-linked services. To that end, it struck a deal with Visa that allowed users to download credit card statements directly into their Quicken applications. Intuit, now a public company, spent $243 million to acquire ChipSoft, a developer of electronic tax return software, and $7.6 million for National Payment Clearinghouse Inc., a processor of electronic transactions.

In 1994 Cook, while retaining his post as chairman, stepped down as CEO in favor of William Campbell, who also assumed the role of president.

Market Forces Driving the Merger/Acquisition

By the mid-1990s, Intuit a represented a portal into the only major software category in which Microsoft did not have a significant presence. Microsoft had been competing successfully with its own personal financial program, Microsoft Money. By 1994, though, that application was serving only 22% of the market, compared to Quicken's 69%.

In addition to adding a popular software program to its offerings, Microsoft would also benefit from Intuit's numerous partnerships with financial institutions. Microsoft was planning to launch an online service, The Microsoft Network, in the spring of 1995. By acquiring Intuit, it would be able to couple its online capabilities with Quicken's applications to provide customers with direct connection to their finan-

cial institutions. The combined company would collect a small royalty for each financial transaction conducted over its service.

Microsoft had another compelling reason to acquire Intuit, and that reason was the force behind most of the industry consolidations that were occurring in the mid-1990s. In the frantic pace of the computer industry, it is cheaper and quicker for many established firms to buy small businesses with cutting-edge technology than to plan, design, and test new software on their own. As reported in *Fortune*, Microsoft executive vice president Mike Maples said, "We finally had to ask ourselves: Do we have the time to build a product and market it on our own, or is the world moving too fast for us?"

Intuit was an anomaly in this industry. Overcrowding in a market usually creates fewer, but larger, companies vying for the same customers. This pressure puts a premium on marketing, and the typical small firm is willing to be acquired in order to capitalize on the marketing and distribution dollars of the larger acquirer. Intuit, however, had not only managed to survive in an industry dominated by giants, it was beating them in its niche market. Cook claimed that the company had not been seeking a merger before it was attracted to Microsoft's "unique" deal.

That's not to say that Intuit wouldn't benefit from a merger. The $1.5 billion price was twice what Intuit's stock was worth. Also, an alignment with the Microsoft name would increase its ability to forge alliances with financial institutions.

Approach and Engagement

On October 13, 1994, Microsoft and Intuit announced their proposed merger. The $1.5 billion deal would be a stock swap transaction in which Microsoft would issue 27 million shares of common stock to Intuit shareholders. Scott Cook would assume the role of Executive Vice President, Electronic Commerce. Microsoft also arranged to sell Microsoft Money to Novell Inc. in order to avert potential antitrust objections.

In November 1994, the U.S. Department of Justice (DoJ) put the merger on hold while continuing its separate antitrust investigation of Microsoft. By this time, the government had been barraged with criticisms of leniency toward the software giant, and felt political pressure to toughen up. Microsoft's settlement was reviewed by a U.S. District Judge, who rejected it in February 1995. Although the decision was unrelated, it sent reverberations through the Microsoft/Intuit deal, which industry watchers began to suspect would be subject to more critical scrutiny.

They were not incorrect. On April 27, 1995, the DoJ filed a lawsuit to block the merger on antitrust grounds. It asserted at the deal would restrict innovation and competition in the personal finance software market, and lead to higher prices. The trial between the companies and the DoJ was scheduled to begin on June 26, 1995.

Memos from within Microsoft and Intuit were used as evidence by the DoJ that the companies had deliberate intentions of establishing a monopoly by eliminating competition. As reported in *Information Week*, memos from Cook to his board of directors referred to Microsoft as "Godzilla," and claimed that a merger would be "eliminating a bloody share war." A Microsoft executive wrote in an internal memo, "I can't imagine anyone would be stupid enough" to buy the Money software after Microsoft and Intuit combine their efforts in Quicken.

At first, both companies were determined to stand up against the DoJ in court. After a short time, however, Microsoft decided at a protracted dispute would not be worth the time and expense. It had already been involved in an antitrust suit for four years, and had learned from experience how draining it can be to engage in battle against the government. On May 20, 1995, Microsoft called off the deal.

Products and Services

Microsoft offered a wide variety of products. Its products fell into a dozen or so types, including business software, operating systems & servers, development tools, Internet technologies, games, kids' tools, home productivity, reference, hardware, Macintosh products, and books.

Of its best-known brands were the Windows family of products, including Windows 98 and 95, Windows NT Workstation, Windows NT Server, and Windows CE. Windows Technologies included Internet Explorer and Windows Media. Products for developers were Microsoft Developer Network, Microsoft Site Builder Network, and Windows Driver Development.

The BackOffice family of servers was built for Microsoft Windows NT operating system. This line of products included Windows NT Server, Exchange Server, Proxy Server, Site Server, Systems Management Server, SNA Server, and SQL Server.

Intuit's products fell into three categories. Personal finance was comprised of Quicken products, such as the best-selling personal finance Quicken application, as well as QuickenMortgage, Quicken InsureMarket, Quicken Financial Planner, and Quicken Lite. Products for small businesses included

The Players

Microsoft Chairman and CEO: Willi4m H. Gates III. Bill Gates has been a computer enthusiast since his youth. Born in 1955 in Seattle, he began programming in the BASIC computer language at the age of fourteen. He and his friend Paul Allen worked on and off as computer consultants throughout high school, but the duo separated when Gates attended Harvard University. He dropped out in his junior year to devote more time to Microsoft, the company that he formed in 1975. Since then he has been on the fast track to success. In 1987, after Microsoft went public, Gates officially became a billionaire. Before the company's initial public offering, Gates' worth was impossible to calculate since most of his holdings were in Microsoft stock. The founder penned his vision of the future of information technology in *The Road Ahead* in 1995, and revised it in 1996 to give further treatment to the Internet. Gates continues to serve as chairman and CEO of his company.

Intuit Chairman of the Executive Committee: Scott D. Cook. Scott Cook's entrepreneurial bent was demonstrated during his studies at the University of Southern California. Cook revitalized the school's ailing ski club by renting out a cabin at a nearby ski area and charging club members a mere $1 per night to use it. The club became one of the most successful organizations on campus, a fact that played an important role in getting him accepted into Harvard's graduate business school after receiving degrees both in math and economics from USC. Cook graduated from Harvard in 1976, and was immediately hired by Ohio-based Procter & Gamble. Upon moving back to California four years later, he took a job with the consulting firm Bain & Co., where he worked in the fields of banking and technology. He applied his experience in these areas, as well as his marketing experience from P&G, to launch Intuit in 1983. At that point he served as president, CEO, and chairman until 1994, when he passed the posts of president and CEO to William Campbell. In 1998 he was made chairman of the executive committee when he stepped down as chairman of the board.

QuickBooks and QuickBooks Pro. Its tax preparation line included TurboTax and ProSeries.

Changes to the Industry

Despite its intention to position Money as a leader in the personal financial software market, Microsoft had been unable to shake Quicken's hold on the market. By early 1999, in fact, Intuit had increased its market share to 80%, followed by Peachtree's 15% stake.

Review of the Outcome

The deal between Microsoft and Intuit incorporated two superlatives. If completed, it would have been the largest software merger in history. Secondly, according to *The National Law Journal*, the government's antitrust lawsuit was the first ever to block a merger based on a threat to a future market rather than to an existing one. Industry analysts were confounded by the suit since an online personal finance market didn't even exist.

Intuit walked away disappointed, but wealthier. It received from Microsoft a break-up fee of $46.25 million, a sizable profit over its merger-related expenses of about $4 million. In 1998, Scott Cook was named chairman of the executive committee, Bill Campbell advanced to chairman of the board, and Bill Harris became president and CEO.

Microsoft renewed efforts to make Microsoft Money a contender. The company hired away a top Intuit salesman and launched a revamped version of Money to be used with Microsoft's long-awaited new operating system, Windows 95, which debuted that August.

Microsoft made determined strides to establish a name in the Internet browser industry. The Microsoft Network and Internet Explorer were included in Windows 95, a fact that didn't escape the notice of the Department of Justice. It accused Microsoft of forcing its licensees, the computer manufacturers, to include Microsoft's Internet Explorer, thereby giving the company an unfair trade advantage over other Internet browsers. Shortly thereafter, a consent decree prohibited Microsoft from requiring manufacturers to license other Microsoft products as part of the Windows package, while permitting Microsoft to continue producing integrated products. The aim of the December 1997 antitrust suit is to force Microsoft either to "unbundle" its browser from its operating system or to offer other browsers inclusion in Windows. In June 1998 the U.S. Court of Appeals overturned the 1997 injunction against Microsoft, although the government's

antitrust case continued ahead. Microsoft concluded its defense in late February 1999, and the trial recessed until mid-April.

Research

Gambon, Jill, Mary E. Thyfault, "Microsoft: Memos, Memos, Memos," in *Information Week*, 15 May 1995. Quotes from the company memos that contributed to the merger's collapse.

"Intuit Inc.," in *International Directory of Company Histories*, Vol. 14, St. James Press: 1996. Narrative account of the company's history beyond the proposed acquisition by Microsoft.

Intuit Inc. Home Page, available at http://www.intuit.com. Official World Wide Web Page for Intuit. Includes press releases, product information, executive biographies, financial reports, and investor information.

"Justice Wants to Stop Microsoft-Intuit Merger," in *Newsbytes*, 28 April 1995. Reports the government's filing of the lawsuit to block the merger.

MacLachlan, Claudia. "Novel Twist in Intuit Lawsuit," in *The National Law Journal*, 15 May 1995. Discusses the legal peculiarities of the government's intention to block the merger due to threats to a non-existent market.

"Microsoft Bails on Intuit Acquisition," in *Information Industry Bulletin*, 22 May 1995. Microsoft withdraws from the deal to avoid a lengthy trial.

"Microsoft to Buy Intuit in Stock Pact," in *The Wall Street Journal*, 14 October 1994. The companies announce their $1.5 billion deal.

"Microsoft Corp," in *Notable Corporate Chronologies*, The Gale Group, 1999. Lists major events in the company's history, including brief coverage of its attempted merger with Intuit.

Microsoft Corp. Home Page, available at http://www.microsoft.com. Official World Wide Web Page for Microsoft. Includes press releases, product information, executive profiles, financial reports, and investor information.

"Microsoft Legal Snag Threatens Intuit Deal," in *San Francisco Examiner*, 16 February 1995. The court's rejection of Microsoft's antitrust settlement, and possible implications to its Intuit acquisition.

Morrissey, Jane. "Microsoft Eyes Electronic Future with Intuit Buyout," in *PC Week*, 17 October 1994. Describes the benefits each company will gain by merging together.

Piven, Joshua. "Bill Gates Gets Intuit for $1.5 Billion in Stock," in *Computer Shopper*, January 1995. Provides details of the proposed stock swap.

Schlender, Brent. "Bill Gates Makes Like J.P. Morgan," in *Fortune*, 14 November 1994. Briefly describes the entry into electronic commerce that spurred Microsoft to acquire Intuit.

KIMBERLY N. STEVENS

MICROSOFT & VERMEER TECHNOLOGIES

nationality: USA
date: February 1996
affected: Microsoft Corp., USA, founded 1975
affected: Vermeer Technologies, Inc., USA, founded 1994

Microsoft Corp.
One Microsoft Way
Redmond, WA 98052-6399
USA

tel: (425)882-8080
fax: (425)936-7329
web: http://www.microsoft.com

Overview of the Acquisition

In 1996 Microsoft, which had fallen behind its rivals in products for Web site creation, made up for lost ground by acquiring Vermeer Technologies, a pioneer in that area. The deal was worth $130 million, a figure representing 13 times that company's annual revenues.

History of Microsoft Corp.

The introduction of the Altair 8800, the first commercial microcomputer, in January 1975 reunited two old friends, William Gates and Paul Allen, who approached Altair's manufacturer, Micro Instrumentation and Telemetry Systems, with the proposal of creating a BASIC interpreter for the system. The offer was met with enthusiasm, and six weeks later the newly formed Microsoft firm delivered. Having had the foresight to retain the rights to their program, they soon began customizing it for other computers, such as those produced by Apple Computer and Commodore. Gates designed the operating system—MS-DOS (short for Microsoft Disk Operating System)—for the 1981 breakthrough, the IBM PC.

In 1982 Microsoft broke into the foreign market by opening Microsoft Ltd. in England. It introduced the Microsoft Mouse, a hand-held pointing device used to move the cursor on the computer screen, as well as the word processing program Microsoft Word.

Microsoft's Windows operating system, introduced in 1985, revolutionized computers by making them more user-friendly by way of a graphical user interface, just as the Macintosh had done for Apple's customers the prior year. The company closed the year with sales of $590 million and a workforce of 2,800. In 1986 Microsoft went public, raising $61 million. It released Excel for Windows, a spreadsheet to compete against Lotus 1-2-3, in 1987; by the end of that year, it was the largest PC software company in the U.S.

Microsoft improved upon itself with the 1990 launch of Windows 3.0. That year, a price war broke out between IBM and Microsoft over their competing operating systems, Microsoft's DOS 5.0 and IBM's OS/2. In 1991 IBM and Apple

The Business

Financials

Revenue (1998): $14.48 billion

Employees (1998): 27,055

SICs / NAICS

sic 7372 - Prepackaged Software

sic 7375 - Information Retrieval Services

naics 511210 - Software Publishers

naics 514191 - On-Line Information Services

announced an alliance to create a new operating system that would allow information to be swapped between the two systems. The move was seen as a way to outflank Microsoft, which was beginning to control the software and operating systems market.

Microsoft's legal troubles began in 1988, when Apple filed suit against the company for stealing the "look and feel" of the Macintosh in its Windows program. In April 1992, the court ruled that the visuals used in Windows 2.03 and Windows 3.0 were not protected under Apple's copyrights. In December of that year, however, the company came under investigation by the Federal Trade Commission (FTC) for allegations of unfair and monopolistic trade practices.

Microsoft and the U.S. Department of Justice reached an agreement in July 1994, when the firm agreed to alter its marketing practices. Critics of this settlement claimed that it failed to curtail the company's alleged anticompetitive practices, and in February 1995 the U.S. District Court rejected the settlement as too lenient. Microsoft and the Department of Justice filed appeals.

Microsoft made determined strides to establish a name in the Internet browser industry. The Microsoft Network and Internet Explorer was included in Windows 95, a fact that didn't escape the notice of the Department of Justice. It accused Microsoft of forcing its licensees, the computer manufacturers, to include Microsoft's Internet Explorer, thereby giving the company an unfair trade advantage over other Internet browsers. Shortly thereafter, a consent decree prohibited Microsoft from requiring manufacturers to license other Microsoft products as part of the Windows package, while permitting Microsoft to continue producing integrated products. The aim of the December 1997 antitrust suit was to force Microsoft either to "unbundle" its browser from its operating system or to offer

other browsers inclusion in Windows. In June 1998 the U.S. Court of Appeals overturned the 1997 injunction against Microsoft, although the government's antitrust case continued ahead. Microsoft concluded its defense in late February 1999, and the trial recessed until mid-April.

History of Vermeer Technologies, Inc.

Vermeer Technologies was founded in April 1994 by Charles Ferguson, an independent computer consultant, and Randy Forgaard, a software designer. This Massachusetts-based startup company pioneered the development of tools for the creation of World Wide Web sites without the need for technical programming language. At this point, only savvy computer technicians were capable of authoring Web sites, using such languages as HyperText Transfer Protocol (HTTP), HyperText Mark-up Language (HTML), and Common Gateway Interface (CGI). Ferguson and Forgaard wanted to make the creation of Web sites available to mainstream computer users.

Vermeer's founders considered the industry for Internet tools on the verge of a growth explosion, and wanted to position their company to leverage that growth when it did occur. According to *The OSINetter Newsletter*, the research firm INPUT estimated that in 1994 the market for Internet products and services represented $1.1 billion; by 1999, INPUT predicted, that market would have grown to $116 billion.

In January 1995 Vermeer obtained its first venture capital investment. This $4 million injection enabled the company to devote more resources to the creation of its first product. On October 16, 1995, after a year and a half of development, that product was released commercially. FrontPage allowed users to design Web sites without entering a single line of code. Its features included: FrontPage Editor, a "what-you-see-is-what-you-get" (WYSIWYG) page creator and editor; FrontPage Explorer, a management tool for complex sites; WebBots, 12 interactive functions, such as capabilities for searching, feedback, and threaded discussions; FrontPage Wizard, customizable templates; and a To Do List, which alerted the user to potential inconsistencies or errors, such as orphaned pages. The initial release of FrontPage was designed for use on Windows 3.1, Windows NT, and Windows 95. A Macintosh version was slated for release in early 1996.

Although FrontPage met competing products from Ceneca Corp., NaviSoft, and Netscape, reviewers noted that FrontPage was the first to market certain technical features, thereby giving it an advantage over its larger rivals.

By November 1995 Vermeer's workforce had grown to 32 employees. Glowing reviews of

FrontPage drew notice from within the industry. That month the company entered into an agreement with BBN Planet Corp., a supplier of Internet hosting services, to resell and support FrontPage as part of BBN's Web Advantage service. In December it released the draft specifications for its Wizard Application Programming Interface (API) to facilitate the customization of FrontPage's functionality. At the end of 1995, its first full year of operation, Vermeer's revenues approached $10 million. One month later, the company was purchased by Microsoft for about $130 million in stock.

Market Forces Driving the Acquisition

By 1995 Microsoft, a leader in most software segments, realized that it had neglected the Web software market. It focused on boosting its presence in that area by modifying its online service, incorporating network features into existing programs, and altering its Visual Basic language to support Internet programming. Yet it still had a gap in its Web product line, a gap that its competitor Netscape Communications Corp. did not have: Web authorship tools. Netscape was poised to launch Navigator Gold, an HTML editor, as well as LiveWire, a Web site management tool.

Vermeer Technologies was a small company that had pioneered this niche area with the launch of FrontPage, a Web site creation program designed for the everyday computer user. With its ready supply of financial resources, Microsoft had both the means and the motivation to snatch up Vermeer in order to plug up the gaping hole in its Web offerings. According to a Microsoft press release, Vermeer's FrontPage product would be a "key component of Microsoft's strategy to provide a full range of tools that put the power of Web publishing, for both the Internet and intranets, in the hands of the broadest range of computer users."

Approach and Engagement

Microsoft was not the only computer software giant with eyes for Vermeer. In mid-1995 Adobe Systems Inc. had considered purchasing the young company, but opted instead for Ceneca Communications Inc., through which it released PageMill and SiteMill. Corel Corp. later entered into talks to license FrontPage, but was knocked out of the running by the aggressive emergence of Microsoft on the scene.

On January 16, 1996, Microsoft announced its acquisition of Vermeer. Terms of the stock swap were not disclosed by either company, but industry analysts estimated the transaction at about $130 million. This figure, valued at about 13 times Vermeer's annual revenues, raised the eyebrows of some experts, but most

The Officers

Chairman and CEO: William H. Gates III

President: Steve Ballmer

Exec. VP, Chief Operating Officer: Bob Herbold

Chief Technology Officer: Nathan Myhrvold

believed that it simply demonstrated Microsoft's eagerness to enter that market segment quickly.

On February 7 Microsoft issued about $92 million in stock for Vermeer, followed less than two weeks later by the remaining balance, at which time Vermeer became part of Microsoft.

Products and Services

Microsoft FrontPage was the world's leading Web site management and creation tool in 1998. It combined ease of use, innovative imaging tools, and seamless integration with the Microsoft Office family of applications. The fifth version of the FrontPage program, Microsoft FrontPage 2000, was scheduled to become commercially available in the second quarter of 1999. The product was also available as Microsoft FrontPage 1.0, Macintosh Edition.

In addition to its FrontPage family, Microsoft offered an array of other products, including business software, operating systems and servers, development tools, games, kids' tools, home productivity software, reference software, hardware, Macintosh products, and books. Among its best-known brands were the Windows family of products, including Windows 98 and 95, Windows NT Workstation, Windows NT Server, and Windows CE. Windows Technologies included Internet Explorer and Windows Media. Products for developers were Microsoft Developer Network, Microsoft Site Builder Network, and Windows Driver Development.

Changes to the Industry

Vermeer's FrontPage product filled out Microsoft's Web creation product lineup. Just prior to the acquisition, Microsoft announced a line of Office Internet Assistants that allowed users to create standalone Web pages using Microsoft Word, Excel, and PowerPoint. FrontPage provided the next step, by incorporating and manipulating such documents into Web sites. Internet Studio rounded out the line by providing a system for more sophisticated Web publishing that could include programming language and interactive multimedia.

The Players

Microsoft Chairman and CEO: William H. Gates III. Bill Gates has been a computer enthusiast since his youth. Born in 1955 in Seattle, he began programming in the BASIC computer language at the age of fourteen. He and friend Paul Allen worked on and off as computer consultants throughout high school. The duo separated when Gates attended Harvard University. He dropped out in his junior year to devote more time to Microsoft, the company he formed in 1975. Since then he has been on the fast track to success. In 1987, after Microsoft went public, Gates officially becomes a billionaire. Before the company's initial public offering, Gates' worth was impossible to calculate since most of his holdings were in Microsoft stock. The founder penned his vision of the future of information technology in *The Road Ahead* in 1995, and revised it in 1996 to give further treatment to the Internet. Gates continues to serve as chairman and CEO of his company.

Vermeer Technologies Cofounder, Chairman, and CEO: Dr. Charles H. Ferguson. Charles Ferguson had been an independent computer consultant and strategist for 12 years before establishing Vermeer. Among his clients were such heavy hitters as Apple, SunOptics, and Intel. In 1993 he joined with Charles R. Morris to pen *Computer Wars: The Fall of IBM and the Future of Global Technology*, which was named by *Business Week* as one of the best business books of the year. Ferguson provided the initial investment for the formation of Vermeer Technologies, a small company he cofounded withy Randy Forgaard. Less than two years after its formation, Vermeer was purchased by Microsoft, and Ferguson's stake was worth $15 million.

Microsoft continued to expand its Internet offerings by acquiring niche companies. At about the same time as its purchase of Vermeer, it acquired Colusa Software, producer of Omniware. That April it acquired Aspect Software Engineering, followed by both eShop and Electric Gravity in June.

Review of the Outcome

Vermeer's 40-employee workforce moved to Microsoft's Washington headquarters and formed the foundation of the company's new Web Authoring Unit, part of the newly reorganized Desktop Applications Division. Chris Peters, the former vice president of Microsoft's Office product segment, became the new unit's vice president. Reporting to Peters was Vermeer's cofounder, Randy Forgaard, who assumed the role of senior program manager. Charles Ferguson cashed out his stake in his company for about $15 million.

Research

Frook, John Evan. "Web Production Gets Boost," in *CommunicationsWeek*, 9 October 1995. Offers a description of FrontPage and competing products in the marketplace.

Mardesich, Jodi. "Microsoft Hot on Trail of Internet Software Companies," in *Computer Reseller News*, 1 July 1996. Describes Microsoft's acquisition of Web-related companies in the months following its purchase of Vermeer.

Mardesich, Jodi, and Debbie Gage. "Microsoft Buys its Way into Web Tools Market," in *Computer Reseller News*, 5 February 1996. Details the acquisition deal.

"Microsoft Corp," in *Notable Corporate Chronologies*, The Gale Group, 1999. Lists major events in the company's history, including brief coverage of its attempted merger with Intuit.

Microsoft Corp. Home Page, available at http://www.microsoft.com. Official World Wide Web Page for Microsoft. Includes press releases, product information, executive profiles, financial reports, and investor information.

Moeller, Michael. "Startup Takes Guesswork out of Web Creation," in *PC Week*, 25 September 1995. Details the newly launched FrontPage product.

Moltzen, Edward F. "Vermeer Leaders Took Home a Bundle in Microsoft Stock Swap," in *Computer Reseller News*, 11 March 1996. Relates the lucrative stock settlements received by Vermeer's founders upon the Microsoft acquisition.

"Special Report: Vermeer Technologies Inc.," in *The OSINetter Newsletter*, May 1995. Profiles Vermeer Technologies.

KIMBERLY N. STEVENS

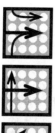

MOBIL & SUPERIOR OIL

nationality: USA
date: September 28, 1984
affected: Mobil Corp., USA, founded 1866
affected: Superior Oil Co., USA

Mobil Corp.
3225 Gallows Rd.
Fairfax, VA 22037-0001
USA

tel: (703)846-3000
fax: (703)846-4666
web: http://www.mobil.com

Overview of the Acquisition

In a family dispute that *Business Week* called "a feud J.R. Ewing would relish," the squabbling among Keck family members over the future of Superior Oil effectively put the company up for sale in the early 1980s. Proxy fights and shifting alliances eliminated many of Superior's takeover defenses, clearing the way for hungry suitors. Mobil was particularly intent on acquiring the company, since it had recently been thwarted by government regulators in its bids for both Conoco and Marathon. Mobil secretly secured the necessary agreements to acquire the exploration and production firm, and in September 1984 completed its $5.7 billion purchase of Superior Oil.

History of Mobil Corp.

In 1866, carpenter and part-time inventor Matthew Ewing devised an innovative method of distilling kerosene from oil by using a vacuum. Although this production method was less successful than he had hoped, his partner, Hiram Bond Everest, noticed that the gummy residue from this process was suitable as a lubricator. Ewing and Everest took out a patent on behalf of Vacuum Oil Co., which was incorporated on October 4, 1866. Ewing later sold his interest in the company in order to focus on experiments in kerosene. The new company soon enjoyed great success due to the demand for heavy vacuum oil, particularly the Gargoyle 600-W Steam Cylinder Oil, by manufacturers of steam engines and the new internal-combustion engines.

John D. Rockefeller's Standard Oil Co. acquired Vacuum Oil in 1879, paying $200,000 for 75% of its stock. Despite its small size, Vacuum was extended a great degree of latitude by Standard's management. In 1886, Everest led Vacuum on an independent course in foreign sales, opening affiliates in Montreal, Canada, and Liverpool, England. By the turn of the century, Vacuum also had operations in France, Germany, Italy, Hungary, India, Singapore, Japan, Australia, New Zealand, and Cuba.

The Business

Financials

Revenue (1998): $53.5 billion

Employees (1998): 41,500

SICs / NAICS

sic 2911 - Petroleum Refining

sic 2992 - Lubricating Oils & Greases

sic 1311 - Crude Petroleum & Natural Gas

sic 1321 - Natural Gas Liquids

sic 5541 - Gasoline Service Stations

sic 2865 - Cyclic Crudes & Intermediates

sic 2869 - Industrial Organic Chemicals Nec

naics 324110 - Petroleum Refineries

naics 324191 - Petroleum Lubricating Oil and Grease Manufacturing

naics 211111 - Crude Petroleum and Natural Gas Extraction

naics 211112 - Natural Gas Liquid Extraction

naics 447110 - Gasoline Stations with Convenience Stores

naics 325110 - Petrochemical Manufacturing

In 1910, Vacuum's holding company, Standard Oil Co. of New Jersey, invested $500,000 to retool its Bayonne, New Jersey, refinery to include the manufacture of Vacuum's lubricants for export. By that time Standard's subsidiaries controlled nearly all of the foreign market, with Socony's affiliates handling about 30% and Vacuum Oil contributing six percent of the total. Socony's domestic operations included five refineries that produced kerosene, gasoline, and naptha for sale in New York and New England through jobbers and a growing number of new roadside stores known as "gas stations."

In 1911, the U.S. Supreme Court ordered the dissolution of Standard of New Jersey, charging violation of the Sherman Antitrust Act. Among the 33 new companies created as a result were Vacuum and Socony. These newly independent companies were cut off from their former sister companies, and spent the next two decades expanding operations to become more self-reliant. Vacuum, which focused on the refinery business, completed construction of a new refinery for export products in 1917. Socony increased its production operations by acquiring 45% of Magnolia Petroleum Co., which owned wells, pipelines, and a Texas refinery, and marketed chiefly in Texas and the Southwest.

Socony purchased the remainder of Magnolia in 1925, and the next year acquired General Petroleum Corp. of California to help supply its large Far East markets. In 1929, Vacuum acquired Lubrite Refining Co., and in 1930 purchased both Wadhams Oil Corp. and White Star Refining Co. Entering the Midwest for the first time in 1930, Socony purchased White Eagle Oil Refining Co., operator of gas stations in 11 states.

Vacuum Oil and Socony merged when Socony purchased the assets of Vacuum in 1931, forming Socony-Vacuum Corp. To supply its Far East markets more efficiently, it joined with Standard of New Jersey to form the Standard-Vacuum Oil Co. (Stanvac) in 1933. The next year Socony-Vacuum Corp. changed its name to Socony-Vacuum Oil Co., Inc. By that time it had become the nation's second-largest oil concern, with nearly $500 million in sales. It also sold a full line of petroleum products in warehouses and gas stations in 43 states, many sporting the Mobil brand name or its winged, red horse logo.

By World War II, Stanvac contributed 35% of Socony-Vacuum's corporate earnings. With 14 refineries and a fleet of 54 ocean-going tankers, Socony-Vacuum's European holdings were vulnerable to intensifying warfare. In 1941 its large refinery in Gravenchon, France, was destroyed by retreating French in a blaze that lasted seven days. Likewise, a $30 million refinery in Palembang, Indonesia, was burned to prevent Japanese control. German submarines destroyed 32 company ships, killing 432 crewmembers. Its capital losses and declining civilian revenue, however, were replaced by increases in military sales.

Capitalizing on the worldwide recognition of the Mobil gasoline brand, the company changed its name to Socony Mobil Oil Co., Inc. in 1955. Egypt's nationalization of the Suez Canal the following year provided one of the many indications that the company's Middle Eastern dependence would prove to be a liability. The canal was reopened in 1957, creating a surplus of oil and a corresponding drop in prices that forced the company to reorganize. As part of that reorganization, Magnolia Petroleum and General Petroleum merged. Also in 1959 the company formed two chief operating divisions: Mobil Oil Co. for North American operations and Mobil International Co. to serve all other parts of the world.

Mobil Chemical Co. was formed as a subsidiary in 1960 to take advantage of the many discoveries in petrochemicals. Six years later Socony Mobil Oil Co. was renamed Mobil Oil Corp., and its red horse logo was retired in favor of a bright red "o" within the Mobil moniker.

By 1966, the Middle East supplied 43% of Mobil's crude production. Massive world consumption of oil surpassed production, shifting the market in favor of the Organization of Petroleum Exporting Countries (OPEC). In 1973, OPEC imposed an embargo on oil shipments to the U.S. for six months and commenced a gradual annexation of U.S.-owned oil properties. The price of oil quadrupled overnight, marking a new era of energy awareness. Sales and profits for all of the major oil companies dramatically increased as an immediate result; Mobil's sales nearly tripled within four years to $32 billion. As its profits reached record heights, Mobil responded to congressional and media criticism by defending the rights of members of the oil industry to conduct business as they deemed appropriate.

However, to protect itself from any anti-oil company backlash, Mobil embarked on a diversification campaign. In 1974, it acquired Marcor, owner of the Montgomery Ward retailer, followed by Container Corp. of America, a paperboard manufacturer. Its hold on these and other extraneous assets was only temporary, and by 1993 it had divested numerous underperforming operations.

Mobil Corp. was formed as a holding company for Mobil Oil Corp. and Mobil Chemical in 1976. In 1981, it was unsuccessful in its attempt to acquire Conoco Inc., a performance that was repeated the following year in its bid for Marathon. In 1984, it purchased Superior Oil Co. for $5.7 billion, gaining extensive reserves of natural gas and oil in Canada and the U.S. Four years later Mobil discontinued retail gasoline businesses in 20 states, deriving 88% of its retail revenue from the remaining 14 states, and cut its oil-related employment by 20%.

The company made determined efforts to increase exploration activities. By 1991, new discoveries enabled Mobil to increase its oil and natural gas production by five percent, to 1.6 million barrels per day. Later that year it acquired Exxon's Australian facilities, and divested its Wyoming coalmine and hundreds of Texas oil wells for a total of $570 million. In 1994, the company signed a production-sharing agreement with Vietnam's state oil company to develop the offshore Blue Dragon field. In October of the following year, it sold its plastics unit, Packaging Corp., maker of Hefty and Baggies products, to Tenneco for $1.27 billion in order to renew its focus on the core areas of oil, gas, and petrochemicals.

In 1996, Mobil and British Petroleum consolidated their European refining, fuel, and gas station operations in a $5 billion agreement. According to the pact's division of labor, BP was responsible for the refining, marketing, and distribution, while Mobil

The Officers

Chairman and CEO: Lucio A. Noto

President and Chief Operating Officer: Eugene A. Renna

Exec. VP and Chief Financial Officer: Harold R. Cramer

Sr. VP and General Counsel: Samuel H. Gillespie III

handled the lubricant portion of the business. Two years later Mobil agreed to be acquired by Exxon Corp. to form Exxon Mobil, the world's largest petroleum company.

History of Superior Oil Co.

By the early 1980s, Superior Oil had become the largest independent petroleum producer in the U.S. Rather than participating in all aspects of the oil businesses, it operated chiefly in North American exploration and production, avoiding refining and marketing activities. Its reserves held the equivalent of about one billion barrels of oil and gas, and revenues in 1982 reached $2 billion.

Superior's founder, William M. Keck, died in 1964, leaving his son Howard B. Keck at the helm. For two decades he steered the company on a successful course, repeatedly rebuffing interested suitors. He retired as chairman in 1981, yet retained much of his control over Superior through his involvement in a number of board committees. With his direct ownership of an 11.5% stake, as well as the authority over another 9.1% interest held in a family trust, Keck had a 20% control of Superior.

It was this influence of Keck on Superior's operations that ignited a bitter family feud. Willametta Keck Day asserted that her brother, in refusing to consider acquisition offers, was protecting his own interests at the expense of Superior's other shareholders. Day, who owned a 3.5% stake in the company, also objected to the low amount in dividends paid to shareholders, as well as Keck's $850,000 salary as the sole guardian of the family trust.

This feud effectively opened the bidding for Superior, as hopeful suitors now stood a greater chance of gaining the acceptance of their acquisition offers. In early March 1983, Mesa Petroleum Co. purchased a 1.6% stake in Superior, and soon increased that interest to 2.5%. Later in March, Day mailed a proxy statement to shareholders, calling for the establishment of a committee, independent of Keck and all other directors, to review and recommend any acceptable offers for at least 45% of the company's stock. This proposal was approved by shareholders in late May.

For the most part, the Keck family remained out of the headlines through the summer. Then, on October 20, 1983, Keck resigned as director of and consultant to Superior, declining to offer an explanation for this sudden move. By that time, he had increased his personal stake in the company to 12.3%.

In November 1983, the saga took a strange twist, as opponents became allies. Keck and Day joined forces against Superior's management, which had recently adopted anti-takeover measures, to put Superior up for sale. The newly adopted defenses consisted of two components. The first, a scorched-earth feature, became effective when a suitor acquired a 35% stake. It would allow shareholders to redeem their stock at the highest price that the suitor had paid for it over the previous two years. This tactic would cost Superior an estimated $2 billion, driving it nearly bankrupt. The second feature was a poison pill that would go into effect should a company make a cash-and-securities offer of varying values, in which case shareholders could demand the higher value for all outstanding stock.

Keck launched a proxy fight on December 1 to overturn the anti-takeover measures. Days later, management rescinded the poison pill, but remained firm in its resolve to keep Superior independent.

The Keck family continued to lobby for the sale of Superior, and in March 1984 agreed to sell out to Mobil Corp. That company also offered to purchase all remaining outstanding stock at $45 per share, an offer that was accepted by the majority of Superior shareholders in September. The deal was completed later that month, and Superior became a subsidiary of Mobil.

Market Forces Driving the Acquisition

The ongoing, well-publicized feuding over the independence of Superior Oil effectively put the company up for sale. For years, Howard Keck steadfastly refused to consider acquisition offers. His sister, Willametta Keck Day, along with a majority of shareholders, opposed that rigid stance, and in 1983 formed a committee for the evaluation of any future offers. Within months, Keck reversed his position, joining with Day to overturn the anti-takeover measures that Superior's management had adopted. They successfully persuaded management to eliminate one such tactic, a poison pill. With the removal of that barrier, hopeful suitors believed that Superior was finally within reach.

Mobil Corp. had been unsuccessful in its bid for Conoco and Marathon in 1981 and 1982, respectively. It desperately sought to increase its domestic reserves, as it found itself in the undesirable position of relying on reserves in the Middle East. Thwarted in its bids for Conoco and Marathon due to antitrust concerns over refining and marketing activities, Mobil desired to acquire a company with few operations in those businesses.

Superior Oil was unique in that respect. Its assets consisted of oil and gas reserves in the U.S. and Canada that would complement Mobil's own operations in North America. The addition of those reserves would increase its global position by 20% and would firmly entrench it as the second-largest oil company in the U.S., after Exxon.

Approach and Engagement

On March 11, 1984, Mobil made a two-part announcement. It disclosed its agreement to purchase a 22% stake in Superior Oil from the Keck family, as well as its offer to purchase the remaining outstanding stock for $45 per share. The announcement stunned Wall Street—an effect that Mobil had taken great pains to ensure in order to prevent Superior's market price from escalating over its bid.

The secret deal involved two nearly simultaneous agreements. By March 8 Mobil's chairman, William Tavoulareas, had secured Howard Keck's commitment to sell his stake in Superior. The company then rapidly obtained the agreements to acquire the interests held by Willametta Day, William Keck II, and six different trusts.

Meanwhile, Mobil had been negotiating with Superior's executives. On March 10, Superior's board approved the $45 per share, or $5.7 billion, acquisition offer. Late the following day, Tavoulareas, checking into a hotel under an alias, obtained the signature of Superior's chairman, Fred Ackman, on an agreement to acquire the company's remaining outstanding stock.

On May 11, Mobil launched its bid, offering $20 in cash and $25 in securities for each Superior share. Days later the U.S. Federal Trade Commission approved the deal. On September 20, nearly 83% of Superior's shareholders voted in favor of the offer. The acquisition was completed shortly thereafter, and Superior became a wholly owned subsidiary of Mobil.

Products and Services

By 1998, Mobil was a major producer, refiner, and marketer of petroleum. Its exploration and production activities focused on locating, developing, and producing hydrocarbon resources worldwide. The company produced the equivalent of 1.7 million barrels of oil per day, and had increased its proven reserves to 7.6 billion barrels of oil equivalent, a 12-year supply.

Mobil's marketing and refining facilities, with refining capacity of 2.2 million barrels of oil per day, operated at a 94% utilization rate in 1998. It sold 144 million gallons of refined products daily in more than 15,000 service stations in 50 countries. Additionally, Mobil lubricants were marketed in more than 100 countries.

Mobil Chemical operated 28 chemical facilities located in 10 countries. Its principal products included basic petrochemicals (ethylene, propylene, benzene, and paraxylene), intermediates (ethylene glycol), and a key derivative (polyethylene).

Changes to the Industry

The acquisition of Superior Oil contributed about one billion barrels of oil equivalent to Mobil's North American reserves, adding 314 million barrels of oil and 4.25 trillion cubic feet of natural gas. The augmentation of those assets increased Mobil's market position in the U.S. by 27% and globally by 20%. The companies' combined revenues of more than $60 billion secured Mobil's position as the nation's second-largest oil company, behind Exxon.

Research

Cole, Robert J. "Superior Oil Gets Offer from Mobil," in *The New York Times*, 12 March 1984. Reveals Mobil's agreements to acquire Superior.

———. "Superior Oil Loses Proxy Vote," in *The New York Times*, 25 May 1983. Reports Day's success in establishing an independent committee for acquisition offer reviews.

"Family Feud at Superior Oil," in *The New York Times*, 30 April 1983. Describes the disputes leading up to Day's proxy fight.

"A Feud J.R. Ewing Would Relish," in *Business Week*, 28 March 1983. Provides a background into the ongoing Keck family disputes.

"Mobil Corp.," in *Notable Corporate Chronologies*, The Gale Group, 1999. Provides a historical review of the company.

Mobil Corp. Home Page, available at http://www.mobil.com. Official World Wide Web Page for Mobil. Includes information on products and services, finances, and employment, as well as news releases, biographies, and a company history.

Potts, Mark. "Founder's Children United against Superior Oil Plan," in *The Washington Post*, 29 November 1983. Details the alliance of Keck and Day against Superior's management.

CAROLINE C. HOBART

MONSANTO & G.D. SEARLE

Monsanto Co.
800 N. Lindbergh Blvd.
St. Louis, MO 63167
USA

tel: (314)694-1000
web: http://www.monsanto.com

nationality: USA
date: October 1, 1985
affected: Monsanto Co., USA, founded 1901
affected: G.D. Searle & Co., USA, founded 1889

Overview of the Acquisition

Monsanto's 1985 acquisition of G.D. Searle provided the company with a much-needed pharmaceutical operation and distribution network. However, the $2.7 billion acquisition proved to be more costly than the purchase price, as Monsanto also inherited hundreds of lawsuits over Searle's Copper 7 intrauterine device.

History of Monsanto Co.

In 1901 John Francis Queeny founded Monsanto Chemical Works, named after his wife's maiden name, for the production of saccharin in St. Louis, Missouri. Its largest customer for the artificial sweetener was Coca-Cola Co. The company added caffeine and vanillin to its product line by 1905. Ten years later its sales surpassed $1 million.

Monsanto opened a branch office in New York in 1913. Four years later the chemical firm began the production of aspirin and remained the nation's largest producer of the pain reliever until the 1980s. In 1918 it acquired Commercial Acid Co. of Illinois in order to widen the scope of Monsanto's factory operations. The following year it expanded overseas with the establishment of a joint venture to form U.K.-based R.A. Graesser Chemical Works, the world's largest producer of phenol and cresol at the time.

The company made its initial public offering in 1927 to reduce the debt that it had accrued during the post-World War I depression. The next year, Monsanto acquired the remaining 50% of Graesser and later renamed it Monsanto Chemicals Ltd. In 1929 Monsanto doubled in size and gained entry into key rubber chemical markets by acquiring Rubber Services Laboratories Co. and Nitro Co. It continued its acquisition spree into the following year, purchasing the Australian-based Southern Cross Chemical Co. Pty. Ltd.

In 1935 the firm, by then named Monsanto Chemical Co., expanded into the soap and detergents industry by acquiring Swann Corp. Three years later it expanded into plastics and resins by purchasing Fiberloid Corp. During World

War II Monsanto became involved in nuclear research by working on the Manhattan Project and then operating research facilities for the government until the 1980s.

In April 1947 the cargo ship *S.S. Grandcamp*, carrying ammonium nitrate fertilizer, exploded in the Texas City harbor, destroying the town and killing 512 people. Two years later Monsanto joined with American Viscose to form the Chemstrand Corp. for the production of synthetic fibers. In 1955, with the acquisition of Lion Oil, Monsanto began providing petrochemical raw materials.

Monsanto laid the foundation for the future success of its agricultural group with the 1956 commercialization of Randox, an herbicide capable of killing weeds before they broke ground. The following year the company expanded into plastic bottle technology with the acquisition of Plax Corp. It diversified into electronics materials in 1959 with the opening of a facility for the production of ultra-pure silicon. Sales exceeded $1 billion for the first time in 1962.

In recognition of the growing diversity of its product line, the company dropped the word "Chemical" from its corporate name in 1964. By that time it was involved in nylon and acrylic fiber production, oil and gas exploration, fabricated plastic production, and the manufacture of thousands of specialty and commodity chemical products, including biodegradable detergents.

Monsanto introduced AstroTurf in 1966 as an artificial playing surface for the Houston Astrodome. In 1969 the company launched Lasso herbicide and formed the Monsanto Enviro-Chem Systems subsidiary. It also acquired the seed producer Farmers Hybrid Co. and the valve and controls systems maker Fisher Governor Co. Due to increased competition from Japan, the company discontinued the production of saccharin in 1972.

In 1977 Monsanto entered into a petrochemical joint venture with Conoco, but sold its stake when DuPont acquired Conoco four years later. This marked the beginning of the firm's move away from commodity chemicals. In 1979, despite its environmental efforts, Monsanto was one of several defendants named in a lawsuit regarding Agent Orange, a defoliant used during the Vietnam War. The suit claimed that the dioxin in Agent Orange caused permanent damage to hundreds of veterans. In 1984 Monsanto and seven other manufacturers agreed to a $180 million settlement of the lawsuit.

In 1980 Monsanto formed a division to focus on gas separation systems; this Permea group was sold in 1991. Company scientists became the first to genetical-

The Business

Financials

Revenue (1998): $8.6 billion

Employees (1998): 31,800

SICs / NAICS

sic 2879 - Agricultural Chemicals Nec

sic 2834 - Pharmaceutical Preparations

sic 8731 - Commercial Physical Research

sic 2899 - Chemical Preparations Nec

naics 325320 - Pesticide and Other Agricultural Chemical Manufacturing

naics 325412 - Pharmaceutical Preparation Manufacturing

naics 541710 - Research and Development in the Physical, Engineering, and Life Sciences

naics 325199 - All Other Basic Organic Chemical Manufacturing

ly modify a plant cell in 1982. That year Monsanto formed Monsanto Hybritech Seed International, and the following year it acquired Jacob Hartz Seed Co. In 1983 Richard Mahoney took the company's helm.

The company expanded into pharmaceuticals and artificial sweeteners with the 1985 acquisition of G.D. Searle & Co. Soon after, hundreds of lawsuits over Searle's Copper 7 intrauterine device became Monsanto's responsibility. In the ensuing reorganization, the company divested many businesses outside its focus on agriculture, pharmaceuticals, and food products.

In 1988 Monsanto acquired Greensweep, maker of lawn and garden products. The following year the firm released Cytotec, the world's first anti-ulcer medication. Simplesse, an all natural fat substitute, was commercialized in 1990. Two years later the company sold its Fisher Controls subsidiary.

By 1993 Monsanto had spent in excess of $300 million over the previous ten years to develop posilac bovine somatotropin (BST), a genetically engineered product similar to the hormone produced in cows that controls milk production. That year it acquired Ortho Consumer Products and formed the Solaris unit to combine Ortho's assets with the Greensweep and Roundup products.

Akzo Nobel NV and Monsanto merged their rubber and chemical operations in 1994 to form Flexsys,

The Officers

Chairman and CEO: Robert B. Shapiro

President: Hendrik A. Verfaillie

Vice Chairman: Richard U. De Schutter

Vice Chairman: Robert W. Reynolds

Sr. VP and Chief Financial Officer: Gary L. Crittenden

the world's largest maker of rubber chemicals. The next year Monsanto purchased Merck & Co.'s specialty chemicals unit, Kelco, for $1.08 billion.

In an unprecedented move, the U.S. Environmental Protection Agency (EPA) granted its approval in 1995 for the growing of plants that had been bioengineered to produce their own pesticide. The EPA permitted Monsanto to plant, but not to sell, potatoes, corn, and cotton crops that had been genetically altered to produce an insecticide. That year the company also purchased a 49.9% stake in Calgene Inc., obtaining the remaining stake in 1997.

In 1996 Monsanto received a patent for synthetic genes that enabled plants to create their own insecticides. The company filed patent infringement suits against rivals Ciba-Geigy AG and Mycogen Corp. for their unauthorized use of this gene. That year Monsanto strengthened its operations in seeds by purchasing Asgrow Agronomics and Monsoy, the second-largest soybean seed marketer in the U.S. and the world, respectively. Monsanto also acquired the plant biotechnology assets of W.R. Grace's Agracetus unit.

The company improved its position in cardiovascular, arthritis, and women's healthcare products in 1996 by acquiring the Latin American-based Biolab Industrias Farmaceuticas S.A. The following year it purchased a stake in Dekalb Genetics, the second-largest seed company in the U.S. The firm also completely exited from the chemicals business by spinning off Solutia Inc.

In 1998 Monsanto terminated a merger agreement with American Home Products Corp. That year it acquired the remainder of DEKALB Genetics, the international seed business of Cargill Inc., and Plant Breeding International Cambridge Ltd. It also entered into a merger agreement with Delta and Pine Land Co., a leading cottonseed producer. With the exception of Roundup, the company's lawn and garden businesses were sold in January 1999 to The Scotts Company for $300 million. The following month saw the U.S. commercial release of the Celebrex arthritis treatment.

History of G.D. Searle & Co.

Gideon D. Searle founded his namesake company in Chicago in 1889. Initially the small firm sold a diverse array of products, but soon began limiting its offerings to specialized, profitable items. Searle established a laboratory for the development of such products, focusing on pharmaceuticals for the treatment of cardiovascular diseases, the central nervous system, and mental disorders. In 1949 the company introduced Dramamine, the first motion sickness pill.

Its reputation as a manufacturer of quality drugs enabled the company to achieve annual revenue increases of $1 million to $2 million, and in 1960 it recorded sales of $37 million. In just four years that figure exploded to $87 million with its greatest innovation to date—"the pill." In 1960 Searle unveiled Enovid, the first oral contraceptive, which became one of the decade's most revolutionary drugs.

Competition in the birth control industry soon arose, reducing Searle's market share. Falling profitability and increasing costs of research and development prompted the company to embark on an acquisition spree. During the remainder of the 1960s, Searle accumulated a diverse mix of companies; some, like nuclear instrumentation and medical electronics, were outside the pharmaceuticals arena. By 1971 about 80% of total profits originated from sales of pharmaceuticals other than oral contraceptives. That year the firm recorded a 12% increase in profitability, but only after using its Puerto Rican operations as a tax shelter; profits before taxes actually dropped $5 million.

By 1973 the sale of Aldactone and Aldactazide, two diuretics used in the treatment of hypertension, accounted for 18% of company revenues, surpassing sales generated from the birth control pill for the first time. The next year Searle released its Copper 7 intrauterine device (IUD), so named because the contraceptive was shaped like the number seven with copper wiring wrapped around its leg.

Meanwhile, Searle awaited approval to market aspartame, an artificial sweetener, as a food additive. This new sweetener lacked the bitter aftertaste of saccharin, as well as 95.5% of the calories of sugar, yet its high cost and relatively short shelf life precluded a speedy acceptance by the profitable soft drink market. Still, Searle persevered in the test marketing of Equal, the consumer brand name for the product.

In December 1975 the Food and Drug Administration (FDA) suspended Searle's permission to market aspartame. This unprecedented move followed allegations by the FDA that the company suppressed laboratory test results regarding the cancer risks of Aldactone and Flagyl, a remedy for reproductive tract infections. This mar on the company's image was compounded by financial difficulties arising from the significant interest charges obtained from loans against the company's Puerto Rican operations.

To turn Searle around, Donald H. Rumsfeld, a former congressman, presidential aide, and defense secretary, was brought in as president and CEO. Rumsfeld immediately sold unprofitable divisions and engaged new management. He also orchestrated the acquisition of Vision Centers, a lucrative eyewear retailer that was later renamed Pearle Vision Centers. By 1981, as Searle obtained FDA approval for aspartame, the company reported the second-highest profit margin among 30 leading U.S. drug firms.

Searle invested heavily in pharmaceutical research to strengthen its production of aspartame. Sales of this sweetener increased from $13 million in 1981 to $74 million the following year. This product received FDA approval to enter the soft drink market, and by the end of 1983, under the consumer name NutraSweet, listed virtually all major bottlers among its customers. Sales of aspartame reached $336 million that year. Generating 47% of total company sales, NutraSweet had become the focus of much of Searle's resources.

By 1984 the Searle family, which held a 34% stake in the company, believed that NutraSweet's market potential had peaked and decided to sell off part of its holdings. However, there were no takers. Other companies steered clear of Searle because the prospects for NutraSweet were limited and because the Internal Revenue Service had launched an investigation into its Puerto Rican subsidiary. The Searle family reduced its stake to 21% by reselling shares back to the company in April 1985. Just after this transaction, chemical firm Monsanto Co. purchased Searle for $2.7 billion. As part of the Searle package, however, Monsanto also inherited the company's tax liabilities as well as the unexpected and massive litigation against Searle's Copper 7 IUD. Faced with hundreds of lawsuits, Searle pulled the IUD from the U.S. market in 1986. The suits and settlements continued throughout the decade.

Meanwhile, Monsanto invested in Searle's research and development program, announcing plans to introduce one important new product each year. In 1987 Searle launched the "Patient Promise" program, which offered refunds for any product that proved ineffective. This program helped enable Searle's blood pressure treatment, Calan SR, to capture a 20% market share in 1990 and to become the company's most profitable product.

The Players

Monsanto Chairman and CEO: Richard J. Mahoney. After earning a chemistry degree from the University of Massachusetts in the 1950s, Richard Mahoney took a job with U.S. Rubber, later known as Uniroyal. After only a couple of months, he moved to Alaska to fulfill his Airforce ROTC duties. He returned to the chemicals industry by gaining employment first at Alco Chemical and then at Shawinigan Resins. When the latter company was acquired by Monsanto, Mahoney moved through the executive ranks there, becoming CEO in 1983. In 1994 he was succeeded as chairman and CEO by Robert B. Shapiro.

G.D. Searle President and CEO: Donald H. Rumsfeld. Born in Chicago in 1932, Donald Rumsfeld interrupted a political career to take the helm of G.D. Searle as president and CEO until 1985. He was a congressman from 1963 to 1969, at which time he became a director of the Office of Economic Opportunity and then of the Cost of Living Council. Rumsfeld was appointed Chief of Staff in 1974, moving on to become the Secretary of Defense in 1975. In 1996 he was named a possible Republican vice presidential candidate.

Market Forces Driving the Acquisition

By the mid-1980s Monsanto was determined to exit the commodity chemicals business. Subject to erratic price fluctuations, bulk chemicals no longer held much growth potential, and chemical producers began moving to related industries. Monsanto had already begun a shift away from bulk chemicals and had built a profitable agricultural chemicals operation. This business, based primarily on its Roundup and Lasso products, generated 65% of total operating earnings in 1984, and made Monsanto the leading U.S. producer of herbicides. Company executives were convinced that continued success in this area was unlikely, however. The patent on Lasso was scheduled to expire in 1988, clearing the way for generic competition. Even more critical was the decreasing importance of traditional chemical research in favor of biotechnology. In that field, Monsanto's direction had first focused on agricultural products, then on animal nutrition, and finally on human healthcare and pharmaceuticals.

It was the latter market segment that held the most appeal for Monsanto. "Our objective is to be one of the four or five major pharmaceutical companies," said president Richard Mahoney in *Forbes*. To this end, G.D. Searle would provide not only an established pharmaceutical division but also a valuable distribution network, contacts with the FDA, and marketing expertise.

As for G.D. Searle, several troublesome situations spurred the company to consider making itself available for acquisition. Its strongest product, NutraSweet, was a source of concern for the pharmaceutical firm. First, its patent was scheduled to expire in 1987, at which time competition could be expected to arise. Second, questions of its side effects were not completely dispelled. And third, the sweetener held most of Searle's interests, as new pharmaceuticals in the development pipeline were practically non-existent.

Approach and Engagement

In September 1984 the Searle family decided to reduce the risk in owning 34% of a company revolved around a single product, NutraSweet, by announcing that it would sell the firm. Monsanto entered into a joint agreement to make an offer for Searle's pharmaceutical and consumer products business, while another company bid on its aspartame division. Searle's board, however, rejected all offers, declaring in March 1985 that the company would remain independent.

The industry was therefore stunned by the July 18 announcement that Monsanto would acquire Searle. Searle's own executives appeared only slightly less surprised by this development. "We closed the window on offers last March," said Searle's president, John Robson, in *The New York Times*. "Unsolicited and unexpected, Monsanto came back."

Monsanto had exited from the artificial sweetener industry some time earlier and, not intending to reenter it, had excluded the aspartame division in its previous bid for Searle. In acquiring the whole company, however, Monsanto would benefit from the profitable NutraSweet business to cover the company while its pharmaceutical products worked their way through the research and development pipeline. "NutraSweet brings a very interesting earnings stream in the time between now and when our biotechnology begins to pay off, so we're going to stick with it," said Mahoney in an August issue of *Business Week*.

The $2.7 billion deal was a cash tender offer for all outstanding Searle shares, followed by a $65 per share exchange for the remaining shares. That $2.7 billion

offer represented about 17 times Searle's estimated 1985 earnings, and the $65 per share price was a $7 premium to the going value of the company's stock.

To finance the deal, Monsanto sold off some assets. In August 1985 it agreed to sell Searle's 40% stake in Pearle Health Services, the nation's leading eyewear retailer, to the U.S. unit of Grand Metropolitan PLC for $386 million. Monsanto also announced that it would divest itself of its oil and gas operations, and possibly its small consumer products division.

By late August Monsanto had acquired 97.5% of Searle's common stock, and on October 1, 1985, completed the acquisition.

Products and Services

In 1998, Monsanto operated in three business sectors:

The Agriculture sector worked to transform the way that food and fiber were produced everywhere in the world. Products included: Roundup brand family of non-selective herbicides, Lasso, Permit, Harness, Avadex, and other selective herbicides; Bollgard and Ingard insect-protected cotton; YieldGard and Maisgard insect-protected corn; NewLeaf insect-protected potatoes; Roundup Ready soybeans, canola, cotton, and other crops resistant to Roundup brand herbicides; Posilac bovine somatotropin; Quantum hybrid wheat; and Bollgard/Roundup Ready stacked-gene cotton. The Agriculture sector generated revenues in excess of $4 billion in 1998.

Searle comprised the Pharmaceutical sector, which discovered, developed, and marketed pharmaceutical products. Such products were divided into four main lines: **Arthritis**: Daypro, a nonsteroidal anti-inflammatory drug (NSAID); Cytotec, an ulcer drug for the prevention of NSAID-induced ulcers; and Arthrotec, a safer NSAID for the treatment of arthritis; **Cardiovascular**: Calan SR and Isoptin, calcium channel blockers for hypertension; Covera HS, a treatment for hypertension; and Aldactone, an aldosterone receptor blocker for hypertension; **Women's Health**: Demulen, Norinyl, and Tri-Norinyl, oral contraceptives; Flagyl, an anti-infective; and Synarel, an endometriosis treatment; and **Sleep**: Ambien, an insomnia treatment. Searle's 1998 revenues were $2.9 billion.

The Nutrition & Consumer sector produced food ingredients, consumer sweeteners, and other consumer products, and served as a bridge between Monsanto's agriculture and pharmaceutical divisions. Its products were divided into three segments: **Food Ingredients**: NutraSweet brand sweetener,

NutraSweet Custom Select line of sweeteners, Keltrol xanthan gum, Kelcogel gellan gum, Manucol and Manugel sodium alginates, Manucolester and Kelcoloid propylene glycol alginates, and Simplesse fat substitute; **Consumer Sweeteners**: Low-calorie aspartame sweeteners: Equal, Canderel, NutraSweet, Chucker, Misura, Flix, Sweet Choice, SweetMate, Sabro, Semble; Mid-calorie sweeteners: Sukari aspartame/sugar blend; and Sugar: Sweet Home pre packaged premium sugar; and **Lawn And Garden**: Roundup herbicide, Weed-B-Gon herbicide, Bug-B-Gon insecticide, Home Defense insecticide, Ant-Stop ant killer, Rose Pride fertilizer and systemic insecticide, Diazinon Plus insecticide, Dursban insecticide, White Swan packaged seeds, and Phostrogen plant foods and garden products. The Nutrition & Consumer sector had revenues of $1.5 billion in 1998.

Review of the Outcome

Monsanto reorganized after its absorption of Searle, taking a $559 million charge in the fourth quarter of 1985. In November it agreed to sell Searle's consumer products division, including the Metamucil laxative and Dramamine motion sickness remedy, to Procter & Gamble. The company combined six units into two new subsidiaries: Monsanto Chemical Co. and Monsanto Agricultural Co., and separated the NutraSweet business from Searle by establishing the NutraSweet Co. The firm also announced a workforce reduction, laying off up to 500 employees and offering early retirement to 3,800 others.

While such moves were typical in the months following a consolidation, Monsanto also inherited some unique problems in its acquisition of Searle. First was the assumption of a possible $499 million in liability from the pharmaceutical company's Puerto Rican tax shelter. Far worse, however, were the unexpected legal problems arising from Searle's Copper 7 intrauterine device (IUD). Released in 1974, the contraceptive was the most popular IUD in the world; more than seven million had been sold by October 1985. By that time, too, hundreds of lawsuits had been filed against Searle by women alleging severe medical, sometimes even lethal, effects from the device. They claimed that the Copper 7 caused the development of pelvic inflammatory disease, which could lead to sterility and possibly death. Moreover, the plaintiffs charged that Searle had

doctored or deleted clinical test data indicating the potential risks of the device. According to *The Wall Street Journal*, a company medical supervisor testified that "to make a 1972 report to the FDA 'more readable,' he cut the number of suspected pelvic disease cases from 2.7% to 1.8%."

Facing a growing number of lawsuits, Searle withdrew the Copper 7 from the U.S. market in January 1986. By 1988 the number of suits surpassed 500. Although not admitting liability, the company acted to settle many of the claims. It wanted to avoid the recent fate of A.H. Robins, which filed for bankruptcy protection due to the litigation costs surrounding its Dalkon Shield intrauterine device.

Research

Chakravarty, Subrata N. "Taking Risks is What They Pay You For," in *Forbes*, 10 February 1986. Provides an overview of Monsanto's goal of becoming a leader in biotech and pharmaceuticals.

Ellis, James E. and Ellyn E. Spragins. "Why Monsanto is Bucking the Odds," in *Business Week*, 5 August 1985. Offers explanation for Monsanto's reentry into the artificial sweeteners business by acquiring Searle.

"G.D. Searle & Company," in *International Directory of Company Histories*, Vol. 12, St. James Press: 1996. Provides a historical review of the company, before and after it became a subsidiary of Monsanto.

Greenhouse, Steven. "Monsanto to Acquire G.D. Searle," in *The New York Times*, 19 July 1985. Details the acquisition offer.

"Monsanto Co.," in *Notable Corporate Chronologies*, The Gale Group, 1999. Profiles the history of Monsanto through and beyond its acquisition of G.D. Searle.

Monsanto Company 1998 Annual Report. Provides a comprehensive account of the company's financial highlights and operating segments.

Monsanto Company Home Page, available at http://www.monsanto.com. Official World Wide Web Page for Monsanto. Includes product descriptions, annual reports and other financial information, and news releases.

Richards, Bill. "Monsanto Inherits a Problem in Searle," in *The Wall Street Journal*, 28 October 1985. Details Searle's Copper 7 litigation that became Monsanto's problem.

Williams, Winston. "Taking Monsanto Another Step Beyond Basic Chemicals," in *The New York Times*, 28 July 1985. Profiles Monsanto's CEO Mahoney as well as his vision of turning the company into a biotechnology leader.

DEBORAH J. UNTENER

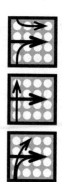

MORGAN STANLEY & DEAN WITTER, DISCOVER

Morgan Stanley Dean Witter & Co.
1585 Broadway
New York, NY 10036
USA

tel: (212)761-4000
fax: (212)761-0086
web: http://www.msdwd.com

nationality: USA
date: May 31, 1997
affected: Morgan Stanley Group Inc., USA, founded 1935
affected: Dean Witter, Discover & Co., USA, founded 1924

Overview of the Merger

The May 1997 merger between Dean Witter, Discover & Co. and Morgan Stanley Group Inc. stunned Wall Street, and not the least because it had been hatched in utter secrecy. The two financial services companies were of vastly different worlds. Morgan Stanley served upper class institutions, and had the corporate culture to go along with that playing field. Dean Witter, along with its Discover card, marketed to members of the middle-class, where the company itself seemed to be comfortable. Wall Street joked that a union between such different cultures should be named "White Shoes & White Socks." Yet it was these differences that made such a marriage logical.

Morgan Stanley Group Inc. specialized in investment banking and institutional sales and trading. Offices in 19 countries created a dispersed global company presence. Its clients included sovereign governments, corporations, institutions, and individuals. With its varied portfolio of products and services, Morgan Stanley provided the "origination" aspect of the merger.

Dean Witter, Discover & Co. was a retailing powerhouse. Its three main businesses—full-service brokerage, asset management, and credit resources—combined to create the third-largest retail brokerage firm. It was the largest credit card issuer in the U.S., with 39 million accounts. The company served the nation's individual investors, a group that had grown increasingly powerful in the market. Dean Witter contributed the "distribution" angle of the merger.

History of Morgan Stanley Group Inc.

The Glass-Steagall Act of 1933 was passed in response to a banking scandal that occurred on the heels of the stock market crash of 1929. The Act required a distinction between commercial and investment banking. As a result, commercial banks spun off their securities underwriting and brokering services. In September 1935 Morgan Stanley & Company was spun off from J.P. Morgan & Co. The new investment banking firm was headed by Harold Stanley and Henry Morgan.

During its first month of operation, the company participated in three major financial underwritings, including $43 million for AT&T. In 1936, its first full year of operation, it managed or co-managed $1.1 billion in public offerings and private placements, capturing a 24% market share. Morgan Stanley soon established a strong presence in such industries as utilities, telecommunications, railroads, and mining. By 1938 it had become the leading issuer of bonds among New York City investment firms.

The Temporary National Economic Committee initiated an examination of monopolistic practices in big business in 1939, and two years later recommended the use of mandatory competitive bidding on new securities issues. This move hurt Morgan Stanley, which depended on its close relations with businesses to secure their contracts.

In 1941 Morgan Stanley reincorporated as a partnership to comply with new membership requirements of the New York Stock Exchange. The U.S. entered World War II, bringing the securities business to a virtual halt. The firm survived on its brokerage commissions, consulting fees, and private placements.

The U.S. Department of Justice filed suit in 1947 against Morgan Stanley and 16 other investment bankers, charging them with illegal restraint of trade in the securities market. The company was cleared of all charges in 1953.

During the 1950s Morgan Stanley secured a reputation as an efficient firm that handled securities issues on its own. Despite having only $3 million in capital, it counted such industrial giants as General Motors, U.S. Steel, and General Electric among its clients.

The 1960s brought rapid expansion in international banking, as Euro markets offered unregulated liquidity. In 1967 it joined with Morgan Guaranty Trust Company and established Morgan & Cie International SA, a French subsidiary to manage and participate in underwritings of foreign securities. By 1975 this office issued $5 billion annually. Two years later it moved to London, which had emerged as the center of the European financial market.

In 1969 the firm entered the commercial real estate business, acquiring a controlling interest in Brooks, Harvey & Company, Inc. The following year it reorganized, shifting its focus from underwriting to such activities as retail banking and provision of venture capital. It also began to pursue foreign customers more actively. Its paid-in capital reached $7.5 million and its workforce numbered 250.

Morgan Stanley reincorporated as Morgan Stanley & Company Inc. in 1971. That year it also ven-

The Business

Financials

Revenue (1998): $16.4 billion

Employees (1998): 45,712

SICs / NAICS

sic 6371 - Pension, Health & Welfare Funds

sic 6211 - Security Brokers & Dealers

sic 6282 - Investment Advice

sic 6153 - Short-Term Business Credit

sic 6722 - Management Investment-Open-End

sic 6726 - Investment Offices Nec

naics 523210 - Securities and Commodity Exchanges

naics 523110 - Investment Banking and Securities Dealing

naics 523120 - Securities Brokerage

naics 522210 - Credit Card Issuing

naics 523140 - Commodity Contracts Brokerage

naics 523920 - Portfolio Management

tured into sales and trading, a move that would alter the company's makeup in future years. It created Morgan Development Company, Inc. to manage and invest in joint real estate development ventures.

Having resisted financing the proliferation of merger and acquisition activity in the previous decade, the company finally relented in 1971 by forming the industry's first mergers and acquisitions department. The following year it established a corporate research department and expanded into equity markets.

In 1974 Morgan Stanley handled its first hostile takeover, International Nickel's purchase of ESB, the world's largest battery manufacturer. The company fully incorporated in 1975 to acquire the large capital base necessary for withstanding the risks inherent in trading. Two years later it established Morgan Stanley Realty Inc. to manage its real estate development operations. The company also began offering its services to individual investment services and individuals for the first time. By the end of the decade, its paid-in capital reached $118 million, and its workforce rose to 1,700.

Competition in investment banking increased throughout the 1980s, as the U.S. government deregulated financial markets and permitted commercial

The Officers

Chairman and CEO: Philip J. Purcell

President, Chief Operating Officer: John J. Mack

Chairman of the Executive Committee: Richard B. Fisher

Exec. VP and Chief Legal Officer: Christine A. Edwards

Exec. VP, Chief Strategic and Administrative Officer: John H. Schaefer

Exec. VP, Chief Financial Officer: Robert G. Scott

banks to enter capital markets. In 1986 the company went public as the Morgan Stanley Group Inc., in which management retained an 81% interest.

The stock market crash of 1987 devastated much of the financial world, but Morgan Stanley fared well, and was the only New York City investment banking firm to record an increase in profits for the year. That year it bought Burlington Industries for $46.3 million in cash and $2.2 billion in debt. It sold off many of Burlington's assets, and took in over $176 million in fees and dividends. By April 1989 the company had become the largest provider of international securities research services to U.S. businesses.

The company's international operations improved through the 1990s. In 1991 it became the first foreign investment bank to lead-manage a bond underwriting in Japan, handling a 50 billion yen transaction for Nippon Telegraph and Telephone Corp. By the end of that year, the company realized 40% of its gross revenues from operations outside the U.S. In 1994 Morgan Stanley was the only foreign securities firm to participate in the formation of the China International Capital Corporation, that country's first joint venture investment bank.

A planned merger with London-based S.G. Warburg and Company Ltd. was called off in 1994. Two years later Morgan Stanley diversified into the individual investor mutual fund market by acquiring Van Kampen/American Capital Inc. for $1.1 billion.

History of Dean Witter, Discover & Co.

Dean Witter & Co. was founded in 1924 in San Francisco by Dean Witter, his brother Guy, and his cousin Jean. The trio started the business as a West Coast securities firm dealing in municipal and corporate bonds. That year the company also opened branches in Seattle and Sacramento.

In 1926 the new firm underwrote the $1.5 million debenture offering of the Boeing Co. In 1928 it pur-

chased a seat on the San Francisco Stock Exchange, and the following year on the New York Stock Exchange. It merged with Duisenberg, Wichman & Co. in 1929. That year, seven months before the stock market crash, Witter warned clients about speculative excess in stocks. Following his own advice, Witter sold most of his own stock, allowing him and his company to escape much of the ensuing economic devastation.

In 1931 Richard S. Reynolds, Jr., Thomas F. Staley, and Charles H. Babcock established Reynolds & Co., a securities brokerage business. Four years later it merged with F.A. Willard & Co., thereby tripling sales and emphasizing underwritings. In 1941 that company acquired Dyer, Hudson & Co.

Dean Witter & Co. acquired Bissinger & Co. in 1939, followed by W.M. Cavalier & Co. the following year, and Lieb, Keyston & Co. in 1941.

Expansion for both Dean Witter and Reynolds picked up after World War II. In 1953 alone, Reynolds acquired three financial services firms. During the 1950s, Dean Witter purchased Harris, Hall & Co., Central Republic Company of Chicago, and Laurence M. Marks & Co. Both companies continued expansion through acquisition into the next decade, with Dean Witter expanding eastward from the west, and Reynolds growing westward from the east.

Dean Witter & Co. incorporated in 1968 as Dean Witter & Co. Inc., with more than $45 million in capital. It made several acquisitions during the 1970s: J. Barth & Co., Laird, Bissel & Meeds, and InterCapital Inc. Reynolds & Co. made its initial public offering in 1971, and Dean Witter followed suit in 1972.

In 1978, in the largest merger in the history of the securities industry at that time, Dean Witter & Co. joined with Reynolds & Co. to form Dean Witter Reynolds, the fifth-largest broker in the U.S. The new company was the first brokerage firm to have offices in all 50 states, and its revenues surpassed $520 million.

By the early 1980s the economy created in the company a need for capital, so in 1981 it sold itself to Sears, Roebuck & Co., the largest retailer in the world, for $600 million. Sears began using its retail store network to open new Dean Witter offices in areas of the country where Dean Witter was nonexistent or poorly represented. The retailer shifted Dean Witter's focus exclusively on individual investors. The strategy was to transform Sears into a financial service "supermarket" aimed at the broad middle consumer market.

In 1986 Sears' financial services operations, which included Dean Witter, posted profits of $80 million. Sears invested $200 million to launch the Discover credit card as a division of Dean Witter. Unlike its rivals Visa and MasterCard, the Discover card had no annual free and offered cashback bonuses and interest-free cash advances. That year Philip J. Purcell became chairman and CEO of Dean Witter Financial Services.

In 1987 Dean Witter's rank in the corporate debt and equity underwriting market slipped from tenth to 15th, and investment banking accounted for less than 10% of its revenues. The Discover card's lukewarm reception by retailers contributed to the Sears financial group's loss of $37 million on sales of $3.5 billion. By the following year, however, the Discover card boasted more than 22 million subscribers and was accepted at 740,000 merchant outlets.

This upswing was short-lived. By 1989 Dean Witter was barely profitable, despite having doubled in size since 1981. Sears announced plans to close 200 of Dean Witter's 650 outlets, primarily those located in department stores. Then the rollercoaster shifted again, and in 1990 Dean Witter posted profits of $109 million. By the following year Discover was the largest single issuer of general purpose credit cards, generating earnings of $174 million from a total of 40 million cards.

Dean Witter introduced a new family of proprietary funds, and its mutual funds assets increased to over $50 billion in 1992. Sears, suffering under a $38 billion debt load, decided to sell its financial services operations. In 1993 Dean Witter, Discover & Co. was formed when Sears spun off the financial services operation's stock into an independent, publicly traded company. During its first year of operation, its revenues rose more than 20% to $4.6 billion as net income reached $600 million.

Now the largest credit card issuer in the U.S., the company joined with NationsBank to introduce a co-branded credit card, Prime OptionSM MasterCard. In 1995 it established the NOVUS credit card network, which launched the Private Issue Card and the BRAVO Card.

In 1996 it entered into an agreement to provide investment, product, and sales support services to Banc One Corp. The company also made a number of moves to capitalize on the Internet. It formed DWD Electronic Financial Services to target consumers seeking the ability to conduct banking and securities transactions online. It then acquired Lombard Brokerage Inc., a provider of securities transactions over the Internet.

Market Forces Driving the Merger

For several decades, investment and commercial banking had been separated by federal regulations.

The Players

Chairman and CEO: Philip J. Purcell. Philip Purcell started out as a consultant at McKinsey & Co. While working there, he met Edward Tellin, the chairman of Sears Roebuck. He was soon hired by Sears as a strategic planner, and spurred the retailer into financial services. Purcell was the force behind that company's acquisition of Dean Witter. He then moved into brokerage operations and encouraged the launch of the Discover card. Purcell took the helm of Dean Witter, Discover & Co. in 1986, and assumed the positions of chairman and CEO upon the formation of Morgan Stanley Dean Witter & Co. in 1997.

President, Chief Operating Officer: John J. Mack. John Mack graduated from Duke University in 1968 and immediately enrolled in a training program at Smith, Barney & Co. After a stint at F.S. Smithers & Co., he joined Morgan Stanley in 1972. There, he moved up the corporate ladder, from managing director in 1979, to head of fixed-income sales in 1984, to chief operating officer in 1992, and president in 1993. He initiated a rapid expansion program, as well as a failed merger attempt with S.G. Warburg. Mack became the president and chief operating officer at the newly formed Morgan Stanley Dean Witter & Co.

The Glass-Steagall Banking Act of 1935 forced companies to limit their activities to only one of those industries. It was for this reason that Morgan Stanley had been established, as a spin-off of J.P. Morgan & Co.

Over the years, a chasm developed between these industries. Institutional investment banks flourished in their lucrative niche of serving corporations rather than individuals. They regarded retail brokerage houses as mass merchandisers peddling middle-of-the-road products.

These retail operations, however, had experienced a growth surge. Increasingly, mainstream Americans were investing in the stock market, and mutual fund and brokerage firms reaped the reward. The traditional order, in which institutions controlled the markets and retail businesses had low-margins, was no longer holding true.

Regulatory changes to the financial services landscape began tearing down the wall between the two segments. In 1988 Glass-Steagall was modified to permit a securities subsidiary of a bank to generate up to 10% of the company's total revenues. This act had relatively little impact on the industry, however, since any worthwhile acquisition would likely cross that threshold. But it did open the door for further liberalization in regulation, and in 1996 that maximum was raised to 25%. This threw commercial and investment banking back into the mix together. Investment bankers like Morgan Stanley would be facing heavy competition from banks, which would almost certainly be seeking securities firms to acquire.

Approach and Engagement

Dean Witter, Discover's initial public offering in 1993 had been handled by Morgan Stanley. These two firms began merger discussion shortly thereafter, but Dean Witter wanted to hold on to its newfound freedom. The companies resumed merger talks in the fall of 1996, and became committed to the idea that December, when John Mack, Morgan Stanley's president and COO, and Philip Purcell, Dean Witter's chairman and CEO, met at a Utah ski resort.

After that, negotiations progressed quickly. The companies conducted their talks in neutral locations, and Morgan Stanley's bankers were excluded until the deal's final stages. So covert were the discussions that it was rumored that Morgan Stanley would soon be launching an acquisition of PaineWebber.

On February 5, 1997, the merger was announced. It was to be a union of equals, with neither firm acquiring the other. The $10.2 billion deal would entail a stock swap of 1.65 shares of Dean Witter for each Morgan Stanley share. The resulting company would be the largest U.S. securities firm, based on its $21 billion in market capitalization.

Morgan Stanley Dean Witter, Discover & Company would be led by the top executives of the individual companies. Both Philip Purcell and John Mack would retain their previous positions at the new company. Richard Fisher, chairman of Morgan Stanley, would become chairman of the Executive Committee of the Board of Directors.

On May 28, 1997, eighty-seven percent of Dean Witter's shareholders approved the merger, as did 83% of Morgan Stanley's shareholders. Three days later, on May 31, the merger was consummated.

Products and Services

The company operates in three business segments: The Securities division was comprised of individual and institutional securities. Its institutional segment could be broken down into investment banking, including advisory services; institutional sales and trading, made up of fixed income, institutional equity, foreign exchange, and commodities; and equity and debt underwriting. The company also offered individual securities services. Securities businesses generated 66%, or $10.8 billion, of the company's total 1998 revenues. Investment/Asset Management was made up of both institutional and individual investment management services. In 1998 this division generated 15%, $2.4 billion, of the company's total revenues in 1998. Credit Services & Electronic Brokerage was comprised of Discover Financial Services and Novus Financial Corp., as well as the Discover Brokerage Direct electronic brokerage. It provided 19%, or $3.2 billion, toward the total company's revenues in 1998.

Changes to the Industry

The Morgan Stanley/Dean Witter merger created an impetus for merger and acquisition activity in the industry. Just weeks after this merger was announced, commercial banks began purchasing securities firms. In April Bankers Trust New York Corp. spent $1.7 billion to acquire Alex Brown & Sons Inc. This deal was followed in rapid succession by other acquisitions by such banks as SBS Warburg, BankAmerica Corp., NationsBank Corp., ING Group, and U.S. Bancorp.

Consolidation and globalization in the industry was expected to continue, as consumers increasingly began to expect financial services firms to meet more of their needs. A successful company would have to offer an array of products and services, as well as the global resources to distribute them. According to *Fortune*, on the day after the Morgan Stanley/Dean Witter merger announcement, House Banking Committee Chairman Jim Leach said, "Yesterday could be the first day of the new financial order."

Review of the Outcome

Morgan Stanley Dean Witter, Discover & Co. immediately had $270 billion in managed assets, 3.2 million retail customers, 28,000 employees, and 409 offices. Its credit card business, which accounted for half of Dean Witter's revenues, generated 25% of the new company's revenues.

Since the two companies had previously operated in different market segments, overlaps were minimal. Still, some positions were redundant, necessitating lay-offs. Just prior to the merger, Dean Witter had laid off 14 people; after the merger it announced that it would let go an additional 200 employees.

The new company closed the year with $14.8 billion in revenues, up from a combined $12 billion in 1996. Its net income also improved, reaching $2.6 billion, an increase from $1.9 billion the previous year. By the end of 1997, the company had also jumped from fifth to third place in U.S. debt and equity underwriting. As Purcell stated in *Institutional Investor*, "The fact that we have factual market data that this merger is working blows me away. I wouldn't have predicted this was possible in six months."

On March 24, 1998, the company shortened its name to Morgan Stanley Dean Witter & Co. In October Chase Manhattan Corp. bought its global custody businesses, Morgan Stanley Trust Co. and Morgan Stanley Bank Luxembourg, S.A. The firm ended 1998 with net income of $3.3 billion on revenues of $16.4 billion. Morgan Stanley Dean Witter ranked second in initial public offerings, high yield debt, and equity research; it ranked third in worldwide mergers & acquisitions transactions, as well as in equity related issues.

Research

"Dean Witter, Discover & Co.," in *Notable Corporate Chronologies*, The Gale Group, 1999. Profiles the company up though the announcement of its merger with Morgan Stanley.

"Dean Witter, Morgan Stanley Stockholders Back Deal," in *American Banker*, 29 May 1997. Reports on the approval of the companies' shareholders for the merger.

Dutt, Jill. "Two Wall St. Giants Plan a Mega-Merger; Dean Witter, Morgan Set $10 Billion Deal," in *The Washington Post*, 6 February 1997. Provides facts on the newly-announced arrangement.

Fox, Justin. "What the Morgan Merger Portends," in *Fortune*, 3 March 1997. Suggests that the merger will be the first of a wave across the industry.

"Making the Merger Work: The Devil's in the Details," in *Investment Dealers' Digest*, 10 February 1997. Speculates about the impact that the merger will have on the industry, as well as what a pooling of resources will mean to the new company.

"Mating Games," in *Institutional Investor*, January 1998. Provides an overview and details of a number of unusual mergers and acquisitions during 1997.

Morgan Stanley, Dean Witter, Discover & Co. 1997 Annual Report. Provides detailed financial highlights and company events.

Morgan Stanley Dean Witter & Co. Home Page, available at http://www.msdwd.com. Official World Wide Web Page for Morgan Stanley Dean Witter. Includes a company history, annual report, products and services, and investor information.

"Morgan Stanley, Dean Witter, Discover & Co.—Company Report," in *Investext*, 1 August 1997. Reports on the layoffs resulting from the merger.

"Morgan Stanley and Dean Witter, Discover in Merger of Equals; Creates Preeminent Global Financial Services Firm," in *Business Wire*, 5 February 1997. Provides details of the merger agreement, from the market forces spurring it to the resources that the united firm will have in its possession.

"Morgan Stanley Group Inc.," in *Notable Corporate Chronologies*, The Gale Group, 1999. Lists major events in the history of the company until its merger with Dean Witter.

Wasserstein, Bruce. *Big Deal: The Battle for Control of America's Leading Corporations*, Warner Books, 1998. Offers an overview of the largest mergers in recent American corporate history.

PATRICIA ARCHILLA

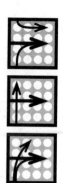

NATIONAL AMUSEMENTS & VIACOM

National Amusements Inc.
200 Elm St.
Dedham, MA 02026-4536
USA

tel: (781)461-1600
fax: (781)461-1412
web: http://www.nationalamusements.com

nationality: USA
date: March 4, 1987
affected: National Amusements Inc., USA
affected: Viacom International Inc., USA, founded 1970

Overview of the Acquisition

In 1986 a team of directors was considering an offer led by a group of Viacom International management to take the company private. In the meantime, National Amusements gradually increased its stake in Viacom, leading to speculation that the movie theater chain would make an acquisition offer for the company. National Amusements made no comment until February 1987, when it launched an unfriendly offer to acquire Viacom. This led to a bidding war with the management group, but National Amusements prevailed the following month.

History of National Amusements, Inc.

After practicing law for 12 years, Sumner Redstone decided that he'd rather become an entrepreneur. So in 1954 he joined his father's theater business, Redstone Management. This company owned and operated 12 drive-in theater in northeastern U.S.

Redstone soon began applying his training as a lawyer to improve not only the business, but also the drive-in theater industry as a whole. At that time, motion picture studios refused to grant drive-ins the first-run rights to movies, making them wait until the films had exhausted their runs at indoor theaters. Redstone filed suit against the studios for this practice, and ultimately won drive-ins the same access to first-runs as indoor theaters enjoyed.

Redstone took notice of the trend toward suburbia and realized that as the audiences were moving away from the cities, so should the movie houses. That notion took shape in Redstone's pioneering of multiple-screen theaters. He even copyrighted the term "Multiplex."

National Amusements, as the company became known, differed from other theater chains in terms of ownership of property. While most movie houses leased their property, National Amusements protected itself from fluctuations in the motion picture industry by owning all of its buildings and land.

Sumner gradually gained control of the company, and guided it from a chain of 59 screens in 1964 to one of 129 screens in 1974. By 1986 National Amusements had about 400 screens and was the nation's eighth-largest theater chain in the U.S. As a privately held company, it didn't disclose its financial results, but analysts estimated its 1986 revenues to be $150 million.

In October of that year National Amusements began increasing its stake in Viacom International, the languishing owner of cable television networks and related ventures. By 1987 National Amusements had launched a full-scale hostile battle for the company, finally having its bid accepted that March.

History of Viacom International Inc.

The Central Broadcasting System (CBS) complied with the Federal Communications Commission's (FCC) regulations barring television networks from owning cable TV systems or from syndicating their own programs in the U.S. by establishing Viacom International Inc. in 1970. The following year CBS spun off Viacom as a separate company to CBS shareholders. That firm's initial annual sales reached $19.8 million. Its 90,000 subscribers made it one of the nation's largest cable systems.

In 1976, to compete with Home Box Office (HBO), the nation's leading cable outlet for films, Viacom created the Showtime movie network as a 50-50 venture with Warner Amex. The next year, despite a federal ruling that removed many restrictions on the choice of programming available on pay-television, Showtime posted a loss of $825,000. Nevertheless, Viacom earned $5.5 million on sales of $58.5 million, mostly from sales of television series such as *I Love Lucy*. Subscription to the company's cable system rose to 350,000.

Viacom reached a deal in 1978 with Teleprompter Corp., the largest cable systems operator in the U.S., whereby Teleprompter offered its customers Showtime rather than HBO. Three years later Viacom acquired Video Corp. of America for $16 million. The company's growth goals included the acquisition of radio and television stations during the 1970s. Those acquisitions proved to be insurance against any possible takeover of the company, since the transfer of broadcast licenses must be overseen by the FCC.

Viacom invested $65 million on its cable infrastructure in 1981. The next year Showtime had 3.4 million subscribers and earned about $10 million on sales of $140 million. Subscriptions to Viacom's cable systems totaled 540,000, making it the ninth-largest cable operator in the U.S.

In 1984 Showtime became a sister station to Warner Amex's The Movie Channel in a move designed to increase sales for both stations. In September of the following year, Viacom purchased

The Business

Financials

Revenue (1998):$2.91 billion

Employees (1998): 116,700

SICs / NAICS

sic 7832 - Motion Picture Theaters Except Drive-In

sic 4841 - Cable & Other Pay Television Services

sic 4833 - Television Broadcasting Stations

sic 7822 - Motion Picture & Tape Distribution

sic 7812 - Motion Picture & Video Production

sic 2731 - Book Publishing

sic 7996 - Amusement Parks

naics 512131 - Motion Picture Theaters (except Drive-Ins)

naics 513210 - Cable Networks

naics 513120 - Television Broadcasting

naics 512120 - Motion Picture and Video Distribution

naics 512110 - Motion Picture and Video Production

naics 511130 - Book Publishers

naics 713110 - Amusement and Theme Parks

Warner Amex's stake in Showtime from Warner Communications, as well as MTV Networks, which included MTV, Nickelodeon, and VH1. Viacom revamped Nickelodeon's image and introduced *Nick at Night*, a block of classic sitcoms aired for an adult audience.

Weakened by the $2 billion debt load it had incurred through its acquisitions, and in part to scare off potential takeovers, Viacom was purchased by National Amusements Inc., a movie theater chain, for about $3.4 billion in March 1987. Sumner M. Redstone, president of National Amusements, assumed the chairmanship of Viacom.

The U.S. Congress passed legislation deregulating the cable industry in 1987, causing prices of cable franchises to soar. Viacom recorded sales in excess of $1 billion for the first time, but the company still posted a loss of approximately $154.4 million.

Viacom sold its cable systems in Long Island, New York, and suburban Cleveland, Ohio, to Cablevision Systems Corp. for $545 million. Cablevision then purchased a five-percent stake in Showtime for $25 million, giving it a tangible interest in the channel's success. Viacom also sold 50% of

The Players

National Amusements CEO, President, and Chief Operating Officer: Sumner M. Redstone. Billionaire Sumner Redstone was never fed with a silver spoon, even after he could afford it. Born in a 1923 Boston tenement, he sped through Harvard in only three years. He then joined an Army Intelligence unit that cracked Japan's World War II codes before acquiring a law degree from Harvard. Redstone practiced law for six years before returning to his father's business, a chain of 12 drive-in theaters. He then revolutionized the theater industry by establishing the multiplex, a term that he later copyrighted.

No profile of Redstone is complete without the tale of the hotel fire that nearly cost him his life. In 1979 he escaped death by hanging by his fingertips from the ledge of the Boston hotel until he was rescued. He sustained severe burns over half his body, and doctors predicted that he would never walk again. Redstone not only recovered, he became a voracious and highly competitive tennis player.

Redstone entered the big leagues with his 1986 investment in Viacom, later winning the company in a heated battle. He emerged victorious in his takeover of Paramount as well. Redstone was still serving as chairman of his media empire in 1999, at age 76.

Showtime's stock to Tele-Communications Inc. (TCI), a cable systems operator with about six million subscribers, for $225 million.

Viacom joined with Hearst Corp. and Capital Cities/ABC Inc. in 1989 to introduce Lifetime Television, a cable channel geared toward women. Viacom established a production company, Viacom Pictures, which made about 10 feature films that year at a cost of about $4 million each.

Viacom filed a $2.4 billion antitrust suit against HBO, alleging that HBO was trying to put Showtime out of business by intimidating cable systems that carried Showtime and by trying to corner the market on Hollywood films to prevent competitors from airing them. The suit was settled out of court in August 1992. Time Warner, HBO's parent, agreed to pay Viacom $75 million and to buy a Viacom cable system in Milwaukee for $95 million. It also agreed to increase its distribution of Showtime and The Movie Channel on its cable networks.

A five-month battle against QVC Inc. for Paramount Communications Inc. was initiated by Viacom's bid in September 1993. To help raise fund for this acquisition, Viacom offered $8.4 billion in stock to acquire Blockbuster Entertainment Corp. Viacom successfully gained control of Paramount in July 1994 and of Blockbuster that September.

Viacom also sold its one-third interest in Lifetime to its partners, and Blockbuster increased its presence in the children's entertainment-center industry by lifting its stake in Discovery Zone from 20% to 50.1%. The following year Viacom sold its Madison Square Garden sports assets.

In January 1995 the company joined with Chris-Craft to launch United Paramount Network (UPN), which targeted viewers aged 18-34. That June Paramount had its most successful motion picture opening, that of *Congo*.

Wal-Mart's William R. Fields was hired to lead Blockbuster Entertainment, which has close to 3,000 video rental stores in the U.S. Fields was fired the following year, however, and was replaced by John F. Antioco as CEO. He was assigned the task of turning around Blockbuster, which had been plagued by sluggish video rentals, management errors, a lack of focus, and problems with a new distribution system. In 1998 Antioco laid off 180 employees, mainly at the company's headquarters; curtailed store expansion; and closed all 17 of Germany's struggling stores. More importantly, he introduced the concept of revenue sharing, enabling the stores to stock more copies of popular titles in exchange for a percentage of the rental revenues to be paid to the movie studios. Blockbuster's revenues in 1998 reached $3.9 billion, strong enough for Viacom to file for its initial public offering in March 1999.

In a $2 billion stock deal with Tele-Communications Inc. (TCI) and its shareholders, Viacom spun off its cable systems in 1996. In a controversial move, Redstone fired Frank J. Biondi Jr. as Viacom CEO and assumed the post himself.

Viacom sold its 10-station radio group to Chancellor Media Corp. in July 1997 for about $1.1 billion in cash. That year it also increased its ownership of Spelling Entertainment Group Inc. to 80%, and acquired full ownership in June 1999.

The hugely successful *Titanic* was released in December 1997, far surpassing even the enormous success of the company's previous hit, *Forrest Gump*.

In October 1998 Viacom sold Blockbuster Music to Wherehouse Entertainment Inc. for $115 million. By the end of the year, Blockbuster's video stores in the U.S. and 25 other countries numbered about 6,000, making it the nation's leading video rental company. Viacom also sold Simon & Schuster's educational, professional, and reference publishing operations to Pearson PLC for $4.6 billion in cash.

Market Forces Driving the Acquisition

Sumner Redstone and his National Amusements company frequently invested in entertainment companies. Over the years he owned stakes in Columbia Pictures, MGM/UA, Time Inc., and Loews Corp. He reportedly rushed out in the middle of a *Star Wars* screening to telephone in an investment in Twentieth Century Fox.

Redstone was constantly on the lookout for burgeoning areas in which to invest. By the mid-1980s cable television was becoming a phenomenon, one that was stealing the audience away from his movie theater chain. Although he knew nothing about the cable industry, Redstone knew that he wanted to be a part of it. "A cable system to me was a wire in the ground and a thingumajiggy pointed at the screen," he admitted in a September 1993 issue of *Time*. "But I saw a vast technology and global revolution that would change the habits of people all over the world, and I saw Viacom at the center of it."

Approach and Engagement

On September 16, 1986, a management group of Viacom International offered $40.50 per share, or about $2.73 billion, to take the company private. National Amusements, which held a 9.9% interest in Viacom, and Coniston Partners, another large shareholder, opposed the offer as inadequate. The group's sweetened offer, to $44 per share or $2.97 billion, was rejected by Viacom's outside directors as well. This led to speculation on Wall Street that another potential bidder was waiting in the wings.

In early October 1986 National Amusements asked for regulatory approval to increase its stake in Viacom to as much as 24.9%. At the same time, it also agreed to purchase part of Coniston Partners' stake that would boost its interest to 18.3%, contingent upon regulatory approval.

After increasing its stake to 18.3% and then to 19.6%, National Amusements filed in December for permission from the Securities and Exchange Commission to increase its interest as high as 49.9%. But the company still refused to comment on its intentions toward Viacom.

In February 1987 National Amusements broke that silence. It launched a counteroffer to the management-led bid by offering about $49.25 per share, compared with management's $47-per-share offer.

Because the competing bids consisted of a complex combination of cash, partial shares of a new issued of preferred, and an equity stake in a newly formed company, their composite value could not be accurately calculated. As a result, the proceedings contained an element of uncertainty in the assessment of the favorability of one bid over the other.

Another point of consideration was the time frame for the deal's completion. The management group was closer to receiving the necessary approval from the Federal Communications Commission, since it had filed sooner than National Amusements for it.

On February 10 National Amusements' bid was rejected on the basis that it "was not more favorable" than the management group's bid. Two weeks later National Amusements slightly sweetened its bid to about $3.2 billion. This offer reflected an increase in the cash portion, as well as an offer to pay interest on payments due to Viacom's shareholders if the transaction wasn't closed by April 30. These features had been added "to address any hypothetical concern you may have as to the timing of our transaction," according to a February issue of *The Wall Street Journal*.

The rival bids were again shot down by Viacom's outside directors, and were once again sweetened. On March 3, 1987, management increased its bid to $3.23 billion and National Amusements offered a slightly higher $3.4 billion. The next day, after a 16-hour meeting that wrapped up at 4:00 a.m., Viacom's special committee of directors accepted National Amusements' bid.

Products and Services

By 1999 National Amusements owned and operated 1,293 motion picture screens in the U.S., the U.K., and Latin America under the brand names of Showcase and Multiplex Cinemas.

Its wholly owned Viacom International company operated in six business segments: cable networks, including MTV, MTV2, Nickelodeon, Nick at Nite, Nick at Nite's TV Land, VH1, Showtime, The Movie Channel, and Flix; motion picture and television production and distribution; Blockbuster Video; Paramount Parks; consumer publishing, including such imprints as Simon & Schuster, Pocket Books, Scribner, and The Free Press; and Viacom Online Services, its interactive businesses.

Review of the Outcome

National Amusements assumed a huge amount of debt to pay for the acquisition. After borrowing

$240 million, thereby raising the company's total debt burden to about $2.8 billion, Redstone admitted that he had taken an enormous chance with his family's fortunes. "If anything happened, it would have taken a long time to dig out a chain of 250 screens from hundreds of millions in debt," he recalled in *Forbes*.

Yet Redstone was determined to do whatever he could to retain the company's holdings in spite of that debt. At that time Viacom was the 10th-largest cable operator, with assets including MTV, Showtime/The Movie Channel, several television and radio stations, and the syndication rights to such shows as *I Love Lucy* and *The Cosby Show*. Soon, Redstone insisted, cable film viewers would not be able to survive without Viacom.

Research

Barnes, Peter W. "National Amusements Boosts Viacom Bid to $3.2 Billion, Increases Cash Amount," in *The Wall Street Journal*, 24 February 1987. Details National Amusements sweetened offer that included payment of interest to Viacom shareholders.

———. "National Amusements, as Expected, Lifts Viacom Bid Again; Move Pressures Rival," in *The Wall Street Journal*, 4 March 1987. Reports the final bids from the rival bidders.

———. "National Amusements Wins Bidding War for Viacom with Its Offer of $3.4 Billion," in *The Wall Street Journal*, 5 March 1987. Describes the acceptance of National Amusements' bid.

Greenwald, John. "The Man with the Iron Grasp," in *Time*, 27 September 1993. Profiles Redstone and his rise from tenement to media empire.

Landro, Laura, and James B. Stewart. "Viacom's Outside Directors Turn Down Management's $2.97 Billion Buyout Bid," in *The Wall Street Journal*, 8 October 1986. Reveals the rejection of a bid from Viacom's management group and the simultaneous intention of National Amusements to increase its stake up to 24.9%.

Lenzner, Robert, and Marla Matzer. "Late Bloomer," in *Forbes*, 17 October 1994. Profiles Sumner Redstone.

Lieberman, David, and Lois Therrien, with Mark Ivey. "Now Redstone is a Media Giant," in *Business Week*, 16 March 1987. Briefly details the victory of National Amusements for Viacom.

National Amusements, Inc. Home Page, available at http://www.nationalamusements.com. Official World Wide Web Page for Viacom. Includes theater locations and show times, the sale of gift certificates, news releases regarding new theater locations, and links to company Websites.

Therrien, Lois. "Sumner Redstone's Idea of a Good Time is Hardnosed Bargaining," in *Business Week*, 20 October 1986. Profiles National Amusements and its possible bid for all of Viacom.

"Viacom International Inc.," in *Notable Corporate Chronologies*, Gale Research, 1999. Lists major events in the history of Viacom.

Viacom International Inc. Home Page, available at http://www.viacom.com. Official World Wide Web Page for Viacom. It includes a description of operations, news releases, executive biographies, annual reports, investor information, and links to company Websites.

DEBORAH J. UNTENER

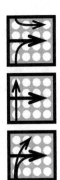

NATIONSBANK & BARNETT BANKS

nationality: USA
date: January 9, 1998
affected: NationsBank Corp., USA, founded 1968
affected: Barnett Banks, Inc., USA, founded 1877

Bank of America Corp.
100 N. Tryon St., 18th Fl.
Charlotte, NC 28255
USA

tel: (704)386-5000
fax: (704)386-6699
web: http://www.bankofamerica.com

Overview of the Acquisition

NationsBank's $15.5 billion acquisition of Barnett Banks in 1997 was the largest banking deal in the history of the U.S., as well as the nation's second-largest corporate deal ever. But the trend of merger and acquisition activity continued, and this record-breaking transaction was soon surpassed in size by First Union's $17 billion acquisition of CoreStates.

History of NationsBank Corp.

NationsBank, which became an acquisition machine in the 1960s, had a modest beginning. In February 1874 a consortium of prominent local citizens formed the Commercial National Bank in Charlotte, North Carolina, with an initial capitalization of $50,000. Meanwhile, in November 1887, Citizens Bank of Savannah opened for business in Georgia with an initial capitalization of $200,000. In 1901 George Stephens established the Southern States Trust Company, which changed its name to the American Trust Company six years later.

In 1906 Citizens Bank of Savannah merged with its cross-town rival, the Southern Bank, to form Citizens and Southern Bank. This operation began opening branches in South Carolina in 1928. In 1940 it spun off its South Carolina branches as Citizens and Southern Bank of South Carolina in anticipation of federal laws barring multistate bank ownership.

In 1957 Commercial National Bank merged with American Trust Company to form American Commercial Bank. Two years later this firm expanded its operations throughout North Carolina by absorbing the First National Bank of Raleigh. In July 1960 it merged with Security National to form the North Carolina National Bank. North Carolina National Bank employed 1,300 workers at 40 offices in 20 cities throughout the state, with assets of $480 million. It expanded aggressively, acquiring nine North Carolina banks during the following eight years.

In 1968 North Carolina National Bank formed NCNB Corp. as a holding company to manage its subsidiary operations. By 1970 it operated 91 offices in 27 North Carolina cities. Its voracious appetite unabated, the firm acquired nine more banks

The Business

Financials

Revenue: $30.5 billion

Employees (1998): 171,000

SICs / NAICS

sic 6021 - National Commercial Banks

sic 6211 - Security Brokers & Dealers

naics 522110 - Commercial Banking

naics 523110 - Investment Banking and Securities Dealing

naics 523120 - Securities Brokerage

during the decade. After NCNB absorbed the Bank of Asheville and Carolina First in 1979, it became the largest financial institution in North Carolina.

In 1982 the federal government lifted its ban on bank holding companies' acquiring failing out-of-state banks. NCNB took advantage of this legislation by making its first purchase in Florida. It became the first non-Florida bank to offer retail services in the state by purchasing the First National Bank of Lake City in January 1982. Later that year it extended its presence in the state by purchasing Gulfstream Banks, Exchange Ban-Corp., and People's Downtown National Bank.

Hugh L. McColl, Jr. became chairman of NCNB in 1983 and led the company on a mission to become the leading bank on the Southeast Coast. The next year NCNB added to its Florida operations, acquiring banks in Boca Raton, Tampa, Miami, and Bradenton. In 1985 it purchased the Pan American Bank of Miami, with assets of $2 billion, and entered the financial market in Georgia with the acquisition of Southern National Bankshares Inc. of Atlanta. NCNB expanded its operations into two new states in 1986, purchasing the Bankers Trust of South Carolina and the Prince William Bank of Virginia. Its purchase of CentraBank of Baltimore the next year gained it entry into Maryland.

NCNB was chosen by the Federal Deposit Insurance Corp. in 1988 to manage the restructuring of the First Republic Bank Corp., Texas's largest, but failing, financial institution. NCNB paid $210 million to acquire a 20% interest in First Republic, with the option to acquire the remaining 80% at a later date. This purchase, questioned by some analysts, proved strategic, as NCNB used First Republic's losses as a tax

shelter. The following year it acquired the remaining interest of First Republic.

In 1989 NCNB launched a hostile takeover of Citizens and Southern Bank, but dropped the attack in the face of regulatory barriers. Instead NCNB acquired University Federal Savings (Texas) and Freedom Savings and Loan Association of Florida. The next year it acquired nine banks from National Bancshares of San Antonio, Texas.

The company paid $4.26 billion to acquire C&S/Sovran in 1991 in order to gain entry into Georgia and Virginia, thereby growing closer to its goal of becoming a national bank. The new entity, renamed NationsBank Corp., became the nation's third-largest bank. Former C&S/Sovran chairman and CEO, Bennett A. Brown, was named NationsBank's chairman, while McColl functioned as the new bank's president and CEO.

The bank diversified into financial businesses, including securities, dividends, and options, with its 1993 acquisition of Chicago Research & Trading in 1993. That year it also formed an alliance with Dean Witter, Discover & Co. to offer brokerage services in its bank branches, but the alliance was terminated the following year upon customer complaints and a Securities and Exchange Commission investigation into NationsBank's misleading sales practices. It paid $30 million to settle the ensuing class action lawsuit.

By 1994 NationsBank was the fourth-largest banking company in the U.S., operating 1,800 offices in nine states and the District of Columbia. It purchased two Florida banks, Intercontinental Bank and CSF Holdings, the parent of Citizens Federal Bank, for $516 million and $218 million, respectively. In 1997 it acquired Boatmen's Bancshares Inc., headquartered in St. Louis, Missouri. This $9.6 billion purchase introduced NationsBank to the Midwest market, and the firm then occupied 16 states.

Later that year it decided to boost its financial securities operations and gain entry into the California market by acquiring San Francisco-based Montgomery Securities. In September it also acquired Barnett Banks, thereby becoming the nation's second-largest commercial bank in terms of market capitalization. The bank then captured the nation's top spot by merging with BankAmerica Corp.; the new entity retained the BankAmerica moniker.

In October 1998 David Coulter, chairman and CEO of the former BankAmerica, resigned as president of the company, and was succeeded by Kenneth Lewis. In December 1998 the firm entered into a merger agreement with BankAmerica Merchant Services, Inc. Also that month it agreed to sell its Alaskan consumer and small business operations to Northrim Bank. In March 1999 it acquired Fleetwood Credit Corp., a subsidiary of Associates First Capital Corp. The next month shareholders approved the company's name change to Bank of America Corp.

History of Barnett Banks, Inc.

In 1877 banker William Boyd Barnett moved his family from Kansas to Jacksonville, Florida, in an effort to improve his wife's health in the mild southern climate. On May 7 of that year he established The Bank of Jacksonville, and in less than seven months the institution boasted $35,000 in capital. In 1888 the bank's name was changed to The National Bank of Jacksonville.

Upon William's death in 1903, his son Bion became president. Five years later the bank emerged from a reorganization as Barnett First National Bank of Jacksonville. The enterprise survived, even flourished, during the stock market crash of 1929. The family formed the Barnett National Securities Corp. as a bank holding company that began acquiring failing local banks. On March 4, 1933, the day before President Franklin Roosevelt's scheduled bank holiday, Barnett's officers devised a strategy to prevent a run on deposits. Tellers were instructed to process withdrawals slowly, using only small bills. As customers witnessed others leaving with large wads of cash, their confidence in the bank's liquidity was restored and many left their deposits intact.

After World War II Florida became a retirement haven, and immigrating seniors brought their savings and pensions to the state's financial institutions. Barnett went public on a limited basis in the mid-1950s, and in 1962 it was listed on the Over-the-Counter Exchange. In the early 1970s Barnett became the southeast's first bank to gain a listing on the New York Stock Exchange.

Guy W. Botts, a local attorney, became president of Barnett First National in 1963. He envisioned an expansion of the bank into a statewide entity, and three years later that regulatory door opened. Barnett National Securities Corp. was transformed from a subsidiary of the bank to its parent company and was thereby legally empowered to purchase other banks. It bought the First National Bank of Winter Park in 1966, and went on to complete the acquisition of seven others by 1969. That year the holding company changed its name to Barnett Banks of Florida, Inc. to reflect its statewide influence.

The entity diversified during the 1970s. It established the state's first credit card franchise, and subsequently founded the Barnett Computing Co. to facilitate credit transactions. In 1971 the Barnett Mortgage

The Officers

Chairman and CEO: Hugh L. McColl Jr.

Vice Chairman and Chief Financial Officer: James H. Hance, Jr.

President: Kenneth D. Lewis

President, Global Corporate & Investment Banking: Michael J. Murray

Corporate Risk Management Executive: F. William Vandiver, Jr.

Co. was formed, followed the next year by the establishment of Barnett Winston Co., an investment vehicle. In 1973 the firm founded Barnett Investment Services, Barnett Leasing Company, and Barnett Banks Trust Company.

Charles E. Rice became president in 1972 and led the company's second wave of acquisitions. Barnett survived the state's real estate crash of the mid-1970s, and by 1975 controlled the largest number of banks of any holding company in Florida. In 1977 Florida's legislation lifted the ban on bank branching. Barnett opened four branches that year, and by 1988 had covered the state with about 240 more branch locations.

Florida lifted its prohibition on interstate banking in 1985. Barnett not only withstood the encroachment on its territory from outsiders, it also began expanding into new regions. In 1986 it purchased the Georgia institution First National Bank of Cobb County. The next year Barnett changed its name to Barnett Banks, Inc., dropping its reference to the state of Florida.

Interest rates dropped in the late 1980s, and bank customers sought higher-interest alternatives to standard savings. In 1988 Barnett introduced the Emerald group of mutual funds. The company was the subject of a class action suit in 1990 that charged Barnett Equity Securities with distorting or failing to disclose vital information to investors. The case was settled two years later for $1.25 million in common shares.

In 1992 Barnett purchased CSX Commercial Services, a student loan holder, and changed its name to BTI Services. The following year, however, it sold this unprofitable subsidiary. In February 1992 it purchased United Savings of America, a failed Florida thrift. That May it paid $800 million to acquire the 144-branch First Florida Banks, the state's last large independent bank. In late 1994 it bought the 34 Florida branches of Glendale Federal Bank.

The Players

NationsBank Chairman and CEO: Hugh L. McColl, Jr. Born in 1935 in South Carolina, Hugh McColl was a fourth-generation banker who broke the mold of traditional Southern charm. His aggressiveness sometimes translated into hostility and abrasiveness. Although these qualities occasionally hurt his business dealings by sending acquisition targets into the arms of white knights, they inspired fierce loyalty among his subordinates. They also built his bank into a national powerhouse. McColl graduated from the University of North Carolina in 1957. After a two-year stint in the Marines, he joined a small Charlotte bank that later became a part of NationsBank's predecessor, NCNB Corp. He was named head of the bank's national division in 1964 and president in 1974. McColl became chairman of NCNB in 1983 and sent the company on a shopping spree that turned it into the nation's third largest bank by the early 1990s. After several other unions, particularly with BankAmerica Corp. in 1998, NationsBank held the country's top spot.

Barnett Banks Chairman and CEO: Charles E. Rice. Charles Rice graduated from the University of Miami and then earned an MBA from Rollins College in 1965. He became president of First National Bank of Winter Park, which was purchased by Barnett Banks in 1966. In 1971 Rice became an executive vice president at Barnett and was named president the following year. He succeeded Guy Botts as CEO in 1979 and as chairman in 1984. After Barnett's acquisition by NationsBank, Rice was named the successor of the company's chairman, Andy Craig, who was scheduled to retire in 1998. In April 1998 he took that post, aware that his tenure would be brief. NationsBank was set to merge with BankAmerica in September, at which time Hugh McColl would become chairman.

In December 1995 the U.S. Department of Justice officially closed its probe into Barnett's alleged racial discriminatory lending practices during 1991-92. The Department had launched an investigation in September 1993, but found no evidence of illegal transgressions.

In early 1995 Barnett bought the mortgage banking firms Loan America Financial and BancPlus Financial Corp., as well as the EquiCredit Corp. consumer finance firm. In March 1996 the U.S. Supreme Court handed down its decision in a case regarding Barnett's attempt to overturn Florida's ban on the sale of insurance by banks. The Court opened the insurance markets to banks in 20 states, including Florida. Later that year Barnett introduced its first global mutual fund, the Emerald International Fund. The company recorded earnings of $564.5 million for the year.

On April 1, 1997, the company paid $670 million for Oxford Resources Corp., the largest independent automobile leasing company in the U.S., thereby gaining entry into 21 states. The next month it entered into an agreement to acquire Republic Banking Corp., but the deal was terminated two weeks later, presumably due to irreconcilable cultural differences. In September it agreed to be acquired by NationsBank in the largest banking deal in U.S. history.

Market Forces Driving the Acquisition

NationsBank had built itself into a banking behemoth by throwing itself into an aggressive acquisition campaign. Under the leadership of its expansion-driven chairman, Hugh McColl, the bank had grown to the nation's fourth-placed position by mid-1997. But the race for market share was unrelenting. A particular rivalry existed between McColl and Edward Crutchfield, chairman of First Union Corp. In 1995 that banking institution bought First Fidelity Corp. for $5.4 billion, breaking the record as the largest banking deal at that time. This record was shattered later that year with Wells Fargo's $10.9 billion purchase of First Interstate Bancorp. NationsBank itself spent $9.6 billion in 1996 to acquire Boatmen's Bancshares Inc.

As the large industry players swallowed more and more banks, the scarcity of the remaining independents drove their prices up. The ever decreasing number of acquisition targets spurred more banks to enter into the bidding, which also pushed up purchase prices. The largest players jockeyed for market positions with their purchases and had to remain on alert for desirable deals that would either boost their own presence or prevent a rival from increasing its position.

By 1997 Barnett Banks was the largest independent bank in Florida and the 20th-largest in the nation. With $44 billion in assets and 600 branches, it had captured a 20% share of the Florida market. Although the real estate crash of the late 1980s had caused Barnett's earnings and stock price to plummet, the company had recovered by the mid-1990s. However, Barnett discovered that it had emerged from the crisis at a distinct disadvantage to its rivals. Barnett's concentration in Florida made it vulnerable to the full force of that state's recession, while banks that operated over a more diverse geographical region were more resilient. And during the time that Barnett was crafting its recovery, these competitors had increased their positions through expansion. The bank's growth in its home state was limited and slow, and an expensive out-of-state acquisition would dilute its value as a leading Florida force. The best option, bank executives believed, was to put Barnett up for sale.

Approach and Engagement

In late August 1997 Charles Rice, Barnett's chairman, initiated a quiet auction for the company. Rice telephoned several potential bidders to inform them that they each had a week to submit an offer. Among the suitors were Banc One Corp., Bank of New York Co., First Union Corp., SunTrust Banks, and Wachovia Corp. NationsBank was the last to submit its bid.

NationsBank's $75.18 per share offer, representing a total of $15.5 billion, astounded the industry. That price was 4.1 times Barnett's book value (its assets minus liabilities). This ratio was unheard of, as about two times book value was considered par. McColl defended the offer in *Institutional Investor*: "Our bid was very aggressive, and we wanted it to be very aggressive." Less than one week after making the offer, NationsBank announced on August 29 Barnett's acceptance of the deal—the largest in U.S. banking history.

By December 10, 1997, both the U.S. Department of Justice and the Florida Attorney General had approved the transaction, with several conditions. NationsBank would have to divest $4.1 billion in deposits, increase its small business lending in Florida, freeze customer account charges through September 1998, and offer jobs to all NationsBank and Barnett employees displaced as a result of the merger. The Federal Reserve Board then granted its approval for the deal, providing that NationsBank sell 67 Barnett branches in Florida and Georgia.

On December 19, 1997, shareholders of each company approved the stock swap, in which each Barnett share would be exchanged for 1.1875 NationsBank share. On January 9, 1998, the acquisition was formally completed.

Products and Services

Bank of America provided a wide range of consumer and corporate banking products and services after the merger. Its 4,700 banking centers and 14,000 ATMs served 30 million households in 22 states, the District of Columbia, and Hong Kong. Its business customers numbered two million, and it operated 37 international offices that conducted business in 190 countries.

Changes to the Industry

The Barnett acquisition propelled NationsBank from the nation's fourth-largest banking firm in terms of assets to the number three spot, behind Chase Manhattan and Citicorp. Measured by market capitalization, it ranked number one, as it also did in terms of common shareholder equity.

Its market share in Florida, the former Barnett Bank's strongest territory, approached 32%, with nearly $60 billion in deposits. This position far outdistanced second-placed First Union, with a 17% share, and SunTrust's 10.4% third-place rank. These two rivals launched heavy print and television advertising campaigns to try to lure customers away from NationsBank and Barnett during their integration. Newly merged banks were most vulnerable to competitive raiding during this period, typically losing about 5% of deposits. First Union also sought to increase its holdings via acquisition. NationsBank's record-breaking acquisition of Barnett was beaten later in 1997 by First Union's $17 billion agreement to acquire CoreStates Financial Corp.

Review of the Outcome

No bank employees lost their jobs as a result of the acquisition. Although more than 200 Florida banks were closed, their workers were promised jobs as the remaining branches expanded their staffs. The same assurance wasn't made for corporate positions, however. In February 1998 NationsBank announced the elimination of about 6,000 redundant positions at its headquarters. Attrition played a significant role in that job reduction as many workers declined to transfer from Florida to NationsBank's North Carolina headquarters.

On October 9, 1998, all remaining Barnett banks in Florida were officially converted to the NationsBank name. This transformation caused a number of problems—long teller lines, computer glitches, and busy phone centers—that NationsBank had not experienced in its history of acquisitions. Chairman McColl attributed the problems to this unique merger situation, in which it marketed both the Barnett and NationsBank brands while trying to retain customers whose accounts were switched to a third bank, Huntington Bank, which had purchased 60 Barnett branches. "We don't go through any merger without making mistakes," he apologized in *Knight-Ridder/Tribune Business News*, "and we made plenty here in Florida."

Research

Bank of America Corp. Home Page, available at http://www.bankofamerica.com. Official World Wide Web Page for Bank of America. Includes news releases, annual reports and other financial information, a branch directory, and online banking capabilities.

"Barnett Banks, Inc.," in *International Directory of Company Histories*, Vol. 9, St. James Press: 1994. Provides an historical review of the company.

Brannigan, Martha, Nikhil Deogun, Eleena de Lisser, and Steven Lippon. "NationsBank Wins Bidding for Barnett," in *The Wall Street Journal*, 2 September 1997. Details the acquisition offer.

Elkins, Ken. "With Barnett in Fold, NationsBank Tops in Many Ways," in *Tampa Bay Business Journal*, 19 September 1997. Describes NationsBank's new market positions as a result of the acquisition.

Harrington, Jeff. "BankAmerica CEO's Sorry for Barnett-NationsBank Merger Problems," in *Knight-Ridder/Tribune Business News*, 26 March 1999. Relates the problems experienced at the newly integrated Florida branches.

"Heart Failure: Bank Mergers," in *The Economist*, 6 September 1997. Describes the concern of some market analysts over the record-breaking value of the deal.

"Mating Games," in *Institutional Investor*, January 1998. Provides an overview and details of a number of unusual mergers and acquisitions during 1997.

Milligan, John W. "Scooping up Banks and Thrifts," in *US Banker*, March 1998. Offers a discussion and ranking of the year's banking unions.

"NationsBank Corp.," in *Notable Corporate Chronologies*, The Gale Group, 1999. Profiles the history of the company.

Wasserstein, Bruce. *Big Deal: The Battle for Control of America's Leading Corporations*, Warner Books, 1998. Offers an overview of the largest mergers in recent American corporate history.

KIMBERLY N. STEVENS

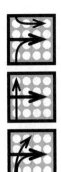

NATIONSBANK & MONTGOMERY SECURITIES

nationality: USA
date: October 1, 1997
affected: NationsBank Corp., USA, founded 1968
affected: Montgomery Securities, USA, founded 1969

Bank of America Corp.
100 N. Tryon St., 18th Fl.
Charlotte, NC 28255
USA

tel: (704)386-5000
fax: (704)386-6699
web: http://www.bankofamerica.com

Overview of the Acquisition

NationsBank's acquisition of Montgomery Securities in 1997 marked the commercial bank's effort to strengthen its financial securities operations. The union was successful in that respect, yet tensions arising from a clash of cultures—as well as a proposed reunion of two bitter rivals—resulted in the exodus of more than 100 former Montgomery Securities employees, including the firm's founder and CEO, Thomas Weisel.

History of NationsBank Corp.

NationsBank, which became an acquisition machine in the 1960s, had a modest beginning. In February 1874 a consortium of prominent local citizens formed the Commercial National Bank in Charlotte, North Carolina, with an initial capitalization of $50,000. Meanwhile, in November 1887, Citizens Bank of Savannah opened for business in Georgia with an initial capitalization of $200,000. In 1901 George Stephens established the Southern States Trust Company, which changed its name to the American Trust Company six years later.

In 1906 Citizens Bank of Savannah merged with its cross-town rival, the Southern Bank, to form Citizens and Southern Bank. This operation began opening branches in South Carolina in 1928. In 1940 it spun off its South Carolina branches as Citizens and Southern Bank of South Carolina in anticipation of federal laws barring multistate bank ownership.

In 1957 Commercial National Bank merged with American Trust Company to form American Commercial Bank. Two years later this firm expanded its operations throughout North Carolina by absorbing the First National Bank of Raleigh. In July 1960 it merged with Security National to form the North Carolina National Bank. North Carolina National Bank employed 1,300 workers at 40 offices in 20 cities throughout the state, with assets of $480 million. It expanded aggressively, acquiring nine North Carolina banks during the following eight years.

In 1968 North Carolina National Bank formed NCNB Corp. as a holding company to manage its subsidiary operations. By 1970 it operated 91 offices in 27 North

The Business

Financials

Revenue (1998): $30.5 billion

Employees (1998): 171,000

SICs / NAICS

sic 6021 - National Commercial Banks

sic 6211 - Security Brokers & Dealers

naics 522110 - Commercial Banking

naics 523110 - Investment Banking and Securities Dealing

naics 523120 - Securities Brokerage

Carolina cities. Its voracious appetite unabated, the firm acquired nine more banks during the decade. After NCNB absorbed the Bank of Asheville and Carolina First in 1979, it became the largest financial institution in North Carolina.

In 1982 the federal government lifted its ban on bank holding companies' acquiring failing out-of-state banks. NCNB took advantage of this legislation by making its first purchase in Florida. It became the first non-Florida bank to offer retail services in the state by purchasing the First National Bank of Lake City in January 1982. Later that year it extended its presence in the state by purchasing Gulfstream Banks, Exchange Ban-Corp., and People's Downtown National Bank.

Hugh L. McColl, Jr. became chairman of NCNB in 1983 and led the company on a mission to become the leading bank on the Southeast Coast. The next year NCNB added to its Florida operations, acquiring banks in Boca Raton, Tampa, Miami, and Bradenton. In 1985 it purchased the Pan American Bank of Miami, with assets of $2 billion, and entered the financial market in Georgia with the acquisition of Southern National Bankshares Inc. of Atlanta. NCNB expanded its operations into two new states in 1986, purchasing the Bankers Trust of South Carolina and the Prince William Bank of Virginia. Its purchase of CentraBank of Baltimore the next year gained it entry into Maryland.

NCNB was chosen by the Federal Deposit Insurance Corp. in 1988 to manage the restructuring of the First Republic Bank Corp., Texas's largest, but failing, financial institution. NCNB paid $210 million to acquire a 20% interest in First Republic, with the option to acquire the remaining 80% at a later date. This purchase, questioned by some analysts, proved strategic, as NCNB used First Republic's losses as a tax shelter. The following year it acquired the remaining interest of First Republic.

In 1989 NCNB launched a hostile takeover of Citizens and Southern Bank, but dropped the attack in the face of regulatory barriers. Instead NCNB acquired University Federal Savings (Texas) and Freedom Savings and Loan Association of Florida. The next year it acquired nine banks from National Bancshares of San Antonio, Texas.

The company paid $4.26 billion to acquire C&S/Sovran in 1991 in order to gain entry into Georgia and Virginia, thereby growing closer to its goal of becoming a national bank. The new entity, renamed NationsBank Corp., became the nation's third-largest bank. Former C&S/Sovran chairman and CEO, Bennett A. Brown, was named NationsBank's chairman, while McColl functioned as the new bank's president and CEO.

The bank diversified into financial businesses, including securities, dividends, and options, with its 1993 acquisition of Chicago Research & Trading in 1993. That year it also formed an alliance with Dean Witter, Discover & Co. to offer brokerage services in its bank branches, but the alliance was terminated the following year upon customer complaints and a Securities and Exchange Commission investigation into NationsBank's misleading sales practices. It paid $30 million to settle the ensuing class action lawsuit.

By 1994 NationsBank was the fourth-largest banking company in the U.S., operating 1,800 offices in nine states and the District of Columbia. It purchased two Florida banks, Intercontinental Bank and CSF Holdings, the parent of Citizens Federal Bank, for $516 million and $218 million, respectively. In 1997 it acquired Boatmen's Bancshares Inc., headquartered in St. Louis, Missouri. This $9.6 billion purchase introduced NationsBank to the Midwest market, and the firm then occupied 16 states.

Later that year it decided to boost its financial securities operations and gain entry into the California market by acquiring San Francisco-based Montgomery Securities. In September it also acquired Barnett Banks, thereby becoming the nation's second-largest commercial bank in terms of market capitalization. The bank then captured the nation's top spot by merging with BankAmerica Corp.; the new entity retained the BankAmerica moniker.

In October 1998 David Coulter, chairman and CEO of the former BankAmerica, resigned as president of the company, and was succeeded by Kenneth

Lewis. In December 1998 the firm entered into a merger agreement with BankAmerica Merchant Services, Inc. Also that month it agreed to sell its Alaskan consumer and small business operations to Northrim Bank. In March 1999 it acquired Fleetwood Credit Corp., a subsidiary of Associates First Capital Corp. The next month shareholders approved the company's name change to Bank of America Corp.

History of Montgomery Securities

In the late 1960s the infant high technology industry was burgeoning on the West Coast. Small computer companies were springing up in Silicon Valley, poised to explode into full-grown industry players. Yet in their start-up stage, they were too small to attract such large financial investment firms as Smith Barney. One employee of that company, Sanford Robertson, quit in 1969 to establish Robertson, Coleman & Siebel to take advantage of the opportunity that he saw in technology companies.

In 1971 Thomas Weisel, a Harvard Business School graduate, joined the firm as the head of institutional sales. Within a couple of years he became a partner and the company was renamed Robertson, Coleman, Siebel & Weisel. The new partnership proved to be short-lived, however, as shortly thereafter it was ripped apart by disputes over its direction. Weisel wanted to increase the firm's trading operations, a move that Robertson believed would result in a loss of its lucrative relationships with the investment banking clients. On October 1, 1978, Robertson and Coleman left to form the predecessor of Robertson, Stephens & Co. Siebel also resigned, and Weisel, the only remaining partner, renamed the firm Montgomery Securities.

During the 1980s these two rival companies vied for business in the same fields—technology, healthcare, and specialty retailing. Robertson Stephens grew slowly yet steadily by forging long-term relationships with clients. Montgomery, on the other hand, grew quickly and aggressively. Its riskiness landed it in some trouble over its trading practices. The firm straightened itself out, however, and received a $10 million equity infusion from the Pritzker family.

As Montgomery offered only a limited amount of services, many of the largest potential clients clung to the Wall Street financial institutions that could offer more of a one-stop shop. To better compete with these big players, Montgomery began increasing its portfolio to include research, corporate finance, and trading capabilities. It occasionally ventured into mergers and acquisitions, and backed First Interstate Bancorp's attempted takeover of BankAmerica Corp. in 1986.

The Officers

Chairman and CEO: Hugh L. McColl, Jr.

Vice Chairman and Chief Financial Officer: James H. Hance Jr.

President: Kenneth D. Lewis

President, Global Corporate & Investment Banking: Michael J. Murray

Corporate Risk Management Executive: F. William Vandiver, Jr.

The 1990s brought booms in initial public offerings (IPOs) and mutual funds, and Montgomery aggressively rode those waves. In 1990 it established Montgomery Asset Management, its mutual-fund and institutional-account management business. This unit introduced its first product, the Small Cap Fund, in November of that year, just in time to take advantage of a surge in the market in 1991. Montgomery Asset Management launched its Emerging Markets Fund, for Third World investing, in 1992.

Montgomery's IPO operations exploded during the early 1990s. In 1990 the firm underwrote three IPOs, and the following year increased that number to 28. By 1994 it ranked third of the nation's leading IPO underwriters, behind only Merrill Lynch and Lehman Brothers. The firm's aggressiveness in this area again landed it in hot water, however. Shareholders of Media Vision Technology filed a suit against Montgomery—one of a half-dozen such suits—alleging inadequate due diligence for failure to discover and report inflated financial facts before taking the company public. By 1995 Montgomery had paid $7 million to settle three of these lawsuits.

In 1996 Montgomery expanded outside San Francisco by opening offices in New York and Boston. Although revenues that year reached $705 million, up from $94 million in 1990, the firm required an influx of capital to continue to compete with the Wall Street leaders. In March 1997 it agreed to sell Montgomery Asset Management to Commerzbank AG. Later that year it agreed to be acquired by NationsBank for $1.2 billion.

Market Forces Driving the Acquisition

NationsBank first began expanding outside of North Carolina after the passage of federal legislation lifting the ban on interstate banking acquisitions in 1982. That year the company quickly gained entry into

The Players

NationsBank Chairman and CEO: Hugh L. McColl, Jr. Born in 1935 in South Carolina, Hugh McColl was a fourth-generation banker who broke the mold of traditional Southern charm. His aggressiveness sometimes translated into hostility and abrasiveness. Although these qualities occasionally hurt his business dealings by sending acquisition targets into the arms of white knights, they inspired fierce loyalty among his subordinates. They also built his bank into a national powerhouse. McColl graduated from the University of North Carolina in 1957. After a two-year stint in the Marines, he joined a small Charlotte bank that later became a part of NationsBank's predecessor, NCNB Corp. He was named head of the bank's national division in 1964 and president in 1974. McColl became chairman of NCNB in 1983 and sent the company on a shopping spree that turned it into the nation's third largest bank by the early 1990s. After several other unions, particularly with BankAmerica Corp. in 1998, NationsBank held the country's top spot.

Montgomery Securities Founder and CEO: Thomas W. Weisel. In the business world, Thomas Weisel was known to be aggressive and cutthroat, qualities that also extended to his athletic endeavors. Born in 1941, this Milwaukee native was a nationally ranked speed skater with Olympic ambitions. After failing to qualify for the 1960 games, however, he graduated in economics from Stanford University before attending Harvard Business School. Upon completion of his studies there, Weisel first took a job at FMC Corp. and then at the William Hutchinson & Co. brokerage firm. In 1971 he joined Robertson Coleman & Siebel, where he soon became partner. A bitter dispute over the firm's direction resulted in the departure of its three other partners. Weisel renamed the remaining firm Montgomery Securities and drove it to become one of the nation's leading investment boutiques. In the meantime his competitive nature spurred him to participate in both amateur skiing and cycling and to chair Empower America, a Republican think-tank. After steering Montgomery into an acquisition by NationsBank, Weisel resigned out of frustration with his company's new parent. In January 1999 he formed a start-up investment house, Thomas Weisel Partners LLC.

the Florida market, and by 1996 the corporation had branches in 16 states. Its growth moved into a new direction in 1997, when the Federal Reserve Board permitted commercial banks to derive up to 25%, rather than only 10%, of their earnings from underwriting and dealing in ineligible securities. This permission spurred the acquisition of mid-sized firms by large banks, which considered acquisition to be the most efficient method of entering that market. They also aspired to become more of a one-stop shop for mid-sized corporate clients. NationsBank's small investment banking unit, NationsBanc Capital Markets, was still too small to make much of an impression in that market, so the firm began pursuing an acquisition as a means of shoring up its position.

Other banks soon began entering into deals to acquire market-savvy investment firms. Bankers Trust united with Alex Brown; then SBC Warburg acquired Dillon, Read & Co., followed by BankAmerica Corp.'s purchase of Robertson Stephens. NationsBank began eyeing Montgomery Securities. This firm, based in San Francisco, would strengthen NationsBank's presence in the California market, where it had only a small capital markets operation. By acquiring Montgomery NationsBank would establish a foundation on which to add other California securities firms.

Although Thomas Weisel, head of Montgomery Securities, had resisted taking his partnership public or allowing it to be bought out, competition drove him to consider the latter option. Without an infusion of funds, Montgomery would continue to lose the biggest deals to its deep-pocketed Wall Street brethren.

Approach and Engagement

On June 30, 1997, NationsBank Corp. announced its proposed acquisition of Montgomery Securities. The $1.2 billion purchase would be comprised of 70% cash and 30% stock, valued at $67.75 per share. In addition, NationsBank would establish a pool of $100 million in cash and stock options to secure the retention of senior Montgomery employees.

After receiving approval from the Federal Reserve Board, NationsBank fully acquired Montgomery Securities on October 1, 1997. Montgomery was folded into NationsBanc Capital Markets, which became known as NationsBanc Montgomery Securities Inc. Thomas Weisel, founder and CEO of Montgomery, was named chairman of the new subsidiary.

Products and Services

After the acquisition, Banc of America Securities offered a range of global debt and equity capital raising and advisory services that included: asset-backed securitization, commercial paper, convertible securities, debt and equity bridge financing, debt and equity private placements, equity derivatives, equity underwriting, financial sponsors, high grade securities, high yield securities, leasing, liability management, M&A advisory, medium-term notes, municipal securities, project finance, real estate finance, senior bank debt, short-term asset sales/bid loans, structured trade finance, and syndicated finance.

Changes to the Industry and Review of the Outcome

Industry analysts correctly anticipated a clash of cultures as a result of NationsBank's acquisition of Montgomery Securities. As was very often the case in unions between banks and securities firms, issues of compensation and business styles came into play. The chairmen of the bank had to deal with the fact that the securities analysts and brokers often made a far greater salary than they did. Commercial bankers also had been trained to conform to strict policy and to avoid risk, while investment bankers developed personal relationships with clients and operated in chancy ventures.

In the case of NationsBank and Montgomery Securities, however, other factors compounded the tension. In April 1998 NationsBank announced its merger agreement with BankAmerica Corp. This move would unite the two securities subsidiaries, NationsBanc Montgomery Securities and BancAmerica Robertson Stephens, which were run by the former partners-turned-rivals, Thomas Weisel and Sanford Robertson. The impending clash between these two firms, as well as the redundancies in their operations, prompted BankAmerica to sell BancAmerica Robertson Stephens to BankBoston Corp. in September 1998. At that point Sanford Robertson resigned to start up his own investment house.

More tension mounted in August 1998, when NationsBank reversed its agreement to allow Montgomery Securities to retain control of its high-yield bond business, a condition for the company's acquisition the previous October. For Weisel, this move was the final straw in what he perceived as an increasing withdrawal of autonomy from his firm's new parent. In late September, just days before NationsBank's merger with BankAmerica, he suddenly resigned to launch a new firm. Within two weeks at least seven other Montgomery employees followed him. By the end of February 1999, more than 100 former Montgomery employees had defected to join Weisel's new firm, Thomas Weisel Partners LLC. This started another feud between Weisel and a former col-

league, this time McColl. The CEO of Bank of America had to spend tens of millions of dollars to fill the gaps in Montgomery's workforce after the departure of workers for Weisel's new firm. As reported in *Fortune*, a Wall Street observer remarked that "McColl is upset about having to pay out so much, but he doesn't want to lose to Weisel."

On May 17, 1999, NationsBanc Montgomery Securities was renamed Banc of America Securities. In 1998 this subsidiary employed more than 4,000 associates and raised $28.5 billion in equity underwritings. It ranked second in IPOs in terms of number of issues, completing 55 transactions, and sixth in common stock offerings, based on number of transactions.

Research

Bank of America Corp. Home Page, available at http://www.bankofamerica.com. Official World Wide Web Page for Bank of America. Includes news releases, annual reports and other financial information, a branch directory, and online banking capabilities.

DeBlasi, Michelle. "Pumping Up," in *Bank Investment Marketing*, September 1997. Describes the industry trend of unions between banks and securities firms.

Friedman, Amy S. "NationsBank Buys Montgomery Securities in $1.2 Billion Deal," in *National Underwriter Life & Health—Financial Services Edition*, 7 July 1997. Details the newly announced acquisition deal.

Haber, Carol. "Montgomery Goes to NationsBank in Rich and Risky Deal, Some Say," in *Electronic News (1991)*, 7 July 1997. Offers the opinion of some analysts that NationsBank overbid for Montgomery.

Koselka, Rita. "Riding the Wave," in *Forbes*, 23 May 1994. Profiles Weisel and Montgomery Securities.

McMurray, Scott. "What Makes Montgomery Run?" in *Institutional Investor*, February 1997. Details the history and growth of Montgomery.

"NationsBank Corp.," in *Notable Corporate Chronologies*, The Gale Group, 1999. Profiles the history of the company.

Schonfeld, Erick. "Married with Children: The BankAmerica Deal Reunites Two Investment Banks Stuck in a 20-Year Sibling Rivalry," in *Fortune*, 11 May 1998. Details the challenge of merging Montgomery Securities and Robertson Stephens after NationsBank's merger with BankAmerica.

Schwartz, Nelson D. "Meet the Man Who's Driving Hugh McColl Nuts: Grudge Matches, Wall Street Division," in *Fortune*, 12 April 1999. Relates the feud between McColl and Weisel after the latter's departure from NationsBanc Montgomery Securities.

Tarquinio, J. Alex. "Montgomery Chief Expected to Start Own Merchant Bank," in *American Banker*, 21 September 1998. Describes the resignation of Weisel following the acquisition.

Wasserstein, Bruce. *Big Deal: The Battle for Control of America's Leading Corporations*, Warner Books, 1998. Offers an overview of the largest mergers in recent American corporate history.

KIMBERLY N. STEVENS

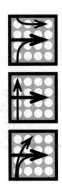

NESTLE & CARNATION

Nestle S.A.
Avenue Nestle 55
Vevey, CH-1800
Switzerland

tel: (021)924-2111
fax: (021)921-1885
web: http://www.nestle.com

nationality: Switzerland
date: January 1985
affected: Nestle S.A., Switzerland, founded 1866
affected: Carnation Co., USA, founded 1899

Overview of the Merger

The $3 billion acquisition of Carnation Co. by Nestle S.A. marked the largest non-oil acquisition in corporate America. Done in an attempt to boost its American presence, to increase revenue, and to compensate for lagging business in Third World countries, the acquisition was projected to double U.S. sales. Revenue was expected to increase by one-third, estimated at $14.78 billion. Nestle was also planning to bolster Carnation's sales overseas by marketing them in 57 countries. The was indicative of Nestle's new strategy to grow by acquiring, broaden product lines, and strengthen existing products.

History of Nestle S.A.

While serving as an American consul in Zurich, Charles Page established Anglo-Swiss Condensed Milk Co. in Cham, Switzerland, in 1866. Page felt that Switzerland would be an ideal place to start the company because of its abundant milk supply and its location in the European market. He chose the name, Anglo-Swiss, to try to appeal to the British. Condensed milk was soon found in cupboards throughout Europe. In 1872 operations expanded beyond the Swiss border with a new factory in Chippenham, England. The next year, George Page took over the company following his brother's death.

Meanwhile, Henri Nestle began marketing Farine Lactee Nestle (a mixture of cow's milk, sugar, and cereal) for infants who refused breast milk. By 1873 the demand for Nestle's product had doubled over the past two years, exceeding production capabilities and resulting in missed delivery dates. Wanting to retire, Nestle accepted a SFr1 million offer from Jules Monnerat, a former member of Parliament who had been eyeballing the company. In 1875 Monnerat became chairman.

Expansion continued for Anglo-Swiss with the purchase of English Condensed Milk Company in London in 1874. Just two years later, sales for Anglo-Swiss had quadrupled. Anglo-Swiss began to broaden its product line to include the manufacture of cheese and milk-based food for babies in 1877; at the same time, Nestle launched a condensed milk product of its own. George Page attempted to purchase Nestle, to no avail, and the two companies began to compete. In 1881 Anglo-Swiss opened its first U.S. factory in Middletown, New York. The factory was a success and began to challenge Borden, the leader in the American condensed milk market. Unfortunately, sales in Europe began to falter as Page spent most of his time in New York. The death of George Page in 1899 brought on the sale of the American business to Borden in order to regain control in Europe.

Not to be outdone by Anglo-Swiss, Nestle acquired a Norwegian condensed milk company in 1898. The next year Nestle opened factories in the U.S., Britain, Germany, and Spain. In 1904 Nestle entered the chocolate business, partnering with the Swiss General Chocolate Co. Anglo-Swiss and Nestle decided to join forces, and merged in 1905. With Emile-Louis Roussy as chairman, the new company included seven factories in Switzerland, six in Great Britain, three in Norway, and one each in the U.S., Germany, and Spain.

The company began to manufacture in Australia with the purchase of Cressbrook Dairy Co. in Brisbane. Sales continued to increase throughout the early years of the 1900s. When World War I broke out in 1914, Nestle was faced with problems because of limited supplies. It responded by expanding in markets less affected by the war. By 1917 Nestle was operating 40 factories. World production had doubled over the past four years, and in 1920 Nestle acquired controlling interests in three Australian companies. Production also began in Latin America.

The 1920s marked change for the company. With more than 80 factories and 12 subsidiaries and affiliates in production, the company's first loss was reported at SFr100 million. In 1922 it closed factories in the U.S., Britain, Australia, Norway, and Switzerland. The company called upon Louis Dapples, a banking expert, to repair the damage. He was able to reduce debt and increase operations in France, Belgium, Italy, Germany, and South Africa. In 1923 Nestle merged with Peter, Cailler, Kohler Chocolats Suisses S.A., adding 13 chocolate plants in Europe, South America, and Australia. New products included malted milk, Milo powdered beverage, and Eledon, a powdered buttermilk for infants with digestive disorders.

The 1930s were tough years for companies around the globe. The Great Depression forced a change in Nestle's game plan. Subsidiaries in Argentina and Cuba were established, as well as production centers in Copenhagen, Moravia, and Czechoslovakia. However, profits were down 13% from the years before. Consumer frugality was a cause for concern until 1933, when new legislation set mini-

The Business

Financials

Revenue (1998): $52.2 billion

Employees (1998): 231,881

SICs / NAICS

sic 2064 - Candy & Other Confectionery Products

sic 2066 - Chocolate & Cocoa Products

mum prices and conditions of sales. This legislation regulated the cutthroat competition that seriously affected Nestle's New York-based subsidiary, which had become known as Nestle's Milk Products Co. By 1936 Nestle was forced to close factories in Cham and Vevey due to the devaluation of currency caused by the depression in Switzerland. The company structure continued to change as interests in more than 20 companies on five continents led Nestle and the Anglo-Swiss Company to become a holding company. A second holding company, Unilac Inc., was created in Panama. In 1937 Louis Dapples died and was succeeded by Edouard Muller and a management team that had been with Nestle for years.

By the end of the 1930s, Nestle had introduced its Crunch candy bar and its first non-milk product, Nescafe instant coffee. This beverage gained a worldwide reputation and experienced increased popularity in the United States. Nevertheless, with the onset of World War II, Nestle's profits plummeted from $20 million to $6 million by 1939. A lack supplies was compounded by food shortages. There was a light at the end of the tunnel, however, and by 1941 demand for Nescafe and evaporated and powdered milk by American armed forces substantially increased sales.

By 1945 sales jumped to $225 million. Two years later, Nestle merged with Alimentana S.A., manufacturer of Maggi seasoning, bouillon, and dehydrated soup. The holding company changed its name to Nestle Alimentana Co. Edouard Muller became its first chairman but died in 1948, at which time Carl Abegg took leadership of the board. In 1950 the company acquired Cross and Blackwell, a British manufacturer of preserves and canned foods. Nestle hoped to use this as a marketing outlet for its Maggi products, but Cross and Blackwell could not compete in the United Kingdom against H.J. Heinz Company. They had similar problems when Nestle bought Findus frozen foods in Scandinavia. They could not compete with the British-Dutch giant, Unilever, so in 1963 the

The Officers

Chairman: Helmut O. Maucher

Vice Chairman: Fritz Gerber

Vice Chairman: Rainer E. Gut

CEO: Peter Brabeck-Letmathe

company merged its German, Italian, and Australian Findus branches with Unilever. In 1966 the first freeze-dried coffee, Taster's Choice, was introduced.

Nestle acquired a U.S. fruit juice maker, Libby, in 1971. Two years later they entered the hotel and restaurant industry with the purchase of Stouffer's. In 1974 Nestle entered the non-food business for the first time by becoming a major shareholder in the L'Oreal cosmetic company. The firm also acquired Alcon Laboratories, a pharmaceutical company, and Burton, Parson and Company Inc., a manufacturer of contact lens products. The company adopted its present name, Nestle S.A., in 1979.

A U.S. boycott of all Nestle products began in 1977. Activists claimed that the company's aggressive promotions of baby food encouraged mothers in developing countries to use the products in any way they could. Infants eventually starved to death when their mothers mixed formula with polluted water or used an insufficient amount of formula to make it last longer. Nestle lost about $40 million in sales. In 1981 Nestle addressed the boycott supporters and complied with the World Health Organization's demand to stop promoting the product through advertising and free samples. Helmut Maucher became the managing director in 1981 and squelched the critics' fears by directly confronting the issue rather than assuming a low profile as Nestle had done in the past.

Maucher proved to be a strong leader and blazed the trail for a series of major acquisitions. In 1984 Nestle acquired Carnation, a U.S. manufacturer of milk, pet, and culinary products. This was the largest takeover in the food industry at the time, worth $3 billion. Ground roast coffee joined Nestle's product line with the purchase of Hills Brothers Inc. in 1985. Acquisitions in 1988 included British chocolate manufacturer, Rowntree PLC and Italian pasta maker, Buitoni SpA.

Nestle S.A. continued its acquisition frenzy, making 31 acquisitions in 1991. In September of that year the firm joined with Coca-Cola to market concentrates for its coffee, tea, and chocolate beverages. In 1992

Nestle launched and won a hostile takeover bid for Source Perrier. The giant also acquired Alpo pet food in 1994, and Ortega Mexican foods in 1995. With factories in 63 countries, Nestle remained the undisputed leader in the industry as the world's largest packaged food manufacturer, coffee roaster, and chocolate maker.

In 1996 Nestle introduced Nescafe ready-to-drink iced coffees, the first single-serve ready-to-drink coffee widely distributed to convenience stores. Nestle also purchased Koala Springs International and laid the groundwork for Nestle Clinical Nutrition, which would provide nutritional assistance to nursing homes and hospitals. The next year, Peter Brabeck-Letmathe became CEO. Maucher remained chairman.

Nestle continued to make changes over the next few years by divesting its Contadina line to Del Monte and by purchasing San Pellegrino. In 1998 it sold Libby's canned meat products to International Home Foods. That same year, Nestle purchased Spillers pet food from Dalgety PLC, which strengthened its position in the European pet food market. The company continued to sell and acquire over the next year in efforts to strengthen its global presence in the food industry.

History of Carnation Co.

Elbridge Amos Stuart and Thomas E. Yerxa purchased a bankrupt condensary in Kent, Washington, in 1899. They called upon John B. Meyenberg, the Swiss inventor of evaporated milk, and paid him $25,000 for his technology. The partners named their company Carnation after a brand of popular cigars, and put significant efforts into marketing their product. The product was slow to take off and in the first year they lost $140,000. They soon discovered, however, that Alaskan gold prospectors valued the product for its nonperishable and transportable qualities. Carnation began to capitalize on that market and soon its sales were up. The company established a sales office in Seattle and a plant in Forest Grove, Oregon, and purchased state-of-the-art equipment.

By 1911 despite the failure of Sanupure, a product formulated for infants, Carnation had already turned down several acquisition offers, including a $1 million offer from Borden. Stuart established Carnation Stock Farms on 750 acres of land in Snoqualmie Valley, Washington. He spent lavishly on prized cattle, making this farm the showpiece of the company. The Carnation cows had become known for setting records in milk and butterfat production. In 1915 Stuart bought a second farm in Oconomowoc, Wisconsin, the location of the eastern division offices.

In 1916, when the company introduced a low cost alternative to condensed milk, the dairymen of the U.S. saw it as a threat. The new product, Hebe, was banned in Ohio. Carnation fought the ban, to no avail. As a result, the government passed the Federal Filled Milk Act in 1923, making it illegal to ship adulterated milk over state lines. Sales remained steady in the Midwest and the East despite the presence of two major competitors, Borden and Pet. The company changed its name to Carnation Milk Products Company in 1916 when it reincorporated in Maine. Stuart opened an office in Chicago, built a can factory in Oconomowoc, and acquired two condensaries. The company was producing more than 530 pounds of evaporated milk and operating 20 facilities.

World War I proved to be profitable for Carnation, as it was able to supply European firms to help alleviate shortages. When the war ended, however, the company was faced with major surpluses. Carnation went overseas and found an affiliate in Pet Milk Company. The joint venture, Branches of American Milk Products Corporation, opened in Paris and Germany. Back in the U.S., Carnation was busy acquiring. In 1922 it bought the Malt-A-Milk Company, and a few years later, it entered the fresh milk industry with the purchase of six diaries in Seattle. Carnation plunged into this market and went on to acquire dairies in Oregon, California, Texas, Oklahoma, and Iowa. In 1929 Stuart bought Albers Brothers Milling Co., taking Carnation outside of the dairy market for the first time by adding cereals and soybean livestock feed to its interests. The company was renamed Carnation Co. to reflect the purchase and the company's diversity.

Elbridge Hadley Stuart took over for his father in 1932. The company lost $660,000 that year, but bounced back the next with earnings of over $1 million on account of Stuart's cost cutting skills. He also worked hard on the company's image, sponsoring *The Contented Hour* on NBC Network and featuring a promotional campaign with the Dionne quintuplets. The babies were to be fed the company's new vitamin D milk. As the firm was pushing to be the first choice for infant milk, it was also involved in research and development for new livestock feed. By the end of 1936, this feed was popular with farms throughout the world. Carnation also introduced Friskies, the first dry dog food, in 1934.

With the onset of World War II, demand for evaporated milk skyrocketed. Sales rose for Carnation as demand increased to as much as 86.6 million cases of the milk. Government rationing and price ceilings kept its profits steady during the war, but in 1946 they rose to $3.2 million. The company celebrated its 50th anniversary in 1949 and saw profits rise to $7.76 mill-

The Players

Chairman of Nestle S.A.: Helmut O. Maucher. Helmut O. Maucher began his illustrious career in business after completing graduate studies at IMEDE, Lausanne. From 1964 to 1975 he held various management positions with the German branch of Nestle. In 1980 he transferred to Nestle in Switzerland where he became executive vice president of Nestle S.A., and one year later, its president and CEO. He became the first German to head Switzerland's largest company.

The 1980s were years of development and growth for Nestle as Maucher spearheaded a series of major acquisitions. Nestle's acquisition of the Carnation Co. that year was the largest non-oil acquisition in American corporate history. The food industry giant went on to acquire Hills Brothers Inc., Rowntree Mackintosh PLC, and Buitoni SpA. Maucher's ideas and innovations went on to change the corporate mindset from conservative to aggressive. He is credited with being a frontrunner in an ever-changing global industry. The 35-year Nestle veteran has led the company to double its profits, triple its American sales, and remain the leader in the food sales industry across the globe.

CEO of Carnation Co.: Timm F. Crull. Crull began his career with the Carnation Co.in 1955 as a trainee in its Grocery Products Marketing division. He worked his way up the ladder of success and was elected a senior vice president and member of the executive committee. He resigned that year and went on to become president and a director of Norton Simon Inc., another company in the food industry.

His leave from the Carnation Company was short lived, and he returned in 1980 as executive vice president. Crull was elected president in 1983 and took over as CEO on February 1, 1985. He led the company through a smooth transition of the mega-merger with Nestle S.A. He was named CEO of Nestle USA Inc. and in 1992 became chairman of the company in addition to becoming an executive vice president of Nestle S.A.'s general management. He was slated to oversee operations in the USA and Canada.

ion. It opened corporate offices that year in Los Angeles, California.

Carnation began the 1950s with a cautious, conservative attitude. In 1953 the company opened a research laboratory in Van Nuys, California, in an effort to increase product development and improve market analysis methods. With demand for evaporated milk plummeting, sales for nonfat dry milk soared, despite its tendencies to have bad flavor and resist dissolution in water. Carnation was not eager to market this product and went out to create a product of its own. In 1954 the company formed the Instant Milk Company with Western Condensing. Western had patented a powdered milk without the inferior qualities that Carnation wanted to avoid. The new company sold the new product under the Carnation name and was a success.

Carnation began to research other powdered foods. In 1956 instant cocoa was introduced, and in 1961 Coffeemate entered the market. Convenience foods became popular in the 1960s and Carnation began to direct its focus on that market. Pet foods were also becoming popular and the company introduced canned cat and dog food in 1959. In 1963 H. Everett Olson became president and lead the way to many acquisitions. The same year that he became president, the company bought Contadina. Three years later it purchased Trenton Foods, one of the largest suppliers of canned meats and sauces.

Under Olson's leadership, the company went on to acquire Reliable Tool and Pronto Pacific, the Western Farmers Association processing plant. It began to delve into genetic research and artificial insemination of livestock. Olson became chairman in 1971, and wanted to further diversify the company. He purchased Herff Jones, a manufacturer of school rings and graduation products. He planned to purchase a trucking company, but a drop in stock forced him to reconsider diversification in that direction. In 1973 Dwight L. Stewart became president of Carnation.

By the end of the 1970s, Carnation was the second-largest producer of pet food; the company's new focus on these products and instant foods made up for the decrease in demand for evaporated milk. Carnation began to cut back on advertising and marketing, as well as on product development. The company's long standing policy of being tight-lipped on plans was beginning to have a negative effect. The government began to investigate possible price fixing and illegal payments to foreign governments. Despite the difficulties, Carnation was still able to pull in a profit.

In 1980 Olson urged the Stuart family trust to dissolve itself. New production increased, but market share in pet foods slipped noticeably. The company opened its first Health and Nutrition Center, which was well received because of its diet programs. In 1983 Timm F. Crull took over as president of Carnation. The next year formal negotiations with Nestle began to evolve. In January of 1985, the $3 billion, $83 per share takeover took place. As a result of Carnation's failure to disclose information to shareholders about the merger, it paid a $13 million settlement in 1987. Crull took over as Olson retired in 1985 and was slated to lead the company in a smooth transition of the takeover.

Market Forces Driving the Merger

Loss of sales in third world countries, competition in the U.S. market, and the need to increase revenue prompted Nestle S.A. to seek out Carnation. Nestle was dealing with a $40 million dollar loss in sales from a boycott that developed in the late 1970s. Aggressive promotion of the company's baby food in developing countries had caused an uproar when it was discovered that the women in those countries were using polluted water to mix with Nestle's formula. The situation was not remedied until the early 1980s, and Nestle needed to gain market share in the U.S. to improve its financial record.

With 73% of revenue stemming from U.S. sales, Carnation seemed to be a perfect fit for Nestle's goals. Carnation's earnings had been consecutively increasing for the last 31 years to $194.8 million in 1983 and Nestle was attracted to the lucrative firm. Nestle would be able to grab larger market shares and edge out competitors, such as General Foods Corp. and Unilever, with the completion of the merger.

Approach and Engagement

Merger talks between Nestle S.A. and Carnation began in the early 1980s. Nestle approached members of the Stuart family, who owned roughly 35% of Carnation stock. A letter promising $82 a share was sent to Carnation management in an effort to push the board to accept the offer. Nestle saw the company as a perfect vehicle in which to gain a strong presence in the U.S. market. "The U.S. is attractive for its free enterprise dynamics," commented Helmut Maucher, CEO of Nestle S.A., in *The Wall Street Journal*. Carnation's directors approved Nestle's offer, and in January of 1985, the Federal Trade Commission gave the go ahead for the merger. With more than 90% of shares tendered to Nestle, this was the largest takeover by a Swiss Company.

Products and Services

After the merger, Nestle incorporated Carnation into its U.S. holding company, which included

Stouffer Corp., Libby McNeil & Libby Inc., and Beech-Nut Corp.. Nestle now had more product lines and its revenue increased by 20% as a result. The company began to push ice cream novelties and its Contadina fresh pasta and cheese products. Nestle also focused on Carnation's food service and potato processing lines. The pet food line remained a high priority. Through the acquisition, Carnation's products became marketable in more than 57 countries around the world.

Changes to the Industry

European interest in acquiring U.S. companies was surging in the 1980s. The $3 billion acquisition of Carnation by Nestle S.A. was just one of the 39 foreign acquisitions of U.S. companies announced in the first quarter of 1984. As public tastes were ever changing, the giant of the food industry would be able to reach more markets with the addition of Carnation's product lines. "Maucher has used acquisitions to help pep up the corporate culture and get the whole organization thinking about growth. He has management thinking about growth rather than just defending market share," said Paul Strebel, a professor at IMEDE in Lausanne, in *The New York Times*. Maucher's mindset and business tactics are credited for beginning a trend towards food industry mergers.

Review of the Outcome

The $3 billion ($83 a share) acquisition of Carnation Co. by Nestle S.A. was the largest takeover by a Swiss company in the world. It reinforced Nestle's efforts to increase sales in the U.S. and kept them in the number one slot as the world's largest food company. Carnation was expected to earn $235 million in 1985, thereby doubling Nestle's U.S. sales. Nestle's overall revenue was projected to increase by a third to $14.78 billion. Nestle also planned to bolster Carnation's sales overseas by heavy market promotion in 57 different countries.

Research

"Business People; Carnation's New Chief," in *The New York Times*, 14 January 1985. Offers information on the appointment of Timm Crull.

"Carnation Corp.," in *International Directory of Corporate Histories*, Vol II, St. James Press: 1990. Lists the company history for Carnation Company.

Greenhouse, Steven. "Nestle's Time to Swagger," in *The New York Times*, 1 January 1989. Provides information on Helmut Maucher.

Hulihan, Maile. "Nestle Offers to Buy Carnation Co. for $83 a Share, or $3 Billion Total," in *Wall Street Journal*, 5 September 1984. Details the planned acquisition.

Metz, Tim. "Nestle May Get a Bargain in Carnation," in *Wall Street Journal*, 6 September 1984. Details the acquisition.

Nestle Home Page, available at http://www.nestle.com. Official World Wide Web Home Page for Nestle. Includes detailed financial, historical, and product information.

"Nestle S.A.," in *Notable Corporate Chronologies*, The Gale Group, 1999. Lists major events in the history of Nestle S.A.

Truell, Peter. "European Firms on Buying Spree in U.S.," in *Wall Street Journal*, 6 September 1984. Explains the trend of European interest in U.S. business.

Wicks, John. "Green Light for Nestle to Take Over Carnation," in *Financial Times (London)*, 7 January 1985. Describes the approved acquisition.

CHRISTINA M. STANSELL

NESTLE & SOURCE PERRIER

Nestle S.A.
Avenue Nestle 55
Vevey, CH-1800
Switzerland

tel: (021)924-2111
fax: (021)921-1885
web: http://www.nestle.com

nationality: Switzerland
date: July 1992
affected: Nestle S.A., Switzerland, founded 1866
affected: Source Perrier, France, founded 1906

Overview of the Merger

The takeover of Source Perrier in 1992 was marked by hostile bidding in a fairly quiet European market. After months of battling between the Agnelli Family and Nestle S.A., Source Perrier became the property of the latter. In July of 1992, the European Commission approved Nestle's bid of $2.6 billion, making the company a powerhouse in the mineral-water market throughout the globe.

History of Nestle S.A.

While serving as an American consul in Zurich, Charles Page established Anglo-Swiss Condensed Milk Co. in Cham, Switzerland, in 1866. Page felt that Switzerland would be an ideal place to start the company because of its abundant milk supply and location in the European market. He chose the name, Anglo-Swiss, to try to appeal to the British. Condensed milk was soon found in cupboards throughout Europe. In 1872 operations expanded beyond the Swiss border with a new factory in Chippenham, England. The next year, George Page took over the company following his brother's death.

Meanwhile, Henri Nestle began marketing Farine Lactee Nestle (a mixture of cow's milk, sugar, and cereal) for infants who refused breast milk. By 1873 the demand for Nestle's product had doubled over the past two years, exceeding production capabilities and resulting in missed delivery dates. Wanting to retire, Nestle accepted a SFr1 million offer from Jules Monnerat, a former member of Parliament who had been eyeballing the company. In 1875 Monnerat became chairman.

Expansion continued for Anglo-Swiss with the purchase of English Condensed Milk Company in London in 1874. Just two years later, sales for Anglo-Swiss had quadrupled. Anglo-Swiss began to broaden its product line to include the manufacture of cheese and milk-based food for babies in 1877; at the same time, Nestle launched a condensed milk product of its own. George Page attempted to purchase Nestle, to no avail, and the two companies began to compete. In 1881 Anglo-Swiss opened its first U.S. factory in Middletown, New York. The factory was a success and began to challenge Borden, the leader in the American condensed milk market. Unfortunately, sales in Europe began to falter as Page spent most of his time in New York. The death of George Page in 1899 brought on the sale of the American business to Borden in order to regain control in Europe.

Not to be outdone by Anglo-Swiss, Nestle acquired a Norwegian condensed milk company in 1898. The next year Nestle opened factories in the U.S., Britain, Germany, and Spain. In 1904 Nestle entered the chocolate business, partnering with the Swiss General Chocolate Co. Anglo-Swiss and Nestle decided to join forces, and merged in 1905. With Emile-Louis Roussy as chairman, the new company included seven factories in Switzerland, six in Great Britain, three in Norway, and one each in the U.S., Germany, and Spain.

The company began to manufacture in Australia with the purchase of Cressbrook Dairy Co. in Brisbane. Sales continued to increase throughout the early years of the 1900s. When World War I broke out in 1914, Nestle was faced with problems because of limited supplies. It responded by expanding in markets less affected by the war. By 1917 Nestle was operating 40 factories. World production had doubled over the past four years, and in 1920 Nestle acquired controlling interests in three Australian companies. Production also began in Latin America.

The 1920s marked change for the company. With more than 80 factories and 12 subsidiaries and affiliates in production, the company's first loss was reported at SFr100 million. In 1922 it closed factories in the U.S., Britain, Australia, Norway, and Switzerland. The company called upon Louis Dapples, a banking expert, to repair the damage. He was able to reduce debt and increase operations in France, Belgium, Italy, Germany, and South Africa. In 1923 Nestle merged with Peter, Cailler, Kohler Chocolats Suisses S.A., adding 13 chocolate plants in Europe, South America, and Australia. New products included malted milk, Milo powdered beverage, and Eledon, a powdered buttermilk for infants with digestive disorders.

The 1930s were tough years for companies around the globe. The Great Depression forced a change in Nestle's game plan. Subsidiaries in Argentina and Cuba were established, as well as production centers in Copenhagen, Moravia, and Czechoslovakia. However, profits were down 13% from the years before. Consumer frugality was a cause for concern until 1933, when new legislation set minimum prices and conditions of sales. This legislation regulated the cutthroat competition that seriously

The Business

Financials

Revenue (1998): $52.2 billion

Employees (1998): 231,881

SICs / NAICS

sic 2064 - Candy & Other Confectionery Products

sic 2066 - Chocolate & Cocoa Products

affected Nestle's New York-based subsidiary, which had become known as Nestle's Milk Products Co. By 1936 Nestle was forced to close factories in Cham and Vevey due to the devaluation of currency caused by the depression in Switzerland. The company structure continued to change as interests in more than 20 companies on five continents led Nestle and the Anglo-Swiss Company to become a holding company. A second holding company, Unilac Inc., was created in Panama. In 1937 Louis Dapples died and was succeeded by Edouard Muller and a management team that had been with Nestle for years.

By the end of the 1930s, Nestle had introduced its Crunch candy bar and its first non-milk product, Nescafe instant coffee. This beverage gained a worldwide reputation and experienced increasing popularity in the United States. Nevertheless, with the onset of World War II, Nestle saw profits plummet from $20 million to $6 million by 1939. A lack of supplies was compounded by food shortages. There was a light at the end of the tunnel, however, and by 1941 demand for Nescafe and evaporated and powdered milk by American armed forces substantially increased sales.

By 1945 sales jumped to $225 million. Two years later, Nestle merged with Alimentana S.A., manufacturer of Maggi seasoning, bouillon, and dehydrated soup. The holding company changed its name to Nestle Alimentana Co. Edouard Muller became its first chairman but died in 1948, at which time Carl Abegg took leadership of the board. In 1950 the company acquired Cross and Blackwell, a British manufacturer of preserves and canned foods. Nestle hoped to use this as a marketing outlet for its Maggi products, but Cross and Blackwell could not compete in the United Kingdom against H.J. Heinz Company. They had similar problems when Nestle bought Findus frozen foods in Scandinavia. They could not compete with the British-Dutch giant, Unilever, so in 1963 the company merged its German, Italian, and Australian Findus branches with Unilever. In 1966 the first freeze-dried coffee, Taster's Choice, was introduced.

The Officers

Chairman: Helmut O. Maucher

Vice Chairman: Fritz Gerber

Vice Chairman: Rainer E. Gut

CEO: Peter Brabeck-Letmathe

Nestle acquired a U.S. fruit juice maker, Libby, in 1971. Two years later they entered the hotel and restaurant industry with the purchase of Stouffer's. In 1974 Nestle entered the non-food business for the first time by becoming a major shareholder in the L'Oreal cosmetic company. The firm also acquired Alcon Laboratories, a pharmaceutical company, and Burton, Parson and Company Inc., a manufacturer of contact lens products. The company adopted its present name, Nestle S.A., in 1979.

A U.S. boycott of all Nestle products began in 1977. Activists claimed that the company's aggressive promotions of baby food encouraged mothers in developing countries to use the products in any way they could. Infants eventually starved to death when their mothers mixed formula with polluted water or used an insufficient amount of formula in order to make it last longer. Nestle lost about $40 million in sales. In 1981 Nestle addressed the boycott supporters and complied with the World Health Organization's demand to stop promoting the product through advertising and free samples. Helmut Maucher became the managing director in 1981 and squelched the critics' fears by directly confronting the issue rather than assuming a low profile as Nestle had done in the past.

Maucher proved to be a strong leader and blazed the trail for a series of major acquisitions. In 1984 Nestle acquired Carnation, a U.S. manufacturer of milk, pet, and culinary products. This was the largest takeover in the food industry at the time, worth $3 billion. Ground roast coffee joined Nestle's product line with the purchase of Hills Brothers Inc. in 1985. Acquisitions in 1988 included British chocolate manufacturer, Rowntree Plc, and Italian pasta maker, Buitoni SpA.

Nestle S.A. continued on its acquisition frenzy, making 31 acquisitions in 1991. In September of that year the firm joined with Coca-Cola to market concentrates for its coffee, tea, and chocolate beverages. In 1992 Nestle launched and won a hostile takeover bid for Source Perrier. The giant also acquired Alpo pet

food in 1994, and Ortega Mexican foods in 1995. With factories in 63 countries, Nestle remained the undisputed leader in the industry as the world's largest packaged food manufacturer, coffee roaster, and chocolate maker.

In 1996 Nestle introduced Nescafe ready-to-drink iced coffees, the first single-serve ready-to-drink coffee widely distributed to convenience stores. Nestle also purchased Koala Springs International and laid the groundwork for Nestle Clinical Nutrition, which would provide nutritional assistance to nursing homes and hospitals. The next year, Peter Brabeck-Letmathe became CEO. Maucher remained chairman.

Nestle continued to make changes over the next few years by selling off its Contadina line to Del Monte, and by purchasing San Pellegrino. In 1998 it sold Libby's canned meat products to International Home Foods. That same year, Nestle purchased Spillers pet food from Dalgety PLC, which strengthened its position in the European pet food market. The company continued to sell and acquire over the next year in efforts to strengthen its global presence in the food industry.

History of Source Perrier

Les Bouillens, "boiling waters" in French, was the name of the spring that was the origin of Perrier. Located in Vergeze, this spring was commonly used by the Romans and Carthaginians dating back to the time of Caesar. Historians found the remains of a stone pool, along with other Roman artifacts, there. In the 17th and 18th centuries, the spring was claimed by Monsieur de Gaude, the Lord of Vergeze, his son-in-law Monsieur de Fayet, the Ursuline Order of Montpellier, and Alphonse Granier. Granier had many difficulties proving ownership, however, so the public routinely drank and bathed from the spring, which was said to have healing properties. In 1847, Granier fenced in the spring and began to seek legal help in declaring the property his own. By 1858, the courts had ruled the property his, and he approached the medical profession to prove the healthful claims of Les Bouillens. Professor Courcieres analyzed the water from the spring and found it to be naturally carbonated.

On June 23, 1863, rights to commercialize the spring were declared by Napoleon III, and Les Bouillens became a health spa complete with hotel and bathing cubicles. The water was bottled that year for the first time, and the name was changed to Societe Anonyme des Eaux Minerales de Vergeze ou des Bouillens. Six years after the founding of the hotel, the site was destroyed by fire and the company faltered. In 1888, it was bought by Monsieur Rouviere.

The spring was damaged severely by the fire and the new owner sought help from Dr. Louis Perrier, director of the Etablissement Thermal d'Euzet-les-Bains. One year after he bought it, Rouviere turned the spring over to the Societe des Eaux Minerales, Boissons et Produits Hygieniques de Bergeze. Dr. Perrier began work on the water and in 1894, he leased the property. He developed a bottling method and sought out a business partner in hopes of buying the spring.

Perrier leased the property and continued to develop a business plan until 1903, when he met Sir John Harmsworth. A member of the English aristocracy, Harmsworth also had a nose for business and was keenly interested in the spring. He bought shares and became completely absorbed in the business venture. In 1906, The Compagnie de la Source Perrier came into existence. Harmsworth built a mansion on the site and got the idea for the distinctive shape of the Perrier bottle from the Indian clubs he used for exercise. In 1910 he built a plant and the company began to bottle and market the mineral water.

The water became well known in London, Delhi, and Singapore first, with supplies being shipped to English military in the British Empire. With the onset of World War I, the water had become a much-needed commodity. By 1914, over 2 million bottles were being produced. In the years that followed, production increased. Over 6 million bottles were shipped out in 1922: 3.7 million exported and 2.3 million for the French. By the 1930s, 18.2 million bottles were in production.

When Sir John Harmsworth died in 1933, he almost took the company with him. Hard times began to invade the prosperous company. Harmsworth's successors faltered, and with the onset of World War II and the seizure of France by the Germans, the company's future was uncertain. Management decided to sell the company, and turned to a bank in Paris owned by the Levin family. Gustave Levin, the son of the owner, went out to the spring to analyze its worth for the purpose of sale. With one look, he decided to purchase the spring himself. He saw enormous potential in the mineral water the spring produced and was certain the market for such a product was on the rise.

Levin began a powerful course of expansion. In 1950 he constructed a new factory that produced 131 million bottles, 25 million for export. Four years later he branched out into sodas and soft drinks with the development of Pschitt and Gini. The company continued to grow, fed by a strong marketing and advertising plan, as well as an increase in the demand for mineral water. In the early 1970s Source Perrier built

The Players

Chairman of Nestle S.A.: Helmut O. Maucher. Helmut O. Maucher began his illustrious career in business after completing graduate studies at IMEDE, Lausanne. From 1964 to 1975 he held various management positions with the German branch of Nestle. In 1980 he transferred to Nestle in Switzerland where he became executive vice president of Nestle S.A., Vevey and one year later, its president and CEO. He became the first German to head Switzerland's largest company.

The 1980s were years of development and growth for Nestle as Maucher spearheaded a series of major acquisitions. Nestle's acquisition of the Carnation Co. that year was the largest non-oil acquisition in American corporate history. The food industry giant went on to acquire Source Perrier, Hills Brothers Inc., Rowntree Mackintosh PLC, and Buitoni SpA. Maucher's ideas and innovations changed the corporate mindset from conservative to aggressive. He is credited with being a frontrunner in an ever-changing global industry. The 35-year Nestle veteran has led the company to double its profits, triple its American sales, and remain the leader in the food sales industry across the globe.

Chairman of Source Perrier: Jacques Vincent. When the founder of Source Perrier, Gustave Levin, stepped down in June 1990, Jacques Vincent was called upon to take over. A graduate of L'Ecole Centrale des Arts et Manufactures in France, Vincent was left with a company trying to recover from a costly recall one of its products and facing hostile takeover bids from Nestle S.A. At the same time, he was also chairman of Exor, a holding company that owned 31% of Perrier. After the acquisition by Nestle S.A., Vincent handed the company to Thierry Chereau, who, after a period of working alongside Vincent, eventually took over completely. The French businessman went on to become president of Exor.

Chairman of Fiat: Gianni Agnelli. Italy's most well known industrialist had been involved in the family dynasty as well as Fiat for over 30 years. Throughout his career, Agnelli carved a prestigious path in the European business world. He is responsible for turning the Fiat's small car company into a world-renowned conglomerate involved in transport, insurance, retailing, and machinery. He also ran the family empire, making strong relationships with large companies and powerful banks. He was the leader in the Agnelli's bid to takeover Source Perrier 1990, but lost out to Nestle S.A. Agnelli stepped down from his post at Fiat in 1994.

another huge plant, integrating bottle manufacturingas well as filling. In order to remain a leader in the industry, French scientists that worked for Source Perrier were continually devising new developments in process of bottling. They developed a system of bottling that captured the water and the natural carbonic gas separately, filtered the two, and then bottled the combination.

Boasting flavors in lemon, lime, and orange, Source Perrier started the 1980s with a bang. With sales skyrocketing, the company acquired Poland Spring Corp. in 1980 in a transaction worth $10 million. By 1984, U.S. sales were at $100 million and expected to double over the next two years. In 1987, Perrier Group of America, Source Perrier's American unit, purchased Arrowhead Drinking Water Company from Beatrice Co. Despite the upturn in business, the next two years proved to be challenging. The company sold its interest in Lindt & Spruengli S.A. and fended off competition from the Adolph Coors Co. PepsiCo withdrew from the French market due to lagging sales, thereby ending a contract with Source Perrier and consequently initiating a court battle between the two. At the same time, PepsiCo was looking to takeover Source Perrier.

Disaster struck in 1990, when the company was forced to pull all of its bottles from shelves across the world when a U.S. laboratory found traces of Benzene, a colorless liquid, in Perrier water. An error in the bottling process in France cost the company over $140 million. Gustave Levin, the founder of the company stepped down that year, replaced by Jacques Vincent. With revenue at $2.7 billion the year before, the company planned for a drastic decrease in sales and profit. Despite Vincent's efforts to turn the company around, Source Perrier became a vulnerable target for a takeover. Several interested parties began vying for the company. The Agnelli Family and Nestle S.A. began hostile negotiations for the company in January of 1992. The summer of that same year marked the takeover by Nestle S.A. of Source Perrier.

Market Forces Driving the Merger

The recall of Perrier in 1990 weakened the company's earnings. Even after it had been put back on the shelves in the U.S., sales were only two-thirds of what they had been. Operating profit and consolidated revenue had fallen 18%. The time had come for Nestle to make a move on the company. "L'eau est le petrole de l'avenir" ("Water is the petrol of the future") said Perrier's Eve Magnant, and Nestle S.A. wanted to cash in on that future. The company was attracted to Source Perrier for its 40% share of France's mineral water market and 20% share of the U.S. market. At the time, Nestle controlled two-fifths of the French market, one-quarter of the U.S. market, and one-fifth of the world market. The desire to become a dominant force in mineral water throughout the globe prompted Nestle S.A. to place a strategic bid on the company. The acquisition would also complete Nestle's efforts to be involved in all aspects of the food industry.

Approach and Engagement

On November 28, 1991, the Agnelli family placed a $930 million bid for Exor, a French holding company that controlled 35% of Perrier. Looking to diversify into the food and beverage industry due to lagging sales at Fiat, the family wanted to gain control of Exor as well as Source Perrier. Nestle S.A. jumped in with a $2.3 billion cash bid to counter the Agnelli offer. On January 5, 1992, Source Perrier sold 13.8% of itself to Saint Louis, a food and paper company, as well as an ally to the Agnelli Family. Nestle was outraged, claiming that the deal took place after Perrier knew of Nestle's offer. Nestle teamed up with BSN, Europe's third-largest food company, to reclaim the takeover attempt. BSN made a FFr6 billion counter offer for Exor and proposed that Exor and Perrier be divided among the three parties. Nestle would get the Perrier brand, the Agnellis would receive Exor's wine and extensive properties, and BSN would keep Volvic, a Perrier water brand.

In March, the courts ruled that the sale to Saint Louis was not valid and the transaction was canceled. Agnelli's voting rights were slashed to 23.7%, and Jacques Vincent, Chairman of Source Perrier, was criticized for the role he played in the deal. He contested the effort of Nestle and BSN claiming that the two were conspiring to tear apart the French mineral water market and divide it between the two companies. The Agnelli family stepped away from the hostile bidding and without the backing of the family, Vincent could do little on his own. By the end of March, Nestle had won the battle and the proposal made by BSN to divide the company prevailed.

Products and Services

After the acquisition, Nestle S.A., the world's largest food and drink company, focused on Source Perrier's U.S. brands Poland Spring, Arrowhead, and Great Bear. The move complemented the company's five units: drinks, milk products, ready meals, chocolates and sweets, and pharmaceuticals. The company was now the dominant force in the French market for bottled waters as well as a leader in the U.S. Nestle would continue with heavy product promotion and focus on innovative advertising for its Perrier brand.

Changes to the Industry

Sales were lagging in the beverage industry in the early 1990s. There was only a .5% increase in bottled water sales in 1991 compared to double-digit gains in the 80s. In 1992, sales increased by only 1.5% from the previous year. The growth trend in the U.S. was likely to resume, especially with the increase interest in health benefits of bottled water. Other companies such as Pepsi, Coca-Cola, and Seagram's were debuting "lighter" drinks. "New age" beverages were being created and marketed versus the typical soda pops. Crystal Pepsi, 2-Calorie Quest by Seagram, Ice Mountain by the Perrier Group of America, and Nordic Mist by Coca-Cola, were all being introduced. Clearly Canadian, with its introduction of fruit flavored "natural" water, saw an increase in sales from $37.5 million in 1990 to $127.4 million in 1991. Innovative marketing and consumer demand for something new and different was credited for the increase. Meanwhile, Europe was becoming more politically and economically sound, and analysts predicted that battles like the Nestle/Perrier transaction would become more commonplace as companies competed for market share.

Review of the Outcome

The European Commission approved Nestle's $2.6 billion bid for Source Perrier in July of 1992. The hostile battle for the company concluded with each of the three parties receiving some benefit. The Agnelli family, which sold Nestle its 35.5% stake in the company, received Exor's property and Chateau Margaux; BSN walked away with Volvic; and Nestle won the Perrier brand. Nestle S.A. was forced to sell 20% of its French market share by disposing of Vichy, Saint Yorre, Thonon, and Pierval brands in order for BSN to receive its rights to Volvic. As a result of the acquisition, Perrier cut 14% of its jobs in 1993. Nestle S.A. saw revenue increase from $37.1 billion in 1992 to $38.6 billion in 1993. Net income also increased by $108 mil-

lion. The the acquisition left Nestle S.A. and BSN with over 67% of the market in bottled water, with Nestle S.A. as the leading supplier of bottled water in the world.

Research

Brasier, Mary. "Finishing Line Nears for Fiat's Driver," in *The Daily Telegraph*, 30 September 1992. Offers insight into the career of Gianni Agnelli.

Bright, Christopher. "Nestle/Perrier: New Issues in EC Merger Control," in *International Financial Law Review*, September 1992. Discusses results of the European Commission's findings about the acquisition.

"BSN and the Agnelli's: Friend or Foe?" in *Economist*, 29 February 1992. Lists details of the takeover attempt by BSN and the Agnelli family.

"Chairman of Perrier Leaves; Post Goes to Vice Chairman," in *The New York Times*, 30 June 1990. Provides information on the career of Jacques Vincent.

Cohen, Roger. "Nestle is Set for Victory," in *The New York Times*, 20 March 1992. Lists details of the events leading up to the acquisition.

Du Preez, Nicky. "Geau for It," in *Accountancy*, July 1992. Explains Perrier's reentry into the market after the recall of 1990.

Lever, Robert. "Nestle Makes Splash in Perrier Acquisition," in *Europe*, May 1992. Discusses key events in the months leading up to the acquisition.

"Nestle Becomes Perrier Owner," in *The New York Times*, 7 April 1992. Explains the Agnelli family decision to not pursue the acquisition.

"Nestle S.A.," in *Notable Corporate Chronologies*, Gale Research 1999. Lists major events in the history of Nestle S.A.

Perrier Home Page, available at http://www.perrier.com. Official World Wide Web Home Page for Perrier. Includes historical and product information.

Prince, Greg. "1992: The Year in Review," in *Beverage World*, December 1992. Describes trends in the beverage industry.

Templeman, John. "Nestle: A Giant in a Hurry," in *Business Week*, 22 March 1993. Discusses Nestle's approach to the upcoming year and changes in the industry.

CHRISTINA M. STANSELL

NEW YORK CENTRAL RAILROAD & ERIE RAILROAD

Conrail Inc.
2001 Market St., 2 Commerce Sq.
Philadelphia, PA 19101
USA

tel: (215)209-4000
web: http://www.conrail.com

nationality: USA
date: canceled July 10, 1868
affected: New York Central Railroad Co., USA, founded 1853
affected: Erie Railroad Co., USA, founded 1832

Overview of the Acquisition

The attempt of Cornelius Vanderbilt to acquire control of the Erie Railroad in order to extend his New York Central Railroad empire resulted in the Erie Wars. Opposing Vanderbilt were three corrupt directors of Erie—Daniel Drew, Jay Gould, and James Fisk. These three men, the Erie Ring, issued fraudulent stock to dilute Vanderbilt's stake, then fled to New Jersey to elude the police. Protected by hired guns, the Erie Ring fought Vanderbilt first in the courts and then in the bribery of state legislators. Vanderbilt finally called a halt to the seemingly endless battle by setting terms with Drew to unload his Erie stock in July 1868.

History of New York Central Railroad Co.

In the early days of the railroad, individual lines were short, typically running for distances under 100 miles. To create extended service, 10 small railroads in New York, running between Albany and Buffalo, banded together to establish the informal Central Line, an alliance that incorporated standardized fares, schedules, and policies to make travel more efficient and therefore better equipped to compete with the Erie Canal. Erastus Corning, president of the 78-mile Utica & Schenectady line, orchestrated the formal merger of these systems in 1853, forming the New York Central Railroad Co.

The new railroad was an immediate success, and with a total capital of $23 million, it caught the eye of Cornelius Vanderbilt. The "Commodore" had acquired control of the New York & Harlem Railroad in 1857 and of the Hudson River Railroad in 1865. With monopolistic ambitions, he sought to gain control of virtually every major line in the state.

Having acquired a stake in New York Central, as well as a representative seat on its board, he forged an agreement that facilitated the transfer of passengers and freight between the Hudson River Railroad and the New York Central where they connected in Albany. Vanderbilt terminated that agreement in 1867, annoyed by the railroad's tendency to send business to the Hudson only when New York Central's steamboats were iced in along the river. Vanderbilt's move meant that passengers and freight had to undertake a two-mile trek to transfer from one line to the other, causing such a mess for New York Central that its stock price began to plummet. Vanderbilt immediately began buying its shares, and before the end of the year he had acquired control of New York Central, extending his empire from New York City to Buffalo.

He then began buying into the Erie Railroad, a competitor that spanned the southern part of New York, and soon acquired a seat on its board. Daniel Drew, head of the Erie, divined Vanderbilt's goal of taking over the company, and, with the help of two shady allies, thwarted Vanderbilt's takeover attempt in 1868, through what became known as the Erie Wars.

Vanderbilt continued to expand his empire, adding to it the Michigan Central in 1871 and the Lake Shore and Michigan Southern Railway two years later. With these purchases, he was able to run trains from New York City to Chicago.

Robert R. Young gained control of New York Central in 1954. By that time, the railroad industry was suffering due to the rise of airplane and automobile travel. In 1968 New York Central merged with the Pennsylvania Railroad Co. to form Penn Central Transportation Co. This merger soon failed, however, and Penn Central entered bankruptcy in June 1970.

The U.S. Congress interceded by establishing the National Railroad Passenger Corp., which assumed control of the nation's rail passenger services in October 1970; this corporation was later renamed Amtrak. New York Central's remaining operations were pooled with those of five other lines to form Consolidated Rail Corp. (Conrail) in April 1976.

History of Erie Railroad Co.

The New York & Erie Railroad Company was chartered in 1832 as a link between the Hudson River and Lake Erie, thereby connecting the Atlantic Ocean with the Great Lakes. Funding was unpredictable and the terrain was troublesome, and the New York & Erie went bankrupt before it was finally completed in May 1851.

Initially, the railroad experienced tremendous success, engendered by its continued expansion along trunk lines and the economic growth of the area that it served. Its revenues lured Daniel Drew to invest in it, and in 1853 he obtained a seat on its board. Drew was known as an unscrupulous "bear" of Wall Street who would use virtually any means at his disposal to capitalize personally from his dealings, regardless of the long-term impact on the companies that he controlled.

By that time, the New York & Erie was once again in financial trouble. As treasurer of the railroad, Drew

The Business

Financials

Revenue (1998): $3.9 billion

Employees (1998): 22,000

SICs / NAICS

sic 4011 - Railroads-Line-Haul Operating

sic 4731 - Freight Transportation Arrangement

sic 6719 - Holding Companies Nec

naics 482111 - Line-Haul Railroads

naics 541614 - Process, Physical Distribution, and Logistics Consulting Services

manipulated company stock, causing it to fluctuate wildly on the market. In 1859 the company, unable to pay both its employees and its bills, went bankrupt for the second time. It began a reorganization that year, emerging as the Erie Railroad in 1862.

Cornelius Vanderbilt, head of the New York Central Railroad, gained a seat on Erie's board as a prelude to obtaining control of the company. Drew knew that with Vanderbilt in control, his days of Erie stock manipulation would be at an end. So he enlisted Jay Gould and Jim Fisk, Erie's president and vice president, respectively, to aid him in thwarting Vanderbilt's plan. These three scoundrels, known as the Erie Ring, printed up 50,000 phony shares of Erie stock, dumping them on the market each time Vanderbilt increased his holdings. When Vanderbilt figured out why his interests were continually diluted, the Erie Ring fled the jurisdiction to escape an arrest warrant. In the middle of the ensuing bribery war, Drew and Vanderbilt made peace. In their agreement, Vanderbilt was paid $4.75 million in cash and bonds for his Erie shares, and Drew resigned from Erie. The pact left Gould and Fisk in charge of the company and Erie $9 million poorer.

Gould and Fisk continued to manipulate Erie's stock. Their effort to corner the gold market led to the financial panic of 1869, touched off on "Black Friday." As a result, the Erie Railroad earned the dubious nickname "The Scarlet Woman of Wall Street." In 1872, Fisk was assassinated by a romantic rival and Gould was ousted from Erie's board.

Erie never quite recovered from the dealings of the Erie Ring. During the 1870s and 1880s, a fierce price war with other railroads resulted in yet another

The Players

New York Central Railroad Co. Chief: Cornelius Vanderbilt. Born in 1794, Cornelius Vanderbilt was the embodiment of the rags-to-riches legend. Coming from an impoverished family, he quit school at age 11 to volunteer in odd jobs on the New York waterfront. At age 16 he borrowed $100 from his parents and purchased a boat, which he used to ferry passengers between Staten Island and New York City. The War of 1812 increased his business, enabling him to amass a small fleet. In 1818, Vanderbilt sold his operations and took a job as a steamship captain for Thomas Gibbons, using his salary to establish his own steamship company in 1829. His new business flourished by undercutting competition, which, at one point, included Daniel Drew. The "Commodore" became a millionaire by 1846. Railroads captured his attention after the Civil War, and Vanderbilt began acquiring stock in various companies, including the New York Central Railroad. Despite his failure to gain control of the Erie Railroad, his railroad empire eventually extended from New York City to Chicago. Throughout his life, Vanderbilt had held his money closely, but in the years immediately preceding his death, he became philanthropic. He donated $1 million to Central University, later renamed Vanderbilt University. Cornelius died in 1877 as the first American to have acquired a personal fortune in excess of $100 million.

Erie Railroad Co. Treasurer: Daniel Drew. Like Vanderbilt, Drew was born in poverty and went on to accumulate a fortune. Yet Drew, as a robber baron, favored much more sinister business practices than his rival. He was as unscrupulous and greedy as he was religious, seldom without a Bible in tote. Born in 1797, Drew began his career as a cattle trader. His affinity for shady business practices was soon revealed, as he earned notoriety by "watering stock," depriving cattle of water during transit, then allowing them to drink their fill just before being weighed for sale. Drew entered the steamboat business in the 1830s and, after being driven out by Vanderbilt, established the Drew, Robinson, and Co. brokerage in 1844. He earned the reputation of a "bear trader," an investor who sold stock on the decline, then scooped it back up at a reduced rate. He gained a seat on the board of the Erie Railroad and became its treasurer, manipulating the company's shares for his own profit. The Erie Wars resulted in the loss of Drew's affiliation with the railroad. In 1876 he went bankrupt, and passed away three years later.

bankruptcy for Erie. After emerging, it passed through several reorganizations before merging with the Delaware, Lackawanna & Western Railroad Co. in 1960. Despite the efficiencies realized by eliminating redundant track, the newly formed Erie Lackawanna entered bankruptcy in 1972. Four years later it became part of Consolidated Rail Corp. (Conrail).

Market Forces Driving the Acquisition

By 1866 Cornelius Vanderbilt had assembled a railroad empire. In successively acquiring control of the New York & Harlem Railroad, the Hudson River Railroad, and the New York Central Railroad, he created a line that connected New York City to Buffalo. Not yet satisfied, he sought both to expand and to eliminate a competitor in his territory, the Erie Railroad. In 1866 Vanderbilt quietly began buying shares in Erie, and soon acquired a seat on its board. There he faced his old rival, Daniel Drew, whom he had bested in their steamship days. Drew, as director and treasurer of Erie, had been manipulating the company's resources to increase his personal wealth, and was fully aware of the threat that Vanderbilt posed to the continuation of his shady enterprise.

Approach and Engagement

Vanderbilt continued to purchase shares in Erie, attempting to increase his holdings to a controlling interest. To prevent this outcome, which would have deprived him of his cash cow, Drew enlisted Jay Gould, Erie's unscrupulous president, and James Fisk, its equally corrupt vice president, to assist him in fending off Vanderbilt. The three men, who became known as the Erie Ring, secured a printing press and issued fraudulent shares of Erie stock each time Vanderbilt increased his holdings. Finally realizing that underhanded forces were conspiring to dilute his interest, Vanderbilt broke character by seeking assistance from the law rather than crushing his enemies single-handedly.

New York's political system at this time was controlled by the corrupt Boss Tweed and Tammany Hall, and Vanderbilt easily persuaded a judge to issue an arrest warrant for Drew, Gould, and Fisk. They quickly grabbed $6 million and fled the jurisdiction, holing up in New Jersey's Taylor Hotel. Fisk nicknamed their refuge Fort Taylor, as it was guarded by hundreds of hired thugs and more than a dozen policemen armed with shotguns, cannons, and brassknuckles.

Vanderbilt and the Erie Ring continually filed injunctions against the other, but neither side was making much headway. The battle then shifted from the courts to the legislature. The Erie Ring bribed politicians to put forth a bill legalizing their fraudulent stock issues, but Vanderbilt paid well to ensure that it was defeated.

Determined not to make the same mistake twice, the Erie Ring dispatched Gould to handle the matter personally. He arrived in Albany with a suitcase stuffed with half a million dollars. Vanderbilt had him arrested, but with a fist full of ready cash, Gould quickly obtained his release on bail. He took a hotel room in Albany, feigning illness while he distributed bribes to secure the bill's repassage by the state senate. Before the vote went before the house of representatives, however, Vanderbilt and Drew called a truce, much to the dismay of the representatives, who had eagerly held their hands out for their turn to be "persuaded" by Gould.

Vanderbilt knew that continuing the war of bribery would be both expensive and lengthy, and with a questionable outcome. He sent a note to Drew, requesting a conference. Vanderbilt threatened to continue his siege against the Erie Ring unless Drew agreed to his proposal. Drew, eager to leave New Jersey and return to Wall Street, accepted the terms. Vanderbilt demanded $4.75 million for his Erie shares, along with the resignation of Drew as both director and treasurer of Erie. On July 10, 1868, the agreement went into effect, leaving Gould and Fisk as Erie's president and chief operating officer, respectively.

Products and Services

In June 1999 Conrail, which had ultimately acquired both New York Central Railroad and the Erie Railroad, was divided into three separate pieces, one of which merged with CSX Corp., another with Norfolk Southern Co., and the third, jointly owned by CSX and Norfolk, bore the Conrail name. CSX became the nation's third-largest rail company, with 22,300 miles of track in 23 states. Norfolk Southern's 21,600-mile system in 22 states made it the fourth-largest railroad in the U.S.

Research

Douglas, George H. *All Aboard! The Railroad in American Life*, Marlowe & Company, 1992. Provides a history of the railroad in the U.S.

"Erie Railroad Co." *Britannica CD 98 Multimedia Edition, 1994-1998*.Encyclopedia Britannica, Inc. Offers a history of Erie.

Gordon, John Steele. *The Scarlet Woman of Wall Street*, Weidenfeld & Nicolson, 1988. Details the colorful Erie Wars and the railroad's role in Gould and Fisk attempt to corner the market on gold.

Jensen, Oliver. *The American Heritage History of Railroads in America*, American Heritage Publishing Co., 1975. A pic

The Players

Erie Railroad Co. President: Jay Gould. Born in 1836, Jay Gould became a surveyor and tanner before speculating in railroads in 1859. He acquired control of several companies, and was named president and director of the Erie Railroad in 1867. Having been enlisted by Daniel Drew to thwart Cornelius Vanderbilt's attempt to acquire the company, Gould thought nothing of issuing fraudulent stock and bribing legislators. After gaining control of Erie upon the resignation of Drew, he joined with James Fisk, William "Boss" Tweed, and Peter Sweeney to corner the market on gold. Their efforts resulted in the financial panic of Black Friday (September 24, 1869). Gould was later ousted from Erie's board. In 1874, he acquired control of the Union Pacific Railroad, where he continued his pattern of stock manipulation. He gained control of the Western Union Telegraph Co. in 1881, the *New York World* newspaper in 1879, and the Manhattan Elevated Railroad monopoly in 1886. Gould remained ruthless and friendless until his death in 1892, having amassed a fortune of $77 million.

Erie Railroad Co. Vice President: James Fisk, Jr. Born in 1834, James Fisk, Jr., was a raider and stock manipulator, yet unlike his cronies at Erie, he was nonetheless well-liked. He held jobs as a circus hand, peddler, and executive before establishing the brokerage firm Fisk, Belden and Co. in 1866. The next year, as vice president and director of Erie Railroad, he joined Daniel Drew and Jay Gould in the battle to keep the company out of Cornelius Vanderbilt's hands. After their victory, Fisk joined Gould and two others in attempting to corner the market on loose gold, causing the financial panic of 1869. Although married at an early age, Fisk was constantly in the company of women, earning him the nickname the "Prince of the Erie." He had a particular fondness for the third-rate actress Josie Mansfield. In 1872 he was shot and killed by Edward Stokes, a rival for the affections of Mansfield. Never having set out to accumulate a huge fortune, Fisk left behind an estate of less than $1 million.

torial and narrative history of the nation's railroad industry.

"New York Central Railroad Co." *Britannica CD 98 Multimedia Edition, 1994-1998.*Encyclopedia Britannica, Inc. Provides a history of the company.

Stover, John F. *Iron Road to the West*, Columbia University Press, 1978. Provides a history of American railroads during the 1850s.

Wasserstein, Bruce. *Big Deal: The Battle for Control of America's Leading Corporations*, Warner Books, 1998. Offers an overview of the largest mergers in American history.

DEBORAH J. UNTENER

NEWMONT MINING & SANTE FE PACIFIC GOLD

nationality: USA
date: May 5, 1997
affected: Newmont Mining Corp., founded 1916
affected: Sante Fe Pacific Gold Corp., founded 1983

Newmont Mining Corp.
1700 Lincoln St.
Denver, CO 80203
USA

tel: 303-863-7414
fax: 303-837-5837
web: http//www.newmont.com

Overview of the Merger

What began as an unsolicited merger attempt by Newmont Mining Corp. turned into a bidding war for control of Sante Fe Pacific Gold. Three days after receiving Newmont's bid, Sante Fe's board announced that it unanimously approved a merger agreement with Homestake Mining Co. After sweetening its bid several times, however, Newmont ultimately emerged victorious, becoming the world's second-largest gold mining company.

History of Newmont Mining Corp.

Newmont Mining Corp. was the result of Colonel William Boyce Thompson's founding of the Newmont Company in 1916. The original purpose of the company was to trade the colonel's oil and mining stocks. Thompson died in 1930, but Newmont continued to grow. It went public in 1925 with a major focus on oil and gold in the U.S. and gas production in the North Sea. Newmont owned 12 gold mines by 1939.

In the first half of the 1960s, Newmont's discovery of disseminated gold at Carlin, Nevada, turned out to be the largest 20th century gold discovery in North America. In 1965 Newmont began mining the site under the name Carlin Gold Mining Co. The name was changed to Newmont Gold in 1986 and became the company's largest subsidiary. Newmont Mining acquired 100% of the gold subsidiary after the 1997 merger with Sante Fe Pacific Gold.

In 1967 Newmont purchased a portion of Foote Mineral, a stake that later increased to over 80% in 20 years. Other acquisitions included the 1969 merger with Magma Copper and the purchase of a portion of Peabody Coal in 1977. After successfully defending itself against several takeover attempts during the 1980s, Newmont spun off its Magma Copper holdings in 1988, its Peabody Coal stake in 1990, and Foote Mineral in 1987. Newmont went through a major restructuring following the dilution of these operations, including the relocation of its headquarters to Denver from New York in 1994. In 1993, Ronald Cambre was appointed vice chairman and chief executive officer.

The Business

Financials

Revenue (1998): $1453.9 million

Employees (1998): 5,700

SICs / NAICS

sic 1041 - Gold Ores

naics 212221 - Gold Ore Mining

The ability to dilute operating expenses and share equipment has made joint mining ventures commonplace during the latter half of the 1990s. In 1993 Newmont began operations in a joint venture with the French government and Peru's Buenaventura. The three companies ran the Yanacocha Mine until 1994, when France tried to transfer its share to an Australian company. By 1998 Newmont held more than 50% of Yanacocha after courts agreed that France was unable to transfer its interest without allowing its partners a chance to purchase the shares first.

Newmont entered into additional joint ventures in 1995 with La Teko Resources in Alaska. In 1996, with Japan's Sumitomo, Newmont began gold exploration on Sumbawa Island in Indonesia. In 1999 Newmont and Barrick Gold Corp. agreed to a land swap in Carlin Trend, creating larger contiguous portions of exploitable land.

Despite its rank as one of the cheapest gold producers, Newmont was forced to reduce its workforce in 1998 and 1999 due to a continued slump in gold prices. Revenues were $1.4 billion in 1998, down 7.6% from the previous year.

History of Sante Fe Pacific Gold Corp.

Sante Fe Pacific Gold was incorporated in 1983. Its headquarters were located in Albuquerque, New Mexico, where it managed operations in the United States, Europe, and Central and South America. Sante Fe's Twin Creeks Mine in Winnemucca, Nevada, was considered to be the third-largest mine in the United States.

In February 1996, Sante Fe began a joint venture with Kyrgyzaltyn, a state-owned mining company in Kyrgyzstan. Sante Fe invested $2.5 million for a 50% interest in the operation. Kyrgyzaltyn paid $10 million for its equal share, but agreed to give 90% interest to Sante Fe after the state-owned operation recouped its investment.

In 1995 Sante Fe's sales began a sharp decline. The company's earnings fell due to lower yields at Twin Creeks, while its third-quarter interest expenses rose $2.2 million over the same period in 1994. The first quarter of 1996 saw an income drop of 50%. The company attributed the decrease to poor heap-leach and lower mill grade ore.

In December of the same year, Sante Fe received merger offers from Newmont Mining Corp. and Homestake Mining. The two companies launched a bidding war, with Newmont ultimately winning. Sante Fe's chairman and CEO, who had been with the company since 1979, left to head Rio Algom Ltd. when the merger was completed in May 1997.

Market Forces Driving the Merger

Gold is typically used as a speculative hedge against rising inflation, and when the U.S. emerged from its recession in 1993, gold demand fell sharply. Companies like Newmont had survived the recession by forward selling gold, or promising to deliver it at a future date for prices locked in at an agreed price regardless of the current market conditions at that future date. Gold prices continued a steady downward spiral, forcing companies to mine at ever-decreasing operating costs. To achieve this, many mining firms entered into joint ventures or mergers.

Approach and Engagement

On December 5, 1996, Newmont's leader, Ronald Cambre, sent a letter to Sante Fe Pacific Gold's CEO, Patrick James, outlining his desire for a stock swap merger. Valued at $2.1 billion, the proposed transaction entailed a stock swap at .33 common shares for each Sante Fe common share.

A few days after receiving Newmont's bid, Sante Fe announced that it had instead accepted a deal with Homestake Mining, which had been secretly negotiating a merger with Sante Fe. Homestake's offer was valued at approximately $2.3 billion, and would give Sante Fe a 50% interest in the company. Newmont's deal, on the other hand, only offered 30%. Aware of possible takeover bids from other companies, Homestake included a caveat in its agreement calling for a $65 million break-up charge if Sante Fe should back out of the deal.

In January 1997, Newmont increased its offer to .4 shares for each Sante Fe share. Sante Fe declined to respond to the offer and continued working on merging with Homestake. Newmont's CEO offered a third bid of .44 shares for each share of Sante Fe, and personally visited Sante Fe shareholders to convince them that Newmont would be the better merger partner. Homestake did not place another bid, stating that a higher price would increase the company's per ounce cost above the current market average. Sante Fe eventually accepted Newmont's offer, and paid the $65 million break-up fee to Homestake according to their agreement.

On May 5, 1997, Sante Fe completed the merger with Newmont Mining. Newmont issued 56.6 million new shares to assume Sante Fe stock. It then transferred the stocks to its Newmont Gold subsidiary in an equal stock swap. Sante Fe's Chairman and CEO Patrick James left the company to head Canada's Rio Algom Ltd.

Products and Services

After the Newmont/Sante Fe merger, the company became the second-largest gold producer worldwide and the largest in the United States. Projected analysis ranked Newmont's gold production at 55 million ounces from 17 open pit and nine underground mines.

In 1998 Newmont Mining operated mines in the United States, Indonesia, Eastern Europe, and Central and South America. In the United States, it operated such mines as Carlin Trend, Twin Creeks, Lone Tree, and Rosebud. The merger with Sante Fe created more mining areas around the Carlin Trend area, considered to be the largest gold discovery of the 20th century.

Most of the company's international operations were run under joint ventures. In Peru Newmont owned a 50% interest in a joint venture at the Yanacocha mine, a 46% share in a Mexico mine, and in Eastern Europe it operated in Uzbekistan and Kyrgyzstan. On the Indonesian island of Sumbawa, Newmont jointly operated the Batu Hijau mine, a large copper and gold open pit mine with projections accessed at 550,000 ounces of gold and 270,000 tons of copper annually.

Changes to the Industry and Review of the Outcome

The Sante Fe Pacific Gold shares that Newmont received in the stock swap helped Newmont take 90% control of its largest subsidiary, Newmont Gold. Newmont eventually acquired 100% of this gold subsidiary.

Newmont suffered a 7.6% decline in revenue for 1998, as the nation's economy suffered little inflationary concern. The company announced planned layoffs in 1999 to keep its per ounce production cost below industry standards. The company turned out over one million ounces from its low cost Peru facility and

The Officers

Chairman, President and Chief Executive Officer: Ronald C. Cambre

Exec. VP and Chief Financial Officer: Wayne W. Murdy

Sr. VP, Exploration: John A.S. Dow

Sr. VP, International Operations: David H. Francisco

planned to continue exploiting its ventures where gold was easy to mine. Newmont's 1999 projections for Yanacocha showed an expected 1.65 million ounces.

At the conclusion of the merger, Newmont's CEO Ronald Cambre remained at the top positions, while many Sante Fe executives accepted newly created board positions. Sante Fe's CEO Patrick James did not join Newmont, and instead went to lead Canadian-based Rio Algom Ltd.

Research

"Cambre Named Chairman of Newmont," in *American Metal Market*, 12 January 1995. Briefly discusses the appointment of Ronald Cambre to Chairman of Newmont.

Green, William. "Will It Recover on May Watch?" in *Forbes*, 1 December 1997. Interview with Cambre regarding gold market prices and the operations of Newmont Mining.

"James to Head Rio Algom Ltd.," in *American Metal Market*, 12 May 1997. Brief article announcing the appointment of Patrick James to president and CEO of Rio Algom after leaving Sante Fe due to the merger with Newmont Mining Corp.

Moody's Industrial Manual, 2 vols. Raeburn, Vicki, publisher. Financial Communications Co., Inc. 1998. Large two-volume reference with financial reports of companies listed on the New York and American Stock Exchanges.

Newmont Mining Corp. Home Page, available at http://www.newmont.com. Official World Wide Web Home Page for The Newmont Mining Corp. Includes press releases, annual report, detailed financial, product, and historical information.

Ozols, Victor. "Newmont-Sante Fe Link OK'd," in *American Metal Market*, 7 May 1997. Examines the initial result of the merger between Newmont and Sante Fe Pacific Gold.

"Sante Fe Helm Passing to James," in *American Metal Market*, 8 November 1994. Announces the appointment of Patrick James to the CEO position as Richard Zitting steps down.

"Sante Fe Pacific Gold Corp. Signs New Joint Ventures in Kyrgyzstan," in *Skillings Mining Review*, 24 February 1996. Focuses on new joint venture for Sante Fe in Eastern Europe.

"Sante Fe Sees Earnings Tumble," in *American Metal Market*, 26 October 1995. Discusses Sante Fe's slumped third quarter 1995 earnings.

Ward, Aaron D. "Homestake Offers $2.3 Billion for Sante Fe," in *American Metal Market*, 10 December 1996. Announces Homestake's merger agreement with Sante Fe days after Newmont offered a unsolicited offer worth $2.1 billion.

———. "Newmont Ups Bid for Sante Fe," in *American Metal Market*, 8 January 1997. Discusses Newmont's counter offer for Sante Fe after news of a merger agreement between Sante Fee and Homestake.

———. "Sante Fe, Newmont Sign $2.5 Billion Merger Agreement," in *American Metal Market*, 11 March 1997.

Announces that Sante Fe's board signed a pact to merger with Newmont in a $2.5 billion deal, terminating its deal with Homestake.

Worthington, Ted. "Homestake Outbids Newmont for Sante Fe," in *Northern Miner*, 16 December 1996. Discusses the initial Homestake bid worth $2.3 billion that was accepted by Sante Fe's board only days after Newmont made an unsolicited offer.

SEAN C. MACKEY

NEWS CORP. & NEW WORLD COMMUNICATIONS

nationality: Australia
date: January 21, 1997
affected: The News Corporation Ltd., Australia, founded 1923
affected: New World Communications Group Inc., USA, founded 1982

The News Corporation Ltd.
2 Holt St.
Sydney, 2010
Australia

tel: 61 2 9288 3000
fax: 61 2 9288 3292
web: http://www.newscorp.com

Overview of the Acquisition

The $3 billion acquisition of New World Communications propelled News Corp. to the position of the leading television station owner in the U.S. As a result, its Fox network, a newcomer to the industry, penetrated nearly 35% of America's homes, beating out such other television groups as Westinghouse, Tribune, NBC, and Disney/ABC.

History of The News Corporation Ltd.

Following his father's death in 1952, Australian Rupert Murdoch inherited two Adelaide newspapers, *News* and *Sunday Mail*. These papers were owned by News Ltd., in which his father was a major shareholder. Four years later Murdoch added the Perth *Sunday Times* to his company.

Patterned after the American *TV Guide*, *TV Week* was launched in 1957. The following year Southern Television Corporation, in which News Ltd. had a 60% stake, gained control of Channel 9, one of the only two TV channels in Adelaide.

In 1960 the firm acquired Cumberland Newspapers, a group of local papers in the Sydney suburbs; among its holdings were the Sydney *Daily* and *Sunday Mirror*. That year Adelaide *News* editor Rohan Rivett was fired five weeks after being acquitted of charges of seditious libel stemming from the newspaper's criticisms of a state government's inquiry into a murder case.

News Ltd. launched *The Australian*, the country's first national newspaper, in 1964. Four years later News Ltd. swapped shares in some of its minor ventures. As a result it gained a 40% stake in the U.K.'s News of the World Organization (NOTW), owner of the *News of the World*, the Bemrose group of local newspapers, the papermakers Townsend Hook, and several other publishing companies.

In 1969 News Ltd. acquired the British daily *The Sun*, and soon after substantially increased the paper's circulation by printing blaring headlines and racy features that were often accompanied by photos of topless women.

The Business

Financials

Revenue (1998): $14 billion

Employees (1998): 30,000

SICs / NAICS

sic 2711 - Newspapers

sic 2721 - Periodicals

sic 2731 - Book Publishing

sic 4833 - Television Broadcasting Stations

sic 4841 - Cable & Other Pay Television Services

sic 7812 - Motion Picture & Video Production

sic 7941 - Sports Clubs, Managers & Promoters

naics 511110 - Newspaper Publishers

naics 511120 - Periodical Publishers

naics 511130 - Book Publishers

naics 513120 - Television Broadcasting

naics 512110 - Motion Picture and Video Production

naics 711211 - Sports Teams and Clubs

With Murdoch as chairman, NOTW purchased an eight-percent stake in London Weekend Television. In 1972 News Ltd. acquired the Sydney *Daily* and *Sunday Telegraph*. It expanded its interests to the U.S. with the 1972 acquisition of three San Antonio, Texas, newspapers. Circulation for *The Sun* reached three million that year.

The New York Post was added to Murdoch's holdings in 1976. The *San Antonio News*, purchased three years earlier, gained brief but worldwide notoriety with the striking but inaccurate headline "Killer Bees Move North."

In 1977 the company purchased The New York Magazine Company, publisher of the magazines *New York* and *Village Voice*. A series of reports on the "Son of Sam" serial killing led to increased circulation of the *Post*. The following year News Ltd. joined forces with the Packer's group as well as Vernons, the British football pools company, to create a New South Wales lottery.

News Ltd. gained a 48.2% interest in Channel TEN-10, a Sydney television station, in 1979. Also that year it took over ATI, a group of airlines and other transport firms. Rupert Murdoch became chief executive of ATI and attempted to share 50-50 ownership of

the company with TNT, another transport group. News Corp. was created as the main holding company of Murdoch's group of companies.

In 1981 the British arm of the Murdoch group, News International, acquired 42% of the voting shares in the British publishers William Collins and Sons, and bought the London *Times*, the *Sunday Times*, the *Times Literary Supplement*, and the *Times Education Supplement* from what later became known as the Thomson Corp.

News Corp. acquired the *Boston Herald*—formerly the *Herald-American*—in 1982. Back in the U.K., *The Sun* remained the biggest-selling daily newspaper in Britain, having offered enthusiastic support to the British forces in the Falklands War.

In 1983 News Corp. was humiliated by the revelation that the secret diaries of Adolf Hitler, which the *Sunday Times* planned to serialize, were forgeries. That year a majority holding in Satellite Television PLC (SATV) was acquired, as well as a stake in Inter-American Satellite Television Network. Twentieth Century Fox Film Corp. became a wholly owned subsidiary. In 1984 the *Chicago Sun-Times* joined the group.

More than 5,000 print workers were fired in 1985 when Murdoch hired the Electrical, Electronic, Telecommunications and Plumbing Union to recruit new production staff. The following year News Ltd. divested itself of Channel Ten-10, ATV 10, a record company, several radio stations, and three newspapers.

A fifth newspaper, *Today*, was acquired in 1987. The takeover of the *Herald* and *Weekly Times* for $A2.3 billion made the News Corp. the largest publisher of English-language newspapers in the world. The chairman of the Australian Press Council resigned in protest over the government's failure to invoke the Foreign Takeovers Acts against Murdoch. The year was rounded out with the purchases of *South China Morning Post* and Harper & Row.

News Corp. purchased American magazine *TV Guide* and Triangle Publications, the company that published it, in 1988. That year the company sold the money-losing *New York Post*. The biggest news of the year, however, was the launch of Fox Broadcasting Co., the first new U.S. TV network in 40 years.

In 1989, having sold 50% of Harper & Row to William Collins and Sons, News International purchased Collins outright, creating HarperCollins Publishers, the largest English-language publisher in the world. Sky Television was established in the U.K. as a four-channel service available on cable and satellite receiver dishes. By the following year, Sky

Television was reaching 1.6 million households. That same year Sky Television merged with its smaller rival, BSB.

Murdoch assumed the leadership of Fox TV after firing the studio's president in 1992 for booking a male stripper at a company executives' meeting—even though the appearance was intended to make a point about censorship. Also that year the company sold the *San Antonio Express-News*.

The next year Murdoch purchased the *New York Post* for the second time. In 1994 Fox Broadcasting signed a $500 million deal with New World Communications Group to create new Fox network affiliates in up to 121 major markets. This resulted in the largest realignment of network affiliation in the 60-year history of American television broadcasting.

News Corp. acquired New World Communications Group from Ronald O. Perelman for $3 billion in 1997. Later that year it purchased Heritage Media Corp..

In November 1998 The Fox Entertainment Group, Inc. filed for its initial public offering; this transaction represented the largest initial public offering of a media company and the third-largest initial public offering in U.S. history. News Corp Europe was also established that month.

To expand its presence in the digital industry, News Corp. announced in April 1999 the formation of e-partners, which will participate in the Internet, inter-active television, and wireless communication. In June 1999 the firm entered into an agreement to purchase the Hearst Book Group, consisting of William Morrow & Company and Avon Books.

History of New World Communications Group Inc.

Epic Productions was founded in 1982 as a film producer and home video distributor. The following year the company acquired New World Entertainment, taking that company's name, from New World Pictures. Ronald Perelman acquired the firm in 1989 and led it into the international movie production market. It soon began expanding into tele-vision, and after acquiring a handful of stations from Storer Communications and Gillette, it took the name New World Communications to reflect its broader media focus.

The firm made its initial public offering in 1994, thereby gaining the funds to acquire four more televi-sion stations during the year. That year New World began its relationship with News Corp. by selling the Australian-based conglomerate a 20% stake for $500

The Officers

Chairman and CEO: K. Rupert Murdoch

President and Chief Operating Officer: Peter Chernin

Co-Chief Operating Officer: Chase Carey

Chief Financial Officer: David F. DeVoe

Group General Counsel: Arthur Siskind

Exec. VP, Corporate Affairs & Communications: Gary Ginsberg

Exec. VP: Leon Hertz

Exec. VP: Martin Pompadur

million; as part of the deal New World also switched most of its stations' affiliations to News Corp.'s Fox network.

In 1995 New World joined with Hachette Filipacchi Magazines to purchase *Premier* magazine. The new owners began interfering in the editorial decisions at that magazine. Such actions included the listing of the name of Perelman's wife on the mast-head and the axing of a story about Planet Hollywood because Perelman was engaged in a deal with the restaurant chain. These actions spurred the resigna-tion of two of its top editors and general resentment by the staff in 1996.

After selling two of its 12 television stations to NBC, New World was acquired by News Corp. for $3 billion in 1997.

Market Forces Driving the Acquisition

Rupert Murdoch had coveted New World Communications for several years. That company's network of a dozen owned-and-operated television stations would give Fox network the leading share of the over-the-air television market in the U.S. It would also endow that unit of News Corp. with the power to command a greater share of programming, particular-ly in sports and entertainment.

News Corp. had acquired an initial stake in New World in May 1994, when it purchased a 20% interest for $500 million. Part of that deal called for New World to switch its stations' affiliations to Fox.

Approach and Engagement

In April 1996 Murdoch approached Ronald Perelman, chairman of New World, to discuss an acquisition deal. The talks deadlocked, however, as Perelman insisted on $29 per share while Murdoch remained firm at $23.

The Players

News Corp. Chairman and CEO: K. Rupert Murdoch. K. Rupert Murdoch, a native of Melbourne, Australia, was educated at Oxford. After returning to Australia, he inherited his father's newspaper, *The News*, and built a global media empire from that one newspaper. In 1985 Murdoch became a U.S. citizen. By 1998 Murdoch ranked 18th on the *Forbes* list of the richest 400 Americans, with a net worth of $5.6 billion.

New World Communications Chairman: Ronald O. Perelman. Billionaire Ronald Perelman, introduced to the business world at an early age, has become a dominant player in the world of takeovers. At age 11, he began sitting in on the board meetings of his father's firm, Belmont Industries. He began working there after graduating from the University of Pennsylvania in 1964. Perelman established his own investment business in 1978, and soon made a name for himself as a financier. He took over struggling companies and divested non-core businesses, restoring them to profitability. Through his MacAndrews & Forbes Holdings company, he has taken interest in a number of companies. Notably, he assumed control of Revlon, Inc. in 1985 and engaged in a highly publicized ownership battle with Carl Icahn over Marvel Entertainment Group Inc. in 1997.

Soon after negotiations ceased, Perelman slyly lured Murdoch back to the table. During the time since the termination of their merger talks, New World had agreed to acquire King World Productions for about $1.5 billion. If that deal were to close, New World would be much more expensive to acquire. Realizing that it was now or never, Murdoch renewed negotiations with Perelman.

On July 17, 1996, Murdoch and Perelman forged a deal. Not surprisingly, its terms were closer to what Perelman had originally been seeking than what Murdoch had been willing to pay. The $3 billion deal called for News Corp. to issue $2.48 billion in stock and assume New World's debt of $540 million. This placed a value of $27 per share for New World stock, which had recently been trading at $21.75.

The U.S. Federal Communications Commission approved the deal in November, the day after it had proposed to ease its duopoly rule barring a company from owning more than one station in a given market. Therefore, the commission exempted News Corp. from rule in regard to the overlap in Milwaukee and Chicago that would result from the proposed acquisition.

On January 21, 1997, News Corp. completed the acquisition of New World Communications.

Products and Services

The News Corporation operated six business segments in 1998:

The **Television** segment received New World's television programming library and production division. This unit included Fox Broadcasting Company, Fox Sports, Fox Television Stations, Inc., Fox Family Worldwide (Fox Kids Network and Fox Family Channel), Twentieth Century Fox Television, Twentieth Television, and Fox Television Studios.

Filmed Entertainment encompassed Twentieth Century Fox Film Corp., Fox Studios Australia, Twentieth Century Home Entertainment (Fox Consumer Products, Twentieth Century Fox Home Entertainment, Fox Interactive, and Twentieth Century Fox Licensing and Merchandising).

Cable & Satellite TV consisted of Fox News, Fox Sports Net, FX Networks, LLC, British Sky Broadcasting Ltd., STAR TV (Zee TV Network, ESPN STAR Sports, Channel, and Phoenix Satellite Television Company Ltd.), ISkyB, Sky PerfecTV!, News Broadcasting Japan, Co., Ltd., News Corporation Limited Japan, Sky Latin America, LLC, and FOXTEL.

Magazine, Book & Digital Publishing included News America Publishing Group (HarperCollins , TV Guide, The Weekly Standard), News America Marketing, and News America Digital Publishing (TV Guide Inc. and News Corporation Music).

The **Newspapers** unit incorporated News International PLC (The Sun, The Times, The Sunday Times, and News of the World), News Limited (*The Australian, Herald Sun, The Advertiser*, and *The Daily Telegraph*), and *New York Post*.

Its sixth segment, **Other & Technology**, encompassed the Los Angeles Dodgers, Inc., Kesmai Corporation, NDS Limited, and PDN Xinren Information Technology Co. Ltd.

Changes to the Industry

With the addition of New World, News Corp. became the leading television station owner in the

U.S. It had a total of 22 stations, 10 of which were obtained from New World after its sale of two to NBC. Those stations brought Fox's penetration to 34.83% of America's households. Westinghouse ranked second, with 14 stations and a coverage of 30.95%. Tribune's 16 stations brought it a 24.96% penetration, just edging out NBC's 24.65% garnered from its 11 stations.

Moreover, nine of the stations that New World contributed were in the nation's top 10 markets. This presence provided Fox with greater bidding power for programming, particularly sports, as the network now had stations in eight of the National Football League's top 10 markets.

Review of the Outcome

Arthur Siskind, News Corp.'s executive vice president, stated that the company would "make necessary changes" in the operations of New World's "underperforming" stations. "It's not a reflection on how we view New World management," he said in *MEDIAWEEK*. "But we'd like to think the Fox O&Os' [owned-and-operated] better performance is due to certain synergies we benefit from in the ownership of the network, production, sports programming, and news-feed services."

In 1997 News Corp. reported third-quarter net income of $256 million, from $197 million in the previ-

ous year. It also recorded a 78% rise in the operating profit of its television division, to $105 million, over the same period. The company attributed those gains to the acquisition and integration of New World.

Research

Brooks, Boliek. "FCC Clears New World Order," in *Hollywood Reporter*, 11 November 1996. Reports the regulatory approval for the acquisition and briefly describes the duopoly rule.

Freeman, Michael. "Rupert Rules: On Top of the World," in *MEDIAWEEK*, 22 July 1996. Describes the newly announced acquisition deal and how the Fox network will benefit from it.

"News Corporation Ltd.," in *Notable Corporate Chronologies*, The Gale Group, 1999. Profiles the history of News Corp.

News Corporation Ltd. Home Page, available at http://www.newscorp.com. Official World Wide Web Page for News Corp. Includes business segment descriptions, annual reports and other financial information, and press releases.

"News Corp. Posts Big 3Q Gain," in *Media Daily*, 8 May 1997. Reports New World's contribution to News Corp.'s finances in late 1997.

Rathbun, Elizabeth A., and Cynthia Littleton. "Murdoch Claims New World," in *Broadcasting & Cable*, 22 July 1996. Details the deal and the share of the market that Fox will have as a result.

DAVIS MCMILLAN

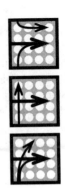

NEWS CORP. & TWENTIETH CENTURY FOX

The News Corporation Ltd.
2 Holt St.
Sydney, 2010
Australia

tel: 61 2 9288 3000
fax: 61 2 9288 3292
web: http://www.newscorp.com

nationality: Australia
date: September 24, 1985
affected: The News Corporation Ltd., Australia, founded 1923
affected: Twentieth Century Fox Film Corp., USA, founded 1935

Overview of the Acquisition

The acquisition of Twentieth Century Fox Film Corp. by The News Corporation Ltd. was a two-part process. In March 1985, The News Corp. acquired a 50% stake in the film studio. Six months later, it made the company a wholly-owned subsidiary by acquiring the remaining interest from owner Marvin Davis.

History of The News Corporation Ltd.

Following his father's death in 1952, Australian Rupert Murdoch inherited two Adelaide newspapers, *News* and *Sunday Mail*. These papers were owned by News Ltd., in which his father was a major shareholder. Four years later Murdoch added the Perth *Sunday Times* to his company.

Patterned after the American *TV Guide*, *TV Week* was launched in 1957. The following year Southern Television Corp., in which News Ltd. had a 60% stake, gained control of Channel 9, one of only two TV channels in Adelaide.

In 1960, the firm acquired Cumberland Newspapers, a group of local papers in the Sydney suburbs; among its holdings were the Sydney *Daily* and *Sunday Mirror*. That year Adelaide *News* editor Rohan Rivett was fired five weeks after being acquitted of charges of seditious libel stemming from the newspaper's criticisms of a state government's inquiry into a murder case.

News Ltd. launched *The Australian*, the country's first national newspaper, in 1964. Four years later, News Ltd. swapped shares in some of its minor ventures. As a result, it gained a 40% stake in the U.K.'s News of the World Organization (NOTW), owner of the *News of the World*, the Bemrose group of local newspapers, the papermakers Townsend Hook, and several other publishing companies.

In 1969, News Ltd. acquired British daily *The Sun* and soon after substantially increased the paper's circulation by printing blaring headlines and racy features that were often accompanied by photos of topless women.

With Murdoch as chairman, NOTW purchased an 8% stake in London Weekend Television. In 1972, News Ltd. acquired the Sydney *Daily* and *Sunday*

Telegraph. It expanded its interests to the U.S. with the 1972 acquisition of three San Antonio, Texas, newspapers. Circulation for *The Sun* reached three million that year.

The New York Post was added to Murdoch's holdings in 1976. The *San Antonio News*, purchased three years earlier, gained brief but worldwide notoriety with the striking but inaccurate headline "Killer Bees Move North."

In 1977, the company purchased The New York Magazine Co., publisher of magazines *New York* and *Village Voice*. A series of reports on the "Son of Sam" serial killing led to increased circulation of the *Post*. The following year, News Ltd. joined forces with the Packer's group as well as Vernons, the British football pools company, to create a New South Wales lottery.

News Ltd. gained a 48.2% interest in Channel TEN-10, a Sydney television station, in 1979. Also that year it took over ATI, a group of airlines and other transport firms. Rupert Murdoch became chief executive of ATI and attempted to share 50-50 ownership of the company with TNT, another transport group. News Corp. was created as the main holding company of Murdoch's group of companies.

In 1981, the British arm of the Murdoch group, News International, acquired 42% of the voting shares in the British publishers William Collins and Sons and bought the London *Times*, the *Sunday Times*, the *Times Literary Supplement*, and the *Times Education Supplement* from what later became known as Thomson Corp.

News Corp. acquired the *Boston Herald*—formerly the *Herald-American*—in 1982. Back in the U.K., *The Sun* remained the biggest-selling daily newspaper in Britain, having offered enthusiastic support to the British forces in the Falklands War.

In 1983, News Corp. was humiliated by the revelation that the secret diaries of Adolf Hitler, which the *Sunday Times* planned to serialize, were forgeries. That year a majority holding in Satellite Television PLC (SATV) was acquired, as well as a stake in Inter-American Satellite Television Network. In 1984, the *Chicago Sun-Times* joined the group.

The firm purchased a 50% stake in Twentieth Century Fox Film Corp. in March 1985, and acquired full control of the company that September. In July of that year, it paid $2 billion for Metromedia's seven television stations, thereby increasing News Corp.'s reach to 18% of America's television viewership.

More than 5,000 print workers were fired in 1985 when Murdoch hired the Electrical, Electronic, Telecommunications and Plumbing Union to recruit

The Business

Financials

Revenue (1998): $14 billion

Employees (1998): 30,000

SICs / NAICS

sic 2711 - Newspapers

sic 2721 - Periodicals

sic 2731 - Book Publishing

sic 4833 - Television Broadcasting Stations

sic 4841 - Cable & Other Pay Television Services

sic 7812 - Motion Picture & Video Production

sic 7941 - Sports Clubs, Managers & Promoters

naics 511110 - Newspaper Publishers

naics 511120 - Periodical Publishers

naics 511130 - Book Publishers

naics 513120 - Television Broadcasting

naics 512110 - Motion Picture and Video Production

naics 711211 - Sports Teams and Clubs

new production staff. The following year News Ltd. divested itself of Channel Ten-10, ATV 10, a record company, several radio stations, and three newspapers.

A fifth newspaper, *Today*, was acquired in 1987. The takeover of the *Herald* and *Weekly Times* for $A2.3 billion made News Corp. the largest publisher of English-language newspapers in the world. The chairman of the Australian Press Council resigned in protest over the government's failure to invoke the Foreign Takeovers Acts against Murdoch. The year was rounded out with the purchases of *South China Morning Post* and Harper & Row.

News Corp. purchased American magazine *TV Guide* and Triangle Publications, the company that published it, in 1988. That year the firm sold the money-losing *New York Post*. The biggest news of the year, however, was the launch of Fox Broadcasting Co., the first new U.S. TV network in 40 years.

In 1989, having sold 50% of Harper & Row to William Collins and Sons, News International purchased Collins outright, creating HarperCollins Publishers, the largest English-language publisher in the world. Sky Television in the U.K. was established as a four-channel service available on cable and satel-

The Officers

Chairman and CEO: K. Rupert Murdoch

President and Chief Operating Officer: Peter Chernin

Co-Chief Operating Officer: Chase Carey

Chief Financial Officer: David F. DeVoe

Group General Counsel: Arthur Siskind

lite receiver dishes. In 1990, Sky Television reached 1.6 million households and merged with its smaller rival, BSB.

Murdoch assumed the leadership of Fox TV after firing the studio's president in 1992 for booking a male stripper at a company executives' meeting—even though the appearance was intended to make a point about censorship. Also that year the company sold the *San Antonio Express-News*.

The next year Murdoch purchased the *New York Post* for the second time. In 1994, Fox Broadcasting signed a $500 million deal with New World Communications Group to create new Fox network affiliates in up to 121 major markets. This resulted in the largest realignment of network affiliation in the 60-year history of American television broadcasting.

News Corp. acquired New World Communications Group from Ronald O. Perelman for $3 billion in 1997. Later that year it purchased Heritage Media Corp.

In November 1998, The Fox Entertainment Group, Inc. filed for its initial public offering; this transaction represented the largest initial public offering of a media company and the third-largest initial public offering in U.S. history. Also that month, News Corp Europe was established.

To expand its presence in the digital industry, News Corp. announced in April 1999 the formation of e-partners, an Internet, interactive television, and wireless communication venture. In June 1999, the firm entered into an agreement to purchase the Hearst Book Group, consisting of William Morrow & Co. and Avon Books.

History of Twentieth Century Fox Film Corp.

William Fox, a 25-year old Hungarian immigrant born as Wilhelm Fried, purchased a nickelodeon in 1904 in New York City. Fox and two partners transformed this single movie theater into a chain of 25 nickelodeons within a few years. They established the Greater New York Film Rental Co., and in 1913 organ-ized the Box Office Attraction Co. for original movie production.

In 1915, Fox founded the Fox Film Corp., one of the first companies that encompassed the production, distribution, and exhibition of movies. The new company was headquartered in California, where Fox believed that film production would be better suited by its temperate climate. It purchased 55% of Loew's Inc., the parent company of MGM, in 1929. The company experienced a series of shake-ups beginning in 1927, and three years later a group of shareholders ousted William Fox.

Twentieth Century Pictures was founded in 1933 by Darryl F. Zanuck, head of production at Warner Bros., and Joseph M. Schenck, head of United Artists. In 18 months, it released 18 movies, including *The House of Rothschild* and *Les Miserables*. In 1935, it merged with Fox Film Corp. to form Twentieth Century Fox Film Corp.

The new studio flourished during the 1940s, producing such winners as *The Grapes of Wrath, How Green Was My Valley, The Snows of Kilimanjaro*, and *All About Eve*. It also tackled such topical social issues as race relations and anti-Semitism with *Pinky* and *Gentleman's Agreement*.

Television viewership took a toll on movie attendance by the early 1950s. Studios could no longer afford to maintain exclusive contracts with actors and directors, and movie production declined. Frustrated by such difficulties, Zanuck resigned from Twentieth Century Fox in 1956 to become an independent film producer in Paris.

Twentieth Century Fox verged on liquidation by the turn of the decade. Between 1959 and 1961, it lost $48.5 million, and in 1962 it lost $39.8 million on revenues of $96.4 million. The production of *Cleopatra* accounted for much of these financial results. That film's budget of $7 million multiplied to $41.5 million, with the studio even resorting to selling 334 acres of land to cover its expenses.

Zanuck, still a major stockholder, returned to Twentieth Century Fox in 1962 to orchestrate its recovery. His reputation bolstered the company's image, and his European production company made *The Longest Day*, which was released through Twentieth Century Fox. This epic was a smash hit, enabling the studio to restart movie production in 1963.

Initially, the company proceeded cautiously, producing movies with modest budgets. Once revenues from these releases began to accumulate, the company reverted to more costly film production in the hope of making another blockbuster. *The Sound of Music*, released in 1964, outgrossed *Gone with the Wind*, the record holder for 27 years.

Twentieth Century Fox Television emerged as one of the largest TV producers in the mid-1960s, producing 12 network shows during the 1966-67 season. It also began distributing its feature films to television, including a deal that leased 17 movies to ABC for $19 million.

Its newfound success in motion pictures and television encouraged the company to continue its lavish spending on film production. That strategy proved nearly disastrous when *Dr. Dolittle* and *Tora! Tora! Tora!* were among Hollywood's all-time biggest box office losers. Twentieth Century Fox's operating losses were $36 million in 1969.

This strain contributed to infighting among the company's leadership. After a proxy fight for control of the firm, Richard Zanuck, son of Darryl, was forced to resign as president. Four months later Darryl himself resigned as chairman. Their successor, Dennis Stanfill, led the company on a diversification path that took it into the record business, broadcasting, film processing, and theme parks.

Stanfill also hired Alan Ladd, Jr., as head of the film division. Under Ladd, Twentieth Century Fox released such successes as *The Poseidon Adventure*, *Young Frankenstein*, and *The Towering Inferno*. These hits were eclipsed in 1977, however, by *Star Wars*, which became the biggest box office success in history at that time.

As profits soared, the company accelerated its diversification program. It purchased Coca-Cola Bottling Midwest; Aspen Skiing, the nation's largest ski resort operator; and Pebble Beach Corp., owner of a California resort. Ladd resigned in 1979, and was replaced by Sherry Lansing, the first female to head the production arm of a major motion picture studio.

The success of such films as *Alien* and *The Empire Strikes Back* was tempered by disappointments like *The Rose* and *I Ought to be in Pictures*. Twentieth Century Fox's operating profit dropped 10% in 1980. Late that year, when investment groups began purchasing large stakes in the company, Stanfill initiated a management-led leveraged buyout to prevent a hostile takeover attempt. He was thwarted, however, when oil magnate Marvin Davis joined with silent partner Marc Rich to form TCF Holdings for the purchase of Twentieth Century Fox for $722 million in June 1981. Stanfill resigned the following month.

The company's financial position deteriorated rapidly in the immediate aftermath of the purchase. Movie success continued to elude the studio. Lansing and other top executives resigned, reportedly over clashes with Davis. And Davis, who had burdened the company with $650 million in debt to pay back TCF's

The Players

The News Corporation Ltd. Chairman and CEO: K. Rupert Murdoch. K. Rupert Murdoch, a native of Melbourne, Australia, was educated at Oxford. After returning to Australia, he inherited his father's newspaper, *The News*, from which he built a global media empire. Murdoch became a U.S. citizen in 1985. In 1998, Murdoch ranked 18th on *Forbes* list of the richest 400 Americans, with a net worth of $5.6 billion.

Twentieth Century Fox Film Corp. Owner: Marvin Davis. Marvin Davis, a wealthy Denver oilman, was intrigued by the prospects of owning a major motion picture studio. When Twentieth Century Fox was engulfed in internal turmoil and a declining market share, Davis decided to move in on the company. He formed a partnership with Marc Rich and purchased the company in June 1981. In doing so, however, he had burdened the studio with an enormous debt load. After buying out Rich, Davis sold a 50% stake to The News Corp. in March 1985. That December he exited the movie industry completely by selling his remaining interest in Twentieth Century Fox to The News Corp.

---

loans, began selling off the company's assets to reduce that load.

In October 1984, Davis paid $116 million to buy out Rich's 50% stake in TCF. That year he also recruited Barry Diller from Paramount to become chairman and CEO of Twentieth Century Fox, guaranteeing him a $3 million salary. Diller began turning around the beleaguered company by increasing film production and by securing financing from diverse sources.

In March 1985, The News Corp., a media company owned by Rupert Murdoch, paid $250 million for half of Davis' interest in Twentieth Century Fox. That September it purchased Davis' remaining interest in the firm for $325 million.

Under its new parent, Twentieth Century Fox began to revive. Among its box office successes in the late 1980s were *Wall Street*, *Big*, and *Die Hard*. Joe Roth was hired as new head of the studio, and led the company to release such hits as *Home Alone* and *Edward Scissorhands*. By 1991, Twentieth Century Fox was the market leader, capturing 18% of the box-office share.

Roth resigned in 1992, and was succeeded by Peter Chernin as president of the film unit. The following year Bill Mechanic became president of Twentieth Century Fox Film Corp.

During the early 1990s, the company ventured into new entertainment ventures. In 1993 it supported the development of pay-per-view television and negotiated a distribution agreement with DirecTV the following year. Also in 1994, it organized an interactive game division, as well as establishing Fox Animation Inc. for the production of animated feature films. In 1995, it formed the Twentieth Century Fox Home Entertainment division for the distribution of its video and interactive products.

Anastasia, the first product of its animated film unit, was released at the box office in 1997 and on pay-per-view in 1998. The release of *Titanic* in 1998 broke all box office attendance records and earned 11 Academy Awards.

Market Forces Driving the Acquisition

Rupert Murdoch envisioned the creation of a vertically integrated media empire. By the mid-1980s, The News Corp. was an international publishing, television, and satellite broadcasting concern. The major piece missing from its entertainment holdings, however, was a Hollywood movie studio. Not only would such a studio round out its holdings, it would give the company's television stations access to a library of valuable films.

Twentieth Century Fox Film Corp. was hurting in the early 1980s. Marvin Davis, its owner, had lured Barry Diller away from Paramount to revive the company's situation. Diller had begun to do so, but the company was in worse shape than even he had realized. In the second half of 1984, Twentieth Century Fox ranked fourth in U.S. box office returns. Its $183 million in revenues, accounting for an 8.8% share, was far outranked by the leaders: Warner Bros., with $441 million or 21.1%; Paramount, with $417 million or 19.9%; and Columbia Pictures, with $392 million or 18.7%. Davis, reluctant to throw good money after bad, decided to reduce his stake rather than make further investments in the company.

Approach and Engagement

According to reports, Davis and Murdoch entered into acquisition discussions in February 1985. Their first deal, which had been hatched in utter secrecy, was announced only after its completion on March 20. On that date The News Corp. paid $250 million to purchase 50% of Davis' stake in TCF Holdings, the parent company of Twentieth Century Fox. Of that amount, $162 million went directly to TCF to retire its debt, with the remaining $88 million going to the movie studio.

Murdoch immediately assumed an active role in the company. When he acquired seven television stations from Metromedia in July, Davis expressed concerns about the company's film operation becoming tied too closely to a television network, so Murdoch offered to buy out Davis completely, and on September 24, 1985, paid $325 million for the remaining 50% interest in Twentieth Century Fox.

Products and Services

The News Corporation operated in six business segments in 1998:

The **Television** segment received New World's television programming library and production division. This unit included Fox Broadcasting Co., Fox Sports, Fox Television Stations, Inc., Fox Family Worldwide (Fox Kids Network and Fox Family Channel), Twentieth Century Fox Television, Twentieth Television, and Fox Television Studios.

Filmed Entertainment encompassed Twentieth Century Fox Film Corp., Fox Studios Australia, Twentieth Century Home Entertainment (Fox Consumer Products, Twentieth Century Fox Home Entertainment, Fox Interactive, and Twentieth Century Fox Licensing and Merchandising).

Cable & Satellite TV was comprised of Fox News, Fox Sports Net, FX Networks, LLC, British Sky Broadcasting Ltd., STAR TV (Zee TV Network, ESPN STAR Sports, Channel[V], and Phoenix Satellite Television Company Ltd.), ISkyB, Sky PerfecTV!, News Broadcasting Japan, Co., Ltd., News Corp. Ltd. Japan, Sky Latin America, LLC, and FOXTEL.

Magazine, Book & Digital Publishing included News America Publishing Group (HarperCollins, TV Guide, The Weekly Standard), News America Marketing, and News America Digital Publishing (TV Guide Inc. and News Corp. Music).

The **Newspapers** unit incorporated News International PLC(*The Sun*, *The Times*, *The Sunday Times*, and *News of the World*), News Limited (*The Australian*, *Herald Sun*, *The Advertiser*, and *The Daily Telegraph*), and *New York Post*.

Its sixth segment, **Other & Technology**, encompassed the Los Angeles Dodgers, Inc., Kesmai Corp., NDS Ltd., and PDN Xinren Information Technology Co. Ltd.

Changes to the Industry and Review of the Outcome

Ownership by The News Corp. had an immediate impact on Twentieth Century Fox. For the year ending June 28, 1986, the film studio recorded its first annual profit since 1981, earning $30.4 million on revenues of $568.3 million. Additionally, the firm posted an operating profit of $51.8 million, reversing the loss of $40 million for the previous year.

Research

Hall, William. "Murdoch Empire's Big-Screen Debut," in *Financial Times (London)*, 22 March 1985. Details the terms of The News Corporation's purchase of the first half of Twentieth Century Fox.

Harmetz, Aljean. "Optimism Among Fox Executives," in *The New York Times*, 22 March 1985. Describes The News Corporation's initial 50% investment in Twentieth Century Fox.

Harris, Kathryn. "20th Century Fox Ends Year Back in the Black," in *Los Angeles Times*, 1 October 1986. Relates the financial results of Twentieth Century Fox after its first year under ownership by The News Corp.

Hayes, Thomas C. "Murdoch Will Buy out Davis's Holdings in Fox," in *The New York Times*, 24 September 1985. Reveals the complete acquisition of Twentieth Century Fox by The News Corp.

"News Corporation Ltd.," in *Notable Corporate Chronologies*, The Gale Group, 1999. Profiles the history of News Corp.

News Corporation Ltd. Home Page, available at http://www.newscorp.com. Official World Wide Web Page for News Corp. Includes business segment descriptions, annual reports and other financial information, and press releases.

"Twentieth Century Fox Film Corporation," in *International Directory of Company Histories*, Vol. 25, St. James Press: 1999. Provides a historical review of the company, before and after it became a subsidiary of The News Corp.

Twentieth Century Fox Film Corp. Home Page, available at http://www.fox.com. Official World Wide Web Page for Twentieth Century Fox Film. Includes film, television, and video information; an online store; news releases; and financial information.

DAVIS MCMILLAN

NORFOLK SOUTHERN, CSX, & CONRAIL INC.

Norfolk Southern Corp.
Three Commercial Pl.
Norfolk, VA 23510-2191
USA

tel: (757)629-2680
fax: (757)664-5069
web: http://www.nscorp.com

CSX Corp.
901 E. Cary St.
Richmond, VA 23219-4031
USA

tel: (804)782-1400
fax: (804)782-6747
web: http://www.csx.com

Conrail, Inc.
2001 Market St., 2 Commerce Sq.
Philadelphia, PA 19101
USA

tel: (215)209-4000
web: http://www.conrail.com

date: June 1, 1999
affected: Norfolk Southern Corp., USA, founded 1982
affected: CSX Corp., USA, founded 1980

Overview of the Merger

On October 15, 1996, CSX announced its proposed merger with Conrail. The $9.5 billion cash and stock trade, totaling $92.50 per share, was to be a merger of equals. Competitor Norfolk Southern (NS) launched an aggressive counter bid of $10.3 billion for Conrail. Conrail's board approved the Norfolk offer on January 17, 1997. This opened the door for Norfolk to discuss a joint venture with CSX, which held a minor share of Conrail stock. Eventually, a joint $10.3 billion acquisition of Conrail was agreed to by CSX and Norfolk; once completed, the deal divided Conrail into three parts.

CSX and NS each obtained two separate parts of Conrail and jointly shared the third. On June 1, 1999, the two companies became the largest competitive operators east of the Mississippi, with lines running from Montreal to Florida. CSX received approximately 4,000 miles of rail and become the nation's third largest rail company. With 22,300 rail miles, CSX served 23 states and become the primary carrier on former Conrail routes East of the Hudson River. Norfolk Southern became the nation's fourth largest railroad company with a 21,600-mile rail system serving 22 states. Both companies shared tracks and facilities in hub cities such as Philadelphia and Detroit.

History of Norfolk Southern Corp.

In 1982 Norfolk & Western Railway Co. (N&W) merged with Southern Railway Co. (SRC) to create Norfolk Southern. Three years later the company diversified with the purchase of North American Van Lines. In 1986 Norfolk created a subsidiary, Triple Crown Services, which was responsible for the company's intermodal transport.

David Goode became Norfolk Southern's CEO in 1992 and revived the business into one of the safest and financial sound rail companies. The wealth and assets of the company allowed Norfolk to offer a $10.3 billion tender purchase of Conrail in 1996, circumventing a proposed merger with CSX. Eventually, Norfolk entered a joint purchase agreement with CSX and obtained a 58% share of Conrail.

History of CSX Corp.

In 1973 the Baltimore & Ohio Railroad (BOR) combined with the Chesapeake & Ohio Railroad (COR) under the control of a holding company called The Chessie System. The Baltimore & Ohio Railroad (BOR) had been created in 1827 to offer a rail and canal system between the eastern seaboard and the industrial centers around the Great Lakes. The COR had been taken over by J.P. Morgan in 1878, after the company suffered great losses and even bankruptcy after the Civil War.

Chessie System Inc. merged with Seaboard Coast Line Industries (SCL) in 1980 creating CSX Corp. Prime F. Osborn became chairman of the new company, while Chessie's Hays T. Watkins was named president. Two years later Watkins also took over as chairman when Osborn retired.

Watkins diversified CSX with a series of acquisitions beginning with the 1983 purchase of Texas Gas Resources. CSX purchased AMR Commercial Lines, Inc. in 1984 and Sea-Land Corp. in 1986. Additionally, CSX entered into the leisure and lodging industry with the acquisition of Rockresorts, Inc. By 1988, however, CSX was forced to sell off many of its recent acquisitions in a corporate restructuring program designed to address complaints about company performance. In 1989 John W. Snow replaced Watkins as president and CEO; he immediately began divesting subsidiaries in an effort to streamline the company.

In October 1996, Conrail accepted CSX's $8.4 billion acquisition bid. The merger would have increased CSX's preeminence in the eastern U.S., with 70% of the market share. Rival company Norfolk Southern fought the proposal and Conrail's board eventually voted against the CSX takeover. Norfolk offered a $10.3 billion tender purchase of Conrail, and the Surface Transportation Board set up a 365-day consideration period. By June 1998, the deal had been forged. CSX acquired 40% of Conrail stock, and Norfolk received the remaining 58% when the deal was completed on June 1, 1999.

History of Conrail, Inc.

In 1976 the U.S. government attempted to revive the nation's struggling east coast rail industry. The government assumed the operations of six failed and bankrupt rail companies and joined them together to form Consolidated Rail Corp. Initially, the government planned to create the company in order to sell it to the private sector, but found no interested parties and began running it under the holding company, Conrail. The six defunct railroad operations that made up Conrail were Penn Central, Central of New Jersey,

The Business

Financials - Norfolk Southern Corp.

Revenue (1998): $4.22 billion

Employees (1998): 24,300

Financials - CSX Corp.

Revenue (1998): $9.8 billion

Employees (1998): 46,147

Financials - Conrail, Inc.

Revenue (1998): $3.86 billion

Employees (1998): 22,000

SICs / NAICS

sic 4011 - Railroads-Line-Haul Operating

sic 4731 - Freight Transportation Arrangement

sic 6719 - Holding Companies Nec

naics 482111 - Line-Haul Railroads

naics 541614 - Process, Physical Distribution, and Logistics Consulting Services

Erie Lackawanna, Lehigh & Hudson River, Lehigh Valley, and Reading.

In 1980 the government deregulated U.S. rail operations with the passage of the Staggers Act. The following year former Southern Railway chairman Stanley Crane became CEO of Conrail. Crane turned the company around and by 1984 was able to make Conrail profitable. In 1987 the government sold its 85% share of Conrail in a $1.6 billion public offering.

In 1996, amidst a financial restructuring, Conrail agreed to a merger with CSX Corp. Norfolk Southern successfully interceded in the merger and eventually created an agreement with CSX to jointly acquire and split Conrail, creating the two largest firms east of the Mississippi River. Both CSX and Norfolk integrated portions of Conrail's operations into their current companies and shared the remaining third of the acquired company, still called Conrail.

Market Forces Driving the Merger

The proposed merger of CSX and Conrail would have boosted annual revenues at CSX to $14 billion. It would have allowed CSX to offer barge, container-shipping, intermodal, and rail services, with operations in 80 countries, and secured for CSX control of 70% of the eastern U.S. market. Management estimat-

The Officers

Norfolk Southern Corp.

Chairman, CEO, and President: David R. Goode

Vice Chairman and Chief Financial Officer: Henry F. Wolf

Vice Chairman and Chief Operations Officer: Stephen C.
Tobias

Vice Chairman and Chief Marketing Officer: L. I. Prillaman

CSX Corp.

Chairman, CEO, and President: John W. Snow

Chief Financial Officer; Executive Vice President, Finance:
Paul R. Goodwin

President and CEO, CSX Transportation: Alvin R. "Pete"
Carpenter

Vice Chairman, CSX Transportation: Gerald L. Nichols
affected: Conrail, Inc., USA, founded 1976

Conrail, Inc.

Chairman and CEO: David M. LeVan

President: Timothy T. O'Toole

Senior VP of Operations: Ronald J. Conway

ed that the firm would save $730 million in elimination of redundancies. The deal also appealed to Conrail, which needed to find a merger partner to reduce costs, increase service and offer more competitive prices to consumers.

Norfolk Southern knew that it would become a minor player in the east if Conrail and CSX merged. To prevent this, Norfolk started a hostile takeover bid after attempts to block the deal in the courts failed. Conrail was an attractive acquisition for any company, because it operated a monopoly in the nation's lucrative northeastern market. A merger with Conrail would also allow Norfolk to reduce operating expenses, as well as line transfers, and open direct line service to many consumers who were currently using non-rail transportation services.

Approach and Engagement

On the morning of October 15, 1996, Norfolk Southern CEO David Goode received a phone call informing him that his long-time merger interest, Conrail, was no longer available. CSX CEO John Snow delivered the message that his company was the lucky partner in a $9.5 billion cash and stock deal with Conrail. Stunned, Goode hung up the phone and then set in motion an aggressive takeover bid.

After filing several court documents to prevent the CSX/Conrail merger, Norfolk offered a $10.3 billion tender deal, surpassing CSX's cash and stock deal by nearly $1.5 billion. With Norfolk's offer on the table, Conrail's board rejected CSX's bid. CSX held 17% of Conrail prior to the Norfolk bid, so it was in a position to negotiate the acquisition deal. After a series of talks, CSX and Norfolk agreed to a split Conrail. They created a joint venture company called Green Acquisition. Norfolk paid $5.9 billion to acquire 58% of Conrail's routes. CSX paid $4.3 billion for the remaining stock. Both companies also decided to share specific facilities, which would operate under the name Conrail beginning on June 1, 1999. All companies maintained their current executive leadership, with the exception of the promotion of Timothy O'Toole as Conrail's president.

The Surface Transportation Board approved the deal, but set up a five-year oversight period to monitor operations. A previous rail merger involving Union Pacific Corp. (UP) cost several million dollars in losses for industries reliant on the railroad when UP's merger created havoc among the two combined operating systems.

Products and Services

CSX and Norfolk Southern provided the first competitive rail market in the northeastern United States after they jointly began operation of acquired Conrail. With 23,100 miles of track CSX became the nation's third largest railroad, providing a vast single line network from Montreal to Florida and New York to the Midwest. CSX offered coal transport from the Mongahela Mine, provided shorter routes to Baltimore, and served 23 states.

Norfolk Southern began using the new operations to compete against railroads and over-the-road trucking companies. The new system allowed the company to offer direct shipping from freight carriers to consumer locations. Consumers benefitted from lower costs due to fewer line switches and extensive intermodal operations. Norfolk Southern also began targeting non-rail consumers and planned to offer the same door-to-door service provided by trucking firms.

Changes to the Industry

CSX and Norfolk Southern's joint acquisition of Conrail broke up a long standing monopoly in the northeastern United States. The new competition promised consumers better pricing, faster service, and expanded service areas throughout the eastern seaboard and Midwest.

Review of the Outcome

When the deal was completed, the two companies became the largest eastern U.S. railroads with extensive service to sites from the Atlantic seaboard to the Mississippi River. The acquired systems were primarily divided in half, with a series of shared facilities to be run under the name Conrail. Each company gained enough new rail routes to increase their overall networks to over 20,000 miles. It's estimated that, by the end of the century, 1,500 union jobs will be cut or transferred and that 1,200 management positions, mostly at Conrail's main office, will be eliminated.

Research

Bemis, Tom. "CSX, Norfolk Southern Dividing Conrail," in *CBS MarketWatch*, 22 May 1999. Discusses how the two companies will divide Conrail and the aspects of the acquisition.

Consolidated Rail Corp. Home Page, available at http://www.conrail.com. World Wide Web site for Conrail. Includes current and archived news; detailed financial, product, historical information; annual reports; and press releases.

"Consolidated Rail Corp.," in *Notable Corporate Chronologies*, The Gale Group, 1999. Lists major events in the history of Conrail.

"CSX Corp.," in *Notable Corporate Chronologies*, The Gale Group, 1999. Profiles major events in the history of CSX Corp.

CSX Corp. Home Page, available at http://www.csx.com. World Wide Web page for CSX Corp. Includes current and archived news; detailed financial, product, and historical information; annual reports; and press releases.

"David M. LeVan," in *Philadelphia Business Journal*, 3 January 1997. Spotlights Conrail's CEO David LeVan.

"Details of the Conrail Deal," by *The Associated Press*, 23 May 1999. Details the new operations to be offered by CSX and Norfolk Southern after June 1, 1999.

Dinsmore, Mylene. "How Norfolk Southern Derailed the Merger of CSX and Conrail," in *Virginian-Pilot*, 5 March 1997. Describes Norfolk's counter offer that the Conrail Board approved over CSX's bid.

Holcomb, Henry J. "Rail Executive Profile: Norfolk Southern's David Goode," in *The Philadelphia Inquirer*, 25 November 1996. Profiless the career of David Goode.

Jesdanun, Anick. "Railroads Ready to Carve Up Conrail," in *The Associated Press*, 23 May 1999. Explains major points that made the Conrail acquisition by CSX and Norfolk Southern possible.

Martin, Justin. "Surviving A Head-on Collision," in *Fortune*, 14 April, 1997. Discusses how Norfolk Southern CEO David Goode fought the merger between CSX and Conrail.

Norfolk Southern Corp. Home Page, available at http://www.nscorp.com. World Wide Web page for Norfolk Southern. Includes current news, as well as detailed financial, product, and historical data. Includes a special site with reports and press releases specifically regarding the Conrail merger.

"People," in *Railway Age*, March 1996. Discusses the career of David LeVan.

The Players

Chairman, CEO and President of Norfolk Southern Corp.: David R. Goode. David R. Goode began his career in the tax department of Norfolk and Western in 1965. He worked his way up the ranks and 25 years later was named vice president. He was named heir apparent and took over as CEO in 1982. In 1996, after hearing about a proposed merger between Norfolk Southern's two largest competitors, CSX and Conrail, Goode led an aggressive counter strike to prevent the deal that would place his company at a tremendous size disadvantage in the lucrative northeastern United States. Eventually Conrail accepted Norfolk's higher cash offer. Goode helped create a joint holding company between Norfolk and CSX, which split control and use of Conrail. Both Norfolk Southern and CSX retained separate leadership ranks.

Chairman, CEO, and President of CSX Corp.: John W. Snow. Former federal highway official John Snow took the helm at CSX in 1989. He approached the struggling rail industry with a no nonsense, back-to-basics mission to help CSX compete successfully against both rail and trucking competitors. In a series of meetings with business and industry operators, he listened to harsh criticism regarding CSX's services. He took their suggestions and was able to increase revenues and stock prices. Snow streamlined intermodal and maritime to rail transfer operations, eliminated several thousand miles of struggling Florida rail line, and reduced rail car turnaround time. As the company grew to the third largest Eastern U.S. rail company, Snow realized the inevitability of a merger to stay competitive. His October 1996 announcement of a proposed deal with fifth ranked Conrail would launch the company into the largest rail operation east of the Mississippi River. Direct competitor Norfolk Southern successfully blocked the merger and was able to wedge out an equal share in the Conrail acquisition. Snow and Norfolk's David Goode worked together to create a joint venture which split Conrail into two separate entities with a third portion of the company being shared by both.

Slack, Charles. "CSX, Norfolk Southern in Accord," in *Richmond Times-Dispatch*, 9 April 1997. Summaries the joint acquisition details of the Conrail merger.

SEAN C. MACKEY

NORTHROP & GRUMMAN

Northrop Grumman Corp.
1840 Century Park E.
Los Angeles, CA 90067
USA

tel: (310)553-6262
fax: (310)201-3023
web: http://www.northgrum.com

nationality: USA
date: April 1994
affected: Northrop Corp., USA, founded 1939
affected: Grumman Corp., USA, founded 1929

Overview of the Acquisition

The acquisition of Grumman Corp. in 1994 had been a tug-of-war between Martin Marietta Corp. and Northrop Corp. These two suitors—one friendly and the other hostile—engaged in a month-long contest for Grumman. Over the course of this battle, tempers flared, feeling were hurt, and lawsuits were filed. In the end, Northrop was the victor, acquiring Grumman for $2.17 billion. The newly formed Northrop Grumman Corp. was a combination of the nation's 2nd- and 12th-largest prime defense contractors.

History of Northrop Corp.

Aerospace engineer and innovator Jack Northrop co-founded Lockheed Aircraft in 1927. He then formed Avion Corp., which was later acquired by United Aircraft and Transportation. In 1932 he established Northrop Corp., which was acquired by Douglas Aircraft in 1938. The following year he formed yet another company, Northrop Aircraft.

Jack Northrop began working on a "Flying Wing" bomber, which he anticipated would be in demand during World War II. The following year, he tested the company's first Flying Wing bomber, the N-1M. He followed that up with other Flying Wings, developing the B-35 and the B-49. Despite Northrop's hopes that the Army Air Corps would make the B-49 its primary bomber, government contracts for development of the aircraft were canceled amid controversial circumstances: the Army's claim that the design was flawed, and Jack Northrop's belief that his company was denied the contract due to his refusal to merge with another company to produce it.

During the 1950s Northrop continued its focus on government defense contracts, relying heavily on its F-89 fighter plane and Snark missile system. In 1958 the company changed its name to Northrop Corp. The company's new president, Thomas V. Jones, steered Northrop on a less volatile course. It began subcontracting to produce components for military and civilian aircraft, missiles, and electronic control systems, and expanding into construction. In 1959 it purchased Page

Communications Engineers to reduce corporate dependence on government contracts. Despite continuing efforts to diversify, Northrop relied on defense contracts, particularly sales of the F-5 and its trainer version, the T-38, during the 1960s.

In 1970 Northrop acquired a 49% interest in Iran Aircraft Industries of Tehran, Iran. The following year it acquired Olson Laboratories, Wilcox Electric, Inc., and World Wide Wilcox, Inc. The company also faced scandal, as Jones was convicted of making illegal contributions to the presidential campaign of Richard Nixon, and the company was found to have paid $30 million in bribes to officials in Indonesia, Iran, and Saudi Arabia. Jones was forced to resign as president, although he remained CEO.

Northrop acquired Berkeley Scientific Laboratories (later known as Northrop Data Systems, Inc.) and a 23% interest in General Energy Resources, Inc. in 1972. It also purchased Page Aircraft Maintenance, Inc., which then changed its name to Northrop Worldwide Aircraft Services, Inc. In 1974 George A. Fuller Co. merged into Northrop. The company then sold Olson Laboratories as well as its interest in Iran Aircraft Industries.

In 1975 Northrop filed suit against McDonnell-Douglas, alleging improprieties in their joint development of the F-18A Hornet. Northrop was awarded $50 million in damages, although McDonnell-Douglas was awarded rights to all future F-18-related contracts.

In 1978 Wilcox Electric acquired Tull Aviation Corp. and its subsidiary, Tull International. The company then embarked on a divestiture program in the 1980s, selling the George A. Fuller Co., Northrop Architectural Systems, World Wide Wilcox, Inc., and Northrop Services, as well as its interests in Wilcox Electric, Inc. and Page Communications Engineers. In 1985 the company incorporated. Five years later, a second scandal came to light. When the company pled guilty to falsifying test results on government projects, it paid $17 million in fines and $18 million in a suit filed by its shareholders.

In 1992 Northrop, the Carlyle Group, and Loral Corp. became partners to purchase the missile and aircraft businesses of LTV Corp. for $475 million. The partnership won a bidding war against Martin-Marietta, Lockheed Corp., and Thompson-CSF of France after a court ruling forbade a foreign firm from purchasing a defense contractor. Later that year, Northrop again was in competition as a suitor, when it and Lockheed Corp. vied to purchase the military aircraft manufacturing operations of General Dynamics Corp.

The Business

Financials

Revenue (1998): $8.9 billion

Employees (1998): 49,600

SICs / NAICS

sic 3694 - Engine Electrical Equipment

sic 3721 - Aircraft

sic 3728 - Aircraft Parts & Equipment Nec

sic 3761 - Guided Missiles & Space Vehicles

sic 3812 - Search & Navigation Equipment

sic 7373 - Computer Integrated Systems Design

sic 7374 - Data Processing & Preparation

naics 334511 - Search, Detection, Navigation, Guidance, Aeronautical, and Systems

naics 336322 - Other Motor Vehicle Electrical and Electronic Equipment Manufacturing

naics 336411 - Aircraft Manufacturing

naics 336413 - Other Aircraft Part and Auxiliary Equipment Manufacturing

naics 336414 - Guided Missile and Space Vehicle Manufacturing

naics 514210 - Data Processing Services

naics 541512 - Computer Systems Design Services

Northrop's net sales for 1992 reached $5.5 billion, and the company employed 33,000 by year's end. However, when government orders for its B-2 bomber were slashed from 132 to 20, Northrop was forced to cut 3,000 jobs. Its 1993 revenues dipped to $5.1 billion.

History of Grumman Corp.

On December 6, 1929, three former employees of the Loening Aircraft Engineering Co.—Roy Grumman, Jake Swirbul, and Bill Schwendler—established an aircraft company. Within three months, Grumman Aircraft Engineering Corp. had a contract to design a U.S. Navy fighter. In 1931 the company unveiled introduced the FF-1, a plane so durable that it earned Grumman the nickname "The Iron Works."

The Grumman Goose, the company's first commercial aircraft, was released in 1937. The following

The Officers

Chairman, President, and CEO: Kent Kresa

Chief Human Resources and Administrative Officer:
   Marvin Elkin

VP and Controller: Nelson F. Gibbs

VP and General Counsel: Richard R. Molleur

VP and Chief Financial Officer: Richard B. Waugh, Jr.

year, Grumman went public and won a contract for 27 F3F-3s, the last of its biplane fighters. In 1941 it delivered its final non-military aircraft, a G-44 Widgeon. The following year it began to focus on building carrier aircraft for the U.S. and the Royal navies. Sales in 1942 reached $143 million, but began to fall in the following years. In 1945, although it had produced over 17,000 aircraft, the sudden termination of government contracts at the end of World War II resulted in a 27% drop in gross sales. In 1946 they plummeted to almost one-tenth of what they had been two years earlier.

By 1947, however, net income and profit margins rose substantially. It began expanding its facilities by purchasing most of the government's plants that had been built during the war. Grumman established the Aerobilt Bodies subsidiary in 1948 to continue the manufacture of aluminum truck bodies, a venture that it had begun in 1930. Sales of such non-aeronautical products as canoes and trucks remained low and constituted only about four percent of total sales.

Grumman accelerated the production of military aircraft following the onset of the Korean War, resulting in a 70% increase in gross sales. Net income in 1950 nearly doubled to $6.2 million. It increased its reliance on sub-contracting, with 50% of the volume in 1951 obtained from outside sources, including the Plymouth Division of the Chrysler Corp. By 1954, sales of the Aerobilt Bodies' subsidiary, the manufacturing arm for truck bodies for Chevrolet, Dodge, Ford, and GMC chassis, had increased from $850,000 to $2.5 million in five years.

In 1954 the F9F-9, the prototype of the first Grumman aircraft to reach supersonic speeds in level flight, made its first flight. Two years later Grumman began the initial development and design of a twin-propeller-turbine executive transport in order to lessen its dependency on its aeronautical activities for the Department of Defense. That year the company also acquired a 50% stake in Dynamic Developments, Inc. In 1958 it released its first corporate jet, the Gulfstream.

Grumman organized a Space Steering Group in 1958 to consolidate company efforts by participating in national programs for space exploration. Two years later it won its first major NASA contract for the design, development, and production of the unmanned Orbiting Astronomical Observatory.

In 1960 Grumman Boats merged with Pearson Boat Corp., a manufacturer of fiberglass power and sailing boats. Three years later Aerobilt Bodies and Pearson merged into a new subsidiary called Grumman Allied Industries. Gross sales that year reached $468 million. In 1963 it began work on the lunar module for the Apollo space mission.

Grumman entered the European market in 1965 through an agreement with Blohm und Voss for the construction of its 90-passenger *Dolphin*. The following year the first Grumman-built satellite, the Spacecraft A-1, was launched. Sales that year surpassed the $1 billion mark for the first time. In 1969 it changed its name to Grumman Corp. and won a contract to build 134 F-14 Tomcats. The costs involved in producing these planes were higher than anticipated, and by 1972 the company was nearly bankrupt. A $75 million loan from the Shah of Iran helped the company improve its financial position.

In 1973 the Grumman American Aviation Corp. was formed through a merger of the company's civil aircraft activities with those of American Aviation Corp., a general aviation manufacturer; this unit was sold in 1978. In 1976 Grumman came under scrutiny regarding the use of commissioned sales representatives and alleged payments to foreign officials. Despite the company's denial, the Securities Exchange Commission investigated and ruled that violation of the laws and regulations had occurred.

In 1978 it acquired the curiously named Flxible Co., a manufacturer of city and suburban buses from Rohr Industries. It also divested itself of Grumman American Aviation. Three years later it faced a hostile takeover attempt by LTV Corp., a steel, electronics, and aircraft conglomerate based in Texas. On the grounds that the takeover would reduce competition in the aerospace and defense industries, a U.S. Court of Appeals rejected LTV's bid.

In 1983 Grumman sold the troubled Flxible bus subsidiary when many of its buses developed cracks in their undercarriage components, prompting such customers as the City of New York to pull all of their Flxible buses out of service. Grumman filed a $500 million suit against Rohr, alleging that details of design flaws were not revealed prior to the sale. The suit was later dismissed in court.

The company sold the unprofitable Pearson Yacht product line in 1986. By 1991 Grumman's business with the U.S. government accounted for 89% of its sales. The following year Grumman and its former chairman of the board, John O'Brien, were targeted by federal prosecutors for criminal charges stemming from alleged illegal political contributions and unethical subcontracting. This $20 million settlement was put on hold in 1993, when NASA initiated investigation into the company for alleged overcharging. That year Grumman had $3 billion in sales and a workforce of 18,000.

Market Forces Driving the Acquisition

By the early 1990s, the U.S. defense industry was faced with the stark reality of a shrinking market. An end of the Cold War deflated the necessity of a large national defense budget, and it soon became apparent that there were too many contractors vying for a reduced number of contracts. Industry players had to make a decision—consolidate or exit.

For most of the large companies in the business, however, the federal government was their prime source of revenue. Northrop, for example, derived only about 10% of it revenue from the commercial airline sector. Worse, even that industry was experiencing a depression, with many contracts reduced, shelved, or canceled outright. To stay in business, therefore, the companies had to look to their peers to form partnerships.

The federal government itself began in 1994 to encourage consolidation within the defense industry. Under the Clinton Administration, an agreement was forged between the Pentagon and the antitrust officials at the Department of Justice and the Federal Trade Commission to extend special consideration to proposed defense-related deals. This accord would allow the government, as its largest customer, to benefit from cost reductions in the defense industry as a result of mergers. Moreover, the issue of consumer protection, the motivating force behind governmental review of proposed mergers, didn't factor into defense, a largely non-commercial industry. Additionally, the matter of national security was of a level of importance unmatched by civilian enterprise.

Northrop had, for some time, been actively seeking a partner. It had been unsuccessful in its efforts to acquire the tactical-aircraft division of General Dynamics, the Federal Systems operations of International Business Machines, and the missiles operations of McDonnell Douglas. Northrop's strength—its B-2 stealth bomber—would be winding down in 1997, when the company was scheduled to deliver the last in its contract with the U.S. Air Force. Northrop had lined up substantial subcontracting work for the McDonnell Douglas F/A-18 Hornet, but

The Players

Northrop Chairman, President, and CEO: Kent Kresa. Kent Kresa is a New York City native who earned several degrees in aeronautics and astronautics: a B.S. in 1959, an M.S. in 1961, and an E.A.A. in 1966. He was involved in ballistic missile defense research and reentry technology at Massachusetts Institute of Technology (M.I.T.) from 1961 to 1968. After working with the Defense Advanced Research Projects Agency, Kresa joined Northrop Corp. in 1975 as a vice president of research and technology. From there he advanced through other executive positions, attaining the roles of company president in 1987, CEO in January 1990, and Chairman in September of that year.

Grumman Chairman and CEO: Renso L. Caporali. Renso Caporali is an aeronautical engineer and ex-Navy bomber pilot. He joined Grumman in 1959 and eventually moved up the company ladder. In 1990 he took the company's helm, replacing John O'Brien, who had pled guilty to a number of illegal activities. Caporali began steering Grumman in a positive direction by trimming company fat, moving into electronics, and expanding into the commercial sector. He took a position on the new company's board after Northrop's acquisition of Grumman. Tensions arising from the companies' integration were said to be the reasons behind his resignation in 1995. In April of that year, he became Raytheon Co.'s senior vice president of government and commercial marketing, a position from which he retired in April 1998.

this job wouldn't come close to filling the void from its B-2 contracts, which accounted for about half of its total revenues.

Grumman had long been a supplier of aircraft for the U.S. Navy, particularly of its F-14 Tomcat fighter. In 1993, however, the Navy declined to order any more F-14s, and Grumman withdrew from the fighter airframe business. It shifted its focus to airborne surveillance systems, defense electronics, and systems integration. It also held contracts with the Navy for the E-2C Hawkeye and with the Air Force for the Joint Surveillance Target Attack Radar Systems (JSTARS) project.

In seeking a merger with Grumman, Northrop was hoping to combine its stealth electronics capabilities with Grumman's electronic defense operations. It also would gain entry to the data processing and systems integration businesses, where Grumman already had experienced success. A combined company would double the respective size of each partner, becoming more of a contender for future government contracts. It would also increase its abilities to provide more extensive subcontracting services, especially if Northrop exercised its option to complete the acquisition of Vought Aircraft, a subcontractor in which Northrop held a 49% stake.

Meanwhile, Martin Marietta was the U.S. Department of Defense's 10th-largest prime contractor, as well as the nation's leading defense electronics contractor. Grumman's prowess in systems integration was particularly appealing to this company. An acquisition of Grumman would also enable Martin Marietta to reenter the airplane manufacturing business, from which it was exited in the 1960s.

Approach and Engagement

Grumman had been rebuffing Northrop's covert acquisition offers since 1993, claiming that it wasn't for sale. Northrop was persistent, however, and continued to initiate negotiations into the following year. On February 23, 1994, it submitted a $50 per share offer, valued at $1.73 billion in cash and stock. Unbeknownst to that company, rival suitor Martin Marietta had submitted a $55 per share offer just two days earlier. This offer, valued at $1.94 billion in cash, came to light on March 7, 1994, when Grumman announced its board's acceptance of the bid.

Kent Kresa, Northrop's chairman, took exception to this shocking turn of events. He wrote a letter to Grumman's chairman, Renso Caporali, expressing distress at what he perceived as a betrayal of the good-faith negotiations in which the two companies had been engaged. As reported in *Flight International*, Kresa wrote, "As early as February 16 your representative asked Martin Marietta, but not us, to submit their highest and best offer. We never received such a request. Never...were we advised that a decision had been made to sell Grumman."

Both Northrop's and Martin's bids were significantly higher than Grumman's trading value, which ranged from $30 to $43 per share. In an attempt to ensure that the purchase price wouldn't be pushed even higher, Norman Augustine, chairman of Martin Marietta, had installed two safeguards in his offer. First, the company insisted on an exclusive negotiation. Its offer would be withdrawn if Grumman were to open negotiations to other parties, thereby turning its acquisition into an auction. Second, it was agreed that Grumman would pay a $55 million penalty and up to $8.8 million in expenses if their deal was terminated.

Northrop wasn't to be deterred so easily, however. On March 10, just three days after Grumman's acceptance of Martin's bid, Northrop launched a hostile bid of $60 per share, or $2.04 billion. This bid was controversial for reasons other than its hostile nature. Northrop and Grumman had had a "standstill" agreement that prohibited Northrop from making unsolicited acquisition offers for Grumman until January 1996. Kresa believed that the $60 per share offer was not in violation of this agreement, since it was clear to Northrop that Grumman was openly seeking suitors.

Augustine disagreed with this interpretation. He was angered at having his offer topped, especially by a company that he considered to be out of the running due to that standstill agreement. According to *The Wall Street Journal*, he issued an ominous warning that Martin would respond to Northrop "in an appropriate manner at the appropriate time."

On March 18, Grumman shareholders filed suit against that company and Martin Marietta for allegedly misleading investors. The suit also called for the dissolution of their $55 million lock-up agreement, a pact that Northrop called "improper and illegal."

Now willing to consider Northrop as an acquirer, Grumman furnished that company with the same financial information that it had supplied to Martin Marietta. In a March 21 letter to Renso Caporali, Grumman's chairman, Augustine charged that the provision of non-public financial data to Northrop was in violation of those two companies' standstill agreement. Caporali disputed this claim two days later, responding that "Grumman has complied and continues to comply with the existing merger agreement between our companies," as reported in *Defense Daily*.

Grumman wanted to cut off what it foresaw as a protracted bidding war. It was already facing a shareholder suit for closing off negotiations to higher bids. It also wanted to avoid an expensive and lengthy period in limbo. So it announced that its future would be determined through a sealed-bid auction in which Martin and Northrop would each submit their best and final offer by 5:00 p.m. EST on March 31.

Northrop rejected the terms of this auction, insisting on an open procedure. According to *Defense Daily*, on March 30 Kresa wrote to Grumman that the arrangement was wholly unfair. "Northrop is now being asked to bid against a purely hypothetical price increase from Martin Marietta without knowledge of whether such an increase is in fact submitted," he wrote. "Grumman is proposing that Northrop bid against itself."

At the same time, his company upped its previous bid to $62 per share, or $2.17 billion, if Grumman abandoned its sealed-bid auction in favor of an open, 24-hour auction. Grumman would be under a deadline to accept this offer, however, as Northrop warned that the sweetened offer would expire at 2:00 p.m. on March 31, three hours before the auction deadline, at which time its $60 per share offer would remain in force. Grumman rejected the terms of this new offer, and held firm to the sealed-bid procedure.

After the auction's completion and the three-day weekend that followed, Grumman announced the winner. On April 4, 1994, its board unanimously accepted Northrop's offer. By April 15, Northrop had acquired 93.4% of Grumman's outstanding shares, and announced that it would immediately move to complete the acquisition. The cash deal would create a new company called Northrop Grumman Corp., which would be headed by Kresa. It would have revenues of $8.3 billion, profits of $220 million, and more than 40,000 employees.

Products and Services

Northrop Grumman was organized into three operational segments:

Integrated Systems & Aerostructures was a systems integration enterprise with capabilities to design, develop, produce, and support fully missionized airborne systems and subsystems. This sector was divided into four major business areas: Aerostructures, Air Combat Systems, Airborne Early Warning & Electronic Warfare Systems, and Airborne Ground Surveillance & Battle Management Systems. In 1998 this sector realized total revenues of just over $5 billion. Of that total, the U.S. government accounted for $3.8 billion and the Boeing Company accounted for $1.08 billion.

Electronic Sensors & Systems designed, developed, produced and supported advanced electronics products for government, industry, commercial, and personal use. It was comprised of four business areas: Aerospace Electronic Systems; Command, Control, Communications, Intelligence & Naval Systems; Defensive Electronic Systems; and miscellaneous operations consolidated as Other. Total revenues for this segment in 1998 were $2.9 billion, with the U.S. government as its largest customer, accounting for $2.01 billion of that total.

Logicon Inc. represented Northrop Grumman's third business sector, Information Technology. It provided advanced information technology systems and services to support national security, civil, and industrial needs. It was organized into three primary business areas: Government Information Technology, Technology Services, and Commercial Information

Technology. Logicon's revenues in 1998 were $1.7 billion, with the U.S. government accounting for $948 million of that amount.

Changes to the Industry

The $2.17 billion union of Northrop and Grumman was not the industry's last, nor largest, merger. Even as that deal was wrapping up, Paul Nisbet, an analyst with JSA Research, predicted a combination of mergers that would once again unite Northrop and Grumman with Martin Marietta. In an April 11, 1994, issue of *Electronic News (1991)*, he suggested that Martin and Lockheed might join forces and then acquire Northrop Grumman. As it turned out, this is exactly what happened—almost. Lockheed and Martin Marietta merged in 1995 to form Lockheed Martin Corp. In 1997 this company entered into a merger agreement with Northrop Grumman, yet terminated the deal the following year in the face of government opposition.

Meanwhile, consolidation in the defense industry was snowballing. Declining defense budgets had spurred the initial push to merge. As the number of industry players was reduced to fewer and larger companies, the remaining firms felt pressure to partner up in order to stay viable and to avoid being bought out themselves. Several large deals followed the formation of Northrop Grumman. Lockheed Martin purchased Loral Corp. in 1996. That year Boeing acquired Rockwell International's defense and aerospace business, and in 1997 it merged with McDonnell Douglas.

Review of the Outcome

Job redundancy as a result of the merger, combined with decreasing sales, prompted Northrop Grumman in September 1994 to announce that it would cut about 9,000 jobs, or 19% of its workforce, by the end of 1995.

Northrop Grumman continued to strengthen the electronics operations that had been held by Grumman prior to the merger. Late in 1994 it bought the remaining shares of Vought Aircraft Co. for $130 million. In 1996 it spent $2.9 billion to purchase the defense and electronics systems business of Westinghouse Electric Corp. In August 1997 it acquired Logicon Inc., a provider of computer systems for scientific and management information. In September 1998 this subsidiary acquired International Research Inc. for $55 million.

In July 1997 it entered into a merger agreement with Lockheed Martin Corp., but this agreement was scrapped a year later when the U.S. government filed suit to block the deal. As a result of the $186 million in the terminated merger-related charges, Northrop Grumman's 1998 net income was $214 million, down from $407 million in 1997. Sales also dipped, from $9.2 billion to $8.9 billion in the same time frame.

Research

Andrews, Walter. "Northrop Wins Bidding for Grumman," in *Electronic News (1991)*, 11 April 1994. Discusses Northrop's victory in the auction for Grumman.

Cole, Jeff. "Northrop Seeks Grumman in Hostile $2.04 Billion Bid," in *The Wall Street Journal*, 11 March 1994. Reports Northrop's and Martin Marietta's mutual accusations of unfairness in light of Northrop's hostile bid.

Deady, Tim. "If It Doesn't Get Grumman, What Will Northrop Do?" in *Los Angeles Business Journal*, 21 March 1994. Explains Northrop's hostile pursuit of Grumman.

"Grumman Gives Potential Buyers Until Thursday to Make Final Bid," in *Defense Daily*, 29 March 1994. Describes Grumman's desire for a quick end to the acquisition saga.

Harris, Roy J., Jr. "Northrop Offers to Sweeten Bid for Grumman," in *The Wall Street Journal*, 31 March 1994. Reports the terms of Northrop's $62 per share bid.

Hord, Christopher. "Northrop, Martin Marietta in Grumman Tug-of-War," in *LI Business News*, 21 March 1994. Discusses the rival bids for Grumman.

"Northrop Calls Grumman's Deadline Unfair," in *Defense Daily*, 30 March 1994. Northrop responds to Grumman's imposition of the sealed-bid auction procedure.

"Northrop Grumman Corp.," in *Notable Corporate Chronologies*, The Gale Group, 1999. Profiles the history of both Northrop and Grumman, and describes major events since the consolidated company's formation.

Northrop Grumman Corp. Home Page, available at http://www.northgrum.com. Official World Wide Web Page for Northrop Grumman. Includes product description, annual reports and other financial information, and news releases.

"Northrop Grumman Cuts Jobs as Sales Fall," in *Flight International*, 28 September 1994. Reports the post-merger job reduction.

"Northrop Says It Received 93.4% of Grumman Shares," in *The Wall Street Journal*, 18 April 1994. Announces Northrop's acquisition of the majority of Grumman's stock.

"Northrop's Bid to Buy Grumman is Illegal," *Defense Daily*, 25 March 1994. Martin Marietta charges Northrop and Grumman with violation of their standstill agreement.

Ricks, Thomas E. "Antitrust Pact Aims to Support Defense Mergers," in *The Wall Street Journal*, 12 April 1994. Describes the government's arrangement to support consolidation in the defense industry.

"US Giants Clash over Control of Grumman," in *Flight International*, 16 March 1994. Northrop launches its hostile bid for Grumman.

Wasserstein, Bruce. *Big Deal: The Battle for Control of America's Leading Corporations*, Warner Books, 1998. Provides insight into the defense industry consolidation wave.

DEBORAH J. UNTENER

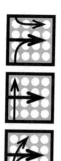

NORTHWEST AIRLINES & REPUBLIC AIRLINES

nationality: USA
date: October 1986
affected: Northwest Airlines Corp., USA, founded 1926
affected: Republic Airlines, USA

Northwest Airlines Corp.
5101 Northwest Dr.
St. Paul, MN 55121-3034
USA

tel: (612)726-2111
fax: (612)727-7795
web: http://www.nwa.com

Overview of the Merger

The $884 million joining of Northwest Airlines and Republic Airlines created the third-largest airline company in the U.S., just behind United Airlines and American Airlines. The deal nearly doubled Northwest's domestic operations and was approved by the Department of Transportation in August of 1986. Spawned from industry deregulation and consolidation, the merger was the largest in airline history at the time.

History of Northwest Airlines Corp.

In 1926, a group of Minnesota and Michigan investors led by Colonel Louis Britton established Northwest Airways (NA) as a Michigan-based company headquartered at Wold-Chamberlain Field, the Minneapolis/St. Paul area. A series of crashes forced Ford Motor Co. to sell its Ford Transport Co. subsidiary to NA, and the company established its first air mail route between Chicago, Illinois, and the Twin Cities of Minnesota. That year, NA introduced the nation's first closed-cabin commercial aircraft, capable of carrying three passengers, and, in 1927, the company carried its first ticketed passenger, from Minneapolis/St. Paul to Chicago.

The newly formed company expanded and, in 1928, began weekly service linking the Twin Cities and Winnipeg, Manitoba, Canada. Its service also included routes to Montana, Iowa, the Dakotas, and Seattle and Tacoma, Washington. In July 1930, a consortium of Twin Cities investors purchased NA, erected the company's first ground radio installation, and moved the company headquarters to the downtown St. Paul airport. Four years later, NA reincorporated as Northwest Airlines, Inc. (NAI), a Minnesota-based company.

In 1934, the U.S. government temporarily suspended all airmail contracts, but NAI survived with its passenger and freight operations and began to use all-weather aircraft for the first time. NAI continued to grow under the leadership of Croil Hunter, the company's first president, and pilots began making expeditions to Alaska, seeking a practical northern air route to east Asia. In 1938, NAI introduced the first practical oxygen mask for high-altitude flight, and one year later, employed its first stewardesses. NAI offered its common stock for public sale in 1941.

The Business

Financials

Revenue (1998): $9 billion

Employees (1998): 50,600

SICs / NAICS

sic 4512 - Air Transportation-Scheduled

naics 481111 - Scheduled Passenger Air Transportation

naics 481112 - Scheduled Freight Air Transportation

NAI was chosen to operate military air supply routes in Alaska and the Aleutian Islands, and company pilots were used to ferry aircraft within the U.S. during World War II. Many of the airlines domestic routes were suspended for the duration of the war. NAI's revenues from passengers exceeded those from mail for the first time and despite the loss of many of its routes, NAI benefitted from the war as government contracts enabled the airline to improve its aircraft and support facilities.

After the war, NAI focused on growth. The company began service linking the Twin Cities to New York City, as well as New Jersey. NAI also offered routes to Anchorage, Alaska, from Seattle. In 1947, the company sought out international options. It introduced service to the Far East, flying to Tokyo, Japan; Seoul, Korea; Shanghai, China; and Manila, The Philippines. One year later, NAI replaced its fleet of DC-3 aircraft with Martin 202 airliners and Boeing 377 Stratocruisers. The Martin 202 soon developed a reputation for malfunctioning, however, and NAI purchased DC-4s instead.

NAI continued to be an innovative airline and in 1949, became the first to offer transcontinental all-coach flights. The company was also the first airline to offer beverage service on its flights. In the early 1950s, NAI included Taiwan and Hong Kong in its service routes. With Donald W. Nyrop in control of the company, he demanded that the company's debt never exceed 10% of its capital. NAI ranked as a leader among debt-free companies in the airline industry as a result.

In 1957, NAI introduced first class service, as well as pioneering effective air turbulence prediction. The company began using DC-8 jet aircraft on its Far East routes and replaced its older aircraft with Boeing 707 and 727 models. The airline also instituted the indus-

try's first jet noise abatement procedures and originated the location and forecasting of wind shears. In 1963, NAI decommissioned its last propeller-driven aircraft, and became the nation's first all-jet fleet. One year later, it received the "Flight Safety Foundation Safety Award," for its wind turbulence research, and also received a Presidential Award for its development of export markets in the Orient.

By 1968, NAI was highly successful and posted the highest net profit in the U.S. airline industry. The company launched service to Honolulu, Hawaii, and was the first airline to use Boeing 747 aircraft on its trans-Pacific routes. In 1971, the company was once again recognized when it was honored for its noise abatement activities by the National Organization to Ensure a Sound-Controlled Environment.

During the 1970s, NAI introduced the industry's first computer-generated ticketing system and first direct computer reservation service. The firm was also the first to be approved by the Federal Aviation Administration (FAA) to conduct its own coordinated flight crew training. In 1979, NAI extended its service to Europe, starting all-cargo service to Glasgow, Scotland. The company also inaugurated all-cargo service to Copenhagen, Denmark and expanded its new European service to include passenger flights to Stockholm, Sweden, and Copenhagen.

In 1980, NAI added routes to Shannon, Ireland; Oslo, Norway; and Hamburg, Germany. Two years later it added Kansas City, Missouri; Wichita, Kansas; and Dallas/Ft. Worth, Texas, to its domestic network. In 1984, the company underwent a restructuring, forming NWA, Inc. as a holding company to manage all corporate operations. That year the company developed Northwest Airlink, a major marketing program involving mutual feeder agreements with small and local airline companies, signing the first such pact with Mesaba Airlines.

The company continued to fare well under the leadership of Steven Rothmeier. Northwest instituted service to Kuala Lumpur, Malaysia, and signed an airlink agreement with America West Airlines. The airline also acquired Mainline Travel, Inc., a Minnetonka, Minnesota-based tour operator. NWA continued to expand its fleet and announced the largest purchase of aircraft in its history, a $2 billion contract for ten Boeing 747-400s, ten Boeing 757s, and three Boeing 747-200s. In 1986, the company formed the Northwest Aerospace Training Corp. That year, NWA also acquired Republic Airlines for $884 million.

Despite the success of the company, contract negotiations with the airline's pilots broke down, and the pilots began working without a contract in 1986.

Analysts speculated that the company had grown too fast with its Republic purchase and could not handle expanded service routes and additional employees. The company was growing increasingly negative in the consumer eye due to several public relations disasters in 1987.

During these setbacks, entrepreneur Marvin Davis made an unsolicited bid to purchase NWA for $90 per share in 1989. At roughly the same time, Pan American Airlines indicated its interest in acquiring all NWA common stock. Their plans were thwarted, however, when Wings Holdings, a corporation organized by KLM Royal Dutch Airlines and Marriott executive Alfred A. Checchi, purchased NWA for $121 per share. Checchi became chairman of NWA, and Frederic V. Malek was named the company's new president. Under the new leadership, the company acquired a 25% interest in Hawaiian Airlines (HA) and entered into a variety of cooperative programs with the airline, including the transfer of HA's Australia routes to NWA. Checchi also implemented a new program to get the company back in the good graces of its customers. He focused on training employees to better serve customers and created a five-year plan to reorganize. Despite the positive changes, NWA reported a $10.4 million net loss for the year, due to increased fuel prices caused by the Iraqi invasion of Kuwait.

Northwest was still experiencing financial problems in 1991. The company contemplated acquiring Midway Airlines, but eventually purchased its facilities at Midway Airport, Chicago, for $21 million. The company began reducing staff to cut costs, laying off 610 employees, including 110 pilots. NWA also sold 18 of its Midway Airport gates to Southwest Airlines for $15 million

By 1993, the company employed 45,000, and maintained hubs in Detroit; Minneapolis/St. Paul; Memphis, Tennessee; and Tokyo, Japan. It had expanded its domestic network to include Raleigh, Durham; Greenville, and Spartanburg, North Carolina; and Reno, Nevada. NWA was the world's fourth largest airline and the oldest U.S. airline operating under its original name. Through its cost cutting efforts, NWA experienced its largest earnings to date in 1997 of $536.1 million.

In 1998, the company paid $519 million in cash and stock to acquire 51% of Continental Airlines. Employees and airplanes were kept separate, but the companies merged their route networks, frequent flyer programs, and advertising. At the same time, negotiations with pilots failed, resulting in a costly, two-week strike. Afterwards, Northwest once again focus efforts on cutting fares and gaining back the customers it had lost.

The Officers

Chairman: Gary L. Wilson

President and CEO: John H. Dasburg

Exec. VP and Chief Operating Officer: Richard H. Anderson

Exec. VP, Marketing and Distribution: J. Timothy Griffin

Exec. VP, International, Sales, and Information Services: Philip C. Haan

Market Forces Driving the Merger

In 1985, United Airlines took over the Pacific routes of Pan American World Airways, threatening to bump Northwest from its leading position in the Pacific market. Northwest, wanting to remain competitive, began looking for a deal that would match United's acquired Pacific service. According to *The New York Times*, Steven Rothmeier had stated that "his airline would be forced to seek to acquire a major domestic airline if United Airlines was allowed to acquire the Pacific routes of Pan American World Airways." In the fall of 1985, the Transportation Department approved United's deal, forcing Rothmeier to seek out a domestic carrier. Northwest could then manipulate that carrier's planes and routes to bolster its Pacific presence.

Meanwhile, Republic Airlines was facing industry consolidation and knew that in order to remain part of the industry, it would have to seek a relationship with a larger company. Stephen Wolf stated in the same *The New York Times* article that "the competitive phenomenon we find ourselves in during the post-deregulation environment requires a carrier, for long term survival, to be of substantial size." The union of Northwest and Republic would suit both companies needs, as well as launch Northwest as the nation's third largest carrier.

Approach and Engagement

Board directors of both NWA, the holding company for Northwest, and Republic Airlines met in January of 1986 in Minneapolis to discuss merger plans. Both companies approved Northwest's bid of $17 per share for Republic and announced the deal in late January. Rothmeier stated in a *The New York Times* article that "bringing together two of the country's medium sized airlines with differing, but complementary, fleets and routes into a single unit will create the economic mass necessary to provide competitive service in this highly competitive industry." He went on to say that joining "together with Northwest's extensive

The Players

President and CEO of Northwest Airlines Corp.: Steven G. Rothmeier. Notre Dame graduate Steven Rothmeier joined Northwest in 1973 after serving as an officer in the U.S. army in Vietnam. In 1978, he was promoted to vice president of finance and chief financial officer. At age 32, he was the youngest CFO in airline history. Rothmeier continued working his way up the ranks and, in 1983, he was elected president and chief operating officer of Northwest. Two years later, he was named president and CEO of NWA and its principal subsidiary, Northwest Airlines. In 1986, he was also elected chairman of the two. Rothmeier left the airline industry in 1989 to join the investment market, where he created Great Northern Capital.

President and CEO of Republic Airlines: Stephen M. Wolf. Stephen Wolf joined American Airlines in 1966. He earned a reputation for turning around troubled airline companies, joining Pan American World Airways in 1981, Continental Airlines in 1982, and Republic in 1984. He was named president and CEO of the faltering company and is credited with saving Republic from bankruptcy. He left the company in 1986, after the deal with NWA.

international operations will result in employment and career opportunities of Republic people beyond those that could be expected if Republic continued on its own." The largest deal in aviation history at the time was completed in October of 1986 after being cleared by the Department of Transportation.

Products and Services

After the merger, Northwest owned 298 aircraft and employed more than 30,000 people. Its service routes included over 100 cities in the U.S., four in Canada, two in Mexico, eight in Europe, and eleven in Asia. In 1998, Northwest had partnerships with KLM Royal Dutch Airlines and Alaska Airlines and served over 400 cities in over 80 countries.

Domestic operations accounted for $6.09 billion in sales, 67% of total revenues. Operations in the Pacific brought in 23% of sales, and the Atlantic region was responsible for the remaining 10%. The company offered passenger services as well as cargo services, owned 296 planes, and leased 113 aircraft. The company's subsidiaries included MLT Inc., a travel and tour

service, Northwest Aerospace Training Corp., and Northwest PARS, Inc.

Changes to the Industry

After the Northwest/Republic deal, many analysts felt that carriers would jump on the consolidation bandwagon as Northwest did. The Airline Deregulation Act of 1978 had caused a major stir in the industry when carriers were allowed to decide where they would fly and how much they would charge. The number of airlines in the U.S. went from 36 in 1978 to 124 in 1984. Consolidation and bankruptcies lowered that number to 74 in 1988.

The merger between Northwest and Republic came on the heels of the consolidation trend as companies were trying to strengthen their position in the market in anticipation of a globalization in the industry. Trans World Airlines teamed up with Ozark and Texas Air bought Eastern Airlines. In 1988, Scandinavian Airline Systems purchased a stake in Texas Air Corp., American Airlines teamed up with Japan Airlines, and Qantas Airlines of Australia bought a stake in Air New Zealand.

At the same time, responsibility for overseeing airline industry mergers was changing hands. On January 1, 1989, the Justice Department took over authority in approving such mergers. In the ten years since the deregulation, the Department of Transportation had overseen 21 mergers, approving them all. In that time, ten large airlines had gained control of 93% of the market. The Justice Department had opposed two—Northwest-Republic and TWA/Ozark—but the Department of Transportation went ahead with their approval.

Review of the Outcome

Upon completion of the deal with Republic, Northwest was positioned as the number three carrier in the nation. The $884 million deal was the largest merger in airline history at the time, and Northwest stood just behind United and American Airlines in terms of revenue based on passenger miles. In October of 1986, Republic's flight schedules were integrated into Northwest's operations. The company gained over 16,000 employees and became the dominant hub in Detroit, Minneapolis-St.Paul, and Memphis. Northwest also gained routes to Toronto, Nashville, New Orleans, Grand Cayman, Greenville/Spartanburg, Baltimore, Green Bay, Houston, Cincinnati, and Birmingham.

Northwest had trouble adapting to its new size and despite a 33.9% increase in net earnings in 1987—up from $76.9 million in 1986 to $103 million in 1987—

the company began experiencing problems relating to the merger. Delays and passenger complaints happened on a daily basis, and employee morale sank as union workers threatened to strike. Republic employees were paid less than Northwest counterparts causing friction within the company. In addition, flights were canceled, baggage was lost, and the company had earned the nickname "Northworst" in the media. To top it off, the airline experienced disaster in 1987 when two separate plane crashes led to the deaths of 165 people and three of its pilots were convicted of flying while intoxicated.

In 1989, a group of executives led by Alfred Checci purchased the ailing company. They formed a $422 million, 5-year program to bring Northwest back on its feet. Part of the new program included refurbishing planes and empowering employees to handle customer complaints. By 1990, Northwest's tarnished image was slowly being forgotten. The company recorded an increase in revenue from $6.57 billion in 1989 to $7.4 billion in 1990, although net income was a negative $361 million.

Research

"After 10 Years, Jury Still Out on Deregulation," in *Los Angeles Times*, 24 October 1988. Discusses the major changes the airline industry went through after the deregulation.

Hamilton, Martha. "Airline Mergers to Land on Other Desks," in *The Washington Post*, 22 December 1988. Discusses the change in authority over approving airline mergers to the Department of Justice.

———. "DOT Approves Airline Merger," in *The Washington Post*, 1 August 1986. Explains the Department of Transportation's approval of the merger with Northwest and Republic.

Marshall, Steve. "After Woes, Northwest Started Rebound," in *USA Today*, 4 December 1990. Explains Northwest's turn-around and new management plan.

"Northwest Airlines Corp.," in *Notable Corporate Chronologies*, The Gale Group, 1999. Lists major events in the history of Northwest Airlines Corp.

Northwest Airlines Corp. Home Page, available at http://www.nwa.com. Official World Wide Web Home Page for Northwest Airlines Corp. Includes historical, financial, and product information, as well as recent news articles.

Salpukas, Agis. "Airline Mergers Expected to Grow," in *The New York Times*, 25 January 1986. Discusses industry speculation that the Northwest deal will spark a wave of mergers.

———. "Northwest to Buy Republic," in *The New York Times*, 24 January 1986. Details the merger between Northwest and Republic.

CHRISTINA M. STANSELL

NOVELL & LOTUS

Novell, Inc.
122 E. 1700 S.
Provo, UT 84606
USA

tel: (801)861-7000
fax: (801)228-7077
web: http://www.novell.com

Lotus Development Corp.
55 Cambridge Pkwy.
Cambridge, MA 02142
USA

tel: (617)577-8500
web: http://www.lotus.com

date: May 19, 1990 (canceled)
affected: Novell, Inc., USA, founded 1980
affected: Lotus Development Corp., USA, founded 1982

Overview of the Merger

The 1990 merger deal between Lotus Development and Novell was designed to create a force capable of challenging their mutual enemy—Microsoft Corp. Unfortunately, their union never came to fruition, as Novell's chairman, Ray Noorda, set last-minute conditions that Lotus' chairman, Jim Manzi, wouldn't accept.

History of Novell, Inc.

Novell Data Systems Inc. was founded in 1980 to manufacture personal computers. Most of its venture capital was spent in research and development, leaving little money for marketing. The following year investment firm Safeguard Scientifics purchased a 51% interest in Novell, providing the start-up with additional capital, yet it still experienced financial difficulties as well as internal turmoil, as it had gone through eight presidents since its formation.

Novell was on the brink of collapse in 1982. Unable to afford a booth at the computer industry's Comdex trade show, the company exhibited its products in a hotel room. Raymond Noorda, a turnaround specialist and electronics engineer, invested $125,000 of his own money and borrowed $1.3 million from investors to gain a 33% stake in the company and become its ninth president. He decided that the company's most valuable product was an operating system that enabled personal computers to share peripherals such as printers and disk drives on a local area network (LAN).

In 1983 the company, now named Novell, Inc., released Btrieve, the first multi-user database application for LANs, and a software package for computers implementing UNIX, an operating system used primarily for math-intensive applications. It then introduced its first software designed to analyze Ethernet networks.

Novell made its first acquisition in 1985, by purchasing Microsource, Inc., a distribution company. That year Novell became the first independent network company to support Microsoft's new DOS 3.1 operating system. It also released a product that permitted the use of Apple computers on Ethernet networks.

Safeguard began selling off its stake in Novell, and the company went public.

To meet its goal of offering complete network systems rather than merely software, Novell acquired Santa Clara Systems Inc. and CXI in 1987. Net income in the following year reached $35.9 million on revenues surpassing $347 million.

The company made its greatest leap forward when it introduced NetWare 386 in 1989. Earlier versions worked only with IBM compatible hardware, while the 386 could serve IBM, UNIX, and Macintosh computers simultaneously. Novell solidified its move from hardware to software with its purchase of Excelan, a specialist in networking software.

In 1990 Novell formed a merger agreement with Lotus Development Corp., one of the largest PC software firms, but later backed out of the deal. Moving to limit Microsoft's power to set standards, IBM decided in 1991 to promote NetWare, boosting Novell's position. Later that year, Hewlett-Packard agreed to collaborate with Novell for the development of network technologies for its computers. Novell purchased Digital Research Inc, whose DR-DOS operating system, similar to Microsoft's MS-DOS, was expected to provide Novell with muscle to develop software for file servers. That operating system proved to be a disappointment, however.

In 1992 the firm signed a marketing and product development agreement that allowed the Lotus Notes networking software to be connected more closely with NetWare. Novell acquired UNIX System Laboratories from AT&T in June 1993. The company also introduced NetWare 4.0, a new version of the original system. By the end of that year, with $1.12 billion in revenues, Novell was the largest computer networking firm in the world, offering operating software and network management software, hardware, and services.

History of Lotus Development Corp.

In April 1982 Mitchell D. Kapor founded Lotus for the development of applications for the emerging personal computer market. The company, named for a Transcendental Meditation term, began operations with eight employees. The following year Kapor partnered with Jonathan Sachs to develop a spreadsheet that translated numbers into graphs. The team leveraged the newly introduced 256K memory on personal computers to develop this program, Lotus 1-2-3, into a fast recalculator. Released on January 26, the spreadsheet surpassed the company's VisiCalc to become the best selling software package. Also that year the company went public, raising a total of $41 million. By the

The Business

Financials - Novell, Inc.

Revenue (1998): $1.08 billion

Employees (1998): 4,500

Financials - Lotus Development Corp.

Revenue (1998): $1.4 billion

Employees (1998): 6,542

SICs / NAICS

sic 7372 - Prepackaged Software

naics 511210 - Software Publishers

end of its first full year of business, Lotus ranked as the second-leading software company, with sales of $53 million and a staff of 300.

In 1984 Kapor became chairman, and Jim P. Manzi was named president. Because Lotus' success was strongly tied to 1-2-3, the company had difficulty matching new products in the market. It began to invest in software start-ups and the creation of new programs, including Symphony, an integrated software package that added word processing, a sophisticated data-management system, and an ability to network other computers to 1-2-3.

Lotus pursued diversifying its product base in 1985 through acquisitions, including Software Arts. The company paid off its $2.2 million debt, which had accumulated after its spreadsheet program. VisiCalc lost market share to 1-2-3. That year the firm also reached an agreement with Apple Computer to develop the Jazz spreadsheet program, intended to attract introductory level users. However, Lotus programmers had difficulty writing Macintosh compatible codes, and even after the bugs were worked out, consumers were not satisfied with the program.

Kapor entered into merger discussions in 1986 with Microsoft's chairman, William Gates, but these discussions fell apart. He then resigned to pursue other projects, leaving Manzi to head the company. Lotus continued to build on 1-2-3's success, selling 750,000 copies, about three times as many copies as its nearest competitor, Microsoft's Multiplan. It also released improved versions of 1-2-3 to compete with Microsoft's Excel, created for the Macintosh market just as 1-2-3 had been created for the IBM market. That year Lotus introduced Graphwriter, a business graph-

The Officers

Novell, Inc.

Chairman and CEO: Dr. Eric Schmidt

Sr. VP and Chief Information Officer: Sheri Anderson

Sr. VP and General Counsel: David Bradford

Sr. VP, Human Resources: Jennifer Konecny-Costa

Sr. VP and Chief Financial Officer: Dennis Raney

Lotus Development Corp.

President and CEO: Jeffery P. Papows

Exec. VP, Strategy: Michael D. Zisman

Sr. VP, Finance and CFO: Karen Fukama

Chief Technology Officer: Nick Shelness

VP, Human Resources: Jeffrey Yanagi

ics tool. It also acquired Human Access Language (HAL) technology, which allowed for natural language commands on its 1-2-3 program.

A merger deal struck with the president of Ashton-Tate Co. was terminated in 1987 by that company's board. That year Lotus introduced the forerunner of Notes, Lotus Express, a stand-alone communication program. The following summer it released Manuscript, a processor for technology professionals, as well as Agenda, the company's first personal information manager. Delays in delivering an upgraded version of 1-2-3 damaged the company's reputation, which took a beating from the press.

Lotus 1-2-3 Version 3 was released in 1989, as were 26 additional programs, including long-promised spreadsheets for mainframes, minicomputers, and workstations. Among those programs was the first version of Notes, a LAN-based communications product, and Magellan, a utility software program. The company invested in Sybase Inc., a database firm, and Rational Systems Inc., a manager of programming software. Due to bitter rivalry between Lotus and Microsoft, Lotus refused to develop products for Microsoft's Windows graphic interface program, thereby missing out on the benefits from the rapidly growing market. Lotus' income rose to $68 million that year.

In 1990 Lotus entered into, and then terminated, a merger agreement with Novell Inc. That year the company finally gave into the success of Windows and began to develop programs within that framework. This project was delayed, however, as Lotus invested

in a new operating system known as OS/2, which proved to be a commercial failure. Also in 1990 Lotus acquired Alpha Software, thereby gaining the AlphaWorks program that led to the development of the LotusWorks suite. Lotus ranked third in the word processing market behind Microsoft and the WordPerfect Corp. Its profit reached $23.3 million on annual sales of $692.2 million.

Lotus acquired cc:Mail, Inc., whose namesake product permitted the exchange of data across all major platforms. Also in 1991 it released the Macintosh version of 1-2-3, as well as the Freelance Graphics program for Windows, OS/2, and DOS. Minor bugs in its most recent version of 1-2-3 resulted in the sale of only about 250,000 copies of the program for 1991, and Lotus was forced to lay off 400 employees, or 10% of its workforce.

In 1992 the company unveiled SmartSuite, a collection that included 1-2-3, Freelance Graphic, and cc:Mail. Although revenue for the year was $900 million, the firm's inability to capture more than 30% of the Windows market damaged its earnings and growth. In 1993 Lotus introduced Ami Pro, a general purpose word and document processor.

Lotus abandoned the Macintosh software market in 1994. Its discontinuation of both Agenda and Improv signaled a trend in the software industry toward more mainstream, less unique products. The next year, the company cut costs, reduced staff, and reorganized product groups. That year IBM Corp. purchased Lotus in a friendly takeover worth $3.5 billion. Jim Manzi resigned soon after, citing differences in opinion over the company's strategy. Michael D. Zisman and Jeffrey Papows were appointed as co-presidents to replace Manzi.

In 1998 Lotus purchased DataBeam and Ubique Ltd. The following year the number of its Notes' customers increased to 34 million, up from only four million before its acquisition by IBM.

Market Forces Driving the Merger

By 1990 both Lotus Development and Novell were regarded by the software industry as one-product companies. Those flagship products, however, dominated their respective markets. Lotus' 1-2-3 program was the leading spreadsheet program, while Novell's NetWare networking program was the favorite among small- and mid-sized corporate clients. By merging, these companies were hoping to combine their technology, talent, client lists, and distribution channels to increase and improve their product lineup.

Lotus was eager to increase its presence in the network arena, which it believed to be the future of the computer software industry. It had only recently expanded into this area with the December 1989 release of Notes, a LAN-based group communication product. For Novell's part, it was hoping that the clout of the Lotus name would persuade software producers to develop programs for Novell's standard rather than Microsoft's.

Aside from these rather vague reasons for joining together (the companies wouldn't elaborate further), analysts were left scratching their heads over the proposed union. The only truly compelling reason, many believed, would be to become a greater rival to Microsoft Corp. Lotus' $559 million in revenues in 1989 would combine with Novell's $422 million to surpass Microsoft's $803 million that year. Yet even this competitive reason made analysts skeptical.

As pointed out by *The Economist*, any supposed synergies of operation, as well as the challenge to Microsoft, could just as easily be achieved through a strategic alliance—perhaps even more easily. Mergers between software companies were typically risky undertakings, as the most valuable resource, the programmers, were apt to leave if they grew disenchanted with management. This was especially true with a divergent meeting of cultures, as with a Lotus/Novel merger. Lotus was a suit-and-tie, MBA-type operation, while Novell was largely comprised of t-shirt and jeans employees. At a loss to understand the rationale, *InfoWorld*'s John Gantry took a humble view: "Since neither company is coming to the other with hat in hand, both companies must see benefits those of us on the outside world don't necessarily see."

Approach and Engagement

Ray Noorda, Novell's chairman, approached Lotus Development in mid-March 1990 to try to recruit W. Frank King III, the senior vice president credited with revitalizing Lotus. When Noorda failed to persuade Lotus to release King, he instead proposed a merger.

On April 6, 1990, Lotus and Novell announced their $1.5 billion merger agreement. The plan called for an exchange of stock whereby Lotus would issue 1.9131 shares for each share of Novell. The new company would retain the Lotus Development Corp. name and Novell would become its subsidiary. Jim Manzi, Lotus' chairman, president, and CEO, would retain those positions, while Noorda would continue as chairman of Novell while taking on the additional post of vice chairman of Lotus. The seven-member board would be comprised of four Lotus directors and three Novell seats.

The Players

Novell Chairman and CEO: Raymond J. Noorda. Raymond Noorda was known to his employees at Novell as "Uncle Ray"; he is known to the industry as the visionary who realized the value of networked computers to business organization. Although he didn't invent the local-area network (LAN), he created a market for it and propelled Novell to the forefront of that market. After joining the Navy during World War II, he earned an engineering degree from the University of Utah. Noorda worked at General Electric before resigning in 1970 to establish a management consulting business that specialized in revitalizing troubled companies. In 1982 he purchased a majority interest in Novell and remained at its helm until his resignation in 1994, just two months after the company acquired WordPerfect.

Lotus Chairman and CEO: Jim P. Manzi. Jim Manzi traded his career as a journalist for a master's degree in economics from Tufts University. After working as a management consultant for McKinsey & Co., he took a job with Lotus in 1983 as a marketing director. He became the company's president in 1984 and chairman two years later. In 1995, just 99 days after Lotus was sold to IBM, Manzi resigned due to clashes with the new parent company over the direction of its software strategy. He went on to become chairman of Nets Inc., a business-to-business Internet marketing service.

Investors clearly disliked the deal. On the day of the announcement, Novell's stock dropped $4 per share and Lotus' slipped $2 per share. Within days, two Novell shareholders filed a class action lawsuit against Novell, claiming breach of fiduciary duties. To them the deal, which offered no premium to Novell shareholders, was tantamount to a buyout rather than a merger of equals, as claimed by the principals. Company executives said that they had been expecting a shareholder suit, but not this quickly.

Still, the deal progressed. On May 16 Lotus and Novell revised their terms to grant Novell more of a management voice. Noorda was to become chairman of the newly renamed Lotus/Novell Corp. Lotus directors approved the deal the following day. On May 18 Novell's board suddenly demanded an additional seat on the board, presumably to placate angry investors. Manzi was stunned, as he claimed to have made clear from the start his resistance to any make-up of the board that would be conducive to frequent deadlocks. Moreover, he said, this matter had never been at issue during the prior months of negotiations. At an impasse, the companies declared their agreement at an end on May 19, 1990.

Products and Services

Novell developed and sold directory services software and network server platforms, and distributed network applications software. In 1998, its products were organized into several segments: Network Operating Systems, which was comprised of its NetWare solutions; Advanced Network Services, which included Novell Replication Services and SFT III for NetWare; Network Clients, composed of Novell Client products; Internet Services, including BorderManager and GroupWise; Network-to-Network Connectivity, which included NetWare Connect; Host Connectivity and TCP/IP and UNIX Connectivity, both of which contained NetWare and intraNetWare products; Directory Services, consisting primarily of NDS solutions; Border Services, comprised of several BorderManager products; E-mail, Calendaring, Scheduling, consisting of GroupWise and Netscape Messaging Server for NetWare; Network Groupware, which contained GroupWise and InForms products; Network Management (NetWare and Windows NT), which included ManageWise and Z.E.N.works; and Developer Tools, containing Novell Developer Kit and Novell AppNotes.

Lotus also produced a wide array of software products: 1-2-3, Approach, BeanMachine, cc:Mail, Components, C++API, Domino Advanced Services, Domino Application Server R5, Domino Application Studio, Domino CAL, Domino.Doc, Domino Designer R5, Domino Enterprise Server R5, Domino Extended Search, Domino Family of Servers R5, Domino Global WorkBench, Domino Instant! Host, Domino Intranet Starter Pack, Domino Mail Server R5, Domino Media Connection Services, Domino Translation Object, Domino.Merchant Server Pack, Domino Tools Zone, Domino Workflow, EasySync for Notes & Organizer, Enterprise Integrator, eSuite, Fax for Domino, FastSite, Freelance Graphics, Instant!TEAMROOM, Intranet products, JDBC Driver, LearningSpace, LN:DI (Lotus Notes: Document Imaging), Lotus Pager Gateway, LotusScript, LotusScript Data Object, LSX Toolkit, Messaging, Migration, Mobile & Wireless Products, MQ Series & CICS Connections, NetObjects Fusion, NetObjects ScriptBuilder, Notes R5, Notes C API, Notes Designer for Domino, Notes MTAs, Notes Reporter, NotesSQL, Notes WAN drivers, Organizer,

QuickPlace, R5 Home, Sametime, ScreenCam, SmartSuite, Soft-Switch products, StreamCam, Wireless Domino Access, and Word Pro.

Review of the Outcome

Ray Noorda appeared to believe that the two companies could renew their relationship and look forward to collaborations on projects in the future, while Jim Manzi obviously felt otherwise. "We're going to have to think twice about what that relationship is going to be," he said in *Business Week*. Novell's sudden change of heart also had implications for alliances beyond Lotus. Given its last-minute pullout of the Lotus deal, potential suitors would be likely to view negotiating with Novell as a risky venture.

Research

Gantz, John. "It's a Safe Bet That Lotus, Novell Know What They're Doing," in *InfoWorld*, 16 April 1990. As analysts struggle to make sense of the merger plans, this column suggests that the rationale might not yet be apparent to observers.

Hammonds, Keith H., Sandra D. Atchison, and Evan Schwartz. "Lotus Isn't Wasting Time Weeping at the Altar," in *Business Week*, 4 June 1990. Describes the merger's formation and collapse, and the companies' return to their respective businesses. Includes a related article on the feud between Manzi and Bill Gates.

Keefe, Patricia, and Jim Nash. "Lotus/Novell Merger Aims at Microsoft," in *Computerworld*, 9 April 1990. Discusses the merger agreement and its almost immediate effect on the companies' stock prices.

"Lotus Development Corporation," in *International Directory of Company Histories*, Vol. 6, St. James Press: 1992. Provides a historical review of the company.

Lotus Development Corp. Home Page, available at http://www.lotus.com. Official World Wide Web Page for Lotus. Features a company history and product information.

"Lotus Eating," in *The Economist*, 14 April 1990. Offers the opinion that a marketing alliance between Lotus and Novell would be more effective against Microsoft than an outright merger.

Markoff, John. "Lotus Plans $1.5 Billion Novell Link," in *The New York Times*, 7 April 1990. Details the newly announced merger agreement.

Nash, Jim. "Miffed Lotus Wonders Why Novell's Condition Changed," in *Computerworld*, 28 May 1990. Reports Jim Manzi's reaction to Novell's sudden balk at merging.

"Novell, Inc.," in *Notable Corporate Chronologies*, The Gale Group, 1999. Profiles the history of the company.

Novell, Inc. Home Page, available at http://www.novell.com. Official World Wide Web Page for Novell. Includes product information, executive biographies, annual reports, and press releases.

Wilke, John R. "Lotus-Novell Plan for Merger is Called off," in *The Wall Street Journal*, 21 May 1990. Describes the collapse of the deal.

PATRICIA ARCHILLA

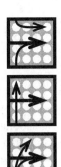

NOVELL & WORDPERFECT

nationality: USA
date: June 27, 1994
affected: Novell, Inc., USA, founded 1980
affected: WordPerfect Corp., USA, founded 1980

Novell Inc.
122 East 1700 South
Provo, UT 84606
USA

tel: (801)861-7000
fax: (801)228-7077
web: http://www.novell.com

Overview of the Acquisition

The 1994 acquisition of WordPerfect by Novell was the largest transaction in the history of the software industry. It created a $1.8 billion company that ranked third, behind Microsoft and Computer Associates. Despite such glimmering prospects, however, the union was considered a failure by industry analysts. This interpretation appeared to be confirmed by Novell, as well, when it sold the Microsoft business to Corel Corp. only a year and a half after acquiring it.

History of Novell Inc.

Novell Data Systems Inc. was founded in 1980 to manufacture personal computers. Most of its venture capital was spent in research and development, leaving little money for marketing. The following year investment firm Safeguard Scientifics purchased a 51% interest in Novell, providing the start-up with additional capital. Yet it still experienced financial difficulties as well as internal turmoil, as it had gone through eight presidents since its formation.

Novell was on the brink of collapse in 1982. Unable to afford a booth at the computer industry's Comdex trade show, the company exhibited its products in a hotel room. Raymond Noorda, a turnaround specialist and electronics engineer, invested $125,000 of his own money and borrowed $1.3 million from investors to gain a 33% stake in the company and become its ninth president. He decided that the company's most valuable product was an operating system that enabled personal computers to share peripherals such as printers and disk drives on a local area network (LAN).

In 1983 the company, now named Novell Inc., released Btrieve, the first multi-user database application for LANs, and a software package for computers implementing UNIX, an operating system used primarily for math-intensive applications. It then introduced its first software designed to analyze Ethernet networks.

Novell made its first acquisition in 1985, by purchasing Microsource, Inc., a distribution company. That year Novell became the first independent network company to support Microsoft's new DOS 3.1 operating system. It also released a

The Business

Financials
Revenue (1998): $1.08 billion

Employees (1998): 4,500

SICs / NAICS
sic 7372 - Prepackaged Software

naics 511210 - Software Publishers

product that permitted the use of Apple computers on Ethernet networks. Safeguard began selling off its stake in Novell, and the company went public.

To meet its goal of offering complete network systems rather than merely software, Novell acquired Santa Clara Systems Inc. and CXI in 1987. Net income in the following year reached $35.9 million on revenues surpassing $347 million.

The company made its greatest leap forward when it introduced NetWare 386 in 1989. Earlier versions worked only with IBM compatible hardware, while the 386 could serve IBM, UNIX, and Macintosh computers simultaneously. Novell solidified its move from hardware to software with its purchase of Excelan, a specialist in networking software.

In 1990 Novell formed a merger agreement with Lotus Development Corp., one of the largest PC software firms. With Lotus designated as the majority owner of the new company, Novell stockholders killed the deal out of the fear of becoming "junior partners."

Moving to limit Microsoft's power to set standards, IBM decided in 1991 to promote NetWare, boosting Novell's position. Later that year, Hewlett-Packard agreed to collaborate with Novell for the development of network technologies for its computers. Novell purchased Digital Research Inc, whose DR-DOS operating system, similar to Microsoft's MS-DOS, was expected to provide Novell with muscle to develop software for file servers. That operating system proved to be a disappointment, however.

In 1992 it signed a marketing and product development agreement that allowed the Lotus Notes networking software to be connected more closely with NetWare. Novell acquired UNIX System Laboratories from AT&T in June 1993. The company also introduced NetWare 4.0, a new version of the original system. By the end of that year, with $1.12 billion in revenues, Novell was the largest computer networking firm in the world, offering operating software and network management software, hardware, and services.

History of WordPerfect Corp.

In 1976 Bruce Bastian, the director of Brigham Young University's marching band, collaborated with the school's computer science professor, Alan Ashton, to design a computer program for the three-dimensional display of band formations. The pair again joined forces in 1979 to develop a word processor system for Data General Corp. They retained the rights to this program and launched their own company to market it.

Satellite Software International (SSI) was established in 1980, and initially relied on word-of-mouth advertising. The company's first release was WordPerfect 1.0, an innovation in word processing in that it kept distractive computer functions off of the computer screen. Once its initial growth was achieved, SSI began to expand. By 1981, with 16 employees, SSI began marketing internationally.

The explosion of the personal computer industry, set off by the new IBM PC, sparked competition in the word processing industry. In November 1982 SSI debuted its first version of WordPerfect for the IBM-compatible MS-DOS system. Revenues that year reached $1 million.

The WordStar program of MicroPro International was the leader of the word processing industry in 1983. SSI introduced a variety of successively enhanced programs to better compete, including WordPerfect 3.0 and Personal WordPerfect, designed for non-business applications. WordStar initiated its own downfall by releasing a version of its word processor that differed significantly from its flagship program. This mistake enabled WordPerfect to increase its market share, and by 1984 it was the number three word processing program. That year it diversified into other types of software, introducing Math Plan, a spreadsheet program. It also began designing programs for nearly every operating system available, including those compatible with Tandy, Apple, and such obscure platforms as Apriocot and DEC Rainbow.

By 1986 WordPerfect was the nation's best-selling word processing software, capturing a third of the market for IBM-compatible word processing software. SSI was propelled to the position of fifth-largest PC software company. That year, as it posted $52 million in revenues, SSI changed its name to WordPerfect Corp. to exploit the popularity of that product.

Microsoft Corp. altered the shape of the PC software industry with its 1990 release of the Windows operating system. That company also released compatible word processing software, Microsoft Word. More than a year later, WordPerfect released its own Windows-compatible program, but by then had lost valuable ground to Microsoft. Of the burgeoning Windows market for word processing software, Microsoft controlled more than half of the market while WordPerfect clung to only one-third.

In March 1992 WordPerfect adopted a seven-member executive committee and began speeding up programming developments and launching increased advertising efforts, including its first national television commercials. It also purchased Deltaware, bringing Adrian Rietveld into the organization. Later that year it released WordPerfect Works, an integrated software package. In 1993 it acquired Reference Software International and Soft Solutions Technology Corp. WordPerfect teamed up with the software developer Borland International Inc. to release its first package of Windows programs, which included WordPerfect's word processor and Borland's spreadsheet.

Competition with Microsoft remained fierce. WordPerfect filed suit to stop Microsoft from advertising that it had "the most popular word processor in the world," a claim disputed by WordPerfect. The firms agreed in an out-of-court settlement that WordPerfect could use the terms "most popular" and "all-time best selling," while Microsoft could call its Word program "best selling."

WordPerfect's 1993 revenues reached $707 million. Ashton stepped down as president and CEO in January 1994, and was succeeded by Adrian Rietveld; Ashton and Bastian continued as co-chairmen.

Market Forces Driving the Acquisition

The computer software industry had become a playground for Microsoft. That company had redefined the market with its revolutionary Windows operating system. Software companies found themselves in a reactionary position, as they were forced to design products to fit the Windows mold. WordPerfect had been slow to do this. Sixteen months after Microsoft's Word for Windows was introduced and began making significant gains in the word processor market, WordPerfect began shipping its first version of WordPerfect for Windows. Thereafter, WordPerfect focused on playing catch-up with Microsoft. It needed financial backing to fuel its continued competitiveness.

Novell, too, was facing stiff competition from Microsoft. Novell had built itself into a dominant force in networking, but watched Microsoft Office grab an increasing share of the corporate market. It needed to

The Officers

Chairman of the Board and CEO: Dr. Eric Schmidt

Sr. VP and Chief Information Officer: Sheri Anderson

Sr. VP and General Counsel: David Bradford

Sr. VP, Human Resources: Jennifer Konecny-Costa

Sr. VP and Chief Financial Officer: Dennis Raney

add to its software applications lineup in order to improve its office suite. The market for network applications was growing, and Raymond Noorda, Novell's president and CEO, believed that Novell was still a strong player. "The era of standalone personal computing is evolving into group collaboration that connects individuals, groups and companies," he said in *EDGE: Work-Group Computing Report*. "Novell's objective is to accelerate this market transition by offering new generations of network applications with the flexibility and freedom of open interfaces and published standards."

Approach and Engagement

Lotus Development had offered $700 million in stock to acquire WordPerfect. After learning of this offer, Novell entered into the bidding by offering to purchase 59 million shares of Novell stock, valued at $1.35 billion. Simultaneously, Novell announced its acquisition of the Quattro Pro spreadsheet business of Borland International for $145 million.

Novell's acquisition of WordPerfect was the largest in the history of the software industry. It would create a $1.8 billion company that ranked third, behind Microsoft and Computer Associates. Both WordPerfect and the Quattro Pro business would be the foundation of Novell's new business unit, the WordPerfect/Novell Applications Group. Adrian Rietveld, WordPerfect's CEO, would become president of this new unit.

Wall Street wasn't pleased with the deal. Novell's investors disapproved of the company's plans to diversify, and began unloading their stock. Novell's stock price plummeted from $24 to $15.25, thereby reducing the value of the deal to $855 million by the time the transaction was completed on June 27, 1994.

Products and Services

Novell developed and sold directory services software and network server platforms, and distributed network applications software. Its products were

The Players

Novell Chairman and CEO: Raymond J. Noorda. Raymond Noorda was known to his employees at Novell as "Uncle Ray"; he is known to the industry as the visionary who realized the value of networked computers to business organization. Although he didn't invent the local-area network (LAN), he created a market for it and propelled Novell to the forefront of that market. After joining the Navy during World War II, he earned an engineering degree from the University of Utah. Noorda worked at General Electric before resigning in 1970 to establish a management consulting business that specialized in revitalizing troubled companies. In 1982 he purchased a majority interest in Novell and remained at its helm until his resignation in 1994, just two months after the company acquired WordPerfect.

WordPerfect President and CEO: Adrian Rietveld. Adrian Rietveld, a native of Holland, moved to the U.S. in the early 1990s. He became part of WordPerfect in 1992 when that company purchased Deltaware, his software distribution company. Rietveld worked as an executive in WordPerfect's European office before becoming company president and CEO just prior to its acquisition by Novell. After the merger, he was selected to preside over the newly formed WordPerfect/Novell Applications Group. In March 1995 Rietveld resigned to return to Holland, where he hoped to serve as a consultant to U.S. software companies trying to get a foothold in the European market.

organized into several segments: Network Operating Systems, which was comprised of its NetWare solutions; Advanced Network Services, which included Novell Replication Services and SFT III for NetWare; Network Clients, composed of Novell Client products; Internet Services, including BorderManager and GroupWise; Network-to-Network Connectivity, which included NetWare Connect; Host Connectivity and TCP/IP and UNIX Connectivity, both of which contained NetWare and intraNetWare products; Directory Services, consisting primarily of NDS solutions; Border Services, comprised of several BorderManager products; E-mail, Calendaring, Scheduling, consisting of GroupWise and Netscape Messaging Server for NetWare; Network Groupware, which contained GroupWise and InForms products;

Network Management (NetWare and Windows NT), which included ManageWise and Z.E.N.works; and Developer Tools, containing Novell Developer Kit and Novell AppNotes.

Changes to the Industry

The day following the acquisition, Novell unveiled PerfectOffice 3.0 at an industry exposition. This product was an office suite that combined WordPerfect's word processor and Presentations graphics software with the Quattro Pro spreadsheet application and other Novell software. Reviewers praised PerfectOffice, claiming that it ranked with Microsoft Office, the market leader. As impressive as the Novell product appeared to be, however, it was meaningless if it wasn't introduced to the consumer. The market release of PerfectOffice had been delayed until that December, enabling Microsoft to increase it market share in the meantime. Added to this were delays in the release of NetWare 4.1, an improved version of the problematic 4.0 version, allowed Microsoft to aggressively market Windows NT, an operating system with networking capabilities. Consequently, Microsoft's market share for suites rose to 90% by mid-1995.

Internal problems within Novell and WordPerfect didn't help. WordPerfect products languished in the warehouse while the Novell sales force, less familiar with those products, neglected to push their sale. At the same time, WordPerfect's worldwide sales force was slashed, with some overseas offices eliminated altogether. The departure of Novell's chairman Raymond Noorda two months after the merger added to the company's difficulties. Moreover, WordPerfect once again missed the competitive boat by failing to have products ready for the release of Windows 95.

With its sales and market share eroding, Novell decided in October 1995 to cut its losses and unload WordPerfect in order to focus on its core networking business. Investors viewed this more as an admission that the previous year's acquisition was a mistake. WordPerfect customers worried that it might signal the eventual demise of the company, and were hesitant to invest in additional WordPerfect products.

Corel Corp., a leader in graphics and design software, purchased WordPerfect in January 1996 for $10.75 million in cash and $112.7 million in stock. Its chairman, Michael Cowpland, planned aggressive marketing and bundling of WordPerfect products, which still generated sales of $300 million per year. He also intended to release a Java version of WordPerfect, which could run on any operating system, not just Microsoft's.

Review of the Outcome

Novell's acquisition of WordPerfect doubled its sales force to about 10,100 and gave it entry into eight additional countries. In August 1994 it announced the reduction of 1,100 positions by that October, and the planned elimination of 650 more in January 1995.

Management underwent considerable shifts in the years following the merger. The first to depart was Novell's chairman Raymond Noorda, who was succeeded in August 1994 by Robert Frankenberg, president and CEO since April. March 1995 brought the resignation of Adrian Rietveld, former CEO of WordPerfect who was most recently the president of WordPerfect/Novell Applications Group; that June he was succeeded by Jeffrey Waxman. In November 1995, one of WordPerfect's founders, Bruce Bastian, resigned. In 1997 Frankenberg was succeeded as CEO by Eric Schmidt, as chairman by John Young, and as president by Joseph Marengi. Frankenberg's resignation in August 1996 was followed by that of WordPerfect's remaining founder, Alan Ashton, that December.

Novell sold WordPerfect and Quattro Pro to Corel Corp. in January 1996 for about $125 million—a loss of about $730 million. It followed up that divestiture with the sale of its Appware division as well as UNIX Systems Laboratories. The disposal enabled Novell to focus on providing Internet-ready products, a vision embraced by Schmidt.

In 1997 Novell reduced its workforce by 19%, or about 1,000 positions. It began to concentrate on new product development, particularly in the directory services arena. In 1998 it unveiled BorderManager, a version of NetWare for Internet and intranet applications, followed by Z.E.N.works, a version for remote management. Revenues increased slightly in 1998 to $1.08 billion, while net income jumped to $102 million from a loss of $78 million in the prior year. In 1999 it introduced Digital Me, a program that enabled users to control information from the Internet.

Research

"Acquisition: Novell to Acquire WordPerfect Corporation and Buy Borland's Quattro Pro Spreadsheet Business," in *EDGE: Work-Group Computing Report*, 28 March 1994. Details the merger agreement and the strengths that each company brought to the table.

Doyle, T.C. "School of Hard Knocks," in *VARbusiness*, 1 June 1996. Suggests the reasons that the merger was considered a failure.

Einstein, David. "The New Novell," in *Marketing Computers*, February 1995. Profiles Novell several months after its acquisition of WordPerfect.

"Merger: Novell Completes WordPerfect Corp. Merger," in *EDGE: Work-Group Computing Report*, 4 July 1994. Describes the completed merger transaction.

"Novell, Inc.," in *Notable Corporate Chronologies*, The Gale Group, 1999. Profiles the history of the company, up through and beyond its acquisition of WordPerfect.

Novell, Inc. Home Page, available at http://www.novell.com. Official World Wide Web Page for Novell. Includes product information, executive biographies, annual reports, and press releases.

"Of Spandex and Software," in *The Economist*, 12 October 1996. Reports Corel's acquisition of WordPerfect from Novell.

Willett, Shawn. "Ray Noorda," in *Computer Reseller News*, 16 November 1997. Profiles the former chairman and CEO of Novell.

Willett, Shawn, and Barbara Darrow. "Novell-WordPerfect Finish Tough Year," in *Computer Reseller News*," 13 March 1995. Reviews Novell's performance in the 12 months following the announced acquisition.

"WordPerfect Corp.," in *International Directory of Company Histories*, Vol. 10, St. James Press: 1995. Provides a historical review of the company, including its acquisition by Novell.

PATRICIA ARCHILLA

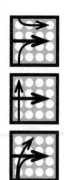

OCCIDENTAL PETROLEUM & DIAMOND SHAMROCK

Occidental Petroleum Corp.
10889 Wilshire Blvd.
Los Angeles, CA 90024-4201
USA

tel: (310)208-8800
web: http://www.oxy.com
e-mail: los_angeles-communications@oxy.com

Ultramar Diamond Shamrock, Inc.
6000 N. Loop 1604 W.
PO Box 696000
San Antonio, TX 78269-6000
USA

tel: (210)592-2000
web: http://www.udscorp.com

date: January 7, 1985 (canceled)
affected: Occidental Petroleum Corp., USA, founded 1920
affected: Ultramar Diamond Shamrock, Inc. (formerly Diamond Shamrock Corp.), USA, founded 1967

Overview of the Merger

In one of the shortest merger accords in history, Occidental Petroleum and Diamond Shamrock agreed to unite in January 1985 to form the eighth-largest oil company in the U.S. The deal was nixed, however, by Diamond's board of directors only hours after the companies' respective chairmen had arrived at terms.

History of Occidental Petroleum Corp.

Occidental Petroleum Co. was founded in 1920 in California to operate as a small exploration and drilling firm. In 1956 its activities came to the attention of investor Armand Hammer, who invested $50,000 in two wells being drilled by the company. By that time, Occidental's net worth was $34,000.

In 1957 Hammer began playing a major role in company operations due to his force of personality and ability to raise funds to finance new exploration. That year he became president of Occidental and began steering the company on a diversification course. In 1959 the firm acquired Gene Reid Drilling Company of Bakersfield, California. It retained the services of Gene Reid and his son, two talented engineers and geologists, by offering them stock in the company. That year Occidental gained a listing on the American Stock Exchange.

Hammer sought international opportunities beginning in 1960 by initiating mineral rights negotiations with the governments of Libya, England, Venezuela, and Saudi Arabia. The following year Occidental discovered California's second-largest gas field. The Lathrop Field, located near San Francisco, was a site where many other companies had failed in their attempts to make a discovery. Company profits that year were $1 million on revenues of $4 million.

In 1963 Occidental acquired Jefferson Lake Sulfur and a fertilizer company, both of which used great quantities of natural gas, thus creating internal demand for the production of the Lathrop Field. On March of the following year, the company was listed on the New York Stock Exchange. Occidental again made a discovery where other companies had failed, uncovering a billion-barrel oil field in Libya in 1966. Libya's King Idris granted Occidental the rights to the new field. It continued diversification, acquiring Garrett Research and Engineering and Permian Corp., a marketer of crude oil. By 1967 it had become one of the largest oil exploration companies in the world. Its stock doubled in value to reach $100 per share.

In 1968 it acquired Island Creek Coal, Hooker Chemical, and the European refining and marketing operations of Signal Oil. The next year King Idris was overthrown by the Revolutionary Command Council, headed by Moammar Khadafi, and Occidental was forced to sell 51% of its holdings to the Libyan government. The company concluded negotiations with the Libyan government in 1970, agreeing to an immediate increase in price per barrel (to be paid to the Libyans) and further increases over the next five years. As other international oil companies followed suit and reached similar agreements with their host countries, petroleum prices rose worldwide.

Occidental turned to Latin America, initiating oil exploration there and purchasing the region's plastics manufacturers. In 1972 despite criticism from the U.S. government, Hammer concluded a $20 billion agreement with the Soviet Union, calling for Occidental to provide phosphate fertilizers to the Soviets in exchange for ammonia and urea. In 1973, a year after beginning oil exploration in the North Sea, Occidental discovered the lucrative Piper Field. Four years later Hooker Chemical acquired Zoecon Corp., a manufacturer of veterinary products and insecticides, for $49 million.

In 1980 the company shifted its focus to domestic exploration. The next year it acquired Iowa Beef Packers for $750 million and entered into a $525 million joint venture with the Italian state energy agency. In 1982 Occidental became the 12th-largest concern in the U.S. with the purchase of Cities Service Co. (CSC) of Oklahoma City for $4 billion. It immediately divested portions of Cities' holdings for $1 billion and reduced its workforce by 16,000. CSC had initially intended to merge with Gulf Oil Corp., but Gulf had backed out of the deal, prompting CSC to sue for $230 million in breach of contract. This case was finally settled in May 1999 with a $935 million reward paid to Occidental by Chevron Corp., which had purchased Gulf in 1984.

Occidental sold its Citgo refining and marketing operations to Southland Corp. in 1983. That year Ray Irani was hired to turn around the company's chemical businesses, which showed a loss of $38 million. Following the discovery of a large oil field in Colombia in 1984, Occidental reached an agreement with Repsol, the Spanish national oil company, whereby Repsol purchased 25% of the Occidental subsidiary responsible for Colombian oil operations.

The Business

Financials - Occidental Petroleum Corp.

Revenue (1998): $6.6 billion

Employees (1998): 9,190

Financials - Ultramar Diamond Shamrock, Inc.

Revenue (1998): $11.1 billion

Employees (1998): 20,000

SICs / NAICS

sic 2911 - Petroleum Refining

sic 5172 - Petroleum Products Nec

sic 5983 - Fuel Oil Dealers

naics 324110 - Petroleum Refineries

naics 422720 - Petroleum and Petroleum Products Wholsesalers

naics 454311 - Heating Oil Dealers

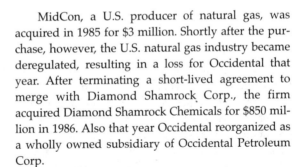

MidCon, a U.S. producer of natural gas, was acquired in 1985 for $3 million. Shortly after the purchase, however, the U.S. natural gas industry became deregulated, resulting in a loss for Occidental that year. After terminating a short-lived agreement to merge with Diamond Shamrock Corp., the firm acquired Diamond Shamrock Chemicals for $850 million in 1986. Also that year Occidental reorganized as a wholly owned subsidiary of Occidental Petroleum Corp.

Occidental's chemical arm, Oxychem, acquired the operations of Shell Oil Co. and DuPont Corp. in 1987. Oxychem's sales that year doubled their 1983 level, approaching $3 billion. The following year it acquired Cain Chemical for $2.2 billion, making Oxychem the sixth-largest chemical producer in the U.S. This division's sales constituted 25% of total corporate revenues.

In 1988 the company's Piper Alpha oil rig exploded in the North Sea, killing 167. Worldwide oil prices rose by $1 per barrel in the wake of the accident as Occidental was forced to close its entire North Sea operation for repair until 1989. That year a restructuring of Occidental's U.S. oil and gas operations resulted in the loss of 900 jobs.

Hammer died in 1990 and was succeeded as CEO by Irani. He instituted a campaign to reduce corporate debt, spinning off its remaining holdings in Iowa Beef

The Officers

Occidental Petroleum Corp.

Chairman and CEO: Ray R. Irani

President and Sr. Operating Officer; Chairman and CEO, Occidental Oil and Gas Corp.: Dale R. Laurance

Chief Financial Officer and Exec. VP, Corporate Development: Stephen I. Chazen

Exec. VP, Secretary, and General Counsel: Donald P. de Brier

Exec. VP, Human Resources: Richard W. Hallock

Ultramar Diamond Shamrock, Inc.

Vice Chairman, President, and CEO: Jean R. Gaulin

Chairman: Roger R. Hemminghaus

Exec. VP, Refining, S&D, and Wholesale: William R. Klesse

Sr. VP, Retail Marketing and Operations: Christopher Havens

Exec. VP and Chief Financial Officer: H. Pete Smith

Exec. VP, Chief Administrative and Legal Officer: Timothy J. Fretthold

Packers, canceling joint ventures with the Soviet Union and People's Republic of China, divesting corporate interests in the North Sea Oil Field, and selling 50% of the company's domestic liquid natural gas operations. These moves, coupled with a 60% reduction in dividends, enabled Occidental to reduce its debt by $3 billion. It continued to restructure for debt release in 1992, selling 12 million shares of Canadian Occidental Petroleum for $241 million, thereby reducing corporate interest in this subsidiary by 30%. By 1993 Occidental demonstrated a renewed commitment to oil and gas exploration and production, chemical manufacture, and coal mining.

In 1994 it acquired interests in 17 Gulf Coast oil and natural gas properties from Agip Petroleum Co. for $195 million. The next year it announced a restructuring plan to consolidate its oil and gas operations into one operating company with four divisions. It also acquired an equity interest in Clark USA Inc., an oil refiner and marketer.

Occidental paid $3.5 billion in February 1998 to acquire the U.S. government's 78% stake in the Elk Hills oil and gas field, one of the top fields in the continental U.S. To help pay for the purchase, it sold its natural gas transmission and marketing subsidiary,

MidCon, to KN Energy for $3.49 billion. By April it had also divested itself of several other assets amounting to $376 million. That May Occidental contributed its ethylene and propylene businesses to Equistar Chemicals LP, a partnership with Lyondell Petrochemicals Co. and Millennium Chemicals Inc. Oxy Vinyls, LP, the largest North American producer of polyvinyl chloride resins, was formed in May 1999 in a joint venture with The Geon Co.

History of Diamond Shamrock, Inc.

Diamond Alkali Co., a Pittsburgh-based soda ash manufacturer, was formed in 1910. Four years later the company began producing large amounts of canning glass and marketing more of its soda ash. By 1915 Diamond Alkali had overproduced and began to utilize excess product in new ways. By combining soda ash with limestone, it manufactured caustic soda, which eventually led to the production of lye, soap, detergents, rayon, and cellophane. In 1925 it again expanded its product line to include calcium carbonates, cement, and coke. Four years later, using the electrolysis of salt process, the company produced caustic soda and discovered two by-products, chlorine and pure hydrogen.

The company established its first research laboratory in 1942. By 1944 Diamond Alkali was operating a plant for magnesium, calcium hypochlorite, and synthetic catalysts in a joint lease with the M.W. Kellogg Co. That year it bought Emeryville Chemical Co. In 1948 company sales surpassed $50 million. The following year it purchased the Martin Dennis Co. and formed an export sales division.

During the 1950s the company's assets included 12 plants responsible for more than 100 various chemicals. In 1950 it bought the chromic acid business from E.I. du Pont de Nemours and Co., entering the organic and agricultural chemicals and plastics areas of business. The next year it entered the organic insecticides and agricultural chemicals field by purchasing Kolker Chemical Works, Inc. In 1953 Diamond purchased Belle Alkali Co., a producer of chemicals used to make silicone resins, solvents, and drugs.

The company bought a 51% interest in Diamond Black Leaf Co. in 1955, making it a wholly owned subsidiary two years later. It entered a consolidation period in the 1960s. In 1960 Diamond merged with Bessemer Limestone & Cement Co. That year it also bought Harte & Co. and the Chemical Process Co. In 1967, after merging with Nopco Chemical Co., Diamond merged with Shamrock Oil and Gas Co., to form Diamond Shamrock Corp. In 1969 it bought Taylor-Evans Seed Co. and Pickland Mather & Co.

Diversifying, the company acquired American Chocolate & Citrus Co. in 1972. It followed up this purchase in 1975 by expanding its market to include commercial baking supplies through its purchase of Federal Yeast Corp., Gold Star Foods Co., and Bakery Products Inc. William H. Bricker became CEO in 1976 and set about focusing Diamond away from chemicals toward oil and gas. In 1979 Diamond bought Falcon Seaboard Inc., a producer of steam coal.

The 1980s brought the diversification strategy to a halt. In 1980 the company created new divisions targeted for divestiture in order to expand into coal. These divisions included plastics, metal coatings, domestic polymers, food-related products, animal nutrition, and medical products. In 1981 Diamond entered the coal industry by purchasing Amherst Coal Co. Two years later it paid $1.4 billion to purchase Natomas Co., thereby gaining oil and gas operations, a geothermal energy business, and wells producing oil in the North Sea, Canada, and the U.S.

Concerned about a possible takeover attempt by Occidental Petroleum Corp., Diamond Shamrock Offshore Partners Ltd. was formed in 1984 to prevent any hostile maneuvers. Rather than become involved in a takeover, however, Occidental and Diamond entered into a very brief merger agreement in 1985. Its termination depressed the value of its stock, leaving Diamond vulnerable to a takeover. In 1986 the company received a $2 billion acquisition offer from T. Boone Pickens in a securities exchange. Diamond rejected Pickens' offer and filed suit against him. Later that year it sold its chemical business to Occidental Petroleum for $850 million. In 1987 Pickens bid on the company again, forcing Diamond to restructure itself for the third time in two years. In April Diamond Shamrock R&M, Inc. became an independent oil refining and marketing company based in San Antonio, Texas, and Diamond Shamrock Corp. became known as Maxus Energy Corp.

In 1988 Diamond Shamrock R&M began focusing on marketing operations in the Southwest by expanding refinery and pipeline capacity and retail presence. The following year it became a 33% partner in Mont Belvieu of Texas, which later grew to become the world's largest storage capacity. In 1989 it formed Diamond Shamrock Natural Gas Marketing Co. as a subsidiary. That year this subsidiary purchased Merit Tank-Testing, Inc. and Petro/Chem Environmental Services, Inc., which merged to form Petro/Chem Environmental Services, Inc.

The company again changed its name in 1990, returning to Diamond Shamrock, Inc. In 1995 it paid $260 million to acquire National Convenience Stores Inc., maintaining the Stop N Go name on its 660 stores.

The Players

Chairman and CEO of Occidental Petroleum Corp.: Armand Hammer. Armand Hammer had a reputation as an aggressive businessman, but only after his death did this character trait prove to be merely the tip of the iceberg. Born in 1898 in New York, Armand Hammer was named by his father, Julius, after the arm and hammer insignia of the Socialist Labor Party, of which he was a member. Julius, a fence for Soviet smuggled diamonds, introduced Armand to shady business activities. While the younger Hammer claimed to have made his fortune by running legitimate businesses, he secretly laundered money for the Soviets to finance espionage and revolution. He allowed his father to take the blame and suffer imprisonment for a botched abortion that Armand had performed while a medical student. Under the guise of respectability, he forged connections with American politicians whose aid he enlisted when his dealings drew suspicion. Hammer operated a successful distillery during World War II, but his spending habits left his personal finances shaky—until he abandoned his wife to marry a wealthy widow, that is. Her money enabled Hammer to invest in Occidental Petroleum in 1956. He gradually gained control of the company through the acquisition of additional stock.

Hammer faced felony charges of obstruction of justice after lying about a $54,000 illegal contribution to Richard Nixon's re-election campaign. He feigned illness to elicit sympathy in order to plead guilty to lesser misdemeanor charges. Hammer later tried to bribe President Reagan $1 million to pardon him; he successfully received that pardon from President Bush, presumably free of charge. Hammer died of cancer at age 92 in 1990, at which point more than 100 lawsuits were filed against his estate.

Chairman and CEO of Diamond Shamrock, Inc.: William H. Bricker. Compared to his counterpart at Occidental, William Bricker led a more ordinary life. After receiving a Masters degree in chemical engineering, he began his career in chemicals by taking a job as a seller of agricultural products. He joined Diamond Shamrock in 1969 and moved through successive executive ranks until he was appointed CEO in 1976. Bricker began restructuring the company away from chemicals toward the energy sector. He became chairman in 1979 and was instrumental in forging the ultimately unsuccessful merger agreement with Occidental Petroleum. In 1997 Bricker became CEO of Petromidia USA, which held a 51% stake in Romania's Petromidia refinery.

In December 1996 Diamond Shamrock merged with Ultramar Corp. to form Ultramar Diamond Shamrock Corp., the third-largest independent petroleum company in the U.S.

Market Forces Driving the Merger

Occidental Petroleum and Diamond Shamrock, while similar enterprises, were moving in opposite directions in the mid-1980s. Occidental viewed Diamond's profitable chemical operations as a valuable supplement to its own, while Diamond was eager to exit the chemicals industry to focus on oil and gas.

Other than the synergies that a combined company would realize, each firm would also receive a capital benefit from a merger. Occidental was still heavily in debt from its recent purchase of Cities Services Co. For Diamond, a merger could boost its depressed stock price, as well as provide the resources to shore up expansion in the energy industry.

Not everyone was enamored of these reasons for a union, however. "I can't believe it will do anything for the common shareholder," said David Murdock, a multi-millionaire who had once been Occidental's largest shareholder, in a January 1985 article in the The Wall Street Journal. Alan Edgar, an analyst with the Schnelder, Bernet & Heckman brokerage firm, concurred. "It's the two ugly ducklings of the oil industry getting together," he said. "Neither company seems to offer much for the other."

Approach and Engagement

On January 2, 1985, Diamond chairman William Bricker flew to California to determine whether Occidental would be willing to serve as a white knight rescuer if Diamond's proposed takeover of a third oil company went awry, making Diamond the target of a takeover instead. These discussions led to the suggestion by Occidental's chairman Armand Hammer of a merger between Diamond and Occidental. That Friday, January 4, the two companies announced that they were negotiating a union that would boost Occidental's position up two notches to the eighth-largest oil company in the U.S. The new company, which would retain the Occidental Petroleum name, would be formed through a $3.3 billion stock swap in which each company would trade their shares for the new company's shares on a one-for-one basis.

On Sunday night the chairmen reached an agreement, and on Monday morning they announced their accord. Each company then held a board meeting, considered merely a formality. The agreement was approved by Occidental's board with only two dissenters. In Diamond's meeting, however, the members unanimously voted against the deal. Later that same day, January 7, the companies released a one-sentence statement that they had terminated their agreement.

Products and Services

Occidental Petroleum's Oil and Gas business had production in nine foreign countries, active exploration projects in eight foreign countries, and production and exploration operations in six U.S. states and the Gulf of Mexico. Its Chemicals operation, OxyChem, manufactured basic chemicals, vinyls, petrochemicals, and specialty products. In 1998 it was the largest merchant marketer of chlorine and caustic soda in the U.S. Its Oxy Vinyls subsidiary was the largest producer of polyvinyl chloride resins and vinyl chloride monomer in North America, and its Equistar Chemicals unit was North America's largest producer of ethylene and certain derivatives.

Having sold its chemicals business to Occidental, Ultramar Diamond Shamrock operated in two main lines of business. Its Marketing segment was comprised of 6,300 retail gasoline outlets in 21 states and six Canadian provinces. The majority of these were branded Diamond Shamrock, Ultramar, Beacon, or Total. It also operated retail stores branded as Corner Store, Stop N Go, Ultramar, Beacon, Total, and Sergaz locations. The company's Refining segment consisted of seven company-owned refineries in Texas, California, Oklahoma, Colorado, Michigan, and Quebec.

Changes to the Industry

The companies walked away from the table amicably, insisting that they were not enemies. Diamond emerged in a more vulnerable state, however. Because of the heavy trading of its stock over the course of the merger discussion, arbitrageurs gained a large portion of Diamond's outstanding shares. This predicament left the company subject to a takeover attempt, as many of those shares could be tendered if a suitor's price was right. Bricker admitted the company's vulnerability to such an attempt, but stated in a January 9 article of The Wall Street Journal, "If anybody tries to take us over, they'll be in for a hell of a fight."

He soon got a chance to prove it. In 1986 T. Boone Pickens made a $2 billion acquisition offer for Diamond Shamrock. The company rejected it, filing suit to stop him. Pickens renewed his efforts in 1987, but was again thwarted. In 1996 Diamond secured its position by merging with Ultramar to form Ultramar Diamond Shamrock.

Review of the Outcome

Both Occidental and Diamond were initially silent on the causes for the sudden collapse of their merger, sending analysts into fits of speculation. Among the conjectures was that of an insurmountable clash of personalities between the strong-willed chairmen. Hammer was to have retained his positions at the new company, while Bricker would have no role whatsoever, receiving a $5 million severance settlement instead. Bricker broke the silence on January 8, dispelling that rumor. He asserted that the merger's abortion had nothing to do with his displacement in the new company, as he had agreed to such terms before taking the deal to Diamond's board.

Bricker attributed the collapse to two other reasons, both of which had also been rumored on Wall Street. The first was the drop in Occidental's share price and the simultaneous rise in Diamond's after news of the merger. Since the transaction was to have been a stock swap, this diluted the benefits of a merger for Diamond's shareholders. Secondly, as they would receive only two seats on the new company's board, Diamond's directors had doubts about whether Occidental's management would be capable of operating the company with such little assistance from Diamond. Bricker had spoken harshly of Occidental's management. He said in a January 8 *The Wall Street Journal* article that with the exception of Hammer and president Ray Irani, "Occidental has a bunch of clerks holding professional positions."

The following year, the two companies again found themselves in negotiations. In May 1986 Occidental joined with Drexel Brunham Lambert, an investment banking concern, to purchase Diamond Shamrock Chemical Company for $800 million and the assumption of $110 million in debt. With this purchase, Occidental became the nation's second-largest producer of chlorine and caustic soda, after Dow Chemical Co.

Research

Castro, Janice. "Jilted; Calling off a Rushed Deal," in *Time*, 21 January 1985. Provides a brief review of the failed merger deal.

Cieply, Michael and Charles F. McCoy. "Occidental, Diamond Shamrock Cancel Merger Plan Hours After Announcing It," in *The Wall Street Journal*, 8 January 1985. Reports on the merger's sudden termination.

———. "Occidental Sets Merger Talks with Oil Firm," in *The Wall Street Journal*, 7 January 1985. Discusses the pros and cons of the merger.

Cieply, Michael, Charles F. McCoy, G. Christian Hill, and John D. Williams. "Diamond Shamrock Chief Says Concern Isn't for Sale, but Notes Vulnerability," in *The Wall Street Journal*, 9 January 1985. Describes the vulnerable position of Diamond due to its stock price in the aftermath of the failed merger.

Cole, Robert J. "Occidental, Shamrock Study Link," in *The New York Times*, 5 January 1985. Reveals that the two companies are engaged in merger negotiations.

"Diamond Shamrock, Inc.," in *International Directory of Company Histories*, Vol. IV, St. James Press: 1991. Provides an historical account of the company.

Kristof, Nicholas D. "Occidental and Drexel in Joint Bid," in *The New York Times*, 22 May 1986. Describes the purchase of Diamond Shamrock Chemical by Occidental.

"Occidental Petroleum Corporation," in *International Directory of Company Histories*, Vol. IV, St. James Press: 1991. Examines the history of Occidental.

Occidental Petroleum Corp. 1998 Annual Report on Form 10-K. Provides a detailed review of company operations during the year.

Occidental Petroleum Corp. Home Page, available at http://www.oxy.com. Official World Wide Web Page for Occidental Petroleum. Includes news releases, a description of operations, and annual reports, and other financial information.

"Ultramar PLC," in *Notable Corporate Chronologies*, The Gale Group, 1999. Profiles the history of Ultramar.

Ultramar Diamond Shamrock Corp. Home Page, available at http://www.udscorp.com. Official World Wide Web Page for Ultramar Diamond Shamrock. This French- and English-language site includes a description of operations, annual reports, and other financial information, and news releases.

Ybarra, Michael. "*Dossier: The Secret History of Armand Hammer*," in *Washington Monthly*, March 1997. A book review of the biography of Occidental's chairman.

DEBORAH J. UNTENER

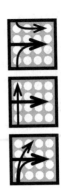

OLIVETTI & TELECOM ITALIA

Olivetti SpA
Via Jervis 77
Ivrea, 10015
Italy

tel: 39-0125-52-00
fax: 39-0125-52-2524
web: http://www.olivetti.it

Telecom Italia SpA
41 Corso d'Italia
Rome, 00198
Italy

tel: 39-06-3600-1273
fax: 39-06-3688-2225
web: http://www.telecomitalia.it

nationality: Italy
date: April 1999 (canceled)
affected: Olivetti SpA, USA, founded 1908
affected: Telecom Italia SpA, Italy, founded 1918

Overview of the Merger

Olivetti SpA rocked the Italian telecommunications industry in February of 1999 when it launched a $40 billion hostile takeover of Telecom Italia SpA, the sixth largest telephone operator in the world and the fourth largest in Europe. Nearly bankrupt less than a year and a half prior to its offer, Olivetti was looking to swallow an industry behemoth nearly seven times its size. To fend off the attack, Telecom Italia sought to make itself prohibitively expensive by offering to repurchase the 40% of Telecom Italia Mobile it had spun off in 1995. Olivetti responded by upping its bid roughly 15% to $58 billion. In April, Telecom Italia thwarted the takeover effort when it reached an $82 billion merger deal with Germany's Deutsche Telekom; if that union is completed, the combined firm will capture the second place spot—behind Japan's Nippon Telegraph and Telephone—among the world's leading telecommunications companies.

History of Olivetti SpA

In 1908, Camillo Olivetti opened his own typewriter manufacturing plant in Ivrea, Italy. Three years later, Olivetti exhibited the first Italian typewriter, the Olivetti M1, at the Turin Universal Exposition. Olivetti's son, Adriano Olivetti, opened the company's first advertising office in 1928 to communicate Olivetti's commitment to aesthetics as well as efficiency. In 1932, the company listed publicly as Ing. C. Olivetti & C., SpA. The following year, a portable variety of the Olivetti typewriter was introduced.

By the mid-1940s, Olivetti employed 4,700 workers, and exported its machines to more than 22 countries. In 1959, Olivetti added the Elea 9003 mainframe, Italy's first computer, to its product line, which included adding machines, teleprinters, and office furniture. After purchasing U.S. typewriter maker Underwood, the firm established a U.S. subsidiary. Adriano Olivetti died in 1960, ending his family's direct management of the firm.

Falling profits plagued Olivetti in the early 1960s. In 1964, the company was rescued by a consortium of Italian banks and industrial concerns. Products included electronic typewriters, banking terminals, telecommunications equipment, and smaller computers such as minicomputers and an early version of the desktop microcomputer. Two new markets were entered with the introductions of the Copia 2000 line of copying machines and industrial automation systems, including robots and precision machine tools. In 1978, Franco and Carlo De Benedetti acquired 14% of Olivetti for about $17 million; Carlo became CEO.

Olivetti introduced its first personal computer, the M20, in 1982. The following year, AT&T Corp. began marketing Olivetti microcomputers under the AT&T name in the U.S., while Olivetti sold AT&T minicomputers outside the U.S. AT&T also agreed to buy a 22% stake in Olivetti, with an option on another 18%. Olivetti launched its first IBM compatible personal computer, the M24, in 1983. Three years later, the firm acquired Triumph-Adler AG from Volkswagen.

After AT&T's sales of Olivetti computers declined in the late 1980s, the two partners nearly ended relations. De Benedetti reaffirmed his faith in Olivetti by upping his share to 20%; this move was also designed to make it more difficult for AT&T to launch a takeover. Falling profits prompted a restructuring in which management created four new and separate companies under the ownership of Olivetti: Olivetti Systems and Networks, makers of personal computers and minicomputers; Olivetti Information Services, providers of computer related services; Olivetti Office, makers of traditional business machines; and Olivetti Technologies Group, 24 ancillary computer hardware manufacturers and developers of large industrial projects.

In 1991, Olivetti suffered its first net loss in 13 years. The following year, the firm introduced its Quaderno notebook personal computer. Digital Equipment Corp., a leading U.S. computer maker, purchased 10% of Olivetti for about $300 million. Furthering its diversification into telecommunications services, in 1994 the company hooked up with Hughes Network System Corp., a unit of General Motors, to provide a pan-European digital satellite communications network.

Losses continued into the mid-1990s. In 1995, Olivetti wrung $1.5 billion in capital out of investors. De Benedetti was forced by institutional shareholders and management to step down as chairman; he was given the title of honorary chairman. Francesco Caio was named CEO and charged with the task of making the company profitable. He orchestrated the firm's 1997 spin-off of its PC operations and refocused Olivetti on telecommunications operations. The following year, Olivetti divested its computer services business. Olivetti initiated a hostile takeover over of Telecom Italia in 1999, but the deal was thwarted

The Business

Financials - Olivetti SpA

Revenue (1998): $4.34 billion

Employees (1998): 17,000

Financials - Telecom Italia SpA

Revenue (1998): $27.5 billion

Employees (1998): 122,300

SICs / NAICS

sic 4813 - Telephone Communications Except Radiotelephone

sic 4812 - Radiotelephone Communications

sic 3661 - Telephone & Telegraph Apparatus

sic 3669 - Communications Equipment Nec

naics 513322 - Cellular and Other Wireless Telecommunications

naics 513321 - Paging

naics 334418 - Printed Circuit Assembly (Electronic Assembly) Manufacturing

when Telecom Italia and Deutsche Telekom agreed to merge.

History of Telecom Italia SpA

In 1933, Societa Finanziaria Telefonica (STET) was created to oversee Italy's telephone operations. STET operated under the umbrella of Italy's state-owned industrial holding company, Instituto per La Ricostruzione Industriale (IRI). Telephone equipment maker TETI came under government control in 1958 and was merged with STET.

STET diversified into satellite communications and data transmission in the 1970s. The advent of fax machines and personal computers in the 1980s threatened STET's monopoly status. As a result, the Italian government decided to privatize STET. In 1994, STET reorganized its five telephone and telecommunication operations companies—SIP, Italcable, Telespazio, Iritel, and SIRM—into Telecom Italia, the sixth largest telecommunications company in the world. SIP was Italy's domestic telephone operator; Italcable specialized in intercontinental telecommunications; Telespazio was a satellite communications company; Iritel was the country's domestic long distance operator; and SIRM offered maritime communications services.

The Officers

Olivetti SpA

Honorary Chairman: Carlo De Benedetti

Chairman: Antonio Tesone

Chief Executive Officer: Roberto Colaninno

Sr. VP, Central Division for Administration, Finance and
Control: Corriado Ariaudo

Sr. VP, Operations and Information Systems: Enzo
Badalotti

Sr. VP, Corporate Finance: Luciano La Noce

Telecom Italia SpA

Chairman: Berardino Libonati

Deputy Chairman: Pier G. Jaeger

Chief Executive Officer: Franco Bernabe

General Manager, Strategy, Business Clients, and
Research: Francesco de Leo

General Manager, Operations Division: Massimo Sarmi

In 1995, the board of directors of Telecom Italia approved the incorporation of Telecom Italia Mobile SpA, which included all of Telecom Italia's radiomobile holdings. Telecom Italia then spun off Telecom Italia Mobile, which was one of two digital mobile service operations in Italy at that time. In 1996, Telecom Italia divested its publishing arm, SEAT, and reduced leased-line tariffs by 35% and residential dial-up Internet rates by 50%. The firm also released ATMosfera, the first Asynchronous Transfer Mode service offered in Italy. Citing antitrust concerns, the Italian government in 1997 blocked Telecom Italia from purchasing Intesa, a communications venture which operated as the service provider for the IBM Global Network in Italy. To speed privatization efforts, the Italian government merged Telecom Italia with STET that year. The entity kept the Telecom Italia name.

In mid-1997, to launch the firm's long awaited privatization, the Italian government sold a 9% stake in Telecom Italia to an investor group made up of Italian insurers and banks. A few months later, the government sold another 34% stake in Telecom Italia for nearly $12 billion. Telecom Italia's privatization, which raised a total of $15.1 billion for the Italian government, was the largest such transaction to take place in Europe and the second largest privatization in the world. In 1998, Telecom Italia, AT&T Corp., and

Unisource agreed to cooperate in Latin American and European markets.

Market Forces Driving the Merger

According to most analysts, two main factors drove Olivetti's bid for Telecom Italia. As explained in an April 1999 *Washington Post* article, "with the advent of deregulation—telecommunications in the 15-nation European Union was largely liberalized last year—and the arrival of the single currency, the euro, companies are rushing to consolidate." The arrival of the euro allayed the currency risks fears of foreign investors, which added to the globalization trend among large European companies in most industries. As a result, during the first three months of 1999, merger and acquisition activity among European countries had reached $345 billion, compared to $145 billion during the first quarter of 1998. Shareholders had seen what consolidation had done to share performance in U.S. markets as merged firms had slashed costs, and they began pressuring European firms for the same results.

Olivetti promised Telecom Italia shareholders savings in the form of 12,000 layoffs and the spin off of peripheral operations if they approved the takeover. In 1988, Olivetti had made a $152 million investment in Omnitel, a cellular phone operation worth roughly $10 billion in 1999. To finance its $40 billion bid for Telecom Italia, the firm planned to sell its Omnitel stake, as well as other telecommunications holdings. Many analysts felt that Olivetti, which had only recently emerged from near insolvency, sought the merger to fuel its own recovery.

Approach and Engagement

Telecom Italia asked shareholders to reject Olivetti's $40 billion takeover bid and announced plans to save $560 million per year by laying off 40,000 employees, nearly one third of the firm's workforce. The stock market regulator of Italy, Consob, bought Telecom Italia some time for a defense maneuver when it ruled on February 22, 1999, that Olivetti's bid was incomplete and, therefore, invalid. Two days later, Olivetti submitted a revised bid.

Telecom Italia employed several tactics to ward off the attack: it converted non-voting shares into common stock, paid shareholders a special divided, and offered to buy the 40% of cellular phone subsidiary Telecom Italia Mobile it didn't own as a means of making itself too expensive for Olivetti. In March, Olivetti upped its offer by 15% to $12.39 per share, worth a whopping $57.3 billion. Telecom Italia's final defensive move was its most noteworthy. In April, the firm agreed to an \$82 billion merger with Germany's Deutsche Telekom.

Products and Services

After divesting it personal computer operations in 1997, Olivetti began focusing more closely on its telecommunications operations, including Infostrada, a fixed-line network operator, and Omnitel, a cellular phone and phone card services provider. Olivetti's Lexikon unit manufactured copiers, fax machines, printers, and related products.

Telecommunications accounted for roughly 89% of Telecom Italia's 1998 revenues. Operations included fixed-line telephone service in Italy; Telecom Italia Mobile, of which Telecom Italia owned 60%; and satellite and digital television services. Other telecommunications subsidiaries included telephone services provider Entel Chile; cellular operator Mobilkom Austria AG; Telekom Austria; and Telekom Serbia. Manufacturing and installation services, including subsidiaries Italtel and Sirti, brought in 6% of sales. FINSIEL, the firm's information technology software and services unit, secured the remainder. International operations accounted for roughly 10% of total revenues.

Changes to the Industry

If the Telecom Italia/Deutsche Telekom deal clears extensive regulatory hurdles, the combined firm will emerge as one of the world's largest telecommunications companies, second only to Japan's Nippon Telegraph and Telephone. With \$65 billion in combined sales and a market value of roughly \$200 billion, the new firm will offer competition to U.S. companies like AT&T Corp. Larger firms will face increased competition, and smaller companies may begin clambering for their own consolidation moves. According to most analysts, the European telecommunications industry will likely see similar effects, even if the Telecom Italia/Deutsche Telekom deal crumbles and Olivetti succeeds in its hostile takeover of Telecom Italia.

Review of the Outcome

Immediately following the announcement of the Olivetti bid, Telecom Italia's shares jumped from euro 9.04 to euro 10.08. Shares were temporarily suspended when trading became too intense. Olivetti's shares, however, tumbled from euro 3.2 to euro 3.11 which reflected investor concern regarding the amount of debt Olivetti would take on if the deal was completed. While the long-term effects of the bid on both firms remain to be seen, most analysts agree that Olivetti's

The Players

CEO of Olivetti SpA: Roberto Colaninno. Roberto Colaninno began working for Fiaam, an Italian auto parts maker, in 1969. After serving as administrative director for three years, he was named CEO of the company. When Fiamm and Britain's Turner & Newall merged, Colaninno became managing director of the new operation. In 1981, he founded his own auto parts manufacturing firm, Sogefi, which he expanded into an international concern with 30 plants scattered throughout 20 countries by the end of the decade. In September of 1996, Olivetti tapped Colaninno as CEO.

CEO of Telecom Italia SpA: Franco Bernabe. After graduating from the University of Turin in 1973, Franco Bernabe accepted a position there as an assistant lecturer. In 1976, he was named senior economist at the OECD Department of Economics and Statistics in Paris. Other academic stints of Bernabe's included heading the economic studies department at FIAT and working as a professor of economic politics at the School of Industrial Administration. Bernabe moved from academia to the corporate world in March of 1983 when he was hired as assistant to the chairman at ENI. Between 1986 and 1992, he served as director of development, planning, and control for the firm. In August of 1992, Bernabe was appointed CEO of ENI, a position he retained until 1998. In November of that year, Bernabe took the helm of Telecom Italia as CEO.

move likely altered the Italian telecommunication industry permanently. According to a February 1999 issue of *Economist*, Olivetti's real achievement may have been "to open up a sheltered part of the European telecoms business."

Research

Ball, Deborah. "Olivetti Seeks to Build on Turnaround with \$58 Billion Offer for Telecom Italia," in *The Wall Street Journal, Europe*, 22 February 1999. Offers an overview of why Olivetti launched its takeover bid for Telecom Italia.

———. "Telecom Italia Continues Push to Fend Off Olivetti," in *The Wall Street Journal, Europe*, 12 March 1999. Explains the defensive maneuvers employed by Telecom Italia to ward off Olivetti's attack.

"Italian Telecoms: Gulp," in *The Economist*, 27 February 1999. Explains how Olivetti's bid for Telecom Italia will likely change the Italian telecommunications industry whether or not it is successful.

Olivetti SpA Home Page, available at http://www.olivetti.com. Official World Wide Web Home Page for Olivetti SpA. Available in both English and Italian. Includes news, as well as financial, product, and historical information.

"Olivetti SpA," in *Notable Corporate Chronologies*, The Gale Group, 1999. Lists major events in the history of Olivetti SpA.

Swardson, Anne. "European Phone Firms Discuss Huge Merger," in *Washington Post*, 20 April 1999. Offers an overview of the merger between Telecom Italia and Deutsche Telekom.

Telecom Italia SpA Home Page, available at http://www.telecomitalia.com. Official World Wide Web Home Page for Telecom Italia SpA. Available in both English and Italian. Includes news, as well as financial, product, and historical information.

"Telecom Italia," in *Notable Corporate Chronologies*, The Gale Group, 1999. Lists major events in the history of Telecom Italia.

Wallace, Charles. "The Takeover Cowboys," in *Time*, 19 April 1999. Explains the reasons for increased merger and acquisition activity, including Olivetti's bid for Telecom Italia, in Europe during the first quarter of 1999.

ANNAMARIE L. SHELDON

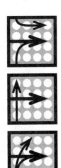

PACIFIC ENTERPRISES & ENOVA

nationality: USA
date: July 7, 1998
affected: Pacific Enterprises, USA, founded 1886
affected: Enova Corp., USA, founded 1881

Sempra Energy
101 Ash St.
San Diego, CA 92101
USA

tel: (619)696-2034
fax: (619)233-6875
web: http://www.sempra.com

Overview of the Merger

In an attempt to capitalize on the energy deregulations enacted by California Governor Pete Wilson, Enova and Pacific Enterprises announced their plans to merge in October 1996. Originally, the deal was to give Enova 48% of Pacific stock for $4.3 billion plus $2.8 billion in assumed debt. The new company would create the nation's largest consumer use utilities firm with 21 million clients.

Rival company Southern California Edison attempted to block the merger, stating it would violate anti-competitive restrictions. Regulatory agencies disagreed, and after several months of delay, the deal was allowed to continue, with some stipulations. Enova was required to divest itself of two electric plants. A year and a half after the merger was set in motion, the deal was finalized, creating Sempra Energy. The new firm acted as the parent company for eight subsidiaries, with assets totaling $10.5 billion.

History of Pacific Enterprises

In 1886, Walter B. Cline and G.O.G. Miller established the Pacific Lighting Co., a San Francisco-based firm renting gas lamps. The company expanded its scope in gas and electric energy services through acquisition, and its sales skyrocketed. In 1907, Pacific incorporated as Pacific Lighting Corp. The company continued to grow in the 1920s with the acquisition of Southern Counties Gas distribution system, Santa Maria Gas, and Southern California Gas. By 1930, Pacific reached nearly two million homes.

In 1889, three years after Pacific was originally founded, it created the Los Angeles Lighting Co. with the purchase of several gas and electric firms. The subsidiary imported gas-powered appliances. In 1890, Pacific Lighting purchased a controlling interest in Los Angeles Electric Co. Pacific combined the lighting and electric operations to form Los Angeles Gas and Electric Co. (LAG&E). By 1915, Los Angeles' utilities were controlled by three unpopular companies, including LAG&E. The city reacted by trying to form a municipal energy system, which the companies fought to prevent. Additionally, in 1917 energy companies finally came under the regulation of the California Public Utilities Commission (CPUC).

Antagonism between LAG&E and the Los Angeles government grew more fervent when the city announced its desire to purchase the company's electric serv-

The Business

Financials

Revenue (1998): $5.4 billion

Employees (1998): 11,148

SICs / NAICS

sic 4911 - Electric Services

sic 4924 - Natural Gas Distribution

sic 4922 - Natural Gas Transmission

naics 221119 - Other Electric Power Generation

naics 221122 - Electric Power Distribution

ices. LAG&E made every effort to avoid the sale, but in 1937 the city got an advantage that forced the $46 million sale. The company needed to have its gas franchise renewed by the city, who would not do it unless LAG&E agreed to sell.

Economic losses were incurred by pipeline damage during heavy rains in 1938. Pacific's attempt in 1940 to merge two of its gas companies was denied by regulators. In 1960, however, changes in utility regulations stabilized prices, allowing Pacific to merge its Southern California Gas and Southern Gas into Southern California Gas Co. (SoCalGas).

Pacfic acquired Terra Resources in 1983, gaining oil and gas operations in 18 states. The firm entered the franchise business with its 1986 acquisition of the Los Angeles Thrifty Corp. retail chain. Two years later, Pacific augmented its oil exploration division with the purchase of Sabine Corp. The 1988 purchase of Pay n' Save and Bi-Mart drug stores prompted Pacific to change its name to Pacific Enterprises. During the first half of the 1990s, however, Pacific divested the retail companies in order to focus on SoCalGas, which had become the nation's largest natural gas distributor. In 1995 Pacific divided its services into four sectors: Energy Distribution Services, Energy Transportation Services, New Product Development, and Pacific Enterprises International.

In 1996, Pacific Enterprises International entered into a joint venture with Enova International Corp. and Mexico's Proxima S.A. de CV. The group obtained the Mexico's first privatized natural gas contract. The following year, Pacific and Enova decided to merge to take advantage of deregulatory opportunities that had recently emerged in California. Despite anti-competitive concerns raised by rival Southern California Edison, the merger was approved by stockholders, UPAC, and anti-trust officials. The new company,

Sempra Energy, provided service to 21 million customers.

History of Enova Corp.

The San Diego Gas and Electric Co. (SDG&E) began in 1881. The company continued to grow throughout the 20th century, providing energy services to Orange County and the surrounding areas of San Diego, California.

SDG&E didn't have the best reputation among its customers, as its rates and services were inconsistent. In the first part of the 1980s, Thomas Page was appointed as CEO. In an effort to improve the company's track record, he decided that SDG&E should provide the lowest rates for energy, avoid competitive prices, and improve its customer service.

Page's goal encountered a major stumbling block in 1991 when Ted and Michelle Zuidema filed a lawsuit, on behalf of their four year old daughter Mallory, against SDG&E. The suit alleged that young Mallory received cancer from electromagnetic field transmissions from SDG&E power lines near their home. The media immediately began a relentless attack on the energy firm, judging them guilty well before the trial. In July of 1993, a jury found in favor the SDG&E, but the damage to its reputation was already done.

As energy regulations in California and across the nation began to loosen in the mid-1990s, SDG&E split its diverse operations into four separate subsidiaries. Enova Corp. was created as a parent company, and SDG&E stock was converted equally into Enova shares. The company began trading on the New York Stock Exchange as ENA.

In 1996, Enova announced its plans to merge with Pacific Enterprises. The deal gave Enova 48% of Pacific shares for $4.3 billion, including $2.8 billion in assumed debt. When the merger was finalized in 1998, the deal was valued at $6 billion. It created Sempra Energy, the nation's largest gas utility company.

Market Forces Driving the Merger

In September 1996, California Governor Pete Wilson passed legislation allowing consumers to choose their utilities provider. This, along with other deregulatory actions, sparked increased competition, which resulted in five gas and electric mergers in 1996.

Energy companies, in an effort to lure new customers from competitors, needed to provide low-cost, efficient, dependable service. By combining gas and electric services for consumers, utility providers hoped to make their services convenient and cost efficient.

Approach and Engagement

In October 1996, Enova Corp. announced its plans to acquire Pacific Enterprises in a deal worth $4.3 billion in cash and assumed debt. Pacific stockholders would sell 48% of the company's stock for $2.8 billion, and Enova would assume $1.5 billion in debt. By the time the deal was finalized in 1998, the value of the transaction increased to $6 billion. Since the merger tested the limits of California's utilities deregulation of 1996, it required close scrutiny before it would be approved.

Southern California Edison, a direct competitor, balked the Enova/Pacific Enterprises deal. In October of 1996, the rival filed a suit to block the merger, stating it would violate anti-competitive regulations. The California Attorney General reviewed the merger proposal and disagreed, pointing out that the state's regulatory requirements were not being violated. While not supporting Edison's concerns, the Attorney General did comment that the Public Utilities Commission might force Enova to sell some intrastate gas transportation lines which would serve competing energy companies. Southern California Edison's protests did delay the deal, and forced the approval deadlines to be pushed back by several months.

The Justice Department finally gave its approval for the merger on March 9, 1998, but only on the condition that Enova sell its two largest electric power plants. Enova agreed to comply with the divestment, and on March 26, 1998 the California Public Utilities Commission gave its final approval. One day later, the Federal Energy Regulatory Commission also accepted the terms of the merger.

On June 25, 1998, the two companies joined under the name Sempra Energy. Sempra became the parent company of eight various subsidiaries, including San Diego Gas & Electric, Southern California Gas & Electric, and various venture, investment, and unregulated enterprises. Pacific Enterprises moved its headquarters to Enova's offices in San Diego.

Products and Services

Sempra Energy took its name from the Latin *semper* which means "always." Sempra was the parent company of eight operations, each with a specific focus in the energy industry. Its two largest subsidiaries were San Diego Gas & Electric (SDG&E), and Southern California Gas (SoCalGas). The remaining subsidiaries supported Sempra and the two utility companies with investment, marketing, financial, development, conservation and international exploration services.

SDG&E served two counties in the San Diego area, providing natural gas and electric distribution.

The Officers

Chairman and CEO: Richard D. Farman

Vice-Chairman, President, and Chief Operating Officer:
  Stephen L. Baum

Group President of Non-Regulated Business Units.:
  Donald E. Felsinger

Its three million customers consumed 1.2 million electric meters and 720,000 natural gas meters.

SoCalGas, the nation's largest utilities provider, served 18 million customers. Its services were divided into two business operations: Energy Distributions Services, serving residential and small commercial customers, and Energy Transportation Services, meeting large commercial needs, including electric generation for other utility providers. SoCalGas covered 23,000 square miles of Southern and Central California.

Sempra Energy Trading, a subsidiary based out of Stamford, Connecticut, was responsible for trading and procurement of natural gas, crude oil and other energy commodities. The trading division used to be known as AIG Trading until it was acquired in 1997, by Pacific Enterprises and Enova, while their merger was being finalized. It served almost every energy company in the United States, with 800 listed clients.

Sempra Energy International reached 2.5 million customers worldwide, with operations in Argentina, Chile, Mexico, Peru and Uruguay. Its Ventures subsidiary sought new markets in the U.S. and Canada currently without natural gas services. Its Solutions division provided retail marketing support for its commercial and retail services.

Changes to the Industry

Four days after the deal was finalized, Sempra began trading on the New York Stock Exchange under the symbol SRE. Enova was forced to sell its two largest electric power plants in order to comply with a settlement agreement with the U.S. Justice Department.

Only weeks after Sempra Energy was formed, the company paid $48 million for CNG Energy Services. The cash deal for the unit of Consolidated Natural Gas Co. opened up natural gas markets on the East coast for the California-based Sempra. The purchase included CNG Energy's gas contracts to utilities and commercial consumers and the right to natural gas storage facilities and pipelines.

The Players

Chairman and CEO of Pacific Enterprises: Richard D. Farman. Richard Farman, a graduate from Stanford University and Law School, began his career with Pacific Enterprises in 1978. He served as president of Pacific's alternate energy subsidiary, before leading Southern California Gas (SoCalGas) in 1987. At SoCalGas, another Pacific subsidiary, Farman served as vice chairman and director for one year, before accepting the chairman and CEO position. In 1993, Farman was appointed president of Pacific Enterprises, and in May 1998 he became CEO. His negotiations with Enova's Stephen Baum led to a merger which created Sempra Energy, the nation's largest gas utility provider. Farman retained his CEO title and was additionally named chairman when the deal was completed. Farman plans to retire in June 2000, at which time he will be succeeded by Stephen Baum.

Chairman and CEO of Enova Corp.: Stephen L. Baum. Stephen Baum began his career as an attorney in 1978. He became an associate at Curtis, Mallet, Prevost, Colt and Mosle in New York, before becoming the general attorney for Orange and Rockland Utilities. In 1982, Baum—a Harvard and University of Virginia Law School graduate—worked as senior vice president and general counsel of the New York Power Authority. Three years later, Stephen Baum joined San Diego Gas & Electric (SDG&E) as vice president and general counsel. He continued moving up the ranks and was eventually named executive vice president in 1993. Baum was later named CEO of Enova Corp., which was created in 1996 as the parent company of SDG&E and other subsidiaries. On January 1, 1998, prior to completion of Enova's merger with Pacific Enterprises, Baum was appointed chairman of Enova. The two companies merged to form Sempra Energy in of June 1998, and Baum became vice chairman, president, and chief operating officer. He is scheduled to replace Richard Farman as chairman and CEO in 2000.

Review of the Outcome

The creation of Sempra Energy from the 1998 merger of Enova Corp. and Pacific Enterprises highlighted the new growth opportunities available for utility companies after California deregulated the industry. The success of their merger may be repeated by other companies in California and the rest of the nation as many states are currently in the process of deregulating electric power industries. Sempra became the nation's largest energy provider with $10.5 billion in assets and 21 million natural gas customers. More than 800 jobs were cut, mostly at the management level.

Research

Barnes, Gregory E. "A Blitz Fails: An Insider Tells How The Zuidema Jury Sided With SDG&E...Despite Unprecedented Media Pressure," in *Public Utilities Fortnightly*, 1 July 1993. Reviews the court case and verdict regarding electromagnetic field transmission and its relation to cancer. SDG&E was the defendant.

"Business In Brief; California Utility To Buy Pacific Enterprises," in *The Atlantic Journal and Constitution*, 15 October 1996. Gives initial financial details of the merger between Enova and Pacific Enterprises.

"California Merger Would Form One of Nation's Largest Utilities," in *The Daily Record*, 16 October 1996. Discusses the deregulations made available by California governor Wilson.

"Company News; Sempra Energy Pays $48 million in Cash for CNG Energy," in *The New York Times*, 22 July 1998. Announces the first acquisition by Sempra after it began operations in June of 1998.

"Enova and Pacific Complete Merger; New Firm Largest U.S. Customer Base," in *Electric Utility Week*, 6 July 1998. Details the completion of the merger between Enova and Pacific Enterprises, with summaries about the firms subsidiary businesses and operations.

"Pacific Enterprises," in *Notable Corporate Chronologies*, The Gale Group, 1999. Lists major events in the history of Pacific Enterprises.

"Pacific Enterprises names Farman CEO," in *Business Wire*, 7 May 1998. Announces the appointment of Richard Farman as CEO of Enova.

Sempra Energy Homepage at http://www.sempra.com. World Wide Web site for Sempra Energy, with links to subsidiaries. Contains detailed financial and investment reports, press releases, and biographical data for top executives.

Sutherland, Billie. "The Changing Future Is Holding For SDG&E," in *San Diego Business Journal*, 1 May 1995. Discusses the creation of Enova in preparation for deregulatory opportunities.

"Utility Is To Sell Two Plants; Government Approves Merger," in *The New York Times*, 10 March 1998. Reports the Justice Department's decision to allow the merger of Enova and Pacific Enterprises to take place if Enova divests two electric plants.

SEAN C. MACKEY

PACKARD BELL & NEC

nationality: USA
date: July 1, 1996
affected: Packard Bell Electronics Inc., USA, founded 1986
affected: NEC Corp., Japan, founded 1899

Packard Bell NEC Inc.
1 Packard Bell Way
Sacramento, CA 95828
USA

tel: (916)388-0101
fax: (916)388-1109
web: http://www.packardbell.com

Overview of the Merger

The 1996 formation of Packard Bell NEC represented the culmination of five years of cross-border alliances between Packard Bell, NEC, and Groupe Bull. These three computer manufacturers, based in the U.S., Japan, and France, respectively, came together to break into new markets by playing off of the strengths of the others. The resulting company immediately became the largest PC manufacturer in the U.S. and the fourth-largest in the world.

History of NEC Corp.

In 1898 Nippon Electric Co. (NEC) was organized as a limited partnership between Japanese investors and U.S.-based Western Electric Co. for the establishment of a telephone network in Japan. The company went public the following year, with Western Electric holding a 54% stake. At first NEC was little more than a distributor of imported telephone equipment from Western Electric and General Electric. By century's end, however, the steady stream of sales and guaranteed business from the government-sponsored telephone network expansion program enabled NEC to embark on an expansion program.

A serious economic recession in 1913 forced the Japanese government to retrench sponsorship of its telephone expansion program. Struggling to survive, NEC quickly turned back to importing; this time it brought in such household appliances as the electric fan, a device never seen before in Japan. After a brief economic recovery, a second recession hit Japan in 1922, but intelligent planning allowed the company to continue its growth. Two years later NEC began to work on radios and transmitting devices. As with the telephone project, the government sponsored the establishment of a radio network, which began operation with Western Electric equipment supplied by NEC.

In 1931 Japan passed legislation that forcedInternational Standard Electric (ISE, formerly International Western Electric) to transfer about 15% of its ownership in NEC to Sumitomo Densen. One decade later, under pressure from the militarists, ISE was obliged to transfer a second block of NEC shares to Sumitomo Densen. With the beginning of war against the Allied powers of World War II, ISE's

The Business

Financials

Revenue (1998): $2.4 billion (est.)

Employees (1998): 2,600

SICs / NAICS

sic 3571 - Electronic Computers

sic 3575 - Computer Terminals

sic 3577 - Computer Peripheral Equipment Nec

sic 5045 - Computers, Peripherals & Software

naics 334111 - Electronic Computer Manufacturing

naics 334113 - Computer Terminal Manufacturing

naics 334119 - Other Computer Peripheral Equipment
    Manufacturing

naics 421430 - Computer and Computer Peripheral
    Equipment and Software Wholesalers

naics 443120 - Computer and Software Stores

remaining 19.7% stake in NEC was confiscated as enemy property. NEC came under full control of Sumitomo and was renamed Sumitomo Communication Industries.

At the end of the war, American occupation forces abolished Japan's zaibatsu, or leadership by family controlled groups. These organizations were outlawed and broken up. In 1945 Sumitomo Communication Industries readopted the name Nippon Electric Co. and its ownership reverted to a government liquidation corporation. The company's leadership was also replaced, and was faced with the challenge of rehabilitating a company paralyzed by war damage, a product line with no demand, and a workforce of 27,000.

In July 1950, eager to reestablish ties with ISE, NEC took steps to ensure that both companies' technologies would be legally protected, no small feat considering that all patented designs had become a "common national asset" during the war. After this accomplishment, the two companies signed new cooperative agreements. The government-sponsored Nippon Telegraph and Telephoneorganization was formed in 1952, and NEC became one of its primary suppliers. The following year NEC advanced in television and microwave communication technologies. In 1954 it initiated research and development activities in the field of computers, and five years later it debuted its transistor-based computer, the NEAC-2201.

With foreign offices in Taiwan, India, and Thailand, NEC established a U.S. office in 1962. International Telephone & Telegraph's interest in NEC (held through ISE) was reduced to 9.3% in 1970; by 1978 it had sold off its remaining stake in NEC.

In an effort to promote Japanese electronics companies, the Japanese government in 1974 pushed through a series of partnership agreements among the big six computer makers: NEC, Fujitsu, Hitachi, Mitsubishi, Oki, and Toshiba. After several years of continued advancements in computers, the company released Japan's first microprocessor in 1974. Having changed its name to NEC Corp. in 1983, the company became the world's leading independent producer of semiconductors in 1985. With the following year's introduction of the industry's first 4-megabit dynamic random access memory (DRAM) chip, NEC surpassed IBM to become Japan's second-ranked computer manufacturer, after Fujitsu.

In 1991 NEC traded its 15% in Bull HN Information Systems for a five-percent share in Groupe Bull of France. Annual sales that year reached an all-time high of $28.4 billion, but net income remained low, at $112 million. By 1993 NEC was the leader in PC sales, generating the second-largest amount of revenue from computers in Japan. Despite its high position in worldwide semiconductor manufacturing, the company's primary market remained domestic, with NTT as its largest customer.

History of Packard Bell Electronics Inc.

In 1985 Beny Alagem bought the rights to the Packard Bell name from Teledyne, which had owned the consumer electronics firm since 1968. Alagem's plan was to use the name to market a personal computer. The following year, as the personal computer industry began to boom, Alagem and his partners, Jason Barzilay and Alex Sandel, established Packard Bell Electronics Inc. They contracted with Asian suppliers to design a product line specifically for their company, and formed an arrangement with Asian manufacturers to build the machines.

The first Packard Bell personal computer was introduced in 1987. As one of numerous IBM clones, the product competed in a crowded market. To distinguish itself from the competition, the company introduced various innovations, including computers equipped with both three-inch and five-and-one-quarter-inch disk drives, a relatively large 40-megabyte hard drive, and pre-installed software.

In 1989 Packard Bell became one of the first PC manufacturers to distribute its products through such mass retail sales channels as discount chains, warehouse stores, and electronics and appliance centers. That year it generated $600 million in sales.

The company expanded overseas in 1991 by selling its PCs in Europe; by the following year, its European operations accounted for 10%, or $100 million, of total company sales. Despite an economic downturn, Packard Bell's sales jumped to $700 million that year. By 1992 it controlled a leading 26% share of the mass-market distribution channel. It unveiled a local area network (LAN) system that, unlike competitors' systems, was ready to hook up and use straight out of the box. It also introduced a new version of the company's top-of-the-line PC, which could be upgraded by plugging in a new central processing unit.

By 1993 Packard Bell operated in 1,500 retail outlets in 13 countries, and sales reached $1.25 billion. Its U.S. market share was 6.7%, making the company the fourth-largest personal computer supplier in the U.S., behind IBM, Apple, and Compaq.

It diversified in 1994 by selling software under the brand name Active Imagination. That year it also introduced its Spectria computer line, which included a full-function multimedia PC, CD player, stereo, FM radio, TV and video player, telephone answering system, and fax/modem. The company jumped ahead of Apple to the number-three position in domestic PC sales. Since the previous year, its production had doubled to 2.1 million units, and gross revenues increased nearly three-fold, to a record $3 billion.

Packard Bell introduced the first PC with dual CD-ROM drives in 1995. It leapt over both Compaq and IBM to take the leading share, 13%, of the U.S. personal computer market. It was also the leading distributor of PCs through mass retail channels, controlling 50% of that market.

Market Forces Driving the Merger

Packard Bell Electronics, Inc., based in Sacramento, had carved out a niche during the late 1980s. It sold low-priced consumer PC systems through the retail market, an innovative distribution channel for computers at that time. But its dominance in the low-end PC market was increasingly challenged by such giants as Compaq and IBM, and the industry was becoming more competitive. To retain its dominance, Packard Bell had to break into new markets, but experienced difficulty in wrenching the grip that the well-established leaders possessed. In order to be successful in such markets, the company required the capital to acquire new technologies and improve marketing. At the same time, the company needed to revitalize the Packard Bell name, which had become tarnished by allegations of poor product quality and

The Officers

President and CEO: Alain Couder

Exec. VP, Manufacturing and Operations: Paul Greenwood

Exec. VP, Service and Support: Zur Feldman

Exec. VP, Human Resources and Administration: Fred Philpott

Exec. VP, Worldwide Finance and Chief Financial Officer: Marvin Burkett

inaccessible customer support services. The company was privately held, and didn't release financial results, but was believed to have been operating in the red for a number of years.

NEC Corp. was the market leader in Japan, where it enjoyed a healthy 40% share. Yet it, along with most other Japanese PC manufacturers at the time, was experiencing difficulty breaking into the U.S. market, which accounted for 40% of the global computer market. NEC would benefit not only from Packard Bell's strong presence in this target market, but also from its manufacturing efficiencies and expertise in the retail segment. In exchange, it would provide Packard Bell with the desperately needed cash infusion and the credibility of the NEC name, which was particularly strong in the corporate computer segment.

The third player, Groupe Bull SA, was more of a silent partner in the alliance. Bull was a leading supplier of business information systems in Europe, and had also injected Packard Bell with capital. It had sold the U.S. company its Zenith Data Systems Inc. subsidiary, an Illinois-based leader in computers for the government and educational market.

Approach and Engagement

The three-way alliance began in 1991, when NEC acquired a five-percent stake in Groupe Bull. Two years later, in June 1993, Groupe Bull acquired a 19.9% interest in Packard Bell for $70 million. After the span of another two years, the three companies became more directly involved with each other. In July 1995, NEC acquired a 19.9% interest in Packard Bell for $170 million. At the same time, in order to retain its 19.9% stake, Groupe Bull paid the company an additional $27 million. That September, NEC raised its interest in Groupe Bull from five-percent to 17%.

Despite the ties that the trio shared, each company remained a competitor of the others, an arrangement that would have been impossible if they operat-

The Players

Former president of NEC: Hisashi Kaneko. Hisashi Kaneko received his Doctor of Engineering Degree from the University of Tokyo. In 1956 he joined the NEC Central Research Laboratories in Kawasaki, Japan. A technical-minded professional who also possessed leadership qualities, he quickly moved up the company ladder. He became general manager of NEC's transmission division in 1979. Five years later he was appointed vice president of that group. In 1985 he was named vice president and director of the transmission and terminals group. From there he moved up to senior vice president and director of NEC Corp. and then to president and chief executive officer of the company's U.S. subsidiary, NEC America. In June 1994 he was promoted to president of NEC Corp., a position he held until his resignation in 1998.

Former chairman, CEO, and president of Packard Bell: Beny Alagem. Beny Alagem, a 32-year-old Israeli immigrant and naturalized U.S. citizen, founded Packard Bell with a pair of partners. In the space of only a couple of years, this computer company became a leading manufacturer of PCs in the U.S. Alagem was an innovative entrepreneur who carved out a niche by selling consumers low-priced computers though retail channels. By the mid-1990s, however, Packard Bell was being pummeled by competition, and turned to NEC Corp. for financial assistance. This assistance carried a price to Alagem, and in 1998 he abruptly resigned. In January 1999 Alagem reentered the computer industry by purchasing a 75% stake in AST Research, a computer manufacturing subsidiary of Samsung.

ed in overlapping markets. Packard Bell, however, focused on the consumer PC market, NEC on the corporate, and Groupe Bull, through its Zenith Data Systems subsidiary, moved in the government/educational segment.

The stakes were raised in February 1996 in a deal worth $650 million. Under this deal, Packard Bell acquired Zenith Data Systems from Groupe Bull in exchange for $400 million in Packard Bell's preferred stock. At the same time, NEC provided $283 million in cash to Packard Bell, also in return for preferred stock. (The acquisition of preferred stock didn't raise their

stake in the company, however, since the additional shares were not common stock.) This newly strengthened alliance, in which Packard Bell absorbed Zenith, formed the world's fourth-largest PC manufacturer. The three companies all gained by consolidating product lines, combining research and development resources, and gaining leverage in purchasing components.

In June 1996 NEC announced the merger of its PC business outside of Japan with Packard Bell to form Packard Bell NEC. The new company, with $8 billion in estimated revenue, would immediately become the leading PC manufacturer in the U.S. The combination of the Packard Bell, NEC, and Zenith brand names would capture a 15.2% share of the U.S. market, jumping over Compaq's 12.3% share. The resulting company, led by Beny Alagem as chairman, CEO, and president, began operations as Packard Bell NEC on July 1, 1996.

Products and Services

Packard Bell designed, manufactured, and marketed a broad range of desktop, notebook, and mobile computers and network servers under the Packard Bell, NEC, and Zenith Data Systems brands. It also offered a variety of monitors and printers. Desktop computers included the Platinum, Multimedia, PackMate, and Legend models.

Changes to the Industry/Review of the Outcome

On paper, the merger seemed like the ideal arrangement. A single company controlled three strong brand names, each of which operated in a distinct market segment, and was based in the largest computer market in the world. Its assets included the technological knowledge of the Japanese partner, the consumer retail manufacturing and marketing expertise of the American company, and the European distribution channel of the French concern.

In reality, though, the outcome was far different. In June 1997 Packard Bell NEC launched a built-to-order direct sales network, cutting out its distributors as middlemen. The company soon recognized that it would not attain the same success that Dell and Gateway enjoyed from this scheme, but when it turned back to its distributors, it realized that it had lost much of their trust.

The company was still plagued by its tarnished name, which suffered another blow in late 1996. The attorneys general of 22 states filed a suit against Packard Bell NEC for reusing certain components from returned PCs. Although the firm admitted no wrongdoing, claiming that it subjected the parts to a series of tests before recycling them, it agreed to pay each of the states $70,000 for their legal expenses. It also began to label the boxes of PCs containing used parts.

Even worse, Packard Bell's association with NEC was bruising the reputation of this once stellar brand name, precisely the opposite of the effect that the companies had been expecting. "NEC, before the merger, was starting to make a bid to become more of a player in the corporate market," remarked Joe Ferlazzo, an analyst with Technology Business Research Inc., in *Computer Reseller News*, "but the merger with Packard Bell killed all that."

Meanwhile, rival manufacturers had entered Packard Bell NEC's territory of low-end PCs. Competition was fierce, and prices dropped. In 1996 the company's domestic market share dropped to 11.4%, behind Compaq's 12.9%. The next year it dropped again, holding an 8.8% share, behind Dell's 9.3% and Compaq's 16%. Its grasp on the worldwide market dropped as well, from a third-place 6.1% share in 1996 to a fifth-place 5.2% share in 1997.

In June 1998, Beny Alagem abruptly resigned, citing irreconcilable differences with NEC and Groupe Bull. Alain Couder, chief operating officer of Groupe Bull, was brought in as interim CEO at Packard Bell NEC. In September 1998 he was officially named the company's president and CEO.

That August NEC and Groupe Bull injected another $225 million and $25 million, respectively, into restructuring Packard Bell NEC. At the same time, although in a separate transaction, NEC exercised stock options to increase its share of common stock from 49% to 52.8%, a controlling interest. With this development, Packard Bell NEC was made a subsidiary of the Japanese corporation.

The cash infusion proved less than enough to turn Packard Bell NEC around, however, and the company was still unprofitable. Its restructuring over the previous year involved the reduction of its workforce from 5,600 to about 3,000. NEC, too, was facing the elimination of about 10% of its 150,000 global workforce. These two companies were expected to post losses for the 1998 year, about $500 million for Packard Bell NEC and $1.25 billion for NEC. These results spurred the resignation of NEC's president, Hisashi Kaneko. Although taking ultimate responsibility for the losses, he attributed partial blame to the depressed Asian economy and to the poor performance of Packard Bell NEC.

In February 1999, NEC again increased it stake in Packard Bell NEC. It purchased the 35% interest formerly held by Beny Alagem for $450 million, and in so doing acquired an 88% stake. The company remained optimistic that the new products under research and development would enable the company to become profitable, a prerequisite for an initial public offering, which would provide a source of new capital. NEC was reportedly also considering phasing out the Packard Bell brand name, replacing it with the sterling NEC name.

Research

Baljko, Jennifer L. "Packard Bell Gets $300M Infusion—Capital Will Be Used to Help Launch New Products," in *Electronic Buyers' News*, 5 January 1998. Reports NEC's acquisition of a 49% stake in Packard Bell.

Bournellis, Cynthia. "Is It a New Packard-Bell?" in *Electronic News (1991)*, 2 February 1998. Discusses the firm's failed attempts to turn a profit and restore reputability to its name.

———. "NEC Plows $225M More into Packard Bell," in *Electronic News (1991)*, 3 August 1998. Describes NEC's acquisition of Packard Bell as a subsidiary.

Caisse, Kimberly, and Jeff Bliss. "NEC Now—Two Years after Its Formation, Has Packard Bell NEC Prospered?" in *Computer Reseller News*, 6 April 1998. Reviews the company's dismal performance since its formation, assigning much of the blame to the Packard Bell reputation.

Ferranti, Marc. "Cash, Zenith Data Boost Packard Bell," in *Electronic News (1991)*, 12 February 1996. Reports the gains that Packard Bell gains through its acquisition of Zenith, and outlines the company's history of investments by NEC and Groupe Bull.

Johnson, Bradley. "New No. 1 Packard Bell NEC Faces Trio of PC Challenges," in *Advertising Age*, 10 June 1996. Predicts the difficulty that the newly merged company will have in aligning the Packard Bell, NEC, and Zenith brands.

Larson, Mark. "Packard Bell Scrambles to Stop Market-Share Slide," in *Sacramento Business Journal*," 24 April 1998. Describes the company's reinstallation of a distributor network and its hopes at going public.

"NEC Corp.," in *Notable Corporate Chronologies*, The Gale Group, 1999. Lists major events in the history of the company.

"Packard Bell Electronics Inc.," in *Notable Corporate Chronologies*, The Gale Group, 1999. Profiles the history of the company though its merger with NEC.

"Packard Bell & NEC Announce Merger of Worldwide PC Operations," in *EDGE: Work-Group Computing Report*, 10 June 1996. Details the synergies of the Packard Bell and NEC union.

Packard Bell NEC, Inc. Home Page, available at http://www.packardbell.com. Official World Wide Web Page for Packard Bell NEC. Includes an online store, news releases, service and support assistance, and product information.

Sperling, Ed. "Beny Alagem," in *Computer Reseller News*, 18 November 1996. Profiles Packard Bell's founder.

WILLIAM P. FREEMAN

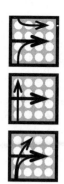

PANHANDLE EASTERN &
ASSOCIATED NATURAL GAS

Duke Energy Corp.
422 S. Church St.
Charlotte, NC 28242
USA

tel: (704)594-6200
fax: (704)382-3814
web: http://www.duke-energy.com

nationality: USA
date: December 15, 1994
affected: Panhandle Eastern Corp., USA, founded 1929
affected: Associated Natural Gas Corp., USA, founded 1983

Overview of the Acquisition

The 1994 acquisition of Associated Natural Gas by Panhandle Eastern created the nation's third-largest natural gas marketing company and the fourth-largest gas gathering company. Not only did the union give Panhandle Eastern entry into those higher growth industry segments, it also helped the firm assimilate its recent merger with Texas Eastern in forming a nationwide distribution network.

History of Panhandle Eastern Corp.

Interstate Pipe Line Co. was formed in 1929 as a subsidiary of a gas pipeline company, Missouri-Kansas Pipe Line Co. (Mo-Kan). Interstate's original network consisted of an 860-mile line feeding the Midwest with gas from the southwest Kansas and Texas panhandle. William G. Maguire, a consultant to Mo-Kan, suggested that Interstate's name be changed to Panhandle Eastern Pipe Line Co. He also recommended that the company expand its network, initially designed to terminate in Minneapolis, into the more populous states along Lake Michigan.

Mo-Kan sold 50% of Panhandle Eastern to rival Columbia Oil and Gasoline Corp. in 1930. Two years later Mo-Kan went bankrupt and was placed in receivership. In 1935 its trustees filed an anti-trust suit against Columbia, claiming bad-faith bargaining that resulted in the collapse of Mo-Kan. The proceedings dragged on until 1943, when Columbia was ordered to sign over its entire stake in Panhandle Eastern to a third party, Phillips Petroleum Co. Phillips then sold half of that stake to Mo-Kan, returning controlling interest in Panhandle Eastern to that company, which had emerged from receivership in 1937.

In 1943 the company launched an ultimately failed attempt to merge Mo-Kan, which served as merely a holding company, with Panhandle Eastern, which held all gas and pipeline assets. The next year a liquidation scheme for Mo-Kan was conceived. This former parent company was eventually merged into Panhandle Eastern and finally dissolved in 1971.

Meanwhile, Maguire had become president of Mo-Kan, and then became chairman and CEO of Panhandle Eastern. In 1939 Panhandle Eastern completed its first pipeline, extending from Illinois to the Texas Panhandle. It founded its second pipeline, Trunkline Gas Co., in 1951 to link the Midwest market with the Gulf Coast. Eight years later Panhandle Eastern established Anadarko Production to develop exploration activity in the gas-laden Anadarko Basin, which sprawled over portions of Texas, Oklahoma, and Kansas. In 1960 Panhandle Eastern joined with National Distillers & Chemical Corp. to form National Helium Corp., which opened the world's largest helium extraction plant three years later.

Governmental price controls on natural gas during the 1970s discouraged producers from exploring for new sources. As the rising demand caught up with the shrinking supply, alternative sources of fuel, such as synthetic fuels, coal gasification, and liquified natural gas, emerged as necessary, but expensive, solutions. In connection with its coal gasification plans, Panhandle Eastern acquired Youghioney and Ohio Coal Co. in 1976. The next year it entered into a long-term contract to purchase liquified natural gas from Enterprise Nationale Sonatrach, the Algerian national energy company.

This contract with Sonatrach, considered a wise investment at the time, proved to be a liability. In 1978 the U.S. government began deregulating natural gas prices, making conventional sources of gas more affordable and unconventional sources expensive and unnecessary. In 1983 the company unilaterally suspended its contract with Sonatrach and was immediately sued by both the Algerian energy company and by Lachmar, Panhandle Eastern's shipping partner. Three years later Panhandle Eastern agreed to purchase the interests of its partners in Lachmar for $32 million.

Panhandle Eastern Corp. was formed in 1981 as a holding company for Panhandle Eastern Pipe Line Co. Between 1977 and 1982 the company had the highest return on equity of any gas producer/pipeliner. Yet that streak came to an end as Panhandle Eastern proved slow in adapting to the increasingly deregulated market environment. Moreover, its 1.5 trillion cubic feet of reserves made it an attractive takeover target. In 1986 Wagner & Brown, an oil and gas firm, offered $2.3 billion for Panhandle Eastern. After rejecting the bid, Panhandle Eastern spun off its Anadarko subsidiary in October 1986.

To avoid future takeover attempts, the company decided to go back on the acquisition trail. In 1989 it paid $3.2 billion for Texas Eastern Corp., outbidding Coastal Corp., which was led by Oscar Wyatt. Texas

The Business

Financials

Revenue (1998): $17.61 billion

Employees (1998): 22,000

SICs / NAICS

sic 4923 - Gas Transmission & Distribution

sic 4925 - Gas Production & Distribution Nec

sic 4911 - Electric Services

sic 1311 - Crude Petroleum & Natural Gas

sic 4822 - Telegraph & Other Communications

sic 4941 - Water Supply

naics 221210 - Natural Gas Distribution

naics 486210 - Pipeline Transportation of Natural Gas

naics 221122 - Electric Power Distribution

naics 221111 - Hydroelectric Power Generation

naics 221112 - Fossil Fuel Electric Power Generation

naics 221113 - Nuclear Electric Power Generation

naics 211111 - Crude Petroleum and Natural Gas Extraction

naics 513310 - Wired Telecommunications Carriers

naics 221310 - Water Supply and Irrigation Systems

Eastern had three times the revenues of Panhandle Eastern, and its northeastern pipeline system could be combined with Panhandle Eastern's Midwest system to create a national network. The purchase, however, proved troublesome, as Panhandle Eastern's debt quadrupled to $2.8 billion, just as increased competition in the industry squeezed profit margins for all players. In 1990 Dennis Hendrix, former CEO of Texas Eastern, assumed that post at Panhandle Eastern. He trimmed operations and redirected the company's focus from production to distribution. The following year, Panhandle Eastern extended its pipeline system to the lucrative Northeast market.

In 1993 earnings rose 30% to $180 million, and the net profit margin increased to 5.7%, the company's highest in six years. The potential for growth, however, had come to a virtual standstill, and Panhandle Eastern looked to add to its operations. In December 1994 the firm acquired Associated Natural Gas Corp., a company operating in the gas gathering and marketing sector. The market position gained through this transaction was not indefinitely stable, and in 1997 Panhandle Eastern, which had become known as PanEnergy Corp., began shopping for another mate.

The Officers

Chairman and CEO: Richard B. Priory

Exec. VP and Chief Financial Officer: Richard J. Osborne

Exec. VP and Chief Administrative Officer: Ruth G. Shaw

Exec. VP, General Counsel and Secretary: Richard W. Blackburn

That year it merged with Duke Power Corp. to form Duke Energy.

History of Associated Natural Gas Corp.

Cortlandt S. Dietler had founded the Western Crude oil company in the mid-1960s and then sold the successful operation to Getty Oil in 1980. In the decade's early years, he realized that the role of natural gas as an energy source was poised to increase dramatically. Beginning in 1983 the Federal Energy Regulatory Commission began passing regulations that opened up interstate pipelines to gas companies that didn't own them. This enabled suppliers to link directly with local gas distributors, utilities, and industrial customers in exchange for a fee for use of the pipelines. To take advantage of this new environment, Dietler formed Natural Gas Associates (NGA) in 1983, with the hope that this young company would be more nimble than its larger peers to exploit the industry's segments.

The company's first natural gas processing and gathering system became operational in March 1983. Its plant in Kersey, Colorado, was part of a system 18 miles long connected to 22 wells. While NGA gradually expanded that system, the company's success was tied to aggressive marketing. It launched its first major marketing campaign, initially targeting potential customers via the Yellow Pages, when its volume exceeded the demand of the local utility companies. This tactic enabled NGA to sustain its early growth and provided the resources for expansion.

In 1986 NGA acquired the Colorado Gathering & Processing Corp., whose system was adjacent to and easily absorbed by NGA's existing system. Later that year it also extended its reach into the gas- and oil-rich Anadarko Basin by purchasing two parallel pipelines in Oklahoma. NGA formed the ATTCO Pipeline Co. subsidiary from these two pipelines, adding to them additional oil gathering systems bought from other companies to transform ATTCO into a 900-mile chain in Oklahoma and Texas.

NGA purchased the Minden gas gathering and processing plant located in Louisiana in February 1987. That October it acquired the Pantera gathering system in Colorado. The following year the newly renamed Associated Natural Gas Corp. (ANG) went public and doubled its revenues to $189 million. These financial resources fueled the company's acquisition streak. In 1988 it purchased the Wilcox gas processing plant in Texas as well as an associated natural gas liquids pipeline. The next year it bought the Milfay gathering and processing system in eastern Oklahoma.

In 1990 ANG purchased the Alabama natural gas gathering systems of Galaxy Energies Inc. and AD-AM Gas Co. ANG's revenues leapt to $292 million, and the firm recorded a $3.3 million profit, up from a slight loss the previous year.

ANG absorbed 940 miles of gas gathering pipelines from MEGA Natural Gas Co. in 1991. That year it also bought the Wattenberg System, consisting of 1,200 miles of pipeline and eight compressor stations, from Panhandle Eastern Corp. for $48 million. ANG acquired Apache Corp.'s Spindle field pipeline gathering and gas processing facilities for $34 million.

During 1992 the company expanded operations in all of its major areas of activity. It added to its Colorado system by acquiring the gas processing and gathering properties of Gerrity Oil & Gas Corp., and enlarged its Oklahoma system with the purchase of 1,900 miles of natural gas pipeline from Phillips Petroleum.

ANG sustained its momentum through 1993. It acquired a gas gathering system from Evergreen Resources, Inc. and four natural gas pipeline systems from Endevco Inc. It also joined with Evergreen Resources to form ANGI Ltd., a gas marketing company in the U.K. That year revenues reached $1.5 billion.

In July 1994 ANG merged with Grand Valley Gas Co., thereby gaining assets in New Mexico, Kansas, Texas, Oklahoma, Wyoming, and Utah. At the same time it formed Associated Gas Services Inc. as a subsidiary to combine ANG's natural gas marketing activities with those of Grand Valley. In October ANG agreed to be acquired by Panhandle Eastern, and in December it became a subsidiary of that company.

Market Forces Driving the Acquisition

Panhandle Eastern had never fully recovered from the oil crisis of the 1970s. A governmentally regulated domestic environment coupled with the Arab oil embargo made Panhandle Eastern a likely target for a takeover. Having thwarted one such attempt in 1986, the company realized it had only two choices:

acquire or be acquired. In 1989 the firm entered into the bidding for Texas Eastern Corp., an operator of pipelines in the northeastern U.S. Panhandle Eastern topped Coastal Corp.'s $2.5 billion hostile bid with a $3.2 billion cash and stock offer. While the acquisition was considered a sound investment over the long haul, Panhandle Eastern's debt load quadrupled as a result, to $2.8 billion.

This purchase, however, not only loaded Panhandle Eastern with massive debt, but it also brought a number of unexpected environmental hurdles to clear. Panhandle Eastern's stock price fell, and after the company cut its dividends by 60% in 1990, its shares nose-dived to a low of $10 each.

Dennis Hendrix, former CEO of Texas Eastern, became CEO of Panhandle Eastern in 1990. As part of his redirection of the company from producer to distributor, he improved the capacity of the company's distribution network while paring down its debt load. In 1993, as the company's revenues decreased, its earnings increased 38% to $180 million.

Yet even the combination of Texas Eastern's distribution network in the Northeast and Panhandle Eastern's system in the Midwest wasn't enough for the company to sustain growth. Industry experts estimated that the annual growth rate for distributors would be between 2% and 4%, not a great forecast for a segment that accounted for 90% of Panhandle Eastern's operating income.

In 1992 the Federal Energy Regulatory Commission lifted some of its restrictions and permitted the industry's distributors to engage in less regulated sectors such as gathering, marketing, and storing gas. It was in these high-growth areas that Associated Natural Gas operated.

Approach and Engagement

On October 11, 1994, Panhandle Eastern announced its proposed acquisition of Associated Natural Gas. The $830 million deal involved a $591 million stock swap and a $239 million assumption of ANG debt. Panhandle Eastern operated four interstate pipelines covering 26,000 miles, while ANG held about 9,400 miles of gas gathering pipes. These systems had little overlap and would therefore extend the combined company's reach. As Paul Anderson, president of Panhandle Eastern, said in *The Oil Daily*, "Panhandle will broaden its service portfolio and access to western markets and supply; Associated will achieve improved access to new high-value markets in the Midwest and Northeast, as well as to Gulf Coast, Canada and Mexican gas supply, along with a portfolio of complementary market services."

The Players

Panhandle Eastern Chairman and President: Dennis R. Hendrix. In 1990 Dennis Hendrix, former CEO of Texas Eastern, assumed the post of CEO at Panhandle Eastern. He retained that position after the acquisition of Associated Natural Gas in 1994. The following April, Hendrix stepped down as CEO in favor of Paul Anderson.

Associated Natural Gas Chairman and CEO: Cortland S. Dietler. Cortland Dietler had a long career in the petroleum industry. By 1987 he had purchased 11 oil companies and established 20 others, including Associated Natural Gas (ANG). After selling ANG to Panhandle Eastern, Dietler and a group of investors reorganized a petroleum services company in April 1995, renaming it TransMontaigne Oil.

The acquisition was completed on December 15, 1994, as Associated Natural Gas became a subsidiary of Panhandle Eastern. Cortland Dietler, ANG's chairman and CEO, became an advisory director to the company's board, while Hendrix retained his position. The presidents of both companies—Don Anderson of ANG and Paul Anderson of Panhandle Eastern—also remained in place in the new company.

Products and Services

Duke Energy operated in four business units:

Energy Services: Duke Energy North America developed, owned, and operated electric generation projects for customers across the U.S. and Canada. Duke Energy Trading and Marketing, one of the nation's five largest energy marketers, delivered electric power and natural gas products to utilities, municipalities, industrials, commercial entities, and other large energy users. Duke Engineering & Services, Inc. was the engineering, energy, and environmental project arm of Duke Energy Corp. Duke Energy International was the international development and asset management unit of Duke Energy Corp. Duke/Fluor Daniel was a joint operation of Duke Energy Corp. and Fluor Daniel, Inc. for the purpose of meeting global power generation needs. DukeSolutions provided custom energy solutions to help organizations improve their competitiveness, productivity, and profitability.

The corporation's transmission and distribution operations fell under its **Energy Transmission** unit, which was comprised of Northeast Natural Gas Pipelines, Maritimes & Northeast Pipeline, SpectrumSM, Algonquin HubLineSM, Cross BaySM Pipeline, LINK System, Duke Electric Transmission, Duke Communication Services, Duke Energy Field Services, and TEPPCO Partners, L.P.

Duke Power, one of the nation's largest investor-owned electric utilities, served nearly two million customers in North Carolina and South Carolina. With its subsidiary, Nantahala Power and Light Company, this unit operated three nuclear generating stations, eight coal-fired stations, 31 hydroelectric stations, and numerous combustion turbine units.

Diversified Businesses consisted of three units. Crescent Resources, Inc. was a real estate development and forest management company. DukeNet Communications, Inc., the telecommunications arm of Duke Energy Corp., met the communication needs of industrial, commercial, and residential customers in the Southeast by developing and managing communications systems, including fiber optic and wireless digital network services. Duke Water Operations provided franchised water services to customers in parts of North Carolina and South Carolina.

Changes to the Industry

By acquiring Associated Natural Gas, which had revenues of $1.5 billion in 1993, Panhandle Eastern became the nation's third-largest marketer and fourth-largest gatherer of natural gas. The new company continued to take advantage of deregulation in the year following the acquisition. As the U.S. gas market became more competitive, some industry players ventured into electric power, which was also undergoing regulatory restructuring. On October 1, 1995, the company's Associated Power Services unit became the first independent gas marketer to provide direct electricity service in the U.S.

As the lines between energy sectors began to blur, so did those between industries that at first blush appeared unrelated. In September 1995 PanEnergy Information Services Co., a unit of Panhandle Eastern, engaged in negotiations with Williams Information & Trading Systems Co. (WIT) to form an alliance combining their electronic information operations. "As the gas, liquid fuels, and electricity markets converge into a common energy marketplace, we fully expect that opportunities to apply a broader range of information and communication technologies will multiply rapidly," said E. Russell Braziel, vice president of WIT, in *The Oil and Gas Journal*.

Review of the Outcome

The newly combined company continued to strengthen its market position through acquisitions. In 1995 Associated Natural Gas acquired the Texas-based Wharton Gas Plant and gathering system, the Wattenberg gas system located in Colorado, and the Canadian gas marketer Continental Energy Marketing Ltd.

In January 1996 Panhandle Eastern changed its name to PanEnergy Corp. to reflect its growth beyond the regional transmission of natural gas. In December 1997 PanEnergy merged with Duke Power, an electric utility, to form Duke Energy Corp., the nation's second-largest investor-owned utility. The following year, Duke Energy increased its stake to 21.1% of TEPPCO Partners L.P., a gas and oil transporter; acquired a 51.5% controlling interest in Electroquil S.A., an electricity generator in Ecuador; and purchased three power plants to compete in the deregulated market of California.

Research

"Associated Natural Gas Corporation," in *International Directory of Company Histories*, Vol. 11, St. James Press: 1995. Profiles the company until its acquisition by Panhandle Eastern.

Connolly, Paul. "Panhandle Acquires Associated Natural Gas, Creating Third-Largest Independent Marketer," in *The Oil Daily*, 16 December 1994. Briefly reports the completion of the deal.

Duke Energy Corp. Home Page, available at http://www.duke-energy.com. Official World Wide Web Page for Duke Energy. Includes business segment descriptions, annual reports and other financial data, executive biographies, press releases, and a brief history of the company's formation.

Osterland, Andrew W. "...Join 'Em: Panhandle Eastern Looks to Tap into Greener, Less Regulated Fields," in *Financial World*, 3 January 1995. Describes the deregulated environment that spurred Panhandle Eastern's acquisition of ANG.

"Panhandle Eastern Agrees to Acquire Associated Gas for $591 Million in Stock," in *The Wall Street Journal*, 11 October 1994. Discloses the acquisition agreement.

"Panhandle Eastern Expanding Power Role," in *The Oil and Gas Journal*, 16 October 1995. Reports Panhandle's foray into electric power.

"Panhandle Eastern Corporation," in *International Directory of Company Histories*, Vol. V, St. James Press: 1992. Offers a narrative account of the company's history.

Walsh, Campion. "Panhandle, ANG Approve $839 Million Merger as Pipelines Look for Nonregulated Assets," in *The Oil Daily*, 12 October 1994. Provides an account of the proposed merger.

DAVIS MCMILLAN

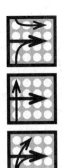

PANTRY PRIDE & REVLON

nationality: USA
date: November 5, 1985
affected: Pantry Pride Inc. (subsidiary of MacAndrews & Forbes Holdings Inc.), USA, founded 1984
affected: Revlon, Inc., USA, founded 1932

MacAndrews & Forbes Holdings Inc.
35 E. 62nd St.
New York, NY 10021
USA

tel: (212)527-688-9000
fax: (212)572-8400

Overview of the Acquisition

Initiating a spirited battle, Pantry Pride launched a hostile bid for Revlon, Inc. in 1985. Determined to remain independent, Revlon threw a number of defensive blockades in front of Pantry Pride, but none deterred Ronald Perelman, Pantry Pride's chairman. As a last resort, Revlon arranged a leverage buyout with Forstmann, Little & Co., an investment banking firm. In their agreement, Revlon agreed to sell certain assets to Forstmann Little at a price below their market value as part of a lock-up agreement to close the bidding to other suitors. In a landmark case, the Delaware Supreme Court nullified this agreement, and Pantry Pride subsequently acquired Revlon for $2.7 billion.

History of MacAndrews & Forbes Holdings Inc.

Ronald O. Perelman earned experience in mergers and acquisitions by working with his father in building a small family conglomerate, Belmont Industries. In 1978 he ventured out on his own, and bought 40% of Cohen-Hatfield Industries, a small jeweler, for $1.9 million in loans. Within a year Perelman had repaid those loans and made a $15 million profit by upping the jeweler's marketing efforts and selling its underperforming stores.

In 1979 he acquired a stake in MacAndrews & Forbes, a supplier of licorice extract, a product used by cigarette makers. After completely acquiring MacAndrews & Forbes the following year, Perelman again took an active role in improving the company's business. Technicolor, a motion picture processor, was purchased in 1982. Six years later, after divesting its unprofitable operations and acquiring other film and video processing companies, Perelman sold Technicolor for $780 million.

MacAndrews & Forbes Holdings, housing Perelman's accumulated assets, was taken private in 1984. That year it acquired Consolidated Cigar. Pantry Pride, a struggling Florida-based supermarket chain, was purchased for $60 million in 1985. Perelman liquidated that company's assets and transformed it into a shell company for the acquisition of other companies.

The Business

SICs / NAICS

sic 2844 - Toilet Preparations

naics 325620 - Toilet Preparation Manufacturing

Pantry Pride's first attempted acquisition, and Perelman's first hostile bid, targeted Revlon Inc. in August 1985. After a protracted battle that ultimately required the intervention of the Delaware Supreme Court, Pantry Pride successfully purchased the cosmetics and healthcare products company that November. In 1986 Pantry Pride changed its name to Revlon Group Inc.

MacAndrews & Forbes was unsuccessful in its later attempts to acquire Gillette and Salomon Brothers. In 1988 however, it completed the lucrative acquisition of five failing Texas savings and loan banks after receiving valuable government incentives. Five years later it sold the group, by then known as First Gibraltar, to BankAmerica.

In 1988 the firm bought the Coleman Co., a manufacturer of camping equipment. It also purchased Marvel Entertainment Group Inc., a comic book publisher, and added trading cards to that company's offerings. When both of these markets collapsed in the mid-1990s, however, Carl Icahn and other shareholders ousted its board after Marvel entered into bankruptcy in 1996.

Perelman purchased New World Entertainment in 1989. This company became New World Communications Group after absorbing other media interests like Guthy-Renker, Genesis Entertainment, and New World Entertainment. It joined with Hachette Filipacchi to purchase *Premiere* magazine in 1995. Two years later New World was sold to News Corp.

Mafco Consolidated Group was formed in 1995 through the combination of Consolidated Cigar, Mafco Worldwide, and Abex. Two years later MacAndrews & Forbes acquired the remaining 15% interest in this company that it didn't already own.

In 1994 First Nationwide, one of the nation's leading savings and loans, was purchased by MacAndrews & Forbes and Gerald J. Ford. This bank paid $1.2 billion for Cal Fed Bancorp in 1997. The next year First Nationwide merged with Golden State Bancorp for $1.8 billion, resulting in the second-largest thrift in the U.S.

MacAndrews & Forbes sold Coleman to Sunbeam Corp. in 1998, the same year that Consolidated Cigar was sold to Societe Nationale d'Exploitation Industrielle des Tabacs et Allumettes (Seita). Also in 1998 the firm purchased a 72% stake in the movie camera manufacturer Panavision. By 1999 MacAndrews & Forbes was one of the nation's largest private companies.

History of Revlon, Inc.

Unemployment during the Great Depression drove Charles Revson to take a job with the Elka company in 1931 to sell nail polish to beauty salons. The next year Revson decided to open his own nail polish company. To do so he joined with his brother Joseph and a nail polish supplier named Charles R. Lachman, best remembered for contributing the letter "L" to the Revlon name.

The young company enjoyed great success as the popularity of beauty salons grew, with the demand for manicures rising along with it. Of even greater importance to its success was the company's use of pigments rather than dyes, lending its products an opaque look in a variety of shades that had previously been unavailable. Sales reached $11,000 in 1933, the year that the company incorporated as Revlon Products Corp.

Revson was a master—and trailblazer—in marketing for the cosmetics industry. He applied evocative names, like Fatal Apple and Kissing Pink, to the company's nail polish. He also targeted affluent customers, placing printed ads in *The New Yorker* and retailing through department stores.

Revlon offered an array of manicure products by 1940, when it unveiled its first lipstick. The success of this new line, designed to match the nail polish, was apparent in the company's sales—$2.8 million that year. After World War II Revlon paid $301,000 for Graef & Schmidt, a cutlery manufacturer that also made manicure instruments.

The firm began launching new color debuts twice a year, tying them into seasonal clothing fashions. One of the company's most successful launches was that of its 1952 Fire and Ice color nail polish and lipstick, which helped push sales that year to $25.5 million.

Three years later Revlon became the sole sponsor of *The $64,000 Question* television show, which had a weekly audience of 55 million. As a result, sales of certain products grew by 500%, with the company's net sales increasing nearly $20 million to $51.6 million.

The company reorganized as Revlon, Inc. in November 1955 and went public the following month.

It was listed on the New York Stock Exchange at the end of 1956. By the end of the decade, Revlon had begun to market its products overseas. Using a unique strategy, it didn't adapt its promotions to specific cultures, instead promoting the American look by using U.S. models.

During the 1960s Revlon increased its marketplace presence by reorganizing its product line into six units, each targeting a different market—Princess Marcella Borghese, Revlon, Etherea, Natural Wonder, Moon Drops, and Ultima. With this move, the company expanded from its traditional base of elite markets into more mainstream areas.

Revlon's initial attempts to diversify through acquisition were unsuccessful and included such companies as Knomark, a shoe-polish company; Ty-D-Bowl, a maker of toilet cleansers; Schick, an electric shaver manufacturer; and Picone, a women's sportswear company. Revlon finally hit success with its 1966 acquisition of U.S. Vitamin & Pharmaceutical Corp. This company provided the basis for Revlon's foray into pharmaceuticals and housed its future acquisitions in this industry.

The company acquired the Mitchum Co., maker of antiperspirants and other toiletries, in 1970. Three years later it launched Charlie, an immensely popular fragrance targeting the young, independent woman. Falling victim to pancreatic cancer, Revson recruited Michel Bergerac as his successor in 1974; the company's founder died the following year.

Bergerac focused the company on improving its profitability, reducing spending and cutting 500 jobs. He also implemented a diversification strategy to reduce the company's dependence on cosmetics, an industry that was becoming increasingly competitive. To this end he purchased Coburn Optical Industries, a manufacturer of ophthalmic equipment, in 1975. The next year Revlon bought Barnes-Hind, the largest U.S. marketer of hard contact lens solutions. Other healthcare acquisitions included the Armour Pharmaceutical Co., a thyroid drug company, and Lewis-Howe Co., maker of the Tums antacid. The acquisition of Technicon Corp., manufacturer of blood analyzers, was controversial due to its $60 million price tag for a marginally profitable company. Revlon's sales exceeded $1 billion in 1977 and reached $1.7 billion in 1979.

By the mid-1980s Revlon's health care operations were outperforming its cosmetics business. As Bergerac had foreseen, the company was losing market share to increasingly stiff competition, such as Estee Lauder and Noxell, maker of the Cover Girl line. Many analysts believed that the company would be worth more if it were broken up and sold piecemeal. With this goal in mind, Ronald Perelman's Pantry

The Officers

Chairman: Ronald O. Perelman

Vice Chairman: Donald G. Drapkin

Vice Chairman: Howard Gittis

President: Bruce Slovin

Exec. VP: Meyer Laskin

Pride company initiated an intense bid to take the company private in 1985. At its conclusion, Perelman, as chairman and CEO, began divesting its healthcare businesses to reduce the company's $2.9 billion in debt. By 1988 he had pared down that load by $1.5 billion. At its same time, he expanded its core cosmetics operations, purchasing Max Factor for $300 million in 1987. Subsequent acquisitions included Yves Saint Laurent fragrances and cosmetics, Charles of the Ritz, Germaine Monteil, Alexandre de Markoff, and Betrix.

Despite these moves, Revlon continued to lose market share. In the early 1990s Perelman was forced to sell Max Factor and Betrix, along with several other Revlon brands. The company finally turned the corner with its 1994 launch of the ColorStay line of cosmetics, followed by the introduction of the Age Defying line. By 1995 it had usurped Maybelline as the industry's leader, with $1.9 billion in sales.

The financial improvements enabled the company to go public in 1996. Two years later Revlon purchased the Cutex nail products brand. In December 1998 it exited from the operation of retail stores by selling its interest in The Cosmetic Center, Inc.

By early 1999 the company's prospects were dimming, as it once again lost the industry's top spot. In January it announced the closure of three factories, calling for a job reduction of 1,200. Mired in $2.7 billion in debt in June 1999, Revlon was the subject of industry speculation about a possible break-up.

Market Forces Driving the Acquisition

By the mid-1980s Revlon was in sore shape. The company's earnings had fallen to $112 million in 1984, down from $192 million in 1980. A number of forces lay behind this decline. Revlon had diversified into healthcare by acquiring manufacturers of contact lenses and blood analyzers. These ventures had only just begun to show even a slight contribution to Revlon's balance sheet, however.

The Players

MacAndrews & Forbes Holdings Chairman and CEO: Ronald O. Perelman. Ronald Perelman learned the business of mergers and acquisitions as partner with his father in the family business. The pair added company after company to the holdings of his father's firm, Belmont Industries. Perelman, a graduate of the University of Pennsylvania, struck out on his own in his mid-30s. As owner of an investment company, he built a reputation— and a profitable business—by purchasing struggling yet valuable companies. Installing himself at the reins of these newly acquired concerns, Perelman would restore profitability by refocusing them on core operations and promoting growth. By the mid-1980s his MacAndrews & Forbes Holdings company had accomplished this with a number of acquisitions. One of his most public and far-reaching purchases was that of Revlon, Inc. in 1985. He later locked horns with corporate raider Carl Icahn over the ownership of Marvel Entertainment Group Inc.

Revlon Chairman and CEO: Michel C. Bergerac. Born in southwest France, Michel Bergerac earned an economics degree at the Sorbonne before moving to the U.S., where he then received an MBA from the University of California at Los Angeles. After taking a variety of far-flung jobs, he settled down as a sales representative for Cannon Electric Company in 1957. Bergerac steadily moved up the corporate ladder, finding himself as head of ITT Europe, a unit of Cannon's parent, ITT Corp. There, he orchestrated more than 100 acquisitions, doubling the company's sales in three years.

These results caught the eye of Charles Revson, Revlon's founder. After five years of pursuit, Revson succeeded in recruiting Bergerac, enticed by a lucrative sign-on bonus, as his successor in 1974. At the company's helm as chairman and CEO, he led the company on a controversial diversification path. After failing to fend off Pantry Pride in its takeover of Revlon in 1985, Bergerac resigned, walking away with some $36 million in stock options and severance pay.

Moreover, its core cosmetics business was losing its grip on the market. For years Revlon had failed to launch a blockbuster product that matched the success of its Charlie perfume or Flex shampoo. Retailers had reduced the selection of Revlon products that they stocked. This was a difficult challenge for the firm, as cosmetics companies relied on slight variations in product color to meet customer demands. The company was also finding itself without a well-defined territory—it was considered not quite glamorous enough for upscale stores yet was undercut by Maybelline and Cover Girl in drugstores and supermarkets.

To some analysts, the pieces of Revlon were more valuable than the whole. Ronald Perelman also believed this to be true. He had built a fortune by purchasing underperforming companies, divesting them of their least profitable businesses, and then setting about improving core operations. This formula had proved to be a success for his MacAndrews & Forbes company, a mini-conglomerate consisting of jewelry, cigars, licorice, and film processing.

Having secured $761 million in financing to pursue a large company, Perelman began searching for a suitable acquisition target. Through the process of elimination, he settled on Revlon. Its financial condition left it vulnerable, as its low stock price might make its shareholders amenable to a premium offer. More importantly, Perelman believed that the company could exact a recovery. The Revlon name was still golden, and its healthcare operations could be sold off at a price well over their original cost, with the profits used to bolster the remaining cosmetics business.

Approach and Engagement

In June 1985 Ronald Perelman contacted Michel Bergerac, Revlon's chairman and CEO, to discuss a deal. Their accounts of this meeting later varied, as Perelman contended that Bergerac had said that Revlon might be for sale at the right price, while Bergerac insisted that he had indicated that the company was decidedly not for sale.

Regardless, Perelman offered $47.50 per share, or $1.8 billion, for Revlon on August 19. This bid was made through Pantry Pride Inc., a shell company that was a subsidiary of MacAndrews & Forbes Holdings.

Revlon rejected the offer and installed a poison pill, a defensive measure that would add millions of dollars in expenses to Revlon if it were purchased. The pill would be triggered if a shareholder acquired 20% of Revlon's shares, at which point its other shareholders would get the right to swap one share for $65 in notes. The company also authorized a stock repurchase for up to 26% of its outstanding shares at $57.50, or $10 more per share than Pantry Pride's bid. Additionally, Revlon announced plans to sell a healthcare unit to finance this repurchase.

On September 13 Pantry Pride countered by reducing its offer to $42 per share. The bid's total value was thereby reduced by $575 million, the same amount that Revlon would take on in debt through its proposed stock buyback. Two weeks later Pantry Pride reversed this stance, increasing its bid to $50 per share in the hopes of enticing shareholders to force Revlon into negotiations. It then sweetened that bid to $53 per share.

On October 2 Revlon requested that Pantry Pride keep that offer open while it considered other proposals, including a leveraged buyout (LBO) and an acquisition by another company. The following day Revlon announced that it had agreed to be taken private through an LBO. Forstmann, Little & Co. would pay $56 per share in cash, or $1.8 billion, and split the company into three pieces. First, Revlon would sell its cosmetics business, along with the Revlon name, to Adler & Shaykin, another LBO firm. Forstmann Little would then sell Revlon's Norcliff Thayer and Reheis Chemicals units to American Home Products Corp. The remaining healthcare company would become the basis for a new company, headed by Bergerac.

The bidding soon escalated. Pantry Pride increased its bid to $56.25 per share, or $1.78 billion in cash, on October 8, and Forstmann Little upped its offer to $57.25 per share on October 13. As part of this sweetened bid from Forstmann Little, Revlon entered into a lock-up agreement consisting of two elements. Not only would Revlon refrain from seeking any better acquisition offers, it would also sell its Vision Care group and National Health Laboratories to Forstmann Little at the bargain price of $525 million if a rival bidder acquired 40% of Revlon's stock. At the same time, Bergerac withdrew his personal investment in the LBO amid mounting criticism that he was looking only to increase his personal interest by agreeing to the LBO. On October 18 Pantry Pride increased its offer to $58 per share, just over $1.8 billion, provided that Revlon terminate this lock-up agreement.

Revlon's plans took a blow on October 23. In a court ruling that had implications for future merger and acquisition activity in the U.S., the Delaware Chancery Court ruled that Revlon had breached its fiduciary duty by forging the lock-up agreement. The Delaware Supreme Court upheld this ruling days later. "A lock-up agreement is not per se illegal," the court wrote, as quoted in *The New York Times*. "A lock-up provision, however, must advance or stimulate the bidding process, not retard it."

On November 1, 1985, Revlon capitulated, stating that it would "do nothing to impede" a takeover by Pantry Pride. Three days later Pantry Pride took Revlon private by acquiring 93% of its shares.

Products and Services

By the late 1990s Revlon was a world leader in cosmetics, skin care, fragrance, personal care and professional products. Its products were sold in approximately 175 countries and territories. Revlon's brands included Revlon, ColorStay, Age Defying, StreetWear, Almay, Ultima II, Flex, Super Lustrous, African Pride, Creme of Nature, Charlie, and Flex.

Changes to the Industry

The drama between Revlon, Pantry Pride, and Forstmann, Little & Co. had a great impact on takeovers throughout the U.S. By invalidating the lock-up agreement between Revlon and Forstmann Little, the Delaware Supreme Court set limits on the defensive tactics that could be used against hostile bidders.

The Court ruled that when Revlon began seeking a white knight, such as Forstmann Little, it had effectively put itself up for sale. At this point, it had the fiduciary responsibility to its shareholders to consider higher offers, such as Pantry Pride's. By this measure, then, its lock-up agreement with Forstmann Little was a breach of duties to Revlon's shareholders, and was therefore invalid.

Review of the Outcome

On November 5, 1985, Perelman replaced Bergerac as Revlon's chairman and CEO. As planned, he immediately proceeded to break up the company. In early December he agreed to sell the Norcliff Thayer health products unit and the Reheis chemicals business to Beecham Group PLC for $395 million. Later that month Rorer Group Inc. agreed to pay $690 million for Revlon's ethical drug business.

The fate of Revlon's cosmetics business remained up in the air for nearly a year. Since the start of his pursuit of Revlon, Perelman had intended to retain that business and divest all others. Forstmann Little, however, had agreed to sell those operations to Adler & Shaykin, focusing instead on Revlon's healthcare operations. In late December 1985 Pantry Pride declared that the agreement between those two companies was void because it had expired, but Adler & Shaykin disputed that claim. The conflict was finally resolved in late October 1986, when Revlon agreed to pay $19.5 million to settle the dispute.

Research

Cole, Robert J. "High Stakes Drama at Revlon," in *The New York Times*, 11 November 1985. Profiles the acquisition, from start to finish.

———. "Pantry Pride Bid is Opposed by Revlon," in *The New York Times*, 20 August 1985. Details Perelman's initial bid for the company.

———. "Takeover Accepted by Revlon," in *The New York Times*, 2 November 1985. Provides a chronology of the battle.

Greenhouse, Steven. "Merger Game Altered by New Rulings," in *The New York Times*, 30 December 1985. Relates the impact that the Revlon battle, along with several other 1985 court rulings, would have on future merger deals.

"Revlon, Inc.," in *International Directory of Company Histories*, Vol. 17, St. James Press, 1997. Profiles the history of the company.

Revlon, Inc. Home Page, available at http://www.revlon.com. Official World Wide Web Page for Revlon. Includes annual reports and other financial information, news releases, and product descriptions.

Rivera, Nancy. "Revlon Board Accepts $1.8 Billion Buy-Out by Forstmann, Little," in *Los Angeles Times*, 4 October 1985. Describes the agreement, including the lock-up arrangement, between Revlon and Forstmann Little.

Wasserstein, Bruce. *Big Deal: The Battle for Control of America's Leading Corporations*, Warner Books, 1998. Offers an overview of the largest mergers in recent American corporate history.

DEBORAH J. UNTENER

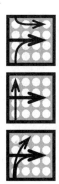

PARAMOUNT & MACMILLAN

nationality: USA
date: February 1994
affected: Paramount Communications Inc. (later acquired by Viacom International Inc.),
USA, founded 1956
affected: Macmillan Inc., USA, founded 1896

Viacom International Inc.
1515 Broadway, 51st Fl.
New York, NY 10036
USA

tel: (212)258-6000
web: http://www.viacom.com
e-mail: info@viacom.com

Overview of the Acquisition

Macmillan Inc., one of the last remaining portions of the bankrupt Maxwell Communications Corp. PLC, was put on the auction block in late 1993. This company, a strong player in textbook, children's, adult trade, and reference book publishing, was sought after by several publishing companies. Paramount Communications paid nearly $554 million for Macmillan the following February, and immediately became the world's second-largest book publisher. The timing of the sale was of interest, as Paramount itself was the subject of a heated acquisition battle between Viacom International and QVC.

History of Paramount Communications, Inc.

After experimenting in the import-export business, Austrian-born Charles George Bluhdorn began searching for a publicly traded company whose stock he could use to buy other companies. In 1956 he secured a controlling interest in Michigan Plating & Stamping and joined its board of directors. The next year Bluhdorn merged Michigan Plating with Beard & Stone Electric Co., a Houston-based auto parts distributor.

In 1958, in deference to the company's location on the Gulf of Mexico and to Bluhdorn's belief that most of its growth would originate in the West, where automobile sales were rapidly increasing, the firm changed its name to Gulf + Western Corp.

Having acquired a number of private auto parts distributors and warehouses, Gulf + Western's annual sales approached $200 million in the mid-1960s. Bluhdorn embarked on a diversification campaign, and in just a matter of days, the company purchased a large amount of stock in New Jersey Zinc, a large mining and chemical company.

The struggling Paramount Pictures Corp. became Bluhdorn's next target. Paying $125 million for the movie company in 1966, Gulf + Western immediately became one of the nation's top manufacturing companies. Sales that year increased from $180 million to nearly $300 million—nearly tripling earnings to $17 million.

The Business

Financials

Revenue (1998): $12.1 billion

Employees (1998): 111,700

SICs / NAICS

sic 4841 - Cable & Other Pay Television Services

sic 4833 - Television Broadcasting Stations

sic 7822 - Motion Picture & Tape Distribution

sic 7812 - Motion Picture & Video Production

sic 2731 - Book Publishing

sic 7996 - Amusement Parks

naics 513210 - Cable Networks

naics 513120 - Television Broadcasting

naics 512120 - Motion Picture and Video Distribution

naics 512110 - Motion Picture and Video Production

naics 511130 - Book Publishers

naics 713110 - Amusement and Theme Parks

Gulf + Western acquired 23 companies in 1968, including Consolidated Cigar, E.W. Bliss, Universal American, Brown Company, and Associates Investment Co. Sales surpassed the $1 billion mark for the first time, reaching $1.3 billion and producing net income of $69.8 million. Paramount became a success story. Nearly bankrupt when purchased, it recorded its highest box-office revenues in history during 1972. Five years later Gulf + Western acquired Madison Square Garden.

In 1969 the company's fast-paced acquisition program ended when Wall Street analysts, congressmen, and the media charged Gulf + Western with manipulating accounting procedures to inflate its earnings. As a result, the company's stock dropped 30 points, costing shareholders $500 million and further reducing its dismal price earnings.

The company's regulatory problems continued in the next decade. In 1975 the U.S. Securities and Exchange Commission (SEC) charged that the company's operations in the Dominican Republic illegally withheld over $38 million in profits owed to the Dominican Republic government. In 1980 the company reached a settlement with the SEC over this matter, whereby Gulf + Western agreed to pay $39 million over seven years in order to fund a social and economic development program in the Dominican Republic.

In 1978, as the company's poor public image continued, Gulf + Western spent $3.3 million to print its annual report in *Time* magazine, hoping to raise its price earning ratio. The next year, the SEC initiated a second investigation, accusing Bluhdorn and executive vice president Don. F. Gatson of misconduct. Among its charges were allegations that the two executives allowed the company's pension fund to make "inappropriate" investments in companies where they had personal investments. In 1981 this investigation was settled, with no restitution called for under the terms of the agreement.

Bluhdorn died of a heart attack in 1983, and was succeeded as CEO by Martin S. Davis. Davis quickly streamlined the company's operations from seven operating groups into three units, focusing on the areas of entertainment, financial services, and consumer products. Within months, Consolidated Cigar was sold, as were 50 other units, including operations in chemicals, concrete equipment, and mechanical presses.

In 1984 Gulf + Western acquired the remaining 73% of Esquire, Inc., as well as the publishers Prentice-Hall and Glen & Company. Divestitures continued, and the company sold its consumer and industrial products to Wickes Co. for $1 billion in cash in 1985. Four years later Gulf + Western changed its name to Paramount Communications. Also that year, the company made an unsuccessful bid for Time Inc.

In 1991 Paramount purchased the television station operator TVX, renaming it Paramount Stations Group, and started a pay-per-view programming and distribution venture with Capital Cities/ABC. It also purchased the Macmillan Computer Publishing division in late 1991 for $157.5 million. The company's revenues increased to $4.3 billion in 1992, due in large part to the success of such movies as *The Addams Family*, *Star Trek VI*, and *Wayne's World*.

Paramount began bypassing television networks in 1993 by taking its TV series *The Untouchables* and *Deep Space Nine* directly into the first-run syndication market. The following year, Paramount was the prize in a heated takeover battle between Viacom Inc. and QVC, and in July 1994 Paramount was acquired by Viacom. Before the battle was over, Paramount acquired Macmillan Inc., thereby becoming the nation's second-largest book publisher.

History of Macmillan Inc.

D. & A. Macmillan was established in 1843 in London by brothers Daniel and Alexander. The following year, on the verge of bankruptcy, the brothers closed the business. They borrowed the capital needed to purchase a small publisher and retailer in Cambridge. This shop's emphasis on educational and socio-political titles was attributed to the tastes of its proprietors and to its proximity to Cambridge University. As a result, it gained a reputation as a leading publisher of textbooks and other educational materials.

In the 1850s the company, since renamed Macmillan & Co., began enjoying success in fictional works. Daniel died in 1857, and the following year Alexander opened a second branch. This London shop had weekly social and intellectual gatherings, attended by such writers as Tennyson, T.H. Huxley, and Herbert Spencer. They, among other great 19th-century English novelists, became part of Macmillan's stable of writers.

Recognizing the importance of the American market, Alexander retained Scribner & Welford as the U.S. agent for Macmillan books. In 1869 he established a New York branch office as a marketer and distributor, and eventually publisher, of Macmillan titles. At the urging of the branch's leader, George P. Brett, Macmillan split into two distinct entities, The Macmillan Company and Macmillan & Co., Ltd., based in New York and London, respectively.

The companies were still joined, however, as the Macmillan family retained majority control of both. They also cooperated in sharing titles and authors, and made use of a common network of international sales offices.

The American company prospered, publishing such titles as *The Call of the Wild*, and pioneering a national distribution network through the establishment of branch offices throughout the country. It fortified its reputation as a leading publisher of college textbooks, and anticipated a growth in children's books by establishing a department for that unit. These successes were overshadowed, however, by its failure to adapt quickly to the emerging popularity of paperbacks. As a consequence, the company slipped back into the middle of the field of U.S. trade, or retail, publishing. Its educational titles generated about two-thirds of the company's total revenues of $13.2 million in 1950.

The Macmillan Company gained complete independence in 1951, when its British owner sold its 61% stake on the open market. During the 1950s even the company's core strengths slowed in growth. Despite a surge in college enrollment, Macmillan's revenues reached only $19.1 million in 1960. That year Crowell-Collier Publishing Co. gained control of Macmillan. The name of the resulting company was changed from Crowell-Collier to Macmillan soon after.

The Officers

Chairman and CEO: Sumner M. Redstone

Deputy Chairman and Exec. VP: Philippe P. Dauman

Deputy Chairman and Exec. VP: Thomas E. Dooley

Macmillan's fortunes changed when in 1963 Raymond C. Hagel succeeded the last of the Bretts as the company's leader. He diversified the firm into retail sales, by acquiring Brentano's; into language schools, through the acquisition of Berlitz Inc.; into musical instruments, through C.G. Conn; and into information services, by acquiring Standard Rate & Data Inc. As a result, Macmillan recorded revenues of $600 million by 1980.

Many of its far-flung assets were sold off after T. Mellon Evans acquired control of the company in 1980. He retained Macmillan's operations in publishing, language schools, and information services, and the company's net income and sales responded favorably.

Macmillan became the target of a bidding war between the Barr brothers, Kohlberg Kravis Roberts & Co., and the British investor Robert Maxwell. Maxwell emerged the victor in 1988 with a bid of $2.6 billion. After his mysterious death by drowning three years later, his media empire was revealed to be a complex, and borderline shady, entanglement of financial maneuvers between the companies that he owned or controlled. His umbrella company, Maxwell Communications Corp. PLC, was placed under supervision of bankruptcy officials in Britain and the U.S., and its assets were liquidated. Paramount Communications purchased the Macmillan Computer Publishing division in late 1991 for $157.5 million.

Market Forces Driving the Acquisition

After the death of Robert Maxwell, the Maxwell Communications media conglomerate was liquidated under the supervision of the U.S. Federal Bankruptcy Court and regulators in London, England. In late 1993 Macmillan Inc. became the last significant component of the empire to be put up for sale.

Several publishing companies were reportedly interested in Macmillan. Among them were Paramount Communications, Harcourt General, Pearson PLC, and K-III Communications Corp. Macmillan's textbook publishing business, ranked seventh in the U.S., was of great appeal to suitors. It also had an enviable backlist of authors, including Ernest Hemingway and F. Scott Fitzgerald.

The Players

Paramount Communications Chairman: Martin S. Davis. Martin Davis, a former publicist, took the helm of the bloated Gulf + Western in 1983. He immediately refocused the company and trimmed expenses, finally completing this task in 1989. That year the company changed its name to Paramount Communications and made a failed attempt to make a hostile takeover of Time Inc. Four years later, Davis found himself on the receiving end of such an attempt, when QVC launched an unfriendly bid to wrest Paramount from its merger agreement with Viacom. That bid was even more distasteful to Davis, as it would place his company in the hands of Barry Diller, whose clashes with Davis had spurred Diller to resign from Paramount in 1983. Ultimately, Viacom succeeded in its bid for Paramount, at which point Davis resigned, although he gained a seat on the board of Viacom's parent, National Amusements, Inc.

In 1994 he established Wellspring Associates, L.L.C., a buyout group specializing in investing in undervalued companies in need of dramatic restructuring. By early 1998, Wellspring had made investments in the bankrupt Discovery Zone, the hockey equipment manufacturer SLM International, and Lionel Trains, a toy company acquired in 1995.

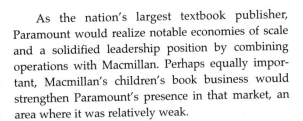

As the nation's largest textbook publisher, Paramount would realize notable economies of scale and a solidified leadership position by combining operations with Macmillan. Perhaps equally important, Macmillan's children's book business would strengthen Paramount's presence in that market, an area where it was relatively weak.

Meanwhile, Paramount itself was the target of an acquisition battle, between Viacom International and QVC. Some analysts speculated that an acquisition of Macmillan in the midst of this tug-of-war might have an effect on the contest, since Paramount might be viewed as a more valuable commodity but with a reduced amount of liquid capital. Most Wall Street analysts rejected that probability, however, suggesting that the successful acquirer of Paramount could easily sell off some of its publishing assets if necessary to reduce the debt accrued in the acquisition.

Approach and Engagement

The auction for Macmillan Inc. ended on November 9, 1993, when sealed bids were submitted to J.P. Morgan & Co. on behalf of the U.S. Bankruptcy Court. The next day Paramount emerged as the high bidder, with an offer of $552.8 million in cash. That price was almost twice Macmillan's fiscal 1993 sales of $290 million, and was considered by some to be excessively high. Yet the consensus held that Paramount's synergies with Macmillan were so great that a reduction of expenses would quickly make up for the purchase price.

Paramount received government approval for the acquisition in early 1994, and closed the deal in late February.

Products and Services

Viacom operated in six business segments:

Networks encompassed its basic cable and premium subscription television program services. These networks included MTV, MTV2, Nickelodeon, Nick at Nite, Nick at Nite's TV Land, VH1, Showtime, The Movie Channel, and Flix. This segment also held the company's interests in Comedy Central, Sundance Channel, and UPN (United Paramount Network). Total revenues in 1998 for the Network segment reached $2.6 billion.

Entertainment housed the company's operations in the production and distribution of motion pictures and television programming, as well as its television stations, international channels, movie theater operations, and music publishing. This segment was comprised of Paramount Pictures, Paramount Television, Spelling Entertainment Group Inc., and the Paramount Stations Group, and generated revenues of $4.8 billion in 1998.

The **Video** segment consisted of Blockbuster Video, a retailer in home videos and games; it produced $3.9 billion in revenues in 1998. The **Parks** segment, comprised of the five regional Paramount Parks, achieved $421 million in 1998 revenues. **Publishing** encompassed such consumer publishing imprints as Simon & Schuster, Pocket Books, Scribner, and The Free Press; this unit generated sales of $564 million in 1998. Finally, **Viacom Online Services**, the company's interactive businesses, produced 1998 revenues of $13.7 million.

Changes to the Industry

After acquiring Macmillan, Paramount became the world's second-largest book publisher, after Bertlesmann AG. Its leading position in textbooks was solidified by the incorporation of Macmillan's titles, and its relatively weak presence in the juvenile market was expanded and given an identity with Macmillan's strong children's operations.

Despite the benefits that Paramount realized, however, to many the acquisition represented a continuation of a particular threat to the publishing industry. The wave of consolidation that was washing over corporate America was viewed with concern by the creative element in the publishing world. Authors and agents saw the shrinking industry in terms of a reduction in the number of available outlets for their work. In addition, others feared as increasing numbers of imprints were incorporated into publishing houses, chances for error in assigning a title to the incorrect imprint was heightened.

Review of the Outcome

The synergies between Paramount and Macmillan that so enthused company executives were a source of worry for employees. Layoffs due to redundancies were inevitable in the wake of any merger, but particularly so when the combining companies overlapped as much as Paramount and Macmillan did. Adding to these concerns was Paramount's track record in dissolving recently acquired imprints. Within two years of its absorption of Prentice Hall in 1984, Paramount eliminated eight imprints and divided up the remaining pieces into new divisions.

In January 1995 Paramount disclosed its plans for the integration of Macmillan. Through a reorganization, Paramount Publishing would reduce the number of imprints and titles, and lay off up to 10% of its total workforce of 10,000. The Macmillan name was dissolved except in the area of reference, where all Paramount imprints were consolidated as Macmillan General Reference. The children's area would be reduced from 18 imprints to seven. Macmillan's other divisions—college textbooks, adult trade, and The Free Press—were incorporated into existing Paramount divisions.

Research

Baker, John, and John Mutter. "The Morning After," in *Publishers Weekly*, 20 December 1993. Describes the consolidation efforts underway at Paramount.

Cox, Meg. "Sealed Offers for Macmillan Are Due Today," in *The Wall Street Journal*, 9 November 1993. Reports the close of the auction and speculation about the identity of eventual winner.

Fabrikant, Geraldine. "Paramount to Acquire Macmillan," in *The New York Times*, 11, November 1993. Details the terms of the newly announced acquisition agreement.

Lyall, Sarah. "Paramount Publishing to Cut Jobs and Books," in *The New York Times*, 24 January 1994. Reveals the newly announced changes planned for Paramount after its acquisition of Macmillan.

———. "Workers Ponder Future after Sale of Macmillan," in *The New York Times*, 12 November 1993. Describes the concerns that Macmillan employees have over the acquisition.

"Macmillan, Inc.," in *International Directory of Company Histories*, Vol. 7, St. James Press: 1993. Profiles the history of Macmillan.

"Paramount Pictures Corp.," in *Notable Corporate Chronologies*, The Gale Group, 1999. Profiles the history of the company.

"Viacom International Inc.," in *Notable Corporate Chronologies*, The Gale Group, 1999. Lists major events in the history of Viacom.

Viacom International Inc. Home Page, available at http://www.viacom.com. Official World Wide Web Page for Viacom. Includes a description of operations, news releases, executive biographies, annual reports, investor information, and links to company Websites.

Wasserstein, Bruce. *Big Deal: The Battle for Control of America's Leading Corporations*, Warner Books, 1998. Provides a detailed overview of Viacom's acquisition of Paramount.

DEBORAH J. UNTENER

PENNSYLVANIA RAILROAD &
NEW YORK CENTRAL RAILROAD

Conrail Inc.
2001 Market St.
2 Commerce Sq.
Philadelphia, PA 19101
USA

tel: (215)209-4000
web: http://www.conrail.com

nationality: USA
date: February 1, 1968
affected: Pennsylvania Railroad Co., USA, founded 1846
affected: New York Central Railroad Co., USA, founded 1853

Overview of the Merger

Penn Central was formed by the Pennsylvania Railroad and New York Central Railroad in the largest merger of the time. It immediately became the nation's largest railroad in history, yet soon became its largest single bankruptcy as well. Only 867 days after its formation, Penn Central went broke. At the root of its web of difficulties were weak finances, operational inefficiencies, mismanagement, and a clash of personalities.

History of Pennsylvania Railroad Co.

The Pennsylvania Railroad Co. was chartered in 1846 to run from Harrisburg to Pittsburgh. Backed by the business community, construction began the following year, and a line connecting Philadelphia and Pittsburgh was completed in 1848.

J. Edgar Thomson became its president in 1852, and the Pennsylvania Railroad expanded during his 22-year tenure. It purchased or leased other railroads, including the Main Line of Public Works, the Pittsburgh, Fort Wayne & Chicago Railroad, and the Panhandle Railway. By 1869 the Pennsylvania had 3,000 miles of line west of Pittsburgh. It also expanded eastward during this time, acquiring an interest in the Philadelphia & Erie Railroad, the Allegheny Valley Railroad, and lines into New Jersey and Washington, D.C.

During the 1880s and 1890s, the Pennsylvania shifted its focus from expansion to the consolidation of its acquisitions and the refinement of its operations. Separate lines were united, forming the Philadelphia, Baltimore & Washington Railroad and the Washington Terminal Co. Expansion into new territory was not neglected during this period, however, and the Pennsylvania obtained lines into Michigan and, with the construction of a tunnel under the Hudson River, into New York City.

By the early 1900s, the Pennsylvania had become a powerful company, dominating much of its territory. It was called "The Standard Railroad of the World." During World War II the Pennsylvania's business multiplied, but slumped again in the post-war period. The railroad industry throughout the nation had begun losing business to the automobile and airplane, and the Pennsylvania failed to respond to these threats adequately. For example, it was slow to dieselize operations and to take up excess trackage. In 1946, the Pennsylvania recorded the first loss in its history.

In 1957, the Pennsylvania entered into discussions to merge with its rival, the New York Central Railroad, and the two companies finally reached an agreement in 1961. The union was delayed for another seven years before being completed in February 1968 to form the Pennsylvania Central Transportation Co.

Penn Central had interests outside of the railroad business, having diversified into real estate, oil refining, and other industries over the years. This ill-advised diversification strategy contributed, but was not wholly responsible for, the rapid decline of Penn Central. Serious management and financial difficulties erupted, and the railroad began bleeding money. In June 1970 it went bankrupt. The U.S. government transferred its passenger business to the newly established National Railway Passenger Corp., later known as Amtrak. President Nixon signed into law the Regional Rail Reorganization Act of 1974, which created the Consolidated Rail Corp. (Conrail). This concern absorbed Penn Central's remaining operations in April 1976.

History of New York Central Railroad Co.

In the early days of the railroad, individual lines were short, typically running for distances under 100 miles. To create extended service, 10 small railroads in New York, running between Albany and Buffalo, banded together to establish the informal Central Line, an alliance that incorporated standardized fares, schedules, and policies to make travel more efficient and therefore better equipped to compete with the Erie Canal. Erastus Corning, president of the 78-mile Utica & Schenectady line, orchestrated the formal merger of these systems in 1853, forming the New York Central Railroad Co.

The new railroad was an immediate success, and with a total capital of $23 million, it caught the eye of Cornelius Vanderbilt. The "Commodore" had acquired control of the New York & Harlem Railroad in 1857 and of the Hudson River Railroad in 1865. With monopolistic ambitions, he sought to gain control of virtually every major line in the state.

The Business

Financials

Revenue (1998): $3.9 billion

Employees (1998): 22,000

SICs / NAICS

sic 4011 - Railroads-Line-Haul Operating

sic 4731 - Freight Transportation Arrangement

sic 6719 - Holding Companies Nec

naics 482111 - Line-Haul Railroads

naics 541614 - Process, Physical Distribution, and Logistics Consulting Services

Having acquired a stake in New York Central, as well as a representative seat on its board, he forged an agreement that facilitated the transfer of passengers and freight between the Hudson River Railroad and the New York Central where they connected in Albany. Vanderbilt terminated that agreement in 1867, annoyed by the railroad's tendency to send business to the Hudson only when New York Central's steamboats were iced in along the river. Vanderbilt's move meant that passengers and freight had to undertake a two-mile trek to transfer from one line to the other, causing such a mess for New York Central that its stock price began to plummet. Vanderbilt immediately began buying its shares, and before the end of the year he had acquired control of New York Central, extending his empire from New York City to Buffalo.

He then began buying into the Erie Railroad Co., a competitor that spanned the southern part of New York, and soon acquired a seat on its board. Daniel Drew, head of the Erie, divined Vanderbilt's goal of taking over the company, and, with the help of two shady allies, thwarted Vanderbilt's takeover attempt in 1868, through what became known as the Erie Wars.

Vanderbilt continued to expand his empire, adding to it the Michigan Central in 1871 and the Lake Shore and Michigan Southern Railway two years later. With these purchases, he was able to run trains from New York City to Chicago.

Robert R. Young gained control of New York Central in 1954. By that time, the railroad industry was suffering due to the rise of airplane and automobile travel. In 1968, New York Central merged with the Pennsylvania Railroad Co. to form Penn Central Transportation Co. This merger soon failed, however, and Penn Central entered bankruptcy in June 1970.

The Officers

Chairman and CEO: David M. LeVan

President: Timothy T. O'Toole

Sr. VP of Operations: Ronald J. Conway

The U.S. Congress interceded by establishing the National Railroad Passenger Corp., which assumed control of the nation's rail passenger services in October 1970; this corporation was later renamed Amtrak. New York Central's remaining operations were pooled with those of five other lines to form Consolidated Rail Corp. (Conrail) in April 1976.

Market Forces Driving the Merger

After the U.S. rail business peaked in 1916, it took a steady decline. In the 1920s the Interstate Commerce Commission was charged with planning mergers and consolidations of the nation's lines. This task proved insurmountable, particularly because its suggestions were often resisted by the rail companies themselves. Healthy companies chose to form alliances of their own design rather than absorb ailing concerns, executives were reluctant to form mergers that might result in the loss of the high-paying positions, and unions were fiercely protective of workers' jobs.

The nation's rail industry recovered briefly during World War II, but declined sharply thereafter. The explosion of travel by automobile and airplane deprived the railroad of both passenger and freight traffic, resulting in less funds to implement the improvements necessary to attract and retain customers. New York Central Railroad verged on bankruptcy, and its competitor, Pennsylvania Railroad, was not faring much better. Railroad executives across the nation realized that consolidation was more crucial to the survival of their companies than ever before.

Approach and Engagement

On November 1, 1957, Alfred Perlman, chairman of New York Central Railroad, and James Symes, CEO of Pennsylvania Railroad, announced that they were considering a merger. However, New York Central didn't enter into negotiations enthusiastically—it was hoping that a more appealing partner would emerge. Both New York Central and the Pennsylvania, in fact, accused the other of secretly negotiating with other companies, and in January 1959 they broke off talks.

In October 1961, they renewed negotiations, and soon arrived at terms. New York Central shareholders would receive 1.3 shares of the new Pennsylvania Railroad, as yet unnamed. The boards of both companies approved the deal in January 1962, as did their shareholders in May.

The Interstate Commerce Commission initiated 14 months of hearings on the proposal. Then, in October 1963, the ICC began a two-and-a-half-year review. Finally, after politicians and unions had approved the deal, the ICC authorized the merger in April 1966.

The deal was finally consummated on February 1, 1969, when the Pennsylvania New York Central Transportation Co. was formed. Saunders became its chairman and Perlman was its president. The new entity changed its name to the Penn Central Co. in May 1968.

Review of the Outcome

Penn Central was born as the largest railroad in the nation's history. It had more than 20,000 miles of track, nearly 100,000 employees, and $4.5 billion in assets.

Yet the new company immediately faced difficulties in operations, finances, and personalities. The New York Central and the Pennsylvania had been bitter rivals, and company loyalties were slow to dissipate. The workplace was rife with animosities, and the situation in the executive suite was not much better. Saunders and Perlman had dissimilar personalities, aside from their mutual distrust of the other. These clashes led to Saunders' replacement of Perlman as president in 1969.

Operationally, integration was a nightmare. The computer systems were incompatible, and the two railroads even used different kinds of spikes. Procedures between the two companies varied, contributing to the culture clash among workers. Such operational problems as these routinely resulted in serious delays and lost shipments. In July 1969, about 16,000 New York commuters were stranded for nearly three hours when the railroad's electrical system shut down. Disruptions such as this ignited sharp criticism of the railroad and a further reduction of business.

Financially, Penn Central started out weak and continued to falter. On the date of its creation, it had railroad assets of $4.5 billion. Yet it had only $13.3 million in cash, an amount that David Bevan, the company's chief financial officer, later estimated should have been $40 million, minimum. Bevan and other executives immediately sought to finance the company through loans, the sale of certain real assets, and the doctoring of the company's ledgers. Bevan also raised about $200 million by selling commercial paper, a risky means of borrowing short-term quickly that was popular among corporations in the 1960s.

Despite these efforts, Penn Central's balance sheet read like the writing on the wall. In its first year, it lost $2.8 million, and in 1969 it lost $83 million. The new year brought even dimmer prospects. "The Penn Central's 1970 first quarter was probably the most disastrous in American railroad history," wrote Daughen and Binzen in *The Wreck of the Penn Central*. "Receipts from rail operations totaled about $5 million a day. But the railroad was admittedly spending more than $6 million a day. Even for the Penn Central, this was an intolerable situation." By the end of 1970, its losses totaled $431 million, the worst annual showing in the nation's railroad industry.

On June 8, 1970, the board of directors ousted Saunders, Perlman, and Bevan. On June 21 Penn Central Transportation Co., the railroad operations, entered bankruptcy; this did not affect the Penn Central Co., its holding company, nor the Pennsylvania Co., which held the railroad's nonrail assets.

On May 1, 1971, the federally established National Railway Passenger Corp., later renamed Amtrak, took over Penn Central's passenger operations. Its remaining assets were reorganized and then assumed by Consolidated Rail Corp. (Conrail) on April 1, 1976.

Research

Daughen, Joseph R., and Peter Binzen. *The Wreck of the Penn Central*, Little, Brown and Co., 1971. Details the rise and fall of the Penn Central.

Douglas, George H. *All Aboard! The Railroad in American Life*, Marlowe & Co., 1992. Provides a history of the railroad in the U.S.

Jacobs, Timothy. *The History of the Pennsylvania Railroad*, Brompton Books, 1988. Offers an illustrated and narrative history of the Pennsylvania, through its demise.

Jensen, Oliver. *The American Heritage History of Railroads in America*, American Heritage Publishing Co., 1975. A pictorial and narrative history of the nation's railroad industry.

"New York Central Railroad Co." *Britannica CD 98 Multimedia Edition, 1994-1998*. Encyclopedia Britannica, Inc. Provides a history of the company.

Stover, John F. *Iron Road to the West*, Columbia University Press, 1978. Provides a history of American railroads during the 1850s.

Wasserstein, Bruce. *Big Deal: The Battle for Control of America's Leading Corporations*, Warner Books, 1998. Offers an overview of the largest mergers in American history.

DEBORAH J. UNTENER

The Players

Pennsylvania Railroad Co. Chairman and CEO: Stuart T. Saunders. Stuart Saunders, a Harvard Law School graduate, practiced law privately for five years before becoming an assistant general solicitor for Norfolk & Western in 1939. He succeeded through various executive positions, achieving the rank of president in 1958, and was instrumental in merging the Nofolk & Western with the Virginian. He became chairman and CEO of Pennsylvania Railroad in October 1963, and set out to complete the merger with New York Central that his predecessor, James Symes, had initiated. Saunders held the positions of chairman and CEO of Penn Central upon its inception. When the railroad declined, he, along with Alfred Perlman and David Bevan, was ousted by the board of directors in June 1970.

New York Central Railroad Co. President: Alfred E. Perlman. Alfred Perlman studied at Massachusetts Institute of Technology (MIT) before joining the Denver & Rio Grande Western. There, he earned a reputation as a turnaround specialist by restoring the four-time bankrupt railroad. He joined the New York Central Railroad in 1954 to work the same magic at that ailing company. After trimming the workforce by 15,000 and taking steps to modernize the railroad, Perlman realized that the success that he had achieved in the West could not be duplicated in the East. He was in favor of a merger, and agreed to a union with the Pennsylvania Railroad. He served as president of Penn Central when it was formed in 1968. Due to repeated clashes with Saunders, principally over the allocation of funds, Perlman was removed from the office of president and relegated to that of vice chairman, a largely ineffectual role, in December 1969. He was one of the three directors ousted by the board the following year.

PEPSICO & TROPICANA PRODUCTS

PepsiCo Inc.
700 Anderson Hill Rd.
Purchase, NY 10577
USA

tel: (914)253-2000
web: http://www.pepsico.com

nationality: USA
date: August 25, 1998
affected: PepsiCo Inc., USA, founded 1965
affected: Tropicana Products Inc., USA, founded 1947

Overview of the Merger

PepsiCo completed the largest acquisition in its history when it purchased Tropicana Products in August 1998. The $3.3 billion purchase made PepsiCo the owner of the world's largest producer of branded juice. In so doing it engaged Coca-Cola in yet another area of competition—juices. Unlike the soft drink market, however, in which Pepsi-Cola had been locked into the second-place position for years, Pepsi immediately dominated over Coke's Minute Maid brand in the chilled orange juice market.

The Tropicana Pure Premium was the fifth-largest brand of all food products sold in U.S. grocery stores. The Tropicana brand name, combined with the clout of the Pepsi-Cola and Frito-Lay names, gave PepsiCo considerable leverage in terms of grocery store shelf space.

Tropicana also extended PepsiCo's reach in international markets. The juice company had the leading position in chilled orange juice in Belgium, Canada, France, and U.K. Its combined annual sales growth in those segments was in the double-digits. It had also been making headway in Asian markets, particularly in Japan, China, Hong Kong, and Taiwan.

History of PepsiCo Inc.

Caleb D. "Doc" Bradham, a pharmacist and drugstore owner, invented a syrup that was a concoction of sugar, vanilla, oils, cola nuts, and other flavorings diluted in carbonated water. In 1898 he named the drink Pepsi-Cola, as it purported to be a remedy for dyspepsia. Four years later, the drink had become so successful that Doc Bradham abandoned the drugstore business to devote himself full-time to the production of the beverage. By 1910 Bradham's annual syrup production exceeded one million gallons.

Wartime rationing in 1920 caused sugar prices to fluctuate from 5.5 cents per pound to 26.5 cents. Bradham, in light of this, stockpiled the commodity as a precaution against higher prices. By the end of the year, however, sugar prices plunged to two cents per pound. In 1923 the company went bankrupt and sold its assets. Roy C. Megargel, a Wall Street investment banker, bought the company trademark and in 1928 reorganized the firm as the National Pepsi-Cola Co.

Megargel didn't have much success with the firm either, and in 1931 the company again went bankrupt. Charles G. Guth, president of Loft Inc., a New York-based candy and fountain store enterprise, entered into an agreement with Megargel to revive Pepsi-Cola. After acquiring 80% of the company's new shares, Guth modified the Pepsi formula and cancelled Loft's contract with Coca-Cola, replacing the soft drink with his own new Pepsi product.

Sales were slow until 1934, when Guth began selling Pepsi in 12-ounce bottles for the same five-cent price as six-ounce bottles of Coke. Sales exploded and the company set about establishing international branches. In 1936 Pepsi became a subsidiary of Loft, Inc. Guth stepped down, and the new president, Walter S. Mack, Jr., initiated a promotion effort to unseat Coca-Cola as the number one soft drink.

Loft and Pepsi merged in 1940, and the newly formed Pepsi-Cola Company went public the following year. Soft drink sales fell during World War II, and in 1950 profits sank to a low of $1.3 million. The proliferation of supermarkets and overseas business developments enabled profits to rebound, and by 1960 they had reached $14.2 million. Diet Pepsi was unveiled four years later.

Pepsi-Cola merged with Frito-Lay in 1965, forming PepsiCo Inc. The new enterprise reported sales of $510 million and a workforce of 19,000 employees. The following year Frito-Lay introduced Doritos brand tortilla chips, destined to become the country's most popular snack chip. PepsiCo diversified outside food and beverage products by purchasing North American Van Lines in 1968 and Wilson Sporting Goods in 1970; both companies were sold in 1985. PepsiCo introduced the industry's first two-liter bottle in 1970.

The firm expanded into the restaurant business by purchasing the Pizza Hut chain of restaurants in 1977 and the Taco Bell fast-food chain the following year. Sales in 1981 exceeded $7 billion.

Caffeine-free colas, Pepsi Free and Diet Pepsi Free, were introduced in 1982. Diet Pepsi was reformulated with 100% Nutrasweet in 1984. That year it introduced Slice and Diet Slice, two soft drink products featuring real fruit juice.

In 1985 PepsiCo was the beverage industry leader, with revenues of over $7.5 billion. The "Cola Wars" heated up that year when Coca-Cola changed its syrup recipe and introduced New Coke. Analysts

The Business

Financials

Revenue (1998): $22.3 billion

Employees (1998): 150,000

SICs / NAICS

sic 2037 - Frozen Fruits & Vegetables

sic 2033 - Canned Fruits & Vegetables

sic 2096 - Potato Chips & Similar Snacks

sic 2086 - Bottled & Canned Soft Drinks

naics 312111 - Soft Drink Manufacturing

naics 311411 - Frozen Fruit, Juice and Vegetable Manufacturing

naics 311421 - Fruit and Vegetable Canning

naics 311919 - Other Snack Food Manufacturing

suggested that the move was merely a publicity ploy to introduce a Pepsi taste-alike. Pepsi jumped on the opportunity to declare itself the better cola, since Coke's attempt at imitation appeared to be such an admission. Coke soon reintroduced its original formula, and New Coke quietly died off the shelves.

PepsiCo reorganized and decentralized in 1986. Beverage operations combined under PepsiCo Worldwide Beverages, and snack food operations under PepsiCo Worldwide Foods. That year the company bought the Kentucky Fried Chicken fast-food chain, Mug Root Beer, the MEI Corp., and Seven-Up International, the third-largest franchise soft drink company outside the U.S.

By 1990 PepsiCo Food Service International was serving 10,000 PepsiCo restaurants, making it the nation's fourth-largest food service distributor. Profits topped $1 billion for the first time in 1991. The following year it entered into an agreement with Thomas J. Lipton Co. to develop and sell tea-based beverages. Coca-Cola, earlier in the year, had entered into a similar contract with Nestle, maker of Nestea.

In 1992 PepsiCo began distributing single-serve juice products made by Ocean Spray Cranberries, Inc. It also launched Crystal Pepsi, a new clear cola, that year. The company united Pizza Hut, Taco Bell, and KFC into a single division, which it spun off as Tricon Global Restaurants, Inc. in 1997, garnering $4.5 billion in the sale.

The Officers

Chairman and CEO: Roger A. Enrico

Vice Chairman: Karl M. von der Heyden

Sr. VP, Personnel: William R. Bensyl

Sr. VP, Public Affairs: Joseph F. McCann

Sr. VP and Chief Financial Officer: Michael D. White

PepsiCo now operated two lines of business—soft drinks and snack foods. Frito-Lay was the world's leading manufacturer of snack foods. PepsiCola held the second-place position in the soft drink industry. PepsiCo's 1997 operating profit was $2.6 billion on net sales of $20.9 billion.

History of Tropicana Products, Inc.

Anthony T. Rossi made a living by selling gift boxes of Florida fruit to such New York department stores as Macy's and Gimbel's. He had been purchasing fruit from retail supermarkets, but in order to save money and obtain fresher supplies, he purchased the Florida-based Overstreet Packing Co. in 1947. This company, renamed Manatee River Packing Co., supplied him with large fruit for his gift boxes, as well as smaller fruit. He hated to see the unused fruit go to waste, and came up with the notion of using them for juice. In 1949 Rossi renamed the company Fruit Industries, Inc. and began selling jars of sectioned fruit and small quantities of juice to hotels and restaurants in northeastern U.S. That year the company also began selling frozen juice concentrate, and registered Tropicana as a trademark.

Rossi realized that there were undeveloped avenues in the juice business, since only two juice options were available at this time—frozen concentrate or home-squeezing fresh fruit. The gap between the two options pointed to fresh chilled juice, but there was no existing way to mass-market it while preserving its freshness.

In 1954 Rossi perfected a technique—flash pasteurization, in which the juice temperature was raised briefly. This method launched the not-from-concentrate juice market. That year the company also developed waxed paper cartons to replace many of the glass jars that it had been using. The new juice product was called Tropicana Pure Premium, and its nationwide success prompted Rossi to change his company's name to Tropicana Products, Inc. in 1957. That year the company also launched the *SS Tropicana*, a juice tank ship running between Florida and New York; this ship would continue to make weekly runs for four years.

The company still used glass jars for long-distance shipping, but couldn't fill them quickly enough to meet demand. Then Tropicana devised a method of high-speed vacuum packing, the first commercially viable method for high-speed glass packaging of food products.

The firm introduced Tropicana Coffee in 1958, and Tropi-Cal-Lo in 1963. It filled its first international order in 1965, selling 14,000 cases of juice to France. Tropicana went public in 1969, the same year that it became the first citrus company to operate its own plastic container manufacturing plant. Three years later it expanded its packaging operations again by making its own boxes.

During the 1970s Tropicana received acquisition overtures from such companies as Philip Morris, PepsiCo, and Kellogg. In 1978, however, it selected Beatrice Foods Co. as its preferred acquirer. This conglomerate's financial resources enabled Tropicana to expand its line in a variety of new products and sizes. It debuted Tropicana Home Style in 1985, and in 1987 its 16-ounce single-serve bottles first appeared in convenience stores.

Kohlberg, Kravis & Roberts (KKR) acquired Beatrice in 1986. KKR then sold Tropicana to The Seagram Company two years later. Tropicana's operations were combined with the Dole Food Company's global juice business, which Seagram acquired in 1995. With this acquisition, it added the brands of Fruvita, Dole, Juice Bowl, and Looza to Tropicana's offerings.

Under Seagram's ownership, Tropicana continued to expand its portfolio, introducing Tropicana Twister, Pure Tropics, Pure Premium Grovestand, Pure Premium Plus, and numerous other Pure Premium varieties. It also expanded internationally, particularly during 1991. That year it launched Pure Premium in Canada, France, and the U.K. It also formed a partnership with Kirin to produce and distribute the Kirin-Tropicana juice brand in Japan.

In October 1996 Tropicana struck a 30-year deal to rename the Thunder-Dome, in Saint Petersburg, Florida, as Tropicana Field. That maneuver shut down concession stand negotiations between Coke and the Devil Rays Major League Baseball team.

Tropicana's 1997 revenues of $1.9 billion made it the world's leading producer and marketer of branded juices.

Market Forces Driving the Acquisition

Seagram had become a major participant in the entertainment industry in 1995 by acquiring MCA

Inc., now called Universal Studios. In 1998 it increased its holdings in that industry by purchasing PolyGram N.V., the world's largest music company, for $10.6 billion. Seagram looked at its three business segments to analyze what could be sold in order to finance that purchase. The company had been built a century earlier on spirits and wine—it was its heritage. Its entertainment holdings, naturally, would be kept relatively intact, as PolyGram would become a link in that chain. Its third business, Tropicana, would be the most logical divestment, since it really didn't enjoy any natural synergies with the other two.

Tropicana, for its part, was an increasingly successful company and brand. It was the leader in practically all of the segments in which it operated. In the $3 billion orange juice market, Tropicana held a 42% market share, while its nearest competitor, Minute Maid, held just over half of that amount, 24%. In a division of that total orange juice market, refrigerated orange juice, Tropicana as a whole captured 40%, with Pure Premium accounting for about 30% of that share; in contrast, Minute Maid held under a 20% share. Additionally, in the not-from-concentrate (NFC) segment, the fastest growing segment of the orange juice market, Tropicana Pure Premium held a 71% share; no other brand came close. In August 1998, for the first time in history, sales in the NFC orange juice segment surpassed those in the concentrate segment. Over the previous year, NFC sales had grown 13.9% to capture 50% of the chilled orange juice market, while from-concentrate orange juice sales increased a mere two percent to hold 49%.

Obviously, Tropicana would be an asset in the hands of the right company, and PepsiCo believed that it fit the bill. This company had spent years trying to usurp Coca-Cola as the leader in soft drinks. Although adding Tropicana to its coffers wouldn't budge their positions in that industry, it would beat Coca-Cola in the orange juice industry, turning the competitive table on Coke, so to speak. Acquisition would also afford PepsiCo entry into the morning "daypart" market, the before-lunch beverage market.

Approach and Engagement

In May 1998 Seagram announced that it planned to spin off Tropicana by taking that company public. It would be the largest public stock offering in U.S. history, with Seagram expecting to raise between $3.5 billion and $4 billion. At the same time as announcing the spin-off, Seagram indicated that it would be receptive to entertaining private acquisition offers for Tropicana.

PepsiCo regarded this as a prime opportunity to acquire the brand leader. Tropicana would enhance

The Players

PepsiCo Chairman and CEO: Roger A. Enrico. Born in Chisholm, Minnesota, Roger Enrico attended Babson College, a business school in Massachusetts, in the 1960s. He joined PepsiCo in 1971 as an associate product manager for Frito-Lay. In 1982 he had become executive vice president of Pepsi-Cola USA. When John Sculley, leader of Pepsi USA, left the company for Apple Computer the next year, Enrico succeeded him. His next step came in 1987, when he was promoted to president and CEO of PepsiCo Worldwide Beverages. He was inducted into the Beverage World Soft Drink Hall of Fame in 1990. Enrico then moved on to head PepsiCo Worldwide Restaurants before succeeding D. Wayne Calloway as chairman and CEO of PepsiCo in April 1996. Enrico is best known as the man who brought stars and glamour to Pepsi's advertising campaigns, including the highly popular commercials featuring Michael Jackson in the 1980s. Enrico also penned a book, *The Other Guy Blinked: How Pepsi Won the Cola Wars*.

Seagram President and CEO: Edgar Bronfman, Jr. Before joining the family business, Edgar Bronfman, Jr., had nurtured a successful career in movie production and songwriting. His father lured him to Seagram, however, in 1982. Starting out as a presidential assistant, he later became managing director of London-based Seagram Europe. In 1984 he was promoted to president of The House of Seagram, a position that he held for four years. Bronfman continued to move up the company ranks, becoming executive vice president of U.S. operations and earning a seat on the board of directors in 1988. From there it was only a matter of time before he took the company's helm as president and chief operating officer. Having held those positions since 1989, Bronfman added the post of CEO to his responsibilities in June 1994.

PepsiCo in at least three areas. It would complement its other food and beverage operations, challenging Coca-Cola in yet another market, and strengthen its product portfolio in the retail, vending, and food service industries.

Shortly after Seagram announced the planned initial public offering, PepsiCo's chairman and CEO,

Roger Enrico, called Seagram's CEO, Edgar Bronfman, to discuss a possible deal. By early July, the terms had been settled, and Tropicana's public offering was canceled.

On October 10, 1998, Ocean Spray Cranberries Inc. filed a suit to block the acquisition. Its motion requested a preliminary injunction against the sale on the grounds that it would violate Ocean Spray's distribution agreement with PepsiCo. According to Ocean Spray, this deal precluded PepsiCo from selling or distributing any single-serve juice in competition with Ocean Spray's single-serve beverages, which are distributed through Pepsi's network.

PepsiCo disputed this claim of conflict of interest. It pointed out that not-from-concentrate juice was distributed through a warehouse and food broker distribution network, not the soft drink network that distributed single-serve juices. Moreover, most of Tropicana's products were marketed in supermarket dairy cases, while Ocean Spray's products were sold in non-chilled shelves.

A federal court apparently agreed with the PepsiCo, and rejected Ocean Spray's request. Just days later, on August 25, PepsiCo completed its $3.3 billion cash purchase of Tropicana.

Products and Services

PepsiCo's operations were divided into three segments, each of which is centered around a distinct company. Beverage operations were handled by Pepsi-Cola Co., Snack Foods were represented in the U.S. by Frito-Lay, Inc., and Juices were comprised of Tropicana Products, Inc.

Pepsi-Cola's brands included Pepsi-Cola, Diet Pepsi, Mountain Dew, Slice, Mug Root Beer, Mug Creme, All Sport, Lipton, Aquafina, Josta, and Frappuccino. In 1998 Pepsi-Cola had $10.6 billion in net sales, $8.3 billion of which originated in North America.

Frito-Lay included the following brands: Baked Lay's brand potato crisps, Baked Tostitos brand tortilla chips, Cheetos brand cheese flavored snacks, Chester's brand popcorn, Doritos brand crackers, Doritos brand dips, Doritos brand tortilla chips, Fritos brand corn chips, Funyons brand onion flavored rings, Grandma's brand cookies, Lay's brand potato chips, Munchos brand potato chips, Rold Gold brand pretzels, Ruffles brand potato chips, Santitas brand tortilla chips, Smartfood brand popcorn, Sunchips brand multigrain snacks, Tostitos brand crackers, Tostitos brand dips, Tostitos brand tortilla chips, and Baken-ets brand fried pork skins. Frito-Lay's 1998

sales totaled $10.9 billion, with North America accounting for $7.4 billion of that figure.

Tropicana Products brands included Tropicana Pure Premium Juices, Tropicana Season's Best Juices, Tropicana Pure Tropics Juices, Tropicana Twister Juice Beverages, Dole Juices, Fruitwise Smoothies and Healthy Shakes, Tropicana 100% Pure Juices, Copella Juices, Fruvita Juices, Hitchcock Juices, Kirin-Tropicana Juices, Looza Juices, Looza Nectars, Juice Bowl Juices, and Juice Bowl Nectars. Tropicana's sales amounted to $722 million in 1998.

Changes to the Industry

Industry experts predicted that Tropicana would continue to reign over the orange juice market. That market had experienced annual growth of about eight percent, and there were no obvious reasons to expect any downturn—just the opposite, many believed. The international markets offered many opportunities for growth. While the average annual consumption of orange juice in the U.S. was 15 gallons, it was only six in Europe and 0.5 in Asia.

Coca-Cola wasn't overtly concerned about PepsiCo's new leading position in the orange juice market. As reported in *Chain Drug Review,* a Coca-Cola spokesman stated, "It is irrelevant which company owns which competitor."

Review of the Outcome

Tropicana Products, Inc. was incorporated into PepsiCo as a separate company, on par with Pepsi-Cola Co. and Frito-Lay, Inc. As Roger Enrico said in *Chain Drug Review,* "This fits in with what we want to be—a company of big brands staying within the beverage and snack business."

At the conclusion of the merger, Tropicana's president and CEO, Ellen R. Marram, stepped down to pursue other opportunities outside the company. She was succeeded by Gary M. Rodkin, who had served as president of Tropicana North America since 1995.

Tropicana continued to expand its operations after the sale. In early November 1998, it entered into an agreement that would introduce Tropicana-branded grapefruit juice to the U.S. market. In January 1999 it gained a stronger presence in Spain by acquiring Alimentos del Valle S.A., a leading Spanish maker of chilled fruit juices and soups.

Pepsi-Cola also made some changes soon after the acquisition. In 1998 it unveiled two new beverages: Storm, a lemon-lime soft drink, and Pepsi One, a one-calorie cola made with the newly approved sweetener Sunett. In January 1999 it announced the initial public offering of The Pepsi Bottling Group, Inc., PepsiCo's wholly-owned subsidiary.

At the end of 1998, Tropicana's operating profit was $40 million, accounting for only about 1.5% of PepsiCo's total operating profit of $2.6 billion. Not surprising, claimed industry experts, since juice can usually be counted on to provide margins between one- and three-percent. It is subject to fluctuations of the commodity market, variations in the weather, crop failure, and the expense of distributing perishable fresh juice. Soda, by comparison, offers margins of about 16%.

Research

"Beverage Wars Intensify as PepsiCo Acquires Tropicana," in *Chain Drug Review*, 10 August 1998. Discusses how Pepsi's rivalry will be affected by the Tropicana acquisition.

Deogun, Nikhil. "Judge Denied Bid by Ocean Spray to Block Tropicana Sale to Pepsi," in *The Wall Street Journal*, 24 August 1998. Ocean Spray fails to prevent the acquisition.

Haber, Gary. "Bradenton, Fla.-Based Tropicana Buys Spanish Company," in *Knight-Ridder/Tribune Business News*, 24 January 1999. Reports Tropicana's completion of the acquisition of Alimentos del Valle.

Lofstock, John. "Pepsi Acquires Tropicana in $3.3 Billion Deal," in *Convenience Store News*, 24 August 1998. Pepsi's purchase of Tropicana gives it entry into the breakfast beverage market.

"PepsiCo to Acquire Seagram's Tropicana, a World Leader in Branded Juices, for $3.3 Billion," in *Food & Drink Weekly*, 27 July 1998. Seagram sells the juice company to fund its acquisition of PolyGram.

"PepsiCo Completes Tropicana Purchase, Names Gary M. Rodkin Tropicana CEO," in *PR Newswire*, 25 August 1998. Offers a brief biographical sketch of Rodkin upon the closing of the deal.

"PepsiCo Inc.," in *Notable Corporate Chronologies*, The Gale Group, 1999. Provides an overview of the company, including its purchase of Tropicana.

PepsiCo, Inc. 1997 Annual Report, Pepsi Co, Inc.: 1998. Provides in-depth review of the company's finances and activities.

PepsiCo, Inc. Home Page, available at http://www.pepsi-co.com. Official World Wide Web Page for PepsiCo. Contains annual reports, press releases, corporate information, career opportunities, and links to Pepsi-Cola Co., Frito Lay, Inc. and Tropicana Products, Inc.

Prince, Greg W. "PepsiCo-Star," in *Beverage World*, January 1998. Offers an account of Roger Enrico's career at Pepsi.

"The Seagram Co., Ltd.," in *Notable Corporate Chronologies*, Gale Research, 1999. Traces the company's chronological development.

Steinriede, Kent. "Pepsi Buys Tropicana," in *Beverage Industry*, 1 September 1998. Provides a report of the merger, Ocean Spray's interference, and PepsiCo's plans to spin off its bottler.

"Tropicana: Pepsi's New 'Weapon'," in *The Food Institute Report*, 3 August 1998. Offers facts on the orange juice industry, including its sales growth, profit margins, and international consumption.

Tropicana Products, Inc. Home Page, available at http://www.tropicana.com. Official World Wide Web Page for Tropicana . It includes a company history, product and nutrition information, news releases, and career opportunities.

DAVIS MCMILLAN

PHARMACIA & UPJOHN

Pharmacia & Upjohn Inc.
95 Corporate Dr.
PO Box 6995
Bridgewater, NJ 08807
USA

tel: (908)306-4400
fax: (908)306-4433
web: http://www.pnu.com

nationality: USA
date: November 1995
affected: The Upjohn Co., USA, founded 1886
affected: Pharmacia AB, Sweden, founded 1911

Overview of the Merger

The 1995 merger between Pharmacia AB and The Upjohn Co. was brought about by industry pressure to consolidate. Pharmaceutical companies were frantically entering into merger or acquisition agreements and leaving non-partnered companies in their dust. This drive toward consolidation was spurred by two primary industrial trends. The first, patent expiration, had affected Upjohn to no small extent during the previous few years. It was losing market share, and its research and development capabilities needed a boost in order to introduce new products quickly. The second industry trend was the growing necessity for non-U.S. firms to establish a beachhead in the U.S. market. Pharmacia, a Swedish company, had no distribution channel in the U.S.

A merger between these two companies would benefit them both. Upjohn's strong U.S. distribution network would afford Pharmacia entry into this market. Pharmacia offered Upjohn its strength in research and development, as well as access into niche markets, Pharmacia's specialty.

History of Pharmacia AB

C. Me Kunwald formulated a recipe for energy pills made from animal products, and in 1910 he patented the drug in Sweden. The following year Pharmacia was formed around this product, and generated a turnover of SKr 20,000 in its first year. This state-owned company quickly readied itself to try its hand at other products, and introduced rheumatism and stomachache remedies in the several years that followed. During the 1920s it expanded into laxatives and vitamins.

Nanna Svatz, a researcher in the field of rheumatic diseases, developed a number of valuable sulpha products that served to increase Pharmacia's profitability, which had become stunted. With the proceeds now available, the company invested in the development of a product based on dextrose, which had been identified and separated in 1941 by a team of researchers. This substance was marketed as Dextran, a plasma substitute, and was put to use during World War II.

The company expanded into the production of research aids after researchers successfully separated pectin in the 1950s. It joined with two companies, AS Pharmacia and Organon, to launch a line of hormones in 1955. As Pharmacia expanded, it licensed the manufacture of its products in foreign countries, allowing for expansion through subsidiaries. To control these subsidiaries and joint ventures, it formed a separate company, Pharmacia International, in 1967.

Despite its leading position in separation and purification technology, an integral component in biotechnology, Pharmacia produced poor financial results through the 1970s and into the 1980s. After relying on loans to pay its employees in 1985, the company became privatized the following year. Jan Ekberg was named its new chairman, and executed the company's turnaround.

U.S. sales counted for approximately 40% of company sales in 1985, and Pharmacia embarked on joint ventures and acquisitions to improve its hold on the American market. It also strengthened its presence in the European market by acquiring German, Scandinavian, and Italian firms in 1988. Two years later it merged with the food-and-drug company Procordia and the food company Provenda. The resulting company retained the Procordia name and integrated all pharmaceutical operations into Pharmacia. Ekberg continued seeking out acquisition properties for Pharmacia, including Italy's Farmitalia Carlo Erba in 1993, until the company ranked third among pharmaceutical companies worldwide. Its sales that year totaled more than $3 billion.

By 1995, however, a wave of industry consolidation had kicked Pharmacia down to the ninth global position. It was prepared to introduce a new drug for the treatment of glaucoma, but realized that it needed a partner with the capabilities for mass marketing in the United States.

History of The Upjohn Co.

In 1885 Dr. William Upjohn, a physician from Hastings, Michigan, was granted a patent on the "friable" pill, so named because it could be easily crumbled; this property allowed it be absorbed readily by the patient, a quality that had been lacking in the pills at the time. He and his brother established The Upjohn Pill and Granule Co. the following year, and sales for the year reached $50,000. It opened its first branch sales office opens in New York City in 1890.

By 1902, the company, now called The Upjohn Co., had become a manufacturer of general pharmaceuticals, as it produced a variety of fluid extracts, tinctures, ointments, elixirs, syrups, and tablets. Sales in 1912 exceeded $1 million for the first time. Upjohn

The Business

Financials

Revenue (1998): $6.7 billion

Employees (1998): 30,000

SICs / NAICS

sic 2833 - Medicinals & Botanicals

sic 2834 - Pharmaceutical Preparations

sic 2835 - Diagnostic Substances

sic 2836 - Biological Products Except Diagnostic

sic 8731 - Commercial Physical Research

naics 325411 - Medicinal and Botanical Manufacturing

naics 325412 - Pharmaceutical Preparation Manufacturing

naics 325413 - In-Vitro Diagnostic Substance
  Manufacturing

naics 325414 - Biological Product (except Diagnostic)
  Manufacturing

naics 541710 - Research and Development in the Physical,
  Engineering, and Life Sciences

hired its first Ph.D. chemist, Fredrick W. Heyl, the following year; Heyl later became the company's first director of research. In 1927 the company established a nutritional research laboratory, and launched a research and development initiative to make vitamin supplements common household items.

Upjohn expanded internationally in 1935 by opening a sales office in Toronto, Canada. Sales that year surpassed the $10 million mark. One year later, researchers combined high quality kaolin with fruit pectin to produce Kaopectate, which would become one of the most widely used nonprescription remedies for diarrhea. In 1940 it introduced another successful product, Unicap multivitamins. Upjohn scientists and engineers made progress in the development of antibiotics and steroids during World War II, with a pilot plant to speed mass production of penicillin for wartime demand.

The company expanded into the veterinary industry with its 1949 release of an estrogenic hormone. In 1952 it became the leader in the steroid market after discovering a new method for harnessing the action of microorganisms to produce cortisone, thereby reducing the cost of steroid drug production. That year Upjohn also entered the plant health field by introducing its first non-medical antibiotic.

The Officers

Chairman: Soren Gyll

CEO: Fred Hassan

Exec. VP and President, Research and Development:
Goran Ando

Exec. VP, Chief Financial Officer: Christopher J. Coughlin

International expansion continued, and the firm opened its first subsidiary outside North America, Upjohn of England, Ltd., in London. In 1958 the company held its initial public offering. At that time Upjohn was the sixth-largest manufacturer of antibiotics, with antibiotics sales of about $22.6 million.

It entered into the production of organic chemicals and their derivatives, including raw materials for urethane foams and plastics, in 1962. Upjohn ventured into the personal health care field with its 1969 purchase of Homemakers, Inc., a temporary help service specializing in home health care workers.

Motrin, a nonsteroidal anti-inflammatory utilizing the active ingredient ibuprofen, had been licensed by Upjohn from The Boots Company PLC. In 1974 this product enjoyed the highest first year sales of any pharmaceutical product and accounted for 40% of company earnings. Other well-known products released in the next several years include Halcion, an insomnia treatment, and Cortaid, a hydrocortisone product—the first to be made available in the U.S. without a prescription.

The Boots Company initiated a price war in 1981 by selling its version of ibuprofen at prices 20-30% lower than Upjohn's, leading to the erosion of Upjohn's dominant market position. In 1984, however, Upjohn launched Nuprin, a nonprescription form of ibuprofen, and recovered some of its losses. That year it also announced its intentions to enter the biotechnology field and to develop genetically engineered products. Its first bioengineered product to be marketed was its 1987 release of Tolvid, a vaccine for swine.

Canadian health authorities approved registration of the Rogaine treatment of male pattern baldness in 1986. Demand for this product appeared to be high, yet sales were disappointing. After three years of lackluster performance, Upjohn began marketing directly to the consumer through an information campaign. This direct campaign increased sales of Rogaine more than one-third from 1989 to 1990, but brought criticism from the U.S. Food and Drug Administration, which disapproved of the company's sidestepping of physicians.

After losing patent protection on a number of its products, Upjohn entered into an agreement in 1992 with Geneva Pharmaceutical, a subsidiary of Ciba-Geigy Ltd., to market generic versions of several Upjohn products. It also worked to speed up its research and development process in order to replace the products it would lose to the generic market. Yet new products were not expected to offset the revenue losses over the long term. By November 1992, Upjohn showed the lowest multiple of all pharmaceutical stocks.

John L. Zabriskie, former executive vice president of Merck & Co., became chairman and CEO in 1994. He instituted cost-cutting measures to improve the company's profitability. These measures increased profits by 25%, yet sales remained mediocre.

Market Forces Driving the Merger

Pharmaceutical companies enjoyed tremendous financial success in the early 1980s. Drug prices increased faster than the rate of inflation, and research and development initiatives produced blockbuster new drugs. As a whole, pharmaceuticals became the most profitable industry in the US. This encouraged more companies and individuals to throw their hat into the ring, either by expanding operations to include pharmaceuticals or by forming start-up pharmaceutical companies.

Then, in the late 1980s, a period of patent expiration impacted the profitability of drug companies. Generic competitors were launched by rival firms, and profits and market share for the firms that held the original patents decreased. Pharmaceutical companies had to release breakthrough drugs to stay ahead of competition, but research and development, at its subsequent governmental approval, can take years. That time span may be reduced by joining with another company to push products through the pipeline.

Intense growth and increasing global competition also stresses the importance of speed-to-market. To move quickly, research and development funds, as well as marketing dollars, must be available. Consolidation, which allows for a pooling of financial and research and development assets, allows pharmaceutical companies to commercialize new products with enhanced speed.

European pharmaceutical companies began showing greater interest in the U.S. This market had two features that made it desirable to industry players. It represented 30% of global pharmaceutical sales and, unlike countries, its drug prices were not regulated by the government. The easiest way to break into the U.S. is through a merger with an American company. The first European giant to crack the market was U.K.-based Beecham PLC, which merged with the U.S.-based SmithKline Beckman in 1989. This deal defined the immediate future of the global pharmaceutical industry, and other consolidations soon followed.

The second wave of pharmaceutical consolidation occurred in mid-1990s in response to increasing costs of product development and delivery. Doctors had less time to research the merits of a particular drug, so pharmaceutical companies employed squads of salespeople to deliver the research for company drugs into their hands. Combining these pools of salespeople would add up to significant marketing savings.

Acquiring a large array of products would also allow for reduced marketing allocations. A company that could meet more pharmaceutical needs of end-customers would be regarded favorably by managed care companies, and the pharmaceutical companies could gain loyalty from these companies by offering volume discounts.

Approach and Engagement

Pharmacia began analyzing prospective U.S. merger partners in 1995. It singled out Upjohn as a prime candidate because of that company's attractive distribution network. Upjohn was also a generalist, a classification that would complement Pharmacia's presence in niche markets. Its vulnerable position, a result of recent patent expirations, would likely make it receptive to a merger offer. It might also be drawn to Pharmacia's strong research and distribution resources, particularly in the areas of cancer and cardiovascular, infectious, and neurological diseases.

Pharmacia's Jan Ekberg initiated merger talks, but it was Upjohn's CEO John Zabriskie who proposed the merger. Ekberg sent a team of analysts to ascertain the state of Upjohn's research and development activities over the course of four months. After finding them viable, he agreed to the merger in August 1995.

The proposed merger was to be a $6 billion stock swap in which Upjohn shareholders received 1.45 shares of the new company, Pharmacia & Upjohn, while Pharmacia shareholders received an even trade. This new company would immediately become the world's ninth-largest pharmaceutical company, with annual sales of $6.9 billion and a research budget of $1.1 billion. It would be headquartered in London, a

The Players

President and CEO: John L. Zabriskie. John Zabriskie was the driving force behind Upjohn's merger with Pharmacia. Although it was Pharmacia's chairman, Jan Ekberg, who initiated merger discussions, Zabriskie was the one to propose the deal. He first joined Upjohn in January 1994 as its chairman and CEO, and immediately set about trying to improve the company's financial standing. Upjohn was just treading water, however, until its 1995 marriage with Pharmacia. After this union, Zabriskie served as Pharmacia's president and CEO. He resigned from the company in 1997, leaving its London headquarters to return to the U.S. Before joining Upjohn, Zabriskie had spent nearly 30 years at Merck & Co. He eventually achieved the positions of executive vice president of Merck and president of its manufacturing unit. He had also been instrumental in coordinating the integration of Medco Containment Services into Merck.

Chairman: Jan Ekberg. Jan Ekberg was inexperienced in pharmaceuticals when he was asked by the Swedish government to take the helm of Pharmacia AB. The recently privatized company required rescue from financial distress, and its new chairman and CEO proved more than capable. Ekberg embarked upon a string of acquisitions and joint ventures to improve the company's geographic coverage, particularly in the lucrative U.S. market. He drove the company to become a market leader, only to watch its position slip as a result of the mega-mergers that had swept through the pharmaceutical industry. He approached Upjohn to discuss a possible merger, a proposition that was well received by that company's chairman and CEO, John Zabriskie. The deal was completed in 1995, and Ekberg became the new company's chairman. He also filled in as president and CEO upon Zabriskie's departure in 1997, the same year that he too would resign.

---

geographically neutral location, and would have operations in Stockholm, Sweden; Kalamazoo, Michigan; and Milan, Italy. Jan Ekberg would be the chairman and Zabriskie would assume the positions of president and CEO. The company would realize about $500 million in annual savings from the elimination of 4,000 of the combined workforce of 34,500.

Regulatory approval was the next step in consummating the merger. The European Commission bestowed its approval in October. The U.S. Federal Trade Commission granted its approval later that month, on the condition that Pharmacia license out a treatment under development that duplicated a similar product being developed by Upjohn.

The final hurdle to clear was obtaining shareholder approval. Upjohn shareholders approved the deal on October 17, 1995, but approval from Pharmacia shareholders could have constituted a problem. Ninety-percent of its shareholders had to approve the deal, and since over 10% of its stock was held by savings associations, it was possible that the proposal would not pass. In early November, however, 96% gave a nod to the deal, and Pharmacia & Upjohn was officially formed. Its shares began trading on the New York Stock Exchange on November 3rd and on the Stockholm Stock Exchange on November 6, 1985.

Products and Services

Pharmacia & Upjohn operates in five main segments. The largest of these was its **Rx Pharma** division, which houses its core prescription pharmaceuticals. This group was subdivided into four categories. General Therapeutics consisted of products used by primary care customers, including Detrol/Detrusitol, for overactive bladders; Edronax, for depression; and Xanax, for anxiety and panic disorder. Specialty Products was organized around peptide hormones and ophthalmology, and includes such products as Genotropin, for growth and metabolic disorders; Xalatan, for glaucoma; and Mirapex/Mirapexin and Cabaser, for Parkinson's disease. Hospital Products centered on such oncological products as Camptosar, for colorectal cancer; Fragmin, and antithrombotic; Rescriptor, an HIV-positive treatment; and Vistide, for viral infections. The fourth product classification was Diversified Products, which contains such products as Depo-Provera, a contraceptive; Caverject, for erectile dysfunction; and Estring, for symptoms of urogenital atrophy.

Consumer Health operations held the company's over-the-counter products. Two of its most popular brands are the Nicorette line of nicotine replacement products and the Rogaine hair-loss treatment.

Animal Health produced a number of pharmaceuticals and feed additives for livestock and pets. Naxcel/Excenel is an antibiotic, Lincomix treats diseases in swine and poultry, and MGA Feed Additive is a growth promotant for heifers.

The **Diagnostics** supplied of in-vitro allergy tests. The company's fifth business operation category was

PCS, its pharmaceutical commercial services, which supplies products to third-party customers.

Review of the Outcome

Pharmacia & Upjohn immediately realized a boost in revenues. Sales for 1995 increased 3.6% to $6.95 billion. Zabriskie announced that in 1996 "we will begin experiencing the benefits of our strengthened global distribution capabilities. We have already refocused our research and development efforts and will invest in the innovative technologies that will drive our growth and leadership positions in important therapeutic areas."

Despite the power of the combined companies, Pharmacia & Upjohn's stock value fell owing to poor earnings and management confusion after the merger. Sales growth slowed, which accounted for some of the disappointing earnings. Moreover, English, Italian, American, and Swedish executives now shared management of the company, and many literally did not speak the same language.

Zabriskie announced his immediate resignation in January 1997, expressing interest in returning to the U.S. Some analysts pointed to the company's disappointing results as the reason for his departure, while others allowed for the chance that Zabriskie was simply homesick for his native country. Ekberg temporarily assumed the vacated posts of president and CEO, and then returned to his position as chairman when the company hired Fred Hassan as the new president and CEO that May.

Hassan initiated a restructuring plan to simplify and streamline structure. He brought the pharmaceutical product centers in Stockholm, Milan, and Kalamazoo together under the worldwide Pharmaceutical Business. These sites continued to house other company operations, however. Hassan also formed two management groups, the Executive Committee and the Operations Group, to focus decision making and increase accountability.

Pharmacia & Upjohn transferred its headquarters from London to New Jersey in 1997 to be at the center of the global pharmaceutical industry. Hassan remarked that this move "will create a strong operational global headquarters for Pharmacia & Upjohn, tightly linked to the marketplace and providing swift, decisive leadership."

In August 1997, Ekberg requested to step down as chairman. He was succeeded by Soren Gyll, and was granted a seat on the company's board of directors. Also in August, Pharmacia & Upjohn merged

Pharmacia Biotech, its biotechnology supply arm, with Amersham Life Science in a stock swap. The resulting company, which was 45% owned by Pharmacia & Upjohn, became the world's largest biotechnology supply firm.

Referring to the changes that he had instituted, Hassan's Letter to Shareholders in the company's 1997 annual report stated, "We acknowledge that some of these changes have been difficult for our employees, who have undergone a challenging transition during the past year. We are indebted to them for their patience, understanding and resilience."

In December 1998 the company's Nutrition business, consisting of a range of products for patients unable to digest an adequate amount of nutrients, was sold to Fresnius AG. The following January, the Swedish government reduced its stake in Pharmacia & Upjohn to 0.9%.

Research

"Pharmacia & Upjohn Inc.," in *International Directory of Company Histories*, Vol. 25. St. James Press: 1999. Provides a narrative account of the history of both Pharmacia and Upjohn, and of the resulting merger.

Pharmacia & Upjohn 1997 Annual Report. Reports financial highlights and describes company operating segments.

Pharmacia & Upjohn Home Page, available at http://www.pnu.com. Official World Wide Web Home Page for Pharmacia & Upjohn. Offers such information as shareholder news and product descriptions.

Reier, Sharon. "Dark Horse," in *Financial World*, 21 November 1995. Treatise on the history of Pharmacia.

Schwartz, Nelson D. "A Tempting Drug Deal," in *Fortune*, 9 June 1997. Discusses Wall Street's reaction, and possible overreaction, to depressed financial reports by the newly-formed company.

"Pharmacia & Upjohn Announces Measures to Improve Performance," in *PR Newswire*, 2 July 1997. Reports Fred Hassan's steps to streamline the company's structure and systems.

"Pharmacia and Upjohn Clear Final Hurdle for Merger," in *The Wall Street Journal, Europe*, 2 November 1995. Pharmacia shareholders approve the deal.

"Pharmacia & Upjohn to Move Headquarters to U.S.," in *Chemical & Engineering News*, 20 October 1997. The company's announced relocation from London to an undetermined U.S. site.

Lerner, Matthew. "Drug Production is Restructuring," in *Chemical Marketing Reporter*, 18 March 1996. Merger activity sweeping through the pharmaceutical industry.

"Pharmacia & Upjohn First Combined Results," in *Marketletter*, 26 February 1996. Sales figures at the close of the new company's first year, and comments from Zabriskie on expected future growth.

"Pharmacia & Upjohn Inc.," in *Notable Corporate Chronologies*, The Gale Group, 1999. Lists major events in the history of The Upjohn Co. and of Pharmacia & Upjohn.

BERTRAM W. ROLAND

PHILADELPHIA NATIONAL BANK &
GIRARD TRUST CORN EXCHANGE BANK

Mellon Bank Corp.
One Mellon Bank Center
Pittsburgh, PA 15258
USA

tel: (412)234-5000
web: http://www.mellon.com

date: June 17, 1963 (canceled)
affected: Philadelphia National Bank, USA
affected: Girard Trust Corn Exchange Bank, USA, founded 1951

Overview of the Merger

The merger between Philadelphia National Bank and Girard Trust Corn Exchange Bank was barred by the U.S. Supreme Court in 1963 in a decision that set precedent for both antitrust law and the banking industry. For the first time, banks were found to be subject to the standards of the Clayton Antitrust Act, from which the industry had long insisted that it was exempt. *Philadelphia National Bank* also expanded on the standard of illegal market concentration set down by *Brown Shoe*, and would, in turn, be expanded upon in *Alcoa-Rome* and *Von's Grocery*.

History of Girard Trust Corn Exchange Bank

The Girard Trust Corn Exchange Bank was formed through the 1951 merger of Girard Bank, which had been established in 1835, and Corn Exchange Bank, founded in 1858. The new concern proceeded to grow, and became an innovative force in the industry. It installed its first computer in 1962, and, over the next 10 years, pioneered the development of the city's automated retail services. Eventually, Girard's automated banking system would be recognized as state of the art.

In 1963, its proposed merger with Philadelphia National Bank was blocked by the U.S. Supreme Court. The Court's decision, the first application of the Clayton Antitrust Act to bank mergers, declared illegal the proposed union based on the 30% combined market share that would result.

Girard Company was established as a holding company in 1970. The Girard Trust Bank changed its name to Girard Bank in 1977. Four years later Girard acquired the Farmers Bank of Delaware, founded in 1807, and renamed it Girard Bank Delaware. The firm subsequently experienced a significant decline in earnings, and was purchased by Mellon Bank in November 1982. Instead of improving Girard's balance sheet, which included a vast stable of delinquent loans, the merger actually worsened it. Girard contributed to a 14% decline in Mellon's earnings in 1984. In response, Mellon fully integrated Girard, dismissing several Girard executives and expunging the Girard name.

Approach and Engagement

The Kennedy Administration filed an antitrust suit to block the pending merger between two small Philadelphia banks, Philadelphia National Bank and Girard Trust Corn Exchange Bank. The case proceeded to the U.S. Supreme Court, which delivered a landmark decision on June 17, 1963, barring the merger and ruling that banks are covered under the Clayton Antitrust Act. This trailblazing decision incorporated several key elements, affecting antitrust law in general as well as mergers in the banking industry.

The *Philadelphia National Bank* decision expanded on the *Brown Shoe* decision of 1962. In barring the merger between Brown Shoe and Kinney Shoe, the Court held that even a merger resulting in a combined market share as small as five percent could be considered anticompetitive if the market was shown to be concentrated.

In *Philadelphia National Bank* the Court decided that a large market share can be assumed to be anticompetitive in and of itself, even in the absence of evidence supporting this claim. To the contrary, the decision suggested that such a union could proceed only if the companies proved that their proposed merger would not restrain competition. Since the combination of Philadelphia National and Girard would have captured 30% of the city's market, it was judged to be illegal. "Without attempting to specify the smallest market share which would still be considered to threaten undue concentration," wrote the majority, "we are clear that 30 percent represents that threat."

The decision was also the first to apply antitrust law to commercial banks. Prior to this case, the banking industry had enjoyed exemption from the Clayton Act, on two counts. First, bankers maintained that the Bank Merger Act of 1960 had been enacted by Congress precisely to protect proposed unions from Justice Department scrutiny. Second, they asserted that the Clayton Act applied to the purchase of assets, not the purchase of stock that is typical in bank deals.

The Court overruled both arguments. "There is no indication in the legislative history to the 1950 amendment of Section 7 [of the Clayton Act] that Congress wished to confer a special dispensation upon the banking industry," wrote the majority.

Changes to the Industry

Brown Shoe determined that in certain circumstances an increase in market share could be consid-

The Business

Financials

Revenue (1998): $390 billion (assets under management)

Employees (1998): 28,000

SICs / NAICS

sic 6021 - National Commercial Banks

sic 6211 - Security Brokers & Dealers

naics 522110 - Commercial Banking

naics 523110 - Investment Banking and Securities Dealing

naics 523120 - Securities Brokerage

ered anticompetitive. *Philadelphia National Bank* expanded on this standard by ruling that a certain market share increase absolutely would be anticompetitive, barring evidence that it would not. The U.S. Supreme Court expanded on that standard in ensuing decisions. In *Alcoa-Rome* the Court ruled in 1964 that even slight increases in market share were illegal in a concentrated market. *Von's Grocery*, set down in 1966, determined that slight share increases were also illegal even if the market was only leaning toward concentration.

In response to *Philadelphia National Bank*, Congress enacted the Bank Merger Act of 1966. This edict specified that a bank merger could not be challenged under Section 7 unless the U.S. Attorney General challenged it within 30 days after it had been approved by the applicable banking regulatory agency. Depending on the circumstances, either the Federal Deposit Insurance Corp., the Federal Reserve System, or the Board of Directors of the Federal Reserve System has authority in examining proposed banking mergers.

Products and Services

Mellon Bank, which had acquired Girard Bank in 1982, offered a variety of personal, small business, and corporate services in the late 1990s. Its Consumer Fee Services included private asset management and mutual funds. Consumer Banking serviced more than 2.5 million customers, and its 400 offices comprised the third-largest retail store network in the Mid-Atlantic States. Its Business Fee Services included investment management, global securities services, foreign exchange, benefits consultancy, retirement services, cash management, and mutual funds.

Research

"High Court Tightens the Antitrust Reins," in *Business Week* 18 June 1966. Analyzes the increasingly stringent standards of illegal market concentration.

"Mellon Bank Corporation," in *International Directory of Company Histories*, Vol. II, St. James Press: 1990. Provides a historical review of the Mellon.

Mellon Bank Corp. Home Page, available at http://www.mellong.com. Official World Wide Web Home Page for Mellon Bank. Includes information on products and services, annual reports and other financial data, an extensive company history, news releases, and executive biographies.

Shanahan, Eileen. "Clayton Act Held Bank-Merger Bar," in *The New York Times*, 18 June 1963. Details the landmark decision.

"Thunderbolt for Bank Mergers," in *Business Week* 22 June 1963. Examines the ruling and its impact on antitrust law in application to the banking industry.

Wasserstein, Bruce. *Big Deal: The Battle for Control of America's Leading Corporations*, Warner Books, 1998. Offers an overview of *Philadelphia National Bank* and other antitrust suits in American corporate history.

PATRICIA ARCHILLA

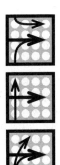

PHILIP MORRIS & KRAFT

nationality: USA
date: November 1988
affected: Philip Morris Companies, Inc., USA, founded 1847
affected: Kraft Inc., USA, founded 1909

Philip Morris Companies, Inc.
120 Park Avenue
New York, NY 10017
USA

tel: (917)663-5000
fax: (917)663-2167
web: http://philipmorris.com

Overview of the Merger

The $13.1 billion acquisition of Kraft Inc. by Philip Morris Companies was the second-largest corporate takeover up to that time. The 1991 union created the world's largest consumer company, incorporating such brands as Maxwell House, Jell-O, Post, Kool-Aid, Parkay, Miracle Whip, and Lender's. Hamish Maxwell, CEO of Philip Morris at the time of the merger, stated in the *Financial Times (London)* that the deal would create "a U.S. based food company that will compete more effectively in the world food markets."

History of Philip Morris Companies, Inc.

In 1847 Philip Morris opened a tobacco shop on Bond St. in a fashionable district of London, England. The shop fared well, and in 1873, when Morris died, his brother and widow inherited the company. In 1902 Philip Morris & Co., Ltd., was incorporated in New York by Gustav Eckmeyer.

By 1911 American Tobacco Trust, which maintained a virtual monopoly on the cigarette industry in the U.S., was dissolved by a court order. George J. Whelan formed a new company called Tobacco Products Corp., which absorbed Melachrino Cigarettes and several other smaller companies. Two leading Melachrino salesmen, Reuben M. Ellis and Leonard B. McKitterick, became vice presidents and stockholders of the new company. In 1919 Whelan bought the U.S. branch of Philip Morris Company and formed Philip Morris & Company Ltd., Inc., to manage its assets. Ellis and McKitterick became part owners and managers of the new Philip Morris brands.

The 1920s were years of growth and change for the company. In 1923 Ellis became president and McKitterick left the company. Two years later Philip Morris introduced the Marlboro brand of cigarettes, which sold for $.20 apiece. The brand was marketed to wealthy, sophisticated women, and by the next year over 500 million Marlboro cigarettes had been sold. Toward the end of the decade, Whelan left Philip Morris because of financial difficulties, and the company began to manufacture its own cigarettes by purchasing a factory in Richmond, Virginia.

The Business

Financials

Revenue (1998): $74,391 million

Employees (1998): 144,000

SICs / NAICS

sic 2021 - Creamery Butter

sic 2022 - Cheese-Natural & Processed

sic 2024 - Ice Cream & Frozen Desserts

sic 2034 - Dehydrated Fruits, Vegetables & Soups

sic 2037 - Frozen Fruits & Vegetables

sic 2043 - Cereal Breakfast Foods

sic 2082 - Malt Beverages

sic 2083 - Malt

sic 2098 - Macaroni & Spaghetti

naics 311512 - Creamery Butter Manufacturing

naics 311513 - Cheese Manufacturing

naics 311423 - Dried and Dehydrated Food Manufacturing

naics 311999 - All Other Miscellaneous Food Manufacturing

naics 311421 - Fruit and Vegetable Canning

naics 311941 - Mayonnaise, Dressing, and Other Prepared
  Sauce Manufacturing

naics 311411 - Frozen Fruit, Juice and Vegetable
  Manufacturing

naics 311942 - Spice and Extract Manufacturing

naics 311213 - Malt Manufacturing

naics 311823 - Dry Pasta Manufacturing

McKitterick returned to Philip Morris in 1930, and with Ellis, began to buy Philip Morris stock from Whelan. After gaining control of the company the following year, they introduced the Philip Morris economy brand cigarette, which had become popular during the Depression. By that time the company also sold pipe tobacco and three types of cigarettes: English Ovals, Marlboro, and Paul Jones. By 1933 the firm introduced a new cigarette called Philip Morris English Blend. Bellhop John Roventini began playing the role of Johnnie Morris and spent years promoting cigarettes on weekly radio shows and at public appearances.

In 1936 Alfred Lyon took control of the company after the deaths of Ellis and McKitterick. Under his control, Philip Morris sold 7.5 billion cigarettes by year-end and became the fourth-largest cigarette company in the country. Lyon also created the industry's largest sales department. Four years later sales hit $64 million. With the onset of World War II, the sale of cigarettes increased dramatically. At the end of the war, however, cigarette consumption dropped significantly. Philip Morris overestimated peacetime demand and the company's net income fell. The company had floated a new bond issue and was forced to withdraw the offering, which damaged its reputation.

To try to remedy falling profits, Philip Morris bought Axton-Fisher Tobacco Co. of Louisville, Kentucky, for $20 million, mainly to acquire its large store of cured tobacco and a second manufacturing plant. In 1948 the company introduced a new advertising campaign, asserting that its English blend cigarettes did not cause "cigarette hangover," a theretofore unheard of problem. Sales increased substantially from this move, but the company still faced hard times. By 1950 the public had become increasingly aware of the health dangers related to smoking, and began opting to buy filtered cigarettes. Philip Morris was slow to recognize this trend, and its sales once again dropped.

To rebound, the company acquired Benson & Hedges in 1954. The next year Philip Morris introduced the Marlboro Man, the quintessential American cowboy, to advertise its new filtered cigarettes. The firm also established an overseas division and adopted Philip Morris Incorporated as its corporate name. In 1957 Joseph Cullman III took over management of the company and increased sales, especially on the international market. By the end of the 1950s, however, the company had slipped to the rank of sixth-largest in the tobacco industry, with its best-selling product in tenth place among leading brands. George Weissman, named director of international operations, focused on making Philip Morris the United States' leading exporter of tobacco products.

Controlling only 9.4% of the tobacco market in 1961, the company spent the next years developing a plan to increase sales and market share. In 1968 it introduced Virginia Slims, a cigarette marketed toward women. Two years later Miller Brewing Co., the country's seventh-largest brewer, was added to Philip Morris' holdings. In 1972 Philip Morris acquired Mission Viejo Co., and by 1973 Marlboro cigarettes had become the second-most popular cigarettes in the country, accounting for two-thirds of the company's tobacco business.

Continuing on its upturn, Philip Morris introduced a new low-tar cigarette called Merit, which became very popular among Americans concerned about the health risks of smoking. In 1976, 94 million Marlboro cigarettes were sold and Philip Morris became the second-largest seller of tobacco in the world, controlling over 25% of the tobacco market. All other competitors, except Reynolds, suffered financial decline that year. Together, those two companies controlled 50% of the market. In 1978 Philip Morris bought the Seven-Up Company for $520 million, and acquired Liggett Group Inc., an international cigarette company.

With the repositioning of High Life Beer and the introduction of the country's first low calorie beer, Miller Lite, Miller became the country's number-two brewer in 1985. That same year Philip Morris bought General Foods Corp. for $5.75 billion to further diversify the company, ensuring a substantial financial base outside the tobacco industry. Philip Morris also developed a holding company that year. By 1987, however, General Foods Corp. was not supplying the large income expected, and 60% of Philip Morris' profits for the year were generated by the sale of Marlboro cigarettes. To further diversify, Philip Morris bought Kraft, Inc. for $12.9 billion in 1988, and in 1990, Jacobs Suchard, a Swiss maker of chocolate and coffee for $4.1 billion. The next year the company acquired Egri Dohangyar, one of Hungary's largest state-owned cigarette makers.

The 1990s were marked by an increase in consumer health awareness and the onset of attacks from health-conscious warriors. In 1994 Philip Morris filed a $10 billion lawsuit against Capital Cities/ABC, claiming that the *Day One* television program falsely reported that Philip Morris manipulated cigarette nicotine levels to foster addiction. In response, the company promoted a newspaper advertising campaign designed to offset recent reports of the negative health effects of second-hand smoke. Chairman and CEO Michael A. Miles resigned that year and was succeeded by Geoffrey C. Bible as president and chairman, and by James J. Morgan as CEO. Philip Morris joined other tobacco companies to block the state of Florida from suing cigarette companies for Medicaid costs incurred in the treatment of smoking-related health problems. The company underwrote the campaign costs of California Proposition 188, which repealed more than 200 local tobacco laws and replaced them with a less strict state statute.

With the tobacco industry under siege, Philip Morris reorganized its food operations, merging Kraft and General Foods to form Kraft Foods in 1995. In the same year international units of Philip Morris and PepsiCo announced a joint venture to market canned, cold coffee in Asia, and the Miller Brewing subsidiary formed a strategic alliance with Costa Rican brewer Cerveceria Americana S.A. to expand its markets in Latin America. Capital Cities/ABC agreed to settle the libel suit brought by Philip Morris by issuing an apol-

The Officers

Chairman and CEO: Geoffrey C. Bible

Vice Chairman, External Affairs and General Counsel: Murray H. Bring

Chief Operating Officer: William H. Webb

Sr. VP and Chief Financial Officer: Louis C. Camilleri

Sr. VP, Corporate Affairs: Steven C. Parrish

Sr. VP, Human Resources and Administration: Timothy A. Sompolski

ogy and admitting error in its reporting. That same year CPC International purchased Philip Morris's baking businesses for $865 million.

Despite efforts to focus on the food industry, the company had to recall more than eight billion cigarettes following the discovery of pesticide residue in some cigarette filters in 1995. The State of Massachusetts sued six tobacco companies that year, including Philip Morris, for more than $1 billion in damages to repay taxpayers for money used to treat indigent patients suffering from smoking-related health problems. In 1996 three former Philip Morris executives testified to a Food and Drug Administration (FDA) panel that the company did in fact manipulate the nicotine levels of its cigarette brands. Philip Morris officials issued a public statement rebutting the allegations. To counter the negative publicity, Philip Morris and the FDA released a joint proposal to ban billboard advertising for tobacco products within 1,000 feet of schoolyards and playgrounds.

The company experienced problems abroad, as well. In 1996 European Union commissioner Karl Van Miert launched a probe of Philip Morris and the tobacco regulatory arm of the Italian government, citing a possible conspiracy to control cigarette sales. Brazil's largest manufacturer of chocolate, Industrias de Chocolate Lacta SA, was acquired that year, as the company decided it needed to focus on growth in other industries. In 1998, Philip Morris cut more than 2,500 overseas jobs at Kraft Foods International and cut the tobacco force by 12%. That same year the company settled the suits brought on by states by agreeing to pay $250 billion over the next 25 years for protection against future suits. Individuals, however, still had the power to pursue legal action against the company, and in 1999, Philip Morris had to pay $25 million to a California smoker and $80 million to an Oregon family who lost a member due to smoking. Tobacco sales continued to decline in 1999, and the company

The Players

Chairman and CEO of Philip Morris Companies, Inc.: Hamish Maxwell. After graduating from Cambridge University in England, Hamish Maxwell joined Thomas Cook Sons & Company. In 1954 he began work as a salesman with Philip Morris. Maxwell made his way through the company ranks, from vice president to executive vice president, and became president and chief operating officer in 1983. The next year he was named CEO, and is credited with expanding the firm into the food industry. Because of his innovative style, the company's product mix generated $51.2 billion in sales in 1990. The following year, at age 65, Maxwell stepped down from his position, but remained chairman of the executive committee.

Chairman and CEO of Kraft, Inc.: John M. Richman. John Richman began his career with Kraft as the company's lawyer in 1954. Named CEO in 1979, he was responsible for the company's growth and diversity during the 1980s. Richman orchestrated the merger in 1980 with Dart Industries, the deal that instantly diversified the company. When Philip Morris bought Kraft in 1988, he was elected to the board of directors and was slated to become a vice chairman.

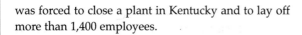

was forced to close a plant in Kentucky and to lay off more than 1,400 employees.

History of Kraft Inc.

In 1903 James L. Kraft established a wholesale cheese distribution system where he delivered cheese to grocer's doors so they wouldn't have to travel to the market everyday. Despite dismal sales in the first few years (Kraft lost his horse and $3,000), his four brothers, Fred, Charles, Norman, and John, joined the business. In 1909 the company was formed as J.L. Kraft & Bros. Company.

The new company focused on product development and innovative advertising. In 1911, Kraft began to mail out circulars and advertising on trains and billboards. The company was also one of the first to place color advertisements in national magazines. In 1912, a New York office was opened to develop international business. Two years later the company opened a fac-

tory in Stockton, Illinois, and sold more than 31 different types of cheeses. By 1915, Kraft had developed pasteurized cheese, whichn't spoil like other cheese products; in 1916 the company patented this new product.

In 1924 the company changed its name to Kraft Cheese Company, offered its shares to the public, and opened its first overseas office in London. Three years later, the Kraft Cheese Company Ltd. was established. Kraft ventured into the German market by opening a sales office in Hamburg. The Phenix Cheese Corp., known for its Philadelphia brand cream cheese, merged with Kraft in 1928. The new company, Kraft-Phenix Cheese Corp., controlled 40% of the cheese market and developed a presence in Canada, Australia, Britain, and Germany.

The 1930s marked a season of change for the cheese company. National Dairy Products Corp. acquired Kraft-Phenix in May of 1930. National acted as a holding company for Kraft's operations. The company went on to introduce Velveeta cheese spread, Miracle Whip salad dressing, and Kraft caramels. The firm marketed its famous macaroni and cheese dinner in 1937, and introduced Parkay margarine in 1940. Kraft emphasized heavy radio promotion to gain public interest in its new products. The company also began a musical review called *Kraft Music Hall* that was broadcast every week and hosted by Bing Crosby.

The onset of World War II prompted Kraft to focus on developing recipes that would work well with wartime shortages. By 1941 four million pounds of cheese were being shipped to Britain. The company became a major supplier to the U.S. government as well. After the war, the company continued to focus on product development and advertising. Kraft Cheese Company became Kraft Foods Company in 1945, and in 1947 the company sponsored and created the *Kraft Television Theatre*, the first commercial network program on television. Sliced cheese made its debut in 1950 and two years later the world was introduced to Cheez Whiz. National Dairy's sales were now over $1 billion.

J.L. Kraft died in 1953, the year after Thomas McInnerney, the leader of National Dairy, passed away. With both founders gone, the company became more centralized. All of its subsidiaries became divisions of a single operating company. In 1956 the company began its diversification process by acquiring Metro Glass, a producer of glass packaging. Kraft introduced its jellies and preserves in 1956, jet puffed marshmallows in 1959, barbecue sauce in 1960, and its famous wrapped cheese slices in 1965. The company continued on its path to growth by introducing many of its products to foreign markets.

The late 1960s brought about yet another name change for the company. In 1969, National Dairy took the name Kraftco Corp. Three years later the company moved its headquarters from New York to Chicago. By 1976, the name had changed once again to Kraft Inc. Management wanted to shift focus to food processing and the internationally known Kraft brand seemed like a good fit for a name. The centralization process that had begun in the 1950s was completed as the company separated into divisions specific to market and product.

The uncertain economy in the 1970s forced Kraft to be conservative. Inflation increased costs and ate up profits, and as a result, the company slowed its new product development and growth. Squeezable Parkay margarine was introduced in 1973, and Breyers yogurt hit the stores in 1977. John M. Richman became the company's CEO in 1979 and wanted the company to grow and diversify. He felt that it had been stagnant for too many years. In 1980, Richman announced the merger with Dart Industries, owner of Tupperware, West Bend Appliances, Duracell batteries, Wilsonart plastics, and Thatcher glass, thereby fulfilling Richman's desire to diversify with just that single deal.

In 1981, the company acquired Hobart Corp., a producer of food service equipment, in a $460 million deal. Kraft's acquisitions slowed down on account of the recession of the early 1980s. Its European operations, the food service business, Dart's plastics, and West Bend appliances, as well as Hobart, were all experiencing sales slumps. Tupperware was also suffering because of a decline in dealers—more women taking jobs outside of the home meant fewer women to market the product.

By 1984, the company had come up with a plan that would put it back on track. It planned to add new products, to extend existing lines, and to initiate an aggressive marketing approach. The company wanted to increase returns from 13.3% to 18%, making it fifth in the consumer products industry.

Michael A. Miles joined the company to help kick off its new sales plan. He reduced costs in the European divisions, added new lines to existing products, and acquired new brands such as Churny Company cheese, Celestial Seasonings herb tea, and Lender's bagels. In 1986, the company spun off Hobart, Tupperware, West Bend, and Wilsonart to form Premark International Inc.

Kraft began a tenacious effort to market and advertise its new products. The company's innovative marketing skills and product development became attractive to Philip Morris, and in 1988 Kraft was purchased. In 1989 Philip Morris merged Kraft and its General Foods division into Kraft General Foods, Inc.

As a result, the company became the largest food marketer in the U.S. Michael Miles took the role of CEO of the new company, which experienced profit growth of over 20% for the first two years.

In the early 1990s the company began to have problems. Internal politics were causing Kraft to introduce new products late. Additionally, the company's new microwave dinner line was a disaster; it was pulled after only six months. Sales in North America only grew by one percent in 1991. The company lost $125 million in profits when its presence in the cheese market faltered. Sales were tumbling in its line of Oscar Meyer processed meats; Kraft tried to battle this by introducing "lighter" products, such as turkey bacon, for its health conscious consumers. The firm eliminated more than 1,000 jobs at its plant in Tulare, California, and discontinued more than 300 products with lagging sales.

Despite the rocky financial climate, Post cereal and Maxwell House were performing well for the company. In 1992, KGF Marketing Services was created to assist with marketing and communication in the different divisions. One year later, Kraft General Foods bought RJR Nabisco's cold cereal line for $450 million.

Market Forces Driving the Merger

Tobacco companies were under fire in the late 1980s. Consumer awareness of the health risks of smoking damaged sales, so Philip Morris planned to decrease its dependence on its tobacco sales. A merger with Kraft would diversify the company and increase marketing potential and financial leverage when dealing with retailers, advertising agencies, and competition. The food industry was also attractive as it was seen to be stable and recession-proof. After the deal, the percentage of sales from tobacco would fall to 39% from 53%, whereas food would increase to 53% from 36%.

The acquisition also raised questions concerning the increase in power the new company would have. Many critics, including Senator Howard Metzenbaum, believed that Philip Morris viewed the merger as a way to protect the cigarette market. With increased leverage as a lobbyist, employer, and advertiser, the giant could throw its weight around to discourage advertisers from printing critical ads about tobacco and to influence company policies about smoking. Philip Morris denied these allegation and agreed to keep tobacco politics out of its advertising decisions and its food divisions.

Approach and Engagement

The bidding for Kraft Inc. created a rather hostile environment between Philip Morris and Kraft. The original offer placed by Philip Morris on October 17, 1988, was $90 a share, or $11.5 billion, in cash. Kraft disputed the offer, claiming that its shares were worth $110. Hamish Maxwell, CEO of Philip Morris, stopped his bidding because he thought Kraft's dividend package was overpriced. John Richman, CEO of Kraft, would not buckle under the pressure, and took offense at Philip Morris's attempts to undervalue Kraft.

With Kraft's stock price fluctuating on account of the merger discussions, Kraft threatened to load itself up with $12 billion in debt in attempt to drive its stock price up. Richman and Hamish, not wanting a drawn out, costly negotiation, agreed to meet in private in the Westin O'Hare Hotel. After four hours of negotiation, a $106 per share deal was reached. Richman then went to his board and the merger agreement was approved.

The merger was completed after the Federal Trade Commission cleared the deal. "Our shareholders are receiving full value, and this merger is the best possible outcome for our employees, customers, and the communities in which we operate," said John Richman, as quoted in *The New York Times*.

Products and Services

The Philip Morris takeover of Kraft, Inc. created the largest food company in the world and brought together such brands such as Velveeta, Parkay, Miracle Whip, Frusen Gladje, Breyers, Sealtest, Maxwell House, Birds Eye, Kool-Aid, Jell-O, Oscar Meyer, Post, and Miller Lite. According to *The New York Times*, Hamish Maxwell believed that the merger created "a U.S. based food company that would compete more effectively in world food markets."

Changes to the Industry

The U.S. food industry, undergoing a reorganization, experienced intense competition companies battled for control of brand names. Buying an established brand was much cheaper than creating a new one—RJR Nabisco was fending off a $20.3 billion offer from Kohlberg Kravis Roberts & Company, and Pillsbury was dealing with offers from Grand Metropolitan of the U.K. The lucrative acquisition process was becoming most popular among companies looking to diversify and take control of market share.

Retailers were also becoming more powerful in the industry. As more brand names competed for shelf space, manufacturers were forced to pay premiums for the space. Computerized check out lanes also helped stores determine which brands were doing well and which brands they could do without. By owning and acquiring more brands, a company owned more shelf space.

The $13.1 billion acquisition of Kraft Inc. by Philip Morris created the world's largest consumer products company by bringing together numerous brand names. The deal provided Philip Morris with and advantage over its competitor Unilever NV and reinforced the company's top ranking among U.S. national advertisers.

Review of the Outcome

Philip Morris planned to take advantage of similar distribution channels that the companies shared. Kraft's cheese products were shipped the same way as Philip Morris's Oscar Meyer meats, and the company was able to combine distribution of the two. Kraft products retained their brand names, as brand image was something that the company wanted to keep intact after the deal. "From the retailer and consumer standpoint, there will be little immediate impact," said Jerry Pinney, vice president of IGA Inc, an organization of over 3,000 grocers, in an interview in *The New York Times*.

Net income for Philip Morris increased from $2.9 billion in 1989 to $3.5 billion in 1990. Revenue went up to $51.2 billion in 1990 from $44.8 billion in 1989.

Research

Brown, Warren. "Marketing Plan for New Acquisitions: Let Brand Names Sell Themselves," in *The Washington Post*, 17 November 1988. Provides insight in the food industry and the trend on buying brand names.

Cole, Robert. "Kraft Being Sold to Philip Morris for $13.1 Billion," in *The New York Times*, 31 October 1988. Lists details of the merger.

Gibbens, Robert. "Kraft Chief Joins Philip Morris Board," in *Financial Times London*, 29 December 1988. Discusses the career of John Richman.

"Kraft General Foods Inc.," in *International Directory of Company Histories*, Vol. 7, St. James Press, 1993. Lists major events in the history of Kraft.

"Kraft and Philip Morris Shares Soar after Deal," in *Financial Times London*, 1 November 1988. Gives financial information upon the announcement of the merger.

"Philip Morris Companies, Inc.," in *Notable Corporate Chronologies*, The Gale Group, 1999. List major events in the history of Philip Morris.

"Philip Morris Elects Chief," in *The New York Times*, 29 April 1991. Details the career of Hamish Maxwell.

"Smoke Clouds a Mega-Merger," in *The New York Times*, 14 November 1988. Discusses possible Philip Morris gains by merging with Kraft.

Stevenson, Richard. "A Muscular New Consumer Giant," in *The New York Times*, 1 November 1988. Lists information on the merger and changes in the industry.

Vamos, Mark. "The Feeding Frenzy Has Its Price," in *Business Week*, 7 November 1988. Describes changes in the food industry and the tendency to buy brand names versus starting new ones.

CHRISTINA M. STANSELL

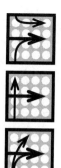

PHYCOR & MEDPARTNERS

date: January 7, 1998 (canceled)
affected: PhyCor, Inc., USA, founded 1988
affected: MedPartners, Inc., USA, founded 1993

PhyCor, Inc.
30 Burton Hills Blvd., Ste. 400
Nashville, TN 37215
USA

tel: (615)665-9066
fax: (615)665-9088
web: http://www.phycor.com

MedPartners, Inc.
3000 Galleria Tower, Ste. 1000
Birmingham, AL 35244
USA

tel: (205)733-8996
fax: (205)982-7709
web: http://www.medpartners.com

Overview of the Acquisition

The proposed merger of PhyCor and MedPartners in October 1997 was designed to form the nation's largest physician practice management company. Wall Street was critical of the deal, however, and the stock prices of both companies took a nose-dive. Less than two months after the merger announcement, the companies jointly terminated the deal, citing cultural and organizational integration difficulties. But analysts suspected that the merger's collapse was rooted in PhyCor's discovery of the poor financial condition of MedPartners. This suspicion was borne out later in 1998, when MedPartners exited the physician practice management business altogether.

History of PhyCor, Inc.

PhyCor, short for The Physicians' Corporation, was founded in 1988 by Joseph Hutts and three partners. The new company was established to provide participating physicians with leverage in dealing with the pressures exacted upon them by health maintenance organizations (HMOs). PhyCor, referring to itself as a physician practice management company (PPM), assumed long-term administrative control over clinics for a percentage of profits, freeing the clinics themselves from such tasks as billing, purchasing, and hiring.

PhyCor grew steadily, operating 11 clinics by 1991. It went public in January of the following year, fueling its continued growth. By early 1997 it managed 44 clinics in 25 states, as well as independent practice associations (IPAs) with more than 8,700 physicians.

In October 1997, PhyCor announced its agreement to acquire MedPartners, Inc., the nation's leading PPM. The combined company would have about 35,000 affiliated physicians in 44 states. In early 1998, however, the companies jointly announced the termination of the deal, citing irreconcilable operational and cultural differences.

PhyCor continued its acquisition strategy, purchasing PrimeCare International, a PPM based in southern California, in May 1998. Two months later

The Business

Financials - PhyCor, Inc.

Revenue (1998): $1.5 billion

Employees (1998): 21,500

Financials - MedPartners, Inc.

Revenue (1998): $2.6 billion

Employees (1998): 19,636

SICs / NAICS

sic 8011 - Offices & Clinics of Medical Doctors

naics 621111 - Offices of Physicians (except Mental Health Specialists)

it acquired three companies: Morgan Health Group, an Atlanta-based IPA; CareWise, Inc., a Seattle firm in the healthcare decision-support field; and First Physician Care, Inc., a physician management company. That October PhyCor entered into a joint venture agreement with Physician Partners Co. to operate a managed care network in the northeastern U.S.

In October 1998, PhyCor denied that it was seriously considering going private through a leveraged buyout, insisting that the company was in good condition. The following summer, however, it agreed to permit E.M. Warburg, Pincus & Co., an investment firm, to increase its 10% stake in PhyCor by investing up to $200 million in its operations.

History of MedPartners, Inc.

Richard M. Scrushy, chairman and CEO of HealthSouth Corp., formed MedPartners in early 1993. Like PhyCor, MedPartners positioned itself as a physician practice management company (PPM), which operated by purchasing the assets of medical practices and assuming their administrative duties.

Led by Larry House, MedPartners embarked on an aggressive acquisition campaign, and by the end of 1994 it managed 25 practices. In February 1995 the company went public, thereby gaining the capital to continue its rapid expansion. Later that year it merged with Mullikin Medical Enterprises, Inc., the nation's largest private PPM. After acquiring Pacific Physician Services, Inc., MedPartners changed its name to MedPartners/Mullikin, Inc.

The company completed the $1.9 billion purchase of Caremark International, Inc. in September 1996, at which point it changed its name back to MedPartners, Inc. The following June it acquired InPhyNet Medical Management, Inc.

In October 1997, MedPartners agreed to be acquired by PhyCor, Inc., the nation's second-largest PPM. Less than two months later, however, the deal was terminated on the claims of overwhelming cultural and organizational differences. Wall Street assigned a different interpretation on the cancellation, and sent the stocks of both companies, particularly that of MedPartners, crashing. In addition, MedPartners recorded a $8.4 million loss in the fourth quarter of the year, prompting the replacement of House by Scrushy as chairman and by Edwin Mac Crawford as president and CEO in early 1998.

MedPartners decided to exit the PPM business in 1998, focusing instead on pharmaceutical services and contract medical services under the brand name Caremark. In January 1999, it divested itself of its government services business for $67 million. That March the company sold its Team Health business for $319 million, and agreed to sell the assets of its PPM business for $89 million. MedPartners recorded $2.6 billion in revenues in 1998, but suffered a net loss of $1.26 billion due to a $1.28 billion charge from discontinued operations, namely its PPM business.

Market Forces Driving the Acquisition

PhyCor and MedPartners had both built themselves into leading PPMs based on a strategy of growth through acquisition. By late 1997, MedPartners was the industry's leader, with PhyCor a close second. The two companies began looking upon each other as potential partners rather than rivals. By pooling their interests, a tactic that had been successful in their previous respective mergers, they would form a company that would be the nation's solid leader.

The combined company would have nearly 35,000 affiliated physicians (21,600 from PhyCor and 13,300 from MedPartners) in 44 states, and achieve $8.4 billion in annual revenues. Since its total number of physicians represented only five percent of the total number of physicians in the U.S., PhyCor and MedPartners perceived that an alliance would be the most efficient means of reaching the remaining 95% through geographic expansion and consolidation of operating expenses.

Approach and Engagement

On October 29, 1997, PhyCor announced its agreement to acquire MedPartners for $8 billion. The transaction called for the exchange of 1.18 shares of PhyCor stock for each share of MedPartners, totaling about $6.8 billion. PhyCor would also assume $1.2 billion in MedPartners debt.

Within a week of the announcement, analysts and investors demonstrated their skepticism of the deal. PhyCor's stock dropped over 20% to $23, and Standard & Poor's placed MedPartners on a watch with "negative implications." Before long, MedPartners' stock also dipped, by about 17%.

Reasons for this lack of confidence varied. Some believed that, at a 13% premium, PhyCor's purchase price was too high. Others believed that the integration of the two companies would be hampered by MedPartners, which was still digesting its sizable acquisition of Caremark.

On January 7, 1998, PhyCor and MedPartners issued a joint statement announcing the termination of their merger. "After a lengthy review and planning process, we determined due to significant operational and strategic differences we would be unable to successfully and effectively integrate the two companies," wrote Joseph Hutts, head of PhyCor. Larry House, chairman of MedPartners, concurred, stating that "it became apparent the differences in the two companies were significant."

Products and Services

As of August 1999, PhyCor managed 48 clinics with 3,076 affiliated physicians. This physician practice management company also operated in 34 independent practice association markets with 26,000 subscribing physicians. Its CareWise, Inc. business provided decision support to more than 3.5 million consumers worldwide.

Having exited the PPM industry, MedPartners operated two main lines of business in 1999. Its Caremark Prescription Services provided clinical care and pharmaceutical health care services by integrating mail service, retail networks, and the delivery of advanced biotech pharmaceutical services. In addition, Caremark Therapeutic Services offered home infusion services for individuals with chronic conditions and diseases.

Review of the Outcome

While analysts agreed that there was some truth to the claims of the difficulties inherent in the integration of the companies, particularly in reference to their computer systems, most believed that there was more behind the merger's cancellation. They surmised that PhyCor had determined that MedPartners was in worse financial condition than it had initially realized.

The Officers

PhyCor, Inc.

Chairman and CEO: Joseph C. Hutts

Vice Chairman: Derril W. Reeves

President and Chief Operating Officer: Thompson S. Dent

Exec. VP and Chief Financial Officer: John K. Crawford

MedPartners, Inc.

President, CEO, and Chairman: Edwin Mac Crawford

Director: Richard M. Scrushy

Director: Larry D. Striplin, Jr.

Director: Charles W. Newhall III

Director: Ted H. McCourtney

This spin on the situation appeared to be justified when MedPartners announced on January 7, the same day that the merger was terminated, that it would fail to meet its earnings projections and would be taking a $145 million fourth-quarter charge. As a result of these combined announcements, MedPartners' stock plummeted 45%. Larry House gave in to the company's request for his resignation as chairman and CEO of MedPartners on January 16. He was succeeded as chairman by Richard Scrushy and as CEO by Edwin Mac Crawford.

By mid-September 1998, MedPartners' stock had dropped to $2, down 90% from its 12-month high of $28.38 on the day after the merger announcement. In November 1998 the company had decided to exit the PPM business altogether, turning to its Caremark pharmaceutical and contract medical services.

Changes to the Industry

The implications of the failed merger, along with the aftershock of the companies' plummeting stock prices and earnings projections, were felt throughout the industry. The PPM business quickly became regarded as risky territory, as the consensus held that its players had overextended themselves by expanding too rapidly. Those companies that relied on growth via geographic expansion consequently spread themselves too thinly to operate effectively in local markets.

PhyCor and MedPartners were not the only PPMs to experience problems in 1998. FPA Medical Management went bankrupt in July. The next month PhyMatrix exited the physician management busi-

The Players

PhyCor President, Chairman, and CEO: Joseph C. Hutts. Joseph C. Hutts joined with three partners to establish PhyCor in 1988. This young company served as an ally for physicians by assuming control of their administrative and organizational affairs, thereby freeing the physicians to devote more of their time to the practice of medicine. Hutts led the company on a slow but steady growth via acquisition. As chairman, president, and CEO of PhyCor, Hutts was to have assumed those same positions upon his company's acquisition of MedPartners.

MedPartners Chairman and CEO: Larry R. House. Larry House founded American Intermedical Resources in 1975. This company, which provided contract respiratory services to hospitals, collapsed when the government reduced reimbursement rates for these services. Richard Scrushy recruited House to work for HealthSouth in 1985. There, he succeeded through corporate ranks, eventually becoming head of MedPartners when it was formed in 1993. He led that company on an aggressive acquisition strategy with the aim of usurping PhyCor as the industry's leader. But House's strategy called for the company to grow too quickly and too expansively. Instead of slowly increasing market share in a given community, he strove to build MedPartners into a nationwide consolidator, a plan that ultimately led to the company's demise in the PPM business. After a two-day battle to oust House, Scrushy persuaded him to resign as chairman and CEO in 1998. House went on to establish his own firm, VentureHouse.

ness, as did Advanced Health in November. By early 1999 only PhyCor remained a major player in the business. While some analysts regarded this mass exodus as the death of the PPM industry, other viewed it instead as a retrenchment of the business. "In the next two years, we'll see the unwinding of companies that are not viable," predicted Ephram Sigel, president of Corporate Research Group, in a January 1999 issue of *Medicine & Health*. "The industry has to shrink before it can grow again."

Research

Freudenheim, Milt. "PhyCor to Buy a Competitor, MedPartners, for $6.8 Billion in Stock," in *The New York Times*, 30 October 1997. Announces the merger deal.

Hudson, Terese. "A Strategy in Plain Sight: PhyCor Says Clues to Its Surprise Purchase of MedPartners Were There All Along," in *Hospitals & Health Networks*, 5 December 1997. Describes the strengths of the uniting companies.

MedPartners, Inc. 1997 Annual Report. Offers detailed financial and operating information.

MedPartners, Inc. Home Page, available at http://www.medpartners.com. Official World Wide Web Page for MedPartners. Includes a description of services, investor information, annual reports, and current news releases.

Morrow, David J. "A Big Merger in Health Care is Called Off," in *The New York Times*, 8 January 1998. Announces the termination of the merger agreement.

PhyCor, Inc. Home Page, available at http://www.phycor.com. Official World Wide Web Page for PhyCor. Offers information on services, investor information, annual reports, and press releases.

"Physician Organizations Struggle over Questions of Size and Structure," in *Medicine & Health*, January 1999. Reviews the difficulties encountered by PPMs during 1998 and provides expert opinions on the future of the industry.

Tokarski, Cathy. "Nation's Two Largest Physician Management Firms Become One," in *American Medical News*, 17 November 1997. Details the characteristics of the proposed combined company.

KIMBERLY N. STEVENS

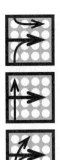

PIRELLI & CONTINENTAL

date: December 1, 1991 (canceled)
affected: Pirelli SpA, Italy, founded 1872
affected: Continental AG, Germany, founded 1871

Pirelli SpA
222 Viale Sarca
Milan, 20126
Italy

tel: 39 02 644 21
fax: 39 02 644 23300
web: http://www.pirelli.com

Continental AG
Vahrenwalder Strasse 9
Hannover, D-30165
Germany

tel: 49 511 938 01
fax: 49 511 938 1766
web: http://www.conti.de
e-mail: mail_service@conti.de

Overview of the Merger

The attempted takeover of Continental AG by Pirelli SpA provided a rare glimpse of Germany's defensive machinery in action against the threat of a hostile takeover. Such attempts were virtually unheard of in that country, and were almost always unsuccessful. The Italian tire company was undeterred, however, and staged a 14-month attempt to acquire control of Continental. It was ultimately unsuccessful, and the fight resulted in the resignation of both companies' chief executives.

History of Pirelli SpA

Engineering graduate Giovanni Battista Pirelli formed Pirelli & C. in 1872 to manufacture rubber sheets, belts, slabs, and vulcanized products. Less than one year after its inception, the company built its first factory, a 1,000-sq.-m. building employing 45 workers. Throughout the decade, production expanded to include sporting goods, haberdashery, and insulated telegraph cable, a venture that will ultimately prove very successful.

Pirelli began the manufacture of rubber strips for carriage wheels in 1885. The following year it expanded production to the newly invented underwater telegraph cables. In 1990 Pirelli produced its first tire, devoting a segment of its rubber department to these "pneumatic tires for bicycles." Tire production expanded to include models for motor cars and motorcycles in 1899.

In 1902 the company established a trend for many Italian companies when it first expanded abroad by establishing a cable and electrical lead factory near Barcelona, Spain. Three years later it began producing automobile and motorcycle tires on an industrial scale, and also launched production of tires for heavy vehicles. In 1915 Pirelli introduced its first pneumatic tires for aircraft.

Pirelli & C. changed its status in 1920 and became Societa Italiana Pirelli, an investment company rather than a production company. At the same time, Societa Italiana Pirelli was incorporated as a holding company to control the group's varied industrial operations based in Italy. Compagnie Internationale Pirelli SA was

The Business

Financials - Pirelli SpA

Revenue (1998): 10.6 billion lira

Employees (1998): 38,209

Financials - Continental AG

Revenue (1998): DM 13.2 billion

Employees (1998): 62,357

SICs / NAICS

sic 3011 - Tires & Inner Tubes

sic 3052 - Rubber & Plastics Hose & Belting

sic 3714 - Motor Vehicle Parts & Accessories

sic 3711 - Motor Vehicles & Car Bodies

sic 2296 - Tire Cord & Fabrics

sic 3357 - Nonferrous Wiredrawing & Insulating

sic 3089 - Plastics Products Nec

naics 326211 - Tire Manufacturing (except Retreading)

naics 326220 - Rubber and Plastics Hoses and Belting Manufacturing

naics 336111 - Automobile Manufacturing

naics 314992 - Tire Cord and Tire Fabric Mills

naics 335921 - Fiber Optic Cable Manufacturing

naics 326199 - All Other Plastics Product Manufacturing

incorporated in Brussels, Belgium, to manage the group's increasing overseas operations, which included factories in Britain, Brazil, Greece, Argentina, Turkey, Spain, and Germany.

The company gained a listing on the Milan Stock Exchange in 1922. Two years later Luigi Emanueli, a Pirelli employee, developed the first commercially viable oil-filled cable, which permitted the transmission of power in excess of one million volts. In 1927 Pirelli supplied oil-filled cables for the electric power grids of New York and Chicago.

The world's first crossply tire, the Superflex Stella Bianca, was launched in 1927 and became the most popular tire of the 1930s. By 1929 about 80% of the cars sold in Italy were equipped with Pirelli tires.

By the onset of World War II, Italy's foreign policy led to a period of economic and political turbulence. To counteract the impending threat of international boycotts, Compagnie Internationale Pirelli was

transferred into Pirelli Holdings SA, a holding company incorporated in Switzerland.

After the devastation of war in Italy, the country's leader initiated a large-scale public investment program. Pirelli responded to the upswing in business in 1953 by producing the first radial tire, the Cintuarto, which revolutionized the tire industry. The company continued to expand on this technology, and in 1968 its production processes were converted from traditional to radial.

Traditionally, Pirelli had eschewed joint ventures and acquisitions garnering the company less than 100% control. In 1971, however, as a defensive measure designed to counter Michelin's introduction of steel-belted radial tires, Pirelli entered into a long-term research and development agreement with Britain's Dunlop Group to produce low-profile tires and revolutionary fiber optics. They went their separate ways in 1980 due to disputes over accounting methods, confirming company executives of the wisdom in insisting upon complete control of strategic partnerships.

Chairman Giovanni Pirelli was killed in a car crash in 1973. His younger brother, Leopoldo Pirelli, was injured in the accident but assumed the chairmanship upon recovery. That year the company introduced the P3, a steel-belted radial for automobiles.

Italy, far more dependent on imported sources of energy than most of Europe, was hit badly by the oil crisis of the mid-1970s. Rampant inflation and a massive drop in the value of the lire ensued.

Pirelli began to experiment with fiber optic technology, testing a one-kilometer-long telephone cable in 1977. Four years later it produced the first fiberoptic cable for on Italy's national telephone network. That year Pirelli underwent an extensive reorganization, resulting in a new management company, Pirelli Societe Generale SA.

In 1983 Pirelli manufactured the industry's first radial for motorcycles. Two yeas later it acquired the share capital of Metzeler Kautschuk, a German company with diversified interests in the rubber industry, leading to a 13% increase in consolidated turnover and reinforcing Pirelli's position in the market for motorcycle tires and automotive components.

The company's shares were restructured again in 1988, as Pirelli SpA acquired Societe Internationale Pirelli's holding in Pirelli Societe Generale; Pirelli SpA thereby accepted direct responsibility for the day-to-day management of the operating companies. The next year it began experimenting in long-distance fiber-optic technology.

Pirelli and Bridgestone launched rival takeover bids for U.S.-based Firestone Tire & Rubber Co. in 1988. Bridgestone emerged the winner, but Pirelli gained ownership of Armstrong Tire, a unit of Firestone. Determined to forge a merger with a tire company, Pirelli initiated a hostile merger for Continental AG of Germany, the world's fourth-largest tire manufacturer, in 1990. Continental board members immediately mounted a massive defense that held Pirelli at bay for 14 months, at which point the suitor dropped its takeover attempt. Due in part to merger-related expenses, Pirelli recorded a net loss of 619 billion lire in 1991.

In February 1992 Leopoldo Pirelli passed the chief executive position to his son-in-law, Marco Tronchetti Provera, the first leader not of the Pirelli family. He immediately set about streamlining the company and refocusing it on its two core businesses, tires and cables. By early 1993 he had sold seven of the nine businesses in the diversified products division, including operations in tennis shoes and bedding. By mid-1997 the fast-growing cable sector accounted for half of the company's revenues, up from one-third in 1991. During that time, Provera had also closed 31 of its 102 factories and cut the workforce by a third. His strategy proved successful, as Pirelli reported a $723 profit on sales of $6.2 billion in 1996.

The company won a contract from the U.S. Department of Energy in October 1998 to produce the world's first superconductor cable for an electric network; Detroit Edison was scheduled to begin using it in 2000. Pirelli also acquired portions of Siemen's energy cable division, with operations in Germany, Hungary, Slovakia, and South Africa.

In February 1999 it entered into a multi-branding alliance with Cooper Tire & Rubber Co. That June the company agreed to purchase a majority stake in Cairo-based Alexandria Tire Co.

History of Continental AG

Continental-Caoutchouc-und Gutta Percha Compagnie (CCGC) was founded in 1871 to produce soft rubber products, rubberized fabrics, and solid bicycle and carriage tires. In 1892 it became the first German company to produce pneumatic bicycle tires. Six years later it initiated production of pneumatic automobile tires, the first models of which were treadless, followed by treaded tires in 1904.

CCGC supplied material for the fuselage and wings of the first airplane to cross the English Channel. Seven years later, in 1921, it became the first German company to use pliable cord fiber fabric in its tires. Also that year it developed the first large pneumatic tires for use on trucks and other commercial vehicles.

The Officers

Pirelli SpA

Chairman and CEO: Marco Tronchetti Provera

Deputy Chairman: Alberto Pirelli

General Manager, Finance and Administration: Carlo Buora

General Manager, General Affairs and Secretary: Adalberto Castagna

Continental AG

Chairman: Stephan Kessel

Executive Board Member, Personnel Director: Klaus Friedland

Executive Board Member, Finance, Control, and Law: Jens P. Howaldt

During the 1920s CCGC experienced a period of growth through horizontal integration within the German economy. In 1928 it absorbed several large German rubber companies, acquiring new plants in Hannover-Limmer and Korbach-Hesse. The following year the firm changed its name to Continental Gummi-Werke AG and launched production of tractor tires.

In 1932 Continental introduced Schwingmetall, a rubber-to-metal bonding agent used to isolate vibrations in supported motors and machinery. A shortage of raw materials prompted the company to increase its use of synthetic materials in producing rubber and rubber products, and in 1936 it produced the first synthetic rubber tire.

Continental established its first foreign operation, in Spain, in 1939. World War II stalled the company's growth, but at its conclusion Continental resumed development of new products. In 1951 it introduced an all-weather tire and began the manufacture of steel cable conveyor belts. Four years later it became the first German company to launch the commercial production of tubeless tires, for which it had received a patent in 1943. In 1960 it produced its first series of radial tires.

The company expanded into retail in 1962 by acquiring an interest in Verglost GmbH, a German chain of retail tire outlets. During the 1970s Continental began increasing its international focus in response to decreased demand in European markets. In 1979 it acquired the European operations of U.S.-

The Players

Pirelli Chairman and CEO: Leopoldo Pirelli. Leopoldo Pirelli, grandson of the company's founder, was employed at the family business for 45 years before retiring as chairman in May 1996. He relinquished the title of chief executive in favor of his son-in-law, Marco Tronchetti Provera, when pressure arising from the failed bid for Continental prompted his resignation in May 1992.

Continental Chairman and CEO: Horst Urban. Employed at Continental for 17 years, Horst Urban resigned from his positions as chief executive and chairman during the takeover attempt by Pirelli. His uncompromising position on the matter, viewed by many as hard-nosed stubbornness, eventually led to his forced resignation in May 1991, when he failed to secure support from the company's board to use any means necessary to retain the company's independence.

based Uniroyal Inc., thereby adding manufacturing facilities in Belgium, Germany, France, Great Britain, and Luxembourg. Six years later it acquired Semperit, an Austrian tire maker with plants in Austria and the Republic of Ireland.

In 1987, as the company shorted its name to Continental AG, it acquired U.S.-based General Tire, Inc., immediately becoming the world's fourth-largest tire manufacturer. It followed up that purchase with its 1988 acquisition of the Anoflex Group, a French manufacturer of hose couplings, and with its 1989 purchase of Mabor, a Portuguese tire maker.

Continental reorganized in 1989, implementing a new logistics and electronic system to link the company's European operations. The following year Italian tire maker Pirelli SpA attempted a hostile takeover of Continental's tire operations. Horst Urban, Continental's chairman and CEO, staunchly refused to entertain the notion, leading to a conflict with the board that resulted in his sudden resignation. Pirelli finally terminated its attempt 14 months after initiated the battle.

In the meantime, Continental acquired National Tyre Service Ltd. of Great Britain and AGES Srl, an Italian manufacturer of automotive rubber products. In 1991 it reorganized its industrial products operations into 21 independent subsidiaries operating

under the ContiTech brand name. The following year it acquired Nivis Tyre AB, Swedish manufacturer of Viking and Gislaved brand tires.

The company entered into a joint venture with Grupo Carso in 1993 to produce and sell tires in Mexico. Five years later Continental increased its Mexican operations by purchasing Grupo Carso's tire business, consisting of two factories and 1,000 outlets.

In 1995, the same year that Continental withdrew from an alliance with Michelin S.A., ContiTech entered into a joint venture with Cooper Tire & Rubber Co. Three years later it paid $1.93 billion to purchase the Automotive Brake and Chassis unit of ITT Industries Inc., absorbing this unit into its Automotive Systems Group as Continental Teves.

Market Forces Driving the Merger

By the beginning of the 1990s, the global tire industry was severely depressed. Consolidation in the automotive industry had resulted in a concentration of power among a reduced number of companies, which used that influence to pressure tire manufacturers to lower prices. Exacerbating the problem was a decrease in demand for U.S. automobile production as well as an increase in cost for crude oil, the raw material for tires. As a result, tire companies were engaged in a fierce price war, thereby cutting their already reduced profitability.

In the midst of this environment, tire companies were consolidating in an attempt to gain market share and reduce expenses. Unfortunately, virtually each of these unions proved to be less than beneficial for the companies involved. Michelin S.A., the market leader with a 24% share, acquired Uniroyal-Goodrich Tire in 1989, and reported a huge loss the following year. Third-placed Bridgestone Corp. purchased Firestone Tire & Rubber Co. in 1989, and suffered much the same fate as Michelin. Continental AG was still feeling the pinch as a result of its 1987 acquisition of General Tire. Even Goodyear Tire & Rubber Co., America's sole remaining large independent, was experiencing a string of losses.

Yet Pirelli SpA, the world's fifth-largest tire manufacturer, still considered consolidation to be the best way to weather the storm. In joining with Continental AG, the fourth-placed company, it would capture a 16% market share and produce a company with annual sales of about 10 trillion lire ($8.6 billion). Pirelli saw complementary operations with Continental from their respective strengths in Europe, South America, and the U.S. Moreover, it believed that a combined company could achieve significant savings in production, distribution, and research and development.

Approach and Engagement

None of these arguments swayed Continental when Pirelli proposed a merger on September 15, 1990. Continental's chairman, Horst Urban, believed that the offer was ill-timed, as neither company could afford expenses arising from a merger at a time when their profitability and share prices were low.

The fiercely independent Continental also objected to the terms of the offer. In what amounted to a reverse acquisition, Pirelli proposed that Continental acquire Pirelli Tyre Holding NV, its tire operations, for DM 2 billion ($1.25 billion). In exchange, Pirelli would take majority control of the merged company. It was this relinquishment of control that Urban found particularly objectionable. In late September Continental rejected the proposal but indicated its willingness to discuss a possible cooperative venture.

Continental, like many German companies, was well fortified against hostile takeovers. Among those defenses was a five-percent limitation on shareholder voting rights, even if the actual stake held exceeded that percentage. In addition, German companies and banks quickly closed ranks to protect any target of such an attempt. These defensive measures proved highly successful, making hostile takeovers extremely rare in Germany.

Continental quickly enlisted powerful allies to block the deal—Deutsche Bank, Volkswagen, and BMW. Each of these companies began purchasing Continental stock in an effort to weaken the threat of Pirelli. In the end, they had accumulated a total of 28%.

Pirelli claimed to have accumulated a majority stake in Continental through a network of shareholders. This tactic presented a possible mean of gaining control by circumventing the voting rights limitation. Such an alliance could collectively vote to overturn Continental's five-percent restriction, freeing Pirelli to install its own management team. Later, that stake was revealed to be 35%, less than a majority but still perhaps enough to make the first step toward takeover by installing new representatives on the board.

On January 12, 1991, Continental broke off negotiations. At that point its shareholders began seeking to overturn the voting right limitation themselves, and were successful at a shareholders' meeting on March 13. Coming in the midst of the takeover attempt, this vote was clearly a sign that Continental's investors were in favor of a merger with Pirelli.

Consequently, Continental's board knew that it had a responsibility to renew talks with Pirelli. Several of the firm's backers, including Deutsche Bank, withdrew support for Urban. The chairman, however, was unrelenting in his staunch opposition to the deal and issued an ultimatum—either the board support his efforts to block Pirelli or he would resign. The board, displeased with this uncompromising stance, accepted Urban's resignation in early May. At that point, Continental's board expressed its intent to wipe the slate clean and begin negotiations with Pirelli anew.

Hubertus von Grunberg, former president and CEO of ITT Automotive Inc., took the helm as chairman in July 1991. Renewed talks with Pirelli were unproductive, however, and on December 1, 1991, Pirelli terminated its immediate pursuit, leaving the door open for a future attempt. As quoted in *The Wall Street Journal*, Leopoldo Pirelli, the company's chairman and CEO, stated, "For now the talks are over...but we think Continental could change its thinking."

Products and Services

Pirelli SpA operated in two principal businesses in 1998. Its Tire Sector, one of the world's top six, offered a product range encompassing tires for cars (standard, high performance, and motorsport), for trucks, buses, agricultural vehicles and earthmovers, and motorcycles and other two-wheeled vehicles. It had a long history of equipping motorsports participants, and was the exclusive supplier of tires to the Ferrari Challenge, the Porsche SuperCup, and the World Sports Car Championship.

Pirelli's Cables and Systems Sector offered a series of integrated components, including products, systems, engineering, and installations for global turnkey projects, particularly in telecommunications and power transmission. Pirelli was engaged in the development of both photonic components and systems, where in 1998 it was the world's leader in amplification systems and WDM.

Continental AG operated in five main divisions in 1998. Passenger Tires included the brands ContiSportContact, EPContiEcoContactCP, ContiEcoContactEP, ContiWinterContact TS 760, ContiWinterContact TS 770, and ContiWinterContact TS 790. Continental's Commercial Vehicle Tires and General Tire divisions produced such models as the AMERI series, the GRABBER series, the GEN SEAL series, and the XP 2000 series.

ContiTech was a specialist in rubber and plastics technology. It supplied functional parts, components, and systems for the automotive industry, mechanical and apparatus engineering, and other markets. Its product range included conveyor belts, materials, printing blankets, engineered products rubber solutions, life rafts, dinghies and utility boats, hoses and hose assemblies, power transmission products, air spring systems, anti-vibration and sealing molded products, extrusions, footwear materials, cushioning products, vinyl coated fabrics and sheeting, car head-liners, and sunscreen and bookbinding materials.

Continental Automotive Systems manufactured the Continental Electronic Chassis Control (CECC), Integrated Starter Alternator Damper (ISAD), Tire Pressure Monitoring System (TPMS), Continental Air Suspension Systems (CASS), and Passive and Active Noise Cancellation (PANC), as well as chassis and tire/wheel units and preassemblies.

Review of the Outcome

Pirelli faced stiff consequences from its failed bid. Merger-related expenses amounted to 350 billion lire ($287 billion). Combined with operating losses and restructuring costs, Pirelli recorded a loss of 670 billion lire for the year. Under pressure, Leopoldo Pirelli stepped down as CEO, although he retained the post of chairman, in favor of his son-in-law, Marco Tronchetti Provera, in February 1992.

After the final collapse of negotiations Continental took the offensive, ultimately killing any likelihood that Pirelli could successfully launch another takeover bid. In May 1992 a German court nullified the 1991 shareholder vote that overturned the five-percent voting rights limitation. It held that Pirelli was in violation of German corporate laws by not disclosing that it was voting on behalf of more than 25.4% of Continental's share capital. Shareholders reversed their previous position by reinstating that limitation on July 3.

In April 1993 Pirelli closed the book on any future acquisition of Continental by selling the 33.4% stake owned by the company and its allies for 330 billion lire ($208 million).

Research

Baldo, Anthony. "The Big Skid," in *Financial World*, 16 October 1990. Describes the failed efforts of consolidation in the tire industry.

Collins, Guy, and Michael C. Bergmeijer. "Pirelli Fails in Attempt to Merge Tire Operations with Continental's," in *The Wall Street Journal*, 2 December 1991. Reports Pirelli's termination of its merger attempt.

Collins, Guy, and Terence Roth. "Pirelli Proposes Tire Merger to Continental," in *The Wall Street Journal*, 18 September 1990. Describes the terms of the newly announced merger offer.

"Continental AG," in *Notable Corporate Chronologies*, Gale Research, 1999. Lists major events in the history of Continental.

Continental AG Home Page, available at http://www.conti.de. Official World Wide Web Page for Continental. This German- and English-language site includes product information, financial results and annual reports, employment information, a company history, press releases, dealer locations, and information on selecting tires.

"Continental Holders Give Pirelli a Boost," in *The Wall Street Journal*, 14 March 1991. Explains the invalidation of Continental's voting rights limitation by its shareholders.

Hicks, Jonathan P. "Continental, Still Digesting General Tire, Battle Pirelli," in *The New York Times*, 25 August 1991. Details Continental's difficult financial condition in the midst of the takeover attempt.

"No Thank You," in *The Economist*, 26 January 1991. Reports Continental's termination of negotiations.

"Pirelli SpA," in *Notable Corporate Chronologies*, The Gale Group, 1999. Profiles the history of the company.

Pirelli SpA Home Page, available at http://www.pirelli.com. Official World Wide Web Page for Pirelli. Includes product information, financial results, employment information, a company history, news releases, information on the Pirelli calendar and the Pirelli-sponsored La Scala Theatrical Museum in Milan, results of motorsports events of cars equipped with Pirelli tires.

Roth, Terence. "Continental AG Chairman Quits as Support Vanishes," in *The Wall Street Journal*, 10 May 1991. Describes the events leading to Urban's resignation.

———. "Uneasy Time for Germany's Continental," in *The Wall Street Journal*, 7 December 1990. Describes the rationale behind Continental's rejection of the merger, and how it might force Pirelli to stage an all-out hostile takeover.

PATRICIA ARCHILLA

PRICE WATERHOUSE & COOPERS & LYBRAND

nationality: USA
date: July 1, 1998
affected: Price Waterhouse L.L.P., USA, founded 1850
affected: Coopers & Lybrand L.L.P., USA, founded 1957

PricewaterhouseCoopers
1301 Avenue of the Americas
New York, NY 10019
USA

tel: (212)596-7000
fax: (212)790-6620
web: http://www.pwcglobal.com

Overview of the Merger

Accounting's Big Six was reduced to five in one fell swoop when two of the industry's leaders joined forces on July 1, 1998. PricewaterhouseCoopers instantly became the world's leading accountancy firm, leapfrogging over a pack that included Andersen Worldwide, Ernst and Young, Deloitte and Touche, and KPMG Peat Marwick.

Fifth-placed Coopers & Lybrand contributed its strengths in human resource consulting and operations in the telecommunications business, while sixth-placed Price Waterhouse brought its strong name recognition and presence in the media and information technology industries. The two companies also combined their geographic dispersion, as Coopers was stronger in Europe while Price Waterhouse laid claim to the Latin American and Southeast Asian areas.

History of Coopers & Lybrand L.L.P.

William Cooper, later joined by his brother Arthur, established an accounting firm in the United Kingdom in 1854. Seven years later, with the addition of two more Cooper brothers, Francis and Ernest, the company adopted the name Cooper Brothers & Co.

Meanwhile, in 1898, the accounting firm Lybrand, Ross Bros. & Montgomery was formed by William M. Lybrand, T. Edward Ross, Adam A. Ross, and Robert H. Montgomery. The following year, the New York Stock Exchange adopted standards for its listees; this "publication of accounts" was a great boon to the business of accounting. In 1912 Robert Montgomery wrote *Montgomery's Auditing*, a book that served as the profession's handbook for many years.

Lybrand began international expansion in 1902 by opening an office in New York City, where many large companies had established their headquarters. Four years later that company began having an impact on issues outside its walls. William Lybrand published an article advocating the adoption by governments of accounting systems similar to those used by businesses, and the Secretary of the Navy appointed Adam Ross to a committee for the investigation into record-keeping methods in several bureaus and throughout the Navy.

The Business

Financials

Revenue (1998): $11.8 billion

Employees (1998): 146,000

SICs / NAICS

sic 8721 - Accounting, Auditing & Bookkeeping

sic 8742 - Management Consulting Services

naics 541211 - Offices of Certified Public Accountants

naics 541611 - Administrative Management and General
Management Consulting Services

naics 541612 - Human Resources and Executive Search
Consulting Services

In 1910 George Cross McDonald established an accounting practice in Canada. The following year, he was joined by his cousin, George Selkirk, and the firm was renamed McDonald, Currie & Co.

Lybrand continued to increase its presence in governmental affairs. In 1913, as a pioneer of tax consulting, it was one of a group of accounting firms to help the U.S. government draft the first general income tax bill. Six years later, due to new developments in government affairs and an increasing number of tax cases, it opened an office in Washington D.C. In 1924 it merged with Klink, Bean & Co., a firm that had acted as its agent in California.

Lybrand expanded overseas by establishing an office in Berlin in 1924, in Paris in 1926, and in London in 1929. That year the company participated in conferences between the New York Stock Exchange and the American Institute of Accountants, as the business world realized that proper accounting methods and independent audits might have prevented some of the financial losses resulting from the stock market crash.

Coopers also expanded internationally, setting up branches in Brussels in 1921, New York in 1926, and Paris in 1930. It later acquired the British firms Alfred Tongue & Co., Aspell Dunn & Co., and Rattray Brothers, Alexander & France.

Peter & Moss, Lybrand's representative in Texas, merged with Lybrand in 1930. In 1952 the company ventured into new businesses by creating a formal management consulting services function, the first accounting company to provide such services.

In 1957 the senior partners of Cooper Brothers, McDonald, Currie & Co., and Lybrand, Ross Bros. & Montgomery agreed to form an international accounting firm comprised of their respective companies. At first, this new firm didn't adopt a single name to represent its 79 offices in 19 countries; it remained an association of autonomous national firms bound together by common policies, procedures, and standards.

Four years later, Lybrand became the first firm to have actuaries and an actuarial benefits consulting practice by acquiring Terriberry Co., the firm that pioneered the concept of long-term disability protection and major medical insurance.

The group merged in 1962 with Scovell, Wellington & Co., a firm with 12 offices and 29 partners; it was considered one of the largest mergers accomplished at this time. It followed that accomplishment up with its 1969 merger with Florida-based Ring, Mahony & Arner.

Following the trend toward globalization, the group adopted Coopers & Lybrand (C&L) as the single name for all of its accounting firms worldwide in 1973. The company introduced the Coopers & Lybrand audit approach, a systems audit approach that recognized the role of effective internal controls in reducing audit risk. The following year C&L led the way in the use of computers by establishing a computer audit assistance group. In 1976 it introduced this audit approach to all international member firms, creating a common approach worldwide. By 1977 C&L was the third-largest accounting firm in the U.S., behind Peat Marwick and Arthur Andersen.

As the auditor for AT&T, C&L played a major supporting role in the telecommunication company's $115 billion divestiture, the largest such breakup in the history of U.S. business. That year, 1982, C&L's worldwide revenues reached the $1 billion mark. Five years later, Prosperity United Firm of Taiwan became an associate firm of C&L (International) and the 100th member of the international network.

After the savings and loan crisis in the 1980s, investors and the government began holding accounting firms liable for the accuracy of the figures that their clients supplied them. The Insiders Trading and Securities Fraud Enforcement Act became law in 1988, increasing senior management's responsibility for detecting and preventing insider trading. During that year, the company also merged with Herman Smith Associates, a full-service international healthcare consulting organization.

Gelfand, Rennert & Feldman, a leading business management firm for the entertainment industry, merged with C&L in 1989 to form a new division. Revenues that year totaled $3 billion.

In April 1990 the company acquired the U.K.-based Deloitte Haskins & Sells, a defector from the international merger between Deloitte Haskins & Sells and Touche Ross. With this merger, C&L controlled Britain's largest accounting and management consulting firm, Coopers & Lybrand Deloitte.

The company entered into a joint venture in 1991, joining with IBM to form Meritus, a company providing full service, organization-wide industrial consulting services for the consumer packaged goods and pharmaceutical/healthcare markets.

Now liable for the content of its clients' financial statements, the company was forced to make a number of costly settlements. In 1991 it paid $20 million to absolve itself in the government's investigation of its audit of Silverado Bank, which went out of business. The next year, it paid $95 million to investors of MiniScribe, a failed disk drive manufacturer.

By 1993, Coopers & Lybrand was the world's fifth-largest accounting firm.

History of Price Waterhouse L.L.P.

Interested in taking advantage of England's recent parliamentary laws requiring the examination of a company's financial statement and records, Samuel Lowell Price established an accounting firm in London in 1850. He took on a partner, Edwin Waterhouse, in 1865.

Having worked primarily on arbitrations, bankruptcies, and liquidations, Price Waterhouse developed a practice of introducing borrowers to prospective lenders in 1870. The company changed its name in 1874 to Price, Waterhouse & Co. By 1887 it had established a reputation in Britain as one of the leaders of auditing, accounting, and financial consulting services. The firm expanded overseas in 1890 by opening an U.S. branch in New York City, followed by a Chicago office the following year.

Its 1902 financial report for client U.S. Steel was the first to include supporting statements and time schedules that reflected significant balance sheet accounts, such as inventories and long-term debt, and provided information on assets, operating funds, and payroll statistics. It was also the first to provide client shareholders with quarterly financial data. In 1913 it expanded its scope once again by offering tax searches immediately after Congress enacted the federal income tax.

The stock market crash of 1929 brought about regulations and standards of audit, and Price

The Officers

Chairman: Nicholas G. Moore

CEO: James J. Schiro

Global Human Resources Leader: William O'Brien

Global Operations Leader: Geoffrey Johnson

Global Risk Management Leader: Ian Brindle

Waterhouse, along with the entire accounting industry, grew quickly. In 1935 it was contracted to handle the balloting of the Academy Awards to assure the honesty of the voting process; it would continue to serve in this capacity throughout the rest of the century. By the end of that decade, the company had 57 offices and 2,500 employees around the world.

In 1945 the Price Waterhouse International Firm was established to promote uniform accounting standards for all of its offices around the world. The company created MCS, a management consulting service, the following year.

During the 1940s, the firm faced its first major crisis when drug wholesaler McKesson & Robbins, Inc. became the victim of an embezzlement scheme. The scheme had eluded detection by Price Waterhouse auditors, and though a subsequent investigation indicated that the firm's auditing procedures were intact, the situation was of concern to both the firm and the industry.

In 1954 Price Waterhouse restructured into four specialized divisions: accounting research, international tax, SEC review, and international operations. By the end of 1959, gross income was $25.8 million.

Dramatic drops in the stock market and futures exchange during the 1970s led to a decade of financial instability. In addition, as competition increased, the company could no longer rely on its reputation to secure accounts, and was forced to develop aggressive hard-sell marketing techniques, expand its range of services, and reduce its fees. To attract new clients, it developed "industry service groups," comprised of specialists with extensive knowledge and experience in various industries.

During the 1980s Price Waterhouse entered into two major merger agreements, both of which failed. In October 1984, it signed a letter of intent to merge with another account giant, Deloitte Haskins & Sells, conditional upon the approval of the partners. When the ballots were counted, the U.S. partners had approved the merger but the British partners had vetoed it. In

The Players

Chairman: Nicholas G. Moore. Nicholas Moore is the recipient of a Bachelor's degree in accounting from St. Mary's College, and of a Doctor of Law degree from Haskings College of Law, University of California at Berkeley. He began his career at Coopers & Lybrand in 1968, and became a partner in 1974. After leading the tax practice at the San Jose office for seven years, he became that office's managing partner. In 1991 he was appointed vice chairman of the company's West Region, and the following year was promoted to client service vice chairman. In 1994 he became the chairman and CEO of the company's U.S. firm, and in 1997 was appointed chairman of Coopers & Lybrand International. He assumed the role of chairman upon the creation of PricewaterhouseCoopers in July 1998.

CEO: James J. Schiro. James Schiro had been with Price Waterhouse for more than 30 years, and continued to hold an executive position with the company after its merger with Coopers & Lybrand. Schiro is a graduate of St. John's University and of the Amos Tuck School Executive Program at Dartmouth College. He took a job with Price Waterhouse in 1967. In 1979 he became a partner and chaired the company's Mining Special Services Group. In 1988 he was named National Director of Mergers & Acquisitions Service, a position that he held until his promotion to vice chairman and managing partner for the New York Metropolitan Region three years later. In 1995 he became chairman and senior partner of the U.S. firm, and CEO of Price Waterhouse in 1997. He assumed the same post at the newly-formed PricewaterhouseCoopers in 1998.

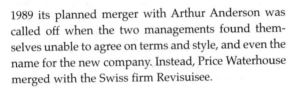

1989 its planned merger with Arthur Anderson was called off when the two managements found themselves unable to agree on terms and style, and even the name for the new company. Instead, Price Waterhouse merged with the Swiss firm Revisuisee.

The early 1990s brought Price Waterhouse a number of legal difficulties. In 1990 the British bank Standard Chartered PLC sued the firm for negligence in failing to provide an accurate financial accounting during the acquisition of United Bank of Arizona; the $338 judgement against Price Waterhouse was later thrown out. The company became involved in another scandal when it was revealed in 1993 that it had charged the government 67 cents per page for a copying job of 10 million documents. Then, the company was sued for $11 billion by Touche Ross to cover the losses of the failed Bank Credit & Commerce International; this amount, too, was later reduced.

In 1996 the company reorganized. It also established two new units: PW Financial Solutions, to provide insurance and accounting services; and an electronic financial services consulting group, to conduct market research and to develop and implement Internet and Web site strategies. The firm also became the first of the world's largest accounting firms to establish operations in China.

Market Forces Driving the Merger

The pressures to consolidate, which had been sweeping through nearly every global industry, again reared its head in the accounting sector. That industry had undergone a wave of merger activity in the 1980s. At that time, the industry had been led by a group of firms known as the Big Eight. Then Deloitte Haskins & Sells merged with Touche Ross & Co. to form Deloitte & Touche, and Ernst & Whinney combined with Arthur Young & Co. to form Ernst & Young.

Those mergers had been driven by a shrinking audit market, and firms became eager to increase their tax resources. Also, the recession of the 1980s created a need to consolidate expenses and pool resources.

The merger of Coopers & Lybrand with Price Waterhouse was motivated by three factors: to increase consultancy services, to offer a portfolio of all-inclusive services, and to operate in an increasingly global market. Gary J. Previts, professor of accountancy at Case Western Reserve University, stated to *Journal of Accountancy*, "It's becoming more expensive for service entities, such as CPA firms, to exist in an increasingly complex global environment. Firms at this international level are still seeking an optimal size—and its size is going to be larger."

Price Waterhouse had been witnessing its position behind Arthur Worldwide slip on an annual basis. Although Price's net gain was increasing, Arthur Worldwide's size was growing at a rate that outpaced it. Part of the reason for Arthur Worldwide's growth was that it had already partially shifted its focus from accounting to consultancy.

Consultancy services were becoming more important to the success of the firms. Accounting services had leveled off, and clients increasingly began turning to pre-packaged computer software and number crunchers such as H&R Block to compile their returns.

Both Coopers and Price were partnerships. As such, they could not raise capital via public offerings or stock splits. The partners themselves had to supply the cash required to improve technology and increase workforce training programs.

Approach and Engagement

On September 18, 1998, the two companies dropped the bombshell of their merger agreement. No one had seen it coming—not even the partners of the two companies. Apparently, the deal had been in the works for two months, strictly guarded in a shroud of secrecy.

The combined company would usurp Arthur Worldwide as the world's largest accounting firm, bypassing Ernst and Young, Deloitte and Touche, and KPMG Peat Marwick. Nicholas Moore, chairman of Coopers & Lybrand, would assume the same post in the new company, as would James Schiro, CEO of Price Waterhouse.

The two firms' partners approved the merger before the end of 1997, with 90% of Coopers' and 94% of Price's voting in favor of the deal. In March 1998, the merger was approved by the U.S. Department of Justice, and in May by the European Commission.

The selection of a name for the new entity was a matter of some importance. Industry watchers delighted in speculation, and some wondered if a disagreement over this matter would contribute to the downfall of the agreement, as it had to the 1989 proposed merger between Price Waterhouse and Arthur Andersen. Finally, the firms revealed that the new company would bear the single-word moniker PricewaterhouseCoopers. The perceived importance of the name is still apparent. On the company's "Frequently Asked Questions" section of its Website, the company answered a question regarding its new name (#5) before it treated the issue of the benefits that clients could expect to see as a result of the merger (#7).

On July 1, 1998, the merger was completed, and the two companies began operating as one. PricewaterhouseCoopers was the largest accounting firm in the world and the second-largest in the U.S. It had 8,500 partners and about 135,000 employees. Its revenues of $11.8 billion surpassed Arthur Worldwide's 1996 revenues of $9.5 billion.

Products and Services

PricewaterhouseCoopers provided six lines of service:

Audit, Assurance and Business Advisory Services

offered solutions to organizations' financial control, regulatory reporting, shareholder value, and technology issues; its 1998 revenues were $6.7 billion.

Business Process Outsourcing covered such areas as finance/accounting, internal audit, tax compliance, applications process, procurement, human resources, and real estate services; its revenues were $40.7 million in 1998.

Financial Advisory Services offered financial, economic, and strategic advice to companies with complex business problems and disputes; its revenues in 1998 were $1.08 billion.

Global Human Resource Solutions provided an array of human resource and insurance management services; its 1998 revenues were $395 million.

Management Consulting Services operated in the areas of strategic change management, process improvement, and technology solutions; its revenues were $3.9 billion.

Tax and Legal Services offered strategies for optimizing taxes, implementing tax planning, and maintaining compliance; its revenues in 1998 were just over $3 billion. The company worked in 23 market sectors that have been grouped into five clusters: Consumer and Industrial Products, Energy and Mining, Financial Services, Service Industries, and Technology Info-Com and Entertainment.

The Consumer and Industrial Products contained the industries of automotive, consumer packaged goods, industrial products, pharmaceuticals, and retail. Energy and Mining contained its mining, oil and gas, and utilities services. Financial Services included such industries as banking, capital markets, insurance, investment companies, and real estate. Service Industries contained the industries of education/not-for-profit, engineering and construction, government, health care, hospitality, posts (postal industry), and transportation. Technology Info-Com and Entertainment contained the sectors of entertainment and media, technology, and telecommunications.

Changes to the Industry

With the Big Six now reduced to the Big Five, many wondered if the future would bring about more attempts at large-scale consolidation in the accounting industry. As it turned out, no one had to wait long for an answer. Only weeks after the announced union between Coopers & Lybrand and Price Waterhouse, Ernst & Young and KPMG Peat Marwick announced their own merger. In February 1998, however, these two firms scrapped their merger plans due to their difficulty in receiving worldwide regulatory approval.

Although this failure at consolidation may have signaled future difficulties in marriages between the world's accountancy leaders, few believe that merger activity within the industry will cease. Consolidation was likely to occur between smaller firms, which were under increasing pressure to acquire or be acquired. The mid-sized firms, too, could form unions that would push them into the industry's highest tiers.

Speculation also abounded regarding the new directions accountancy firms seem to be evolving, and whether mergers would get them there more quickly. With consultancy having become a more important segment for accountancy firms, such businesses, especially the larger ones, may have to begin acquiring consulting firms.

Review of the Outcome

The merger that created PricewaterhouseCoopers was completed fairly seamlessly. No lay-offs were necessary; in fact, the new firm citing the likelihood of adding to its workforce, as "the need for more resources and staff to meet out growth is one of the drivers of the merger," according to the company's Website.

The new company did not operate out of a single headquarters. Instead, its global leadership was based in New York, Frankfurt, and London. In 1998, PricewaterhouseCoopers had a workforce of 146,000 people in 148 countries.

Research

"And Then There Were Five," in *Journal of Accountancy*, December 1997. Discusses the driving forces behind the Price/Coopers merger.

Berton, Lee. "From Big 6 to Big 5: Not Business as Usual," in *Accounting Today*, 6 October 1997. Suggests why the proposed merger is a good fit between the two companies.

"Coopers & Lybrand," in *Notable Corporate Chronologies*, The Gale Group, 1999. Profiles the history of the company until its merger with Price Waterhouse.

MacDonald, Elizabeth. "Coopers, Price Waterhouse Get Merger Backing," in *The Wall Street Journal*, 1 December 1997. Partners at the two firms overwhelmingly approve the union.

Miller, Tracey L. "Coopers, Price Merger Scheme Rocks Industry," in *Accounting Today*, 6 October 1997. Provides an in-depth look at the proposed merger, from the strengths each company will contribute to speculations on the industry's future consolidation.

"Price-C&L Deal OK'd," in *Information Week*, 16 March 1998. Ernst & Young and KPMG Peat Marwick call off their merger just as Price and Coopers receive U.S. regulatory approval to pursue a union.

"Price Waterhouse, Coopers and Lybrand Bring Different Strengths to Merger," in *Petroleum Finance Week*, 6 October 1997. Brief account of the merging companies and of the global rank that the new company will have.

"Price Waterhouse L.L.P.," in *Notable Corporate Chronologies*, The Gale Group, 1999. Gives an account of the company's history until the 1998 merger.

PricewaterhouseCoopers Home Page, available at http://www.pwcglobal.com. Official World Wide Web Page for PricewaterhouseCoopers. Includes investor information, news releases, description of services, a brief company history, executive biographies, and career opportunities.

"PW and Coopers Merger Set for July Launch Date," in *Management Consultant International*, 1 May 1998. The union receives approval from the European Commission, the last regulatory hurdle.

"Soon There Will Be Five, Four," in *The Practical Accountant*, November 1997. The changes to the industry as a result of the Price/Coopers and Ernst & Young/KPMG Peat Marwick mergers.

DEBORAH J. UNTENER

PRIMERICA & TRAVELERS

nationality: USA
date: December 31, 1993
affected: Primerica Corp., USA, founded 1901
affected: Travelers Corp., USA, founded 1864

Citigroup Inc.
153 E. 53rd St.
New York, NY 10043
USA

tel: (212)559-1000
fax: (212)793-3946
web: http://www.citi.com

Overview of the Acquisition

Primerica strengthened its position as a leading financial services and insurance provider by acquiring The Travelers Companies in 1993. The new company, which took the name The Travelers Companies, immediately ranked among the nation's leading financial services companies.

History of Primerica Corp.

The American Can Co. incorporated in New Jersey in 1901. By 1920 American Can and Continental Can were the "twin giants" of the canmaking industry. Throughout the next two decades, canning became the most effective way of containing, preserving, and storing industrial and consumer goods, especially during the Great Depression. During the 1940s, despite wartime rationing measures and unpredictable supplies of metal resources, American Can continued to prosper.

The company and its chief competitor were so invaluable that they were able to offer large volume discounts to the major can customers. In 1950, however, a federal court struck down the volume discount practice employed by American Can and Continental, reducing the leverage of the two canmakers over their smaller rivals and altering the complexion of the canmaking industry. No longer able to receive volume discounts on containers, customers began manufacturing their own cans.

During the 1950s increased competition, loss of revenue, and higher labor costs due to unionization led to lower profit margins and serious difficulties for American Can. Since technological changes and innovations in the industry required large capital outlays, the company was forced to diversify to remain viable.

In 1957 the company purchased the forest products operations of Dixie and Marathon paper products, the business that produced Dixie Cups, Brawny, and Aurora paper towels and toilet tissue. To American Can executives, the growth potential of the paper industry appeared more favorable than that of the can and container industry.

The Business

Financials

Revenue (1998): $76.4 billion

Employees (1998): 173,000

SICs / NAICS

sic 6321 - Accident & Health Insurance

sic 6324 - Hospital & Medical Service Plans

sic 8011 - Offices & Clinics of Medical Doctors

naics 524114 - Direct Health and Medical Insurance
    Carriers

naics 621491 - HMO Medical Centers

The pop-top, or ring-tab, can opener was introduced in 1963, thereby revolutionizing the beverage can business and ushering in the era of the six-pack. Beer and soft drink sales increased markedly, and canmakers enjoyed their most profitable decade ever. However, American Can realized the need to diversify further out of the can business, as it had lost a good portion of market share due to "in-house" can operations and increased competition.

In 1970 American Can recognized the need for a new approach to diversification and the business of canmaking. William May, the company's chief executive, undertook the task of reorientation, calling for a corporate "think tank" and hiring a group of talented business theorists. Based on the recommendations of the new leadership, the firm planned to venture into areas of aluminum recycling and resource recovery. It also pursued investment in such smaller businesses as records and mail order retail products in order to benefit from short-term returns.

Although May aspired to reduce the container manufacturing operations to less than 50% of the company's total business, he recognized the company's dependency on canmaking operations to secure capital for new investments. He therefore took steps to modernize the canmaking network by selling and closing plants considered antiquated, supplementing the remaining plants with a network of 62 new facilities.

American Can launched on a diversification program. In 1975 it acquired Pickwick, the world's largest distributor and retailer of record albums. Three years later it purchased the Fingerhut direct marketing company. Fingerhut secured a sizeable market, catering to low-to-medium-income households by developing computerized profiles of its four million customers and marketing products corresponding to their likely requirements.

During the 1980s American Can continued its can modernization measures, but still lagged behind Continental Can and others in the shift away from steel to aluminum and plastics. In 1980 the company sold off its forest operations for $423 million, a figure far below what most analysts estimated them to be worth. The following year it purchased Associated Madison Insurance for $140 million. This purchase triggered a string of insurance acquisitions over the next several years, including American General Capital Corp., which ran $4.3 billion worth of mutual funds. In 1984 American Can reported $4.1 billion in revenues and $100 million in net income.

In 1986 Triangle Industries, National Can's parent firm, offered a deal to purchase all of American Can's U.S. packaging businesses, earning the company $600 million. With that divestiture, American Can became primarily a financial services and specialty retail firm, and changed its name to Primerica. In 1987 the company purchased the securities operation Smith Barney, Inc., as well as A.L. Williams Insurance, a term life insurance company.

Commercial Credit, headed by Sanford I. Weill, acquired Primerica in 1988. Weill engineered a plan to form the company into a diversified financial business akin to American Express. Weill, now the company's chairman and CEO, sold Primerica's Musicland retail operation and decreased its ownership of Fingerhut through public offering of its stock. A.L. Williams was renamed Primerica Financial Services.

In 1992 Primerica acquired a 27% stake in Travelers Corp. In July 1993 it paid $1.15 to purchase the Shearson Lehman retail brokerage firm from American Express Company. This business was folded into its Smith Barney subsidiary, forming the nation's second-largest securities broker. In December 1993 Primerica acquired Travelers Corp. and changed its name to Travelers Inc. The merged company was bought by Citicorp in 1998.

History of Travelers Inc.

In 1863 James G. Batterson and nine others petitioned the Connecticut legislature for permission to form an accident insurance corporation. The following year the Travelers Insurance Co. opened for business. In 1865 it began writing life insurance, thereby becoming the first company to offer more than one line of insurance. It introduced its retirement income contract in 1884. Travelers diversified into liability, automobile, and health insurance in the late 1890s.

The company established the branch office system in 1902, setting up an administrative system to support its agents. The first branch office opened in New York, and its responsibilities included servicing existing policyholders, overseeing sales operations, and providing inspection and investigation services. The following year the company founded the industry's first vocational school for insurance agents.

After expanding into workers' compensation insurance in 1911, the company pioneered group life insurance with a policy written for the Ohio Electric Railway Co. In 1915, the cruiseliner *Lusitania*, with 17 Travelers policyholders onboard, was sunk by a German submarine. Travelers demanded $426,000 from the German government, but received nothing.

In May 1919 the company began offering comprehensive insurance that included life, public liability, workers' compensation, and passenger accident policies. Travelers' stock holdings were transferred into U.S. government bonds, one of the safest investments available, just two days before the stock market crashed in 1929. Although Travelers escaped financial ruin, the Depression caused a dramatic decline in premiums as many life insurance policyholders committed suicide. Other policyholders threatened similar action and demanded that Travelers loan them money against their policies, but Travelers rejected those demands.

By 1955 the Homeowners Policy had grown to include insurance for fire, personal liability, windstorm, medical coverage for those injured on the property, and living expenses should a home become inhabitable. Four years later, after losing money in its automobile accident insurance division for a number of years due to the increase in automobile use and, thus, accidents, Travelers began basing auto insurance rates on a driver's safety record.

Travelers reorganized its capital structure in 1965, becoming The Travelers Corp., a holding company for Travelers Insurance Co. and its former subsidiary, Travelers Indemnity Co. The following year Medicare went into effect, making nearly 20 million Americans eligible for federally funded hospital and medical care. That year Travelers acquired the Phoenix Insurance Co., the 29th-largest U.S. property and casualty insurer. In 1967 the company entered the mutual funds arena with the founding of Travelers Equity Fund.

The company restructured its departments in 1974, splitting the property and casualty division along individual and business lines, while its health, life, and financial services divisions remained intact. In 1980 it acquired Keystone Life Insurance Co. The next year it established the Travelers Lloyds Insurance

The Officers

Co-Chairman and Co-CEO: John S. Reed

Co-Chairman and Co-CEO: Sanford I. Weill

Vice Chairman: Paul J. Collins

Vice Chairman: Deryck C. Maughan

Chief Financial Officer: Heidi G. Miller

Co., followed by the Provident Travelers Mortgage Securities Corp. in 1983.

Travelers purchased the Bankers and Shippers Insurance Company of New York in 1984. The next year it established Travelers Keystone Fixed Income Advisors and Travelers Plan Administrators. In 1986 it became a principal contender in the securities market by purchasing Dillon, Reed, and Co., one of Wall Street's oldest investment banking firms, for $157.5 million.

As health care costs continued to grow, it increased its interests in HMOs, which were expected to keep health care costs in check. In 1987 it acquired a major HMO from Whittaker Corp., as well as Health Plan of Virginia. The following year more than 880 employees were trimmed from the workforce as part of a cost reduction effort. The HMO segment didn't perform as expected. In 1989, after losing $18 million on its HMOs, it sold five such operations for $1 apiece and cut 225 additional jobs.

In 1992, as Travelers continued to struggle with its billions of dollars of laggard real estate, it announced a workforce reduction of 5,000 jobs by the end of 1994. Primerica acquired a 27% stake in the company for $722 billion in 1992, and in September of the following year, it purchased the remainder of Travelers.

Market Forces Driving the Acquisition

Primerica and Travelers held very different, yet complementary, missions in the early 1990s. Primerica aimed to build itself into a financial services supermarket, operating on a level competitive with such leaders as Aetna Life & Casualty Company and Merrill Lynch & Company. It had just completed a significant leap in that direction in July 1993, when it purchased the Shearson Lehman retail brokerage operation. Primerica folded this business into its Smith Barney company to form the second-largest securities company in the U.S. Earlier, in 1992, Primerica had purchased a 27% stake in Travelers Corp., a move that some analysts believed to foreshadow its intention of acquiring the entire company.

For Travelers, the urge to merge was less ambitious as it was necessary. Travelers' real estate portfolio was languishing, and was weighing heavily upon its other businesses. Additionally, its group health insurance operations were on uncertain ground as the government considered the national health care reform issue. By joining with a robust company like Primerica, Travelers could insulate itself from potentially devastating blows from either of those markets.

Approach and Engagement

In September 1993, Primerica and Travelers announced an agreement in which Primerica would acquired the remaining 73% of Travelers stock that it didn't already own. The $4.2 billion transaction would be a stock swap in which each Travelers share would be converted to 0.80423 share of Primerica.

The new company would take the familiar Travelers name, and would be led as chairman and CEO by Sanford Weill, who held those positions at Primerica. His counterpart at Travelers, Edward Budd, would become chairman of the new company's insurance operations. Robert Lipp, Primerica's vice chairman, would assume the post of CEO of the Travelers insurance business.

With $95 billion in assets and $10 billion in equity, the new company would become the fifth-largest financial services company, behind Federal National Mortgage Association, American Express, Solomon Brothers, and Merrill Lynch.

In November 1993 both Primerica and Travelers announced their respective company reorganizations in anticipation of the merger. Primerica made some changes to its senior management team, naming James Dimon to the newly created post of chief operating officer, and establishing a four-person office of the chairman. Travelers, on the other hand, announced that it would trim its workforce by about 300 corporate staff positions.

On December 30, 1993, shareholders of each company approved the deal, and the following day Travelers Inc. was officially formed. The new company began trading on the New York Stock Exchange on January 3, 1994.

Products and Services

Citigroup, which purchased Travelers in 1998, operated in both the insurance and financial services industries. Through Travelers Group Inc. it offered commercial loans, mutual funds, life insurance, credit card issuance, life and long-term care insurance, and personal and commercial insurance. It also offered asset management services through such subsidiaries as Citibank Global Asset Management, Salomon Brothers Asset Management, and Smith Barney Asset Management.

Review of the Outcome

Travelers merged its ailing group health business with that of Metropolitan Life Insurance Co. in 1995 to form MetraHealth Companies, Inc., which was sold to United HealthCare Corp. later that year. In 1996 it acquired the property casualty lines of Aetna, and merged them with Travelers' to create the Travelers/Aetna Property Casualty Corp. The company's core insurance and financial businesses at that time included: Smith Barney, an investment services provider; Commercial Credit, which offered consumer finance services; Travelers Bank, a credit card issuer; Primerica Financial Services, which dealt with mutual funds; and Travelers/Aetna Property Casualty Corp. and Travelers Indemnity, which sold property casualty and other types of insurance.

In 1997 it purchased Salomon and combined it with Smith Barney to form Salomon Smith Barney Holdings. On October 8, 1998, Travelers completed its merger with Citicorp to form Citigroup Inc., the world's largest financial services company.

Research

Connolly, Jim. "Analysts: New Travelers Will Be More Competitive," in *National Underwriter Life & Health-Financial Services Edition*, 4 October 1993. Offers analysts' reactions to the newly announced merger agreement.

Connolly, Jim. "Primerica Buys Travelers for $4.2 Billion," in *National Underwriter Life & Health-Financial Services Edition*, 27 September 1993. Describes the terms of the deal, and offers reasons why the two companies wanted to merge.

Greenwald, Judy. "Merger Will Strengthen Travelers, Analysts Say," in *Business Insurance*, 27 September 1993. Comments on the strengths of Primerica that should assist Travelers.

"Primerica Announces Management Changes," in *Federal & State Insurance Week*, 8 November 1993. Briefly describes the changes to Primerica's executive team prior to the merger.

"Primerica Corp.," in *Notable Corporate Chronologies*, The Gale Group, 1999. Provides a history of the company.

"Primerica, Travelers Seal Merger Pact: Takeover May Speed Insurer's Recovery," in *The Wall Street Journal*, 24 September 1993. Details the terms of the deal, and outlines how Travelers will benefit.

"Travelers Inc.," in *Notable Corporate Chronologies*, Gale Research, 1999. Lists major events in the history of the company.

"Travelers to Cut 300 Corporate Staff Jobs," in *The New York Times*, 5 November 1993. Announces the company's workforce reduction before completion of the merger.

BERTRAM W. ROLAND

PROCTER & GAMBLE & CLOROX

nationality: USA
date: August 1, 1957
affected: The Procter & Gamble Co., USA, founded 1837
affected: The Clorox Co., USA, founded 1913

The Procter & Gamble Co.
One Procter & Gamble Plz.
PO Box 599
Cincinnati, OH 45201
USA

tel: (513)983-1100
fax: (513)983-2060
web: http://www.pg.com.

The Clorox Co.
1221 Broadway
Oakland, CA 94612
USA

tel: (510)271-7000
fax: (510)832-1463
web: http://www.clorox.com
e-mail: info@clorox.com

Overview of the Acquisition

The 1957 acquisition of The Clorox Chemical Co. by Procter & Gamble is significant not because of the transaction itself, but because it was followed by 10 years of litigation that resulted in a landmark ruling by the U.S. Supreme Court regarding antitrust violation. The Supreme Court ruled that although Procter & Gamble didn't operate in the bleach market itself, its enormous advertising budget and merchandising clout created an unfair and anticompetitive advantage for Clorox in that field, and forced the company to divest itself of Clorox.

History of Procter & Gamble Co.

In 1837, William Procter and James Gamble formed Procter & Gamble, a partnership in Cincinnati, Ohio, to manufacture and sell candles and soap. This unlikely product combination was formed on the basis that candlemaking and soapmaking both required the use of lye. The company grew quickly, as it was well-situated to take advantage of rail and river transportation.

The famous moon-and-stars trademark symbol was created in 1851 to distinguish the company's products. According to lore, the symbol evolved from a simple cross, to a cross with an encircled star, with Procter eventually adding 13 stars, representing the original 13 colonies, and the man in the moon. (This logo would later be altered due to false yet ongoing allegations that the company endorsed Satanism.) By 1859, Proctor & Gamble's sales surpassed $1 million, and the firm employed 80 workers.

In 1860, on the brink of the Civil War, Procter & Gamble began stockpiling rosin, one of the main components of its business. When wartime shortages forced competitors to cut production, the company continued to prosper, supplying the Union Army with soap and candles. As the continued war effort resulted in a shrinking stockpile of raw materials, the company was forced to discover new methods of manufacturing. It developed a method to produce stearic acid using tallow, and then experimented with silicate of soda, an item that later became a key ingredient in modern soaps and detergents.

The Business

Financials - The Procter & Gamble Co.

Revenue (1999): $38.2 billion

Employees (1999): 110,000

Financials - The Clorox Co.

Revenue (1998): $2.7 billion

Employees (1998): 11,000

SICs / NAICS

sic 2035 - Pickles, Sauces & Salad Dressings

sic 2045 - Prepared Flour Mixes & Doughs

sic 2079 - Edible Fats & Oils Nec

sic 2095 - Roasted Coffee

sic 2096 - Potato Chips & Similar Snacks

sic 2676 - Sanitary Paper Products

sic 2834 - Pharmaceutical Preparations

sic 2841 - Soap & Other Detergents

sic 2842 - Polishes & Sanitation Goods

sic 2844 - Toilet Preparations

sic 5141 - Groceries-General Line

naics 311941 - Mayonnaise, Dressing, and Other Prepared
Sauce Manufacturing

naics 311822 - Flour Mixes and Dough Manufacturing from
Purchased Flour

naics 311222 - Soybean Processing

naics 311225 - Fats and Oils Refining and Blending

naics 311920 - Coffee and Tea Manufacturing

naics 311919 - Other Snack Food Manufacturing

naics 322291 - Sanitary Paper Product Manufacturing

naics 325412 - Pharmaceutical Preparation Manufacturing

naics 325611 - Soap and Other Detergent Manufacturing

naics 325612 - Polish and Other Sanitation Good
Manufacturing

naics 325620 - Toilet Preparation Manufacturing

naics 422410 - General Line Grocery Wholesalers

The company hired its first full-time chemist in 1875 to assist in developing new products. Three years later, Clorox introduced White Soap, soon renamed Ivory Soap. This classic product was created when a worker accidentally left a soap mixer on during his lunch break, causing extra air to be mixed in. As people begin requesting "the floating soap," the board of directors embarked on the risky venture of advertising. In 1882, an annual advertising budget of $11,000 was approved, and the slogan "99 44/100% pure" soon became synonymous with Ivory Soap.

In 1889, Lenox soap was introduced and marketed as a heavy-duty product. This yellow soap helped the company achieve revenues in excess of $3 million that year. Procter & Gamble incorporated the following year, with William Alexander Procter serving as its first president. In 1904, a second plant was opened, in Kansas City, Missouri, followed by Port Ivory on Staten Island, New York.

Crisco shortening was introduced in 1911 after years of research with hydrogenation processes. Four years later the company expanded internationally by entering Canada. Ivory Flakes was put on the market in 1919, followed by Chipso soap flakes for industrial laundry machines in 1921, Camay facial soap in 1926, and Oxydol cleanser in 1929. Dreft, the first synthetic detergent for home use, was introduced in 1933.

In 1933, Procter & Gamble became a key sponsor of radio's daytime serials, soon known as "soap operas." By the end of the decade it sponsored 21 radio programs, spending $9 million on this sort of promotion. The company expanded into television advertising in 1939, when sports commentator Red Barber plugged Ivory soap during the first television broadcast of a major league baseball game.

During World War II, the U.S. government requested the company to oversee the construction and operation of ordnance plants. Procter & Gamble Defense Corp. operated as a subsidiary and filled contracts for 60-millimeter mortar shells. Procter & Gamble was one of the largest manufacturers of glycerin, which became key to the war effort for its use in explosives and medicine.

The company introduced Tide detergent to great fanfare in 1947. Backed by a $21 million advertising budget, it became the number-one laundry detergent in 1949, outselling even the company's own Oxydol and Duz brands. Cheer was introduced as bluing detergent in 1950, followed by Dash detergent in 1954. After five years of research, the company firmly established itself in the toiletries business by creating Crest toothpaste in 1955. It was developed using stannous fluoride, a compound of fluorine and tin, that could substantially reduce the occurrence of cavities.

W.T. Young Foods, a Kentucky-based nut company, was acquired in 1955. The next year Procter & Gamble acquired Consolidated Mills Co., owner of the Duncan Hines product line. In 1957, it acquired both

Charmin Paper Company and Clorox Chemical Company, producer of a single product—bleach. White Cloud toilet paper was introduced in 1958, followed by Puffs tissues two years later.

Pampers disposable diapers were released in the early 1960s and was met with great demand. Bold detergent was introduced in 1965. Two years later the U.S. Supreme Court ordered the divestiture of Clorox on the basis on antitrust violations.

Bounce fabric softener for the dryer was released in 1972, as was Sure antiperspirant and Coast soap two years later. In 1976, it unveiled Luvs, its premium disposable diaper brand. The next year, after three years of test marketing, Rely tampons were introduced and gained rapid acceptance. In 1980, however, the Centers for Disease Control published a report showing a statistical link between the usage of Rely and a rare but often fatal disease known as toxic shock syndrome. The company suspended further sales of Rely tampons, and took a $75 million write-off on the product.

Procter & Gamble entered the over-the-counter drug market with the 1982 purchase of Norwich-Eaton Pharmaceuticals, maker of Pepto Bismol and Chloraseptic. Three years later it completed its largest purchase to date by paying $1.2 billion for Richardson-Vicks Co. Its additional purchase of the Dramamine and Metamucil brands from G.D. Searle & Co. propelled the firm to a leadership position in over-the-counter drug sales.

In 1988, Procter & Gamble ventured into the cosmetics business with the purchase of Noxell Corp., the maker of Noxzema products and Cover Girl cosmetics, in a $1.3 billion stock swap. That year it also purchased Blendax, a European health-and-beauty-care goods manufacturer, as well as the Bain de Soleil suncare product line. In 1991, it acquired Max Factor and Betrix of Germany from Revlon.

After 25 years of research, Procter & Gamble's olestra, a controversial fat-free substitute fortified with vitamins A, D, E, and K, was approved by the U.S. Food & Drug Administration in 1996. The FDA required that foods incorporating it be labeled with a warning of the potential side effects, which included stomach cramping and loose bowels.

The company purchased the Eagle Snacks brand from Anheuser-Busch and spent $1.84 billion in 1997 to acquire Tambrands, Inc., the maker of the Tampax brand. In 1998, with sales of $37.15 billion, Procter & Gamble initiated a restructuring centered on seven business units: Baby Care, Beauty Care, Fabric & Home Care, Feminine Protection, Food & Beverage, Health Care & Corporate New Ventures, and Tissues & Towels.

The Officers

The Procter & Gamble Co.

Chairman, President, CEO, and COO: Durk I. Jager

Exec. VP; President, North America: Wolfgang C. Berndt

Exec. VP; President, Europe, Middle East, and Africa: Harald Einsmann

Exec. VP; President, Asia: Alan G. Lafley

Exec. VP; President, Latin America: Jorge P. Montoya

The Clorox Co.

Chairman & CEO: G. Craig Sullivan

President and COO: Gerald E. Johnston

Sr. VP, Secretary, and General Counsel: Peter D. Bewley

VP and Chief Operating Officer: Karen M. Rose

VP: Peter N. Louras, Jr.

In 1999, it entered into agreements to purchase certain brands of Brothers Gourmet Coffees and to sell the Hawaiian Punch name to Cadbury Schweppes. It also paid $2.3 billion for The Iams Company, a pet health and nutrition company.

History of The Clorox Co.

In 1913, five California businessmen invested $100 each in a venture to produce sodium hypochlorite bleach from ocean water using an electrolytic process. The Electro-Alkaline Co. soon began production of Clorox Liquid bleach, which was used to clean and disinfect such facilities as dairies, breweries, and laundries. Later that year, an initial stock issue of 750 shares provided the company $75,000 in start-up capital.

The company registered the Clorox brand name and diamond-shaped trademark in 1914. Two years later it developed a less concentrated liquid bleach product for household use and sold in amber glass pint bottles. The firm's name was changed to Clorox Chemical Co. in 1922. By that time its plant produced 2,000 cases, or 48,000 bottles, of bleach per day. The firm went public in 1928.

The onset of World War I reduced the availability of chlorine, a key ingredient in Clorox bleach. In response, the government permitted bleach manufacturers to reduce the concentration of sodium hypochlorite in their products. Clorox, however, elected to decrease production rather than change the quality of its bleach and jeopardize customer satisfaction.

In 1957, Clorox, still a one-product company, held the largest share of the domestic market for household bleach. The Procter & Gamble Co., a successful manufacturer of consumer products, viewed Clorox bleach as a compatible addition to its existing line of laundry products, and acquired the firm, changing the name of its new subsidiary to The Clorox Co. Within three months of this purchase, the U.S. Federal Trade Commission raised anti-trust concerns and asserted that the acquisition could create a monopoly on household liquid bleaches. After nearly a decade of litigation, the U.S. Supreme Court upheld the FTC's order that Procter & Gamble divest itself of the Clorox operation. Clorox was spun off as a public company in January 1969.

As a newly independent company, Clorox embarked on a campaign of acquisition and internal development. In 1969, it purchased Jiffee Chemical, maker of Liquid-Plumr; Shelco, maker of Jifoam oven cleaner; and the 409 division of Harrell International, producer of Formula 409 spray cleaner. The next year it ventured into the dry, nonchlorine segment of the bleach market by introducing Clorox 2.

In 1971, it purchased McFadden Industries, maker of Litter Green cat litter, as well as Grocery Store Products Co., manufacturer of such specialty food products as B&B mushrooms, Kitchen Bouquet gravy thickener, and Cream of Rice cereal. It added a line of salad dressings and party dips to the Grocery Store Products operation when it bought Hidden Valley Ranch Food Products in 1972, the same year that it purchased Nesbitt Food Products, a soft drink maker. Kingsford Corp., maker of charcoal briquettes, was purchased in 1973.

A civil antitrust suit was filed against Clorox and Procter & Gamble by Purex Corp., a bleach competitor, in 1975. The suit sought over $520 million in damages, which Purex claimed resulted from Procter & Gamble's acquisition of Clorox. Both a federal court and federal appeals court ruled that Purex failed to prove that it suffered any loss of business. The company finally admitted defeat in 1982, when the U.S. Supreme Court refused to hear the case.

In 1979, acknowledging that its aggressive growth plan had been unsuccessful, Clorox sold its Martin-Brower subsidiary to Dalgety PLC, and Country Kitchen Foods to H.J. Heinz Co., Ltd. These divestitures gave Clorox a rich pool of capital to use in its search for niches in the consumer packaged-goods market, in which the company hoped to develop its own products and capture a dominant share.

In 1981, Clorox acquired Comerco, producer of stains and wood preserves marketed under the Olympic brand name. Clorox faced its toughest competitive challenge when Procter & Gamble launched Vibrant, its own bleach product, the next year. Clorox responded quickly, introducing Wave.

The company purchased Lucite house paints from E.I. Du Pont de Nemours Co. in 1983. Four years later Clorox began diversifying into bottled-water by purchasing a number of companies, including the Deer Park Spring Water Co. and Deep Rock Water Co. It added to those purchases in 1988 by acquiring the Aqua Pure Water Co. and Emerald Coast Water Co.

Clorox took the competitive offensive against Procter & Gamble in 1989, when it introduced Clorox Super Detergent brand of laundry soap powder in four western states. That year Procter & Gamble's new Tide With Bleach debuted, a preemptive move intended to cut off Clorox in the laundry detergent market. In 1989, Procter & Gamble withdrew its bleach product due to poor sales, while Clorox continued to face an uphill battle against entrenched detergent brands. In 1991, Clorox pulled out of the laundry detergent business, unable to compete adequately with Procter & Gamble and Unilever.

A restructuring in early 1994 involved a workforce reduction, divestiture of underperforming assets, and development of new core products. It also moved to increase its presence internationally, and spent $1 billion to acquire 26 companies, 23 of which were located outside the U.S., between 1993 and 1997. Of its notable acquisitions during this period were Black Flag, Lestoil, and Armor All. In 1999, it purchased First Brands, gaining brands in cat litter, car care, and plastic wrap.

Market Forces Driving the Acquisition

By the mid-1950s Procter & Gamble (P&G) had become a major conglomerate. Established as a maker of soap, the company had expanded into food products, laundry detergents, toiletries, and paper products. It had achieved this diversification through internal product development as well as the acquisition of small companies already entrenched in a given field. Beginning in 1955, it began considering the purchase of The Clorox Chemical Co., a single-product firm that held the dominant share, 48.8%, of the U.S. bleach market. P&G reasoned that bleach, a popular clothes whitening agent, served as a logical extension of its own laundry products. Moreover, it believed that bleach was a growth market, since the product was particularly popular among young women, and was used more often in the newer, automatic washing machines than in conventional machines. P&G also calculated that purchasing Clorox outright would be more cost effective than developing a bleach product of its own and then attempting to wrest share from the market leaders.

Approach and Engagement

By 1957, Procter & Gamble had decided to acquire The Clorox Chemical Co. to grasp an immediate lead in its entry into the bleach field. The deal, a stock swap valued at $30.3 million, was completed on August 1, 1957. The Clorox Chemical Co., renamed simply The Clorox Co., became a wholly-owned subsidiary of Procter & Gamble.

Products and Services

By the late 1990s, Procter & Gamble was the largest maker of household products in the U.S., selling more than 300 brands to nearly five billion consumers in over 140 countries. It operated in five primary business segments: Beauty Care, Food/Beverage, Health Care, Laundry/Cleaning, and Paper. Among its most popular brands were Tide, Always, Downey, Folgers, Head & Shoulders, Ivory, Cascade, Comet, Pepto Bismol, Nyquil, Scope, Cover Girl, Secret, Jif, and Zest.

In the late 1990s, The Clorox Co.'s products were divided into 10 categories: Laundry Additives (including the brands Clorox, Clorox 2, and Stain Out), Household Cleaners (such as Formula 409, Liquid-Plumr, Lestoil, Pine-Sol, Soft Scrub, S.O.S, and Tilex), Automotive Care (including Armor All and Rain Dance), Charcoal (Kingsford and Match Light), Insecticides (Black Flag, Roach Motel, Combat, and Maxforce), Bags, Wraps and Containers (Glad), Cat Litter (Ever Fresh, Jonny Cat, Scoop Away, and Fresh Step), Dressings and Sauces (Hidden Valley and K.C. Masterpiece), Water Filtration (Brita), and Home Fireplace (HearthLogg and StarterLogg).

Changes to the Industry

In September 1957, the U.S. Federal Trade Commission (FTC) challenged the purchase on antitrust grounds. These claims became more assertive in the 1960s, when an FTC hearing examiner, Everett Haycraft, ruled that P&G's advertising and merchandising clout provided Clorox with an unfair advantage in the bleach market, where even the leading players were of relatively small size with correspondingly low advertising budgets. He asserted that P&G, the nation's largest single advertiser, was using its marketing muscle to force rival bleach companies to consolidate in order to compete. Clorox had also derived benefits from P&G's scale by realizing volume discounts in broadcast and print advertising. As evidence of its newfound power, Haycraft cited the test marketing of Purex Corp., Clorox's closest rival, in Erie, Pennsylvania. Clorox, which held a 50% share in that market, nullified Purex's efforts by launching an aggressive advertising campaign that knocked Purex

from its newly acquired 30% share down to seven percent.

The FTC was not persuaded by Haycraft's arguments, however, and instructed him in July 1961 to obtain more data. He did so, and in December 1963 the FTC ordered P&G to sell the Clorox Co. It cited five factors in its ruling: the size of P&G compared to other bleach manufacturers, Clorox's dominant position in a concentrated market, the elimination of P&G as a potential competitor by its decision not to manufacture its own bleach, P&G's leading presence in other markets, and the economies that the companies received as a result of the merger. Moreover, the FTC determined that since all bleach products are chemically identical, advertising plays a key role in consumer preference and allegiance.

"In short," the decision read, "the barriers to entry, already very high, have been markedly heightened by the merger—to the point at which few firms indeed would have the temerity or resources to attempt to surmount them." The acquisition, the FTC concluded, constituted a violation of Section 7 of the Clayton Antitrust Act, since its effect "may be substantially to lessen competition, or to tend to create a monopoly" in liquid household bleaches.

P&G appealed, and in the spring of 1966 a U.S. Court of Appeals dismissed the FTC's complaints, commenting that they were based on conjecture and general distaste for large companies. The FTC, in turn, appealed to the U.S. Supreme Court, which unanimously upheld the FTC order to dissolve the merger. The April 11, 1967, decision ruled that, in general, a conglomerate merger is illegal if the acquired company is a major player in a market with few leaders, and if the acquiring company operates in a closely-related field. Specifically, the Court ruled that, P&G harmed competition in three ways in its decision not to enter the bleach market through internal expansion. First, it was far wealthier than any of its rivals in the concentrated market, spending 20 times more on advertising than Clorox had as an independent company. Second, it was a powerful force that inhibited entry into the market through the internal expansion of any outsider, as was demonstrated by the Purex test market case. Finally, before the acquisition, P&G had had an outside influence on competition in the bleach market, since those manufacturers kept prices and profits low so as not to attract entry by such giants as P&G.

Review of the Outcome

On January 2, 1969, The Clorox Co. was spun off as an independent public company, and quickly embarked on a program of vigorous growth. It established a three-pronged strategic plan aimed at the acquisition and internal development of a line of non-food grocery products, the acquisition of a food specialty business, and the development of a line of institutional food and cleaning products. Clorox plunged into this plan immediately, and within a year had acquired such companies as Jiffee Chemical Corp., Shelco, and the 409 division of Harrell International.

Research

"The Clorox Co.," in *International Directory of Company Histories*, Vol. 22, St. James Press: 1998. Provides a historical review of the company.

The Clorox Co. 1998 Annual Report. Presents detailed financial and operating information.

The Clorox Co. Home Page, available at http://www.clorox.com. Official World Wide Web Page for Clorox. Offers product and financial information, press releases, news releases, and employment opportunities.

"FTC Blames Ad Discounts for Aiding Brand Monopoly," in *Editor & Publisher*, 21 December 1963. Provides excerpts from the FTC's order dissolve the merger.

"High Court Backs FTC; Orders P&G to Drop Clorox," in *Advertising Age*, 15 April 1967. Describes the U.S. Supreme Court ruling; includes a related article providing the text of the decision.

"High Court Dissolves a Sudsy Conglomerate," in *Business Week*, 15 April 1967. Details the decision of the U.S. Supreme Court.

"P&G Is Told It Must Sell Clorox," in *Business Week*, 21 December 1963. Reports on the FTC's order calling for the divestiture of Clorox.

"P&G Must Dispose of Clorox, FTC Is Told," in *Advertising Age*, 11 July 1960. Describes the ruling of the FTC hearing examiner.

"The Procter & Gamble Co.," in *International Directory of Company Histories*, Vol. 26, St. James Press: 1999. Presents a chronology of the company's history.

The Procter & Gamble Co. 1998 Annual Report. Offers detailed financial and operating information.

The Procter & Gamble Co. Home Page, available at http://www.pg.com. Official World Wide Web Page for Procter & Gamble. Includes product descriptions, financial information, news releases, and employment opportunities.

DEBORAH J. UNTENER

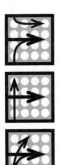

PRUDENTIAL INSURANCE & THE BACHE GROUP

nationality: USA
date: June 12, 1981
affected: The Prudential Insurance Co. of America, USA, founded 1873
affected: The Bache Group, USA, founded 1879

The Prudential Insurance Co. of America
751 Broad St.
Newark, NJ 07102-3777
USA

tel: (973)802-6000
fax: (973)367-8204
web: http://www.prudential.com

Overview of the Merger

Prudential's $385 million acquisition of the Bache Group in June of 1981 set the stage for a wave of financial industry mergers. Acting as a white knight, Prudential, the nation's largest insurance company, saved Bache, the eighth largest brokerage firm, from a takeover by the Belzberg brothers from Canada, who owned 22% of Bache's shares and who sought control of the company.

History of Prudential

In 1873 the Widows and Orphans Society was founded by John F. Dryden to provide low-cost policies to industrial workers that would pay for their burial and would leave a small sum for their widows. Two years later the firm changed its name to The Prudential Friendly Society, and once again in 1877 to the Prudential Insurance Company of America.

By the late 1890s, Prudential reported 422,000 policies in force, with assets of $1.3 million. The company had over 3,000 field agents in eight states and was selling more than 2,000 ordinary policies a year. In 1896 the logo "The Prudential has the strength of Gibraltar" was created. With nearly 6.5 million policies in force and assets of $102 million by 1899, the insurance industry came under investigation for violating customer interests, but Prudential was cleared of any charges.

Because of an influenza epidemic, Prudential paid out over $20 million for flu-related deaths in 1918. Two years later Forrest Dryden, son of the founder, resigned as president following another legislative investigation into the insurance industry and his failure to satisfactorily explain a conflict of interest he had with certain stocks holdings.

The following years were prosperous for the company. Corporate assets exceeded $830 million, and in 1924 the company began offering group insurance coverage to home office staff, as well as group health insurance the following year. By 1935 policies in force had grown to $1.5 billion. In 1942 the Pru's conversion to a mutual company was completed.

The Business

Financials

Revenue (1998): $271 billion

Employees (1998): 50,000

SICs / NAICS

sic 6311 - Life Insurance

naics 524113 - Direct Life Insurance Carriers

Carroll M. Shanks took office as the company's youngest CEO in 1946, leading Prudential into a new era with a parade of new products and innovative investment strategies. Eight regional home offices were opened across the nation, the first one in Los Angeles, California. In 1949 group life sales exceeded $589 million, a record for both the Pru and the industry. Two years later the company's district agents voted to strike, bringing on the nation's first formal job action by a white collar union. The strike lasted for three months.

Shank's era of diversification ended when he retired in 1960. He was replaced by Louis R. Menagh, Jr., who retired two years later. Orville E. Beal, who took over when Menagh retired in 1962, wanted to pursue Shank's diversification plan. In 1964 Prudential sold its first group variable annuity policy. Three years later the Pru surpassed Metropolitan Life Insurance as the world's largest insurance company, with total assets of $23.6 billion.

The company discontinued its pay-by-the-week policies in 1968 and the PIC Realty Corp. was established as a wholly owned subsidiary to own or lease commercial real estate through joint ventures with established real estate developers. Donald MacNaughton replaced Orville E. Beal as president that year. With total assets of over $25 billion, Prudential entered the property and casualty insurance business and signed a contract with Kemper Insurance to set up business in 26 states. Because of the costly nature of training certified agents, the company dropped its agreement with Kemper in 1972 and continued its interests in casualty and fire through its holding company subsidiary, Prudential Property and Casualty Insurance Company. One year later the Pru formed Prudential Reinsurance Company (PRURE) to insure other insurance companies against extraordinary losses.

Prudential continued to grow and, in 1974, the company acquired CNA Nuclear Leasing, renaming it Prudential Lease. In 1976 Prudential entered the international market by acquiring Hanbro Life Assurance Ltd. of Britain. PIC Realty Canada Ltd. was created, as well as Prudential Health Care Plan and Pru Capital Management. MacNaughton retired as the company reported $35.8 billion in assets, and Robert Beck was named as his replacement. In 1979 the Pru formed Dryden and Co. and Gibraltar Casualty Co. to sell coverage of unusual and difficult insurance risks. It also entered a joint venture with Sony Corp. to sell life insurance in the Japanese market.

The 1980s were important growth years for the company. In 1981 Prudential acquired the Bache investment and brokerage house. Property Investment Separate Account was formed as well. Under the leadership of Robert C. Winters, Prudential Realty Group reorganized into four new groups in 1987: Prudential Property Company; Prudential Acquisition and Sales Group; Prudential Mortgage Capital Company; and the Investment Service Group. The Pru also sold its shares in Sony-Prudential to Sony.

In 1990 Prudential acquired the real estate business of Merrill Lynch. The company also introduced a Living Needs program that allowed prepayment of death benefits to policyholders impoverished by medical expenses to use for their current needs. In 1994 Prudential conceded that it improperly inflated the value of two real-estate funds. Under fire for its unethical business tactics, the firm planned to embark on an aggressive cost-cutting plan that would affect 2,500 of its employees and slash expenses by $800 million over the next 18 months. In May of 1996 London Life Insurance Co. acquired $4.2 billion of Pru's life insurance business. In June of that year, Prudential once again became the target of a number of investigations and lawsuits.

In March of 1997, a New Jersey U.S. district court judge upheld a class-action settlement against Prudential for deceptive sales practices which would require the company to pay from $410 million to $1.7 billion depending on the number of claims. Several lawyers appealed the settlement, claiming the amount was too low. The company mailed out a statement to all customers who bought policies between 1982 and 1995, encouraging them to claim any reparation they believed was due. Prudential launched plans in late 1998 to become a publicly traded company. Wanting to focus on insurance, the Pru decided to sell its health care interest to Aetna.

History of The Bache Group

In 1880 Jules Bache joined his uncle's firm, Leopold Cahn & Co. Bache quickly became treasurer of the company and three years later was named partner. By 1890 the firm had expanded, adding offices in New York City and Albany. With clients such as John Rockefeller, Jay Gould, and Edward H. Harriman, Leopold Cahn & Co. soon set itself apart from its competitors and became a leader in the financial industry.

In 1892 the company's name was changed to J.S. Bache & Co. Under the leadership of Jules Bache, the company grew significantly, adding eight more branches in the U.S. and founding operations in London and Paris. By 1896 the company had seats on the New York Stock Exchange, the New York Cotton Exchange, the New York Produce Exchange, the Chicago Board of Trade, and the Philadelphia Stock Exchange.

During World War I, J.S. Bache & Co. purchased materials for the American, British, and French military and also sold Liberty Bonds. During the 1920s J.S. Bache forged important relationships with leaders in the railroad and automobile industries. The company was key in the development of the Chrysler Corp. and was one of the financiers of the New York subway development.

Strategic management allowed the firm to remain strong during the stock market crash of 1929. The company began a period of growth, acquiring companies that faltered during the crash. J.S. Bache developed relations in Tokyo, Hong Kong, Singapore, Berlin, and Amsterdam, as well as furthered its expansion in the United States and Canada. The company again supported the Allied troops during World War II by selling government bonds and by employing women for the first time to fill in for men called off to the war. J.S. Bache was also the first company to implement a program of profit sharing to its employees.

In 1944 Harold Bache took over the company and changed its name to Bache & Co. Continuing with expansion, overseas operations that were halted during the war were reestablished and new offices were opened across the United States, as well as in Geneva, Frankfurt, and Rome. During the 1940s and 1950s, the firm was a frontrunner in the industry due to its creative innovations. Bache & Co. was the first to sponsor a financial news program on television.

In 1971 Bache and Co. went public. This move cemented the company's position as an industry leader in securities by raising over $40 million in capital. Two years later, the company merged with Halsey, Stuart & Co., a well-known investment bank-

The Officers

Chairman and CEO: Arthur F. Ryan

President and CEO, Prudential Property & Casualty: Ed Rafter

CEO, Prudential Investments: E. Michael Caulfield

CEO, Prudential Insurance: John V. Scicutella

President and CEO, Prudential Healthcare Group: Steven Shulman

ing company, to become Bache Halsey Stuart Inc. In 1975 the Bache Group Inc. was formed as a holding company. Bache acquired Shield Model Roland and changed its name to Bache Halsey Stuart Shield Inc., the eventual moniker of Bache Group's brokerage and banking subsidiary. The company also went on to acquire Harrison & Co. and the Albert M. Bender Co. In 1981 The Prudential Insurance Company of America acquired the Bache Group.

Market Forces Driving the Merger

Prudential's interest in acquiring the Bache Group stemmed from ten years of expansion into leasing, international sales, property insurance, and casualty insurance. The Pru's long standing desire to become a leader in the financial services industry would be somewhat quenched with the acquisition of Bache. In an article in *The New York Times*, Prudential CEO Robert Beck was quoted as stating, "Acquiring Bache will be a very significant step in our strategic plan to offer a broad range of financial services. From our standpoint, it is an extension of a program we have already been on."

With over $60 billion in assets, Prudential led the U.S. insurance industry. It was 25% larger than Metropolitan Life Insurance Co., its closest competitor, and 75% larger than Equitable Life, its third largest competitor. Prudential's life insurance operations brought in the highest revenue at $7.6 billion in 1980, and the company had the financial means to expand and diversify.

Meanwhile, the Bache Group was fending off unwanted takeover attempts from the Belzberg family of Canada. The group had become a target due to financial problems and the fall of the silver market. The company had narrowly escaped bankruptcy when the Hunt brothers of Dallas, who used Bache as their broker, failed to covers loans the company had made. Prudential was immediately interested in the company, as it would help complete the insurance

The Players

CEO of The Prudential Insurance Co. of America: Robert A. Beck. As a graduate from Syracruse, Robert Beck began his career working in the finance department of Ford Motor Co. He joined Prudential one year later as a sales agent. In 1974 he was named president of the company and four years later was elected chairman and CEO. Beck led the company through an expansion phase into residential home sales, the credit card industry, group health insurance, homeowners and auto insurance, and reinsurance. He is credited for orchestrating the purchase of the Bache Group Inc. in 1981. Beck retired as CEO in 1987, but remained a board member and continued to sell insurance to high-profile professionals. In May of 1997, Beck died of cancer of the esophagus.

President and CEO of The Bache Group Inc.: Harry A. Jacobs. Harry A. Jacobs graduated from Dartmouth College in 1942. After serving with the U.S. Army Air Force for five years, he was honorably discharged as a First Lieutenant. He joined Bache & Co. in 1946 as a member of the research team and soon was in charge of the research and investment departments. Jacobs was named president of the company in 1968. In 1978 he was elected CEO of the Bache Group and its subsidiary, Bache Halsey Stuart Shields, Inc. Four years later he took over as chairman of Prudential Bache Securities, Inc., which was formed after Prudential purchased Bache in 1981. Jacobs held that position until 1986 when he retired. He was also named chairman of the Democratic Business Council for two consecutive years in 1985 and 1986.

company's diversification process. Bache encouraged the sale, eyeballing Prudential as a source of capital.

Approach and Engagement

First Boston Corp., financial advisor to the Bache Group, was given orders to find a merger partner for the company when it looked certain that the Belzberg family, consisting of brothers Samuel, Hyman, and William, would gain control of the company unless defensive measures were taken. With 22.6% ownership of Bache and failed attempts to gain two board seats, the Belzberg's had been buying stock in the company since 1979 and threatened a takeover in

1981. In March of that year, First Boston called upon Prudential and within two weeks, a cash merger of $385 million was proposed. The friendly deal called for Prudential to pay $32 a share for more than 51% of Bache's outstanding stock, which traded at $29.75 per share upon announcement of the deal.

Prudential planned to make Bache a subsidiary and keep its operations intact. Management was expected to remain without change. In June of 1981, the deal was approved by shareholders and finalized.

Products and Services

After folding Bache's operations into Prudential by forming the Prudential Bache Securities subsidiary, the insurance giant could now offer its customers a full line of financial portfolio management services through Bache's existing 193 offices. Later named Prudential Securities, the subsidiary was part of a diversified array of services the Prudential Insurance Co. provided, including securities brokerage.

With operations in Italy, Japan, South Korea, Taiwan, and the U.S., Prudential had 8,777 domestic insurance agents; 6,128 domestic financial advisors; 2,332 international financial advisors; and 456 international life planners in 1998. Through the company's diversified group, it offered banking and real estate information. The Individual Insurance Group offered individual and group life, property and casualty insurance, annuities, mutual funds, and pensions. The Prudential Healthcare Group offered group life, health products, and HMO. Prudential Investments handled individual and corporate investment management.

Changes to the Industry

According to an article in *The New York Times*, Wall Street saw the deal between Prudential and Bache as "the first signs of major confrontation between insurance companies and banks to compete in the investment business." The growing trend in the industry was to form a "financial supermarket" for consumers. The concept of one-stop shopping for financial services was becoming a popular goal for companies wanting to become major players in the industry.

In *Big Deal: The Battle for Control of America's Leading Corporations*, Bruce Wasserstein described the reasoning behind marriages of insurance companies and brokerage firms as reasonable. "The brokerage operations would provide new distribution channels for the insurance companies' mutual funds and other products. In return, the insurance companies would provide capital for expansion and technological improvements." Such was the case in the Prudential deal, and many other similar acquisitions followed. The Kemper Group acquired five brokerage firms in just two years, John Hancock Mutual Life Insurance Co. purchased Tucker Anthony Holding Corp. in 1982, Travelers Corp. merged with Securities Settlement Corp., Penn Mutual Life Insurance acquired Janney, Montgomery Scott Inc., and American Express paid $864 million for Shearson Loeb Rhoades Inc.

Review of the Outcome

The deal allowed Prudential to sell money market funds, mutual funds, tax shelters, real estate partnerships, as well as stocks and bonds. George L. Ball was named CEO of Prudential Bache Securities in 1982 to help integrate the two companies. In 1984, the unit posted a $104.8 million net loss in the first nine months of the year and received an additional $100 million in capital from Prudential. Wall Streets analysts hinted that Prudential had possible plans for selling off the securities firm, but CEO Robert Beck firmly denied any such plans.

Prudential Bache concentrated on growth in the 1980s, developing an Electronic Retrieval Assistant (ERA) that was advanced compared with competitors' information systems. With the acquisition of Thomson McKinnon in 1989, Prudential-Bache became the third largest brokerage company in the United States. Two years later, Prudential-Bache changed its name to Prudential Securities Inc. With over 6,000 financial advisors and assets of $202 billion, the securities firm remained a strong contender in the industry in the late 1990s.

Research

Arenson, Karen. "Prudential is Branching Out," in *The New York Times*, 8 April 1981. Discusses Prudential's plan to buy the Bache Group.

Cole. Robert. "First Boston Sparked by Bache Tie," in *The New York Times*, 20 March 1981. Details the deal between Prudential and Bache.

"Mutual Funds by Prudential," in *The New York Times*, 26 November 1981. Explains Prudential's plans to integrate some of Bache's mutual funds into its insurance business.

Prudential Insurance Co. of America Home Page, available at http://www.prudential.com. Official World Wide Web Home Page for Prudential Insurance Co. Includes historical, financial, and product information, as well as recent news articles.

"Prudential Insurance Co. of America," in *Notable Corporate Chronologies*, The Gale Group, 1999. Lists major events in the history of Prudential Insurance Co.

"Pru-Bache Not For Sale," in *Financial Times London*, 8 December 1984. Comments on the faltering performance of Prudential's securities unit.

"Recent Insurer-Broker Mergers," in *The New York Times*, 6 November 1984. Discusses the recent mergers of insurance companies and brokerage firms.

Rowe, James. "Prudential Announces Plan to Buy Bache Group," in *The Washington Post*, 20 March 1981. Explains Prudential's white knight approach in thwarting the Belzberg's plan to takeover Bache Group.

Wasserstein, Bruce. *Big Deal: The Battle for Control of America's Leading Corporations*, Warner Books, 1998. Offers an overview of the largest mergers in recent American corporate history.

CHRISTINA M. STANSELL

QUAKER OATS & SNAPPLE

The Quaker Oats Co.
321 N. Clark St.
PO Box 049001
Chicago, IL 60604-9001
USA

tel: (312)222-7111
fax: (312)222-8323
web: http://www.quakeroats.com

nationality: USA
date: November 3, 1994
affected: The Quaker Oats Co., USA, founded 1901
affected: Snapple Beverage Corp., USA, founded 1972

Overview of the Merger

Michael Mauboussin, an analyst with First Boston Corporation, summed up Wall Street's impression of Quaker Oats' acquisition of Snapple as "one of the worst, costliest, strategic blunders in the history of the food industry." This may sound like hyperbole, but Quaker Oats shareholders were in complete agreement. In November 1994, when Quaker Oats purchased Snapple for the incredible price of $1.7 billion, both Wall Street and Quaker Oats shareholders emitted a collective gasp. As reported in *Crain's New York Business*, that enormous sum was estimated by NatWest Securities analyst Michael Branca to be about 17 times Snapple's annual cash flow. If that were the end of this story, shareholders could possibly view the purchase price as an investment, albeit a large one, that would be recouped during upcoming years. The bitter pill was the fact that Snapple's sales growth was on the decline, and newly-introduced competition from heavy-hitters Coke and Pepsi would only drive profit margins down further.

Still, perhaps the purchase wasn't entirely folly. After all, it positioned Quaker Oats as the nation's third-largest producer of non-alcoholic beverages, behind Coke and Pepsi. Quaker Oats chairman and CEO William Smithburg was confident that Snapple would align neatly with the Gatorade operations. At the same time, he envisioned that Snapple would benefit from Gatorade's efficient supermarket distribution system, while Gatorade would gain from Snapple's strength in the small grocery store market.

Despite such optimism, industry experts were correct in their labeling of the deal as disastrous. In March 1997, Smithburg finally gave in to pressure and sold Snapple to Triarc Companies for $300 million—a fraction of what it had paid for it only two-and-a-half years earlier.

History of Quaker Oats

Ferdinand Schumacher established the German Mills American Oatmeal Factory in 1856. In 1877 Henry Seymour, owner of the Quaker Mill Co., introduced the trademark of a man dressed in Quaker garb—the first trademark ever registered for a breakfast cereal. Two years later, Robert Stuart and George Douglas opened the Imperial Mill Oatmeal facility. Henry Crowell purchased the Quaker Mill Co. from Seymour in 1881. Seven years later, these four oatmeal manufacturers—Schumacher, Stewart, Douglas, and Crowell—joined with three others in forming the American Cereal Co.. Stuart and Crowell subsequently assumed control of the company, and in 1901 incorporated it as the Quaker Oats Co. Its campaign to promote the healthful virtues of oatmeal proved successful, as sales at the end of its first year were $16 million.

The new company began to grow through diversification, acquisition, and new product introduction. In 1905 it established an animal feed business, and in 1909 introduced Quaker Puffed Rice and Puffed Wheat. Two years later, when it acquired Mother's Oats, the company owned roughly half of all milling operations east of the Rocky Mountains. In 1916, just after it posted net earnings of $3 million, it introduced its famous cylindrical packaging. In 1922 nearly 25% of its total sales originated from abroad.

Quaker Oats purchased Aunt Jemima Mill's Co. in 1925, and Ken-L Ration Dog Foods in 1942. In the mid-1960s it introduced two of its most popular products: Cap'n Crunch cereal and Instant Quaker Oatmeal. It continued to diversify, acquiring Fisher-Price Toys in 1969, as well as a restaurant and candy business.

Following the election of William Smithburg as CEO, Quaker Oats acquired Stokely-Van Camp Inc. in 1983 for $238 million. With that company came the Gatorade sports drink, which held an 83% share of the isotonic drink market. Three years later it acquired two companies: the Golden Grain Macaroni Co., maker of such brands as Rice-A-Roni, and Anderson, Clayton & Co., which produced Seven Seas salad dressings, Chiffon margarine, Gaines dog food, and Igloo coolers. Quaker added to its healthy food line by acquiring the Chico-San rice cake brand from Heinz in 1993.

In 1994 the company expanded its beverages product line by acquiring Snapple for $1.7 billion. This ill-fated purchase would drive the company to divest more businesses, call for the resignation of several key executives (including both the company president and CEO), and ultimately take an enormous loss in selling off Snapple.

History of Snapple Beverage Corp.

Snapple inadvertently defined—and dominated—a niche market in the early 1970s. In 1972 brothers-in-law Leonard Marsh and Hyman Golden were window washers in New York. Marsh's long-time

The Business

Financials - Snapple Beverage Corp.

Revenue (1998): $4.84 billion

Employees (1998): 11,860

SICs / NAICS

sic 2043 - Cereal Breakfast Foods

sic 2086 - Bottled & Canned Soft Drinks

sic 2099 - Food Preparations Nec

naics 311230 - Breakfast Cereal Manufacturing

naics 311999 - All Other Miscellaneous Food Manufacturing

naics 312111 - Soft Drink Manufacturing

friend, Arnold Greenberg, operated a natural food store. Greenberg's customers asked him repeatedly for all-natural juice products, so the three friends joined together to make juice for sale to local health food stores through their newly-formed Unadulterated Food Products Co. Several years later, they were approached by a man who purchased 400 cases of juice with the intention of selling them to local groceries. Thinking that they had gotten the better half of the deal, the partners were astounded when the man returned later that week to purchase a trailer-full of more juice. As Marsh was quoted in *Beverage Industry*, "At that point, we realized we had a business."

While experimenting in creating an apple soft drink, the partners arrived at the name "Snapple." They bought the name in 1978 from a Texan entrepreneur who owned the rights to it. The company made an early attempt at franchising, but this venture soon failed. As a result, the company's 12 distributors were left without a product to sell. In order to maintain good relations with these distributors, Snapple supplemented their commissions with the commissions that had been allocated for its franchisors. The distributors were not only appeased, they were delighted. Unfortunately, this delight soon faded as sales dropped off, and only a handful of distributors stuck it out. Snapple learned through focus groups that though the product still appealed to customers' sense of taste, the bottles themselves disturbed their sense of aesthetics. The company quickly redesigned the bottles in 1986 and watched sales of natural soft drinks, introduced in 1983, triple.

For the previous few years, the partners, who still held part-time jobs outside of Snapple, had been try-

The Officers

Snapple Beverage Corp.

Chairman, President, and CEO: Robert S. Morrison

Sr. VP, Chief Financial Officer: Robert S. Thomason

Sr. VP, Human Resources: Douglas J. Ralston

ing to perfect an iced tea product. The industry's standard cold-bottling method utilized preservatives, which not only went against company image, but also produced an odd-tasting beverage. In 1987 they hit on the solution—hot-bottling. The success of the new tea product prompted the partners to abandon their other jobs and devote themselves to Snapple full-time. Having introduced fruit flavor into the teas, that product line accounted for 55% of company sales in 1993.

In March 1992 the trio sold a majority interest in Snapple to the Thomas H. Lee Co. for $130 million. That December the company went public, with each of the partners hanging onto an 8.5% stake. Shares during the initial public offering went for $20 each; less than a year later they were going for more than $50.

Later in the year, however, increased competition in the bottled iced tea market caused share prices to dip. In April 1993 a joint venture between Pepsi-Cola Co. and Unilever debuted Lipton Original, while Coca-Cola Co. followed by joining with Nestle S.A. to market Nestea products. Still, Snapple held on to its 33% share of the $1.6 billion bottled iced tea market. Sales continued to grow, only at a slower rate.

When Quaker Oats swooped down with a bushel of money in 1994, Snapple allowed itself to be acquired at the pretty price of $1.7 billion. Marsh became executive vice president of strategic planning for Quaker Oats' Beverage unit. Golden and Greenberg retired upon completion of the acquisition. However, the marriage of the two companies was problematic and short-lived. On March 27, 1997, Quaker Oats sold Snapple to Triarc Companies Inc. for $300 million.

Market Forces Driving the Merger

Coca-Cola and Pepsi-Cola were making waves in the turfs of both Quaker Oats and Snapple. Quaker's cornerstone beverage product, Gatorade, held nearly 90% of the isotonic drink market. Snapple's ready-to-drink iced tea line held about 33% of its market. Yet the cola producers were expected to grab at least part

of those shares with their new product introductions. In the sports drink arena, PowerAde and All Sport, produced by Coke and Pepsi, respectively, had made small impressions. And the mid-1993 debut of their ready-to-drink iced tea products would also introduce new threats. Lipton Original, the product resulting from a partnership between Pepsi and Unilever, was launched that April, and Coke's joint venture with Nestle S.A. introduced a Nestea product soon after.

A union of the two companies, executives believed, would allow each to draw off of the strengths of the other, especially in terms of distribution. Snapple's recent decline in sales growth was interpreted by Quaker Oats CEO William Smithburg as a sign that it was ready for Quaker's efficient, highly-computerized distribution network. For Quaker Oats, on the other hand, the acquisition of Snapple would fuel its entry into the delicatessen and small grocery store market, Snapple's homebase.

Combined, the two companies would create the third-largest non-alcoholic beverage company, a rank that would strengthen its ability to compete with the heavy-hitting cola companies.

Approach and Engagement

Quaker Oats and Snapple announced the acquisition on November 2, 1994. The following day, Quaker began its cash tender offer of $14 per share, and concluded the deal only a day later, on November 4th.

Almost immediately, Snapple shareholders objected to the purchase. On November 3rd, more than a dozen filed suit against the company, demanding their right to vote on whether to approve or reject the acquisition. Their complaint was that Quaker was paying $2 less per share than the current going rate. Shares were valued at $11.50 on October 5th, but had risen to $16 based on rumors of the acquisition.

Meanwhile, Quaker's shareholders were doing some grumbling of their own. The $1.7 billion purchase price seemed extraordinarily high in itself, but given the fact that Snapple's sales growth had slowed, having dropped six percent from the previous year's level, it seemed incomprehensible. Even worse for Smithburg, shareholders soon discovered that he had passed on the opportunity to purchase Snapple two years earlier—for only $200 million.

Products and Services

Quaker Oats operated in two main categories: foods and beverages. Food sales dropped slightly in 1998 to $2.93 billion compared to the previous year's total of $2.94 billion. Operating income also fell slightly, dipping two percent to $394 million.

Since its divestiture of Snapple, Quaker's Beverage unit consisted solely of Gatorade. That one product, in various flavors and formats, held the number-one U.S. market share in isotonic beverages—82%. In 1997 it introduced Gatorade Frost, a product similar to the original Gatorade but with new flavors and colors designed to appeal to a wider audience. This product garnered sales of $150 million in its first year.

Food products centered on grains. Its Hot Cereals operations included such brands as Old Fashioned Quaker Oats, Quick Quaker Oats, Quaker Instant Oatmeal, and Quaker Quick n' Hearty Microwave Oatmeal. These products were given a boost in January 1997 by the U.S. Food and Drug Administration, which made the first food-specific health claim in a release that read, "Soluble fiber from oatmeal, as part of a low saturated fat, low cholesterol diet, may reduce the risk of heart disease." That year, Quaker held the nation's leading market share, 60%, for that category.

Quaker captured the nation's fourth-largest market share, eight percent, in ready-to-eat cereals in 1997. Its strongest products in that category include Cap'n Crunch, Life, Quaker Oatmeal Squares, Quaker Toasted Oatmeal, and Quaker Puffed Rice Cereals.

Its Golden Grain division in 1997 included Rice-A-Roni, Pasta Roni, and Near East grain and pasta products. That year it held the number-one market share position, 40%, in value-added rice, while holding the number-two slot, 38%, in value-added pasta.

The Grain-Based Snacks operations held the nation's leading market share in rice cakes, at 67%, and granola bars, at 37%. These products included Quaker Rice Cakes, Quaker Chewy Granola Bars, and Quaker Fruit & Oatmeal bars.

Changes to the Industry

By creating the nation's third-largest non-alcoholic beverage company, Quaker Oats intended to position itself as formidable competition to Coke and Pepsi. This required a concentration of company resources to that end, and the company proceeded to divest itself of non-food and -beverage operations. Sales proceeds also helped to pay for the acquisition of Snapple.

In 1995, Quaker Oats sold its pet foods, Pritikin, Mexican chocolates, Wolf/VanCamps bean and chili, and Dutch honey businesses. It continued divestiture into the following year, selling off its Italian oils and frozen foods operations.

The Players

Snapple President: Leonard Marsh. Leonard Marsh was a New York window washer in 1972. Inspired by an acquaintance in the budding health food industry, Marsh teamed up with his brother-in-law and a friend to produce all-natural juices. The idea was ripe for the times, and this niche market company soon grew into a powerhouse. When Snapple was acquired by Quaker Oats just a little over two decades after it was founded, each of the three partners walked away with $130.5 million in stock. Marsh was the only one to follow his company to its new parent, where he assumed the position of executive vice president for strategic planning of the Quaker Oats Beverage division.

CEO and Chairman: William D. Smithburg. William Smithburg's 16-year tenure as Quaker Oats' CEO may have bought him some time at the company after the Snapple acquisition, but that time did eventually run out. Unable to get the newly-acquired beverage company to show a healthy profit, angry shareholders and the board of directors were instrumental in affecting his "resignation" in 1997. His departure came on the heels of an exodus of the half-dozen or so other Quaker executives, among them company present Phil Marineau. Smithburg announced his exit in April 1997, and the following November was succeeded by Robert Morrisson, former chairman and CEO of Kraft Foods Inc.

Review of the Outcome

In light of dissatisfaction with the merger, the pressure would soon mount on Smithburg to prove that his judgment was intact, and that Quaker Oats would have the last laugh over industry skeptics. However, the company's absorption of Snapple was not seamless, and a major glitch over distribution served only to justify popular sentiment.

Quaker Oats didn't realize just how different the two companies' distribution methods were until after the acquisition was completed. While Gatorade's distributors delivered to customers' warehouses, Snapple's delivered directly to the stores. On top of that logistical headache, Quaker demanded that Gatorade's distributors handle all large supermarket customers while Snapple's deal only in small convenience store accounts. The Snapple distributors refused and Quaker finally relented, but valuable time had been lost in the conflict. In the end, Quaker was able to pull it together and improve Snapple's system. Delivery time to distributors was reduced from three weeks to just three days, allowing for reduced inventories and faster delivery to customers.

By late 1995, however, the damage had been done. Sales for Snapple in 1994 were $670 million. In 1995, its first full year under Quaker Oats ownership, sales dropped five percent to $640 million. Quaker Oats' sales in 1995 dropped from $6.2 billion to $5.9 billion.

Quaker Oats' executives began to feel the heat. In 1995, Philip A. Marineau, president and CEO, was forced to resign. The board of directors denied chairman William D. Smithburg a bonus and a raise. It repeated this action in 1996, the same year that it fired Don Uzzi, president of the beverage division. In April 1997, Smithburg also was forced to resign. His successor, Robert S. Morrison, was appointed chairman, president, and CEO in October of that year.

In 1997 the company decided that it had had enough. On March 27th it sold Snapple to Triarc Companies Inc. for $300 million. In shedding this business, Quaker Oats hoped to squash the possibility of a takeover by a larger company. Its relatively low stock value could appeal to such companies as Nestle, Cadbury Schweppes, Philip Morris, and Coca-Cola.

Following the sale, Quaker Oats continued its divestiture of non-core operations by ridding itself of its frozen bagels business, and its Richardson's dessert toppings and condiment lines.

In 1998 it reorganized by combining its food and beverage (now consisting solely of Gatorade) operations to strengthen its realignment on grain and Gatorade. It sold Continental Coffee Products Co., Ardmore Juice, Nile Spice soup business, and Liqui-Dri Foods Inc., a foodservice pastry mix unit.

Research

"Distribution Issues Surround Quaker-Snapple Merger," in *Beverage Industry*, November 1994. Differences between Snapple's and Gatorade's distribution systems.

Frank, John N. "The Kings of New Age: At Snapple, Everything Old is New Age Again," in *Beverage Industry*, March 1993. Snapple's history and 1993 financials.

"He Who Laughs Last," in *Forbes*, 1 January 1996. With the distribution glitch successfully resolved, some experts admit that perhaps the Snapple purchase wasn't altogether a bad idea for Quaker.

LaFemina, Lorraine. "Snapple's Liquid Assets Slakes Quaker's Thirst," in *LI Business News*, 21 November 1994. Snapple's shareholders express dissatisfaction with the price that Quaker paid for the company.

Prince, Greg. "Dream Team III," in *Beverage World*, January 1995. Lengthy treatment of the plans for successful integration of Snapple into Quaker's operations.

The Quaker Oats Company 1997 Annual Report. Reports financial highlights and describes company operating segments.

The Quaker Oats Company Home Page, available at http://www.quakeroats.com. Official World Wide Web Home Page for Quaker Oats. Offers limited company information, such as shareholder news, brief history, product overview, and employment opportunities.

"Quaker Reports 22 Percent Increase in Diluted EPS for 1998, 36 Percent for Fourth Quarter, Before Unusual Items," in *PR Newswire*, 4 February 1999. Year-end results for Quaker Oats.

Rewick, C.J. "Quaker Gets Snappled," in *Crain's Chicago Business*, 1 June 1998. Brief summary of Quaker's sale of Snapple.

"The Story of Snapple," in *Tea & Coffee Trade Journal*, October 1995. Speech by Snapple co-founder Leonard Marsh to members of the tea industry. He discusses Snapple's establishment, perfection of tea recipes, and methods for building brand image.

Willis, Gerri. "Founders Snapping up Big Profits in Takeover," in *Crain's New York Business*, 7 November 1994. Earnings for Snapple's three co-founders from its acquisition by Quaker.

Zbar, Jeffery D. "Quaker's Great Expectations: Analysts, Shareholders Question Snapple's Future Growth," in *Advertising Age*, 21 November 1994. Shareholders question Quaker's purchase of Snapple.

BERTRAM W. ROLAND

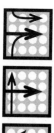

QUAKER OATS & STOKELY-VAN CAMP

nationality: USA
date: July 1983
affected: The Quaker Oats Co., USA, founded 1901
affected: Stokely-Van Camp Inc., USA, founded 1898

The Quaker Oats Co.
321 N. Clark St.
PO Box 049001
Chicago, IL 60604-9001
USA

tel: (312)222-7111
fax: (312)222-8323
web: http://www.quakeroats.com

Overview of the Acquisition

Considered to be one of the best deals of the 1980s, the acquisition of Stokely-Van Camp by Quaker Oats was completed in July 1983. The $230 million purchase price, believed by industry analysts and investors to be too generous, was considered by Quaker executives fair for the acquisition of the strong yet underdeveloped Gatorade brand. Under its new parent, Gatorade vigorously increased its presence in the market, both nationally and internationally, thereby vindicating Quaker chairman William Smithburg. Moreover, after the sale of inconsequential Stokely-Van Camp businesses, the $230 million price was reduced to a mere $95 million.

History of The Quaker Oats Co.

Ferdinand Schumacher established the German Mills American Oatmeal Factory in 1856. In 1877 Henry Seymour, owner of the Quaker Mill Co., introduced the trademark of a man dressed in Quaker garb—the first trademark ever registered for a breakfast cereal. Two years later, Robert Stuart and George Douglas opened the Imperial Mill Oatmeal facility. Henry Crowell purchased the Quaker Mill Co. from Seymour in 1881. Seven years later, these four oatmeal manufacturers—Schumacher, Stewart, Douglas, and Crowell—joined with three others in forming the American Cereal Co.. Stuart and Crowell subsequently assumed control of the company, and in 1901 incorporated it as the Quaker Oats Co. Its campaign to promote the healthful virtues of oatmeal proved successful, as first year sales reached $16 million.

The new company began to grow through diversification, acquisition, and new product introduction. In 1905 it established an animal feed business and in 1909 introduced Quaker Puffed Rice and Puffed Wheat. Two years later, when it acquired Mother's Oats, the company owned roughly half of all milling operations east of the Rocky Mountains. In 1916, just after it posted net earnings of $3 million, the firm introduced its famous cylindrical packaging. In 1922 nearly 25% of its total sales originated from abroad.

Quaker Oats purchased Aunt Jemima Mill's Co. in 1925, and Ken-L Ration Dog Foods in 1942. In the mid-1960s it introduced two of its most popular prod-

The Business

Financials

Revenue (1998): $4.84 billion

Employees (1998): 11,860

SICs / NAICS

sic 2043 - Cereal Breakfast Foods

sic 2086 - Bottled & Canned Soft Drinks

sic 2099 - Food Preparations Nec

naics 311230 - Breakfast Cereal Manufacturing

naics 311999 - All Other Miscellaneous Food Manufacturing

naics 312111 - Soft Drink Manufacturing

ucts: Cap'n Crunch cereal and Instant Quaker Oatmeal. It continued to diversify, acquiring Fisher-Price Toys in 1969, as well as a restaurant and candy business.

William Smithburg became CEO in 1981 and chairman in 1983. Under his leadership, Quaker reverted to a focus on grocery products. It began selling off such non-food operations as chemicals, video games, and restaurants. At the same time, it sought to add to its core businesses through strategic acquisitions.

Quaker Oats acquired Stokely-Van Camp in 1983 for $230 million. With that company came the Gatorade sports drink, which held an 83% share of the isotonic drink market. Three years later the firm acquired two companies: Golden Grain Macaroni Co., maker of such brands as Rice-A-Roni, and Anderson, Clayton & Co., which produced Seven Seas salad dressings, Chiffon margarine, Gaines dog food, and Igloo coolers. Quaker added to its healthy food line by acquiring the Chico-San rice cake brand from Heinz in 1993.

In 1994 the company expanded its beverages product line by acquiring Snapple Beverage Corp. for $1.7 billion. By creating the nation's third-largest non-alcoholic beverage company, Quaker Oats intended to position itself as formidable competition to Coke and Pepsi. This required a concentration of company resources to that end, and the company proceeded to divest itself of non-food and non-beverage operations. Sales proceeds also helped to pay for the acquisition of Snapple.

In 1995 Quaker Oats sold its pet foods, Pritikin, Mexican chocolates, Wolf/VanCamps bean and chili,

and Dutch honey businesses. It continued divestitures into the following year, selling off its Italian oils and frozen foods operations.

That year, however, in its first full year under Quaker Oats ownership, Snapple's sales dropped 5% to $640 million, while Quaker Oats' overall sales dropped from $6.2 billion to $5.9 billion. Quaker Oats' executives began to feel the heat. In 1995 Philip A. Marineau, president and CEO, was forced to resign. The board of directors denied chairman William D. Smithburg a bonus and a raise, repeating this action in 1996, the same year it fired Don Uzzi, president of the beverage division. In April 1997, Smithburg also was forced to resign. His successor, Robert S. Morrison, was appointed chairman, president, and CEO in October of that year.

On March 27, 1997, the company sold Snapple to Triarc Companies Inc. for $300 million. In shedding this business, Quaker Oats hoped to quash the possibility of a takeover as its relatively low stock value could appeal to such companies as Nestle, Cadbury Schweppes, Philip Morris, and Coca-Cola. Following this sale, Quaker Oats continued its divestiture of non-core operations by ridding itself of its frozen bagels business, as well as its Richardson's dessert toppings and condiment lines.

In 1998 Quaker Oats reorganized by combining its food and beverage (now consisting solely of Gatorade) operations to strengthen its realignment on grain and Gatorade. It sold Continental Coffee Products Co., Ardmore Juice, Nile Spice soup business, and Liqui-Dri Foods Inc., a foodservice pastry mix unit.

History of Stokely-Van Camp Inc.

Based in Indianapolis, Stokely-Van Camp was founded in 1898. The food processing company had become an American institution by the early 1980s, marketing such best-sellers as Van Camp's pork and beans, the market leader with a 34% share. Stokely also offered frozen fruits and vegetables, consumer vegetable oil products, popcorn, and vegetable-based industrial products.

The biggest star in its showcase, however, was Gatorade. This sports beverage was developed in 1965 by Michael Cade to rehydrate the University of Florida Gators football players. After tinkering with its flavoring, Cade began selling the product to local football coaches. In 1967 Stokely purchased the rights to the Gatorade Thirst Quencher. Under its new parent, Gatorade's visibility was increased, but it remained a regional product lacking major promotion.

Chairman William B. Stokely III, grandson of the company's founder, organized a management group in November 1982 to take Stokely private through a leveraged buyout. This group, SVC Acquiring Corp., offered $50 per share, or $136.5 million, for the company. Shareholders filed suit to block the deal, citing its low price. SVC Acquiring subsequently increased its offer to $55 per share, a bid that was accepted by Stokely's board in June 1983.

As the company was clearly for sale at that point, other suitors appeared. Among the rival bidders were Pillsbury Co. and Quaker Oats Co. Ultimately, Quaker Oats emerged the victor, gaining control of Stokely in July 1983.

Market Forces Driving the Acquisition

The U.S. food industry had reached a plateau in the early 1980s. The nation's population level was on a slow but steady decline, and the industry was considered mature. Moreover, food wholesales and retailers were wielding greater power over price control, forcing the average food company's profit margin down to only 4.7% in 1982. Growth opportunities were limited to new product introductions, geographic expansion, and alliances.

Quaker Oats was one such company on the acquisition path. It had recently redefined its focus away from a diverse array of ventures toward core food operations and was actively looking for companies to bolster those businesses. Similarly, Stokely-Van Camp had fine-tuned its holdings, divesting its inefficient and low profit seasonal fruits and vegetables operations. This streamlined firm, flush with cash from the divestiture of such lines, was appealing to Quaker Oats.

Particularly attractive was Stokely's Gatorade brand. This beverage accounted for 37% of Stokely's total profit of $15.3 million for the fiscal year ending May 31, 1983. This return, while impressive enough, was believed by Quaker officials to be only the tip of the iceberg. Gatorade was distributed only regionally, and had never been marketed aggressively. Quaker was certain that it could apply its well-developed advertising capabilities along with its national and international distribution network to introduce that product to new markets.

Approach and Engagement

In June 1983 Stokely-Van Camp's board of directors put the company in play by accepting a leveraged buyout bid of $55 per share, or $136.5 million, from SVC Acquiring Corp., a management group led by company chairman William Stokely. On July 5, however, Pillsbury Co. commenced a hostile tender offer of $62 per share, or $170 million. Pillsbury had recently purchased a 6.1% stake in Stokely held by Esmark, which had briefly considered acquiring Stokely itself. Pillsbury had then purchased additional shares to gain an 18% stake in Stokely.

Stokely terminated its agreement with SVC, which had declined to increase its buyout offer. The company then filed suit to block its acquisition by Pillsbury, citing antitrust issues in the canned beans and sauce market that would arise as a result of a completed merger. It also sought offers from white knight suitors.

Quaker Oats Co. soon emerged in that role, and on July 17 the two companies announced a merger agreement. Quaker's tender offer of $77 per share, or $230 million, was accompanied by a second agreement that would allow it to purchase the Gatorade subsidiary for $110 million at any time before July 15, 1985, even if its acquisition of Stokely failed.

In light of this backup agreement, Pillsbury withdrew its offer on July 19, claiming that it wasn't interested in entering a bidding war; however, analysts believed that Pillsbury simply wasn't interested in Stokely without Gatorade. With no other contenders beating its offer, Quaker Oats walked away the winner of Stokely-Van Camp.

Products and Services

In 1999 Quaker Oats operated in two main categories: foods and beverages. Food sales dropped slightly in 1998 to $2.93 billion compared to the previous year's total of $2.94 billion. Operating income also fell slightly, dipping 2% to $394 million.

After its 1997 divestiture of Snapple, Quaker's Beverage unit consisted solely of Gatorade. That one product, in various flavors and formats, held the number-one U.S. market share in isotonic beverages—82%. In 1997 the firm introduced Gatorade Frost, a product similar to the original Gatorade but with new flavors and colors designed to appeal to a wider audience. This product garnered sales of $150 million in its first year.

The Officers

Chairman, President, and CEO: Robert S. Morrison
Sr. VP, Chief Financial Officer: Robert S. Thomason
Sr. VP, Human Resources: Douglas J. Ralston

The Players

Quaker Oats Co. Chairman and CEO: William D. Smithburg. William Smithburg took the helm of Quaker Oats as CEO in 1981. Two years later, having added the additional post of chairman, he realigned core grocery businesses while divesting unrelated operations. Smithburg scored a major coup by orchestrating the purchase of Stokely-Van Camp in 1983. In the face of Wall Street skepticism, he demonstrated the wisdom of the purchase, which was later cited as one of the best of the decade.

In an attempt to bolster the company's beverage line, Smithburg directed Quaker's purchase of Snapple Beverage in 1994. This acquisition proved to be remarkably unsuccessful, and became known as one of the worst of the 1990s. Under pressure from shareholders and the board of directors, Smithburg announced his exit in April 1997. That November he was succeeded by Robert Morrisson, former chairman and CEO of Kraft Foods Inc.

Stokely-Van Camp Inc. Chairman and CEO: William B. Stokely III. William Stokely III, a grandson of one of the company's founders, initiated the sale of Stokely-Van Camp by launching a management-led leveraged buyout offer for the company in November 1982. This put Stokely on the auction block, ultimately landing in the hands of Quaker Oats. In August 1983 William Stokely resigned and walked away with $42 million from the sale of his 20% company stake.

Food products centered on grains. The Hot Cereals operations included such brands as Old Fashioned Quaker Oats, Quick Quaker Oats, Quaker Instant Oatmeal, and Quaker Quick n' Hearty Microwave Oatmeal. These products were given a boost in January 1997 by the U.S. Food and Drug Administration, which made the first food-specific health claim in a release that read, "Soluble fiber from oatmeal, as part of a low saturated fat, low cholesterol diet, may reduce the risk of heart disease." That year, Quaker held the nation's leading market share, 60%, for that category.

Quaker captured the nation's fourth-largest market share, 8%, in ready-to-eat cereals in 1997. Its strongest products in that category included Cap'n Crunch, Life, Quaker Oatmeal Squares, Quaker Toasted Oatmeal, and Quaker Puffed Rice Cereals.

The Golden Grain division in 1997 included Rice-A-Roni, Pasta Roni, and Near East grain and pasta products. That year the firm held the number one market share position, 40%, in value-added rice, while holding the number two slot, 38%, in value-added pasta.

The Grain-Based Snacks operations held the nation's leading market share in rice cakes, at 67%, and granola bars, at 37%. These products included Quaker Rice Cakes, Quaker Chewy Granola Bars, and Quaker Fruit & Oatmeal bars.

Changes to the Industry and Review of the Outcome

Many Wall Street analysts were skeptical, if not downright critical, of Quaker Oats' acquisition of Stokely-Van Camp. They believed that the purchase price was far higher than the value any possible synergies could produce. Even the company's announced plans to invest heavily in the Gatorade brand by devising new flavors, marketing aggressively, and distributing globally were scoffed at by analysts, who claimed that Gatorade, while a strong brand, had peaked. Some believed that Quaker would have been better served by investing in its own businesses, as company sales had recently dipped.

Quaker, however, persevered under the guidance of William Smithburg. When the dust had settled, the acquisition was touted as one of the best of the 1980s. *The Washington Post* referred to Stokely-Van Camp, particularly the Gatorade line, as an "untapped goldmine."

Under Quaker Oats, Gatorade introduced new flavors and varieties, unveiled new packaging, and launched a national marketing campaign. As a result, Gatorade achieved average annual unit volume sales increases of 20% throughout the remainder of the decade. "Gatorade is the biggest single brand in Quaker's portfolio today," remarked a company spokesperson in *M&A Europe*.

The payoff of the acquisition was even greater after Quaker Oats began divesting those Stokely operations outside of Gatorade and pork and beans. The firm sold Pomona Products, which offered canned specialty products, in April 1984, followed by the Capital City vegetable oil division that December. The third remaining division of the former Stokely-Van Camp, the popcorn and dry cereal manufacturer Purity Mills, was absorbed into Quaker. After these divestitures, Quaker Oats had purchased the strongest elements of Stokely for only $95 million.

Flush with success over this coup, Smithburg attempted a repeat performance by merging with

Snapple Beverage Corp. in 1994. In stark contrast to the Gatorade acquisition, however, the Snapple purchase proved disastrous. Distribution problems and increased competition from soft drink rivals compromised the value of Snapple, leading to falling sales and the departure of high-ranking company executives, including chairman Smithburg.

Research

"Is Stokely Worth Quaker's Lofty Bid?" in *Business Week*, 1 August 1983. Offers criticism of the deal, as well as Smithburg's justification for it.

"Pillsbury Halts Offer for Stokely," in *The New York Times*, 20 July 1983. Announces Pillsbury's withdrawal from the bidding.

Potts, Mark. "Quaker Oats is Buying Back into Its Basic Business," in *The Washington Post*, 12 April 1987. Describes Quaker's efforts to commit to the grocery market.

"Quaker 'Insurance' on Bid for Stokely," in *The New York Times*, 19 July 1983. Reveals Quaker's backup agreement to acquire the Gatorade division regardless of the turnout of its acquisition of Stokely.

The Quaker Oats Company 1997 Annual Report. Reports financial highlights and describes company operating segments.

The Quaker Oats Company Home Page, available at http://www.quakeroats.com. Official World Wide Web Home Page for Quaker Oats. Offers limited company information, such as shareholder news, brief history, product overview, and employment opportunities.

Rappaport, Alfred, and Elizabeth A. Friskey. "The Quaker-Stokely Deal: Boosting Shareholder Value through M&A," in *M&A Europe*, March/April 1990. Provides a detailed analysis of the effects of the merger on investors, with a brief discussion of the merger transaction.

"Robust Growth of Gatorade Nets a Payoff to Quaker," in *M&A Europe*, March/April 1990. Briefly relates the investments in Gatorade and the divestiture of former Stokely operations that proved a success for Quaker Oats.

"Stokey Approves Quaker Bid," in *The New York Times*, 18 July 1983. Announces the terms of the acquisition offer.

BERTRAM W. ROLAND

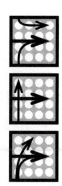

RALSTON PURINA & DRAKE BAKERIES

Ralston Purina Co.
Checkerboard Square
St. Louis, Missouri 63164-0001
USA

tel: (314)982-1000
fax: (314)982-2134
web: http://www.ralston.com

nationality: USA
date: July 1986
affected: Ralston Purina Co., USA, founded 1894
affected: Drake Bakeries, USA, founded 1888

Overview of the Merger

Ralston's $115 million purchase of Drake Bakeries gave the company an opportunity to become the largest manufacturer and producer of snack cakes and pies in the United States. Ralston's plan to fold Drake's operations into Continental Baking Co., a subsidiary of Ralston famous for marketing Hostess products, would send the company's market share to over 70% in New York City, 64% in Boston, and 62% in New England.

Tasty Baking Co. filed a federal complaint in August of 1986 on anti-trust violations. In February of 1987, Ralston's integration of its bakery units came to a halt on account of the anti-trust suit. In July of 1987, one year after it had purchased Drake, Ralston sold the bakery to Rock Capital Partners L.P., and Drake management to put an end to the anti-trust litigation.

History of Ralston Purina Co.

In 1894, William Henry Danforth and two church associates, George Robinson and William Andrews, began the Robinson-Danforth Commission Co. to mix and sell feed for mules and horses. The blend of oats and corn, billed as "cheaper than oats and safer than corn," sold well among farmers along the Mississippi River. Two years later, Danforth became president after buying the controlling interest of the company. Just after the purchase, a tornado destroyed the company's mill, forcing Danforth to secure a $25,000 rebuilding loan from Walker Hill, president of a local bank and a personal friend.

In 1898, Danforth discovered a Kansas miller who had found a way to prevent wheat from turning rancid, and introduced the miller's hot breakfast cereal made from cracked wheat. It was sold under the name Purina Whole Wheat Cereal. "Purina" was coined from the company slogan, "where purity is paramount." Danforth persuaded Dr. Ralston, author of the book *Life Building* to endorse the Purina cereal. He agreed only on the condition that the cereal be renamed Ralston Cereal.

Offering both the cereal and feeds, Danforth renamed the company Ralston Purina in 1902. He also adopted the famous checkerboard logo, based on his recollection of a family in his town who were easily identified by their checkered clothing. By 1904, the Louisiana Purchase Exposition drew thousands of people to St. Louis and acquainted many new people to the checkerboard products. The company's product line included Purina Pancake Flour, Ralston Breakfast Food, and Purina Whole Wheat Flour.

Danforth contributed to World War I by going to France as YMCA secretary for the troops of the Third Army Division. While there, he observed that soldiers referred to rations as "chow." After returning to the U.S., Danforth began to call his animal feeds "chows." He forced the use of the term by fining each employee who used the word "feed" 25 cents. (The proceeds went to charity.) In 1920, Danforth's son, Donald Danforth, joined the company. The two implemented a technique picked up in England by which feed was compressed into cubes. His pellet-shaped feed revolutionized the industry.

Danforth reluctantly purchased a research farm outside St. Louis at the request of his son in 1926. They tested innovative farm management methods, sanitation techniques, and new feed products, including feeds with non-grain ingredients like animal by-products and vitamins. While other feed companies diversified, Danforth invested profits into Purina chows, buying mills nationwide so he could adapt his mixtures to the climate-related needs of farmers in each region. By 1930, Ralston Purina's sales exceeded $60 million.

During the Great Depression, farmers could no longer afford commercial feed. To compensate for this loss, Danforth persuaded the country's most popular cowboy, Tom Mix, to lend his name to the advertising for Ralston Cereal. The inexpensive cereal, which had been losing money, began to generate a profit. When Donald Danforth became president in 1932, William Danforth split his time between contributing to Ralston Purina and running the Danforth Foundation, an organization created to build chapels on college campuses and in hospitals and to raise and donate funding towards churches, colleges, and universities.

With the onset of World War II, farmers increasingly relied on commercially prepared feeds. Ralston Purina's sales more than tripled and, despite price controls, net profits rose nearly 150%. The company implemented a program to train its local salespeople in the basics of farming so that they would be able advise customers. During the war years, Ralston Purina demonstrated, through its experimental farm, that the nutritional balance offered by Purina chows could produce bigger, healthier animals for less money. As more sophisticated feed supplements became available, the company added them to its

The Business

Financials

Revenue (1998): $4.6 billion

Employees (1998): 22,435

SICs / NAICS

sic 2051 - Bread, Cake & Related Products

sic 2043 - Cereal Breakfast Foods

sic 2041 - Flour & Other Grain Mill Products

sic 2047 - Dog & Cat Food

sic 2032 - Canned Specialties

sic 3691 - Storage Batteries

sic 3629 - Electrical Industrial Apparatus Nec

sic 2048 - Prepared Feeds Nec

naics 311812 - Commercial Bakeries

naics 311211 - Flour Milling

naics 311111 - Dog and Cat Food Manufacturing

naics 311422 - Specialty Canning

naics 311999 - All Other Miscellaneous Food Manufacturing

naics 335999 - All Other Miscellaneous Electrical Equipment and Component Manufacturing

naics 311611 - Animal (except Poultry) Slaughtering

naics 335911 - Storage Battery Manufacturing

chows, while carefully maintaining the homespun image its customers had come to trust.

After the war, grain prices began to rise sharply. The company was forced to go public in 1945 in order to raise the necessary operating capital. By 1947, chow sales had reached $200 million. Three years later Purina developed a highly nutritious and palatable dog food that was to be sold through grocery outlets.

William Danforth died in 1955. His son, Donald, became chairman of the board, and Raymond E. Rowland became president. The company began international expansion by becoming co-owner of feed companies in France, West Germany, and Italy, and by purchasing plants in Mexico, Guatemala, Colombia, Venezuela, and Argentina.

Purina Dog Chow was introduced to the market at the end of the 1950s, and within 16 months it passed Gaines as the market leader. In January of 1962 the company's stock was listed on the New York Stock Exchange. That same day, a fire destroyed a large port

The Officers

Chairman: William P. Stiritz

Co-President and Co-CEO; President and CEO, Pet
    Products Group: W. Patrick McGinnis

Co-President and Co-CEO; Chairman and CEO, Eveready
    Battery: J. Patrick Mulcahy

VP and Chief Financial Officer: James R. Elsesser Mannix

VP and Controller: Anita M. Wray

ion of the St. Louis plant. Despite the destruction, Ralston Purina continued to expand in its customer goods sector, increasing its penetration of the U.S. supermarket with Chex cereals and Purina Dog Chow.

Ralston acquired Van Camp Seafood Co., its first major domestic acquisition, for 1.9 million shares of stock in 1963. Donald Danforth retired that year with R. Hal Dean becoming president. When Dean became chairman in 1968, he began a program of acquisitions with the purchase of Foodmaker Inc., a restaurant franchising company. He also acquired the St. Louis hockey franchise, the Blues, and renamed the stadium the Checkerdome. He went on to purchase Green Thumb, a houseplant retailer, for $45 million, and Bremner Biscuit Co., maker of Cookie Crisp cereal. A well-known life sciences testing lab merged with Ralston Purina's lab in 1968, becoming the WARF Institute.

When William P. Stiritz took over as chairman in 1981, he immediately had to deal with a Kentucky soybean processing plant leaking a solvent into local sewers. The resulting explosion caused few injuries but cost the company over $40 million in reparations, plus an indictment and fine for failing to notify the proper officials of the leak.

With sales totaling $4.8 billion in 1982 and net income equaling $91 million, Stiritz began a plan to diversify. In 1984 he paid International Telephone and Telegraph (ITT) $475 million for Continental Baking Co., home of Wonder Bread and Hostess brand snack cakes (including Twinkies). The following year, sales exceeded $5 billion for the first time. The company sold Foodmaker, its restaurant operations, for $450 million. The cash from the sale was used toward the $1.4 billion purchase of Union Carbide Corp.'s battery division, manufacturers of Eveready and Energizer brand batteries. This acquisition made Ralston Purina the world's leading battery producer. Less than two weeks later, the company purchased Drake Bakeries, an important competitor in baked snacks, for $115 mil-

lion. In 1986, British Petroleum purchased Purina Mills' chows business in hopes of gaining a steady earner in the fluctuating U.S. agricultural industry.

Stiritz had reshaped the company's product lines and priorities by aggressively buying back 50 million shares of the company's own stock, and by selling its less profitable subsidiaries such as the St. Louis Blues, its fleet of tuna boats, fresh mushroom operations, and soybean processing business. In 1987, an antitrust action persuaded Ralston to sell Drake Bakeries in 1987, resulting in an after-tax profit of $43 million; net income reached a company high of $526 million on sales of $5.8 billion. Ralston also went on to sell its Van Camp Seafood division to a group of investors led by a privately held Indonesian concern for $260 million.

By the early 1990s, Ralston Purina was the world's largest producer of pet foods and dry cell battery products, as well as the largest fresh product wholesale baker in the U.S. Sales surpassed $7 billion and, with efforts underway to continue downsizing, Ralston Purina spun off the company's baby food, cereal, crackers and ski resorts businesses as a subsidiary called Ralcorp Holdings Inc. The company also sold Continental Baking Co. to former rival Interstate Bakeries Corp. for $560 million in an effort to pare down its business scope. Kellogg agreed to purchase Purina's sole cereal plant in South Korea, ending Purina's cereal business in that region.

The Eveready Battery Co. planned to build a $70 million plant that would produce lithium-ion rechargeable batteries for computers and hand-held electronics, prompted by the growth in portable computer sales in 1996. Ralston spun off its animal-feed division to shareholders in 1998. The company planned to split into two separate companies in 1999, allowing its Eveready Battery division to focus on the Energizer brand.

History of Drake Bakeries

Drake Bakeries was founded in 1888 in Wayne, New Jersey. The company became famous in the Northeast for marketing such snack cake products as Devil Dogs, Ring Dings, Yodels, and Yankee Doodles. Operating as a division of Borden, Inc., Drake Bakeries posted sales of $125 million in 1985 and operated three bakeries: one in Tennessee and two in New York.

The latter half of the 1980s proved to be changing times for the company. In 1986, Ralston Purina purchased Drake. The next year, because of anti-trust claims, the bakery management, with the help of Rock Capital Partners L.P., purchased the company back from Ralston for $176 million. That same year the company had to deal with hostile contract negotiations with its delivery truck drivers.

Culinar Inc., a Canadian company, purchased Drake on New Years Eve in 1990 for $35 million. Drake entered into a period of financial difficulty, and in 1994 experienced a $14 million loss, nearly destroying Culinar. The company began marketing on the West Coast and Canada to increase its presence in 14 Northeastern states, Florida, and Phoenix. In 1997, Rosie O'Donnell began promoting Yodel's on her hit television show. Before long, the company was getting free publicity on such programs as *Seinfeld*, *Friends*, and *The Nanny*. Culinar saw a resulting five-percent increase in sales in its Drake unit.

Drake was also involved in the fight against cystic fibrosis. In 1998, it developed a new product, Chocolate Mousse Ring Dings, and donated proceeds from the sale of this product to the cystic fibrosis cause. Later that year, Interstate Bakeries Corp. bought Drake, which was producing $115 million in sales per year.

Market Forces Driving the Merger

Ralston Purina's cash flow was estimated to be over $1 billion by 1988. Stiritz, the company's chairman, felt Ralston would be flagged as a takeover target if he didn't take action to ward off potential buyers and decrease cash flow. He implemented a stock buyback program in 1983 to increase long term debt, and was looking into acquisitions to do the same. With the purchase of Union Carbide's battery division, announced just before the Drake purchase, the company's total debt load would rise to $1.8 billion. Stiritz also focused on restructuring the company and on expanding its base in the consumer goods business. With the purchase of Continental, the nation's largest baking company, Ralston's strategy of delving further into packaged consumer goods was taking shape.

Approach and Engagement

Wanting to expand and diversify further in the consumer goods market, Ralston approached Borden in 1985 regarding its Drake Bakeries division. In July of 1986 the two announced that Ralston was purchasing the company for $115 million. Drake was set to pair up with Continental Baking Co., a subsidiary of Ralston. Continental was the leader of fresh baked goods in the U.S., with 46 bakeries and sales of $1.6 billion in 1985. Drake's products, such as Yodels and Ring Dings, would add to Continental's Hostess snack products and to its Wonder, Home Pride, and Beefsteak breads.

The Players

Chairman and CEO of Ralston Purina Co.: William P. Stiritz. After graduating from Northwestern University in 1959, William Stiritz went to work for the Pillsbury Co. After four years at Pillsbury, and following a brief sting at Gardner Advertising Co., he joined Ralston Purina and quickly became a group vice president. Stiritz is credited with returning the company to profitability at the beginning of 1980s. Named president and CEO of Ralston Purina in 1981, Stiritz was also elected Chairman of Ralcorp Holdings Inc., a spin off of Ralston, in 1994. He is well respected by his peers and known throughout the industry as an innovative and knowledgeable leader.

President and CEO of Drake Bakeries: Christos Christodoulou. Christos Christodoulou was at the helm of Drake Bakeries through its tumultuous times in the 1980s. He oversaw the company's change in ownership several times and was a key player in resolving contract negotiations with the company's truck drivers in 1987.

One month after the deal took place, Tasty Baking Co. filed a complaint in Federal District Court against Ralston's plans to merge the two baking companies together. Tasty's president and CEO Nelson Harris stated in a company news release, "Unless Ralston Purina and Continental are restrained, the acquisition of Drake will substantially lessen competition and tend to create a monopoly in many regions of the snake cake and pie industry. And this is wrong."

Harris was also concerned that Ralston's financial power would enable the company to gain leverage in supermarkets across the United States to increase shelf space unfairly. According to the same news release, the complaint asked that "while court action is pending, Ralston Purina and Continental be restrained from implementing the transfer of Drake's assets to Ralston Purina and Continental, in any way integrating the operations of Drake into those of Continental, or from disposing of any of the assets of Drake." Drake would continue to sell it products in the same manner as it had in the past, remaining in competition with Ralston and Continental.

In February of 1987, Ralston was halted in its efforts to combine its two subsidiaries. One year after it purchased Drake, Ralston sold it back to Drake management and Rock Capital Partners L.P. in order to appease the anti-trust suit.

Products and Services

At the time of the merger, Ralston Purina was the largest producer of fresh bakery products in the United States. Through its subsidiary, Continental Baking, Ralston owned 46 bakeries across the U.S. and posted sales of $1.6 billion from its baking business. Drake had three baking outlets in New York and Tennessee and sales of $125 million.

In 1998 Ralston Purina was focused on its pet products and battery division. Upon completion of the acquisition of Union Carbide's battery division just after the Drake purchase, Ralston Purina gained 60% of the market share for batteries. With the brand names of Energizer and Eveready, battery products accounted for 45% of total sales for the company in 1998. Ralston remained a leader in the pet products industry as well. Leading brands included Tidy Cat and Tidy Cat Scoop cat litter, Meow Mix cat food, Purina Dog Chow, Purina Cat Chow, Tender Vittles, and Field 'n Farm. With sales of $2.6 billion in 1998, pet products accounted for 55% of total sales. Ralston serviced the United States, Europe, Asia, and South and Central America.

Changes to the Industry

Consolidation was a growing trend in the food business industry. The desire of large companies to diversify into different types of products and services was becoming more commonplace. Philip Morris's purchase of General Foods in 1985 and Kraft in 1988 were examples of how quickly a company could become an industry leader simply by purchasing companies.

Ralston's leap into the battery industry also demonstrated a trend in diversification. The battery industry was growing at more than five percent each year, spurred by the intensifying popularity of portable radios and tape players, as well as electronic games and toys. Companies in the packaged consumer goods industry were looking to break into that market. Ralston, which specialized in pet products, and Kraft, known throughout the world for its cheese products, were two examples of company diversification efforts to capitalize on growth in different markets.

Review of the Outcome

Faced with the anti-trust suit, Ralston was forced to sell off Drake Bakeries to Rock Capital Partners, an investment firm, and Drake management. The $176 million deal led to an after-tax gain of $43 million in net income in 1987 for Ralston. Drake was later purchased by Culinar Inc. in 1990 and Interstate Bakeries Corp. in 1998.

Ralston slowly started to remove itself from the food industry by selling its Van Camp Seafood division in 1988, spinning off its baby food and cereal business as Ralcorp Holdings, and selling Continental in 1995. Ralston's focus was on its battery and pet food operations in the mid-1990s. Ralston Purina became the world's largest manufacturer of dry cell battery products after its 1986 merger with Union Carbide, with its Energizer and Eveready brand names. Ralston's Purina brand was the largest producer of dog and cat foods, marketed in more than 160 countries. In 1998, 55% of sales were from its pet products, with its battery division accounting for the remaining 45% of sales. With a net profit margin of 23.8%, Ralston posted revenues of $4.6 billion and employed 22,435 people.

Research

Greenhouse, Steven. "British Concern to Buy Ralston Feed Business," in *The New York Times*, 11 July 1986. Discusses Ralston's recent plans to diversify, its merger with Union Carbide, and its purchase of Drake Bakeries.

"Interstate Bakeries to Acquire Drake," in *Los Angeles Times*, 24 June 1998. Announces the purchase of Drake by Interstate Bakeries.

"Judge Blocks Bakery Merger Plan," in *The Washington Post*, 28 February 1987. Details the anti-trust suit brought against Ralston.

"Philadelphia.," in *PR Newswire*, 21 August 1986. Discusses Tasty Baking Co.'s reasons for filing suit against Ralston.

"Ralston Purina Co.," in *Notable Corporate Chronologies*, The Gale Group, 1999. Lists major events in the history of Ralston Purina Co.

"Ralston Purina Co.," in *Wall Street Journal*, 24 August 1987. Discusses Ralston's sale of Drake Bakeries.

Ralston Purina Co. Home Page, available at http://www.ralston.com. Official World Wide Web Home Page for Ralston Purina Co. Includes current and archived news, and detailed financial and product information.

"Ralston Purina Co. Reports Earnings," in *The New York Times*, 4 November 1988. Lists earnings in 1988 compared to 1987.

Shalom, Francois. "How a Sappy Talk Show Sweetened Sales for a Sugary Snack," in *The Gazette Montreal*, 5 April 1997. Discusses Drake products' recent popularity on hit television shows.

CHRISTINA M. STANSELL

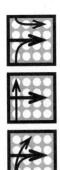

RALSTON PURINA & UNION CARBIDE

nationality: USA
date: July 1986
affected: Ralston Purina Co., USA, founded 1894
affected: Union Carbide Corp., USA, founded 1876

Ralston Purina Co.
Checkerboard Square
St. Louis, Missouri 63164-0001
USA

tel: (314)982-1000
fax: (314)982-2134
web: http://www.ralston.com

Overview of the Merger

The $1.4 billion cash purchase of Union Carbide's battery products division by the Ralston Purina Co. was an act of diversification as well as the first step of Union Carbide's restructuring. Ralston received the brand names Eveready and Energizer as part of the deal. As a manufacturer, Eveready controlled 60% of the U.S. market as well as 30% of the world market with over $1 billion in sales in 1985. Ralston planned to operate the new acquisition as the Eveready Battery Co. in the United States.

History of Ralston Purina

In 1894, William Henry Danforth and two church associates, George Robinson and William Andrews, began the Robinson-Danforth Commission Co. to mix and sell feed for mules and horses. The blend of oats and corn, billed as "cheaper than oats and safer than corn," sold well among farmers along the Mississippi River. Two years later, Danforth became president after buying the controlling interest of the company. Just after the purchase, a tornado destroyed the company's mill, forcing Danforth to secure a $25,000 rebuilding loan from Walker Hill, president of a local bank and a personal friend.

In 1898, Danforth discovered a Kansas miller who had found a way to prevent wheat from turning rancid, and introduced the miller's hot breakfast cereal made from cracked wheat. It was sold under the name Purina Whole Wheat Cereal. "Purina" was coined from the company slogan, "where purity is paramount." Danforth persuaded Dr. Ralston, author of the book *Life Building* to endorse the Purina cereal. He agreed only on the condition that the cereal be renamed Ralston Cereal.

Offering both the cereal and feeds, Danforth renamed the company Ralston Purina in 1902. He also adopted the famous checkerboard logo, based on his recollection of a family in his town who were easily identified by their checkered clothing. By 1904, the Louisiana Purchase Exposition drew thousands of people to St. Louis and acquainted many new people to the checkerboard products. The company's product line included Purina Pancake Flour, Ralston Breakfast Food, and Purina Whole Wheat Flour.

The Business

Financials

Revenue (1998): $4.6 billion

Employees (1998): 22,435

SICs / NAICS

sic 2051 - Bread, Cake & Related Products

sic 2043 - Cereal Breakfast Foods

sic 2041 - Flour & Other Grain Mill Products

sic 2047 - Dog & Cat Food

sic 2032 - Canned Specialties

sic 3691 - Storage Batteries

sic 3629 - Electrical Industrial Apparatus Nec

sic 2048 - Prepared Feeds Nec

naics 311812 - Commercial Bakeries

naics 311211 - Flour Milling

naics 311111 - Dog and Cat Food Manufacturing

naics 311422 - Specialty Canning

naics 311999 - All Other Miscellaneous Food Manufacturing

naics 335999 - All Other Miscellaneous Electrical Equipment and Component Manufacturing

naics 311611 - Animal (except Poultry) Slaughtering

naics 335911 - Storage Battery Manufacturing

Danforth contributed to World War I by going to France as YMCA secretary for the troops of the Third Army Division. While there, he observed that soldiers referred to rations as "chow." After returning to the U.S., Danforth began to call his animal feeds "chows." He forced the use of the term by fining each employee who used the word "feed" 25 cents. (The proceeds went to charity.) In 1920, Danforth's son, Donald Danforth, joined the company. The two implemented a technique picked up in England by which feed was compressed into cubes. His pellet-shaped feed revolutionized the industry.

Danforth reluctantly purchased a research farm outside St. Louis at the request of his son in 1926. They tested innovative farm management methods, sanitation techniques, and new feed products, including feeds with non-grain ingredients like animal by-products and vitamins. While other feed companies diversified, Danforth invested profits into Purina chows, buying mills nationwide so he could adapt his mix-

tures to the climate-related needs of farmers in each region. By 1930, Ralston Purina's sales exceeded $60 million.

During the Great Depression, farmers could no longer afford commercial feed. To compensate for this loss, Danforth persuaded the country's most popular cowboy, Tom Mix, to lend his name to the advertising for Ralston Cereal. The inexpensive cereal, which had been losing money, began to generate a profit. When Donald Danforth became president in 1932, William Danforth split his time between contributing to Ralston Purina and running the Danforth Foundation, an organization created to build chapels on college campuses and in hospitals and to raise and donate funding towards churches, colleges, and universities.

With the onset of World War II, farmers increasingly relied on commercially prepared feeds. Ralston Purina's sales more than tripled and, despite price controls, net profits rose nearly 150%. The company implemented a program to train its local salespeople in the basics of farming so that they would be able advise customers. During the war years, Ralston Purina demonstrated, through its experimental farm, that the nutritional balance offered by Purina chows could produce bigger, healthier animals for less money. As more sophisticated feed supplements became available, the company added them to its chows, while carefully maintaining the homespun image its customers had come to trust.

After the war, grain prices began to rise sharply. The company was forced to go public in 1945 in order to raise the necessary operating capital. By 1947, chow sales had reached $200 million. Three years later Purina developed a highly nutritious and palatable dog food that was to be sold through grocery outlets.

William Danforth died in 1955. His son, Donald, became chairman of the board, and Raymond E. Rowland became president. The company began international expansion by becoming co-owner of feed companies in France, West Germany, and Italy, and by purchasing plants in Mexico, Guatemala, Colombia, Venezuela, and Argentina.

Purina Dog Chow was introduced to the market at the end of the 1950s, and within 16 months it passed Gaines as the market leader. In January of 1962 the company's stock was listed on the New York Stock Exchange. That same day, a fire destroyed a large portion of the St. Louis plant. Despite the destruction, Ralston Purina continued to expand in its customer goods sector, increasing its penetration of the U.S. supermarket with Chex cereals and Purina Dog Chow.

Ralston acquired Van Camp Seafood Co., its first major domestic acquisition, for 1.9 million shares of stock in 1963. Donald Danforth retired that year with R. Hal Dean becoming president. When Dean became chairman in 1968, he began a program of acquisitions with the purchase of Foodmaker Inc., a restaurant franchising company. He also acquired the St. Louis hockey franchise, the Blues, and renamed the stadium the Checkerdome. He went on to purchase Green Thumb, a houseplant retailer, for $45 million, and Bremner Biscuit Co., maker of Cookie Crisp cereal. A well-known life sciences testing lab merged with Ralston Purina's lab in 1968, becoming the WARF Institute.

When William P. Stiritz took over as chairman in 1981, he immediately had to deal with a Kentucky soybean processing plant leaking a solvent into local sewers. The resulting explosion caused few injuries but cost the company over $40 million in reparations, plus an indictment and fine for failing to notify the proper officials of the leak.

With sales totaling $4.8 billion in 1982 and net income equaling $91 million, Stiritz began a plan to diversify. In 1984 he paid International Telephone and Telegraph (ITT) $475 million for Continental Baking Co., home of Wonder Bread and Hostess brand snack cakes (including Twinkies). The following year, sales exceeded $5 billion for the first time. The company sold Foodmaker, its restaurant operations, for $450 million. The cash from the sale was used toward the $1.4 billion purchase of Union Carbide Corp.'s battery division, manufacturers of Eveready and Energizer brand batteries. This acquisition made Ralston Purina the world's leading battery producer. Less than two weeks later, the company purchased Drake Bakeries, an important competitor in baked snacks, for $115 million. In 1986, British Petroleum purchased Purina Mills' chows business in hopes of gaining a steady earner in the fluctuating U.S. agricultural industry.

Stiritz had reshaped the company's product lines and priorities by aggressively buying back 50 million shares of the company's own stock, and by selling its less profitable subsidiaries such as the St. Louis Blues, its fleet of tuna boats, fresh mushroom operations, and soybean processing business. In 1987, an antitrust action persuaded Ralston to sell Drake Bakeries in 1987, resulting in an after-tax profit of $43 million; net income reached a company high of $526 million on sales of $5.8 billion. Ralston also went on to sell its Van Camp Seafood division to a group of investors led by a privately held Indonesian concern for $260 million.

By the early 1990s, Ralston Purina was the world's largest producer of pet foods and dry cell battery products, as well as the largest fresh product wholesale baker in the U.S. Sales surpassed $7 billion and, with efforts underway to continue downsizing,

The Officers

Chairman: William P. Stiritz

Co-President and Co-CEO; President and CEO, Pet Products Group: W. Patrick McGinnis

Co-President and Co-CEO; Chairman and CEO, Eveready Battery: J. Patrick Mulcahy

VP and Chief Financial Officer: James R. Elsesser

VP and Controller: Anita M. Wray

Ralston Purina spun off the company's baby food, cereal, crackers and ski resorts businesses as a subsidiary called Ralcorp Holdings Inc. The company also sold Continental Baking Co. to former rival Interstate Bakeries Corp. for $560 million in an effort to pare down its business scope. Kellogg agreed to purchase Purina's sole cereal plant in South Korea, ending Purina's cereal business in that region.

The Eveready Battery Co. planned to build a $70 million plant that would produce lithium-ion rechargeable batteries for computers and hand-held electronics, prompted by the growth in portable computer sales in 1996. Ralston spun off its animal-feed division to shareholders in 1998. The company planned to split into two separate companies in 1999, allowing its Eveready Battery division to focus on the Energizer brand.

History of Union Carbide Corp.

In 1876, the first carbon arc streetlight was used in Cleveland, Ohio, with the help of Charles F. Brush. As a result of Brush's invention, the National Carbon Co. was formed to make street light carbons and later, carbon electrodes for electric furnaces. Eventually, the Eveready trademark became a part of this company. In 1890, National Carbon produced the first dry cell battery. Meanwhile, in North Carolina, Thomas L. Wilson and Major James T. Morehead produced calcium carbide, resulting in acetylene. These two chemicals were considered mere laboratory curiosities at the time, but Morehead convinced several Chicago entrepreneurs of the uses for acetylene in city and home lighting.

National Carbon built one of the first industrial research laboratories in the country in 1894, and The Union Carbide Co. was formed to manufacture calcium carbide in 1898. Electric lighting was starting to become practical during this time, eliminating any expansion hopes for Union Carbide's acetylene lighting business, but the calcium carbide plants began to

The Players

Chairman and CEO of Ralston Purina Co.: William P. Stiritz. After graduating from Northwestern University in 1959, William Stiritz went to work for the Pillsbury Co. After four years at Pillsbury, and following a brief stint at Gardner Advertising Co., he joined Ralston Purina and quickly became a group vice president. Stiritz is credited with returning the company to profitability at the beginning of 1980s. Named president and CEO of Ralston Purina in 1981, Stiritz was also elected Chairman of Ralcorp Holdings Inc., a spin off of Ralston, in 1994. He is well respected by his peers and known throughout the industry as an innovative and knowledgeable leader.

President and CEO of Union Carbide Corp.: Robert D. Kennedy. Cornell University graduate Robert Kennedy joined Union Carbide in 1955. He took on many different roles in management and engineering before being named named president, CEO, and chairman in 1986. Kennedy successfully reorganized the company, and in 1995 received the Chemical Industry Medal from the American chapter of the Society of Chemical Industry for his foresight and contributions to the industry. He also received the Kavaler Award for chief executive excellence from chemical industry security analysts that year. Although Kennedy retired from Union Carbide in 1995, he remained a member of the board of directors.

operate in Sault Ste. Marie, Michigan, and Niagara Falls, New York. By the turn of the century, capital stock of Union Carbide was $6 million. Charles F. Dieterich served as president, with George O. Knapp as vice president and A.B. Proal as secretary and treasurer.

In 1906, Union Carbide's main office was located in Chicago, Illinois. The company purchased an alloy business and a metals research laboratory, and established a separate division to produce alloys for steelmaking. Under the direction of chief metallurgist Dr. Fredrick M. Becket, the new company began a line of alloying metals, such as low-carbon ferrochrome, which resulted in the development of modern stainless steels. The discovery in France of a hot metal-cutting flame resulted from burning acetylene in oxygen, creating a demand for such resources. By 1907,

Charles Brush had interested several electrode producers in forming the first oxygen-producing company. This company would later become the corporation's Linde Division.

Union Carbide bought an interest in the oxygen company, bringing together for the first time the carbon and carbide interests. Union Carbide's major competitor during this period was the Prest-O-Lite Co., the largest single purchaser of calcium carbide for acetylene lamps for automobiles. Prest-O-Lite hired Dr. George O. Curme, Jr., to find an alternative form of acetylene. He consulted scientists from the Linde Co. and Union Carbide to conduct research on the gas. In 1917, the cooperative efforts resulted in the formation of the Union Carbide and Carbon Corp.

The government's need for ethylene during World War I regenerated interest in hydrocarbon byproducts, and in 1919 the first production of synthetic ethylene began. America's petrochemical industry and the corporation's chemicals business were established. With combined research efforts, new developments occurred rapidly. New products included ethylene glycol (today's Prestone anti-freeze and coolant), batteries for portable radios, quiet flickerless carbons used for the first sound movies, and ferroalloys to improve the steels used to build skyscrapers, bridges, and cars. By 1920, the company's technology included the production of corrosion-resistant and heat-resistant alloys.

The firm acquired vanadium interests on the Colorado Plateau, which eventually supplied the uranium for atomic energy in 1926. Two years later, graphite skills were added to the company's carbon activities with the Acheson Graphite Corp. In 1933, the Chicago World's Fair enabled Union Carbide to exhibit more than half of the known chemical elements to the public. With the advent of World War II, Union Carbide focused its attention on developing raw material resources and utilization of by-products. The company resumed its butadiene studies, begun years before, to succeed in developing a synthetic rubber, and soon acquired the Bakelike Corp., increasing its technology in the field of plastics. Carbide was also responsible for research on vanadium that eventually involved the firm in government atomic energy development.

Having demonstrated that gaseous diffusion can be used to separate quantities of uranium-235, Union Carbide and the Manhattan Engineer District entered into a contract to operate the Oak Ridge Gaseous Diffusion Plant. Linde perfected a refining process for treating uranium concentrates, and a plant was built and operated by the Electro Metallurgical Co. (eventually the Metals Division) to provide extensive emergency metallurgical research and to manufacture uranium. Graphite products and special carbons were developed and manufactured by National Carbon. In 1943, uranium-bearing materials were provided by U.S. Vanadium; Union Carbide and Carbon Research Laboratories contributed to the development of the atomic weapon itself.

In 1945, following the war, the company expanded. Polyethylene, a plastic used in squeeze bottles, as well as in films and sheeting, became its largest dollar-volume product. Other materials, such as gases and carbon products, also continued to succeed. In 1948, Union Carbide celebrated its 50th anniversary, and, as the decade progressed, Union Carbide began restructuring. Interest in new fields of technology began to emerge. The Metals Division was established to handle worldwide ore procurement, and a food casings business, the Visking Co., was also established. By this point, Union Carbide had established some 400 plants in the U.S. and Canada, in addition to overseas affiliates. With the public's increasing awareness of its activities, the company decided to delete "carbon" from its official title and take the name of Union Carbide Corp.

By 1959, consumer products such as Eveready batteries and Prestone anti-freeze continued to increase in sales. To accommodate this, a separate division for consumer products was established. Early in the new decade, the Glad line of plastic wraps, bags, and straws was introduced. The company continued to grow; it acquired the Englander Company Inc., a bedding manufacturer, in 1964 and purchased Neisler Laboratories in 1965. International operations were restructured to accommodate new subsidiaries, including Union Carbide Pan America Inc., Union Carbide Europe Inc., Union Carbide Eastern Inc., Union Carbide Africa and Middle East Inc., and Union Carbide Canada Ltd. (a 75% owned subsidiary). In 1969, the Visking casings business became the new Films-Packaging Division, consolidating activities in food casings and related products.

During the next few years, Union Carbide decided to sell and dissolve some of its businesses in order to concentrate on further expansion of certain industries. Among the businesses sold were Neisler Laboratories, the Stellite, or Materials Systems Division, Ocean Systems, Inc., and The Englander Co. The firm also sold off most of its oil and gas interests, a pollution-monitoring devices business, a plastic container line, a fibers business, a jewelry line, and an insect repellant business. In 1971, the company formed a New Business Development Department and merged it with the Corporate Technology Department. The next year a comprehensive long-term program was established with the following

objectives: "Strengthening the assignment of individual responsibilities and accountabilities, strengthening business management methods, allocating resources selectively in strategic planning units, and practicing good corporate citizenship at home and abroad."

With the advent of new strategies came new materials and processes, including molecular sieve adsorbents and catalysts, specialized electronic materials, foamed plastics, biomedical systems, pollution abatement systems, energy conversion, miniature batteries, chemicals to increase food yields, and Thornel carbon-graphite fibers. By 1975, Union Carbide had approached authorities in New Delhi, India, with an offer to build a pesticides plant in the city of Bhopal. The offer was gladly accepted as India's "Green Revolution" included the increased use of pesticides and fertilizers to boost harvests. Later that year, the Indian government granted Union Carbide a license to manufacture pesticides, and a plant was built with the company owning 51% of the business and India's private companies owning the remaining 49%. Local residents were hired for management positions. Although the plant was located on the outskirts of the city, an area that was not densely populated, the construction brought more residents. More than 900,000 people eventually lived in this capital of Madhya Pradesh. Union Carbide increased its ties with local government and even helped the city to build a park.

The firm had held an impressive safety record within the chemical industry up to this point. In December of 1984, however, a massive disaster at Union Carbide's Bhopal plant led to the deaths of more than 2,500 people. Called "the worst industrial accident in history" by *Newsweek* magazine, the incident was caused by a deadly leak of methyl isocyanate gas (MIC). Union officials claimed that at least five tons of MIC seeped out in the 30 minutes before the tank was sealed. The effects of the chemical on humans were said to resemble those of nerve gas. Following the accident, Bhopal police arrested five senior Indian executives of Union Carbide. In a written statement, Arjun Singh, chief minister of the Madhya Pradesh state, charged Warren Anderson, chairman of Union Carbide's board, with "corporate and criminal liability," and accused company management of "cruel and wanton negligence."

By 1985, many class action suits were filed against the company. Business shut down at the India facility, and Union Carbide stopped production and distribution of MIC at their plant in Institute, West Virginia. Stock prices plunged by 12 points, and the company's reputation was significantly damaged. GAF, a chemical and roofing materials firm, tried to take over Union Carbide. Responding to the takeover threat, the company went into debt by $3 billion in order to buy back 55% of its stock. In an effort to regain profitability and pare down operations, the battery division, including Eveready, was sold to Ralston Purina, the agricultural products operation was sold to Rhone-Poulenc, and the home and auto products business was sold to First Brands. The company was restructured to focus on chemicals, plastics, industrial gases, and carbon products.

In 1989, Union Carbide was ordered to pay a $470 million settlement in India's Supreme Court. One year later Union Carbide sold its urethane polyols and propylene glycols businesses to Arco Chemical and sold 50% of its carbon business to Mitsubishi. In 1991, the company flirted with disaster again when an explosion at the company's Seadrift plant in Texas contributed to an annual loss of $116 million. Union Carbide announced plans to sell its half interest in Union Carbide India, Ltd., the largest maker of dry cell batteries in India, in April of 1992. The firm also announced the establishment of a charitable trust of $17 million to ensure funding of a hospital in Bhopal; the company initially offered to underwrite the hospital in 1986. Funding for the trust came from UCC's $16 million in common shares in UCIL.

The company also introduced the development of a new lubricant that represented a step forward in the quest to phase out ozone-destroying chlorofluorocarbons. Union Carbide was the first U.S.-based firm to develop and market this type of product. UCON Refrigeration Lubricant 488 was a synthetic material from the polymer family. The item would enable car makers to convert to the new refrigerant without having to make major modifications to existing A/C systems.

By August of 1994, plans were underway to form a joint venture with EniChem SpA of Milan, Italy, to produce polyethylene for the European market. If approved, the joint venture would enable the companies to build an additional polyethylene facility in Priolo, Italy. The company invested $200 million in new capacity, including a $1.5 billion Kuwait petrochemical plant slated to be completed in 1997. The next year Union Carbide was investing aggressively in its core businesses, including several European joint ventures that Carbide expected would make it the largest global polyethylene producer. The firm was emerging as the low-cost producer of polyethylene and ethyl glycol.

After a drastic, long-term restructuring following the Bhopal tragedy in 1984, Union Carbide consolidated its assets in North America and reduced employment from 100,000 in the early 1980s to 12,000. Sales dropped from approximately $10 billion in the mid-

1980s to roughly $5 billion, but the company's profitability and stock price remained strong. In 1995, Chairman Robert D. Kennedy retired and CEO William H. Joyce succeeded him. One year later Union Carbide completed the purchase of Shell Oil Co.'s polypropylene plastic assets, which Shell was forced to sell by the U.S. Federal Trade Commission to encourage competition in the polypropylene market. The acquisition gave Union Carbide the remaining 50% of a joint polypropylene business that it ran jointly with Shell. In April of 1996, the Nova Corp. of Alberta and Union Carbide planned to build a $825 million ethylene plant in Joffre, Alberta, to meet the growing global demand for ethylene. Nova officials were optimistic that this venture would enable them to produce about 2.4 million tons of ethylene per year, about 10% of the total world production.

Union Carbide, which had cut operating expenses $575 million since 1991, was planning another $637 million in cuts by the year 2000. It also planned to focus on its core chemical business by investing $282 million into those operations. The company formed a joint venture with Shanghai Petrochemical to build a new petrochemical plant in China.

Union Carbide pursued partnerships in the late 1990s, including relationships with Exxon Univation Technologies to make low-cost polyethylene, and with Tosco to produce polypropylene. The company also planned to build a plant in Malaysia with Petronas.

Market Forces Driving the Merger

Ralston Purina's cash flow was estimated to be over $1 billion by 1988. Stiritz, the company's chairman, felt Ralston would be flagged as a takeover target if he didn't take action to ward off potential buyers and decrease cash flow. He implemented a stock buyback program in 1983 to increase long term debt, and was looking into acquisitions to do the same. By purchasing Union Carbide's battery division, the company's total debt load would rise to $1.8 billion.

At the same time, Union Carbide was looking for a buyers to snatch up its consumer products business. In an attempt to thwart another takeover attempt by GAF, a specialty chemical and building materials company, Carbide was selling this division in hopes of increasing shareholder value. The company planned to rid itself of Eveready and Energizer, which Ralston eagerly agreed to purchase, and other products such as Prestone antifreeze and Glad plastic bags. The sale of these brands was expected to bring in over $2.3 billion for Carbide, helping Carbide to fend off future attempts by GAF and raising the value of its stock.

Approach and Engagement

With Ralston looking to purchase and Union Carbide pushing to sell, the two joined up to lessen risks of takeover. In January, GAF launched a hostile takeover bid of Carbide. Carbide loaded itself up with $4.1 billion in debt when it took out loans to buy back 116 million shares of its own stock in order to fend off the chemical giant, and wanted to sell off some of its assets to pay off that debt and increase share value. At the same time, Ralston was swimming in excess cash flow. The company wanted to increase its debt as the abundant reserves made it a target for takeover, as well.

In April of 1986 Ralston announced that it would buy Union Carbide's Eveready and Energizer battery division for $1.4 billion, ending its search for a lucrative business deal that would increase debt, yet still be economically sound in the long run. Stiritz was quoted in *The New York Times* as stating "I've never seen an opportunity such as this. There is real quality and value. Eveready has a market share that exceeds 60%. It's in a market that has only two competitors—itself and Dart & Kraft's Duracell."

Products and Services

Upon completion of the acquisition of Union Carbide's battery division, Ralston Purina gained 60% of the market share for batteries. With the brand names of Energizer and Eveready, battery products accounted for 45% of total sales for the company in 1998. Ralston remained a leader in the pet products industry as well. Leading brands included Tidy Cat and Tidy Cat Scoop cat litter, Meow Mix cat food, Purina Dog Chow, Purina Cat Chow, Tender Vittles, and Field 'n Farm. With sales of $2.6 billion in 1998, pet products accounted for 55% of total sales. Ralston serviced the United States, Europe, Asia, and South and Central America.

Changes to the Industry

Union Carbide ended its run in the consumer products industry in July of 1986 when it sold its battery division to Ralston and spun off its other home and automotive products to a group led by First Boston Corp. for $800 million. The two competing companies left standing in the industry were Ralston Purina with Eveready and Energizer, and Dart & Kraft with Duracell.

The battery industry was growing at a rate of more than 5% per year with the steady popularity of portable radios and tape players, as well as electronic games and toys. Companies in the packaged consumer goods industry were looking to break into that market. Ralston, which specialized in pet products, and Kraft, known throughout the world for its cheese, were two examples of company diversification to capitalize on growth in different markets.

Review of the Outcome

After the merger, Ralston Purina became the world's largest manufacturer of dry cell battery products. It was also the largest producer of dog and cat foods, sold under the name of Purina.

Upon completion of the merger, J. Patrick Mulahy was named chairman and CEO of Ralston's new Eveready Battery Co. Over 90% of the company's earning were now coming from packaged consumer goods products. In 1987, the company earned net income of $526.4 million, boasted 58,298 employees, and operated in more than 160 countries.

Research

Cuff, Daniel. "Sale by Carbide Seen," in *The New York Times*, 18 April 1986. Explains Union Carbide's interest in selling off its consumer products business.

Dreyfack, Kenneth. "What Purina Really Wanted from Carbide," in *Business Week*, 21 April 1986. Discusses Ralston's motive for the acquisition.

Greenhouse, Steven. "Ralston Aiming at New Area," in *The New York Times*, 8 April 1986. Reports Ralston's plans to diversify into the battery industry.

Hiltzik, Michael. "Union Carbide Plans to Sell off $1 Billion More of Assets," in *Los Angeles Times*, 8 April 1986. Details Ralston's purchase and Carbide's efforts to ward off takeover attempts.

"Ralston Purina Acquires Carbide Battery Division," in *Financial Times London*, 19 April 1986. Lists details of the acquisition.

"Ralston Purina Co.," in *Notable Corporate Chronologies*, The Gale Group, 1999. List major events in the history of Ralston Purina Co.

Ralston Purina Co. Home Page, available at http://www.ralston.com. Official World Wide Web Home Page for Ralston Purina Co. Includes current and archived news, and detailed financial and product information.

"Robert D. Kennedy Named to the Board of General Signal," in *Business Wire*, 21 October 1996. Discusses the career of Robert Kennedy.

"Union Carbide Acts," in *The San Diego Union-Tribune*, 15 July 1986. Details Union Carbide's sale of consumer products assets.

"Union Carbide Corp.," in *Notable Corporate Chronologies*, The Gale Group, 1999. Lists major events in the history of Union Carbide Corp.

CHRISTINA M. STANSELL

RAYTHEON & HUGHES AIRCRAFT

Raytheon Co.
141 Spring St.
Lexington, MA 02421
USA

tel: (781)862-6600
fax: (781)860-2172
web: http://www.raytheon.com

nationality: USA
date: October 1997
affected: Raytheon Co., USA, founded 1922
affected: Hughes Aircraft Co., USA, founded 1913

Overview of the Merger

The agreement to purchase Hughes Aircraft was the fourth purchase by Raytheon in a little more than a year-and-a-half, having acquired E-Systems for $2.3 billion, the Chrysler Defense Business for $475 million, and Texas Instruments Defense Group for $2.95 billion.

Raytheon's acquisition of Hughes Aircraft was seen as a highlight of the many defense industry mergers and acquisitions that took place worldwide during 1997. The company's 1997 missile sales were expected to be more than all of Europe's missile manufacturers combined, and almost twice that of its nearest rival, Lockheed.

History of Raytheon

Incorporated as the American Appliance Co. in 1922, Raytheon was, by the mid-1990s, one of the largest and most diversified American companies. In addition to facilities in 28 states and Washington, D.C., it had offices and manufacturing facilities in Europe, the Middle East, and the Pacific Rim.

Growing consumer demand for radios and other electronic products in the early 1920s was the impetus for the creation of the American Appliance Company. Laurence Marshall, a civil engineer, physicist Charles Smith, and MIT's Dr. Vannevar Bush originally formed a partnership to pursue development of home refrigeration, but soon recognized that some of Smith and Bush's earlier inventions could be patented to take advantage of increasing interest in radios. The development of the S-tube, which converted AC to DC, created a market for smaller radios than had been possible when both A and a high-voltage B battery had been required.

By 1926 Raytheon (Greek for "god of life") was a major source of S-tubes. However, the next year RCA, one of the radio manufacturers for whom Raytheon was a prime supplier, announced that it would begin producing its own S-tubes.

Rather than quietly accept being shut out of RCA's market, Raytheon diversified, acquiring Acme-Delta Company, a producer of electronic auto parts, transformers, and power equipment. Later in the 1920s, National Carbon Co. took an equity position in the company to market replacement Eveready-Raytheon radio tubes; National Carbon's option to acquire Raytheon lapsed in 1938.

During the Second World War Raytheon was a leading producer of radar (Radio Detection and Ranging) tubes as well as complete radar systems, and following the War it was a leading pioneer in the development of missile guidance. One of its best known products is the Patriot missile system, which is thus far the only such combat-proven system.

Among the other defense equipment manufactured through the Raytheon Electronic Systems division are the Hawk ground-launched missile, ground-based phased-array radars, and the Advanced Medium Range Air-to-Air Missile.

Its Raytheon E-Systems division, acquired in May 1995, is a $2 billion defense and government electronics company. This division specializes in intelligence, reconnaissance, and surveillance systems, command and control, specialized aircraft maintenance and modification, guidance, navigation and control communications, and data systems. Raytheon has expanded from its defense activities into the air traffic control, environmental monitoring, transportation, and data management markets.

Ranked as the country's fifth-largest defense contractor, Raytheon also holds that status in the rankings of appliance manufacturers. Among its consumer items are Caloric cooking ranges, Speed Queen washers and dryers, and Amana microwave ovens. Its general aviation line, led by Beech Aircraft Corp., manufactures a broad line of general aviation products.

History of Hughes Aircraft

Hughes Aircraft, despite the name, hasn't been involved in manufacturing airplanes since the 1950s. Instead, it develops advanced radar and navigation systems. Because of its connection with Howard Hughes, the man who developed the company, though, it is perhaps inevitable that when one hears "Hughes Aircraft" one thinks of planes and the pilot who broke transcontinental and world speed records.

When he was 19, Howard Hughes inherited a family fortune, part of which he used to gain control of the business his father had started in 1913, the Hughes Tool Company. As a manufacturer of oil industry drill bits, the company had become very profitable, and continued to be so after the young Hughes took over.

The Business

Financials

Revenue (1998): $19.5 billion

Employees (1998): 108,000

SICs / NAICS

sic 3812 - Search & Navigation Equipment

sic 3721 - Aircraft

naics 334511 - Search, Detection, Navigation, Guidance, Aeronautical, and Systems

naics 336411 - Aircraft Manufacturing

Soon bored with tools, though, Hughes had a brief fling with Hollywood. Unsatisfied with the performance of several of the stunt pilots in the only successful film he produced, *Hell's Angels*, Hughes performed several feats himself. This proved to be the springboad for his next adventure: aviation.

In the early 1930s, Noah Dietrich, an accountant friend of Hughes, set up Hughes Aircraft Co. mainly to humor Hughes. As a copilot for American Airways, however, Hughes had learned all aspects of the airline business, and soon he collaborated on racing plans and set new transcontinental and world speed records.

Hughes's piloting ability—and his inherited fortune—soon caught the attention of the president of TWA, Jack Frye. Using a $1.6 million loan from Hughes, Frye quickly turned TWA into a world-class airline with the purchase of Boeing 307 Stratoliners.

Then followed a string of unsuccessful military aircraft ventures. The most infamous was the huge flying boat dubbed the *Spruce Goose*, completed two years after the end of the war for which it had been designed. Later, Howard Hughes survived the crash an experimental plane in 1946 and became ever more elusive. He did, however, continue to make increasing amounts of money from Hughes Tool Company, Hughes Aircraft, and TWA.

Meanwhile, the Hughes Aircraft managers were working on armament and military aircraft. At the war's conclusion, the company continued applying the skills it had acquired during the war to the military applications of radar. Originally designed to enable pilots to detect targets when they couldn't see them, radar made the precise firing of fire-guided missiles possible under less-than-optimum conditions.

The Officers

Chairman: Dennis J. Picard

President and CEO: Daniel P. Burnham

Exec. VP; President and COO, Raytheon Systems: Kenneth C. Dahlberg

Exec. VP; Chairman and CEO, Raytheon Systems: William H. Swanson

Exec. VP, Business Development; Chairman, Raytheon International: John C. Weaver

Exec. VP; Chairman and CEO, Raytheon Aircraft: Arthur E. Wegner

In 1947 Hughes introduced its first radar product, won an exploratory development contract for a guided missile, and received an Atomic Energy Commission contract to design and build an electronic measuring instrument for experiments with high explosives.

Six years later the Hughes Medical Institute was created to promote medical research and to be the recipient of all of stock in the newly developed Hughes Aircraft Company, formed from the Aircraft Division of Hughes Tool Company.

Market Forces Driving the Merger

The merger of Hughes Aircraft with Raytheon was based on a shrinking market in the late 1990s for defense industry products. Defense procurement spending had fallen from a peak of $127 billion in 1985 to $43 billion in 1997, a drop of 66 percent. Raytheon's chairman and CEO said: "It is clear that the end of the Cold War, and the resulting decline in the U.S. defense procurement budget, have brought about fundamental changes to the defense industry requiring continued consolidation." Similarly, Hughes Electronics chairman and CEO C. Michael Armstrong said, "For Hughes Aircraft to remain competitive in a shrinking market, there was a need to increase its participation in the industry consolidation."

Approach and Engagement

The Chairman of General Motors, John F. Smith, Jr., announcement the Hughes Aircraft merger with Raytheon in January 1997. General Motors had purchased Hughes Aircraft in 1985, combining it with subsidiary Delco Electronics to form GM Hughes Electronics. At the time of that merger, it was said that the two entities would be independently managed. When Hughes merged with Raytheon, Delco was transferred back to GM, where it became a part of Delphi.

The combined GM spin-off of Hughes Aircraft Co. from Hughes Electronics and the tax-free merger with Raytheon had an indicated total value of $9.5 billion to GM and its stockholders. The $9.5 billion was comprised of approximately $5.1 billion in common stock and $4.4 billion in debt. On a 1996 pro-forma basis, the combined company had revenues of approximately $21 billion, of which over $13 billion was in defense electronics.

Hughes Aircraft incurred between $3.7 billion and $4.7 billion of new debt immediately before the spin off. The proceeds were used primarily to fund Hughes Electronics telecommunications and space businesses.

The Justice Department agreed to allow the merger if Raytheon divested itself of two defense electronics businesses that produced electro-optical equipment for Army ground vehicles. The divestment was necessary, according to the Justice Department, "in order to preserve competition in sophisticated technology for U.S. weapon systems." While it had conditionally approved the merger, under antitrust law the Department was required to file suit in federal court to make legally binding the agreement in which Raytheon pledged to divest two technology businesses.

The agreement also forbade Raytheon and Hughes from disclosing information—to each other and to Raytheon's senior management—on the development and production of a new antitank missile for the Army. Raytheon and Hughes were both competing for the Army's Follow-On to TOW (FOTT) contract.

In addition, the Justice's Antitrust agency also approved another agreement with Raytheon regarding pricing on its Advanced Medium-Range Air-to-Air Missile (AMRAAM). The Air Force, whose approval was a condition of the Raytheon Hughes merger, had feared that, by consolidating AMRAAM suppliers, it could be forced to pay higher prices in the future. When Raytheon agreed to firm pricing for AMRAAM, the Air Force granted its approval and the U.S. Department of Justice gave its consent to merger on October 16, 1997.

Products and Services

Raytheon has five subsidiaries: Aircraft Products, Commercial Group, Engineers & Constructors, Raytheon Systems Company, and Raytheon Systems

Limited. Its electronic products, among them air defense and traffic control systems, marine electronics, missile (Hawk, Patriot, and Tomahawk) systems, and weather detection systems, account for 76% of its sales. Its aircraft, including Beech Baron personal and business aircraft and the T-1A Jayhawk military training jet, is responsible for another 13% of sales, and the balance (11%) comes from the engineering and construction sector that designs, constructs, and maintains heavy industrial plans.

Raytheon Systems has five segments: Defense Systems; Sensors and Electronic Systems; Command, Control and Communications (C3) Systems; Intelligence, Information and Aircraft Integration systems; and Training and Services. Each is managed by a Raytheon Systems Executive Vice President. The company's contribution to Raytheon Company's 1998 $20 billion revenues was approximately $14.5.

Changes to the Industry

The $9.5 billion merger reduced competition, generating both positive (including some from competitor Lockheed) and negative reactions. One area of agreement upon which both camps agreed was that Raytheon's acquisition of Hughes Aircraft highlighted the late 1990s wave of defense industry acquisitions and mergers.

Some, like Lockheed Martin CEO Norman Augustine, quoted in *Defense Daily*, believed that the deal would be good for the industry. He wished "the market were big enough to support both a Raytheon and a Hughes, but it's not and so I think it's inevitable. It can either be done now logically and proactively, or we can wait until both companies grind down in terms of defense capabilities until they are both very weak. It's the right thing to do. It will make a tougher competitor for us and that's okay."

On the other side, critics claimed that the combination of Raytheon with Hughes would create an air-to-air missile producer monopoly. The two companies were the only makers of air-launched anti-aircraft missiles. Government officials, financial analysts, and Pentagon spokespeople said that prices were bound to rise with only one supplier.

Raytheon Systems was expected to be a leader in several markets, with 80% of the country's missile market, 60% of the electro-optics market, and 50% each of the radar and air traffic control markets. The combined technical and business skills of Hughes with Raytheon made the company able to compete for large contracts independently rather than the teaming up that each had been forced to do in the past.

The Players

Raytheon Chairman and CEO: Dennis J. Piccard. Piccard was chief of Raytheon at the time of the Hughes Aircraft merger. He had been president and a director since 1989, and CEO since 1991.

Raytheon Systems Chairman and CEO: William H. Swanson. Prior to assuming his CEO duties at Raytheon Systems, Mr. Swanson had, since 1995, been Executive Vice President and General Manager of Raytheon Electronic Systems Division. He also served as Senior Vice President and General Manager of the company's Missile System Division.

General Motors Chairman, CEO, and President: John F. Smith, Jr. Board Chairman Smith is CEO and President as well as a member of the Board's Finance Committee. He is also on the boards of Hughes Electronics Corp., Electronic Data Systems Corp., and Proctor and Gamble.

Review of the Outcome

Raytheon doubled its size in 1997 when it bought Texas Institute's missile and defense electronics, along with Hughes Electronics' defense business, Hughes Aircraft.

In 1998 the company cut approximately 14,000 defense jobs (16% of its defense workforce) and announced that it would close 28 defense facilities within two years. Additionally, it let 1,000 engineering and construction workers go.

Considering the lay-offs, the report that Raytheon chief executive Daniel P. Burnham had received $26.8 million during the preceding year did not sit well with government officials and some compensation experts. Combined with the annual salary and bonus of $4.5 million given to Burnham's predecessor Daniel P. Picard, executive pay seemed excessive to many who felt that the money would be better used to rehire employees.

Research

Drosnin, Michael. *Citizen Hughes*, Rinehart and Winston, 1985.

"GM Hughes Electronic Corp.," in *International Directory of Company Histories*, Vol. 2, St. James Press: 1990.

Kerber, Ross. "Burham Well-Paid in 1998," in *Boston Globe*, 31 March 1999.

Macrae, Dunan. "Raytheon-Hughes Building Electronics Dream Team?" in *Interavia Business & Technology*, May 1997.

Muradian, Vago, "Justice Files Suit Seeking Raytheon-Hughes Merger Approval," in *Defense Daily* 20 October 1997.

"Raytheon Company," in *International Directory of Company Histories*, Vol. 11, St. James Press: 1995.

Sutton, Oliver, "Raytheon Completes Hughes Merger," in *Interavia Business & Technology*, January 1998.

BARBARA J. KELLY

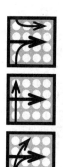

REED ELSEVIER & MEAD DATA CENTRAL

nationality: United Kingdom
date: December 1994
affected: Reed Elsevier PLC, United Kingdom, founded 1993
affected: TheMead Corp., USA, founded 1846

Reed Elsevier PLC
25 Victoria St.
London, SW1H 0EX
United Kingdom

tel: 44 (0)171 222 8420
fax: 44 (0)171 227 5799
web: http://www.reed-elsevier.com

Overview of the Acquisition

Reed Elsevier, an Anglo-Dutch publishing company, forged entry into the electronic publishing arena by acquiring Mead Data Central in 1994. This unit was comprised of a number of electronic information services, namely LEXIS and NEXIS. Reed Elsevier took advantage of that product name recognition and renamed the unit LEXIS-NEXIS. It also injected it with the resources to capture the new technology that it required to remain at the top of its field.

History of Reed Elsevier PLC

Elsevier NV, the first large Dutch publishing company, was formed in 1880 as a pooling of the interests of several publishers and booksellers. It initially focused on small-scale publishing for the general trade market. The company's name became well known as the publisher of Dutch translations of the novels by Jules Verne.

Meanwhile Albert Reed established a newsprint manufacturing facility in Kent, England, in 1894. In 1903 that concern, Albert E. Reed & Co., incorporated as a public company. In 1929 it diversified into the manufacture of packaging and multiwall paper products, and formed the Medway Corrugated Paper Co. Elsevier diversified as well, entering the scientific publishing field in the 1930s, and into consumer magazines, newspapers, business manuals, and commercial printing after World War II.

In 1954 Reed entered the building products field with the manufacture of pitch fiber pipes. It expanded into New Zealand the following year, followed by Canada in 1960. Reed acquired Wall Paper Manufacturers Ltd. in 1965 and General Paint in 1966. In 1970 it also acquired International Publishing Corporation Ltd., Mirror Group Newspaper, and 29% of Cahners Publishing. The firm changed its name twice that year, first to Reed Group Ltd. and then to Reed International PLC, to reflect its geographical expansion and diversified product range. By 1971 the company was recognized as one of the U.K.'s largest conglomerates, with a workforce of 84,000 and turnover of GBP 502 million.

The Business

Financials

Revenue (1998): GBP 3.2 billion

Employees (1998): 26,100

SICs / NAICS

sic 7375 - Information Retrieval Services

sic 2721 - Periodicals

sic 2731 - Book Publishing

sic 2741 - Miscellaneous Publishing

naics 514191 - On-Line Information Services

naics 511120 - Periodical Publishers

naics 511130 - Book Publishers

naics 511140 - Database and Directory Publishers

Elsevier entered the U.S. market in 1979 with the purchase of Congressional Information Service. This acquisition contributed to the company's strategy of becoming a leader in publishing and information for the English-language markets. To further this end, Elsevier divested itself of its commercial printing and book publishing operations.

By the early 1980s, Reed's diversification strategy proved to be a burden, as the company experienced difficulty in coordinating its activities. The company decided to focus on its core publishing business, selling off the Mirror Group to Robert Maxwell in 1984. By 1987 it had divested all other nonpublishing and nonpaper businesses. It continued to expand its core operations through acquisitions. Reed purchased the publisher R.R. Bowker in 1985; the second-largest book publisher in the U.K., Octopus Publishing, in 1987; TV Times and Travel Information Group in 1989; and Martindale-Hubbell in 1990.

During this time, Elsevier was involved in a number of takeovers. In 1987 it launched a hostile bid for Kluwer, the third-largest publisher in The Netherlands, but was defeated by Wolters Samson when the two merged to form Wolters Kluwer. Robert Maxwell initiated a takeover bid for Elsevier in 1988, but was thwarted when Elsevier arranged a merger with Pearson, a U.K.-based publisher. This merger later failed, and in 1991 Elsevier purchased Pergamon Press from Maxwell. By 1992 Elsevier was the world's leader in scholarly journal publication.

On January 1, 1993, Reed International and Elsevier NV created Reed Elsevier as a joint venture to house their publishing and information businesses. At the same time, those two parent companies also formed Elsevier Reed Finance BV to hold their finance activities. That year Reed Elsevier purchased the France-based legal publisher Editions Techniques and Robert Maxwell's Official Airlines Guides (OAG). By the end of that year it had generated revenues of GBP 2.7 billion.

Reed International and Elsevier NV both gained listings on the New York Stock Exchange in 1994 to increase their presence in the U.S. market. The following year, Reed Elsevier purchased the Mead Data Central unit of Mead Corp. At that time, with over $9 billion in capital, Reed Elsevier was recognized as the third-largest publishing and information company in the world.

History of The Mead Corp.

Colonel Daniel Mead and his partners formed Ellis, Chafflin & Co. in 1846. The enterprise produced book and other printing papers at a mill in Dayton, Ohio. It succeeded through a number of owners and company names, until in 1882 it became the Mead Paper Co. Under the leadership of Daniel Mead's sons, Charles and Harry Mead, the company floundered beneath rising debts. Banks began calling in the company's loans due to the losses it had incurred by 1902. Two years later Mead became a trustee of several bankers. In 1905 they turned to George Mead, Harry Mead's business-minded son, requesting that he take the helm of Mead. George reorganized the firm as the Mead Pulp and Paper Co., instituting production efficiencies and raising funds through an initial public offering. Profits reached almost $25,000 in 1908, marking the beginning of long-term prosperity for the company.

Mead began expanding through acquisition, purchasing the Peerless Paper Co. in 1917. The following year, the company began marketing its engineering services to other paper companies. Mead diversified into white paper production and the manufacture of paperboard in 1923. Four years later the Mead Paperboard Corp. was founded as a holding company for its paperboard operations, which included Sylvia Paperboard Co., The Harriman Co., The Southern Extract Co., and the Chillicothe Co.

Its acquisitions of Dill & Collins and the George W. Wheelwright Co. in the early 1930s provided Mead with established names and well-developed distribution systems. In 1936 it joined with Scott Paper Co. to build the Brunswick Pulp & Paper Co. to reduce its dependence on imported pulp and to enter the kraft linerboard business. In 1942 Mead purchased a small white-paper mill from the Escanaba Paper Co; this mill became one of Mead's largest operations.

Mead purchased the Manistique Pulp and Paper Co. in 1943 and the Columbia Paper Co. three years later. The mid-1950s marked the beginning of a growth period for Mead, as the company diversified beyond its traditional paper products. It entered the container business with the acquisition of Jackson Box Co., the specialty paper industry with the purchase of Hurlbut Paper, and the wholesale distribution business with the acquisition of Cleveland Paper Co. The packaging business that it entered with the purchase of the Atlanta Paper Co. later invented the familiar paper six-pack carrier for bottled beverages.

In 1966 Mead acquired Westab, an educational products supplier. Two years later it purchased the Woodward Corp., a maker of pipe and pipe fittings, castings, and chemicals. It also paid $6 million to acquire the computer software producer Data Corp. as a hedge in the possible evolution from paper-based to electronic publishing.

Mead's acquisition spree came to a halt in 1971, when the company was hit by an economic recession. As a result of declining profits, Mead began to sell off some of its earlier acquisitions, and by 1976 had divested itself of $80 million worth of interests in low-growth markets. That year Mead Data Central was formed as a subsidiary whose primary products were LEXIS, a computer-assisted legal research service, and NEXIS, a news and business information database.

By 1975 sales and profits were on the upturn. Two years later, in one of the largest price-fixing lawsuits in U.S. legal history, Franklin Container Corp. and Tim-Bar Corp. filed a $1.2 billion antitrust suit against Mead and eight other box makers for allegedly fixing prices and driving smaller operations out of business. Mead was found not guilty of the criminal charges but guilty of civil charges, for which it agreed in 1982 to pay $45 million in settlement.

A depressed paper industry caused Mead to report a loss of $86 million in 1982, its first such loss since 1938. It initiated a divestiture program to reduce its debt load by selling off products outside of its focus on forest products and electronic publishing, while adding to operations in those core areas. It acquired the Micromedex medical database in 1985, the office supply producer Ampad in 1986, the paper distributor Zellerbach in 1988, and The Michie Co., a legal publisher of state statutes, in 1989.

Business began to improve in 1984 as its electronic information-retrieval services became profitable. Mead Data Central was growing at a rate of 43% per year and captured about 75% of the computerized legal research market by decade's end. That unit had negotiated in the previous year to secure exclusive license for the archives of *The New York Times*, gaining

The Officers

Non-Executive Chairman: Morris Tabaksblat

Co-Chief Executive Officer: Herman Bruggink

Co-Chief Executive Officer: Nigel Stapleton

Chief Financial Officer: Mark Armour

Executive Director: Onno Laman Trip

Executive Director: Herman Spruijt

NEXIS the perpetual rights to its content. The success of LEXIS sparked a 1988 lawsuit by West Publishing Co., which claimed copyright infringement, to which Mead responded by filing an antitrust countersuit; the settlement granted Mead Data Central the rights to offer West-copyrighted material on LEXIS.

In 1991, although its sales approached $4.6 billion, Mead's earnings suffered in the recessionary economy. The company refocused on paper business, selling Micromedex, Ampad, and Mead Data Central. In 1994 it acquired Hilroy, a school and office products producer in Canada. In 1998 Mead sold its Zellerbach distribution business to International Paper and its Mead Ink Products company to Alper Ink Group.

Market Forces Driving the Acquisition

By the mid-1990s, many publishing companies regarded the future of much of the industry being played out on the Information Superhighway. Publishers in increasing numbers were issuing electronic version of their products, releasing them online as well as on CD-ROM and diskette. One such publisher was Reed Elsevier. This Anglo-Dutch company was a world-leading publisher and information provider for the scientific, professional, and business communities. Its strengths were primarily in its numerous print products, and it was seeking entry into the electronic publishing arena. It also wanted to increase its presence in English-speaking countries, particularly the U.S., as well as to enhance revenues in subscription-based operations.

Meanwhile, just as the online revolution was sweeping through the world, the Mead Corp. wanted out of this area. Mead was a huge paper products concern, noted as a leader in school supplies. Mead Data Central (MDC), which housed the company's electronic information operations, had been build as a hedge against a paperless future. By the mid-1990s, however, Mead perceived a perpetual demand for forest products, and wanted to return to those roots, so to speak. By selling off MDC, Mead could use the pro-

The Players

Reed Elsevier Chairman: Pierre Vinken. Pierre Vinken was co-chairman of Reed Elsevier from 1993 until he retired from that post in 1995. At that time he was appointed Chairman of the Supervisory Board of Elsevier. In April 1999, Vinken and Loek van Vollenhoven resigned as directors of Reed Elsevier. Previously, Vinken was a director of Pearson PLC and The Economist Group, and served on the board of Logica Netherlands and Logica PLC.

Mead Data Central President: Rodney L. Everhart. After earning a degree in management from the University of Illinois, Rodney Everhart held jobs at Systems & Computer Technology Corp. and General Electric Co. He joined Mead Data Central in 1989 as a Vice President of Financial Resources and Administration. He became president of that unit of Mead Corp. in 1992, and oversaw its acquisition by Reed Elsevier in 1994. Upon completion of the merger, Everhart served as president and COO of the unit, renamed LEXIS-NEXIS, until he resigned in March 1995. At that point he joined the communications software company Bellcore as senior Vice President and Chief Financial Officer.

ceeds to reduce debt and add to its core forest product operations, including pulp, paper, packaging, paperboard, containerboard, and school and office supplies.

During the time that Mead had wavered over the focus of its future, it had been reluctant to inject MDC with the resources required to stay on top of emerging technology. MDC was still the world's largest legal and news service, but was witnessing competitors gain on it. The WESTLAW Service of West Publishing rivaled LEXIS, MDC's legal online information service. In 1993 LEXIS was the industry leader, capturing a 42.9% market share, with WESTLAW a not-too-distant rival with a 31.8% share. While both services were about equal in terms of case law information, state statutes, and public records, WESTLAW 's synopses and natural language search software enabled it to capture a growing edge. LEXIS was also facing competition from the government sector. Circuit courts were beginning to release free daily electronic opinions, and federal court information was to be released by the Justice Department under the Freedom of Information Act.

Their respective goals and visions suggested that Reed Elsevier and MDC would be a good match. In coming together, these two companies would also realize strategic synergies. Reed Elsevier's entry into electronic publishing would enable it to apply this technology to offer document delivery of its existing library of titles or to fold its products into the LEXIS or NEXIS services. MDC would be in the hands of a company willing to invest in the technology that it had been deprived of under Mead. It would also gain entry into international markets. "Mead Corporation has been a good parent for the last 25 years...but they are not in our business," said Rod Everhart, president of Mead Data Central, in *Searcher*. "We have greater needs for more technology, content, and funding."

Approach and Engagement

On May 16, 1994, the Mead Corp. announced that it was putting Mead Data Central on the auction block. Rumors regarding the identities of potential buyers were compounded by the confidential nature of the sale. Suitors submitted sealed bids to Goldman, Sachs & Co., which would open the bids and declare the winner.

The simplicity of this arrangement was marred by speculation over the role of *The New York Times* in it. This newspaper had the option of terminating its long-time licensing agreement with MDC in the event of a buyout. Without *The New York Times* content, the NEXIS service was far less valuable. This situation may have given the paper the clout to veto the purchase by any company not meeting with its favor, such as the parent of a competing paper. Some industry analysts even suggested that *The New York Times* itself might be a bidder, but many rejected this notion because the paper would have little use for the rest of the MDC package.

On October 4, 1994, Reed Elsevier's bid of $1.5 billion was announced to be the highest, beating out such companies as Thomson Corp. and Times Mirror. That purchase price, representing 2.7 times the amount of MDC's 1993 sales, was pulled together from the company's cash reserves and about $1 billion in financing. In early December, after concluding new licensing agreements with *The New York Times* and other content providers, the acquisition was completed.

MDC's name was changed to LEXIS-NEXIS, but most other elements remained the same. Rodney Everhart continued as president of the unit, which remained located in Dayton, Ohio.

The unit itself was comprised of the LEXIS legal document search service; the NEXIS full-text newspaper and magazine service; the Jurisoft legal citations service; The Michie Company, a legal material publisher; Folio Corp., a full-text retrieval company; and LEXIS Counsel Connect, an online communication vehicle for attorneys.

Products and Services

Reed Elsevier was grouped into three business units:

The **Business Segment** was comprised of two subsegments. Reed Exhibition Companies served the exhibition market by providing event organization services. The other subsegment, comprised of Cahners Business Information, Elsevier Business Information, and Reed Business Information, provided magazines, reference products, and online services to the business community. As a whole, the Business Segment had turnover of GBP 1.4 billion in 1998, representing 44% of total company revenues.

The **Professional Segment** was divided into three units. LEXIS-NEXIS, serving the U.S., and The Reed Elsevier Legal Division, serving areas outside the U.S., provided legal, business, and public records in the form of online databases, reference products, law reports, and journals. In addition to its flagship LEXIS and NEXIS products, the LEXIS-NEXIS group included Martindale Hubbell, Matthew Bender, and Shepard's. The Reed Elsevier Legal Division included Butterworths, Tolley Publishing, Editions du Juris-Classeur, and Verlag Orac. Reed Educational & Professional Publishing served the educational market with books and learning resources, and was comprised of Heinemann, Ginn, Rigby, and Elsevier Opleidingen, which provided courses for the tuition market in Belgium and The Netherlands. In 1998, the Professional Segment generated GBP 1.2 billion in turnover, or 36% of Reed Elsevier's total revenues.

The **Scientific Segment** had two primary subsections. Elsevier Science produced scientific journals, online databases, and reference products. The company's medical publishing and communications businesses together served the medical community by providing conferences, journals, reference products, and online services; these businesses included Excerpta Medica, *The Lancet*, Springhouse Corporation, and Editions Scientifiques et Medicales Elsevier. Turnover for the Scientific Segment reached GBP 622 million in 1998, representing 20% of total company sales.

Changes to the Industry

The post-merger market position of LEXIS-NEXIS didn't change—it remained the world's largest provider of full-text online information. In fact, as the business and professional communities increasingly looked to the Internet for their information needs, LEXIS-NEXIS grew. Its 1998 revenues climbed 13% from the previous year to reach GBP 741 million. Yet as that environment became more lucrative, it also became more competitive. As stated in Reed Elsevier's *Annual Review 1998*, "LEXIS-NEXIS is responding vigorously through the launch of new products and expansion of its sales and marketing activities, together with investment in content and enhanced capabilities to search, link and present information."

Review of the Outcome

In 1995 Reed Elsevier sold Bonaventura's consumer magazines, Cahners Consumer Magazines, Dagbladumie newspapers, and Reed Regional Newspapers. The following year, it purchased the tax and legal publisher Tolley, as well as a 50% stake in the Shepard's Company, a U.S. legal citation service. In 1997 Reed Elsevier acquired the Chilton magazine operations from The Walt Disney Co. That year it announced a merger agreement with Wolters Kluwer NV, but in 1998 the deal was terminated by the boards of Reed International and Elsevier.

In July 1998 it acquired Matthew Bender & Company Inc., a U.S. publisher of legal analysis, and the remaining 50% interest in Shepard's that it didn't already own, thereby strengthening the presence of LEXIS-NEXIS in the U.S. legal market. By the end of that year, Reed Elsevier had completely exited the consumer publishing industry with its sale of IPC Magazines. Turnover at the end of 1998 rose six percent from the previous year to GBP 3.2 billion. In April 1999, a unitary management structure was adopted for Reed International, Elsevier, and Reed Elsevier, whereas the boards of these three companies would be identical. That same month, Pierre Vinken resigned from the board due to its failure to fill the newly created CEO position after an eight-month search.

Research

"Information Industry Mega-Sales: Mead Data Central, Ziff-Davis, et al.," in *Searcher*, July 1994. Profiles the pending acquisition of MDC as well as several other deals in the publishing industry.

"Mead Corp.," in *Notable Corporate Chronologies*, The Gale Group, 1999. Provides historical highlights of the company, including its divestiture of Mead Data Central.

"Mead to Divest Mead Data Central," in *Information Industry Bulletin*, 15 May 1994. Announces the planned sale of MDC, and describes that unit's growth under Mead Corp.

Pemberton, Jeff. "Who Will Buy Mead Data Central...How Much Will They Pay? The New York Times Holds the Key to a News Analysis of the Mead Data Central Sale," in *Online*, July 1994. Speculates on the clout that *The New York Times* might wield in determining the winner of MDC.

"Reed Closes Mead Data Deal, Renegotiates with NY Times," in *Media Daily*, 2 December 1994. Briefly reports the closure of the acquisition deal.

Reed Elsevier Annual Review 1998. Covers financial highlights and describes company operating segments.

"Reed Elsevier PLC," in *Notable Corporate Chronologies*, The Gale Group, 1999. Profiles the history of the company, through and beyond it acquisition of Mead Data Central.

Reed Elsevier PLC Home Page, available at http://www.reed-elsevier.com. Official World Wide Web Page for Reed Elsevier. Includes organizational and product information, press releases, annual reports, and other financial information.

"Reed Elsevier to Spend $1.5 Billion for Mead Data Central," in *Electronic Information Report*, 7 October 1994. Describes the MDC package, and why it appealed to Reed Elsevier.

"Reed to Pay $1.5 Billion for Mead Data Central," in *Information Industry Bulletin*, 13 October 1994. Describes where MDC will fit in at Reed Elsevier.

—DEBORAH J. UNTENER

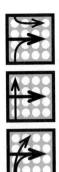

REED ELSEVIER & WOLTERS KLUWER

date: March 9, 1997 (canceled)
affected: Reed Elsevier PLC, United Kingdom, founded 1993
affected: Wolters Kluwer NV, The Netherlands, founded 1987

Reed Elsevier PLC
25 Victoria St.
London, SW1H 0EX
United Kingdom

tel: 44 (0)171 222 8420
fax: 44 (0)171 227 5799
web: http://www.reed-elsevier.com

Wolters Kluwer NV
Stadhouderskade 1, PO Box 818
Amsterdam, NL-1000 AV
The Netherlands

tel: 31 (0)20-60 70 400
fax: 31 (0)20-60 70 490
web: http://www.wolters-kluwer.com
e-mail: info@wolterskluwer.com

Overview of the Merger

In 1997 Reed Elsevier and Wolters Kluwer announced a merger that would have formed the world's largest scientific publishing and information group. Reed Elsevier's strength in scientific publishing and Wolters Kluwer's prowess in the areas of taxation and law would have been complementary—a little too complementary for the comfort of the European Commission. When that government agency ruled that the combined company would have to divest itself of a number of assets, Wolters Kluwer sought to renegotiate the terms of the merger deal. Reed Elsevier refused, and the companies terminated their accord.

History of Reed Elsevier PLC

Elsevier NV, the first large Dutch publishing company, was formed in 1880 as a pooling of the interests of several publishers and booksellers. It initially focused on small-scale publishing for the general trade market. The company's name became well known as the publisher of Dutch translations of the novels by Jules Verne.

Meanwhile Albert Reed established a newsprint manufacturing facility in Kent, England, in 1894. In 1903 that concern, Albert E. Reed & Co., incorporated as a public company. In 1929 it diversified into the manufacture of packaging and multiwall paper products, and formed the Medway Corrugated Paper Co. Elsevier diversified as well, entering the scientific publishing field in the 1930s, and into consumer magazines, newspapers, business manuals, and commercial printing after World War II.

In 1954 Reed entered the building products field with the manufacture of pitch fiber pipes. It expanded into New Zealand the following year, followed by Canada in 1960. Reed acquired Wall Paper Manufacturers Ltd. in 1965 and General Paint in 1966. In 1970 it also acquired International Publishing Corporation Ltd., Mirror Group Newspaper, and 29% of Cahners Publishing. The firm changed its name twice that year, first to Reed Group Ltd. and then to Reed International PLC, to reflect its geographical expansion and diversified product range. By 1971 the company was recognized as one of the U.K.'s largest conglomerates, with a workforce of 84,000 and turnover of GBP 502 million.

The Business

Financials - Reed Elsevier PLC

Revenue (1998): GBP 3.2 billion

Employees (1998): 26,100

Financials - Wolters Kluwer NV

Revenue (1998): Dfl 6.04 billion

Employees (1998): 17,431

SICs / NAICS

sic 7375 - Information Retrieval Services

sic 2721 - Periodicals

sic 2731 - Book Publishing

sic 2741 - Miscellaneous Publishing

naics 514191 - On-Line Information Services

naics 511120 - Periodical Publishers

naics 511130 - Book Publishers

naics 511140 - Database and Directory Publishers

Elsevier entered the U.S. market in 1979 with the purchase of Congressional Information Service. This acquisition contributed to the company's strategy of becoming a leader in publishing and information for the English-language markets. To further this end, Elsevier divested itself of its commercial printing and book publishing operations.

By the early 1980s, Reed's diversification strategy proved to be a burden, as the company experienced difficulty in coordinating its activities. The company decided to focus on its core publishing business, selling off the Mirror Group to Robert Maxwell in 1984. By 1987 it had divested all other nonpublishing and nonpaper businesses. It continued to expand its core operations through acquisitions. Reed purchased the publisher R.R. Bowker in 1985; the second-largest book publisher in the U.K., Octopus Publishing, in 1987; TV Times and Travel Information Group in 1989; and Martindale-Hubbell in 1990.

During this time, Elsevier was involved in a number of takeovers. In 1987 it launched a hostile bid for Kluwer, the third-largest publisher in The Netherlands, but was defeated by Wolters Samson when the two merged to form Wolters Kluwer. Robert Maxwell initiated a takeover bid for Elsevier in 1988, but was thwarted when Elsevier arranged a merger with Pearson, a U.K.-based publisher. This merger

later failed, and in 1991 Elsevier purchased Pergamon Press from Maxwell. By 1992 Elsevier was the world's leader in scholarly journal publication.

On January 1, 1993, Reed International and Elsevier NV created Reed Elsevier as a joint venture to house their publishing and information businesses. At the same time, those two parent companies also formed Elsevier Reed Finance BV to hold their finance activities. That year Reed Elsevier purchased the France-based legal publisher Editions Techniques and Robert Maxwell's Official Airlines Guides (OAG). By the end of that year it had generated revenues of GBP 2.7 billion.

Reed International and Elsevier NV both gained listings on the New York Stock Exchange in 1994 to increase their presence in the U.S. market. The following year, Reed Elsevier purchased the Mead Data Central unit of Mead Corp. At that time, with over $9 billion in capital, Reed Elsevier was recognized as the third-largest publishing and information company in the world.

The first few years of the newly formed Reed Elsevier involved the continuation of the acquisition and divestiture strategies of its parent companies. In 1995 it sold Bonaventura's consumer magazines, Cahners Consumer Magazines, Dagbladumie newspapers, and Reed Regional Newspapers. The following year, it purchased the tax and legal publisher Tolley, as well as a 50% stake in the Shepard's Company, a U.S. legal citation service. In 1997 Reed Elsevier acquired the Chilton magazine operations from The Walt Disney Co.

History of Wolters Kluwer NV

J.B. Wolters founded the Schoolbook publishing house in 1836 in Groningen, The Netherlands, to produce educational and instructional materials. After the company passed to his brother-in-law, E.B. ter Horst, in 1860, it underwent a period of expansion, adding a printing shop and bindery to its operations. The company, now known as J.B. Wolters Publishing Co., was incorporated in 1882. Just after the turn of the century, it reorganized as a corporation and brought in the first directors from outside the family.

The new management served Wolters well, and it opened offices in The Hague and in what is now known as Jakarta, Indonesia, to provide books for the Dutch population there. The Great Depression, a modernization of Dutch grammar and spelling, and World War II caused setbacks for the company, but it rebounded after the war.

A postwar wave of mergers affected the Dutch publishing industry. The Noordoff publishing house, founded in 1858 by P. Noordoff to serve the educational and vocational market, was located directly next door to Wolter's office in Groningen. Noordoff and Wolters decided to join forces to increase their competitiveness against the industry's increasingly large publishing companies, and in 1968 completed a merger. Four years later, it merged again, with Information and Communication Union (ICU).

ICU had its roots with Nicolas Samson, who in 1883 established a publishing house for new administrative forms made necessary by the modernization of Dutch law. The company's output gradually came to include periodicals and books for the administrative market, and in 1920 it began offering educational materials. Samson's firm continued to prosper, achieving a national reputation. In 1970 it merged with the publisher A.W. Sijthoff to form ICU. This company itself merged with Wolters Noordoff in 1972, and the combined entity changed its name to Wolters Samson in 1983.

The fourth and final principal component of the modern Wolters Kluwer NV was founded in the 1880s by A.E. Kluwer. This bookseller-turned-author entered the publishing industry in 1892 with the publication of one of the first trade papers aimed at the educational market. It expanded to include business, tax, and professional publications. The company flourished through domestic and international expansion, and by 1986 it was The Netherlands' third-largest publisher.

In 1987 Elsevier NV, the nation's largest publisher, announced a hostile bid for Kluwer. When it was unable to talk Elsevier out of its bid, Kluwer approached Wolters Samson to discuss a friendly merger between the two. Wolters Samson agreed, thereby setting off a race between it and Elsevier to acquire the majority of Kluwer's stock. Elsevier came very close on August 3, 1987, when it captured 48.2%, but on August 14 Wolters Samson acquired a 50.9% controlling interest. The new company was called Wolters Kluwer NV, of which Elsevier eventually sold off its 33% stake.

Wolters Kluwer immediately became second-largest publisher in The Netherlands, and began a period of foreign expansion through acquisition. By 1989 about 44% of its revenues were generated internationally. It moved to focus on the lucrative tax and legal markets, dropping most trade and consumer operations. Seeking to increase its presence in the U.S., it paid $250 million in 1990 to purchase J.B. Lippincott & Co. from HarperCollins. The opening of the European borders in 1992 spurred the company to devote more operations toward the translation of new laws and regulations into a variety of languages.

The Officers

Reed Elsevier PLC

Non-Executive Chairman: Morris Tabaksblat

Co-Chief Executive Officer: Herman Bruggink

Co-Chief Executive Officer: Nigel Stapleton

Chief Financial Officer: Mark Armour

Executive Director: Onno Laman Trip

Executive Director: Herman Spruijt

Wolters Kluwer NV

Chairman, Executive Board: Caspar H. van Kempen

Deputy Chairman, Executive Board: R. Pieterse

CFO and Corporate Director, Finance & Accounting: J.E. M. van Dinter

Corporate Director, Technology: A.S. F. Kuipers

Corporate Director, Human Resources: M. H. Sanders

Wolters Kluwer increased the holdings in its core businesses, adding Commerce Clearing House (CCH), a U.S.-based publisher of tax guides, in 1995.

Market Forces Driving the Merger

Consolidation in the publishing industry continued at a rapid pace in the 1990s. Reed Elsevier and Wolters Kluwer, both of which had been formed through mergers themselves, joined the ranks of the world's leaders by acquiring small- and mid-sized publishing houses. Such acquisition activity enabled the large companies to get even larger, thereby widening the gap between the giants and the rest of the pack. To stay competitive, the leaders were forced to continue to form unions, lest they become potential takeover targets themselves.

Both Reed Elsevier and Wolters Kluwer possessed rich histories in professional and scientific publishing. Wolters Kluwer was the world's second-largest publishing concern, with particular strengths in the tax, legal, and medical segments. Reed Elsevier was the third-largest publisher, delivering strong products in science and business, and controlling the LEXIS-NEXIS online law and business information services. A combined company, with sales in the professional market of $4.66 billion in 1996, would usurp The Thomson Corp., which had professional revenues of $3.39 billion, as the world's largest professional publisher. McGraw-Hill would become a distant third, with $1.37 billion in professional revenues in 1996.

The Players

Reed Elsevier Co-Chairman: Nigel Stapleton. Nigel Stapleton joined Reed International as a finance director in 1986. He became deputy chairman of that company in 1994, moving up to chairman in 1997. Meanwhile, he was named co-chairman of Reed Elsevier in 1996. Had the merger with Wolters Kluwer gone through, Stapleton would have become the new company's co-deputy chief executive. In August 1998 he was named co-chief executive of Reed Elsevier.

Wolters Kluwer Chairman: Cornelis J. Brakel. Cornelis Brakel became chairman of Wolters Kluwer upon the retirement of M. Ververs on May 1, 1995. He was named the chief executive of the new company formed by the planned merger between his company and Reed Elsevier. On September 1, 1999, Brakel resigned as chief executive and was succeeded by Caspar van Kempen.

A union would also enable the companies to share both content and technology. In early 1997, Wolters Kluwer licensed some of its CCH tax databases to LEXIS-NEXIS. Such content sharing could be expected to increase as a result of a merger, particularly among those two titles. Yet the companies stressed that shared technology was an even greater incentive to merge. The combined company predicted that it would generate about 30% of its revenues from non-print operations. Nigel Stapleton, co-chairman of Reed Elsevier, commented in *Information Today* that the merger "is about new technology and the need for scale. This is more an online story than a story about publishers merging."

Approach and Engagement

On October 13, 1997, Reed Elsevier and Wolters Kluwer surprised the industry, as well as some of their employees, with their $8.8 billion merger announcement. The new company, to be named Elsevier Wolters Kluwer, would realize combined 1996 revenues of $7.8 billion. Of that amount, $4.6 billion would originate from the professional market, making the company the largest professional publisher in the world, with significant strengths in legal, medical, scientific, and technical fields. It would be headed by Cornelis Brakel, chairman of Wolters Kluwer, while Herman Bruggink and Nigel Stapleton, co-chairmen of Reed Elsevier, would become co-deputy chief executives.

The transaction would take place as a stock swap. Reed Elsevier itself didn't offer any stock; it was owned by the shareholders of Reed International and Elsevier. In this merger, Reed International's shareholders would control 38.3% of the newly formed entity, Elsevier's would own 34.2%, and Wolters Kluwer's would hold 27.5%. Shareholders of the three companies were scheduled to vote on the deal in April 1998.

Before they had the opportunity to do so, however, the deal hit an antitrust snag. On February 20, 1998, the European Commission issued a formal statement of its objections. It believed that the proposed merger would restrict competition in the area of legal and scientific publishing, and would put the company in a position to control prices. It would also create near-monopolies in the medical and legal arenas, especially in such European markets as France, The Netherlands, and Britain. As a result, the Commission required substantial divestiture of a number of Wolters Kluwer's tax, medical, and legal publications, which controlled a market share of about 90% in certain areas.

Since the burden of divestiture fell on Wolters Kluwer, it wanted to renegotiate the terms of the merger. It demanded a greater stake in the merged company, asserting that the Commission's demands would have a negative impact for its shareholders. Reed International and Elsevier disputed that argument, claiming that the divestitures would impact the company as a whole, not merely Wolters Kluwer. They countered that any changes to the merger terms would have an adverse effect on their own shareholders.

Reed Elsevier and Wolters Kluwer met over the March 7-8 weekend to discuss the possibility of a renegotiation. Each company held its ground, however, and on March 9, 1998, the boards of Reed International, Elsevier, and Wolters Kluwer terminated their agreement. "We could not agree to their demand for a greater slice of the pie," explained Paul Richardson, Reed Elsevier's VP of Finance, in *Electronic Information Report.*

Products and Services

Reed Elsevier was grouped into three business units:

The **Business Segment** was comprised of two subsegments. Reed Exhibition Companies served the exhibition market by providing event organization services. The other subsegment, comprised of Cahners Business Information, Elsevier Business Information, and Reed Business Information, provided magazines, reference products, and online services to the business community. As a whole, the Business Segment had turnover of GBP 1.4 billion in 1998, representing 44% of total company revenues.

The **Professional Segment** was divided into three units. LEXIS-NEXIS, serving the U.S., and The Reed Elsevier Legal Division, serving areas outside the U.S., provided legal, business, and public records in the form of online databases, reference products, law reports, and journals. In addition to its flagship LEXIS and NEXIS products, the LEXIS-NEXIS group included Martindale Hubbell, Matthew Bender, and Shepard's. The Reed Elsevier Legal Division included Butterworths, Tolley Publishing, Editions du Juris-Classeur, and Verlag Orac. Reed Educational & Professional Publishing served the educational market with books and learning resources, and was comprised of Heinemann, Ginn, Rigby, and Elsevier Opleidingen, which provided courses for the tuition market in Belgium and The Netherlands. In 1998, the Professional Segment generated GBP 1.2 billion in turnover, or 36% of Reed Elsevier's total revenues.

The **Scientific Segment** had two primary subsections. Elsevier Science produced scientific journals, online databases, and reference products. The company's medical publishing and communications businesses together served the medical community by providing conferences, journals, reference products, and online services; these businesses included Excerpta Medica, *The Lancet*, Springhouse Corporation, and Editions Scientifiques et Medicales Elsevier. Turnover for the Scientific Segment reached GBP 622 million in 1998, representing 20% of total company sales.

Wolters Kluwer was divided into six subject areas:

Legal and Tax Publishing included such operations as Kluwer Law International, CCH, Lamy Juridique, Herman Luchterhand Verlag, IPSOA Editore, ABC Dom Wydawniczy, and Norstedts Juridik; this segment had sales of Dfl 2.7 billion in 1998.

Business Publishing included Bohmann Group, Kluwer Editorial, Dalian Professionnel, Teleroute Medien, ten Hagen & Stam, Samsom, Croner Publications, and Aspen Publishers; this segment generated Dfl 1.2 billion in 1998.

Medical Publishing included Adis International, Liber, and Lippincott Williams & Wilkins. Scientific Publishing was comprised of Akadémiai Kiado and Kluwer Academic Publishers. (The Medical and Scientific units had combined sales in 1998 of Dfl 1.1 billion.)

Educational Publishing included Bohmann/Jugend und Volk, Educatieve Partners Nederland, Wolters-Noordhoff, Wolf Verlag, and Stanley Thornes Publishers. Professional Training was comprised of such units as Kluwer Opleidingen, The Financial Training Company, Blessing/White-IEC, and Krauthammer International. (The Educational and Professional Training segment had combined 1998 sales of Dfl 888 million.)

Changes to the Industry

The merger's failure caused libraries and other customers of professional publications to heave a collective sigh of relief. They had been concerned that a combination of two of their largest suppliers would ultimately restrict innovation and raise prices. "If Reed Elsevier and Wolters Kluwer continue to compete, that can only be good news for the end-uses of their products," commented Maureen Fleming, an analyst with The Gartner Group, in *Folio: The Magazine for Magazine Management*.

Review of the Outcome

Reed Elsevier and Wolters Kluwer resumed their roles as competitors and immediately picked up from where they had left off—making acquisitions. In July 1998 Reed acquired Matthew Bender and Co., a U.S. publisher of legal analysis, and the remaining 50% interest in Shepard's that it didn't already own, thereby strengthening the presence of LEXIS-NEXIS in the U.S. legal market. By the end of that year, Reed Elsevier had completely exited the consumer publishing industry with its sale of IPC Magazines. Turnover at the end of 1998 rose six percent from the previous year to GBP 3.2 billion. In April 1999, a unitary management structure was adopted for Reed International, Elsevier, and Reed Elsevier, whereas the boards of these three companies would be identical.

In November 1997, while the merger with Reed Elsevier was still on track, Wolters Kluwer purchased Wiley Law Publications from John Wiley & Sons. It purchased the Thomson Science unit of Thomson International Publishing in March 1998. That May it acquired Baltimore-based Waverly Inc. for $375 million, followed in July by the acquisition of New York-based Plenum Publishing Corp., a publisher of scientific, medical and technical journals and books. It expanded activities in the U.K. by acquiring Hawksmere Group Ltd. in November 1998, the same month that it acquired New York-based Ovid Technologies, Inc., a provider of subscription based electronic information services. Wolters Kluwer exited the trade market in favor of providing publications and services for the professional market in April 1999 with the sale of its Veen Uitgevers Groep and Van Dale Lexicografie units.

Research

Fontes, Robyn. "Euro Trade Merger Falls Apart," in *Folio: The Magazine for Magazine Management,* Spring 1998. Offers the opinions of industry analysts that the merger's failure was inevitable.

Reed Elsevier Annual Review 1998. Provides financial details and describes company operating segments.

"Reed Elsevier PLC," in *Notable Corporate Chronologies,* The Gale Group, 1999. Profiles the history of the company.

Reed Elsevier PLC Home Page, available at http://www.reed-elsevier.com. Official World Wide Web Page for Reed Elsevier. Includes organizational and product information, press releases, annual reports, and other financial information.

"Reed Elsevier, Wolters Kluwer Call off Merger Amid Antitrust Concerns," in *Electronic Information Report,* 13 March 1998. Details the reasons for the termination of the deal.

"Reed Elsevier, Wolters Kluwer to Merge into Megapublisher," in *Information Today,* November 1997. Describes the technological incentives for their recently announced merger agreement.

"Reed Elsevier-Wolters Kluwer Merger Creates New Prof'l Leader," in *BP Report,* 27 October 1997. Reports the surprising merger announcement.

Wolters Kluwer Annual Report 1998. Provides detailed financial analysis and highlights of the year.

"Wolters Kluwer NV," in *International Directory of Company Histories,* Vol. 14, St. James Press: 1996. Provides a historical review of the company.

Wolters Kluwer NV Home Page, available at http://www.wolters-kluwer.com. Official World Wide Web Page for Wolters Kluwer. Features information on its subsidiaries, annual reports, and press releases.

DEBORAH J. UNTENER

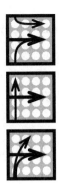

REED INTERNATIONAL & ELSEVIER

nationality: United Kingdom
date: January 1, 1993
affected: Reed International PLC, United Kingdom, founded 1894
affected: Elsevier NV, The Netherlands, founded 1880

Reed Elsevier PLC
25 Victoria St.
London, SW1H 0EX
United Kingdom

tel: 44 (0)171 222 8420
fax: 44 (0)171 227 5799
web: http://www.reed-elsevier.com

Overview of the Merger

When Dutch scientific journal publisher Elsevier and British trade, consumer, and business magazine publisher Reed International merged in 1993, they formed a $4.8 billion global media group, Reed Elsevier, that soon became the third-largest publishing and information company in the world. The two firms kept separate headquarters, stock, and management, which caused integration problems soon after the merger. However, the size of the new firm enabled it to pursue larger mergers, including its $1.5 billion takeover of Mead Data Central in late 1994, which brought with it electronic information services LEXIS and NEXIS. Reed Elsevier's next attempt at major growth, the planned $8.8 billion merger with Wolters Kluwer NV, fell apart in 1997 due to restrictions posed by the European Commission.

History of Reed International

Albert Reed established a newsprint manufacturing facility in Kent, England, in 1894. In 1903 that concern, Albert E. Reed & Co., incorporated as a public company. In 1929, it diversified into the manufacture of packaging and multiwall paper products, and formed the Medway corrugated Paper Co. Elsevier diversified as well, entering the scientific publishing field in the 1930s, and into consumer magazines, newspapers, business manuals, and commercial printing after World War II.

In 1954, Reed entered the building products field with the manufacture of pitch fiber pipes. It expanded into New Zealand the following year, followed by Canada in 1960. Reed acquired Wall Paper Manufacturers Ltd. in 1965 and General Paint in 1966. In 1970, it also acquired International Publishing Corporation Ltd., Mirror Group Newspaper, and 29% of Cahners Publishing. The firm changed its name twice that year, first to Reed Group Ltd. and then to Reed International, to reflect its geographical expansion and diversified product range. By 1971, the company was recognized as one of the U.K.'s largest conglomerates, with a workforce of 84,000 and turnover of GBP 502 million.

The Business

Financials

Revenue (1998): GBP 3.2 billion

Employees (1998): 26,100

SICs / NAICS

sic 7375 - Information Retrieval Services

sic 2721 - Periodicals

sic 2731 - Book Publishing

sic 2741 - Miscellaneous Publishing

naics 514191 - On-Line Information Services

naics 511120 - Periodical Publishers

naics 511130 - Book Publishers

naics 511140 - Database and Directory Publishers

By the early 1980s, Reed's diversification strategy proved to be a burden, as the company experienced difficulty in coordinating its activities. The company decided to focus on its core publishing business, selling off the Mirror Group to Robert Maxwell in 1984. By 1987, it had divested all other nonpublishing and nonpaper businesses. It continued to expand its core operations through acquisitions. Reed purchased publisher *R.R. Bowker* in 1985; the second-largest book publisher in the U.K., Octopus Publishing, in 1987; TV Times and Travel Information Group in 1989; and Martindale-Hubbell in 1990.

On January 1, 1993, Reed International and Elsevier NV created Reed Elsevier as a joint venture to house their publishing and information businesses. At the same time, those two parent companies also formed Elsevier Reed Finance BV to hold their finance activities. That year, Reed Elsevier purchased the France-based legal publisher Editions Techniques and Robert Maxwell's Official Airlines Guides (OAG). By the end of that year, the firm had generated revenues of GBP 2.7 billion.

Reed International and Elsevier NV both gained listings on the New York Stock Exchange in 1994 to increase their presence in the U.S. market. The following year, Reed Elsevier purchased the Mead Data Central unit of Mead Corp. At that time, with over $9 billion in capital, Reed Elsevier was recognized as the third-largest publishing and information company in the world.

The first few years of the newly formed Reed Elsevier involved the continuation of the acquisition and divestiture strategies of its parent companies. Consumer publishing assets were let go in favor of business, legal, and scientific acquisitions, as well as electronic operations. In 1995, the firm sold Bonaventura's consumer magazines, Cahners Consumer Magazines, Dagbladumie newspapers, and Reed Regional Newspapers. The following year, Reed Elsevier purchased the tax and legal publisher Tolley, as well as a 50% stake in Shepard's Co., a U.S. legal citation service.

In 1997, Reed Elsevier acquired the Chilton magazine operations from The Walt Disney Co. A planned $8.8 billion merger with Wolters Kluwer fell apart in 1998. Later that year, Reed Elsevier bought the remainder of Shepard's, as well as Matthew Bender and Co. The firm also sold its IPC consumer magazines division for $860 million. Rumors of a potential takeover of Reed Elsevier began to circulate in the late 1990s.

History Elsevier NV

Elsevier NV, the first large Dutch publishing company, was formed in 1880 as a pooling of the interests of several publishers and booksellers. The firm initially focused on small-scale publishing for the general trade market. The company's name became well known as the publisher of Dutch translations of the novels by Jules Verne.

Elsevier entered the U.S. market in 1979 with the purchase of Congressional Information Service. This acquisition contributed to the company's strategy of becoming a leader in publishing and information for the English-language markets. To further this end, Elsevier divested itself of its commercial printing and book publishing operations.

During this time, Elsevier was involved in a number of takeovers. In 1987, it launched a hostile bid for Kluwer, the third-largest publisher in The Netherlands, but was defeated by Wolters Samson when the two merged to form Wolters Kluwer. Robert Maxwell initiated a takeover bid for Elsevier in 1988, but was thwarted when Elsevier arranged a merger with Pearson, a U.K.-based publisher. This merger later failed, and in 1991 Elsevier purchased Pergamon Press from Maxwell. By 1992 Elsevier was the world's leader in scholarly journal publication. On January 1, 1993, Reed International and Elsevier merged to form Reed Elsevier as a joint venture to house their publishing and information businesses.

Market Forces Driving the Merger

In the early 1980s, Reed International operated in printing, paper, and packaging, as well as publishing.

Its diversification strategy of the 1970s had spread the firm too thin, and management was unable to coordinate and integrate operations as it had planned. After deciding to refocus on its core publishing operations, Reed launched a divestiture campaign that included sell its Mirror Group assets in 1984. By 1987, the firm had divested all other peripheral businesses. Elsevier followed a similar strategy in the 1980s. It had moved into the U.S. market with its 1979 purchase of Congressional Information Service, which fueled the company's efforts to dominate English-language publishing and information markets, and prompted its sale of commercial printing and book publishing assets.

According to a September 1992 article in *The Economist*, these strategies had positioned each firm for the 1993 merger. "Elsevier became the world's biggest publisher of scientific journals. Reed became one of the world's biggest and most competitive publishers of business magazines.... In the late 1980s both were itchy to grow."

Prior to the merger, Reed, with $2.5 billion in annual sales, was struggling with falling advertising revenues, which were the result of economic downturns in both the U.S. and the U.K. Because the firm relied on advertising for roughly 40% of its sales, it needed to expand into less cyclical markets. Elsevier's 20% operating profit margin—which had grown fourfold during the 1980s—on sales of $1.3 billion, would help lessen Reed's dependence on advertising revenues. Reed also wanted to increase its U.S. presence, a market Elsevier had successfully penetrated via its scientific and medical publishing operations.

Elsevier's reasons for pursuing a marriage with Reed were the subject of some debate. Elsevier management asserted that the maturity of the scientific and medical markets was at the root of the firm's efforts to diversify into segments, like the business and professional markets in which Reed was entrenched. Some analysts felt, though, that Elsevier chairman Pierre Vinken, after experiencing the collapse of two previous merger attempts while at the helm of Elsevier, was determined to complete a major deal before retiring.

Approach and Engagement

In September of 1992, Reed International and Elsevier announced their plans to merge. The deal was unusual in that the two firms agreed to retain separate headquarters and leaders—Reed chairman Peter Davis and Elsevier chairman Pierre Vinken would jointly run the company from London and Amsterdam, respectively—as well as two sets of stock. On January 1, 1993, Reed International and Elsevier

The Officers

Non-Executive Chairman: Morris Tabaksblat

Co-Chief Executive Officer: Herman Bruggink

Co-Chief Executive Officer: Nigel Stapleton

Chief Financial Officer: Mark Armour

Executive Director: Onno Laman Trip

Executive Director: Herman Spruijt

jointly created an equally owned holding company, Reed Elsevier PLC, under which each began operating as a separate entity. Reed ended up owning 5.8% of Elsevier. Terms of the agreement stipulated that when Vinken retired in 1995, Davis would takeover as sole chairman.

Products and Services

By the late 1990s, Reed Elsevier was grouped into three business units:

The **Business Segment** consisted of two subsegments. Reed Exhibition Companies served the exhibition market by providing event organization services. The other subsegment—comprised of Cahners Business Information, Elsevier Business Information, and Reed Business Information—provided magazines, reference products, and online services to the business community. As a whole, the Business Segment had turnover of GBP 1.4 billion in 1998, representing 44% of total company revenues.

The **Professional Segment** was divided into three units. LEXIS-NEXIS, serving the U.S., and Reed Elsevier Legal Division, serving areas outside the U.S., provided legal, business, and public records in the form of online databases, reference products, law reports, and journals. In addition to its flagship LEXIS and NEXIS products, the LEXIS-NEXIS group included Martindale Hubbell, Matthew Bender, and Shepard's. The Reed Elsevier Legal Division included Butterworths, Tolley Publishing, Editions du Juris-Classeur, and Verlag Orac. Reed Educational & Professional Publishing, the third unit, served the educational market with books and learning resources and was comprised of Heinemann, Ginn, Rigby, and Elsevier Opleidingen, which provided courses for the tuition market in Belgium and The Netherlands. In 1998, the Professional Segment generated GBP 1.2 billion in turnover, or 36% of Reed Elsevier's total revenues.

The Players

Chairman of Reed International PLC: Peter Davis. Peter Davis headed the Sainsbury supermarket chain prior to his appointment at Reed International. When Reed merged with Elsevier in 1993, Davis accepted the post of co-chairman of Reed Elsevier. Management disputes at the new firm prompted Davis to resign in 1994. That year, he was tapped by Prudential Co., the largest life insurer in Britain, as CEO.

Chairman of Elsevier NV: Pierre Vinken. Prior to his career at Elsevier, Pierre Vinken worked as a director of Pearson PLC and The Economist Group, and served on the boards of Logica Netherlands and Logica PLC. When Elsevier merged with Reed in 1993, Vinken began serving as co-chairman of Reed Elsevier, a post he held until his retirement in 1995. At that time, he was appointed chairman of the Supervisory Board of Elsevier. In April 1999, Vinken resigned as director of Reed Elsevier.

The **Scientific Segment** had two primary subsections. Elsevier Science produced scientific journals, online databases, and reference products. The company's medical publishing and communications businesses together served the medical community by providing conferences, journals, reference products, and online services; these businesses included Excerpta Medica, *The Lancet*, Springhouse Corporation, and Editions Scientifiques et Medicales Elsevier. Turnover for the Scientific Segment reached GBP 622 million in 1998, representing 20% of total company sales.

Changes to the Industry

After the merger's completion, Reed Elsevier was considered by many analysts to be "one of the few companies large enough to be a contender to buy Ziff Communications Co., a media company with a nearly $2 billion price tag, and Mead Corp.'s $1 billion Lexis/Nexis electronic information services" wrote *Folio: the Magazine for Magazine Management* in September of 1994. Almost as if on cue, Reed Elsevier paid $1.5 billion for Mead Data Central in December of 1994, gaining access to the electronic information services market via the Lexis and Nexis operations.

Both deals fueled growth in the rapidly consolidating global publishing and information industry. In an effort to retain a leadership position, particulary in the business publishing sector, Reed Elsevier paid $447 million in 1997 for Walt Disney's Chilton Business Group, which it merged with its Cahners Publishing Co. to form U.S.-based Reed Elsevier Business Information, a new subsidiary with more than 100 titles and annual sales of roughly $1 billion.

Later that year, Reed Elsevier and Wolters Kluwer proposed an $8.8 billion merger. The resulting company, with combined sales in the professional market of $4.66 billion, would have dethroned The Thomson Corp. as the world's largest professional publisher. However, the deal fell apart in 1998 after the European Commission imposed several conditions on both firms. Undaunted, Reed Elsevier purchased Matthew Bender and Co., as well as the 50% of Shepard's that it didn't already own from Times Mirror for $1.65 billion.

Review of the Outcome

The deal's unusual structuring, which kept the management and stock of both firms separated, caused problems for Reed Elsevier. Co-chairman Peter Davis, who was slated to take over as sole chairman in 1995, resigned in July of 1994 after a fierce power struggle which culminated in a plan to institute an executive committee consisting of four people. He was replaced by Ian Irvine, former deputy chairman of Reed International.

Despite management shakeups, however, consolidation and cost cutting efforts resulted in a 30% increase of pretax profits, which totaled $801 million, in 1993. Profits grew in 1994 to $957 million. According to industry analyst, David Leibowitz, as quoted in *Folio*, the merger "worked out a lot better than naysayers had envisioned."

Research

"Bigger, Better?" in *Economist*, 19 September 1992. Explains why Reed and Elsevier decided to merger.

"Elsevier, Reed Publishers Merge," in *American Libraries*, November 1992. Offers an overview of the terms of the merger.

Evans, Richard. "Playing House," in *FW*, 1 August 1995. Describes the problems Reed and Elsevier have had since they decided to merge.

Hochwald, Lambeth. "Reed Elsevier: The Dancing Elephant," in *Folio: The Magazine for Magazine Management*, 1 September 1994. Offers a profile of Reed Elsevier two years after the merger.

Reed Elsevier Annual Review 1998. Provides financial details and describes company operating segments.

Reed Elsevier PLC Home Page, available at http://www.reed-elsevier.com. Official World Wide Web Page for Reed Elsevier. Includes organizational and product information, press releases, annual reports, and other financial information.

"Reed Elsevier PLC," in *Notable Corporate Chronologies*, The Gale Group, 1999. Profiles the history of the company.

JEFF ST. THOMAS

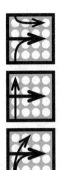

RENAULT & VOLVO

date: December 1, 1993 (canceled)
affected: Regie Nationale des Usines-Renault S.A., France, founded 1899
affected: AB Volvo, Sweden, founded 1915

Regie Nationale des Usines-Renault S.A.

34, quai du Point du Jour
Boulogne-Billancourt, 92109 Cedex
France

tel: 33 1 41 04 50 50
fax: 33 1 41 04 67 90
web: http://www.renault.com

AB Volvo
Goteborg, S-405 08
Sweden

tel: 46 31 59 00 00
fax: 46 31 54 57 72
web: http://www.volvo.com

Overview of the Merger

The collapse of the union between Renault and Volvo brought an end to their three-year engagement. The two companies had formed an alliance in 1990, and in 1993 set their official merger date as January 1, 1994. Before they could complete the union, however, Volvo managers and shareholders voiced their objections to the terms of the agreement, pressuring Volvo's president, Soren Gyll, to terminate the deal.

History of Regie Nationale des Usines-Renault S.A.

After persuading his brothers, Fernand and Marcel, to invest FFr30,000 in his automobile company, Louis Renault formed Renault Freres in 1899 and produced the world's first sedan. Only two years later, the company had become the eighth-largest firm in the automobile industry. The Renault brothers became competitive race car drivers to promote their company's products. Consequently, Marcel Renault was killed in 1903 while competing in the Paris-Madrid car race.

Taxicabs had become Renault's best-selling product by 1905. The company began experimenting with aircraft engines, particularly in the pursuit of the development of light-weight, air-cooled motors. After Fernand left the business in 1908, Louis renamed the company La Societe Louis Renault. It began exporting in 1912. At that time, nearly 100 Renault cabs were in service in Mexico City, and Renault cabs outnumbered all other types of cabs in Melbourne, Australia. By 1914 the firm had 31 dealers in foreign countries.

The Renault factory expanded after World War I, yet Renault's reluctance to apply new organizational ideas resulted in stagnated growth. At the conclusion of World War II, Louis Renault was imprisoned on charges of Nazi collaboration, and died in prison while awaiting trial. The de Gualle provisional government nationalized Renault's company, which it renamed as Regie Nationale des Usines-Renault S.A. It operated the company along commercial lines, building up its internal production of machine tools and making it the first in Europe to use automation.

The Business

Financials - Regie Nationale des Usines-Renault S.A.

Revenue (1998): FFr 195 billion

Employees (1998): 138,321

Financials - AB Volvo

Revenue (1998): SEK 212.9 billion

Employees (1998): 79,820

SICs / NAICS

sic 3711 - Motor Vehicles & Car Bodies

sic 3713 - Truck & Bus Bodies

sic 6141 - Personal Credit Institutions

sic 3531 - Construction Machinery

sic 3728 - Aircraft Parts & Equipment Nec

sic 3519 - Internal Combustion Engines Nec

naics 336111 - Automobile Manufacturing

naics 336112 - Light Truck and Utility Vehicle Manufacturing

naics 336120 - Heavy Duty Truck Manufacturing

naics 336211 - Motor Vehicle Body Manufacturing

naics 522291 - Consumer Lending

naics 333120 - Construction Machinery Manufacturing

naics 336413 - Other Aircraft Part and Auxiliary Equipment Manufacturing

naics 333618 - Other Engine Equipment Manufacturing

In 1948 Renault manufactured a miniature car called the Quatre Chevaux (4 CV or hp), which had been developed secretly during the war by Renault technicians. Two years later it released the Dauphine, manufactured to fit into the market opening between the inexpensive economy models and the higher priced models. For five years, the Dauphine outsold all other models.

Renault, which was strongly export-minded, was one of the first companies in the international automobile industry to make a serious effort to develop a sales organization in the U.S. By 1959 it ranked as the sixth-largest automobile manufacturer in the world. As the American market began to shrink in the 1970s, however, sales of the Dauphine dropped 33%. Renault adjusted its products to meet specific requirements of the American motorist, and began production of the four-cylinder R-16.

In 1976 Renault merged its Peugeot-Citroen truck subsidiary with its own Saviem truck company, thereby creating the largest truck producer in France, Renault Vehicles Industriels. Three years later American Motors Corp. (AMC) agreed to become the exclusive North American importer and distributor of Renault cars, while Renault agreed to market AMC products in France and other countries.

In 1980 Renault purchased 46.4% of AMC. In the years that followed, both AMC and Renault suffered from an industry slump and increased competition from Japanese automakers. Renault recorded a loss of $1.5 billion in 1984. George Besse took the company's helm in 1985, and set about instituting a cost-reduction program that cut staff and encouraged the concept of profit to the state-owned company. He was assassinated by terrorists the following year, and was succeeded by Raymond Levy, who continued the program that Besse had initiated.

In March of 1987 Renault withdrew from the U.S. market by selling its stake in AMC to Chrysler Corp. for $200 million. It formed a partnership with AB Volvo in 1990 to cooperate in international auto and truck operations. Three years later, these partners began developing a new line of luxury executive cars for the European market, raising speculation of a full merger between the two companies. Such an alliance was attempted in 1993, but fell apart when Volvo's shareholders and management rejected the deal. As a result, the companies terminated their partnership and sold their respective stock interests in each other.

Renault edged toward privatization as the French government reduced its stake in the company from 80% to 52% in 1995, and then to 46% in 1996. The firm forged a relationship with the Italian car manufacturer Fiat SpA in 1998, when it arranged to acquire part of Fiat's Teksid subsidiary. The two companies also joined their bus making businesses the following year. In May 1999 Renault acquired a 36.8% stake in Nissan for $5.4 billion.

History of AB Volvo

AB Volvo was formed in 1915 as a subsidiary of AB Svenska Kullagerfabriken, a Swedish ball bearing manufacturer. It began the assembly of cars in 1927 and of trucks in 1928. Two years later it acquired the means to safeguard the delivery of engines by purchasing a majority interest in AB Pentaverken. In 1934 Volvo began the production of bus chassis and marine engines. The following year the company gained a listing on the Stockholm Stock Exchange.

Volvo acquired a majority interest in the Swedish precision engineering company Svenska Flygmotor AB, later known as Volvo Aero. In 1942 it purchased Kopings Mekaniska Verkstad AB, Sweden's leading gearbox manufacturer. That year the company produced its first bogie axle, thus increasing the load capacity of its trucks. Its first tractor was unveiled in 1943, and by 1947 Volvo was recognized as one of the largest companies in Sweden.

Volvo entered the 1950s by acquiring AB Bolinder-Munktell, a Swedish manufacturer of farm machinery with its own line of diesel engines. This unit eventually became part of the VME Group, later renamed Volvo Construction Equipment. By 1951 the company concentrated on tractor production, and was named CEO in 1971, and proceeded to lead the company on a campaign to diversify outside of automobiles, where it had slim chance of ever becoming a true leader. Volvo also began adding to its heavy truck holdings.

The VESC, or Volvo Experimental Safety Car, was unveiled in 1972. With low profits and an inability to finance a comprehensive product modernization program, Volvo explored a possible merger in 1977 with Saab-Scania, Sweden's other car manufacturer. Three months following the announcement, however, plans were abandoned due to heavy opposition.

In 1981 Volvo diversified into the oil industry with the acquisition of Beijerinvest Group, a Swedish company with interests in oil, food, finance, and trading. It also bought the truck operations of U.S.-based White Motors, later providing the basis for Volvo GM Heavy Truck Corp. In 1982 it introduced Duoprop, an airplane part featuring two counter-rotating propellers To provide 30% faster acceleration and 10% better fuel efficiency. Two years later Volvo entered into a joint venture with U.S.-based Clark Equipment Co., thereby creating the world's third-largest construction equipment company.

U.K.-based Leyland Bus Group Ltd. was acquired in 1988. Two years later Volvo sold its food and pharmaceutical interests for a share of the government-controlled holding company, Procordia. Also, Volvo initiated a stock swap with Renault SA and began the production of cars in the Netherlands in a joint venture with Mitsubishi Motors and the Dutch government. In the largest industrial overhaul in Swedish history, Volvo spent $2 billion in 1991 to update its plants and develop the 800 series of performance-oriented family sedans.

A failed merger with Renault SA prompted the resignation of Gyllenhammar. Soren Gyll, his successor, began selling off the company's non-core businesses. In 1995 Volvo acquired the remaining 50% of

The Officers

Regie Nationale des Usines-Renault S.A.

Chairman and CEO: Louis Schweitzer

Exec. VP, Worldwide Sales and Marketing: Patrick Faure

Exec. VP: Carlos Ghosn

Chief Financial Officer: Christian Dor

AB Volvo

Chairman: Hakan Frisinger

President and CEO: Leif Johansson

Deputy CEO and Exec. VP: Lennart Jeansson

Exec. VP: Arne Wittlov

Volvo Construction Equipment, as well as a 51% stake in Prevost Car Inc., a Canadian bus manufacturer.

The company introduced the Volvo B7R bus chassis and the Volvo 770 truck to the North American market in 1997. Gyll resigned suddenly and was replaced by Leif Johansson. The next year Volvo paid $570 million to acquire the construction equipment business of Samsung Heavy Industries, and also purchased Mexicana de Autobuses, a Mexico-based bus manufacturer.

Volvo sold its automobile operations to Ford Motor Co. in 1999, leaving the company with operations in only heavy-duty vehicles, including heavy trucks, buses, construction equipment, marine and industrial engines, and aerospace vehicles. Flush with capital from the sale to Ford, Volvo bought an unfriendly 20% stake in Scania AB, a Swedish heavy-truck rival.

Market Forces Driving the Merger

By 1990 Sweden's export sales had begun to slow. As a result, many of the nation's automotive companies were squeezed financially. One such firm, SAAB, reacted by entering into an alliance with General Motors whereby GM gained effective control of the company. Volvo, too, looked for foreign assistance. That year it entered into a complex arrangement with France-based Renault to share the increasingly high costs of research and product development. The market decline continued, however, and Volvo recorded a loss of $469 million in 1992.

Moreover, the industry showed no signs of rebounding in the immediate future. West European car sales dropped 16.5% in the first eight months of

The Players

Renault Chairman and CEO: Louis Schweitzer. Louis Schweitzer, the grandnephew of Dr. Albert Schweitzer, began his career at Renault in 1986 as chief financial officer. He was named president in 1990 and chairman in 1992. Before joining the company, he was a chief of staff to the Socialist Prime Minister, Laurent Fabius. In 1995 his service in that governmental post caught up with him, as he was indicted for involvement in the alleged telephone-tapping of leading figures, including journalists, between 1983 and 1986. Schweitzer emerged from the scandal fairly unscathed, however, and continued his tenure as leader of Renault.

Volvo President: Soren Gyll. Soren Gyll joined Volvo in 1990, and was named its president in 1992. Although he didn't orchestrate the merger pact with Renault, he was instrumental in terminating it. As a result of that collapse, Pehr Gyllenhammar resigned as CEO in December 1993 and Gyll assumed the vacated post. In 1997 Gyll resigned suddenly and was succeeded by Leif Johansson. That August he became the non-executive chairman of the board of Pharmacia & Upjohn.

1993. And increased competition would soon arise from Japanese manufacturers, as the limitations on European imports were scheduled to be lifted by the European Union in 1999.

Hoping to strengthen its position, Volvo entered into a merger agreement with Renault in September 1993. The combined company would be the world's sixth-largest car manufacturer, after General Motors, Ford, Toyota, Volkswagen, and Nissan. It hoped to achieve gains in that sector by reaping the rewards from cross-marketing in luxury cars, Volvo's strength, as well as compact cars, Renault's specialty. Yet the merged company's biggest impact would be in commercial vehicles, as the separate companies had substantial operations in Europe and the U.S. They would rank the combined firm second in that industry, behind Mercedes-Benz.

Approach and Engagement

On September 6, 1993, Renault and Volvo announced their merger accord. Renault was a state-owned company, which meant that the French gov-

ernment would hold a stake in the combined enterprise. This brought a patriotic tremble to those vested in Volvo, a Swedish company. And that tremble developed into an outright shudder when the details of the merger deal were revealed.

While Volvo would hold a direct interest of 18% in the new company, to be named Renault-Volvo RVA, the French government would directly control a 47% stake. The remaining 35% share would be held by RVC, a holding company in which France would also hold a 51% interest.

On October 6 the Swedish Shareholders Association, an alliance of individual investors who owned a combined 10% of Volvo, voiced its objections to the deal. This group was headed by Lars-Erik Forsgardh, who was the first to speak out against the merger. "From a shareholder's point of view, I couldn't think of a worse arrangement," he said in *Business Week*.

Three points in particular disturbed Forsgardh. First, the deal gave the French government a "golden share," which enabled it to restrict the voting rights of any investor, including Volvo, to 20%. Secondly, the companies failed to produce compelling benefits arising from a merger that could not be achieved from a continuation of their partnership. Finally, France remained elusive about the date that it planned to privatize Renault; until that time the merger's benefits to Swedish shareholders would be limited. *The Economist* wrote that France promised to do as "as soon as the car and financial markets allowed—probably in late 1994."

Forsgardh's voice of dissension emboldened Volvo's managers to speak their minds as well—or at least leak confidential information in the hopes of squelching the deal. Reports of the operations on the production floor indicated a lack of cooperation between the companies' employees, as well as a growing resentment from Volvo's research and development staff over a perceived imbalance of information sharing.

The companies tried to quell the growing number of oppositionists. Volvo issued a revised statement of the merger's projected savings, reporting that they would be $7.4 billion, up from the $4.8 billion that had been earlier reported. But that didn't explain the source of those extra savings. In another vague statement, the French government expressed its assurance that it would not abuse its golden share rights.

These efforts to charm investors and managers proved ineffective, and on November 30 the last straw broke. A leaked financial report indicated that while Volvo's monthly earnings increased markedly,

Renault's dropped sharply. Soren Gyll, Volvo's CEO, quickly conducted an informal poll of the company's 25 senior managers, who overwhelmingly declared that the merger wouldn't work. Gyll telephoned Volvo's chairman, Pehr Gyllenhammar, who was in the U.S. at the time, and informed him of the developments. Gyllenhammar terminated the deal and resigned the following day.

Products and Services

Renault was divided into two main segments. Passenger Cars included such brands as Clio II, Espace, Kangoo, Laguna, Megane, Scenic, Nevada, Safrane, Twingo, and Spider. Commercial Vehicles was comprised of vehicles for long-haul goods transport, distribution transport, and passenger transport, as well as construction trucks, public service vehicles, and military vehicles.

Volvo operated in five segments: Volvo Buses, Volvo Trucks, Volvo Construction Equipment Group, Volvo Penta Corp. (marine and industrial engines), and Volvo Aero.

Review of the Outcome

The breakup didn't just bring about an end to the merger deal, it also terminated their previous partnership. Volvo and Renault dissolved their joint purchasing and quality control accords. They also surrendered most of the seats held on the other's board; Renault's chairman Louis Schweitzer, however, retained his seat on Volvo's board. Renault reduced its stake in Volvo to 3.45% on February 3, 1994, and Volvo sold its 11.38% interest in Renault to the Union Bank of Switzerland on July 31, 1997.

Research

"AB Volvo," in *Notable Corporate Chronologies*, The Gale Group, 1999. Profiles the history of the company.

AB Volvo Home Page, available at http://www.volvo.com. Official World Wide Web Page for Volvo. Offers product and financial information, a company history, and press releases.

Dwyer, Paula. "Why Volvo Kissed Renault Goodbye," in *Business Week*, 20 December 1993. Chronicles the objections that brought about the collapse of the deal.

"A Marriage of Necessity," in *Fortune*, 15 November 1993. Describes the merger deal and the driving forces behind it.

"Regie Nationale des Usines-Renault S.A.," in *Notable Corporate Chronologies*, The Gale Group, 1999. Reports significant events in the history of Renault.

Regie Nationale des Usines-Renault S.A. Home Page, available at http://www.renault.com. Official World Wide Web Page for Renault. This French- and English-language site presents information on products and services, financial data, and press releases.

"Who's Driving Renault-Volvo?" in *Economist*, 11 September 1993. Provides reasons why the two companies agreed to merge.

DAVIS MCMILLAN

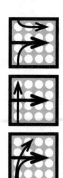

RHODIA & PAARMAL

Rhodia
25, Quai Paul Doumer
Courbevoie, 92408 Cedex
France

tel: 33 1 47 68 12 34
fax: 33 1 47 68 19 11
web: http://www.rhodia.com

nationality: France
date: December 22, 1997
affected: Rhodia, France, founded 1998
affected: Paarmal, Mexico

Overview of the Acquisition

Rhodia Brasil, a unit of the specialty chemicals manufacturer Rhodia, acquired the Mexican-based chemicals manufacturer Paarmal in late 1997 to facilitate the expansion of its presence in the Latin American market. Paarmal produced specialty surfactants for various industries, including the high-growth cosmetics sector.

History of Rhodia

In 1858 Etienne Poulenc, a French pharmacist, opened an apothecary in Paris and began to manufacture drugs. At the turn of the century, Poulenc's brothers joined his pharmaceutical business to form Etablissement Poulenc-Freres. This new company soon began working with Comptoir des Textiles Artificielles (CTA). In 1922 the firm acquired May and Baker, a pharmaceutical company based in the U.K.

Meanwhile, in 1895, the Societe Chimiques des Usines du Rhone was formed in Lyon, France, for the manufacture of dyestuffs and perfumes. By the end of the century, German companies dominated the European production of chemicals, particularly dyestuffs, so completely that French companies could not profit. As a result, the Usines du Rhone discontinued its dyestuffs operations and was taken over by French banks. In 1919 Usines du Rhone formed a perfume company in Brazil, Rhodia SA; its Rodo perfume garnered almost 75% of the company's profits. In 1922 CTA and Usines du Rhone merged certain operations to form Rhodiaceta. Through the interactions of both Usines du Rhone and Poulenc-Freres with CTA, the two companies developed close ties.

In 1928 they decided to make it official. Societe des Usine Chimiques Rhone-Poulenc was formed that year through the merger of Societe Chimiques des Usines du Rhone and Etablissement Poulenc-Freres. At the same time, it established two subsidiaries: Prolabo, to develop new ways to make artificial textiles, and Specia, to develop specialty pharmaceuticals. The following year, however, worldwide economic difficulties forced Rhone-Poulenc to reduce its number of labs to two and its factories to three.

By the end of World War II, Rhone-Poulenc had suffered from the German occupation and the ensuing supply limitations. Despite the diminished research and development of the previous years, it produced nylon and became the first French company to produce penicillin. In 1953 it began the manufacture of its products in the U.S. Three years later it acquired a health products company, Theraplix.

In 1961 the company established a holding company, Rhone-Poulenc SA, to oversee the operations of its various subsidiaries. In the late 1960s it made several acquisitions: Pechiney-Saint-Gobain, maker of agricultural and basic chemicals; Progil, a chemical company; a 50% interest in Institut Merieux; and a majority stake in the research facility Laboratoire Roger Bellon. By 1969 Rhone-Poulenc was the largest company in France, and the following year it became the third-largest chemical company in Europe.

In the early 1970s, France's high tariffs limited foreign expansion. Though the company tried to expand globally, its efforts proved ill timed, as little market share was left for which to compete. To add to Rhone-Poulenc's financial woes, the French government's attempts to decrease inflation were detrimental to business, and forced the company to lay off 20,000 employees.

By the latter part of the decade, the company had recovered. In 1979 its U.S. subsidiary, Rhone-Poulenc Inc., acquired 58% of Anken Industries. Two years later, Rhone-Poulenc purchased P.B.U.S.A. Co. and the agricultural chemicals business of Mobil Chemical Corp. In October of that year, the Socialist Mitterand party gained control of the French government and began to nationalize most of the country's companies. When Rhone-Poulenc was nationalized in 1982, the new French government installed Loik Le Floch-Prigent as its chairman. This year the company increased its revenues by making a number of acquisitions. But due to continued unprofitability, it lost its status as the country's largest chemical company. It later discontinued the production of fertilizers and petrochemicals.

In 1983 Floch-Prigent returned profitability to the company for the first time in four years by reducing the workforce and eliminating ailing operations. Two years later Siltec Corp., in which Rhone-Poulenc owned stock, agreed to make silicon wafers with Rhone-Poulenc. It also entered into a joint venture with Mitsui Petrochemical for the manufacture of computer boards.

Jean-Rene Fourtou replaced Floch-Prigent as chairman in 1986. The company's farm chemicals business improved through the acquisition of the agrichemicals business of Union Carbide Corp. The fol-

The Business

Financials

Revenue (1998): 5.53 billion Euros (FrF 36.3 billion)

Employees (1998): 23,500

SICs / NAICS

sic 2833 - Medicinals & Botanicals

sic 2834 - Pharmaceutical Preparations

sic 2865 - Cyclic Crudes & Intermediates

sic 2821 - Plastics Materials & Resins

sic 2823 - Cellulosic Manmade Fibers

sic 2841 - Soap & Other Detergents

sic 2844 - Toilet Preparations

sic 2879 - Agricultural Chemicals Nec

naics 325411 - Medicinal and Botanical Manufacturing

naics 325412 - Pharmaceutical Preparation Manufacturing

naics 325110 - Petrochemical Manufacturing

naics 325211 - Plastics Material and Resin Manufacturing

naics 325221 - Cellulosic Manmade Fiber Manufacturing

naics 325611 - Soap and Other Detergent Manufacturing

naics 325620 - Toilet Preparation Manufacturing

naics 325320 - Pesticide and Other Agricultural Chemical Manufacturing

lowing year, the company acquired the industrial chemicals business of Stauffer, and Fourtou began advocating privatization. In 1989 net income exceeded FrF 3 billion on sales greater than FrF 73 billion.

In 1990 the company purchased 66% of Rhone-Poulenc Rorer Inc., a merger of R-P's human pharmaceuticals business with U.S.-based pharmaceuticals company, the Rorer Group Inc. This acquisition increased Rhone-Poulenc's North American sales with such products as Maalox, the world's best selling antacid. The following year it formed Pateur Merieux Serums et Vaccins, a joint venture with Merck & Co. for the manufacture of children's multi-vaccines. The company continued a divestiture program of non-core businesses. In 1991 alone its divestitures brought in more than $700 million. By 1992 Rhone-Poulenc was the world's eighth-largest chemical company, as well as France's largest chemical and veterinary pharmaceutical company.

The Officers

Chairman and CEO: Jean-Pierre Tirouflet

Deputy Chairman, Fine Organics Division: Jean-Claude Bravard

Deputy Chairman, Human Resources and Communications: Bernard Chambon

Deputy Chairman, Consumer Products Specialties Division: David Eckert

Deputy Chairman, Polyamide Division: Pierre Levi

Deputy Chairman, Acetow and Polyester Activities and Competitivity and Progress Programs: Michel Ybert

In December 1993 Rhone-Poulenc became privatized when the French government sold its majority interest. Earlier that year the company had expanded into biotechnology by purchasing 37% of Applied Immune Science in a joint research venture in cell and gene therapy. In 1994 the company acquired Cooperation Pharmaceutique Francaise, the nation's second-largest over-the-counter drug distributor. In 1995 its Rhone-Merieux subsidiary acquired Sanofi's animal health activities in North American, South America, and Asia.

On July 31, 1997, Rhone-Poulenc merged Rhone-Merieux with Merck & Co.'s animal health business to form Merial Ltd., the world's leader in animal health and poultry genetics. Later that year it acquired full ownership of Rhone-Poulenc Rorer for FrF 27 billion. By the end of 1997, Rhone-Poulenc generated net sales of FrF 90 billion and had a workforce of 68,377.

In January 1998, the company formed Rhodia, one of the world's leaders in specialty chemicals, by combining its chemical operations with its fibers and polymers businesses. Only days before its official formation, Rhodia's Brazilian unit acquired Mexico-based Paarmal.

As part of a strategy to focus on its core specialty chemicals business, Rhodia divested itself of 16 companies during the year, including operations in polyester and sodium bicarbonate production. It also sought to strengthen its presence in foreign markets, acquiring Slovakia-based Chenllon, as well as entering into joint ventures with Poland-, Japan-, and China-based partners.

Market Forces Driving the Acquisition

Rhodia, a company that housed the specialty chemicals business of Rhone-Poulenc, sought to expand its specialty surfactants operations in global markets. Rhone-Poulenc had recently made investments in the Asian market, namely China, Japan, and Thailand, and wanted to increase its presence in Latin America, where it operated a manufacturing plant in Brazil. Operations at this Brazilian plant would be facilitated by the establishment of a second business in the region, as free trade zone arrangements opened up the market for increased import and export activity.

The Latin American cosmetics sector in particular was a high-growth market. According to a Rhodia official, the Brazilian retail market for cosmetics and toiletries was expanding at a rate of 16% annually, and was worth $4.8 billion in 1997.

Approach and Engagement

On December 22, 1997, Rhodia's Brazilian unit, Rhodia Brasil Ltd., acquired Paarmal for an undisclosed sum. This Mexican company operated in the specialty surfactants sector, manufacturing such products as amphoteric, ethoxylates, sulphosuccinates, and Sorbitan derivatives. Operating out of facilities in Cuernaraca and Veracruz (Mexico), Paarmal served a variety of industries, including personal care, agrochemicals, polymerization, oil fields, metal treatment, and institutional and industrial detergents.

Products and Services

In 1998 Rhodia was the world's third-largest specialty chemicals group. It was comprised of five divisions: Fine Organics, Consumer Products Specialties, Industrial Products Specialties, Polyamide, and Services and Specialties:

Fine Organics manufactured active agents and intermediate products, primarily for the pharmaceutical, agricultural chemical, and perfume markets. This division accounted for 18% of Rhodia's total revenues in 1998.

Consumer Products Specialties manufactured additives and specialties for the food, cosmetic, detergent, and industrial process industries. In 1998 it was the world's leader in phosphates, guar gum, and stain repellent polymers, and was number-two in lactic ferments and xanthane. This division generated 19% of total 1998 revenues for Rhodia.

Industrial Products Specialties operated in three primary activities, Paper, Paint, and Construction Materials; Silicones, and Tire and Rubber. The world leader in high-dispersability silicas and adhesion promoters, this division also ranked second worldwide in Tolonate and third in emulsions. It accounted for 19% of total company revenues in 1998.

Polyamide was the world's second-largest producer of polyamide, involved at every stage of the production process, from raw material through such finished products as textile and industrial yarns, engineering plastics, and fibers for the construction, textile, and automotive industries. This unit accounted for 20% of Rhodia's 1998 revenues.

Services and Specialties consisted of three main divisions. Eco Services provided manufacturers with chemical expertise to assist them in controlling the impact of their activities in the environment. Acetow, the third-largest producer of cellulose acetate in the world and the largest in Europe for cigarette filters, was a supplier to major global customers. Finally, Rare Earths was the leading producer of separated rare earths, and served high-technology industries ranging from computers and cellular telephones to catalytic converters, and from plastic coloration to the glass industry. This division accounted for 16% of Rhodia's revenues in 1998.

Research

"Rhodia Brasil Buys Mexico's Paarmal," in *Chemical Market Reporter*, 8 June 1998. Briefly describes the Latin American cosmetics market that will be served by Rhodia's acquisition of Paarmal.

Rhodia Home Page Available at http://www.rhodia.com. Official World Wide Web Page for Rhodia. This French- and English-language site includes product information, press releases, executive biographies, and financial and investor information.

The Players

Rhodia Chairman and CEO: Jean-Pierre Tirouflet. Born in 1950, Jean-Pierre Tirouflet earned a degree in economics from the University of Paris II Assas. After continuing his education at the Ecole Nationale d'Administration, he took a job in 1978 as the Commercial Attache for the French Representation at the EEC Brussels. He left that position after three years, briefly heading the African Division of the government's Economic External Relations Department. In 1983 Tirouflet joined Rhone-Poulenc as the Corporate Finance Director, and passed through successive executive ranks. After serving as the Chairman and President of the company's Fibers and Polymers sector, he was named Rhodia's Chairman and CEO upon the company's formation in 1998.

"Rhone-Poulenc SA," in *Notable Corporate Chronologies*, The Gale Group, 1999. Lists major events in the company's history.

Rhone-Poulenc SA, 1997 Annual Report. Details the company's finances and operating segments.

KIMBERLY N. STEVENS

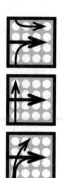

RHONE-POULENC & RORER

Rhone-Poulenc Rorer Inc.
500 Arcola Rd.
PO Box 1200
Collegeville, PA 19426-0107
USA

tel: (610)454 8000
web: http://www.rp-rorer.com

nationality: USA
date: August 1, 1990
affected: Rhone-Poulenc SA, France, founded 1928
affected: Rorer Group Inc., USA, founded 1909

Overview of the Merger

The 1990 merger of Rorer Group Inc. and the pharmaceutical business of Rhone-Poulenc formed Rhone-Poulenc Rorer Inc., the world's sixth-largest pharmaceutical company. For U.S.-based Rorer, best known for its Maalox antacid, the deal provided the security and resources to compete against the largest players in a rapidly consolidating industry. France-based Rhone-Poulenc gained immediate entry into the world's two largest pharmaceuticals markets, the U.S. and Japan.

History of Rhone-Poulenc SA

In 1858 Etienne Poulenc, a French pharmacist, opened an apothecary in Paris and began to manufacture drugs. At the turn of the century, Poulenc's brothers joined his pharmaceutical business to form Etablissement Poulenc-Freres. This new company soon began working with Comptoir des Textiles Artificielles (CTA). In 1922 the firm acquired May and Baker, a pharmaceutical company based in the U.K.

Meanwhile, in 1895, the Societe Chimiques des Usines du Rhone was formed in Lyon, France, for the manufacture of dyestuffs and perfumes. By the end of the century, German companies dominated the European production of chemicals, particularly dyestuffs, so completely that French companies could not profit. As a result, the Usines du Rhone discontinued its dyestuffs operations and was taken over by French banks. In 1919 Usines du Rhone formed a perfume company in Brazil, Rhodia SA; its Rodo perfume garnered almost 75% of the company's profits. In 1922 CTA and Usines du Rhone merged certain operations to form Rhodiaceta. Through the interactions of both Usines du Rhone and Poulenc-Freres with CTA, the two companies developed close ties.

In 1928 they decided to make it official. Societe des Usine Chimiques Rhone-Poulenc was formed that year through the merger of Societe Chimiques des Usines du Rhone and Etablissement Poulenc-Freres. At the same time, it established two subsidiaries: Prolabo, to develop new ways to make artificial textiles, and Specia, to develop specialty pharmaceuticals. The following year, however, worldwide economic difficulties forced Rhone-Poulenc to reduce its number of labs to two and its factories to three.

By the end of World War II, Rhone-Poulenc had suffered from the German occupation and the ensuing supply limitations. Despite the diminished research and development of the previous years, it produced nylon and became the first French company to produce penicillin. In 1953 it began the manufacture of its products in the U.S. Three years later it acquired a health products company, Theraplix.

In 1961 the company established a holding company, Rhone-Poulenc SA, to oversee the operations of its various subsidiaries. In the late 1960s it made several acquisitions: Pechiney-Saint-Gobain, maker of agricultural and basic chemicals; Progil, a chemical company; a 50% interest in Institut Merieux; and a majority stake in the research facility Laboratoire Roger Bellon. By 1969 Rhone-Poulenc was the largest company in France, and the following year it became the third-largest chemical company in Europe.

In the early 1970s, France's high tariffs limited foreign expansion. Though the company tried to expand globally, its efforts proved ill timed, as little market share was left for which to compete. To add to Rhone-Poulenc's financial woes, the French government's attempts to decrease inflation were detrimental to business, and forced the company to lay off 20,000 employees.

By the latter part of the decade, the company had recovered. In 1979 its U.S. subsidiary, Rhone-Poulenc Inc., acquired 58% of Anken Industries. Two years later, Rhone-Poulenc purchased P.B.U.S.A. Co. and the agricultural chemicals business of Mobil Chemical Corp. In October of that year, the Socialist Mitterand party gained control of the French government and began to nationalize most of the country's companies. When Rhone-Poulenc was nationalized in 1982, the new French government installed Loik Le Floch-Prigent as its chairman. This year the company increased its revenues by making a number of acquisitions. But due to continued unprofitability, it lost its status as the country's largest chemical company. It later discontinued the production of fertilizers and petrochemicals.

In 1983 Floch-Prigent returned profitability to the company for the first time in four years by reducing the workforce and eliminating ailing operations. Two years later Siltec Corp., in which Rhone-Poulenc owned stock, agreed to make silicon wafers with Rhone-Poulenc. It also entered into a joint venture with Mitsui Petrochemical for the manufacture of computer boards.

The Business

Financials

Revenue (1998): $4.95 billion (FrF 29.2 billion)

Employees (1998): 26,000

SICs / NAICS

sic 2834 - Pharmaceutical Preparations

naics 325412 - Pharmaceutical Preparation Manufacturing

Jean-Rene Fourtou replaced Floch-Prigent as chairman in 1986. The company's farm chemicals business improved through the acquisition of the agri-chemicals business of Union Carbide Corp. The following year, the company acquired the industrial chemicals business of Stauffer, and Fourtou began advocating privatization. In 1989 net income exceeded FrF 3 billion on sales greater than FrF 73 billion.

In 1990 the company purchased 66% of Rhone-Poulenc Rorer Inc., a merger of R-P's human pharmaceuticals business with U.S.-based pharmaceuticals company, the Rorer Group Inc. This acquisition increased Rhone-Poulenc's North American sales with such products as Maalox, the world's best selling antacid. The following year it formed Pateur Merieux Serums et Vaccins, a joint venture with Merck & Co. for the manufacture of children's multi-vaccines. The company continued a divestiture program of non-core businesses. In 1991 alone its divestitures brought in more than $700 million. By 1992 Rhone-Poulenc was the world's eighth-largest chemical company, as well as France's largest chemical and veterinary pharmaceutical company.

In December 1993 Rhone-Poulenc became privatized when the French government sold its majority interest. Earlier that year the company had expanded into biotechnology by purchasing 37% of Applied Immune Science in a joint research venture in cell and gene therapy. In 1994 the company acquired Cooperation Pharmaceutique Francaise, the nation's second-largest over-the-counter drug distributor. In 1995 its Rhone-Merieux subsidiary acquired Sanofi's animal health activities in North American, South America, and Asia.

On July 31, 1997, Rhone-Poulenc merged Rhone-Merieux with Merck & Co.'s animal health business to form the world's leader in animal health and poultry genetics. Later that year it acquired full ownership of Rhone-Poulenc Rorer for FrF 27 billion. By the end of

The Officers

Chairman and CEO: Michel de Rosen

Sr. VP and General Counsel: Rick Boardman

Sr. VP and CFO: Guillaume Prache

VP, Communications: Marie-Dominique de La Salle

Sr. VP, Human Resources: Jean le Dain

1997, Rhone-Poulenc generated net sales of FrF 90 billion and had a workforce of 68,377.

In January 1998, the company formed Rhodia, one of the world's leaders in specialty chemicals, by combining its chemical operations with its fibers and polymers businesses. It operated in two main businesses: Life Sciences, comprised of pharmaceuticals and animal health units, and Specialty Chemicals, operating as Rhodia. In December of that year, Rhone-Poulenc announced a proposed merger with Hoescht AG to form Aventis SA, expected to be the world's largest life sciences company. In December 1998, the two companies evaluated the feasibility of speeding up the proposed merger to consummate it sometime in 1999, rather than the planned completion target date of 2001.

History of Rorer Group Inc.

The William H. Rorer pharmaceutical company was established in Pennsylvania in 1909. This small business began to experience significant growth under the leadership of Gerald Rorer when he assumed the helm of the family business in the 1950s. Maalox, which would remain the company's flagship product throughout the remainder of the century, was developed in the early 1950s. Rorer achieved immediate success with this antacid, yet Gerald realized that overdependence on that single product left the company vulnerable.

This prompted Rorer to diversify into agricultural and specialty chemicals by acquiring Amchem Products, Inc. in 1968. Two years later Rorer-Amchem recorded sales of $133 million, attributed in large part to the company's penetration into foreign markets. As a result, the company had the capital to increase its investments in research and development, expand its sales force, and secure more acquisitions.

While Rorer-Amchem's pharmaceutical business, especially Maalox, were highly profitable, the chemicals operations languished and drove down the firm's overall earnings and stock price. So in 1976 the com-

pany sold its Amchem division to Union Carbide. With an improved balance sheet, Rorer made several acquisitions that helped to boost its revenues in 1979 to $260.5 million, a 16.1% annual increase.

Meanwhile, the company introduced several notable new drugs, including Ascriptin, a Maalox-aspirin combination, and Slo-Phyllin, a treatment for asthma. Rorer eventually pulled Quaalude, the notorious sedative-hypnotic product, from the market amid adverse publicity arising from its appeal to illicit drug users. It manufactured such ontological products as hip, knee, and ankle replacements, and its surgical products division included such subsidiaries as Sonometrics Inc., Dyonics Inc., and Cryomedics Inc.

With sales of $475 million in 1982, Rorer continued to expand through acquisitions. It purchased Kremers-Urban, Omni Hearing Aid Systems, and the medical products division of Black & Decker.

The company's chairman, John Eckman, claimed that virtually each major pharmaceutical company had made acquisition overtures to Rorer at some point. He had rejected these proposals, and instituted defensive measure to thwart any hostile takeover attempt. In 1983, when a group of shareholders representing 13% of the company's stock began shopping for a potential buyer for Rorer, Eckman increased the firm's authorized shares by 66%, thereby making Rorer prohibitively expensive to acquire.

Two years later the company faced another takeover challenge. Parker Montgomery, chairman of Cooper Laboratories, launched a proxy fight to gain control of Rorer's board. In response, Rorer's shareholders adopted a "poison pill." When triggered, this defensive tactic froze the hostile suitor's stake in the company while allowing its other shareholder to purchase Rorer stock at a much-reduced price, thereby diluting the value of the raider's stake. Montgomery was unsuccessful in his attempt to enlist Rorer shareholders to revoke the poison pill and eventually terminated his takeover attempt.

Robert Cawthorn succeeded Eckman as CEO in May 1985 and began making significant changes at Rorer. He divested the company of its surgical products business, installed a new management team, and increased the company's research and development (R&D)budget from a mere $18 million in 1985 to $125 million in 1989. The purchase of Revlon, Inc.'s ethical drug division from Pantry Pride Inc. for $690 million nearly doubled Rorer's sales, which reached $845 million in 1986.

In June 1987 Rorer offered to acquire A.H. Robins Co., the bankrupt manufacturer of the faulty Dalkon Shield intrauterine device (IUD). American Home

Products launched a rival bid, however, and ultimately won Robins for $3.3 billion.

Rorer's sales in 1989 reached $1.1 billion, yet its acquisition spree and investments into marketing and R&D left the company highly leveraged, and therefore vulnerable to a takeover. In early 1990 it entered into friendly merger negotiations with Rhone-Poulenc S.A.; Rhone-Poulenc Rorer was formed that August.

Market Forces Driving the Merger

The pharmaceutical industry experienced a wave of consolidation activity beginning in the late 1980s. For many companies, impending patent expiry on their blockbuster drugs would permit competitors to introduce generic version of the products, with the likelihood of undercutting prices in order to steal the market from the brand name product. New breakthrough drugs were needed, but many potential blockbusters were tied up in the companies' research and development pipelines. They could remain there for years before emerging and enter another waiting period, this time from government regulators.

The year 1988 saw the first of the industry's large-scale mergers. A hostile takeover attempt by Roche drove Sterling Drug into the arms of Eastman Kodak in a $5.1 billion deal. Also that year, American Home Products beat Sanofi in a contest for A.H. Robins Co. The stakes got even higher in 1989. SmithKline Beckman merged with Beecham for $16 billion, and Bristol-Myers and Squibb teamed up in a $12 billion deal.

The pressure to form unions was particularly intense for European pharmaceutical companies. Despite the fact that they filled out the ranks of the world's largest players, most had little, if any, presence in the U.S. market, the industry's largest. Moreover, their relatively secure positions in their home territories was facing the threat of increased cross-border competition arising from the European Commission's elimination of internal trade barriers in 1992.

Rorer Group, a medium-sized U.S. pharmaceutical firm, wanted to remain independent. Its strategy had been to increase its strength through acquisitions, notably its 1985 acquisition of Revlon's pharmaceutical operations, which doubled the company's size. Under chairman Robert Cawthorn, Rorer had recently begun increasing its research and development budget, up from $18 million in 1985 to $125 million four years later. Despite these improvements, Rorer remained a vulnerable takeover target. Its acquisition campaign had left the company saddled with debt, thereby restricting its ability to engage in future high-priced acquisitions.

The Players

Rorer Group Chairman and CEO: Robert E. Cawthorn. English-born Robert Cawthorn was an 18-year veteran of Pfizer. After joining the startup Biogen, he became president of the Rorer Group's international unit in 1982. In May 1985 he became the company's CEO, and led it on a successful campaign to focus on core businesses and reduce its dependence on Maalox by investing serious amounts of money into research and development. He then orchestrated the 1990 merger with Rhone-Poulenc's pharmaceuticals business.

In April 1995 Cawthorn passed the post of CEO to Michael de Rosen, and one year later resigned as chairman, as well. In early 1997 Cawthorn became one of the three directors of the newly formed Global Healthcare Partners, a healthcare investment firm of Donaldson, Lufkin & Jenrette.

Approach and Engagement

In May 1989 Rorer's chairman Robert Cawthorn announced that he would be willing to entertain the notion of a merger if a suitable partner should come forth. That sent the message that Rorer was up for sale, and Wall Street abounded with speculation about potential suitors. Yet by autumn none had emerged.

On January 15, 1990, Rorer disclosed that it had been engaged since December in merger negotiations with an undisclosed company. Three days later it revealed that Rhone-Poulenc S.A. had agreed to merge most of its pharmaceutical operations into Rorer. The $3.15 billion deal, which was still just a preliminary agreement, called for Rhone-Poulenc to acquire a 68% stake in Rorer in exchange for a cash-and-stock package worth about $73 per share.

The newly formed company, which would be based in the U.S., would become the world's sixth-largest pharmaceutical firm. Cawthorn would remain its chairman and CEO, but its board would be controlled by Rhone-Poulenc. Not included in the deal were Rhone-Poulenc's valuable chemical business, nor its serum and vaccine operations.

A delay in arriving at definitive terms was attributed by the companies to complexity of the multi-step transaction and to the arduous task of auditing Rhone-Poulenc's pharmaceutical operations as separate from its chemicals business. On March 12, 1990, the firms declared a definitive pact. The previously announced elements of the deal remained intact, but details as to the mechanics of the transaction were revealed.

First, Rhone-Poulenc would make a cash tender offer at $78 per share for 50.1% of Rorer's stock, totaling $1.68 billion. In the second step, Rhone-Poulenc would increase its stake to 68% by offering Rorer shareholders stock in the new company, plus contingent-value rights ensuring reimbursement from Rhone-Poulenc if the new company's stock price fell below a specified level over its first three years of operation.

Rhone-Poulenc completed its tender offer in May. Following Rorer shareholders' approval of the remainder of the deal, Rhone-Poulenc Rorer was formed on August 1, 1990. The 32% stake not held by Rhone-Poulenc was listed on the New York Stock Exchange.

Products and Services

Rhone-Poulenc Rorer stated that its principal objectives were to improve the quality of human health through the discovery, development, manufacture, and marketing of innovative medicines that meet patient needs in three targeted therapeutic areas—respiratory/allergy, oncology, and thrombosis/cardiology. In 1998 the firm was among the top pharmaceutical companies in the world, and one of the top three in Europe. It marketed its products in 140 countries and had manufacturing operations in 30 countries.

Changes to the Industry/Review of the Outcome

At the end of 1992 Rhone-Poulenc Rorer's sales surpassed $4 billion. Its research and development budget had increased four-fold since 1989, and the company's pipeline contained several potential blockbusters. It had significantly increased its global presence, as sales from the U.S. accounted for only 22% of total revenues.

Part of these results were attributed to cost savings arising from consolidating operations. Rhone-Poulenc Rorer closed five European factories, thereby eliminating 22,500 positions. It also refocused on pharmaceuticals and hospital products by selling off noncore businesses.

The new company continued in the tradition of Rorer by forming strategic partnerahips. In 1994 it formed Centeon LLC with Hoescht to produce hemophilia treatments. In 1995, the same year that Michael de Rosen succeeded Cawthorn as CEO, the firm purchased Brazil-based Rhodia Farma and the U.K. pharmaceutical company Fisons plc. In September 1997 Rhone-Poulenc Rorer became a wholly owned subsidiary of Rhone-Poulenc when the French company acquired the 32% stake that it didn't already own for FrF 27 billion.

Research

Koenig, Richard. "Rhone-Poulenc, Rorer Set Linkup Pact That They Value at About $3.15 Billion," in *The Wall Street Journal*, 13 March 1990. Details the definitive agreement.

———. "Rhone-Poulenc Unit to Merge with Rorer," in *The Wall Street Journal*, 19 January 1990. Describes the terms of the preliminary merger agreement.

Novack, Janet. "Please Pass the Maalox," in *Forbes*, 7 August 1989. Details the advancements that Rorer had achieved since Cawthorn took the helm.

Rhone-Poulenc Rorer Inc. Home Page, available at http://www.rp-rorer.com. Official World Wide Page for Rhone-Poulenc Rorer. Includes financial, product, and employment information, news releases, and a directory of offices.

"Rhone-Poulenc SA," in *Notable Corporate Chronologies*, The Gale Group, 1999. Lists major events in the company's history.

Rhone-Poulenc SA, 1997 Annual Report. Details the company's finances and operating segments.

"Rorer Group," in *International Directory of Company Histories*, Vol. I, St. James Press: 1988. Provides a narrative account of the company's history.

Weber, Joseph, and Charles Hoots. "What a Difference a Merger Makes," in *Business Week*, 7 December 1992. Describes the successful of the merged company at the end of its second year in operation.

KIMBERLY N. STEVENS

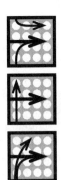

RITE AID & REVCO

date: April 25, 1996 (canceled)
affected: Rite Aid Corp., USA, founded 1962
affected: CVS Corp. (parent of Revco D.S. Inc.), USA, founded 1947

Rite Aid Corp.
30 Hunter Ln.
Camp Hill, PA 17011-2404
USA

tel: (717)761-2633
web: http://www.riteaid.com

CVS Corp.
One CVS Dr.
Woonsocket, RI 02895
USA

tel: (401)765-1500
fax: (401)762-2137
web: http://www.cvs.com

Overview of the Merger

On November 30, 1995, Rite Aid and Revco announced their $1.8 billion merger agreement. The combined company, which was to operate under the Rite Aid name, would bring in about $9.95 billion in annual sales, closing the gap between it and Walgreen's, the nation's leader, with sales of $10.4 billion. Hopes of going for that gold, however, were dashed on April 24, 1996, when the Federal Trade Commission announced its intention of seeking federal injunction of the deal. Rather than fight in what would likely be a losing battle, Rite Aid withdrew its acquisition offer the following day. The two companies retired to their separate corners to resume business as usual, a concept that had been put on hold for several months in anticipation of the merger.

History of Rite Aid

Alex Grass founded Rack Rite Distributors in 1958 to supply grocery stores with such non-food products as health and beauty aids. In 1962 Grass opened the Thrif D discount drugstore in Scranton, Pennsylvania. By the end of that year, the store was earning $25,000 per week. Grass expanded his business into New York in 1963 and into New Jersey and Virginia in 1964. Two years later he introduced a pharmacy in one of his 36 stores.

Grass changed the company name to Rite Aid in 1968. That year the company made its initial public offering and began expansion through acquisition, starting with the 11-store Martin's chain. It followed up this purchase with an average of about one chain each year throughout the 1970s.

In 1969 Rite Aid also began diversification by acquiring Immuno Serums and Sero-Genics. Two years later it added to its medical holdings by purchasing Sera-Tec Biologicals. In 1980 Rite Aid became one of the nation's leading plasma suppliers with the opening of its sixth plasmapheresis center.

The company's drugstore operations experienced even greater growth, and in 1981 it became the nation's third-largest retail drug chain. It began diversifying into other retail industries by purchasing Circus World Toy Stores in 1982 and

The Business

Financials - Rite Aid Corp.

Revenue (1998): $11.4 billion

Employees (1998): 83,000

Financials - CVS Corp.

Revenue (1998): $15.3 billion

Employees (1998): 80,000

SICs / NAICS

sic 5912 - Drug Stores & Proprietary Stores

naics 446110 - Pharmacies and Drug Stores

American Discount Auto Parts and Encore Books in 1984. That year it spun off its wholesale grocery business, Super Rite.

Rite Aid continued to add to its drugstore chain through a string of acquisitions: SupeRx in 1987, Begley Co. and Gray Drug Fair in 1988, a number of Wellby Super Drug and Reliable Drug stores in 1993, and the LaVerdiere's Enterprises and Perry Drugs chains in 1994. In 1992 it made acquisition overtures for the bankrupt Revco chain, but withdrew when the bidding escalated too high. In 1994 Rite Aid refocused on its core business by beginning to divest itself of all non-drugstore operations. The company also launched Eagle Managed Care, a pharmacy benefits management (PBM) company. At the end of fiscal 1994, Rite Aid operated 2,690 stores in 23 states, and generated $4.06 billion in sales.

History of Revco D.S.

Bernard Shulman opened the Regal drugstore in 1947 in Detroit. In 1956 the four-store chain transformed itself into a discount drugstore operation. Six years later Regal, which operated 24 Michigan stores, expanded into Ohio by acquiring the 40-unit Standard Drug chain. In 1964 the company, now known as Revco D.S., made its initial public offering. The capital generated from the offering enabled it to expand further, and it acquired the Peck Drug and Patterson Drug chains in 1967. Revco diversified with its 1974 launch of the Revco Optical Center. The company became the nation's largest drugstore chain based on number of stores, as it opened its 1,000th unit in 1978. Five years later it increased that total to 1,700.

Just as it was enjoying its leading position, the company suffered a devastating blow when a vitamin produced by its Carter-Glogau Laboratories subsidiary was shown to have contributed to the deaths of 38 children. The ensuing federal investigation caused Revco stock to plummet. To thwart possible takeover attempts, CEO Sidney Dworkin traded $113 million in Revco stock, a 12% stake, for ownership of Odd Lot Trading, run by Bernard Marden and Issac Perlmutter. Unfortunately, this safety net disintegrated when those partners attempted a takeover of Revco themselves. The company bought them out and executed a leveraged buyout in 1986, accumulating debt of $1.1 billion in the process. It hung on for over a year, but in 1988 it filed for bankruptcy and began to close or sell almost 900 stores.

In 1992 Sam Zell and other investors bailed out Revco, and it emerged from bankruptcy. D. Dwayne Hoven became CEO the following year, and in 1994 the company bought the 1,100-store Hook SupeRx chain for $600 million. Fiscal 1994 results demonstrated that Revco appeared to be on the path to recovery, as sales were $2.5 billion and net income was $38.7 million.

Market Forces Driving the Merger

Managed care had altered the face of the chain drugstore industry by the mid-1990s. Drugstores found themselves at an increasingly competitive disadvantage against pharmacy benefit management (PBM) companies. Many of these operations are administered by their drug company parents, such as Merck & Co., Smithkline Beecham, or Eli Lilly & Co. These vertically integrated prescription networks control the distribution of drugs, from their manufacture to public consumption. In dictating where the public can go to get a prescription filled, PBMs have a stronghold on managed pharmacy care that is very difficult for chain drug retailers to penetrate. They controlled the distribution network, and in so doing can effectively control the price of drugs. PBMs offer prescription benefits plans to large third-party companies, whose employees are allowed to fill their prescriptions only at those drugstores so authorized by that particular PBM. In exchange for these participation rights, retailers are charged fees by the PBMs. These fees are sometimes so oppressive that the pharmacy accounts for less and less of drugstore profits.

Eagle Managed Care, Rite Aid's small PBM, was still too lightweight to compete with the PBM giants for third-party contracts. But through expansion, the drug store chain would acquire more resources to develop this network and secure exclusive managed care contracts. It would still be much smaller than the others, but at least it would be operating on a more level playing field.

A boost for such an aspiring drugstore chain would be to increase its geographic coverage, giving it more clout in securing contracts. Rather than spread itself thinly over a large territory, Rite Aid realized that the smarter option would be to intensify its coverage in the same area, becoming more convenient to end-customers and therefore more attractive to third-party companies.

With this in mind, Rite Aid viewed Revco as a prime acquisition. Except for the state of Illinois, the two companies operated in the same 20 eastern and midwestern states. Revco's prescription mail order operations would also increase Rite Aid's leverage. Based on number of stores, the 2,700-unit Rite Aid was the largest drugstore chain in the U.S., while Revco's 2,100 stores ranked it second. Upon acquisition, Rite Aid would increase its coverage from 13 markets to 36 markets. The two combined companies would operate 4,800 stores and generate revenues of about $9.95 billion, right behind the industry leader, Walgreen, which had $10.4 billion in sales. Looking ahead, Rite Aid chairman and CEO Martin Grass was quoted in a December 1995 issue of *Drug Store News* as saying, "We will be the best-positioned drug store chain to compete with the large, vertically integrated pharmacy management systems owned by the pharmaceutical companies."

Approach and Engagement

Martin Grass approached Revco board member David Schulte in August 1995 to discuss a possible acquisition. Schulte was a partner of the Zell/Chilmark Fund, Revco's largest stockholder, with a 19.7% interest. Interested, he arranged a formal meeting between Grass's team and two Revco board members. Schulte, with the approval of the board, agreed to tender the fund's stake.

On November 30, 1995, Rite Aid and Revco announced their $1.8 billion merger agreement. Under the terms, Rite Aid would acquire 50.1% of Revco's outstanding stock. Revco's shareholders were offered a choice between cashing in their stock at $27.50 per share or tendering them later in exchange for Rite Aid stock. At completion of the merger, any remaining Revco stock would be converted to Rite Aid interests.

During 1996, the first three tender deadlines were missed and then extended, yet by early April Rite Aid still didn't have enough of the necessary shares. During this time, the Federal Trade Commission (FTC) was investigating the deal for possible antitrust violations. In March, Rite Aid rejected its right to the imposition of a time limit for the FTC inquiry, confident that federal approval would soon be forthcoming. On April 10th, however, with a decision still pending, Rite

The Officers

Rite Aid Corp.

Chairman and CEO: Martin L. Grass

President and Chief Operating Officer: Timothy J. Noonan

Vice Chairman: Franklin C. Brown

Exec. VP and CFO: Frank M. Bergonzi

CVS Corp.

Chairman: Stanley P. Goldstein

President and CEO, CVS Corp. and CVS/pharmacy, Inc.: Thomas M. Ryan

Exec. VP and CFO, CVS Corp. and CVS/pharmacy, Inc.: Charles C. Conaway

Exec. VP, Corporate Development: Lawrence Zigerelli

Aid drew a line in the sand: unless it received the FTC's decision by April 29th it would withdraw its acquisition offer.

The ultimatum didn't produce the result the company had been expecting. On April 17, 1996, the FTC announced that its five commissioners had unanimously voted to block the acquisition in federal court. Attorney generals of the states of Ohio, Pennsylvania, New York, and West Virginia followed suit, announcing that they would seek their own injunctions to stop the deal. On April 18, 1996, Rite Aid followed through on its promise and called off the merger.

In a strategy that can often alleviate FTC antitrust concerns, Rite Aid had previously offered to close 340 stores. Given the concentration of the two chains, however, the FTC found the overlap too great, and had countered by recommending the closure of 650-700 units, as well as all Revco outlets in Ohio, South Carolina, and West Virginia. This counter-offer was too much for the companies to accept, and the two sides had reached an impasse.

The FTC reasoned that the merger would have created a company with enough of a hold on its markets to influence drug prices. According to the commission, by controlling the majority of chain drugstores in a market, the business could decline to participate in a given managed care program, putting it in a position to demand higher reimbursement rates from PBMs, who would then pass those extra expenses on to the consumer.

The Players

Rite Aid Chairman and CEO: Martin L. Grass. Martin Grass took the helm of Rite Aid in March 1995 upon his father's retirement. Alex Grass, the chain's founder, chairman, and CEO, passed the reins to Martin, who had served as president and chief operating officer since 1989. A future at Rite Aid had been essentially mapped out for Martin throughout his adult life. As a teenager, he worked at the chain after school and on vacations. He went on to graduate from the University of Pennsylvania in 1976 and earn a Master's degree in business administration from Cornell University two years later. At that time, he joined the company full-time and moved through successive executive positions.

Revco President and CEO: D. Dwayne Hoven. D. Dwayne Hoven is credited with revitalizing Revco and instilling in it a sense of direction. In July 1992, one month after the company emerged from bankruptcy, Hoven was promoted from executive vice president and chief operating officer to president. Earnings for his first fiscal year at the helm skyrocketed 224% from $10.8 million to $35 million. In September 1993 he added the position of CEO to his responsibilities. Hoven's climb to the top of Revco came about fairly quickly. He had joined the firm in 1987 as a senior vice president of distribution, and from there moved through various executive positions. His background prior to Revco included executive positions at Sav-A-Stop and TG&Y Stores & Co.

Review of the Outcome

Disappointed and stunned at the collapse of their plans, Rite Aid and Revco hitched up their boots and threw themselves back into their respective businesses. After months of regarding each other as eventual partners, each chain had to return to considering the other as a competitor.

The companies learned their lesson about the FTC's objection to large mergers within overlapping markets, yet still recognized that consolidation was the most feasible method of competing in a managed care environment. As an illustration of its commitment in this arena, Revco chairman and CEO D. Dwayne Hoven said in a prepared statement, "The FTC's ruling in this case does not preclude further consolidation in the retail drugstore business."

That statement proved to be prophetic, as Revco purchased the 400-unit Big B drugstore chain for $380 million in 1996. Then, on May 29, 1997, Revco itself was purchased by CVS Inc. for $2.8 billion. Upon this acquisition, that company, later renamed CVS Revco D.S. Inc., became the nation's largest drug store chain, with 3,888 units in 24 states.

Martin Grass, too, endorsed Hoven's views on consolidation by stating at Rite Aid's annual meeting in June 1996, "Our acquisition strategy will be to continue to look for chains both in our trading area and, now, outside our trading area." True to its word, the company expanded into western U.S. by acquiring the 1,000-store Thrifty Pay Less chain for $2.3 million before the end of 1996. Rite Aid continued to expand in 1997 and 1998, acquiring K&B, Harco Drug, and PCS Health Systems.

Research

Fried, Lisa I. "Clout! What Martin Will Do," in *Drug Store News*, 11 December 1995. How Martin Grass set up the acquisition of Revco.

———. "Inside the Mind of the FTC: Will the Rite Aid/Revco Deal Survive?" in *Drug Store News*, 29 April 1996. After the FTC's announcement to block the deal, industry experts wonder if Rite Aid will be able to negotiate a settlement.

———. "Rite Aid Shifts Growth Strategy," in *Drug Store News*, 8 July 1996. Brief mention of Rite Aid's plans in the dust of the failed merger.

"FTC Moves to Block Rite Aid-Revco Deal," in *Chain Drug Review*, 6 May 1996. Discussion of the FTC's inquiry and ultimate decision in prohibiting the merger.

Griffen, Marie. "Industry Mulls Impact of Massive Merger Plan," in *Drug Store News*, 11 December 1995. The effects that the merger would have on competition.

"Hoven Gets CEO Post at Revco," in *Chain Drug Review*, 13 September 1993. Summary of D. Dwayne Hoven's career at Revco.

Mooney, Barbara. "Revco Still Ripe to Merge," in *Crain's Cleveland Business*, 29 April 1996. Possible future plans for Revco in the fall-out of the blocked merger.

Rite Aid 1998 Annual Report. Lists in-depth financial news and announcements.

"Rite Aid Corp.," in *Notable Corporate Chronologies*, The Gale Group, 1999. Lists major events in the company's history.

"Rite Aid Merger with Revco Changes Face of the Industry," in *Chain Drug Review*, 6 May 1996. Highlights of the impact that the merger would have on the pharmacy benefits management environment. Although dated after the merger was called off, this article is written as though it was still going to survive.

Ukens, Carol. "Rite Aid Abandons Its Plans to Purchase Revco," in *Drug Topics*, 20 May 1996. Reasons why the FTC blocked the deal, and statements from both companies' CEOs on what it meant for their respective businesses.

Wilson, Marianne. "Groomed for Succession," in *Chain Store Age Executive*, April 1995. The challenges faced by Martin Grass as he assumes the positions of chairman and CEO of Rite Aid.

WILLIAM P. FREEMAN

R.J. REYNOLDS & NABISCO BRANDS

nationality: USA
date: July 1985
affected: R.J. Reynolds Industries Inc., USA, founded 1874
affected: Nabisco Brands, Inc., USA, founded 1898

Nabisco Group Holdings Corp.
1301 Avenue of the Americas
New York, NY 10019
USA

tel: (212)258-5600
fax: (212)969-9173
web: http://www.rjrnabisco.com

Overview of the Acquisition

The 1985 acquisition of Nabisco Brands by R.J. Reynolds formed RJR Nabisco, the largest consumer products company in the U.S. This deal represented the highest ever paid for a food products company at that time, but was considered well worth the $4.9 billion price tag. Nabisco offered valuable brand names, a dominant share in several markets, and an international distribution network, as well as critical protection in the form of diversification for the tobacco-dependent Reynolds.

History of R.J. Reynolds Industries Inc.

In 1874, after selling his interest in his father's tobacco business, Richard Joshua Reynolds moved to Winston, North Carolina, the heart of the bright leaf tobacco area. He invested $7,500 in land, and built a small factory in which to manufacture flat plug chewing tobacco. In the first year of operation, the establishment produced 150,000 pounds of tobacco.

The R.J. Reynolds Tobacco Co. was incorporated in North Carolina in 1879. It faced stiff competition from manufacturers in Winston and its neighboring city of Salem. In 1884, R.J.'s brother, William Neal Reynolds, joined the firm. Initially, Reynolds' products were sold to jobbers who distributed chewing tobacco under their own brand names.

In 1885, R.J. Reynolds introduced Schnapps, his own brand of chewing tobacco, which soon gained popularity. The next year he registered "R.J.R." as his trademark and had an elaborate RJR design affixed to his carriage. These ornate initials became the company's symbol and remained such until they were redesigned in 1961. The company issued its first stock in 1890, with the firm's founder owning nearly 90%. R.J. Reynolds was elected president and his brother served as vice president. A sales department was created, as was a systematic national advertising program.

Reynolds was one of the first companies to introduce saccharin as a sweetening agent in chewing tobacco. The company also adopted many laborsaving devices and experienced a 400% production increase over the next six years.

The Business

Financials

Revenue (1998): $17 billion

Employees (1998): 80,400

SICs / NAICS

sic 2064 - Candy & Other Confectionery Products

sic 2052 - Cookies & Crackers

sic 2067 - Chewing Gum

sic 2068 - Salted & Roasted Nuts & Seeds

sic 2035 - Pickles, Sauces & Salad Dressings

naics 311330 - Confectionery Manufacturing from Purchased Chocolate

naics 311340 - Non-Chocolate Confectionery Manufacturing

naics 311821 - Cookie and Cracker Manufacturing

naics 311919 - Other Snack Food Manufacturing

naics 311911 - Roasted Nuts and Peanut Butter Manufacturing

naics 311941 - Mayonnaise, Dressing, and Other Prepared Sauce Manufacturing

Reynolds began experimenting with smoking tobacco in 1894 to compete with James Buchanan Duke's profitable brands as well as to turn scrap tobacco into a paying product. The next year the company introduced its first smoking tobacco brand, Naturally Sweet Cut Plug.

Although company assets were valued at over $1 million, its considerable expansion late in the decade brought about a need for large amounts of capital. Reluctantly, Reynolds sought help from rival James Duke. Duke's American Tobacco Co. had established a subsidiary, Continental Tobacco Co., in an effort to monopolize the nation's chewing tobacco business. Reynolds sold two-thirds of his stock to Continental, but retained his position as president of the R.J. Reynolds Tobacco Co. Reynolds tried to maintain his independence in Duke's tobacco trust and was determined not to be swallowed up by his rival. Duke extended Reynolds this independence as long as he acquired chewing tobacco companies in the Virginia and Carolina areas for the trust. Reynolds proceeded to buy ten such companies.

R.J. Reynolds demonstrated his independence from the trust in 1905 by producing five brands of smoking tobacco. Two years later Prince Albert smoking tobacco, a unique mixture of burley and flue-cured tobacco, was introduced by Reynolds. The product achieved instant success with the slogan "It can't bite your tongue."

The tobacco trust, like most trusts during this period, proved unpopular. In 1911, a U.S. Circuit Court ordered the dissolution of the American Tobacco Co. Since American was forced to divest itself of all Reynolds stock, R.J. Reynolds and members of his family reacquired some of the firm's stock. During the trust's years, Reynolds expanded facilities, hired aggressive management, and increased production and sales almost five-fold.

In 1912, R.J. regained control of the company, at a time when Reynolds Tobacco was the smallest of the big four tobacco manufacturers. The company again considered the production of cigarettes because of the great success experienced by its Prince Albert brand. Profits that year reached $2.75 million.

After manufacturing the company's first cigarette, Reynolds decided to produce three different cigarette brands simultaneously to see which one had the greatest public appeal. R.J. personally selected the blend of Turkish, burley, and flue-cured tobaccos, along with the new name of the brand that would prove most popular, Camel. The item became instantly successful due to its blend, low price, and advertising. In 1915, in fact, Reynolds spent more than $2 million in an aggressive national advertising campaign.

William Neal Reynolds assumed the presidency after the death of R.J. Reynolds in 1918. At that time the company employed 10,000 people in 121 buildings in the Winston-Salem area. Four years later its preferred stock was listed on the New York Stock Exchange.

Sales rose to nearly $24 million in 1924, largely because of the phenomenal success of Camel. The firm's net profits surpassed those of the nation's largest manufacturer, the American Tobacco Co. At that time the majority of the company's voting stock was in the hands of employees. Over the past several years, employees had been encouraged, via a company bylaw, to purchase voting stock, and had even been allowed to borrow from surplus funds and profits to do so. In 1927, the company's common stock was publicly listed for the first time.

Bowman Gray, Sr., became chairman in 1931. Under his direction, the firm introduced a moisture-proof cellophane wrapper to preserve freshness in cigarettes, an innovation other companies soon adopted. The company also began manufacturing its own tin foil and paper from factories in North Carolina to reduce dependence on foreign supplies, and it developed a new sales policy stressing mass sales based on brand name loyalty and recognition.

In 1948, in a major antitrust suit against the tobacco industry, several Reynolds officers were convicted and fined on charges of monopolistic practices; the company itself was also found guilty. The next year Reynolds introduced a major new cigarette brand, Cavalier. The product never won a wide acceptance, however, and lost a total of $30 million over five years.

An article entitled "Cancer by the Carton" appeared in *Reader's Digest* in 1952, and the tobacco industry began to experience, for the first time, critical attacks centering on the issue of smoking and health. The next year the Sloan-Kettering Cancer Institute announced that its research showed a relationship between cancer and tobacco. The development of filter-tipped cigarettes was, in part, a response to such health concerns.

Winston, the company's first filter-tipped cigarette, was introduced in March 1954 to compete directly with Brown & Williamson's Viceroy brand. With such catchy slogans as "Winston tastes good like a cigarette should" and "It's what's up front that counts," the cigarette was quickly accepted, selling 40 billion in its first year alone.

Two years later Reynolds began marketing Salem, the industry's first king-size, filter-tipped menthol cigarette. The new brand went on to reap tremendous profits, but Camel remained the industry leader through the beginning of the next decade.

In 1957, the board of directors responded to increasing health concerns by appointing a diversification committee to study possible investment in nontobacco areas and to consider expansion of tobacco operations overseas. Alexander H. Galloway became president in 1960 and, along with Chairman Bowman Gray, Jr., led the company into a period of unparalleled growth and diversification. Its diversification strategy initially focused on acquisitions in food-related industries. Reynolds bought a controlling interest in Haus Neuerburg, one of West Germany's leading cigarette manufacturers, thereby marking the beginning of international tobacco operations for Reynolds.

All cigarette manufacturing was centralized in 1961 with the opening of a massive, modern factory in Winston-Salem, North Carolina. Two years later Reynolds bought Pacific Hawaiian Products.

The U.S. surgeon general issued a report linking smoking with lung cancer and heart disease in 1964. The next year U.S. Congress passed the Cigarette Advertising and Labeling Act, requiring tobacco companies to place health warnings on cigarette packs.

The Officers

Chairman, President, and CEO: Steven F. Goldstone

Sr. VP, Human Resources and Administration: Gerald I. Angowitz

Sr. VP and General Auditor: Jeffrey A. Kuchar

Sr. VP, Associate General Counsel, and Secretary: H. Colin McBride

Sr. VP, Strategy and Business Development: Lionel L.Nowell III

Reynolds acquired Chun King for $63 million in 1966. R.J. Reynolds Foods, a subsidiary, was created to encompass all of the organization's non-tobacco companies. Two years later R.J. Reynolds International was established to develop foreign tobacco markets.

In June 1970, all tobacco operations became a subsidiary of R.J. Reynolds Industries; thus the word "tobacco," now with questionable connotations, was removed from the firm's name. A.H. Galloway became the new company's first chairman and CEO. Under the holding company structure, Reynolds Industries provided coordinated and centralized financial, administrative, personnel, public relations, and other services, as well as overall management, for the subsidiaries.

Later that year, Reynolds Industries acquired American Independent Oil Co. (Aminoil), an independent producer and refiner whose principal sales were to other oil companies. Also, Vantage brand cigarettes were first marketed.

In 1971, cigarette advertising was banned from radio and television. Three years later Winston Lights, a low "tar" and nicotine version of the original Winston cigarette, went on sale. The company acquired one of Canada's largest tobacco manufacturers, Macdonald Tobacco Inc., which had been the sole Canadian distributor of RJR cigarette brands.

In addition to governmental pressure, Reynolds faced intense competition, primarily from Philip Morris, and marketing strategies focused on luring customers away from competitors instead of attracting new smokers. Philip Morris' Marlboro brand surpassed Winston in domestic sales in 1976. The next year Reynolds introduced its Real brand cigarette to appeal to the back-to-nature movement; sales proved disastrous, and within three years the product was discontinued.

The Players

R.J. Reynolds Industries Inc. Chairman and CEO: J. Tylee Wilson. J. Tylee Wilson took the helm of R.J. Reynolds in September 1983, and proceeded to shed the company of its expensive oil and gas businesses in order to focus on consumer brands. Although he remained the company's chairman and CEO after its merger with Nabisco Brands, F. Ross Johnson, his second in command, was largely running the company within a month. Less than a year later the board of directors replaced Wilson with Johnson

Nabisco Brands CEO: F. Ross Johnson. F. Ross Johnson, born in Winnipeg, Canada, and educated as an accountant, made a career out of crafting deals for the companies that employed him. In 1981, as president of Standard Brands, he orchestrated the company's merger with Nabisco. Then, as president of Nabisco, he sold the company to RJR Reynolds four years later. He was named president of the newly merged company and added the title of CEO in 1987. In 1988, he put RJR Nabisco in play by attempting to take it private, against the wishes of its board, through a leveraged buyout. When the company went to Kohlberg Kravis Roberts instead, Johnson resigned.

R.J. Reynolds acquired produce giant Del Monte Corp. in 1979. The next year Reynolds was the first U.S. company to reach an agreement with the People's Republic of China to manufacture and sell cigarettes there. Late in 1980 the firm announced an ambitious $2 billion, ten-year construction and plant modernization plan.

The federal cigarette tax doubled in 1983. Reynolds acquired Heublein Inc., a well-known manufacturer of wines and spirits. It also began manufacturing the novel 25-cigarette-per-pack Century brand. Most consumers, however, preferred the traditional 20-cigarette pack. That year competitor Philip Morris usurped Reynolds as the leader in domestic sales.

In 1984, with the sale of Aminoil to Phillips Petroleum for $1.7 billion, Reynolds completed the divestiture of all transportation and energy operations.

In one of the largest acquisitions in corporate history, R.J. Reynolds purchased Nabisco Brands, Inc. for $4.9 billion in 1985. F. Ross Johnson, a Nabisco veter-

an, was appointed president and COO of the new firm, RJR Nabisco Holdings Corp.

In 1986, Johnson assumed the position of CEO. He continued the policy of returning the company to its core business by selling off more than half the corporation's subsidiaries. Headquarters were moved from Winston-Salem to Atlanta, Georgia. The next year Reynolds began test-marketing a smokeless cigarette, Premier, in response to mounting pressure to make smoking more acceptable; the item was a colossal failure, however. That same year, Heublein was sold to Grand Metropolitan.

At a meeting of the board of directors in 1988, Johnson proposed a leveraged buyout to take the company private. The directors, alienated by Johnson's proposal, opened the door to other bidders, and ultimately accepted the $25 billion offer by Kohlberg Kravis Roberts & Co.; this was the largest leveraged buyout in U.S. history.

RJR Nabisco Holdings Corp. was established as the parent company of RJR Nabisco, Inc. After F. Ross Johnson resigned, KKR selected Louis Gerstner, Jr., to take over as CEO. He immediately instituted cost cutting measures, including an 11.5% personnel cutback in tobacco operations. Corporate headquarters relocated to New York and Nabisco's European food business was divested.

In 1990, Del Monte's processed foods operation was sold, along with selected facets of Nabisco. RJR's attempts to target specific consumer groups with new cigarette brands failed. The company did, however, succeed in penetrating the Soviet market.

Sales of the company's three most popular brands, Camel, Winston, and Salem, accounted for 28% of 1991 revenues. By that time debt had been reduced to about $17 billion from $25 billion at the time of the buyout. The company once again went public with a new issue of stock; the action put approximately 25% of the firm back in public hands with KKR retaining roughly 65%. Also that year the company was criticized by the American Medical Association for marketing to minors through its ad campaign featuring a cartoon-type character called Joe Camel.

By May 1993, RJR Nabisco was facing cash-flow problems due to price competition in the cigarette industry and a proposed increase in the cigarette tax. The firm also lost CEO Louis V. Gerstner, Jr., who resigned to take the top job at IBM. Mike Harper, noted for developing ConAgra into a strong company, took the helm as CEO of RJR Nabisco.

In November 1995, investors Bennett S. LeBow and Carl Icahn purchased 4.8% of RJR Nabisco in a bid to force the company to split its food and tobacco businesses through a proxy battle. The following April, having defeated LeBow and Icahn, RJR Nabisco re-elected its board of directors and rejected a spin-off of its food operations. The company eliminated 6,000 jobs and took a charge of $428 million in 1996. This action was repeated in 1998 due to soft sales, resulting in another 6,500 job cuts and a charge of $530 million.

In May 1999, RJR Nabisco completed the sale of its international tobacco business to Japan Tobacco, Inc. for $8 billion. The following month the company's tobacco and food businesses were split, and RJR Nabisco was renamed Nabisco Group Holdings Corp.

History of Nabisco Brands, Inc.

The National Biscuit Co. was formed through the 1898 merger of the American Biscuit Co. and New York Biscuit. The new company's product lineup included such recognizable fare as Fig Newton cookies, invented in 1891; Nabisco Graham Crackers, developed in 1829 by Sylvester Graham; and Premium Soda Crackers, which later became known as Premium Saltines.

Chairman Aldolphus Green directed the company on a path of product and brand development. National Biscuit introduced the Uneeda Biscuit, a soda cracker that, unlike its predecessors, was packaged in a paper box. It became an immediate success, selling 10 million packages annually. Barnum's Animal Crackers were introduced in 1902, as were Oreo cookies in 1913. The firm expanded internationally in 1925 by launching operations in Canada.

National Biscuit began expanding through the acquisition of smaller companies. In 1928, it purchased the Shredded Wheat Co., maker of Triscuit Wafers and Shredded Wheat Cereal. Three years later it diversified into pet products by acquiring Bennett Biscuit, maker of Milk-Bone dog biscuits.

National Biscuit also continued to grow through internal product development. In November 1934, it introduced the Ritz Cracker, which, due to heavy demand, was distributed nationally the following year. The company changed its name to Nabisco in 1941, and during the 1950s focused on international expansion.

Nabisco purchased the Cream of Wheat Co. in 1962. It introduced Chips Ahoy! chocolate chip cookies in 1963 and Honey Maid graham crackers three years later. By the end of the 1960s the company was the leading manufacturer in crackers and cookies not only in the U.S., but also in Canada, France, and Scandinavian countries, and was a major supplier to many other European and South American nations. Sales surpassed $1 billion for the first time in 1971.

In 1981, it acquired the LifeSavers Co. and merged with Standard Brands Inc., maker of Chase & Sanborn coffee, Fleischmann gin and yeast, Royal baking powder, and Planters nuts. Standard's chairman, F. Ross Johnson, became head of the newly renamed Nabisco Brands, Inc.

Johnson orchestrated Nabisco's purchase by R.J. Reynolds in 1985 in the most expensive acquisition of a food product company to date.

Market Forces Driving the Acquisition

By mid-1985 R.J. Reynolds was a consumer products conglomerate, manufacturing such offerings as Winston and Camel cigarettes, Del Monte fruits and vegetables, Smirnoff vodka, and Kentucky Fried Chicken. Yet the nation's second-largest tobacco company was ultimately dependent on cigarettes for about 75% of its earnings, a risky situation given the increasingly aggressive anti-smoking movement sweeping through the nation. To protect itself from fallout, the company's chairman, J. Tylee Wilson, sought to increase Reynolds' presence in consumer foods, ideally through the purchase of a company already firmly entrenched in that market.

Nabisco Brands, the nation's fifth-largest food manufacturer, was one such acquisition candidate. With such products as Fig Newtons and Oreo cookies, Nabisco held a 40% share of the cookie market. Its other products, like Ritz and Premium crackers, Life Savers and Baby Ruth candy, and Planters nuts, enjoyed priceless brand recognition, enabling the company's sales to grow at twice the industry average. Moreover, Nabisco was stronger than Reynolds was internationally, with foreign sales accounting for 37% and 21% of total revenue, respectively. Its extensive overseas marketing and distribution network would enable Reynolds to boost its presence globally.

Approach and Engagement

Reynolds chairman, J. Tylee Wilson, met with Nabisco's CEO, F. Ross Johnson, in April 1985. They soon began discussing a possible union, and on June 2, 1985, announced a deal. Under its terms, R.J. Reynolds would pay $85 per share, or $4.9 billion, to acquire Nabisco, forming the nation's largest consumer products company. This purchase price represented three-times Nabisco's book value, and was the highest ever paid for a food company. Wilson defended this premium, stating in *Business Week*, "You don't buy a Cadillac at Chevrolet prices."

With no overlap in the merging companies' product areas, the deal quickly gained approval, and was completed in July 1985.

Products and Services

Nabisco Group Holdings Corp.'s products in 1998 included the brand names SnackWell, Oreo, Teddy Grahams, A1, Triscuit, Breath Savers, CareFree, Now 'N Later, Life Savers, Planters, Chips Ahoy!, Barnum's Animals, and Knox.

Changes to the Industry

The combined company, named RJR Nabisco, emerged as the nation's leading consumer products company. With $19.2 billion in sales, it easily usurped $13 billion Procter & Gamble from that position. RJR Nabisco had a stable of nearly bulletproof brands, a large share in several key markets, and an extensive vehicle for promoting international growth. "It's a perfect fit," commented Wilson in *Industry Week*. "We're going to look awesome on the grocery store shelves."

Review of the Outcome

J. Tylee Wilson retained his position as chairman and CEO of the combined company, and F. Ross Johnson was named president and chief operating officer. Within a month, however, Johnson claimed that he had effectively taken the company's reins. In less than a year, the board, whose directors could not be counted among Wilson's friends, gave the chairman and CEO role to Johnson.

Once in charge, Johnson trimmed corporate staff from 1,000 to 350, and moved RJR Nabisco's headquarters out of tobacco country in North Carolina to Atlanta, Georgia. He set about streamlining the company's business, selling off more than 30 underperforming operations by mid-1988. Among those sales were Kentucky Fried Chicken, Canada Dry, and Heublein liquors. The impact was positive for the company's food business, which had an overall gross profit margin of 10%, compared to the industry's average of seven percent.

Research

Goldstein, Mark L. "Cookies and Tobacco; J. Tylee Wilson's Building a Global Empire," in *Industry Week*, 5 August 1985. Offers industry reaction to the deal.

"Nabisco Brands, Inc.," in *International Directory of Company Histories*, Vol. II, St. James Press: 1990. Provides a historical review of the company.

Nabisco Group Holdings Corp.: http://www.rjrnabisco.com. Includes new releases and investor information.

Nabisco Group Holdings Corp.: http://www.nabisco.com. Dedicated to Nabisco products, this site offers product information, recipes, and promotions.

"RJR Nabisco Holdings Corp.," in *Notable Corporate Chronologies*, The Gale Group, 1999. Offers a history of the company.

Saporito, Bill. "The Tough Cookie at RJR Nabisco," in *Fortune*, 18 July 1988. Profiles Ross Johnson and the changes he had instilled in the immediate post-merger years.

Scredon, Scott, and Amy Dunkin. "Why Nabisco and Reynolds Were Made for Each Other," in *Business Week*, 17 June 1985. Details the terms of the agreement and the strengths of each company.

"Taking a $4.9 Billion Bite," in *Time*, 17 June 1985. Offers a brief description of the acquisition agreement.

"Wedding Bells for Corporate Giants," in *U.S. News & World Report*, 17 June 1985. Briefly describes two mammoth deals, Reynolds' acquisition of Nabisco and General Motors' purchase of Hughes Aircraft.

SAMANTHA MORRISON

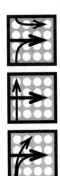

ROCHE HOLDING & GENENTECH

nationality: Switzerland
date: September 7, 1990
affected: Roche Holding AG, Switzerland, founded 1896
affected: Genentech, Inc., USA, founded 1976

Roche Holding AG
Basel, CH-4070
Switzerland

tel: 41 61 688 11 11
fax: 41 61 691 93 91
web: http://www.roche.com

Overview of the Acquisition

Roche entered the biotechnology arena in 1990 with its purchase of a 60% stake in Genentech, the leading U.S. biotech firm. This acquisition united a wealthy Swiss pharmaceutical company in possession of few new products with a product-rich U.S. firm having limited capital resources for its research and development.

History of Roche Holding AG

On October 1, 1896, Fritz Hoffmann-La Roche joined with his ex-business partner Max Carl Traub to form F. Hoffmann-La Roche & Co. Ltd. Based in Basel, Switzerland, this chemicals and pharmaceuticals manufacturing company hired Dr. Emil Christoph Barell as a chemist, whose work would gain Roche its first patent.

Slow business made a financial restructuring a painful necessity, and the young company took on various investors in 1987. This influx of capital enabled Roche to establish subsidiaries in Milan and Grenzach. The following year the company developed its first successful product, the non-prescription cough syrup Sirolin.

In 1904 Roche introduced Digalen, the first consistently safe dosage of digitalis for the treatment of heart diseases. A subsidiary in New York was established the following year to serve as the basis for the company's extensive American marketing and production operations. In 1909 the firm introduced Pantopon, a remedy for a variety of mild conditions. This product would prove to be the company's longest selling product, as it was still marketed in the late-1990s.

By 1911 Roche had expanded worldwide with subsidiaries in Paris, Vienna, London, St. Petersburg, and Yokohama, Japan. During World War I, trade with the neighboring countries Germany and France was closed off, demonstrating the need for Roche to establish its own production facilities. By 1919 the company's financial state was dire, so Fritz Hoffmann-La Roche provided 75% of the SFr4 million needed to restructure Roche as a limited company; Dr. Barell, two associates, and Fritz's brother-in-law provided the remaining 25%. This brother-in-law, Rudolf

The Business

Financials

Revenue (1998): $17.9 billion

Employees (1998): 66,700

SICs / NAICS

sic 2833 - Medicinals & Botanicals

sic 2834 - Pharmaceutical Preparations

sic 2836 - Biological Products Except Diagnostic

sic 2899 - Chemical Preparations Nec

sic 3841 - Surgical & Medical Instruments

naics 325411 - Medicinal and Botanical Manufacturing

naics 325412 - Pharmaceutical Preparation Manufacturing

naics 325414 - Biological Product (except Diagnostic) Manufacturing

naics 325199 - All Other Basic Organic Chemical Manufacturing

naics 339112 - Surgical and Medical Instrument Manufacturing

Adolf Koechler-Hoffmann, became chairman of F. Hoffmann-La Roche Ltd. Co.

Dr. Barell became the company president upon the death of Fritz Hoffmann-La Roche in 1920. That year the introduction of its first hypnotics, such as Somnifen, marked the company's shift from drug extraction to the synthesis of chemical therapeutics.

Due to the financial difficulties incurred as a result of World War I and the threat of another war in Europe, Roche established Sapac Corporation Ltd. in 1927 as a separate company comprised of several of the group's operating units. That year it obtained the commercial right to produce thyroxine, a thyroid hormone. In 1929 Roche transferred its New York operations to Nutley, New Jersey; this became Roche's American headquarters. Sales that year reached SFr50.4 million, up from SFr18.2 million in 1921.

Roche first synthesized ascorbic acid, a source of vitamin C, in 1933, leading to the introduction of the company's first vitamin specialty product, Redoxin. This discovery was followed two years later with the development of synthesized vitamin B1. At the outbreak of World War II, Roche moved its headquarters to Lausanne, Switzerland. The company also consoli- dated all associated companies outside continental Europe into Sapac.

Roche introduced its first cosmetic, Panteen hair tonic, in 1944. Its success led to the formation of Panteen AG by the end of that same year. In 1949 Roche entered the antimicrobial market with the launch of Gantrisin, a treatment for urinary tract infections. Three years later, to great fanfare, it released Rimifon as a treatment for tuberculosis. This product also led to the development of antidepressants, as mood elation was a side effect of the drug.

In 1953 synthetic vitamin K was launched as Konakion. Two years later Roche established a department of experimental medicine, consisting of its work on pharmacology and chemotherapy. In 1956 it synthesized the cancer drug 5-fluorouracil, which served as the basis for the development of future cancer drugs. Two years later Roche expanded its non-prescription operations by acquiring Laboratoires Sauter SA, whose product line included anti-inflammatories, digestives, adhesive bandages, and suppositories.

In 1960 Roche introduced Librium, a benzodiazepine tranquilizer, that later became America's best-selling prescription drug. The next year the company forayed into tropical disease treatment with the release of Astiban, for the treatment of the parasitic disease schistosomiasis.

Roche had a successful year in 1963. It introduced the hugely successful benzodiazepine tranquilizer Valium. Also that year Roche acquired Givaudan SA, a perfume and flavoring manufacturer that comprised the core of Roche's Fragrances and Flavors division.

In 1965 Dr. Walter Adolf Jann became chairman and CEO, and led the company on a diversification campaign that took it into such new fields as bioelectronics, publishing, agrochemicals, and liquid crystal displays (used in consumer products like clocks and calculators).

The company expanded into diagnostics in 1969 with the formation of a division to develop, produce, and sell equipment and materials that contribute to diagnosis of disease. That year sales of Valium exceeded those of Librium for the first time. That same year Roche acquired a stake in the agrochemicals firm Dr. R. Maag AG; this company was absorbed into Roche eight years later. By 1971 Roche's vitamins accounted for more than 50% of worldwide production.

In 1973 British authorities insisted upon pricing controls, to which Roche finally relented in 1975. In addition to the negative reaction from this well-publicized battle, Roche suffered several other public relations blows. In 1975 a former Roche employee, Stanley Adams, waged a media war against the company for offering illegal discounts to customers. The following year, a chemical cloud released by its Italian fragrance subsidiary Icmesa caused skin damage to residents of neighboring communities and necessitated the destruction of produce, farm animals, and contaminated buildings. Roche paid over SFr300 million in compensation.

Fritz Gerber was named chairman and CEO in 1978 to improve the company's business and reputation. He set about reversing the diversification efforts of the past in order to focus on core strengths. In 1982 the company formed Roche Biomedical Laboratories by acquiring Biomedical Reference Laboratories, Inc. and Consolidated Biomedical Laboratories, Inc. That year it sold the Panteen cosmetics company to Richardson-Vicks Inc.

In 1981 Roche released Imadyl, its first drug in the rheumatology segment. That year SmithKline's Tagamet drug overtook Valium as the world's best-selling prescription pharmaceutical. In 1982, with few products in the R&D pipeline, and no expected blockbusters, Gerber formed an agreement to market Glaxo Holdings' Zantac product. Rocephin, Roche's first injectable cephalosporin antibiotic, was also introduced. Sales that year were $7.1 billion with net income of $281 million.

Roche Research Foundation was formed in 1983 by merging Roche Study Foundation, Emil Barell Foundation, Fritz Hoffmann-La Roche Foundation, and Roche Foundation for Scientific Exchange and Biomedical Collaboration with Switzerland. The company acquired American Diagnostics, Inc. in 1984 and Productor Kaspe SA the following year. The U.S. patent for Valium expired in 1985, and as a result the company's pharmaceutical sales were cut in half by competition from cheaper generic imitations.

In June 1986 Roche acquired the licensing rights to market Genentech's treatment for hairy cell leukemia. This product, sold under the name Roferon-A, marked Roche's foray into genetically engineered pharmaceuticals. U.S.-based ICN Pharmaceuticals, Inc. was thwarted in its attempted takeover Roche in 1987. The next year Roche embarked on a hostile takeover attempt of its own, bidding $4.2 billion for Sterling Drug Inc., but was topped by Eastman Kodak.

Roche Holding Ltd. emerged from a 1989 company restructuring as the holding company for F. Hoffmann-La Roche Ltd., its main operations arm. Acquisitions that year included Eupharma GmbH; Priorin AG; Institut Virion AG and its marketing company Dinalar AG; Roche Lipid Technologies Ltd.; Givaudan Aromen GmbH; and 60% of Laboratoires ACS.

The Officers

Chairman: H.C. Fritz Gerber

Vice-Chairman: Andres F. Leuenberger

Vice-Chairman: Rolf Hanggi

Chairman, Executive Committee: Franz B. Humer

President and CEO, Hoffmann-La Roche: Patrick J. Zenner

Roche's Plant Protection Division was divested with the sales of La Quinoleine et ses Derives and Dr. R. Maag to Ciba-Geigy Ltd. in 1990. That September the firm strengthened its presence in biotechnology by acquiring 60% of Genentech, Inc., a U.S.-based research and manufacturing company, for $2.1 billion. Also in 1990 Roche acquired Fritzsche, Dodge & Olcott Inc., a New York-based flavorings and fragrances company.

In 1991 the company paid $821 million for Nicholas, the European over-the-counter drug business of Sara Lee. It also acquired the marketing rights to polymerase chain reaction (PCR) technology from Chiron Corp. Neupogen, a product for treating cancer patients, was introduced that year.

The U.S. Food and Drug Administration (FDA) approved Roche's AIDS treatment dideoxycytidine in 1992. That year Roche ranked first in world vitamin sales and second in fragrances. Roche purchased the struggling drug maker Syntex Corp. for $5.3 billion. It later sold Syntex's women's healthcare product lines and its animal health business.

Roche Biomedical Laboratories merged with National Health Laboratories Holdings in 1995 to form Laboratory Corporation of America, the nation's largest operator of medical lab tests. That year the FDA approved the sale of Roche's AIDS drug, Invirase. Its introduction of CellCept, an agent for the prevention of transplant rejections, marked Roche's entry into the field of transplant medicine.

In 1996 the company bought out Procter & Gamble's interest in their joint venture, thereby gaining control of such products as Aleve and Femstat. That year Roche sold its namatic liquid crystal chemical business to Merck & Co., although it continued to conduct research in that field. Roche strengthened its German over-the-counter position by acquiring Rhone-Poulenc Rorer's vitamin and tonic brands in Europe.

The Players

Roche Chairman and CEO: Fritz Gerber. Fritz Gerber joined Switzerland's Federal Department of Economic Affairs after receiving an education in law. In 1958 he took a job with Zurich Insurance, where he earned a reputation by turning around the troubled company. In 1974 he was appointed to chairman of the firm, a position he held until 1995. His success at Zurich Insurance convinced Roche that he could fulfill the same purpose there, and he was named chairman and CEO of the pharmaceutical company in 1978. In those roles, Gerber successfully set the company on a course consistent with its core products. He turned over the role of CEO to Franz Humer in 1998 and announced in March 1999 his decision to step down as chairman in 2001.

Genentech CEO and President: G. Kirk Raab. G. Kirk Raab's tenure at Genentech ranged from huge success to embarrassing controversy. In 1985 he left Abbott Laboratories to join Genentech, and five years later added the position of CEO to his role as president. By 1995 he had resuscitated Genentech, nearly doubling its revenues, tripling its earnings, and increasing the number of new products under development. Yet personal transgressions coincided with each of the two acquisition negotiations with Roche. In 1990 his wife was indicted for giving insider information of the deal to her brother. In 1995, while renegotiating the pact, Raab asked Roche to secure a $2 million personal loan needed to settle his tax liabilities. He didn't get that loan; what he got instead was an ouster by the board.

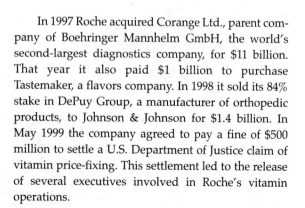

In 1997 Roche acquired Corange Ltd., parent company of Boehringer Mannheim GmbH, the world's second-largest diagnostics company, for $11 billion. That year it also paid $1 billion to purchase Tastemaker, a flavors company. In 1998 it sold its 84% stake in DePuy Group, a manufacturer of orthopedic products, to Johnson & Johnson for $1.4 billion. In May 1999 the company agreed to pay a fine of $500 million to settle a U.S. Department of Justice claim of vitamin price-fixing. This settlement led to the release of several executives involved in Roche's vitamin operations.

History of Genentech, Inc.

In 1976 biochemist Dr. Herbert Boyer and geneticist Stanley Cohen pioneered the field of recombinant DNA technology, also known as gene splicing. Venture capitalist Robert Swanson was enthusiastic about the technology's prospects, and joined with Boyer to found Genentech on April 7, 1976. Thomas J. Perkins, a partner at an investment firm, became the new company's chairman.

To avoid high research and development costs, Genentech decided to contract with the City of Hope National Medical Center for its first research project. The first genetically engineered human protein, somatostatin, was produced within seven months by splicing human hormones into the cells of E. coli bacteria where replication of the protein occurred. This venture was not lucrative but did earn industry respect and credibility for Genentech.

After expenditures of about $100 million, Genentech scientists successfully cloned human insulin in 1978. The next year the company developed genetically engineered human growth hormone (HGH), a product that prevented dwarfism in children. In its public offering on October 14, 1980, Genentech's stock price jumped from $35 to $88 per share. Through this offering, the company amassed $35 million in capital to fund further research and development (R&D).

In 1982 the U.S. Food and Drug Administration (FDA) approved Genentech's human insulin product, the first recombinant DNA drug to be sold in America. As the company had no desire to compete with Eli Lilly & Co., which held 75% of the American insulin market, it arranged a licensing agreement under which Lilly would market the product under the name Humulin. Revenues in 1983 rose $13 million to $42 million; net income, however, remained flat at $1 million.

Genentech produced Factor VIII, a blood clotting agent for hemophiliacs, in 1984. It sold the product's worldwide manufacturing and sales rights to Cutter Biological (later known as Miles, Inc.) The following year Genentech manufactured and sold its own product, Protropin, an injectable human growth hormone for children with insufficient HGH production. This product was the first recombinant DNA pharmaceutical made and marketed by a biotechnology company.

In 1986 the company introduced the Uninsured Patients Program, which dispensed necessary drugs to uninsured, financially disadvantaged patients. That year Genentech granted Roche the marketing rights to interferon alpha-2a, a treatment for hairy cell leukemia. In 1987, after five years and $200,000 in

R&D, Genentech introduced Activase, a tissue-plasminogen activator (tPA) to prevent blood clotting in heart attack victims. Its licensing agreement with Eli Lilly garnered $5 million annually.

Activase's $180 million in sales in 1988 represented the largest first-year sales figure of any new drug. In 1990 Roche Holding acquired a 60% share of Genentech, Inc. for $2.1 billion. Also in 1990 the firm introduced Actimmune, a gamma-1b-interferon for treating a rare immunodeficiency.

Genentech entered into joint ventures with Glycomed, Inc. and Xenova Ltd in 1991. The following year it formed an agreement with Roche for the European marketing of Pulmozyme, a treatment for respiratory infection and cystic fibrosis. It also entered into a venture with DePuy Inc. to develop Transforming Growth Factor Beta for use against bone diseases.

In 1992 the Founders Research Center, the world's largest biotechnology research factory, was opened. The following year the company established Genentech Europe Ltd. as part of its agreement with Roche. Roche increased its stake in Genentech to 66% in 1994. That year a Genentech sales executive and a Minneapolis physician were indicted for unethically marketing growth hormone drugs. In January 1995 Genentech and Eli Lilly settled all pending litigation against each other, with Lilly agreeing to pay Genentech $145 million.

In 1995 the FDA launched another investigation into Genentech's marketing practices, this time of the human growth hormone drug Protropin. The company's reputation continued to suffer as CEO G. Kirk Raab was ousted in July 1995 for secretly asking Roche to guarantee a $2 million personal loan. Research and development chief, biochemist Arthur Levinson, was appointed his successor.

The company continued to acquire FDA approval for new drugs and new applications of previously released drugs. For example, in 1996 Genentech received approval to market Nutropin AQ, the first liquid recombinant human growth hormone. In 1997 the company received a unique honor when the city of South San Francisco changed the name of a block of Genentech's street to DNA Way in recognition of the firm's contribution to the biotechnology industry.

In 1998 Genentech entered into a joint venture with DAKO A/S to develop a diagnostic kit, HercepTest, for the screening of breast cancer patients. Its new manufacturing facility in Vacaville began operation as the world's largest biotechnology manufacturing facility. Meanwhile, Genentech settled patent infringement suits levied against it by Novo

Nordisk A/S and Biogen, Inc. The company paid $50 million in 1999 to settle a suit filed by a U.S. Attorney for Genentech's promotion of HGH.

Market Forces Driving the Acquisition

Genentech was squeezed between financial pressures originating from inside and outside the company by the late 1980s. The U.S. biotechnology firm, despite $400 million in revenues in 1989, was in need of additional funding for its research and development activities. The process of bringing a new product to market was long and filled with pitfalls at the hands of regulatory agencies and environmental groups. Robert Fildes, founder of the biotech firm Cetus Corp., estimated in *Newsweek* that the entire process took about 10 years and $150 million per product.

Externally, Wall Street was insistent on steadily increasing company profits. Biotechnology had fallen into disfavor among investors during the mid-1980s. Moreover, Genentech's heart attack drug, tPA, posted lower than expected sales during its first year on the market, sending the company's stock plummeting in 1988. Disappointing sales also meant less funding for R&D, which laid claim to about 40% of Genentech's revenues. Top executives finally acknowledged that independence would no longer sustain the firm.

Roche was the polar opposite of Genentech. The Swiss pharmaceutical firm had bushels of money but few new products in the works. Between 1975 and 1985 it had launched only three semi-successful products. Roche was eager to expand into biotechnology and viewed Genentech as the brightest player in that field. Moreover, it saw promise in several products in Genentech's pipeline, including treatments for AIDS, cancer, and difficult child delivery.

Approach and Engagement

After realizing that it would have to form an alliance in order to remain a viable competitor, Genentech began looking for an American partner in early 1989. Failing that, it enlisted Frederick Frank, an investment banker, to help in the search. Frank arranged a meeting between the executives of Genentech and Roche on October 21, 1989. The attraction was mutual, and the firms conducted covert negotiations in the months that followed.

On February 2, 1990, the companies announced a deal. Roche would acquire 60% of Genentech for $2.1 billion in cash. At $36 per share, that purchase price represented a premium of 65% over Genentech's stock price. Included in the deal was the option for Roche to purchase the rest of Genentech over five years at a per share price based on a scale that increased each quarter. This scale ranged from $38 per share in 1990 to $60 on April 1, 1995. This option was scheduled to expire on June 30, 1995. In addition, the company could opt to purchase as much as an additional 15% of Genentech on the open market before 1995. Genentech's founder Robert Swanson said in *Newsweek* that the deal "gives us the resources to accomplish the dream that I set out to do."

That June 97% of Genentech's shareholder voted in favor of the transaction. The following month the Federal Trade Commission (FTC) granted its approval, provided that Genentech sell its 50% interest in GLC Associates, a vitamin C producer, and Roche divest itself of research operations for a certain human growth hormone.

Products and Services

In 1998, Roche Holding operated in four main business units:

Roche Pharmaceuticals was divided into two segments. The Prescription sector developed and marketed drugs in the areas of the central nervous system, infectious diseases, oncology, virology, cardiovascular diseases, inflammatory and autoimmune diseases, dermatology, metabolic disorders, and respiratory diseases. Its Nonprescription segment produced such brands as Aleve, Aspro 500, Bepanthen, Bepanthen Plus, Bepanthen Lotion, Berocca Calcium and Magnesium, Elevit Pronatal, Ephynal, Pretuval, Pretuval C, Supradyn, Redoxon, Rennie, and Saridon.

Roche Vitamins and Fine Chemicals produced and sold ingredients that impacted nutrition, health maintenance, and disease prevention in humans and animals. The product range consisted of vitamins, carotenoids, medicinal feed additives, amino acids, feed enzymes, citric acid, polyunsaturated fatty acids, UV filters, emulsifiers, and antitussives.

Roche Diagnostics focused on diagnostic systems for the in-vitro diagnostic market, for the patient self-monitoring sector, and for the research community. It operated four business units: Roche Molecular Biochemicals, Roche Molecular Systems, Roche Laboratory Systems, and Roche Patient Care.

The **Fragrances and Flavors Division** served luxury perfume makers, the cosmetics industry, consumer goods manufacturers, the food and beverages industries, and the pharmaceuticals industry. The Fragrances operation produced ingredients for luxury perfumes, toilet waters, cosmetics, soaps, and other household products. The Flavors unit focused on natural and synthetic flavor additives for beverages, foods, pharmaceuticals, oral hygiene products, and animal feeds.

Changes to the Industry

By November 1994 Roche had increased its stake in Genentech to 66%. In May 1995 the two companies agreed to extend Roche's option to buy the rest of the company until June 30, 1999. A price schedule was again implemented, with the highest per share price set at $82.50. Roche was also extended the option to increase its stake to 79.9% by purchasing shares on the open market. An additional term in the new deal gave Genentech shareholders the right to force Roche to purchase for $60 any shares still outstanding by the new expiration date. Genentech's non-Roche shareholders approved the deal on October 25, 1995.

Roche and Genentech stated that they had sought this extension in order to preserve Genentech's autonomy. This hands-off relationship had been key to Genentech's original agreement to sell a majority stake to Roche. Only with this independence—and a steady supply of R&D funds—could Genentech's scientists remain unfettered in their development of successful new products. Burdening them with undue corporate bureaucracy would only quash their drive.

This arrangement enabled Genentech to post a profit in 1991, up from a $98 million loss in 1990. By 1994 the firm had the industry's strongest pipeline, with such drugs as DNase, a cystic fibrosis treatment. The firm's stock price was also on the rise, surpassing $48 by mid-1994.

Roche's investment not only had a direct impact on Genentech's success, it also seemed to have improved the perception of the value of the biotechnology field as a whole. This newfound respectability, combined with a string of product innovations, sent other small biotech firms into the arms of pharmaceutical giants. Such significant deals included Sandoz's purchase of Genetic Therapy in 1995, the same year as Ciba-Geigy's acquisition of 49% of Chiron; the 1996 purchase of Plant Genetic Systems by Agrevo, a joint venture between Hoechst and Schering; and the proposed $7.7 billion merger of E.I. du Pont de Nemours & Co. and Pioneer Hi-Bred International Inc. in May 1999.

Review of the Outcome

Genentech remained an independent entity after Roche's acquisition of a majority stake. None of its facilities, nor any of its 1,200-person workforce, were eliminated. However, about 200 scientists and researchers did resign, either because they no longer felt the same entrepreneurial charge by working for a corporate giant or because they had become wealthy as a result of the stock buyout. The ranks of the company's leadership were also altered. Thomas Perkins was succeeded as chairman by Robert Swanson and G. Kirk Raab was promoted from president to CEO.

Raab's tenure with Genentech was not long lasting, however, as he was ousted in July 1995. Genentech had been involved in several embarrassing incidents under Raab's leadership. Among these were the insider trading charges filed against his wife by the Securities and Exchange Commission in 1990. The final straw was Raab's request of Roche to secure a $2 million personal loan. This quiet request took place while the two companies were renegotiating their pact in 1995 and was considered both inappropriate and a conflict of interest. Raab was replaced by Dr. Arthur Levinson, a company researcher.

Research

Chase, Marilyn. "Genentech Plans to Sell 60% Stake to Roche Holding for $2.1 Billion," in *The Wall Street Journal*, 5 February 1990. Details the terms of the acquisition.

"Genentech Inc," in *International Directory of Company Histories*, Vol. 8, St. James Press: 1994. Profiles of the history of the company.

Grabarek, Brooke H. "Genentech: Still Nowhere But Up?" in *Financial World*, 21 June 1994. Describes Genentech's upturn since Roche acquired its majority stake.

McCoy, Charles. "Genentech to Extend Pact with Roche," in *The Wall Street Journal*, 2 May 1995. Describes the deal that extended the alliance until June 1999.

Peyer, Hans Conrad. *Roche: A Company History, 1896-1996*, Basel, 1996. Provides a detailed chronology of the history of Roche.

"Roche Holding AG," in *Notable Corporate Chronologies*, The Gale Group, 1999. Lists major events in the history of Roche.

Roche Holding AG Home Page, available at http://www.roche.com. Official World Wide Web Page for Roche. This English- and German-language site offers news releases, financial information and annual reports, links to affiliated divisions and companies, and product information.

Schwartz, John. "Deep Pockets for Biotech," in *Newsweek*, 19 February 1990. Relates the rationale for the acquisition of the majority stake.

"Why Genentech Ditched the Dream of Independence," in *Business Week*, 19 February 1990. Describes the strengths and weaknesses of the companies.

RICHARD BARROW

ROCHE HOLDING & SYNTEX

Roche Holding AG
Basel, CH-4070
Switzerland

tel: 41 61 688 11 11
fax: 41 61 691 93 91
web: http://www.roche.com

nationality: Switzerland
date: September 12, 1994
affected: Roche Holding AG, Switzerland, founded 1896
affected: Syntex Corp., USA, founded 1944

Overview of the Acquisition

The acquisition of Syntex by Roche Holding in 1994 formed the world's fourth-largest drug company. Due to a low stock price and the effects of patent expiration on a best-selling product, Syntex was in desperate need of capital to maintain research and development activities. Roche Holding, a source of such capital, was willing to inject Syntex with the resources necessary to develop the promising new products in its pipeline.

History of Roche Holding AG

On October 1, 1896, Fritz Hoffmann-La Roche joined with his ex-business partner Max Carl Traub to form F. Hoffmann-La Roche & Co. Ltd. Based in Basel, Switzerland, this chemicals and pharmaceuticals manufacturing company hired Dr. Emil Christoph Barell as a chemist, whose work would gain Roche its first patent.

Slow business made a financial restructuring a painful necessity, and the young company took on various investors in 1987. This influx of capital enabled Roche to establish subsidiaries in Milan and Grenzach. The following year the company developed its first successful product, the non-prescription cough syrup Sirolin.

In 1904 Roche introduced Digalen, the first consistently safe dosage of digitalis for the treatment of heart diseases. A subsidiary in New York was established the following year to serve as the basis for the company's extensive American marketing and production operations. In 1909 the firm introduced Pantopon, a remedy for a variety of mild conditions. This product would prove to be the company's longest selling product, as it was still marketed in the late-1990s.

By 1911 Roche had expanded worldwide with subsidiaries in Paris, Vienna, London, St. Petersburg, and Yokohama, Japan. During World War I, trade with the neighboring countries Germany and France was closed off, demonstrating the need for Roche to establish its own production facilities. By 1919 the company's financial state was dire, so Fritz Hoffmann-La Roche provided 75% of the SFr4 million needed to restructure Roche as a limited company; Dr. Barell, two associates, and Fritz's brother-in-law provided the remaining 25%. This brother-in-law, Rudolf Adolf Koechler-Hoffmann, became chairman of F. Hoffmann-La Roche Ltd. Co.

Dr. Barell became the company president upon the death of Fritz Hoffmann-La Roche in 1920. That year the introduction of its first hypnotics, such as Somnifen, marked the company's shift from drug extraction to the synthesis of chemical therapeutics.

Due to the financial difficulties incurred as a result of World War I and the threat of another war in Europe, Roche established Sapac Corporation Ltd. in 1927 as a separate company comprised of several of the group's operating units. That year it obtained the commercial right to produce thyroxine, a thyroid hormone. In 1929 Roche transferred its New York operations to Nutley, New Jersey; this became Roche's American headquarters. Sales that year reached SFr50.4 million, up from SFr18.2 million in 1921.

Roche first synthesized ascorbic acid, a source of vitamin C, in 1933, leading to the introduction of the company's first vitamin specialty product, Redoxin. This discovery was followed two years later with the development of synthesized vitamin B1. At the outbreak of World War II, Roche moved its headquarters to Lausanne, Switzerland. The company also consolidated all associated companies outside continental Europe into Sapac.

Roche introduced its first cosmetic, Panteen hair tonic, in 1944. Its success led to the formation of Panteen AG by the end of that same year. In 1949 Roche entered the antimicrobial market with the launch of Gantrisin, a treatment for urinary tract infections. Three years later, to great fanfare, it released Rimifon as a treatment for tuberculosis. This product also led to the development of antidepressants, as mood elation was a side effect of the drug.

In 1953 synthetic vitamin K was launched as Konakion. Two years later Roche established a department of experimental medicine, consisting of its work on pharmacology and chemotherapy. In 1956 it synthesized the cancer drug 5-fluorouracil, which served as the basis for the development of future cancer drugs. Two years later Roche expanded its non-prescription operations by acquiring Laboratoires Sauter SA, whose product line included anti-inflammatories, digestives, adhesive bandages, and suppositories.

In 1960 Roche introduced Librium, a benzodiazepine tranquilizer, that later became America's best-selling prescription drug. The next year the company forayed into tropical disease treatment with the release of Astiban, for the treatment of the parasitic disease schistosomiasis.

The Business

Financials

Revenue (1998): $17.9 billion

Employees (1998): 66,700

SICs / NAICS

sic 2833 - Medicinals & Botanicals

sic 2834 - Pharmaceutical Preparations

sic 2836 - Biological Products Except Diagnostic

sic 2899 - Chemical Preparations Nec

sic 3841 - Surgical & Medical Instruments

naics 325411 - Medicinal and Botanical Manufacturing

naics 325412 - Pharmaceutical Preparation Manufacturing

naics 325414 - Biological Product (except Diagnostic) Manufacturing

naics 325199 - All Other Basic Organic Chemical Manufacturing

naics 339112 - Surgical and Medical Instrument Manufacturing

Roche had a successful year in 1963. It introduced the hugely successful benzodiazepine tranquilizer Valium. Also that year Roche acquired Givaudan SA, a perfume and flavoring manufacturer that comprised the core of Roche's Fragrances and Flavors division.

In 1965 Dr. Walter Adolf Jann became chairman and CEO, and led the company on a diversification campaign that took it into such new fields as bioelectronics, publishing, agrochemicals, and liquid crystal displays (used in consumer products like clocks and calculators).

The company expanded into diagnostics in 1969 with the formation of a division to develop, produce, and sell equipment and materials that contribute to diagnosis of disease. That year sales of Valium exceeded those of Librium for the first time. That same year, Roche acquired a stake in the agrochemicals firm Dr. R. Maag AG; this company was absorbed into Roche eight years later. By 1971 Roche's vitamins accounted for more than 50% of worldwide production.

In 1973 British authorities insisted upon pricing controls, to which Roche finally relented in 1975. In addition to the negative reaction from this well-publicized battle, Roche suffered several other public rela-

The Officers

Chairman: H.C. Fritz Gerber

Vice-Chairman: Andres F. Leuenberger

Vice-Chairman: Rolf Hanggi

Chairman, Executive Committee: Franz B. Humer

President and CEO, Hoffmann-La Roche: Patrick J. Zenner

tions blows. In 1975 a former Roche employee, Stanley Adams, waged a media war against the company for offering illegal discounts to customers. The following year, a chemical cloud released by its Italian fragrance subsidiary Icmesa caused skin damage to residents of neighboring communities and necessitated the destruction of produce, farm animals, and contaminated buildings. Roche paid over SFr300 million in compensation.

Fritz Gerber was named chairman and CEO in 1978 to improve the company's business and reputation. He set about reversing the diversification efforts of the past in order to focus on core strengths. In 1982 the company formed Roche Biomedical Laboratories by acquiring Biomedical Reference Laboratories, Inc. and Consolidated Biomedical Laboratories, Inc. That year it sold the Panteen cosmetics company to Richardson-Vicks Inc.

In 1981 Roche released Imadyl, its first drug in the rheumatology segment. That year SmithKline's Tagamet drug overtook Valium as the world's best-selling prescription pharmaceutical. In 1982, with few products in the R&D pipeline, and no expected blockbusters, Gerber formed an agreement to market Glaxo Holdings' Zantac product. Rocephin, Roche's first injectable cephalosporin antibiotic, was also introduced. Sales that year were $7.1 billion with net income of $281 million.

Roche Research Foundation was formed in 1983 by merging Roche Study Foundation, Emil Barell Foundation, Fritz Hoffmann-La Roche Foundation, and Roche Foundation for Scientific Exchange and Biomedical Collaboration with Switzerland. The company acquired American Diagnostics, Inc. in 1984 and Productor Kaspe SA the following year. The U.S. patent for Valium expired in 1985, and as a result the company's pharmaceutical sales were cut in half by competition from cheaper generic imitations.

In June 1986 Roche acquired the licensing rights to market Genentech's treatment for hairy cell leukemia. This product, sold under the name Roferon-A, marked Roche's foray into genetically engineered

pharmaceuticals. U.S.-based ICN Pharmaceuticals, Inc. was thwarted in its attempted takeover Roche in 1987. The next year Roche embarked on a hostile takeover attempt of its own, bidding $4.2 billion for Sterling Drug Inc., but was topped by Eastman Kodak.

Roche Holding Ltd. emerged from a 1989 company restructuring as the holding company for F. Hoffmann-La Roche Ltd., its main operations arm. Acquisitions that year included Eupharma GmbH; Priorin AG; Institut Virion AG and its marketing company Dinalar AG; Roche Lipid Technologies Ltd.; Givaudan Aromen GmbH; and 60% of Laboratoires ACS.

Roche's Plant Protection Division was divested with the sales of La Quinoleine et ses Derives and Dr. R. Maag to Ciba-Geigy Ltd. in 1990. That September the firm strengthened its presence in biotechnology by acquiring 60% of Genentech, Inc., a U.S.-based research and manufacturing company, for $2.1 billion. Also in 1990 Roche acquired Fritzsche, Dodge & Olcott Inc., a New York-based flavorings and fragrances company.

In 1991 the company paid $821 million for Nicholas, the European over-the-counter drug business of Sara Lee. It also acquired the marketing rights to polymerase chain reaction (PCR) technology from Chiron Corp. Neupogen, a product for treating cancer patients, was introduced that year.

The U.S. Food and Drug Administration (FDA) approved Roche's AIDS treatment dideoxycytidine in 1992. That year Roche ranked first in world vitamin sales and second in fragrances. Roche purchased the struggling drug maker Syntex Corp. for $5.3 billion. It later sold Syntex's women's healthcare product lines and its animal health business.

Roche Biomedical Laboratories merged with National Health Laboratories Holdings in 1995 to form Laboratory Corporation of America, the nation's largest operator of medical lab tests. That year the FDA approved the sale of Roche's AIDS drug, Invirase. Its introduction of CellCept, an agent for the prevention of transplant rejections, marked Roche's entry into the field of transplant medicine.

In 1996 the company bought out Procter & Gamble's interest in their joint venture, thereby gaining control of such products as Aleve and Femstat. That year Roche sold its namatic liquid crystal chemical business to Merck & Co., although it continued to conduct research in that field. Roche strengthened its German over-the-counter position by acquiring Rhone-Poulenc Rorer's vitamin and tonic brands in Europe.

In 1997 Roche acquired Corange Ltd., parent company of Boehringer Mannhelm GmbH, the world's second-largest diagnostics company, for $11 billion. That year it also paid $1 billion to purchase Tastemaker, a flavors company. In 1998 it sold its 84% stake in DePuy Group, a manufacturer of orthopedic products, to Johnson & Johnson for $1.4 billion. In May 1999 the company agreed to pay a fine of $500 million to settle a U.S. Department of Justice claim of vitamin price-fixing. This settlement led to the release of several executives involved in Roche's vitamin operations.

History of Syntex Corp.

In 1944 Russell E. Marker, a chemist from Penn State University, discovered a method of synthesizing progesterone from the roots of the barbasco plant. That year he took a sample of it to two scientists working at Laboratorios Hormona in Mexico City, and the three joined together to establish Syntex Corp. In 1951 Charles Allen, Jr., chief partner of a leading investment banking company, became half-owner of Ogden Corp., which then acquired Syntex as a subsidiary.

By that time Syntex had hired European chemists who helped redirect the company's focus from the manufacture of bulk steroids to the development of oral contraceptives. In 1956 Syntex received a patent for a progesterone product essential to three of its first four oral contraceptives. This drug would later be supplied to such pharmaceutical giants as Eli Lilly & Co., Johnson & Johnson, Schering, and Ciba-Geigy in return for a share of the profits earned from resultant products. The profits from the Eli Lilly arrangement alone paid for 50% of certain Syntex research costs.

In June 1957 Ogden incorporated Syntex in Panama for tax purposes. The next year Ogden spun off Syntex to shareholders for $2 per share. Allen & Co., the investment firm headed by Charles Allen, retained more than one million of the 4.5 million outstanding shares, giving him a 40% interest.

Syntex introduced the Norinyl birth control pill in 1964. Public acceptance of contraceptives pushed the company's stock price to $190 per share, giving it a market value of $855 million though its annual sales were only $16 million.

In 1966 the company introduced its first diagnostic product, the Syva drug-monitoring system. By that time birth control products accounted for 47% of company profits. In 1970, however, the U.S. Senate began hearings on the side effects related to oral contraceptive use. As a result, Syntex's revenues dropped significantly, causing its stock price to fall below $20 per share. Management became disillusioned about relying almost entirely on contraceptive sales, and implemented a program for expanded research and development.

The Players

Roche Chairman and CEO: Fritz Gerber. Fritz Gerber joined Switzerland's Federal Department of Economic Affairs after receiving an education in law. In 1958 he took a job with Zurich Insurance, where he earned a reputation by turning around the troubled company. In 1974 he was appointed to chairman of the firm, a position that he held until 1995. His success at Zurich Insurance convinced Roche that he could fulfill the same purpose there, and Gerber was named chairman and CEO of the pharmaceutical company in 1978. In those roles Gerber successfully set the company on a course consistent with its core products. He turned over the role of CEO to Franz Humer in 1998 and announced in March 1999 his decision to step down as chairman in 2001.

Syntex Chairman and CEO: Paul E. Freiman. Paul Freiman began his 32-year career with Syntex as a drug salesman. He moved up the company ladder, becoming CEO in 1989. After orchestrating the company's acquisition by Roche, Freiman resigned on February 1, 1995. He immediately became involved in the leadership of several other biotechnology firms, sitting on the boards of three privately held firms before his resignation from Syntex even became effective. He joined Minerva Pharmaceuticals as co-CEO and then was named CEO of Neurobiological Technologies, Inc. after being asked to join its board in 1997.

Birth control pill sales accounted for only 28% of company sales by 1972. The next year Syntex organized a marketing team of 400 salespeople to handle its expanded product lineup, which had grown to include Aarane, an asthma drug, and Naproxen, an anti-inflammatory to reduce arthritic pain. By that time, the company had diversified into animal health division and dental equipment.

In May 1976 Naproxen was marketed in the U.S. as Naprosyn. Later that year, however, Syntex came under pressure from the FDA regarding Naprosyn's safety, and was obligated to conduct a 24-month replacement study in support of the product. This controversy affected sales for five consecutive quarters. In 1978 Syntax began promoting Naprosyn in the U.S. again, bringing sales to record levels of $400 million.

Syntex completed a merger with a dental equipment manufacturer, Den-Tal-Ez, in June 1979. Later that year an investigation into the company's baby formulas resulted in product recalls and the initiation of a five-year study by the National Institute of Health. Also that year a group of British women filed a lawsuit seeking redress for harmful side effects from Syntex's oral contraceptives.

In 1980 the company entered into an agreement with several Seattle microbiologists, whereby Syntex paid $3 million for their research in exchange for the rights to manufacture and market tests developed for sexually transmitted diseases. Three years later this venture resulted in four successful products.

Syntex acquired Laroche Navarron, a French pharmaceuticals manufacturer, in 1985. That year an Illinois court awarded two boys $27 million for suffering brain damage as a result of Syntex's baby foods. By that time the company had already settled more than 100 similar cases, but it decided to appeal this decision.

In anticipation of the expiration of Naprosyn's U.S. patent, Syntex formed a joint venture with Procter & Gamble in 1988 to manufacture and market an over-the-counter (OTC) version of the drug. The following year Syntex introduced Cardene, a calcium-channel blocker antihypertensive; Cytovene, an antiviral drug; and Toradol, an injectable pain reliever. Annual sales rose to $1.3 million and net income surpassed $300 million.

In 1992 the company announced the closure of its Palo Alto manufacturing factory and the corresponding loss of 1,000 jobs. In December 1993 the U.S. patents on its Naproxen-based products, Naprosyn and Anaprox, expired, leaving the market open to generic competition. Net income that year was $290 million on sales of $2.12 billion.

In January 1994 the FDA approved the commercial release of Aleve, a generic form of Naprosyn produced through its venture with P&G. Later that year Syntex entered into a joint venture with Genemedicine Inc. to develop gene therapies for certain inflammatory and immunological diseases. In September Syntex was acquired by pharmaceutical giant Roche Holding for $5.3 billion.

Market Forces Driving the Acquisition

Syntex had a number of compelling reasons to seek a union in the early 1990s. First was the expiration on the patent for its flagship anti-inflammatory, Naprosyn, in December 1993. The company had prepared for this event by forming an alliance with Procter & Gamble to beat competitors to market with a generic version of the drug, branded as Aleve. Even so, the introduction of other companies' generic ver-

sions cut into Syntex's sales. Its stock price fell from a high of $56 in early 1992 to the mid-teens by May 1994.

Secondly, the changes to the healthcare field overall, particularly the managed care aspect, impacted the earnings of drug companies and reduced the amount of funding they could devote to research and development. This lead to the third motivating factor. Lowered earnings potential in the domestic market highlighted the importance of a global reach. Aside from the U.S., however, Syntex operated only in Canada and Mexico.

Roche Holding, a Swiss pharmaceutical giant, became interested in Syntex when its stock price began falling. Although the commercial value of Naprosyn had diminished, Syntex had a number of promising new products in its pipeline, including treatments for AIDS, transplant rejections, angina, male sexual dysfunction, Lou Gehrig's disease, osteoporosis, and chemotherapy-related nausea. Moreover, Syntex's presence in North America would complement Roche's strength in Europe and Asia.

The purchase of U.S. firms by Swiss corporations surged in 1994, spurred by an impending change in the International Accounting Standards. Transactions completed before the beginning of 1995 would involve a tax advantage that would be eliminated after January 1. Swiss companies were particularly capable of entering to such unions, as many held large amounts cash that enabled them to conduct acquisitions in record time.

Approach and Engagement

On May 2, 1994, Roche announced its proposed acquisition of Syntex. The $5.3 billion cash deal represented a per share price of $24, a 57% premium over Syntex's stock value. Although neither company offered details of their courtship, the June 1994 issue of *Drug & Cosmetic Industry* reported that Syntex had considered a possible takeover by several other companies before settling on Roche as a preferred suitor.

The tender offer was scheduled to expire on June 6, but a request from the Federal Trade Commission (FTC) for additional information in its antitrust investigation necessitated the extension of the deadline to July 1. That deadline was bumped two more times, to August 3 and then to August 24, to accommodate the FTC's methodical review. Finally, in early September the FTC granted its approval to the deal on the condition that Syntex divest itself of Syva Co., a medical diagnostics business. Having received the approval of the European Commission in June, Roche completed the acquisition on September 12, 1994.

Products and Services

In 1998, Roche Holding operated in four main business units:

Roche Pharmaceuticals was divided into two segments. The Prescription sector developed and marketed drugs in the areas of the central nervous system, infectious diseases, oncology, virology, cardiovascular diseases, inflammatory and autoimmune diseases, dermatology, metabolic disorders, and respiratory diseases. Its Nonprescription segment produced such brands as Aleve, Aspro 500, Bepanthen, Bepanthen Plus, Bepanthen Lotion, Berocca Calcium and Magnesium, Elevit Pronatal, Ephynal, Pretuval, Pretuval C, Supradyn, Redoxon, Rennie, and Saridon.

Roche Vitamins and Fine Chemicals produced and sold ingredients that impacted nutrition, maintenance of health, and prevention of disease in humans and animals. The product range consisted of vitamins, carotenoids, medicinal feed additives, amino acids, feed enzymes, citric acid, polyunsaturated fatty acids, UV filters, emulsifiers, and antitussives.

Roche Diagnostics focused on diagnostic systems for the in-vitro diagnostic market, for the patient self-monitoring sector, and the research community. It operated four business units: Roche Molecular Biochemicals, Roche Molecular Systems, Roche Laboratory Systems, and Roche Patient Care.

The **Fragrances and Flavors Division** served luxury perfume makers, the cosmetics industry, manufacturers of consumer goods, the food and beverages industries, and the pharmaceuticals industry. The Fragrances operation produced ingredients for luxury perfumes, toilet waters, cosmetics, soaps, and other household products. The Flavors unit focused on natural and synthetic flavor additives for beverages, foods, pharmaceuticals, oral hygiene products, and animal feeds.

Changes to the Industry

The union of Roche and Syntex created the world's fourth-largest drug company. This deal continued the trend of large-scale consolidation in the pharmaceutical industry, as it was followed by the $14.2 billion alliance between Glaxo and Wellcome into Glaxo Wellcome PLC. It also perpetuated the trend, begun by Roche in 1990 through its acquisition of Genentech, for the marriage between large, well-financed pharmaceutical companies and small, innovative biotechnology firms. This trend was demonstrated by the 1996 purchase by Hoescht AG and Schering's joint venture company, Agrevo, of Plant Genetic Systems in 1996 and DuPont's $7.7 billion bid for Pioneer Hi-Bred International Inc. in 1999.

Review of the Outcome

The integration of Syntex into Roche resulted in a reorganization that eliminated 5,000 positions in the areas of research, production, and marketing. About 70% of those jobs affected Roche's U.S. subsidiaries, Syntex and Hoffman-La Roche. Paul Freiman, chairman and CEO of Syntex, resigned on February 1, 1995.

Syntex was integrated into the pharmaceuticals division of Roche as Roche Bioscience, a new research and development operation focusing on inflammatory diseases, osteoporosis, and the peripheral nervous system. In compliance with the FTC's order, Roche divested itself of Syva, selling it to the Behring Group, a subsidiary of Hoescht AG, in 1995. It also agreed to sell Syntex's animal health business to American Home Products Corp., as well as to sell its women's healthcare product lines to GD Searle Inc., a subsidiary of Monsanto Co. In September 1996 Ornead Inc. agreed to buy Syntex's commercial and clinical manufacturing and pharmaceutical formulation development operations.

Research

Chase, Marilyn. "Switzerland's Roche to Buy Syntex Corp. for $5.3 Billion," in The Wall Street Journal, 3 May 1994. Details the acquisition agreement.

Davey, Tom. "Delays Raise Questions on Planned Merger of Syntex, Roche," in The Business Journal, 22 August 1994. Chronicles the FTC's repeated delays in approving the deal.

"Genentech Inc," in International Directory of Company Histories, Vol. 8, St. James Press: 1994. Profiles the history of the company.

Roche Holding AG Home Page, available at http://www.roche.com. Official World Wide Web Page for Roche. This English- and German-language site offers news releases, financial information and annual reports, links to affiliated divisions and companies, and product information.

"Roche Holding AG," in Notable Corporate Chronologies, The Gale Group, 1999. Lists major events in the history of Roche.

"Roche-Syntex Deal to Cut 5,000 Jobs," in Modern Healthcare, 31 October 1994. Briefly relates the elimination of jobs after the acquisition of Syntex.

Templeman, John. "The Swiss Are Coming! The Swiss Are Coming!" in Business Week, 6 June 1994. Details the reasons for 1994's flurry of U.S. acquisitions by Swiss firms.

RICHARD BARROW

ROCKWELL INTERNATIONAL & AEROSPACE TECHNOLOGIES OF AUSTRALIA

Rockwell International Corp.
600 Anton Blvd., Ste. 700
Costa Mesa, CA 92628-5090
USA

tel: (714)424.4200
fax: (714)424.4251
web: http://www.rockwell.com

nationality: USA
date: June 1995
affected: Rockwell International Corp., USA, founded 1973
affected: AeroSpace Technologies of Australia, Pty. Ltd., Australia, founded 1986

Overview of the Acquisition

Rockwell International's purchase of AeroSpace Technologies of Australia in 1995 rescued the Australian aerospace company from possible financial ruin. It had long been a money-losing venture while under government ownership, and its recent transformation into an independent firm had not improved its position.

History of Rockwell International Corp.

In 1919 Colonel Willard F. Rockwell reorganized Wisconsin Parts Co., a bankrupt axle company in Oshkosh, Wisconsin. By 1921, however, the company once again faced bankruptcy, and in 1929 Wisconsin Parts was purchased by Timken-Detroit Axle Co. Rockwell became president of Timken-Detroit in 1933. In 1953 Timken merged with Standard Steel Spring Co. to form Rockwell Spring and Axle Co. Rockwell Spring and Axle changed its name in 1958 to Rockwell-Standard Corp., and embarked on a program of diversification within the automotive industry. By 1967 Rockwell-Standard ranked as a major international producer of automotive components, with annual sales exceeding $600 million.

Meanwhile, North American Aviation, Inc. (NAA) was founded by Clement Melville Keys in 1928 as a holding company for his aviation assets. Its operations were hit hard by the Great Depression, and corporate debt mounted. J. H. Kindelberger became president of NAA in 1932, and began aggressively pursuing government and defense contracts. In 1934 NAA became an independent operating company that manufactured aircraft. The next year General Motors Corp. purchased NAA, which retained its corporate autonomy after the buyout. NAA secured a contract in 1935 to produce 85 trainer aircraft for the U.S. Army. It divested itself of its Eastern Airlines unit in 1936 in response to a government investigation of monopolistic practices in the aircraft and airline industries.

NAA's business boomed during World War II, as it produced 42,000 military aircraft. After the war ended, though, sales dropped. NAA decided not to reenter the commercial aviation market, concentrating instead on continued pursuit of defense contracts and diversification into production of rockets, electronics, space systems, and nuclear energy equipment. In 1947 it divested itself of its last commercial aviation operations.

General Motors spun off NAA in 1948. The newly independent company created Rocketdyne, Autotecnics, and Atomics International as subsidiaries. Benefiting from German data captured after World War II, NAA made numerous aerospace breakthroughs during the 1950s, including the F-86 Sabre fighter jet and the X-15 hypersonic research aircraft.

Despite delays caused by the U.S. Justice Department, which first judged the proposed merger to be "anticompetitive", NAA merged with Rockwell-Standard in 1967 to form North American Rockwell Corp. The following year the company produced *Saturn V* rocket and *Apollo* capsules for NASA. Disaster struck in 1969, when three *Apollo* astronauts were killed inside one such space capsule. Northern American Rockwell was the subject of negative publicity, as shoddy workmanship was suspected to have been the cause.

North American Rockwell and Rockwell Manufacturing Co. merged in 1973 to form Rockwell International Corp. The new company absorbed Collins Radio Co., whose military communications technology was later leveraged into the commercial market, providing the basis for computer and fax modem technology in the 1990s.

Robert Anderson, president and CEO of the former Rockwell Manufacturing Co., was appointed to those positions of Rockwell International in 1973. He moved to streamline and diversify the company's operations. That year Rockwell purchased the consumer electronics manufacturer Admiral Co. and formed a joint venture to produce oilfield equipment with the British firm of Pegler Hattersley. By 1977 Anderson's streamlining program had improved the company's debt-to-equity ratio from 90% in 1974 to 50%. Rockwell received a blow, however, when the U.S. government canceled the B-1 Bomber program; the program was not reinstated until 1982.

Anderson succeeded Willard Rockwell, Jr., as chairman in 1979. That year the company formed Astrotech, a venture to purchase and privatize the NASA space shuttle program. In 1985 Rockwell was implicated in fraud for illegal overcharges in government contracts, and was banned from receiving further defense work. After Anderson vowed to fire all personnel involved in the fraudulent overcharging, the U.S. government reinstated Rockwell as an approved defense contractor. Also in 1985 the company acquired the industrial electronics concern Allen-Bradley Co. for $1.7 billion.

The Business

Financials

Revenue (1998): $6.8 billion

Employees (1998): 40,000

SICs / NAICS

sic 3714 - Motor Vehicle Parts & Accessories

sic 3823 - Process Control Instruments

sic 3661 - Telephone & Telegraph Apparatus

sic 3621 - Motors & Generators

naics 336350 - Motor Vehicle Transmission and Power Train Part Manufacturing

naics 334513 - Instruments for Measuring and Displaying Industrial Process Variables

naics 334418 - Printed Circuit Assembly (Electronic Assembly) Manufacturing

naics 335312 - Motor and Generator Manufacturing

The 1986 explosion of the space shuttle *Challenger* brought the Astrotech venture to an end. Rockwell acquired Electronics Corp. of America, a manufacturer of photoelectric controls. The next year, the company increased its commercial operations by forming joint ventures with Scripps Howard for the production and marketing of newspaper mailroom components and systems, and with TDK Corp. for the production and marketing of ferrite magnets.

Donald R. Beall, president of Rockwell's Electronics Division, succeeded Anderson as chairman and CEO in 1988. He began to change Rockwell's focus from defense contracts to production of electronics, and moved to streamline company organization. Government contracts that year represented 50% of company sales. That year Rockwell established a European center in France, sold its measurement and flow control operations to BTR Dunlop, and acquired Baker Perkins, a printing machine operator based in the U.K.

A downturn in U.S. economy in 1990 slowed Rockwell's reorganization. The company allocated $250 million to its Allen-Bradley division for the development of a new generation of factory automation products. It sold its industrial tools division to Cooper Industries, and divested itself of its fiber-optic transmission systems division in 1991. That year it delivered the space shuttle *Endeavor* to NASA. By 1993

The Officers

Chairman and CEO: Don H. Davis Jr.

Sr. VP, Finance and CFO: W. Michael Barnes

Sr. VP, General Counsel, and Secretary: William J. Calise, Jr.

Sr. VP, Human Resources: Joel R. Stone

Sr. VP, Marketing & Communication: Earl S. Washington

government contracts accounted for 23% of Rockwell's sales, and its workforce was reduced by 40,000. It purchased Sprecher + Schuh, an industrial automotive supplier.

In 1994 the company joined with Actel and Brooktree to purchase an equity position in a semiconductor manufacturing facility in Singapore. It sold its automotive plastics operations to Cambridge Industries. The following year Rockwell purchased Aerospace Technologies of Australia and Reliance Electric Co. Reliance and Allen-Bradley provided the core of the newly formed Rockwell Automation division, which made Rockwell the leading U.S. manufacturer of industrial automation. By 1995 the transition into a commercial company had had virtually no effect on its revenues, as it had replaced the $4 billion lost in government contracts since 1986 with about that amount of civilian business.

Rockwell spent $1.2 billion to modernize and expand its semiconductor plant in Colorado Springs, Colorado in 1996. That year it acquired Brooktree Corp., a manufacturer of computer chips, for $275 million, and divested itself of its graphics business. It also completely exited the defense and aerospace business by selling those operations to Boeing Co. for $3.2 billion.

In 1997 Beall stepped down as CEO in favor of Don Davis, who also succeeded him as chairman in February 1998. In December 1997 Rockwell spun off its automotive component business as Meritor Automotive Inc. It acquired the in-flight entertainment business of Hughes-Avicom International for $157 million, renaming the unit Rockwell Collins Passenger Systems.

Rockwell announced a restructuring in June 1998 that was to be completed by late 1999. This reorganization was expected to result in the closure of a number of facilities and the elimination of about 3,000 jobs. That November the company acquired Anorad Corp., the world's leader in linear motor technology.

As a result of a soft personal computer market, Rockwell spun off its semiconductor systems operations in January 1999 as Conexant Systems, Inc. That month it agreed to acquire EJA Engineering Ltd., a U.K.-based manufacturer of safety products. In February it announced a relocation of the company's headquarters from Costa Mesa to Milwaukee. This move, scheduled for completion by year-end 1999, was made in order to move closer to its business center, the Midwest. In April Rockwell Colllins purchased Flight Dynamics, producer of aircraft guidance systems. Also that month Rockwell Automation agreed to purchase ETG, a software company based in Pittsburgh.

History of AeroSpace Technologies of Australia, Pty. Ltd.

AeroSpace Technologies of Australia (ASTA) was formed in 1986 out of the state-owned Government Aircraft Factories (GAF). This company had had an extremely narrow focus. It depended heavily on domestic defense work, rarely, if ever, stretching beyond those industrial and geographic boundaries. As other aerospace companies throughout the world evolved into global, diversified operations, GAF was left behind. Moreover, it had been unprofitable for years, a position that compounded its competitive disadvantage.

In October 1987 ASTA completed a restructuring aimed at making it more independent and profitable. The government, which still held 100% of its interests, appointed an independent board of directors and cut its workforce by 10%, to 1,800. ASTA was also split into several market-specific units. At the end of its first year, it showed a profit, of A$276,000.

ASTA also began forging international alliances. It joined with Chinese, French, and Singaporean manufacturers to develop a new generation of light helicopters, of which 400 were to be built by ASTA. It later entered into an agreement with BP to manufacture advanced composite products.

Boeing aircraft were somewhat of a specialty of ASTA, as the company manufactured a variety of its parts, including flaps and inspar ribs. In October 1988 it began work on a three-year contract to provide maintenance services for Continental Airline's Boeing 747s. In January 1992 it won a subcontracting job to provide 16 sets of Boeing 747 aileron hinge fittings for Fuji Heavy Industries of Japan.

In April 1994 the Australian government decided to complete the transformation of ASTA into an independent enterprise by offering its shares to the public. This move "transformed the former Government

Aircraft Factories from a defense-focused facility, which relied on significant commonwealth subsidies, to a company that now has an aggressive commercial and international focus," said Australian Defense Minister Bob Ray in *Defense & Aerospace Electronics*.

Market Forces Driving the Acquisition

Despite its efforts to become profitable, AeroSpace Technologies of Australia was still losing money—a lot of it. For fiscal 1994 it lost A$60 million on revenues just short of A$159 million. As a company no longer subsidized by the government, those figures threatened its very existence, let alone its ability to compete in an increasingly global environment. As its spin-off into a public company had not yet been initiated, and financial results such as those would be unlikely to attract private investors, the government decided to put ASTA up for sale.

Approach and Engagement

By October 1994 two firms, one Australian and the other foreign, had expressed interest in acquiring ASTA. By year's end, however, as the company continued to lose money, the government began to consider breaking ASTA into separate units to make the pieces more valuable than the whole.

Rockwell International emerged as the Australian government's preferred acquirer of ASTA. This American giant was not interested in the entire company, however. It declined to purchase ASTA Aircraft Services, which contained the company's civil transport maintenance center, an airport, and a New Zealand subsidiary.

In June 1995 Rockwell completed its purchase of ASTA for A$40 million ($29 million). Included in the package were ASTA's aircraft engineering and servicing operations, aircraft and automotive manufacturing capabilities, submarine communications equipment unit, and industrial automation businesses.

Products and Services

Rockwell International operated in four main business segments:

Rockwell Automation was a leading supplier of industrial automation products, systems, and software in North America. With total sales in excess of $4.5 billion, it was comprised of two subsections: Rockwell Automation Control Systems provided customer solutions for integrated sequential, motion, drive system, process, and information applications by supplying controllers, input/output systems, drives, sensors, power devices, packaged control

products, and services under the Allen-Bradley and Rockwell Software brand names. Rockwell Automation Power Systems provided Dodge brand gear reducers, mounted bearings, power transmission components, network monitoring products, and Reliance Electric motors.

Rockwell Collins was a leading supplier of commercial avionics and military electronics systems, as well as service and support solutions. By providing flight deck avionics and in-flight entertainment electronics to airlines worldwide, and integrated communication, navigation, and situational awareness systems for military and business aircraft, Rockwell Collins generated annual sales of $2 billion.

Rockwell Electronic Commerce supplied customer interaction technologies such as automatic call distributors, computer telephony integration software, information collection, reporting, and management systems, and call center consulting and systems integration services for a variety of commercial industries.

The Rockwell Science Center conducted research on projects ranging from disruptive technologies to technology application. It employed 400 people and maintained partnerships with over 200 universities, national laboratories, and research organizations of other companies to provide access to leading edge technologies worldwide.

Review of the Outcome

As part of its plan to improve ASTA's manufacturing capabilities, Rockwell immediately transferred about A$50 million in work to the newly acquired Australian company. "By merging Rockwell's and ASTA's extensive commercial aerostructures and military-aircraft modification experience, we build critical mass that opens up opportunities which we couldn't pursue individually," commented John McLuckey, Rockwell Defense Systems president, in *Flight International*.

Research

"Aerospace Deal Will Net Gov't $40 M," in *Australian Financial Review*, 28 June 1995. Explains the acquisition agreement.

"ASTA—Future in Doubt," in *Aerospace (Asia-Pacific)*, December 1994. Describes ASTA's financial difficulties that may impede its purchase as a whole.

"ASTA Gains Foothold in International Market for Civil, Military Aerospace Products," in *Aviation Week & Space Technology*, 4 July 1988. Profiles ASTA and its current projects.

"Australia Seeks Friendly Trade Environment," in *Defense & Aerospace Electronics*, 4 April 1994. Includes a brief description of ASTA's intention to go public.

"Rockwell International Corp.," in *International Directory of Company Histories*, Vol. 11, St. James Press: 1995. Profiles the history of the company prior to its acquisition of Reliance.

Rockwell International Corp. Home Page, available at http://www.rockwell.com. Official World Wide Web Page for Rockwell. Includes a description of operations, news releases, executive biographies, and investor information.

"Rockwell Ties up Australian ASTA Purchase," in *Flight International*, 5 July 1995. Briefly describes the acquisition's completion.

—DAVIS MCMILLAN

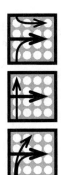

ROCKWELL INTERNATIONAL & RELIANCE ELECTRIC

nationality: USA
date: January 1995
affected: Rockwell International Corp., USA, founded 1973
affected: Reliance Electric Co., USA, founded 1904

Rockwell International Corp.
600 Anton Blvd., Ste. 700
Costa Mesa, CA 92628-5090
USA

tel: (714)424-4200
fax: (714)424-4251
web: http://www.rockwell.com

Overview of the Acquisition

Reliance Electric and General Signal entered into a merger agreement in 1994. Before that deal had progressed, however, Rockwell International threw its hat into the ring by outbidding General Signal for Reliance. General Signal refused to enter into a bidding war, allowing Rockwell to complete negotiations with Reliance. In 1995 the $1.6 billion acquisition was completed, and Reliance consolidated with Allen-Bradley to form Rockwell Automotive.

History of Rockwell International Corp.

In 1919 Colonel Willard F. Rockwell reorganized Wisconsin Parts Co., a bankrupt axle company in Oshkosh, Wisconsin. By 1921, however, the company once again faced bankruptcy, and in 1929 Wisconsin Parts was purchased by Timken-Detroit Axle Co. Rockwell became president of Timken-Detroit in 1933. In 1953 Timken merged with Standard Steel Spring Co. to form Rockwell Spring and Axle Co. Rockwell Spring and Axle changed its name in 1958 to Rockwell-Standard Corp. and embarked on a program of diversification within the automotive industry. By 1967 Rockwell-Standard ranked as a major international producer of automotive components, with annual sales exceeding $600 million.

Meanwhile, North American Aviation, Inc. (NAA) was founded by Clement Melville Keys in 1928 as a holding company for his aviation assets. Its operations were hit hard by the Great Depression, and corporate debt mounted. J. H. Kindelberger became president of NAA in 1932 and began aggressively pursuing government and defense contracts. In 1934 NAA became an independent operating company that manufactured aircraft. The next year General Motors Corp. purchased NAA, which retained its corporate autonomy after the buyout. NAA secured a contract in 1935 to produce 85 trainer aircraft for the U.S. Army. It divested itself of its Eastern Airlines unit in 1936 in response to a government investigation of monopolistic practices in the aircraft and airline industries.

The Business

Financials

Revenue (1998): $6.8 billion

Employees (1998): 40,000

SICs / NAICS

sic 3714 - Motor Vehicle Parts & Accessories

sic 3823 - Process Control Instruments

sic 3661 - Telephone & Telegraph Apparatus

sic 3621 - Motors & Generators

naics 336350 - Motor Vehicle Transmission and Power Train Part Manufacturing

naics 334513 - Instruments for Measuring and Displaying Industrial Process Variables

naics 334418 - Printed Circuit Assembly (Electronic Assembly) Manufacturing

naics 335312 - Motor and Generator Manufacturing

NAA's business boomed during World War II, as it produced 42,000 military aircraft. After the war ended, though, sales dropped. NAA decided not to reenter the commercial aviation market, concentrating instead on continued pursuit of defense contracts and diversification into production of rockets, electronics, space systems, and nuclear energy equipment. In 1947 it divested itself of its last commercial aviation operations.

General Motors spun off NAA in 1948. The newly independent company created Rocketdyne, Autotecnics, and Atomics International as subsidiaries. Benefitting from German data captured after World War II, NAA made numerous aerospace breakthroughs during the 1950s, including the F-86 Sabre fighter jet and the X-15 hypersonic research aircraft.

Despite delays caused by the U.S. Justice Department, which first judged the proposed merger to be anti-competitive, NAA merged with Rockwell-Standard in 1967 to form North American Rockwell Corp. The following year the company produced the *Saturn V* rocket and *Apollo* capsules for NASA. Disaster struck in 1969, when three *Apollo* astronauts were killed inside one such space capsule. Northern American Rockwell was the subject of negative publicity, as shoddy workmanship was suspected to have been the cause.

North American Rockwell and Rockwell Manufacturing Co. merged in 1973 to form Rockwell

International Corp. The new company absorbed Collins Radio Co., whose military communications technology was later leveraged into the commercial market, providing the basis for computer and fax modem technology in the 1990s.

Robert Anderson, president and CEO of the former Rockwell Manufacturing Co., was appointed to those positions at Rockwell International in 1973. He moved to streamline and diversify the company's operations. That year Rockwell purchased the consumer electronics manufacturer Admiral Co. and formed a joint venture to produce oilfield equipment with the British firm of Pegler Hattersley. By 1977 Anderson's streamlining program had improved the company's debt-to-equity ratio from 90% in 1974 to 50%. Rockwell received a blow, however, when the U.S. government canceled the B-1 Bomber program; the program was not reinstated until 1982.

Anderson succeeded Willard Rockwell, Jr., as chairman in 1979. That year the company formed Astrotech, a venture to purchase and privatize the NASA space shuttle program. In 1985 Rockwell was implicated in fraud for illegal overcharges in government contracts and was banned from receiving further defense work. After Anderson vowed to fire all personnel involved in the fraudulent overcharging, the U.S. government reinstated Rockwell as an approved defense contractor. The company also acquired the industrial electronics concern Allen-Bradley Co. for $1.7 billion.

The 1986 explosion of the space shuttle *Challenger* brought the Astrotech venture to an end. Rockwell acquired Electronics Corp. of America, a manufacturer of photoelectric controls. The next year, the company increased its commercial operations by forming joint ventures with Scripps Howard for the production and marketing of newspaper mailroom components and systems and with TDK Corp. for the production and marketing of ferrite magnets.

Donald R. Beall, president of Rockwell's Electronics Division, succeeded Anderson as chairman and CEO in 1988. He began to change Rockwell's focus from defense contracts to production of electronics, and he moved to streamline company organization. Government contracts that year represented 50% of company sales. Rockwell also established a European center in France, sold its measurement and flow control operations to BTR Dunlop, and acquired Baker Perkins, a printing machine operator based in the U.K.

A downturn in the U.S. economy in 1990 slowed Rockwell's reorganization. The company allocated $250 million to its Allen-Bradley division for the development of a new generation of factory automation products. It sold its industrial tools division to Cooper Industries and divested itself of its fiber-optic transmission systems division in 1991. That year it delivered the space shuttle *Endeavor* to NASA. By 1993 government contracts accounted for 23% of Rockwell's sales and its workforce was reduced by 40,000. The firm also purchased Sprecher + Schuh, an industrial automotive supplier.

In 1994 the company joined with Actel and Brooktree to purchase an equity position in a semiconductor manufacturing facility in Singapore. It sold its automotive plastics operations to Cambridge Industries. The following year Rockwell purchased AeroSpace Technologies of Australia, Pty. Ltd. and Reliance Electric Co. Reliance and Allen-Bradley provided the core of the newly formed Rockwell Automation division, which made Rockwell the leading U.S. manufacturer of industrial automation. By 1995 the transition into a commercial company had virtually no effect on its revenues, as it had replaced the $4 billion lost in government contracts since 1986 with about that amount of civilian business.

Rockwell spent $1.2 billion to modernize and expand its semiconductor plant in Colorado Springs, Colorado in 1996. That year it acquired Brooktree Corp., a manufacturer of computer chips, and divested itself of its graphics business. The firm also completely exited the defense and aerospace business by selling those operations to Boeing Co. for $3.2 billion.

In 1997 Beall stepped down as CEO in favor of Don Davis, who also succeeded him as chairman in February 1998. In December 1997 Rockwell spun off its automotive component business as Meritor Automotive Inc. It acquired the in-flight entertainment business of Hughes-Avicom International for $157 million, renaming the unit Rockwell Collins Passenger Systems.

Rockwell announced a restructuring in June 1998 that was to be completed by late 1999. This reorganization was expected to result in the closure of a number of facilities and the elimination of about 3,000 jobs. That November the company acquired Anorad Corp., the world's leader in linear motor technology.

As a result of a soft personal computer market, Rockwell spun off its semiconductor systems operations in January 1999 as Conexant Systems, Inc. That month it agreed to acquire EJA Engineering Ltd., a U.K.-based manufacturer of safety products. In February it announced a relocation of the company's headquarters from Costa Mesa to Milwaukee. This move, scheduled for completion by year-end 1999, was made in order to move closer to its business center, the Midwest. In April Rockwell Collins purchased Flight Dynamics, producer of aircraft guidance sys-

The Officers

tems. Also that month Rockwell Automation agreed to purchase ETG, a software company based in Pittsburgh.

History of Reliance Electric Co.

In 1904 inventor John Lincoln and industrialist Peter Hitchcock established a partnership to develop, manufacture, and market an arc-type light bulb invented by Lincoln. When Thomas Edison's superior incandescent bulb was developed, however, Lincoln's invention became obsolete. So the partners chose to focus on another of Lincoln's inventions, the first adjustable speed direct current (D-C) motor. They shipped their first motor in 1905 and named their company Lincoln Electric Motor Works.

Control of the company passed to Hitchcock's sons in 1907, upon Peter's death and Lincoln's exit from the business. They brought in Clarence Collins as president, a role in which he served for 40 years. The company changed its name that year to Reliance Electric and Engineering Co. to avoid confusion with another Lincoln Electric company in the area.

Reliance introduced its second product, a T-line D-C motor, in 1913, and entered into the market for alternating current (A-C) motors during the 1920s. Because it was entering that field relatively late and would be going up against such heavy hitters as General Electric and Westinghouse Electric, Reliance decided to carve out a niche that it could dominate. It focused on supplying industrial motors, with an emphasis on the applied engineering aspect of the project.

In 1927 Reliance provided a custom modified fan-cooled motor for General Motors, for which it received a lucrative contract. This provided the impetus for growth, and by 1929 sales reached $3 million. Government contracts for military motors during World War II furnished the capital to build several new plants. In the 1950s Reliance expanded through such technological advances as semiconductors, tran-

The Players

Rockwell International Chairman and CEO: Donald R. Beall. Donald Beall studied metallurgical engineering at San Jose State University and then received an MBA from the University of Pittsburgh. Even before the end of the Cold War, he was emphatic about turning Rockwell into a commercial enterprise. By 1978 he was president of Rockwell's electronics division. In 1988 he became the company's chairman and CEO. In April 1995 Beall received the Navy League's Nimitz award for his contributions to U.S. maritime strength and national security. He also oversaw the purchase of Reliance that year. In September 1997 Beall stepped down as CEO, and in February 1998 he gave up the chairmanship.

Reliance Electric President and CEO: John B. Morley. John Morley was appointed president and CEO of Reliance in 1980. Six years later, he led the leveraged buyout of the company that transferred its ownership from Exxon to Citicorp, Prudential, two New York investment firms, and Reliance management. Morley returned the company's stock to the public equity markets in February 1992. This move was made in part to reduce the company's debt to a manageable level. When Reliance was acquired by Rockwell in 1995, Morely retired.

---

sistors, and digital equipment, as well as through such acquisitions as Reeves Pulley Co. and Master Electric Co. Reliance was listed on the New York Stock Exchange in 1957, as its sales reached $100 million. Two years later it established a Canadian subsidiary.

By the mid-1960s, however, growth had slowed due to Reliance's introduction of complex products that were commercial failures. To change that tide, it reorganized in 1967 to focus on industrial automation. It acquired Dodge Manufacturing Co. and the Toledo Scale Co. that year, followed by Custom Engineering Corp., Applied Dynamics, and two European firms before the decade's end.

Reliance diversified into telecommunications in 1973 with the purchase of Lorain Products Corp., a manufacturer of power equipment for the communications industry. It added to its operations in that area with the purchase of Continental Telephone Electronic Co. in 1977, and then of Utility Products Co., Federal

Pacific Co., and Kato Engineering. In 1979 it purchased Federal Pacific Electric (FPE), but divested it in the late 1980s after discovering that FPE had deceived Underwriters Laboratory to get approval for its circuit breakers.

In December 1979 the Exxon Corp. purchased Reliance for $1.24 billion in order to develop and manufacture an experimental alternating current synthesizer (ACS). This device would use current only when needed, thereby saving the U.S. up to one million barrels of oil each day. By 1981, however, the project was scrapped due to the expense and unreliability of the device. These efforts, combined with the impact of a recession, contributed to consecutive years of losses for Reliance in the early 1980s. Between 1982 and 1984 it was forced to cut 27% of its workforce.

Reliance purchased Inertia Dynamics in 1985. The following year it became the nation's largest industrial motor manufacturer upon its acquisition of the Medium A-C Motor Division from Westinghouse Electric.

Exxon gave up ownership of Reliance in 1986, when a $1.35 billion leveraged buyout placed the company in the hands of Citicorp (43%), Prudential Bache Securities (13%), Reliance management (15%), and institutional investors. The following year Reliance posted a $4 million profit on $1.17 billion in sales and had pared its debt to $969 million. Selling Toledo Scale in 1989 reduced that debt load further, enabling Reliance to invest in research and development (R&D) and expansion.

Citibank liquidated its interest in Reliance in 1991. Unable to find a new primary investor, management took Reliance public in 1992. The following year its revenues reached $1.6 billion. In August 1994 it entered into a deal to merge with General Signal, but those plans were interrupted when Rockwell International launched a counter bid. Reliance was folded into Rockwell in early 1995.

Market Forces Driving the Acquisition

The end of the Cold War greatly reduced government contracts for U.S. defense suppliers. With that major source of revenue diminished, these companies came under pressure to generate sales from other sources. Some rushed to enter the commercial sector where feasible. Others looked to combine operations with similarly situated firms to increase their capabilities and size in competing for a greater share of the remaining government contracts. The government itself encouraged unions between the defense contractors by passing relaxed antitrust guidelines for this sector in 1993.

To Rockwell International's chairman, Donald Beall, this turn of events came as no surprise. Although the company had made the occasional foray into commercial ventures, only when Beall became president in the mid-1980s did Rockwell make aggressive strides to reduce its dependence on defense work. By acquiring such companies as Allen-Bradley and then investing in research and development, Rockwell had cut its revenues from government contracts to 39% in 1983 from 64% ten years earlier.

Beall aimed to improve such operations in order to position Rockwell to exit the defense industry altogether. Strategic acquisitions would expand its product line as well as add to its technological applications across existing businesses. For three years it had weighed the possible purchase of Reliance Electric, a diversified electrical products manufacturer. In 1994 Rockwell was spurred into action upon news of Reliance's merger agreement with General Signal.

Approach and Engagement

On August 30, 1994, General Signal and Reliance Electric announced their $1.35 billion, or $26 per share, stock swap agreement. On October 21 Donald Beall sent a letter to Reliance's president and CEO, John Morley, announcing Rockwell's all-cash tender offer for Reliance at $30 per share. Days later, General Signal announced that it refused to raise its bid, confident that U.S. regulators would reject Rockwell's bid on antitrust grounds. In early November, however, the U.S. Department of Justice cleared the way for Rockwell, having found no cause for antitrust concerns.

Meanwhile, Reliance Electric hadn't taken any position on the competing offers. Its hesitation was due to uncertainties about its future with Rockwell, as well as a $50 million breakup fee, plus $5.15 million in expense reimbursement, to be paid to General Signal upon termination of their accord. Rockwell was growing impatient. Its bid was scheduled to expire on November 18, and as that date drew closer, Rockwell revealed that although it preferred a friendly deal, it was prepared to acquire Reliance by other means if necessary.

On November 17 the three companies called a four-day truce, with General Signal permitting Rockwell and Reliance to try to work out an arrangement. "While our board of directors has made no decision to sell Reliance, the board has a duty to examine all proposals the company receives," said Morley in *Electronic News (1991)*. "Accordingly, we appreciate the constructive approach General Signal has taken in permitting Reliance to explore with Rockwell their latest acquisition proposal."

On November 21 Rockwell and Reliance emerged from negotiations with an agreement, which had been revised to $31 per share, or $1.6 billion. At that time General Signal withdrew its offer and quickly received a $55.15 million check from Rockwell. By the end of that day, 61.2% of Reliance's shares had been tendered, and in January 1995 the company was fully acquired.

Products and Services

In 1998, Rockwell International operated in four main business segments:

Rockwell Automation—formed in 1995 after Reliance was folded into Rockwell's Allen-Bradley unit—was a leading supplier of industrial automation products, systems, and software in North America. With total sales in excess of $4.5 billion, it was comprised of two subsections: Rockwell Automation Control Systems provided customer solutions for integrated sequential, motion, drive system, process, and information applications by supplying controllers, input/output systems, drives, sensors, power devices, packaged control products, and services under the Allen-Bradley and Rockwell Software brand names. Rockwell Automation Power Systems provided Dodge brand gear reducers, mounted bearings, power transmission components, network monitoring products, and Reliance Electric motors.

Rockwell Collins was a leading supplier of commercial avionics and military electronics systems, as well as service and support solutions. By providing flight deck avionics and in-flight entertainment electronics to airlines worldwide, and integrated communication, navigation, and situational awareness systems for military and business aircraft, Rockwell Collins generated annual sales of $2 billion.

Rockwell Electronic Commerce supplied customer interaction technologies such as automatic call distributors, computer telephony integration software, information collection, reporting, and management systems, and call center consulting and systems integration services for a variety of commercial industries.

The Rockwell Science Center conducted research on projects ranging from disruptive technologies to technology application. It employed 400 people and maintained partnerships with over 200 universities, national laboratories, and research organizations of other companies to provide access to leading edge technologies worldwide.

Changes to the Industry

By acquiring Reliance Electric, Rockwell became the largest industrial automation company in the U.S.

The combined firm had sales of $12.6 billion, of which 30%, or about $3.5 billion, was generated from industrial automation. This sales volume made Rockwell a contender for a global leadership position, as one of its top rivals, Siemens, had sales of $4 billion.

Reliance's industrial motors, controls, generators, transformers, and mechanical transmissions businesses were combined with the Allen-Bradley unit, manufacturer of automation control equipment, to form Rockwell Automation. This unit played a key role in Rockwell's goal of transformation from an aerospace concern into an electronics and industrial automation conglomerate.

By mid-1995 Rockwell had already made significant accomplishments in that arena. It provided about 80% of all fax and modem chips used in Japanese fax machines. Its printing presses were utilized by two-thirds of all U.S. daily newspapers. And its axles were part of two out of every three trucks built in North America.

Rockwell continued to concentrate on commercial industries by shedding non-core operations and making strategic acquisitions. In 1996 it exited the aerospace and defense industry by selling those businesses to Boeing for $3 billion. That year it purchased Brooktree for $275 million. In 1997 it spun off its $3.3 billion automotive component unit as Meritor Automotive.

Review of the Outcome

Reliance Electric's 14,000 employees increased Rockwell's headcount to 27,200. In June 1995 Rockwell sold Reliance's telecommunications equipment unit, Reliance Comm/Tec, to Kohlberg, Kravis and Roberts, marking that group's foray into telecommunications.

In 1998 Reliance's headquarters in Cleveland were consolidated into Rockwell's South Carolina office. This move resulted in the reduction of about 140 positions.

Research

Franson, Paul. "Rockwell Dangerfield," in *Electronic Business*, March 1998. Describes Wall Street's skepticism of Rockwell's transformation into an electronic company.

Haber, Carol. "Rockwell Takes Reliance in $1.6B Sweep: GS Out," in *Electronic News (1991)*, 28 November 1994. Details Rockwell's capture of Reliance.

Lubove, Seth. "New-Tech, Old-Tech," in *Forbes*, 17 July 1995. Describes Rockwell's diverse electronic business, which made it resilient to reductions in defense work.

Perry, Nancy J. "Getting out of Rocket Science," in *Fortune*, 4 April 1994. Describes Beall's efforts to move Rockwell away from the defense industry.

"Reliance Electric Agrees to Deal with Rockwell," in *The New York Times*, 22 November 1994. Announces Reliance's agreement to unite with Rockwell.

"Reliance Electric Co.," in *International Directory of Company Histories*, Vol. 9, St. James Press: 1994. Provides an historical review of the company until its acquisition by Rockwell.

"Rockwell International Corp.," in *International Directory of Company Histories*, Vol. 11, St. James Press: 1995. Profiles the history of the company prior to its acquisition of Reliance.

Rockwell International Corp. Home Page, available at http://www.rockwell.com. Official World Wide Web Page for Rockwell. Includes a description of operations, news releases, executive biographies, and investor information.

"Rockwell is Trying to Sell Aerospace, Defense Assets," in *The Wall Street Journal*, 20 March 1996. Relates Rockwell's search for a buyer for its defense and aerospace division.

DAVIS MCMILLAN

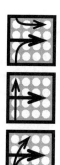

ROYAL DUTCH/SHELL GROUP & SHELL OIL

nationality: Netherlands
date: June 1985
affected: Royal Dutch/Shell Group, The Netherlands, founded 1907
affected: Shell Oil Co., USA, founded 1915

Royal Dutch/Shell Group
30, Carel van Bylandtlaan
The Hague, 2596 HR
The Netherlands

tel: (31)70-377-3395
fax: (31)70-377-3115
web: http://www.shell.com

Overview of the Merger

After seventeen months of battling Shell's shareholders, Royal Dutch/Shell Group completed the $5.7 billion merger in June of 1985. At an ultimate price of $60 per share for the remaining 30.6% of Shell that Royal Dutch did not already own, the deal strengthened the company's control over Shell's cash income and large oil and natural gas reserves. Shell became a wholly owned subsidiary of Royal Dutch/Shell Group as a result of the acquisition.

History of Royal Dutch/Shell Group

In 1870 Marcus Samuel, Sr., founder of a British trading company, died leaving his two sons Samuel and Marcus Samuel, Jr., to continue his activities of trading goods in the Far East. Eight years later, the pair formed two partnerships, Marcus Samuel & Company in London, England, and Samuel Samuel & Company in Japan. As a leading shipping and trading enterprise in the Far East, the brothers business expanded to include the selling of Russian oil produced by the Rothschild family's businesses.

To exploit the discovery of oil in the Dutch East Indies, The Royal Dutch Petroleum Company was established in The Hague under the direction of J.B. August Kessler in 1890. Just two years later, Royal Dutch exported its oil for the first time. Under fears that Russian supplies might be reduced, Samuel Samuel began to search for a secure source of oil nearer to his Far Eastern markets in 1897. The Shell Transport and Trading Company PLC was formed. It was named for the products Marcus Samuel, Sr., began selling when he founded the business, boxes that were made from shells from the Far East. In 1898 Shell discovered a major oil field in Dutch Borneo. The company began growing rapidly, owning oil fields and a refinery in Borneo and a fleet of oil tankers. By 1901 Henri Deterding, originally a bookkeeper, became Royal Dutch's chief executive.

The next year had a rough start when Shell made a costly mistake by agreeing to buy the oil produced by a Texaco well which subsequently ran dry shortly after being discovered. In 1903, as part of Deterding's strategy to build a company capa-

The Business

Financials

Revenue (1998): $93,692 million

Employees (1998): 102,000

SICs / NAICS

sic 2911 - Petroleum Refining

sic 2999 - Petroleum & Coal Products Nec

sic 1311 - Crude Petroleum & Natural Gas

sic 1321 - Natural Gas Liquids

sic 1382 - Oil & Gas Exploration Services

sic 2810 - Industrial Inorganic Chemicals

sic 2820 - Plastics Materials & Synthetics

sic 2870 - Agricultural Chemicals

sic 1099 - Metal Ores Nec

sic 3334 - Primary Aluminum

sic 1200 - Coal Mining

naics 324199 - All Other Petroleum and Coal Products Manufacturing

naics 211111 - Crude Petroleum and Natural Gas Extraction

naics 211112 - Natural Gas Liquid Extraction

naics 213112 - Support Activities for Oil and Gas Field Operations

naics 212299 - Other Metal Ore Mining

naics 331312 - Primary Aluminum Production

ble of rivaling the world's largest oil enterprises, such as Rockefeller's Standard Oil Company, the Asiatic Petroleum Company was established as a marketing company owned jointly by Royal Dutch, Shell, and members of the Rothschild family. The formation of Asiatic Petroleum left Royal Dutch in control of Shell's sales in the East. In 1907 the Royal Dutch/Shell Group was formed by the merger of Royal Dutch Petroleum Company and The "Shell" Transport and Trading Company PLC, with each company retaining its separate identity and headquarters. Shell was in such financial trouble that Deterding was able to arrange for Royal Dutch to hold a 60% majority stake to Shell's 40% share in the new company. He was also made chief executive of Royal Dutch/Shell.

By 1913 the group owned major production facilities in Russia and Venezuela. The company's first move into the U.S. came with the formation of Roxana Petroleum Company in Oklahoma, and California

Oilfields, Ltd., was acquired. Within two years, Royal Dutch/Shell was producing nearly 6 million barrels of crude oil per year in the U.S. alone. Continuing in the growth process, Deterding initiated an agreement with a U.K. government representative to provide an internal rearrangement of the group and to allow U.K. interests majority control in 1919. The agreement was never implemented, however, chiefly because of the delays caused by incoherence and confusion in the official U.K. oil policy. Shell purchased the large Mexican oil fields controlled by the U.K. oil company, Mexican Eagle, instead.

The Shell Union Oil Corporation was established in the U.S. to consolidate Shell interests there with those of the Union Oil Company of Delaware in 1923. Thirty percent of the new company was owned by U.S. shareholders. With over-capacity plaguing the oil industry, Deterding was prompted to organize a meeting in Achnacarry, Scotland, with the heads of Standard Oil of New Jersey and the Anglo-Persian Oil Company, to form a worldwide oil cartel. Despite the meeting, the oil companies were unable to control all sources of supply in the world, and the agreement did not last long. To compensate for problems caused by the over-capacity, Royal Dutch/Shell made its first venture into the chemicals business in 1929 when it formed NV Mekog in the Netherlands to manufacture nitrogeneous fertilizer from coke oven gases. The Shell Chemical Company was established in the U.S. to manufacture nitrogeneous fertilizer from natural gas.

Tumultuous times were ahead for the company and in 1940 German forces invaded the Netherlands forcing head offices of Dutch companies to move to Curacao in the Dutch West Indies. During the war, Royal Dutch/Shell refineries in the U.S. produced large quantities of high-octane aviation fuel, and Shell Chemical manufactured butadiene for synthetic rubber products. In addition, all the group's tankers were placed under U.K. government control. After the war, the company rebounded and was able to focus on development. In 1959 a joint Shell/Esso venture found a natural gas field in Groningen, the Netherlands, which became one of the world's largest natural gas fields, capable of supplying about 50% of the natural gas consumed in Europe.

By the 1970s the group was actively pursuing ways to diversify and grow. The company acquired the Billiton mining and metals business in the United Kingdom and in 1971 Shell continued active exploration of the North Sea and struck oil in its northern waters. A major offshore gas discovery was made on the northwest shelf of Australia as well. In 1973 the Organization of Petroleum Exporting Countries (OPEC) unilaterally raised crude oil prices, beginning the worldwide oil and energy crisis. Oil companies were faced with difficult political decisions on how to allocate their scarce oil supplies. Royal Dutch/Shell diversified into nuclear energy interests in response to the crisis in 1974, and also acquired coal and metals interests leading to the formation of Shell Coal International.

Over-capacity became a problem once again for the company when the chemical industry was hit prompting Shell Chemicals to restructure itself in order to reduce capacity. Despite the changes and cutbacks, the group remained the world leader in production of petrochemicals and a leading supplier of agrochemicals. By 1982 Royal Dutch/Shell recorded sales of $83.8 billion and net income of $3.5 billion during its 75th anniversary year. Continuing with its tenacious efforts to grow, Royal Dutch/Shell's stake in the Shell Oil Company of the U.S. was increased to 100% in 1985, making it a wholly owned subsidiary. Group sales totaled $81.56 billion resulting in net income of $3.87 billion.

Royal Dutch/Shell had to deal with rising problems in the latter half of the 1980s. The group's activities in South Africa involved oil supply to the Rhodesian government, and as a result, U.S. labor groups and antiapartheid organizations mobilized a consumer boycott of the group. In 1988 an explosion occurred at one of Shell Oil's refineries in Norco, Louisiana, causing profits to drop and prompting lawsuits from injured parties and families of the deceased. Group sales remained stable, however, at $78.39 billion, and net income eclipsed $5 billion for the first time.

By 1993 the group's three holding companies, The Shell Petroleum Co. Ltd. (U.K.), Shell Petroleum NV (the Netherlands), and Shell Petroleum Inc. (U.S.), were the individual leading companies in their respective countries. The Royal Dutch/Shell Group emerged as a powerhouse employing over 130,000 people, exploring for, refining, and marketing oil and natural gas across the globe, and operating the world's largest tanker fleet. The group was the number one petroleum and natural gas company in terms of sales and revenue and second in terms of production, and remained among the world's top five industrial companies.

In 1995, under pressure from the public and environmental organizations, the company decided not to sink an oil platform, called the Brent Spar platform, in the Atlantic Ocean. Royal Dutch/Shell was criticized by many for its inaction in Nigeria before the execution of nine pro-democracy campaigners in the country. Ken Saro-Wiwa, one of the activists, had protested that environmental damage to the Niger delta area

The Officers

Chairman and Group Managing Director: Mark Moody-Stuart

Vice Chairman and Group Managing Director: Maarten A. van Den Bergh

was caused by the company. Despite these attacks, the group continued to thrive. In 1996 Mobil Oil Corporation and Royal Dutch/Shell agreed to jointly develop Peru's Camisea gas field. The company opened a refinery in Thailand and planed to build more than 50 gas stations in Spain. The group also purchased Chevron's 445 gas stations in the U.K. in late 1997. One year later, Royal Dutch/Shell partnered with Texaco to form Equilon Enterprises. With the century coming to a close, the group remained a leader in the industry and gained controlling interest in Brazil's largest natural gas company, Comgas.

History of Shell Oil Co.

In order to take advantage of the increased interest in automobiles in the U.S., Royal Dutch/Shell began to sell gasoline that was imported from Sumatra in 1912. The group formed the American Gasoline Company and Roxana Petroleum Company, and opened refineries in Louisiana and Illinois. Royal Dutch then set its eyes on California Oilfields, Ltd. The company was attractive due to its ownership of gasoline in the U.S. The group acquired the company in 1913, alleviating the need to import gasoline. American gasoline changed its name to Shell Company of California in 1915, and opened its first gas station.

The company's site in California was abundant in the early 1920s, making it easy for the company to penetrate the Los Angeles area. Sales of Shell gasoline and petroleum products allowed the company to grow. In 1922 Roxana Petroleum and Shell Company of California merged with Union Oil Company of Delaware and formed a holding company. The new entity, Shell Union Oil Corporation, had 65% of its shares owned by the Royal Dutch/Shell Group. Shell continued to grow and in 1927, the Shell Pipe Line Corporation was established with the acquisition of Ozark Pipe Line Corporation, to oversee the transport of oil from Texas to its Wood River refinery. A new refinery in Houston also emerged, supplying products to the East Coast and overseas and in 1929 Shell Petroleum Corporation bought the New Orleans Refining Company.

The Players

Managing Director of Royal Dutch/Shell Group: Sir Peter Baxendell. Sir Peter Baxendell began his career as a petroleum engineer in 1946. After graduating from London University, he started working for Royal Dutch. His forty-nine year stint with the company led to such roles as managing director of Shell-BP Nigeria, managing director of Royal Dutch/Shell Group, London, chairman of Shell U.K., and chairman of Shell Transport & Trading Company PLC. He retired from the company in late 1985 and became chairman of Hawker Siddeley Group PLC, Inchcape PLC, and Sun Life Assurance Company.

President and CEO of Shell Oil Co.: John F. Bookout. University of Texas graduate John F. Bookout began his career in 1950 with Shell Oil Company working as a geologist. He worked in that position for nine years and then went into management and exploration for the company. Bookout took on several different roles in the 1960s and 70s and became president and CEO of Shell Oil Company in 1976. He remained a strong leader for the company until 1988 when he retired. He went on to serve as a member of the board for McDermott International Inc., an energy services company, until 1997, and was president and CEO of Kelly Oil and Gas Corporation. In 1990, he was awarded the "Gold Medal for Distinguished Achievement" by the petroleum trade association. Bookout is credited with being a leader in the oil industry for his knowledge and understanding of the world's energy markets.

Shell began the 1930s focused on research and development. The creation of Shell Development Company brought about research in petrochemicals, which led the Shell Chemical Company to begin manufacturing operations. Shell gasoline was now being sold throughout the United States and the company fared well in the unsettling economy the industry was faced with. The company opened two more plants dedicated to chemical research, the manufacturing of synthetic ammonia, and synthetic glycerin.

Continuing with its efforts to develop, Shell became able to synthesize 100-octane fuel and became the leading supplier of aviation fuel. With the onset of World War II, the company helped others in the industry aid the U.S. government by sharing its technology,

and also supplied butadiene, a chemical necessary to make synthetic rubber. Shell Oil Company of California eventually merged with Shell Petroleum Corporation, forming the Shell Oil Company, Inc. With offices in San Francisco, St. Louis, and New York City, the company was able to meet increasing needs of the public and continue developing new products. Emerging new developments in epoxy resins, ethylene, synthetic rubber, detergent alcohol, and other chemicals, enabled the company to become a leader in the industry.

Shell Oil Company also effectively introduced new fuel products such as jet fuel and high octane, unleaded gasoline for automobiles. By 1958, the company redesigned its gas stations in an effort to gain control of the market. This ranch style station became its leading retail outlet and in 1971, the self-service station was introduced. By becoming user friendly, accepting competitor's credit cards, and introducing travel and entertainment cards, Shell was able to realize its goals and gained large shares of the market.

Shell kicked off the 1960s by becoming a company concerned with environmental issues. Major investments in pollution reduction and energy conservation were made. The company published books for consumers on car maintenance and ways to save energy. Shell also turned its efforts to offshore drilling of oil and natural gas, focusing on Alaska and the Gulf of Mexico. Its enhanced and expert techniques led to one of its biggest strikes at the Bullwinkle prospect in the Gulf of Mexico. The discovery was expected to lead to more than 100 million barrels of oil.

Shell Oil delved into the coal production industry and in 1974 formed the Shell Mining Company. Two years later, John F. Bookout was named president of the company. The industry began to see hard times with high prices and little increase in demand. Bookout led the company through a phase of increased efficiency and re-evaluated its less profitable service stations. In 1979 the company purchased Belridge Oil Company. The new company, Kernridge Oil Company, was able to increase Shell's oil reserves when the rest of the industry was struggling with drilling opportunities.

In 1984, Royal Dutch/Shell Group began efforts to buy the remaining shares of Shell Oil Company. The battle became quite hostile, with quarrels over share price. Royal Dutch eventually offered $60 per share and the takeover was completed in June of 1985. The next year the company was criticized for Royal Dutch/Shell Group's involvement in South Africa. Because of the alleged unfair treatment of South African workers, the AFL-CIO, United Mineworkers, National Education Association, and the Free South

Africa Movement joined together to boycott the company. Soon efforts in Berkley and Boston were underway as protestors tried to stop Shell purchases. In 1989, Shell was under scrutiny as well for the cleanup of the Rocky Mountain Arsenal in Colorado. Shell had produced pesticides there and had allegedly dumped carcinogens on the grounds. The cleanup efforts cost upwards of $250 million for the company.

By the late 1980s Shell Oil was faring well, despite these setbacks. Bookout retired leaving Frank H. Richardson in charge. He led the company to see increasing cash flows and reduction of long term debt. There were problems with production, however, and the number of barrels produced on a daily basis were decreasing. The number fell from 531,000 in 1988 to 398,000 per day in 1994. Coupled with a recession in the early 1990s, Shell began to experience difficulties. Revenues declined from $24.79 billion in 1990 to $21.09 billion in 1993. Shell reduced its work force in response to the decline by cutting more than 7,000 jobs that year.

In the meantime, Shell's engineers were developing an Auger platform used in deep sea drilling in the Gulf of Mexico. In April of 1994, the oil found there could be extracted and production reached 55,000 barrels a day. In 1997 Shell partnered with Amoco to form Altura Energy, a research and development venture. The company also sought out relationships with Mobil and Exxon. Shell Oil continued to look to acquisitions and ventures in the late 1990s positioning itself to remain a leader in the oil industry as well as the number one gasoline marketer in the United States.

Market Forces Driving the Merger

By acquiring the remaining shares of Shell that it did not own, Royal Dutch/Shell Group would be positioned to take advantage of the United State's increasing role in the oil industry. In *The New York Times*, Sir Peter Baxendell, the managing director of Royal Dutch, stated that the deal "would also enable Royal Dutch/Shell Group investments and operations to take place, whether in the United States or elsewhere, without any possible inhibitions arising out of the existence of a minority interest."

Oil companies were also faced with declining reserves, stagnant demand, and price cuts. OPEC ordered a 15% price cut in March of 1983, resulting in weakening prices. Domestic oil demand fell to 15.3 million barrels per day in 1982 from 18.4 million in 1977. Reserves were also falling from 33.5 billion in 1977 to 27.9 billion in 1982. The price of oil stocks was faltering as a result. To top it off, the industry was experiencing a slowdown in discoveries and exploration. One unsuccessful attempt in Alaska reinforced

thoughts of alternative ways to expand reserves. Mr. Von Metzch, executive of the Wellington Management Company, was quoted in *The New York Times* as stating "Seeing $1.6 billion go into one massive unsuccessful venture made a lot of people think twice about the prospects of replacing reserves through exploration."

With the industry facing these pitfalls, Royal Dutch saw a premium opportunity to snatch up the remaining 30% shares of Shell. The acquisition would put Royal Dutch at the advantage of increased reserves without having to shell out billions in exploration. The company had seen a decline in its reserves over the past five years and Shell was attractive for its 2.2 billion barrels of oil that would come relatively cheap compared to average $12 per barrel cost of new exploration. Most of Shell's oil was located in the U.S., lowering tax cost, and making it a reliable, controllable, supply.

Approach and Engagement

On January 24, 1984, Royal Dutch/Shell Group made a $55 per share bid for 100% interest in Shell Oil Company. In April of 1984, Royal Dutch/Shell Group increased its bid to $58 per share after the original bid of $55 was declined. Shareholders had no interest in the new bid as well stating that it was "inadequate and certainly not in the best interest of the company and its public shareholders." They felt that $75 per share was a fair price and were in an uproar claiming that Royal Dutch was using its leverage to try to get Shell "on the cheap." In *Business Week*, Fayez Sarofim, a three million shareholder of Shell, stated "we think Shell is one of the best managed oil companies and should demand a premium multiple." Royal Dutch defended its offer claiming that it was one third over Shell's market value at the time of the original offer and that it planned to leave the company intact.

Shell prompted its shareholders to decide for themselves whether or not to sell their shares as Royal Dutch was firm in stating it would not pay more for at least one year. By late April, Shell stock was up to $58.125, and in May many shareholders tendered under fear that Royal would not only refuse to raise the price, but that it would fall to $40 per share. In a court order issued that month, shareholders were allowed to take back shares as the Delaware Chancery Court concluded that Royal Dutch had left out pertinent information to Morgan Stanley & Company, the company's financial advisors, when they were evaluating for a fair offer. Goldman Sachs & Company, Shell's advisors, thought $75 per share would be a fair price for Royal to offer.

Royal Dutch did not falter due to the fact that it did not have any "legal duty" under Delaware law to increase its offer. The two would have to officially merge before the courts had power and even then, shareholders who wanted to sue would have to wait for the merger to take place and then file for an appraisal proceeding in order to benefit. Nevertheless, the merger was put on hold until Royal Dutch could provide sufficient evidence to back up its offer. In June of 1984, Morgan Stanley & Company re-evaluated the offer and concluded that the original offer was fair.

By November of that year, stockholder litigation was still holding back the merger. Shell stock had fallen to $55.125 per share. Only 363,000 of 78.3 million shares had been taken back since May and Royal Dutch owned 94.6% of Shell. Despite the large amount of shareholder support, seven separate lawsuits consolidated into one, *Jane Joseph v. Shell Oil Company*, were still holding up the deal, complaining the offer was not fair. In April of 1985, the court rewarded a $190 million settlement to shareholders, with Royal Dutch having to wait 30 days for appeals before it could proceed with the merger. On May 21, the shareholders appealed claiming that new information on the value of Shell stock increased its value. The company's reserves in the Gulf of Mexico were said to have increased. On June 6, 1985, the court dismissed the motion on grounds that it was not valid and Royal Dutch was free to complete the merger at $60 per share. Shell became a wholly owned subsidiary merged into SPNV Holdings, another wholly owned subsidiary of Royal Dutch/Shell Group.

Products and Services

With operations in over 100 countries, Royal Dutch/Shell Group led the oil and gas industry. After the merger, Royal was exposed to Shell reserves, increasing its ability to strengthen its U.S. presence. In 1997, operations in the U.S. accounted for 22% of total sales for the company with earnings of $28,668 million. The company also spent $10,790 million on exploration and production that year.

Shell Oil continued its operations after the merger in the United States and also delved into other countries as well. Brazil, Yemen, China, and Cameroon, were included in Shell's ventures. By 1997, the company operated over 9,300 gas stations in 40 states and the District of Columbia, and had refineries in Texas, Illinois, Alabama, California, and Louisiana. The company focused on oil products, exploration, production, chemicals, and gas, and had over 40 subsidiaries.

Changes to the Industry

Mega-mergers were the wave of the future in the 1980s, spawning heated debate among industry offi-

cials. Many felt that competition would be reduced, power would be in the hands of a few strong companies, and consumers would bear the brunt having to pay more for each gallon of gas purchased. Mobil's purchase of Superior Oil for $5.7 billion, the merging of Standard Oil and Gulf Oil, and Texaco's buyout of Getty Oil, proved that larger companies were looking to buy reserves rather than spend the time and money on exploration. Analysts feared that interest rates would skyrocket and that there would be less competition in the industry as eight giants controlled almost 60% of the market.

Low-priced oil coming from the Persian Gulf sent chills throughout small oil companies in 1986. Large, strong companies fared well as cash flows diminished, but small companies like Global Marine, Inc. were forced to declare bankruptcy as they were loaded down with debt. This was another opportunity for the strong to get stronger as companies with substantial cash flows could buy up failing companies cheaply. The industry began to become more concentrated with fewer competitors in production, refining, and marketing.

Review of the Outcome

After battling for almost a year and a half, Royal Dutch completed its purchase of Shell Oil in June of 1985. Second only to Exxon, the company gained considerable reserves as a result of the deal and sweetened its position in the United States, where Royal Dutch's management felt the future of the industry would play out. The company went on to purchase 50% of Occidental's interest in a billion-barrel oilfield in Columbia for $1 billion, strengthening its reserves even further. The company also purchased 400 U.S. gas stations owned by Arco. In the first quarter of 1986, Royal Dutch/Shell reported a 16.6% decline in profits blaming the drop in global crude oil prices. Net income fell to $1 billion from $1.2 billion in the first quarter of 1985. The slump in price affected the industry as a whole as companies like Pennzoil and British Petroleum reported drastic losses as well.

Research

"Api to Honor Bookout and Hartley," in *The Oil Daily*, 13 November 1990. Discusses career of John Bookout.

Cole, Robert. "Parent Bids $5.2 Billion for the Rest of Shell Oil," in *The New York Times*, 25 January 1984. Discusses Royal Dutch's plan to purchase remaining Shell shares.

"Earnings: Profits at Royal Dutch-Shell Decline," in *Los Angeles Times*, 16 May 1986. Describes the recent drop in profits for prominent oil companies.

Greenhouse, Steven. "An Unsettling Shift in Big Oil," in *The New York Times*, 11 March 1984. Explains emerging trends in the oil industry.

Hargreaves, Ian. "Flexibility Keeps Royal Dutch/Shell in Good Shape," in *Financial Times, London*, 10, July 1985. Discusses Royal Dutch's position in the changing oil industry.

Rothschild, Edwin. "The Fear of Concentration is Justified," in *The New York Times*, 18 March, 1984. Reports recent changes in the oil industry.

Royal Dutch/Shell Group Home Page, available at http://www.shell.com. Official World Wide Web Home Page for Royal/Dutch Shell Group. Includes historical, financial, and product information, as well as recent news articles.

"Royal Dutch/Shell Group," in *Notable Corporate Chronologies*, The Gale Group, 1999. Lists major events in the history of Royal Dutch/Shell Group.

"Shell Oil Company," in *International Directory of Corporate Histories, Volume 14*, St. James Press, 1996.

"Shell Says Merger Bid is Still Inadequate," in *The Washington Post*, 6 April 1984. Details Royal Dutch's bid for Shell.

"The Shell Buyout Becomes a Family Feud," in *Business Week*, 16 April 1984. Discusses the battle over share price between Royal Dutch and Shell's shareholders.

CHRISTINA M. STANSELL

SANDOZ & CIBA-GEIGY

Novartis International AG
Basel, CH-4002
Switzerland

tel: 41 61 324 8000
fax: 41 61 321 0985
web: http://www.novartis.com

nationality: Switzerland
date: December 20, 1996
affected: Sandoz Ltd., Switzerland, founded 1886
affected: Ciba-Geigy Ltd., Switzerland, founded 1758

Overview of the Merger

The largest merger in corporate history was completed in 1996. Novartis AG was formed by the union of Sandoz Ltd. and Ciba-Geigy Ltd., two Swiss pharmaceutical giants. Upon completion of the deal, Novartis immediately became the world's second-largest pharmaceutical company and the largest agrochemicals firm.

Ciba-Geigy was the larger of the two uniting companies. Its sales in 1995 amounted to CHF 20.7 billion, compared to Sandoz's CHF 15.2 billion. However, Ciba's structure was highly bureaucratic, and the number of new products in its research and development pipeline had been virtually depleted. Moreover, the impending expiration of patents left a number of its products unprotected, namely Voltaren, its most profitable drug.

Sandoz, on the other hand, had a healthy number of promising new products in its pipeline. It had recently restructured and trimmed management, creating a more sound balance sheet. In addition, Sandoz's net income in 1995 was CHF 2.06 billion, or 13.5% of sales, while Ciba's was CHF 2.16 billion, of only 10.4% of sales. Return on equity illustrated an even greater discrepancy: Sandoz's was 26.7% compared to Ciba's 13.3%.

History of Sandoz Ltd.

In 1886 Edouard Sandoz, a businessman, and Dr. Alfred Kern, a color chemist, formed Chemical Company Kern & Sandoz to manufacture synthetic dyes. Problems arose for the partnership when Kern's previous partner refused to let them make a dye that he had he helped to develop, and when another dye caused an explosion during production. Despite these difficulties, by the following year the company made 13,000 kilograms of six different dyes.

The company was renamed Sandoz & Co. in 1893 upon the death of Kern. Two years later it incorporated and introduced its first pharmaceutical product, a fever reducer. It diversified into the sweeteners market by beginning production of saccharin in 1899. In 1911 the company established its first subsidiary, in

England. Sandoz gained a listing on the Basel Stock Exchange the following year. In 1913 its profits totaled CHF 500,000.

During World War I, Germany controlled supplies and access to customers, forcing Sandoz to develop new chemical processes and business tactics to remain viable and profitable. These innovations enabled the company to compete effectively with the previously dominant German dye and chemical companies during the war. Sandoz hired a prominent European chemist, Dr. Arthur Stoll, to organize the firm's first pharmaceuticals division.

Sandoz refused to join the German cartel I.G. Farben, instead joining with Ciba and Geigy in 1918 to form Basel AG. This cartel enabled the companies to cooperate in factory construction and operation, and also to avoid bankruptcy through a profit sharing scheme.

Sandoz formed a New York subsidiary in 1919. During the 1920s the textile industry experienced a depression, causing similar financial woes for dependent dye companies. In response, the company established subsidiaries globally and increased diversification into chemicals to be used by leather, paper, and textile businesses. Its new products included industrial cleaners, soaps, softening agents, mercerizers, and bleaches.

In 1929 Basel AG merged with I.G. Farben, and later with the French and British counterparts. This new organization was destroyed during World War II, with only Basel AG surviving. In 1951 this cartel, too, was dismantled.

Sandoz and Geigy formed a joint venture in 1930 that led to the formation of the Cincinnati Chemical Works, a tariff-free operation. In 1939 Sandoz ventured into agrobusiness; its first product of this line, a pesticide, was introduced in 1943.

In 1942 Albert Hofmann, a Sandoz chemist working on pharmaceuticals for psychiatric use, developed lysergic acid dyethilamide, or LSD 25. The company marketed it as Delysid to psychiatrists engaged in research because of its ability to produce "model psychosis." By 1961 LSD had been produced for illicit use throughout the U.S. and Canada. It developed mescaline and psilocybin, strong hallucinogens, from cactus and mushrooms, respectively. In 1958 Sandoz introduced Melleril, one of the company's first psychotropic pharmaceuticals.

Sandoz ventured into biotechnology with its 1963 acquisition of Biochemie GmbH. Sales the following year exceeded CHF 1 billion. The company diversified into nutritionals by merging in 1967 with Wander Ltd., gaining a product line that included Ovaltine.

The Business

Financials

Revenue (1998): CHF 31.7 billion

Employees (1998): 85,000

SICs / NAICS

sic 2834 - Pharmaceutical Preparations

sic 3253 - Ceramic Wall & Floor Tile

sic 2879 - Agricultural Chemicals Nec

sic 8731 - Commercial Physical Research

sic 2032 - Canned Specialties

sic 2023 - Dry, Condensed & Evaporated Dairy Products

naics 325412 - Pharmaceutical Preparation Manufacturing

naics 541710 - Research and Development in the Physical, Engineering, and Life Sciences

naics 325320 - Pesticide and Other Agricultural Chemical Manufacturing

naics 311514 - Dry, Condensed, and Evaporated Dairy Product Manufacturing

naics 311422 - Specialty Canning

The company acquired the dye manufacturer Durand & Huguenin in 1969, followed by the food company Delmark in 1972. By the middle of the decade, the oil crisis-induced global recession forced Sandoz to institute overhead reduction, operational efficiency, and personnel cutback programs to minimize losses. Diversification and acquisitions continued, however, including the purchase of Rogers Seed Co. and Northrup, King & Co., a seed company in the U.S.

It continued its policy of acquisition into the 1980s with the purchases of U.S. seed company, McNair; French dye company, SA Cardoner; U.S. pharmaceutical company, Ex-Lax; Swiss crispbread manufacturer, Svenska Knacker AB; and Swedish crispbread producer, Wasa. Sandoz expanded into chemicals designed for the construction industry in 1985, when it purchased Master Builders Group, a division of Martin Marietta.

A fire struck one of Sandoz's plants in 1986. When firefighters tried to contain the blaze, toxic chemicals were flushed into the Rhine River. Wildlife from Switzerland to Germany died as a result, spurring citizens to protest the use of such chemicals.

The Officers

Honorary Chairman: Alex Krauer

Chairman, CEO, and Managing Director: Daniel Vasella

Head, Finance: Raymond Breu

Head, Human Resources: Norman Walker

Head, Strategic Planning and Organization: Wolfdietrich Schutz

Sales exceeded CHF 10 billion in 1988. Two years later Cartapip, the company's first biochemical product, was marketed. That year it formed the subsidiary McLaren/Hart Environmental Engineering Corp., one of the top five such companies in the U.S.

In 1990 the company restructured itself as the holding company Sandoz Ltd., owner of six operating companies: Sandoz Chemicals Ltd., Sandoz Pharma Ltd., Sandoz Agro Ltd., Sandoz Seeds Ltd., Sandoz Nutrition Ltd., and MBT Holding Ltd.

The following year it acquired 60% of SyStemix and six percent of Genetic Therapy. By 1992 Sandoz Ltd. was among the top 10 worldwide pharmaceutical companies, and ranked second globally in seed production. It acquired Gerber Products Co. in 1994. The next year it spun off its chemicals division as Clariant Ltd., thereby enabling Sandoz to focus on drug and nutrition operations. In the largest merger in corporate history, Sandoz merged with Ciba-Geigy Ltd. in 1996 to form Novartis.

History of Ciba-Geigy Ltd.

In 1758 Johann Rudolf Geigy began manufacturing and selling drugs, dyes, and spices. Soon after, he merged his operations with that of Nicolaus Bernoulli to form J.R. Geigy SA for the production of such products as opium, gum arabic, and dyewoods. When Geigy died in 1793, the company was disbanded. It was reborn in 1840, however, under Carl Geigy and Leonhard Bernoulli, sons of Geigy's founders. Having expanded into silk manufacturing, Geigy entered the dyestuff industry in 1883. Geigy became a public limited company in 1901, and in 1914 changed its name to J.R. Geigy Ltd.

Meanwhile, Alexander Clavel, a French silk maker and dyer, moved to Switzerland in 1859 to establish a dyeworks. In 1873 he sold his dye factory to Bindschedler & Busch. Three years later, this company had operations in Germany, France, England, Italy, Russia, and the U.S. It transformed into

Gesellschaft fur Chemische Industrie Basel in 1884. This joint-stock company's abbreviation, Ciba, became so popular that the company adopted it as its official name in 1945.

By the turn of the century, Ciba was Switzerland's largest chemical company. The firm expanded into pharmaceuticals with the introduction of the antiseptic Vioform and the antirheumatic Salen.

In 1913 both Ciba and Geigy established factories in Germany to avoid the Swiss labor shortage and the pollution laws. In order to compete with the well-established German companies, they agreed to focus production on expensive specialty dyes in favor of the German specialty, bulk dye manufacturing. By the following year, the outbreak of war in Europe forced Basel dye factories to cease production. Meanwhile, German troops seized Swiss factories in Germany and forced a trade embargo. Ciba and Geigy agreed to give the British preferential treatment in exchange for raw materials, and they took over the German companies' export duties to the U.K. and the U.S.

Ciba, Geigy, and Sandoz joined together in 1918 to form Basel AG. This profit-sharing cartel enabled the companies to cooperate in factory construction and operation. In 1929 Basel AG merged with I.G. Farben, and later with the French and British counterparts. This new organization was dismantled during World War II, as was Basel AG in 1951.

In 1921 Ciba's profits dropped to CHF 1 million from CHF 15 million in 1917. That year it entered the U.S. market with the acquisition of Aniline Dyes & Chemicals. The Swiss companies diversified into textiles, first by Geigy in 1925 and then by Ciba in 1928. Geigy joined with Sandoz in 1930 to establish a joint venture that led to the formation of the Cincinnati Chemical Works.

Ciba began making synthetic hormones in 1934 when company scientists discovered how to isolate progesterone in pure crystalline form. The following year, Geigy ventured into the production of insecticides, with Ciba following suit in 1954.

In 1938 Geigy began pharmaceuticals production, manufacturing such products as sleeping pills, anticoagulants, and anti-tuberculosis drugs. Two years later, one of its scientists, Dr. Paul Hermann Muller, discovered the insecticidal properties of DDT. The company originally believed the chemical was safe enough to be sprayed directly on humans for de-lousing. Later research on the substance led to Privine, a hayfever treatment, and Nupercaine, a spinal anesthetic for use during childbirth. Dr. Muller received a Nobel Prize for this work in 1948.

In 1949 Geigy introduced its first major pharmaceutical, Butazolidin, a substance used to fight gout and rheumatoid arthritis. By the following year, Ciba's sales were CHF 531 million; Geigy's sales were CHF 26 million. In 1958 Geigy introduced its first successful psychotropic drug, Tofranil.

Ciba and Geigy merged in 1970, forming Ciba-Geigy Ltd. To gain U.S. regulatory approval for the merger, Ciba divested its U.S. dyeworks while Geigy sold off its U.S. pharmaceutical companies. Four years later, Ciba-Geigy diversified into the seeds business by acquiring Funk Seeds International.

In 1978 an anti-diarrhea drug manufactured by Ciba-Geigy was linked to the deaths of more than 1,000 people in Japan. In 1980 Ciba-Geigy acquired the Mettler Group, an electronics manufacturer. It also established a biotechnology division. Four years later, Ciba-Geigy generated sales in excess of CHF 17 billion.

It formed a joint venture in 1986 with the U.S.-based Chiron Corp. to develop and sell genetically engineered vaccines. The following year, Ciba-Geigy established its Ciba-Vision subsidiary. The firm purchased Maag AG, an agrochemical company, in 1990. The next year it entered into a joint venture with Netherlands-based Affymax to research drugs for cancer, arthritis, and immune system diseases. That year Ciba-Geigy introduced Habitrol, a nicotine patch designed to help smokers quit; it quickly gained 60% of the U.S. market.

The U.S. government fined Ciba-Geigy $18 million in 1992 for damage and clean-up costs brought on by toxic waste spills at its plants in New Jersey and Alabama. By the following year, Ciba-Geigy was the fourth-largest pharmaceutical company in the world, and ranked number one in the production of agrochemicals and textile dyes.

In 1994 it paid $2.1 billion for 49.9% of Chiron, its diagnostics business, and its stake in the two companies' joint vaccine venture. That year it also acquired the Maalox antacid from Rhone-Poulenc. In 1995 the U.S. Environmental Protection Agency granted approval of plants that had been bioengineered to produce their own pesticide. Ciba-Geigy was permitted to plant, but not sell, potatoes, corn, and cotton crops that had been genetically altered to produce an insecticide.

Market Forces Driving the Merger

Pharmaceutical companies enjoyed tremendous financial success in the early 1980s. Drug prices increased faster than the rate of inflation, and research and development initiatives produced blockbuster new drugs. As a whole, pharmaceuticals became the most profitable industry in the U.S. As a result, the

The Players

Honorary Chairman: Alex Krauer. Alex Krauer obtained a doctorate in economics, and in 1956 began working in the finance department of Ciba Limited. In 1957 he became a member of the company's management team and headed the Finance Function, and in 1972 was named Head of the Control and Management Services Function. Krauer was appointed a member of the Executive Committee in 1976 and became deputy chairman in 1982. He became chairman and CEO of Ciba in 1987. Krauer was appointed chairman of Novartis upon that company's formation in 1996. In April 1999 he stepped down as chairman in favor of Daniel Vasella, and was named honorary chairman.

Chairman and CEO: Daniel L. Vasella. Dr. Daniel Vasella began his professional career in a variety of medical positions at such Swiss hospitals as Waid Hospital in Zurich, University Hospital in Bern, and at the University of Bern Institute of Pathology. In 1988 Vasella joined the Sandoz Pharmaceuticals Corp. in the U.S., moving up the ranks from a market research analyst to the Director of Special Project Marketing. In 1993 he was appointed head of Corporate Marketing. After holding the position of chief operating officer of Sandoz Pharma, he was appointed CEO, a position that he held at Novartis when it was established. In 1999 Vasella added the post of chairman to his duties, succeeding the departing Alex Krauer.

industry swelled with the entry of companies expanding operations to include pharmaceuticals or forming start-up pharmaceutical companies.

Then, in the late 1980s, a period of patent expiration impacted the profitability of drug companies. Generic competitors were launched by rival firms, and profits and market share for the firms that held the original patents decreased. Pharmaceutical companies had to release breakthrough drugs to stay ahead of competition, but research and development, and the subsequent review by governmental agencies, often took years. That time span could be reduced, however, by joining with another company. Consolidation would made available additional research and development funds, as well as marketing dollars.

A second wave of pharmaceutical consolidation occurred in mid-1990s in response to the growth of managed care, increasing costs of product development and delivery, and further patent expiration. Offering a large array of products would allow for reduced marketing allocations. It would also translate into increased leverage in negotiations with managed care organizations. A company that could meet more of the pharmaceutical needs of end-customers would be regarded favorably by managed care companies, and the pharmaceutical companies would gain loyalty from these companies by offering volume discounts.

Approach and Engagement

Merger talks were conducted in secrecy, and the March 7, 1996, announcement of the merger was big news in the industry. It was not so much a shock that the two companies would want to link lots; rather, it was the record-breaking size of the deal that made headlines. The $27 billion deal represented the largest corporate merger in history at that time.

The new company would be called Novartis AG, from the Latin term *novae artes*, meaning "new arts" or "new skills." The transaction would consist of a stock swap in which Ciba shareholders received 1.066 shares of Novartis stock for each Ciba share, while Sandoz's shares were traded evenly. The shareholders of each company approved the merger in late April.

On July 17, 1996, the European Union granted approval to the deal. The last regulatory hurdle to clear was the U.S. Federal Trade Commission (FTC). This agency granted its approval to the merger on December 17, but only with several caveats. The companies were forced to divest their U.S. corn herbicide business, as well as their U.S. flea and tick control products. In addition, the FTC laid down the condition that Novartis make available to all players its research in gene therapy. This was a controversial requirement because no products based on that science were in existence; the FTC had extended its reach to the laboratory. The companies complied, however, and three days later, on December 20, 1996, Novartis AG was officially formed.

Products and Services

Novartis operated in three primary divisions:

Healthcare consisted of pharmaceutical, consumer health, generic, and vision care products and services. It operated in 126 affiliates in 63 countries and generated total sales of CHF 17.5 billion in 1998. This division was subdivided into three components: Novartis Pharma developed and manufactured prescription medications, and contributed CHF 14.5 billion in revenues. CIBA Vision offered optical and ophthalmic products and services, and was the second-largest provider of contact lenses and lens care products in the world, with CHF 1.5 billion in 1998; and Novartis Generics was one of the largest generic pharmaceutical organizations in the world, with 1998 sales of CHF 1.5 billion.

Agribusiness focused on the discovery and development of solutions for sustainable agriculture, crop protection, resilient seed strains, and animal health. Its 116 affiliates in 50 countries generated total 1998 revenues of CHF 8.4 billion, and was comprised of three segments: Novartis Crop Protection sold CHF 6 billion in such products as insecticides, fungicides, herbicides, seed treatment, turf and ornamentals, plant care products, and plant activators. Novartis Animal Health was centered on products designed to maintain and improve the health and welfare of animals, both pets and food-producing animals, and produced sales of CHF 901 million. Novartis Seeds developed and produced genetically enhanced seed and plants, and with sales of CHF 1.4 billion, was the world's second-largest seed producer.

Consumer Health centered on consumer self-care, health, and medical nutrition needs, and generated 1998 sales of CHF 5.8 billion. It operated affiliates in 42 countries in three main areas of healthcare. Self-medication healthcare generated revenues of CHF 1.7 billion, and offered such over-the-counter products as Desenex athlete's foot treatment, ExLax laxative, Gas-X anti-gas remedy, Maalox antacid, Nicotinell/Habitrol smoking cessation agents, Tavist allergies treatment, Theraflu/Neocitran cold remedies, and Triaminic cough and cold medicine. Health and Functional Food included food beverages, baked goods, health food, sport nutrition, sweeteners, sugar-free confectionery, nutritional supplements, and products for infants and babies. Medical Nutrition developed products designed to meet the special needs of patients and convalescents in hospitals, nursing homes, and at home, and offered such brands as Resource. Combined, the company's health and functional food and its medical nutrition businesses generated 1998 sales of CHF 3.6 billion.

Changes to the Industry

Novartis became the second-largest pharmaceutical company, behind Glaxo-Wellcome. It was also the world's leader in agrochemicals, and ranked second in animal health and in seeds. Based on combined 1995 figures of the Ciba and Sandoz, Novartis had CHF 35.9 billion in sales and CHF 4.2 billion in net income. The new company estimated that it would realize CHF 2 billion in savings over three years.

Upon formation, the new company divested itself of non-core businesses to focus on three areas—healthcare, agrochemicals, and nutrition. Novartis began shedding its non-core businesses, a program that Sandoz had initiated prior to the merger agreement. In 1995 it had spun off its chemicals division as Clariant Ltd., thereby enabling the firm to focus on drug and nutrition operations. Ciba, in turn, spun off its Specialty Chemicals division in March 1997. To comply with the FTC decree, Novartis sold its corn herbicides business to BASF for $778 million, and its flea and tick products to Central Garden for $42 million.

Review of the Outcome

Despite little overlap in product lines, a workforce and facility redundancy was unavoidable. At the time of the merger announcement, the companies anticipated the closure of five manufacturing plants and a 10% reduction in its total workforce, or about 12,000 positions. By February 1997, it had reduced its worldwide staff to 90,200, more than double the anticipated percentage of reduction. At the same time, however, it had hired 2,400 additional employees in specialized positions by year-end 1997.

For the year 1997, its first full year of operation, Novartis had total revenues of CHF 31.1 billion and net income of CHF 5.2 billion. By segment, its healthcare division, comprising pharmaceuticals, consumer health, generics, and CIBA Vision, contributed most to those sales, CHF 18.7 billion. Agribusiness, made up of crop protection, seeds, and animal health operations, accounted for CHF 8.3 billion. The Nutrition division, its healthcare and baby food businesses, contributed CHF 4.1 billion to the company's total sales.

In July 1997, Novartis acquired the crop protection business of Merck & Co. for $910 million. The following year it merged its over-the-counter (OTC) drug operation with its nutrition business into a new Consumer Health division, which became one of the leading three OTC drug and specialty nutrition companies. In 1998 it also acquired Young's Animal Health business in Australia and New Zealand. That year it sold its Italian sugar-free business as well as the snack food company Roland Murten and the U.S. medical supplies company Red Line HealthCare Corp.

Novartis began 1999 with a number of divestitures. In January it agreed to sell its stakes in two joint ventures centered on the OLW snack food brand. That March it confirmed the sale of its Wasa crispbread unit and its Eden nutrition operations. In April 1999, chairman Alex Krauer stepped down as chairman. He was named honorary chairman, and CEO Daniel Vasella assumed the vacated post.

Research

"The Behemoth from Basle: Drug Mergers," in *The Economist*, 9 March 1996. Describes the market pressures that contributed to the union.

Chapman, Peter. "Novartis Gets Green Light from US FTC," in *Chemical Market Reporter*, 23 December 1996. Reports the conditions laid down by the FTC for its approval of the merger.

"Drug Suppliers Consolidate," in *Chain Drug Review*, 4 November 1996. Details the anticipated workforce reduction resulting from the merger.

"EC Merger Regulation: Decision—Ciba-Geigy/Sandoz," in *Business Law Europe*, 31 July 1996. Describes the areas of concern to the European Commission in approving the merger.

Giddings, Sharon. "Taking Stock," in *Pharmaceutical Executive*, February 1997. Discusses the stock swap in detail, offering rationale for the differences in the specifics between Ciba and Sandoz shares.

"Late News...Sandoz and Ciba Agree Merger," in *OTC News & Market Report*, 1 April 1996. Provides a break-down of 1995 financial figures for both Ciba and Sandoz.

"No Hidden Surprises from US FTC for Birth of Novartis," in *Marketletter*, 6 January 1997. Reports the divestiture of the corn herbicide and animal health business in compliance with the FTC.

"Novartis AG," in *Notable Corporate Chronologies*, The Gale Group, 1999. Lists major events in the histories of both Sandoz and Ciba-Geigy, and in the time period after the formation of Novartis.

Novartis International AG, 1997 Annual Report. Covers financial highlights and describes company operating segments.

Novartis International AG Home Page, available at http://www.novartis.com. Official World Wide Web Page for Novartis. Includes access to product information, press releases, a company history, executive biographies, and investor information.

"Novartis to Sell Wasa and Eden Units," in *Nutraceuticals International*," March 1999. Reports Novartis' intention to divest its Wasa and Eden nutritional units.

Young, Ian. "Ciba Spin-Off Enters Final Stretch," in *Chemical Week*, 26 February 1997. Describes the upcoming spin-off of Ciba, and what that new company could expect from the future.

DEBORAH J. UNTENER

SANDOZ & GERBER PRODUCTS

Novartis International AG
Basel, CH-4002
Switzerland

tel: 41 61 324 8000
fax: 41 61 321 0985
web: http://www.novartis.com

nationality: Switzerland
date: August 1994
affected: Sandoz Ltd., Switzerland, founded 1886
affected: Gerber Products Co., USA, founded 1901

Overview of the Merger

The acquisition of Gerber by Sandoz in 1994 spun on one key concept—distribution. The U.S. baby food manufacturer had gone about as far as it could domestically, where it dominated the market with a 71% share. International expansion was progressing sluggishly, and Gerber needed to find a vehicle to deliver swifter growth.

Likewise, Sandoz needed entry into the U.S. market. This Swiss giant had established a presence in the U.S. with its pharmaceuticals and chemicals, but its fledgling nutrition division required a boost from an insider to get its products on grocery store shelves.

A combined distribution network would provide inroads into areas where the respective companies had been experiencing growing pains. Sandoz flourished in Europe and Asia, while Gerber had strong bases in the U.S. and Latin America. Moreover, Sandoz would benefit from Gerber's century of experience in manufacturing baby food, along with its advanced processing and packaging technologies.

History of Sandoz Ltd.

In 1886 Edouard Sandoz, a businessman, and Dr. Alfred Kern, a color chemist, formed Chemical Company Kern & Sandoz to manufacture synthetic dyes. Problems arose for the partnership when Kern's previous partner refused to let them make a dye that he had he helped to develop, and when another dye caused an explosion during production. Despite these difficulties, by the following year the company made 13,000 kilograms of six different dyes.

The company was renamed Sandoz & Co. in 1893 upon the death of Kern. Two years later it incorporated and introduced its first pharmaceutical product, a fever reducer. It diversified into the sweeteners market by beginning production of saccharin in 1899. In 1911 the company established its first subsidiary, in England. Sandoz gained a listing on the Basel Stock Exchange the following year. In 1913 its profits totaled CHF 500,000.

During World War I, Germany controlled supplies and access to customers, forcing Sandoz to develop new chemical processes and business tactics to remain viable and profitable. These innovations enabled the company to compete effectively with the previously dominant German dye and chemical companies during the war. Sandoz hired a prominent European chemist, Dr. Arthur Stoll, to organize the firm's first pharmaceuticals division.

Sandoz refused to join the German cartel I.G. Farben, instead joining with Ciba and Geigy in 1918 to form Basel AG. This cartel enabled the companies to cooperate in factory construction and operation, and also to avoid bankruptcy through a profit sharing scheme.

Sandoz formed a New York subsidiary in 1919. During the 1920s the textile industry experienced a depression, causing similar financial woes for dependent dye companies. In response, the company established subsidiaries globally and increased diversification into chemicals to be used by leather, paper, and textile businesses. Its new products included industrial cleaners, soaps, softening agents, mercerizers, and bleaches.

In 1929 Basel AG merged with I.G. Farben, and later with the French and British counterparts. This new organization was destroyed during World War II, with only Basel AG surviving. In 1951 this cartel, too, was dismantled.

Sandoz and Geigy formed a joint venture in 1930 that led to the formation of the Cincinnati Chemical Works, a tariff-free operation. In 1939 Sandoz ventured into agrobusiness; its first product of this line, a pesticide, was introduced in 1943.

In 1942 Albert Hofmann, a Sandoz chemist working on pharmaceuticals for psychiatric use, developed lysergic acid dyethilamide, or LSD 25. The company marketed it as Delysid to psychiatrists engaged in research because of its ability to produce "model psychosis." By 1961 LSD had been produced for illicit use throughout the U.S. and Canada. It developed mescaline and psilocybin, strong hallucinogens, from cactus and mushrooms, respectively. In 1958 Sandoz introduced Melleril, one of the company's first psychotropic pharmaceuticals.

Sandoz ventured into biotechnology with its 1963 acquisition of Biochemie GmbH. Sales the following year exceeded CHF 1 billion. The company diversified into nutritionals by merging in 1967 with Wander Ltd., gaining a product line that included Ovaltine.

The company acquired the dye manufacturer Durand & Huguenin in 1969, followed by the food company Delmark in 1972. By the middle of the

The Business

Financials

Revenue (1998): CHF 31.7 billion

Employees (1998): 85,000

SICs / NAICS

sic 2834 - Pharmaceutical Preparations

sic 3253 - Ceramic Wall & Floor Tile

sic 2879 - Agricultural Chemicals Nec

sic 8731 - Commercial Physical Research

sic 2032 - Canned Specialties

sic 2023 - Dry, Condensed & Evaporated Dairy Products

naics 325412 - Pharmaceutical Preparation Manufacturing

naics 541710 - Research and Development in the Physical, Engineering, and Life Sciences

naics 325320 - Pesticide and Other Agricultural Chemical Manufacturing

naics 311514 - Dry, Condensed, and Evaporated Dairy Product Manufacturing

naics 311422 - Specialty Canning

decade, the oil crisis-induced global recession forced Sandoz to institute overhead reduction, operational efficiency, and personnel cutback programs to minimize losses. Diversification and acquisitions continued, however, including the purchase of Rogers Seed Co. and Northrup, King & Co., a seed company in the U.S.

It continued its policy of acquisition into the 1980s with the purchases of U.S. seed company, McNair; French dye company, SA Cardoner; U.S. pharmaceutical company, Ex-Lax; Swiss crispbread manufacturer, Svenska Knacker AB; and Swedish crispbread producer, Wasa. Sandoz expanded into chemicals designed for the construction industry in 1985, when it purchased Master Builders Group, a division of Martin Marietta.

A fire struck one of Sandoz's plants in 1986. When firefighters tried to contain the blaze, toxic chemicals were flushed into the Rhine River. Wildlife from Switzerland to Germany died as a result, spurring citizens to protest the use of such chemicals.

Sales exceeded CHF 10 billion in 1988. Two years later Cartapip, the company's first biochemical product, was marketed. That year it formed the subsidiary

The Officers

Honorary Chairman: Alex Krauer

Chairman, CEO, and Managing Director: Daniel Vasella

Head, Finance: Raymond Breu

Head, Human Resources: Norman Walker

Head, Strategic Planning and Organization: Wolfdietrich Schutz

McLaren/Hart Environmental Engineering Corp., one of the top five such companies in the U.S.

In 1990 the company restructured itself as the holding company Sandoz Ltd., owner of six operating companies: Sandoz Chemicals Ltd., Sandoz Pharma Ltd., Sandoz Agro Ltd., Sandoz Seeds Ltd., Sandoz Nutrition Ltd., and MBT Holding Ltd.

The following year it acquired 60% of SyStemix and six percent of Genetic Therapy. By 1992 Sandoz Ltd. was among the top 10 worldwide pharmaceutical companies, and ranked second globally in seed production. It acquired Gerber Products Co. in 1994. The next year it spun off its chemicals division as Clariant Ltd., thereby enabling Sandoz to focus on drug and nutrition operations. In the largest merger in corporate history, Sandoz merged with Ciba-Geigy Ltd. in 1996 to form Novartis.

History of Gerber Products Co.

In March 1901 Frank Gerber and his father began packaging peas, beans, and fruits at the Fremont Canning Co. in Fremont, Michigan. The company became fairly successful, and by 1914 its plant had been expanded to permit year-round production. Three years later, annual sales exceeded $1 million for the first time. In 1926, Frank's son, Daniel, became assistant general manager. His wife, Dorothy Gerber, had been hand-straining solid food for their seven-month old daughter based on her pediatrician's recommendation. In the summer of 1927, she pointed out to Daniel that this messy and time-consuming chore could be done at the cannery. After trying his own hand at the task, he agreed.

Frank and Daniel undertook extensive preliminary research before launching the concept, thoroughly testing the products, contacting nutrition experts, distributing thousands of samples, and conducting follow-up market research interviews. In 1928 the company successfully introduced a baby food line, consisting of strained peas, prunes, carrots, spinach, and beef vegetable soup.

At this time, canned baby food produced for the mass market was unheard of, and both consumers and grocers were wary of the product. Fremont Canning enticed them by placing advertisements, featuring the "Gerber Baby" logo, in such magazines as *Good Housekeeping*. The ads stressed the nutritional and timesaving value of Gerber's foods, and included an offer of six cans of food in exchange for $1.00 and the name of a preferred grocer. Within six months, the company had convinced enough grocers of the product's market to enable the young firm to go national. Its revenues at the end of that first year were $345,000 on sales of 590,000 cans.

By 1931 Fremont had its own fleet of delivery trucks featuring the Gerber Baby on their back windows and horns that played the "Rock-a-Bye-Baby" tune. The following year it introduced canned cereal as well as new varieties of canned vegetables, including tomatoes, green beans, and beets. The company expanded internationally in 1933 by selling its products in Canada.

Competition stepped up rapidly. By 1935 more than 60 other manufacturers had introduced strained, pressure-cooked baby foods. They couldn't shake Gerber's market dominance, however. The company had already established trust in the consumer, possessed a widely recognized logo, and published numerous pamphlets on parenting and child-care. In addition, Dorothy Gerber served as a spokesperson, personally answering customers' questions and writing a newspaper column.

Sales of strained baby foods exceeded $1 million in 1938. Two years later, because its baby food production of one million cans per week far exceeded its adult foods production, the company was renamed Gerber Products Co. In 1943 it discontinued production of adult foods completely. That year the company acquired Elmhurst Packers, Inc. and opened a second baby food factory in Oakland, California. By 1949 sales exceeded $39 million from its 40 varieties of strained and junior foods.

Daniel assumed the presidency of Gerber upon Frank's death in 1952, and embarked on a program of expansion and diversification. Gerber became the first baby food company to advertise on television. In 1955 the company introduced a line of toys, and the following year it obtained a listing on the New York Stock Exchange. Gerber then initiated a program of aggressive international expansion. It established a Mexican subsidiary in 1959, and sales for that year topped $126 million. During the 1960s it entered into an agreement with CPC International to distribute its products in the U.K., France, Germany, and Italy. It later founded a Puerto Rican distribution center, purchased a major interest in a food processing plant in Venezuela, and established new operations in Costa Rica.

During the 1960s Gerber introduced a large line of baby-related products, such as bottles and teethers. It had also introduced safety caps for its jars, the first tamper-evident packaging of its kind. The company diversified into life insurance with the 1967 establishment of Gerber Life Insurance Co., a direct response marketing insurance company and provider of juvenile life insurance. By the end of the decade, the company manufactured about 80 food products and generated net sales of $222 million.

Gerber continued on its diversification program. In 1970 it purchased both Jack & Jill School, a national chain of baby-watching and nursery school training facilities, and Hanskraft Company Inc., maker of children's specialties, vaporizers, and humidifiers. The following year it acquired Spartan Graphics, a provider of photographic, design, and printing services. In July 1974 it purchased Walter W. Moyer Company Inc., a maker of children's knit under- and outer-garments.

A five-year price war on baby food finally ended in 1974. During that time, Gerber had increased its domestic market share from 53% to 70%. Its annual sales reached $278 million. In 1977 Anderson, Clayton, and Co., a food producer, attempted a takeover of Gerber, but ceased action upon threat of lengthy legal proceedings. By the end of that year, Gerber manufactured about 150 food products and generated sales of $405 million.

To offset expected declines in birth rates, Gerber embarked upon a fervent diversification campaign in 1979, when it acquired CW Transport, a freight carrier. Three years later it formed a children's furniture division. In 1983 it purchased WeatherTamer Inc., Walter International, and Buster Brown Apparel, Inc.

The company experienced the first of its public relations crises in 1984, when reports of glass in Gerber baby juice jars caused company to recall 550,000 jars throughout 15 states. Because of its prompt action in remedying the problem, it temporarily lost only four percent in sales. In 1986 a second glass scare was reported through 645 complaints in 40 states. This crisis was handled quite differently than the previous scare. Now headed by William L. McKinley, Gerber chose to remain silent and take no action other than to cooperate with federal investigators. Although absolved of blame, the company's pol-

icy of silence and inactivity contributed to a $15 million drop in profits from the previous year.

In 1987 McKinley resigned. David W. Johnson assumed his role, and aggressively reemphasized Gerber as a major food company. By 1989 the company had reversed its diversification strategy that began a decade ago. Having shed many non-core businesses, it was better able to focus on baby food, care, and clothing lines. In 1992 Gerber introduced the 23-item Gerber Graduates line, a variety of foods for children older than 15 months. It also became the largest baby food producer in Central Europe by purchasing 60% of the Polish producer of food and juices, Alima S.A.

In the early 1990s, Heinz and Beech-Nut participated in intense price wars, undercutting Gerber's prices by up to 28 cents per jar. By September 1993, Gerber's market share had slipped to 67.6%, and its stock value declined accordingly. It redoubled its efforts to vigorously promote itself. It pumped $15 million into the marketing of Gerber Graduates, whose revenues of $58 million in 1994 more than doubled those of the previous year. In December 1994, Gerber was acquired by the Swiss drug giant Sandoz Ltd.

During the next two years, Gerber's public relations took a number of hits. In 1996 the Center for Science in the Public Interest disputed some of the health claims made by Gerber's advertising. Later that year, under pressure from consumers, Gerber announced that it would discontinue adding starch and sugar to its products. In 1997 the Federal Trade Commission accused Gerber of distorting advertising claims that four out of five pediatricians recommended Gerber products. The company's settlement with the FTC barred Gerber from making unfounded claims in the future. In October 1997 it debuted Tender Harvest, its first organic baby food line.

Market Forces Driving the Merger

Gerber was struggling to expand globally. The domestic market had been pretty much tapped out, as the company already enjoyed a dominant 71% market share. Gerber's annual growth rate in the U.S. was below five percent. In addition, declining birth rates in the U.S. pointed to the likelihood of depressed future sales.

The international market, however, was untapped in many areas. Parents were frequently wary of pre-packaged baby food, believing that homemade food was fresher and healthier. While American parents purchased 49 dozen jars of baby food per birth each year, Japanese parents purchased five dozen, and Polish parents only one dozen. Of

Gerber's total 1993 sales of $1.3 billion, only 16.6%, or $216.1 million, originated abroad.

The only foreign market in which Gerber had established a beachhead was Latin America, specifically Puerto Rico, Mexico, and Venezuela. In fact, Puerto Rican families consumed 58 dozen jars of baby food per year, even more than Americans.

In the European countries where jarred baby food was accepted, brutal competition effectively blocked Gerber from making much headway. H.J. Heinz, Nestle, and Danone were aggressive rivals, particularly Heinz, which dominated the European market with a 25% share. "You'd be foolish to compete with us there," warned Heinz's chairman Anthony O'Reilly in *Business Week*.

Sandoz, meanwhile, was a three-legged Swiss giant. This company was the third-largest pharmaceutical and chemical company in Europe. It wanted to expand its nutrition business to even out revenues from its three operating segments. Sandoz also sought to strengthen the footing of its nutrition line in the U.S. market, where it held little presence. This nutrition unit didn't manufacture baby food, but it did produce baby cereals and formulas in Spain and Switzerland. It also possessed the strong health food brands of Ovaltine, Wasa crispbread, and Isostar sports drink.

Along with its general nutrition business, Sandoz wanted to strengthen its position in nutraceuticals, natural substances possessing medicinal properties. This was a ripe new market being targeted by food and drug companies alike. Large companies such as these were on the prowl for smaller firms that had carved out a presence in this category.

An impending change in the International Accounting Standards spurred European companies to complete takeovers before the end of 1994. Until that time, Europeans could continue to write off goodwill—the difference between the purchase price and the value of the acquired company—against that year's taxes. As of 1995, however, they would have to write off goodwill over 20 years, thereby evening out the playing field a bit with U.S. companies, which were required to write it off over 40 years. Completing a deal before year-end, therefore, would reduce equity, while a deal conducted after January 1, 1995, would reduce earnings.

This time limit prompted a surge in European takeover activity, especially by the Swiss. These companies tended to embrace the fiscal responsibility that many parents had attempted to impress upon their children—save up your money and then you can buy what you want. Many Swiss companies had accumulated and been sitting on cash hoards. This ready supply of capital enabled them to conduct transactions in record time, since they didn't have to work out deals with banks. On May 2, 1994, Roche Holding Ltd., a Swiss pharmaceutical company, bid $5.3 billion in cash for Syntex Corp., a U.S. drug firm. Just weeks later, Sandoz followed suit in its quest for Gerber.

Approach and Engagement

Marc Moret, Sandoz's chairman, had approached Gerber Products in the mid-1980s with acquisition overtures. He wanted to build his company's nutrition business, and Gerber seemed an ideal company to help Sandoz do just that. The U.S. company, however, passed on the offer. It maintained independence until 1994, when it put itself on the auction block.

Sandoz jumped at the opportunity to acquire the long-desired asset. The timing was right for its purchase, in light of the upcoming changes in accounting rules and the company's wish to strengthen and expand its nutrition business.

On May 21 Gerber's board of directors approved the deal, and three days later the merger was announced. The terms of the deal stunned the industry. The $3.7 billion cash purchase price was valued at $53 per share, an amount 53% higher than Gerber's current market value. "We took the market by surprise, no doubt," remarked Raymond Breu, chief financial officer of Sandoz, in *Financial World*. This high bid effectively eliminated competing bids, however. After gaining the requisite regulatory approvals, Sandoz completed the purchase in August 1994.

Sandoz merged with Ciba-Geigy, another Swiss pharmaceutical giant, in 1996 to form Novartis. This $36 billion merger combined the two Swiss pharmaceutical manufacturers to create the world's largest life sciences company. Upon formation, the new company divested itself of non-core businesses to focus on three areas—healthcare, agrochemicals, and nutrition.

Products and Services

Novartis operated in three primary divisions:

Healthcare consisted of pharmaceutical, consumer health, generic, and vision care products and services. It operated in 126 affiliates in 63 countries, and generated total sales of CHF 17.5 billion in 1998. This division was subdivided into three components: Novartis Pharma developed and manufactured prescription medications, and contributed CHF 14.5 billion in revenues. CIBA Vision offered optical and ophthalmic products and services, and was the second-largest provider of contact lenses and lens care products in the world, with CHF 1.5 billion in 1998; and Novartis Generics was one of the largest generic pharmaceutical organizations in the world, with 1998 sales of CHF 1.5 billion.

Agribusiness focused on the discovery and development of solutions for sustainable agriculture, crop protection, resilient seed strains, and animal health. Its 116 affiliates in 50 countries generated total 1998 revenues of CHF 8.4 billion, and was comprised of three segments: Novartis Crop Protection sold CHF 6 billion in such products as insecticides, fungicides, herbicides, seed treatment, turf and ornamentals, plant care products, and plant activators. Novartis Animal Health was centered on products designed to maintain and improve the health and welfare of animals, both pets and food-producing animals, and produced sales of CHF 901 million. Novartis Seeds developed and produced genetically enhanced seed and plants, and with sales of CHF 1.4 billion, was the world's second-largest seed producer.

Consumer Health centered on consumer self-care, health, and medical nutrition needs, and generated 1998 sales of CHF 5.8 billion. It operated affiliates in 42 countries in three main areas of healthcare. Self-medication healthcare generated revenues of CHF 1.7 billion, and offered such over-the-counter products as Desenex athlete's foot treatment, ExLax laxative, Gas-X anti-gas remedy, Maalox antacid, Nicotinell/Habitrol smoking cessation agents, Tavist allergies treatment, Theraflu/Neocitran cold remedies, and Triaminic cough and cold medicine. Health and Functional Food included food beverages, baked goods, health food, sport nutrition, sweeteners, sugar-free confectionery, nutritional supplements, and products for infants and babies. Medical Nutrition developed products designed to meet the special needs of patients and convalescents in hospitals, nursing homes, and at home, and offered such brands as Resource. Combined, the company's health and functional food and its medical nutrition businesses generated 1998 sales of CHF 3.6 billion.

Changes to the Industry

Sandoz immediately realized a doubling of its nutrition business with the addition of Gerber. It also increased that division's contribution toward total company revenues to 20%. This was an important step for the company, which wanted to make nutrition its second priority, after pharmaceuticals. Chemicals had become more of a sideline than a focus for Sandoz.

In March 1995, the company announced that it would shed the chemical division to concentrate on pharmaceuticals and nutrition. While construction chemicals, agrochemicals, and seed businesses were retained, Sandoz divested its textile dyestuff, leather and paper treatment chemicals, and pigments and additives operations. In 1995 it spun off these operations as Clariant Ltd.

The merger with Sandoz enabled Gerber to expand outside the baby food market. In 1995 it made its first foray into the adult nutrition market in the U.S. by introducing Resource, a nutritional supplement drink for adults 55 and older. It was modeled after a product that Sandoz had marketed to hospitals and nursing homes.

Review of the Outcome

Gerber employees were relieved to see the company go to an international firm with minimal presence in the U.S. If it had been acquired by RJR Nabisco, or a similar U.S.-based firm that had been rumored to be interested, huge job losses would have been likely upon consolidation. As it turned out, fewer than 100 employees were displaced by the deal.

The acquisition of Gerber contributed to a six-percent rise in Sandoz's turnover. In the half-year period ending June 30, 1995, turnover reached SF 8.7 billion, up from SF 8.2 billion over the same period in the previous year.

Research

"Gerber Buy Boost Sandoz' Sales," in *ECN—European Chemical News*, 17 July 1995. Reports the sales growth by Sandoz in the months following the Gerber acquisition.

Gerber Home Page, available at http://www.gerber.com. Official World Wide Web Page for Gerber. Includes access to product information, a brief company history, research data, and information on phases of child development.

"Gerber Products Co.," in *Notable Corporate Chronologies*, The Gale Group, 1999. Profiles the company from its foundation through its acquisition by Sandoz.

"Gerber Products Company," in *International Directory of Company Histories*, Vol. 21, St. James Press, 1994. Profiles of the history of Gerber through its acquisition by Sandoz.

"Novartis AG," in *Notable Corporate Chronologies*, The Gale Group, 1999. Lists major events in the histories of both Sandoz and Ciba-Geigy, and since the time period after the formation of Novartis.

Novartis International AG Home Page, available at http://www.novartis.com. Official World Wide Web Page for Novartis. Includes access to product information, press releases, a company history, executive biographies, and investor information.

Reingold, Jennifer. "The Pope of Basel," in *Financial World*, 18 July 1995. Profiles Sandoz's Marc Moret and his acquisition strategy to pump up nutrition businesses.

Rickard, Leah, and Laurel Wentz. "Sandoz Opens World for Gerber: But Some Lands Wary of Jar Baby Food," in

Advertising Age, 30 May 1994. Describes the obstacles in introducing pre-packaged baby food in global markets.

"Sandoz Completes $3.7 Billion Acquisition of Gerber," in *The New York Times*, 26 August 1994. Announces the completed deal.

Spethmann, Betsy. "Sandoz Gerber Formula is a Baby Step into Nutraceuticals," in *Brandweek*, 30 May 1994. Describes the efforts of food and drug companies to enter the nutraceutical market.

Templeman, John. "The Swiss Are Coming! The Swiss Are Coming!" in *Business Week*, 6 June 1994. Details the reasons for 1994's flurry of U.S. acquisitions by Swiss firms.

Woodruff, David, John Templeman, and Keith L. Alexander. "Strained Peas, Strained Profits?" in *Business Week*, 6 June 1994. Describes the difficulties Gerber might experience in global expansion.

DEBORAH J. UNTENER

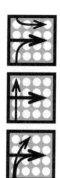

SANPAOLO IMI & BANCA DI ROMA

nationality: Italy
date: April 1999 (canceled)
affected: Sanpaolo IMI SpA, Italy, founded 1998
affected: Banca di Roma SpA, Italy, founded 1992

Sanpaolo IMI SpA
Piazza San Carlo, 156
Turin, 10121
Italy

tel: 39 011 555 1
web: http://www.sanpaolo.it

Banca di Roma SpA
Via M. Minghetti, 17
Rome, 00187
Italy

tel: 39 06 670 71
fax: 39 06 544 53154
web: http://www.bancaroma.it

Overview of the Merger

The adoption of the euro in January 1999 tore down economic trade barriers between European countries. As a result, companies could more easily expand into new territories, all the while trying to defend their own markets from other companies doing likewise. Italy's banking industry was particularly vulnerable to foreign competitors, as even the largest of its banks were far smaller than its European counterparts.

Consolidation of these firms was the most feasible means of growing quickly. Following this logic, Sanpaolo IMI proposed a merger with Banca di Roma in March 1999. This union, which would have created one of Europe's top 10 banks, was rejected by Banca di Roma's shareholders and the country's mergers authority because of the bid's hostile nature.

History of Sanpaolo IMI SpA

On January 3, 1994, the privatization of the Instituto Mobilaire Italiano (IMI) initiated when its shares were offered to the public. In July 1995, in a private placement, 19% of IMI's share capital was placed into a joint trust shared by three banks, each of which boosted its stake to 10% as a result: Instituto Bancario San Paolo di Torini (San Paolo), Cassa di Risparmio delle Provincie Lombarde, and Monte dei Paschi di Siena. One year later the Italian Treasury completed IMI's privatization by selling its remaining 6.93% stake.

Instituto Bancario San Paolo di Torini, one of IMI's shareholders, was moving closer to independence itself. Its owner, the local government foundation Compagnie di San Paolo, completed a secondary offering of the bank's shares in May 1997. This sale followed the bank's 1992 initial public offering.

In April 1998 San Paolo and IMI agreed to merge, solidifying San Paolo as the nation's largest bank while combining its retail banking services with the financial services business of IMI. On November 11, 1998, the transaction was competed, and San Paolo IMI SpA became the combined company's identity.

In February 1999 the U.S. Federal Reserve Board approved San Paolo IMI's request for a Section 20 license, which permitted the bank to engage in nonbank-

The Business

Financials - Sanpaolo IMI SpA

Revenue (1998): 118.3 billion euro (229,148 billion lire) in assets

Employees (1998): 24,527

Financials - Banca di Roma SpA

Revenue (1998): 201,917 billion lire in assets

Employees (1998): 29,400

SICs / NAICS

sic 6029 - Commercial Banks Nec

sic 6211 - Security Brokers & Dealers

naics 522110 - Commercial Banking

naics 522120 - Savings Institutions

naics 523120 - Securities Brokerage

ing activities in the U.S.; this was the first such license approved for an Italian bank. The following month San Paolo IMI proposed a merger with Banca di Roma, but was rejected both by Banca di Roma's shareholders and by Italy's central bank, the Banca d'Italia.

History of Banca di Roma SpA

Benito Mussolini established the Istituto per la Ricostruzione Industriale (IRI) in 1933 to bolster Italy's economy. The following year this state-owned organization absorbed the Banco di Roma, established in 1880, and in 1935 acquired the Banco di Santo Spirito, established in 1605.

IRI flourished, controlling nearly half of the nation's leading companies by the 1960s. Its usefulness waned in the ensuing decades, however, and by the 1980s it was dragging down, rather than supporting, the economy.

In April 1989 the Cassa di Risparmio di Roma, established in 1836, acquired Banco di Santo from IRI. Cassa transferred its banking operations to its new property the following year.

Sta. Italiana di Partecipazioni Bancarie, later renamed Cassa di Risparmio di Roma Holding, was established by Cassa in 1991. That year both founding companies transferred their banking operations into the new firm—IRI its 55% stake in Banco di Roma, and Cassa its 71% interest in Banco di Santo. The newly

merged company, which took the Banco di Santo Spirito name, gained a listing on the Milan Stock Exchange in April 1991. The merger was completed the following year, at which time the firm changed its name to Banca di Roma.

The newly formed company experienced financial difficulties from the outset. The three united banks were each relatively weak; together they formed a weak company of greater size. Still, it fared better than most Italian banks, ranking second in 1993, behind Sanpaolo Group, with 1993 revenues of $10.9 billion.

Banca di Roma sought to expand out of central Italy through acquisitions. It paid $625 million in early 1995 for Banca Nazionale dell' Agricoltura, Italy's 13th-largest bank. In October 1996 it was granted permission by the U.S. Federal Reserve Board to establish branches in New York, Chicago, San Francisco, and Houston.

The Italian Treasury ordered the dismantling of IRI beginning in 1997 and finalizing by 2000. Banca di Roma was the first unit to be broken off, no doubt due, in part, to its burden of continued unprofitability. In September the bank posted a half-year net loss of 3 trillion lire ($1.7 billion). Two months later IRI put its 36.5% stake in Banca di Roma on the public market. At the end of 1997 the retail bank had assets of 207 trillion lire and 1,600 branches.

The newly independent bank soon sought a merger partner and began pursuing Banca Commerciale Italiana (BCI), Italy's sixth-largest bank. That potential partner was less than enthusiastic about the prospects of joining with Banca di Roma, however. Negotiations were sporadic, and by late 1998 they had stalled.

In March 1999 ABN AMRO Bank N.V., a Dutch bank, became the first foreign institution to acquire a core stake in Banca di Roma when it purchased an 8.8% stake. That same month Sanpaolo IMI SpA proposed a merger with the bank. The following month its bid was rejected by Banca di Roma's shareholders and blocked by Banca d'Italia, the nation's central bank.

Market Forces Driving the Merger

The introduction of a single European currency, the euro, on January 1, 1999, pulled down many of the economic trade barriers between the countries. A wealth of new opportunities was opened up, and companies quickly began expanding outside of their domestic markets. Yet this open market also brought increased competition. European companies no longer faced merely domestic rivals, they were forced to compete with foreign competitors encroaching upon their territory.

This new environment brought significant pressure on Italy's banks, which were dwarfed by such European giants as Germany's Deutsche Bank. A March 1999 issue of *The Economist* reported that San Paolo IMI, Italy's largest, ranked 58th among Europe's top banks. "The euro zone needs euro-sized players. Italian banks do not have the critical mass to be aggressive," remarked Rainer Masera, San Paolo IMI's managing director.

Italy's position could be changed through consolidation. A combination of San Paolo IMI, which possessed a strong presence in corporate and investment banking, with Banca di Roma, a retail banking operation, would create one of Europe's top ten banks. It would have a network of 3,000 branches throughout Italy, and would control assets in excess of 670 trillion lire.

Approach and Engagement

On March 21, 1999, San Paolo IMI launched a $9.7 billion bid for Banca di Roma. This offer represented a 19.2% premium over Banca di Roma's current trading value.

Despite this premium, shareholders of Banca di Roma rejected the offer in mid-April, citing unsatisfactory terms and their resentment of the hostile tone of the offer. To defend itself against another takeover bid, the bank authorized a share buyback of up to 10% of its outstanding stock.

In late April Italy's central bank brought an end to the takeover attempt. The Banca d'Italia possessed the authority (or "delusions of grandeur," as *The Economist* phrased it) to reject proposed mergers and acquisitions based on its own judgement. It agreed with Banca di Roma's shareholders' interpretation of the bid as hostile, and had previously stated that it would not endorse such maneuvers in the Italian market.

Products and Services

Sanpaolo IMI was Italy's leader in mutual funds and bancassurance in 1998. In retail savings, it operated a network of nearly 1,300 branches in Italy and a financial services salesforce of almost 4,000. Sanpaolo had offices and subsidiaries around the world: Amsterdam, Athens, Bangkok, Beijing, Bombay/Mumbai, Brussels, Budapest, Dublin, Frankfurt, Istanbul, London, Los Angeles, Luxembourg, Moscow, Munich, Nassau (Bahamas), New York, Paris, Sao Paulo, Shanghai, Singapore, Stockholm, Tokyo, Toronto, and Warsaw.

In 1998 Banca di Roma was present in 20 countries outside Italy, with 17 affiliates and eight repre-

The Officers

Sanpaolo IMI SpA

Chairman: Luigi Arcuti

General Manager and CEO: Luigi Maranzana

General Manager and CEO: Rainer Stefano Masera

Deputy General Manager: Piero Gavazzi

Banca di Roma SpA

Chairman and President: Cesare Geronzi

CEO: Antonio Nottola

Exec. VP and Branch Manager: Alexander Zoller

Sr. VP and Deputy Manager: Romeo Collina

VP and Deputy Manager: Augustino Cacace

sentative offices. Its network covered a wide range ofcountries, including the U.S., China, Great Britain, and Japan. The whole of its direct and indirect shareholdings involved 200 companies, both in the financial and service sectors.

Research

"2 Big Banks in Italy Plan a Merger," in *The New York Times*, 18 February 1999. Details the proposed merger deal.

Banca di Roma Home Page, available at http://www.bancaroma.it. Official World Wide Web Page for Banca di Roma. This Italian- and English-language Web site provides access to news releases, branch locations, banking services, and financial and investor information.

"Bank of Italy: Sic Transit Gloria," in *The Economist*, 8 May 1999. Offers criticism of Banca d'Italia's authority in merger proposals.

"Italian Banking: Spaghetti Junction," in *The Economist*, 27 March 1999. Describes the details and the rationale for Sanpaolo IMI's bid for Banca di Roma.

Lane, David. "Rome-Based Bank IMI Sold," in *Privatisation International*, August 1996. Explains the privatization of IMI from the Italian Treasury.

Sanpaolo IMI SpA Home Page, available at http://www.sanpaolo.it. Official World Wide Web Page for Sanpaolo IMI. This Italian- and English-language Web site offers news releases, branch locations, and financial and investor information.

Sullivan, Ruth. "Italy Seeks Sale of the Century," in *The European*, 18 September 1997. Relates the proposed dissolution of IRI, starting with the spin-off of Banca di Roma.

RICHARD BARROW

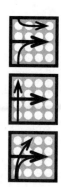

SARA LEE & AKZO CONSUMENTEN PRODUKTEN

Sara Lee Corp.
3 First National Plz.
Chicago, IL 60602-4260
USA

tel: (312) 726-2600
fax: (312)726-3712
web: http://www.saralee.com

nationality: USA
date: December 1987
affected: Sara Lee Corp., USA, founded 1939
affected: Akzo Consumenten Produkten NV (a division of Akzo NV), The Netherlands, founded 1969

Overview of the Acquisition

The sale of Akzo Consumenten Produkten NV, the consumer products division of the Dutch chemicals giant Akzo Nobel NV, was another step in that company's shift in focus to higher value-added segments in chemicals and fibers. Completed in December 1987 for $612 million, this acquisition represented the largest in the history of Sara Lee Corp. at that time.

History of Sara Lee Corp.

Nathan Cummings borrowed $5.2 million to buy the C.D. Kenny Company, a small wholesaler of coffee, tea, and sugar, in 1939. Two years later the C.D. Kenny Co. was incorporated. In 1942, after the purchase of Sprague, Warner & Co., a distributor of canned and packaged food, the company changed its name to Sprague Warner-Kenny Corp. It launched an aggressive acquisition campaign that would become the hallmark of its expansion strategy over the decades.

After acquiring several grocery chains in 1945, the company changed its name to Consolidated Grocers Corp. Consolidated went public in 1946, and sales that year increased $123 million over the previous year. In 1954 stockholders voted to change the company's name to Consolidated Foods Corp. to reflect its diverse presence in food processing, packaging, and distribution. In 1956 the firm acquired the Kitchens of Sara Lee, a five-year-old maker of frozen baked goods, that was founded by Charles Lubin and named after his daughter. That year Consolidated also entered the retail food business by acquiring 34 Piggly Wiggly supermarkets.

International expansion began in 1960 with Consolidated's purchase of a controlling interest in a Venezuelan vinegar company. It increased its global expansion two years later, acquiring the Dutch canner Jonker Fris. In 1961 the company acquired the Eagle supermarket chains. In compliance with an order by the Federal Trade Commission, Consolidated divested its Eagle and Piggly Wiggly supermarkets in 1966. That year the company expanded outside the food industry by acquiring Oxford Chemical Corp.; it also purchased E. Kahn's Sons Co., its first meat company.

Acquisitions in 1968 bought Consolidated entry into several new industries including apparel. The firm also acquired Bryan Foods, Inc. in 1968 and Aris Gloves, later renamed Aris Isotoner, the following year. Hillshire Farm and Rudy's Farm were acquired in 1971. Consolidated entered the personal care business the next year by purchasing Erdal, a Dutch company later renamed Intradal.

Durable goods accounted for nearly two-thirds of corporate profits in 1975. For this reason the company began focusing on non-food merchandise, believing that federal restraints on the food industry would continue to impede growth in that area. That year John H. Bryan became CEO, and initiated the divestiture of more than 50 small companies purchased in the 1960s. Sales for 1975 reached $2.4 billion.

In 1978 Consolidated acquired Chef Pierre, a frozen desserts manufacturer, and invested in Douwe Egberts, a coffee, tea, and tobacco company based in Holland. The next year it completed the hostile takeover of Hanes Corp., a family-owned undergarment manufacturer whose brands included L'eggs, Bali, and Hanes. Consolidated also acquired Superior Tea and Coffee Co., a distributor of coffee and tea for the foodservice industry, as well as Gallo Salame, Inc., a manufacturer of Italian sausage products.

The Spanish household products company Productos Cruz Verde was purchased in 1980 and contributed to the company's record sales of $5 billion that year. Two years later Consolidated acquired meat processor Standard Meat Co., and added to its meat holdings with the 1984 purchase of Jimmy Dean Meat Co. For $330 million, it acquired the foreign subsidiaries of Nicholas Kiwi Limited, an Australian maker of various shoe care products, medicines, cleaners, and cosmetics.

Consolidated changed its name to Sara Lee Corp. in 1985, using one of its most prominent brand names to enhance public awareness of the company. That year the company purchased Coach Leatherware Co., a manufacturer of high-quality leather handbags and other accessories. In 1987 Sara Lee acquired Akzo Consumenten Produkten, a maker of food, household, and personal care products in Holland. Sara Lee was one of the largest U.S. multinationals, with foreign revenues reaching nearly $2 billion that year.

The company continued to increase its global presence by purchasing a 25.1% interest in Delta-Galil, a leading Israeli textile company, in 1988. It also gained entry into the men's sock market by purchasing Adams-Millis Corp. In 1989 it acquired Dim, S.A., the leading producer of hosiery and underwear in France and of Champion athletic knitwear in the U.S. Also that year Sara Lee acquired Hygrade Products,

The Business

Financials

Revenue (1999): $20 billion

Employees (1999): 139,000

SICs / NAICS

sic 2095 - Roasted Coffee

sic 2053 - Frozen Bakery Products Except Bread

sic 2013 - Sausages & Other Prepared Meats

sic 2251 - Women's Hosiery Except Socks

sic 2252 - Hosiery Nec

sic 2254 - Knit Underwear Mills

sic 2322 - Men's/Boys' Underwear & Nightwear

sic 2342 - Bras, Girdles & Allied Garments

sic 2341 - Women's/Children's Underwear

sic 2842 - Polishes & Sanitation Goods

sic 5963 - Direct Selling Establishments

sic 5046 - Commercial Equipment Nec

naics 311920 - Coffee and Tea Manufacturing

naics 311813 - Frozen Cakes, Pies, and Other Pastries Manufacturing

naics 311613 - Rendering and Meat By-product Processing

naics 315111 - Sheer Hosiery Mills

naics 315119 - Other Hosiery and Sock Mills

naics 315192 - Underwear and Nightwear Knitting Mills

naics 315221 - Men's and Boys' Cut and Sew Underwear and Nightwear Manufacturing

naics 315231 - Women's and Girls' Cut and Sew Lingerie, Loungewear and Nightwear Manufacturing

naics 325612 - Polish and Other Sanitation Good Manufacturing

naics 311612 - Meat Processed from Carcasses

naics 454390 - Other Direct Selling Establishments

naics 421440 - Other Commercial Equipment Wholesalers

maker of Ball Park hot dogs, and completed the divestiture of its food service operations.

In 1991 the company sold its European over-the-counter drug business to Roche Holding AG. That year Sara Lee purchased Playtex Apparel, Inc., manufacturer of intimate apparel, and Rinbros, Mexican-based maker of men's and boys' underwear.

The Officers

Chairman and CEO: John H. Bryan

President and Chief Operating Officer: C. Steven McMillan

Exec. VP: Frank L. Meysman

Exec. VP and Chief Financial Officer: Judith A. Sprieser

Acquisitions in 1992 included BP Nutrition's Consumer Foods Group, Giltex Hosiery, Bessin Corp., the furniture care operations of SC Johnson Wax, and certain properties of Mark Cross, Inc. The European bath and body care business of SmithKline Beecham PLC was purchased in 1993.

A restructuring in 1994 called for the closure of several factories and the loss of 8,500 jobs. That year Imperial Meats was acquired, and Sara Lee's sales exceeded $15 billion. In 1997 the company initiated its "de-verticalization" plan, a restructuring that included the divestiture of non-core businesses and the elimination of 90 manufacturing and distribution facilities.

In July 1998 Sara Lee divested its international tobacco operations by selling Amphora, Drum, and Van Nelle to Imperial Tobacco for $1.1 billion. Later that year the company acquired the Continental Coffee Products Co. from Quaker Oats Co. Sara Lee recalled certain hot dogs and packaged meats that were linked to 24 deaths due to food poisoning. In June 1999 the company announced its planned merger with Chock Full o' Nuts Corp.

History of Akzo Nobel NV

Akzo Nobel was formed in 1994 by the merger of two Dutch companies with long histories. Akzo's history began in 1835, when Ketjen, one of the businesses that would later comprise Akzo, was founded in the Netherlands. The ensuing decades saw the consolidation of several Dutch companies, including Ketjen, Noury & Van der Lande, Zwanenberg, Vereinigte Glanzstoff Fabriken, Nederlandse Kunstzijdefabriek Enka, Koninklijke Nederlandse Zoutindustrie, and Organon. Finally, in 1969, Akzo NV was formed as a result of the merger of Koninklijke Zout Organon and Algemene Kunstzijde Unie. In late 1987 Akzo sold Akzo Consumenten Produkten NV, its consumer products unit operated in partnership with Shell Petroleum NV, to Sara Lee Corp.

Nobel, too, can trace its roots to the 19th century. In 1863 Alfred Nobel invented the blasting cap, which enabled the detonation of nitroglycerin to be controlled. The next year, with the assistance of J.W. Smitt,

a Stockholm merchant, Nobel established Nitroglycerin Ltd. to manufacture the liquid. Nobel continued his research and experimentation with nitroglycerin, and invented dynamite in 1867. Nitroglycerin Ltd. introduced blasting gelatin in 1875 and smokeless gunpowder in 1877. The company acquired A.B. Bofors-Gullspang, a Swedish munitions factory, in 1894.

Nobel died in 1895. His will called for the distribution of annual prizes bearing his name "to those who, during the preceding year, shall have conferred the greatest benefit on mankind." The five prizes, which were first awarded in 1901, were the Nobel Prize for Physics, the Nobel Prize for Chemistry, the Nobel Prize for Physiology or Medicine, the Nobel Prize for Literature, and the Nobel Prize for Peace; in 1969 a sixth prize was added, the Prize for Economic Sciences in Memory of Alfred Nobel.

Nitroglycerin Ltd. gained international recognition by manufacturing the 40-mm anti-aircraft gun used by both the U.S. and the U.K. during World War II. In 1965 the company changed its name to Nitro Nobel. Five years later it was purchased by the KemaNord chemical group and renamed KemaNobel.

Having bought numerous shares in Bofors and KemaNobel over the previous decade, businessman Erik Penser gained control of Bofors in 1982. Two years later he took over KemaNobel and merged it with Bofors to form Nobel Industries AB. In 1986 the company acquired the Swedish defense electronics firm Pharos. Four years later, after the purchase of the Spectro-Physics subsidiary of Ciba-Geigy Ltd. and the U.K.'s Continental Microwave, Pharos changed its name to Spectra-Physics.

Bofors was accused in 1986 of paying $60 million in kickbacks to middlemen in connection with a sale to India. The charges were dropped two years later, but Penser's troubles were only beginning. Years of risky investments resulted in the collapse of his finances in 1991. All of his holdings were taken over by Securum, a government-owned holding company.

In 1992 Nobel sold its Consumer Goods business to Henkel, the German chemicals group, in order to offset the nearly $1 billion that the company had lost during the previous year. Continuing to raise funds through divestitures, Nobel sold its interest in Swedish Ordnance to Celsius Industrier AB, which also bought Nobel's Defense Electronics Business in 1993.

Akzo Nobel NV was formed in early 1994 when Akzo NV acquired the Nobel shares owned by Securum and bid for the remaining shares. The new company, with annual sales of $10 billion, was the ninth-largest chemical concern in the world. It employed 70,000 people in 50 countries, and manufactured and marketed basic and specialty chemicals, salt, man-made fibers, coatings, and healthcare products.

In 1997 the company spun off its fiber operations as a joint venture with the Turkish company Sabanci, and sold its North American salt division to Cargill. In July 1998 Akzo Nobel acquired Courtaulds, a leading chemical company involved in high-tech industrial coatings and man-made fibers, changing that unit's name to Akzo Nobel UK. Akzo Nobel planned to integrate its fiber operations with those of this new unit to form Acordis as a separate company. It also divested other Akzo Nobel UK businesses, including window and high-tech films and aerospace coating and sealing products. By 1999 Akzo Nobel was the world's largest paint maker and a world leader in chemical manufacturing and salt production.

Market Forces Driving the Acquisition

By the late 1980s Akzo NV had been shifting its corporate focus toward such value-added areas of the chemical and fiber industries as pharmaceuticals, specialty chemicals, advanced fibers, and special coatings. In so doing, it began eliminating its non-core businesses to raise money for strategic expansion and acquisition. In previous years, the company had formed a consumer products division, known as Akzo Consumenten Produkten NV, in partnership with Shell Petroleum NV, the Dutch unit of Royal Dutch/Shell Group. This unit, which produced personal care products, cleaning agents, snack foods, and pesticides, experienced a 13% decline in sales, to Fl 1.25 billion, in 1986. Akzo NV perceived that the time was right to find a buyer for the division.

For Sara Lee Corp., an acquisition of Akzo Consumenten Produkten would be in line with two of the company's strategies. Sara Lee was a conglomerate whose diverse array of offerings would be complemented by the product line of the Dutch company. In purchasing that unit, Sara Lee would gain such foods as soups, nuts, and sauces under brand names that included Temana and Heidelberg. Moreover, Akzo Consumenten Produkten would strengthen Sara Lee's already broad global reach, as its products were sold in 13 countries in Western Europe.

Approach and Engagement

On September 17, 1987, Akzo NV and Sara Lee Corp. announced their acquisition agreement. The U.S. company would purchase Akzo Consumenten Produkten NV, the consumer products division of Akzo NV, for Fl 1.25 billion ($612 million). Shell Petroleum NV, partial owner of the unit, had previously granted its approval for the sale.

Because the deal called for the exchange of ready cash and stock, it didn't require third-party involvement. Its rapid completion was further facilitated by the European business environment, which was more personal and less litigious than that of the U.S. In December 1987 the acquisition was successfully completed.

Products and Services

In 1999 Sara Lee Corp. was a global consumer packaged goods company operating in more than 40 countries. It was divided into five business segments.

Sara Lee Foods was the world's leading packaged meats company, offering such brands such as Ball Park, Bryan, Hillshire Farm, Jimmy Dean, and Justin Bridou. In 1999 this unit had sales of $5.2 billion.

The **Coffee and Tea** segment, which contributed $2.6 billion in sales in 1999, included such brands as Douwe Egberts, Maison du Cafe, Marcilla, and Merrild.

Household and Body Care, accounting for $2 billion in sales, included branded household and body care products branded as Sanex, Duschdas, Badedas, Radox, Delial, and others. This segment also housed Sara Lee's Direct Selling division, which distributed cosmetics, fragrances, jewelry, toiletries, and apparel products directly to consumers' doors.

The **PYA/Monarch Foodservice Division**, with 1999 sales of $2.7 billion, was the fourth-largest full-line foodservice company in the U.S. It distributed paper supplies, foodservice equipment, and dry, refrigerated, and frozen foods to institutional customers and restaurants.

Branded Apparel, whose sales totaled $7.4 billion in 1999, was comprised of three subsegments. Intimate Apparel and Accessories offered such brands as Bali, Dim, Hanes Her Way, Just My Size, Playtex, and Wonderbra, as well as its newly licensed Ralph Lauren Intimates collection. Knit Products offered the Hanes, Hanes Her Way, Champion, Dim, Just My Size, Rinbros, Abanderado, and Princesa brands. Legwear, the U.S. leader in sheer hosiery, offered Hanes, L'eggs, Donna Karan, and DKNY brands.

Review of the Outcome

Akzo Consumenten Produkten NV was merged into Douwe Egberts NV, Sara Lee's Dutch subsidiary. This unit produced such items as toothpaste and shoe polish and processed coffee, tea, and tobacco. With the acquisition of the Dutch division, Douwe Egberts' sales totaled Fl 5.5 billion. Sara Lee announced that about 4% of that unit's workforce of 11,300 would be cut by 1991.

Research

Akzo Nobel NV. Home Page, available at http://www.akzonobel.com. Official World Wide Web Home Page for Akzo Nobel NV. Includes news releases, financial and product information, and an historical review of the company.

"Akzo Nobel NV," in *Notable Corporate Chronologies*, The Gale Group, 1999. Provides a history of the company.

Lyne, Barbara. "Cooking Up Deals at Sara Lee," in *Lyne, Barbara*, April 1988. Profiles Sara Lee in terms of its recent acquisitions and divestitures.

Raun, Laura. "Akzo Confirms Deal with Sara Lee," in *Financial Times (London)*, 18 September 1987. Briefly relates the terms of the deal.

———. "Akzo Puts Consumer Division up for Sale," in *Financial Times (London)*, 17 September 1987. Reports rumors regarding the sale of the division to Sara Lee.

Sara Lee Corp. Home Page, available at http://www.sar-alee.com. Official World Wide Web Home Page for Sara Lee. Includes news releases, financial data, product information, and an historical review of the company.

"Sara Lee Corp.," in *Notable Corporate Chronologies*, The Gale Group, 1999. Offers a chronology of Sara Lee's history.

"Sara Lee to Buy Dutch Unit," in *The New York Times*, 18 September 1987. Describes the recently announced acquisition agreement.

DAVIS MCMILLAN

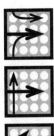

SBC COMMUNICATIONS & AMERITECH

nationality: USA
date: 1999
affected: SBC Communications Inc., USA, founded 1984
affected: Ameritech Corp., USA, founded 1984

SBC Communications Inc.
175 E. Houston
PO Box 2933
San Antonio, TX 78299-2933
USA

tel: (210)821-4105
fax: (210)351-2071
web: http://www.sbc.com

Ameritech Corp.
30 S. Wacker Dr., 34th Fl.
Chicago, IL 60606
USA

tel: (312)750-5000
fax: (312)207-1601
web: http://www.ameritech.com

Overview of the Merger

In a deal that would be the largest in telecommunications history, SBC Communications and Ameritech proposed a merger in 1998. These companies were two of the original seven RHCs (regional holding companies) formed by the 1984 break-up of AT&T, and a combination would reduce the number of remaining RHCs to four. Never louder were the cries denouncing a merger between the RHCs. Critics lamented that the deal was another step toward a recreation of the anti-competitive Ma Bell. By April 1999 these claims had been dismissed by half of the regulatory agencies whose approval was necessary for completion of the deal. Both the Federal Communications Commission and the Illinois Commerce Commission were expected to arrive at their decisions in June 1999.

History of SBC Communications Inc.

In 1982 American Telephone & Telegraph Corp. (AT&T) agreed to break up its monopoly by forming seven regional holding companies (RHCs); among them, Southwestern Bell Corp. as the holding company for Southwestern Bell Telephone Co. On January 1, 1984, the ownership of Southwestern Bell Telephone was officially transferred to Southwestern Bell Corp. The parent also held three other subsidiaries: Southwestern Bell Publications, Inc., a directory publisher; Southwestern Bell Mobile Systems, Inc., a mobile telephone operator; and Southwestern Bell Telecommunications, Inc., a marketer of telephone equipment to business customers.

It acquired the cellular and paging business of Metromedia Inc. in 1987, thereby becoming the third-largest cellular communications company in the U.S., behind McCaw Cellular and Pacific Telesis. These operations were increased the following year, when it bought Omni Communications' paging business.

In 1990 its subsidiary, Southwestern Bell International Holdings Corp., joined a group that purchased 20.4% of total equity and 51% of the shares in Telefonos de Mexico, S.A. de C.V., Mexico's newly privatized telephone company. That year it also agreed to purchase West Midlands Cable Communications, owner of the largest cable television franchise in the U.K. It acquired Hauser Communications

The Business

Financials - SBC Communications Inc.

Revenue (1998): $28.8 billion

Employees (1998): 129,850

Financials - Ameritech Corp.

Revenue (1998): $17.2 billion

Employees (1998): 70,525

SICs / NAICS

sic 2741 - Miscellaneous Publishing

sic 3661 - Telephone & Telegraph Apparatus

sic 4812 - Radiotelephone Communications

sic 4813 - Telephone Communications Except
     Radiotelephone

naics 334210 - Telephone Apparatus Manufacturing

naics 511199 - All Other Publishers

naics 513310 - Wired Telecommunications Carriers

naics 513321 - Paging

naics 513322 - Cellular and Other Wireless
     Telecommunications

naics 513330 - Telecommunications Resellers

naics 513340 - Satellite Telecommunications

Corporation's two cable systems in 1993 for $650 million.

To reflect a less regional focus, the corporation changed its name to SBC Communications Inc. in 1994. The following year it became the first RHC to receive approval from the Federal Communications Commission (FCC) to integrate cellular and local phone service outside of its service region, and formed SBMS New York Services, Inc. to operate in New York. It also became the first RHC to open retail outlets.

SBC purchased 40% of VTR, a Chilean telecommunications company, in 1995. That year it joined with Cable & Wireless PLC and Corporate Africa Ltd. to form New Africa Communications for the purpose of bidding on the installation of one million new telephone lines.

The Telecommunications Act of 1996 stipulated that RHCs could enter the long distance market outside of their operating region only if they first allowed other local telephone companies to compete in their local telephone territories. In response, SBC entered into a network interconnection agreement with U.S. Long Distance Corp. to provide competing local telephone service in its five-state service area: Kansas, Texas, Missouri, Oklahoma, and Arkansas.

In 1996 it merged its phone equipment division, Southwestern Bell Telecom, with its phone service subsidiary, Southwestern Bell Telephone Co. In April 1997 it merged with Pacific Telesis Group, creating the second-largest telecommunications company in the U.S. It then entered into discussions to merge with AT&T, but dropped the plan after realizing the improbability of gaining regulatory approval. Later that year, it exited the cable business by agreeing to sell its two Washington D.C. cable systems and its interest in Prime Cable of Chicago. That year it also increased its international operations, first by entering into an alliance to form Cegetel, a long distance carrier to compete with France Telecom, then by entering into a joint venture with six Swiss utilities to form Diax, a company to build a digital telecommunications network in that country, and finally by purchasing a 30% stake in Telkom South Africa.

The Oklahoma Corporation Commission supported SBC's bid to offer long distance service in that state, but the FCC rejected the proposal. In 1998 it filed applications to compete in the long distance markets of Kansas, Texas, and Arkansas. That year, it became the first RHC to enter the long distance market by acquiring Connecticut-based Southern New England Telecommunications Corp. for $4.4 billion in stock. It also agreed to merge with Ameritech, thereby forming the largest U.S. local telephone company; the deal was expected to close in mid-1999. In 1999 it agreed to buy Comcast's cellular business. In February of that year, it announced an agreement under which Williams Communications would serve as SBC's long distance provider.

History of Ameritech Corp.

American Information Technologies Corp. incorporated as one of the first regional holding companies (RHCs) in 1983. That year it began trading on the New York Stock Exchange. In 1984 this company became one of the seven communications companies to begin operations as a result of the breakup of AT&T. Serving the Great Lakes region, Ameritech was the parent company of Illinois Bell Telephone Co., Indiana Bell Telephone Co., Michigan Bell Telephone Co., Ohio Bell Telephone Co., and Wisconsin Bell.

In 1985 the firm ventured into office automation systems by acquiring Real Com, an IBM Satellite Business Systems subsidiary. That year it purchased Purchasing Directories, Inc. and began publishing telephone directories in Ohio, Illinois, Indiana, and Michigan. In 1986 it bought Old Heritage Advertising & Publishing, expanding its coverage to 90 telephone directories in 15 states.

The company diversified into computer-generated data and storage in 1986 by acquiring Applied Data Research, Inc., a database management software producer for IBM mainframe computers, as well as Speech Plus, Inc., a developer of speech-synthesis technology. That year it also became the first RHC authorized by the FCC to enter international telecommunications as well as the international manufacturing and non-telecommunications businesses.

In 1987 its Wisconsin Bell subsidiary proposed two experimental ventures with Warner Cable Communications of Milwaukee, and launched a six-month trial pay-per-view cable television channel. Through a joint venture, Ameritech announced iNet, the first computer-based information management service offered in the U.S. This service was available through data terminals, personal computers, and word processors equipped with a telephone line and modem.

In 1988 Ameritech Mobile Communications acquired the paging assets of Multicom, Inc. from sibling Pacific Telesis and of A Beeper Co. from Bell Atlantic. It also acquired Tigon Corp., a voice-mail company. The Tigon subsidiary soon negotiated a multimillion-dollar deal to supply Texas Instruments with voice-mail capable of reaching 140 national and international locations.

In 1989 Illinois Bell participated part in the first installation of ISDN service, linking the Andersen Consulting offices of Chicago and Tokyo. The following year the company formed Ameritech International to develop business opportunities outside the U.S. Advancing in fiber optics, Ameritech initiated the nation's first passive optic network. Ameritech, Bell Atlantic, and two New Zealand companies purchased Telecom New Zealand, the national telephone system, in 1990. That year the company acquired Wer Leifert Was? (Who Supplies What?), the leading German industrial yellow pages directory publisher.

American Information Technologies Corp. officially changed its name to Ameritech in 1991. That year it purchased 94% of outstanding shares of Knowledge Data Systems, Inc., a provider of integrated multi-application data processing systems and related services to health-care institutions and independent medical laboratories.

By 1991 Ameritech Mobile was the largest paging service provider in the Midwest, with 319,000 pagers in service. The following year it joined with Bell

The Officers

SBC Communications Inc.
Chairman and CEO: Edward E. Whitacre, Jr.

President, SBC Operations: Royce S. Caldwell

Sr. Exec. VP, External Affairs: Cassandra S. Carr

President, SBC International: J. Cliff Eason

Sr. Exec. VP and General Counsel: James D. Ellis

Ameritech Corp.
Chairman and CEO: Richard C. Notebaert

Exec. VP: Barry K. Allen

Exec. VP: W. Patrick Campbell

Sr. VP of Human Resources: Walter M. Oliver

Exec. VP and Chief Financial Officer: Oren G. Shaffer

Atlantic Mobile Systems, Contel Cellular Inc., GTE Mobilenet, and NYNEX Mobile Communications to form a nationwide mobile telephone network for sending and receiving cellular calls anywhere in the U.S.

In 1992 Ameritech and France Telecom entered into an agreement with Polish Post, Telegraph and Telephone to construct and operate Centertel, a nationwide cellular system in Poland. By the following year, Ameritech serviced about 75% of the Great Lakes' population.

Ameritech received approval for price rather than profit regulation for intrastate revenues in its five-state territory in 1993. In return, Ameritech agreed to cap rates on basic services for two to six years and to reduce rates in 1995. That year it signed a four-year pact with Northern Telecom to acquire up to $200 million in switching equipment for upgrading more than 270 facilities. An Ameritech-led international consortium won the rights in 1995 to acquire slightly less than half of the Belgium state-owned telephone company. Ameritech and the German company Deutsche Telekom announced that they would spend $850 million to expand their interests in the Hungarian national telephone company from 30% to 67%.

In 1996 Ameritech became the nation's second-largest provider of security monitoring services by purchasing National Guardian and SecurityLink. The following year it purchased a 50% stake in Belgacom SA, a Belgian telecommunications company. In 1998 it bought 40% of Tele Danmark while shedding its interests in its New Zealand holdings.

The Players

SBC Chairman and CEO: Edward E. Whitacre, Jr. Edward Whitacre earned a Bachelor's degree in industrial engineering in 1964 from Texas Tech University. He began his affiliation with the company when he joined its operational departments in Arkansas, Kansas, and Texas. Whitacre moved from Southwestern Bell Telephone Co. to SBC when that company was formed in 1984. There he progressed through the positions of group vice president, vice president of revenues and public affairs, vice chairman, and chief financial officer before being appointed chairman and CEO in 1990.

Ameritech Chairman and CEO: Richard C. Notebaert. Richard Notebaert received a Bachelor of Arts degree from the University of Wisconsin in 1969, the same year that he took a job at Wisconsin Bell. He joined Ameritech Communications as vice president of marketing and operations in 1983, just as he earned an MBA from his alma mater. Notebaert became president of Ameritech Mobile Communications in 1986, and then of Indiana Bell and Ameritech Services. In January 1993 he became vice chairman, followed in June by appointments to president and chief operating officer. In January 1994 he added the post of CEO to his duties as president, and that April he traded his responsibilities as president for those of chairman.

Market Forces Driving the Merger

After the government-imposed break-up of AT&T in 1984, the telecommunications industry became regulated. Long distance carriers and local telephone carriers were restricted as to the types of services they offered as well as to the areas in which they operated. Then came the Telecommunications Act of 1996. This legislation broke the boundaries between local telephone, long distance telephone, and cable television companies by permitting them to conduct business in each other's markets.

A rapid industry shake-up soon followed. The large, yet previously limited, local service providers realized that the quickest way to gain entry into a new market was to form strategic alliances with other companies. In April 1996 SBC Communications announced its merger with Pacific Telesis, another RHC. This announcement was followed only weeks later by the proposed merger of two other RHCs, Bell Atlantic and NYNEX. Both deals were closed in mid-1997. The following year SBC completed another high profile acquisition, that of Southern New England Telecommunications Corp. Yet SBC was still not satisfied.

Ameritech, an RHC operating in five Great Lakes states, claimed that its very survival hinged upon the formation of an alliance with a large telecommunications company. Barry Allen, company executive vice president, stated in *The Business Journal-Milwaukee*, "We can't compete globally if we don't grow." He even suggested that if left alone, Ameritech would be vulnerable to a hostile takeover attempt.

Approach and Engagement

In May 1998 SBC Communications and Ameritech announced a merger agreement. The $62 billion deal was significant for a number of reasons. It would be the largest deal in the history of the telecommunications industry and the second-largest corporate deal ever, behind the pending $70 billion merger between CitiCorp and Travelers Group. It would also create the largest national telecommunications company offering local telephone service, as the combined company would control about one-third of all local phone lines in the U.S. The deal would also reduce the original seven RHCs to four—Bell Atlantic, BellSouth, SBC, and U S West.

Under the terms of the accord, each Ameritech share would be converted to 1.316 shares of SBC stock. This valued Ameritech's stock at $55.77 per share, a 57% premium to its closing price just prior to the merger announcement. Ameritech would become a subsidiary of SBC. Whether Richard Notebaert, chairman and CEO of Ameritech, would retain his job after the merger was undetermined, but Edward Whitacre, Jr., would continue as chairman and CEO of SBC.

According to a news release announcing the deal, the "industry-transforming merger [would] create a new type of telecommunications company with a 'national-local' focus...to compete against incumbent local telecommunications companies, competitive local exchange carriers, long distance companies and global competitors." The companies claimed that the deal would encourage competition since they would invest in building networks to enter and introduce competition in new territories. It would also become more competitive internationally, as the new company would have stakes in the French, Swiss, Danish, Belgian, British, and Hungarian telecommunication markets.

It wasn't long before critics voiced their objections. Consumer advocate groups, local telephone companies, and cable television operators banded together with such giants as AT&T to oppose the merger, hoping to influence the public and, more importantly, the regulators. The fact that the merger would put one out of every three telephone lines under control of SBC was the primary cause for their concern. They noted that the proposed market concentration exceeded the merger guidelines of the U.S. Department of Justice. The groups also opposed the deal based on the outcome of similar deals in the past. They pointed their fingers at the SBC/Pacific Telesis union of the previous year, claiming that the resulting company had proposed to raise, not lower, its prices and that the quality of its customer service had declined; SBC denied the latter charge.

The opposition also noted Ameritech's track record regarding competition, claiming that the company was deficient in opening its market to competitors despite a Federal Communications Commission (FCC) requirement to do so. As reported in *The Business Journal-Milwaukee*, "Ameritech has done nothing to encourage local competition," said Steve Hinker, executive director of the Wisconsin Citizens Utility Board, Madison. "It's dangerous to let them merge and get so big and powerful that they will have even less reason to be responsive."

The companies' financial results for 1998 were touted by critics as further evidence that neither company was ailing, and therefore had little compelling reason to join forces. For that year, SBC's net income skyrocketed 140% to $4.02 billion on revenues that increased 7.9% to $28.8 billion, while Ameritech's earnings rose 11.4% to $2.6 billion on a 7.2% increase in revenues to $17.2 billion.

Despite the opposition, however, the merger slowly accumulated regulatory approval. Because of the companies' stakes in European markets, the approval of the European Union was required—and granted in July 1998. That December shareholders of each company overwhelmingly approved the deal. The U.S. Department of Justice, which decided whether antitrust laws would be violated due to the merger, approved it on March 23, 1999. One of the Department's conditions was that the companies shed their overlapping cellular phone operations in Chicago and St. Louis. In early April, Ameritech agreed to sell those businesses to a venture of GTE for $3.3 billion.

In early April 1999, the FCC, the agency that considered whether a merger would be in the consumers' best interest, asked the companies for additional information. SBC and Ameritech grudgingly agreed to cooperate, puzzled as to why the FCC would require more information after eight months of review. The

FCC expected to deliver its decision on the merger by the end of June.

On April 8, 1999, the Public Utilities Commission of Ohio cleared the deal. The only remaining authority, other than the FCC, whose approval was required was the Illinois Commerce Commission (ICC). In mid-April, two of its examiners recommended the Commission's approval, but only if the companies would agree to refund 100% of the merger savings in Illinois. SBC and Ameritech found that condition to be unnecessary, illegal, and unrelated to the merger. The companies would obviously attempt to dissuade the Commission from that condition. Like the FCC, the ICC had until the end of June to arrive at a final decision.

Products and Services

SBC was organized into four main operational segments. The Wireline unit provided landline telecommunications services, including local, network access and long distance services, messaging, and Internet services. It also sold customer premise and private business exchange equipment. Its principal subsidiaries in this segment were Southwestern Bell Telephone Co., Pacific Bell, The Southern New England Telephone Co., and Nevada Bell. Wireline operations generated revenues of $22.2 billion in 1998. The Wireless segment provided wireless telecommunications services, including local and long distance services, and sold wireless equipment. Its principal subsidiaries were Southwestern Bell Mobile Systems, Inc., Pacific Bell Mobile Services, and SNET Cellular, Inc. This segment realized $4.2 billion in revenues in 1998. The Directory segment sold advertising for and publication of yellow pages and white pages directories and electronic publications. It operated under the subsidiaries Southwestern Bell Yellow Pages, Inc., Pacific Bell Directory, and SNET Information Services, Inc. Directory operations generated revenues of $2.4 billion in 1998. The fourth unit included SBC's international investments and miscellaneous domestic operating subsidiaries. In 1998 this unit generated $85 million in revenues.

Ameritech offered five primary services. Local Phone Services were offered under the Ameritech brand, serving 11.1 million residences and one million businesses in Illinois, Indiana, Michigan, Ohio, and Wisconsin. Cellular and Personal Communication Services (PCS) were offered to 3.6 million customers in Illinois, Indiana, Michigan, Missouri, Ohio, Wisconsin, Kentucky, and Hawaii under the Ameritech brand. The company's Paging Services were offered under the Ameritech brand to 1.5 million customers in Illinois, Indiana, Michigan, Minnesota, Missouri,

Ohio, and Wisconsin. Its Advertising operations produced printed Ameritech Yellow Pages directories in Illinois, Indiana, Michigan, Ohio, and Wisconsin, as well as global access to Internet Yellow Pages. Capital Services provided leasing and other equipment financing solutions under the Ameritech Capital Services brand to 7,000 businesses and government units in the U.S., Europe, and Asia.

Research

"Ameritech Corp.," in *Notable Corporate Chronologies*, The Gale Group, 1999. Profiles the history of the company.

Ameritech Corp. Home Page, available at http://www.ameritech.com. Official World Wide Web Page for Ameritech. Includes executive biographies, annual reports, press releases, and product and service information.

"FCC Considers Placing Conditions on SBC-Ameritech Merger," in *Communications Daily*, 2 April 1999. Deep into the review period, the FCC asks the companies for additional information. This article describes the Commission's concerns with the merger.

"Justice Dept. Approves SBC-Ameritech Merger with Conditions," in *Communications Daily*, 24 March 1999. Outlines the conditional approval of the Department of Justice for the deal.

Meyers, Jason. "How Big is Too Big? SBC/Ameritech Move Raises Local Strategy Questions," in *Telephony*, 18 May 1998. Describes the possible impact that the merger may have on competitive local exchange carriers.

Millard, Pete. "Ameritech Says Acquisition is Key to Survival," in *The Business Journal-Milwaukee*, 18 December 1998.

"SBC Communications Inc.," in *Notable Corporate Chronologies*, The Gale Group, 1999. Provides historical highlights of the company.

SBC Communications Inc. 1998 Annual Report. Covers financial highlights and describes company operating segments.

SBC Communications Inc. Home Page, available at http://www.sbc.com. Official World Wide Web Page for SBC. Includes organizational and product information, annual reports, press releases, and other financial information.

KIMBERLY N. STEVENS

SBC COMMUNICATIONS & PACIFIC TELESIS

nationality: USA
date: April 1, 1997
affected: SBC Communications Inc., USA, founded 1984
affected: Pacific Telesis Group, USA, founded 1984

SBC Communications Inc.
175 E. Houston
PO Box 2933
San Antonio, TX 78299-2933
USA

tel: (210)821-4105
fax: (210)351-2071
web: http://www.sbc.com

Overview of the Merger

Twelve years after the break-up of AT&T into seven regional holding companies, the pieces began to reconnect with each other. The first of these reunions was that of SBC Communications and Pacific Telesis. That $16.6 merger was the largest telecommunications deal ever completed in the U.S., and was the third-largest transaction in the nation's history. It formed the second-largest telephone company, although the new company didn't enjoy that position for long.

History of SBC Communications Inc.

In 1982 American Telephone & Telegraph Corp. (AT&T) agreed to break up its monopoly by forming seven regional holding companies (RHCs); among them, Southwestern Bell Corp. as the holding company for Southwestern Bell Telephone Co. On January 1, 1984, the ownership of Southwestern Bell Telephone was officially transferred to Southwestern Bell Corp. The parent also held three other subsidiaries: Southwestern Bell Publications, Inc., a directory publisher; Southwestern Bell Mobile Systems, Inc., a mobile telephone operator; and Southwestern Bell Telecommunications, Inc., a marketer of telephone equipment to business customers.

It acquired the cellular and paging business of Metromedia Inc. in 1987, thereby becoming the third-largest cellular communications company in the U.S., behind McCaw Cellular and Pacific Telesis. These operations were increased the following year, when it bought Omni Communications' paging business.

In 1990 its subsidiary, Southwestern Bell International Holdings Corp., joined a group that purchased 20.4% of total equity and 51% of the shares in Telefonos de Mexico, S.A. de C.V., Mexico's newly privatized telephone company. That year it also agreed to purchase West Midlands Cable Communications, owner of the largest cable television franchise in the U.K. It acquired Hauser Communications Corporation's two cable systems in 1993 for $650 million.

The Business

Financials

Revenue (1998): $28.8 billion

Employees (1998): 129,850

SICs / NAICS

sic 2741 - Miscellaneous Publishing

sic 3661 - Telephone & Telegraph Apparatus

sic 4812 - Radiotelephone Communications

sic 4813 - Telephone Communications Except Radiotelephone

naics 334210 - Telephone Apparatus Manufacturing

naics 511199 - All Other Publishers

naics 513310 - Wired Telecommunications Carriers

naics 513321 - Paging

naics 513322 - Cellular and Other Wireless Telecommunications

naics 513330 - Telecommunications Resellers

naics 513340 - Satellite Telecommunications

To reflect a less regional focus, the corporation changed its name to SBC Communications Inc. in 1994. The following year it became the first RHC to receive approval from the Federal Communications Commission (FCC) to integrate cellular and local phone service outside of its service region, and formed SBMS New York Services, Inc., to operate in New York. It also became the first RHC to open retail outlets.

SBC purchased 40% of VTR, a Chilean telecommunications company, in 1995. That year it joined with Cable & Wireless PLC and Corporate Africa Ltd. to form New Africa Communications for the purpose of bidding on the installation of one million new telephone lines.

The Telecommunications Act of 1996 stipulated that RHCs could enter the long distance market outside of their operating region only if they first allowed other local telephone companies to compete in their local telephone territories. In response, SBC entered into a network interconnection agreement with U.S. Long Distance Corp. to provide competing local telephone service in its five-state service area: Kansas, Texas, Missouri, Oklahoma, and Arkansas.

In 1996 it merged its phone equipment division, Southwestern Bell Telecom, with its phone service

subsidiary, Southwestern Bell Telephone Co. In April 1997 it merged with Pacific Telesis Group, creating the second-largest telecommunications company in the U.S. It then entered into discussions to merge with AT&T, but dropped the plan after realizing the improbability of gaining regulatory approval. Later that year, it exited the cable business by agreeing to sell its two Washington D.C. cable systems and its interest in Prime Cable of Chicago. That year it also increased its international operations, first by entering into an alliance to form Cegetel, a long distance carrier to compete with France Telecom, then by entering into a joint venture with six Swiss utilities to form Diax, a company to build a digital telecommunications network in that country, and finally by purchasing a 30% stake in Telkom South Africa.

The Oklahoma Corporation Commission supported SBC's bid to offer long distance service in that state, but the FCC rejected the proposal. In 1998 it filed applications to compete in the long distance markets of Kansas, Texas, and Arkansas. That year, it became the first RHC to enter the long distance market by acquiring Connecticut-based Southern New England Telecommunications Corp. for $4.4 billion in stock. It also agreed to merge with Ameritech, thereby forming the largest U.S. local telephone company; the deal was expected to close in mid-1999. In 1999 it agreed to buy Comcast's cellular business. In February of that year, it announced an agreement under which Williams Communications would serve as SBC's long distance provider.

History of Pacific Telesis Group

Following the U.S. District court's divestiture of American Telephone and Telegraph Co. (AT&T) in 1983, Pacific Telesis Group (PacTel) incorporated in Nevada as the western holding company of the massive Bell telephone network. The following year it began operations as the owner of Pacific Bell and its fully owned subsidiary Nevada Bell.

PacTel Mobile Access launched the first cellular service in the Los Angeles area, coinciding with the 1984 Olympics. The next year Pacific Telesis International (PTI) was launched to offer telecommunications and information systems and services outside the U.S., and PacTel Properties was created to develop a diversified investment portfolio of properties. In 1985 the California Public Utilities Commission (CPUC) granted Pacific Bell Directory permission to operate as a separate subsidiary; by 1987 it was the largest producer of printed directories in California.

PacTel gained access to cellular and paging operations outside of its territory by acquiring

Communications Industries, Inc., in 1986 for $431 million. That year PTI became licensed to install the first digital display paging system in Bangkok, Thailand. In 1988 PTI and Jones Intercable, Inc., acquired a principal interest in a London-based cable television and telephone company, East London Telecommunications, Ltd.

PacTel Business Systems, Inc., was formed in 1989 to market and service telecommunications systems to businesses in California and Nevada. Under the new regulatory framework, the CPUC ordered Pacific Bell to cut annual telephone rates by $391 million the following year in order to bring the company's authorized rate of return to 11.5%. PacTel Cable was formed in 1990 to oversee its foreign and domestic cable interests.

The company advanced its wireless business in 1991 when PacTel received an experimental license from the FCC to conduct a far-reaching set of advanced wireless communications experiments in San Francisco, Dallas, Chicago, Los Angeles, and New York. That year it joined its cellular operations in San Francisco, San Jose, Dallas, and Kansas City with those of McCaw Cellular Communications in a 99-year joint venture.

PacTel Wireless Data division was created in 1992 to develop and sell wireless data communications services over its cellular network. That year PTI formed an agreement with one of France's largest public companies to acquire a 20% interest in a Public Access Mobile Radio operation, a form of mobile communications used primarily for dispatch. In 1993 it acquired a majority stake in NordicTel Holding, a Swedish cellular services company.

In 1994 it spun off its Airtouch cellular operations to join with those of U S West in the formation of a national service. The following year the company entered the Personal Communications Services (PCS) market by obtaining licenses to provide wireless voice and data services throughout California and Nevada. This occurred just as it began losing wireline customers, as the CPUC had opened the toll market in California to long distance carriers.

In 1996 PacTel became the first regional Bell company to offer Internet access services to business customers. It also agreed to purchase wireless transmission capacity from WinStar Communications, Inc., to cope with heavy Internet usage.

Market Forces Driving the Merger

The Telecommunications Act of 1996 broke the boundaries between local telephone, long distance telephone, and cable television companies by permit-

The Officers

Chairman and CEO: Edward E. Whitacre, Jr.

President, SBC Operations: Royce S. Caldwell

Sr. Exec. VP, External Affairs: Cassandra S. Carr

President, SBC International: J. Cliff Eason

Sr. Exec. VP and General Counsel: James D. Ellis

ting them to conduct business in each other's markets. It also made provisions affecting broadcast media, relaxing the rules of television, radio, and cable system ownership, and deregulating cable service rates.

As a result of the opportunities created by these deregulatory policies, some telecommunications companies began expanding into new geographic markets, while others aimed to offer bundled services—packages of local, long distance, and wireless telephone services, as well as Internet, paging, and cable television services. To overcome the hurdles of efficiently entering new markets, businesses sought to acquire or merge with an existing company in the target area.

By the end of 1995, SBC Communications was one of the world's largest telecommunications companies, with more than 16.7 million customers. It had diversified over the years, becoming the nation's second-largest wireless company, deriving about 37% of its revenues from such non-traditional operations. Yet this diversification had occurred at the expense of its basic wireline business. The company had fallen behind others in terms of digital switching and high-speed lines, technology that was becoming increasingly important for the use of telephone lines computer transmissions.

SBC's territory in five southwestern states—Texas, Oklahoma, Missouri, Arkansas, and Kansas—was strategically located near international markets, namely Mexico and Latin America. The company also owned a stake in Telefonos de Mexico. By the end of 1995, SBC ranked second of the RHCs based on market capitalization, behind BellSouth.

While SBC held a leadership position in the market, Pacific Telesis was bringing up the rear. Its market capitalization and revenues in 1995 were both dead last among the RHCs. It was not realizing its potential in the lucrative California market, due in large part to the increased competition in that state. To SBC, California would be an enviable jewel in its crown, as its own territory lacked a comparable major market.

The Players

SBC Chairman and CEO: Edward E. Whitacre, Jr. Edward Whitacre earned a Bachelor's degree in industrial engineering in 1964 from Texas Tech University. He began his affiliation with the company when he joined its operational departments in Arkansas, Kansas, and Texas. Whitacre moved from Southwestern Bell Telephone Co. to SBC when that company was formed in 1984. There he progressed through the positions of group vice president, vice president of revenues and public affairs, vice chairman, and chief financial officer before being appointed chairman and CEO in 1990.

An even greater incentive to a merger with PacTel, however, was its similar connection with Mexico, which would complement and strengthen SBC's operations there. Like SBC's region, the territory of PacTel was a main origin of long distance calls to Latin America. This pointed to significant growth potential, as long distance profit margins were six times greater than those of local service.

Approach and Engagement

On April 1, 1996, SBC Communications and Pacific Telesis announced their merger agreement. Upon conclusion of the transaction, SBC would become the nation's second-largest telecommunications company, behind AT&T. The $16.6 billion deal would be a stock swap in which each PacTel share would be converted to 0.733 share of SBC. Edward Whitacre would retain his post as chairman and CEO, and PacTel's chairman and CEO, Philip Quigley, would become vice chairman of SBC.

On July 31, 1996, the shareholders of each company voted overwhelmingly in favor of the merger. The U.S. Department of Justice raised no objection, and in November granted its approval to the first major merger between RHCs. In December the Nevada Public Service Commission followed suit, as did the Federal Communications Commission in January 1997. The only regulatory impediment arose with the California Public Utilities Commission (CPUC), which demanded that the companies refund $590 million to California customers at conclusion of the deal. The CPUC later granted its approval to a compromise that reduced that amount to $341 million. On April 1, 1997, exactly one year after its announcement, the merger was completed.

Products and Services

SBC was organized into four main operational segments:

The **Wireline** unit provided landline telecommunications services, including local, network access and long distance services, messaging, and Internet services. It also sold customer premise and private business exchange equipment. Its principal subsidiaries in this segment were Southwestern Bell Telephone Co., Pacific Bell, The Southern New England Telephone Co., and Nevada Bell. Wireline operations generated revenues of $22.2 billion in 1998.

The **Wireless** segment provided wireless telecommunications services, including local and long distance services, and sold wireless equipment. Its principal subsidiaries were Southwestern Bell Mobile Systems, Inc., Pacific Bell Mobile Services, and SNET Cellular, Inc. This segment realized $4.2 billion in revenues in 1998.

The **Directory** segment sold advertising for and publication of yellow pages and white pages directories and electronic publications. It operated under the subsidiaries Southwestern Bell Yellow Pages, Inc., Pacific Bell Directory, and SNET Information Services, Inc. Directory operations generated revenues of $2.4 billion in 1998.

The **Other** unit included SBC's international investments and miscellaneous domestic operating subsidiaries. In 1998 this unit generated $85 million in revenues.

Changes to the Industry

The SBC/PacTel merger triggered a series of consolidations in the telecommunications industry. In April 1996, just weeks after this merger was announced, the RHCs Bell Atlantic and NYNEX announced their own accord, valued at $22.1 billion. Like the SBC deal, this proposal obtained easy, unconditional approval from the Department of Justice (DoJ).

This rapid approval tendency of the federal government spurred zealousness for other major industry deals. At the same time, negative press and public outcry caused the DoJ to reevaluate its stance for future deals. Analysts suspected that the agency would begin to demand significant concessions from any proposed similar transactions. This prediction proved incorrect, however, as in March 1999 the DoJ approved SBC's acquisition of Ameritech Corp. with only minor concessions.

Review of the Outcome

The new SBC became the nation's second-largest telecommunications company, with a market value of $47.9 billion and revenues of $23.5 billion. It operated in seven of the nation's top 10 markets, as well as select international markets. SBC began focusing on traditional services, stepping back from such costly ventures as fiber optics, video, and cable.

The merger's benefits to customers were unclear even in the year following the deal's consummation. For the most part, rates remained unchanged, and an increase in the number of complaints suggested that the quality of customer service had fallen. Customer service representative claimed that they were forced to become sales representatives, and that the company employed hard-sell tactics to push expensive add-on services, sometimes misleading the customer in the process. According to reports, the newly merged company even sold Caller-ID services to a blind person.

Indeed, the most apparent effects of the merger were internal. PacTel's 35 corporate offices were reduced to 13, and a new organizational structure was implemented in July 1997, reducing the number of existing PacTel managers in high executive positions. By the end of that year, PacTel had lost its three leading executives—Philip Quigley, chairman and CEO; David Dorman, Pacific Bell's CEO; and Michael Fitzpatrick, PacTel Enterprises' CEO. Moreover, significant PacTel departments were transferred to SBC, including auditing, accounting, human resources, marketing, research and development, and public relations. On the other hand, however, Pacific Bell increased its California workforce by about 4,000, four times as many as had been anticipated.

In 1998 net income rose 140% to $4.02 billion on revenues of $28.8 billion. At the end of that year, SBC had 37.2 million network access lines in service and 6.8 million wireless customers.

Research

Cohen, Warren, and Robin Knight. "Look Who's Talking: The First Baby Bell Merger Should Lead to More Telecom Deal Discussions," in *U.S. News & World Report*, 15 April 1996. Describes the possible future of the telecommunications industry in light of the SBC merger.

Ginsberg, Steve, and Lorna Fernandes. "Merger with SBC Rang Hollow for Many at Pacific Telesis," in *Business First-Columbus*, 15 May 1998. Discusses changes to the organization following the merger.

Kupfer, Andrew. "A Whirlwind Romance Leads to Wedding Bells," in *Fortune*, 29 April 1996. Briefly describes the strengths and weaknesses SBC and PacTel.

"Pacific Telesis Group," in *Notable Corporate Chronologies*, The Gale Group, 1999. Profiles the company up to its merger with SBC.

Palmeri, Christopher. "Bully Bell," in *Forbes*, 22 April 1996. Offers reasons for SBC's merger with PacTel.

Pearce, Alan. "Learning to Say 'No,'" in *America's Network*, 15 June 1998. Describes the criticisms against the DoJ due to its ready approval of telecom mergers.

"SBC Communications Inc.," in *Notable Corporate Chronologies*, The Gale Group, 1999. Provides historical highlights of the company, including its merger of PacTel.

SBC Communications Inc., available at http://www.sbc.com. Official World Wide Web Page for SBC. Includes organizational and product information, press releases, annual reports, and other financial information.

SBC Communications Inc. 1998 Annual Report. Provides financial information and describes company operating segments.

"SBC/PacTel Merger Completed; NYNEX Bell Atlantic Accept Commission Terms," in *Communications Today*, 2 April 1997. Reports developments in two mergers between RHCs.

KIMBERLY N. STEVENS

SCOTTISH POWER & PACIFICORP

Scottish Power PLC
One Atlantic Quay
Glasgow, Strathclyde G28SP
United Kingdom

tel: 44-141-248-8200
fax: 44-141-248-8300
web: http://www.scottishpower.PLC.uk

PacifiCorp
700 NE Multnomah
Portland, OR 97232
USA

tel: (503)813-5000
fax: (503)813-7247
web: http://www.pacificorp.com

date: 1999
affected: Scottish Power PLC, United Kingdom, founded 1954
affected: PacifiCorp, USA, founded 1910

Overview of the Merger

When United Kingdom-based Scottish Power PLC and PacifiCorp, a Portland, Oregon-based electricity firm, complete their $7.3 billion merger in late 1999, the combined company will serve seven million customers in the U.S., the U.K., and Australia. Scottish Power, an electricity, gas, telephone, and water utility provider will become the first foreign company to purchase a U.S. utility.

History of Scottish Power PLC

In 1882, Parliament passed the Electric Lighting Act, the first public measure to deal with matters concerning the new industry of electrical supply. The Act allowed the establishment of electricity generating companies within prescribed areas, but also gave local authorities the right to purchase company undertakings after a period of only 21 years. A new Electric Lighting Act, passed in 1888, extended the purchase period from 21 to 42 years. This encouraged investors and more electricity companies began to form.

By the turn of the century, more than 400 electricity companies were operating in the U.K. All were small undertakings as the existing legislation discouraged amalgamation and restricted the areas of operation. The companies had diverse system characteristics, and voltage and frequency differed considerably. In 1919, the new Electricity (Supply) Act established the Electricity Commissioners, a body responsible for securing reorganization on a regional basis by voluntary means in an effort to increase standardization and coordination in the industry. A new Act of Parliament in 1926 established the Central Electricity Board, which was charged with constructing a national grid of main transmission lines, over which electricity generated at selected power stations could be supplied wholesale to local distributors for retailing to customers. Less than a decade later, a Grid system, operating at 132 kV, served most parts of England.

A Government White Paper proposed that the Electricity Commissioners prepare schemes for the integration of distribution companies into larger groups to improve efficiency and economy. However, the advent of World War II delayed any further legislation. In 1947, the government nationalized the electricity supply industries of England, Wales, and southern Scotland with a new Electricity Act. The 560 existing companies were integrated into 14 area electricity boards. An Act of Parliament in 1954 reorganized electricity supply in Scotland. A new statuary body, the South of Scotland Electricity Board (SSEB) was formed to handle generation, main transmission, and distribution.

In 1989, an Act of Parliament established the legal framework for the privatization of the assets of the old South of Scotland Electricity Board and the granting of licenses to a new private company of the same name. A few months later, the new company's name was changed to ScottishPower PLC. The electrical appliance retail shops, previously owned by the SSEB, became an independently-managed division within Scottish Power. In June of 1991, ScottishPower offered publicly 814.81 million ordinary shares at 2.4 British pounds per share.

During the early 1990s, the company secured a contract to supply electricity to ICI's Teeside complex; launched a new joint venture with Utilicorp; and established a new company, Caledonian Gas, to sell gas to industrial and commercial customers. In 1995, Scottish Power won a 1.13 billion British pounds takeover bid for Manweb, obtaining over 60% of the regional electrical company. Four years later, the firm agreed to buy PacifiCorp, a Portland, Oregon-based electricity firm.

History of PacifiCorp

In 1910, after acquiring various small utility company in the western U.S., Electric Bond & Share established Pacific Power & Light. The parent company developed its new subsidiary by pursuing new acquisitions and purchasing power lines. The Public Utility Holding Company Act of 1935 was at the root of Electric Bond & Share's divestment of Pacific Power & Light in 1950. Mountain States Power and Pacific Power & Light joined forced three years later. The merger allowed Pacific Power & Light to move into three new states: Montana, Idaho, and Wyoming.

The firm acquired California Oregon Power, which boasted nearly 1.5 billion tons in coal reserves, in the early 1960s. The following decade, Pacific Power & Light purchased two telephone companies: Washington-based local provider Telephone Utilities and Alaska-based long distance operator Alascom. The Northern Energy Resources Co. was established to oversee all coal mining operations. Pacific Power & Light changed its name to PacifiCorp in 1983. Telephone operations were consolidated into a new unit, named Pacific Telecom. PacifiCorp acquired Utah Power in 1987.

The Business

Financials - Scottish Power PLC

Revenue (1998): $5.1 billion

Employees (1998): 14,300

Financials - PacifiCorp

Revenue (1998): $5.5 billion

Employees (1998): 9,000

SICs / NAICS

sic 4911 - Electric Services

sic 4924 - Natural Gas Distribution

naics 221111 - Hydroelectric Power Generation

naics 221112 - Fossil Fuel Electric Power Generation

naics 221113 - Nuclear Electric Power Generation

During the mid-1990s, PacifiCorp underwent a reorganization. Pacific Telecom became a separate, autonomous subsidiary. Also, the firm's utility holdings were divided into three segments: generation, retail sales, and transmission. AT&T Corp. bought the Alascom long distance assets.

PacifiCorp acquired Powercor in 1995. Two years later, the firm bought TPC, a natural gas concern. PacifiCorp's $9.6 billion bid for Energy Group, of the United Kingdom, was thwarted by a higher offer from Texas Utilities. Century Telephone bought Pacific Telecom. Hurt by its inability to meet power demands during a long, hot summer in the western U.S., PacifiCorp began divesting assets in 1999, including TPC, which was sold to NIPSCO for $132.5 million. That year, the firm agreed to be acquired by Scottish Power.

Market Forces Driving the Merger

PacifiCorp was struggling in the late 1990s. Plans made in 1997 to acquire United Kingdom-based Energy Group for roughly $9.6 billion fell apart in 1998, resulting in a $67 million loss. Because the firm couldn't keep up with energy demands during a heat wave in the western U.S. in the summer of 1998, it faced another loss, this one worth $151 million. Consequently, Fred Buckman, CEO since 1994, resigned. His successor, Keith McKennon, began an overhaul of PacifiCorp that included divesting non-core assets, such as its coal mining operations and

The Officers

Scottish Power PLC

Chairman: Murray Stuart

CEO: Ian Robinson

Executive Director: Alan Richardson

Deputy Chief Executive and Director Finance: Ian Russell

PacifiCorp

Chairman, CEO, and President: Keith R. McKennon

Exec. VP and Chief Operating Officer: Richard T. O'Brien

Sr. VP and General Counsel: Verl R. Topham

Controller and Chief Accounting Officer: Robert R. Dalley

international power plants. As part of its retrenchment, PacifiCorp agreed to be acquired by Scottish Power. According to McKennon in a June 1999 news release, the deal, if approved, will allow PacfiCorp to "pursue more effectively our strategy of focusing on our core electricity business in the West. The combined company will have a better opportunity to take advantage of the ongoing changes in the U.S. utilities market, thereby enhancing growth prospects for both partners in the long term."

Despite the questionable performance of other U.S./European utilities linkups (between 1990 and 1999, U.S. companies bought eight regional electric companies in Britain), Scottish Power was looking to move into the U.S. market, mainly because most of the companies there weren't performing well. According to a December 1998 article in *The European*, "the main attraction for Europeans is that the American market has been regulated in a way that has not inspired good management. The utility business is dominated by the need to prevent the companies involved from overexploiting the dependency of their customers. Regulation in America controls the profits a company can make, whereas in Britain it controls the prices a company can charge." Because this type of regulation tended to reduce motivation to cut costs at U.S. utility firms like PacifiCorp, European companies like Scottish Power saw room for improvement.

Approach and Engagement

Secret negotiations between Scottish Power and PacifiCorp began in November of 1998. Determined to keep the deal quiet to avoid the stock fluctuations rumors of a deal might breed, Scottish Power took on

the code name Sapphire, while PacifiCorp was dubbed Pegasus. Plans to merge became known as Project Jet. After two weeks of shredding documents, drawing blinds, and checking for bugs, an agreement to merge was finalized on December 2. Clandestine board meetings were completed, and a deal was signed on December 6; plans to merge were made public on the following day.

In June of 1999, shareholders of both companies voted in favor of the deal. According to the terms of the agreement, PacifiCorp shareholders will receive either 2.32 common shares or 0.58 of an American Depository Share of Scottish Power for each PacifiCorp share held. Scottish Power will also assume PacifiCorp's $4.9 billion in debt. Scottish Power shareholders will end up with roughly 64% of the firm, while PacifiCorp shareholders will hold 36%. The deal is contingent upon approval from the Federal Energy Regulatory Commission and state regulatory commissions in the western U.S.

PacifiCorp will remain fairly autonomous, operating as a "sister company" to Scottish Power under a new holding company, named HoldCo. The U.S. utility will maintain its headquarters operations in Portland, Oregon. Scottish Power executive director Alan Richardson will move to Portland to take over as CEO.

Products and Services

Scottish Power offers electricity, gas, telephone, and water service to roughly five million customer in the United Kingdom. The firm's largest areas of operation are southern Scotland; southern England, served by the Southern Water unit; and northwestern England, served by the Manweb unit.

PacifiCorp offers electricity services to 1.5 million customers in California, Idaho, Oregon, Utah, Washington, and Wyoming, as well as to 560,000 households in Australia's Victoria and New South Wales. The firm also operates one of the largest electricity transmission networks in the U.S. and owns roughly 8,400 megawatts of thermal and hydroelectric generation.

Changes to the Industry

If the merger is completed, Scottish Power will become one of the world's top ten utilities, serving seven million customers in the United Kingdom, the U.S., and Australia. Employees will total 23,500. Scottish Power will also become the first foreign company to acquire a major U.S. utility.

Research

Fadness, Gene. "Scottish Utility Seeks Merger with Portland,Ore.-Based PacifiCorp," in *Knight Ridder/Tribune Business News*, 13 June 1999. Discusses the industry conditions that prompted the deal.

———. "Utilities ScottishPower, PacifiCorp Seal Deal in Secret," in *Knight Ridder/Tribune Business News*, 15 June 1999. Details the negotiation process of PacifiCorp and Scottish Power.

PacifiCorp Home Page, available at http://www.pacificorp.com. Official World Wide Web Home Page for PacifiCorp. Includes news, financial, product, employment, and historical information.

"PacifiCorp," in *International Directory of Company Histories*, Vol. V, St. James Press, 1992. Offers a detailed history of PacifiCorp.

"PacifiCorp Shareholders Overwhelmingly Approve Merger with Scottish Power," in *Business Wire*, 17 June 1999. Explains why shareholders approved the deal.

Scottish Power PLC Home Page, available at http://www.scottishpower.com. Official World Wide Web Home Page for Scottish Power. Includes financial, product, employment, and historical information.

"Scottish Power PLC," in *Notable Corporate Chronologies*, The Gale Group, 1999. Lists major events in the history of Scottish Power PLC.Shelton, Ed.

"Scottish Goes West for Fresh Opportunities," in *The European*, 14 December 1998. Explains why Scottish Power was interested in purchasing a U.S. utility.

THERA WILLIAMS

The Players

CEO of Scottish Power PLC: Ian Robinson. Ian Robinson left Trafalgar House, where he served as a board director and as CEO of John Brown, in March of 1995 to accept the top spot at Scottish Power. When the merger with PacifiCorp is completed, Robinson will remain at the helm of Scottish Power and become chairman of PacifiCorp's board.

Chairman, CEO, and President of PacifiCorp: Keith R. McKennon. Former chairman of Dow Corning Corp., Keith McKennon was named CEO of PacifiCorp in October of 1998. He oversaw the firm's negotiations with Scottish Power in late 1998 and early 1999. When the merger is completed, McKennon will step down as CEO, handing the reins of PacifiCorp, which will remain a separate entity, to Scottish Power executive director, Alan Richardson.

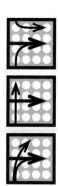

SEAGATE TECHNOLOGY & CONNER PERIPHERALS

Seagate Technology, Inc.
920 Disc Dr.
Scotts Valley, CA 95066
USA

tel: (408)438-8111
fax: (408)429-6356
web: http://www.seagate.com

nationality: USA
date: February 5, 1996
affected: Seagate Technology, Inc., USA, founded 1979
affected: Conner Peripherals, Inc., USA, founded 1985

Overview of the Merger

The 1996 merger between Seagate and Conner Peripherals reunited two old friends. Alan Shugart and Finis Conner, business partners turned rivals, were the founders and leaders of their respective disk drive manufacturing companies. Seagate, which held the number-two market position, and Conner Peripherals, which ranked third, combined to form the new world's leader in the industry. It also expanded Seagate into areas where Conner Peripherals had created a stronghold. Seagate had exited the personal computer (PC) disk drive market a few years prior to the merger in order to focus on the more lucrative high-capacity segment. Conner Peripherals had captured a leading share of that PC segment, as well as such other data storage businesses as tape drives, subsystems, and software. The combination of the two businesses created a company that was not only the market leader in disk drives, but also supplied customers with a variety of products to meet their data storage needs.

History of Seagate Technology, Inc

The PC industry was in its infant stage in 1979, when a small group including Alan Shugart and Finis Conner established Shugart Technology to develop hard drives for PCs. The company, later known as Seagate Technology, supplied PC users with triple the capacity of the multiple floppy drives that they had been adding to their machines. Seagate's banner product, the industry's first 5.25-inch disk drive, was incorporated into IBM's PCs the following year. The firm went public in 1981, and by 1982 it captured half of the market for small disk drives. Sales reached $344 million in 1984.

Three-quarters of Seagate's output was going to IBM, and in 1984 it paid for putting so many of its eggs in one basket. An industry-wide slump decreased demand and prices, and Seagate was forced to lay off 900 of its 1,600 employees. Conner insisted that the company would be wise to begin buying parts from other manufacturers rather than build the drives from scratch. He also wanted the company to diversify, and after sparring with the company's other executives, he resigned.

Sales continued to slump, so Seagate shifted production overseas and began to expand through acquisition. It acquired Grenex, a manufacturer of thin-film media, in 1984. Three years later it acquired Aeon Corporation, a manufacturer of aluminum substrates for thin-film media, and Integrated Power Systems, maker of custom semiconductors. The 5.25-inch drive began losing market share to the recently developed 3.5-inch drive (invented by Finis Conner's new company). After losing IBM as a customer of its 5.25-inch drives, Seagate introduced its first 3.5-inch drive in 1988. It gained entry into high-capacity drives, used in mainframes, by acquiring Imprimis Technology Inc. in 1989. Seagate instantly became the world's leading independent drive manufacturer.

It introduced a 2.5-inch disk drive, for laptop and notebook computers, in 1990. Sales doubled over the previous year, reaching a new height of $2.4 billion—more than all of its U.S. competitors combined. Company president David "Tom" Mitchell was ousted in 1991 by Shugart, who wanted the firm to focus on product innovation for the lucrative mainframe and notebook markets. Shugart's strategy worked, as the company was the first to market with its 3.5-inch drive for workstations.

Seagate's vertical integration, the organization that Conner had fought to change, enabled it to be the only drive manufacturer to show a profit in 1993, the height of an industry slump. It launched a software expansion initiative, acquiring Crystal Computer Services and Palindrome Corporation in 1994, and Network Computing Inc., Netlabs Inc., CIT Inc., and Frye Computer Systems in 1995. It formed Seagate Enterprise Management Software (SEMS) that year to hold Network Computing, Netlabs, and Frye.

After acquiring Conner Peripherals in 1996, it merged its software businesses, which now included Conner's Arcada Holdings subsidiary, to form Seagate Software, Inc. Later that year it acquired Creative Interaction Technologies, OnDemand Software, and Calypso Software, and merged these new additions with SEMS to form Seagate Software, Network, and Systems Management Group (NSMG).

Expansion continued in 1997, and it bought Quinta Corporation for $230 million. That year it not only shipped its 100 millionth disk drive, it unveiled the Elite 47; with 47 gigabytes, it is the world's highest capacity drive.

Another industry slump hit in 1998, forcing a layoff of 20% of its workforce and the dismissal of Shugart. Stephen L. Luczo replaced him as chairman and CEO just weeks after the company reported its fiscal 1998 revenues of $6.8 billion, but a net loss of $530 million. In October the company announced the sale

The Business

Financials

Revenue (1998): $6.8 billion

Employees (1998): 87,000

SICs / NAICS

sic 3572 - Computer Storage Devices

sic 5045 - Computers, Peripherals & Software

sic 7372 - Prepackaged Software

naics 334112 - Computer Storage Device Manufacturing

naics 421430 - Computer and Computer Peripheral Equipment and Software Wholesalers

naics 511210 - Software Publishers

of NSMG to VERITAS Software Corporation for $1.6 billion in stock. Seagate would hold a 35% stake in VERITAS, which would become the world's largest independent storage management software company.

History of Conner Peripherals, Inc.

Finis Conner left Seagate Technology in 1984 after fighting with Alan Shugart over the direction that the company should take. Conner wanted to diversify into other products and to begin outsourcing the manufacture of parts, while Shugart held fast to Seagate's vertical integration. He created Conner Peripherals in 1985, and the following year merged it with Co-Data Memory. Co-Data was founded by John Squires, who had recently invented the 3.5-inch disk drive.

The new company was hungry for start-up capital, and in 1986 persuaded Compaq Computer Corporation to invest $6 million in Conner. Compaq invested another $6 million the following year, giving that company a 49% stake in Conner Peripherals. By the end of 1987, its first full year of business, Conner reported sales of $113.2 million, surpassing Compaq's record for a manufacturing start-up.

By 1988 Conner Peripherals dominated the 3.5-inch drive market, and began expanding into the laptop and notebook computer segment. After raising $40 million in its initial public offering, it purchased 49% of the failing Olivetti disk drive subsidiary, renaming the Italian company Conner Peripherals Europe. In 1989 it increased its stake in Conner Peripherals Europe to a 51% controlling interest. That year it also debuted the first 2.5-inch drives, a year before its com-

The Officers

President and Chief Executive Officer: Stephen J. Luczo

Sr. VP and Chief Financial Officer: Charles C. Pope

Exec. VP and Chief Technical Officer: Townsend H. Porter, Jr.

Exec. VP and Chief Administrative Officer: Donald L. Waite

Exec. VP and Chief Operating Officer: William D. Watkins

petitors would introduce theirs. That same year Compaq reduced its stake in Conner Peripherals to 25%. As an indication of its meteoric rise, this three-year-old company was listed on the *Fortune 500* in 1989. About this time, Connor entertained the notion of acquiring Seagate. Sales in 1990 where $1.3 billion, making it the fastest-growing manufacturing start-up in U.S. history.

Conner Peripherals made its first major acquisition in 1990 by purchasing the disk coating operations of Domain Technology. By the following year, Conner was manufacturing 85% of all 2.5-inch drives, and found itself unable to keep up with demand. So it purchased VISqUS Corporation, a head-to-media firm that gave Conner access to liquid-bearing technology for increasing disk capacity.

In 1992 the company bought back Compaq's remaining 20% stake, purchased 16% of the disk head maker Sunward Technologies, and introduced its 1.8-inch removable drive for hand-held computers. It also stunned the industry by acquiring Archive Corporation for entry into the tape drive, subsystem, software, and storage distribution markets.

Conner's outsourcing strategy caused it, along with every other drive maker except Seagate, to record a loss in 1993 due to an explosion in PC demand that far surpassed supply of components. By April of that year, Conner was forced to layoff 1,200 employees. It reinforced its position in the software industry by establishing Arcada Software to devise data management software for client/server networks. The company returned to profitability in 1994, earning $109 million on sales of $2.36 billion. Yet it felt vulnerable to takeover, and adopted a poison pill plan late that year.

In 1995 company president and chief operating officer David "Tom" Mitchell, who had been ousted from Seagate in 1991, suddenly resigned from Conner Peripherals, and Finis Conner assumed the vacated roles in addition to carrying on as chairman and CEO. In the summer of 1995, Seagate approached Conner with an acquisition offer, and the following February completed the transaction.

Market Forces Driving the Merger/Acquisition

Competition in the computer industry, while good for consumers, can be devastating for the companies involved. The industry was volatile, full of ups and downs, and in 1995 it had taken a downturn. Price wars and a shortage of components contributed to falling profitability for computer businesses. Conner Peripherals, a leading manufacturer of disk and tape drives, storage systems, and software, was considering breaking apart its company and selling off the pieces. It was struggling, but not failing: 1994 revenues were $2.36 billion, and for the first six months of 1995, it held a second-place, 13% market share, for disk drives.

Seagate Technology was the world's leading independent manufacturer of hard disk drives, holding a 20% market share in the first half of 1995. Yet the company found it increasingly difficult to hang on to its profitability. Its customers, computer manufacturers, were demanding more and more capability for lower prices. And since Seagate operated primarily in this one business, it had to succumb to such demands.

By acquiring a more diverse company like Conner, Seagate would gain entry into the tape drive, subsystem, and software industries. It would also strengthen its share of the hard drive market. Seagate's focus on high-capacity drives would be augmented by Conner Peripheral's strength in the PC market. The combined company would hold nearly a third of the $25 billion industry, usurping Quantum Corporation's 22.3% leading market share.

Approach and Engagement

Seagate made acquisition overtures to Conner Peripherals in the summer of 1995, and on September 20th the companies announced that they were involved in merger negotiations. On October 3rd, they announced a finalized deal. The $1.4 billion transaction would be a stock swap, with Conner Peripherals shareholders receiving a 0.442 share of Seagate for each Conner share.

U.S. regulators raised no objections to the deal. Although the two companies do overlap in the hard drive market, they serve different segments—Seagate concentrated on the high-capacity segment, for servers and mainframes, while Conner Peripherals focused on the portable/notebook and desktop segments. On November 24th, the proposed merger was approved by the European Commission.

In January 1996, Seagate announced plans to acquire Arcada Software, Conner Peripheral's software subsidiary. Conner Peripherals' 69% stake in Arcada would become Seagate's upon completion of the merger, and Seagate arranged a stock swap to acquire the remaining outstanding interest. Shareholders of both Seagate and Conner approved their merger deal on February 2, 1996. Three days later, the acquisition was completed for $1.4 billion in stock. Alan Shugart assumed the chairman and CEO positions. Finis Conner remained with the company during a brief transition period, then exited the firm.

Products and Services

Seagate's products fell into three general categories: hardware, components, and software. Its core hardware business included disk drives with capacities ranging from 2 to 50 gigabytes. The Seagate Removable Storage Solutions unit offered a wide variety of tape drive solutions, serving everything from portable PCs to networks. The acquisition of Quinta Corporation gained Seagate the technology for integrating optical, magnetic, and telecommunications technologies to develop new levels of disk drive capacity.

Seagate's components operations encompassed Recording Media Operations, the world's leading supplier of disk media, develops read/write heads for disk and tape drives. The unit's proprietary MINT (Magnetic Information Technology) system produced the industry's lowest-cost, highest-density of magnetic disks for hard drives.

Seagate Software Inc. was the company's majority-owned subsidiary, holding Seagate's software acquisitions: Crystal Services, Palindrome Corp., Network Computing, NetLabs, Frye Computer Systems, Creative Interaction Technologies, OnDemand Software, Arcada Software, Calypso, and Holistic Systems. This subsidiary was divided into two subgroups. Information Management Group offers Business Intelligence solutions for accessing, analyzing, and sharing information. The Network and Storage Management Group (NSMG) developed a variety of desktop and server-based products for controlling network and system behavior. On October 5, 1998, Seagate announced that NSMG would be acquired by VERITAS Software Corporation for $1.6 billion.

Changes to the Industry

The merger between Seagate and Conner Peripherals created the world's largest independent disk drive manufacturer. After acquiring Conner Peripherals in February 1996, Seagate held a 27.5% share of the global disk drive market.

This new company also became a one-stop shop for storage products. Seagate was now able to supply

The Players

Seagate Chairman and CEO Alan F. Shugart. Alan Shugart didn't originally set out to found the world's leader in disk drive manufacturing. Born in 1930 in a suburb of Los Angeles, he earned a degree in engineering physics at the University of Redlands. Not one to let the grass grow under his feet, he got a job the day after graduation, fixing punch-card tabulating devices at IBM. He was transferred in 1955 to the company's research facility, where he designed the production model of the computer that incorporated the industry's first disk drive. He stuck with IBM until 1969, when he resigned and moved on to the Memorex Corporation. He, along with a group of about 200 fellow engineers from IBM, established an engineering division for the manufacture of computer peripherals. Three years later he resigned and became one of the founders of Shugart Associates, a manufacturer of floppy disks. The company failed to become profitable, and the start-up's venture capitalists dismissed Shugart in 1974. He vanished from the computer industry for the next five years, during which he opened a bar and bought a salmon-fishing boat. Computers reappeared in his life in 1978, when Finis Conner approached him with the idea of forming a company for the development of small disk drives for PCs. Shugart Technology Inc. was thus born. Later known as Seagate Technology, this company became a world leader in disk drives. He added the title of president to his roles as chairman and CEO in 1991, and continued as chairman and CEO after the acquisition of Conner Peripherals in 1996. In June of 1998, however, he was ousted by the board directors, and was succeeded by then-president and chief operating officer, Stephen J. Luczo.

customers with entry-level tape and disk drive products, high-end magneto-resistive head drives, and management and backup software.

The Conner name was no longer used on any of its products, although the brand names were retained. Name changes also occurred on its software products. After combining Arcada Software with Palindrome to create Software Storage Management Group, the company substituted the Seagate name for the Arcada and Palindrome product names.

The Players

Conner Peripherals Chairman and CEO: Finis F. Conner. Finis Conner has worked with, or for, Alan Shugart for most of his career in the computer industry. He began this association at IBM, where he first served as Shugart's gofer shortly after that computer engineer joined the firm in the 1950s. Conner was one of the 200 engineers who followed Shugart from IBM to Memorex in 1969. Three years later Conner, Shugart, and a handful of ex-Memorex employees founded the floppy disk pioneer Shugart Associates, where Conner started out as a salesman. He continued with the company after Shugart was ousted in 1974. Four years later Conner lured Shugart back into the computer business with his idea of forming a company for the production of disk drives for PCs. Originally called Shugart Technology, Seagate Technology was the industry leader by 1984. That year was Conner's last at Seagate, as he wanted the firm to expand into different products and begin buying rather than making parts. In 1986 Conner was able to put his plan into play. With the backing from Compaq Computer Corporation, he formed Conner Peripherals and continued to run that successful firm for a decade. Upon the 1996 merger with Seagate, he left the company after signing a two-year non-compete agreement. Just months after satisfying those terms, Conner co-founded Conner Technology PLC. Incorporated in England but headquartered in California, this start-up company aimed to be the first to focus on disk drives for the low-cost PC industry.

Review of the Outcome

Two main problems resulted from the merger. Workforce redundancy in the areas of engineering and corporate staff called for the lay-off of 500 employees in April 1996. Some Conner employees had anticipated this before the merger, however, and had already secured jobs at other computer companies, making the number of lay-offs lower than it might have been.

The second problem was excess inventory from the combined companies. Its solution to this problem was a headache for distributors. They claimed that Seagate coerced them into taking 30% more inventory than they usually carried, just to improve the company's bottom line for fiscal 1996, which ended on June 28th. An estimated $100 million of inventory was stuck in the distribution channel. With more than 90 days of inventory in stock, many distributors were compelled to sell at or below cost.

Despite a $242 million restructuring charge from the Conner Peripherals merger, Seagate recorded a net profit of $230 million on sales of $8.6 billion in fiscal 1996. Both figures increased in 1997, but took a sudden dive in 1998. The company ended that year on July 3rd with sales of $6.8 billion and a net loss of $530 million. That net loss was attributed to a $347 million restructuring charge and a $223 million write-off from its acquisition of Quinta. The board of directors decided that new blood was needed at the company's helm, and replaced Shugart with Stephen J. Luczo.

Research

Balch, Karen. "Finis Conner: An Interview," in *VARbusiness*, May 1993. Conner answers technical questions about Conner Peripherals and the company's value-added products.

——. "Meet Father Storage," in *VARbusiness*, 15 April 1996. Technical interview with Alan Shugart after the Conner acquisition.

Burrows, Peter. "The Man in the Disk Driver's Seat," in *Business Week*, 16 March 1996. Discussion of Shugart and his company upon acquiring Conner Peripherals.

"Conner Peripherals, Inc.," in *Notable Corporate Chronologies*, Gale Research, 1999. Provides an overview of the company until its absorption into Seagate.

Hachman, Mark. "Conner Comes Back," in *Electronic Buyers' News*, 28 September 1998. Conner's newest company, Conner Technology PLC.

Longwell, John. "Alan Shugart," in *Computer Reseller News*, 16 November 1997. Shugart's biography and business career.

Moltzen, Edward F. "Seagate Acquisition of Conner on Track, Hits Homestretch," in *Computer Reseller News*. 27 November 1995. Remarks from both Shugart and Conner as the merger nears completion.

Pereira, Pedro. "Seagate Looking to Beef up Profits with Stuffing," in *Computer Reseller News*. 17 June 1996. Seagate's jamming of its distribution channel with excess inventory after the merger.

"Seagate, Conner May Merge as Drive Vendors Struggle," in *InfoWorld*, 25 September 1995. Brief article containing latest revenue and market share figures prior to the merger.

"Seagate Technology Inc.," in *Notable Corporate Chronologies*, The Gale Group, 1999. Lists major events in the history of the company.

Seagate Technology, Inc. Home Page, available at http://www.seagate.com. Official World Wide Web Page for Seagate Technology. Includes access to a brief overview and history of the company, the 1998 annual report, and recent news.

DEBORAH J. UNTENER

SEAGRAM & DOLE FOOD

nationality: Canada
date: June 1995
affected: The Seagram Company Ltd., Canada, founded 1924
affected: Dole Food Company, Inc., USA, founded 1851

The Seagram Company Ltd.
1430 Peel St.
Montreal, PQ H3A 1S9
Canada

tel: (514)849-5271
fax: (514)987-5224
web: http://www.seagram.com

Overview of the Merger

Seagram's acquisition of the beverage operations of Dole Foods strengthened the third leg of the Canadian company's operational segments. Seagram had been an established name in the distilled alcohol industry for over a century, and had recently forayed into the entertainment industry with its acquisition of an interest in Time Warner. Its acquisition of Tropicana in 1988 gave it entry into the fruit juice market, a segment strengthened by Dole's fruit juice business. Tropicana, already the leading U.S. maker of ready-to-serve orange juice, gained an international presence with Dole's manufacturing plants in Europe, as well as its joint ventures in Asia. Seagram and Tropicana's extensive distribution networks would enable the company to introduce the Dole brand name efficiently into international markets, a situation that would benefit both companies.

History of The Seagram Company Ltd.

Joseph E. Seagram & Sons, Ltd., a distilling company, was founded in Waterloo, Ontario, Canada, in 1857. By the turn of the century, the company had become a leading Canadian rye producer with two popular brands: Seagram's '83 and V.O.

In 1916, when Prohibition became effective in parts of Canada, Samuel Bronfman purchased the Bonaventure Liquor Store Co., conveniently located near the downtown railway in Montreal. People traveling to the "dry" west could stock up on liquor before boarding the train. Two years later, Sam's brother, Harry, ventured into the drug business. He purchased a Dewar's whiskey contract from the Hudson Bay Co., and began selling liquor through drugstores and to processors who made "medicinal" mixtures.

The Volstead Act instituted Prohibition in the U.S. in 1919. Soon the Bronfmans imported 300,000 gallons of alcohol from the United States for the manufacture of 800,000 gallons of whiskey. In 1924 the Bronfmans opened their first distillery in La Salle, across the St. Lawrence River from Montreal, and incorporated under the name Distillers Corporation Ltd.

The Business

Financials

Revenue (1998): US$9.7 billion

Employees (1998): 24,200

SICs / NAICS

sic 2086 - Bottled & Canned Soft Drinks

sic 2037 - Frozen Fruits & Vegetables

sic 2033 - Canned Fruits & Vegetables

sic 2084 - Wines, Brandy & Brandy Spirits

sic 7812 - Motion Picture & Video Production

sic 7822 - Motion Picture & Tape Distribution

sic 7829 - Motion Picture Distribution Services

naics 312111 - Soft Drink Manufacturing

naics 311421 - Fruit and Vegetable Canning

naics 312130 - Wineries

naics 512110 - Motion Picture and Video Production

naics 512120 - Motion Picture and Video Distribution

naics 311411 - Frozen Fruit, Juice and Vegetable
Manufacturing

The company ventured overseas in 1926 when the Bronfman family sold a 50% interest in Distillers Co. to an amalgamation of British distillers that controlled more than half of the world's Scotch market. In exchange, the British Enterprise gave the Bronfmans the Canadian distribution rights for its brands, including Haig, Black & White, Dewar's, and Vat 69. Two years later Distillers Corp. acquired all of the stock in Joseph E. Seagram & Sons, Ltd. The merged company went public under the name Distillers Corp.-Seagram Ltd.

During the 1930s, the border between Canada and the U.S. became dangerous for illegal alcohol transport, so trading was accomplished mostly by sea under the cover of night. Sam Bronfman attempted to eradicate the somewhat dubious image of whiskey that developed during the bootlegging era by extensively promoting the virtue and quality of his whiskey. The company also revolutionized liquor marketing by selling their products to distributors already bottled, while other distillers sold their products in barrel consignments, thereby losing control over the quality of the final product.

Prohibition in the United States ended in 1933. The company acquired 20% of Schenley, whose prod-

uct line included the well-known Golden Wedding brand of rye whiskey. Sam Bronfman informed the Distillers Co. board of the acquisition and requested an increase in prices. When the board denied his request, the Bronfman brothers raised $4 million and bought out the Distillers Co.'s holding in Distillers Corp.-Seagrams Ltd. Sam Bronfman assumed the post of president.

The company purchased the Rossville Union Distillery in Lawrenceburg, Indiana, in 1933, and established Joseph E. Seagram & Sons Inc. to operate it. The following year, it purchased Maryland Distillers, Inc. Seagram began to import its own aged Canadian stock to blend with its new American distillates, resulting in products known under the Five Crown and Seven Crown labels.

In 1934, after the end of Prohibition, the head the Canadian Conservative Party launched an investigation into the liquor smuggling industry. The Bronfmans were arrested and tried, but the case was later thrown out of court. That year the company also introduced Seagram's V.O. Canadian Whiskey.

The firm made its first foreign acquisition in 1935 with the purchase of Robert Brown Ltd. (Scotch whiskey); its name was subsequently changed to Seagram Distillers PLC. By the following year, Seagram's sales had grown to $60 million in the United States, with another $10 million in Canada.

Impressed by the British aristocracy, in 1939 Sam Bronfman blended 600 samples of whiskey before creating the prestigious Crown Royal brand, in honor of the Canadian visit of George VI and Queen Elizabeth. Later that year, the company purchased the Chivas distillery in Aberdeen, Scotland.

During World War II, the company imported rum from Puerto Rico and Jamaica. It also acquired several West Indies distilleries, which would later introduce such labels as Captain Morgan, Myer's, Woods, and Trelawny. Seagram also purchased Mumm's Champagne, Perrier-Jouet Champagne, Barton & Guestier, and Augier Freres. In 1942 it entered the wine market through a partnership with German vintners Fromm & Sichel to purchase the Paul Masson Vineyards in California.

The firm established Captain Morgan Rum Co. in 1944. Five years later it purchased Chivas Brothers Ltd. (Scotch whiskey); in 1950 it bought a majority interest in Fromm & Sichel; in 1952 it acquired G.H. Mumm & Cie and Perrier-Jouet S.A. (Champagne); and in 1954 it purchased Barton & Guestier S.A. (wine). At the same time, the company also began diversifying into natural resources. It invested in the Alberta oil company Royalite in 1950, and three years later it formed the Frankfort Oil Co. for future oil investments. In 1963 the company acquired the Texas Pacific Coal and Oil Co.

Sam Bronfman's son, Edgar, became president in 1957. He expanded Seagram's brands of rum, Scotch, and bottled mixed drinks, and began importing wine on a larger scale. By 1965 the company was operating in 119 countries and had surpassed $1 billion in sales.

The company made its first, albeit short-lived, foray into the entertainment industry in 1969, when Edgar Bronfman bought $40 million of MGM stock and replaced Robert O'Brien as the studio's chairman. The following year MGM lost $25 million, and Edgar Bronfman resigned from the studio.

During the early 1970s, the company increased its international presence. It formed Kirin-Seagram Ltd. in Japan, a joint venture with Kirin Brewery Co., Ltd., and acquired two German producers of spirits, distilled spirits, and liqueurs: Seagram Spirituosen GmbH and Weichsler GmbH. It also formed another joint venture, with Industria de Licores Internacionales, SA, in the Dominican Republic.

In 1975 the company changed its name to The Seagram Co. Ltd. That year earnings slipped nine percent to $74 million. Edgar Bronfman reorganized the company's board of directors and management. In two years, net income rebounded to $84 million on sales of $2.2 million.

Seagram acquired the prestigious Glenlivet Distillers Ltd. of Scotland, a producer of single malt Scotch whiskey, in 1978. In 1980 it sold Texas Pacific to the Sun Co. for $2.3 billion, and began to invest extensively in other companies. It made a significant investment in 1981 by acquiring 27.9 million shares of Conoco Inc. for $2.6 billion, then traded that interest to E.I. du Pont de Nemours and Co. for a 20.2% stake in that company. During the next several years, Seagrams also acquired Geo. G. Sandeman Sons & Co., Ltd. (ports, sherries, and brandy); the British retail chain Oddbins Ltd.; Sterling Vineyards; and 11.6% of Biotechnical International.

In 1985 the company underwent reorganization of its companies, brands, and personnel. It also launched Seagram's Coolers in the U.S. That same year Edgar Bronfman requested television networks to suspend their ban on advertising for distilled spirits, but all three major networks refused to air a commercial comparing the alcohol content of whiskey, wine, and beer.

During 1988 it acquired Tropicana Products Inc., a major fruit juice and juice beverage manufacturer. Three years later it reorganized Tropicana into Tropicana Canada and two European companies, Tropicana United Kingdom Ltd. and Tropicana Europe SA.

The Officers

Chairman: Edgar M. Bronfman

Co-Chairman: Charles R. Bronfman

President and CEO: Edgar Bronfman, Jr.

Vice Chairman and Chief Financial Officer: Robert W. Matschullat

Exec. VP, Human Resources: John D. Borgia

The firm expanded into the entertainment business in 1993 by acquiring 15% of Time Warner. The following year, Edgar Bronfman, Jr., succeeded his father as CEO.

History of Dole Food Company, Inc.

In 1851 Samuel Castle formed a partnership in Hawaii with missionary colleague Amos Cooke for the management of their church's depository, a provider of staple goods to missionaries in outlying posts. The following year the partners added a store in Honolulu, selling goods to the general public. By 1853 Cooke & Castle was Hawaii's fourth-largest company. The two men decided to enter the sugar business by forming the Haiku Sugar Company in 1858.

In 1899 James Drummond Dole, a 21-year-old graduate of Harvard's School of Horticulture and Agriculture, arrived in Hawaii, determined to become successful through the marketing of the still-exotic pineapple. Two years later he purchased 60 acres of land in Wahiawa, just north of Honolulu, to grow Cayenne pineapple, a smoother and more palatable variety than that which grows wildly on the Hawaiian islands. The Hawaiian Pineapple Co. was thus formed.

Dole harvested his first crop in 1903 and started selling his product canned, thereby avoiding the problem of spoilage inherent in the shipping of fresh fruit to market. Later that year, he constructed a cannery in Wahiawa. Dole packed 1,893 cases of the fruit and sold every one via a food broker in San Francisco. In only two years, he began shipments of 25,000 cases of canned pineapple. This sales increase was due, in part, to the presence of a new railroad reaching from Dole's estate in Wahiawa to Honolulu.

Output stood at 32,000 cases by 1906. The following year, he moved his pineapple cannery to Honolulu, where cheap labor was in ample supply.

The Players

Seagram President and CEO: Edgar Bronfman, Jr. Edgar Bronfman, Jr., first joined Seagram in 1982 as a presidential assistant, and later became managing director of London-based Seagram Europe. In 1984 he was promoted to president of The House of Seagram, a position that he held for four years. Bronfman continued to move up the company ranks, becoming executive vice president of U.S. operations and earning a seat on the board of directors in 1988. From there it was only a matter of time before he took the company's helm as president and chief operating officer. Having held those positions since 1989, Bronfman added the post of CEO to his responsibilities in June 1994.

Dole Foods Chairman and CEO: David H. Murdock. David Murdock was born in Ohio to a family of modest means. He quit school at age nine, and went off on his own at 17. Three years later he landed in Detroit, where his friend was working in a small restaurant. This friend kept Murdock in free meals until the owner cut him off, demanding that he either start paying for the food or buy the restaurant. So Murdock, with only six cents in his pocket, secured financing and purchased the business for $1,200. He sold it a little over a year later, and took his $900 profit to Arizona. There he built a multimillion dollar empire in real estate, only to lose it all in 1962. When he rebuilt his fortune, he took care to diversify his holdings. Among other roles at his various companies, Murdock is the chairman and CEO of Dole Foods and the leader of the Castle & Cooke real estate development company.

That year he also launched one of America's first nationwide consumer advertising campaigns. By 1915 the Hawaiian Pineapple Co. was Hawaii's second-largest industry. Three years later it ranked as the world's biggest pineapple producer and processor, packaging over one million cases for that year.

Dole raised expansion capital in 1922 by selling a one-third interest in the company to Castle & Cooke. With this money, he expanded operations by purchasing the island of Lana'i, where he erected a new pineapple plantation.

The Great Depression decreased demand for pineapple, and in the first nine months of 1932,

Hawaiian Pineapple lost over $5 million. That year Castle & Cooke acquired an additional 21% stake, giving it a majority interest. It took over Hawaiian Pineapple and relegated Jim Dole to a figurehead position as chairman. The new owners successfully managed to reverse the downward sales trend through aggressive advertising of pineapple juice.

The repeal of Prohibition in 1933 increased consumption of pineapple juice, as Castle & Cooke immediately began to promote pineapple juice as an excellent mixer for drinks. By 1936 the company had once again established a profitable footing.

In 1948 Castle & Cooke diversified into the tuna packing business by acquiring a 41% stake in Hawaiian Tuna Packers, and a few years later it increased that stake to 97%. In 1956 Castle & Cooke traded its ownership in this company for a 12% interest in Columbia Rivers Packers Association, the producers of Bumble Bee Seafood brand; two years later this stake was increased to a 30% share. In 1958 the company, now known as Castle & Cooke, merged with Helemano Company, Ltd.

In 1961 the three companies—Castle & Cooke, Hawaiian Pineapple, and Columbia River—merged. Drawing on the popularity of the strength of the new company's brandnames, Hawaiian Pineapple was renamed Dole Pineapple and Columbia River Packers Association became Bumble Bee Seafood, Inc.

The company diversified into bananas in 1964 by acquiring Standard Fruit of New Orleans. Three years later this company established Stanfilco in the Philippines to supply East Asian markets.

The Castle & Cooke Foods division was established in 1972 to hold the company's food operations, with the exception of sugar. The following year, the company acquired West Foods, Inc., the leading mushroom producer in the western U.S. Blue Grass Growers, a citrus company, was acquired by the Dole Fresh Fruit Company subsidiary in 1984.

After two takeover attempts, Castle & Cooke agreed to merge with Flexi-Van Corp., a transportation equipment leasing firm, in July 1985. This acquisition reintroduced financial stability to Castle & Cooke. Flexi-Van's owner, David H. Murdock, took the company's helm as chairman and CEO.

Murdock began a divestiture program that would allow the company to focus on its fruit and real estate businesses. In 1986 it sold Bumble Bee, and the following year sold Flexi-Van's leasing business. At the same time, the company began strengthening its food operations by acquiring the agricultural business of Tenneco West and the agricultural properties and operations of Apache Corp. In 1988 it purchased the raisin operations of Bonner Packing, while selling off House of Almonds, Inc. The following year it purchased the apple producers Wells and Wade Fruit Co. and Beebe Orchard Co.

Castle & Cooke also launched new product introductions. In 1988 it unveiled a line of dried fruits and nuts, and two years later debuted a line of value-added packaged fresh vegetable products, including pre-cut vegetables and salads.

Murdock terminated the pineapple operation on Lana'i, turning the company's properties there into tourist resorts. It established the Lodge at Koele and the Lodge at Manele Bay, as well as the development of 775 luxury homes. By 1991 Dole was the third-largest landowner in the state of Hawaii.

Dole Foods Co., Inc. was formed when Castle & Cooke stockholders approved the company's name change in 1991. That year Dole embarked upon an expansion program into Eastern Europe, South Korea, and the Middle East, and the company became the world's largest producer of fresh fruit and vegetables.

The following year, Dole acquired SAMICA, a European dried fruits and nuts marketer. In 1994 the company acquired the Dromedary date producer and the Made in Nature organic produce company, as well as a stake in U.K.-based Jamaica Fruit Distributors.

In 1995 the company reorganized, with Dole Food Company, Inc., holding its food producing and distribution businesses, and Castle & Cooke, Inc., maintaining its real estate and resort operations. The following year Dole acquired Pascual Hermanos, Spain's largest fruit and vegetable grower. Dole diversified into flowers in 1998 with the acquisitions of Sunburst Farms, the largest importer of fresh cut flowers to the U.S.; Finesse Farms, an importer of roses; Four Farmers, a bouquet firm; and CCI Farms, a fresh cut flower company.

Market Forces Driving the Acquisition

A number of factors spurred Seagram's 1995 acquisition of Dole's juice businesses. First, the company increased its global presence with the addition of the Dole's manufacturing plants in Europe and the U.S., and its joint ventures in China and Japan. The international market for juice and juice products was still largely untapped and was growing at a rate of about 5% annually. Tropicana reported that in 1996, North Americans far outdrank international populations in juice, consuming 46 liters per capita, as stated in *Food Processing*. The closest group abroad was Western Europeans, with 22 liters, followed by Latin Americans with 12, and Asians with a mere two.

A second force driving the acquisition was Tropicana's push to challenge Coke's leading rank in the U.S. juice market. By late 1994 Coca-Cola Co., with its leading brands of Minute Maid and Hi-C, captured the top 19.5% market share. At the same time, Tropicana controlled 13.1% and Dole had 2.5%. PepsiCo's distribution agreement with Ocean Spray enabled it to place third, with a 10% share.

Changing consumer tastes also encouraged the growth of juice operations. The iced tea market, which had been carved out by Snapple Corp., had taken a downturn. Consumers were increasingly opting for juice beverages, particularly those with lighter tastes in ready-to-go containers. Blended juice combinations, too, appealed to palettes. With Dole's juice operations, Tropicana would fortify its presence in all of these directions.

Additionally, Tropicana was driven by a need to expand its product line. This company was primarily a citrus juice company, with strong orange and grapefruit brands. Such brands included Tropicana Pure Premium Original Orange Juice, Tropicana Pure Premium Grovestand Orange Juice, Tropicana Pure Premium Grapefruit Juice, Season's Best, and Tropicana Twister. Dole was known more as a pineapple and blended fruit juice maker. A combination of the two would strengthen both beverage businesses and enable the company to concentrate its advertising efforts into more focused markets.

Approach and Engagement

Seagram announced its acquisition of Dole's fruit juice business on January 5, 1995. The $285 million cash deal was completed without incident five months later.

The transferred operations had annual sales of $320 million. They included the U.S. brands of Dole, Juice Bowl, and Looza; the European brands of Fruvita, Dole, Juice Bowl, and Looza; and the Asian brand of Dole. Also included in the deal were Dole's manufacturing plants in the U.S. and Europe, and its interest in joint ventures in China and Japan.

Not included in the sale were Dole's canned pineapple juice operations, although the companies agreed to a long-term supply contract for pineapple juice concentrate. By hanging onto this business, Dole was keeping a hand in the blended juice industry, in which pineapple juice is a key ingredient.

Products and Services

The Seagram Spirits and Wine Group had global responsibility for all production, brand management and marketing, sales, and distribution of The Seagram

Company Ltd.'s beverage alcohol brands throughout more than 150 countries and territories. It was comprised of Seagram Americas, Seagram Asia Pacific, Seagram Europe & Africa, Seagram's Martell Mumm Group, Chivas Brothers Ltd. Similarly, The Seagram Beverage Company was responsible for the development, production, and marketing of Seagram's premium low- and no-alcohol beverages. Its main brands included Seagram's Coolers and Seagram's Mixers.

Seagram's entertainment holdings consisted of a number of sub-units under the Universal Studios umbrella: Universal Pictures, which created and distributed theatrical and non-theatrical filmed entertainment; Universal Television & Networks Group, an international production, distribution, and networks operation; Universal Studios Recreation Group, the company's destination-based entertainment (theme park) business; Universal Music Group, encompassing MCA Records, MCA Records Nashville, Decca Records, GRP Recording Company, Geffen/DGC Records, Universal Records, Interscope Records, Hip-O Records, Universal Music & Video Distribution, Universal Music International, Universal Music Special Markets, MCA Music Publishing, and Universal Concerts; Universal Studios New Media Group, which developed and promoted Universal's properties for the global digital consumer market; Universal Studios Consumer Products Group, its global licensing division; and Spencer Gifts, retail store businesses operating under the Spencer Gifts, Dapy, and Glow! names.

Changes to the Industry

With the deal, Tropicana Products Inc. became the largest U.S. maker of ready-to-serve orange juice, with annual sales of $1.5 billion and a 41% share of the nation's orange juice market. Overall, the acquisition gave Tropicana a 15.6% share of the U.S. fruit juice market, behind Coke's 19.5% share. Tropicana immediately began working to close that gap by investing in high-visibility promotional campaigns. It launched a tie-in with the video release of *Apollo 13*, followed by a promotion with the movie *Twister*. In October 1996, it struck a 30-year deal to rename the Thunder-Dome, in Saint Petersburg, Florida, as Tropicana Field. That maneuver shut down concession stand negotiations between Coke and the Devil Rays Major League Baseball team.

Review of the Outcome

Upon completion of the acquisition in June 1995, Seagram reorganized its beverage operations into domestic and international units: Tropicana Dole Beverages North America was based in Bradenton, Florida, and Tropicana Dole Beverages International, was headquartered in Brussels, Belgium.

After its acquisition of the Dole juice unit, Seagram solidified its presence in the entertainment industry in a big way. Later in 1995 it acquired 80% of MCA, renaming it Universal Studios the following year. It increased its interest in USA Networks by 50% in 1997, and then took a 45% stake in the newly-formed television joint venture USA Networks, Inc. The following year it acquired the remaining 75% interest in PolyGram for $10.2 billion. To finance this acquisition, it sold Tropicana to PepsiCo for $3.3 billion.

At the time of the sale to Pepsi, Tropicana Dole held a 16.4% market share for U.S. fruit beverages. In the span of only about three years, Seagram had closed the gap between it and Coke, the industry leader with a 17% market share.

Research

Berne, Steve. "Pure Premium Maneuvers," in *Prepared Foods*, November 1996. An interview with Jack Jost, VP of engineering at Tropicana Dole Beverages North America.

Blamey, Pamela. "Seagram Buys Most of Dole Juice Units," in *Supermarket News*, 19 June 1995. Describes the integration of the acquisition into Tropicana.

Buss, Dale D. "Fresh Markets for Tropicana," in *Food Processing*, November 1996. Examines the effects of the acquisition one year after its completion, with a brief account of the history of the Tropicana company.

"Dole Food Co. Inc.," in *Notable Corporate Chronologies*, The Gale Group, 1999. Provides an overview of the company beyond the acquisition of its juice business by Seagram.

"Mergers Unleash Flow of Mass Distribution; Marketing Muscle Gives Beverages Significant Presence at Discount," in *Discount Store News*, 20 February 1995. The changing beverage preferences of the U.S. consumer, and how retailers must react to recent mergers within the industry.

"Seagram Acquiring Dole's Juice Unit," in *The New York Times*, 6 January 1995. Describes how the newly-announced merger will affect the U.S. juice market share.

"Seagram to Buy Dole Food's Fruit Juice for $285 Million," in *Food & Drink Daily*, 6 January 1995. Describes the recently announced acquisition deal.

"The Seagram Co., Ltd.," in *Notable Corporate Chronologies*, The Gale Group, 1999. Traces the company's chronological development.

The Seagram Co., Ltd. Home Page, available at http://www.seagram.com. Official World Wide Web Page for Seagram. Includes a financial information, news releases, description of products and services, company history, and executive biographies.

DAVIS MCMILLAN

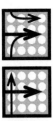

SEAGRAM & MCA

nationality: Canada
date: June 5, 1995
affected: The Seagram Company Ltd., Canada, founded 1924
affected: MCA Inc., USA, founded 1924

The Seagram Company Ltd.
1430 Peel St.
Montreal, PQ H3A 1S9
Canada

tel: (514)849-5271
fax: (514)987-5224
web: http://www.seagram.com

Overview of the Merger

By the mid-1990s, the Matsushita Electric Industrial Co. wanted out of the entertainment industry. Under its previous president, the company had diversified beyond consumer electronics by purchasing the U.S. entertainment company MCA Inc. in 1991. By 1994, changes in Matsushita's leadership, an economic recession, and internal strife made it long to return to basics.

MCA's assets were varied and valuable. Its Universal Pictures movie production arm generated $2.7 billion in revenues in 1994. Its music operations, operating as Geffen Records, MCA Records, and GRP Records, generated revenues of $1.3 billion. Its two theme parks accounted for $245 million in revenues, while Putnam Berkeley Group Publishing generated $278 million.

Seagram, or at least its president, wanted to make a big splash in the entertainment industry. It had a small, but limited, stake in Time Warner, and was looking to increase its footing in the industry. Its controversial method of raising the purchase price, however, drew criticism from shareholders. They expected that the return on the company's investment in MCA would not come close to the profits that it already earned from its stake in duPont.

History of The Seagram Company Ltd.

Joseph E. Seagram & Sons, Ltd., a distilling company, was founded in Waterloo, Ontario, Canada, in 1857. By the turn of the century, the company had become a leading Canadian rye producer with two popular brands: Seagram's '83 and V.O.

In 1916, when Prohibition became effective in parts of Canada, Samuel Bronfman purchased the Bonaventure Liquor Store Co., conveniently located near the downtown railway in Montreal. People traveling to the "dry" west could stock up on liquor before boarding the train. Two years later, Sam's brother, Harry, ventured into the drug business. He purchased a Dewar's whiskey contract from the Hudson Bay Co., and began selling liquor through drugstores and to processors who made "medicinal" mixtures.

The Business

Financials

Revenue (1998): US$9.7 billion

Employees (1998): 30,000

SICs / NAICS

sic 2086 - Bottled & Canned Soft Drinks

sic 2037 - Frozen Fruits & Vegetables

sic 2033 - Canned Fruits & Vegetables

sic 2084 - Wines, Brandy & Brandy Spirits

sic 7812 - Motion Picture & Video Production

sic 7822 - Motion Picture & Tape Distribution

sic 7829 - Motion Picture Distribution Services

naics 312111 - Soft Drink Manufacturing

naics 311421 - Fruit and Vegetable Canning

naics 312130 - Wineries

naics 512110 - Motion Picture and Video Production

naics 512120 - Motion Picture and Video Distribution

naics 311411 - Frozen Fruit, Juice and Vegetable
Manufacturing

The Volstead Act instituted Prohibition in the U.S. in 1919. Soon the Bronfmans imported 300,000 gallons of alcohol from the United States for the manufacture of 800,000 gallons of whiskey. In 1924 the Bronfmans opened their first distillery in La Salle, across the St. Lawrence River from Montreal, and incorporated under the name Distillers Corporation Ltd.

The company ventured overseas in 1926 when the Bronfman family sold a 50% interest in Distillers Co. to an amalgamation of British distillers that controlled more than half of the world's Scotch market. In exchange, the British Enterprise gave the Bronfmans the Canadian distribution rights for its brands, including Haig, Black & White, Dewar's, and Vat 69. Two years later Distillers Corp. acquired all of the stock in Joseph E. Seagram & Sons, Ltd. The merged company went public under the name Distillers Corp.-Seagram Ltd.

During the 1930s, the border between Canada and the U.S. became dangerous for illegal alcohol transport, so trading was accomplished mostly by sea under the cover of night. Sam Bronfman attempted to eradicate the somewhat dubious image of whiskey that developed during the bootlegging era by exten-

sively promoting the virtue and quality of his whiskey. The company also revolutionized liquor marketing by selling their products to distributors already bottled, while other distillers sold their products in barrel consignments, thereby losing control over the quality of the final product.

Prohibition in the United States ended in 1933. The company acquired 20% of Schenley, whose product line included the well-known Golden Wedding brand of rye whiskey. Sam Bronfman informed the Distillers Co. board of the acquisition and requested an increase in prices. When the board denied his request, the Bronfman brothers raised $4 million and bought out the Distillers Co.'s holding in Distillers Corp.-Seagrams Ltd. Sam Bronfman assumed the post of president.

The company purchased the Rossville Union Distillery in Lawrenceburg, Indiana, in 1933, and established Joseph E. Seagram & Sons Inc. to operate it. The following year, it purchased Maryland Distillers, Inc. Seagram began to import its own aged Canadian stock to blend with its new American distillates, resulting in products known under the Five Crown and Seven Crown labels.

In 1934, after the end of Prohibition, the head the Canadian Conservative Party launched an investigation into the liquor smuggling industry. The Bronfmans were arrested and tried, but the case was later thrown out of court. That year the company also introduced Seagram's V.O. Canadian Whiskey.

The firm made its first foreign acquisition in 1935 with the purchase of Robert Brown Ltd. (Scotch whiskey); its name was subsequently changed to Seagram Distillers PLC. By the following year, Seagram's sales had grown to $60 million in the United States, with another $10 million in Canada.

Impressed with the British aristocracy in 1939, Sam Bronfman blended 600 samples of whiskey before creating the prestigious Crown Royal brand, in honor of the Canadian visit of George VI and Queen Elizabeth. Later that year, the company purchased the Chivas distillery in Aberdeen, Scotland.

During World War II, the company imported rum from Puerto Rico and Jamaica. It also acquired several West Indies distilleries, which would later introduce such labels as Captain Morgan, Myer's, Woods, and Trelawny. Seagram also purchased Mumm's Champagne, Perrier-Jouet Champagne, Barton & Guestier, and Augier Freres. In 1942 it entered the wine market through a partnership with German vintners Fromm & Sichel to purchase the Paul Masson Vineyards in California.

The firm established Captain Morgan Rum Co. in 1944. Five years later it purchased Chivas Brothers Ltd. (Scotch whiskey); in 1950 it bought a majority interest in Fromm & Sichel; in 1952 it acquired G.H. Mumm & Cie and Perrier-Jouet S.A. (Champagne); and in 1954 it purchased Barton & Guestier S.A. (wine). At the same time, the company also began diversifying into natural resources. It invested in the Alberta oil company Royalite in 1950, and three years later it formed the Frankfort Oil Co. for future oil investments. In 1963 the company acquired the Texas Pacific Coal and Oil Co.

Sam Bronfman's son, Edgar, became president in 1957. He expanded Seagram's brands of rum, Scotch, and bottled mixed drinks, and began importing wine on a larger scale. By 1965 the company was operating in 119 countries and had surpassed $1 billion in sales.

The company made its first, albeit short-lived, foray into the entertainment industry in 1969, when Edgar Bronfman bought $40 million of MGM stock and replaced Robert O'Brien as the studio's chairman. The following year MGM lost $25 million, and Edgar Bronfman resigned from the studio.

During the early 1970s, the company increased its international presence. It formed Kirin-Seagram Ltd. in Japan, a joint venture with Kirin Brewery Co., Ltd., and acquired two German producers of spirits, distilled spirits, and liqueurs: Seagram Spirituosen GmbH and Weichsler GmbH. It also formed another joint venture, with Industria de Licores Internacionales, SA, in the Dominican Republic.

In 1975 the company changed its name to The Seagram Co. Ltd. That year earnings slipped nine percent to $74 million. Edgar Bronfman reorganized the company's board of directors and management. In two years, net income rebounded to $84 million on sales of $2.2 million.

Seagram acquired the prestigious Glenlivet Distillers Ltd. of Scotland, a producer of single malt Scotch whiskey, in 1978. In 1980 it sold Texas Pacific to the Sun Co. for $2.3 billion, and began to invest extensively in other companies. It made a significant investment in 1981 by acquiring 27.9 million shares of Conoco Inc. for $2.6 billion, then traded that interest to E.I. du Pont de Nemours and Co. for a 20.2% stake in that company. During the next several years, Seagram also acquired Geo. G. Sandeman Sons & Co., Ltd. (ports, sherries, and brandy); the British retail chain Oddbins Ltd.; Sterling Vineyards; and 11.6% of Biotechnical International.

In 1985 the company underwent reorganization of its companies, brands, and personnel. It also launched Seagram's Coolers in the U.S. That same

The Officers

Chairman: Edgar M. Bronfman

Co-Chairman: Charles R. Bronfman

President and CEO: Edgar Bronfman, Jr.

Vice Chairman and Chief Financial Officer: Robert W. Matschullat

Exec. VP, Human Resources: John D. Borgia

year Edgar Bronfman requested television networks to suspend their ban on advertising for distilled spirits, but all three major networks refused to air a commercial comparing the alcohol content of whiskey, wine, and beer.

During 1988 it acquired Tropicana Products Inc., a major fruit juice and juice beverage manufacturer. Three years later it reorganized Tropicana into Tropicana Canada and two European companies, Tropicana United Kingdom Ltd. and Tropicana Europe SA.

The firm expanded into the entertainment business in 1993 by acquiring 15% of Time Warner. The following year, Edgar Bronfman Jr. succeeded his father as CEO.

History of MCA Inc.

In the early 1920s Jules C. Stein worked his way through medical school by playing violin and saxophone in a band. When the band began to generate more bookings than it could handle, Stein began earning a commission by booking other bands. This turned out to be a very profitable business, and Stein gave up his ophthalmology studies. In 1924 Stein and William Goodheart formed the Music Corporation of America (MCA).

MCA grossed over $30,000 in its first year. By 1927 the company represented about 40 bands. Three years later it persuaded Lucky Strike to sponsor a radio program that featured a different MCA band each night. The show caused musicians to flock to MCA, and by the end of the decade the company had signed about 65% of the nation's major bands.

The company began to diversify outside the music business into other forms of entertainment. In 1937 MCA moved to Hollywood. There, Lew Wasserman became the first agent to negotiate for his clients a percentage of a movie's earnings rather than

The Players

Seagram President and CEO: Edgar Bronfman, Jr. Edgar Bronfman, Jr., had a taste for the entertainment industry even as a teenager. He wrote and developed screenplays, and by age 16 was working with producer Bruce Stark. Bronfman skipped college to pursue other opportunities in that industry. He became a producer in his own right, as well as an accomplished songwriter. His father lured him into the company business in 1982 as a presidential assistant. He later became managing director of London-based Seagram Europe. In 1984 he was promoted to president of The House of Seagram, a position that he held for four years. Bronfman continued to move up the company ranks, becoming executive vice president of U.S. operations and earning a seat on the board of directors in 1988. From there it was only a matter of time before he took the company's helm as president and chief operating officer. Having held those positions since 1989, Bronfman added the post of CEO to his responsibilities in June 1994.

Matsushita President: Yoichi Morishita. Yoichi Morishita had been with Matsushita for 35 years when he was called upon to succeed Akio Tanii, who had served as the company president for seven years. Morishita had worked primarily in company sales. He climbed onto the first rung of the executive ladder by becoming managing director of the Consumer Product Sales Division in 1989. He was promoted to senior manager the following year, and then was chosen to head the Living Business Group in late 1991. Morishita was named an executive VP in December 1992. Upon the sudden resignation of Tanii in 1993, Morishita became company president, and set about refocusing the company on its core electronics business.

a straight salary. MCA purchased other agencies, among them the Hayward-Deverich Agency in 1945. This acquisition brought such clients as Henry Fonda, Greta Garbo, and Joseph Cotton to MCA, making it the nation's premier talent agency.

Wasserman became president of MCA in 1946, while Stein assumed the chairmanship. Three years later Wasserman took MCA into television show production. In 1952 its newly formed division, Revue Productions, began selling reruns to local stations. In

1954 MCA purchased United Television Programs, a syndicator dealing primarily in reruns. By the late 1950s MCA produced and co-produced more series, including *General Electric Theater* and *Alfred Hitchcock Presents*, than any of its rivals. For the first time, MCA's agency commissions where exceeded by its income from TV film rentals.

MCA purchased the TV rights to Paramount's pre-1948 library of 750 feature films for $35 million in 1958. The following year it acquired the 420-acre back lot of Universal Studios for $11 million. In 1959 MCA Inc. was formed as the new parent company, and went public the same year.

By then MCA was both the largest representative and employer of show business talent. As a result, the company often hired its own clients, a practice deplored by other industry members. In 1962, when MCA bought Decca Records, Inc., the company that owned Universal Pictures, Inc., the Justice Department forced it to choose whether to operate as a talent agency or a film-production concern. The company decided to divest itself of its talent agency and concentrate on feature-film production under the Universal Pictures name.

During the late 1960s MCA diversified by acquiring Columbia Savings & Loan Association of Colorado, a financial services firm, and Spencer Gifts, a small retail chain. It would later move into publishing by purchasing G.P. Putnam's Sons and Grosset & Dunlap, Inc. In 1973 Wasserman became chairman and appointed Sidney J. Steinberg as president and chief operating officer.

After a slow start in the motion picture business, MCA finally hit the big time in the mid-1970s with such movies as *Jaws* and *The Deer Hunter*. Its film revenues now surpassed television revenues. By 1975 the theatrical films and Universal Television operations reported combined revenues of $364 million. MCA Records generated $127 million, MCA Recreation tallied $10 million, and MCA Financial generated $44 million. Four years later, total revenues reached $1.1 billion.

In 1980 MCA had more than 20 films, 11 hours of television a week, 90 record albums, and nearly 700 books scheduled for production. But cost overruns and a number of unsuccessful movie releases contributed to a drop in operating income and rumors of a possible takeover. To shield itself from any such takeover attempt, MCA slashed Universal's film budget and amended its bylaws to require approval of 75% of the company's stockholders for any takeover.

In 1981 it acquired a 33% interest in USA Networks, a partnership with Time and Paramount. It also purchased a lot in Orlando, Florida, where it planned to build a theme park to compete with Disney/MGM Studio.

After several successful movie releases in the early 1980s, including *E.T.* and *Back to the Future*, MCA again experienced disappointing results in the latter part of the decade with such films as *Howard the Duck*. Thomas Pollock, an entertainment lawyer, was hired to head the film division. Pollock brought with him the directors Steven Spielberg, Ron Howard, and George Lucas.

MCA completed a series of acquisitions in the late '80s. It purchased 50% of Cineplex Odeon Corp., a chain of movie theaters, in 1986, followed the next year by New York's "superstation" WWOR-TV. In 1987 Time withdrew from USA Networks, and MCA increased its stake in that venture to 50%. Three years later it acquired Geffen Records and GRP Records.

In 1991 the Matsushita Electric Industrial Co. purchased MCA for $6.1 billion. This Japanese consumer electronics manufacturer hoped to capitalize on the increasing popularity of American entertainment in international markets. The same hopes were shared by Sony, which had just purchased Columbia Pictures for $4.8 billion.

Market Forces Driving the Merger/Acquisition

Just after Matsushita's acquisition of MCA, Japan experienced a stock market crash. This, combined with the resulting recession, made Matsushita less capable of injecting MCA with the expansion capital that Wasserman had been counting on by selling MCA.

Matsushita management grew increasingly wary of its new subsidiary, as it watched Sony struggle with its own foray into the American motion picture industry. The heads of Columbia spent Sony's money freely, and the studio turned out a string of expensive flops. In 1994 that company began to right itself, dumping the Columbia management team and taking a $3.2 billion write-off.

The U.S. motion picture business had become costlier and riskier than ever. In 1994 the average cost of producing and marketing a movie rose 15% to $50.4 million. At the same time, the big studios were increasing the number of films they released. That year they released 185 films, up from 161 the year earlier. Adding to MCA's troubles was the departure of both Steven Spielberg and David Geffen, who left to join Jeffrey Katzenberg in forming DreamWorks SKG.

MCA's hands were tied by Matsushita's tight purse strings. It had been prevented from joining its rivals in increasing its television and cable holdings. It hadn't been permitted to purchase Virgin Records, among other companies. And its hopes to open retail stores along the lines of Disney's had been quashed.

The conflict over spending created a feud between the Japanese parent and the American entertainment firm. MCA's leaders claimed that Matsushita was stingy, while that company accused MCA of operating without a clear strategy. In 1994 the conflict became public, with Wasserman and Steinberg demanding an investment into MCA, else they would refuse to renew their expiring contracts.

Akio Tanii, the president who had led Matsushita into purchasing MCA, resigned in 1993 under the cloud of a loan fraud scandal, faulty refrigerators, and financial difficulties. Yoichi Morishita succeeded him, and initiated a program of refocusing on electrical consumer goods. Revitalizing that area of business, however, required the capital to overhaul factories and redevelop international sales networks.

Edgar Bronfman, Jr., Seagram's president, was interested in MCA. Seagram already had a stake in the entertainment industry, 15% of Time Warner, but was prevented by a poison pill from adding to that interest. Bronfman personally relished the notion of becoming a major player in that industry. He had forgone attending college in order to pursue career opportunities in movies and songwriting, and he regularly mixed in Hollywood circles.

According to *Hollywood Reporter*, the company's leaders—Edgar Sr., Charles, and Edgar Jr.—signed a letter addressed to Seagram shareholders. It referred to the MCA deal as "a rare opportunity both to unlock the value of a minority investment and to take a position in the ninth-largest, fifth-fastest growing industry in the United States."

Approach and Engagement

Matsushita sought a quick sale. It didn't want to waste much time in the approval process, so it was looking for a buyer that wouldn't raise regulatory objections. It also wanted payment in cash, and therefore needed a suitor with access to ready capital. In Seagram it found a willing suitor that met these requirements. For this reason it granted Seagram an exclusive two-week negotiating window in March 1995.

Seagram had access to the cash required to close the sale, but it would have to liquidate its valuable du Pont stock to get it. The company's 24.9% stake in E.I. du Pont de Nemours & Co. generated about 70% of Seagram's earnings. Shareholders, therefore, were less than enthusiastic about unloading it. Bronfman reassured them of the wisdom in the deal, and sold the company's 156 million shares back to du Pont for $8.8 billion on April 6, 1995.

Three days later, on April 9, Seagram and Matsushita announced their $5.7 billion deal, in which Seagram acquired 80% of MCA Inc. The agreement stipulated that MCA would be debt-free upon its transfer to Seagram. This meant that Matsushita would not only assume $1.2 billion in existing MCA debt, it would also assume the costs already incurred in the production of *Waterworld*. This $175 million movie, which was in the post-production stage, was the most expensive movie ever made at that time. Seagram would have to invest only in marketing the film, yet would keep all of its profits.

Products and Services

The Seagram Spirits and Wine Group had global responsibility for all production, brand management and marketing, sales, and distribution of The Seagram Company Ltd.'s beverage alcohol brands throughout more than 150 countries and territories. It was comprised of Seagram Americas, Seagram Asia Pacific, Seagram Europe & Africa, Seagram's Martell Mumm Group, and Chivas Brothers Ltd. Similarly, The Seagram Beverage Company was responsible for the development, production, and marketing of Seagram's premium low- and no-alcohol beverages. Its main brands include Seagram's Coolers and Seagram's Mixers.

Universal Studios was comprised of a number of sub-units: Universal Pictures, which created and distributed theatrical and non-theatrical filmed entertainment; Universal Television & Networks Group, an international production, distribution, and networks operation; Universal Studios Recreation Group, the company's destination-based entertainment (theme park) business; Universal Music Group, encompassing MCA Records, MCA Records Nashville, Decca Records, GRP Recording Company, Geffen/DGC Records, Universal Records, Interscope Records, Hip-O Records, Universal Music & Video Distribution, Universal Music International, Universal Music Special Markets, MCA Music Publishing, and Universal Concerts; Universal Studios New Media Group, which developed and promoted Universal's properties for the global digital consumer market; Universal Studios Consumer Products Group, its global licensing division; and Spencer Gifts, retail store businesses operating under the Spencer Gifts, Dapy, and Glow! names.

Review of the Outcome/Changes to the Industry

On June 5, 1995, Seagram assumed ownership of MCA Inc. Bronfman had been negotiating to put

Michael Ovitz, a powerful agent, in the company's top position, but negotiations broke down, presumably due to a steep asking price on Ovitz's part. Instead, Frank Biondi was named chairman and CEO, and Ron Meyer was appointed president and chief operating officer. MCA Inc.'s name was changed to Universal Studios, Inc. in 1996.

In the months following the acquisition, industry watchers seemed to take more of an interest in the performance of duPont's stock than the performance of MCA. An April 1997 *Forbes* article reported that duPont's stock had doubled since Seagram had sold its stake. Much of that increase, however, was a direct result of Seagram's sale of it. DuPont's absorption of those shares put fewer in circulation, thereby increasing their value.

In April 1995, just after the acquisition deal was announced, Seagram filed suit against Viacom Inc. for violating their partnership in the USA Network by launching a competing cable network. In 1997 the companies settled, with Seagram purchasing Viacom's 50% interest for $1.7 billion. The company combined its domestic television operations with USA Networks, and then sold this business to Home Shopping Network. Seagram received a 45% equity interest in the new company, which was named USA Networks Inc.

Seagram made several other significant acquisitions and divestitures in the following years. In 1996 it sold Putnam Berkeley Publishing Group to Pearson PLC for $336 million in cash. That year it acquired a 50% interest in Interscope Records. In 1997 it acquired Multimedia Entertainment and a majority interest in October Films. In October 1998 it purchased Wet 'n Wild, Inc., the world's largest independent water park company. On Nov. 16, 1998 Frank Biondi Jr. was ousted as Universal's chairman and CEO as part of Seagram's reorganization into three areas: music, movies and theme parks, and beverages.

Seagram formed the world's largest music group in 1998 when it purchased PolyGram for $10.4 billion, and merged it with Universal Music Group. To pay for the acquisition, it sold Tropicana Products to PepsiCo for $3.3 billion, relinquished most of Polygram's film library to MGM, and divested itself of its Time Warner stock.

Universal ranked ninth among studios based on its 1998 market share of 5.5%. By comparison, Buena Vista ranked first with a 16% market share, a slight lead over Paramount's 15.8%.

Research

Daniels, Jeffrey. "Seagram Tries to Quell Investor Ire over MCA Buy," in *Hollywood Reporter*, 12 May 1995.

Provides quotes from the letter that Seagram's leader addressed to its shareholders.

"Expensive Flops: Ego and Inexperience among Studio Buyers Add up to Big Losses," in *The Wall Street Journal*, 10 April 1995. Rising production costs cause trouble for many large studios.

Koselka, Rita, and Randall Lane. "What Matsushita Left on the Table," in *Forbes*, 3 July 1995. Puts forth reasoning as to the wisdom of the MCA purchase, despite the outcry from Seagram's shareholders.

"MCA Inc.," in *International Directory of Company Histories*, Vol. II, St. James Press: 1990. Narrative account of the company's history through 1988.

"Retreat from Tinseltown: Matsushita and Hollywood," in *The Economist*, 8 April 1995. Provides an account of how MCA had fared under Matsushita ownership, and ventures guesses as to possible suitors.

Roberts, Johnnie L. "Hey Edgar, Why MCA?" in *Newsweek*, 17 April 1995. Provides an account of MCA's troubles at Matsushita, as well as Seagram's own history of scandals and feuds.

Rose, Frank. "The Love Song of E. Bronfman Jr.," in *Esquire*, June 1997. Offers a detailed account of Edgar Bronfman Jr., from his early years in the entertainment to his re-entry into Hollywood via the MCA acquisition.

"Seagram Buys 80% of MCA at $5.7 Bil," in *The Wall Street Journal*, 10 April 1995. Seagram announces its acquisition of MCA.

"Seagram Closes Deal to Take over MCA," in *Newsbytes*, 7 June 1995. Seagram releases 1994 revenue figures for MCA's operating segments.

"The Seagram Co., Ltd.," in *Notable Corporate Chronologies*, The Gale Group, 1999. Traces the company's chronological development.

The Seagram Co., Ltd. Home Page, available at http://www.seagram.com. Official World Wide Web Page for Seagram. Includes a financial information, news releases, description of products and services, company history, and executive biographies.

Siklos, Richard. "Edgar in the Land of TV Moguls," in *The Financial Post*, 9 November 1996. Provides details of the fall-out between Seagram and Viacom.

"Studio Scorecard, in *Entertainment Weekly*, 5 February 1999. Ranks the top ten movies studios based on their 1998 performance.

DAVIS MCMILLAN

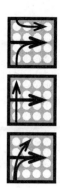

SEARS, ROEBUCK & DEAN WITTER REYNOLDS

Sears, Roebuck & Co.
3333 Beverly Road
Hoffman Estates, IL 60179
USA

tel: (847)286-2500
fax: (847)286-7829
web: http://www.sears.com

Morgan Stanley Dean Witter & Co.
1585 Broadway
New York, NY 10036
USA

tel: (212)761-4000
fax: (212)761-0086
web: http://www.msdw.com

nationality: USA
date: December 1981
affected: Sears, Roebuck & Co., USA, founded 1886
affected: Morgan Stanley Dean Witter & Co. (formerly Dean Witter Reynolds), USA, founded 1924

Overview of the Merger

Upon completion of the merger with Dean Witter Reynolds, Sears, Roebuck & Co. was able to fulfill its goal of becoming a leader in the nation's consumer financial services industry. The retail giant purchased the financial company for $607 million, and with 859 retail stores and 25 million credit card customers, planned to offer an array of financial specialties within its retail outlets.

History of Sears, Roebuck & Co.

In 1886 Richard W. Sears, a railway agent in Minnesota, purchased a shipment of unwanted watches from a local jeweler, and founded the R.W. Sears Watch Co. The next year Sears moved to Chicago, Illinois, and hired Indiana watchmaker Alvah C. Roebuck. In 1888 Sears published the first of its famous mail-order catalogs, consisting of 80 pages of watch and jewelry advertisements. The watch business did not fare well, however, and Sears sold the watch business the next year.

Sears and Roebuck formed a mail-order business in 1891, offering farmers an alternative to high-priced rural stores. The U.S. post office's rural free delivery system made it affordable for the company to mail orders to remote locations. Three years later the company adopted the name Sears, Roebuck & Co., with sales topping $400,000. In 1895 the firm produced a 532-page general merchandise catalog, offering shoes, women's garments, wagons, fishing tackle, stoves, furniture, china, musical instruments, saddles, firearms, buggies, bicycles, and glasses in addition to watches and jewelry. Roebuck grew nervous about the business and sold his shares of the company, remaining on as a repairman. Sears replaced his partner with entrepreneur Arron Neusbaum, but the relationship was short-lived. In 1901 Neusbaum sold his interest for $1.25 million after clashing with Sears.

Sears went on to sell common and preferred stock on the open market to raise money for expansion in 1906. The company opened a mail-order plant in Chicago and its first branch office in Dallas. Sears resigned as president in 1908 when his conservative financial leadership stalled the company's progress. Julius Rosenwald was elected president and Sears was appointed chairman, but never attended a meeting; he finally retired in 1913. Under new management Sears began offering credit to customers at a time when even banks would not consider lending to consumers. It also established a research laboratory to set minimum standards for products and to spot-check mail-order merchandise.

An economic depression in 1921 caused Sears to post a loss of $16.4 million and to omit its quarterly dividend for the first time. Rosenwald responded by cutting executive salaries, eliminating his own salary, and donating 50,000 shares from his personal holdings to the company treasury. He retired four years later, with Charles Kittle taking over as president and Robert Wood as vice president. Under the leadership of the two, Sears opened its first retail shop in Chicago, and seven more stores followed. The company also introduced a line of tires under the name Allstate. By 1927 Sears operated 27 retail stores.

Continuing with expansion, Sears arranged a merger between two of its suppliers, Upton Machine and Nineteen Hundred Washer Co. to form Nineteen Hundred Corporation, which would become the Whirlpool Corporation in 1929. Two years later the company diversified further and took advantage of the growing popularity of the automobile by expanding Allstate into an auto insurance company. At the same time, Sears' retail outlets surpassed mail-order sales for the first time, with stores accounting for 53.4% of the year's $180 million in sales.

Lessing Rosenwald replaced his father in 1932 as chairman. Under his lead, Sears established a store-planning and display department to focus on tables, fixtures, space requirements, customer flow, and width of aisles. Instead of fitting merchandise into their surroundings, buildings were built around merchandise. In 1933 Allstate installed sales locations in Sears stores. With the onset of World War II, sales benefited from increases in military spending, rising 30% to reach $975 million.

With sales reaching $1 billion, Sears expanded internationally by opening a store in Havana, Cuba, and in Mexico City, Mexico, in 1947. Sears also joined a pioneer Canadian merchandising company, Simpsons, Ltd., to form Simpsons-Sears, Ltd. in 1953. Sears was quickly becoming an industry leader, posting sales of $3 billion in 1954, while rival Montgomery Ward achieved only $1 billion in sales. Its Allstate operations expanded into life insurance and developed an auto club, and in 1960 the company created its own shopping center development subsidiary, Homart Development.

Sales increased to $5.1 billion in 1963, and surveys showed that one out of five U.S. consumers shopped at Sears regularly. By 1970 construction was underway

The Business

Financials - Sears, Roebuck & Co.

Revenue (1998): $41,322 million

Employees (1998): 324,000

SICs / NAICS

sic 5311 - Department Stores

sic 6211 - Security Brokers & Dealers

sic 5961 - Catalog & Mail-Order Houses

naics 523999 - Miscellaneous Financial Investment
    Activities

Financials - Morgan Stanley Dean Witter & Co.

Revenue (1998): $31,131 million

Employees (1998): 45,712

SICs / NAICS

sic 6211 - Security Brokers & Dealers

naics 523999 - Miscellaneous Financial Investment
    Activities

on the 110-story Sears Tower in Chicago. Three years later the tower, housing the Sears headquarters, was completed—at 1,454 feet it was the tallest building in the world. Sears' good fortune did not last long, however, as a recession caused by skyrocketing oil prices led to a $170 million drop in profits for 1974. By 1977 the company was facing strong competition from the K Mart Corporation. Edward Telling took over the next year as chairman, centralizing all buying and merchandising operations. As a result of restructuring, the retail business was renamed the Sears Merchandising Group, and the insurance business was renamed Allstate Insurance Group. In an effort to increase sales outside of its faltering retail operations, Sears acquired Los Angeles-based Coldwell Banker Co., the largest real estate brokerage in the U.S., and securities from Dean Witter Reynolds, Inc. in late 1981.

In 1982 Sears introduced the Financial Network Centers in its stores. Three years later, under the leadership of Edward Brennan, the company introduced the Discover Card, a combined credit and financial services card that also offered savings accounts through the Greenwood Trust Co.. In 1986 Sears vowed to refocus on its retail efforts, as the catalog and direct mail division were losing up to $100 million

The Officers

Morgan Stanley Dean Witter & Co.

Chairman and CEO: Philip J. Purcell

President and Chief Operating Officer: John J. Mack

Exec. VP, Chief Strategic and Administrative Officer: John H. Schaefer

Exec. VP and Chief Financial Officer: Robert G. Scott

Controller and Principal Accounting Officer: Eileen K. Murray

Sears, Roebuck & Co.

Chairman and CEO: Arthur C. Martinez

Exec. VP and Chief Financial Officer: Julian Day

Exec. VP, Marketing: Mark A. Cohen

Exec. VP, Logistics: William G. Pagonis

Exec. VP, Secretary, and General Counsel: Anastasia Kelly

Sr. VP and Chief Information Officer: Gerald N. Miller

per year. One year later The Merchandise Group launched a new strategy to turn Sears into a collection of specialty superstores. Sears acquired Eye Care Centers of America and Pinstripes Petites. In 1988 the company acquired Western Auto Supply and its chain of 405 stores. Brennan announced a new, "everyday low price" retail strategy, reducing the number of sales and promotions.

Sears was faced with problems in the early 1990s. The company purchased a savings and loan enterprise in order to begin issuing VISA cards, a move that Visa USA challenged in court. Brennan took control of operations, carrying out several cost-cutting measures including the elimination of over 43,000 jobs. In 1992 Sears Auto Centers in California was accused of over-billing customers, and the next year the company announced that it was discontinuing its mail-order catalog. The company also spun off its Dean Witter and Discover units. Two years later shareholders over-whelmingly defeated a proposal calling for Sears to spin off its 80% interest in the Allstate Corporation insurance unit.

In an effort to boost home furnishings sales, Sears combined its furniture and electronics departments to form Sears HomeLife Furniture and Brand Central. Arthur C. Martinez became the new CEO of the company and divided Home Group back into two units. Pier 1 Imports began selling its products in Sears' Puerto Rico stores, and Sears sold Homart Development Corporation to General Growth Properties. The company also sold the famed Sears Tower to AEW Partners LP in 1995.

Continuing problems spread through the company. Its venture with IBM failed, forcing the two to sell Prodigy, their online information service, to International Wireless for $250 million. Sears also sold its 80% share in the Allstate Insurance Co. It continued to divest portions of itself in an attempt to regain control of its finances. In the latter half of 1998, several top executives left the company as Sears focused its efforts on restructuring its automotive operations as well as its marketing plans.

History of Dean Witter Reynolds

Dean Witter & Co. was founded in San Francisco by Dean Witter, his brother Guy, and his cousin Jean in 1924. The trio started the business as a West Coast securities firm dealing in municipal and corporate bonds. In 1928 the company purchased a seat on the San Francisco Stock Exchange, which was later incorporated into the Pacific Stock Exchange. One year later it opened a New York office and purchased a seat on the New York Stock Exchange as well.

In 1931 Richard S. Reynolds, Jr., Thomas F. Stanley, and Charles H. Babcock, all members of the Reynolds family, launched Reynolds & Co., a securities brokerage business. Dean Witter continued to post yearly profits despite the Depression-era securities industry shakeout in 1939. The company fared well in the 1950s and 60s. In 1970, one year after Dean Witter died, Guy Witter retired and William M. Witter, Jean Witter's son, became CEO. Two years later Dean Witter went public with an offering of 1.5 million shares on the New York Stock Exchange.

The latter half of the 1970s were strong years for the company, as it purchased InterCapital Inc., an investment management firm with $200 million in assets. In 1978, in the largest merger in the history of the U.S. securities industry, Dean Witter & Co. joined with Reynolds & Co. to form Dean Witter Reynolds, the fifth-largest broker in the U.S.

In 1981 Sears, Roebuck & Co., the largest retailer in the world, purchased Dean Witter Reynolds for $607 million. Philip J. Purcell, a strategic planner at the Sears Chicago headquarters, was chosen to head Dean Witter. Sears began using its retail store network to open new Dean Witter offices in areas of the country where Dean Witter was nonexistent or poorly represented. Sears also decided that Dean Witter was to make a major shift in corporate strategy by focusing exclusively on individual investors. The theory was that Sears would create a sort of financial services supermarket aimed at the broad middle consumer market.

By 1986 Sears' financial services operations, which included Dean Witter, posted profits of $80 million. Sears invested $200 million to launch the Discover credit card as a division of Dean Witter. Unlike competitors Visa and MasterCard, the Discover card was free and offered cashback bonuses and interest-free cash advances. By 1987, however, Dean Witter's rank in the corporate debt and equity underwriting market slipped from tenth to 15th, and investment banking accounted for less than 10% of its revenues. The Discover card's poor performance contributed to the Sears financial group's loss of $37 million on sales of $3.5 billion.

After early losses and an initially lukewarm reception by retailers, the Discover card boasted more than 22 million subscribers and was accepted at 740,000 merchant outlets in 1988. One year later, Sears announced plans to close 200 of Dean Witter's 650 outlets, primarily those located in department stores. Dean Witter was barely profitable, despite having doubled in size since 1981.

In the early 1990s, Dean Witter staged a major comeback, posting profits of $109 million. By 1991 Discover was the largest single issuer of general purpose credit cards, generating earnings of $174 million from a total of 40 million cards. Net income from Dean Witter and its Discover division rose to $171 million and $173 million, respectively, and combined sales soared to a record $3.35 billion. In keeping with its emphasis on mutual funds, Dean Witter introduced a new family of proprietary funds (funds managed in-house). Its total net income surpassed $400 million on revenues of $3.7 billion, and its mutual funds assets increased to over $50 billion.

Suffering under a $38 billion debt load, Sears decided to sell its financial services operations. In 1993 Dean Witter, Discover & Co. was formed when Sears spun off the financial services operation as an independent, publicly traded company. During its first year of operation, its revenues rose more than 20% to $4.6 billion as net income reached $600 million. Now the largest credit card issuer in the U.S., the company introduced a new credit card, Prime Option in 1994. In February of 1996 the new company entered into an agreement to provide investment, product, and sales support services to Banc One Corp. One year later Dean Witter merged with Morgan Stanley Group Inc.

The new company, Morgan Stanley Dean Witter & Co., began immediate restructuring, paring down its operations and focusing on high profit margin units. The company remained focused on entering the European market with the purchase of Spain's largest brokerage firm, AB Asesores, in 1999.

The Players

Chairman and CEO of Sears, Roebuck & Co.: Edward R. Telling. Telling began his career with Sears in 1946. He worked his way through the ranks and was elected chairman and CEO in 1978. Credited with diversifying and restructuring the world's largest retailer, Telling also served as a director of Cox Communications Inc. and Dean Witter Intercapital Funds. He retired from Sears in 1986.

Vice Chairman of Dean Witter Reynolds: Robert M. Gardiner. Princeton graduate Robert Gardiner was named vice chairman and chief operating officer of Dean Witter after it merged with Reynolds Securities in 1978. Upon completion of Sears' purchase of the company, Gardiner was named chairman and CEO of Dean Witter Financial Services Group. He retired in 1986 after a prominent run in the security interest field. He was also served as a director and vice chairman for the New York Stock Exchange; as governor, director, and first chairman of the Securities Industry Association; and as president and chairman for the National Association of Securities Dealers.

Market Forces Driving the Merger

Major mergers in the financial industry were sparking interest among those wanting to create large financial institutions that they could call their own. Prudential Insurance Co., the largest insurance company in the nation, purchased Bache Group Inc., the sixth-largest brokerage firm in the nation. American Express Co. joined forces with Shearson Loeb Rhoades, the second-largest broker in the U.S., and Phibro Corporation, a commodities trading company, bought out Salomon Brothers.

Sears held such a dominant position in merchandising that its future growth would be slim, according to analysts. This forced the company to look at other methods of achieving growth and diversity. In May of 1981 Sears decided that it wanted to enter the financial services industry. According to the *Washington Post*, Sears' Chairman Edward Telling declared that "The world's largest retailer is determined to become the nation's largest consumer-oriented financial service entity."

Dean Witter had come into financial trouble and needed capital. It was attracted to a deal with Sears because of the retailer's huge customer base, its 25 million cardholders, and the potential for sharing information with Allstate and Coldwell, Banker & Co. Combined with Dean Witter, these latter two assets could form the largest financial force in the industry.

Approach and Engagement

In October of 1981 Sears announced plans to purchase Dean Witter for $607 million. Gaining the support of both boards, the tender offer consisted of a purchase of up to 5,463,213 of Dean Witter's outstanding shares of common stock at $50 a share. The deal, orchestrated in the same time frame as Sears' purchase of Coldwell, Banker & Co., would launch the retail giant into financial services. The merger was completed soon after shareholders approved the deal in December of 1981.

Products and Services

According to a popular company slogan, "You can always find it at Sears." After Sears finalized the deal with Dean Witter and purchased Coldwell, Banker & Co., the company was positioned to be a leading provider of financial services. In an article in the *Financial Times (London)*, Philip Purcell, president of Dean Witter, stated "Just imagine, with the virtual one-stop shopping a customer could find and buy a house—through Sears—finance and insure it—with Sears—arrange for the sale of the old house and move to the new one—through Sears—furnish, decorate it, fill it with well-serviced appliances—from Sears—and later he or she could obtain a second mortgage to remodel the kitchen or build an addition, purchase insurance to cover the second mortgages, and then buy the paint, tools, and cabinets for that home improvement—all from Sears."

After the deal, Sears opened eight "financial supermarkets" in Virginia, Atlanta, Dallas, Houston, Chicago, Denver, Los Angeles, and San Francisco in its stores. The Sears Financial Networks bought and sold homes, stocks, bonds, and money market funds, and opened IRAs and wrote insurance for cars and homes.

In 1988 Sears focused on its retail operation once again. Merchandise sales and services accounted for 89% of total sales with credit accounting for 11%. Selling popular brands such as Craftsman, DieHard, Kenmore, Canyon River Blues, and Fieldmaster, Sears operated over 850 department stores. The company also had specialty stores NTB National Tire & Battery and Sears Hardware.

Morgan Stanley Dean Witter had over 450 offices in the U.S. and 30 overseas. The company offered service in mergers and acquisitions, insurance, brokerage, asset management, consumer credit, home equity loans, and mutual funds.

Changes to the Industry

There was increased pressure in the early- to mid-1980s for retailers to jump into the financial services ring. Following Sears' acquisition of Dean Witter and a series of mergers in the financial industry, J.C. Penney Co. joined forces with First National Savings to offer financial services to its credit card customers. The Kroger Co. also began offering services in its supermarkets. The growing trend was that consumers did not have to go to "banks" to take care of their financial needs.

Increased costs in advancing computer technology for financial communication and growing competition in the industry caused many companies to merge. Only companies who offered a full range of services felt assured that they could remain competitive in the future. According to an article in *The New York Times*, "the trend toward financial conglomeration is real and is likely to continue for the foreseeable future."

Review of the Outcome

Deadset on leading the financial industry, Sears launched the Sears Financial Network in 1982. It was faced with the challenge of sparking interest in its financial services to its customers. Many analysts in the industry were skeptical about Sears' plan to meld financial services into a retail shopping experience. While Sears' retail operations were experiencing large gains, a 28.5% increase in net income in the third quarter of 1982, its financial services were faltering. Dean Witter lost $4.1 million in July of 1982.

In 1983, Sears dissolved its Allstate Financial Corporation into the Dean Witter Financial Services Group, transferring its $720 million consumer auto and home improvement loan operations. Although net income was up 89% in the first nine months of 1983, Dean Witter's brokerage net was disappointing due to lower volume in the securities market. In 1989, however, the Discover Card was doing remarkably well and became a business unit of Dean Witter Financial Services.

Sears opted to introduce Dean Witter Financial Services as an independent, publicly owned company, re-named Dean Witter, Discover & Co., in 1992. The next year Sears sold 20% of its equity in DWD to the public and spun off the remaining shares to Sears shareholders. Unable to find the right mix between retail and finance, Sears would benefit more from the sale, rather than the retention, of its financial services. Sears began to refocus its efforts on merchandising when its venture in financial services came to a close in 1993. According to Sears' 1993 annual report, the decision was based on "harvesting the value of the financial-services businesses" while at the same time putting an emphasis on "key skills in merchandising."

In 1997 Dean Witter, Discover & Co. merged with Morgan Stanley. One year later its name was changed to Morgan Stanley Dean Witter & Co. The company had over 45,000 employees and net income of over $3,275 million. Its stock closed at 69.63, up from 54.31 the year before.

Research

Barmash, Isadore. "Sears Profit Grows 73% on Gains in Retailing," in *The New York Times*, 25 October 1983. Discusses Sears gains in the third quarter of 1983 and nine month results for the year.

Bennett, Robert A. "A Bank, By Any Other Name," in *The New York Times*, 27 December 1981. Comments on recent trends in the retail and financial industries and offers a look current mergers and purchases of large financial companies.

Betts, Paul. "A Keen Watch on Sears Roebuck Developments," in *Financial Times London*, 8 December 1982. Explains Dean Witter's and Sears' perspective on what the future will hold for the company with its expanded financial services.

"Dean Witter, Discover & Co.," in *Notable Corporate Chronologies*, The Gale Group, 1999. Lists major events in the history of Dean Witter, Discover & Co.

Knight, Jerry. "Sears is Planning Super Credit Card for Transactions," in *The Washington Post*, 26 February 1982. Explains Telling's outlook for Sears' future.

Lascelles, David. "Retail Side Boosts Sears by 22%," in *Financial Times London*, 29 July 1982. Reports second quarter results for Sears in 1982.

Morgan Stanley Dean Witter & Co. Home Page, available at http://www.msdw.com. Official World Wide Web Home Page for Morgan Stanley Dean Witter & Co. Includes current and archived news; detailed financial, product, and historical information; and annual reports.

Rowe, James L. "Sears is Building a Tower to Carry out New Strategy," in *The Washington Post*, 11 October 1981. Discusses Sears' quest to become a leader in the financial services industry.

———. "Sears Make Bid to Buy Dean Witter Reynolds," in *The Washington Post*, 9 October 1981. Explains the acquisition of Dean Witter by Sears.

Sears Roebuck & Co. Home Page, available at http://www.sears.com. Official World Wide Web Home Page for Sears Roebuck & Co. Includes current and archived news; detailed financial, product, and historical information; and annual reports.

"Sears Roebuck & Co.," in *Notable Corporate Chronologies*, The Gale Group, 1999. Lists major events in the history of Sears Roebuck & Co.

Wiggins, Phillip H. "Penney and Thrift Unit Plan Financial Services," in *The New York Times*, 7 December 1982. Discusses recent trends for retailers to dive into the financial services industry.

CHRISTINA M. STANSELL

SERVICE CORPORATION INTERNATIONAL &
THE LOEWEN GROUP

Service Corporation International
1929 Allen Pkwy.
PO Box 130548
Houston, TX 77219-0548
USA

tel: (713)522-5141
fax: (713)525-5308
web: http://www.sci-corp.com
e-mail: sciinfo@sci-corp.com

The Loewen Group Inc.
4126 Norland Ave.
Burnaby, BC V5G 3S8
Canada

tel: (604)299-9321
web: http://www.loewengroup.com

date: January 7, 1997 (canceled)
affected: Service Corporation International, USA, founded 1962
affected: The Loewen Group Inc., Canada, founded 1985

Overview of the Acquisition

The North American funeral services industry was rocked with the hostile bid of Service Corporation International (SCI), the leader, for its closest rival, The Loewen Group. The acquisition was never consummated, however, as Loewen resisted the takeover with a number of defensive tactics. In early 1997, four months after launching it, SCI withdrew its bid, claiming that Loewen's tactics made the company less attractive as an acquisition candidate. The funeral services industry later experienced a slump, and both companies were adversely affected. In early 1999 Loewen announced that it would consider takeover bids, but by that time SCI was no longer interested.

History of Service Corporation International

Inspired by McDonald's revolution of the food industry, Robert Waltrip began to transform his single, family-owned Houston funeral home, the Heights Undertaking Co., into a chain of funeral homes. Believing that shared facilities, vehicles, equipment, and personnel was the key to increased efficiency and lower overhead costs, Waltrip founded Southern Capital Co. in July 1962 to facilitate acquisitions. It maintained community loyalty by retaining the individual styles of its acquisitions rather than redesigning them to fit some corporate mold.

In 1968 it purchased Chicago-based Drake and Son, Inc., its first acquisition outside of Texas. The company expanded internationally the following year by acquiring Clark Leatherdale Ltd. of Winnipeg, Canada. It changed its name to Service Corporation International (SCI) to reflect its expansion. To secure the capital to support further expansion, SCI went public, first on the American Stock Exchange in 1970 and then on the New York Stock Exchange in 1974. SCI acquired Kinney Services, a 26-funeral home business operating in three states, in 1971.

During the mid-1970s, the company experienced trouble with the Federal Trade Commission (FTC). In 1975 this agency ordered SCI to refund patrons the company had overcharged for flowers, cremation, obituary notices, and similar services between 1971 and 1975; reimbursement costs ranged $135,000-$175,000 per customer. The following year the FTC filed a new complaint that included such allegations as charging cremation customers for caskets, paying medical examiners to help generate business, paying hospital employees or police to inform the company when deaths occurred, failing to share volume discounts and other rebates with customers, and misinforming customers about casket sealing devices. The FTC later dropped those charges, but informed local law officials of the allegations.

In 1977 SCI introduced a "pre-need" funeral services program, in which customers paid current prices for their future funeral services. In 1981 the company acquired International Funeral Industries Inc., the industry's second-largest company, with 91 funeral homes and 22 cemeteries in the U.S. and Canada. SCI embarked on a diversification program in 1982, opening a quick-service floral chain to sell flowers in 15 funeral homes and at 15 independent stores. Four years later it acquired Amedco, the nation's second-largest maker of caskets and a leading supplier of embalming fluids, burial clothing, and mortuary furniture. It established the Provident Services, Inc. subsidiary to provide capital financing to independent funeral homes and cemeteries.

In 1989, based on meager earnings that year, the company refocused on its two core businesses, funeral homes and cemeteries, and announced plans to expand internationally. The following year it sold Amedco and divested its two insurance businesses. It established Equity Corporation International (ECI) in 1991 to hold about 70 of its rural funeral homes; SCI sold its 40% stake in ECI in 1996, only to buy back the entire company in 1999.

SCI expanded outside of North America in 1993 by acquiring Australian-based Pine Grove Funeral Group. Its acquisition of Melbourne-based Le Pine Holdings Proprietary Ltd. the following year led to the formation of the SCI-Australia subsidiary.

In 1994 it expanded into Europe by purchasing the United Kingdom's two largest publicly traded funeral service providers, Great Southern Group plc and Plantsbrook Group plc. With those companies' 534 funeral homes and 13 crematoria, SCI captured a 15% share of the British market. In July 1995 it acquired two divisions of the French conglomerate Lyonnaise des Eaux, which included Pompes Funebres Generales, the leading funeral service organization in Europe. This purchase provided 950 funeral homes in France, as well as properties in Switzerland, Italy, Belgium, the Czech Republic, and Singapore.

History of The Loewen Group Inc.

Raymond Loewen inherited his father's Manitoba funeral home, which had opened its doors

The Business

Financials - Service Corporation International

Revenue (1998): $2.9 billion

Employees (1998): 27,618

Financials - The Loewen Group Inc.

Revenue (1998): $1.14 billion

Employees (1998): 16,700

SICs / NAICS

sic 7261 - Funeral Services & Crematories

sic 6311 - Life Insurance

sic 6553 - Cemetery Subdividers & Developers

sic 6141 - Personal Credit Institutions

naics 812210 - Funeral Homes and Funeral Services

naics 812220 - Cemeteries and Crematories

naics 524113 - Direct Life Insurance Carriers

naics 522291 - Consumer Lending

in 1961. During that decade, Ray attempted to persuade other funeral home operators to join him in establishing a national chain. As the holder of a degree in theology, not business, he was unaware of compelling arguments related to economies of scale, and was therefore unable to be very persuasive.

Discouraged, Ray and his family moved to British Columbia, where he acquired several funeral homes. In 1975 he abruptly left the business to pursue a political career, and won a seat on the provincial legislature. In 1979 he abandoned that profession as well, and turned to real estate. His timing proved unfortunate, as the market entered a slump in the early 1980s. It was then that he returned to the funeral business.

Ray's dream of building a chain of funeral homes was facilitated, ironically, by Service Corporation International (SCI), its future archenemy. When SCI moved into Canada to add to its own chain of funeral services operations, previously resistant funeral directors began to consider selling their operations. Loewen revived acquisition overtures and exploited the patriotism of the independents, as many proved more willing to be bought by a Canadian than an American company.

The Loewen Group was incorporated in October 1985, and in two years had acquired 45 funeral homes in western Canada. Ray had also learned the meaning

The Officers

Service Corporation International

Chairman, CEO, Interim President, and Chief Operating Officer: Robert L. Waltrip

Sr. Exec. VP: Jerald L. Pullins

Exec. VP, Operations: W. Blair Waltrip

Exec. VP, Special Services: John W. Morrow, Jr.

Chief Financial Officer: George R. Champagne

President, Provident Services, Inc.: Henry M. Nelly III

The Loewen Group Inc.

Chairman: John S. Lacey

President and CEO: Robert B. Lundgren

Chairman, Loewen Group International, Inc.: Timothy R. Hogenkamp

Chief Operating Officer and Exec. VP, Operations: Paul Wagler

Exec. VP, Administration, Accounting and Control and Chief Administrative Office: Michael G. Weedon

of economies of scale, and had centralized the firm's purchase of such items as embalming fluid, coffins, and advertising.

Revenues in 1987 reached $14 million. Ray wanted to expand more quickly than its earning of $786,000 would support, however. So he took the company public that year, earning $4.6 million to further acquisitions. He also introduced the concept of budgets to the operators, who were usually the previous owners of the funeral homes. Loewen's post-acquisition policy was to retain a funeral home's name and management, as well as provide funeral directors with stock options.

The company continued its acquisition spree in the early 1990s. By September 1995 it owned 764 funeral homes and 172 cemeteries, up from 98 and five, respectively, at the end of 1987. One of those acquisition deals went sour, however, and nearly broke the company. When Loewen backed out of an agreement to purchase two Mississippi funeral homes owned by Jerry O'Keefe, former mayor of Biloxi, it was sued for fraud and antitrust violations. The jury awarded O'Keefe $500 million in damages. When Loewen revealed that it might be forced to seek bankruptcy protection to pay that charge, the parties reached an out-of-court settlement for $175 million.

Although Loewen's stock plummeted from $41 to $8 per share during the litigation, it continued its acquisition efforts. In 1995 and 1996, it purchased several companies, including Osiris Holding Co., MHI Group, Inc., Shipper Group, and Ourso Investment Corp., adding a total of 32 funeral homes and 35 cemeteries from those deals.

Market Forces Driving the Acquisition

By mid-1996, the U.S. funeral services industry was in the midst of a consolidation. Even though about 85% of the industry's 22,000 funeral homes were independently owned, several large corporations were gobbling them up in increasing numbers. Cemeteries and funeral services operations were also prime targets for these companies, which aimed to realize savings by combining such assets as hearses and embalming facilities to serve a number of their properties.

Two such acquirers were Service Corporation International (SCI) and The Loewen Group, the industry's first- and second-ranked companies, respectively. Both had been engaged in a campaign of growth through acquisition. By the end of 1995, SCI owned 2,832 funeral homes, 331 cemeteries, and 146 crematoria in North America, Europe, and Australia, and drew sales of $1.6 billion. Loewen owned a fraction of those assets, 923 funeral homes and 263 cemeteries in North America and Puerto Rico, and generated revenues of $600 million. Stewart Enterprises was a distant third, with 211 funeral homes, 114 cemeteries, and $320 million in sales.

Not only were SCI and Loewen in competition with each other, their chairmen were also unamicable. Different business styles contributed to their rivalry. Loewen had a reputation as a nice-guy owner, typically retaining existing management at the properties it acquired. "Money is not the only motivation in life," said president and founder Ray Loewen in *Maclean's*. "We are not a slash-and-burn company." SCI, on the other hand, substituted its own corporate management at newly acquired properties. The company was also open about its aggressive pursuit of target companies. "We'd like to try to negotiate something that's a good deal for everybody," said president William Heiligbrodt in that same *Maclean's* article. "But we also have a tradition of doing hostile deals."

In September 1996 SCI demonstrated that posture in its quest for Loewen. To SCI, Loewen appeared ripe for a takeover. In November 1995, that company had lost a breach of contract suit filed by a Mississippi funeral home owner, and was ordered to pay $500 million. Although that amount was later reduced to $175 million, the negative publicity associated with the settlement caused Loewen's stock value to plummet, making it attractive to SCI.

Approach and Engagement

On September 17, 1996, Loewen's board was in the midst of a meeting regarding its proposed acquisition of Rose Hills Memorial Park. Those discussions came to a halt when a news report interrupted them, announcing SCI's takeover bid for Loewen. This news report included the text of a letter that SCI had sent to Loewen and to the press simultaneously. SCI's deal presented a swap stock valued at $43 per share, or $2.8 billion. That price, the letter pointed out, represented a 48.9% premium over Loewen's stock price 30 days earlier, or 27.4% over its current trading value.

On October 24 Loewen's board unanimously rejected SCI's offer. Loewen believed that it had successfully emerged from the Mississippi crisis and that its stock price would soon rebound. It had also recently gained acquisition momentum, completing the purchase of the funeral services company Prime Succession Inc., as well as Rose Hills, the second-largest cemetery in the U.S. Loewen aimed to continue this aggressive acquisition streak, thereby hoping to convince shareholders that greater growth could be achieved through current management than through SCI.

Swaying its shareholders was vital in fending off SCI. Under British Columbian rules, a suitor could take control of Loewen upon the acquisition of 75% of its stock. Since Raymond Loewen held a 15% interest, a takeover through that route was unlikely but not impossible. To increase its defenses, therefore, Loewen implemented a poison pill and staggered the terms of its directors. It also enhanced employee severance packages and executive golden parachutes, which would add an expense of about $30 million to SCI in the event of a takeover.

On September 28 the state of Florida launched an antitrust probe into the deal, since it proposed to put 25% of the state's funeral homes under SCI ownership. Regardless of whether or not Loewen actually encouraged such an investigation, as SCI suspected, it certainly was eager to cooperate with the regulators. Similar inquiries by 11 other states and the Federal Trade Commission were also embraced by Loewen as a means of discouraging SCI.

SCI upped its offer to $45 per share in stock on October 2, 1996. It also added that it would be willing to sweeten that $2.9 billion bid if Loewen voluntarily gave SCI 90% of its stock. Loewen again rejected the offer, and the two companies took their case to the courts. Loewen filed an antitrust suit against SCI,

The Players

Service Corporation International Chairman and CEO: Robert L. Waltrip. When his father died in 1953, Robert Waltrip forfeited a college athletic scholarship and took over the family's funeral home business. He envisioned the concept of a chain of funeral homes and services, and in 1962 founded the company that would become known as Service Corporation International. Under Waltrip's leadership, the firm expanded nationally and internationally, pursuing acquisition quarry aggressively, sometimes even ruthlessly. In under three decades, Waltrip had built his company into the world's leading funeral services provider.

The Loewen Group President, CEO, and Co-Chairman: Raymond Loewen. Like his nemesis, Robert Waltrip, Raymond Loewen entered the business by inheriting the family's funeral home. Loewen, a theology graduate, had no intention of entering that line of work, but when his father's health failed him, Loewen took control of the Manitoba funeral home. After growing discouraged at his failure to persuade other funeral home owners to join him in establishing a chain, he threw his hat in the political ring and served on British Columbia's legislature. He returned to the funeral services industry, and soon created North America's second-largest operator in that industry. His company experienced serious financial difficulties in 1998, and Loewen resigned, breaking all ties with the company by selling his 14% stake.

maintaining that SCI intended to eliminate competition by acquiring its closest rival. SCI filed a countersuit, holding that Loewen had no basis for trying to block the takeover on antitrust grounds.

The matter rested there until January 7, 1997, when SCI withdrew its bid. In a company press release, Waltrip stated, "The cumulative effect of actions taken by Loewen since our offer was announced, and the disclosure of details related to certain of Loewen's other transactions, have adversely impacted SCI's view of Loewen's value to SCI shareholders."

Products and Services

Two of companies' three main lines of business in 1998 were identical. In the Funerals segment, SCI's

1998 revenues reached $1.8 billion, while Loewen's totaled $631.2 million. In the Cemetery business, SCI's sales were $846.6 million; Loewen's sales were $408.5 million. The third primary business, however, differed. SCI's Financial Services operations provided loans to independent funeral home operators through its Provident Services subsidiary; revenues in this segment reached $199.3 million in 1998. Loewen's third area of operation was Insurance, which sold industrial life and ordinary life insurance policies, generating sales of $96.5 million in 1998.

Review of the Outcome

Both companies resumed expansion activity in the immediate aftermath of the takeover attempt. In 1997 alone, SCI acquired 294 funeral homes, 51 cemeteries, and 19 crematoria. In September 1998 it purchased the pre-need funeral division of American Annuity Group Inc. for $164 million. In January 1999 it absorbed its Equity Corporation International subsidiary, increasing its portfolio to about 3,700 funeral locations and 500 cemeteries in 18 countries. Although SCI's overall 1998 net income rose to $342 million on revenues that climbed 13.4% to $2.9 billion, the company's fourth-quarter net income dropped 35.6%. As a result of this poor performance, attributed by the company to declining death rates, its president and chief operating officer William Heiligbrodt resigned in February 1999.

Loewen's performance was even dimmer than SCI's in the years following the attempted takeover. Like SCI, Loewen started out strong, acquiring 138 funeral homes and 171 cemeteries in 1997. In October 1998, as the company hit the same market slump that had affected SCI, Ray Loewen resigned. He sold his 14% stake in his company for only $9 per share, far lower than the price that SCI had offered only two years earlier. Loewen was succeeded as president, CEO, and co-chairman by Robert Lundgren.

Loewen's revenues inched up 2.1% to $1.1 billion in 1998. Its net income, however, indicated severe financial difficulties, as the profit of $41.8 million that the company had posted in 1997 became a loss of $599 million in 1998. This figure included a loss of $334 million from continuing operations and a charge of $315.2 million for the writedown of portions of its Prime Succession and Rose Hills acquisitions. In January 1999 Loewen announced that it would entertain takeover bids, either for the company as a whole or in pieces; SCI stated that it was no longer interested in an acquisition. Later that month, John Lacey was appointed chairman. In March it sold off 22%, or 124, of its cemetery properties to the McDown De Leeuw & Co. buyout group for $193 million in cash.

Research

"Dust Up in 'Death Services'," in *Business Week*, 7 October 1996. Profiles the offer and rejection of the takeover bid.

England, Robert Stowe. "Die Hard: The Loewen Group Snatches Victory from the Jaws of Defeat," in *CFO, The Magazine for Senior Financial Executives*, March 1997. Describes Loewen's successful evasion of the takeover.

"The Loewen Group, Inc.," in *International Directory of Company Histories*, Vol. 16, St. James Press: 1997. Provides a historical review of the company.

The Loewen Group Inc. 1997 Annual Report. Covers financial highlights and describes company operating segments.

The Loewen Group Inc. Home Page, available at http://www.loewengroup.com. Official World Wide Web Page for The Loewen Group. Includes financial information, executive biographies, press releases, and product and services information.

"Loewen Spurns a $3-Billion Hostile Bid," in *Maclean's*, 30 September 1996. Offers statements from SCI and Loewen in reflection of their different business styles.

Schreiner, John. "Ray Loewen Busts His Ghost," in *The Financial Post*, 11 January 1997. Provides an overview of the merger after its termination.

"Service Corp. Ends Takeover Offer for Loewen Group," in *The Wall Street Journal*, 8 January 1997. SCI withdraws its bid after Loewen's defensive tactics prove overwhelming.

"Service Corporation International," in *Notable Corporate Chronologies*, The Gale Group, 1999. Profiles the history of the company, including its bid for Loewen.

Service Corporation International 1997 Annual Report. Presents detailed financial and operating information.

Service Corporation International Home Page, available at http://www.sci-corp.com. Official World Wide Web Page for Service Corp. Includes a company history, financial information, press releases, and product and services information.

"Service Corp. Seeks Loewen in $2.8 Billion Stock Deal," in *The Wall Street Journal*, 18 September 1996. Reports SCI's hostile takeover bid.

—PATRICIA ARCHILLA

SHELL OIL & BELRIDGE OIL

nationality: USA
date: September 1979
affected: Shell Oil Co., USA, founded 1915
affected: Belridge Oil Co., USA, founded 1911

Shell Oil Co.
One Shell Plaza
Houston, TX 77002
USA

tel: (713)241-6161
fax: (713)241-4044
web: http://www.countonshell.com

Overview of the Merger

In September of 1979, Shell Oil Co. won the rights to purchase Belridge Oil, beating out rival suitors Mobil and Texaco. Its bid of $3.6 billion topped other offers by $500 million and was the largest acquisition to date in corporate America. The deal marked the beginning of a revolution in the oil industry and lit the flame under other mega-mergers in 1980s.

History of Shell Oil Co.

In order to take advantage of the increased interest in automobiles in the U.S., Royal Dutch/Shell began to sell gasoline that was imported from Sumatra in 1912. The group formed the American Gasoline Company and Roxana Petroleum Company, and opened refineries in Louisiana and Illinois. Royal Dutch then set its eyes on California Oilfields, Ltd. This company was attractive because of its ownership of gasoline in the U.S. The group acquired the company in 1913, alleviating the need to import gasoline. American gasoline changed its name to Shell Company of California in 1915, and opened its first gas station.

In 1922 Roxana Petroleum and Shell Company of California merged with Union Oil Company of Delaware and formed a holding company. The new entity, Shell Union Oil Corporation, had 65% of its shares owned by the Royal Dutch/Shell Group. In 1927, the Shell Pipe Line Corporation was established with the acquisition of Ozark Pipe Line Corporation for the purpose of overseeing the transport of oil from Texas to its Wood River refinery. A new refinery in Houston also emerged, supplying products to the East Coast and overseas. In 1929 Shell Petroleum Corporation bought the New Orleans Refining Company.

Shell began the 1930s committed to research and development. The creation of Shell Development Company brought about research in petrochemicals, which led the Shell Chemical Company to begin manufacturing operations. Shell gasoline was now being sold throughout the United States and the company fared well in the unsettling economy that faced the industry. Shell opened two more plants dedicated to chemical research and the manufacturing of synthetic ammonia and synthetic glycerin.

The Business

Financials

Revenue (1998): $15,451 million

Employees (1998): 19,800

SICs / NAICS

sic 2911 - Petroleum Refining

sic 2999 - Petroleum & Coal Products Nec

sic 1311 - Crude Petroleum & Natural Gas

sic 1321 - Natural Gas Liquids

sic 1382 - Oil & Gas Exploration Services

sic 2810 - Industrial Inorganic Chemicals

sic 2820 - Plastics Materials & Synthetics

sic 2870 - Agricultural Chemicals

sic 1099 - Metal Ores Nec

sic 3334 - Primary Aluminum

sic 1200 - Coal Mining

naics 324199 - All Other Petroleum and Coal Products Manufacturing

naics 211111 - Crude Petroleum and Natural Gas Extraction

naics 211112 - Natural Gas Liquid Extraction

naics 213112 - Support Activities for Oil and Gas Field Operations

naics 212299 - Other Metal Ore Mining

naics 331312 - Primary Aluminum Production

Continuing with its development efforts, Shell gained the skills to synthesize 100-octane fuel and became the leading supplier of aviation fuel. With the onset of World War II, the company helped the U.S. government by sharing its technology with others in the industry; it also supplied butadiene, a chemical necessary to make synthetic rubber. Shell Oil Company of California eventually merged with Shell Petroleum Corporation, forming the Shell Oil Company, Inc. With offices in San Francisco, St. Louis, and New York City, the company was able to meet the increasing needs of the public and to continue developing new products. Emerging new developments in epoxy resins, ethylene, synthetic rubber, detergent alcohol, and other chemicals enabled the company to become a leader in the industry.

Shell Oil Company also effectively introduced new fuel products, such as jet fuel and high octane, unleaded gasoline for automobiles. By 1958, the com-

pany redesigned its gas stations in an effort to gain control of the market. This ranch-style station became its leading retail outlet, and in 1971, the self-service station was introduced. By becoming user-friendly, accepting competitors' credit cards, and introducing travel and entertainment cards, Shell was able to realize its goal to gain a large share of the market.

Shell kicked off the 1960s by becoming a company concerned with environmental issues. Major investments in pollution reduction and energy conservation were made. The company published books on car maintenance and energy conservation. Shell also turned its efforts to offshore drilling of oil and natural gas, focusing on Alaska and the Gulf of Mexico. Its enhanced and expert techniques led to one of its biggest strikes, at the Bullwinkle prospect in the Gulf of Mexico. The discovery was expected to lead to over 100 million barrels of oil.

Shell Oil delved into the coal production industry, and in 1974 formed the Shell Mining Company. Two years later, John F. Bookout was named president of the company. The industry began to see hard times with high prices and little increase in demand. Bookout led the company through a phase of increased efficiency, and it began re-evaluating its less profitable service stations. In 1979 the company purchased Belridge Oil Company. The new company, Kernridge Oil Company, was able to increase Shell's oil reserves when the rest of the industry was struggling with drilling opportunities.

In 1984, Royal Dutch/Shell Group began efforts to buy the remaining shares of Shell Oil Company. The battle became quite hostile, with quarrels over share price. Royal Dutch eventually offered $60 per share, and the takeover was completed in June of 1985. The next year the company was criticized for Royal Dutch/Shell Group's involvement in South Africa. The protests over alleged unfair treatment of South African workers became widespread when the AFL-CIO, United Mineworkers, National Education Association, and the Free South Africa Movement joined together to boycott the company. Soon, efforts in Berkley and Boston were underway as protestors tried to stop Shell purchases. In 1989, Shell was under additional scrutiny for the cleanup of the Rocky Mountain Arsenal in Colorado, where its pesticide production operation had allegedly dumped carcinogens on the grounds. The cleanup efforts cost upwards of $250 million for the company.

Despite these setbacks, Shell Oil was faring well by the late 1980s. Bookout retired, leaving Frank H. Richardson in charge. He led the company to see increased cash flows and the reduction of long term debt. There were problems with production, however, and the number of barrels produced on a daily basis was decreasing. That number fell to 398,000 per day in 1994, from 531,000 in 1988. Coupled with a recession in the early 1990s, Shell began to experience difficulties. Revenues declined from $24.79 billion in 1990 to $21.09 billion in 1993. In response to the decline, Shell reduced its workforce by more than 7,000 jobs that year.

In the meantime, Shell's engineers were developing an Auger platform used in deep sea drilling in the Gulf of Mexico. In April of 1994, the oil found there produced 55,000 barrels a day. In 1997 Shell partnered with Amoco to form Altura Energy, a research and development venture. The company also sought out relationships with Mobil and Exxon. Shell Oil continued to look to acquisitions and ventures in the late 1990s, positioning itself to remain a leader in the oil industry as well as the number-one gasoline marketer in the United States.

History of Belridge Oil Co.

Belridge Oil Company, founded in 1911 by the Greene, Whittier, and Buck families, began its business in Kern County, California. The company grew to deal in oil, cotton, citrus, almonds, and various crops. Belridge's 20,000 acres of land steadily became a hot commodity, as the little known company became more popular because of its large reserves of heavy crude.

With the original founders owning 55% of the company and Mobil Corp. and Texaco Inc. owning 34%, Belridge became subject to a takeover attempt in the late 1970s. By that time, it was producing over 40,000 barrels of oil a day and had 376 million barrels of reserves. In 1978 the company earned more than $156 million in sales, almost double what it had been making in the past. The founders put the company up for auction after Mobil and Texaco threatened a takeover; Shell Oil Company won with a bid of $3.6 billion in September of 1979. The sale of the reserves in California broke up the family ownership and became a landmark event in the oil industry.

Market Forces Driving the Merger

The mindset of the players in the oil industry at the time leading up to the purchase of Belridge was that they needed to have as much oil as possible for the future and that the discovery of new reserves was vital. With net income largely increasing in the industry, from $11.7 billion in 1972 to $16.4 billion in 1974, the oil giants had money to spend for exploration, diversification, and acquisitions. Shell decided to pursue all three of these options.

The Officers

Chairman and Group Managing Director: Mark Moody-Stuart

President and CEO: Jack E. Little

VP, Corporate Affairs: Susan Borches

VP, Human Resources: B.W. Levan

In 1979 Shell's oil refinery runs were down to 950,000 barrels a day, compared to 1.1 million in the past year. A Shell spokesman was quoted in *The Washington Post* as stating "We're crude poor at the moment; sometimes we run 100,000 barrels a day below capacity." Belridge was attractive to the company for its crude oil reserves as well as its ability to produce well into the next century.

Shell had developed a process by which Belridge's thick oil could be easily extracted. With the use of steam, the reserves could be tapped into and taken advantage of, whereas competing companies had not yet developed a process to accomplish this cost effectively. Shell believed that with Belridge's supply and the company's technology, they could produce more than the 40,000 barrels a day that were currently being produced there.

Approach and Engagement

With Mobil and Texaco owning 34% of Belridge Oil, the two plotted together to buy out the other shareholders. The two companies approached the three families that founded the company individually, in an attempt to negotiate with them to lower the buyout price. The trio staunchly refused, irate over the business tactics used to try to sway them separately.

They decided to put Belridge up for auction, with the oil rich company going to the highest bidder. Shell entered into the fray, and in September of 1979, outbid its opponents by $500 million. Under the terms of the $3.6 billion deal, the largest to date in American business, owners of the 996,800 shares of Belridge would receive either $3,665 in cash per share, or $916 in cash and the rest in an installment note, in exchange for 376 million barrels in oil reserves on 20,000 acres of California land. Mobil and Texaco filed suit in December of that year claiming that Shell planned to liquidate the company in an unfair manner. The companies eventually gave in and sold their interest to Shell.

The Players

President and CEO of Shell Oil Co.: John F. Bookout. University of Texas graduate John F. Bookout began his career in 1950 with Shell Oil Co. as a geologist. He worked in that position for nine years, and then went into management and exploration for the company. Bookout took on several different roles in the 1960s and 1970s, and became president and CEO of Shell Oil in 1976. He remained a strong leader for the company until his retirement in 1988. He went on to serve as a member of the board for McDermott International Inc., an energy service company, until 1997, and was president and CEO of Kelly Oil and Gas Corp. In 1990, he was awarded the "Gold Medal for Distinguished Achievement" by the petroleum trade association. Bookout is credited as a leader in the oil industry for his knowledge and understanding of the world's energy markets.

Executive of Belridge Oil Co.: Joseph Greene. As a member of one of the founding families of Belridge, Joe Greene led the company to double its income in the late 1970s. He played a key role in the auction of the company in 1979, when Shell Oil took over its oil reserves.

Products and Services

After the buyout, Shell was able to produce 53,000 barrels a day from the Belridge property. Total production of oil and condensates were upwards of 165 million barrels in 1980. Its natural gas reserves rose by 85 billion cubic feet to top out at 7.41 trillion cubic feet that same year. Shell's liquid reserves of oil and natural gas liquids had also reached record levels at 2.39 billion barrels by the end of 1980.

Shell Oil continued its operations in the United States, and delved into other countries as well. Brazil, Yemen, China, and Cameroon were included in Shell's ventures. By 1997, the company operated over 9,300 gas stations in 40 states and the District of Columbia, and owned refineries in Texas, Illinois, Alabama, California, and Louisiana. The company focused on oil products, exploration, production, chemicals, and gas, and had more than 40 subsidiaries.

Changes to the Industry

Belridge "set off a bruising competitive atmosphere," wrote Bruce Wasserstein in *Big Deal: The Battle for Control of America's Leading Corporations*. Megamergers were the wave of the future in the 1980s, spawning heated debate among industry officials. Many felt that competition would be reduced, power would be restricted to a few strong companies, and consumers would bear the brunt by having to pay more for each gallon of gas purchased. When Conoco, the world's ninth-largest oil company, became a takeover target in 1981, it reinforced the stage that the Belridge deal had set for the major merger boom of the 1980s. Mobil's purchase of Superior Oil for $5.7 billion, the merging of Standard Oil and Gulf Oil, and Texaco's buyout of Getty Oil, proved that larger companies were looking to buy reserves rather than spend the time and money on exploration. Analysts feared that interest rates would skyrocket and that there would be less and less competition in the industry, as eight giants controlled almost 60% of the market.

Low-priced oil coming from the Persian Gulf also sent chills throughout small oil companies in 1986. Large, strong companies fared well as cash flows diminished, but small companies like Global Marine, Inc. were forced to declare bankruptcy as a result of their debt burdens. This was another opportunity for the strong to get stronger, as companies with substantial cash flows could buy up failing companies cheaply. The industry began to become more concentrated, with fewer competitors in production, refining, and marketing.

Review of the Outcome

"This is going to be a crown jewel for Shell," said Robert LeVine, an analyst with E.F. Hutton & Co., speaking of the company's recent purchase of Belridge Oil. With production rising by eight percent in 1980, that statement held true for Shell. In the second quarter of 1980, its revenues rose by 44% to $4.9 billion, and the company's earnings topped out at $407 million. With Shell's steam technology, production nearly tripled at the Belridge site. Wasserstein wrote, "Mr. Bookout had bought himself a bargain and earned the reputation for being one of the smartest men in the industry."

Decontrol of crude oil prices also helped Shell in 1980. This move benefited domestic oil companies and was credited for increasing Shell's revenue by $204 million in the second quarter of 1980. Shell bagged 56% more in earnings in the first half of 1980 than it did in the previous year's first half. However, the same decontrol was responsible for a 3.2% decline in net profit in the first quarter of 1981, as well as a decrease in demand for petroleum products.

Research

"Belridge Suits," in *The Washington Post,* 13 December 1979. Explains Mobil and Texaco's plans for filing suit against Belridge.

Martin, Douglas. "Shell Slips 3.2%," in *The New York Times,* 28 April 1981. Offers insight to industry trends on decreasing profits.

Parisi, Anthony. "Shell Reports 46.9% Gain," in *The New York Times,* 26 July 1980. Details Shell's second quarter results in 1980.

Rich, Spencer. "Shell to Purchase Calif. Oil Land for $3.65 Billion," in *The Washington Post,* 30 September 1979. Explains the details of Shell's bid for Belridge.

"Shell Buys Belridge Oil," in *The Washington Post,* 17 October 1979. Discusses details of the merger.

Shell Oil Co. Home Page, available at http://www.counton-shell.com. Official World Wide Web Home Page for Shell Oil Co. Includes historical, financial, and product information, as well as recent news articles.

"Shell Oil Company," in *International Directory of Corporate Histories,* Vol. 14, St. James Press, 1996.

"Shell Output up 8% in Year," in *The New York Times,* 31 March 1981. Discusses output at the Belridge property in 1981, as well as output in Shell's other interests.

Wasserstein, Bruce. *Big Deal: The Battle for Control of America's Leading Corporations,* Warner Books, 1998. Offers an overview of the largest mergers in recent American corporate history.

CHRISTINA M. STANSELL

SIEMENS & NIXDORF

Siemens AG
Wittelsbacherplatz 2
Munich, D-80333
Germany

tel: 49 89 636 33032
fax: 49 89 636 32825
web: http://www.siemens.de

nationality: Germany
date: October 1, 1990
affected: Siemens AG, Germany, founded 1847
affected: Nixdorf AG, Germany, founded 1952

Overview of the Acquisition

Nixdorf AG, which once enjoyed an enviable and predictable pattern of profitability, experienced a dramatic drop in earnings at the end of the 1980s. This computer hardware and software manufacturer, Germany's pride and joy, was in deep trouble due to an industry collapsed by declining prices for computers, coupled with increasing costs for their components. Nixdorf had no clear choice other than to put itself up for sale, but patriotism demanded that it remain in German hands. Siemens AG fit the bill as an acquirer, and, in late 1990, spun off its computer operations and combined them with Nixdorf. The resulting subsidiary, Siemens Nixdorf Informationssysteme AG, was Europe's largest software company and its second-largest hardware manufacturer.

History of Siemens AG

Werner Siemens and J. G. Halske founded Siemens & Halske in 1847 in Berlin, Prussia, to produce and install telegraphy systems. The young company received its first major contract the next year, commissioning it to establish a telegraphic link between Berlin and Frankfurt.

Siemens & Halske prospered amid a general boom in the communications industry. In 1853 it received a contract to establish a telegraph network in Russia, and two years later it opened a Russian office. The company began cooperating in the development of the world's first deep-sea underwater telegraph cable in 1857.

The next year, as part of a joint venture with Newall & Co., the company's London office was transformed into a subsidiary under the direction of Wilhelm Siemens. Its British operations grew significantly, incorporating as Siemens Brothers in 1865.

In 1867 the firm received a contract to lay an 11,000-mile telegraph line linking London and Calcutta, India. Halske retired that year, but the company retained his name. At the same time Werner Siemens discovered the electrodynamics principle, enabling electric current to be produced without the use of a permanent magnet.

Growth was rapid in the 1870s. Siemens laid the first transatlantic cable linking Ireland and the U.S., and then built Europe's first electric power transmission system. In 1879 it created the world's first electric railway at a trade fair in Berlin.

In 1881 the company obtained a license to manufacture light bulbs from the patent holder, Thomas Edison. A disagreement between Edison and Werner Siemens resulted in different wiring standards for Europe and the U.S., 220 and 110 volts, respectively.

Werner Siemens retired in 1890 and the company became a limited partnership operated by his sons, Wilhelm and Arnold Siemens, and his brother, Carl Siemens. Six years late it obtained the patent for an X-ray tube.

In 1903 the firm absorbed Eletrizitats-AG vorm Schuckert. Also that year, as it created Siemens-Schuckertwerke GmbH as an electric power engineering subsidiary, Siemens & Halske ranked the largest German electrical engineering company.

During World War I, the British government took control of Siemens Brothers, selling its assets to various British industrial and engineering interests. Likewise, as the Bolsheviks seized control of Russia, the company's St. Petersburg subsidiary was nationalized, resulting in a loss of Rb50 million to the company. At the conclusion of the war, Britain retained control of Siemens Brothers, but reestablished limited business ties between the two concerns.

The company initiated the commercial production of radio receivers in 1923. That year it also formed Fuji Electric as a joint venture with Furukawa Electric. In 1925 Siemens acquired Reininger, Gebbert & Schall, thereby expanding its presence in the medical equipment business. Three years later it merged its carbon and graphite electrode production activities with those of Rutgerswerke to form Siemens-Plania. By the end of the 1920s, Siemens & Halske controlled one-third of Germany's electrical manufacturing capacity.

During World War II the company received military contracts to manufacture automatic-pilot systems and other high-tech devices. Repulsed at the rise of anti-Semitism in Germany, Carl Siemens retired in 1940, appointing Hermann von Siemens to succeed him as board chairman. Four years later Siemens & Halske contributed to the development and production of the V-2 rocket, the world's first ballistic missile. In 1945 the company's principal facilities were overrun and dismantled by the Red Army. Hermann von Siemens was arrested by American occupation authorities for war crimes committed by the company. Such allegations included the company's importation of slave labor from occupied countries and the supply of

The Business

Financials

Revenue (1998): DM 118 billion

Employees (1998): 400,000

SICs / NAICS

sic 3571 - Electronic Computers

sic 3641 - Electric Lamps

sic 3651 - Household Audio & Video Equipment

sic 3661 - Telephone & Telegraph Apparatus

sic 3612 - Transformers Except Electronic

naics 334111 - Electronic Computer Manufacturing

naics 335110 - Electric Lamp Bulb and Part Manufacturing

naics 334310 - Audio and Video Equipment Manufacturing

naics 334210 - Telephone Apparatus Manufacturing

naics 335311 - Power, Distribution, and Specialty Transformer Manufacturing

gas chamber equipment to death camps. They could not be proven, however, and Hermann von Siemens was released and permitted to resume his post as board chairman.

During the 1950s Siemens diversified from consumer electronics and power generating products into railroad, medical, and telephone equipment. The firm's research into computers led to its 1951 development of a method of producing silicates of sufficient quality for use in semiconductors. Four years later the company unveiled its first mainframe computer, as well as the first international automatic telephone dialing system. Hermann von Siemens retired in 1956, and was succeeded by Ernst von Siemens as chairman.

The company's first nuclear power plant went into service at Munich-Garching in 1959. Five years later Siemens' technology was incorporated into the *Mariner IV* mission to Mars. In 1965 its Model 03 high-speed passenger train began service for the German Federal Railway.

Siemens reorganized in 1966, changing its name to Siemens AG and bringing all subsidiaries under direct company control. The following year the firm joined with Bosch to form Bosch-Siemens Hausgerate, a manufacturer of household appliances.

The company's nuclear power operations were spun off into Kraftwerk Union, a joint venture with

The Officers

Chairman, Supervisory Board: Karl-Hermann Baumann

President and CEO: Heinrich v. Pierer

Chief Financial Officer: Heinz-Joachim Neuberger

AEG, in 1969. AEG and Siemens AG also joined assets to form Transformatoren Union AG, a producer of transformers.

The 1970s were a prosperous decade for the company, as it took advantage of protectionist German trade policies to grow despite a slow global economy that forced the company to cut its workforce in selected areas. Siemens' profits in 1976 reached DM 606 million on sales of DM 20.7 billion.

Siemens increased its stakes in its joint ventures with AEG in 1977. It purchased an additional 25% interest in Transformatoren Union for $20.2 million and acquired a 50% interest in Kraftwerk Union for $255.8 million. Also that year it joined with Allis-Chalmers, creating Siemens-Allis Inc. to market turbine generators in the U.S. In 1978 Siemens surpassed Westinghouse Corp. as the world's second-largest manufacturer of electrical equipment.

In 1979 it acquired a 55% interest in Norwesco AS, a Norwegian manufacturer of electrical equipment and installations. It also entered the microcircuit technology business by spending $1 billion to establish a research and development program in the field, acquiring shares of Advanced Micro Devices and Litronix, and forming a joint venture with Phillips of the Netherlands. In 1980 Siemens acquired the nuclear power and radiation and ultrasound medical diagnostic imaging equipment operations of G.D. Searle & Co.

Bernard Plettner became chairman in 1981, marking the first time that the company was not under the direct control of the Siemens family. Six years later Siemens' electronic components operations continued to lose money, and the company was forced to buy technology from Toshiba in order to meet its obligations. In 1988 it acquired Bendix Electronics and the telecommunications operations of Plessey Ltd. The company also purchased Rolm Systems, a struggling subsidiary of IBM, for $844 million, thereby gaining control of the third-largest supplier of telephone switching equipment in North America.

By 1988 expenditures on research/development and acquisitions, which amounted to more than $24 billion over the preceding five years, forced the company's earnings to decline sharply, necessitating a reduction in dividend payments. Siemens reorganized the following year, transferring complete responsibility for all operations to units engaged in manufacturing related product lines. Its passive components businesses were also spun off as Siemens Matsushita GmbH & Co.

In 1990 Siemens merged its computer operations with those of Nixdorf, a German computer company, to form Siemens-Nixdorf. Siemens retained a 78% interest in the newly formed company, which reported a loss of $583 million for the year. Also that year the firm acquired 11 businesses in the former East Germany. Siemens purchased IN2, a French computer manufacturer, and Stromberg-Carlson, becoming the third-largest telecommunications equipment supplier in North America.

The company entered into a joint agreement with Toshiba and IBM in 1981 to produce a 256-megabit computer chip within six years. It also joined with Olivetti SpA of Italy and Groupe Bull of France to design a pan-European computer network. Later that year it purchased the outstanding shares of Siemens-Nixdorf for $474 million.

Cardion Electronics, a U.S. radar manufacturer, was acquired in 1991. By 1994 Siemens was Germany's third-largest public corporation, and the world's third-largest manufacturer of electrical equipment and power generation systems. Siemens Nixdorf Informationssysteme AG, the computer unit of Siemens AG, had its first profitable year in 1995, reporting net profit of DM 23 million on sales of DM 12.8 billion.

Siemens Rolm Communications, Inc., a unit located in Santa Clara, California, signed an agreement with MCI Communications Corp. in 1996 to offer services and discounts to each other's customers. In addition, the two companies jointly planned to develop new products and applications for voice and data networks. Siemens also formed a new alliance with Canadian-based Newbridge Networks Corp. to develop high-speed communications networks for telecommunications carriers.

In 1998 Siemens sold its defense electronics business to British Aerospace PLC and Daimler-Benz AG and traded its stake in the largest telecommunications equipment supplier, GPT Holdings, for General Electric's 50% interest in Siemens GEC Communications Systems. The company also acquired the power generation operations of CBS for $1.2 billion. In order to digest these recent acquisitions, Siemens Nixdorf Informationssysteme reorganized its information and communications holdings, spinning off its semiconductor operations as its Infineon Technologies subsidiary.

History of Nixdorf AG

Heinz Nixdorf was born in Paderburn, Germany, in 1925. After studying physics and business at Frankfort University, he started his own company, Labor fur Impulstechnik, in a basement workshop in 1952. It developed a calculator that was sold to West Germany's largest electrical utility, Pheinische Westfalische Elektrizitatswerke. As word spread of Nixdorf's innovative products, his company began supplying leading utilities throughout Europe.

The firm lost a large customer when France's Groupe Bull was acquired by General Electric Co. in 1964. At that point the company ceased to rely on industrial giants as its primary customer base, and instead began manufacturing and selling its own equipment. It even purchased one of its best customers, Wanderer Werke, in 1967. Through this acquisition, Nixdorf gained extensive production facilities and a worldwide sales force, with which it set about revolutionizing the use of computers in the small business and banking sectors.

During the mid-1960s, Nixdorf, as the company was now known, deliberately established a manufacturing and marketing stance opposed to that of IBM Corp. While IBM designed powerful computers for large companies, Nixdorf targeted smaller companies requiring more versatile, custom-made computers. In 1968 it unveiled its 820 general-purpose minicomputer. The success of this product, particularly with the small, family-owned firms typical in Germany, helped drive company sales to DM 263 million in 1970, up from DM 28 million four years earlier.

Nixdorf expanded internationally by selling 1,000 terminals to Swedish banks. By 1972 it had formed sales offices in 22 countries. In the U.S., however, it was unable to establish a significant presence, acquiring a peak market share of only one percent throughout the company's existence. Still, in 1978 the company's sales exceeded DM 1 billion and its workforce numbered 10,000.

Nixdorf engaged in negotiations with several suitors eager to buy a stake in the private company, but Heinz Nixdorf was determined not to relinquish control of his company. Even so, he wanted to get an injection of capital from an investor and sold a 25% stake to Deutsche Bank AG in 1979.

In 1982 the company created Germany's first digital telephone switching system. By the end of that year it provided information services to the small business, banking, retail, and telecommunications industries. Nixdorf predicted that telecommunications would be the company's largest growth sector, and he sought additional capital to enable it to increase its operations in that area. Hence, in 1984 the firm went public.

Heinz died of an unexpected heart attack in 1986 and was replaced as chairman by Klaus Luft. The company, as Europe's largest seller of software and a leading manufacturer of hardware, had enjoyed two decades of remarkable, steady growth. In 1988, however, this streak ended, as profits fell 90% to DM 26 million. The situation worsened in 1989, when the company recorded a significant loss in both halves of the year.

Four main reasons were behind this sudden collapse. Increased competition in the industry lowered computer prices. At the same time, the price of computer chips skyrocketed. Nixdorf had allowed its rivals to gain ground on it in the open operating systems market. Finally, the company's customer base had shifted from the high-margin banking sector to the low-margin office and retail areas.

The company needed a buyer, preferably a fellow German company. In 1990 Siemens AG paid $350 million for Nixdorf. Siemens merged its computer operations with Nixdorf to form Siemens Nixdorf Informationssysteme AG.

Market Forces Driving the Acquisition

By 1989 the global computer industry was severely depressed. Intense competition drove down the price of computers, while the cost of the chips that went into their manufacture skyrocketed. For large, diverse companies like Siemens AG, this decline could be braced by solid performances of the firm's healthier units. However, for a smaller concern like Nixdorf, whose operations centered solely on computers, the blow was devastating. "The problem is that Nixdorf is a smaller organization that doesn't have deep pockets to ride out the rough times," summarized Patricia Meagher Davis, an analyst with James Capel & Co., in *Business Week*.

External factors were not solely to blame for this downturn though. Nixdorf had been slow to move into the open operating systems, like Unix, that had swept the industry. More nimble competitors got a head start in that market, leaving Nixdorf behind.

All the more difficult for Nixdorf, as well as Germany itself, to swallow was that this company decline was an abrupt departure from the stellar performance the firm had enjoyed for decades. Since its inception in 1952, Nixdorf's innovations had resulted in steady sales growth. Its revenues in 1984 reached DM 3.27 billion, and increased annually by 20% in the following years. In 1988, however, profits dropped 90% over the previous year, reaching DM 26 million.

The downward spiral continued in 1989, dragging earnings into the red. That year Nixdorf recorded a loss of DM 700 million on revenues of DM 5.4 billion. As a result, chairman Klaus Luft resigned in November 1989 and was succeeded by a couple of interim leaders.

Clearly, Nixdorf needed help. The company had great potential, if only it could weather the storm. It had carved out a niche in minicomputers and had a strong sales force and loyal customer base, particularly outside of its home territory of Germany. For these reasons, a number of companies from various countries regarded Nixdorf as an attractive acquisition.

Not just any suitor would do, however. In the eyes of Germany and the Deutsche Bank, which held a 25% stake in Nixdorf, only a German acquirer would be acceptable. The U.S. and Japanese giants had already squeezed out or absorbed so many other European companies that patriotism became a ruling factor in determining a suitable acquirer.

Siemens AG appeared to be an acceptable candidate. Not only was that company of German origin, but it also had operations that would benefit from Nixdorf's. The electrical conglomerate operated its computer business with staid conservatism, unlike Nixdorf's freewheeling atmosphere that, like the Silicon Valley models, fostered innovation and ingenuity. Nixdorf's strength in custom-designed products for mid-sized markets complemented Siemens' strength in mainframes for large companies.

Approach and Engagement

On January 10, 1990, Siemens acquired a 51% controlling stake in Nixdorf for $350 million in the first step toward complete absorption of the company. After it received German and European regulatory approval, Siemens completed the transaction. It merged its computer business into its new acquisition, forming Siemens Nixdorf Informationssysteme AG on October 1, 1990.

Products and Services

By 1998 Siemens AG was a diverse electrical conglomerate organized into eight business segments: Energy, Industry, Information and Communications, Health Care, Transportation, Components, Lighting, Financial Services, and Household Appliances. Siemens Nixdorf Informationssysteme (SNI), the subsidiary formed through the acquisition of Nixdorf, was part of the company's Information and Communications segment. SNI was Europe's largest information technology company, operating 250 business units in 58 countries and recording earnings of DM 68 in 1998.

Review of the Outcome

In January 1990, shortly after the deal was completed, Nixdorf announced a workforce reduction of nearly 5,000 of its 30,000 positions as part of a restructuring started prior to the merger. That summer, however, the company reduced the number of those cuts to 3,500 in light of employee pressure. In August 1991 the newly formed Siemens Nixdorf Informationssysteme (SNI) announced that it would reduce its 52,000 jobs by 3,000 by year-end.

These cuts were made in attempts to improve the profitability of computer operations. SNI lost DM 780 million in 1991, in part due to costs associated with the merger and an initial restructuring. The subsidiary's CEO, Hans-Dieter Wiedig, attributed the continued unprofitability to industry pressures, the cultural differences at the combined companies, and incompatible administrative and computer systems that resulted in lost and delayed orders. By the mid-1990s the situation had improved somewhat, and SNI was back in the black. In 1998 that unit recorded a profit of DM 68.

Research

"The Cellar Revisited," in *The Economist*, 3 December 1988. Reports the falling profitability of Nixdorf.

Collier, Andrew. "Siemens, Nixdorf Deal: Banking on Packs, Money," in *Electronic News*, 22 January 1990. Describes the newly announced acquisition deal.

"Europe's Computer Champion on the Ropes," in *Financial Times (London)*, 14 May 1992. Details the unprofitability of Siemens Nixdorf Informationssysteme in the years after its formation.

"Nixdorf Computer AG," in *International Directory of Company Histories*, Vol. III, St. James Press, 1991. Provides an historical review of the company, including its acquisition by Siemens.

Reichlin, Igor, and Thane Peterson. "Why Siemens Wrote Such a Big Check," in *Business Week*, 22 January 1990. Briefly describes the hidden strengths of Nixdorf.

Schares, Gail E. "This German Company's Days of Freedom May Be Numbered," in *Business Week*, 4 December 1989. Reports Nixdorf's poor performance and suggests possible acquirers of the struggling company.

Siemens AG 1998 Annual Report. Includes financial highlights and describes company operating segments.

Siemens AG Home Page, available at http://www.siemens.de. Official World Wide Web Page for Siemens. This German- and English-language site includes information on products and services, annual reports and other financial data, and press releases.

"Siemens AG," in *Notable Corporate Chronologies*, The Gale Group, 1999. Provides historical highlights of Siemens.

PATRICIA ARCHILLA

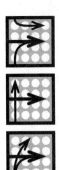

SIERRA HEALTH SERVICES &
PHYSICIAN CORPORATION OF AMERICA

date: March 19, 1997 (canceled)
affected: Sierra Health Services, Inc., USA, founded 1984
affected: Physician Corporation of America, USA, founded 1985

Humana Inc.
500 W. Main St.
Louisville, KY 40202
USA

tel: (502)580-1000
fax: (502)580-1441
web: http://www.humana.com

Overview of the Merger

Already dominating the Nevada market, Sierra Health Services would have acquired a company with a strong presence in Florida, Texas, and Puerto Rico had the merger with Physician Corporation of America been completed. It would have created the nation's eighth largest publicly held managed care company, and the 12th-largest publicly traded managed care firm.

Physician Corporation of America (PCA) had been losing money since early 1995, as a result of difficulty in controlling medical costs. In 1996 it had losses of $95.44 million in the third quarter, or $2.44 a share, on revenues of $362.1 million. Its financial condition made it attractive to suitors, including Sierra.

Financial markets did not respond well to Sierra's proposal to purchase Physician Corporation of America. Adding to merger concerns was the investigation by Florida officials into a 1991 misdemeanor conviction of Anthony Marlon, Sierra's chairman and CEO, for falsifying documents. Florida law forbade its Medicare program from dealing with any plan that had an officer having a record of a criminal violation.

History of Physician Corporation of America

Physician Corporation of America (PCA), a comprehensive health care services organization with 1.15 million members by 1997, was founded in Kansas in 1985 by Dr. Kardatze. It opened HMOs in Texas and Puerto Rico in the late 1980s, and in Florida in 1990; its Texas and Puerto Rico operations were profitable, its Florida HMO was not. In addition to operating and managing HMOs, PCA provided administrative, management, and workers' compensation services for health-related insurance matters to its members.

In 1997, the year that its acquisition by Sierra was canceled, PCA was Florida's largest provider of health services to poor and disabled people. However, it had suffered since 1995 from cuts in Medicaid reimbursements as well as higher-than-

The Business

Financials

Revenue (1998): $9.8 billion

Employees (1998): 16,300

SICs / NAICS

sic 6324 - Hospital & Medical Service Plans

naics 524114 - Direct Health and Medical Insurance
    Carriers

expected medical expenses. It took an $80 million charge to cover claims from workers' compensation, and lost $121 million in 1996.

One of its Florida subsidiaries, PCA Property & Casualty Insurance, was placed under administrative supervision and ordered to stop selling or renewing policies. In May, the day after a request from state regulators was received to take over PCA Property and Casualty, a judge approved an agreement giving the company an extra month to fix its problems.

Since April 1997, however, PCA had been pressured by its lenders to address its growing losses, having reported a 1996 fourth quarter loss of $182.5 million on revenues of $365.1 million. Its options were limited, including only selling off assets, issuing junk bonds, or finding another buyer. Kardatzke said at the time that "several parties have expressed an interest in a transaction with PCA," and that the company was looking for buyers.

In November 1997 a class action lawsuit on behalf of purchasers of PCA's common stock was filed in the U.S. District Court for the South District of Florida. The complaint, in which the corporation as well as some of its current and fomer officers were named as defendants, alleged that the defendants had violated several sections of the federal securities laws and common law by misrepresenting and/or omitting financial information on PCA's condition. It also alleged that the price of PCA was artificially inflated as a result of the defendant's conduct. The price of PCA's stock declined with the disclosure of the misrepresentation.

History of Sierra Health Services, Inc.

Sierra, the oldest and largest HMO in Nevada, was one of the nation's leading examples of this type

of insurer and occupied the dominant market position in the state. Health Plan of Nevada was established in 1981, and had been enrolling members for approximately two years by the time it was taken over by Sierra.

In what appeared to be prime time for HMOs, the early 1980s proved to be fraught with difficulties for Sierra and many other similar companies. Perceived by many as offering second-rate (or lower) programs, many potential customers took their business elsewhere. Although Sierra had Health Plan of Nevada's client core in place, it, like other HMOs, had to overcome the negative image of a plan that offered a limited number of physicians and less-than-first-class care.

One plan of attack that Sierra employed to attract customers (which instead contributed to negative earnings) was to expand outside of Nevada. During 1984 it established HMO plans in the neighboring states of New Mexico, Colorado, and Arizona. At the same time, perhaps because of its Las Vegas location, Sierra was willing to gamble on going public; it began selling common shares in 1985.

Expanding and going public proved almost fatal. In its first year as a publicly owned corporation it lost almost $9 million, and the following year earned only a small profit.

In 1987, in an effort to stem losses, Sierra reduced its holdings once again to only Nevada facilities. As much of its clientele came from the gambling casinos in and around Las Vegas, this strategy successfully moved the company's earnings into the profit column by the end of the year. The company was also helped by the solid reputation it held based on its connection with Health Plan of Nevada, Inc.

In addition to divesting itself of the unprofitable out-of-state facilities (in 1987 alone, the facilities in New Mexico, Colorado, and Arizona lost a combined $3.7 million), Sierra put other cost-containing measures in place. By combining controls and incentives, it hoped to turn its poor performance around. Yet 1988 proved to be another bad year with a $3.4 million loss on a rather modest gain in revenue.

Despite the dollar losses, there were some positive aspects of the business that kept investors' hopes alive at the end of the 1980s. Among them was the fact that its medical loss ratio—the percentage of its revenue spent on medical expenses—was considerably lower than other HMOs. Also, its Nevada operation was strong; it was, in fact, the largest HMO in the state. Through its Southwest Medical Associates subsidiary it had 123,000 enrollees, as well as 1,600 employer groups.

Whether it was the climate of the 1980s or growing pains that had caused Sierra's difficulties is hard to measure, but the 1990s were far more advantageous to the company. The first five years saw consistent sales, growth in profits, and a rejuvenation of the company's image. Capitalizing on this positive environment, Sierra's income increased in each year from 1990 to 1994, breaking company records at $22.2 million in 1994, and earning revenue of $269.3 million that same year.

By the mid-1990s, almost all of Sierra subsidiaries were doing well. As an example, Southwest Medical Associates, which by 1994 was Nevada's largest multi-specialty medical group practice, opened its tenth medical facility in Las Vegas that year. By the beginning of the next, it began construction of a new outpatient surgery center.

These results did not go unnoticed by the stock market. Shares sold at an all-time high, and $45 million flowed into waiting coffers from a stock offering. This money could be used to fund expansion, such as the proposed merger with PCA, and develop new business.

Market Forces Driving the Merger

During the 1980s the number of individuals enrolled in health maintenance organizations (HMOs) quadrupled. At the beginning of the decade less than ten million people had this type of health coverage; by 1990 more than 35 million, or roughly 15% of the U.S. population, did. Faced with continually escalating charges, managed care programs that limited costs were appealing to many people during a time when individuals, businesses, and government organizations were beginning to turn away from traditional fee-for-service ways of paying for health care.

Rising health costs were a public, and thus a governmental, concern in the early 1990s, and were a major feature of 1992 election campaigns. Many people saw HMOs, with their selected lists of hospitals and physicians, as a possible solution to ever-increasing medical charges. Accordingly, HMO companies were created, merged, and dropped in a continuing swirl of buy-outs, staff changes, and acquisitions.

Approach and Engagement

Sierra made its original offer to purchase PCA in November 1996. The all-stock deal would have involved a swap of 0.45 shares of Sierra for every share of Physician Corporation of America. Sierra said it anticipated the merger would generate $10 million to $15 million in annual cost savings.

The Officers

Chairman and Co-Founder: David A. Jones

Chief Operating Officer, President, and CEO: Gregory H. Wolf

Sr. VP, Sales, Marketing, and Business Development: Kenneth J. Fasola

Sr. VP and Chief Information Officer: Bruce J. Goodman

Sr. VP and Chief Financial Officer: James E. Murray

But after Sierra announced its purchase intentions, its shares dropped $5, or 17%. This decline was much steeper than that which often accompany acquiring companies. At the time Ria Marie Carlson, Sierra's vice president for investor relations, said that "the decision [to acquire PCA] had been made for more than just the short term." She added that the drop in Sierra's stock prices would not alter the terms of the transaction.

The financial community, however, was almost uniformly negative. Most analysts felt similar to Lori Price at Oppenheimer & Company who said in the *New York Times*: "The problem is that Sierra's stock will incur a lot of dilution over the next year or so. They are almost doubling their numbers of shares outstanding for a company that is just approaching the break-even point for the first time in 19 months. That is a high price to pay."

At $11.81/share, or $453.1 million, Sierra's offer was triple Physicians' closing price the day before, or $4.06/share. Analysts said Sierra was paying too much for a troubled company, since turnaround time for Physicians was expected to take up to two years.

In February 1997 Sierra said that it was "seriously evaluating" its options following the news that PCA would take a fourth quarter charge against earnings of $60 million in connection to cover claims for workers' compensation policies that it had issued. This $60 million later turned out to be $80.

The approval of the Florida Department of Insurance was also necessary for the merger to go ahead. In May 1997, just as there was to have been a ruling on a request by state regulators to take over PCA Property & Casualty, the judge instead approved an agreement between the state and the company allowing it an extra month to fix its workers' compensation problems. However, the combination of regulatory objections to the merger and financial concerns caused Sierra to cancel its proposed acquisition. It ended its bid to buy PCA on March 19, 1997. This left PCA is default of $102 million in bank debt.

The Players

Physician Corporation of America Chairman and CEO: E. Stanley Kardatzke. E. Stanley Kardatzke received a B.A. from Anderson College and his M.D. from Indiana University Medical School. He served as medical director and chairman of Health Care Plus of America, an HMO in Kansas and Oklahoma, before his association with Physician Corporation of America (PCA), and founded Kardatzke Management, Inc. after his tenure at PCA. On April 22, 1998, following a loan of $1.6 million from Kardatzke Management, Kardatzke became chairman and CEO of Integrated Medical Resources, Inc.

Sierra Health Services Chairman and CEO: Anthony M. Marlon. Anthony Marlon, M.D., head of Southwest Medical Associates, a group medical practice in Nevada, founded Sierra Health as a holding company in 1984 specifically to acquire Health Plan of Nevada, Ltd. and its four affiliated corporations. By the end of 1995, The Marlon Family Trust held roughly 6.5 million Sierra shares. Marlon owned these shares indirectly in his capacity as co-trustee of this trust.

Humana CEO: Gregory H. Wolf. Humana Inc. appointed Greg Wolf as the firm's new CEO on January 1, 1998. He assumed that post while maintaining his responsibilities and job title as president of Humana and simultaneously joining the firm's board. Analysts regarded Wolf as an excellent choice because he possessed the skills both to gather a strong management team and to reduce expenses.

After Sierra dropped its purchase plans, PCA filed a lawsuit against it in Federal Court in Miami seeking monetary and other damages for Sierra's "willfully breaching and terminating the merger agreement." PCA also said it was in a "financial covenant default" under its bank debt agreement, but that its bankers were willing to give the company time to work through its problems.

Review of the Outcome

Humana acquired PCA in September 1997 for $290 cash and the assumption of $121 million in debt generated from workers' compensation claims. Based in Louisville, Ky., Humana was one of the nation's largest publicly-traded managed health care companies. It had 5.9 million health plan members located primarily in 17 states and Puerto Rico, and offered health care through a variety of delivery systems: HMOs, preferred provider organizations, point-of-service plans, and administrative services products.

PCA had 324,000 of its 1.1 million members in Florida where Humana, with its 1.1 Florida members, wanted to increase its market share. It also wanted to add PCA's 323,000 members in Texas to its existing base there of 337,000.

Humana's President and Chief Operating Officer Gregory H. Wolf was quoted in *PR Newswire* as saying, "Our strategy to achieve critical mass and concentration in select markets is greatly enhanced by our acquisition of PCAM. This transaction clearly advances our long-term objectives by adding significant membership to our Florida and Texas markets, where in major metropolitan areas such as Miami, Tampa, San Antonio and Austin, Humana is now the largest HMO.

"In just over three months, we have successfully guided the PCAM acquisition to a close and we are pleased to welcome 1.1 million new members, including our new membership in Puerto Rico, to the Humana family of health plans," added Wolf. "Using the detailed integration plans we have developed, we will move expeditiously to fold PCAM members and operations into the Humana system and begin building upon the critical mass and synergistic opportunities now available."

Humana's offer of about $400 million, $7/share for $270 million plus $130 million in debt, was 68% less than Sierra's had been.

The Wall Street Journal on November 17, 1998, reported rumors that Humana was looking to expand its then current holdings, and that Gregory H. Wolf, president and CEO of Humana Inc., was talking with Prudential Insurance Co. about acquiring Prudential's healthcare division.

Research

"Integrated Medical Resources Announces Appointment of New Chairman & CEO Dr. E. Stanley Kardatzke in Connection with Additional Financing Commitment," in *PR Newswire*, 22 April 1998.

"PCA, Sierra Merger: It Doesn't Look Good," in *South Florida Business Journal*, 3 February 1997.

"PCA Signs Definitive Merger Agreement with Humana; Enters Reinsurance Agreement for PCA P&C," in *PR Newswire*, 3 June 1997.

"Sierra Ends Planned Purchase of Physician Corp.," in *The New York Times*.

"Sierra Health Services," in *International Directory of Company Histories*, Vol. 15, St. James Press: 1995. Background information on HMOs, why they are desirable, their problems, their advantages, and the history of Sierra.

"Sierra Health Services Announces Staff Reorganization and Promotions," in *Business Wire*, 7 January 1993.

"Sierra Health Stock Falls on Acquisition Announcement," in *The New York Times*.

"Sierra Reconsiders Offer for Physician Corporation," in *The New York Times*.

—BARBARA J. KELLY

SMITHKLINE BECKMAN & BEECHAM GROUP

SmithKline Beecham PLC
1 New Horizons Ct.
Brentford, Middlesex TW8 9EP
United Kingdom

tel: 44-181-975-2000
fax: 44-181-975-2090
web: http://www.sb.com

nationality: United Kingdom
date: July 26, 1989
affected: SmithKline Beckman Corp., USA, founded 1830
affected: Beecham Group PLC, U.K., founded 1847

Overview of the Merger

The July 1989 merger of SmithKline Beckman Corp. and Beecham Group PLC created the second largest drug company in the world. Valued at $16 billion, the merger was the largest cross-border deal of the 1980s. Besides its hefty valuation, the deal was noteworthy because it reflected current pharmaceutical industry trends and set the stage for the market's first consolidation flurry.

History of Beecham Group PLC

In 1847, Thomas Beecham began selling herbal remedies and pills (mostly laxatives) to people in England. A decade later, Beecham was concentrating his efforts on cough tablets and Beecham's Pills, his famous laxatives. He also launched his first advertising campaign, selling his pills through mail order and in the apothecary shop. In 1888, Beecham's pills were distributed in the United States for the first time, and two years later, Beecham established manufacturing operations in New York City.

Financier and land developer, Philip Hill acquired the Beecham estate, including the pill business, from the Beecham family in 1924. Four years later, he incorporated the pill operations as Beecham's Pills and acquired new products such as Yeast Vite, Iron Jelloids, Phosferine, and Phylosan; he also acquired new companies such as Prichard and Constance, makers of Amami shampoo, and a toiletries manufacturer.

Beecham continued its expansion efforts throughout the 1930s, buying several companies: toothpaste maker, Macleans Ltd.; County Perfumery, makers of Brylcreem; and an antacid manufacturer, Eno Proprietaries. The company also began making health drinks. Beecham Research Laboratories Ltd. was established to develop new food products and pharmaceuticals in 1944. To reflect its recent product line expansions, Beecham's Pills changed its name to Beecham Group Ltd. the following year. The research division began focusing exclusively on pharmaceuticals in an effort to propel the company further into the field of medicinal products. By acquiring C.L. Bencard, an allergy vaccine company, Beecham established a strong base for entering the prescription drugs market in 1949.

In 1957, Beecham scientists isolated 6-APA, the penicillin nucleus, a discovery that allowed them to develop all kinds of antibiotics. Two year later, when Beecham's labs produced the world's first partly synthetic penicillins, Broxil (phenethicillin) and Celbenin (methicillin), the problem of bacterial strains immune to widely used vaccines was overcome. The firm acquired Ribena blackcurrant juice, Shloer apple and grape drinks, and PLJ to expand its line of consumer brand health drinks.

Beecham opened a U.S.-based factory designed especially for antibiotics production in 1967. The company bought Horlicks brand milk drinks in 1969 and S.E. Massengill, a U.S.-based feminine hygiene products maker, in 1970. Two years later, the U.K. government forbade the proposed merger of Beecham and the Glaxo Group, its largest competitor, fearing the deal would decrease research efforts in the pharmaceutical industry. By the mid-1970s, the firm was selling its Norval antidepressant and Pollinex allergy vaccine, as well as three new antibiotics: amoxicillin, flucloxacillin, and ticarcillin.

In 1977, Beecham paid $76 million for Sucrets brand cough drops and bought Calgon's line of bath products. The company diversified into perfumes in 1979 with the $85 million purchase of U.S.-based Jovan. A year later, Beecham entered the foods market with its purchase of Bovril.

In the early 1980's Beecham continued its acquisition spree by purchasing J.B. Williams—which gave the firm access to Geritol vitamin supplements, Sominex sleeping pills, and Aqua Velva after shave lotion—for $100 million. Despite sagging ampicillin sales caused by increased competition and government attempts to restrict profits of pharmaceutical companies, Beecham also bought several drug companies in France, West Germany, and Italy. The firm paid $369 million for Norcliff Thayer, makers of Tums and other over-the-counter drugs, and also acquired the cosmetics and fragrance products of BAT in 1985. A year later, the firm began divesting non-core operations.

In July of 1989, Beecham merged with SmithKline Beckman to become SmithKline Beecham PLC, based in London, England. In 1990, net income exceeded $1 billion for the first time. A year later, SmithKline Beecham unveiled its first major drug since the merger, Seroxat, an antidepressant. The company developed several new drugs in the early 1990s, including Relafen, an arthritis drug with $40 million in sales; Paxil, an antidepressant; and the world's first hepatitis A vaccine, Havrix. SmithKline Beecham was number one in acne remedies (Oxy brands), number two in antiulcer drugs, and number three in prescription

The Business

Financials

Revenue (1998): $13.4 billion

Employees (1998): 58,300

SICs / NAICS

sic 2834 - Pharmaceutical Preparations

sic 2833 - Medicinals & Botanicals

sic 8071 - Medical Laboratories

naics 325412 - Pharmaceutical Preparation Manufacturing

naics 325411 - Medicinal and Botanical Manufacturing

naics 621512 - Diagnostic Imaging Centers

naics 621511 - Medical Laboratories

drugs and toothpaste (Aquafresh). The firm expanded its global distribution network in 1994 when it bought the over-the-counter unit of Sterling Winthrop, and paid $2.3 billion for United HealthCare Corp.'s pharmacy-benefit services unit. SmithKline Beecham then divested its animal health division for $1.5 billion and the U.S. over-the-counter operations of Sterling Winthrop to Bayer AG for $1 billion.

In 1995, over-the-counter sales of Tagamet HB for heartburn and acid indigestion were approved by the FDA. The drug faced direct competition from Johnson & Johnson's Pepcid AC, which was approved for nonprescription use at roughly the same time. SmithKline Beecham and Johnson and Johnson became involved in a $200 advertising war that eventually prompted a New York judge to order both firms to withdraw specific advertisements for their new heartburn drugs, due to their unsubstantiated claims. Later that year, SmithKline Beecham received FDA approval to market its hepatitis A vaccine and to sell a tablet form of Kytril, an anti-nausea drug for cancer patients.

The FDA approved Nicorette gum as an over-the-counter product in early 1996. Also, Hycamtin was approved by the FDA for patients whose ovarian cancer had not responded to other treatments. SmithKline Beecham filed a total of 154 new product approvals in 1996; although new product sales grew by 37%, sales of Tagamet fell 41%. In January of 1997, the firm announced its intention to merge with American Home Products. Less than two weeks later, SmithKline Beecham decided Glaxo Wellcome was a more attractive partner and ended its discussions with American Home Products. SmithKline Beecham and

The Officers

Chairman: Sir Peter Walters Jr.

Chief Executive Officer: Jan Leschly

Chief Operating Officer and President, Pharmaceuticals and Consumer Health Care: Jean-Pierre Garnier

Exec. VP and Chief Financial Officer: Andrew Bonfield

Glaxo Wellcome executives couldn't agree on how to best run the new company, though, and that deal was called off in late February. After deciding to refocus on core operations, SmithKline put its clinical laboratory and diversified pharmaceuticals operations up for sale in early 1999.

History of SmithKline Beckman Corp.

The SmithKline pharmacy opened in Philadelphia, Pennsylvania, in 1830. In 1846, SmithKline supplied quinine to American soldiers during the war with Mexico. The company also supplied spirits of ammonia to U.S. troops in World War I. By the mid-1930s, SmithKline had developed into a major pharmaceuticals firm; it introduced the Benzedrine Inhaler in 1936 and the first timed-release capsule, Dexedrine, in 1944. The firm introduced the world's first day-long cold remedy, Contac, in 1960. In 1976, SmithKline launched Tagamet, the world's first drug able to heal peptic ulcers; by 1981, it had become the world's number one selling drug.

The following year, SmithKline used its Tagamet revenues to acquire Beckman Instruments, maker of medical supplies such as the pH meter and the spectrophotometer. The firm changed its name to SmithKline Beckman Corp. In 1987, SmithKline's second leading drug, Dyazide, lost its patent, allowing other companies to make generics. Reliance on a few blockbuster products began taking its toll on the company's bottom line.

The firm's hypertension drug, Selacryn, was accused of causing liver damage. SmithKline had to pay $100 million to a child abuse program, and three executives were ordered to do 200 hours of community service as punishment for 36 deaths and 34 counts of failing to immediately inform the FDA of side effects. In July of 1989, SmithKline Beckman merged with Beecham Group PLC to become SmithKline Beecham PLC, based in London, England.

Market Forces Driving the Merger

Throughout the 1980s, pharmaceutical firms were able to stay a step ahead of inflation by upping prescription costs and launching blockbuster new drugs. The industry was among the most profitable in America at that time. By the decade's end, however, many firms faced patent expiry on major drugs. Increased competition was also eroding profits. In particular, SmithKline Beckman's best-selling drug, Tagamet, was facing direct competition from Glaxo's anti-ulcer medication Zantac.

To remain competitive, firms needed to develop new drugs, which required deep research and development pockets. According to Bruce Wasserstein, author of *Big Deal: The Battle for Control of America's Leading Corporations*, "Drug companies already spent a much higher percentage of revenues on R&D than other kinds of companies. The expectation was that a major drug company would need to spend more than $500 million a year on research to be successful. Few companies in the industry could afford that level of expenditure on their own."

SmithKline had developed no major products since Tagamet; with sales declining and patent protection on the drug expiring throughout Europe in 1992, analysts began speculating that the firm would likely be taken over. United Kingdom-based Beecham seemed to have exactly what SmithKline needed: a strong over-the-counter product line, as well as several new drugs in various stages of the development and approval process. Furthermore, Beecham wanted to strengthen its position in the U.S. market, which accounted for approximately 30% of global pharmaceutical sales at that time. The U.S. market was also attractive to foreign companies because, unlike many other markets, drug prices were not limited there.

Approach and Engagement

In early 1989, the stock prices of struggling SmithKline Beckman began climbing amidst speculation that the firm would be taken over by Beecham. The two firms announced their $16 billion stock swap a few weeks later. SmithKline chairman Henry Wendt would takeover as chairman of the new firm; Beecham chairman Robert Bauman would become CEO. The new company would change its name to SmithKline Beecham PLC and be based in London, England. Shareholders overwhelmingly approved the deal, and the merger of equals was finalized on July 26, 1989.

Products and Services

SmithKline Beecham earned $12.8 billion in revenues in 1997. Pharmaceuticals accounted for 59% of total sales and included five antibiotics—Augmentin (the company's best selling drug), Amoxcil, Bactroban, Famvir, and Timentin—as well as cholesterol reducer Baycol, heart medication Dyazide, ovarian cancer treatment Hycamtin, pediatric vaccine Infanrix, congestive heart failure treatment Kredex, antinausea drug Kytril, Lyme disease vaccination Lymerix, arthritis drug Relifex, and hypertension treatment Teveten. Consumer healthcare products, including Aquafresh toothpaste, NicoDerm CQ, Nicorette, Philips Milk of Magnesia, Sucrets, Tagamet HB, and Tums, earned 30% of total sales. Clinical laboratories brought in the remaining 11%.

Subsidiaries included Beecham Group PLC; Belgian pharmaceutical business Fournex S.A.; Colombian consumer healthcare unit Instituto Farmacologico Colombiano S.A.; Portugese pharmaceutical company Instituto Luso-Farmaco Lda.; 70% owned consumer health care concern PT Sterling Products Indonesia; United Kingdom-based Saxet Ltd.; pharmaceutical firm SmithKline & French Laboratories Ltd.; 55% owned Sino-American Tianjin SmithKline & French Laboratories Ltd.; 75% owned SmithKline & French of Pakistan Ltd.; and Austrian consumer health care operation SmithKline Beecham Markenartikel.

Changes to the Industry

Beecham was the first European pharmaceutical company to successfully secure a noteworthy foothold in the U.S. drug market. When the merger was completed, SmithKline Beecham became the second largest drug company in the world, with combined sales of $6.9 billion, behind only Merck & Co., Inc. Most analysts credited the deal for sparking the first wave of pharmaceutical industry consolidation. In 1990, France's Rhone-Poulenc spent $2 billion for U.S.-based Rorer Group Inc. Dow Chemical Co. began its lengthy takeover of Marion Laboratories. Also, Bristol-Myers Squibb Co. was formed via the $12 billion joining of Bristol Myers and Squibb. The firms that chose not to merge, such as Merck & Co., pursued strategic joint ventures with other leading players. Despite the flurry of consolidation during the late 1980s and early 1990s, each of the top five companies in the pharmaceuticals industry held less five percent of worldwide market share, leaving the industry open for future consolidation.

Review of the Outcome

Within five years of the deal, sales at SmithKline Beecham had grown to roughly $10 billion. Shareholders saw their investments in the company double in the years following the merger. Stock prices before the merger peaked at $12.25 per share. In 1992, they reached $24 per share, and three years later, they were up to $27.50 per share. According to an April 1993 article in the *Financial Times*, the new firm was

The Players

Chairman of Beecham Group PLC: Robert P. Bauman. Robert Bauman worked for General Foods, Avco, and Textron before he became the first American to run U.K.-based Beecham Group in 1986 with his appointment as chairman of the board. When Beecham and SmithKline Beckman merged in July of 1989, Bauman took over as CEO and president, posts he held until his retirement in early 1993, when he was succeeded by current SmithKline Beecham CEO Jan Leschly.

Chairman of SmithKline Beckman Corp.: Henry Wendt. Henry Wendt was CEO of SmithKline Beckman when Tagamet became the world's best selling drug in the early 1980s. Credited for steering the firm's merger with Beecham Group, he served as chairman of the board of the new company after the 1989 deal was finalized. Wendt resigned in early 1993 and was replaced by current SmithKline Beecham chairman Sir Peter Walters.

transformed "from an insignificant pharmaceutical company into a world leader in the industry." To retain its competitive edge, SmithKline began seeking merger partners again in the late 1990s, eventually turning down deals with both American Home Products and Glaxo Wellcome. The firm then changed tactics by shunning consolidation and announcing its intent to refocus on core operations by divesting its clinical laboratory and diversified pharmaceuticals operations in early 1999.

Research

Abrahams, Paul. "Patient Responds to a Successful Prescription," in *The Financial Times*, 27 April 1993. Discusses the departure of chairman Henry Wendt and CEO Robert Bauman from SmithKline Beecham, four years after the merger.

Duncan, Gordon. "Two Men, One Vision," in *Acquisitions Monthly*, November 1994. Details the outcome of the merger between SmithKline Beckman and Beecham Group.

Green, Daniel. "Prescription for Future," in *The Financial Times*, 2 February 1998. Explains the planned merger between Glaxo Wellcome and SmithKline Beecham after SmithKline Beecham ended discussions with AHP.

SmithKline Beecham PLC Home Page, available at http://www.sb.com. Official World Wide Web Home Page for SmithKline Beecham PLC. Includes news, financial, product, and historical information.

"SmithKline Beecham PLC," in *Notable Corporate Chronologies*, The Gale Group, 1999. Lists major events in the history of SmithKline Beecham PLC, including the merger between Beecham Group and SmithKline Beckman.

Wasserstein, Bruce. *Big Deal: The Battle for Control of America's Leading Corporations*, Warner Books, 1998. Offers an overview of the largest mergers in recent American corporate history, including the merger of SmithKline Beckman and Beecham Group.

JEFF ST. THOMAS

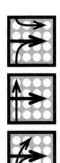

SMITHKLINE BEECHAM & DIVERSIFIED PHARMACEUTICALS SERVICES

nationality: United Kingdom
date: May 1994
affected: SmithKline Beecham PLC, United Kingdom, founded 1830
affected: Diversified Pharmaceutical Services Inc., USA, founded 1977

SmithKline Beecham PLC
1 New Horizons Ct.
Brentford, Middlesex TW89EP
United Kingdom

tel: (44)181-975-2000
fax: (44)181-975-2090
web: http://www.sb.com

Overview of the Merger

SmithKline Beecham expanded into healthcare management in the U.S. when it acquired Diversified Pharmaceutical Services Inc. (DPS) from United HealthCare Corp. for $2.3 billion in May 1994. Already a giant in the British-American pharmaceuticals industry, SmithKline positioned itself among the leaders of comprehensive healthcare services by teaming up with one of the largest pharmaceutical benefit managers (PBMs) in the U.S. Driving the deal was the increased pressure in the industry for pharmaceutical companies to pair up with PBMs as a means of providing one-stop-shopping to large corporations. When the anticipated synergies didn't emerge, however, SmithKline sold DPS for $700 million in June 1999, taking a $713 million hit on the deal.

History of SmithKline Beecham PLC

The SmithKline pharmacy opened in Philadelphia, Pennsylvania, in 1830. In 1846, SmithKline supplied quinine to American soldiers during the war with Mexico. The company also supplied spirits of ammonia to U.S. troops in World War I. By the mid-1930s, SmithKline had developed into a major pharmaceuticals firm; it introduced the Benzedrine Inhaler in 1936 and Dexedrine in 1944. In 1976, SmithKline introduced Tagamet, the world's first drug able to heal peptic ulcers; by 1981, it had become the world's number one selling drug.

The following year, SmithKline used its Tagamet revenues to acquire Beckman Instruments, maker of medical supplies such as the pH meter and the spectrophotometer; the firm then changed its name to SmithKline Beckman Corp. 1987 was a less than stellar year for the company. Its second leading drug, Dyazide, lost its patent, allowing other companies to make generics. The firm's hypertension drug, Selacryn, was accused of causing liver damage. As a result, SmithKline had to pay $100 million to a child abuse program, and three executives were ordered to do 200 hours of community service as punishment for 36 deaths and 34 counts of failing to immediately inform the FDA of side effects.

The Business

Financials

Revenue (1998): $13.4 billion

Employees (1998): 58,300

SICs / NAICS

sic 2834 - Pharmaceutical Preparations

sic 2833 - Medicinals & Botanicals

sic 2835 - Diagnostic Substances

sic 2844 - Toilet Preparations

sic 2835 - Diagnostic Substances

naics 325412 - Pharmaceutical Preparation Manufacturing

naics 325411 - Medicinal and Botanical Manufacturing

naics 325412 - Pharmaceutical Preparation Manufacturing

naics 325413 - In-Vitro Diagnostic Substance
    Manufacturing

SmithKline's other half, Beecham, was founded in 1847, when Thomas Beecham began selling herbal remedies and pills (mostly laxatives) in England. A decade later, Beecham was concentrating his efforts on cough tablets and Beecham's Pills, his famous laxatives. He also launched his first advertising campaign, distributing his pills through mail order sales as well as in the apothecary shop. In 1888, Beecham's pills were sold in the United States for the first time; two years later, Beecham established manufacturing operations in New York City.

Financier and land developer Philip Hill acquired the Beecham estate, including the pill business, from the Beecham family in 1924. Four years later, he incorporated the pill operations as Beecham's Pills and acquired new products such as Yeast Vite, Iron Jelloids, Phosferine, and Phylosan; he also acquired the Prichard and Constance companies.

Beecham continued its expansion efforts throughout the 1930s, buying several companies: Macleans Ltd., a toothpaste maker; County Perfumery, the creator of Brylcreem; and Eno Proprietaries, an antacid manufacturer. Beecham Research Laboratories Ltd. was established in 1944 to develop new food products and pharmaceuticals. To reflect its recent product line expansions, Beecham's Pills changed its name to Beecham Group Ltd. the following year. The research division began focusing exclusively on pharmaceuticals in an effort to propel the company further into the field of medicinal products. By acquiring C.L. Bencard, an allergy vaccine company, Beecham established a strong base for entering the prescription drugs market in 1949.

In 1957, Beecham scientists isolated 6-APA, the penicillin nucleus, a discovery that allowed them to develop a variety of antibiotics. Two year later, when Beecham's labs produced the world's first partly synthetic penicillins, Broxil (phenethicillin) and Celbenin (methicillin), the problem of bacterial strains immune to widely used vaccines was overcome. The firm acquired Ribena blackcurrant juice, Shloer apple and grape drinks, and PLJ to expand its line of consumer brand health drinks.

Beecham opened a U.S.-based factory designed for antibiotics production in 1967. The company bought Horlicks milk drinks in 1969 and S.E. Massengill, a U.S.-based feminine hygiene products maker, in 1970. Two years later, the U.K. government forbade a proposed merger between Beecham and the Glaxo Group, its largest competitor, fearing the deal would decrease research efforts in the pharmaceutical industry. By the mid-1970s, the firm was selling its Norval antidepressant and Pollinex allergy vaccine, as well as three new antibiotics: amoxicillin, flucloxacillin, and ticarcillin. In 1977, Beecham paid $76 million for Sucrets brand cough drops and bought Calgon's line of bath products. The company diversified into perfumes in 1979 with the $85 million purchase of U.S.-based Jovan. A year later, Beecham entered the foods market with its purchase of Bovril.

In the early 1980s, Beecham continued its acquisition spree by purchasing J.B. Williams—which gave the firm access to Geritol vitamin supplements, Sominex sleeping pills, and Aqua Velva after shave lotion—for $100 million. Despite sagging ampicillin sales caused by increased competition and government attempts to restrict profits of pharmaceutical companies, Beecham also bought several drug companies in France, West Germany, and Italy. The firm paid $369 million for Norcliff Thayer, makers of Tums and other over-the-counter drugs, and also acquired the cosmetics and fragrance products of BAT in 1985. A year later, the firm began divesting non-core operations.

In July of 1989, Beecham merged with SmithKline Beckman to become SmithKline Beecham PLC, based in London, England. The newly merged firm placed number two, after Merck & Co., among world drug companies with $6.9 billion in combined annual sales. In 1990, net income exceeded $1 billion for the first time. A year later, SmithKline Beecham unveiled its first major drug since the merger, Seroxat, an antidepressant.

The company developed several new drugs in the early 1990s, including Relafen, an arthritis drug with $40 million in sales; Paxil, an antidepressant; and Havris, the world's first hepatitis A vaccine. SmithKline Beecham ranked number one in acne remedies (Oxy brands), number two in antiulcer drugs, and number three in prescription drugs and toothpaste (Aquafresh). The firm expanded its global distribution network in 1994 when it bought the over-the-counter unit of Sterling Winthrop, and paid $2.3 billion for United Health Care's pharmacy-benefit services unit. SmithKline Beecham then divested its animal health division for $1.5 billion and the U.S. over-the-counter operations of Sterling Winthrop to Bayer AG for $1 billion.

In 1995, the FDA approved over-the-counter sales of Tagamet HB for heartburn and acid indigestion. The drug faced direct competition from Johnson & Johnson's Pepcid AC, which was approved for non-prescription use at roughly the same time. SmithKline Beecham and Johnson and Johnson became involved in a $200 advertising war that eventually prompted a New York judge to order both firms to withdraw specific advertisements for their new heartburn drugs, due to their unsubstantiated claims. Later that year, SmithKline Beecham received FDA approval to market its hepatitis A vaccine and to sell a tablet form of Kytril, an anti-nausea drug for cancer patients.

In 1996 the FDA allowed Nicorette gum to be sold as an over-the-counter product and approved Hycamtin for patients whose ovarian cancer had not responded to other treatments. Altogether, SmithKline Beecham filed a total of 154 new product approvals in 1996; although new product sales grew by 37%, sales of Tagamet fell 41%. In January of 1997, the firm announced its intention to merge with American Home Products. Less than two weeks later, SmithKline Beecham decided Glaxo Wellcome was a more attractive partner and ended its discussions with American Home Products. SmithKline Beecham and Glaxo Wellcome executives couldn't agree on how to best run the new company, though, and that deal was called off in late February.

History of Diversified Pharmaceuticals Services Inc.

United HealthCare Corp. was incorporated in 1977 in Minnetonka, Minnesota. The owner and manager of HMOs, it expanded through acquisitions and development of its management services, controlled 11 HMOs in ten states by 1984. United created Diversified Pharmaceutical Services (DPS) during this period of expansion. Operating as a subsidiary, DPS provided managed care drug services.

The Officers

Chairman: Sir Peter Walters, Jr.

CEO: Jan Leschly

Chief Operating Officer and President, Pharmaceuticals and Consumer Healthcare: Jean Pierre Garnier

Exec. VP and Chief Financial Officer: Andrew Bonfield

Sr. VP, Corporate Affairs: James Hill

United continued with its expansion efforts and went public in 1984. It began to implement national expansion plans by creating new HMOs and acquiring multi-state organizations. In 1985 the company acquired Share Development Corp. for $60 million. The deal allowed United and its subsidiaries to become active in 22 states with 822,400 members in company-owned and -managed health plans. One year later United purchased Peak Healthcare Inc. for $83 million. By the end of 1986 the company served roughly 1.6 million people.

United began a restructuring program in 1987. Operating expenses were increasing dramatically, offsetting the firm's substantial sales increases. The company sold off unrewarding businesses and had to forego several HMO startups and health plans. In 1988 United sold Peak Health Care for $41.5 million. The restructuring efforts paid off, and by 1989 the company was once again profitable and one of the largest publicly traded HMOs in the U.S., serving one million people in 15 states.

Under the leadership of Dr. William McGuire, United purchased PrimeCare Health Plan Inc. in 1990 to work hand in hand with DPS. Enrollment in DPS programs surged from three million to 14 million. In 1993 the subsidiary began targeting more of the public sector market, including state and federal government health insurance programs. United anticipated strong demand for the specialty services of DPS and restructured its product lines to increase its competitive stance in the industry.

SmithKline Beecham (SB) began pursuing DPS in 1994, and in May of that year United sold its subsidiary to the giant pharmaceutical firm for $2.3 billion. DPS was integrated into SB; in 1996 its services were combined with Clinical Labs, Diversified Prescription Delivery, and Health Management Services to form SmithKline Beecham Healthcare Services. In June 1999 SB sold its interest in DPS to Express Scripts in order to focus on its core operations as well as to streamline and consolidate manufacturing efforts.

The Players

CEO of SmithKline Beecham: Jan Leschly. Jan Leschly, once the 10th-ranked tennis player in the world, exchanged his athletic career for a position at Novo, a Danish pharmaceutical company. In 1979 he took a job with Squibb, pioneering the introduction of Capoten, the second largest selling prescription medication in the world. In 1988 he was elected president and chief operating officer of the company. He left when Squibb was sold to Bristol Meyers and joined SmithKline Beecham in 1990. In April of 1994 he was named CEO of the company. Leschly oversaw SmithKline's diversification by orchestrating a number of acquisitions, including the 1994 purchase of Diversified Pharmaceutical Services from United Healthcare. Highly regarded in the healthcare industry, he received the Pharmacy Practitioner of the Year Award from the International Pharmaceutical Federation Foundation for Education and Research in 1995.

President of United HealthCare Corp.: William W. McGuire, M.D. Dr. McGuire left his post as president and chief operating officer of Peak Health Plan in 1988 when he joined United HealthCare Corp. as an executive vice president. One year later he was named president chief operating officer. In February of 1991 McGuire was elected CEO of United. Three years later, he oversaw United's sale of subsidiary Diversified Pharmaceutical Services to SmithKline Beecham.

Market Forces Driving the Merger

In the early 1990s the U.S. healthcare industry was bombarded with the emergence of pharmaceutical benefit managers (PBMs). These companies managed the drug costs of employers who offered health insurance to employees. Because PBMs were so prominent, they could negotiate discounts with drug companies by purchasing in bulk and then offering lower prices to their members. By 1994, PBMs boasted a client base of over 50 million Americans.

Rather than trying to compete with PBMs, large pharmaceutical companies were looking to join forces with them. Merck & Co., the world's largest drug company, purchased Medco, the largest PBM, in November of 1993. Pressured by Merck's purchase, SmithKline began to seek out a possible merger with a PBM. In an article in *The Times*, SmithKline's CEO Jan Leschly said, "We all know the environment in which

we work is changing rapidly. The winners will position themselves to capitalize on change. Those who fail to adapt will lose."

By merging with DPS, SmithKline would be able to compete with Merck, and could promote a more cost effective form of medical treatment. The deal would strengthen SmithKline's position in the industry, allowing it to continue in its research and development areas.

Approach and Engagement

DPS became attractive to SmithKline in early 1994. As one of the country's largest PBMs, managing drug benefits for nearly 11 million people, DPS could transform SmithKline into a frontrunner in the burgeoning industry.

In May of that year, United HealthCare sold its Diversified Pharmaceutical Services unit to SmithKline for $2.3 billion. Some analysts thought the price was a bit steep, given the company's sales of $142.1 million and its operating income of $39.9 million in 1993. However, SmithKline believed the cost was justified because it would gain access to the pharmaceutical benefits market. According to an article in the *Financial Times (London)*, Jan Leschly viewed the deal as "a vital part of his efforts to move the group from being a manufacturer selling pills to a supplier of total pharmaceutical care."

United HealthCare secured a six-year alliance as part of the deal. United would continue to provide administrative and management services to DPS, and SmithKline would have exclusive rights to United's data on 1.6 million members of its HMOs. United agreed to use DPS as its pharmaceutical benefit manager for its operations and also agreed not to create a competitor to DPS for six years.

Products and Services

By acquiring DPS, SmithKline had gained one of the largest pharmaceutical benefit managers in the U.S. DPS serviced health plans, government health programs, and employers. With over 14 million enrolled in its program, DPS had a presence in over 30,000 pharmacies across the United States.

With operations in over 39 countries throughout the world, SmithKline Beecham was one of the largest drug companies in the world. Sales from pharmaceuticals accounted for 60% of total sales (or $7.7 billion) in 1997. Pharmaceutical products included Amoxil, an antibiotic; Hycamtin, used for ovarian cancer; Kytril, anti-nausea medication for cancer patients; Seroxat/Paxil, an antidepressant; and Baycol, a cholesterol controller, just to name a few. The company's wide variety of consumer products (accounting for about 30% of sales) included such brands as Nicorette, a nicotine gum; Geritol, a diet supplement; Contac, a cold treatment; Aquafresh, a toothpaste; Tums, an antacid; and OXY, used for facial skin care.

Changes to the Industry

The rise of health management organizations (HMOs) and PBMs in the 1990s sparked an intense wave of mergers in the healthcare industry. Merck's takeover of Medco in 1993 served as the impetus for other large companies to merge. Eli Lilly & Co. purchased PCS Health Systems, the benefits division of McKesson Corp.; Pfizer Inc., Rhone-Poulenc Rohr, and Bristol-Myers Squibb Co. also joined forces to form an alliance with Caremark International, Inc., a managed care company. The drug industry had moved from dictating prices to dealing with generic alternatives and the increasing power of PBMs.

According to Bruce Wasserstein in *Big Deal: The Battle for Control of America's Leading Corporations,* "The rationale behind this rash of deals was simple; drug companies saw their control of the distribution channel for pharmaceuticals slipping away, along with their favorable margins. By acquiring the big pharmacy benefits companies, the drug companies hoped to recapture the initiative."

The mid-1990s also saw small U.S. firms being gobbled up by stronger foreign companies: Roche, a Swiss-based company, purchased Syntex Corp., a drug maker, in 1994. Biotech companies became targets, as well. When a patent expired on a brand name, drug competitors could recreate generic versions, which drove down prices. Companies could either spend a fortune on research and development of new drugs or acquire biotech companies to gain access to promising new drugs.

Review of the Outcome

Although SmithKline Beecham's deal with United HealthCare's DPS unit followed the trend of marriages between drug companies and PBMs, SmithKline was not allowed to use DPS to boost sales of its own products because of a ruling by the U.S. Federal Trade Commission after the merger. This was a minor setback however, and in 1995 the company saw a large increase in net income from the previous year.

SmithKline continued its attempt to become the largest healthcare provider after its purchase of DPS. Although it was outbid for American Cyanamid Co. (by American Home Products Corp.), it purchased Sterling Health in 1994, becoming the world's largest

over-the-counter medicine producer. That same year, the company sold its animal healthcare business to Pfizer Inc. for $1.45 billion, furthering its efforts to focus on health care business for humans.

By April of 1995 DPS had increased its clientele by 17% and served over 16.2 million people. Although many analysts claimed the purchase was a horrible mistake and that benefits of the deal had not yet proved their worth in dollars, Leschly was confident in DPS's operations. He contended that DPS's operations allowed the company to forge valuable relationships with healthcare buyers and to track data on drug consumption.

In 1999 SmithKline began a reorganization process that would allow the company to focus on pharmaceutical and consumer healthcare businesses. It eliminated 3,000 jobs and sold Clinical Laboratories to Quest Diagnostics Inc. for $1.27 billion. Leschly finally admitted that SmithKline's purchase of DPS hadn't produced the anticipated synergies; in fact, the unit was losing money. DPS was sold to Express Scripts Inc. for $700 million in June 1999. SmithKline lost a total $713.6 million on the deal.

Research

Bagnall, Sarah. "SmithKline Broadens U.S. Base with $2.3 Bn Buy," in *The Times,* 4 May 1994. Explains SB's move to acquire a PBM.

"Express Scripts Public Offering," in *Wall Street Journal,* 14 June 1999. Details the sale of SmithKline's DPS unit to Express Scripts.

Olmos, David. "Drug Makers Can't Beat 'Em So They Join Managed Care," in *Los Angeles Times,* 4 May 1994. Discusses recent trends in the drug and health care industry.

SmithKline Beecham PLC Home Page, available at http://www.sb.com. Official World Wide Web Home Page for SmithKline Beecham PLC. Includes historical, financial, and product information, as well as recent news articles.

"SmithKline Beecham," in *Notable Corporate Chronologies,* The Gale Group, 1999. Lists major events in the history of SmithKline Beecham.

"SmithKline to Sell Two Units, Eliminate 3,000 Jobs," in *The Buffalo News,* 10 February 1999. Discusses SB's plans to reorganize and sell DPS as well as Clinical Laboratories.

"SmithKline's Well-Sugared Pill," in *Financial Times (London),* 22 February 1997. Reports SmithKline's financial position in 1996 and results of the DPS deal.

Wasserstein, Bruce. *Big Deal: The Battle for Control of America's Leading Corporations,* Warner Books, 1998. Offers an overview of the largest mergers in recent American corporate history.

Wighton, David. "SmithKline's Deal Brings An Explosive Bargain," in *Financial Times London,* 4 May 1994. Examines the deal between SmithKline and United HealthCare.

CHRISTINA M. STANSELL

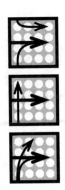

SOCIÉTÉ NATIONALE ELF AQUITAINE & TEXASGULF

Tour Elf
Paris La Défense Cedex, 92078
France

tel: 33 01 47 44 45 46
fax: 33 01 47 44 73 66
web: http://www.elf.fr and http://www.elfadr.com

nationality: France
date: September 1981
affected: Société Nationale Elf Aquitaine, France, founded 1976
affected: Texasgulf Inc., USA, founded 1950s

Overview of the Merger

Société Nationale Elf Aquitaine's $4.3 billion acquisition of Texasgulf Inc. in September 1981 was one of the largest cross-border deals of the 1980s. The transaction was actually a three-way deal between Elf and Canada Development Corporation. The U.S. company learned of its fate the very day that the takeover began, and was unable to stop it. Within a month it found itself not only in the hands of the French oil company, but also without its Canadian operations—accounting for 42% of its assets and about half of its employees.

History of Société Nationale Elf Aquitaine

Régie Autonome des Pétroles (RAP) was established by the French government in 1939 to mine the gas of a newly discovered field in France. Two years later France formed the public, yet state-majority-owned, Société Nationale des Pétroles d'Aquitaine (SNPA) for oil exploration in France. In 1945 the government formed the Bureau de Recherches de Pétrole (BRP) for two main purposes: to serve as a holding company for RAP and SNPA, and to seek out and financially support oil projects beyond the country's borders.

In 1951 SNPA discovered a large gas field at Lacq, and the company launched chemicals operations to develop the resources mined there. Through this and the following decade, France's natural resources companies continued to explore and make discoveries in various parts of the world. Now assured that its resources needs would be met, France expanded into refining. In 1960 it formed Union Générale des Pétroles (UGP), a state-owned holding company for BRP's subsidiaries, as well as the Union Industrielle des Pétroles, jointly-owned by UGP, Texaco, and Standard Oil.

In 1966 BRP and RAP merged to form Enterprise de Recherches d'Activitiés Pétrolières (ERAP), a holding company for France's various natural resources companies. SNPA was kept a distinct company, even though the government's holdings in it were absorbed into ERAP. The following year, ERAP integrated the group's seven logos and brand names as Elf, a word selected by a computer because of its easy pronunciation in any language.

Aquitaine Total Organico, ERAP's first petrochemicals company, was established in 1969. ERAP increased its market share in oil to 25% the following year by acquiring a majority stake in the Antar group. In 1971 it joined with Total Chimie to form the chemicals company Ato Chimie. Two years later it diversified into pharmaceuticals by founding Sanofi, which immediately launched a strategy of expansion through acquisition of small pharmaceuticals and cosmetics companies.

Finally, on September 1, 1976, France's natural resources companies were completely integrated when ERAP merged with SNPA to form Société Nationale Elf Aquitaine, in which the state held a 70% interest. Albin Chalandon became the new company's chairman in 1977, the same year that Elf expanded its chemical operations into the U.S. by acquiring M&T Chemicals.

Elf's interest in U.S. companies would not end with M&T Chemicals, as Texasgulf was soon to learn. Politics, particularly the threat of nationalization, would spur Elf to acquire greater interests in American companies, the assets of which would be protected from the French government.

After its 1981 acquisition of Texasgulf, Elf Aquitaine continued to cement its hold on the oil, gasoline, chemicals, and health industries. Atochem, a chemicals subsidiary, was formed on October 1, 1983. In 1989 Elf purchased U.S.-based Pennwalt Corporation for $1 billion. Sanofi, which by 1987 held Elf's bio industrial activities, acquired several prestigious perfume companies, including the Nina Ricci Group in 1988, followed by the Yves Saint Laurent Group in 1993. The following year, Sanofi acquired the U.S. pharmaceuticals company Sterling Winthrop.

Privatization occurred in 1994, with the French government's stake reduction from 51.5% to 13.3% through an initial public offering. That year the company recorded its first net income loss—FF 5.4 billion. The following year, however, it bounced back into the black, reporting FF 5 billion in net income on revenues of FF 208.3 billion. In 1995 it sold Texasgulf to Potash Corporation of Saskatchewan for $180 million.

History of Texasgulf Inc.

Texas Gulf Sulphur Company was a chemicals company involved in solely in sulphur in the mid-20th century. Its focus on only one product made it appealing to other, more diverse companies. In 1959 Tenneco approached it with a merger offer. Charles Fogarty, vice president of exploration, developed a strategic

The Business

Financials

Revenue (1997): FF 254.3 billion ($42.3 million)

Employees (1997): 83,700

SICs / NAICS

sic 2911 - Petroleum Refining

sic 1311 - Crude Petroleum & Natural Gas

sic 5541 - Gasoline Service Stations

sic 2834 - Pharmaceutical Preparations

sic 2865 - Cyclic Crudes & Intermediates

sic 2874 - Phosphatic Fertilizers

sic 2844 - Toilet Preparations

sic 2891 - Adhesives & Sealants

naics 324110 - Petroleum Refineries

naics 211111 - Crude Petroleum and Natural Gas Extraction

naics 447190 - Other Gasoline Stations

naics 325412 - Pharmaceutical Preparation Manufacturing

naics 325110 - Petrochemical Manufacturing

naics 325312 - Phosphatic Fertilizer Manufacturing

naics 325620 - Toilet Preparation Manufacturing

naics 325520 - Adhesive and Sealant Manufacturing

plan for diversification without benefit of a partnership with another company, so Texas Gulf's board rejected Tenneco's offer. That year the firm generated earnings of $13.4 million on revenues of $63.6 million.

The company's diversification led it into other natural resources industries such as metals, including copper, zinc, and silver; as well as such chemicals as phosphate, potash, and soda ash. Its foray into phosphate was a natural fit with its core sulphur operations, since both chemicals are key ingredients in the fertilizer industry.

Unfortunately for Texasgulf, as the company was now known, its independence was again challenged in 1973. The Canada Development Corporation (CDC) had been formed the previous year by the Canadian government for the purpose of investing in and developing Canadian companies. On July 24, 1973, CDC initiated a tender offer for Texasgulf. Three days later Texasgulf filed a lawsuit to block the takeover, alleging that CDC was in violation of U.S. antitrust laws. The court dismissed the complaint, pointing out that the matter of antitrust was not an issue due to the fact

The Officers

Chairman and Chief Executive Officer : Philippe Jaffré

Executive VP, Exploration and Production: Jean-Luc Vermeulen

Executive VP, Refining, Marketing and Trading: Bernard de Combret

Executive VP, Health: Jean-Francois Dehecq

Executive VP, Chemicals: Jacques Puéchal

that Texasgulf and CDC do not operate in the same industry. Although losing the lawsuit, Texasgulf still gained from the takeover delay. On September 14, 1973, the two companies reached a deal limiting CDC's acquisition to a 32% minority interest.

In 1979 Texasgulf was enjoying continued success—earnings were $115 million on $760 million in sales. The diversification plan developed by Fogarty, who was now chairman and CEO, had reduced sulphur's contribution to only 20% of total operating income. The company's metals operations generated the lion's share, 51%, with other chemicals accounting for less than 40%. Its entry into the coal business would be facilitated by its 1978 purchase of a Colorado coalmine.

Texasgulf's complacency was about to be shattered, however. In June 1981 it would face a sudden betrayal by CDC and resulting takeover by the French company Société Nationale Elf Aquitaine. This marriage would prove to be relatively short-lived, however, as Texasgulf would be sold to the Potash Corporation of Saskatchewan in 1995.

Market Forces Driving the Merger/Acquisition

By 1981 Société Nationale Elf Aquitaine owned 75% of the oil and gas enterprise Aquitaine Company of Canada. This company was Elf's largest North American foothold. Canadian politics, however, were creating a market of increasing difficulty for foreign competition. Under the "Canadization" part of the country's National Energy Program, the government provided large subsidies to companies having Canadian-held majority interests. Elf and other foreign-owned enterprises were being driven out, sometimes forced to sell their interests to Canadians at severely undervalued prices.

Elf and other French companies were also eager to acquire U.S. companies to maintain operations out-side the realm of state intervention. Elf itself was 67% state-owned at this time, and was one of the companies threatened by the government to undergo complete nationalization. As Chalandon told *Fortune*, "Above all, we needed a place where we could make profits and raise funds and send them wherever we wanted to support our operations outside France."

In order to maintain a North American presence while evacuating Canada, Elf began eyeing Texasgulf Inc., an American company that was 37% owned by the Canada Development Corporation (CDC). CDC had been formed in 1972 by the national government to fund the development of Canadian companies. In 1973 it had made a hostile takeover bid on Texasgulf, finally settling for a 32% minority interest.

Focusing on companies operating on its homeland, CDC was interested in acquiring Elf's interest in the Aquitaine Company of Canada. The leaders of the two companies—Albin Chalandon, of Société Nationale Elf Aquitaine, and H. Anthony Hampson, of CDC—pursued the possibility of arranging a mutually beneficial deal.

Approach and Engagement

Negotiations between Elf and CDC were kept secret, and Texasgulf's chairman Richard D. Mollison suspected that they had been initiated more than a year prior to the announcement. Yet regardless of the time frame of the negotiations, the news came as a complete surprise to Texasgulf. On June 26, 1981, Hampson telephoned Mollison to break the news of the takeover. Within the month, Elf had acquired 87% of Texasgulf's stock.

The deal arranged by Elf and CDC was a complex, three-way transaction. Elf would sell its 75% stake in Aquitaine Company of Canada to CDC for $994 million in cash. CDC would transfer its 37% stake in Texasgulf to Elf in exchange for Texasgulf's Canadian assets, which include the Kidd Creek field, the world's largest silver and zinc mine. Because Texasgulf's Canadian properties were worth more than CDC's share of Texasgulf, CDC would also pay Elf an additional $500 million. The deal would make CDC the 12th-largest oil company in Canada.

Texasgulf didn't passively submit to this raid. Unable to gain the support of the U.S. Department of Justice or the Federal Trade Commission, Mollison enlisted the aid of the Committee on Foreign Investment in the U.S. This agency, established to look out for American companies with foreign investors, wrote a letter to the French ambassador in Washington, D.C., requesting a suspension of the merger until it could analyze its implication to the U.S.

economy. As reported in *Fortune*, France's president, François Mitterrand, responded nearly two weeks later, "I hereby confirm that this is purely a commercial transaction. Therefore the French government has no intention of intervening." This brought the matter to rest, as Texasgulf failed to muster more powerful support from within the U.S. government.

Products and Services

By 1997 Elf had four operating divisions: Upstream, Downstream, Chemicals, and Health.

Upstream, its oil and gas exploration and production operations, was Elf's principal business, accounting for 67%, or FF 17.1 billion, of total company operating income. It made Elf the fourth-largest producer of natural gas in Europe. Exploration activities took place in 28 countries and production concentrated in 15 countries.

Downstream was comprised of refining and marketing enterprises, as well as international trading activities. Generating operating income of FF 2.2 billion, or 9% of the company's total, this division operated 5,000 service stations in Europe and West Africa. Its assets included the Heron network in the U.K. and British Petroleum's African refining and marketing assets. It owned a 43.3% stake in Cepsa, Spain's second-largest oil company.

Chemicals generated 16%, or FF 4.1 billion, of total operating income, making Elf the world's 13th-largest chemicals company. It was divided into three segments. Basic chemicals was the largest, comprised of such businesses as petrochemicals, chlorochemicals, and fertilizers. The performance products segment involved adhesives, electroplating, and performance polymers. Intermediates and fine chemicals included such specialty chemicals as acrylics, fluorochemicals, peroxides, and thiochemicals; it was the world's leading producer of the latter, as well as of electroplating products.

Its smallest division, **Health**, contributed FF 2.1 billion, or 8% of total operating income. This division was comprised of Sanofi, which was 55% owned by Elf. This subsidiary operated in two segments: health and beauty. Health was concerned with pharmaceuticals, mainly in the therapeutic classes of cardiovascular disease, internal medicine, oncology, and central nervous system disorders. Sanofi was the world's 23rd-largest pharmaceutical company. In addition, its beauty operations included the trademarks of Parfuns Yves Saint Laurent, Oscar de la Renta, Roger & Gallet, and Yves Rocher (Nina Ricci had been sold in January 1998).

The Players

Société Nationale Elf Aquitaine Chairman: Albin Chalandon. Politics was an arena that suited Albin Chalandon well. During World War II, he had been a leader of the French resistance. He later provided support for Charles de Gaulle's return to power in 1957. Under this administration and the Georges Pompidou regime that succeeded it, Chalandon held numerous cabinet posts. Under President Valéry Giscard d'Estaing, he was given the chief executive position at Elf in 1977 with the mission of revitalizing the company and operating it similarly to a private firm. Having taken the independence directive a bit too far for governmental comfort, the Minister of Industry twice asked for his resignation—and was twice refused. But as Elf's largest shareholder, the French government had little to complain about financially. In 1978, the year after Chalandon took the helm, Elf's common stock was trading at FF 300; two years later it was valued at FF 1,545.

Texasgulf Inc. Chairman: Richard D. Mollison. Richard Mollison began working at Texasgulf in 1948. He was primarily involved in exploration, and contributed to the company's famed Kidd Creek Mine in Timmons, Ontario. He eventually came in from the fields as he received various promotions, ultimately attaining the position of vice chairman. In February 1981, he suddenly found himself the company's leader when Charles Fogarty was one of six company executives killed in a plane crash. Mollison had been planning to retire in only a few months but put those plans on hold for two years. Then, just as he was settling in to his new job, he would be challenged by an undesired acquisition by Elf Aquitaine just four short months after assuming control.

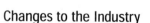

Changes to the Industry

Elf's acquisition of Texasgulf tripled its U.S. operations. It became the world's largest producer of sulphur, and a major player in phosphate mining and fertilizer production.

Albin Chalandon, aware of the discontent that Texasgulf harbored due to its takeover, signed a pledge with the company to retain all of its executives—at their current salaries—as well as the company's name and traditions. This gesture served to pour oil over troubled waters, but Mollison and other executives had been resentful not of Elf, but of CDC.

In the eyes of many Texasgulf executives, CDC had betrayed the company by secretly selling it out. In an August 1981 *Forbes* article, Mollison stated, "We were misled." In that same article, CDC chairman H. Anthony Hampson insisted that its transfer of Texasgulf ownership "didn't involve Texasgulf." Determined to make the best of its situation, the U.S. company resolved to get along with its new parent.

The loss of its Canadian properties to CDC represented 42% of its assets and approximately half of its 6,700 employees. But balancing that loss was the gain in other operations from Elf. Texasgulf absorbed three of Elf's U.S. subsidiaries: a New Jersey chemical company, a Houston oil- and gas-exploration operation, and a Denver uranium exploration business. Combined, the U.S. company would have revenues of about $380 million.

Review of the Outcome

Valued at $4.3 billion, the Elf Aquitaine/Texasgulf merger was one of the ten largest international deals of the 1980s. In 1985 Elf sold a 15% stake in Texasgulf to The Williams Companies Inc. in exchange for that company's Agrico subsidiary. Elf hung onto its 85% interest for another decade, until it came to the realization that this subsidiary would never be as profitable as its other operations. Moreover, Texasgulf's businesses really didn't fit in with Elf's principal operations.

Elf and The Williams Companies planned in February 1995 to sell all of their shares in Texasgulf through an initial public offering of that company. One month later, however, they cancelled the offering when the Potash Corporation of Saskatchewan (PCS)

offered to purchase Texasgulf for $810 million—twice what Elf had estimated to earn from the IPO. The purchase doubled PCS's assets and employees, and, with its subsequent purchase of White Springs Agricultural Chemicals, made PCS the world's third-largest producer of phosphate fertilizer.

Research

Blyskal, Jeff. "The Takeover Nobody Noticed," in *Forbes*, 31 August 1981. A brief review of the impending merger, focusing on the Canada Development Corporation angle.

Cook, James. "How Texasgulf Kept Its Independence," in *Forbes*, 21 January 1980. Overview of Texasgulf's history and success at deflecting CDC's 1973 takeover attempt—ironic in light of the upcoming year's transaction.

"PCS's 'Superb Acquisition': Texasgulf for $835 Million," in *Chemical Week*, 15 March 1995. Short article describing the Potash Corporation of Saskatchewan's closing of the Texasgulf purchase.

"Societe Nationale Elf Aquitaine," in *Notable Corporate Chronologies*, The Gale Group, 1999. Lists major events in the history of the company.

Société Nationale Elf Aquitaine 1997 Annual Report. Lists in-depth financial news and announcements.

Société Nationale Elf Aquitaine 1997 Data Book. Covers financial highlights and describes company operating segments.

Société Nationale Elf Aquitaine Home Page, available at http://www.elf.fr and http://www.elfadr.com. Official World Wide Web Page for Elf Aquitaine. Includes access to a brief overview and history of the company, summary financial information, and recent news.

"Texasgulf Hopes to Raise $396M with IPO," in *Going Public, the IPO Reporter*, 6 February 1995. Announcement of Elf's plans to spin off Texasgulf.

Tinnin, David B. "Elf's Adventures in the U.S.A." in *Fortune*, 7 September 1981. Reports the background and follow-through of the merger.

KIMBERLY N. STEVENS

SONY & COLUMBIA PICTURES ENTERTAINMENT

nationality: Japan
date: November 6, 1989
affected: Sony Corp., Japan, founded 1946
affected: Columbia Pictures Entertainment, Inc., USA, founded 1924

The Sony Corp.
7-35, Kitashinagawa, 6-chome
Shinagawa-ku
Tokyo, 141
Japan

tel: 81-3-5448-2111
fax: 81-3-5448-2183
web: http://world.sony.com

Overview of the Merger

With its 1989 acquisition of Columbia Pictures Entertainment, Inc., Sony Corp. became the largest Japanese company in the U.S. Sony gained an extensive library containing 2,770 film titles, as well as 23,000 episodes of 260 popular television series. It also gained control over Loews Theater Management Corp., a leading American cinema chain operating in 220 locations. After the acquisition, the name of Columbia Pictures Entertainment was changed to Sony Pictures Entertainment. Although Sony profited from the recordings of such artists as Bruce Springsteen, its involvement in film production proved unprofitable. In 1994, Sony wrote off its $2.7 billion investment in film studios, which resulted in a stunning quarterly loss of $3.2 billion for the firm.

History of Sony Corp.

Sony was founded by Masaru Ibuka and Akio Morita, two men who became acquainted while designing radar equipment for the Japanese military during World War II. In 1946, drawing upon the equivalent of $500 in capital, Ibuka and Morita incorporated the Tokyo Telecommunications Engineering Co. with the express purpose of developing innovative consumer electronic products for an international market. In war-devastated Japan, scarcity drove innovation in the development of the first Japanese tape recorder. In the absence of vinyl, Ibuka and Morita were forced to develop a delicate and high-precision machine that could capture sound on paper recording tape without causing tape breakage. Initially sold for entertainment uses, the recorder was more successfully marketed for use in Japanese schools and courtrooms. In 1953, Ibuka and Morita purchased a license to make transistors, the components necessary for the production of miniature electrical circuits and portable radios. In 1955, a design team led by Ibuka produced a portable, all-transistor radio for the Japanese market. Three years later, Ibuka and Morita made Sony the official name of their company.

With the establishment of the Sony Corp. of America in 1960, as well as the sale of two million shares of Sony common stock to American interests, Ibuka and Morita made their first significant moves towards establishing an international

The Business

Financials

Revenue (1999): $1.5 billion

Employees (1999): 177,000

SICs / NAICS

sic 3651 - Household Audio & Video Equipment

sic 3695 - Magnetic & Optical Recording Media

sic 5045 - Computers, Peripherals & Software

naics 334612 - Prerecorded Compact Disc (except
    Software), Tape, and Record Reproducing

naics 334613 - Magnetic and Optical Recording Media
    Manufacturing

market. After 1960, the goal of pioneering consumer electronics for a global market drove Sony's expansion. In 1962, Sony introduced the first in a long series of superlative products when it placed the world's smallest and lightest all-transistor TV on the market. One year later, Sony introduced the first portable all-transistor video tape recorder for industrial use, a move that was followed five years later by Sony's development of Trinitron color television picture tube. Sony expanded its international market and production base, not only by outpacing other companies in product development, but also by entering joint ventures with American companies such as CBS for the purpose of marketing U.S. goods in Japan. In 1970, Sony listed its depository shares on the New York Stock Exchange.

Throughout the 1980s, Sony's expansion was marked by two primary emphases: innovative product design and increased involvement in the software and entertainment industries. By miniaturizing products, Sony hoped to create a new relationship between machines and consumers. Sony's most popular portable entertainment systems were the Sony Walkman and the Video Walkman. In the late 1970s, Morita and Ibuka responded to the increasing popularity of pop music among Japanese youth by developing a portable stereo for individual use. By 1984, the popularity of the Walkman had spread from Japan to the U.S., despite the stereo's lack of recording capability. Shortly after, Sony produced a Video Walkman, a pocket-sized VCR with an attached TV screen. The Video Walkman was an immense success with Japanese commuters, and in 1988, it was marketed in the U.S. These and other products proved profitable

because competitors found it difficult to replicate Sony's technologically advanced components quickly and easily.

Sony's expansion in the 1980s was based not only on the popularity of portable entertainment systems, but also on the diversification of the company's product line to include entertainment software. Intensive diversification began with Sony's failure to successfully market the Betamax home videocassette recorder, first produced in 1975. The world's first videocassette recorder for home use, the Betamax represented an enormous technological accomplishment. Its popularity, however, was curtailed when Japan's entertainment industry began mass-producing recording tape in VHS format, and consumers correspondingly began buying VHS machines produced by Japanese competitors. By 1988, Sony was forced by this market pressure to relent and produce VHS tapes and recording machines.

Due to the failure of the Betamax, Sony's executives learned that consumer demand for Sony electronic hardware and corporate profitability ultimately depended on the availability of compatible software products. In late 1987, Sony took its first significant step into the entertainment business by purchasing CBS Records for $2 billion. In buying CBS Records, Sony executives hoped to gain control over the production of records, compact discs, and tapes that would stimulate the consumption of Sony stereos and recorders. In 1989, Sony further invested in the entertainment industry by purchasing Columbia Pictures Entertainment, Inc. and gaining rights to the holdings of the Columbia's vast library.

In 1994, Sony began to write off its investment in film studios because of the declining profitability of Sony Pictures Entertainment. By that time, Sony had entered the market for personal computers. Noting the complementarity of innovation in consumer electronics and computer industries, Sony's executives began experimenting with high-definition televisions designed to convey enhanced special effects, and filmless cameras that electronically stored images on floppy disks. In 1996, Sony introduced a desktop computer to the American market, and by 1998, it was experimenting with zip drives. Since entering the desktop computer market, Sony has had to both cooperate and compete with Microsoft Corp. in its production of network technologies and computer components. In April of 1998, Microsoft and Sony announced plans to work together in developing standard technology for digital television. In 1999, the two companies discussed options regarding the production of compatible Sony software and Microsoft network technology.

Since the late 1980s, Sony's position as a producer of consumer electronics was transformed by developments in digital technology and competition with Microsoft. Questions arose as to whether Sony's partial redirection of capital investments from consumer electronics to digital network services would prove profitable, as Microsoft and Intel expanded into interactive cable television, direct broadcasting satellite TV, and entertainment systems. In April of 1999, Sony announced a 19.4% decline in its fiscal earnings relative to the previous year and its first quarterly net loss in four years. Only one month earlier, Sony had announced a plan to eliminate 10% of its total work force, or about 17,000 jobs, and to shut down 15 manufacturing plants around the world during the next three years.

History of Columbia Pictures Entertainment, Inc.

Columbia Pictures started as a tiny studio founded by Harry Cohn in 1924. Initially dismissed as the "Poverty Row Studio," Columbia Pictures was a dominant force in the entertainment industry by the 1930s. Noted for its two-reel comedies and particularly for its production of *Three Stooges* films, Columbia Pictures also produced such classics as *It Happened One Night*, *The Caine Mutiny*, and *On the Waterfront* in the first three decades of its existence.

In the early 1980s, the film industry took a downturn. In 1982, in an effort to diversify its investments, Coca-Cola Co. purchased Columbia Pictures, founded Tri-Star, and bought two notable television companies, Embassy Communications and Merv Griffin Enterprises. For seven years, Coca-Cola sustained Columbia through adept financing that protected the studio from market fluctuations. However, the studio failed to produce highly successful films and, ultimately, Coca-Cola proved incapable of boosting the profits of Columbia's film studios, although Columbia's television division maintained profitability under Coca-Cola's ownership.

In 1987, Coca-Cola made its first attempts to reverse its diversification efforts. After merging Columbia with Tri-Star Pictures Inc. to form Columbia Pictures Entertainment, Inc., Coca-Cola executives sold stock in the combined company to Coke shareholders. In doing so, they reduced the company's stake in Columbia to 49%. In 1988, the profits of Columbia and Tri-Star continued to decline. That year, Columbia films accounted for only 9.9% of American and Canadian theater ticket sales, having dropped from the 10.7% level of 1987. In 1989, following a series of box office disappointments including *Ghostbusters II* and *The Karate Kid III*, Coca-Cola sold its stake in Columbia Pictures Entertainment to Sony Corp.

The Officers

Chairman and CEO: Norio Ohga

Chief Human Resources Officer: Tsunao Hashimoto

President and Co-CEO: Nobuyuki Idei

Exec. Deputy President and CFO: Tamotsu Iba

Exec. Deputy President: Minoru Morio

Market Forces Driving the Merger

Sony's purchase of Columbia Pictures Entertainment took place in conjunction with global trends toward market deregulation and within the context of growing public debates about levels of foreign investment in American companies. Along with other electronic hardware companies, Sony chose to tap into expanding European and Asian markets for American entertainment by purchasing a Hollywood studio.

By the late 1980s, American producers had already developed extensive foreign alliances in attempts to maintain profits and boost foreign ticket sales in the face of grossly inflated movie budgets. The impetus to invest in film studios was particularly great for Japanese firms during this period, given recent innovations in satellite broadcasting, which made 24-hour television reception possible in even the remotest of Japanese villages. In addition, the mid-1980s breakup of the state-owned Nippon Telephone and Telegraph Co., the extension of cable networks in Japan, and the increasing affordability of rooftop satellite dishes fostered the growth of consumer demand for more varied American entertainment.

A pressing need to diversify its product line also motivated Sony's acquisition of Columbia Pictures. By producing films, television series, and music in formats compatible with its electronic hardware, Sony hope to stimulate demand for its audio and visual equipment. This need had its origins in the sharp division of intellectual and technological labor that developed between East and West in the decades following World War II. After 1945, the U.S. simultaneously abandoned production of electronic hardware to Japan and other Asian nations and established dominance in the mass entertainment and computer software industries.

Approach and Engagement

With its $3.4 billion acquisition of Columbia Pictures Entertainment Inc., Sony Corp. became the largest Japanese company in the U.S. On November 6,

The Players

Sony Corp. Chairman: Akio Morita. As a co-founder of Sony Corp. with Masaru Ibuka, Akio Morita oversaw Sony's rise from a small appliance repair shop to a global enterprise with a leading position in the consumer electronics, entertainment, and computer markets. From the late 1940s, Morita distinguished himself in the Japanese business community through his unusual efforts to establish a product niche in European and American markets. One of Morita's most fortuitous decisions in establishing Sony's international market was to hire Norio Ohga. While a student of opera at Berlin's Kunst Universitaet, Ohga had written a detailed letter to Morita to express his dissatisfaction with the quality of Sony's magnetic tape recorders. Impressed with Ohga's sophisticated grasp of electronic technology, Morita offered to subsidize Ohga's musical training in Europe in exchange for information regarding European recorders and recording processes. Morita's creative hiring strategies paid off well. In 1959, after two years of part-time consulting, Ohga accepted a full-time position in Sony's design center, and during the next 20 years, worked with Morita to establish CBS/Sony, the first major American-Japanese joint corporate venture and Japan's biggest record company. In the late 1980s, as president of Sony, Ohga assisted Morita's efforts to diversify production through the acquisition of American entertainment companies, including CBS Records and Columbia Pictures Entertainment Inc. Noted for his cosmopolitan outlook and innovative business strategies, Morita served an ambassadorial role for Japan as chairman of the Japan-U.S. Business Council, an organization founded to promote economic cooperation between East and West. Despite his international outlook, Morita occasionally alienated the American business community, most notably in 1991, when he co-authored *The Japan That Can Say No*. By advocating an aggressive Japanese approach to the American market, and by criticizing U.S. economic shortsightedness, Morita tarnished Sony's reputation in the United States. By promoting shorter working hours and better pay for Sony's workers, Morita simultaneously challenged members of the Japanese business community who supported increased liberalization of the Japanese economy. In 1994, the widely respected Morita cited health reasons in resigning as chairman.

1989, when the acquisition was finalized, Columbia Pictures became a subsidiary of Sony Corp. under the name Sony Pictures Entertainment.

According to the merger agreement, Sony paid $27 for each outstanding share of Columbia, including the $1.46 billion block of shares representing the Coca-Cola Co.'s 49% stake in Columbia. Sony also assumed Columbia's $1.4 billion debt, making Columbia the most expensive American company ever purchased by a Japanese concern. Through this purchase, Sony gained rights to the extensive holdings of a library containing 2,770 film titles, including *Kramer vs. Kramer*, *The Natural*, and *Gandhi*, as well as rights to 23,000 episodes of 260 popular television series. The rights to Columbia's library holdings, in addition to continued film production at Columbia studios, allowed Sony to control the format and to produce and market music and film in ways that boosted consumer demand for Sony stereos and video recorders. Through the acquisition of Columbia, Sony also gained control over Loews Theater Management Corp., a leading American cinema chain operating in 220 locations.

Sony's acquisition of Columbia Pictures took place in the context of widespread public debates about foreign investment the U.S. and, more specifically, about economic rivalry between the U.S. and Japan. In this context, opponents of Sony's purchase of Columbia frequently linked issues related to cultural protectionism with questions surrounding the U.S. position in the global economy. In some cases, American network executives opposed the acquisition on the grounds that it would create unfair advantages for foreign corporations exempt from antitrust laws preventing mergers between American television networks and film studios. Negative American responses to the takeover of Columbia pictures were widely communicated throughout American and Japanese media. At the same time, most senior U.S. officials, including John Robson, Deputy Secretary of the Treasurer, welcomed Japanese investment, arguing that it would reinvigorate the film industry and create additional American jobs.

Although federal officials did not challenge the combination of Sony and Columbia on antitrust grounds because the companies' product lines did not significantly overlap, Sony's acquisition of Columbia Pictures was nevertheless marred by legal questions. These questions concerned Sony's executives' bid to acquire the talents of producers to manage Columbia Pictures. In July 1989, at an international executive board meeting, Morita and Ohga announced they would approve the acquisition of Columbia Pictures if suitable managers could be found for the company. After a two-month search, Michael Schulhof, president of Sony Corp. of America, approached Peter Guber and Jon Peters, two prominent Hollywood producers noted for their work on *Batman*, *Rain Man*, and *Flashdance*.

At the time of the acquisition, Guber and Peters owned their own company, Guber-Peters Entertainment Co., but were also under contract to produce films exclusively for Warner Bros. Nevertheless, in September of 1989, Sony began negotiating salary terms with Guber and Peters, and on October 10, 1989, Sony executives announced that they had hired Guber and Peters. Three days later, Warner Bros. filed a $1 billion lawsuit against Sony Corp. for unlawful recruitment and incitement to breach of contract. In mid-November, Warner agreed to the release of Gubers and Peters in return for financial compensation. Shortly thereafter, Sony purchased Guber-Peters Entertainment Co. for $200 million, securing the services of Peters and Guber for $2.75 million a year for the first 30 months of a five-year contract and $2.9 million a year for the remaining 30 months. While resolved from a legal standpoint, Sony's recruitment of Peters and Guber generated a certain resentment of Sony's acquisition of Columbia in Hollywood circles. From a financial standpoint, Sony's entrance into the film industry had been costly. According to *Variety* magazine, Columbia Pictures Entertainment and the services of Guber and Peters had cost Sony approximately $6 billion.

Products and Services

In 1989, after 40 years of specializing in consumer electronic hardware, Sony entered the entertainment industry on the grounds that innovations in electronics were driven by developments in software and entertainment. In the mid-1990s, a decline in the profits of its film studios led Sony to redirect its capital investment into the computer industry. Emphasizing the links between innovation in electronic and computer industries, Sony executives promoted the development of high-definition televisions that could convey sharper images and enhanced special effects and filmless cameras that stored stores images electronically on floppy disks.

In 1996, Sony introduced a desktop computer to the American market, and in 1998, began developing zip drives. Although Sony faced difficult competition from Microsoft in the market for home computers and network technology, it made attempts to coordinate its production of computer software with developments in Microsoft network technology and to provide digital network services. In April 1998, Microsoft and Sony announced plans to coordinate the production of Microsoft software and Sony electronic hardware and

The Players

Columbia Pictures Entertainment, Inc. President: Victor Kaufman. Born in New York City in 1943, Kaufman received a degree from New York University School of Law in 1967. After teaching criminal law at UCLA, Kaufman joined the Wall Street law firm Simpson, Thatcher, & Bartlett. In 1974, he became a general legal advisor to Columbia Pictures, and one year later, he assumed the position of Columbia's chief legal counselor. During the next several years, Kaufman quickly rose through the executive ranks at Columbia to become vice chairman in 1976. As vice chairman, he managed Columbia's motion picture division and, in 1982, initiated a joint venture between Coca-Cola Corp., Time Inc., and CBS Inc. to establish Tri-Star Pictures. When Tri-Star merged with Columbia Pictures in 1987, Kaufman became president of the newly formed Columbia Pictures Entertainment. Dissatisfied with the terms of Sony's 1989 takeover of Columbia Pictures Entertainment, he resigned his executive position and began teaching classes in entertainment industry finance at New York University's School of Law. In 1992, Kaufman returned to the film industry and established Savoy Pictures Entertainment, a marketing and distribution company dealing primarily in independent features.

to work together in developing technology standards for digital television.

Changes to the Industry

In acquiring Columbia Pictures Entertainment, Inc., Sony Corp. became the first Japanese company to control the integrated production of both hardware and software. The acquisition represented the beginning of a trend toward the consolidation of diverse production units under a single corporate ownership. Corporate consolidations and mergers raised many troubling questions in Hollywood and elsewhere about the future of independent film production. As the power of production and distribution became concentrated in fewer companies, independent filmmakers began to express concerns about committing to work with smaller and possibly less viable studios, those that have traditionally supported smaller, independent film producers. Small film producers increasingly feared that such studios would not remain viable for the two years required for film production and distribution.

At the time of the merger, anticipated profits from the release of syndicated television series exceeded $500 million. By 1994, it had become clear that Columbia's television archives and studios represented the greatest source of potential profit. Conversely, Sony's film studios experienced a steady decline in profits and after five disappointing years, Sony Corp. began to write off its investments in film and transfer its capital into the computer industry.

Review of the Outcome

In the six months following the acquisition of Columbia Pictures Entertainment, Sony Corp.'s overall profits rose 68.1% to 49.06 billion yen ($340 million) from 29.18 billion yen ($202 million) in the same period as the previous year. In the late 1980s, Sony was well entrenched in both the hardware and software markets. In addition to its immensely successful Walkman, Sony marketed compacts discs and CD players, taking advantage of a recording business booming from the popularity of Michael Jackson and Bruce Springsteen.

The returns on Sony's investment in films were less than spectacular. In 1994, Sony underwent a corporate makeover, redirecting its capital away from film production and into the development of computers. The success of Sony's diversification efforts has been limited by fluctuations in the value of the yen against the dollar and by competition from Microsoft and Intel.

Sony's entrance into the American computer market has required a corporate overhaul in many respects. Traditionally run by the coordinated efforts of a relatively small executive corps, Sony recently began to grant autonomy to various production units in order to foster responsiveness to local markets without completely dismantling the vertically integrated structure of the various branches of the corporation. In

March of 1999, Sony announced a plan to eliminate 10% of its total workforce, or about 17,000 jobs, and to shut down 15 manufacturing plants around the world by 2003. One month later, Sony announced a 19.4% decline in fiscal earnings from the previous year and its first quarterly net loss in four years.

Research

Castro, Janice. "From Walkman to Showman," in *Time*, 9 October 1989. Provides a basic overview of the terms of Sony's acquisition of Columbia and an introduction to public debates surrounding cultural protectionism and U.S.-Japanese economic rivalry.

Easton, Nina J. "Behind the Scenes of the Big Deal," in *Los Angeles Times*, 31 December 1989. Discusses the personalities of lawyers and executives involved in Warner/Sony conflict over the Peter and Guber breach of contract.

Griffin, Nancy, and Kim Masters. *Hit & Run: How Jon Peters and Peter Guber Took Sony for a Ride in Hollywood*, Simon & Schuster, 1996. Traces the careers of Jon Peters and Peter Guber, taking frequent detours into the sensationalistic gossip and culture surrounding Hollywood's film industry in the late 1980s.

Grover, Ronald. "When Columbia Met Sony: A Love Story," in *Business Week*, 9 October 1989. Outlines details related to the merger, focusing on potential profits secured by Sony through the acquisition of Columbia's film library.

Morita, Akio and Reingold, Edwin. *Made in Japan: Akio Morita and Sony*, Dutton, 1986. Biography of Sony's co-founder and chairman, Akio Morita. Covers a variety of topics ranging from post war reconstruction of Japan to Morita's business philosophy.

Nathans, Leah, J. "The Leading Man in the Sony-Columbia Deal," in *Business Week*, October 1989. Traces the career of Michael Schulhof, the vice-president of Sony Corp. of America who negotiated the Sony-Columbia deal.

Sanger, David E. "Sony's Norio Ohga: Building Smaller, Buying Bigger," in *The New York Times*, 18 February 1990. Concise yet comprehensive history of Sony Corp. detailing Ohga's business philosophy and personal characteristics. Outlines the market forces and innovative steps that produced Sony's trademark compact electronic equipment.

ALICE M. RITSCHERLE

SOUTHERN & SOUTHWESTERN ELECTRICITY

nationality: USA
date: September 1995
affected: Southern Co., USA, founded 1906
affected: Southwestern Electricity PLC, England

Southern Co.
270 Peachtree St. NW
Atlanta, GA 30303
USA

tel: (404)506-5000
fax: (404)506-0598
web: http://www.southernco.com

Overview of the Merger

After months of heated price wars, Southern Co. announced that Southern Electric International, its subsidiary, had reached an agreement to purchase Southwestern Electricity PLC for $1.8 billion in September of 1995. The deal marked yet another foreign interest venture by the growing global electric firm. Southern also gained considerable revenue and a customer base of more than 1.3 million as a result of the deal. The merger was one of many U.S./British deals to come about due to deregulation and privatization in the utilities industry.

History of Southern Co.

The foundation of the Southern Company dates back to 1906, when W.P. Lay founded the Alabama Power Company. The small company grew in its early years, and in 1912, was taken over by James Mitchell. He reorganized the company as Alabama Traction Light & Power and added various Alabama utilities to the firm.

In 1920, the company changed its name to Southeastern Power & Light. Alabama Power, Georgia Power, Gulf Power, and Mississippi Power were folded into its operations, with Southeastern acting as a holding company. The integration was beneficial to all of the units, increasing cash flow for development, creating reliable services, and capitalizing on the expertise of engineers throughout the company.

Southeastern started the next decade by purchasing Penn-Ohio Edison and forming the Commonwealth & Southern Corp. The new company had 11 different northern and southern utilities firms. The Public Utility Holding Company Act of 1935 was the demise of Commonwealth however, and, in the late 1940s, the company was dissolved due to the lack of integration of its different units. Four of its southern companies, Alabama Power, Georgia Power, Gulf Power, and Mississippi Power, were able to stay together and a new holding company, Southern Co., was formed to oversee the operations of the southern utilities. It was incorporated in 1945, and four years later the company was operating at full force. Southern Company Services was also formed to provide technical and specialized services for its holding company as well as the other companies in the organization.

The Business

Financials

Revenue (1998): $11.4 billion

Employees (1998): 31,848

SICs / NAICS

sic 4911 - Electric Services

naics 221111 - Hydroelectric Power Generation

naics 221112 - Fossil Fuel Electric Power Generation

naics 221113 - Nuclear Electric Power Generation

naics 221119 - Other Electric Power Generation

naics 221121 - Electric Bulk Power Transmission and Control

naics 221122 - Electric Power Distribution

In the 1970s, the utilities industry was in turmoil. Energy shortages and political interference led to the near bankruptcy of Georgia Power. Alabama Power was forced to lay off over 4,000 employees, and new development came to a standstill. Southern Co. finally received a break from its financial woes when the Securities and Exchange Commission allowed the company to form a new, unregulated subsidiary. In 1982, Southern Energy was formed.

The new subsidiary focused on distribution, generation, integrated operations, marketing, new projects, and investing in independent firms. In 1985, Southern Co. Energy Solutions was created to focus on research and development, as well as searching for new business opportunities. With the purchase of Savannah Electric in 1988, Southern owned five operating companies and continued to grow.

In the 1990s, the industry was changing dramatically with companies searching to expand outside of their territories. Southern sold one of its Georgia plants and bought 50% of Freeport Power in the Bahamas. Southern continued expanding in foreign interests, and by 1994, had interests in Trinidad and Tobago as well. The company, attracted to Britain's deregulated market, partnered up with PP&L Resources to purchase Southwestern Electricity in 1995.

Southern continued to partner with overseas companies and, in 1997, had complete ownership of Consolidated Electric Power Asia in Hong Kong. The firm also became the first U.S. company to gain interest in German utilities when it purchased a 25% stake in Bewag.

By 1998, Southern had heavy interests in its U.S. operations and had expanded into California and the Northeast. The company struck deals with Commonwealth Energy, Eastern Utilities, ConEd, and PG&E in order to expand its operations in these new territories. In 1999, Southern planned to sell its interests in Argentina and Chile. The company, along with PP&L Resources, which owned a 51% stake in Southern's British interests, decided to sell SWEP's supply business to London Electricity. Southern was positioned to enter the next millennium as one of the globe's leading independent power producers and the largest producer in the U.S.

Market Forces Driving the Merger

Southern Co. had been feeding its long-term plans of entering the foreign utilities market since deregulation in 1990 had allowed companies to seek interests abroad. Southern had already acquired interest in Edelnor in Chile, hydroelectric plants in Argentina, power projects in Trinidad and Tobago, and Freeport Power in the Bahamas. The company saw striking up a deal with Southwestern Electricity PLC (SWEP) as the perfect way to enter the British market, which had been privatized in 1990.

By acquiring SWEP, the company would have a leg up in what was considered to be a market that was more advanced than its U.S. counterpart. Thomas Boren explained in an article in the *The Financial Times London* that Southern was attracted to the British firm because of its "political stability relative to other areas of the world," and because it "had a market capitalization small enough to make it a manageable entity." Other factors motivating the purchase were the similarities in both firms operations, and Southern's financial stability and customer service record, which would benefit SWEP's 1.3 million customers.

Approach and Engagement

The battle for SWEP began in July 1995, when Southern Electric International (SEI) purchased an 11.2% interest in the company. In the weeks to follow, SWEP was bombarded by a hostile Pounds 1 billion offer from SEI. Southern Electric, another U.K.-based company, entered into the fray as well by offering Pounds 10 per share, beating SEI's offer by Pounds 1. Although talks with the British Southern Electric fell through, Maurice Warren saw the opportunity for increased bidding and urged his shareholders to "take no action and not allow SWEP to be bought on the cheap," according to a *Financial Times London* article.

By August, SEI had revamped its offer to $14.96 per share (Pounds 9.65 per share) and had successfully increased its interest to 29.9%, making it SWEP's largest shareholder. The two companies finally agreed on the $1.8 billion offer (Pounds 1.1 billion). According to a press release issued by the Southern Co., Thomas Boren stated that "we are very pleased to receive the recommendations of the SWEP board for the terms of our revised offer. We are offering a premium price but are confident that we can add value to SWEP's business." On September 18, 1995, Southern Co. gained full control of the British company.

Products and Services

After the deal with SWEP, Southern continued on its journey to become a global force. In 1998, the company was the leading producer of electricity in the U.S. and had over $35 billion in assets. It operated Alabama Power, Georgia Power, Gulf Power, Mississippi Power, and Savannah Electric. While its U.S. operations accounted for 85% of total sales, its foreign interests included Argentina, the Bahamas, Chile, China, India, the Philippines, Trinidad and Tobago, and the U.K.

Southern Company also had subsidiaries, including Southern Energy; Southern LINC, which offered wireless communications; Southern Nuclear; and Southern Company Energy Solutions, the marketing arm of the company. In 1998, the company operated over 41,000 megawatts in the U.S. alone, more than any U.S. electric firm. Residential utility operations accounted for 28% of total revenues in 1998, commercial services brought in 24%, and wholesale ventures secured 8%. Other electrical interests accounted for the remaining 20%.

Changes to the Industry

The Southern/SWEP deal took place just before a major interest in British utilities broke out. According to Bruce Wasserstein, author of *Big Deal: The Battle for Control of America's Leading Corporations*, American companies were faced with increased competition and were focusing on foreign investments. "One manifestation of this trend has been the race to invest in projects in the emerging markets of South America and China. Another has been a rush by U.S. utilities into the UK market," he noted.

From 1995 to 1997, U.S. utility companies began a feverish race to grab one of the 12 regional British utilities firms that had been privatized in 1990. U.K. firms had become attractive due to recent deregulation and advanced growth. Such deals included Dominion Resource's $2.2 billion purchase of East Midlands, Entergy's $2.1 billion merger with London Electricity, and CalEnergy's $1.3 billion takeover of Northern Electric.

The Officers

Chairman: A. W. Dahlberg

President and CEO: S. Marce Fuller

Exec. VP and CEO, Southern Energy: Thomas G. Boren

Exec. VP and CEO, Southern Company Services: Paul J. DeNicola

Chief Financial Officer: Larry Westbrook

By June of 1998 however, seven of the eight regional electricity companies that Americans had recently purchased were again for sale. U.S. shareholders were displeased with financial returns, and the imposition of a British windfall-profits tax on the companies that were sold. According to industry analysts, most companies were discouraged by their British investments and were looking to other parts of the world for higher returns.

Among the U.S. companies unloading its British concerns was Entergy and Dominion Resources. By this time, analysts were speculating that other U.S. companies would also put their newly acquired properties, once considered to be hot prospects, up for sale.

Review of the Outcome

Southern Co., the largest of the U.S. firms that had invested in a British utility, had fared well with its purchase. The company had seen a rise in revenue of 12.8% in 1996 due to its operations with SWEP. That year, PP&L Resources, which generated and sold electricity, purchased a 25% stake in SWEP Holdings, and in 1998 increased that interest to 51%. Thomas Boren backed the move in a press release issued on June 18, 1998, stating that "this transaction reflects our practice of seeking strong business partners in our international investments—partners who share our long-term commitment to customers and the communities we serve. Since PP&L's initial investment in SWEP Holdings two years ago, our companies have developed a strong working relationship based on a mutual pursuit of operational excellence."

As a result of the deal, SWEP's reliability increased by 34%, the company was able to reduce its prices on four separate occasions, and it had the fewest customer complaints of any electric company in the U.K. in 1997. Southern Co., along with PP&L Resources, decided to sell SWEP's supply business to London Electricity in order to focus on its distribution functions in 1998.

Research

"Futile Feuding," in *Financial Times London*, 14, July 1995. Discusses relations between Southern Co. and SWEP during merger talks.

Gottschalk, Arthur. "Southern Co.'s British Bid Kicks Off Expansion Abroad," in *Journal of Commerce*, 16 August 1995. Desribes Southern Co.'s plans for purchasing SWEP.

Quinn, Matthew. "Britain Just Part of Southern Co. Game Plan for Overseas Growth," in *The Atlanta Journal and Constitution*, 15 August 1995. Details Southern Co.'s plans for foreign ventures.

Smith, Michael. "Southern Electric in Bid Talks With SWEP," in *Financial Times London*, 11 August 1995. Explains Southern Co.'s bid for SWEP.

———. "Southern of U.S. Locks Horns with SWEP as UK Talks Fail," in *Financial Times London*, 15 August 1995. Discusses Southern Electric's involvement in the bidding process for SWEP.

———. "Step Right Up for the Main Attraction," in *Financial Times London*, 14 July 1995. Details Southern Co.'s interest in obtaining SWEP.

Southern Co. Home Page, available at http://www.southernco.com. Official World Wide Web Home Page for Southern Co. Includes historical, financial, and product information, as well as recent news articles and press releases.

Wasserstein, Bruce. *Big Deal: The Battle for Control of America's Leading Corporations*, Warner Books, 1998. Offers an overview of the largest mergers in recent American corporate history.

CHRISTINA M. STANSELL

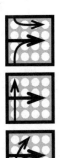

SOUTHWESTERN BELL & COX ENTERPRISES

date: April 5, 1994 (canceled)
affected: SBC Communications Inc., USA, founded 1984
affected: Cox Enterprises, Inc., USA, founded 1964

SBC Communications Inc.
175 E. Houston, PO Box 2933
San Antonio, TX 78299-2933
USA

tel: (210)821-4105
fax: (210)351-2071
web: http://www.sbc.com

Cox Enterprises, Inc.
1400 Lake Hearn Dr.
Atlanta, GA 30319
USA

tel: (404)843-5000
fax: (404)843-5142

Overview of the Merger

In the race to build an interactive telephone/cable company, Southwestern Bell Corp. and Cox Enterprises Inc. agreed in late 1993 to form a joint venture that would operate in both industries. Within months after announcing the $4.9 billion deal, the companies scuttled their plans, as did other telephone and cable operators that had proposed alliances. The fallout of these mergers was blamed by the companies on the Federal Communications Commission's mandate for a rate decrease by all cable systems.

History of Southwestern Bell Corp.

In 1982 American Telephone & Telegraph Corp. (AT&T) agreed to break up its monopoly by forming seven regional holding companies (RHCs), among them Southwestern Bell Corp. as the holding company for Southwestern Bell Telephone Co. On January 1, 1984, the ownership of Southwestern Bell Telephone was officially transferred to Southwestern Bell Corp. The parent also held three other subsidiaries: Southwestern Bell Publications, Inc., a directory publisher; Southwestern Bell Mobile Systems, Inc., a mobile telephone operator; and Southwestern Bell Telecommunications, Inc., a marketer of telephone equipment to business customers.

The firm acquired the cellular and paging business of Metromedia Inc. in 1987, thereby becoming the third-largest cellular communications company in the U.S., behind McCaw Cellular and Pacific Telesis. These operations were increased the following year, when Southwestern Bell bought Omni Communications' paging business.

In 1990 its subsidiary, Southwestern Bell International Holdings Corp., joined a group that purchased 20.4% of total equity and 51% of the shares in Telefonos de Mexico, S.A. de C.V., Mexico's newly privatized telephone company. That year it also agreed to purchase West Midlands Cable Communications, owner of the largest cable television franchise in the U.K. The firm acquired Hauser Communications Corp.'s two cable systems in 1993 for $650 million.

The Business

Financials - SBC Communications Inc.

Revenue (1998): $28.8 billion

Employees (1998): 129,850

SICs / NAICS

sic 2741 - Miscellaneous Publishing

sic 3661 - Telephone & Telegraph Apparatus

sic 4812 - Radiotelephone Communications

sic 4813 - Telephone Communications Except
    Radiotelephone

sic 4841 - Cable & Other Pay Television Services

sic 4832 - Radio Broadcasting Stations

sic 4833 - Television Broadcasting Stations

sic 2711 - Newspapers

sic 5012 - Automobiles & Other Motor Vehicles

naics 334210 - Telephone Apparatus Manufacturing

naics 511199 - All Other Publishers

naics 513310 - Wired Telecommunications Carriers

naics 513321 - Paging

naics 513322 - Cellular and Other Wireless
    Telecommunications

naics 513330 - Telecommunications Resellers

naics 513340 - Satellite Telecommunications

naics 513210 - Cable Networks

naics 513112 - Radio Stations

naics 513120 - Television Broadcasting

naics 511110 - Newspaper Publishers

naics 421110 - Automobile and Other Motor Vehicle
    Wholesalers

To reflect a less regional focus, the corporation changed its name to SBC Communications Inc. in 1994. The following year it became the first RHC to receive approval from the Federal Communications Commission (FCC) to integrate cellular and local phone service outside of its service region, and formed SBMS New York Services, Inc. to operate in New York. It also became the first RHC to open retail outlets.

SBC purchased 40% of VTR, a Chilean telecommunications company, in 1995. That year it joined with Cable & Wireless PLC and Corporate Africa Ltd. to form New Africa Communications for the purpose of bidding on the installation of one million new telephone lines.

The Telecommunications Act of 1996 stipulated that RHCs could enter the long distance market outside of their operating region only if they first allowed other local telephone companies to compete in their local telephone territories. In response, SBC entered into a network interconnection agreement with U.S. Long Distance Corp. to provide competing local telephone service in its five-state service area: Kansas, Texas, Missouri, Oklahoma, and Arkansas.

In 1996 it merged its phone equipment division, Southwestern Bell Telecom, with its phone service subsidiary, Southwestern Bell Telephone Co. In April 1997 the firm merged with Pacific Telesis Group, creating the second-largest telecommunications company in the U.S. It then entered into discussions to merge with AT&T, but dropped the plan after realizing the improbability of gaining regulatory approval. Later that year, it exited the cable business by agreeing to sell its two Washington D.C. cable systems and its interest in Prime Cable of Chicago. That year it also increased its international operations, first by entering into an alliance to form Cegetel, a long distance carrier to compete with France Telecom, then by entering into a joint venture with six Swiss utilities to form Diax, a company to build a digital telecommunications network in that country, and finally by purchasing a 30% stake in Telkom South Africa.

The Oklahoma Corporation Commission supported SBC's bid to offer long distance service in that state, but the FCC rejected the proposal. In 1998 it filed applications to compete in the long distance markets of Kansas, Texas, and Arkansas. That year, it became the first RHC to enter the long distance market by acquiring Connecticut-based Southern New England Telecommunications Corp. for $4.4 billion in stock. It also agreed to merge with Ameritech Corp., thereby forming the largest U.S. local telephone company; the deal was expected to close in mid-1999. SBC also offered that year to buy Comcast Corp.'s cellular business and announced an agreement under which Williams Communications would serve as SBC's long distance provider.

History of Cox Enterprises, Inc.

In 1898 James Middleton Cox purchased his first newspaper, the *Dayton Evening News*, in Dayton, Ohio, for $26,000, and then changed the name of the paper to the *Dayton Daily News*. Cox bought the *Springfield Press-Republic* in 1905, renaming it the *Springfield Daily News*. With that purchase, he established the News League of Ohio newspaper chain.

Cox embarked on a political career in 1909, when he was elected to represent Ohio's third district in U.S. Congress. Four years later he became governor of Ohio. Cox failed to get reelected in 1915, but again became governor in 1917. In 1920, as the Democratic Party's presidential candidate with running mate Franklin D. Roosevelt, Cox lost to publisher Warren G. Harding.

He then turned his attention back to his newspaper interests. In 1923 Cox acquired the *Canton News* of Canton, Ohio, as well as the *Miami Metropolis* of Miami, Florida. Seven years later he sold the Canton paper and purchased the *Springfield Sun*, another Ohio paper.

After a brief return to politics with his 1933 appointment as delegate to the World Monetary and Economic Conference, Cox remained committed to his business activities. He entered the broadcasting industry in 1934 by founding WHIO, the first radio station in Dayton, Ohio. In 1939 he acquired *The Atlanta Journal* and WSB, the first AM radio station of Georgia, which had been founded in 1922 as the South's first radio station.

Cox expanded into the television industry in 1948 by acquiring WSB, the first TV station in the South. That year he also established WSB as the first FM radio station in the South. His enterprise continued to grow in 1949 by purchasing *The Journal Herald* of Dayton and by establishing WHIO, the call letters for the first TV station and FM radio station in Dayton.

In 1950 the company purchased *The Atlanta Constitution*, which joined *Atlanta Journal* in producing a Sunday edition. Seven years later James Cox died, passing the family business to his son, James M. Cox Jr.

In 1962 Cox became one of the first broadcasting businesses to invest in cable television by purchasing a cable system in Lewistown, Pennsylvania. The Cox family created Cox Broadcasting Corp. two years later to hold its broadcasting operations, with its newspaper interests run by Cox Enterprises. While Cox Enterprises remained private, Cox Broadcasting went public on the New York Stock Exchange, although the family maintained its controlling interest.

Cox Broadcasting expanded by adding a business and technical publishing division in 1966. The next year that company entered the motion picture industry by joining with Bing Crosby Productions to release such movies as *Ben*, *Walking Tall*, and *The Reincarnation of Peter Proud*.

The Cox companies were again reorganized in 1968. All of its newspapers were organized as Cox Enterprises, Inc., and Cox Cable Communications Inc. was created as a subsidiary of Cox Broadcasting.

The Officers

SBC Communications Inc.

Chairman and CEO: Edward E. Whitacre, Jr.

President, SBC Operations: Royce S. Caldwell

Sr. Exec. VP, External Affairs: Cassandra S. Carr

President, SBC International: J. Cliff Eason

Sr. Exec. VP and General Counsel: James D. Ellis

Cox Enterprises, Inc.

Chairman and CEO: James C. Kennedy

President and Chief Operating Officer: David E. Easterly

Sr. VP and Chief Financial Officer: Robert O'Leary

Sr. VP Administration: Timothy W. Hughes

Cox Broadcasting diversified into the automobile-auction business with the acquisition of auction facilities in Pennsylvania, New Jersey, and Virginia. As with its television and radio properties, the company continued to add auction houses to its holdings over the decades.

Cox purchased TeleRep, a national television advertising sales firm, in 1972. It also created a programming division, Television Program Enterprises, to sell such syndicated programming as *Entertainment Tonight*, *Star Search*, and *Lifestyles of the Rich and Famous*. That same year, Cox Cable announced plans to merge with American Television and Communications Corp., but terminated the deal the following year when the U.S. Justice Department filed suit to block it on antitrust grounds.

In 1972 James M. Cox, Jr., broke with the family's Democratic tradition, not to mention journalistic impartiality, by endorsing President Richard M. Nixon for re-election and demanding that Cox's newspapers do likewise. Two editors resigned in disagreement to his imposition of political affiliation on newspapers.

After the death of James Cox, Jr., in 1974, his brother-in-law, Garner Anthony, succeeded him as director. Two years later Cox purchased four Texas newspapers: the *Austin American-Statesman*, the *Waco Tribune-Herald*, the *Port Arthur News*, and the *Lufkin Daily News*.

In 1977 the Cox Cable subsidiary, which operated in nine states and had 500,000 subscribers, was merged with Cox Broadcasting. Over the next few years Cox Broadcasting added 26 cable franchises to the group. Cox ceased activities in the motion picture

The Players

Southwestern Bell Corp. Chairman and CEO: Edward E. Whitacre, Jr. Edward Whitacre earned a Bachelor's degree in industrial engineering in 1964 from Texas Tech University. He began his affiliation with the company when he joined its operational departments in Arkansas, Kansas, and Texas. Whitacre moved from Southwestern Bell Telephone Co. to Southwestern Bell Corp. when that company was formed in 1984. There he progressed through the positions of group vice president, vice president of revenues and public affairs, vice chairman, and chief financial officer before being appointed chairman and CEO in 1990.

Cox Enterprises, Inc. Chairman and CEO: James C. Kennedy. James Kennedy is the latest in a long tradition of family leadership of Cox companies. Kennedy is the grandson of its founder and stepson of Barbara Cox's husband, Garner Anthony. He became the chairman of Cox Enterprises upon Anthony's resignation from that post in 1987. More than a decade later, Kennedy remains at the head of Cox Enterprises.

industry in 1979. That year the Cox family entered into negotiations for the sale of Cox Broadcasting to General Electric Co. These talks terminated, however, due to concern by the Federal Communication Commission over GE's extensive holdings.

In 1980 Cox Broadcasting sold its business and technical division to the Hearst Corp. in an effort to focus on broadcasting and cable operations. The annual revenues of Cox Enterprises and Cox Broadcasting tripled during the next decade. Cox Broadcasting was renamed Cox Communications in 1982.

Cox Communications continued its acquisition of auction facilities, a business that it had retained because of its high profitability. In 1985 Cox Enterprises purchased Cox Communications for $75 a share, forming Cox Enterprises, Inc., the 13th-largest media firm in the U.S.

In 1986, without pre-approval from the U.S. Securities and Exchange Commission (SEC), Cox invested $101 million in a fellow communications company, Knight-Ridder. As a result, the U.S. Justice Department sued Cox in 1991 for $3.67 million. Lawyers for Cox maintained that the shares were

bought for investment purposes only and therefore did not constitute a violation of antitrust law.

James Kennedy, the founder's grandson and Anthony's stepson, was named chairman when Anthony resigned from his post in 1987. Cox Enterprises also sold its Datext unit, which stored the firm's financial information on compact discs, to Lotus Development Corp.

In 1989 the company acquired an equity stake in Blockbuster Entertainment Corp., becoming a franchisee of Blockbuster Video stores. That same year, Cox purchased Trader Publications, The Clipper, Inc., The Stuffit Co., Main Street Advertising USA, Cox In-Store Advertising, and an interest in IP Services, Inc. It also formed a joint venture with Picture Classified Network (PCN) to market the PCN Gold Book. By 1990 Cox was the 14th-largest U.S. media company and the country's 69th-largest privately held company.

Cox put its Blockbuster stores up for sale in 1991. That year the company merged its Manheim Auction operations with the auto auction businesses of Ford Motor Credit Co. and GE Capital to form the world's largest auto auction company. It also purchased Val-Pak Direct Marketing, a direct mail coupon business, and negotiated plans to develop the first all-local cable channel.

Cox acquired a 50.1% controlling share in Teleport Communications Group, a fiber optics company, in 1991. That year Cox joined with Tele-Communications to develop technology that would compete with local phone companies. By then, as a shareholder in The Discovery Channel, Viewer's Choice, and Movietime, Cox was the nation's sixth-largest cable operator.

In early 1993 it joined with Southwestern Bell Corp. to offer cable television in Britain. That December those two companies agreed to form a $4.9 billion cable joint venture, but terminated the deal in April 1994.

The company joined with Sprint, Tele-Communications, and Comcast in a $3 billion joint venture called Sprint Spectrum LP. This company was formed to compete with local phone service providers by offering a new type of wireless phone service, Personal Communications Service (PCS); Cox sold its interest in this venture to Sprint in 1999.

It acquired Times Mirror's cable television operations in a $2.3 billion deal in 1994, forming the new Cox Communications Inc. Two years later Cox made its foray into the Internet by establishing Cox Interactive Media. In May 1999 Cox Communications agreed to acquire TCA Cable for $4 billion.

Market Forces Driving the Merger

By the mid-1990s technological advances pointed to a telecommunication revolution. Broad-based, fiber-optic cable was capable of delivering voice, data, and video over the same line. Since local telephone and cable television companies were both connected to the customer via a direct line; they were natural partners for combining their networks and conducting operations in both industries.

Several such partnerships had been planned in early 1993. Tele-Communications Inc., the nation's largest cable operator, agreed to a $30 billion merger with Bell Atlantic Corp., and U.S. West agreed to purchase 25% of Time Warner Entertainment Co. for $2.5 billion.

Cox Enterprises wanted to participate in an industry that promised to be highly lucrative and competitive. Already the nation's sixth-largest cable operator, Cox sought to achieve explosive growth that would transform it into an even bigger player. To accomplish this, it required a partner with deep pockets, such as a regional Bell local telephone company. After considering all seven regional Bell companies, Cox decided that Southwestern Bell, its partner in a British cable venture, made the most strategic sense.

Southwestern Bell was a willing partner. It had been watching its brother Baby Bells enter into alliances with cable companies and didn't want to miss an opportunity to forge a similar partnership of its own. It already owned two small cable systems in Washington DC, but by joining with Cox, the nation's sixth-largest cable operator, Southwestern Bell would immediately be propelled into the industry's top ranks.

Approach and Engagement

On December 7, 1983, Southwestern Bell and Cox Enterprises announced the formation of a joint venture, Cox Cable. In the $4.9 billion agreement, Southwestern Bell would contribute $1.6 billion in cash for a 40% stake. Cox would receive a 60% interest in exchange for $3.3 billion in cable assets, or 21 of its 24 cable systems. The new company would be privately owned and would be operated as a 50/50 partnership between its parents.

The cash infusion from Southwestern Bell was earmarked solely for acquisitions. Cox Cable's initial strategy would be to double in size, aiming to become the nation's third-largest operator. Unlike the Bell Atlantic/TCI and U S West/Time Warner partnerships, Cox Cable planned to build its subscription base before investing heavily in new technology.

The U.S. Federal Communications Commission enacted regulation that altered the landscape of the cable industry in early 1994. Two years earlier, Congress had re-regulated the industry amid customer complaints of the excessively high prices imposed by cable operators, which were essentially monopolies. Since then, the cable companies had been gradually raising their prices. In February 1994 the FCC took a firmer approach with them, mandating a 7% cut in cable rates nationwide.

Suddenly, cable companies looked less attractive to their marriage partners. Later in February, Bell Atlantic and TCI terminated their merger agreement, citing the reduction in TCI's cash flow that would result from the rate cuts. Those cuts also drove Southwestern Bell and Cox back to the negotiating table to revise the terms of their agreement. On April 5, 1994, however, they canceled their deal altogether.

Like Bell Atlantic and TCI, they attributed the deal's termination to the FCC mandate, as well as to uncertainty over future regulations. "The Federal Communications Commission has a budget to hire 250 people whose mandate it is to regulate the industry," said James Kahan, senior vice-president at Southwestern Bell, in *The New York Times*. "Those people are not just going to come to work and play checkers."

The telephone companies had also relished entry into an unregulated industry, unlike their own, and its demise further reduced the appeal of their proposed ventures. In addition, industry analysts suggested a third possible reason for the termination of the Southwestern Bell/Cox deal. With the collapse of the Bell Atlantic/TCI merger, which would have created a powerhouse, other telephone and cable companies no longer felt as much pressure to rush into mergers in order to remain competitive.

Products and Services

In the late 1990s SBC was organized into four main operational segments:

- The **Wireline** unit provided landline telecommunications services, including local, network access and long distance services, messaging, and Internet services. It also sold customer premise and private business exchange equipment. Its principal subsidiaries in this segment were Southwestern Bell Telephone Co., Pacific Bell, The Southern New England Telephone Co., and Nevada Bell. Wireline operations generated revenues of $22.2 billion in 1998.

- The **Wireless** segment provided wireless telecommunications services, including local and long distance services, and sold wireless equipment. Its principal subsidiaries were Southwestern Bell Mobile Systems, Inc., Pacific Bell Mobile Services, and SNET Cellular, Inc. This segment realized $4.2 billion in revenues in 1998.

- The **Directory** segment sold advertising for and publication of yellow pages and white pages directories and electronic publications. It operated under the subsidiaries Southwestern Bell Yellow Pages, Inc., Pacific Bell Directory, and SNET Information Services, Inc. Directory operations generated revenues of $2.4 billion in 1998.

- The **Other** unit included SBC's international investments and miscellaneous domestic operating subsidiaries. In 1998 this unit generated $85 million in revenues.

By mid-1999 Cox Enterprises published 16 daily and 15 weekly newspapers. Its interests also included ownership of 11 television and more than 50 radio stations. Cox Communications was one of the nation's largest cable systems, and Manheim Auctions was the leading used-car auction company in the U.S.

Research

Andrews, Edmund L. "Southwestern Bell and Cox Plan a $4.9 Billion Venture," in *The New York Times*, 8 December 1993. Describes the planned merger.

Fabrikant, Geraldine. "$4.9 Billion Cable Deal Called Off," in *The New York Times*, 6 April 1993. Provides details of the termination of the merger.

Haddad, Charles. "Deal to Double Cox Cable's Size," in *The Atlanta Journal and Constitution*, 8 December 1993. Details the terms of the merger agreement.

SBC Communications Inc. Home Page, available at http://www.sbc.com. Official World Wide Web Page for SBC. Includes organizational and product information, press releases, annual reports, and other financial information.

"SBC Communications Inc.," in *Notable Corporate Chronologies*, The Gale Group, 1999. Provides historical highlights of the company, including its merger of PacTel.

SBC Communications Inc. 1998 Annual Report. Provides financial information and describes company operating segments.

Stroud, Jerri. "SW Bell, Cox Are Revising Deal after Cable Rate Cut," in *St. Louis Post-Dispatch*, 12 March 1994. Briefly relates the companies' return to negotiations.

KIMBERLY N. STEVENS

SOUTHWESTERN BELL & METROMEDIA

nationality: USA
date: October 1987
affected: Southwestern Bell Corp., USA, founded 1984
affected: Metromedia Inc., USA, founded 1959

SBC Communications Inc.
175 E. Houston
PO Box 2933
San Antonio, TX 78299-2933
USA

tel: (210)821-4105
fax: (210)351-2071
web: http://www.sbc.com

Overview of the Merger

Southwestern Bell became the nation's largest investor in cellular telephones with its $1.38 billion purchase of most of the assets of Metromedia Inc. in 1986. The acquisition came at time of feverish diversification in the telecommunications industry, as companies were swiftly positioning themselves to operate in a variety of arenas. By 1995 Southwestern Bell, later renamed SBC Communications Inc., had earned the reputation as the most diverse of the Baby Bells.

History of Southwestern Bell Corp.

In 1982 American Telephone & Telegraph Corp. (AT&T) agreed to break up its monopoly by forming seven regional holding companies (RHCs), among them Southwestern Bell Corp. as the holding company for Southwestern Bell Telephone Co. On January 1, 1984, the ownership of Southwestern Bell Telephone was officially transferred to Southwestern Bell Corp. The parent also held three other subsidiaries: Southwestern Bell Publications, Inc., a directory publisher; Southwestern Bell Mobile Systems, Inc., a mobile telephone operator; and Southwestern Bell Telecommunications, Inc., a marketer of telephone equipment to business customers.

The firm acquired the cellular and paging business of Metromedia Inc. in 1987, thereby becoming the third-largest cellular communications company in the U.S., behind McCaw Cellular and Pacific Telesis. These operations were increased the following year, when Southwestern Bell bought Omni Communications' paging business.

In 1990 its subsidiary, Southwestern Bell International Holdings Corp., joined a group that purchased 20.4% of total equity and 51% of the shares in Telefonos de Mexico, S.A. de C.V., Mexico's newly privatized telephone company. That year it also agreed to purchase West Midlands Cable Communications, owner of the largest cable television franchise in the U.K. The firm acquired Hauser Communications Corp.'s two cable systems in 1993 for $650 million.

The Business

Financials

Revenue (1998): $28.8 billion

Employees (1998): 129,850

SICs / NAICS

sic 2741 - Miscellaneous Publishing

sic 3661 - Telephone & Telegraph Apparatus

sic 4812 - Radiotelephone Communications

sic 4813 - Telephone Communications Except
        Radiotelephone

naics 334210 - Telephone Apparatus Manufacturing

naics 511199 - All Other Publishers

naics 513310 - Wired Telecommunications Carriers

naics 513321 - Paging

naics 513322 - Cellular and Other Wireless
        Telecommunications

naics 513330 - Telecommunications Resellers

naics 513340 - Satellite Telecommunications

To reflect a less regional focus, the corporation changed its name to SBC Communications Inc. in 1994. The following year it became the first RHC to receive approval from the Federal Communications Commission (FCC) to integrate cellular and local phone service outside of its service region, and formed SBMS New York Services, Inc. to operate in New York. It also became the first RHC to open retail outlets.

SBC purchased 40% of VTR, a Chilean telecommunications company, in 1995. That year it joined with Cable & Wireless PLC and Corporate Africa Ltd. to form New Africa Communications for the purpose of bidding on the installation of one million new telephone lines.

The Telecommunications Act of 1996 stipulated that RHCs could enter the long distance market outside of their operating region only if they first allowed other local telephone companies to compete in their local telephone territories. In response, SBC entered into a network interconnection agreement with U.S. Long Distance Corp. to provide competing local telephone service in its five-state service area: Kansas, Texas, Missouri, Oklahoma, and Arkansas.

In 1996 it merged its phone equipment division, Southwestern Bell Telecom, with its phone service

subsidiary, Southwestern Bell Telephone Co. In April 1997 the firm merged with Pacific Telesis Group, creating the second-largest telecommunications company in the U.S. It then entered into discussions to merge with AT&T, but dropped the plan after realizing the improbability of gaining regulatory approval. Later that year, it exited the cable business by agreeing to sell its two Washington D.C. cable systems and its interest in Prime Cable of Chicago. That year it also increased its international operations, first by entering into an alliance to form Cegetel, a long distance carrier to compete with France Telecom, then by entering into a joint venture with six Swiss utilities to form Diax, a company to build a digital telecommunications network in that country, and finally by purchasing a 30% stake in Telkom South Africa.

The Oklahoma Corporation Commission supported SBC's bid to offer long distance service in that state, but the FCC rejected the proposal. In 1998 it filed applications to compete in the long distance markets of Kansas, Texas, and Arkansas. That year, it became the first RHC to enter the long distance market by acquiring Connecticut-based Southern New England Telecommunications Corp. for $4.4 billion in stock. It also agreed to merge with Ameritech Corp., thereby forming the largest U.S. local telephone company; the deal was expected to close in mid-1999. SBC also offered that year to buy Comcast Corp.'s cellular business and announced an agreement under which Williams Communications would serve as SBC's long distance provider.

History of Metromedia Inc.

In 1946 John W. Kluge, a German immigrant, invested the $7,000 in poker winnings that he had accumulated while attending Columbia University into the purchase of a radio station in Silver Spring, Maryland. Over the years he added other radio stations to his holdings.

Kluge's business interests were far flung, and in 1951 he launched a food brokerage that eventually became Baltimore's largest. In 1959 he paid $4 million for a 24% stake in Metropolitan Broadcasting Corp., whose assets included television and radio stations. Kluge took the firm public and renamed it Metromedia, Inc. in 1961. He acquired additional independent television stations, and when he reached the Federal Communication Commission's ownership limit of seven, he began trading them for increasingly larger ones.

During the 1960s he continued his ventures into other diverse industries, such as magazines and poster concessions. Metromedia's balance sheet and stock price suffered, however, and Kluge shed these interests. In the mid-1970s the independent television industry boomed on increased advertising revenues. Metromedia's net profits were $55 million on sales of $450 million in 1980.

The company added to its broadcasting holdings, and by the early 1980s had stations in seven of the nation's top ten markets, including New York, Washington D.C., Los Angeles, and Boston. It also owned 14 radio stations, the Harlem Globetrotters, and the Ice Capades. Metromedia jumped into the burgeoning cellular telephone business by purchasing franchises in New York, Chicago, and Boston in 1983. It added seven additional cellular and paging companies the following year.

Kluge and a group of investors took Metromedia private through a $1.6 billion leveraged buyout in 1984. The heavy debt load accrued in the process necessitated the sale of company assets. Metromedia sold six television stations to Rupert Murdoch and its seventh to Hearst Corp. in 1985 for a total of $2 billion. The next year it raised $1 billion by selling nine radio stations, the Harlem Globetrotters, and the Ice Capades. In 1987 the company sold most of its cellular assets to Southwestern Bell Corp. for $1.38 billion and divested its remaining interests in 1990. By then Kluge had become the nation's second-richest individual.

Kluge led Metromedia into a dramatic departure from media when it purchased the Ponderosa Steak House chain in 1988. The next year he bought USA Cafes, operator of the Bonanza restaurants. These two chains formed Metromedia Steakhouses Inc. To this unit he added S&A Restaurant Corp., owner of the Steak & Ale and Bennigan's restaurant chains.

In 1988 Kluge played the role of white knight to Orion Pictures Corp. by purchasing a 70% interest in the motion picture company to save it from a hostile acquisition by National Amusement Corp. A string of box office flops drove Orion into bankruptcy in 1991. It emerged the next year, but continued to lose money. In 1994 Kluge merged Orion with Actava Group, a lawn mower manufacturer, and Metromedia Inc., the group's investment arm, to form Metromedia International Marketing Inc.

Kluge acquired ITT Corp.'s long-distance telephone operations in 1989, renaming the division Metromedia Communications Corp. In September 1993 this company merged with Resurgens Communication Group Inc. and LDDS Communications Inc. to form one of the nation's leading long-distance providers. In 1995 its name was changed to WorldCom Inc., of which Kluge sold his 16% stake to the public later that year.

In 1998 Metromedia announced an aggressive plan to refurbish its restaurants and restore their prof-

The Officers

Chairman and CEO: Edward E. Whitacre, Jr.

President, SBC Operations: Royce S. Caldwell

Sr. Exec. VP, External Affairs: Cassandra S. Carr

President, SBC International: J. Cliff Eason

Sr. Exec. VP and General Counsel: James D. Ellis

itability and image, both of which had been suffering for years.

Market Forces Driving the Acquisition

The cellular telephone industry was on the verge of an explosion in the mid-1980s. The image of the cellular telephone was shifting from simply a toy for the rich to a piece of standard business equipment. As greater numbers of consumers bought into cellular telephony, the costs for its technology and services inched down, enabling more customers to afford it. In 1986 the industry had 462,000 subscribers in 83 markets, generating revenues of $650 million annually, according to consultant Herschel Shosteck in *The Washington Post*. Most analysts and industry executives predicted that cellular use would experience strong growth in future years.

When the federal government first established regulations for the cellular industry, it awarded two licenses in every territory, one for the Baby Bell in that territory and the other to an independent operator. In limited supply, therefore, those licenses had been valuable since their beginning. In February 1986 the government increased their value to Baby Bells by ruling that those telephone companies could purchase the licenses held by independent owners outside of their operating region, launching a stampede across the nation to snap them up.

Metromedia Inc. held interests in eight cellular systems, six of which were in major cities: New York, Chicago, Boston, Washington D.C./Baltimore, Philadelphia, and Dallas. Metromedia, owned by billionaire entrepreneur John Kluge, had been divesting its assets ever since it had been taken private through a leveraged buyout in 1984. Its cellular and paging interests represented its last remaining large group of assets.

Approach and Engagement

On June 30, 1986, Southwestern Bell Corp. announced its agreement to purchase Metromedia's

The Players

Southwestern Bell Corp. Chairman and CEO: Edward E. Whitacre, Jr. Edward Whitacre earned a Bachelor's degree in industrial engineering in 1964 from Texas Tech University. He began his affiliation with the company when he joined its operational departments in Arkansas, Kansas, and Texas. Whitacre moved from Southwestern Bell Telephone Co. to Southwestern Bell Corp. when that company was formed in 1984. There he progressed through the positions of group vice president, vice president of revenues and public affairs, vice chairman, and chief financial officer before being appointed chairman and CEO in 1990.

Metromedia Inc. Chairman: John W. Kluge. John Warren Kluge was born in Germany in 1914 and at age eight immigrated to the U.S. He earned a scholarship to Columbia University, where he secured an economics degree and about $7,000 in poker winnings. After graduating in 1937, he invested in a paper company in Detroit, doubling the small company's sales in four years. He then pursued a variety of business ventures, including radio, food brokerage, and hotels. Kluge kept getting drawn back into broadcasting, however, and in 1959 purchased a group of television and radio stations that would form the basis for his media empire. Metromedia was gradually pared down through the sale of its assets, earning Kluge billions and making him one of the wealthiest people in America. (He earned $1.4 billion on the sale of Metromedia's cellular assets to Southwestern Bell alone.) After the company's assets had dwindled down to next to nothing, Kluge began building them up again in a variety of new businesses, including restaurants, movies, and long-distance telephony.

cellular and paging business for $1.65 billion in cash. At that price, Southwestern Bell was paying $45 to $55 per potential customer, or about three times higher than the going rate. In so doing, however, the telephone company would become the nation's largest investor in the cellular industry.

On September 11, 1986, Metromedia withdrew three licenses from the deal because LIN Broadcasting Corp. was a partner with Metromedia in the New York, Dallas, and Philadelphia markets, and had declined to sell them to Southwestern Bell Corp.

Without those licenses, the price of the acquisition was reduced to $1.38 billion.

On September 22, 1987, over a year later, the companies finally received regulatory approval from Federal Judge Harold H. Greene, best known for breaking up American Telephone & Telegraph Corp. in 1982. The acquisition was completed shortly thereafter.

Products and Services

In the late 1990s SBC was organized into four main operational segments:

The **Wireline** unit provided landline telecommunications services, including local, network access and long distance services, messaging, and Internet services. It also sold customer premise and private business exchange equipment. Its principal subsidiaries in this segment were Southwestern Bell Telephone Co., Pacific Bell, The Southern New England Telephone Co., and Nevada Bell. Wireline operations generated revenues of $22.2 billion in 1998.

The **Wireless** segment provided wireless telecommunications services, including local and long distance services, and sold wireless equipment. Its principal subsidiaries were Southwestern Bell Mobile Systems, Inc., Pacific Bell Mobile Services, and SNET Cellular, Inc. This segment realized $4.2 billion in revenues in 1998.

The **Directory** segment sold advertising for and publication of yellow pages and white pages directories and electronic publications. It operated under the subsidiaries Southwestern Bell Yellow Pages, Inc., Pacific Bell Directory, and SNET Information Services, Inc. Directory operations generated revenues of $2.4 billion in 1998.

The **Other** unit included SBC's international investments and miscellaneous domestic operating subsidiaries. In 1998 this unit generated $85 million in revenues.

Changes to the Industry and Review of the Outcome

Criticism of the price that Southwestern Bell had paid for Metromedia's assets was stifled in the years following the deal. Those properties, acquired for about $45 per potential customer—the record high at that time—were worth about $300 per customer by 1995. SBC Communications, as Southwestern Bell had been renamed, enjoyed the cellular industry's highest market penetration. Its wireless subscribers numbered 2.9 million, and in 1994 its 7.4% sign-up rate surpassed the 5% industry average.

Research

Burrows, Peter. "Pick of the Litter: Why SBC is the Baby Bell to Beat," in *Business Week*, 6 March 1995. Reviews SBC's progress in the cellular and other telecommunications industries.

"Metromedia Companies," in *International Directory of Company Histories*, Vol. 14, St. James Press, 1996. Traces the history of the company.

SBC Communications Inc. 1998 Annual Report. Provides financial information and describes company operating segments.

SBC Communications Inc. Home Page, available at http://www.sbc.com. Official World Wide Web Page for SBC. Includes organizational and product information, press releases, annual reports, and other financial information.

"SBC Communications Inc.," in *Notable Corporate Chronologies*, The Gale Group, 1999. Provides historical highlights of the company.

Sims, Calvin. "Metromedia to Sell Mobile Phone Operations," in *The New York Times*, 1 July 1986. Describes the terms of the deal.

———. "Metromedia Limits Sales of Mobile Phone Stakes," in *The New York Times*, 12 September 1986. Reports of the reduction of the number of licenses that SBC was to acquire from Metromedia.

Tucker, Elizabeth. "Mobile Phone Rivals Are Being Consolidated; Regional Bell Systems Buying up Licenses from Nontelephone Companies," in *The Washington Post*, 11 August 1986. Describes the open field of the cellular industry as local telephone companies scrambled to acquire cellular licenses.

KIMBERLY N. STEVENS

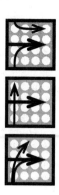

STANDARD OIL COMPANY OF NEW YORK & VACUUM OIL

Mobil Corp.
3225 Gallows Rd.
Fairfax, VA 22037-0001
USA

tel: (703)846-3000
fax: (703)846-4666
web: http://www.mobil.com

nationality: USA
date: July 1931
affected: Standard Oil Company of New York, USA, founded 1882
affected: Vacuum Oil Co., USA, founded 1866

Overview of the Merger

In the first alliance between members of J.D. Rockefeller's former Standard Oil of New Jersey monopoly, Standard Oil of New York (Socony) and Vacuum Oil merged in 1931. A constant and desperate need for new sources of crude provided mutual impetus for the merger. Socony was heavily dependent on large quantities of crude for its sizable fuel and lubricants business, and Vacuum specialized in a wide variety of lubricants.

History of Standard Oil Company of New York

Standard Oil Company of New York (Socony) was created alongside the formation of John D. Rockefeller's Standard Oil Company of New Jersey in 1882. Socony served as both the legal domicile for the company's New York assets and the administrative and banking center for the Standard Oil Trust. William Rockefeller, J.D.'s younger brother, remained Socony's president until 1911.

Socony was also established to handle the trust's growing foreign sales. It gained control of Meissner, Ackermann & Co., a merchant firm with offices in New York and Germany, as well as agents throughout Europe. Standard Oil increasingly established foreign subsidiaries, and by 1910 Socony's affiliates handled about 30% of the company's total foreign sales. These sales were among the largest of any Standard company. The firm also held responsibility for administering most of the Standard group's internal affairs. Through these roles, it enjoyed a large degree of intimacy with its immediate parent, Standard Oil of New Jersey.

By 1910, Socony's domestic operations included five refineries that produced kerosene, gasoline, and naptha for sale in New York and New England through jobbers and a growing number of new roadside stores known as "gas stations."

In 1911, the U.S. Supreme Court ordered the dissolution of Standard of New Jersey, charging violation of the Sherman Antitrust Act. Among the 33 new companies created as a result were Socony. Cut off from its former affiliates' supply of crude oil, of which it had a great need for crude due to its large-scale production of oil-based fuels and lubricants, Socony fervently began expanding operations to become more self-reliant.

In 1918, Socony increased its production operations by acquiring 45% of Magnolia Petroleum Co., which owned wells, pipelines, and a Texas refinery, and marketed chiefly in Texas and the Southwest. It purchased the remainder of Magnolia in 1925, and the next year acquired General Petroleum Corp. of California to help supply its large Far East markets. Entering the Midwest for the first time in 1930, Socony purchased White Eagle Oil Refining Co., operator of gas stations in 11 states.

Socony purchased the assets of Vacuum Oil in 1931, forming Socony-Vacuum Corp. To supply its Far East markets more efficiently, the firm joined with Standard Oil of New Jersey to form the Standard-Vacuum Oil Co. (Stanvac) in 1933. The next year Socony-Vacuum Corp. changed its name to Socony-Vacuum Oil Co., Inc. By that time it had become the nation's second-largest oil concern and operated warehouses and gas stations in 43 states, many sporting the Mobil brand name or its winged, red horse logo.

By World War II, Stanvac contributed 35% of Socony-Vacuum's corporate earnings. With 14 refineries and a fleet of 54 ocean-going tankers, Socony-Vacuum's European holdings were vulnerable to intensifying warfare. Nazis assumed control of several Stanvac refineries in Western Europe, using them to service the Third Reich. In 1941, its large refinery in Gravenchon, France, was destroyed in a seven-day blaze. Likewise, a $30 million refinery in Palembang, Indonesia, was burned to the ground to prevent Japanese control. German submarines destroyed 32 company ships, killing 432 crewmembers. Capital losses and declining civilian revenue, however, were replaced by increases in military sales.

Capitalizing on the worldwide recognition of the Mobil gasoline brand, the company changed its name to Socony Mobil Oil Co., Inc. in 1955. Sales were $2.8 billion in 1958, and reached $6.5 billion in 1967. Egypt's nationalization of the Suez Canal the following year provided one of the many indications that the company's Middle Eastern dependence would prove to be a liability, but little could be done to reduce this dependence. The canal was reopened in 1957, creating a surplus of oil and a corresponding drop in prices that forced the company to reorganize. As part of that reorganization, Magnolia Petroleum and General Petroleum merged. Also in 1959, the company formed two chief operating divisions: Mobil Oil Co. for North American operations and Mobil International Co. to serve all other parts of the world.

The Business

Financials

Revenue (1998): $53.5 billion

Employees (1998): 41,500

SICs / NAICS

sic 2911 - Petroleum Refining

sic 2992 - Lubricating Oils & Greases

sic 1311 - Crude Petroleum & Natural Gas

sic 1321 - Natural Gas Liquids

sic 5541 - Gasoline Service Stations

sic 2865 - Cyclic Crudes & Intermediates

sic 4925 - Gas Production & Distribution Nec

sic 5169 - Chemicals & Allied Products Nec

sic 2869 - Industrial Organic Chemicals Nec

naics 324110 - Petroleum Refineries

naics 324191 - Petroleum Lubricating Oil and Grease Manufacturing

naics 211111 - Crude Petroleum and Natural Gas Extraction

naics 211112 - Natural Gas Liquid Extraction

naics 447110 - Gasoline Stations with Convenience Stores

naics 325110 - Petrochemical Manufacturing

naics 221210 - Natural Gas Distribution

naics 422690 - Other Chemical and Allied Products Wholesalers

Mobil Chemical Co. was formed as a subsidiary in 1960 to take advantage of the many discoveries in the field of petrochemicals. Six years later Socony Mobil Oil Co. was renamed Mobil Oil Corp., and its red horse logo was retired in favor of a bright red "o" within the Mobil moniker.

By 1966, the Middle East, principally Saudi Arabia, supplied 43% of Mobil's crude production. Massive world consumption of oil surpassed production, shifting the market in favor of the Organization of Petroleum Exporting Countries (OPEC). In 1973, OPEC imposed an embargo on oil shipments to the U.S. for six months, and commenced a gradual annexation of U.S.-owned oil properties. The price of oil quadrupled virtually overnight, marking a new era of energy awareness. Sales and profits for all of the major oil companies dramatically increased as an immediate result; Mobil's sales nearly tripled within four years to $32 billion in 1977. As its profits reached record

The Officers

Chairman and CEO: Lucio A. Noto

President and Chief Operating Officer: Eugene A. Renna

Exec. VP and Chief Financial Officer: Harold R. Cramer

Sr. VP and General Counsel: Samuel H. Gillespie III

heights, Mobil responded to congressional and media criticism by defending the rights of members of the oil industry to conduct business as they deemed appropriate.

However, to protect itself from any anti-oil company backlash, Mobil embarked on a diversification campaign. In 1974, it acquired Marcor, owner of the Montgomery Ward retailer, and then Container Corp. of America, a paperboard manufacturer. Mobil's hold on these and other extraneous assets was only temporary, and by 1993 the firm had divested numerous underperforming operations.

Mobil Corp. was formed as a holding company for Mobil Oil Corp. and Mobil Chemical in 1976. An unsuccessful attempt to acquire Conoco Inc. in 1981 was followed the next year when a bid for Marathon Oil Co. fell through. In 1984, Mobil purchased Superior Oil Co. for $5.7 billion, gaining extensive reserves of natural gas and oil in Canada and the U.S. Four years later, Mobil discontinued retail gasoline businesses in 20 states, deriving 88% of its retail revenue from the remaining 14 states. It also cut its oil-related employment by 20%.

The company made determined efforts to increase exploration activities. By 1991, new discoveries enabled Mobil to increase its oil and natural gas production by five percent, to 1.6 million barrels per day. Later that year, the firm acquired Exxon's Australian facilities, and divested its Wyoming coalmine and hundreds of Texas oil wells for a total of $570 million. In 1994, the company signed a production-sharing agreement with Vietnam's state oil company to develop the offshore Blue Dragon field. In October of the following year Mobil sold its plastics unit, Packaging Corp., maker of Hefty and Baggies products, to Tenneco Inc. for $1.27 billion in order to renew its focus on the core areas of oil, gas, and petrochemicals.

In 1996, Mobil and British Petroleum PLC consolidated their European refining, fuel, and gas station operations in a $5 billion agreement. According to the pact's division of labor, British Petroleum was responsible for the refining, marketing, and distribution, while Mobil handled the lubricant portion of the business. Two years later, Mobil agreed to be acquired by Exxon Corp. to form Exxon Mobil, the world's largest petroleum company.

History of Vacuum Oil Co.

In 1866, carpenter and part-time inventor Matthew Ewing devised an innovative method of distilling kerosene from oil by using a vacuum. Although this production method was less successful than he had hoped, his partner, Hiram Bond Everest, noticed that the gummy residue from this process was suitable as a lubricator. Ewing and Everest took out a patent on behalf of Vacuum Oil Co., which was incorporated on October 4, 1866. Ewing later sold his interest in the company in order to focus on experiments in kerosene. The new company soon enjoyed great success due to the demand for heavy vacuum oil, particularly the Gargoyle 600-W Steam Cylinder Oil, by manufacturers of steam engines and the new internal-combustion engines.

In 1879, John D. Rockefeller's Standard Oil Co. acquired 85% of Vacuum Oil for $200,000. Despite its small size, Vacuum was extended a great degree of latitude by Standard's management. In 1886, Everest led Vacuum on an independent course in foreign sales, opening affiliates in Montreal, Canada, and Liverpool, England. By the turn of the century, Vacuum also had operations in France, Germany, Italy, Hungary, India, Singapore, Japan, Australia, New Zealand, and Cuba. It became the leader among Standard companies in the use of efficient marketing and sales techniques, packaging its lubricants in attractive tins, operating an well-organized sales force, and, when necessary, consulting a lubricants specialist to assist customers in selecting the most suitable oil.

In 1910, Vacuum's holding company, Standard Oil Co. of New Jersey, invested $500,000 to retool its Bayonne, New Jersey, refinery to include the manufacture of Vacuum's lubricants for export. By that time Standard's subsidiaries controlled nearly all of the foreign market, accounting for six percent of the total. Its Mobil Oil products had become well-known on five continents.

In 1911, the U.S. Supreme Court ordered the dissolution of Standard of New Jersey, charging violation of the Sherman Antitrust Act. Among the 33 new companies created as a result were Vacuum and Standard Oil Company of New York (Socony). These newly independent companies were cut off from their sister companies' supply of crude oil, and spent the next two decades expanding operations to become more self-reliant. Vacuum, which focused on the refinery business, completed construction of a new refinery for export products in 1917. In 1929, Vacuum acquired Lubrite Refining Co., and in 1930 purchased both Wadhams Oil Corp. and White Star Refining Co. Vacuum Oil and Socony merged when Socony purchased the assets of Vacuum in 1931, forming Socony-Vacuum Corp.

Market Forces Driving the Merger

Standard Oil Company of New York (Socony) and Vacuum Oil Company had both been part of the huge Standard Oil Trust that monopolized the nation's oil industry. When the U.S. Supreme Court ordered the dissolution of this behemoth, 33 independent companies were created, among them Socony and Vacuum. Each of the newly independent firms was allotted varying proportions of the three basic oil assets—crude production, refining, and marketing—but neither Socony nor Vacuum ended up with any sources of crude. Both companies were strong marketers and refiners, so they occupied themselves in searching for enough crude oil to keep their plants and salesmen busy.

By the early 1930s, both Socony and Vacuum had increased their supply through strategic acquisitions, but continued to operate under a chronic shortage of crude. The two firms were similar in profile and were complementary in product offerings, and also had a practical, working knowledge of the other through their previous affiliation under the Standard Oil Trust. They, therefore, decided to consolidate their operations through a merger.

Approach and Engagement

In 1930, Socony and Vacuum announced their intention to merge, the first such reunion of the 33 companies that had been divested by the Standard Oil Trust in 1911. Government regulators, naturally, were not eager to begin rebuilding what they had labored to break up, however. In July 1930, the government filed suit to block the merger as a violation of the Sherman Antitrust Act.

The companies argued that the oil industry had changed significantly since the Trust days. In the two decades since the dissolution, many new rivals had arisen, so their proposed merger would not restrain healthy competition. In this environment, Socony and Vacuum argued, they had as much right as any other company to form unions that would not restrain trade.

The government appealed a court decision approving the merger, but in February 1931 the Federal Circuit Court of Appeals upheld the lower court's ruling. In June the government dropped its plan to appeal to the U.S. Supreme Court.

Shareholders approved the deal in late July, and Socony-Vacuum Corp. was subsequently created.

Products and Services

A major producer, refiner, and marketer of petroleum, Mobil had exploration and production activities focused on locating, developing, and producing hydrocarbon resources worldwide. In 1998, the company produced the equivalent of 1.7 million barrels of oil per day and had reserves of 7.6 billion barrels of oil equivalent, a 12-year supply.

Mobil's marketing and refining facilities, with refining capacity of 2.2 million barrels of oil per day, operated at a 94% utilization rate in 1998. The firm sold 144 million gallons of refined products daily in more than 15,000 service stations in 50 countries. Additionally, Mobil lubricants were marketed in more than 100 countries.

Mobil Chemical operated 28 chemical facilities located in 10 countries. Its principal products included basic petrochemicals (ethylene, propylene, benzene, and paraxylene), intermediates (ethylene glycol), and a key derivative (polyethylene).

Review of the Outcome

The union of Socony and Vacuum formed a company with formidable refining and marketing strengths, both domestically and internationally. To supply its Far East markets more efficiently, the firm joined with Standard Oil of New Jersey to form the Standard-Vacuum Oil Co. (Stanvac) in 1933. By the following year Socony-Vacuum had become the nation's second-largest oil concern, with nearly $500 million in sales, and sold a full line of petroleum products in warehouses and gas stations in 43 states.

Research

Abels, Jules. *The Rockefeller Billions*, The Macmillan Co., 1965.

Mobil Corp. Home Page, available at http://www.mobil.com. Official World Wide Web Page for Mobil. Includes information on products and services, finances, and employment, as well as news releases, biographies, and a company history.

"Mobil Corporation," in *International Directory of Company Histories*, Vol. IV, St. James Press, 1991. Profiles of the history of Mobil.

Nevins, Allan. *Study in Power: John D. Rockefeller, Industrialist and Philanthropist*, 2 volumes, Charles Scribner's Sons, 1953.

Tarbell, Ida. *History of the Standard Oil Company*, Peter Smith, 1904.

Yergin, Daniel. *The Prize: The Epic Quest for Oil, Money, and Power*, Simon & Schuster, 1991.

CAROLINE C. HOBART

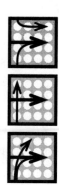

STAPLES & OFFICE DEPOT

Staples, Inc.
One Research Dr.; PO Box 5114
Westborough, MA 01581-5114
USA

tel: (508)370-8500
fax: (508)370-8989
web: http://www.staples.com

Office Depot, Inc.
2200 Old Germantown Rd.
Delray Beach, FL 33445
USA

tel: (561)278-4800
fax: (561)265-4001
web: http://www.officedepot.com

date: April 4, 1997 (canceled)
affected: Staples, Inc., USA, founded 1985
affected: Office Depot, Inc., USA, founded 1986

Overview of the Merger

The two leading office supply retailers announced a $4.3 billion merger agreement in September 1996. In linking lots, Staples and Office Depot would form a company twice their respective sizes. The combined company would pass on to customers the savings it would realize as a greater force in purchasing and distribution, as well as the lower costs of advertising since the separate companies would no longer be in competition with each other. The FTC, however, didn't see the situation quite that way.

Based on the belief that the combined company would drive prices up, not down, the FTC blocked the merger on antitrust grounds. Staples and Office Depot decided to fight the commission in federal court, but lost the preliminary round in June 1997. Sensing that a continued battle would be both expensive and futile, the companies scrubbed their merger agreement.

The FTC challenge and subsequent ruling by the federal court puzzled consumers, industry experts, and Wall Street. The combined company would have had only about a six-percent share of the U.S. office supply market—hardly a percentage that should raise antitrust objections. Moreover, the two companies overlapped in only 30 markets, and had even identified 63 stores that they would close upon completion of a merger. The FTC was not swayed, and was subsequently labeled in a *Forbes* article as "moronic, high-handed, [and] arbitrary."

History of Staples, Inc.

The fruitless search for a printer ribbon over the July Fourth weekend in 1985 gave Thomas Stemberg the idea for an office supply superstore. That notion fermented in his mind for months, and when he was dismissed from his supermarket job in December, Stemberg seized the opportunity to develop his idea. The approach was to apply the supermarket model to office supplies, stocking large quantities of merchandise and passing the bulk prices on to small businesses, which typically do not buy large enough quantities to receive discounts from manufacturers.

In October 1985, Stemberg and Leo Kahn, along with the backing of venture capitalists, established Staples, Inc. It opened its first store in May 1986 in Brighton, Massachusetts. Failing to attract initial customers, the company invested $1 million to develop a database of local small businesses, a system that was then used to track their purchases once telemarketing programs lured them in. That November Staples opened its second store, in Woburn, Massachusetts.

The chain expanded into Rhode Island and New York in 1987 with its next two openings. Pennsylvania and District of Columbia outlets opened the following year. In 1989 it introduced a generic line of merchandise and held its initial public offering. By the end of the year, its 38 operations generated revenues of $182 million, but it had slipped from the nation's top spot, landing behind Office Depot.

In 1990 Staples expanded to California with the opening of three stores. It also launched two new concepts: Staples Direct, a direct mail catalog business, and Staples Express, a compact version of the prototype store for urban markets. Acquisition and investment marked the next couple of years. The 10-unit HQ Office Supplies Warehouse, a bankrupt California company, was purchased in 1991, as was as a stake in Business Depot, Ltd., a new Canadian office superstore. The company gained entry into the European market with its 1992 acquisition of 40% of Germany-based MAXI-Papier-Markt-GmbH and a partnership with U.K.-based Kingfisher PLC. That year it also spent $3.1 million for the purchase of Office Mart Holdings Corporation. In 1993 it opened its 200th store and recorded revenues in excess of $1 million for the first time.

Staples acquired National Office Supply Company, Spectrum Office Products, the seven-store Office America chain, and full ownership of Business Depot in 1994. That year it entered the contract stationer business, which serves large companies.

After terminating its merger with Office Depot in 1996, it acquired full-ownership of MAXI-Papier and increased its stake in its U.K. joint-venture to 92%. In 1997 it opened 128 new stores. Martin Hanaka resigned as president and COO under allegations of an improper relationship with an employee, and was succeeded by Ronald Sargent in 1998. It purchased Quill Corporation, a mail-order office supply operation, in May 1998 for $690 million.

At the end of fiscal 1997, Staples operated 742 stores in 32 states, the District of Columbia, Canada, the U.K., and Germany. Net income of $131 million on sales of $5.2 billion made it the nation's second-largest office supply operator.

The Business

Financials - Staples, Inc.

Revenue (1999): $7.12 billion

Employees (1999): 21,580

Financials - Office Depot, Inc.

Revenue (1998): $8.98 billion

Employees (1998): 44,000

SICs / NAICS

sic 5943 - Stationery Stores

sic 5712 - Furniture Stores

sic 5961 - Catalog & Mail-Order Houses

naics 453210 - Office Supplies and Stationery Stores

naics 442110 - Furniture Stores

naics 454110 - Electronic Shopping and Mail-Order Houses

History of Office Depot, Inc.

Before 1986, the office supply industry was dominated by small, independent operators selling products at prices close to the manufacturers' suggested prices. That October Patrick Sher, Stephen Dougherty, and Jack Kopkin opened the Office Depot warehouse-style store in Florida. Purchasing products in large volumes enabled it to offer its wares to consumers at prices lower than its competitors. In less than two months, it opened two more stores in Florida.

In 1987 David I. Fuente, former president of Sherwin-Williams' paint store division, joined Office Depot as chairman and CEO. Venture capital provided the resources for expansion, and by the end of the year it opened seven more stores, expanding into Georgia, and generated sales of $33 million. Its initial public offering in 1988 fueled faster expansion, as did a $41 million investment by the French Carrefour chain. That year it ventured into Kentucky, North Carolina, Tennessee, and Texas. It reached Alabama, Missouri, Indiana, Louisiana, Oklahoma, and South Carolina in 1989. By the end of that year, the company's 67 stores generated sales of $314 million and net income of $6 million.

Personal computers and peripherals were added to its offerings in 1990. That year it opened its first stores in Kansas, Maryland, Mississippi, Nebraska, Ohio, Pennsylvania, and Wisconsin. Office Depot gained entry into nine western states by purchasing

The Officers

Staples, Inc.

Chairman and CEO: Thomas G. Stemberg

President: Ronald L. Sargent

Exec. VP and Chief Administrative Officer: John J. Mahoney

Exec. VP, Merchandising: Richard R. Gentry

Exec. VP, Human Resources: Susan S. Hoyt

Office Depot, Inc.

Chairman and CEO: David I. Fuente

Vice-Chairman of the Board and Chairman, Viking Office Products: Irwin Helford

President and Chief Operating Officer: John C. Macatee

President, Office Depot International: Bruce Nelson

Chief Financial Officer and Exec. VP, Finance: Barry J. Goldstein

Exec. VP, Human Resources: Thomas Kroeger

the 51-unit Office Club chain in April 1991 for $246 million in stock. Office Club's president and founder, Mark Begelman, became president and COO of Office Depot. Carrefour invested another $40 million, bringing its stake in Office Depot to 18%. By the end of 1991, the company was North America's largest office products retailer. Its 228 stores in 29 states earned $38 million on sales of $1.3 billion.

The firm expanded beyond the U.S. borders with its 1992 acquisition of the Great Canadian Office Supplies Warehouse. It gained entry into Columbia and Israel the following year by entering into licensing agreements to open Office Depot stores in those countries. It also entered the contract stationer industry, which caters to large companies, by acquiring Wilson Stationery & Printing Company and Eastman Office Products. Begelman resigned in 1995, and Fuente assumed the vacated post of president. By the end of that year, the chain consisted of 504 stores generating sales of $5.3 billion.

Office Depot continued expansion on its own after the 1996 dissolution of its merger agreement with Staples. In August 1998 it acquired the 26-unit Viking Office Products for $2.7 billion, gaining entry into several additional countries. By year-end 1998, Office Depot operated 726 stores in the U.S., Canada, and France. Licensing agreements also lent the company's operations to sixteen other countries. It ended the year as the leading office supply retailer in the U.S.

Market Forces Driving the Merger

Office Depot and Staples decided in the autumn of 1996 to merge. By the end of that year, Office Depot, the industry leader, would have 570 stores and sales of $6 billion. The second-place company, Staples, would have 557 stores bringing in revenues of nearly $4 billion. In combining the two, a superforce in the office supply industry would be created, dwarfing its nearest competitor, Office Max.

Additionally, by combining their operations, the merged company would realize about $4 billion in savings. The consumer would benefit from reduced overhead, as part of the savings would be passed along as reduced retail prices. Staples' chairman and CEO, Thomas Stemberg, also wanted to absorb Office Depot in order to learn from and incorporate into the chain its efficient and productive operating practices. Office Depot's chairman David Fuente remarked at the press conference announcing the merger, "We're a lot happier to be together with Staples than competing against them," according to *Discount Store News*.

Even the number-three company, Office Max, gave its seal of approval to the merger. It saw the upcoming couple of years of post-merger transition between its two rivals as the perfect window of opportunity to step up and snatch part of its market share.

The companies' chairmen believed that any merger between the companies must be enacted soon, before the individual chains grew too large. They overlapped in only 30 markets, or 20% of their stores. Staples' territory is mainly in the Northeast and southern California, while Office Depot's major markets are the Southeast, the Midwest, and California. If a merger was delayed much longer, it was likely that their overlap would be increased, making a merger trickier. Governmental approval would be more difficult to obtain, and more of their stores would probably have to be sold or closed to satisfy antitrust regulations.

Approach and Engagement

Merger talks between the two companies began in mid-August 1996. On September 4th, Stemberg and Fuente held a press conference announcing their $3.6 billion proposed merger. Under the deal, each company would purchase up to 19.9% of the other's outstanding stock. Office Depot shareholders would receive 1.14 shares of Staples stock for each of their Office Depot shares.

The new company would be called Staples/ Office Depot Inc., and the stores would operate under the moniker Staples: The Office Depot. It would hold only a six-percent share of the office supply market.

The company would be based in Staples' headquarters site at Westborough, Massachusetts. David Fuente, Office Depot's chairman and CEO, was named the new company's chairman, and Staples' chairman and CEO, Thomas Stemberg, was slated to assume the post of CEO of the combined company.

The chains knew that as leaders of the industry, they would be subject to close governmental scrutiny before receiving approval to merge. They were confident, though, that antitrust concerns would be alleviated upon realization by the Federal Trade Commission (FTC) that their geographic markets had relatively low overlap—only 20% of their stores operated in the same market. The new company's planned for translating savings in purchasing, distribution, operations, and marketing into product savings for the consumer should also convince the government to approve the merger.

In November the FTC requested additional information from the retailers in its investigation of the proposed deal. This move indicated that the deal would probably have about even chances for receiving approval, according to statistics on the FTC's previous record.

The FTC was expected to release its determination of the deal in January 1997. By mid-February it had still not come to a decision, and Staples and Office Depot agreed to extend the deadline to March 5th. The retailers launched an advertising campaign addressing the FTC's concerns about higher retail pricing as a probable result of the merger. Full-page ads run in large newspapers featured consumer testimonials in favor of the merger, and presented such headlines as, "What happens when two low-price leaders combine? Prices get lower."

Meanwhile, an organization affiliated with consumer advocate Ralph Nader purportedly proved otherwise. At the request of FTC staffers, the Consumer Project on Technology initiated a two-day study of the price of thermal fax paper at 15 Staples and 17 Office Depot locations. It found that the prices were cheaper whenever the two chains occupied the same market. The FTC considered the findings to be evidence proving its suspicions about higher pricing, while the retailers objected to the study's obvious flaws. It had been conducted on only one product, over only a two-day period, and was conducted not through store visits, but over the telephone.

The FTC deadline was again extended, until March 13th. On March 10th the agency announced that it would seek a federal court order to block the merger. It reasoned that the deal would reduce competition and lead to higher prices in parts of 17 states and the District of Columbia. In going to court, the

The Players

Staples CEO and Chairman: Thomas G. Stemberg. Thomas Stemberg defined a niche retail market when he and Leo Kahn opened the first office products superstore. This Harvard Business School graduate was employed as an executive at First National Supermarkets until his dismissal in December 1985. Drawing off of his knowledge of the supermarket business, the 36-year-old applied the grocery store model to office supplies retailing. Six months later, he opened the Staples superstore in Brighton, Massachusetts. His company quickly grew into a powerhouse, and by 1996 was the nation's second-largest office products company. That year he engineered a merger with the nation's leader, Office Depot. Had the merger been completed, Stemberg would have served as the CEO of the $10 billion combined company.

Office Depot CEO and Chairman: David I. Fuente. David Fuente, a 41-year-old native of Chicago, was sought out by a headhunter in 1987 to join the ten-store Office Depot chain as chief executive. At that time he was happily serving as president of the Sherwin-Williams' paint store division, and was not interested in switching jobs. That changed when he walked into one of the office products stores and marveled at both the concept and the crowds. Later that year one of the company's founders, Pat Sher, died of leukemia, and Fuente came aboard as chairman and CEO. Less than a decade later, Office Depot agreed to merge with its closest competitor, Staples. Fuente was slated to assume the role of chairman of the combined company.

FTC would seek a preliminary injunction, followed by an administrative trial to block the merger.

Staples and Office Depot announced on March 26th their agreement to sell 63 of their stores to Office Max, hoping to appease the FTC by eliminating some of their overlap markets. This divestiture, although recommended by FTC staffers, was dismissed by the commissioners as inadequate. On April 4th the commissioners voted 4-to-1 against the merger.

The retailers weren't giving up, however. As reported in Business Wire, Stemberg optimistically said, "We believe an unbiased court of law will understand the merits of our case. The FTC clearly lacks an understanding of the office products industry." So they accepted the FTC's challenge, and extended the terms of their merger agreement until June 30th. On that day, their agreement suffered the fatal blow. Federal district judge Thomas Hogan granted the FTC's injunction. Portions of his opinion was reported in *Computer Retail Week*, and can be summarized as "consumers would be at risk of serious anti-competitive harm" if the merger was successful.

The retailers regretfully accepted that it would be futile to pursue the merger at trial. They had already lost months in putting the deal together, and each had spent a small fortune in getting only to this point. Staples had incurred costs of $29.6 million, while Office Depot had spent over $16 million. They terminated their merger agreement and went back to their respective operations.

Products and Services

Both companies offered a wide range of office products, including general office supplies, furniture, computer hardware and software, photocopiers, fax machines, telephones, briefcases and attaches, and accounting supplies.

Review of the Outcome

Critics of the ban of the Staples/Office Depot merger not only condemned the irrationale of the FTC block, they feared that they had witnessed the writing on the wall for future merger attempts. Except for extreme cases, in which the threat of a monopoly is indeed looming, the FTC usually approved merger propositions. In this case, it not only challenged the merger (for shaky reasons), but it actually won federal court approval to halt the merger. Perhaps the focus of the government's antitrust investigations was shifting from the size of the resulting company's market share to simply the market rank of the proposed partners. The result of this case was sure to have an impact on merger speculations within other industries.

The two retailers brushed off the dust of their failed merger and resumed business as usual. Staples hadn't stagnated during the waiting period of the previous nine months. During its first quarter, which ended May 3, 1997, it opened 42 new stores and increased sales by 26%.

Office Depot, however, had a tougher time picking up the pieces. With the expected move of its headquarters to the Staples' site, it had lost number of executives. Moreover, it experienced slowed expansion and revenues. In its first quarter, ending March 29,

1997, it opened only one store and recorded a nine-percent sales increase. Chairman Fuente believed that although the chain did have some lost ground to recover, at least a couple of good things developed from the merger process. The analysis of its business preparatory to the merger revealed improvements that could be implemented in terms of systems, service, and inventory management. Because its information systems were to serve as the platform for the combined company, they had undergone enhancements that could be utilized in strengthening the Office Depot operation.

Research

Forbes, Steve. "Daft," in *Forbes*, 5 May 1997. Offers a negative opinion of the FTC's ban on the merger.

Harrington, Mark. "Mega Merger Scrutinized by Nader, Wall St.," in *Computer Retail Week*, 3 March 1997. Results of, and response to, the pricing study conducted by the Consumer Project on Technology.

Liebeck, Laura. "FTC Nixes Staples/Office Depot," in *Discount Store News*, 14 April 1997. The companies evaluate their options after the FTC blocks their merger.

———. "Staples/Office Depot Merger Delayed Pending FTC Approval," in *Discount Store News*, 3 March 1997. Staples' advertising campaign to sway the public and the FTC to approve the merger.

Moukheiber, Zina. "A Lousy Day for Golf," in *Forbes*, 9 May 1994. History of Office Depot since David Fuente joined as CEO.

"Office Depot, Inc.," in *Notable Corporate Chronologies*, The Gale Group, 1999. Lists major events in the history of the company.

Office Depot, Inc. Home Page, available at http://www.officedepot.com. Official World Wide Web Page for Office Depot. It includes an online store, a store directory, company history, executive biographies, annual reports, and investor information.

Olenick, Doug. "Office Depot, Staples Remain Just Arch Rivals; Federal Judge Backs FTC to Block Merger," in *Computer Retail Week*, 7 July 1997. Selected readings from U.S. District Judge Thomas Hogan's opinion in granting the FTC injunction.

"Staples, Inc.," in *Notable Corporate Chronologies*, The Gale Group, 1999. Profiles the history of the company.

"Staples/Office Depot Merger: The Timing is Right," in *Discount Store News*, 16 September 1996. Discusses the reasons that the merger is well-timed, and outlines how the transaction will be completed.

"Staples and Office Depot to Vigorously Contest FTC Ruling," in *Business Wire*, 7 April 1997. Comments from the chairmen on their expectations of taking on the FTC in federal court.

"Staples: Thomas Stemberg, Chief Executive Officer," in *Computer Retail Week*, 18 November 1996. Stemberg's conceptualization and establishment of Office Depot.

DEBORAH J. UNTENER

STONE CONTAINER & CONSOLIDATED BATHURST

nationality: USA
date: March 1989
affected: Stone Container Corp., USA, founded 1926
affected: Consolidated Bathurst Inc., USA

Smurfit-Stone Container Corp.
150 N. Michigan Ave.
Chicago, IL 60601
USA

tel: (312)346-6600
fax: (312)580-2272
web: http://www.smurfit-stone.com

Overview of the Merger

In March of 1989, Stone Consolidated made its largest purchase to date when it paid $2.2 billion for Consolidated Bathurst. The Power Corp., which had a 40% stake in the company, Kuwait Investment Office, which owned 10%, and Daily Mail and General Trust, which claimed ownership of 14.8% of the company, tendered their stock upon announcement of the deal. When the transaction was completed, Stone Container became the second largest producer of pulp and paper in the world, as well as a major player in the newsprint industry.

History of Stone Container Corp.

In 1926, Joseph Stone founded J.H. Stone & Sons, with his sons Norman and Marvin, as a jobber of packing materials and office supplies. After emigrating from Russia to the U.S., Stone had created the company using savings of $1,500. The business proved immediately successful, with sales of $68,000 and profits of $13,500 for the first full year. In 1928, Jerome Stone, the youngest of the three Stone brothers, entered the family business as well. As the business progressed and Joseph decreased his involvement, the three sons took on additional responsibility, using a simple management system of majority rule among themselves.

With the onset of The Great Depression in 1933, J.H. Stone & Sons was forced into manufacturing. The National Recovery Act, signed into law by President Roosevelt, outlawed price-cutting, which meant that jobbers would no longer get their merchandise at a discount. Stone's customers would now have to pay a premium for the company's services. Needing a cheaper source of supplies, the company bought five pieces of old equipment that converted corrugated sheets into boxes. A second-hand corrugator was also purchased for $20,000.

As the company began to grow, it moved to increasingly larger quarters, eventually ending up on 74th Street in Chicago, with 55,000 square feet. In 1938, the Stones decided to erect their own plant; the 150,000-square-foot Chicago building was the first plant anywhere devoted exclusively to the manufacture of corrugated boxes. The company reached $1 million in sales for the first time in 1939.

The Business

Financials

Revenue (1998): $3.46 billion

Employees (1998): 38,000

SICs / NAICS

sic 2631 - Paperboard Mills

sic 2621 - Paper Mills

sic 2611 - Pulp Mills

sic 2679 - Converted Paper Products Nec

naics 322121 - Paper (except Newsprint) Mills

naics 322122 - Newsprint Mills

naics 322211 - Corrugated and Solid Fiber Box
Manufacturing

naics 322222 - Coated and Laminated Paper Manufacturing

naics 322299 - All Other Converted Paper Product
Manufacturing

naics 322231 - Die-Cut Paper and Paperboard Office
Supplies Manufacturing

Stone continued to see good fortune during World War II, when the government was sending aid and arms overseas. Nearly everything sent was packed in corrugated boxes. Since the company's war priority rating was high, it had no problem with material shortages. Stone & Sons continued to expand in the face of a good market, and in 1943, Light Corrugated Box Co., of Philadelphia, Pennsylvania, was acquired for $1.2 million. The first non-family member, David Lipper, became general manager at the newly purchased facility. In 1945, the business incorporated, changing its name to Stone Container Corp.

After the war, demand skyrocketed and raw materials grew short. CEO Norman Stone saw the opportunity for expansion, as well as a need to monitor raw materials. Under his leadership the company acquired two mills, a $1.2 million box-board mill in Franklin, Ohio, and a $575,000 mill in Coshocton, Ohio, that produced corrugating medium (the fluted material sandwiched between linerboard layers in corrugated containers) from straw. In 1947, the firm issued 250,000 shares of common stock and became a publicly owned company. No longer completely family-owned, the brothers began working to attract outsiders to management positions.

The 1950s saw a huge expansion of supermarkets and self-service outlets in the retail sector. As containers became pieces of advertising, as well as a means of conveying merchandise, Stone pioneered the use of ads on box exteriors. The company also began a hefty expansion plan, acquiring several companies such as W.C. Ritchie & Co. and Acme Carton Co., both of Chicago, Illinois; the Western Paper Box Co. of Detroit, Michigan; Campbell Box & Tag Co. of South Bend, Indiana; and Delmar Paper Box Co.

In addition to manufacturing and selling corrugated containers and paperboard, Stone Container began selling folding cartons, folding cartons, fiber cans and tubs, tags, and special paper packages as a result of the Ritchie & Co. acquisition. In 1961, jute linerboard was losing ground to the lighter, stronger kraft linerboard. To stay competitive, the company had to purchase kraft linerboard from other paper companies. Consequently, Stone took a 65% equity share in South Carolina Industries (SCI), through which the firm planned the construction of a new kraft linerboard mill in Florence, South Carolina. This mill would be capable of producing 400 tons of board a day.

In 1962, the company was listed for the first time on the New York Stock Exchange. Construction began on the SCI mill in the midst of an economic recession, and the project was financed through Northwestern Mutual Life Insurance at a cost of $24 million, a sum greater than Stone's entire net worth. When the mill was completed in 1964, Stone became a fully integrated company, supplying virtually all of its own raw materials.

Throughout the late 1960s and early 1970s, the company kept growing, spending $35 million in capital expansion and diversifying with a plastics packaging division. By 1975, the Stone family's ownership in the company was at 62%.

In the 1980s, Stone Container focused on growth. The company purchased an equity position in the Dean-Dempsy Corp., a wood-chip fiber source, becoming the 13th-largest producer of boxes in the U.S. Three years later, the company paid $510 million for Continental Group's containerboard and brown-paper operations. Because an industry downturn had left Continental in desperate need of cash, Stone was able to buy three highly efficient paper mills, 15 corrugated box plants, five bag plants, and the cutting rights to 1.45 million acres of timberland for about one-third of the replacement value of the mills alone. The $600 million loan Stone used to finance the deal boosted debt to 79% of capital. To pay some of the deficit down, Stone conducted its first equity offering since 1947. The Continental purchase also doubled

Stone's annual capacity to 2.3 million tons and made Stone Container the nation's second-largest producer of brown paper behind International Paper Co.

With containerboard prices on the rise, Stone was able to significantly reduce debt and continued on acquisition spree. In 1985, Stone paid $457 million to buy three containerboard mills and 52 box-and-bag plants from Champion International Corp. With this purchase, Stone's debt again soared, to about 70% of capitalization. Two years later, Southwest Forest Industries (SFI), a containerboard company that also made newsprint, was purchased for $760 million, making Stone the nation's largest producer of brown paper, including corrugated boxes, paper bags, liner-board, and kraft paper.

In 1989, Stone made its biggest acquisition yet, paying $2.2 million in cash and securities for Consolidated Bathurst Inc. (CB), Canada's fifth-largest pulp-and-paper company. The purchase made Stone the world's second-largest producer of pulp, paper, and paperboard, as well as a major player in the newsprint industry.

In the mid-1990s, weak pricing, heavy debt, and falling liner-board prices took a toll on Stone's bottom line. To make matters worse, an explosion at Stone's mill in Panama City, Florida, killed two people and left four injured and one missing. In 1995, Stone Consolidated, a subsidiary of Stone Container, merged with Rainy River Forest Products Inc., based in Toronto. This added three North American paper mills and the output of a fourth to Stone Consolidated's mill system, making the company the world's largest marketer of newsprint and ground-wood paper. That same year, the company announced capacity expansion projects for seven of its twelve U.S. containerboard mills. The projects were slated to add 704 tons per day to the company's linerboard and cor-rugating medium capacity.

In 1997, Stone Consolidated merged with Abitibi-Price, a Canadian company, to form Abitibi-Consolidated, in which Stone Container held a 25% stake. Later that year, however, Stone sold its interest in its Canadian subsidiary, including its stake in Abitibi, in an effort to increase cash flow. Stone was forced to look to merge as a means of staying afloat, and in November of 1998, Stone Container merged with Jefferson Smurfit Corp. to form Smurfit-Stone Container Corp.

Market Forces Driving the Merger

After purchasing Stone Forest Industries in 1988, Stone Container set its sights on becoming a major force in the packaging, newsprint, and market pulp industry. Since 1983, the company had grown over

The Officers

Chairman: Michael W.J. Smurfit

President and CEO: Ray Curran

VP and General Manager, Corrugated Container Division: Peter F. Dages

VP and General Manager, Specialty Packaging: James D. Duncan

VP and Chief Financial Officer: Patrick J. Moore

eight times its original size and had spent billions of dollars, thanks to an aggressive acquisition strategy led by Roger Stone. Stone wanted to grow in the inter-national market as well. He predicted that the change in Europe economics that would occur in 1992 would springboard the packaging industry's revenues as more people would be shipping overseas. Stone would be able to feed off of that trend as his company stood poised with a large manufacturing pool and large claims to raw materials.

Consolidated Bathurst had operations in the UK, West Germany, and the Netherlands. Stone had already began moving into the Pacific Rim with deals in Japan and China set up for exporting. The company wanted to manufacture overseas as well. By striking a deal with the Canadian company, Stone could gain valuable market share, access to Bathurst's European production facilities, and additional newsprint and pulp making capacity. The deal would also place Stone in a very comfortable number two position in the paper industry in terms of pulp and paper pro-duced in tonnage.

Approach and Engagement

In the spring of 1988, Roger Stone began dis-cussing merger plans with Consolidated Bathurst. In January 1989, Stone Container announced that it had formed an agreement with Consolidated Bathurst's three major shareholders to purchase the paper com-pany for $2.2 billion. The Power Corp. in Canada, led by Paul Desmarais, agreed to sell its 40% stake in the company, as did Daily Mail and General Trust, and the Kuwait Investment Office. Together, the three owned roughly 65% of the company. Under the terms of the deal, Stone would have to spend $1 billion in Canadian operations in the next five years, and the company would not be able to lay-off any Consolidated Bathurst employees as a result of the merger.

The Players

Chairman and CEO of Stone Container Corp.: Roger W. Stone. Roger Stone graduated from the Wharton School in 1957 and began to work for the family container business as a sales representative. He held several positions in sales and marketing before holding the title of corporate vice president in 1969. In 1975, he was named president of Stone Container and four years later, took on the role of CEO as well. Stone was named chairman of the container company in 1983. He is credited with leading the company's growth into one of the largest producers of cardboard and corrugated boxes in the world.

Chairman of Power Corp. (parent company of Consolidated Bathurst Inc.): Paul Desmarais. Canadian businessman Paul Desmarais began his career owning a bus company in Sudbury, Ontario. He went on to own large stakes in the Power Corp. of Canada, Consolidated Bathurst, the Montreal Trust Co., and Gesca. He was eventually elected chairman of Power Corp. and orchestrated several deals from that position, including Stone Container's purchase of the Consolidated Bathurst unit. In 1990, he also became chairman of Pargesa, a Dutch holding company.

Investment Canada, led by Harvie Andre, approved the deal in March 1989. In an article in *The Toronto Star*, Andre stated that the deal would create "a world-scale pulp and paper company better able to compete in the increasingly competitive international environment." The same article also mentioned that "opposition members slammed the Progressive Conservative government's open-door investment policy," claiming that the recent foreign deals in Canada would "lead to increased foreign ownership of the Canadian economy." Investment Canada had approved every foreign merger placed before it, and the Stone-Bathurst deal was the 4th major foreign merger deal to appear before the board within a one-week time frame in January.

Products and Services

After the deal with Bathurst, Stone was able to compete more effectively in the global market using Bathurst's paper and packaging units. The company was the second largest producer of pulp and paper, just behind International Paper Co. In 1998, after Stone Container merged with the Jefferson Smurfit Corp., the new company—Smurfit-Stone Container Corp.—owned more than 300 facilities in the U.S. and around the globe.

Paperboard and packaging products produced $2.93 billion in sales in 1997, 91% of total revenues; newsprint accounted for $302 million, bringing in the remaining 9%. Smurfit-Stone also provided services such as printing, laminating, photography, and design consultation. The company's products included boxboard, consumer packaging, kraft paper, newsprint, labels, corrugated shipping containers and pallets, and folding cartons.

Changes to the Industry

At the time of the Stone/Bathurst deal, the paper industry was in the midst of consolidation, and many companies were spending money on foreign interests. Several mergers followed Stone's lead, including International Paper's purchase of Aussedat-Ret from France, and Ciba-Geigy's purchase of Ilford's photographic products (in addition to its 51% stake in Zanders, a West German paper interest). James River Corp. from the U.S., Nokia of Finland, and Feruzzi of Italy, also formed a joint venture together.

Stone Container also pursued future deals. In 1997, its Consolidated unit merged with Abitibi-Price Inc., the largest newsprint producer in the world. Stone Container was left with a 25% interest in the merged company, Abitibi-Consolidated. Later in 1997, Stone Container, $4 million in debt, sold all of its Canadian interests including Abitibi-Consolidated, into which the Bathurst operations had been folded. In 1998, Stone Container merged with Jefferson Smurfit to form the Smurfit-Stone Container Corp.

Review of the Outcome

The purchase of Bathurst made Stone the world's second-largest producer of pulp, paper, and paperboard, as well as a major force in the newsprint industry. However, debt soared to 70% of capital, and at the time of the deal, the newsprint market was tumbling. While some analysts applauded Stone's efforts to become an international company, others were worried about the company's debt load, and stock price plummeted.

The firm's net income fell to $22 million in 1990 from $36 million in 1989. By 1991, net income was a negative $77 million, caused by weak pricing, heavy debt, and falling liner-board sales. Eventually, Stone was forced to divest the Bathurst assets in an effort to boost cash flow.

Research

"Abitibi-Price, Stone Consolidated to Merge," in *Los Angeles Times*, 15 February 1997. Provides details on the merger of Stone Consolidated and Abitibi-Price.

Cole, Robert. "Stone Agrees to Acquire Paper Maker," in *The New York Times*, 27 January 1989. Details Stone's decision to merge with the Canadian company.

Hargreaves, Deborah. "Bathurst Gives Stone a European Sprinboard," in *Financial Times London*, 7 February 1989. Discusses Stone's interest in acquiring Bathurst's European operations.

McCarthy, Shawn. "Stone Container Makes $1 Billion Promise," in *The Toronto Star*, 2 March 1989. Reports Investment Canada's approval of the Stone/Bathurst deal.

McGovern, Sheila. "Stone Container Bailing Out," in *The Gazette Montreal*, 28 October 1997. Describes Stone's sale of its Canadian subsidiaries.

Owen, David. "Stone to Acquire Bathurst," in *Financial Times (London)*, 27 January 1989. Details Stone's purchase of Consolidated Bathurst.

Smurfit-Stone Container Corp. Home Page, available at http://www.smurfit-stone.com. Official World Wide Web Home Page for Smurfit-Stone Container Corp. Includes historical, financial, and product information, as well as recent news articles.

"Stone Container Corp.," in *Notable Corporate Chronologies*, The Gale Group, 1999. Lists major events in the history of Stone Container Corp.

Urry, Maggie. "World Pulp and Paper Industry 2," in *Financial Times (London)*, 13 December 1989. Examines industry and recent mergers following the Bathurst deal.

CHRISTINA M. STANSELL

STROH COMPANIES & G. HEILEMAN

Pabst Brewing Co. (purchased The Stroh Brewery Co. in 1999)
P.O. Box 1661
San Antonio, TX 78296
USA

tel: (210)226-0231
web: www.pabst.com

nationality: USA
date: July 1996
affected: The Stroh Companies, Inc., USA, founded 1850
affected: G. Heileman Brewing Co., USA, founded 1853

Overview of the Acquisition

Stroh's 1996 acquisition of G. Heileman Brewing Co. joined the nation's fourth and fifth largest brewing operations. Stroh acquired all of Heileman's assets: its five breweries and all its brands, including Old Style, Henry Weinhard's, Schmidt's, Lone Star, Colt 45, and Mickey's. The purchase also increased Stroh's distribution and export capabilities.

History of Stroh Brewery History

Begun in the United States by Bernhard Stroh following his emigration from Germany, the company has always been family held. While its names have changed from Lion's Head, to B. Stroh Brewing Co., to The Stroh Products Co. and finally to The Stroh Brewery Co., the tradition of family ownership has remained constant.

One has to wonder what Bernhard Stroh, who founded Lion's Head Brewery in Detroit in 1850, would think of the incarnations his brewery has undergone in the century-and-a-half of its existence. The last remaining brewery to make fire-brewed beer, Stroh has a history that reflects this country's changing attitudes toward beer consumption.

Bernhard Stroh, who had learned the brewing trade from his father, first took advantage of refrigerated rail cars, and the then-new process of pasteurization, to ship beer out of Michigan. His brother Julius also expanded the company's horizons when, during Prohibition, he started producing such non-alcoholic products as soft drinks, or "near beer." He also diversified into ice cream; Stroh Ice Cream still can be found in retail grocery stores and ice-cream stores in Michigan.

A 1958 Michigan beer strike, along with the emergence of Miller and Anheuser-Busch as serious competitors, changed Stroh's profile in the second half of the 20th century. The strike had made it possible for out-of-state breweries to capture a large share of the Michigan beer traffic, and ten years later, while it was still the largest brewery in the state, it had not fully recovered from the strike.

Peter Stroh, grandson of Julius, recognized as president in 1968 that a larger-than-Michigan vision was necessary if Stroh were to maintain its leadership position in the industry. He changed the company's marketing vision, and by 1971 Stroh held 13th place in the national market. It moved into the top ten the following year.

Competition was heating up, however. Anheuser-Bush was the nation's dominant brewer and wanted to remain in that position. Seventh-placed Miller was actively attempting to overtake Anheuser, and the competition between the two drove many smaller breweries out of business. Not so Stroh. Peter Stroh expanded the company's product line with Stroh Light in 1978, gained additional facility space, brands, and distribution with the purchase of F&ampM Schaefer Brewing Corporation, and held Stroh's place as the seventh-largest beer seller.

Stroh moved from seventh to third place with its takeover of Schlitz Brewing Co. in 1982. Schlitz had fought the takeover, but acquiesced when Stroh increased its offer of $16 per share to $17. The U.S. Justice Department required Stroh to sell either the Schlitz brewery in Tennessee or North Carolina, but otherwise approved the merger.

In 1985 business was going well for the regional-gone-national brewery: It followed first-and second-place sellers Anheuser-Busch and Miller with 12% of the U.S. beer market, and had active advertising and corporate-sponsorship programs in place. But five years later, burdened by heavy debt due to efforts to keep its original Detroit brewery going, increasing raw material costs, rising advertising costs, and diversification efforts, the company's fortunes had turned.

William E. Henry, the first non-Stroh to be president of the company, and chairman Peter Stroh implemented three strategies to turn those failing fortunes around: expansion of product lines and of overseas distribution, and contract brewing. Stroh was quickly successful in the non-alcoholic beer, ice beer, and packaged draft beer markets, increasing its international sales by 50% by 1995. It then launched an active plan to purchase smaller specialty breweries. The purchase of microbreweries along with production of their products proved profitable for Stroh; by the mid-1990s about 30% of Stroh's output was for beers such as Pete's Wicked Ale and Samuel Adams.

Another prong of the turn-around strategies was acquisition. Stroh had been after G. Heileman for several years, and finally was successful in its ownership bid in 1996.

History of G. Heileman Brewing Company, Inc.

Like Stroh's, Heileman's brewing history goes back almost one hundred and fifty years. Founded as the City Brewery in LaCross, Wisconsin, by a German

The Business

Financials

Revenue (1999): $500 million (est.)

Employees (1999): 1,500

SICs / NAICS

sic 2082 - Malt Beverages

naics 312120 - Breweries

immigrant. Gottlieb Heileman joined with a local brewer to form G. Heileman, which bumped along from mid-century to mid-century, reflecting many of the same highs and lows as did the Stroh operation. By the middle of the 20th century, though, it was hurting.

The 1960s saw one of what would be Heileman's many turnarounds. As its sales and profits grew, it joined the top 20 American breweries and acquired Blatz, a nationally recognized company. Added to the regional breweries the company had acquired during the decade, its outlook was promising.

The 1970s continued the upswing. Russell Clearly, son-in-law of the man who had been president since 1956, continued the policy of acquiring regional breweries. The company's sales improved due to falling sales of Schlitz and strike-induced losses at Anheuser-Busch, and increased revenues from its bakery division enabled it to make significant acquisitions of breweries located in larger beer-drinking areas. In the late-1970s Heileman was the seventh-largest brewer in the country.

The 1980s, however, were cruel to Heileman. Even though it eventually won an antitrust suit that had been filed by Stroh and Schmidt brewers, it was an expensive win. Strong in the 15-state region bounded by Pennsylvania on the northeast, the Dakotas on the west, and Missouri to the south, Heileman had to lower prices and spend considerable advertising dollars to increase its market share in the southeast.

Chief Executive Russell Clearly's strategy of acquisitions worked to keep Heileman strong during a time when revenues alone would have made it weak. Other regional breweries were finding it difficult to stay open. Clearly added several plants and brands to the Heileman portfolio, allowing it to survive and prosper despite sagging sales. The strategy was successful enough to attract the interest of overseas venture capitalists. In 1987 Clearly sold the company to Australian businessman Alan Bond for over $1 billion.

The Players

The Stroh Companies, Inc. and The Stroh Brewery Co. Chairman: Peter W. Stroh. Peter Stroh retired at the end of 1997 as board chairman of both family-owned companies, handing over management to John W. Stroh, son of Peter's cousin. The transfer moved leadership control of the company to the fifth generation of Strohs. A member of the Stroh family has always headed the parent company, and ten family members sat on the company's board of directors, and/or held management positions, at the time of the merger.

G. Heileman Brewing Co. Founder: Russell G. Cleary. Russell Cleary, the brewing executive best known for building the G. Heileman Brewing Co. into an industry power, died in May 1997 of complications from heart surgery. At the time of his death, Mr. Cleary was president of the Cleary Management Co., a development company.

When Cleary retired in 1989, Heileman fell upon hard times. The firm went bankrupt and was bought by Hicks, Muse & Co. which, attempting to turn the company around through rapid brand expansion, brought about disastrous results instead.

The 1990s were even more difficult for Heileman. The brewery emerged from bankruptcy in 1991 after its ill-fated takeover and was sold two years later for $428 million to a private Dallas investment company. It was hurt, too, by high aluminum prices and lower-than-expected revenue from contract brewing.

Stroh, selling off its operations nationwide at the end of the decade, left the old La Crosse Heileman brewery in limbo, eliminating one of Western Wisconsin's biggest and oldest employers. Stroh officials said they would look for a buyer for the plant which it had purchased for about $290 million in 1996, but for employees, most of who had worked there had more than 20 years, it was not a good time. Mr. Cleary returned briefly in 1993 to oversee the resuscitation efforts, but Heileman again entered Chapter 11.

Hicks, Muse Hicks, Music, Tate & Furst, which ranked in 1997 as the nation's leading leveraged buyout conglomerate, bought then-bankrupt Heileman for $390 million in 1994. It hired an outside management firm with no beer industry experience to oversee the introduction of 150 new products with costly consequences: After Heileman racked up losses of $37

million in 1994 and $64 million 1995, Hicks, Muse sold it to Stroh Brewery for a reported $290 million.

Approach and Engagement

Acquisition of Heileman was a long-time goal of Stroh President and CEO William Henry, who regarded Heileman's brands and breweries as very attractive purchase targets. Looking to strengthen Stroh's position in a very competitive market, Henry felt that Heileman assets would help Stroh both domestically and internationally.

Muse, Tate & Furst, Inc., which had held the controlling interest in Heileman since 1994, had grown tired of waiting for improvements in the beer industry and in Heileman's financial performance. It wanted to focus its efforts elsewhere and, accordingly, to divest itself of the disappointing brewery. Heileman, which had had to fight both an antitrust suit when it had acquired Pabst in the early 1980s and a takeover attempt by Australian conglomerate Bond Corporation Holdings, Ltd. later in that decade, was weak financially.

After purchasing Heileman for $290 million in early July 1996, Stroh retired Heileman's bank debt, assumed all its trade and other specified liabilities, and issued a combination of Stroh debt and equity securities that Heileman could exchange for its outstanding bonds and common stock.

Products and Services

Heileman's brands included Special Export, Old Style, Rainier, Henry Weinhard, Schmidt's, Lone Star, Champale, Colt 45, and Mickey's.

Stroh brewed Samuel Adams for the Boston Brewing Co., Pete's Wicked Ale for Pete's Brewing Co., and several brands for Portland Brewing Co. Among its own brands were Old Milwaukee and Old Milwaukee Light, Rainier, Stroh's, and Schlitz Malt Liquor.

Changes to the Industry

The 1996 acquisition of Heileman put Stroh into debt from which it could not escape. In 1999 president and CEO John W. Stroh III, great-great-grandson of founder Bernhard who had been named to those positions in 1997, sold the family-owned brewery to the smaller Pabst Brewing Co. Pabst, in turn, agreed to sell some of Stroh's malt liquor brands to the Miller Brewing Co.

Miller had replaced Stroh as Pabst's contract brewer the year before, resulting in Stroh's decision to shut one of its breweries. The company then pumped money into its Rainier brewery in Seattle to expand its production of specialty and contract beers, but such efforts couldn't save the company. Seattle feared, with the sale of Stroh to Pabst, that its landmark brewery would close. Pabst, which paid about $500 million for Stroh's beer brands and its Pennsylvania brewery, was expected to keep most of the brands and sell a few to Miller. It was expected to close Stroh's Detroit headquarters.

Part of Stroh's lower sales-in 1998 it was in fourth place behind Anheuser, Miller and Coors with 7% of the market—was blamed on brewers of high-priced brands who, as the century drew to a close, lowered their prices. This made them able to effectively compete with Stroh's lower-end brands like Old Milwaukee and Colt 45.

Review of the Outcome

Stroh president William Henry's remarks in the November 15, 1996 issue of *Beverage World* sum up the reasons Stroh went after its competitor and pursued it even when the going got rough: "Putting Stroh and Heileman together makes us stronger. It doesn't answer all the questions; we know that. But as we start off, we can use some of the cost savings of putting the two companies together to support our brands more effectively, and we'll reap other synergies that show allow us to compete more effectively. We want to get bigger. We look to do that by growing our own brand portfolio and, if the opportunity presents itself, to grow through additional acquisitions."

Research

Baron, Stanley W. *Brewed in America: A History of Beer and Ale in the U.S.*, Arnold Press, 1972.

Harrington, Patrick. "Sale Likely Means Goodbye to Rainier Brewery," in *Seattle Times*, 9 February 1999.

"Stroh to Acquire Heileman," in *Midwest Beer Notes*, 5 October 1998.

"Stroh Acquires Heileman," in *Celebrator Beer News*, 7 January 1999.

"The Stroh Brewery Corporation," in *International Directory of Company Histories*, Vol. 18, St. James Press: 1997.

"Targeting Efficiency," in *Beverage World*, 15 November 1996.

"Trouble Brews after Bitter Year for Stroh," in *Associated Press*, 31 January 1999.

Waldsmith, Lynn. "Peter Stroh To Retire; Control Stays in Family," in *The Detroit News*, 14 August 1997.

BARBARA J. KELLY

SWISS BANK & UNION BANK OF SWITZERLAND

UBS AG
Bahnhofstrasse 45, PO Box
Zurich, CH-8098
Switzerland

tel: 41 1 234 41 00
fax: 41 1 234 34 15
web: http://www.ubs.com

nationality: Switzerland
date: June 29, 1998
affected: Swiss Bank Corp., Switzerland, founded 1872
affected: Union Bank of Switzerland, Switzerland, founded 1912

Overview of the Acquisition

The 1998 acquisition of Union Bank of Switzerland by Swiss Bank Corporation created UBS AG, the largest bank in Europe, as well as the largest asset manager and the second-largest bank in the world. Sparked by the industry's move toward consolidation and globalization, the deal represented the first step by European concerns to break the mold by joining in such trends, which had been sweeping through U.S. institutions for most of the decade.

History of Swiss Bank Corporation

The Basler Bankverein was established in 1854 by six private bankers in response to the credit needs of Switzerland's railroad and manufacturing industries. The Swiss government made Basler Bank the official Swiss bank of issue for the French national loan and for the financing of the growing textile and metal industries in France. By 1872, as a number of new competitors had entered the market, Basler Bank became a joint stock company.

Basler Bank merged with the Zurcher Bankverein in 1895, changing its name to Basler and Zurcher Bankverein. Two years later it purchased both the Schweizerische Unionbank in St. Gall, Switzerland, and the Basler Depositenbank. The new entity began operating as Schweizerischer Bankverein Societe de Banque Suisse (Swiss Bank Corporation).

At the onset of World War I, Swiss Bank discontinued its support of the government's efforts to buy back the country's major railroads from foreign competitors. It began offering loans to foreign countries in 1924, as well as acting as a depository of foreign funds for investors threatened by inflation and political instability in their own countries. In 1929, Swiss Bank helped to establish the Bank for International Settlements, an institution designed to mediate the payment of war reparations.

In 1939, Swiss Bank established an agency in New York City to store assets in the event of a Nazi invasion of its property. At the conclusion of World War II, with its assets totaling CHF2 billion, the bank returned to focusing on private rather than political matters. It opened a San Francisco office in 1965, the same year that it became one of the first European financial companies to establish an office in Tokyo, Japan. The Swiss Bank and Trust Corporation, Ltd. was formed on Grand Cayman Island in 1972.

In 1982, as one of the world's largest private gold dealers, Swiss Bank joined with Union Bank of Switzerland and Credit Suisse to form Premex AG, a brokerage house designed to reinforce gold bullion trading activity in Zurich, Switzerland. Three years later, due to the Japanese government's unfair treatment of foreign banks, Swiss Bank, Union Bank, and Credit Suisse united to oppose Swiss franc note issues managed by the Swiss units of two leading Japanese banks. Also that year Switzerland's highest court ordered Swiss Bank to release information about an account allegedly used to deposit a $2.9 million ransom for the Irish Republican Army.

In 1987, Swiss Bank's investment banking subsidiary acquired Savory Milln, a London, England-based securities broker. The subsidiary also acquired Banque Stern and a controlling interest in the Paris, France-based brokerage house of Ducatel-Duval. The next year Swiss Bank, Union Bank, and Credit Suisse became embroiled in a $1 billion money laundering scheme operated by a Lebanese-Turkish drug syndicate. Although Swiss Bank did hold accounts for some of the principals involved, it claimed that those accounts were legitimate.

As one of the underwriters of Swiss franc bonds issued by RJR Nabisco, Swiss Bank attempted in February 1989 to force the company to redeem those notes due to an impending buyout by Kohlberg Kravis Roberts & Co. According to the provisions of the issue, the bondholders were entitled to the return of their investment in the event of a reorganization. The lawsuits filed by the bank on the behalf of its bondholders were settled later that month, before the ultimate sale of RJR Nabisco.

The Canadian government excluded Swiss Bank from participating in the issue of C$500 million in Eurobonds in 1989 because of the suspicion of business dealings with South African authorities. By 1991, the bank's assets of about $151.89 billion ranked it 32nd among the world's top commercial banks. Only two years later, it ascended to the position of the second-largest bank in Switzerland and one of the largest financial institutions in the world.

During the 1990s, the bank increased its money management properties. In 1992, it purchased O'Connor Associates, a Chicago-based investment house. It followed up that acquisition by purchasing the London investment bank SG Warburg in 1995; Brinson Partners, a U.S. money management firm, in

The Business

Financials

Revenue (1998): CHF23.3 billion in operating income

Employees (1998): 48,011

SICs / NAICS

sic 6021 - National Commercial Banks

sic 6081 - Foreign Banks-Branches & Agencies

sic 6082 - Foreign Trade & International Banks

sic 6211 - Security Brokers & Dealers

naics 522110 - Commercial Banking

naics 522293 - International Trade Financing

naics 523110 - Investment Banking and Securities Dealing

1996; and the U.S. investment house Dillon Read in 1997.

In December 1997, it announced its agreement to acquire Union Bank of Switzerland, a deal that formed UBS AG in June 1998.

History of Union Bank of Switzerland

The Bank of Winterthur and Toggenburger Bank, both formed in the 1860s, merged in 1912 to form Union Bank of Switzerland, with dual headquarters in the cities of Winterthur and St. Galen. Initially, it confined its operations to its regulatory strongholds in the east and northeast of the country. By 1929, however, its operations had expanded to include new branches, acquisitions of local banks, and the addition of markets in Aaragau, Bern, and Ticino. Assets that year totaled CHF992 million.

Despite Switzerland's neutrality, World War II damaged the bank by virtually shutting down international businesses. Only a few months after Germany's defeat, however, it resumed its growth by acquiring Eidgenossische Bank, a prominent Zurich financial institution. This purchase pushed its assets to CHF1 billion and established it as one of Switzerland's three largest banks.

Also in 1946 it established its presence in the U.S. for the first time by opening a representative office in New York City. By 1962, the bank had 81 branch offices and assets of CHF7 billion. Three years later, substantial withdrawals in British pound sterling were initiated by nervous investors making a run on the British pound to be sold on the currency markets,

The Officers

President and CEO: Marcel Ospel

CEO Private & Corporate Clients: Stephan Haringer

CEO Private Banking: Rudi Bogni

CEO Warburg Dillon Read: Markus Granziol

CEO UBS Brinson: Peter Wuffli

and Swiss banks invested $80 million into stopping the panic.

In 1967, Union Bank acquired Interhandel, a Swiss financial company. That year it also opened its first foreign branch office, in London, England. Two years later it diversified into consumer lending, leasing, and factoring through the acquisition of four domestic financial companies: Banque Orca, Abri Bank Bern, Aufina Bank, and AKO Bank. Union Bank became the last of the three largest Swiss banks to establish a branch office in the U.S. when it formed one in New York City in 1970.

In 1985, in an attempt to become a leading European underwriter, it bought major bond issues worth a total of $850 million for Nestle, Rockwell, IBM, and Mobil to market at unusually low yields. These low yields were designed to attract corporate customers who embraced the prospect of paying lower interest rates on their issues.

Anticipating the deregulation of Britain's financial markets, it acquired the London brokerage house Phillips & Drew Ltd. in 1985. The next year it purchased the West German bank Deutsche Landerbank, which was renamed Schweizerische Bankgesellschaft. Also in 1986 it established a Phillips & Drew office in Tokyo, Japan. The worldwide stock market crash of 1987 resulted in a GBP48 million loss for Phillips & Drew. It sought to solidify its position in the London markets with a bid to take over the British merchant banker, Hill Samuel. This deal fell through, though, because Union Bank refused to accept Hill Samuel's shipbrokering and insurance services in the deal. As a solution to the repeated problems associated with it, Phillips & Drew was merged with UBS Securities Ltd. in London in 1982.

Union Bank's assets in 1992 eclipsed the CHF200 billion mark for the first time, and net income was nearly CHF1 billion. By 1993 Union Bank continued to be the largest banking company in Switzerland.

In 1991, it acquired the money management operations of Chase Manhattan Corp. Five years later it

rejected a $47 billion merger proposal by CS Holding, a deal that would have produced the second-largest lending bank in the world and the largest lender in Europe. Also in 1996 it reported a loss of $338 million, its first full-year loss since World War II. It took a one-time $2.3 billion charge to settle loan problems.

Union Bank faced a public relations disaster beginning in January 1997, when Christoph Meili, a night watchman, discovered Nazi-era documents about to be shredded by the firm. He confiscated several ledgers containing records of accounts held by Jewish victims of the holocaust and their survivors. Meili turned them over to a Jewish cultural organization, which in turn submitted them to the police as evidence that the bank had violated a national law prohibiting the destruction of documents relevant to an ongoing investigation into the Switzerland's dealings with Nazis during World War II. Meili was subsequently fired, and, after receiving large volumes of hate mail and numerous death threats by anti-Semites, fled with his family to the U.S. President Clinton granted permanent resident status to the family, the only Swiss nationals ever to received political asylum in the U.S.

Although it denied that it was harboring such assets, Union Bank joined with Credit Suisse and Swiss Bank Corporation in February 1997 in establishing a $70.1 million fund for victims. The U.S., however, deemed unacceptable the bank's denial and offer of compensation. Banks in five states, plus the city of New York, threatened to boycott American branches of Swiss banks, resulting in the withdrawal of $11 billion on March 31, 1998, unless the country's major banks reached a global settlement. The banks reluctantly agreed, and in August 1998 set aside $1.25 billion to be paid over the course of four years.

Meanwhile, Union Bank had been acquired by Swiss Bank Corporation in June 1998, forming UBS AG.

Market Forces Driving the Acquisition

The intense wave of consolidation sweeping through the U.S. banking industry that began in the early 1990s had created behemoths in both size and global reach. Such merger deals grew increasingly large, from BankAmerica's 1991 acquisition of Security Pacific Corp. for $4.2 billion, to NationsBank's 1997 merger with Barnett Banks for $14.8 billion in 1997. As the breadth of American banks grew, so did their competitive pressure on European institutions, which had long enjoyed the top positions in the world's banking industry. European firms, traditionally more conservative in matters of consolidation than their U.S. counterparts, had little choice than to enter into unions of their own in response to escalating competition as well as the ongoing globalization and deregulation in the financial services industry.

By late 1997 Switzerland had three large banks: Swiss Bank Corporation (SBC), Union Bank of Switzerland, and Credit Suisse Group. By joining forces, any two of these firms could be expected to realize significant cost savings through the elimination of duplicate branches and jobs positions, as well as the combination of information technology and other operational systems.

Although both SBC and Credit Suisse had considered acquiring their smaller rival, in the end Union Bank formed an alliance with SBC. Separately, these two concerns had considerable presence in asset management and private banking; together, they would form the world's largest asset manager, with CHF1.3 trillion under management. A combination would emerge as a leading player in virtually all areas of private banking, and would be the top European investment banking house, well-poised for international growth. Overall, this union would create the largest bank in Europe and the second-largest worldwide.

Approach and Engagement

On December 5, 1997, the boards of Union Bank of Switzerland and Swiss Bank Corporation approved a merger agreement. The announcement, made three days later, was met with widespread praise, not only for this deal specifically, but as a breakthrough for the European banking industry as a whole. "This is the first step in a radical transformation of the European banking market," said Philip Middleton, head of banking strategy at KPMG, in *European Banker*. "There are too many financial institutions in the European market and this could be the beginning of a final shake-out."

The new bank was initially to be named United Bank of Switzerland, but that moniker already belonged to an existing institution. Selecting the name UBS AG instead, the boards named Mathis Cabiallavetta, CEO of Union Bank, as its new chairman, and Marcel Ospel, CEO of SBC, as its CEO.

Under its terms, the agreement called for the exchange of five shares of UBS for each Union Bank bearer share and one share for each Union Bank registered share. Each SBC share would be exchanged for 1.08 shares of UBS. Ultimately, Union Bank shareholders would own 60% of UBS, with SBC shareholders owning the remaining 40%.

By February 4, 1998, shareholders of each bank had approved the deal, which was also approved by

the European Commission one month later. The final regulatory approval was received by the U.S. Federal Reserve Board on June 8, with the condition that UBS divest itself of its U.S. merchant banking business. On June 29, 1998, UBS AG formally began business.

Products and Services

In 1998, UBS was one of the world's leading financial services groups, operating in five primary sectors. Private Banking, had CHF607 billion in assets under management, in 1998, and held the leading position in the global private banking industry. Institutional Asset Management, operating as UBS Brinson, had CHF360 billion in institutional assets under management and an additional CHF171 billion in mutual funds. Investment Banking, operating as UBS Warburg Dillon Read, delivered debt and equity financing, advisory services, global research, securities and foreign exchange execution, and risk management services to major corporations, institutions, and public entities around the world. The Private and Corporate Clients Division, operating in the retail and commercial clients sector, had CHF434 billion in assets under management and a loan portfolio to CHF165 billion in 1998. Private Equity, principally UBS Capital, operated a network of more than 30 countries in Western Europe, the Americas, and Asia Pacific.

Changes to the Industry

The formation of Europe's largest bank was expected to be the pioneering deal in a wave of consolidation within the European banking industry. This breakthrough added to the pressure from U.S. banks that forced consolidation as a means of remaining competitive and participating effectively in the industry's growing globalization. "The real import of the merger was not so much what it said about the present, as what it said about the likely course of future events," wrote Bruce Wasserstein in *Big Deal: The Battle for Control of America's Leading Corporations*. The creation of UBS "crystallized the inevitability of a global consolidation. The leapfrog to $100 billion in market capitalization had started."

Review of the Outcome

UBS faced increasing public relations difficulties before it was even officially formed. Swiss banks had been embroiled in an international scandal over their retention of assets belonging to Nazi-persecuted Jews. Added to this was the domestic outcry over the combining banks' planned reduction of 13,000 positions, with the bulk occurring through the closure of about 250 branches in Switzerland.

The completion of the merger brought little relief from further scandal. In September 1998 Long-Term Capital Management LP, a hedge fund, collapsed under $90 billion in losses. As a result, UBS took a charge of $696 million due to its investments in the fund. Although the bank failed to uncover any gross negligence on the part of its risk management assessment, its board implemented changes in UBS's executive ranks. Mathis Cabiallavetta resigned as chairman, and was succeeded by vice chairman Alex Krauer. Three other executives of the former Union Bank also left the company by mutual agreement.

By the end of the year, the newly formed bank appeared to have recovered well enough to continue efforts in integration and growth. In January 1999, it consolidated six independent, private banks of the merged firms into a newly formed Private Banking division. In March, UBS strengthened that division by agreeing to purchase the European and Asian private banking business of Bank of America. In September, it added to those operations by entering into an agreement to purchase GAM Global Asset Management.

In March 1999, it announced the sale of its non-Swiss trade finance business to Standard Chartered PLC for CHF300 million, as well as the sale of its 75% stake in the precious metals processor Argor-Heraeus SA. On June 1, 1999, Warburg Dillon Read, the firm's investment banking division, opened a new trading floor, the largest in continental Europe.

Research

Lefevere, Patricia. "Bank Guard Enters Ranks of 'Righteous Gentiles'," in *National Catholic Reporter*, 16 April 1999. Provides a chronology of the discovery of hidden Jewish assets at Union Bank, as well as a profile of Christoph Meili.

"Swiss Bank Corporation," in *Notable Corporate Chronologies*, The Gale Group, 1999. Offers an historical review of the bank.

"Then There Were Two Swiss Giants," in *The Banker*, January 1998. Details the acquisition agreement.

"Union Bank of Switzerland," in *Notable Corporate Chronologies*, The Gale Group, 1999. Provides a chronology of the firm's history.

"United Bank of Switzerland: The Shape of Things to Come," in *European Banker*, 1 December 1997. Offers analyses of the newly announced deal in respect to Europe's banking industry.

UBS AG Home Page, available at http://www.ubs.com. Official World Wide Web Page for UBS. This multi-language site offers news releases, information on products and services, and financial data.

"UBS (Union Bank of Switzerland) and Swiss Bank Corporation (SBC) to Merge," through *PR Newswire*, 8 December 1997. Describes the terms of the deal, as well as the strengths of the combining firms.

Wasserstein, Bruce. *Big Deal: The Battle for Control of America's Leading Corporations*, Warner Books, 1998. Offers an overview of the largest mergers in recent corporate history.

DEBORAH J. UNTENER

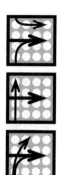

TELLABS & CIENA

nationality: USA
date: September 14, 1998 (canceled)
affected: Tellabs, Inc., USA, founded 1975
affected: Ciena Corp., USA, founded 1992

Tellabs, Inc.
4951 Indiana Ave.
Lisle, IL 60532-1698
USA

tel: (630)378-8800
fax: (630)852-7346
web: http://www.tellabs.com

Ciena Corp.
1201 Winterson Rd.
Linthicum, MD 21090
USA

tel: (410)865-8500
fax: (410)694-5750
web: http://www.ciena.com

Overview of the Merger

In June of 1998, Ciena Corp. and Tellabs, Inc. agreed to a $7.1 billion merger. AT&T's sudden decision to abandon its testing of Ciena's wavelength division multiplexing (WDM) system caused a significant drop in the firm's share price. As a result, the two companies agreed in September to a reduced price of $4.6 billion. Shortly thereafter, however, Pirelli Cable opted to license WDM systems from Digital Telepoint Inc. instead of Ciena. After Ciena's stock tumbled for a second time, the deal was called off. When the dust settled, Ciena's share price had reached a low of $13 per share, nearly 77% less than its price prior to the deal's announcement.

History of Tellabs, Inc.

In 1975, Michael Birck and a group of five men experienced in electrical engineering and sales raised $110,000 to found Tellabs Inc., a telecommunications company, in Illinois. The firm's first product was an echo suppressor designed for independent telephone companies. By the end of the year, employees totaled 20 and sales reached $312,000. Within two years, Tellabs had secured Western Union as a client and a permanent headquarters was established in Lisle, Illinois.

Tellabs established its first subsidiary, Tellabs Communications Canada Ltd., in 1979. The following year, the firm opened a Texas plant and listed publicly for the first time. It continued to pour money into research and development, designing intricate networking systems and a line of digital communications systems for phone companies, as well as large computer systems.

In 1983, Tellabs established its fourth operation, this one in Puerto Rico. After the Bell System monopoly was disbanded in 1984, Tellabs faced increased competition from new companies pursuing contracts with the regional "Baby Bell" firms. Sales grew to $100 million in 1985; however, profits faltered as competitors continued to emerge. Tellabs responded by overhauling its system of management and increasing its research and development budget by roughly 40%.

In 1986, Tellabs secured a long-term contract with AT&T Corp. to supply net-

The Business

Financials - Tellabs, Inc.

Revenue (1998): $1.66 billion

Employees (1998): 4,980

Financials - Ciena Corp.

Revenue (1998): $508.1 million

Employees (1998): 1,380

SICs / NAICS

sic 3661 - Telephone & Telegraph Apparatus

sic 3613 - Switchgear & Switchboard Apparatus

sic 3669 - Communications Equipment Nec

naics 335313 - Switchgear and Switchboard Apparatus
Manufacturing

working multiplexers. In a contract worth $10 million, the company agreed in 1987 to supply Sprint Corp. with a complete optical fiber network, including echo suppressors. Sales jumped 18% to $136.1 million; net income climbed 27% to $10.7 million. An international expansion program was initiated, and by the end of the decade, Tellabs operated sales offices in London, Australia, and Hong Kong.

The firm diversified into signaling and conversion systems by acquiring Delta Communications, based in Shannon, Ireland, in 1989; the new subsidiary was renamed Tellabs Ltd. In 1991, Tellabs unveiled its TITAN 5500 digital cross-connect system, as well as a new line of digital echo suppressors developed exclusively for the new fiber optics platform. International operations had grown to include Belgium, New Zealand, Korea, and Mexico. Sales of digital echo suppressors reached $40 million in 1992. That year, Tellabs diversified into high-bit-rate digital subscriber line (HDSL) equipment.

In 1993, Tellabs purchased Martis Oy, a Finnish telecommunications company, for $70 million and began marketing the Martis digital cross-connect system. Sales leapt by 90% to a record $320 million; net income totaled $32 million. Stock prices soared to $69 per share. A year later, the firm introduced CABLESPAN 2300 Universal Telephony Distribution System and the Alta 2600, an asynchronous transfer mode product. Digital cross-connect system sales grew another 37% in 1995, surpassing $300 million and accounting for almost half of Tellabs' annual revenues.

Steinbrecher Corp., a wideband wireless communications systems provider, was added to the mix in 1996 for $76 million. Stock split two-for-one that year. As part of its plan to launch a wavelength division multiplexing (WDM) product by 1999, Tellabs acquired IBM Corp.'s optical networking team, including several patents related to WDM technology, for $6 million in 1997. Total revenue exceeded $1 billion that year due mainly to sales of the TITAN and Martis digital cross-connect systems, which increased 54% and 48%, respectively. Also, as a means of gaining access to the hybrid fiber/coax networks (HFC) market, Tellabs founded the Broadband Media Group.

Between 1992 and 1997, Tellabs stock earned higher returns than nearly any other U.S. stock. In 1998, the firm paid $860 million for Coherent Communications Systems Corp., a designer, maker, and marketer of echo cancellation and conference products. That year, Tellabs and Ciena Corp. announced plans for a $7 billion merger; the deal crumbled shortly after Ciena lost two major accounts, which caused its share price to tumble.

History of Ciena Corp.

In 1992, the former optical research lab manager of General Instrument, David Huber, founded what would become Ciena Corp. to manufacture and sell optical fiber systems that allowed increased data, voice, and graphic transmissions along existing lines. Within two years, Huber had secured financial backing from Sevin Rosen Funds and had hired Patrick Nettles to manage his new firm.

Sprint was the first major client to purchase Ciena's dense-wavelength division multiplexing (DWDM) system, called MultiWave, in 1995. Two years later, Ciena listed publicly. The firm launched the MultiWave Sentry and the MultiWave Firefly, a short-distance DWDM system. Disagreements with Nettles over the technology Ciena should pursue prompted Huber to leave the firm that year.

In 1998, Ciena paid $30 million to settle a patent infringement lawsuit with Pirelli SpA. Tellabs and Ciena Corp. announced plans for a $7 billion merger, but the deal fell apart shortly after Ciena lost two major accounts, making the company less valuable. To strengthen its presence in the fiber optics network market, Ciena agreed in 1999 to pay $520 million for Lightera Networks and $430 million for Omnia Communications.

Market Forces Driving the Merger

According to a June 1998 article in *Information Week*, the increased consolidation in the networking industry in the late 1990s was due to "intense competition in the market for equipment that can squeeze more capacity out of existing public networks." The networking industry as a whole saw two of its largest acquisitions to date unfold in 1997: the $6.6 billion merger of 3COM Corp. and U.S. Robotics Corp., which joined the LAN and WAN vendors, allowed for comprehensive networking capabilities; and the $3.7 billion merger of Ascend Communications Inc. and Cascade Communications Inc., which joined a WAN core switching technology provider with a WAN access provider.

In June of 1998 France's Alcatel Alsthom SA, the world's fourth-largest telecommunications equipment maker announced its intent to double its presence in the U.S. telecommunications market by acquiring U.S.-based switching equipment technology manufacturer DSC Communications Corp. for approximately $4.4 billion. Tellabs, Inc. and Ciena Corp. inked their deal at roughly the same time.

Tellabs needed access to Ciena's wave division multiplexing technology, which was able to expand network capacity by 40 times the normal amount. Mainly a manufacturer of digital network connectivity equipment, Tellabs also needed to expand its product line, and a deal with Ciena would give Tellabs access to the fiber optics market. At the same time, Ciena recognized that it needed to grow to remain competitive in the rapidly consolidating market.

Approach and Engagement

On June 3, 1998, Ciena Corp. agreed to a $7.1 billion takeover by Tellabs, Inc. According to the terms of the agreement, Ciena shareholders would receive one share of Tellabs stock for each Ciena share. However, AT&T's sudden decision to abandon its testing of Ciena's wavelength division multiplexing (WDM) system on August 21 caused a 45% drop in the firm's stock price, which tumbled from $56.78 to $31.25 per share in just a few days. Angry shareholders filed suit against the company, alleging that Ciena had issued "false and misleading" statements that had inflated share prices in July to a high of $92.37.

Tellabs' board of directors met for six hours on August 26 to discuss a reduced offer for Ciena. The two firms agreed in September to a reduced price of $4.6 billion. Ciena shareholders would receive .8 of a Tellabs share for each Ciena share owned. Shortly thereafter, however, Pirelli Cable opted to license WDM systems from Digital Telepoint Inc. instead of Ciena. As a result, Ciena's stock tumbled for a second time, the deal with Tellabs was called off on September 14, 1998.

The Officers

Tellabs, Inc.

President and CEO: Michael J. Birck

Exec. VP, Chief Operating Officer, and Treasurer: Peter A. Guglielmi

Exec. VP and President, Global Systems and Technology: Brian J. Jackman

President, Tellabs Global Sales and Service: John E. Vaughan

Sr. VP and General Manager, Digital Systems Division: Richard T. Taylor

Ciena Corp.

Chairman: John W. Bayless

President and CEO: Patrick H. Nettles

Sr. VP, Strategy and Corporate Development: Steve W. Chaddick

Chief Financial Officer and Sr. VP, Finance: Joesph R. Chinnici

Products and Services

In 1998, Tellabs earned nearly 57% of its sales from digital cross-connect systems, which included the TITAN system. Managed digital networks, such as CROSSNET multiplexers and Martis DXX managed access and transport network systems, secured 25%. Network access systems, including CABLESPAN—which allowed cable systems to offer phone services—and digital signal processing equipment such as echo suppressors and voice compression products, brought in 11%. International sales accounted for roughly 30% of total annual revenue.

Ciena's products in 1998 included the MultiWave 1600, 4000, and Sentry systems which offered dense-wavelength division multiplexing (DWDM) functions to long-distance fiber optic telecommunications providers. The firm also made the MultiWave Firefly, a short distance DWDM system, MultiWave Metro, MultiWave Optical, and WaveWatcher, network management software.

Review of the Outcome

After announcing that the deal with Tellabs was off, Ciena's share price tumbled to a low of $13 per share, nearly 77% less than its price prior to the deal's announcement. Many analysts believed that the firm's

The Players

President and CEO of Ciena Corp.: Patrick H. Nettles. After earning his B.S. degree from the Georgia Institute of Technology and his Ph.D. from the California Institute of Technology, Dr. Patrick Nettles went to work for Optilink, a venture start-up that was acquired by DSC Communications, as chief financial officer. Between 1990 and 1992, Nettles served as president and chief executive officer of Protocol Engines Inc., an offshoot of Silicon Graphics Inc. He then worked as executive vice president and chief operating officer of Blyth Holdings Inc., a client/server software vendor, until 1994, when he was hired to run upstart Ciena Corp. When Ciena's planned merger with Tellabs, Inc. fell apart in 1998, Nettles began focusing Ciena on growth via acquisition.

President and CEO of Tellabs, Inc.: Michael J. Birck. After working for several telecommunications companies, including Bell Labs, electrical engineer Michael Birck founded Tellabs in 1975. He spearheaded the firm's impressive growth record through the 1980s and 1990s. After the takeover of Ciena Corp. was canceled in 1998, Birck refocused his firm on developing its own version of Ciena's technology. In 1999, he owned nearly 10% of Tellabs.

low share price might make it a takeover target. Instead, a restructuring helped the firm recover, and Ciena agreed in early 1999 to pay a total of $850 million for two fiber optic network firms.

Tellabs' stock also plunged in the months during negotiations with Ciena. When the deal was announced, share prices rose to a record high in the upper 80s. By the time plans were nixed in September,

though, stock prices had plummeted to the low 30s. The firm then focused on developing its own network capacity expanding technology—what it would have gained access to by acquiring Ciena—and by early 1999, share prices had rebounded.

Research

Ciena Corp. Home Page, available at http://www.ciena.com. Official World Wide Web Home Page for Ciena Corp. Includes press releases, as well as financial, product, and investor information.

"Ciena Shareholders Charged Company Thurs. With 'False and Misleading' Statements," in *Communications Daily*, 28 August 1998. Details the charges made by Ciena shareholders after share prices tumbled in the wake of AT&T's decision to stop testing Ciena technology.

Crockett, Roger O. "Tellabs Has a Really Bad Day," in *Business Week*, 7 September 1998. Explains why the merger of Tellabs and Ciena is at risk.

Fischer, Lawrence M. "Outlook Brightens for Ciena after Catastrophic '98 Drop," in *The New York Times*, 22 February 1999. Discusses Ciena's recovery after its takeover by Tellabs crumbled and its stock prices plummeted.

Mehta, Stephanie N. "Tellabs Reaches Pact to Acquire Ciena in Stock Swap Valued at $6.9 Billion," in *The Wall Street Journal*, 4 June 1998. Details the original agreement between Ciena and Tellabs in June of 1998.

"Tellabs, Inc.," in *Notable Corporate Chronologies*, The Gale Group, 1999. Lists major events in the history of Tellabs, Inc.

Tellabs, Inc. Home Page, available at http://www.tellabs.com. Official World Wide Web Home Page for Tellabs, Inc. Includes current news and financial, product, historical, and investor information.

Thyfault, Mary E. "Major Mergers in Telecom Equipment," in *InformationWeek*, 8 June 1998. Discusses the industry conditions prompting Tellabs' offer for Ciena.

Upjohn, Bruce. "Survival Technique: Paranoia," in *Forbes*, 18 May 1998. Offers an overview of the success of Tellabs prior to its offer for Ciena.

Wirbel, Loring. "Canceled Merger with Tellabs Drives Down Ciena Stock—Now Flying Solo, Ciena Attempts to Right Itself," in *Electronic Engineering Times*, 21 September 1998. Explains how and why the deal between Tellabs and Ciena fell apart.

JEFF ST. THOMAS

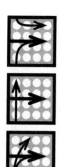

TEXACO & GETTY OIL

nationality: USA
date: February 13, 1984
affected: Texaco Inc., USA, founded 1901
affected: Getty Oil Co., USA

Texaco Inc.
2000 Westchester Ave.
White Plains, NY 10650
USA

tel: (914)253-4000
fax: (914)2537753
web: http://www.texaco.com

Overview of the Merger

Texaco's $10.8 billion purchase of Getty Oil in 1984 came at the height of the 1980s merger boom in the oil industry. By topping Pennzoil's offer, Texaco pulled off one of the largest deals of its time. Pennzoil's ensuing claim of interference in its negotiations brought on years of legal battle. The two sparring companies finally agreed on a $3 billion settlement, but only after Texaco had suffered major losses and a bout with bankruptcy.

History of Texaco Inc.

In 1901, Joseph S. Cullinan organized the Texas Fuel Co., following an explosion earlier that year that resulted in the discovery of oil, forever changing Texas' economy. Requiring a larger company to carry out his plans, Cullinan sought additional financial assistance, and with $3 million in capital, incorporated The Texas Co. The company built 36 storage tanks and laid a 20-mile pipeline to transport the crude from oil fields to harbor facilities at Port Arthur, Texas. Within a five-year span, operations began in the European market, Texaco was registered as the company's trademark (although the name was not officially changed for nearly 50 years), and sales operations in the U.S. covered all areas except five Western states.

Texaco continued to flourish and in 1928 acquired California Petroleum Corp., extending its operations to 48 states. By that time, the company owned or leased more than 4,000 stations. Texaco "Fire Chief" gasoline was introduced in 1932, and one year later, Texaco's *Giliasso*, the industry's first submersible drilling barge, went into service at Lake Pelto in coastal Louisiana. Texaco also held a 50% interest in Caltex and its Suez Canal concentration, and a 50% interest in California Arabian Standard Oil Co. In 1938, the company introduced a premium gasoline, "Texaco Sky Chief."

Throughout the 1940s, Texaco continued to become a recognized name across the U.S. and abroad. In 1940, it sponsored the live Saturday afternoon radio broadcasts of the Metropolitan Opera. During the war, Texaco also supplied the government with aviation fuel and lubricants, gasoline, lubricating oils, fuel oils, and

The Business

Financials

Revenue (1998): $30.9 billion

Employees (1998): 24,628

SICs / NAICS

sic 2911 - Petroleum Refining

petrochemicals. In 1945, refining facilities were expanded at Bahrain. A large refinery at Ras Tanura, Saudi Arabia, was also completed. Texaco introduced such new products as a new and improved "Havoline Motor Oil," Texaco Anti-Freeze, and Texamatic Fluid for automatic transmissions.

The company purchased Trinidad Oil in 1956 and Seaboard Oil Co. two years later. With products like Advanced Havoline Motor Oil, heavy-duty diesel lubricants, fuels and lube oils for jet aircraft, and Petrox, an additive for gasoline, the company's name was officially changed to Texaco in 1959. That year, Texaco also purchased the Paragon group of companies.

In 1962, Texaco bought White Fuel Corp., as well as the mineral rights from TXL Oil Corp. for almost two million largely-undeveloped acres in west Texas. Fuel Chief heating oils, oil burners, and heating equipment were added to the company's product line. The company was also focusing efforts abroad, and in 1966, opened its first European Chemical plant in Ghent, Belgium. It acquired the bulk of the capital stock of West German's Deutsche Erdol A.G. One year later, Texaco subsidiaries acquired assets and businesses representing one-half of Caltex's interests in 12 European countries and one-half of its worldwide marine operations. In 1969, Columbia's Trans-Andean crude pipeline, spanning 193 miles of mountains and jungles, was completed. Texaco's worldwide operating volumes more than doubled, with gross production that exceeded three million barrels a day.

Texaco acquired a two-third interest in Refineria Panama S.A., which operated a 70,000-barrel-a-day refinery near Colon, Republic of Panama, in 1971. Continuing to focus on growth, the company also purchased Jefferson Chemical. Despite a drop in net income, Texaco forged ahead with its growth plan. In 1978, a new 95,000-barrel-a-day refinery in Nanticoke, Canada, began operations. One year later, Texaco's crude oil supplies in the Western Hemisphere were

further diversified with the completion of the 300-mile-long Trans-Ecuadorian pipeline crossing the Andes.

In 1980, the company acquired full ownership of Neches Butane Products Co. Jefferson Chemical merged into the new Texaco Chemical Co. Texaco also began a reorganization process and divided into three segments—Texaco U.S.A., Texaco Europe, and Texaco Latin America/West Africa. In 1981, a new logo emerged, introducing Texaco's System 2000 Stations with self-service gasoline, food marts, and car washes. Despite its good fortune, a recession hit in the early 1980s, forcing the company to close and sell six refineries. Texaco looked for a boost overseas and formed Texaco Middleast/Far East to take advantage of supplies in that region.

Getty Oil Co. was acquired in February 1984. The deal brought on a harsh battle with Pennzoil, who had also bid on the company. In 1985, Texaco lost a lawsuit filed by Pennzoil Co., which alleged that Texaco interfered with an agreement for Pennzoil to acquire three-sevenths of Getty's shares. After several years of legal intervention, Texaco and Pennzoil finally agreed on a $3 billion settlement.

By 1991, Texaco operated more than 22,000 retail locations worldwide. In 1994, the company and three other oil giants formed a unit to explore and develop huge fields beneath the isolated tundra of Russia's Arctic Circle. Texaco was faced with problems within the company when a group of employees filed a discrimination lawsuit against the company. In 1996, the group presented to the U.S. District Court a taped conversation of senior executives who, during a 1994 meeting, conspired to destroy documents that could be used against them in the case. Texaco chairman, Peter Bijur, expressed outrage after listening to the tapes. He suspended two employees and reduced the financial and insurance benefits of two retirees who were reportedly involved in the conspiracy to destroy documents. To settle the lawsuit, Texaco agreed in principle to pay $115 million, plus a one-time salary increase of 11% to the group.

In 1997, MAPCO Inc. joined Texaco Inc. in building and operating the Discovery Producer Services LLC, a company that would construct, own and operate the Discovery Project, a major natural gas pipeline, processing, and fractionation complex located in Louisiana. One year later, when the oil industry suffered a downturn, Texaco and Shell merged some of their operations to form Equilon. The two also paired with Saudi Aramco to form Motiva. Texaco remained focus on its efforts overseas in 1999 to combat the downturn the industry was facing.

Market Forces Driving the Merger

Throughout the early 1980s, the oil industry was facing major change. A wave of consolidation was set off by the Belridge/Shell Oil deal in 1979. According to Bruce Wasserstein, author of *Big Deal: The Battle for Control of America's Leading Corporations*, "Belridge set off a bruising competitive atmosphere." Major oil companies were looking for ways to cheaply expand reserves and avoid high exploration costs. The battle for Conoco, U.S. Steel's deal with Marathon, and the pairing up of Superior Oil and Mobil set the stage for further merger deals.

Not to be outdone, Texaco was looking for a partner as well. The company needed to expand on its oil and gas reserves. An article in *The New York Times* stated that one reason for Texaco's desire to seek out a partner was that it "had failed to keep pace with the huge exploration budgets of other major oil companies during the 1970s. As a result Texaco has suffered a rapid decline in its worldwide reserves."

Getty Oil, on the other hand, was looking for a partner that could increase its market value. Gordon Getty had long since been looking for a deal that would sweeten his family trust. The company was faced with depleting reserves and a low stock value, and Gordon Getty was not pleased with the performance of company CEO, Sidney Petersen. Pennzoil made a $1.6 billion offer for a portion of Getty stock when the tumultuous relationship between the two executives became public.

Approach and Engagement

Pennzoil's offer entailed a leveraged buyout in which it and the family trust, Sarah C. Getty Trust, would take Getty Oil private by buying 60% of the outstanding shares for $110 a share. Shareholders urged Gordon to auction the company to a high bidder, but agreed to the Pennzoil offer.

On January 6, 1984, Texaco put an offer on the table to purchase the 11.8% stake owned by the J. Paul Getty Museum for $125 a share, and later in the day announced that it planned to buy the company for nearly $10 billion, making the proposed offer the largest corporate acquisition at that time. Texaco would gain a great deal from Getty Oil, including an increase in assets of 37% and a doubling of its oil reserves, and Getty stood to make a larger profit by paring up with Texaco. Pennzoil's chairman, J. Hugh Liedtke, was furious with Texaco's advances. He threatened to file suit if his company's previous offer was not honored, and claimed that a union of Texaco and Getty Oil would raise significant anti-trust issues.

The Officers

Chairman and CEO: Peter I. Bijur

Sr. VP and Chief Financial Officer: Patrick J. Lynch

Sr. VP: C. Robert Black

Sr. VP; President, Texaco Worldwide Exploration and Production: John J. O'Conner

Sr. VP, Global Business: Glenn F. Tilton

On January 11, 1984, Pennzoil filed suit in a Delaware court to block Texaco's deal with Getty on the grounds that its deal with Getty had already been accepted. Getty Oil struck back, claiming that there was no valid merger contract between the two. Meanwhile, family members were battling over the deal as well, some siding with Pennzoil, others with Texaco.

Texaco raised its bid to $128 per share on January 23rd. This $10.8 billion offer satisfied all family members and angered Pennzoil further. The company's frustration mounted when, on February 5th, a federal judge ruled against Pennzoil's efforts to block the deal. Later that month, the U.S. Federal Trade Commission approved Texaco's purchase of Getty Oil with the stipulation that Texaco rid itself of certain assets. On February 13, 1984, Texaco went ahead with the largest corporate acquisition of its time.

According to Wasserstein, "the deal made sense. Texaco had been depleting reserves at a rapid pace. The company's total reserves declined by 1.4 billion barrels between 1978 and 1983, leaving it with just 1 billion barrels in the ground. If the trend continued, Texaco would be out of business in just a few short years. Furthermore, the company's finding cost had soared to roughly $21 a barrel. Even with the premium paid for Getty, Texaco was buying several billion barrels for less than $5 a barrel."

Products and Services

After the deal, Texaco stood as the third-largest oil company in the U.S., just behind Exxon and Mobil. In 1998, its U.S. operations accounted for 18% of total sales, with its foreign interests accounting for 82%. With operations in over 150 countries, Texaco focused its exploration and production efforts in Europe, the Far and Middle East, Latin America, the North Sea, the Gulf of Mexico and the U.S.

Manufacturing, marketing, and distribution efforts accounted for 66% of total sales in 1998. Exploration and production brought in 20% of sales,

The Players

President of Texaco Inc.: John K. McKinley. John McKinley was elected president of Texaco in 1971, after nearly thirty years of working his way though various positions in the company. He implemented a reorganization plan that refocused company efforts on exploration and growth, after being named chairman and CEO of the company in 1980. His next big move came when he organized Texaco's purchase of Getty Oil in 1984. At the time of the deal, he was known throughout the oil industry for his quiet, yet strong, approach to oil mergers.

Trustee of the Sarah C. Getty Trust: Gordon P. Getty. This University of San Francisco literature graduate joined the family business, Getty Oil Co., in 1958, working as a consultant in Saudi Arabia and Kuwait. He had little interest in pursuing a career in oil, as his interests led him to become a benefactor of the San Francisco Opera and chairman of L.S.B. Leakey Foundation, an anthropological organization. After the death of his step-brother, who had planned to take over the family business, Gordon was forced to take the role vacated by J. Paul Getty, his father, upon his death in 1976. He did not pursue an active role in the company until the death of C. Lansing Hays, Jr., a co-trustee, in 1982.

Getty stood as the sole trustee of the family's 40.2% stake in the company and had to contend with chairman and CEO, Sidney R. Peterson, in making decisions for the company. Getty sought to maximize the value of his interests, and, after a long battle among Getty Oil's management as well as Pennzoil, Gordon Getty sold the family business, doubling his trust.

while gas was responsible for 14%. Texaco also had interests in aviation, lubricants, and marine fuels, and was involved in refining ventures with Caltex Petroleum, Equilon Enterprises, and Motiva Enterprises.

Changes to the Industry

Mega-mergers were the wave of the future in the early 1980s, spawning heated debate among industry officials. Many felt that competition would be reduced, power would be in the hands of a few strong companies, and consumers would bear the brunt by having to pay more for each gallon of gas purchased. The deals leading up to, including, and following the Texaco deal, proved that larger companies were looking to buy reserves rather than spend the time and money on exploration. Analysts feared that interest rates would skyrocket and that there would be less and less competition in the industry, as eight giants controlled almost 60% of the market.

After the Texaco deal, other large mergers were announced. Chevron bought out Gulf in a deal worth over $13.2 billion. Philips Petroleum was forced to fend off takeover attempts, as was Unocal, forcing other companies to look into protecting themselves from future takeover attempts. ARCO, Royal Dutch/Shell, British Petroleum, and Exxon spent money on reinvesting in ventures they were already a part of and implemented stock repurchase programs.

According to Wasserstein, "the 1985 collapse in oil prices put added pressures on Big Oil. Profits plummeted; shareholders began to revolt. It was at this point that the diversification efforts of most oil companies were unwound." Low-priced oil coming from the Persian Gulf also sent chills throughout small oil companies in 1986. Large, strong companies fared well as cash flows diminished, but small companies like Global Marine, Inc., were forced to declare bankruptcy as a result of their debt burdens. This was another opportunity for the strong to get stronger, as companies with substantial cash flows could buy failing companies cheaply. The industry began to become more concentrated, with fewer competitors in production, refining, and marketing.

Review of the Outcome

In the years following the Getty deal, Texaco faced the legal battles with Pennzoil, as well as fending off takeover attempts. It bought the Bass family's stake in the company for $50 a share in March of 1984 in an effort to diminish takeover rumors. Even after the FTC gave its final approval in July, Pennzoil went ahead with legal action, and in a Texas court sued Texaco for billions of dollars in damages. Texaco's earnings in 1984 were $306 million, falling 75.2% from the previous year.

In November of 1985, the Texas jury assigned to the Texaco/Pennzoil feud awarded $10.53 billion in damages to the spurned Getty bidder, believing that Texaco wrongfully enticed Getty away from Pennzoil. In April of 1986, Texaco filed for bankruptcy and finally settled the case for $3 billion in damages, prompted by Carl Icahn, who had been purchasing Texaco stock while it was cheap. Texaco's worries of takeover were calmed when Icahn sold his interest in the company after it settled with Pennzoil and issued a special dividend, leaving him with a $500 million profit.

In 1987, Texaco stocked closed at $18.63 a share, while in 1988, it climbed to $25.56 a share. Net income finally came into the positive in 1988, reaching $1,304 million.

Research

"Earnings: Texaco Suffers $522 Million Loss in 4th Quarter, " in *Los Angeles Times*, 30 January 1985. Discusses Texaco's financial situation after the Getty deal.

"Getty Agrees to $10 billion Texaco Deal," in *The San Diego Union-Tribune*, 7 January 1984. Reports the terms of the Texaco/Getty deal.

Hayes, Thomas. "Gordon Getty's Goal Realized," in *The New York Times*, 10 January 1984. Details Gordon Getty's career and his involvement in Texaco's purchase of Getty Oil.

Lippman, Thomas. "Jury Awards $10.53 Billion to Pennzoil in Texaco Case," in *The Washington Post*, 20 November 1985. Reports the verdict of the Pennzoil/Texaco case.

Lueck, Thomas. "Texaco's Aggressive Leader," in *The New York Times*, 12 January 1984. Explains Texaco's motives concerning the Getty purchase as well as the career of John McKinley.

"Pennzoil Sues to Halt Texaco-Getty Merger," in *The Washington Post*, 18 January 1984. Discusses Pennzoil's suit against Texaco.

Potts, Mark. "Pennzoil Seeks to Block Merger," in *The Washington Post*, 11 January 1984. Explains Pennzoil's involvement in Texaco's purchase of Getty Oil.

"Texaco Inc.," in *Notable Corporate Chronologies*, The Gale Group, 1999. Lists major events in the history of Texaco Inc.

Texaco Inc. Home Page, available at http://www.texaco.com. Official World Wide Web Home Page for Texaco Inc. Includes historical, financial, and product information, as well as recent news articles.

Wasserstein, Bruce. *Big Deal: The Battle for Control of America's Leading Corporations*, Warner Books, 1998. Offers an overview of the largest mergers in recent American corporate history.

CHRISTINA M. STANSELL

TEXAS PACIFIC & DEL MONTE FOODS

Texas Pacific Group
201 Main St., Ste. 2420
Fort Worth, TX 76102
USA

tel: (817)871-4000
fax: (817)871-4010

Del Monte Foods Co.
1 Market St.
San Francisco, CA 94105
USA

tel: (415)247-3000
fax: (415)247-3565
web: http://www.delmonte.com

nationality: USA
date: April 18, 1997
affected: Texas Pacific Group, USA, founded 1993
affected: Del Monte Foods Co., USA, founded 1916

Overview of the Acquisition

The 1997 acquisition of Del Monte by Texas Pacific Group marked the conclusion of more than a decade of ownership changes and reorganizations that had left the canned food company loaded with debt. Texas Pacific, an investment firm known for restoring profitability to underperforming businesses, revitalized Del Monte, enabling it to go public in early 1999. The proceeds from that stock offering provided Del Monte, the largest U.S. producer of canned fruits and vegetables, with the resources to trim its debt and launch marketing campaigns.

History of Texas Pacific Group

In 1992 David Bonderman, an intuitive dealmaker for billionaire Robert M. Bass, ventured out on his own. His ten-year employment with Bass had resulted in triple-digit annual returns on some of his deals. During that tenure, Bonderman's modus operandi was to target for acquisition undervalued or otherwise financially troubled companies, as well as those in such emerging industries as cable television. These companies were an eclectic mix, ranging from hotels to savings and loans. When Bonderman tried to sell the idea of investing in Continental Airlines, however, Bass balked. That company was mired in bankruptcy for the second time in a decade, and the airline industry was in the midst of a depression.

Confident that the airline's prospects were solid, Bonderman joined with another Bass advisor, James G. Coulter, to form Air Partners, which acquired a 42% controlling stake in Continental in April 1993. In late 1994, as the airline had recently been driven to the brink of collapse through unsuccessful promotional strategies, Bonderman replaced management and restructured the firm. By 1997 Continental, the nation's fifth-largest airline, was posting operating income of $716 million, up from an operating loss of $108 million in 1992.

In the meantime, Air Partners had increased its interest in the industry by purchasing America West Airlines in August 1994. When Air Partners sold its stake in Continental in November 1998, the annual rate on the company's original investment was 106%, a figure similar to its return on the America West venture.

In 1993 Bonderman and Coulter decided to make their partnership formal by establishing Texas Pacific Group, a name referring to Bonderman's base in Fort Worth and the company's headquarters in San Francisco. The new firm added William Price and Richard Schifter as partners.

Texas Pacific purchased a 50.1% controlling interest in the managed care company PPOM in October 1994; it sold this interest three years later. In January 1995 it invested $50.2 million in Allied Waste Industries. That June it joined with real estate investment firm Colony Capital to purchase Britain's 116-unit movie theater chain MGM Cinemas for $320 million. On September 25, 1995, Texas Pacific acquired a 78% stake in Kraft Food's confection division, which made marshmallow, caramel, peanut brittle, and mint products; this unit operated as Favorite Brands International. Also in September the company acquired the telecommunications company St. Joe Communications for $113 million. In December Texas Pacific invested $40 million in Denbury Resources, an oil and gas exploration firm in Dallas.

Sensing that the demand for wine would experience growth in upcoming years, Texas Pacific began investing in this industry. In January 1996 the firm joined with Silverado Partners to pay $395 million for Wine World Estates, the wine division of Nestle. It added to the operations of this company, which had been renamed Beringer Wine Estates Holdings, with the April acquisition of Chateau St. Jean Vineyards and Wineries for $30 million. Texas Pacific then purchased Paradyne, a subsidiary of Lucent Technologies, for $175 million in September 1996. It also acquired 51% of Ducati Motor SpA, an ailing Italian motorcycle manufacturer; the remaining shares of Ducati were purchased in July 1998.

By 1997 the stock market had climbed out of its slump, making valuable but undervalued properties more difficult to locate. For this reason, Texas Pacific's investments became riskier. The firm also began scrutinizing foreign markets more closely and opened an office in London. In April 1997 the company purchased Del Monte Foods Co. That October, after a failed attempt to purchase the New York retailer Barney's, Texas Pacific paid $560 million for 88% of the clothing catalog retailer J. Crew Group.

Texas Pacific acquired 90% of ZiLOG Inc., a supplier of semiconductor products, in February 1998. The following month it injected $350 million into Oxford Health Plans, a troubled HMO. In February 1999 Texas Pacific parted with 38% of Del Monte via that company's initial public offering. It increased its

The Business

Financials - Del Monte Foods Co.

Revenue (1998): $1.3 billion

Employees (1998): 13,400

SICs / NAICS

sic 6799 - Investors Nec

sic 2033 - Canned Fruits & Vegetables

naics 311421 - Fruit and Vegetable Canning

naics 523910 - Miscellaneous Intermediation

stake in Denbury Resources from 32% to 60% in April. The next month Texas Pacific entered into an agreement to purchase the Semiconductor Components Group of Motorola for $1.6 billion.

History of Del Monte Foods Company

The history of Del Monte is rooted in the development of cannery operations in western U.S. Francis Cutting pioneered the West Coast canning of fruits and vegetables in 1858. The brand name Del Monte, which means "of the mountain," first appeared in 1886 as the name for a premium blend of coffee offered by Frederick Tillman's Oakland Preserving Company for the prestigious Del Monte Hotel in Monterey, California. Three years later, 18 Pacific Coast canning operations, including the companies of Cutting and Tillman, joined together to form the California Fruit Canners Association. Given this organization's wide area of operations and the strong wills of its various principals, true integration of the canneries never materialized. The retention of a large number of name brands prevented it from developing a strong, cohesive marketing presence in its early years. Despite this, the cannery prospered, and Del Monte emerged as its premier brand.

In 1916 the California Fruit Packing Corporation, which had been established in 1875 by Dr. James Dawson, merged with the California Fruit Canners Association to form the California Packing Corp., or CalPak for short. Holding the companies together was the understanding that CalPak was intended to present a solid front in the market place. The one premium CalPak label, Del Monte, was promoted as a standard of uniformly high quality. The company made promotional history by placing its first Del Monte advertisement in the *Saturday Evening Post* in 1917. At that

The Officers

Texas Pacific Group

CEO and Managing Partner: David Bonderman

Managing Director: James G. Coulter

Managing Director: William S. Price

Managing Director: Richard P. Schifter

Chief Financial Officer: James O'Brien

Del Monte Foods Co.

Chairman: Richard W. Boyce

CEO: Richard G. Wolford

Chief Operating Officer: Wesley J. Smith

Chief Financial Officer and Exec. VP, Administration: David L. Meyers

Exec. VP, Sales: Glynn M. Phillips

Exec. VP, Marketing: Brent D. Bailey

point, the new company embarked on an acquisition strategy.

CalPak expanded into the Midwest as well as the lucrative corn and pea canning segments with its 1925 purchase of the Illinois-based Rochelle Canneries. It ventured into the sardine and tuna canning business by acquiring Pacific Fish Company in 1926, the same year that it established British Sales Ltd., its first overseas marketing affiliate. During the Great Depression, CalPak's earnings tumbled from $6.19 to $0.09 per share. In 1932, as its losses reached $8.9 million, the company suspended dividends and cut salaries. Profitability was restored two years later, but only upon the onset of World War II did growth reach its previous level. However, increased labor and material costs caused profit margins to drop. The removal of wartime price controls and restrictions in 1947 enabled CalPak's sales that year to rise 35% while its earnings quadrupled.

Deemed the most successful new product in its CalPak's history, Del Monte Pineapple Grapefruit Drink was introduced in 1956 and soon outsold all other Del Monte products. That year CalPak also acquired 64.9% of Canadian Canners Ltd., the second-largest canner in the world. This purchase gave CalPak entry into the British market, and the company began exploring other international markets. By 1965 the company's exports had quintupled, to $96 million. CalPak changed its name to Del Monte Corp. in 1967. Five years later, it became the first major U.S.

food processor to include nutrition labels on its products.

In February 1979 Del Monte was purchased by R.J. Reynolds Industries Inc. as part of that company's diversification program. Under this new parent, Del Monte benefitted from additional food lines, but suffered from managerial impulses. It underwent four reorganizations and a succession of managers before R.J. Reynolds was purchased by the leveraged buyout firm Kohlberg Kravis Roberts & Co. in 1989. In order to finance this $24 million deal, the newly named RJR Nabisco began selling off pieces of Del Monte, including its Hawaiian Punch brand and tropical fruit unit.

In 1990 Del Monte management joined with Merrill Lynch & Co. to salvage the remainder of the business via another leveraged buyout. The cost of the deal was $1.4 billion, 80% of which was financed with outside capital, leaving the company laden with debt. To reduce that load, Del Monte began consolidating facilities, reducing freight and logistical costs, reevaluating its product line, and moving to smaller standard can sizes. It also divested its dried fruit operations and its pudding division.

After trying to sell the company for several years, the owners of Del Monte agreed in 1994 to sell the firm to Mexican financier Carlos Cabal Peniche for $1 billion. That deal soured, however, when Cabal became a fugitive from the Mexican government. Del Monte finally found a buyer when Texas Pacific Group purchased a majority stake in the company in 1997.

Market Forces Driving the Acquisition

Del Monte had been an independent company for over half a century before it was acquired by R.J. Reynolds Industries in 1979. Over the following ten years, it was reorganized multiple times and fell victim to a succession of management changes. In 1989 Kohlberg Kravis Roberts & Co. affected the largest leveraged buyout in U.S. history by purchasing RJR-Nabisco, as Del Monte's parent had become known, for $24 million. In order to reduce the substantial debt incurred in the transaction, KKR sold off Del Monte assets.

In 1990 Del Monte management joined with Merrill Lynch & Co., Huff Asset Management Co., and Citibank to salvage the remainder of the business by conducting another leveraged buyout. The cost of this acquisition was $1.48 billion. Eighty percent of that purchase price was financed with outside capital, leaving Del Monte with an enormous debt load.

The company embarked on a streamlining strategy to reduce its financial liabilities, but could not emerge from its debt. Its owners soon began shopping around for an acquirer for the food canning company. In 1994 Del Monte entered into a $1 billion acquisition agreement with Mexican financier Carlos Cabal Peniche, owner of the Del Monte Fresh Produce Company (no affiliation to Del Monte Foods). The deal was called off, however, when Cabal went on the lam after being charged with fraud by the Mexican government. In 1996 the company, still seeking a buyer, announced the elimination of 150 positions, or 20% of its full-time workforce.

In early 1997 two companies were rumored to be considering a purchase of Del Monte. Tri-Valley Growers was the leading contender, but many analysts predicted that a union of these companies would raise anti-trust concerns, as they were the two largest canned fruit and vegetable companies in California. The other possible acquirer named was the investment firm Hicks, Muse, Tate & Furst Inc., yet this company was beat out by another investment firm, Texas Pacific Group.

Approach and Engagement

In 1995 Richard Wolford, a venture capitalist and ex-Dole Foods executive, sought reentry into the canned food industry by acquiring Del Monte. Certain that the company had great potential, he aimed to revive it via marketing, higher-margin products, strategic acquisitions, and expanded distribution. Wolford convinced David Bonderman, head of Texas Pacific Group, of his vision. This investment firm had carved a reputation as a turnaround company for underperforming companies. As it already had investments in other food and beverage businesses, Wolford believed that the firm might be willing to gamble on Del Monte.

Wolford was correct, and on February 28, 1997, Texas Pacific announced its acquisition deal. On April 18, 1997, the $840 cash transaction was completed. Texas Pacific assured Del Monte's 2,100 full-time employees, who were suffering from an already low level of morale, that no jobs would be lost as a result of the deal—except for top management, that is. As was Texas Pacific's practice, the top executives of an acquired property were dismissed and replaced with a new team. Del Monte's co-CEOs, Paul Mullan and Bryan Hycox, were succeeded by Wolford as CEO and by Wesley Smith, another former executive of Dole, as chief operating officer.

Products and Services

Del Monte's products offerings fell into four main categories. **Fruits**: apricots, cherries, chunky mixed fruit, citrus fruit, fruit cocktail, fruit cup, Fruit

The Players

Texas Pacific Group CEO and Managing Partner: David Bonderman. David Bonderman was a man with a variety of talents and a Midas touch. Graduating from the University of Washington with a degree in Russian studies in 1963, he earned a Harvard law degree three years later. After teaching law for a year at Tulane University, "Mondo," as he was known to friends, took a job at the civil rights division of the U.S. Department of Justice. A Democrat, Bonderman left that post when Nixon became president. He then joined the law firm of Arnold & Porter, where his pro bono work drew the attention of billionaire Robert Bass. Impressed with Bonderman's work on the protection of Fort Worth's historic district, Bass hired him as his lead financial advisor. Despite his lack of experience in this field, Bonderman orchestrated a number of fortune-making deals. In 1992 he struck out on his own, and soon formed Texas Pacific Group as an investment partnership.

Del Monte Foods CEO: Richard G. Wolford. Richard Wolford was responsible for the engineering of Texas Pacific Group's acquisition of Del Monte Foods. This venture capitalist, who had served as president of Dole Foods' packaged foods division, knew the food industry well. In 1995 he viewed the debt-laden Del Monte as rich with potential. He soon sold fellow investor David Bonderman on the idea, and in 1997 Texas Pacific purchased Del Monte. Wolford was installed as CEO, and he immediately began to improve the company's performance.

Pleasures, Fruitrageous, Orchard Select, pears, pineapple, tropical fruit, yellow cling peaches, and yellow freestone peaches. **Vegetables**: asparagus, beets, carrots, cream style corn, green beans, Italian beans, lima beans, mixed vegetables, peas and carrots, sweet peas, potatoes, sauerkraut, spinach, wax beans, whole kernel corn, and zucchini. **Beverages**: Fruit Smoothie Blenders concentrate, pineapple juice, tomato juice, and vegetable blended cocktail. **Tomatoes**: chunky tomatoes, crushed tomatoes, diced tomatoes, ketchup, tomato paste, chili sauce, seafood cocktail sauce, tomato sauce, tomato wedges, sloppy joe sauces, spaghetti sauces, and stewed tomatoes.

Changes to the Industry and Review of the Outcome

The infusion of cash and new management had an almost immediate effect on Del Monte. In 1997 its market share of canned fruit reached 42%, compared to the 40% held by private label brands. The company began introducing new products with a more hip style to revive its dusty old image. By 1998 such offerings included ginger-flavored pears, Fruitrageous lunchbox-sized fruit cups, and Orchard Select jar-packed fruit. Wolford also prepared the launch of the company's first advertising campaign in over eight years.

In canned vegetables, where Del Monte's 20% market share trailed far behind the 44% hold of private labels, the company initiated a strategy of growth via acquisition. In December 1997 it paid $195 million for the Contadina brand of canned tomato products from Nestle S.A., adding a product line, as well as processing facilities in concert with its own tomato operations. As part of the synergies realized from this facility consolidation, Del Monte announced the closure of two plants and the corresponding elimination of about 1,000 jobs, planned for 1999 and 2000.

In March 1998 Del Monte filed plans with the Securities Exchange Commission for a $250 million initial public offering in order to pare down some of its debt. Those plans were postponed for nearly a year, however, as the market suddenly became disenchanted with food stocks. By early 1999 the market had stabilized, and on February 5 Del Monte raised $300 million through the issue of 16.7 million shares. Through this offering, Texas Pacific Group reduced its stake in the company by 38% to 46.7%.

Research

Angwin, Julia. "Texas Group to Acquire Del Monte," in *San Francisco Chronicle*, 1 March 1997. Announces the acquisition agreement.

Atlas, Riva. "Thrills! Chills! Spills? Mondo Bondo," in *Institutional Investor*, January 1999. Offers a detailed account of Texas Pacific's history.

Barron, Kelly. "Breathing New Life into a Tired Old Brand," in *Forbes*, 30 November 1998. Reviews Del Monte's progress during the year after its acquisition by Texas Pacific.

"Del Monte Foods Company," in *International Directory of Company Histories*, Vol. 23, St. James Press: 1998. Provides a narrative account of the company's history.

Del Monte Foods Company Home Page, available at http://www.delmonte.com. Official World Wide Web Home Page for Del Monte. Includes a company history, product information, press releases, recipes, and games and food facts geared toward children.

Pierce, Ellise. "Mondo Bondo: These Days It's Fort Worth Financier David Bonderman's World," in *Texas Monthly*, February 1996. Profiles Texas Pacific's founder.

"Texas Pacific Group Completes Acquisition of Del Monte Foods Company," in *Business Wire*, 18 April 1997. Reports the closure of the deal.

Zellner, Wendy. "Flying High—And Against the Wind," in *Business Week*, 6 May 1996. Describes the success of Texas Pacific since its formation.

DEBORAH J. UNTENER

TEXTRON & AMERICAN WOOLEN

nationality: USA
date: February 24, 1955
affected: Textron Inc., USA, founded 1923
affected: American Woolen Co., USA

Textron Inc.
40 Westminster St.
Providence, RI 02903
USA

tel: (401)421-2800
fax: (401)421-2878
web: http://www.textron.com

Overview of the Merger

In a deal that *Fortune* dubbed a "demonstration of business judo," Textron forged a three-way merger with American Woolen and Robbins Mills. The primary goal of Royal Little, chairman and founder of Textron, was American Woolen, a failing textile manufacturer that held a cash surplus that could be used to propel Little's diversification goals.

American Woolen was resistant to Textron's overtures, and put up a struggle to retain its independence. The ensuing 14-month battle included shareholders' fights, third-party alliances, and even forgery. In the end, the deal was completed by engaging Robbins Mills as a principal in a three-way merger that formed Textron American, Inc. This arrangement worked for each company because, as a Textron representative summarized in *Time*, "Textron has the management, Robbins has the plants, and American Woolen has the money."

History of Textron Inc.

Royal Little founded the Boston textile firm Special Yarns Corp. in 1923. Facing bankruptcy, Special Yarns merged with Franklin Rayon Dyeing Co. to become Franklin Rayon Corp. in 1928. Ten years later, once headquartered in Providence, Rhode Island, the company changed its name to Atlantic Rayon.

Atlantic Rayon expanded during World War II to keep up with government orders for parachutes. In 1944, the company renamed itself Textron Inc., a moniker derived from "textile products made from synthetics." It developed into an integrated textile company operating in all aspects of the business, from raw material to finished product. The industry slumped, however, in the period following World War II.

In 1952, Textron embarked on an aggressive acquisition strategy, purchasing over 40 various companies by the end of the decade in order to diversify beyond the volatile textile industry. It made its first non-textile acquisition the following year, purchasing Burkart Manufacturing Co., supplier of automotive cushioning materials. In 1955, the company orchestrated a three-way merger with American

The Business

Financials

Revenue (1998): $9.7 billion

Employees (1998): 64,000

SICs / NAICS

sic 3721 - Aircraft

sic 3694 - Engine Electrical Equipment

sic 6211 - Security Brokers & Dealers

naics 336411 - Aircraft Manufacturing

naics 336413 - Other Aircraft Part and Auxiliary Equipment Manufacturing

naics 336412 - Aircraft Engine and Engine Parts Manufacturing

naics 336322 - Other Motor Vehicle Electrical and Electronic Equipment Manufacturing

naics 523110 - Investment Banking and Securities Dealing

Woolen and Robbins Mills. By 1956, with Rupert Thompson overseeing acquisitions, Textron had become known as the world's first conglomerate. Its purchases during this period included the autoparts manufacturer Randall; E-Z-Go, a maker of golf carts; and Bell Aerospace, which included Bell Helicopter, thereby gaining entry into the aerospace industry.

Textron completely exited the textile industry by selling the underperforming Amerotron in 1962. During the first half of the 1960s the company acquired 20 more companies, including the watchband maker Speidel and the stapler manufacturer Bostich. In 1968, Thompson retired and was succeeded by G. William Miller. After Textron's failed attempt to take over United Fruit, Miller aspired to the acquisition of smaller firms, such as zipper and fastener manufacturers.

Another takeover plan failed when Textron was outbid by another company in its attempt to acquire healthcare manufacturer Kendall Co. in 1971, as did its attempt to acquire Lockheed Corp. three years later. The company successfully acquired the lawn care equipment maker Jacobsen Manufacturers in 1978. Miller resigned that year to assume the positions of Chairman of the U.S. Federal Reserve and Secretary of the U.S. Treasury Department under the Carter administration.

Under president B. F. Dolan, Textron sold its less profitable operations, including zipper, snowmobile, and machine tool manufacturers. In 1984, it was the target of a hostile takeover attempt by Chicago Pacific Corp. Although it successfully fending off that suitor, Textron realized that it must resume its acquisition strategy to avoid being acquired itself. That year it acquired Avco Corp., a finance and insurance company. Textron shocked its stockholders when management announced in 1985 that it was considering the sale of its main operating division, Bell Aerospace. The company's financial position improved, however, and Bell was retained and reorganized as Bell Aerospace and Textron Marine Systems. In 1986 Ex-Cell-O, a defense and auto parts manufacturer, was acquired.

The firm purchased Avdel, a U.K.-based manufacturer of metal fastening systems, in 1989. In 1992, under the leadership of James Hardymon, Textron purchased Cessna Aircraft Co. for $600 million. In 1994 it acquired Orag Inter AG of Switzerland, the leading distributor of golf and turf-care equipment in Europe. During the next two years it purchased Household Finance of Australia, Elco Industries, Boesner, and Valois.

In 1996, Bell Helicopter Textron and The Boeing Co. began the development of a commercial tilt-rotor aircraft—a nine-passenger vehicle that would rise from the ground like a helicopter and then reposition its propellers 90 degrees for forward flight. That year it divested a large portion of its aircraft wing business, and acquired fuel tank manufacturer Kautex Werke Reinold Hagen AG. In 1997 it sold its majority interest in Paul Revere Corp. to insurance provider Provident. The next year it sold Speidel and purchased both Ransomes PLC and David Brown Group PLC.

Textron sold Avco Financial Services in 1999, acquiring the funds to purchase Flexalloy, ALSTOM Gears, and the Fluid Systems operation of LCI Corp. That year Lewis B. Campbell added the position of chairman to his responsibilities as CEO. Textron also entered into agreements to purchase the construction equipment manufacturer Omniquip International and the automation systems developer Aylesbury Automation Ltd.

History of American Woolen Co.

By the mid-1950s American Woolen was the world's largest maker of woolens and worsteds. It operated dozens of small mills in New England, as well as two obsolete plants in the southern part of the country, where the center of the textile industry was emerging.

Throughout its history, American Woolen was highly profitable during wartime, including both World Wars and the Korean Conflict. Yet in times of peace the company's inefficiency and often idle mills could not effectively compete with the southern companies. It also suffered from its failure to diversify into other fibers. Sales plummeted from $253 million in 1951 to $28 million in 1954, and losses over that period totaled over $30 million.

Market Forces Driving the Merger

The textile industry was highly volatile, fluctuating from enormous success during periods of war, but remaining unpredictable in other years. It was at the mercy of rapid changes in fashion trends, which dictated preferred fabrics as well as styles. Most textile companies suffered from such pressures, but American Woolen was in particularly sore shape. In early 1955, it was had obsolete, inflexible facilities, as well as 13 idle plants that were losing about $40,000 each month. Overall, the company was losing about $1 million monthly.

In 1952, Textron initiated a strategy of diversification out of textiles to insulate it from the industry's fluctuations. On this basis, it seemed an unlikely suitor of American Woolen, which was not only a textile company, but also one of the industry's worst performers. Yet that firm was sitting on $28 million in cash and government bonds that Textron could use to fuel its diversification plans. Royal Little, Textron's chairman and founder, also believed that he could improve American Woolen's balance sheet by updating, moving, or closing its plants.

Approach and Engagement

In December 1953, American Woolen announced a plan, to be voted on by shareholders the following month, in which it would close 11 plants and repurchase about $20 million of its shares. A group of dissidents, including then-director Joseph Ely, opposed this application of funds that could be used instead for mill refurbishment. With this rift in the board, Royal Little saw his opportunity to propose a merger. Referring to American Woolen in *Fortune*, he later said, "If it hadn't been such a God-awful mess, I couldn't have picked it up."

Little proposed a cash-and-stock purchase of American Woolen common shares. The directors resisted the offer, fearing that Little simply wanted to get his hands on American Woolen's capital and to move its New England operations south. On the day before the stockholder vote that would decide the company's proposal, Little dispatched lawyers to locate an

The Officers

Chairman and CEO: Lewis B. Campbell

President and Chief Operating Officer: John A. Janitz

Exec. VP Government, International, Communications and Investor Relations: Mary L. Howell

Exec. VP and General Counsel: Wayne W. Juchatz

Exec. VP and Chief Financial Officer: Stephen L. Key

American Woolen shareholder who would be willing to file for a temporary injunction against the meeting. They finally located one, and obtained his signature by hiring a private plane, the only means fast enough to return in time to file the injunction request in court the following morning.

On February 3, the day after the restraining order had expired, American Woolen's shareholders overwhelmingly approved management's plan. This vote was immediately stalled, however, by a second injunction that was filed by a shareholder who found fault with the tally.

During this time, only a trickling of American Woolen shares were tendered to Textron's offer. On April 5, the date of the offer's deadline, Textron accepted the 175,000 shares offered, even though the company had required a minimum of 300,000 tendered shares.

Meanwhile, American Woolen had sidled up to Bachmann Uxbridge Worsted Corp. In early April, American Woolen offered to sell $14 million of its stock to Bachmann Uxbridge. If accepted, the deal would have given Bachmann Uxbridge a greater stake in American Woolen than Textron held, an outcome that Little desperately wanted to avoid.

Both American Woolen and Textron sought to elect their own slate of directors to the four seats that became vacant in late April. American Woolen succeeded, but a handwriting analysis indicated that 75,000 of the proxies had been forged. A court subsequently threw out the results of the meeting.

With the Bachmann Uxbridge threat still looming, Little moved to lock up his control of American Woolen quickly. Textron, however, was short on cash, and had few assets that could be sold. After obtaining a loan on May 24, Textron offered to purchase 100,000 shares of American Woolen at $23. With that offer still pending, it also purchased 460,000 shares, or a 47% stake, thereby effectively killing any chance of a deal with Bachmann Uxbridge. Ely relented by giving

The Players

Textron Chairman: Royall Little. After acquiring a Harvard degree in 1919, Royal Little worked for Cheney Brothers, the nation's leading silk manufacturer. In 1923, he borrowed $10,000 to establish Special Yarns Corp., New England's first synthetic yarn processor, that was later known as Textron Inc. The cyclicity of the textile industry inspired Little to embark on a strategy of "unrelated diversification," and Textron soon emerged as the first true conglomerate. He retired as chairman in 1960, and successively took the helm of various companies, including Amtel Inc., before becoming a mergers and acquisitions consultant. He was elected to *Fortune*'s U.S. Business Hall of Fame in 1975, and later published *How to Lose $100,000,000 and Other Valuable Advice*. Little passed away in January 1989 in The Bahamas.

American Woolen President: Joseph B. Ely. The Democratic ex-governor of Massachusetts, Joseph Ely had served on the board of directors of American Woolen for many years before becoming its president in May 1954. The company that he inherited was cash-rich, but overwhelmed by losses and an array of idle or underperforming textile mills. Earlier in 1954, Ely had been one of several directors who opposed the company's plan to repurchase its shares rather than invest in operations. This dissention among the ranks provided Textron the opening it sought to make its merger offer, a proposition that Ely resisted because of Textron's clear goal of obtaining American Woolen's cash hoard. To thwart this threat, he entered into an agreement with Bachmann Uxbridge Worsted Corp., but to no avail. When Textron ultimately merged with American Woolen and Robbins Mills, Inc., Ely assumed the post of chairman of the executive committee of the newly formed Textron American, Inc.

three board seats to Textron, but refused to grant Little an executive position.

In July 1954, Textron learned that Robbins Mills, a nearly bankrupt manufacturer of synthetics, had been put up for sale. This company had modern, flexible facilities, but had lost about $10 million over the previous three years. Textron acquired a 42% stake in that company, and initially negotiated to sell Robbins' stock and Textron's southern mills in a deal that would give him four additional seats, constituting a majority, on American Woolen's board. After that proposal hit several snags, Little suggested a three-way merger. The strengths and weaknesses of the three companies complemented each other well. American Woolen held the capital needed to improve business, but had obsolete mills. Robbins Mills had modern plants and the capabilities to produce a variety of fabrics, but was broke. Textron had up-to-date facilities and savvy management, but limited cash.

Finally, on December 15, 1954, an agreement was reached. In February 1955 the board of each company approved the merger, a stock swap of Textron shares for American Woolen and Robbins Mills stock. On February 24, 1955, the merger was completed, and Textron, the surviving entity, was renamed Textron American, Inc.

Products and Services

In 1998, Textron operated in four primary business areas. The Aircraft division, which accounted for 33% of total revenues, manufactured commercial and military helicopters, tiltrotor aircraft, business jets, and single-engine piston aircraft; its operating companies were Bell Helicopter Textron and Cessna Aircraft Co. Automotive, operating as Textron Automotive Co, generated 25% of company revenues through the manufacture of instrument panels, interior and exterior plastic trim and fuel tanks, and functional components and systems. The Industrial segment, which generated 38% of revenues, consisted of Textron Fastening Systems; Golf, Turf Care and Specialty Products; Fluid and Power Systems; and Industrial Components. The Finance division, accounting for four percent of revenues, operated as TFC, which provided diversified commercial finance supporting the sale of Textron and third-party products.

Review of the Outcome

Textron American emerged as the nation's sixth-largest textile company, with $160 million in assets, a workforce of 13,600, and 43 plants. Royal Little retained his post as chairman of the new company. Joseph Ely became chairman of the executive committee, and Robert L. Huffines, Jr., president of both Robbins Mills and Textron, was named president of Textron American.

Textron set about on the expansion and diversification plan that it had envisioned. It built the world's largest woolen mill in South Carolina, where it consolidated all of American Woolen's operations, thereby cutting off the company's $1 million monthly loss. With these savings, as well as American Woolen's capital and tax benefits, Textron "was affluent for the first time in its life," wrote Little in *How to Lose $100,000,000 and Other Valuable Advice*. Between April and October of 1955, Textron spent 80% of its surplus cash in purchasing five companies.

Royal Little attributed much of Textron's future success as a conglomerate to its union with American Woolen and Robbins Mills. "Without the American Woolen merger, Textron would never have amounted to anything," he wrote in his book. "It would have been a very small company with three or four diversified operations still primarily in textiles."

Research

"Down to Business," in *Newsweek*, 21 February 1955. Describes the proposed merger deal.

Little, Royal. "Conglomerates Are Doing Better Than You Think," in *Fortune*, 28 May 1984. Textron's founder defends the nature of the conglomerate, a entity that had not found favor on Wall Street.

———. *How to Lose $100,000,000 and Other Valuable Advice*, Little, Brown and Co., 1979. A tongue-in-cheek account of the history of Textron, and the errors that Little had made along the way.

Saunders, Dero A. "The Stormiest Merger Yet," in *Fortune*, April 1955. Provides a detailed chronology of the 14-month battle for American Woolen.

"Textron American, Inc. Votes First Common Dividend of 10 Cents," in *The Wall Street Journal*, 25 February 1955. Relates the completion of the merger.

Textron Inc. Home Page, available at http://www.textron.com. Official World Wide Web Page for Textron. Includes a description of products and services, annual reports and other financial information, news releases, executive biographies, and a company history.

"Through a Stone Wall," in *Time*, 28 February 1955. Describes the recently announced three-way merger deal.

KIMBERLY N. STEVENS

TEXTRON & CHICAGO PACIFIC

Textron Inc.
40 Westminster St.
Providence, RI 02903
USA

tel: (401)421-2800
fax: (401)421-2878
web: http://www.textron.com

date: 1984 (canceled)
affected: Textron Inc., USA, founded 1923
affected: Chicago Pacific Corp., USA, founded 1984

Overview of the Merger

Four-month-old Chicago Pacific Corp., the remnant of the bankrupt Chicago, Rock Island, & Pacific Railroad, attempted to take over the much larger Textron, Inc.—a $5.5 billion, 25-company conglomerate—in 1989. The $1.6 billion deal fell apart, however, when Textron turned down the $43 per share offer and shunned further negotiations. Chicago Pacific went on to be acquired by Maytag Corp. in 1989.

History of Textron, Inc.

In 1923, the Boston, Massachusetts-based textile business, Special Yarns Corp., was founded by Royal Little. To avoid bankruptcy, Special Yarns merged with Franklin Rayon Dyeing Co. in 1928 to become Franklin Rayon Corp. After moving its headquarters to Providence, Rhode Island, the company changed its name to Atlantic Rayon in 1938. The firm expanded during World War II to keep up with government orders for parachutes. By the war's end, Atlantic Rayon had renamed itself Textron Inc., which was derived from the phrase, "textile products made from synthetics."

To diversify beyond the textile industry, Textron began an acquisition campaign in the early 1950s that resulted in the purchase of over 40 companies. In 1955, the firm completed a hostile takeover of American Woolen and also purchased the Homelite chainsaws line. Autoparts manufacturer Randall joined Textron in 1959. By the end of the decade, Textron had transformed itself into one of the world's first conglomerates.

In 1960, the company entered the aerospace industry with the purchase of helicopter manufacturer Bell Aircraft Co.; E-Z-Go, a maker of golf carts, was also acquired. Two years later, Textron sold Amerotron, its last textile holding, due to poor performance. The Spiedel watchbands line was acquired in 1964. By 1966, Bell Aircraft's sales accounted for 41% of Textron's revenues. An effort to take over United Fruit failed in 1968, and Textron's attempt to acquire healthcare manufacturer Kendall Co. fell apart in 1971. Three years later, the firm was forced to abandon merger negotiations with a reluctant Lockheed Corp., due to pressure from Wall Street. In 1978, lawn care equipment maker Jacobsen Manufacturers joined Textron.

Textron fended off three hostile takeovers attempts in the early 1980s, including a $1.6 billion bid by Chicago Pacific Corp. in 1984. Avco, a finance and insurance company, was acquired that year. In 1985, Textron shocked stockholders by announcing plans to sell off its main operating division, Bell Aerospace. Zipper, snowmobile, and machine tool making operations had already been divested. When the company's financial position improved, however, Bell was retained and reorganized into Bell Aerospace and Textron Marine Systems. Textron bought Ex-Cell-O, a defense and auto parts manufacturer, in 1986.

In 1991, the FTC challenged Textron's 1989 purchase of Avdel, a British-based manufacturer of metal fastening systems. The following year, the firm paid $600 million for Cessna Aircraft. Europe's largest distributor of golf and turf-care equipment, Orag Inter AG, was added to Textron's mix in 1994. Acquisitions the following year included Elco Industries and Boesner, both fastening systems manufacturers, as well as Household Finance of Australia. In 1996, Bell Helicopter Textron and Boeing Co. begin joint development of a commercial tilt-rotor aircraft. The firm also increased its fastener operations with the $120 acquisition of France's Valois, paid $308 million for plastic fuel tank maker Kautex Werke Reinold Hagen AG, and divested a large chunk of its aircraft wing business.

Textron exited the watchband and jewelry market, as well as the insurance sector, in 1997. The launch of an upgraded Cessna 172 marked the firm's reentry into the general aviation industry. Associates First Capital paid $3.9 billion for Textron's Avco Financial Services unit in 1999. The firm planned to use the capital to fund future acquisitions.

History of Chicago Pacific Corp.

In 1975, the struggling Chicago, Rock Island, & Pacific Railroad filed bankruptcy. After efforts to continue operations failed, a bankruptcy judge decreed that the company be liquidated. The resulting $204 million in cash and $140 million in tax credits were used to found Chicago Pacific Corp. in June of 1984. David Murdock and Chicago's Crown family jointly owned 20% of the new firm.

Harvey Kapnick was hired to mold Chicago Pacific into a holding company. After attempts to takeover Textron and Scovill Inc. were thwarted, Chicago Pacific set its sights on Hoover Co. in October

The Business

Financials

Revenue (1998): $9.6 billion

Employees (1998): 64,000

SICs / NAICS

sic 3721 - Aircraft

sic 3724 - Aircraft Engines & Engine Parts

sic 2396 - Automotive & Apparel Trimmings

sic 5013 - Motor Vehicle Supplies & New Parts

sic 3492 - Fluid Power Valves & Hose Fittings

sic 6159 - Miscellaneous Business Credit Institutions

sic 3965 - Fasteners, Buttons, Needles & Pins

sic 3524 - Lawn & Garden Equipment

sic 3511 - Turbines & Turbine Generator Sets

sic 3711 - Motor Vehicles & Car Bodies

naics 336411 - Aircraft Manufacturing

naics 336412 - Aircraft Engine and Engine Parts Manufacturing

naics 332912 - Fluid Power Valve and Hose Fitting Manufacturing

naics 522000 - Credit Intermediation and Related Activities

naics 339993 - Fastener, Button, Needle, and Pin Manufacturing

naics 333112 - Lawn and Garden Tractor and Home Lawn and Garden Equipment Manufacturing

naics 333611 - Turbine and Turbine Generator Set Unit Manufacturing

naics 336112 - Light Truck and Utility Vehicle Manufacturing

of 1985. After upping its initial offer of $497.1 million to $535 million, Chicago Pacific completed the deal, gaining access to the international appliance market. In 1986, the firm diversified into the furniture industry by purchasing a few furniture makers. It also paid $74 million for Rowenta, an appliance manufacturer based in West Germany. To pay down debt, Chicago Pacific sold Rowenta for $50 million in 1988.

In January of 1989, Chicago Pacific was acquired by Maytag Corp. for $960 million. Chicago Pacific's appliance operations were folded into its new parent company; the furniture assets were divested for $213.4 million.

The Officers

Chairman and CEO: Lewis B. Campbell

President and Chief Operating Officer: John A. Janitz

Exec. VP and Chief Financial Officer: Stephen L. Key

Exec. VP, Administration: John D. Butler

Exec. VP, Government, International, Communications,
   and Investor Relations: Mary L. Howell

Market Forces Driving the Merger

According to *Financial Times (London)*, Chicago Pacific was looking to become a holding company of diverse industrial operations. With roughly $350 million in its coffers, the firm "said it was aiming to take over sector leaders, and indicated that it wanted companies with strong managements that could be retained. It added that it wanted to avoid high risk situations, and might sell off divisions or acquisitions if they were not performing satisfactorily." Textron seemed to meet all of these requirements. The firm boasted several profitable divisions, including the Bell Helicopter unit, as well as several businesses that could be divested as a means of paying down debt. Most analysts believed the firm was back on track after a couple of sluggish years that left it vulnerable to takeover attacks in the early 1980s.

Approach and Engagement

Chicago's Pacific's $43 per share bid, launched in October of 1984, was the third such bid received by Textron that year. In a letter to Textron, Chicago Pacific CEO Harvey Kapnick explained that the bid was certainly negotiable. Backed by Citibank, the firm was planning to take on a 4.5 to 1 debt to equity ratio to finance the $1.6 billion deal.

Although the offer reflected a significant premium over Textron's 12-month high of $35.33 and record high of $38.50, Textron rejected the bid as too low and indicated that it was not interested in pursuing further negotiations. Chicago Pacific agreed to not purchase any shares of the conglomerate without its consent.

Products and Services

The appliance and furniture operations of Chicago Pacific were split apart in 1989 after the firm was acquired by Maytag Corp. In 1985, Textron began a series of divestitures that left it with four major product groups by the late 1990s: aircraft, which accounted for 30% of sales; industrial, 29%; automotive, 25%; and

finance, 4%. North American operations brought in 72% of revenues, while businesses in Europe, Canada, and Asia secured the remainder.

Textron's aircraft division included two units: Bell, which manufactured helicopters, and Cessna, which made business jets and general aviation aircraft.

Industrial product units included Cone Drive Textron and Maag Pump Systems Textron, both makers of gears; E-Z-Go Textron, a golf carts and utility vehicles manufacturer; Greenlee, a supplier of powered equipment, electrical test instruments, and hand tools; HR Textron, an aircraft control systems designer; Jacobsen Textron, a mowing and turf maintenance equipment maker; Ransomes plc, a manufacturer of lawn care machinery; Textron Fastening Systems; Textron Logistics Corp.; Textron Lycoming, a supplier of piston aircraft engines; Textron Marine & Land Systems; and Turbine Engine Components.

Automotive businesses included engine camshafts maker CWC Castings; plastic fuel tank systems manufacturer Kautex Werke Reinold Hagen AG; machine tool supplier Micromatic; fuel filler systems designer Randall; Textron Automotive Trim Operations; and McCord Winn, a maker of seating, windshield and headlamp washer systems, and DC motor armatures.

After selling the Avco Financial Services unit in 1999, Textron's financial arm consisted of Textron Financial Corp., a commercial finance operation.

Review of the Outcome

In 1985, Textron began selling off several assets, including its Jones & Lamson machine tool business and its specialty chemicals subsidiary. The firm even put its lucrative Bell Helicopter on the block, although financial improvements allowed the firm to hang on to the unit. According to a March 1985 article in *Business Week*, Textron was reacting to the three hostile bids its had defended itself against in 1984 by "doing pretty much what the raiders, and many stockholders, wanted: raising return on equity from 9% in 1984 and selling off the dogs."

Still determined to make a major acquisition, Chicago Pacific bought Hoover in 1985 for $535 million. Four years later, the firm was purchased by Maytag for $960 million.

Research

Beam, Alex. "As the Sharks Circle, Textron Sheds Its Losers," in *Business Week*, 18 March 1985. Explains how Textron strengthened itself in 1985 by selling off assets.

Brenner, Brian. "How Chicago Pacific Became a Tantalizing Target," in *Business Week*, 30 January 1989. Discusses why Maytag Corp. decided to purchase Chicago Pacific in 1989. Includes a brief history of Chicago Pacific.

Dodsworth, Terry. "Chicago Pacific's Rocky Road to Riches; A Revamped U.S. Railway Makes a Dramatic Takeover Move," in *Financial Times (London)*, 30 October 1984. Describes how Chicago Pacific plans to finance its $1.6 billion takeover of the much larger Textron.

Textron, Inc. Home Page, available at http://www.textron.com. Official World Wide Web Page for Textron, Inc. Includes product, corporate, historical, and employ-ment information, along with current news.

"Textron, Inc.," in *International Directory of Company Histories*, Vol. 1, St. James Press, 1988. Details the history of Textron, Inc.

"Textron, Inc.," in *Notable Corporate Chronologies*, The Gale Group, 1999. Lists major events in the history of Textron, Inc.

"Textron Rejects a Merger Bid," in *Business Week*, 12 November 1984. Offers an overview of Textron's rejection of Chicago Pacific's takeover bid.

JEFF ST. THOMAS

THOMSON & DAEWOO

Thomson S.A.
173 Haussmann Blvd.
Cedex 08, Paris, F-75008
France

tel: (33)1-53-77-80-00
fax: (33)1-53-77-83-00

Daewoo Corp.
541 Namdaemunno 5-ga
Chung-gu, Seoul
South Korea

tel: (82)2-759-2114
fax: (82)2-753-9489
web: http://www.dwc.co.kr

date: 1996 (canceled)
affected: Thomson S.A., France, founded 1893
affected: Daewoo Corp., South Korea, founded 1967

Overview of the Merger

In October of 1996, the French government announced its plans to sell Thomson S.A. to the Lagardere Groupe for a symbolic FFr 1. Beating out Alcatel Alsthom SA, Lagardere would gain control of Thomson-CSF, the defense subsidiary of the company, to create Europe's largest defense electronics company, equal in size to Hughes Aircraft Co. of the U.S., and second only to Lockheed Martin Loral in defense electronics.

Lagardere had arranged to divest Thomson Multimedia, the company's consumer electronics division, to Daewoo Corp. of South Korea. The plan sparked a xenophobic reaction, as well as heated debate, throughout France during November 1996. France's Privatisation Commission was concerned that Daewoo would not follow through with promises of increased jobs and profits and would somewhat tarnish Thomson's high quality image. In December of 1996, the Commission turned down the sale.

History of Thomson S.A.

In 1893, Thomson-Houston Electric Corp., established a French subsidiary, Compagnie Francaise Thomson-Houston, to handle sales and administration for the company. In 1903, Compagnie Francaise Thomson-Houston became a private, French-owned company after General Electric Co. (GE) bought its parent, Thomson-Houston, only to sell the French subsidiary to a group of French businessmen. The company's primary operations were the manufacturing of power equipment, much of which was under license from GE.

In 1904, Thomson-Houston bought telephone equipment manufacturing operations. Eight years later, the company began making lamps and light bulbs. In 1918, Thomson-Houston bought l'Eclairage Electrique in order to expand its power generating equipment production capability. Two years later, Pied-Selle, a home appliance manufacturer, was acquired. In 1922, the lamp and light bulb business grew with the formation of a joint venture with CGE, called Compagnie des Lampes. Five years later, another joint venture, with the Societe Alsacienne de

Construction Mecanique, created Alsthom, an electrical equipment manufacturer. The same year, International Telephone & Telegraph (ITT) bought Thomson-Houston's telephone equipment manufacturing operations.

During the 1930s, the company continued to grow through acquisition. Thomson-Houston acquired a manufacturer of radio receivers and helped establish Compagnie Generale de Radiologie. In 1936, radio transmitting equipment operations were purchased, and one year later, manufacturing of radio tubes began. In 1938, Thomson-Houston fully acquired Compagnie Generale de Radiologie.

During the war in 1941, the French government attempted to thwart the impending German invasion by creating an industrialization plan. However, by 1945, Thomson-Houston plants, like most French manufacturing plants, were occupied by German troops and were forced to work for the German war effort. Advances in consumer products, including many of Thomson's, were almost completely halted during World War II. At the war's conclusion, however, the French government persuaded Thomson to focus more on refurbishing the country's infrastructure and industry even though consumer demands were still high.

By 1953, Thomson-Houston's desire for independence from GE was reinforced by its emergence as a major industrial and military supplier and France's growing need for secrecy about its nuclear technology. As a result, Thomson-Houston discontinued its 50-year licensing agreement with GE. The company also profited from increased orders from the French government to support their renewed colonial interests. In 1960, Thomson-Houston created Sodeteg to operate its nuclear and civil engineering businesses. Six years later, the company bought Hotchkiss-Brandt, a maker of appliances, defense electronics, cars, and postal equipment. Now called Thomson-Brandt, the company formed a subsidiary, Thomson-CSF, when its electronics operations merged with another French communications company, Compagnie Generale de Telegraphie Sans Fils. Thomson-CSF became France's number one maker of high-tech electronics for professional use. In 1969, CGE allowed Thomson-Brandt the household appliances and data processing business in France due to government restructuring that gave them Thomson-Brandt's subsidiary, Alsthom, an electric power generation equipment and power plant construction businesses.

By 1976, Thomson-Brandt operated businesses throughout Europe, Asia, Africa, and North America. Despite this expansion, the company struggled financially, at least in part due to inefficient management. In

The Business

Financials - Thomson S.A.
Revenue (1997): $12.7 billion
Employees (1997): 90,000

Financials - Daewoo Corp.
Revenue (1998): $30.5 billion
Employees (1997): 15,000

SICs / NAICS

sic 3730 - Ship & Boat Building & Repairing
sic 3320 - Iron & Steel Foundries
sic 3710 - Motor Vehicles & Equipment
sic 3720 - Aircraft & Parts
sic 3651 - Household Audio & Video Equipment
sic 3821 - Laboratory Apparatus & Furniture
sic 3663 - Radio & T.V. Communications Equipment
sic 3674 - Semiconductors & Related Devices
sic 3699 - Electrical Equipment & Supplies Nec
sic 3631 - Household Cooking Equipment
sic 3632 - Household Refrigerators & Freezers
sic 3633 - Household Laundry Equipment
sic 3639 - Household Appliances Nec

naics 339111 - Laboratory Apparatus and Furniture Manufacturing
naics 334412 - Bare Printed Circuit Board Manufacturing
naics 333319 - Other Commercial and Service Industry Machinery Manufacturing
naics 333618 - Other Engine Equipment Manufacturing
naics 333992 - Welding and Soldering Equipment Manufacturing
naics 335129 - Other Lighting Equipment Manufacturing
naics 335999 - All Other Miscellaneous Electrical Equipment and Component Manufacturing
naics 335221 - Household Cooking Appliance Manufacturing
naics 335222 - Household Refrigerator and Home and Farm Freezer Manufacturing
naics 335224 - Household Laundry Equipment Manufacturing
naics 335212 - Household Vacuum Cleaner Manufacturing
naics 327211 - Flat Glass Manufacturing
naics 331312 - Primary Aluminum Production
naics 339914 - Costume Jewelry and Novelty Manufacturing
naics 315212 - Women's, Girls', and Infants' Cut and Sew Apparel Contractors
naics 331311 - Alumina Refining
naics 325211 - Plastics Material and Resin Manufacturing
naics 523999 - Miscellaneous Financial Investment Activities

The Officers

Thomson S.A.

Chairman: Thierry Breton

President and CEO: Denis Ranque

Chief Financial Officer: Frank Dangeard

Chairman, President, and CEO, Thomson-CSF: Francois Gayet

Director of Human Resources: Paul Calandra

Daewoo Corp.

Chairman: Suh Hyung-Suk

President and CEO: Chang Byung-Ju

Chief Financial Officer: Kim Seong-Sik

Director of Human Resources: M. H. Chae

1981, Socialists attained government control and nationalized Thomson-Brandt nationalized. Alain Gomez, a Harvard graduate who worked for Saint Gabon, replaced Jean Pierre Bouyssonnie as chairman. Gomez lessened the company's financial woes by hiring a finance officer to pinpoint profitable and unprofitable divisions.

In September 1982, Thomson S.A., a holding company, was formed to oversee the old Thomson-Brandt operations. In an attempt to nationalize French electronics production, Thomson gave Compagnie Generale d'Elcectricite (CGE) its telecommunications and cable manufacturing business in exchange for CGE's military and consumer electronics operations. Thomson attempted to take over Grundig, a West German electronics company, but the West German government blocked the acquisition in 1984. Thomson and Gomez settled for purchasing Telefunken, which controlled about 25% of the West German consumer electronics market. Gomez was satisfied with the concession because Thomson gained a strong marketing network to avoid West German import restrictions. In 1985, Thomson-CSF and General Telephone & Electronics Corp. (GTE) secured a $4.3 billion military communications equipment contract, the largest deal from the Pentagon for non-American technology.

In the latter half of the 1980s, Thomson focused once again on acquisitions. The company purchased most of semiconductor manufacturer Mostek's assets. In 1987, Thomson bought the consumer electronics operations of Thorn-EMI PLC and also acquired all of GE's consumer electronics division, including RCA and GE brand names, in exchange for Compagnie Generale de Radiologie and $800 million in cash. This acquisition made Thomson number two in world production and number one in television production. That same year, Thomson's semiconductor business and STET's subsidiary, SGS Microelettronica, formed SGS-Thomson Microelectronics. Thomson also signed a three-year deal with GE USA: GE acquired 19.9% of Thomson Consumer Electronics Inc. in exchange for 19.9% of GE CGR SA.

In 1990, Thomson worked with Philips and GE-owned television network NBC to develop high-definition televisions. Thomson-CSF traded shares of its finance division for a 15.5% stake in Credit Lyonnais. Philips's defense electronics company, TRT, was bought and the Ferranti Thomson Sonar Systems partnership was formed. In December of 1991, the French government planned to merge Thomson Consumer Electronics with the country's nuclear technology interest, Commisariat a l'Energie Atomique (CEA). The intention was to use the profits from CEA to subsidize the semiconductor subsidiaries also involved in the merger. Dissent among French politicians about this plan prevented it from being executed.

Thomson went on to buy 50% of Pilkington Optronics, the makers of laserand optical guidance systems. The company also began joint ventures with the Boeing Co. to make aerospace products and with Aerospatiale and a Daimler-Benz subsidiary to make missiles. Thomson-CSF teamed with GEC-Marconi to make radar equipment for aircraft. In 1992, the research firm that had developed virtual reality computer technology failed to repay loans provided by Thomson-CSF. Because the company used the patent rights as collateral, the patents were given to Thomson-CSF. Three years later Thomson, Matsushita Electric Industrial Co., and Pioneer Electronic Corp. agreed to support a digital video disk player format presented by Toshiba Corp. to compete with the alliance of Sony Corp. and Philips Electronics NV.

As part of a defense industry downsizing effort, France announced that it planned to privatize Thomson through a direct sale to investors by the end of 1996. Lagardere Groupe and Alcatel Alsthom were competing for the company. In October, the French government approved the sale of Thomson to defense and publishing group Lagardere, whose plans included selling Thomson Multimedia to Daewoo Electronics. In December, an independent privatization commission spoke out against the sale of Thomson Multimedia to Daewoo and convinced the French government to rescind its approval of the sale of Thomson to Lagardere. One year later, a Socialist government was elected in France, halting plans for the sale of Thomson to Alcatel Alsthom and Dassault Industrie SA. The government announced that it intended to sell only roughly 20% of Thomson to Alcatel Alsthom and Dassault. In 1998, Microsoft Corp., NEC Corp., Alcatel, and DirecTV each gained 7.5% of Thomson Multimedia.

History of Daewoo Corp.

In 1967, Woo Choong Kim and Dae Do To invested the equivalent of $18,000 as capital for a new company called Daewoo. The name, derived from their given names, meant "Great Universe." Daewoo began concentrating on the labor intensive clothing and textile industries that would provide relatively high profits while utilizing South Korea's large workforce. The company also benefitted from cheap government-sponsored loans for exports.

Daewoo Corp., the major company in the Daewoo group, was licensed as a trading company by the government. In exchange for promoting Korean goods abroad, it received preferential loan agreements, reduced foreign exchange requirements, and improved government advice on exporting and marketing abroad. In 1980, Daewoo was forced into the shipbuilding industry against Kim's wishes when the government made the company take over the world's biggest dockyard at Okpo, South Korea.

In 1986, the government changed its attitude toward business, vowing to support only large companies that were instantly competitive and could further an equitable distribution of income. Daewoo responded with the establishment of several joint ventures including a 50-50 venture with Sikorsky Aerospace, a subsidiary of United Technologies to manufacture S-76 helicopters, and a 50-50 venture with General Motors Corp. and Daewoo Motor to manufacture the Pontiac LeMans in Korea. Later that year, the company launched a $40 million Eurobond issue in order to expand exports of machine tools, defense products, and aerospace interests. The group also acquired a controlling interest in ZyMOS Corp. In 1987, Daewoo and Carrier Corp., another United Technologies subsidiary, formed a joint venture to manufacture air-conditioner equipment. Daewoo Motor proved to be the group's most profitable venture with a foreign company.

In 1989, Daewoo Shipbuilding and Heavy Machinery suffered heavy losses, making servicing the group's loans increasingly difficult. Daewoo workers protested against years of long hours and low pay and finally received pay raises of more than 20%. Despite these problems, the group reported record sales of W4.79 trillion and net income of W215 billion, an increase of almost 700%. In 1991, Daewoo Motor's waning sales and the rumored friction between Daewoo and General Motors management led to talks

The Players

President of Thomson Multimedia: Alain Prestat. Formerly a senior advisor to the French prime minister, Alain Prestat was appointed chairman of Thomson Consumer Electronics in 1992. He played a key role in the French government's attempt to privatize the company in 1996; however, the company remained a state-owned unit.

President and CEO of Daewoo Corp.: Bae Soon Hoon. Massachusetts Institute of Technology doctoral graduate Bae Soon Hoon, worked for eight years as the head of Daewoo Corp. Under his leadership the company expanded operations in the U.S. as well as across the globe. In 1997, he was named Information and Communications Minister of South Korea. Under fire for public criticisms he made about the government, Bae Soon Hoon resigned after eight months of service.

of dissolving the partnership. One year later, Daewoo agreed to buy out General Motors' half of Daewoo Motor for $170 million. The company also reached an agreement with Honda Motor to begin production of Honda Legends and merged its ship building subsidiaries. In 1995, Daewoo announced plans to quadruple its annual auto output by the year 2000 to 2.2 million vehicles, with 5% of the production located outside of Korea. The firm also agreed to invest $1.1 billion for 60% ownership of Poland's state owned FSO automobile factory and planned to further its interest in the United States and Europe as well. Efforts to acquire Thomson Multimedia fell through in 1996.

Market Forces Driving the Merger

Daewoo Corp. was looking to increase its presence in Europe and the United States in the mid-1990s. The company planned on spending $1.5 billion in France by the year 2000 as part of a $2.6 billion plant construction program. According to an article in *The Indianapolis Star*, Daewoo "wanted to boost its presence in the United States and gain a foothold in high-tech production," and "planned to boost research and development investment by almost 100% in the coming year." The South Korean company also had a strong emphasis on simple products such as televisions, which accounted for 80% of the global consumer electronics market. The acquisition of Thomson

Multimedia would give Daewoo 15% of the television market and would strategically enhance its aggressive plans for growth by combining the French company's popular brand names of RCA, GE, and ProScan with Daewoo's manufacturing and appliance operations. The agreement would also cinch Daewoo's position as one of the world's largest home electronics firms.

At the same time, the French government was looking to privatize Thomson, as part of its plan to restructure the French defense industry, and seeking a buyer who wanted the defense unit of Thomson, which was swimming in FFr 25 billion in debt, as well as the firm's multimedia assets. Lagardere sought Thomson's defense operations as a means of becoming Europe's largest defense electronics company with French ties. To gain those operations, Lagardere was willing to also take on the multimedia business, which it planned to divest to Daewoo.

Approach and Engagement

In October of 1996, the French government entered into a deal with Lagardere, agreeing to sell the state-owned Thomson group to the French defense company for a symbolic FFr1. Under the terms of the deal, the French government would give FFr11 billion to Thomson to relieve some of the firm's debt and Lagardere would give Thomson CSF minority shareholders, who owned 42% of the company, FFr156 per share. Lagardere was only interested in the defense unit of Thomson and planned to sell Thomson Multimedia to Daewoo Corp. for FFr1. In turn, Daewoo promised to protect 5,000 jobs in France and to create 5,000 additional positions. The company also planned to invest heavily in its venture by spending upwards of $1 billion.

By November, Thomson workers were protesting the deal. Although the French government backed the venture, the approval of the Privatisation Commission in France was also necessary. While there were no problems with Lagardere purchasing Thomson CSF, the commission found fault with its plan to sell Thomson Multimedia to Daewoo. Thomson was regarded a French jewel, and Daewoo had a reputation in France for manufacturing lower quality products. The commission was also reluctant to allow the deal because of the transfer of technology that would occur, as well as the doubt that Daewoo would keep its promises of jobs and investments.

In November, the South Korean company began an aggressive ad campaign in France, asking "Do you know the dwarf Daewoo? The 34th biggest world company?" The campaign was part of an effort to counter French resentment that a small Asian company was buying a famous French unit for only FFr1.

The ad pushed the fact that both companies had similar sales and that, unlike Thomson, Daewoo made a profit.

In December 1996, the commission officially canceled the deal. The announcement came at a time when the French government was trying to enhance its reputation in Asia, so the Privatisation Commission ran the risk that its decision might hinder other Asian companies from entering the European market.

Products and Services

In 1998, Thomson S.A. major consumer electric brands included General Electric, RCA, ProScan, Saba, Thomson, and Telefunken. Thomson CSF, the company's defense segment, had products in missile systems and air security, naval systems, communication systems, avionics, and space. Thomson Multimedia, the company's other segment, manufactured televisions, VCRs, DVD players, camcorders, and communications equipment.

In 1998, Daewoo imported and exported over 3,000 items in 165 countries throughout the world. With over 2,000 subsidiaries, the company had a hand in everything from cars to movies. It involved itself with the entertainment industry, international finance, resource development, and the telecommunications industry. Daewoo divisions included machinery, chemical, textile, energy, steel and metal, and media electronics.

Changes to the Industry

According to the *Financial Times (London)*, there were "growing pressures on French authorities to revert to nationalistic industrial policies at the expense of commercial good sense." When French trade unions and socialist parties protested Daewoo's involvement in the Thomson deal, it furthered the pressure. Although the government had been delving into restructuring the state sector by announcing plans to privatize France Telcom and the railways and the nuclear sector, the unrest from the Daewoo deal was a setback.

Other deals were also under scrutiny. Air Liberte, a French airline, was bid on by British Airways, and Britian's GEC was showing interest in Framatome, a French nuclear engineering company. Even though these French-owned companies were not profitable, nationalistic throwbacks saw them as France's pride and joy. By 1997, however, the government continued its efforts to ward off xenophobic tendencies. Korean companies Daewoo, Hyundai Electronics, and Pacific Chemicals had a presence in France. Other large investors in the country included the U.S., Germany, the U.K., the Netherlands, Italy, and Japan.

Review of the Outcome

After announcing that the deal with Daewoo and Thomson Multimedia was off, the French government visited Seoul in January of 1997 in an effort to strengthen relations that had been strained. South Koreans saw the dismissal of the deal as being blatant prejudice against Korean companies trying to invest in France. Later that year, the French government decided to begin a privatization process of the two segments of Thomson separately. In 1998, 26% of Thomson CSF was sold to Alcatel, Dassault Industries, and Aerospatiale Matra. Later that year Microsoft, NEC, Alcatel, and DirecTV each bought a 7.5% interest in Thomson Multimedia.

Research

"Cold Feet in France," in *Financial Times (London)*, 30 October 1996. Discusses rising protest of the Thomson Multimedia sale to Daewoo.

"Daewoo Corp.," in *Notable Corporate Chronologies*, The Gale Group, 1999. Lists major events in the history of Daewoo Corp.

Daewoo Corp. Home Page, available at http://www.dwc.co.kr. Official World Wide Web Home Page for Daewoo Corp. Includes press releases, as well as financial, product, historical, and investor information.

"Daewoo Takes No-Frills Path," in *Financial Times (London)*, 22 October 1996. Explains Daewoo's interest in Thomson Multimedia.

"French Try to Mend Korea Ties," in *Financial Times London*, 8 January 1997. Discusses French concern for Korean outlook in French investments.

Kukolla, Steve. "Analysts Don't Fear Thomson Purchase," in *The Indianapolis Star*, 18 October 1996. Reports U.S. interest in the Thomson Multimedia and Daewoo deal.

"Thomson S.A.," in *Notable Corporate Chronologies*, The Gale Group, 1999. Lists major events in the history of Thomson S.A.

"Tripped on the Way to Market," in *Financial Times (London)*, 5 December 1996. Explains the French government's position in the Daewoo deal.

CHRISTINA M. STANSELL

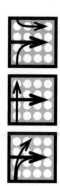

THOMSON & WEST PUBLISHING

Thomson Corp.
Toronto Dominion Bank Tower, Ste. 2706
PO Box 24, Toronto-Dominion Centre
Toronto, ON M5K 1A1
Canada

tel: (416)360-8700
fax: (416)360-8812
web: http://www.thomcorp.com

nationality: Canada
date: June 1996
affected: Thomson Corp., Canada, founded 1934
affected: West Publishing Co., USA, founded 1872

Overview of the Acquisition

The legal publishing field underwent significant consolidation when Thomson Corporation acquired West Publishing Company in 1996. The number of the industry's leaders shrank from three to two, intensifying the rivalry between Thomson and Reed Elsevier. Because of this result, the deal raised numerous objections from competitors, state attorneys general, and the U.S. Department of Justice. After several concessions, the acquisition was approved and completed in June 1996, although some of its elements were argued well into the following year.

History of Thomson Corp.

After trying a variety of professions, Roy Thomson entered into a franchise arrangement in 1930 to sell radios in the remote town of North Bay, Ontario. Two years later he borrowed money to launch a new radio station, CFCH. By 1934 Thomson had acquired additional Ontario radio stations in Kirkland Lake and Timmins. That year he founded Thomson Newspapers by purchasing the *Timmins Press*.

During the 1940s Thomson focused on the newspapers while his new partner, Jack Kent Cooke, assumed management of the radio stations. By 1944 the company's holdings included five newspapers and eight radio stations. Five years later Thomson made his first newspaper purchase outside Ontario, at the same time dissolving the partnership with Cooke.

In 1951 Thomson diversified, acquiring several insurance agencies and folding them together to form the Scottish & York Group. The following year he purchased his first non-Canadian newspaper, *The Independent* of St. Petersburg, Florida, bringing the total newspapers owned to 13.

Thomson purchased the *Scotsman*, Scotland's leading newspaper, in 1953. By then he had moved to Scotland, leaving North American operations in the hands of his son, Kenneth R. Thomson. His residence in Scotland enabled him to move quickly when the U.K. first allowed commercial television broadcasting in 1957, and Thomson established Scottish Television Ltd. (STV). Using the profits from

STV Thomson bought London's leading Sunday paper, *The Sunday Times*, and 17 other local papers from the Kemsley family to form International Thomson Organisation. Kemsley Newspapers, in turn, bought STV in exchange for Kemsley shares—the first "reverse takeover" in the U.K.'s business history. In the end, Thomson controlled 70% of the combined businesses.

The company entered the book and magazine publishing industry in 1961 by purchasing the Illustrated London News Co. Three years later Roy Thomson adopted British citizenship and accepted a seat in the House of Lords as Lord Thomson of Fleet. When international travel became popular in Britain, Thomson bought three package tour companies and a small airline, Britannia Airways, to form Thomson Travel in 1965. By that time, Thomson had acquired Thomas Nelson & Sons, George Rainbird, Hamish Hamilton, and Derwent Publications. It had also launched four new newspapers and had started publishing *Family Circle* and *Living* magazines, as well as a color magazine for the *Sunday Times*. Thomson bought *The Times of London* in 1966, the same year that it formed Sphere, the company's first paperback imprint.

In 1971 the company diversified again, into oil exploration. That year it paid about $5 million to join a North Sea oil drilling venture with Occidental Petroleum, Getty Oil, and Allied Chemical. Two years later the oil consortium struck oil in the Piper field, which drew 800 million barrels of oil. Thomson rebuffed his partners' offer to buy out his 20% stake. In 1974 the venture struck oil in the Claymore field, bringing in 400 million barrels. In 1976 oil accounted for most of the company's profits.

By 1974 the company owned more than 100 newspapers. Two years later Lord Kenneth Thomson assumed control of the family business upon the death of his father. In 1977 the company sold its remaining stake in STV.

The company reorganized in 1978 as International Thomson Organisation Ltd. (ITOL). It was comprised of two main operating subsidiaries: Thomson British Holdings Ltd. and International Thomson Holdings Inc. ITOL made its first acquisition in North America by purchasing the college textbook publisher Wadsworth Inc. in 1979. This purchase was quickly followed by the acquisition of other business and professional publishers, including Callaghan & Company, Van Nostrand Reinhold, Linguistics International, and Thomas Nelson International.

In 1980 Thomson acquired FP Publications' chain of newspapers serving large cities in Canada. That year Thomson Travel was the number-one tour opera-

The Business

Financials

Revenue (1998): US$6.3 billion

Employees (1998): 48,000

SICs / NAICS

sic 2711 - Newspapers

sic 2721 - Periodicals

sic 2731 - Book Publishing

sic 2741 - Miscellaneous Publishing

sic 7375 - Information Retrieval Services

naics 511110 - Newspaper Publishers

naics 511120 - Periodical Publishers

naics 511130 - Book Publishers

naics 511140 - Database and Directory Publishers

naics 514191 - On-Line Information Services

tor in the U.K. and the owner of the country's largest charter airlines. After losing $36 million, the *Times* of London was sold to Australian Rupert Murdoch for GBP 12 million. In 1982 oil field production provided about 75% of ITOL's profits. That year the company was renamed International Thomson Organisation PLC.

The company embarked on a shift from advertising-based publications to more recession-proof, subscription-based publications. To this end it purchased the *American Banker* and *Bond Buyer* financial publications in 1983. Two years later it acquired Gale Research, Inc., a reference book publisher. In 1986 it acquired America's largest business textbook publisher, South-Western Publishing, followed by the Associated Book Publishers, a British producer of legal information and textbooks.

In 1988 Thomson Travel acquired rival Horizon Travel Group. The next year Thomson Newspapers Ltd. and International Thomson Organisation merged to form The Thomson Corp. After witnessing its oil ventures lose money over the past several years, Thomson sold its remaining oil and gas holdings, enabling the company to focus its resources on publishing and information services.

Thomson Newspapers made its largest purchase at that time, that of five U.S. newspapers and weekly publications, as well as eight Canadian papers and the *Financial Times of Canada*. In 1991 it purchased

The Officers

Chairman: Kenneth R. Thomson

President and CEO: Richard J. Harrington

Exec. VP and Chief Operating Officer: David H. Shaffer

Chief Financial Officer: Robert D. Daleo

Exec. VP, Human Resources: Theron H. Hoffman

Maxwell's Macmillan Professional and Business Reference Publishing for $57 million. The following year it bought JPT Publishing for its 40 journals and the Institute for Scientific Information, the world's number-one commercial scientific research database. That year Thomson ventured into nonpublishing forms of media by releasing a total of 190 online services, 161 CD-ROM products, and other software.

In 1994 it purchased Information Access Company (IAC), a database provider of full-text online articles from periodicals, for $465 million. The next year it sold numerous newspaper holdings in Ontario and Canada's Atlantic provinces to Hollinger Inc. It continued to dispose of its newspaper assets, selling more than 40 during 1996. That year it added to its non-print holdings by acquiring Medstat Group, an electronic supplier of healthcare information. It also attempted to purchase Mead Data Central, producer of LEXIS-NEXIS, but lost out to rival Reed Elsevier.

History of West Publishing Co.

In 1872 John B. West, Sr., an entrepreneur and traveling book salesman, established John B. West Publisher and Bookseller, targeting lawyers who needed law treatises, legal forms, dictionaries, and general office supplies. Realizing that no single publishing company offered expedient and accurate case reporting, West took on the task of making available new and previous court reports.

Four years later his brother, accountant Horatio West, joined the company to record Minnesota Supreme Court rulings. By that time the firm's principal product was *The Syllabi*, an eight-page weekly pamphlet containing legal excerpts from Minnesota and Wisconsin cases. West soon established a reputation as a reliable source of information and supplies for the legal community.

In 1876 the company launched *The North Western Reporter*, which covered everything in *The Syllabi* as well as Minnesota U.S. Circuit Court decisions, select Minnesota and Wisconsin lower court cases, and abstracts from select cases throughout the U.S. West introduced a new series, the *North Western*, in 1879 to provide full coverage of current decisions in Minnesota, Wisconsin, Michigan, Nebraska, Iowa, and the Dakota Territory.

West introduced the *Federal Reporter* in 1880 for information on decisions by U.S. District and Circuit Courts around the country. Two years later it launched the *U.S. Supreme Court Reporter* In 1887 the company expanded the *Reporter* to provide coast-to-coast coverage by introducing the *Pacific, Atlantic, South Western, South Eastern,* and *Southern*.

In 1890 West introduced the *American Digest System*, comprised of listings and synopses of federal and state cases dating back to 1638. This new publication implemented the Key Number System, categorizing cases by topic, subtopic, and headnote. That year it also purchased John A. Mallory's *Complete Digest*, a potential competitor, and hired Mallory to perfect the Key Number System. In 1896 Volume One of the *Century Digest*, the definitive encyclopedia of all existing case law, was unveiled at the annual convention of the American Bar Association.

West expanded into the publication of law textbooks in 1910. By that time the company was so influential that it had not only reconstructed the field of legal reference publishing, but also had the ability to alter the manner in which law was taught. In 1927 West was commissioned by a congressional joint committee on law revision to join with the Edward Thompson Co. in publishing the *United States Code Annotated*. The original set consisted of 61 volumes, and eventually grew to 215 permanent hardcovers that were continually updated with pamphlets and statutory supplements.

The company continued to expand during the 1940s and 1950s. In 1945 it employed 645 people; by 1950 that number had multiplied to 1,172. In 1956 West implemented teletypesetting for the first time. Printing quality and efficiency improved with the 1962 installation of its first web offset press. In 1968 Dwight D. Opperman became president.

Computers began impacting the publishing business during the 1970s, pointing to the direction of the future. In 1973 one of West's major competitors, Mead Data Central, introduced its LEXIS computer-assisted legal research service. Two years later West followed suit, unveiling its own computer assisted legal research service, WESTLAW. In 1992 this service introduced WIN, a simplified natural language search and retrieval process.

In 1993 West introduced state statutes and *United States Code Annotated* on CD-ROM. That year it acquired both the Bank-Baldwin Law Publishing Company and Tailored Solutions, an applications software company. The following year WESTLAW became the first online legal research service to offer voice recognition capabilities. West also acquired the Rutter Group, a publisher of California legal materials, and Information America, Inc., a provider of public record information and investigative tools.

West opened its first International Information Center in London, England, in 1995. That year the company entered into a licensing agreement with Dow Jones to be the exclusive online provider of *The Wall Street Journal* aside from the Dow Jones News/Retrieval Service.

Market Forces Driving the Acquisition

By 1996 Thomson Corp. was a diversified conglomerate in the publishing industry. The Canadian company produced newspapers and reference products for the educational, legal, business, and general information segments. Although its content base was strong, it lacked an efficient means of electronic distribution.

Thomson had made an effort to acquire such a distribution system in 1994, when it bid for Mead Data Central, producer of the popular LEXIS-NEXIS online legal and business information service. It lost out to Reed Elsevier, an Anglo-Dutch company that used the purchase to strengthen its own legal publishing operations, thereby becoming an even larger rival to Thomson.

West Publishing announced in 1995 that it was putting itself up for sale. This Minnesota-based company published a number of legal resources, but its most valuable asset was the WESTLAW online information provider. This service was a strong competitor of LEXIS-NEXIS, and would increase Thomson's position against Reed Elsevier PLC. At the same time, the acquisition of West by Thomson would eliminate West as a competitor in the legal publishing field, reducing the segment's leading companies from three to two. Most important to Thomson, however, was West's ready distribution system. Because it lacked an electronic system of its own, Thomson relied on LEXIS for distribution of its legal products, an undesirable situation since it was owned by a competitor. By acquiring West, not only could Thomson's legal holdings become available through WESTLAW, that service's technology could be applied to other, non-legal divisions within Thomson. For these reasons, plus its previous loss in purchasing Mead Data Central, Thomson bid heavily for West.

The Players

Thomson Chairman: Kenneth R. Thomson. In 1953, 30-year old Kenneth R. Thomson took the helm of the company's North American operations from his father, Roy Thomson. In 1976 he succeeded his father as head of the company. Still serving as chairman of the empire, Thomson is also the chairman of The Woodbridge Company Ltd.

West Publishing Chairman and CEO: Dwight D. Opperman. Dwight Opperman succeeded Lee Slater as president of West Publishing in 1968. He remained at the head of the company for more than a quarter of a decade. When his company was acquired by Thomson in 1996, Opperman was named chairman emeritus.

Approach and Engagement

In February 1996 Thomson announced its planned acquisition of West Publishing in a cash deal of $3.425 billion. The size of this deal, which would be Thomson's largest acquisition to date, surprised industry analysts, many of whom believed the price to be too high. It was more than four times West's 1995 revenues of $825 million and 17 times its operating profits of $200 million. Yet given the WESTLAW assets, and what they would mean to Thomson, most admitted that the deal might be worth the hefty price. This was especially true in consideration of Thomson's recent loss in its pursuit for LEXIS-NEXIS. As Andrew Prozes, divisional president of Southam Inc., said in *Maclean's*, "I think they were determined not to be shut out this time."

Others, however, questioned the wisdom of investing so much in a system that was facing increased competition. WESTLAW was an online database of a hundred years' worth of legal statutes, cases, codes, and regulations. The company editorially enhanced those elements, adding such features as cross-indexing and annotations, but the basic information was part of the public domain, and therefore was freely available from the government. The proliferation of the Internet, moreover, could facilitate the introduction of electronic versions of this information in competition with WESTLAW. Thomson dismissed this threat, confident that WESTLAW's value-added elements would be difficult to duplicate.

On June 19, 1996, the U.S. Department of Justice approved the deal, provided that the companies agreed to divest more than 50 legal titles, valued at a total of $275 million and accounting for about four percent of West's revenues. The acquisition was completed shortly thereafter.

During the 60-day comment period that followed, three competitors, Reed Elsevier among them, voiced disapproval of the government's settlement. They considered the conditions to be too lax. The stipulations, they believed, would have little impact on addressing competition in the online legal publishing market as they required Thomson to shed only its least profitable titles. In response, the Department of Justice and the attorneys general of seven states filed suit in September 1996 to block the merger.

The government sought a revised agreement in which Thomson and West would charge reduced fees for competitors who wished to use West's controversial Star Pagination system. This citation system was developed by West and had become the legal system's standard for citing case law. The controversy over the system arose over its copyright. West's copyright claim had been challenged several times in court, with rulings in West's favor most of the time, but the matter was not finally resolved. With West's claim undetermined, its right to charge companies for a licensing fee to utilize the system was questionable.

To resolve that issue for their pending merger, Thomson and West agreed to lower their licensing fees, while spreading out fee increases over a greater number of years. This pricing arrangement encouraged would-be competitors to introduce their products in the market more easily. In late December 1996, however, a U.S. Court reversed the agreement, claiming that the Star Pagination system should be made available to all comers for free, not merely at reduced prices, since West's copyright claim had not been judicially resolved. In a subsequent settlement of this matter, the parties agreed that West would defer licensing fees until December 31, 2000, or a final Supreme Court decision on the issue, which ever came first.

On March 31, 1997, the Department of Justice and the state attorneys general granted their final approval to the deal that had for all intents and purposes been concluded ten months earlier.

Products and Services

Thomson served five core market sectors:

The Legal and Regulatory Group provided information and software-based solutions to law, tax, accounting, corporate finance, and human resource professionals. Its principal businesses and activities included West Group, serving the legal information marketplace; RIA Group, delivering solutions for the accounting, tax, corporate finance, and human resource marketplaces; Thomson Legal and Professional Group, serving the needs of legal, tax, and business professionals outside the Americas; and Thomson & Thomson Group, provider of trademark information to corporate and law firm attorneys, intellectual property professionals, and trademark agents. The Legal and Regulatory Group generated revenues in excess of US $2.2 billion in 1998.

Thomson Financial provided proprietary information services and work solutions to the global financial community. Its markets included retail and investment banks, institutional investment firms, securities brokers and dealers, corporations, underwriters of municipal bonds and syndicated loans, and consumers. The group's operating brands and businesses included American Banker/Bond Buyer, Faulkner & Gray, First Call Corp., ILX Systems, The Investext Group, Securities Data Co., Thomson Electronic Settlements Group, and Thomson Investment Software. Sales in this group surpassed US $1 billion for the first time in 1998, registering US $1.2 billion.

Thomson Learning provided courseware, primarily textbooks and related multimedia products, designed to provide total teaching and learning solutions. Its principal brands and businesses included Brooks/Cole Publishing, Delmar Publishers, International Thomson Publishing, ITP Nelson, and Wadsworth Publishing Co. These operations accounted for US $736 million in sales during 1998.

Reference, Scientific & Healthcare provided information and services to researchers in specific segments of healthcare, academic, business, scientific, and government marketplaces. Principal brands and businesses included Information Access Company (IAC), Gale Research, Physicians' Desk Reference, Primary Source Media, The Medstat Group, Institute for Scientific Information, Derwent Information, Jane's Information Group, and Mitchell International. This group generated 1998 revenues of US $1.03 billion.

Thomson Newspapers was comprised of 68 daily newspapers, ranking it third in the industry in terms of newspaper ownership, and with a total daily circulation of 1.9 million, it ranked ninth in circulation. The company also produced numerous non-daily newspapers and more than 250 advertising and specialty publications in both print and electronic formats. Its five newspapers with daily circulation in excess of 75,000 were *The Globe and Mail, Connecticut Post, Winnipeg Free Press, Phoenix Tribune Suburban,* and *Victoria Times Colonist.* This group generated sales of US $951 million in 1998.

Review of the Outcome

In January 1997 West Publishing was joined with the Thomson Legal Publishing unit to form West Group. Maintaining the headquarters of the former West Publishing, the new unit had revenues of $1.1 billion and 9,500 employees, and was the foremost provider of U.S. legal information.

In May 1997 Thomson announced the elimination of 231 West employees, the majority of which were employed at two satellite keyboarding offices. Later that year, West Group joined with a London-based Thomson subsidiary to enter the European online legal market by launching WESTLAW Europe.

With the merger integration completed, Thomson resumed its acquisition of companies in line with its core operations. Among its purchases during 1998 were Tudor House Publications Ltd., Computer Language Research Inc., and digiTRADE. Company revenues for 1998 totaled US $6.3 billion.

Research

Faustmann, John. "Buying Legal History: Thomson's Biggest Takeover Draws Mixed Reaction," in *Maclean's*, 11 March 1996. Profiles Thomson and its quest for electronic distribution resources.

Griffith, Cary. "Thomson Corporation Acquires West Publishing," in *Information Today*, April 1996. Offers explanations for Thomson's acquisition of West.

———. "The Thomson/West Merger Takes a Short Breath," in *Information Today*, February 1997. Details the controversial pagination system and the Court's objection to the terms of its licensing.

Hellwege, Jean. "West-Thomson Merger Hits Snag over Pagination Copyright Claim," in *Trial*, March 1997. Outlines the Court's objections to the merger accord.

Sileo, Lorraine. "Analysis: Thomson Pays Big to Finally Own Online Network," in *Media Daily*, 26 February 1996. Briefly describes Thomson's need for technology.

"Thomson Acquires West Publishing for $3.425 Billion," in *Online Newsletter*, 1 April 1996. Describes the terms of the merger.

"The Thomson Corp.," in *Notable Corporate Chronologies*, The Gale Group, 1999. Provides a history of the company.

Thomson Corp. Home Page, available at http://www.thomcorp.com. Official World Wide Web Page for Thomson. Includes annual reports, press releases, and product information.

"West Publishing Co.," in *Notable Corporate Chronologies*, The Gale Group, 1999. Offers an account of the company's history.

PATRICIA ARCHILLA

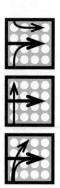

3COM & U.S. ROBOTICS

3Com Corp.
5400 Bayfront Plaza
Santa Clara, CA 95052-8145
USA

tel: (408)326-5000
fax: (408)326-5001
web: http://www.3com.com

nationality: USA
date: June 12, 1997
affected: 3Com Corp., USA, founded 1979
affected: U.S. Robotics Inc., USA, founded 1975

Overview of the Merger

The $8.5 billion merger of 3Com Corp. and U.S. Robotics Corp in 1997, the largest merger in the history of the computer networking sector, created a networking industry giant second only to Cisco Systems. Sales at 3Com grew by 31% to $5.6 billion after the joining of the LAN (local area network) and WAN (wide area network) vendors, who immediately began working on integrating their 800 plus products to meet client demand for end-to-end networking capabilities. The 3Com product line grew from network interface cards and enterprise systems to include remote access networking products and modems. Despite increased revenues, 3Com posted a $51.2 million loss in the first quarter of 1998, due mainly to severe inventory problems, a result of the merger.

History of 3Com Corp.

In 1973, while employed by Xerox, Robert Metcalfe and a group of engineers invented Ethernet, a local area network (LAN) system which linked computers and similar equipment within a building. Six years later, Metcalfe left Xerox to establish 3Com Corp., a computer network technology consulting firm. The name stood for computer, communication, and compatibility. After securing $1.1 million in backing, Metcalfe and his three partners began manufacturing LAN equipment with Ethernet technology. In 1981, 3Com introduced an Ethernet transceiver and adapter, its first product.

Two years later, 3Com achieved profitability for the first time. In March of 1984, the company went public, raising $10 million in capital. As the networking industry took off in the mid 1980s, 3Com grew at a rate of 300% annually and established a new software division for the development of complex network software. In 1985, the company began marketing its 3Server computer, which functioned as a server with a client-server platform; within a year, it accounted for 32% of 3Com's total revenue. Although it held eight percent of the LAN market, 3Com recognized that competitors like IBM were incorporating LAN hardware and software into their computer packages, and the firm began developing and marketing more comprehensive computer network systems.

Because it sought to market computers that functioned as clients within a client-server platform, 3Com agreed to merge with Convergent Technologies Inc., a maker of UNIX-based workstations, in 1986. However, the deal fell through when 3Com's investment banker raised concerns about the transaction. During the year, 3Com also introduced 3+, its first network operating system software. In 1987, 3Com began reorganizing itself as a workgroup computing company that manufactured and marketed personal computer network systems; new network servers, software programs, and network adapter cards were launched. 3Com acquired Bridge Communications Inc. for $151 million to become the largest independent networking manufacturer in the world and the second leading computer network provider, trailing only Digital Equipment Corp. The company also established a joint venture with Microsoft Corp. to make and market LAN Manager network software for the OS/2 platform; less than a year later, 3Com introduced 3+Open, its own version of Microsoft's LAN Manager.

Despite the launch of Bridge Communication's new inter-networking products, earnings fell in 1990, due mainly to intense competition in the network operating system market. As a result, 3Com shifted its focus away from client/server networking and towards comprehensive networking and inter-network connections. The LAN Manager marketing agreement with Microsoft was terminated, and the 3Com's five divisions were condensed into three groups: product development, internal operations, and sales. Eric Benhamou was tapped to return the company to profitability.

Benhamou first established a Network Adapter Division to market Ethernet cards and a Networks Systems Division which encompassed three previous product-oriented groups: enterprise systems; distributed systems; and management, messaging, and connectivity. After losing market share to Novell for three consecutive years, the company halted its network operating system software operations in 1991. The firm also laid off roughly 12% of its workforce and posted an annual loss of $33 million.

In 1992, sales bounced back as restructuring efforts began to pay off. 3Com purchased the Data Networks unit of BICC PLC, gaining access to the LinkBuilder ECS, an Ethernet chassis hub. A year later, 3Com diversified into Token-Ring network technology with the purchase of Star-Tek Inc. Acquisitions during 1994 included Synernetics, a LAN switches maker; Centrum Communications Inc., a provider of remote network access products; and NiceCom Ltd., an ATM technology firm. As revenues moved toward the $1 billion mark, 3Com became a *Fortune* 500 company

The Business

Financials

Revenue (1998): $5.42 billion

Employees (1998): 12,920

SICs / NAICS

sic 3577 - Computer Peripheral Equipment Nec

sic 3661 - Telephone & Telegraph Apparatus

naics 334119 - Other Computer Peripheral Equipment
    Manufacturing

and stock prices reached a record of $68.25 per share. Growth continued with the 1995 purchases of AccessWorks, an ISDN modem maker; Sonix Communications, an ISDN inter-networking operation; Primary Access, a remote access system provider; and Chipcom, a maker of chassis hubs and switches.

3Com reorganized into two units in 1996: 3Com Systems, which manufactured switches, hubs, and routers; and 3Com Interface Products, which made adapter cards and related products. The company continued it acquisition spree with the $65 million purchase of Axon, a maker of remote network management software, and the $245 million purchase of OnStream Networks. In February of 1997, 3Com and U.S. Robotics announced their impending $8.5 billion merger, which was finalized on June 12, 1997.

History of U.S. Robotics Inc.

In 1975, Casey Cowell teamed up with two former classmates, Paul Collard and Steve Muka, to build a keyboard and acoustic coupler for communication over phone lines via handsets. They named their new enterprise U.S. Robotics. The company began selling a range of equipment made by DEC, General Electric, Applied Digital Data Televideo, and Perkin-Elmer in 1976. A 1979 FCC ruling allowed AT&T products to be plugged directly into phone lines; this prompted U.S. Robotics to move into modem technology. Three years later, the firm launched Password, the industry's first 1200-bps auto-dial modem to use standard, off-the-shelf microprocessors.

In 1984, U.S. Robotics relocated to a large factory in Skokie, a suburb north of Chicago, to manufacture its modems, which operated eight times faster than they had been only a few years prior. Within a year, U.S. Robotics had launched the first affordable 2400-

The Officers

Chairman of the Board and Chief Executive Officer: Eric A. Benhamou

President and Chief Operating Officer: Bruce Claflin

VP and Chief Financial Officer: Christopher B. Paisley

Sr. VP and Chief Technical Officer: John H. Hart

bps modem, the Courier 2400; in 1987, the firm introduced the Courier HST 9600-bps, which became the first high-speed model designed for personal computer and business workstation environments to sell for under $1,000.

An acquisition spree was launched in 1989 with the purchase of Miracom Technology Ltd., based in the United Kingdom. Communications Research Group, maker of BLAST communications products, was acquired in 1990. U.S. Robotics also introduced the Courier V.32bis modem. Net sales for the year jumped 50% to $56.4 million. U.S. Robotics became one of the main players in portable-to-WAN network access via its acquisition of Touchbase Systems, Inc. in 1991. The firm also established U.S. Robotics, S.A. in Europe, and in 1992, entered the LAN-WAN connectivity market with the unveiling of Shared Access remote LAN access products. A joint venture with Sears Technology and IBM Corp. to supply Total Control WAN Hub technology gave U.S. Robotics access to the WAN marketplace.

The firm acquired France-based P.N.B., S.A., a designer and manufacturer of data communications products for IBM-compatible personal computers and workstations, in 1993. A year later, U.S. Robotics launched Shared Access Fax Server for both Ethernet and Token-Ring networks; the server supported OCR, email routing of faxes, and sophisticated management utilities. Purchases during 1995 included ISDN Systems, for $40 million, and Palm Computing Inc. U.S. Robotics considered acquiring its rival in the modem market, Hayes Microcomputer Products Inc., but the deal later fell apart. By 1996, U.S. Robotics held a 30% market share of the modem industry and reached nearly $2 billion in revenues. Along with other telecommunications companies, U.S. Robotics formed the ISDN Forum to facilitate the use of integrated services digital networks (ISDN) by service providers and end users.

In February of 1997, U.S. Robotics shipped its new x2 56K modems. At roughly the same time, CEO Casey Cowell began discussing merger plans with 3Com; the $8.5 billion deal was completed on June 12, 1997.

Market Forces Driving the Merger

The networking industry as a whole saw an unprecedented level of consolidation in 1997. Nearly as noteworthy as the $8.5 billion 3Com and U.S. Robotics union, was the $3.7 billion merger of Ascend Communications Inc. and Cascade Communications Inc., which combined a WAN access provider with a WAN core switching technology provider; it was second largest merger in networking history. This industry's consolidation was mainly market driven: network equipment providers scrambled to offer Internet Service Providers (ISPs) comprehensive and integrated technologies, allowing the ISPs to distinguish their services from the growing number of start-up operations. Enterprise carriers, who made up the other major client base of the networking industry, were also demanding integrated end-to-end networking products.

The CEOs of both 3Com and U.S. Robotics—Eric Benhamou and Casey Cowell, respectively—pointed to these client demands as the major factor for their merger. U.S. Robotics, a leader in WAN equipment, lacked the LAN technology offered by 3Com. Cowell realized that U.S. Robotics' product line was too limited to sustain a competitive edge in the rapidly consolidating market, particularly with industry giants like Cisco Systems marketing comprehensive, integrated connectivity equipment to corporate clients. At the same time, along with gaining access to the WAN technology of U.S. Robotics, Benhamou recognized that 3Com—which served mainly a corporate market—would secure inroads to two new distribution channels: Internet access companies and retail outlets. Because sales of networking products to small businesses and consumers had begun growing more rapidly than traditional networking markets, access to the burgeoning retail market, in particular, would offer 3Com yet another competitive edge.

Industry analysts pointed to two additional motives, not only for the merger itself, but also for the speediness of the deal and the $68.25 per share price to which Cowell agreed. Less than a year prior to the merger, U.S. Robotics' stock had traded for $100 a share, yet Cowell accepted the low offer from 3COM despite the fact that U.S. Robotics had just shipped its new x2 56K modems, which could transmit data at roughly twice the speed of earlier modems. This led many analysts to suspect that Cowell was concerned about the success of the x2 technology. Both Motorola Inc. and Rockwell International Corp. had announced plans to introduce 56K modems shortly after U.S.

Robotics launched its x2 technology. Another factor, according to Salomon Brothers Inc., was the five percent loss in remote access products market share U.S. Robotics had experienced during the twelve months preceding the merger.

Approach and Engagement

Recognizing that his firm's lack of LAN capability was turning into "an uphill battle," U.S. Robotics CEO Cowell approached 3Com in January of 1997 hoping to hammer out a merger deal; roughly one month later, the two companies reached an agreement in which shareholders of U.S. Robotics would receive 1.75 shares of 3Com stock for each U.S. Robotics share they held. In the week following the announcement, U.S. Robotics stock dropped eight percent and 3Com stock tumbled 15% to roughly $33 per share.

U.S. Robotics shareholders protested the deal, mainly because it offered no easy out to U.S. Robotics if 3Com stock continued to lose value. In fact, the terms of the agreement stipulated that U.S. Robotics would be fined $75 million for terminating the deal to considering alternative offers, as well as another $75 million if they were sold to a rival bidder. Six shareholders filed suit in Delaware Chancery Court, but the charges were later dismissed.

The value of the merger, originally $7.35 billion, dropped to $6.71 billion during the months following the announcement; however, by June of 1997, when shareholders of both companies approved the deal, it was valued at $8.5 billion based on 3Com's stock price of $45 per share.

While announcing the completion of the transaction, Benhamou told shareholders, "The next wave of growth in networking will be led by companies that offer faster access to the network, that build more intelligence into the network, and that lower the cost of network ownership. The new 3Com is now best positioned to meet and surpass these requirements and deliver our solutions to the broadest set of customers in the industry." On the same day, Cowell told his shareholders: "3Com and U.S. Robotics can now accomplish together things that no other networking company in the industry can achieve alone." Cowell also later noted that the 800 plus products of the two companies would need to be integrated as quickly as possible to meet the goal of offering clients "the benefits of integrated end-to-end systems."

Products and Services

After completion of the merger, 3Com reorganized into three units: Enterprise Systems, Client Access, and Carrier Systems. **Enterprise Systems**

The Players

Chairman and CEO of 3Com Corp.: Eric A. Benhamou. Between 1981 and 1987, Stanford graduate Eric Benhamou served as vice president of engineering for Bridge Communications, a networking firm he co-founded in the early 1980s. Bridge Communications merged with 3Com Corp. in 1987. Three years later, after posting a year-end loss of $27.7 million, 3Com tapped Benhamou as CEO, assigning him the task of returning the company to profitability. Under Benhamou's tutelage, 3Com achieved Fortune 500 status in 1994 with revenues of $617 million. In 1992, he was awarded the President's Environment and Conservation Challenge Award, the most prestigious environmental award in the United States, and in 1997, Benhamou was named to the President's Information Technology Advisory Committee.

Chairman and CEO of U.S. Robotics Inc.: Casey Cowell. In 1976, a year after graduating from the University of Chicago with a bachelor's degree in economics, Casey Cowell co-founded U.S. Robotics. During his 20 year tenure at U.S. Robotics, Cowell transformed the fledgling networking operation into a leader in remote access networking technology and modem manufacturing, with roughly $2 billion in sales. Recognized as a pioneer in the technology industry, Cowell was named one of *Business Week*'s "25 Top Managers" in 1995 and the *Crain's Chicago Business* "Executive of the Year" in 1996. When U.S. Robotics merged with 3Com Corp. in 1997, Cowell took on the non-managerial role of vice chairman.

makes and manufactures network control devices, switches, routers, and network management software. 3Com is the world's leading manufacturer of ethernet hubs, fast ethernet hubs, stackable hubs, and desktop switching devices. The firm's LAN switching technology holds the number two market share spot.

Client Access makes LAN and WAN access devices, including modems and network interface cards (NICs). 3Com's 56Kbps modems, 10 Mbps NICs, and 10/100 Mbps NICs all secure more market share than competing products.

Carrier Systems designs remote access communications equipment for Internet Service Providers

(ISPs) and other carriers. 3Com is the major vendor serving nine out of the ten largest ISPs in North America, including America Online and Compuserve. It is also a major supplier to leading ISPs in Europe, Latin America, and Asia.

Changes to the Industry

According to an article in *Network World*, the 3Com and U.S. Robotics merger created a new dividing line between networking industry players: those with sales in excess of $5 billion, namely 3Com and Cisco; and those will lesser revenues, such as Cabletron Systems and Bay Networks. With sales reaching less than half those of 3Com and Cisco, companies like Cabletron and Bay were left scrambling to find strategic partners. Most analysts believed that the 3Com merger would likely spawn additional industry consolidation, as evidenced by the $3.6 billion joining of Ascend Communications and Cascade Communications Corp. only three weeks after the finalization of the 3Com merger.

Review of the Outcome

As predicted by several analysts, 3Com struggled in the months following the merger. The firm faced the daunting task of integrating over 800 products, and an inventory glut caused stock prices to tumble. The company posted a $51.2 million loss in the first quarter of 1998. It took over a year for 3Com to get back on track; in the first quarter of 1999, share prices beat forecasts for the first time since the merger with U.S. Robotics was completed.

In an October edition of *PC Week*, Benhamou detailed the reason for 3Com's turnaround: "We're seeing an expansion of what used to be referred to as the networking industry. We used to only deal with enterprise customers and carriers and IPSs. Now there are two major new constituencies that have emerged as two full-fledged market segments. One is small and medium size businesses and the other is networking products for consumers and SOHO (small offices/home offices). 3Com is the first to address the fullness of the four major components." In fact, 3Com's traditional competitors—Cisco, Bay Networks, and Cabletron—didn't have the toehold in these new markets that 3Com boasted after the merger, which positioned the firm as the only supplier offering end-to-end connectivity to all four of the networking industry's strategic markets.

Research

"3 Com Corp.," in *Notable Corporate Chronologies*, The Gale Group, 1999. Lists major events in the history of 3Com Corp., including the merger.

"3Com Corp. Briefing Book," in *The Wall Street Journal Online*, available at http://www.wsj.com. This section of *The Wall Street Journal Online* offers a company overview, stock charts, links to archived articles, financials, and press releases.

3Com Corp. Home Page, available at http://www.3com.com. Official World Wide Web Home Page for 3Com Corp. Includes news, financial, product, historical, and employment information.

Berinato, Scott. "3Com-USR Merger Goes Forward," in *PC Week*, 23 June 1997. Outlines the challenges 3Com faces in integrating its products with those of U.S. Robotics.

Cahill, Joseph B. "Why Fear Led U.S. Robotics to Sell Now," in *Crain's Chicago Business*, 3 March 1997. Explores U.S. Robotics CEO Cowell's motives for approaching 3Com, as well as his reasons for moving quickly and agreeing to a price that some analysts found surprisingly low.

Carlton, Jim. "3Com Earnings, Topping Forecasts, Suggests a Rebound," in *The Wall Street Journal*, 23 September 1998. Discusses 3Com's strong quarterly performance and examines the reason for 3Com's turnaround.

"Let the Good Times Roll," in *PC Week*, 5 October 1998. In an interview, CEO Eric Benhamou details 3Com's post-merger struggles and the company's strengths nearly a year and a half after the merger.

Mills, Elinor. "3Com Beats Estimates at 36 Cents Per Share," in *Network World*, 4 January 1999. Discusses 3Com's first strong quarter since the merger.

Petrovsky, Mary. "Consolidation Breeds Interesting Times," in *Network World*, 26 January 1998. The impact of recent consolidation—including the 3Com and U.S. Robotics merger—on the networking industry as a whole is discussed in this article.

Reinhardt, Andy. "One David Taking on Two Goliaths," in *Business Week*, 19 May 1997. Explains that not only does CEO Benhamou have to seamlessly integrate 3Com and U.S. Robotics, but he also must fend off competitors Cisco and Intel at the same time.

"U.S. Robotics Inc.," in *Notable Corporate Chronologies*, The Gale Group, 1999. Lists major events in the history of U.S. Robotics Inc. before the merger.

Wallace, Bob. "3Com Unveils Reorganization" in *Computerworld*, 21 April 1997. Details the reorganization of 3Com in 1996, as well as its plans for reorganization upon finalization of the merger.

ANNAMARIE L. SHELDON

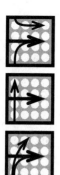

TIME & WARNER

nationality: USA
date: August 1989
affected: Time Inc., USA, founded 1923
affected: Warner Communications, USA, founded 1922

Time Warner Inc.
75 Rockefeller Plaza
New York, NY 10019
USA

tel: (212)484-8000
fax: (212)956-2847
web: http://www.timewarner.com

Overview of the Merger

The merger of Time Inc. and Warner Communications in 1989 was, as Bruce Wasserstein, author of *Big Deal: The Battle For Control of America's Leading Corporations*, wrote, "the capstone of the 1980s vertical integration movement." The deal, forged after numerous battles with Paramount, was finally completed in August 1989, forming a $15.2 billion media giant with interests in cable, movie and television production, book and magazine publishing, and record/music businesses.

History of Time Inc.

In 1923, two Yale University sophomores, Briton Hadden and Henry Robinson Luce, founded Time Inc. That year, the pair published the first weekly issue of *Time* magazine. With Hadden as editor and Luce acting as the business manager, the first magazine was 32 pages long and included postcard inserts soliciting subscribers. It had 30,000 subscribers after only one year of circulation.

Luce and Hadden launched a second publication in 1924, *The Saturday Review of Literature*. Time's printing operations moved to R.R. Donnelly in Chicago and editorial moved back to New York. Hadden assumed the duties of business manager, and Luce took command of the journalistic direction of *Time*. In 1929, Hadden died at the age of 31, and in order to protect ownership of the company, Luce and other Time employees purchased most of Hadden's shares of company stock.

Throughout the 1930s, Time introduced several popular magazines, including *Fortune* and *Life*. The company also dove into radio shows with the *The March of Time* show, which re-enacted historical events. In 1937, Luce created the company's divisional system with each fundamental publication receiving its own publisher, managing editor, and advertising director. Although the company had come far since its inception, *Time* magazine was in trouble. In 1938, the company acquired *Literary Digest* to battle against *Time*'s circulation problems. About 60% of the new magazine's subscribers transferred subscriptions to *Time*.

The Business

Financials

Revenue (1998): $14,582.0 million

Employees (1998): 67,500

SICs / NAICS

sic 2721 - Periodicals

sic 4832 - Radio Broadcasting Stations

sic 4833 - Television Broadcasting Stations

sic 2731 - Book Publishing

sic 7812 - Motion Picture & Video Production

sic 2782 - Blankbooks & Looseleaf Binders

sic 5961 - Catalog & Mail-Order Houses

naics 513111 - Radio Networks

naics 513112 - Radio Stations

naics 323116 - Manifold Business Form Printing

naics 323118 - Blankbook, Loose-leaf Binder and Device
  Manufacturing

By 1941, *Time*'s circulation approached one million and *Life* had weekly sales of 3.3 million magazines. Upon retirement of Luce, Time reorganized operations under C.D. Jackson. Luce had redefined the job of publisher and appointed James A. Linen III to the position. In 1949, Edward K. Thompson began serving as managing editor of *Life*. He dismantled the periodical's divisional structure and led the magazine to its most successful decade.

Time Inc. continued to grow in the 1950s. The company created *House and Home* as a compliment to *Forum*. It also founded the Time-Life Broadcast subsidiary with 50% interest in KOB and KOB-TV in Albuquerque, New Mexico. In 1953, Time launched *Life en Espanol* as a companion to *Life International*. One year later the company acquired KLZ-AM and KLZ-TV of Denver, Colorado, its first wholly-owned and-operated station. In another attempt to diversify, Time launched *Sports Illustrated*.

In 1961, Time created Time-Life Books. The company's sales were skyrocketing, as management continued to make such innovative purchases as textbook publisher Silver Burdett, acquired in a $6 million stock swap. Time initiated a joint venture with General Electric and General Learning Corp. to sell learning tools in 1966.

Time announced plans to sell broadcast properties to concentrate on cable television in 1970. Two years later, the company ceased publication of *Life* magazine, which was later reintroduced as a monthly magazine, and launched *Money* magazine. Time also made another diversification move and merged with Temple Industries, a producer of lumber, plywood, and other building materials, for $129 million. The company ended the decade by furthering its diversification efforts and introducing *People* magazine.

In 1980, Time launched Cinemax, a pay television service. By 1983, in an effort to focus interests on its video and print businesses, Time divested some of its units by forming Temple-Inland, which was spun off to Time shareholders. Time now focused on its seven magazines, HBO, Cinemax, and Time-Life Books. In 1987, Time acquired a stake in Turner Broadcasting System Inc. and one year later added four new magazine titles, bringing the total number of published magazines to 24. It also paid $185 million for a 50% interest in Whittle Communications.

In 1990, Time Inc. merged with Warner Communications for $14 billion, creating the world's largest entertainment and media concern. The Time-Warner Inc. combination was almost thwarted by an unsolicited $10.7 billion bid for Time by Paramount Pictures. The new company, Time Warner, began integrating the two companies' operations. Warner Publishing was created to oversee all magazine and book publishing operations. *Entertainment Weekly* was launched, and management planned to open a nationwide chain of retail stores to sell merchandise featuring Looney Toons characters.

Time Warner formed Time Warner Entertainment to oversee its cable and film operations, and made several key acquisitions in the 1990s, including TBS in 1996. The company formed relationships with TCI, which allowed its WB network to reach nearly all of the U.S. In 1998, Time Warner owned rights to the television show *ER*, and cable syndication rights for *Seinfeld*. The company remained focused on its broadcasting concerns in cable and television networks, as well as Internet interests.

History of Warner Communications

In 1922, brothers Harry, Jack, Abe, and Sam Warner opened their first West Coast studio, Warner Brothers. One year later, Warner Bros. incorporated. In 1925, the company went public and obtained exclusive rights to the Vitaphone, enabling music and effects to be synchronized to silent film. Just five years into its inception, Warner Bros. produced the first talking feature film, *The Jazz Singer*.

During the 1930s and '40s, Warner Bros. stood as one of the largest film studios, producing more than 50 films a year. The company owned nearly a quarter of all movie theaters in the U.S. and saw revenues climb with the introduction of *Bugs Bunny* and *Rin-Tin-Tin*. The company was showing some of the best films ever made, including *Casablanca* and *The Maltese Falcon*, and was also remaking movies.

Despite its success, Warner's golden image began to tarnish when, in 1950, production of *A Streetcar Named Desire* marked a change in how film actors, directors, and designers were hired. Warner had long since used full-time employees to create its films, but the new trend was to hire for each individual project, meaning that most of the crew would not be under Warner contract. The increasing popularity of television brought on problems as well, as movie attendance began to drop. In 1949, an anti-trust action brought on by the government forced Warner and the other big film companies to give up their theater chains. Warner suffered from a drop in revenues, as well as artistic decline.

Under the leadership of Jack Warner, the company continued its downhill slide. In 1966, Jack sold his shares to Seven Arts Productions, and three years later, left the company. Under new management, Warner-Seven Arts made the major purchase of Atlantic Records in 1967. The firm was still floundering, however, and in 1969, Steven Ross bought Warner for $17 million.

Ross began working to turn the company around and renamed it Warner Communications. He oversaw the release of two major hits, *All The President's Men* and *The Exorcist*. Ross also began a diversification strategy and acquired a toy company, cable-television interests, record companies, publishing firms, and a magazine distribution unit. In 1976, Warner also acquired Atari, which led to huge increases in revenue. The company formed Warner Home Video, and established a joint venture with American Express to form Warner Amex, which launched the Nickelodeon cable channel.

In 1981, Warner launched MTV, a cable channel featuring music videos. The company began to focus on its core business and sold Atari, whose sales had plummeted due to losses in the game industry. Warner slowly began to see profits again, and in 1986, the firm acquired the American Express share of Warner Amex and sold MTV. One year later, Warner bought Chappell & Co., thereby becoming the world's largest music publisher. The company also purchased Teldec and Lorimar in 1989.

In 1990, Time Inc. joined forces with Warner Communications in a deal worth nearly $14 billion,

The Officers

Chairman and CEO: Gerald M. Levin

Vice Chairman: Ted Turner

President: Richard D. Parsons

Exec. VP and Chief Financial Officer: Joseph Ripp

Exec. VP, Secretary and General Counsel: Peter R. Haje

creating the world's largest entertainment and media concern. The Time Warner Inc. combination was almost thwarted by an unsolicited bid for Time by Paramount Pictures for $10.7 billion. However, in August 1989, the deal was cleared to go through.

Market Forces Driving the Merger

Throughout the 1980s, the communications and media industry was being overrun by globalization and the desire to grow dramatically. Sony's purchase of CBS Records and Robert Murdoch's purchase of Twentieth Century Fox, among other television stations, clearly demonstrated that media concerns would have to continue to grow themselves, join forces with others, or risk takeover.

The desire to have content and distribution walk hand-in-hand continued as Time Inc. snatched up a piece of Turner Broadcasting. Management had long since been looking at entertainment prospects and set their sights on Warner Communications. According to Wasserstein, Time looked to the deal to "better control the content provided over its cable channels, which included HBO and Cinemax, use Warner's assets as a stepping-stone to position itself for the increasing globalization of the media business," and "Warner's key assets were simply growing faster than Times."

Warner also saw the union as lucrative. Steven Ross was quoted in *The New York Times* as stating "Only strong American companies will survive after the formation of a unified European market in 1992." The same article also pointed out that "the merger would insure Time Warner a place in the 1990s as one of a handful of global media giants able to produce and distribute information in virtually any medium."

Approach and Engagement

Discussion between the two companies started in 1987. The talks were called off early by Warner due to disagreements in how the management structure would be placed. Time wanted control of the CEO position but Warner chairman Steven Ross wanted

The Players

Chairman of Warner Communications: Steven J. Ross. Steven Ross began his career in the early 1960s working for a mortuary business that he had married into. He soon diversified the family business, Kinney Services, and set his sights on acquiring a major motion picture studio. In 1969, he purchased Warner Bros.-Seven Arts. Renaming the company Warner Communications, Ross is credited for leading the company through positive changes such as its entrance into the cable industry, as well as the negative publicity, received for its alleged insider trading involvement, takeover threats, and ties with organized crime. He played a key role in the merger with Time Inc. and remained chairman of merged company until 1993, when he died of cancer.

Chairman of Time Inc.: J. Richard Munro. Columbia University graduate J. Richard Munro joined Time Inc. in 1957. Three years later he was elected to the board of directors and was eventually named chairman and CEO of the company. Under his leadership, Time Inc. saw success in its HBO cable channel and grew to be a major media company. After serving briefly as co-CEO of Time Warner, Munro stepped down shortly after the merger. In 1997, he stood as chairman of Genentech, and was a director of Sensormatic Electronics Corp., Mobil Corp., Kellogg Co., as well as the Kmart Corporation.

that position to go to his company. A compromise of co-CEOs was finally reached, and in March 1989, the stock-for-stock deal was announced.

Paramount, however, had different plans. In June, just before Time shareholders' were to approve the deal, it made an offer of $175 per share for Time. The company's stock price went up $9.25 to $116.75 per share upon Paramount's bid. The company turned down the cash offer, however, which Paramount then upped to $200 per share. Time again declined and found itself in a court battle with Paramount. A judge in Delaware sided with Time, and, when appealed to the Delaware Supreme Court, Time again was cleared to continue plans with Warner. In August 1989, the two companies completed the $14 billion deal.

Products and Services

After the merger, Warner looked to capitalize on Time's distribution channels for its media. In 1998,

Time Warner had interests in publishing, music, cable networks, film, and cable. Its publishing concerns accounted for 16% of total sales, putting out such magazines as *Fortune, Entertainment Weekly, People, Time, Sports Illustrated,* and *In Style.* Time Warner's music operations brought in 15% of sales, and cable networks cinched 12% with such popular networks as HBO, Cinemax, Cartoon Network, CNN, and the TBS SuperStation.

While its U.S. operations accounted for 42% of sales, Time Warner also had operations in the U.K., France, Germany, and Canada. It operated many entertainment divisions, including Castle Rock Entertainment, Warner Bros. Studio stores, and the WB television network. The company also owned 50% of Columbia House, Warner Music Group, Sire Records Group, and the Atlantic Group.

Changes to the Industry

The union of Time and Warner was followed by a desire for vertical integration throughout the industry. As new technologies—like cable and satellite—surfaced, distribution companies continued to search for viable content companies. Matsushita of Japan purchased MCA, and Sony joined forces with Columbia House as U.S. entertainment was growing internationally.

After the Matsushita/MCA deal, Toshiba and C. Itoh formed a joint venture with Time Warner. A recession slowed down the merger deals, however, in the early 1990s, but they sparked up again in 1993. According to Bruce Wasserstein, "the 1993 no-holds barred fight for Paramount Communications Inc. ushered in a new period of large-scale media deals. By combining Viacom, Blockbuster, and Paramount, Sumner Redstone," Viacom's leader, "put cable channels, television, and movie production, video distribution and publishing all under one roof."

Developments in technology and changes in industry regulations created a wave of diversity in the media market, such as Warner and Paramount's creation of their own networks and ABC's merger with Disney. The deals, however, were different than those of the 1980s and early '90s. Japanese interest in American media had slowed dramatically, and large U.S.-based companies were teaming up with other American-owned companies.

Review of the Outcome

Ten months after the Time Warner deal, Steven Ross took over as chairman and co-CEO with Nick Nicolas. Unhindered by the company's growing debt, he orchestrated such deals as a publishing company for $225 million, part of a cellular phone company for $13.3 million, a stake in Six Flags amusement parks, and Pathe Communications and UA Films. Time and Warner also combined their cable operations and publishing interests.

Despite internal enthusiasm concerning the recent union, many analysts believed that Time should have accepted Paramount's offer. A May 9, 1990, article in *USA Today* stated that, "one big, gray cloud in this rosy picture is Time Warner's stock price. The shares closed at $94 Tuesday, well below the $200 a share that Paramount offered Time shareholders last summer." The article went on to say, "Time Warner stock wasn't expected to equal the $200 price for several years, but it is trading well below even the more modest expectations."

After the $13.9 billion purchase, the newly-formed company suffered net losses, although operating income increased 17% in the fourth quarter of 1989, and 16% in the first quarter of 1990. Revenue increased in 1990 to $11.5 billion from $7.6 billion in 1989.

Research

Antilla, Susan. "Time-Paramount Battle is a Nasty One," in *USA Today*, 19 June 1989. Discusses Paramount's advances towards Time.

Guy, Pat. "The Honeymoon Continues," in *USA Today*, 9 May 1990. Explains Time Warner position nearly one year after the merger.

Lohr, Steve. "Media Mergers: An Urge to Get Bigger and More Global," in *The New York Times*, 19 March 1989. Lists recent changes in media industry.

McClintick, David. "The Man Who Swallowed Time Inc.," in *The New York Times*, 10 April 1994. Discusses the career of Steven Ross and the merger of Time and Warner.

Norris, Floyd. "Time Inc. and Warner to Merge, Creating Largest Media Company," in *The New York Times*, 5 March 1989. Lists reasons that Time and Warner planned to merge.

Richter, Paul. "Shares of Time Soar $9.25 Amid Takeover Talk," in *Los Angeles Times*, 8 March 1989. Discusses a possible takeover attempt that would thwart Time and Warner's plans to merge.

"Time Warner Inc.," in *Notable Corporate Chronologies*, The Gale Group, 1999. Lists major events in the history of Time Warner.

Time Warner Home Page, available at http://www.time-warner.com. Official World Wide Web Home Page for Time Warner. Includes historical, financial, and product information, as well as recent news articles.

Wasserstein, Bruce. *Big Deal: The Battle for Control of America's Leading Corporations*, Warner Books, 1998. Offers an overview of the largest mergers in recent American corporate history.

CHRISTINA M. STANSELL

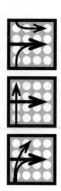

TIME WARNER &
TURNER BROADCASTING SYSTEM

Time Warner Inc.
75 Rockefeller Plz.
New York, NY 10019
USA

tel: (212)484-8000
fax: (212)956-2847
web: http://www.timewarner.com

nationality: USA
date: October 10, 1996
affected: Time Warner Inc., USA, founded 1990
affected: Turner Broadcasting System Inc., USA, founded 1961

Overview of the Acquisition

The world's largest media company was formed in 1996 through the acquisition of Turner Broadcasting System by Time Warner. This $7.6 billion deal had been fraught with shareholder entanglements that led to lawsuits and regulatory complications.

History of Time Warner Inc.

Warner Bros. opened its first West Coast movie studio in 1922. Three years later it went public and obtained exclusive rights to the Vitaphone, enabling music and effects to be synchronized to silent film. In 1927 the company produced the first talking feature film, *The Jazz Singer*.

Warner Bros. produced its first television series in 1954 and founded Warner Bros. Records in 1958. In 1967 it purchased Seven Arts and renamed the company Warner-Seven Arts, which in turn purchased Atlantic Records. It sold Warner Seven Arts in 1969 to the Kinney National Co., a conglomerate built by Steven Ross. Two years later, Kinney became known as Warner Communications Inc. Warner acquired its first cable systems in 1971.

Warner Bros. changed its name to Warner Communications Inc. in 1972. In 1979 the firm formed Warner Home Video. It also established a joint venture with American Express Co. to form Warner Amex, which launched the Nickelodeon cable channel. Warner expanded its cable offerings by launching MTV in 1981. Two years later Warner Amex and Viacom International merged Showtime with The Movie Channel. Warner acquired the American Express share of Warner Amex in 1986, at which point it sold MTV. In 1987 Warner became the world's largest music publisher by acquiring Chappell & Co.

Meanwhile, Time Inc. was formed in 1923, the same year that it published the first weekly issue of *Time* magazine. *Time*'s subscriber numbered 30,000 after only one year of circulation. The company launched a second publication, *The Saturday*

Review of Literature in 1924, followed by *Fortune* in 1930. The firm ventured into radio in 1931 with *The March of Time* show, which re-enacted historical events.

Life magazine premiered in 1936 and began showing a profit three years later. By 1941 *Time*'s circulation approached one million; *Life* had weekly sales of 3.3 million magazines; and *Fortune* had a small but influential readership of 160,000. It launched *Money* magazine in 1972 and *People* magazine two years later.

Time founded the Time-Life Broadcast subsidiary in 1952 with a 50% interest in KOB-AM and KOB-TV in Albuquerque, New Mexico. Two years later it acquired KLZ-AM and KLZ-TV of Denver, Colorado, the company's first wholly owned and operated stations. Time also launched *Sports Illustrated* that year.

In 1970 Time announced plans to sell broadcast properties to concentrate on cable television. Two years later it launched the pay television service Home Box Office Inc. (HBO) through the Time subsidiary, Sterling Information Services Ltd. In 1980 Time launched Cinemax, another pay television service. In 1987 it acquired a stake in Turner Broadcasting System, Inc.

Time Inc. merged with Warner Communications for $14 billion in 1990, creating the world's largest entertainment and media concern. The creation of this enterprise had nearly been thwarted by a $10.7 billion unsolicited bid for Time by Paramount Pictures. Later that year it launched *Entertainment Weekly* and revealed plans to open a nationwide chain of retail stores to sell merchandise featuring Looney Tunes characters.

The Warner Music Group acquired a half-interest in America's leading music club, Columbia House Co., in 1991. That same year Time Warner Cable introduced the world's first 150-channel interactive television system. It also completed the largest rights offering in U.S. history, raising $2.7 billion and paying off 23% of its debt.

In 1993 the company premiered *Vibe*, an urban music and culture magazine founded by Quincy Jones. Three years later it purchased Turner Broadcasting System. In 1998 it received a record setting $850 million from the television network NBC for the rights to broadcast *ER*. Later that year TBS acquired the syndication rights to *Seinfeld* from Columbia Tristar for $1 million per episode. In 1999 it entered into an agreement to allow AT&T to offer local telephone services via Time Warner's cable network.

History of Turner Broadcasting System Inc.

In 1961 Robert Edward "Ted" Turner III became president and chief operating officer of a $1 million

The Business

Financials

Revenue (1998): $14.6 billion

Employees (1998): 67,500

SICs / NAICS

sic 2721 - Periodicals

sic 4832 - Radio Broadcasting Stations

sic 4833 - Television Broadcasting Stations

sic 4841 - Cable & Other Pay Television Services

sic 7812 - Motion Picture & Video Production

sic 7941 - Sports Clubs, Managers & Promoters

naics 511120 - Periodical Publishers

naics 513112 - Radio Stations

naics 513120 - Television Broadcasting

naics 513210 - Cable Networks

naics 513220 - Cable and Other Program Distribution

naics 512110 - Motion Picture and Video Production

naics 711211 - Sports Teams and Clubs

Billboard enterprise, Turner Advertising Co., upon his father's death. This firm merged in 1970 with Rice Broadcasting Co., Inc., a small Atlanta UHF television station. That transaction took the resulting company public, with Turner as majority stockholder, under the new name Turner Communications Corp. Later that year the company bought the rights to broadcast the Atlanta Braves major league baseball games. In 1976, as the Braves franchise ran into financial problems and was on the verge of transferring to another city, Turner purchased the team.

Turner expanded his station's audience in 1976 by transmitting its signal nationwide through a cable satellite. The result was the development of the SuperStation WTBS network. The following year, Turner increased his sports presence by acquiring the controlling interest in the National Basketball Association's Atlanta Hawks.

In 1980 Turner created the Cable News Network (CNN) subsidiary to broadcast news around-the-clock. The live, 24-hour format offered a more direct and unedited presentation of the news than the networks provided, as well as the instant availability of news at the viewer's convenience. On its first day, CNN reached about 1.7 million cable households. In

The Officers

Chairman and CEO: Gerald M. Levin

Vice Chairman: Robert Edward Turner III

President: Richard D. Parsons

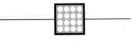

1982 CNN Radio launched a 24-hour, all-news format in the radio market. Sales the following year reached $224 million, with net income of $3 million.

TBS filed a preliminary exchange offer with the Securities and Exchange Commission (SEC) in 1985 for the acquisition of CBS. That network immediately bought back about six million shares of its common stock, forcing TBS to withdraw its offer. The aborted bid cost the company about $20 million in underwriting, legal, and accounting fees.

Its ventures into original programming were dwarfed by its 1986 acquisition of the film company MGM/UA Entertainment. To meet the financial requirements for the deal, Turner was forced to sell all MGM assets except the film library.

The Color Classics arm of TBS debuted in 1986 with the world premiere of a patented "colorized" version of the Oscar-winning movie *Yankee Doodle Dandy*. In 1987, still troubled by the MGM purchase, Turner sold about 37% of TBS to a group of 31 cable operators, including Tele-Communications Inc. (TCI). This capital secured Turner's control of voting stock and introduced new directors to Turner operations, including John Malone, president of TCI; Michael Fuchs, chairman of HBO; and Jim Gray, chairman of Warner Cable.

By 1988 SuperStation TBS reached a 50% penetration of all U.S. television households. That year a new cable channel, TNT, was launched in 17 million cable homes—the largest network launch in cable history. The network debuted with the first cable-exclusive telecast of *Gone With the Wind*. The next year TNT and TBS licensed the largest film package in basic-cable history—1,000 feature-film titles from Columbia Pictures Television, Inc. Sales exceeded $1 billion, and net income rose to $28 million.

Turner sponsored the Goodwill Games beginning in 1990. The Games, which were held every four years, generated about $60 million in subscription and advertising revenues, but created production costs of nearly $95 million. Later that year TBS instituted a $1-per-viewer surcharge to cable operators for carrying the Games, resulting in a blackout of TBS for nearly 17% of the 54 million households receiving the net-work. Ratings for the Goodwill Games still fell short of expectations.

Turner continued to create specialized networks for particular markets, launching the Airport Channel and the Checkout Channel in 1991. The Airport Channel was broadcast in strategic airport locations, and its programming consisted of a 30-minute loop of live news and features lifted from CNN, as well as several advertising spots. Revenues in its first year approached $10 million.

TBS purchased Hanna-Barbera Productions for $320 million in 1991. That company's popular characters, including *Yogi Bear*, *The Flintstones*, *Scooby Doo*, and *The Jetsons*, spurred the launch of the Cartoon Network, a 24-hour animation channel for basic cable systems. In 1995 TBS agreed to be purchased by Time Warner, a transaction that was completed in October of the following year.

Market Forces Driving the Acquisition

Time Warner became straddled with debt from the 1990 deal that formed it from a merger of Time Inc. and Warner Communications. That debt load weighed in at about $15 billion by mid-decade, even though the company had such well-performing assets as Warner Bros. film and television studios, the Home Box Office and Cinemax premium cable operations, and *Time*, *People*, and *Sports Illustrated* magazines. Time Warner's debt load remained enormous due to its unwillingness, not its inability, to pare it down.

Gerald Levin, Time Warner's CEO, had envisioned the company as evolving into a vertically integrated multimedia behemoth. He was particularly fascinated with cable television, which he wanted to use as a distribution channel for his company's valuable programming interests. He was also keen on the idea of using cable wires to provide other telecommunications services, including Internet access and local telephone services, directly to the customer. For those reasons, Levin continued to invest company profits into new ventures and acquisitions. As a result, Time Warner's stock performed poorly. Peaking at $45 in the 1980s, it registered at only the mid-30s by October 1996.

Approach and Engagement

On August 19, 1995, Gerald Levin strode up to Ted Turner's Montana ranch to broach the subject of a union between their companies. Turner's initial reaction was dismissive, but the more that he listened and considered the idea, the better it sounded. A combination of Time Warner and Turner Broadcasting System (TBS) would create the largest media empire on the planet, and Turner would become one of its leaders and its largest shareholder. TBS's properties would blend nicely with those of Time Warner, creating an enterprise that would control both content and distribution of television and movie interests, as well as significant assets in music, publishing, and other entertainment.

On September 29, after five weeks spent in negotiations with John Malone, TBS's largest shareholder, Time Warner and TBS announced their agreement. The $7.6 billion deal called for an exchange of stock valued at $35 per share, almost one-third more than TBS's going rate of $24. Ted Turner personally would own 11% of the combined company, and John Malone, president of the Tele-Communications Inc. (TCI) cable company, would own 9.2%. Most principals were pleased with the deal.

U S West was another matter, however. In 1993 this Baby Bell had acquired 25.5% of Time Warner Entertainment (TWE), comprised of its parent's movie studio, HBO cable channels, and its cable systems. If the acquisition of TBS was completed, Levin revealed that he intended to reorganize Time Warner by combining TBS and TWE's movie studio and HBO operations. TWE would then be comprised solely of cable systems, in which Levin said that he would seek an investment from AT&T. U S West was resistant to such an arrangement for two reasons: it would no longer hold a stake in the valuable movie and HBO assets, and it would become an unwilling partner with a potential rival in the local telephone market, AT&T. Just hours after the merger announcement, therefore, U S West filed suit to block it. This attempt failed when, in June 1996, a Delaware court ruled that Time Warner didn't need the permission of U S West to acquire TBS.

In July the Federal Trade Commission (FTC) finally approved the union, with several cable-related conditions. The FTC had been troubled by TCI's stake in TBS, and feared that a combination of these two interests with Time Warner would create an anticompetitive force in that industry. To alleviate those concerns, it ordered TCI to spin off its 9.2% stake in the new company into a trust entity held by its subsidiary, Liberty Media Corp. That interest would have no voting power nor management authority. Additionally, Time Warner and TBS agreed to refrain from bundling programs to cable systems operations so as not to exert excessive pricing pressure on them. The companies also agreed to offer on their cable systems a news channel in competition with CNN.

On October 10, 1996, more than a year after it had been announced, the acquisition was completed. Jerry Levin retained his positions as chairman and CEO of

The Players

Time Warner Chairman and CEO: Gerald M. Levin. A graduate of University of Pennsylvania Law School, Levin practiced law before joining Home Box Office in 1972. After rising through HBO's ranks, he became Time Warner's CEO in 1992 and chairman in 1993. In the immediate years after his ascension to the company's helm, Levin was criticized by Wall Street as an uninspired, unassertive man who appeared more willing to let his company lead him than to take the lead himself. The acquisition of TBS, however, turned the tide, and by 1999 investors and analysts loved Levin, the company, and its stock.

Turner Broadcasting System Chairman and CEO: Robert Edward (Ted) Turner III. Ted Turner took control of his family's billboard advertising company upon his father's death in 1963. He ventured into broadcasting by purchasing a small UHF television station in Atlanta in 1970. Five years later, having renamed the station WTBS (or TBS, for Turner Broadcasting System), he introduced it to cable television. Expanding on the success of his cable venture, he formed the Cable News Network (CNN) in 1980, followed by Turner Network Television (TNT) in 1988; the Cartoon Network in 1992; CNN International in 1993; and Turner Classic Movies (TCM) in 1994. Aside from his cable ventures, Turner also had a hand in the movie industry. In 1986 he purchased the MGM/UA Entertainment Company, acquiring its movie library of more than 4,000 titles. A sore point with the film industry, he proceeded to "colorize" many black-and-white classics. The year 1993 marked his expansion into film production with the acquisition of two movie studios: Castle Rock Entertainment and New Line Cinema. After the sale of his company in 1996, Turner became vice-chairman of Time Warner.

Time Warner, and Ted Turner assumed the post of vice chairman.

Products and Services

After absorbing TBS, Timer Warner reorganized from three operating divisions to four: cable networks, publishing, entertainment and cable systems.

Cable Networks was comprised of two segments. Home Box Office (HBO) included HBO, Cinemax, and the Comedy Channel; and New Line Cinema holdings. TBS, Inc. incorporated CNN, TBS SuperStation, Turner Network Television, Cartoon Network, and Turner Classic Movies networks, as well as interests in the Atlanta Braves, Atlanta Hawks, Atlanta Thrashers, World Championship Wrestling, and Goodwill Games.

The **Publishing** unit operated as Time Inc., which offered such magazines as *Time, People, Sports Illustrated, Fortune, Life, Money, Parenting, In Style,* and *Entertainment Weekly.*

Entertainment was comprised of two companies. Warner Bros. held the Warner Bros. branded movie and television production houses, video company, and retail stores, as well as Castle Rock Entertainment and the WB Television Network. Warner Music Group encompassed such music labels as Atlantic, Elektra, Warner Bros., and Sire.

Cable Systems consisted of Time Warner Cable, which served more than 12.6 million subscribers by year-end 1997.

Review of the Outcome

Time Warner became the world's largest media company by acquiring Turner Broadcasting System. By year-end 1997, its first full year of combined operations, Time Warner's stock rose 65%, from $37.50 per share in December 1996 to $62. Revenues that year increased to $24.6 billion, and the company had even managed to reduce its debt by $850 million. In 1999 its stock price approached 70, and many analysts predicted that it could easily reach the 80s by the end of that year.

Research

Deutschman, Alan. "The Ted and Jerry Show," in *GQ,* December 1997. Reviews the company's performance during the first year after its acquisition of TBS, and profiles Levin's career at Time Warner.

Oneal, Michael, with Catherine Arnst and Peter Burrows. "The Baby Bell in Jerry Levin's Soup," in *Business Week,* 4 December 1995. Describes the U S West factor in the proposed acquisition deal.

Roberts, Johnnie L. "Time's Uneasy Pieces," in *Newsweek,* 2 October 1995. Reports the acquisition agreement and cites the assets that each company would bring to the table.

"Time Warner Inc." in *Notable Corporate Chronologies,* The Gale Group, 1999. Profiles Time Warner, including its acquisition of TBS.

Time Warner Inc., 1997 Annual Report. Includes financial highlights and describes company operating segments.

Time Warner Inc. Home Page, available at http://www.timewarner.com. Official World Wide Web Page for Time Warner. Provides access to information on products and services, press releases, and investor information.

"Turner Broadcasting System Inc." in *Notable Corporate Chronologies,* The Gale Group, 1999. Offers a historical review of TBS.

Valdmanis, Thor. "Humpty-Dumpty: Why Time Warner's Attempt at World Media Domination May Come Crashing Down," in *Financial World,* 2 January 1996. Relates regulatory objections to the acquisition deal.

Yang, Catherine, and Elizabeth Lesly. "Time Warner-Turner: Ready for Prime Time," in *Business Week,* 29 July 1996. Reports the FTC's conditions for approving the transaction.

LAURA BRYSON

TRACOR & AEL INDUSTRIES

nationality: United Kingdom
date: February 22, 1996
affected: Tracor Inc., USA, founded 1955
affected: AEL Industries, USA

The General Electric Company PLC
One Brouton St.
London, W1X8AQ
United Kingdom

tel: (44)171-493-8484
fax: (44)171-493-1974
web: http://www.gec.com

Overview of the Merger

Tracor's $94.4 million purchase of AEL Industries in 1995 reflected an industry-wide consolidation trend in defense electronics. The deal was only part of Tracor's fevered acquisition program, through which it purchased over 10 major companies in just two years. The merger solidified Tracor's position as one of the leading defense contractors in the U.S. and put its sales over the $1 billion mark for the first time in 1996.

History of Tracor Inc.

The foundation for Tracor Inc. was created in 1955, when Jess Stanbrough, Chester McKinney, Richard Lanc, and Frank McBee turned an idea into a business venture. The four studied acoustical research and decided to turn their efforts into profits. With the help of attorney Harry Polland, they named their enterprise Associated Consultants and Engineers, and quickly received their first contract, an industrial noise abatement project for Eastern State Petroleum & Chemical Company.

Over the next two years, the company locked in several other projects and formed a reliable reputation. In 1957, the name was changed to Texas Research Associates and the firm received a $200,000 grant from Union Carbide to develop liquid transmitters. The company also remained focused on acoustical and sonar technology. Texas Research soon had to hire a staff and purchase computers, supplies, and office facilities. Contracts from the U.S. Navy became steady and Texas Research began to grow by leaps and bounds.

Meanwhile, Textran Corporation, similar to Texas Research in that it, too, had been formed by four men, was growing in the field of defense electronics. It had contracts with the U.S. Armed Forces and was one of the fastest growing defense firms in the country. In 1962, the eight men that had formed both companies decided to merge their interests together as Tracor Inc.

The newly formed company began an aggressive plan of growth by acquisition. Its first purchase was Rudmose Associates, a well-known manufacturer of

The Business

Financials

Revenue (1998): $18.6 billion

Employees (1998): 71,963

SICs / NAICS

sic 3812 - Search & Navigation Equipment

sic 8711 - Engineering Services

naics 334511 - Search, Detection, Navigation, Guidance, Aeronautical, and Systems

audiometers. With the help of that company's famed leader, Wayne Rudmose, Tracor was soon receiving larger contracts from the U.S. Department of Defense.

Throughout the 1960s, Tracor continued to grow. The company issued its first public offering in 1964, in order to help fund its purchase of Sulzer Laboratories. The offer was highly successful, as were the rest of Tracor's ventures throughout the decade. The company was focused on acquisition to broaden its interests in the defense industry, and purchased many leaders in the manufacture and design of electronic components for the automobile, electronics, and home appliances.

Tracor was an innovative leader, and began introducing such products as graphic display software and noise monitoring systems for the U.S. Navy. It continued to make acquisitions, but sold off some of its less successful ventures to concentrate on its core defense interests. By 1975, Tracor had increased its domestic market share, reported sales of over $100 million, and begun to plan its entrance into foreign markets.

The election of Ronald Reagan as U.S. President brought a focus on military and defensive strength during the 1980s that furthered Tracor's successes. Its foreign ventures had proved to be profitable with new customers in Europe and the Middle East. Despite its untainted record of success, however, the company was purchased by Westmark Systems Inc. in 1987 through a leveraged buyout that Tracor's management was unable to deter. The $900 million deal led to the appointment of Bobby Inman, who was elected to run the company. The former deputy director of the CIA had no formal corporate experience, and soon faced major problems.

Under his leadership, Tracor's manufacturing operations began to falter, the company experienced

high costs, there was a decrease in sales, and the U.S. government began to spend less on defense as the Cold War was coming to a close. By 1989, Tracor was unable to pay off the large debt it had assumed during the buyout.

In 1990, Inman was replaced by James Skaggs. With over 37 years of experience in computer-based electronics systems, he began to sell off unprofitable units, restructure management, consolidate operations, and implemente quality control measures. Tracor also began to reorganize under Chapter 11 of the Bankruptcy Code. In 1991, Tracor emerged from the restructuring, without Westmark. Tracor became the defense arm and Littlefuse focused on electronics.

In 1992, Tracor shares began trading again, doubling in value by 1993 to $9 a share. The company made two key acquisitions that year—GDE Systems and Vitro Corporation. With the integration of those companies, Tracor's sales increased by 28% and the company was back on track after its bout with major debt and near collapse.

By 1995, Tracor received the majority of its contracts from the U.S. government, including the Department of Defense and the Armed Services. The company developed key technology in the Polaris, Poseidon, and Trident missile systems. With its acquisition of AEL Industries in 1996, Tracor furthered its efforts in becoming a leader in providing engineering and support services for the U.S. Department of Defense.

Tracor continued to design, develop, manufacture, install, and maintain advanced radio communications for the U.S. Navy, as well as avionics systems for the U.S. Air Force and 16 foreign air forces. It was responsible for the electronics systems on the F-16 fighter jet, the C-17 transport, and the B-2 bomber. After its purchase of AEL, the company received a major contract to design the Explosive Standoff Minefield Breacher system for the U.S. Army and Marines.

Protected from cuts in the defense budget with its focus on maintenance and operation of defense mechanisms, Tracor continued to be a leader in the defense industry. In 1998, the company joined The General Electric Company PLC (GEC) and became part of Marconi North America Inc.

Market Forces Driving the Merger

Consolidation was sweeping through the defense industry in the mid-1990s. Due in part to cuts in defense spending by the U.S. government, major defense contractors were either merging into larger entities or gobbling up smaller companies. As an example, Magnavox Electronics Systems Co. was sold on the auction block in September of 1995. An article in *The Washington Post* stated that the deal was "evidence that the wave of Pentagon contractor mergers will continue cresting through 1996." The article went on to claim that the market was "hottest for defense electronics firms, whose prospects for Pentagon sales are better than for 'metal bending' companies that build jets and ships."

Tracor, whose focus was on electronics and maintenance rather than the actual defense vehicles themselves, was somewhat shielded from the cuts in spending. Nevertheless, its aggressive acquisition strategy was helping it get back on its feet after its bout with bankruptcy. Beginning in 1993, Tracor began its plan to purchase computer/electronics defense companies with its acquisition of Vitro Systems. In 1994, it bought GDE Systems, and one year later, a Lundy manufacturing unit, a division of Convair, and a division of Munitions.

By purchasing AEL Industries, Tracor would continue its plan of building a huge base of electronic warfare systems. In February 1996, James B. Skaggs stated that "the addition of AEL is expected to push us over the $1 billion mark in sales for 1996." He went on to say Tracor believed that "AEL's long-term electronic warfare production programs will strengthen Tracor's sales and market growth potential, while substantially broadening our customer set."

Approach and Engagement

Tracor first bid on AEL in October of 1995. The $155 million offer included the purchase of all 4.1 million shares of AEL for $28 a share. AEL's experience in radio frequency, antenna and microwave technologies made it particularly attractive to Tracor. Upon announcement of the deal, AEL's shares rose 2.9% to $27 a share, while Tracor's slipped 3.8% to $15.875 per share.

The deal was contingent on Tracor's financial arrangements with Bankers Trust New York, and needed regulatory approval. By January 1996, Tracor lowered its bid to $24.50 a share. The decreased bid of $99.4 million reflected AEL's poor performance in the third quarter, which led to a loss of $1.1 million. On February 22, 1996, AEL shareholders approved the deal, and Tracor was free to go ahead with its planned purchase.

Products and Services

After the deal, Tracor stood strong as one of the largest defense contractors in the U.S. When it joined GEC in 1998, its operations were folded into one of

The Officers

Chairman: Sir Roger Hurn

Vice Chairman: M. Lester

Manging Director and CEO: Lord Simpson

Managing Director, GEC-Marconi: P.O. Gershon

Director of Finance: John Mayo

GEC's subsidiaries, Marconi North America. Marconi North America focused on operations in several different areas. Its Integrated Systems network was comprised of four different group including Imagery & Information Systems, Mission Management Systems, Test & Space Systems, and a Products Group.

The Imagery & Information sector was responsible for digital systems that supported military and commercial efforts across the globe, and included Archive and Dissemination Systems, Commercial Remote Sensing, Exploitation Systems, Ground Station Systems, and Precision Imagery programs. The Mission Management unit focused on military decision support and information processing systems, and included such systems as IMPULSE, STP, APS, CESAR, JTW, MALD, OMM, STS, SWPS, TBMCS, and Global Hawk Mission Planning. Marconi's Test & Space Systems division developed sensors used aboard aircraft and spacecraft, and had programs including Agile Support, Atlas & Titan Space Launch Vehicle, CSOSS, and various other satellite programs. Its Products Group included Talisin, a business area focused on providing services to non-military groups. Products in this group included Commercial Mapping (LH-Systems), Dodger, GEONAME, RapidScene, SOCET SET, VITec Cobra, and VETec Electronic Light Table.

GEC had operations across the globe in 1998. Operations in Europe claimed 44% of total sales, the United Kingdom took 17%, North and South America claimed 18%, and Africa, Australia, and Asia were responsible for 6% of total sales. Marconi Electronic Systems and GEC's Alstom operations contributed 33% of total 1998 sales, Industrial Electronics accounted for 19%, and Marconi Communications took 9% of sales.

Changes to the Industry

The Tracor/AEL deal came at a time when the industry was consolidating. Tracor continued to purchase other companies, including a division of Aegis in June 1996, a division of Shelter and Westmark in

The Players

Chairman, President and CEO of Tracor Inc.: James B. Skaggs. James Skaggs joined NASA in 1964, beginning his career in defense programs. Working his way through NASA's management positions, he assumed a senior appointment with System Development Corp. and worked for the computer-service company from 1971 to 1982, holding such positions as chief operating officer and president. In 1982, Skaggs joined AMEX Systems and successfully led the company through its merger with Allied-Signal Corp. In 1984, he was named president of the new company, Allied-Signal Electronic Systems Co. He left the company in 1986 to become a consultant to NASA. In 1990, he was elected chairman, president, and CEO of Tracor Inc. Known throughout the industry for his expertise, he helped Tracor reorganize after declaring Chapter 11 bankruptcy.

July, and Cordant in September of that year. Mid-sized companies were joining larger companies in the hope that the move would ensure government contracts for the future.

Peter Kusek, Cordant's chairman and CEO, was quoted in *The Washington Post* stating that "in order to continue the type of growth we had been experiencing in the past couple of years and to be a really effective competitor as out industry continues to consolidate, we needed to align ourselves with another company." The overwhelming belief among defense industry companies was that the larger the company, the better the chance of gaining lucrative government contracts.

Review of the Outcome

Tracor continued to grow at a rapid pace after the AEL deal. Sales exceeded $1 billion in 1996, and Tracor stood as one of the 15 largest defense electronics firms in the U.S. The company sold off unprofitable divisions of AEL to SIMCO in June 1996 in order to focus on strategic operations. In 1997, AEL was folded into Tracor Aerospace, later known as Tracor Aerospace Electronic Systems Inc. By April of that year, Tracor reported sales of $297.5 million in the first quarter, an increase of 30% over 1996 results. Tracor also won a $51 million, five-year contract from the Defense Special Weapons Agency, a $35 million contract from the Australian Defense Forces, and several other lucrative contracts in the U.S. and abroad.

In 1998, Tracor became an attractive company to GEC in the United Kingdom. Tracor joined the company in a $1.4 billion deal that year. It became part of Marconi North America Inc. a subsidiary of GEC, as well as clinching the position as the 9th-largest U.S. Defense Department contractor.

Research

Chandrasekaran, Rajiv. "Defense Contractor to Buy Cordant," in *The Washington Post*, 4 September 1996. Explains trends in the defense industry and Tracor's purchase of Cordant.

GEC PLC Home Page, available at http://www.gec.com. Official World Wide Web Home Page for GEC PLC. Includes historical, financial, and product information, as well as recent news articles and archived press releases.

"James B. Skaggs Named President and CEO of Tracor," in *Business Wire*, 14 December 1990. Details Skaggs' career.

Marconi North America Home Page, available at http://www.tracor.com. Official World Wide Web Home Page for Marconi North America. Includes historical, financial, and product information, as well as recent news articles and archived press releases.

"Mergers in Arms' Way," in *The Washington Post*, 24 August 1995. Discusses the consolidation trend in the defense industry.

"Purchase of AEL Planned for About $115 Million," in *The Wall Street Journal*, 3 October 1995. Discusses Tracor's bid for AEL Industries.

"Tracor Inc.," in *International Directory of Corporate Histories*, Volume 17, St. James Press, 1997. Lists major events in the history of Tracor, Inc.

"Tracor Inc.," in *New York Times*, 11 January 1996. Explains Tracor's lowered bid for AEL Industries.

Vogel, Steve. "Employees at Tracor Get Pledge; Takeover Won't Cost Jobs," in *The Washington Post*, 9 July 1998. Discusses GEC's purchase of Tracor Inc.

CHRISTINA M. STANSELL

TRAVELERS & METROPOLITAN LIFE INSURANCE

nationality: USA
date: January 3, 1995
affected: Travelers Inc., USA, founded 1864
affected: Metropolitan Life Insurance Co., USA, founded 1863

United HealthCare Group
300 Opus Ctr., 9900 Bren Rd. E.
Minnetonka, MN 55343
USA

tel: (612)936-1300
fax: (612)936-7430
web: http://www.unitedhealthgroup.com

Overview of the Merger

The 1995 New Year rang in the birth of a new company. MetraHealth Companies Inc. was formed as a joint venture for the group health insurance operations of Travelers Inc. and Metropolitan Life Insurance Co. It immediately became the largest health insurer in the U.S. in terms of premiums held. Yet even with that strong position and the powerful backing of its parent companies, MetraHealth's growth was sluggish, and it was sold to United HealthCare Corp. before the ball dropped to herald 1996.

History of Travelers Inc.

In 1863 James G. Batterson and nine others petitioned the Connecticut legislature for permission to form an accident insurance corporation. The following year the Travelers Insurance Co. opened for business. In 1865 it began writing life insurance, thereby becoming the first company to offer more than one line of insurance. It introduced its retirement income contract in 1884. Travelers diversified into liability, automobile, and health insurance in the late 1890s.

The company established the branch office system in 1902, setting up an administrative system to support its agents. The first branch office opened in New York, and its responsibilities included servicing existing policyholders, overseeing sales operations, and providing inspection and investigation services. The following year the company founded the industry's first vocational school for insurance agents.

After expanding into workers' compensation insurance in 1911, the company pioneered group life insurance with a policy written for the Ohio Electric Railway Co. In 1915, the cruiseliner *Lusitania*, with 17 Travelers policyholders onboard, was sunk by a German submarine. Travelers demanded $426,000 from the German government, but received nothing.

In May 1919 the company began offering comprehensive insurance that included life, public liability, workers' compensation, and passenger accident policies. Travelers' stock holdings were transferred into U.S. government bonds, one of

The Business

Financials

Revenue (1998): $17.4 billion

Employees (1998): 31,000

SICs / NAICS

sic 6321 - Accident & Health Insurance

sic 6324 - Hospital & Medical Service Plans

sic 8011 - Offices & Clinics of Medical Doctors

naics 524114 - Direct Health and Medical Insurance Carriers

naics 621491 - HMO Medical Centers

the safest investments available, just two days before the stock market crashed in 1929. Although Travelers escaped financial ruin, the Depression caused a dramatic decline in premiums as many life insurance policyholders committed suicide. Other policyholders threatened similar action and demanded that Travelers loan them money against their policies, but Travelers rejected those demands.

By 1955 the Homeowners Policy had grown to include insurance for fire, personal liability, windstorm, medical coverage for those injured on the property, and living expenses should a home become inhabitable. Four years later, after losing money in its automobile accident insurance division for a number of years due to the increase in automobile use and, thus, accidents, Travelers began basing auto insurance rates on a driver's safety record.

Travelers reorganized its capital structure in 1965, becoming The Travelers Corp., a holding company for Travelers Insurance Co. and its former subsidiary, Travelers Indemnity Co. The following year Medicare went into effect, making nearly 20 million Americans eligible for federally funded hospital and medical care. That year Travelers acquired the Phoenix Insurance Co., the 29th-largest U.S. property and casualty insurer. In 1967 the company entered the mutual funds arena with the founding of Travelers Equity Fund.

The company restructured its departments in 1974, splitting the property and casualty division along individual and business lines, while its health, life, and financial services divisions remained intact. In 1980 it acquired Keystone Life Insurance Co. The

next year it established the Travelers Lloyds Insurance Co., followed by the Provident Travelers Mortgage Securities Corp. in 1983.

Travelers purchased the Bankers and Shippers Insurance Company of New York in 1984. The next year it established Travelers Keystone Fixed Income Advisors and Travelers Plan Administrators. In 1986 it became a principal contender in the securities market by purchasing Dillon, Reed, and Co., one of Wall Street's oldest investment banking firms, for $157.5 million.

As health care costs continued to grow, it increased its interests in HMOs, which were expected to keep health care costs in check. In 1987 it acquired a major HMO from Whittaker Corp., as well as Health Plan of Virginia. The following year more than 880 employees were trimmed from the workforce as part of a cost reduction effort. The HMO segment didn't perform as expected. In 1989, after losing $18 million on its HMOs, it sold five such operations for $1 apiece and cut 225 additional jobs.

In 1992, as Travelers continued to struggle with its billions of dollars of laggard real estate, it announced a workforce reduction of 5,000 jobs by the end of 1994. Primerica acquired a 27% stake in the company for $722 billion in 1992, and in September of the following year, it purchased the remainder of Travelers.

Travelers merged its ailing group health business with that of Metropolitan Life Insurance Co. in 1995 to form MetraHealth Companies, Inc., which was sold to United HealthCare Corp. later that year. In 1996 it acquired the property casualty lines of Aetna, and merged them with Travelers' to create the Travelers/Aetna Property Casualty Corp. The company's core insurance and financial businesses at that time included: Smith Barney, an investment services provider; Commercial Credit, which offered consumer finance services; Travelers Bank, a credit card issuer; Primerica Financial Services, which dealt with mutual funds; and Travelers/Aetna Property Casualty Corp. and Travelers Indemnity, which sold property casualty and other types of insurance.

In 1997 it purchased Salomon and combined it with Smith Barney to form Salomon Smith Barney Holdings. On October 8, 1998, Travelers completed its merger with Citicorp to form Citigroup Inc., the world's largest financial services company. Dips in the domestic and foreign economies slowed the company's growth. These, added to the sizeable burden of integrating merged operations, necessitated a company reorganization, which eliminated more than 10,000 positions.

History of Metropolitan Life Insurance Co.

The National Union Life and Limb Insurance Company was chartered in 1863 to underwrite Union soldiers during the Civil War. Two years later it began to offer life insurance to civilians, and changed it name to National Life and Travelers' Insurance Co. In 1866 the company reorganized, separating its life and casualty lines into two companies—National Life Insurance Co. and National Travelers' Insurance Co. On March 24, 1868, National Travelers' reorganized as Metropolitan Life Insurance Co. The following year it wrote 2,930 policies, valued at over $4.8 million.

Metropolitan Life began issuing industrial, or workingman's, insurance in 1870. It established its first Canadian district office in 1885, and in 1901 opened its first office on the West Coast. By 1909 Metropolitan was the nation's largest life insurance company, with $2 billion of insurance in force.

It introduced the first group surgical policy in 1938. In 1952 it began offering personal hospital and surgical expense policies for individuals and families. Six years later it became the first U.S. life insurance company to make insurance available locally to members of the U.S. armed forces by opening a service center in Europe. Its gain in life insurance in force of $9.9 billion in 1969 was the highest in the industry.

The company established Metropolitan Property and Liability Insurance Company in 1972 to provide automobile and homeowner's insurance. The following year, as regional service centers opened in Oklahoma, and Rhode Island, the company had over $198 billion of life insurance in force. In 1976 it founded Metropolitan Insurance and Annuity Co. as a subsidiary for health reinsurance. Two years later Metropolitan Reinsurance Company began operations marketing property and casualty insurance.

In 1981 Metropolitan became the first insurer to pay $100 billion in benefits to policyholders and beneficiaries. Company assets that year passed the $50 billion mark. It formed a joint venture with Metropolitan Structures to create one of the nation's largest commercial real estate development organizations. The company opened more than 300 branch offices throughout the U.S. and Canada in 1982, bringing its network of sales offices to more than 1,000.

Metropolitan acquired Cross & Brown, a major management and leasing firm, in 1984. That year it launched a new mortgage banking company, MetFirst Financial, and a new slogan: "Get Met. It Pays." In 1985 it introduced HMOs. Acquisitions that year included Century 21 Real Estate Corp., CrossLand Capital Corp., Albany Life Assurance Co., Ltd., and Litton Industries Credit Corp. In 1986 it formed a

The Officers

Chairman, President, and CEO: William W. McGuire

Chief Operating Officer: Stephen J. Hemsley

Chief Financial Officer: Arnold H. Kaplan

Canadian holding company, Metropolitan Life Holdings Ltd.

The company assumed the assets of Baldwin-United Insurance subsidiaries in 1987. The following year it acquired the group life and health business of Allstate Insurance Co. In 1989 it acquired the property and casualty insurance portfolio of J.C. Penney Casualty Insurance Co., as well as the operations of United Resources Insurance Services, Inc. MetLife became the first North American company to have $1 trillion of life insurance in force in 1991.

In 1994 a class action lawsuit was filed against MetLife for allegedly engaging in deceptive sales practices, resulting in fine, fees, and refunds totaling $100 million. In January 1995 MetLife merged its health insurance operations with those of Travelers to form MetraHealth Companies Inc. MetraHealth was subsequently purchased by United HealthCare Corp. later in the year. Also in 1995 MetLife merged with New England Mutual, forming a company with assets totaling $146.9 billion. That year it sold Metmor Financial Inc. and Century 21 Real Estate Corp.

MetLife assumed 25,000 policies and contracts from Heritage Life Insurance Co. in 1996. The following year it acquired Security First Group. The company streamlined its business in 1998, divesting its Canadian and U.K. insurance businesses, and reducing its workforce by 10%. In 1998 it disclosed that it was considering making an initial public offering before year-end 1999.

Market Forces Driving the Merger

By the mid-1990s the U.S. health insurance industry was well entrenched in managed care. Traditional indemnity coverage, under which an insurer paid for any reasonable claim, was being steadily replaced by managed care systems as the plan of choice for insurers, if not for enrollees. Under managed care, an insurer operated a network of plan doctors and/or medical facilities that agreed to provide services in line with the network's rules.

The health operations of both Metropolitan Life and Travelers were far behind their competitors in managed care. A combination of the two would have

391,000 managed care enrollees in 1993, compared to Cigna's 3.1 million, Prudential's 1.5 million, and Aetna's 1.2 million. However, a combined company would lead the pack in terms of 1993 premiums. Together, MetLife and Travelers had $17.6 billion in total health premiums, with Cigna at $16.5 billion, Aetna at $15.3 billion, and Prudential at $10.6 billion. The combining companies were hoping to leverage those funds to boost its presence in the managed care environment.

Some analysts were skeptical about the proposed company's success in that arena. MetLife had managed care operations in 39 states, while Travelers had them in 27 states. Their combined presence in 42 states was considered by some to be spread too thin to be an effective contender. "If you don't have the density in a market, you don't have the clout to negotiate favorable contracts with providers in order to build a profitable network," explained Eleanor Kerns, an analyst at Alex. Brown and Sons, in *National Underwriter Life & Health-Financial Services Edition*.

Approach and Engagement

On June 14, 1994, Travelers and Metropolitan Life agreed to combine their group health insurance operations in a 50-50 joint venture. The new company, MetraHealth Companies Inc., would be the nation's largest health insurer, with premiums totaling $17.6 billion. Kennett L. Simmons, former chairman and CEO of United HealthCare Corp., would become the new company's CEO.

Travelers would contribute $370 million to the venture, while MetLife, which would contribute more managed care assets to the company, would pay $280 million. Additionally, MetraHealth would pay Travelers $350 million to acquire its non-medical group business, including dental, vision, disability, and accident insurance. Approval for the deal was obtained relatively quickly, and on January 3, 1995, MetraHealth was established.

Products and Services

United HealthCare Group operated several business units. UnitedHealthcare was its health care services segment, composed of UnitedHealthcare and Ovations: UnitedHealthcare operated locally based organized health systems that served employers and individuals enrolled in Medicare and Medicaid programs; and Ovations offered health and well-being products and services for older Americans. The company's Uniprise segment managed health benefits for customers in the large-scale, multi-site employer and labor union segment. Specialized Care Services offered specialized benefits, networks, services, and

resources, including employee assistance, mental health, organ transplant, dental, and personal health advisory services. The Ingenix segment was an information, analytic, research, and consulting enterprise.

Review of the Outcome

MetraHealth hit the ground running. On January 31, 1995, it announced that it would acquire HealthSpring, a company operating group practices that contracted with health maintenance organizations (HMOs) in three states. This deal gained MetraHealth a cheaper means of increasing its managed care enrollment than by purchasing HMO plans.

Despite this quick move to bolster its managed care operations, the company was ailing by mid-year. MetraHealth had tried to convert its indemnity business to managed care, but discovered that accomplishing this task was more difficult than anticipated. It enrolled only four percent, or 450,000, of its members into managed care plans. Meanwhile it had lost five percent of its members outright.

In September 1995, MetraHealth agreed to be acquired by United HealthCare Corp. for $1.65 billion. The following month, the transaction was completed. With revenues exceeding $8 billion, United became the largest health care management services company in the U.S.

Research

Cerne, Frank. "Big Deal: Can United HealthCare Make a Silk Purse out of a Sow's Ear?" in *Hospitals & Health Networks*, 5 September 1995. Describes United's acquisition and integration of MetraHealth.

Jones, David C. "Met/Travelers Deal Creates a Player," in *National Underwriter Life & Health-Financial Services Edition*, 20 June 1994. Offers industry reaction to the newly announced merger.

"MetraHealth Makes Its Opening Move," in *Health Alliance Alert*, 10 February 1995. Briefly describes MetraHealth's acquisition of HealthSpring.

"Metropolitan Life Insurance Co.," in *Best's Review—Life-Health Insurance Edition*, November 1994. Provides a brief description of the terms of the merger.

"Metropolitan Life Insurance Co.," in *Notable Corporate Chronologies*, The Gale Group, 1999. Describes the history of MetLife.

Roush, Chris. "Reality Plays Matchmaker," in *Business Week*, 27 June 1994. Describes the industry position of the proposed joint venture.

"Travelers Inc.," in *Notable Corporate Chronologies*, The Gale Group, 1999. Lists major events in the history of the company.

UnitedHealth Group Home Page, available at http://www.unitedhealthgroup.com. Official World Wide Web Page for United HealthCare. Includes annual reports, press releases, and product information.

BERTRAM W. ROLAND

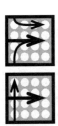

TURNER BROADCASTING SYSTEM & CBS

date: August 7, 1985 (canceled)
affected: Turner Broadcasting System Inc., (subsidiary of Time Warner Inc.), USA, founded 1961
affected: CBS Inc., USA, founded 1927

Turner Broadcasting System Inc.
75 Rockefeller Plz.
New York, NY 10019
USA

tel: (212)484-8000
fax: (212)956-2847
web: http://www.timewarner.com

CBS Inc.
51 W. 52nd St.
New York, NY 10019
USA

tel: (212)975-4321
fax: (212)975-4516
web: http://www.cbs.com

Overview of the Acquisition

Ted Turner's quest for CBS in 1985 was spurred by his desire to gain access to a steady source of revenue to support the cable television operations of Turner Broadcasting System. His hostile bid was defeated by anti-takeover defenses erected by CBS, including a plan to buy back a large portion of its outstanding stock and the adoption of corporate provisions that made Turner's all-stock bid nearly impossible to complete. Four months after launching the takeover, Turner terminated his offer in favor of acquiring MGM/UA Entertainment.

History of Turner Broadcasting System Inc.

In 1961, Robert Edward "Ted" Turner III became president and chief operating officer of a $1 million billboard enterprise, Turner Advertising Co., upon his father's death. This firm merged in 1970 with Rice Broadcasting Co., Inc., a small Atlanta UHF television station. That transaction took the resulting company public, with Turner as majority stockholder, under the new name Turner Communications Corp. Later that year the company bought the rights to broadcast the Atlanta Braves major league baseball games. In 1976, as the Braves franchise ran into financial problems and was on the verge of transferring to another city, Turner purchased the team.

Turner expanded his station's audience in 1976 by transmitting its signal nationwide through a cable satellite. The result was the development of the SuperStation WTBS network. The following year, Turner increased his sports presence by acquiring the controlling interest in the National Basketball Association's Atlanta Hawks.

In 1980, Turner created the Cable News Network (CNN) subsidiary to broadcast news around-the-clock. The live, 24-hour format offered a more direct and unedited presentation of the news than the networks provided, as well as the instant availability of news at the viewer's convenience. On its first day, CNN reached about 1.7 million cable households. In 1982, CNN Radio launched a 24-hour, all-news format in the radio market. Sales the following year reached $224 million, with net income of $3 million.

The Business

Financials - Turner Broadcasting System Inc.

Revenue (1998): $14.6 billion

Employees (1998): 67,500

Financials - CBS Inc.

Revenue (1998): $6.8 billion

Employees (1998): 46,100

SICs / NAICS

sic 2721 - Periodicals

sic 4832 - Radio Broadcasting Stations

sic 4833 - Television Broadcasting Stations

sic 4841 - Cable & Other Pay Television Services

sic 7812 - Motion Picture & Video Production

sic 7941 - Sports Clubs, Managers & Promoters

naics 511120 - Periodical Publishers

naics 513112 - Radio Stations

naics 513120 - Television Broadcasting

naics 513210 - Cable Networks

naics 513220 - Cable and Other Program Distribution

naics 512110 - Motion Picture and Video Production

naics 711211 - Sports Teams and Clubs

TBS filed a preliminary exchange offer with the Securities and Exchange Commission (SEC) in 1985 for the acquisition of CBS. That network immediately bought back about six million shares of its common stock, forcing TBS to withdraw his offer. The aborted bid cost the company about $20 million in underwriting, legal, and accounting fees.

Its ventures into original programming were dwarfed by its 1986 acquisition of the film company MGM/UA Entertainment. To meet the financial requirements for the deal, Turner was forced to sell all MGM assets except the film library.

Its Color Classics arm debuted in 1986 with the world premiere of a patented "colorized" version of the Oscar-winning movie *Yankee Doodle Dandy*. In 1987, still troubled by the MGM purchase, Turner sold about 37% of TBS to a group of 31 cable operators, including TeleCommunications Inc. (TCI). This capital secured Turner's control of voting stock and introduced new directors to Turner operations, including John Malone, president of TCI; Michael Fuchs, chairman of HBO; and Jim Gray, chairman of Warner Cable.

By 1988, SuperStation TBS reached a 50% penetration of all U.S. television households. That year a new cable channel, TNT, was launched in 17 million cable homes—the largest network launch in cable history. The network debuted with the first cable-exclusive telecast of *Gone With the Wind*. The next year TNT and TBS licensed the largest film package in basic-cable history—1,000 feature-film titles from Columbia Pictures Television, Inc. Sales exceeded $1 billion, and net income rose to $28 million.

Turner sponsored the Goodwill Games beginning in 1990. The Games, which were held every four years, generated about $60 million in subscription and advertising revenues, but created production costs of nearly $95 million. Later that year, TBS instituted a $1-per-viewer surcharge to cable operators for carrying the Games, resulting in a blackout of TBS for nearly 17% of the 54 million households receiving the network. Ratings for the Goodwill Games still fell short of expectations.

Turner continued to create specialized networks for particular markets, launching the Airport Channel and the Checkout Channel in 1991. The Airport Channel was broadcast in strategic airport locations, and its programming consisted of a 30-minute loop of live news and features lifted from CNN, as well as several advertising spots. Revenues in its first year approached $10 million.

TBS purchased Hanna-Barbera Productions for $320 million in 1991. That company's popular characters, including *Yogi Bear*, *The Flintstones*, *Scooby Doo*, and *The Jetsons*, spurred the launch of the Cartoon Network, a 24-hour animation channel for basic cable systems. In 1995, TBS agreed to be purchased by Time Warner, a transaction that was completed in October of the following year.

History of CBS Inc.

United Independent Broadcasters, Inc. was founded by Arthur Judson, impresario of the Philadelphia and New York Philharmonic orchestras, in 1927 as a radio broadcasting company designed to promote classical music. Financing for the new company was spotty, and after several difficult months, Judson entered into a partnership with Columbia Phonograph. Columbia purchased UIB's operating rights for $163,000, renaming the new company the Columbia Phonograph Broadcasting System. Its operating rights were resold back to the broadcasting company the following year, and the company's name was shortened to Columbia Broadcasting System (CBS).

Radio advertiser William Paley purchased $400,000 worth of CBS stock in 1928. He became president, and earnings tripled during his first year at that position. Paley's success was based in his strategy to offer programming free to prospective affiliates, a practice that contradicted NBC's policy of charging affiliates for all programming. In exchange for the free programming, CBS affiliate stations offered airtime to the parent network for its sponsored broadcasts. By 1936, CBS had 97 affiliate stations and was the country's largest radio network.

Instead of challenging NBC's dominance in entertainment, CBS opted to make a name for itself in news and public affairs. In 1933, it formed Columbia News Service, the first radio network news operation of its kind. Five years later Edward R. Murrow launched the first international radio news broadcast with reports from Vienna, Paris, Berlin, and Rome. Also in 1938 CBS purchased the American Recording Corp., which was later renamed the Columbia Recording Corp.

CBS transmitted the world's first experimental color TV broadcast in 1940, and the next year began weekly broadcasts of black-and-white television programs. It acquired the nickname the Tiffany Network as a reference to its quality programming, which now included such star performers as Jack Benny, Edgar Bergen, Red Skelton, George Burns, and Gracie Allen. Its popular TV quiz show, *$64,000 Question*, became embroiled in the national game show scandal in 1956 when it was revealed to have supplied contestants with the correct answers to posed questions.

CBS introduced lighter forms of entertainment in 1959, thereby doubling profits in only two years. Fare like *The Beverly Hillbillies*, *Mr. Ed*, and *The Munsters* helped make CBS the nation's best-rated network. It maintained that lead through the 1970s with such shows as *The Mary Tyler Moore Show* and *All in the Family*.

CBS entered the video industry by joining with Twentieth Century Fox-Video in 1982 to form CBS/Fox, a distributor of videocassettes. The next year it acquired the music publishing operations of United Artists Corp. and created Tri-Star Pictures as a joint venture with Columbia Pictures and HBO. In 1985, CBS fought off a hostile takeover attempt by Turner Broadcasting Service. It also purchased the consumer magazine publishing operations of Ziff-Davis Publishing Co. for $362.5 million.

In 1986, Laurence Tisch became CEO. He launched drastic cost-cutting strategies that included the reduction of the news division budget by $30 million, the elimination of 1,200 jobs, and the sale of several CBS publishing concerns. CBS also began divesting its music and professional interests, including the

The Officers

Turner Broadcasting System Inc.

Chairman and CEO: Gerald M. Levin

Vice Chairman: Robert Edward Turner III

President: Richard D. Parsons

Chairman and CEO, Home Box Office: Jeffrey L. Bewkes

Chairman and CEO, Time Warner Cable: Joseph J. Collins

CBS Inc.

Chairman: David McLaughlin

President and CEO: Mel Karmazin

Exec. VP and Chief Financial Officer: Fredric Reynolds

Exec. VP and General Counsel: Louis Briskman

highly criticized sale of CBS Records to Sony for $2 billion.

The network acquired Midwest Communications, a broadcast and sports programming company, in 1991. Three years later, the up and coming Fox Network acquired the rights to Monday Night Football, a former staple of CBS, as well as several of CBS's broadcasting affiliates, sending the company scrambling for replacement affiliates. CBS soon slipped to third-place, behind NBC and ABC. In 1995, it was purchased by Westinghouse Electric Corp. for $5.4 billion.

Westinghouse changed its name to CBS Corp. and continued to divest the network's non-broadcasting operations. CBS acquired an additional 90 radio stations by purchasing American Radio Systems in 1998. Later that year it reduced its stake in Infinity by spinning off 20% of that unit through an initial public offering. In 1999, it agreed to purchase King World Productions.

Market Forces Driving the Acquisition

Cable television had become formidable competition to broadcast television networks by the mid-1980s. By 1984, the networks reached an audience of 75% of U.S. homes, down from 92% just eight years earlier. Moreover, Federal Communications Commission (FCC) regulations forbade the networks from both owning and broadcasting most prime-time programming, restrictions that were not levied against cable systems. Because of these factors, the stock prices of the networks were depressed, setting the stage for potential takeovers.

The Players

Turner Broadcasting System Chairman and CEO: Robert Edward (Ted) Turner III. Ted Turner took control of his family's billboard advertising company upon his father's death in 1963. He ventured into broadcasting by purchasing a small UHF television station in Atlanta in 1970. Five years later, having renamed the station WTBS (or TBS, for Turner Broadcasting System), he introduced it to cable television. Expanding on the success of his cable venture, he formed the Cable News Network (CNN) in 1980, followed by Turner Network Television (TNT), 1988; the Cartoon Network, 1992; CNN International, 1993; and Turner Classic Movies (TCM), 1994. Aside from his cable ventures, Turner also had a hand in the movie industry. In 1986 he purchased the MGM/UA Entertainment Company, acquiring its movie library of more than 4,000 titles. A sore point with the film industry, he proceeded to "colorize" many black-and-white classics. The year 1993 marked his expansion into film production with the acquisition of two movie studios: Castle Rock Entertainment and New Line Cinema. After the sale of his company in 1996, Turner became vice-chairman of Time Warner.

Yet the cable television industry was not without problems of its own. Aside from such pay-cable stations as HBO and Showtime, most cable systems relied on advertiser revenues, a source that was largely inadequate for covering broadcasting and operational expenses. Advertisers were reluctant to pay a premium because the demographics of cable audiences were largely unknown.

In response to this advertising income problem, cable systems began eyeing the networks as sources of steady streams of revenue. The big three networks—ABC, CBS, and NBC—enjoyed powerful name recognition, valuable affiliate stations, and programming capabilities in sports and news. In March 1985, ABC agreed to a friendly takeover by Capital Cities. This deal immediately heightened speculation over the future of the two remaining networks. Rumors of a takeover of CBS gained intensity, and its stock price soared. A group of political conservatives led by Jesse Helms announced its intention to take over CBS to eliminate the "liberal bias" of its news programming, but this threat was not taken seriously by the industry. Meanwhile, Ivan Boesky acquired nine percent of

CBS's stock on the open market. At the same time, Ted Turner was rumored to be interested in acquiring the network as well.

Approach and Engagement

On April 18, 1985, Ted Turner put forth an unsolicited bid for CBS. He offered to acquire the network in exchange for Turner Broadcasting System stocks and "junk" bonds. Turner valued the deal at $175 per share, although analysts pegged its value between $150 and $160 per share. The offer required the approval of both the Federal Communications Commission (FCC) and the Securities and Exchange Commission (SEC) before it could be put to shareholders.

Turner announced that he was interested only in the network's television business. He planned to sell CBS's recording, toy, and publishing operations, as well as its radio stations. He also disclosed that he intended to assume control of the company's board and then merge CBS with Turner Broadcasting.

As expected, CBS rejected the deal on April 22, citing the excessive debt that Turner's deal would place on the network. On June 3, CBS intensified its position by arguing before the FCC that Turner's offer would destroy the company. The petition argued that the amount of debt that CBS would shoulder as a result of a completed merger, about $4.5 billion, would make it unable to support it programming, leading to a "death spiral" of lower ratings, reduced advertising revenues, and fewer affiliated stations. Ultimately, CBS requested the FCC to reject Turner's offer.

Turner responded by filing a petition with the FCC that detailed his plans to reduce that debt load through the sale of various CBS assets, namely all non-television properties. With those divestitures, Turner claimed, he would have enough capital to sustain the network for nearly a decade. Later that week, on June 21, he received SEC approval to pursue CBS.

On July 3, CBS announced a plan that proved to be an insurmountable defense against Turner's advances. The network would buy back 21% of its outstanding stock for $150 per share, $40 in cash and $110 in notes. In addition, CBS adopted provisions limiting the amount of debt that it could carry on its books, an amount, coincidentally, would be exceeded by Turner's plan.

Turner immediately asked the FCC to block this plan, arguing that CBS's proposed transfer of stock from shareholders to the company's board was subject to the same FCC regulations as Turner's own bid. He also requested an accelerated review of his offer by the

FCC so that his appeal to CBS shareholders would coincide with that of the network.

Turner's offer effectively died on July 30, however, when a federal court denied his request to block the CBS buyback. Yet Turner refused to admit defeat, and insisted that he would make another run for CBS once he had secured the financial backing of an investor in order to extend an offer that included a cash portion.

But on August 7, 1985, Turner officially dropped his pursuit of CBS. This decision was made in light of his takeover of another company, MGM/UA Entertainment Co. Turner's friendly acquisition of MGM/UA was favorable to that of CBS because it afforded Turner the opportunity "to acquire one of the world's major motion picture studios in a friendly deal that had a much higher probability of succeeding," as reported in *The Washington Post*.

Products and Services

In mid-1999 CBS's television offerings included: *48 Hours, 60 Minutes, CBS Evening News with Dan Rather, Chicago Hope, Cosby, Diagnosis Murder, Early Edition, Everybody Loves Raymond, LA Doctors, Late Show with David Letterman, Martial Law, Nash Bridges, Touched by an Angel, Unsolved Mysteries*, and *Walker, Texas Ranger*. In addition, it owned 14 television stations; 80% of Infinity Broadcasting, which owned a collection of 160 radio stations; and the cable networks The Nashville Network and Country Music Television.

Time Warner, which acquired Turner Broadcasting System in 1996, was organized in four operating divisions in late 1999:

Cable Networks was comprised of two segments. Home Box Office (HBO) included HBO, Cinemax, and the Comedy Channel; and New Line Cinema holdings. TBS, Inc. incorporated CNN, TBS SuperStation, Turner Network Television, Cartoon Network, and Turner Classic Movies networks, as well as interests in the Atlanta Braves, Atlanta Hawks, Atlanta Thrashers, World Championship Wrestling, and Goodwill Games.

The **Publishing** unit operated as Time Inc., which offered such magazines as *Time, People, Sports Illustrated, Fortune, Life, Money, Parenting, In Style*, and *Entertainment Weekly*.

Entertainment was comprised of two companies. Warner Bros. held the Warner Bros. branded movie and television production houses, video company, and retail stores, as well as Castle Rock Entertainment and the WB Television Network. Warner Music Group encompassed such music labels as Atlantic, Elektra, Warner Bros., and Sire.

Cable Systems consisted of Time Warner Cable, which served more than 12.6 million subscribers by year-end 1997.

Research

CBS Corp. Home Page, available at http://www.cbs.com. Official World Wide Web Page for CBS. Offers the television programming line-up for CBS.

"CBS Inc.," in *Notable Corporate Chronologies*, The Gale Group, 1999. Provides the history of the company.

Smith, Sally Bedell. "CBS Asks Government to Deny Turner's Bid," in *The New York Times*, 4 June 1985. Describes CBS's appeal to the FCC to reject Turner's bid.

Smith, Sally Bedell. "Turner Makes Offer for CBS; Wall St. Skeptical on Success," in *The New York Times*, 19 April 1985. Announces the launch of Turner's hostile bid for CBS.

Time Warner Inc. 1997 Annual Report. Covers financial highlights and describes company operating segments.

Time Warner Inc. Home Page, available at http://www.time-warner.com. Official World Wide Web Page for Time Warner. Includes access to information on products and services, press releases, and investor information.

"Turner Broadcasting System Inc." in *Notable Corporate Chronologies*, The Gale Group, 1999. Provides a historical review of TBS.

Vise, David A. "Judge Rejects Turner Request on CBS; Broadcaster Vows to Continue Takeover Fight," in *The Washington Post*, 31 July 1985. Describes the federal court's denial of Turner's request to block the stock buyback of CBS.

Vise, David A. "Turner Drops Hostile Bid for CBS," in *The Washington Post*, 8 August 1985. Announces Turner's termination of the CBS bid in favor of his deal with MGM/UA.

Vise, David A. "Turner Seeks to Halt CBS Stock Buyback Plan; Asks FCC to Hasten Review of Takeover Bid," in *The Washington Post*, 6 July 1985. Detail's CBS's anti-takeover plan, including its stock buyback and debt limit.

LAURA BRYSON

TURNER BROADCASTING SYSTEM &
MGM/UA ENTERTAINMENT

Time Warner Inc.

75 Rockefeller Plz.

New York, NY 10019

USA

tel: (212)484-8000

fax: (212)956-2847

web: http://www.timewarner.com

nationality: USA

date: March 25, 1986

affected: Turner Broadcasting System Inc., USA, founded 1961

affected: MGM/UA Entertainment Co., USA, founded 1981

Overview of the Acquisition

Bruised from his battle to acquire CBS, Ted Turner immediately entered into another acquisition deal, for MGM/UA Entertainment Co. This $1.5 billion deal, unlike that for CBS, was a friendly, all-cash offer. However, difficulties in securing the necessary financing led to two separate revisions in the terms, which ultimately dropped the value of the deal to $1.25 billion in cash and stock.

Even under these reduced terms, Turner's investment bankers were still concerned about his ability to finance the deal. As incentive, they gave him a year to pare down the company's debt from the $2 billion it would carry at the deal's completion to $1.1 billion. Otherwise, Turner would be forced to relinquish control of his company by distributing dividends to shareholders in the form of company stock, thereby diluting his own stake below a 50% majority ownership. He narrowly avoided this occurrence by selling off all of MGM's assets except for its prized film library.

History of Turner Broadcasting System Inc.

In 1961, Robert Edward "Ted" Turner III became president and chief operating officer of a $1 million billboard enterprise, Turner Advertising Co., upon his father's death. This firm merged in 1970 with Rice Broadcasting Co., Inc., a small Atlanta UHF television station. That transaction took the resulting company public, with Turner as majority stockholder, under the new name Turner Communications Corp. Later that year the company bought the rights to broadcast the Atlanta Braves major league baseball games. In 1976, as the Braves franchise ran into financial problems and was on the verge of transferring to another city, Turner purchased the team.

Turner expanded his station's audience in 1976 by transmitting its signal nationwide through a cable satellite. The result was the development of the SuperStation WTBS network. The following year, Turner increased his sports presence by acquiring the controlling interest in the National Basketball Association's Atlanta Hawks.

In 1980, Turner created the Cable News Network (CNN) subsidiary to broadcast news around-the-clock. The live, 24-hour format offered a more direct and unedited presentation of the news than the networks provided, as well as the instant availability of news at the viewer's convenience. On its first day, CNN reached about 1.7 million cable households. In 1982, CNN Radio launched a 24-hour, all-news format in the radio market. Sales the following year reached $224 million, with net income of $3 million.

TBS filed a preliminary exchange offer with the Securities and Exchange Commission (SEC) in 1985 for the acquisition of CBS Inc. That network immediately bought back about six million shares of its common stock, forcing TBS to withdraw his offer. The aborted bid cost the company about $20 million in underwriting, legal, and accounting fees.

Its ventures into original programming were dwarfed by its 1986 acquisition of the film company MGM/UA Entertainment. To meet the financial requirements for the deal, Turner was forced to sell all MGM assets except the film library.

Its Color Classics arm debuted in 1986 with the world premiere of a patented "colorized" version of the Oscar-winning movie *Yankee Doodle Dandy*. In 1987, still troubled by the MGM purchase, Turner sold about 37% of TBS to a group of 31 cable operators, including Tele-Communications Inc. (TCI). This capital secured Turner's control of voting stock and introduced new directors to Turner operations, including John Malone, president of TCI; Michael Fuchs, chairman of HBO; and Jim Gray, chairman of Warner Cable.

By 1988, SuperStation TBS reached a 50% penetration of all U.S. television households. That year a new cable channel, TNT, was launched in 17 million cable homes—the largest network launch in cable history. The network debuted with the first cable-exclusive telecast of *Gone With the Wind*. The next year TNT and TBS licensed the largest film package in basic-cable history—1,000 feature-film titles from Columbia Pictures Television, Inc. Sales exceeded $1 billion, and net income rose to $28 million.

Turner sponsored the Goodwill Games beginning in 1990. The Games, which were held every four years, generated about $60 million in subscription and advertising revenues, but created production costs of nearly $95 million. Later that year, TBS instituted a $1-per-viewer surcharge to cable operators for carrying the Games, resulting in a blackout of TBS for nearly 17% of the 54 million households receiving the network. Ratings for the Goodwill Games still fell short of expectations.

The Business

Financials

Revenue (1998): $14.6 billion

Employees (1998): 67,500

SICs / NAICS

sic 2721 - Periodicals

sic 4832 - Radio Broadcasting Stations

sic 4833 - Television Broadcasting Stations

sic 4841 - Cable & Other Pay Television Services

sic 7812 - Motion Picture & Video Production

sic 7941 - Sports Clubs, Managers & Promoters

naics 511120 - Periodical Publishers

naics 513112 - Radio Stations

naics 513120 - Television Broadcasting

naics 513210 - Cable Networks

naics 513220 - Cable and Other Program Distribution

naics 512110 - Motion Picture and Video Production

naics 711211 - Sports Teams and Clubs

Turner continued to create specialized networks for particular markets, launching the Airport Channel and the Checkout Channel in 1991. The Airport Channel was broadcast in strategic airport locations, and its programming consisted of a 30-minute loop of live news and features lifted from CNN, as well as several advertising spots. Revenues in its first year approached $10 million.

TBS purchased Hanna-Barbera Productions for $320 million in 1991. That company's popular characters, including *Yogi Bear*, *The Flintstones*, *Scooby Doo*, and *The Jetsons*, spurred the launch of the Cartoon Network, a 24-hour animation channel for basic cable systems. In 1995, TBS agreed to be purchased by Time Warner, a transaction that was completed in October of the following year.

History of MGM/UA Entertainment Co.

MGM/UA Entertainment Company was formed in 1981 through the merger of Metro-Goldwyn-Mayer (MGM) and United Artists Corp. (UA). Each company had been operating in the motion picture industry for decades.

United Artists Corp. was formed in 1919 by Mary Pickford, Charlie Chaplin, Douglas Fairbanks, and

The Officers

Chairman and CEO: Gerald M. Levin

Vice Chairman: Robert Edward Turner III

President: Richard D. Parsons

Chairman and CEO, Home Box Office: Jeffrey L. Bewkes

Chairman and CEO, Time Warner Cable: Joseph J. Collins

D.W. Griffith. These well-known artists joined together to establish a motion picture company in which they, rather than powerful Hollywood magnates, would have creative control.

The young company did not operate a studio, nor did it have actors or directors under contract. Instead, it was a cooperative distributor of pictures that were made by independent producers who financed their own production and paid UA a percentage of their profits.

During the company's first five years, it released an average of only eight pictures per year, the first of which was *His Majesty, the American*, starring Douglas Fairbanks. Financing was difficult, since UA remained privately held. In 1924, Joseph Schenck became president and reorganized the company. He recruited such stars as Buster Keaton and Gloria Swanson, as well as producer Sam Goldwyn. As a result, UA's production schedule improved. In 1927, its *Two Arabian Knights* garnered the company's first Academy Award.

In order to compete with the leading studios for the declining audiences during the Great Depression, Schenck led UA into financing the production of films for a cut of their revenues. He also joined with Darryl Zanuck to form Twentieth Century Pictures. This independent production company eventually accounted for nearly half of UA's films, yet UA's partners would not give up any of their shares in UA to Twentieth Century. Consequently, Schenck and Zanuck resigned and merged Twentieth Century with the Fox Film Corp.

Although UA worked with such producers as Walt Disney, Alexander Korda, and Sam Goldwyn, and its attendance was healthy, it continued to lag behind MGM, Warner Brothers, and Paramount. Financial difficulties and internal disputes resulted in the departure of Goldwyn, who had made 50 films during his 14 years at UA.

Movie attendance picked up during World War II, but UA's shortage of films for distribution prompted it to lower its production standards, which harmed the company's reputation. After the war, attendance dropped again. David O. Selznick, the independent producer who had released MGM's *Gone With the Wind* through United Artists, left UA in 1946. By the end of the decade the company repeatedly failed to show a profit.

In July 1950, UA's remaining owners, Chaplin and Pickford, brought in new management. The first team was replaced within months by Arthur Krim and Robert Benjamin. Chaplin and Pickford had agreed to give these two film veterans half of UA if they could make it profitable within ten years. After securing a $3 million loan from Fox Films, the company released the highly successful *High Noon* and *African Queen*. Within a year UA was back in the black.

UA's success continued during the 1950s, when its roster included such stars as John Wayne and Bob Hope. In 1955, Chaplin sold his 25% interest in UA to Krim and Benjamin, who gained full ownership of the company when Pickford did the same the following year. UA went public in 1957, bringing in $17 million.

UA thrived during the 1960s. Its profitability had been solidified through its stock offering, and its reputation for quality films had been salvaged. That decade its films earned 11 Academy Awards, five of them for Best Picture. In 1963 *Dr. No*, the first James Bond movie, was distributed through UA, and touched off what would become one of the company's most successful series.

Transamerica Corp. purchased 98% of UA in 1967. Krim and Benjamin were replaced as the company's leaders in 1969, only to be brought back when UA lost $35 million in 1970. Three years later UA purchased the distribution rights to MGM's films for ten years while that company focused on building the MGM Grand Hotel in Las Vegas.

UA released a number of box office hits in the late 1970s, including *One Flew Over the Cuckoo's Nest*, *Rocky*, and *Annie Hall*. In 1978, however, Krim left after a dispute with Transamerica leader John Beckett. He was soon joined by Benjamin and Eric Pleskow, UA's president. These three men then joined together to form Orion Pictures Corp.

UA faced leadership problems in the wake of their departure. Transamerica's James Harvey became chairman and Andy Albeck was promoted to president. UA experienced its most successful season in 1979, with such hits as *Rocky II*, *Manhattan*, *Moonraker*, and *The Black Stallion*. The next year, however, *Heaven's Gate* nearly brought the company to its knees. This western, directed by Michael Cimino, went over budget, ultimately costing $44 million to produce, yet brought in only $1.5 million. These results prompted the resignation of Albeck, who was replaced by Norbert Auerbach. In May 1981, Auerbach announced that UA had been purchased by MGM.

MGM had been formed in 1924 through the merger of three motion picture studios—Metro Pictures, Goldwyn Picture Corp., and Louis B. Mayer Pictures. The union had been orchestrated by Marcus Loew, chief of Loew's, Inc., one of the nation's largest theater chains, in order to secure an adequate supply of quality films for exhibition at his theaters. Mayer was selected as head of the new studio, which became a subsidiary of Loew's.

In its first two years, MGM released more than 100 motion pictures, one of which was the hugely successful *Ben Hur* in 1925. Although movie attendance dropped during the Depression, MGM remained a leader in the industry, and continued as such when the country emerged from the economic crisis. Its reputation for such well regarded films as *The Wizard of Oz* and *Boys Town* was supplemented by its quality shorts, including "Our Gang," "Laurel and Hardy," and the "Tom and Jerry" cartoons.

The U.S. motion picture industry reached its epitome in 1939. That year, MGM released such blockbusters as *Stagecoach, Mr. Smith Goes to Washington, Of Mice and Men,* and *Gunga Din.* Yet even these hits were eclipsed by its release of the record-breaking *Gone With the Wind.* Strangely, this film had not even been produced by MGM. Rather, it was the product of United Artists' David Selznick. Selznick insisted that the movie star Clark Gable, who was under contract with MGM. In order to use him, then, UA agreed to pay MGM half of the film's profits and release it through MGM.

MGM's reign was threatened by the boom in television viewership in the late 1940s and early 1950s. Executives scrambled to produce fare that audiences didn't have access to through television, and settled on musicals. MGM produced such hits as *Easter Parade, Annie Get Your Gun, Show Boat, Singin' in the Rain, An American in Paris,* and *Seven Brides for Seven Brothers.*

In 1952, the government ordered the dissolution of the monopoly of motion picture production and exhibition channels, and forced the split between studios and theaters. After Loew's was separated from MGM, the studio no longer had a guaranteed market. In 1957, it recorded its first net loss, but bounced back the next year. By the end of the 1960s, however, MGM lost its leadership position, as independent production became the standard.

By this time, the major studios were being purchased by large corporations. In 1970, investor Kirk

The Players

Turner Broadcasting System Chairman and CEO: Robert Edward (Ted) Turner III. Ted Turner took control of his family's billboard advertising company upon his father's death in 1963. He ventured into broadcasting by purchasing a small UHF television station in Atlanta in 1970. Five years later, having renamed the station WTBS (or TBS, for Turner Broadcasting System), he introduced it to cable television. Expanding on the success of his cable venture, he formed the Cable News Network (CNN) in 1980, followed by Turner Network Television (TNT), 1988; the Cartoon Network, 1992; CNN International, 1993; and Turner Classic Movies (TCM), 1994. Aside from his cable ventures, Turner also had a hand in the movie industry. In 1986, he purchased the MGM/UA Entertainment Company, acquiring its movie library of more than 4,000 titles. A sore point with the film industry, he proceeded to "colorize" many black-and-white classics. The year 1993 marked his expansion into film production with the acquisition of two movie studios: Castle Rock Entertainment and New Line Cinema. After the sale of his company in 1996, Turner became vice-chairman of Time Warner.

Tracinda Corp. President: Kirk Kerkorian. Kirk Kerkorian chose commercial aviation over a high school diploma. After earning his wings as a pilot, he formed the Los Angeles Air Service, which was soon renamed Trans International Airlines Corp. Kerkorian took a leap into Hollywood by purchasing controlling ownership of MGM in 1969, and orchestrated the company's merger with United Artists in 1981. Five years later he sold MGM/UA to Turner Broadcasting but repurchased United Artists, which he kept privately held. Frustrated with the company's poor financial performance, he sold it to Pathe Communications in 1990. That year he launched a failed takeover of Chrysler Corp., but walked away with about $3 billion in Chrysler stock. Kerkorian returned to the motion picture industry by repurchasing United Artists, then known as MGM/UA Communications, in 1996.

Kerkorian gained control of MGM. He sold off many of its assets, including its overseas theaters, its record company, and parts of its lot. In 1973, MGM sold its entire distribution business to United Artists. Continuing to invest in operations outside of the unpredictable motion picture industry, MGM pulled in more revenues from its MGM Grand Hotels in Las Vegas and Reno than from its movie operations. In 1981, however, it changed direction back into motion pictures, and purchased United Artists.

The MGM/UA Entertainment Co. was formed at a time when movie libraries became valuable assets in the cable television and videocassette markets. In 1983, Kerkorian attempted to take the company private by purchasing the shares of MGM/UA that he didn't already own, but was defeated. Two years later, Ted Turner agreed to buy the company, whose movie library would plug a shortage of content for the cable operations of Turner Broadcasting System. As part of the agreement, Turner resold United Artists to Kerkorian, thereby reverting UA into a separate company. UA proceeded to purchase from Turner additional assets, including the production and distribution units, the MGM/UA Home Entertainment Group, and the UA film library.

United Artists changed its name to MGM/UA Communications Co. in 1986. The company had only volatile success, and a frustrated Kerkorian soon began shopping for potential buyers. An agreement to sell off a 25% stake in July 1988 fell through, and company executives began resigning. MGM lost $88 million in 1987 and $48.7 million the following year. A deal to sell the company to Qintex Australia Ltd. was canceled in October 1989.

Led by Italian tycoon Giancarlo Paretti, Pathe Communications purchased MGM/UA in 1990. Paretti drove MGM nearly bankrupt, and Credit Lyonnais foreclosed on it and assumed control. It began looking for buyers, and in 1996 Kerkorian was again attracted to the company. He formed a group of investors that included MGM chief Frank Mancuso and Australian-based Seven Network to purchase MGM.

MGM/UA went public in 1997, thereby gaining the funds to buy Orion Pictures, Goldwyn Entertainment, and Motion Picture Corporation of America. Kerkorian purchased an additional 25% in MGM from one of his partners in 1998, giving his Tracinda company a 90% interest. MGM paid $250 million for PolyGram's movie library in 1999. That year it also terminated its agreement that gave Time Warner distribution rights to MGM's videos.

Market Forces Driving the Acquisition

By July 1985, Ted Turner was losing in his attempt to acquire CBS Inc. That network would have boosted the languishing revenues of Turner Broadcasting System by providing a steady source of advertising income, as well as supplying news and sports programming capabilities. The fiercely independent CBS threw several blockades before Turner, however. These anti-takeover measures included a stock buyback plan and a cap on the amount of debt it could shoulder, an amount that, not coincidentally, would have been exceeded if Turner's bid was successful. Faced with these impediments, Turner dropped his initial offer for CBS in late July, but vowed that he would make another run for the network after securing additional financing.

But Turner realized that the writing was on the wall, and that a future attempt for CBS would face additional obstacles. So in early August he entered into negotiations with Kirk Kerkorian, the majority owner of MGM/UA Entertainment Co. This conglomerate had a number of prized assets, including a movie production studio and a global distribution network. Of particular interest to Turner, though, was its library of 3,600 films, including *Gone With the Wind* and *The Wizard of Oz.*

Meanwhile, Kerkorian was frustrated with MGM/UA's profitability. He had attempted to take the company private in 1983, but was challenged by high criticism and a lawsuit. Although dropping this idea at the time, he continued to desire the company's privatization. When Turner approached him in August, Kerkorian saw the opportunity to retain a piece, which would become privately owned, of MGM/UA.

Approach and Engagement

On July 25, 1985, only days before canceling his offer for CBS, Ted Turner entered into negotiations with Kirk Kerkorian to purchase MGM/UA Entertainment Co. Talks proceeded quickly, and on August 7 an acquisition agreement was announced. At the same time, Turner officially abandoned his quest for CBS.

The $29 per share cash offer was valued at $1.5 billion. Under it, Turner would also assume $578 million in MGM debt. As part of the complex deal, Turner agreed to sell United Artists, including its film library, back to Kerkorian for $470 million, thereby reducing Turner's cash purchase to about $1 billion. Yet Turner Broadcasting System didn't have even this sum, so it had to seek financing from outside sources.

Skepticism over his ability to raise the necessary financing caused Turner and Kerkorian to revise the terms of their deal on October 2. Although still valued at $29 per share, the offer was modified from an all-cash bid to $25 in cash plus one share of new issue TBS stock.

Meanwhile, another stumbling block arose. Rainbow Services Company, a cable operator, had recently entered into an agreement for the rights to broadcast certain MGM films on its American Movie Classics cable channel. On October 19 Turner and Kerkorian reached a settlement with the cable company. Rainbow would receive payment totaling $50 million, of which $32.5 million would be paid by United Artists with the remaining $17.5 million paid by TBS after completion of the acquisition.

This extra payment exacerbated the financial difficulties Turner was facing. In early November he thought that his problems were solved when Viacom International Inc. entered into negotiations to purchase a large portion of MGM's studio, videocassette, and film distribution businesses for an estimated $300 million. These talks broke off, however, in mid-December.

Turner also terminated discussions to sell 50% of his Cable News Channel (CNN) to NBC when he refused to relinquish editorial control over it. This deal would have garnered Turner about $300 million to help pay for MGM, as well as make a preemptive strike against a 24-hour cable news channel planned by NBC.

On January 16, 1986, Turner and Kerkorian again revised their deal. Under the new terms, Turner would pay $20 per share in cash plus one share of TBS preferred stock, dropping the total value to $25 per share, or $1.25 billion. Analysts believed that under these terms, Turner finally had a viable chance at financing the deal. They were correct, and on March 25, 1986, Turner completed the acquisition of MGM/UA Entertainment.

Products and Services

Time Warner, which acquired Turner Broadcasting System in 1996, was organized in four operating divisions in late 1999:

Cable Networks was comprised of two segments. Home Box Office (HBO) included HBO, Cinemax, and the Comedy Channel; and New Line Cinema holdings. TBS, Inc. incorporated CNN, TBS SuperStation, Turner Network Television, Cartoon Network, and Turner Classic Movies networks, as well as interests in the Atlanta Braves, Atlanta Hawks, Atlanta Thrashers, World Championship Wrestling, and Goodwill Games.

The **Publishing** unit operated as Time Inc., which offered such magazines as *Time, People, Sports Illustrated, Fortune, Life, Money, Parenting, In Style,* and *Entertainment Weekly.*

Entertainment was comprised of two companies. Warner Bros. held the Warner Bros. branded movie and television production houses, video company, and retail stores, as well as Castle Rock Entertainment and the WB Television Network. Warner Music Group encompassed such music labels as Atlantic, Elektra, Warner Bros., and Sire.

Cable Systems consisted of Time Warner Cable, which served more than 12.6 million subscribers by year-end 1997.

Changes to the Industry

The acquisition of MGM/UA by Turner Broadcasting Service (TBS) marked Ted Turner's foray into Hollywood. More importantly, it provided the company with the access to content for which it had been starved. Turner's 24-hour cable station, SuperStation WTBS, gained thousands of movie classics for broadcast in their original format. MGM's library also provided new opportunities for content. Some of its films could serve as the basis for television spin-off series. Many also lent themselves to "colorization," a controversial process of adding color to black-and-white movies. These assets came at a huge price, however, and in the end, Turner was forced to sell of all but that single piece of MGM.

Review of the Outcome

The acquisition left Turner with almost $2 billion in debt. Annual payments on that load would reach as high as $750 million in 1988, while the combined TBS/MGM was expected to earn less than $200 million in 1986.

Devising a method of reducing that debt load was not only a matter of finance, it was the only way for Turner to retain control of his beloved company. According to the terms of January's revised deal, Turner was required by his investment banking house, Drexel Burnham Lambert Inc., to reduce his debt load to $1.1 billion before he could pay cash dividends. If he failed to do so, Turner would be forced to issue those dividends in TBS stock, thereby diluting his own 80% stake. The agreement gave him up to a year to accomplish this debt reduction.

On June 6, 1986, TBS announced two separate sales of MGM assets for a total of $490 million. Lorimar-Telepictures Inc. agreed to purchase MGM's 44-acre lot for $190 million. United Artists Corp. agreed to pay $300 million for MGM's film and television production operations, its home video unit, its 50% stake in the MGM/UA distribution company, and the MGM logotype. With that sale, TBS retained only one MGM asset—its film library.

Nearly one year later, on June 3, 1987, Turner narrowly escaped losing majority ownership of TBS. On that date, a group comprised of Time Inc., Tele-Communications Inc. (TCI), and 25 other cable television operators paid $562.5 million for 37% of TBS. This sale left Turner with slightly over 50% of his company, enough to retain control.

Research

Dodsworth, Terry. "Ted Turner's Celluloid Dream," in *Financial Times (London)*, 9 August 1985. Describes the reasons that MGM and TBS came together.

Engardio, Pete, with Mark Ivey and Ellen Farley. "It's December. Does Turner Know Where His MGM Bid Is?" in *Business Week*, 16 December 1985. Describes Turner's attempts to raise financing for his acquisition.

Fabrikant, Geraldine. "Ted Turner's Screen Test," in *The New York Times*, 30 March 1986. A lengthy article providing a chronology of the transaction.

———. "Turner to Sell MGM Assets," in *The New York Times*, 7 June 1986. Describes Turner's sale of the last of the MGM properties.

"MGM/UA Communications Co.," in *International Directory of Company Histories*, Vol. II, St. James Press: 1990. Provides a historical review of both MGM and UA.

Stevenson, Richard W. "Turner and MGM/UA Alter Deal," in *The New York Times*, 3 October 1985. Details the first revision to the deal, as well as the Rainbow snag.

Time Warner Inc. 1997 Annual Report. Covers financial highlights and describes company operating segments.

Time Warner Inc. Home Page, available at http://www.time-warner.com. Official World Wide Web Page for Time Warner. Includes access to information on products and services, press releases, and investor information.

"Turner Broadcasting System Inc." in *Notable Corporate Chronologies*, The Gale Group, 1999. Provides a historical review of TBS.

Vise, David A. "Turner Drops Hostile Bid for CBS," in *The Washington Post*, 8 August 1985. Announces Turner's termination of the CBS bid in favor of his deal with MGM/UA.

LAURA BRYSON

TYCO INTERNATIONAL & AMP

nationality: USA
date: April 2, 1999
affected: Tyco International Ltd., USA, founded 1960
affected: AMP Inc., USA, founded 1941

Tyco International Ltd.
The Gibbons Bldg.
10 Queen St., Ste. 301
Hamilton, HM11
Bermuda

tel: (441)292-8674
web: http://www.tyco.com

Overview of the Acquisition

In August 1998 AlliedSignal launched a hostile takeover for AMP, the leading manufacturer of electrical, electronic, fiber optic, and wireless interconnection products. AMP responded by throwing every type of blockade it could muster at AlliedSignal, including the Pennsylvania state legislature. Those impediments proved an annoyance, but not a deterrent, to AlliedSignal.

Determined to outmaneuver AlliedSignal, AMP turned to Tyco International as a white knight, a preferred acquirer. Tyco, the world's leader in fire protection systems, electronic security, and flow control valves, brought an end to the battle by offering a price for AMP that AlliedSignal considered to be out of proportion to the value of the target company.

History of Tyco International Ltd.

Arthur J. Rosenberg established the Materials Research Laboratory in 1960, and began conducting experimental work for the government. That year it formed Tyco, Inc. as a holding company for both the laboratory and the newly formed Tyco Semiconductor unit. In 1962 Rosenberg incorporated his enterprise as Tyco Laboratories, into which the Material Research Laboratory and Tyco Semiconductor were merged.

Tyco went public in 1964 and began branching into the commercial sector, employing a team of top researchers to develop high-tech products for the marketplace. By 1965 the company had developed a silicon carbide laser and the Dynalux battery charger, and had made advances in fluid controls, microcircuitry, and fuel cell catalysts.

The company embarked on an aggressive acquisition campaign in 1966 in order to expand its development and distribution network. That year it purchased Mule Battery Manufacturing Co., Industrionics Control, Inc., and Custom Metal Products, Inc. By the end of 1968, Tyco had acquired 16 companies, including those added that year: Electralab Electronics Corp., Air Spec, Inc., Explosive Fabricators Corp., Coating Products, Inc., and Digital Devices, Inc.

The Business

Financials

Revenue (1998): $12.3 billion

Employees (1998): 87,000

SICs / NAICS

sic 3678 - Electronic Connectors

sic 3679 - Electronic Components Nec

sic 2676 - Sanitary Paper Products

sic 2821 - Plastics Materials & Resins

sic 7382 - Security Systems Services

sic 3669 - Communications Equipment Nec

sic 3823 - Process Control Instruments

sic 3357 - Nonferrous Wiredrawing & Insulating

naics 334417 - Electronic Connector Manufacturing

naics 334418 - Printed Circuit Assembly (Electronic Assembly) Manufacturing

naics 339113 - Surgical Appliance and Supplies Manufacturing

naics 322291 - Sanitary Paper Product Manufacturing

naics 325211 - Plastics Material and Resin Manufacturing

naics 334290 - Other Communications Equipment Manufacturing

naics 561621 - Security Systems Services (except Locksmiths)

naics 334513 - Instruments for Measuring and Displaying Industrial Process Variables

naics 335921 - Fiber Optic Cable Manufacturing

With total sales of $41 million, Tyco purchased five additional companies in 1969, the same year that it reorganized its businesses into units and divested a number of unprofitable companies. Under the leadership of Joseph P. Gaziano, Tyco gained a listing on the New York Stock Exchange in 1974. Gaziano completed Tyco's most ambitious acquisition yet, that of the $22 million cash purchase of the Simplex Wire and Cable Co., a manufacturer of undersea fiber optic cable.

In 1976 Tyco purchased Grinnell Fire Protection Systems, a subsidiary of International Telephone and Telegraph (ITT) and a market leader in automatic sprinklers. Later that year it acquired a 13% stake in the process control designer and manufacturer Leeds & Northrup Co. Soon thereafter, Tyco announced its intention to buy more of Leeds' stock, and over the next two years embarked on a hostile takeover battle for the company. In January 1978, having acquired only 19% of Leeds, Tyco gave up its effort and sold its interest to Cutler-Hammer Inc.

Tyco acquired Armin Plastics, a leader in the production of polyethylene films, for $27 million in September 1979. Two years later it spent $97 million to purchase Ludlow Corp., a maker of packaging and other materials. Tyco's revenues surpassed $500 million in 1982.

The company reorganized in 1983 into three main units: fire protection and plumbing, electronics, and packaging. It disposed of corporate jets and apartments, trimmed corporate staff, and instituted a compensation program under which employees were rewarded in proportion to the profits that their units generated. Three years later Tyco reorganized again, this time into four segments: disposable and specialty products; fire and security systems; flow control; and electrical and electronic components. Also in 1986 it acquired Grinnell Corp.

Tyco continued its acquisition strategy, which enabled it to post sales in excess of $1 billion in 1987. It acquired Allied Tube and Conduit in 1988 and Mueller Co., a water and gas manufacturer, the following year. Its purchases in 1990 included National Pipe and Tube Co. as well as the fire production operations of Wormald International Ltd. In 1992 Tyco acquired Neotecha, a producer of Teflon-lined components.

L. Dennis Kozlowski was appointed CEO in 1993, the same year that the company changed its name to Tyco International Ltd. as a reflection of its global reach. Tyco's acquisitions in 1994 included three disposable medical product manufacturers: Classic Medical, Uni-Patch, and Promeon. Its 1995 purchases included Graphics Controls Corp., Stant Corp, and Kendall International Inc., maker of Curad brand bandages and other disposable medical products.

Tyco purchased James Jones Co. and Edward Barber & Co., Ltd., along with the waterworks valve businesses of Watts Industries, Inc., in 1996, and acquired American Pipe & Tube, ADT Ltd., Keystone International, and Inbrand Corp. in 1997. The following year it purchased Confab, Wells Fargo Alarm, United States Surgical Corp., Signal Circuits, Graphics Controls Corp., and Sherwood-Davis & Geck. Tyco also acquired the largest contract in its history, a $1.2 billion contract for the Pacific Crossing project, the first dense wavelength division multiplexed undersea fiber optic connection between Japan and the U.S., in 1988.

Tyco beat out AlliedSignal for the acquisition of AMP Inc., a deal that was completed in April 1999. Also that month, Tyco and Johnson & Johnson agreed to settle their three pending patent infringement lawsuits against each other. During the first half of 1999 Tyco agreed to acquire Raychem Corp., Central Sprinkler Corp., and certain subsidiaries of the Metals Processing Division belonging to Glynwed International. By that time Tyco was the world's leader in fire protection systems, electronic security, and flow control valves.

The Officers

Chairman and CEO: L. Dennis Kozlowski

Exec. VP and Chief Corporate Counsel: Mark A. Belnick

Secretary: Michael Jones

Exec. VP and Chief Financial Officer: Mark H. Swartz

VP: Joshua M. Berman

History of AMP Inc.

U.A. Whitaker, an engineer, entered into a business alliance in 1940 with S.N. Buchanan, inventor of a solderless method for crimping terminals to electric wires. Lacking startup capital, the partners received investments from the Hixon family's Midland Investment Company. In September 1941 they established Aero-Marine Products, Inc., a company specializing in solderless, uninsulated electrical connections for aircraft and boat manufacturers. Only months later the partners split up, and Buchanan cashed in his stock in the newly formed enterprise.

Aero-Marine thrived during World War II with its new preinsulated electrical terminal and unique crimping tool. Revenues in 1943 doubled to $2.2 million. After the war, however, the termination of government contracts caused the company's profits to drop sharply. Aero-Marine quickly turned its focus to civilian markets. In 1948 it introduced strip-form terminals and semi-automatic machines for high-volume customer use.

The firm expanded its product line and geographic presence. In 1952 it created a marketing unit called AMP Special Industries and established an affiliate, Pamcor, Inc., in Puerto Rico. Four years later, with sales of $32 million, the company went public and shortened its name to AMP Inc. It entered Japan with a wholly-owned manufacturing subsidiary, AMP Japan.

By 1959, having established subsidiaries in Australia, Britain, the Netherlands, Italy, Mexico, France, Canada, and West Germany, AMP gained a listing on the New York Stock Exchange. After establishing a plant in Greensboro, North Carolina, AMP formed AMP Air, a company airline offering commuter flights between its facilities. In 1965 it entered the ranks of the *Fortune 500* with sales of $142 million.

During the 1970s and 1980s AMP diversified into new markets by unveiling products for the computer, telecommunication, and home entertainment industries. In 1985 the company spent over $100 million in the development of fiber optics technology. Two years later it introduced "smart" connectors and undercarpet flat cables for offices, and formed the Automotive/Consumer and Aerospace/Government Systems business units in the U.S.

To expand its aerospace business, AMP acquired Matrix Science in 1988. Two years later it acquired Kaptron Inc., a maker of opto-electronic components, and entered into a joint venture with AKZO Nobel, a Dutch chemical company, to produce additive-type printed circuit boards. In 1995 AMP-AKZO became a wholly-owned unit of AMP following the company's buyout of the joint venture with AKZO Nobel. AMP-AKZO's name was later changed to AMP Circuits, which became a division of AMP. The following year it acquired the privately-held HTS Electrotechnik GmbH, a manufacturer of heavy-duty, metal-shell connectors located in Neunkirchen, Germany.

Falling revenues in 1997 prompted the company to reorganize for the second time in three years. That year it acquired El-Con and El-form, two Poland-based companies. By the end of 1997 AMP was the world's leading manufacturer of electrical, electronic, fiber optic, and wireless interconnections products. It emlpoyed 48,300 people in 53 countries and posted revenues of $5.75 billion.

Its falling profitability persisted in 1998, as the Asian economy continued its downturn. In response AMP announced the closure of three factories and the elimiation of 3,500 jobs. The following month AMP became the target of a hostile takeover attempt by AlliedSignal. Tyco International came to AMP's rescue by announcing its friendly purchase of the company in November 1998. Robert Ripp resigned as AMP president the day before the acquisition was completed in April, and was succeeded by Juergen Gromer.

Market Forces Driving the Acquisition

Tyco International Ltd. responded to a plea from AMP Inc. for a white knight to rescue it from a hostile

The Players

Tyco International Ltd. Chairman and CEO: L. Dennis Kozlowski. L. Dennis Kozlowski was appointed to the position of CEO of Tyco in 1993, and continued the company's aggressive acquisition campaign. Under Kozlowski, Tyco had acquired nearly 90 companies, quadrupling revenues from $3 billion to $13 billion, by the time the company closed the deal with AMP.

AMP Inc. Chairman and CEO: Robert Ripp. Robert Ripp left a long career at IBM to join AMP in 1994 as chief financial officer, a position that he held until he became executive vice president in charge of AMP's global businesses in 1998. In August 1999 Ripp was selected by the company's board to replace William Hudson as CEO to spearhead the company's battle against AlliedSignal. On April 1, 1999, just hours after AMP's shareholders voted in favor of the merger with Tyco International, Ripp announced his resignation effective at the end of that month.

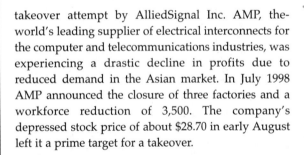

takeover attempt by AlliedSignal Inc. AMP, the world's leading supplier of electrical interconnects for the computer and telecommunications industries, was experiencing a drastic decline in profits due to reduced demand in the Asian market. In July 1998 AMP announced the closure of three factories and a workforce reduction of 3,500. The company's depressed stock price of about $28.70 in early August left it a prime target for a takeover.

For Tyco International, an acquisition of AMP was right in line with its aggressive acquisition campaign over the previous years. This strategy had boosted its revenues from $2 billion in 1992 to $12.3 billion in 1998. L. Dennis Kozlowski, Tyco's chairman and CEO, remarked in a company press release that the acquisition of AMP would meet "all of Tyco's previously stated strategies for adding to our business."

Tyco and AMP were compatible in a number of lines of operation. Although Tyco didn't have operations in the connector business, both companies produced backplanes and printed circuit boards. Tyco would also be able to leverage AMP's technological expertise in such areas as semiconductors, microwave components, memory modules, fiber optics, and network systems.

Approach and Engagement

AMP's vulnerability to a takeover was borne out on August 4, 1998, when AlliedSignal announced that it would be launching a cash offer of $44.50 per share for all outstanding AMP stock. AlliedSignal publicized this $9.8 billion unsolicited offer after AMP's board of directors refused to consider its earlier offers. On August 21 AMP's board rejected this bid as well, calling it "inadequate" and citing a lack of perceived synergies between the two companies. At the same time, it named Robert Ripp, a company vice president, to the posts of chairman and CEO to help it fend off AlliedSignal.

The takeover attempt grew increasingly hostile, as each company took its case to the courts. AlliedSignal filed suit to challenge the legality of AMP's dead-hand poison pill, which served as a defense mechanism against unfriendly takeovers by diluting the suitor's stake in the target company should it acquire more than a 20% interest. In addition, the dead-hand provision intensified this defense by ensuring that only those board members who were in place while the poison pill was adopted could vote to revoke it; a hostile suitor could, therefore, not redeem the pill by gaining control of the company's boarde. AMP had installed the dead-hand clause after AlliedSignal filed a consent solicitation with the Securities and Exchange Commission to install 17 new members to AMP's current 11-seat board. AMP countered by filing a suit to stop AlliedSignal from doing just that.

In September AMP revised its poison pill to trigger at a 10% limit, not 20%. AlliedSignal disclosed that it intended to acquire nine percent of the company's stock, just under that threshold, and then remove the pill. At the end of that month AMP joined in the bidding for its own stock, announcing its plan to repurchase up to 30 million shares at $55 each.

The battle moved to the Pennsylvania legislature in October 1998. AMP introduced a bill that would protect it, and all other companies incorporated in Pennsylvania, from hostile attacks by disallowing its shareholders to take part in a consent vote for 12 months after a hostile bid was launched. After the state senate approved the bill, the house tacked on several amendments, some irrelevant to the bill itself, before approving and returning it to the senate for reapproval. By that time, however, the senate was out of session, and the bill consequently stalled.

On October 8 the U.S. District Court rejected both of AlliedSignal's claims, forbidding that company to pack AMP's board with its own nominees and rejected its challenge of the legality of the poison pill. AlliedSignal received another blow on November 19, when the court enjoined it to solicit shareholder consent to expand AMP's board to 28 members, 17 of which would be allies of AlliedSignal.

Despite these legal victories, AMP still felt vulnerable to AlliedSignal and sought a white knight. Tyco International emerged in that capacity on November 23, when it announced a definitive agreement to acquire AMP. The stock swap agreement was based on a sliding scale dependent on Tyco's average stock price during the three-week period preceding AMP's shareholder vote on the deal. At the time of the acquisition announcement, the deal was valued at $11.3 billion, or $51 per share. At the completion of the transaction on April 2, 1999, AMP shareholders received 0.7507 shares of Tyco stock, valuing the deal at $12.25 billion, or $55.95 per share.

The deal was unchallenged by AlliedSignal, which withdrew from the bidding in November, stating that Tyco's purchase price far exceeded AlliedSignal's estimation of the value of AMP.

Products and Services

Tyco International operated in four business segments: Disposable and Specialty Products, Fire and Security Services, Flow Control, and Electrical and Electronic Components.

The **Disposable and Specialty Products** segment manufactured a wide range of products used in packaging including polyethylene films, laminated and coated products, a wide range of disposable medical products, and other specialty products. Its operating units included: Accurate Forming, ADT Automotive, A&E Products, Armin Plastics, Carlisle Plastics, Inc., Graphic Controls, Kendal Healthcare Products, Kendall International, Ludlow Coated Products, Ludlow Technical Products, Sherwood-Davis & Geck, Tyco Adhesives (formerly Kendall-Polyken), Uni-Patch, and U.S. Surgical. Earnings for this segment in 1998 increased 42% to $643.7 million on sales of $3.45 billion.

The **Fire and Security Services** unit in 1998 was the world's largest manufacturer, installer, and servicer of fire protection and life safety systems and services. Its operating units were: ADT, Ansul, Atlas Fire Engineering, Automatic Sprinkler, Bon + Naga, CIPE, Fire Control, Fire Defender, Grinnell Corporation, Interco Alarms, Lintott Process System, Mather & Platt, Modern, National Fire & Security, O'Donnell Griffin, Olsen Engineering, OPPI, Quintrix Communications, SEPCI, Sonitrol, Thorn Security, Total Walther, Tyco Building Products, Tyco Engineering and Construction, Vigilant, Wormald

Ansul (UK), and Wormald Fire Systems. This segment recorded a 45% increase in earnings in 1998, to $654.9 million, on sales of $4.74 billion.

The **Flow Control** segment manufactured and distributed products that moved, controlled, and sampled liquids, gases, powders, and other substances. These products included valves, pipe, couplings, fittings, meters, pipe hangers, steel fence posts, steel channel, and other related products. Operating units included: Allied Tube and Conduit, American Tube & Pipe, Anderson Greenwood, Bayard, Belgicast, Biffi, Canvil, Century Valve, Crosby, Debro Engineering & Presswork, Earth Tech, Goliath Engineering, Grinnell, Hancock, Henry Pratt Company, Hindle Valves, J.B. Smith Co., Intecva, James Jones, Keystone, Morin Actuators, Mueller Co., Neotecha, Sempell, Star Sprinkler, T.J.Cope, Unistrut, Valvtron, Vanessa, Winn Valves, and Yarway. In 1998 this segment posted earnings of $325.9 million on revenues of $2.34 billion.

The **Electrical and Electronic Components** segment, into which AMP was merged, manufactured a variety of products, including undersea fiber optic cable for telecommunications; multi-layer printed circuit boards for telecommunications, military, and computer applications; and electrical conduit. Its operating units in 1998 included: Allied Tube & Conduit, The Rochester Corporation, Simplex Technologies, Tyco Printed Circuit Group, Inc., and Tyco Submarine Systems, Ltd. In 1998, before the addition of AMP, this segment's earnings increased 131% to $367.5 million on revenues that reached $1.78 billion.

Review of the Outcome

Job cuts began almost immediately after Tyco merged AMP into its Electrical and Electronic Components unit. In fact, the workforce changes began only hours after AMP's shareholders approved the deal on April first. At that time Robert Ripp, AMP's chairman and CEO, announced his resignation effective April 30, 1999. Ripp had been slated to become president of AMP under Tyco, and was also to serve on the parent company's board of directors. In his statement, Ripp cited his resignation as a means to pursue "a number of other exciting opportunities." Some industry analysts, however, suggested that his exit was spurred by disagreements with Tyco over the scope of the impending job cuts.

This theory appeared even more plausible following the announcement of the planned cuts on April 6. Tyco eliminated about 30 executive positions as well as a 29-person AMP operation at Harrisburg International Airport. These cuts were the first of the planned reduction of about 8,000 AMP employees as part of a program to save Tyco an estimated $1 billion through the year 2001.

Research

"AMP Inc.," in *Notable Corporate Chronologies*, The Gale Group, 1999. Offers a chronology of the major events in AMP's history, until its acquisition by Tyco.

AMP Inc. Home Page, available at http://www.amp.com. Official World Wide Web Page for AMP. Includes annual reports and other financial data, business segment and product information, company history, news releases, and employment information.

Dochat, Tom. "AMP Shares Valued at Top Dollar in Tyco Deal," in *Knight-Ridder/Tribune Business News*, 29 March 1999. Details the sliding scale of the value of the Tyco offer.

———. "Bermuda-Based Tyco Optimistic about Savings at Recently Acquired Firm," in *Knight-Ridder/Tribune Business News*, 20 April 1999. Describes the restructuring program planned in the wake of the acquisition.

Liotta, Bettyann. "AMP, AlliedSignal Do Battle in Court," in *Electronic Buyers' News*, 31 August 1998. Details the legal maneuverings of AlliedSignal and AMP.

Quan, Margaret. "Connector Giant Staves off AlliedSignal with $11.3 Billion Deal, Tyco Merger Saves AMP from Hostile Takeover," in *Electronic Engineering Times*, 30 November 1998. Relates the terms of the Tyco/AMP agreement.

Richtmyer, Richard. "With Tyco's Bid, AMP Can Now Focus on Turnaround Plan—Back to Business," in *Electronic Buyers' News*, 30 November 1998. Describes the benefits that Tyco and AMP expect to realize from their union.

"Tyco International Ltd.," in *Notable Corporate Chronologies*, The Gale Group, 1999. Profiles the history of the company until its acquisition of AMP.

Tyco International Ltd. 1998 Annual Report, Tyco International Ltd., 1998. Provides in-depth financial results and an annual overview of the company's activities.

Tyco International Ltd. Home Page, available at http://www.tycoint.com. Official World Wide Web Page for Tyco International. Includes annual reports and other financial information, business segment and product information, a company history, links to Tyco subsidiaries, and news releases.

DEBORAH J. UNTENER

UAL MANAGEMENT AND EMPLOYEES & UAL

date: October 1989 (canceled)
affected: UAL Corp., USA, founded 1928

UAL Corp.
1200 E. Algonquin Rd.
Elk Grove Township, IL 60007
USA

tel: (847)700-4000
fax: (847)700-5229
web: http://www.ual.com

Overview of the Buyout

The $6.75 billion buyout of UAL Corp., the parent company of United Airlines, by management and employees in September of 1989 would have created the world's largest employee-owned company. The original deal called for United Airlines pilots to own 75% of the firm, management to retain 10%, and British Airways PLC to pay $750 million for the remaining 15%. The deal fell apart when Citicorp and Chase Manhattan were unable to raise the $7.2 billion loan sought by the airline to fund the buyout and cover anticipated cash flow requirements. After several rounds of buyout negotiations with unions, UAL shareholders agreed in 1994 to sell a 55% stake of the firm to employees for $5 billion.

History of UAL Corp.

The U.S. government privatized its air mail operations, with national routes divided into twelve regional segments, in 1925. The following year, Walter T. Varney formed Varney Air Lines to deliver mail between Elko, Nevada, and Pasco, Washington. Also, Vern Gorst established Pacific Air Transport to deliver mail between Los Angeles, California, and Seattle, Washington. In 1927, William Boeing formed Boeing Air Transport Co. (BAT) as a subsidiary of Boeing Airplane Co., and took over air mail service linking Chicago, Illinois, and San Francisco, California.

On October 28, 1928, United Aircraft and Transportation Corp. (UATC) was founded as a holding company for various Boeing enterprises, including Boeing Airplane Co., Boeing Air Transport, Pratt and Whitney, and Pacific Air Transport, which BAT had acquired earlier that year. BAT became the first airline to offer flight attendant services in 1929. A year later, UATC acquired Varney Air Lines. UATC incorporated United Air Lines Inc. in 1931, as a management company to oversee its airline operations.

United Airlines took delivery of the Boeing 247, its first all-metal, low-wing passenger aircraft, in 1933. The following year, United Airlines became a separate business entity and began offering flights to Canada. Publicity surrounding airplane crashes caused a decline in business in the mid-1930s; United Airlines

The Business

Financials

Revenue (1998): $17.56 billion

Employees (1998): 95,035

SICs / NAICS

sic 4512 - Air Transportation-Scheduled

sic 6719 - Holding Companies Nec

naics 481111 - Scheduled Passenger Air Transportation

naics 551112 - Offices of Other Holding Companies

responded by creating and implementing more rigid safety codes. The airline also established the industry's first flight kitchen.

During World War II, United Airlines participated in military contract operations for the Air Transport Command and gained experience in flying from the mainland U.S. to Hawaii. Service linking Honolulu, Hawaii, and San Francisco, California, began in 1947. The firm also began experimenting with jet passenger and cargo airplanes, and aircraft maintenance operations were centralized in San Francisco. In 1953, United Airlines joined with RCA Corp. to develop airborne weather-mapping radar. By the end of the decade, United Airlines became the first airline to make use of flight simulators in pilot training and testing programs; began offering the first nonstop service between New York, New York, and San Francisco; and entered the jet age with the purchase of 30 DC-8 jet aircraft at a cost of $175 million.

Despite these accomplishments, UA's position within the industry began to decline. In 1961, the airline merged with Capital Airlines, as a means of expanding its position in the eastern U.S. When the deal was completed, United Airlines became the world's largest airline. In December of 1964, United Airlines became the first U.S. airline to install fully automated, all-weather landing systems in its aircraft. The famous "fly the friendly skies" slogan was launched in 1965. Revenues exceeded $1 billion in 1967. United Airlines then created UAL as a subsidiary to manage the company's non-airline businesses; eventually, United Airlines became a subsidiary of UAL.

In 1970, UAL acquired Western International Hotels. Six years later, the firm established a computerized reservation system for use by travel agents and

agreed to pay $1 million to settle back-pay claims in a suit filed by minority and female employees. A dispute with the pilots union was settled quickly in 1979 when UAL agreed to job security provisions in exchange for increased flexibility in work rules. That year, the firm posted a loss of $72 million for the fiscal year. Acquisitions included Mauna Kea Properties and Olohana Corp., both based in Hawaii, for a total of $78 million.

Service to Mexico was offered by United Airlines for the first time in 1980. The Mileage Plus frequent flier program was launched a year later. In 1983, United Airlines received clearance to offer its first scheduled flights outside of North America and initiated routes to Hong Kong and Japan from the Pacific Northwest. The airline also established San Francisco as its West Coast hub. UAL bought rental car giant Hertz Corp. in 1985. That year, American Airlines usurped United Airlines as the world's largest airline. Early in 1986, United Airlines paid $715.5 million for the Pacific Division of Pan American Airlines, gaining 18 jet aircraft, 2,700 employees, 65,000 route miles, and 30 Asian destinations. The airline also established an East Coast hub at Dulles International Airport outside Washington, D.C., and formed United Express as a joint venture with small commuter airlines including Air Wisconsin, Aspen, and Westair.

UAL changed its name to Allegis, a computer-generated amalgam of allegiance and aegis, in 1987. Later that year, Coniston Partners acquired a 13% share of Allegis and announced its intention to take over the company. Allegis responded by assigning Boeing Co. a 16% stake in corporate stock in exchange for a $2.1 billion order for new aircraft, but the attempt to avert the takeover by Coniston Partners failed. In 1987, Allegis restructured to streamline operations, announcing its intention to divest all non-airline holdings. When the overhaul was completed in May of 1988, Allegis changed its name back to UAL Corp. After thwarting a hostile takeover bid by billionaire Marvin Davis, United Airlines management and pilots attempted a buyout of the firm. The deal crumbled, however, when financial backing for the purchase failed to materialize.

In the early 1990s, United Airlines began offering service from Chicago, Illinois, and Washington, D.C., to Frankfurt, Germany, as well as nonstop service between Chicago and Tokyo. The firm also bought the Pan American's hub operations at Heathrow Airport in England. In 1993, United Airlines entered into a cooperative arrangement with Deutsche Lufthansa AG, wherein the companies shared airport facilities at Chicago; Washington, D.C.; and Frankfurt, Germany. Although UAL refused a buyout offer made by airline unions that year, the unions persisted in their efforts to purchase the company. In 1994, employees purchased 55% of UAL for roughly $5 billion. The firm posted an $11 million fourth quarter profit, its first final quarter profit since 1989.

A planned merger with USAir Inc. fell apart in late 1995. UAL cited USAir's high labor costs as the chief obstacle to the purchase. Profits jumped 45% in 1996 to $960 million. International air freight service to Asia was launched that year. Delta Airlines and United Airlines agreed to merge frequent flier programs in 1998. In the first three months of 1999, UAL stock vaulted 252% as industrywide labor disputes abated. United Airlines announced plans to build a new 250,000-square-foot headquarters building at Chicago's O'Hare International Airport.

Market Forces Driving the Buyout

UAL's diversification into car rental and hotel operations in the mid-1980s had weakened its performance, leaving the firm vulnerable to Coniston Partners, which secured a 13% stake of UAL in 1987 and threatened to take over the firm. That year, the new majority shareholder led a successful effort to oust CEO Richard Ferris in favor of Stephen Wolf.

It was amidst this management scuffle that the pilots of United Airlines made their first buyout offer for UAL, which UAL turned down. It wasn't until oil and real estate billionaire Marvin Davis launched a $240 per share bid in August of 1989 for UAL that the firm began to seriously consider an employee buyout. "Compared to Davis, who might have wanted the airline simply for the resale value to its planes, the pilots began to look more attractive," wrote *Newsweek* in September of 1989.

A consortium comprised of management, pilots, and British Airways countered on September 15 with a $300 per share bid, and after two years of negotiations, it looked like the pilots were finally going to be successful in their efforts to buyout UAL. According to *Newsweek*, "The pilot offer had two big advantages over Davis's plan: the insider team could bring the airline $250 million-per-year savings in wage concessions, and they could give the corporation the tax benefits that the government affords employees stockownership plans."

British Airlines agreed to help fund the buyout as a means of securing its position as the world's leading international carrier. As owner of a 15% stake in UAL, British Airlines would gain access to the worldwide hubs, routes, and reservations systems of United Airlines, the second largest U.S. airline. Combined, British Airlines and United Airlines would have access to roughly 50% of the global air travel market.

The Officers

Chairman and CEO, UAL and United Airlines: Gerald Greenwald

President and Chief Operating Officer, United Airlines: James E. Goodwin

Exec. VP, UAL; Exec. VP of Corporate Affairs, United Airlines: Stuart I. Oran

Sr. VP and Chief Financial Officer, UAL and United Airlines: Douglas A. Hacker

Sr. VP, Secretary, and General Counsel, UAL and United Airlines: Francesca M. Maher

Approach and Engagement

Within a month of the August 4 bid by Davis, UAL stock had jumped from $164.50 per share to a whopping $290 per share. When UAL management, pilots, and British Airways launched their counterbid on September 14, stock was hovering at $279 per share. According to the terms of the $6.75 billion agreement, United Airline pilots would own 75% of UAL, management would retain a 10% stake, and British Airways would pay $750 million for a 15% stake. Almost immediately, UAL accepted the employee offer.

To fund the purchase, United Airlines approached a consortium of banks—led by Citicorp and Chase Manhattan—which was planning to loan out a total of $3 billion and raise another $4.2 billion from leading Japanese banks. However, the Japanese lenders balked at the financial framework of the agreement and refused to approve a loan that size. With UAL unable to raise the $7.2 billion needed to fund the buyout, as well as expected cash flow needs, the transaction ground to a halt, and stock plummeted to $198 per share. Davis withdrew his bid for UAL, and British Airways rescinded its offer to participate in the buyout, causing stock to tumble to $166.50 on October 20.

Products and Services

By the late 1990s, United Airlines, the main business of parent company UAL, offered services to nearly 150 U.S. destinations and 29 international destinations. The airline operated hubs in Chicago, Denver, San Francisco, and Washington, D.C., as well as in Tokyo and London. Domestic operations accounted for 68% of sales.

The Players

Chairman and CEO of UAL Corp.: Stephen M. Wolf. Once the chief executive at Flying Tigers, a cargo carrier, Stephen Wolf took the helm at UAL in 1987 after CEO Richard Ferris resigned amidst a management shakeup instigated by the firm's largest shareholder, Coniston Partners. Wolf divested the hotels and car rental operations acquired by UAL while Ferris was in charge. He led an unsuccessful buyout effort by UAL management and employees in 1989. In 1994, after UAL stockholders agreed to sell a 55% chunk of UAL to employees, Wolf resigned. He joined USAirways Group, Inc. as CEO in January of 1996.

Changes to the Industry

According to Bruce Wasserstein, author of *Big Deal: The Battle for Control of America's Leading Corporations*, the deal fell apart in the midst of a junk bond crisis. "Reflecting the turmoil in the junk bond market, UAL intended to raise the money entirely from a syndicate of banks." Ironically, the collapse of the agreement also helped heighten the market's disorder. When the UAL deal dissolved after the loan failed to emerge, "both the stock and junk bond markets reacted sharply downward."

Review of the Outcome

Negotiations between UAL and various airline unions continued during the early 1990s, during which time the firm laid off a substantial portion of its employee base and slashed executive salaries and fees. UAL sold the kitchen operations of United Airlines to Dobbs Houses in 1993, resulting in the loss of 5,800 union jobs. In 1994, UAL applied for and receives Securities and Exchange Commission approval for an employee (pilots and machinists, but not flight attendants) takeover of UAL, with a price tag set at $5 billion. Shareholders approved the purchase of a 55% interest in UAL by its employees, and the deal was completed later that year.

Research

Buchan, James. "UAL Struggles for Buy-Out Partner as BA Withdraws, in *Financial Times (London)*, 21 October 1988. Discusses UAL's options after the firm failed to get financing for its employee buyout and partner British Airways decided against participating in a future deal.

Carroll, Doug. "UAL Drops; Bid Is Still Up in the Air," in *USA Today*, 18 October 1989. Offers an overview of the wild ride of UAL stock during takeover negotiations in 1989.

Schwartz, John. "Giving 'United' a New Meanings," in *Newsweek*, 25 September 1989. Explains why UAL agreed to an employee takeover and why British Airways agreed to act as a partner in the deal.

UAL Corp. Home Page, available at http://www.ual.com. Official World Wide Web Page for UAL Corp. Includes product, corporate, and employment information, as well as current news and annual reports.

"UAL Corp.," in *Notable Corporate Chronologies*, The Gale Group, 1999. Covers major events in the history of UAL Corp.

Wasserstein, Bruce. *Big Deal: The Battle for Control of America's Leading Corporations*, Warner Books, 1998. Offers an overview of the largest mergers in recent American corporate history.

THERA WILLIAMS

ULTRAMAR & DIAMOND SHAMROCK

nationality: USA
date: December 3, 1996
affected: Ultramar Corp., USA, founded 1935
affected: Diamond Shamrock Inc., USA, founded 1967

Ultramar Diamond Shamrock Corp.
6000 N. Loop 1604 W.
PO Box 696000
San Antonio, TX 78269-6000
USA

tel: (210)592-2000
web: http://www.udscorp.com/

Overview of the Merger

The 1996 merger of Ultramar Corp. and Diamond Shamrock Inc. formed the third-largest independent petroleum company in the U.S. The new firm had oil refineries and retail units in Canada and much of the U.S.

History of Ultramar Corp.

The Ultramar Exploration Company, Ltd. (UEC) was founded in 1935 by four South African mining groups—Consolidated Gold Fields, Selection Trust, Central Mining, and Union Corp.—to discover and develop oil fields in Venezuela. Three years later it merged with Caracas Petroleum Co., an earlier Venezuelan oil field venture financed by the same companies that founded Ultramar Exploration, to form Caracas Petroleum Sociedad Anonima (CPSA). This transaction moved the company's headquarters from England to New York City, where it would be in a better position to develop close working relationships with U.S. oil companies.

In 1941 CPSA transferred the operation of most of its concessions in central Venezuela to Texaco and its subsidiaries, while retaining ownership of its land and drilling equipment. The alliance between CPSA and Texaco proved beneficial to the company, which gained access to technologies that would otherwise have been unavailable. That year it reorganized as Ultramar Company, Ltd., a holding company to manage the company's oil assets and equipment, which were almost exclusively operated by Texaco.

Ultramar began construction in 1943 of a 150-mile pipeline to link its Mercedes oil field at Guarico, Venezuela, with the sea. Three years later, the company's performance began to slump as the development of Venezuelan oil fields proved very capital intensive. Its financial position was further compromised in 1948, when production at the Mercedes oilfield increased more slowly than planned. The following year Union Corp. and Central Mining withdrew their support of Ultramar, selling their shares in the company to the public.

Finally, in 1950 the Mercedes oil field began producing according to plan, reaching a peak of 30,000 barrels of crude oil and 80 million cubic feet of natural

The Business

Financials

Revenue (1998): $11.1 billion

Employees (1998): 20,000

SICs / NAICS

sic 2911 - Petroleum Refining

sic 5172 - Petroleum Products Nec

sic 5983 - Fuel Oil Dealers

naics 324110 - Petroleum Refineries

naics 422720 - Petroleum and Petroleum Products
   Wholsesalers

naics 454311 - Heating Oil Dealers

gas per day. In 1952, fearing political instability in Venezuela, Ultramar began exploration in western Canada, creating Canpet Exploration Ltd. Ultramar joined with the Atlantic Refining Company in 1954 to explore and develop the Oritupana area in eastern Venezuela. The next year the company took on new shareholders, including a subsidiary of Consolidated Gold Fields, to raise capital for new exploration efforts. In 1957 it established Caracas Petroleum U.S. Ltd. to carry out joint exploration efforts in the U.S. with the Texkan Oil Co. The next year it formed Ultramar Canada, Ltd. as a wholly owned subsidiary to manage its Canadian operations.

In 1959 Texaco announced that it would no longer purchase all of Ultramar's Venezuelan oil. So the next year the company began to develop its own refining and marketing operations to make up for Texaco's reduced role. It purchased the Panama Refining and Petrochemical Company, itself the owner of the Golden Eagle Refining Company (GER), with refining and marketing activities in California. The U.S. government imposed new quotas and restrictions on importation of petroleum products shortly after the acquisition, lessening its profitability and closing off Golden Eagle as an outlet for Ultramar's Venezuelan crude.

GER concentrated on production of aviation fuel and low-sulfur fuel oil, and in 1962 became the largest independent supplier of jet fuel to the U.S. military in California. Four years later Ultramar established Golden Eagle Exploration as a subsidiary to conduct petroleum exploration in western Canada. By 1967 Ultramar had become one of the largest importers of

petroleum products in Canada. Its increased presence in Canada occurred just in time, as its Venezuelan operations were experiencing difficulty. Political pressures to nationalize the Venezuela's oil fields mounted, and increasingly heavy taxes were levied against foreign companies operating in the country.

Ultramar expanded into the United Kingdom's petroleum market in 1968, when it purchased the Herts & Beds Petroleum Co. and its network of gas stations. This set off a pattern of acquiring small gas station management companies and heating oil distributors in the UK throughout the 1970s. In 1971 Ultramar began to develop a network of gas stations in eastern Canada; by 1975 it operated 1,500 gas stations there.

It sold its production facilities at the Mercedes field in Venezuela in 1972. The following year Venezuela nationalized its petroleum industry, and Ultramar lost its concessions at the Mercedes field and its 50% interest in the Oritupana oil field. By mid-decade a worldwide tanker surplus and the inaccessibility of Ultramar's Quebec refinery to supertankers led the company to withdraw from the shipbuilding business.

It purchased Canadian Fuel Marketers, an oil marketing and storage company with 40 gas stations in eastern Canada, in 1979, followed by Beacon Oil, an operator of 300 gas stations in central and northern California, two years later. In 1982 the company changed its name to Ultramar PLC. The next year it purchased Pittston Petroleum, a leading marketer and distributor of heating oils in the northeastern U.S. and eastern Canada.

The company entered a period of financial difficulties in 1985, as crude oil prices collapsed amid a worldwide glut on the petroleum market. That year it reported net profits of GBP 71 million, a 50% decline from the previous year's level. In 1986 it acquired the marketing operations of Gulf Canada. At the same time it divested itself of Ultramar Petroleum Inc., its marketing subsidiary in the northeastern U.S. Operating profits rebounded to GBP 136 million.

Ultramar doubled its U.K. holdings in 1988 by acquiring Blackfriars Oil & Gas from Associated Newspaper Holdings. It also shored up its operations in the western U.S., purchasing the Wilmington Refinery in California for GBP 260 million. Having closed its California refinery, the company was forced to supply its western U.S. distributors using oil bought in public markets. In 1989 it acquired the U.S. oil and gas properties of ENSTAR, in partnership with Union Texas, gaining production facilities in the U.S. to complement its refining and marketing operations.

The Persian Gulf War improved Ultramar's global position, as it conducted no business in the Middle East. In 1990 it purchased 62 gas stations in California from Conoco, and acquired 200 Canadian gas stations and a refinery in Nova Scotia from Texaco. That year it transferred its interests in the Indonesian consortium to the Virginia Indonesia Co., a joint venture it created with Union Texas.

Lasmo PLC purchased a 54% interest in Ultramar in 1991 and announced that it would sell off select portions of the company's Canadian operations. The following year Texaco emerged as the front-runner to acquire Ultramar's refinery operations in Quebec. Lasmo PLC spun off the U.S. operations of Ultramar PLC as Ultramar Corp., a separate company with headquarters in New York City. By 1994 Ultramar PLC had been stripped of its North American operations but retained significant holdings in the North Sea and Indonesia.

History of Diamond Shamrock Inc.

Diamond Alkali Co., a Pittsburgh-based soda ash manufacturer, was formed in 1910. Four years later the company began producing large amounts of canning glass and marketing more of its soda ash. By 1915 Diamond Alkali had overproduced, and began to utilize excess product in new ways. By combining soda ash with limestone, it manufactured caustic soda, which eventually led to the production of lye, soap, detergents, rayon, and cellophane. In 1925 it again expanded its product line to include calcium carbonates, cement, and coke. Four years later, using the electrolysis of salt process, the company produced caustic soda and discovered two by-products, chlorine and pure hydrogen.

The company established its first research laboratory in 1942. By 1944 Diamond Alkali was operating a plant for magnesium, calcium hypochlorite, and synthetic catalysts in a joint lease with the M.W. Kellogg Co. That year it bought Emeryville Chemical Co. In 1948 company sales surpassed $50 million. The following year it purchased the Martin Dennis Co. and formed an export sales division.

During the 1950s the company's assets included 12 plants responsible for more than 100 various chemicals. In 1950 it bought the chromic acid business from E.I. du Pont de Nemours and Co., entering the organic and agricultural chemicals and plastics areas of business. The next year it entered the organic insecticides and agricultural chemicals field by purchasing Kolker Chemical Works, Inc. In 1953 Diamond purchased Belle Alkali Co., a producer of chemicals used to make silicone resins, solvents, and drugs.

The Officers

Vice Chairman, President, and CEO: Jean R. Gaulin

Chairman: Roger R. Hemminghaus

Exec. VP, Refining, S&D, and Wholesale: William R. Klesse

Exec. VP and Chief Financial Officer: H. Pete Smith

Exec. VP, Chief Administrative and Legal Officer: Timothy J. Fretthold

The company bought a 51% interest in Diamond Black Leaf Co. in 1955, making it a wholly owned subsidiary two years later. It entered a consolidation period in the 1960s. In 1960 Diamond merged with Bessemer Limestone & Cement Co. That year it also bought Harte & Co. and the Chemical Process Co. In 1967, after merging with Nopco Chemical Co., Diamond merged with Shamrock Oil and Gas Co., to form Diamond Shamrock Corp. In 1969 it bought Taylor-Evans Seed Co. and Pickland Mather & Co.

Diversifying, the company acquired American Chocolate & Citrus Co. in 1972. It followed up this purchase in 1975 by expanding its market to include commercial baking supplies through its purchase of Federal Yeast Corp., Gold Star Foods Co., and Bakery Products Inc. In 1979 Diamond bought Falcon Seaboard Inc., a producer of steam coal.

The 1980s brought the diversification strategy to a halt. In 1980 the company created new divisions targeted for divestiture in order to expand into coal. These divisions included plastics, metal coatings, domestic polymers, food-related products, animal nutrition, and medical products. In 1981 Diamond entered the coal industry by purchasing Amherst Coal Co. Two years later it merged with Natomas Co., gaining oil and gas operations, a geothermal energy business, and wells producing oil in the North Sea, Canada, and the U.S.

Concerned about a possible takeover attempt by Occidental Petroleum Corp., Diamond Shamrock Offshore Partners Ltd. was formed in 1984 to prevent any hostile maneuvers. In 1986 the company received a $2 billion acquisition offer from T. Boone Pickens in a securities exchange. Diamond rejected Pickens' offer and filed suit against him. Later that year it sold its chemical business to Occidental Petroleum for $850 million. In 1987 Pickens bid on the company again, forcing Diamond to restructure itself for the third time in two years. In April Diamond Shamrock R&M, Inc. became an independent oil refining and marketing company based in San Antonio, Texas, and Diamond

Shamrock Corp. became known as Maxus Energy Corp.

In 1988 Diamond Shamrock R&M began focusing on marketing operations in the Southwest by expanding refinery and pipeline capacity and retail presence. The following year it became a 33% partner in Mont Belvieu of Texas, which later grew to become the world's largest storage capacity. In 1989 it formed Diamond Shamrock Natural Gas Marketing Co. as a subsidiary. That year this subsidiary purchased Merit Tank-Testing, Inc. and Petro/Chem Environmental Services, Inc., which merged to form Petro/Chem Environmental Services, Inc.

The company again changed its name in 1990, returning to Diamond Shamrock, Inc. In 1995 it paid $260 million to acquire National Convenience Stores Inc., maintaining the Stop N Go name on its 660 stores.

Market Forces Driving the Merger

When the U.S. oil and gas industry experienced a consolidation trend in the 1990s, Ultramar and Diamond Shamrock felt obligated to participate. By uniting, these two petroleum companies would create the largest independent oil refiner and marketer, capable of operating on all three national coasts—the Atlantic, Pacific, and Gulf. The new company would benefit from geographic expansion and synergies of operation.

Ultramar operated in California, the northeast U.S., and eastern Canada. It possessed two oil refineries, one in California and the other in Quebec, that had a combined capacity of 250,000 barrels per day. Diamond Shamrock's strengths were in the southwest U.S., where it operated a large retail network. This network was comprised of 2,700 outlets under the names of Corner Store, Stop N Go, and Diamond Shamrock. It had captured the leading market share of gasoline in Texas, and held the second-place position in Colorado and New Mexico.

"By joining together, we will leverage both our companies' considerable strengths in petroleum refining and marketing and create new opportunities for cost savings and strategic expansion," explained Roger Hemminghaus, head of Diamond Shamrock, in *National Petroleum News*.

Approach and Engagement

On September 22, 1996, Ultramar and Diamond Shamrock entered into a merger agreement. Announced on the following day, the news was met with differing opinions from industry analysts. While there was consensus that the combined company would realize cost savings, the opinions varied regarding its strategic advantages. Some analysts believed that the deal would enable the company to expand its geographic reach efficiently. Others questioned the logic in forming a union between two companies that operated in distinct territories, as they would receive no synergies from overlap.

Ultramar Diamond Shamrock Corp. would be formed through a stock swap in which each share of Diamond Shamrock would be converted to 1.02 shares of Ultramar Diamond Shamrock, while each Ultramar share would be translated on a share-for-share basis.

The new company would be headquartered at Diamond Shamrock's base in San Antonio, Texas, with about 200 jobs cut as a result of the displacement and job duplication. Roger Hemminghaus, Diamond Shamrock's chairman, CEO, and president, would take the helm of the new firm as chairman and CEO. Jean Gaulin, Hemminghaus' counterpart at Ultramar, would assume the roles of vice chairman, president, and chief operating officer.

On December 3, 1996, Ultramar Diamond Shamrock was officially formed and began trading on the New York Stock Exchange.

Products and Services

Ultramar Diamond Shamrock operated in two main lines of business. Its Marketing segment was comprised of 6,300 retail gasoline outlets in 21 states and six Canadian provinces. The majority of these were branded Diamond Shamrock, Ultramar, Beacon, or Total. It also operated retail stores branded as Corner Store, Stop N Go, Ultramar, Beacon, Total, and Sergaz locations. The company's Refining segment consisted of seven company-owned refineries in Texas, California, Oklahoma, Colorado, Michigan, and Quebec. With a total throughput capacity rated at 662,000 barrels per day, these refineries converted their raw material input into high-value products, primarily gasoline, diesel, and jet fuels.

Changes to the Industry

Ultramar Diamond Shamrock immediately became the nation's third-largest independent petroleum refiner and marketer. Its capacity of 475,000 barrels per day (b/d) was surpassed only by Sun Oil's capacity of 700,000 b/d and Koch Industries' 485,000 b/d. The new company had revenues of $8 billion and an equity market value of $2.3 billion, putting it in a favorable position to continue to expand through acquisitions and partnerships. This, claimed Hemminghaus, was exactly what the company planned to do.

True to that prediction, the new company wasted little time before entering into alliances. In September 1997 it acquired Total Petroleum (North America) Ltd., gaining a strong foothold in the Rocky Mountain and western plans region. In early 1998 it entered into an agreement to merge with Petro-Canada Inc., but the companies terminated discussion that June due to strong opposition by Canadian antitrust regulators. In October 1998 Ultramar Diamond Shamrock entered into an agreement with Phillips Petroleum Company to form a joint venture of their North American refining and marketing operations, but terminated negotiations in March 1999.

Review of the Outcome

As a result of combined operations, the new company's capital spending in 1997 dropped to $285 million from a combined total of $430 million in 1996. At the end of 1997, its first full year of operation, Ultramar Diamond Shamrock reported net income of $154.8 million on revenues of $10.9 billion.

At the conclusion of the merger, the newly formed company anticipated a reduction of 200 jobs. In January 1999 it announced plans to restructure retail marketing and refining operations, closing about 14% of its stores and eliminating 300 more positions. With those additional job cuts, the total workforce reduction since the formation of Ultramar Diamond Shamrock reached 1,300. On January 1, 1999, Jean Gaulin, vice chairman and president, added the post of CEO to his responsibilities; Roger Hemminghaus retained his role as chairman.

Research

"Diamond Shamrock, Inc.," in *Notable Corporate Chronologies*, The Gale Group, 1999. Profiles the company until its merger with Ultramar.

Francella, Barbara Grondin. "Diamond Shamrock, Ultramar to Merge to Form Oil Giant," in *Convenience Store News*, 20 October 1996. Describes the terms of the merger.

Pools, Jessica Johns. "This Big Texan Just Got Bigger," in *National Petroleum News*, November 1996. Profiles the two merging companies, with an emphasis on Diamond Shamrock.

Ultramar Diamond Shamrock Corp. Home Page, available at http://www.udscorp.com. Official World Wide Web Page for Ultramar Diamond Shamrock. Includes description of operations, annual reports and other financial information, and news releases.

"Ultramar, Diamond Shamrock to Merge," in *The Wall Street Journal*, 24 September 1996. Details the newly announced merger.

"Ultramar, Diamond Shamrock Merger 'Unique'," in *National Petroleum News*, November 1996. Details the merger agreement and provides comments from analysts.

"Ultramar PLC," in *Notable Corporate Chronologies*, The Gale Group, 1999. Provides an historical account of the company.

"Ultramar-Shamrock-Total Merger Creates Rockies Power," in *Octane Week*, 21 April 1997. Describes the company's acquisition of Total Petroleum just months after completing its own formation.

DAVIS MCMILLAN

UNICREDITO ITALIANO &
BANCA COMMERCIALE ITALIANA

UniCredito Italiano SpA
Piazza Cordusio 2
Milan, 20123
Italy

tel: 39 02 8862 1
fax: 39 02 8862 3967
web: http://www.credit.it

Banca Commerciale Italiana
Piazza Della Scala 6
Milan, 20121
Italy

tel: 39-02-88-501
fax: 39-02-88-503-026
web: http://www.bci.it

date: May 1999 (canceled)
affected: UniCredito Italiano SpA, Italy, founded 1870
affected: Banca Commerciale Italiana, Italy, founded 1862

Overview of the Merger

The planned merger between Italy's fourth-largest bank, Banca Commerciale Italiana SpA (BCI), and Italy's second-largest bank, UniCredito Italiano (UCI), would have created a new leader in Italy's financial services industry—called Eurobanca—with assets of nearly Lr500 trillion ($280 billion) and 4,200 branches in operation. The largest takeover bid in Italian corporate history, the $16.5 billion stock offer was rejected by BCI's board of directors in May of 1999. Despite the deal's failure, most analysts believe consolidation in the Italian banking industry will increase over the next few years as players reposition themselves to compete in the increasingly global marketplace.

History of UniCredito Italiano SpA

In 1870, Banca di Genova (BG) was founded. The Italian economy, although still essentially agricultural, underwent rapid industrial development for the next two decades. In 1893, a banking crisis was caused by the combination of the end of Italy's era of industrialization, agricultural failure in southern Italy, overextension of financial resources to fund building in the North, and a worldwide economic depression. Within two years, the Italian banking system was completely reorganized, and BG became Credito Italiano (CI), with most of its capital provided by German banks.

Caisse Commerciale de Bruxelles, Credit Liegiois, and Comptoir National d'Escompte de Paris acquired equity in CI in 1898, strengthening the bank's ties outside Italy. CI then began a twenty-year period of steady growth and expansion. In 1907, CI increased its capitalization with the financial support of the Banque Francaise pour le Commerce et l'Industrie and the Banque del'Union Parisienne. Three years later, CI joined Societe Generale de Belgique to found Banca Brasiliana Italo-Belgia (BBIB). The Italo-Turkish War put great strain on the Italian economy, with increased government expenditures triggering inflation.

In 1911, CI established a branch in London, which later in the year was named Correspondent to the Royal Treasury. World War I began in 1914. CI facilitated imports of grain, raw materials, and other essential goods using its international influence. The Italian government averted financial panic immediately after the War's outbreak by allowing banks to collaborate in meeting depositors' demands. CI entered another period of growth, particularly in its investment banking operations, as Italian banks became increasingly competitive in a booming industrial market fueled by the war effort.

In 1916, CI forged a joint venture with Lloyds Bank and London County and Westminster Bank, forming nonbanking subsidiaries Italian Corp. in London and Compagnia Italo-Britannica in Italy. The bank opened a representative office in New York City in 1917. The following year, the four largest Italian banks, including CI, formed a cartel to avoid competition and better regulate the rationing of industrial credit. CI established the Banca Unione di Credito in 1919 and acquired an interest in the Banque Generale des Pays Roumains and several other Austrian and Czechoslovak banks.

CI's activities during the early 1920s included joining the Italian Ministry of Foreign Affairs and a group of Chinese investors to form the Banca Italo-Cinese; helping establish the Banca Italo-Viennese and the Tiroler Hauptbank; opening branch offices in Paris and Berlin; and acquiring an equity interest in the Banco Italo-Egiziano. In 1925, a consortium of Italian and foreign banks, including CI, created the National Bank of Albania. CI also acquired equity interests in the Regional Bank of Erzegovina and the Istituto Nazionale per il Lavoro Italiano all'Estero. The following year, the Italian government imposed new regulations, forcing banks to obtain Ministry of Finance consent before amalgamating branches or opening new ones. CI continued to expand overseas despite the onset of the Great Depression, setting up several investment banking ventures including Societe Financiere Italo-Suisse-Geneva, Societe Financiere et Industrielle d'Egypte, Steweag-Sterische Wasserkraft und Elektizitat Graz, and the Societa Elettrica Italo-Albanese.

CI absorbed the Banca Nazionale di Credito in 1930 and gained three new foreign affiliates: Banque Italo-Francaise de Credit, Banca Coloniale di Credito, and Banca Dalmata di Sconto. Three years later, the Italian government reorganized the national banking industry, creating the Istituto per la Ricostruzione Industriale (IRI) to buy the long- and medium-term assets of the main commercial banks and become their main shareholder. In 1936, the government declared

The Business

Financials - UniCredito Italiano SpA

Revenue (1998): Lr133 trillion in assets

Employees (1998): 35,600

Financials - Banca Commerciale Italiana

Revenue (1998): Lr218 trillion in assets

Employees (1998): 28,479

SICs / NAICS

sic 6029 - Commercial Banks Nec

sic 6211 - Security Brokers & Dealers

sic 6021 - National Commercial Banks

sic 6282 - Investment Advice

naics 522110 - Commercial Banking

naics 522120 - Savings Institutions

naics 523120 - Securities Brokerage

naics 523930 - Investment Advice

CI to be a bank of national interest and barred the bank from engaging in investment banking.

World War II left CI stripped of its overseas assets and the Italian economy in shambles. The Allied occupational government moved to privatize IRI, but the company was in such disarray that a reorganization proved impossible. CI resumed international operations in 1946, reopening its offices in London, Zurich, Paris, and New York City, and establishing new offices in Frankfurt, Buenos Aires, and Sao Paolo. In conjunction with Banca Commerciale Italiana and Banco di Roma, CI founded the Metrobanca Banca di Credito Finanziario SpA, a provider of medium-term credit and merchant banking services.

Growth of the Italian export economy in the early 1950s turned CI's focus to domestic reorganization and development for the next two decades. In 1969, the U.S. Federal Reserve Board instituted a policy of monetary restraint, causing funds to flow into the U.S. and breeding a capital shortage in Italy and many other countries. IRI-controlled banks, including CI, were allowed to offer significant amounts of their stock for public sale to raise capital.

Italian businesses continued to expand their export trade and to demand increased services abroad during the early 1970s. CI once again began to emphasize expanding its international network; acquired an

The Officers

UniCredito Italiano SpA

Chairman: Lucio Rondelli

Deputy Chairman: Paolo Biasi

Deputy Chairman: Fabrizio Palenzona

CEO: Alessandro Profumo

Banca Commerciale Italiana

Chairman: Luigi Lucchini

Vice Chairman: Gianfranco Gutty

Co-CEO and Managing Director: Alberto Abelli

Co-CEO and Managing Director: Pier Saviotti

Chief Financial Officer: Alberto Varesco

interest in Orion Bank Ltd.; purchased a 50% interest in Credit Factoring International SpA, a British credit factoring operation in Italy; and acquired Libra Bank Ltd. Investments in the domestic economy remained low, and a three-month long strike in 1972 by bank employees resulted in increased operating costs. Rising energy prices touched off inflation in 1973, leading to a balance of payments that jeopardized Italian currency reserves. The following year, CI acquired the Banque Transatlantique. The value of the lira plummeted in relation to that of the dollar, causing economic instability, and in 1979, CI and the other national Italian banks were increasingly forced to invest in many unprofitable state-owned companies.

In 1982, IRI allowed banks of national interest to raise 41% of their own capital, easing restrictions in return for the continued support of the banks in propping up unsuccessful state-owned industries. Two years later, CI established Credito Italiano International Ltd. as a wholly owned merchant banking subsidiary operating out of London, England. The 1987 U.S. stock market crash hit CI's newly expanded securities operations hard, and the bank as a whole suffered a 33% drop in profits. However, the decreasing value of the dollar in relation to the lira and a worldwide drop in oil prices boosted the Italian economy. In 1988, CI doubled the size of its securities department. The following year, CI entered into a distribution agreement with Commercial Union of Britain, a composite insurer, to broaden its range of banking services and acquired a 35% interest in the Bank CIC-Union Europeene AG. CI also purchased a 4% share of Banca Nazionale dell'Agricoltura (BNA), Italy's largest private bank, and a 20% stake in

Bonifiche Siele, BNA's largest shareholder, for a total of Lr227 billion.

CI bought a 5% stake in Banque Commerciale du Maroc in 1990. Three years later, the Italian government privatized CI. In 1995, CI and Rolo Banca merged under the umbrella of Credito Italiano Group. The following year, the two banks began to form Credit Rolo Gestione SIM, a new company in which to consolidate all asset management activities. On October 23, 1998, Credito Italiano Group and Unicredito merged to form UniCredito Italiano, the second largest banking group in Italy. Plans to merge with Banca Commerciale Italiana to become the number one bank in Italy crumbled in mid-1999.

History of Banca Commerciale Italiana

In 1862, Societa Generale di Credito Mobiliare (SGCM) was founded to provide funding for industrial development following the unification of Italy. The bank prospered, lending primarily to the iron and steel industries. Financial crisis struck the Italian economy in the early 1890s, and in 1894, SGCM was declared insolvent and was reorganized as a private, joint-stock bank called Banca Commerciale Italiana (BCI) by a consortium of German banks. BCI was structured like a German bank and began floating both short- and long-term loans, specializing in financing shipping, textile, and electrical ventures.

The Italian economy suffered another depression in 1906 and once again BCI's investments in the iron and steel industries became untenable. A consortium led by the Bank of Italy stepped in and averted disaster by lending additional funds to iron and steel concerns. Five years later, BCI opened its first foreign branch in London, England, and began a two-year period of rapid growth. The end of World War I left many industrial concerns with surplus capacity, which hurt the banks' ability to lend to heavy industries. BCI formed a cartel with Credito Italiano (CI), Banco di Roma (BR), and Banca Italiana di Sconto (BIS) to coordinate loans to industrial firms. The bank also opened its second foreign branch, this one in New York City.

The Great Depression left many firms unable to repay their loans. By the early 1930s, BCI and many other Italian banks faced serious financial difficulties. To stave off insolvency, the Italian government created an agency called Instituto per la Ricconstruzione Industriale (IRI), which became the sole owner of BCI, CI, and BR and also acquired all of their industrial holdings. In 1936, IRI sold most of its industrial assets, but retained control of BCI. The bank became a short-term lender to comply with new government regulations differentiating short-, medium-, and long-term lending. BCI, CI, and BR were declared banks of national interest by the government in 1937.

Much of Italy's industrial capacity was destroyed during World War II. The Allied Control Commission, the governing body for occupied territories, took control of IRI and began to investigate the agency for alleged participation in war crimes. IRI was eventually cleared of these charges. In 1946, Mediobanca (MB), a medium-term credit institution, was created as a joint venture by BCI, CI, and BR. The Italian economy then entered a period of rapid growth, particularly in exports. BCI grew steadily throughout the 1950s, becoming more involved in domestic finance and opening few overseas branches.

The bank continued to grow slowly but steadily throughout the 1960s, despite a chronic shortage of capital. In 1969, BCI was allowed to sell some shares of its stock to raise capital, although IRI retained its controlling interest in the bank. A worldwide rise in petroleum prices created an energy crisis in 1973, and the Italian government moved to restrict the Italian money supply by imposing strict credit ceilings. Six years later, the same authorities restricted international expansion by Italian banks.

In 1982, BCI became the second-largest commercial bank in Italy when it acquired Litco Bancorp., owner of the Long Island Trust Co. in New York City, for $93 million. That year, the Italian government lifted credit ceilings, allowing greater competition in the banking industry and forcing the banks of national interest to re-evaluate their practices. BCI and Assicurazioni Generali SpA (AG), a large insurance company, formed GenerComit Gestione SpA, an investment management company. By the end of the decade, BCI had also created BCI (Suisse) and BCI of Canada; sold 51% of North American Bancorp (NAB) (formerly Litco) to the Bank of New York; created Fin. Comit SpA, a wholly owned subsidiary providing financial services, with branches in Munich and Shanghai; acquired Finservizi SpA (FS); created the BCI Funding Co.; helped to establish the Banca Internazionale Lombardia; and acquired a 2% interest in the Compagnie Financiere de Paribas.

BCI divested another 25% of its interest in NAB in 1990. The bank also created BCI Capital Corp. in Wilmington, Delaware, as a securities trader, and Comit Finance (Jersey) to collect funds through issuance of Eurobonds. In 1991, BCI acquired the Banque Sudameris France SA, renaming it Banca Commerciale Italiana (France) SA. Three years later, BCI was privatized. The bank acquired a 20% share of Cassa di Risparmio di Biella e Vercelli in 1997; a year later, that stake was increased to 40%. BCI also secured

controlling interests of Central-European International Bank of Budapest and Banco America do Sul Sao Paulo. Negotiations to merge with UniCredito Italiano into Italy's largest bank came to a halt in mid-1999.

Market Forces Driving the Merger

The advent of a standard European currency, the euro, on January 1, 1999, eliminated many major economic trade barriers between European countries. As a result, companies began expanding outside of their domestic markets, and international competition intensified. This new environment placed significant pressure on Italy's banks, which were dwarfed by such European giants as Germany's Deutsche Bank AG. A March 1999 issue of *The Economist* reported that San Paolo IMI, Italy's largest bank—formed by the 1998 merger of IMI Group and Istituto Bancario San Paolo di Torino—ranked only 58th among Europe's top banks. "The euro zone needs euro-sized players. Italian banks do not have the critical mass to be aggressive."

Rather than wait to be acquired, many Italian banks began pursuing deals, hoping to become hunters themselves, rather than targets. For example, on March 21, 1999, San Paolo IMI, which possessed a strong presence in corporate and investment banking, agreed to merge with Banca di Roma, a retail banking operation, to form one of Europe's top ten banks, with a network of 3,000 branches throughout Italy and assets in excess of 670 trillion lire. On the same day, Italy's fourth-largest bank, Banca Commerciale Italiana (BCI)—which had recently ended negotiations with Banca di Roma, Italy's fifth-largest bank—announced its intent to merge with UniCredito Italiano, the second-largest bank in Italy, formed by the 1998 merger of Credito Italiano Group and Unicredito.

According to a November 1998 article in *Institutional Investor*, Italian banks had been "merging at a dizzying pace in a much-needed consolidation ahead of the euro's introduction." BCI, which had yet to seal a deal of its own, needed to merge if it was going to compete globally. When BCI's negotiations with Banca di Roma dissolved in the wake of Dutch bank ABN AMRO's purchase of 8.8% of Banca di Roma, BCI became vulnerable to takeover attacks. Recognizing this, UniCredito moved in with a friendly offer. Acquiring BCI would allow UniCredito to cut costs by laying off an estimated 3,700 employees; increase sales, enabling the bank to spend more on things like innovative technology and marketing efforts; and enhance market capitalization, shoring up UniCredito's position as a global banking force.

Approach and Engagement

UniCredito Italiano offered eight shares for every five shares of Bance Commerciale Italiana (BCI). Worth $16.5 billion, the offer was the largest to date in Italian corporate history. Most analysts believed the deal would proceed fairly smoothly; however, in May of 1999, a new shareholder group gained control of the board of BCI in an effort to halt the merger. The dissident group successfully rejected the takeover offer that month and elected a new board of directors in June.

Products and Services

In 1999, UniCredito Italiano operated 2,700 branches and held a 12.5% share of Northern Italy's banking services market. Along with traditional banking products and services, the bank also offered equipment leasing, factoring, assets management, consumer credit, and insurance products and services and served the retail, corporate, and investment banking markets.

Banca Commerciale Italiana operated roughly 1,500 branches—1,100 units in Italy and 400 international units spanning 40 countries. Services included retail banking, leasing, factoring, securities intermediation, securities custody and settlement, securities lending, portfolio management, and investment and merchant banking. The bank also sold insurance policies.

Review of the Outcome and Changes to the Industry

According to *American Banker* in March 1999, most analysts believed the merger plans between UniCredito Italiano and Banca Commerciale Italiana (BCI) would "trigger other in-market deals across Europe and set the stage for larger crossborder transactions." Accordingly, after the deal with UniCredito

was nixed, BCI and Banca Intesa, formed by the 1998 merger of Banco Ambrosiano Weneto and Cariplo, began merger negotiations.

Research

Ball, Deborah. "Board of BCI Names Civaschi Chief Executive," in *The Wall Street Journal*, 22 June 1999. Explains how the deal fell apart.

Banca Commerciale Italiana Home Page, available at http://www.bci.it. Official World Wide Web Page for Banca Commerciale Italiana. Available in both Italian and English, this Web site houses news releases, branch locations, banking services, and financial and investor information.

"Banca Commerciale Italiana," in *Notable Corporate Chronologies*, The Gale Group, 1999. Offers a summary of events in the history of Banca Commerciale Italiana.

Colby, Laura. "BCI's On-Again, Off-Again Marriage," in *Institutional Investor International Edition*, November 1998. Discusses the industry conditions leading up to the merger negotiations.

"Credito Italiano SpA," in *Notable Corporate Chronologies*, The Gale Group, 1999. Offers a summary of events in the history of Credito Italiano SpA prior to its merger with Unicredito.

"Italian Banking: Spaghetti Junction," in *The Economist*, 27 March 1999. Explains why UniCredito Italiano was looking to merge again so soon after completing its own merger.

Kraus, James R. "Big Italy Deals Seen Spurring More in Europe," in *American Banker*, 23 March 1999. Predicts the outcome of the proposed mergers among Italy's top banks.

Lane, David. "Visions of Grandeur," in *The Banker*, May 1999. Discusses merger and acquisition activity in the Italian banking industry in early 1999.

UniCredito Italiano SpA Home Page, available at http://www.credit.it. Official World Wide Web Page for UniCredito Italiano SpA. Available in both Italian and English, this Web site houses news releases, branch locations, banking services, and financial and investor information.

ANNAMARIE L. SHELDON

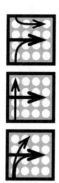

UNION PACIFIC & SOUTHERN PACIFIC TRANSPORTATION

nationality: USA
date: September 11, 1996
affected: Union Pacific Corp., USA, founded 1862
affected: Southern Pacific Transportation Corp., USA, founded 1866

Union Pacific Corp.
1416 Dodge St.
Omaha, NE 68179
USA

tel: (402)271-5000
web: http://www.up.com

Overview of the Acquisition

The 1996 acquisition of Southern Pacific by Union Pacific, which formed the nation's largest railroad company, was at the root of one of the worst railroad debacles in U.S. history. The integration of the two systems caused such serious congestion, delays, and accidents that the federal government declared it a "transportation emergency." Union Pacific finally began to emerge from the crisis in 1998, having cost the U.S. economy an estimated $2 billion in lost production due to the tie-ups on its lines.

History of Union Pacific Corp.

On July 2, 1862, President Abraham Lincoln signed the Pacific Railroad Act, which directed two companies, Union Pacific (UP) and Central Pacific (CP), to build a transcontinental railroad. UP broke ground the following year at Omaha, Nebraska, to commence westward construction, but was delayed by the Civil War and insufficient finances. On July 10, 1985, it laid its first rail at Omaha.

On May 10, 1869, the "golden spike" was driven at Promontory Summit, Utah, linking the converged lines and marking the completion of the first transcontinental railroad in the U.S. Despite its title, however, the railway extended only halfway across the continental U.S., from Omaha to the Pacific Coast.

The Credit Mobiler scandal came to light in 1872. In this racket, various UP officials received $23 million in dividends from a bogus construction company, Credit Mobiler, and gave a portion of its stock to members of Congress. Jay Gould bought into UP the following year, rescuing the railroad from near bankruptcy. During the following five years, he confounded his critics by providing the railroad with the strong leadership that it desperately needed, rather than using the company for his own profit as he had been charged earlier in connection with the Erie Railroad.

UP acquired the Kansas Pacific and the Denver Pacific railroads. In 1884 it completed the Oregon Short Line, gaining access into Portland, Oregon. Its first subsidiary, Union Pacific Coal Co., was established in 1890 to supply coal from Wyoming coalmines to fuel UP's steam locomotives.

The Business

Financials

Revenue (1998): $10.6 billion

Employees (1998): 65,000

SICs / NAICS

sic 4011 - Railroads-Line-Haul Operating

sic 4013 - Switching & Terminal Services

sic 4213 - Trucking Except Local

sic 7372 - Prepackaged Software

naics 482111 - Line-Haul Railroads

naics 482112 - Short Line Railroads

naics 484122 - General Freight Trucking, Long-Distance,
Less Than Truckload

naics 511210 - Software Publishers

Jay Gould died in 1892, and was succeeded at the company's helm by George Gould. The next year UP filed for bankruptcy due to residual effects of the Credit Mobiler scandal and lingering debt. In November 1897 UP, bankrupt and in receivership, was sold for $110 million to a group of investors at an Omaha auction. One of the investors was Edward H. Harriman, president of the Illinois Central Railroad. Harriman and Judge Robert S. Lovett soon dominated UP management.

In 1901 it attempted to buy Central Pacific Railroad from its parent company, Southern Pacific Railroad (SP), but the attempt was rebuffed. So UP purchased 38% of SP's stock and assumed control over the company. The Pacific Fruit Express was created in 1906 as a joint subsidiary of UP and SP, with an initial fleet of 6,000 iced refrigerator cars to haul fruits and vegetables to market. This company was dissolved in 1978 and its assets were split equally between UP and SP.

Lovett became chairman upon the death of Harriman in 1909. Four years later the U.S. Supreme Court ordered UP to sell its 46% stake in SP on antitrust grounds. UP completed a management reorganization in 1920 in which the Union Pacific Company was limited to major financial matters, major policy decisions, and government relations; all other management decisions were made in Omaha at Union Pacific Railroad headquarters. The U.S. Interstate Commerce Commission (ICC) was formed in 1920 to regulate the railroad industry by overseeing nearly every aspect of the business, including pricing, routes, and lines.

Union Pacific Stages introduced the nation's first transcontinental bus service in a joint venture with Chicago & Northwestern Railroad (C&NW) in 1929. Five years later UP inaugurated the nation's first streamliner, the M-10000, which introduced luxury passenger service. In December 1936 the company opened the Sun Valley Ski Resort, the nation's first ski resort, containing the first ski lift with chairs.

Cecil B. DeMille's motion picture *Union Pacific* premiered in Omaha during the four-day "Golden Spike Day" celebration in April 1939. Two years later the No. 400, the largest steam locomotive ever built and the first of the Big Boy class, went into service in Wyoming. In 1944 UP took delivery of its last steam passenger locomotive.

The company gained a connection with the Canadian Pacific Railway by acquiring Spokane International in 1958. Two years later it filed with the ICC to acquire the Chicago, Rock Island & Pacific Railroad (CRI&P). This filing set off the longest and most bitterly contested railroad merger proposal in the nation's history. Fifteen years later, ICC finally approved the deal, but UP terminated its offer three months later as a result of CRI&P's continued decline in fortunes.

UP acquired the Mount Hood Railroad in 1968. The following year Union Pacific Corporation was established as a New York-based holding company with Union Pacific Railroad as one of its operating companies, based in Omaha.

In 1980 President Ronald Reagan signed the Staggers Rail Act, which once again deregulated the industry and began allowing mergers between the nation's railroad companies. In September of that year UP filed with the ICC to acquire the Missouri Pacific Railroad (MP) and the Western Pacific Railroad. The ICC approved this deal in December 1981.

UP purchased Overnite Transportation Co., a nationwide trucking company, in 1986 as a further investment into intermodal service. Drew Lewis became CEO the next year. He moved rapidly in conjunction with president Michael Walsh to trim costs arising from the assimilation of MP and WP.

In 1988 it acquired the Missouri-Kansas-Texas Railroad, also known as the Katy Railroad. The next year it opened the Harriman Dispatching Center in Omaha, Nebraska, thereby centralizing all train dispatching for the entire railroad in one location. It also purchased 25% of Chicago & North Western Railroad (C&NW); this interest was held in trust awaiting regulatory approval of the deal. In 1994 the ICC granted its approval, and UP gained minority control of the railroad. In 1995 UP acquired the remainder of C&NW's stock and absorbed the company. In the months that followed, UP was plagued by problems arising from the incorporation of the railroad.

UP embarked on a strategy to refocus on its core railroad business. To this end it sold USPCI, Inc., its waste management business, in 1994. In October 1995 it completed the spin-off of its natural resources business, Union Pacific Resource Group, Inc. through an initial public offering. The company then divested Skyway Freight Systems, Inc., its logistics business, in 1998. UP postponed its public offering, planned for July 1998, of Overnite Transportation due to depressed market conditions.

UP and Burlington Northern Railroad entered into a bidding war for Atchison, Topeka & Santa Fe Railroad (the Santa Fe) in 1994. The next year it terminated its bid, thereby allowing for the formation of Burlington Northern Santa Fe Corp.

In September 1996 UP acquired SP to reclaim the title of the largest railroad company in the U.S. The integration of this company was so disastrous that it required federal assistance to emerge from the crisis two years later.

UP absorbed the Missouri Pacific Railroad on January 1, 1997. Later that year it invested $525 million for a 25% stake in the Mexico City Terminal Company and for a concession to operate the Pacific-North and Chihuahua Pacific lines in Mexico. In April 1999 UP announced another move of its corporate headquarters, to Omaha from Dallas, where it had relocated in 1997.

History of Southern Pacific Transportation Corp.

The Central Pacific Railroad of California (CP) was established in June 1861 by four investors. Formed with the hopes of creating a link between California and the eastern part of the U.S., CP was granted government approval to do just that the following year. President Abraham Lincoln signed the Pacific Railroad Act, directing CP to join with Union Pacific (UP) to form a transcontinental railroad. CP began constructing eastward from Sacramento while UP initiated westward construction from Omaha Nebraska. These lines were united in 1869 with the driving of the "golden spike" in Promontory Summit, Utah.

The U.S. government commissioned the formation of the Southern Pacific Railroad (SP) in 1866 for the construction of an east-west line in California. CP

The Officers

Chairman, President, and CEO: Richard K. Davidson

Vice Chairman, Union Pacific Railroad Co.: Jerry R. Davis

President and Chief Operating Officer, Union Pacific Railroad Co.: Ike Evans

Chairman and CEO, Overnite Transportation Co.: Leo H. Suggs

Exec. VP, Finance: Gary M. Stuart

gained control of SP two years later as part of its campaign to create a railroad monopoly in the state. By 1877 the company controlled 85% of California's rail traffic and had extended its reach to New Orleans.

In 1884 the partners formally merged the two railroads as Southern Pacific Company. It was incorporated in Kentucky, thereby shielding the enterprise from California's laws of incorporation, under which stockholders' liability was unlimited.

SP grew into a behemoth untouchable by even the government. The state of California established a railroad commission as a legal recourse against allegations against SP of such practices as bribery and intimidation of government officials, discriminatory pricing, and monopolistic grip. Nearly 10% of California's population signed a petition requesting that the federal government assume control of the railroad. The federal government declined, but targeted SP in the early 1890s, not only for these allegations but also because the 30-year government loans that CP and UP had been granted for their initial construction were scheduled to expire in the mid-1890s. As SP had made no provision to repay those huge debts, instead funneling its profits into the pockets of the partners, the government extended the deadline for repayment until 1909.

This debt was paid off on schedule, due in large part to SP's acquisition by rival UP in 1901. Under UP's chairman, Edward H. Harriman, financial credibility was implemented in SP through conservative and prudent leadership. However, in 1913 the U.S. Supreme Court ordered the break-up of this union on antitrust grounds, and UP sold much of its 46% stake to the Pennsylvania Railroad Co.

The nation's railroad industry suffered a decline in the 1920s, as shippers increasingly opted for truck and auto transport of goods. SP embarked on an expansion program to reverse its falling profitability. In 1932 it acquired the St. Louis Southwestern Railroad, nicknamed the Cotton Belt. SP also estab-

The Players

Union Pacific Chairman and CEO: Richard K. Davidson. Richard Davidson began his career in railroading in 1960, when he took a job as a brakesman with Missouri Pacific. Its steady work and good pay prompted him to choose the railroad over a career in law. By age 27 he was a division superintendent, and by the time that Union Pacific merged with Missouri Pacific in 1982, Davidson had reached the rank of vice president of operations. In July 1996 he was elected president and chief operating officer. That November he succeeded the retiring Drew Lewis as chairman and CEO.

Southern Pacific Chairman: Philip F. Anschutz. Philip Anschutz has been on the move ever since he assumed control of his family's oil rig outfit at age 20. He sold the company for $10 million, and used the proceeds to purchase ranches in Utah and Wyoming. In 1979 Amoco discovered that one of his ranches contained one of the 50 largest gas fields in U.S. Anschutz sold half of his interest in that field to Mobil for $500 million.

In 1984 he purchased the small Rio Grande Railroad for $500 million, and four years later added to it the struggling Southern Pacific railroad. In 1996 Anschutz agreed to sell SP to Union Pacific Corp. He became a vice chairman of UP and cleared about $1.6 billion on the deal.

The Denver billionaire was considered by many to be ill-advised when he announced his intent to build a fifth nationwide fiber-optic network against such competitors as AT&T, MCI Communications, LDDS WorldCom, and Sprint. Ignoring the criticism, he invested $55 million in 1995 to launch the telecommunications company that would become known as Qwest Communication International. In June 1999 that company went head-to-head with the nation's leading telecom companies, as it embarked on an attempt to acquire U S West and Frontier Corp.

lished the Pacific Motor Transport Company as a short-haul trucking company to transport goods between rail depots and customer warehouses. It even launched a campaign for passenger business, but failed in competition against the cheaper and more direct offerings of airlines and automobiles.

The outbreak of World War II ushered in a period of prosperity for SP, whose net income reached a record high of $80 million in 1942. This good fortune continued in the following years, as the nation's railroad industry was permitted to thrive due to the ban on mergers and price wars among competing lines by the Interstate Commerce Commission (ICC).

That same government agency also regulated pricing and the market area of the nation's railroads, so SP looked to technological innovation and consequent labor reductions to increase profitability. By 1969 SP was guided by a single computer system designed to increase efficiency. As a result, its workforce was reduced from 76,000 in the mid-1950s to 45,000 in 1970; by 1990 that level was down to 21,000.

SP diversified during the 1970s, first into telecommunications and then into real estate. It began offering long-distance telecommunications services under the name Sprint. In 1979 it acquired Ticor, the nation's largest title insurer. Neither venture was particularly successful, however, and both were eventually sold.

President Ronald Reagan deregulated the railroad industry in 1980, and SP soon faced competitive pressures arising from that open environment. In 1982 UP and Missouri Pacific announced a merger pact that would create the largest railroad concern in the U.S. SP began scouting for partner of its own, and in 1983 announced its merger with Santa Fe Industries. Four years later, however, the ICC nixed this deal on antitrust grounds.

In October 1988 Philip Anschutz, a Denver businessman, paid $1 billion for the acquisition of SP and assumed the post of chairman. The railroad was incorporated into Anschutz's Rio Grande Industries, owner of the Denver and Rio Grande Western Railroad. Profitability of the railroad fell in the wake of the merger, but the company was buoyed by the proceeds from Rio Grande's real estate operations.

The company implemented an expensive reduction program in 1993, slashing its workforce by 5,000 and investing in more efficient locomotives through 1995. Also in 1995 Jerry Davis succeeded Ed Moyers as CEO and president. That August SP and UP announced their merger, a deal that was completed in September of the following year.

Market Forces Driving the Acquisition

The U.S. railroad industry of the 1990s differed vastly from that of the 1970s. Before deregulation, railroads were relatively insulated from competitive pressures arising from the industry. The Interstate Commerce Commission (ICC) regulated the pricing and territorial aspects of the business, disallowing large-scale consolidation and price wars. With the

Staggers Rail Act of 1980, that safe environment disappeared. Suddenly mergers became available as an option to increase the breadth of a line, forcing other railroads to enter into similar unions to stay competitive. Between 1980 and 1995, the number of Class 1 railroads in the U.S. shrank from 40 to 10 as a result of such consolidation.

Moreover, there was more at stake in the railroad industry by the mid-1990s. Shipping business had returned to the industry after having defected to air and truck transport for much of the century, particularly in the 1960s and 1970s. Between 1980 and 1996, rail-ton miles increased 33%. This surge in demand spurred railroads to enter into unions to gain additional track, territory, and customers.

Despite this favorable market condition, SP had been failing financially for a number of years. It was immersed in a vicious cycle. Although it had good routes, its lack of capital restricted its investment in the improvement of tracks, cars, and computer systems. These deficiencies reduced its appeal to customers, thereby driving down capital intake even farther. SP viewed its future as an independent company so bleakly that reported in a statement to the U.S. Surface Transportation Board (STB) that without a merger it would be forced "to reduce service quality to the bare minimum needed to let the customer survive," as reported in *Traffic World*.

For UP, consolidation was less a financial necessity than an issue of competition and pride. This railroad company had been the largest in North America until it was usurped by the $3.85 billion merger of Burlington Northern Inc. and Santa Fe Pacific Corp. These companies united to form Burlington Northern Santa Fe Corp. on September 22, 1995. UP itself had been in the bidding for Santa Fe, but had dropped out as the price escalated. Industry analysts predicted that since it lost out on the Santa Fe, it was only a matter of time before UP would seek to secure the only remaining major railroad in the West, Southern Pacific.

Approach and Engagement

On August 3, 1995, Union Pacific and Southern Pacific announced their $5.4 billion acquisition accord. UP would pay $4 billion in cash and stock and would assume about $1.4 billion in SP debt. The combined company would have about 36,000 miles of track in 25 states, Canada, and Mexico. It would control about 99% of the railroad traffic in Utah, 89% in Nevada, 70% in California, and 50% in Colorado and Oregon. It would also control most of the nation's access into Mexico.

Needless to say, this kind of power stirred up ardent opposition. Rival competitors, union leaders, and major shippers cried foul, and launched campaigns to derail the acquisition. Other opponents were those who feared that a union of this magnitude, which would create a giant that would force other railroads to merge, might also prompt the federal government to consider re-regulating the industry.

The government, however, had not reached a consensus of opinion about the deal. In late August 1995 the ICC informally approved the deal. But the U.S. Department of Justice disclosed its vehement opposition to it. The ICC was scheduled for termination as of March 1996, to be succeeded by the Surface Transportation Board (STB). As with the ICC, the STB was the final word on issues dealing with the railroad industry, and exempted railroads from the antitrust laws affecting other industries.

Still, the STB did take into consideration opinions from other branches of the government. In an attempt to alleviate those concerns, as well as those from civilian opponents, UP announced on September 27 a track-sharing agreement with Burlington Northern Santa Fe (BNSF). In exchange for BNSF's support of the UP/SP merger, the combined company would sell 335 miles of track to BNSF and allow it to share about 3,800 miles of track.

On November 30, 1995, UP filed with the ICC its formal application to acquire SP. Along with the application, the railroad included the endorsement of some 1,060 shippers, seven state governors, 40 short-line railroads, and 220 legislatures and other state officials. In March, after the Texas Railroad Commission voiced its opposition to the deal, UP filed additional statements of support, bringing the total to nearly 1,800 filings.

The opposition continued to mount, however. After the Department of Justice filed its official statement of protest with the STB, UP and SP issued a statement on April 29 in defense of the deal. Conrail, one of the most vociferous critics of the deal, made repeated offers to purchase the eastern lines of SP in order to allow UP to placate opposition, not to mention improve its own position. In June UP rejected Conrail's most recent $1.9 billion offer, reiterating that its track-sharing deal with BNSF would be adequate to satisfy the STB.

This optimism proved to be well-founded, as the STB voted to approve the transaction on July 3, 1996. The board believed that the union would encourage, not prevent, reduced rates, since it estimated that the combined company would realize $627 million in annual expenses. The only condition that it imposed on the companies was that they grant trackage rights through certain areas in Texas to the Texas Mexican Railway.

The combined company would also be required to submit regular reports on operations to the STB, which would retain oversight of the new railroad for five years. On August 12 the STB issued its formal written approval of the acquisition. UP and SP were officially united on September 11, 1996. At that time SP became a subsidiary of UP and Philip Anschutz, chairman of the former SP, became vice chairman of UP.

Products and Services

Union Pacific Corporation was composed of three operating companies:

Union Pacific Railroad, with the acquisition of the Missouri Pacific and Western Pacific railroads in 1982, the Missouri-Kansas-Texas Railroad in 1988, the Chicago & North Western in 1995, and the Southern Pacific in 1996, operated a 36,000-mile rail network linking 23 states from the Midwest to the West and Gulf Coasts. This company posted net income of $27 million in 1998.

Overnite Transportation, the nation's sixth-largest freight trucking company, served all 50 states and Canada with more than 150 terminals, specializing in less-than-truckload shipments. This company posted net income of $40 million in 1998.

Union Pacific Technologies provided computer software and technological support to the corporation and the other operating companies, marketing its systems and services to the transportation industry. In 1998 this unit completed the installation of the corporation's Transportation Control System on the lines of the former Southern Pacific.

Changes to the Industry

The railroad industry held its breath during the fallout of the Union Pacific/Southern Pacific merger. So disastrous was its consolidation that railroad companies feared that the U.S. government would become increasingly heavy handed in its dealings with the industry. Some believed that it might cause the government to limit or revoke the free rein of deregulation. Others were concerned that it would prompt the government to curtail future merger and acquisition activity.

Proposed consolidation in the eastern U.S. was the first to test the regulatory waters. In March 1997 Conrail agreed to be split up between CSX Corp. and Norfolk Southern Corp., leaving only four major railroad companies in the country—CSX, Norfolk Southern, Union Pacific, and Burlington Northern Santa Fe. By June 1998, when the deal was approved by the STB, regulatory delays had already cost the companies millions of dollars. Their transaction was concluded in June 1999, making CSX and Norfolk Southern the nation's third-and fourth-largest railroad companies. By the middle of that month, however, delays and other problems began emerging, reminiscent of the problems experienced by Union Pacific in its acquisition of Southern Pacific.

Review of the Outcome

Union Pacific was determined to avoid the problems that it had faced during the integration of Chicago & North Western in 1995. Crew and diesel shortages caused month of delays, for which the company had apologized to its customers. With the acquisition of South Pacific, the firm vowed not to rush the implementation, laying out a four-step plan. Beginning in 1997 it would combine operations in the Central Corridor, followed by the rest of the system at intervals through mid-1998. "This will be the best-planned and best-executed merger in North American railroading," promised UP chairman Richard Davidson in *Traffic World*.

That prediction could not have been more inaccurate. By the summer of 1997 it had become apparent that UP was experiencing serious difficulties. A number of collisions between the company's railroad cars resulted in the deaths of several employees. On September 10, 1997, the Federal Railroad Administration (FRA) completed its investigation into the company's safety practices, and demanded that UP take immediate steps to improve conditions. Among the FRA's findings were defective locomotives, insufficient training of dispatchers, intimidation of employees to quash reports of problems, and violation of the Hours of Service Act that limited the number of hours worked by crew members. As reported in *HazMat Transport News*, the FRA attacked UP for "widespread safety deficiencies in the areas of training, dispatching and employee fatigue." UP agreed to make the requested improvements.

UP's problems were just beginning, however. SP had operated an inefficient computer system and switching yard at Englewood, Texas, but its personnel were knowledgeable in their effective operation. UP was certain that its own employees could operate and even improve the system, and either laid off or disregarded the advice of SP workers familiar with it. As a result, Englewood became the epicenter of a congestion nightmare that disrupted the U.S. economy for months.

In an attempt to improve efficiency at the yard, UP brought more cars into it. The company didn't realize that it didn't have enough crew members or locomotives to move the additional cars, and the yard became increasingly clogged with idle cars. UP couldn't send excess cars to its other yards, since they were already filling with petrochemical and Mexico-bound shipments. For lack of anywhere else to stop, trains began filling into the sidings alongside the main rails. When they became full, trains had to stop on the main lines, thereby effectively shutting down transportation to or from the area. Soon the rails throughout Texas were blocked.

The desperate need for experienced crew was compounded by UP's compliance with the government's restriction of work shifts to 12 hours. Crews stranded in traffic at the end of their shift had no choice but to abandon the trains where they stood, since the company was short-handed in replacement workers. As UP brought in more help and locomotives from nearby states, they got stuck also, and the problems spread throughout the system. "We had westbound trains lined up all the way to Phoenix and Tucson waiting to get into Southern California," UP admitted in *Fortune*.

The ensnarlement caused shipments to take three or four times as long to reach destination as they had in the past. In addition, cargoes and rail cars were lost or misdirected.

The snafu impacted a multitude of industries, as electric utilities grew short on coal, manufactured products piled up at plants, and food products rotted awaiting transport Petrochemical plants were hit particularly hard. Normally they stored their finished products on rail cars. But since the availability of empty cars decreased and the filled cars were entangled in traffic, the plants were forced to scale back or shut down production altogether.

On October 31, 1997, the STB stepped in and made the unprecedented move of declaring a "transportation emergency" on UP. It ordered the Texas Mexican Railway to do what ever it could to clear out Houston. The UP filed a Service Recovery Plan with the STB to move 40,000 cars off the rails, acquire 500 locomotives, hire and train additional crew, and temporarily divert traffic to the rail lines of BNSF, Illinois Central, and various regional railroads.

UP reported a fourth-quarter 1997 deficit of $152 million, five times worse than expected. It also announced the reduction of dividends by 50% in the issue of $1 billion in securities to raise emergency funds.

By March 1998 economists at the University of North Texas estimated that the railroad mess had cost the U.S. economy $2 billion in lost production. NAFTA trade was also imperiled, since UP controlled most of the access into Mexico. In late March, with 5,500 cars awaiting entry into Mexico, UP announced that it would no longer accept southbound shipments until the line was cleared.

UP showed signs of recovery in May 1998. Its train speeds were up marginally since the height of the crisis, while delays and trapped cars were down. The company filed with the STB a five-year plan to spend $800 million on track and $600 million on other capacity improvements. The STB agreed that the worst was over, and declined to renew the emergency service order when it expired on August 2, 1998.

The company reverted to a decentralized system later that autumn. It formed northern, southern, and western divisions, as well as 22 local offices. It also formed joint dispatch centers in Fort Worth, Texas; Kansas City, Missouri; and San Bernardino, California, to replace the single dispatch center in Omaha.

By the end of 1998 UP had terminated 2,400 employees and relocated 3,800 others due to redundancies. At the same time it had hired 6,400 workers. In December it announced a plan to hire an additional 60,000 people over the next 12 years.

Research

Burke, Jack. "SP Spell out Doomsday Scenario Should Merger with UP Be Rejected," in *Traffic World*, 6 May 1996. Relates SP's arguments for the necessity of a merger.

"FRA Assails Union Pacific, Tells Carrier to Improve Safety Program," in *HazMat Transport News*, 1 September 1997. Reports the conclusion of the government's investigation into UP's safety condition.

Keefe, Kevin P. and David Lustig. "For Union Pacific, the "Natural" Merger Partner," in *Trains Magazine*, November 1995. Details the market grasp that the combined company would hold in the western U.S.

O'Reilly, Brian. "The Wreck of the Union Pacific," in *Fortune*, 30 March 1998. Provides a detailed look at the problems arising from the merger.

"Old Rivals Join Forces," in *American Metal Market*, 11 August 1995. Details the terms of the newly announced merger.

Palmeri, Christopher, and Ann Marsh. "Can Drew Lewis Drive the Golden Nail?" in *Forbes*, 18 December 1995. Describes the opposition to the SP/UP deal in the rapidly consolidating industry.

Schulz, John D. "Don't Worry, Be Happy," in *Traffic World*, 25 November 1996. Describes the company's optimism about the recently completed acquisition.

"Southern Pacific Transportation Company," in *International Directory of Company Histories*, Vol. V, St. James Press: 1992. Provides a historical review of the company through 1990.

"Union Pacific Corp.," in *Notable Corporate Chronologies*, The Gale Group, 1999. Profiles the history of Union Pacific.

Union Pacific Corporation Home Page, available at http://www.up.com. Official World Wide Web Page for Union Pacific. Includes annual reports and other financial information, business segment and product information, company history, news releases, and links to the corporation's operating companies.

DEBORAH J. UNTENER

UNION PACIFIC RESOURCES & PENNZOIL

Union Pacific Resources Group Inc.
777 Main St.
PO Box 7
Fort Worth, TX 76101-0007
USA

tel: (817)321-6000
web: http://www.upr.com

PennzEnergy Co.
700 Milam
PO Box 4616
Houston, TX 77210-4616
USA

tel: (713)546-6000
fax: (713)546-6589
web: http://www.pennzenergy.com

date: November 17, 1997 (canceled)
affected: Union Pacific Resources Group Inc., USA, founded 1987
affected: PennzEnergy Co. (formerly Pennzoil Co.), USA, founded 1889

Overview of the Acquisition

After failed attempts to enter into friendly negotiations to acquire Pennzoil, Union Pacific Resources launched a hostile takeover for the company in 1997. The battle took place in the public forum, as the chairmen engaged in a heated exchange of letters and advertising campaigns designed to sway Pennzoil's shareholders. In effect, however, the wishes of shareholders themselves were not considered by Pennzoil's board of directors, which refused to put UPR's offer to a shareholder vote. After five months UPR withdrew its offer.

Pennzoil's shareholders responded that the board acted with indifference to their wishes. They filed numerous lawsuits, and one shareholder even vowed to overturn the company's poison pill by launching a proxy fight to gain a seat on the board. As a compromise, Pennzoil made its poison pill "chewable," a new feature that established specific circumstances under which a hostile offer could bypass the pill's defenses.

History of Union Pacific Resources Group Inc.

President Abraham Lincoln signed the Pacific Railroad Act in 1862 to establish the nation's first transcontinental railroad. The two companies charged with that mission were Central Pacific and Union Pacific Corp. (UP). The government also gave UP a 7.5 million-acre tract of land in Utah, Colorado, and Wyoming to sell off in order to raise capital for its railroad operations. At that time, though, this land was located too far west to be in great demand, so UP simply held on to it.

That tract happened to hold plentiful natural reserves, and by the 1930s UP was drawing a sizable portion of income from its oil and gas operations. During the following decades the company came to rely on those operations more heavily, as the railroad business was steadily losing customers to the trucking industry.

UP acquired Champlin Petroleum Co. for $240 million in 1970, and the next year merged its oil and gas operations by folding them into Champlin. Also in 1971 UP established Rocky Mountain Energy for its minerals business.

The lucrative energy market of the 1970s brought good fortune to Champlin, which had revenues of $4.4 billion in 1983. After that, however, the market bottomed out. UP combined Champlin with Rocky Mountain Energy to form Union Pacific Resources Group (UPR) in 1987. Revenues of this natural resources unit reached only $822 million in 1988.

That subsidiary experienced a change for the better when Jack Messman became CEO of UPR. Messman, who was a newcomer to the energy industry, began leading the firm with a general business sense rather than the conventional operational practices of the industry. Typically, when energy prices were low, exploration and production companies sat still and waited for them to rise. Messman immediately recognized that this was a poor business practice, since pricing was the one thing that the company could not control.

He reorganized the company into five units and eliminated 200 positions, or 13% of its workforce. He reviewed the returns on UPR's Canadian operations, something that the previous executives had never thought to do, and began divesting them after discovering that they were earning below 10% on capital. Messman also focused operations in the domestic market while larger rivals concentrated on territories overseas. In March 1992 he formed an agreement to develop acreage in Wyoming owned by Amoco in return for share of the production.

Messman repeatedly tried to persuade Union Pacific to transform UPR into a separate company, and in 1995 he finally succeeded. That October UPR was spun off through an initial public offering.

Just prior to that time, Pennzoil Co. had offered to buy the unit. In 1997 those roles were reversed, as UPR launched an unsolicited $6.4 billion bid for Pennzoil. The battle was long and acrimonious, and in November 1997 UPR finally admitted defeat.

In March 1998 UPR paid $3.5 billion to acquire Norcen Energy Resources Ltd., a Canadian-based energy firm with operations in western Canada, the Gulf of Mexico, Guatemala, and Venezuela. That December UPR entered into a development and operational agreement with the Brazilian oil company Petroleo Brasileiro S.A. It also announced the planned reduction of its corporate staff by 14%. On March 31, 1999, UPR sold its natural gas gathering and processing, along with its natural gas liquid pipeline, businesses to Duke Energy Field Services Inc. for $1.35 billion.

History of Pennzoil Co.

In 1889 the South Penn Oil Co., the earliest predecessor to Pennzoil, was formed by a unit of John D.

The Business

Financials - Union Pacific Resources Group Inc.

Revenue (1998): 1.8 billion

Employees (1998): 2,900

Financials - PennzEnergy Co.

Revenue (1998): $837.4 million

Employees (1998): 1,100

SICs / NAICS

sic 1311 - Crude Petroleum & Natural Gas

sic 1321 - Natural Gas Liquids

sic 1381 - Drilling Oil & Gas Wells

sic 1241 - Coal Mining Services

sic 1474 - Potash, Soda & Borate Minerals

sic 2992 - Lubricating Oils & Greases

naics 211111 - Crude Petroleum and Natural Gas Extraction

naics 211112 - Natural Gas Liquid Extraction

naics 213111 - Drilling Oil and Gas Wells

naics 213113 - Support Activities for Coal Mining

naics 212391 - Potash, Soda, and Borate Mineral Mining

naics 324191 - Petroleum Lubricating Oil and Grease Manufacturing

Rockefeller's Standard Oil Co. to participate in oil production in Pennsylvania. By 1898 South Penn was the leader among Standard interests, with output of 7.6 million barrels per year.

The next year Standard Oil reorganized, and all of its affiliated companies became subsidiaries of the newly enlarged Standard Oil Co. (New Jersey). In 1911 the Supreme Court ordered the dissolution of that firm, and South Penn became an independent company.

In 1913 Charles Suhr, president and partner of the automobile lubricant producer Pennsylvania Refining Co., invested in Penn-American Refining Co., a California-based distributor of its lubricants. That company introduced the brand name Pennzoil a few years later. In 1921, to capitalize on Pennzoil's growing popularity, Suhr changed the name of his two marketing companies to the Pennzoil Co. (California) and the Pennzoil Co. (Pennsylvania). Three years later Penn-American and its marketing companies, now

The Officers

Union Pacific Resources Group Inc.

Chairman and CEO: Jack L. Messman

President and Chief Operating Officer: George Lindahl III

VP, People: Anne M. Franklin

VP, General Counsel, and Secretary: Joseph A. LaSala, Jr.

VP and Chief Financial Officer: Morris B. Smith

PennzEnergy Co.

Chairman: James L. Pate

President and CEO: Stephen D. Chesebro

Exec. VP: Donald A. Frederick

Sr. VP, Legal: John B. Chapman

Treasurer and Senior VP, Finance: Bruce K. Misamore

including Pennzoil Co. (New York), merged into an umbrella concern called Pennzoil Company.

Pennzoil, weak in crude production capacity, began negotiations with South Penn in 1925 about a possible merger, since South Penn was relatively limited in its refining and marketing capability. Instead of a union, South Penn purchased 51% of Pennzoil's stock, purchasing the remainder in 1955.

Zapata Petroleum Corp. was founded in 1953 by J. Hugh Liedtke, Bill Liedtke, and George Bush. During its first year of operation, the company drilled 127 successful wells. In 1958 Bush purchased a subsidiary of Zapata and eventually left the business to pursue a career in politics, ultimately becoming president of the U.S.

In 1959 the Liedtkes began purchasing large quantities of South Penn stock, buying out majority stockholder J. Paul Getty within a couple of years. In 1963 South Penn merged with Zapata to form Pennzoil Co. Sales that year reached $77 million, with net profits at $7 million.

In an early example of corporate raiding, whereby a smaller company gained control of a much larger but underperforming competitor, the Liedtkes purchased 42% of United Gas Pipe Line Co. in 1965. Sales reached $700 million in 1970, as the absorption of United Gas transformed Pennzoil into a large and diversified natural resources company. Its Duval Corp. mining subsidiary made a series of quick strikes in sulfur, potash, copper, gold, and silver. To keep natural gas production up, Pennzoil created two companies, Pennzoil Offshore Gas Operators and Pennzoil Louisiana & Texas Offshore, Inc.

After divesting itself of most of United Gas's assets, Liedtke sold the remaining United Gas Pipe Line Co. in 1974. According to Pennzoil, this sale was necessitated by government regulations that inhibited Pennzoil's operation of both production and distribution concerns. However, the Liedtkes faced several lawsuits and an investigation by the Federal Power Commission as a result of the deal, and agreed to pay $100,000 to Pennzoil stockholders. In 1980, with sales in excess of $2 billion, Pennzoil became the second-largest seller of motor oil.

In 1984, after calculating that Getty Oil Co.'s stock was undervalued, Pennzoil entered into an agreement with Gordon Getty to acquire three-sevenths of the company for $3.9 billion. Later that year, however, Texaco Inc. announced its agreement to buy all of Getty's stock at $128 per share. Pennzoil sued Texaco for tortuous interference of Pennzoil's prior contract with Getty. A Texas jury decided in favor of Pennzoil, requiring a payment of $10.5 billion by Texaco to Pennzoil for real and punitive damages, the highest such award to date. Upon appeal, the award was lowered to $8.5 billion, but the verdict was upheld. That amount was further reduced to $3 billion after Texaco sought bankruptcy protection.

Pennzoil became the leading seller of motor oil in the U.S. in 1986, and would hold this position for over a decade. The following year it began selling its various mining interests, with the exception of sulfur. The company also spent $2.1 billion in cash for 8.8% of Chevron Corp., which immediately filed suit against Pennzoil to prevent a possible hostile takeover. This suit was dismissed in 1990, at which time Pennzoil increased its interest to 9.4%.

In 1988 Pennzoil purchased Facet Enterprises, a producer of automotive filters, for $233 million. This company, which was renamed Purolator, Inc., proved to be a money-losing enterprise, and Pennzoil soon sought to unload it. After reorganizing the firm to improve its bottom line, Pennzoil spun off Purolator as an independent company in 1992.

In 1990 Pennzoil purchased an 80% stake in Jiffy Lube International, Inc. for $43.5 million and appointed James L. Pate as CEO of Pennzoil. With almost 100% of its energy reserves in the U.S., Pennzoil began in 1993 to focus more on the exploration of overseas fields, particularly in Western Siberia. The following year Pate added the role of chairman to his existing positions as chief executive and president. That same year, Pennzoil Canada paid $225 million to acquire Co-enerco Resources Ltd. of Calgary, Alberta.

In 1995 Pennzoil offered to acquire Union Pacific Resources Group, but was rebuffed. The company began shifting its focus back to its core motor oil business while maintaining a large oil exploration program. It received permission from the Egyptian government to form a joint venture with International Egyptian Oil Co. for the exploration of the West Feiran Block.

The following year it entered into a joint venture with LUKAgip NV, LUKoil International Ltd., Agip Azerbaijan BV, and Socar to drill for oil beneath the Caspian Sea. Pennzoil also sold its oil and gas interests in western Canada to Gulf Canada Resources Ltd. for $151 million. For the 11th consecutive year, Pennzoil motor oil was the nation's top-selling brand.

The company became the target of a five-month, $6.4 billion hostile takeover bid from Union Pacific Resources in 1997. Pennzoil's board managed to hold off the suitor through the use of a poison pill defense, despite the fact that a majority of its shareholders wanted the deal to go through.

In 1998 Quaker State Corp. merged with Pennzoil Products Group to form Pennzoil-Quaker State Co. Pennzoil's remaining operations, its exploration and production activities, were renamed PennzEnergy Co. In May 1999 PennzEnergy entered into an agreement to be acquired by Devon Energy Corp.; the merger was scheduled for completion in the third quarter of 1999.

Market Forces Driving the Acquisition

Union Pacific Resources Group (UPR) began eyeing Pennzoil's domestic assets in the latter half of the 1990s. Under the leadership of Jack Messman, UPR had focused its oil and gas exploration and production activities in the U.S., and viewed Pennzoil's lubricating oil, petroleum refineries, and quick-service oil change operations as valuable and complementary assets.

It saw a combined company as the nation's undisputed leader in exploration and production. UPR would apply its drilling expertise and technology, notably horizontal and 3-D seismic technology, to gain the most from Pennzoil's properties. The company also expected to achieve efficiencies in the operating and administrative corners, and could invest those capital savings in further expanding its operations.

The Economist (US) offered a different theory of UPR's rationale for acquiring Pennzoil—its strong brand name. "Many consumers, it appears, still think UPR is a railway. UPR believes that, thanks to its prey's ubiquitous motor oils, Pennzoil is just the name it needs."

The Players

Union Pacific Resources Group Chairman and CEO: Jack L. Messman. Jack Messman took a job as a salesman at Union Carbide upon graduation from the University of Delaware. After earning a Harvard MBA in the 1970s, he gained a reputation as a turnaround specialist. Drew Lewis, a fellow turnaround specialist, hired Messman in 1988 to head Union Pacific's hazardous waste disposal business. In 1991 Messman was promoted to CEO of Union Pacific Resources, even though he had had no experience in the energy industry. This lack of experience proved to be an asset to the company, as Messman applied business practices that were unconventional in the industry in order to trim the company's expenses and improve its growth.

Pennzoil Chairman and CEO: James L. Pate. After completing graduate studies in economics at Indiana University, James Pate became a professor of economics at Monmouth College. He later worked as a senior economist at the Federal Reserve Bank of Cleveland, and then as chief economist for the B. F. Goodrich Co. In 1974 President Ford appointed him to the position of Assistant Secretary of Commerce, in which capacity Pate was the chief economist of the Department of Commerce. The following year he became a special adviser to the White House. In 1976 Pate traded a career in government for commercial ventures. That year he joined Pennzoil Co. and quickly succeeded through executive positions. In 1990 he first became chief operating officer and then president and CEO. Four years later he was elected chairman.

Approach and Engagement

Union Pacific Resources Group first made acquisition overtures to Pennzoil in April 1997, offering $80 per share for the underperforming company. Pennzoil's board rejected the offer, citing the implementation of a five-year turnaround plan that it expected to outvalue UPR's purchase price.

The suitor refused to accept this rejection, and on June 23, 1997, made public its $6.4 billion unsolicited offer. The two-tiered deal offered $84 per share in cash for 50.1% of Pennzoil's outstanding shares, followed by a stock swap for the remaining shares. That share price reflected a 41% premium over Pennzoil's closing price on June 20. Additionally, about $2.2 billion of the total purchase price consisted of UPR's assumption of Pennzoil debt.

In announcing the offer, Jack Messman, UPR's chairman and CEO, sent a strongly worded letter to James Pate, his counterpart at Pennzoil. As quoted in a company press release, this communique berated Pennzoil for declining to take UPR's previous offers to Pennzoil's shareholders and for refusing to divulge the details of the company's turnaround plan. "Frankly, we do not see how any existing or newly created longer-range plan from you can compare favorably, or compete economically, with our proposal for Pennzoil," he wrote. "In my view, your repeated rejections of our efforts to initiate discussions regarding a merger have been a delaying tactic, providing time to allow you to try to develop yet another strategic plan."

On the same day as its announcement, UPR filed suit in three states seeking to force Pennzoil to revoke its poison pill, a defense measure that dilutes the value of its stock in the hands of a hostile suitor. In addition, Pennzoil's board members had staggered terms, making it virtually impossible for UPR to gain control of the board through a proxy fight. On June 25 Pennzoil increased its defensive stance. It filed suit against UPR, charging that the company had failed to disclose the negative financial repercussions that it would face by acquiring Pennzoil.

Pennzoil's board rejected UPR's hostile offer on July 1 as "inadequate." As reported in *Gas Daily*, Pate stated that "Pennzoil has undergone a major restructuring in the last few years and is only now beginning to realize for its shareholders the tremendous values that it will unlock."

UPR responded with a press release of its own. "Pennzoil's rejection of UPR's offer amounts to another 'dry hole' for Pennzoil shareholders. It is clear that Pennzoil is trying to hide from its shareholders behind a classic 'just say no' defense." In UPR's view, Pennzoil's management had failed its shareholders in that it had an "abysmal record" for producing "virtually zero value in the company" by having "squandered away [and] mismanaged its capital resources."

Unlike its board, Pennzoil's shareholders were strongly in favor of the company's acquisition. By July 21, about 61.5% of Pennzoil's shares had been tendered. "Now that their shareholders have spoken, the spotlight turns to Pennzoil's Board of Directors," stated UPR in a press release.

Pennzoil put a different interpretation on the tender. "Given the two-tiered, coercive nature of the UPR proposal, it is not surprising to us that 61.5% of our shareholders felt they had no choice but to tender their shares in an attempt to protect themselves from being forced into accepting all stock in the backend of a transaction that is highly uncertain and of questionable value," Pate said in *The Oil Daily*.

By September both companies had taken their war of words to the media. UPR placed a series of full-page ads in national newspapers comparing Pennzoil's turnaround plan to such fictional characters as Big Foot and the Tooth Fairy. Pennzoil's newspaper ads called UPR a "valley of despair," a term that UPR had used in a 1996 deposition to the IRS in reference to its decline in production, from which it had since claimed to have emerged.

Pennzoil's lawsuit seeking additional disclosure from UPR was dismissed as moot on September 10, as UPR had already voluntarily released the six internal financial documents in question. Pate issued a letter to Pennzoil's shareholders asserting that those documents revealed that UPR was in a worse financial condition than it had indicated. He also sent a letter to 10 members of UPR's board, asserting that these documents contradicted the company's statements "concerning its own business, the premise of UPR's unsolicited offer for Pennzoil, and UPR's statements concerning the value of Pennzoil," as quoted in *Gas Daily*.

Seeking to eliminate the question of the value of its stock as a reason for rejecting the deal, UPR revised its offer to an all-cash proposal on October 6, 1997. One week later Pennzoil's board rejected this offer as well. "Our track record over the last two years demonstrates that Pennzoil's turnaround is well under way, as UPR itself has acknowledged," said Pate in *The Oil Daily*. In a sharply worded response, UPR called the refusal "an appalling and arrogant rejection of its shareholders' interests." The press release went on to state that "Pennzoil is obviously afraid to let its shareholders choose between UPR's $84 per share offer and Pennzoil's secret strategic plan."

After several extensions of its tender deadline, UPR established November 17 as the final date for the offer. When Pennzoil declined to negotiate, UPR terminated its acquisition attempt on that date.

Products and Services

Union Pacific Resources Group, Inc. was a large independent oil and gas exploration and production company, particularly active in Latin America. Claiming to be the most active driller in the United States since 1991, UPR was well-known as the leader in horizontal drilling. In addition, the company engaged in the hard minerals business through joint ventures and royalty interests in several coal and trona mines.

UPR was organized into three main business segments. Its Canadian activities, concentrated in western Canada, represented the company's largest business segment. The U.S. segment, divided into onshore and offshore units, operated in Texas, Louisiana, Wyoming, Utah, Kansas, and Colorado; it was also the 15th-largest operator of production in the Gulf of Mexico. UPR's International segment was active in Guatemala, Venezuela, Brazil, and Argentina.

PennzEnergy was one of the largest independent exploration and production companies in the U.S. in 1998. Its activities consisted of two main segments, U.S. and International. The company's U.S. onshore initiatives were located in areas of South Texas, South Louisiana, East Texas, West Texas, Mississippi, southern Colorado, and northern New Mexico. Offshore, the Gulf of Mexico was one of PennzEnergy's primary domestic focus areas, accounting for about 47% of the company's total U.S. production volumes. It held the 16th-largest acreage position in the Gulf, with 585,000 net acres.

Internationally, PennzEnergy focused its worldwide exploration and production efforts on basins where significant hydrocarbons had been discovered. In 1998 such areas consisted of South America, Caspian Sea, and Middle East/North Africa.

Review of the Outcome

As UPR withdrew, Pennzoil faced another battle, this time from within. By December, as the company's stock price slipped to the mid-60s, angry shareholders had filed suit against Pennzoil for denying them the opportunity to accept the lucrative acquisition offer. Guy P. Wyser-Pratte, owner of one percent of Pennzoil's stock, took the matter even farther. He sought to alter the company's defensive tactics, threatening to launch a proxy fight for a board seat if necessary to do so.

In early April 1998 Pennzoil and Wyser-Pratte resolved their differences. Among other changes, Pennzoil made its poison pill "chewable." Under the terms of this relatively unique feature, the pill would not be triggered if an offer was made in all cash at a value of at least 35% over the company' s 20-day stock price.

Despite these modifications, some industry analysts believed that Pennzoil had missed the boat by rejecting UPR's offer. By autumn 1998 Pennzoil's stock had plummeted to $35 per share. Referring to the company as "a horror story for investors," a June 1999 article in *Fortune* suggested that "if the share price doesn't rebound, many investors think a buyer will swoop in, and this time management may not be able to say no." That prediction proved accurate, as in 1999 PennzEnergy, as the company had become called, agreed to be acquired by Devon Energy Corp.

Research

Davies, Erin. "Tight-Lipped Pennzoil Goes It Alone," in *Fortune*, 29 December 1997. Describes the displeasure of Pennzoil's shareholder in the months immediately following the UPR offer.

McLean, Bethany. "Pennzoil Shareholders May Finally Get a Payback," in *Fortune*, 7 June 1999. Briefly suggests that Pennzoil's stock plunge may leave it vulnerable to another takeover attempt.

"Name Games: Marketing Energy," in *The Economist (US)*, 28 June 1997. Reviews the importance of a strong brand name to U.S. oil companies.

PennzEnergy Co. 1998 Annual Report, PennzEnergy Co., 1998. Offers a detailed review of PennzEnergy's annual operations.

PennzEnergy Co. Home Page, available at http://www.pennzenergy.com. Official World Wide Web Home Page for PennzEnergy. Includes news releases, financial data, product and services information, locations, and a historical review of the company.

"Pennzoil Board Rejects Hostile Takeover Bid," in *Gas Daily*, 2 July 1997. Relates Pennzoil's rejection of UPR's stock-and-cash offer.

"Pennzoil Chief Targets UPR Board Members," in *Gas Daily*, 22 September 1997. Quotes Pate's letter to UPR's board members.

"Pennzoil Co.," in *Notable Corporate Chronologies*, The Gale Group, 1999. Lists major events in the history of the company.

Shook, Barbara. "Pennzoil Continues to Withstand Pressure from UPR, Shareholders," in *The Oil Daily*, 16 October 1997. Describes Pennzoil's reaction to UPR's all-cash offer.

———. "UPR Leaps First Hurdle in Bid for Pennzoil," in *The Oil Daily*, 23 July 1997. Reports on Pennzoil's interpretation of the tender of a majority of its shares to UPR.

Stickel, Amy I. "Will Chewable Pills Catch On?" in *Mergers & Acquisitions Report*, 27 July 1998. Discusses the introduction and future of the "chewable" form of the poison pill.

"Union Pacific Corp.," in *Notable Corporate Chronologies*, The Gale Group, 1999. Profiles the history of Union Pacific.

Union Pacific Resources Group Inc. 1998 Annual Report, Union Pacific Resources Group Inc., 1998. Provides an in-depth review of the company's operations over the year.

Union Pacific Resources Group Inc. Home Page, available at http://www.upr.com. Official World Wide Web Page for UPR. Includes investor information, annual reports, press releases, annual reports, and job opportunities.

DEBORAH J. UNTENER

UNITED HEALTHCARE & HUMANA

United HealthCare Group

300 Opus Ctr.

9900 Bren Rd. E.

Minnetonka, MN 55343

USA

tel: (612)936-1300

fax: (612)936-7430

web: http://www.unitedhealthgroup.com

Humana Inc.

500 W. Main St.

Louisville, KY 40202

USA

tel: (502)580-1000

fax: (502)580-1441

web: http://www.humana.com

date: August 10, 1998 (canceled)

affected: United HealthCare Group, USA, founded 1974

affected: Humana Inc., USA, founded 1961

Overview of the Merger

The largest managed care company in the U.S. was almost formed in 1998 by a merger between United HealthCare Corp. and Humana Inc. That deal was killed, however, when United reported a loss that caused its stock price to plummet, thereby devaluing the merger. After holding emergency meetings, the boards of the two companies agreed to terminate the merger.

History of United HealthCare Group

United HealthCare was founded in 1974 by Richard Burke as a for-profit company to manage the newly created, non-profit Physicians Health Plan of Minnesota. Three years later it incorporated as United HealthCare Corp. By 1984, through a strategy of expansion and acquisition, the company was operating 11 HMOs in ten states. In order to support further expansion efforts, the company went public that year.

United HealthCare acquired the Indiana-based Share Development Corp., which operated HMOs in several states, through a $60 million stock swap. After this acquisition, United HealthCare operated in 22 states, covering 822,400 members through company-owned or -managed health plans. Later in 1985 it formed the United Behavioral Systems subsidiary. In 1986 it paid $83 million to acquire the Colorado-based Peak Health Care, Inc., a four-state HMO network.

In 1987, with a large annual loss looming, it approached New York investment group Warburg, Pincus Capital Company L.P., which agreed to purchase $9.8 million of newly issued preferred voting stock to take a 39.5% interest in the company. That year, although revenues doubled to more than $440 million, higher operating expenses resulted in a loss of $15.8 million. It consequently abandoned several marginal HMO startups. United HealthCare sold its interest in Peak for $41.5 million in 1988, and raised another $31.6 million through a secondary public stock offering. As part of a restructuring program designed to restore profitability, it divested itself of several unpromising businesses.

In 1989 Dr. William McGuire, a former Peak Health Care president, was promoted to president of United HealthCare. He launched a new expansion and acquisition program that focused on geographic areas in which the company is already operating. Earnings that year reached $13.6 million on revenues of $412 million. The company was one of the largest publicly traded HMOs in the U.S., serving about one million people in 15 states.

The company raised $100 million for acquisitions and expansion through a secondary public offering in 1990. That year it acquired Premature Health Plan Inc., a Milwaukee-based HMO with 103,000 members. This acquisition complemented the services of its growing subsidiary, Diversified Pharmaceutical Services, Inc., a provider of managed-care drug services to 200,000 members of various Wisconsin HMOs. United HealthCare became the first managed health care company to market its services to clients already associated with other HMOs.

In 1991 it acquired the Institute of Human Resources, an employee assistance company based in Rockville, Maryland, and merged it with its own employee assistance operation, Employee Performance Design. It also acquired Samaritan Health Plan Insurance Corp., a hospital-sponsored HMO based in Wisconsin, and Ocean State Physicians Health Plan, an HMO based in Rhode Island. Also that year, the company began trading on the New York Stock Exchange.

The firm acquired Physicians Health Plan of Ohio, HealthPro, Inc., and a 50% stake in Physicians Health Plan of North Carolina in 1992. That year it raised another $200 million via a secondary public stock offering. As a result of acquisitions, enrollment growth, and increased sales in specialty operations, revenues jumped 70% to $1.4 billion, with income rising 54% to $111.5 million.

United HealthCare became Ohio's major HMO in 1993 when it acquired Western Ohio Health Care Corporation of Dayton for $100 million. That year it also formed the largest managed care health system in Chicago by acquiring HMO America, Inc. in a stock swap valued at more than $370 million.

It sold Diversified Pharmaceutical Services, Inc., a wholly owned subsidiary, to SmithKline Beecham Corp. in 1994 for $2.3 billion in cash. Net earnings surpassed $1 million for the first time, registering at $1.6 million, on sales of $3.7 billion. The following year it acquired GenCare Health Systems, Inc., a St. Louis-based health plan, and Group Sales and Services of Puerto Rico, Inc., a health plan based in San Juan, Puerto Rico. It also acquired MetraHealth Companies, Inc., which was formed by a combination

The Business

Financials - United HealthCare Group

Revenue (1998): $17.4 billion

Employees (1998): 31,000

Financials - Humana Inc.

Revenue (1998): $9.8 billion

Employees (1998): 16,300

SICs / NAICS

sic 6321 - Accident & Health Insurance

sic 6324 - Hospital & Medical Service Plans

sic 8011 - Offices & Clinics of Medical Doctors

naics 524114 - Direct Health and Medical Insurance Carriers

naics 621491 - HMO Medical Centers

of the group health care operations of Metropolitan Life Insurance Co. and The Travelers Insurance Group.

Acquisitions continued in 1996. It agreed to acquire HealthWise of America, Inc. and its related health plan operations in Arkansas, Tennessee, Maryland, and Kentucky. It purchased PHP, Inc., a health plan based in North Carolina for which United HealthCare had provided administrative services. It also completed its acquisition of Community Health Network of Louisiana by purchasing the remaining 50% interest in a stock transaction valued at $50 million. That year revenues surpassed $10 billion for the first time, with net income of $355.6 million.

In 1997 it merged United Behavioral Systems with U.S. Behavioral Health, which was obtained through its acquisition of MetraHealth, to form United Behavioral Health, Inc., a provider of employee assistance and managed behavioral health services.

After its 1998 merger agreement with Humana fell apart, United decided to scale back its Medicare operations in about 40 counties. On August 12, 1998, it acquired Principal Health Care of Texas. The following year it purchased ClinPharm International, a contract research company in the U.K.

History of Humana Inc.

In 1961 two lawyers, Wendell Cherry and David Jones, built Heritage House, a nursing home in

The Officers

United HealthCare Group

Chairman, President, and CEO: William W. McGuire

Chief Operating Officer: Stephen J. Hemsley

Chief Financial Officer: Arnold H. Kaplan

Humana Inc.

Chairman and Co-founder: David A. Jones

Chief Operating Officer, President, and CEO: Gregory H. Wolf

Sr. VP and Chief Information Officer: Bruce J. Goodman

Sr. VP and Chief Financial Officer: James E. Murray

Louisville, Kentucky. Seven years later their venture incorporated as Extendicare. The company went public and acquired its first hospital late in the year. Sales reached $7.7 million, enabling Extendicare to expand its holdings. By 1970 the firm had acquired nine more hospitals, and began divesting itself of its nursing home operations. In 1973 the company changed its name to Humana and recorded sales of $106 million.

As the nation's third-largest hospital management chain, Humana acquired American Medicorp, the second-largest, in 1978. This purchase doubled Humana's size and greatly increased its debt load. In 1982 the company established specialty care centers for neuroscience, diabetes, spinal injuries, and artificial-heart research and surgery. By that time Humana had 90 hospitals. The company launched Humana Health Care, offering medical insurance plans, in 1984.

By 1986 the company began to experience financial difficulties as a result of underpriced premiums, doctor resentment, and plan patients who elected to attend non-referred hospitals. Net income plunged nearly 75% over the previous two years. In 1987 some of the company's clinics closed. Meanwhile, Medicare prepayment of bills ceased, which slowed cash flow for Humana significantly.

Humana recovered in 1988, and the following year its health plan division made its first operating profit in over five years. Two years later the firm announced its intention to acquire the Chicago-based Michael Reese Health Plan Inc., a hospital and medical center. On March 1, 1993, Humana split into two publicly held companies: a health-plan concern and a hospital concern called Gale Health Care Inc. That year

Humana also agreed to buy Washington HMO Group Health Association for $50 million.

In 1994 Humana received $71 million in tax refunds for a settlement with the IRS related to the timing of medical claims deductions and the deductibility of intangible amortization for 1988 through 1991. Coastal Healthcare Group Inc. signed a five-year agreement with Humana to provide physician services to 65,000 Humana health plan members in Florida. Also in 1994 the company was the subject of an investigation, and it agreed to pay $6.3 million to settle allegations that it overcharged thousands of health care consumers. Federal investigators also probed eight cases of allegedly insufficient patient care by Humana.

Humana signed a definitive agreement in 1995 to acquire CareNetwork Inc. in a $123 million cash transaction. Plunging into the small group insurance market, Humana purchased Emphesys Financial Group Inc. of Green Bay, Wisconsin, for $650 million. It also purchased 47 Florida health centers from Coastal Physician Group Inc. for $50 million. Also in 1995 Humana received a $3.78 billion government contract to provide health care to the military in several southern states for five years.

After an outsider purchased 15% of its outstanding shares, Humana amended its stockholder rights plan in 1996, adopting a poison pill. During 1997 it acquired Health Direct, Inc. for $23 million, Physician Corporation of America for $411 million, and ChoiceCare Corporation for $250 million. That December David Jones stepped down as CEO in favor of Gregory Wolf; Jones retained his position as chairman.

In May 1998 it announced its merger with United HealthCare Corp., but the deal was scrapped that August. In light of the failed merger, Humana announced its withdrawal from five markets: Puerto Rico, two Florida markets, and two Missouri markets. Meanwhile, in June, Humana completed the largest pharmacy benefits conversion in U.S. history when it converted its pharmacy benefits management business to PCS Health Systems.

In October of 1998 Humana was ordered to pay $13 million in damages for refusing to perform a doctor-recommended hysterectomy on a woman with cancer of the cervix. Two months later it sold its Humana MedPay Inc. subsidiary. In January 1999 the U.S. Supreme Court ruled that Humana could be held liable under the federal Racketeer Influenced and Corrupt Organizations Act for allegedly acquiring "illicit profit" from its group insurance operations in Nevada.

Market Forces Driving the Merger

In 1998 United HealthCare and Humana were the second- and fourth-largest public managed care companies in the U.S. Seeking security in their market positions, therefore, was not the underlying motivation for their decision to merge. Rather, the decision was driven by synergies. The two companies intended to consolidate corporate overhead, merge overlapping businesses, and cross-promote their products and services.

Approach and Engagement

On May 27, 1998, United HealthCare and Humana announced their $6.2 billion merger agreement. The new company would operate under the United HealthCare name, and it would be based at that company's current headquarters. The deal would consist of a $5.5 billion stock swap in which every two shares of Humana would be exchanged for a single share of United. In addition, United would assume $850 million in Humana debt.

By July the antitrust red flags were waving, as the union would create the country's largest managed care company. State hospital associations as well as state and federal regulatory agencies were reviewing the deal. The companies were confident, however, that they would be able to resolve any noncompetitive concerns. But they never even got the chance.

On August 6 United announced that it would report a $900 million restructuring charge in its second quarter in order to reorganize and exit specific markets. Shocked investors rushed to shed their United stock, driving down its value 28% during that day alone. That decline dropped the value of the stock swap from $5.5 billion to $4 billion. The boards of both companies held emergency meetings over that weekend, and on August 10, 1998, announced their mutual agreement to terminate the merger.

Products and Services

Humana offered two main lines of products and services. The Medical Products sector included HumanaHMO and HumanaHMO Plus medical plans; HumanaPPO medical insurance plans; HumanaTraditional Indemnity medical insurance plans; HumanaFreedom and HumanaFreedom Plus health plans; HumanaValue Ultra & Premier medical insurance plans; and HumanaValue Classic medical insurance plans. Specialty Products encompassed HumanaLife insurance plans, Humana Short-term Income Protection Plans, and HumanaDental insurance.

United HealthCare Group operated several business units. UnitedHealthcare was its health care services segment, composed of UnitedHealthcare and Ovations: UnitedHealthcare operated locally based organized health systems that served employers and individuals enrolled in Medicare and Medicaid programs; and Ovations offered health and well-being products and services for older Americans. The company's Uniprise segment managed health benefits for customers in the large-scale, multi-site employer and labor union segment. Specialized Care Services offered specialized benefits, networks, services, and resources, including employee assistance, mental health, organ transplant, dental, and personal health advisory services. The Ingenix segment was an information, analytic, research, and consulting enterprise.

Research

"Humana Inc.," in *Notable Corporate Chronologies*, Gale Research, 1999. Profiles the history of Humana.

Humana Inc. Home Page, available at http://www.humana.com. Official World Wide Web Page for Humana. It includes product and service description, annual reports and other financial information, and news releases.

Rauber, Chris. "The Going Get Tough: United-Humana Deal Draws Federal, State Scrutiny," in *Modern Healthcare*, 20 July 1998. Provides an account of the ongoing antitrust review.

Rauber, Chris. "Picking up the Pieces: United, Humana Cope with Fallout from Failed Merger," in *Modern Healthcare*, 17 August 1998. Describes the collapse of the deal.

"Supreme Court Allows RICO Lawsuit against Health Insurer," in *Federal & State Insurance Week*, 25 January 1999. Details the suit against Humana and the Court's ruling holding the company subject to federal law.

UnitedHealth Group Home Page, available at http://www.unitedhealthgroup.com. Official World Wide Web Page for United HealthCare. It includes annual reports, press releases, and product information.

"United HealthCare Corp.," in *Notable Corporate Chronologies*, Gale Research, 1999. Provides a history of the company.

"United HealthCare-Humana Merger Forms Monolith That's Tops in 13 States," in *Managed Care Week*, 8 June 1998. Describes the newly announced merger agreement.

DAVIS MCMILLAN

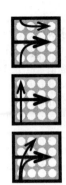

U.S. STEEL & MARATHON OIL

USX Corp.
600 Grant St.
Pittsburgh, PA 15219
USA

tel: (412)433-1121
fax: (412)433-4818
web: http://www.usx.com

nationality: USA
date: March 11, 1982
affected: U.S. Steel Corp., USA, founded 1901
affected: Marathon Oil Corp., USA, founded 1887

Overview of the Acquisition

In a battle that ended up in the U.S. Supreme Court, the takeover of the Marathon Oil Co. involved two rivals: U.S. Steel Corp. and Mobil Corp. In the end, U.S. Steel won the company for $6.5 billion—one of the largest takeovers in history at that time, second only to Du Pont's $7.3 billion acquisition of Conoco in the summer of 1981.

The combination of U.S. Steel and Marathon formed the nation's 13th-largest industrial concern and was a major step in U.S. Steel's desire to diversify outside of the steel industry. That diversification was a key factor in shutting out rival bidder Mobil, the nation's second-largest oil company. Decisions handed down by the Federal Trade Commission and several courts had asserted that Mobil would violate antitrust law if it were to acquire Marathon.

History of U.S. Steel Corp.

Carnegie Steel, Federal Steel Co., and eight other industrial concerns merged in 1901 to form the United States Steel Corp. (USS), the largest company ever formed, with initial capitalization of $1.4 billion. The merger was part of a plan by Federal Steel owner J.P. Morgan to dominate the steel market by creating a centralized combine, or trust, in the industry. Later that year USS purchased Shelby Steel Tube Co. and the Bessemer Steamship company. Sales in 1902, the first full year of operation, reached $423 million, and the company held 66% of the nation's steel market.

Company president Charles M. Schwab resigned in 1903 over disagreements with board chairman Elbert Henry Gary, leaving Gary in control of USS. Gary's stated intent was not to establish a trust, but rather to build an efficient company able to compete on product quality and price.

USS acquired the Union Steel Co. in 1903 and the Clairton Steel Co. the next year. In 1905 the U.S. government launched an antitrust investigation of the company's competitive practices. USS continued its expansion while this probe was conducted. In 1906 it began construction of a new steel mill and a model city, Gary,

Indiana. The following year it acquired Tennessee Coal, Iron and Railroad Co., the largest steel producer in the South. USS expanded into the West with the 1910 purchase of Columbia Steel Co. Gary, though opposed to unionization of workers, led a movement in 1911 to reduce the standard 12-hour day in the steel industry.

The antitrust investigation ended in 1911, when the government brought monopoly charges against USS. The U.S. Court of Appeals ruled in favor of USS four years later, deciding that the company's market position was a direct result of its competitiveness.

The steel industry boomed during World War I and USS's sales doubled their 1915 level. In 1919 steelworkers engaged in a strike for a reduction of hours, along with other considerations. This strike ended the following year, with none of the workers' demands having been met.

Myron C. Taylor became chairman of the board in 1932 and began a total overhaul of USS. Taking advantage of plant closings during the Great Depression, Taylor retooled the company by closing or modernizing old plants and building new facilities. He also changed its focus to the production of lighter steel for consumer products. In 1933, however, sales reached an all-time low of $288 million. Taylor resigned in 1938, and was replaced as chairman by Edward R. Stettinius, Jr. That year approximately 75% of USS's product lines were different, or produced using different techniques, than they were in 1927. At the same time, the firm began losing its hold of the domestic steel market, as its share dropped to 33%.

In 1940 Stettinius resigned, and Irving S. Olds became chairman. The company's growth was dramatically improved during World War II, and United States Steel Supply was created as a subsidiary in 1943. Six years later USS initiated the construction of a steel plant in Pennsylvania to penetrate the Eastern steel market dominated by Bethlehem Steel. In 1951 the company launched a reorganization designed to streamline its administration by combining its four operational subsidiaries into a single company. Sales that year topped $3.5 billion, representing a 400% increase since 1938.

In 1952 steelworkers prepared to strike, demanding wage increases and an enhancement of union influence in the industry. Before that strike could occur, U.S. President Harry S. Truman nationalized the steel industry to ensure production of military supplies for the Korean War, but the U.S. Supreme Court ruled that this action was unconstitutional. The steelworkers' strike commenced later that year and was settled two months later. Olds resigned and was succeeded first by Benjamin F. Fairless and then by Roger M. Bough.

The Business

Financials

Revenue (1998): $27.8 billion

Employees (1998): 45,000

SICs / NAICS

sic 2911 - Petroleum Refining

sic 3312 - Blast Furnaces & Steel Mills

sic 4612 - Crude Petroleum Pipelines

sic 4613 - Refined Petroleum Pipelines

sic 5541 - Gasoline Service Stations

sic 4923 - Gas Transmission & Distribution

sic 1222 - Bituminous Coal-Underground

naics 324110 - Petroleum Refineries

naics 331111 - Iron and Steel Mills

naics 486110 - Pipeline Transportation of Crude Oil

naics 486910 - Pipeline Transportation of Refined Petroleum Products

naics 447110 - Gasoline Stations with Convenience Stores

naics 221210 - Natural Gas Distribution

naics 212110 - Coal Mining

In 1958 USS absorbed its subsidiaries Universal Atlas Cement Co., Union Supply Co., and Homewood Stores Co. to further streamline the corporate management structure. Profits began to fall due to rising production costs and increased competition from foreign steelmakers. The company's share of the U.S. steel market in 1961 fell to 25%.

The firm attempted to raise its prices in April 1962, but reversed that decision after being sternly criticized by U.S. President John F. Kennedy. The next year USS again reorganized, centralizing its steelmaking divisions and sales operations in order to direct more management resources into sales and customer services. In 1964 it established the Pittsburgh Chemical Co. to function as its chemical division. This division was superseded two years later by the creation of the United States Steel Chemicals Division.

In 1973 Edgar B. Speer became chairman and launched the company on a program of diversification into nonsteel businesses. Over the next five years, the company closed or sold many of its interests in steel, cement, and mining, but capital expenditures remained high due to new environmental regulations.

The Officers

Chairman and CEO: Thomas J. Usher

Vice Chairman and Chief Financial Officer: Robert M. Hernandez

Secretary, General Counsel, and Sr. VP, Human Resources and Public Affairs: Daniel D. Sandman

VP, Strategic Planning: Albert E. Ferrara, Jr.

VP and Treasurer: Edward F. Guna

David M. Roderick replaced Speer as chairman in 1979. He announced the liquidation of 13 unprofitable steel mills for a write-off of $809 million. Despite this move, and the sale of Universal Atlas Cement, the company reported losses of $293 million for the year.

USS acquired the Marathon Oil Co. for $6.4 billion in 1982, thereby doubling the company's size while reducing steel's contribution to 40% of company sales. Two years later its planned purchase of National Steel Corp., the steel operations of National Intergroup, Inc., was frowned upon by federal regulators, and the two companies terminated their agreement.

Under Roderick, the company had closed down more than 150 facilities, reduced its management workforce by 54%, cut its overall workforce by 100,000, and sold $3 billion of assets by 1985. The next year USS changed its name to USX Corp. It continued to diversify with the acquisition of Texas Oil & Gas Corp. USX divested itself of United States Steel Supply and the United States Steel Chemicals Division later that year.

In 1986 corporate raider Carl Icahn bid $7.1 billion for USX, but his takeover attempt was thwarted when Roderick borrowed $3.4 billion to retire corporate debt. Icahn abandoned his takeover attempt in 1987, but retained a large interest in the company and continued advocating a corporate restructuring and the divestiture of all steelmaking facilities.

USX and Armco Inc. formed National Oilwell Inc., a joint venture in oilfield supplies, in 1987. USX shut down 25% of its remaining steelmaking capacity, and by 1988 its remaining steel facilities were among the most efficient in the world. That year it also sold its interest in Transtar, a domestic transportation subsidiary.

Roderick was replaced as chairman by Charles A. Corry in 1989. USX sold some of Texas Oil & Gas' energy reserves to raise capital for debt retirement and stock buybacks. The company also sold its Lorain,

Ohio, plant to Kobe Steel Co., and divested itself of the Quebec Cartier Mining Co. In 1990 Texas Oil & Gas was merged into Marathon Oil as a cost-cutting measure. USX entered into a joint venture that year with Kobe Steel to produce hot-dipped galvanized steel for the automotive industry.

In 1991 USX recapitalized by issuing separate classes of stock for its two new divisions, USX-U.S. Steel Group and USX-Marathon Group. It reported losses of $587 million for the year, reflecting further capital investments in the company's steelmaking operations. That same year, Corry concluded a three-year agreement with the United Steelworkers Union (USW) and removed Icahn from the corporate picture through a $1 billion buyout.

USX formed a corporate information technologies unit to market systems integration, consulting services, and computer resources to other businesses in 1992. It also unveiled a state-of-the-art continuous steel casting facility in Pittsburgh, Pennsylvania. The company recorded losses of $1.8 billion for 1992. That same year, USX joined a consortium of U.S. steelmakers to bring suit against foreign competitors, claiming unfair trading practices. This case was settled in 1993, when the U.S. Commerce Department ruled in favor of domestic steel producers, imposing heavy duties on imported steel. In 1994 a joint venture between Lone Star Steel Co. and Metallia USA Inc. offered to purchase USX's abandoned steel-producing facilities at Baytown, Texas.

In 1996 USX and Armco Inc. sold National Oilwell for $180 million to a partnership of that company's management. The Delhi Gas Pipeline Corp. was sold to Koch Industries in late 1997. Also in 1998 Marathon joined with Ashland Inc. to form Marathon Ashland Petroleum LLC, a refining, marketing, and transportation company. The following year Marathon purchased Tarragon Oil & Gas, a Canadian concern, thereby increasing its reserves by 20%. In June 1999 USX agreed to sell Carnegie Natural Gas Co. to Equitable Resources, Inc.

History of Marathon Oil Corp.

In 1887, The Ohio Oil Co. was formed by 14 independent oilmen who wanted to create a rival to Standard Oil, the industry's leader. The new concern grew rapidly, and was purchased by Standard Oil two years after its formation.

Ohio Oil regained its independence when the U.S. Government ordered the break-up of the Standard Oil trust in 1911. The company began expanding outside of Ohio into Kentucky, Louisiana, Texas, and Wyoming. It also began diversifying by purchasing Lincoln Oil Refining in 1924. Ohio Oil began international operations three years later, joining with Continental Oil and Amerada Hess to launch exploration activities in Africa, South America, and Central America.

In 1962, after purchasing Plymouth Oil, the company changed its name to Marathon Oil Co. This name had been used as the brand name for its automobile fuel since the 1930s. The company continued to expand its operations in exploration, production, refining, transportation, and marketing.

A dramatic battle for the acquisition of Marathon in 1981 involved the rival suitors U.S. Steel Corp. and Mobil Corp. The following year U.S. Steel purchased Marathon for $6.5 billion, a price that was second only to Du Pont's acquisition of Conoco the previous year. At the conclusion of its merger with U.S. Steel, Marathon's operations were divided into two groups, both subsidiaries of its new parent. Marathon Oil Co. held domestic exploration and production operations, and Marathon Petroleum Co. housed all other oil activities.

In 1990 U.S. Steel Corp., which had become known as USX Corp., merged Texas Oil & Gas into Marathon. The next year USX was separated into two divisions, USX-U.S. Steel Group and USX-Marathon Group, each with its own class of stock. USX-Marathon merged its domestic refining, marketing, and transportation activities with those of Ashland Inc. in 1998, forming Marathon Ashland Petroleum LLC. Later that year USX-Marathon agreed to buy Tarragon Oil & Gas, a Canadian concern, thereby increasing its reserves by 20%. In June 1999 it agreed to sell Carnegie Natural Gas Co. to Equitable Resources, Inc.

Market Forces Driving the Acquisition

U.S. Steel's diversification outside the steel industry had begun during the 1970s. By the early 1980s, steel was one of the nation's least profitable industries. The market was compressed, labor costs increased, and foreign competition, particularly from Japan and Germany, had reduced the domestic industry's returns to 4%-5%, less than half for manufacturing overall.

Under Chairman David Roderick, U.S. Steel intensified its diversification efforts. By 1981 the company operated four divisions: steel, chemicals, natural resources, and manufacturing. In the third quarter of that year, steel accounted for only 40% of U.S. Steel's operating profit.

While most industry analysts agreed with U.S. Steel's decision to continue to diversify, many ques-

The Players

U.S. Steel Corp. Chairman: David M. Roderick. After earning a degree in economics from the University of Pittsburgh, David Roderick took a job with Gulf Oil Corp. He then worked for U.S. Steel as a comptroller of its railroads and took a position in the company's accounting department in 1959. Twenty-one years after first joining the company, Roderick ascended to the chairmanship in 1979. Once in that position, he led the company on an aggressive diversification path outside of the steel industry. He trimmed operations and the workforce in an effort to accumulate funds to make strategic purchases. While still remaining committed to that industry, Roderick acquired operations in chemicals, natural resources, and manufacturing. Most importantly, however, he plunged U.S. Steel deep into oil by purchasing Marathon Oil Co. in 1982 and followed up that acquisition with the purchase of Texas Oil & Gas Corp. four years later. In 1989 Roderick was succeeded as chairman by Charles A. Corry.

tioned the wisdom of moving into the oil industry, where the steel giant had no experience. Moreover, the oil industry was somewhat depressed, as a glut in the market had driven down prices.

The U.S. government, in particular, was displeased when U.S. Steel threw its hat into the ring for Marathon Oil. Yielding to pleas from the nation's steel companies, Congress had granted them numerous concessions, enabling them to afford plant and equipment modernization in order to compete more effectively against foreign players. Such concessions included tax incentives, lenient environmental laws, and a measure of protection against imports. U.S. Steel's purchase of Marathon using those savings "won't help the steel company to compete more effectively, won't add one drop of oil to our nation's resources, and won't help in any way to alleviate the nation's economic ills," argued Howard M. Metzenbaum, Ohio Senator, in *The New York Times*.

Mobil Corp. was interested in Marathon because it had recently lost in the battle for another oil company, Conoco, to Du Pont. As the nation's second-largest oil company, after Exxon Corp., Mobil fervently sought to broaden its domestic reserves, since it was heavily dependent on oil from Saudi Arabia. Marathon Oil was the nation's 17th-largest oil company, and possessed nearly a one-half interest in the Yates oil field. This field in western Texas was, after Alaska's Prudhoe Bay, the nation's second-largest reserve.

Approach and Engagement

On October 31, 1981, Mobil offered $85 per share, or $5.1 billion, for Marathon. Marathon rejected the offer, wishing to remain independent. It also filed a suit to block Mobil from pursuing its bid, citing antitrust concerns in the marketing of products in the Midwest that would result from the proposed merger. Marathon also began the search for a white knight, or preferred acquirer, to make an alternate offer.

After rejecting other large oil companies like Gulf and Texaco for the same anti-competitive reasons cited against Mobil, Marathon decided on U.S. Steel. This conglomerate was large enough to top Mobil's bid and was diverse enough to dispel any antitrust concerns. Of equal—or even greater—importance was U.S. Steel's promise to retain Marathon's headquarters in Findlay, Ohio, home to about 2,300 of Marathon's employees.

On November 19, U.S. Steel and Marathon announced their agreement. U.S. Steel offered a total of $6.3 billion in a two-step transaction: it would pay $125 per share, or $3.75 billion, in cash for 51% of Marathon's stock, as well as exchange $100 worth of 12.5%, 12-year notes for the remaining shares. Moreover, Marathon agreed to sell to U.S. Steel its interest in the Yates oil field for $2.8 billion if another suitor were to acquire control of Marathon. Mobil responded by upping its bid to $6.5 billion, offering $126 per share in cash for at least 51% of Marathon and $90 in debentures for all remaining shares.

Over the course of the quest for Marathon, the competing companies filed various court motions to block or restrain the other, and each won small victories. However, a major blow to Mobil came on December 8, when the Federal Trade Commission blocked its proposed acquisition of Marathon. It indicated a willingness to reconsider its ruling if the company eliminated the Commission's antitrust concerns by arranging to sell Marathon's Midwest marketing and transportation operations. Meanwhile, U.S. Steel announced that 90% of Marathon's shares had been tendered into its offer.

Mobil fought back by announcing in December that it planned to buy 25% of U.S. Steel, presumably as a bargaining chip to trade for Marathon assets if those two companies combined. Mobil also revealed that Amerada Hess Corp. had agreed to buy Marathon's Midwest businesses if Mobil acquired Marathon.

On January 6, 1982, Chief Justice Warren Berger of the U.S. Supreme Court declined to block the U.S. Steel bid and to set aside the lower court antitrust rulings that blocked Mobil's own bid for Marathon. On February 3 Mobil gave up, dropping its pursuit of Marathon along with its plans to buy a large stake in U.S. Steel. On February 23 the U.S. Supreme Court refused to hear Mobil's final appeal to block the U.S. Steel's acquisition. Although the ruling had no practical effect on Mobil's terminated bid for Marathon, it finally and formally closed the matter.

On March 11, after more than two-thirds of Marathon's shareholders approved the deal, U.S. Steel acquired Marathon Oil.

Products and Services

In 1999 USX Corp. was a major worldwide producer of oil and natural gas, and the nation's largest producer of steel products. It functioned as two separate businesses, each with its own management, who operated under the USX board of directors.

The USX-Marathon Group was involved in global crude oil and natural gas exploration, production and transportation, and in the domestic refining, marketing, and transportation of crude oil and petroleum products. Its Marathon Ashland Petroleum unit had seven refineries that accounted for 6% of total U. S. refining capacity. Its gas stations were branded under the names Marathon, Ashland, Speedway, Starvin' Marvin, United, Bonded, SuperAmerica, and Rich Oil.

The USX-U.S. Steel Group manufactured and marketed a variety of steel mill products, coke, and taconite pellets; it also operated in a diverse array of other businesses, including coal mining, mineral resources management, real estate development, engineering and consulting services, technology licensing, and leasing and financial services.

Changes to the Industry and Review of the Outcome

With the acquisition of Marathon, U.S. Steel immediately gained a strong position in the oil industry. It doubled its size and became the nation's 17th-largest oil company, as well as the 12th-largest industrial concern, as its revenues reached $23.5 billion. About 40% of U.S. Steel's assets were based in steel, 40% in oil and gas, and the remaining in such miscellaneous operations as chemicals, natural resources, utilities, and transportation.

This major move by U.S. Steel out of the steel industry brought an immediate benefit for the company. The industry continued its decline, resulting in losses of millions of dollars for several major steel companies, including National Steel, for the second quarter of 1982. Although U.S. Steel recorded a shocking 97.4% decline in profits for that quarter, its Marathon operations enabled it to remain in the black, with a profit of $4.3 million.

In July 1982 Marathon's domestic exploration and production operations were transferred to U.S. Steel Holdings, which was renamed Marathon Oil Co. Its refining, marketing, transportation, and international exploration and production operations were renamed Marathon Petroleum Co.

Research

Cole, Robert J. "U.S. Steel Agrees to Pay $6.3 Billion for Marathon Oil," in *The New York Times*, 20 November 1981. Reveals the terms of U.S. Steel's first offer.

———. "Mobil Increases Bid to Buy Marathon, Topping U.S. Steel," in *The New York Times*, 26 November 1981. Details the escalating bidding war.

Greenhouse, Linda. "U.S. Steel Cleared to Buy Marathon," in *The New York Times*, 7 January 1982. Provides an overview of the contest, including Chief Justice Berger's refusal to block U.S. Steel's bid.

Marbach, William D. and Hope Lambert. "Battle of the Behemoths," in *Newsweek*, 21 December 1981. Describes Mobil's surprise plan to purchase shares of U.S. Steel.

Pauly, David and Hope Lambert, Richard Manning, and Jerry Buckley. "U.S. Steel to the Rescue," in *Newsweek*, 30 November 1981. Describes the circumstances and market conditions spurring U.S. Steel's initial bid.

USX Corp. Home Page, available at http://www.usx.com. Official World Wide Web Page for USX Corp. Includes brief organizational and product descriptions, press releases, financial and investor information, and links to USX-Marathon and USX-U.S. Steel Web pages.

"USX Corp.," in *Notable Corporate Chronologies*, The Gale Group, 1999. Profiles the history of the company, through and beyond it acquisitions of Marathon and Texas Oil & Gas.

—J.M. WEBER

U.S. STEEL & NATIONAL STEEL

U.S. Steel Corp.
600 Grant St.
Pittsburgh, PA 15219
USA

tel: (412)433-1121
fax: (412)433-4818
web: http://www.usx.com

National Steel Corp.
McKesson Plz.
One Post St.
San Francisco, CA 94104-5296
USA

tel: (415)983-8300
fax: (415)983-7160
web: http://www.mckhboc.com

date: March 9, 1984 (canceled)
affected: U.S. Steel Corp. (now part of USX Corp.), USA, founded 1901
affected: National Steel Corp. (now part of McKesson HBOC, Inc.), USA, founded 1929

Overview of the Acquisition

The proposed acquisition of National Steel Corp. by U.S. Steel Corp. in early 1984 was a response to the depressed U.S. oil industry. Both U.S. Steel and National Intergroup, National Steel's parent, considered the deal to be advantageous. U.S. Steel would enjoy economies of scale and a strong position in flat-rolled steel, while the merger would provide National Intergroup with a lucrative departure from the steel industry. Two months after fashioning the deal, however, the companies terminated it in light of a U.S. Justice Department ruling against another proposed merger between U.S. steel companies.

History of U.S. Steel Corp.

Carnegie Steel, Federal Steel Co., and eight other industrial concerns merged in 1901 to form the United States Steel Corp. (USS), the largest company ever formed, with initial capitalization of $1.4 billion. The merger was part of a plan by Federal Steel owner J.P. Morgan to dominate the steel market by creating a centralized combine, or trust, in the industry. Later that year USS purchased Shelby Steel Tube Co. and the Bessemer Steamship company. Sales in 1902, the first full year of operation, reached $423 million, and the company held 66% of the nation's steel market.

Company president Charles M. Schwab resigned in 1903 over disagreements with board chairman Elbert Henry Gary, leaving Gary in control of USS. Gary's stated intent was not to establish a trust, but rather to build an efficient company able to compete on product quality and price.

USS acquired the Union Steel Co. in 1903 and the Clairton Steel Co. the next year. In 1905 the U.S. government launched an antitrust investigation of the company's competitive practices. USS continued its expansion while this probe was conducted. In 1906 it began construction of a new steel mill and a model city, Gary, Indiana. The following year it acquired Tennessee Coal, Iron and Railroad Co., the largest steel producer in the South. USS expanded into the West with the 1910 purchase of Columbia Steel Co. Gary, though opposed to unionization of workers, led a movement in 1911 to reduce the standard 12-hour day in the steel industry.

The antitrust investigation ended in 1911, when the government brought monopoly charges against USS. The U.S. Court of Appeals ruled in favor of USS four years later, deciding that the company's market position was a direct result of its competitiveness.

The steel industry boomed during World War I and USS's sales doubled their 1915 level. In 1919 steelworkers engaged in a strike for a reduction of hours, along with other considerations. This strike ended the following year, with none of the workers' demands having been met.

Myron C. Taylor became chairman of the board in 1932 and began a total overhaul of USS. Taking advantage of plant closings during the Great Depression, Taylor retooled the company by closing or modernizing old plants and building new facilities. He also changed its focus to the production of lighter steel for consumer products. In 1933, however, sales reached an all-time low of $288 million. Taylor resigned in 1938, and was replaced as chairman by Edward R. Stettinius, Jr. That year approximately 75% of USS's product lines were different, or produced using different techniques, than they were in 1927. At the same time, the firm began losing its hold of the domestic steel market, as its share dropped to 33%.

In 1940 Stettinius resigned, and Irving S. Olds became chairman. The company's growth was dramatically improved during World War II, and United States Steel Supply was created as a subsidiary in 1943. Six years later USS initiated the construction of a steel plant in Pennsylvania to penetrate the Eastern steel market dominated by Bethlehem Steel. In 1951 the company launched a reorganization designed to streamline its administration by combining its four operational subsidiaries into a single company. Sales that year topped $3.5 billion, representing a 400% increase since 1938.

In 1952 steelworkers prepared to strike, demanding wage increases and an enhancement of union influence in the industry. Before that strike could occur, U.S. President Harry S. Truman nationalized the steel industry to ensure production of military supplies for the Korean War, but the U.S. Supreme Court ruled that this action was unconstitutional. The steelworkers' strike commenced later that year and was settled two months later. Olds resigned and was succeeded first by Benjamin F. Fairless and then by Roger M. Bough.

In 1958 USS absorbed its subsidiaries Universal Atlas Cement Co., Union Supply Co., and Homewood Stores Co. to further streamline the corporate manage-

The Business

Financials - U.S. Steel Corp.
Revenue (1998): $27.8 billion

Employees (1998): 45,000

Financials - National Steel Corp.
Revenue (1998): $20.8 billion

Employees (1998): 25,000

SICs / NAICS
sic 5122 - Drugs, Proprietaries & Sundries

sic 5047 - Medical & Hospital Equipment

sic 2911 - Petroleum Refining

sic 3312 - Blast Furnaces & Steel Mills

sic 4612 - Crude Petroleum Pipelines

sic 4613 - Refined Petroleum Pipelines

sic 5541 - Gasoline Service Stations

sic 4923 - Gas Transmission & Distribution

sic 1222 - Bituminous Coal-Underground

naics 324110 - Petroleum Refineries

naics 331111 - Iron and Steel Mills

naics 486110 - Pipeline Transportation of Crude Oil

naics 486910 - Pipeline Transportation of Refined Petroleum Products

naics 447110 - Gasoline Stations with Convenience Stores

naics 221210 - Natural Gas Distribution

naics 212110 - Coal Mining

naics 422210 - Drugs and Druggists' Sundries Wholesalers

naics 421450 - Medical, Dental and Hospital Equipment and Supplies Wholesalers

ment structure. Profits began to fall due to rising production costs and increased competition from foreign steelmakers. The company's share of the U.S. steel market in 1961 fell to 25%.

The firm attempted to raise its prices in April 1962, but reversed that decision after being sternly criticized by U.S. President John F. Kennedy. The next year USS again reorganized, centralizing its steelmaking divisions and sales operations in order to direct more management resources into sales and customer services. In 1964 it established the Pittsburgh Chemical Co. to function as its chemical division. This

The Officers

U.S. Steel Corp.

Chairman and CEO: Thomas J. Usher

Vice Chairman and Chief Financial Officer: Robert M. Hernandez

Secretary, General Counsel, and Sr. VP, Human Resources and Public Affairs: Daniel D. Sandman

VP, Strategic Planning: Albert E. Ferrara, Jr.

VP and Treasurer: Edward F. Guna

National Steel Corp.

Chairman: Alan Seelenfreund

Co-CEO: John H. Hammergren

Co-CEO: David L. Mahoney

Acting Chief Financial Officer: Heidi Yodowitz

Group President, Retail Business: Mark Majeske

division was superseded two years later by the creation of the United States Steel Chemicals Division.

In 1973 Edgar B. Speer became chairman and launched the company on a program of diversification into nonsteel businesses. Over the next five years, the company closed or sold many of its interests in steel, cement, and mining, but capital expenditures remained high due to new environmental regulations. David M. Roderick replaced Speer as chairman in 1979. He announced the liquidation of 13 unprofitable steel mills for a write-off of $809 million. Despite this move, and the sale of Universal Atlas Cement, the company reported losses of $293 million for the year.

USS acquired Marathon Oil Co. for $6.4 billion in 1982, thereby doubling the company's size while reducing steel's contribution to 40% of company sales. Two years later its planned purchase of National Steel Corp., the steel operations of National Intergroup, Inc., was frowned upon by federal regulators, and the two companies terminated their agreement.

Under Roderick, the company had closed down more than 150 facilities, reduced its management workforce by 54%, cut its overall workforce by 100,000, and sold $3 billion of assets by 1985. The next year USS changed its name to USX Corp. It continued to diversify with the acquisition of Texas Oil & Gas Corp. USX divested itself of United States Steel Supply and the United States Steel Chemicals Division later that year.

In 1986 corporate raider Carl Icahn bid $7.1 billion for USX, but his takeover attempt was thwarted when Roderick borrowed $3.4 billion to retire corporate debt. Icahn abandoned his takeover attempt in 1987, but retained a large interest in the company and continued advocating a corporate restructuring and the divestiture of all steelmaking facilities.

USX and Armco Inc. formed National Oilwell Inc., a joint venture in oilfield supplies, in 1987. USX shut down 25% of its remaining steelmaking capacity, and by 1988 its remaining steel facilities were among the most efficient in the world. That year it also sold its interest in Transtar, a domestic transportation subsidiary.

Roderick was replaced as chairman by Charles A. Corry in 1989. USX sold some of Texas Oil & Gas' energy reserves to raise capital for debt retirement and stock buybacks. The company also sold its Lorain, Ohio, plant to Kobe Steel Co., and divested itself of the Quebec Cartier Mining Co. In 1990 Texas Oil & Gas was merged into Marathon Oil as a cost-cutting measure. USX entered into a joint venture that year with Kobe Steel to produce hot-dipped galvanized steel for the automotive industry.

In 1991 USX recapitalized by issuing separate classes of stock for its two new divisions, USX-U.S. Steel Group and USX-Marathon Group. It reported losses of $587 million for the year, reflecting further capital investments in the company's steelmaking operations. That same year, Corry concluded a three-year agreement with the United Steelworkers Union (USW) and removed Icahn from the corporate picture through a $1 billion buyout.

USX formed a corporate information technologies unit to market systems integration, consulting services, and computer resources to other businesses in 1992. It also unveiled a state-of-the-art continuous steel casting facility in Pittsburgh, Pennsylvania. The company recorded losses of $1.8 billion for 1992. That same year, USX joined a consortium of U.S. steelmakers to bring suit against foreign competitors, claiming unfair trading practices. This case was settled in 1993, when the U.S. Commerce Department ruled in favor of domestic steel producers, imposing heavy duties on imported steel. In 1994 a joint venture between Lone Star Steel Co. and Metallia USA Inc. offered to purchase USX's abandoned steel-producing facilities at Baytown, Texas.

In 1996 USX and Armco Inc. sold National Oilwell for $180 million to a partnership of that company's management. The Delhi Gas Pipeline Corp. was sold to Koch Industries in late 1997. Also in 1998 Marathon joined with Ashland Inc. to form Marathon Ashland Petroleum LLC, a refining, marketing, and transportation company. The following year Marathon purchased Tarragon Oil & Gas, a Canadian concern, thereby increasing its reserves by 20%. In June 1999 USX agreed to sell Carnegie Natural Gas Co. to Equitable Resources, Inc.

History of National Steel Corp.

The National Steel Corp. was formed in 1929 through the merger of Great Lakes Steel Co., Hanna Iron Ore Co., and the Weirton Steel Co. The new company enjoyed fairly steady success through the 1960s, but in the late 1970s the steel industry entered a slump. Declining profits spurred Chairman Howard Love to lead National Steel on an aggressive diversification path.

The company formed National Intergroup, Inc. (NII) in late 1983 as an umbrella holding company for current operating companies as well as future acquisitions. It consisted of six business groups, one of which was National Steel. A $575 million offer by U.S. Steel Corp. for National Steel in 1984 was dropped due to the U.S. Department of Justice's apparent opposition to such mergers in the industry. NII then reached out to Nippon Kokan K.K., Japan's second-largest steelmaker, to begin negotiations of a possible deal. Later in 1984 NII sold 50% of National Steel to that company, later known as NKK Corp., for $322 million.

Behind Love's diversification plan was a move into the more stable, less capital intensive, wholesale pharmaceutical industry. After a failed merger attempt with healthcare products distributor Bergen Brunswig Corp. in 1985, NII successfully acquired FoxMeyer Corp., the nation's third-largest drug distributor and operator of the Health Mart and Ben Franklin drugstore chains.

NII's acquisitions proved troublesome, as both oil and pharmaceutical prices dropped. By early 1987 these financial difficulties, combined with operating problems in its steel businesses, left NII with a debt load of $600 million. Despite the sale of half of Permian Corp. and the reduction of 25% of its operating expenses, NII was unable to secure credit, as bankers found the company's performance risky.

Laurence Farley became president of NII in 1988 and directed the company toward initial recovery by focusing on FoxMeyer. This company represented 85% of NII's $3 billion in sales, yet had profit margins half the industry's average. In mid-1998 Farley staged a coup against Love, who he felt wasn't improving NII quickly enough. Farley proposed to the company's board that he become CEO, relegating Love to the largely ceremonial role of chairman. On March 21, however, the board decided in favor of Love and hired James Pasman Jr. as Farley's replacement.

The Players

U.S. Steel Corp. Chairman: David M. Roderick. After earning a degree in economics from the University of Pittsburgh, David Roderick took a job with Gulf Oil Corp. He then worked for U.S. Steel as a comptroller of its railroads, and took a position in the company's accounting department in 1959. Twenty-one years after first joining the company, Roderick ascended to the chairmanship in 1979. Once in that position, he led the company on an aggressive diversification path outside of the steel industry. He trimmed operations and the workforce in an effort to accumulate funds to make strategic purchases. While still remaining committed to that industry, Roderick acquired operations in chemicals, Rnatural resources, and manufacturing. Most importantly, however, he plunged U.S. Steel deep into oil by purchasing Marathon Oil Co. in 1982, and followed up that acquisition with the purchase of Texas Oil & Gas Corp. four years later. In 1989 Roderick was succeeded as chairman by Charles A. Corry.

National Steel Corp. Chairman and CEO: Howard M. Love. Howard Love, the son of long-time National Steel executive George Love, became CEO of National Steel Corp. in March 1980. He developed a diversification plan that would move the company away from steel into other industries, particularly into wholesale pharmaceuticals. This strategy proved unprofitable in the 1980s, and National Steel remained in the red for several consecutive years. In July 1990 a dissident shareholder group ousted Love from the company's board.

Pasman, like Farley, concentrated on improving the FoxMeyer operations. In addition, he began to explore the sale of the company's steel and aluminum businesses. So, in late 1989, NII sold its aluminum rolling and extrusion divisions, followed the next year by its majority stake in an aluminum smelter. NII also announced major restructuring plans to fend off a hostile takeover by a group of dissident shareholders, operating as Centaur Partners, which held a 16.5% stake in the company. Among the changes announced were the sale of the Ben Franklin chain of stores and the relocation of company headquarters from Pittsburgh to Dallas. That July Centaur won control of the board and ousted Love. That same year, Nippon

Kokan increased its stake in National Steel to 87%. For fiscal 1990 NII finally showed a profit, $55.7 million.

In 1991 the company sold Permian Corp. to Ashland Oil, and also sold 30% of FoxMeyer stock to the public. In 1994 FoxMeyer Corp. merged with its parent company, National Intergroup, to form FoxMeyer Health Corp. Two years later the firm separated its failing pharmaceuticals distribution from the parent company, selling FoxMeyer Drug to McKesson HBOC. FoxMeyer Health Corp. was renamed Avatex Corp. as a holding company for diverse interests in real estate.

Market Forces Driving the Acquisition

A depressed U.S. steel industry in the early 1980s served as the impetus for a rash of merger and acquisition activity by steelmakers. Labor costs were high, plants were aging, and, most pressing, imports were squeezing the sales and profitability of domestic companies. The percentage of total U.S. steel consumption increased from 15.2% in 1979 to 20.5% in 1983, yet the net income of the nation's seven largest steel producers fell, from a total profit of $800 million in 1979 to a loss of $2.8 billion in 1983.

By purchasing National Steel Corp., the steel operations of National Intergroup, Inc., U.S. Steel would increase its overall market share from 17.5% to 23%. It would also control 25% of the nation's flat-rolled market. U.S. Steel would be able to trim expenditures by combining overlapping facilities, which could be purchased from National Steel for a fraction of what they would cost to construct from scratch.

For National Intergroup, a sale of its steel operations would enable it to focus on its other businesses, including financial services, aluminum, distribution, and an array of other diversified operations. National Intergroup was also carrying a sizable debt load, an impediment in pursuing its diversification strategy.

Approach and Engagement

On February 1, 1984, National Intergroup, Inc. announced the sale of National Steel Corp. to U.S. Steel Corp. The price tag for the subsidiary was $575 million, plus the assumption of $460 in debt.

A cloud soon settled over this agreement, however. On February 15 the U.S. Department of Justice announced its opposition to the proposed acquisition of Republic Steel Corp. by LTV Corp., both large U.S. steelmakers, on antitrust grounds. Concerned about the implications of this decision for their own merger plans, the chairmen of U.S. Steel and National Intergroup met with officials at the Justice Department in early March.

One option offered by the government as a way to obtain clearance was the divestiture of several major plants. This suggestion was unacceptable to U.S. Steel, which cited the addition of those plants as a motivation for the acquisition in the first place.

On March 9, 1984, the companies canceled their acquisition agreement. "Obviously we're disappointed," said David Roderick, chairman of U.S. Steel, in *The New York Times*. "It would have been a marvelous fit. We called it off because the Justice Department very clearly put such onerous, economically punitive conditions on a solution that we obviously couldn't proceed."

Products and Services

In 1999 USX Corp. was a major worldwide producer of oil and natural gas, and the nation's largest producer of steel products. It functioned as two separate businesses, each with its own management, who operated under the USX board of directors.

The USX-Marathon Group was involved in global crude oil and natural gas exploration, production and transportation, and in the domestic refining, marketing, and transportation of crude oil and petroleum products. Its Marathon Ashland Petroleum unit had seven refineries that accounted for six percent of total U. S. refining capacity. Its gas stations were branded under the names Marathon, Ashland, Speedway, Starvin' Marvin, United, Bonded, SuperAmerica, and Rich Oil.

The USX-U.S. Steel Group manufactured and marketed a variety of steel mill products, coke, and taconite pellets; it also operated in a diverse array of other businesses, including coal mining, mineral resources management, real estate development, engineering and consulting services, technology licensing, and leasing and financial services.

In the late 1990s McKesson HBOC, which had purchased FoxMeyer Drug Corp. (formerly National Intergroup) in 1996, had three operating segments. Pharmaceutical Services encompassed BioServices, Healthcare Delivery Systems, J Knipper, and Technology Solutions units. Information Technologies provided software systems. Finally, Supply Management included Automated Healthcare, BakerAPS, and Red Line Extended Care.

Changes to the Industry and Review of the Outcome

National Intergroup immediately found another buyer for National Steel. On April 24 Nippon Kokan agreed to purchase 50% of National Steel for $292 million, thereby giving Japan's second-largest steel producer access to the U.S. market. Once it had divested its steel holdings, the firm began targeting the wholesale pharmaceutical industry. After failing to merge with healthcare products distributor Bergen Brunswig Corp. in 1985, National Intergroup acquired FoxMeyer Corp., the nation' s third-largest drug distributor. Eventually, FoxMeyer became National Intergroup's core focus.

Recognizing that acquisitions in the steel industry would likely continue to be heavily regulated, U.S. Steel continued the diversification it had launched with its 1982 purchase of Marathon Oil. In 1986, the firm bought Texas Oil & Gas Corp., moving into the natural gas market for the first time.

Research

Arenson, Karen W. "U.S. Steel and National Drop Plan to Merge Steel Divisions," in *The New York Times*, 10 March 1984. Details the termination of the merger and the Justice Department's ruling on the LTV/Republic accord.

Cuff, Daniel F. "New Emphasis for Intergroup," *The New York Times*, 2 February 1984. Relates the terms of the merger accord.

"For Steelmakers, No Mergers May Mean More Bankruptcies," in *Business Week*, 5 March 1984. Describes the impact on the industry of the Justice Department's ruling.

"High Hurdles Ahead for U.S. Steel and National," in *Business Week*, 20 February 1984. Describes the strengths and weaknesses of the combining operations.

"National Intergroup, Inc.," in *International Directory of Company Histories*, Vol. IV, St. James Press, 1991. Provides an historical review of the company.

USX Corp. Home Page, available at http://www.usx.com. Official World Wide Web Page for USX Corp. Includes brief organizational and product descriptions, press releases, financial and investor information, and links to USX-Marathon and USX-U.S. Steel Web pages.

"USX Corp.," in *Notable Corporate Chronologies*, The Gale Group, 1999. Profiles the history of the company.

J.M. WEBER

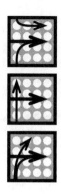

U.S. STEEL & TEXAS OIL

USX Corp.
600 Grant St.
Pittsburgh, PA 15219
USA

tel: (412)433-1121
fax: (412)433-4818
web: http://www.usx.com

nationality: USA
date: February 11, 1986
affected: U.S. Steel Corp. (now part of USX Corp.), USA, founded 1901
affected: Texas Oil & Gas Corp., USA

Overview of the Acquisition

Playing on the success of its 1982 acquisition of Marathon Oil, U.S. Steel continued its quest to increase its presence in the oil industry by purchasing Texas Oil & Gas in 1986. The timing of the deal was slightly unfortunate, as the natural gas industry continued its depression after the acquisition was completed. U.S. Steel, however, improved the situation by folding Texas Oil into its Marathon holdings in 1990.

History of U.S. Steel Corp.

Carnegie Steel, Federal Steel Co., and eight other industrial concerns merged in 1901 to form the United States Steel Corp. (USS), the largest company ever formed, with initial capitalization of $1.4 billion. The merger was part of a plan by Federal Steel owner J.P. Morgan to dominate the steel market by creating a centralized combine, or trust, in the industry. Later that year USS purchased Shelby Steel Tube Co. and the Bessemer Steamship company. Sales in 1902, the first full year of operation, reached $423 million, and the company held 66% of the nation's steel market.

Company president Charles M. Schwab resigned in 1903 over disagreements with board chairman Elbert Henry Gary, leaving Gary in control of USS. Gary's stated intent was not to establish a trust, but rather to build an efficient company able to compete on product quality and price.

USS acquired the Union Steel Co. in 1903 and the Clairton Steel Co. the next year. In 1905 the U.S. government launched an antitrust investigation of the company's competitive practices. USS continued its expansion while this probe was conducted. In 1906 it began construction of a new steel mill and a model city, Gary, Indiana. The following year it acquired Tennessee Coal, Iron and Railroad Co., the largest steel producer in the South. USS expanded into the West with the 1910 purchase of Columbia Steel Co. Gary, though opposed to unionization of workers, led a movement in 1911 to reduce the standard 12-hour day in the steel industry.

The antitrust investigation ended in 1911, when the government brought monopoly charges against USS. The U.S. Court of Appeals ruled in favor of USS four years later, deciding that the company's market position was a direct result of its competitiveness.

The steel industry boomed during World War I and USS's sales doubled their 1915 level. In 1919 steelworkers engaged in a strike for a reduction of hours, along with other considerations. This strike ended the following year, with none of the workers' demands having been met.

Myron C. Taylor became chairman of the board in 1932 and began a total overhaul of USS. Taking advantage of plant closings during the Great Depression, Taylor retooled the company by closing or modernizing old plants and building new facilities. He also changed its focus to the production of lighter steel for consumer products. In 1933, however, sales reached an all-time low of $288 million. Taylor resigned in 1938, and was replaced as chairman by Edward R. Stettinius, Jr. That year approximately 75% of USS's product lines were different, or produced using different techniques, than they were in 1927. At the same time, the firm began losing its hold of the domestic steel market, as its share dropped to 33%.

In 1940 Stettinius resigned, and Irving S. Olds became chairman. The company's growth was dramatically improved during World War II, and United States Steel Supply was created as a subsidiary in 1943. Six years later USS initiated the construction of a steel plant in Pennsylvania to penetrate the Eastern steel market dominated by Bethlehem Steel. In 1951 the company launched a reorganization designed to streamline its administration by combining its four operational subsidiaries into a single company. Sales that year topped $3.5 billion, representing a 400% increase since 1938.

In 1952 steelworkers prepared to strike, demanding wage increases and an enhancement of union influence in the industry. Before that strike could occur, U.S. President Harry S. Truman nationalized the steel industry to ensure production of military supplies for the Korean War, but the U.S. Supreme Court ruled that this action was unconstitutional. The steelworkers' strike commenced later that year and was settled two months later. Olds resigned and was succeeded first by Benjamin F. Fairless and then by Roger M. Bough.

In 1958 USS absorbed its subsidiaries Universal Atlas Cement Co., Union Supply Co., and Homewood Stores Co. to further streamline the corporate management structure. Profits began to fall due to rising production costs and increased competition from foreign steelmakers. The company's share of the U.S. steel market in 1961 fell to 25%.

The Business

Financials

Revenue (1998): $27.8 billion

Employees (1998): 45,000

SICs / NAICS

sic 2911 - Petroleum Refining

sic 3312 - Blast Furnaces & Steel Mills

sic 4612 - Crude Petroleum Pipelines

sic 4613 - Refined Petroleum Pipelines

sic 5541 - Gasoline Service Stations

sic 4923 - Gas Transmission & Distribution

sic 1222 - Bituminous Coal-Underground

naics 324110 - Petroleum Refineries

naics 331111 - Iron and Steel Mills

naics 486110 - Pipeline Transportation of Crude Oil

naics 486910 - Pipeline Transportation of Refined Petroleum Products

naics 447110 - Gasoline Stations with Convenience Stores

naics 221210 - Natural Gas Distribution

naics 212110 - Coal Mining

The firm attempted to raise its prices in April 1962, but reversed that decision after being sternly criticized by U.S. President John F. Kennedy. The next year USS again reorganized, centralizing its steelmaking divisions and sales operations in order to direct more management resources into sales and customer services. In 1964 it established the Pittsburgh Chemical Co. to function as its chemical division. This division was superseded two years later by the creation of the United States Steel Chemicals Division.

In 1973 Edgar B. Speer became chairman and launched the company on a program of diversification into nonsteel businesses. Over the next five years, the company closed or sold many of its interests in steel, cement, and mining, but capital expenditures remained high due to new environmental regulations. David M. Roderick replaced Speer as chairman in 1979. He announced the liquidation of 13 unprofitable steel mills for a write-off of $809 million. Despite this move, and the sale of Universal Atlas Cement, the company reported losses of $293 million for the year.

USS acquired Marathon Oil Co. for $6.4 billion in 1982, thereby doubling the company's size while

The Officers

Chairman and CEO: Thomas J. Usher

Vice Chairman and Chief Financial Officer: Robert M. Hernandez

Secretary, General Counsel, and Sr. VP, Human Resources and Public Affairs: Daniel D. Sandman

VP, Strategic Planning: Albert E. Ferrara, Jr.

VP and Treasurer: Edward F. Guna

reducing steel's contribution to 40% of company sales. Two years later its planned purchase of National Steel Corp., the steel operations of National Intergroup, Inc., was frowned upon by federal regulators, and the two companies terminated their agreement.

Under Roderick, the company had closed down more than 150 facilities, reduced its management workforce by 54%, cut its overall workforce by 100,000, and sold $3 billion of assets by 1985. The next year USS changed its name to USX Corp. It continued to diversify with the acquisition of Texas Oil & Gas Corp. USX divested itself of United States Steel Supply and the United States Steel Chemicals Division later that year.

In 1986 corporate raider Carl Icahn bid $7.1 billion for USX, but his takeover attempt was thwarted when Roderick borrowed $3.4 billion to retire corporate debt. Icahn abandoned his takeover attempt in 1987, but retained a large interest in the company and continued advocating a corporate restructuring and the divestiture of all steelmaking facilities.

USX and Armco Inc. formed National Oilwell Inc., a joint venture in oilfield supplies, in 1987. USX shut down 25% of its remaining steelmaking capacity, and by 1988 its remaining steel facilities were among the most efficient in the world. That year it also sold its interest in Transtar, a domestic transportation subsidiary.

Roderick was replaced as chairman by Charles A. Corry in 1989. USX sold some of Texas Oil & Gas' energy reserves to raise capital for debt retirement and stock buybacks. The company also sold its Lorain, Ohio, plant to Kobe Steel Co., and divested itself of the Quebec Cartier Mining Co. In 1990 Texas Oil & Gas was merged into Marathon Oil as a cost-cutting measure. USX entered into a joint venture that year with Kobe Steel to produce hot-dipped galvanized steel for the automotive industry.

In 1991 USX recapitalized by issuing separate classes of stock for its two new divisions, USX-U.S. Steel Group and USX-Marathon Group. It reported losses of $587 million for the year, reflecting further capital investments in the company's steelmaking operations. That same year, Corry concluded a three-year agreement with the United Steelworkers Union (USW) and removed Icahn from the corporate picture through a $1 billion buyout.

USX formed a corporate information technologies unit to market systems integration, consulting services, and computer resources to other businesses in 1992. It also unveiled a state-of-the-art continuous steel casting facility in Pittsburgh, Pennsylvania. The company recorded losses of $1.8 billion for 1992. That same year, USX joined a consortium of U.S. steelmakers to bring suit against foreign competitors, claiming unfair trading practices. This case was settled in 1993, when the U.S. Commerce Department ruled in favor of domestic steel producers, imposing heavy duties on imported steel. In 1994 a joint venture between Lone Star Steel Co. and Metallia USA Inc. offered to purchase USX's abandoned steel-producing facilities at Baytown, Texas.

In 1996 USX and Armco Inc. sold National Oilwell for $180 million to a partnership of that company's management. The Delhi Gas Pipeline Corp. was sold to Koch Industries in late 1997. Also in 1998 Marathon joined with Ashland Inc. to form Marathon Ashland Petroleum LLC, a refining, marketing, and transportation company. The following year Marathon purchased Tarragon Oil & Gas, a Canadian concern, thereby increasing its reserves by 20%. In June 1999 USX agreed to sell Carnegie Natural Gas Co. to Equitable Resources, Inc.

Market Forces Driving the Acquisition

The same market conditions that had spurred U.S. Steel's foray into the oil industry in 1982 continued into the following years. With its purchase of Marathon Oil Co., the company took a big leap outside of the steel industry, which had been crippled by stiff competition from foreign competition, high labor costs, and a compressed market for steel. To protect itself from such conditions, which showed no sign of improving, U.S. Steel decided to transform itself into an energy company, of which steel operations would constitute only a portion.

With the acquisition of Marathon, U.S. Steel immediately doubled its size and became the nation's 17th-largest oil company. About 40% of its assets were based in steel, 40% in oil and gas, and the remaining in such diverse operations as chemicals, natural resources, utilities, and transportation. Its shift in focus was fortuitous, as the steel industry continued its downward decline. The nation's largest steelmakers recorded net losses in the second quarter of 1982, while U.S. Steel managed to squeak by with a small profit due to the performance of its oil interests.

The steel decline continued. In 1985 Wheeling-Pittsburgh Corp. filed for bankruptcy and Bethlehem Steel withheld its quarterly dividend for the first time in nearly half a century. The industry's other large players were also trapped in a cycle of plunging profitability and the resulting inability to expand or invest in plant modernization, thereby perpetuating their decline. U.S. Steel was one of the few players still able to afford to increase its holdings outside the industry. Because oil operations had proven to be a life raft for the company, it decided to increase its presence in that industry, as well as move in the natural gas sector, with the purchase of Texas Oil & Gas Corp.

Approach and Engagement

On October 30, 1985, U.S. Steel agreed to acquire Texas Oil & Gas Corp. for $3.6 billion. This company was a large natural gas producer and gatherer, but had experienced slightly depressed profits as a result of falling gas prices. David Roderick, chairman of U.S. Steel, was confident that the gas market would rebound, and that the acquisition of Texas Oil would be strategic over the long term. "Ultimately, natural gas in the country is going to be in short supply," he said in *Newsweek*. "That [oversupply] bubble is going to burst sooner than people think."

The acquisition agreement consisted of a stock exchange of .6333 of a U.S. Steel share, valued at $17, for each Texas Oil share. Some analysts and shareholders criticized the deal, claiming that the price offered by U.S. Steel was too low given Texas Oil's future prospects. The majority of shareholders, however, were pleased with the terms. On February 11, 1986, shareholders of each company overwhelmingly approved the acquisition, and the deal was completed that same day.

Products and Services

In 1999 USX Corp. was a major worldwide producer of oil and natural gas and the nation's largest producer of steel products. It functioned as two separate businesses, each with its own management, who operated under the USX board of directors.

The USX-Marathon Group was involved in global crude oil and natural gas exploration, production and transportation, and in the domestic refining, marketing, and transportation of crude oil and petroleum products. Its Marathon Ashland Petroleum unit had seven refineries that accounted for six percent of total

The Players

U.S. Steel Corp. Chairman: David M. Roderick. After earning a degree in economics from the University of Pittsburgh, David Roderick took a job with Gulf Oil Corp. He then worked for U.S. Steel as a comptroller of its railroads and took a position in the company's accounting department in 1959. Twenty-one years after first joining the company, Roderick ascended to the chairmanship in 1979. Once in that position, he led the company on an aggressive diversification path outside of the steel industry. He trimmed operations and the workforce in an effort to accumulate funds to make strategic purchases. While still remaining committed to that industry, Roderick acquired operations in chemicals, natural resources, and manufacturing. Most importantly, however, he plunged U.S. Steel deep into oil by purchasing Marathon Oil Co. in 1982, and followed up that acquisition with the purchase of Texas Oil & Gas Corp. four years later. In 1989 Roderick was succeeded as chairman by Charles A. Corry.

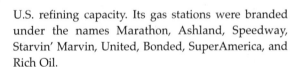

U.S. refining capacity. Its gas stations were branded under the names Marathon, Ashland, Speedway, Starvin' Marvin, United, Bonded, SuperAmerica, and Rich Oil.

The USX-U.S. Steel Group manufactured and marketed a variety of steel mill products, coke, and taconite pellets; it also operated in a diverse array of other businesses, including coal mining, mineral resources management, real estate development, engineering and consulting services, technology licensing, and leasing and financial services.

Changes to the Industry and Review of the Outcome

After the acquisition of Texas Oil & Gas, U.S. Steel lessened its dependence on steel to 25% from 32% of sales. Its doubled its presence in the gas industry and immediately became the 13th-largest industrial concern in the nation. The gas industry, however, continued its decline, and Texas Oil & Gas failed to show a profit for several years after its acquisition. Although these results had little impact on USX's overall profitability—its net income quadrupled in the first half of 1988 to $370 million—the company decided to take steps to improve its balance sheet. In 1989 it sold certain energy reserves of Texas Oil, as well as such assets as its Lorain, Ohio, plant and the Quebec Cartier Mining Co. In 1990 Texas Oil & Gas was merged into Marathon Oil as a further cost-cutting measure.

Research

Cuff, Daniel F. "U.S. Steel to Acquire Texas Oil and Gas in $3.6 Billion Deal," in *The New York Times*, 31 October 1985. Describes the terms of the deal, as well as industry conditions surrounding it.

———. "Shareholders Clear U.S. Steel Merger," in *The New York Times*, 12 February 1986. Briefly reports the share-holder approval and completion of the deal.

Dodsworth, Terry. "Stepping on the Gas; U.S. Steel in Transition," in *Financial Times (London)*, 11 December 1985. Describes the performance of steel companies in the collapsed industry.

Nicholson, Tom and Mark Miller. "U.S. Steel's Big Energy Play," in *Newsweek*, 11 November 1985. Reviews the recently announced acquisition agreement.

USX Corp. Home Page, available at http://www.usx.com. Official World Wide Web Page for USX Corp. Includes brief organizational and product descriptions, press releases, financial and investor information, and links to USX-Marathon and USX-U.S. Steel Web pages.

"USX Corp.," in *Notable Corporate Chronologies*, The Gale Group, 1999. Profiles the history of the company, through and beyond it acquisitions of Marathon and Texas Oil & Gas.

—J.M. WEBER

U S WEST & CONTINENTAL CABLEVISION

nationality: USA
date: November 1996
affected: U S West Inc., USA, founded 1984
affected: Continental Cablevision, Inc., USA, founded 1963

U S West Inc.
1801 California St., Ste. 5200
Denver, CO 80244
USA

tel: (800)879-4357
web: http://www.uswest.com

Overview of the Merger

The merger between U S West and Continental Cablevision was the first combination of local telephone and cable television since the passage of the Telecommunications Act of 1996. At a time when other telephone companies were shedding their cable ventures, U S West remained committed to the media. It was confident that the future of telecommunications was in the provision of a combination of voice, data, and video transmission, all of which required a direct pipeline to the consumer.

History of U S West Inc.

U S West was established as one of seven regional holding companies (RHCs) created from the 1984 breakup of AT&T's Bell Telephone System. Its holdings included Northwest Bell Telephone Co., Mountain States Telephone & Telegraph Co., and Pacific Northwest Bell Telephone Co. Its territory consisted of Arizona, Colorado, Idaho, Iowa, Minnesota, Montana, New Mexico, Nebraska, North and South Carolina, Oregon, Utah, Washington, and Wyoming.

Later that year, U S West moved into financial services, buying a commercial real estate funding company and the Kansas City operations of Control Data Corporation's Commercial Credit Co. In addition, the company began investing in cellular telephone services and directory publishing. In 1985 the company reorganized into a decentralized structure with its three local phone companies and new subsidiaries operating as separate entities.

U S West acquired Applied Communications Inc. for $120 million in 1986. That year it formed a commercial real estate subsidiary, Beta West Properties. The company's two equipment-marketing subsidiaries, First Tel Information Systems and Interline Communication Services, were combined into a new subsidiary, U S Information Systems.

By 1987 eleven of the 14 states the company serviced had loosened regulation, freeing U S West to price new services such as central phone switching, cellular phones, and private lines. The next year it acquired two reinsurance companies for

The Business

Financials

Revenue (1998): $12.4 billion

Employees (1998): 54,483

SICs / NAICS

sic 2741 - Miscellaneous Publishing

sic 3661 - Telephone & Telegraph Apparatus

sic 4812 - Radiotelephone Communications

sic 4813 - Telephone Communications Except
    Radiotelephone

sic 4841 - Cable & Other Pay Television Services

naics 334210 - Telephone Apparatus Manufacturing

naics 511199 - All Other Publishers

naics 513310 - Wired Telecommunications Carriers

naics 513321 - Paging

naics 513322 - Cellular and Other Wireless
    Telecommunications

naics 513330 - Telecommunications Resellers

naics 513340 - Satellite Telecommunications

naics 513220 - Cable and Other Program Distribution

$50 billion. U S West, along with the other RHCs, won court permission to enter into new information services, such as voice mail and database transmission, as long as they didn't create or manipulate the data themselves.

The company acquired Financial Security Assurance, Inc. in 1989. That year its cable television division invested in two British cable companies, London South Partnership and Cable London. By 1990, U S West had invested $1.05 billion overseas, and became the first RHC in Eastern Europe by acquiring a 49% stake in a Hungarian cellular telephone project. That year it invested $35 million to develop "self-healing" phone networks in five cities, using loops of fiber-optic cable to prevent disruption of service.

A relaxation of federal restrictions in 1991 spurred the firm to introduce a number of services, including long distance services across state lines and the manufacture of telecommunications equipment. It also entered into a joint venture with the cable company Tele-Communications Inc. to combine their European cable TV and telephone operations.

It forged a 10-year alliance in 1992 with

Motorola's Cellular Infrastructure Group to upgrade U S West's cellular operations using Motorola's Narrow-band Advanced Mobile Phone Service, which boosted cellular cell capacity and improved transmission quality. The following year it acquired a 25.5% stake in Time Warner Entertainment, which controlled most of Time Warner's cable operations as well as the Warner Brothers movie studio and the Home Box Office cable channel. This investment gave U S West access to more cable television outlets than any other Bell company. Its harmony with Time Warner was short-lived, however, as in 1995 it filed suit against the company over its proposed purchase of the Turner Broadcasting System, Inc. on the grounds that the acquisition violated the terms of U S West's 25% investment in Time Warner Entertainment.

In 1995 U S West split into two publicly traded units, U S West Media Group and U S West Communications. The Media Group was involved in domestic and international cable and telephony, wireless communications, and directory and information services, while U S West Communications provided telecommunications services. Also that year, the company won approval from the U.S. Department of Justice for extra-regional marketing, allowing it to provide long distance telephone service via cable television systems to states outside its 14-state operating region. In 1996 U S West expanded its cable holdings by acquiring Continental Cablevision.

History of Continental Cablevision

Amos Hostetter, an employee of Boston-based Cambridge Capital, became involved in a proposition to finance a cable television system for industry pioneer Bill Daniels in 1962. Hostetter recommended that Cambridge help finance the deal. Hostetter developed a personal interest in cable television and invited a Harvard classmate, Irving Grousbeck, to join him in bidding on other franchises.

The next year Hostetter and Grousbeck pooled $3,000 and devised a plan to serve areas that were underserved by conventional television. They settled upon two rural communities in northwestern Ohio that were unable to receive a decent signal from major cities without the help of a cable system. The two men negotiated franchises to serve the area but required an additional $650,000 to construct the system. After securing the backing from Boston Capital, they returned to Ohio to discover that the local authorities had grown impatient with them and had awarded a competing franchise to a local radio station that had already begun construction. Hostetter and Grousbeck eventually reached an agreement to buy out the competitor for $80,000. With only a few thousand customers, the two men officially began business.

In 1965 the partners expanded their Continental Cablevision venture to Illinois. Grousbeck handled the Illinois operations while Hostetter managed the Ohio properties. Four years later they appointed new managers for their businesses and returned to Boston, where they established the company's headquarters. By 1970 Continental served 65,000 subscribers. Its growth slowed, however, when banks and venture capitalists grew wary of the cable industry in the face of possible competition from telephone companies, the apparent exhaustion of undeveloped franchises, and the threat of overbuilding.

Through conservative financial management and a measured construction schedule, Continental remained strong. In fact, because some companies were forced to sell off portions of their systems, it became a buyer's market for the stronger, smaller companies in the industry, such as Continental. During the 1970s Hostetter became an outspoken advocate for the cable industry, strongly opposing any federal regulation that threatened to impede its growth.

By 1978 Continental had more than 200,000 subscribers. The following year, Hostetter helped to establish C-SPAN, a cable network devoted to televising congressional proceedings. Dow Jones & Co., Inc. purchased a 25% share in Continental for $80 million in 1981. This investment provided Continental with enough capital to bid on or buy out franchises in lucrative suburban markets around Boston, Cleveland, Detroit, Chicago, and St. Louis. Three years later the company scored its first major acquisition when it purchased a mismanaged, 82,000-subscriber system in Jacksonville, Florida.

Continental marked its one-millionth customer with the 1985 opening of a 1,000-mile cable system in St. Paul, Minnesota. In 1986 the company sold its troublesome cellular telephone operations to Colony Communications. In exchange, Continental received cash and several of Colony's cable systems in eastern Massachusetts.

In 1988, the year after Irving Grousbeck resigned, Continental purchased American Cablesysems. Its largest acquisition to date, the transaction brought 900,000 customers in greater Los Angeles. The following year, Continental began making large investments in programming from Turner Broadcasting System, Inc. and the Viewers Choice pay-per-view network.

Abuse in the cable industry led the U.S. Congress to enact legislation regulating the cable television industry in 1992. By that time, Continental Cablevision was the nation's third-largest Multiple System Operator, serving 2.9 million subscribers in 16 states.

The Officers

President and CEO: Solomon D. Trujillo

Exec. VP, Retail Markets: Betsy Bernard

VP and Chief Information Officer: Dave R. Laube

Exec. VP and Chief Financial Officer: Allan Spies

Exec. VP, Operations and Technologies: Greg M. Winn

In 1994 the company acquired the cable systems of Providence Journal Co. for $1.4 billion and the assumption of $755 million in debt. The following year Continental began testing cable modems that transmitted data up to 1,000 times faster than any telephone-based systems. Also in 1995 it received permission from the California Public Utilities Commission to offer local telephone service in 10 counties.

Continental entered into an agreement in 1996 with Tele-Communications Inc. to swap several systems representing about 200,000 subscribers in three states. That year, Continental was acquired by U S West.

Market Forces Driving the Merger

Just as the Telecommunications Act of 1996 deregulated the local and long distance telephone industries, it impacted cable television in the same way. Each of these three telecommunications segments became relatively free to enter into one another's market, both product and geographic. While local and long distance industries were sometimes considered the logical and complementary extension of the other, in some ways local telephone and cable television were more suitable partners. Technologically speaking, they had more in common with each other than either had with the long distance segment. Although they transmitted different media, both had direct connection with the customer, something that long distance carriers lacked. "The wire to your home or business doesn't care if it carries voice, video, or data," remarked Dave Otto, an analyst with Edward D. Jones & Co., in *InfoWorld*. "And eventually, that's what a communications company's going to be about: voice, video, and data."

Some of the Bell regional holding companies (RHCs) had anticipated such an open market, and had already formed ventures into the cable industry prior to deregulation. In 1993 Southwestern Bell spent $650 million to acquire Hauser Communications, a cable system in Washington, D.C. This move piqued the interest of other RHCs, who soon followed with similar deals themselves. Later that year, U S West and

The Players

U S West Media Group President and CEO: Charles M. Lillis. Charles Lillis spent a significant portion of his adult life in universities. He earned a bachelor's degree and an MBA from the University of Washington, before receiving a PhD from the University of Oregon in 1972. He became a business professor at Washington State University, and then the Dean of the University of Colorado Business School. In 1985 Lillis joined U S West as a vice president of strategic marketing. After receiving several executive promotions, he was appointed president and CEO of U S West Media Group in 1995. When the company's cable and wireless operations were spun off from U S West in 1997, Lillis became chairman and CEO of the new group, MediaOne.

Continental Chairman and CEO: Amos Hostetter, Jr. Amos "Bud" Hostetter, Jr., a Harvard Business School graduate, was a banker and corporate financier by training. He became involved in the cable television industry in 1962, forming Continental Cablevision the following year, and went on to become an industry advocate. In 1972 Hostetter became chairman of the National Cable Television Association. Three years later he joined the board of the Corporation for Public Broadcasting, and in 1980 joined the board of the Children's Television Workshop. He fueled his company's acquisition by U S West in 1996. In August of the following year, however, Hostetter resigned out of feelings of frustration over Continental's relocation from Massachusetts to Colorado.

Time Warner formed a partnership with the intention of delivering a combination of their strengths—voice, video, and data.

Now the ball was rolling. Southwestern Bell formed a cable alliance with Cox Enterprises, and BellSouth entered into an accord to invest in Prime Cable. Bell Atlantic unveiled its $21 billion acquisition of both Tele-Communications Inc. (TCI), the largest cable company, and Liberty Media, a television programmer.

Then the U.S. government intervened. Between 1984, when the cable industry became deregulated, and 1992, the rates of cable companies rose about 60%. The Federal Communications Commission (FCC) passed the Cable Act of 1992 to regulate the rates of basic cable service. The following year it imposed a 10% rate reduction, followed by a seven-percent reduction in 1994.

Suddenly the cable market was less appealing to RHCs. In February 1994 Bell Atlantic dropped its alliance with TCI after the cable company's cash flow fell 15%. That April, the deal between Southwestern Bell and Cox disintegrated.

U S West remained the only RHC committed to cable along with its core local telephone business. It chose to stick it out in cable rather than venturing into wireless offerings, like direct broadcast satellite (DBS), as other telephone companies were doing. Such one-way delivery would not be capable of providing the two-way, high-speed connection required for the transmission of data over the Internet, a service that cable had the possibility to begin offering. U S West's patience paid off, as the Telecommunications Act of 1996 removed the rate caps that had been imposed in the 1992 legislation.

To make a significant foray into cable, U S West wanted to go big. The company already held 25.5% of Time Warner Entertainment, which had about 11.5 million subscribers, and MediaOne, a Georgia-based cable system with about 525,000 subscribers. By acquiring Continental Cablevision, U S West would gain 4.2 million cable subscribers, as well as direct access into their homes for potential telephone service. U S West's footprint—its area of geographic coverage—had a relatively low density, as its territory of 14 western states had few major markets. The acquisition of the Boston-based cable company would gain it entry into five major markets—New England, California, Chicago, Florida, and Michigan/Ohio.

Continental was eager to gain access to the deep pockets of U S West. The task of upgrading its wiring to offer high-speed transmission was expensive, requiring hundreds of millions of dollars. The company's COO estimated that it would take Continental about six years to raise the necessary funds. In fact, the firm had scheduled a $345 million initial public offering in February 1996, but canceled it when merger talks with U S West grew serious.

Approach and Engagement

On February 27, 1996, U S West and Continental Cablevision announced a merger that would create the nation's third-largest cable company, behind TCI and Time Warner. This deal was the first such union announced since the passage of the Telecommunications Act just one month earlier. The $10.8 billion offer would consist of $5.3 billion in cash and stock (valued at $24.50 per share) and $5.5 in assumed debt.

The cable company would be absorbed by U S West Media Group, the unit of U S West holding its media and wireless properties. Amos Hostetter, Jr., Continental's chairman and CEO, would lead the company's cable operations, while Charles Lillis would retain his role as president and CEO of U S West Media Group.

In July 1996 U S West's stock price plummeted to $14.38, rising back to only about $17 by October. Under the terms of the deal, Continental could back out if Stroh's stock dropped below $20.83 per share, but it chose not to terminate the deal. Not only were no other deep-pocketed suitors beating down its door, but in the time period since U S West had made its bid, Continental had accrued an additional $1 billion in debt from system upgrades. The cable company wanted to continue to advance its network, so it accepted a revised deal in which U S West's stock was valued at $21 per share. This reduced the deal's value to $11.3 billion, yet Continental's additional debt bounced it up even higher, to $12.3 billion.

The FCC approved the merger on October 18, 1996, as did the Department of Justice on November 5th. The FCC ordered the company to divest cable properties in Iowa, Minnesota, and Idaho. The Department of Justice gave Continental until the end of December 1998 to shed its 11.2% interest in Teleport Communications Group Inc., a local telephone service provider in New York. The companies agreed to the terms, and concluded their merger in mid-November 1996.

Products and Services

U S West Inc. provided telecommunications services in 14 states: Arizona, Colorado, Idaho, Iowa, Minnesota, Montana, Nebraska, New Mexico, North Dakota, Oregon, South Dakota, Utah, Washington, and Wyoming. It also operated in several business segments. Voice encompassed its retail and wholesale telephone services; Data consisted of its Internet access services; Wireless telephone reached six major western markets; Directories consisted of its Dex directory publishing arm; and Video offered cable-like video services.

Review of the Outcome

In the summer of 1997, U S West Media Group lost one of Continental's most valuable assets—its management team. Amos Hostetter, its founder and chairman, resigned out of anger at the company's relocation from Boston to Denver. Under assurances by Lillis, Hostetter had promised Continental's staff that a post-merger relocation would not occur. His resignation was fol-

lowed by that of William Schleyer, the unit's president, as well as a number of other executives.

As Hostetter and the other managers walked out the door, so did U S West's cable expertise. Jan Peters, a U S West veteran but a cable neophyte, replaced Hostetter. Capital Research & Management, a large stockholder of the group, was so disenchanted with the change in management that it unloaded a significant block of its shares.

In October 1997 U S West announced that it would split into two independent companies. U S West Inc. would hold all telephony operations, while MediaOne Group would contain its cable and wireless operations. According to Charles Lillis, the split would affect several benefits. It would provide regulatory separation and technological distinction for its telephone and cable operations. This separation would better serve the company, as those segments had revealed themselves to be more difficult to co-manage than expected. The split would also allow the company to retain some of the cable operations that it had been ordered by the FCC to divest.

On March 22, 1999, MediaOne Group announced a merger agreement with Comcast Corp. The stock swap would combine the third- and fourth-largest cable systems, respectively, to create the world's largest broadband communications provider.

Research

Cauley, Leslie. "U S West Takes over a Huge Cable Firm, Then Angers Its Brass," in *The Wall Street Journal*, 29 August 1997. Describes the mass-exit of Continental management after the relocation is announced.

"Continental Cablevision, Inc.," in *Notable Corporate Chronologies*, The Gale Group Research, 1999. Profiles the company up to its acquisition by U S West.

Grover, Ronald, and Peter Burrows. "U S West Can't Take Its Eyes off TV," in *Business Week*, 24 March 1997. Describes the U S West as the only RHC committed to cable.

Higgins, John M. "Continental Settles for Less," in *Multichannel News*, 14 October 1996. Relates how the drop in the price of U S West's stock and the accrued debt of Continental affected the price of the deal.

"U S West Communications Group Inc.," in *Notable Corporate Chronologies*, The Gale Group, 1999. Profiles the history of the company, up through and beyond its acquisition of Continental Cablevision.

U S West Inc., available at http://www.uswest.com. Official World Wide Web Page for U S West. Includes organizational and product information, annual reports, press releases, and other financial information.

"U S West Pursues Cable Strategy with $10.8 Billion Continental Cablevision Acquisition," in *Electronic Marketplace Report*, 5 March 1996. Describes the newly announced merger deal.

"U S West Seeks to Delay Compliance with Merger Order;

Point Moot," in *Communications Today*, 25 November 1997. Briefly describes the separation of the company's cable and wireless operations, resulting in an automatic fulfillment of the FCC merger conditions.

Wilen, John. "Deregulation Shakes up Entire Industry," in *InfoWorld*, 21 October 1996. Details the effects that the Telecommunications Act of 1996 has had on the industry in only the first few months after its passage.

DAVIS MCMILLAN

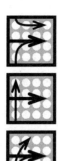

USA WASTE SERVICES & WASTE MANAGEMENT

nationality: USA
date: July 16, 1998
affected: USA Waste Services Inc., USA, founded 1987
affected: Waste Management, Inc., USA, founded 1968

Waste Management Inc.
1001 Fannin, Ste. 4000
Houston, TX 77002
USA

tel: (713)512-6200
fax: (713)512-6299
web: http://www.wm.com

Overview of the Acquisition

The world's largest waste service provider, Waste Management, was in severe financial trouble in 1998. Years of overextension and failed diversification efforts, combined with an enormous write-off due to inflated accounting practices, had sent the company's stock price plunging. USA Waste, the third-largest industry player, was on an active acquisition campaign, and took the opportunity to capture the lead position by acquiring Waste Management, despite the fact that Waste Management was three times its size.

History of USA Waste Services Inc.

In September 1987 the waste services provider USA Waste was founded in Oklahoma. It went public the following year, providing the capital needed for expansion through acquisition. During 1989 the company purchased two refuse collection firms for a total of $4.4 million. The following January it expanded into Texas with the acquisition of Texas Medical Environmental Disposal, Inc. Later that year Donald Moorehead bought a controlling interest in USA Waste and moved the company to Dallas. USA Waste increased its growth efforts under Moorehead. Among its purchases in the early 1990s were Mission Disposal, Big Dipper Enterprises, and North Shore Waste Control.

In May 1994 Moorehead offered the job of chairman and CEO to John Drury, former president of the nation's second-largest waste company, Browning-Ferris Industries, Inc. With Drury at the helm, USA Waste grew quickly by acquiring firms operating in the waste collection and disposal industry. He was adamant about sticking to core businesses—the point of contention with his former boss at BFI that eventually cost him his job there.

In June 1995 the company paid $725 million for Chambers Development Corp., owner of 50 collection operations on the East Coast. In May 1996 it entered the California market by buying Western Waste Industries for $525 million. Three months later it purchased Sanifill Inc., its closest competitor, for $1.3 billion. Following that purchase, USA Waste moved its headquarters to Houston.

The Business

Financials

Revenue (1998): $12.7 billion

Employees (1998): 68,000

SICs / NAICS

sic 4212 - Local Trucking Without Storage

sic 4953 - Refuse Systems

naics 562111 - Solid Waste Collection

naics 562212 - Solid Waste Landfill

USA Waste acquired the Canadian Waste unit of Allied Waste Industries in March 1997. That August it completed its largest acquisition to date, a $2.2 billion deal for United Waste Systems Inc. This purchase helped to increase USA Waste's revenues that year to $2.6 billion.

In July 1998 USA Waste acquired Waste Management Inc. (WMI) and adopted its name. That December the new company and its auditor, Arthur Anderson LLP, agreed to a $220 million settlement for a shareholder class action suit that arose out of the former WMI's accounting debacle revealed in 1997.

That settlement was not the end of the controversy, however. In an unusual move, WMI's board withheld $40 million in pension funds due to several executives who had been in charge during the years affected by the accounting mess. By May 1999 the matter had not yet been settled, but several members of its 14-person board strongly believed that some or all of that amount should go toward the $220 million settlement, of which WMI was responsible for about $145 million.

History of Waste Management, Inc.

Dean L. Buntrock assumed control of his in-law's business, Ace Scavenger Service, 1956. This company, founded in 1894 as Chicago's first garbage hauler, had 12 waste collection vehicles and $750,000 in revenues. The post-war consumerism and the development of new packaging and disposable products generated growing levels of garbage and, consequently, growing need for refuse collectors.

Buntrock moved aggressively to expand the business through acquisition and formation of other companies. After Ace expanded into Wisconsin, Buntrock entered into merger talks with his cousin, H. Wayne Huizenga, who operated a small collection company in Florida. Their negotiations became serious after the U.S. Congress passed the Solid Waste Disposal Act of 1965. Drawn up in response to a growing need for safe, efficient waste removal, the act required collection companies to meet new standards of hygiene. In so doing, it effectively forced out of business many of the oldest and least sophisticated companies. Aware of the opportunities that consolidation would afford them, Buntrock and Huizenga united their companies three years later as Waste Management, Inc. (WMI).

The new firm went public in 1971 in order to raise the funds to transform WMI into a national enterprise. It pursued that goal aggressively, purchasing 75 companies over the ensuing 18 months. During that decade WMI grew at a rate of 48% per year. In 1977 it became the world's first international supplier of sanitation services by winning a contract to serve Riyadh, Saudi Arabia.

During the 1970s WMI also sought expansion outside of its non-hazardous core operations. The proliferation of oil-based plastics and other industrial chemicals spurred the company to expand its waste handling capabilities in those directions. Passage of the Resource Conservation and Recovery Act in 1976 regulated the disposal of toxic and chemical waste. This act intimidated many smaller companies, thereby clearing the field for such companies as WMI that were willing to pursue the business. By 1980 WMI's subsidiary, Chemical Waste Management, Inc., had acquired enough large toxic landfills to rank as the recycling industry's leader.

WMI pursued further international expansion during the 1980s, and by the end of the decade it had secured contracts in Argentina, Venezuela, Australia, Hong Kong, and a number of European countries. In 1993 Huizenga retired and Phillip B. Rooney became president. That year net income was $120 million on sales that surpassed $1 billion for the first time.

In March 1983 a widely publicized lawsuit was brought against WMI arising from the discovery that its oil waste landfill in Vickery, Ohio, contained 135,000 gallons of material contaminated with polychlorinated biphenyls (PCBs). Both the state of Ohio and the Environmental Protection Agency brought suit against WMI. During the two years following the discovery, WMI faced suits alleging illegal dumping in at least six states. It reacted by installing environmental compliance officers in management positions and adopting stricter safety measures.

The company's most significant acquisition in the 1980s was that of a 60% stake in SCA Services Inc., a Boston-based company ranking third in the waste treatment industry. This 1984 purchase added about

$200 million to WMI's revenue, provided entry into 43 new markets, and increased its total number of landfills to 89.

During the decade WMI diversified outside of its three core businesses—solid waste collection, chemical waste treatment, and international waste services. A particularly aggressive area of expansion was recycling. In 1986 the company acquired Envirotech Operating Services, the nation's leading supplier of waste and wastewater treatment services. Two years later it purchased 22% of Wheelabrator Technologies, Inc., a group that encompassed a number of companies involved in the waste-to-energy business; WMI acquired controlling interest in Wheelabrator in 1990.

Expansion in recycling continued into the early 1990s. In 1990 the formed recycling joint ventures with E.I. du Pont de Nemours & Co. and with American National Can Co. The following year WMI joined with Stone Container Corp. to create Paper Recycling International LP for the marketing of recycled paper products back to Stone Container as well as to other manufacturers. Sales that year reached $7.5 billion, but net income dropped to $606 million.

To reflect its diversification, WMI was renamed WMX Technologies Inc. in 1993. That year it spun off Rust International Inc., its engineering and construction subsidiary that it had gained through the acquisition of Wheelabrator. By 1995 WMX conducted solid waste management, recycling, and related operations in 48 states, the District of Columbia, four Canadian provinces, Mexico, and a number of other foreign countries.

The company began to experience serious problems, however, as a result of its diversification program. Earnings were sporadic and its stock plunged in value to roughly $25 per share from over $45 per share in early 1992. In June 1996 Rooney became CEO, and he and chairman Buntrock unveiled a plan to return WMX to its garbage hauling roots.

In 1997 WMX reverted to its previous name, Waste Management. In February it announced that it would eliminate up to 3,000 jobs, sell $1.5 billion in assets, buy back 50 million of its shares, and retrench its overseas operations. Yet the company's stock price continued to drop, and Rooney resigned from the pressure. Ronald LeMay succeeded him, but left after only three months. Buntrock, who had retired earlier that year, filled in as temporary CEO. In late October 1997, turnaround specialist Robert S. Miller became interim chairman and CEO until a permanent successor could be located.

Miller inherited a company more troubled than he and its investors realized. On February 24, 1998,

The Officers

Chairman: Robert S. Miller

CEO: John E. Drury

President and Chief Operating Officer: Rodney R. Proto

Exec. VP and Chief Financial Officer: Earl E. DeFrates

Miller revealed that WMI had been grievously overstating assets and undervaluing liabilities in order to cast a better light on its financial situation. He was forced to restate company earnings for the period from 1992 through the first three quarters of 1997, taking a $3.5 billion charge in the process. WMI posted a net loss of $1.2 billion on revenues of $9.2 billion in 1997. The following March, it agreed to be acquired by USA Waste, a company about one-third its size.

Market Forces Driving the Acquisition

By 1998 Waste Management Inc. (WMI) was a deeply troubled company. Its stock had plummeted, its management had been shuffled several times, and its accounting irregularities had resulted in a $3.5 billion charge to correct its books. Investors were ill-tempered and impatient for a drastic change. WMI's temporary chairman and CEO was Richard Miller, a turnaround specialist. He had discovered those questionable accounting practices five months after taking charge and quickly realized that the company would not survive on its own.

Not all of WMI's problems originated internally, however. The waste industry overall had experienced a decline, as competition drove prices down while a surplus of dump space and general inefficiencies kept costs high and profits restrained. One solution was for a waste-hauling company to own more of its dumping sites rather than pay its competitors fees for use of their sites. In order to do this, though, a company needed enough market share in a given area to make ownership of a dump worthwhile.

This was the rationale behind USA Waste's aggressive acquisition campaign. Not only did it gain ownership of more dump sites, it amassed a fleet of trucks that could be pared down to reduce costs. It also increased its regional and local concentration, capturing a greater market share and reducing driving time, thereby creating additional efficiencies. This program caused USA Waste's share price to rise, which provided the company with the resources to make additional acquisitions, thereby continuing its cycle of growth.

The Players

USA Waste Services Chairman and CEO: John E. Drury. John Drury was born to a Milwaukee garbage collector. He followed in his father's footsteps beginning at age 14, when he became a driver for his father's company, which was later purchased by Browning-Ferris Industries in 1970. Drury spent 21 years at that company, where he became president and chief operating officer in 1972. The beginning of the end of his career at BFI was marked by the entrance of William D. Ruckelshaus as the company's chairman and CEO in 1988. This newcomer was a former Environmental Protection Agency chief who wanted to steer BFI into the recycling business, a direction that Drury was dead-set against. After repeated clashes, Drury resigned from both BFI and the waste business in 1990. He spent the next four years as an investment banker, and then reentered the industry by becoming CEO of USA Waste in 1994. He added the post of chairman the following year.

Waste Management Chairman: Robert S. Miller. Robert S. (Steve) Miller was recruited as interim chairman of Waste Management in October 1997, when the company was in the throes of financial and managerial distress. After five months on the job, this turnaround specialist agreed to allow USA Waste to acquire Waste Management. Miller's first major experience with corporate turnarounds was at Chrysler Corp., where as its chief financial officer and vice chairman he negotiated the firm's financial restructuring with the federal government. He also served as chairman of Morrison Knudsen Corp. from 1995 to 1996 upon the resignation of its chairman and CEO.

Acquiring WMI would be quite a coup for USA Waste. With revenues of $9.2 billion, WMI was the world's largest waste services company. USA Waste was the nation's third-largest, but its balance sheet and stock price were far healthier than those of WMI. In fact, USA Waste had been eyeing WMI for months. Watching its stock price drop, it finally made a move in October 1997 after Ronald LeMay's departure caused its stock to dip to the low-20s. The next day, USA Waste joined with the investment group Relational Investors LLC to purchase WMI's stock, eventually accumulating a stake of 13 million of WMI's 455 million outstanding shares.

Approach and Engagement

The chiefs at USA Waste and Waste Management first entered into merger negotiations due to the matchmaking efforts of Jerome York, a board member of USA Waste. He contacted Robert Miller on October 30, 1997, the day after Miller took the temporary helm of WMI. York suggested that Miller meet with his counterpart at USA Waste, John Drury. On March 11, 1998, the two firms announced their acquisition agreement.

In a transaction valued at $13.5 billion, WMI agreed to be acquired by USA Waste though a stock swap in which each WMI share would be exchanged for 0.725 shares of USA Waste. In addition, the deal included the assumption of $7 billion in WMI debt by USA Waste. The agreement also left a 60% controlling interest in the hands of shareholders, although USA Waste would manage the new company. On July 16, 1998, the acquisition was completed.

Products and Services

After the merger, USA Waste (later renamed Waste Management) was the largest solid waste company in the world, providing collection, transfer, landfill, recycling, and waste-to-energy services to residential, commercial, and industrial customers throughout the United States, Canada, Mexico, Puerto Rico, and 13 foreign countries.

Changes to the Industry

The newly formed company, which retained the Waste Management name, also retained the industry's top spot. This move strengthened its position over Browning-Ferris Industries, now a far more distant second. The new WMI controlled nearly 25% of the U.S. market. It operated a total of 319 landfills (182 from USA Waste; 137 from the former WMI), 650 collection operations (250 from USA Waste; 400 from WMI), and 339 transfer stations (175 from USA Waste; 164 from WMI).

In compliance with federal regulators, WMI divested itself of certain assets that had raised antitrust concerns. In October 1998 it sold 16 landfills, 11 transfer stations, and 136 collection routes to Republic Services Inc. for $500 million.

Review of the Outcome

USA Waste changed its name to Waste Management Inc. and the former Waste Management was renamed Waste Management Holdings, Inc. The headquarters remained at USA Waste's Houston site, where about 150 of WMI's corporate workforce of 1,600 was to be added to USA Waste's staff of about 100. John Drury retained the position of CEO, and Robert Miller became its non-executive chairman. Other top management positions were rounded out by USA Waste executives. Rodney Proto retained his posts as president and chief operating officer, and Earl DeFrates continued as chief financial officer.

The new company expected to realize annual savings of $800 million from combined operations. Those savings were planned to be experienced beginning in 1999, its first full year of operation. About $400 million of the savings was expected to arise from consolidation of routes, transfer stations, and other operational facilities. Reduced administrative staff and overhead was expected to generate $225 million in savings. The remaining $175 million was to be gained from savings on dumping fees at competitors' sites, since the new company was more efficiently concentrated in that respect.

Research

Bailey, Jeff. "In USA Waste Deal, York Shows His Face Again," in *The Wall Street Journal*, 12 March 1998. Relates the matchmaking efforts of Jerome York, and details the savings expected from the combined company.

————. "Scandal at Waste Management Risks Payout for Retired CEO," in *The Wall Street Journal*, 19 May 1999. Describes the drama over the WMI executive pension payments.

————. "Under Merger Plan, USA Waste is to Run Waste Management," in *The Wall Street Journal*, 11 March 1998. Details the newly announced deal.

Melcher, Richard A. "Can Waste Management Climb out of the Muck?" in *Business Week*, 23 March 1998. Describes the accounting irregularities discovered at WMI before the merger deal.

"Waste Management: In the Boardroom," in *The Economist*, 7 March 1998. Describes the shakeup of WMI management in the short time preceding the merger agreement.

"Waste Management, Inc.," in *International Directory of Company Histories*, Vol. V: St. James Press: 1992. Provides an historical review of the company through 1990.

Waste Management, Inc. Home Page, available at http://www.wm.com. Official World Wide Web Page for WMI. Includes financial information, descriptions of services, a directory of operations, and news releases.

DEBORAH J. UNTENER

VIACOM & BLOCKBUSTER

Viacom International Inc.
1515 Broadway, 51st Fl.
New York, NY 10036
USA

tel: (212)258-6000
web: http://www.viacom.com
e-mail: info@viacom.com

nationality: USA
date: September 29, 1994
affected: Viacom International Inc., USA, founded 1970
affected: Blockbuster Entertainment Corp., USA, founded 1982

Overview of the Acquisition

The 1994 acquisition of Blockbuster by Viacom was forged as a strategy to enable Viacom to succeed in its bidding war for Paramount Communications. The battle against QVC had depleted Viacom's coffers, and it desperately needed Blockbuster's $1.25 billion in cash flow.

Viacom's steady drop in stock price nearly killed the acquisition, however, as Blockbuster shareholders watched the value of their deal decline. Viacom eventually rebounded, but after the acquisition was completed, Blockbuster suffered a decline of its own. Two years later, the company's revolutionary revenue sharing concept revitalized the video chain, making it a candidate for an initial public offering in 1999.

History of Viacom International Inc.

The Central Broadcasting System (CBS) complied with the Federal Communications Commission's (FCC) regulations barring television networks from owning cable TV systems or from syndicating their own programs in the U.S. by establishing Viacom International Inc. in 1970. The following year CBS spun off Viacom as a separate company to CBS shareholders. That firm's initial annual sales reached $19.8 million. Its 90,000 subscribers made it one of the nation's largest cable systems.

In 1976, to compete with Home Box Office (HBO), the nation's leading cable outlet for films, Viacom created the Showtime movie network as a 50-50 venture with Warner Amex. The next year, despite a federal ruling that removed many restrictions on the choice of programming available on pay-television, Showtime posted a loss of $825,000. Nevertheless, Viacom earned $5.5 million on sales of $58.5 million, mostly from sales of television series such as *I Love Lucy*. Subscription to the company's cable system rose to 350,000.

Viacom reached a deal in 1978 with Teleprompter Corp., the largest cable systems operator in the U.S., whereby Teleprompter offered its customers Showtime rather than HBO. Three years later Viacom acquired Video Corp. of America for

$16 million. The company's growth goals included the acquisition of radio and television stations during the 1970s. Those acquisitions proved to be insurance against any possible takeover of the company, since the transfer of broadcast licenses must be overseen by the FCC.

Viacom invested $65 million on its cable infrastructure in 1981. The next year Showtime had 3.4 million subscribers and earned about $10 million on sales of $140 million. Subscriptions to Viacom's cable systems totaled 540,000, making it the ninth-largest cable operator in the U.S.

In 1984 Showtime became a sister station to Warner Amex's The Movie Channel in a move designed to increase sales for both stations. In September of the following year, Viacom purchased Warner Amex's stake in Showtime from Warner Communications, as well as MTV Networks, which included MTV, Nickelodeon, and VH1. Viacom revamped Nickelodeon's image and introduced *Nick at Night*, a block of classic sitcoms aired for an adult audience.

Weakened by the $2 billion debt load it had incurred through its acquisitions, and in part to scare off potential takeovers, Viacom was purchased by National Amusements Inc., a movie theater chain, for about $3.4 billion in March 1987. Sumner M. Redstone, president of National Amusements, assumed the chairmanship of Viacom.

The U.S. Congress passed legislation deregulating the cable industry in 1987, causing prices of cable franchises to soar. Viacom recorded sales in excess of $1 billion for the first time, but the company still posted a loss of approximately $154.4 million.

Viacom sold its cable systems in Long Island, New York, and suburban Cleveland, Ohio, to Cablevision Systems Corp. for $545 million. Cablevision then purchased a five-percent stake in Showtime for $25 million, giving it a tangible interest in the channel's success. Viacom also sold 50% of Showtime's stock to Tele-Communications Inc. (TCI), a cable systems operator with about six million subscribers, for $225 million.

Viacom joined with Hearst Corp. and Capital Cities/ABC Inc. in 1989 to introduce Lifetime Television, a cable channel geared toward women. Viacom established a production company, Viacom Pictures, which made about 10 feature films that year at a cost of about $4 million each.

Viacom filed a $2.4 billion antitrust suit against HBO, alleging that HBO was trying to put Showtime out of business by intimidating cable systems that carried Showtime and by trying to corner the market on

The Business

Financials

Revenue (1998): $12.1 billion

Employees (1998): 111,700

SICs / NAICS

sic 4841 - Cable & Other Pay Television Services

sic 4833 - Television Broadcasting Stations

sic 7822 - Motion Picture & Tape Distribution

sic 7812 - Motion Picture & Video Production

sic 2731 - Book Publishing

sic 7996 - Amusement Parks

naics 513210 - Cable Networks

naics 513120 - Television Broadcasting

naics 512120 - Motion Picture and Video Distribution

naics 512110 - Motion Picture and Video Production

naics 511130 - Book Publishers

naics 713110 - Amusement and Theme Parks

Hollywood films to prevent competitors from airing them. The suit was settled out of court in August 1992. Time Warner, HBO's parent, agreed to pay Viacom $75 million and to buy a Viacom cable system in Milwaukee for $95 million. It also agreed to increase its distribution of Showtime and The Movie Channel on its cable networks.

A five-month battle against QVC Inc. for Paramount Communications Inc. was initiated by Viacom's bid in September 1993. To help raise funds for this acquisition, Viacom offered $8.4 billion in stock to acquire Blockbuster Entertainment Corp. Viacom successfully gained control of Paramount in July 1994 and of Blockbuster that September.

Viacom sold its one-third interest in Lifetime to its partners. Blockbuster increased its presence in the children's entertainment-center industry by lifting its stake in Discovery Zone from 20% to 50.1%. The following year Viacom sold its Madison Square Garden sports assets.

In January 1995 the company joined with Chris-Craft to launch United Paramount Network (UPN), which targeted viewers aged 18-34. That June Paramount had its most successful motion picture opening, *Congo*.

The Officers

Chairman and CEO: Sumner M. Redstone

Deputy Chairman and Exec. VP: Philippe P. Dauman

Deputy Chairman and Exec. VP: Thomas E. Dooley

Wal-Mart's William R. Fields was hired to lead Blockbuster Entertainment, which has close to 3,000 video rental stores in the U.S. Fields was fired the following year, however, and was replaced by John F. Antioco as CEO. He was assigned the task of turning around Blockbuster, which had been plagued by sluggish video rentals, management errors, a lack of focus, and problems with a new distribution system. In 1998 Antioco laid off 180 employees, mainly at the company's headquarters; curtailed store expansion; and closed all 17 of Germany's struggling stores. More importantly, he introduced the concept of revenue sharing, enabling the stores to stock more copies of popular titles in exchange for a percentage of the rental revenues to be paid to the movie studios. Blockbuster's revenues in 1998 reached $3.9 billion, strong enough for Viacom to file for its initial public offering in March 1999.

In a $2 billion stock deal with Tele-Communications Inc. (TCI) and its shareholders, Viacom spun off its cable systems in 1996. In a controversial move, Redstone fired Frank J. Biondi Jr. as Viacom CEO and assumed the post himself.

Viacom sold its 10-station radio group to Chancellor Media Corp. in July 1997 for about $1.1 billion in cash. That year it also increased its ownership of Spelling Entertainment Group Inc. to 80%, and acquired full ownership in June 1999.

The hugely successful *Titanic* was released in December 1997, far surpassing even the enormous success of the company's previous hit, *Forrest Gump*.

In October 1998 Viacom sold Blockbuster Music to Wherehouse Entertainment Inc. for $115 million. By the end of the year, Blockbuster's video stores in the U.S. and 25 other countries numbered about 6,000, making it the nation's leading video rental company. Viacom also sold Simon & Schuster's educational, professional, and reference publishing operations to Pearson PLC for $4.6 billion in cash.

History of Blockbuster Entertainment Corp.

David P. Cook founded Cook Data Services in Dallas, Texas, in 1982. This company offered software and computing services to the oil and gas industries. An ensuing decline in the energy business prompted Cook to diversify into video rentals. The company opened its first Blockbuster Entertainment store in October 1985. The following year, when 18 new retail outlets opened, the company changed its name to Blockbuster Entertainment.

H. Wayne Huizenga, former president and chief operating officer of Waste Management, Inc., invested $18 million in Blockbuster in 1987, and by the end of the year had bought out Cook. Huizenga led the company on an acquisition strategy to achieve growth. During that year, the acquisitions of Southern Video Partnership and Movies to Go brought the total number of Blockbuster stores to 130. The number of outlets tripled by the end of 1988, after Blockbuster purchased the Video-Library chain.

Blockbuster gained a listing on the New York Stock Exchange in 1989, the same year that it acquired Major Video and Video Superstore MLP. It followed up those purchases with the acquisitions of Applause Video, Video Express, Movie Emporium, and other chains in Arizona, California, and Texas. The number of company stores exceeded 1,500 in 1990, and it had begun to expand internationally. It operated units in Puerto Rico and established agreements to open stores in Japan, Mexico, and Australia. Blockbuster purchased the nation's third-largest video chain, Erol's, in 1990 and became the largest video renter in the United Kingdom after it purchased the Cityvision chain of 875 stores in February 1992.

The company began diversifying in 1992. That December it forayed into the music industry when it purchased two of the biggest music retailers, Sound Warehouse and Music Plus. Revenues that year rose 38% to $1.2 billion.

Blockbuster purchased 35% of movie producer Republic Pictures Corp. and a majority stake in Spelling Entertainment in 1993. The company reorganized into six divisions: domestic home video, international home video, domestic music retailing, international music retailing, new technology ventures, and other entertainment areas. By the end of that year it had 3,127 video and 253 music stores in 48 states, Puerto Rico, Guam, and 13 foreign countries.

Viacom agreed to purchase Blockbuster for $8.4 billion in January 1994, but a decline in Viacom's stock dropped the value of the deal to $7.65 by its completion that September.

Market Forces Driving the Acquisition

In coming together with Blockbuster, Viacom's Sumner Redstone spoke enthusiastically about vertical integration. He highlighted that the new company would control not only entertainment content but also its video distribution channel—and the nation's leader, at that.

But few analysts bought that logic. As *The Economist* wrote, "The truth is that the Viacom-Blockbuster deal has only one rationale: cash." Viacom was in the throes of the fiercely competitive, and expensive, battle against QVC for the acquisition of Paramount Communications. Both bidders had scraped together whatever funding they could muster to top the other's bids. Viacom had even received a $600 million investment from Blockbuster in the autumn of 1993 to boost Viacom's financial arsenal. Soon after, however, its investment had fallen short of the amount needed to outbid QVC, and Viacom looked longingly at Blockbuster's cash flow.

Blockbuster was the nation's leading video retailer, with healthy income and revenue levels. However, the landscape of the video market was changing, as rumblings of movies-on-demand and other interactive television technology threatened the growth of the industry. Although the company rejected the seriousness of this threat, Blockbuster had begun hedging its bets. By 1994 it had diversified into music retailing and video software. The appeal of adding cable to its interests made Viacom look like a suitable partner. And if its acquisition of Paramount was successful, Viacom would add movie and television production, publishing, and amusement parks to its holdings.

Approach and Engagement

Coming in the final stages of the battle for Paramount, negotiations between Viacom and Blockbuster necessitated utmost secrecy. Redstone, Blockbuster chairman H. Wayne Huizenga, and a team of advisers locked themselves in a hotel suite for a weekend. On January 7, 1994, the companies announced their deal, whereby Viacom would acquire Blockbuster for $8.4 billion in stock. This arrangement enabled Viacom to raise its bid for Paramount through a cash infusion of $1.25 billion from Blockbuster. And on February 15, 1994, Viacom emerged victorious in that deal.

Although they understood the market pressures bearing down on Blockbuster, many analysts were mystified as to why Huizenga would agree to relinquish control of his company, as he was slated to step down to the position of vice chairman of Viacom. He admitted in *Time* magazine, "While it may not be a great victory for me, it's a very, very great victory for the Blockbuster shareholders."

The Players

Viacom Chairman: Sumner M. Redstone. Billionaire Sumner Redstone was never fed with a silver spoon, even after he could afford it. Born in a 1923 Boston tenement, he sped through Harvard in only three years. He then joined an Army Intelligence unit that cracked Japan's World War II codes before acquiring a law degree from Harvard. Redstone practiced law for six years before returning to his father's business, a chain of 12 drive-in theaters. He then revolutionized the theater industry by establishing the multiplex, a term that he later copyrighted.

No profile of Redstone is complete without the tale of the hotel fire that nearly cost him his life. In 1979 he escaped death by hanging by his fingertips from the ledge of the Boston hotel until he was rescued. He sustained severe burns over half his body, and doctors predicted that he would never walk again. Redstone not only recovered, he became a voracious and highly competitive tennis player.

Redstone entered the big leagues with his 1986 investment in Viacom, later winning the company in a heated battle. He emerged victorious in his takeover of Paramount as well. Redstone was still serving as chairman of his media empire in 1999, at age 76.

H. Wayne Huizenga. Harry Wayne Huizenga has become a billionaire through a string of successes in garbarge collection, video rental, sports, and automobile dealerships. After dropping out of college, he purchased and began making rounds with a single garbarge truck. In 1968 he joined with his cousin and fellow garbage collector, Dean L. Buntrock, to form Waste Management, Inc. This firm, briefly known as WMX Technologies, soon became the nation's largest collection chain. Huizenga left the company in 1993, and four years later secured control of Blockbuster Entertainment. He resigned after the purchase of his company by Viacom in 1994, and went on to become chairman of Republic Industries, Inc.. Under that parent company, he established AutoNation, Inc., a national chain of no-haggle automobile dealerships. During the 1990s Huizenga was also the owner of three Florida professional sports teams: the Florida Panthers, Miami Dolphins, and Florida Marlins.

Those investors, along with Huizenga, began to question the value of the deal in the aftermath of Viacom's acquisition of Paramount. During the five-month battle, Viacom's Class B shares plummeted from 55 to 28 by late February 1994. As Blockbuster was to be purchased with Viacom stock, the value of the deal to Blockbuster's shareholders dropped accordingly. Even the contingent value right (CVR) in place didn't placate them. This CVR called for Viacom to compensate Blockbuster shareholders if Viacom's stock dipped over a period of one year after the completion of their deal. It made no provision for Viacom's decline in stock before that completion, however. Huizenga warned that Viacom would have to sweeten its offer unless it experienced a dramatic turnaround.

That turnaround remained elusive through early summer. As Viacom's stock continued its downward spiral, talks between the two companies stalled. Huizenga announced at the company's annual shareholder meeting in May that, should the deal come down to a shareholder vote, Blockbuster's board would not vote in favor of it.

In July, however, just as the value of the proposed merger had sunk below $5 billion, Viacom's stock unexpectedly began to rebound. Part of this turnaround could be attributed to the disclosure that financier Kirk Kerkorian had acquired a five-percent stake in Viacom. This show of confidence in the company was contagious on Wall Street, and the value of the deal gained lost ground, soon reaching $6.8 billion.

Blockbuster's board consequently reversed its decision to vote against the deal. On September 29, 1994, 70% of Blockbuster's shareholdes voted in favor of the $7.65 billion merger. The transaction was completed that same day.

Products and Services

Viacom operated in six business segments:

Networks encompassed its basic cable and premium subscription television program services. These networks included MTV, MTV2, Nickelodeon, Nick at Nite, Nick at Nite's TV Land, VH1, Showtime, The Movie Channel, and Flix. This segment also held the company's interests in Comedy Central, Sundance Channel, and UPN (United Paramount Network). Total revenues in 1998 for the Network segment reached $2.6 billion.

Entertainment housed the company's operations in the production and distribution of motion pictures and television programming, as well as its television stations, international channels, movie theater operations, and music publishing. This segment was comprised of Paramount Pictures, Paramount Television,

Spelling Entertainment Group Inc., and the Paramount Stations Group, and generated revenues of $4.8 billion in 1998.

The **Video** segment consisted of Blockbuster Video, a retailer in home videos and games; it produced $3.9 billion in revenues in 1998. The **Parks** segment, comprised of the five regional Paramount Parks, achieved $421 million in 1998 revenues. **Publishing** encompassed such consumer publishing imprints as Simon & Schuster, Pocket Books, Scribner, and The Free Press; this unit generated sales of $564 million in 1998. Finally, **Viacom Online Services**, the company's interactive businesses, produced 1998 revenues of $13.7 million.

Review of the Outcome

Blockbuster did not fare well after its acquisition by Viacom. Huizenga resigned after a brief transition period, and a string of CEOs succeeded through the unit. In addition to its leadership difficulties, it was experiencing sluggish video revenues. This depression was interpreted as a foretelling of the future of the video retail industry, many analysts believed.

Things began turning around in July 1997, when John F. Antioco was recruited as CEO. Antioco had made a name for himself as chief of Taco Bell, and immediately began applying his business acumen to Blockbuster.

In addition to slashing expenses and refocusing the company on its core rental business, Antioco revolutionized the video rental industry with the concept of revenue sharing. A common problem in the video rental business was a supply falling short of demand. Customers frequently walked out empty-handed when all of the available copies of the video of choice were already rented. This was an unfortunate reality in the industry, since the retailers paid $65 to $80 per copy of each video. Antioco changed that reality by using a model borrowed from movie theaters.

With revenue sharing, video retailers would pay a much reduced price per video copy, between $3 and $8, but return about 40% of the rental price back to the movie studios. This let Blockbuster keep customers happy and cash registers ringing by enabling it to stock more copies of popular titles. Other rental chains soon adopted the concept.

The revenue sharing strategy was just the boost that Blockbuster needed. *Business Week* reported that by March 1999 the company's stock had jumped over 200% since the previous year, garnering a 30% share of the market and a 37% rise in revenues, to $3.9 billion. Its forecast appeared so favorable to its parent, that in 1999 Viacom filed for Blockbuster's initial public offering.

Research

"Another Fine Mess," in *The Economist*, 15 January 1994. Offers rationale for Viacom's acquisition of Paramount and Blockbuster.

"Blockbuster Entertainment Corp.," in *Notable Corporate Chronologies*, The Gale Group, 1999. Profiles the history of the company.

"Blockbuster Finally Gets It Right," in *Business Week*, 8 March 1999. Describes the revenue sharing concept and its effect on Blockbuster's performance.

Gunther, Marc. "Viacom: Redstone's Ride to the Top," in *Fortune*, 26 April 1999. Offers a detailed profile of Sumner Redstone and of his successful acquisitions of Paramount and Blockbuster.

McCarroll, Thomas. "A Blockbuster Deal for Beavis and Butt-Head," in *Time*, 17 January 1994. Details the newly announced acquisition agreement.

Taub, Stephen. "Redstone in Motion," in *Financial World*, 6 December 1994. Profiles Viacom after its acquisitions of Paramount and Blockbuster.

"Viacom International Inc.," in *Notable Corporate Chronologies*, The Gale Group, 1999. Lists major events in the history of Viacom.

Viacom International Inc. Home Page, available at http://www.viacom.com. Official World Wide Web Page for Viacom. Includes a description of operations, news releases, executive biographies, annual reports, investor information, and links to company Websites.

Wasserstein, Bruce. *Big Deal: The Battle for Control of America's Leading Corporations*, Warner Books, 1998. Provides a detailed overview of Viacom's acquisition of Paramount.

DEBORAH J. UNTENER

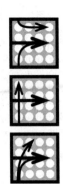

VIACOM & CBS

Viacom International Inc.
1515 Broadway, 51st Fl.
New York, NY 10036
USA

tel: (212)258-6000
web: http://www.viacom.com
e-mail: info@viacom.com

CBS Corp.
51 W. 52nd St.
New York, NY 10019
USA

tel: (212)975-4321
fax: (212)975-4516
web: http://www.cbs.com

nationality: USA
date: 1999
affected: Viacom International Inc., USA, founded 1970
affected: CBS Corp., USA, founded 1927

Overview of the Merger

The $34.5 billion merger of Viacom International and CBS, announced in September of 1999 and scheduled to be completed early in the year 2000, will push The Walt Disney Co. into the third place spot among worldwide media leaders. The new Viacom, valued at $80 billion, will remain second only to Time Warner. Viacom International head Sumner Redstone will remain at the helm of Viacom as CEO and chairman, while CBS CEO Mel Karmazin will take over as president and chief operating officer. If approved, the deal will mark the largest transaction in the history of the media industry.

History of Viacom International Inc.

The Central Broadcasting System (CBS) complied with the Federal Communications Commission's (FCC) regulations barring television networks from owning cable TV systems or from syndicating their own programs in the U.S. by establishing Viacom International Inc. in 1970. The following year, CBS spun off Viacom as a separate company to CBS shareholders. That firm's initial annual sales reached $19.8 million. Its 90,000 subscribers made it one of the nation's largest cable systems.

In 1976, to compete with Home Box Office (HBO), the nation's leading cable outlet for films, Viacom created the Showtime movie network as a 50-50 venture with Warner Amex. The next year, despite a federal ruling that removed many restrictions on the choice of programming available on pay-television, Showtime posted a loss of $825,000. Nevertheless, Viacom earned $5.5 million on sales of $58.5 million, mostly from sales of television series such as *I Love Lucy*. Subscription to the company's cable system rose to 350,000.

Viacom reached a deal in 1978 with Teleprompter Corp., the largest cable systems operator in the U.S., whereby Teleprompter offered its customers Showtime rather than HBO. Three years later, Viacom acquired Video Corp. of America for $16 million. The company's growth goals included the acquisition of radio and television stations during the 1970s. Those acquisitions proved to be insurance against any possible takeover of the company, since the transfer of broadcast licenses had to be overseen by the FCC.

Viacom invested $65 million on its cable infrastructure in 1981. The next year, Showtime had 3.4 million subscribers and earned about $10 million on sales of $140 million. Subscriptions to Viacom's cable systems totaled 540,000, making it the ninth-largest cable operator in the U.S. In 1984, Showtime became a sister station to Warner Amex's The Movie Channel in a move designed to increase sales for both stations. In September of the following year, Viacom purchased Warner Amex's stake in Showtime from Warner Communications, as well as MTV Networks, which included MTV, Nickelodeon, and VH1. Viacom revamped Nickelodeon's image and introduced *Nick at Night*, a block of classic sitcoms aired for an adult audience.

Weakened by the $2 billion debt load it had incurred through its acquisitions, and in part to scare off potential takeovers, Viacom was purchased by National Amusements Inc., a movie theater chain, for about $3.4 billion in March 1987. Sumner M. Redstone, president of National Amusements, assumed the chairmanship of Viacom. The U.S. Congress passed legislation deregulating the cable industry that year, causing prices of cable franchises to soar. Viacom recorded sales in excess of $1 billion for the first time, but the company still posted a loss of approximately $154.4 million.

Viacom sold its cable systems in Long Island, New York, and suburban Cleveland, Ohio, to Cablevision Systems Corp. for $545 million in 1989. Cablevision also purchased a 5% stake in Showtime for $25 million, gaining a tangible interest in the channel's success. Also that year, Viacom sold 50% of Showtime's stock to Tele-Communications Inc. (TCI), a cable systems operator with about six million subscribers, for $225 million; joined with Hearst Corp. and Capital Cities/ABC Inc. to introduce Lifetime Television, a cable channel geared toward women; established a production company, Viacom Pictures, which made about 10 feature films at a cost of about $4 million each; and filed a $2.4 billion antitrust suit against HBO, alleging that HBO was trying to put Showtime out of business by intimidating cable systems that carried Showtime and by trying to corner the market on Hollywood films to prevent competitors from airing them. The suit was settled out of court in August 1992. Time Warner, HBO's parent, agreed to pay Viacom $75 million and to buy a Viacom cable system in Milwaukee for $95 million. Time Warner also agreed to increase its distribution of Showtime and The Movie Channel on its cable networks.

The Business

Financials - Viacom International Inc.

Revenue (1998): $12.1 billion

Employees (1998): 111,700

Financials - CBS Corp.

Revenue (1998): $6.8 billion

Employees (1998): 46,100

SICs / NAICS

sic 4841 - Cable & Other Pay Television Services

sic 4833 - Television Broadcasting Stations

sic 7822 - Motion Picture & Tape Distribution

sic 7812 - Motion Picture & Video Production

sic 2731 - Book Publishing

sic 7996 - Amusement Parks

sic 4832 - Radio Broadcasting Stations

naics 513210 - Cable Networks

naics 513120 - Television Broadcasting

naics 512120 - Motion Picture and Video Distribution

naics 512110 - Motion Picture and Video Production

naics 511130 - Book Publishers

naics 713110 - Amusement and Theme Parks

A five-month battle against QVC Inc. for Paramount Communications Inc. was initiated by Viacom's bid in September 1993. To help raise funds for this acquisition, Viacom offered $8.4 billion in stock to acquire Blockbuster Entertainment Corp.. Viacom successfully gained control of Paramount in July 1994 and of Blockbuster that September.

Also in 1994, Viacom sold its one-third interest in Lifetime to its partners. Blockbuster increased its presence in the children's entertainment-center industry by lifting its stake in Discovery Zone from 20% to 50.1%. The following year, Viacom sold its Madison Square Garden sports assets.

In January 1995, the company joined with Chris-Craft to launch United Paramount Network (UPN), which targeted viewers aged 18-34. That June, Paramount conducted its most successful motion picture opening, that of *Congo*.

Also in 1995, Wal-Mart's William R. Fields was hired to lead Blockbuster Entertainment. Fields was

The Officers

Viacom International Inc.

Chairman and CEO: Sumner M. Redstone

Deputy Chairman and Exec. VP: Philippe P. Dauman

Deputy Chairman and Exec. VP: Thomas E. Dooley

Chairman and CEO of the Blockbuster Entertainment
Group: John F. Antioco

Chairman of the Viacom Entertainment Group: Jonathan L.
Dolgen

CBS Corp.

Chairman: David McLaughlin

President and CEO: Mel Karmazin

Exec. VP and Chief Financial Officer: Fredric Reynolds

Exec. VP and General Counsel: Louis Briskman

fired the following year, however, and was replaced as CEO by John F. Antioco, who was assigned the task of turning around Blockbuster, which had been plagued by sluggish video rentals, management errors, a lack of focus, and problems with a new distribution system. In 1998, Antioco laid off 180 employees, mainly at the company's headquarters; curtailed store expansion; and closed all 17 of Germany's struggling stores. More importantly, he introduced the concept of revenue sharing, enabling the stores to stock more copies of popular titles in exchange for a percentage of the rental revenues to be paid to the movie studios. Blockbuster's revenues in 1998 reached $3.9 billion, strong enough for Viacom to file for its initial public offering in March 1999.

In a $2 billion stock deal with Tele-Communications Inc. (TCI) and its shareholders, Viacom spun off its cable systems in 1996. In a controversial move, Redstone fired Frank J. Biondi, Jr., as Viacom CEO and assumed the post himself.

Viacom sold its 10-station radio group to Chancellor Media Corp. in July 1997 for about $1.1 billion in cash. That year, it also increased its ownership of Spelling Entertainment Group Inc. to 80% and acquired full ownership in June 1999.

The hugely successful *Titanic* was released in December 1997, far surpassing even the enormous success of the company's previous hit, *Forrest Gump*. In October 1998, Viacom sold Blockbuster Music to Wherehouse Entertainment Inc. for $115 million. By the end of the year, Blockbuster's video stores in the

U.S. and 25 other countries numbered about 6,000, making it the nation's leading video rental company. Also in 1998, Viacom sold Simon & Schuster's educational, professional, and reference publishing operations to Pearson PLC for $4.6 billion in cash. In September 1999, CBS and Viacom announced their mammoth merger.

History of CBS Corp.

Arthur Judson, impresario of the Philadelphia and New York Philharmonic Orchestras, founded United Independent Broadcasters, Inc. in 1927 as a radio broadcasting company designed to promote classical music via the airing of orchestral performances. After several difficult months, Judson entered into a partnership with Columbia Phonograph. Columbia purchased UIB's operating rights for $163,000 and the new company was renamed the Columbia Phonograph Broadcasting System.

The next year, operating rights were resold back to the broadcasting company, whose name was shortened to Columbia Broadcasting System (CBS). Also in 1928, radio advertiser William Paley bought $400,000 worth of CBS stock. He became president, and earnings tripled in his first year of tenure.

Paley fostered success by offering to prospective affiliates the young network's complete, unsponsored schedule for free; this was in stark contrast to the practice of competing network NBC, which charged affiliates for all programming. In exchange for the free programs, CBS affiliate stations offered airtime to the parent network for its sponsored broadcasts. By 1936, CBS had 97 affiliate stations and was the country's largest radio network.

The company began to carve out a niche in news and public affairs, leaving NBC to continue its dominance in the entertainment front. It formed Columbia News Service, the first radio network news operation of its kind, in 1933. Five years later, broadcast journalist Edward R. Murrow initiated the first international radio news broadcast with reports from Vienna, Paris, Berlin, and Rome. That year, CBS purchased the American Recording Corp., which was later renamed as Columbia Recording Corp.

CBS transmitted the world's first experimental color TV broadcast in 1940. The following year it began weekly broadcasts of black-and-white television programs. As it became successful in luring from NBC such star performers as Jack Benny, Edgar Bergen, Red Skelton, George Burns, and Gracie Allen, CBS became known as the Tiffany Network, which made reference to its quality programming.

In 1956, the popular TV quiz show *$64,000 Question* became embroiled in the national game show scandal of unfairly briefing contestants prior to the show. Three years later, president James Aubrey introduced lighter fare into the network's entertainment lineup, and doubled profits in his first two years at the helm of CBS. Such shows as *The Beverly Hillbillies, Mr. Ed,* and *The Munsters* helped make CBS the best-rated network. It maintained that lead through the 1970s with hit shows including *The Mary Tyler Moore Show* and *All in the Family.*

In 1982, CBS and Twentieth Century Fox-Video combined forces to form CBS/Fox, a distributor of videocassettes. The following year, the firm acquired the music publishing portion of United Artists Corp. and created Tri-Star Pictures as a joint venture with Columbia Pictures and Home Box Office. In 1985, CBS purchased the consumer magazine publishing operations of Ziff-Davis Publishing Co. for $362.5 million.

Laurence Tisch became CEO in 1986 and began drastic cost-cutting measures that included the reduction of the news division budget by $30 million; the lay-off of 1,200 employees; and the sale of several CBS publishing concerns. CBS also began divesting its music and professional interests, including CBS Records to Sony Corp. for $2 billion, a sale most industry analysts sharply criticized.

CBS acquired Midwest Communications, a broadcast and sports programming company, in 1991. Three years later, the Fox Network acquired the rights to air Monday Night Football, a former staple of CBS. Fox also acquired several of CBS's broadcasting affiliates, sending the company scrambling for replacement affiliates in such large markets as Detroit, Michigan. In 1995, CBS was acquired by Westinghouse Electric Corp. for $5.4 billion. Westinghouse acquired Infinity Broadcasting in 1996, gaining a dominant share of the U.S. radio market. During the mid-1990s, Westinghouse divested most of its non-broadcasting operations, and in December 1997, the firm changed its name to CBS Corp. to reflect its new focus. CBS gained an additional 90 radio stations by purchasing American Radio Systems in 1998. Later that year, the company reduced its stake in Infinity by spinning off 20% of that unit through an initial public offering. In 1999, CBS agreed to purchase King World Productions and to merge with Viacom International.

Market Forces Driving the Merger

Motion picture studios and television networks had been prohibited from operating in each other's markets since the financial interest/syndication, or fin/syn, rules had been established by the U.S. Federal Communications Commission in 1970. The legislation

The Players

Chairman of Viacom International Inc.: Sumner M. Redstone. Born in a 1923 Boston tenement, Sumner Redstone earned a Harvard degree in just three years. After serving in an Army Intelligence unit that deciphered Japan's World War II codes, Redstone returned to his alma mater to earn a law degree. He practiced law for six years before returning to his father's business, a chain of 12 drive-in theaters. While running the family business, Redstone pioneered the theater industry's multiplex, a term he later copyrighted. Redstone's 1986 investment in Viacom propelled him into the big leagues, and he later won the company in a heated battle. He emerged victorious in the bidding war for Paramount as well. Redstone was still serving as chairman of his media empire in 1999, at age 76, when he orchestrated a merger with CBS Corp., the largest media deal to date in history.

CEO of CBS Corp.: Mel Karmazin. After graduating from Pace University, Mel Karmazin launched his career in radio as an advertising salesman. He took a position at Metromedia in 1970. Eleven years later, Karmazin founded Infinity Broadcasting, the firm that hired and eventually syndicated shock jock Howard Stern after NBC dropped him. When Infinity was acquired by Westinghouse (later renamed CBS Corp.) in January of 1997, Karmazin took over as CEO of radio and television operations. CBS Corp. brought Karmazin on as chief operating officer in April of 1998. He replaced Michael Jordan as CEO in January of 1999. By the year's end, Karmazin had negotiated the blockbuster merger deal with Viacom.

barred television networks, which broadcasted to about 95% of homes, from making a profit on both program ownership and syndication. Consequently, studios ended up controlling content, while networks grabbed hold of distribution.

The dawn of cable television, coupled with the growing popularity of VCRs during the 1980s, created sudden, intense competition for the networks. Viewership began dwindling, undercutting the value of commercial spots, and networks began pressuring the government to remove the fin/syn rules. However, studios fought to keep their near-monopoly on television show production. The Reagan Administration quelled efforts to relax the rules, and for a while, the studios were victorious.

In 1991, under increasing pressure, the FCC did loosen the restrictions. Dissatisfied, the networks pushed for complete removal of the fin/syn rules. Two years later, a judge ordered the removal of the regulation, beginning September 1995. The acquisition of Capital Cities/ABC by The Walt Disney Co. in 1996 marked the first major move between a movie studio and television. The deal, as well as the legislation itself, sparked similar consolidation efforts in the industry, as other movie studios followed Disney's lead and began hunting for a distribution channel for their content. For example, later that year, the world's largest media company was formed when Turner Broadcasting System Inc. was acquired by Time Warner Inc.

With media companies continuing to grow in size, most analysts believed CBS needed to pursue a deal of its own as a means of remaining competitive. A merger with Viacom would not only give Viacom a leading distribution channel—it would also catapult both firms into the second-place spot among global media companies, behind Time Warner.

Approach and Engagement

CBS first approached Viacom in August of 1999 to discuss the possible sale of television stations. Both sides began discussing an outright merger, and within a few weeks, they had reached a $34.5 billion agreement in which shareholders would receive 1.085 Viacom class B shares for each CBS share held.

Scheduled for completion early in the year 2000, the merger is subject to regulatory approval, and analysts point to several issues that might cause problems for the firms. For example, combining the 20 television stations of CBS with the 18 stations owned by Viacom's Paramount unit would result in a market share significantly higher than the 35% currently allowed. Also, because Viacom holds a 50% stake in the UPN television network, a merger with CBS would violate laws that forbid ownership of more than one television network.

Products and Services

In 1999, Viacom operated in six business segments:

Networks encompassed basic cable and premium subscription television program services. These networks included MTV, MTV2, Nickelodeon, Nick at Nite, Nick at Nite's TV Land, VH1, Showtime, The Movie Channel, and Flix. This segment also held the company's interests in Comedy Central, Sundance Channel, and UPN (United Paramount Network). Total revenues in 1998 for the Network segment reached $2.6 billion.

Entertainment housed the company's operations in the production and distribution of motion pictures and television programming, as well as its television stations, international channels, movie theater operations, and music publishing. This segment was comprised of Paramount Pictures, Paramount Television, Spelling Entertainment Group Inc., and the Paramount Stations Group, and generated revenues of $4.8 billion in 1998.

The **Video** segment consisted of Blockbuster Video, a retailer in home videos and games; it produced $3.9 billion in revenues in 1998. The **Parks** segment, comprised of the five regional Paramount Parks, achieved $421 million in revenues that year. **Publishing** encompassed such consumer publishing imprints as Simon & Schuster, Pocket Books, Scribner, and The Free Press; this unit generated sales of $564 million. Finally, **Viacom Online Services**, the company's interactive businesses, produced revenues of $13.7 million.

Among CBS's television offerings were: *48 Hours, 60 Minutes, CBS Evening News with Dan Rather, Chicago Hope, Diagnosis Murder, Early Edition, LA Doctors, Martial Law, Nash Bridges, Touched by an Angel,* and *Walker, Texas Ranger.*

In addition, the company also owned 14 television stations; 80% of Infinity Broadcasting, which owned a collection of 160 radio stations; and the cable networks The Nashville Network and Country Music Television.

Research

CBS Corp. Home Page, available at http://www.cbs.com. Official World Wide Web Page for CBS. Provides information on the programming of the Web site visitor's local CBS affiliate.

"CBS Inc.," in *Notable Corporate Chronologies*, The Gale Group, 1999. Profiles the history of the company.

Gunther, Marc. "Viacom: Redstone's Ride to the Top," in *Fortune*, 26 April 1999. Offers a detailed profile of Sumner Redstone and of his successful acquisitions of Paramount and Blockbuster.

Haddad, Charles. "CBS-Viacom Merger Further Narrows Media," in *Knight-Ridder/Tribune Business News*, 10 September 1999. Describes the industry conditions that prompted the deal.

Kurtz, Howard. "Good News for CBS? Observers Split on Merger," in *The Washington Post*, 8 September 1999. Explains why the two firms decided to merge and how analysts are viewing the deal.

Schwartz, John. "Mel Karmazin's Signal Achievement," in *The Washington Post*, 8 September 1999. Profiles the career of Mel Karmazin.

"Viacom Acquiring CBS in $80 Billion Deal," in *Communications Daily*, 8 September 1999. Covers the terms of the transaction, as well as the regulatory hurdles the deal may face.

Viacom International Inc. Home Page, available at http://www.viacom.com. Official World Wide Web Page for Viacom International Inc. Includes a description of operations, news releases, executive biographies, annual reports, investor information, and links to company Websites.

"Viacom International Inc.," in *Notable Corporate Chronologies*, The Gale Group, 1999. Lists major events in the history of Viacom.

ANNAMARIE L. SHELDON

VIACOM & PARAMOUNT

Viacom International Inc.
1515 Broadway, 51st Fl.
New York, NY 10036
USA

tel: (212)258-6000
web: http://www.viacom.com
e-mail: info@viacom.com

nationality: USA
date: July 1994
affected: Viacom International Inc., USA, founded 1970
affected: Paramount Communications Inc., USA, founded 1956

Overview of the Acquisition

The battle over the acquisition of Paramount in the early 1990s captured headlines for five months. The rival bidders, Viacom and QVC, volleyed escalating billion-dollar bids for the movie and TV producer ultimately valued in excess of $10 billion. Each of the suitors bid with a portion of money that they had to acquire from outside sources. Both turned to other companies for investments, and QVC even closed a whirlwind merger with Blockbuster Entertainment to gain access to the video retailer's cash flow. Added to the volatile mix were the personalities, egos, and relationships of the companies' leaders: QVC's Barry Diller, Paramount's Martin Davis, and Viacom's Sumner Redstone.

In the end, Viacom emerged the victor when QVC finally declined to increase its bid farther. Viacom had its prize, but many analysts and investors criticized Redstone for overpaying. Viacom's debt load was a staggering $10 billion, and Blockbuster was seriously underperforming. Within only a couple of years, though, Viacom reduced that debt burden significantly and turned the video chain around, prompting Wall Street to tout the shrewdness of Redstone once again.

History of Viacom International Inc.

The Central Broadcasting System (CBS) complied with the Federal Communications Commission's (FCC) regulations barring television networks from owning cable TV systems or from syndicating their own programs in the U.S. by establishing Viacom International Inc. in 1970. The following year CBS spun off Viacom as a separate company to CBS shareholders. That firm's initial annual sales reached $19.8 million. Its 90,000 subscribers made it one of the nation's largest cable systems.

In 1976, to compete with Home Box Office (HBO), the nation's leading cable outlet for films, Viacom created the Showtime movie network as a 50-50 venture with Warner Amex. The next year, despite a federal ruling that removed many restrictions on the choice of programming available on pay-television, Showtime posted a loss of $825,000. Nevertheless, Viacom earned $5.5 million on sales of $58.5 million, mostly from sales of television series such as *I Love Lucy*. Subscription to the company's cable system rose to 350,000.

Viacom reached a deal in 1978 with Teleprompter Corp., the largest cable systems operator in the U.S., whereby Teleprompter offered its customers Showtime rather than HBO. Three years later Viacom acquired Video Corp. of America for $16 million. The company's growth goals included the acquisition of radio and television stations during the 1970s. Those acquisitions proved to be insurance against any possible takeover of the company, since the transfer of broadcast licenses must be overseen by the FCC.

Viacom invested $65 million on its cable infrastructure in 1981. The next year Showtime had 3.4 million subscribers and earned about $10 million on sales of $140 million. Subscriptions to Viacom's cable systems totaled 540,000, making it the ninth-largest cable operator in the U.S.

In 1984 Showtime became a sister station to Warner Amex's The Movie Channel in a move designed to increase sales for both stations. In September of the following year, Viacom purchased Warner Amex's stake in Showtime from Warner Communications, as well as MTV Networks, which included MTV, Nickelodeon, and VH1. Viacom revamped Nickelodeon's image and introduced *Nick at Night*, a block of classic sitcoms aired for an adult audience.

Weakened by the $2 billion debt load it had incurred through its acquisitions, and in part to scare off potential takeovers, Viacom was purchased by National Amusements Inc., a movie theater chain, for about $3.4 billion in March 1987. Sumner M. Redstone, president of National Amusements, assumed the chairmanship of Viacom.

The U.S. Congress passed legislation deregulating the cable industry in 1987, causing prices of cable franchises to soar. Viacom recorded sales in excess of $1 billion for the first time, but the company still posted a loss of approximately $154.4 million.

Viacom sold its cable systems in Long Island, New York, and suburban Cleveland, Ohio, to Cablevision Systems Corp. for $545 million. Cablevision then purchased a five-percent stake in Showtime for $25 million, giving it a tangible interest in the channel's success. Viacom also sold 50% of Showtime's stock to Tele-Communications Inc. (TCI), a cable systems operator with about six million subscribers, for $225 million.

Viacom joined with Hearst Corp. and Capital Cities/ABC Inc. in 1989 to introduce Lifetime Television, a cable channel geared toward women. Viacom established a production company, Viacom Pictures, which made about 10 feature films that year at a cost of about $4 million each.

The Business

Financials

Revenue (1998): $12.1 billion

Employees (1998): 111,700

SICs / NAICS

sic 4841 - Cable & Other Pay Television Services

sic 4833 - Television Broadcasting Stations

sic 7822 - Motion Picture & Tape Distribution

sic 7812 - Motion Picture & Video Production

sic 2731 - Book Publishing

sic 7996 - Amusement Parks

naics 513210 - Cable Networks

naics 513120 - Television Broadcasting

naics 512120 - Motion Picture and Video Distribution

naics 512110 - Motion Picture and Video Production

naics 511130 - Book Publishers

naics 713110 - Amusement and Theme Parks

Viacom filed a $2.4 billion antitrust suit against HBO, alleging that HBO was trying to put Showtime out of business by intimidating cable systems that carried Showtime and by trying to corner the market on Hollywood films to prevent competitors from airing them. The suit was settled out of court in August 1992. Time Warner, HBO's parent, agreed to pay Viacom $75 million and to buy a Viacom cable system in Milwaukee for $95 million. It also agreed to increase its distribution of Showtime and The Movie Channel on its cable networks.

A five-month battle against QVC Inc. for Paramount Communications Inc. was initiated by Viacom's bid in September 1993. To help raise funds for this acquisition, Viacom offered $8.4 billion in stock to acquire Blockbuster Entertainment Corp. Viacom successfully gained control of Paramount in July 1994 and of Blockbuster that September.

Viacom sold its one-third interest in Lifetime to its partners. Blockbuster increased its presence in the children's entertainment-center industry by lifting its stake in Discovery Zone from 20% to 50.1%. The following year Viacom sold its Madison Square Garden sports assets.

In January 1995 the company joined with Chris-Craft to launch United Paramount Network (UPN),

The Officers

Chairman and CEO: Sumner M. Redstone
Deputy Chairman and Exec. VP: Philippe P. Dauman
Deputy Chairman and Exec. VP: Thomas E. Dooley

which targeted viewers aged 18-34. That June Paramount had its most successful motion picture opening, *Congo*.

Wal-Mart's William R. Fields was hired to lead Blockbuster Entertainment, which has close to 3,000 video rental stores in the U.S. Fields was fired the following year, however, and was replaced by John F. Antioco as CEO. He was assigned the task of turning around Blockbuster, which had been plagued by sluggish video rentals, management errors, a lack of focus, and problems with a new distribution system. In 1998 Antioco laid off 180 employees, mainly at the company's headquarters; curtailed store expansion; and closed all 17 of Germany's struggling stores. More importantly, he introduced the concept of revenue sharing, enabling the stores to stock more copies of popular titles in exchange for a percentage of the rental revenues to be paid to the movie studios. Blockbuster's revenues in 1998 reached $3.9 billion, strong enough for Viacom to file for its initial public offering in March 1999.

In a $2 billion stock deal with Tele-Communications Inc. (TCI) and its shareholders, Viacom spun off its cable systems in 1996. In a controversial move, Redstone fired Frank J. Biondi Jr. as Viacom CEO and assumed the post himself.

Viacom sold its 10-station radio group to Chancellor Media Corp. in July 1997 for about $1.1 billion in cash. That year it also increased its ownership of Spelling Entertainment Group Inc. to 80%, and acquired full ownership in June 1999.

The hugely successful *Titanic* was released in December 1997, far surpassing even the enormous success of the company's previous hit, *Forrest Gump*.

In October 1998 Viacom sold Blockbuster Music to Wherehouse Entertainment Inc. for $115 million. By the end of the year, Blockbuster's video stores in the U.S. and 25 other countries numbered about 6,000, making it the nation's leading video rental company. Viacom also sold Simon & Schuster's educational, professional, and reference publishing operations to Pearson PLC for $4.6 billion in cash.

History of Paramount Communications, Inc.

After experimenting in the import-export business, Austrian-born Charles George Bluhdorn began searching for a publicly traded company whose stock he could use to buy other companies. In 1956 he secured a controlling interest in Michigan Plating & Stamping and joined its board of directors. The next year Bluhdorn merged Michigan Plating with Beard & Stone Electric Co., a Houston-based auto parts distributor.

In 1958, in deference to the company's location on the Gulf of Mexico and to Bluhdorn's belief that most of its growth would originate in the West, where automobile sales were rapidly increasing, the firm changed its name to Gulf + Western Corp.

Having acquired a number of private auto parts distributors and warehouses, Gulf + Western's annual sales approached $200 million in the mid-1960s. Bluhdorn embarked on a diversification campaign, and in just a matter of days, the company purchased a large amount of stock in New Jersey Zinc, a large mining and chemical company.

The struggling Paramount Pictures Corp. became Bluhdorn's next target. Paying $125 million for the movie company in 1966, Gulf + Western immediately became one of the nation's top manufacturing companies. Sales that year increased from $180 million to nearly $300 million—nearly tripling earnings to $17 million.

Gulf + Western acquired 23 companies in 1968, including Consolidated Cigar, E.W. Bliss, Universal American, Brown Company, and Associates Investment Co. Sales surpassed the $1 billion mark for the first time, reaching $1.3 billion and producing net income of $69.8 million. Paramount became a success story. Nearly bankrupt when purchased, it recorded its highest box-office revenues in history during 1972. Five years later Gulf + Western acquired Madison Square Garden.

In 1969 the company's fast-paced acquisition program ended when Wall Street analysts, congressmen, and the media charged Gulf + Western with manipulating accounting procedures to inflate its earnings. As a result, the company's stock dropped 30 points, costing shareholders $500 million and further reducing its dismal price earnings.

The company's regulatory problems continued in the next decade. In 1975 the U.S. Securities and Exchange Commission (SEC) charged that the company's operations in the Dominican Republic illegally withheld over $38 million in profits owed to the Dominican Republic government. In 1980 the company reached a settlement with the SEC over this matter, whereby Gulf + Western agreed to pay $39 million over seven years in order to fund a social and economic development program in the Dominican Republic.

In 1978, as the company's poor public image continued, Gulf + Western spent $3.3 million to print its annual report in *Time* magazine, hoping to raise its price earning ratio. The next year, the SEC initiated a second investigation, accusing Bluhdorn and executive vice president Don. F. Gatson of misconduct. Among its charges were allegations that the two executives allowed the company's pension fund to make "inappropriate" investments in companies where they had personal investments. In 1981 this investigation was settled, with no restitution called for under the terms of the agreement.

Bluhdorn died of a heart attack in 1983, and was succeeded as CEO by Martin S. Davis. Davis quickly streamlined the company's operations from seven operating groups into three units, focusing on the areas of entertainment, financial services, and consumer products. Within months, Consolidated Cigar was sold, as were 50 other units, including operations in chemicals, concrete equipment, and mechanical presses.

In 1984 Gulf + Western acquired the remaining 73% of Esquire, Inc., as well as the publishers Prentice-Hall and Glen & Company. Divestitures continued, and the company sold its consumer and industrial products to Wickes Co. for $1 billion in cash in 1985. Four years later Gulf + Western changed its name to Paramount Communications. Also that year, the company made an unsuccessful bid for Time Inc.

In 1991 Paramount purchased the television station operator TVX, renaming it Paramount Stations Group, and started a pay-per-view programming and distribution venture with Capital Cities/ABC. It also purchased the Macmillan Computer Publishing division in late 1991 for $157.5 million. The company's revenues increased to $4.3 billion in 1992, due in large part to the success of such movies as *The Addams Family*, *Star Trek VI*, and *Wayne's World*.

Paramount began bypassing television networks in 1993 by taking its TV series' *The Untouchables* and *Deep Space Nine* directly into the first-run syndication market. The following year, Paramount was the prize in a heated takeover battle between Viacom Inc. and QVC, and in July 1994 Paramount was acquired by Viacom. Before the battle was over, Paramount acquired Macmillan Inc., thereby becoming the nation's second-largest book publisher.

The Players

Viacom Chairman: Sumner M. Redstone. Billionaire Sumner Redstone was never fed with a silver spoon, even after he could afford it. Born in a 1923 Boston tenement, he sped through Harvard in only three years. He then joined an Army Intelligence unit that cracked Japan's World War II codes before acquiring a law degree from Harvard. Redstone practiced law for six years before returning to his father's business, a chain of 12 drive-in theaters. He then revolutionized the theater industry by establishing the multiplex, a term that he later copyrighted.

No profile of Redstone is complete without the tale of the hotel fire that nearly cost him his life. In 1979 he escaped death by hanging by his fingertips from the ledge of the Boston hotel until he was rescued. He sustained severe burns over half his body, and doctors predicted that he would never walk again. Redstone not only recovered, he became a voracious and highly competitive tennis player.

Redstone entered the big leagues with his 1986 investment in Viacom, later winning the company in a heated battle. He emerged victorious in his takeover of Paramount as well. Redstone was still serving as chairman of his media empire in 1999, at age 76.

Market Forces Driving the Acquisition

According to Sumner Redstone, Viacom's chairman, content is king. Paramount was a major producer of movies and television shows, and also possessed the Simon & Schuster publishing house as well as the New York Knickerbockers and Rangers. Added to Viacom's cable channels, such as MTV, VH1, Nickelodean, and Showtime, a combined company would become the nation's second-largest entertainment company. It would also be in a position to become a major content provider for the multiple entertainment distribution channels expected in the near future—500-channel digital cable systems, video-on-demand, and global satellite television. With a combined 11 TV stations, it might also launched a fifth network.

Redstone's vision for Viacom was that the "exploitation of our copyrights in every window provided by each technology and the control of software...would be the key to success regardless of the

The Players

Paramount Communications Chairman: Martin S. Davis. Martin Davis, a former publicist, took the helm of the bloated Gulf + Western in 1983. He immediately refocused the company and trimmed expenses, finally completing this task in 1989. That year the company changed its name to Paramount Communications and made a failed attempt to make a hostile takeover of Time Inc. Four years later, Davis found himself on the receiving end of such an attempt, when QVC launched an unfriendly bid to wrest Paramount from its merger agreement with Viacom. That bid was even more distasteful to Davis, as it would place his company in the hands of Barry Diller, whose clashes with Davis had spurred Diller to resign from Paramount in 1983. Ultimately, Viacom succeeded in its bid for Paramount, at which point Davis resigned, although he gained a seat on the board of Viacom's parent, National Amusements, Inc. In 1994 he established Wellspring Associates, L.L.C., a buyout group specializing in investing in undervalued companies in need of dramatic restructuring. By early 1998, Wellspring had made investments in the bankrupt Discovery Zone, the hockey equipment manufacturer SLM International, and Lionel Trains, a toy company acquired in 1995.

QVC Chairman: Barry Diller. Born in Beverly Hills, California, Barry Diller rose from the ranks of the mail room at a talent agency to a revolutionary who turned the entertainment industry on its ear. After being promoted to agent at the William Morris Agency, he gained a job at age 24 as an executive at ABC, where he launched the hugely successful *Movie of the Week* and the miniseries concept. After Diller took the helm at Paramount in 1974, he and his team, known as "Killer Dillers," produced such hits as *Star Trek*, *Raiders of the Lost Ark*, and *Saturday Night Fever*. In 1983 he left Paramount after clashing with its new CEO, Martin Davis. At Twentieth Century Fox, Diller launched the Fox Network, the nation's first new television network in 40 years. He suddenly resigned in February 1992, and went on to purchase QVC, a cable shopping channel. That company lost out on two acquisitions in as many years, Paramount and CBS, and in 1994 Diller sold his stake in QVC. Diller then became chairman of Silver King Communications, which he merged with the Home Shopping Network. After gaining control of USA Networks Inc., Diller embarked on a plan to create a new network. In mid-1999 he embarked on plans to form USA-Lycos Interactive Network by merging parts of USA Networks with the Web portal Lycos Inc.

distribution system and with or without the information superhighway," as reported by *Financial World*.

By late 1993 Paramount was one of the two remaining major independent movie studios. Since the other, Walt Disney Co., was unlikely to need or want a merger, Paramount represented the last chance for media companies to grab a major stake in movie production. Viacom was not the first to realize this. Among Paramount's reported suitors were Tele-Communications Inc. (TCI), ABC, NBC, and Ted Turner. Each had been rebuffed by Paramount's chairman, Martin Davis, based on the purchase price or some measure of the relinquishment of control by Davis. Paramount was still under pressure to compete with the large conglomerants poised to control the industry.

In early 1993 Davis had heard a rumor that QVC's chairman, Barry Diller, was preparing a takeover attempt for Paramount. Davis and Diller became enemies when Davis forced Diller out of Paramount a number of years earlier. This hostility and mistrust lingered, and Davis presumed that he would be sent packing should Diller gain control of Paramount. Upon confrontation by Davis, Diller quietly denied any truth to the rumor, but Davis reportedly shouted, "I know you're coming after me!" That June, Paramount and Viacom entered into serious negotiations.

Approach and Engagement

On September 13, 1993, Viacom and Paramount announced their $8.2 billion merger agreement. It was comprised of a cash payment of $9.10 per share plus Viacom stock valued at $60 per share. Davis would play CEO to Redstone's chairman. *The Economist* reported that Davis was willing to take a backseat because he feared that Viacom might merge with another company if he refused. "Davis realized that no 'ideal partnership' was available, but that Viacom looked as close as he would get."

One week later, on September 20, QVC proposed a $9.5 billion merger with Paramount. The deal was not only about $2 billion higher than Viacom's, as a fall in its stock price over the previous week devalued Viacom's offer, it offered a larger cash portion per share, $30. QVC would help finance its bid through the investment of $500 million each from Comcast and from John Malone's Liberty Media Corp. and TCI.

Davis's reluctance to enter into a deal with Diller, despite his company's premium over Viacom's bid, compelled him to consider it thoroughly—and slowly. Diller grew tired of waiting and went over the head of Paramount's board by launching a cash tender offer.

The offer was contingent, however, on the removal of Paramount's poison pill and lockup provisions, including a breakup fee to be paid to Viacom; these defensive measures have been adopted upon the company's agreement with Viacom to deter rival bidders.

In response, Viacom raised its bid to $80 per share in cash for 51% of Paramount's stock, with the remainder at $80 per share in Viacom stock. This $9.5 billion deal, now equal to QVC's, was financed in part by a $600 million investment from Blockbuster Entertainment and a $1.2 billion investment from NYNEX, a New York Baby Bell.

The battle then shifted to the courtroom. Viacom successfully convinced the courts that John Malone's investment in QVC was an antitrust violation, as Liberty Media's partial ownership of QVC constituted a monopolistic attempt to control the cable industry. QVC, however, replaced Malone's $500 million investment with a $1.5 billion investment from BellSouth Corp.

QVC won the next legal round. The courts ruled that the Viacom/Paramount deal was an acquisition, not a merger, and as such, the bidding should be open to all comers. Paramount was forbidden to use its poison pill and lockup provisions in favor of Viacom.

Forced to conduct an auction, Davis called for the bidders to submit their final offers by December 20. By that time, Viacom's $9.6 billion offer was edged out by QVC's $9.8 billion bid, which had been modified with an increase in cash to $92 per share with an equal reduction in the stock portion. Paramount's board appropriately endorsed the higher bid, as the courts had directed, but Davis still hoped for a higher bid from Viacom.

On January 7, 1994, Viacom announced its $8.4 billion acquisition of Blockbuster Entertainment. Redstone emphasized the strategic benefits inherent in a Viacom/Paramount/Blockbuster union, but analysts suspected that the underlying reason was the $1.25 billion that Blockbuster would provide Viacom in its quest for Paramount. As Viacom would purchase Blockbuster in stock, this capital infusion enabled it to increase the cash portion of its bid for Paramount to $105 per share. At the same time it reduced the stock component to value the total deal at $9.4 billion, $400 million lower than QVC's pending offer.

Aware that the increased cash component might entice Paramount's shareholders, Diller charged that Viacom's deal violated auction rules. Paramount's board agreed and rejected it, thereby keeping the auction open for an extended time, until February 1.

Viacom then revealed its "Diller killer"—an offer of $107 per share in cash with the remainder in stock,

a deal valued at $9.8 billion. It also included a contingent value right (CVR), which guaranteed to Paramount's shareholders an award if Viacom's shares should fail to attain a specific value over the next three years.

Diller refused to get caught up in the emotions of the battle by paying more than he valued Paramount simply in order to win. He left his last offer on the table and up to the vote of Paramount's shareholders.

On February 15, 1994, nearly 75% of Paramount's shares had been tendered to Viacom, marking the end of the contest. Bruce Wasserstein, author of *Big Deal: The Battle for Control of America's Leading Corporations*, revealed the statements of the rival, and equally weary, suitors upon the news. Redstone raised his glass and toasted with relief, "Here's to us. We won." Diller also offered a five-word reaction: "They won. We lost. Next."

In early July 1994, upon the approval of their stockholders, Viacom and Paramount completed their union.

Products and Services

Viacom operated in six business segments:

Networks encompassed its basic cable and premium subscription television program services. These networks included MTV, MTV2, Nickelodeon, Nick at Nite, Nick at Nite's TV Land, VH1, Showtime, The Movie Channel, and Flix. This segment also held the company's interests in Comedy Central, Sundance Channel, and UPN (United Paramount Network). Total revenues in 1998 for the Network segment reached $2.6 billion.

Entertainment housed the company's operations in the production and distribution of motion pictures and television programming, as well as its television stations, international channels, movie theater operations, and music publishing. This segment was comprised of Paramount Pictures, Paramount Television, Spelling Entertainment Group Inc., and the Paramount Stations Group, and generated revenues of $4.8 billion in 1998.

The **Video** segment consisted of Blockbuster Video, a retailer in home videos and games; it produced $3.9 billion in revenues in 1998. The Parks segment, comprised of the five regional Paramount Parks, achieved $421 million in 1998 revenues. **Publishing** encompassed such consumer publishing imprints as Simon & Schuster, Pocket Books, Scribner, and The Free Press; this unit generated sales of $564 million in 1998. Finally, **Viacom Online Services**, the company's interactive businesses, produced 1998 revenues of $13.7 million.

Changes to the Industry

Viacom immediately became the nation's second-largest media company, behind Time Warner Inc., as it had annual revenues in excess of $10 billion. As summed up in *Kiplinger's Personal Finance Magazine*, Viacom "made itself into what Disney and Westinghouse would like to become: a vertically integrated company that can take a creative idea and turn it into a film at its own studio (Paramount), show it on one of its own cable channels (Showtime and the Movie Channel), publish it as a book through its own imprint (Simon & Schuster), rent out the video at its own store (Blockbuster), then roll out the spinoff characters at one of its regional theme parks (Paramount)."

Review of the Outcome

The downside to its enviable presence in the entertainment industry was a debt load of $10 billion. In addition, its stock was plummeting, largely due to the newly acquired Blockbuster. This troubled unit was flailing in an industry that experts believed was shrinking in the face of such higher-tech offerings as satellite television and movies-on-demand. After bringing in new talent and revamping the operation, Blockbuster improved its financial performance well enough for Viacom to consider taking it public in March 1999.

In the meantime, Viacom had shed several assets in order to relieve its debt burden. In March 1995 it sold Madison Square Garden, including its sports teams, for $1 billion. It reduced debt by $1.7 billion in July 1996 by selling its stake in the USA and Sci-Fi cable networks. One year later it received $1.1 billion for the sale of its radio business. And in May 1998 it sold the non-consumer business of Simon & Schuster for $4.6 billion. Despite these reductions in assets, Viacom recorded a 13% increase in revenues in 1998, to $12.1 billion. The company also reported an interest in buying CBS; if the acquisition is completed, it could be the largest media deal to date.

Research

"Another Fine Mess," in *The Economist*, 15 January 1994. Offers rationale for Viacom's acquisition of Paramount and Blockbuster.

Cook, William J., and Linda Grant. "An Ace in the Hole," in *U.S. News & World Report*, 11 October 1993. Describes the value that Viacom and QVC viewed in Paramount.

Greenwald, John. "The Deal that Forced Diller to Fold," in *Time*, 28 February 1994. Details Viacom's victory over QVC.

Gunther, Marc. "Viacom: Redstone's Ride to the Top," in *Fortune*, 26 April 1999. Offers a detailed profile of Sumner Redstone and of his successful acquisitions of Paramount and Blockbuster.

"Indecent Proposals," in *The Economist*, 25 September 1993. Relates the beginning of the bidding war for Paramount.

Moreau, Dan. "Memo to Michael Eisner: Viacom Beat You to the Finish," in *Kiplinger's Personal Finance Magazine*, October 1995. Offers a financial analysis of Viacom's performance in the year after its acquisition of Paramount.

"Of Paramount Importance," in *The Economist*, 18 December 1993. Relates the ruling that forced Paramount to drop its poison pill in defense against QVC.

"Paramount Pictures Corp.," in *Notable Corporate Chronologies*, The Gale Group, 1999. Profiles the history of the company.

Taub, Stephen. "Redstone in Motion," in *Financial World*, 6 December 1994. Profiles Viacom after its acquisitions of Paramount and Blockbuster.

"Viacom International Inc.," in *Notable Corporate Chronologies*, The Gale Group, 1999. Lists major events in the history of Viacom.

Viacom International Inc. Home Page, available at http://www.viacom.com. Official World Wide Web Page for Viacom. Includes a description of operations, news releases, executive biographies, annual reports, investor information, and links to company Websites.

Wasserstein, Bruce. *Big Deal: The Battle for Control of America's Leading Corporations*, Warner Books, 1998. Provides a detailed overview of Viacom's acquisition of Paramount.

"When Sumner Met Marty," in *The Economist*, 18 September 1993. Details the newly announced acquisition agreement.

DEBORAH J. UNTENER

VODAFONE GROUP & AIRTOUCH COMMUNICATIONS

nationality: United Kingdom
date: 1999
affected: Vodafone Group PLC, United Kingdom, founded 1984
affected: AirTouch Communications, Inc., USA, founded 1984

Vodafone Airtouch PLC
The Courtyard, 2-4 London Rd.
Newbury, Berkshire RG14 1JX
United Kingdom

tel: 44-1635-33-251
fax: 44-1635-550-779
web: http://www.vodafone-airtouch-plc.com

Overview of the Merger

United Kingdom-based cellular phone leader Vodafone Group rocked the global telecommunications industry in early 1999 when it bested Bell Atlantic's $45 billion bid for California-based AirTouch Communications, the number two U.S. cellular service provider, behind AT&T Wireless Services. When the $60 billion deal—the largest cross-border merger in global corporate history—was completed in mid-1999, Vodafone AirTouch usurped behemoth Deutsche Telekom AG as the largest telecommunications group in Europe. With 28 million customers spanning 23 countries and five continents, the new firm, valued at roughly $110 billion, also became the largest cellular phone service provider in the world, as well as the 20th-largest public company in the U.S. and the third-largest such company in Britain

History of Vodafone Group PLC

In 1985, Racal Electronics Ltd. established Racal Telecommunications Group Ltd. to develop the first cellular phone network in the U.K. As one of two contenders in the new and relatively unregulated new industry, the fledgling operation was well positioned for rapid growth. Despite this, the new firm posted a loss of 10 million pounds in its first year of operation.

Within two years, Vodac, Vodata, and Vodapage divisions were established to offer new products under the Vodafone name. By 1988, thanks to explosive growth in the U.K. cellular communications market, Racal Telecommunications had become the most successful operation of Racal Electronics. That year, roughly 20% of Racal Telecommunications shares were floated publicly. The company held a 56% share of the U.K.'s mobile telecommunications market by 1990.

Racal Electronics spun off Racal Telecommunications as Vodafone Group Ltd. in 1991. Vodafone used the Global System for Mobile Communications, a digital system that permitted calls between member countries, for its EuroDigital network, which allowed subscribers to make calls throughout Europe and Scandinavia. The following year, Vodafone launched Safelink, a service offered in

The Business

Financials

Revenue (1999): $5.41 billion

Employees (1999): 12,642

SICs / NAICS

sic 4812 - Radiotelephone Communications

sic 4899 - Communications Services Nec

naics 513322 - Cellular and Other Wireless
    Telecommunications

naics 513321 - Paging

conjunction with local police departments to grant subscribers access to the police; Callsafe, which allowed stranded drivers to phone for assistance; and Recall, the largest voice messaging service in the world.

After competitor Mercury Communications launched its One-2-One personal communications network in London in 1993, Vodafone began offering new services such as Low Call, which lowered rental costs while increasing call fees, and MetroDigital, which provided lower rates for users calling from a limited "home cell" area. Vodafone also began developing digital technology, which was rapidly replacing the traditional analog systems. Also, the company provided emergency mobile phone services to rescue workers in the aftermath of the Braer tanker wreck in the Shetland Islands, and Vodafone International secured a license to operate Australia's third mobile phone network.

In 1994, the company acquired 10% of Globalstar, an international cartel with the goal of developing a satellite-based network allowing mobile telecommunications to take place worldwide by the end of the century. Vodafone paid $52.2 million in 1996 for the 66% of Talkland International's General Mobile Corporate Ltd. that it didn't already own. That year, Sir Gerald Whent retired as CEO; he was replaced by Chris Gent.

Vodafone reached the four million worldwide subscriber mark in 1997. Overseas customers made up 28% of the firm's customer base. As part of a new corporate identity program launched that year, the firm announced that all Vodafone products would bear the Vodafone brand name. Vodafone also acquired the

80% of Astec Communications Ltd. that it didn't already own. In 1998, Sir Ernest Harrison was succeeded by Lord Ian MacLaurin as chairman. The firm sold its French operations to Investel; acquired a 30% stake in Misrfone, based in Egypt; and paid $375 million for BellSouth New Zealand.

Vodafone challenged Bell Atlantic's $45 billion bid for AirTouch in early 1999 with a $60 billion bid of its own. AirTouch eventually accepted the larger bid, and the deal was completed in mid-1999.

History of AirTouch

PacTel Corp. was established as a subsidiary of Pacific Telesis Group in 1984. It founded PacTel Cellular to provide telecommunications services to the Los Angeles Olympic Games. Within a year, PacTel Cellular served 15,000 cellular telephone service subscribers in southern California. In 1986, Pacific Telesis Group acquired Communications Industries, which was reorganized to form PacTel Paging. The following year, PacTel opened an international subsidiary offering regional paging services in Bangkok, Thailand.

In 1991, PacTel began regional marketing of pagers, reaching nontraditional users of wireless telecommunications by opening retail outlets, and formed a joint venture to provide international long-distance communications service to Japan. That same year, Pacific Telesis Group formed PacTel Teletrac to provide tracking services on stolen vehicles for commercial automobile and truck fleets.

In a move designed to take advantage of changes in telecommunications regulations, PacTel Cellular announced its intention in 1992 to spin off from PacTel Corp. to form an independent company called AirTouch Communications. AirTouch pioneered the use of Code Division Multiple Access (CDMA) digital cellular technology, which increased the company's call-handling capacity by 2,000%. The firm invested $50 million to install CDMA technology in California and Georgia, and patented its microcell transceiver, which improved cellular service in obstructed areas, including major cities.

AirTouch's initial public offering in 1993 raised $1.38 billion, the third largest IPO in American corporate history. (Pacific Telesis retained an 88% interest in the company.) In 1994, the spin-off of AirTouch from Pacific Telesis was completed. AirTouch formed a joint venture with Belgacom, the Belgian state telecommunications company, to provide mobile communications services. It also acquired a nationwide two-way radio frequency paging license at a Federal Communications Commission auction, gaining access to new paging systems and services. That year, the firm introduced AirTouch One Number Service, enabling customers to consolidate multiple numbers, and Display Messaging, equipping cellular phones to accept messages while in use. AirTouch also formed a joint cellular venture with U S West and diversified into personal communications services (PCS) by establishing PrimeCo, a PCS joint venture with Bell Atlantic Corp., NYNEX, and U S West.

In 1995, AirTouch announced its intention to invest $275 million in Globalstar, a satellite-based mobile telephone system scheduled to begin operation in 1998. The company also divested PacTel Teletrac and launched cellular operations in Italy and Spain via its new AirTel subsidiary. By the following year, the company had expanded operations into Brazil, the Czech Republic, Poland, and Taiwan, and international sales accounted for 25% of the corporate total. U S West Cellular adopted the AirTouch brand name in anticipation of a planned merger of the two companies, which was called off in 1997 after Congress voted to eliminate the "Morris Trust" tax exemption on large corporate transactions. In 1996, AirTouch also acquired the outstanding interest in Cellular Communications Inc.; forged informal ties with Vodafone of the United Kingdom to increase penetration of European cellular telecommunications markets; and began offering paging services in New York City.

Targets of a 1997 class action price-fixing lawsuit in Southern California, both AirTouch and L.A. Cellular agreed to a $165 million settlement. In 1998, AirTouch and MediaOne (formerly U S West Media) rekindled their merger plans. AirTouch paid $5.9 billion for the New Vector cellular operations of MediaOne, including its stake in PrimeCo, to become the second-largest wireless service provider in the U.S. Late in the year, Bell Atlantic bid $45 billion for AirTouch; Vodafone topped the offer with a $60 billion bid in early 1999, to which AirTouch agreed.

Market Forces Driving the Merger

Many Wall Street analysts expressed surprise that a relatively unknown British firm was able to wrest AirTouch from the altar of its marriage with Bell Atlantic. According to an April 1999 article in *Europe*, however, Vodafone was better positioned for a major coup than most U.S. telecommunications firms, particularly in the worldwide cellular arena. "Vodafone's success springs from the fact that Europe, and to a lesser extent Asia, are ahead of the United States in wireless telecommunications." This is mainly because European cellular technology revolves around the digital standard, GSM, while the U.S. market is fragmented by companies using a variety of cellular technologies. As a result, cellular phone use grew by 10% in Europe in 1998, compared to only 5% in the U.S.

The Officers

Chairman: Sam Ginn

Deputy Chairman: Lord Ian MacLaurin

CEO: Christopher C. Gent

Managing Director, Vodafone UK: Peter R. Bamford

Managing Director, Vodafone Retail Holdings: Ian Gray

In 1998, consolidation in the U.S. telecommunications market had reached a feverish pitch: AT&T bought cable giant Tele-Communications Inc., WorldCom Inc. and MCI Communications completed their union, and Bell Atlantic inked a $70 billion agreement to take over GTE Corp. Cellular telecommunications remained one of the major untapped markets. According to technology research firm Yankee Group, the number of worldwide cellular phone users was expected to triple by 2005. While many regional U.S. players had secured chunks of market share in the late 1990s, most analysts predicted that the larger mobile telephony firms would be better poised to capitalize on this explosive growth.

The reason for this was fairly straightforward: industry competition heated up significantly in 1997, which forced companies like AirTouch to lower rates. In fact, according a February 1998 *Forbes* article, AirTouch's average monthly bill dropped 38% between 1992 and 1997. To improve earnings in the face of perpetually declining rates, companies needed to secure new customers quickly; major mergers afforded easy access to new subscriber bases.

AirTouch made its first major move in 1998 by acquiring the New Vector cellular operations of MediaOne, which allowed the firm to shore up its position in the U.S. wireless market by nearly doubling its existing base of 3.9 million customers and increasing its reach to 17 states. Bell Atlantic's $60 billion bid in late 1998 for AirTouch was designed to "create a seamless American mobile-telephone venture that could have offered customers a nationwide mobile-telephone network," wrote *South China Morning Post*. The deal would have allowed AirTouch to become even more competitive within the U.S. However, a merger with Vodafone would, according to CEO Sam Ginn, allow AirTouch to grow into "an international wireless company and position ourselves as the strongest in the world."

Approach and Engagement

Bell Atlantic bid $45 billion for AirTouch in late 1998. Vodafone topped the offer with a $60 billion,

The Players

CEO of Vodafone Airtouch PLC: Christopher Gent. Chris Gent joined the board of Vodafone in 1985 at the age of 50. He worked as managing director of Vodafone Ltd., the U.K. network operator of Vodafone Group, until his appointment as CEO in January of 1997. Almost immediately, Gent launched a restructuring at Vodafone that included opening retail stores, increasing advertising, and tightening up distribution operations. Within two years, Vodafone customers had more than doubled, from 4.2 million to 9.1 million. After the firm's takeover of AirTouch, Gent took the helm of Vodafone AirTouch.

Chairman of Vodafone AirTouch PLC: Sam Ginn. In 1994, Pacific Telesis CEO Sam Ginn became chairman and CEO of AirTouch, which was formed when Pacific Telesis spun off its cellular phone and paging operations, known as PacTel Cellular, into an independent company. Ginn oversaw his firm's acquisition of the New Vector cellular operations of MediaOne (formerly U.S. West Media) in 1998 and accepted the post of non-executive chairman after Vodafone's takeover of AirTouch.

roughly $97 per share, in early 1999, and AirTouch accepted the offer, which reflected a $19 per share premium. As reported in a February 1999 *Forbes* article, the CEOs of each firm negotiated their deal over the New Year's holiday via cell phones. AirTouch CEO Sam Ginn was vacationing in Hawaii, while Vodafone CEO Chris Gent was relaxing in Australia.

According to the terms of the agreement, AirTouch CEO Ginn would become non-executive chairman, while Vodafone CEO Gent would take the helm of the new firm, to be called Vodafone AirTouch. Vodafone paid AirTouch shareholders .5 of a Vodafone AirTouch ADS, which is equal to the value of five Vodafone AirTouch common shares, and $9 in cash for each common AirTouch share held. (If the deal had fallen apart, AirTouch would have been required to pay Vodafone a $1 billion termination fee.) Headquarters remained at Vodafone's main office in Newbury, England. U.S. and Asia-Pacific operations continued to be run from AirTouch's San Francisco base.

Products and Services

As the largest cellular phone operator in the U.K., with roughly four million subscribers, Vodafone secured roughly 72% of its 1998 sales from U.K. businesses. However, the firm also operated in Australia, Egypt, Fiji, France, Germany, Greece Malta, the Netherlands, New Zealand, South Africa, Sweden, and Uganda. Along with cellular phone services, Vodafone offered messaging services via its Vodafone Connect unit, paging services by way of its Vodafone Paging unit, and mobile data services by way of its Vodafone Value Added and Data Services unit. The firm also operated retails outlets throughout the U.K.

In 1999, AirTouch offered cellular telephone services, paging, and personal communications services (PCS) in the United States and 12 other countries. AirTouch Cellular included Cellular Communications Inc. and CMT Partners, a 50-50 joint venture with AT&T Wireless. Internationally, AirTouch owned minority stakes in the following cellular operations: Spain's Airtel Movil, Belgacom Mobile, Cellular Communications India Ltd., Central Japan Digital Phone Co., Japan's Digital TU-KA, Sweden's Europolitan, Japan's Kansai Digital Phone Co., Germany's Mannesmann Mobilfunk GmbH, Romania's MobilFon, Omnitel-Pronto Italia, Poland's Polkomtel, India's RPG Cellcom Ltd., South Korea's Shinsegi Telecommunications, Portugal's Telecel, and Tokyo Digital Phone Co.

Upon completion of its 1998 merger with the cellular holdings of MediaOne, AirTouch's stake in PrimeCo Personal Communications, LP had jumped from 25% to 50%. AirTouch also owned six percent of the Globalstar satellite-based network service; 10% of International Digital Communications, a long-distance provider; 49% of Northstar Paging Holdings Ltd., based in Canada; 18% of Sistelcom-Telemensaje SA, a paging equipment and services provider based in Spain; and 51% of Telechamada-Servico de Chamada de Pessoas SA, a paging equipment and services provider based in Portugal.

Review of the Outcome and Changes to the Industry

The announcement of the deal in early 1999 sent telecommunications stock soaring. The new firm is the first cellular operation ever to reach nearly all of Europe, several large U.S. markets, and major Asian markets. As a result, cellular operators in both Europe and the U.S., including AT&T, have announced their intent to position themselves as global cellular communications players.

The mammoth merger received mixed reviews from industry analysts. Some saw the link up of

Vodafone and AirTouch as a necessary step in the quest for the development of a standard global cellular technology, with Vodafone AirTouch positioned as the worldwide cellular leader. Others predicted that Vodafone AirTouch, which wouldn't be profitable for at least three years following the costly deal, faced grave technological and operational obstacles in the integration of their operations.

Research

"AirTouch Communications Inc.," in *Notable Corporate Chronologies*, The Gale Group, 1999. Covers major historical milestones in the history of AirTouch Communications.

Barnard, Bruce. "Vodafone-AirTouch: Europe's Largest Transatlantic Takeover," in *Europe*, April 1999. Offers a detailed look at the industry conditions that allowed Vodafone to launch a successful bid for AirTouch.

Goldsmith, Charles. "Vodafone Reflects Its Dashing, Daring CEO," in *The Wall Street Journal*, 7 January 1999. Discusses how Chris Gent transformed Vodafone prior to its bid for AirTouch.

Guyon, Janet. "Dial 'T' for Trouble," in *Forbes*, 15 February 1999. Describes potential problems with the Vodafone/AirTouch merger.

"Vodafone Deal Threatens to Tear Fabric of Alliances," in *South China Morning Post*, 18 January 1999. Explains how the merger of AirTouch and Vodafone will impact the worldwide mobile telecommunications industry.

"Vodafone Group PLC," in *Notable Corporate Chronologies*, The Gale Group, 1999. Covers major historical milestones in the history of Vodafone Group PLC.

Vodafone AirTouch PLC Home Page, available at http://www.vodafone-airtouch-plc.com. Official World Wide Web Home Page for Vodafone AirTouch PLC. Includes current and archived press releases and historical information, as well as news, product, and employment information.

"Vodafone Merger with AirTouch," in *Business Wire*, 22 April 1999. Details the terms of the agreement between Vodafone and AirTouch.

ANNAMARIE L. SHELDON

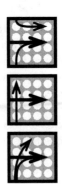

VOLKSWAGEN & ROLLS-ROYCE

Volkswagen AG
Brieffach 1848-2
Wolfsburg, D-38436
Germany

tel: 49 5361 90
fax: 49 5361 928282
web: http://www.vw-online.de

nationality: Germany
date: July 3, 1998
affected: Volkswagen AG, Germany, founded 1938
affected: Rolls-Royce Motor Cars Ltd., England, founded 1906

Overview of the Acquisition

Volkswagen jumped into the luxury car market by beating out BMW in the bidding for Rolls-Royce Motors in 1998. Yet a strange twist to the acquisition left the valuable Rolls-Royce marque in the hands of BMW, not Volkswagen, since Rolls-Royce PLC, the parent of Rolls-Royce Motors and owner of the Rolls-Royce name and logo, preferred to see those assets in the possession of a fellow luxury car maker than a manufacturer of economy class cars. BMW extended a license permitting Volkswagen to use the Rolls-Royce name until January 1, 2003, when it would revert to BMW's exclusive use. Volkswagen would retain all other components of the Rolls-Royce acquisition—the Bentley luxury brand name and the manufacturing facility in Crewe, England.

History of Volkswagen AG

In January 1934, Ferdinand Porsche, an engineer and automobile designer, sent a design for a "people's car," the Volkswagen, to the new German Reich government. Porsche received approval and an investment from the government to develop a prototype for the car within 10 months. Technical difficulties resulted in a 12-month delay, but the first prototype was finally unveiled in October 1935. The introduction of this car had a two-pronged purpose: to develop the German automotive industry and to enable more people to purchase cars, as only one in 49 Germans in 1936 were car owners.

The government granted its approval for the prototypes in 1937, and Porsche secured financial backing from Adolf Hitler. The GEZUVOR (Gesellschaft zur Vorbereitung des Volkswagens), or The Company for the Development of People's Cars, was formed in May 1938, and construction began on a factory. The first Volkswagen rolled off the line in July 1938, and was dubbed the "Beetle" by *The New York Times*. In September 1938 the company was renamed Volkswagenwerk GmbH.

World War II halted production of Volkswagens in favor of military armament. By the end of 1939, the company had lost five million Reichsmark. Although the company's focus remained on military needs for the duration of the war, the first series production of Volkswagen began in 1941. Two years later, more than 26,000 Volkswagens were produced.

In 1944, although bombings had destroyed two-thirds of the factory's buildings, the company produced nearly 21,000 Volkswagens. The Allies took control of the German company at the end of World War II. With little interest in restoring the facilities and in production of the Volkswagen itself, the British relinquished control of the company's factory in Wolfsburg. In September 1945, the British military placed an order for 20,000 Volkswagens.

The first civilian Beetles were produced in 1946, but they were still not available to the general public. Instead they were earmarked only for reparation to the Allies and for such German institutions as the Post Office and the Red Cross. In October of that year, the 10,000th Beetle since the end of the war was produced.

Volkswagen began exporting the car in 1947 by establishing a dealership in The Netherlands. That year the British began searching for a German to whom they could hand over the company. In 1948 they selected Heinz Nordhoff, a former employee of Adam Opel Co., which was owned by General Motors. Nordhoff applied managerial strategies to transform Volkswagen into a largely profitable operation. He established a sales and service network, both domestically and internationally. By mid-year, the 25,000th Volkswagen was produced, and by the end of the year operations had expanded into Denmark, Luxembourg, Sweden, Belgium, and Switzerland. Exports accounted for 23% of company sales, and Volkswagen's market share in Germany reached 63.5%.

In 1949, Volkswagen's Wolfsburg factory was turned over by the Allies to the German government. That year the first Beetle was shipped to the U.S., but was met with reserve and distrust. The four-seater VW Convertible was introduced in 1949, and would prove to be the world's most popular and longest produced convertible. The 100,000th Volkswagen was produced in March 1950. That year the company also unveiled the VW Transporter, a new type of commercial vehicle that was also available as a minibus.

By 1951, Volkswagen was exporting to 29 countries. The next year the company developed the synchromesh gearbox, which eliminated the need to double de-clutch for a smooth, silent gear change. The company formed the Volkswagen Canada Ltd. subsidiary in Toronto.

In 1953, the Beetle underwent its first significant visual modification in 20 years when the split rear

The Business

Financials

Revenue (1998): $80.5 billion

Employees (1998): 298,000

SICs / NAICS

sic 3711 - Motor Vehicles & Car Bodies

naics 336111 - Automobile Manufacturing

window was replaced with a solid glass component. In October 1954, the 100,000th Transporter was produced, and construction of a separate Transporter factory began. The next year the one-millionth Volkswagen came down the production line. As U.S. sales quadrupled to 35,800 vehicles, the U.S. became Volkswagen's most important export market, and the Volkswagen of America distribution unit was established.

The two-seater VW Karmann Ghia Cabriolet was presented at the Frankfurt International Motor Show in 1957. Volkswagen finally began to overcome its image associated with the Nazis when Doyle Dane Bernbach took over the company's advertising promotions in 1959, introducing such slogans as "Think Small" and "Ugly Is Only Skin-Deep."

The company was partially privatized in 1960 when 60% of its stock was sold to the public, with the remaining 40% divided between the federal government and the government of Lower Saxony. Two years later the VW Variant was introduced. Also in 1962 the one-millionth Transporter was produced and the U.S. imported its one-millionth Volkswagen. In 1964, the company acquired a stake in Auto-Union GmbH from Daimler Benz AG, later acquiring full control of the company in 1966.

The 10 millionth Volkswagen since the end of World War II was produced in 1965. That year Auto Union introduced the Audi. In 1969, Auto Union GmbH merged with NSU Motorenwerke AG to form Audi NSU Auto Union AG. Initially Volkswagen held a 59.5% interest in the new company, but would eventually increase its stake to 99%.

In 1970, Volkswagen acquired Selbstfahrer-Union, the largest car rental company, and later renamed it interRent. Two years later, with production of the 15,007,034th unit, the Beetle surpassed Ford's Model T as the most produced car in history.

The Officers

Chairman and CEO: Ferdinand Piech

Manager, Controlling and Accounting: Bruno Adelt

Manager, Sales and Marketing: Robert Buechelhofer

Manager, Human Resources: Peter Hartz

Manager, Group Strategy, Treasury, Legal Matters, and
Organization: Jens Neumann

The 1973 introduction of the Passat marked the first of the new model generation geared toward the custom-production of Volkswagen automobiles. By 1974 the public regarded the Beetle as outdated, and Volkswagen discontinued its production at Wolfsburg, limiting its European production to plants at Emden and Brussels. The Beetle was succeeded by the Golf, which heralded the introduction of the compact class of car. Volkswagen also introduced the Scirocco, a sports coupe with a large tailgate and transverse engine. In January 1975, the Golf was unveiled in the U.S. as the Rabbit.

In 1976, after only 31 months of production, the one-millionth Golf was produced. Two years later, European production of the Beetle ceased, and was limited to production in Mexico only. In 1979, Volkswagen acquired a stake in Chrysler Motors do Brasil, later known as Volkswagen Caminhoes Ltda. Sao Paulo, as well as a majority interest in Triumph-Adler AG.

During the late 1970s and early 1980s Volkswagen was adversely affected by diminishing sales, rising labor costs, increasing competition from the Japanese automakers, and the end of fixed exchange rates. In 1981, Volkswagen's U.S. workforce was cut from 10,000 to 6,000 and a plant in Michigan was sold to Chrysler.

The Volkswagen Polo Coupe and the Volkswagen Caddy, a pick-up truck, were introduced in 1982. By the end of that year Volkswagen was the world's largest manufacturer of diesel-engined vehicles. In 1984, the new Volkswagen Jetta was introduced, equipped with a 132 kW water-cooled engine with supercharger. the company changed its name to Volkswagen AG in 1985, the same year that its sales rose 25% and it earned the rank as the leading European automaker.

In 1986, Volkswagen acquired a 51% interest in the Spanish car manufacturer Sociadad Espanola de Automoviles de Turismo, S.A. (SEAT). It also exchanged its interest in Triumph Adler for a five-per-cent share of the voting capital in Ing. C. Olivetti C. Sp.A. In 1989, the first VW Taro was released, the product of a two-year old joint venture with Toyota. Volkswagen acquired Skoda, a Czech automaker, from the Czech government the following year.

Volkswagen underwent a restructuring in 1991 that separated central management from the respective management of Volkswagen, Audi, and Skoda. That year Volkswagen and Ford entered a joint venture to produce a multi-purpose vehicle in Setubal, Portugal. Ferdinand Piech took the reins of Volkswagen in 1993, after the company reported a loss of over $1 billion. He cut costs and revitalized the Seat and Skoda brands.

Volkswagen shares slumped in 1994 after a German prosecutor investigating industry espionage brought charges against company production chief J. Ignacio Lopez de Arriortua, a former purchasing manager at General Motors, after the discovery of GM information at Volkswagen's headquarters and in the homes of Volkswagen executives.

In 1995, Audi announced a venture with Chinese auto maker First Automobile Works to produce a model of the Audi-100. That year European Union officials investigated Volkswagen and its Italian car dealerships for possible antitrust violations. The EU claimed that it had received many complaints that Volkswagen's Italian dealerships refused to sell cars to non-Italian EU citizens who wanted to take advantage of the devaluation of the lira.

Volkswagen began increasing its presence in the luxury car market in 1998. It purchased Rolls-Royce Motor Cars and the Cosworth engine manufacturer from Vickers PLC, with the agreement to relinquish use of the Rolls-Royce brand name and logo to rival bidder BMW beginning in 2003. Also in 1998 Volkswagen purchased two Italian luxury car manufacturers, Bugatti and Lamborghini Automobil. That year it unveiled the New Beetle, the Rolls-Royce Silver Seraph, the Bentley Arnage, and the Bentley Continental SC.

In mid-1998, Volkswagen finally folded under pressure to establish a fund to compensate the 15,000 slave laborers that it employed during World War II; Volkswagen had resisted doing so because it claimed that the German government had the sole responsibility for such compensation.

History of Rolls-Royce Motor Cars Ltd.

Frederick Henry Royce, an engineer, established the electric crane manufacturer Royce Ltd. in Manchester, England, in 1884. In 1904, he purchased a two-cylinder car, a French Decauville. Dissatisfied with its performance, Royce built his own model in April of that year. His two-cylinder, 10-horsepower cars were characterized by their silent and vibration-free ride.

Royce's automobiles came to the attention of Charles Steward Rolls, an automobile dealer and engineer. The two men entered into an informal partnership to produce cars equipped with more than two cylinders. They soon released four-cylinder, 20-horsepower automobiles that won several important races. These custom-built cars soon became popular luxury items for an increasingly exclusive clientele.

The partners formalized their alliance by establishing Rolls-Royce Ltd. in March 1906. The company's first product made its debut at the Paris Motor Show later that year. The six-cylinder car was nicknamed the "Silver Ghost" due to its metallic appearance and the ghostlike silence of its engine.

Rolls-Royce ventured into the manufacture of small aircraft engines in 1907. Three years later, Charles Rolls was killed in an airplane crash. As a symbol of mourning, the company's intertwined "RR" logo was changed from red to black. The distinctive arched top radiator on Rolls-Royce cars was further enhanced by the introduction of the "Spirit of Ecstasy" statuette on the 1911 Silver Ghost. The electric starter was incorporated into the company's cars beginning in 1919. Rolls-Royce continued to serve the aeronautics industry, and during World War I supplied half of Britain's total aircraft engine output.

Having been released in more than 6,000 models, the Silver Ghost went out of production in 1925. It was replaced by the Phantom, which was later equipped with a 12-cylinder engine. In 1931, Rolls-Royce acquired Bentley Motor Ltd., an English manufacturer of high-performance automobiles. Two years later, Henry Royce died after a long illness.

Rolls-Royce ceased production of automobiles during World War II, focusing instead on that of aircraft engines. By war's end more than 150,000 of its Merlin engines had been used to power the Supermarine Spitfire and Hawker Hurricane, the primary fighters of the Royal Air Force. The company expanded into commercial aircraft with its introduction of the industry's first turboprop engine. During the 1950s, it modified its Avon jet engine for commercial use, and unveiled the Conway, specifically designed for the American Douglas DC-8 and the Boeing 707.

Although its aircraft division had traditionally accounted for about 80% of total company revenues, Rolls-Royce intended to increase that proportion by entering into the U.S. aircraft engine market. In 1966,

The Players

Volkswagen AG Chairman and CEO: Ferdinand Piech. Ferdinand Piech was the grandson of Volkswagen's founder, Ferdinand Porsche. Following his family's tradition in automobiles, Piech joined Audi in 1972 after earning an education in engineering. He succeeded through various executive positions at Volkswagen before becoming its chairman in 1993. To address the company's problems with high costs and inefficient plants, he implemented streamlining efforts and steered the release of new models of Golf, Audi, and the Beetle. Under his leadership, Volkswagen's revenues jumped from $44 billion in 1994 to $62.7 billion in 1997. In the late 1990s, Piech directed the company into new markets by orchestrating the purchase of the luxury car manufacturers Rolls-Royce, Lamborghini, and Bugatti.

it unveiled the RB211 engine. In order to beat out General Electric in supplying an order of 555 engines to Lockheed Corp., Rolls-Royce severely undercut the price of the RB211s, necessitating a transfer of funds from its automotive division to cover production expenses in its aircraft division.

Several design flaws first became apparent when construction of the RB211 commenced in the summer of 1969. Production was delayed to correct these problems, and the company was forced to pay penalties to its awaiting customers. In November 1970, the British government extended a GBP 60 million loan to Rolls-Royce to cover anticipated losses on the RB211 project as well as overall operating expenses. That same year, the government nationalized Rolls-Royce.

Britain continued to meet Rolls-Royce's financial obligations and oversee its reorganization. Once completed, the government decided to restore privatization to the company's automotive division, which was considered a source of national pride as a symbol of prosperity and luxury. In 1973, Rolls-Royce Motors Ltd. was created as a private company, while the aircraft engine division remained under government control.

The new company launched a modernization program that included a GBP 20 million investment in new plants and equipment. It also increased its annual output to 3,500 cars, up from 2,000. Despite these improvements, Rolls-Royce fell victim to a diminished demand for automobiles due to high interest rates in 1979. Once again, it approached bankruptcy. In

September 1980, Vickers PLC, a British engineering firm and defense contractor, acquired 90% of Rolls-Royce's stock, making it a subsidiary.

Britain's economic recession continued, however, and Rolls-Royce's production in 1983 was nearly half, about 1,500, of its 1980 level. As a result, the company laid off 1,000 employees and lowered the price of its automobiles.

Rolls-Royce faced disaster again in 1991, when an economic recession hit all of its major markets simultaneously. Moreover, the U.S., its leading market, instituted a luxury tax that depressed demand for Rolls-Royce products. The number of cars the company sold that year plummeted to 1,700 from 3,300 in 1990. In response, the company reorganized, slashing its workforce from 5,700 to 2,300. It also streamlined its assembly process to turn out its custom-built cars in 30 days, down from 61. Despite these improvements, Rolls-Royce lost a total of $150 million in 1991 and 1992.

In 1993, Rolls-Royce showed a modest profit, but still could not afford to introduce sorely needed new models. Vickers admitted that Rolls-Royce would require a partner in order to develop any new cars, and officials stated that the company might be for sale at the right price. In December 1994, it entered into an alliance whereby Bayerische Motoren Werke AG (BMW) would supply the V-8 and V-12 engines for Rolls-Royce's next generation of cars, thereby relieving the British company of the expense of designing new engines.

Rolls-Royce continued its streamlining in 1997, when, for the first time in its history, it implemented automated assembly systems for certain processes. This innovation, while applicable to only one percent of its total manufacturing process, shaved production down to 17.5 days.

Pressure from competition and continued financial difficulties led Vickers to put Rolls-Royce Motor Cars up for sale in October 1997. In March 1998, BMW and Volkswagen vied for ownership of the company, with Volkswagen emerging as the winner in July. In a strange twist, however, BMW secured the right to the Rolls-Royce name and logo, and beginning in 2003 Volkswagen would be left with only the Bentley name and the Crewe manufacturing facilities.

Market Forces Driving the Acquisition

Rolls-Royce Motor Cars had only begun to emerge from the financial crisis that left it verging on bankruptcy in 1991. That year's economic recession crippled the sale of luxury cars, and Rolls-Royce found it necessary to retrench in order to stay afloat. It slashed its workforce by 60%, introduced automated

assembly for the first time, and contracted BMW to supply it with new engines. These changes, however, provided Rolls-Royce with the funds only to invest in refurbishing its equipment and plants, not to design new cars. For that, company officials stated, Rolls-Royce would need a partner or a new owner. In October 1997, Vickers PLC put the British luxury car maker up for sale.

Meanwhile, Volkswagen AG sought to offer brands in virtually all automobile classes with a goal of ultimately usurping Toyota Motor Company as the world's third-leading car manufacturer. To do this, CEO Ferdinand Piech intended to acquire Sweden-based Scania, which would add heavy trucks to its offerings. More importantly, he wanted to plunge Volkswagen into the luxury car market, a wide departure from the economy market that the company had been founded to offer. Rolls-Royce Motor Cars produced automobiles under such luxury brands as Rolls-Royce and Bentley. When that company's owner put Rolls-Royce up for sale, Volkswagen seized the opportunity to acquire these two leading luxury car brand names.

Approach and Engagement

In March 1998, BMW decided to complete its alliance with Rolls-Royce by offering to purchase the company for GBP 340 million. Vickers PLC, the owner of Rolls-Royce Motor Cars, supported the offer and advised its shareholders to accept it.

In early May, however, Volkswagen launched an unsolicited bid of GBP 430 million for the company. On May 7 Vickers reversed its decision to support BMW's offer and opted for the higher bid. Rolls-Royce PLC, the aeronautical engines maker that had once been joined with Rolls-Royce Motor Cars, owned the rights to the Rolls-Royce name. This company was displeased with Vickers' support of the Volkswagen bid. It wanted the Rolls-Royce marque to go to BMW, but announced that it would defer to the wishes of Vickers' shareholders.

BMW, however, did not shoulder its disappointment so bravely. The German company announced that it would terminate its agreement to supply engines to Rolls-Royce if it lost in the bidding for the company. To lessen the impact of this threat as a potential dealbreaker, Volkswagen revised its offer on June 4. It agreed to purchase the Cosworth high-performance engine manufacturer from Vickers for GBP 120 million once its acquisition of Rolls-Royce was completed.

Volkswagen's sweetened offer of GBP 479 million, which reflected a slight increase in the value of Rolls-Royce's assets since the initial round of bidding, was approved in June and completed on July 3, 1998. The deal was not finalized on that date, however, as Rolls-Royce PLC still retained ownership of the Rolls-Royce name and logo.

On July 28, BMW, Volkswagen, and Rolls-Royce shocked the industry by announcing an agreement that settled the matter. Under its terms, BMW paid GBP 40 million to Rolls-Royce PLC for the rights to the Rolls-Royce brand and logo. In turn, it would grant Volkswagen a license to use the brand through the end of 2002. As of January 1, 2003, BMW would become the exclusive producer of the Rolls-Royce, and Volkswagen would retain only the Bentley name, the Cosworth subsidiary, and the Crewe manufacturing facility, where both Rolls-Royce and Bentley were produced.

Products and Services

After the acquisition of Rolls-Royce Motor Cars, Volkswagen unveiled the Silver Seraph, the first new Rolls-Royce model in nearly two decades. Aside from its other primary luxury marque, Bentley, Volkswagen offered cars branded as Lupo, Polo, Golf, New Beetle, Bora, Passat, and Sharan.

Review of the Outcome

Immediately after acquiring Rolls-Royce, Volkswagen moved to strengthen its newly established luxury car operations by purchasing Lamborghini Automobil, an Italian company that manufactured about 200 automobiles per year, as well as Bugatti, another Italian luxury car maker. Volkswagen also entered into a joint venture with Porsche to produce luxury sport utility vehicles beginning in 2002.

In October 1998, Volkswagen invested GBP 500 million to upgrade the Crewe factory in anticipation of accelerating production of Bentleys from 1,400 to 9,000 within five years. It also planned to introduce new models, including the Bentley Hunaudieres and the Silver Seraph, the first new Rolls-Royce model in nearly two decades.

Sales of Rolls-Royce and Bentley cars increased a total of 13.2% for the first six months of 1999. Sales rose 84.7% in North America alone, a performance accredited by the company to a new advertising campaign and to a reorganization that included the transfer of Rolls-Royce's U.S. headquarters from New Jersey to Detroit.

Research

Andrews, Edmund L. "A Volkswagen with Class; German Car Maker is Going Upscale," in *The New York Times*, 17 July 1998. Describes the company's growth under Ferdinand Piech, and his direction for the future of Volkswagen in luxury cars.

Fisher, Andrew, and Graham Bowley. "VW in GBP 430m Bid for R-R Motors," in *Financial Times (London)*, 8 May 1998. Reports Volkswagen's unsolicited bid.

Kurylko, Diana T. "Heights of Success: Rolls-Royce Needs a Boost from a Partner to Regain the Pinnacle of High Technology," in *Automotive News*, 18 July 1994. Describes Rolls-Royce's turnaround efforts since 1991, as well as the unlikelihood of a full recovery as an independent company.

Rolls-Royce & Bentley Motor Cars Limited Home Page, available at http://www.rolls-royceandbentley.co.uk/home.html. Official World Wide Web Page for Rolls-Royce & Bentley. Includes worldwide office locations and company press releases.

"Rolls-Royce Motors Ltd.," in *International Directory of Company Histories*, Vol. I, St. James Press: 1988. Provides a historical review of the company.

"The Silver Lady is Captivated by BMW's Charms," in *Financial Times (London)*, 29 July 1998. Details the agreement that granted the Rolls-Royce brand to BMW.

"Volkswagen AG," in *Notable Corporate Chronologies*, The Gale Group, 1999. Describes the history of Volkswagen.

Volkswagen AG 1997 Annual Report. Presents detailed financial and operating information.

DAVIS MCMILLAN

VON'S GROCERY & SHOPPING BAG FOOD STORES

Safeway Inc.
5918 Stoneridge Mall Rd.
Pleasanton, CA 94588
USA

tel: (925)467-3000
web: http://www.safeway.com

nationality: USA
date: March 28, 1960
affected: The Von's Companies, Inc., USA, founded 1906
affected: Shopping Bag Food Stores, USA

Overview of the Merger

The merger of Von's Grocery Co. with Shopping Bag Food Stores resulted in a landmark U.S. Supreme Court decision six years later. Expanding on several other rulings, the *Von's Grocery* decision found illegal any horizontal merger in a given market that is becoming increasingly concentrated. Based on those standards, it found the Von's/Shopping Bag union illegal, even though the combined company held only a 7.5% share of the Los Angeles grocery retail market, and ordered Von's to divest itself of the Shopping Bag stores.

History of Von's Grocery Co.

With start-up capital of $1,200, entrepreneur Charles T. Von der Ahe opened Von's Groceteria in Los Angeles, California, in 1906. The small grocery store soon expanded, opening several additional branches over the next few years. Von der Ahe also instilled a number of innovative strategies that fueled dynamic growth. He was the first to offer cash-and-carry and self-service. He also paved the way for the supermarket concept by leasing his open storefronts to produce vendors and butchers. In 1929, Von der Ahe sold his 87 stores to McMarr Stores, narrowly escaping the property value plummet brought on by the stock market crash.

Von der Ahe reentered the grocery business three years later by forming a partnership with his sons, Ted and Wil. They established a new chain of stores in the Los Angeles area, and in 1948 opened a 50,300-sq.-ft. unit, a prototype of the modern supermarket. By 1958 the Von's Grocery Co. operated 28 stores and was the third-largest retailer in the Los Angeles area.

In 1960, Von's merged with Shopping Bag Food Stores, the fifth-largest grocer in the area. The U.S. Justice Department challenged the merger on antitrust grounds that same year, and in 1966 the U.S. Supreme Court ordered the immediate divestiture of the Safeway stores.

Von's was purchased by the Household Finance Corp., later known as Household International, in 1969, and was incorporated into the company's Household Merchandising division. The grocery chain flourished under its new parent, expanding into the San Diego and Fresno areas during the 1970s and 1980s. It also diversified into wholesale marketing and fast-food chains. In the mid-1970s it established Value Centers, a food-and-drug retailer that evolved into the Pavilions chain in 1987.

Von's was designated the official supermarket of the Los Angeles Olympics in 1984. In return for the provision and preparation of food for 12,000 athletes, coaches, and trainers, Von's received exclusive merchandising and advertising rights.

Management of the Household Merchandising unit completed a $757 million leveraged buyout of the division in early 1986. The deal, which was the largest retail buyout in the U.S. at that time, was orchestrated by Roger E. Strangelove, head of the Von's operations since 1982. He became chairman of the newly independent Von's Companies, and William S. Davila served as its president.

In December 1986, burdened with a heavy debt load from the buyout, Von's entered into a $700 million merger agreement with Allied Supermarkets, Inc. By uniting with the Detroit-area chain, Von's regained its status as a public company, and, after selling its Detroit assets, remained focused in California.

Observing that California's Latino population was growing, Von's opened the first Tianguis store in January 1987. Catering to the specific needs of Latino customers, this store featured bilingual signs and employees, an extensive selection of Mexican imports, and wide aisles to promote more socialization between customers.

In August 1988 Von's acquired 172 of Safeway's southern California stores in exchange for $297 million in cash and 11.67 million shares of common stock. Von's immediately set about refashioning the stores, and by late 1990 had increased the sales per square foot at the former Safeway stores from $447 to $615, well above the $550 industry average. Von's also improved its profitability, recording earnings of $50 million in 1990, up from a $25 million loss the previous year.

The company acquired the 18-unit Williams Brothers Markets for $58 million in January 1992. The next year Von's faced a public relations disaster when three children died from ingesting Jack-in-the-Box hamburgers contaminated with the E. coli bacteria. Von's was the meat processor for the fast-food chain, and one of its suppliers was traced by health authorities to be the source of the contaminated beef. Years of litigation ensued, culminating in a $58.5 million settlement in 1998.

In 1997 Safeway paid $2 billion to purchase the remaining 65% of Von's that it didn't already own,

The Business

Financials

Revenue (1998): $24.5 billion

Employees (1998): 170,000

SICs / NAICS

sic 5411 - Grocery Stores

naics 445110 - Supermarkets and Other Grocery (except Convenience) Stores

making it a wholly owned subsidiary. Von's purchased eight stores from Ralphs Grocery in 1998, and agreed to purchase four Albertson's stores the following year.

Market Forces Driving the Merger

Von's Grocery, a 28-unit chain operating in and around the Los Angeles area, was the area's third-largest grocery retailer based on sales. Fifth-placed Shopping Bag Food Stores operated 38 stores in the same market. By merging, the two companies would form the area's second-largest chain, based on combined sales of $185 million, and capture 7.5% of Los Angeles' retail grocery market.

Approach and Engagement

On January 26, 1960, the boards of Von's and Shopping Bag entered into a merger agreement, which was approved by their shareholders in mid-March. Under its terms, Shopping Bag stock would be exchanged for Von's stock on a share-for-share basis. Charles Von der Ahe, president of Von's, would become chairman of the new company, which would retain the Von's Grocery name. Ted Von der Ahe would serve as its president, and W.R. Hayden, president of Shopping Bag, would become its senior vice president. The existing Shopping Bag stores would retain their name, but any stores opened in the future would bear the Von's name. The merger was completed on March 28, 1960.

Products and Services

Safeway Inc. was one of the largest food and drug retailers in North America based on sales. As of January 2, 1999, it operated 1,497 stores, including 324 Von's stores and 114 Dominick's stores, in the western,

The Officers

Chairman, President, and CEO: Steven A. Burd

Exec. VP: Kenneth W. Oder

Exec. VP and Chief Financial Officer: David G. Weed

Sr. VP, Finance and Control: David F. Bond

Sr. VP and Chief Information Officer: David T. Ching

southwestern, Rocky Mountain, midwestern, and mid-Atlantic regions of the United States. Its Canadian operations were primarily located in western Canada, in the provinces of British Columbia, Alberta, and Manitoba/Saskatchewan. It also held a 49% interest in Casa Ley, S.A. de C.V. Safeway's retail grocery business accounted for 98% of total company sales.

Additionally, Safeway held operations in manufacturing, food processing, and distribution. Since its introduction in 1993, its Safeway SELECT brand name had offered about 900 products. It also offered 2,500 products marketed under the Safeway, Lucerne, and Mrs. Wright's banners.

Changes to the Industry

In late March 1960 the U.S. Department of Justice filed a civil antitrust suit to block the merger, claiming that it would inhibit competition in the market. On June 14 a U.S. district court denied this motion. The case was appealed, and was ultimately heard by the U.S. Supreme Court. In June 1966 the Court upheld the Justice Department's challenge to the Von's/Shopping Bag merger. The landmark case expanded the *Brown Shoe*, *Philadelphia National Bank*, and *Alcoa-Rome* decisions defining the standards for determining the illegality of horizontal mergers in a given product and geographic market.

In *Brown Shoe*, the Court decided in 1962 that a horizontal merger could be anticompetitive, even if the resulting company held only a five-percent market share, as long as certain conditions existed in its product and geographic market. The *Philadelphia National Bank* decision the following year expanded on *Brown Shoe* by suggesting that certain market concentrations would, in fact, inhibit competition, and should be considered illegal in the absence of evidence to the contrary. The 1964 *Alcoa-Rome* decision took the standard a step farther, ruling that even a slight increase in share would be anticompetitive in a highly concentrated market.

In *Von's Grocery*, the Supreme Court expanded on *Alcoa* by ruling that slight increases in share are anticompetitive in a market that is evolving into a concentrated industry, even if that market is currently highly competitive. Its analysis of the Los Angeles market during the 1950s revealed that single-store owners declined from 5,365 in 1950 to 3,818 in 1959, while owners of two or more stores increased from 96 to 150.

The 66-unit Von's chain captured 7.5% of the city's grocery market, a relatively small share. Yet, as reported in *Business Week*, the Court's majority stated, "It is enough for us that Congress feared that a market marked...by both a continuous decline in the number of small businesses and a large number of mergers would, slowly but inevitably, gravitate from a market of many small competitors to one dominated by one or a few giants."

Consequently, Von's was forced to divest itself of its Safeway stores.

Research

"Antitrust Suit Aimed at Merger of Von's, Shopping Bag Markets," in *The Wall Street Journal*, 28 March 1960. Briefly describes the Justice Department's initial challenge to the merger.

"High Court Bars Merger of Rivals," in *Business Week*, 4 June 1966. Discloses the Supreme Court's ruling.

"Holders of Two Food Chains Vote Merger in Los Angeles," in *The Wall Street Journal*, 21 March 1960. Describes the terms of the merger agreement.

Safeway Home Page, available at http://www.safeway.com. Official World Wide Web Home Page for Safeway. Offers news releases, financial information, a store directory, and such shopping features as recipes and advertised sales.

"The Vons Companies, Incorporated," in *International Directory of Company Histories*, Vol. 7, St. James Press: 1993. Provides a historical review of the company.

Wasserstein, Bruce. *Big Deal: The Battle for Control of America's Leading Corporations*, Warner Books, 1998. Offers an review of the *Von's Grocery* decision.

—SAMANTHA MORRISON

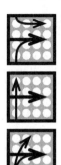

WALT DISNEY & ABC

nationality: USA
date: February 9, 1996
affected: The Walt Disney Co., USA, founded 1923
affected: ABC Inc., USA, founded 1943

The Walt Disney Co.
500 S. Buena Vista St.
Burbank, CA 91521
USA

tel: (818)560-1000
fax: (818)560-1930
web: http://www.disney.com

Overview of the Merger

The acquisition of Capital Cities/ABC by The Walt Disney Co. in 1996 marked the first major move by a movie studio toward vertical integration since the removal of the government's ban on joint-ownership of movie and television companies. The deal created a trend in the industry, as other movie studios followed Disney's lead and began hunting for a distribution channel for their content.

History of The Walt Disney Co.

Walt Elias Disney, a twenty-one-year old aspiring cartoonist, left Chicago in 1923 and headed for Hollywood, where he and his brother Roy established the Disney Brothers Cartoon Studio. The following year it released the first Alice Comedy, *Alice's Day at Sea*. In 1928 it released the first film featuring Mickey Mouse, *Plane Crazy*, followed later in the year by *Steamboat Willie*, the industry's first film to incorporate fully synchronized sound.

The company's name became Walt Disney Productions the following year. Over the next several years it began marketing Mickey Mouse merchandise, such as a comic strip, the *Mickey Mouse Book*, and watches. This character's popularity spawned the creation of other well-known characters, including Minnie Mouse, Donald Duck, and Goofy.

Among Disney's releases during the 1930s were the Academy Award winners *Flowers and Trees*, the first full-color cartoon, and *The Three Little Pigs*. The industry's first full-length feature film, *Snow White and the Seven Dwarfs*, debuted in 1937. Disney suspended commercial production for the duration of World War II in order to produce films featuring Disney characters for the promotion of public wartime conscientiousness.

Increased labor costs during the late 1940s prompted the company to expand into live-action productions, releasing *Seal Island* in 1948. The following year the Walt Disney Music Company was founded, followed by WED Enterprises (later known as Walt Disney Imagineering) in 1952. It introduced its first television show, *One Hour in Wonderland*, in 1950.

The Business

Financials

Revenue (1998): $23 billion

Employees (1998): 117,000

SICs / NAICS

sic 2711 - Newspapers

sic 4832 - Radio Broadcasting Stations

sic 4833 - Television Broadcasting Stations

sic 5947 - Gift, Novelty & Souvenir Shops

sic 7375 - Information Retrieval Services

sic 7812 - Motion Picture & Video Production

sic 7822 - Motion Picture & Tape Distribution

sic 7996 - Amusement Parks

naics 453220 - Gift, Novelty and Souvenir Stores

naics 511110 - Newspaper Publishers

naics 512110 - Motion Picture and Video Production

naics 512120 - Motion Picture and Video Distribution

naics 513112 - Radio Stations

naics 513120 - Television Broadcasting

naics 514191 - On-Line Information Services

naics 713110 - Amusement and Theme Parks

The *Disneyland* television series premiered in 1954. This show, which ran for 29 years, proved to be the longest-running prime-time series in history; in 1997, it was reborn on ABC as the *Wonderful World of Disney*. In 1955, the Disneyland park opened in Anaheim, California, and *The Mickey Mouse Club* debuted on ABC.

In August 1964 Disney released *Mary Poppins*, destined to become one of the top-grossing films in movie history. Two years later Walt Disney died of lung cancer and was succeeded as chairman by his brother Roy O. Disney. *The Love Bug* was released in 1969 and became the second-highest grossing film in Disney's history.

Walt Disney World opened in Orlando, Florida, in 1971, just as Disneyland welcomed its 100 millionth guest. That year Roy O. Disney died, and E. Cardon Walker became Disney's president. Roy's son, Roy E. Disney, was named vice president of the animation division and inherited principal shareholdership from his father. In 1980 Walker was promoted to CEO, and Walt Disney's son, Ron Miller, was named president

and COO. The EPCOT Center opened in Orlando, Florida, in October 1982.

Tokyo Disneyland opened in 1983, the same year that the Disney Channel premiered on cable television. The company founded Touchstone Pictures in 1984 for the production of more adult entertainment than the standard Disney fare. That studio's first film release was *Splash*, Disney's first major hit at the box office since *The Love Bug*.

The company experienced internal management difficulties in 1984. Disney paid $325.4 million for Saul Steinberg's 11.1% controlling interest, which he had acquired in alliance with Roy E. Disney. Disney stockholders filed suit against the Disney and Steinberg's Reliance Group, charging its managers with lowering the stock value to secure their positions. In the ensuing management shakeout, Michael Eisner became CEO and Frank Wells became president. The stockholder suit was finally settled in 1989 as the two companies agreed to pay $45 million to stockholders.

The company increased its presence in television in 1985 by debuting Saturday morning cartoons and premiering the *Golden Girls* situation comedy. The next year it premiered *The Disney Sunday Movie*, and began airing syndicated features and television shows. Also in 1986 the company shortened its name to The Walt Disney Co.

The first Disney store opened its doors in 1987. The following year Disney/MGM Studios completed its first filming project. Undertaking steps to take full advantage of the growing cable television and home video industries, Eisner directed Disney in 1988 to sign an agreement with Showtime Networks, Inc., through which that network gained exclusive rights to Touchstone and Disney productions through 1996. Eisner also embarked on plans to secure new markets for old Disney films through television syndication.

Disney's Hollywood Pictures was established in 1989, the same year that the Disney/MGM Studio Theme Park and Pleasure Island opened near Orlando. Also that year, Disney's animated film *The Little Mermaid*, won an Academy Award. In 1990 Hollywood Pictures released its first film, *Arachnophobia*. Disney's 1991 release of *The Beauty and the Beast* surpassed previous records as the most successful animated film.

EuroDisney opened in 1992 outside of Paris, France; initial revenues for the new attraction were disappointing. That year Disney produced the hit situation comedy *Home Improvement*. In 1993 the company acquired Miramax Films. Disney entered into a joint venture with three Baby Bells—Ameritech, BellSouth, and Southwestern Bell—to offer video programming. Michael Ovitz, co-founder of Creative Artists Agency, became president of Disney in 1995, only to leave two years later. In 1996 the company acquired Capital Cities/ABC Inc.

History of ABC Inc.

In order to reduce the possibility of an NBC monopoly of the broadcasting industry, the FCC directed that company in 1941 to divest itself of one of its two networks. Two years later NBC sold its Blue network to Edward J. Noble, who renamed it the American Broadcasting Company (ABC).

In 1953 ABC merged with United Paramount Theatres, Paramount Picture's movie theater division, to form American Broadcast-Paramount Theatres. This new company began operations with 355 radio network affiliates, 14 primary TV affiliates, as well as TV stations, radio stations, and theaters nationwide. Leonard Goldenson, Paramount's president, became its president.

This merger gave ABC access to capital, and in 1954 it loaned the Walt Disney Company $4.5 million for the construction of Disneyland in exchange for a Disney television show. That year ABC, the broadcasting division, expanded its TV programming to 35 hours per week. *The Mickey Mouse Club* debuted on ABC in 1955. By 1957 the ABC division surpassed the company's theater segment as the largest revenue producer.

ABC entered the sports broadcasting arena in 1960, when it won the TV rights to NCAA college football and basketball games. ABC Sports was founded in 1961. That year's Thanksgiving broadcast of the Texas-Texas A&M football games featured the first instant replay.

ABC experienced financial difficulties during the 1960s, losing a total of more than $120 million. In 1965 the company announced plans to merge with International Telephone and Telegraph Corp. Although the Federal Communications Commission approved the merger, the U.S. Department of Justice delayed its decision so long that ITT eventually opted out of the deal. Instead, that company loaned ABC $25 million to help the network convert to color broadcasting.

In 1968 ABC divided into three separate divisions: entertainment, sports, and news. Four years later the network became profitable for the first time in a decade, as earnings exceeded $35 million on revenues of $800 million.

In 1975 ABC hired two important personalities: Barbara Walters, the first full-time female news anchor

The Officers

Chairman and CEO: Michael D. Eisner

Vice Chairman of the Board: Roy E. Disney

Sr. Exec. VP and Chief of Corporate Operations: Sanford M. Litvack

Exec. VP, Corporate Affairs: John F. Cooke

Exec. VP and Chief Financial Officer: Thomas O. Staggs

on any network, and the famous mass-media programmer Fred Silverman. Within one year of Silverman's arrival, ABC moved into first place in prime-time ratings. In 1978, however, he was lured away from ABC by NBC. The late-night news show *Nightline* was born in 1979 as an offshoot of the network's coverage of the Iran hostage crisis. In 1984 it purchased the ESPN sports cable network. By the following year ABC had fallen behind both CBS and NBC in ratings although it remained ahead of them in terms of profits.

Capital Cities Communications, Inc., a company with one-quarter of ABC's sales, purchased ABC for $3.5 billion in 1985. The name of the combined operation was changed to Capital Cities/ABC Inc. Budget trimming began as a result of the company's substantial loss in the following year. In 1987 ABC's ratings edged past those of CBS, but the network was still a distant second to NBC.

Roseanne debuted in 1988 and became one of the top-ranked programs on network TV. That year ABC made its first significant offshore investment, in a satellite-delivered sports programming service available throughout Western Europe. The following year Ultra Entertainment was formed to create and program primarily for U.S. cable services and the international television market.

The company purchased HBJ Farm Publications from Harcourt Brace Jovanovich in 1991. *World News Now* debuted the following year. In 1993 Capital Cities/ABC formed a venture capital unit, Capital Cities Capital, to offer new and emerging companies airtime for commercials in exchange for equity stakes in the companies. That year the company began aggressive promotion of its new sports channel, ESPN2, and signed deals with a number of cable services to carry the programming.

During the 1990s ABC's news reporting experienced several setbacks and lawsuits. In 1993 Tyson Foods Inc. asked a court to bar the television program

The Players

Disney's Chairman and CEO: Michael D. Eisner. Michael Eisner began working in the entertainment industry as an usher for NBC during the summer months. Upon graduation from Denison University in 1964, he found himself successively employed by each of the three major networks. After six weeks as an FCC logging clerk at NBC, he moved to the programming department of CBS. Still dissatisfied, Eisner mailed out hundreds of resumes. The only response that he received was from Barry Diller, who hired Eisner as an assistant to the national programming director at ABC. He passed through various vice president positions before accepting an offer from Barry Diller, who was then working for Paramount, to become president and chief operating officer of Paramount Pictures in 1976. Eisner joined Disney in 1984 as its chairman and CEO. In those positions he revitalized the studio's movie operations and made the company an enviable force in the industry.

Capital Cities/ABC Chairman: Thomas Murphy. Thomas Murphy, a graduate of Harvard Business School, assumed control of a bankrupt UHF television station in Albany, New York, in 1954. After orchestrating that station's recovery, Murphy brought in his friend, Daniel Burke, as partner. The duo built their station into a print and broadcast empire known as Capital Cities through a policy of conservative money management and calculated acquisitions.

Berkshire Hathaway CEO: Warren E. Buffett. Warren Buffett worked for neither Disney nor Capital Cities/ABC, yet he was the matchmaker for the two. This so-called "Sage of Omaha" made a fortune by investing in undervalued companies and then helping them achieve their worth. His highly regarded financial acumen is a combination of his education at Columbia Business School and an innate sense about business dealings. His Berkshire Hathaway was a holding company for diverse interests, including a 13% interest in Capital Cities/ABC.

20/20 from sneaking hidden cameras into Tyson's poultry plant. The following year John Prozeralik, a restaurant owner who was misidentified as a mob figure in local TV and radio news broadcasts, won an $11.5 million libel verdict against ABC. In 1995 Capital Cities/ABC settled a $10 billion libel lawsuit by the Philip Morris Cos. with public apologies for "a mistake" it made in a 1994 broadcast on the *Day One* news magazine about the calculated use of nicotine by the cigarette industry. Also that year, the firm was sued by supermarket chain Food Lion Inc. for *Prime Time Live* reports that claimed that the Food Lion engaged in unsanitary food-handling methods and unfair labor practices.

In 1994 the company joined with the Washington Post Co. and Oracle Corp. to develop electronic services that included news-on-demand. That year it also acquired a minority stake in Alpha Software Corp. In one of the most ambitious plans to date to link television and computer services, America Online Inc. and Capital Cities/ABC began offering online subscribers ABC newswire, celebrity "chat," and interactive games from ABC Sports.

In partnership with the Hearst Corp., Capital Cities/ABC bought one-third of Lifetime cable from Viacom Inc. for $317.6 million in 1994. The following year, the Walt Disney Co. announced its acquisition of Capital/Cities ABC Inc. for $19 billion in cash and stock.

Market Forces Driving the Merger

For decades, motion picture studios and television networks were forbidden to operate in each other's business. The financial interest/syndication, or fin/syn, rules had been enacted by the U.S. Federal Communications Commission in 1970. They prevented the networks, which controlled access to about 95% of homes, from profiting on both program ownership and syndication. The result from this regulation was that the studios controlled the content while the networks controlled the distribution.

The advent of cable television and the proliferation of the VCR during the 1980s suddenly created competition for the networks. Advertising comprised the bulk of their revenues, and as their viewership declined, so did the value of their commercial spots. The networks fought with the studios and the government to remove the fin/syn rules, but the studios resisted forfeiture of their near-monopoly on television show production. The interests of the studios were protected by Ronald Reagan, a former Hollywood actor, who quashed an attempt to lift the regulation.

Still, the FCC relaxed the rules a bit in 1991, but the networks sought absolute repeal. Two years later they won a lawsuit, winning removal of the fin/syn rules effective September 1995. Networks and studios sprang into action, and both Warner Brothers and

Paramount studios founded television networks as their captive distribution outlets.

The Walt Disney Company instead chose to acquire an established network. The movie studio had had an on again/off again relationship with ABC for decades. The television network would now be a compatible partner for the distribution of Disney's movie and television content. Disney would gain an outlet for new shows, as well as stakes in the ESPN, Arts & Entertainment, and Lifetime cable networks. It would also acquire television and radio stations, and publishing operations that included newspapers and magazines.

In turn, Disney would provide ABC with original television shows, some likely to feature proven Disney characters and movie hits. The network would benefit from Disney's expert marketing prowess, sorely needed by ABC, which was struggling to improve its position against NBC and CBS. Moreover, ABC would receive the advantage of product promotion at Disney's international chain of retail stores.

Approach and Engagement

In mid-July 1995, a media conference in Idaho brought together the three key players that would craft the Disney/Capital Cities merger. Michael Eisner, chairman of Walt Disney, ran into Warren Buffet, the largest shareholder of Capital Cities/ABC. Eisner asked Buffet whether the two companies "could do something together," according to *Maclean's*. The pair went in search of Thomas Murphy, chairman of Capital Cities/ABC, of whom Eisner asked, "We're buying. Are you selling?" Eisner got his answer, and in just eight days the men had hammered out a deal.

On July 31, 1995, The Walt Disney Company announced its proposed acquisition of Capital Cities/ABC. The $19 billion deal would be the nation's second-largest, after the $25 billion acquisition of RJR Nabisco by Kohlberg, Kravis & Roberts in 1988. Disney would pay $65 in cash plus one share of Disney stock for each share of Capital Cities/ABC. Warren Buffet's holding company, Berkshire Hathaway Inc., owned 13% of Capital Cities/ABC. That stake translated into 20 million shares, worth about $2 billion.

In August, Disney recruited as company president Michael Ovitz, chairman and co-founder of Hollywood's leading talent agency, Creative Artists Agency. Four months later, Disney lured Geraldine Laybourne away from her post as president of the Nickelodeon cable network to become president of Disney/ABC Cable Networks.

In early January 1996, the companies' shareholders approved the acquisition. The U.S. Department of Justice then granted its approval, contingent upon Disney's divestiture of a Los Angeles television station that competed against a Capital Cities/ABC station in the same market. On February 8, 1996, the Federal Communications Commission cleared the deal, which was completed the following day.

Products and Services

Disney's **Creative Content** division included The Walt Disney Studios, Consumer Products, television production and distribution, Buena Vista Internet Group, Fairchild Publications, and Disney Televentures. This segment also included the Buena Vista Music Group, which was comprised of Walt Disney Records, Hollywood Records, Lyric Street Records, and Mammoth Records. The Creative Content division contributed $10.3 billion of the company's total revenues in 1998.

The **Broadcasting** segment encompassed the cable network, the ABC Television Network, television and radio stations, and the radio networks. The ABC Television Network's hits for the 1998-99 season were *Drew Carey, NYPD Blue, Spin City, Dharma & Greg*, and *Monday Night Football*, as well as the new comedies *The Hughleys* and the critically-acclaimed *Sports Night*. The Broadcasting segment accounted for $7.1 billion of total 1998 revenues.

Theme Parks and Resorts consisted of Disney Resorts in California, Florida, Paris, and Tokyo. It also included the Disney Vacation Club, Walt Disney Imagineering, and sports interests (the Mighty Ducks of Anaheim and the Anaheim Angels). Disney Regional Entertainment opened a second Club Disney location (and announced two more) and opened the first DisneyQuest and ESPNZone locations. The opening of Disney's Animal Kingdom in 1997 brought the number of Disney theme parks operating worldwide to seven, with two more under construction. The Theme Parks and Resorts segment contributed $5.5 billion of the company's total revenues in 1998.

Changes to the Industry

The Disney/Capital Cities merger changed the industry overnight—literally. On August 1, 1995, the day after Disney made its merger announcement, Westinghouse Electric Corporation announced its planned acquisition of CBS Inc. for $5.4 billion. The following month, Time Warner and Turner Broadcasting Systems announced a merger accord. Disney's demonstration of the creation of a vertically integrated entertainment company had not been lost on the industry's largest players. Disney's trailblazing in this arena "left the rest of the industry scrambling to catch up with the Magic Kingdom," said *Maclean's*.

Review of the Outcome

In June of 1996 Capital Cities/ABC and the Walt Disney Co. consolidated their international TV operations into a single division, Disney/ABC International Television. That October Capital Cities/ABC shortened its name to ABC Inc.

The Southern Baptist Convention boycotted Disney films and products in 1996 largely because of the company's policy of offering benefits to the partners of gay employees, as well as for producing adult movies through its units. Disney reportedly responded that the company found "it curious that a group that claims to espouse family would vote to boycott the world's largest producer of wholesome family entertainment."

In 1997 Disney divested itself of four ABC-owned newspapers. In April 1997 Disney purchased a majority interest in Starwave Corp., a Web developer that designed the ABC Web site. Later that year it joined with Starwave to launch the ABCNews.com Web site.

Disney paid $92 billion in 1998 to renew ABC's license to carry *Monday Night Football* through the year 2005. That year Patricia Fili-Krushel became the first woman at the helm of a major network when she was named president of ABC Television. Also in 1998 Disney merged its live-action film production units— Walt Disney Pictures, Hollywood Pictures, and Touchstone—to form Buena Vista Motion Pictures Group. Disney's Animal Park, a 500-acre theme park in Walt Disney World opened, and the Disney Cruise Line made its maiden voyage. Disney acquired a 43% interest in Infoseek Corp. for the development of an Internet portal combining Infoseek's search technology with Disney's content.

The company made expansion plans for its three Regional Entertainment businesses: Club Disney, an interactive entertainment venue for children; ESPNZone, a sports-theme dining and entertainment center; and DisneyQuest, an "eatertainment" facility featuring video games and rides. Revenues in 1998 increased slightly to $22.9 billion and net income reached $1.85 billion.

Research

"ABC Inc.," in *Notable Corporate Chronologies*, The Gale Group, 1999. Offers a history of the company.

Fennell, Tom. "'We're Buying': Disney Expands the Kingdom," in *Maclean's*, 14 August 1995. Describes the events leading up to the merger deal.

Garneau, George. "Disney Enters News Business," in *Editor & Publisher*, 5 August 1995. Outlines the holdings of each of the merging companies.

Sherman, Stratford. "Why Disney Had to Buy ABC," in *Fortune*, 4 September 1995. Describes the telecommunications industry in terms of content versus distribution.

"Wall St. Stunned," in *The New York Times*, 1 August 1995. Details the shocking merger announcement.

"The Walt Disney Co.," in *Notable Corporate Chronologies*, The Gale Group, 1999. Profiles the history of the company, through and beyond its acquisition of Capital Cities/ABC.

The Walt Disney Co. Home Page, available at http://www.disney.com. Official World Wide Web Page for Disney. As part of the GO Network, this site features information on the company's holdings, annual reports and other financial information, press releases, and links to other Disney Web sites.

Wasserstein, Bruce. *Big Deal: The Battle for Control of America's Leading Corporations*, Warner Books, 1998. Offers an overview of the changes affecting the telecommunications industry in the 1990s.

KIMBERLY N. STEVENS

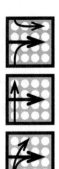

WALT DISNEY & INFOSEEK

nationality: USA
date: November 18, 1998
affected: The Walt Disney Co., USA, founded 1923
affected: Infoseek Corp., USA, founded 1994

The Walt Disney Co.
500 S. Buena Vista St.
Burbank, CA 91521
USA

tel: (818)560-1000
fax: (818)560-1930
web: http://www.disney.com

Infoseek Corp.
1399 Moffett Park Dr.
Sunnyvale, CA 94089
USA

tel: (408)543-6000
fax: (408)734-9350
web: http://info.infoseek.com
e-mail: info@infoseek.com

Overview of the Acquisition

In 1998 Mickey Mouse finally got married, but not to Minnie—to a computer mouse instead. The Walt Disney Company forged an alliance with Infoseek, an Internet search engine, to increase the media conglomerate's presence on the World Wide Web. These two companies created the GO Network, an Internet portal.

History of The Walt Disney Co.

Walt Elias Disney, a twenty-one-year old aspiring cartoonist, left Chicago in 1923 and headed for Hollywood, where he and his brother Roy established the Disney Brothers Cartoon Studio. The following year it released the first Alice Comedy, *Alice's Day at Sea*. In 1928 it released the first film featuring Mickey Mouse, *Plane Crazy*, followed later in the year by *Steamboat Willie*, the industry's first film to incorporate fully synchronized sound.

The company's name became Walt Disney Productions the following year. Over the next several years it began marketing Mickey Mouse merchandise, such as a comic strip, the *Mickey Mouse Book*, and watches. This character's popularity spawned the creation of other well-known characters, including Minnie Mouse, Donald Duck, and Goofy.

Among Disney's releases during the 1930s were the Academy Award winners *Flowers and Trees*, the first full-color cartoon, and *The Three Little Pigs*. The industry's first full-length feature film, *Snow White and the Seven Dwarfs*, debuted in 1937. Disney suspended commercial production for the duration of World War II in order to produce films featuring Disney characters for the promotion of public wartime conscientiousness.

Increased labor costs during the late 1940s prompted the company to expand into live-action productions, releasing *Seal Island* in 1948. The following year the Walt Disney Music Company was founded, followed by WED Enterprises (later known as Walt Disney Imagineering) in 1952. It introduced its first television show, *One Hour in Wonderland*, in 1950.

The Business

Financials - The Walt Disney Co.

Revenue (1998): $23 billion

Employees (1998): 117,000

Financials - Infoseek Corp.

Revenue (1998): $50.7 million

Employees (1998): 325

SICs / NAICS

sic 2711 - Newspapers

sic 4832 - Radio Broadcasting Stations

sic 4833 - Television Broadcasting Stations

sic 5947 - Gift, Novelty & Souvenir Shops

sic 7375 - Information Retrieval Services

sic 7812 - Motion Picture & Video Production

sic 7822 - Motion Picture & Tape Distribution

sic 7996 - Amusement Parks

naics 453220 - Gift, Novelty and Souvenir Stores

naics 511110 - Newspaper Publishers

naics 512110 - Motion Picture and Video Production

naics 512120 - Motion Picture and Video Distribution

naics 513112 - Radio Stations

naics 513120 - Television Broadcasting

naics 514191 - On-Line Information Services

naics 713110 - Amusement and Theme Parks

The *Disneyland* television series premiered in 1954. This show, which ran for 29 years, proved to be the longest-running prime-time series in history; in 1997, it was reborn on ABC as the *Wonderful World of Disney*. In 1955, the Disneyland park opened in Anaheim, California, and *The Mickey Mouse Club* debuted on ABC.

In August 1964 Disney released *Mary Poppins*, destined to become one of the top-grossing films in movie history. Two years later Walt Disney died of lung cancer and was succeeded as chairman by his brother Roy O. Disney. *The Love Bug* was released in 1969 and became the second-highest grossing film in Disney's history.

Walt Disney World opened in Orlando, Florida, in 1971, just as Disneyland welcomed its 100 millionth guest. That year Roy O. Disney died, and E. Cardon

Walker became Disney's president. Roy's son, Roy E. Disney, was named vice president of the animation division and inherited principal shareholdership from his father. In 1980 Walker was promoted to CEO, and Walt Disney's son, Ron Miller, was named president and COO. The EPCOT Center opened in Orlando, Florida, in October 1982.

Tokyo Disneyland opened in 1983, the same year that the Disney Channel premiered on cable television. The company founded Touchstone Pictures in 1984 for the production of more adult entertainment than the standard Disney fare. That studio's first film release was *Splash*, Disney's first major hit at the box office since *The Love Bug*.

The company experienced internal management difficulties in 1984. Disney paid $325.4 million for Saul Steinberg's 11.1% controlling interest, which he had acquired in alliance with Roy E. Disney. Disney stockholders filed suit against the Disney and Steinberg's Reliance Group, charging its managers with lowering the stock value to secure their positions. In the ensuing management shakeout, Michael Eisner became CEO and Frank Wells became president. The stockholder suit was finally settled in 1989 as the two companies agreed to pay $45 million to stockholders.

The company increased its presence in television in 1985 by debuting Saturday morning cartoons and premiering the *Golden Girls* situation comedy. The next year it premiered *The Disney Sunday Movie*, and began airing syndicated features and television shows. Also in 1986 the company shortened its name to The Walt Disney Co.

The first Disney store opened its doors in 1987. The following year Disney/MGM Studios completed its first filming project. Undertaking steps to take full advantage of the growing cable television and home video industries, Eisner directed Disney in 1988 to sign an agreement with Showtime Networks, Inc., through which that network gained exclusive rights to Touchstone and Disney productions through 1996. Eisner also embarked on plans to secure new markets for old Disney films through television syndication.

Disney's Hollywood Pictures was established in 1989, the same year that the Disney/MGM Studio Theme Park and Pleasure Island opened near Orlando. Also that year, Disney's animated film *The Little Mermaid*, won an Academy Award.

EuroDisney opened in 1992 outside of Paris, France, but initial revenues for the new attraction were disappointing. That year Disney produced the hit situation comedy *Home Improvement*. In 1993 the company acquired Miramax Films. Disney entered into a joint venture with three Baby Bells—Ameritech,

BellSouth, and Southwestern Bell—to offer video programming. Michael Ovitz, co-founder of Creative Artists Agency, became president of Disney in 1995, only to leave two years later.

In 1996 the company acquired Capital Cities/ABC Inc. That year Metro-Goldwyn-Mayer Inc. filed a lawsuit against Disney, claiming that the company broke a licensing contract for possible theme park ventures in Europe. In the meantime, Disney and Oriental Land Co. moved closer to developing a second theme park in Tokyo, tentatively entitled Tokyo Disneysea.

The Southern Baptist Convention boycotted Disney films and products in 1996 largely because of the company's policy of offering benefits to the partners of gay employees, as well as for producing adult movies through its units. Disney reportedly responded that the company found "it curious that a group that claims to espouse family would vote to boycott the world's largest producer of wholesome family entertainment."

In April 1997 Disney purchased a majority interest in Starwave Corp., a Web developer that designed the ABC Web site. In 1998 Disney merged its live-action film production units—Walt Disney Pictures, Hollywood Pictures, and Touchstone—to form Buena Vista Motion Pictures Group. Disney's Animal Park, a 500-acre theme park in Walt Disney World, opened, and the Disney Cruise Line made its maiden voyage in 1998, as well. Disney acquired a 43% interest in Infoseek for the development of the GO Network, an Internet portal combining Infoseek's search technology with Disney's content.

The company continued to expand its three Regional Entertainment businesses: Club Disney, an interactive entertainment venue for children; ESPNZone, a sports-theme dining and entertainment center; and DisneyQuest, an "eatertainment" facility featuring video games and rides. Revenues in 1998 increased slightly to $22.9 billion and net income reached $1.85 billion.

History of Infoseek Corp.

Steven Kirsch, the inventor of the optical mouse, founded Mouse Systems in 1982, followed by the software company Frame Technology four years later. In 1993 he anticipated that the Internet would experience a runaway explosion in information. He also realized that the World Wide Web would soon require an accurate search mechanism. In January 1994 Kirsch founded Infoseek Corp. as a search engine to harness the Internet.

The Officers

The Walt Disney Co.

Chairman and CEO: Michael D. Eisner

Vice Chairman of the Board: Roy E. Disney

Sr. Exec. VP and Chief of Corporate Operations: Sanford M. Litvack

Exec. VP, Corporate Affairs: John F. Cooke

Exec. VP and Chief Financial Officer: Thomas O. Staggs

Infoseek Corp.

President and CEO: Harry M. Motro

Exec. VP, Products: Patrick Naughton

Sr. VP, Chief Administrative Officer, and Chief Financial Officer: Les Wright

Sr. VP, Advertising Sales and Strategic Partnerships: Beth Haggerty

Sr. VP and General Manager, Commerce: Baghwan D. Goel

The company was among the first to recognize the commercial possibilities of the World Wide Web. It developed and patented the technology that counted the number of times users clicked on "banner" advertisements, thereby tracking the success of a particular ad and its relative monetary value. In June 1996 Infoseek held its initial public offering.

Harry Motro joined the company as president and CEO in April 1997. That September Infoseek received a patent for its search technology. It acquired WBS.net, a provider of online community services, in April 1998. Later that year, the company announced a joint venture agreement with Deutsche Telekom, Axel Springer Verlag, and Verlagsgruppe Georg von Holtzbrinck to launch Infoseek Germany by mid-1999. In January 1999 Infoseek acquired Quando Inc., an Internet company specializing in directories and custom guides, for $17 million in stock.

With a background in online media, Harry Motro envisioned Infoseek as a service providing the consumer with all of his daily resource needs, including news, weather, sports, shopping, and entertainment. To achieve that goal, the company needed a trusted, well-established brand that was willing to invest in an online venture. In June 1998 it found such a company—Walt Disney. The two companies formed an alliance for the creation of a Web portal that would use Infoseek's search technology to direct users to Disney's other online ventures.

The Players

Infoseek President and CEO: Harry M. Motro. Harry Motro spent most of his professional life involved in media. After receiving a Bachelor of Science degree from the University of Virginia, he handled telecommunications clients for Coopers & Lybrand. From that company he moved to Turner Broadcasting, where he was involved in the company's mergers and acquisitions strategy. Motro then joined CNN, where, as senior vice president in charge of interactive business development, he launched CNN.com, CNNfn, and All Politics. He joined Infoseek in April 1997 and steered the company's transformation into a global media network.

Buena Vista Internet Group Chairman: Jacob J. Winebaum. Jacob Winebaum founded *Family Fun* magazine. Disney acquired both the magazine and Winebaum's services as an online visionary. Although he had little technological know-how, he had marketing savvy and could steer Disney's online ventures. Winebaum launched the Disney.com site, followed by ABCNews.com, the Disney Store Online, and the Disney Daily Blast sites. He orchestrated the company's purchase of Starwave, and developed the GO Network portal idea with Infoseek's leader, Harry Motro.

Market Forces Driving the Acquisition

By the late 1990s the Internet had revealed itself to be a force so powerful that it could not be ignored, not even by a media behemoth with interests in movies, television, retail, theme parks, and restaurants. And Disney had not exactly been a Johnny Come Lately to the Internet, either. It maintained the Web sites ABC.com, ESPN.com, ABCNEWS.com, Disney.com, Disney's Blast Online (a subscription site for children), and the official sites of the NFL, the NBA, and NASCAR. Yet the company wanted to capture an even wider online audience.

Other Hollywood studios had the same mission. One of the first to buy a piece of the Web was NBC, which agreed in early November 1998 to purchase 60% of CNet, provider of the Snap! online service. Disney aimed to make a similar alliance, and then take it to the next level.

The first step would be to acquire a search engine, such as Infoseek, that could be used as a springboard to the development of a portal. (A portal is an entry point to the Web where the user can get email, read current news and weather, and search the Web.) Disney hoped to design a portal that would also create traffic to its other Web sites. "We are a content company," said Disney's CEO Michael Eisner in *Fortune*. "But without distribution at the early stage of this business, we are going to find ourselves in second position."

Approach and Engagement

On June 18, 1998, The Walt Disney Company and Infoseek announced their strategic alliance. The somewhat complicated deal would be a stock and cash transaction in which Disney would acquire a 43% majority interest in Infoseek. In exchange, Disney would pay Infoseek $70 million in cash plus its majority stake in Starwave. Additionally, Infoseek would pay $165 million to Disney for the provision of promotional support for the new portal service.

Under the deal, Infoseek Corp. would retain its name and personnel. It would reincorporate as a holding company for its two subsidiaries: Starwave and Infoseek. The proposition raised no regulatory eyebrows. In November shareholders approved the alliance, and on November 18, 1998, the transaction was completed.

Products and Services

Disney and Infoseek came together for the purpose of creating an Internet portal service, and on January 12, 1999, the GO Network (www.go.com) was launched. It debuted as the fourth most popular Web domain, behind yahoo.com, aol.com, and msn.com. According to an Infoseek press release dated February 22, 1999, "GO Network is the first Internet portal built from the ground up to deliver the diversity of the Web by combining many of the most popular Web sites and leading consumer brands with innovative services."

Like any other search engine, the Go Network utilized search and indexing technologies to enable the user to conduct searches over the Web. In addition, this portal featured 18 content centers, including GO News, GO Sports, GO Money, and GO Kids and Family, that relied on other Disney properties, such as ABC News, ESPN, and Disney Online. Each of these channels contained sub-portals to sites and chat rooms related to that channel's content.

In February 1999 the GO Shop network was launched. This online shopping site provided links to the sites of retails offering everything from apparel and baby products to flowers and computer hardware. The companies planned to launch GO Auction and GO Stores before Christmas 1999. Also in

February, GoTo.com filed suit against Disney and Infoseek to require them to change GO Network's logo, which, the company claimed, was similar enough to the GoTo.com logo to infringe on its trademark.

In April 1999 Disney disclosed that it was considering spinning off its Internet holdings as a separately traded company. These holdings would include its Disney Online assets along with its stake in Infoseek.

Research

"Infoseek/Disney Pact a Done Deal," in *Newsbytes*, 19 November 1998. Reports the completion of the merger.

"It's Official—Disney Buying Piece of Infoseek," in *Newsbytes*, 18 June 1998. Describes Disney's newly announced arrangement to purchase a stake in Infoseek.

Moody, Glyn. "Old Media Gets Cozy with New for Mutual Benefit," in *Computer Weekly*, 4 February 1999. Details the technological aspects of the GO Network.

Orwall, Bruce, and Kara Swisher. "Disney Weighs Joining Internet Assets with 43% Infoseek Stake for an IPO," in *The Wall Street Journal*, 12 April 1999. Reports Disney's consideration of a spin-off of its online ventures.

Rose, Frank. "Mickey Online," in *Fortune*, 28 September 1998. Profiles the Disney team devoted to the development of the GO Network.

"The Walt Disney Co.," in *Notable Corporate Chronologies*, The Gale Group, 1999. Profiles the history of the company.

The Walt Disney Co. Home Page, available at http://www.disney.com. Official World Wide Web Page for Disney. As part of the GO Network, this site features information on the company's holdings, annual reports and other financial information, press releases, and links to other Disney Web sites.

Wasserstein, Bruce. *Big Deal: The Battle for Control of America's Leading Corporations*, Warner Books, 1998. Offers an overview of the changes affecting the telecommunications industry in the 1990s.

DAVIS MCMILLAN

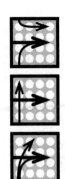

WESTINGHOUSE ELECTRIC & CBS

CBS Corp.
51 W. 52nd St.
New York, NY 10019
USA

tel: (212)975-4321
fax: (212)975-4516
web: http://www.cbs.com

nationality: USA
date: November 28, 1995
affected: Westinghouse Electric Corp., USA, founded 1886
affected: CBS Inc., USA, founded 1927

Overview of the Acquisition

When they came together in 1995, Westinghouse Electric and CBS Inc. were both struggling enterprises. Westinghouse was burdened with a huge debt load and an array of weak interests. CBS had been slipping steadily farther behind its rivals NBC and ABC and was facing increased competition from the Fox Network as well. Industry analysts believed that a merger of such companies would be quite risky, but the combined company surprised them. After shedding non-core interests while adding core assets, CBS emerged as the nation's best-rated network in the 1998/99 television season.

History of CBS Inc.

Arthur Judson, impresario of the Philadelphia and New York Philharmonic Orchestras, founded United Independent Broadcasters, Inc. in 1927 as a radio broadcasting company designed to promote classical music via the airing of orchestral performances. After several difficult months, Judson entered into a partnership with Columbia Phonograph. Columbia purchased UIB's operating rights for $163,000 and the new company was renamed the Columbia Phonograph Broadcasting System.

The next year its operating rights were resold back to the broadcasting company, whose name was shortened to Columbia Broadcasting System (CBS). Also in 1928 radio advertiser William Paley bought $400,000 worth of CBS stock. He became president, and earnings tripled in his first year of tenure.

Paley fostered success by offering to prospective affiliates the young network's complete, unsponsored schedule for free; this was in stark contrast to the practice of competing network NBC, which charged affiliates for all programming. In exchange for the free programs, CBS affiliate stations offered airtime to the parent network for its sponsored broadcasts. By 1936 CBS had 97 affiliate stations and was the country's largest radio network.

The company began to carve out a niche in news and public affairs, leaving NBC to continue its dominance in the entertainment front. It formed Columbia News Service, the first radio network news operation of its kind, in 1933. Five years later broadcast journalist Edward R. Murrow initiated the first international radio news broadcast with reports from Vienna, Paris, Berlin, and Rome. That year CBS purchased the American Recording Corp., which was later renamed as Columbia Recording Corp.

CBS transmitted the world's first experimental color TV broadcast in 1940. The following year it began weekly broadcasts of black-and-white television programs. As it became successful in luring from NBC such star performers as Jack Benny, Edgar Bergen, Red Skelton, George Burns, and Gracie Allen, CBS became known as the Tiffany Network as a reference to its quality programming.

In 1956 its popular TV quiz show, *$64,000 Question*, became embroiled in the national game show scandal of unfairly briefing contestants prior to the show. President James Aubrey introduced lighter fare into the network's entertainment lineup in 1959, and doubled profits in his first two years of tenure. Such shows as *The Beverly Hillbillies*, *Mr. Ed*, and *The Munsters* helped make CBS the best-rated network. It maintained that lead through the 1970s with such shows as *The Mary Tyler Moore Show* and *All in the Family*.

CBS and Twentieth Century Fox-Video combined forces in 1982 to form CBS/Fox, a distributor of videocassettes. The following year it acquired the music publishing portion of United Artists Corp. and created Tri-Star Pictures as a joint venture with Columbia Pictures and Home Box Office. In 1985 it purchased the consumer magazine publishing operations of Ziff-Davis Publishing Co. for $362.5 million.

Laurence Tisch became CEO in 1986, and began drastic cost-cutting measures that included the reduction of the news division budget by $30 million; the lay-off of 1,200 employees; and the sale of several CBS publishing concerns. It also began divesting its music and professional interests, including the highly criticized sale of CBS Records to Sony for $2 billion.

CBS acquired Midwest Communications, a broadcast and sports programming company, in 1991. Three years later, the Fox Network acquired the rights to air Monday Night Football, a former staple of CBS. It also acquired several of CBS's broadcasting affiliates, sending the company scrambling for replacement affiliates in such large markets as Detroit, Michigan. In 1995 CBS was acquired by Westinghouse Electric Corp. for $5.4 billion.

The Business

Financials

Revenue (1998): $6.8 billion

Employees (1998): 46,100

SICs / NAICS

sic 4832 - Radio Broadcasting Stations

sic 4833 - Television Broadcasting Stations

naics 513112 - Radio Stations

naics 513120 - Television Broadcasting

History of Westinghouse Electric Corp.

In 1886 George Westinghouse founded the Westinghouse Electric Co. in Pittsburgh. He began developing an economical system of transmission using alternating current (AC). At the time, direct current (DC), championed by Thomas Edison, was the only form of electrical power in common use. In 1891 Westinghouse installed the nation's first AC power system, in Telluride, Colorado. Two years later it provided the generating system that powered the World's Fair in Chicago.

By 1896 Westinghouse had spent a small fortune accumulating patents, and by 1909 the company was unable to produce the necessary cash to pay its $14 million worth of debt. Westinghouse was placed in receivership, and the bankers who reorganized it appointed a new board of directors. The company recovered, and in 1919 joined RCA, General Electric, United Fruit, AT&T, and Wireless Specialty Co. in a series of cross-licensing agreements that paved the way for the commercial introduction of radio. The following year Westinghouse established the Pittsburgh radio station KDKA, which made the nation's first commercial radio broadcast.

In 1930 it ventured into consumer appliance by introducing a line of electric refrigerators. After the entrance of the U.S. into World War II, Westinghouse forayed into the military electronics business, and became one of the nation's largest radar contractors. Because it was slow to target other areas of the armed forces, however, it ranked only 25th in sales among defense contractors by 1957.

During the 1960s the company diversified into such disparate businesses as soft-drink bottling, car rental, motels, land development, and mail-order record clubs. In 1974 it obtained an order for 12

The Officers

Chairman: David McLaughlin

President and CEO: Mel Karmazin

Exec. VP and Chief Financial Officer: Fredric Reynolds

Exec. VP and General Counsel: Louis Briskman

nuclear power systems from France's state-run nuclear power agency; this was the largest single order for nuclear equipment in history. During the 1980s, Westinghouse implemented a "back to basics" strategy, and began divesting its unprofitable businesses. By 1987 it had sold off 70 less profitable businesses, replacing them with 55 acquisitions that complemented existing operations.

In the largest merger between communications companies in U.S. history, Westinghouse Broadcasting expanded its cable television operations by acquiring Teleprompter Corp. in 1981. Three years later annual sales surpassed $10 billion as net income exceeded $500 million.

Michael H. Jordan became CEO in 1993 and began strengthening its assets by refocusing on its broadcasting roots. Two years later it acquired CBS Inc. for $5.4 billion, and the following year purchased Infinity Broadcasting, thereby gaining the dominant share of the U.S. radio market. Westinghouse continued to divest its non-broadcasting operations, and in December 1997 changed its name to CBS Corp. to reflect its new focus. It gained an additional 90 radio stations by purchasing American Radio Systems in 1998. Later that year it reduced its stake in Infinity by spinning off 20% of that unit through an initial public offering. In 1999 it agreed to purchase King World Productions.

Market Forces Driving the Acquisition

Westinghouse Electric had built itself from a broadcasting pioneer in the 1890s to a diversified conglomerate a century later. It had strayed far from those roots into consumer appliances, financial services, and nuclear power plants, among other industries. In the process it had accrued an enormous debt load of nearly $10 billion in 1991, which it had reduced to $2.5 billion by 1995. Yet the company still had the remains of its broadcasting interests, held in its Group W arm. And it was this unit that Chairman Michael Jordan wanted to use as the cornerstone for a new Westinghouse. He looked to CBS Inc. as the foundation for the company's return to a broadcasting empire.

That television network had troubles of its own, however. Once known as the Tiffany Network, it had become entrenched in the third-place ratings slot behind NBC and ABC, both of which appealed to younger audiences. Yet Jordan still saw the glimmer of a jewel in the network, and intended to polish it to its former brilliance.

He was particularly interested in CBS's radio and television stations. Those stations, when added to Group W, would give Westinghouse a collection of 15 stations in seven of the nation's largest markets and reaching one-third of the nation's homes. Those operations would also account for about 80% of Westinghouse's total operating profits.

Approach and Engagement

On August 1, 1995, Westinghouse Electric announced its $5.4 billion agreement to acquire CBS Inc. The deal, valued at $81 per share, boosted Westinghouse's debt load to about $8 billion. Jordan planned to trim that amount by shedding the company's non-core operations. Shareholders expressed their confidence in the strategy by approving the deal in November 1995. After gaining the approval of the Federal Communications Commission, Westinghouse and CBS completed the transaction on November 28, 1995.

Products and Services

Among CBS's television offerings were: *48 Hours*, *60 Minutes*, *CBS Evening News with Dan Rather*, *Chicago Hope*, *Diagnosis Murder*, *Early Edition*, *LA Doctors*, *Martial Law*, *Nash Bridges*, *Touched by an Angel*, and *Walker, Texas Ranger*.

In addition, the company also owned 14 television stations; 80% of Infinity Broadcasting, which owned a collection of 160 radio stations; and the cable networks The Nashville Network and Country Music Television.

Review of the Outcome

Analysts who had been pessimistic about the deal from the beginning saw their skepticism justified in the immediate wake of the acquisition. Audience levels dropped 20% in 1995, and operating earnings plummeted 98% over the previous year. As David Letterman's late-night talk show, one of the network's prizes, slipped behind Jay Leno's, the host grumbled about quitting when his contract expired. CBS's highly rated *60 Minutes* was mired in controversy over its journalistic standards when it refused to air an interview with a tobacco industry whistle-blower for fear of legal repercussions. A change in the programming schedule caused *Murder, She Wrote* to drop from ninth place to 59th place. And the network's launch of 11 new shows produced no winners.

All that soon changed, however. Westinghouse installed a new management team at CBS. It secured a two-year, multi-million dollar television contract with Bill Cosby. And it began shedding its non-broadcasting businesses, reducing its debt load and gaining the resources to strengthen its core interests. It acquired a dominant share of the nation's radio market by purchasing Infinity Broadcasting for $5.4 billion in 1996. It solidified this hold in 1998 with the purchase of American Radio Systems, thereby adding 90 radio stations to its collection.

In the 1996/97 television season, CBS broke out of its third-place rank by slipping past ABC. In the 1998/99 season, it regained the title of the highest rated network in the U.S. Executives at Westinghouse, now known as CBS Corp., were more than pleased that they had brought about this impressive turnaround in such a short time.

Research

Baker, Stephen, and Michael Oneal, with Ronald Grover. "Too Big a Stretch?" in *Business Week*, 31 July 1995. Discusses the financial strain that a purchase of CBS would place on Westinghouse.

"CBS Inc.," in *Notable Corporate Chronologies*, The Gale Group, 1999. Profiles the history of the company.

CBS Corp. Home Page, available at http://www.cbs.com. Official World Wide Web Page for CBS. Provides information on the programming of the Web site visitor's local CBS affiliate.

Labich, Kenneth. "Maybe Jordan Does Know What He's Doing at Westinghouse," in *Fortune*, 22 July 1996. Offers reasons why the CBS purchase may have been a strategic move after all.

Robins, J. Max. "Westinghouse Gives CBS Cause for Optimism," in *Variety*, 4 December 1995. Relates the investments that Westinghouse made in the newly acquired CBS to ensure its turnaround.

The Players

Westinghouse Electric Chairman and CEO: Michael H. Jordan. Michael Jordan, an 18-year veteran of PepsiCo, became CEO of Westinghouse in 1993 and refocused the company on its broadcasting roots rather than the diverse array of holdings that had spread Westinghouse's assets over a wide range of industries. Critics were highly skeptical of his purchase of CBS, but his vision proved beneficial for both struggling companies. In 1999 Jordan was succeeded as chairman by David McLaughlin and as CEO by Mel Karmazin.

CBS Inc. Chairman and CEO: Laurence Tisch. The Lowes Corp., headed by Laurence Tisch, began buying CBS stock in 1985, at which time Tisch joined the network's board of directors. He was named CEO of CBS in 1986, and instituted drastic cost-cutting measures designed to reduce expenses and increase profitability at the ailing network. As part of that program, he sold the profitable CBS Records to Sony in 1988, a move for which he was sternly criticized. He resigned from CBS in 1995.

Rozansky, Michael L., and Stephen Seplow. "Westinghouse Agrees to Buy CBS for $5.4 Billion," in *Knight-Ridder/Tribune News Service*, 1 August 1995. Details the acquisition agreement.

"Westinghouse Electric Corp.," in *Notable Corporate Chronologies*, The Gale Group, 1999. Details the history of Westinghouse.

RICHARD BARROW

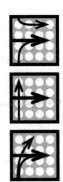

WINGS HOLDING & NORTHWEST AIRLINES

Northwest Airlines Corp.
5101 Northwest Dr.
St. Paul, MN 55121-3034
USA

tel: (612)726-2111
fax: (612)727-7795
web: http://www.nwa.com

nationality: USA
date: July 27, 1989
affected: Wings Holding Inc., USA
affected: Northwest Airlines, Inc., USA, founded 1926

Overview of the Merger

When Northwest Airlines was under siege by a hostile bidder in early 1989, several other suitors emerged as white knight rescuers of the troubled airline. The winning offer of $3.65 billion came from Wings Holding Inc., an investment group organized by Alfred Checchi. When he took control of the newly private company that July, critics expected him to worsen NWA's already tarnished reputation and sagging balance sheet. Within a year, however, Checchi actually improved the company's situation.

History of Northwest Airlines Corp.

Northwest Airways was established in 1926 by a group of Minnesota and Michigan investors led by Colonel Louis Britton. Based in Michigan, the company's headquarters were at Wold-Chamberlain Field, Minneapolis/St. Paul. The airline carried its first air mail, between Chicago, Illinois, and Minneapolis/St. Paul (Twin Cities). It also introduced the nation's first closed-cabin commercial aircraft, which was capable of carrying three passengers. The young company added to its assets before the end of its first year, acquiring the Ford Transport Co., a subsidiary of Ford Motor Co.

The airline carried its first ticketed passenger, from Minneapolis/St. Paul to Chicago, in July 1997. The next year Northwest Airways launched weekly service linking the Twin Cities and Winnipeg, Manitoba, Canada. It also looked to expand its service to include Montana, Iowa, the Dakotas, and Seattle and Tacoma, Washington. In July 1930 a consortium of Twin Cities investors purchased Northwest Airways and moved it headquarters to the downtown St. Paul airport. Under its new owner, the airline's first ground radio installation was erected.

Northwest Airways reincorporated as Northwest Airlines, Inc. (NAI) in 1934. That year the U.S. government temporarily suspended all airmail contracts, but NAI survived through its passenger and freight operations. It also began to use all-weather aircraft for the first time. In 1938 NAI introduced the first practical oxygen mask for high-altitude flight, and the next year employed its first stewardesses.

NAI went public in 1941. During World War II it was selected by the government to operate military air supply routes in Alaska and the Aleutian Islands, and company pilots were used to ferry aircraft within the U.S. Although many of the airline's domestic routes were suspended for the duration of the war, its revenues from passengers exceeded those from mail for the first time.

Expansion of its domestic routes in the latter 1940s included the introduction of service to New York City, New Jersey, Washington D.C., and Anchorage, Alaska. It also expanded to the Far East, flying to Tokyo, Japan; Seoul, Korea; Shanghai, China; and Manila, The Philippines. In 1949 NAI became the first airline to offer transcontinental all-coach flights and to offer beverage service on its flights.

Donald W. Nyrop became president in 1954. His insistence that the company's debt never exceed 10% of its capital made NAI one of the most debt-free companies in the airline industry. Two years later it consolidated its administrative operations at a new, $17.5 million facility at Wold-Chamberlain Field in St. Paul. In 1957 the airline introduced first class service. It also pioneered effective air turbulence prediction, and in 1962 originated a system to locate and forecast wind shears. In 1964 NAI received the Flight Safety Foundation Safety Award for its wind turbulence research.

NAI became the nation's first all-jet airline by decommissioning its last propeller-driven aircraft in 1963. The next year it received a Presidential Award for its development of export markets in the Orient. The company's service grew to include Philadelphia and Honolulu during the 1960s. In 1968 NAI posted the highest net profit in the U.S. airline industry.

In September 1970 NAI was the first airline to use Boeing 747 aircraft on its Trans-Pacific routes. The next year the infamous D.B. Cooper hijacked an NAI airliner in Washington, D.C., demanding $200,000 and two parachutes. He then parachuted out of the aircraft over Washington state, and was never found.

The airline introduced the industry's first computer-generated ticketing system and the first direct computer reservation service in 1973. Nyrop became chairman in 1976, and two years later challenged the airline pilots' union by establishing a mutual fund with 15 other airlines to enable the companies to withstand strikes. Nyrop retired in 1979, and his successor inherited poor labor relations arising from Nyrop's actions. That year NAI extended its service to Europe, starting all-cargo service to Glasgow, Scotland and to Copenhagen, Denmark. European expansion occurred rapidly, and in 1980 alone the airline added routes to Shannon, Ireland; Oslo, Norway; and Hamburg, Germany.

The Business

Financials

Revenue (1998): $9 billion

Employees (1998): 50,600

SICs / NAICS

sic 4512 - Air Transportation-Scheduled

naics 481111 - Scheduled Passenger Air Transportation

naics 481112 - Scheduled Freight Air Transportation

In 1984 the company reorganized, forming NWA, Inc. as a holding company to manage all corporate operations. Steven G. Rothmeier added the post of chairman to his presidential responsibilities that year. NWA inaugurated Northwest Airlink, a major marketing program involving mutual feeder agreements with small and local airline companies and acquired Mainline Travel, Inc., a Minnesota-based tour operator. The airline also announced its largest aircraft purchase in its history—a $2 billion contract for ten Boeing 747-400s, ten Boeing 757s, and three Boeing 747-200s.

NWA acquired Republic Airlines for $884 million in 1986, the same year that it purchased a 50% interest in the PARS computer reservation system operated by Trans World Airlines. Negotiations with the airline's pilots broke down, and the pilots began working without a contract. Two years later NWA became the first U.S. airline to ban smoking on all domestic flights.

In 1989 oil billionaire Marvin Davis made a hostile bid to purchase NWA for $90 per share. Several other suitors, including Pan America Airlines, joined in the bidding. In the end, Wings Holdings, an investment firm organized by Alfred A. Checchi that included KLM Royal Dutch Airlines, purchased NWA for $121 per share. Checchi installed himself as chairman, with fellow-investor Frederic V. Malek as president.

NWA acquired a 25% interest in Hawaiian Airlines in 1990. It entered into a variety of cooperative programs with the airline, including the assumption of Hawaiian Airlines' Australia routes. That year it merged its PARS computer system with Delta Airline's DATAS II system to form WorldSpan. NWA recorded a $10.4 million net loss for 1990, largely due to increased fuel prices caused by the Iraqi invasion of Kuwait.

The Officers

Chairman: Gary L. Wilson

President and CEO: John H. Dasburg

Exec. VP and Chief Operating Officer: Richard H. Anderson

Exec. VP, Marketing and Distribution: J. Timothy Griffin

Exec. VP, International, Sales, and Information Services: Philip C. Haan

In 1991 the airline entered into a joint venture with KLM to provide service from the Twin Cities to Amsterdam, Netherlands. NWA also became the first U.S. airline to contract for service to Ho Chi Minh City, Vietnam. Also in 1991 it signed a $20 million deal with America West Airlines, helping the troubled Phoenix, Arizona-based airline out of debt in exchange for its route from Honolulu to Nagoya, Japan. NWA considered acquiring Midway Airlines, but instead opted to purchase its facilities at Midway Airport, Chicago, for $21 million. NWA also paid $35.5 million for valuable gates and landing rights at Washington National Airport.

The WorldPerks frequent flier program was established with KLM in 1992. That year NWA began implementing cost reductions. It trimmed staff by laying off 610 employees, including 110 pilots, and sold 18 of its Midway Airport gates to Southwest Airlines for $15 million.

The airline's tenure as a private company under the Checchi team ended in 1996, when the company went public as Northwest Airlines Corp. That year bad weather forced NWA to make full use of replacement aircrews, resulting in a pilot shortage that caused the cancellation of more than 500 flights systemwide. Earnings for 1996 reached $536.1 million, a record high for the company.

Checchi resigned in 1997 to pursue a political career. Incompatible corporate cultures and management styles led to conflicts that threatened to end the alliance between NWA and KLM, and in 1998 KLM sold back its stake in NWA. The two companies, however, agreed to extend their partnership for 10 years.

In early 1998 NWA paid $519 million in cash and stock to acquire 51% of Continental Airlines. Their employees and airplanes were kept separate, but they merged their route networks, frequent flyer programs, and advertising. Service across the airline shut down in August 1998, when 6,100 of its pilots went on strike. The strike ended two weeks later, with a resolution of contract negotiations.

Market Forces Driving the Merger

Northwest Airlines was experiencing difficulties in its digestion of Republic Airlines. Although the nation's third-largest carrier posted a 34% increase in earnings in 1987, it was met with a string of snags that earned it the dubious nickname "Northworst." Flight delays and cancellations occurred on a daily basis, and luggage was continually lost. Internal friction between the employees of the merged companies squelched morale. The company's long history of troubled relationships with pilots' and machinists' unions were not improved, either. But the most serious damage to NWA's image occurred in 1987, when two airline crashes killed a total of 165 people, and three of its pilots were convicted of flying while intoxicated.

Consequently, the airline's falling stock price left it vulnerable to a takeover. On March 30, 1989, oil billionaire Marvin Davis launched a $2.7 billion hostile bid to take NWA private. He also waged a proxy fight to replace members of the company's board with his own slate of directors. NWA Inc., the holding company of Northwest Airlines, Inc., rejected the offer and invited other bidders to make counteroffers.

Approach and Engagement

By mid-May four known bidders were vying for NWA. Pan Am Corp. topped Davis' bid with a $3.3 billion offer, and NWA's machinists' union had made an offer of an undisclosed amount. The fourth suitor was Wings Holding Inc., a consortium organized by Alfred A. Checchi. This group also included as investors KLM Royal Dutch Airlines; Bankers Trust New York, the nation's ninth-largest bank; Elders IXL Ltd., an Australian brewing company; and Fred Malek, Robert Blum, and Gary Wilson, three friends of Checchi.

On June 5 NWA's board rejected all offers and invited the submission of sweetened bids by June 16. Three days later, Wings Holding was announced to be the winner, with an offer of $121 per share, or $3.65 billion. Checchi installed a new seven-member board on July 27, even though the acquisition would not be formalized until it received the approval of the U.S. Department of Transportation.

The Transportation Department granted its conditional approval for the takeover on September 29, 1989. Federal regulations limited foreign ownership of a U.S. airline carrier to 25%. Despite the fact that the combined interest of KLM and Elders IXL represented only a 20% stake, the Department decided to impose a limitation on their cash investment as well, in an effort to curtail any attempt, particularly by KLM, to exercise control over NWA. To meet these impositions, Checchi agreed to cut KLM's $400 million investment to $175 million, and later secured other investments to make up the difference.

Products and Services

In 1999 Northwest Airlines served more than 400 cities in over 80 countries on six continents. It offered more than 1,700 flights daily, and also operated more than 130 nonstop flights between the U.S. and Asia each week. Its hub cities were Detroit, Memphis, Minneapolis/St. Paul, and Tokyo.

The airline had a fleet of more than 400 aircraft, including Boeing 727s, 747s, and 757s, McDonnell-Douglas DC-9s and DC-10s, and Airbus A320s. Northwest was also one of the world's largest cargo airlines, operating a dedicated fleet of eight B747 freighters.

Review of the Outcome

Checchi had never run a large company before taking control of NWA, so critics expected him to fail. Indeed, many of NWA's problems, especially its tarnished image, were not immediately corrected when he bought the company. If anything, the airline suffered additional headaches as a result of skyrocketing fuel prices and escalating fare wars.

Despite these obstacles, Checchi's team quickly began turning around the company. It implemented a $422 million, five-year improvement program. Most impressive, however, was Checchi's ability to reduce the company's debt under the airline's difficult circumstances. By December 1990 he had reduced the $3.1 billion in takeover-related debt to $1.5 billion. He accomplished this by selling airplanes, refinancing land in Japan, and obtaining loans and investments from a variety of sources. All the more remarkable was the airline's ability to afford to make strategic purchases, including a 25% stake in Hawaiian Airlines, as well as airport facilities in Chicago and Washington D.C.. In 1990 NWA's revenues climbed to $7.4 billion from $6.6 billion for the previous year.

Research

Cauchon, Dennis. "The Players Behind Bid for NWA," in *USA Today*, 21 June 1989. Offers a brief biographical sketch of the investors in Wings Holding.

Grover, Ronald, with Leah J. Nathans and Seth Payne. "Checchi and Wilson Are Old Hands at Corporate Dealmaking," in *Business Week*, 24 April 1989. Profiles both Al Checchi and Gary Wilson.

Kelly, Kevin, with Seth Payne. "Al Checchi's Steady Course through the Maelstrom," in *Business Week*, 27 May 1991. Reviews the airline's performance over the year since Checchi's takeover.

The Players

Director of Wings Holding Inc.: Alfred A. Checchi. Alfred Checchi returned to big-time dealmaking with his leveraged buyout of NWA in 1989. That transaction also reunited him with his friend and mentor, Gary L. Wilson. Wilson had first met 16-year-old Checchi while working at his uncle's economic consulting firm, and the two were involved in a number of business dealings in the years since. After graduating from Harvard Business School in 1976, Checchi was hired by Wilson, then company treasurer, to work at Marriott Corp. as his assistant. Together, the duo increased Marriott's market value 20 times over by selling hotels to private investors while continuing to manage them under contract. Checchi attempted to persuade J.W. Marriott Jr. to purchase an airline, convinced that a hotel/restaurant/travel company would be a strategic combination. Marriott, while respectful of Checchi's intelligence and business acumen, would not be swayed.

In 1982 Checchi became a financial consultant to the Fort Worth investors Sid R. Bass and Lee M. Bass. He advised the brothers on deals that included Texaco Inc., Arvida Corp., and Walt Disney Co., in which they purchased a 25% stake, and established Airlie Group L.P. as an investment group dealing in high-yield, high-risk junk bonds. After earning millions for himself, and even more for the Basses, Checchi resigned in 1986. Checchi took a low profile after leaving the Basses. He worked on a city panel formed to study the long-range problems of Los Angeles and even established Bedford Group for the development of government-subsidized housing. Checchi also considered a career in politics, but was disenchanted by the amount of time required to achieve a position that he believed suited his abilities.

In 1989 Checchi organized a group of investors to participate in the bidding for Northwest Airlines. After beating out several other suitors, Checchi gained control of the company and took the chairmanship. He tapped into innovative sources for acquiring outside investment in the company, and in only a year had retired $1.6 billion of the company's acquisition-related debt.

Politics continued to call to Checchi, so he resigned as chairman in April 1997 to pursue a candidacy for the Democratic governor of California. After spending $35 million of his own money in campaign funds, however, Checchi lost in the June 1998 primaries.

"Northwest Airlines Corp.," in *Notable Corporate Chronologies*, The Gale Group, 1999. Provides a history of the company.

Northwest Airlines Corp. Home Page, available at http://www.nwa.com. Official World Wide Web Home Page for Northwest Airlines Corp. Offers historical, financial, and route information; news releases; and an online flight reservation service.

Rosenblatt, Robert A. "U.S. Approves Northwest Deal, Sets Conditions," in *Los Angeles Times*, 30 September 1989. Describes the terms set by the Transportation Department in approving the acquisition.

KIMBERLY N. STEVENS

WORLDCOM & MCI COMMUNICATIONS

nationality: USA
date: September 14, 1998
affected: WorldCom Inc., USA, founded 1983
affected: MCI Communications Corp., USA, founded 1968

MCI WorldCom, Inc.
515 E. Amite St.
Jackson, MS 39201-2702
USA

tel: (601)360-8600
fax: (601)974-8350
web: http://www.mciworldcom.com

Overview of the Acquisition

MCI Communication's merger agreement with British Telecommunications (BT) was shattered by WorldCom's surprise bid for MCI. The stakes were raised even higher when GTE Corp. launched a bid of its own. When WorldCom raised its offer, BT backed down and GTE held firm. Ultimately, MCI's shareholders opted for WorldCom's $37 billion stock offer, and MCI WorldCom was formed in September 1998.

History of WorldCom Inc.

WorldCom, which began as a small company with a huge appetite, is the product of a September 1983 meeting between Bernard J. Ebbers, Bill Fields, David Singleton, and Murray Waldron. The founders met at a Mississippi coffeeshop, where they discussed the formation of a long-distance telephone company. A waitress suggested the name for their company—Long Distance Discount Service, shortened to LDDS.

The plan entailed reselling long-distance service to local businesses. The partners borrowed $500,000 and purchased a small phone company. That November LDDS received permission from the Mississippi Public Service Commission to offer long-distance service and soon landed the University of Southern Mississippi as its first customer.

Ebbers assumed the role of CEO in April 1985. He realized that the company would achieve quicker growth by building a network of existing carriers rather than signing up customers piecemeal. He also sought to concentrate on the largely ignored small business market.

Because the young company lacked the capital to purchase carriers outright, it instead completed acquisitions by offering company stock. This successful strategy would become a hallmark of the company, enabling it to purchase much larger companies without straining its debt load.

By 1989 LDDS had purchased several companies with a total value of about $35 million. In August of that year it merged with Advantage Companies, Inc.,

The Business

Financials

Revenue (1998): $30.4 billion

Employees (1998): 70,000

SICs / NAICS

sic 4813 - Telephone Communications Except
     Radiotelephone

naics 513310 - Wired Telecommunications Carriers

going public in the process. The combined companies served 11 states in the southern and midwestern U.S. By 1991 several other acquisitions had extended LDDS into 27 states.

Advanced Telecommunications Corp. was acquired in 1992 for $850 million in stock. This company brought coverage in 26 states, and made LDDS the nation's fourth-largest long-distance carrier. In September 1993 a three-way merger united LDDS with Metromedia Communications Corp. and Resurgens Communication Group Inc. The resulting company was named LDDS Communications, Inc., of which Ebbers was CEO and John Kluge, chairman of Metromedia, became chairman.

LDDS merged with IDB Communications Group, Inc. in December 1994. This company brought to LDDS a domestic and international network providing long-distance, fax, data, television and radio transmission, and mobile satellite communications services. LDDS changed its name to WorldCom, Inc. the next year. The company also paid $2.5 billion to acquire WilTel Network Services, the network services operations of Williams Telecommunications Group, Inc. This acquisition added 11,000 miles of fiber optic capabilities on a global scale.

WorldCom became the first company to offer both local and long-distance services in the U.S. since 1984's break-up of AT&T. It merged with MFS Communications Co., Inc. in December 1996, thereby extending its fiber optic network in the U.S. and Europe. The $12 billion merger also brought in MFS's recently acquired subsidiary, UUNET Technologies, Inc., the world's largest Internet services provider (ISP). James Crowe, chairman of MFS, replaced the departing Kluge as chairman of WorldCom. The company now had a presence, albeit a small one, in the

local, long-distance, and data telecommunication segments. A much stronger presence was only an acquisition away.

In October 1997 WorldCom offered to purchase MCI Communications Corp., which had already agreed to merge with British Telecommunications PLC (BT). GTE entered into the bidding as well, but WorldCom was ultimately successful. The formation of MCI WorldCom Inc. was completed in September 1998.

Meanwhile, the company merged with Brooks Fiber Properties, Inc., in January 1998, adding 40 new local markets to its coverage. Two days later, on January 31, WorldCom acquired CompuServe Corp. and ANS Communications, Inc., the Internet and networking divisions of America Online, Inc.

In March 1999 MCI WorldCom announced a plan to double its pan-European fiber optic network to provide national coverage to Great Britain, France, and Germany. That November it became the first foreign-owned company to provide Type 1 telephone service in Japan.

MCI WorldCom moved to focus on its core communications business by selling MCI's investment in News Corp. for $1.39 billion in April 1999. As part of the same strategy, it also sold MCI Systemhouse, an information technology services company, to EDS.

In May 1999 MCI WorldCom agreed to acquire SkyTel Communications, Inc. The following month it invested in the formation of a fiber optic submarine cable system connecting Africa, Europe, and Asia. The company sold its 25% stake in New Zealand's Clear Communications to BT.

History of MCI Communications Corp.

In 1968 John Goeken and William G. McGowan founded Microwave Communications Inc., a microwave radio system to handle telephone calls between Chicago, Illinois, and St. Louis, Missouri. Later that year McGowan became chairman while Goeken left to pursue new opportunities, eventually forming Airfone.

The Federal Communications Commission (FCC) granted Microwave Communications the authorization to begin operations the following year, but the company received no assurance that it could expand its network or connect with existing AT&T lines. AT&T sued Microwave, blocking the new company from providing service.

Microwave Communications hired Kenneth Cox in 1971 to spearhead its legal drive to dismantle

AT&T's monopoly on telephonic communications. That year the company received final approval to begin providing services along the Chicago-St. Louis route, and officially opened for business as MCI Communications.

MCI issued public stock in June 1972, raising more than $100 million in capital. The following year the company reorganized as MCI Communications Corp., and began providing commercial private line service between Chicago and St. Louis. It faced financial difficulties, however, and was forced to appeal to the FCC for permission to route FX calls through AT&T's switched network.

The beginning of the end of the AT&T monopoly occurred in 1974. After MCI filed a civil antitrust suit against AT&T, the U.S. Department of Justice (DoJ) filed an antitrust suit designed to break up AT&T's system of Bell Telephone companies.

AT&T volleyed against MCI with a protest of its own. It asked the FCC to force MCI to cease offering its long-distance service for businesses, Execunet, which was in direct competition with AT&T. The FCC ruled for AT&T in 1975, but an Appeals court found for MCI the following year, requiring AT&T to reconnect Execunet to its network.

MCI also won the right to use AT&T switching equipment, but AT&T tripled its tariffs for MCI, ensuring that MCI's service remained more expensive. MCI sued AT&T for this practice, and in 1978 the U.S. Supreme Court ruled in favor of MCI. Two years later the courts also ruled in favor of MCI in its civil antitrust suit against AT&T. In 1982 AT&T settled the antitrust suit brought against it by the DoJ, agreeing to divest itself of its Bell Telephone subsidiaries. Two years later the break-up of the AT&T system was completed, forming several regional telephone operating companies (RBOCs).

In 1980 MCI entered the personal long-distance business, becoming a full-scale competitor with AT&T, and its revenues began to rise rapidly, approaching $1 billion in 1981. The following year it paid $195 million to acquire WUI Inc., a holding company for several communications subsidiaries, including Western Union International. In 1983 MCI became the first U.S. company aside from AT&T to offer international long-distance service.

In 1985 IBM agreed to purchase an 18% interest in MCI in order to supply MCI with the capital to expand its national network and to launch an aggressive marketing campaign. That year AT&T reduced its rates, crippling MCI's earnings and causing the company's stock to lose 65% of its value.

The Officers

Chairman: Bert C. Roberts, Jr.

President and CEO: Bernard J. Ebbers

President and CEO of MCI WorldCom International: Gerald H. Taylor

President and CEO of MCI WorldCom Internet/Technology and Solutions: John Sidgmore

President and CEO of MCI WorldCom U.S.: Tim Price

Chief Financial Officer: Scott D. Sullivan

MCI acquired Satellite Business Systems, a long-distance and data transmission company, in 1986. The company posted a net loss of $448.4 million that year, but rebounded the following year with net earnings of $85 million. In 1988 it acquired RCA Global Communications, Inc., a company providing worldwide fax, telex, and high-speed data transmission services. By 1989 long-distance telephone service accounted for 90% of corporate revenues.

In 1990 the company entered into an agreement to lay a transatlantic fiber optic cable in conjunction with British Telecommunications PLC (BT). That year MCI also purchased a 25% interest in INFONET Services Corp., a provider of international data services, and acquired the whole of Telecom*USA, the fourth-largest long-distance company in the U.S.

In 1991 it acquired Overseas Telecommunications Inc., an international leader in digital satellite services, giving MCI a 16% share of the U.S. domestic long-distance market. It also introduced its popular Friends and Family discount long-distance service for residential customers. McGowan retired that year, and was succeeded as chairman and CEO by Bert C. Roberts, Jr. At that time, the company maintained a 32,000-mile digital network, including analog capability.

BT purchased a 20% stake in MCI for $4.3 billion in 1993, and the two companies established Concert Communications Services as a global telecommunications joint venture. By 1994 MCI was the second-largest long-distance telephone service company in the U.S., with international service to 196 countries worldwide and diversified capabilities including fax and electronic mail services.

In 1995 MCI acquired SHL Systemhouse Inc. and agreed to purchase Darome Teleconferencing Inc., an audio and video conferencing service. It also invested $1 billion in News Corp. for the development of a direct broadcast satellite (DBS) system.

The Players

WorldCom Chairman and CEO: Bernard J. Ebbers. Bernard Ebbers, a native of Alberta, Canada, moved to Mississippi when he won a basketball scholarship at Mississippi College. He graduated in 1967 with a degree in physical education and took a job as a high school basketball coach. Ebbers remained there only briefly before passing onto careers as a garment warehouse manager and owner of nine Best Western hotels. In 1983 he joined with three friends to form LDDS, the predecessor of WorldCom. Ebbers became CEO and directed the company on its highly successful strategy of acquiring telecommunications through the issue of company stock rather than cash deals. He orchestrated the merger with MCI in 1998, at which time he became president and CEO of MCI WorldCom, Inc.

MCI Communications Chairman and CEO: Bert C. Roberts, Jr. Bert Roberts, Jr. graduated from John Hopkins University with a degree in electrical engineering. He began his long career with MCI Communications in 1972, and quietly moved through the executive ranks. In 1991 Roberts was appointed CEO, and the following year, upon the death of William G. McGowan, he assumed the post of chairman. In that role, he led MCI into the markets of data communications and integration, and helped the company record revenues of $13.3 billion in 1994. Roberts orchestrated MCI's merger with British Telecommunications, and then with WorldCom when that company offered a competing bid. Upon the formation of MCI WorldCom, Inc., Roberts became chairman.

The following year MCI entered into a definitive merger agreement with BT to create the world's first global communications company, to be called Concert PLC. MCI announced a realignment of its senior executives in anticipation of this deal. However, after MCI reported a loss of $800 million from its local operations in 1997, BT cut its offer by 20%, making MCI vulnerable to bids from other companies. Both WorldCom and GTE entered into the bidding, with WorldCom ultimately emerging victorious. The resulting company, MCI WorldCom, was formed in September 1998.

Market Forces Driving the Acquisition

By 1997 WorldCom, Inc. had grown into one of the world's most diverse telecommunication companies. Ever since Bernard Ebbers had assumed the post of CEO of the young company, it had undertaken an aggressive strategy of expansion by acquisition. Through strategic purchases, which numbered more than 40 since 1993, WorldCom had broken into the local, long-distance, international, and Internet telecommunications segments. Despite its integrated presence in the industry, WorldCom was by no means a household name, as it was still a relatively small player in each segment. Internet services was the exception, where it was the global leader.

MCI was the second-largest long-distance provider in the U.S., but its services were carried over an aging network that was no match against the high-capacity networks of strong newcomers like Qwest. Investment into the updating of its network would be costly, especially since growth in that segment was slow. Its efforts to break into the local market were repeatedly blocked by regulatory impediments at the hands of the territorial Baby Bells.

British Telecommunications PLC (BT) had purchased a 20% stake in MCI in 1993, and the 1997 the two companies agreed to a full-fledged merger. BT sought to leverage MCI's presence in the U.S. market in order to develop a global one-stop telecommunications service. MCI looked favorably upon BT's technology and financial strength as a means of finally establishing itself in the American local market.

To many analysts, however, a union with WorldCom made more strategic sense for MCI than one with BT. The synergies between the two were far greater than MCI could hope for with BT, as both companies already had capabilities for local and long-distance services. By combining those operations, the combined company would be the nation's second-largest long-distance carrier, a formidable force against such giants as AT&T, Sprint, and the Baby Bells.

Moreover, a union between WorldCom and MCI would control about 55% of all U.S.-originated Internet traffic, the fastest growing telecommunications segment. *Time* magazine called this telecommunication environment "one of those great turning points in business history: telecommunication companies fear being left behind at a time when data and Internet traffic has begun to surpass the volume of voice calls." It was growing so rapidly that "e-mail, video and other data could account for 99% of all telecommunications traffic by 2004."

Approach and Engagement

In November 1996 MCI and BT agreed to a merger that would form a company called Concert PLC. The agreement called for BT to pay $21 billion in cash and stock for the 80% of MCI that it didn't already own. The deal began to crumble the following summer, however, when MCI's losses in the local market were twice the anticipated amount and its growth in the long-distance market had dropped. As a result, MCI's share price kept falling. BT's investors grew uneasy, and BT reduced its purchase price by 20% in August 1997. This angered MCI's shareholders and opened the door to rival bidders.

On October 1, 1997, WorldCom announced its offer of $30.5 billion for MCI. Valued at $41.50 per share of WorldCom stock, the deal represented a 41% premium to MCI's stock price. Although the BT deal consisted partly of a cash offer, which investors typically find more appealing than a stock swap, WorldCom stock was no ordinary stock. According to *The Economist*, its average annual return during the 1990s was 55.8%, compared to BT's 9.4% and MCI's 4.3%.

Moreover, the WorldCom deal offered MCI shareholders a 45% stake in the new company, significantly higher than the 25% stake offered by BT. WorldCom also expected remarkable savings in synergies between the two companies. It estimated savings of $2.5 billion in the first year alone, growing to $5 billion in the fifth year. BT had projected savings of $850 million starting in the fifth year.

A third eligible suitor entered the scene on October 15, when GTE Corp. launched a $28 billion, all-cash bid. This represented $40 per share, in between BT's cash and stock deal and WorldCom's stock offer.

The idea of a bidding war made BT's "risk averse shareholders," as the company's CEO Sir Peter Bonfield referred to them in *Computergram International*, nervous, so BT stepped out of the bidding, holding onto its previously acquired 20% stake in MCI.

WorldCom sweetened its offer by 20% to $51 per share, or a total of $37 billion. GTE's stock price had fallen due to the $30 billion in additional debt it would take on in acquiring MCI. The company left its offer on the table, just in case WorldCom's stock should plummet, thereby making a guaranteed cash price more appealing to MCI's shareholders.

On November 10, 1997, WorldCom and MCI agreed to merge; BT gave its blessing to the union as well. The merging companies' shareholders approved the deal in March 1998. At the same time, however, the deal showed the first sign of trouble. Mounting criticism over the creation of an Internet monopoly surfaced, although many analysts believed that the issue wouldn't become a regulatory deal breaker. They suggested that the demand for Internet services far outweighed supply, and that a monopoly could rapidly be shattered at the introduction of new ISPs.

Still, the European Commission granted its approval in early July with the condition that the combined company shed MCI's Internet operations. Cable & Wireless PLC agreed to purchase the divested property for $1.75 billion. The U.S. Department of Justice agreed to those terms, granting its approval that same month. The Federal Communications Commission (FCC) extended its approval on September 14, 1998, and the deal was completed that same day.

Products and Services

Globally, MCI WorldCom was the second-largest long-distance carrier in the U.S. in 1998, and was a leader in providing integrated voice, Internet, and data communications services. It served millions of U.S. business and residential customers over a 45,000-mile, all-fiber high capacity nationwide network. The company operated in four primary business sectors:

The **Voice** segment offers local and long-distance services to customers in the U.S. In 1998 it was a $20 billion business that had grown nine percent since 1997.

Data offers high bandwidth services that include private line circuits, ATM, and frame relay services. This segment in 1998 generated over $6 billion in annual revenues, and had grown 28% over the previous year.

The **Internet** segment was the fastest growing sector in 1998. Having grown 69% since 1997, this group represented over $2.6 billion in annual revenues. Its primary operating companies were UUNET and MCI WorldCom Advanced Networks.

International operations recorded revenues of $1.3 billion in 1998, a 56% increase over the previous year. MCI WorldCom operated on a global basis, offering services in Mexico, Latin America, Europe, and the Asia-Pacific region.

Changes to the Industry

The newly formed MCI WorldCom emerged as the second-largest long-distance carrier in the U.S., with nearly a 25% market share. Of even greater importance to the firm was its ability to offer a greater package of integrated services. By bundling its local, long-distance, and Internet services to its customers, it could serve as a one-stop telecommunications shop. This capability would not only provide the convenience of seamless service, it would also likely be offered for lower rate.

MCI WorldCom immediately took steps toward that end. Only two weeks after this new company was formed, it announced On-Net for business customers. The service was the first wholly-owned "local to global to local" network for both voice and data. Bernie Ebbers said in *The Red Herring* that "having your own end-to-end network, without needing to go through different companies, in different countries, is very important in ensuring high-quality service for data."

Other telecommunication companies announced similar services at about the same time. Sprint revealed ION, a network based on ATM technology, and AT&T announced its Integrated Network Connection Service, scheduled for release in late 1999. In addition, AT&T acquired IBM's Global Network in December 1998, and merged with TCI the following March, gaining access to a cable network.

Not everyone agreed about the appeal of the consolidation of telecommunication companies to form integrated service providers. Just after the FCC approved the formation of MCI WorldCom, the commission's chairman William Kennard brought into question the approval of such mergers in the future. Referring to the WorldCom/MCI deal in *Network World*, he said "Once this merger is consummated, the industry will once again be...just a merger away from undue concentration."

Review of the Outcome

As part of the merger's approval, the newly formed company sold its Internet business to Cable & Wireless for $1.6 billion. MCI also exited from its Concert joint venture by selling its 25% stake to its partner, BT, for $1 billion.

About 2,000 positions were eliminated in the wake of the merger. Completion of the union also brought the departure of two MCI executives: Gerald Taylor, its CEO and a founder, and Lance Boxer, its chief information officer.

MCI WorldCom entered into an agreement with Bell Atlantic in February 1999 to begin offering residential telephone services in New York. This was the first in a series of agreements to lease local services from Baby Bells until the company's own network could be built.

Research

"BT's Bonfield Blames MCI Failure on Shareholders," in *Computergram International,* 26 November 1997. Briefly relates the reluctance of BT's shareholders to raise the company's bid.

Dodge, John. "Started in a Coffee Shop and Named by a Waitress," in *PC Week,* 20 October 1997. Profiles the history of WorldCom.

Greenwald, John. "Bernie's Deal," in *Time,* 13 October 1997. Profiles WorldCom and its chief, Bernard Ebbers.

Greenwald, John, and Bruce van Voorst. "Dial M for Merger," in *Time,* 27 October 1997. Describes how the boom in data services sparked consolidation in the telecom industry.

"MCI Communications Corp." in *Notable Corporate Chronologies,* The Gale Group, 1999. Lists major events in the history of MCI.

MCI WorldCom, Inc. Home Page, available at http://www.mciworldcom.com. Official World Wide Web Page for MCI WorldCom. Includes financial information, descriptions of services, news releases, and career opportunities.

Pappalardo, Tim, and Denise Greene. "Telecom Mega-Mergers Not All Bad," in *Network World,* 28 September 1998. Offers varying opinions of the consolidation occurring in the telecom industry.

WorldCom, Inc. 1997 Annual Report, WorldCom, Inc., 1997. Provides a detailed review of WorldCom's annual operations.

"WorldCom Tucks in—Again," in *The Economist,* 4 October 1997. Describes the reasons that WorldCom and MCI sought a union.

Zerega, Blaise. "The Next Ma Bell," in *The Red Herring,* May 1999. Explains the importance of data services in the telecommunications industry, with an emphasis on MCI WorldCom.

RICHARD BARROW

CONTRIBUTORS

Patricia Archilla received an MBA from Colorado University. As a board member of several major U.S. corporations, she lends her expertise to the business community as a consultant and occasional writer for consumer and trade publications.

Richard Barrow, a graduate of University of California-Los Angeles (UCLA), is a freelance writer and editor. He is currently working on various scripts, as well as a full-length novel. He lives with his wife Kara and their three children in Santa Monica.

Sean C. Mackey received his Bachelor's of Art in Writing and Literature from the Naropa Institute. He is a freelance writer, adult education instructor in accounting and English, and a volunteer scoutmaster for an inner-city Boy Scout Troop in Denver, Colorado.

Davis McMillan has nearly 20 years of experience in scholarly and professional writing. The recipient of a bachelor's degree in journalism, he has written numerous journal and newspapers articles, many of which have reached a nationwide audience.

Samantha Morrison was a gerontology student before becoming a musician and process server. She works as a freelance writer on a part-time basis in the Denver area.

Alice M. Ritscherle received a B.A. in History and Literature from the University of Wisconsin-Madison and an M.A. in History from the University of North Carolina at Chapel Hill. As a doctoral student of European History at the University of Michigan-Ann Arbor, she is conducting research for a dissertation related to post-1945 Britain. She is also working on a novel-length piece of fiction.

AnnaMarie L. Sheldon earned a B.S. in English Language and Literature at Eastern Michigan University and an M.A. in Composition Theory from Wayne State University. She is currently working as a freelance business writer/editor and community college writing teacher in Orlando, Florida.

Christina M. Stansell received her Bachelor's of Art in Interdisciplinary Studies with a concentration in Business, Communication, and Spanish from Eastern Michigan University. She is a freelance business writer living in Detroit, Michigan.

Kimberly N. Stevens earned degrees in economics and history from Michigan State University. She has taught at the community college level for seven years.

Deborah J. Untener received a bachelor's degree in anthropology from Oakland University. She worked as an editor for Gale Research for five years before becoming a freelance writer and editor in Colorado. She volunteers as an editor for the wolf restoration organization Sinapu and as a fingerprinter for the Broomfield Police Department.

Thera Williams earned an M.A. in business education from the University of Central Florida. She teaches business and marketing classes at the community college level and also works as a freelance business writer.

CHRONOLOGY

1868	New York Central Railroad & Erie Railroad (canceled)
1930	Exxon & Anglo-American Oil
1931	Standard Oil Company of New York & Vacuum Oil
1955	Textron & American Woolen
1957	Procter & Gamble & Clorox
1960	Von's Grocery & Shopping Bag Food Stores
1963	Philadelphia National Bank & Girard Trust Corn Exchange Bank (canceled)
1965	Consolidated Foods & Gentry (canceled)
1966	Gulf + Western & Paramount Pictures
1967	Gillette & Braun
1968	General Mills & Gorton's
1968	LTV & Jones & Laughlin
1968	Pennsylvania Railroad & New York Central Railroad
1970	ITT & Hartford Fire Insurance
1974	International Nickel & ESB
1975	Gulf + Western & Simon & Schuster
1977	C. Itoh & Ataka
1979	Shell Oil & Belridge Oil
1980	Grand Metropolitan & Liggett
1981	Du Pont & Conoco
1981	Prudential Insurance & The Bache Group
1981	Sears, Roebuck & Dean Witter Reynolds
1981	Société Nationale Elf Aquitaine & Texasgulf
1982	Allied & Bendix
1982	Anheuser-Busch & Campbell Taggart
1982	Gulf Oil & Cities Service (canceled)
1982	Insurance Company of North America & Connecticut General
1982	Mesa Petroleum & Cities Service (canceled)
1982	U.S. Steel & Marathon Oil
1983	GTE & Sprint
1983	Quaker Oats & Stokely-Van Camp
1984	Champion International & St. Regis Paper
1984	General Motors & Electronic Data Systems
1984	Gulf + Western & Prentice-Hall
1984	The Limited & Carter Hawley Hale (canceled)
1984	Mesa Petroleum & Phillips Petroleum (canceled)
1985	Mobil & Superior Oil
1984	Texaco & Getty Oil
1984	Textron & Chicago Pacific (canceled)

1984 U.S. Steel & National Steel (canceled)

1985 Baxter Travenol & American Hospital Supply

1985 Chevron & Gulf Oil

1985 Coastal & American Natural Resources

1985 Cooper Industries & McGraw-Edison

1985 General Motors & Hughes Aircraft

1985 Sir James Goldsmith & Crown Zellerbach

1985 Hasbro Industries & Milton Bradley

1985 Carl Icahn & Trans World Airlines

1985 InterNorth & Houston Natural Gas

1985 Johnson Controls & Hoover Universal

1985 Mesa Petroleum & Unocal (canceled)

1985 Monsanto & G.D. Searle

1985 Nestle & Carnation

1985 News Corp. & Twentieth Century Fox

1985 Occidental Petroleum & Diamond Shamrock (canceled)

1985 Pantry Pride & Revlon

1985 R.J. Reynolds & Nabisco Brands

1985 Royal Dutch/Shell & Shell Oil

1985 Turner Broadcasting System & CBS (canceled)

1986 Bertelsmann & Doubleday

1986 Bertelsmann & RCA/Ariola International

1986 Burroughs & Sperry

1986 Campeau & Allied Stores

1986 Citicorp & Quotron Systems

1986 General Electric & RCA

1986 GTE Sprint Communications & United Telecommunications

1986 James River & Crown Zellerbach

1986 Kohlberg Kravis Roberts & Beatrice

1986 Kohlberg Kravis Roberts & Safeway Stores

1986 Northwest Airlines & Republic Airlines

1986 Ralston Purina & Drake Bakeries

1986 Ralston Purina & Union Carbide

1986 Turner Broadcasting System & MGM/UA Entertainment

1986 U.S. Steel & Texas Oil

1987 British Petroleum & Standard Oil of Ohio

1987 Fujitsu & Fairchild Semiconductor International (canceled)

1987 Hoechst & Celanese

1987 Klynveld Main Goerdeler & Peat Marwick Mitchell

1987 Manpower & Blue Arrow

1987 National Amusements & Viacom

1987 Sara Lee & Akzo Consumenten Produkten

1987 Southwestern Bell & Metromedia

1988 Amoco & Dome Petroleum

1988 Asea & BBC Brown Boveri

1988 BAT Industries & Farmers Group

1988 Bridgestone & Firestone

1988 Credit Suisse & First Boston

1988 Eastman Kodak & Sterling Drug

1988 Federal Express & Tiger International

1988 ICN Pharmaceuticals & Roche Holding (canceled)

1988 Kohlberg Kravis Roberts & RJR Nabisco

1988 MacAndrews & Forbes & Marvel Entertainment

1988 Marks & Spencer & Brooks Brothers

1988 Philip Morris & Kraft

1989 Bristol-Myers & Squibb

1989 Coastal & Texas Eastern (canceled)

1989 Deloitte Haskins & Sells & Touche Ross

1989 Ernst & Whinney & Arthur Young

1989 Fletcher Challenge & Rural Banking and Finance

1989 Grand Metropolitan & Pillsbury

1989 Marion Laboratories & Merrell Dow Pharmaceuticals

1989 SmithKline Beckman & Beecham Group

1989 Sony & Columbia Pictures Entertainment

1989 Stone Container & Consolidated Bathurst

1989 Time & Warner

1989 UAL Management and Employees & UAL (canceled)

1989 Wings Holding & Northwest Airlines

1990	ConAgra & Beatrice
1990	Forstmann Little & General Instrument
1990	Forstmann Little & Gulfstream Aerospace
1990	Georgia-Pacific & Great Northern Nekoosa
1990	Gillette & Wilkinson Sword
1990	Matsushita Electric Industrial & MCA
1990	McCaw Cellular Communications & LIN Broadcasting
1990	Michelin & Uniroyal Goodrich
1990	Novell & Lotus (canceled)
1990	Rhone-Poulenc & Rorer
1990	Roche Holding & Genentech
1990	Siemens & Nixdorf
1991	AT&T & NCR
1991	Cadence Design & Valid Logic
1991	General Cinema & Harcourt Brace Jovanovich
1991	GTE & Contel
1991	Pirelli & Continental (canceled)
1992	Kyoei Steel & Florida Steel
1992	Nestle & Source Perrier
1993	Cadbury Schweppes & A&W Brands
1993	Costco & Price
1993	Cyprus Minerals & Amax
1993	Merck & Medco Containment Services
1993	Primerica & Travelers
1993	Reed International & Elsevier
1993	Renault & Volvo (canceled)
1994	Adobe Systems & Aldus
1994	Akzo & Nobel Industries
1994	American Home Products & American Cyanamid
1994	AT&T & McCaw Cellular Communications
1994	Bell Atlantic & TCI (canceled)
1994	Columbia Healthcare & Hospital Corp. of America
1994	Conseco & Kemper (canceled)
1994	Eli Lilly & PCS Health Systems
1994	Federated Department Stores & R.H. Macy

1994	Forstmann Little & Ziff-Davis
1994	Hollinger & Sun-Times
1994	Kohlberg Kravis Roberts & Borden
1994	Northrop & Grumman
1994	Novell & WordPerfect
1994	Panhandle Eastern & Associated Natural Gas
1994	Paramount & Macmillan
1994	Quaker Oats & Snapple
1994	Reed Elsevier & Mead Data Central
1994	Roche Holding & Syntex
1994	Sandoz & Gerber Products
1994	SmithKline Beecham & Diversified Pharmaceuticals Services
1994	Southwestern Bell & Cox Enterprises (canceled)
1994	Viacom & Blockbuster
1994	Viacom & Paramount
1995	Burlington Northern & Santa Fe Pacific
1995	Cadbury Schweppes & Dr. Pepper/Seven Up
1995	Glaxo Holdings & Wellcome
1995	Hoechst & Marion Merrell Dow
1995	IBM & Lotus
1995	ING & Barings
1995	Ingersoll-Rand & Clark Equipment
1995	Interbrew & Labatt Brewing
1995	Interstate Bakeries & Labatt Brewing
1995	Kirk Kerkorian, Lee Iacocca & Chyrsler
1995	Kimberly-Clark & Scott Paper
1995	Lockheed & Martin Marietta
1995	Microsoft & Intuit (canceled)
1995	Pharmacia & Upjohn
1995	Rockwell International & AeroSpace Technologies of Australia
1995	Rockwell International & Reliance Electric
1995	Seagram & Dole Food
1995	Seagram & MCA
1995	Southern & Southwestern Electricity
1995	Travelers & Metropolitan Life Insurance

1995	Westinghouse Electric & CBS
1996	Aetna & U.S. Healthcare
1996	Allegheny Ludlum & Teledyne
1996	Chase Manhattan & Chemical Bank
1996	Crown Cork and Seal & Carnaud Metalbox
1996	Ensco International & Dual Drilling
1996	First Chicago & NBD Bancorp
1996	First Union & First Fidelity
1996	Fleet Financial Group & National Westminster Bancorp
1996	Gillette & Duracell
1996	Hilton Hotels & Bally Entertainment
1996	Johnson & Johnson & Cordis Corp.
1996	Lockheed Martin & Loral
1996	Lucas Industries & Varity
1996	Microsoft & Vermeer Technologies
1996	Packard Bell & NEC
1996	Rite Aid & Revco (canceled)
1996	Sandoz & Ciba-Geigy
1996	Seagate Technology & Conner Peripherals
1996	Stroh Companies & G. Heileman
1996	Thomson & Daewoo (canceled)
1996	Thomson & West Publishing
1996	Time Warner & Turner Broadcasting System
1996	Tracor & AEL Industries
1996	Ultramar & Diamond Shamrock
1996	Union Pacific & Southern Pacific Transportation
1996	U S West & Continental Cablevision
1996	Walt Disney & ABC
1997	Apple Computer & NeXT Software
1997	Ashland Coal & Arch Mineral
1997	Bell Atlantic & NYNEX
1997	Bergen Brunswig & IVAX (canceled)
1997	Boeing & McDonnell Douglas
1997	British Telecommunications & MCI WorldCom (canceled)
1997	Canal Plus & NetHold

1997	Credit Suisse & Winterthur
1997	CUC International & HFS
1997	Dominion Resources & East Midlands Electricity
1997	Duke Power & PanEnergy
1997	Filipacchi Medias & Hachette Filipacchi Press
1997	Grand Metropolitan & Guinness
1997	James River & Fort Howard
1997	Jefferson-Pilot & Chubb Life Insurance
1997	Mattel & Tyco Toys
1997	McKesson & General Medical
1997	Merck & Rhone-Poulenc
1997	Morgan Stanley & Dean Witter Discover
1997	NationsBank & Montgomery Securities
1997	Newmont Mining & Sante Fe Pacific Gold
1997	News Corp. & New World Communications
1997	Raytheon & Hughes Aircraft
1997	Reed Elsevier & Wolters Kluwer (canceled)
1997	Rhodia & Paarmal
1997	SBC Communications & Pacific Telesis
1997	Service Corporation International & The Loewen Group (canceled)
1997	Sierra Health Services & Physician Corporation of America (canceled)
1997	Staples & Office Depot (canceled)
1997	Texas Pacific & Del Monte Foods
1997	3Com & U.S. Robotics
1997	Union Pacific Resources & Pennzoil (canceled)
1998	AirTouch & MediaOne
1998	American Home Products & Monsanto (canceled)
1998	American Home Products & SmithKline Beecham (canceled)
1998	Banc One & First Chicago NBD
1998	Bank of Montreal & Royal Bank of Canada (canceled)
1998	Berkshire Hathaway & General Re
1998	Bertelsmann & Random House

1998	British Petroleum & Amoco
1998	Citicorp & Travelers
1998	Compaq Computer & Digital Equipment
1998	CVS & Arbor Drugs
1998	Daimler-Benz & Chrysler
1998	Ernst & Young & KPMG Peat Marwick (canceled)
1998	First Union & CoreStates Financial
1998	Halliburton & Dresser Industries
1998	ITT & Starwood
1998	Lockheed Martin & Northrop Grumman (canceled)
1998	NationsBank & Barnett Banks
1998	Pacific Enterprises & Enova
1998	PepsiCo & Tropicana Products
1998	PhyCor & MedPartners (canceled)
1998	Price Waterhouse & Coopers & Lybrand
1998	Swiss Bank & Union Bank of Switzerland
1998	Tellabs & Ciena (canceled)
1998	United HealthCare & Humana (canceled)
1998	USA Waste Services & Waste Management
1998	Volkswagen & Rolls-Royce
1998	Walt Disney & Infoseek
1998	WorldCom & MCI Communications
1999	Aerospatiale & Dassault Aviation
1999	Allied Waste & Browning-Ferris
1999	AlliedSignal & Honeywell
1999	America Online & Netscape Communications

1999	Astra & Zeneca
1999	AT&T & TCI
1999	Banco Central Hispanoamericano & Banco Santander
1999	Banque Nationale de Paris & Paribas
1999	Bell Atlantic & GTE
1999	British Aerospace & Marconi Electronic Systems
1999	British American Tobacco & Rothmans International
1999	Du Pont & Herberts
1999	Exxon & Mobil
1999	Ford & Volvo
1999	General Dynamics & Newport News Shipbuilding (canceled)
1999	LVMH Moet Hennessy Louis Vuitton & Gucci (canceled)
1999	Norfolk Southern, CSX & Conrail Inc.
1999	Olivetti & Telecom Italia
1999	Sanpaolo IMI & Banca di Roma (canceled)
1999	SBC Communications & Ameritech
1999	Scottish Power & PacifiCorp
1999	Tyco International & AMP
1999	UniCredito Italiano & Banca Commerciale Italiana (canceled)
1999	Viacom & CBS
1999	Vodafone Group & AirTouch Communications
2000	AT&T & MediaOne
2000	Dow Chemical & Union Carbide

INDUSTRY INDEX

PETROLEUM AND COAL PRODUCTS

RUBBER AND MISCELLANEOUS PLASTICS PRODUCTS

STONE, CLAY, GLASS, AND CONCRETE PRODUCTS

PRIMARY METAL INDUSTRIES

FABRICATED METAL PRODUCTS

INDUSTRIAL MACHINERY AND EQUIPMENT

ELECTRICAL AND ELECTRONIC EQUIPMENT

TRANSPORTATION EQUIPMENT

MEASURING, ANALYZING, AND CONTROLLING INSTRUMENTS

Industry Index

Industry Index

General Index

General Index

General Index

General Index

Q

R

General Index

U

V

General Index